Gun Digest® Book of

MODERN GUN VALUES

W9-ALM-952

The Shooter's Guide to Guns 1900 to Present

17th Edition

Edited By

Richard A. Mann and Jerry Lee

Copyright ©2013 F+W Media, Inc.

All rights reserved. No portion of this publication may be reproduced or transmitted in any form or by any means, electronic or mechanical, including photocopy, recording, or any information storage and retrieval system, without permission in writing from the publisher, except by a reviewer who may quote brief passages in a critical article or review to be printed in a magazine or newspaper, or electronically transmitted on radio, television, or the Internet.

Published by

Gun Digest® Books, an imprint of F+W Media, Inc.
Krause Publications • 700 East State Street • Iola, WI 54990-0001
715-445-2214 • 888-457-2873
www.krausebooks.com

To order books or other products call toll-free 1-800-258-0929
or visit us online at www.gundigeststore.com.

ISBN-13: 978-1-4402-3746-1
ISBN-10: 1-4402-3746-8

Cover & Interior Design by Tom Nelsen

Edited by Richard A. Mann, Jerry Lee, and Jennifer L.S. Pearsall

Printed in the United States of America

GunDigest® Book of

MODERN GUN VALUES

17th Edition

Table of Contents

Introduction 4

Inspection Guide to Used Guns 6

Guide to Evaluating Firearms Condition 17

Illustrated Guide to Condition 25

Firearms Restoration 27

Better Than Book: Factors that Increase A Gun's Value 30

Arms Pricing & Reference

GUNDEX® 32

Directory of Handgun Manufacturers 83

Handgun Listings 84

Directory of Rifle Manufacturers 265

Rifle Listings 266

Today's Guns for Tomorrow's Collector 433

Directory of Shotgun Manufacturers 480

Shotgun Listings 481

Directory of Commemorative Years 675

Introduction to Commemoratives & Limited Editions 676

Commemoratives Listings 677

Firearms Trade and Proprietary Names 706

Introduction

Welcome to the 17th Edition of the *Gun Digest Book of Modern Gun Values*. In this book you will find historical data, photographs, detailed descriptions, technical information, and estimated values of virtually every handgun, rifle, and shotgun of the modern smokeless-powder era, generally defined as those manufactured or imported into the United States since 1900. More than 8,500 firearms are profiled in these pages, including many newer models that the gun companies have introduced since the last edition was published in 2011. Estimated values have been revised for more than 1,500 models or variations, most on the upside and a few downward, as the popularity and demand for certain models have changed. Economic conditions seem to have improved somewhat since the last edition went to press, which has pushed up values, especially for higher-priced collectable models.

Modern Gun Values profiles the products of all major U.S. gun manufacturers and importers and, in most cases, every model variation that appeared in the company's catalogs. Not every prototype or projected new introduction is included, such as the occasional model that was shown at trade shows, but, for whatever reason, never went into production. Still, for their historical value, some prototypes or models with very limited runs are listed.

This book is primarily designed for the gun owner or potential buyer who wants a handy source for the estimated values and descriptions of the models likely to be seen in gun stores, at gun shows, or auction sites. Some military-issue weapons are included but, for the most part, *Modern Gun Values* focuses on firearms produced for the general civilian market. We also limit listings for made-to-order custom firearms, especially those produced by one- or two-man shops that turn out only a handful of guns each year. For those interested in a wider range of firearms or a more in-depth look at specific categories, we call the reader's attention to these other Krause publications: *Standard Catalog of Firearms*, *Flayderman's Guide to Antique American Firearms*, *Standard Catalog of Military Firearms*, and *Gun Digest Buyer's Guide to Tactical Rifles*. The company also publishes books that focus exclusively on the firearms of a specific manufacturer, such as *Standard Catalog of Colt Firearms*, *Standard Catalog of Browning Firearms*, and similar titles covering the guns of Winchester, Smith & Wesson, and others.

THE TACTICAL BOOM

Since the previous edition of this book went to press, the subject of firearms has been almost continuously in the news, and much of the media attention has had an effect on both supply and demand. During a contentious general election campaign in 2012 that lasted way too long, there were fears among many gun owners that a continuation of the Obama administration would bring about new gun legislation. Well before the election was over, many were very worried about what the future held and rushed to gun stores and shows in response to the "get 'em while you can" warnings from sellers. The results were no surprise: shortages in certain models, mostly high-capacity semi-auto rifles and pistols. Notable mass shootings in 2011 and 2012 kept guns in the headlines and brought even more calls for stronger gun controls, which again pushed up the demand for AR-15 type models. Prices at the retail level began to exceed MSRP, and manufacturers increased their production to keep up with the demand. When President Obama was re-elected, that demand increased exponentially.

In December 2012, the massacre at an elementary school in New Town, Connecticut, shocked the nation, and restrictive legislation on military-style firearms was quickly passed in several states. Gun control advocates renewed their efforts for more federal gun laws through Congress. All this occurred in spite of the fact that most experts—including those on the anti-gun side—admitted that the laws being passed would not have prevented the New Town shootings.

For several months, prices for military-style rifles went even higher, and ammunition for all types of guns began to disappear from gun store shelves. Hoarding, whether for fear of continuing shortages, or greed from speculators looking for reselling opportunities, continued into the spring of 2013. Then, by mid-summer, the tactical gun price bubble began to deflate. Production had caught up with demand, as the now more than 100 AR-type manufacturers, large and small, began to catch up with their orders. One could again buy a new AR-style rifle for the manufacturer's suggested retail price and, in some instances, below MSRP. Ammo shortages began to end for the same reasons, though there are still limits on purchases in many areas, especially for .22 rimfire.

The initial plans for this book included expectations for higher values for new or used tactical-style rifles, especially AR-15 types, but that turned out not to be the case. Some models are more popular (and pricier) than others, but, as we go to press, the shelves of gun stores across the country have, for the most part, returned to normal. Of course, no one can predict what the future holds for the values of firearms, gold, art, or any other investment or collectible. Or stocks or real estate. But, for those of us who just happened to love the look and feel of a fine firearm, we like the fact that such a purchase might turn out to be a good investment, and, if it doesn't, well, you just can't have too many guns.

HOW TO USE THIS EDITION

Modern Gun Values is divided into four major sections - Handguns, Rifles, Shotguns and Commemoratives. Within each of these sections the individual firearms entries are listed in numerical model, then alphabetical, order. (A valuable reference section is also included in the back pages of this book.)

Readers can locate a particular gun in three ways: by browsing through the sections and alphabetical manufacturers' listings; by consulting the comprehensive "GUNDEX" index section; or by consulting the "Manufacturers' Directory" that precedes each respective section of the book. We have attempted to improve the illustrations shown in this book wherever possible and especially in those cases in which illustrations help the reader to differentiate between similar models.

We have established a three-tiered pricing approach for each firearm based on the six NRA Modern Condition Pricing Standards: New, Perfect, Excellent, Very Good, Good and Fair. Each firearm has been evaluated to determine which three NRA standards most accurately reflect the condition in which the particular firearm is most likely to be found on the used market; the firearm is priced accordingly. For example, firearms currently on the retail market, or manufactured in the last four years, will most always be found in New or Perfect condition on the used market, while most older firearms will rarely be found in any condition exceeding Very Good. The three pricing levels we provide reflect current observations of prices seen at gun shows, in the gun shops or in the various periodicals, dealer's catalogs or at auction sales.

There are three primary factors that are key to establishing a firearm's value. These are demand, availability and condition.

DEMAND AND AVAILABILITY

One of the factors driving demand – and thus the value of a particular firearm – is availability. When demand exceeds availability, the price of the firearm increases. This pertains not only to collectibles but to shooting guns as well. For example, it is not unusual for a current-production firearm in limited supply to sell in the marketplace for prices considerably above the manufacturer's suggested list price. Even some Colt and Smith & Wesson models have enjoyed such run-ups. However, realize that in this case when supply finally catches up with demand prices will dip.

Some older firearms may be in scarce supply yet are not in demand by collectors. Without demand, regardless of availability, the dollar value of the firearm will be low.

CONDITION

Of the three factors used to establish value, condition is perhaps the most important and certainly the factor most frequently used by shooters as well as collectors for determining the price of a firearm. A "like new" example of a relatively common older Colt, Smith & Wesson, Luger or other arm popular with collectors can bring up to twice the price of another that easily ranks as "Excellent." On the other end of the scale, a scarce, popular collectible in "Poor" or even "Fair" condition often will go begging at a fraction of its value in more acceptable shape.

Of course, neither condition nor pricing is ever absolute. There is no such thing as a fixed price. It's an axiom among gun enthusiasts that there are only two conditions any two collectors can agree upon and those are "New" and "Junk"; everything in between is highly subjective and subject to debate. For example, a shooter looking at a potential acquisition might rate a gun with little finish but mechanically tight and with a fine bore, "Excellent"; to the collector that same firearm would rate only a "Good" or possibly "Very Good." An old Luger with most of its original blue but with the bore badly pitted from corrosive ammunition would rate an "Excellent" from most collectors but only a "Fair" from a shooter. Collectors and shooters alike find the line between "Good" and "Very

Good" or "Very Good" and "Excellent" a fuzzy one.

GUNS AND THE INTERNET

It is very important to educate one's self on the particular gun models that pique your interest, whether you're a buyer or seller. And if you want to build a serious collection, you need to become a true student of the gun. In addition to books like *Modern Gun Values*, the internet is a great source for information on firearms. Note in particular the auction houses that are listed below. Their websites provide not only a place to participate in the buying or selling of guns at their auctions, but also a way to track the asking and the selling prices of individual firearms.

The internet makes everyone a seller and everyone a buyer. It has infused an enormous volume of fresh blood into the hobby. In the past, a shooter or collector had to comb the classifieds, drive to every retail shop in the county, and attend gun shows to find a rare or scarce model. Nowadays virtually any gun can be found after a few minutes' searching online. The result? For newer guns, it's a buyer's market. For scarce vintage or antique models, it's a seller's market, at least as far as the internet is concerned.

At any rate, the effect of the internet on firearms pricing can neither be ignored nor overestimated. The worldwide web is the single greatest influence on modern gun values, and we can all use it to our advantage, either as buyers or sellers.

These are the most prominent auction houses that specialize in firearms and armory.

Amoskeag Auctions: www.amoskeag-auction.com

Bonhams and Butterfields: www.bonhams.com

Heritage Auctions: www.ha.com

James D. Julia, Inc.: www.juliaauctions.com

Little John's Auctions: www.littlejohnsauctions.com

Rock Island Auction Co.: www.rockislandauction.com

A REMINDER

Remember that the values shown here should be taken as guidelines, not absolutes. When a rarely seen gun that you've been wanting for a long time shows up at a price somewhat higher than we indicate, it still may be worth buying because the pleasure of ownership is often well worth the higher price. Many collectors freely admit they rarely regret the firearms they buy, but all too often regret the ones they didn't buy. On the other hand, don't be too quick to buy a common gun that you'd like to have when you see it at market price, since one will likely show up sooner or later at a lower price.

From the buyer's standpoint, pricing at the extreme ends of the condition scale (New to Poor) generally reflects the most you might consider paying for a particular firearm in a particular condition. From the seller's standpoint, these values reflect ballpark figures where you might start your pricing, leaving yourself ample room for negotiation. In a bidding or other competitive situation, however, all bets are off. Whoever wants the item the most, and can reinforce his sentiments with his checkbook, will ultimately obtain it. The sky's the limit.

With any luck, however, the buyer's and the seller's comfort zones will overlap at a certain point, and that will be the figure for which the firearm is sold.

RESTORATION

For collectors in particular, there's another important aspect of condition that needs to be addressed and that is restoration. As the demand for many collectible arms has exceeded the supply of those in "acceptable" condition, many rare, and even not so rare, firearms have been restored. Pitted areas built up by welding, missing or damaged parts remade, obliterated markings re-rolled, grips and stocks with re-cut checkering, or the metal polished and refinished using the techniques of the original maker are some examples of the restoration work possible. A first-class restoration is an expensive proposition, but if properly done is often difficult to tell from original factory work.

But how does the value of a restored firearm compare with that of an original in like condition? A truly first-class job can bring close to the price of an original-condition example; however, very few restorations are that good. Generally, a very good restoration is usually worth at best half as much as a nice original. Two warnings: First, beware of restorations passed off as original. Second, be extra aware of a common model that's "restored" into a rare variation by modifying markings, barrel length or the like. When in doubt, ask an expert and refer to the NRA's Code of Ethics. Misrepresentation can be fraud.

NRA CODE OF ETHICS

A listing of practices considered unethical and injurious to the best interests of the collecting fraternity.

1. The manufacture or sale of a spurious copy of a valuable firearm. This shall include the production of full-scale replicas of historic models and accessories, regardless of easily effaced modern markings, and it also shall include the rebuilding of any authentic weapon into a rarer and more valuable model. It shall not include the manufacture or sale of firearms or accessories which cannot be easily confused with the rare models of famous makers. Such items are: plastic or pottery products, miniatures, firearms of original design, or other examples of individual skill, plainly stamped with the maker's name and date, made up as examples of utility and craftsmanship, and not representative of the designs or models of any old-time arms maker.

2. The alteration of any marking or serial number, or the assembling and artificially aging of unrelated parts for the purpose of creating a more valuable or unique firearm with or without immediate intent to defraud. This shall not include the legitimate restoration or completion of missing parts with those of original type, provided that such completions or restorations are indicated to a prospective buyer.

3. The refinishing (bluing, browning, or plating) or engraving of any collector's weapons, unless the weapons may be clearly marked under the stocks or elsewhere to indicate the date and nature of the work, and provided the seller unequivocally shall describe such non-original treatment to a buyer.*

4. The direct or indirect efforts of a seller to attach a spurious historical association to a firearm in an effort to inflate its fair value; efforts to "plant" a firearm under circumstances which are designed to inflate the fair value.

5. The employment of unfair or shady practices in buying, selling, or trading at the expense of young and inexperienced collectors or anyone else; the devious use of false appraisals, collusion and other sharp practices for personal gain.

6. The use of inaccurate, misleading, or falsified representations in direct sales or in selling by sales list, catalog, periodical advertisement and other media; the failure to make prompt refunds, adjustments or other proper restitution on all just claims which may arise from arms sales, direct or by mail.

*When the NRA formulated this Code of Ethics many years ago restoration was rarer than it is today and some restoration was indeed marked. However, such marking is rarely if ever done today and restoration is not only considered ethical but desirable when appropriate. Furthermore, for many, a restorer's mark in even the most inconspicuous internal location would detract from originality.

Fortunately, many knowledgeable collectors and dealers are able to distinguish even the best restoration work from "factory original." In addition, in the current marketplace it is not at all unusual for an owner or seller to not only admit restoration, but to state with pride that a certain arm was restored by a specific well-known restorer.

Ethically, of course, the fact that restoration work has been done and to what extent should always be disclosed to a prospective purchaser. Not to do so has, in the case of some very valuable collectibles, resulted in expensive and embarrassing legal actions.

NRA MODERN CONDITION STANDARDS

To give a firm foundation for the pricing structure of this edition, it is essential to establish a set of condition standards by which a firearm can be judged. We have adopted the well-respected and popular National Rifle Association's Modern Condition Standards as a guideline to the various grades of condition but have made slight modifications (italics) to further help readers determine condition degrees.

New: In same condition as current factory production, with original box and accessories.

Perfect: In new condition in every respect, but may be lacking box and/or accessories.

Excellent: Near new condition, used but little, no noticeable marring of wood or metal, bluing perfect (except at muzzle or sharp edges).

Very Good: In perfect working condition, no appreciable wear on working surfaces, visible finish wear but no corrosion or pitting, only minor surface dents or scratches.

Good: In safe working condition, minor wear on working surfaces, no corrosion or pitting that will interfere with proper functioning.

Fair: In safe working condition, but well worn, perhaps requiring replacement of minor parts or adjustments, no rust, but may have corrosion pits which do not render article unsafe or inoperable.

The editors want to thank you for your interest in firearms, whether as a collector, hunter, competitive shooter, casual plinker, or simply one who is fascinated by the world of the gun. We especially thank you for your support of our corner of that world, the world of gun books!

—Jerry Lee and
Richard A. Mann, Editors

Inspection Guide To Used Guns

by Patrick Sweeney

While the satisfaction of buying a new firearm, from the standpoint of warranty and features, appeals to many shooters and collectors, sometimes "used" is the only route. After all, how many new-in-the-box Winchester pre-64s still exist? Sometimes the only way to acquire the firearm model, or the firearm with the features you desire, is by buying it used. We all have budgets, and purchasing a used gun is much easier on them! Read on and learn how to buy "used" – safely.

If at all possible buy from an established dealer, with a track record and reputation. Even better, a dealer who has an in-house gunsmith who inspects all their used firearms and makes sure no lemons slip through. In the event one does, a reputable dealer will take it back or make it right.

What should the dealer warranty? The normal and expected performance and durability of that model firearm, and that he presented it correctly as to its features and performance. If you buy a plain old used 30-30 and find it shoots three- to four-inch groups at 100 yards, don't expect to be able to return it. If, however, it shoots those groups four feet to the left or right, you have every right to return it. An as-new benchrest rifle better do well under an inch with its provided ammo, or you may have cause to return it (assuming you can shoot that well). If the dealer doesn't have a written warranty, ask what the return policy is.

If you are not buying from a dealer, you have the standard business-school Latin to guide you – Caveat Emptor: "Let the buyer beware." One approach that some of my customers took – and more should have – was to have their purchase inspected by a pro. If you have any doubts about an attractive purchase, take it to a gunsmith and explain things. Don't just drop it off for a "strip and clean" and count on him (or her) uncovering hidden problems.

Come right out and explain: You just bought it, and you want it inspected for safety, durability, function and headspace. If there is a limited return time, the gunsmith needs to know in order to inspect it within the allotted time. Many gunsmiths are booked solid for months and may not get it back to you in time if you leave your purchase for what the 'smith understands is just a "regular cleaning." By explaining your inspection period time constraint you can get your new purchase back in time to meet the refund terms of the sale, should you need to return the gun.

General Inspection of a Used Firearm

To start, give the firearm in question a quick visual inspection. I call it the "tire tracks and hammer marks" look, and it is the same regardless of the type you are thinking of buying. The inspection of a firearm to determine the percentage of finish remaining is covered elsewhere. The purpose of this initial inspection is to uncover damage, repairs or abuse. Is the stock straight and clean? Is the barrel straight? Are the sights centered? Are there dents, scratches, cracks or repairs to be seen? Does the bluing have the right color? Are the barrel markings clean and crisp, or are they blurry or smeared? Is the barrel, the correct length? Is the muzzle uniform? Does the chambering marked on, the barrel match what the seller tells you it shoots? Try to get a "feel" for the history and typical condition of the gun you are looking at. Does it match the description of the one the seller is trying to sell you? A firearm that doesn't match what the seller describes is probably best left on the table.

Just because you are looking at a worn, used-to-gray rifle the seller describes as "the best he's seen" doesn't mean he's fibbing. If you are holding a Remington 700 in 308 Winchester – yes, he is. On the other hand, if you are holding a pre-'64 M-70 in 300 Savage – no, he isn't.

RIFLES

Open the action. With a light or reflector – and with the action open and bolt removed if appropriate – look down the bore. Clean, shiny and clear of obstructions, right? If not, let the bargaining begin!

While many rifles will shoot accurately with a slightly pitted bore, some won't – and all will require more frequent cleaning. Work the action and see if there are any binding spots or if the action is rough. Ask if you can dry fire it to check the safety.

Some people do not like to have any gun in their possession dry-fired; others don't care. If you cannot, you may have to pass on the deal. Or, you can assure the owner that you will restrain the cocking piece to keep the striker from falling.

Close the action and dry-fire it. How much is the trigger pull? Close the action, push the safety to *ON*, and pull the trigger. It should stay cocked. Let go of the trigger and push the safety *OFF*. It should stay cocked. Now, dry-fire it. Is the trigger pull different than it was before? If the pull is now lighter, the safety is not fully engaging the cocking piece, and you'll have to have someone work on it to make it safe. If the rifle fires at any time while manipulating the safety (even without your having touched the trigger) it is unsafe until a gunsmith repairs it.

While you were checking the safety, just what was the trigger pull? A very light trigger pull is not always bad, but may need adjustment. As an example, if you are handling a Remington 700 or Winchester 70, and the trigger pull is one pound, someone may have adjusted the trigger mechanism. If you are handling a Winchester '94 and the trigger pull is a pound, someone has been stoning the hammer or sear. On the first two, you or your gunsmith can adjust the weight back to normal ranges. On the '94 you may have to buy a new hammer or sear – or both – to get the pull back into the normal range.

Inspect the action and barrel channel. Is the gap between the barrel and the channel uniform? Ordoes the forearm bend right or left? Changes in humidity can warp aforearm and, if the wood touches the barrel, alter accuracy. The owner may be selling it because the accuracy has *"gone south,"* and not know that some simple bedding work can cure it.

Look at the action where it meets the stock. Is the wood/metal edge clean and uniform? Or do you see traces of epoxy bedding compound? Epoxy could mean a bedding job,and it could mean a repair of a cracked stock. Closely inspect the wrist of the stock, right behind the tang. Look for cracks and repairs.

Turn the rifle over and look at the action screws. Are the slots clean, or are they chewed up? Mangled slots indicates a rifle that has been taken apart many times – and at least a few of those times with a poorly-fitting screwdriver.

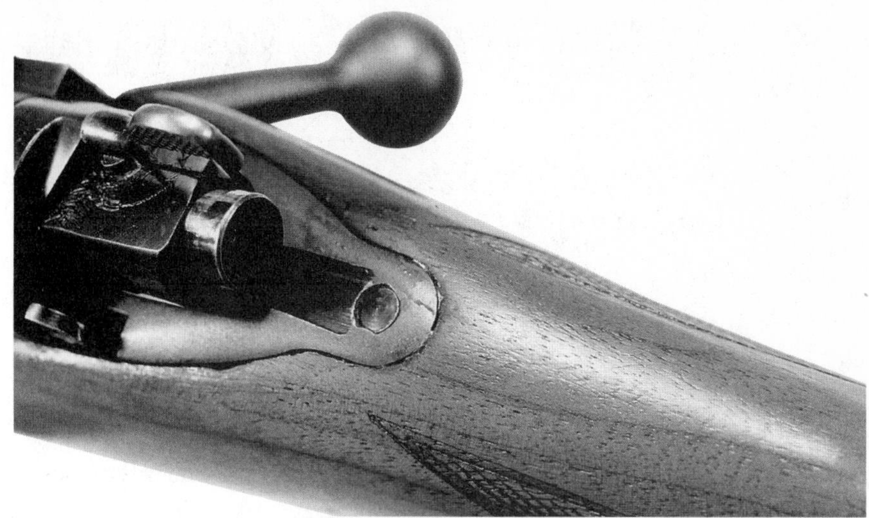

A rifle fired with a poorly-fitted stock, or one dried out from decades of storage, will often crack light behind the tang. Look closely for cracks or repairs.

Are the screw slots clean, or are they chewed up? This screw is just tolerable. Any worse and it would indicate abuse instead of 59 years of indifferent attention.

Check the edges of the stock where the action rests for signs of glass bedding. Bedding is not bad; in fact, it can be good. But don't pay collectors' prices for a working tool that has been modified.

Be sure of the chambering, and be sure it is clearly marked. This Marlin was not a 38-55 when it left the factory; but is now and is clearly so marked.

Consider rarity when assessing condition. A 30-06 with signs of honest use and hunting wear is a tool. This same rifle, were the barrel marked "300 Savage" or "35 Remington," would be a collector's dream.

Remove the bolt if you can. If not, use a reflector or light to illuminate the bore. Is the bore clean and bright? Look at the bore near the muzzle. Do you see jacket fouling or lead deposits? Many an "*inaccurate*" rifle can be made accurate again simply by cleaning the jacket fouling out of the bore. While looking down the bore, hold the barrel so a vertical or horizontal bar in a window reflects down the bore. If the reflection of the bar has a 'break' in it, the barrel is bent. Sight down the outside of the barrel and see if you can spot it. A slightly bent barrel can still be accurate, but will walk its shots when it heats up. A severely bent barrel must be replaced.

SHOTGUNS

Pump-Action & Autoloading Shotguns

Pumps and autoloaders require the same safety check as rifles do, with a few additions. Safety on, pull the trigger, let go, safety off. Dry fire and see if the weight of the trigger pull changes.

When inspecting the barrel, look for dents or creases. Also, inspect the rib (if there is one) to see if it has been dented. While a dented barrel or rib can be repaired so the damage is almost unnoticeable, you can still see evidence of the repair.

Remove the barrel to inspect the bore. Is the bore clean of plastic? Is the choke clean? If not, swab them clean. If there are screw-in chokes, do they unscrew easily and smoothly? While you have the forearm off an autoloader, look at the gas system. Is it clean? Or is it crusty from powder residue? Powder residue can be wiped off, but rust requires more a vigorous remedy, and may leave the shotgun as a non-cycling autoloader.

Double-Barrel Shotguns

Doubles require a different inspection. While looking over the barrels, look to see that the side or bottom ribs are smoothly attached along their length. A lifted rib that has been repaired will have a different appearance at the repair.

Open and close the action. Does the lever move smoothly into place, or do you have to push it the last fraction to fully close it? How far does the lever move? Levers are initially positioned to not go fully to the centerline. As the action wears, the lever moves further and further, taking up the wear. A shotgun with a lever too far past the centerline may have been shot a great deal, or been taken apart and put back together with the lever mis-timed.

Next, check to see the barrels are tight. Often, the forearm will put enough pressure on the action to make it seem tight. Remove the forearm and then check barrel

Are screw-in chokes easy to remove? Or do you have to wrestle with them? A bulged choke may mean a ruined barrel. Always unscrew the chokes to make sure they work as intended.

The screw-in chokes in this barrel, while functional, doom the barrel for resale. The wall was cut too thin on one side and chipped out. The owner will never be able to sell the barrel, for who would buy it? You might, if you neglected to check.

tightness. Does the barrel assembly move or wobble when closed? Can you see the joint at the action changing size when you try to move the barrel? A loose barrel is an expensive repair, so be sure to check. Pull or twist the barrel in all three axes; attempt to move the rear side to side, lift as if you were opening the action (but not pushing the lever), and pull the barrels forward. The action should be as tight as a bank vault.

Next, the triggers. You'll need snap caps and the owner's permission. Insert the snap caps and close the action. Put the safety on. If the double is a twin trigger, check to make sure the safety blocks both triggers. If it is a single trigger, make sure the safety blocks the trigger when the barrel selector is set to each barrel in turn.

Push the safety to *OFF* and snap one of the barrels. Open the action *(keep your hand over the action to stop the snap cap from being launched across the room)* then close it and select the other barrel. Snap that barrel and open the action again, stopping the snap cap from being ejected. Both barrels work? Good. Close the action, snap one of the barrels, and then slap the butt of the shotgun with your hand. If the shotgun has a non-inertial trigger – like the Ruger Red Label – you can forego the slapping. Does the second barrel now fire when you pull the trigger? If so, the inertial trigger is working. If not, you may have to slap it harder, or the inertia weight needs adjusting.

HANDGUNS

Handguns come in two types: revolvers and autoloading pistols, and each has sub-types with their own peculiarities. The four types we'll cover are the **single-action revolver** and **double-action revolver**, **single-action autoloading pistol** and **double-action autoloading pistol**.

Single-Action Revolvers

The single-action revolver is known by many as the *cowboy* revolver. Your quick visual inspection of the exterior should start with the sights, to make sure they are straight, and the grips to make sure they are without cracks or dents. Also look at the exterior edge of the muzzle, and the corners of the frame, for signs of dropping. Bent sights and cracked grips indicate a dropped handgun. Dropping can bend the barrel, warp the frame or throw off the timing.

Hold the revolver up to the light, sideways, and look at the cylinder gap. There should be daylight, but not too much of it. The SA comes in the Colt pattern, old Ruger, and the new Ruger.

In Colts and old Rugers, open the loading gate, cock the hammer back to the *(half-cock)* notch that frees the cylinder, and rotate the cylinder. Look to see that it isn't loaded. On new Rugers, opening the loading gate frees the cylinder to rotate. To close up both action "systems," close the loading gate, cock the hammer and, with your thumb on the hammer spur, pull the trigger and ease the hammer forward while holding the trigger back. Check the cylinder for play.

For those who may not know, spinning the cylinder at high speed, or fanning the hammer are both considered abusive handling, and will likely end the sale before it starts. Don't do either!

Does the cylinder move back and forth? Called *endshake*, it can be easily fixed, but if there is too much it indicates a revolver that has seen a lot of use. On a Colt-pattern revolver it could mean that the cylinder has been replaced and not properly fitted, or the bushing is worn – or peened – from heavy loads.

The wood on this shotgun can be repaired, but what caused it? If a previous owner used magnum shells in a non-magnum-capable gun, the action may be loose. Check the tightness of the barrels to the receiver.

On doubles, check to see if the top lever is easy to move and the action easy to open.

You must remove the forearm before checking a double for tightness. If you don't, the forearm's support may mask any looseness present in the action.

Does the top lever go past center? As the locking surfaces wear the lever moves farther and farther. When it reaches the far side of the top strap, it needs to be refitted.

Does it wobble from side to side? The cylinder stop may be worn, or the slots may be worn or too large. Look at the slots. If they have been abused, the edges will be chewed up. If they appear sharp and clean, the cylinder stop may be worn or its spring weak. A worn or abused cylinder is expensive, while a new cylinder stop or spring is relatively cheap.

Slowly cock the revolver, watching the cylinder. Does it come fully into position? Or do you have to push the cylinder around the last fraction of an inch to get it to lock? A cylinder failing to carry up will require a new hand – or require that the old one be "stretched."

Check each chamber. It isn't unusual for a revolver to have one chamber that has a slightly different timing on the *carry up* than the others do. Once you've checked *carry-up*, test the trigger pull. If the owner is leery of letting you dry fire, catch the hammer with your other hand each time you cock it and pull the trigger. Is the pull within normal limits? A heavy pull may indicate someone has fussed with the trigger – as would a very light pull.

While a trigger is relatively cheap, they can be salvaged only sometimes. The hammer is expensive, but you can often have the notch re-stoned (properly, of course) or in extreme cases, welded and re-cut. If the trigger pull has been "messed with," what was done? You can't tell without getting out a screwdriver set and disassembling the revolver there and then. You will have to either take the risk, or insist on a return/refund option if your gunsmith finds something too expensive to fix.

To continue inspecting the Single Action, open the loading gate, release and pull the center pin, roll the freed-up cylinder out of the frame *(to the right)* and inspect the front and rear of the cylinder. On the rear, is the bluing of the ratchet that the hand pushes against evenly worn white? *(A difficult inspection on a stainless or nickel gun, but you can see the wear if you look closely.)* Each chamber should be clean, their edges unmarred. On the front face of the cylinder, check to see if there are marks from the cylinder face rubbing against the rear of the barrel. A cylinder with *endshake* may rub. The rubbing may even be only partial. Don't worry unless the rubbing has been hard or extensive enough to have marred the face of the cylinder.

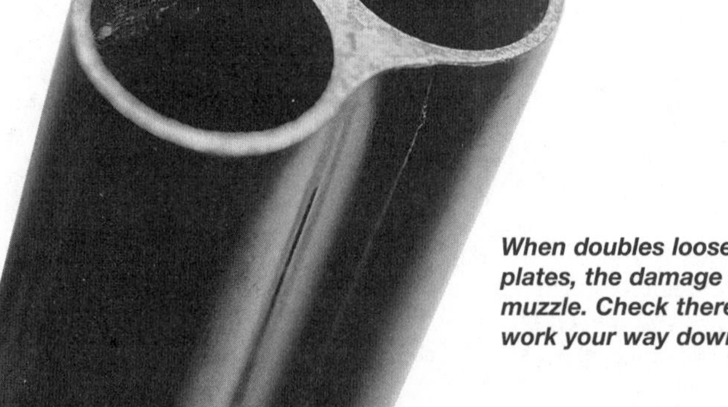

When doubles loosen their ribs and plates, the damage often starts at the muzzle. Check there first, and then work your way down the barrels.

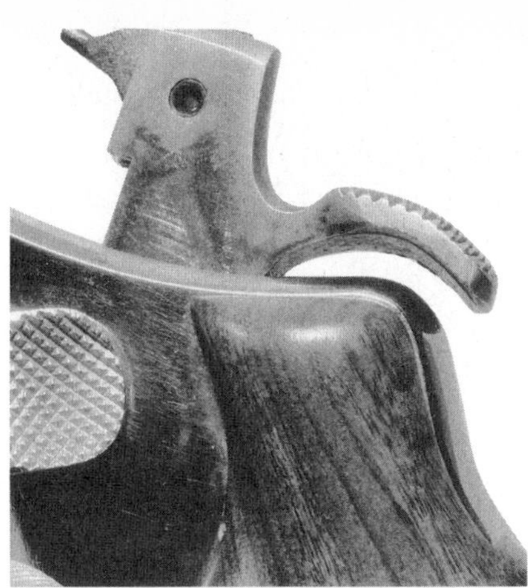

Hammer clearance on a revolver in single action mode is important. You can see here the hammer may bind on the frame if the spur is bent.

Look at the rear of the barrel. Is the end even and square to the bore? Or has someone been stoning or filing the rear face for some reason? Is the forcing cone clean and smooth?

A revolver that has been fired with lead alloy bullets will often have a forcing cone crusted with lead, even when the rest of the barrel is clean.

A revolver that has seen a lot of jacketed magnum-level loads will show the wear in the forcing cone, the edges of which will be slightly rounded from the heat and abrasion.

Look down the bore. Is it clean and are the lands and grooves smooth and shiny? A pitted bore means the barrel must be replaced. If you see a dark ring (or *donut*) that indicates a "ringed barrel," the barrel may still be accurate but will probably lead quickly. A bullet stopping partway down the bore, and then being jolted out by the next round fired, causes a "ringed" barrel. The bulge may not show on the outside.

Double-Action Revolvers

The quick exterior inspection should include the hammer spur. Dropping a DA revolver can bend the spur, keeping the hammer from being cocked. Your inspection will reveal this, so be prepared when you get there.

Push the cylinder latch and open the cylinder. Does the latch move smoothly? Does the cylinder move without binding or catching? Check by opening the cylinder at each of its six (or five, seven or eight) positions. A dropped DA revolver can have a bent center pin, and the bend will interfere with opening at only one chamber. On a DA revolver, opening and closing it Hollywood-style, by flicking the wrist, is flagrant handling abuse which will get it snatched out of your hands by many owners.

To check single action engagement, cock the hammer and push the hammer forward with one thumb. Again, ten pounds is all you need.

Check *carry-up*, both in single action and double action modes. You may have to ride your offhand thumb on the hammer as you slowly do the double-action check, to keep the hammer (and the trigger) from jerking to the end of the DA stroke and thus hiding improper carry-up. If the revolver has been dropped and the hammer spur bent, this is when you'll find out. A bent spur can still work fine in double action, but the hammer goes back farther in cocking for single action. A bent spur may bind against the frame and not allow the revolver to be cocked. With the hammer cocked, put your thumb behind it and give it a gentle push… no more than ten pounds worth. The hammer should stay cocked.

Years ago I had a run-in with a desk sergeant at a local police department about proper testing for push-off *(my home state of Michigan requires a safety inspection for the sale of a handgun)*. He was pushing for all he was worth, with both thumbs, and rejecting every revolver my customers came in

Does the cylinder unlatch smoothly and easily? Binding or requiring force to move is a bad sign, usually indicating a bent crane or bent center pin.

Close the cylinder, dry fire and hold the trigger back. Check the cylinder for wobble: front-to-back and side-to-side. Then release the trigger and try again. The cylinder shouldn't move at all when the trigger is held back, and only a little when released.

A peened cylinder locking slot indicates heavy use, either many rounds or magnum loads. Peened slots can't be fixed, and require a new cylinder, a major cost.

with. I finally had to bring in the S&W Armorers Manual, and show him and his supervisor what the factory-accepted test was. If the revolver you are testing pushes off at ten pounds or less, the single-action notch is worn – or has been worked on. Depending on theremedy required, it may be expensive to fix; sometimes requiring a new hammer.

Check cylinder tightness with the trigger held back, as with the SA revolver, checking for play side-to-side and front-to-back. As on the SA revolver, side-to-side play can be caused by peened locking slots in the cylinder, which is expensive to repair. Or, it can be caused by a worn cylinder stop (less expensive), or a tired cylinder stop spring (cheap to fix).

Endshake is a sign of use with heavy or magnum loads.

Endshake is easy and inexpensive to fix by stretching the crane or installing shims, but both increase cylinder gap at the rear of the barrel. If removing *endshake* increases the gap beyond tolerances, you'll have to have the barrel set back, a moderately expensive fix.

Open the action and look at the front and rear of the cylinder. The front of the cylinder should not show rub marks from the rear of barrel. If it does, it is a sign of excessive *endshake*, which must be fixed. The rear of the chambers should have clean ninety-degree edges. Some shooters bevel the rear opening of the chambers to make speedloading faster and easier. Properly done, beveling does speed reloads but, improperly done, it can cause improper ejection.

If you see beveling, look closely at the ejector star. Has the star been beveled, too? A proper job bevels the cylinder but not the ejector. A beveled ejector that improperly ejects (the empties will not be fully ejected) is a moderately expensive repair.

Inspect the forcing cone. Is it clean, with sharp edges? A revolver that has seen a lot of magnum loads, especially jacketed ones, will have an eroded forcing cone. A worn forcing cone can cause *spitting* and a loss of accuracy. A worn forcing cone can be fixed, but only by setting the barrel back and cutting a new cone in fresh steel. The gunsmith will also have to shorten the ejector rod and center pin, and will have to remove *endshake* to do the job properly and the cost will be moderate to moderately high.

Look down the bore. Clean, shiny and straight? Good. If it is pitted, or ringed from a bullet having been lodged in the bore, you'll need a new barrel.

The last check concerns the crane. The swing-out crane makes loading and unloading easier, but it is relatively fragile and can be bent by being dropped, or being flipped open Hollywood-style.

Gently close the cylinder, and see how much thumb pressure it takes to lock up. Does the cylinder swing

The crane on a DA revolver is easily bent from abuse, dropping or incorrect gunsmithing.

into place and click shut without force? Great. Try it on all chambers, as a bent crane can be offset by other tolerances, and may be hidden on one or more chambers. If you find you need moderate thumb pressure to get the cylinder to lock in place, the crane may be bent.

A bent crane and its repair are brand-dependent. Rugers are so stoutly built that you need a ball-peen hammer to bend the crane. You also need one to straighten it. A S&W crane is more fragile and more sensitive to misalignment, but a simple job to straighten. The Colt system is less sensitive than the S&W, not as stout as the Ruger, and a more involved job to fix.

Autoloading Pistols, Single-Action

The icon of single-action autoloading pistols is the 1911 pistol. Of all handguns, this one is the most likely to be assembled from parts, played with, experimented upon – and had parts swapped in and out. Any used pistol requires a close inspection to ensure you don't end up with a pig in a poke.

On your exterior visual inspection, don't be put off by parts of different colors. The government never cared about matching the color of Parkerized parts on military-issue 45s, and many shooters through the years have come to favor deliberately two-toned pistols. It is not at all unusual to find a 1911 with a blued slide and nickeled or stainless frame, or blued or Parkerized parts on a hard-chromed gun.

Check the muzzle end of the slide for dings and gouges indicating it has been dropped. Look at the magazine well. A dropped pistol can crack at the magazine well if the well has been beveled for fast magazine insertion. You may see a crack on the frame forward of the slide stop lever. Pay it no mind. A cracked dustcover on high-mileage auto-pistols is not rare. If you see the crack and the owner says it has never been shot, be suspicious. ***Any crack in a slide is grounds for immediate rejection.*** Cracked slides cannot be repaired, cannot be trusted, and must be replaced.

Give the pistol a brief visual check for signs of dropping, or tool marks from previous experimenting. Work the slide. Does it move smoothly? It should move its full travel without catching, binding or hesitating. A binding slide could be a bent slide, dented frame rails, or a mis-fit replacement barrel. All will be moderately expensive to fix. Or, it could simply be a replacement slide that was not fully lapped to fit – which is cheap to fix.

Flip the thumb safety up and down. It should move smoothly and snap from one setting to another. Check the grip safety. It should move in and out without binding, and its spring should snap it back out when released. A grip safety that doesn't move should set off alarm bells in your head. It was popular in competition circles a decade or more ago to pin down grip safeties so they would not move. A pistol with a pinned grip safety is probably a high-mileage competition gun that has seen tens of thousands of rounds. Even if it has seen only light use, you will have to have the grip safety unpinned and properly tuned.

Now check the function of the safeties. Happily, owners of the 1911 are much less prone to the *"don't dry fire"* attitude. Check to

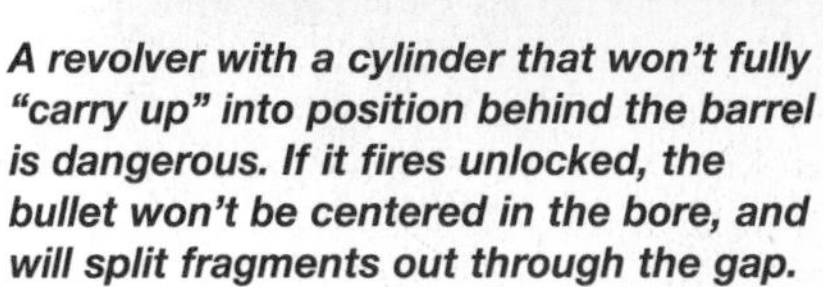

A revolver with a cylinder that won't fully "carry up" into position behind the barrel is dangerous. If it fires unlocked, the bullet won't be centered in the bore, and will split fragments out through the gap.

A dropped revolver can bend the center pin where it protudes into the frame. It cannot be straightened and must be replaced.

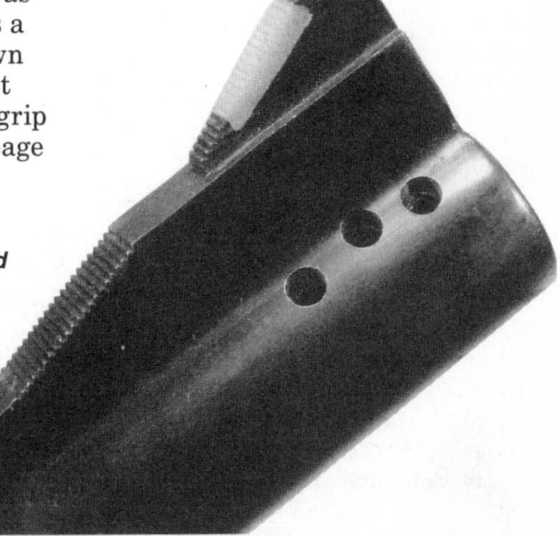

Some home gunsmithing is beyond the pale. These home-drilled "ports" on this revolver have ruined the barrel. If the seller won't subtract the cost of a new barrel and installation from the cost, pass it up.

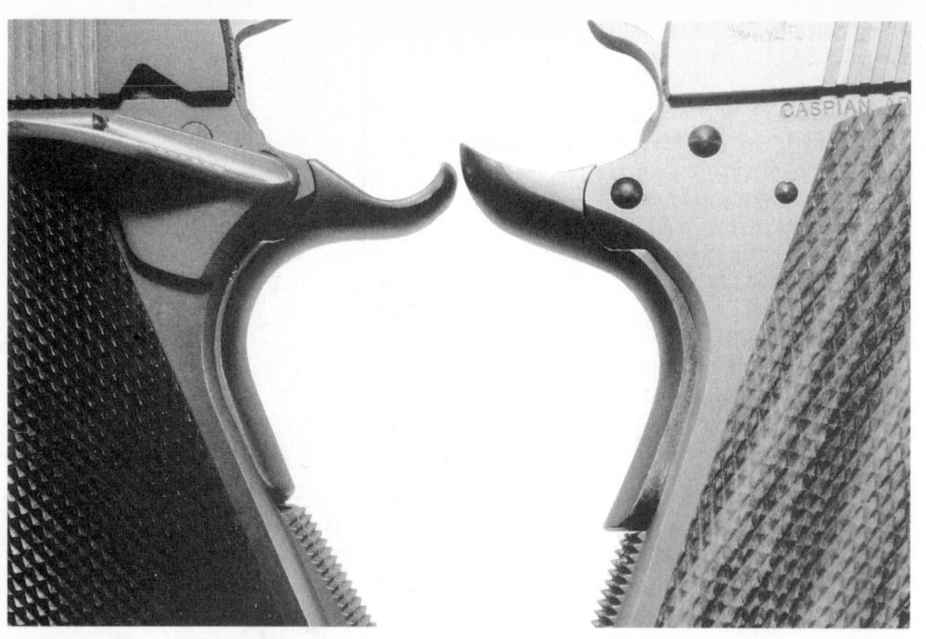

The grip safety on the left has been pinned down, and doesn't work. Don't buy a 1911 with a pinned grip safety unless it can be unpinned and tested for function.

make sure the pistol isn't loaded, then cycle the slide and dry fire it. Hold the trigger back and work the slide. It should move smoothly. A pistol that is hard to cycle with the trigger held back could have disconnector problems – or an improperly adjusted trigger binding the disconnector. With the slide cycled back and forth, does the hammer stay cocked *(It better, or you will be facing expensive repairs)?* Next, push the thumb safety *ON*. Pull the trigger (using no more than ten pounds pressure), release the trigger and push the safety *OFF*. If the hammer falls, the safety isn't blocking the sear's movement. I've seen pistols that would fire when the safety was ON and the trigger was pulled. Not very safe and, potentially, an expensive repair.

If the hammer stays back, you now listen. Lift the pistol to

Does the thumb safety move smoothly, or do you need to force it? Forcing is bad, and indicates a poorly fitted thumb safety.

Once the safety is on, pull the trigger with about 10 pounds of force. Then push the safety off and listen to the sear.

your ear, and gently thumb back the hammer. If you hear nothing *(assuming you have properly worn hearing protection during all those years of shooting)* then the thumb safety is fine. If you hear a little metallic "*tink*" then the safety needs adjustment. If the safety blocks the sear – but not entirely – the sear can move minutely when you pull the trigger. The "*tink*" is the sear tip snapping back into the bottom of the hammer hooks when the spring pressure is released. If the thumb safety passes the "listen" test, you're on to the grip safety.

Cock the hammer and hold the pistol so you don't grip the grip safety. Pull the trigger. The test, and "listen," are the same as the thumb safety test, looking for the same problems. Now start looking for signs of abuse or experimentation.

To check the grip safety's function you have to hold the pistol so you don't depress the safety. Then pull the trigger.

Hold the slide partway back and look at the feed ramp. It should be clean and shiny. There should be a gap between the ramp on the frame and the ramp on the barrel. If someone has polished them to be an uninterrupted surface, they have decreased feeding reliability. An improperly polished or ground ramp is expensive to fix.

Should you check barrel fit? Checking won't tell you much. The customary check is to press down on the chamber area to see if it moves, and having moved, if it springs back. The problem is, it doesn't tell you much. I've seen apparently loose pistols that shot quite accurately, and tight pistols that wouldn't shoot worth a darn.

There are some indications that something is amiss. If you are looking at a custom competition gun with a name-brand barrel fitted, and the fit is loose, be suspicious. The barrel may have been simply dropped in (with no attempt at properly fitting it), or it may have been shot tens of thousands of rounds until it wore loose.

If you have a pistol with a plain barrel, tightly fitted, and the front

To check the disconnector: dry fire, hold the trigger down and slowly cycle the slide.

sight is very short, something is up. The barrel may be tight simply because the owner has fitted a long link to the barrel. In which case the link is propping the barrel up to be tight, and the front sight had to be shortened to get the sights to line up with the groups.

Lock the slide open and look down the bore. More so than many other pistols, the 1911 can be a high-mileage survivor. Is the bore clean, or fouled with lead or copper? Is the muzzle worn from cleaning? Is there heavy brass "marking" behind the ejection port? Signs of high mileage are not a reason to pass, but if the pistol is offered as "new" or "like new" and you see signs of bore wear, hold on to your money.

On the subject of the cost of repairs to a 1911, the same symptoms can be cheap – or expensive – depending whether the parts involved merely need adjustment, or must be replaced. Accept a dysfunctional 1911 into your home only after careful consideration and acceptance of potentially high repair costs.

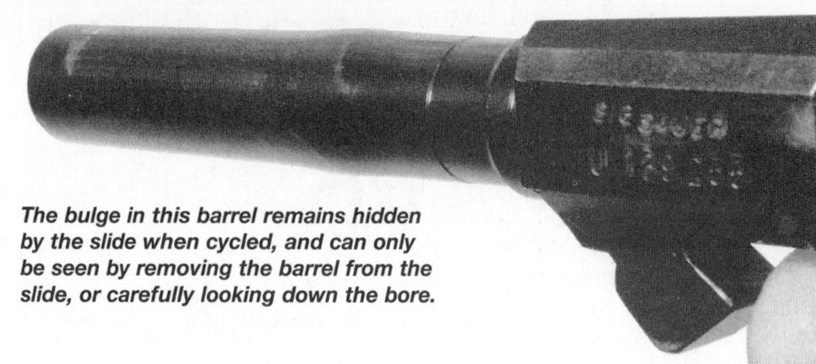

The bulge in this barrel remains hidden by the slide when cycled, and can only be seen by removing the barrel from the slide, or carefully looking down the bore.

Autoloading Pistols, Double-Action

Your visual inspection for the DAs will be the same as with the 1911, except that more of the DAs will have alloy frames. You must take a closer look, especially at a police trade-in, to check for signs of dropping. If you have a pistol with worn bluing, but new grips, look closely. New grips go on only when the old ones are too far gone to be presentable. Police guns get dropped, whacked into car doors and frames, door jambs, light poles, vending machines and seat belt buckles – and that is just when holstered!

Check the frame closely for cracks and signs of dropping, and pass on cracked frames. Glocks get an automatic "passing grade" here, as you can't do more than cosmetic damage, even by throwing one into a cement mixer. Do the dry fire and slide cycle test just as you would with the 1911. Hammerless guns, or DA-only guns, where the hammer follows the slide down, obviously won't show you a cocked hammer to manually manipulate. Dry fire them, cycle the slide, and dry fire again.

The safety check is less involved than with the 1911, and is dependent on design. On Glocks, cycle the action and attempt to press the trigger back without depressing the centrally-mounted trigger safety. On DA guns, drop a pencil down the muzzle, eraser end first, and point up.

Push the safety lever to *SAFE,* or use the de-cocking lever. The pencil shouldn't move. Don't pay attention to vibrations. If the safety isn't blocking the firing pin, the pencil will get launched out and upwards.

Buying a used firearm can be rewarding, fun and educational. By taking a few precautions, and using the inspection procedures outlined, you can avoid buying a walnut and blue steel lemon. Have fun and stay safe! ★

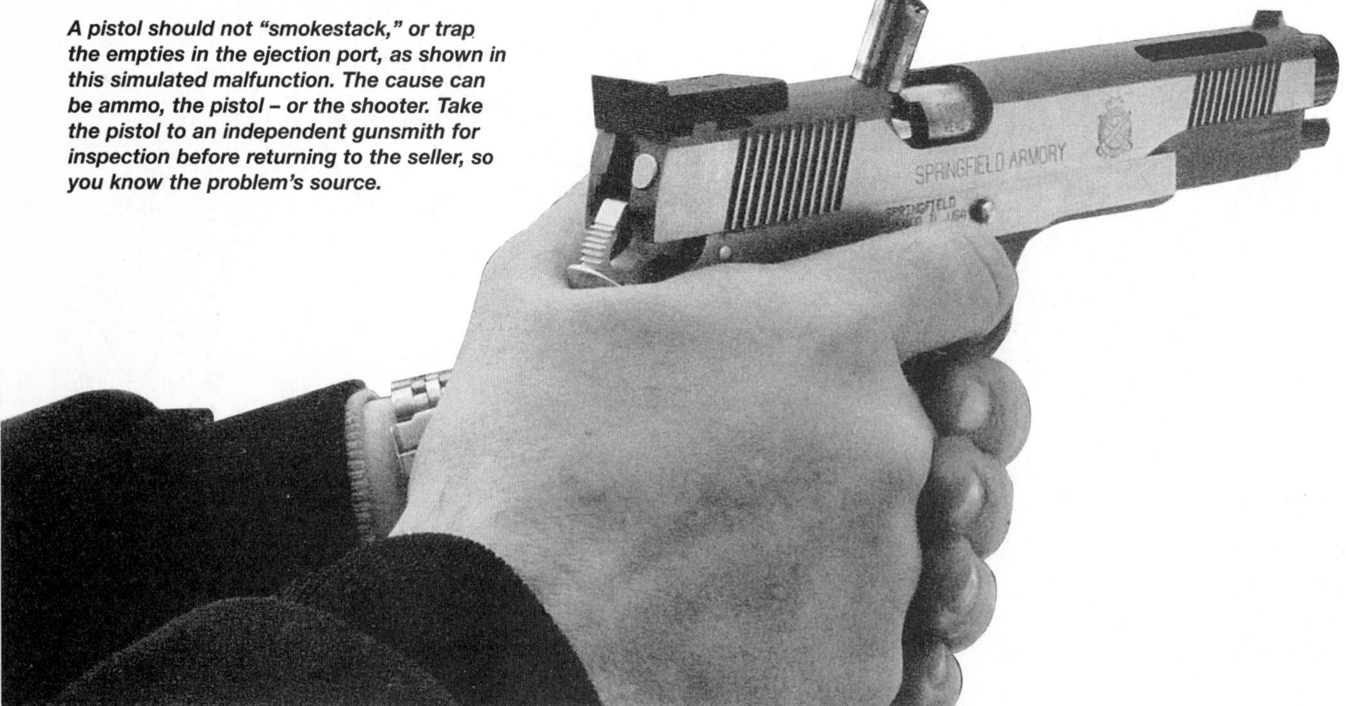

A pistol should not "smokestack," or trap the empties in the ejection port, as shown in this simulated malfunction. The cause can be ammo, the pistol – or the shooter. Take the pistol to an independent gunsmith for inspection before returning to the seller, so you know the problem's source.

Guide to Evaluating Arms Condition

Before a firearm-pricing guide can be effectively used, the condition of the given firearm must be properly evaluated. The following examples provide perspective on establishing a realistic condition assessment of a firearm. Modern Gun Values uses the widely accepted grading criteria developed by the National Rifle Association for modern firearms. For more information, read the Introduction that begins on page 4.

NRA Modern Condition Standards

Here are the NRA guidelines; we have made slight modifications (italics) to further help readers determine degrees of condition.

New: In same condition as current factory production, ***with original box and accessories.***

Perfect: In new condition in every respect, ***but may be lacking box and/or accessories.***

Excellent: Near new condition, used but little, no noticeable marring of wood or metal. Bluing perfect (except at muzzle or sharp edges).

Very Good: In perfect working condition, no appreciable wear on working surfaces, ***visible finish wear*** but no corrosion or pitting, only minor surface dents or scratches.

Good: In safe working condition, minor wear on working surfaces, no corrosion or pitting that will interfere with proper functioning.

Fair: In safe working condition, but well worn, perhaps requiring replacement of minor parts, or adjustments; no rust, but may have corrosion pits which do not render article unsafe or inoperable.

S&W Highway Patrolman, Model 28

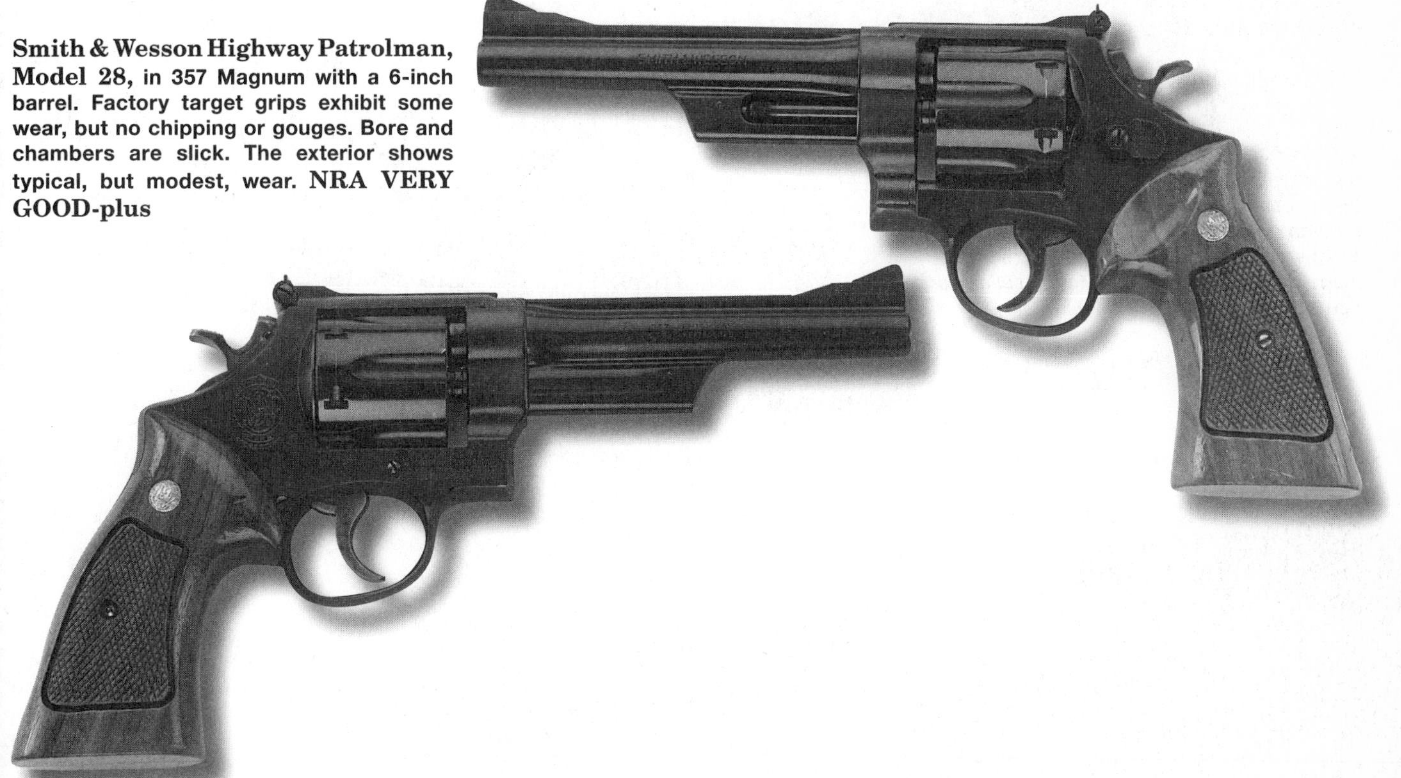

Smith & Wesson Highway Patrolman, Model 28, in 357 Magnum with a 6-inch barrel. Factory target grips exhibit some wear, but no chipping or gouges. Bore and chambers are slick. The exterior shows typical, but modest, wear. NRA VERY GOOD-plus

Colt Police Positive Special

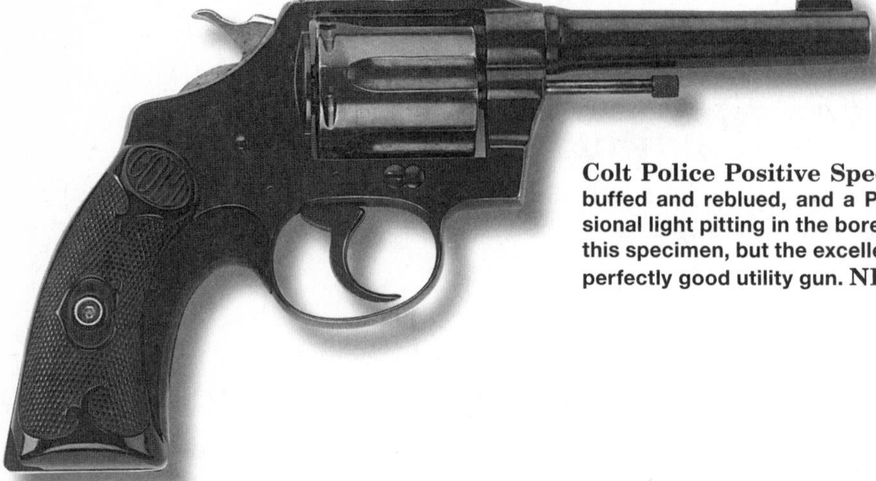

Colt Police Positive Special, 38 Special. This revolver has been buffed and reblued, and a Pachmayr grip-filler added. There is occasional light pitting in the bore and chambers. A collector would pass on this specimen, but the excellent mechanics & reliable function make it a perfectly good utility gun. NRA GOOD

Winchester Model 94 XTR Big Bore

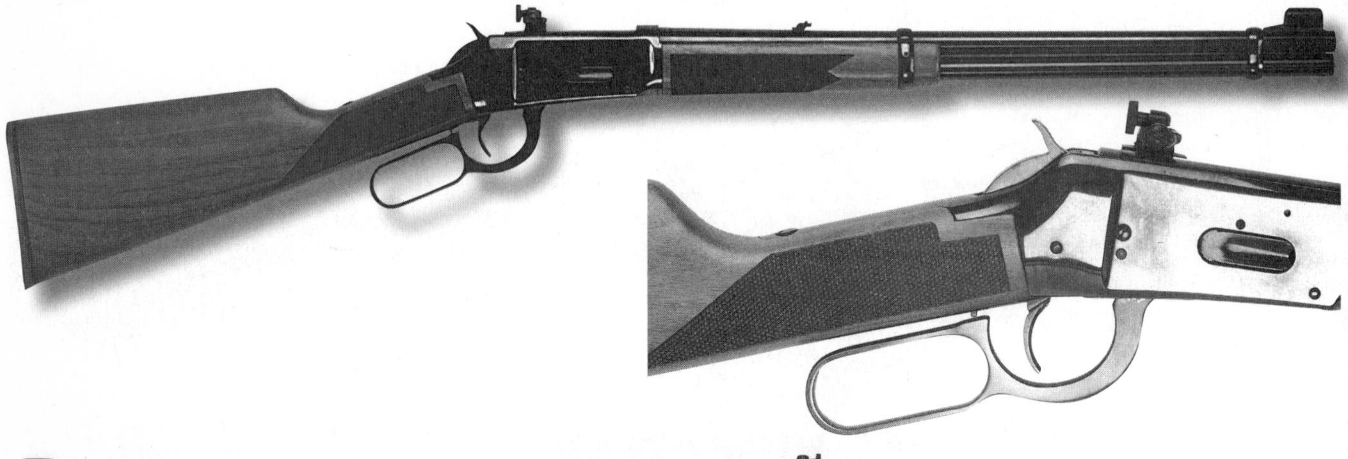

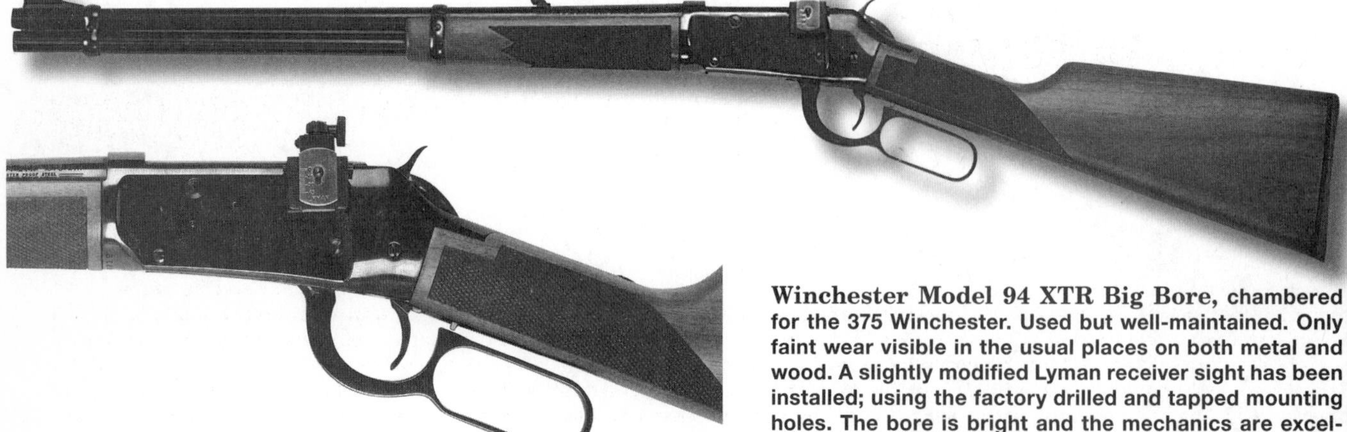

Winchester Model 94 XTR Big Bore, chambered for the 375 Winchester. Used but well-maintained. Only faint wear visible in the usual places on both metal and wood. A slightly modified Lyman receiver sight has been installed; using the factory drilled and tapped mounting holes. The bore is bright and the mechanics are excellent. NRA EXCELLENT

Stevens Favorite No. 26 Crack Shot

Stevens Favorite No. 26 Crack Shot with a 22-inch barrel chambered for the 22LR. Well-used, with obvious wear–but mechanically sound. NRA GOOD

BSA Model 12/15 Match

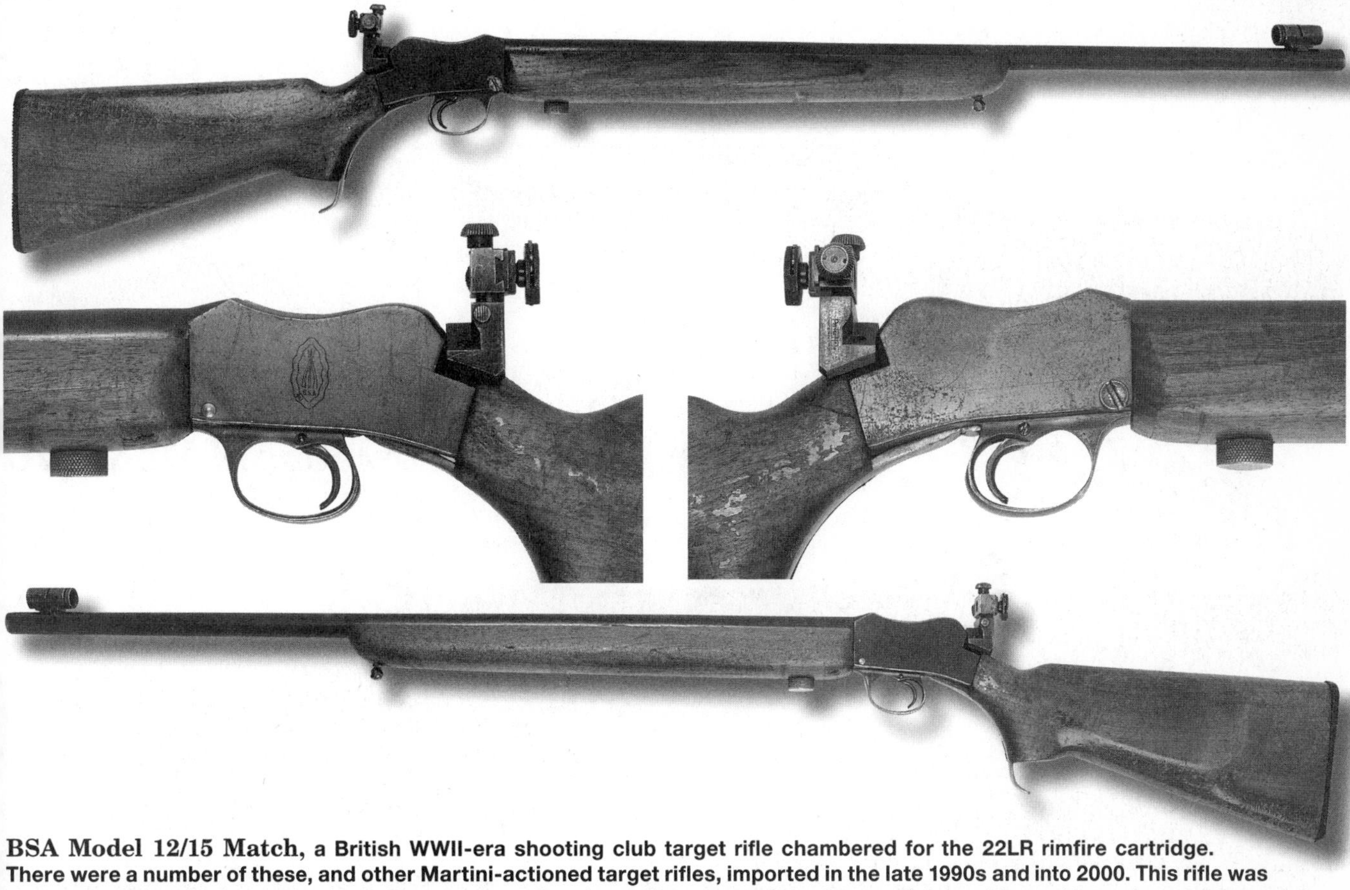

BSA Model 12/15 Match, a British WWII-era shooting club target rifle chambered for the 22LR rimfire cartridge. There were a number of these, and other Martini-actioned target rifles, imported in the late 1990s and into 2000. This rifle was obviously well used, but maintained. The stock retains about 60 percent of the factory finish, with an old repair – and a ragged hole *(likely from a sling swivel stud that took a bit too much stress)* – at the rear of the forearm. The barrel, receiver and trigger/lever assembly are worn but retain about 80 percent of the original bluing that is thinning in places and turning brown in others. There are no mechanical problems; the reliable Martini action cycles and extracts flawlessly and the trigger breaks cleanly and consistently. The bore is bright, with strong rifling. The Parker-Hale micrometer rear sight is interesting in that the base is drilled through, matching a hole in the receiver that is in alignment with the rifle's bore. Remove the breechblock assembly and the bore can be cleaned from the breech-end, with the sight base serving as the cleaning rod guide. NRA GOOD

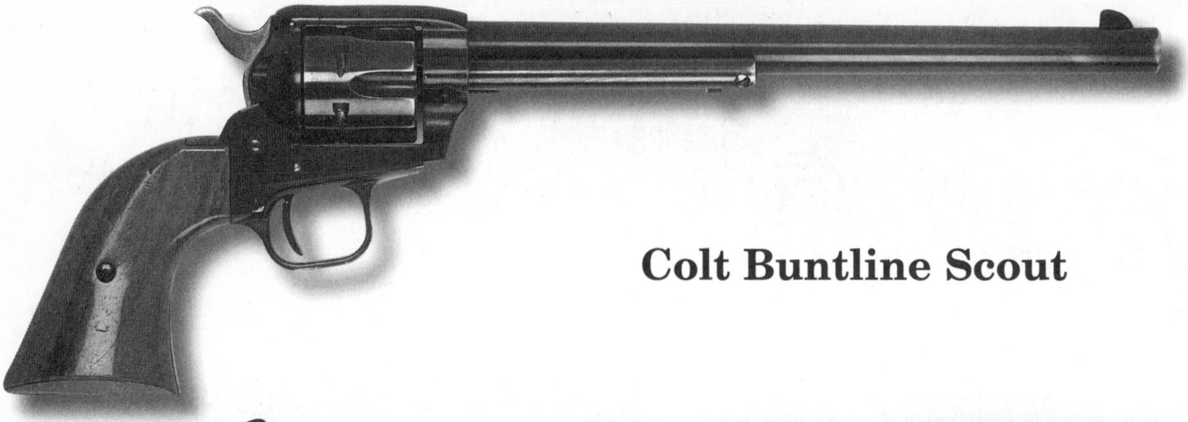

Colt Buntline Scout

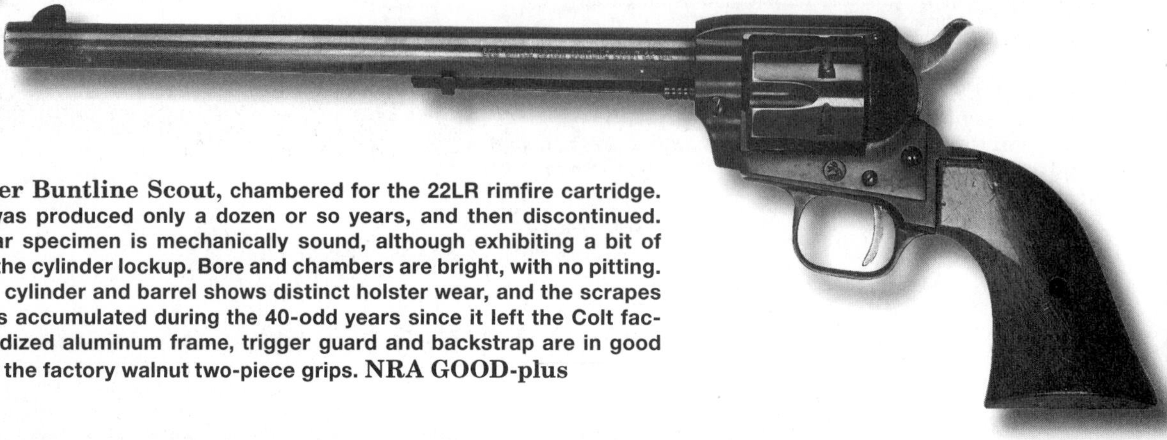

Colt Frontier Buntline Scout, chambered for the 22LR rimfire cartridge. This model was produced only a dozen or so years, and then discontinued. This particular specimen is mechanically sound, although exhibiting a bit of looseness in the cylinder lockup. Bore and chambers are bright, with no pitting. Bluing on the cylinder and barrel shows distinct holster wear, and the scrapes and scratches accumulated during the 40-odd years since it left the Colt factory. The anodized aluminum frame, trigger guard and backstrap are in good shape, as are the factory walnut two-piece grips. **NRA GOOD-plus**

S&W Highway Patrolman, Model 28

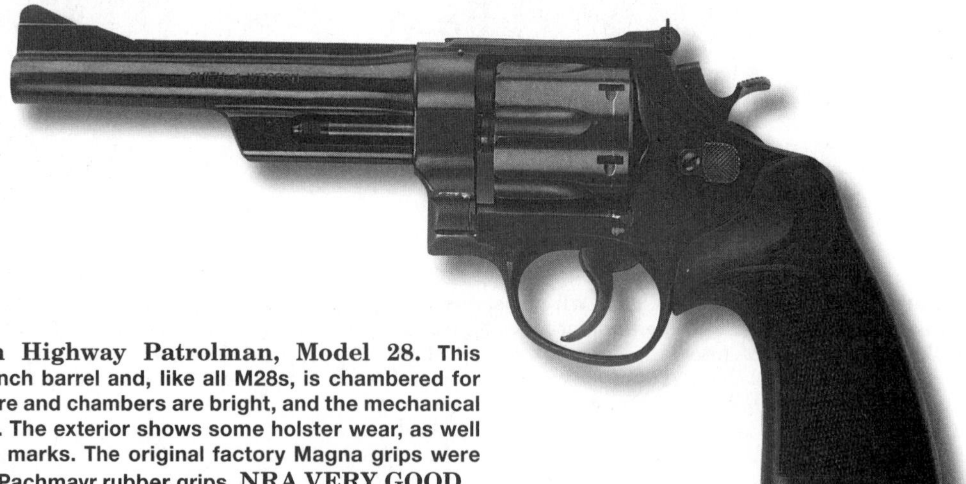

Smith & Wesson Highway Patrolman, Model 28. This revolver wears a 6-inch barrel and, like all M28s, is chambered for the 357 Magnum. Bore and chambers are bright, and the mechanical function is excellent. The exterior shows some holster wear, as well as a few other wear marks. The original factory Magna grips were replaced by a set of Pachmayr rubber grips. **NRA VERY GOOD**

Winchester Model 70 Deluxe

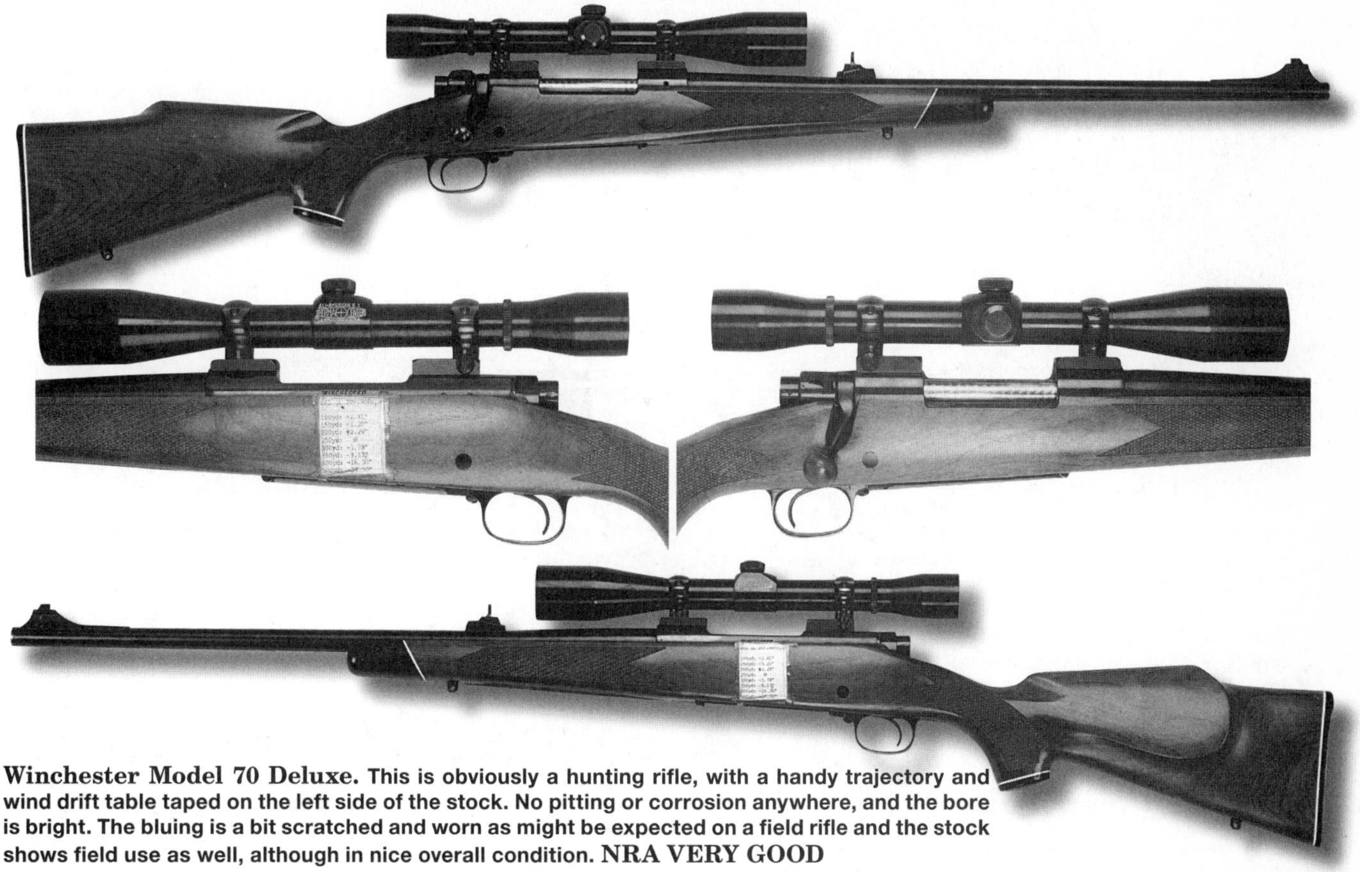

Winchester Model 70 Deluxe. This is obviously a hunting rifle, with a handy trajectory and wind drift table taped on the left side of the stock. No pitting or corrosion anywhere, and the bore is bright. The bluing is a bit scratched and worn as might be expected on a field rifle and the stock shows field use as well, although in nice overall condition. NRA VERY GOOD

High Standard Sentinel Mark IV

High Standard Sentinel Mark IV, 22WMR with a 2-inch barrel. There is external wear, and the common bolt drag ring around the cylinder. Excellent function. NRA VERY GOOD

Winchester Model 52A

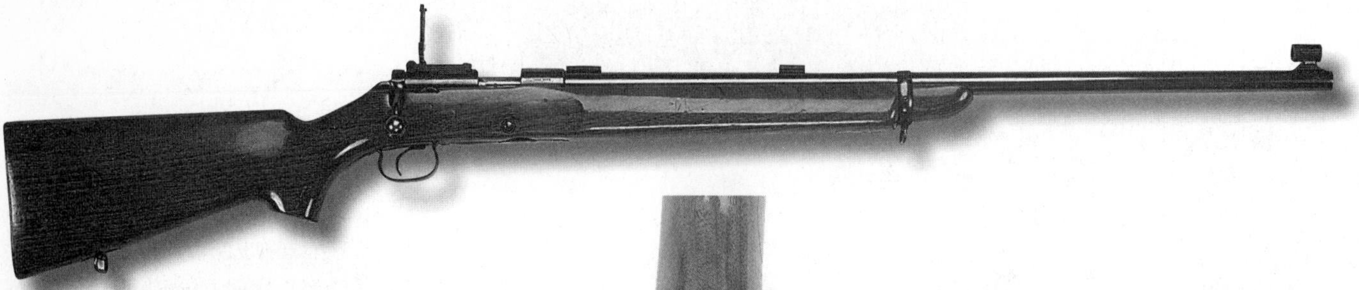

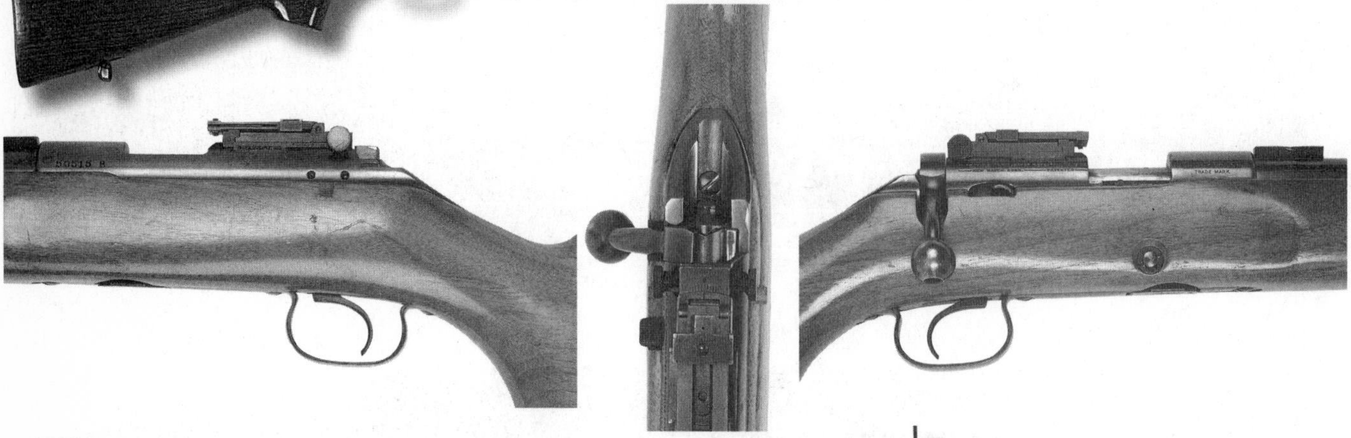

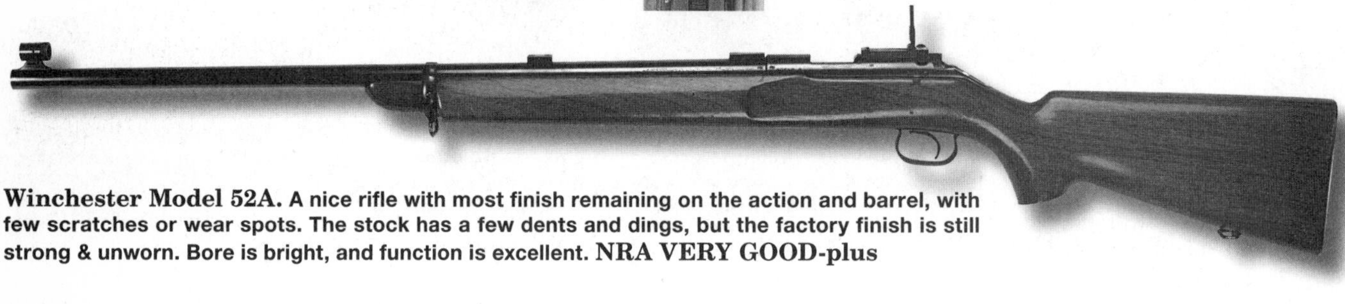

Winchester Model 52A. A nice rifle with most finish remaining on the action and barrel, with few scratches or wear spots. The stock has a few dents and dings, but the factory finish is still strong & unworn. Bore is bright, and function is excellent. **NRA VERY GOOD-plus**

Remington Model 14

Remington Model 14. This particular specimen, fitted with a Williams receiver sight, is chambered for the 30 Remington cartridge and exhibits the wear typical of a well-used but well-maintained hunting rifle. **NRA GOOD**

Remington Model 11A

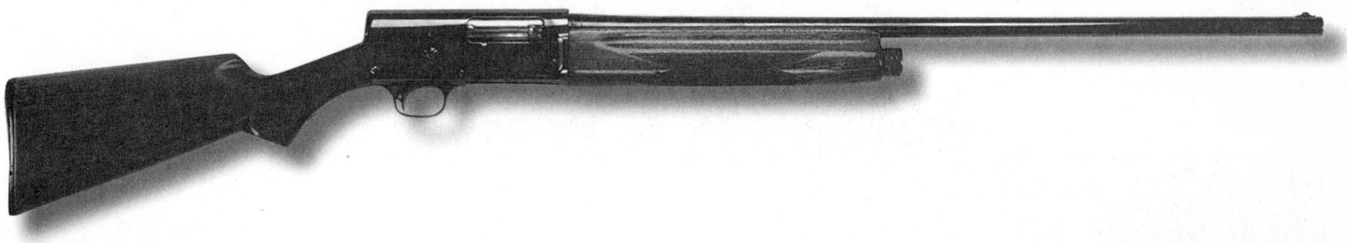

Remington Model 11A, in 20-gauge with a Modified choke. The gun has been buffed and reblued. The stock is refinished and shows an amateurish attempt to expand upon the factory wrist checkering. The front sight has been replaced with a white bead. Bore is bright and function is excellent. Not much collector value here, but a good find for a hunter. NRA GOOD

Sturm, Ruger Blackhawk New Model

Sturm, Ruger Blackhawk New Model, 45 Colt, with 7 1/2-inch barrel. The gun has been fired a fair amount, but is well-maintained. The grips are intact and retain the factory finish. The exterior shows light wear only, and the typical bolt drag ring on the cylinder. Excellent function. NRA VERY GOOD-plus

Savage Model 99C

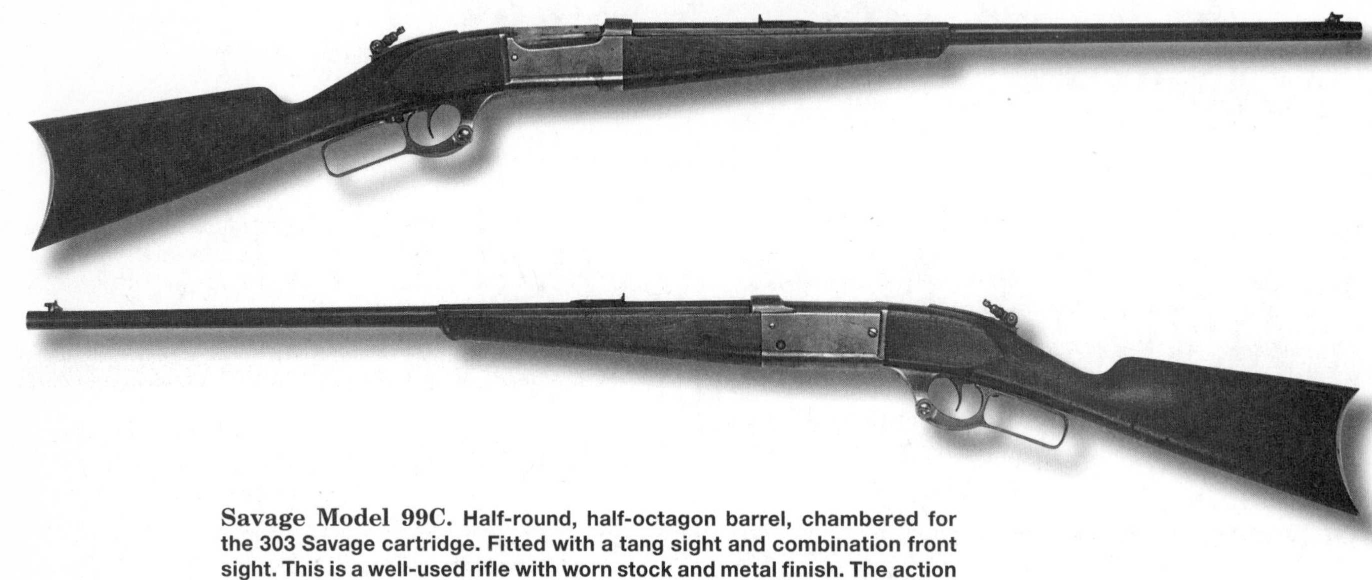

Savage Model 99C. Half-round, half-octagon barrel, chambered for the 303 Savage cartridge. Fitted with a tang sight and combination front sight. This is a well-used rifle with worn stock and metal finish. The action works smoothly and this rifle still has plenty of hunts in it. **NRA FAIR**

Lefever Nitro Special

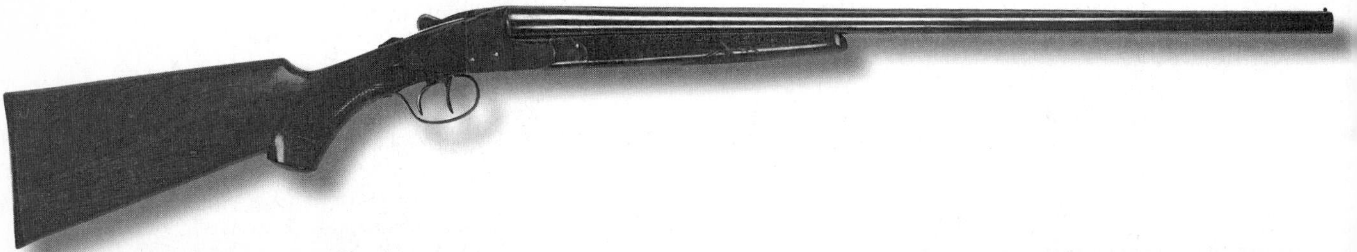

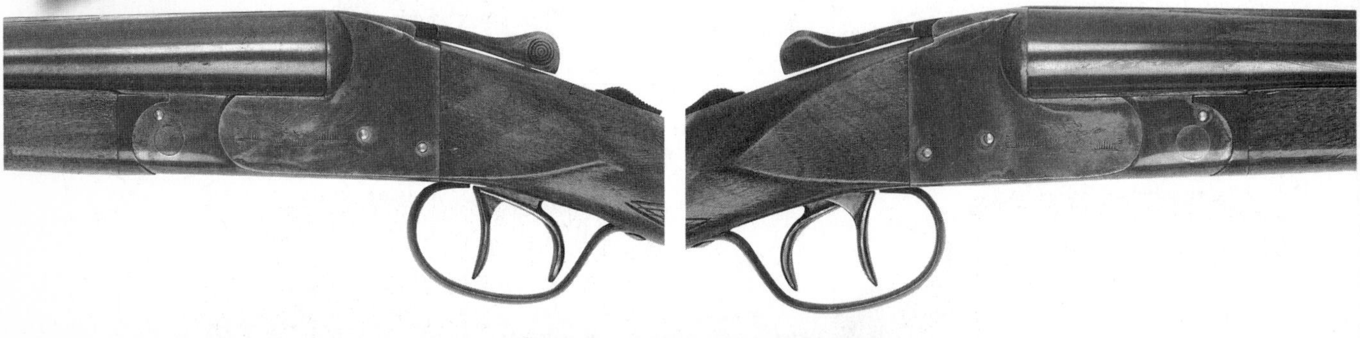

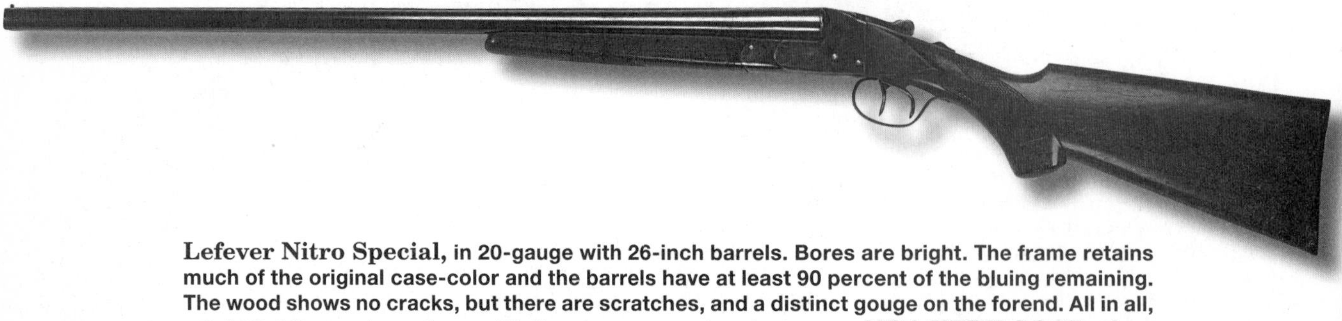

Lefever Nitro Special, in 20-gauge with 26-inch barrels. Bores are bright. The frame retains much of the original case-color and the barrels have at least 90 percent of the bluing remaining. The wood shows no cracks, but there are scratches, and a distinct gouge on the forend. All in all, a tight lightly-used specimen with the wear appropriate for its age. **NRA VERY GOOD-plus**

An Illustrated Guide To Condition

by Joseph Schroeder

To further clarify the standard classifications of "Excellent" through "Fair," we present the following photographs. Since "New" means just that—new, in the original box with all papers and accessories and perfect means the gun is new but the original box and/ or accessories may be missing, we do not show those classifications. All other classifications are subjective, and subject to argument!

Excellent

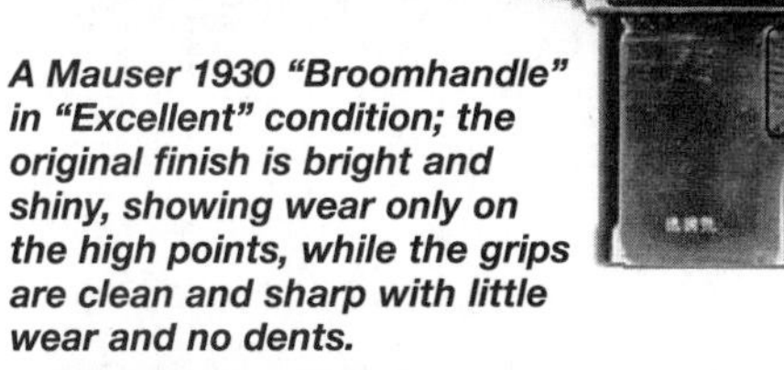

A Mauser 1930 "Broomhandle" in "Excellent" condition; the original finish is bright and shiny, showing wear only on the high points, while the grips are clean and sharp with little wear and no dents.

The left side of the "Excellent" Mauser 1930; note the tight fit of the magazine bottom. The Chinese characters translate to "Made In Germany" and add 5 to 10 percent to the value as compared to the same model without markings.

Very Good

A Mauser Model 1930, this one about "Very Good." Note the finish, though almost all there, has dull areas with some light rust "freckling," and shows more high point wear.

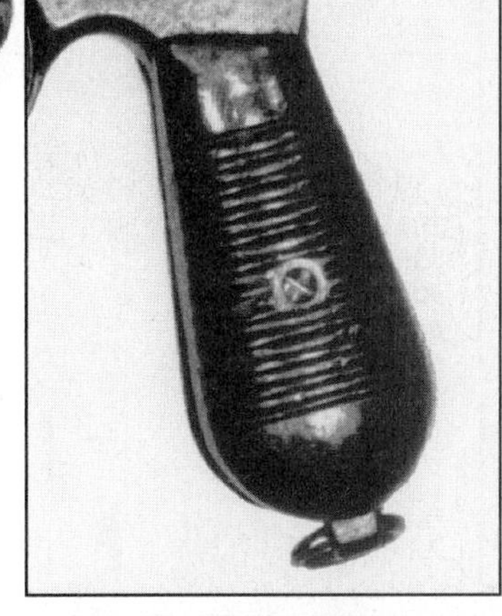

Though the grip grooves are still deep and sharp on this "Very Good" Model 1930, the wood does show the nicks and scratches that come from use.

Excellent

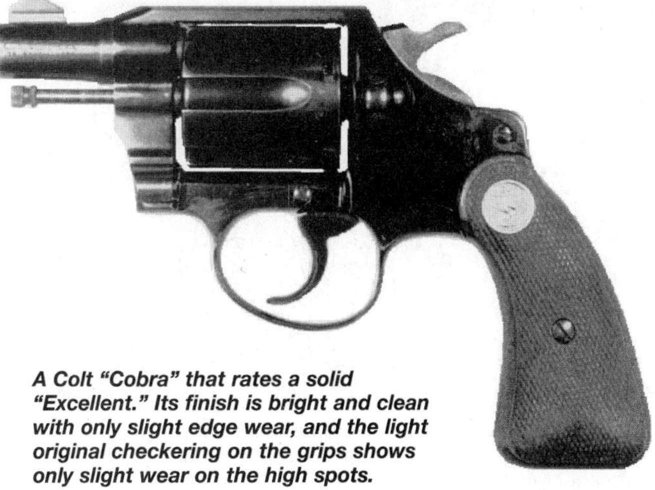

A Colt "Cobra" that rates a solid "Excellent." Its finish is bright and clean with only slight edge wear, and the light original checkering on the grips shows only slight wear on the high spots.

Very Good

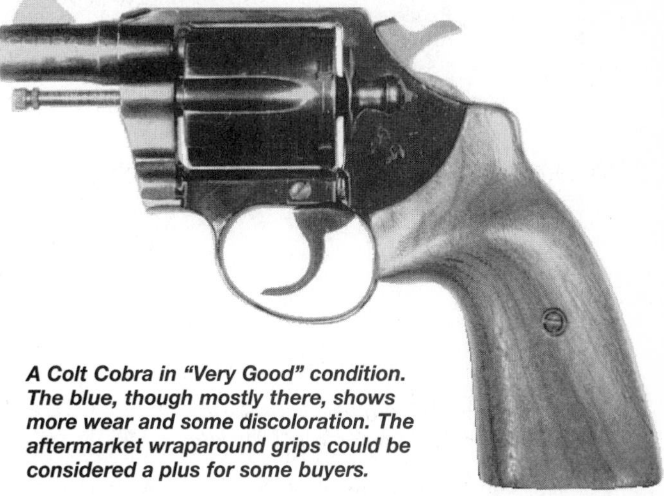

A Colt Cobra in "Very Good" condition. The blue, though mostly there, shows more wear and some discoloration. The aftermarket wraparound grips could be considered a plus for some buyers.

Import Markings

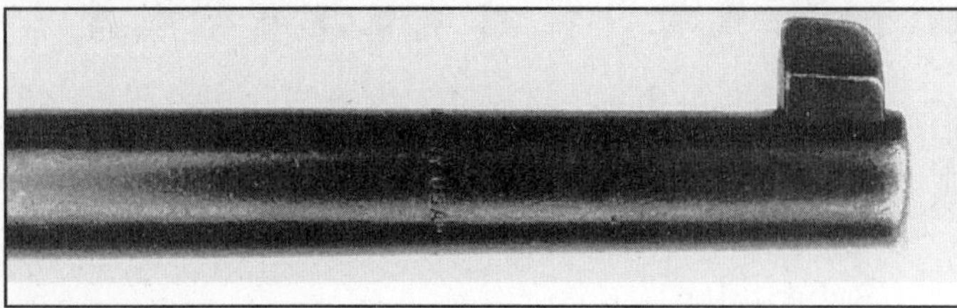

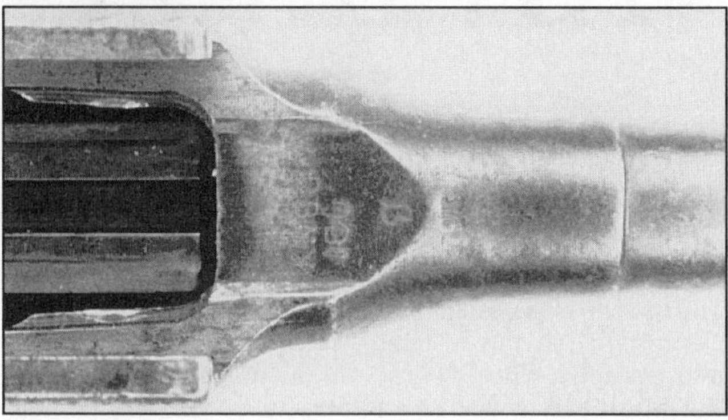

Two examples of the import markings now required on all firearms imported into the U.S. The OBI OBNY under the Mauser chamber (right) indicates the importer was Oyster Bay Industries in Oyster Bay, New York. Oyster Bay also marked some Mausers by rolling their marking around the barrel (above). Guns without import markings such as those brought back by GIs bring a premium from collectors.

Good

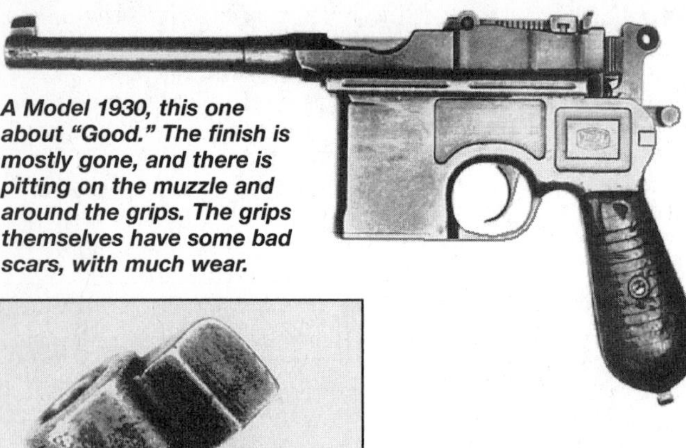

A Model 1930, this one about "Good." The finish is mostly gone, and there is pitting on the muzzle and around the grips. The grips themselves have some bad scars, with much wear.

The muzzle of the "Good" Mauser; in addition to the deep pitting, the muzzle crown is also worn almost flat.

Fair

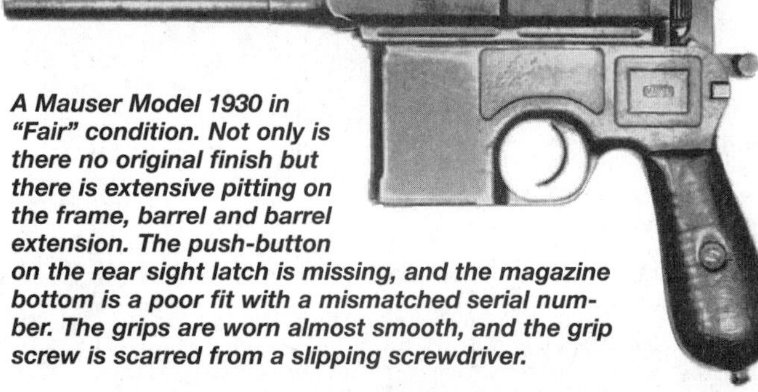

A Mauser Model 1930 in "Fair" condition. Not only is there no original finish but there is extensive pitting on the frame, barrel and barrel extension. The push-button on the rear sight latch is missing, and the magazine bottom is a poor fit with a mismatched serial number. The grips are worn almost smooth, and the grip screw is scarred from a slipping screwdriver.

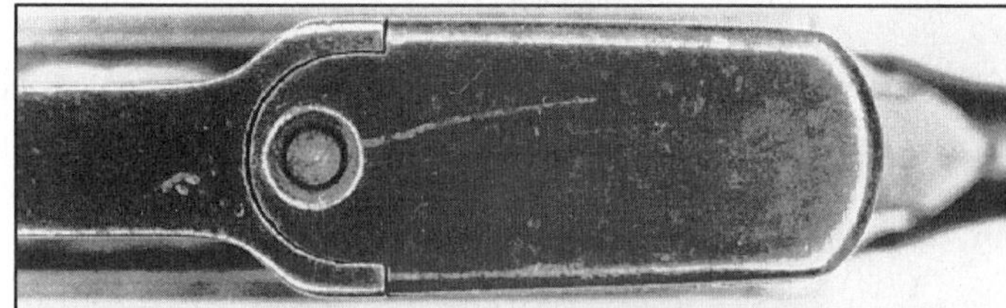

The underside of the "Fair" Mauser; the magazine bottom is a poor fit in the gun, showing an irregular gap between parts. The scratch is from careless use of a screwdriver during removal.

Good

A Colt Cobra that would rate a high "Good." There is a good deal of blue wear with some light rust freckling, and the frame has been drilled just above the hammer for a hammer shroud (missing). The grips are so worn that the original checkering is entirely gone.

The cylinder of the "Good" condition Colt Cobra. Note the fingerprint etched into the cylinder by perspiration and the pits on the adjacent chamber.

Firearms Restoration

by Peter Koppmann

What is firearms restoration – making old guns look new? That definition is close, but not completely accurate. Restoration of anything (cars, boats, paintings, furniture – even airplanes) is the careful re-construction of that particular item to as close to new condition as possible.

The most important factors in any type of restoration project are time, price, and the skill and resources of the restorer. The factor that surprises most people is the cost of a full, high-quality restoration project. High-quality restoration takes a great deal of skill and knowledge; the ability of the restorer to deliver the highest quality restoration possible should be the foremost concern.

Refinishing vs. Restoration

The terms **refinishing** and **restoration** are sometimes used interchangeably, although there is considerable difference between the two. **Refinishing** is just what the name implies, applying a new finish to an existing piece with little or no concern for the underlying surface or internal condition. Think of refinishing as what you do when you repaint a room; you are basically putting a new finish over the old. **Restoration** is refinishing taken to the highest level.

When restoring firearms, the gun must not only look good but it must be safe to shoot. Any mechanical problems should be corrected before any other work is started. If the mechanical problems cannot be fixed at a reasonable cost, this a good time to decide whether to proceed with the restoration. Once the mechanical issues have been addressed, work on the outside of the gun can begin.

The key to any restoration project is the surface preparation of either the wood or the metal – or both. One of the most overlooked details of modern firearms manufacturing is the fit and finish of the final product. The degree to which most early firearms were finished is one of the reasons they are so desirable. In a restoration project, however, the aspects that generally receive the most attention are the preparation of both the wood and metal surfaces.

Value of Restored Firearms

For whatever reason, firearms restoration has long been looked upon as an undesirable practice. The commonly-held view is that a restored gun is not worth as much as an untouched original gun. That view would be accurate only if you could find an original gun in "as-new condition." In most cases restoration of a firearm will improve the condition and value of the firearm – providing the restoration is done correctly.

Reasons for Restoration

Restoration offers the shooter the opportunity to own a firearm (often historical) that is as close to factory original as possible. Firearms have played an important role in shaping and protecting this country and certain models are important pieces of history that should be preserved.

In some instances, the costs involved in restoration greatly exceed the value of the finished gun. Remember, the value of the gun is what you would expect to pay for the same gun–if and when you could find it. In some cases the gun may have belonged to a family member—or hold some other sentimental value. A sentimental restoration can return a piece of family history to the current generation or fulfill a desire to own a firearm with particular significance.

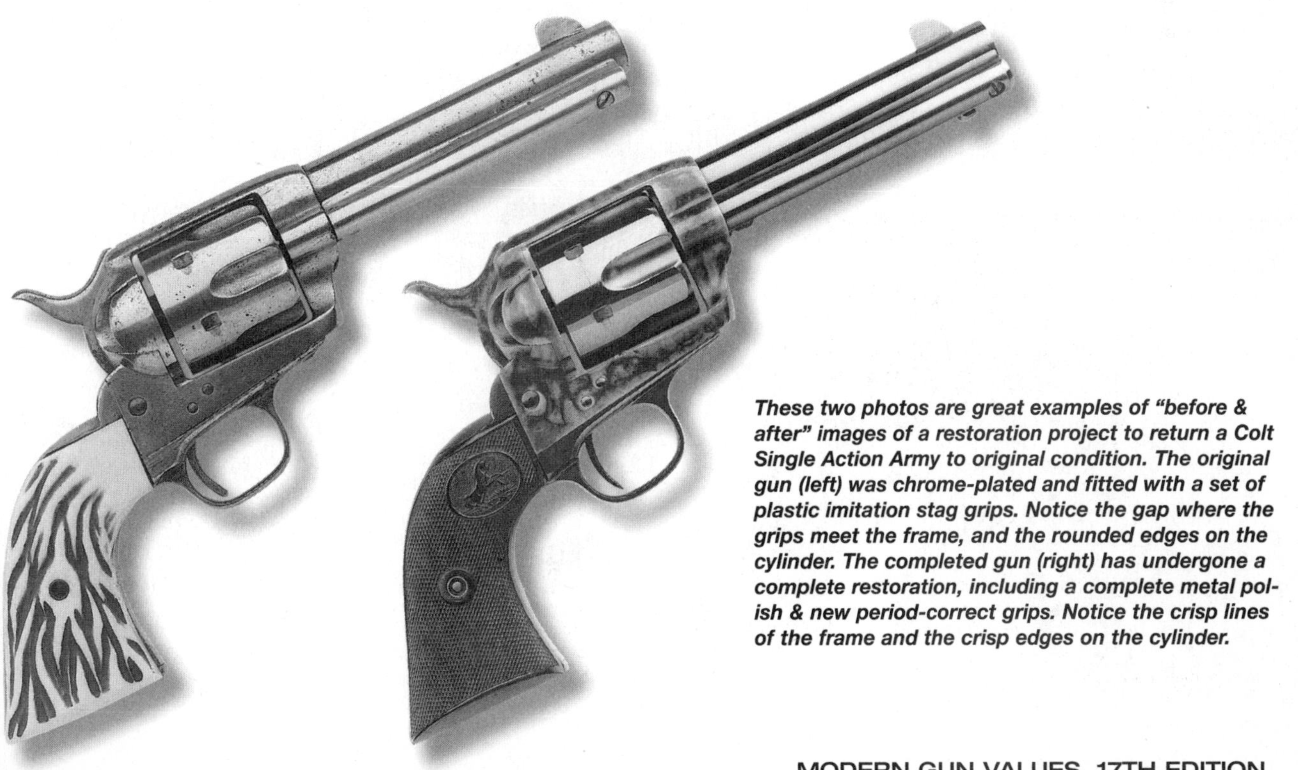

These two photos are great examples of "before & after" images of a restoration project to return a Colt Single Action Army to original condition. The original gun (left) was chrome-plated and fitted with a set of plastic imitation stag grips. Notice the gap where the grips meet the frame, and the rounded edges on the cylinder. The completed gun (right) has undergone a complete restoration, including a complete metal polish & new period-correct grips. Notice the crisp lines of the frame and the crisp edges on the cylinder.

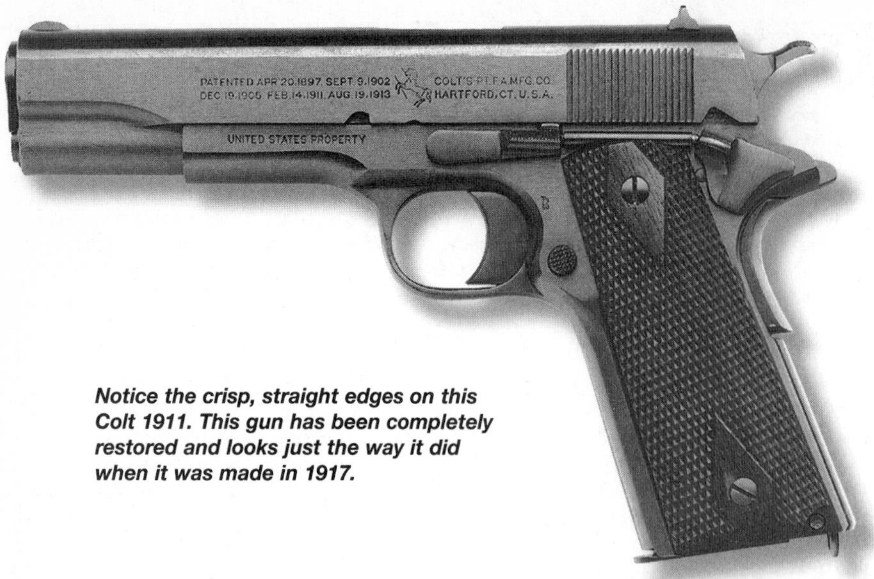

Notice the crisp, straight edges on this Colt 1911. This gun has been completely restored and looks just the way it did when it was made in 1917.

Metal Polishing

The degree and direction of polish on metal parts in a restoration is one of the things that differentiate a restored gun from a refinished gun. Remember, a **restoration** is trying to return that firearm to as close to original condition as possible. A **refinished** gun may receive only a minimal amount of metal polishing before the final finishes are applied. In contrast, some restorations may require as many as 40 or 50 hours of polish time to prepare the surface for final finishing. Metal polishing, if done correctly, will never be noticed; if done incorrectly, however, the deficiency will stick out like a sore thumb.

True metal polishing is a lost art. Most people think of polishing as machine-buffing the part until you can see your reflection. Polishing is not just about making the metal shiny. The order, direction and degree of the polish are just as important as (in most cases, more important than) getting the metal bright and shiny. One of the most critical areas in the polishing sequence is the restoration of the edges. The transition between flat and round surfaces should be sharp and crisp, with the correct direction and degree of polish. The early gunmakers were masters at keeping the edges sharp, crisp and straight.

Another area where the early gunmakers excelled was the polishing of large flat areas leaving few, if any, flaws in the surface. Remember, the surface has to be completely flat, with no ripples or flaws; it's not as easy as it may sound. The skill and talent required to correctly polish these areas cannot be understated.

Stock Work

The marriage of wood to metal is one of the most complex and sometimes frustrating aspects of gunmaking. A restoration may involve only the refinishing of the wood to return it to the correct color. It may also involve the repair of dents, scratches, cracks or splits in the wood. Some restorations may require the complete restocking of the gun, starting with a blank that must be cut and shaped to duplicate the original piece. The type of wood, direction of the grain and the color of the wood are just a few of the variables in constructing a stock from scratch.

Restocking is the last resort in the restoration of a firearm. If the original wood can be saved it can significantly reduce the cost of the project.

The new stock must be cut and shaped from a block of wood, then married to the action in a process known as inletting. Once the inletting is complete, shaping the stock – an art – to final dimensions can begin.

Once the stock has been shaped, sanded and finished, the process of checkering can begin. Checkering is the cutting of lines into the wood to form small diamonds so the shooter has a textured stock surface to grip. Checking comes in many shapes and styles, from basic to elaborate patterns with carving; in some cases ebony, brass, and gold – even ivory – may be inletted in and around the checkering. Checkering can add great beauty to the stock as well as being a truly functional part of the gun.

Metal Finishing

Metal finishing comes in many different variations. We are all familiar with the bluing on a gun. But did

Checkering patterns come in many forms. This Parker A1 Special is an example of a very elaborate checkering pattern that combines standard checkering with woodcarving. This type of work takes a keen eye for detail, and a very steady hand.

This Winchester 1873 features a color case-hardened receiver, one of the most beautiful of the old-time firearm finishes. Due to the varying composition of steel, no two guns ever have the same pattern.

you know that bluing comes in many different varieties and color shades and is specific to certain parts of the gun? For example, Winchester rifles used three different types of bluing on rifle and shotgun barrels throughout the years. The original gunmakers, to harden steel, used color case-hardening. Today we use its vivid colors and unique patterns on the frames of shotguns, rifles and handguns.

Without going into the specifics of each process, the biggest mistake do-it-yourself gun restorers make is using the wrong finish for a particular firearm. For example, one of the simplest methods of bluing is hot bluing, also referred to as salt bluing. Hot bluing is used by almost every modern gunmaker because it is very easy to do and requires only a small amount of specialized equipment. If you can read a thermometer, you can hot blue! The problem is that hot bluing was not used until the mid-1940s. One of the most common mistakes we see as professional gun restorers is the incorrect use of finishes on vintage firearms. That said, some guns were reblued before they became so highly collectible.

Do-It-Yourself vs. Professional Restoration

Most firearm owners do some form of gunsmithing at some point. One of the most important things to remember about working on your own firearm is to know your limitations and to be careful. The last thing you want to do is something detrimental to you or the firearm.

aIf you decide to restore your own firearm, pay attention to such details as wood-to-metal fit, direction and degree of the metal polish, barrel and frame markings (these may need to be re-cut or re-applied) and, of course, the correct final finishes. The restoration of a firearm can be a very satisfying and rewarding undertaking, whether you chose to do the work yourself or have it done by a professional. The reasons for restoring firearms vary greatly. Maybe you want to restore your father's old gun, or you just like the look and feel of a classic firearm. Whatever the reason, firearms restoration is a great way to preserve these important pieces of history for future generations. ★

Author Peter Koppmann is the shop manager at Turnbull Restorations, which specializes in the refurbishment of American firearms made from 1870 to 1940; to include Colt, Winchester, Marlin, Parker, Fox, L.C. Smith and Ithaca. Specializing in historically-correct metal finishes, including bone color case-hardening, charcoal bluing, rust bluing, nitre bluing and hot bluing, Turnbull Restoration also offers complete metal polishing services and has a complete wood department for restocking and repairs – all under one roof.

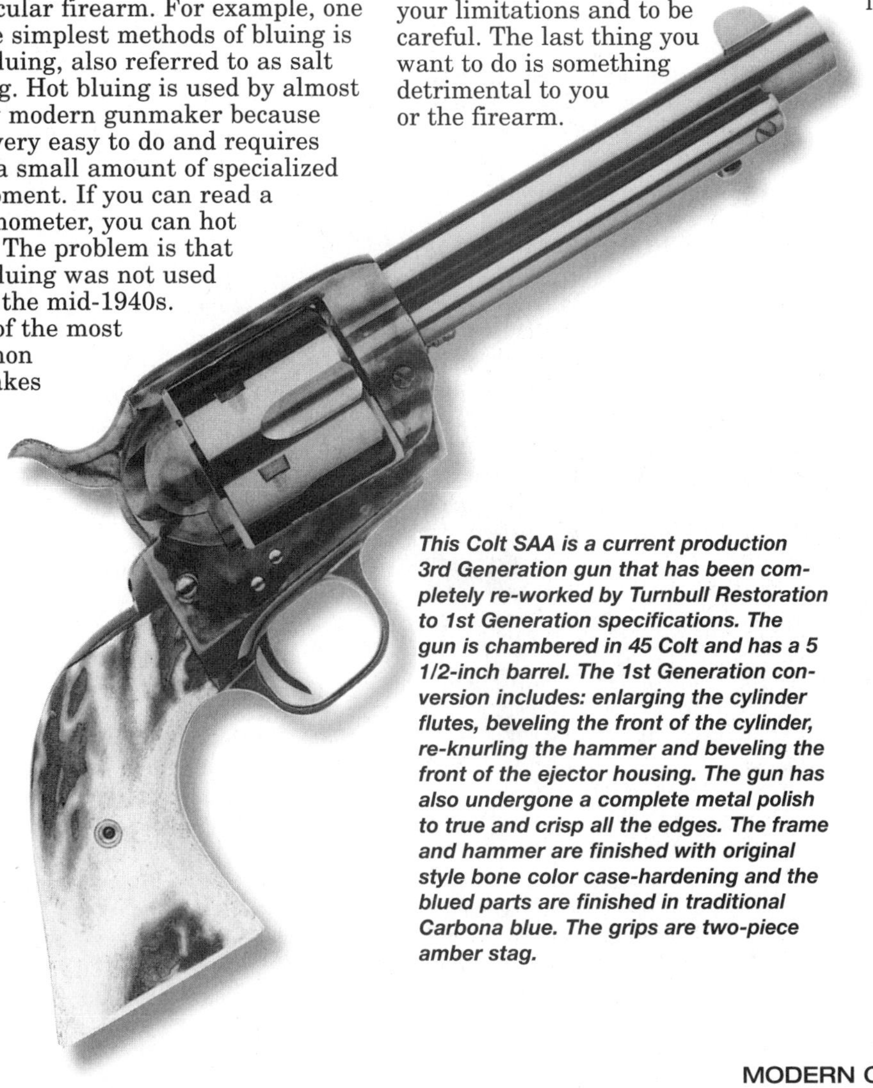

This Colt SAA is a current production 3rd Generation gun that has been completely re-worked by Turnbull Restoration to 1st Generation specifications. The gun is chambered in 45 Colt and has a 5 1/2-inch barrel. The 1st Generation conversion includes: enlarging the cylinder flutes, beveling the front of the cylinder, re-knurling the hammer and beveling the front of the ejector housing. The gun has also undergone a complete metal polish to true and crisp all the edges. The frame and hammer are finished with original style bone color case-hardening and the blued parts are finished in traditional Carbona blue. The grips are two-piece amber stag.

Better than Book:

Factors that Add to the Value of a Firearm

By Phillip Peterson

We all know that non-factory alterations can reduce the value of a collectible firearm. Aftermarket chokes, cutdown stocks, recoil pads and other "improvements" may have looked good in their day, but for the most part they leave today's collectors cold. (How many Winchester Model 12s have you seen with those hideous adjustable chokes hanging off them?)

Recently, however, it was suggested to me that there might also be items or features that could add value to a given firearm. So true.

There are many factors that can be used to arrive at a price for a gun. Some reduce the price, some add to it. In fact, almost any of the factors I just mentioned that can lower the price can add to it as well. It really depends on the intended use for the firearm. Certainly, if you repair a broken gun to make it usable again, that will add to the value of that gun. It might hurt the value in the eyes of a collector or investor but not the hunter who wants a functional tool to use in the field. The collector probably would not have wanted that particular firearm anyway. If it was in need of repair it likely was not in good enough condition to appeal to discriminating collectors or investors. Thus it still comes down to the seller and potential buyer agreeing on a price.

Here, the, are just a few of the factors that can add to the value of a firearm:

Scopes & Sights

Many add-on accessories and customizations found on firearms are there to make aiming the piece easier and increase the chance of hitting the target. After all, that is the ultimate use for any firearm. So, the holes that are drilled in the receiver of, say, a Winchester Model 75 bolt action .22 to allow the mounting of a scope might not hurt its value at all. In fact, if a hunter wants that model with a scope he will likely be more interested in it. Yes, it is still reduced in value to a collector, but the hunter's cash is just as spendable. Of course, if a "gunsmith" drilled seven off-center holes in the receiver before he got four to match the mounts he had, the gun just looks bad. You can take a good thing too far.

When a rifle or shotgun is offered with a scope already installed, the value of the scope should be included in the overall value of the gun. How much are used scopes worth? I figure current production optics at about one third to one half of retail price when attached to a gun. That way, if the buyer does not want the particular scope they can negotiate a price reduction with the scope removed. Or they can sell it themselves and buy the scope that suits their needs. Older, out of production scopes have become collectibles in their own right. The long target scopes as made by Unertl, Fecker, Winchester and others can be worth hundreds of dollars. Some firearms manufacturers, such as Marlin and Mossberg, actually used to make their own scopes or had scopes made for them that had their name on it.

Many times I have bought a used Stevens or Mossberg .22 rifle with an old scope on it that is worth more than the gun. I suggest consulting the book *Old Rifle Scopes* by Nick Stroebel when attempting to price older optics. Always check the scope for damage if it is adding to the price of the gun. Make sure the optics are clear, glass lenses have no chips or scratches, crosshairs are intact, and adjusting knobs are working. Getting a broken scope fixed is possible but expensive. Original replacement parts are hard to come by.

In addition to scopes, metallic sights of several configurations will be found. The most popular of these is the tang sight. This is a peep sight that mounts on the tang or back of the receiver of many guns. These were frequently found on Winchester, Sharps, Remington, and other quality sporting rifles. The tang sights made by a gun manufacturer are especially desirable. Winchester-made sights are among the most valuable as collectibles. Other tang sight makers include Marble and Lyman.

Besides tang sights, there are peep sights that mount on the side of a firearm. These were offered by companies like Mossberg, Redfield, Williams, and Lyman. When a firearm is offered that has an older metallic sight, I refer the reader to the book *Old Gunsights*, also by Nick Stroebel. This fine book lists the metallic sights by maker and model number.

Some of the old aftermarket tang or peep sights required the gun to be drilled and tapped to install the sight. This sort of modification usually reduces the price of a firearm. On the other hand, a Winchester Model 1886 that has had its receiver drilled to install a newer Marbles sight might be worth less to some buyers, but if a period, i.e., vintage, sight is present it could add to the value. Depends on the buyer.

All Scratched Up

Fine engraving on a firearm definitely adds to its value. The amount of coverage can range from a fine highlight on the edges all the way to fully engraved hunting scenes complete with gold inlay. If the work is done by a known engraver, pricing the firearm becomes more akin to pricing a piece of art than a useful tool. As with a fine painting or sculpture, when a known engraver dies, examples of his or her work will skyrocket in price. Some gun makers offered engraving as a special order option on their products. The factory engraved Colts and Winchesters done in the late 1800s by artists such as Nimschke and Ulrich will bring several times their book value. Indeed, many books are devoted solely to this subject.

Engraving done by an amateur or unknown craftsman will be judged solely on its attractiveness on a particular firearm. If you are contemplating the purchase of an engraved firearm, look closely at the work. Some engraving I have seen was cut too deep and really did not look pleasing. Or there were errors in the pattern that the engraver tried to blend in. After all, an apprentice engraver had to perfect his craft somewhere. The "practice" pieces frequently were sold to buyers who did not spot the defects.

Sometimes the style of engraving may make a gun more (or less) attractive to a given buyer. For example, Germanic-style engraving, with its deep-cut oak-leaf patterns and dramatic portraiture, may turn off some buyers but attract others.

Got Wood?

Walnut was the primary type of wood used to make factory gunstocks in America through the WW II era. The massive production of rifles for military use reduced the stands of available walnut trees and set the industry on a quest to find acceptable substitutes that cost less. In the 1950s, many of the less expensive firearms began being equipped with birch, ash or particle wood stocks. When a model that was once offered with a walnut stock is then sold with a cheaper kind of wood, the older walnut stocked models can bring a higher price. A good example of this is the Ruger 10-22 semi automatic rifle. When introduced in 1964, it sported a walnut stock. In the early 1980s a birch stock replaced the walnut. So a 10-22 with a walnut stock can be worth as much as $75 more than a recent birch stocked rifle.

The grain structure or pattern in nice walnut stocks can add a lot to the price of a long gun. When walnut stock blanks are sold to gun makers there is a grading system based on the attractiveness of the wood. They use terms like AAA or AA Fancy down to field or utility grade. Very desirable is a striped pattern in the buttstock. This can look like the stripes on a tiger or it might be a pattern of wavy lines of coloration. The finest grade AAA walnut stock blanks can be priced at over $1000 just for an unshaped wood blank. Imagine how much that finished stock would add to the value of a pre 1964 Winchester Model 70. It could quickly make that $750 rifle in to a $4500 rifle.

I have seen many mid-grade stocks on field-grade shotguns and rifles. Mid-grade walnut might have some tiger stripe pattern near the butt end but standard grain in the rest. These are fairly common so they don't attract the high rollers who want the AAA fancy wood. There is no set way to calculate the additional value in stock appearance. It is a very subjective thing, attractiveness of a piece of wood. But it can add to the price of a gun for someone who likes it.

Any discussion of stock materials must also consider synthetics. Some synthetics can add significantly to the value of a gun. A Remington Nylon 66 .22 rifle with Seneca Green stock can bring twice as much as an otherwise identical model in Mohawk Brown.

Get a Grip

Grip materials can also add to the value of a handgun. A S&W First Model .32 Hand Ejector with factory pearl grips can bring 50 percent more than an otherwise identical gun with hard rubber grips. In fact, in some cases factory pearls are worth more than the gun itself! None-factory aftermarket grips, no matter how nice, do not generally add to the value of a gun. Quite the contrary.

Previous Ownership

Previous ownership of a gun can also add significantly to its value. One of John Wayne's Great Western revolvers, for example, can bring many times as much as a similar model owned by Joe Blow. But such enhanced value depends on the celebrity status of the previous owner. A Colt SAA owned by Mel Torme might not be particularly attractive to a younger buyer ("Mel *Who*?").

Note that previous ownership of a gun always depends on provenance, i.e., the paper trail that proves such ownership. Without provenance, claims of previous ownership are merely talk, and worth about just as much.

Potential Historical Association

Sometimes a gun is worth more merely because it was produced during a historically-relevant era. A Colt SAA whose serial number places it in the range of those used by the U.S. Army at the Battle of Little Big Horn, for example, is automatically more valuable than one outside that range. It doesn't matter if it can't be proven that the gun in question was carried during the battle–although that would be nice. The mere fact that it *might* have been significantly adds to its value.

Wrapping It Up

Another item that will add to the price of an older gun is the original box and paperwork that came with a gun when sold new. On vintage Colts or Smith & Wessons a box and papers could almost double the price of the gun. Of course, the Commemorative guns as made by Colt and Winchester in the 1960s and 70s have to be unfired and have their boxes and literature to be worth full book price. Even utility grade firearms sold as recently as five or 10 years ago can be enhanced by having the box with them.

Finally, there are any number of add-on accessories that might come with a used gun that can add to the value for a prospective buyer: Slings, holsters, extra magazines, boxes of ammunition or brass, scope covers, bi-pods, cases, or any other accessory that was purchased and installed by the owner. All of these cost money. I frequently buy guns, then the owner brings in another $50 or 100 worth of stuff and says "here, these were with that gun." Every little bit helps.

When acquiring or selling firearms, it pays to remember that not everyone wants a museum-quality collectible. Some want hunting guns, some want shooters. Some want guns from a specific period in history. Any factor that caters to any of these interests can add to the value of a gun – sometimes a little, sometimes a lot. ★

GUNDEX®

A listing of all MODERN GUN VALUES, 17TH EDITION firearms by type and manufacturer in numeric/alpha order.
HANDGUNS, pg.32; RIFLES, pg. 47; SHOTGUNS, pg. 65

HANDGUNS

A.A. ARMS
A.A. ARMS AP9 .84
A.A. ARMS AP9 TARGET .84

ACCU-TEK
ACCU-TEK MODEL AT-9SS .84
ACCU-TEK MODEL AT-25SS .84
ACCU-TEK MODEL AT-25AL .84
ACCU-TEK MODEL AT-25SSB .84
ACCU-TEK MODEL AT-32SS .84
ACCU-TEK MODEL AT-32SSB .84
ACCU-TEK MODEL AT-40SS .84
ACCU-TEK MODEL AT-45SS .84
ACCU-TEK MODEL AT-380SS/SSB .84
ACCU-TEK MODEL AT-380 LADY .84
ACCU-TEK BL-9 AUTO PISTOL .84
ACCU-TEK BL-380 .84
ACCU-TEK MODEL CP-9SSAUTO PISTOL .84
ACCU-TEK CP-40SS AUTO PISTOL .84
ACCU-TEK CP-45SS AUTO PISTOL .84
ACCU-TEK MODEL HC-380SS .85

ACTION ARMS
ACTION ARMS AT-84 .85
ACTION ARMS AT-84P .85
ACTION ARMS AT-88S .85
ACTION ARMS AT-88H .85
ACTION ARMS AT-88P .85
ACTION ARMS UZI PISTOL .85

ADVANTAGE ARMS
ADVANTAGE ARMS MODEL 442 .85

AGNER
AGNER MODEL 80 .85

AIR MATCH
AIR MATCH 500 .85

A.J. ORDNANCE
A.J. ORDNANCE THOMAS 45 .85

AKDAL
AKDAL GHOST TR SERIES .85

ALAMO
ALAMO RANGER .85

ALKARTASUNA
ALKARTASUNA RUBY .85

ALCHEMY ARMS
ALCHEMY ARMS SPECTRE STANDARD ISSUE .85
ALCHEMY ARMS SPECTRE SERVICE GRADE (SG & SGC) .85
ALCHEMY ARMS SPECTRE TITANIUM EDITION .85

ALLEN
ALLEN 1875 ARMY OUTLAW .86
ALLEN BUCKHORN .86
ALLEN BUCKHORN BUNTLINE MODEL .86
ALLEN BUCKHORN TARGET MODEL .86
ALLEN CATTLEMAN .86
ALLEN CATTLEMAN BUNTLINE MODEL .86
ALLEN CATTLEMAN SHERIFF'S MODEL .86
ALLEN CATTLEMAN TARGET MODEL .86
ALLEN 1871 ROLLING BLOCK TARGET PISTOL .86

AMERICAN ARMS
AMERICAN ARMS BUCKHORN .86
AMERICAN ARMS CX-22 .86
AMERICAN ARMS CXC-22 .86
AMERICAN ARMS EP-380 .86
AMERICAN ARMS ESCORT .86
AMERICAN ARMS MATEBA AUTO/REVOLVER .86
AMERICAN ARMS MODEL P-98 .87
AMERICAN ARMS PK-22 .87
AMERICAN ARMS PX-22 .87
AMERICAN ARMS PX-25 .87
AMERICAN ARMS REGULATOR .87
AMERICAN ARMS REGULATOR DELUXE .87
AMERICAN ARMS BISLEY SINGLE-ACTION REVOLVER .87
AMERICAN ARMS SPECTRE .87
AMERICAN ARMS TT-9MM TOKAREV .87
AMERICAN ARMS ZC-380 .87

AMERICAN DERRINGER
AMERICAN DERRINGER COP 357 .87
AMERICAN DERRINGER COP MINI .87
AMERICAN DERRINGER DA 38 .87
AMERICAN DERRINGER STANDARD DERRINGER .87
AMERICAN DERRINGER LADY DERRINGER .88
AMERICAN DERRINGER MODEL 1 .88
AMERICAN DERRINGER MODEL 1 TEXAS COMMEMORATIVE .88
AMERICAN DERRINGER MODEL 3 .88
AMERICAN DERRINGER MODEL 4 .88
AMERICAN DERRINGER MODEL 4 ALASKAN SURVIVAL MODEL .88
AMERICAN DERRINGER MODEL 6 .88
AMERICAN DERRINGER MODEL 7 ULTRA LIGHTWEIGHT .88
AMERICAN DERRINGER MODEL 10 LIGHTWEIGHT .88
AMERICAN DERRINGER MODEL 11 .88
AMERICAN DERRINGER SEMMERLING LM-4 .88

AMERICAN FIREARMS
AMERICAN FIREARMS 25 .88
AMERICAN FIREARMS 380 .89
AMERICAN FIREARMS DERRINGER .89

AMERICAN FRONTIER
AMERICAN FRONTIER 1851 NAVY CONVERSION .89
AMERICAN FRONTIER 1851 NAVY RICHARDS & MASON CONVERSION .89
AMERICAN FRONTIER REMINGTON NEW ARMY CAVALRY .89
AMERICAN FRONTIER RICHARDS 1860 ARMY .89
AMERICAN FRONTIER 1871-1872 POCKET MODEL REVOLVER .89
AMERICAN FRONTIER REMINGTON NEW MODEL REVOLVER .89
AMERICAN FRONTIER POCKET RICHARDS & MASON NAVY .89
AMERICAN FRONTIER 1871-1872 OPEN-TOP REVOLVERS .89

AMT AUTOMAG
AMT AUTOMAG II .89
AMT AUTOMAG III .89
AMT AUTOMAG IV .90
AMT AUTOMAG V .90
AMT BACKUP .90
AMT BACKUP II .90
AMT BACKUP DOUBLE-ACTION-ONLY .90
AMT BULL'S-EYE TARGET .90
AMT BULL'S-EYE TARGET REGULATION .90
AMT COMBAT GOVERNMENT .90
AMT HARDBALLER .90
AMT HARDBALLER LONG SLIDE .90
AMT JAVELINA .90
AMT LIGHTNING .90
AMT ON DUTY .90
AMT SKIPPER .91
AMT SKIPPER COMBAT .91

ANSCHUTZ
ANSCHUTZ EXEMPLAR .91
ANSCHUTZ MODEL 64P SPORT/TARGET .91
ANSCHUTZ MODEL 17 LP .91

ARCUS-94
ARCUS-94 AUTO PISTOL .91
ARCUS-94C COMPACT AUTO PISTOL .91

ARGENTINE
ARGENTINE FM HI-POWER 9MM .91
ARGENTINE FM HI-POWER DETECTIVE MODEL .91

ARMALITE
ARMALITE AR-24 PISTOL .91
ARMALITE AR-24 TACTICAL CUSTOM .91

ARMINEX
ARMINEX TRI-FIRE .91
ARMINEX TRI-FIRE TARGET MODEL .91

ARMINIUS
ARMINIUS MODEL 3 .91
ARMINIUS MODEL 8 .91
ARMINIUS MODEL 9 .91
ARMINIUS MODEL 9A .91
ARMINIUS MODEL 10 .91
ARMINIUS MODEL TP1 .92
ARMINIUS MODEL TP2 .92

ARMSCOR
ARMSCOR MODEL 38 .92
ARMSCOR MODEL 200P .92
ARMSCOR MODEL 200SE .92
ARMSCOR MODEL 200TC .92
ARMSCOR MODEL 202 .92
ARMSCOR MODEL 206 .92
ARMSCOR MODEL 210 .92
ARMSCOR MAP1 FS .92
ARMSCOR MAPP1 FS .92
ARMSCOR/ROCK ISLAND ARMORY MAP1 & MAPP1 PISTOLS .92
ARMSCOR/ROCK ISLAND ARMORY XT22 PISTOL .92

ARM TECH
ARM TECH DERRINGER .92

ASTRA
ASTRA A-70 .92
ASTRA A-75 DECOCKER .92
ASTRA A-80 .93
ASTRA A-90 .93
ASTRA A-100 .93
ASTRA CADIX .93
ASTRA CONSTABLE .93
ASTRA A-60 CONSTABLE .93
ASTRA CONSTABLE STAINLESS .93

ASTRA CONSTABLE SPORT 93
ASTRA CUB (2000). 93
ASTRA CAMPER (2000) 93
ASTRA MODEL 41 93
ASTRA MODEL 44 93
ASTRA MODEL 45 93
ASTRA MODEL 200 FIRECAT 93
ASTRA MODEL 300 93
ASTRA MODEL 357 94
ASTRA MODEL 400 94
ASTRA MODEL 600 94
ASTRA MODEL 800 CONDOR. 94
ASTRA MODEL 900 94
ASTRA MODEL 1911 25 94
ASTRA MODEL 1911 32 94
ASTRA MODEL 1915/1916 94
ASTRA MODEL 3000 94
ASTRA MODEL 4000 FALCON 94

AUTAUGA

AUTAUGA MK II 94

AUTO MAG

AUTO MAG. 94

AUTO-ORDNANCE

AUTO-ORDNANCE MODEL 1911C. 94
AUTO-ORDNANCE MODEL 1911CAF 94
AUTO-ORDNANCE 1911A1. 94
AUTO-ORDNANCE 1911A1 40 S&W 95
AUTO-ORDNANCE 1911A1 COMPETITION MODEL. 95
AUTO-ORDNANCE 1911A1 CUSTOM HIGH POLISH 95
AUTO-ORDNANCE 1911A1 GENERAL MODEL. 95
AUTO-ORDNANCE ZG-51 PIT BULL 95
AUTO-ORDNANCE THOMPSON CUSTOM 1911 95

AWA

AWA MATEBA AUTO REVOLVER. 95

BAER

BAER 1911 BULLSEYE WADCUTTER. 95
BAER 1911 CONCEPT SERIES I-X PISTOLS 95
BAER 1911 CUSTOM CARRY 95
BAER 1911 NATIONAL MATCH HARDBALL 95
BAER 1911 PREMIER II 96
BAER 1911 PROWLER III. 96
BAER 1911 TARGET MASTER 96
BAER 1911 ULTIMATE MASTER COMBAT 96
BAER 1911 ULTIMATE MASTER "STEEL SPECIAL" 96
BAER MODEL 1911 TWENTY-FIFTH ANNIVERSARY 96
BAER ULTIMATE RECO 96

BAFORD ARMS

BAFORD ARMS THUNDER DERRINGER 96

BAIKAL

BAIKAL IZH-35M 96
BAIKAL IJ-70 96
BAIKAL IJ-70HC. 97
BAIKAL IJ-70HC, 380 ACP 97

BAUER

BAUER 25 97
BAUER 25 ACP BICENTENNIAL MODEL 97
BAUER RABBIT DERRINGER 97

BAYARD

BAYARD MODEL 1908 POCKET AUTOMATIC 97
BAYARD MODEL 1923 POCKET AUTOMATIC (LARGE MODEL) 97
BAYARD MODEL 1923 POCKET AUTOMATIC (SMALL MODEL) 97
BAYARD MODEL 1930 POCKET AUTOMATIC. 97

BEEMAN

BEEMAN P-08 97
BEEMAN P-08 MINI 97
BEEMAN SP DELUXE 97
BEEMAN SP STANDARD. 97
BEEMAN SP/SPX. 97
BEEMAN MODEL SPX DELUXE 97

BEHOLLA

BEHOLLA POCKET AUTO. 97

BENELLI

BENELLI B76 97
BENELLI B-76S TARGET 98
BENELLI MODEL B-77. 98
BENELLI MODEL B-80. 98
BENELLI MODEL B-80S TARGET 98
BENELLI MP90S MATCH. 98
BENELLI MP95E MATCH. 98

BERETTA

BERETTA 85FS CHEETAH 98
BERETTA 9000S. 98
BERETTA MODEL 20 98
BERETTA MODEL 21A BOBCAT 98
BERETTA LADY BERETTA 98
BERETTA MODEL 70 98
BERETTA MODEL 70S. 98
BERETTA MODEL 70T 98
BERETTA MODEL 71 98
BERETTA MODEL 71 JAGUAR 98
BERETTA MODEL 72 JAGUAR 99
BERETTA MODEL 76 99
BERETTA MODEL 81 99
BERETTA MODEL 82 99
BERETTA MODEL 84 CHEETAH 99
BERETTA MODEL 84F 99
BERETTA MODEL 85 CHEETAH. 99
BERETTA MODEL 85F 99
BERETTA MODEL 86 CHEETAH 99
BERETTA MODEL 87 CHEETAH 99
BERETTA MODEL 87 TARGET. 99
BERETTA MODEL 89 99
BERETTA MODEL 89 GOLD STANDARD PISTOL 99
BERETTA MODEL 90 99
BERETTA 90-TWO 99
BERETTA MODEL 92 100
BERETTA MODEL 92S (SECOND ISSUE). 100
BERETTA MODEL 92SB-P (THIRD ISSUE). 100
BERETTA MODEL 92SB-P COMPACT 100
BERETTA MODEL 92D. 100
BERETTA MODEL 92FS. 100
BERETTA M9 SPECIAL EDITION PISTOL 100
BERETTA MODEL 92F COMPACT 100
BERETTA MODEL 92F STAINLESS PISTOL. 100
BERETTA MODEL 92FCM 100
BERETTA MODEL 92FS CENTURION 100
BERETTA MODEL 92FS STAINLESS 100
BERETTA MODEL 92F-EL 100
BERETTA 92 STEEL-I. 100
BERETTA M9A1 100
BERETTA MODEL 96 101
BERETTA MODEL 96 BRIGADIER 101
BERETTA MODEL 96 CENTURION 101
BERETTA MODEL 96D. 101
BERETTA MODEL 318 101
BERETTA MODEL 418 101
BERETTA MODEL 420 101
BERETTA MODEL 421 101
BERETTA MODEL 948 101
BERETTA MODEL 949 TIPO OLIMPIONICO 101
BERETTA MODEL 950B JETFIRE 101
BERETTA MODEL 950B MINX M2 101
BERETTA MODEL 950CC MINX M4 101
BERETTA MODEL 950BS. 101
BERETTA MODEL 951 BRIGADIER 101
BERETTA MODEL 1915 101
BERETTA MODEL 1919 101
BERETTA MODEL 1923 101
BERETTA MODEL 1931 102
BERETTA MODEL 1934 102
BERETTA MODEL 1935 102
BERETTA MODEL 3032 TOMCAT 102
BERETTA MODEL 8000 COUGAR. 102
BERETTA MODEL 8000/8040 MINI COUGAR. 102
BERETTA MODEL 8000D COUGAR 102
BERETTA MODEL 8040 COUGAR. 102
BERETTA MODEL 8040D COUGAR 102
BERETTA PX4 STORM. 102
BERETTA PX4 STORM .45ACP 102
BERETTA PX4 STORM SD (SPECIAL DUTY) 102
BERETTA STAMPEDE 102
BERETTA STAMPEDE BISLEY. 102
BERETTA LARAMIE 102
BERETTA U22 NEOS 102
BERETTA U22 NEOS DLX 103
BERETTA U22 NEOS DLX INOX 103
BERETTA U22 NEOS INOX 103

BERGMANN

BERGMANN MODEL 1903 "MARS" 103
BERGMANN SPECIAL. 103
BERGMANN VEST POCKET MODELS. 103
BERGMANN-BAYARD MODEL 1908 103
BERGMANN-BAYARD MODEL 1910/21 TOJHUS. 103

BERNARDELLI

BERNARDELLI MODEL 60. 103
BERNARDELLI MODEL 68. 103
BERNARDELLI MODEL 69 TARGET 103
BERNARDELLI MODEL 80. 103
BERNARDELLI MODEL 90. 103
BERNARDELLI MODEL 100 TARGET 103
BERNARDELLI MODEL AMR. 103
BERNARDELLI MODEL BABY. 104
BERNARDELLI MODEL PO10 TARGET. 104
BERNARDELLI MODEL PO18 104
BERNARDELLI MODEL PO18 COMPACT 104
BERNARDELLI MODEL USA 104
BERNARDELLI P. ONE 104
BERNARDELLI P. ONE PRACTICAL VB PISTOL 104
BERNARDELLI STANDARD 104
BERNARDELLI VEST POCKET MODEL. 104

BERSA

BERSA FIRESTORM 104
BERSA MODEL 23. 104
BERSA MODEL 83. 104
BERSA MODEL 85. 104
BERSA MODEL 86. 105
BERSA MODEL 95 SERIES 105
BERSA MODEL 223. 105
BERSA MODEL 224. 105
BERSA MODEL 225. 105
BERSA MODEL 226. 105
BERSA MODEL 383. 105
BERSA MODEL 383DA 105
BERSA THUNDER 9. 105
BERSA THUNDER 9 ULTRA COMPACT 105
BERSA THUNDER 9 AND 40 PRO SERIES PISTOLS 105
BERSA THUNDER 9 AND 40 PRO ULTRA COMPACT PISTOLS 105
BERSA THUNDER 9/40 HIGH CAPACITY SERIES 105
BERSA THUNDER 22. 105
BERSA THUNDER 45 PRO 105
BERSA THUNDER 380. 105
BERSA THUNDER 380 PLUS 106

BF

BF SINGLE SHOT (E. A. BROWN) 106
BF SINGLE SHOT ULTIMATE SILHOUETTE. 106

BOBERG

BOBERG BR9-S PLATINUM 106

BOND ARMS

BOND ARMS TEXAS DEFENDER 106
BOND ARMS COWBOY DEFENDER. 106
BOND ARMS SNAKE SLAYER IV. 106

BREN TEN

BREN TEN 106

BREN TEN POCKET MODEL . . . 106
BREN TEN SPECIAL FORCES MODEL . . . 106

BRNO
BRNO ZBP 99 . . . 106

BROLIN
BROLIN LEGEND L45 STD . . . 106
BROLIN LEGEND L45C COMPACT . . . 106
BROLIN L45T COMPACT . . . 106
BROLIN TAC SERIES SERVICE MODEL . . . 106
BROLIN TAC SERIES FULL SIZE . . . 107
BROLIN TAC SERIES COMPACT DA . . . 107
BROLIN TAC SERIES BANTAM DA . . . 107
BROLIN TAC SERIES MODEL TAC-11 . . . 107

BRONCO
BRONCO MODEL 1918 . . . 107
BRONCO VEST POCKET AUTOMATIC . . . 107

BROWN
BROWN CLASSIC . . . 107
BROWN EXECUTIVE TARGET . . . 107
BROWN EXECUTIVE ELITE . . . 107
BROWN EXECUTIVE CARRY . . . 107
BROWN SPECIAL FORCES . . . 107

BROWNING
BROWNING 25 BABY . . . 107
BROWNING 25 LIGHTWEIGHT . . . 107
BROWNING 25 RENAISSANCE MODEL . . . 107
BROWNING 380 STANDARD . . . 107
BROWNING 380 RENAISSANCE . . . 107
BROWNING BDA . . . 107
BROWNING BDA 380 . . . 108
BROWNING BDM . . . 108
BROWNING BUCK MARK . . . 108
BROWNING BUCK MARK FIELD 5.5 . . . 108
BROWNING BUCK MARK MICRO . . . 108
BROWNING BUCK MARK MICRO PLUS . . . 108
BROWNING BUCK MARK PLUS . . . 108
BROWNING BUCK MARK SILHOUETTE . . . 108
BROWNING BUCK MARK BULLSEYE . . . 108
BROWNING BUCK MARK TARGET 5.5 . . . 108
BROWNING BUCK MARK UNLIMITED MATCH . 108
BROWNING BUCK MARK UNLIMITED SILHOUETTE . . . 108
BROWNING BUCK MARK VARMINT . . . 108
BROWNING BUCK MARK BULLSEYE TARGET STAINLESS . . . 108
BROWNING BUCK MARK BULLSEYE TARGET URX . . . 108
BROWNING BUCK MARK CONTOUR 5.5 URX . . . 108
BROWNING BUCK MARK CONTOUR LITE 5.5 URX . . . 108
BROWNING BUCK MARK FLD PLUS ROSEWOOD UDX . . . 108
BROWNING BUCK MARK LITE SPLASH 5.5 URX . . . 108
BROWNING BUCK MARK MICRO STANDARD STAINLESS URX . . . 109
BROWNING BUCK MARK MICRO BULL . . . 109
BROWNING BUCK MARK PLUS STAINLESS UDX . . . 109
BROWNING BUCK MARK STANDARD STAINLESS URX . . . 109
BROWNING BUCK MARK PLUS STAINLESS BLACK LAMINATED UDX . . . 109
BROWNING BUCK MARK PLUS UDX . . . 109
BROWNING FULL LINE DEALER BUCK MARK PLUS ROSEWOOD UDX . . . 109
BUCK MARK CAMPER . . . 109
BUCK MARK CAMPER COCOBOLO UDX . . . 109
BUCK MARK PRACTICAL URX FIBER OPTIC . . . 109
BROWNING CHALLENGER . . . 109
BROWNING CHALLENGER II . . . 109
BROWNING CHALLENGER III . . . 109
BROWNING CHALLENGER III SPORTER . . . 109
BROWNING CHALLENGER GOLD MODEL . . . 109
BROWNING HI-POWER . . . 109
BROWNING HI-POWER 40 S&W MARK III . . . 109
BROWNING HI-POWER CAPITAN . . . 109
BROWNING HI-POWER HP-PRACTICAL . . . 109
BROWNING HI-POWER LOUIS XVI . . . 110
BROWNING HI-POWER RENAISSANCE . . . 110
BROWNING MEDALIST . . . 110
BROWNING MEDALIST GOLD MODEL . . . 110
BROWNING MEDALIST INTERNATIONAL . . . 110
BROWNING MEDALIST RENAISSANCE MODEL . . . 110
BROWNING MODEL 1911 . . . 110
BROWNING 1911-22 A1 . . . 110
BROWNING NOMAD . . . 110
BROWNING RENAISSANCE CASED SET . . . 110
BROWNING (FN) HI-POWER 9MM . . . 110
BROWNING (FN) MODEL 1900 . . . 110
BROWNING (FN) MODEL 1903 . . . 110
BROWNING (FN) MODEL 1906 . . . 110
BROWNING (FN) MODEL 1910 . . . 110
BROWNING (FN) MODEL 1922 . . . 111

BRYCO
BRYCO MODEL J-25 . . . 111
BRYCO MODEL M-38 . . . 111
BRYCO MODEL M-48 . . . 111
BRYCO MODEL 58 . . . 111
BRYCO MODEL M-59 . . . 111

BUDISCHOWSKY
BUDISCHOWSKY TP-70 . . . 111

BUSHMASTER
BUSHMASTER CARBON-15 TYPE 21 PISTOL . . . 111
BUSHMASTER CARBON-15 TYPE 97 PISTOL . . . 111

BUTLER
BUTLER DERRINGER . . . 111

CABANAS
CABANAS SINGLE-SHOT . . . 111

CALICO
CALICO MODEL M-100 . . . 111
CALICO MODEL M-950 . . . 111

CAMPO-GIRO
CAMPO-GIRO MODEL 1913 . . . 111
CAMPO-GIRO MODEL 1913-16 . . . 111

CARBON-15
CARBON-15 . . . 111

CENTURY
CENTURY FEG P9R . . . 112
CENTURY FEG P9RK . . . 112
CENTURY MODEL 100 . . . 112

CHARLES DALY
CHARLES DALY M-1911-A1P . . . 112
CHARLES DALY 1911-A1 FIELD EFS . . . 112
CHARLES DALY 1911-A1 FIELD ECS COMPACT . . . 112
CHARLES DALY 1911-A1 EMPIRE EFS . . . 112
CHARLES DALY 1911-A1 EMPIRE ECS COMPACT . . . 112
CHARLES DALY HP . . . 112
CHARLES DALY EMPIRE HP . . . 112
CHARLES DALY M-5 . . . 112
CHARLES DALY MODEL 1873 . . . 112
CHARLES DALY MODEL 1873 STAINLESS . . . 112

CHARTER ARMS
CHARTER ARMS BONNIE & CLYDE SET . . . 112
CHARTER ARMS BULLDOG . . . 112
CHARTER ARMS BULLDOG PUG . . . 112
CHARTER ARMS CHIC LADY . . . 112
CHARTER ARMS COUGAR UNDERCOVER LITE . . . 113
CHARTER ARMS CRIMSON UNDERCOVER . . . 113
CHARTER ARMS DIXIE DERRINGER . . . 113
CHARTER 2000, INC. DIXIE DERRINGER . . . 113
CHARTER ARMS MAG PUG (2006) . . . 113
CHARTER ARMS EXPLORER II . . . 113
CHARTER ARMS LADY ON DUTY . . . 113
CHARTER ARMS MAGNUM PUG . . . 113
CHARTER ARMS MODEL 40 . . . 113
CHARTER ARMS MODEL 79K . . . 113
CHARTER ARMS OFF-DUTY . . . 113
CHARTER PANTHER BRONZE/ BLACK STANDARD . . . 113
CHARTER ARMS PATHFINDER . . . 113
STAINLESS PATHFINDER WITH 3-1/2-INCH SHROUDED BARREL . . . 113
CHARTER ARMS PIT BULL . . . 113
CHARTER ARMS 9 MM PITBULL RIMLESS REVOLVER . . . 113
CHARTER ARMS .40 PITBULL, MATTE STANDARD . . . 114
CHARTER ARMS POLICE BULLDOG . . . 114
CHARTER ARMS POLICE BULLDOG STAINLESS . . . 114
CHARTER ARMS TARGET PATHFINDER COMBO . . . 114
CHARTER ARMS TARGET BULLDOG . . . 114
CHARTER ARMS TARGET BULLDOG STAINLESS . . . 114
CHARTER ARMS UNDERCOVER . . . 114
CHARTER ARMS UNDERCOVERETTE . . . 114
CHARTER ARMS PINK LADY . . . 114
CHARTER ARMS GOLDFINGER . . . 114
CHARTER ARMS PATRIOT . . . 114
CHARTER ARMS UNDERCOVER LITE . . . 114

CHIAPPA
CHIAPPA M FOUR-22 . . . 114
CHIAPPA M9-22 STANDARD . . . 114
CHIAPPA RHINO 60DS . . . 114

CHIPMUNK
CHIPMUNK SILHOUETTE MODEL . . . 114

CIMARRON
CIMARRON 1873 PEACEMAKER . . . 114
CIMARRON 1873 PEACEMAKER SHERIFF'S MODEL . . . 115
CIMARRON 1875 REMINGTON . . . 115
CIMARRON 1890 REMINGTON . . . 115
CIMARRON 1911 . . . 115
CIMARRON NEW THUNDERER . . . 115
CIMARRON MAN WITH NO NAME . . . 115
CIMARRON PEACEKEEPER . . . 115
CIMARRON ROOSTER SHOOTER . . . 115
CIMARRON THUNDERSTORM . . . 115
CIMARRON U.S. ARTILLERY MODEL . . . 115
CIMARRON U.S. CAVALRY MODEL . . . 115
CIMARRON 8TH ARTILLERY CASED SET . . . 115
CIMARRON ROUGH RIDER ARTILLERY MODEL SINGLE-ACTION . . . 115

CLARIDGE
CLARIDGE HI-TEC MODEL L-9 . . . 115
CLARIDGE HI-TEC S-9 . . . 115
CLARIDGE HI-TEC T-9 . . . 115
CLARIDGE M . . . 116

CLASSIC ARMS
CLASSIC ARMS SOUTHERN DERRINGER . . . 116
CLASSIC ARMS TWISTER . . . 116

CLERKE
CLERKE FIRST MODEL . . . 116

COBRA
COBRA SHADOW . . . 116
COBRA TITAN . . . 116

COLT
COLT 22 AUTOMATIC PISTOL . . . 116
COLT 22 TARGET PISTOL . . . 116
COLT 70 SERIES MODEL O . . . 116
COLT 175TH ANNIVERSARY SINGLE ACTION ARMY . . . 116
COLT ACE . . . 116
COLT ACE SERVICE MODEL . . . 116
COLT ALL AMERICAN MODEL 2000 . . . 116
COLT CHALLENGER . . . 116

COLT COMBAT COMMANDER (PRE-1970) .116
COLT COMBAT COMMANDER MKIV SERIES 70 .116
COLT COMBAT COMMANDER LIGHTWEIGHT MKIV SERIES 70 .117
COLT COMBAT COMMANDER MKIV SERIES 80 .117
COLT COMBAT ELITE MKIV SERIES 80 .117
COLT COMBAT GOVERNMENT MKIV SERIES 70 .117
COLT COMBAT GOVERNMENT MKIV SERIES 80 .117
COLT COMMANDER LIGHTWEIGHT MKIV SERIES 80 .117
COLT DEFENDER .117
COLT DELTA ELITE .117
COLT DELTA GOLD CUP .117
COLT DOUBLE EAGLE COMBAT COMMANDER MKII SERIES 90 .117
COLT DOUBLE EAGLE MKII SERIES 90 .117
COLT DOUBLE EAGLE OFFICER'S MODEL MKIV SERIES 90 .117
COLT GOLD CUP NATIONAL MATCH MKIII .118
COLT GOLD CUP NATIONAL MATCH MKIV SERIES 70 .118
COLT GOLD CUP NATIONAL MATCH MKIV SERIES 80 .118
COLT GOLD CUP TROPHY .118
COLT GOVERNMENT MODEL MKIV SERIES 70 .118
COLT GOVERNMENT MODEL MKIV SERIES 80 .118
COLT GOVERNMENT MODEL 380 MKIV SERIES 80 .118
COLT HUNTSMAN, TARGETSMAN .118
COLT JUNIOR .118
COLT MODEL 1900 .118
COLT MODEL 1900 ARMY .118
COLT MODEL 1900 USN .118
COLT MODEL 1902 MILITARY .119
COLT MODEL 1902 SPORTING .119
COLT MODEL 1903 POCKET HAMMER .119
COLT MODEL 1903 POCKET HAMMERLESS (FIRST ISSUE) .119
COLT MODEL 1903 POCKET HAMMERLESS (SECOND ISSUE) .119
COLT MODEL 1903 POCKET HAMMERLESS (THIRD ISSUE) .119
COLT MODEL 1903 POCKET HAMMERLESS (FOURTH ISSUE) .119
COLT MODEL 1905 .119
COLT MODEL 1908 POCKET HAMMERLESS (FIRST ISSUE) .119
COLT MODEL 1908 POCKET HAMMERLESS (SECOND ISSUE) .119
COLT MODEL 1908 POCKET HAMMERLESS (THIRD ISSUE) .119
COLT MODEL 1911 COMMERCIAL .119
COLT MODEL 1911 BRITISH 455 .119
COLT MODEL 1911 MILITARY .119
COLT MODEL 1911 RUSSIAN .120
.38 SUPER (2007) .120
COLT MODEL 1911A1 .120
COLT NATIONAL MATCH .120
COLT NEW FRONTIER .120
COLT SUPER 38 .120
COLT SUPER 38 NATIONAL MATCH .120
COLT MODEL 1991A1 .120
COLT MODEL 1991A1 COMPACT .120
COLT MUSTANG .120
COLT MUSTANG PLUS II .120
COLT MUSTANG POCKETLITE .120
COLT CZ40 .121
COLT OFFICER'S ACP MKIV SERIES 80 .121
COLT PONY .121
COLT PONY POCKETLITE LIGHTWEIGHT .121
COLT 1911 MARINE PISTOL .121
COLT 1911 – WWI REPLICA .121
COLT CONCEALED CARRY .121
COLT .38 SUPER (2006) .121
COLT WOODSMAN (FIRST ISSUE) .121
COLT WOODSMAN (FIRST ISSUE) SPORT MODEL .121
COLT WOODSMAN (FIRST ISSUE) MATCH TARGET .121
COLT WOODSMAN (SECOND ISSUE) .121
COLT WOODSMAN (SECOND ISSUE) SPORT MODEL .121
COLT WOODSMAN (SECOND ISSUE) MATCH TARGET 4-1/2-INCH .121
COLT WOODSMAN (SECOND ISSUE) MATCH TARGET 6-INCH .121
COLT WOODSMAN (THIRD ISSUE) .121
COLT WOODSMAN (THIRD ISSUE) SPORT MODEL .122
COLT WOODSMAN (THIRD ISSUE) MATCH TARGET 4-1/2-INCH .122
COLT WOODSMAN (THIRD ISSUE) MATCH TARGET 6-INCH .122
COLT 3RD MODEL DERRINGER .122
COLT 38 SF-VI .122
COLT PYTHON ELITE .122
COLT 357 MAGNUM .122
COLT AGENT (FIRST ISSUE) .122
COLT AGENT (SECOND ISSUE) .122
COLT AGENT (THIRD ISSUE) .122
COLT ANACONDA .122
COLT ARMY SPECIAL .122
COLT BANKER'S SPECIAL .122
COLT BISLEY .122
COLT BUNTLINE SPECIAL .123
COLT CAMP PERRY MODEL (FIRST ISSUE) .123
COLT CAMP PERRY MODEL (SECOND ISSUE) .123
COLT COBRA (FIRST ISSUE) .123
COLT COBRA (SECOND ISSUE) .123
COLT COMMANDO .123
COLT COMMANDO SPECIAL .123
COLT DETECTIVE SPECIAL (FIRST ISSUE) .123
COLT DETECTIVE SPECIAL (SECOND ISSUE) .123
COLT DETECTIVE SPECIAL (THIRD ISSUE) .123
COLT DETECTIVE SPECIAL (FOURTH ISSUE) .123
COLT DIAMONDBACK .123
COLT FRONTIER SCOUT .123
COLT FRONTIER SCOUT BUNTLINE .124
COLT KING COBRA .124
COLT MAGNUM CARRY REVOLVER .124
COLT LAWMAN MKIII .124
COLT LAWMAN MKV .124
COLT METROPOLITAN MKIII .124
COLT MODEL 1877 LIGHTNING .124
COLT MODEL 1877 THUNDERER .124
COLT MODEL 1878 FRONTIER .124
COLT MODEL 1905 MARINE CORPS .124
COLT MODEL 1917 ARMY .124
COLT NAVY MODEL 1889 (FIRST ISSUE) .124
COLT NAVY MODEL 1892-1903 (SECOND ISSUE) .124
COLT SPECIAL GOVERNMENT COMBAT .124
COLT XSE SERIES .124
COLT NEW FRONTIER .124
COLT NEW FRONTIER BUNTLINE SPECIAL .125
COLT NEW FRONTIER 22 .125
COLT NEW POCKET MODEL .125
COLT NEW POLICE .125
COLT NEW POLICE TARGET .125
COLT NEW SERVICE .125
COLT NEW SERVICE SHOOTING MASTER .125
COLT NEW SERVICE TARGET .125
COLT OFFICER'S MODEL TARGET (FIRST, SECOND, THIRD ISSUES) .125
COLT OFFICER'S MODEL MATCH .125
COLT OFFICER'S MODEL SPECIAL .125
COLT OFFICIAL POLICE .125
COLT OFFICIAL POLICE MKIII .126
COLT PEACEKEEPER .126
COLT PEACEMAKER 22 .126
COLT POCKET POSITIVE .126
COLT POLICE POSITIVE .126
COLT POLICE POSITIVE SPECIAL (FIRST, SECOND, THIRD ISSUES) .126
COLT POLICE POSITIVE TARGET .126
COLT PYTHON .126
COLT PYTHON STAINLESS .126
COLT SINGLE ACTION ARMY .126
COLT SINGLE ACTION (CURRENT PRODUCTION) .127
COLT COWBOY .127
COLT TROOPER .127
COLT TROOPER MKIII .127
COLT TROOPER MKV .127
COLT VIPER .127

COMANCHE

COMANCHE I .127
COMANCHE II .127
COMANCHE III .127
COMANCHE SUPER COMANCHE .127

COMPETITION ARMS

COMPETITION ARMS COMPETITOR .127

COMPETITOR

COMPETITOR SINGLE SHOT .128

COONAN

COONAN 357 MAGNUM .128
COONAN 357 MAGNUM CLASSIC .128
COONAN 357 MAGNUM COMPACT CADET .128
COONAN 357 MAGNUM COMPENSATED MODEL .128

CUMBERLAND MOUNTAIN ARMS

CUMBERLAND MOUNTAIN ARMS THE JUDGE SINGLE SHOT .128

CVA

CVA OPTIMA MUZZLELOADING PISTOL .128

CZ

CZ/ADCO 1911-A1 .128
CZ MODEL 22 .128
CZ MODEL 24 .128
CZ MODEL 27 .128
CZ MODEL 38 .128
CZ MODEL 50 .128
CZ MODEL 52 .128
CZ MODEL 75 .128
CZ 75 COMPACT .129
CZ 75 COMPACT SDP .129
CZ 75 SEMI-COMPACT .129
CZ 75 SHADOW .129
CZ 75 SP-01 SHADOW .129
CZ 75 SP-01 ACCU-SHADOW .129
CZ 75 STAINLESS .129
CZ 75 TACTICAL SPORT .129
CZ 75 TS CZECHMATE .129
CZ MODEL 83 .129
CZ MODEL 83 9X18MM MAKAROV .129
CZ MODEL 85 .129
CZ MODEL 85 COMBAT .129
CZ 97 B .129
CZ 100 AUTO PISTOL .129
CZ MODEL 1945 .129
CZ P-07 DUTY .129
CZ P-09 DUTY .130
CZ POCKET DUO .130
CZ-TT .130
CZ-T POLYMER COMPACT .130

DAEWOO

DAEWOO DH40 .130
DAEWOO DH380 .130
DAEWOO DP51 .130
DAEWOO DP51C .130
DAEWOO DP51S .130
DAEWOO DP52 .130

DAKOTA

DAKOTA 1873 PREMIER .130
DAKOTA 1875 REMINGTON OUTLAW MODEL .130
DAKOTA 1890 REMINGTON POLICE MODEL .130
DAKOTA BISLEY MODEL .131
DAKOTA HARTFORD MODEL .131
DAKOTA HARTFORD MODEL PINKERTON .131
DAKOTA NEW MODEL SINGLE ACTION .131
DAKOTA OLD MODEL SINGLE ACTION .131
DAKOTA SHERIFF'S MODEL .131

DAN WESSON

DAN WESSON ELITE SERIES HAVOC .131
DAN WESSON ELITE SERIES MAYHEM .131
DAN WESSON ELITE SERIES TITAN .131
DAN WESSON VALOR 1911 .131
DAN WESSON VH8 .131
DAN WESSON RZ-10 .131

DAVIS

DAVIS BIG-BORE DERRINGERS .131
DAVIS D-SERIES DERRINGERS .132
DAVIS LONG-BORE DERRINGERS .132
DAVIS P-32 .132
DAVIS P-380 .132

DESERT INDUSTRIES

DESERT INDUSTRIES DOUBLE DEUCE .132
DESERT INDUSTRIES TWO-BIT SPECIAL .132
DESERT INDUSTRIES WAR EAGLE .132

DETONICS

DETONICS COMBAT MASTER MARK I .132
DETONICS COMBAT MASTER MARK V .132
DETONICS COMBAT MASTER MARK VI .132
DETONICS COMBAT MASTER MARK VII .132
DETONICS COMPMASTER .132
DETONICS MARK I .132
DETONICS MARK II .132
DETONICS MARK III .132
DETONICS MARK IV .132
DETONICS MILITARY COMBAT MC2 .132
DETONICS POCKET 9 .133
DETONICS POCKET 9LS .133
DETONICS POCKET 380 .133
DETONICS POWER 9 .133
DETONICS SCOREMASTER .133
DETONICS SERVICEMASTER .133
DETONICS SERVICEMASTER II .133

DIAMONDBACK

DIAMONDBACK DB380 .133
DIAMONDBACK DB9 .133

DOWNSIZER

DOWNSIZER WSP .133

D-MAX

D-MAX SIDEWINDER .133

DREYSE

DREYSE MODEL 1907 .133
DREYSE VEST POCKET MODEL .133
DREYSE MODEL 1910 .133

DWM

DWM POCKET MODEL .133

DSA

DSA B&T TP9 TACTICAL PISTOL .133

E.A.A.

E.A.A. BIG BORE BOUNTY HUNTER .133
E.A.A. BOUNTY HUNTER .133
E.A.A. EA22T TARGET .134
E.A.A. EUROPEAN 320 .134
E.A.A. EUROPEAN 380/DA .134
E.A.A. EUROPEAN 380 LADIES .134
E.A.A. WINDICATOR STANDARD GRADE .134
E.A.A. WINDICATOR TACTICAL GRADE .134
E.A.A. WINDICATOR TARGET GRADE .134
E.A.A. WITNESS .134
E.A.A. WITNESS COMPACT .134
E.A.A. WITNESS GOLD TEAM .134
E.A.A. WITNESS SILVER TEAM .134
E.A.A. WITNESS ELITE MATCH .135
E.A.A. WITNESS FCP .135
E.A.A. ZASTAVA EZ PISTOL .135

ED BROWN

ED BROWN KOBRA CARRY LW .135

ENTRÉPRISE

ENTRÉPRISE ELITE P500 .135
ENTRÉPRISE TACTICAL P500 .135
ENTRÉPRISE MEDALIST P500 .135
ENTRÉPRISE BOXER P500 .135
ENTRÉPRISE TOURNAMENT SHOOTER MODEL I .135

ERMA

ERMA ER 772 .135
ERMA ER 773 .135
ERMA ER 777 .135
ERMA ESP-85A SPORTING/MATCH TARGET .135
ERMA ESP-85A GOLDEN TARGET .135
ERMA ESP-85A JUNIOR MATCH .136
ERMA KGP68A .136
ERMA KGP69 .136
ERMA LA 22 .136
ERMA RX 22 .136

ERL SVENDSEN

ERL SVENDSEN FOUR ACES MODEL 1 .136
ERL SVENDSEN FOUR ACES MODEL 2 .136
ERL SVENDSEN FOUR ACES MODEL 3 .136
ERL SVENDSEN FOUR ACES MODEL 4 .136
ERL SVENDSEN LITTLE ACE DERRINGER .136
ERL SVENDSEN POCKET PONY .136

FALCON

FALCON PORTSIDER .136

FAS

FAS MODEL 601 MATCH .136
FAS MODEL 602 MATCH .136
FAS MODEL 603 MATCH .136
FAS MODEL 607 MATCH .136

FEATHER

FEATHER GUARDIAN ANGEL .136

FEDERAL ORDNANCE

FEDERAL ORDNANCE RANGER ALPHA .137
FEDERAL ORDNANCE RANGER G.I. MODEL .137
FEDERAL ORDNANCE RANGER G.I. MODEL, AMBO .137
FEDERAL ORDNANCE RANGER G.I. MODEL, EXTENDED .137
FEDERAL ORDNANCE RANGER G.I. MODEL, LITE .137
FEDERAL ORDNANCE RANGER G.I. MODEL, TEN AUTO .137
FEDERAL ORDNANCE RANGER SUPERCOMP .137

FEGYVER

FEGYVER ÉS GÉPGYÁR-BADUPEST, HUNGARY (FEG) B9R .137

FEG

FEG FP9 .137
FEG GKK-40C .137
FEG GKK-45C .137
FEG GKK-92C .137
FEG MARK II AP PISTOL .137
FEG MARK II AP22 PISTOL .138
FEG MBK-9HP .138
FEG MBK-9HPC .138
FEG P9R .138
FEG PJK-9HP .138
FEG PMK-380 .138
FEG SMC-22 .138
FEG SMC-380 .138
FEG SMC-918 .138

FELK

FELK MTF 450 AUTO PISTOL .138

F.I.E.

F.I.E. ARMINIUS MODEL 222 .138
F.I.E. ARMINIUS MODEL 232 .138
F.I.E. ARMINIUS MODEL 357 .138
F.I.E. ARMINIUS MODEL 357T .138
F.I.E. ARMINIUS MODEL 382TB .139
F.I.E. ARMINIUS MODEL 384TB .139
F.I.E. ARMINIUS MODEL 386TB .139
F.I.E. ARMINIUS MODEL 522TB .139
F.I.E. ARMINIUS MODEL 532TB .139
F.I.E. ARMINIUS MODEL 722 .139
F.I.E. ARMINIUS MODEL 732B .139
F.I.E. ARMINIUS MODEL N-38 .139
F.I.E. ARMINIUS STANDARD MODEL .139
F.I.E. ARMINIUS ZEPHYR .139
F.I.E. ARMINIUS ZEPHYR LADY .139
F.I.E. BUFFALO SCOUT E15 .139
F.I.E. COWBOY .139
F.I.E. GOLD RUSH .139
F.I.E. HOMBRE .139
F.I.E. KG-99 PISTOL .139
F.I.E. LEGEND .140
F.I.E. LITTLE RANGER .140
F.I.E. MODEL 722 TP SILHOUETTE PISTOL .140
F.I.E. MODEL D38 .140
F.I.E. MODEL D86 .140
F.I.E. SPECTRE PISTOL .140
F.I.E. SSP MODEL .140
F.I.E. SSP MODEL LADY .140
F.I.E. SUPER TITAN II E32 .140
F.I.E. TITAN A27 .140
F.I.E. TITAN E27 .140
F.I.E. TITAN E38 .140
F.I.E. TITAN II E22 .140
F.I.E. TITAN II E22 LADY .140
F.I.E. TITAN II E32 .140
F.I.E. TZ-75 .140
F.I.E. TZ-75 SERIES 88 .140
TZ-75 SERIES 88 COMPENSATED .141
F.I.E. TZ-75 SERIES 88 GOVERNMENT MODEL .141
F.I.E. TZ-75 SERIES 88 PORTED .141
F.I.E. TEXAS RANGER .141
F.I.E. YELLOW ROSE .141

FIRESTORM

FIRESTORM .32 .141
FIRESTORM 1911 MIL-SPEC STANDARD GOVERNMENT .141

FNH

FNH MODEL FORTY-NINE .141
FNH FNS .141
FNH FNX .141
FNH FNX-45 TACTICAL .141
FNP-45 COMPETITION .141
FNH THE FN FIVE-SEVEN .141

FORT WORTH

FORT WORTH HSO .141
FORT WORTH HSS .142
FORT WORTH HSSK .142
FORT WORTH HST TARGET PISTOL .142
FORT WORTH HSC TARGET PISTOL .142
FORT WORTH HSV TARGET PISTOL .142
FORT WORTH MATCHMASTER STANDARD PISTOL .142
FORT WORTH MATCHMASTER DELUXE PISTOL .142
FORT WORTH MATCHMASTER DOVETAIL PISTOL .142

FRASER

FRASER AUTOMATIC .142

FREEDOM ARMS

FREEDOM ARMS MODEL 83 .142
MODEL 83 .500 WYOMING EXPRESS .142
FREEDOM ARMS 44 MAGNUM SILHOUETTE .142
FREEDOM ARMS 454 CASULL .142
FREEDOM ARMS 454 CASULL SILHOUETTE MODEL .143
FREEDOM ARMS MODEL 83 .500 WYOMING EXPRESS .143
FREEDOM ARMS BOOT GUN .143
FREEDOM ARMS FA-S-22LR .143
FREEDOM ARMS FA-S-22M .143
FREEDOM ARMS MINI REVOLVER .143

FREEDOM ARMS MODEL 97
MID FRAME REVOLVER .143
FREEDOM ARMS MODEL 252
VARMINT .143
FREEDOM ARMS MODEL 353 .143
FREEDOM ARMS MODEL 353
SILHOUETTE .143
FREEDOM ARMS MODEL 555 .143

FROMMER

FROMMER
BABY POCKET MODEL .143
FROMMER
LILIPUT POCKET MODEL .143
FROMMER
STOP POCKET MODEL .143

FTL

FTL AUTO NINE .143
FTL POCKET PARTNER .144

GAL

GAL COMPACT AUTO PISTOL .144

GALESI

GALESI MODEL 6 .144
GALESI MODEL 9 .144

GAMBA

GAMBA SAB G90 STANDARD .144
GAMBA SAB G90 COMPETITION .144
GAMBA SAB G91 COMPACT .144
GAMBA SAB G91 COMPETITION .144
GAMBA TRIDENT FAST ACTION .144
GAMBA TRIDENT MATCH 900 .144
GAMBA TRIDENT SUPER .144

GARCIA

GARCIA REGENT .144
GARCIA/FI MODEL D .144

GAUCHER

GAUCHER GN1 SILHOUETTE .144
GAUCHER GP SILHOUETTE .144
GAUCHER RANDALL SINGLESHOT .144

GIRSAN

GIRSAN MC27E .144

GLOCK

GLOCK MODEL 17 .144
GLOCK MODEL 17L COMPETITION .144
GLOCK 17 25TH ANNIVERSARY
LIMITED EDITION .144
GLOCK MODEL 19 .145
GLOCK MODEL 20 .145
GLOCK 20 GEN 4 .145
GLOCK MODEL 21 .145
GLOCK 21 SF .145
GLOCK MODEL 22 .145
GLOCK MODEL 23 .145
GLOCK MODEL 24 COMPETITION .145
GLOCK 26, 27 .145
GLOCK MODEL 28 .145
GLOCK 29, 30 .145
GLOCK 29 GEN 4 .145
GLOCK 30S GEN 4 .145
GLOCK 31 .145
GLOCK 31C .146
GLOCK 32 .146
GLOCK 32C .146
GLOCK 33 .146
GLOCK 33 GEN 4 .146
GLOCK 34 .146
GLOCK 35 .146
GLOCK MODEL 37 .146
GLOCK MODEL 38 .146
GLOCK MODEL 39 .146

GOLAN

GOLAN .146

GREAT WESTERN

GREAT WESTERN DERRINGER .146
GREAT WESTERN FRONTIER .146

GRENDEL

GRENDEL P-10 .146
GRENDEL P-12 .146
GRENDEL P-30 .146
GRENDEL P-30L .146
GRENDEL P-30M .146
GRENDEL P-31 .146

GUARDIAN

GUARDIAN-SS .147

GUNWORKS

GUNWORKS MODEL 9 DERRINGER .147

HAMMERLI

HAMMERLI MODEL 33MP .147
HAMMERLI MODEL 100
FREE PISTOL .147
HAMMERLI MODEL 101 .147
HAMMERLI MODEL 102 .147
HAMMERLI MODEL 103
FREE PISTOL .147
HAMMERLI MODEL 104 MATCH .147
HAMMERLI MODEL 105
MATCH .147
HAMMERLI MODEL 106
MATCH .147
HAMMERLI MODEL 107 .147
HAMMERLI MODEL 120 .147
HAMMERLI MODEL 120-1
FREE PISTOL .147
HAMMERLI MODEL 120-2 .147
HAMMERLI MODEL 120
HEAVY BARREL .147
HAMMERLI MODEL 150
FREE PISTOL .147
HAMMERLI MODEL 151
FREE PISTOL .147
HAMMERLI MODEL 152 MATCH .148
HAMMERLI MODEL 160
FREE PISTOL .148
HAMMERLI MODEL 162
FREE PISTOL .148
HAMMERLI MODEL 206
INTERNATIONAL .148
HAMMERLI MODEL 207
INTERNATIONAL .148
HAMMERLI MODEL 208
INTERNATIONAL .148
HAMMERLI MODEL 208S
INTERNATIONAL .148
HAMMERLI MODEL 209
INTERNATIONAL .148
HAMMERLI MODEL 210
INTERNATIONAL .148
HAMMERLI MODEL 211 .148
HAMMERLI MODEL 212 HUNTER .148
HAMMERLI MODEL 215 .148
HAMMERLI MODEL 230-1 .148
HAMMERLI MODEL 230-2 .148
HAMMERLI MODEL 232-1 .148
HAMMERLI MODEL 232-2 .148
HAMMERLI MODEL 280 TARGET .149
HAMMERLI SP 20 TARGET .149
HAMMERLI VIRGINIAN .149
HAMMERLI-WALTHER MODEL 200
OLYMPIA .149
HAMMERLI-WALTHER MODEL 201 .149
HAMMERLI-WALTHER MODEL 202 .149
HAMMERLI-WALTHER MODEL 203 .149
HAMMERLI-WALTHER MODEL 204 .149
HAMMERLI-WALTHER MODEL 205 .149

HARRINGTON & RICHARDSON

HARRINGTON & RICHARDSON
22 SPECIAL .149
HARRINGTON & RICHARDSON
YOUNG AMERICAN .149
HARRINGTON & RICHARDSON
AUTOMATIC EJECTING MODEL .149
HARRINGTON & RICHARDSON
BOBBY MODEL .149
HARRINGTON & RICHARDSON
EXPERT .149
HARRINGTON & RICHARDSON
HUNTER MODEL .150
HARRINGTON & RICHARDSON
MODEL 4 .150
HARRINGTON & RICHARDSON
MODEL 5 .150
HARRINGTON & RICHARDSON
MODEL 6 .150
HARRINGTON & RICHARDSON
MODEL 40 HAMMERLESS .150
HARRINGTON & RICHARDSON
MODEL 50 HAMMERLESS .150
HARRINGTON & RICHARDSON
MODEL 504 .150
HARRINGTON & RICHARDSON
MODEL 532 .150
HARRINGTON & RICHARDSON
MODEL 586 .150
HARRINGTON & RICHARDSON
MODEL 603 .150
HARRINGTON & RICHARDSON
MODEL 604 .150
HARRINGTON & RICHARDSON
MODEL 622 .150
HARRINGTON & RICHARDSON
MODEL 623 .150
HARRINGTON & RICHARDSON
MODEL 632 GUARDSMAN .150
HARRINGTON & RICHARDSON
MODEL 633 .150
HARRINGTON & RICHARDSON
MODEL 649 .150
HARRINGTON & RICHARDSON
MODEL 650 .151
HARRINGTON & RICHARDSON
MODEL 666 .151
HARRINGTON & RICHARDSON
MODEL 676 .151
HARRINGTON & RICHARDSON
MODEL 686 .151
HARRINGTON & RICHARDSON
MODEL 732 .151
HARRINGTON & RICHARDSON
MODEL 733 .151
HARRINGTON & RICHARDSON
MODEL 766 .151
HARRINGTON & RICHARDSON
MODEL 826 .151
HARRINGTON & RICHARDSON
MODEL 829 .151
HARRINGTON & RICHARDSON
MODEL 830 .151
HARRINGTON & RICHARDSON
MODEL 832 .151
HARRINGTON & RICHARDSON
MODEL 833 .151
HARRINGTON & RICHARDSON
MODEL 900 .151
HARRINGTON & RICHARDSON
MODEL 901 .151
HARRINGTON & RICHARDSON
MODEL 903 .152
HARRINGTON & RICHARDSON
MODEL 904 .152
HARRINGTON & RICHARDSON
MODEL 905 .152
HARRINGTON & RICHARDSON
MODEL 922 .152
HARRINGTON & RICHARDSON
MODEL 922 BANTAMWEIGHT .152
HARRINGTON & RICHARDSON
MODEL 922 CAMPER .152
HARRINGTON & RICHARDSON
MODEL 923 .152
HARRINGTON & RICHARDSON
MODEL 925 .152
HARRINGTON & RICHARDSON
MODEL 926 .152
HARRINGTON & RICHARDSON
MODEL 929 .152
HARRINGTON & RICHARDSON
MODEL 930 .152
HARRINGTON & RICHARDSON
MODEL 939 .152
HARRINGTON & RICHARDSON
MODEL 939 PREMIER .152
HARRINGTON & RICHARDSON
MODEL 940 .152
HARRINGTON & RICHARDSON
MODEL 949 .153
HARRINGTON & RICHARDSON
MODEL 949 WESTERN .153
HARRINGTON & RICHARDSON
MODEL 950 .153
HARRINGTON & RICHARDSON
MODEL 976 .153
HARRINGTON & RICHARDSON
MODEL 999 .153
HARRINGTON & RICHARDSON
MODEL 999 SPORTSMAN .153
HARRINGTON & RICHARDSON
NEW DEFENDER .153
HARRINGTON & RICHARDSON
NO. 196 .153
HARRINGTON & RICHARDSON
NO. 199 .153
HARRINGTON & RICHARDSON
PREMIER MODEL .153

HARRINGTON & RICHARDSON SELF-LOADING 25 .153
HARRINGTON & RICHARDSON SELF-LOADING 32 .153
HARRINGTON & RICHARDSON TRAPPER MODEL .153
HARRINGTON & RICHARDSON USRA MODEL .153
HARRINGTON & RICHARDSON VEST POCKET MODEL .154

HARRIS-MCMILLAN

HARRIS-MCMILLAN SIGNATURE JR. LONG RANGE .154
HARRIS-MCMILLAN WOLVERINE .154

HARTFORD

HARTFORD TARGET AUTOMATIC .154
HARTFORD TARGET SINGLE SHOT .154

HASKELL

HASKELL JS-45 .154

HAWES

HAWES DEPUTY MARSHAL .154
HAWES DEPUTY MARSHAL, DENVER MODEL .154
HAWES DEPUTY MARSHAL, MONTANA MODEL .154
HAWES DEPUTY MARSHAL, SILVER CITY MODEL .154
HAWES DEPUTY MARSHAL, TEXAS MODEL .154
HAWES FAVORITE .154
HAWES MARSHAL, CHIEF MODEL .154
HAWES MARSHAL, FEDERAL MODEL .154
HAWES MARSHAL, MONTANA MODEL .154
HAWES MARSHAL, SILVER CITY MODEL .154
HAWES MARSHAL, TEXAS MODEL .154
HAWES MARSHAL, WESTERN MODEL .155
HAWES MEDALLION MODEL .155
HAWES TROPHY MODEL .155
HAWES/SIG-SAUER P220 .155

HECKLER & KOCH

HECKLER & KOCH HK4 .155
HECKLER & KOCH MARK 23 .155
HECKLER & KOCH P7 K3 .155
HECKLER & KOCH P7 M8 .155
HECKLER & KOCH P7 M10 .155
HECKLER & KOCH P7 M13 .155
HECKLER & KOCH P7 PSP .155
HECKLER & KOCH P9S .155
HECKLER & KOCH P9S COMPETITION KIT .155
HECKLER & KOCH P9S TARGET .155
HECKLER & KOCH P30L SERIES .156
HECKLER & KOCH SP 89 .156
HECKLER & KOCH USP .156
HECKLER & KOCH USP COMPACT AUTO PISTOL .156
HECKLER & KOCH USP45 COMPACT .156
HECKLER & KOCH USP45 COMPACT TACTICAL .156
HECKLER & KOCH USP45 MATCH .156
HECKLER & KOCH USP45 TACTICAL .156
HECKLER & KOCH USP EXPERT .156
HECKLER & KOCH USP ELITE .156
HECKLER & KOCH VP 70Z .156
HECKLER & KOCH P2000 .156
HECKLER & KOCH HK45 .156
HECKLER & KOCH HK45 COMPACT .156
HECKLER & KOCH P30 .156

HELWAN

HELWAN 9MM .156

HERITAGE

HERITAGE MODEL HA25 .157
HERITAGE H25S AUTO PISTOL .157
HERITAGE ROUGH RIDER .157
HERITAGE ROUGH RIDER .32 .157
HERITAGE ROUGH RIDER BIG-BORE SERIES .157
HERITAGE SENTRY .157
HERITAGE STEALTH AUTO PISTOL .157

HI-POINT FIREARMS

HI-POINT FIREARMS JS-9MM .157
HI-POINT FIREARMS JS-9MM COMPACT .157
HI-POINT FIREARMS JS-40 S&W .157
HI-POINT FIREARMS JS-45 .157
HI-POINT FIREARMS MODEL 9MM COMPACT PISTOL .157
HI-POINT FIREARMS MODEL 380 POLYMER PISTOL .157
HI-POINT .380 ACP .158

HIGH STANDARD

HIGH STANDARD SEMI-AUTOMATIC PISTOLS HIGH STANDARD CITATION (FIRST MODEL 102 SERIES) .158
HIGH STANDARD CITATION (103 SERIES) .158
HIGH STANDARD CITATION (104 SERIES) .158
HIGH STANDARD CITATION (106 SERIES) .158
HIGH STANDARD CITATION (107 SERIES) .158
HIGH STANDARD CITATION (ML SERIES) .158
HIGH STANDARD CITATION (SEVEN NUMBER SERIES) .158
HIGH STANDARD CITATION II (SH SERIES) .158
HIGH STANDARD CITATION II SURVIVAL PACK .158
HIGH STANDARD CUSTOM 10-X .158
HIGH STANDARD CUSTOM 10-X TARGET .158
HIGH STANDARD DURA-MATIC .158
HIGH STANDARD FIELD KING (FIRST MODEL) .158
HIGH STANDARD FIELD KING (101 SERIES) .159
HIGH STANDARD FLITE KING (FIRST MODEL) .159
HIGH STANDARD FLITE KING (102 SERIES) .159
HIGH STANDARD FLITE KING (103 SERIES) .159
HIGH STANDARD MODEL A .159
HIGH STANDARD MODEL B .159
HIGH STANDARD MODEL C .159
HIGH STANDARD MODEL D .159
HIGH STANDARD MODEL E .159
HIGH STANDARD MODEL G-380 .159
HIGH STANDARD MODEL G-B .159
HIGH STANDARD MODEL G-D .159
HIGH STANDARD MODEL G-E .159
HIGH STANDARD MODEL H-A .159
HIGH STANDARD MODEL H-B (FIRST MODEL) .160
HIGH STANDARD MODEL H-B (2ND MODEL) .160
HIGH STANDARD MODEL H-D .160
HIGH STANDARD MODEL H-D U.S.A. .160
HIGH STANDARD H-D U.S.A. MILITARY .160
HIGH STANDARD MODEL H-E .160
HIGH STANDARD MODEL S-B .160
HIGH STANDARD OLYMPIC (FIRST MODEL) .160
HIGH STANDARD OLYMPIC (SECOND MODEL) .160
HIGH STANDARD OLYMPIC (THIRD MODEL) .160
HIGH STANDARD OLYMPIC (102 SERIES) .160
HIGH STANDARD OLYMPIC (103 SERIES) .160
HIGH STANDARD OLYMPIC (104 SERIES) .160
HIGH STANDARD OLYMPIC (106 SERIES MILITARY) .160
HIGH STANDARD OLYMPIC ISU (102 SERIES) .160
HIGH STANDARD OLYMPIC ISU (103 SERIES) .161
HIGH STANDARD OLYMPIC ISU (104 SERIES) .161
HIGH STANDARD OLYMPIC ISU (106 SERIES MILITARY) .161
HIGH STANDARD OLYMPIC ISU MILITARY .161
HIGH STANDARD OLYMPIC ISU STANDARD .161
HIGH STANDARD PLINKER .161
HIGH STANDARD SHARPSHOOTER .161
HIGH STANDARD SPORT KING (FIRST MODEL) .161
HIGH STANDARD SPORT KING (101 SERIES) .161
HIGH STANDARD SPORT KING LIGHTWEIGHT (101 SERIES) .161
HIGH STANDARD SPORT KING (102 SERIES) .161
HIGH STANDARD SPORT KING (103 SERIES) .161
HIGH STANDARD SPORT KING (106 SERIES MILITARY MODEL) .161
HIGH STANDARD SUPERMATIC (FIRST MODEL) .161
HIGH STANDARD SUPERMATIC (101 SERIES 2ND MODEL) .161
HIGH STANDARD SUPERMATIC CITATION .162
HIGH STANDARD SUPERMATIC TROPHY .162
HIGH STANDARD SUPERMATIC TOURNAMENT .162
HIGH STANDARD SUPERMATIC TOURNAMENT (102 SERIES) .162
HIGH STANDARD SUPERMATIC TOURNAMENT (103 SERIES) .162
HIGH STANDARD SUPERMATIC TOURNAMENT (106 SERIES MILITARY) .162
HIGH STANDARD SUPERMATIC TROPHY (102 SERIES) .162
HIGH STANDARD SUPERMATIC TROPHY (103/104 SERIES) .162
HIGH STANDARD SUPERMATIC TROPHY (106/107 SERIES) .162
HIGH STANDARD SUPERMATIC TROPHY (ML SERIES) .162
HIGH STANDARD SUPERMATIC TROPHY (SEVEN NUMBER SERIES) .162
HIGH STANDARD SUPERMATIC TROPHY (SH SERIES) .162
HIGH STANDARD VICTOR (FIRST MODEL 107 SERIES) .162
HIGH STANDARD VICTOR (ML SERIES) .162
HIGH STANDARD VICTOR (SEVEN NUMBER SERIES) .162
HIGH STANDARD VICTOR (SH SERIES) .162
HIGH STANDARD VICTOR TARGET .163
HIGH STANDARD CAMP GUN .163
HIGH STANDARD CRUSADER .163
HIGH STANDARD DERRINGER .163
HIGH STANDARD DOUBLE-NINE .163
HIGH STANDARD DOUBLE-NINE CONVERTIBLE .163
HIGH STANDARD DURANGO .163
HIGH STANDARD HIGH SIERRA .163
HIGH STANDARD KIT GUN .163
HIGH STANDARD LONGHORN .163
HIGH STANDARD LONGHORN CONVERTIBLE .163
HIGH STANDARD MARSHALL .163
HIGH STANDARD NATCHEZ .163
HIGH STANDARD POSSE .163
HIGH STANDARD SENTINEL .164
HIGH STANDARD SENTINEL DELUXE .164
HIGH STANDARD SENTINEL IMPERIAL .164
HIGH STANDARD SENTINEL MARK I .164
HIGH STANDARD SENTINEL MARK II .164
HIGH STANDARD SENTINEL MARK III .164
HIGH STANDARD SENTINEL MARK IV .164
HIGH STANDARD SENTINEL SNUB .164

HJS

HJS ANTIGUA DERRINGER .164
HJS FRONTIER FOUR DERRINGER .164

HJS LONE STAR DERRINGER 164

HUNGARIAN

HUNGARIAN T-58 164

IAI

IAI AUTOMAG III. 164
IAI AUTOMAG IV 164
IAI BACKUP 164
IAI JAVELINA 165
IAR MODEL 1873. 165
IAR MODEL 1872 DERRINGER 165
IAR MODEL 1888
DOUBLE DERRINGER. 165

IBERIA FIREARMS

IBERIA FIREARMS JS-40 S&W 165

INDIAN ARMS

INDIAN ARMS STAINLESS. 165

INTERARMS

INTERARMS VIRGINIAN
DRAGOON. 165
INTERARMS VIRGINIAN
DRAGOON DEPUTY MODEL 165
INTERARMS VIRGINIAN
DRAGOON ENGRAVED. 165
INTERARMS VIRGINIAN
DRAGOON SILHOUETTE 165
INTERARMS VIRGINIAN
22 CONVERTIBLE 165

INTRATEC

INTRATEC CATEGORY 9 165
INTRATEC CAT 45 165
INTRATEC PROTEC-25 166
INTRATEC TEC-9C. 166
INTRATEC TEC-22T 166
INTRATEC TEC-22TK. .166
INTRATEC TEC-DC9 166
INTRATEC TEC-DC9S .166
INTRATEC TEC-DC9K .166
INTRATEC TEC-DC9M. 166
INTRATEC TEC-DC9MK. 166
INTRATEC TEC-DC9MS. 166

ITHACA

ITHACA MODEL 20 166
ITHACA X-CALIBER. 166

IVER JOHNSON

IVER JOHNSON 22 SUPERSHOT 166
IVER JOHNSON 22 SUPERSHOT
MODEL 90 166
IVER JOHNSON 22 SUPERSHOT
SEALED EIGHT (FIRST MODEL) 166
IVER JOHNSON 22 SUPERSHOT
SEALED EIGHT (SECOND MODEL) 166
IVER JOHNSON 22 SUPERSHOT
SEALED EIGHT (THIRD
MODEL 844) 167
IVER JOHNSON ARMSWORTH
MODEL 855 167
IVER JOHNSON BULLDOG. 167
IVER JOHNSON CATTLEMAN
MAGNUM 167
IVER JOHNSON CATTLEMAN
BUCKHORN MAGNUM. 167
IVER JOHNSON CATTLEMAN
BUCKHORN BUNTLINE 167
IVER JOHNSON CATTLEMAN
TRAILBLAZER 167
IVER JOHNSON CHAMPION
MODEL 822 167
IVER JOHNSON COMPACT. 167
IVER JOHNSON COMPACT ELITE 167
IVER JOHNSON DELUXE STARTER
MODEL 69 167
IVER JOHNSON ENFORCER
MODEL 3000/IVER JOHNSON
SUPER ENFORCER MODEL PP30 167
IVER JOHNSON HIJO
QUICKBREAK 1961 .168
IVER JOHNSON MODEL 50
SIDEWINDER. 168
IVER JOHNSON MODEL 55 TARGET 168
IVER JOHNSON MODEL 55A 168
IVER JOHNSON MODEL 55S
CADET 168
IVER JOHNSON MODEL 55S-A
CADET 168
IVER JOHNSON MODEL 56 I J
STARTER REVOLVER 168
IVER JOHNSON MODEL 56A
I J STARTER REVOLVER 168
IVER JOHNSON MODEL 57
TARGET 168
IVER JOHNSON MODEL 57A
TARGET 168
IVER JOHNSON MODEL 1900. 168
IVER JOHNSON MODEL 1900
TARGET 168
IVER JOHNSON MODEL 1900
TARGET MODELS 69 & 79 168
IVER JOHNSON MODEL 1908
PETITE HAMMERLESS 168
IVER JOHNSON
PROTECTOR SEALED
EIGHT MODEL 84 169
IVER JOHNSON ROOKIE. 169
IVER JOHNSON SAFETY
AUTOMATIC HAMMER
(SECOND MODEL) .169
IVER JOHNSON SAFETY
AUTOMATIC HAMMER
(THIRD MODEL). 169
IVER JOHNSON SAFETY
HAMMERLESS
(SECOND MODEL) .169
IVER JOHNSON
SAFETY HAMMERLESS
(THIRD MODEL). 169
IVER JOHNSON
SEALED 8 SNUB
MODEL 68S. 169
IVER JOHNSON
SECRET SERVICE SPECIAL
MODELS 1917 & 1923. 169
IVER JOHNSON
TARGET SEALED 8
(FIRST MODEL) 169
IVER JOHNSON TARGET SEALED 8
(SECOND MODEL) .169
IVER JOHNSON TP22 .169
IVER JOHNSON TP25 .170
IVER JOHNSON TRAILSMAN 170
IVER JOHNSON TRAILSMAN
MODEL 66 170
IVER JOHNSON TRAILSMAN
SNUB MODEL 66S .170
IVER JOHNSON TRIGGER COCKING
MODEL 36T 170
IVER JOHNSON U.S. REVOLVER CO.
AUTOMATIC HAMMER MODEL 170
IVER JOHNSON U.S. REVOLVER CO.
AUTOMATIC HAMMERLESS
MODEL 170
IVER JOHNSON U.S. REVOLVER CO.
DOUBLE ACTION 170
IVER JOHNSON VIKING MODEL 67 170
IVER JOHNSON VIKING SNUB
MODEL 67S. 170
IVER JOHNSON X300 PONY. 170

JANA

JANA BISON 171

JANZ

JANZ JTL-S 171

JENNINGS/BRYCO

JENNINGS/BRYCO
MODEL J-22 171
JENNINGS/BRYCO
MODEL J-25 171
JENNINGS/BRYCO
MODEL M-38. 171

JENNINGS

JENNINGS MODEL M-48. 171

JERICHO

JERICHO MODEL 941 .171

JSL

JSL SPITFIRE. 171

KAHR

KAHR CM SERIES 171
KAHR CM45. 171
KAHR CW380. 171
KAHR E9. 171
KAHR K9, K40 171
KAHR KS40 SMALL FRAME PISTOL. 172
KAHR MK9 MICRO-
COMPACT PISTOL .172
KAHR MODEL 1911 STANDARD 172
KAHR MODEL 1911C. .172
KAHR MODEL 1911WGS DELUXE 172
KAHR P45 172
KAHR P380 172
KAHR PM 45 172

KAREEN

KAREEN MKII AUTO PISTOL. 172
KAREEN MKII COMPACT 172

KASSNAR

KASSNAR M-100D. 172
KASSNAR MODEL M-100TC. 172
KASSNAR PJK-9HP. 172

KBI

KBI PSP-25 172

KEL-TEC

KEL-TEC P-11 172
KEL-TEC P-32 172
KEL-TEC P-3AT 173
KEL-TEC P-40 173
KEL-TEC PF-9 173
KEL-TEC PLR-22 173
KEL-TEC PMR-30 173

KIMBER

KIMBER CLASSIC 45 CUSTOM 173
KIMBER CLASSIC 45
GOLD MATCH 173
KIMBER CLASSIC 45
POLYMER FRAME. .173
KIMBER CLASSIC 45 ROYAL 173
KIMBER COMPACT 45
AUTO PISTOL 173
KIMBER CUSTOM TARGET
AUTO PISTOL 173
KIMBER GOLD MATCH
TARGET PISTOL 173
KIMBER PRO COVERT II 174
KIMBER ULTRA COVERT II 174
KIMBER ULTRA AEGIS II 174
KIMBER MASTER CARRY CUSTOM. 174
KIMBER MICRO CDP .380 ACP 174
KIMBER PREDATOR HUNTER. 174
KIMBER PREDATOR SUPERGRADE. 174
KIMBER SOLO CARRY 174
KIMBER SOLO CARRY DC 174
KIMBER SUPER CARRY HD SERIES 174
KIMBER ROYAL II. 174
KIMBER WARRIOR SOC 174

KIMEL

KIMEL AP9. 174
KIMEL AP9 MINI. 174
KIMEL AP9 TARGET. .174

KLEINGUENTHER

KLEINGUENTHER R-15. 174

KORRIPHILA

KORRIPHILA HSP 701 175
KORRIPHILA HSP 701 ODIN'S EYE
(DAMASCUS). 175

KORTH

KORTH COMBAT MODEL
REVOLVER. 175
KORTH SPORT MODEL
REVOLVER. 175
KORTH MATCH MODEL REVOLVER. 175
KORTH REVOLVER 175
KORTH SEMI-AUTOMATIC
(OLD MODEL) 175
KORTH SEMI-AUTOMATIC
(NEW MODEL) 175

LAHTI

LAHTI FINNISH MODEL L-35. 175
LAHTI SWEDISH MODEL 40 175

L.A.R.

L.A.R. GRIZZLY WIN. MAG.
MARK I. 175
L.A.R. GRIZZLY WIN. MAG.
MARK I, 8-INCH, 10-INCH 176

L.A.R. GRIZZLY WIN. MAG. MARK II .176
L.A.R. GRIZZLY 44 MAG. MARK IV .176
L.A.R. GRIZZLY 50 MARK V .176

LASERAIM ARMS

LASERAIM ARMS SERIES I .176
LASERAIM ARMS SERIES II .176
LASERAIM ARMS SERIES III .176
LASERAIM ARMS SERIES IV .176

LE FRANCAIS

LE FRANCAIS ARMY MODEL .176
LE FRANCAIS POCKET MODEL .176
LE FRANCAIS POLICEMAN MODEL .176

LES BAER

LES BAER 1911 .38 SUPER STINGER .176
LES BAER BAER 1911 BOSS .45 .176
LES BAER 1911 HEMI "572" .177
LES BAER 1911 ULTIMATE TACTICAL CARRY 5" MODEL .177
LES BAER CUSTOM CENTENNIAL MODEL 1911 .177

LES INCORPORATED

LES INCORPORATED ROGAK P-18 .177

LIBERTY

LIBERTY MUSTANG .177

LIGNOSE

LIGNOSE MODEL 2 POCKET .177
LIGNOSE MODEL 2A EINHAND .177
LIGNOSE MODEL 3 POCKET .177
LIGNOSE MODEL 3A EINHAND .177

LILIPUT

LILIPUT 4.25 .177
LILIPUT 25 ACP .177

LJUTIC

LJUTIC LJ II .177

LLAMA

LLAMA IIIA SMALL FRAME .177
LLAMA VIII .177
LLAMA IX LARGE FRAME .177
LLAMA IX-A LARGE FRAME .178
LLAMA IX-B COMPACT FRAME .178
LLAMA IX-C NEW GENERATION LARGE FRAME .178
LLAMA IX-D NEW GENERATION COMPACT FRAME .178
LLAMA XA SMALL FRAME .178
LLAMA XI .178
LLAMA XV SMALL FRAME .178
LLAMA COMANCHE .178
LLAMA COMANCHE I .178
LLAMA COMANCHE II .178
LLAMA COMANCHE III .178
LLAMA MARTIAL .178
LLAMA MARTIAL DELUXE .179
LLAMA MAX-I .179
LLAMA MAX-I NEW GENERATION LARGE FRAME .179
LLAMA MAX-I NEW GENERATION COMPACT FRAME .179
LLAMA MICROMAX 380 .179
LLAMA MINIMAX SERIES .179
LLAMA MINIMAX-II .179
LLAMA MODEL 82 .179
LLAMA MODEL 87 COMPETITION MODEL .179
LLAMA OMNI .179
LLAMA SUPER COMANCHE IV .179
LLAMA SUPER COMANCHE V .179

LORCIN

LORCIN L-9MM .179
LORCIN L-22 .179
LORCIN L-25 .180
LORCIN LADY LORCIN .180
LORCIN L-32 .180
LORCIN L-380 .180
LORCIN LH-380 .180
LORCIN LT-25 .180
LORCIN O/U DERRINGER .180

LUGER

LUGER MODEL 1900 COMMERCIAL .180
LUGER MODEL 1900 SWISS .180
LUGER MODEL 1900 EAGLE .180
LUGER MODEL 1902 .180
LUGER MODEL 1902 CARBINE .180
LUGER MODEL 1906 NAVY .180
LUGER MODEL 1906 .180
LUGER MODEL 1908 .181
COMMERCIAL .181
ARMY .181
BULGARIAN CONTRACT .181
NAVY .181
LUGER MODEL 1914 MILITARY .181
LUGER MODEL 1914 ARTILLERY .181
LUGER MODEL 1914 NAVY .181
LUGER MODEL 1920 MILITARY .181
LUGER MODEL 1920 COMMERCIAL .181
LUGER MODEL 1923 COMMERCIAL .181
LUGER SIMSON & CO. .181
LUGER SWISS MANUFACTURE .181
LUGER MAUSER COMMERCIAL .181
LUGER MAUSER MILITARY (P.08) .181
LUGER KRIEGHOFF .182
LUGER MAUSER POST-WAR MANUFACTURE .182
LUGER "MAUSER PARABELLUM" COMMEMORATIVES .182

LUNA

LUNA MODEL 200 FREE PISTOL .182
LUNA MODEL 300 FREE PISTOL .182

MAB

MAB MODEL A .182
MAB MODEL B .182
MAB MODEL C .182
MAB MODEL D .182
MAB MODEL E .182
MAB MODEL F .182
MAB MODEL PA-15 .182

MAGNUM RESEARCH

MAGNUM RESEARCH BABY EAGLE 9MM .182
MAGNUM RESEARCH BABY EAGLE 9MM MODEL F .183
MAGNUM RESEARCH BFR .183
MAGNUM RESEARCH DESERT EAGLE .183
MAGNUM RESEARCH LITTLE MAX REVOLVER .183
MAGNUM RESEARCH LONE EAGLE .183
MAGNUM RESEARCH MOUNTAIN EAGLE .183
MAGNUM RESEARCH MOUNTAIN EAGLE COMPACT EDITION .183
MAGNUM RESEARCH MOUNTAIN EAGLE TARGET EDITION .183

MANDALL/CABANAS

MANDALL/CABANAS PISTOL .183

MAKAROV

MAKAROV SPECIAL EDITION PISTOL .183

MANURHIN

MANURHIN MODEL 73 CONVERTIBLE .183
MANURHIN MODEL 73 DEFENSE .183
MANURHIN MODEL 73 GENDARMERIE .183
MANURHIN MODEL 73 SILHOUETTE .184
MANURHIN MODEL 73 SPORT .184
MANURHIN MODEL MR .32 MATCH .184
MANURHIN MODEL MR .38 .184
MANURHIN MODEL PP .184
MANURHIN MODEL PPK/S .184

MAUSER

MAUSER MODEL 1896 CONEHAMMER .184
MAUSER MODEL 1896 CONEHAMMER 6-SHOT .184
MAUSER MODEL 1896 CONEHAMMER 20-SHOT .184
MAUSER MODEL 1896 "FLATSIDE" .184
MAUSER MODEL 1899 "FLATSIDE" ITALIAN NAVY .184
MAUSER MODEL 1896 LARGE RING HAMMER .184
MAUSER MODEL 1896 PRE-WAR BOLO .184
MAUSER MODEL 1896 6-SHOT .184
MAUSER MODEL 1896 PRE-WAR COMMERCIAL .185
MAUSER MODEL 1896 9MM EXPORT .185
MAUSER MODEL 1896 CARBINE .185
MAUSER MODEL 1916 "RED 9" .185
MAUSER MODEL 1896 WEIMAR REWORK .185
MAUSER MODEL 1896 "FRENCH GENDARME" .185
MAUSER MODEL 1896 POSTWAR BOLO .185
MAUSER MODEL 1930 .185
MAUSER CHINESE COPIES OF THE MODEL 1896 .185
TAKU NAVAL DOCKYARD .185
MAUSER CHINESE SMALL RING HAMMER COPIES .185
MAUSER SHANSEI 45 COPY .185
MAUSER MODEL 1910 .185
MAUSER MODEL 1914 .185
MAUSER MODEL 1910/1934 .186
MAUSER MODEL 1914 .186
MAUSER WTP .186
MAUSER WTP II .186
MAUSER HSC .186
MAUSER HSC POST-WAR .186
MAUSER HSC SUPER (GAMBA) .186
MAUSER MODEL 80 .186
MAUSER MODEL 90 .186
MAUSER MODEL 90 COMPACT .186

MEDUSA

MEDUSA MODEL 47 REVOLVER .186

METRO ARMS

METRO ARMS MAC 3011 SSD .186

MERRILL

MERRILL SPORTSMAN .186

MITCHELL ARMS

MITCHELL ARMS 45 GOLD SERIES (HIGH STANDARD/SIGNATURE SERIES) .186
MITCHELL ARMS 45 GOLD SERIES (HIGH-STANDARD/SIGNATURE SERIES) WIDE-BODY .187
MITCHELL ARMS AMERICAN EAGLE LUGER .187
MITCHELL ARMS BAT MASTERSON MODEL .187
MITCHELL ARMS CITATION II .187
MITCHELL ARMS DERRINGER .187
MITCHELL ARMS GUARDIAN II .187
MITCHELL ARMS GUARDIAN III .187
MITCHELL ARMS MODEL 57A .187
MITCHELL ARMS MODEL 70A .187
MITCHELL ARMS MODEL 1875 REMINGTON .187
MITCHELL ARMS OFFICERS MODEL 88A .187
MITCHELL ARMS OLYMPIC II I.S.U. .187
MITCHELL ARMS ROLLING BLOCK TARGET .187
MITCHELL ARMS SHARPSHOOTER II .187
MITCHELL ARMS SINGLE ACTION ARMY .188

MITCHELL ARMS SINGLE ACTION ARMY, U.S. ARMY MODEL . . . 188
MITCHELL ARMS SINGLE ACTION ARMY, CAVALRY MODEL . . . 188
MITCHELL ARMS SINGLE ACTION ARMY, COWBOY MODEL . . . 188
MITCHELL ARMS SPORT KING II . . . 188
MITCHELL ARMS TITAN II . . . 188
MITCHELL ARMS TITAN III . . . 188
MITCHELL ARMS TROPHY II . . . 188
MITCHELL ARMS VICTOR II . . . 188

MKE KIRIKKALE

MKE KIRIKKALE . . . 188

MOA

MOA MAXIMUM . . . 188

MORINI

MORINI MODEL CM-80 . . . 188
MORINI MODEL CM-80 SUPER COMPETITION . . . 189
MORINI MODEL 84E FREE PISTOL . . . 189

MOSSBERG

MOSSBERG ABILENE . . . 189
MOSSBERG BROWNIE . . . 189

MPA

MPA 380 . . . 189

NAGANT

NAGANT MODEL 1895 . . . 189
NAGANT MODEL 1895 TRAINING MODEL . . . 189

NAMBU

NAMBU MODEL 1902 FIRST TYPE ("GRANDPA") . . . 189
NAMBU MODEL 1902 SECOND TYPE ("PAPA") . . . 189
NAMBU MODEL 1902 7MM ("BABY") . . . 189
NAMBU TYPE 14 (1925) . . . 189
NAMBU TYPE 26 REVOLVER . . . 189
NAMBU TYPE 94 . . . 189

NAVY ARMS

NAVY ARMS 1873 SINGLE-ACTION REVOLVER . . . 189
NAVY ARMS BISLEY MODEL SINGLE-ACTION REVOLVER . . . 189
NAVY ARMS FLAT TOP TARGET MODEL REVOLVER . . . 190
NAVY ARMS FRONTIER MODEL . . . 190
NAVY ARMS FRONTIER, BUNTLINE MODEL . . . 190
NAVY ARMS GRAND PRIX . . . 190
NAVY ARMS HIGH POWER . . . 190
NAVY ARMS LUGER . . . 190
NAVY ARMS MODEL 1873 . . . 190
NAVY ARMS MODEL 1873, ECONOMY MODEL . . . 190
NAVY ARMS MODEL 1875 REMINGTON . . . 190
NAVY ARMS MODEL 1875 SCHOFIELD WELLS FARGO MODEL . . . 190
NAVY ARMS MODEL 1875 SCHOFIELD U.S. CAVALRY MODEL . . . 190
NAVY ARMS MODEL 1890 REMINGTON . . . 190
NAVY ARMS "PINCHED FRAME" SINGLE-ACTION REVOLVER . . . 190
NAVY ARMS ROLLING BLOCK . . . 190
NAVY ARMS TT-OLYMPIA . . . 190
NAVY ARMS TU-90 . . . 190
NAVY ARMS TU-711 MAUSER . . . 191
NAVY ARMS U.S. GOVERNMENT MODEL . . . 191

NEW ADVANTAGE

NEW ADVANTAGE DERRINGER . . . 191

NEW DETONICS

NEW DETONICS LADIES ESCORT . . . 191

NEW ENGLAND FIREARMS

NEW ENGLAND FIREARMS LADY ULTRA . . . 191
NEW ENGLAND FIREARMS MODEL R73 . . . 191
NEW ENGLAND FIREARMS MODEL R92 . . . 191
NEW ENGLAND FIREARMS SINGLE SHOT . . . 191
NEW ENGLAND FIREARMS ULTRA . . . 191

NORINCO

NORINCO MODEL 1911A1 . . . 191
NORINCO MODEL 77B . . . 191
NORINCO TYPE 54-1 TOKAREV . . . 191
NORINCO TYPE 59 MAKAROV . . . 192

NORTH AMERICAN ARMS

NORTH AMERICAN ARMS GUARDIAN . . . 192
NORTH AMERICAN ARMS MINI-MASTER BLACK WIDOW . . . 192
NORTH AMERICAN ARMS MINI-MASTER TARGET . . . 192
NORTH AMERICAN ARMS MODEL 22 LR . . . 192
NORTH AMERICAN ARMS MODEL 22 MAGNUM . . . 192
NORTH AMERICAN ARMS MODEL 22 MAGNUM CONVERTIBLE . . . 192
NORTH AMERICAN ARMS SINGLE ACTION REVOLVER . . . 192
NORTH AMERICAN ARMS VIPER BELT BUCKLE . . . 192

ODI

ODI VIKING . . . 192

OLYMPIC ARMS

OLYMPIC ARMS OA-96 AR PISTOL . . . 192
OLYMPIC ARMS SCHUETZEN PISTOL WORKS BIG DEUCE . . . 192
OLYMPIC ARMS SCHUETZEN PISTOL WORKS CREST SERIES . . . 192
OLYMPIC ARMS SCHUETZEN PISTOL WORKS GRIFFON . . . 193
OLYMPIC ARMS WOLVERINE . . . 193

ONE PRO

ONE PRO .45 AUTO . . . 193
ONE PRO 9 AUTO . . . 193

ORTGIES

ORTGIES POCKET PISTOL . . . 193
ORTGIES VEST POCKET PISTOL . . . 193

PACHMAYR

PACHMAYR DOMINATOR . . . 193

PARA-ORDNANCE

PARA-ORDNANCE P-12.45 . . . 193
PARA-ORDNANCE P-13.45 . . . 194
PARA-ORDNANCE P-14.40 . . . 194
PARA-ORDNANCE P-14.45 . . . 194
PARA-ORDNANCE P-15.40 . . . 194
PARA-ORDNANCE P-16.40 . . . 194
PARA-ORDNANCE S-SERIES LIMITED PISTOLS . . . 194
PARA-ORDNANCE WARTHOG . . . 194
PARA-ORDNANCE NITE HAWG . . . 194
PARA-ORDNANCE SLIM HAWG . . . 194
PARA-ORDNANCE LTC . . . 195

PARA USA

PARA USA GI EXPERT SERIES . . . 195
PARA USA WARTHOG SERIES . . . 195
PARA USA PXT TACTICAL SERIES . . . 195

PARDINI

PARDINI GP RAPID FIRE MATCH . . . 195
PARDINI GP RAPID FIRE MATCH SCHUMAN . . . 195
PARDINI K50 FREE PISTOL . . . 195
PARDINI MODEL HP TARGET . . . 195
PARDINI MODEL SP LADIES . . . 196
PARDINI MODEL SP TARGET . . . 196

PETERS STAHL

PETERS STAHL PS-07 COMBAT COMPENSATOR . . . 196

PHELPS

PHELPS EAGLE I . . . 196
PHELPS GRIZZLY . . . 196
PHELPS HERITAGE I . . . 196
PHELPS PATRIOT . . . 196

PHOENIX ARMS

PHOENIX ARMS HP22 . . . 196
PHOENIX ARMS HP25 . . . 196
PHOENIX ARMS MODEL RAVEN . . . 196

PLAINFIELD

PLAINFIELD MODEL 71 . . . 196
PLAINFIELD MODEL 72 . . . 196

PSA-25

PSA-25 AUTO POCKET PISTOL . . . 196

PUMA

PUMA BOUNTY HUNTER . . . 197
PUMA MODEL 1873 . . . 197

QFI

QFI DARK HORSEMAN . . . 197
QFI HORSEMAN . . . 197
QFI MODEL LA380 . . . 197
QFI MODEL LA380 TIGRESS . . . 197
QFI MODEL SA25 . . . 197
QFI MODEL SA25 TIGRESS . . . 197
QFI MODEL SO38 . . . 197
QFI PLAINS RIDER . . . 197
QFI RP SERIES . . . 197
QFI WESTERN RANGER . . . 197

RG

RG 14 . . . 197
RG 16 . . . 197
RG 17 . . . 198
RG 23 . . . 198
RG 25 . . . 198
RG 26 . . . 198
RG 30 . . . 198
RG 31 . . . 198
RG 38S . . . 198
RG 39 . . . 198
RG 40 . . . 198
RG 42 . . . 198
RG 57 . . . 198
RG 63 . . . 198
RG 66 . . . 198
RG 74 . . . 198
RG 88 . . . 198

RADOM

RADOM P-35 . . . 198

RAM-LINE

RAM-LINE EXACTOR TARGET . . . 198
RAM-LINE RAM-TECH . . . 199

RANDALL

RANDALL CURTIS E. LEMAY FOUR-STAR MODEL . . . 199
RANDALL RAIDER/SERVICE MODEL C . . . 199
RANDALL SERVICE MODEL . . . 199

RAVEN

RAVEN MP-25 . . . 199
RAVEN P-25 . . . 199

RECORD-MATCH

RECORD-MATCH MODEL 200 FREE PISTOL . . . 199
RECORD-MATCH MODEL 210 FREE PISTOL . . . 199
RECORD-MATCH MODEL 210A FREE PISTOL . . . 199

REISING

REISING TARGET MODEL . . . 199

REMINGTON

REMINGTON MODEL 51 .199
REMINGTON MODEL 95 .199
REMINGTON MODEL 1901 TARGET .199
REMINGTON MODEL 1911 MILITARY .199
REMINGTON MODEL 1911 R1 .199
REMINGTON MODEL 1911 R1 ENHANCED .200
REMINGTON MODEL 1911 R1 CARRY .200
REMINGTON XP-22R .200
REMINGTON XP-100 HUNTER PISTOL .200
REMINGTON XP-100 CUSTOM HB LONG RANGE PISTOL .200
REMINGTON XP-100 SILHOUETTE .200
REMINGTON XP-100 VARMINT SPECIAL .200
REMINGTON XP-100R .200

REPUBLIC

REPUBLIC PATRIOT .200

REXIO

REXIO PUCARA M224 REVOLVER .200
REXIO PUCARA M324 REVOLVER .200
REXIO PUCARA M384 REVOLVER .200

ROCK RIVER ARMS

ROCK RIVER ARMS PRO CARRY .200
ROCKY MOUNTAIN ARMS 1911A1-LH .200
ROCKY MOUNTAIN ARMS PATRIOT .201

ROSSI

ROSSI CYCLOPS REVOLVER .201
ROSSI LADY ROSSI .201
ROSSI MODEL 31 .201
ROSSI MODEL 51 .201
ROSSI MODEL 68 .201
ROSSI MODEL 68S .201
ROSSI MODEL 69 .201
ROSSI MODEL 70 .201
ROSSI MODEL 84 STAINLESS .201
ROSSI MODEL 88 STAINLESS .201
ROSSI MODEL 89 STAINLESS .201
ROSSI MODEL 94 .201
ROSSI MODEL 511 SPORTSMAN .201
ROSSI MODEL 515 .201
ROSSI MODEL 518 .201
ROSSI MODEL 720 .202
ROSSI MODEL 720C .202
ROSSI MODEL 851 .202
ROSSI MODEL 877 REVOLVER .202
ROSSI MODEL 941 .202
ROSSI MODEL 951 .202
ROSSI MODEL 971 .202
ROSSI MODEL 971 COMP GUN .202
ROSSI MODEL 971 STAINLESS .202
ROSSI MODEL 971 VRC REVOLVER .202
ROSSI MATCHED PAIR PISTOL .202
ROSSI RANCH HAND .202
ROSSI WIZARD .202

ROYAL

ROYAL .202

RPM

RPM XL SINGLE SHOT .202
RPM XL HUNTER SINGLE SHOT .202

SAFARI ARMS

SAFARI ARMS BLACK WIDOW .203
SAFARI ARMS COHORT PISTOL .203
SAFARI ARMS ENFORCER .203
SAFARI ARMS ENFORCER CARRYCOMP II .203
SAFARI ARMS G.I. SAFARI .203
SAFARI ARMS MATCHMASTER .203
SAFARI ARMS MATCHMASTER CARRYCOMP I .203
SAFARI ARMS MODEL 81 .203
SAFARI ARMS MODEL 81BP .203
SAFARI ARMS MODEL 81L .203
SAFARI ARMS MODEL 81NM .203
SAFARI ARMS MODEL 81 SILUETA .203
SAFARI ARMS OA-93 .203
SAFARI ARMS RELIABLE PISTOL .203
SAFARI ARMS RELIABLE 4-STAR PISTOL .203
SAFARI ARMS RENEGADE .204
SAFARI ARMS UNLIMITED .204

SAKO

SAKO TRIACE MATCH .204

SARSILMAZ

SARSILMAZ KAMA SPORT .204

SAUER

SAUER MODEL 28 .204
SAUER MODEL 38H .204
SAUER MODEL 1913 .204
SAUER MODEL 1913 POCKET .204
SAUER MODEL 1930 (BEHORDEN MODEL) .204
SAUER WTM .204

SAVAGE

SAVAGE AUTOMATIC PISTOL .204
SAVAGE MODEL 101 .204
SAVAGE MODEL 1907 .205
SAVAGE MODEL 1907 U.S. ARMY TEST TRIAL .205
SAVAGE MODEL 1915 HAMMERLESS .205
SAVAGE MODEL 1917 .205
SAVAGE STRIKER BOLT-ACTION HUNTING HANDGUN .205

SCCY

SCCY CPX GEN 2 .205

SECURITY INDUSTRIES

SECURITY INDUSTRIES MODEL PM357 .205
SECURITY INDUSTRIES MODEL PPM357 .205
SECURITY INDUSTRIES MODEL PSS38 .205

SEDCO

SEDCO MODEL SP-22 .205

SEDGELY

SEDGELY BABY HAMMERLESS MODEL .205

SEECAMP

SEECAMP LWS 25 ACP MODEL .205
SEECAMP LWS 32 .205

SHERIDAN

SHERIDAN KNOCABOUT .205

SIG

SIG P210-2 .206
SIG P210-1 .206
SIG P210-5 .206
SIG P210-6 .206

SIG-HAMMERLI

SIG-HAMMERLI MODEL P240 .206

SIG SAUER

SIG SAUER P210 LEGEND .206
SIG SAUER P220 "AMERICAN" .206

SIGARMS

SIGARMS MPX 9 .206
SIGARMS P220 COMBAT .206
SIGARMS P220 MATCH .206
SIGARMS P220 COMPACT .206
SIGARMS P220 ELITE .206
SIGARMS P220 ELITE STAINLESS .207
SIGARMS P220 CARRY ELITE STAINLESS .207
SIGARMS P220 PLATINUM ELITE .207
SIG SAUER P225 .207
SIG SAUER P226 .207
SIGARMS P 226 SAO .207
SIGARMS P226 SCT .207
SIGARMS P226 ELITE .207
SIGARMS P226 ELITE STAINLESS .207
SIGARMS P226 PLATINUM ELITE .207
SIGARMS P 227 .207
SIG SAUER P228 .207
SIG SAUER P229 .207
SIG SAUER P229 S AUTO PISTOL .207
SIGARMS P229 ELITE .207
SIGARMS P229 PLATINUM ELITE .208
SIGARMS 1911 C3 .208
SIGARMS 1911 PLATINUM ELITE .208
SIGARMS 1911 PLATINUM ELITE CARRY .208
SIG SAUER P230 .208
SIG SAUER P230 SL STAINLESS .208
SIG SAUER P232 PERSONAL SIZE PISTOL .208
SIG SAUER P238/P238 EXTREME .208
SIG SAUER P-238 EQUINOX .208
SIG SAUER P-238 STAINLESS .208
SIG SAUER P239 PISTOL .208
SIGARMS P250 COMPACT .208
SIG SAUER P290 .208
SIG SAUER MOSQUITO .208
SIG SAUER P522 .208
SIG SAUER P522 SWAT .208
SIG SAUER P556 .208
SIG SAUER P556 SWAT .208
SIGARMS REVOLUTION COMPACT SAS .209
SIGARMS REVOLUTION COMPACT C3 .209

SMITH & WESSON

SMITH & WESSON 22 STRAIGHT LINE .209
SMITH & WESSON 32 DOUBLE ACTION .209
SMITH & WESSON 32 SAFETY HAMMERLESS .209
SMITH & WESSON 38 DOUBLE ACTION .209
SMITH & WESSON 38 DOUBLE ACTION PERFECTED MODEL .209
SMITH & WESSON 38 SAFETY HAMMERLESS (NEW DEPARTURE) .209
SMITH & WESSON 38 SINGLE ACTION THIRD MODEL (MODEL 1891) .210
SMITH & WESSON 44 DOUBLE ACTION FIRST MODEL .210
SMITH & WESSON 44 DOUBLE ACTION FAVORITE .210
SMITH & WESSON NEW MODEL NO. 3 .210
SMITH & WESSON NEW MODEL NO. 3 FRONTIER .210
SMITH & WESSON NEW MODEL NO. 3 TARGET .210
SMITH & WESSON NEW MODEL NO. 3 WINCHESTER .210
SMITH & WESSON SINGLE SHOT FIRST MODEL .210
SMITH & WESSON SINGLE SHOT SECOND MODEL .210
SMITH & WESSON SINGLE SHOT THIRD MODEL (PERFECTED SINGLE SHOT) .210
SMITH & WESSON 22 WMR SERVICE KIT GUN (MODEL 650) .210
SMITH & WESSON 22/32 KIT GUN .210
SMITH & WESSON 22/32 KIT GUN (MODEL 34) .210
SMITH & WESSON 22/32 TARGET .210
SMITH & WESSON 32 HAND EJECTOR FIRST MODEL (MODEL OF 1896) .211
SMITH & WESSON 32 HAND EJECTOR (MODEL 30) .211
SMITH & WESSON 38 REGULATION POLICE (MODEL 31) .211
SMITH & WESSON 38 REGULATION POLICE TARGET MODEL .211
SMITH & WESSON 38 REGULATION POLICE (MODEL 33) .211
SMITH & WESSON 1960 22/32 KIT GUN WMR (MODEL 51) .211
SMITH & WESSON 1977 22/32 KIT GUN WMR (MODEL 63) .211
SMITH & WESSON AIRWEIGHT KIT GUN (MODEL 43) .211
SMITH & WESSON BODYGUARD 380 .211

SMITH & WESSON BODYGUARD (MODEL 49) .211
SMITH & WESSON BODYGUARD (MODEL 649) .211
SMITH & WESSON BODYGUARD AIRWEIGHT (MODEL 38) .211
SMITH & WESSON CENTENNIAL (MODEL 40) .211
SMITH & WESSON CENTENNIAL (MODEL 640) .212
SMITH & WESSON CENTENNIAL (MODEL 940) .212
SMITH & WESSON CENTENNIAL AIRWEIGHT (MODEL 42) .212
SMITH & WESSON CENTENNIAL AIRWEIGHT (MODEL 442) .212
SMITH & WESSON CENTENNIAL AIRWEIGHT (MODEL 642) .212
SMITH & WESSON MODEL 642 POWERPORT PRO SERIES .212
SMITH & WESSON CHIEF'S SPECIAL (MODEL 36) .212
SMITH & WESSON CHIEF'S SPECIAL AIRWEIGHT (MODEL 37) .212
SMITH & WESSON MODEL 637 AIRWEIGHT REVOLVER .212
SMITH & WESSON CHIEF'S SPECIAL STAINLESS (MODEL 60) .212
SMITH & WESSON MODEL 60 .357 MAGNUM CHIEFS SPECIAL .212
SMITH & WESSON MODEL 60 PRO SERIES .212
SMITH & WESSON LADYSMITH (MODEL 36-LS) .212
SMITH & WESSON LADYSMITH (MODEL 60-LS) .212
SMITH & WESSON MODEL 60 3-INCH FULL LUG .213
SMITH & WESSON MODEL 651 .213
SMITH & WESSON TARGET MODEL 1953 (MODEL 35) .213
SMITH & WESSON TERRIER (MODEL 32) .213
SMITH & WESSON K AND L MEDIUM FRAME REVOLVERS .213
SMITH & WESSON 32-20 HAND EJECTOR .213
SMITH & WESSON 38 MILITARY & POLICE .213
SMITH & WESSON 38 MILITARY & POLICE VICTORY MODEL .213
SMITH & WESSON K-22 OUTDOORSMAN .213
SMITH & WESSON K-22 SECOND MODEL .213
SMITH & WESSON K-32 FIRST MODEL .213
SMITH & WESSON MODEL 10 MILITARY & POLICE .213
SMITH & WESSON MODEL 10 MILITARY & POLICE HEAVY BARREL .214
SMITH & WESSON MODEL 12 MILITARY & POLICE AIRWEIGHT .214
SMITH & WESSON MODEL 13 H.B. MILITARY & POLICE .214
SMITH & WESSON MODEL 14 K-38 MASTERPIECE .214
SMITH & WESSON MODEL 14 K-38 MASTERPIECE FULL LUG .214
SMITH & WESSON MODEL 14 K-38 MASTERPIECE SINGLE ACTION .214
SMITH & WESSON MODEL 15 38 COMBAT MASTERPIECE .214
SMITH & WESSON MODEL 16 K-32 MASTERPIECE .214
SMITH & WESSON MODEL 16 K-32 MASTERPIECE FULL LUG .214
SMITH & WESSON MODEL 17 K-22 MASTERPIECE .214
SMITH & WESSON MODEL 17 K-22 MASTERPIECE FULL LUG .214
SMITH & WESSON MODEL 18 22 COMBAT MASTERPIECE .215
SMITH & WESSON MODEL 19 COMBAT MAGNUM .215
SMITH & WESSON MODEL 48 K-22 MASTERPIECE WMR .215
SMITH & WESSON MODEL 53 .215
SMITH & WESSON MODEL 64 .215
SMITH & WESSON MODEL 65 .215
SMITH & WESSON MODEL 65LS LADYSMITH .215
SMITH & WESSON MODEL 66 COMBAT MAGNUM .215
SMITH & WESSON MODEL 67 K-38 COMBAT MASTERPIECE .215
SMITH & WESSON MODEL 547 .215
SMITH & WESSON MODEL 317 AIRLITE, 317 LADYSMITH .215
SMITH & WESSON MODEL 317 AIRLITE KIT GUN .216
SMITH & WESSON MODEL 586 DISTINGUISHED COMBAT MAGNUM .216
SMITH & WESSON MODEL 610 CLASSIC HUNTER REVOLVER .216
SMITH & WESSON MODEL 617 K-22 MASTERPIECE FULL LUG .216
SMITH & WESSON MODEL 651 .216
SMITH & WESSON MODEL 657 .216
SMITH & WESSON MODEL 696 .216
MODEL 396 NIGHT GUARD .216
SMITH & WESSON MODEL 640 CENTENNIAL .216
SMITH & WESSON MODEL 442 CENTENNIAL AIRWEIGHT .216
SMITH & WESSON MODEL 642 AIRWEIGHT .216
SMITH & WESSON MODEL 642LS LADYSMITH .216
SMITH & WESSON MODEL 648 K-22 MASTERPIECE WMR .216
SMITH & WESSON MODEL 681 .216
SMITH & WESSON MODEL 686 .217
SMITH & WESSON MODEL 686 MAGNUM PLUS .217
SMITH & WESSON MODEL 686 MIDNIGHT BLACK .217
SMITH & WESSON 38/44 HEAVY DUTY (MODEL 20) .217
SMITH & WESSON 38/44 OUTDOORSMAN (MODEL 23) .217
SMITH & WESSON MODEL 57 .217
SMITH & WESSON MODEL 58 .217
SMITH & WESSON 44 HAND EJECTOR 1ST MODEL (TRIPLE LOCK, NEW CENTURY) .217
SMITH & WESSON 44 HAND EJECTOR 2ND MODEL .217
SMITH & WESSON 44 HAND EJECTOR 3RD MODEL .217
SMITH & WESSON 44 MAGNUM (MODEL 29) .217
SMITH & WESSON 44 MAGNUM MODEL 29 CLASSIC .218
SMITH & WESSON 44 MAGNUM MODEL 29 CLASSIC DX .218
SMITH & WESSON 44 MAGNUM MODEL 29 SILHOUETTE .218
SMITH & WESSON 44 MAGNUM MODEL 629 .218
SMITH & WESSON 44 MAGNUM MODEL 629 CLASSIC .218
SMITH & WESSON 44 MAGNUM MODEL 629 CLASSIC DX .218
SMITH & WESSON 357 MAGNUM (PRE-WAR REGISTERED) .218
SMITH & WESSON 357 MAGNUM (POST-WAR/MODEL 27) .218
SMITH & WESSON 1950 44 MILITARY (MODEL 21) .218
SMITH & WESSON MODEL 27 (1991 REINTRODUCTION) .218
MODEL 627 PRO SERIES .218
SMITH & WESSON 455 HAND EJECTOR 1ST MODEL .218
SMITH & WESSON 455 HAND EJECTOR 2ND MODEL .218
SMITH & WESSON 1950 ARMY (MODEL 22) .218
SMITH & WESSON 1950 44 TARGET (MODEL 24) .219
SMITH & WESSON MODEL 24 TARGET (1983 REINTRODUCTION) .219
SMITH & WESSON 1950/1955 45 TARGET (MODEL 25 & 26) .219
SMITH & WESSON HIGHWAY PATROLMAN (MODEL 28) .219
SMITH & WESSON MILITARY MODEL OF 1917 .219
SMITH & WESSON MODEL 25 .219
SMITH & WESSON MODEL 625 .219
SMITH & WESSON MODEL 25-5 .219
SMITH & WESSON MODEL 610 .219
SMITH & WESSON MODEL 624 .219
SMITH & WESSON MODEL 625-2 .219
SMITH & WESSON MODEL 1926 44 MILITARY .219
SMITH & WESSON MODEL 1926 44 TARGET .220
SMITH & WESSON MODEL 500 .220
SMITH & WESSON MODEL 460V .220
SMITH & WESSON MODEL 22 – THUNDER RANCH .45 ACP .220
SMITH & WESSON FIFTIETH ANNIVERSARY MODEL 29 .220
SMITH & WESSON M&P340 .220
SMITH & WESSON MODEL 325 NIGHT GUARD .220
SMITH & WESSON MODEL 327 NIGHT GUARD .220
SMITH & WESSON MODEL 329 NIGHT GUARD .220
SMITH & WESSON M&P340CT .220
SMITH & WESSON M&P360 .220
SMITH & WESSON MODEL 315 NIGHT GUARD .38 .220
SMITH & WESSON MODEL 637 POWER PORT PRO SERIES .220
SMITH & WESSON M&PR8 .220
SMITH & WESSON MODEL 60 WITH HI-VIZ SIGHT .220
SMITH & WESSON MODEL 386 SC/S .220
SMITH & WESSON MODEL 686 PLUS .220
SMITH & WESSON MODEL 36 CLASSIC .220
SMITH & WESSON MODEL 21 CLASSIC .221
SMITH & WESSON MODEL 22 CLASSIC .221
SMITH & WESSON MODEL 22 OF 1917 CLASSIC .221
SMITH & WESSON MODEL 29 CLASSIC .221
SMITH & WESSON MODEL 32 AUTO .221
SMITH & WESSON MODEL 35 .221
SMITH & WESSON 38 TARGET AUTO (MODEL 52) .221
SMITH & WESSON MODEL 39 9MM AUTO .221
SMITH & WESSON MODEL 59 9MM AUTO .221
SMITH & WESSON MODEL 439 .221
SMITH & WESSON MODEL 457 .221
SMITH & WESSON MODEL 459 .221
SMITH & WESSON MODEL 469 .221
SMITH & WESSON MODEL 539 .222
SMITH & WESSON MODEL 559 .222
SMITH & WESSON MODEL 639 .222
SMITH & WESSON MODEL 645 .222
SMITH & WESSON MODEL 659 .222
SMITH & WESSON MODEL 669 .222
SMITH & WESSON MODEL 745 .222
SMITH & WESSON MODEL 356 TSW LIMITED .222
SMITH & WESSON MODEL 356 TSW COMPACT .222
SMITH & WESSON MODEL 410 DA .222
SMITH & WESSON MODEL 411 .222
SMITH & WESSON MODEL 908 .222
SMITH & WESSON MODEL 909 .222
SMITH & WESSON MODEL 910 .223
SMITH & WESSON MODEL 915 .223

SMITH & WESSON MODEL 1006 .223
SMITH & WESSON MODEL 1026 .223
SMITH & WESSON MODEL 1046 .223
SMITH & WESSON MODEL 1066 .223
SMITH & WESSON MODEL 1066-NS .223
SMITH & WESSON MODEL 1076 .223
SMITH & WESSON MODEL 1086 .223
SMITH & WESSON MODEL 3904 .223
SMITH & WESSON MODEL 3906 .223
SMITH & WESSON MODEL 3913 .223
SMITH & WESSON MODEL 3913 LADYSMITH .223
SMITH & WESSON MODEL 3913-NL .223
SMITH & WESSON MODEL 3913TSW/3953TSW AUTO PISTOLS .224
SMITH & WESSON MODEL 3914 .224
SMITH & WESSON MODEL 3914 LADYSMITH .224
SMITH & WESSON MODEL 3914-NL .224
SMITH & WESSON MODEL 3953 .224
SMITH & WESSON MODEL 3954 .224
SMITH & WESSON MODEL 4006 .224
SMITH & WESSON MODEL 4043 .224
SMITH & WESSON MODEL 4013 .224
SMITH & WESSON MODEL 4053 TSW .224
SMITH & WESSON MODEL 4014 .224
SMITH & WESSON MODEL 4046 .224
SMITH & WESSON MODEL 4053 .224
SMITH & WESSON MODEL 4054 .225
SMITH & WESSON MODEL 4505 .225
SMITH & WESSON MODEL 4506 .225
SMITH & WESSON MODEL 4513TSW/4553TSW .225
SMITH & WESSON MODEL 4516 .225
SMITH & WESSON MODEL 4526 .225
SMITH & WESSON MODEL 4536 .225
SMITH & WESSON MODEL 4546 .225
SMITH & WESSON MODEL 4556 .225
SMITH & WESSON MODEL 4566 .225
SMITH & WESSON MODEL 4567-NS .225
SMITH & WESSON MODEL 4576 .225
SMITH & WESSON MODEL 4586 .225
SMITH & WESSON MODEL 5903 .226
SMITH & WESSON MODEL 5904 .226
SMITH & WESSON MODEL 5905 .226
SMITH & WESSON MODEL 5906 .226
SMITH & WESSON MODEL 5924 .226
SMITH & WESSON MODEL 5926 .226
SMITH & WESSON MODEL 5943 .226
SMITH & WESSON MODEL 5943-SSV .226
SMITH & WESSON MODEL 5944 .226
SMITH & WESSON MODEL 5946 .226
SMITH & WESSON MODEL 6904 .226
SMITH & WESSON MODEL 6906 .226
SMITH & WESSON MODEL 6926 .226
SMITH & WESSON MODEL 6944 .226
SMITH & WESSON MODEL 6946 .227
SMITH & WESSON SIGMA SW9F .227
SMITH & WESSON SIGMA SW9C .227
SMITH & WESSON SIGMA SW40F .227
SMITH & WESSON SIGMA SW40C .227
SMITH & WESSON SIGMA SW380 .227
SMITH & WESSON 22 AUTO TARGET (MODEL 41) .227
SMITH & WESSON 22 AUTO MATCH (MODEL 41) .227
SMITH & WESSON MODEL 41 FIFTIETH ANNIVERSARY EDITION .227
SMITH & WESSON 22 AUTO TARGET (MODEL 46) .227
SMITH & WESSON ESCORT MODEL 61 .227
SMITH & WESSON MODEL 422 .227
SMITH & WESSON MODEL 622 .228
SMITH & WESSON MODEL 2206 .228
SMITH & WESSON MODEL 2206 TARGET .228
SMITH & WESSON MODEL 2213 .228
SMITH & WESSON MODEL 2214 SPORTSMAN .228
SMITH & WESSON MODEL 22A SPORT .228
SMITH & WESSON MODEL 22S SPORT .228
SMITH & WESSON MODEL 22A TARGET .228
SMITH & WESSON MODEL 22S TARGET PISTOL .228
SMITH & WESSON GOVERNOR .228
SMITH & WESSON M&P 9 .228
SMITH & WESSON MODEL M&P9-JG .228
SMITH & WESSON MODEL M&P9 PRO SERIES .228
SMITH & WESSON MODEL M&P9L .228
SMITH & WESSON M&P 40 .228
SMITH & WESSON M&P .357 SIG .229
SMITH & WESSON M&P45 .229
SMITH & WESSON M&P9C .229
SMITH & WESSON M&P40C .229
SMITH & WESSON M&P357C .229
SMITH & WESSON SW9VE ALLIED FORCES .229
SMITH & WESSON SW40VE ALLIED FORCES .229
SMITH & WESSON MODEL SW1911 .229
SMITH & WESSON MODEL SW1911 PD .229
SMITH & WESSON MODEL SW1911 PD GUNSITE COMMEMORATIVE .229
SMITH & WESSON SW1911 TACTICAL RAIL .229
SMITH & WESSON MODEL SW1911 – ROLLING THUNDER COMMEMORATIVE .229
SMITH & WESSON MODEL SW1911 PRO SERIES .229
SMITH & WESSON SD9 .229

SOKOLOVSKY

SOKOLOVSKY 45 AUTOMASTER .229

SPECIALIZED WEAPONS

SPECIALIZED WEAPONS SPECTRE FIVE .229

SPHINX

SPHINX AT-380 .229
SPHINX AT-2000S .229
SPHINX AT-2000C COMPETITOR .230
SPHINX AT-2000GM GRAND MASTER .230
SPHINX AT-2000H .230
SPHINX AT-2000P .230
SPHINX AT-2000PS .230
SPHINX 3000 .230

SPORTARMS

SPORTARMS MODEL HS21S .230
SPORTARMS MODEL HS38S .230
SPORTARMS TOKAREV MODEL 213 .230

SPRINGFIELD ARMORY

SPRINGFIELD ARMORY M6 .230
SPRINGFIELD ARMORY MODEL 1911-A1 .230
SPRINGFIELD ARMORY MODEL 1911-A1 BASIC COMPETITION .231
SPRINGFIELD ARMORY MODEL 1911-A1 BULLSEYE WADCUTTER .231
SPRINGFIELD ARMORY MODEL 1911-A1 WADCUTTER ENTRY LEVEL .231
SPRINGFIELD ARMORY MODEL 1911-A1 CHAMPION .231
SPRINGFIELD ARMORY MODEL 1911A1 DEFENDER PISTOL .231
SPRINGFIELD ARMORY MODEL 1911-A1 COMMANDER .231
SPRINGFIELD ARMORY MODEL 1911-A1 COMBAT COMMANDER .231
SPRINGFIELD ARMORY MODEL 1911-A1 COMPACT .231
SPRINGFIELD ARMORY MODEL 1911-A1 COMPACT V10 ULTRA .231
SPRINGFIELD ARMORY MODEL 1911-A1 COMPETITION .231
SPRINGFIELD ARMORY MODEL 1911-A1 CUSTOM CARRY .231
SPRINGFIELD ARMORY MODEL 1911-A1 CUSTOM COMPACT .232
SPRINGFIELD ARMORY MODEL 1911-A1 DISTINGUISHED .232
SPRINGFIELD ARMORY MODEL 1911-A1 EXPERT PISTOL .232
SPRINGFIELD ARMORY MODEL 1911-A1 FACTORY COMP .232
SPRINGFIELD ARMORY MODEL 1911-A1 HIGH CAPACITY .232
SPRINGFIELD ARMORY MODEL V10 ULTRA COMPACT PISTOL .232
SPRINGFIELD ARMORY TRP PISTOLS .232
SPRINGFIELD ARMORY MODEL 1911-A1 N.M. HARDBALL .232
SPRINGFIELD ARMORY MODEL 1911-A1 N.R.A. PPC .232
SPRINGFIELD ARMORY MODEL 1911-A1 PRODUCT IMPROVED DEFENDER .232
SPRINGFIELD ARMORY MODEL 1911-A1 TROPHY MASTER COMPETITION PISTOL .232
SPRINGFIELD ARMORY MODEL 1911-A1 TROPHY MASTER COMPETITION EXPERT PISTOL .233
SPRINGFIELD ARMORY MODEL 1911-A1 TROPHY MATCH .233
SPRINGFIELD ARMORY MODEL 1911-A1 '90S EDITION .233
SPRINGFIELD ARMORY MODEL 1911-A1 '90S EDITION CHAMPION COMP .233

SPRINGFIELD ARMORY MODEL 1911-A1 '90S EDITION CHAMPION XM4 HIGH CAPACITY 233
SPRINGFIELD ARMORY MODEL 1911-A1 '90S EDITION COMBAT COMMANDER 233
SPRINGFIELD ARMORY MODEL 1911-A1 '90S EDITION COMMANDER 233
SPRINGFIELD ARMORY MODEL 1911-A1 '90S EDITION COMPACT 233
SPRINGFIELD ARMORY MODEL 1911-A1 '90S EDITION COMPACT COMP 233
SPRINGFIELD ARMORY MODEL 1911-A1 '90S EDITION STAINLESS 233
SPRINGFIELD ARMORY MODEL 1911-A2 S.A.S.S. 233
SPRINGFIELD ARMORY BOBCAT 233
SPRINGFIELD ARMORY FIRECAT 233
SPRINGFIELD ARMORY LYNX 233
SPRINGFIELD ARMORY MODEL P9 233
SPRINGFIELD ARMORY MODEL P9 COMPACT 234
SPRINGFIELD ARMORY MODEL P9 FACTORY COMP 234
SPRINGFIELD ARMORY MODEL P9 SUBCOMPACT 234
SPRINGFIELD ARMORY MODEL P9 ULTRA LSP 234
SPRINGFIELD ARMORY OMEGA 234
SPRINGFIELD ARMORY OMEGA MATCH 234
SPRINGFIELD ARMORY PANTHER 234
SPRINGFIELD ARMORY XD 45ACP 234
SPRINGFIELD ARMORY LIGHTWEIGHT OPERATOR 234
SPRINGFIELD ARMORY LIGHTWEIGHT CHAMPION OPERATOR 234
SPRINGFIELD ARMORY ENHANCED MICRO PISTOL (EMP) 234
SPRINGFIELD ARMORY XD(M) 234

STAR

STAR FIRESTAR 234
STAR FIRESTAR M45 235
STAR FIRESTAR PLUS 235
STAR MEGASTAR 235
STAR MODEL 28 235
STAR MODEL 30M 235
STAR MODEL 31P 235
STAR MODEL 31PK 235
STAR MODEL A 235
STAR MODEL B 235
STAR MODEL BKM 235
STAR MODEL BKS STARLIGHT 235
STAR MODEL BM 235
STAR MODEL CO POCKET 235
STAR MODEL CU STARLET 235
STAR MODEL DK 235
STAR MODEL F 236
STAR MODEL F SPORT 236
STAR MODEL F TARGET 236
STAR MODEL FM 236
STAR MODEL FR 236
STAR MODEL FRS 236
STAR MODEL FS 236
STAR MODEL H 236
STAR MODEL HK LANCER 236
STAR MODEL HN 236
STAR MODEL I 236
STAR MODEL IN 236
STAR MODEL M 236
STAR MODEL OLYMPIC 236
STAR MODEL P 236
STAR MODEL PD 236
STAR MODEL S 236
STAR MODEL SI 236
STAR MODEL SUPER A 236
STAR MODEL SUPER B 236
STAR MODEL SUPER M 236
STAR MODEL SUPER P 237
STAR MODEL SUPER S 237
STAR MODEL SUPER SI 237
STAR SUPER SM 237
STAR MODEL SUPER TARGET 237
STAR ULTRASTAR 237

STERLING

STERLING MODEL 283 237
STERLING MODEL 284 237
STERLING MODEL 285 237
STERLING MODEL 286 237
STERLING MODEL 295 237
STERLING MODEL 300 237
STERLING MODEL 302 237
STERLING MODEL 400 237
STERLING MODEL 402 237
STERLING X-CALIBER 237

STEVENS

STEVENS CONLIN NO. 38 238
STEVENS DIAMOND NO. 43 238
STEVENS GOULD NO. 37 238
STEVENS LORD NO. 36 238
STEVENS NO. 10 238
STEVENS NO. 35 OFF-HAND TARGET 238
STEVENS NO. 35 AUTOSHOT 238
STEVENS TIP-UP NO. 41 238

STEYR

STEYR C-A1 238
STEYR GB 238
STEYR M-A1 238
STEYR MODEL SP 238
STEYR SSP 238
STEYR MANNLICHER MODEL 1901 238
STEYR MANNLICHER MODEL 1905 238
STEYR 1907 (ROTH STEYR) 238
STEYR 1911 (STEYR HAHN) 238

STI

STI EAGLE 5.1 PISTOL 238
STI TRUSIGHT 239
STI DUTY CT 239
STI LEGACY 239
STI RANGEMASTER II 239
STI GP6 239
STI SENTINEL PREMIER 239
STI STEELMASTER 239
STI TRUBOR 239

STOEGER

STOEGER AMERICAN EAGLE LUGER 239
STOEGER AMERICAN EAGLE LUGER NAVY MODEL 239
STOEGER COMPACT COUGAR 239
STOEGER LUGER 239
STOEGER LUGER TARGET 239

STRUM RUGER

STRUM RUGER 22/45 LITE 239
STURM RUGER BEARCAT (FIRST ISSUE) 239
STURM RUGER BEARCAT (SECOND ISSUE) SUPER BEARCAT 239
STURM RUGER BEARCAT (THIRD ISSUE) NEW SUPER BEARCAT 240
STURM RUGER BISLEY 240
STURM RUGER BISLEY SMALL FRAME 240
STURM RUGER BLACKHAWK 240
STURM RUGER BLACKHAWK CONVERTIBLE 240
STURM RUGER BLACKHAWK FLAT-TOP 240
STURM RUGER BLACKHAWK FLAT-TOP 44 MAGNUM 240
STURM RUGER BLACKHAWK NEW MODEL 240
STURM RUGER BLACKHAWK NEW MODEL 357 MAXIMUM 240
STURM RUGER BLACKHAWK NEW MODEL CONVERTIBLE 240
STURM RUGER FIFTIETH ANNIVERSARY .44 MAGNUM FLATTOP NEW MODEL BLACKHAWK 240
STURM RUGER GP-100 240
STURM RUGER HAWKEYE 240
STRUM RUGER LCR (LIGHTWEIGHT COMPACT REVOLVER) 240
STURM RUGER POLICE SERVICE-SIX MODEL 107 241
STURM RUGER POLICE SERVICE-SIX MODEL 108 241
STURM RUGER POLICE SERVICE-SIX MODEL 109 241
STURM RUGER POLICE SERVICE-SIX MODEL 707 241
STURM RUGER POLICE SERVICE-SIX MODEL 708 241
STURM RUGER REDHAWK 241
STURM RUGER REDHAWK 4-INCH .45 COLT 241
STURM RUGER S ECURITY-SIX MODEL 117 241
STURM RUGER SECURITY-SIX MODEL 717 241
STURM RUGER SINGLE-SIX 241
STURM RUGER SINGLE-SIX CONVERTIBLE 241
STURM RUGER SUPER SINGLE SIX 241
STURM RUGER SINGLE SIX SSM 241
STURM RUGER SP101 241
STURM RUGER SP101 DOUBLE-ACTION-ONLY REVOLVER 241
STRUM RUGER SR 22 241
STRUM RUGER SR 45 241
STRUM RUGER SR1911 COMMANDER 242
STURM RUGER SUPER BLACKHAWK 242
STURM RUGER SUPER BLACKHAWK HUNTER 242
STURM RUGER SUPER REDHAWK 242
STURM RUGER SUPER REDHAWK ALASKAN. .242
STURM RUGER VAQUERO 242
STURM RUGER BISLEY VAQUERO 242
STURM RUGER "COWBOY PAIR" 242
STURM RUGER 50TH ANNIVERSARY MATCHED SET .357 AND .44 MAGNUM 242
STURM RUGER 22/45 KP4 MARK II 242
STURM RUGER 22/45 KP512 MARK II 242
STURM RUGER 22/45 P512 BULL BARREL MARK II 242
STURM RUGER MARK I STANDARD MODEL 242
STURM RUGER MARK I TARGET MODEL 242
STURM RUGER MARK II STANDARD MODEL 242
STURM RUGER MARK II BULL BARREL 243
STURM RUGER MARK II GOVERNMENT MODEL TARGET 243
STURM RUGER MARK II GOVERNMENT MODEL STAINLESS 243
STURM RUGER MARK II TARGET 243
STURM RUGER MK-4B COMPACT 243
STURM RUGER MARK III STANDARD MODEL 243
STURM RUGER MARK III HUNTER 243
STURM RUGER MARK III COMPETITION 243
STURM RUGER MARK III 512 PISTOL 243
STURM RUGER 22/45 MARK III HUNTER 243
STURM RUGER CHARGER 243
STURM RUGER P85 MARK II 243
STURM RUGER P89 243
STURM RUGER P89D DECOCKER 243
STURM RUGER P89/DAO 244
STURM RUGER P90 244
STURM RUGER P91 DC DECOCKER 244
STURM RUGER P93 COMPACT 244
STURM RUGER P94 244
STURM RUGER P94L 244
STURM RUGER KP94 244
STURM RUGER P95 SEMI-AUTO PISTOL 244
STURM RUGER SR9 244
RUGER LC9 244
STURM RUGER LCP (LIGHTWEIGHT COMPACT PISTOL) 244
RUGER LCR 244

SUNDANCE

SUNDANCE MODEL A-25 .244
SUNDANCE MODEL BOA .245
SUNDANCE LASER 25 .245
SUNDANCE POINT BLANK .245

SUPER SIX

SUPER SIX GOLDEN BISON .245
SUPER-SIX LTD. BISON BULL .245

TANARMI

TANARMI MODEL BTA 90 .245
TANARMI MODEL TA 22 .245
TANARMI MODEL TA 38 OVER/UNDER DERRINGER .245
TANARMI MODEL TA 41 .245
TANARMI MODEL TA 41 SS .245
TANARMI MODEL TA 76 .245
TANARMI MODEL TA 90 .245
TANARMI MODEL TA 90 SS .245

TARGA

TARGA MODEL GT 22 .245
TARGA MODEL GT 22 TARGET .245
TARGA MODEL GT 26 .245
TARGA MODEL GT 27 .245
TARGA MODEL GT 32 .246
TARGA MODEL GT 32 XE .246
TARGA MODEL GT 380 .246
TARGA MODEL GT 380 XE .246

TAURUS

TAURUS MILLENNIUM G2 .246
TAURUS MODEL 44 .246
TAURUS MODEL 65 .246
TAURUS MODEL 66 .246
TAURUS MODEL 73 SPORT .246
TAURUS MODEL 74 SPORT .246
TAURUS MODEL 76 .246
TAURUS MODEL 80 .246
TAURUS MODEL 82 .246
TAURUS MODEL 83 .246
TAURUS MODEL 84 .247
TAURUS MODEL 85 .247
TAURUS MODEL 85CH .247
TAURUS MODEL 85 HY-LITE MAGNESIUM .247
MODEL 850 CIA .247
TAURUS MODEL 86 TARGET MASTER .247
TAURUS MODEL 94 .247
TAURUS MODEL 94 UL .247
TAURUS MODEL 96 SCOUT MASTER .247
TAURUS MODEL 431 .247
TAURUS MODEL 441 .247
TAURUS MODEL 445, 445CH .247
TAURUS MODEL RAGING BULL .247
TAURUS RAGING BULL 500 S&W .247
TAURUS MODEL 605 .247
TAURUS MODEL 607 .248
TAURUS MODEL 608 .248
TAURUS MODEL 617, 606CH .248
TAURUS MODEL 669 .248
TAURUS MODEL 689 .248
TAURUS MODEL 709 G2 SLIM .248
TAURUS MODEL 740 G2 SLIM .248
TAURUS MODEL 741 .248
TAURUS MODEL 761 .248
TAURUS MODEL 809 COMPACT .248
TAURUS MODEL 827 .248
TAURUS MODEL 941 .248
TAURUS TRACKER 10MM 10TSS4 .249
TAURUS TRACKER 10SS8 .249
TAURUS TRACKER .45 .249
TAURUS JUDGE .249
TAURUS TRACKER .45 .249
TAURUS TRACKER 4410 10TKR2SS .249
TAURUS GAUCHO S/A-357-B, S/SM, S/S, CHSA .249
TAURUS GAUCHO S/A-44-40B, S/SM, S/S, CHSA .249
TAURUS GAUCHO S/A-45-B12, S/SM12, S/S12, CHSA12 .249
TAURUS MODEL PT 22 .249
TAURUS MODEL PT 25 .249
TAURUS MODEL PT 58 .249
TAURUS MODEL PT 91AF .249
TAURUS MODEL PT 92AF .249
TAURUS MODEL PT 92AFC .249
TAURUS MODEL PT 99AF .249
TAURUS MODEL PT 100 .250
TAURUS MODEL PT 101 .250
TAURUS MODEL PT-111 MILLENNIUM .250
TAURUS MODEL PT 908 .250
TAURUS MODEL PT-911 .250
TAURUS MODEL PT-938 .250
TAURUS 800 SERIES .250
TAURUS MODEL PT-940 .250
TAURUS MODEL PT-945 .250
TAURUS PT24/7LS-9SS-17 .250
TAURUS PT24/79SSC-17 .250
TAURUS PT24/7PLS-9SSPTI-17 .251
TAURUS PT24/7PLS-9SSCTI-17 .251
TAURUS PT1911B .251
TAURUS PT-745GB .251
TAURUS PT745B/SS-LS .251
TAURUS PT917 B20 .251
TAURUS PT609TI-13 .251
TAURUS PT59B/SS-15 .251
TAURUS 24/7OSS .251

TEXAS ARMORY

TEXAS ARMORY DEFENDER .251

TEXAS LONGHORN

TEXAS LONGHORN GROVER'S IMPROVED NO. 5 .251
TEXAS LONGHORN JEZEBEL .251
TEXAS LONGHORN SOUTH TEXAS ARMY .251
TEXAS LONGHORN TEXAS BORDER SPECIAL .251
TEXAS LONGHORN WEST TEXAS FLATTOP TARGET .251

THOMAS

THOMAS 45 .251

THOMPSON/CENTER

THOMPSON/CENTER CONTENDER .251
THOMPSON/CENTER CONTENDER BULL BARREL ARMOUR ALLOY II .251
THOMPSON/CENTER CONTENDER STAINLESS .251
THOMPSON/CENTER CONTENDER VENT RIB BARREL .252
THOMPSON/CENTER CONTENDER VENT RIB BARREL ARMOUR ALLOY II .252
THOMPSON/CENTER CONTENDER HUNTER .252
THOMPSON/CENTER ENCORE .252
THOMPSON/CENTER SUPER CONTENDER SUPER 14, SUPER 16 .252
THOMPSON/CENTER SUPER CONTENDER ARMOUR ALLOY II .252
THOMPSON/CENTER CONTENDER SUPER 14, SUPER 16 STAINLESS .252
THOMPSON/CENTER SUPER CONTENDER VENT RIB BARREL .252

THUNDER FIVE

THUNDER FIVE .252
THUNDER FIVE T-70 .252

TISAS

TISAS FATIH 13 .252
TISAS KANUNI 16 .252
TISAS KANUNI S .252
TISAS ZIGANA M16 .252
TISAS ZIGANA K .252
TISAS ZIGANA T .252
TISAS ZIGANA SPORT .252
TISAS ZIGANA C45 .252
TISAS ZIGANA F .252

TMI

TMI SINGLE SHOT .252

TOKAREV

TOKAREV TT-1930 .253
TOKAREV TT-33 .253
TOKAREV POST-WAR .253

TRADITIONS

TRADITIONS 1873 .253
TRADITIONS 1894 BISLEY .253
TRADITIONS THUNDERER REVOLVER .253
TRADITIONS 1875 SCHOFIELD .253
TRADITIONS 1851 NAVY CONVERSION .253

TURNBULL

TURNBULL MODEL 1911 CENTENNIAL .253

UBERTI

UBERTI 1871 ROLLING BLOCK .253
UBERTI 1873 CATTLEMAN .253
UBERTI 1873 BUCKHORN .253
UBERTI 1873 CATTLEMAN, SHERIFF'S MODEL .253
UBERTI 1873 CATTLEMAN, TARGET .253
UBERTI 1873 CATTLEMAN, BUNTLINE .253
UBERTI 1873 COLT STALLION .253
UBERTI 1875 REMINGTON OUTLAW .253
UBERTI 1890 ARMY OUTLAW .254
UBERTI BUCKHORN .254
UBERTI INSPECTOR .254
UBERTI PHANTOM SILHOUETTE MODEL .254
UBERTI SCHOFIELD .254

ULTRA LIGHT ARMS

ULTRA LIGHT ARMS MODEL 20 HUNTER .254
ULTRA LIGHT ARMS MODEL 20 RIMFIRE .254

UNIQUE

UNIQUE KRIEGSMODELL .254
UNIQUE MODEL 2000-U MATCH .254
UNIQUE MODEL B/CF .254
UNIQUE MODEL D2 .254
UNIQUE MODEL D6 .254
UNIQUE DES/32U TARGET .254
UNIQUE MODEL DES/32U .254
UNIQUE DES/69U TARGET .254
UNIQUE MODEL DES/69U MATCH .254
UNIQUE MODEL 96U TARGET .255
UNIQUE MODEL DES/823-U RAPID FIRE MATCH .255
UNIQUE MODEL L .255
UNIQUE MODEL MIKROS POCKET .255
UNIQUE MODEL RR .255

UNITED SPORTING ARMS

UNITED SPORTING ARMS SEVILLE .255
UNITED SPORTING ARMS SEVILLE SHERIFF'S MODEL .255
UNITED SPORTING ARMS SEVILLE SILHOUETTE .255

UNITED STATES FIRE ARMS

UNITED STATES FIRE ARMS CUSTOM CUSTER BATTLEFIELD GUN .255
UNITED STATES FIRE ARMS ACE .255
UNITED STATES FIRE ARMS SUPER .38 .255
UNITED STATES FIRE ARMS SINGLE ACTION ARMY .255
UNITED STATES FIRE ARMS BISLEY .255
UNITED STATES FIRE ARMS FLATTOP TARGET REVOLVER .255
UNITED STATES FIRE ARMS NETTLETON CAVALRY REVOLVER .255
UNITED STATES FIRE ARMS BIRD'S HEAD MODEL REVOLVER .255
UNITED STATES FIRE ARMS RODEO/RODEO II .255

UNIVERSAL FIREARMS

UNIVERSAL FIREARMS ENFORCER PISTOL, MODEL 3000 .256

USELTON ARMS

USELTON ARMS ULTRA COMPACT CLASSIC .256

UZI

UZI EAGLE AUTO PISTOL .256

VEGA
VEGA STAINLESS 45 .256

VOERE
VOERE VEC-95CG .256
VOERE VEC-RG REPEATER .256

WALTHER
WALTHER MODEL 1 .256
WALTHER MODEL 2 .256
WALTHER MODEL 3 .256
WALTHER MODEL 4 .256
WALTHER MODEL 5 .256
WALTHER MODEL 6 .256
WALTHER MODEL 7 .256
WALTHER MODEL 8 .256
WALTHER MODEL 8 LIGHTWEIGHT .256
WALTHER MODEL 9 .256
WALTHER MODEL HP .256
WALTHER MODEL PP .256
WALTHER MODEL PP LIGHTWEIGHT .257
WALTHER MODEL PP MARK II .257
WALTHER MODEL PP POST-WWII .257
WALTHER MODEL PPK .257
WALTHER MODEL PPK AMERICAN .257
WALTHER MODEL PPK LIGHTWEIGHT .257
WALTHER MODEL PPK MARK II .257
WALTHER MODEL PPK MARK II LIGHTWEIGHT .257
WALTHER MODEL PPK POST-WWII .257
WALTHER MODEL PPK/S (GERMAN) .257
WALTHER MODEL PPK/S (AMERICAN) .257
WALTHER PPK/S (ENGRAVED) .257
WALTHER MODEL TPH .257
WALTHER MODEL TP .257
WALTHER SPORT MODEL 1926 .258
WALTHER OLYMPIA SPORT MODEL .258
WALTHER OLYMPIA FUNKAMPF MODEL .258
WALTHER OLYMPIA HUNTING MODEL .258
WALTHER OLYMPIA RAPID FIRE MODEL .258
WALTHER OSP RAPID-FIRE .258
WALTHER FREE PISTOL .258
WALTHER GSP MATCH .258
WALTHER GSP-C MATCH .258
WALTHER P-5 .258
WALTHER P22 .258
WALTHER P22 TARGET .258
WALTHER MODEL P-38 .258
WALTHER P-38 POST-WAR .258
WALTHER P-1 POST-WAR .258
WALTHER P-38IV .258
WALTHER P-38K .258
WALTHER P-88 COMPACT .259
WALTHER PP SUPER .259
WALTHER P99 .259
WALTHER 75TH ANNIVERSARY PPK .259
WALTHER MODEL SP22-M1 .259
WALTHER MODEL SP22-M2 .259
WALTHER MODEL SP22-M3 .259
WALTHER MODEL SP22-M4 .259

WARNER
WARNER INFALLIBLE .259

WEATHERBY
WEATHERBY MARK IV SILHOUETTE .259
WEATHERBY MARK V CFP PISTOL .259

WEBLEY
WEBLEY-FOSBERY AUTOMATIC REVOLVER .259
WEBLEY GOVERNMENT MODEL .259
WEBLEY MARK I, II, III, IV, V REVOLVERS .259
WEBLEY MARK III POLICE MODEL .259
WEBLEY MARK III POLICE MODEL TARGET .260
WEBLEY MARK IV POLICE MODEL .260
WEBLEY MARK IV WAR MODEL .260
WEBLEY MARK IV TARGET MODEL .260
WEBLEY MARK IV 32 POLICE .260
WEBLEY MARK IV MILITARY REVOLVER .260
WEBLEY MARK VI .260
WEBLEY 1905 POCKET 32 .260
WEBLEY MODEL 1907 HAMMER MODEL .260
WEBLEY MODEL 1909 .260
WEBLEY MODEL 1909 TARGET PISTOL .260
WEBLEY MODEL 1910 .260
WEBLEY MODEL 1910 HIGH VELOCITY .260
WEBLEY MODEL 1911 .260
WEBLEY MODEL 1913 (NAVY MODEL 455) .260
WEBLEY MODEL 1912 HAMMERLESS .261
WEBLEY MODEL 1922 .261
WEBLEY NO. 2 BRITISH BULLDOG .261
WEBLEY R.I.C. (ROYAL IRISH CONSTABULARY) .261
WEBLEY WP WEBLEY POCKET .261

WESSON FIREARMS
WESSON FIREARMS 45 PIN GUN .261
WESSON FIREARMS ACTION CUP/PPC .261
WESSON FIREARMS FB14-2 .261
WESSON FIREARMS FB15, FB715 .261
WESSON FIREARMS FB44 .261
WESSON FIREARMS FB744 .261
WESSON FIREARMS HUNTER SERIES .261
WESSON FIREARMS MODEL 8-2 .262
WESSON FIREARMS MODEL 9-2H .262
WESSON FIREARMS MODEL 9-2V .262
WESSON FIREARMS MODEL 9-2HV .262
WESSON FIREARMS MODEL 11 .262
WESSON FIREARMS MODEL 12 .262
WESSON FIREARMS MODEL 14 .262
WESSON FIREARMS MODEL 14-2 .262
WESSON FIREARMS MODEL 15 .262
WESSON FIREARMS MODEL 15-1 .262
WESSON FIREARMS MODEL 15-2 .262
WESSON FIREARMS MODEL 15-2H .262
WESSON FIREARMS MODEL 15-2HV .262
WESSON FIREARMS MODEL 15 GOLD SERIES .262
WESSON FIREARMS MODEL 715VH .262
WESSON FIREARMS MODEL 22 .262
WESSON FIREARMS MODEL 22 SILHOUETTE .262
WESSON FIREARMS MODEL 32M .263
WESSON FIREARMS MODEL 40 SILHOUETTE .263
WESSON FIREARMS MODEL 41V .263
WESSON FIREARMS MODEL 44V .263
WESSON FIREARMS MODEL 45V .263
WESSON FIREARMS MODEL 322 .263
WESSON FIREARMS MODEL 738P .263
WESSON FIREARMS MODEL 7322 .263
WESSON FIREARMS .455 SUPERMAG .263
WESSON FIREARMS PPC .263

WHITNEY
WHITNEY WOLVERINE .263

WICHITA
WICHITA CLASSIC SILHOUETTE .263
WICHITA INTERNATIONAL .263
WICHITA MASTER .263
WICHITA SILHOUETTE PISTOL .264

WILDEY
WILDEY AUTOMATIC PISTOL .264
WILDEY HUNTER .264
WILDEY PIN GUN .264
WILDEY JAWS VIPER .264

WILKINSON
WILKINSON DIANE .264
WILKINSON LINDA .264
WILKINSON SHERRY .264

WILSON COMBAT
WILSON COMBAT ADP 9MM .264
WILSON COMBAT COMPACTS .264
WILSON COMBAT KZ 9MM .264
WILSON COMBAT SENTINELS .264
WILSON COMBAT SUPERGRADES .264
WILSON COMBAT X-TAC .264

WYOMING ARMS
WYOMING ARMS PARKER AUTO .264

RIFLES

A.A. ARMS
A.A. ARMS AR9 .266

AAO
AAO MODEL 2000 50 CALIBER .266

ACKLEY
ACKLEY OLYMPUS GRADE .266
ACKLEY OLYMPUS GRADE II .266
ACKLEY STANDARD MODEL .266
ACKLEY VARMINT SPECIAL .266

ACTION ARMS
ACTION ARMS TIMBERWOLF .266

ALPHA
ALPHA ALASKAN .266
ALPHA BIG-FIVE .266
ALPHA CUSTOM MODEL .266
ALPHA GRAND SLAM .266
ALPHA JAGUAR GRADE I .266
ALPHA JAGUAR GRADE II .266
ALPHA JAGUAR GRADE III .266
ALPHA JAGUAR GRADE IV .266

ALPINE
ALPINE SPORTER .266

AMAC
AMAC TARGETMASTER .266
AMAC WAGONMASTER .267

AMERICAN ARMS
AMERICAN ARMS AKY 39 .267
AMERICAN ARMS EXP-64 SURVIVAL RIFLE .267
AMERICAN ARMS MINI-MAX .267
AMERICAN ARMS RS COMBO .267
AMERICAN ARMS SM-64 .267

AMERICAN FIREARMS
AMERICAN FIREARMS STAINLESS MODEL .267

AMT
AMT LIGHTNING 25/22 .267
AMT LIGHTNING SMALL-GAME HUNTING RIFLE (HUNTER) II .267
AMT MAGNUM HUNTER .267

ANSCHUTZ
ANSCHUTZ ACHIEVER .267
ANSCHUTZ ACHIEVER ST SUPER TARGET .267
ANSCHUTZ BR-50 .267

ANSCHUTZ KADETT 268
ANSCHUTZ MARK 525 DELUXE AUTO 268
ANSCHUTZ MARK 525 CARBINE 268
ANSCHUTZ MARK 2000 268
ANSCHUTZ MODEL 54.18MS 268
ANSCHUTZ MODEL 54.18MS ED 268
ANSCHUTZ MODEL 54.18MS FORTNER SILHOUETTE RIFLE 268
ANSCHUTZ MODEL 54.18MS REP 268
ANSCHUTZ MODEL 54.18MS REP DELUXE 268
ANSCHUTZ MODEL 64 268
ANSCHUTZ MODEL 64MS 268
ANSCHUTZ MODEL 64MS-FWT 268
ANSCHUTZ MODEL 64MS LEFT-HAND SILHOUETTE 268
ANSCHUTZ 64-MSR SILHOUETTE RIFLE 268
ANSCHUTZ MODEL 64S 268
ANSCHUTZ MODEL 520/61 269
ANSCHUTZ MODEL 1403B BIATHLON 269
ANSCHUTZ MODEL 1403D MATCH 269
ANSCHUTZ MODEL 1407 269
ANSCHUTZ MODEL 1408 269
ANSCHUTZ MODEL 1408ED 269
ANSCHUTZ MODEL 1411 269
ANSCHUTZ MODEL 1413 269
ANSCHUTZ MODEL 1416D KL CLASSIC 269
ANSCHUTZ MODEL 1416D CUSTOM 269
ANSCHUTZ MODEL 1416D DELUXE 270
ANSCHUTZ MODEL 1416D FIBERGLASS 270
ANSCHUTZ MODEL 1418D 270
ANSCHUTZ MODEL 1422D CLASSIC 270
ANSCHUTZ MODEL 1422D CUSTOM 270
ANSCHUTZ MODEL 1432 CLASSIC 270
ANSCHUTZ MODEL 1432 CUSTOM 270
ANSCHUTZ MODEL 1433D 270
ANSCHUTZ MODEL 1449 YOUTH 270
ANSCHUTZ MODEL 1450B BIATHLON 270
ANSCHUTZ MODEL 1451D KL CLASSIC 270
ANSCHUTZ MODEL 1451D KL MONTE CARLO CLASSIC 270
ANSCHUTZ MODEL 1451R SPORTER TARGET 271
ANSCHUTZ MODEL 1451ST R 271
ANSCHUTZ MODEL 1502 D HB CLASSIC 271
ANSCHUTZ MODEL 1516D CLASSIC 271
ANSCHUTZ MODEL 1516D CUSTOM 271
ANSCHUTZ MODEL 1516D DELUXE 271
ANSCHUTZ MODEL 1518D 271
ANSCHUTZ MODEL 1518D DELUXE 271
ANSCHUTZ 1518D LUXUS BOLT-ACTION RIFLE 271
ANSCHUTZ MODEL 1522D CLASSIC 271
ANSCHUTZ MODEL 1522D CUSTOM 271
ANSCHUTZ MODEL 1533D 271
ANSCHUTZ MODEL 1700D BAVARIAN 271
ANSCHUTZ MODEL 1700D BAVARIAN MEISTERGRADE 271
ANSCHUTZ MODEL 1700D CLASSIC 271
ANSCHUTZ MODEL 1700D CLASSIC MEISTERGRADE 271
ANSCHUTZ MODEL 1700D CUSTOM 271
ANSCHUTZ MODEL 1700D CUSTOM GRAPHITE 271
ANSCHUTZ MODEL 1700D CUSTOM MEISTERGRADE 272
ANSCHUTZ MODEL 1700D FEATHERWEIGHT 272
ANSCHUTZ MODEL 1700D FEATHERWEIGHT DELUXE 272
ANSCHUTZ MODEL 1700D GRAPHITE HORNET 272
ANSCHUTZ MODEL 1702 D HB CLASSIC 272
ANSCHUTZ MODEL 1710D CUSTOM RIFLE 272
ANSCHUTZ MODEL 1712 SILHOUETTE SPORTER 272
ANSCHUTZ MODEL 1733D MANNLICHER 272
ANSCHUTZ MODEL 1740 CUSTOM RIFLE 272
ANSCHUTZ MODEL 1743D BOLT-ACTION RIFLE 272
ANSCHUTZ MODEL 1803D 272
ANSCHUTZ MODEL 1808D RT 272
ANSCHUTZ MODEL 1808ED SUPER 272
ANSCHUTZ MODEL 1827B BIATHLON 272
ANSCHUTZ MODEL 1827BT FORTNER BIATHLON 272
ANSCHUTZ MODEL 1903 MATCH 273
ANSCHUTZ MODEL 1907 MATCH 273
ANSCHUTZ MODEL 1907-L MATCH 273
ANSCHUTZ MODEL 1910 SUPER MATCH II 273
ANSCHUTZ MODEL 1911 PRONE MATCH 273
ANSCHUTZ 1912 SPORT RIFLE 273
ANSCHUTZ MODEL 1913 SUPER MATCH 273
ANSCHUTZ SUPER MATCH 2007 ISU STANDARD 273
ANSCHUTZ 2012 SPORT RIFLE 273
ANSCHUTZ SUPER MATCH 2013 273
ANSCHUTZ WOODCHUCKER 273
ANSCHUTZ MODEL 1907 CLUB 273
ANSCHUTZ MODEL 1710 D HB CLASSIC 150 YEARS ANNIVERSARY VERSION 273

ARMALITE

ARMALITE AR-7 CUSTOM 273
ARMALITE AR-7 EXPLORER 273
ARMALITE AR-10 (T) RIFLE 274
ARMALITE AR-10A4 SPECIAL PURPOSE RIFLE 274
ARMALITE M15A2 CARBINE 274
ARMALITE M15A4 274
ARMALITE M15A4(T) 274

ARMSCOR

ARMSCOR MODEL 14D 274
ARMSCOR MODEL 14P 274
ARMSCOR MODEL 20C 274
ARMSCOR MODEL 20P 274
ARMSCOR MODEL 50S 274
ARMSCOR MODEL 1400SC (SUPER CLASSIC) 274
ARMSCOR MODEL 1400LW 274
ARMSCOR MODEL 1500S 274
ARMSCOR MODEL 1500LW 274
ARMSCOR MODEL 1500SC (SUPER CLASSIC) 274
ARMSCOR MODEL 1600 274
ARMSCOR MODEL 1600R 275
ARMSCOR MODEL 2000SC (SUPER CLASSIC) 275
ARMSCOR MODEL AK22 275

ARMSPORT

ARMSPORT 1866 SHARPS RIFLE 275
ARMSPORT 1866 SHARPS CARBINE 275
ARMSPORT 2800 SERIES 275
ARMSPORT 4000 SERIES 275
ARMSPORT 4500 SERIES 275
ARMSPORT TIKKA 4600 SERIES 275

ARNOLD ARMS

ARNOLD ARMS ALASKAN RIFLE 275
ARNOLD ARMS ALASKAN GUIDE RIFLE 275
ARNOLD ARMS GRAND ALASKAN RIFLE 275
ARNOLD ARMS ALASKAN TROPHY RIFLE 275
ARNOLD ARMS SAFARI RIFLE 276
ARNOLD ARMS AFRICAN TROPHY RIFLE 276
ARNOLD ARMS GRAND AFRICAN RIFLE 276

A-SQUARE

A-SQUARE CAESAR 276
A-SQUARE GENGHIS KHAN 276
A-SQUARE HAMILCAR "SMALL BORE" RIFLE 276
A-SQUARE HANNIBAL "BIG BORE" RIFLE 276

AUTO-ORDNANCE

AUTO-ORDNANCE 1927 A1 THOMPSON 276
AUTO-ORDNANCE 1927 A1C THOMPSON 276
AUTO-ORDNANCE 1927A1 COMMANDO 276
AUTO-ORDNANCE 1927A3 276
AUTO-ORDNANCE THOMPSON M1 276
AUTO-ORDNANCE M1 CARBINE 276

BALLARD

BALLARD NO. 1-3/4 FAR WEST 276
BALLARD NO. 4 PERFECTION 276
BALLARD NO. 5 PACIFIC SINGLE-SHOT 277
BALLARD NO. 7 LONG RANGE 277
BALLARD NO. 8 UNION HILL 277
BALLARD MODEL 1885 HIGH WALL SINGLE SHOT 277

BARRETT

BARRETT MODEL 82A-1 277
BARRETT MODEL 90 277
BARRETT MODEL 95 277
BARRETT MODEL 99 SINGLE SHOT 277

BAYARD

BAYARD SEMI-AUTOMATIC MODEL 277

BEEMAN

BEEMAN/HW 60 277
BEEMAN/HW 60J-ST 277
BEEMAN/HW 660 MATCH 277

BENELLI

BENELLI R1 277

BENTON & BROWN

BENTON & BROWN MODEL 93 278

BERETTA

BERETTA AR-70 278
BERETTA MATO DELUXE 278
BERETTA MATO SYNTHETIC 278
BERETTA MODEL 455 278
BERETTA MODEL 500 278
BERETTA MODEL 500 S 278
BERETTA MODEL 500 DL 278
BERETTA MODEL 500 DLS 278
BERETTA MODEL 500 EELL 278
BERETTA MODEL 500 EELLS 278
BERETTA MODEL 501 (MEDIUM-LENGTH ACTION) 278
BERETTA MODEL 501 S 278
BERETTA MODEL 501 DL 278
BERETTA MODEL 501 DLS 278
BERETTA MODEL 501 EELL 278
BERETTA MODEL 501 EELLS 278
BERETTA MODEL 502 (LONG ACTION) 278
BERETTA MODEL 502 DL 278
BERETTA MODEL 502 DLS 278
BERETTA MODEL 502 EELL 278
BERETTA MODEL 502 EELLS 278
BERETTA MODEL 502 S 278
BERETTA MODEL S689 278
BERETTA MODEL S689E 278
BERETTA SPORTING CARBINE 278
BERETTA SSO EXPRESS 279
BERETTA SSO5 EXPRESS 279
BERETTA SSO6 EXPRESS CUSTOM 279
BERETTA STORM CX4 CARBINE 279
BERNARDELLI CARBINE 279
BERNARDELLI EXPRESS VB 279
BERNARDELLI MINERVA 279
BERNARDELLI MODEL 120 279
BERNARDELLI MODEL 190 279
BERNARDELLI MODEL 2000 279

BIG HORN

BIG HORN CUSTOM 279

BLASER

BLASER K77A 279
BLASER K95 279
BLASER R84 279
BLASER R93 279
BLASER R93 LONG RANGE RIFLE 279
BLASER R93 SAFARI 280
BLASER R93 SYNTHETIC 280
BLASER ULTIMATE BOLT ACTION 280

BORTMESS

BORTMESS BIG HORN 280
BORTMESS CLASSIC MODEL 280
BORTMESS OMEGA 280

BRNO

BRNO 500 COMBINATION GUN 280
BRNO CZ 98 HUNTER CLASSIC 280
BRNO CZ 99 PRECISION 22 280
BRNO CZ 537 SPORTER 280
BRNO CZ 550 280
BRNO ZH 300 COMBINATION GUN 280
BRNO HORNET 281
BRNO MODEL 1 281
BRNO MODEL 2 281
BRNO MODEL 3 281
BRNO MODEL 4 281
BRNO MODEL 5 281
BRNO MODEL 21H 281
BRNO MODEL 22F 281
BRNO MODEL ZG-47 281
BRNO MODEL ZKM-456 281
BRNO MODEL ZKM-456 L TARGET 281
BRNO MODEL ZKM-456 MATCH 281
BRNO SUPER EXPRESS 281
BRNO SUPER SAFARI 281
BRNO ZBK 110 SINGLE SHOT RIFLE 281
BRNO ZKB 527 FOX 281
BRNO ZKB 680 FOX 281
BRNO ZKK 600 281
BRNO ZKK 601 281
BRNO ZKK 602 281
BRNO ZKM 452 STANDARD 281
BRNO ZKM 452 DELUXE 281
BRNO ZKM 611 281

BRONCO

BRONCO 281

ED BROWN

ED BROWN SAVANNAH 282
ED BROWN DAMARA 282
ED BROWN COMPACT VARMINT 282

BROWN

BROWN MODEL ONE 282
BROWN MODEL 97D 282

BROWNING

BROWNING A-BOLT HUNTER 282
BROWNING A-BOLT HUNTER, LEFT-HAND 282
BROWNING A-BOLT CAMO STALKER 282
BROWNING A-BOLT COMPOSITE STALKER 282
BROWNING A-BOLT EURO-BOLT 282
BROWNING A-BOLT GOLD MEDALLION 282
BROWNING A-BOLT MEDALLION 282
BROWNING A-BOLT MEDALLION LEFT-HAND 282
BROWNING A-BOLT MICRO MEDALLION 282
BROWNING A-BOLT STAINLESS STALKER 282
BROWNING A-BOLT 22 282
BROWNING A-BOLT 22 GOLD MEDALLION 283
BROWNING A-BOLT II HUNTER 283
BROWNING A-BOLT II MICRO HUNTER 283
BROWNING A-BOLT II COMPOSITE STALKER 283
BROWNING EURO-BOLT II 283
BROWNING A-BOLT II GOLD MEDALLION 283
BROWNING A-BOLT II HUNTER SHORT ACTION **283**
BROWNING A-BOLT II MEDALLION **283**
BROWNING A-BOLT II MEDALLION SHORT ACTION 283
BROWNING A-BOLT II MICRO MEDALLION 283
BROWNING A-BOLT II STAINLESS STALKER 283
BROWNING A-BOLT II VARMINT 284
BROWNING NRA A-BOLT WILDLIFE CONSERVATION COLLECTION 284
BROWNING A-BOLT SPECIAL HUNTER RMEF 284
BROWNING A-BOLT WHITE GOLD RMEF 284
BROWNING X-BOLT COMPOSITE STALKER 284
BROWNING X-BOLT STAINLESS STALKER 284
BROWNING X-BOLT HUNTER 284
BROWNING X-BOLT MEDALLION 284
BROWNING X-BOLT MICRO MIDAS 284
BROWNING ACERA STRAIGHT-PULL 284
BROWNING BBR 284
BROWNING MODEL 52 284
BROWNING (FN) HIGH-POWER SAFARI 284
BROWNING (FN) HIGH-POWER SAFARI-GRADE MEDIUM-ACTION 284
BROWNING (FN) HIGH-POWER SAFARI-GRADE SHORT-ACTION 284
BROWNING (FN) HIGH-POWER SAFARI MEDALLION-GRADE 284
BROWNING (FN) HIGH-POWER SAFARI OLYMPIAN-GRADE 285
BROWNING T-BOLT MODEL T-1 285
BROWNING T-BOLT MODEL T-2 285
BROWNING T-BOLT (2006) 285
BROWNING T-BOLT COMPOSITE HUNTER 285
BROWNING T-BOLT COMPOSITE TARGET/VARMINT 285
BROWNING T-BOLT SPORTER 285
BROWNING T-BOLT TARGET/ VARMINT STAINLESS 285
BROWNING AUTO 22 GRADE I 285
BROWNING AUTO 22 GRADE II 285
BROWNING AUTO 22 GRADE III 285
BROWNING AUTO 22 GRADE VI 285
BROWNING BAR 285
BROWNING BAR-22 285
BROWNING BAR MARK II SAFARI 286
BROWNING BAR MARK II LIGHTWEIGHT 286
BROWNING BAR MARK II SAFARI MAGNUM 286
BROWNING BAR STALKER 286
BROWNING BAR SHORTTRAC 286
BROWNING BAR LONGTRAC 286
BROWNING BAR SHORTTRAC STALKER 286
BROWNING BAR LONGTRAC STALKER 286
BROWNING BUCK MARK SEMI-AUTO RIFLE 286
BROWNING B-92 CARBINE 286
BROWNING BL-22 286
BROWNING BL-22 NRA GRADE 1 286
BROWNING BL-22 GRAY LAMINATE STAINLESS 286
BROWNING MODEL 53 286
BROWNING MODEL 65 GRADE I 287
BROWNING MODEL 65 HIGH GRADE 287
BROWNING MODEL 71 RIFLE AND CARBINE 287
BROWNING MODEL 81 BLR 287
BROWNING MODEL 81 BLR LONG ACTION 287
BROWNING BLR LIGHTWEIGHT TAKEDOWN 287
BROWNING BLR LIGHTWEIGHT 81 STAINLESS TAKEDOWN 287
BROWNING MODEL 1886 RIFLE AND CARBINE 287
BROWNING MODEL 1886 RIFLE AND CARBINE, HIGH GRADE 287
BROWNING MODEL 1895 287
BROWNING MODEL 1885 HIGH WALL 287
BROWNING MODEL 1885 BPCR (BLACK POWDER CARTRIDGE RIFLE) 287
BROWNING MODEL 1885 LOW WALL 287
BROWNING MODEL 1885 LOW WALL TRADITIONAL HUNTER 287
BROWNING MODEL 78 288
BROWNING MODEL B-78 288
BROWNING BPR 288
BROWNING BPR-22 288
BROWNING CONTINENTAL 288
BROWNING EXPRESS 288

BSA

BSA CENTURION 288
BSA CF-2 CARBINE 288
BSA CF-2 HEAVY BARREL 288
BSA CF-2 SPORTER/CLASSIC 288
BSA CF-2 STUTZEN 288
BSA CF-2 VARMINTER 288
BSA CFT TARGET 288
BSA IMPERIAL 288
BSA MAJESTIC DELUXE 288
BSA MAJESTIC DELUXE FEATHERWEIGHT 288
BSA MARTINI INTERNATIONAL ISU MATCH 288
BSA MARTINI INTERNATIONAL MATCH 288
BSA MARTINI INTERNATIONAL MATCH LIGHT 288
BSA MARTINI INTERNATIONAL MATCH MARK II 289
BSA MARTINI INTERNATIONAL MATCH MARK III 289
BSA MARTINI INTERNATIONAL MATCH MARK V 289
BSA MODEL 12/15 MATCH 289
BSA MODEL 12/15 289
BSA MODEL 13 289
BSA MODEL 13 SPORTER 289
BSA MODEL 15 289
BSA MONARCH DELUXE 289
BSA MONARCH DELUXE VARMINT 289
BSA NO. 12 289

BUSHMASTER

BUSHMASTER 308 HUNTER 289
BUSHMASTER ACR SERIES 289
BUSHMASTER ACR ENHANCED 289
BUSHMASTER M17S BULLPUP RIFLE 289
BUSHMASTER SHORTY XM15 E2S CARBINE 289
BUSHMASTER XM15 E2S DISSIPATOR CARBINE 289
BUSHMASTER XM15 E25 AK SHORTY CARBINE 289
BUSHMASTER XM15 E2S TARGET MODEL RIFLE 289
BUSHMASTER DCM COMPETITION RIFLE 289
BUSHMASTER XM15 E2S V-MATCH RIFLE 290
BUSHMASTER VARMINTER RIFLE 290
BUSHMASTER CARBON 15 9MM CARBINE 290
BUSHMASTER CARBON 15 QUAD RAIL FLAT TOP 290
BUSHMASTER CARBON 15 TOP LOADING RIFLE 290
BUSHMASTER PREDATOR 290
BUSHMASTER CARBON 15 .22 RIMFIRE RIFLE 290
BUSHMASTER BA50 .50 BMG RIFLE 290
BUSHMASTER BA50 .50 BMG CARBINE 290

CABANAS

CABANAS ESPRONCEDA 290
CABANAS LASER RIFLE 290
CABANAS LEYRE 290
CABANAS MASTER 290
CABANAS MINI-82 YOUTH PONY 290

CABANAS PHASER 290
CABANAS R83 290
CABANAS TASER 290
CABANAS VARMINT 290

CABELA'S

CABELA'S 1858 HENRY REPLICA 290
CABELA'S 1866 WINCHESTER REPLICA 290
CABELA'S 1873 WINCHESTER REPLICA 290
CABELA'S 1873 WINCHESTER REPLICA SPORTING MODEL 290
CABELA'S CATTLEMAN'S CARBINE 290
CABELA'S SHARPS SPORTING RIFLE 291

CALICO

CALICO LIBERTY 50 CARBINE 291
CALICO LIBERTY 100 CARBINE 291
CALICO MODEL M-100 CARBINE 291
CALICO M-100FS CARBINE 291
CALICO MODEL M-105 SPORTER 291
CALICO MODEL M-900 CARBINE 291
CALICO MODEL M-951 TACTICAL CARBINE 291
CALICO MODEL M-951S TACTICAL CARBINE 291

CARL GUSTAF

CARL GUSTAF 2000 291
CARL GUSTAF GRADE II 291
CARL GUSTAF GRADE II, MAGNUM MODEL 291
CARL GUSTAF GRADE III 291
CARL GUSTAF GRADE III, MAGNUM MODEL 291
CARL GUSTAF GRAND PRIX 291
CARL GUSTAF "SWEDE" STANDARD 291
CARL GUSTAF "SWEDE" DELUXE 291
CARL GUSTAF "SWEDE" STANDARD, MONTE CARLO MODEL 292
CARL GUSTAF VARMINT T ARGET MODEL 292

CENTURY

CENTURY CENTURION P14 SPORTER 292
CENTURY CUSTOM SPORTING RIFLE 292
CENTURY DELUXE CUSTOM SPORTER 292
CENTURY ENFIELD SPORTER NO.4 292
CENTURY INTERNATIONAL FAL SPORTER 292
CENTURY INTERNATIONAL M-14 292
CENTURY MAUSER 98 SPORTER 292
CENTURY SWEDISH SPORTER #38 292
CENTURY TIGER DRAGUNOV 292
CENTURY WEEKENDER 292

CHAPUIS

CHAPUIS AGEX EXPRESS SERIES 292
CHAPUIS BOXLOCK DOUBLE RIFLE 292
CHAPUIS OURAL EXEL 292
CHAPUIS RGEX EXPRESS 292

CHIPMUNK

CHIPMUNK SINGLE SHOT 292
CHIPMUNK TM (TARGET MODEL) 293

CHRISTENSEN ARMS

CHRISTENSEN ARMS CARBON ONE HUNTER 293
CHRISTENSEN ARMS CARBON RANGER REPEATER 293
CHRISTENSEN ARMS CARBON RANGER SINGLE SHOT 293
CHRISTENSEN ARMS CARBON ONE BOLT-ACTION RIFLE 293

CHURCHILL

CHURCHILL HIGHLANDER 293
CHURCHILL REGENT 293
CHURCHILL REGENT COMBO 293

CIMARRON

CIMARRON 1860 HENRY REPLICA 293
CIMARRON 1866 WINCHESTER REPLICA 293
CIMARRON 1866 WINCHESTER REPLICA CARBINE 293
CIMARRON 1866 WINCHESTER REPLICA CARBINE, INDIAN MODEL 293
CIMARRON 1866 WINCHESTER REPLICA CARBINE, TRAPPER MODEL 293
CIMARRON 1873 SADDLE SHORTY 293
CIMARRON 1873 WINCHESTER REPLICA SPORTING RIFLE 293
CIMARRON 1873 WINCHESTER REPLICA, LONG RANGE MODEL 293
CIMARRON 1873 WINCHESTER REPLICA, SADDLE RING CARBINE 293
CIMARRON 1873 WINCHESTER REPLICA, SHORT MODEL 293
CIMARRON 1873 WINCHESTER REPLICA, TRAPPER CARBINE 293
CIMARRON BILLY DIXON 1874 SHARPS SPORTING RIFLE 293
CIMARRON QUIGLEY MODEL 1874 SHARPS SPORTING RIFLE 294
CIMARRON SILHOUETTE MODEL 1874 SHARPS SPORTING RIFLE 294
CIMARRON MODEL 86/71 LEVER ACTION 294
CIMARRON MODEL 1885 HIGH WALL RIFLE 294

CITADEL

CITADEL M-1 CARBINE 294

CLARIDGE

CLARIDGE HI-TEC C CARBINE 294
CLARIDGE HI-TEC MODEL LEC-9 CARBINE 294
CLARIDGE HI-TEC MODEL ZLEC-9 CARBINE 294

CLAYCO

CLAYCO MODEL 4 294

CLERKE

CLERKE HI-WALL 294
CLERKE HI-WALL DELUXE 294

COLT

COLT 57 294
COLT AR-15A2 CARBINE 294
COLT AR-15A2 RIFLE 294
COLT COLTEER 294
COLT COLTEER 1-22 294
COLT COLTSMAN STANDARD 294
COLT COLTSMAN CUSTOM 295
COLT COLTSMAN DELUXE 295
COLT COLTSMAN LONG-ACTION SAKO CUSTOM 295
COLT COLTSMAN LONG-ACTION SAKO STANDARD 295
COLT COLTSMAN MEDIUM-ACTION SAKO CUSTOM 295
COLT COLTSMAN MEDIUM-ACTION SAKO STANDARD 295
COLT COLTSMAN SHORT-ACTION SAKO CUSTOM 295
COLT COLTSMAN SHORT-ACTION SAKO DELUXE 295
COLT COURIER 295
COLT LIGHT RIFLE 295
COLT LIGHTNING 295
COLT LIGHTNING BABY CARBINE 295
COLT LIGHTNING CARBINE 295
COLT LIGHTNING SMALL FRAME 295
COLT MATCH TARGET RIFLE 295
COLT ACCURIZED RIFLE 295
COLT MATCH TARGET HBAR RIFLE 295
COLT SPORTER TARGET 295
COLT SPORTER COMPETITION HBAR 296
COLT SPORTER COMPETITION HBAR RANGE SELECTED 296
COLT SPORTER LIGHTWEIGHT 296
COLT SPORTER MATCH DELTA HBAR 296
COLT SPORTER MATCH HBAR 296
COLT SPORTER MATCH TARGET COMPETITION HBAR II 296
COLT STAGECOACH 296
COLT-SAUER SPORTER 296
COLT-SHARPS FALLING BLOCK 296

COMMANDO ARMS

COMMANDO ARMS MARK 9 296
COMMANDO ARMS MARK 45 296

COOPER ARMS

COOPER ARMS MODEL 21 VARMINT EXTREME 296
COOPER ARMS MODEL 21 BENCHREST 296
COOPER ARMS MODEL 22 PRO VARMINT EXTREME 296
COOPER ARMS MODEL 22 BENCHREST 296
COOPER ARMS MODEL 36 CENTERFIRE SPORTER 296
COOPER ARMS MODEL 36 RIMFIRE SPORTER 297
COOPER ARMS MODEL 36 RF CUSTOM CLASSIC 297
COOPER ARMS MODEL 36 RF FEATHERWEIGHT 297
COOPER ARMS MODEL 38 CENTERFIRE SPORTER 297
COOPER ARMS MODEL 40 CENTERFIRE SPORTER 297
COOPER ARMS MODEL 40 CUSTOM CLASSIC 297
COOPER ARMS MODEL 40 CLASSIC VARMINTER 297
COOPER MODEL 56 297
COOPER ARMS MODEL 57-M BOLT-ACTION RIFLE 297
COOPER ARMS MODEL BR-50 297
COOPER ARMS MODEL TRP-1 ISU STANDARD 297

CUMBERLAND MOUNTAIN ARMS

CUMBERLAND MOUNTAIN ARMS ELK RIVER 297
CUMBERLAND MOUNTAIN ARMS PLATEAU 297

CVA

CVA ACCURA MR 297
CVA OPTIMA V2 297

CZ

CZ MODEL 3 298
CZ 452 AMERICAN CLASSIC BOLT-ACTION RIFLE 298
CZ 452 FS 298
CZ 452 LUX BOLT-ACTION RIFLE 298
CZ 452 SCOUT 298
CZ 452 SILHOUETTE 298
CZ 452 STYLE 298
CZ 452 TRAINING RIFLE 298
CZ 452 VARMINT RIFLE 298
CZ-USA 455 AMERICAN 298
CZ-USA 455 VARMINT TACTICOOL 298
CZ-USA 455 VARMINT THUMBHOLE SST FLUTED 298
CZ 511 AUTO RIFLE 298
CZ MODEL 512 RIFLE 298
CZ 513 BASIC 298
CZ-USA 527 AMERICAN 298
CZ 527 CARBINE 298
CZ-USA 527 VARMINT 298
CZ 527 LUX BOLT-ACTION RIFLE 299
CZ 527 FS 299
CZ 527 VARMINT KEVLAR 299
CZ 527 VARMINT LAMINATE 299
CZ 527 VARMINT WALNUT 299
CZ 527 PRESTIGE 299
CZ 550 AMERICAN CLASSIC BOLT-ACTION RIFLE 299
CZ 550 LUX BOLT-ACTION RIFLE 299
CZ 550 FS 299
CZ 550 MAGNUM (AMERICAN SAFARI MAGNUM) 299
CZ 550 MAGNUM (MEDIUM MAGNUM) 299

CZ 550 MAGNUM (SAFARI MAGNUM) 299
CZ 550 VARMINT KEVLAR. 299
CZ 550 VARMINT LAMINATE. 299
CZ 550 VARMINT WALNUT 299
CZ 550 ULTIMATE HUNTING RIFLE 299
CZ 700 M1 SNIPER RIFLE. 300
CZ 750 SNIPER 300
CZ 584 SOLO COMBINATION GUN 300
CZ 589 STOPPER OVER/UNDER GUN. 300

D-MAX

D-MAX AUTO CARBINE. 300

DAEWOO

DAEWOO DR200 VARMINT. 300

DAISY LEGACY

DAISY LEGACY MODEL 2201/2211. 300
DAISY LEGACY MODEL 2202/2212 300
DAISY LEGACY MODEL 2203/2213 300
DAISY V/L. 300
DAISY V/L COLLECTOR KIT 300
DAISY V/L PRESENTATION 301

DAKOTA

DAKOTA 10 SINGLE SHOT 301
DAKOTA 22 SPORTER. 301
DAKOTA 76 AFRICAN 301
DAKOTA 76 ALPINE. 301
DAKOTA 76 CLASSIC 301
DAKOTA 76 CLASSIC SHORT ACTION. 301
DAKOTA 76 SAFARI 301
DAKOTA 76 TRAVELER TAKEDOWN RIFLE 301
DAKOTA 76 VARMINT 301
DAKOTA LIMITED EDITION .30-06 MODEL 76 301
DAKOTA LIMITED EDITION .30-06 MODEL 10 301
DAKOTA 97 LIGHTWEIGHT HUNTER 301
DAKOTA 97 LONG RANGE HUNTER RIFLE 301
DAKOTA DOUBLE RIFLE. 301
DAKOTA LONGBOW TACTICAL E.R. RIFLE 301

CHARLES DALY

CHARLES DALY BOLT ACTION (EARLY) 302
CHARLES DALY BOLT-ACTION CENTERFIRE RIFLE, FIELD GRADE 302
CHARLES DALY BOLT-ACTION CENTERFIRE RIFLE, FIELD GRADE, MAGNUM 302
CHARLES DALY BOLT-ACTION CENTERFIRE RIFLE, SUPERIOR GRADE 302
CHARLES DALY BOLT-ACTION CENTERFIRE RIFLE, SUPERIOR GRADE, MAGNUM. 302
CHARLES DALY BOLT-ACTION CENTERFIRE RIFLE, EMPIRE GRADE 302
CHARLES DALY BOLT-ACTION CENTERFIRE RIFLE, EMPIRE GRADE, MAGNUM 302
CHARLES DALY BOLT-ACTION 22-CALIBER RIFLE, FIELD GRADE 302
CHARLES DALY BOLT-ACTION 22-CALIBER RIFLE, SUPERIOR GRADE 302
CHARLES DALY BOLT-ACTION 22-CALIBER RIFLE, EMPIRE GRADE 302
CHARLES DALY SUPERIOR COMBINATION GUN 302
CHARLES DALY EMPIRE COMBINATION GUN. 302
CHARLES DALY FIELD GRADE AUTO RIFLE. 302
CHARLES DALY EMPIRE GRADE AUTO RIFLE. 302
CHARLES DALY TRUE YOUTH BOLT-ACTION RIFLE 302

DAN WESSON

DAN WESSON COYOTE CLASSIC BOLT-ACTION RIMFIRE RIFLE 302
DAN WESSON COYOTE TARGET BOLT-ACTION RIMFIRE RIFLE 302

DIANA

DIANA MODEL 820F MATCH. 302
DIANA MODEL 820K 303
DIANA MODEL 820L 303
DIANA MODEL 820S 303
DIANA MODEL 820SF 303

DIXIE

DIXIE MODEL 1873 RIFLE. 303
DIXIE MODEL 1873 CARBINE 303
DIXIE 1874 SHARPS BLACKPOWDER SILHOUETTE. 303
DIXIE 1874 SHARPS LIGHTWEIGHT HUNTER/TARGET 303
DIXIE REMINGTON CREEDMORE LONG RANGE 303

DPMS

DPMS 6.8 HUNTER 303
DPMS 3G2 303
DPMS 300 AAC BLK PERSONAL DEFENSE WEAPON 303
DPMS PANTHER ARMS A-15 RIFLES 303
DPMS PANTHER RACE GUN 303
DPMS PANTHER TUBER. 304
DPMS SINGLE SHOT RIFLE 304
DPMS PANTHERA PARDUS 304
DPMS PANTHER 20TH ANNIVERSARY RIFLE 304
DPMS PANTHER MARK 12 304
DPMS PANTHER SDM-R. 304
DPMS LRT-SASS 304
DPMS LR-260 304
DPMS LR-243 304
DPMS LR-204 304

DSA

DSA SA58 CARBINE 304
DSA SA58 MEDIUM CONTOUR 304
DSA SA58 MEDIUM CONTOUR TACTICAL 304
DSA SA58 STANDARD. 304
DSA SA58 T48 TACTICAL 304
DSA SA58 BULL BARREL 304

DUBIEL

DUBIEL CUSTOM 304

DUMOULIN

DUMOULIN AMAZONE 304
DUMOULIN BAVARIA DELUXE 304
DUMOULIN CENTURION. 305
DUMOULIN CENTURION CLASSIC. 305
DUMOULIN DIANE. 305
DUMOULIN PIONEER EXPRESS. 305
DUMOULIN SAFARI 305
DUMOULIN SIDELOCK PRESTIGE 305

E.A.A.

E.A.A./ANTONIO ZOLI EXPRESS RIFLE 305
E.A.A./BAIKAL IZH-94 COMBINATION GUN. 305
E.A.A./HW 660 MATCH 305
E.A.A./IZHMASH BIATHLON TARGET RIFLE. 305
E.A.A./IZHMASH BIATHALON BASIC TARGET RIFLE. 306
E.A.A./SABATTI MODEL 1822 306
E.A.A./SABATTI ROVER 870 306
E.A.A./SAIGA SEMI-AUTO RIFLE 306
E.A.A./WEIHRAUCH HW 60. 306

EAGLE ARMS

EAGLE ARMS EA-15 306
EAGLE ARMS EA-15 ACTION MASTER 306
EAGLE ARMS EA-15 EAGLE SPIRIT 306
EAGLE ARMS EA-15 GOLDEN EAGLE 306
EAGLE ARMS EA-15A2 POST-BAN HEAVY BARREL 306
EAGLE ARMS EA-15E2 CARBINE. 306
EAGLE ARMS EA-15E2 H-BAR 306
EAGLE ARMS M15A3 POST-BAN PREDATOR 306
EAGLE ARMS EA-15A3 EAGLE EYE 306
EAGLE ARMS M15A3 S.P.R. 306

E.M.F.

E.M.F. 1860 HENRY 307
E.M.F. 1866 YELLOWBOY RIFLE. 307
E.M.F. 1866 YELLOW BOY CARBINE 307
E.M.F. MODEL 1873 RIFLE 307
E.M.F. MODEL 1873 CARBINE. 307
E.M.F. PREMIER MODEL 1873 CARBINE/RIFLE 307
E.M.F. MODEL 1892 RIFLE 307
E.M.F MODEL 1892 CARBINE. 307
E.M.F. REMINGTON-STYLE ROLLING-BLOCK RIFLE 307
E.M.F. REMINGTON-STYLE ROLLING-BLOCK CARBINE 307
E.M.F. SHARPS RIFLE 307
E.M.F. SHARPS CARBINE 307
E.M.F. TEXAS REMINGTON REVOLVING CARBINE. 307

ERMA

ERMA EG72 307
ERMA EG73 307
ERMA EG712 307
ERMA MODEL EG712 L. 307
ERMA EGM1 307
ERMA EM1 307
ERMA ESG22 CARBINE. 308

FAJEN

FAJEN ACRA M-18 308
FAJEN ACRA RA 308
FAJEN ACRA S-24. 308
FAJEN ACRA VARMINT 308

FEATHER

FEATHER AT-9 CARBINE 308
FEATHER AT-22 CARBINE 308
FEATHER MODEL F2 CARBINE. 308
FEATHER MODEL F9 CARBINE. 308

FEDERAL ENGINEERING

FEDERAL ENGINEERING XC222. 308
FEDERAL ENGINEERING XC450. 308
FEDERAL ENGINEERING XC900. 308

FEDERAL ORDNANCE

FEDERAL ORDNANCE M14SA TARGET 308
FEDERAL ORDNANCE MODEL 713 MAUSER CARBINE, DELUXE GRADE 308
FEDERAL ORDNANCE MODEL 713 MAUSER CARBINE, FIELD GRADE 308

FEG

FEG SA-85M 308

FEINWERKBAU

FEINWERKBAU MODEL 2000 MATCH. 309
FEINWERKBAU MODEL 2000 METALLIC SILHOUETTE 309
FEINWERKBAU MODEL 2000 MINI-MATCH 309
FEINWERKBAU MODEL 2000 UNIVERSAL. 309
FEINWERKBAU MODEL 2600 ULTRA FREE RIFLE. 309
FEINWERKBAU MODEL 2600 UNIVERSAL. 309

FERLACH

FERLACH CUSTOM DRILLING 309
FERLACH DOUBLE RIFLE. 309

F.I.E.

F.I.E. GR-8 BLACK BEAUTY. 309
F.I.E. MODEL 122 309
F.I.E. MODEL 322 309

F.I.E. MODEL 422 310
F.I.E./FRANCHI PARA CARBINE 310

FINNISH LION

FINNISH LION CHAMPION MODEL 310
FINNISH LION ISU TARGET MODEL 310
FINNISH LION MATCH MODEL 310
FINNISH LION STANDARD TARGET MODEL 310

F.N.

F.N. DELUXE MAUSER 310
F.N. DELUXE MAUSER, PRESENTATION GRADE 310
F.N. SUPREME MAUSER 310
F.N. SUPREME MAUSER, MAGNUM MODEL 311

FNH-USA

FNH-USA 2000 TACTICAL AND CQB 311
FNH-USA AR STANDARD AND HEAVY 311
FNH-USA BALLISTA 311
FNH-USA PS90 311
FNH-USA SCAR 16S AND 17S 311
FNH-USA SPR A1, A1A, A3G AND A5M 311
FNH-USA TSR XP AND TSR XP USA 311

FORBES

FORBES RIFLE MODEL 24B 311

FOX

FOX MODEL FB-1 311

FRANCOTTE

FRANCOTTE, AUGUSTE 311
FRANCOTTE BOXLOCK DOUBLE 312
FRANCOTTE CARPATHE MOUNTAIN 312
FRANCOTTE RIMAG 312
FRANCOTTE SIDELOCK DOUBLE 312

GALIL

GALIL SPORTER 312

GAMBA

GAMBA BAYERN 88 312
GAMBA MUSTANG 312
GAMBA RGZ 1000 312
GAMBA RGZ 1000 GAME 312
GAMBA SAFARI EXPRESS 312

GARBI

GARBI EXPRESS DOUBLE RIFLE 312

GARCIA

GARCIA MUSKETEER 312

GARRETT ARMS

GARRETT ARMS ROLLING BLOCK 312

GEVARM

GEVARM E-1 AUTOLOADING 312
GEVARM MODEL A2 312

GOLDEN EAGLE

GOLDEN EAGLE MODEL 7000 GRADE I 312
GOLDEN EAGLE MODEL 7000 GRADE I, AFRICAN 313
GOLDEN EAGLE MODEL 7000 GRADE II 313

GREIFELT

GREIFELT DRILLING 313
GREIFELT SPORT MODEL 313

GRENDEL

GRENDEL R-31 CARBINE 313
GRENDEL SRT-20F COMPACT RIFLE 313

HAENEL

HAENEL '88 MAUSER SPORTER 313
HAENEL MAUSER MANNLICHER 313
HAENEL MODEL 900 MATCH 313

HAMMERLI

HAMMERLI MODEL 45 MATCH 313
HAMMERLI MODEL 54 MATCH 313
HAMMERLI MODEL 503 FREE RIFLE 313
HAMMERLI MODEL 505 MATCH 313
HAMMERLI MODEL 506 MATCH 313
HAMMERLI MODEL 1954 22 MATCH 313
HAMMERLI MODEL OLYMPIA 313
HAMMERLI-TANNER 300 METER 313

HARRINGTON & RICHARDSON

HARRINGTON & RICHARDSON MODEL 60 REISING 313
HARRINGTON & RICHARDSON MODEL 65 314
HARRINGTON & RICHARDSON MODEL 150 314
HARRINGTON & RICHARDSON MODEL 151 314
HARRINGTON & RICHARDSON MODEL 165 314
HARRINGTON & RICHARDSON MODEL 360 314
HARRINGTON & RICHARDSON MODEL 361 314
HARRINGTON & RICHARDSON MODEL 700 314
HARRINGTON & RICHARDSON MODEL 700 DELUXE 314
HARRINGTON & RICHARDSON MODEL 755 314
HARRINGTON & RICHARDSON MODEL 760 314
HARRINGTON & RICHARDSON MODEL 800 314
HARRINGTON & RICHARDSON MODEL 058 314
HARRINGTON & RICHARDSON MODEL 155 SHIKARI 314
HARRINGTON & RICHARDSON MODEL 157 314
HARRINGTON & RICHARDSON MODEL 158 TOPPER 314
HARRINGTON & RICHARDSON MODEL 158 MUSTANG 314
HARRINGTON & RICHARDSON MODEL 158 TOPPER JET 314
HARRINGTON & RICHARDSON MODEL 163 315
HARRINGTON & RICHARDSON MODEL 164 315
HARRINGTON & RICHARDSON MODEL 171 315
HARRINGTON & RICHARDSON MODEL 171 DELUXE 315
HARRINGTON & RICHARDSON MODEL 172 315
HARRINGTON & RICHARDSON MODEL 173 315
HARRINGTON & RICHARDSON MODEL 178 315
HARRINGTON & RICHARDSON MODEL 258 HANDY GUN II 315
HARRINGTON & RICHARDSON MODEL 422 315
HARRINGTON & RICHARDSON MODEL 424 315
HARRINGTON & RICHARDSON MODEL 749 315
HARRINGTON & RICHARDSON ULTRA HEAVY BARREL 22 MAG RIFLE 315
HARRINGTON & RICHARDSON ULTRA HUNTER 315
HARRINGTON & RICHARDSON ULTRA VARMINT 315
HARRINGTON & RICHARDSON ULTRA COMP RIFLE 315
HARRINGTON & RICHARDSON BUFFALO CLASSIC 315
HARRINGTON & RICHARDSON CR CARBINE 316
HARRINGTON & RICHARDSON SYNTHETIC HANDI-RIFLE 316
HARRINGTON & RICHARDSON SPORTSTER 316
HARRINGTON & RICHARDSON STAINLESS HANDI-RIFLE 316
HARRINGTON & RICHARDSON SUPERLITE HANDI-RIFLE COMPACT 316
HARRINGTON & RICHARDSON SYNTHETIC HANDI-RIFLE/SLUG GUN COMBO 316
HARRINGTON & RICHARDSON MODEL 250 316
HARRINGTON & RICHARDSON MODEL 251 316
HARRINGTON & RICHARDSON MODEL 265 316
HARRINGTON & RICHARDSON MODEL 265 TARGETEER JR. 316
HARRINGTON & RICHARDSON MODEL 300 ULTRA 316
HARRINGTON & RICHARDSON MODEL 301 ULTRA 316
HARRINGTON & RICHARDSON MODEL 317 ULTRA 316
HARRINGTON & RICHARDSON MODEL 317P ULTRA 316
HARRINGTON & RICHARDSON MODEL 330 316
HARRINGTON & RICHARDSON MODEL 333 316
HARRINGTON & RICHARDSON MODEL 340 316
HARRINGTON & RICHARDSON MODEL 365 316
HARRINGTON & RICHARDSON MODEL 370 ULTRA 316
HARRINGTON & RICHARDSON MODEL 450 316
HARRINGTON & RICHARDSON MODEL 451 317
HARRINGTON & RICHARDSON MODEL 465 317
HARRINGTON & RICHARDSON MODEL 750 317
HARRINGTON & RICHARDSON MODEL 751 317
HARRINGTON & RICHARDSON MODEL 765 317
HARRINGTON & RICHARDSON MODEL 852 317
HARRINGTON & RICHARDSON MODEL 865 317
HARRINGTON & RICHARDSON MODEL 866 317
HARRINGTON & RICHARDSON MODEL 5200 SPORTER 317
HARRINGTON & RICHARDSON MODEL 5200 MATCH 317

HARRIS-MCMILLAN

HARRIS-MCMILLAN ANTIETAM SHARPS 317
HARRIS-MCMILLAN LONG RANGE RIFLE 317
HARRIS-MCMILLAN M-86 SNIPER 317
HARRIS-MCMILLAN M-87 318
HARRIS-MCMILLAN M-87R 318
HARRIS-MCMILLAN M-89 SNIPER 318
HARRIS-MCMILLAN M-92 BULLPUP 318
HARRIS-MCMILLAN M-93 318
HARRIS-MCMILLAN NATIONAL MATCH 318
HARRIS-MCMILLAN SIGNATURE CLASSIC SPORTER 318
HARRIS-MCMILLAN SIGNATURE ALASKAN 318
HARRIS-MCMILLAN SIGNATURE CLASSIC STAINLESS SPORTER 318
HARRIS-MCMILLAN SIGNATURE SUPER VARMINTER 318
HARRIS-MCMILLAN SIGNATURE TITANIUM MOUNTAIN RIFLE 318
HARRIS GUNWORKS SIGNATURE VARMINTER 318
HARRIS-MCMILLAN TALON SAFARI 318
HARRIS-MCMILLAN TALON SPORTER 318

HECKLER & KOCH

HECKLER & KOCH HK91 A-2 319
HECKLER & KOCH HK91 A-3 319
HECKLER & KOCH HK93 A-2 319
HECKLER & KOCH HK93 A-3 319
HECKLER & KOCH HK94 A-2 319

HECKLER & KOCH HK94 A-3 319
HECKLER & KOCH HK270. 319
HECKLER & KOCH HK300. 319
HECKLER & KOCH HK630. 319
HECKLER & KOCH HK770. 319
HECKLER & KOCH HK940. 319
HECKLER & KOCH HK940K 319
HECKLER & KOCH MR556A1 319
HECKLER & KOCH PSG-1 MARKSMAN 319
HECKLER & KOCH SLB 2000 RIFLE 319
HECKLER & KOCH SL6. 319
HECKLER & KOCH SL7. 320
HECKLER & KOCH SL8-1 320
HECKLER & KOCH SR9. 320
HECKLER & KOCH SR9 (T) TARGET. 320
HECKLER & KOCH SR9 (TC) TARGET. 320
HECKLER & KOCH USC CARBINE. 320

HENRY

HENRY LEVER-ACTION 22 320
HENRY LEVER-ACTION FRONTIER 320
HENRY BIG BOY LEVER-ACTION RIFLE. 320
HENRY BIG BOY DELUXE ENGRAVED .44 MAGNUM 320
HENRY BIG BOY .44 MAGNUM "WILDLIFE EDITION". 320
HENRY BIG BOY .45 COLT "COWBOY EDITION". 320
HENRY GOLDEN BOY 22 LEVER-ACTION. 321
HENRY DELUXE ENGRAVED GOLDEN BOY MAGNUM 321
HENRY "MINI" BOLT 22. 321
HENRY PUMP-ACTION 22 321
HENRY PUMP ACTION .22 OCTAGON 321
HENRY U.S. SURVIVAL RIFLE .22. 321

HEYM

HEYM MODEL 55SS 321
HEYM MAGNUM EXPRESS. 321
HEYM MODEL 22S SAFETY COMBO. 321
HEYM MODEL 33. 321
HEYM MODEL 33 DELUXE 321
HEYM MODEL 37B DOUBLE RIFLE DRILLING. 322
HEYM MODEL 37B DELUXE 322
HEYM MODEL 37 SIDELOCK DRILLING 322
HEYM MODEL 55B 322
HEYM MODEL 55BF O/U COMBO 322
HEYM MODEL 55BW. 322
HEYM MODEL 55FW O/U COMBO. 322
HEYM MODEL 77B 322
HEYM MODEL 77BF 322
HEYM MODEL 88B 322
HEYM MODEL 88B SAFARI. 322
HEYM MODEL 88BSS 322
HEYM MODEL SR20 TROPHY 322
HEYM MODEL SR20 ALPINE. 322
HEYM MODEL SR20 CLASSIC SAFARI. 323
HEYM MODEL SR20 CLASSIC SPORTSMAN. 323
HEYM MODEL SR40 323
HEYM-RUGER MODEL HR30 323
HEYM-RUGER MODEL HR30G. 323
HEYM-RUGER MODEL HR38 323
HEYM-RUGER MODEL HR38G. 323

HI-POINT

HI-POINT 9MM CARBINE 323
HI-POINT .40 S&W CARBINE 323

HI-STANDARD

HI-STANDARD FLITE KING 323
HI-STANDARD HI-POWER FIELD 323
HI-STANDARD HI-POWER FIELD DELUXE 323
HI-STANDARD SPORT KING FIELD. 323
HI-STANDARD SPORT KING CARBINE. 324
HI-STANDARD SPORT KING DELUXE. 324
HI-STANDARD SPORT KING SPECIAL 324

HOENIG

HOENIG ROTARY ROUND ACTION DOUBLE RIFLE 324
HOENIG ROTARY ROUND ACTION COMBINATION 324

HOLLAND & HOLLAND

HOLLAND & HOLLAND BEST QUALITY 324
HOLLAND & HOLLAND DELUXE. 324
HOLLAND & HOLLAND NO. 2 MODEL 324
HOLLAND & HOLLAND ROYAL. 324
HOLLAND & HOLLAND ROYAL DELUXE. 324

HOWA

HOWA CLASSIC LAMINATE THUMBHOLE VARMINTER. 324
HOWA HEAVY BARREL VARMINT. 324
HOWA LIGHTNING 324
HOWA LIGHTNING WOODGRAIN. 325
HOWA M-1500 ULTRALIGHT. 325
HOWA M-1500 VARMINTER AND VARMINTER SUPREME RIFLES 325
HOWA MODEL 1500 HUNTER. 325
HOWA MODEL 1500 TROPHY. 325
HOWA REALTREE CAMO 325

HULDRA

HULDRA ARMS CARBINE. 325
HULDRA ARMS TACTICAL ELITE 325
HULDRA ARMS TACTICAL EVO 326
HULDRA ARMS TACTICAL EVO FLUTED BARREL. 326

HUSQVARNA

HUSQVARNA HI-POWER. 326
HUSQVARNA MODEL 456. 326
HUSQVARNA MODEL 1950. 326
HUSQVARNA MODEL 1951. 326
HUSQVARNA MODEL 8000. 326
HUSQVARNA MODEL 9000. 326
HUSQVARNA SERIES 1000. 326
HUSQVARNA SERIES 1100. 326
HUSQVARNA SERIES 3000. 326
HUSQVARNA SERIES 3100. 326
HUSQVARNA SERIES 4000. 326
HUSQVARNA SERIES 4100. 326
HUSQVARNA SERIES 6000. 327
HUSQVARNA SERIES 7000. 327
HUSQVARNA SERIES P-3000. 327

IAI

IAI M-333 M1 GARAND 327
IAI M-888 M1 CARBINE SEMI-AUTOMATIC RIFLE 327
IAR MODEL 1873 REVOLVING CARBINE. 327

IBUS

IBUS M17S 223 BULLPUP 327

INTERARMS

INTERARMS MARK X ALASKAN. 327
INTERARMS MARK X AMERICAN FIELD 327
INTERARMS MARK X CAVALIER. 327
INTERARMS MARK X CONTINENTAL CARBINE 327
INTERARMS MARK X LIGHTWEIGHT. 327
INTERARMS MARK X MARQUIS. 327
INTERARMS MARK X MINI 327
INTERARMS MARK X REALTREE 327
INTERARMS MARK X VISCOUNT 327
INTERARMS MARK X WHITWORTH 327
INTERARMS WHITWORTH EXPRESS. 328
INTERARMS WHITWORTH MANNLICHER-STYLE CARBINE. 328

ISSC

ISSC SPA STRAIGHT PULL ACTION RIFLE. 328

ITHACA

ITHACA MODEL LSA-55 328
ITHACA MODEL LSA-55 DELUXE. 328
ITHACA MODEL LSA-55 HEAVY BARREL. 328
ITHACA MODEL LSA-55 TURKEY GUN 328
ITHACA MODEL LSA-65 328
ITHACA MODEL LSA-65 DELUXE. 328
ITHACA MODEL 49 SADDLEGUN. 328
ITHACA MODEL 49 DELUXE 328
ITHACA MODEL 49 PRESENTATION. 328
ITHACA MODEL 49 SADDLEGUN REPEATER. 328
ITHACA MODEL 49 SADDLEGUN YOUTH. 328
ITHACA MODEL 72 SADDLEGUN. 328
ITHACA MODEL 72 SADDLEGUN DELUXE 328
ITHACA MODEL X5-C 328
ITHACA MODEL X5-T 328
ITHACA MODEL X15 328

IVER JOHNSON

IVER JOHNSON 22 CARBINE MODEL EWHBA 328
IVER JOHNSON LI'L CHAMP 329
IVER JOHNSON MODEL 2-X. 329
IVER JOHNSON MODEL 2-XA. 329
IVER JOHNSON MODEL 1003 UNIVERSAL CARBINE. 329
IVER JOHNSON MODEL 1256 UNIVERSAL CARBINE. 329
IVER JOHNSON MODEL 5100 SPECIAL APPLICATION RIFLE 329
IVER JOHNSON MODEL X (EARLY MODEL). 329
IVER JOHNSON MODEL X (LATE MODEL). 329
IVER JOHNSON PLAINFIELD MODEL M1 CARBINE 329
IVER JOHNSON SURVIVAL CARBINE 329
IVER JOHNSON TARGETMASTER EW22HBP 329
IVER JOHNSON TRAILBLAZER MODEL IJ22HBA. 329
IVER JOHNSON WAGONMASTER EW22HBL 329
IVER JOHNSON WAGONMASTER JUNIOR MODEL EW22HBLY. 329
IVER JOHNSON UNIVERSAL PARATROOPER. 329

JAEGER

JAEGER AFRICAN MODEL 330
JAEGER ALASKAN MODEL. 330
JAEGER HUNTER MODEL. 330

KBI

KBI SA-85M SEMI-AUTO RIFLE 330

KDF

KDF K15. 330
KDF K15 DANGEROUS GAME MODEL. 330
KDF K15 FIBERSTOCK PRO-HUNTER MODEL 330
KDF K15 IMPROVED MODEL 330
KDF K15 SWAT MODEL. 330
KDF K22. 330
KDF K22 DELUXE 330

KEL TEC

KEL TEC RFB HUNTER 330
KEL-TEC SU-16. 330
KEL-TEC SU-16B LIGHTWEIGHT 331
KEL-TEC SU-16C CARBINE 331
KEL-TEC SUB2000 CARBINE 331
KEL-TEC RFB RIFLE 331

KIMBER

KIMBER 22 331
KIMBER 22 SUPERAMERICA 331
KIMBER 22 SVT (SHORT VARMINT/TARGET) 331
KIMBER 22 HS (HUNTER SILHOUETTE) 331
KIMBER MODEL 82 331

KIMBER MODEL 82 ALL-AMERICAN MATCH . . . 331
KIMBER MODEL 82 CONTINENTAL . . . 331
KIMBER MODEL 82 GOVERNMENT TARGET . . . 331
KIMBER MODEL 82 HUNTER . . . 332
KIMBER MODEL 82 MINI CLASSIC . . . 332
KIMBER MODEL 82 SPORTER . . . 332
KIMBER MODEL 82 SUPERAMERICA . . . 332
KIMBER MODEL 82 VARMINTER . . . 332
KIMBER MODEL 82C CLASSIC . . . 332
KIMBER MODEL 82C CUSTOM MATCH . . . 332
KIMBER MODEL 82C SUPERAMERICA . . . 332
KIMBER MODEL 82C SUPERAMERICA CUSTOM . . . 332
KIMBER MODEL 82C SUPERCLASSIC . . . 332
KIMBER MODEL 82C VARMINT . . . 332
KIMBER MODEL 84 . . . 332
KIMBER MODEL 84 CONTINENTAL MODEL . . . 332
KIMBER MODEL 84 CUSTOM CLASSIC MODEL . . . 332
KIMBER MODEL 84 HUNTER MODEL . . . 332
KIMBER MODEL 84 SPORTER MODEL . . . 332
KIMBER MODEL 84 SUPERAMERICA . . . 332
KIMBER MODEL 84 SUPER GRADE . . . 332
KIMBER MODEL 84 ULTRA VARMINTER . . . 333
KIMBER MODEL 84M . . . 333
KIMBER MODEL 84M LPT TACTICAL . . . 333
KIMBER MODEL 8400 SERIES . . . 333
KIMBER MODEL 8400 CLASSIC . . . 333
KIMBER MODEL 8400 MONTANA . . . 333
KIMBER MODEL 8400 SUPERAMERICA . . . 333
KIMBER 8400 CLASSIC SELECT GRADE . . . 333
KIMBER MODEL 8400 TACTICAL . . . 333
KIMBER MODEL 8400 ADVANCED TACTICAL . . . 333
KIMBER MODEL 89 . . . 333
KIMBER MODEL 89 AFRICAN . . . 333
KIMBER MODEL 89 FEATHERWEIGHT DELUXE . . . 334
KIMBER MODEL 89 HEAVYWEIGHT DELUXE . . . 334
KIMBER MODEL 89 HUNTER . . . 334
KIMBER MODEL 89 MEDIUM WEIGHT DELUXE . . . 334
KIMBER MODEL 89 SUPER GRADE . . . 334

KIMEL

KIMEL AR9 . . . 334

KINTREK

KINTREK MODEL KBP-1 . . . 334

KLEINGUENTHER

KLEINGUENTHER K-15 . . . 334
KLEINGUENTHER K-22 . . . 334

KODIAK

KODIAK MK. IV DOUBLE RIFLE . . . 334

KRICO

KRICO CARBINE . . . 334
KRICO MODEL 120M . . . 334
KRICO MODEL 260 . . . 334
KRICO MODEL 300 . . . 334
KRICO MODEL 300 DELUXE . . . 334
KRICO MODEL 300 SA . . . 334
KRICO MODEL 300 STUTZEN . . . 334
KRICO MODEL 302 . . . 334
KRICO MODEL 302DR C . . . 335
KRICO MODEL 302E . . . 335
KRICO MODEL 304 . . . 335
KRICO MODEL 311 . . . 335
KRICO MODEL 320 . . . 335
KRICO MODEL 330S MATCH . . . 335
KRICO MODEL 340 . . . 335
KRICO MODEL 340 KRICOTRONIC . . . 335
KRICO MODEL 340 MINI-SNIPER . . . 335
KRICO MODEL 352E . . . 335
KRICO MODEL 360S BIATHLON . . . 335
KRICO MODEL 360S2 BIATHLON . . . 335
KRICO MODEL 400 . . . 335
KRICO MODEL 400E . . . 335
KRICO MODEL 400L . . . 335
KRICO MODEL 400 MATCH . . . 335
KRICO MODEL 420L . . . 335
KRICO MODEL 500 KRICOTRONIC MATCH . . . 335
KRICO MODEL 600 . . . 336
KRICO MODEL 600 EAC . . . 336
KRICO MODEL 600 DELUXE . . . 336
KRICO MODEL 600 MATCH . . . 336
KRICO MODEL 600 SINGLE SHOT . . . 336
KRICO MODEL 600 SNIPER . . . 336
KRICO MODEL 620 . . . 336
KRICO MODEL 640S . . . 336
KRICO MODEL 640 VARMINT . . . 336
KRICO MODEL 650S . . . 336
KRICO MODEL 650S2 . . . 336
KRICO MODEL 650 SUPER SNIPER . . . 336
KRICO MODEL 700 . . . 336
KRICO MODEL 700 DELUXE . . . 336
KRICO MODEL 700 STUTZEN . . . 336
KRICO MODEL 720 . . . 336
KRICO SPORTER . . . 336
KRICO VARMINT MODEL . . . 336

KRIEGHOFF

KRIEGHOFF CLASSIC DOUBLE RIFLE . . . 336
KRIEGHOFF CLASSIC BIG FIVE DOUBLE RIFLE . . . 337
KRIEGHOFF HUBERTUS SINGLE-SHOT RIFLE . . . 337
KRIEGHOFF NEPTUN . . . 337
KRIEGHOFF TECK COMBO . . . 337
KRIEGHOFF TECK DOUBLE RIFLE . . . 337
KRIEGHOFF TRUMPF . . . 337
KRIEGHOFF ULM COMBO . . . 337
KRIEGHOFF ULM DOUBLE RIFLE . . . 337
KRIEGHOFF ULM-PRIMUS . . . 337

LAKEFIELD ARMS

LAKEFIELD ARMS MARK I . . . 337
LAKEFIELD ARMS MARK II . . . 337
LAKEFIELD ARMS MODEL 64B . . . 337
LAKEFIELD ARMS MODEL 90 BIATHLON . . . 338
LAKEFIELD ARMS MODEL 91T . . . 338
LAKEFIELD ARMS MODEL 91TR . . . 338
LAKEFIELD ARMS MODEL 92S SILHOUETTE . . . 338
LAKEFIELD ARMS MODEL 93M . . . 338

L.A.R.

L.A.R. GRIZZLY 50 BIG BOAR . . . 338

LEBEAU-COURALLY

LEBEAU-COURALLY BOXLOCK . . . 338
LEBEAU-COURALLY EXPRESS RIFLE SXS . . . 338
LEBEAU-COURALLY SIDELOCK . . . 338

LEGACY SPORTS INTERNATIONAL

LEGACY SPORTS INTERNATIONAL M-1500 CUSTOM RIFLES . . . 338
LEGACY SPORTS INTERNATIONAL TEXAS SAFARI RIFLES . . . 338
LEGACY SPORTS INTERNATIONAL MAUSER 98 RIFLE . . . 339

LES BAER

LES BAER CUSTOM ULTIMATE AR 223 RIFLE . . . 339
LES BAER LBC CUSTOM SPECIAL TACTICAL RIFLE . . . 339
LES BAER MID-LENGTH MONOLITH .308 SWAT MODEL . . . 339

LJUTIC

LJUTIC SPACE GUN . . . 339

MAGNUM RESEARCH

MAGNUM RESEARCH MAGNUMLITE TACTICAL RIFLE . . . 339
MAGNUM RESEARCH MAGNUMLITE GRAPHITE RIFLE . . . 339
MAGNUM RESEARCH MAGNUMLITE MLR-1722 RIFLE . . . 339
MAGNUM RESEARCH MAGNUMLITE MLR-1722 .17 MACH-2 RIFLE . . . 339
MAGNUM RESEARCH MAGNUMLITE MLR-1722 .22 WMR GRAPHITE RIFLE . . . 339
MAGNUM RESEARCH MAGNUMLITE MLR-1722 .17 HMR GRAPHITE RIFLE . . . 339
MAGNUM RESEARCH MAGNUMLITE MLR-1722 .17 HMR STAINLESS STEEL RIFLE . . . 339

MAGTECH

MAGTECH MODEL 122.2R . . . 339
MAGTECH MODEL 122.2S . . . 339
MAGTECH MODEL 122.2T . . . 340
MAGTECH MODEL MT-122C . . . 340
MAGTECH MODEL MT-122T . . . 340
MAGTECH MODEL MT-52-T TARGET . . . 340
MAGTECH MODEL MT-66 . . . 340
MAGTECH MT 7022 AUTO RIFLE . . . 340

MANNLICHER-SCHOENAUER

MANNLICHER-SCHOENAUER HIGH VELOCITY . . . 340
MANNLICHER-SCHOENAUER MODEL 1903 CARBINE . . . 340
MANNLICHER-SCHOENAUER MODEL 1905 CARBINE . . . 340
MANNLICHER-SCHOENAUER MODEL 1908 CARBINE . . . 340
MANNLICHER-SCHOENAUER MODEL 1910 CARBINE . . . 340
MANNLICHER-SCHOENAUER MODEL 1924 CARBINE . . . 340
MANNLICHER-SCHOENAUER MODEL 1950 . . . 340
MANNLICHER-SCHOENAUER MODEL 1950 CARBINE . . . 340
MANNLICHER-SCHOENAUER MODEL 1950 CARBINE 6.5 . . . 340
MANNLICHER-SCHOENAUER MODEL 1952 IMPROVED . . . 340
MANNLICHER-SCHOENAUER MODEL 1952 IMPROVED CARBINE . . . 340
MANNLICHER-SCHOENAUER MODEL 1952 IMPROVED CARBINE 6.5 . . . 341
MANNLICHER-SCHOENAUER MODEL 1956 . . . 341
MANNLICHER-SCHOENAUER MODEL 1956 CARBINE . . . 341
MANNLICHER-SCHOENAUER MODEL 1956 MAGNUM . . . 341
MANNLICHER-SCHOENAUER MODEL 1961 MCA . . . 341
MANNLICHER-SCHOENAUER 1961 MCA CARBINE . . . 341

MAPIZ

MAPIZ ZANARDINI OXFORD . . . 341

MARATHON

MARATHON CENTERFIRE . . . 341
MARATHON SUPER SHOT 22 . . . 341

MARCEL

MARCEL THYS KING ROYAL . . . 341
MARCEL THYS LIEGE ROYAL LUX . . . 341

MARLIN

MARLIN MODEL 9 CAMP CARBINE . . . 341
MARLIN MODEL 9N . . . 341
MARLIN MODEL 45 CAMP CARBINE . . . 341
MARLIN MODEL 49 . . . 341
MARLIN MODEL 49DL . . . 341
MARLIN MODEL 50 . . . 341
MARLIN MODEL 50E . . . 342
MARLIN MODEL 60 . . . 342
MARLIN MODEL 60SS . . . 342
MARLIN MODEL 60SN . . . 342
MODEL 60S-CF . . . 342
MARLIN MODEL 70HC . . . 342

MARLIN MODEL 70P PAPOOSE . . . 342
MARLIN MODEL 70PSS . . . 342
MARLIN MODEL 75C . . . 342
MARLIN MODEL 88C . . . 342
MARLIN MODEL 88DL . . . 342
MARLIN MODEL 89C . . . 342
MARLIN MODEL 89DL . . . 342
MARLIN MODEL 98 . . . 342
MARLIN MODEL 99 . . . 343
MARLIN MODEL 99C . . . 343
MARLIN MODEL 99DL . . . 343
MARLIN MODEL 99G . . . 343
MARLIN MODEL 99M1 CARBINE . . . 343
MARLIN MODEL 922 MAGNUM . . . 343
MARLIN MODEL 989M2 CARBINE . . . 343
MARLIN MODEL 990 . . . 343
MARLIN MODEL 990L . . . 343
MARLIN MODEL 995 . . . 343
MARLIN MODEL 995SS . . . 343
MARLIN MODEL 7000 AUTO RIFLE . . . 343
MARLIN MODEL 795 AUTO RIFLE . . . 343
MARLIN MODEL 795SS AUTO RIFLE . . . 343
MARLIN MODEL A-1 . . . 344
MARLIN MODEL A-1C . . . 344
MARLIN MODEL A-1DL . . . 344
MARLIN MODEL A-1E . . . 344
MARLIN MODEL 15 . . . 344
MARLIN MODEL 15Y LITTLE BUCKAROO . . . 344
MARLIN MODEL 15YN LITTLE BUCKAROO . . . 344
MARLIN MODEL 15YS . . . 344
MARLIN MODEL 17V HORNADY MAGNUM . . . 344
MARLIN MODEL 17VS . . . 344
MARLIN MODEL 25 . . . 344
MARLIN MODEL 25M . . . 344
MARLIN MODEL 25MB MIDGET MAGNUM . . . 344
MARLIN MODEL 25MN . . . 344
MARLIN MODEL 25MNC . . . 344
MARLIN MODEL 25N . . . 344
MARLIN MODEL 25NC . . . 344
MARLIN MODEL 65 . . . 345
MARLIN MODEL 65E . . . 345
MARLIN MODEL 80 . . . 345
MARLIN MODEL 80C . . . 345
MARLIN MODEL 80DL . . . 345
MARLIN MODEL 80E . . . 345
MARLIN MODEL 81 . . . 345
MARLIN MODEL 81C . . . 345
MARLIN MODEL 81DL . . . 345
MARLIN MODEL 81E . . . 345
MARLIN MODEL 83TS BOLT-ACTION RIFLE . . . 345
MARLIN MODEL 100 . . . 345
MARLIN MODEL 100S . . . 345
MARLIN MODEL 100SB . . . 345
MARLIN MODEL 101 . . . 345
MARLIN MODEL 101DL . . . 345
MARLIN MODEL 122 . . . 345
MARLIN MODEL 322 . . . 345
MARLIN MODEL 455 . . . 345
MARLIN MODEL XL7 . . . 346
MODEL XL7C . . . 346
MARLIN MODEL 780 . . . 346
MARLIN MODEL 781 . . . 346
MARLIN MODEL 782 . . . 346
MARLIN MODEL 783 . . . 346
MARLIN MODEL 880 . . . 346
MARLIN MODEL 880SS . . . 346
MARLIN MODEL 880SQ SQUIRREL RIFLE . . . 346
MARLIN MODEL 881 . . . 346
MARLIN MODEL 882 . . . 346
MARLIN MODEL 882L . . . 346
MARLIN MODEL 882SS . . . 346
MARLIN MODEL 882SSV . . . 347
MARLIN MODEL 883 . . . 347
MARLIN MODEL 883SS . . . 347
MARLIN MODEL 915Y COMPACT . . . 347
MARLIN MODEL 915YS COMPACT . . . 347
MARLIN MODEL 917 . . . 347
MARLIN MODEL 917VST . . . 347
MARLIN MODEL 917VT . . . 347
MARLIN MODEL 925 . . . 347
MARLIN MODEL 925C . . . 347
MARLIN MODEL 925R . . . 347
MARLIN MODEL 980 . . . 347
MARLIN MODEL 980S . . . 347
MARLIN MODEL 980S-CF . . . 347
MARLIN MODEL 981T . . . 347
MARLIN MODEL 982VS . . . 347
MARLIN MODEL 982VS-CF . . . 347
MARLIN MODEL 983 . . . 347
MARLIN MODEL 983T . . . 347
MARLIN MODEL 983S . . . 347
MARLIN MODEL 2000 . . . 347
MARLIN MODEL 2000A . . . 347
MARLIN MODEL 2000L . . . 347
MARLIN MODEL 18 . . . 348
MARLIN MODEL 20 . . . 348
MARLIN MODEL 25 . . . 348
MARLIN MODEL 27 . . . 348
MARLIN MODEL 27S . . . 348
MARLIN MODEL 30AS . . . 348
MARLIN MODEL 32 . . . 348
MARLIN MODEL 36 RIFLE AND CARBINE . . . 348
MARLIN MODEL 36-DL DELUXE RIFLE . . . 348
MARLIN MODEL 36-DL CARBINE . . . 348
MARLIN MODEL 36RC . . . 348
MARLIN MODEL 38 . . . 348
MARLIN MODEL 39 . . . 348
MARLIN MODEL 39A . . . 348
MARLIN MODEL 39A GOLDEN . . . 348
MARLIN MODEL 39A MOUNTIE . . . 348
MARLIN MODEL 39A MOUNTIE CARBINE . . . 348
MARLIN MODEL 39D . . . 348
MARLIN MODEL 39M . . . 348
MARLIN MODEL 39M OCTAGON . . . 349
MARLIN MODEL 39TDS CARBINE . . . 349
MARLIN MODEL 39AS GOLDEN . . . 349
MARLIN MODEL 56 LEVERMATIC . . . 349
MARLIN MODEL 56 CLIPPER KING LEVERMATIC . . . 349
MARLIN MODEL 57 LEVERMATIC . . . 349
MARLIN MODEL 57M LEVERMATIC . . . 349
MARLIN MODEL 62 LEVERMATIC . . . 349
MARLIN MODEL 92 . . . 349
MARLIN MODEL 93 . . . 349
MARLIN MODEL 93 CARBINE . . . 349
MARLIN MODEL 93SC . . . 349
MARLIN MODEL 94 . . . 349
MARLIN MODEL 95 . . . 349
MARLIN MODEL 97 . . . 349
MARLIN MODEL 336C . . . 350
MARLIN MODEL 336 COWBOY . . . 350
MARLIN MODEL 336A-DL . . . 350
MARLIN MODEL 336CC . . . 350
MARLIN MODEL 336CS . . . 350
MARLIN MODEL 336 ER (EXTRA-RANGE) . . . 350
MARLIN MODEL 336SS . . . 350
MARLIN MODEL 336W . . . 350
MARLIN MODEL 336 MARAUDER . . . 350
MARLIN MODEL 336 OCTAGON . . . 350
MARLIN MODEL 336 SPORT CARBINE . . . 350
MARLIN MODEL 336SC ZIPPER . . . 350
MARLIN MODEL 336SD . . . 350
MARLIN MODEL 336T TEXAN . . . 350
MARLIN MODEL 336TS TEXAN . . . 350
MARLIN MODEL 336Y . . . 350
MARLIN MODEL 336XLR . . . 350
MARLIN MODEL 375 . . . 351
MARLIN MODEL 444 . . . 351
MARLIN MODEL 444 SPORTER . . . 351
MARLIN MODEL 444P OUTFITTER . . . 351
MARLIN MODEL 444SS . . . 351
MARLIN MODEL 1894 . . . 351
MARLIN MODEL 1894C . . . 351
MARLIN MODEL 1894CL CLASSIC . . . 351
MARLIN MODEL 1894CS CARBINE . . . 351
MARLIN MODEL 1894FG . . . 351
MARLIN MODEL 1894M . . . 351
MARLIN MODEL 1894P/1894CP CARBINE . . . 351
MARLIN MODEL 1894 COWBOY . . . 351
MARLIN MODEL 1894 COWBOY COMPETITION RIFLE . . . 352
MARLIN MODEL 1894 OCTAGON . . . 352
MARLIN MODEL 1894 SPORTER . . . 352
MARLIN MODEL 1894S . . . 352
MARLIN MODEL 1894SS . . . 352
MARLIN MODEL 1895 . . . 352
MARLIN MODEL 1895 COWBOY . . . 352
MARLIN MODEL 1895G GUIDE GUN . . . 352
MARLIN MODEL 1895GS GUIDE GUN . . . 352
MARLIN MODEL 1895M . . . 352
MARLIN MODEL 1895S . . . 352
MARLIN MODEL 1895SS . . . 352
MARLIN MODEL 1895XLR . . . 352
MARLIN MODEL 444XLR . . . 352
MARLIN MODEL 1897 COWBOY . . . 352
MARLIN MODEL 1897T . . . 352
MARLIN-GLENFIELD MODEL 15 . . . 353
MARLIN-GLENFIELD MODEL 20 . . . 353
MARLIN-GLENFIELD MODEL 30 . . . 353
MARLIN-GLENFIELD MODEL 30A . . . 353
MARLIN-GLENFIELD MODEL 30GT . . . 353
MARLIN-GLENFIELD MODEL 60 . . . 353
MARLIN-GLENFIELD MODEL 70 . . . 353
MARLIN-GLENFIELD MODEL 75C . . . 353
MARLIN-GLENFIELD MODEL 81G . . . 353
MARLIN-GLENFIELD MODEL 101G . . . 353
MARLIN-GLENFIELD MODEL 989G . . . 353
MARLIN MODEL XT-17 . . . 353
MARLIN MODEL XT-22 SERIES . . . 353

MAUSER

MAUSER MODEL 10 VARMINTER . . . 353
MAUSER MODEL 66 . . . 353
MAUSER MODEL 66 SAFARI . . . 353
MAUSER MODEL 66 STUTZEN . . . 353
MAUSER MODEL 66SP MATCH . . . 354
MAUSER MODEL 77 . . . 354
MAUSER MODEL 77 BIG GAME . . . 354
MAUSER MODEL 77 MAGNUM . . . 354
MAUSER MODEL 77 MANNLICHER . . . 354
MAUSER MODEL 77 SPORTSMAN . . . 354
MAUSER MODEL 77 ULTRA . . . 354
MAUSER MODEL 83 . . . 354
MAUSER MODEL 83 SINGLE SHOT . . . 354
MAUSER MODEL 83 MATCH UIT . . . 354
MAUSER MODEL 86-SR SPECIALTY RIFLE . . . 354
MAUSER MODEL 98 STANDARD . . . 354
MAUSER MODEL 99 . . . 354
MAUSER MODEL 107 . . . 354
MAUSER MODEL 201 . . . 354
MAUSER MODEL 201 LUXUS . . . 355
MAUSER MODEL 225 . . . 355
MAUSER MODEL 660 . . . 355
MAUSER MODEL 660 SAFARI . . . 355
MAUSER MODEL 660 ULTRA . . . 355
MAUSER MODEL 660P TARGET . . . 355
MAUSER MODEL 660S DELUXE . . . 355
MAUSER MODEL 660SH . . . 355
MAUSER MODEL 660T CARBINE . . . 355
MAUSER MODEL 2000 . . . 355
MAUSER MODEL 3000 . . . 355
MAUSER MODEL 4000 VARMINT . . . 355
MAUSER MODEL DSM34 . . . 355
MAUSER MODEL EL320 . . . 355
MAUSER MODEL EN310 . . . 355
MAUSER MODEL ES340 . . . 355
MAUSER MODEL ES340B . . . 355
MAUSER MODEL ES350 . . . 355
MAUSER MODEL ES350B . . . 355
MAUSER MODEL KKW . . . 355
MAUSER MODEL MM410 . . . 356
MAUSER MODEL MM410B . . . 356
MAUSER MODEL MS350B . . . 356
MAUSER MODEL MS420 . . . 356
MAUSER MODEL MS420B . . . 356
MAUSER SPORTER (EARLY) . . . 356
MAUSER SPORTER CARBINE . . . 356
MAUSER SPORTER, MILITARY MODEL . . . 356
MAUSER SPORTER, SHORT MODEL . . . 356
MAUSER SPECIAL BRITISH MODEL TYPE A . . . 356
MAUSER SPECIAL BRITISH MODEL TYPE A MAGNUM . . . 356
MAUSER SPECIAL BRITISH MODEL TYPE A SHORT . . . 356
MAUSER TYPE B . . . 356

MCMILLAN

MCMILLAN 300 PHOENIX LONG RANGE RIFLE . . . 356
MCMILLAN M-40 SNIPER MODEL . . . 356
MCMILLAN M-86 SNIPER . . . 356
MCMILLAN M-87 . . . 356
MCMILLAN M-87R . . . 357
MCMILLAN M-89 SNIPER . . . 357

MCMILLAN M-92 BULLPUP . . . 357
MCMILLAN M-93 . . . 357
MCMILLAN NATIONAL MATCH . . . 357
MCMILLAN SIGNATURE ALASKAN . . . 357
MCMILLAN SIGNATURE CLASSIC SPORTER . . . 357
MCMILLAN SIGNATURE CLASSIC SPORTER STAINLESS . . . 357
MCMILLAN SIGNATURE TITANIUM MOUNTAIN . . . 357
MCMILLAN SIGNATURE VARMINTER . . . 357
MCMILLAN STANDARD SPORTER . . . 357
MCMILLAN TALON SAFARI . . . 357
MCMILLAN TALON SAFARI SUPER MAG . . . 357
MCMILLAN TALON SPORTER . . . 358

MERKEL

MERKEL MODEL 90S DRILLING . . . 358
MERKEL MODEL 90K DRILLING . . . 358
MERKEL MODEL 95S DRILLING . . . 358
MERKEL MODEL 95K DRILLING . . . 358
MERKEL MODEL 96K DRILLING . . . 358
MERKEL MODEL 140-1 DOUBLE RIFLE . . . 358
MERKEL MODEL 140-1.1 DOUBLE RIFLE . . . 358
MERKEL MODEL 150-1 DOUBLE RIFLE . . . 358
MERKEL MODEL 150-1.1 DOUBLE RIFLE . . . 358
MERKEL MODEL 160 DOUBLE RIFLE . . . 358
MERKEL MODEL 210E COMBINATION GUN . . . 358
MERKEL MODEL 211E COMBINATION GUN . . . 358
MERKEL MODEL 213E COMBINATION GUN . . . 358
MERKEL MODEL 220E DOUBLE RIFLE . . . 358
MERKEL MODEL 221E DOUBLE RIFLE . . . 358
MERKEL MODEL 223E DOUBLE RIFLE . . . 359
MERKEL MODEL 313E COMBINATION GUN . . . 359
MERKEL MODEL 323E DOUBLE RIFLE . . . 359
MERKEL MODEL K-1 LIGHTWEIGHT STALKING RIFLE . . . 359

MIDLAND

MIDLAND 1500S SURVIVOR . . . 359
MIDLAND MODEL 1500C SURVIVOR . . . 359

MITCHELL

MITCHELL 1858 HENRY REPLICA . . . 359
MITCHELL 1866 WINCHESTER REPLICA . . . 359
MITCHELL 1873 WINCHESTER REPLICA . . . 359
MITCHELL AK-22 . . . 359
MITCHELL CAR-15/22 . . . 359
MITCHELL GALIL/22 . . . 359
MITCHELL HIGH STANDARD 15/22 . . . 359
MITCHELL HIGH STANDARD 15/22D . . . 359
MITCHELL HIGH STANDARD 20/22 . . . 360
MITCHELL HIGH STANDARD 20/22D . . . 360
MITCHELL HIGH STANDARD 20/22 SPECIAL . . . 360
MITCHELL HIGH STANDARD 9301 . . . 360
MITCHELL HIGH STANDARD 9302 . . . 360
MITCHELL HIGH STANDARD 9303 . . . 360
MITCHELL HIGH STANDARD 9304 . . . 360
MITCHELL HIGH STANDARD 9305 . . . 360
MITCHELL M-16A1 . . . 360
MITCHELL MAS/22 . . . 360
MITCHELL PPS/50 . . . 360

MONTANA ARMORY

MONTANA ARMORY MODEL 1885 HIGH WALL . . . 360

MOSSBERG

MOSSBERG 464 SPC .22 LR . . . 361
MOSSBERG 464 SPX .30-30 . . . 361
MOSSBERG ATR NIGHT TRAIN . . . 361
MOSSBERG MMR HUNTER . . . 361
MOSSBERG MMR TACTICAL . . . 361
MOSSBERG MODEL 10 . . . 361
MOSSBERG MODEL 14 . . . 361
MOSSBERG MODEL 20 . . . 361
MOSSBERG MODEL 21 . . . 361
MOSSBERG MODEL 25 . . . 361
MOSSBERG MODEL 25A . . . 361
MOSSBERG MODEL 26B . . . 361
MOSSBERG MODEL 26C . . . 361
MOSSBERG MODEL 26T TARGO RIFLE/SHOTGUN . . . 361
MOSSBERG MODEL 30 . . . 361
MOSSBERG MODEL 34 . . . 361
MOSSBERG MODEL 35 . . . 361
MOSSBERG MODEL 35A . . . 361
MOSSBERG MODEL 35A-LS . . . 361
MOSSBERG MODEL 40 . . . 361
MOSSBERG MODEL 42 . . . 361
MOSSBERG MODEL 42A . . . 361
MOSSBERG MODEL L42A . . . 362
MOSSBERG MODEL 42B . . . 362
MOSSBERG MODEL 42C . . . 362
MOSSBERG MODEL 42M . . . 362
MOSSBERG MODEL 42M (A), 42M (B), 42M (C) . . . 362
MOSSBERG MODEL 42MB . . . 362
MOSSBERG MODEL 42TR TARGO RIFLE/SHOTGUN . . . 362
MOSSBERG MODEL 42T TARGO RIFLE/SHOTGUN . . . 362
MOSSBERG MODEL 43 . . . 362
MOSSBERG MODEL L43 . . . 362
MOSSBERG MODEL 43B . . . 362
MOSSBERG MODEL 44B . . . 362
MOSSBERG MODEL 44US . . . 362
MOSSBERG MODEL 44US(A), 44US(B), 44US(C), 44US(D) . . . 362
MOSSBERG MODEL 45 . . . 362
MOSSBERG MODEL 45A . . . 362
MOSSBERG MODEL 45AC . . . 362
MOSSBERG MODEL 45B . . . 363
MOSSBERG MODEL 45C . . . 363
MOSSBERG MODEL L45A . . . 363
MOSSBERG MODEL 46 . . . 363
MOSSBERG MODEL 46A . . . 363
MOSSBERG MODEL 46AC . . . 363
MOSSBERG MODEL 46A-LS . . . 363
MOSSBERG MODEL 46B . . . 363
MOSSBERG MODEL 46BT . . . 363
MOSSBERG MODEL 46C . . . 363
MOSSBERG MODEL 46M . . . 363
MOSSBERG MODEL 46M(A), 46M(B) . . . 363
MOSSBERG MODEL 46T . . . 363
MOSSBERG MODEL L46A-LS . . . 363
MOSSBERG MODEL 140B . . . 363
MOSSBERG MODEL 140K . . . 363
MOSSBERG MODEL 142 . . . 363
MOSSBERG MODEL 142K . . . 363
MOSSBERG MODEL 144 . . . 363
MOSSBERG MODEL 144LS . . . 363
MOSSBERG MODEL 144LS-A . . . 363
MOSSBERG MODEL 144LS-B (TARGET) . . . 363
MOSSBERG MODEL 146B . . . 363
MOSSBERG MODEL 146B-A . . . 363
MOSSBERG MODEL 320B . . . 363
MOSSBERG MODEL 320K . . . 364
MOSSBERG MODEL 320K-A . . . 364
MOSSBERG MODEL 320TR TARGO RIFLE/SHOTGUN . . . 364
MOSSBERG MODEL 321B . . . 364
MOSSBERG MODEL 321K . . . 364
MOSSBERG MODEL 340B, 340B-A . . . 364
MOSSBERG MODEL 340K, 340K-A . . . 364
MOSSBERG MODEL 340M . . . 364
MOSSBERG MODEL 340TR TARGO RIFLE/SHOTGUN . . . 364
MOSSBERG MODEL 341 . . . 364
MOSSBERG MODEL 342 . . . 364
MOSSBERG MODEL 342K, 342K-A . . . 364
MOSSBERG MODEL 344 . . . 364
MOSSBERG MODEL 344K . . . 364
MOSSBERG MODEL 346B . . . 364
MOSSBERG MODEL 346K, 346K-A . . . 364
MOSSBERG MODEL 620K, 620K-A . . . 364
MOSSBERG MODEL 640K . . . 364
MOSSBERG MODEL 640KS . . . 364
MOSSBERG MODEL 640M . . . 364
MOSSBERG MODEL 642K . . . 364
MOSSBERG MODEL 800 . . . 364
MOSSBERG MODEL 800D SUPER GRADE . . . 364
MOSSBERG MODEL 800M . . . 365
MOSSBERG MODEL 800SM . . . 365
MOSSBERG MODEL 800VT . . . 365
MOSSBERG MODEL 810, 810A . . . 365
MOSSBERG MODEL 810ASM . . . 365
MOSSBERG MODEL 810B . . . 365
MOSSBERG MODEL 810BSM . . . 365
MOSSBERG MODEL 810C . . . 365
MOSSBERG MODEL 810D . . . 365
MOSSBERG MODEL 1500 MOUNTAINEER . . . 365
MOSSBERG MODEL 1500 MOUNTAINEER DELUXE . . . 365
MOSSBERG MODEL 1500 MOUNTAINEER VARMINT DELUXE . . . 365
MOSSBERG MODEL 1550 . . . 365
MOSSBERG MODEL 1700LS . . . 365
MOSSBERG MODEL B . . . 365
MOSSBERG MODEL C . . . 365
MOSSBERG MODEL C-1 . . . 365
MOSSBERG MODEL R . . . 365
MOSSBERG MODEL RM-7A . . . 365
MOSSBERG MODEL RM-7B . . . 366
MOSSBERG MODEL 50 . . . 366
MOSSBERG MODEL 51 . . . 366
MOSSBERG MODEL 51M . . . 366
MOSSBERG MODEL 151K . . . 366
MOSSBERG MODEL 151M . . . 366
MOSSBERG MODEL 151M(A), 151M(B), 151M(C) . . . 366
MOSSBERG MODEL 152 . . . 366
MOSSBERG MODEL 152K . . . 366
MOSSBERG MODEL 333 . . . 366
MOSSBERG MODEL 350K, 350K-A . . . 366
MOSSBERG MODEL 351K, 351K-A . . . 366
MOSSBERG MODEL 351C . . . 366
MOSSBERG MODEL 352 . . . 366
MOSSBERG MODEL 352K, 352K-A, 352K-B . . . 366
MOSSBERG MODEL 353 . . . 366
MOSSBERG MODEL 377 . . . 367
MOSSBERG MODEL 380, 380S . . . 367
MOSSBERG MODEL 430 . . . 367
MOSSBERG MODEL 432 . . . 367
MOSSBERG MODEL 400 PALOMINO . . . 367
MOSSBERG MODEL 402 PALOMINO . . . 367
MOSSBERG MODEL 472 CARBINE . . . 367
MOSSBERG MODEL 472 BRUSH GUN . . . 367
MOSSBERG MODEL 472 RIFLE . . . 367
MOSSBERG MODEL 472 "1 OF 5000" . . . 367
MOSSBERG MODEL 479PC . . . 367
MOSSBERG MODEL 479PCA . . . 367
MOSSBERG MODEL 479RR ROY ROGERS . . . 367
MOSSBERG MODEL 479SC . . . 367
MOSSBERG MODEL 464 LEVER ACTION CENTERFIRE RIFLE . . . 367
MOSSBERG MODEL 464 LEVER ACTION RIMFIRE RIFLE . . . 367
MOSSBERG MODEL K . . . 367
MOSSBERG MODEL L . . . 368
MOSSBERG MODEL L-1 . . . 368
MOSSBERG MODEL M . . . 368
MOSSBERG MODEL S . . . 368
MOSSBERG/NEW HAVEN MODEL 220K . . . 368
MOSSBERG/NEW HAVEN MODEL 240K . . . 368
MOSSBERG/NEW HAVEN MODEL 246K . . . 368
MOSSBERG/NEW HAVEN MODEL 250K . . . 368
MOSSBERG/NEW HAVEN MODEL 250KB . . . 368
MOSSBERG MODEL 702 PLINKSTER . . . 368
MOSSBERG MODEL 802 PLINKSTER BOLT ACTION . . . 368
MOSSBERG MODEL 817 PLINKSTER . . . 368
MODEL 817 VARMINT . . . 368
MOSSBERG MVP FLEX . . . 368
MOSSBERG MVP PATROL . . . 369
MOSSBERG MVP PREDATOR/ VARMINT . . . 369

MOSSBERG MVP THUNDER RANCH SERIES....369
MOSSBERG SSI-ONE....369
MOSSBERG MODEL 100 ATR (ALL TERRAIN RIFLE)....369
MOSSBERG 100 ATR SUPER BANTAM....369
MOSSBERG 4X4 RIFLE....369

MOUNTAIN EAGLE

MOUNTAIN EAGLE MAGNUM LITE RIFLE....369

M-S SAFARI ARMS

M-S SAFARI ARMS 1000-YARD MATCH MODEL....369
M-S SAFARI ARMS SILHOUETTE MODEL....369
M-S SAFARI ARMS VARMINT MODEL....370

MUSGRAVE

MUSGRAVE PREMIER NR5....370
MUSGRAVE RSA SINGLE SHOT NR1....370
MUSGRAVE VALIANT NR6....370

NAVY ARMS

NAVY ARMS 45-70 MAUSER RIFLE....370
NAVY ARMS 45-70 MAUSER CARBINE....370
NAVY ARMS 1860 HENRY RIFLE....370
NAVY ARMS 1860 HENRY MILITARY RIFLE....370
NAVY ARMS 1860 HENRY CARBINE....370
NAVY ARMS 1860 HENRY IRON FRAME....371
NAVY ARMS 1860 HENRY TRAPPER MODEL....371
NAVY ARMS MODEL 1866 WINCHESTER-STYLE RIFLE....371
NAVY ARMS MODEL 1866 CARBINE....371
NAVY ARMS MODEL 1866 TRAPPER....371
NAVY ARMS MODEL 1866 YELLOWBOY....371
NAVY ARMS MODEL 1866 YELLOWBOY CARBINE....371
NAVY ARMS 1873 SPRINGFIELD INFANTRY RIFLE....371
NAVY ARMS 1873 SPRINGFIELD CAVALRY CARBINE....371
NAVY ARMS 1873 WINCHESTER-STYLE RIFLE....371
NAVY ARMS 1873 WINCHESTER-STYLE SPORTING RIFLE....371
NAVY ARMS 1873 WINCHESTER-STYLE CARBINE....371
NAVY ARMS 1874 SHARPS CAVALRY CARBINE....371
NAVY ARMS 1874 SHARPS BUFFALO RIFLE....371
NAVY ARMS SHARPS PLAINS RIFLE....371
NAVY ARMS SHARPS SPORTING RIFLE....371
NAVY ARMS 1874 SHARPS INFANTRY RIFLE....371
NAVY ARMS 1874 SHARPS SNIPER RIFLE....371
NAVY ARMS 1885 HIGH WALL RIFLE....371
NAVY ARMS 1892 RIFLE....372
NAVY ARMS 1892 STAINLESS CARBINE....372
NAVY ARMS 1892 SHORT RIFLE....372
NAVY ARMS 1892 STAINLESS RIFLE....372
NAVY ARMS EM-331....372
NAVY ARMS MARTINI....372
NAVY ARMS REVOLVING CARBINE....372
NAVY ARMS ROLLING BLOCK BABY CARBINE....372
NAVY ARMS ROLLING BLOCK BUFFALO RIFLE....372
NAVY ARMS ROLLING BLOCK BUFFALO CARBINE....372
NAVY ARMS ROLLING BLOCK RIFLE....372
NAVY ARMS "JOHN BODINE" ROLLING BLOCK RIFLE....373
NAVY ARMS ROLLING BLOCK #2 CREEDMORE....373
NAVY ARMS SHARPS NO. 3 LONG RANGE RIFLE....373
NAVY ARMS SHARPS PLAINS RIFLE....373
NAVY ARMS TU-33/40 CARBINE....373
NAVY ARMS TU-KKW SNIPER TRAINER....373

NEW ENGLAND FIREARMS

NEW ENGLAND FIREARMS HANDI-RIFLE....373
NEW ENGLAND FIREARMS SUPER LIGHT RIFLE....373
NEW ENGLAND FIREARMS SPORTSTER SINGLE-SHOT RIFLE....373
NEW ENGLAND FIREARMS SURVIVOR RIFLE....373

NEW ULTRA LIGHT ARMS

NEW ULTRA LIGHT ARMS MODEL 20....373
NEW ULTRA LIGHT ARMS MODEL 20 SHORT....373
NEW ULTRA LIGHT ARMS MODEL 20 RIMFIRE....373
NEW ULTRA LIGHT ARMS MODEL 24....373
NEW ULTRA LIGHT ARMS MODEL 28....373
NEW ULTRA LIGHT ARMS MODEL 40 MAGNUM....373

NEWTON

NEWTON BUFFALO SPORTER....374
NEWTON-MAUSER SPORTER....374
NEWTON STANDARD SPORTER (TYPE I)....374
NEWTON STANDARD SPORTER (TYPE II)....374

NOBLE

NOBLE MODEL 10....374
NOBLE MODEL 20....374
NOBLE MODEL 33....374
NOBLE MODEL 33A....374
NOBLE MODEL 222....374
NOBLE MODEL 235....374
NOBLE MODEL 275....374
NOBLE MODEL 285....374

NORINCO

NORINCO MAK 90....374
NORINCO MODEL ATD....374
NORINCO MODEL EM-321....374
NORINCO MODEL JW-14....374
NORINCO MODEL JW-15....374
NORINCO MODEL JW-27....374
NORINCO TYPE EM-332....375

NORRAHAMMAR

NORRAHAMMAR MODEL N-900....375

NOSLER

NOSLER CUSTOM MODEL 48 SPORTER....375
NOSLER MODEL 48 VARMINT RIFLE....375

NS FIREARMS

NS FIREARMS MODEL 522....375

OLYMPIC ARMS

OLYMPIC ARMS AR-15 MATCH....375
OLYMPIC ARMS CAR-97 RIFLES....375
OLYMPIC ARMS INTERCONTINENTAL MATCH....375
OLYMPIC ARMS INTERNATIONAL MATCH....375
OLYMPIC ARMS UM-1P....375
OLYMPIC ARMS UM-1....375
OLYMPIC ARMS SM-1P....375
OLYMPIC ARMS SM-1....375
OLYMPIC ARMS ML-1....375
OLYMPIC ARMS ML-2....375
OLYMPIC ARMS MODEL K8....376
OLYMPIC ARMS MODEL K8-MAG....376
OLYMPIC ARMS K3B....376
OLYMPIC ARMS K3B-M4....376
OLYMPIC ARMS K3B-CAR....376
OLYMPIC ARMS K3B-FAR....376
OLYMPIC ARMS K4B....376
OLYMPIC ARMS K4B-A4....376
OLYMPIC ARMS LTF....376
OLYMPIC ARMS LT-M4....376
OLYMPIC ARMS K16....376
OLYMPIC ARMS GI-16....376
OLYMPIC ARMS K30....376
OLYMPIC ARMS K9/K10/K40/K45....376
OLYMPIC ARMS K9-GL/K40-GL....376
OLYMPIC ARMS PLINKER PLUS....376
OLYMPIC ARMS PLINKER PLUS 20....376
OLYMPIC ARMS K7 ELIMINATOR....376
OLYMPIC ARMS K-4 AR-15....376
OLYMPIC ARMS MULTIMATCH....376
OLYMPIC ARMS PCR-1....376
OLYMPIC ARMS PCR-2....376
OLYMPIC ARMS PCR-3....376
OLYMPIC ARMS PCR-4....377
OLYMPIC ARMS PCR-5....377
OLYMPIC ARMS PCR-6....377
OLYMPIC ARMS PCR-9....377
OLYMPIC ARMS PCR-10....377
OLYMPIC ARMS PCR-40....377
OLYMPIC ARMS PCR-45....377
OLYMPIC ARMS SERVICE MATCH....377
OLYMPIC ARMS ULTRAMATCH....377

OMEGA

OMEGA III....377

PARKER-HALE

PARKER-HALE MODEL 81 CLASSIC....377
PARKER-HALE MODEL 81 CLASSIC AFRICAN....377
PARKER-HALE MODEL 85 SNIPER RIFLE....377
PARKER-HALE MODEL 87 TARGET....377
PARKER-HALE MODEL 1000....378
PARKER-HALE MODEL 1000 CLIP....378
PARKER-HALE MODEL 1100 LIGHTWEIGHT....378
PARKER-HALE MODEL 1100M AFRICAN....378
PARKER-HALE MODEL 1200 SUPER....378
PARKER-HALE MODEL 1200P PRESENTATION....378
PARKER-HALE MODEL 1200V VARMINTER....378
PARKER-HALE MODEL 1300C SCOUT....378
PARKER-HALE MODEL 2100 MIDLAND....378
PARKER-HALE MODEL 2600 MIDLAND....378
PARKER-HALE MODEL 2700 LIGHTWEIGHT MIDLAND....378
PARKER-HALE MODEL 2800 MIDLAND....378

PEDERSEN

PEDERSEN MODEL 3000....378
PEDERSEN MODEL 3500....378
PEDERSEN MODEL 4700....378

PERUGINI-VISINI

PERUGINI-VISINI BOXLOCK EXPRESS....379
PERUGINI-VISINI BOXLOCK MAGNUM....379
PERUGINI-VISINI EAGLE....379
PERUGINI-VISINI MODEL SELOUS....379
PERUGINI-VISINI PROFESSIONAL....379
PERUGINI-VISINI PROFESSIONAL DELUXE....379
PERUGINI-VISINI SIDELOCK EXPRESS....379
PERUGINI-VISINI VICTORIA....379

PHILLIPS & RODGERS

PHILLIPS & RODGERS WILDERNESS EXPLORER....379

PLAINFIELD

PLAINFIELD M-1 CARBINE....379

PLAINFIELD M-1 CARBINE, COMMANDO OR PARATROOPER MODEL . . . 379
PLAINFIELD M-1 CARBINE, DELUXE SPORTER . . . 379
PLAINFIELD M-1 CARBINE, MILITARY SPORTER . . . 379

PROFESSIONAL ORDNANCE

PROFESSIONAL ORDNANCE CARBON 15 (TYPE 97) . . . 379
PROFESSIONAL ORDNANCE CARBON 15 TYPE 97S (INSULATED FOREND, OTHER IMPROVEMENTS) . . . 379

PUMA

PUMA BOUNTY HUNTER . . . 379

PURDEY

PURDEY BIG GAME SPORTER . . . 379
PURDEY DOUBLE RIFLE . . . 379

QUALITY PARTS/ BUSHMASTER

QUALITY PARTS/ BUSHMASTER V MATCH . . . 379

REMINGTON

REMINGTON MODEL 7400D PEERLESS . . . 380
REMINGTON MODEL 7400F PREMIER . . . 380
REMINGTON MODEL 7400F PREMIER GOLD . . . 380
REMINGTON MODEL 7400 SPECIAL PURPOSE . . . 380
REMINGTON MODEL 750 WOODSMASTER . . . 380
REMINGTON MODEL 750 SYNTHETIC . . . 380
REMINGTON MODEL R15 VTR PREDATOR RIFLE . . . 380
REMINGTON MODEL R15CS VTR PREDATOR CARBINE . . . 380
REMINGTON MODEL R15 VTR PREDATOR CARBINE . . . 380
REMINGTON “NYLON” SERIES .22 RIFLES . . . 380
REMINGTON NYLON 10 . . . 380
REMINGTON NYLON 10-C . . . 380
REMINGTON NYLON 11 . . . 380
REMINGTON NYLON 12 . . . 380
REMINGTON NYLON 66 . . . 380
REMINGTON NYLON 76 . . . 380
REMINGTON NYLON 77 . . . 380
REMINGTON NYLON 77 APACHE . . . 380
MODEL 597 TVP (TARGET/VARMINT/PLINKER) . . . 380
REMINGTON MODEL 597 YELLOW JACKET . . . 380
REMINGTON MODEL 597 BLAZE CAMO . . . 380
REMINGTON MODEL 597 PINK CAMO . . . 380
REMINGTON BOLT-ACTION RIFLES REMINGTON MODEL 30A . . . 380
REMINGTON MODEL 30R CARBINE . . . 380
REMINGTON MODEL 30S SPORTING . . . 380
REMINGTON MODEL 33 . . . 380
REMINGTON MODEL 33 NRA JUNIOR . . . 381
REMINGTON MODEL 34 . . . 381
REMINGTON MODEL 34 NRA . . . 381
REMINGTON MODEL 37 RANGEMASTER . . . 381
REMINGTON MODEL 37 OF 1940 . . . 381
REMINGTON MODEL 40X . . . 381
REMINGTON MODEL 40X CENTERFIRE . . . 381
REMINGTON MODEL 40X STANDARD . . . 381
REMINGTON MODEL 40-XB RANGEMASTER RIMFIRE . . . 381
REMINGTON MODEL 40-XB RANGEMASTER CENTERFIRE . . . 381
REMINGTON MODEL 40-XB RANGEMASTER REPEATER . . . 381
REMINGTON MODEL 40-XB RANGEMASTER VARMINT SPECIAL KS . . . 381
REMINGTON MODEL 40-XB-BR . . . 381
REMINGTON MODEL 40-XB-BR KS . . . 381
REMINGTON MODEL 40-XC NATIONAL MATCH . . . 381
REMINGTON MODEL 40-XC KS NATIONAL MATCH . . . 382
REMINGTON MODEL 40-XR . . . 382
REMINGTON MODEL 40-XR CUSTOM SPORTER . . . 382
REMINGTON MODEL 40-XR KS . . . 382
REMINGTON MODEL 40-XR KS SPORTER . . . 382
REMINGTON MODEL 41A TARGETMASTER . . . 382
REMINGTON MODEL 41AS . . . 382
REMINGTON MODEL 41P . . . 382
REMINGTON MODEL 41SB . . . 382
REMINGTON MODEL 78 SPORTSMAN . . . 382
REMINGTON MODEL 341A . . . 382
REMINGTON MODEL 341P . . . 382
REMINGTON MODEL 341SB . . . 382
REMINGTON MODEL 510A . . . 382
REMINGTON MODEL 510P . . . 382
REMINGTON MODEL 510SB . . . 382
REMINGTON MODEL 510X . . . 382
REMINGTON 510X-SB . . . 382
REMINGTON MODEL 511A . . . 382
REMINGTON MODEL 511P . . . 382
REMINGTON MODEL 511SB . . . 382
REMINGTON MODEL 511X . . . 382
REMINGTON MODEL 512A . . . 382
REMINGTON MODEL 512P . . . 382
REMINGTON MODEL 512SB . . . 382
REMINGTON MODEL 512X . . . 382
REMINGTON MODEL 513S SPORTER . . . 383
REMINGTON MODEL 513TR MATCHMASTER . . . 383
REMINGTON MODEL 514 . . . 383
REMINGTON MODEL 514P . . . 383
REMINGTON MODEL 514SB . . . 383
REMINGTON MODEL 521T . . . 383
REMINGTON MODEL 540X . . . 383
REMINGTON MODEL 540XR . . . 383
REMINGTON MODEL 540XR JR . . . 383
REMINGTON MODEL 541S . . . 383
REMINGTON MODEL 541T . . . 383
REMINGTON MODEL 541T HB . . . 383
REMINGTON MODEL XR-100 RANGEMASTER . . . 383
REMINGTON MODEL 580 . . . 383
REMINGTON MODEL 580BR “BOYS’ RIFLE” . . . 383
REMINGTON MODEL 580SB . . . 383
REMINGTON MODEL 581 . . . 383
REMINGTON MODEL 581 SPORTSMAN . . . 384
REMINGTON MODEL 582 . . . 384
REMINGTON MODEL 591 . . . 384
REMINGTON MODEL 592 . . . 384
REMINGTON MODEL 504 . . . 384
REMINGTON MODEL 547 . . . 384
REMINGTON MODEL FIVE . . . 384
REMINGTON MODEL 600 . . . 384
REMINGTON MODEL 600 MAGNUM . . . 384
REMINGTON MODEL 600 MOHAWK . . . 384
REMINGTON MODEL 660 . . . 384
REMINGTON MODEL 660 MAGNUM . . . 384
REMINGTON MODEL 673 . . . 384
REMINGTON MODEL 700 ADL . . . 384
REMINGTON MODEL 700 ADL SYNTHETIC . . . 384
REMINGTON MODEL 700 ADL SYNTHETIC YOUTH . . . 384
REMINGTON MODEL 700 APR AFRICAN PLAINS RIFLE . . . 385
REMINGTON MODEL 700 AS . . . 385
REMINGTON MODEL 700 AWR ALASKAN WILDERNESS RIFLE . . . 385
REMINGTON MODEL 700 BDL . . . 385
REMINGTON MODEL 700 BDL 50TH ANNIVERSARY EDITION . . . 385
REMINGTON MODEL 700 LSS . . . 385
REMINGTON MODEL 700 BDL DM . . . 385
REMINGTON MODEL 700 BDL EUROPEAN . . . 385
REMINGTON MODEL 700 BDL LIMITED CLASSIC . . . 385
REMINGTON MODEL 700 BDL MOUNTAIN RIFLE . . . 385
REMINGTON MODEL 700 BDL MOUNTAIN CUSTOM KS WOOD GRAINED . . . 385
REMINGTON MODEL 700BDL MOUNTAIN STAINLESS . . . 385
REMINGTON MODEL 700 BDL SAFARI . . . 386
REMINGTON MODEL 700 BDL SAFARI CUSTOM KS . . . 386
REMINGTON MODEL 700 BDL SAFARI CUSTOM KS STAINLESS . . . 386
REMINGTON MODEL 700 BDL SS . . . 386
REMINGTON MODEL 700 BDL SS DM . . . 386
REMINGTON MODEL 700 BDL VARMINT SPECIAL . . . 386
REMINGTON MODEL 700 BDL VARMINT SYNTHETIC . . . 386
REMINGTON MODEL 700 C . . . 386
REMINGTON MODEL 700D PEERLESS . . . 386
REMINGTON MODEL 700F PREMIER . . . 386
REMINGTON MODEL 700 CAMO SYNTHETIC RIFLE . . . 386
REMINGTON 700 CDL CLASSIC DELUXE . . . 386
REMINGTON MODEL 700 CLASSIC . . . 386
REMINGTON MODEL 700 CUSTOM MOUNTAIN KS . . . 386
REMINGTON MODEL 700 MOUNTAIN . . . 387
REMINGTON MODEL 700 LSS MOUNTAIN RIFLE . . . 387
REMINGTON MODEL 700 FS . . . 387
REMINGTON MODEL 700LS . . . 387
REMINGTON MODEL 700 MTN DM . . . 387
REMINGTON MODEL 700 MTRSS . . . 387
REMINGTON MODEL 700 RS . . . 387
REMINGTON MODEL 700 SENDERO . . . 387
REMINGTON MODEL 700 SPS TACTICAL (16 INCH) . . . 387
REMINGTON MODEL 700 SPS WOOD TECH . . . 387
REMINGTON MODEL 700 SENDERO SF . . . 387
REMINGTON MODEL 700 TITANIUM . . . 387
REMINGTON MODEL 700 VLS (VARMINT LAMINATED STOCK) . . . 387
REMINGTON MODEL 700 VS (VARMINT SYNTHETIC) . . . 387
REMINGTON MODEL 700 VSSF . . . 387
REMINGTON MODEL 700 ETRONX (ELECTRONIC IGNITION RIFLE) . . . 387
REMINGTON MODEL 700 RMEF . . . 388
REMINGTON MODEL 700 SENDERO SF-II . . . 388
REMINGTON MODEL 700 CDL . . . 388
REMINGTON MODEL 700 CDL SF LIMITED . . . 388
REMINGTON MODEL 700 VTR (VARMINT TACTICAL) . . . 388
REMINGTON 700 XCR II . . . 388
REMINGTON MODEL 700 XCR II RMEF LIMITED EDITION . . . 388
REMINGTON MODEL 710 . . . 388
REMINGTON MODEL 770 YOUTH . . . 388
REMINGTON MODEL 715 SPORTSMAN . . . 388
REMINGTON MODEL 720A . . . 388
REMINGTON MODEL 720R . . . 388
REMINGTON MODEL 720S . . . 388
REMINGTON MODEL 721A . . . 388
REMINGTON MODEL 721A MAGNUM . . . 388
REMINGTON MODEL 721 ADL . . . 388
REMINGTON MODEL 721 ADL MAGNUM . . . 388
REMINGTON MODEL 721 BDL . . . 388
REMINGTON MODEL 721 BDL MAGNUM . . . 388
REMINGTON MODEL 722A . . . 388
REMINGTON MODEL 722 ADL . . . 389
REMINGTON MODEL 722 BDL . . . 389
REMINGTON MODEL 725 ADL . . . 389
REMINGTON MODEL 725 ADL KODIAK MAGNUM . . . 389
REMINGTON MODEL 783 . . . 389

REMINGTON MODEL 788 389
REMINGTON MODEL 788 CARBINE 389
REMINGTON MODEL 788 LEFT-HAND 389
REMINGTON MODEL INTERNATIONAL FREE RIFLE 389
REMINGTON MODEL INTERNATIONAL MATCH FREE RIFLE 389
REMINGTON MODEL SEVEN 389
REMINGTON MODEL SEVEN CUSTOM KS 389
REMINGTON MODEL SEVEN CUSTOM MS 389
REMINGTON MODEL SEVEN FS 389
REMINGTON MODEL SEVEN LS 389
REMINGTON MODEL SEVEN SS 389
REMINGTON MODEL SEVEN LSS 390
REMINGTON MODEL SEVEN YOUTH 390
REMINGTON MODEL SEVEN CDL 390
REMINGTON MODEL SEVEN XCR CAMO 390
MODEL SEVEN PREDATOR 390
REMINGTON MODEL SEVEN 25TH ANNIVERSARY VERSION 390
REMINGTON MODEL 770 390
REMINGTON MODEL 798 390
REMINGTON MODEL 798 STAINLESS LAMINATE 390
MODEL 798 SAFARI 390
MODEL 798 SPS 390
REMINGTON MODEL 799 390
REMINGTON-LEE SPORTER 390
REMINGTON-LEE SPORTER DELUXE 390
REMINGTON MODEL SIX 390
REMINGTON MODEL 12, 12A 391
REMINGTON MODEL 12B 391
REMINGTON MODEL 12C 391
REMINGTON MODEL 12CS 391
REMINGTON MODEL 14, 14A 391
REMINGTON MODEL 14R CARBINE 391
REMINGTON MODEL 14-1/2 391
REMINGTON MODEL 14-1/2 CARBINE 391
REMINGTON MODEL 25, 25A 391
REMINGTON MODEL 25R CARBINE 391
REMINGTON MODEL 76 SPORTSMAN 391
REMINGTON MODEL 121A FIELDMASTER 391
REMINGTON MODEL 121S 391
REMINGTON MODEL 121SB 391
REMINGTON MODEL 141, 141A GAMEMASTER 391
REMINGTON MODEL 141R CARBINE 391
REMINGTON MODEL 572A FIELDMASTER 391
REMINGTON MODEL 572 FIELDMASTER 391
REMINGTON MODEL 572 BDL DELUXE 391
REMINGTON MODEL 572 SB 391
REMINGTON MODEL 572 BDL SMOOTHBORE (2007) 392
REMINGTON MODEL 760 392
REMINGTON MODEL 760 ADL 392
REMINGTON MODEL 760 BDL 392
REMINGTON MODEL 760 CARBINE 392
REMINGTON MODEL 760 CDL 392
REMINGTON MODEL 760D PEERLESS 392
REMINGTON MODEL 760F PREMIER 392
REMINGTON MODEL 760F PREMIER GOLD 392
REMINGTON MODEL 7600 392
REMINGTON MODEL 7600 CARBINE 392
REMINGTON 7600 SPECIAL PURPOSE 392
REMINGTON 7600D PEERLESS 392
REMINGTON 7600F PREMIER 392
REMINGTON 7600F PREMIER GOLD 392
REMINGTON 7600P PATROL RIFLE 392
REMINGTON MODEL 7615 TACTICAL PUMP CARBINE 392
REMINGTON MODEL 7615 SPECIAL PURPOSE SYNTHETIC 392
REMINGTON MODEL 7615 CAMO HUNTER 392
REMINGTON MODEL 7615 RANCH CARBINE 392
REMINGTON BABY CARBINE 392
REMINGTON NO. 1 ROLLING BLOCK MID-RANGE SPORTER 392
REMINGTON NO. 2 392
REMINGTON NO. 3 393
REMINGTON NO. 3 HIGH POWER 393
REMINGTON NO. 4 393
REMINGTON NO. 4-S MILITARY 393
REMINGTON NO. 5 393
REMINGTON NO. 5 MILITARY 393
REMINGTON NO. 6 393
REMINGTON NO. 7 393
REMINGTON MODEL SPR18 393
REMINGTON MODEL SPR94 COMBO GUN 393
REMINGTON MODEL 412 393
REMINGTON R15 MOE 393

RIGBY

RIGBY 350 MAGNUM 394
RIGBY 416 MAGNUM 394
RIGBY BEST QUALITY 394
RIGBY BIG GAME BOLT ACTION 394
RIGBY SECOND QUALITY 394
RIGBY STANDARD BOLT ACTION 394
RIGBY STANDARD LIGHTWEIGHT 394
RIGBY THIRD QUALITY 394

RIZZINI

RIZZINI EXPRESS 90L DOUBLE RIFLE 394

ROSS

ROSS MODEL 1905 MARK II 394
ROSS MODEL 1910 MARK III 394

ROSSI

ROSSI MATCHED PAIR CENTERFIRE RIFLE/SHOTGUN 394
ROSSI MATCHED PAIR RIMFIRE RIFLE/SHOTGUN 394
ROSSI MODEL 59 SA 394
ROSSI MODEL 62 SA 395
ROSSI MODEL 62 SAC CARBINE 395
ROSSI MODEL 62 SA STAINLESS 395
ROSSI MODEL 65 SRC 395
ROSSI MODEL 92 SRC 395
ROSSI MODEL 92 SRS PUMA SHORT CARBINE 395
ROSSI SINGLE SHOT CENTERFIRE RIFLE 395

SAKO

SAKO CLASSIC 395
SAKO FIBERGLASS 395
SAKO FIBERGLASS CARBINE 395
SAKO FINNBEAR SPORTER 395
SAKO FINNFIRE 395
SAKO FINNFIRE HUNTER 395
SAKO FINNFIRE SPORTER 395
SAKO FINNSPORT MODEL 2700 395
SAKO FINNWOLF 395
SAKO FORESTER SPORTER 396
SAKO FORESTER SPORTER CARBINE 396
SAKO FORESTER SPORTER HEAVY BARREL 396
SAKO HUNTER 396
SAKO HUNTER CARBINE 396
SAKO HUNTER LS 396
SAKO LIGHTWEIGHT DELUXE 396
SAKO MANNLICHER CARBINE 396
SAKO MAUSER 396
SAKO MAUSER MAGNUM 396
SAKO MODEL 72 396
SAKO MODEL 73 396
SAKO MODEL 74 396
SAKO MODEL 74 CARBINE 396
SAKO 75 HUNTER 396
SAKO 75 HUNTER LEFT-HAND 397
SAKO 75 HUNTER STAINLESS 397
SAKO 75 DELUXE 397
SAKO 75 FINNLIGHT 397
SAKO 75 SINGLE SHOT CUSTOM 397
SAKO 75 STAINLESS SYNTHETIC 397
SAKO 75 VARMINT 397
SAKO 75 VARMINT STAINLESS LAMINATED 397
SAKO MODEL 78 397
SAKO 85 HUNTER 397
SAKO 85 STAINLESS SYNTHETIC 397
SAKO 85 FINNLIGHT 397
SAKO 85 VARMINT 397
SAKO 85 LAMINATED SS VARMINT 397
SAKO QUAD 397
SAKO PPC MODEL 397
SAKO SAFARI GRADE 397
SAKO STANDARD SPORTER 397
SAKO STANDARD SPORTER CARBINE 398
SAKO STANDARD SPORTER CLASSIC 398
SAKO STANDARD SPORTER DELUXE 398
SAKO STANDARD SPORTER HEAVY BARREL 398
SAKO STANDARD SPORTER SAFARI 398
SAKO STANDARD SPORTER SUPER DELUXE 398
SAKO STANDARD SPORTER VARMINT HEAVY BARREL 398
SAKO TRG-21 398
SAKO TRG-22 398
SAKO TRG-S 398
SAKO TRG-42 BOLT-ACTION RIFLE 398
SAKO VIXEN SPORTER 398
SAKO VIXEN SPORTER CARBINE 398
SAKO VIXEN SPORTER HEAVY BARREL 398

SAUER

SAUER DRILLING 398
SAUER MAUSER SPORTER 399
SAUER MODEL 90 399
SAUER MODEL 90 LUX 399
SAUER MODEL 90 SAFARI 399
SAUER MODEL 90 SAFARI LUX 399
SAUER MODEL 90 STUTZEN 399
SAUER MODEL 90 STUTZEN LUX 399
SAUER MODEL 90 SUPREME 399
SAUER MODEL 200 399
SAUER MODEL 200 CARBON FIBER 399
SAUER MODEL 200 LUX 399
SAUER MODEL 202 399
SAUER MODEL 202 ALASKA 399
SAUER MODEL 202 HUNTER MATCH 399
SAUER 202 TR TARGET 399
SAUER MODEL SSG 2000 399

SAVAGE

SAVAGE AXIS SERIES 399
SAVAGE CUB 399
SAVAGE MODEL CUB-T 399
SAVAGE MARK I 400
SAVAGE MARK II 400
SAVAGE MARK II-LV HEAVY BARREL 400
SAVAGE MODEL MARK II CLASSIC 400
SAVAGE MODEL 3 400
SAVAGE MODEL 3S 400
SAVAGE MODEL 3ST 400
SAVAGE MODEL 4 400
SAVAGE MODEL 4M 400
SAVAGE MODEL 4S 400
SAVAGE MODEL 5 400
SAVAGE MODEL 5S 400
SAVAGE MODEL10FM SIERRA ULTRA LIGHT 400
SAVAGE MODEL10FCM SCOUT ULTRA LIGHT 400
SAVAGE MODEL 19 400
SAVAGE MODEL 19H 401
SAVAGE MODEL 19L 401
SAVAGE MODEL 19M 401
SAVAGE MODEL 19 NRA 401
SAVAGE MODEL 23A 401
SAVAGE MODEL 23AA 401
SAVAGE MODEL 23B 401
SAVAGE MODEL 23C 401
SAVAGE MODEL 23D 401
SAVAGE MODEL 30 STEVENS FAVORITE 401
SAVAGE MODEL 34 401
SAVAGE MODEL 34M 401
SAVAGE MODEL 35 401
SAVAGE MODEL 35M 401
SAVAGE MODEL 36 401
SAVAGE MODEL 40 401

SAVAGE MODEL 40 VARMINT HUNTER 401
SAVAGE MODEL 45 402
SAVAGE MODEL 46 402
SAVAGE MODEL 63 402
SAVAGE MODEL 63M 402
SAVAGE MODEL 65 402
SAVAGE MODEL 65M 402
SAVAGE MODEL 93 MAGNUM 402
SAVAGE MODEL 93 CLASSIC THUMBHOLE 402
SAVAGE MODEL 93FSS MAGNUM 402
SAVAGE MODEL 93XP 402
SAVAGE MODEL 93FVSS MAGNUM 402
SAVAGE MODEL 93BTVS 402
SAVAGE MODEL 93R17 CLASSIC 402
SAVAGE MODEL 10 PREDATOR HUNTER 402
SAVAGE MODEL 10FP TACTICAL RIFLE 402
SAVAGE MODEL 10FCP-HS PRECISION 402
SAVAGE MODEL 10FCP CHOATE 402
SAVAGE MODEL 10FCP MCMILLAN 402
SAVAGE MODEL 110 402
SAVAGE MODEL 110B 402
SAVAGE MODEL 110B LAMINATE 402
SAVAGE MODEL 110C 403
SAVAGE MODEL 110CY LADIES/YOUTH 403
SAVAGE MODEL 110D 403
SAVAGE MODEL 110E 403
SAVAGE MODEL 110ES 403
SAVAGE 110F 403
SAVAGE 110FNS 403
SAVAGE MODEL 110FP 403
SAVAGE MODEL 110FP POLICE 403
SAVAGE MODEL 110FP TACTICAL 403
SAVAGE MODEL 110G 403
SAVAGE 110GC 403
SAVAGE MODEL 110GCXP3 PACKAGE 403
SAVAGE 110GLNS 404
SAVAGE 110GNS 404
SAVAGE 110GV VARMINT 404
SAVAGE MODEL 110GXP3 PACKAGE 404
SAVAGE MODEL 110K 404
SAVAGE MODEL 110M 404
SAVAGE MODEL 110MC 404
SAVAGE MODEL 110P PREMIER GRADE 404
SAVAGE MODEL 110PE PRESENTATION GRADE 404
SAVAGE MODEL 110S 404
SAVAGE MODEL 110V 404
SAVAGE 110WLE LIMITED EDITION ONE OF ONE THOUSAND 404
SAVAGE MODEL 110 - FIFTIETH ANNIVERSARY 404
SAVAGE MODEL 111 CHIEFTAIN 404
SAVAGE MODEL 111 HUNTER 404
SAVAGE MODEL 11 HUNTER 404
SAVAGE MODEL 11FYCAK 404
SAVAGE MODEL 111FYCAK 404
SAVAGE MODEL 11BTH 404
SAVAGE MODEL 111F CLASSIC HUNTER 404
SAVAGE MODEL 111G CLASSIC HUNTER 405
SAVAGE MODEL 12 LONG RANGE 405
SAVAGE MODEL 12 LONG RANGE PRECISION VARMINTER (LRPV) 405
SAVAGE MODEL 12VSS VARMINTER RIFLE 405
SAVAGE MODEL 12BTCSS 405
SAVAGE MODEL 12 F/TR F-CLASS TARGET RIFLE 405
SAVAGE MODEL 112 LONG RANGE 405
SAVAGE MODEL 112BV 405
SAVAGE MODEL 112BT COMPETITION GRADE 405
SAVAGE MODEL 112FV VARMINT 405
SAVAGE MODEL 112FVSS 405
SAVAGE MODEL 112FVSS-S 405
SAVAGE MODEL 112R 405
SAVAGE MODEL 112V 405
SAVAGE MODEL 112 VARMINT LOW PROFILE 405
SAVAGE MODEL 14 CLASSIC 405
SAVAGE MODEL 14 EURO CLASSIC 405
SAVAGE MODEL 114 CLASSIC 405
SAVAGE MODEL 114U ULTRA RIFLE 405
SAVAGE MODEL 114CU CLASSIC ULTRA 405
SAVAGE MODEL 114 EURO CLASSIC 405
SAVAGE MODEL 116FSS WEATHER WARRIOR 405
SAVAGE MODEL 116FHSS 406
SAVAGE MODEL 116FSAK 406
SAVAGE MODEL 116FSK 406
SAVAGE MODEL 116FHSAK 406
SAVAGE MODEL 16FHSAK 406
SAVAGE MODEL 116SE SAFARI EXPRESS 406
SAVAGE MODEL 16FSS 406
SAVAGE MODEL 16 FHSS 406
SAVAGE MODEL 16 FLHSS WEATHER WARRIOR 406
SAVAGE MODEL 116US ULTRA STAINLESS RIFLE 406
SAVAGE MODEL 25 LIGHTWEIGHT VARMINTER 406
SAVAGE MODEL 25 CLASSIC SPORTER 406
SAVAGE MODEL 25 LIGHTWEIGHT VARMINTER THUMBHOLE 406
SAVAGE MODEL 340 406
SAVAGE MODEL 340C 406
SAVAGE MODEL 340S DELUXE 406
SAVAGE MODEL 340V 406
SAVAGE MODEL 342 406
SAVAGE MODEL 342S DELUXE 406
SAVAGE MODEL 1904 406
SAVAGE MODEL 1905 406
SAVAGE MODEL 1920 406
SAVAGE MODEL 1920 (1926 VERSION) 407
SAVAGE MODEL 25 407
SAVAGE MODEL 29 407
SAVAGE MODEL 29-G 407
SAVAGE MODEL 99 (MODEL 1899, ORIGINAL VERSION) 407
SAVAGE MODEL 99-358 407
SAVAGE MODEL 99-375 407
SAVAGE MODEL 99A (EARLY MODEL) 407
SAVAGE MODEL 99A (LATE MODEL) 407
SAVAGE MODEL 99B 407
SAVAGE MODEL 99C 407
SAVAGE MODEL 99CD 407
SAVAGE MODEL 99DE CITATION 407
SAVAGE MODEL 99DL 407
SAVAGE MODEL 99E (EARLY MODEL) 407
SAVAGE MODEL 99E (LATE MODEL) 407
SAVAGE MODEL 99EG (EARLY MODEL) 407
SAVAGE MODEL 99EG (LATE MODEL) 407
SAVAGE MODEL 99F CARBINE 407
SAVAGE MODEL 99F FEATHERWEIGHT (EARLY MODEL) 407
SAVAGE MODEL 99F FEATHERWEIGHT (LATE MODEL) 407
SAVAGE MODEL 99G 407
SAVAGE MODEL 99H 407
SAVAGE MODEL 99K 407
SAVAGE MODEL 99PE 408
SAVAGE MODEL 99R (EARLY MODEL) 408
SAVAGE MODEL 99R (LATE MODEL) 408
SAVAGE MODEL 99RS (EARLY MODEL) 408
SAVAGE MODEL 99RS (LATE MODEL) 408
SAVAGE MODEL 99T FEATHERWEIGHT 408
SAVAGE MODEL 170 408
SAVAGE MODEL 170C CARBINE 408
SAVAGE MODEL 1903 408
SAVAGE MODEL 1909 408
SAVAGE MODEL 1914 408
SAVAGE MODEL 6 408
SAVAGE MODEL 6P 409
SAVAGE MODEL 6S 409
SAVAGE MODEL 7 409
SAVAGE MODEL 7S 409
SAVAGE MODEL 24 409
SAVAGE MODEL 24C CAMPER'S COMPANION 409
SAVAGE MODEL 24D 409
SAVAGE MODEL 24DL 409
SAVAGE MODEL 24F 409
SAVAGE MODEL 24F-12T TURKEY GUN 409
SAVAGE MODEL 24FG 409
SAVAGE MODEL 24 FIELD 409
SAVAGE MODEL 24MDL 409
SAVAGE MODEL 24MS 409
SAVAGE MODEL 24S 409
SAVAGE MODEL 24V 409
SAVAGE MODEL 24VS 409
SAVAGE MODEL 60 409
SAVAGE MODEL 64 409
SAVAGE MODEL 64FV 409
SAVAGE MODEL 64FVSS 410
SAVAGE MODEL 64 BTV 410
SAVAGE MODEL 88 410
SAVAGE MODEL 90 CARBINE 410
SAVAGE MODEL 219 410
SAVAGE MODEL 219L 410
SAVAGE MODEL 221 410
SAVAGE MODEL 222 410
SAVAGE MODEL 223 410
SAVAGE MODEL 227 410
SAVAGE MODEL 228 410
SAVAGE MODEL 229 410
SAVAGE MODEL 389 410
SAVAGE MODEL 980DL 410
SAVAGE MODEL 1912 410
SAVAGE-ANSCHUTZ MARK 10 410
SAVAGE-ANSCHUTZ MARK 10D 410
SAVAGE-ANSCHUTZ MARK 12 411
SAVAGE-ANSCHUTZ MODEL 54 411
SAVAGE-ANSCHUTZ MODEL 54M 411
SAVAGE-ANSCHUTZ MODEL 141 411
SAVAGE-ANSCHUTZ MODEL 153 411
SAVAGE-ANSCHUTZ MODEL 164 411
SAVAGE-ANSCHUTZ MODEL 164M 411
SAVAGE-ANSCHUTZ MODEL 184 411
SAVAGE-ANSCHUTZ MODEL 1410 411
SAVAGE-ANSCHUTZ MODEL 1418 SPORTER 411
SAVAGE-ANSCHUTZ MODEL 1518 SPORTER 411
SAVAGE-STEVENS MODEL 35 411
SAVAGE-STEVENS MODEL 35M 411
SAVAGE-STEVENS MODEL 36 411
SAVAGE-STEVENS MODEL 72 CRACKSHOT 411
SAVAGE-STEVENS MODEL 73 411
SAVAGE-STEVENS MODEL 73Y 411
SAVAGE-STEVENS MODEL 74 411
SAVAGE-STEVENS MODEL 80 411
SAVAGE-STEVENS MODEL 88 411
SAVAGE-STEVENS MODEL 89 CRACKSHOT 412
SAVAGE-STEVENS MODEL 120 412
SAVAGE-STEVENS MODEL 125 412

SCHULTZ & LARSEN

SCHULTZ & LARSEN MODEL 47 412
SCHULTZ & LARSEN MODEL 54 412
SCHULTZ & LARSEN MODEL 54J 412
SCHULTZ & LARSEN MODEL 61 412
SCHULTZ & LARSEN MODEL 62 412
SCHULTZ & LARSEN MODEL 68 412

SEDGELY

SEDGELY SPRINGFIELD SPORTER 412
SEDGELY SPRINGFIELD SPORTER CARBINE 412

SERRIFLE

SERRIFLE SCHUETZEN MODEL 412

C. SHARPS ARMS

C. SHARPS ARMS MODEL 1874 SPORTING 412
C. SHARPS ARMS NEW MODEL 1874 OLD RELIABLE 412
C. SHARPS ARMS NEW MODEL 1875 RIFLE 412
C. SHARPS ARMS NEW MODEL 1875 CLASSIC 413
C. SHARPS ARMS NEW MODEL 1875 TARGET & LONG RANGE 413
C. SHARPS ARMS NEW MODEL 1885 HIGH WALL 413

SHILEN
SHILEN DGA SPORTER 413
SHILEN DGA BENCHREST 413
SHILEN DGA SILHOUETTE 413
SHILEN DGA VARMINTER 413

SHILOH
SHILOH SHARPS MODEL 1874 BUSINESS RIFLE 413
SHILOH SHARPS MODEL 1874 CARBINE 413
SHILOH SHARPS MODEL 1874 JAEGER 413
SHILOH SHARPS MODEL 1874 LONG RANGE EXPRESS 413
SHILOH SHARPS MODEL 1874 MILITARY 413
SHILOH SHARPS MODEL 1874 MILITARY CARBINE 413
SHILOH SHARPS MODEL 1874 MONTANA ROUGHRIDER 413
SHILOH SHARPS MODEL 1874 NO. 1 SPORTING 413
SHILOH SHARPS MODEL 1874 NO. 2 SPORTING 413
SHILOH SHARPS MODEL 1874 NO. 3 SPORTING 413
SHILOH SHARPS MODEL 1874 SADDLE RIFLE 413
SHILOH SHARPS 1874 QUIGLEY 413
SHILOH SHARPS 1874 CREEDMOOR TARGET 414

SIGARMS
SIGARMS M400 PREDATOR VARMINTER 414
SIGARMS 716 PATROL 414
SIGARMS SHR 970 414
SIGARMS SIG 556 414
SIGARMS SIG 556 DMR 414
SIGARMS SIG 556 HOLO 414
SIGARMS SAUER SSG 3000 414
SIGARMS SSG 3000 PATROL RIFLE 414

SMITH & WESSON
SMITH & WESSON MODEL 125 414
SMITH & WESSON MODEL 1500 414
SMITH & WESSON MODEL 1500 DELUXE 415
SMITH & WESSON MODEL 1500 MOUNTAINEER 415
SMITH & WESSON MODEL 1500 VARMINT DELUXE 415
SMITH & WESSON MODEL 1700LS CLASSIC HUNTER 415
SMITH & WESSON MODEL A 415
SMITH & WESSON MODEL B 415
SMITH & WESSON MODEL C 415
SMITH & WESSON MODEL D 415
SMITH & WESSON MODEL E 415
SMITH & WESSON M&P15 MILITARY AND POLICE TACTICAL RIFLE 415
SMITH & WESSON M&P 15 PC 415

SOVEREIGN
SOVEREIGN TD 22 415

SPRINGFIELD
SPRINGFIELD INC. BM-59 (ITALIAN MODEL) 415
SPRINGFIELD INC. BM-59 ALPINE PARATROOPER 415
SPRINGFIELD INC. BM-59 NIGERIAN MODEL 415
SPRINGFIELD INC. M-1 GARAND 415
SPRINGFIELD INC. M1A 416
SPRINGFIELD INC. M1A MATCH 416
SPRINGFIELD INC. M1A SCOUT SQUAD RIFLE 416
SPRINGFIELD INC. M1A SOCOM RIFLE 416
SPRINGFIELD ARMORY M1A SOCOM 16 416
SPRINGFIELD INC. M1A SUPER MATCH 416
SPRINGFIELD INC. M1A/M21 TACTICAL 416
SPRINGFIELD INC. M1A/M21 LAW ENFORCEMENT 416
SPRINGFIELD INC. M1A/M21 SNIPER 416
SPRINGFIELD INC. M1A/M25 CARLOS HATHCOCK MODEL 416
SPRINGFIELD INC. M-6 SCOUT RIFLE/SHOTGUN 416
SPRINGFIELD INC. MODEL 700 BASR 416
SPRINGFIELD INC. SAR-8 SPORTER 416
SPRINGFIELD INC. SAR-4800 416
SPRINGFIELD INC. SAR-4800 22 416
SPRINGFIELD INC. SAR-4800 BUSH 416

SQUIRES
SQUIRES BINGHAM MODEL 14D 416
SQUIRES BINGHAM MODEL 15 417
SQUIRES BINGHAM MODEL M16 417
SQUIRES BINGHAM MODEL M20D 417

STAG ARMS
STAG ARMS STAG-15 MODEL 1 PRE-BAN 417
STAG ARMS STAG-15 MODEL 2 PRE-BAN 417
STAG ARMS STAG-15 MODEL 2 T 417
STAG ARMS STAG-15 MODEL 3 PRE-BAN 417
STAG ARMS STAG-15 MODEL 4 PRE-BAN 417
STAG ARMS STAG 6.8 MODEL 5 PRE-BAN 417
STAG ARMS STAG-15 MODEL 6 PRE-BAN SUPER VARMINTER 417
STAG ARMS MODEL 3 417
STAG ARMS MODEL 8T & 8TL 417

STANDARD ARMS
STANDARD ARMS MODEL G 417
STANDARD ARMS MODEL M 417

STEVENS
STEVENS BUCKHORN MODEL 053 417
STEVENS BUCKHORN MODEL 53 417
STEVENS BUCKHORN MODEL 056 417
STEVENS BUCKHORN MODEL 56 417
STEVENS BUCKHORN MODEL 066 418
STEVENS BUCKHORN MODEL 66 418
STEVENS BUCKHORN NO. 057 418
STEVENS BUCKHORN NO. 57 418
STEVENS BUCKHORN NO. 076 418
STEVENS BUCKHORN NO. 76 418
STEVENS MODEL 15 418
STEVENS MODEL 15Y 418
STEVENS MODEL 66 418
STEVENS MODEL 76 418
STEVENS MODEL 84 418
STEVENS MODEL 84S 418
STEVENS MODEL 85 418
STEVENS MODEL 85K 418
STEVENS MODEL 85S 418
STEVENS MODEL 86 418
STEVENS MODEL 86S 418
STEVENS MODEL 87, 87A 418
STEVENS MODEL 87K 418
STEVENS MODEL 87S 418
STEVENS MODEL 110E 419
STEVENS MODEL 110ES 419
STEVENS MODEL 120 419
STEVENS MODEL 125 419
STEVENS MODEL 322 419
STEVENS MODEL 322S 419
STEVENS MODEL 325 419
STEVENS MODEL 325S 419
STEVENS MODEL 416-2 419
STEVENS NO. 419 JUNIOR TARGET 419
STEVENS FAVORITE NO. 17 419
STEVENS FAVORITE NO. 18 419
STEVENS FAVORITE NO. 19 419
STEVENS FAVORITE NO. 20 419
STEVENS FAVORITE NO. 26 CRACKSHOT 419
STEVENS FAVORITE NO. 26-1/2 CRACKSHOT 419
STEVENS FAVORITE NO. 27 419
STEVENS FAVORITE NO. 28 419
STEVENS FAVORITE NO. 29 419
STEVENS FAVORITEMODEL 30 419
STEVENS IDEAL NO. 44 419
STEVENS IDEAL NO. 44-1/2 419
STEVENS IDEAL NOS. 45 THROUGH 56 420
STEVENS NO. 70 VISIBLE LOADER 420
STEVENS NO. 414 ARMORY 420
STEVENS NO. 417 WALNUT HILL 420
STEVENS NO. 417-1 WALNUT HILL 420
STEVENS NO. 417-2 WALNUT HILL 420
STEVENS NO. 417-3 WALNUT HILL 420
STEVENS NO. 417-1/2 WALNUT HILL 420
STEVENS NO. 418 WALNUT HILL 420
STEVENS NO. 418-1/2 WALNUT HILL 420
STEVENS SPRINGFIELD MODEL 15 420
STEVENS SPRINGFIELD MODEL 82 420
STEVENS SPRINGFIELD MODEL 83 420
STEVENS SPRINGFIELD MODEL 084 421
STEVENS SPRINGFIELD MODEL 84 421
STEVENS SPRINGFIELD MODEL 085 421
STEVENS SPRINGFIELD MODEL 85 421
STEVENS SPRINGFIELD MODEL 086 421
STEVENS SPRINGFIELD MODEL 86 421
STEVENS SPRINGFIELD MODEL 087 421
STEVENS SPRINGFIELD MODEL 87 421
STEVENS MODEL 200 421
STEVENS CADET MINI-YOUTH 421
STEVENS MODEL 315 YOUTH 421
STEVENS MODEL 310 421
STEVENS MODEL 310 HEAVY BARREL 421
STEVENS MODEL 300 421
STEVENS MODEL 305 421

STEYR
STEYR A.U.G.-SA 421
STEYR CLASSIC MANNLICHER SBS RIFLE 421
STEYR MODEL 90 CARBINE 421
STEYR MODEL 95 421
STEYR-MANNLICHER JAGD MATCH 421
STEYR-MANNLICHER MATCH SPG-UIT 421
STEYR-MANNLICHER MODEL L 421
STEYR-MANNLICHER MODEL L CARBINE 421
STEYR-MANNLICHER MODEL L LUXUS 421
STEYR-MANNLICHER MODEL L LUXUS CARBINE 422
STEYR-MANNLICHER MODEL L VARMINT 422
STEYR-MANNLICHER MODEL M 422
STEYR-MANNLICHER MODEL M CARBINE 422
STEYR-MANNLICHER MODEL M LUXUS 422
STEYR-MANNLICHER MODEL M LUXUS CARBINE 422
STEYR-MANNLICHER MODEL M PROFESSIONAL 422
STEYR-MANNLICHER MODEL MIII PROFESSIONAL 422
STEYR-MANNLICHER MODEL M72 L/M 422
STEYR-MANNLICHER MODEL M72 MODEL L/M CARBINE 422
STEYR-MANNLICHER MODEL S 422
STEYR SBS FORESTER 422
STEYR SBS PROHUNTER 423
STEYR SCOUT 423
STEYR SSG 08 423

STEYR-MANNLICHER MODEL SL 423
STEYR-MANNLICHER MODEL SL CARBINE 423
STEYR-MANNLICHER MODEL SL VARMINT 423
STEYR-MANNLICHER MODEL SSG 423
STEYR-MANNLICHER MODEL SSG MATCH 423
STEYR-MANNLICHER MODEL SSG MATCH UIT 423
STEYR-MANNLICHER SSG P-II 423
STEYR-MANNLICHER SSG P-IIK 423
STEYR-MANNLICHER SSG P-III 423
STEYR-MANNLICHER SSG P-IV 423
STEYR-MANNLICHER MODEL S/T 423
STEYR-MANNLICHER MODEL S LUXUS 423

STI

STI SPORTING COMPETITION 423

STONER

STONER SR-15 M-5 RIFLE 423
STONER SR-15 MATCH RIFLE 424
STONER SR-25 MATCH 424
STONER SR-25 MATCH LIGHTWEIGHT 424
STONER SR-25 SPORTER 424
STONER SR-25 CARBINE 424

STEYR

STEYR SSG08 424

STRUM RUGER

STRUM RUGER AMERICAN 424
STRUM RUGER AMERICAN COMPACT 424
STURM RUGER DEERFIELD 99/44 CARBINE 425
STRUM RUGER GUIDE GUN 425
STURM RUGER GUNSITE SCOUT 425
STURM RUGER MINI-14 425
STURM RUGER MINI-14 RANCH 425
STURM RUGER MINI-14 STAINLESS 425
STURM RUGER MINI-14 WITH FOLDING STOCK 425
STURM RUGER MINI 14/5 425
STURM RUGER MINI-14 TARGET RIFLE 425
STURM RUGER NRA MINI-14 425
STURM RUGER MINI THIRTY 425
STURM RUGER MODEL 10/22 CARBINE 425
STURM RUGER MODEL 10/22 DELUXE SPORTER 425
STURM RUGER MODEL 10/22 INTERNATIONAL 425
STURM RUGER 10/22 RIFLE 426
STURM RUGER MODEL 10/22 SPORTER 426
STURM RUGER 10/22T TARGET RIFLE 426
STURM RUGER 10/22 ALL-WEATHER RIFLE 426
STURM RUGER 10/22 CRR COMPACT RIFLE 426
STURM RUGER K10/22T RUGER 10/22 TARGET STAINLESS 426
STURM RUGER 10/22-T 426
STRUM RUGER 10-22 TAKEDOWN 426
STURM RUGER 10/22 MAGNUM AUTOLOADING CARBINE 426
STURM RUGER MODEL 44 CARBINE 426
STURM RUGER MODEL 44 INTERNATIONAL 426
STURM RUGER MODEL 44RS 426
STURM RUGER MODEL 44 SPORTER 426
STRUM RUGER 77/357 426
STURM RUGER MODEL 77R 426
STURM RUGER MODEL 77RL ULTRA LIGHT 427
STURM RUGER MODEL 77RS 427
STURM RUGER MODEL 77RS TROPICAL 427
STURM RUGER MODEL 77 ROUND TOP MAGNUM 427
STURM RUGER MODEL 77V VARMINT 427
STURM RUGER MODEL 77 RSI INTERNATIONAL 427
STURM RUGER MODEL 77 RLS ULTRA LIGHT CARBINE 427
STURM RUGER MODEL 77R MARK II 427
STURM RUGER MODEL 77R MARK II EXPRESS 427
STURM RUGER MODEL 77R MARK II MAGNUM 427
STURM RUGER MODEL 77 MARK II ALL-WEATHER STAINLESS 427
STURM RUGER M77VT MARK II TARGET RIFLE 427
STURM RUGER M77 MKII FRONTIER RIFLE 427
STURM RUGER HM77R HAWKEYE 427
STURM RUGER HK77RFP HAWKEYE 427
STURM RUGER HM77RSPHAB HAWKEYE ALASKAN 428
STURM RUGER HKM77PRCM HAWKEYE COMPACT MAGNUM 428
STURM RUGER HKM77RCM HAWKEYE COMPACT MAGNUM 428
STURM RUGER HM77RSPHAB HAWKEYE AFRICAN 428
STURM RUGER MODEL 77/17 428
STURM RUGER MODEL 77/22 428
STURM RUGER MODEL 77/22 HORNET 428
STURM RUGER MODEL 77/22MP 428
STURM RUGER MODEL 77/22RM 428
STURM RUGER MODEL 77/22RMP 428
STURM RUGER MODEL 77/22RP 428
STURM RUGER MODEL 77/22RS 428
STURM RUGER MODEL 77/22RSH HORNET 428
STURM RUGER MODEL 77/22RSM 428
STURM RUGER MODEL 77/22 RSMP 428
STURM RUGER MODEL 77/22 RSP 428
STURM RUGER MODEL 77/22 VH 428
STURM RUGER MODEL 77/44 BOLT-ACTION RIFLE 428
STURM RUGER MODEL 96/22 429
STURM RUGER MODEL 96/17 429
STURM RUGER MODEL 96/22M 429
STURM RUGER MODEL 96/44M 429
STURM RUGER NO. 1B STANDARD SINGLE SHOT 429
STURM RUGER NO. 1A LIGHT SPORTER 429
STURM RUGER NO. 1S MEDIUM SPORTER 429
STURM RUGER NO. 1H TROPICAL 429
STURM RUGER NO. 1 RSI INTERNATIONAL 429
STURM RUGER NO. 1V SPECIAL VARMINTER 429
RUGER NO. 1 LIGHT STANDARD 1-AB 429
STURM RUGER NO. 3 429
STURM RUGER PC4 CARBINE 429
STURM RUGER PC9 CARBINE 430
STURM RUGER SR 22 430
STURM RUGER SR 556 430

SURVIVAL ARMS

SURVIVAL ARMS AR-7 EXPLORER 430
SURVIVAL ARMS AR-7 SPORTER 430
SURVIVAL ARMS AR-7 WILDCAT 430

SWISS

SWISS K-31 TARGET MODEL 430

TANNER

TANNER 50-METER FREE RIFLE 430
TANNER 300-METER FREE RIFLE 430
TANNER 300-METER UIT STANDARD FREE RIFLE 430

TAURUS

TAURUS CT G2 CARBINE 430
TAURUS MODEL 62 PUMP RIFLE 430
TAURUS MODEL 62LAR LEVER RIFLE 430
TAURUS MODEL 72 PUMP RIFLE 430
TAURUS THUNDERBOLT 431
TAURUS MODEL 63 SEMI-AUTOMATIC RIFLE 431

THOMPSON/CENTER

THOMPSON/CENTER CONTENDER CARBINE 431
THOMPSON/CENTER CONTENDER CARBINE RYNITE 431
THOMPSON/CENTER CONTENDER CARBINE STAINLESS 431
THOMPSON/CENTER CONTENDER CARBINE SURVIVAL SYSTEM 431
THOMPSON/CENTER CONTENDER CARBINE YOUTH MODEL 431
THOMPSON/CENTER CUSTOM SHOP TCR '87 431
THOMPSON/CENTER ENCORE 431
THOMPSON/CENTER STAINLESS ENCORE RIFLE 431
THOMPSON/CENTER TCR '83 HUNTER 431
THOMPSON/CENTER TCR '87 HUNTER 431
THOMPSON/CENTER 22 CLASSIC 431
THOMPSON/CENTER 22 BENCHMARK 431
THOMPSON/CENTER SILVER LYNX 431
THOMPSON/CENTER ICON 431
THOMPSON/CENTER ICON CLASSIC LONG ACTION 432
THOMPSON/CENTER ICON WEATHERSHIELD MEDIUM ACTION 432
THOMPSON/CENTER TRIUMPH 432
THOMPSON/CENTER PRO HUNTER 432

TIKKA

TIKKA MODEL 07 432
TIKKA MODEL 55 432
TIKKA MODEL 55 DELUXE 432
TIKKA MODEL 55 SPORTER 432
TIKKA MODEL 65 432
TIKKA MODEL 65 DELUXE 432
TIKKA MODEL 65 TARGET 432
TIKKA MODEL 77K 432
TIKKA MODEL 412S DOUBLE RIFLE 432
TIKKA MODEL 512S COMBINATION GUN 432
TIKKA MODEL 512S DOUBLE RIFLE 432
TIKKA PREMIUM GRADE 432
TIKKA SPORTER RIFLE 449
TIKKA STANDARD 449
TIKKA T3 HUNTER 449
TIKKA T3 LAMINATED STAINLESS 449
TIKKA T3 LITE 449
TIKKA T3 LITE STAINLESS 449
TIKKA T3 TACTICAL 449
TIKKA T3 VARMINT 449
TIKKA T3 VARMINT STAINLESS 449
TIKKA WHITETAIL/BATTUE 449
TIKKA WHITETAIL HUNTER BOLT-ACTION RIFLE 449
TIKKA CONTINENTAL VARMINT RIFLE 449
TIKKA WHITETAIL HUNTER DELUXE 449
TIKKA WHITETAIL HUNTER SYNTHETIC RIFLE 450
TIKKA CONTINENTAL LONG RANGE HUNTING 450
TIKKA WHITETAIL HUNTER STAINLESS SYNTHETIC 450

TRADEWINDS

TRADEWINDS HUSKY MODEL 5000 450

TRADEWINDS MODEL 260-A 450
TRADEWINDS MODEL 311-A 450

TRADITIONS

TRADITIONS 1874 SHARPS DELUXE RIFLE 450
TRADITIONS 1874 SHARPS SPORTING DELUXE RIFLE 450
TRADITIONS 1874 SHARPS STANDARD RIFLE 450
TRADITIONS ROLLING BLOCK SPORTING RIFLE 450

TRISTAR

TRISTAR 1860 HENRY RIFLE 450
TRISTAR 1860 HENRY TRAPPER CARBINE 450
TRISTAR 1874 SHARPS SPORTING RIFLE 450
TRISTAR 1885 SINGLE SHOT 450

TYROL

TYROL CUSTOM CRAFTED MODEL 451

UBERTI

UBERTI HENRY RIFLE 451
UBERTI HENRY CARBINE 451
UBERTI HENRY TRAPPER 451
UBERTI MODEL 1866 SPORTING RIFLE 451
UBERTI MODEL 1866 YELLOWBOY CARBINE 451
UBERTI MODEL 1866 TRAPPER CARBINE 451
UBERTI MODEL 1873 BUCKHORN 451
UBERTI MODEL 1873 CATTLEMAN 451
UBERTI MODEL 1873 SPORTING RIFLE 451
UBERTI MODEL 1873 SPORTING CARBINE 451
UBERTI MODEL 1873 SPORTING CARBINE, TRAPPER MODEL 451
UBERTI MODEL 1875 ARMY TARGET 451
UBERTI ROLLING BLOCK BABY CARBINE 451

ULTIMATE ACCURACY

ULTIMATE ACCURACY MODEL 5100A1 LONG-RANGE RIFLE 451
ULTIMATE ACCURACY MODEL 5100A1 IMPROVED MODEL 451

ULTRA-HI

ULTRA-HI MODEL 2200 451

UNIQUE

UNIQUE MODEL G.21 452
UNIQUE MODEL T AUDAX 452
UNIQUE MODEL T DIOPTRA 452
UNIQUE MODEL T/SM 452
UNIQUE MODEL T/SM BIATHALON JUNIOR 452
UNIQUE MODEL T/SM MATCH JUNIOR 452
UNIQUE MODEL T.66 MATCH 452
UNIQUE MODEL T.791 BIATHLON 452
UNIQUE MODEL X51 BIS 452

UNIVERSAL

UNIVERSAL MODEL 1000 452
UNIVERSAL MODEL 1002 452
UNIVERSAL MODEL 1003 452
UNIVERSAL MODEL 1005 DELUXE 452
UNIVERSAL MODEL 1010 452
UNIVERSAL MODEL 1015 452
UNIVERSAL MODEL 1020 452
UNIVERSAL MODEL 1025 452
UNIVERSAL MODEL 1256 FERRET 452

VALMET

VALMET HUNTER MODEL 452
VALMET MODEL 412 DOUBLE RIFLE 452
VALMET MODEL 412S COMBO GUN 452

VARNER

VARNER FAVORITE HUNTER 452
VARNER FAVORITE SCHEUTZEN 453

VEKTOR

VEKTOR H5 SLIDE-ACTION RIFLE 453
VEKTOR BUSHVELD BOLT-ACTION RIFLE 453
VEKTOR MODEL 98 453

VICKERS

VICKERS EMPIRE MODEL 453
VICKERS JUBILEE MODEL 453

VOERE

VOERE MODEL 1007 453
VOERE MODEL 1013 453
VOERE MODEL 2107 453
VOERE MODEL 2107 DELUXE 453
VOERE MODEL 2114S 453
VOERE MODEL 2115 453
VOERE MODEL 2150 453
VOERE MODEL 2155 454
VOERE MODEL 2165 454
VOERE MODEL 2185 454
VOERE MODEL 2185 MATCH 454
VOERE TITAN 454
VOERE TITAN MENOR 454
VOERE VEC-91 LIGHTNING 454
VOERE VEC-91BR 454
VOERE VEC-91HB VARMINT SPECIAL 454
VOERE VEC-91SS 454

WALTHER

WALTHER MODEL 1 454
WALTHER MODEL 2 454
WALTHER MODEL 2 LIGHTWEIGHT 455
WALTHER MODEL G22 455
WALTHER MODEL GX-1 MATCH 455
WALTHER MODEL KK/MS METALLIC SILHOUETTE 455
WALTHER MODEL KKJ 455
WALTHER MODEL KKJ-HO 455
WALTHER MODEL KKJ-MA 455
WALTHER MODEL KKM MATCH 455
WALTHER MODEL KKM-S 455
WALTHER MODEL KKW 455
WALTHER MODEL PRONE 400 455
WALTHER MODEL SSV VARMINT RIFLE 455
WALTHER MODEL V 455
WALTHER MODEL V MEISTERBUSCHE 455
WALTHER MOVING TARGET MODEL 455
WALTHER OLYMPIC MODEL 456
WALTHER RUNNING BOAR MODEL 500 456
WALTHER U.I.T. BV UNIVERSAL 456
WALTHER U.I.T. MATCH MODEL 456
WALTHER U.I.T.-E MATCH MODEL 456

WEATHERBY

WEATHERBY CLASSICMARK I 456
WEATHERBY CLASSICMARK II 456
WEATHERBY CLASSICMARK II SAFARI CLASSIC 456
WEATHERBY DELUXE (EARLY) 456
WEATHERBY DELUXE MAGNUM (EARLY) 456
WEATHERBY MARK V ACCUMARK 456
WEATHERBY MARK V ACCUMARK RC 456
WEATHERBY MARK V ACCUMARK ULTRA LIGHTWEIGHT 456
WEATHERBY MARK V OUTFITTER (CUSTOM) 456
WEATHERBY MARK V SVM SUPER VARMINT MASTER 457
WEATHERBY MARK V FIBERMARK 457
WEATHERBY MARK V FIBERMARK ALASKAN 457
WEATHERBY MARK V CROWN CUSTOM MODEL 457
WEATHERBY MARK V CUSTOM MODEL 457
WEATHERBY MARK V DANGEROUS GAME 457
WEATHERBY MARK V DELUXE 457
WEATHERBY MARK V EUROMARK 457
WEATHERBY MARK V EUROSPORT 457
WEATHERBY MARK V LAZERMARK 457
WEATHERBY MARK V ROYAL CUSTOM 458
WEATHERBY MARK V SAFARI GRADE CUSTOM 458
WEATHERBY MARK V TRR CUSTOM MAGNUM & TRR RC VERSION 458
WEATHERBY MARK V SPORTER 458
WEATHERBY MARK V STAINLESS 458
WEATHERBY MARK V SLS STAINLESS LAMINATE SPORTER 458
WEATHERBY MARK V SUPER BIG GAME MASTER DEER RIFLE 458
WEATHERBY MARK V SYNTHETIC 458
WEATHERBY MARK XXII CLIP 458
WEATHERBY MARK XXII TUBULAR 458
WEATHERBY MARK XXII BOLT ACTION RIFLE (2007) 458
WEATHERBY THREAT RESPONSE RIFLES (TRR) SERIES 458
WEATHERBY ULTRAMARK 459
WEATHERBY VANGUARD 459
WEATHERBY VANGUARD ALASKAN 459
WEATHERBY VANGUARD BACK COUNTRY SERIES 2 459
WEATHERBY VANGUARD CLASSIC I 459
WEATHERBY VANGUARD CLASSIC II 459
WEATHERBY VANGUARD FIBERGUARD 459
WEATHERBY VANGUARD SERIES 2 CARBINE 459
WEATHERBY VANGUARD SERIES 2 DELUXE 459
WEATHERBY VANGUARD SERIES 2 SPORTER & SPORTER DBM 459
WEATHERBY VANGUARD SERIES 2 STAINLESS SYNTHETIC 459
WEATHERBY VANGUARD SERIES 2 SYNTHETIC 459
WEATHERBY VANGUARD SERIES 2 SYNTHETIC DBM 459
WEATHERBY VANGUARD SERIES 2 SYNTHETIC YOUTH 459
WEATHERBY VANGUARD SERIES 2 VARMINT SPECIAL 460
WEATHERBY VANGUARD STAINLESS 460
WEATHERBY VANGUARD SYNTHETIC 460
WEATHERBY VANGUARD TRR RC & SERIES 2 TRR RC 460
WEATHERBY VANGUARD VGL LIGHTWEIGHT RIFLE 460
WEATHERBY VANGUARD VGS 460
WEATHERBY VANGUARD VGX 460
WEATHERBY VANGUARD WEATHERGUARD 460
WEATHERBY VANGUARD SPORTER STAINLESS 460
WEATHERBY VANGUARD VARMINT SPECIAL 460
WEATHERBY VANGUARD SUB-MOA VARMINT SPECIAL 460
WEATHERBY VANGUARD SUB-MOA MATTE OR STAINLESS 460
WEATHERBY VANGUARD DELUXE 460
WEATHERBY VANGUARD COMPACT 460
WEATHERBY VANGUARD YOUTH COMPACT 460
WEATHERBY VANGUARD SAGE COUNTRY CUSTOM 460
WEATHERBY VANGUARD BACK COUNTRY CUSTOM 460
WEATHERBY WEATHERMARK 460

WEATHERBY WEATHERMARK ALASKAN . . . 460

WEIHRAUCH

WEIHRAUCH MODEL HW 60 . . . 461
WEIHRAUCH MODEL HW 60J . . . 461
WEIHRAUCH MODEL HW 66 . . . 461
WEIHRAUCH MODEL HW 660 MATCH . . . 461

WESSON & HARRINGTON

WESSON & HARRINGTON BUFFALO CLASSIC . . . 461
WESSON & HARRINGTON 38-55 TARGET CLASSIC RIFLE . . . 461

WESTLEY

WESTLEY RICHARDS DOUBLE . . . 461
WESTLEY RICHARDS MAGAZINE MODEL . . . 461

WHITWORTH

WHITWORTH EXPRESS . . . 461
WHITWORTH EXPRESS CARBINE . . . 461
WHITWORTH SAFARI EXPRESS . . . 461

WICHITA

WICHITA CLASSIC MODEL . . . 461
WICHITA SILHOUETTE MODEL . . . 461
WICHITA STAINLESS MAGNUM . . . 461
WICHITA VARMINT MODEL . . . 461

WICKLIFFE

WICKLIFFE MODEL 76 . . . 461
WICKLIFFE MODEL 76 DELUXE . . . 461
WICKLIFFE STINGER . . . 462
WICKLIFFE STINGER DELUXE . . . 462
WICKLIFFE TRADITIONALIST . . . 462

WILKINSON

WILKINSON LINDA CARBINE . . . 462
WILKINSON TERRY CARBINE . . . 462

WINCHESTER

WINCHESTER LEE MUSKET . . . 462
WINCHESTER LEE SPORTER . . . 462
WINCHESTER MODEL 43 . . . 462
WINCHESTER MODEL 43 SPECIAL GRADE . . . 462
WINCHESTER MODEL 47 . . . 462
WINCHESTER MODEL 52 (EARLY PRODUCTION) . . . 462
WINCHESTER MODEL 52 SPORTER . . . 462
WINCHESTER MODEL 52A . . . 462
WINCHESTER MODEL 52A HEAVY BARREL . . . 462
WINCHESTER MODEL 52A SPORTER . . . 462
WINCHESTER MODEL 52B . . . 462
WINCHESTER MODEL 52B BULL GUN . . . 462
WINCHESTER MODEL 52B HEAVY BARREL . . . 462
WINCHESTER MODEL 52B SPORTER . . . 462
WINCHESTER MODEL 52B SPORTER (1993) . . . 463
WINCHESTER MODEL 52C . . . 463
WINCHESTER MODEL 52C BULL GUN . . . 463
WINCHESTER MODEL 52C HEAVY BARREL . . . 463
WINCHESTER MODEL 52C SPORTER . . . 463
WINCHESTER MODEL 52D . . . 463
WINCHESTER MODEL 52D INTERNATIONAL MATCH . . . 463
WINCHESTER MODEL 52D INTERNATIONAL PRONE . . . 463
WINCHESTER MODEL 54 . . . 463
WINCHESTER MODEL 54 CARBINE . . . 463
WINCHESTER MODEL 54 IMPROVED . . . 463
WINCHESTER MODEL 54 IMPROVED CARBINE . . . 463
WINCHESTER MODEL 54 NATIONAL MATCH . . . 463
WINCHESTER MODEL 54 SNIPER'S RIFLE . . . 463
WINCHESTER MODEL 54 SUPER GRADE . . . 463
WINCHESTER MODEL 56 . . . 463
WINCHESTER MODEL 57 . . . 463
WINCHESTER MODEL 58 . . . 464
WINCHESTER MODEL 59 . . . 464
WINCHESTER MODEL 60 . . . 464
WINCHESTER MODEL 60A . . . 464
WINCHESTER MODEL 67 . . . 464
WINCHESTER MODEL 67 JUNIOR (BOY'S RIFLE) . . . 464
WINCHESTER MODEL 68 . . . 464
WINCHESTER MODEL 69, 69A . . . 464
WINCHESTER MODEL 69 MATCH . . . 464
WINCHESTER MODEL 69 TARGET . . . 464
WINCHESTER MODEL 70 . . . 464
WINCHESTER MODEL 70 (1936-1963) . . . 464
PRE-WWII (1936-1945) . . . 464
POST-WWII (1946-1963) . . . 464
WINCHESTER MODEL 70 ALASKAN . . . 465
WINCHESTER MODEL 70 BULL GUN . . . 465
WINCHESTER MODEL 70 CARBINE . . . 465
WINCHESTER MODEL 70 FEATHERWEIGHT . . . 465
WINCHESTER MODEL 70 NATIONAL MATCH . . . 465
WINCHESTER MODEL 70 SUPER GRADE . . . 465
WINCHESTER MODEL 70 SUPER GRADE AFRICAN . . . 465
WINCHESTER MODEL 70 SUPER GRADE FEATHERWEIGHT . . . 465
WINCHESTER MODEL 70 TARGET . . . 465
WINCHESTER MODEL 70 V ARMINT . . . 465
WINCHESTER MODEL 70 (1964-1971) . . . 465
WINCHESTER MODEL 70 AFRICAN . . . 466
WINCHESTER MODEL 70 DELUXE . . . 466
WINCHESTER MODEL 70 INTERNATIONAL ARMY MATCH . . . 466
WINCHESTER MODEL 70 MAGNUM . . . 466
WINCHESTER MODEL 70 MANNLICHER . . . 466
WINCHESTER MODEL 70 TARGET . . . 466
WINCHESTER MODEL 70 (1972 TO PRESENT) . . . 466
WINCHESTER MODEL 70 BLACK SHADOW . . . 466
WINCHESTER MODEL 70 CLASSIC CUSTOM GRADE . . . 466
WINCHESTER MODEL 70 CLASSIC CUSTOM GRADE FEATHERWEIGHT . . . 466
WINCHESTER MODEL 70 CLASSIC CUSTOM GRADE SHARPSHOOTER . . . 466
WINCHESTER MODEL 70 CLASSIC CUSTOM GRADE SPORTING SHARPSHOOTER . . . 467
WINCHESTER MODEL 70 CLASSIC DBM (DETACHABLE BOX MAGAZINE) . . . 467
WINCHESTER MODEL 70 CLASSIC DBM-S . . . 467
WINCHESTER MODEL 70 CLASSIC FEATHERWEIGHT . . . 467
WINCHESTER MODEL 70 CLASSIC FEATHERWEIGHT COMPACT . . . 467
WINCHESTER MODEL 70 CLASSIC SAFARI EXPRESS . . . 467
WINCHESTER MODEL 70 CLASSIC SM . . . 467
WINCHESTER MODEL 70 CLASSIC SPORTER . . . 467
WINCHESTER MODEL 70 CLASSIC SPORTER LT . . . 467
WINCHESTER MODEL 70 CLASSIC STAINLESS . . . 467
WINCHESTER MODEL 70 CLASSIC SUPER GRADE . . . 467
WINCHESTER MODEL 70 CLASSIC SUPER EXPRESS MAGNUM . . . 467
WINCHESTER MODEL 70 COYOTE . . . 467
WINCHESTER MODEL 70 CUSTOM SHARPSHOOTER . . . 467
WINCHESTER MODEL 70 DBM . . . 468
WINCHESTER MODEL 70 FEATHERWEIGHT WINTUFF . . . 468
WINCHESTER MODEL 70 HEAVY BARREL VARMINT . . . 468
WINCHESTER MODEL 70 HEAVY VARMINT . . . 468
WINCHESTER MODEL 70 LIGHTWEIGHT . . . 468
WINCHESTER MODEL 70 LIGHTWEIGHT CARBINE . . . 468
WINCHESTER MODEL 70 RANGER . . . 468
WINCHESTER MODEL 70 RANGER YOUTH/LADIES RIFLE . . . 468
WINCHESTER MODEL 70 SHB (SYNTHETIC HEAVY BARREL) . . . 468
WINCHESTER MODEL 70 SPORTER SSM . . . 468
WINCHESTER MODEL 70 SPORTER WINTUFF . . . 468
WINCHESTER MODEL 70 STEALTH . . . 468
WINCHESTER MODEL 70 SYNTHETIC HEAVY VARMINT . . . 468
WINCHESTER MODEL 70 TARGET . . . 468
WINCHESTER MODEL 70 VARMINT . . . 468
WINCHESTER MODEL 70 WINLITE . . . 469
WINCHESTER MODEL 70 XTR . . . 469
WINCHESTER MODEL 70 XTR FEATHERWEIGHT . . . 469
WINCHESTER MODEL 70 XTR FEATHERWEIGHT EUROPEAN . . . 469
WINCHESTER MODEL 70 XTR SPORTER . . . 469
WINCHESTER MODEL 70 XTR SUPER EXPRESS MAGNUM . . . 469
WINCHESTER MODEL 70 SHADOW ELITE STAINLESS . . . 469
WINCHESTER MODEL 70 SHADOW ELITE CAMO STAINLESS . . . 469
WINCHESTER MODEL 70 PRO SHADOW BLUED . . . 469
WINCHESTER MODEL 70 PRO SHADOW STAINLESS . . . 469
WINCHESTER MODEL 70 LAMINATED COYOTE OUTBACK STAINLESS . . . 469
WINCHESTER MODEL 70 LAMINATED COYOTE GRAY OR BROWN STAINLESS . . . 469
WINCHESTER MODEL 70 FEATHERWEIGHT DELUXE (2008 PRODUCTION) . . . 469
WINCHESTER MODEL 70 SPORTER DELUXE (2008 PRODUCTION) . . . 469
WINCHESTER NEW MODEL 70 SUPER GRADE SPECIAL LIMITED EDITION . . . 469
WINCHESTER MODEL 70 EXTREME WEATHER SS (2008 PRODUCTION) . . . 469
WINCHESTER MODEL 70A . . . 469
WINCHESTER MODEL 72 . . . 470
WINCHESTER MODEL 72 GALLERY . . . 470
WINCHESTER MODEL 72 TARGET . . . 470
WINCHESTER MODEL 75 SPORTER . . . 470
WINCHESTER MODEL 75 TARGET . . . 470
WINCHESTER MODEL 99 THUMB TRIGGER . . . 470
WINCHESTER MODEL 121 . . . 470
WINCHESTER MODEL 131 . . . 470
WINCHESTER MODEL 141 . . . 470
WINCHESTER MODEL 310 . . . 470
WINCHESTER MODEL 320 . . . 470
WINCHESTER WILDCAT . . . 470
WINCHESTER MODEL 670 . . . 470
WINCHESTER MODEL 670 MAGNUM . . . 470
WINCHESTER MODEL 677 . . . 471
WINCHESTER MODEL 697 . . . 471
WINCHESTER MODEL 770 . . . 471
WINCHESTER MODEL 770 MAGNUM . . . 471
WINCHESTER MODEL 1900 . . . 471
WINCHESTER MODEL 1902 . . . 471
WINCHESTER MODEL 1904 . . . 471
WINCHESTER MODEL 1904/1899 THUMB TRIGGER . . . 471
WINCHESTER MODEL 1904-A . . . 471

WINCHESTER MODEL 53 471
WINCHESTER MODEL 55 CENTERFIRE 471
WINCHESTER MODEL 64 (EARLY PRODUCTION) 471
WINCHESTER MODEL 64 (LATE PRODUCTION) 471
WINCHESTER MODEL 64 DEER RIFLE 471
WINCHESTER MODEL 64 ZIPPER 472
WINCHESTER MODEL 65 472
WINCHESTER MODEL 71 472
WINCHESTER MODEL 71 CARBINE 472
WINCHESTER MODEL 71 DELUXE 472
WINCHESTER MODEL 88 472
WINCHESTER MODEL 88 CARBINE 472
WINCHESTER MODEL 94 (POST-1964 PRODUCTION) 472
WINCHESTER MODEL 94 ANTIQUE 472
WINCHESTER MODEL 94 CLASSIC 472
WINCHESTER MODEL 94 DELUXE 472
WINCHESTER MODEL 94 LEGACY 472
WINCHESTER MODEL 94 LIMITED EDITION CENTENNIAL GRADE I 472
WINCHESTER MODEL 94 LIMITED EDITION CENTENNIAL HIGH GRADE RIFLE 473
WINCHESTER MODEL 94 LIMITED EDITION CENTENNIAL HIGH GRADE CUSTOM 473
WINCHESTER MODEL 94 RANGER 473
WINCHESTER MODEL 94 RANGER COMPACT 473
WINCHESTER MODEL 94 SADDLE RING CARBINE 473
WINCHESTER MODEL 94 TIMBER CARBINE 473
WINCHESTER MODEL 94 TRADITIONAL 473
WINCHESTER MODEL 94 TRAILS END 473
WINCHESTER MODEL 94 TRAPPER 473
WINCHESTER MODEL 94 WIN-TUFF 473
WINCHESTER MODEL 94 WRANGLER 473
WINCHESTER MODEL 94 WRANGLER II 473
WINCHESTER MODEL 94 WRANGLER LARGE LOOP 473
WINCHESTER MODEL 94 XTR 473
WINCHESTER MODEL 94 XTR BIG BORE 473
WINCHESTER MODEL 94 XTR DELUXE 474
WINCHESTER MODEL 150 474
WINCHESTER MODEL 250 474
WINCHESTER MODEL 250 DELUXE 474
WINCHESTER MODEL 255 474
WINCHESTER MODEL 255 DELUXE 474
WINCHESTER MODEL 1873 474
WINCHESTER MODEL 1873 CARBINE 474
WINCHESTER MODEL 1873 MUSKET 474
WINCHESTER MODEL 1873 RIMFIRE 474
WINCHESTER MODEL 1873 SPECIAL 474
WINCHESTER MODEL 1876 474
WINCHESTER MODEL 1876 CARBINE 474
WINCHESTER MODEL 1876 MUSKET 474
WINCHESTER MODEL 1885 HIGH WALL 474
WINCHESTER MODEL 1885 HIGH WALL DELUXE GRADE 474
WINCHESTER MODEL 1885 HIGH WALL SCHUETZEN 474
WINCHESTER MODEL 1885 LOW WALL SPORTER 475
WINCHESTER MODEL 1885 LOW WALL RIMFIRE (RECENT MANUFACTURE) 475
WINCHESTER MODEL 1885 LOW WALL WINDER MUSKET 475
WINCHESTER MODEL 1885 HIGH WALL HUNTER 475
WINCHESTER MODEL 1885 .30-06 CENTENNIAL HIGH WALL HUNTER 475
WINCHESTER MODEL 1885 LOW WALL 17 MACH 2 475
WINCHESTER MODEL 1886 475
WINCHESTER MODEL 1886 CARBINE 475
WINCHESTER MODEL 1886 LIGHTWEIGHT 475
WINCHESTER MODEL 1886 MUSKET 475
WINCHESTER MODEL 1886 TAKEDOWN 475
WINCHESTER MODEL 1886 LEVER-ACTION RIFLE (RECENT MANUFACTURE) 475
WINCHESTER MODEL 1892 475
WINCHESTER MODEL 1892 CARBINE 475
WINCHESTER MODEL 1892 MUSKET 475
WINCHESTER MODEL 1892 TRAPPER'S CARBINE 476
WINCHESTER MODEL 1894 476
WINCHESTER MODEL 1894 CARBINE 476
WINCHESTER MODEL 1894 TRAPPER CARBINE 476
WINCHESTER MODEL 1895 476
WINCHESTER MODEL 1895 CARBINE 476
WINCHESTER MODEL 1895 LIMITED EDITION (RECENT PRODUCTION) 476
WINCHESTER MODEL 1895 MUSKET 476
WINCHESTER MODEL 1895 NRA MUSKET 476
WINCHESTER MODEL 1895 SADDLE RING CARBINE (RECENT MFR.) 476
WINCHESTER MODEL 9417 476
WINCHESTER MODEL 9422 476
WINCHESTER MODEL 9422 HIGH GRADE 476
WINCHESTER MODEL 9422 LEGACY 476
WINCHESTER MODEL 9422 MAGNUM 476
WINCHESTER MODEL 9422 WIN-CAM 476
WINCHESTER MODEL 9422 WIN-TUFF 476
WINCHESTER MODEL 9422 XTR CLASSIC 476
WINCHESTER MODEL 55 RIMFIRE 477
WINCHESTER MODEL 63 (1933-1958) 477
WINCHESTER MODEL 63 (1997-1998) 477
WINCHESTER MODEL 74 477
WINCHESTER MODEL 77 CLIP 477
WINCHESTER MODEL 77 TUBE 477
WINCHESTER MODEL 100 477
WINCHESTER MODEL 100 CARBINE 477
WINCHESTER MODEL 190 477
WINCHESTER MODEL 290 477
WINCHESTER MODEL 290 DELUXE 477
WINCHESTER MODEL 490 477
WINCHESTER MODEL 1903 477
WINCHESTER MODEL 1905 478
WINCHESTER MODEL 1907 478
WINCHESTER MODEL 1910 478
WINCHESTER MODEL SXR SUPER X RIFLE 478
WINCHESTER COMBINATION GUN SUPER GRADE 478
WINCHESTER DOUBLE EXPRESS RIFLE 478
WINCHESTER MODEL 61 478
WINCHESTER MODEL 61 MAGNUM 478
WINCHESTER MODEL 62 478
WINCHESTER MODEL 270 478
WINCHESTER MODEL 270 DELUXE 478
WINCHESTER MODEL 275 478
WINCHESTER MODEL 275 DELUXE 479
WINCHESTER MODEL 1890 479
WINCHESTER MODEL 1906 479
WINCHESTER MODEL 1906 EXPERT 479
WINCHESTER CUSTOM SHOP MODEL 70 CUSTOM 100TH ANNIVERSARY .30-06 479
WINCHESTER CUSTOM SHOP MODEL 70 CUSTOM SPECIAL "70 YEARS OF THE MODEL 70" 479
WINCHESTER CUSTOM SHOP MODEL 70 CUSTOM MAPLE 479
WINCHESTER CUSTOM SHOP MODEL 70 CUSTOM CONTINENTAL HUNTER 479
WINCHESTER CUSTOM SHOP MODEL 70 CUSTOM STAINLESS LAMINATE 479

WINSLOW

WINSLOW BOLT-ACTION SPORTER 479

ZOLI

ZOLI COMBINATO 479
ZOLI MODEL AZ-1900 CLASSIC 479
ZOLI MODEL AZ-1900M 479
ZOLI SAVANA DOUBLE RIFLE 479

SHOTGUNS

AMERICAN ARMS

AMERICAN ARMS BRISTOL 481
AMERICAN ARMS BRITTANY 481
AMERICAN ARMS DERBY 481
AMERICAN ARMS EXCELSIOR 481
AMERICAN ARMS FS200 COMPETITION 481
AMERICAN ARMS FS300 COMPETITION 481
AMERICAN ARMS FS400 COMPETITION 481
AMERICAN ARMS FS500 COMPETITION 481
AMERICAN ARMS GENTRY 481
AMERICAN ARMS GRULLA #2 481
AMERICAN ARMS LINCE 481
AMERICAN ARMS ROYAL 481
AMERICAN ARMS SHOTGUN 481
AMERICAN ARMS SILVER I 481
AMERICAN ARMS SILVER II 481
AMERICAN ARMS SILVER II UPLAND LIGHT 482
AMERICAN ARMS SILVER SPORTING 482
AMERICAN ARMS SILVER SPORTING SKEET 482
AMERICAN ARMS SILVER SPORTING TRAP 482
AMERICAN ARMS SILVER WS/OU 12 482
AMERICAN ARMS SILVER WT/OU 10 482
AMERICAN ARMS TS/OU 12 482
AMERICAN ARMS TS/SS 12 DOUBLE 482
AMERICAN ARMS TS/SS 10 DOUBLE 482
AMERICAN ARMS WS/SS 10 482
AMERICAN ARMS YORK 482

APOLLO

APOLLO TR AND TT SHOTGUNS 482

ARIZAGA

ARIZAGA MODEL 31 482

ARMALITE

ARMALITE AR-17 GOLDEN GUN 482

ARMSCOR

ARMSCOR MODEL 30D 483
ARMSCOR MODEL 30D/IC 483
ARMSCOR MODEL 30DG 483
ARMSCOR MODEL 30FS 483
ARMSCOR MODEL 30K 483
ARMSCOR MODEL 30P 483
ARMSCOR MODEL 30R 483
ARMSCOR MODEL 30RP 483

ARMSCOR M-30F
FIELD PUMP SHOTGUN . . . 483

ARMSPORT

ARMSPORT MODEL 1032
GOOSE GUN . . . 483
ARMSPORT MODEL 1040 . . . 483
ARMSPORT MODEL 1041 . . . 483
ARMSPORT MODEL 1042 . . . 483
ARMSPORT MODEL 1043 . . . 483
ARMSPORT MODEL 1050 SERIES . . . 483
ARMSPORT MODEL 1212
WESTERN . . . 483
ARMSPORT MODEL 1626 . . . 483
ARMSPORT MODEL 1628 . . . 483
ARMSPORT MODEL 1726 . . . 483
ARMSPORT MODEL 1728 . . . 483
ARMSPORT MODEL 1810 . . . 483
ARMSPORT MODEL 2526 . . . 483
ARMSPORT MODEL 2528 . . . 484
ARMSPORT MODEL 2626 . . . 484
ARMSPORT MODEL 2628 . . . 484
ARMSPORT MODEL 2697 . . . 484
ARMSPORT MODEL 2698 . . . 484
ARMSPORT MODEL 2699 . . . 484
ARMSPORT MODEL 2700
GOOSE GUN . . . 484
ARMSPORT MODEL 2700 SERIES . . . 484
ARMSPORT MODEL 2701, 2702 . . . 484
ARMSPORT MODEL 2703, 2704 . . . 484
ARMSPORT MODEL 2705 . . . 484
ARMSPORT MODEL 2706
COMMANDER . . . 484
ARMSPORT MODEL 2707 . . . 484
ARMSPORT MODEL 2708
SLUG GUN . . . 484
ARMSPORT MODEL 27 16, 2717 . . . 484
ARMSPORT MODEL 2718, 2719 . . . 484
ARMSPORT MODEL 2720 . . . 484
ARMSPORT MODEL 2725 . . . 484
ARMSPORT MODEL 2730 . . . 484
ARMSPORT MODEL 2731 . . . 484
ARMSPORT MODEL 2733 . . . 484
ARMSPORT MODEL 2734 . . . 484
ARMSPORT MODEL 2735 . . . 484
ARMSPORT MODEL 2736 . . . 484
ARMSPORT MODEL 2741 . . . 485
ARMSPORT MODEL 2742
SPORTING CLAYS . . . 485
ARMSPORT MODEL 2744
SPORTING CLAYS . . . 485
ARMSPORT MODEL 2746 . . . 485
ARMSPORT MODEL 2747 . . . 485
ARMSPORT MODEL 2750
SPORTING CLAYS . . . 485
ARMSPORT MODEL 2751
SPORTING CLAY . . . 485
ARMSPORT MODEL 2751 . . . 485
ARMSPORT MODEL 2755 . . . 485
ARMSPORT MODEL 2900
TRI-BARREL . . . 485
ARMSPORT MODEL 2901 TRI-BARREL . . . 485
ARMSPORT MODEL 3030
DELUXE GRADE TRAP . . . 485
ARMSPORT MODEL 3032
DELUXE GRADE TRAP . . . 485
ARMSPORT MODEL 3101
DELUXE MONO TRAP . . . 485
ARMSPORT MODEL 3102
DELUXE MONO TRAP SET . . . 485
ARMSPORT MODEL 3103
DELUXE MONO TRAP . . . 485
ARMSPORT MODEL 3104
DELUXE MONO TRAP . . . 485
ARMSPORT MODEL 4000
EMPEROR OVER/UNDER . . . 485
ARMSPORT MODEL 4010
EMPEROR SIDE-BY-SIDE . . . 485
ARMSPORT MODEL 4031 . . . 485
ARMSPORT MODEL 4032
MONO TRAP . . . 485
ARMSPORT MODEL 4033
MONO TRAP . . . 485
ARMSPORT MODEL 4034
MONO TRAP SET . . . 485
ARMSPORT MODEL 4034
O/U TRAP SET . . . 485
ARMSPORT MODEL 4035
MONO TRAP SET . . . 486
ARMSPORT MODEL 4035
O/U TRAP SET . . . 486
ARMSPORT MODEL 4040 PREMIER
SLUG . . . 486
ARMSPORT MODEL 4041 PREMIER
SLUG . . . 486
ARMSPORT MODEL 4046 MONO
TRAP . . . 486
ARMSPORT MODEL 4047 MONO
TRAP . . . 486
ARMSPORT MODEL 4048 MONO
TRAP SET . . . 486
ARMSPORT MODEL 4049 MONO
TRAP SET . . . 486
ARMSPORT SINGLE . . . 486

ARRIETA

ARRIETA SIDELOCK DOUBLE
SHOTGUNS . . . 486

ASTRA

ASTRA MODEL 650 . . . 487
ASTRA MODEL 750 . . . 487

AYA

AyA AUGUSTA . . . 487
AyA BOLERO . . . 487
AyA CORAL . . . 487
AyA COSMOS . . . 487
AyA IBERIA . . . 487
AyA IBERIA/E . . . 487
AyA IBERIA II . . . 487
AyA MATADOR . . . 487
AyA MATADOR II . . . 487
AyA MODEL 4 DELUXE . . . 487
AyA MODEL 37 SUPER . . . 487
AyA MODEL 53-E . . . 487
AyA MODEL 56 . . . 488
AyA MODEL 106 . . . 488
AyA MODEL 107 . . . 488
AyA MODEL 107LI . . . 488
AyA MODEL 110 . . . 488
AyA MODEL 112 . . . 488
AyA MODEL 116 . . . 488
AyA MODEL 117 . . . 488
AyA MODEL 931 . . . 488
AyA MODEL XXV/SL . . . 488
AyA MODEL XXV/BL . . . 489
AyA NO. 1 . . . 489
AyA NO. 2 . . . 489
AyA MODEL 3-A . . . 489
AyA NO. 4 . . . 489
AyA YEOMAN . . . 489

BAIKAL

BAIKAL 66 COACH GUN . . . 489
BAIKAL IJ-18 . . . 489
BAIKAL IJ-18EM . . . 489
BAIKAL IJ-18M . . . 489
BAIKAL IJ-25 . . . 489
BAIKAL IJ-27 . . . 489
BAIKAL IJ-27EIC . . . 490
BAIKAL IJ-27EM . . . 490
BAIKAL IJ-27M . . . 490
BAIKAL IJ-43 . . . 490
BAIKAL IJ-43EM . . . 490
BAIKAL IJ-43M . . . 490
BAIKAL IJ-58M . . . 490
BAIKAL MC-5 . . . 490
BAIKAL MC-6 . . . 490
BAIKAL MC-7 . . . 490
BAIKAL MC-8 . . . 490
BAIKAL MC-10 . . . 490
BAIKAL MC-21 . . . 490
BAIKAL MC-109 . . . 490
BAIKAL MC-110 . . . 490
BAIKAL MC-111 . . . 490
BAIKAL TOZ-34P . . . 490
BAIKAL TOZ-66 . . . 490

BAKER

BAKER BATAVIA EJECTOR . . . 490
BAKER BATAVIA LEADER . . . 491
BAKER BATAVIA SPECIAL . . . 491
BAKER BLACK BEAUTY SPECIAL . . . 491
BAKER GRADE R . . . 491
BAKER GRADE S . . . 491

BEEMAN

BEEMAN FABARM . . . 491

BENELLI

BENELLI CORDOBA . . . 491
BENELLI BLACK EAGLE . . . 491
BENELLI BLACK EAGLE
COMPETITION . . . 491
BENELLI BLACK EAGLE COMPETITION
"LIMITED EDITION" . . . 491
BENELLI BLACK EAGLE
SLUG GUN . . . 491
BENELLI BLACK EAGLE SUPER . . . 492
BENELLI BLACK EAGLE
SUPER SLUG . . . 492
BENELLI EXECUTIVE SERIES . . . 492
BENELLI EXTRALUXE . . . 492
BENELLI LEGACY . . . 492
BENELLI SPORT . . . 492
BENELLI M1 FIELD . . . 493
BENELLI M2 FIELD . . . 493
BENELLI M2 TACTICAL . . . 493
BENELLI M2 PRACTICAL . . . 493
BENELLI M1 SUPER 90 . . . 493
BENELLI M1 SUPER 90 DEFENSE . . . 493
BENELLI M1 SUPER 90 ENTRY . . . 493
BENELLI M1 SUPER 90
MONTEFELTRO . . . 493
BENELLI M1 SUPER 90
MONTEFELTRO 20-GAUGE
LIMITED EDITION . . . 493
BENELLI M1 SUPER 90 MONTEFELTRO,
LEFT-HAND . . . 493
BENELLI M1 SUPER 90 MONTEFELTRO
UPLANDER . . . 493
BENELLI M1 SUPER 90
MONTEFELTRO SLUG . . . 493
BENELLI M1 SUPER 90 SLUG . . . 493
BENELLI M1 SUPER 90
SPORTING SPECIAL . . . 493
BENELLI M1 SUPER 90 TACTICAL . . . 494
BENELLI M1 TACTICAL . . . 494
BENELLI M1 PRACTICAL . . . 494
BENELLI MONTEFELTRO
SHOTGUN . . . 494
BENELLI M2 FIELD WITH
COMFORTECH . . . 494
BENELLI M2 FIELD WITHOUT
COMFORTECH . . . 494
BENELLI M3
CONVERTIBLE . . . 494
BENELLI M4 . . . 494
BENELLI NOVA PUMP . . . 494
BENELLI NOVA PUMP SLUG GUN . . . 495
BENELLI NOVA PUMP
RIFLED SLUG GUN . . . 495
BENELLI SUPER VINCI . . . 495
BENELLI VINCI . . . 495
BENELLI SUPERNOVA . . . 495
BENELLI SUPERNOVA
STEADYGRIP . . . 495
BENELLI SUPERNOVA
TACTICAL . . . 495
BENELLI SL-121 . . . 495
BENELLI SL-123 . . . 495
BENELLI SL-201 . . . 496
BENELLI ULTRA LIGHT . . . 496

BERETTA

BERETTA (DR. FRANCO)
ARIETE STANDARD . . . 496
BERETTA (DR. FRANCO) ARIETE . . . 496
BERETTA A-301 FIELD . . . 496
BERETTA A-301 MAGNUM . . . 496
BERETTA A-301 SKEET . . . 496
BERETTA A-301 SLUG . . . 496
BERETTA A-301 TRAP . . . 496
BERETTA A-302 . . . 496
BERETTA A-303 . . . 496
BERETTA A-303 MATTE FINISH . . . 496
BERETTA A-303 SPORTING CLAYS . . . 496
BERETTA A-303 UPLAND MODEL . . . 496
BERETTA A-303 YOUTH . . . 496
BERETTA A391 XTREMA 3.5 . . . 496
BERETTA A391 XTREMA2 . . . 497
BERETTA A391 XTREMA2
SLUG GUN . . . 497
BERETTA A400 XPLOR LIGHT . . . 497
BERETTA AL-2 . . . 497
BERETTA AL-3 . . . 497
BERETTA GOLD LARK . . . 497
BERETTA MODEL 390
FIELD GRADE . . . 497
BERETTA MODEL 390 FIELD GRADE
GOLD MALLARD . . . 497
BERETTA MODEL 390 FIELD GRADE
SILVER MALLARD . . . 497
BERETTA MODEL 390 FIELD GRADE
SILVER SLUG . . . 497
BERETTA MODEL 390 COMPETITION
SKEET SPORT . . . 497

BERETTA MODEL 390 COMPETITION SKEET SPORT SUPER . . . 497
BERETTA MODEL 390 COMPETITION SPORTING . . . 497
BERETTA MODEL 390 COMPETITION TRAP SPORT . . . 497
BERETTA MODEL 390 COMPETITION TRAP SUPER . . . 497
BERETTA AL391 URIKA . . . 497
BERETTA AL391 URIKA GOLD AND GOLD SPORTING AUTO SHOTGUNS . . . 498
BERETTA AL391 URIKA SPORTING AUTO SHOTGUNS . . . 498
BERETTA AL391 URIKA TRAP AND GOLD TRAP AUTO SHOTGUNS . . . 498
BERETTA AL391 URIKA PARALLEL TARGET RL AND SL AUTO SHOTGUNS . . . 498
BERETTA AL391 URIKA YOUTH SHOTGUN . . . 498
BERETTA AL391 TEKNYS . . . 498
BERETTA AL391 TEKNYS GOLD . . . 498
BERETTA AL391 TEKNYS GOLD TARGET . . . 498
BERETTA 3901 TARGET RL . . . 498
BERETTA MODEL 1200F . . . 498
BERETTA MODEL 1200FP . . . 498
BERETTA MODEL 1201F . . . 498
BERETTA MODEL 1201FP . . . 498
BERETTA MODEL 1201FP3 . . . 498
BERETTA MODEL 1201FP GHOST RING AUTO SHOTGUN . . . 499
BERETTA PINTAIL . . . 499
BERETTA RUBY LARK . . . 499
BERETTA SILVER LARK . . . 499
BERETTA TX4 STORM . . . 499
BERETTA AL391 URIKA 2 . . . 499
BERETTA AL391 URIKA 2 X-TRA GRAIN . . . 499
BERETTA AL391 URIKA 2 GOLD . . . 499
BERETTA AL391 URIKA 2 KICK-OFF . . . 499
BERETTA AL391 URIKA 2 GOLD SPORTING . . . 499
BERETTA AL391 URIKA 2 PARALLEL TARGET X-TRA GRAIN . . . 499
BERETTA AL391 URIKA 2 GOLD PARALLEL TARGET . . . 499
BERETTA ASE 90 PIGEON . . . 499
BERETTA ASE 90 GOLD SKEET . . . 499
BERETTA ASE 90 GOLD SPORTING CLAYS . . . 499
BERETTA ASE 90 GOLD TRAP . . . 499
BERETTA ASE 90 GOLD TRAP COMBO . . . 499
BERETTA ASEL . . . 499
BERETTA BL-1 . . . 499
BERETTA BL-2 . . . 499
BERETTA BL-2/S . . . 500
BERETTA BL-3 . . . 500
BERETTA BL-4 . . . 500
BERETTA BL-5 . . . 500
BERETTA BL-6 . . . 500
BERETTA DT10 TRIDENT . . . 500
BERETTA GOLDEN SNIPE . . . 500
BERETTA GOLDEN SNIPE DELUXE . . . 500
BERETTA GRADE 100 . . . 500
BERETTA GRADE 200 . . . 500
BERETTA MODEL 57E . . . 501
BERETTA SERIES 682 GOLD E SKEET, TRAP, SPORTING O VER/UNDERS . . . 501
BERETTA MODEL 682 COMPETITION GOLD SKEET . . . 501
BERETTA MODEL 682 COMPETITION GOLD SKEET SUPER . . . 501
BERETTA MODEL 682 COMPETITION GOLD SPORTING . . . 501
BERETTA MODEL 682 COMPETITION GOLD SPORTING PORTED . . . 501
BERETTA MODEL 682 COMPETITION GOLD SPORTING SUPER . . . 501
BERETTA MODEL 682 COMPETITION GOLD TRAP SUPER . . . 501
BERETTA MODEL 682 COMPETITION GOLD TRAP LIVE BIRD . . . 501
BERETTA MODEL 682 COMPETITION GOLD TRAP MONO . . . 501
BERETTA MODEL 682 COMPETITION GOLD TRAP MONO SUPER . . . 502
BERETTA MODEL 682 COMPETITION GOLD TRAP SUPER . . . 502
BERETTA MODEL 682 COMPETITION SPORTING CONTINENTAL COURSE . . . 502
BERETTA MODEL 685 . . . 502
BERETTA MODEL 686 COMPETITION SKEET SILVER PERDIZ . . . 502
BERETTA MODEL 686 COMPETITION SPORTING COLLECTION SPORT . . . 502
BERETTA MODEL 686 COMPETITION SPORTING ONYX . . . 502
BERETTA MODEL 686 COMPETITION SPORTING ONYX ENGLISH COURSE . . . 502
BERETTA MODEL 686 COMPETITION SPORTING SILVER PERDIZ . . . 502
BERETTA MODEL 686 COMPETITION SPORTING SILVER PIGEON . . . 502
BERETTA MODEL 686 COMPETITION TRAP INTERNATIONAL . . . 502
BERETTA MODEL 686 FIELD EL GOLD PERDIZ . . . 502
BERETTA MODEL 686 FIELD ESSENTIAL . . . 502
BERETTA MODEL 686 FIELD ONYX . . . 502
BERETTA MODEL 686 FIELD ONYX MAGNUM . . . 502
BERETTA MODEL 686 FIELD SILVER PERDIZ . . . 503
BERETTA MODEL 686 FIELD SILVER PIGEON . . . 503
BERETTA MODEL 686 FIELD ULTRALIGHT . . . 503
BERETTA MODEL S686 WHITEWING AND BLACKWING . . . 503
BERETTA S686 ONYX . . . 503
BERETTA S686 SILVER PIGEON O/U SHOTGUN . . . 503
BERETTA MODEL 687 COMPETITION SKEET EELL DIAMOND PIGEON . . . 503
BERETTA MODEL 687 COMPETITION SPORTING EELL DIAMOND PIGEON . . . 503
BERETTA MODEL 687 COMPETITION SPORTING EL GOLD PIGEON . . . 503
BERETTA MODEL 687 COMPETITION SPORTING L SILVER PIGEON . . . 503
BERETTA MODEL 687 COMPETITION SPORTING SILVER PERDIZ ENGLISH COURSE . . . 503
BERETTA MODEL 687 COMPETITION TRAP EELL DIAMOND PIGEON . . . 503
BERETTA MODEL 687 COMPETITION TRAP EELL DIAMOND PIGEON COMBO . . . 503
BERETTA MODEL 687 COMPETITION TRAP EELL DIAMOND PIGEON MONO . . . 503
BERETTA MODEL 687 FIELD EELL DIAMOND PIGEON . . . 503
BERETTA MODEL 687 FIELD EL GOLD PIGEON . . . 503
BERETTA MODEL 687 FIELD EL ONYX . . . 504
BERETTA MODEL 687 FIELD GOLDEN ONYX . . . 504
BERETTA MODEL 687 FIELD L ONYX . . . 504
BERETTA MODEL 687 FIELD L SILVER PIGEON . . . 504
BERETTA SILVER PIGEON S . . . 504
BERETTA SILVER PIGEON S COMBO . . . 504
BERETTA 687 SILVER PIGEON V . . . 504
BERETTA S-55B . . . 504
BERETTA S-56E . . . 504
BERETTA S-58 SKEET . . . 504
BERETTA S-58 TRAP . . . 504
BERETTA SILVER SNIPE . . . 504
BERETTA SPORTING CLAYS . . . 504
BERETTA SO-2 PRESENTATION . . . 504
BERETTA SO-3 . . . 504
BERETTA SO-4 . . . 505
BERETTA SO-5 . . . 505
BERETTA SO-6 . . . 505
BERETTA SO-6 EELL . . . 505
BERETTA SO-7 . . . 505
BERETTA SO-9 . . . 505
BERETTA ULTRALIGHT . . . 505
BERETTA ULTRALIGHT DELUXE . . . 505
BERETTA OVER/UNDER FIELD SHOTGUNS . . . 506
BERETTA GR-2 . . . 506
BERETTA GR-3 . . . 506
BERETTA GR-4 . . . 506
BERETTA MODEL 409PB . . . 506
BERETTA MODEL 410 . . . 506
BERETTA MODEL 410E . . . 506
BERETTA MODEL 411E . . . 506
BERETTA MODEL 424 . . . 506
BERETTA MODEL 426 . . . 506
BERETTA MODEL 452 CUSTOM . . . 506
BERETTA MODEL 452 EELL . . . 507
BERETTA MODEL 626 . . . 507
BERETTA MODEL 626 ONYX . . . 507
BERETTA MODEL 627 EL . . . 507
BERETTA MODEL 627 EELL . . . 507
BERETTA MODEL 470 SILVER HAWK . . . 507
BERETTA SILVER HAWK FEATHERWEIGHT . . . 507
BERETTA SILVER HAWK MAGNUM . . . 507
BERETTA MODEL 471 . . . 507
BERETTA DT 10 TRIDENT TRAP TOP SINGLE SHOTGUN . . . 507
BERETTA FS-1 . . . 507
BERETTA GOLD PIGEON . . . 507
BERETTA MARK II . . . 507
BERETTA MODEL 680 COMPETITION MONO TRAP . . . 507
BERETTA MODEL 680 COMPETITION TRAP . . . 507
BERETTA MODEL 680 COMPETITION TRAP COMBO . . . 507
BERETTA MODEL 680 COMPETITION SKEET . . . 508
BERETTA RUBY PIGEON . . . 508
BERETTA SILVER PIGEON . . . 508
BERETTA SL-2 . . . 508
BERETTA TR-1 . . . 508
BERETTA TR-2 . . . 508

BERNARDELLI

BERNARDELLI OVER/UNDER SHOTGUNS . . . 508
BERNARDELLI MODEL 115 . . . 508
BERNARDELLI MODEL 115E . . . 508
BERNARDELLI MODEL 115L . . . 508
BERNARDELLI MODEL 115S . . . 508
BERNARDELLI MODEL 115 TARGET . . . 508
BERNARDELLI MODEL 115E TARGET . . . 508
BERNARDELLI MODEL 115L TARGET . . . 508
BERNARDELLI MODEL 115S TARGET . . . 508
BERNARDELLI MODEL 115S TARGET MONOTRAP . . . 508
BERNARDELLI MODEL 190 . . . 508
BERNARDELLI MODEL 190MC . . . 508
BERNARDELLI MODEL 190 SPECIAL . . . 508
BERNARDELLI MODEL 190 SPECIAL MS . . . 508
BERNARDELLI MODEL 192 . . . 508
BERNARDELLI MODEL 192MS MC . . . 508
BERNARDELLI MODEL 192MS MC WF . . . 508
BERNARDELLI MODEL 220MS . . . 508
BERNARDELLI 9MM GARDEN GUN . . . 508
BERNARDELLI BRESCIA . . . 509
BERNARDELLI ELIO . . . 509
BERNARDELLI GAMECOCK . . . 509
BERNARDELLI HEMINGWAY . . . 509
BERNARDELLI HEMINGWAY DELUXE . . . 509
BERNARDELLI HOLLAND VB . . . 509
BERNARDELLI ITALIA . . . 510
BERNARDELLI ITALIA EXTRA . . . 510
BERNARDELLI LAS PALOMAS . . . 510
BERNARDELLI MODEL 112 . . . 510
BERNARDELLI MODEL 112EM . . . 510
BERNARDELLI MODEL 112EM MC . . . 510
BERNARDELLI MODEL 112EM MC WF . . . 510
BERNARDELLI ROMA 3 . . . 510
BERNARDELLI ROMA 3E . . . 510
BERNARDELLI ROMA 3EM . . . 510
BERNARDELLI ROMA 3M . . . 510
BERNARDELLI ROMA 4 . . . 510
BERNARDELLI ROMA 4E . . . 510
BERNARDELLI ROMA 4EM . . . 510
BERNARDELLI ROMA 4M . . . 510
BERNARDELLI ROMA 6 . . . 510
BERNARDELLI ROMA 6E . . . 511
BERNARDELLI ROMA 6EM . . . 511

BERNARDELLI ROMA 6M 511
BERNARDELLI ROMA 7. 511
BERNARDELLI ROMA 8. 511
BERNARDELLI ROMA 9. 511
BERNARDELLI S. UBERTO 1. 511
BERNARDELLI S UBERTO 1E 511
BERNARDELLI S. UBERTO 1EM 511
BERNARDELLI S. UBERTO 1M 511
BERNARDELLI S. UBERTO 2. 511
BERNARDELLI S UBERTO 2E 511
BERNARDELLI S. UBERTO 2EM 511
BERNARDELLI S. UBERTO 2M 511
BERNARDELLI S. UBERTO FS 511
BERNARDELLI S UBERTO FSE. 511
BERNARDELLI S. UBERTO FSEM. 511
BERNARDELLI S. UBERTO FSM. 511
BERNARDELLI SLUG GUN 511
BERNARDELLI SLUG LUSSO 511
BERNARDELLI SLUG LUSSO M 511
BERNARDELLI SLUG M GUN 511
BERNARDELLI XXVSL 511

BLASER

BLASER F3 SUPERSPORT 512

BOSS

BOSS SIDE-BY-SIDE 512
BOSS OVER/UNDER 512

BREDA

BREDA AUTOLOADER. 512
BREDA AUTOLOADER MAGNUM 12 512
BREDA VEGA SPECIAL 512
BREDA VEGA SPECIAL TRAP 512
BREDA VEGA LUSSO 512
BREDA SIRIO STANDARD 512
BREDA PEGASO HUNTER 512
BREDA PEGASO SPORTING CLAYS 512
BREDA ANDROMEDA SPECIAL 512

BRETTON

BRETTON BABY 512
BRETTON BABY DELUXE 512
BRETTON SPRINT DELUXE. 512
BRETTON FAIR PLAY. 512

BRI

BRI SPECIAL MODEL 512

BRNO

BRNO CZ-581 512
BRNO MODEL 500. 512
BRNO SUPER 512
BRNO ZBK 100 SINGLE BARREL SHOTGUN. 512
BRNO ZH-301 SERIES. 513
BRNO ZH 300 OVER/UNDER SHOTGUN. 513
BRNO ZP-49 513
BRNO ZP-149 513
BRNO ZP-349 513
BRNO 501.2 OVER/UNDER SHOTGUN. 513

BROWNING

BROWNING A-500G 513
BROWNING A-500G BUCK SPECIAL. 513
BROWNING A-500G SPORTING CLAYS 513
BROWNING A-500R. 513
BROWNING A-500R BUCK SPECIAL. 513
BROWNING AUTO-5 (1900-1940) 513
BROWNING AUTO-5 (1900-1940) GRADE III. 513
BROWNING AUTO-5 (1900-1940) GRADE IV. 513
BROWNING AUTO-5 AMERICAN GRADE I (1940-1949) 513
BROWNING AUTO-5 AMERICAN SPECIAL (1940-1949) 514
BROWNING AUTO-5 AMERICAN SPECIAL SKEET (1940-1949) 514
BROWNING AUTO-5 AMERICAN UTILITY FIELD MODEL (1940-1949) 514
BROWNING AUTO-5 BELGIUM STANDARD (1947-1953) 514
BROWNING AUTO-5 CLASSIC 514
BROWNING AUTO-5 CLASSIC GOLD. 514
BROWNING AUTO-5 LIGHT (FN). 514
BROWNING AUTO-5 LIGHT (MIROKU). 514
BROWNING AUTO-5 LIGHT BUCK SPECIAL (MIROKU) 514
BROWNING AUTO-5 LIGHT SKEET (FN) 514
BROWNING AUTO-5 LIGHT SKEET (MIROKU). 514
BROWNING AUTO-5 LIGHT STALKER 514
BROWNING AUTO-5 SWEET 16 (FN) 514
BROWNING AUTO-5 SWEET 16 (MIROKU). 514
BROWNING AUTO-5 TRAP (FN) 514
BROWNING AUTO-5 MAGNUM (FN) 514
BROWNING AUTO-5 MAGNUM (MIROKU). 514
BROWNING AUTO-5 MAGNUM STALKER 515
BROWNING A5 HUNTER. 515
BROWNING B-80. 515
BROWNING B-80 UPLAND SPECIAL 515
BROWNING B-2000. 515
BROWNING B-2000 BUCK SPECIAL 515
BROWNING B-2000 MAGNUM 515
BROWNING B-2000 SKEET. 515
BROWNING B-2000 TRAP. 515
BROWNING DOUBLE AUTO 515
BROWNING DOUBLE AUTO TWELVETTE. 515
BROWNING DOUBLE AUTO TWENTYWEIGHT 515
BROWNING GOLD. 515
BROWNING GOLD RIFLED DEER HUNTER 515
BROWNING GOLD DEER STALKER 516
BROWNING GOLD SPORTING CLAYS 516
BROWNING GOLD SPORTING GOLDEN CLAYS. 516
BROWNING GOLD LADIES/YOUTH SPORTING CLAYS 516
BROWNING GOLD MICRO 516
BROWNING GOLD STALKER 516
BROWNING GOLD MOSSY OAK® SHADOW GRASS 516
BROWNING GOLD MOSSY OAK® BREAK-UP. 516
BROWNING GOLD CLASSIC HUNTER 516
BROWNING GOLD CLASSIC STALKER 516
BROWNING GOLD FUSION 516
BROWNING NWTF GOLD TURKEY STALKER 516
BROWNING GOLD TURKEY/ WATERFOWL CAMO. 517
BROWNING GOLD NWTF TURKEY SERIES CAMO 517
BROWNING GOLD UPLAND SPECIAL 517
BROWNING GOLD SUPERLITE HUNTER 517
BROWNING GOLD SUPERLITE FIELD HUNTER 517
BROWNING GOLD SUPERLITE MICRO. 517
BROWNING GOLD 10 517
BROWNING GOLD 10-GAUGE AUTO COMBO. 517
BROWNING GOLD LIGHT 10-GAUGE. 517
BROWNING GOLD 10 STALKER. 517
BROWNING SILVER HUNTER 517
BROWNING SILVER STALKER 517
BROWNING SILVER MOSSY OAK. 517
BROWNING SILVER MICRO 517
BROWNING SILVER SPORTING MICRO. 517
BROWNING SILVER NWTF 518
BROWNING SILVER RIFLED DEER. 518
BROWNING BSS 518
BROWNING BSS SPORTER 518
BROWNING B-SS SPORTER GRADE II 518
BROWNING BSS SIDELOCK. 518
BROWNING CITORI (HUNTING) MODELS 518
BROWNING CITORI SATIN HUNTER. 518
BROWNING CITORI LIGHTNING (HUNTING). 518
BROWNING CITORI GRAN LIGHTNING (HUNTING). 518
BROWNING CITORI LIGHTNING MICRO (HUNTING) 518
BROWNING CITORI HUNTING SPORTER 518
BROWNING CITORI SPORTING HUNTER 518
BROWNING CITORI HUNTING SUPERLIGHT. 519
BROWNING CITORI LIGHTNING FEATHER 519
BROWNING CITORI SKEET, SPECIAL SKEET, ULTRA XS SKEET, XS SKEET 519
BROWNING CITORI ULTRA XS SKEET 519
BROWNING CITORI ULTRA XT TRAP 519
BROWNING CITORI ULTRA XS SPORTING 519
BROWNING CITORI FEATHER XS 519
BROWNING CITORI HIGH GRADE. 519
BROWNING CITORI XS SPORTING CLAYS 519
CITORI 525 FEATHER 520
CITORI 625 SPORTING 520
CITORI 625 FIELD 520
CITORI MODEL 725 520
CITORI ULTRA XS PRESTIGE 520
BROWNING SPECIAL SPORTING CLAYS 520
BROWNING LIGHTNING SPORTING CLAYS 520
BROWNING LIGHT SPORTING 802 ES O/U. 520
BROWNING CITORI SPORTING CLAYS 325. 520
BROWNING CITORI SPORTING CLAYS 325 GOLDEN CLAYS 520
BROWNING CITORI SPORTING CLAYS 425. 520
BROWNING CITORI SPORTING CLAYS 425 GOLDEN CLAYS 520
BROWNING CITORI SPORTING CLAYS 425 WSSF 520
BROWNING CITORI SPORTING CLAYS GTI 520
BROWNING CITORI SPORTING CLAYS LIGHTNING 520
BROWNING CITORI SPECIAL SPORTING CLAYS 521
BROWNING CITORI SPORTING CLAYS ULTRA SPORTER 521
BROWNING CITORI TRAP, SPECIAL TRAP, ULTRA XT AND XT 521
BROWNING CITORI TRAP PLUS. 521
BROWNING CITORI XT TRAP OVER/UNDER 521
BROWNING LIEGE. 521
BROWNING ST-100 521
BROWNING SUPERPOSED. 521
BROWNING SUPERPOSED BROADWAY TRAP. 521
BROWNING SUPERPOSED DIANA GRADE. 521
BROWNING SUPERPOSED GRADE I LIGHTNING MODEL. 521
BROWNING SUPERPOSED MAGNUM 522
BROWNING SUPERPOSED MIDAS GRADE 522
BROWNING SUPERPOSED PIGEON GRADE 522
BROWNING SUPERPOSED SKEET 522
BROWNING SUPERPOSED PRESENTATION SUPERLIGHT 522
BROWNING SUPERPOSED PRESENTATION SUPERLIGHT BROADWAY TRAP. 522
BROWNING SUPERPOSED PRESENTATION SUPERLIGHT LIGHTNING SKEET 522
BROWNING SUPERPOSED PRESENTATION SUPERLIGHT LIGHTNING TRAP 522

BROWNING SUPERPOSED PRESENTATION SUPERLIGHT MAGNUM 522
BROWNING SUPERPOSED SUPERLIGHT 523
BROWNING CYNERGY CLASSIC FIELD 523
BROWNING CYNERGY CLASSIC SPORTING 523
BROWNING CYNERGY SPORTING, ADJUSTABLE COMB 523
BROWNING CYNERGY FEATHER 523
CYNERGY FEATHER COMPOSITE 523
BROWNING CYNERGY EURO SPORTING 523
BROWNING CYNERGY CLASSIC TRAP UNSINGLE COMBO 523
BROWNING A-BOLT HUNTER 523
BROWNING A-BOLT STALKER 523
BROWNING BPS 523
BROWNING BPS ALL WEATHER HIGH CAPACITY 523
BROWNING BPS BUCK SPECIAL 523
BROWNING BPS GAME GUN DEER SPECIAL 523
BROWNING BPS GAME GUN TURKEY SPECIAL 524
BROWNING BPS LADIES & YOUTH MODEL 524
BROWNING BPS PIGEON GRADE 524
BROWNING BPS STALKER 524
BROWNING BPS NWTF TURKEY SERIES 524
BROWNING BPS UPLAND SPECIAL 524
BROWNING BPS MICRO 524
BROWNING BPS WATERFOWL 10-GAUGE 524
BROWNING BPS WATERFOWL CAMO 524
BROWNING BPS 10 GAUGE SHOTGUNS 524
BROWNING BPS 10-GAUGE CAMO PUMP 524
BROWNING MAXUS ALL-PURPOSE 524
BROWNING MAXUS HUNTER 524
BROWNING MAXUS MOSSY OAK BOTTOMLAND 524
BROWNING MAXUS MOSSY OAK DUCK BLIND 524
BROWNING MAXUS SPORTING 524
BROWNING MAXUS SPORTING CARBON FIBER 524
BROWNING MAXUS RIFLED DEER STALKER 524
BROWNING MODEL 12 525
BROWNING MODEL 42 525
BROWNING RECOILLESS TRAP 525
BROWNING RECOILLESS TRAP MICRO 525
BROWNING SINGLE SHOT SHOTGUNS
BROWNING BT-99 MAX 525
BROWNING BT-99 TRAP 525
BROWNING BT-99 PLUS 525
BROWNING BT-99 PLUS MICRO 525
BROWNING BT-100 TRAP 525

CAESAR

CAESAR GUERINI ELLIPSE LIMITED 525

CAPRINUS

CAPRINUS SWEDEN 525

CARLO CASARTELLI

CARLO CASARTELLI 526

CENTURION ORDNANCE

CENTURION ORDNANCE POSEIDON 526

CENTURY

CENTURY KHAN ARTHEMIS (SUPER ARTHEMIS) 526
CENTURY PHANTOM 526
CENTURY SAS-12 526
CENTURY COACH GUN 526
CENTURY MODEL YL12 526
CENTURY CENTURION (OLD MODEL) 526
CENTURY CENTURION (NEW MODEL) 526
CENTURY BLACK DIAMOND 526
CENTURY TOZ MODEL 34 526

CHAPUIS

CHAPUIS PROGRESS RBV 526
CHAPUIS PROGRESS RG 526
CHAPUIS PROGRESS SLUG 526
CHAPUIS ST. BONETT 526
CHAPUIS O/U 526

CHARLES DALY

CHARLES DALY AUTO 526
CHARLES DALY DIAMOND GRADE 526
CHARLES DALY DIAMOND-REGENT GRADE 526
CHARLES DALY DIAMOND DL DOUBLE SHOTGUN 526
CHARLES DALY DIAMOND REGENT DL DOUBLE SHOTGUN 526
CHARLES DALY DIAMOND REGENT GTX DL HUNTER O/U 527
CHARLES DALY DIAMOND GTX SPORTING O/U SHOTGUN 527
CHARLES DALY DIAMOND GTX TRAP AE-MC O/U SHOTGUN 527
CHARLES DALY DIAMOND GTX DL HUNTER O/U 527
CHARLES DALY DIAMOND GRADE (1984) 527
CHARLES DALY DIAMOND SKEET (1984) 527
CHARLES DALY DIAMOND TRAP (1984) 527
CHARLES DALY EMPIRE DOUBLE 527
CHARLES DALY EMPIRE EDL HUNTER O/U 527
CHARLES DALY EMPIRE SPORTING O/U 527
CHARLES DALY EMPIRE QUALITY TRAP 527
CHARLES DALY EMPIRE TRAP AE MC 527
CHARLES DALY FIELD AUTO 527
CHARLES DALY FIELD GRADE 527
CHARLES DALY FIELD GRADE (1989) 528
CHARLES DALY FIELD GRADE DELUXE (1989) 528
CHARLES DALY FIELD III 528
CHARLES DALY FIELD HUNTER DOUBLE SHOTGUN 528
CHARLES DALY FIELD HUNTER OVER/UNDER SHOTGUN 528
CHARLES DALY FIELD HUNTER AE SHOTGUN 528
CHARLES DALY SUPERIOR HUNTER AE SHOTGUN 528
CHARLES DALY FIELD HUNTER AE-MC 528
CHARLES DALY SUPERIOR SPORTING 528
CHARLES DALY HAMMERLESS DRILLING 528
CHARLES DALY HAMMERLESS OVER/UNDER 528
CHARLES DALY HAMMERLESS SIDE-BY-SIDE 528
CHARLES DALY LUX OVER/UNDER 528
CHARLES DALY LUX SIDE-BY-SIDE 528
CHARLES DALY MODEL 100 COMMANDER 528
CHARLES DALY MODEL 200 COMMANDER 528
CHARLES DALY MODEL DSS 529
CHARLES DALY MODEL DSS 529
CHARLES DALY MULTI-XII 529
CHARLES DALY NOVAMATIC LIGHTWEIGHT 529
CHARLES DALY NOVAMATIC LIGHTWEIGHT MAGNUM 529
CHARLES DALY NOVAMATIC LIGHTWEIGHT TRAP 529
CHARLES DALY NOVAMATIC LIGHTWEIGHT SUPER 529
CHARLES DALY PRESENTATION GRADE 529
CHARLES DALY SEXTUPLE TRAP 529
CHARLES DALY SUPERIOR GRADE OVER/UNDER 529
CHARLES DALY SUPERIOR GRADE SIDE-BY-SIDE 529
CHARLES DALY SUPERIOR HUNTER DOUBLE SHOTGUN 529
CHARLES DALY EMPIRE HUNTER DOUBLE SHOTGUN 529
CHARLES DALY MODEL 306 529
CHARLES DALY SUPERIOR II 529
CHARLES DALY SUPERIOR SINGLE TRAP 529
CHARLES DALY SUPERIOR TRAP AE MC 529
CHARLES DALY VENTURE GRADE 530
CHARLES DALY MODEL 105 530
CHARLES DALY MODEL 106 530
CHARLES DALY FIELD HUNTER SEMI-AUTO LEFT HAND 530
CHARLES DALY FIELD HUNTER SEMI-AUTO BLACK CHROME TACTICAL 530
CHARLES DALY FIELD HUNTER VR-MC 530
CHARLES DALY HUNTER VR-MC YOUTH 530
CHARLES DALY SUPERIOR II HUNTER 530
CHARLES DALY SUPERIOR II SPORT 530
CHARLES DALY SUPERIOR II TRAP 530
CHARLES DALY FIELD HUNTER MAXI-MAG VR-MC SEMI-AUTO 530
CHARLES DALY FIELD HUNTER PUMP 530
CHARLES DALY FIELD BLACK CHROME TACTICAL PUMP 530
CHARLES DALY FIELD NICKEL TACTICAL PUMP 530
CHARLES DALY FIELD HUNTER 20-GA. YOUTH PUMP 530
CHARLES DALY FIELD HUNTER MAXI-MAG VR-MC PUMP 530

CHIPMUNK

CHIPMUNK .410 YOUTH SHOTGUN 530

CHURCHILL, E.J.

CHURCHILL, E.J., CROWN 530
CHURCHILL, E.J., FIELD 530
CHURCHILL, E.J., HERCULES 531
CHURCHILL, E.J., IMPERIAL 531
CHURCHILL, E.J., PREMIER 531
CHURCHILL, E.J., PREMIER QUALITY 531
CHURCHILL, E.J., REGAL 531
CHURCHILL, E.J., UTILITY 531

CHURCHILL

CHURCHILL DEERFIELD SEMI-AUTO 531
CHURCHILL REGENT IV S/S BOXLOCK 531
CHURCHILL REGENT VI S/S SIDELOCK 531
CHURCHILL REGENT V O/U 532
CHURCHILL REGENT O/U COMPETITION 532
CHURCHILL REGENT O/U FLYWEIGHT 532
CHURCHILL REGENT O/U TRAP/SKEET 532
CHURCHILL REGENT VII O/U 532
CHURCHILL REGENT SEMI-AUTO 532
CHURCHILL ROYAL 532
CHURCHILL TURKEY AUTOMATIC SHOTGUN 532
CHURCHILL WINDSOR O/U III 532
CHURCHILL WINDSOR IV O/U 532
CHURCHILL WINDSOR O/U FLYWEIGHT 532
CHURCHILL WINDSOR O/U SPORTING CLAYS 532
CHURCHILL WINDSOR S/S 532
CHURCHILL WINDSOR S/S II 532
CHURCHILL WINDSOR SEMI-AUTO 532

CITADEL

CITADEL LE TACTICAL . . . 533

CLAYCO

CLAYCO MODEL 6. . . 533

COGSWELL & HARRISON

COGSWELL & HARRISON AMBASSADOR . . . 533
COGSWELL & HARRISON AVANT TOUT KONOR . . . 533
COGSWELL & HARRISON AVANT TOUT REX . . . 533
COGSWELL & HARRISON AVANT TOUT SANDHURST . . . 533
COGSWELL & HARRISON HUNTIC MODEL . . . 533
COGSWELL & HARRISON MARKOR MODEL . . . 533
COGSWELL & HARRISON PRIMAC MODEL . . . 533
COGSWELL & HARRISON VICTOR MODEL . . . 533

COLT

COLT COLTSMAN PUMP. . . 533
COLT COLTSMAN PUMP CUSTOM . . . 533
COLT CUSTOM DOUBLE BARREL . . . 533
COLT MAGNUM AUTO . . . 533
COLT MAGNUM AUTO CUSTOM . . . 533
COLT SAUER DRILLING . . . 533
COLT ULTRA LIGHT AUTO . . . 533
COLT ULTRA LIGHT AUTO CUSTOM . . . 533

CONNECTICUT

CONNECTICUT SHOTGUN MANUFACTURING CO. MODEL 21 . . . 534
CONNECTICUT SHOTGUN MANUFACTURING MODEL 21-1 . . . 534
CONNECTICUT SHOTGUN MANUFACTURING MODEL 21-5 . . . 534
CONNECTICUT SHOTGUN MANUFACTURING MODEL 21-6 . . . 534
CONNECTICUT SHOTGUN MANUFACTURING MODEL 21 GRAND AMERICAN. . . 534
CONNECTICUT VALLEY CLASSICS CLASSIC SPORTER . . . 534
CONNECTICUT VALLEY CLASSICS CLASSIC FIELD WATERFOWLER . . . 534

COSMI

COSMI SEMI-AUTOMATIC . . . 534
COSMI ALUMINUM MODEL . . . 534
COSMI TITANIUM MODEL. . . 534

CROSSFIRE

CROSSFIRE SHOTGUN/RIFLE . . . 534

CRUCELEGUI

CRUCELEGUI HERMANOS MODEL 150. . . 534

CZ

CZ 581 SOLO OVER/UNDER SHOTGUN. . . 534
CZ 912 . . . 534
CZ GROUSE. . . 534
CZ SPORTING . . . 534
CZ WINGSHOOTER. . . 534
CZ-712/720 . . . 534

DAKOTA

DAKOTA PREMIER GRADE SHOTGUNS. . . 534
DAKOTA LEGEND . . . 534

DARNE

DARNE MODEL R11 BIRD HUNTER. . . 534
DARNE MODEL R15 PHEASANT HUNTER. . . 535
DARNE MODEL V19 QUAIL HUNTER SUPREME. . . 535
DARNE MODEL MAGNUM R16. . . 535
DARNE MODEL V22. . . 535

DAVIDSON

DAVIDSON MODEL 63B . . . 535
DAVIDSON MODEL 63B MAGNUM. . . 535
DAVIDSON MODEL 69SL. . . 535
DAVIDSON MODEL 73. . . 535

DESERT

DESERT INDUSTRIES BIG TWENTY . . . 535

DIAMOND

DIAMOND 12-GA. PUMP SHOTGUN . . . 535

DUMOULIN

DUMOULIN EUROPA. . . 535
DUMOULIN LIEGE . . . 535

EAA/BAIKAL

EAA/BAIKAL IZH-43 BOUNTY HUNTER. . . 535
EAA/BAIKAL IZH-43K BOUNTY HUNTER. . . 535
EAA/BAIKAL IZH-18 SINGLE BARREL. . . 535
EAA/BAIKAL IZH-18MAX SINGLE BARREL. . . 535
EAA/BAIKAL MP-133 PUMP. . . 536
EAA/BAIKAL MP-153 AUTO . . . 536
EAA/BAIKAL MP-213. . . 536
EAA/BAIKAL BOUNTY HUNTER MP-213 COACH GUN . . . 536
EAA/BAIKAL MP-233 OVER/UNDER . . . 536
EAA/BAIKAL IZH-27 OVER/UNDER . . . 536
EAA IZH-27 SPORTING O/U . . . 536
E.A.A./SABATTI FALCON-MON . . . 536
E.A.A./SABATTI SABA-MON DOUBLE . . . 536
E.A.A./SABATTI SPORTING CLAYS PRO-GOLD . . . 536
EAA/SAIGA AUTO SHOTGUN . . . 536

E.M.F.

E.M.F. HARTFORD MODEL COWBOY. . . 536
E.M.F. STAGECOACH MODEL. . . 536
E.M.F. MARK V CONQUEST . . . 536

ERA

ERA BIRD HUNTER . . . 536
ERA FULL LIMIT. . . 537
ERA WINNER . . . 537

ERBI

ERBI MODEL 76AJ. . . 537
ERBI MODEL 76ST. . . 537
ERBI MODEL 80. . . 537

ESCORT

ESCORT MODEL AS . . . 537
ESCORT SERIES . . . 537
ESCORT AVERY WATERFOWL EXTREME . . . 537

EXEL

EXEL MODEL 101 . . . 537
EXEL MODEL 102 . . . 537
EXEL MODEL 103 . . . 537
EXEL MODEL 104 . . . 537
EXEL MODEL 105 . . . 537
EXEL MODEL 106 . . . 537
EXEL MODEL 107 . . . 537
EXEL MODEL 201 . . . 537
EXEL MODEL 202 . . . 537
EXEL MODEL 203 . . . 537
EXEL MODEL 204 . . . 537
EXEL MODEL 205 . . . 537
EXEL MODEL 206 . . . 538
EXEL MODEL 207 . . . 538
EXEL MODEL 208 . . . 538
EXEL MODEL 209 . . . 538
EXEL MODEL 210 . . . 538
EXEL MODEL 240 . . . 538
EXEL MODEL 251 . . . 538
EXEL MODEL 281 . . . 538
EXEL SERIES 300. . . 538

FABARM

FABARM CAMO TURKEY MAG . . . 538
FABARM ULTRA CAMO. . . 538
FABARM CLASSIC LION DOUBLE . . . 538
FABARM FIELD PUMP. . . 538
FABARM FP6 PUMP . . . 539
FABARM GOLD LION MARK II AUTO. . . 539
FABARM CAMO LION AUTO. . . 539
FABARM SPORTING CLAYS EXTRA AUTO. . . 539
FABARM MAX LION OVER/UNDER . . . 539
FABARM MAX LION PARADOX . . . 539
FABARM MONOTRAP . . . 539
FABARM RED LION . . . 539
FABARM SILVER LION OVER/UNDER . . . 539
FABARM SILVER LION CUB OVER/UNDER . . . 539
FABARM ULTRA CAMO MAG LION. . . 539
FABARM SPORTING CLAYS COMPETITION EXTRA O/U. . . 539
FABARM TACTICAL SEMI-AUTOMATIC . . . 540

FAUSTI

FAUSTI CALEDON . . . 540
FAUSTI DEA . . . 540

FERLACH

FERLACH CONSTANT COMPANION. . . 540

FERLIB

FERLIB MODEL F VII . . . 540
FERLIB MODEL F VII/SC . . . 540
FERLIB MODEL F VII SIDEPLATE . . . 540
FERLIB MODEL F VII SIDEPLATE SC . . . 540

FIAS

FIAS MODEL SK-1 . . . 540
FIAS MODEL SK-3. . . 540
FIAS MODEL SK-4 . . . 540
FIAS MODEL SK-4D. . . 540
FIAS MODEL SK-4S. . . 540
FIAS MODEL SK-4T. . . 540

F.I.E.

F.I.E. BRUTE. . . 540
F.I.E. CBC. . . 540
F.I.E. HAMILTON & HUNTER . . . 540
F.I.E. S.O.B. . . 540
F.I.E. S.S.S. MODEL . . . 541
F.I.E. STURDY. . . 541
F.I.E. STURDY DELUXE PRITI . . . 541
F.I.E. STURDY MODEL 12 DELUXE. . . 541

FOX FA-1

FOX FA-1 . . . 541
FOX FP-1 . . . 541

STEVENS/FOX

STEVENS/FOX MODEL B . . . 541
STEVENS/FOX MODEL B-DE . . . 541
STEVENS/FOX MODEL B-DL . . . 541
STEVENS/FOX MODEL B-SE . . . 541
STEVENS/FOX MODEL B-ST. . . 541

A.H. FOX

A.H. FOX MODEL B LIGHTWEIGHT. . . 541
A.H. FOX HAMMERLESS DOUBLE BARREL (1902-1905). . . 541
A.H. FOX HAMMERLESS DOUBLE BARREL (1905-1946). . . 541
A.H. FOX HAMMERLESS DOUBLE BARREL A GRADE. . . 542
A.H. FOX HAMMERLESS DOUBLE BARREL AE GRADE. . . 542
A.H. FOX HAMMERLESS DOUBLE BARREL B GRADE. . . 542
A.H. FOX HAMMERLESS DOUBLE BARREL BE GRADE. . . 542
A.H. FOX HAMMERLESS DOUBLE BARREL C GRADE. . . 542
A.H. FOX HAMMERLESS DOUBLE BARREL CE GRADE . . . 542

A.H. FOX HAMMERLESS DOUBLE BARREL D GRADE....542
A.H. FOX HAMMERLESS DOUBLE BARREL DE GRADE....542
A.H. FOX HAMMERLESS DOUBLE BARREL F GRADE....542
A.H. FOX HAMMERLESS DOUBLE BARREL FE GRADE....542
A.H. FOX HAMMERLESS DOUBLE BARREL GE GRADE....542
A.H. FOX HAMMERLESS DOUBLE BARREL SKEETER....542
A.H. FOX HAMMERLESS DOUBLE BARREL TRAP GRADE....542
A.H. FOX HAMMERLESS DOUBLE BARREL XE GRADE....542
A.H. FOX HAMMERLESS DOUBLE BARREL (CURRENT PRODUCTION)....542
A.H. FOX SIDE-BY-SIDE SHOTGUNS....542
A.H. FOX SINGLE-BARREL TRAP....542
A.H. FOX SP GRADE....543
A.H. FOX SPE GRADE....543
A.H. FOX SPE SKEET GRADE....543
A.H. FOX SPE SKEET AND UPLAND GAME GUN....543
A.H. FOX SPR GRADE....543
A.H. FOX STERLINGWORTH....543
A.H. FOX STERLINGWORTH BRUSH....543
A.H. FOX STERLINGWORTH DELUXE....543
A.H. FOX STERLINGWORTH DELUXE EJECTOR....543
A.H. FOX STERLINGWORTH EJECTOR....543
A.H. FOX STERLINGWORTH FIELD....543
A.H. FOX STERLINGWORTH SKEET....543
A.H. FOX STERLINGWORTH SKEET EJECTOR....543
A.H. FOX STERLINGWORTH STANDARD....543
A.H. FOX STERLINGWORTH TRAP....543
A.H. FOX STERLINGWORTH WILDFOWL....543
A.H. FOX SUPER-FOX....543

FRANCHI

FRANCHI BLACK MAGIC 48/AL....543
FRANCHI BLACK MAGIC GAME....543
FRANCHI BLACK MAGIC SKEET....544
FRANCHI BLACK MAGIC TRAP....544
FRANCHI CROWN GRADE....544
FRANCHI DIAMOND GRADE....544
FRANCHI ELDORADO....544
FRANCHI ELITE....544
FRANCHI HUNTER....544
FRANCHI HUNTER MAGNUM....544
FRANCHI IMPERIAL GRADE....544
FRANCHI LAW-12....544
FRANCHI MODEL 500....544
FRANCHI MODEL 520 DELUXE....545
FRANCHI MODEL 520 ELDORADO GOLD....545
FRANCHI MODEL 530....545
FRANCHI 612 AND 620....545
FRANCHI 612 DEFENSE....545
FRANCHI 612 SPORTING....545
FRANCHI 620 SHORT STOCK....545
FRANCHI 720....545
FRANCHI 712 RAPTOR....545
FRANCHI MODEL 720 RAPTOR....545
FRANCHI 912....545
FRANCHI PRESTIGE....545
FRANCHI SKEET GUN....545
FRANCHI SLUG GUN....545
FRANCHI 48AL....545
FRANCHI STANDARD 48/AL....546
FRANCHI STANDARD 48/AL MAGNUM....546
FRANCHI 48AL DELUXE....546
FRANCHI 48AL ENGLISH....546
FRANCHI 48AL SHORT STOCK....546
FRANCHI VARIOMAX 912....546
FRANCHI VARIOMAX 912 CAMO....546
FRANCHI VARIOMAX 912 STEADYGRIP....546
FRANCHI VARIOPRESS 612 SPORTING....546
FRANCHI VARIOPRESS 612 FIELD....546
FRANCHI VARIOPRESS 612 DEFENSE....546
FRANCHI VARIOPRESS 620 FIELD....546
FRANCHI VARIOPRESS 620 SHORT STOCK....546
FRANCHI SPAS-12....546
FRANCHI TURKEY GUN....546
FRANCHI I-12....546
FRANCHI I-12 WHITE GOLD....546
FRANCHI ALCIONE....546
FRANCHI ALCIONE SL....547
FRANCHI ALCIONE FIELD....547
FRANCHI SX....547
FRANCHI ALCIONE SPORT SL....547
FRANCHI ALCIONE TITANIUM....547
FRANCHI ARISTOCRAT....547
FRANCHI ARISTOCRAT DELUXE....547
FRANCHI ARISTOCRAT IMPERIAL....547
FRANCHI ARISTOCRAT MAGNUM....547
FRANCHI ARISTOCRAT MONTE CARLO....547
FRANCHI ARISTOCRAT SILVER-KING....547
FRANCHI ARISTOCRAT SKEET....547
FRANCHI ARISTOCRAT SUPREME....547
FRANCHI ARISTOCRAT TRAP....547
FRANCHI BLACK MAGIC LIGHTWEIGHT HUNTER....547
FRANCHI BLACK MAGIC SPORTING HUNTER....547
FRANCHI FALCONET....547
FRANCHI FALCONET INTERNATIONAL SKEET....548
FRANCHI FALCONET INTERNATIONAL TRAP....548
FRANCHI FALCONET SKEET....548
FRANCHI FALCONET SUPER....548
FRANCHI FALCONET TRAP....548
FRANCHI FALCONET 2000....548
FRANCHI MODEL 2000 SPORTING....548
FRANCHI MODEL 2003 TRAP....548
FRANCHI MODEL 2004 TRAP....548
FRANCHI MODEL 2005 COMBINATION TRAP....548
FRANCHI MODEL 2005/3 COMBINATION TRAP....548
FRANCHI MODEL 3000/2....548
FRANCHI PEREGRIN MODEL 400....548
FRANCHI PEREGRIN MODEL 451....548
FRANCHI VELOCE OVER/UNDER....549
FRANCHI VELOCE ENGLISH OVER/UNDER....549
FRANCHI RENAISSANCE FIELD....549
FRANCHI RENAISSANCE CLASSIC....549
FRANCHI RENAISSANCE ELITE....549
FRANCHI RENAISSANCE SPORTING....549
FRANCHI SIDE-BY-SIDE SHOTGUNS FRANCHI AIRONE....549
FRANCHI ASTORE....549
FRANCHI ASTORE S....549
FRANCHI ASTORE II....549
FRANCHI CUSTOM SIDELOCK....549
FRANCHI SAS-12....549

FRANCOTTE

FRANCOTTE BOXLOCK....550
FRANCOTTE JUBILEE....550
FRANCOTTE KNOCKABOUT....550
FRANCOTTE MODEL 9/40E/38321....550
FRANCOTTE MODEL 9/40SE....550
FRANCOTTE MODEL 10/18E/628....550
FRANCOTTE MODEL 11/18E....550
FRANCOTTE MODEL 120.HE/328....550
FRANCOTTE MODEL 4996....550
FRANCOTTE MODEL 6886....550
FRANCOTTE MODEL 6930....551
FRANCOTTE MODEL 6982....551
FRANCOTTE MODEL 8446....551
FRANCOTTE MODEL 8455....551
FRANCOTTE MODEL 8457....551
FRANCOTTE MODEL 9261....551
FRANCOTTE MODEL 10594....551
FRANCOTTE MODEL SOB.E/11082....551
FRANCOTTE SIDELOCK....551

GALEF

GALEF COMPANION....551
GALEF MONTE CARLO TRAP....551
GALEF/ZABALA....551
GALEF/ZOLI GOLDEN SNIPE....552
GALEF/ZOLI SILVER HAWK....552
GALEF/ZOLI SILVER SNIPE....552
GALEF/ZOLI SILVER SNIPE TRAP....552
GALEF/ZOLI SILVER SNIPE SKEET....552

GAMBA

GAMBA 2100....552
GAMBA AMBASSADOR....552
GAMBA AMBASSADOR EXECUTIVE....552
GAMBA DAYTONA....552
GAMBA DAYTONA SL....552
GAMBA DAYTONA GRADE 4....552
GAMBA DAYTONA GRADE 5/5E....552
GAMBA DAYTONA GRADE 6/6SCE....552
GAMBA DAYTONA GRADE 7....552
GAMBA DAYTONA GRADE 8....553
GAMBA DAYTONA SL HH....553
GAMBA DAYTONA SL....553
GAMBA DAYTONA GRADE ROYALE....553
GAMBA DAYTONA GRADE PURDEY....553
GAMBA DAYTONA SLE TIGER....553
GAMBA DAYTONA SLE BEST....553
GAMBA DAYTONA SLE VENUS....553
GAMBA DAYTONA GRADE 1 SL....553
GAMBA DAYTONA GRADE 2 SL....553
GAMBA DAYTONA GRADE 3 SL....553
GAMBA DAYTONA COMPETITION....553
GAMBA EDINBURGH SKEET....553
GAMBA EDINBURGH TRAP....553
GAMBA EUROPA 2000....553
GAMBA GRIFONE....553
GAMBA GRINTA SKEET....553
GAMBA GRINTA TRAP....553
GAMBA HUNTER SUPER....553
GAMBA LONDON....553
GAMBA LS2000....553
GAMBA MILANO....553
GAMBA OXFORD 90....553
GAMBA PRINCIPESSA....553
GAMBA VICTORY SKEET....553
GAMBA VICTORY TRAP....554

GARBI

GARBI MODEL 51A....554
GARBI MODEL 51B....554
GARBI MODEL 60A....554
GARBI MODEL 60B....554
GARBI MODEL 62A....554
GARBI MODEL 62B....554
GARBI MODEL 71....554
GARBI MODEL 100....554
GARBI MODEL 100 DOUBLE....554
GARBI MODEL 101....554
GARBI MODEL 102....554
GARBI MODEL 103A....554
GARBI MODEL 103B....554
GARBI MODEL 103B ROYAL....554
GARBI MODEL 110....554
GARBI MODEL 200....554
GARBI MODEL 300....555
GARBI SPECIAL MODEL....555

GARCIA

GARCIA BRONCO....555
GARCIA BRONCO .22/.410....555

GOLDEN EAGLE

GOLDEN EAGLE MODEL 5000 GRADE I FIELD....555
GOLDEN EAGLE MODEL 5000 GRADE II FIELD....555
GOLDEN EAGLE MODEL 5000 GRADE I TRAP....555
GOLDEN EAGLE MODEL 5000 GRADE II TRAP....555
GOLDEN EAGLE MODEL 5000 GRADE I SKEET....555
GOLDEN EAGLE MODEL 5000 GRADE II SKEET....555
GOLDEN EAGLE MODEL 5000 GRADE III....555

GOROSABEL

GOROSABEL 501....555
GOROSABEL 502....555
GOROSABEL 503....555
GOROSABEL BLACKPOINT....555
GOROSABEL SILVERPOINT....555

GREENER

GREENER CROWN GRADE DH75....555
GREENER EMPIRE....555
GREENER EMPIRE DELUXE....556

GREENER FAR-KILLER 556
GREENER GENERAL PURPOSE 556
GREENER JUBILEE GRADE DH35 556
GREENER SOVEREIGN GRADE DH40 556

GREIFELT

GREIFELT GRADE NO. 1 556
GREIFELT GRADE NO. 3 556
GREIFELT MODEL 22. 556
GREIFELT MODEL 22E 556
GREIFELT MODEL 103. 556
GREIFELT MODEL 103E 556
GREIFELT MODEL 143E 556

HANUS, BILL

BILL HANUS BIRDGUN 556

HARRINGTON & RICHARDSON

HARRINGTON & RICHARDSON FOLDING MODEL 556
HARRINGTON & RICHARDSON MODEL 088 556
HARRINGTON & RICHARDSON MODEL 088 JUNIOR 557
HARRINGTON & RICHARDSON MODEL 099 DELUXE 557
HARRINGTON & RICHARDSON MODEL 159 GOLDEN SQUIRE 557
HARRINGTON & RICHARDSON MODEL 162 SLUG GUN 557
HARRINGTON & RICHARDSON MODEL 176 557
HARRINGTON & RICHARDSON MODEL 176 SLUG GUN 557
HARRINGTON & RICHARDSON MODEL 348 GAMESTER 557
HARRINGTON & RICHARDSON MODEL 349 GAMESTER DELUXE 557
HARRINGTON & RICHARDSON MODEL 351 HUNTSMAN 557
HARRINGTON & RICHARDSON MODEL 400 557
HARRINGTON & RICHARDSON MODEL 401 557
HARRINGTON & RICHARDSON MODEL 402 557
HARRINGTON & RICHARDSON MODEL 403 557
HARRINGTON & RICHARDSON MODEL 404 557
HARRINGTON & RICHARDSON MODEL 404C. 558
HARRINGTON & RICHARDSON MODEL 440 558
HARRINGTON & RICHARDSON MODEL 442 558
HARRINGTON & RICHARDSON MODEL 459 GOLDEN SQUIRE JUNIOR 558
HARRINGTON & RICHARDSON MODEL 1212 558
HARRINGTON & RICHARDSON MODEL 1212 WATERFOWLER 558
HARRINGTON & RICHARDSON NO. 1 HARRICH. 558
HARRINGTON & RICHARDSON NO. 3 558
HARRINGTON & RICHARDSON NO. 5 558
HARRINGTON & RICHARDSON NO. 6 558
HARRINGTON & RICHARDSON NO. 7 BAY STATE 558
HARRINGTON & RICHARDSON NO. 8 558
HARRINGTON & RICHARDSON NO. 48 TOPPER 559
HARRINGTON & RICHARDSON N.W.T.F. SHOTGUNS. 559
HARRINGTON & RICHARDSON N.W.T.F TURKEY 559
HARRINGTON & RICHARDSON N.W.T.F. TURKEY YOUTH 559
HARRINGTON & RICHARDSON SB2-980 ULTRA SLUG 559
HARRINGTON & RICHARDSON MODEL 928 ULTRA SLUG HUNTER DELUXE 559
HARRINGTON & RICHARDSON TAMER. 559
HARRINGTON & RICHARDSON TOPPER MODEL 058 559
HARRINGTON & RICHARDSON TOPPER MODEL 098 559
HARRINGTON & RICHARDSON TOPPER JUNIOR 098 559
HARRINGTON & RICHARDSON TOPPER MODEL 098 CLASSIC YOUTH. 559
HARRINGTON & RICHARDSON TOPPER MODEL 098 DELUXE 559
HARRINGTON & RICHARDSON TOPPER MODEL 098 DELUXE RIFLED SLUG GUN. 559
HARRINGTON & RICHARDSON TOPPER MODEL 098 JUNIOR 559
HARRINGTON & RICHARDSON TOPPER MODEL 148 560
HARRINGTON & RICHARDSON TOPPER MODEL 158 560
HARRINGTON & RICHARDSON TOPPER MODEL 188 DELUXE 560
HARRINGTON & RICHARDSON TOPPER MODEL 198 DELUXE 560
HARRINGTON & RICHARDSON TOPPER MODEL 480 JUNIOR 560
HARRINGTON & RICHARDSON TOPPER MODEL 488 DELUXE 560
HARRINGTON & RICHARDSON TOPPER MODEL 490 JUNIOR 560
HARRINGTON & RICHARDSON TOPPER MODEL 490 GREENWING. 560
HARRINGTON & RICHARDSON TOPPER MODEL 580 JUNIOR 560
HARRINGTON & RICHARDSON TOPPER MODEL 590 JUNIOR 560

HATFIELD

HATFIELD UPLANDER. 560
HATFIELD'S UPLANDER 28. 560

HEYM

HEYM MODEL 55 F 560
HEYM MODEL 55 SS. 560
HEYM MODEL 200. 560

HHF

HHF (HUGLU) MODEL 101 B 12 AT-DT. 561
HHF MODEL 101 B 12 ST TRAP 561
HHF (HUGLU) MODEL 103 B 12 ST 561
HHF (HUGLU) MODEL 103 C 12 ST 561
HHF (HUGLU) MODEL 103 D 12 ST 561
HHF MODEL 103 F 12 ST 561
HHF (HUGLU) MODEL 104 A 12 ST 561
HHF (HUGLU) MODEL 200 A 12 ST DOUBLE. 561
HHF (HUGLU) MODEL 202 A 12 ST. 561

HI-STANDARD

HI-STANDARD FLITE-KING BRUSH 561
HI-STANDARD FLITE-KING BRUSH DELUXE 561
HI-STANDARD FLITE-KING BRUSH (1966) 561
HI-STANDARD FLITE-KING BRUSH DELUXE (1966). 561
HI-STANDARD FLITE-KING DELUXE RIB 561
HI-STANDARD FLITE-KING DELUXE (1966) 562
HI-STANDARD FLITE-KING DELUXE RIB (1966) 562
HI-STANDARD FLITE-KING DELUXE SKEET (1966) 562
HI-STANDARD FLITE-KING DELUXE TRAP (1966) 562
HI-STANDARD FLITE-KING FIELD. 562
HI-STANDARD FLITE-KING SKEET 562
HI-STANDARD FLITE-KING SPECIAL 562
HI-STANDARD FLITE-KING TRAP 562
HI-STANDARD FLITE-KING TROPHY 562
HI-STANDARD SHADOW AUTO 562
HI-STANDARD SHADOW INDY 562
HI-STANDARD SHADOW SEVEN 563
HI-STANDARD SUPERMATIC DEER 563
HI-STANDARD SUPERMATIC DELUXE. 563
HI-STANDARD SUPERMATIC DELUXE RIB 563
HI-STANDARD SUPERMATIC DUCK. 563
HI-STANDARD SUPERMATIC DUCK DELUXE 563
HI-STANDARD SUPERMATIC DUCK RIB 563
HI-STANDARD SUPERMATIC DUCK RIB DELUXE. 563
HI-STANDARD SUPERMATIC FIELD 563
HI-STANDARD SUPERMATIC SKEET 563
HI-STANDARD SUPERMATIC SKEET DELUXE. 563
HI-STANDARD SUPERMATIC SPECIAL 563
HI-STANDARD SUPERMATIC TRAP 563
HI-STANDARD SUPERMATIC TRAP DELUXE. 564
HI-STANDARD SUPERMATIC TROPHY 564

HOENIG

HOENIG ROTARY ROUND ACTION GAME GUN 564

HOLLAND & HOLLAND

HOLLAND & HOLLAND BADMINTON 564
HOLLAND & HOLLAND BADMINTON GAME GUN. 564
HOLLAND & HOLLAND CAVALIER 564
HOLLAND & HOLLAND CAVALIER DELUXE 564
HOLLAND & HOLLAND DOMINION GAME GUN 564
HOLLAND & HOLLAND NORTHWOOD. 564
HOLLAND & HOLLAND NORTHWOOD DELUXE 564
HOLLAND & HOLLAND NORTHWOOD GAME MODEL 564
HOLLAND & HOLLAND NORTHWOOD PIGEON MODEL. 564
HOLLAND & HOLLAND NORTHWOOD WILDFOWL MODEL 564
HOLLAND & HOLLAND RIVIERA. 564
HOLLAND & HOLLAND ROYAL. 564
HOLLAND & HOLLAND ROYAL GAME GUN 564
HOLLAND & HOLLAND ROYAL GAME GUN DELUXE. 565
HOLLAND & HOLLAND ROYAL OVER/UNDER 565
HOLLAND & HOLLAND ROYAL OVER/UNDER (NEW MODEL). 565
HOLLAND & HOLLAND ROYAL OVER/UNDER GAME GUN 565
HOLLAND & HOLLAND SINGLE BARREL TRAP. 565
HOLLAND & HOLLAND SPORTING OVER/UNDER 565
HOLLAND & HOLLAND SPORTING OVER/UNDER DELUXE. 565
HOLLAND & HOLLAND SUPER TRAP. 565

HUNTER

HUNTER FULTON 565
HUNTER SPECIAL. 565

IGA

IGA COACH MODEL 565
IGA CONDOR 565
IGA CONDOR I. 565
IGA CONDOR II 565
IGA CONDOR I SPECIAL. 565
IGA CONDOR SUPREME. 565
IGA CONDOR SUPREME DELUXE 565
IGA HUNTER CLAYS MODEL 565
IGA TURKEY SERIES. 565
IGA WATERFOWL SERIES. 565
IGA ERA 2000. 565
IGA REUNA 565
IGA UPLANDER 566

INDUSTRIAS

INDUSTRIAS DANOK
RED PRINCE 566

ITHACA

ITHACA MAG-10 566
ITHACA MAG-10 DELUXE 566
ITHACA MAG-10 SUPREME 566
ITHACA MAG-10 ROADBLOCKER 566
ITHACA MODEL 51 566
ITHACA MODEL 51A 566
ITHACA MODEL 51A DEERSLAYER 566
ITHACA MODEL 51A MAGNUM 566
ITHACA MODEL 51A MAGNUM
WATERFOWLER 566
ITHACA MODEL 51A
PRESENTATION. 566
ITHACA MODEL 51A
SUPREME SKEET 566
ITHACA MODEL 51A
SUPREME TRAP 566
ITHACA MODEL 51 DEERSLAYER 566
ITHACA MODEL 51 FEATHERLIGHT 566
ITHACA MODEL 51 FEATHERLIGHT
DELUXE TRAP 566
ITHACA MODEL 51 MAGNUM. 566
ITHACA MODEL 51 SKEET 566
ITHACA MODEL 51 TRAP 566
ITHACA MODEL 51 TURKEY 566
ITHACA MODEL 300 566
ITHACA MODEL 900 DELUXE 566
ITHACA MODEL 900 DELUXE SLUG. 567
ITHACA MODEL XL 300. 567
ITHACA MODEL XL 900. 567
ITHACA MODEL XL 900 SLUG GUN 567
ITHACA MODEL 37 567
ITHACA MODEL 37 $3000 GRADE 567
ITHACA MODEL 37 BASIC
FEATHERLIGHT 567
ITHACA MODEL 37D
FEATHERLIGHT 567
ITHACA MODEL 37 DEERSLAYER 567
ITHACA MODEL 37 DELUXE
FEATHERLIGHT 567
ITHACA MODEL 37DV
FEATHERWEIGHT 567
ITHACA MODEL 37 ENGLISH
ULTRALIGHT 567
ITHACA MODEL 37 FEATHERLIGHT 567
ITHACA MODEL 37 FEATHERLIGHT
PRESENTATION. 568
ITHACA MODEL 37 FIELD GRADE 568
ITHACA MODEL 37 FIELD GRADE
MAGNUM 568
ITHACA MODEL 37R 568
ITHACA MODEL 37R DELUXE. 568
ITHACA MODEL 37S
SKEET GRADE 568
ITHACA MODEL 37
SUPER DEERSLAYER 568
ITHACA MODEL 37
SUPREME GRADE 568
ITHACA MODEL 37T TARGET
GRADE. 568
ITHACA MODEL 37T TRAP GRADE. 568
ITHACA MODEL 37 ULTRA-LIGHT 568
ITHACA MODEL 37V
FEATHERWEIGHT 568
ITHACA MODEL 37 DELUXE PUMP 568
ITHACA MODEL 37 NEW CLASSIC. 568
ITHACA MODEL 37 WATERFOWLER 568
ITHACA MODEL 37
DEERSLAYER II 568
ITHACA MODEL 37
DEERSLAYER III 568
ITHACA MODEL 37
RUFFED GROUSE
SPECIAL EDITION 568
ITHACA ELLETT SPECIAL
MODEL 37 TURKEYSLAYER. 568
ITHACA QUAD BORE
MODEL 37 TURKEYSLAYER. 569
ITHACA MODEL 37 ULTRALIGHT
DELUXE. 569
ITHACA MODEL 66 569
ITHACA MODEL 66 LONG TOM 569
ITHACA MODEL 66RS
BUCK BUSTER 569
ITHACA MODEL 66 VENT RIB. 569
ITHACA MODEL 66 YOUTH MODEL. 569
ITHACA MODEL 87 569
ITHACA MODEL 87 CAMO 569
ITHACA MODEL 87 COMBO 569
ITHACA MODEL 87 DEERSLAYER 569
ITHACA MODEL 87 DEERSLAYER II 569
ITHACA MODEL 87 DEERSLAYER II
FAST TWIST. 569
ITHACA MODEL 87 DEERSLAYER
DELUXE. 569
ITHACA MODEL 87 DEERSLAYER
DELUXE COMBO. 569
ITHACA MODEL 87 DELUXE 569
ITHACA MODEL 87 DELUXE
COMBO 569
ITHACA MODEL 87 DELUXE
MAGNUM 569
ITHACA MODEL 87 ENGLISH 570
ITHACA MODEL 87 M&P 570
ITHACA MODEL 87 SUPREME 570
ITHACA MODEL 87
TURKEYGUN. 570
ITHACA MODEL 87 ULTRA
DEERSLAYER 570
ITHACA MODEL 87 ULTRALIGHT 570
ITHACA MODEL 87
ULTRALIGHT DELUXE. 570
ITHACA HOMELAND SECURITY
GUNS. 570
ITHACA CLASSIC DOUBLES
SPECIAL FIELD GRADE SXS 570
ITHACA CLASSIC DOUBLES
GRADE 4E CLASSIC SXS
SHOTGUN 570
ITHACA CLASSIC DOUBLES
GRADE 7E CLASSIC SXS
SHOTGUN 570
ITHACA CLASSIC DOUBLES
SOUSA SPECIAL GRADE SXS
SHOTGUN 570
ITHACA CRASS MODEL NO. 1 570
ITHACA CRASS MODEL NO. 1
SPECIAL 570
ITHACA CRASS MODEL NO. 1-1/2. 570
ITHACA CRASS MODEL NO. 2 570
ITHACA CRASS MODEL NO. 3 570
ITHACA CRASS MODEL NO. 4 570
ITHACA CRASS MODEL NO. 5 570
ITHACA CRASS MODEL NO. 6 570
ITHACA CRASS MODEL NO. 7 570
NEW ITHACA DOUBLE (NID)
FIELD GRADE 570
NEW ITHACA DOUBLE (NID)
SKEET MODEL FIELD GRADE 571
NEW ITHACA DOUBLE (NID) NO. 2. 571
NEW ITHACA DOUBLE (NID) NO. 3. 571
NEW ITHACA DOUBLE (NID) NO. 4. 571
NEW ITHACA DOUBLE (NID) NO. 5. 571
NEW ITHACA DOUBLE (NID) NO. 7. 571
NEW ITHACA DOUBLE (NID)
SOUSA SPECIAL. 571
ITHACA FLUES MODEL
FIELD GRADE 571
ITHACA FLUES MODEL NO. 1. 571
ITHACA FLUES MODEL NO. 1
SPECIAL 571
ITHACA FLUES MODEL NO. 1-1/2 571
ITHACA FLUES MODEL NO. 2. 571
ITHACA FLUES MODEL NO. 2
KRUPP PIGEON GUN 571
ITHACA FLUES MODEL NO. 3. 571
ITHACA FLUES MODEL NO. 4. 571
ITHACA FLUES MODEL NO. 5. 571
ITHACA FLUES MODEL NO. 6. 571
ITHACA FLUES MODEL NO. 7. 571
ITHACA FLUES ONE-BARREL
TRAP GUN NO. 4 571
ITHACA FLUES ONE-BARREL
TRAP GUN NO. 5 571
ITHACA FLUES ONE-BARREL
TRAP GUN NO. 6 571
ITHACA FLUES ONE-BARREL
TRAP GUN NO. 7 571
ITHACA FLUES ONE-BARREL
TRAP GUN SOUSA SPECIAL 571
ITHACA FLUES ONE-BARREL
TRAP GUN VICTORY GRADE 571
ITHACA KNICKERBOCKER
ONE-BARREL TRAP GUN
NO. 4 571
ITHACA KNICKERBOCKER
ONE-BARREL TRAP NO. 5 572
ITHACA KNICKERBOCKER
ONE-BARREL TRAP NO. 6 572
ITHACA KNICKERBOCKER
ONE-BARREL TRAP NO. 7 572
ITHACA KNICKERBOCKER
ONE-BARREL TRAP SOUSA
SPECIAL 572
ITHACA KNICKERBOCKER
ONE-BARREL TRAP VICTORY
GRADE. 572
ITHACA KNICKERBOCKER
ONE-BARREL TRAP $1000
GRADE. 572
ITHACA MINIER MODEL
FIELD GRADE 572
ITHACA MINIER MODEL NO. 1 572
ITHACA MINIER MODEL NO. 1
SPECIAL 572
ITHACA MINIER MODEL NO. 1-1/2. 572
ITHACA MINIER MODEL NO. 2 572
ITHACA MINIER MODEL NO. 2
KRUPP PIGEON GUN 572
ITHACA MINIER MODEL NO. 3 572
ITHACA MINIER MODEL NO. 4 572
ITHACA MINIER MODEL NO. 5 572
ITHACA MINIER MODEL NO. 6 572
ITHACA MINIER MODEL NO. 7 572
ITHACA LEWIS MODEL NO. 1. 572
ITHACA LEWIS MODEL NO. 1
SPECIAL 572
ITHACA LEWIS MODEL NO. 1-1/2 572
ITHACA LEWIS MODEL NO. 2. 573
ITHACA LEWIS MODEL NO. 3. 573
ITHACA LEWIS MODEL NO. 4. 573
ITHACA LEWIS MODEL NO. 5. 573
ITHACA LEWIS MODEL NO. 6. 573
ITHACA LEWIS MODEL NO. 7. 573
ITHACA LSA-55 TURKEY GUN 573
ITHACA SINGLE BARREL 5E
CUSTOM TRAP. 573

IVER JOHNSON

IVER JOHNSON CHAMPION
MATTED RIB MODEL 573
IVER JOHNSON CHAMPION
MODEL 36 573
IVER JOHNSON CHAMPION
MODEL 36 JUNIOR 573
IVER JOHNSON CHAMPION
MODEL 39 573
IVER JOHNSON CHAMPION
MODEL 39 JUNIOR 573
IVER JOHNSON CHAMPION
TOP SNAP 573
IVER JOHNSON CHAMPION
TOP SNAP NEW MODEL 573
IVER JOHNSON CHAMPION
TOP SNAP NEW MODEL
JUNIOR 573
IVER JOHNSON
EJECTOR SINGLE. 573
IVER JOHNSON EJECTOR SINGLE
JUNIOR 574
IVER JOHNSON HAMMERLESS
DOUBLE BARREL. 574
IVER JOHNSON HERCULES GRADE
HAMMERLESS DOUBLE BARREL 574
IVER JOHNSON HERCULES GRADE
HAMMERLESS SUPERTRAP 574
IVER JOHNSON SEMI-OCTAGON
BARREL. 574
IVER JOHNSON SILVER SHADOW 574
IVER JOHNSON SKEET-ER 574
IVER JOHNSON SPECIAL TRAP
MODEL 574
IVER JOHNSON TRIGGER ACTION
EJECTOR SINGLE. 574
IVER JOHNSON TRIGGER ACTION
EJECTOR SINGLE JUNIOR. 574

KASSNAR

KASSNAR FOX. 575
KASSNAR GRADE I 575
KASSNAR GRADE II. 575
KASSNAR OMEGA. 575
KASSNAR OMEGA PUMP 575
KASSNAR OMEGA SXS. 575
KASSNAR OMEGA
SINGLE BARREL. 575
KASSNAR OMEGA STANDARD
FOLDING SINGLE BARREL. 575
KASSNAR DELUXE
FOLDING SINGLE BARREL. 575

KAWAGUCHIYA

KAWAGUCHIYA FG 575
KAWAGUCHIYA M-250 575

KAWAGUCHIYA M-250 DELUXE . . . 575
KAWAGUCHIYA OT-SKEET E1 . . . 575
KAWAGUCHIYA OT-SKEET E2 . . . 575
KAWAGUCHIYA OT-TRAP E1 . . . 575
KAWAGUCHIYA OT-TRAP E2 . . . 575

KDF

KDF BRESCIA . . . 575
KDF CONDOR . . . 575
KDF CONDOR TRAP . . . 575

KEL-TEC

KEL-TEC KSG BULLPUP TWIN-TUBE . . . 576

KEMEN

KEMEN KM-4 OVER/UNDER . . . 576

KESSLER

KESSLER MODEL 28 THREE-SHOT REPEATER . . . 576
KESSLER MODEL 50 LEVER-MATIC . . . 576

KIMBER

KIMBER AUGUSTA SHOTGUN . . . 576
KIMBER VALIER GRADE I . . . 576
KIMBER VALIER GRADE II . . . 576
KIMBER MARIAS GRADE I . . . 576
KIMBER MARIAS GRADE II . . . 576

KOLAR

KOLAR SPORTING CLAYS . . . 576
KOLAR AAA COMPETITION TRAP . . . 576
KOLAR AAA COMPETITION SKEET . . . 576

KRIEGHOFF

KRIEGHOFF K-80 LIVE BIRD . . . 576
KRIEGHOFF K-80 LIVE BIRD LIGHTWEIGHT . . . 576
KRIEGHOFF K-80 SKEET . . . 577
KRIEGHOFF K-80 SKEET FOUR-BARREL SET . . . 577
KRIEGHOFF K-80 SKEET INTERNATIONAL . . . 577
KRIEGHOFF K-80 SKEET LIGHTWEIGHT . . . 577
KRIEGHOFF K-80 SKEET LIGHTWEIGHT TWO-BARREL SET . . . 577
KRIEGHOFF K-80 SKEET SPECIAL . . . 577
KRIEGHOFF K-80 SPORTING CLAYS . . . 577
KRIEGHOFF K-80 SINGLE BARREL TRAP GUN . . . 577
KRIEGHOFF K-80 TRAP . . . 577
KRIEGHOFF K-20 . . . 577
KRIEGHOFF K-80 TRAP COMBO . . . 577
KRIEGHOFF K-80 TRAP TOP SINGLE . . . 577
KRIEGHOFF K-80 TRAP UNSINGLE . . . 578
KRIEGHOFF KS-5 TRAP . . . 578
KRIEGHOFF KS-5 SPECIAL . . . 578
KRIEGHOFF KX-5 TRAP GUN . . . 578
KRIEGHOFF MODEL 32 . . . 578
KRIEGHOFF MODEL 32 FOUR-BARREL SKEET SET . . . 578
KRIEGHOFF MODEL 32 SINGLE-BARREL TRAP . . . 578
KRIEGHOFF NEPTUN . . . 578
KRIEGHOFF NEPTUN PRIMUS . . . 578
KRIEGHOFF PLUS . . . 578
KRIEGHOFF TECK . . . 578
KRIEGHOFF TECK COMBINATION . . . 578
KRIEGHOFF TRUMPF . . . 578
KRIEGHOFF ULM . . . 578
KRIEGHOFF ULM COMBINATION . . . 578
KRIEGHOFF ULM-PRIMUS . . . 579
KRIEGHOFF ULM-PRIMUS COMBINATION . . . 579
KRIEGHOFF ULTRA COMBINATION . . . 579
KRIEGHOFF ULTRA-B COMBINATION . . . 579
KRIEGHOFF VANDALIA TRAP . . . 579

LANBER

LANBER 82 . . . 579
LANBER 87 DELUXE . . . 579
LANBER 97 SPORTING CLAYS . . . 579
LANBER MODEL 844 . . . 579
LANBER MODEL 844 EST . . . 579
LANBER MODEL 844 MST . . . 579
LANBER MODEL 2004 LCH . . . 579
LANBER MODEL 2004 LCH SKEET . . . 579
LANBER MODEL 2004 LCH TRAP . . . 579
LANBER MODEL 2008 LCH . . . 579
LANBER MODEL 2009 LCH . . . 579

LARRANAGA, MIGUEL

MIGUEL LARRANAGA TRADITIONAL . . . 579

LAURONA

LAURONA 82 SUPER GAME . . . 579
LAURONA 82 TRAP COMPETITION . . . 580
LAURONA 83 SUPER GAME . . . 580
LAURONA 84 SUPER GAME . . . 580
LAURONA 84 SUPER TRAP . . . 580
LAURONA 85 SUPER GAME . . . 580
LAURONA 85 SUPER SKEET . . . 580
LAURONA 85 SUPER TRAP . . . 580
LAURONA GRAND TRAP GTO COMBO . . . 580
LAURONA GRAND TRAP GTU COMBO . . . 580
LAURONA SILHOUETTE 300 SPORTING CLAYS . . . 580
LAURONA SILHOUETTE 300 TRAP . . . 580
LAURONA SILHOUETTE SINGLE BARREL TRAP . . . 580
LAURONA SILHOUETTE ULTRA-MAGNUM . . . 580

LEBEAU-COURALLY

LEBEAU-COURALLY BOSS-VEREES O/U . . . 580
LEBEAU-COURALLY BOXLOCK . . . 580
LEBEAU-COURALLY BOXLOCK SXS SHOTGUN . . . 580
LEBEAU-COURALLY MODEL 1225 . . . 580
LEBEAU-COURALLY SIDELOCK . . . 580
LEBEAU-COURALLY SIDELOCK SXS SHOTGUN . . . 580

LEFEVER ARMS

LEFEVER ARMS AUTOMATIC HAMMERLESS DOUBLES . . . 580
LEFEVER ARMS AUTOMATIC HAMMERLESS DOUBLE GRADE I . . . 581
LEFEVER ARMS AUTOMATIC HAMMERLESS DOUBLE GRADE A . . . 581
LEFEVER ARMS AUTOMATIC HAMMERLESS DOUBLE GRADE AA . . . 581
LEFEVER ARMS AUTOMATIC HAMMERLESS DOUBLE GRADE B . . . 581
LEFEVER ARMS AUTOMATIC HAMMERLESS DOUBLE GRADE BE . . . 581
LEFEVER ARMS AUTOMATIC HAMMERLESS DOUBLE GRADE C . . . 581
LEFEVER ARMS AUTOMATIC HAMMERLESS DOUBLE GRADE CE . . . 581
LEFEVER ARMS AUTOMATIC HAMMERLESS DOUBLE GRADE D . . . 581
LEFEVER ARMS AUTOMATIC HAMMERLESS DOUBLE GRADE DE . . . 581
LEFEVER ARMS AUTOMATIC HAMMERLESS DOUBLE GRADE DS . . . 581
LEFEVER ARMS AUTOMATIC HAMMERLESS DOUBLE GRADE DSE . . . 581
LEFEVER ARMS AUTOMATIC HAMMERLESS DOUBLE GRADE E . . . 581
LEFEVER ARMS AUTOMATIC HAMMERLESS DOUBLE GRADE EE . . . 581
LEFEVER ARMS AUTOMATIC HAMMERLESS DOUBLE GRADE F . . . 581
LEFEVER ARMS AUTOMATIC HAMMERLESS DOUBLE GRADE FE . . . 581
LEFEVER ARMS AUTOMATIC HAMMERLESS DOUBLE GRADE G . . . 581
LEFEVER ARMS AUTOMATIC HAMMERLESS DOUBLE GRADE GE . . . 581
LEFEVER ARMS AUTOMATIC HAMMERLESS DOUBLE GRADE H . . . 581
LEFEVER ARMS AUTOMATIC HAMMERLESS DOUBLE GRADE HE . . . 581
LEFEVER ARMS AUTOMATIC HAMMERLESS DOUBLE OPTIMUS . . . 581
LEFEVER ARMS AUTOMATIC HAMMERLESS DOUBLE THOUSAND DOLLAR GRADE . . . 581
LEFEVER GRADE A . . . 581
LEFEVER GRADE A SKEET . . . 582
LEFEVER LONG RANGE . . . 582
LEFEVER NITRO SPECIAL . . . 582
LEFEVER SINGLE BARREL TRAP . . . 582
D.M. LEFEVER HAMMERLESS DOUBLE . . . 582
D.M. LEFEVER HAMMERLESS DOUBLE GRADE NO. 4, AA . . . 582
D.M. LEFEVER HAMMERLESS DOUBLE GRADE NO. 5, B . . . 582
D.M. LEFEVER HAMMERLESS DOUBLE GRADE NO. 6, C . . . 582
D.M. LEFEVER HAMMERLESS DOUBLE GRADE NO. 8, E . . . 582
D.M. LEFEVER HAMMERLESS DOUBLE GRADE NO. 9, F . . . 582
D.M. LEFEVER HAMMERLESS DOUBLE GRADE O EXCELSIOR . . . 582
D.M. LEFEVER HAMMERLESS DOUBLE UNCLE DAN GRADE . . . 582
D.M. LEFEVER SINGLE BARREL TRAP . . . 582

LJUTIC

LJUTIC BI-GUN . . . 582
LJUTIC BI-GUN COMBO . . . 583
LJUTIC BI-GUN FOUR-BARREL SKEET . . . 583
LJUTIC BI-MATIC . . . 583
LJUTIC DYNA TRAP . . . 583
LJUTIC LM-6 . . . 583
LJUTIC LM-6 COMBO . . . 583
LJUTIC LM-6 FOUR-BARREL SKEET SET . . . 583
LJUTIC LM-6 SUPER DELUXE . . . 583
LJUTIC OVER/UNDER COMBO . . . 583
LJUTIC MODEL X-73 . . . 583
LJUTIC MONO GUN . . . 583
LJUTIC MONO GUN ADJUSTABLE BARREL . . . 583
LJUTIC MONO GUN LTX . . . 583
LJUTIC MONO GUN LTX SUPER DELUXE . . . 583
LJUTIC LTX PRO 3 DELUXE MONO GUN . . . 583
LJUTIC SPACE GUN . . . 583

LUGER

LUGER CLASSIC O/U SHOTGUNS . . . 583
LUGER SEMI-AUTO SHOTGUN . . . 583

MAGTECH

MAGTECH MT-151 . . . 584
MAGTECH MODEL MT-586.2 . . . 584
MAGTECH MODEL MT-586.2-VR . . . 584
MAGTECH MODEL MT-586 SLUG . . . 584
MAGTECH MODEL MT-586P . . . 584

MANUFRANCE

MANUFRANCE AUTO . . . 584
MANUFRANCE FALCOR COMPETITION TRAP . . . 584
MANUFRANCE FALCOR PHEASANT GUN . . . 584
MANUFRANCE FALCOR SKEET . . . 584
MANUFRANCE FALCOR TRAP . . . 584
MANUFRANCE ROBUST . . . 584
MANUFRANCE ROBUST DELUXE . . . 584

MARLIN

MARLIN MODEL 16 . . . 584
MARLIN MODEL 17 . . . 584
MARLIN MODEL 17 BRUSH . . . 584
MARLIN MODEL 17 RIOT . . . 584
MARLIN MODEL 19 . . . 584
MARLIN MODEL 21 TRAP . . . 584
MARLIN MODEL 24 . . . 585
MARLIN MODEL 25MG GARDEN GUN SHOTGUN . . . 585
MARLIN MODEL 26 . . . 585
MARLIN MODEL 26 BRUSH . . . 585
MARLIN MODEL 26 RIOT . . . 585
MARLIN MODEL 28 . . . 585
MARLIN MODEL 28T . . . 585
MARLIN MODEL 28TS . . . 585
MARLIN MODEL 30 . . . 585
MARLIN MODEL 30 FIELD . . . 585
MARLIN MODEL 31 . . . 585
MARLIN MODEL 31 FIELD . . . 585

MARLIN MODEL 42A 585
MARLIN MODEL 43A 585
MARLIN MODEL 43T 585
MARLIN MODEL 43TS 586
MARLIN MODEL 44A 586
MARLIN MODEL 44S 586
MARLIN MODEL 49 586
MARLIN MODEL 50 586
MARLIN MODEL 53 586
MARLIN MODEL 55 586
MARLIN MODEL 55 GOOSE GUN 586
MARLIN MODEL 55 SWAMP GUN 586
MARLIN MODEL 55S SLUG 586
MARLIN MODEL 59 OLYMPIC 586
MARLIN MODEL 59 OLYMPIC JUNIOR 586
MARLIN MODEL 60 586
MARLIN MODEL 63A 586
MARLIN MODEL 63T 587
MARLIN MODEL 63TS TRAP SPECIAL 587
MARLIN MODEL 90 587
MARLIN MODEL 90-DT 587
MARLIN MODEL 90-ST 587
MARLIN MODEL 120 MAGNUM 587
MARLIN MODEL 120 TRAP 587
MARLIN MODEL .410 587
MARLIN LEVER ACTION .410 (RECENT) 587
MARLIN MODEL 512 SLUGMASTER 587
MARLIN MODEL 1898 587
MARLIN MODEL 5510 GOOSE GUN 587
MARLIN PREMIER MARK I 587
MARLIN PREMIER MARK II 587
MARLIN PREMIER MARK IV 588
MARLIN-GLENFIELD MODEL 55G 588
MARLIN-GLENFIELD MODEL 60G 588
MARLIN-GLENFIELD MODEL 60G JUNIOR 588
MARLIN-GLENFIELD MODEL 778 588

MAROCCHI

MAROCCHI AMERICA 588
MAROCCHI AVANZA 588
MAROCCHI AVANZA SPORTING CLAYS 588
MAROCCHI CONQUISTA SKEET 588
MAROCCHI CONQUISTA SPORTING CLAYS 588
MAROCCHI CONQUISTA TRAP 588
MAROCCHI LADY SPORT 588
MAROCCHI CONTRAST 588
MAROCCHI CONQUISTA USA MODEL 92 SPORTING CLAYS 589
MAROCCHI MODEL 99 SPORTING TRAP AND SKEET 589
MAROCCHI SM-28 SXS 589
MAROCCHI PRITI 589

MAUSER

MAUSER MODEL CONTEST 589
MAUSER-BAUER MODEL 71E 589
MAUSER-BAUER MODEL 72E 589
MAUSER-BAUER MODEL 496 589
MAUSER-BAUER MODEL 496 COMPETITION GRADE 589
MAUSER-BAUER MODEL 580 ST. VINCENT 589
MAUSER-BAUER MODEL 610 PHANTOM 589
MAUSER-BAUER MODEL 610 SKEET 589
MAUSER-BAUER MODEL 620 589

MAVERICK

MAVERICK MODEL 60 590
MAVERICK MODEL 88 590
MAVERICK MODEL 88 COMBAT 590
MAVERICK MODEL 88 SECURITY 590
MAVERICK MODEL 91 ACCU-MAG 590
MAVERICK MODEL 95 590

MERCURY

MERCURY MAGNUM 590

MERKEL

MERKEL MODEL 8 590
MERKEL MODEL 47E 590
MERKEL MODEL 47LSC SPORTING CLAYS 590
MERKEL MODEL 47S 590
MERKEL MODEL 47SL, 147SL SIDE-BY-SIDES 590
MERKEL MODEL 280EL AND 360EL SHOTGUNS 590
MERKEL MODEL 280SL AND 360SL SHOTGUNS 590
MERKEL MODEL 100 591
MERKEL MODEL 101 591
MERKEL MODEL 101E 591
MERKEL MODEL 122 591
MERKEL MODEL 127 591
MERKEL MODEL 130 591
MERKEL MODEL 147 591
MERKEL MODEL 147E 591
MERKEL MODEL 147S 591
MERKEL MODEL 200 591
MERKEL MODEL 200E 591
MERKEL MODEL 200E SKEET 591
MERKEL MODEL 200ET TRAP 591
MERKEL MODEL 200SC SPORTING CLAYS 591
MERKEL MODEL 201 591
MERKEL MODEL 201E 591
MERKEL MODEL 201E (RECENT) 592
MERKEL MODEL 201ES 592
MERKEL MODEL 201ET 592
MERKEL MODEL 202 592
MERKEL MODEL 202E 592
MERKEL MODEL 202E (RECENT) 592
MERKEL MODEL 203 592
MERKEL MODEL 203E 592
MERKEL MODEL 203ES 592
MERKEL MODEL 203ET 592
MERKEL MODEL 204E 592
MERKEL MODEL 210 592
MERKEL MODEL 247S 592
MERKEL MODEL 300 592
MERKEL MODEL 300E 592
MERKEL MODEL 301 592
MERKEL MODEL 301E 592
MERKEL MODEL 302 592
MERKEL MODEL 303E 592
MERKEL MODEL 304E 592
MERKEL MODEL 310E 592
MERKEL MODEL 347S 592
MERKEL MODEL 400 593
MERKEL MODEL 400E 593
MERKEL MODEL 410 593
MERKEL MODEL 410E 593
MERKEL MODEL 447S 593
MERKEL MODEL 2001EL 593
MERKEL MODEL 303EL 593
MERKEL MODEL 2002 EL 593
MERKEL 1622 593
MERKEL 1622E 593
MERKEL 1622EL 593
MERKEL 2000CL 593
MERKEL 2000CL SPORTER 593

MIIDA

MIIDA MODEL 612 593
MIIDA MODEL 2100 SKEET 593
MIIDA MODEL 2200S SKEET 593
MIIDA MODEL 2200T TRAP 593
MIIDA MODEL 2300S SKEET 593
MIIDA MODEL 2300T TRAP 593
MIIDA MODEL GRANDEE GRS SKEET 594
MIIDA MODEL GRANDEE GRT TRAP 594

MITCHELL

MITCHELL HIGH STANDARD MODEL 9104 594
MITCHELL HIGH STANDARD MODEL 9104-CT 594
MITCHELL HIGH STANDARD MODEL 9105 594
MITCHELL HIGH STANDARD MODEL 9108-B 594
MITCHELL HIGH STANDARD MODEL 9108-BL 594
MITCHELL HIGH STANDARD MODEL 9108-CT 594
MITCHELL HIGH STANDARD MODEL 9108-HG-B 594
MITCHELL HIGH STANDARD MODEL 9108-HG-BL 594
MITCHELL HIGH STANDARD MODEL 9109 594
MITCHELL HIGH STANDARD MODEL 9111-B 594
MITCHELL HIGH STANDARD MODEL 9111-BL 594
MITCHELL HIGH STANDARD MODEL 9111-CT 594
MITCHELL HIGH STANDARD MODEL 9113-B 594
MITCHELL HIGH STANDARD MODEL 9114-PG 594
MITCHELL HIGH STANDARD MODEL 9115 595
MITCHELL HIGH STANDARD MODEL 9115-CT 595
MITCHELL HIGH STANDARD MODEL 9115-HG 595

MONTE CARLO

MONTE CARLO SINGLE 595

MOSSBERG

MOSSBERG MODEL 1000 595
MOSSBERG MODEL 1000 JUNIOR 595
MOSSBERG MODEL 1000 SKEET 595
MOSSBERG MODEL 1000 SLUG 595
MOSSBERG MODEL 1000 SUPER 595
MOSSBERG MODEL 1000 SUPER SKEET 595
MOSSBERG MODEL 1000 SUPER TRAP 595
MOSSBERG MODEL 1000 SUPER WATERFOWLER 595
MOSSBERG MODEL 5500 595
MOSSBERG MODEL 5500 MKII 595
MOSSBERG MODEL 5500 MARK II CAMO 595
MOSSBERG MODEL 6000 595
MOSSBERG MODEL 9200 CROWN GRADE 595
MOSSBERG MODEL 9200 CROWN GRADE CAMO 595
MOSSBERG MODEL 9200 NWTF EDITION 596
MOSSBERG MODEL 9200 REGAL 596
MOSSBERG MODEL 9200 USST 596
MOSSBERG SLIDE-ACTION SHOTGUNS 596
MOSSBERG HOME SECURITY 410 596
MOSSBERG MODEL HS410 SHOTGUN 596
MOSSBERG MODEL 200D 596
MOSSBERG MODEL 200K 596
MOSSBERG MODEL 500 596
MOSSBERG MODEL 500AGVD 596
MOSSBERG MODEL 500AHT (HI-RIB TRAP) 596
MOSSBERG MODEL 500AHTD (HI-RIB TRAP) 596
MOSSBERG MODEL 500ALD 596
MOSSBERG MODEL 500 ALMR (HEAVY DUCK) 596
MOSSBERG MODEL 500ALS SLUGSTER 596
MOSSBERG MODEL 500ASG SLUGSTER 596
MOSSBERG MODEL 500APR PIGEON GRADE TRAP 596
MOSSBERG MODEL 500 BANTAM 596
MOSSBERG MODEL 500 BULLPUP 596
MOSSBERG MODEL 500 CAMO 596
MOSSBERG MODEL 500 CAMPER 597
MOSSBERG MODEL 500CLD 597
MOSSBERG MODEL 500CLDR 597
MOSSBERG MODEL 500CLS SLUGSTER 597
MOSSBERG MODEL 500E 597
MOSSBERG MODEL 500EGV 597
MOSSBERG MODEL 500EL 597
MOSSBERG MODEL 500ELR 597
MOSSBERG MODEL 500 GHOST RING 597
MOSSBERG MODEL 500 INTIMIDATOR 597
MOSSBERG MODEL 500 MARINER 597
MOSSBERG MODEL 500 MEDALLION 597
MOSSBERG MODEL 500 MUZZLELOADER COMBO 597

MOSSBERG MODEL 500 PERSUADER . . . 597
MOSSBERG MODEL 500 SECURITY SERIES . . . 597
MOSSBERG MODEL 500 SPECIAL PURPOSE . . . 597
MOSSBERG MODEL 500 SUPER GRADE . . . 597
MOSSBERG MODEL 500 TROPHY SLUGSTER . . . 598
MOSSBERG MODEL 500 TURKEY . . . 598
MOSSBERG MODEL 500 ROLLING THUNDER . . . 598
MOSSBERG MODEL 500 JIC (JUST IN CASE) . . . 598
MOSSBERG 510 MINI BANTAM . . . 598
MOSSBERG MODEL 590 SPECIAL PURPOSE SHOTGUNS . . . 598
MOSSBERG MODEL 590 . . . 598
MOSSBERG 590DA DOUBLE-ACTION PUMP SHOTGUN . . . 598
MOSSBERG MODEL 590 BULLPUP . . . 598
MOSSBERG MODEL 590 GHOST RING . . . 598
MOSSBERG MODEL 590 INTIMIDATOR . . . 598
MOSSBERG MODEL 590 MARINER . . . 598
MOSSBERG 930 SPECIAL PURPOSE SERIES . . . 598
MOSSBERG MODEL 930 TACTICAL . . . 598
MOSSBERG MODEL 935 MAGNUM . . . 599
MOSSBERG MODEL 835 AMERICAN FIELD . . . 599
MOSSBERG MODEL 835 ULTI-MAG . . . 599
MOSSBERG MODEL 835 ULTI-MAG CROWN GRADE . . . 599
MOSSBERG MODEL 835 ULTI-MAG . . . 599
MOSSBERG 835 ULTI-MAG SPECIAL PURPOSE SERIES . . . 599
MOSSBERG MODEL 835 SYNTHETIC STOCK . . . 599
MOSSBERG 835 ULTI-MAG THUMBHOLE TURKEY . . . 599
MOSSBERG 835 ULTI-MAG TACTICAL TURKEY . . . 599
MOSSBERG MODEL SA-20 . . . 599
MOSSBERG MODEL 70 . . . 599
MOSSBERG MODEL 73 . . . 599
MOSSBERG MODEL 75 . . . 599
MOSSBERG MODEL 80 . . . 599
MOSSBERG MODEL 83D . . . 600
MOSSBERG MODEL 85 . . . 600
MOSSBERG MODEL 85D . . . 600
MOSSBERG MODEL 173 . . . 600
MOSSBERG MODEL 173Y . . . 600
MOSSBERG MODEL 183D . . . 600
MOSSBERG MODEL 183K . . . 600
MOSSBERG MODEL 185D . . . 600
MOSSBERG MODEL 185K . . . 600
MOSSBERG MODEL 190D . . . 600
MOSSBERG MODEL 190K . . . 600
MOSSBERG MODEL 195D . . . 600
MOSSBERG MODEL 195K . . . 600
MOSSBERG MODEL 385K . . . 600
MOSSBERG MODEL 390K . . . 600
MOSSBERG MODEL 395K . . . 600
MOSSBERG MODEL 695 SLUGSTER . . . 600
MOSSBERG SSI-ONE 12-GAUGE SLUG . . . 600
MOSSBERG SSI-ONE TURKEY SHOTGUN . . . 600
MOSSBERG ONYX RESERVE SPORTING . . . 600
MOSSBERG SILVER RESERVE SIDE-BY-SIDE . . . 600
MOSSBERG ONYX RESERVE SPORTING SXS . . . 600
MOSSBERG SILVER RESERVE FIELD OVER/UNDER . . . 600
ONYX RESERVE SIDE-BY-SIDE . . . 600

NAVY ARMS

NAVY ARMS MODEL 83 BIRD HUNTER . . . 600
NAVY ARMS MODEL 93 . . . 600
NAVY ARMS MODEL 95 . . . 601
NAVY ARMS MODEL 96 . . . 601
NAVY ARMS MODEL 100 SXS . . . 601
NAVY ARMS MODEL 100 O/U . . . 601
NAVY ARMS MODEL 105 . . . 601
NAVY ARMS MODEL 105 DELUXE . . . 601
NAVY ARMS MODEL 150 . . . 601
NAVY ARMS MODEL 600 . . . 601
NEW ENGLAND FIREARMS
NEW ENGLAND FIREARMS CAMO TURKEY SHOTGUNS . . . 601
NEW ENGLAND FIREARMS HANDI-RIFLE . . . 601
NEW ENGLAND FIREARMS PARDNER . . . 601
NEW ENGLAND FIREARMS PARDNER DELUXE . . . 601
NEW ENGLAND FIREARMS PARDNER SPECIAL PURPOSE . . . 601
NEW ENGLAND FIREARMS PARDNER YOUTH . . . 601
NEW ENGLAND FIREARMS SPECIAL PURPOSE SHOTGUNS . . . 601
NEW ENGLAND FIREARMS SURVIVOR . . . 601
NEW ENGLAND FIREARMS TRACKER SLUG GUN . . . 601
NEW ENGLAND FIREARMS TRACKER II SLUG GUN . . . 601
NEW ENGLAND FIREARMS TURKEY/GOOSE GUN . . . 601
NEW ENGLAND FIREARMS TURKEY/GOOSE N.W.T.F. . . . 601
NEW ENGLAND FIREARMS TURKEY/GOOSE SPECIAL . . . 601
NEW ENGLAND FIREARMS/H&R 1871 TOPPER . . . 601
NEW ENGLAND FIREARMS TOPPER DELUXE CLASSIC . . . 601
NEW ENGLAND FIREARMS TOPPER DELUXE . . . 602
NEW ENGLAND FIREARMS TOPPER JUNIOR . . . 602
NEW ENGLAND FIREARMS TOPPER JUNIOR CLASSIC . . . 602
NEW ENGLAND FIREARMS EXCELL . . . 602
NEW ENGLAND FIREARMS EXCELL WATERFOWL . . . 602
NEW ENGLAND FIREARMS EXCELL TURKEY . . . 602
NEW ENGLAND FIREARMS EXCELL COMBO . . . 602
NEW ENGLAND FIREARMS PARDNER PUMP WALNUT . . . 602
NEW ENGLAND FIREARMS PARDNER PUMP SYNTHETIC . . . 602
NEW ENGLAND FIREARMS PARDNER PUMP FIELD . . . 602
NEW ENGLAND FIREARMS PARDNER PUMP COMPACT FIELD . . . 602
NEW ENGLAND FIREARMS PARDNER PUMP COMPACT WALNUT SHOTGUN . . . 602
NEW ENGLAND FIREARMS P ARDNER PUMP COMPACT SYNTHETIC . . . 602
NEW ENGLAND FIREARMS PARDNER PUMP COMBO . . . 602
NEW ENGLAND FIREARMS SPECIAL PURPOSE . . . 602
NEW ENGLAND FIREARMS PARDNER PUMP PROTECTOR . . . 602
NEW ENGLAND FIREARMS PARDNER PUMP COMBO . . . 602
NEW ENGLAND FIREARMS PARDNER PUMP TURKEY . . . 602

NEW HAVEN

NEW HAVEN MODEL 273 . . . 602
NEW HAVEN MODEL 283 . . . 602
NEW HAVEN MODEL 285 . . . 602
NEW HAVEN MODEL 290 . . . 602
NEW HAVEN MODEL 295 . . . 602
NEW HAVEN MODEL 495 . . . 602
NEW HAVEN MODEL 600 . . . 603
NEW HAVEN MODEL 600AST SLUGSTER . . . 603
NEW HAVEN MODEL 600ETV . . . 603
NEW HAVEN MODEL 600K . . . 603

NOBLE

NOBLE MODEL 40 . . . 603
NOBLE MODEL 50 . . . 603
NOBLE MODEL 60 . . . 603
NOBLE MODEL 60ACP . . . 603
NOBLE MODEL 60AF . . . 603
NOBLE MODEL 65 . . . 603
NOBLE MODEL 66CLP . . . 603
NOBLE MODEL 66RCLP . . . 603
NOBLE MODEL 66RLP . . . 603
NOBLE MODEL 66XL . . . 603
NOBLE MODEL 70 . . . 603
NOBLE MODEL 70CLP . . . 603
NOBLE MODEL 70RCLP . . . 603
NOBLE MODEL 70RLP . . . 603
NOBLE MODEL 70X . . . 604
NOBLE MODEL 70XL . . . 604
NOBLE MODEL 80 . . . 604
NOBLE MODEL 160 DEERGUN . . . 604
NOBLE MODEL 166L DEERGUN . . . 604
NOBLE MODEL 390 DEERGUN . . . 604
NOBLE MODEL 420 . . . 604
NOBLE MODEL 420EK . . . 604
NOBLE MODEL 450E . . . 604
NOBLE MODEL 520 . . . 604
NOBLE MODEL 550 . . . 604
NOBLE MODEL 602 . . . 604
NOBLE MODEL 602CLP . . . 604
NOBLE MODEL 602RCLP . . . 604
NOBLE MODEL 602RLP . . . 604
NOBLE MODEL 602XL . . . 604
NOBLE MODEL 662 . . . 604
NOBLE MODEL 757 . . . 604
NOBLE SERIES 200 . . . 604
NOBLE SERIES 300 . . . 605
NOBLE SERIES 400 . . . 605

NORINCO

NORINCO TYPE HL12-203 . . . 605
NORINCO MODEL 99 COACH GUN . . . 605
NORINCO MODEL 87L . . . 605
NORINCO MODEL 2000 FIELD . . . 605
NORINCO MODEL 2000 DEFENSE . . . 605
NORINCO TYPE HL12-102 . . . 605
NORINCO MODEL 984/985/987 . . . 605
NORINCO MODEL 97W HAMMER . . . 605
NORINCO MODEL 97T TRENCH GUN . . . 605
NORINCO MODEL 981/982T . . . 605
NORINCO MODEL 983 . . . 605

OMEGA

OMEGA FOLDING OVER/UNDER . . . 605
OMEGA FOLDING OVER/UNDER DELUXE . . . 605
OMEGA FOLDING SIDE-BY-SIDE . . . 605
OMEGA FOLDING SIDE-BY-SIDE DELUXE . . . 605
OMEGA FOLDING SINGLE BARREL . . . 605
OMEGA FOLDING SINGLE BARREL DELUXE . . . 605

PARKER

PARKER HAMMERLESS DOUBLE . . . 605
PARKER SINGLE-BARREL TRAP . . . 606
PARKER TROJAN . . . 606
PARKER REPRODUCTIONS GRADE A-1 SPECIAL . . . 606
PARKER REPRODUCTIONS GRADE BHE . . . 606
PARKER REPRODUCTIONS GRADE DHE . . . 606

PARKER-HALE

PARKER-HALE MODEL 630 . . . 606
PARKER-HALE MODEL 640A . . . 607
PARKER-HALE MODEL 640E . . . 607
PARKER-HALE MODEL 640M . . . 607
PARKER-HALE MODEL 640 SLUG . . . 607
PARKER-HALE MODEL 645A . . . 607
PARKER-HALE MODEL 645E . . . 607
PARKER-HALE MODEL 645E-XXV . . . 607
PARKER-HALE MODEL 650A . . . 607
PARKER-HALE MODEL 650E . . . 607
PARKER-HALE MODEL 655A . . . 607
PARKER-HALE MODEL 655E . . . 607
PARKER-HALE MODEL 670E . . . 607
PARKER-HALE MODEL 680E-XXV . . . 607

PARQUEMY

PARQUEMY MODEL 48 . . . 607

PARQUEMY MODEL 48E . . . 607

PEDERSEN

PEDERSEN MODEL 1000 . . . 607
PEDERSEN 1000 MAGNUM . . . 607
PEDERSEN MODEL 1000 SKEET . . . 607
PEDERSEN MODEL 1000 TRAP . . . 607
PEDERSEN MODEL 1500 . . . 607
PEDERSEN MODEL 1500 SKEET . . . 608
PEDERSEN MODEL 1500 TRAP . . . 608
PEDERSEN MODEL 2000 . . . 608
PEDERSEN MODEL 2500 . . . 608
PEDERSEN MODEL 4000 . . . 608
PEDERSEN MODEL 4000 TRAP . . . 608
PEDERSEN MODEL 4500 . . . 608
PEDERSEN MODEL 4500 TRAP . . . 608

PERAZZI

PERAZZI COMPETITION I SINGLE BARREL TRAP . . . 608
PERAZZI COMPETITION I SKEET . . . 608
PERAZZI COMPETITION I TRAP . . . 608
PERAZZI COMPETITION IV TRAP . . . 608
PERAZZI DB81 SPECIAL AMERICAN TRAP COMBO . . . 608
PERAZZI DB81 SPECIAL AMERICAN TRAP SINGLE BARREL . . . 608
PERAZZI DB81 SPECIAL TRAP O/U . . . 608
PERAZZI GRAND AMERICAN 88 SPECIAL AMERICAN TRAP COMBO . . . 609
PERAZZI GRAND AMERICAN 88 SPECIAL AMERICAN TRAP SINGLE BARREL . . . 609
PERAZZI GRAND AMERICAN 88 SPECIAL TRAP O/U . . . 609
PERAZZI LIGHT GAME MODEL . . . 609
PERAZZI MIRAGE CLASSIC SPORTING O/U . . . 609
PERAZZI MIRAGE LIVE BIRD (EARLY MFG.) . . . 609
PERAZZI MIRAGE SKEET (EARLY MFG.) . . . 609
PERAZZI MIRAGE TRAP (EARLY MFG.) . . . 609
PERAZZI MIRAGE PIGEON-ELECTROCIBLES O/U . . . 609
PERAZZI MIRAGE SKEET O/U . . . 609
PERAZZI MIRAGE TRAP O/U . . . 609
PERAZZI MIRAGE SPECIAL PIGEON-ELECTROCIBLES O/U . . . 609
PERAZZI MIRAGE SPECIAL SKEET O/U . . . 610
PERAZZI MIRAGE SPECIAL SPORTING O/U . . . 610
PERAZZI MIRAGE SPECIAL TRAP O/U . . . 610
PERAZZI MT-6 SKEET . . . 610
PERAZZI MT-6 TRAP . . . 610
PERAZZI MT-6 TRAP COMBO . . . 610
PERAZZI MX1B PIGEON-ELECTROCIBLES O/U . . . 610
PERAZZI MX1B SPORTING O/U . . . 610
PERAZZI MX3 SPECIAL AMERICAN TRAP COMBO . . . 610
PERAZZI MX3 SPECIAL AMERICAN TRAP SINGLE BARREL . . . 610
PERAZZI MX3 SPECIAL SKEET O/U . . . 610
PERAZZI MX3 SPECIAL SPORTING O/U . . . 611
PERAZZI MX3 SPECIAL TRAP O/U . . . 611
PERAZZI MX6 AMERICAN TRAP SINGLE BARREL . . . 611
PERAZZI MX6 SKEET O/U . . . 611
PERAZZI MX6 SPORTING O/U . . . 611
PERAZZI MX6 TRAP O/U . . . 611
PERAZZI MX7 AMERICAN TRAP SINGLE BARREL . . . 611
PERAZZI MX7 SKEET O/U . . . 611
PERAZZI MX7 SPORTING O/U . . . 611
PERAZZI MX7 TRAP O/U . . . 611
PERAZZI MX8 OVER/UNDER SHOTGUNS . . . 611
PERAZZI MX8 GAME O/U . . . 611
PERAZZI MX8 SKEET O/U . . . 611
PERAZZI MX8 TRAP O/U . . . 611
PERAZZI MX8 TRAP COMBO . . . 611
PERAZZI MX8/MX8 SPECIAL TRAP, SKEET . . . 612
PERAZZI MX8 SPECIAL SKEET OVER/UNDER . . . 612
PERAZZI MX8/20 OVER/UNDER SHOTGUN . . . 612
PERAZZI MX8 SPECIAL AMERICAN TRAP COMBO . . . 612
PERAZZI MX8 SPECIAL AMERICAN TRAP SINGLE BARREL . . . 612
PERAZZI MX8 SPECIAL SKEET O/U . . . 612
PERAZZI MX8 SPECIAL SPORTING O/U . . . 612
PERAZZI MX8 SPECIAL TRAP O/U . . . 612
PERAZZI MX9 AMERICAN TRAP COMBO . . . 612
PERAZZI MX9 AMERICAN TRAP SINGLE BARREL . . . 612
PERAZZI MX9 TRAP O/U . . . 612
PERAZZI MX10 OVER/UNDER SHOTGUN . . . 613
PERAZZI MX10 AMERICAN TRAP COMBO . . . 613
PERAZZI MX10 AMERICAN TRAP SINGLE BARREL . . . 613
PERAZZI MX10 PIGEON-ELECTROCIBLES O/U . . . 613
PERAZZI MX10 SKEET O/U . . . 613
PERAZZI MX10 SPORTING O/U . . . 613
PERAZZI MX10 TRAP O/U . . . 613
PERAZZI MX11 AMERICAN TRAP COMBO . . . 613
PERAZZI MX11 AMERICAN TRAP SINGLE BARREL . . . 613
PERAZZI MX11 PIGEON-ELECTROCIBLES O/U . . . 613
PERAZZI MX11 SKEET O/U . . . 613
PERAZZI MX11 SPORTING O/U . . . 613
PERAZZI MX11 TRAP O/U . . . 613
PERAZZI MX12 HUNTING OVER/UNDER . . . 613
PERAZZI MX20 HUNTING OVER/UNDER . . . 613
PERAZZI MX12 GAME O/U . . . 613
PERAZZI MX14 AMERICAN TRAP SINGLE BARREL . . . 613
PERAZZI MX20 GAME O/U . . . 613
PERAZZI MX28, MX410 GAME O/U SHOTGUNS . . . 614
PERAZZI MX28 GAME O/U . . . 614
PERAZZI MX410 GAME O/U . . . 614
PERAZZI SINGLE BARREL TRAP . . . 614
PERAZZI TM1 SPECIAL AMERICAN TRAP SINGLE BARREL . . . 614
PERAZZI TMX SPECIAL AMERICAN TRAP SINGLE BARREL . . . 614

PERUGINI-VISINI

PERUGINI-VISINI CLASSIC DOUBLE . . . 614
PERUGINI-VISINI LIBERTY DOUBLE . . . 614
PERUGINI-VISINI AUSONIA . . . 614
PERUGINI-VISINI REGINA . . . 614
PERUGINI-VISINI ROMAGNA HAMMER GUN . . . 614
PERUGINI-VISINI NOVA . . . 614

PIOTTI

PIOTTI BOSS OVER/UNDER . . . 614
PIOTTI KING NO. 1 . . . 614
PIOTTI KING NO. 1 EELL . . . 614
PIOTTI KING NO. 1 EXTRA . . . 614
PIOTTI LUNIK . . . 615
PIOTTI MONTE CARLO . . . 615
PIOTTI PIUMA . . . 615
PIOTTI WESTLAKE . . . 615
PIOTTI HAMMER GUN . . . 615
PIOTTI KING EXTRA . . . 615

PRECISION SPORTS

PRECISION SPORTS MODEL 640A . . . 615
PRECISION SPORTS MODEL 640E . . . 615
PRECISION SPORTS MODEL 600 ENGLISH SERIES . . . 615
PRECISION SPORTS MODEL 640M BIG TEN . . . 615
PRECISION SPORTS MODEL 640 SLUG GUN . . . 615
PRECISION SPORTS MODEL 645A . . . 615
PRECISION SPORTS MODEL 645E . . . 615
PRECISION SPORTS MODEL 645E-XXV . . . 615
PRECISION SPORTS MODEL 650A . . . 615
PRECISION SPORTS MODEL 650E . . . 615
PRECISION SPORTS MODEL 655A . . . 616
PRECISION SPORTS MODEL 655E . . . 616
PRECISION SPORTS MODEL 800 AMERICAN SERIES . . . 616

PREMIER

PREMIER AMBASSADOR . . . 616
PREMIER BRUSH KING . . . 616
PREMIER CONTINENTAL . . . 616
PREMIER MONARCH SUPREME . . . 616
PREMIER PRESENTATION CUSTOM GRADE . . . 616
PREMIER REGENT . . . 616
PREMIER REGENT MAGNUM . . . 616

PURDEY

PURDEY SIDE-BY-SIDE . . . 616
PURDEY OVER/UNDER . . . 616
PURDEY SINGLE BARREL TRAP . . . 616

REMINGTON

REMINGTON MODEL 11A . . . 617
REMINGTON MODEL 11B SPECIAL . . . 617
REMINGTON MODEL 11D TOURNAMENT . . . 617
REMINGTON MODEL 11E EXPERT . . . 617
REMINGTON MODEL 11F PREMIER . . . 617
REMINGTON MODEL 11R RIOT GUN . . . 617
REMINGTON MODEL 11-48A . . . 617
REMINGTON MODEL 11-48A RIOT . . . 617
REMINGTON MODEL 11-48B SPECIAL . . . 617
REMINGTON MODEL 11-48D TOURNAMENT . . . 617
REMINGTON MODEL 11-48F PREMIER . . . 617
REMINGTON MODEL 11-48 RSS SLUG GUN . . . 617
REMINGTON MODEL 11-48SA SKEET . . . 617
REMINGTON MODEL 11-87 PREMIER . . . 617
REMINGTON MODEL 11-87 PREMIER 175TH ANNIVERSARY . . . 617
REMINGTON MODEL 11-87 PREMIER N.W.T.F. . . . 617
REMINGTON MODEL 11-87 PREMIER SKEET . . . 617
REMINGTON MODEL 11-87 PREMIER SPECIAL PURPOSE DEER GUN . . . 617
REMINGTON MODEL 11-87 PREMIER SPECIAL PURPOSE MAGNUM . . . 617
REMINGTON MODEL 11-87 PREMIER SPECIAL PURPOSE SYNTHETIC CAMO . . . 618
REMINGTON MODEL 11-87 PREMIER SPORTING CLAYS . . . 618
REMINGTON MODEL 11-87 SP AND SPS SUPER MAGNUM SHOTGUNS . . . 618
REMINGTON MODEL 11-87 PREMIER SPS-BG-CAMO DEER/TURKEY . . . 618
REMINGTON MODEL 11-87 PREMIER SPS CANTILEVER . . . 618
REMINGTON MODEL 11-87 PREMIER SPS-DEER . . . 618
REMINGTON MODEL 11-87 SPS CANTILEVER SHOTGUN . . . 618
REMINGTON MODEL 11-87 PREMIER SPS-T CAMO . . . 618
REMINGTON MODEL 11-87 SPS-T TURKEY CAMO . . . 618
REMINGTON MODEL 11-87 SPS-T SUPER MAGNUM SYNTHETIC CAMO . . . 618
REMINGTON MODEL 11-87 PREMIER TRAP . . . 618
REMINGTON MODEL 11-87 UPLAND SPECIAL . . . 619

REMINGTON MODEL 11-87 SPORTSMAN . . . 619
REMINGTON MODEL 11-87 SPORTSMAN NRA EDITION . . . 619
REMINGTON MODEL 11-87 SPORTSMAN CAMO . . . 619
REMINGTON MODEL 11-87 SPORTSMAN CAMO RIFLED . . . 619
REMINGTON MODEL 11-87 SPORTSMAN CAMO YOUTH . . . 619
REMINGTON MODEL 11-87 SPS SUPER MAGNUM WATERFOWL . . . 619
REMINGTON MODEL 11-87 SP-T THUMBHOLE . . . 619
REMINGTON MODEL 11-87 SP THUMBHOLE . . . 619
REMINGTON MODEL 11-87 SPS-T SUPER MAGNUM . . . 619
REMINGTON MODEL 11-87 SPORTSMAN SUPER MAG SHURSHOT TURKEY . . . 619
REMINGTON MODEL 11-87 SPORTSMAN SUPER MAGNUM WATERFOWL . . . 619
REMINGTON MODEL 11-87 SPORTSMAN SHURSHOT CANTILEVER . . . 619
REMINGTON MODEL 11-96 EURO LIGHTWEIGHT . . . 619
REMINGTON MODEL 878A AUTOMASTER . . . 619
REMINGTON MODEL 1100D TOURNAMENT . . . 619
REMINGTON MODEL 1100 DEER . . . 620
REMINGTON MODEL 1100 DEER SPECIAL PURPOSE . . . 620
REMINGTON MODEL 1100 DEER CANTILEVER 20-GAUGE . . . 620
REMINGTON MODEL 1100F PREMIER . . . 620
REMINGTON MODEL 1100F PREMIER GOLD . . . 620
REMINGTON MODEL 1100 FIELD . . . 620
REMINGTON MODEL 1100 FIELD COLLECTORS EDITION . . . 620
REMINGTON MODEL 1100 SPECIAL FIELD . . . 620
REMINGTON MODEL 1100 LIGHTWEIGHT MAGNUM . . . 620
REMINGTON MODEL 1100 LT-20 . . . 620
REMINGTON MODEL 1100 LT-20 SYNTHETIC . . . 620
REMINGTON MODEL 1100 YOUTH GUN LT-20 . . . 620
REMINGTON MODEL 1100 YOUTH SYNTHETIC TURKEY CAMO . . . 620
REMINGTON MODEL 1100 LT-20 SYNTHETIC DEER . . . 620
REMINGTON MODEL 1100 SYNTHETIC . . . 620
REMINGTON MODEL 1100 LT-20 TOURNAMENT SKEET . . . 620
REMINGTON MODEL 1100 MAGNUM DUCK GUN . . . 621
REMINGTON MODEL 1100 MAGNUM SPECIAL PURPOSE . . . 621
REMINGTON MODEL 1100 SPORTING 28 . . . 621
REMINGTON MODEL 1100 SPORTING 20 . . . 621
REMINGTON MODEL 1100 CLASSIC TRAP . . . 621
REMINGTON MODEL 1100 SPORTING 12 . . . 621
REMINGTON MODEL 1100 SYNTHETIC DEER . . . 621
REMINGTON MODEL 1100SA SKEET . . . 621
REMINGTON MODEL 1100SC SKEET . . . 621
REMINGTON MODEL 1100TA TRAP . . . 621
REMINGTON MODEL 1100TB TRAP . . . 621
REMINGTON MODEL 1100TD TRAP TOURNAMENT . . . 621
REMINGTON MODEL 1100 YOUTH . . . 621
REMINGTON MODEL 1100 TACTICAL SPEEDFEED IV . . . 621
REMINGTON MODEL 1100 TACTICAL STANDARD STOCK . . . 621
REMINGTON MODEL 1100 G3 . . . 621
REMINGTON MODEL 1100 COMPETITION . . . 622
REMINGTON MODEL 1100 PREMIER SPORTING . . . 622
REMINGTON MODEL 105CTI . . . 622
REMINGTON SP-10 MAGNUM . . . 622
REMINGTON SP-10 MAGNUM CAMO . . . 622
REMINGTON SP-10 MAGNUM TURKEY COMBO . . . 622
REMINGTON MODEL SP-10 MAGNUM WATERFOWL . . . 622
REMINGTON MODEL SP-10 MAGNUM THUMBHOLE CAMO . . . 622
REMINGTON VERSA MAX . . . 622
REMINGTON SPORTSMAN AUTO . . . 622
REMINGTON SPORTSMAN MODEL 48A . . . 622
REMINGTON SPORTSMAN MODEL 48B SPECIAL . . . 622
REMINGTON SPORTSMAN MODEL 48D TOURNAMENT . . . 622
REMINGTON SPORTSMAN MODEL 48F PREMIER . . . 623
REMINGTON SPORTSMAN MODEL 48SA SKEET . . . 623
REMINGTON SPORTSMAN MODEL 48SC SKEET TARGET . . . 623
REMINGTON MODEL 48SF SKEET PREMIER . . . 623
REMINGTON SPORTSMAN MODEL 58ADL . . . 623
REMINGTON SPORTSMAN MODEL 58BDL DELUXE SPECIAL . . . 623
REMINGTON SPORTSMAN MODEL 58D TOURNAMENT . . . 623
REMINGTON SPORTSMAN MODEL 58F PREMIER . . . 623
REMINGTON SPORTSMAN MODEL 58SA SKEET . . . 623
REMINGTON SPORTSMAN MODEL 58SC SKEET TARGET . . . 623
REMINGTON SPORTSMAN MODEL 58SD SKEET TOURNAMENT . . . 623
REMINGTON SPORTSMAN MODEL 58SF SKEET PREMIER . . . 623
REMINGTON MODEL 10A . . . 623
REMINGTON MODEL 17A . . . 623
REMINGTON MODEL 29A . . . 623
REMINGTON MODEL 29S TRAP SPECIAL . . . 623
REMINGTON MODEL 31A . . . 623
REMINGTON MODEL 31B SPECIAL . . . 623
REMINGTON MODEL 31D TOURNAMENT . . . 623
REMINGTON MODEL 31E EXPERT . . . 623
REMINGTON MODEL 31F PREMIER . . . 623
REMINGTON MODEL 31H HUNTER'S SPECIAL . . . 623
REMINGTON MODEL 31R RIOT GUN . . . 624
REMINGTON MODEL 31S TRAP SPECIAL . . . 624
REMINGTON MODEL 31 SKEET . . . 624
REMINGTON MODEL 31TC TRAP . . . 624
REMINGTON MODEL 870ADL WINGMASTER . . . 624
REMINGTON MODEL 870 ALL-AMERICAN TRAP . . . 624
REMINGTON MODEL 870AP WINGMASTER . . . 624
REMINGTON MODEL 870AP WINGMASTER MAGNUM . . . 624
REMINGTON MODEL 870AP WINGMASTER MAGNUM DELUXE . . . 624
REMINGTON MODEL 870BDL WINGMASTER . . . 624
REMINGTON MODEL 870 BRUSHMASTER DELUXE . . . 624
REMINGTON MODEL 870 COMPETITION TRAP . . . 624
REMINGTON MODEL 870 EXPRESS . . . 624
REMINGTON MODEL 870 EXPRESS SYNTHETIC 18-INCH . . . 624
REMINGTON MODEL 870 SPS SUPER SLUG DEER GUN . . . 624
REMINGTON MODEL 870 EXPRESS YOUTH GUN . . . 624
REMINGTON MODEL 870 EXPRESS RIFLE-SIGHTED DEER GUN . . . 624
REMINGTON MODEL 870 EXPRESS DEER CANTILEVER . . . 625
REMINGTON MODEL 870 EXPRESS HD . . . 625
REMINGTON MODEL 870 EXPRESS SYNTHETIC . . . 625
REMINGTON MODEL 870 EXPRESS TURKEY . . . 625
REMINGTON MODEL 870 EXPRESS YOUTH . . . 625
REMINGTON MODEL 870 EXPRESS TURKEY/ EXPRESS YOUTH . . . 625
REMINGTON MODEL 870 EXPRESS SUPER MAGNUM . . . 625
REMINGTON MODEL 870 EXPRESS DEER/TURKEY COMBO . . . 625
REMINGTON MODEL 870 WINGMASTER . . . 625
REMINGTON MODEL 870 50TH ANNIVERSARY CLASSIC TRAP SHOTGUN . . . 625
REMINGTON MODEL 870 MARINE MAGNUM . . . 625
REMINGTON MODEL 870 WINGMASTER LW SMALL BORE . . . 625
REMINGTON MODEL 870 WINGMASTER SUPER MAGNUM . . . 626
REMINGTON MODEL 870 SPS-T SYNTHETIC CAMO . . . 626
REMINGTON MODEL 870 SPS SUPER MAGNUM CAMO . . . 626
REMINGTON MODEL 870 FIELD WINGMASTER . . . 626
REMINGTON MODEL 870 LIGHTWEIGHT . . . 626
REMINGTON MODEL 870 LIGHTWEIGHT MAGNUM . . . 626
REMINGTON MODEL 870 MAGNUM DUCK GUN . . . 626
REMINGTON MODEL 870 MARINE MAGNUM . . . 626
REMINGTON MODEL 870 POLICE . . . 626
REMINGTON MODEL 870SA SKEET . . . 626
REMINGTON MODEL 870SC SKEET TARGET . . . 626
REMINGTON MODEL 870SD SKEET TOURNAMENT . . . 626
REMINGTON MODEL 870SF SKEET PREMIER . . . 626
REMINGTON MODEL 870 SPECIAL FIELD . . . 626
REMINGTON MODEL 870 SPECIAL PURPOSE . . . 626
REMINGTON MODEL 870 SPECIAL PURPOSE DEER GUN . . . 626
REMINGTON MODEL 870 SPECIAL PURPOSE SYNTHETIC CAMO . . . 627
REMINGTON MODEL 870 SPS-BG-CAMO DEER/TURKEY . . . 627
REMINGTON MODEL 870 SPS CANTILEVER . . . 627
REMINGTON MODEL 870 SPS DEER . . . 627
REMINGTON MODEL 870 SPS SPECIAL PURPOSE MAGNUM . . . 627
REMINGTON MODEL 870 SPS-T CAMO . . . 627
REMINGTON MODEL 870TA TRAP . . . 627
REMINGTON MODEL 870TB TRAP . . . 627
REMINGTON MODEL 870TC TRAP . . . 627
REMINGTON MODEL 870 XCS MARINE MAGNUM . . . 627
REMINGTON MODEL 870 SPS MAX GOBBLER . . . 627
REMINGTON MODEL 870 TAC-2 SPECOPS . . . 627
REMINGTON MODEL 870 TAC-3 SPEEDFEED IV . . . 627
REMINGTON MODEL 870 TAC-3 FOLDER . . . 627
REMINGTON MODEL 870 SP-T THUMBHOLE . . . 627
REMINGTON MODEL 870 SPS-T SUPER MAG . . . 627
REMINGTON MODEL 870 SPS-T/20 . . . 627

REMINGTON MODEL 870 WINGMASTER NRA EDITION . . . 627
REMINGTON MODEL 870 SPECIAL PURPOSE THUMBHOLE . . . 627
REMINGTON MODEL 870 WINGMASTER 100TH ANNIVERSARY . . . 628
REMINGTON MODEL 870 EXPRESS MAGNUM SHURSHOT TURKEY . . . 628
REMINGTON MODEL 870 EXPRESS MAGNUM SHURSHOT CANTILEVER . . . 628
REMINGTON MODEL 870 EXPRESS SUPER MAGNUM WATERFOWL . . . 628
REMINGTON MODEL 870 SPS SHURSHOT TURKEY . . . 628
REMINGTON MODEL 870 TACTICAL DESERT RECON . . . 628
REMINGTON SPORTSMAN . . . 628
REMINGTON SPORTSMAN PUMP . . . 628
REMINGTON 90-T SUPER SINGLE . . . 628
REMINGTON RIDER NO. 3 . . . 628
REMINGTON RIDER NO. 9 . . . 628
REMINGTON MODEL 32A . . . 628
REMINGTON MODEL 32D TOURNAMENT . . . 629
REMINGTON MODEL 32 EXPERT . . . 629
REMINGTON MODEL 32F PREMIER . . . 629
REMINGTON MODEL 32 SKEET GRADE . . . 629
REMINGTON MODEL 32TC TRAP . . . 629
REMINGTON MODEL 332 . . . 629
REMINGTON MODEL 3200 . . . 629
REMINGTON MODEL 3200 COMPETITION SKEET . . . 629
REMINGTON MODEL 3200 COMPETITION TRAP . . . 629
REMINGTON MODEL 3200 MAGNUM . . . 629
REMINGTON MODEL 3200 SKEET . . . 629
REMINGTON MODEL 3200 SPECIAL TRAP . . . 629
REMINGTON MODEL 3200 TRAP . . . 629
REMINGTON PREMIER STS COMPETITION . . . 629
REMINGTON PREMIER FIELD GRADE . . . 629
REMINGTON PREMIER UPLAND GRADE . . . 630
REMINGTON MODEL 1882 . . . 630
REMINGTON MODEL 1889 . . . 630
REMINGTON MODEL 1894 . . . 630
REMINGTON MODEL 1894 TRAP . . . 630
REMINGTON MODEL 1900 . . . 630
REMINGTON PARKER AAHE 28 GAUGE OVER/UNDER SHOTGUN . . . 630
REMINGTON MODEL 1900 TRAP . . . 630
REMINGTON PEERLESS . . . 630

RHODE ISLAND ARMS

RHODE ISLAND ARMS MORONNE MODEL 46 . . . 630

RICHLAND

RICHLAND MODEL 200 . . . 630
RICHLAND MODEL 202 . . . 630
RICHLAND MODEL 707 DELUXE . . . 630
RICHLAND MODEL 711 MAGNUM . . . 631
RICHLAND MODEL 808 . . . 631
RICHLAND MODEL 828 . . . 631
RICHLAND MODEL 844 . . . 631

RIGBY

RIGBY BEST QUALITY SIDELOCK . . . 631
RIGBY SIDELOCK DOUBLE . . . 631
RIGBY BOXLOCK DOUBLE . . . 631

RIZZINI

RIZZINI S790 EMEL OVER/UNDER . . . 631
RIZZINI S792 EMEL OVER/UNDER . . . 631
RIZZINI UPLAND EL OVER/UNDER . . . 631
RIZZINI ARTEMIS OVER/UNDER . . . 631
RIZZINI S782 EMEL OVER/UNDER . . . 631
RIZZINI BOXLOCK . . . 631
RIZZINI SIDELOCK . . . 632

ROSSI

ROSSI MATCHED PAIR SINGLE-SHOT SHOTGUN/RIFLE . . . 632
ROSSI OVERLAND . . . 632
ROSSI SINGLE-SHOT SHOTGUN . . . 632
ROSSI TURKEY GUN . . . 632
ROSSI SQUIRE . . . 632

ROTTWEIL

ROTTWEIL MODEL 72 AMERICAN SKEET . . . 632
ROTTWEIL MODEL 72 AMERICAN TRAP SINGLE . . . 632
ROTTWEIL MODEL 72 AMERICAN TRAP COMBO . . . 632
ROTTWEIL MODEL 72 AMERICAN TRAP DOUBLE . . . 632
ROTTWEIL MODEL 72 FIELD SUPREME . . . 632
ROTTWEIL MODEL 72 INTERNATIONAL SKEET . . . 632
ROTTWEIL MODEL 72 INTERNATIONAL TRAP . . . 633
ROTTWEIL PARAGON OVER/UNDER . . . 633

ROYAL ARMS

ROYAL ARMS MODEL 87SC . . . 633
ROYAL ARMS MODEL 87T TRAP . . . 633

SAE

SAE MODEL 66C . . . 633
SAE MODEL 70 . . . 633
SAE MODEL 70 MULTICHOKE . . . 633
SAE MODEL 209E . . . 633
SAE MODEL 210S . . . 633
SAE MODEL 340X . . . 633

SAN MARCO

SAN MARCO 10-GAUGE . . . 633
SAN MARCO FIELD SPECIAL . . . 633
SAN MARCO WILDFOWLER . . . 633

SARASQUETA

SARASQUETA BOXLOCK DOUBLE . . . 633
SARASQUETA MODEL 119E . . . 633
SARASQUETA SIDELOCK DOUBLE . . . 633
SARASQUETA SUPER DELUXE . . . 634

SARRIUGARTE

SARRIUGARTE MODEL 101DS . . . 634
SARRIUGARTE MODEL 101E . . . 634
SARRIUGARTE MODEL 101E DS . . . 634
SARRIUGARTE MODEL 200 TRAP . . . 634
SARRIUGARTE MODEL 501E SPECIAL . . . 634
SARRIUGARTE MODEL 501E SPECIAL EXCELSIOR . . . 634
SARRIUGARTE MODEL 501E SPECIAL NIGER . . . 634

SARSILMAZ

SARSILMAZ SEMI-AUTOMATIC SHOTGUN . . . 634
SARSILMAZ PUMP SHOTGUN . . . 634
SARSILMAZ OVER/UNDER SHOTGUN . . . 634

SAUER

SAUER ARTEMIS MODEL . . . 634
SAUER MODEL BBF . . . 634
SAUER MODEL 66 FIELD . . . 635
SAUER MODEL 66 TRAP . . . 635
SAUER MODEL 66 SKEET . . . 635
SAUER ROYAL MODEL . . . 635

SAUER/FRANCHI

SAUER/FRANCHI STANDARD GRADE . . . 635
SAUER/FRANCHI SKEET . . . 635
SAUER/FRANCHI SPORTING S . . . 635
SAUER/FRANCHI TRAP . . . 635

SAVAGE

SAVAGE MODEL 24 . . . 635
SAVAGE MODEL 24DL . . . 635
SAVAGE MODEL 24M . . . 635
SAVAGE MODEL 24MDL . . . 635
SAVAGE MODEL 28A . . . 635
SAVAGE MODEL 28B . . . 635
SAVAGE MODEL 28D . . . 635
SAVAGE MODEL 30 . . . 635
SAVAGE MODEL 30AC . . . 636
SAVAGE MODEL 30ACL . . . 636
SAVAGE MODEL 30D . . . 636
SAVAGE MODEL 30FG . . . 636
SAVAGE MODEL 30 SLUG GUN . . . 636
SAVAGE MODEL 30T . . . 636
SAVAGE MODEL 210F MASTER SHOT SLUG GUN . . . 636
SAVAGE MODEL 220 . . . 636
SAVAGE MODEL 220AC . . . 636
SAVAGE MODEL 220L . . . 636
SAVAGE MODEL 220P . . . 636
SAVAGE MODEL 242 . . . 636
SAVAGE MODEL 312 FIELD . . . 636
SAVAGE MODEL 312SC SPORTING CLAYS . . . 636
SAVAGE MODEL 312T TRAP . . . 636
SAVAGE MODEL 320 . . . 636
SAVAGE MODEL 330 . . . 636
SAVAGE MODEL 333 . . . 636
SAVAGE MODEL 333T TRAP . . . 636
SAVAGE MODEL 420 . . . 636
SAVAGE MODEL 430 . . . 637
SAVAGE MODEL 440 . . . 637
SAVAGE MODEL 440T TRAP . . . 637
SAVAGE MODEL 444 DELUXE . . . 637
SAVAGE MODEL 550 . . . 637
SAVAGE MODEL 720 . . . 637
SAVAGE MODEL 726 . . . 637
SAVAGE MODEL 740C . . . 637
SAVAGE MODEL 745 LIGHTWEIGHT . . . 637
SAVAGE MODEL 750 . . . 637
SAVAGE MODEL 750AC . . . 637
SAVAGE MODEL 750SC . . . 637
SAVAGE MODEL 755 . . . 637
SAVAGE MODEL 755SC . . . 637
SAVAGE MODEL 775 LIGHTWEIGHT . . . 637
SAVAGE MODEL 775SC LIGHTWEIGHT . . . 638
SAVAGE MODEL 2400 COMBO . . . 638
SAVAGE MILANO . . . 638

SCATTERGUN

SCATTERGUN TECHNOLOGIES TACTICAL RESPONSE TR-870 . . . 638
SCATTERGUN TECHNOLOGIES K-9 . . . 638
SCATTERGUN TECHNOLOGIES SWAT . . . 638
SCATTERGUN TECHNOLOGIES URBAN SNIPER . . . 638

W&C SCOTT

W&C SCOTT (GUNMAKERS) LTD. BLENHEIM . . . 638
W&C SCOTT (GUNMAKERS) LTD. BOWOOD DELUXE . . . 638
W&C SCOTT (GUNMAKERS) LTD. CHATSWORTH GRANDELUXE . . . 638
W&C SCOTT (GUNMAKERS) LTD. CROWN . . . 638
W&C SCOTT (GUNMAKERS) LTD. KINMOUNT . . . 638
W&C SCOTT (GUNMAKERS) LTD. TEXAN . . . 639
W&C SCOTT & SON MONTE CARLO B . . . 639
W&C SCOTT & SON PIGEON CLUB GUN . . . 639
W&C SCOTT & SON PREMIER HAMMERLESS . . . 639
W&C SCOTT & SON IMPERIAL PREMIER HAMMERLESS . . . 639
W&C SCOTT & SON PREMIER QUALITY HAMMER . . . 639
W&C SCOTT & SON RELIANCE/CONTINENTAL . . . 639
W&C SCOTT & SON SINGLE BARREL TRAP . . . 639

SECOLO

SECOLO MODEL 250 . . . 639
SECOLO MODEL 530 . . . 639
SECOLO MODEL 540 MONO TRAP . . . 639
SECOLO MODEL 550 TRAP . . . 639

SECOLO MODEL 560 SKEET 639

SENATOR

SENATOR FOLDING MODEL 639

SIGARMS

SIGARMS APOLLO TR AND TT SHOTGUNS 639
SIGARMS SA 3 640
SIGARMS SA 5 640

SILE

SILE SKY STALKER 640

SILMA

SILMA MODEL 70 640
SILMA MODEL 70EJ DELUXE 640
SILMA MODEL 70 EJ SUPERLIGHT 640
SILMA MODEL 70 EJ STANDARD 640

SKB

SKB MODEL 300 640
SKB MODEL 900 DELUXE 640
SKB MODEL 900 DELUXE SLUG 640
SKB MODEL 1300 UPLAND MAG 640
SKB MODEL 1900 FIELD 640
SKB MODEL 1900 TRAP 640
SKB MODEL XL 100 640
SKB MODEL XL 300 641
SKB MODEL XL 900 641
SKB MODEL XL 900 SKEET 641
SKB MODEL XL 900 SLUG GUN 641
SKB MODEL XL 900 TRAP 641
SKB MODEL 500 641
SKB MODEL 500 MAGNUM 641
SKB MODEL 500 SKEET 641
SKB MODEL 505 DELUXE 641
SKB MODEL 505 SKEET 641
SKB MODEL 505 SKEET SET 641
SKB MODEL 505 TRAP 641
SKB MODEL 505 TRAP COMBO 641
SKB MODEL 585 FIELD 641
SKB MODEL 585 GOLD PACKAGE 641
SKB MODEL 585 SKEET 641
SKB MODEL 585 SPORTING CLAYS 641
SKB MODEL 585 TRAP 642
SKB TWO-BARREL COMBO 642
SKB MODEL 585 WATERFOWLER 642
SKB MODEL 585 YOUTH 642
SKB MODEL 600 642
SKB MODEL 600 MAGNUM 642
SKB MODEL 600 SKEET GRADE 642
SKB MODEL 600 SMALL BORE 642
SKB MODEL 600 TRAP GRADE 642
SKB MODEL 605 FIELD 642
SKB MODEL 605 SKEET 642
SKB MODEL 605 SPORTING CLAYS 642
SKB MODEL 605 TRAP 642
SKB MODEL 680 ENGLISH 642
SKB MODEL 685 FIELD 642
SKB MODEL 685 SPORTING CLAYS 642
SKB MODEL 685 TRAP 642
SKB MODEL 685 SKEET 642
SKB MODEL 700 SKEET 643
SKB MODEL 700 TRAP 643
SKB MODEL 785 FIELD 643
SKB MODEL 785 SKEET 643
SKB MODEL 785 SPORTING CLAYS 643
SKB MODEL 785 TRAP 643
SKB MODEL 800 FIELD 643
SKB MODEL 800 SKEET 643
SKB MODEL 800 TRAP 643
SKB MODEL 880 CROWN GRADE 643
SKB MODEL 885 FIELD 643
SKB MODEL 885 SPORTING CLAYS 643
SKB MODEL 885 SKEET 643
SKB MODEL 885 TRAP 643
SKB MODEL 5600 643
SKB MODEL 5700 643
SKB MODEL 5800 643
SKB MODEL 85 TSS TRAP 644
SKB 85TSS UNSINGLE COMBO 644
SKB MODEL 100 644
SKB MODEL 150 644
SKB MODEL 200E 644
SKB MODEL 200E SKEET GRADE 644
SKB MODEL 200 MAGNUM 644
SKB MODEL 280 644
SKB MODEL 385 644
SKB MODEL 385 SPORTING CLAYS 644
SKB MODEL 485 644
SKB MODEL 400E 644
SKB MODEL 400E SKEET GRADE 644
SKB MODEL 480 644
SKB CENTURY 644
SKB CENTURY II 644
SKB MODEL 7300 644
SKB MODEL 7900 TARGET GRADE 644

S&M

S&M 10-GAUGE 645

L.C. SMITH

L.C. SMITH HAMMERLESS DOUBLE BARRELS (1890-1912) 645
L.C. SMITH HAMMERLESS DOUBLE BARREL NO. 00 (1890-1912) 645
L.C. SMITH HAMMERLESS DOUBLE BARREL NO. 0 (1890-1912) 645
L.C. SMITH HAMMERLESS DOUBLE BARREL NO. 1 (1890-1912) 645
L.C. SMITH HAMMERLESS DOUBLE BARREL PIGEON GUN (1890-1912) 645
L.C. SMITH HAMMERLESS DOUBLE BARREL NO. 2 (1890-1912) 645
L.C. SMITH HAMMERLESS DOUBLE BARREL NO. 3 (1890-1912) 646
L.C. SMITH HAMMERLESS DOUBLE BARREL NO. 4 (1890-1912) 646
L.C. SMITH HAMMERLESS DOUBLE BARREL A1 GRADE (1890-1912) 646
L.C. SMITH HAMMERLESS DOUBLE BARREL NO. 5 (1890-1912) 646
L.C. SMITH HAMMERLESS DOUBLE BARREL MONOGRAM (1890-1912) 646
L.C. SMITH HAMMERLESS DOUBLE BARREL A2 GRADE (1890-1912) 646
L.C. SMITH HAMMERLESS DOUBLE BARREL A3 GRADE (1890-1912) 646
L.C. SMITH HAMMERLESS DOUBLE BARRELS (1913-1945) 646
L.C. SMITH HAMMERLESS DOUBLE BARREL FIELD GRADE (1913-1945) 646
L.C. SMITH HAMMERLESS DOUBLE BARREL IDEAL GRADE (1913-1945) 646
L.C. SMITH HAMMERLESS DOUBLE BARREL TRAP GRADE (1913-1945) 646
L.C. SMITH HAMMERLESS DOUBLE BARREL SKEET SPECIAL (1913-1945) 646
L.C. SMITH HAMMERLESS DOUBLE BARREL OLYMPIC GRADE (1913-1945) 646
L.C. SMITH HAMMERLESS DOUBLE BARREL SPECIALTY GRADE (1913-1945) 646
L.C. SMITH HAMMERLESS DOUBLE BARREL EAGLE GRADE (1913-1945) 647
L.C. SMITH HAMMERLESS DOUBLE BARREL CROWN GRADE (1913-1945) 647
L.C. SMITH HAMMERLESS DOUBLE BARREL MONOGRAM GRADE (1913-1945) 647
L.C. SMITH HAMMERLESS DOUBLE BARREL PREMIER GRADE (1913-1945) 647
L.C. SMITH HAMMERLESS DOUBLE BARREL DELUXE GRADE (1913-1945) 647
L.C. SMITH HAMMERLESS DOUBLE BARREL LONG RANGE WILD FOWL GUN (1913-1945) 647
L.C. SMITH HAMMERLESS DOUBLE BARRELS (1945-1950) 647
L.C. SMITH HAMMERLESS DOUBLE BARREL FIELD GRADE (1945-1950) 647
L.C. SMITH HAMMERLESS DOUBLE BARREL IDEAL GRADE (1945-1950) 647
L.C. SMITH HAMMERLESS DOUBLE BARREL SPECIALTY GRADE (1945-1950) 647
L.C. SMITH HAMMERLESS DOUBLE BARREL CROWN GRADE (1945-1950) 647
L.C. SMITH HAMMERLESS DOUBLE BARREL PREMIER SKEET GRADE (1945-1950) 647
L.C. SMITH HAMMERLESS DOUBLE BARREL FIELD GRADE (1967-1971) 647
L.C. SMITH HAMMERLESS DOUBLE BARREL FIELD GRADE DELUXE 647
L.C. SMITH SINGLE-BARREL TRAP GUN 647

SMITH & WESSON

SMITH & WESSON MODEL 916 648
SMITH & WESSON MODEL 916T 648
SMITH & WESSON MODEL 1000 648
SMITH & WESSON MODEL 1000 MAGNUM 648
SMITH & WESSON MODEL 1000S 648
SMITH & WESSON MODEL 1000 TRAP 648
SMITH & WESSON MODEL 1000 WATERFOWLER 648
SMITH & WESSON MODEL 3000 648
SMITH & WESSON MODEL 3000 WATERFOWLER 648
SMITH & WESSON ELITE GOLD 648

SPORTING ARMS

SPORTING ARMS SNAKE CHARMER 648
SPORTING ARMS SNAKE CHARMER II 648
SPORTING ARMS SNAKE CHARMER II NEW GENERATION 648

STEVENS

STEVENS MODEL 22-410 648
STEVENS MODEL 58 648
STEVENS MODEL 59 649
STEVENS MODEL 67 649
STEVENS MODEL 67 SLUG 649
STEVENS MODEL 67 VRT-K CAMO 649
STEVENS MODEL 67 VRT-Y 649
STEVENS MODEL 69 RXL 649
STEVENS MODEL 77 649
STEVENS MODEL 77SC 649
STEVENS MODEL 79-VR 649
STEVENS MODEL 94C 649
STEVENS MODEL 94Y 649
STEVENS MODEL 107 649
STEVENS MODEL 124 649
STEVENS MODEL 240 649
STEVENS MODEL 258 649
STEVENS MODEL 311 650
STEVENS MODEL 520 650
STEVENS MODEL 530 650
STEVENS MODEL 530M 650
STEVENS MODEL 530ST 650
STEVENS MODEL 620 650
STEVENS MODEL 621 650
STEVENS MODEL 675 650
STEVENS MODEL 5151 650
STEVENS MODEL 5151-ST 650
STEVENS MODEL 9478 SUPER VALUE 650

STOEGER

STOEGER P-350 650
STOEGER P-350 DEFENSE 650
STOEGER/IGA UPLANDER 650
STOEGER/IGA ENGLISH STOCK SIDE-BY-SIDE 651
STOEGER UPLAND SHORT STOCK SIDE-BY-SIDE 651
STOEGER MODEL 2000 651
STOEGER SILVERADO COACH 651

STOEGER COACH GUN SUPREME 651
STOEGER UPLANDER 651
STOEGER UPLANDER SUPREME 651
STOEGER 2002 SINGLE-SHOT 651
STOEGER CONDOR 651
CONDOR SPECIAL 652
CONDOR COMBO 652
CONDOR SUPREME 652
CONDOR YOUTH 652
STOEGER CONDOR COMPETITION 652
STOEGER CONDOR COMPETITION COMBO 652
STOEGER CONDOR OUTBACK 652
STOEGER MODEL 3500 652

STURM RUGER

STURM RUGER GOLD LABEL 652
STURM RUGER KTS-1234-BRE RED LABEL TRAP MODEL 652
STURM RUGER RED LABEL 652
RUGER ENGRAVED RED LABEL 652
STURM RUGER RED LABEL SPORTING CLAYS 652
STURM RUGER RED LABEL SPORTING CLAYS 20-GAUGE 652
STURM RUGER RED LABEL WOODSIDE 652

TAR-HUNT

TAR-HUNT RSG-12 PROFESSIONAL 652
TAR-HUNT RSG-12 PROFESSIONAL MATCHLESS MODEL 653
TAR-HUNT RSG-12 PROFESSIONAL PEERLESS MODEL 653
TAR-HUNT RSG-12 TURKEY MODEL 653
TAR-HUNT RSG-20 MOUNTAINEER SLUG GUN 653

TECHNI-MEC

TECHNI-MEC MODEL 610 653
TECHNI-MEC MODEL SPL 640 653
TECHNI-MEC MODEL SPL 642 653
TECHNI-MEC MODEL SR 690 SKEET 653
TECHNI-MEC MODEL SR 690 TRAP 653
TECHNI-MEC MODEL SR 692 EM 653

THOMPSON/CENTER

THOMPSON/CENTER CUSTOM SHOP TCR '87 HUNTER 653
THOMPSON/CENTER ENCORE RIFLED SLUG GUN 653
THOMPSON/CENTER ENCORE TURKEY GUN 653

TIKKA

TIKKA MODEL 77 653
TIKKA MODEL 412S FIELD GRADE 653
TIKKA MODEL 412S SPORTING CLAYS 654
TIKKA MODEL 412ST SKEET 654
TIKKA MODEL 412ST SKEET GRADE II 654
TIKKA MODEL 412ST TRAP 654
TIKKA MODEL 412ST TRAP GRADE II 654

TOLEDO

TOLEDO ARMAS VALEZQUEZ 654

TRADEWINDS

TRADEWINDS H-170 654

TRADITIONS

TRADITIONS ALS 2100 SERIES 654
TRADITIONS ALS 2100 TURKEY 654
TRADITIONS ALS 2100 WATERFOWL 654
TRADITIONS ALS 2100 HUNTER COMBO 654
TRADITIONS CLASSIC SERIES 654
TRADITIONS ELITE SERIES 654
TRADITIONS MAG 350 SERIES 655

TRIDENT

TRIDENT SUPERTRAP II 655

TRISTAR

TRISTAR BRITTANY 655
TRISTAR BRITTANY CLASSIC 655
TRISTAR TSA FIELD 655
TRISTAR TSA SYNTHETIC AND SYNTHETIC MAG 655
TRISTAR DERBY CLASSIC 655
TRISTAR MODEL 1887 655
TRISTAR PHANTOM 655
TRISTAR PHANTOM HP 655
TRISTAR YORK 655
TRISTAR ROTA MODEL 411 655
TRISTAR ROTA MODEL 411D 655
TRISTAR ROTA MODEL 411R COACH GUN 656
TRISTAR ROTA MODEL 411F 656
TRISTAR SILVER SPORTING 656
TRISTAR SILVER II 656
TRISTAR TR-SC "EMILIO RIZZINI" 656
TRISTAR TR-ROYAL "EMILIO RIZZINI" 656
TRISTAR TR-L "EMILIO RIZZINI" 656
TRISTAR TR-I, II "EMILIO RIZZINI" 656
TRISTAR TR-MAG "EMILIO RIZZINI" 656
TRISTAR TR SL "EMILIO RIZZINI" 657
TRISTAR WS 657
TRISTAR HUNTER LITE 657
TRISTAR HUNTER 657
TRISTAR FIELD HUNTER 657
TRISTAR VIPER G2 657

UGARTECHEA

UGARTECHEA 10-GAUGE MAGNUM 657

UNION

UNION ARMERA LUXE 657
UNION ARMERA WINNER 657

UNIVERSAL FIREARMS

UNIVERSAL FIREARMS AUTO WING 657
UNIVERSAL FIREARMS DOUBLE WING 657
UNIVERSAL FIREARMS DUCK WING 657
UNIVERSAL FIREARMS MODEL 101 657
UNIVERSAL FIREARMS MODEL 202 657
UNIVERSAL FIREARMS MODEL 203 657
UNIVERSAL FIREARMS MODEL 2030 657
UNIVERSAL FIREARMS OVER WING 657
UNIVERSAL FIREARMS SINGLE WING 658

URBIOLA

URBIOLA MODEL 160E 658

VALMET

VALMET LION 658
VALMET MODEL 412K 658
VALMET MODEL 412KE 658
VALMET MODEL 412S AMERICAN 658
VALMET MODEL 412STSKEET 658
VALMET MODEL 412ST SKEET GRADE II 658
VALMET MODEL 412ST TRAP 658
VALMET MODEL 412ST TRAP GRADE II 658

VENTURA

VENTURA AVANTI SMALL GAUGE 658
VENTURA AVANTI SMALL GAUGE EXTRA LUSSO 658
VENTURA CONTENTO 658
VENTURA CONTENTO EXTRA LUSSO 658
VENTURA CONTENTO LUSSO GRADE 658
VENTURA MODEL 51 658
VENTURA MODEL 53 658
VENTURA MODEL 62 658
VENTURA MODEL 64 659
VENTURA MODEL 66 659
VENTURA MODEL XXV 659
VENTURA REGIS MODEL 659
VENTURA VICTRIX 659
VENTURA VICTRIX EXTRA LUSSO 659

VERONA

VERONA LX501 HUNTING 659
VERONA LX692 GOLD HUNTING 659
VERONA LX680 SPORTING 659
VERONA LX680 SKEET/ SPORTING, TRAP 659
VERONA LX692 GOLD SPORTING 659
VERONA LX680 COMPETITION TRAP 659
VERONA LX702 GOLD TRAP COMBO 659
VERONA MODEL SX400 SEMI-AUTO SHOTGUN 659

WEATHERBY

WEATHERBY ATHENA SIDE-BY-SIDE 659
WEATHERBY ATHENA GRADE IV 659
WEATHERBY ATHENA GRADE V CLASSIC FIELD 660
WEATHERBY ATHENA III CLASSIC FIELD 660
WEATHERBY ATHENA SINGLE BARREL TRAP 660
WEATHERBY CENTURION 660
WEATHERBY CENTURION DELUXE 660
WEATHERBY CENTURION TRAP 660
WEATHERBY MODEL EIGHTY-TWO 660
WEATHERBY MODEL EIGHTY-TWO BUCKMASTER 660
WEATHERBY MODEL EIGHTY-TWO TRAP 660
WEATHERBY MODEL NINETY-TWO 660
WEATHERBY MODEL NINETY-TWO BUCKMASTER 660
WEATHERBY MODEL NINETY-TWO TRAP 660
WEATHERBY OLYMPIAN 660
WEATHERBY OLYMPIAN TRAP 660
WEATHERBY ORION I 660
WEATHERBY ORION I SPORTING CLAYS 661
WEATHERBY ORION UPLAND 661
WEATHERBY ORION II 661
WEATHERBY ORION II CLASSIC 661
WEATHERBY ORION II CLASSIC SPORTING CLAYS 661
WEATHERBY ORION II SPORTING CLAYS 661
WEATHERBY ORION III 661
WEATHERBY ORION III CLASSIC 661
WEATHERBY ORION GRADE III FIELD 661
WEATHERBY ORION GRADE III CLASSIC FIELD 661
WEATHERBY ORION III ENGLISH FIELD 661
WEATHERBY ORION GRADE II CLASSIC FIELD 661
WEATHERBY ORION GRADE I FIELD 661
WEATHERBY ORION SIDE-BY-SIDE 661
WEATHERBY ORION D'ITALIA 661
WEATHERBY ORION SSC 661
WEATHERBY ATHENA D'ITALIA 662
WEATHERBY ATHENA D'ITALIA PG 662
WEATHERBY ATHENA D'ITALIA DELUXE 662
WEATHERBY PATRICIAN 662
WEATHERBY PATRICIAN DELUXE 662
WEATHERBY PATRICIAN TRAP 662
WEATHERBY REGENCY 662
WEATHERBY REGENCY TRAP 662
WEATHERBY SAS (SEMI-AUTOMATIC SHOTGUN) SPORTING CLAYS/SLUG GUN 662
WEATHERBY SA-08 UPLAND 662
WEATHERBY SA-08 YOUTH 663
WEATHERBY PA-08 SERIES 663
WEATHERBY PA-08 UPLAND 663
WEATHERBY PA-08 KNOXX STRUTTER X 663
WEATHERBY PA-08 KNOXX HD 663
WEATHERBY SA-08 SERIES 663

WESSON & HARRINGTON

WESSON & HARRINGTON LONG TOM CLASSIC SHOTGUN. 663

WESTERN ARMS

WESTERN ARMS LONG RANGE HAMMERLESS 663

WESTLEY RICHARDS

WESTLEY RICHARDS BEST QUALITY BOXLOCK 663
WESTLEY RICHARDS BEST QUALITY SIDELOCK. 663
WESTLEY RICHARDS BOXLOCK MODEL DELUXE QUALITY 663
WESTLEY RICHARDS MODEL B. 663
WESTLEY RICHARDS OVUNDO 663

WINCHESTER

WINCHESTER MODEL 40 663
WINCHESTER MODEL 40 SKEET 663
WINCHESTER MODEL 50 663
WINCHESTER MODEL 50 FEATHERWEIGHT 664
WINCHESTER MODEL 50 PIGEON. 664
WINCHESTER MODEL 50 SKEET 664
WINCHESTER MODEL 50 TRAP 664
WINCHESTER MODEL 59 664
WINCHESTER MODEL 1400 664
WINCHESTER MODEL 1400 DEER GUN 664
WINCHESTER MODEL 1400 MARK II 664
WINCHESTER MODEL 1400 SKEET 664
WINCHESTER MODEL 1400 TRAP 664
WINCHESTER MODEL 1400 (RECENT). 664
WINCHESTER MODEL 1400 CUSTOM (RECENT) 664
WINCHESTER MODEL 1400 SLUG HUNTER (RECENT). 664
WINCHESTER MODEL 1500 XTR 664
WINCHESTER MODEL 1911 664
WINCHESTER MODEL 1911 FANCY FINISHED 664
WINCHESTER MODEL 1911 PIGEON. 664
WINCHESTER MODEL 1911 TRAP 665
WINCHESTER SUPER-X MODEL 1. 665
WINCHESTER SUPER-X MODEL 1 SKEET. 665
WINCHESTER SUPER-X MODEL 1 TRAP. 665
WINCHESTER SUPER X2 665
WINCHESTER SUPER X2 SPORTING CLAYS 665
WINCHESTER SUPER X2 FIELD 3-INCH 665
WINCHESTER SUPER X3 665
WINCHESTER SUPER X3 "FLANIGUN" EXHIBITION/SPORTING 665
WINCHESTER SUPER X3 CLASSIC FIELD 665
WINCHESTER SUPER X3 TURKEY. 665
WINCHESTER MODEL 12 665
WINCHESTER MODEL 12 FEATHERWEIGHT 665
WINCHESTER MODEL 12 HEAVY DUCK 665
WINCHESTER MODEL 12 PIGEON. 665
WINCHESTER MODEL 12 RIOT 665
WINCHESTER MODEL 12 SKEET. 665
WINCHESTER MODEL 12 SUPER PIGEON 666
WINCHESTER MODEL 12 TRAP 666
WINCHESTER MODEL 12 (1972). 666
WINCHESTER MODEL 12 (1993). 666
WINCHESTER MODEL 12 SKEET (1972). 666
WINCHESTER MODEL 12 TRAP (1972). 666
WINCHESTER MODEL 25 666
WINCHESTER MODEL 25 RIOT 666
WINCHESTER MODEL 42 666
WINCHESTER MODEL 42 DELUXE. 666
WINCHESTER MODEL 42 SKEET 666
WINCHESTER MODEL 42 TRAP 666
WINCHESTER MODEL 42 HIGH GRADE (1993) 666
WINCHESTER MODEL 1200 666
WINCHESTER MODEL 1200 DEER. 666
WINCHESTER MODEL 1200 MAGNUM 666
WINCHESTER MODEL 1200 SKEET 666
WINCHESTER MODEL 1200 TRAP 666
WINCHESTER MODEL 1300 DEFENDER PUMP. 667
WINCHESTER MODEL 1300 STAINLESS MARINE PUMP 667
WINCHESTER MODEL 1300 CAMP DEFENDER. 667
WINCHESTER MODEL 1300 WALNUT FIELD PUMP 667
WINCHESTER MODEL 1300 UPLAND PUMP 667
WINCHESTER MODEL 1300 BLACK SHADOW 667
WINCHESTER MODEL 1300 BLACK SHADOW DEER 667
WINCHESTER MODEL 1300 BLACK SHADOW TURKEY. 667
WINCHESTER MODEL 1300 N.W.T.F. SERIES I. 667
WINCHESTER MODEL 1300 N.W.T.F. SERIES II 667
WINCHESTER MODEL 1300 N.W.T.F. SERIES III. 667
WINCHESTER MODEL 1300 N.W.T.F. SERIES IV. 667
WINCHESTER MODEL 1300 RANGER 667
WINCHESTER MODEL 1300 RANGER COMBO 667
WINCHESTER MODEL 1300 RANGER DEER 668
WINCHESTER MODEL 1300 RANGER LADIES/YOUTH. 668
WINCHESTER MODEL 1300 REALTREE TURKEY GUN 668
WINCHESTER MODEL 1300 SLUG HUNTER 668
WINCHESTER MODEL 1300 STAINLESS MARINE 668
WINCHESTER MODEL 1300 TURKEY. 668
WINCHESTER MODEL 1300 TURKEY AND UNIVERSAL HUNTER MODELS 668
WINCHESTER MODEL 1300 XTR 668
WINCHESTER MODEL 1300 XTR DEER GUN. 668
WINCHESTER MODEL 1300 XTR DEFENDER 668
WINCHESTER MODEL 1300 XTR FEATHERWEIGHT 668
WINCHESTER MODEL 1300 XTR LADIES/YOUTH. 668
WINCHESTER MODEL 1300 XTR WALNUT 668
WINCHESTER MODEL 1300 XTR WATERFOWL. 668
WINCHESTER SPEED PUMP SERIES. 668
WINCHESTER SPEED PUMP WALNUT FIELD 669
WINCHESTER SPEED PUMP BLACK SHADOW FIELD 669
WINCHESTER SPEED PUMP DEFENDER 669
WINCHESTER SXP CAMP/ FIELD COMBO. 669
WINCHESTER MODEL 1893 669
WINCHESTER MODEL 1897 669
WINCHESTER MODEL 1897 BRUSH 669
WINCHESTER MODEL 1897 PIGEON 669
WINCHESTER MODEL 1897 SPECIAL TRAP . . . 669
WINCHESTER MODEL 1897 STANDARD TRAP 669
WINCHESTER MODEL 1897 TOURNAMENT . . . 669
WINCHESTER MODEL 1897 TRAP 669
WINCHESTER MODEL 1897 TRENCH 669
WINCHESTER MODEL 101 669
WINCHESTER MODEL 101 MAGNUM 669
WINCHESTER MODEL 101 PIGEON GRADE . . . 669
WINCHESTER MODEL 101 SKEET 669
WINCHESTER MODEL 101 TRAP 669
WINCHESTER MODEL 101 TRAP SINGLE BARREL. 669
WINCHESTER MODEL 101 WATERFOWL. 669
WINCHESTER MODEL 101 DIAMOND GRADE SKEET. 669
WINCHESTER MODEL 101 DIAMOND GRADE TRAP. 670
WINCHESTER MODEL 101 DIAMOND GRADE TRAP COMBO 670
WINCHESTER MODEL 101 DIAMOND GRADE TRAP SINGLE. 670
WINCHESTER MODEL 101 XTR 670
WINCHESTER MODEL 101 XTR AMERICAN FLYER LIVE BIRD. 670
WINCHESTER MODEL 101 XTR AMERICAN FLYER LIVE BIRD. 670
WINCHESTER MODEL 101 XTR PIGEON GRADE FEATHERWEIGHT 670
WINCHESTER MODEL 101 XTR PIGEON GRADE LIGHTWEIGHT. 670
WINCHESTER MODEL 101 XTR PIGEON GRADE SKEET 670
WINCHESTER MODEL 101 XTR PIGEON GRADE TRAP 670
WINCHESTER MODEL 101 XTR QUAIL SPECIAL. 670
WINCHESTER MODEL XTR WATERFOWL 670
WINCHESTER MODEL 501 GRAND EUROPEAN 670
WINCHESTER MODEL 1001 670
WINCHESTER SELECT MODEL 101 FIELD (2007) 670
MODEL 101 PIGEON GRADE TRAP 671
WINCHESTER SUPREME 671
WINCHESTER XPERT MODEL 96 671
WINCHESTER XPERT MODEL 96 SKEET 671
WINCHESTER XPERT MODEL 96 TRAP 671
WINCHESTER SELECT DELUXE FIELD 671
WINCHESTER SELECT PLATINUM FIELD 671
WINCHESTER SELECT PLATINUM SPORTING. 671
WINCHESTER SELECT MIDNIGHT 671
WINCHESTER SELECT WHITE FIELD. 671
WINCHESTER MODEL 21 671
WINCHESTER MODEL 21 CUSTOM. 671
WINCHESTER MODEL 21 DUCK. 671
WINCHESTER MODEL 21 GRAND AMERICAN. 671
WINCHESTER MODEL 21 PIGEON. 672
WINCHESTER MODEL 21 SKEET 672
WINCHESTER MODEL 21 TRAP 672
WINCHESTER MODEL 23 CLASSIC 672
WINCHESTER MODEL 23 CUSTOM. 672
WINCHESTER MODEL 23 XTR 672
WINCHESTER MODEL 23 XTR GOLDEN QUAIL. 672
WINCHESTER MODEL 23 XTR HEAVY DUCK 672
WINCHESTER MODEL 23 XTR LIGHT DUCK 672
WINCHESTER MODEL 23 XTR PIGEON GRADE 672
WINCHESTER MODEL 23 XTR PIGEON GRADE LIGHTWEIGHT. 672
WINCHESTER MODEL 23 XTR TWO-BARREL SET 672
WINCHESTER MODEL 24 672
WINCHESTER MODEL 20 673
WINCHESTER MODEL 36 673
WINCHESTER MODEL 37 673
WINCHESTER MODEL 37A 673
WINCHESTER MODEL 37A YOUTH 673
WINCHESTER MODEL 41 673
WINCHESTER MODEL 370 673
WINCHESTER MODEL 370 YOUTH 673
WINCHESTER MODEL 1885 SINGLE SHOT 673
WINCHESTER MODEL 1887 673
WINCHESTER MODEL 1887 DELUXE. 673
WINCHESTER MODEL 1901 673
WINCHESTER MODEL 9410 LEVER-ACTION SHOTGUN. 673

WOODWARD

WOODWARD BEST QUALITY DOUBLE 674
WOODWARD BEST QUALITY OVER/UNDER 674
WOODWARD SINGLE BARREL TRAP. 674

ZABALA

ZABALA DOUBLE 674

ZANOLETTI, PIETRO

PIETRO ZANOLETTI MODEL 2000 FIELD. 674

ZOLI

ZOLI DELFINO 674
ZOLI GOLDEN SNIPE. 674
ZOLI SILVER FALCON 674
ZOLI SILVER FOX. 674
ZOLI UPLANDER 674
ZOLI WOODSMAN. 674
ZOLI Z90 MONO-TRAP 674
ZOLI Z90 SKEET MODEL. 674
ZOLI Z90 SPORTING CLAYS. 674
ZOLI Z90 TRAP 674

MODERN GUN VALUES
HANDGUNS
DIRECTORY OF MANUFACTURERS

A.A. ARMS . . . 84
ACCU-TEK . . . 84
ACTION ARMS . . . 85
ADVANTAGE ARMS . . . 85
AGNER . . . 85
AIR MATCH 500 . . . 85
A.J. ORDNANCE . . . 85
AKDAL . . . 85
ALAMO . . . 85
ALKARTASUNA . . . 85
ALCHEMY ARMS . . . 85
ALLEN . . . 86
AMERICAN ARMS . . . 86
AMERICAN DERRINGER . . . 87
AMERICAN FIREARMS . . . 88
AMERICAN FRONTIER . . . 89
AMT . . . 89
ANSCHUTZ . . . 91
ARCUS . . . 91
ARGENTINE . . . 91
ARMALITE . . . 91
ARMINEX . . . 91
ARMINIUS . . . 91
ARMSCOR . . . 92
ARMSCOR/ROCK ISLAND ARMORY . . . 92
ARM TECH . . . 92
ASTRA . . . 92
AUTAUGA . . . 94
AUTO MAG . . . 94
AUTO-ORDNANCE . . . 94
AWA . . . 95
BAER . . . 95
BAFORD ARMS . . . 96
BAIKAL . . . 96
BAUER . . . 97
BAYARD . . . 97
BEEMAN . . . 97
BEHOLLA . . . 97
BENELLI . . . 97
BERETTA . . . 98
BERGMANN . . . 103
BERGMANN-BAYARD . . . 103
BERNARDELLI . . . 103
BERSA . . . 104
BF . . . 106
BOBERG . . . 106
BOND ARMS . . . 106
BREN TEN . . . 106
BRNO 99 . . . 106
BROLIN . . . 106
BRONCO . . . 107
BROWN . . . 107
BROWNING . . . 107
BRYCO . . . 111
BUDISCHOWSKY . . . 111
BUSHMASTER . . . 111
BUTLER . . . 111
CABANAS . . . 111
CALICO . . . 111
CAMPO-GIRO . . . 111
CARBON-15 . . . 111
CENTURY . . . 112
CHARLES DALY . . . 112
CHARTER ARMS . . . 112
CHIAPPA . . . 114
CHIPMUNK . . . 114
CIMARRON . . . 114
CLARIDGE . . . 115
CLASSIC ARMS . . . 116
CLERKE . . . 116
COBRA . . . 116
COLT . . . 116
COMANCHE . . . 127
COMPETITION ARMS . . . 127
COMPETITOR . . . 128
COONAN . . . 128
CUMBERLAND MOUNTAIN ARMS . . . 128
CVA . . . 128
CZ/ADCO . . . 128
CZ . . . 128
DAEWOO . . . 130
DAKOTA . . . 130
DAN WESSON . . . 131
DAVIS . . . 131
DESERT INDUSTRIES . . . 132
DETONICS . . . 132
DIAMONDBACK . . . 133
DOWNSIZER . . . 133
D-MAX . . . 133
DREYSE . . . 133
DWM . . . 133
DSA . . . 133
E.A.A. . . . 133
ED BROWN . . . 135
ENTRÉPRISE P500 . . . 135
ERMA . . . 135
ERL . . . 136
FALCON . . . 136
FAS . . . 136
FEATHER . . . 136
FEDERAL ORDNANCE . . . 137
FEG . . . 137
FELK . . . 138
F.I.E. . . . 138
FIRESTORM . . . 141
FNH . . . 141
FORT WORTH . . . 141
FRASER . . . 142
FREEDOM ARMS . . . 142
FROMMER . . . 143
FTL . . . 143
GAL . . . 144
GALESI . . . 144
GAMBA . . . 144
GARCIA . . . 144
GAUCHER . . . 144
GIRSAN . . . 144
GLOCK . . . 144
GOLAN . . . 146
GREAT WESTERN . . . 146
GRENDEL . . . 146
GUARDIAN . . . 147
GUNWORKS . . . 147
HAMMERLI . . . 147
HAMMERLI-WALTHER . . . 149
HARRINGTON & RICHARDSON . . . 149
HARRIS-MCMILLAN . . . 154
HARTFORD . . . 154
HASKELL . . . 154
HAWES . . . 154
HECKLER & KOCH . . . 155
HELWAN . . . 156
HERITAGE . . . 157
HI-POINT FIREARMS . . . 157
HIGH STANDARD . . . 158
HJS . . . 164
HUNGARIAN . . . 164
IAI . . . 164
IAR . . . 165
IBERIA FIREARMS . . . 165
INDIAN ARMS . . . 165
INTERARMS . . . 165
INTRATEC . . . 165
ITHACA . . . 166
IVER JOHNSON . . . 166
JANA . . . 171
JANZ . . . 171
JENNINGS/BRYCO . . . 171
JENNINGS . . . 171
JERICHO . . . 171
JSL . . . 171
KAHR . . . 171
KAREEN . . . 172
KASSNAR . . . 172
KBI . . . 172
KEL-TEC . . . 172
KIMBER . . . 173
KIMEL . . . 174
KLEINGUENTHER . . . 174
KORRIPHILA 701 . . . 175
KORTH . . . 175
LAHTI . . . 175
L.A.R. . . . 175
LASERAIM ARMS . . . 176
LE FRANCAIS . . . 176
LES BAER . . . 176
LES INCORPORATED . . . 177
LIBERTY . . . 177
LIGNOSE . . . 177
LILIPUT . . . 177
LJUTIC . . . 177
LLAMA . . . 177
LORCIN . . . 179
LUGER . . . 180
LUNA . . . 182
MAB . . . 182
MAGNUM RESEARCH . . . 182
MANDALL/CABANAS . . . 183
MAKAROV . . . 183
MANURHIN . . . 183
MAUSER . . . 184
MEDUSA . . . 186
METRO ARMS . . . 186
MERRILL . . . 186
MITCHELL ARMS . . . 186
MKE KIRIKKALE . . . 188
MOA . . . 188
MORINI . . . 188
MOSSBERG . . . 189
MPA . . . 189
NAGANT . . . 189
NAMBU . . . 189
NAVY ARMS . . . 189
NEW ADVANTAGE . . . 191
NEW DETONICS . . . 191
NEW ENGLAND FIREARMS . . . 191
NIGHTHAWK CUSTOM . . . 191
NIGHTHAWK . . . 191
NORINCO . . . 191
NORTH AMERICAN ARMS . . . 192
ODI . . . 192
OLYMPIC ARMS . . . 192
ONE PRO . . . 193
ORTGIES . . . 193
PACHMAYR . . . 193
PARA-ORDNANCE . . . 193
PARA USA . . . 195
PARDINI . . . 195
PETERS . . . 196
PHELPS . . . 196
PHOENIX ARMS . . . 196
PLAINFIELD . . . 196
PSA . . . 196
PUMA . . . 197
QFI . . . 197
RG . . . 197
RADOM . . . 198
RAM-LINE . . . 198
RANDALL . . . 199
RAVEN . . . 199
RECORD-MATCH . . . 199
REISING . . . 199
REMINGTON . . . 199
REPUBLIC . . . 200
REXIO PUCARA . . . 200
ROCK RIVER ARMS . . . 200
ROCKY MOUNTAIN ARMS . . . 200
ROSSI . . . 201
ROYAL . . . 202
RPM . . . 202
SAFARI ARMS . . . 203
SAKO . . . 204
SARSILMAZ . . . 204
SAUER . . . 204
SAVAGE . . . 204
SCCY . . . 205
SECURITY INDUSTRIES . . . 205
SEDCO . . . 205
SEDGELY . . . 205
SEECAMP . . . 205
SHERIDAN . . . 205
SIG . . . 206
SIG-HAMMERLI . . . 206
SIG SAUER . . . 206
SMITH & WESSON . . . 209
SOKOLOVSKY . . . 229
SPECIALIZED WEAPONS . . . 229
SPHINX . . . 229
SPORTARMS . . . 230
SPRINGFIELD ARMORY . . . 230
STAR . . . 234
STERLING . . . 237
STEVENS . . . 238
STEYR . . . 238
STI . . . 238
STOEGER . . . 239
STRUM RUGER . . . 239
SUNDANCE . . . 244
SUPER SIX . . . 245
TANARMI . . . 245
TARGA . . . 245
TAURUS . . . 246
TEXAS ARMORY . . . 251
TEXAS LONGHORN . . . 251
THOMAS . . . 251
THOMPSON/CENTER . . . 251
THUNDER . . . 252
THUNDER . . . 252
TISAS . . . 252
TMI . . . 252
TOKAREV . . . 253
TRADITIONS . . . 253
TURNBULL . . . 253
UBERTI . . . 253
ULTRA LIGHT ARMS . . . 254
UNIQUE . . . 254
UNITED SPORTING ARMS . . . 255
UNITED STATES FIRE ARMS . . . 255
UNIVERSAL FIREARMS . . . 256
USELTON ARMS . . . 256
UZI . . . 256
VEGA 45 . . . 256
VOERE . . . 256
WALTHER . . . 256
WARNER . . . 259
WEATHERBY . . . 259
WEBLEY-FOSBERY . . . 259
WEBLEY . . . 259
WESSON FIREARMS . . . 261
WHITNEY . . . 263
WICHITA . . . 263
WILDEY . . . 264
WILKINSON . . . 264
WILSON COMBAT . . . 264
WYOMING ARMS . . . 264

A.A. Arms AP9

Accu-Tek AT-9SS

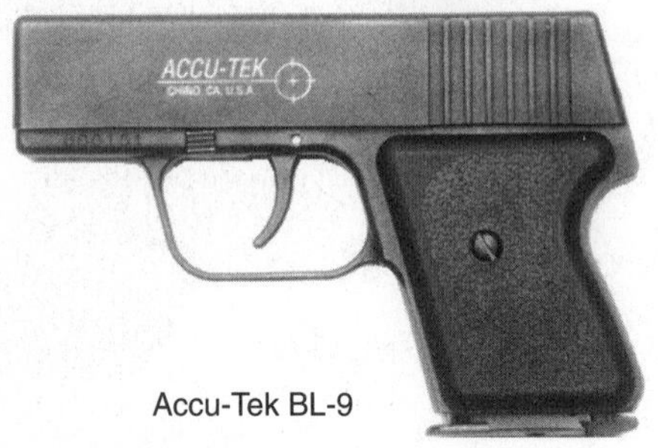
Accu-Tek BL-9

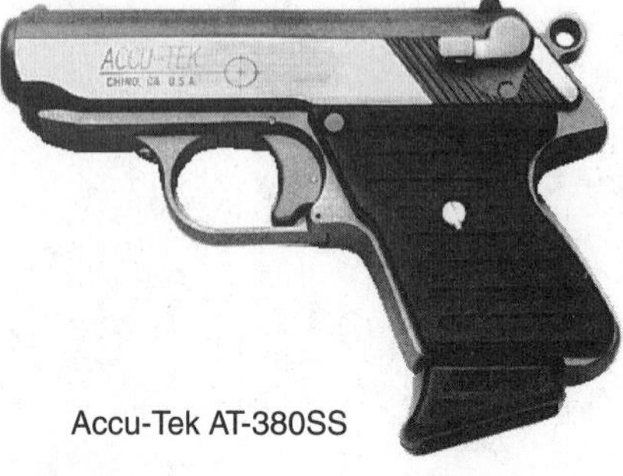
Accu-Tek AT-380SS

Accu-Tek HC-380SS

A.A. ARMS AP9

Semi-automatic; 9mm Para.; 20-shot magazine; 5-inch barrel; 11-13/16-inch overall length; weighs 3-1/2 lbs.; adjustable post front sight in ring, open fixed rear; vented barrel shroud; checkered plastic grips; lever safety; fires from closed bolt; 3-inch barrel available; matte blue-black or nickel finish. Introduced 1988; dropped 1999.

Perf: $425 **Exc:** $375 **VGood:** $250

Nickel finish

Perf: $500 **Exc:** $450 **VGood:** $325

A.A. ARMS AP9 TARGET

Same specs as the AP9 except 12-inch barrel; grooved forend; blue finish. No longer in production. Was marketed by Kimel Industries.

Perf: $425 **Exc:** $375 **VGood:** $250

ACCU-TEK MODEL AT-9SS

Semi-automatic; double-action-only; 9mm Para.; 8-shot magazine; 3-1/4-inch barrel; 6-1/4-inch overall length; weighs 28 oz.; black checkered nylon grips; blade front sight, windage-adjustable rear; three-dot system; stainless steel construction; firing pin block with no external safeties. Made in U.S. by Accu-Tek. Introduced 1992, dropped 1996.

New: $295 **Perf:** $205 **Exc:** $175

ACCU-TEK MODEL AT-25SS

Semi-automatic; single action; 25 ACP; 7-shot magazine; 2-3/4-inch barrel; 6-inch overall length; weighs 28 oz.; blade front sight, windage-adjustable rear; checkered black composition grips; external hammer; manual thumb safety; firing pin block; trigger disconnect; satin stainless steel finish. Made in U.S. by Accu-Tek. Introduced 1991; dropped 1995.

Perf: $165 **Exc:** $125 **VGood:** $105

ACCU-TEK MODEL AT-25AL

Same specs as AT-25SS except aluminum frame and slide with 11-oz. weight. Made in U.S. by Accu-Tek. Introduced 1991; dropped 1995.

Perf: $175 **Exc:** $135 **VGood:** $115

ACCU-TEK MODEL AT-25SSB

Same specs as Model AT-25SS except matte black finish over stainless steel. Introduced 1991; dropped 1995.

Perf: $200 **Exc:** $160 **VGood:** $135

ACCU-TEK MODEL AT-32SS

Semi-automatic; single action; 32 ACP; 5-shot magazine; 2-3/4-inch barrel; 6-inch overall length; weighs 28 oz.; blade front sight, windage-adjustable rear; checkered black composition grips; external hammer; manual thumb safety; firing pin block; trigger disconnect. Satin stainless steel finish. Made in U.S. by Accu-Tek. Introduced 1991; dropped 2003.

Perf: $245 **Exc:** $225 **VGood:** $200

ACCU-TEK MODEL AT-32SSB

Same specs as Model AT-32SS except matte black finish over stainless steel. Introduced 1991; dropped 2003.

Perf: $195 **Exc:** $160 **VGood:** $135

ACCU-TEK MODEL AT-40SS

Semi-automatic; double-action-only; 40 S&W; 7-shot magazine; 3-1/4-inch barrel; 6-1/4-inch overall length; weighs 28 oz.; black checkered nylon grips; blade front sight, windage-adjustable rear; three-dot system; stainless steel construction; firing pin block with no external safeties. Similar to Model CP-9SS. Made in U.S. by Accu-Tek. Introduced 1992; dropped 1996.

New: $295 **Perf:** $205 **Exc:** $175

ACCU-TEK MODEL AT-45SS

Semi-automatic; double-action-only; 45 ACP; 6-shot magazine; 3-1/4-inch barrel; 6-1/4-inch overall length; weighs 28 oz.; blade front sight, windage-adjustable rear; three-dot sight system; stainless steel construction; firing pin block with no external safeties. Similar to Model AT-40SS. Made in U.S. by Accu-Tek. Introduced 1995; dropped 1996.

New: $295 **Perf:** $205 **Exc:** $175

ACCU-TEK MODEL AT-380SS/SSB

Semi-automatic; single action; .380 ACP; 5-shot magazine; 2-3/4-inch barrel; 5-5/8-inch overall length; weighs 16 oz.; blade front sight, windage-adjustable rear; black combat or wood stocks; external hammer; manual safety with firing pin block, trigger disconnect; black (discontinued 1999), chrome or chrome with black slide. Alloy (discontinued 1991) or stainless steel construction. Made in U.S. by Accu-Tek. Introduced 1990.

Perf: $195 **Exc:** $160 **VGood:** $120

ACCU-TEK MODEL AT-380 LADY

Same specs as Accu-Tek 380; chrome finish; gray bleached oak stocks. Introduced 1990; dropped 1991.

Perf: $195 **Exc:** $160 **VGood:** $120

ACCU-TEK BL-9 AUTO PISTOL

Caliber: 9mm Para., 5-shot magazine. Barrel: 3-inch. Weight: 22 oz. Length: 5.6-inch overall. Carbon steel construction. Stocks: Black composition. Sights: Fixed. Features: Double action only; black finish. Was furnished with lockable case. Introduced 1997; dropped 2002.

New: $295 **Perf:** $205 **Exc:** $175

ACCU-TEK BL-380

Same as the BL-9 except chambered for 380 ACP. Introduced 1997. Made in U.S. by Accu-Tek; Introduced 1997; dropped 1999.

Perf: $195 **Exc:** $160 **VGood:** $120

ACCU-TEK MODEL CP-9SS AUTO PISTOL

Caliber: 9mm Para., 8-shot magazine. Barrel: 3.2-inch. Weight: 28 oz. Length: 6.25-inch overall. Stocks: Black checkered nylon. Sights: Blade front, rear adjustable for windage; three-dot system. Features: Stainless steel construction. Double action only. Firing pin block with no external safeties. Lifetime warranty. Introduced 1992. Made in U.S. by Accu-Tek; dropped 1999.

New: $295 **Perf:** $205 **Exc:** $175

ACCU-TEK CP-40SS AUTO PISTOL

Same as the Model CP-9SS except chambered for 40 S&W, 7-shot magazine. Introduced 1992; dropped 1999.

New: $250 **Perf:** $200 **Exc:** $165

ACCU-TEK CP-45SS AUTO PISTOL

Same as the Model CP-9SS except chambered for 45 ACP, 6-shot magazine. Introduced 1995; dropped 1999. Made in U.S. by Accu-Tek.

New: $295 **Perf:** $205 **Exc:** $175

Action Arms AT-84

Agner Model 80

Alkartasuna Ruby

Action Arms Uzi Pistol

Akdal Ghost TR Series

Advantage Arms Model 442

ACCU-TEK MODEL HC-380SS

Semi-automatic; single action; 380 ACP, 10-shot magazine; 2-3/4-inch barrel; 6-inch overall length; weighs 28 oz.; checkered black composition grips; blade front sight, windage-adjustable rear; external hammer; manual thumb safety with firing pin and trigger disconnect; bottom magazine release; stainless finish. Made in U.S. by Accu-Tek. Introduced 1993; dropped 2003.

New: $210 **Perf:** $175 **Exc:** $155

ACTION ARMS AT-84

Semi-automatic; double action; 9mm Para., 41 Action Express; 15-shot magazine (9mm), 10-shot (41 AE): 4-3/4-inch barrel; 8-1/16-inch overall length; weighs 35-1/2 oz.; drift-adjustable rear sight, blade front; polished blued finish. Made in Switzerland. Introduced 1987; dropped 1989.

Perf: $500 **Exc:** $465 **VGood:** $395

ACTION ARMS AT-84P

Same specs as Model AT-84 except 13-shot (9mm Para.), 8-shot (41 AE); 3-11/16-inch barrel; weighs 32 oz. Prototype only.

ACTION ARMS AT-88S

Semi-automatic; double action; 9mm Para., 41 Action Express; 10-shot magazine; 4-3/4-inch barrel; 8-1/8-inch overall length; weighs 35-1/2 oz.; blade front sight, drift-adjustable rear; checkered walnut grips; polished blue finish; originally marketed with both barrels. Made in Switzerland. Introduced 1987; importation dropped 1990.

Perf: $550 **Exc:** $500 **VGood:** $475

ACTION ARMS AT-88H

Same specs as AT-88S except 10-shot (9mm Para.), 7-shot (41 Action Express) magazine; 3-1/2-inch barrel; 6-7/8-inch overall length; weighs 30-1/2 oz. Introduced 1989; importation dropped 1990.

Perf: $550 **Exc:** $500 **VGood:** $475

ACTION ARMS AT-88P

Same specs as AT-88S except 13-shot (9mm Para.), 8-shot (41 Action Express) magazine; 3-11/16-inch barrel; 7-5/16-inch overall length; weighs 32 oz. Introduced 1989; importation dropped 1990.

Perf: $550 **Exc:** $500 **VGood:** $475

ACTION ARMS UZI PISTOL

Semi-automatic; single action; 9mm Para., 45 ACP; 20-shot magazine; 4-1/2-inch barrel; 9-1/2-inch overall length; weighs 3-1/2 lbs.; black plastic grip; post front sight with white dot, open fully click-adjustable rear, two white dots; semi-auto blowback action; fires from closed bolt; floating firing pin; comes in molded plastic case. Imported from Israel by Action Arms. Introduced 1984; dropped 1993.

Perf: $1300 **Exc:** $1100 **VGood:** $895

ADVANTAGE ARMS MODEL 442

Derringer; break-top action; 22 LR, 22 WMR; 4-shot; 2-1/2-inch barrel; 4-1/2-inch overall length; weighs 15 oz.; smooth walnut stocks; fixed sights; double-action trigger; rotating firing pin; spring-loaded extractors; nickel, blued or black finish. Introduced 1983; dropped 1987. Reintroduced 1989 by New Advantage Arms Corp.; no longer in production.

Perf: $150 **Exc:** $125 **VGood:** $115

Add $10 to above prices for .22 WMR chambering.

AGNER MODEL 80

Semi-automatic; 22 LR; 5-shot magazine; 5-15/16-inch barrel; 9-1/2-inch overall length; weighs 36 oz.; adjustable French walnut stocks; fixed blade front sight, adjustable rear; safety key locks trigger, slide, magazine; dry fire button; right- or left-hand models. Made in Denmark. Introduced 1984; dropped 1987; was imported by Beeman.

Perf: $1,125 **Exc:** $1,040 **VGood:** $950

Add $100 to above prices for left-hand action.

AIR MATCH 500

Single-shot; 22 LR; 10-7/16-inch barrel; weighs 28 oz.; match grip of stippled hardwood; left- or right-hand; match post front sight, adjustable match rear; adjustable sight radius; marketed in case with tools, spare sights. Made in Italy. Introduced 1984; dropped 1987; was imported by Kendall International Arms.

Perf: $550 **Exc:** $495 **VGood:** $450

A.J. ORDNANCE THOMAS 45

Semi-automatic; double action; 45 ACP; 6-shot magazine; 3-1/2-inch barrel; 6-1/2-inch overall length; windage-adjustable rear sight, blade front; checkered plastic grips; blued finish; matte sighting surface. Introduced 1977; discontinued 1978.

Perf: $1100 **Exc:** $975 **VGood:** $675

Chrome finish

Perf: $1175 **Exc:** $1050 **VGood:** $750

AKDAL GHOST TR SERIES

In 9mm (TR01) or .380 ACP (TR03) with 15-round double-stacked magazine. Barrel: 4.45 inches, overall length 7.5 inches, weight 29 oz. Polymer frame, striker-fired with short recoil operation and locking breech. Black finish frame, matte stainless slide, Picatinny rail.

Perf: $450 **Exc:** $385 **VGood:** $335

ALAMO RANGER

Double-action revolver formerly manufactured in Spain; resembles Colt SAA; .38 Spl.

Perf: $295 **Exc:** $275 **VGood:** $200

ALKARTASUNA RUBY

Semi-automatic; 32 ACP; 9-shot magazine; 3-3/8-inch barrel; 6-3/8-inch overall length; checkered hard rubber or wooden stocks; blued finish; fixed sights. Manufactured in Spain, 1917 to 1922; distributed primarily in Europe; some used by French army in World Wars I, II.

Exc: $200 **VGood:** $160 **Good:** $125

ALCHEMY ARMS SPECTRE STANDARD ISSUE

Semi-automatic; 9mm Para., .40 S&W, .45 CP; 10-shot double column magazine; 4-1/2-inch barrel; single-action; 32 oz.; linear action trigger; aluminum receiver; keyed internal locking device; tactical rail; lowered ejection port. Introduced 2000.

Exc: $675 **VGood:** $585 **Good:** $525

ALCHEMY ARMS SPECTRE SERVICE GRADE (SG & SGC)

Similar to Spectre Standard Issue, except does not have tactical rail or rounded trigger guard. SGC is designed as a Colt Commander-style pistol with 4-inch barrel, weighing 27 oz. SG introduced 2000; SGC introduced 2001.

Exc: 675 **VGood:** $585 **Good:** $525

ALCHEMY ARMS SPECTRE TITANIUM EDITION

Another in the Spectre series with difference being a titanium lide with an aluminum receiver. Introduced 2000.

Exc: $895 **VGood:** $775 **Good:** $675

Allen Buckhorn Target

Allen 1875 Army Outlaw

Allen Cattleman

American Arms Escort

American Arms CX-22

ALLEN 1875 ARMY OUTLAW

Revolver; single action; 357 Mag., 44-40, 45 Colt; 6-shot cylinder; 7-1/2-inch barrel; 13-3/4-inch overall length; weighs 44 oz.; notch rear sight, blade front; uncheckered walnut stocks; brass triggerguard; color case-hardened frame, rest blued. Copy of Model 1875 Remington. Made in Italy by Uberti. Introduced 1986; importation dropped 1987. Importaton resumed 2001 by Uberti USA, Inc.; dropped 2002.

Perf: $395 **Exc:** $295 **VGood:** $225

Add $45 to above prices for models with convertible cylinder (.45LC/.45ACP).

ALLEN BUCKHORN

Revolver; single-action; 44 Mag., 44 Spl., 44-40; 6-shot cylinder; 4-3/4-inch, 6-inch, 7-1/2-inch barrel; grooved rear sight, blade front; one-piece uncheckered walnut stocks; steel or brass backstrap, triggerguard; color case-hardened frame; blued cylinder, barrel. Made in Italy by Uberti. Formerly imported by Iver Johnson. Reintroduced 1986; importation dropped by Allen Fire Arms 1987. Importation resumed by Uberti USA, Inc. but dropped in 2002.

Perf: $350 **Exc:** $300 **VGood:** $275

Add $70 to above prices for converticle cylinder; add $40 for Target Model.

ALLEN BUCKHORN BUNTLINE MODEL

Same specs as Buckhorn except 18-inch barrel. Was imported by Allen up to 1989; resume by Uberti USA, Inc. in 2001; dropped 2002.

Perf: $400 **Exc:** $350 **VGood:** $325

Add $40 to above prices for target sights; add $40 for extra .44-40 WCF cylinder combo; add $125 for detachable shoulder stock; subtract $50 for brass frame.

ALLEN BUCKHORN TARGET MODEL

Same specs as Buckhorn except flat-top frame; adjustable rear sight ramp front. No longer imported by Allen.

Perf: $425 **Exc:** $375 **VGood:** $350

Convertible cylinder model

Perf: $475 **Exc:** $425 **VGood:** $400

ALLEN CATTLEMAN

Revolver; single action; 22 LR, 22 WMR, 38 Spl., 357 Mag., 44-40, 45 Colt; 6-shot cylinder; 4-3/4-inch, 5-1/2-inch, 7-1/2-inch barrel; fixed groove rear sight, blade front; one-piece uncheckered walnut stocks; brass or steel backstrap and triggerguard; blued barrel, cylinder; case-hardened frame; polished hammer flats. Made in Italy by Uberti. Formerly imported by Iver Johnson. Reintroduced 1986; no longer imported by Allen Fire Arms. Reintroduced by A. Uberti USA 2001; dropped 2002.

Perf: $335 **Exc:** $295 **VGood:** $255

Add $50 to above prices for convertible cylinder (.45LC/45ACP).

Add $10 for chambering in 44 Spl. or 44-40 WCF.

Add $75 for nickel finish (New Model) or Old West (Old Model) finish.

ALLEN CATTLEMAN BUNTLINE MODEL

Same specs as Cattleman except 18-inch barrel; 22 LR/22WMR combo, 357, 44-40, 45 Colt only. No longer imported by Allen.

Perf: $425 **Exc:** $375 **VGood:** $325

ALLEN CATTLEMAN SHERIFF'S MODEL

Same specs as Cattleman except 3-inch or 4-inch barrel; 44-40, 45 Colt only. No longer imported by Allen. Importation discontinued 2002.

Perf: $350 **Exc:** $300 **VGood:** $275

ALLEN CATTLEMAN TARGET MODEL

Same specs as Cattleman except flat-top frame; fully-adjustable rear sight. No longer imported by Allen. Importation discontinued 1990.

Perf: $315 **Exc:** $275 **VGood:** $250

Add $25 to above prices for steel backstrap and trigger guard.

Add $60 for stainless steel construction.

ALLEN 1871 ROLLING BLOCK TARGET PISTOL

Single shot; 22 LR, 22 WMR, 22 Hornet, 357 Mag., 45 Colt (Navy Model with open sights manufactured from 1992 to 1995); 9-7/8-inch half-round, half-octagon barrel; 14-inch overall length; weighs 44 oz.; fully-adjustable rear sight, blade front; walnut stocks, forend; brass triggerguard; color case-hardened frame, blued barrel. Replica of 1871 target rolling block. Made in Italy by Uberti. Introduced 1986; no longer imported by Allen Fire Arms; importation resumed by Uberti USA in 2002; dropped 2002. Add 10% for centerfires.

Perf: $450 **Exc:** $400 **VGood:** $350

AMERICAN ARMS BUCKHORN

Revolver; single action; 44 Mag.; 4-3/4-inch, 6-inch, 7-1/2-inch barrel; 11-inch overall length; weighs 44 oz. (6-inch barrel); smooth walnut grips; blade front sight, groove rear; blued barrel and cylinder; brass triggerguard and backstrap. Imported from Italy by American Arms, Inc. from 1993; dropped 1996.

Perf: $350 **Exc:** $300 **VGood:** $275

AMERICAN ARMS CX-22

Semi-automatic; double action; 22 LR; 8-shot magazine; 3-5/16-inch barrel; 6-5/16-inch overall length; weighs 22 oz.; blade front sight, windage-adjustable rear; checkered black polymer grips; manual hammer-block safety; firing pin safety; alloy frame; blue-black finish. Resembles Walther PPK externally. Introduced 1990; dropped 1995.

Perf: $225 **Exc:** $175 **VGood:** $150

AMERICAN ARMS CXC-22

Same specs as CX-22 except chromed slide. Introduced 1990; dropped 1990.

Perf: $225 **Exc:** $175 **VGood:** $150

AMERICAN ARMS EP-380

Semi-automatic; double action; 380 ACP; 7-shot magazine; 3-1/2-inch barrel; 5-1/2-inch overall length; weighs 25 oz.; checkered wood stocks; fixed sights; slide-mounted safety; made of stainless steel. Manufactured in West Germany. Introduced 1988; dropped 1990.

Perf: $375 **Exc:** $325 **VGood:** $300

AMERICAN ARMS ESCORT

Semi-automatic; double-action-only; 380 ACP; 7-shot magazine; 3-3/8-inch barrel; 6-1/8-inch overall length; weighs 19 oz.; soft polymer grips; blade front sight, windage-adjustable rear; stainless steel construction; chamber-loaded indicator. Marketed by American Arms, Inc. Introduced 1995; dropped 1997.

New: $285 **Perf:** $230 **Exc:** $220

AMERICAN ARMS MATEBA AUTO/REVOLVER

Caliber: 357 Mag., 44 mag., 6-shot. Barrel: 4-inch. Weight: 2.75 lbs. Length: 8.77-inch overall. Stocks: Smooth walnut. Sights: Blade on ramp front,

American Arms PK-22

American Arms Regulator

American Arms PX-22

American Arms ZC-380

American Arms P-98

adjustable rear. Features: Double or single action. Cylinder and slide recoil together upon firing. All-steel construction with polished blue finish. Introduced 1997. Imported from Italy by American Arms, Inc.

New: $1300 **Perf:** $1100 **Exc:** $925

AMERICAN ARMS MODEL P-98

Semi-automatic; double action; 22 LR; 8-shot magazine; 5-inch barrel; 8-1/8-inch overall length; weighs 25 oz.; blade front sight, windage-adjustable rear; grooved black polymer grips; magazine disconnect safety; hammer-block safety; alloy frame; blue-black finish. Has external appearance of Walther P.38. Introduced 1989; dropped 1996.

Perf: $250 **Exc:** $200 **VGood:** $175

AMERICAN ARMS PK-22

Semi-automatic; double action; 22 LR; 8-shot magazine; 3-5/16-inch barrel; 6-5/16-inch overall length; weighs 22 oz.; fixed rear sight; checkered plastic grips; slide-mounted safety; polished blue finish. From American Arms, Inc. Introduced 1989; dropped 1996.

Perf: $225 **Exc:** $175 **VGood:** $150

AMERICAN ARMS PX-22

Semi-automatic; double action; 22 LR; 7-shot magazine; 2-15/16-inch barrel; 5-3/8-inch overall length; weighs 15 oz.; checkered black plastic stocks; fixed sights; polished blued finish. From American Arms, Inc. Introduced 1989; dropped 1995.

Perf: $225 **Exc:** $175 **VGood:** $150

AMERICAN ARMS PX-25

Semi-automatic; double action; 25 ACP; 7-shot magazine; 2-3/4-inch barrel; 5-3/8-inch overall length; weighs 15 oz.; checkered black plastic stocks; fixed sights; blued finish. Introduced 1990; dropped 1991.

Perf: $225 **Exc:** $175 **VGood:** $150

AMERICAN ARMS REGULATOR

Revolver; single action; 357 Mag., 44-40, 45 Colt; 4-3/4-inch, 5-1/2-inch, 7-1/2-inch barrel; 8-1/6-inch overall length (4-3/4-inch barrel); weighs 32 oz. (4-3/4-inch barrel); smooth walnut grips; blade front sight, groove rear; blued barrel and cylinder, brass triggerguard and backstrap. Imported from Italy by American Arms, Inc. Introduced 1992; dropped 2000.

New: $345 **Perf:** $295 **Exc:** $250

Dual cylinder (44-40/44 Spl. or 45 Colt/45 ACP), or DLX all-steel model

Perf: $355 **Exc:** $340 **VGood:** $275

AMERICAN ARMS REGULATOR DELUXE

Similar to Regulator except 45 LC only; all blue charcoal finish (mfd. 1996 to 1997); or color case hardened frame (introduced 1998); steel trigger guard and back strap. Importation dropped in 1992; resumed from 1994 to 2000.

Perf: $325 **Exc:** $300 **VGood:** $280

AMERICAN ARMS BISLEY SINGLE-ACTION REVOLVER

Similar to the Regulator except has Bisley-style grip with steel backstrap and trigger guard, Bisley-style hammer. Color case-hardened steel frame. Hammer block safety. Available with 4-3/4-inch, 5-1/2-inch, 7-1/2-inch barrel, 45 Colt only. Imported from Italy by American Arms, Inc.; introduced 1997; dropped 1998.

New: $395 **Perf:** $375 **Exc:** $350

AMERICAN ARMS SPECTRE

Semi-automatic; double action; 9mm Para., .40 S&W (1991 only), 45 ACP; 30-shot magazine; 6-inch barrel; 13-3/4-inch overall length; weighs 4 lbs., 8 oz.; black nylon grip; fully-adjustable post front sight, fixed U-notch rear; blowback action fires from closed bolt; ambidextrous safety and decocking levers; matte black finish; comes with magazine loading tool. For standard velocity ammunition only. Was marketed by American Arms, Inc.; Introduced 1990; dropped 1993.

9mm & .40 S&W calibers

Perf: $450 **Exc:** $350 **VGood:** $300

45 ACP caliber

Perf: $475 **Exc:** $375 **VGood:** $325

AMERICAN ARMS TT-9MM TOKAREV

Semi-automatic; single action; 9mm Para.; 9-shot magazine; 4-1/2-inch barrel; 8-inch overall length; weighs 32 oz.; grooved plastic stocks; fixed sights; blued finish. Copy of Russian Tokarev, made in Yugoslavia. Introduced 1988; dropped 1990.

Perf: $500 **Exc:** $425 **VGood:** $350

AMERICAN ARMS ZC-380

Semi-automatic; single action; 380 ACP; 7-shot magazine; 3-3/4-inch barrel; 6-1/2-inch overall length; weighs 26 oz.; checkered plastic stocks; fixed sights; polished, blued finish. Made in Yugoslavia. Introduced 1988; dropped 1990.

Perf: $250 **Exc:** $225 **VGood:** $200

AMERICAN DERRINGER COP 357

Derringer; double-action-only; 4-shot; 38 Spl., 357 Mag.; 3-1/8-inch barrel; 5-1/2-inch overall length; weighs 16 oz.; rosewood grips; fixed sights; stainless steel construction. Made in U.S. by American Derringer Corp. Introduced 1990; no longer in production. Add 15 percent for Cop, Inc./Torrance, CA production.

Perf: $900 **Exc:** $725 **VGood:** $400

AMERICAN DERRINGER COP MINI

Same specs as COP 357 except 22 WMR; 2-7/8-inch barrel; 4-15/16-inch overall length; double action; automatic hammer-block safety; rosewood, walnut or other hardwood grips. Made in U.S. by American Derringer Corp. Introduced 1990; dropped 1994.

Perf: $800 **Exc:** $625 **VGood:** $300

AMERICAN DERRINGER DA 38

Derringer; double action; 22 LR, 38 Spl., 357 Mag., 9mm Para., 40 S&W; 3-inch over/under barrels; 4-13/16-inch overall length; weighs 14-1/2 oz.; rosewood, walnut or other hardwood grips; fixed sights; manual safety; made of satin-finished stainless steel, aluminum. Introduced 1989; still in production.

Perf: $360 **Exc:** $250 **VGood:** $200

Add $10 to above prices for 9mm Para., $15 for 357 Mag., and $40 for 40 S&W.

AMERICAN DERRINGER STANDARD DERRINGER

Derringer; double action; 22 LR, 22 WMR; 2-shot; 3-1/2-inch barrel; 5-1/8-inch overall length; weighs 11 oz.; hammer-block safety; blued finish. Direct copy of original High Standard derringer. Reintroduced 1990; dropped 1995. Reintroduced 1998; dropped 2002.

Perf: $320 **Exc:** $245 **VGood:** $185

American Derringer
Lady Derringer

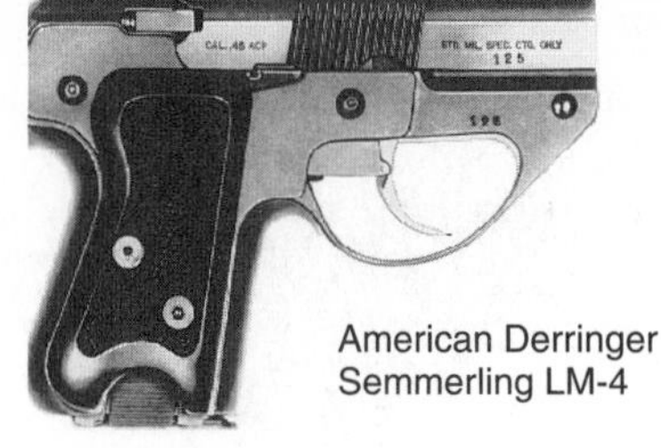
American Derringer
Semmerling LM-4

American Derringer
Model 1 Texas
Commemorative

American Derringer
Model 4

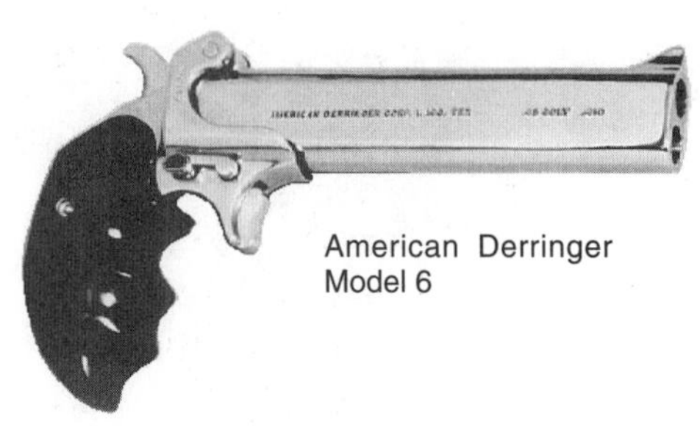
American Derringer
Model 6

AMERICAN DERRINGER LADY DERRINGER

Derringer; over/under; 32 H&R Mag., 38 Spl., 22 LR, 22 WMR, 380 ACP, 357 Mag., 9mm Para., 45 ACP, 45 Colt/.410 shotshell; 2-shot; tuned action; scrimshawed synthetic ivory grips; deluxe grade polished; also deluxe engraved version with 1880s-style engraving. Marketed in fitted box. Introduced 1991; still in production on limited basis.

Perf: $325 **Exc:** $300 **VGood:** $255

Deluxe grade

Perf: $350 **Exc:** $275 **VGood:** $200

Deluxe engraved

Perf: $650 **Exc:** $500 **VGood:** $400

AMERICAN DERRINGER MODEL 1

Derringer; over/under; 22 LR, 22 WMR, 22 Hornet, 223 Rem., 30 Luger, 30-30, 32 ACP, 38 Super, 380 ACP, 38 Spl., 9x18, 9mm Para., 357 Mag., 41 Mag., 44-40, 44 Spl., 44 Mag., 45-70 Govt., 45 Colt/.410; 2-shot; break action; 3-inch barrel; 4-13/16-inch overall length; weighs 15-1/2 oz. (38 Spl.); rosewood, zebra wood stocks; blade front sight; stainless steel with high-polish or satin finish; manual hammer-block safety. Made in U.S. by American Derringer Corp. Introduced 1980; still in production on limited basis.

Regular calibers

Perf: $295 **Exc:** $235 **VGood:** $185

Large caliber

Perf: $345 **Exc:** $285 **VGood:** $205

Add $30 to above prices for high polish finish.

AMERICAN DERRINGER MODEL 1 TEXAS COMMEMORATIVE

Same specs as Model 1 except solid brass frame; stainless steel barrel; rosewood grips; 38 Spl., 44-40 Win., 45 Colt. Made in U.S. by American Derringer Corp. Introduced 1987; still in production on limited basis.

38 Special caliber

Perf: $385 **Exc:** $340 **VGood:** $250

44-40 or 45 Colt caliber

Perf: $470 **Exc:** $415 **VGood:** $250

32 Mag caliber

Perf: $265 **Exc:** $245 **VGood:** $220

AMERICAN DERRINGER MODEL 3

Derringer; single shot; 32 Mag. 38 Spl.; 2-1/2-inch barrel; 4-15/16-inch overall length; weighs 8-1/2 oz.; rosewood grips; blade front sight; stainless steel construction; manual hammer-block safety. Made in U.S. by American Derringer Corp. Introduced 1985; dropped 1994.

Perf: $250 **Exc:** $225 **VGood:** $200

AMERICAN DERRINGER MODEL 4

Derringer; over/under; 357 Mag., 357 Max., 45-70/.410/3-inch, 45 Colt/.410/3-inch, 45 ACP, 44 Mag.; 2-shot; break-action; 4-1/8-inch barrel; 6-inch overall length; weighs 16-1/2 oz.; stainless steel construction. Made in U.S. by American Derringer Corp. Introduced 1985; still in production.

Perf: $375 **Exc:** $290 **VGood:** $230

AMERICAN DERRINGER MODEL 4 ALASKAN SURVIVAL MODEL

Same specs as Model 4 except upper barrel chambered for 45-70 or 44 Mag. Made in U.S. by American Derringer Corp. Introduced 1980; still in limited production.

Perf: $525 **Exc:** $450 **VGood:** $400

AMERICAN DERRINGER MODEL 6

Derringer; over/under; 45 LC/410 3-inch, 22 WMR, 357 Mag., 45 ACP; 2-shot; 6-inch barrels; 8-1/4-inch overall length; weighs 21 oz.; rosewood stocks; manual hammer-block safety. Made in U.S. by American Derringer Corp. Introduced 1986; still in limited production.

Perf: $355 **Exc:** $250 **VGood:** $200

Add $10 to above prices for 45 LC/410 shotshell chambering.
Add $15 for satin finish (discontinued in 1994).
Add $40 for high polish finish.
Add $50 for oversized grips (discontinued in 1994 but reinstated 1998-99).

AMERICAN DERRINGER MODEL 7 ULTRA LIGHTWEIGHT

Derringer; over/under; 22 LR, 22 WMR, 32 H&R Mag., 380 ACP, 38 Spl., 44 Spl.; 2-shot; break-action; 3-inch barrel; 4-7/8-inch overall length; weighs 7-1/2 oz.; high strength aircraft aluminum construction; rosewood, zebra wood stocks; blade front sight; stainless steel; manual hammer-block safety. Made in U.S. by American Derringer Corp. Introduced 1986; still in production.

Perf: $275 **Exc:** $185 **VGood:** $145

44 Spl. caliber

Perf: $450 **Exc:** $395 **VGood:** $300

AMERICAN DERRINGER MODEL 10 LIGHTWEIGHT

Derringer; over/under; 38 Special, 45 ACP, 45 Colt; 2-shot; break-action; 3-inch barrels; 4-13/16-inch overall length; weighs 10 oz.; aluminum frame; matte gray finish. Introduced 1990; still in production.

45 Colt

Perf: $3850 **Exc:** $315 **VGood:** $280

38 Special

Perf: $300 **Exc:** $250 **VGood:** $200

45 ACP

Perf: $325 **Exc:** $275 **VGood:** $225

AMERICAN DERRINGER MODEL 11

Derringer; over/under; 22 LR, 22 WMR, 32 H&R Mag., .380 ACP, 38 Spl.; 2-shot; break-action; 3-inch barrel; 4-13/16-inch overall length; weighs 11 oz.; aluminum barrels; matte gray frame. Introduced 1990.

Perf: $300 **Exc:** $230 **VGood:** $195

AMERICAN DERRINGER SEMMERLING LM-4

Derringer; manually-operated repeater; 9mm Para., 45 ACP; 7-shot (9mm), 5-shot (45 ACP) magazine; 3-inch barrel; 5-1/4-inch overall length; weighs 24 oz.; height 3-3/4-inch; width 1 inch; checkered plastic grips (blued finish), rosewood (stainless finish); open fixed sights. Was sold with manual, leather carrying case, spare stock screws, wrench. Limited manufacture in U.S. by American Derringer Corp.; dropped 2003.

Perf: $2390 **Exc:** $2045 **VGood:** $1876

Stainless steel

Perf: $2450 **Exc:** $2250 **VGood:** $2050

AMERICAN FIREARMS 25

Semi-automatic; 25 ACP; 8-shot magazine; 2-1/8-inch barrel; 4-7/16-inch overall length; fixed sights; walnut grips; blued ordnance steel or stainless

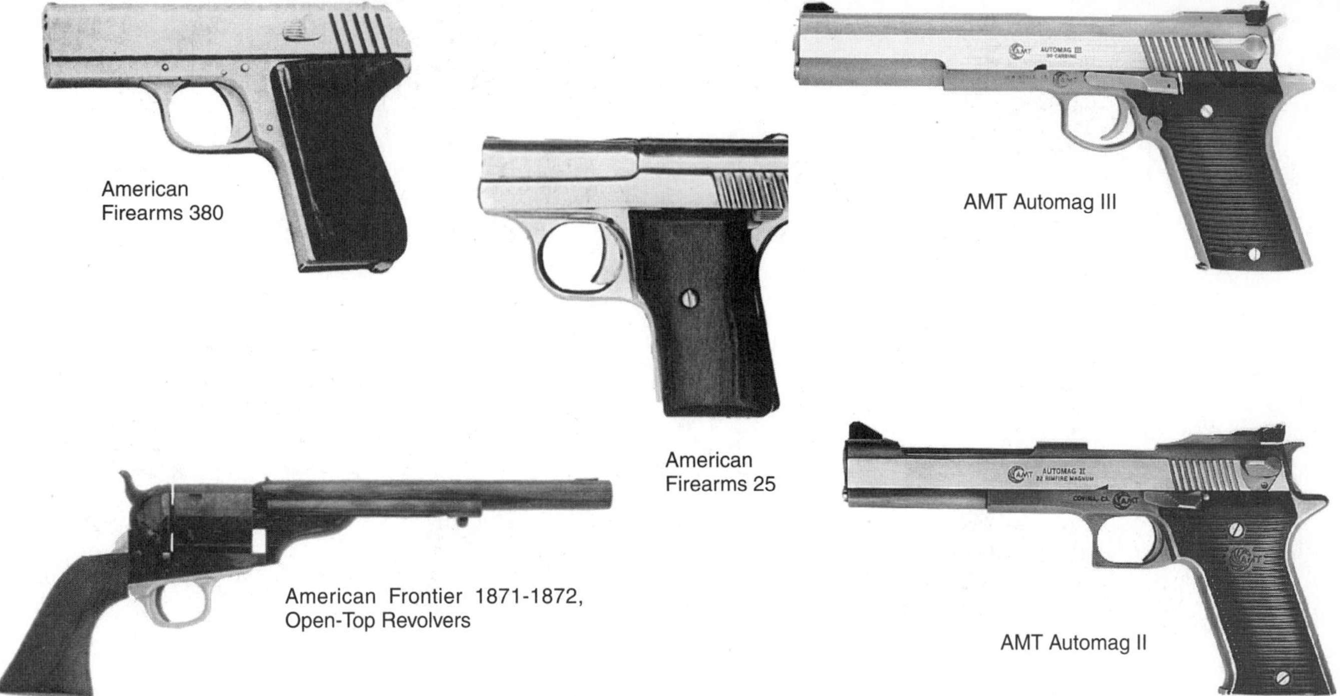
American Firearms 380

American Firearms 25

AMT Automag III

American Frontier 1871-1872, Open-Top Revolvers

AMT Automag II

steel. Manufactured by American Firearms Co., Inc. Introduced 1966; dropped 1974.

Perf: $225 **Exc:** $175 **VGood:** $150

Stainless steel

Perf: $275 **Exc:** $225 **VGood:** $200

AMERICAN FIREARMS 380

Semi-automatic; 380 ACP; 8-shot magazine; 3-1/2-inch barrel; 5-1/2-inch overall; stainless steel; smooth walnut stocks. Limited manufacture 1972.

Perf: $395 **Exc:** $325 **VGood:** $225

AMERICAN FIREARMS DERRINGER

Derringer; over/under; 38 Spl., 22 LR, 22 WMR; 2-shot; 3-inch barrel; fixed open sights; checkered plastic grips; stainless steel construction; spur trigger, half-cock safety. Introduced 1972; dropped 1974.

Perf: $225 **Exc:** $175 **VGood:** $135

AMERICAN FRONTIER 1851 NAVY CONVERSION

Revolver; single action; 38, 44. Barrel: 4-3/4-inch, 5-1/2-inch, 7-1/2-inch, octagon. Weight: NA. Length: NA. Stocks: Varnished walnut, Navy size. Sights: Blade front, fixed rear. Features: Shoots metallic cartridge ammunition. Non-rebated cylinder; blued steel backstrap and trigger guard; color case-hardened hammer, trigger, ramrod, plunger; no ejector rod assembly. Introduced 1996; discontinued 2000. Imported from Italy by American Frontier Firearms Mfg.

Perf: $575 **Exc:** $400 **VGood:** $275

AMERICAN FRONTIER 1851 NAVY RICHARDS & MASON CONVERSION

Similar to the 1851 Navy Conversion except has Mason ejector assembly. Introduced 1996; discontinued 2000. Imported from Italy by American Frontier Firearms Mfg.

Perf: $575 **Exc:** $400 **VGood:** $275

AMERICAN FRONTIER REMINGTON NEW ARMY CAVALRY

Revolver; single action; 38, 44, 45. Barrel: 5-1/2-inch, 7-1/2-inch, 8-inch. Weight: NA. Length: NA. Stocks: Varnished walnut Sights: Blade front, fixed rear. Features: High polish blue finish; color case-hardened hammer. Has ejector assembly, loading gate. Government inspector's cartouche on left grip, sub-inspector's initials on various parts. Introduced 1997; discontinued 2000. Imported from Italy by American Frontier Firearms Mfg.

Perf: $575 **Exc:** $400 **VGood:** $275

AMERICAN FRONTIER RICHARDS 1860 ARMY

Revolver; single action; 38 Spl., 44 Spl. Barrel: 4-3/4-inch, 5-1/2-inch, 7-1/2-inch, round. Weight: NA. Length: NA. Stocks: Varnished walnut, Army size. Sights: Blade front, fixed rear. Features: Shoots metallic cartridge ammunition. Rebated cylinder; available with or without ejector assembly; high-polish blue including backstrap; silver-plated trigger guard; color case-hardened hammer and trigger. Introduced 1996; discontinued 2000. Imported from Italy by American Frontier Firearms Mfg.

Perf: $575 **Exc:** $400 **VGood:** $275

AMERICAN FRONTIER 1871-1872 POCKET MODEL REVOLVER

Revolver; single action; 32, 5-shot cylinder. Barrel: 4-3/4-inch, 5-1/2-inch round. Weight: NA. Length: NA. Stocks: Varnished walnut or Tiffany. Sights: Blade front, fixed rear. Features: Based on the 1862 Police percussion revolver converted to metallic cartridge. High polish blue finish with silver-plated brass backstrap and trigger guard, color case-hardened hammer. Introduced 1996; discontinued 2000. Imported from Italy by American Frontier Firearms Mfg.

Perf: $395 **Exc:** $295 **VGood:** $205

AMERICAN FRONTIER REMINGTON NEW MODEL REVOLVER

Revolver; single action; 38, 44.; 5-1/2-inch, 7-1/2-inch barrel; varnished walnut grips; blade front, fixed rear sights; replica of the factory conversions by Remington between 1863 and 1875; high polish blue or silver finish with color case-hardened hammer; has original loading lever and no gate or ejector assembly. Introduced 1996; discontinued 2000. Imported from Italy by American Frontier Firearms Mfg.

Perf: $400 **Exc:** $300 **VGood:** $275

AMERICAN FRONTIER POCKET RICHARDS & MASON NAVY

Revolver; single action; 32; 5-shot cylinder; 4-3/4-inch, 5-1/2-inch barrel; varnished walnut stocks; blade front, fixed rear sights; shoots metallic-cartridge ammunition; non-rebated cylinder; high-polish blue; silver-plated brass backstrap and trigger guard; ejector assembly; color case-hardened hammer and trigger. Introduced 1996; discontinued 2000. Imported from Italy by American Frontier Firearms Mfg.

Perf: $400 **Exc:** $300 **VGood:** $275

AMERICAN FRONTIER 1871-1872 OPEN-TOP REVOLVERS

Revolver; single action; 38 Spl., 44 Spl.; 4-3/4-inch, 5-1/2-inch, 7-1/2-inch, 8-inch round barrel; varnished walnut grips; blade front, fixed rear sights; reproduction of the early cartridge conversions from percussion; made for metallic cartridges; high polish blued steel; silver-plated brass backstrap and trigger guard; color case-hardened hammer; straight non-rebated cylinder with naval engagement engraving; stamped with original patent dates; does not have conversion breechplate. Introduced 1996; discontinued 2000. Imported from Italy by American Frontier Firearms Mfg.

Perf: $575 **Exc:** $400 **VGood:** $275

Tiffany model with Tiffany grips, silver and gold finish with engraving

Perf: $895 **Exc:** $695 **VGood:** $450

AMT AUTOMAG II

Semi-automatic; 22 WMR; 9-shot magazine, 7-shot (3-3/8-inch barrel); 3-3/8-inch, 4-1/2-inch, 6-inch barrel; 9-3/4-inch overall length; weighs 23 oz.; Millett adjustable rear sight, blade front; grooved black composition stocks; squared triggerguard; stainless steel construction; gas-assisted action; brushed finish on slide flats, rest sandblasted. Introduced 1987; discontinued 2001.

Perf: $650 **Exc:** $600 **VGood:** $550

AMT AUTOMAG III

Semi-automatic; single action; 30 Carbine, 9mm Win. Mag.; 8-shot magazine; 6-3/8-inch barrel; 10-1/2-inch overall length; weighs 43 oz.; carbon fiber grips; blade front sight, adjustable rear; stainless steel construction; hammer-drop safety; brushed finish on

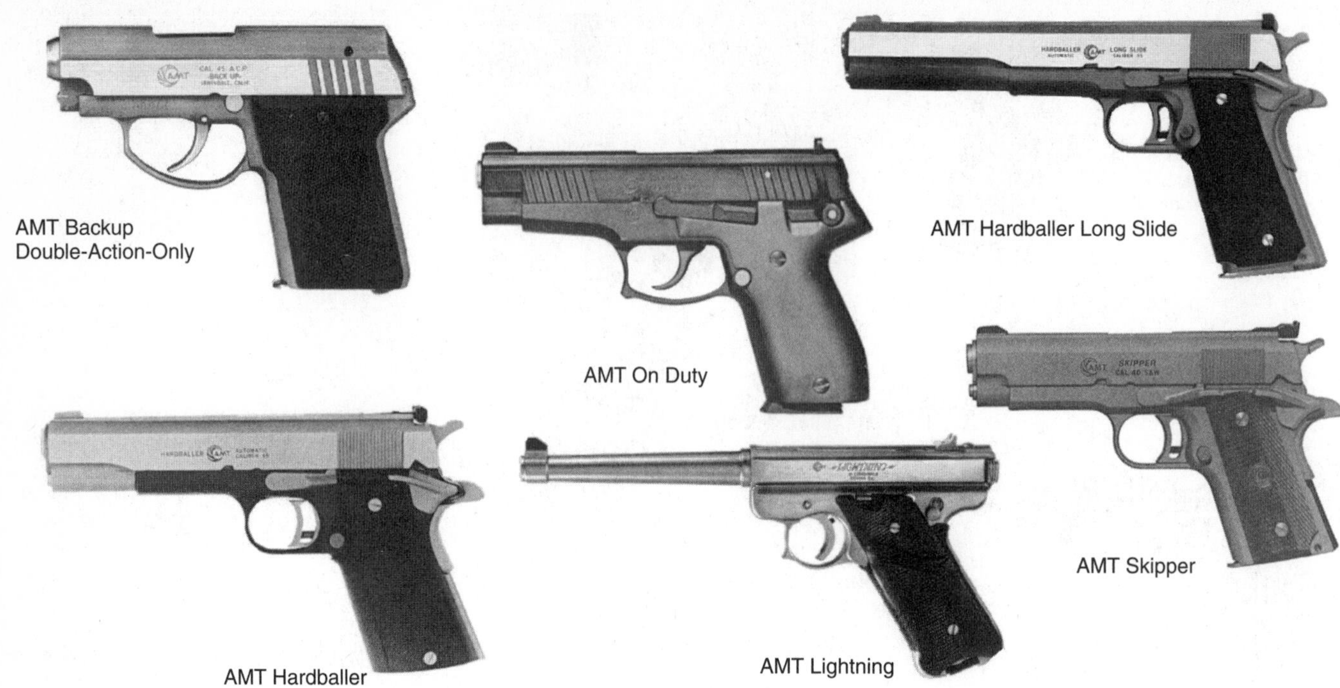
AMT Backup Double-Action-Only

AMT Hardballer Long Slide

AMT On Duty

AMT Skipper

AMT Hardballer

AMT Lightning

slide flats, rest sandblasted. Made in U.S. by AMT. Introduced 1989; discontinued 2001.

Perf: $750 **Exc:** $650 **VGood:** $550

AMT AUTOMAG IV

Semi-automatic; single action; 10mm (discontinued 1993) or 45 Winchester Mag.; 7-shot magazine; 6-1/2-inch barrel; 10-1/2-inch overall length; weighs 46 oz.; carbon fiber grips; blade front sight, adjustable rear; stainless steel construction with brushed finish. Made in U.S. by AMT. Introduced 1990; discontinued 2001.

Perf: $750 **Exc:** $650 **VGood:** $550

AMT AUTOMAG V

Semi-automatic; single action; 50 AE; 5-shot magazine; 6-1/2-inch barrel; 10-1/2-inch overall length; weighs 46 oz.; carbon fiber grips; blade front sight, adjustable rear; stainless steel construction with brushed finish. Made in U.S. by AMT. Introduced 1990; dropped 1995.

Perf: $850 **Exc:** $775 **VGood:** $695

AMT BACKUP

Semi-automatic; double action; 22 LR (discontinued 1987), 357 SIG (from 1996), 380 ACP, 38 Super (from 1995), 9mm Para. (from 1995), 40 S&W (from 1995), 400 Cor-Bon (from 1997); 8-shot (22 LR), 5-shot (380 ACP & 40S&W) magazine; 2-1/2-inch barrel; 5-inch overall length; weighs 17 oz.; smooth wood stocks; fixed open sights; concealed hammer; manual grip safeties; blowback operated; stainless steel. 380 ACP introduced 1974; 22 introduced 1982. No longer in production. (22 LR & 380 ACP), $349 (9mm Para., 40 S&W & 45 ACP), $389 (357 SIG, 38 Super, 400 Cor-Bon).

22 LR

Perf: $250 **Exc:** $190 **VGood:** $145

380 ACP

Perf: $250 **Exc:** $190 **VGood:** $145

9mm Para., 40 S&W & 45 ACP

Perf: $250 **Exc:** $190 **VGood:** $145

357 SIG, 38 Super & 400 Cor-Bon

Perf: $375 **Exc:** $320 **VGood:** $275

AMT BACKUP II

Same specs as standard Backup except single action; 380 ACP only with 5-shot magazine; carbon fiber grips; weighs 18 oz. Introduced 1993; dropped 1998.

Perf: $260 **Exc:** $200 **VGood:** $175

AMT BACKUP DOUBLE-ACTION-ONLY

Same specs as standard Backup except 9mm Para., 38 Super, 40 S&W, 45 ACP; double-action-only; enlarged triggerguard; slide rounded at rear; 5-shot magazine. Made in U.S. by AMT. Introduced 1992. No longer in production.

Perf: $260 **Exc:** $200 **VGood:** $175

AMT BULL'S-EYE TARGET

Semi-automatic; 40 S&W; 8-shot magazine; 5-inch barrel; 8-1/2-inch overall length; weighs 38 oz.; Millett adjustable rear sight; neoprene wrap-around grips; stainless steel construction; long grip safety; wide adjustable trigger; beveled magazine well. Introduced 1991; dropped 1992.

Perf: $400 **Exc:** $340 **VGood:** $295

AMT BULL'S-EYE TARGET REGULATION

Same specs as Bull's-Eye Target except 22 LR; 5-inch, 6-1/2-inch, 8-1/2-inch, 10-1/2-inch, 12-1/2-inch bull or tapered barrel; adjustable sights; vent rib; wooden target grips. Manufactured 1986 only.

Perf: $425 **Exc:** $350 **VGood:** $285

AMT COMBAT GOVERNMENT

Semi-automatic; single action; 45 ACP; 5-inch barrel; 8-1/2-inch overall length; stainless steel construction; extended combat safety; adjustable target-type trigger; flat mainspring housing; custom-fitted barrel bushing; fixed combat sights; checkered walnut grips. Introduced 1978; dropped 1980.

Perf: $450 **Exc:** $365 **VGood:** $295

AMT HARDBALLER

Semi-automatic; 45 ACP; 5-inch barrel; 8-1/2-inch overall length; weighs 39 oz.; stainless steel construction; extended combat safety; serrated matted slide rib; long grip safety; beveled magazine well; grooved front, back straps; adjustable trigger; custom barrel bushing; adjustable combat sights; checkered walnut or wrap-around rubber grips. Introduced 1978; dropped 2001.

New.: $525 **Exc:** $425 **VGood:** $300

AMT HARDBALLER LONG SLIDE

Same specs as Hardballer except 7-inch barrel; was available in 400 Cor-Bon; 10-1/2-inch overall length; fully-adjustable micro rear sight. Introduced 1977; discontinued in 2001. Add 125% for Arcadia, California, address.

Perf: $800 **Exc:** $625 **VGood:** $425

Add $50 to above prices for 400 Cor-Bon chambering.

Add $300 for 5-inch Longslide conversion kit (discontinued 1997).

AMT JAVELINA

Semi-automatic; single action; 10mm Auto; 8-shot magazine; 7-inch barrel; 10-1/2-inch overall length; weighs 40 oz.; wrap-around rubber grips; blade front sight, Millett adjustable rear; all stainless construction, brushed finish. Made in U.S. by AMT. Introduced 1989; dropped 1992.

Perf: $560 **Exc:** $460 **VGood:** $400

AMT LIGHTNING

Semi-automatic; 22 LR; 10-shot magazine; 6-1/2-inch, 8-1/2-inch, 10-1/2-inch, 12-1/2-inch tapered barrels; 5-inch, 6-1/2-inch, 8-1/2-inch, 10-1/2-inch, 12-1/2-inch bull barrels; 10-3/4-inch overall length 6-1/2-inch barrel); weighs 45 oz.; checkered wrap-around rubber stocks; blade front sight, fixed rear; adjustable rear at extra cost; stainless steel; Clark trigger with adjustable stops; receiver grooved for scope; interchangeable barrels. Introduced 1984; dropped 1989.

Perf: $350 **Exc:** $250 **VGood:** $175

Adjustable Sights

Perf: $375 **Exc:** $350 **VGood:** $285

AMT ON DUTY

Semi-automatic; double action; 9mm Para., 40 S&W, 45 ACP; 15-shot (9mm), 11-shot (40 S&W), 9-shot (45 ACP) magazine; 4-1/2-inch barrel; 7 3/4-inch overall length; weighs 32 oz.; smooth carbon fiber grips; blade front sight, windage-adjustable rear; three-dot system; choice of DA with decocker or double-action-only; inertia firing pin, trigger disconnector safety; aluminum frame with steel recoil shoulder, stainless steel slide and barrel. Made in U.S. by AMT. Introduced 1991; dropped 1994.

Perf: $385 **Exc:** $300 **VGood:** $275

45 ACP caliber

Perf: $445 **Exc:** $360 **VGood:** $335

Arminex Tri-Fire

Arcus Model 94C Compact

Arcus 94 Auto Pistol

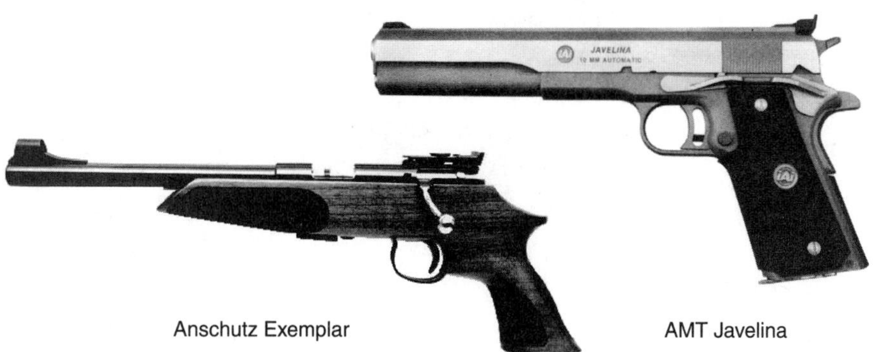
Anschutz Exemplar

AMT Javelina

Armalite AR-24

AMT SKIPPER

Semi-automatic; 45 ACP, 40 S&W; 7-shot magazine; 4-1/4-inch barrel; 7-inch overall length; weighs 33 oz.; Millet adjustable rear sight; checkered walnut grips; matte stainless steel construction. Introduced 1978; dropped 1984.

Perf: $500 **Exc:** $400 **VGood:** $300

AMT SKIPPER COMBAT

Same specs as standard Skipper except fixed sights. Discontinued 1984.

Perf: $500 **Exc:** $400 **VGood:** $300

ANSCHUTZ EXEMPLAR

Bolt action; 22 LR, 22 Hornet; 5-shot magazine; 10-inch, 14-inch barrel; 17-inch overall length; weighs 56 oz.; open-notch adjustable rear sight, hooded front on ramp; European walnut stock, stippled grip, forend; built on Anschutz Match 64 rifle action with left-hand bolt; Anschutz #5091 two-stage trigger; receiver grooved for scope mount. Made in Germany. Introduced 1987; dropped 1997.

Perf: $600 **Exc:** $525 **VGood:** $300

22 Hornet

Perf: $835 **Exc:** $685 **VGood:** $575

ANSCHUTZ MODEL 64P SPORT/TARGET

Bolt action; 22 LR, 22 WMR, 5-shot magazine. Barrel: 10-inch. Weight: 3 lbs., 8 oz. Length: 18-1/2-inch overall. Stock: Choate Rynite. Sights: None furnished; grooved for scope mounting. Features: Right-hand bolt; polished blue finish. Introduced 1998; dropped 2003. Imported from Germany by AcuSport.

Perf: $700 **Exc:** $585 **VGood:** $400

ANSCHUTZ MODEL 17 LP

Similar to Model 64LP except 17 HMR; 4-shot magazine. Importation began 2003.

Perf: $700 **Exc:** $585 **VGood:** $400

ARCUS-94 AUTO PISTOL

Caliber: 9mm Para., 10-shot magazine. Barrel: 5.24-inch. Weight: 32 oz. Length: 8 inches overall. Stocks: Textured rubber. Sights: Blade front, rear adjustable for windage. Features: Single-action trigger. Available in blued, brushed chrome and two-tone finishes. Compact and double-action versions also available. Introduced 1998. Previously imported from Bulgaria by Miltex, Inc. (from 1998 to 2000).

Perf: $285 **Exc:** $250 **VGood:** $225

ARCUS-94C COMPACT AUTO PISTOL

Similar to Arcus-94 except compact version with overall length 7-1/2-inch; Barrel length 4-3/4-inch; weight 2 lbs.

Perf: $285 **Exc:** $250 **VGood:** $225

ARGENTINE FM HI-POWER 9MM

Semi-automatic; single action; 9mm Para.; 10-shot magazine; 4-21/32-inch barrel; 7-3/4-inch overall length; weighs 32 oz.; blade front sight, adjustable rear; checkered walnut grips; licensed copy of Browning Hi-Power made by FM Fray Luis Beltrain. Previously imported from Argentina by Century International Arms, Inc. Introduced 1990; imported by Sarco, Inc. and Pacific Armament Corp.

Perf: $300 **Exc:** $250 **VGood:** $200

Add $150 to above price for Detective Model conversion kit.

ARGENTINE FM HI-POWER DETECTIVE MODEL

Same specs as standard model except 3-13/16-inch barrel; 6-15/16-inch overall length; weighs 33 oz.; finger-groove, checkered soft rubber grips; matte black finish. Formerly imported by Century International Arms, Inc., Sarco, Inc. and Pacific Armament Corp.

New: $275 **Perf:** $250 **Exc:** $200

ARMALITE AR-24 PISTOL

Single-/double-action semi-auto pistol chambered in 9mm Parabellum; based on CZ-75 design. Steel slide and frame; 5.26" (Full-Size) and 3.89" (Compact) barrel lengths. Blue-black finish. Fixed- and adjustable-sight models available. Introduced in 2007. Deduct 15 percent for Compact model.

NIB: $425 **Exc:** $395 **VGood:** $300

ARMALITE AR-24 TACTICAL CUSTOM

Similar to above with tactical refinements including stippled front and back straps, 3-dot luminous sights, etc. Also available inW compact version (shown).

NIB: $475 **Exc:** $445 **VGood:** $350

ARMINEX TRI-FIRE

Semi-automatic; single action; 9mm Para., 38 Super, 45 ACP; 9-shot (9mm), 7-shot (45 ACP) magazine; 5-inch, 6-inch, 7-inch barrel; 8-inch overall length; weighs 38 oz.; smooth contoured walnut stocks; interchangeable post front sight, adjustable rear; slide-mounted firing pin safety; contoured backstrap; blued or electroless nickel finish; convertible by changing barrel, magazine, recoil spring. Introduced 1982; dropped 1987.

Perf: $750 **Exc:** $650 **VGood:** $475

Presentation cased

Perf: $800 **Exc:** $700 **VGood:** $525

With conversion unit

Perf: $880 **Exc:** $780 **VGood:** $605

ARMINEX TRI-FIRE TARGET MODEL

Same specs as Tri-Fire except 1-inch longer slide; 6-inch or 7-inch barrel. Introduced 1982; dropped 1987.

Perf: $850 **Exc:** $725 **VGood:** $550

ARMINIUS MODEL 3

Revolver; double action; 25 ACP; 5-shot; 2-inch barrel; hammerless; safety catch; folding trigger. Produced by Friedrick Pickert, Arminius Waffenwerk. Not currently imported into U.S.

Perf: $175 **Exc:** $135 **VGood:** $125

ARMINIUS MODEL 8

Revolver; double action; 320, 32 ACP; 5-shot; 2-inch, 5-1/2-inch barrel; hammerless; safety catch; folding trigger. Produced by Friedrick Pickert, Arminius Waffenwerk. Not currently imported into U.S.

Perf: $175 **Exc:** $135 **VGood:** $125

ARMINIUS MODEL 9

Revolver; double action; 320, 32 ACP; 5-shot; 2-5/16-inch barrel; hammer model. Produced by Friedrick Pickert, Arminius Waffenwerk. Not currently imported into U.S.

Perf: $185 **Exc:** $140 **VGood:** $130

ARMINIUS MODEL 9A

Same specs as Model 9 except 3-1/8-inch barrel.

Perf: $185 **Exc:** $135 **VGood:** $110

ARMINIUS MODEL 10

Revolver; double action; 320, 32 ACP; 5-shot; 2-5/16-inch barrel; hammerless; safety catch; folding

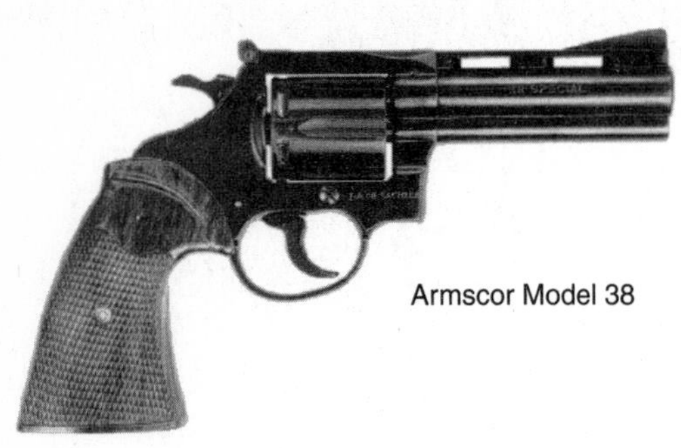
Armscor Model 38

Armscor Model 200SE

Astra A-100

Astra A-70

Armscor MAP1FS

trigger. Produced by Friedrick Pickert, Arminius Waffenwerk. Not currently imported into U.S.

Perf: $165 **Exc:** $145 **VGood:** $125

ARMINIUS MODEL TP1

Single shot; 22 LR; adjustable sights; drop-down action; hammer fired. Target pistol produced by Friedrick Pickert, Arminius Waffenwerk. Not currently imported into U.S.

Perf: $400 **Exc:** $325 **VGood:** $275

ARMINIUS MODEL TP2

Similiar to Model TP1 except double-set trigger; concealed hammer. Target pistol produced by Friedrick Pickert, Arminius Waffenwerk. Not currently imported into U.S.

Perf: $500 **Exc:** $425 **VGood:** $325

ARMSCOR MODEL 38

Revolver; double action; 38 Spl.; 6-shot cylinder; 4-inch barrel; weighs 32 oz.; windage-adjustable rear sight, ramp front; checkered Philippine mahogany stocks; vent rib; polished blue finish. Made in the Philippines. Introduced 1986; dropped 1999; reintroduced 2001.

Perf: $175 **Exc:** $135 **VGood:** $110

ARMSCOR MODEL 200P

Revolver; double action; 38 Spl.; 6-shot cylinder; 2-1/2-inch, 4-inch barrel; 8-7/8-inch overall length (4-inch barrel); weighs 26 oz.; ramp front sight, fixed rear; checkered mahogany or rubber grips; blued finish. Made in the Philippines. Introduced 1990; dropped 1999; reintroduced 2001.

Perf: $175 **Exc:** $135 **VGood:** $110A

ARMSCOR MODEL 200SE

Same specs as Model 200P except 22 LR, 22 WMR, 38 Spl.; 2-inch, 3-inch, 6-inch barrel; overall length 9-1/4 inches (4-inch barrel); weighs 36 oz.; Introduced 1989; dropped 1999; reintroduced 2001.

Perf: $200 **Exc:** $175 **VGood:** $150

ARMSCOR MODEL 200TC

Same specs as Model 200P except 22 LR, 22 WMR, 38 Spl.; full shroud barrel; adjustable rear sight; checkered wood grips. Introduced 1990; dropped 1999; reintroduced 2001.

Perf: $225 **Exc:** $200 **VGood:** $175

ARMSCOR MODEL 202

Similar to Model 200, except does not have barrel shroud. Imported from 2001.

Perf: $175 **Exc:** $150 **VGood:** $125

ARMSCOR MODEL 206

Similar to Model 200, except has 2-inch barrel, weighs 24 oz. Imported from 2001.

Perf: $175 **Exc:** $150 **VGood:** $125

ARMSCOR MODEL 210

Similar to Model 200, except has 4-inch vent-rib barrel, and adjustable rear sight. Weight: 28 oz. Imported from 2001.

Perf: $175 **Exc:** $150 **VGood:** $125

ARMSCOR MAP1 FS

Single/double-action 9mm semi-auto with 16+1 capacity. Fixed sights, 4.45-inch barrel, 40.5 oz. nickel alloy steel frame and slide. (Shorter, lighter MS model has 3.66-inch barrel.) Introduced 2006.

NIB: $425 **Exc:** $350 **VGood:** $275

ARMSCOR MAPP1 FS

Single/double-action 9mm semi-auto with 16+1 capacity. Fixed sights, 4.45-inch barrel, 40.5 oz. polymer frame with integrated accessory rail, and nickel alloy steel slide. (Shorter, lighter MS model has 3.66-inch barrel.)

NIB: $435 **Exc:** $365 **VGood:** $285

ARMSCOR/ROCK ISLAND ARMORY MAP1 & MAPP1 PISTOLS

Caliber: 9mm, 16-round magazine. Browning short-recoil action, nickel steel alloy frame with Parkerized finish. Double-action/single-action with frame-mounted safety, combat slide stop, accessory rail. Tangfolio design manufactured by Armscor in the Philippines. New in 2011.

Price: N/A

ARMSCOR/ROCK ISLAND ARMORY XT22 PISTOL

Caliber: 22 LR, 15-round magazine. Full-size 1911 design with 5-inch barrel, weight 38 oz. Forged steel slide and one-piece chrome moly barrel. Introduced in 2011.

Perf: $435 **Exc:** $365 **VGood:** $315

ARM TECH DERRINGER

Derringer; double-action-only; 22 LR, 22 WMR; 2-5/8-inch barrel; 4-5/8-inch overall length; weighs 19 oz.; fixed sights; hard rubber or walnut stocks; stainless steel; blued model available. Introduced 1983; no longer in production.

Perf: $175 **Exc:** $150 **VGood:** $125

ASTRA A-70

Semi-automatic; double action; 9mm Para., 40 S&W; 8-shot (9 mm), 7-shot (40 S&W) magazine; 3-1/2-inch barrel; weighs 29 oz.; 6-1/2-inch overall length; checkered black plastic grips; blade front sight, windage-adjustable rear; all steel frame and slide; checkered grip straps and trigger guard; nickel or blue finish. Imported from Spain by European American Armory. Introduced 1992; dropped 1996.

New: $300 **Perf:** $250 **Exc:** $225

Nickel finish

New: $325 **Perf:** $300 **Exc:** $250

Stainless steel

New: $350 **Perf:** $325 **Exc:** $275

ASTRA A-75 DECOCKER

Semi-automatic; double action; 9mm Para., 40 S&W, 45 ACP; 8-shot (9mm), 7-shot (40 S&W) magazine; 3-1/2-inch barrel; 6-1/2-inch overall length; weighs 29 oz. (Featherweight, 23-1/2 oz.); contoured pebble-grain grips; blade front sight, windage-adjustable rear; all steel frame and slide; checkered grip straps, triggerguard; nickel or blue finish; ambidextrous decocker system. Imported from Spain by European American Armory. Introduced 1993; dropped 1997.

Blue finish

New: $300 **Perf:** $265 **Exc:** $240

Nickel finish

New: $325 **Perf:** $275 **Exc:** $255

Stainless finish MSR $485

New: $400 **Perf:** $350 **Exc:** $325

Featherweight, 9mm Para.

New: $420 **Perf:** $370 **Exc:** $345

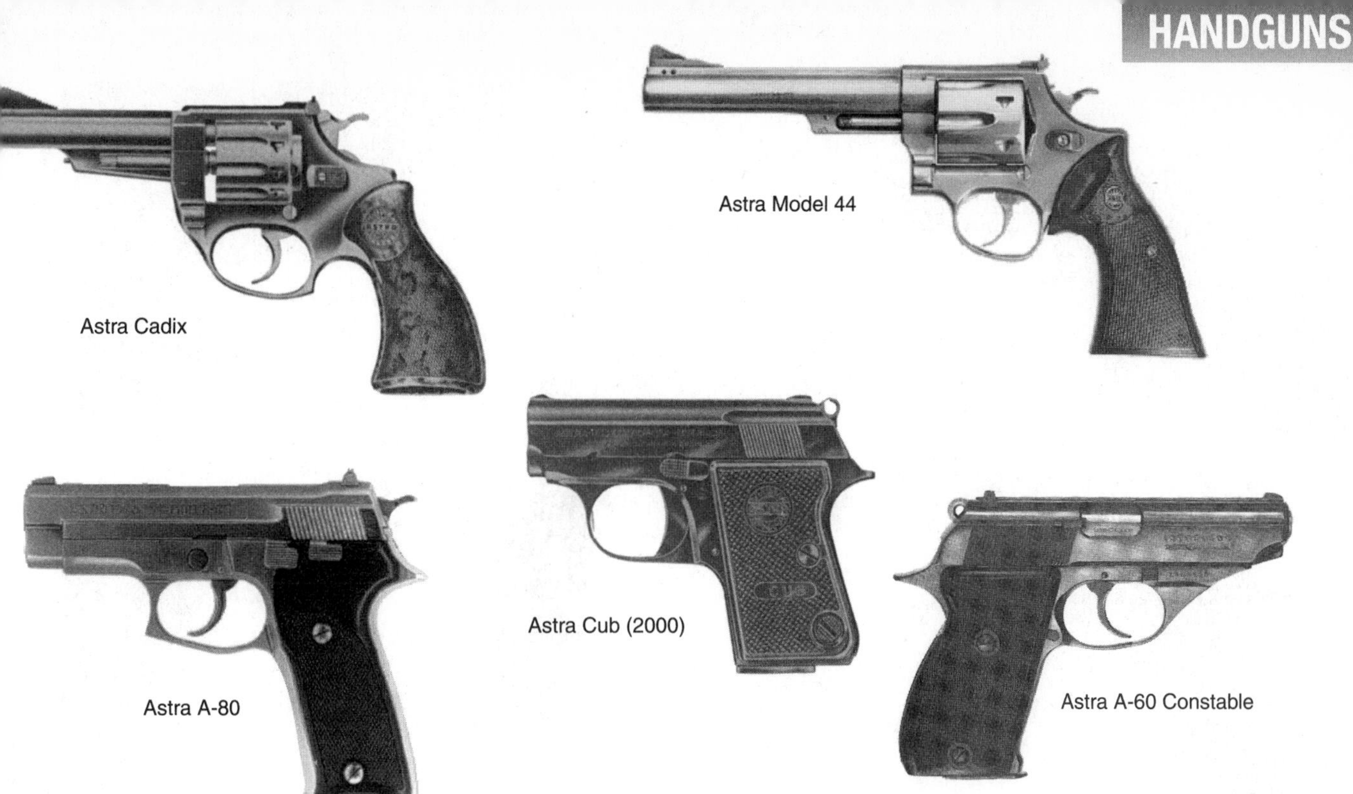
Astra Cadix

Astra Model 44

Astra Cub (2000)

Astra A-80

Astra A-60 Constable

ASTRA A-80

Semi-automatic; double action; 9mm Para., 38 Super, 45 ACP; 15-shot (9mm, 38 Super), 9-shot (45 ACP); 3-3/4-inch barrel; 7-inch overall length; weighs 40 oz.; checkered black plastic stocks; square blade front sight, drift-adjustable square notch rear; loaded-chamber indicator; combat-style triggerguard; optional right-side slide release; automatic internal safety; decocking lever; blued or chrome finish. Imported from Spain by Interarms. Introduced 1982; dropped 1989.

Blue finish
Perf: $350 **Exc:** $300 **VGood:** $285

Chrome finish
Perf: $385 **Exc:** $335 **VGood:** $325

ASTRA A-90

Semi-automatic; double action; 9mm Para., 45 ACP; 14-shot (9mm), 8-shot (45 ACP); 3-3/4-inch barrel; 7-inch overall length; weighs 48 oz.; checkered black plastic stocks; square blade front sight, square notch windage-adjustable rear; double or single action; loaded chamber indicator; optional right- or left-side slide release; combat-type triggerguard; auto internal safety; decocking lever. Made in Spain. Introduced 1985; dropped 1990. Replaced by Model A-100.

Perf: $375 **Exc:** $325 **VGood:** $300

ASTRA A-100

Semi-automatic; double action; 9mm Para., 40 S&W; 45 ACP; 10-shot (9mm, 40 S&W), 9-shot (45 ACP) magazine; 3-15/16-inch barrel; 7-1/16-inch overall length; weighs 29 oz.; checkered black plastic grips; blade front sight, interchangeable rear blades for elevation, screw-adjustable for windage; decocking lever permits lowering hammer onto locked firing pin; automatic firing pin block; side button magazine release. Imported from Spain by European American Armory. Introduced 1993; dropped 1997.

Blue finish
New: $375 **Perf:** $325 **Exc:** $300

Nickel finish
New: $400 **Perf:** $350 **Exc:** $325

For pistols made for the Turkish police add 50 percent.

ASTRA CADIX

Revolver; double action; 22 LR, 38 Spl.; 9-shot (22), 5-shot (38 Spl.); 4-inch, 6-inch barrel; blued finish; adjustable rear sight, ramp front; checkered plastic stocks. Manufactured 1960 to 1968.

Perf: $250 **Exc:** $200 **VGood:** $150

ASTRA CONSTABLE

Semi-automatic; double action; 22 LR, 32 ACP, 380 ACP; 10-shot (22 LR), 8-shot (32 ACP), 7-shot (380 ACP) magazine; 3-1/2-inch barrel; adjustable rear sight, fixed front; molded plastic grips; exposed hammer; non-glare rib on slide; quick, no-tool take-down feature; blued or chrome finish except 32. Was imported by Interarms. Introduced 1969; dropped 1990.

Perf: $295 **Exc:** $250 **VGood:** $210

Chrome finish or wood grips
Perf: $305 **Exc:** $260 **VGood:** $220

Blue, engraved
Perf: $350 **Exc:** $325 **VGood:** $275

Chrome, engraved
Perf: $395 **Exc:** $325 **VGood:** $300

Add $20 to above prices for 22 LR chambering or checkered wood grips.

ASTRA A-60 CONSTABLE

Semi-automatic; double action; 380 ACP; 13-shot magazine; 3-1/2-inch barrel; adjustable rear sight, fixed front; molded plastic grips; slide mounted ambidextrous safety; blued steel only. Made in Spain. Introduced 1986; dropped 1991.

Perf: $395 **Exc:** $325 **VGood:** $280

ASTRA CONSTABLE STAINLESS

Same specs as Constable except 380 ACP only; stainless steel finish. Manufactured 1986.

Perf: $350 **Exc:** $300 **VGood:** $250

ASTRA CONSTABLE SPORT

Same specs as Constable except 6-inch barrel; blue finish; weighs 35 oz. Manufactured 1986-1987.

Perf: $325 **Exc:** $250 **VGood:** $225

ASTRA CUB (2000)

Semi-automatic; 22 Short, 25 ACP; 6-shot magazine; 2-1/2-inch barrel; 4-7/16-inch overall length; fixed sights; blued or chrome finish; plastic grips. Introduced 1957; still in production, but U.S. importation dropped 1968.

Perf: $250 **Exc:** $190 **VGood:** $140

Chrome finish
Perf: $315 **Exc:** $235 **VGood:** $175

Engraved
Perf: $375 **Exc:** $290 **VGood:** $225

ASTRA CAMPER (2000)

Semi-automatic; 22 Short; 4-inch barrel; 6-1/4-inch overall length; fixed sights; blued or chrome finish; plastic grips. Manufactured 1953 to 1960.

Perf: $375 **Exc:** $325 **VGood:** $275

ASTRA MODEL 41

Revolver; double action; 41 Mag.; 6-shot; 6-inch barrel only; 11-3/8-inch overall length; weighs 2-3/4 lbs. Introduced 1980; no longer manufactured.

Perf: $275 **Exc:** $250 **VGood:** $200

ASTRA MODEL 44

Revolver; double action; 44 Mag.; 8-1/2-inch barrel. Introduced 1980; importation dropped 1990.

Perf: $300 **Exc:** $275 **VGood:** $250

Stainless, 6-inch barrel
Perf: $350 **Exc:** $300 **VGood:** $275

ASTRA MODEL 45

Revolver; double action; 45 Colt; 6-shot; 6-inch barrel. Manufactured in Spain. Introduced 1980; dropped 1987.

Perf: $325 **Exc:** $275 **VGood:** $220

ASTRA MODEL 200 FIRECAT

Semi-automatic; 25 ACP, 6-shot magazine; 2-1/4-inch barrel; 4-3/8-inch overall length; fixed sights; blued finish; plastic grips. Introduced in 1920; U.S. importation dropped 1968.

Perf: $250 **Exc:** $190 **VGood:** $165

Engraved Model 200 Firecat
Perf: $375 **Exc:** $285 **VGood:** $250

ASTRA MODEL 300

Semi-automatic; 32 ACP, 380 ACP; 4-inch barrel; 5-3/8-inch overall length; hard rubber grips. Introduced 1922; dropped 1947.

Perf: $600 **Exc:** $500 **VGood:** $350

With Nazi proofmarks
Perf: $700 **Exc:** $600 **VGood:** $500

Lightly engraved Astra Model 300
Perf: $1700 **Exc:** $1300 **VGood:** $900

Astra Model 800 Condor

Astra Model 1915

Astra Model 357

Auto Mag

Auto-Ordnance ZG-51 Pit Bull

Astra Model 900

Deeply engraved Astra Model 300

Perf: $2550 **Exc:** $1950 **VGood:** $1350

ASTRA MODEL 357

Revolver; 357 Mag.; 6-shot swing-out cylinder; 3-inch, 4-inch, 6-inch, 8-1/2-inch barrel; integral rib, ejector rod; click-adjustable rear sight, ramp front; target hammer; checkered walnut grips; blued. Imported by Interarms. Introduced 1972; importation dropped 1990.

Perf: $250 **Exc:** $215 **VGood:** $185

Stainless, 4-inch barrel

Perf: $370 **Exc:** $300 **VGood:** $265

ASTRA MODEL 400

Semi-automatic; 9mm Bergmann-Bayard/9mm Largo; 9-shot magazine; 6-inch barrel; 10-inch overall length; fixed sights; blowback action; some will also chamber and fire 9mm Para. and 38 ACP but it isn't recommended; blued finish; hard rubber or walnut grips. Introduced 1921; dropped 1946.

Exc: $425 **VGood:** $350 **Good:** $200

Navy Model

Exc: $1275 **VGood:** $975 **Good:** $690

With Nazi proof marks

Exc: $700 **VGood:** $600 **Good:** $450

ASTRA MODEL 600

Semi-automatic; 9mm Luger; 8-shot; 5-1/4-inch barrel, 8-inch overall length; fixed sights; blued finish; hard rubber or walnut grips. Military, police issue. Introduced 1942; dropped 1946.

Exc: $450 **VGood:** $400 **Good:** $350

With Nazi proofmarks

Exc: $700 **VGood:** $600 **Good:** $500

ASTRA MODEL 800 CONDOR

Semi-automatic; 9mm Para.; 8-shot magazine; 5-5/16-inch barrel; 8-1/4-inch overall length; fixed sights; blued finish; grooved plastic grips; tubular-type design. Based on Model 400 design. Introduced 1958; dropped 1968. Few imported; produced primarily for European police, military use.

Exc: $1200 **VGood:** $950 **Good:** $650

ASTRA MODEL 900

Semi-automatic; 7.63mm Mauser; 10-shot fixed magazine; 5-1/2-inch barrel; 11-1/2-inch overall length; adjustable rear sight, fixed front; small ring hammer on early models, larger hammer on later; grooved walnut grips; lanyard ring. Resembles design of "broomhandle" Mauser, but has barrel, barrel extension as two parts rather than one as in German Mauser, different lockwork, etc. Introduced 1927; dropped 1940. Originally priced at $37; has collector value. Add $600 for proper Astra holster-stock. Add 50 percent for early Bolo grips. Add 20 percent for those marked with Japanese characters.

Exc: $1200 **VGood:** $800 **Good:** $650

ASTRA MODEL 1911 25

Semi-automatic; 25 ACP; 6-shot; 2-inch barrel; 4-1/8-inch overall length; fixed sights; horn grips; external hammer, loaded indicator on top; marked "Victoria Patent." Rare.

Exc: $365 **VGood:** $265 **Good:** $175

ASTRA MODEL 1911 32

Semi-automatic; 32 ACP; 7-shot; 3-3/16-inch barrel; 5-1/2-inch overall length; weighs 21 oz.; black horn grips; blued finish. Similar to the Browning Model 1903 with internal hammer; marked "Victoria Patent." Manufactured until 1916.

Exc: $365 **VGood:** $265 **Good:** $175

ASTRA MODEL 1915/1916

Semi-automatic; 32 ACP; 9-shot magazine; 3-1/4-inch barrel; 5-3/4-inch overall length; fixed sights; checkered wood or horn grips. Actually introduced in 1911 as the "Victoria," first marked "Astra" in 1915; dropped after WWI.

Exc: $350 **VGood:** $265 **Good:** $175

ASTRA MODEL 3000

Semi-automatic; 32 ACP; 380 ACP; 6-shot, 7-shot magazine; 4-inch barrel; fixed sights; plastic grips; blued finish. Introduced 1948; dropped 1956.

Perf: $550 **Exc:** $425 **VGood:** $350

Engraved

Perf: $1300 **Exc:** $1000 **VGood:** $610

ASTRA MODEL 4000 FALCON

Semi-automatic; 22 LR, 32 ACP, 380 ACP; 10-shot (22 LR), 8-shot (32 ACP), 7-shot (380 ACP) magazine; 3-1/2-inch barrel; 6-1/2-inch overall length; thumb safety; exposed hammer; fixed sights; checkered black plastic grips; blued. Introduced 1956; U.S. importation dropped 1968.

Perf: $550 **Exc:** $425 **VGood:** $350

22 LR

Perf: $825 **Exc:** $637 **VGood:** $495

With caliber conversion kit in factory box

Perf: $1250 **Exc:** $950 **VGood:** $750

AUTAUGA MK II

Semi-automatic; double action only; 32 ACP, 6-shot magazine. Barrel: 2-inch. Weight: 11.3 oz. Length: 4.3-inch overall. Stocks: Black polymer. Sights: Fixed. Features: Double-action-only mechanism. Stainless steel construction. Uses Winchester Silver Tip ammunition. Introduced in 1996; dropped 2000. Clone of the Seecamp.

Perf: $225 **Exc:** $200 **VGood:** $150

AUTO MAG

Semi-automatic; 357 Auto Mag., 44 Auto Mag.; 7-shot magazine; 6-1/2-inch barrel; 11-1/2-inch overall length; short recoil; rotary bolt system; stainless steel construction; checkered plastic grips; fully-adjustable rear sight, ramp front. Manufactured by Auto Mag. Corp. and TDE Corp. 1970 to 1982.

Original Pasadena manufacture

Perf: $2500 **Exc:** $2300 **VGood:** $1995

TDE North Hollywood marked

Perf: $2275 **Exc:** $1850 **VGood:** $1700

AUTO-ORDNANCE MODEL 1911C

.45 ACP semi-auto with fixed sights and 7+1 capacity. Stainless frame and slide. 5-inch barrel, 39 oz. Laminate grips.

NIB: $400 **Exc:** $350 **VGood:** $295

AUTO-ORDNANCE MODEL 1911CAF

.45 ACP semi-auto with fixed sights and 7+1 capacity. Aluminum frame and stainless slide. 5-inch barrel, 31.5 oz. Laminate grips.

NIB: $400 **Exc:** $350 **VGood:** $295

AUTO-ORDNANCE 1911A1

Semi-automatic; 9mm Para., 38 Super, 10mm, 41 AE 45 ACP; 7- shot (45 ACP), 8-shot (41 AE), 9-shot (others); 5-inch barrel; 8-1/2-inch overall length;

Auto-Ordnance Model 1911A1

Baer 1911 Bullseye Wadcutter

AWA Mateba Auto Revolver

Auto-Ordnance Thompson Custom 1911

Baer Custom Carry

Baer Concept Series I-X

weighs 39 oz.; blade front sight, windage-adjustable rear; parts interchangeable with original Colt Gov't. Model; blued, non-glare finish. Made in U.S. by Auto-Ordnance Corp. Introduced 1983; still in production except for 10mm and 41 AE.

Perf: $445 **Exc:** $365 **VGood:** $29

AUTO-ORDNANCE 1911A1 40 S&W

Same specs as standard Auto-Ordnance 1911A1, except 4-1/2-inch barrel; 7-3/4-inch overall length; weighs 37 oz.; 40 S&W; 8-shot magazine; black rubber wrap-around grips; 3-dot sight system. Introduced 1991; no longer in production.

Perf: $445 **Exc:** $365 **VGood:** $295

AUTO-ORDNANCE 1911A1 COMPETITION MODEL

Same specs as 1911A1 except 45 ACP (38 Super version produced in 1996 only); black textured, rubber wrap-around grips; fully-adjustable rear sight with three-dot system; machined compensator; Commander combat hammer; flat mainspring housing; low-profile magazine funnel; magazine bumper; high-ride beavertail grip safety; full-length recoil spring guide system; extended slide stop, safety and magazine catch; Videcki adjustable speed trigger; extended combat ejector. Made in U.S. by Auto-Ordnance Corp. Introduced 1994; dropped 1996.

New: $525 **Perf:** $450 **Exc:** $425

AUTO-ORDNANCE 1911A1 CUSTOM HIGH POLISH

Similar to the standard 1911A1 except has a Videcki speed trigger, extended thumb safety, flat mainspring housing, Acurod recoil spring guide system, osewood grips, custom combat hammer, beavertail grip safety. High-polish blue finish. Introduced 1998. Made in U.S. by Auto-Ordnance Corp.; dropped 1999.

New: $485 **Perf:** $395 **Exc:** $300

AUTO-ORDNANCE 1911A1 GENERAL MODEL

Same specs as 1911A1 except 45 ACP (38 Super version produced in 1996 only); 4-1/2-inch barrel; 7-3/4-inch overall length; weighs 37 oz.; three-dot sight system; black textured, rubber wrap-around grips with medallion; full-length recoil guide; blue finish.

New: $385 **Perf:** $325 **Exc:** $300

AUTO-ORDNANCE ZG-51 PIT BULL

Semi-automatic; single action; 45 ACP; 7-shot magazine; 3-1/2-inch barrel; 7-1/4-inch overall length; weighs 36 oz. Introduced 1989; dropped 1999.

Perf: $385 **Exc:** $310 **VGood:** $275

AUTO-ORDNANCE THOMPSON CUSTOM 1911

Semi-automatic; single action; 45 ACP; stainless steel construction; Series 80 design; barrel; 7-shot; grip safety; checkered laminate grips with medallion; skeletonized trigger; combat hammer; low profile sights; 39 oz.; Thompson bullet logo on left side of double serrated slide.

Perf: $625 **Exc:** $525 **VGood:** $450

AWA MATEBA AUTO REVOLVER

Calibers: 357, 44 Magnum, 44 Special, and 454 Casull. Barrel: 4, 5, 6 or 8-3/8 inches. Barrel aligns with bottom chamber of 6-round cylinder. Unique operating system uses recoil to rotate the cylinder and cock the hammer. When gun is fired, upper assembly (barrel, cylinder and frame) recoils approximately 7/8 inch to actuate the operating system. Weight is 47 oz. (4" bbl.), length 10.8 inches. Blue or matte nickel finish.

Perf: $1650 **Exc:** $1375 **VGood:** $1050

BAER 1911 BULLSEYE WADCUTTER

Semi-automatic; single action; 45 ACP; 7-shot magazine; 5-inch barrel; 8-1/2-inch overall length; weighs 37 oz.; Baer dovetail front sight with undercut post, low-mount Bo-Mar rear with hidden leaf rear; checkered walnut grips; polished feed ramp and barrel throat; Bo-Mar rib on slide; full-length recoil rod; Baer speed trigger; Baer deluxe hammer and sear; Baer beavertail grip safety with pad; flat mainspring housing checkered 20 lpi; blue finish. Made in U.S. by Les Baer Custom, Inc.

New: $1500 **Perf:** $1200 **Exc:** $1100

BAER 1911 CONCEPT SERIES I-X PISTOLS

Semi-automatic; single action; 45 ACP; 7-shot magazine; 5-inch barrel; 8-1/2-inch overall length; weighs 37 oz.; checkered rosewood grips; Baer dovetail front sight, Bo-Mar deluxe low-mount rear with hidden leaf; Baer forged steel frame, slide and barrel with Baer stainless bushing; slide fitted to frame; double serrated slide; Baer beavertail grip safety; checkered slide stop; tuned extractor; extended ejector; deluxe hammer and sear; match disconnector; lowered and flared ejection port; fitted recoil link; polished feed ramp, throated barrel; Baer fitted speed trigger; flat serrated mainspring housing; blue finish. Aluminum frame, stainless slide, BoMar and Novak sights and smaller Commanche frame sizes compose the Series I-X.

New: $1800 **Perf:** $1475 **Exc:** $1000

BAER 1911 CUSTOM CARRY

Semi-automatic; single action; 45 ACP; 7- or 10-shot magazine; 5-inch barrel; 8-1/2-inch overall length; weighs 37 oz.; checkered walnut grips; Baer improved ramp-style dovetailed front sight, Novak low-mount rear; Baer forged NM frame, slide and barrel with stainless bushing; fitted slide to frame; double serrated slide (full-size only); Baer speed trigger with 4-lb. pull; Baer deluxe hammer and sear; tactical-style extended ambidextrous safety; beveled magazine well; polished feed ramp and throated barrel; tuned extractor; Baer extended ejector; checkered slide stop; lowered and flared ejection port; full-length recoil guide rod; recoil buff. Made in U.S. by Les Baer Custom, Inc.

Standard size, blued

New: $1400 **Perf:** $1100 **Exc:** $1000

Standard size, stainless

New: $1500 **Perf:** $1200 **Exc:** $1100

Commanche size, blued

New: $1600 **Perf:** $1100 **Exc:** $1000

Commanche size, stainless

New: $1700 **Perf:** $1200 **Exc:** $1100

Commanche size, aluminum frame, blued slide

New: $1700 **Perf:** $1200 **Exc:** $1100

Commanche size, aluminum frame, stainless slide

New: $1800 **Perf:** $1300 **Exc:** $1200

BAER 1911 NATIONAL MATCH HARDBALL

Semi-automatic; single action; 45 ACP; 7-shot magazine; 5-inch barrel; 8-1/2-inch overall length; weighs 37 oz.; Baer dovetail front sight with undercut post, low-mount Bo-Mar rear with hidden leaf rear; checkered walnut grips; Baer NM forged steel frame, double serrated slide and barrel with stainless steel

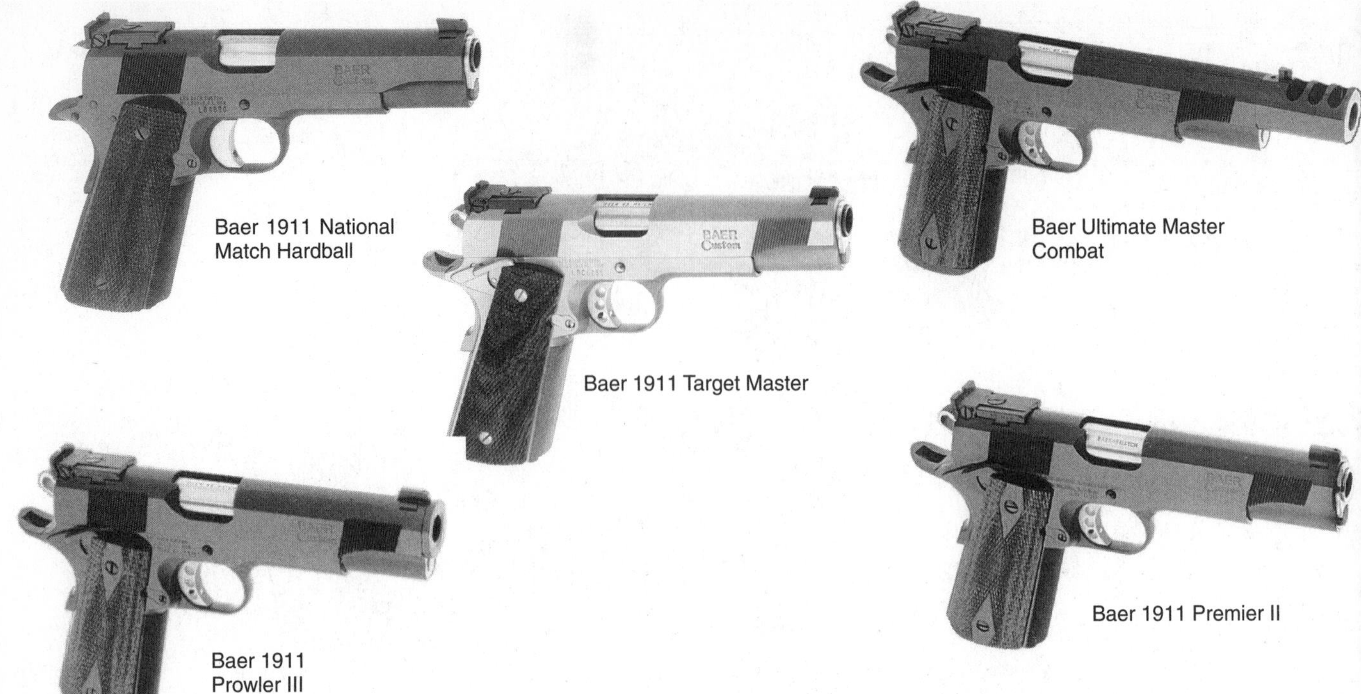
Baer 1911 National Match Hardball

Baer 1911 Target Master

Baer Ultimate Master Combat

Baer 1911 Prowler III

Baer 1911 Premier II

bushing; slide fitted to frame; Baer match trigger with 4-lb. pull; polished feed ramp; throated barrel; checkered frontstrap; arched mainspring housing; Baer beveled magazine well; lowered, flared ejection port; tuned extractor; Baer extended ejector; checkered slide stop; recoil buff. Made in U.S. by Les Baer Custom, Inc.

New: $1100 **Perf:** $875 **Exc:** $725

BAER 1911 PREMIER II

Semi-automatic; single action; 45 ACP; 7-shot magazine; 5-inch barrel; 8-1/2-inch overall length; weighs 37 oz.; Baer dovetail front sight with undercut post, low-mount Bo-Mar rear with hidden leaf rear; checkered rosewood grips with double diamond pattern; Baer NM forged steel frame and barrel with stainless steel bushing; slide fitted to frame; double serrated slide; aluminum speed trigger with 4-lb. pull; deluxe Commander hammer and sear; polished feed ramp; throated barrel; checkered frontstrap; flat mainspring housing; Baer beveled magazine well; lowered, flared ejection port; tuned, polished extractor; Baer extended ejector; checkered slide stop. Made in U.S. by Les Baer Custom, Inc.

Blued

New: $1800 **Perf:** $1200 **Exc:** $975

Stainless stee4

New: $2000 **Perf:** $1395 **Exc:** $1100

BAER 1911 PROWLER III

Semi-automatic; single action; 45 ACP, 7- or 10-shot magazine; 5-inch barrel; 8-1/2-inch overall length; weighs 37 oz.; checkered rosewood grips with double diamond pattern; Baer dovetailed front sight, low-mount Bo-Mar rear with hidden leaf; Baer NM forged steel frame and barrel with stainless bushing; slide fitted to frame; double serrated slide; lowered, flared ejection port; tuned, polished extractor; Baer extended ejector; checkered slide stop; aluminum speed trigger with 4-lb. pull; deluxe Commander hammer and sear; beavertail grip safety with pad; beveled magazine well; extended ambidextrous safety; flat mainspring housing; polished feed ramp and throated barrel; 30 lpi checkered frontstrap; tapered cone stub weight and reverse recoil plug. Made in U.S. by Les Baer Custom, Inc. Still in production.

Standard or Commanche size, blued

New: $1700 **Perf:** $1625 **Exc:** $1500

Standard or Commanche size, stainless

New: $1800 **Perf:** $1725 **Exc:** $1600

BAER 1911 TARGET MASTER

Semi-automatic; single action; 45 ACP; 7-shot magazine; 5-inch barrel; 8-1/2-inch overall length; weighs 37 oz.; checkered walnut grips; Baer post-style dovetail front sight, low-mount Bo-Mar rear with hidden leaf; Baer NM forged steel frame; double serrated slide and barrel with stainless bushing; slide fitted to frame; standard trigger; polished feed ramp; throated barrel; checkered frontstrap; flat serrated mainspring housing; Baer beveled magazine well; lowered, flared ejection port; tuned extractor; Baer extended ejector; checkered slide stop; recoil buff. Made in U.S. by Les Baer Custom, Inc. Still in production.

New: $1850 **Perf:** $1495 **Exc:** $1000

BAER 1911 ULTIMATE MASTER COMBAT

Semi-automatic; single action; 45 ACP (others available); 10-shot magazine; 5-inch Baer NM barrel; 8-1/2-inch overall length; weighs 37 oz.; checkered rosewood grips; Baer dovetail front sight, low-mount Bo-Mar rear with hidden leaf; Baer forged NM blued steel frame and double serrated slide; Baer triple port, tapered cone compensator; fitted slide to frame; lowered, flared ejection port; Baer reverse recoil plug; full-length guide rod; recoil buff; beveled magazine well; Baer Commander hammer and sear; Baer extended ambidextrous safety, extended ejector; checkered slide stop; beavertail grip safety with pad; extended magazine release button; Baer speed trigger. Made in U.S. by Les Baer Custom, Inc. Still in production.

Compensated, open sights

New: $1900 **Perf:** $1795 **Exc:** $1650

Uncompensated "Limited" Model

New: $1800 **Perf:** $1695 **Exc:** $1550

Compensated, with Baer optics mount

New: $2300 **Perf:** $2250 **Exc:** $2100

BAER 1911 ULTIMATE MASTER "STEEL SPECIAL"

Same specs as Ultimate Master except scope and Baer scope mount; bushing-type compensator; fitted slide to frame; lowered, flared ejection port; Baer reverse recoil plug; two-piece guide rod. Designed for maximum 150 Power Factor; hard chrome finish. Still in production.

New: $2500 **Perf:** $2425 **Exc:** $2350

BAER MODEL 1911 TWENTY-FIFTH ANNIVERSARY

Custom-engraved limited collector edition .45 ACP semi-auto. Built on fully functional, fully equipped Baer Premier II. Hand engraved, both sides of slide and frame. Les Baer signature. Inlaid with white gold. Ivory grips. Deep blue finish. Presentation box.

NIB: $6100 **Exc:** $5200 **VGood:** $3950

BAER ULTIMATE RECO

Semi-auto with integral Picatinny rail, 5-inch barrel, .45 ACP. Blue or chrome. Comes with SureFire X-200 light. Fixed sights. 4-pound trigger. Two 8-round magazines. Cocobolo grips.

NIB: $2700 **Exc:** $1850 **VGood:** $1450

BAFORD ARMS THUNDER DERRINGER

Derringer; .410 2-1/2-inch shotshell/44 Spl.; insert sleeves available for 22 Short, 22 LR, 25 ACP, 32 ACP, 32 H&R Mag., 30 Luger, 380 ACP, 38 Super, 38 Spl., 38 S&W, 9mm Para.; barrel lengths vary with caliber inserts; weighs 8-1/2 oz., sans inserts; no sights; uncheckered walnut stocks; blued steel barrel, frame; polished steel hammer, trigger; side-swinging barrel; positive lock, half-cock safety; roll block safety. Introduced 1986; dropped 1991.

Perf: $130 **Exc:** $110 **VGood:** $100

Extra barrel inserts

Perf: $75 **Exc:** $65 **VGood:** $50

BAIKAL IZH-35M

Semi-automatic 22 target pistol with fully adjustable walnut target grip; 6-inch hammer forged barrel; adjustable trigger; integral grip safety; 5-shot; weighs 2.3 lbs.; cocking indicator; detachable scope mount. Imported from Russia.

Perf: $325 **Exc:** $305 **VGood:** $275

BAIKAL IJ-70

Semi-automatic; double action; 9x18mm Makarov; 8-shot magazine; 4-inch barrel; 6-1/4-inch overall length; weighs 25 oz.; checkered composition grips; blade front sight, fully-adjustable rear; all-steel construction; frame-mounted safety with decocker. Comes with two magazines, cleaning rod, universal tool. Imported from Russia by Century International

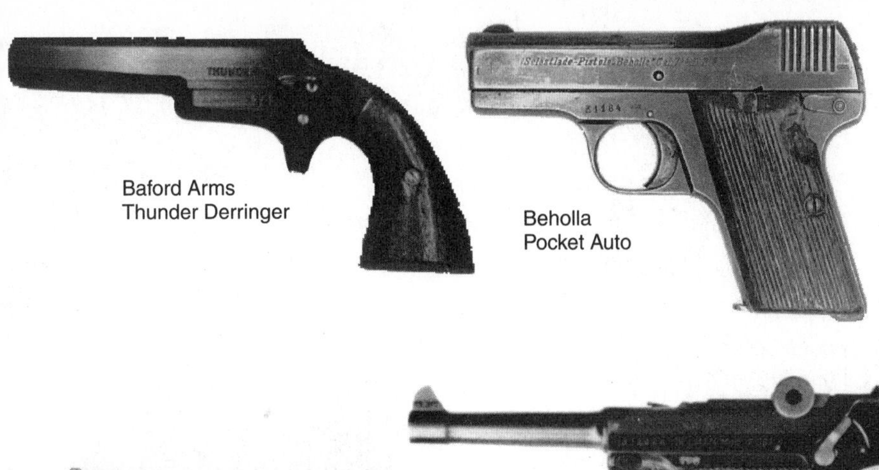
Baford Arms Thunder Derringer

Beholla Pocket Auto

Benelli B76

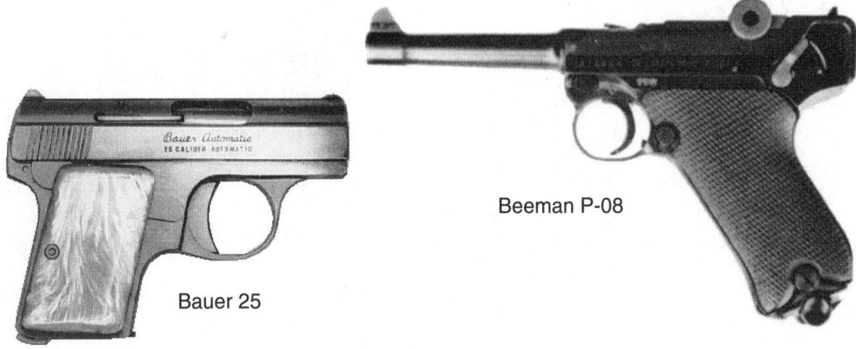
Beeman P-08

Bauer 25

Bayard Model 1908 Pocket Automatic

Arms, K.B.I., Inc. Introduced 1994; dropped 1996. Add 20% for nicke4l finish.

New: $325 **Perf:** $275 **Exc:** $200

BAIKAL IJ-70HC

Same specs as IJ-70 except 10-shot magazine. Introduced 1994; dropped 1996.

New: $300 **Perf:** $275 **Exc:** $225

BAIKAL IJ-70HC, 380 ACP

Same specs as IJ-70HC except 380 ACP. Importation ceased in 1996.

New: $325 **Perf:** $275 **Exc:** $225

BAUER 25

Semi-automatic; 25 ACP; 6-shot magazine; 2-1/8-inch barrel; 4-inch overall length; stainless steel construction; fixed sights; plastic pearl or checkered walnut grips; manual, magazine safeties. Identical to Baby Browning except for stainless construction. Introduced 1973; dropped 1984.

Perf: $240 **Exc:** $185 **VGood:** $150

BAUER 25 ACP BICENTENNIAL MODEL

Identical to standard Bauer 25 except with engraving and packaged with buckle in display case.

Perf: $300 **Exc:** $200 **VGood:** $150

BAUER RABBIT DERRINGER

Over/under derringer in 22 LR and 410 bore shotshell; all metal construction. Introduced 1982; dropped 1984.

Perf: $300 **Exc:** $250 **VGood:** $190

BAYARD MODEL 1908 POCKET AUTOMATIC

Semi-automatic; 25 ACP, 32 ACP, 380 ACP; 6-shot magazine; 2-1/4-inch barrel; 4-7/8-inch overall length; fixed sights, blued finish; hard rubber grips. Introduced 1908; dropped 1923.

25-caliber

Exc: $385 **VGood:** $220 **Good:** $175

32-caliber

Exc: $350 **VGood:** $250 **Good:** $165

380-caliber

Exc: $350 **VGood:** $250 **Good:** $165

Note: Model marked with an Imperial Eagle command 25 percent additional; factory engraved specimens command 200 percent more.

BAYARD MODEL 1923 POCKET AUTOMATIC (LARGE MODEL)

Semi-automatic; 32 ACP, 380 ACP; 6-shot magazine; 3 -5/16-inch barrel; 4-5/16-inch overall length; fixed sights; blued finish; checkered grips of hard rubber. Introduced 1923; dropped 1940.

32 cal.

Exc: $375 **VGood:** $295 **Good:** $225

380 ACP Model

Exc: $750 **VGood:** $590 **Good:** $450

BAYARD MODEL 1923 POCKET AUTOMATIC (SMALL MODEL)

Semi-automatic; 25 ACP only; 2-1/2-inch barrel; 4-5/16-inch overall length; fixed sights, blued finish; checkered grips of hard rubber. Scaled-down model of large Model 1923. Introduced 1923; dropped 1930.

Exc: $350 **VGood:** $295 **Good:** $225

BAYARD MODEL 1930 POCKET AUTOMATIC

Semi-automatic; 25 ACP; 6-shot; 2-1/8-inch barrel; 5-15/16-inch overall length; fixed sights; blued finish; checkered hard rubber grips. Similar to small Model 1923 auto pistol with improvements in finish, internal mechanism. Introduced 1930; dropped 1940.

Exc: $350 **VGood:** $250 **Good:** $200

BEEMAN P-08

Semi-automatic; 22 LR; 8-shot magazine; 4-inch barrel; 7 3/4-inch overal length; weighs 25 oz.; checkered hardwood stocks; fixed sights; based on original Luger design; Luger-type toggle action. Made in Germany. Introduced 1989; importation dropped 1990.

Perf: $325 **Exc:** $295 **VGood:** $245

BEEMAN P-08 MINI

Same specs as P-08 except 380 ACP or .32 ACP; 5-shot magazine; 3-1/2-inch barrel; weighs 22-1/2 oz.; magazine and sear disconnect safeties. Made in Germany. Introduced 1989; importation dropped 1990.

Exc: $450 **VGood:** $375 **Good:** $300

BEEMAN SP DELUXE

Single shot; 22 LR; 8-inch, 10-inch, 11-3/16-inch, 15-inch barrel; European walnut stocks; adjustable palm rest; blade front sight, adjustable notch rear; detachable forend, barrel weight; standard version has no forend or weight. Imported by Beeman. Introduced 1984; dropped 1987.

Perf: $600 **Exc:** $550 **VGood:** $500

BEEMAN SP STANDARD

Single shot; 22 LR; sidelever action; 8-inch, 10-inch, 12-inch, or 15-inch barrel; adjustable sights; walnut grips. Made in West Germany. Imported 1985-1986 only.

Perf: $300 **Exc:** $250 **VGood:** $220

BEEMAN SP/SPX

Single shot; 22 LR; made for silhouette shooting; 10-inch bull barrel; blued metal parts; burwood stock and forearm; aperture sights; 3.9 lbs. Dropped 1994.

Perf: $625 **Exc:** $550 **VGood:** $475

BEEMAN MODEL SPX DELUXE

Similar to Model SPX, except has matte chrome metal finish; hand stippled walnut grips; Anshutz rear sight. Introduced 1993; dropped 1994.

Perf: $800 **Exc:** $725 **VGood:** $650

BEHOLLA POCKET AUTO

Semi-automatic; 32 ACP; 7-shot magazine; 3-inch barrel; 5-1/2-inch overall length; fixed sights; grooved hard rubber or wooden stocks; blued finish. German-made. Manufactured 1915 to 1925.

Exc: $225 **VGood:** $170 **Good:** $150

BENELLI B76

Semi-automatic; 9mm Para.; 8-shot magazine; 4-1/4-inch chrome-lined barrel; 8-1/16-inch overall length; weighs 34 oz. (empty); walnut stocks with cut checkering and high gloss finish; blade front sight with white face, windage-adjustable; fixed barrel, locked breech; stainless steel inertia firing pin and loaded chamber indicator; blued finish with internal parts hard chrome plated; all steel construction. Introduced 1979; dropped 1990.

Perf: $700 **Exc:** $575 **VGood:** $400

Beretta Model 20

Beretta Model 70S

Beretta Model 76

Beretta Model 21A Bobcat

Beretta Model 70

Beretta Model 85FS Cheetah

BENELLI B-76S TARGET

Similar to B-76 except has 5-1/2-inch barrel; target grips; adjustable rear sight; 9mm Para. Importation dropped 1990.

Perf: $725 **Exc:** $600 **VGood:** $450

BENELLI MODEL B-77

Semi-automatic; selective double action; 32 ACP; all steel construction; 4-1/4-inch barrel; 8-shot magazine. Importation dropped 1995.

Perf: $395 **Exc:** $350 **VGood:** $295

BENELLI MODEL B-80

Semi-automatic; selective double action; 32 ACP; all steel construction; 4-1/4-inch barrel; 8-shot magazine; 34 oz. Importation dropped 1995.

Perf: $395 **Exc:** $350 **VGood:** $295

BENELLI MODEL B-80S TARGET

Similar to B-80 except has 5-1/2-inch barrel; target grips; adjustable rear sight. Importation dropped 1995.

Perf: $500 **Exc:** $450 **VGood:** $375

BENELLI MP90S MATCH

Semi-automatic; single action; 22 Short, 22 LR, 32 S&W wadcutter; 5-shot magazine; 4-3/8-inch barrel; 11-7/8-inch overall length; weighs 39 oz.; stippled walnut match-type grips with fully-adjustable palm shelf, anatomically shaped; match type, blade front sight, fully click-adjustable rear; removable trigger fully-adjustable for pull and position; special internal weight box on sub-frame below barrel; comes with loading tool, cleaning rod. Imported from Italy by European American Armory. Introduced 1993; still imported.

Perf: $1050 **Exc:** $900 **VGood:** $850

Add $105 to above prices for 32 S&W Wadcutter chambering.

BENELLI MP95E MATCH

Semi-automatic; single action; 22 LR, 32 S&W WC; 9-shot magazine; 4-3/8-inch barrel; 11-7/8-inch overall length; weighs 39 oz.; checkered walnut match-type grips, anatomically shaped; blade front sight, fully click-adjustable match-type rear; removable, adjustable trigger; special internal weight box on sub-frame below barrel; cut for scope rails. Imported from Italy by European American Armory. Introduced 1993; still imported.

Blue finish

New: $645 **Perf:** $575 **Exc:** $495

Chrome finish

New: $700 **Perf:** $625 **Exc:** $550

Add $120 to above prices for 32 S&W Wadcutter chambering.

BERETTA 85FS CHEETAH

Caliber: 380 ACP with 8-round magazine. Barrel is 4.45 inches, weight 21 oz. Open slide design with aluminum alloy frame. Three-dot sight system, plastic or wood grips. Available in black or nickel finish.

Perf: $650 **Exc:** $550 **VGood:** $475

BERETTA 9000S

9mm double action or DAO (D model) pistol. 3 ½ inch barrel. 10 or 12 round magazine. Unique design with black polymer frame with molded rubber grip. Weighs 26 oz. Mfg. 2000 – 2005.

Perf: $475 **Exc:** $425 **VGood:** $375

Add 10 percent for nickel finish

BERETTA MODEL 20

Semi-automatic; double action; 25 ACP; 8-shot magazine; 2-1/2-inch barrel; 4-1/2-inch overall length; weighs 11 oz.; fixed sights; plastic or walnut stocks. Made in Italy. Introduced 1984; dropped 1986.

Perf: $275 **Exc:** $200 **VGood:** $150

BERETTA MODEL 21A BOBCAT

Semi-automatic; double action; 22 LR, 25 ACP; 7-shot (22 LR), 8-shot (25 ACP); 2-1/2-inch barrel; 4-15/16-inch overall length; weighs 11-1/2 oz.; fixed sights; thumb safety; half-cock safety; hinged tip-up barrel; blued, nickel or matte finish; checkered walnut or plastic grips. Introduced 1985; still in production. Made in the U.S.

New: $300 **Exc:** $190 **VGood:** $145

Nickel finish

New: $310 **Exc:** $215 **VGood:** $165

Matte finish

New: $300 **Exc:** $175 **VGood:** $140

Engraved

New: $400 **Exc:** $225 **VGood:** $200

BERETTA LADY BERETTA

Semi-automatic; double action; 22 LR; 7-shot; 2-1/2-inch barrel; 4-15/16-inch overall length; weighs 11-1/2 oz.; fixed sights; thumb safety; half-cock safety; hinged tip-up barrel; similar to Model 21A except gold etching on top of frame and side of slide. Introduced 1990; dropped 1990.

Perf: $295 **Exc:** $215 **VGood:** $160

BERETTA MODEL 70

Semi-automatic; double action; 32 ACP; 8-shot magazine; 3-1/2-inch barrel; 6-5/16-inch overall length; 23-1/2 oz.; fixed sights; plastic grips; crossbolt safety; blue or chrome finish. Replaced Model 948; has hold-open device and push-button magazine release. Alloy frame 32 ACP marketed in U.S. as the New Puma. Introduced 1958; dropped 1968.

Perf: $385 **Exc:** $325 **VGood:** $275

Chrome finish

Perf: $395 **Exc:** $335 **VGood:** $285

BERETTA MODEL 70S

Same specs as Beretta Model 70 except 380 ACP, 22 LR; weighs 18 oz. (22 LR), magazine safety; steel frame; fixed sights (380 ACP); adjustable rear (22 LR); checkered plastic wrap-around grips with thumbrest; blued. Steel frame 380 ACP marketed in U.S. as the Cougar. Introduced 1977; dropped 1985.

Perf: $385 **Exc:** $325 **VGood:** $275

BERETTA MODEL 70T

Same specs as Beretta Model 70 except 9-shot magazine; 32 ACP; 6-inch barrel; 8-1/2-inch overall length; adjustable rear sight, fixed front; slide stays open after last shot; checkered plastic wrap-around grips. Introduced 1969; dropped 1975.

Perf: $385 **Exc:** $325 **VGood:** $275

BERETTA MODEL 71

Semi-automatic; single action; 22 LR; 8-shot magazine; 6-inch barrel only; 8-3/4-inch overall length; adjustable rear sight; wrap-around checkered plastic grips; lever thumb safety. Imported 1987 only.

Perf: $385 **Exc:** $325 **VGood:** $275

BERETTA MODEL 71 JAGUAR

Semi-automatic; 22 LR; 8-shot magazine; 3-1/2-inch barrel; windage-adjustable rear sight, fixed front; checkered plastic grips; blued. Marketed in U.S. as Jaguar. Introduced 1956; dropped 1968.

Perf: $385 **Exc:** $325 **VGood:** $275

Beretta Model 84F

Beretta Model 84 Cheetah

Beretta Model 85F

Beretta Model 89

Beretta Model 89 Gold Standard Pistol

Beretta Model 90

BERETTA MODEL 72 JAGUAR

Semi-automatic; 22 LR; 8-shot magazine; 3-1/2-inch, 6-inch interchangeable barrels; windage-adjustable rear sight, fixed front; checkered plastic grips; blued finish. Introduced 1956; dropped 1968.

Perf: $325 **Exc:** $250 **VGood:** $200

BERETTA MODEL 76

Semi-automatic; single action; 22 LR only; 10-shot magazine; 6-inch barrel; 9-1/2-inch overall length; adjustable rear sight, interchangeable blade front; non-glare, ribbed slide; heavy barrel; external hammer; checkered wrap-around plastic (76P) or wood (76W) grips; blued. Also known as New Sable. Introduced 1971; dropped 1985.

Perf: $350 **Exc:** $300 **VGood:** $275

With wood grips

Perf: $400 **Exc:** $350 **VGood:** $325

BERETTA MODEL 81

Semi-automatic; double action; 32 ACP; 12-shot magazine; 3-13/16-inch barrel; 6-13/16-inch overall length; blued finish; fixed sights; plastic or wood stocks. Introduced 1976; dropped 1981.

Perf: $375 **Exc:** $250 **VGood:** $200

Nickel finish

Perf: $425 **Exc:** $340 **VGood:** $290

With wood grips

Perf: $395 **Exc:** $275 **VGood:** $225

Beretta Model 81BB

Perf: $300 **Exc:** $275 **VGood:** $225

BERETTA MODEL 82

Semi-automatic; double action; 32 ACP; 9-shot straightline magazine; 3-13/16-inch barrel; 6-13/16-inch overall length; weighs 17 oz.; non-reversible magazine release; blued finish; fixed sights; wood grips. Introduced 1977; dropped 1984.

Perf: $295 **Exc:** $250 **VGood:** $225

Nickel finish

Perf: $355 **Exc:** $325 **VGood:** $300

BERETTA MODEL 84 CHEETAH

Semi-automatic; double action; 380 ACP; 10-shot magazine; 3-7/8-inch barrel; 6-13/16-inch overall length; weighs 23 oz.; black plastic (84P) or wood (84W) grips; fixed front sight, drift-adjustable rear; blue finish; squared trigger guard; exposed hammer. Imported from Italy by Beretta U.S.A. Introduced 1977.

Perf: $400 **Exc:** $325 **VGood:** $275

Blue, wood grips

Perf: $375 **Exc:** $350 **VGood:** $300

Nickel, wood grips

Perf: $475 **Exc:** $400 **VGood:** $325

BERETTA MODEL 84F

Same specs as Model 84 except combat-style frame; grooved triggerguard; plastic grips; manual safety; decocking device; matte finish. Made in Italy. Introduced 1990; still in production.

Perf: $395 **Exc:** $330 **VGood:** $300

BERETTA MODEL 85 CHEETAH

Semi-automatic; double action; 380 ACP; 8-shot straightline magazine; 3-7/8-inch barrel; 6-13/16-inch overall length; weighs 23 oz.; black plastic (85P) or wood (85W) grips; fixed front sight, drift-adjustable rear; non-reversible magazine release; blue finish; squared triggerguard; exposed hammer. Imported from Italy by Beretta U.S.A. Introduced 1977; still imported.

Perf: $450 **Exc:** $350 **VGood:** $295

Blue, wood grips

Perf: $485 **Exc:** $385 **VGood:** $330

Nickel, wood grips

Perf: $530 **Exc:** $430 **VGood:** $375

BERETTA MODEL 85F

Same specs as Model 85 except combat-type frame; grooved triggerguard; plastic grips; matte black finish; manual safety; decocking device. Made in Italy. Introduced 1990; dropped 1990.

Perf: $375 **Exc:** $325 **VGood:** $275

BERETTA MODEL 86 CHEETAH

Semi-automatic; double action; 22 LR; 8-shot magazine; 4-7/16-inch barrel; 7-5/16-inch overall length; weighs 23-1/2 oz.; fixed sights; tip-up barrel; checkered walnut grips; matte finish; gold trigger. Importation began 1991.

Perf: $450 **Exc:** $375 **VGood:** $300

BERETTA MODEL 87 CHEETAH

Semi-automatic; double action; 22 LR; 7-shot magazine; 3-7/8-inch barrel; 6-13/16-inch overall length; weighs 21 oz.; black plastic grips; fixed front sight, drift-adjustable rear; blue finish; squared trigger guard; exposed hammer. Imported from Italy by Beretta U.S.A. Introduced 1977; dropped 1990.

Perf: $450 **Exc:** $375 **VGood:** $300

BERETTA MODEL 87 TARGET

Same specs as Model 87 except single action; 6-inch barrel with counterweight; wood grips. Made in Italy. Introduced 1977; importation began in 1986; dropped 1994; importation resumed 2000.

Perf: $600 **Exc:** $465 **VGood:** $380

BERETTA MODEL 89

Semi-automatic; single-action only; 22 LR; 8-shot magazine; 6-inch barrel; 9-1/2-inch overall length; weighs 41 oz.; interchangeable front sight, fully-adjustable rear; semi-anatomical walnut grips; fixed monoblock barrel machined from forged steel block; aluminum alloy frame; manual safety on either side. Made in Italy. Introduced 1977. Importation began 1986; still imported.

Perf: $600 **Exc:** $500 **VGood:** $400

BERETTA MODEL 89 GOLD STANDARD PISTOL

Caliber: 22 LR, 8-shot magazine. Barrel: 6. Weight: 41 oz. Length: 9-1/2-inch overall. Stocks: Target-type walnut with thumbrest. Sights: Interchangeable blade front, fully adjustable rear. Features: Single action target pistol. Matte black, Bruniton finish. Imported from Italy by Beretta U.S.A.

Perf: $650 **Exc:** $510 **VGood:** $410

BERETTA MODEL 90

Semi-automatic; double action; 32 ACP; 8-shot magazine; 3-5/8-inch barrel; 6-3/4-inch overall length; weighs 19 oz.; fixed sights, matted rib on slide; chamber-loaded indicator; external hammer; stainless steel barrel; molded plastic wrap-around grips; blued. Introduced 1969; dropped 1982.

Perf: $350 **Exc:** $275 **VGood:** $200

BERETTA 90-TWO

Wrap-around polymer grip, standard or slim. Single/double-action semi-auto in 9mm (10+1, 15+1 or 17+1

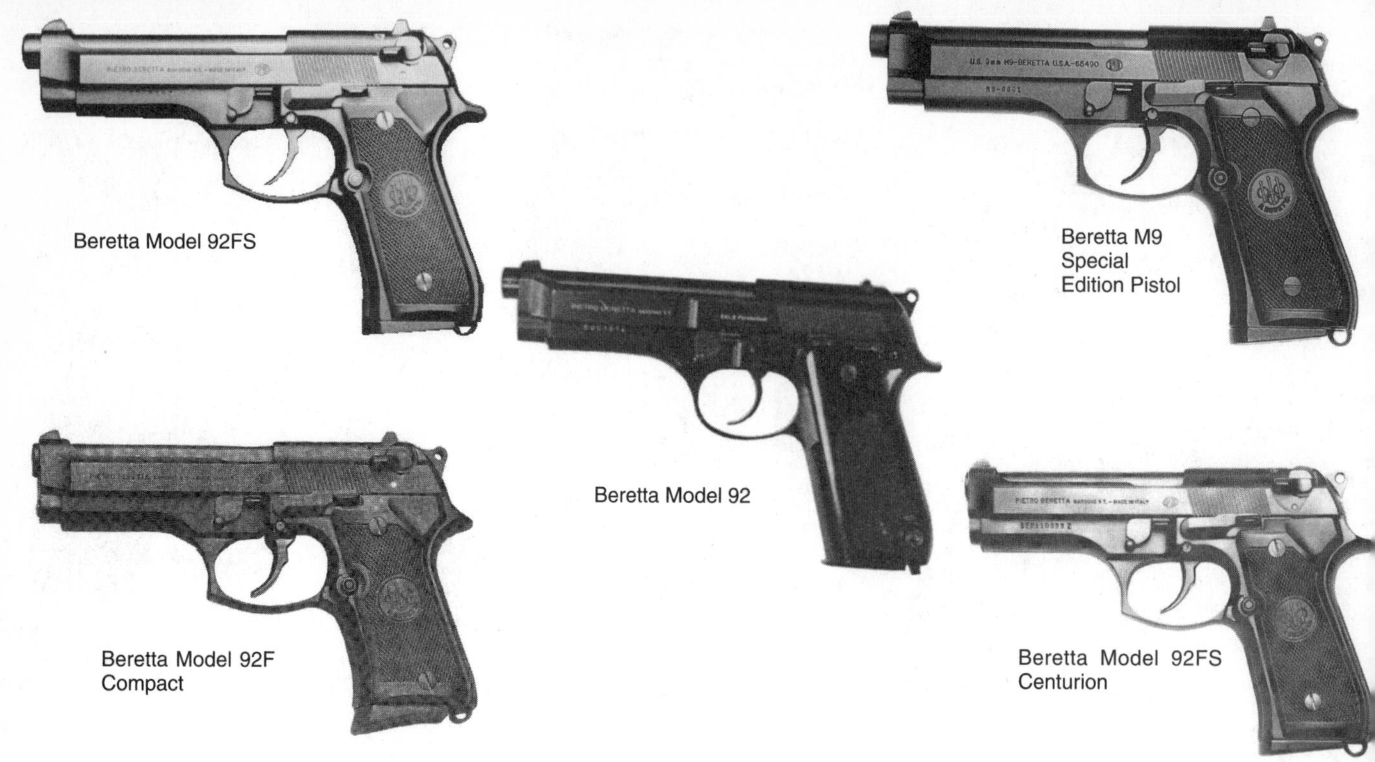
Beretta Model 92FS

Beretta M9 Special Edition Pistol

Beretta Model 92

Beretta Model 92F Compact

Beretta Model 92FS Centurion

capacity) or .40 S&W (10+1 or 12+1 capacity). Types D, F or G. Fixed sights. 4.9-inch barrel, 32.5 oz.

NIB: $685 **Exc:** $575 **VGood:** $400

BERETTA MODEL 92

Semi-automatic, double action; 9mm Para.; 15-shot magazine; 5-inch barrel; 8-1/2-inch overall length; blued finish; fixed sights; plastic grips. Updated version of the Model 951. Introduced 1976; dropped 1981.

Perf: $750 **Exc:** $600 **VGood:** $450

BERETTA MODEL 92S (SECOND ISSUE)

Semi-automatic; double action; 9mm Para.; 15-shot magazine; 5-inch barrel; 8-1/2-inch overall length; fixed sights; plastic grips; blued finish. Variant of Model 92 with safety catch on side. Discontinued.

Perf: $575 **Exc:** $475 **VGood:** $400

BERETTA MODEL 92SB-P (THIRD ISSUE)

Automatic; double action; 9mm Para.; 16-shot magazine; 5-inch barrel; 8-1/2-inch overall length; weighs 34-1/2 oz.; blade front sight, windage-adjustable rear; black plastic or wood grips. Developed for U.S. Army pistol trials of 1979-1980. Introduced 1979; dropped 1985.

Perf: $525 **Exc:** $425 **VGood:** $395

Wood grips

Perf: $550 **Exc:** $450 **VGood:** $400

BERETTA MODEL 92SB-P COMPACT

Same specs as Model 92SB-P except 4-5/16-inch barrel, 14-shot magazine; plastic grips. Introduced 1977; dropped 1985.

Perf: $500 **Exc:** $450 **VGood:** $400

Wood grips

Perf: $525 **Exc:** $475 **VGood:** $425

BERETTA MODEL 92D

Semi-automatic; double-action only; 9mm Para.; 10-shot magazine; 5-inch barrel; 8-1/2-inch overall length; weighs 34 oz.; bobbed hammer; no external safety; plastic grips; three-dot sights. Also offered with Trijicon sights. From Beretta U.S.A. Introduced 1992; dropped 1998.

New: $475 **Perf:** $400 **Exc:** $350

BERETTA MODEL 92FS

Semi-automatic; double action; 9mm Para.; 15-shot magazine; 5-inch barrel; 8-1/2-inch overall length; matte black finish; squared triggerguard; grooved front backstraps; inertia firing pin; extractor acts as chamber loaded indicator; wood or plastic grips. Adopted 1985 as official U.S. military sidearm. Introduced 1984; still produced by Beretta USA.

Perf: $595 **Exc:** $500 **VGood:** $450

Add $25 to above prices for olive drab finish
Add $465 for 22 LR conversion kit
Add $395 for 9mm Competition Conversion kit

Stainless steel barrel and slide (92F)

Perf: $635 **Exc:** $550 **VGood:** $400

BERETTA M9 SPECIAL EDITION PISTOL

Copy of the U.S. M9 military pistol. Similar to the Model 92FS except has special M9 serial number range; one 15-round (pre-ban) magazine; dot-and-post sight system; special M9 military packaging; Army TM 9-1005-317-10 operator's manual; M9 Special Edition patch; certificate of authenticity; Bianchi M12 holster, M1025 magazine pouch, and M1015 web pistol belt. Introduced 1998; dropped 2000. From Beretta U.S.A.

Perf: $850 **Exc:** $700 **VGood:** $550

BERETTA MODEL 92F COMPACT

Same specs as Beretta Model 92FS except cut down frame; 4-3/8-inch barrel; 7-7/8-inch overall length; 13-shot magazine; weighs 3-1/2 oz.; Trijicon sights and wood grips optionally available. From Beretta U.S.A. Introduced 1989; no longer in production.

Perf: $500 **Exc:** $450 **VGood:** $400

Wood grips

Perf: $525 **Exc:** $475 **VGood:** $425

BERETTA MODEL 92F STAINLESS PISTOL

Same as the Model 92FS except has stainless steel barrel and slide, and frame of aluminum-zirconium alloy. Has three-dot sight system. Introduced 1992.

Perf: $635 **Exc:** $500 **VGood:** $400

Add $90 for specimens with Tritium or Trijicon night sight system

BERETTA MODEL 92FCM

Same specs as Model 92F Compact except thinner grip; straightline 8-shot magazine; weighs 31 oz.; 1-1/4-inch overall width; plastic grips. From Beretta U.S.A. Introduced 1989; no longer in production.

Perf: $575 **Exc:** $465 **VGood:** $415

BERETTA MODEL 92FS CENTURION

Same specs as Model 92FS except 4-3/8-inch barrel shorter slide; Trijicon or three-dot sights; plastic or wood grips; 9mm Para. only. From Beretta U.S.A. Introduced 1992.

With plastic grips, three-dot sights

New: $550 **Perf:** $500 **Exc:** $450

With wood grips

New: $575 **Perf:** $525 **Exc:** $475

Add $90 to above prices for Tritium sight system (available 1994-1998)

BERETTA MODEL 92FS STAINLESS

Same specs as Model 92FS except for stainless steel satin finish; groove in slide rail; larger hammer pin head; modified to meet special-use military specs. Introduced 1990.

Perf: $620 **Exc:** $500 **VGood:** $450

BERETTA MODEL 92F-EL

Same specs as Model 92FS Stainless except gold trim on safety levers, magazine release, trigger and grip screws; gold inlaid Beretta logo top of barrel; P. Beretta signature inlaid in gold on slide; contoured walnut grips with Beretta logo engraved; high-polish blued finish on barrel, frame, slide. Introduced 1991; dropped 1994.

Perf: $685 **Exc:** $600 **VGood:** $500

BERETTA 92 STEEL-I

Steel-frame semi-auto in 9mm or .40 S&W. Single- or single/double-action. 15+1 capacity, 4.7-inch barrel, 42.3 oz. IDPA certified. Fixed, 3-dot sights.

NIB: $950 **Exc:** $825 **VGood:** $675

BERETTA M9A1

Semi-auto, single/double-action in 9mm developed for U.S. Marine Corps. Capacity 10+1 or 15+1. Fixed sights.

NIB: $700 **Exc:** $595 **VGood:** $425

Beretta M9A1

Beretta Model 96D

Beretta Model 96 Brigadier

Beretta Model 949 Tipo Olimpionico

Beretta 950B Jetfire

Beretta Model 418

Beretta Model 950BS (2½" barrel)

BERETTA MODEL 96

Semi-automatic; double action; 40 S&W; 10-shot magazine; 5-inch barrel; 8-1/2-inch overall length; weighs 34 oz.; ambidextrous triple safety with passive firing pin catch; slide safety/decocking lever; trigger bar disconnect; plastic grips; blued finish. Introduced 1992. Add 40 percent for Steel Target version.

New: $595 **Perf:** $500 **Exc:** $430

BERETTA MODEL 96 BRIGADIER

Same specs as Model 96 except removable front sight; reconfigured high slide wall profile; 10-shot magazine; three-dot sights system; 4-15/16-inch barrel; weighs 35 oz.; matte black Bruniton finish. From Beretta U.S.A. Introduced 1995; still in production.

New: $645 **Perf:** $550 **Exc:** $450

BERETTA MODEL 96 CENTURION

Same specs as Model 96 except 4-3/8-inch barrel; shorter slide; Trijicon or three-dot sights; plastic or wood grips; 40 S&W only. From Beretta U.S.A. Introduced 1992.

New: $550 **Perf:** $500 **Exc:** $400

With three-dot sights, plastic grips

New: $650 **Perf:** $600 **Exc:** $500

BERETTA MODEL 96D

Same specs as Model 96 except double-action-only; three-dot sights. From Beretta U.S.A. Introduced 1992.

New: $600 **Perf:** $550 **Exc:** $450

BERETTA MODEL 318

Semi-automatic; 25 ACP; 8-shot magazine; 2-1/2-inch barrel; 4-1/2-inch overall length; weighs 14 oz.; blued finish, fixed sights; plastic grips. Sold in the U.S. as the Panther. Manufactured 1934 to 1946.

Exc: $275 **VGood:** $225 **Good:** $175

BERETTA MODEL 418

Semi-automatic; 25 ACP; 8-shot magazine; 3-1/2-inch barrel; 5-3/4-inch overall length; fixed sights; plastic grips; blued finish; grip safety redesigned to match contour of backstrap. Introduced 1946; dropped 1958.

Exc: $250 **VGood:** $175 **Good:** $150

BERETTA MODEL 420

Semi-automatic; 25 ACP; 8-shot magazine; 3-1/2-inch barrel; 5-inch overall length; fixed sights; plastic grips; chrome-plated, engraved version of the Model 418.

Exc: $250 **VGood:** $200 **Good:** $150

BERETTA MODEL 421

Semi-automatic; 25 ACP; 8-shot magazine; 3-1/2-inch barrel; 5-inch overall length; fixed sights; plastic grips; gold-plated, elaborately engraved version of the Model 418.

Exc: $500 **VGood:** $350 **Good:** $250

BERETTA MODEL 948

Semi-automatic; double action; 22 LR; 3-5/16-inch, 6-inch barrel; fixed sights; hammer; grip displays "BERETTA" across top instead of earlier "PB" monogram. Sold in U.S. as Featherweight or Plinker.

Exc: $250 **VGood:** $225 **Good:** $195

BERETTA MODEL 949 TIPO OLIMPIONICO

Semi-automatic; 22 Short; 6-shot magazine; 8-3/4-inch barrel; 12-1/2-inch overall length; target sights; adjustable barrel weight; muzzle brake; hand-checkered walnut thumbrest grips; blued. Introduced 1949; dropped 1968.

Exc: $575 **VGood:** $400 **Good:** $300

BERETTA MODEL 950B JETFIRE

Semi-automatic; single action; 22 Short (discontinued 1992); 25 ACP; 7-shot magazine; 2-3/8-inch barrel; 4-1/2-inch overall length; weighs 9-1/2 oz.; tip-up barrel; rear sight milled in slide, fixed front; black plastic or wood grips; blue or nickel finish. Introduced 1950; imported from Italy until 1968, made in U.S. from 1968; dropped 2002.

Exc: $225 **VGood:** $185 **Good:** $165

BERETTA MODEL 950B MINX M2

Semi-automatic; 22 Short; 6-shot magazine; 2-3/8-inch barrel; 4-1/2-inch overall length; rear sight milled in slide, fixed front; black plastic grips; blued. Introduced 1950; importation dropped 1968.

Exc: $225 **VGood:** $200 **Good:** $175

BERETTA MODEL 950CC MINX M4

Same specs as Model M2 except 3-3/4-inch barrel. Introduced 1956. Not imported since 1968.

Exc: $225 **VGood:** $200 **Good:** $175

BERETTA MODEL 950BS

Semi-automatic; single action; 22 Short, 25 ACP; 8-shot magazine; 2-1/2-inch, 4-inch (22) barrel; 4-1/2-inch overall length; weighs 10 oz. (25 ACP); checkered plastic or walnut grips; fixed sights; thumb safety, half-cock safety; hinged barrel for single loading, cleaning; blued, nickel or matte finish. Made by Beretta USA. Introduced 1982; dropped 2002.

Perf: $180 **Exc:** $145 **VGood:** $125

4-Inch Barrel

Perf: $225 **Exc:** $200 **VGood:** $150

BERETTA MODEL 951 BRIGADIER

Semi-automatic; 9mm Para.; 8-shot magazine; 4-1/2-inch barrel; 8-inch overall length; external hammer; crossbolt safety; slide stays open after last shot; fixed sights; molded grooved plastic grips; blued. Advertised originally as Brigadier model. Introduced 1951; no longer in production.

Exc: $550 **VGood:** $400 **Good:** $325

BERETTA MODEL 1915

Semi-automatic; 32 ACP, 9mm Glisenti; 8-shot magazine; 6-inch overall length; 3-5/16-inch barrel; blued finish; fixed sights; grooved wooden grips. Smaller caliber manufactured 1915 to 1930; 9mm Glisenti, 1915 to 1918.

32 ACP

Exc: $400 **VGood:** $275 **Good:** $225

9mm Glisenti

Exc: $675 **VGood:** $525 **Good:** $400

BERETTA MODEL 1919

Semi-automatic; 25 ACP; 8-shot magazine; 3-1/2-inch barrel; 5-3/4-inch overall length; hammerless; grip safety on frame backstrap; fixed sights; wood (early models), pressed sheet steel or plastic grips; blued finish. Introduced in 1919, went through several modifications to be designated as Model 318; dropped 1939.

Exc: $400 **VGood:** $350 **Good:** $275

BERETTA MODEL 1923

Semi-automatic; 9mm Glisenti; 8-shot magazine; 4-inch barrel; 6-1/2-inch overall length; 28 oz.; ring-type external hammer; blued finish; fixed sights; pressed steel or wood grips. Manufactured 1923 to 1936.

Exc: $600 **VGood:** $450 **Good:** $300

Beretta PX4 Storm

Beretta Model 1931

Beretta U22 NEOS

Beretta Model 3032 Tomcat

Beretta Model 8000 Cougar

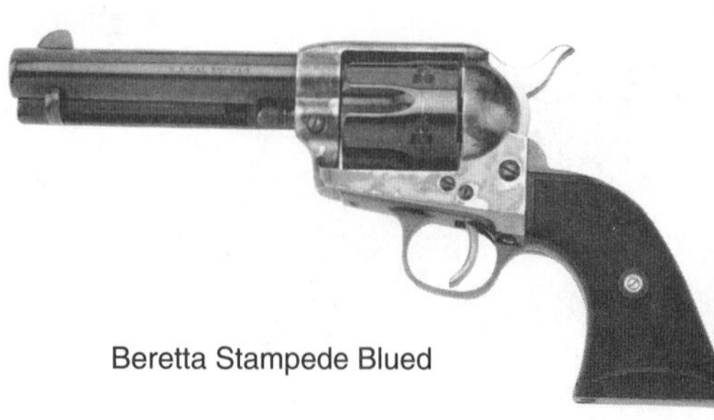
Beretta Stampede Blued

BERETTA MODEL 1931

Semi-automatic; double-action; 32 ACP; 8-shot magazine; 3-1/2-inch barrel; 6-inch overall length; weighs 22-1/2 oz.; fixed sights; walnut grips; blued finish. Italian Navy issue bears medallion with "R/Anchor/M" emblem. Commercial issue has standard "PB" embossed black plastic grips.

Exc: $650 **VGood:** $575 **Good:** $400

BERETTA MODEL 1934

Semi-automatic; 380 ACP; 7-shot magazine; 3-3/8-inch barrel; 5-7/8-inch overall length; weighs 28-1/8 oz.; fixed sights; plastic grips; thumb safety; blued or chrome finish. Official Italian service sidearm in WWII; military versions marked "RE," "RA" or "RM" for the army, air force and navy respectively. Police versions marked "PS" on rear of frame. Wartime version lacks quality of commercial model. Introduced 1934.

Exc: $400 **VGood:** $350 **Good:** $275

BERETTA MODEL 1935

Semi-automatic; double action; 32 ACP; 7-shot magazine; 3-3/8-inch barrel; 5-7/8-inch overall length; fixed sights; plastic grips; thumb safety; blued or chrome finish. Italian service pistol during WWII; frame markings "RA" or "RM" on frame for the air force and navy respectively. Commercial version after 1945 known as Model 935.

Exc: $400 **VGood:** $350 **Good:** $275

BERETTA MODEL 3032 TOMCAT

Semi-automatic; 32 ACP, 7-shot magazine. Barrel: 2.45-inch. Weight: 14.5 oz. Length: 5 inches overall. Stocks: Checkered black plastic. Sights: Blade front, drift-adjustable rear. Features: Double action with exposed hammer; tip-up barrel for direct loading/unloading; thumb safety; polished or matte blue finish. Made by Beretta U.S.A. Introduced 1996.

Perf: $300 **Exc:** $245 **VGood:** $165

BERETTA MODEL 8000 COUGAR

Semi-automatic; double action; 9mm Para.; 10-shot magazine; 3-1/2-inch barrel; 7-inch overall length; weighs 33-1/2 oz.; textured composition grips; blade front sight, drift-adjustable rear; slide-mounted safety; exposed hammer; matte black Bruniton finish. Imported from Italy by Beretta U.S.A. Introduced 1994. A Turkish-made version under thje Stoeger name was introduced c. 2008 and is worth approximately 35% less.

New: $615 **Perf:** $555 **Exc:** $420

BERETTA MODEL 8000/8040 MINI COUGAR

Similar to the Model 8000/8040 Cougar except has shorter grip frame and weighs 27.6 oz. Introduced 1998. Imported from Italy by Beretta U.S.A.

Perf: $600 **Exc:** $550 **VGood:** $400

BERETTA MODEL 8000D COUGAR

Same specs as Model 8000 except double-action-only trigger mechanism. Imported from Italy by Beretta U.S.A. Introduced 1994.

New: $550 **Perf:** $500 **Exc:** $400

BERETTA MODEL 8040 COUGAR

Semi-automatic; double action; 40 S&W; 10-shot magazine; 3-1/2-inch barrel; 7-inch overall length; weighs 33-1/2 oz.; textured composition grips; blade front sight, drift-adjustable rear; slide-mounted safety; exposed hammer; matte black Bruniton finish. Imported from Italy by Beretta U.S.A. Introduced 1994.

Exc: $615 **Perf:** $555 **Exc:** $525

BERETTA MODEL 8040D COUGAR

Same specs as Model 8040 except double-action-only trigger mechanism. Imported from Italy by Beretta U.S.A. Introduced 1994.

Exc: $615 **Perf:** $555 **Exc:** $525

BERETTA PX4 STORM

A semi automatic single or double action pistol available in 9mm, .40 S&W. Polymer frame. New rotating barrel locking system. Matte black finish. Accessory rail on frame. Standard model has a 4 inch barrel. The compact model has a 3.2 inch barrel. Magazine capacity is 12 – 17 rounds, based on caliber and standard or compact frame. Weighs approx 27 oz. New in 2005.

Perf: $550 **Exc:** $475 **VGood:** $400

BERETTA PX4 STORM .45ACP

New in 2007

Perf: $625 **Exc:** $575 **VGood:** $500

BERETTA PX4 STORM SD (SPECIAL DUTY)

.45 caliber single or double action. 4 inch barrel. Brown polymer frame with accessory rail. 9 or 10 rd magazines. Weighs 28 oz.

Perf: $850 **Exc:** $750 **VGood:** $600

BERETTA STAMPEDE

Single action revolver patterned after the Colt Single Action Army; 357 Mag; 44-40 (mfd. in 2003), 45 LC; transfer bar; half cock safety; 6-shot; 4-3/4-inch, 5-1/2-inch, 7-1/2-inch barrel; 37 oz. Made by Aldo Uberti in Italy, which is owned by Beretta.

Stampede Blue

Exc: $395 **Perf:** $345 **VGood:** $300

Stampede Brushed Nickel

Exc: $415 **Perf:** $365 **VGood:** $330

Stampede Stainless (Inox)

Exc: $510 **Perf:** $460 **VGood:** $400

Stampede Marshal

Exc: $415 **Perf:** $365 **VGood:** $330

Stampede Deluxe

Exc: $510 **Perf:** $460 **VGood:** $400

BERETTA STAMPEDE BISLEY

Single action 6-shot Bisley replica revolver in .45 Colt or .357 Magnum. Blued with 4-3/4-inch, 5-1/2-inch or 7-1/2-inch barrel.

NIB: $425 **Exc:** $385 **VGood:** $350

BERETTA LARAMIE

Break-open single-action revolver reminiscent of S&W #3 chambered for.45 LC or .38 Special. Six-shot cylinder. Adjustable rear sight. 5-inch or 6-1/2-inch barrels.

NIB: $800 **Exc:** $700 **VGood:** $595

BERETTA U22 NEOS

Semi automatic .22LR. 10 round magazine. 4 ½ or 6 inch barrel. Full length sight rail. Interchangable grip frames in aqua, grey and black. Base model gun is black. Weighs 31 to 36 oz. New 2002.

Perf: $275 **Exc:** $225 **VGood:** $175

Bergmann-Bayard Model 1908
Bergmann Special
Bergmann Vest Pocket
Bergmann Model 1903 "Mars"
Bernardelli Model AMR
Bernardelli Model 80
Bernardelli Model 68

BERETTA U22 NEOS DLX

U22 with adjustable trigger and interchangeable front and rear sights. Six included. 6 or 7 ½ inch barrel. Mfg 2002-2007.

Perf: $300 **Exc:** $250 **VGood:** $200

BERETTA U22 NEOS DLX INOX

The Neos DLX with stainless steel finish.

Perf: $325 **Exc:** $275 **VGood:** $225

BERETTA U22 NEOS INOX

The U22 with stainless steel finish.

Perf: $325 **Exc:** $275 **VGood:** $225

BERGMANN MODEL 1903 "MARS"

Semi-automatic; 9mm Bergmann-Bayard; 6-, 10-shot magazine; 4-inch barrel; 10-inch overall length; checkered wood grips. Marked "Bergmann Mars Pat. Brev. S.G.D.G." on locking block top. About 1,000 made in Germany before rights were sold to Pieper in Belgium where, with a few minor changes, it was made as the Bergmann-Bayard.

Exc: $5500 **VGood:** $4250 **Good:** $3000

BERGMANN SPECIAL

Semi-automatic; double action; 32 ACP; 8-shot magazine; 3-7/16-inch barrel; 6-3/16-inch overall length; checkered plastic wrap-around grips. Rare double-action competitor to Walther's Model PP, actually made by Menz but sold under Bergmann's name.

Exc: $1200 **VGood:** $850 **Good:** $500

BERGMANN VEST POCKET MODELS

Semi-automatic; 25 ACP; 6-, 9-shot magazine; 2-1/8-inch barrel; 4-3/4-inch overall length; checkered hard rubber or wood (rare) grips. Both conventional and one-hand-cocked ("Einhand") models later marketed under the Lignose name (see Lignose).

Conventional

Exc: $300 **VGood:** $200 **Good:** $125

Einhand

Exc: $500 **VGood:** $400 **Good:** $250

32 or 380 Einhand

Cataloged but apparently never made.

BERGMANN-BAYARD MODEL 1908

Semi-automatic; 9mm Bergmann-Bayard; 6-shot magazine; 4-inch barrel; 10-inch overall length; checkered wood or hard rubber (rare) grips. Marked "ANCIENS ESTABLISSEMENTS PIEPER" on side. Made under contract for the Spanish and Danish armies as well as commercial sale.

Exc: $2300 **VGood:** $1900 **Good:** $1500

Spanish contract (tiny circle with three-line proofmark)

Exc: $1500 **VGood:** $1250 **Good:** $750

Shoulder stock slot in backstrap

Exc: $2400 **VGood:** $1800 **Good:** $1450

BERGMANN-BAYARD MODEL 1910/21 TOJHUS

Semi-automatic; 9mm Bergmann-Bayard; 6-shot magazine; 4-inch barrel; 10-inch overall length. Made under contract for Danish army but reworked post-WWI models with oversize wood or plastic grips; screw-retained instead of latched sideplate; stamped "1910/21" on side. After WWI when Pieper could no longer supply pistols to Denmark, the Danes produced about 2200 Model 1910/21 pistols in their own arsenals.

Exc: $2150 **VGood:** $1800 **Good:** $1450

BERNARDELLI MODEL 60

Semi-automatic; 22 LR, 32 ACP, 380 ACP; 10-shot (22 LR), 9-shot (32 ACP), 7-shot (380 ACP); 3-1/2-inch barrel; 6-1/2-inch overall length; weighs 26-1/2 oz.; ramp front sight, adjustable white-outlined rear; checkered plastic grips, thumbrest; hammer-block slide safety; loaded chamber indicator; dual recoil buffer springs; serrated trigger, inertia-type firing pin. Made in Italy. Introduced 1978; no longer imported.

Perf: $250 **Exc:** $195 **VGood:** $180

BERNARDELLI MODEL 68

Semi-automatic; 22 Short, 22 LR; 6-shot; 2-inch barrel; 4-1/8-inch overall length; weighs 8-1/2 oz.; plastic grips; blued finish. A replacement for the Vest Pocket Model with rounded slide, loaded chamber indicator, optional extended magazine. Discontinued 1970.

Perf: $195 **Exc:** $150 **VGood:** $125

BERNARDELLI MODEL 69 TARGET

Semi-automatic; 22 LR; 10-shot magazine; 5-15/16-inch barrel; 9-inch overall length; weighs 38 oz.; interchangeable target sights; wrap-around hand-checkered walnut stocks; thumbrest; meets UIT requirements; manual thumb safety, magazine safety; grooved trigger. Made in Italy. Introduced 1987.

Perf: $575 **Exc:** $475 **VGood:** $400

BERNARDELLI MODEL 80

Semi-automatic; 22 LR, 32 ACP, 380 ACP; 10-shot (22 LR), 8-shot (32 ACP, 380 ACP); 3-1/2-inch barrel; 6-1/2-inch overall length; adjustable rear sight, white dot front; plastic thumbrest stocks; blued finish;. Introduced 1968 as modification of Model 60 to meet U.S. import requirements; dropped 1988.

Perf: $185 **Exc:** $160 **VGood:** $150

BERNARDELLI MODEL 90

Semi-automatic; 22 LR, 32 ACP; 10-shot (22 LR), 8-shot (32 ACP); 6-inch barrel; 9-inch overall length; adjustable rear sight, white dot front; plastic thumbrest stocks; blued finish. Introduced 1968; dropped 1988.

Perf: $210 **Exc:** $185 **VGood:** $170

BERNARDELLI MODEL 100 TARGET

Semi-automatic; 22 LR; 10-shot magazine; 6-inch barrel; 9-inch overall length; adjustable rear sight, interchangeable front; checkered walnut thumbrest stocks; blued finish. Introduced in 1969 as Model 68; dropped 1983.

Perf: $395 **Exc:** $325 **VGood:** $295

BERNARDELLI MODEL AMR

Semi-automatic; single action; 22 LR, 32, 380 ACP; 6-inch barrel; target sights. Similar to the Model USA. Introduced 1989; dropped 1991. Was imported by Magnum Research.

Perf: $395 **Exc:** $325 **VGood:** $275

Bernardelli Model Baby

Bernardelli Model PO18

Bernardelli Model PO10

Bernardelli Model USA

Bernardelli Vest Pocket Model

BERNARDELLI MODEL BABY

Semi-automatic; 22 Short; 22 LR; 2-1/8-inch barrel; fixed sights; plastic grips; blued finish. This was the first of Bernardelli's 22 pistols and was largely the Vest Pocket Model altered to handle rimfire cartridges. Introduced 1949; discontinued 1968.

Perf: $295 **Exc:** $225 **VGood:** $175

BERNARDELLI MODEL PO10 TARGET

Semi-automatic; single action; 22 LR; 5- or 10-shot magazine; 6-inch barrel; weighs 40-1/2 oz.; walnut thumbrest stocks; fully-adjustable target-type sights; external hammer with safety notch; pivoted adjustable trigger; matte black finish. Made in Italy. Introduced 1989; importation dropped 1990.

Perf: $475 **Exc:** $405 **VGood:** $355

BERNARDELLI MODEL PO18

Semi-automatic; double action; 9mm Para; 16-shot magazine; 4-7/8-inch barrel; 6-3/16-inch overall length; weighs 36-1/3 oz.; low-profile combat sights; checkered, contoured plastic or optional walnut stocks; manual thumb safety, half-cock, magazine safeties; ambidextrous magazine release; auto-locking firing pin block safety. Made in Italy. Introduced 1987; was imported by Armsport and by Magnum Research, Inc.; no longer imported.

Perf: $485 **Exc:** $400 **VGood:** $350

Walnut grips

Perf: $525 **Exc:** $450 **VGood:** $375

Add $60 to above prices for chrome finish

BERNARDELLI MODEL PO18 COMPACT

Same specs as standard PO18 except 4-1/8-inch barrel; 14-shot magazine. Introduced 1987; was imported by Armsport and by Magnum Research, Inc.; no longer imported.

Perf: $545 **Exc:** $450 **VGood:** $400

Walnut stocks

Perf: $550 **Exc:** $500 **VGood:** $450

Add $55 to above prices for chrome finish

BERNARDELLI MODEL USA

Semi-automatic; 22 LR, 380 ACP; 10-shot (22 LR), 7-shot (380 ACP) magazine; 3-1/2-inch barrel, 6-1/2-inch overall length; weighs 26-1/2 oz.; ramp front sight; fully-adjustable white-outline rear; checkered plastic stocks, thumbrest; serrated trigger; inertia-type firing pin; hammer-block safety; loaded chamber indicator. Made in Italy. Introduced 1989; was imported by Armsport and by Magnum Research, Inc.; no longer imported.

Perf: $380 **Exc:** $300 **VGood:** $275

BERNARDELLI P. ONE

Semi-automatic; double action; 9mm Para., 40 S&W; 16-shot (9mm), 10-shot (40 S&W) magazine; 4-7/8-inch barrel; 8-3/8-inch overall length; weighs 34 oz.; checkered black plastic grips; blade front sight, fully adjustable rear; three-dot system; forged steel frame and slide; full-length slide rails; reversible magazine release; thumb safety/decocker; squared triggerguard; blue/black finish. Imported from Italy by Armsport. Introduced 1994; no longer imported.

Perf: $580 **Exc:** $495 **VGood:** $400

Chrome finish

Perf: $575 **Exc:** $500 **VGood:** $450

Add $40 to above prices for wood grips

BERNARDELLI P. ONE PRACTICAL VB PISTOL

Same specs as P. One except 9x21mm; two- or four-port compensator; straight trigger; micro-adjustable rear sight. Imported from Italy by Armsport. Introduced 1994; dropped 1997.

New: 900 **Perf:** $850 **Exc:** $750

Add $60 to above price for 4-port compensator.
Add $60 to above price for chrome finish

BERNARDELLI STANDARD

Semi-automatic; 22 LR; 10-shot magazine; 6-inch, 8-inch, 10-inch barrel; 13-inch overall length (10-inch barrel); target sights; adjustable sight ramp; walnut target grips; blued. Simply the Pocket Model adapted for 22 LR cartridge. Introduced 1949; no longer imported. Smallest 25 Auto ever mfd.

Perf: $225 **Exc:** $200 **VGood:** $175

BERNARDELLI VEST POCKET MODEL

Semi-automatic; 25 ACP; 5-shot; 8-shot extension magazine also available; 2-1/8-inch barrel; 4-1/8-inch overall length; no sights, but sighting groove milled in slide; plastic grips; blued finish. Introduced 1948; U.S. importation dropped 1968.

Exc: $250 **VGood:** $195 **Good:** $165

BERSA FIRESTORM

SA/DA operation. .380 or .22LR caliber. 3 ½ inch barrel. Duo tone or matte black finish. Rubber grips. 7 rd magazine for .380. The 22LR holds 10 rds. Weighs 20 oz. Current model.

Perf: $300 **Exc:** $250 **VGood:** $200

BERSA MODEL 23

Semi-automatic; double action; 22 LR; 10-shot magazine; 3-1/2-inch barrel; 6-1/2-inch overall length; weighs 24-1/2 oz.; walnut grips with stippled panels; blade front sight, notch windage-adjustable rear; three-dot system; firing pin, magazine safeties; blue or nickel finish. Made in Argentina; distributed by Eagle Imports, Inc. Introduced 1989; dropped 1994.

Blue finish

Perf: $230 **Exc:** $195 **VGood:** $155

Nickel finish

Perf: $250 **Exc:** $215 **VGood:** $175

BERSA MODEL 83

Semi-automatic; double action; 380 ACP; 7-shot magazine; 3-1/2-inch barrel; 6-1/2-inch overall length; weighs 25-3/4 oz.; stippled walnut grips; blade front sight, notch windage-adjustable rear; three-dot system; firing pin, magazine safety systems; blue or nickel finish. Imported from Argentina; distributed by Eagle Imports, Inc. Introduced 1989; dropped 1994.

Blue finish

Perf: $235 **Exc:** $180 **VGood:** $150

Nickel finish

Perf: $270 **Exc:** $235 **VGood:** $185

BERSA MODEL 85

Semi-automatic; double action; 380 ACP; 13-shot magazine; 3-1/2-inch barrel; 6-1/2-inch overall length; weighs 25-3/4 oz.; stippled walnut grips; blade front sight, notch windage-adjustable rear; three-dot system; firing pin, magazine safety systems; blue or nickel finish. Imported from Argentina; distributed by Eagle Imports, Inc. Introduced 1989; dropped 1994.

Blue finish

Perf: $285 **Exc:** $245 **VGood:** $220

Bersa Model 83

Bersa Model 95 Series

Bersa Model 223

Bersa Model 23

Bersa Model 225

Bersa Thunder 380

Nickel finish
Perf: $340 **Exc:** $295 **VGood:** $270

BERSA MODEL 86

Semi-automatic; double action; 380 ACP; 13-shot magazine; 3-1/2-inch barrel; 6-1/2-inch overall length; weighs 22 oz.; wrap-around textured rubber grips; blade front sight, windage-adjustable rear; three-dot system; firing pin, magazine safeties; combat-style triggerguard; matte blue or satin nickel finish. Imported from Argentina; distributed by Eagle Imports, Inc. Introduced 1992; dropped 1994.

Blue finish
Perf: $315 **Exc:** $265 **VGood:** $225

Nickel finish
Perf: $345 **Exc:** $295 **VGood:** $255

BERSA MODEL 95 SERIES

Semi-automatic; double action; 380 ACP; 7-shot magazine; 3-1/2-inch barrel; 6-1/2-inch overall length; weighs 22 oz.; blade front sight, windage-adjustable rear; three-dot system; firing pin and magazine safeties; combat-style triggerguard; wrap-around textured rubber grips; matte blue or satin nickel. Imported from Argentina; distributed by Eagle Imports, Inc. Introduced 1992.

Matte blue finish
New: $250 **Perf:** $200 **Exc:** $150

Satin nickel finish
New: $250 **Perf:** $240 **Exc:** $175

BERSA MODEL 223

Semi-automatic; double action; 22 LR; 11-shot magazine; 3-1/2-inch barrel; weighs 24-1/2 oz; blade front sight, square-notch windage-adjustable rear; checkered target-type nylon stocks; thumbrest; blowback action; squared-off triggerguard; magazine safety; blued finish. Made in Argentina. Introduced 1984; dropped 1987.

Perf: $250 **Exc:** $200 **VGood:** $150

BERSA MODEL 224

Semi-automatic; single action; 22 LR; 11-shot magazine; 4-inch barrel; weighs 26 oz; blade front sight, square-notch windage-adjustable rear; checkered target-type nylon stocks; thumbrest; blowback action; combat-type triggerguard; magazine safety; blued finish. Made in Argentina. Introduced 1984; dropped 1987.

Perf: $250 **Exc:** $200 **VGood:** $150

BERSA MODEL 225

Semi-automatic; single action; 22 LR; 10-shot magazine; 5-inch barrel; weighs 26 oz.; blade front sight, square-notch windage-adjustable rear; checkered target-type nylon stocks; thumbrest; blowback action; combat-type triggerguard; magazine safety; blued finish. Made in Argentina. Introduced 1984; dropped 1987.

Perf: $275 **Exc:** $200 **VGood:** $150

BERSA MODEL 226

Semi-automatic; single action; 22 LR; 10-shot magazine; 6-inch barrel; weighs 26 oz; blade front sight, square-notch windage-adjustable rear; checkered target-type nylon stocks; thumbrest; blowback action; combat-type triggerguard; magazine safety; blued finish. Made in Argentina. Introduced 1984; dropped 1987.

Perf: $200 **Exc:** $170 **VGood:** $150

BERSA MODEL 383

Semi-automatic; single action; 380 ACP; 9-shot magazine; 3-1/2-inch barrel; weighs 25 oz.; square-notch windage-adjustable rear sight, blade front; target-type black nylon stocks; blowback action; combat-type trigger guard; magazine safety; blued finish. Made in Argentina. Introduced 1984; dropped 1987.

Perf: $250 **Exc:** $200 **VGood:** $150

BERSA MODEL 383DA

Same specs as Model 383 except double action.

Perf: $150 **Exc:** $135 **VGood:** $125

BERSA THUNDER 9

Semi-automatic; double action; 9mm; barrel length 3.6"; alloy frame; weight 23 oz.; 6.53" overall length; polymer grips; capacity 10+1; fixed sights. Imported from Argentina. 1993-1995.

New: $375 **Perf:** $300 **Exc:** $250

BERSA THUNDER 9 ULTRA COMPACT

Available blued or stainless with 10- or 13-round capacity. Double-action chambered for 9mm. 3.5-inch barrel, 25 oz., fixed sights and polymer grips.

New: $375 **Perf:** $300 **Exc:** $250

BERSA THUNDER 9 AND 40 PRO SERIES PISTOLS

Semi automatic SA/DA action. 4 ¼ inch barrel. Alloy frame with accessory rail. Steel slide. Matte black or Duo tone finish. 9mm 17 rd or .40S&W 13rd magazine. Weighs 30 oz. Current model.

Perf: $425 **Exc:** $400 **VGood:** $350

BERSA THUNDER 9 AND 40 PRO ULTRA COMPACT PISTOLS

Semi automatic SA/DA action. 3 ¼ inch barrel. Alloy frame with accessory rail. Steel slide. Matte black or Duo tone finish. 9mm 13 rd or .40S&W 10rd magazine. Weighs 23 oz. Current model.

Perf: $425 **Exc:** $400 **VGood:** $350

BERSA THUNDER 9/40 HIGH CAPACITY SERIES

Double-action semi-autos available chambered for 9mm (17-rd.) or .40 S&W (13-rd.) and in matte blued or satin nickel-plate. Fixed sights and polymer grips. LOA 7 1/2-inch, 4 1/4-inch barrel, 26 oz.

New: $375 **Perf:** $300 **Exc:** $250

BERSA THUNDER 22

Semi-automatic; double action; 22 LR; 10+1 capacity; 3-1/2" barrel; alloy frame; polymer grips; 6-1/2" overall length. Introduced 1995; dropped 1996.

New: $230 **Perf:** $200 **Exc:** $175

Nickel finish
New: $250 **Perf:** $225 **Exc:** $200

BERSA THUNDER 45 PRO

As above in .45 caliber. 3.6 inch barrel. 7rd magazine. Weighs 27 oz. Current model.

Perf: $425 **Exc:** $400 **VGood:** $350

BERSA THUNDER 380

Semi-automatic; double action; 380 ACP; 7-shot magazine; 3-1/2-inch barrel; 6-1/2-inch overall length; weighs 25-3/4 oz.; black rubber grips; blade front sight, notch windage-adjustable rear; three-dot system; firing pin and magazine safeties; blue, nickel or duo-tone finish. Imported from Argentina; distributed by Eagle Imports, Inc. Introduced 1995; dropped 1998.

New: $235 **Perf:** $200 **Exc:** $175

Bond Arms Snake Slayer IV

Boberg BR9-S Platinum

Bren Ten

Bond Arms Texas Defender

BF Single Shot

Nickel finish

New: $255 **Perf:** $225 **Exc:** $200

Duo-tone finish

New: $255 **Perf:** $220 **Exc:** $200

BERSA THUNDER 380 PLUS

Same specs as Thunder 380 except 10-shot magazine. Imported from Argentina; distributed by Eagle Imports, Inc. Introduced 1995; dropped 1998.

New: $265 **Perf:** $210 **Exc:** $175

Nickel finish

New: $300 **Perf:** $250 **Exc:** $225

Duo-tone finish

New: $275 **Perf:** $225 **Exc:** $200

BF SINGLE SHOT (E. A. BROWN)

Single shot; 22 LR, 357 Mag., 44 Mag., 7-30 Waters, 30-30 Win., 375 Win., 45-70; custom chamberings from 17 Rem. through 45-cal.; 10-inch, 10-3/4-inch, 12-inch, 15+-inch barrel lengths; weighs about 52 oz.; custom Herrett finger-groove grip, forend; undercut Patridge front sight, 1/2-MOA match-quality fully-adjustable RPM Iron Sight rear; barrel or receiver mounting; drilled and tapped for scope mounting; rigid barrel/receiver; falling block action with short lock time; automatic ejection; air-gauged match barrels by Wilson or Douglas; matte black oxide finish standard, electroless nickel optional. Guns with RPM sights worth slightly more. Made in U.S. by E.A. Brown Mfg. Introduced 1988;.

New.: $700 **Exc:** $600 **VGood:** $450

BF SINGLE SHOT ULTIMATE SILHOUETTE

Same specs as standard model except 10-3/4-inch heavy barrel; special forend; RPM rear sight; hooded front; gold-plated trigger. Made in U.S. by E.A. Brown Mfg. Introduced 1988; still in production.

New.: $750 **Exc:** $650 **VGood:** $500

BOBERG BR9-S PLATINUM

Semi-automatic, striker fired 9mm Luger. 3.35 inch barrel with a rotating barrel - locked breach action. 5.1 inches long. Weight: 17.5 ounces. Aluminum frame, stainless steel slide with fixed low profile sights. +P rated. Polymer grips and 7+1 capacity. Made in the U.S.A. Introduced 2013.

Perf: $1250 **Exc:** $1150 **VGood:** $1075

BOND ARMS TEXAS DEFENDER

Over-Under; 9mm Para, 38 Spec./357 Mag., 44 Spec./44 Mag., 45 Colt/410 shotshell. Barrel: 3-1/2-inch. Weight: 21 oz. Length: 5-inch overall. Stocks: Laminated black ash or rosewood. Sights: Blade front, fixed rear. Features: Interchangeable barrels; retracting firing pins; rebounding firing pins; cross-bolt safety; removable trigger guard; automatic extractor for rimmed calibers. Stainless steel construction with blasted/polished and ground combination finish. Introduced 1997. Made in U.S. by Bond Arms, Inc.

New: $400 **Perf:** $345 **Exc:** $260

BOND ARMS COWBOY DEFENDER

Similar to Texas Defender except designed for Cowboy Action Shooting without trigger guard. Introduced 2000.

New: $400 **Perf:** $345 **Exc:** $260

Add $20 to above prices for left-hand model

BOND ARMS SNAKE SLAYER IV

Modern variation of the Remington over/under derringer. Interchangeable 4.5-inch barrel assemblies, rosewood grip panels, stainless finish, fixed sights. Chambered for .410-bore shotshell/.45 LC, 9mm, 10mm, .40 S&W, .45 ACP.

NIB: $435 **Exc:** $395 **VGood:** $295

BREN TEN

Semi-automatic; 10mm Auto; 11-shot magazine; 5-inch barrel; 8-3/4-inch overall length; textured black nylon stocks; adjustable, replaceable combat sights; double- or single-action; stainless steel frame; blued slide; reversible thumb safety, firing pin block. Made by Dornaus & Dixon. Introduced 1983; dropped 1986. Deduct 25 percent if missing magazine or with non-factory magzine.

Perf: $1775 **Exc:** $1300 **VGood:** $1100

Military/Police black matte finish model

Perf: $1700 **Exc:** $1300 **VGood:** $1100

Dual presentation 10mm and 45 ACP

Perf: $4200 **Exc:** $3300 **VGood:** $2500

BREN TEN POCKET MODEL

Same specs as Bren Ten except 4-inch barrel; 7-3/8-inch overall length; weighs 28 oz.; 9-shot magazine; chrome slide.

Perf: $1775 **Exc:** $1400 **VGood:** $1200

BREN TEN SPECIAL FORCES MODEL

Same specs as Pocket Model except standard grip frame; 11-shot magazine; weighs 33 oz.; black or natural light finish. Introduced 1984; dropped 1986.

Perf: $2400 **Exc:** $1800 **VGood:** $1400

Light finish

Perf: $2400 **Exc:** $1800 **VGood:** $1400

BRNO ZBP 99

Semi-automatic; 9mm. Para., 40 S&W, 10-shot magazine. Barrel: 4-inch. Weight: 27.5 oz. Length: 7.2-inch overall. Stocks: Black composition. Sights: Blade front, rear adjustable for elevation; three-dot system. Features: Double action mechanism; polymer frame; chamber loaded indicator. Announced 1998. Was to be imported from The Czech Republic by Euro-Imports.

BROLIN LEGEND L45 STD

Semi-automatic; 45 ACP, 7-shot magazine. Barrel: 5-inch. Weight: 35.9 oz. Length: 8-1/2 inches overall. Stocks: Checkered walnut. Sights: Millett High Visibility front, white outline fixed rear. Features: Throated match barrel; polished feed ramp; lowered and flared ejection port; beveled magazine well; flat top slide; flat mainspring housing; lightened aluminum match trigger; slotted Commander hammer; matte blue finish. Introduced 1996; dropped 1998.

New: $425 **Perf:** $365 **Exc:** $325

BROLIN LEGEND L45C COMPACT

Similar to the L45 Standard pistol except has 4-inch barrel with conical lock up; overall length 7-1/2 inches; weighs 32 oz. Matte blue finish. Introduced 1996; dropped 1998.

New: $440 **Perf:** $380 **Exc:** $330

BROLIN L45T COMPACT

Same as the L45 Legend except uses compact slide on the standard-size frame. Has 4-inch barrel, weighs 33.9 oz., and is 7-1/2 inches overall. Introduced 1996; dropped 1998.

New: $440 **Perf:** $380 **Exc:** $330

BROLIN TAC SERIES SERVICE MODEL

Semi-automatic; double action; 45 ACP, 8-shot magazine. Barrel: 5-inch. Weight: 23 oz. Length: 8-inch overall. Stocks: Checkered black plastic. Sights: Blade front, drift adjustable rear. Features:

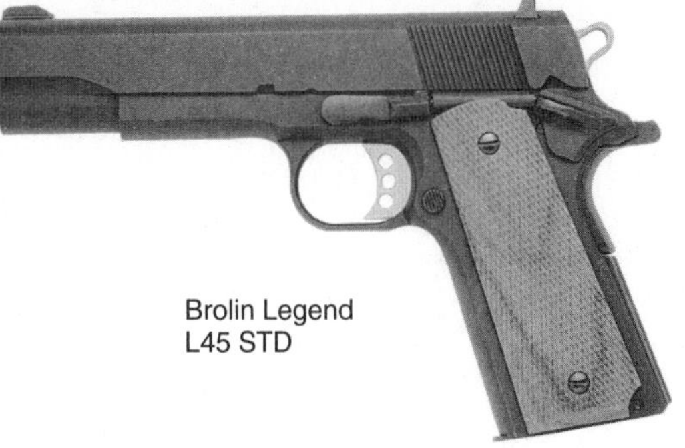
Brolin Legend L45 STD

Bronco Model 1918

Brown Executive Elite

Bren Ten Special Forces Model

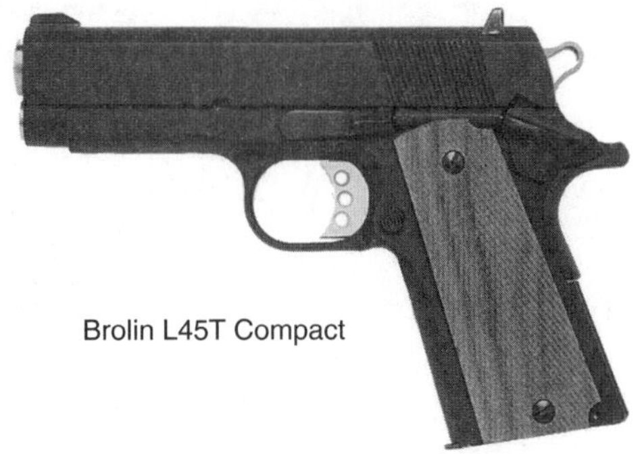
Brolin L45T Compact

Brown Executive Carry

Skeletonized hammer; low-profile three-dot sight system. Introduced 1998; dropped 1998. By Brolin Industries.

New: $360 **Perf:** $315 **Exc:** $285

BROLIN TAC SERIES FULL SIZE

Similar to the Service Model except available in 9mm Para. 40 S&W (10- shot), and 45 ACP (8-shot). Checkered walnut or plastic grips, checkered full-length slide rib. Introduced 1998; dropped 1998. By Brolin Industries.

New: $360 **Perf:** $315 **Exc:** $285

Add $90 to above prices for specimens with Tritium sights

BROLIN TAC SERIES COMPACT DA

Similar to the Service Model except has 3-1/2-inch barrel, 6-1/2-inch overall length, and weighs 19 oz. Available in 9mm Para. or 40 S&W only. Introduced 1998; dropped 1998. By Brolin Industries.

New: $360 **Perf:** $315 **Exc:** $285

BROLIN TAC SERIES BANTAM DA

Similar to the Compact pistol except has shorter grip frame for 4-inch overall height. Has 3-1/2-inch barrel, 6-1/4-inch overall length, and weighs 17 oz. Chambered for the 9mm Para. and 40 S&W; 6-shot magazine; concealed hammer. Introduced 1998; dropped 1998. By Brolin Industries.

New: $375 **Perf:** $325 **Exc:** $275

BROLIN TAC SERIES MODEL TAC-11

Semi-automatic; 45 ACP, 8-shot magazine. Barrel: 5-inch; conical match design. Weight: 35.1 oz. Length: 8.5 inches overall. Stocks: Black rubber contour. Sights: Ramp front, Novak Low Profile Combat Sight or Novak tritium. Features: Throated Conical barrel; polished feed ramp; lowered and flared ejection port; beveled magazine well; flat-top slide; flat mainspring housing; front strap high relief cut; lightened aluminum match trigger; slotted commander hammer; custom beavertail grip safety; Brolin "Iron Claw" extractor. Introduced 1997; dropped 1998. Made in the U.S. by Brolin Industries.

New: $595 **Perf:** $465 **Exc:** $425

BRONCO MODEL 1918

Semi-automatic; 32 ACP; 6-shot magazine; 2-1/2-inch barrel; 5-inch overall length; blued finish; fixed sights; hard rubber stocks. Manufactured in Spain 1918 to 1925.

Exc: $175 **VGood:** $125 **Good:** $100

BRONCO VEST POCKET AUTOMATIC

Semi-automatic; 6.35; small frame. Discontinued.

Exc: $160 **VGood:** $125 **Good:** $110

BROWN CLASSIC

Single-shot; 17 Ackley Hornet through 45-70 Govt. Barrel: 15-inch air gauged match grade. Weight: About 3 lbs., 7 oz. Stocks: Walnut; thumbrest target style. Sights: None furnished; drilled and tapped for scope mounting. Features: Falling block action gives rigid barrel-receiver mating; hand-fitted and headspaced. Introduced 1998. Made in U.S. by E.A. Brown Mfg.

New: $525 **Perf:** $450 **Exc:** $300

BROWN EXECUTIVE TARGET

1911 Executive Elite modified for target/range with adjustable BoMar rear sight, ambidextrous safety. 38 oz. 5-inch barrel chambered for .45 ACP. 7-round magazine.

NIB: $2200 **Exc:** $1800 **VGood:** $1350

BROWN EXECUTIVE ELITE

Government model 5-inch barrel, 38 oz., chambered for .45 ACP. 7-round magazine. Fixed sights. Blue/blue, stainless/blue or all-stainless.

NIB: $2050 **Exc:** $1650 **VGood:** $1225

BROWN EXECUTIVE CARRY

A 4.25-inch commander model .45 ACP with Ed Brown Bobtail. 38 oz. 7-round magazine, fixed sights. Blue/blue, stainless/blue or all-stainless.

NIB: $2200 **Exc:** $1800 **VGood:** $1350

BROWN SPECIAL FORCES

Blue/blue 1911 semi-auto with 5-inch barrel and fixed 3-dot night sights. Chambered for .45 ACP. 38 oz.; 7-round magazine. Cocobolo grips.

NIB: $1900 **Exc:** $1575 **VGood:** $1150

BROWNING 25 BABY

Semi-automatic; 25 ACP; 6-shot magazine; 2-1/8-inch barrel; 4-inch overall length; fixed sights, hard rubber grips; blued finish. Introduced ca. 1936; dropped 1968, not currently importable.

Browning Arms Co. marked

Perf: $475 **Exc:** $375 **VGood:** $250

FN marked

Perf: $500 **Exc:** $440 **VGood:** $375

Built-up model marketed by Iver Johnson 2007

Perf: $425 **Exc:** $395 **VGood:** $300

BROWNING 25 LIGHTWEIGHT

Same specs as Browning 25 except chrome-plated; polymer pearl grips; alloy frame. Introduced 1954; dropped 1968.

Perf: $450 **Exc:** $365 **VGood:** $325

BROWNING 25 RENAISSANCE MODEL

Same specs as standard Browning 25 except chrome-plated finish; polyester pearl grips; full engraving. Introduced 1954; dropped 1968.

Perf: $975 **Exc:** $750 **VGood:** $550

BROWNING 380 STANDARD

Semi-automatic; 380 ACP, 32 ACP; 9-shot magazine; 3-7/16-inch barrel; 6-inch overall length; pre-'68 models have fixed sights, later adjustable; hard rubber grips; blued finish. Redesigned 1968; dropped 1974. Last models had 4-1/2-inch barrel; 7-inch overall length.

Perf: $300 **Exc:** $250 **VGood:** $200

BROWNING 380 RENAISSANCE

Same specs as standard Browning 380 Standard except chrome-plated finish; full engraving; polyester pearl grips. Introduced 1954; dropped 1981.

Perf: $900 **Exc:** $800 **VGood:** $700

BROWNING BDA

Semi-automatic; 9mm Para., 38 Super, 45 ACP; 9-shot magazine (9mm, 38 Super), 7-shot (45 ACP); 4-7/16-inch barrel; 7-13/16-inch overall length; fixed sights; plastic stocks; blued finish. Manufactured by Sauer; same as SIG-Sauer P220. Imported 1977 to 1981.

9mm, 45 ACP

Perf: $550 **Exc:** $450 **VGood:** $375

38 Super

Perf: $650 **Exc:** $575 **VGood:** $495

Browning Buck Mark Target 5.5

Browning BDA 380

Browning Buck Mark Lite Splash

Browning Buck Mark Micro

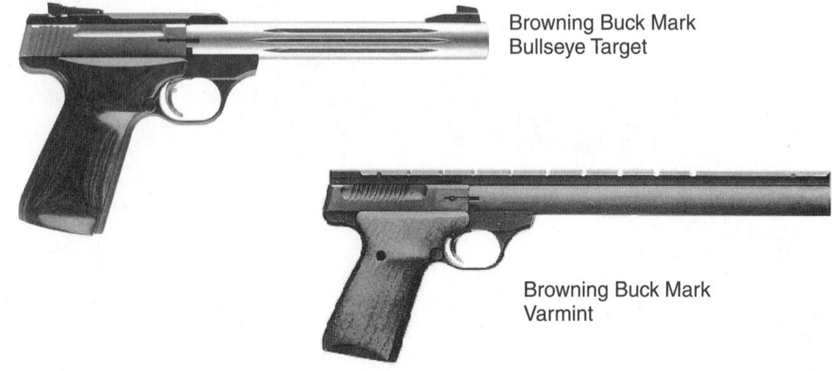

Browning Buck Mark Bullseye Target

Browning Buck Mark Varmint

BROWNING BDA 380

Semi-automatic; 380 Auto; 12-shot magazine; 3-13/16-inch barrel; 6-3/4-inch overall length; blade front sight, windage-adjustable rear; combination safety; de-cocking lever; inertia firing pin; uncheckered walnut grips. Manufactured in Italy by Beretta. Introduced 1978; dropped 1997.

Perf: $450 **Exc:** $350 **VGood:** $300

Add $30 to above prices for nickel finish

BROWNING BDM

Semi-automatic; double action; 9mm Para.; 15-shot magazine; 4-3/4-inch barrel; weighs 31 oz; low-profile removable blade front sight, windage-adjustable rear; checkered black molded composition grips, thumbrest on both sides; all-steel frame; matte black finish; two safety systems; mode selector for switching from DA auto to revolver mode. Introduced 1991; dropped 1997.

Perf: $500 **Exc:** $400 **VGood:** $365

BROWNING BUCK MARK

Semi-automatic; 22 LR; 10-shot magazine; 5-1/2-inch barrel; 9-inch overall length; weighs 32 oz.; adjustable rear sight, ramp front; skip-line checkered molded black composition stocks; all-steel construction; gold-colored trigger; matte blue finish. Introduced 1985; still in production.

Perf: $245 **Exc:** $195 **VGood:** $160

Add $60 to above prices for nickel finish

BROWNING BUCK MARK FIELD 5.5

Same specs as Buck Mark except 9-7/8-inch barrel; matte blue finish only; hoodless ramp-type front sight, low profile rear; contoured or finger-groove walnut stocks. Introduced 1991; still in production.

Perf: $400 **Exc:** $295 **VGood:** $240

BROWNING BUCK MARK MICRO

Same specs as Buck Mark except 4-inch barrel; 16-click Pro Target rear sight; blue or nickel finish. From Browning. Introduced 1992.

Perf: $295 **Exc:** $245 **VGood:** $195

Nickel finish

Perf: $325 **Exc:** $275 **VGood:** $230

BROWNING BUCK MARK MICRO PLUS

Same specs as Buck Mark Micro except laminated wood grips. From Browning. Introduced 1992; still in production.

New: $300 **Perf:** $250 **Exc:** $175

BROWNING BUCK MARK PLUS

Same specs as Buck Mark except laminated wood stocks. Introduced 1985; still in production.

Perf: $325 **Exc:** $275 **VGood:** $230

BROWNING BUCK MARK SILHOUETTE

Same specs as Buck Mark except 9-7/8-inch heavy barrel; hooded sights; interchangeable posts; black, laminated wood grip and forend. Introduced 1987; dropped 1999.

Perf: $450 **Exc:** $350 **VGood:** $300

BROWNING BUCK MARK BULLSEYE

Similar to the Buck Mark Silhouette except has 7-1/4-inch heavy barrel with three flutes per side; trigger is adjustable from 2-1/2 to 5 lbs.; specially designed rosewood target or three-finger-groove stocks with competition-style heel rest, or with contoured rubber grip. Overall length is 11-5/16-inch, weighs 36 oz. Introduced 1996. Made in U.S. From Browning.

Perf: $450 **Exc:** $350 **VGood:** $300

BROWNING BUCK MARK TARGET 5.5

Same specs as Buck Mark except 5-1/2-inch barrel with .900-inch diameter hooded sights; adjustable post front; contoured walnut target grips; matte blue or gold anodized finish; 10-shot magazine. Introduced 1990; still in production.

Perf: $370 **Exc:** $300 **VGood:** $250

Gold anodized

Perf: $355 **Exc:** $325 **VGood:** $300

Add $55 to above prices for nickel finish

BROWNING BUCK MARK UNLIMITED MATCH

Same specs as Buck Mark except 14-inch heavy barrel; 15-inch sight radius. Introduced 1991; dropped 1999.

Perf: $425 **Exc:** $350 **VGood:** $300

BROWNING BUCK MARK UNLIMITED SILHOUETTE

Same as the Buck Mark Silhouette except has 14-inch heavy barrel. Conforms to IHMSA 15 maximum sight radius rule. Introduced 1991; dropped 1999.

New: $450 **Per.:** $400 **Exc:** $350

BROWNING BUCK MARK VARMINT

Same specs as Buck Mark except 9-7/8-inch heavy barrel; full-length scope base; no sights; black laminated wood stocks, optional forend; weighs 48 oz. Introduced 1987; dropped 1999.

Perf: $365 **Exc:** $310 **VGood:** $250

BROWNING BUCK MARK BULLSEYE TARGET STAINLESS

Blowback, single action .22 LR semi-auto. Matte blued, heavy 7.25-inch round and fluted stainless bull barrel. Laminated rosewood grip, adjustable sights.

NIB: $575 **Exc:** $515 **VGood:** $495

BROWNING BUCK MARK BULLSEYE TARGET URX

Blowback, single-action semi-auto in .22LR. Matte blued, heavy 7.25-inch round and fluted bull barrel. Grooved, rubberized grip, 39 oz., adjustable sights.

NIB: $470 **Exc:** $425 **VGood:** $315

BROWNING BUCK MARK CONTOUR 5.5 URX

Blowback, single-action .222 semi-auto. Matte blued, contoured 5.5-inch barrel. Full-length scope base, 36 oz., adjustable sights. (Multiple barrel lengths and options.)

NIB: $460 **Exc:** $410 **VGood:** $300

BROWNING BUCK MARK CONTOUR LITE 5.5 URX

.22 LR blowback, single-action semi-auto. Matte blued, contoured 5.5-inch barrel. Full-length scope base, 28 oz. Adjustable sights. (Multiple barrel lengths and options.)

NIB: $425 **Exc:** $400 **VGood:** $300

BROWNING BUCK MARK FLD PLUS ROSEWOOD UDX

.22 LR blowback single-action semi-auto. "FLD" sculpted grip with rosewood panels. Blued, contoured 5.5-inch barrel, 34 oz., adjustable rear sight, fiber optic front sight. (Multiple barrel lengths and options.)

NIB: $425 **Exc:** $400 **VGood:** $300

BROWNING BUCK MARK LITE SPLASH 5.5 URX

Blowback single-action semi-auto. Matte blued finish, gold splash anodizing. Chambered for .22 LR, 5.5-inch barrel. Rubberized ambidextrous grip.

Buck Mark Camper Cocobola UD

Browning Buck Mark Plus UDX

Browning Challenger Gold Model

Browning Buck Mark Plus Stainless Black Laminted UDX

Browning Buck Mark Micro Standard Stainless URX

Browning Full Line Dealer Buck Mark Plus Rosewood UDX

Adjustable sights; fiber optic front sight. 28 oz. (Also available with 7 1/2-inch barrel.)

NIB: $400 **Exc:** $375 **VGood:** $285

BROWNING BUCK MARK MICRO STANDARD STAINLESS URX

With a 4-inch stainless barrel, this .22 LR weighs 32 oz. Ambidextrous rubberized grip and adjustable sights. (Also available in alloy steel.)

NIB: $375 **Exc:** $350 **VGood:** $275

BROWNING BUCK MARK MICRO BULL

4-inch stainless bull barrel; .22 LR; weight 33 oz. Plastic grip panels and adjustable sights.

NIB: $250 **Exc:** N/A **VGood:** N/A

BROWNING BUCK MARK PLUS STAINLESS UDX

.22 LR semi-auto with finger-grooved wood grips. 5.5-inch barrel, 34 oz. Adjustable sights, fiber optic front sight. (Also available blued alloy steel.)

NIB: $425 **Exc:** $375 **VGood:** $295

BROWNING BUCK MARK STANDARD STAINLESS URX

.22 LR semi-auto. 5.5-inch stainless bull barrel; 34 oz. Ambidextrous rubberized grip and adjustable sights. (Also available in alloy steel.)

NIB: $375 **Exc:** $335 **VGood:** $295

BROWNING BUCK MARK PLUS STAINLESS BLACK LAMINATED UDX

Similar to Buck Mark Standard Stainless UDX but with ambidextrous grips.

NIB: $450 **Exc:** $395 **VGood:** $310

BROWNING BUCK MARK PLUS UDX

Similar to Buck Mark FLD Plus but with ambidextrous walnut grips.

NIB: $400 **Exc:** $335 **VGood:** $285

BROWNING FULL LINE DEALER BUCK MARK PLUS ROSEWOOD UDX

Similar to Buck Mark Plus UDX but with ambidextrous rosewood grips. Available only to full-line and Medallion-level Browning dealers.

NIB: $400 **Exc:** $350 **VGood:** $285

BUCK MARK CAMPER

This model is fitted with a heavy 5.5" barrel and has a matte blue finish. Ten-round magazine capacity. Weight is about 34 oz. Introduced in 1999. Add $50 for stainless.

NIB: $300 **Exc:** $265 **VGood:** $225

BUCK MARK CAMPER COCOBOLO UDX

Similar to above but with cocobolo Ultra DX grips and TruGlo front sight. Introduced 2008.

NIB: $360 **Exc:** $310 **VGood:** $285

BUCK MARK PRACTICAL URX FIBER OPTIC

Matte grey finish, 5.5-inch tapered bull barrel, Ultragrip RX ambi grips, adjustable ProTarget rear sight with TruGlo fiber optic front sight. Introduced 2008.

NIB: $350 **Exc:** $300 **VGood:** $2755

BROWNING CHALLENGER

Semi-automatic; 22 LR; 10-shot magazine; 4-1/2-inch, 6 3/4-inch barrels; overall length 11-7/16 inches (6-3/4-inch barrel); screw-adjustable rear sight, removable blade front; hand-checkered walnut grips; gold-plated trigger; blued finish. Introduced 1962; dropped 1974.

Perf: $375 **Exc:** $315 **VGood:** $275

BROWNING CHALLENGER II

Same specs as Challenger except changed grip angle; impregnated hardwood stocks. Introduced 1975; replaced by Challenger III, 1982.

Perf: $275 **Exc:** $225 **VGood:** $195

BROWNING CHALLENGER III

Same specs as Challenger except 5-1/2-inch heavy bull barrel; 9-1/2-inch overall length; weighs 35 oz.; lightweight alloy frame; improved sights; smooth impregnated hardwood grips; gold-plated trigger. Introduced 1982; dropped 1985.

Perf: $350 **Exc:** $295 **VGood:** $225

BROWNING CHALLENGER III SPORTER

Same specs as Challenger III except 6-3/4-inch barrel; 10-7/8-inch overall length; weighs 29 oz.; all-steel construction; blade ramped front sight, screw-adjustable rear, drift-adjustable front. Introduced 1982; dropped 1985.

Perf: $300 **Exc:** $190 **VGood:** $170

BROWNING CHALLENGER GOLD MODEL

Same specs as Challenger except gold wire inlays in metal; figured hand-carved, checkered walnut grips. Introduced 1971; dropped 1974.

Perf: $1450 **Exc:** $1250 **VGood:** $850

BROWNING CHALLENGER RENAISSANCE MODEL

Same specs as Challenger except satin nickel finish; full engraving; top-grade hand-carved, figured walnut grips. Introduced 1971; dropped 1974.

Perf: $1450 **Exc:** $1250 **VGood:** $850

BROWNING HI-POWER

Semi-automatic; 9mm para.; 13-shot magazine; 4 5/8" barrel; fixed sights; checkered walnut (pre-1986) or moulded grips; ambidextrous safety added in '80s; blued finish. Introduced 1954; still in production.

Perf: $675 **Exc:** $600 **Vgood:** $470

Limited Edition Digital Camo version

Perf: $900 **Exc:** $800 **Vgood:** $700

BROWNING HI-POWER 40 S&W MARK III

Same specs as standard Hi-Power except 40 S&W; 10-shot magazine; weighs 35 oz.; 4-3/4-inch barrel; matte blue finish; low profile front sight blade, drift-adjustable rear; ambidextrous safety; molded polyamide grips with thumbrest. Imported from Belgium by Browning. Introduced 1993; still imported.

New: $650 **Perf:** $575 **Exc:** $445

BROWNING HI-POWER CAPITAN

Same specs as standard Hi-Power except adjustable tangent rear sight authentic to early-production model; Commander-style hammer; checkered walnut grips; polished blue finish. Imported from Belgium by Browning. Reintroduced 1993; dropped 2000.

New: $700 **Perf:** $625 **Exc:** $500

BROWNING HI-POWER HP-PRACTICAL

Same specs as standard Hi-Power except silver-chromed frame, blued slide; wrap-around Pachmayr rubber grips; round-style serrated hammer; removable front sight, windage-adjustable rear. Introduced 1981; still in production.

Perf: $700 **Exc:** $625 **VGood:** $500

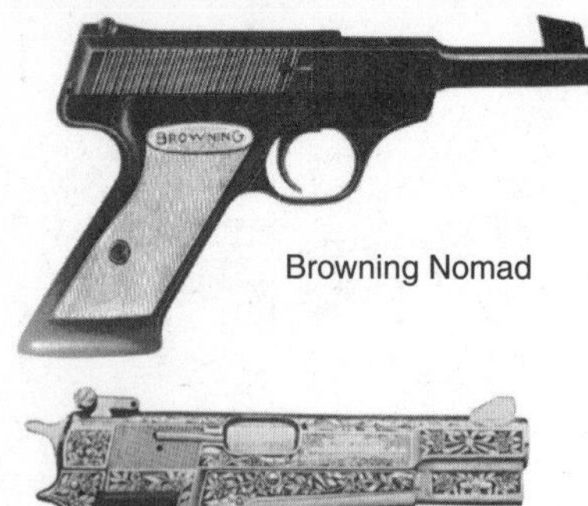
Browning Nomad

Browning Renaissance Cased Set

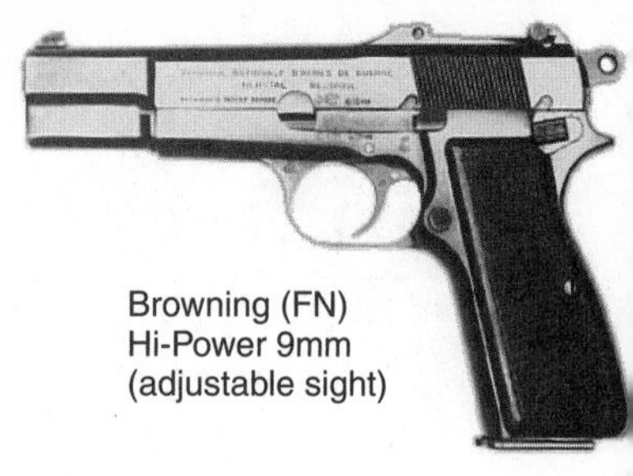
Browning (FN) Hi-Power 9mm (adjustable sight)

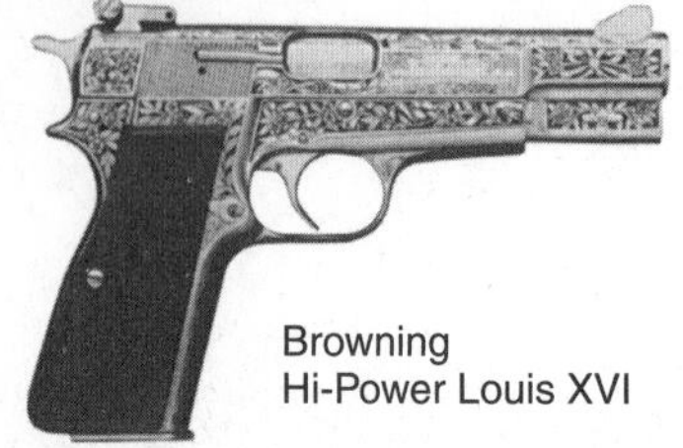
Browning Hi-Power Louis XVI

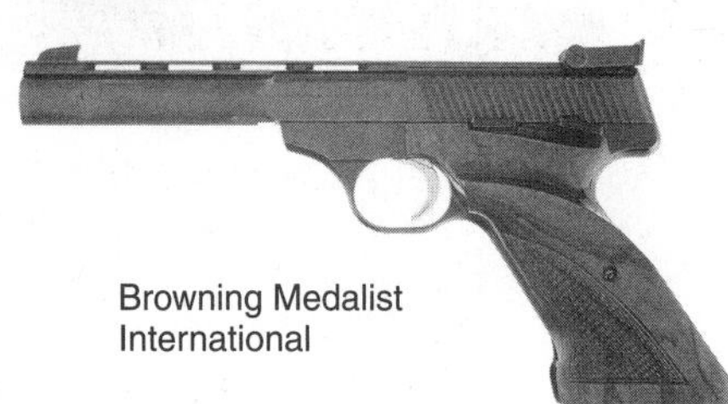
Browning Medalist International

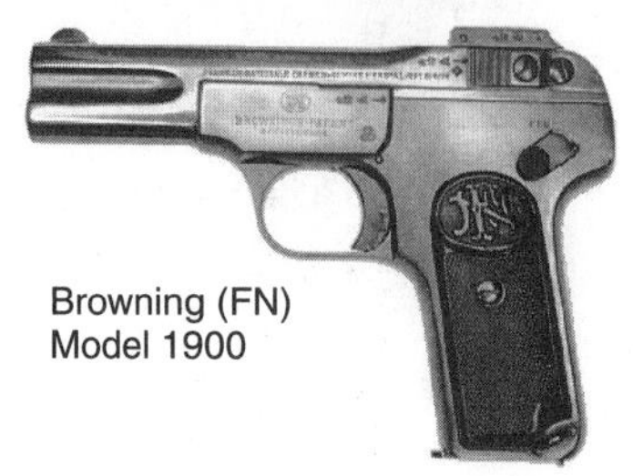
Browning (FN) Model 1900

Browning (FN) Model 1910

BROWNING HI-POWER LOUIS XVI

Same specs as standard Hi-Power 9mm except fully engraved silver-gray frame, slide; gold-plated trigger; hand checkered walnut grips; issued in deluxe walnut case. Introduced 1981; dropped 1984.

Perf: $2300 **Exc:** $1770 **VGood:** $1050

BROWNING HI-POWER RENAISSANCE

Same specs as standard Hi-Power except chrome-plated finish; full engraving; polyester pearl grips. Introduced 1954; dropped 1982.

Perf: $2500 **Exc:** $2200 **VGood:** 1675

Add $200 to above prices for internal extractor

Add $300-$500 for coin finish

BROWNING MEDALIST

Semi-automatic; 22 LR only; 10-shot magazine; 6-3/4-inch barrel; 11-1/8-inch overall length; vent rib; full wrap-around grips of select walnut, checkered with thumbrest; matching walnut forend; left-hand model available; screw-adjustable rear sight, removable blade front; dry-firing mechanism; blued finish. Introduced 1962; dropped 1974.

Perf: $900 **Exc:** $750 **VGood:** $595

BROWNING MEDALIST GOLD MODEL

Same general specs as Browning Medalist except gold wire inlays; better wood in grip. Introduced 1963; dropped 1974.

Perf: $1950 **Exc:** $1400 **VGood:** $1000

BROWNING MEDALIST INTERNATIONAL

Same specs as Medalist except sans forend; 5-15/16-inch barrel; 10-15/16-inch overall length; meets qualifications for International Shooting Union regulations. Introduced 1964; dropped 1974.

Perf: $615 **Exc:** $550 **VGood:** $500

Browning Medalist International (early model)

Perf: $850 **Exc:** $700 **VGood:** $550

BROWNING MEDALIST RENAISSANCE MODEL

Same specs as Medalist except finely figured, hand-carved grips; chrome plating; full engraving. Introduced 1964; dropped 1974.

Perf: $2350 **Exc:** $1750 **VGood:** $1250

BROWNING MODEL 1911

New in 2011 to commemorate the 100th anniversary of John Brownings' invention of the M 1911. .45 caliber with a 5 inch barrel. Blued steel frame and slide.

Price: N/A

BROWNING 1911-22 A1

Caliber: 22 LR on scaled-down Model 1911 design. Magazine capacity is 10 rounds. Barrel length, 4.25 inches; weight, 16 oz., overall length, 7.1 inches. Alloy frame, brown composite grips, fixed sights. Blowback action with standard 1911 controls. Compact model has 3.6-inch barrel. New in 2011.

Perf: $510 **Exc:** $450 **VGood:** $395

BROWNING NOMAD

Semi-automatic; 22 LR; 10-shot magazine; 4-1/2-inch, 6-3/4-inch barrel; 8-15/16-inch overall length (4-1/2-inch barrel); screw-adjustable rear sight, removable blade front; brown plastic grips; blued finish. Introduced 1962; dropped 1973.

Perf: $325 **Exc:** $295 **VGood:** $250

Add 10 percent to above prices for alloy frame

BROWNING RENAISSANCE CASED SET

Includes Renaissance versions of Hi-Power 9mm, 380 Automatic, 25 ACP in a specially fitted walnut case. Oddly, value depends to a degree upon condition of the case. Introduced 1954; dropped 1968.

Perf: $4000 **Exc:** $3300 **VGood:** $2500

Add 20 percent to above prices for coin finish and early walnut case

Add $100 to above prices for "St. Louis" slide address

Add $100 for old style extractor

BROWNING (FN) HI-POWER 9MM

Semi-automatic; 9mm Para.; 13-shot magazine; 4-5/8-inch barrel; 7-3/4-inch overall length; based on Browning-Colt 45 ACP; adjustable or fixed rear sight; checkered walnut grips; thumb, magazine safeties; external hammer with half-cock safety feature; blued finish. Pre-WWII-made and Nazi occupation marked models have collector value. Introduced 1935; still in production.

Pre-War Commercial Adjustable Sight

Exc: $950 **VGood:** $750 **Good:** $450

Pre-War Military Contact

Exc: $1000 **VGood:** $850 **Good:** $700

WWII Production (Fixed sights, Nazi proofed)

Exc: $500 **VGood:** $400 **Good:** $300

Post-War Production (Adjustable sights)

Exc: $750 **VGood:** $600 **Good:** $500

Post-War Production (Fixed sights)

Exc: $600 **VGood:** $465 **Good:** $395

BROWNING (FN) MODEL 1900

Semi-automatic; 32 ACP; 7-shot magazine; 4-inch barrel; 6-3/4-inch overall length; checkered hard rubber stocks; fixed sights; blued finish. Manufactured in Belgium, 1899 to 1910.

Exc: $450 **VGood:** $375 **Good:** $300

Add about 50 percent to above prices for factory nickel finish

BROWNING (FN) MODEL 1903

Semi-automatic; 9mm Browning Long; 7-shot magazine; 5-inch barrel; 8-inch overall length; hard rubber checkered stocks; fixed sights; blued finish. Designed primarily for military use. Manufactured 1903 to 1939.

Exc: $500 **VGood:** $400 **Good:** $325

BROWNING (FN) MODEL 1906

Semi-automatic; 25 ACP; 6-shot magazine; 2-inch barrel; 4-1/2-inch overall length; weighs 12-1/2 oz.; fixed sights; blued or nickel finish; hard rubber grips. At about production number 100,000, a safety lever was fitted to left rear of frame. Almost identical to Colt Vest Pocket 25 semi-auto. Introduced 1906; dropped 1940.

Exc: $325 **VGood:** $295 **Good:** $225

BROWNING (FN) MODEL 1910

Semi-automatic; 32 ACP, 380 ACP; 7-shot magazine (32), 6-shot (380); 3-1/2-inch barrel; 6-inch overall length; weighs 20-1/2 oz.; hard rubber stocks; fixed sights; blued finish. Made in Belgium. Introduced 1910; dropped 1983.

Exc: $350 **VGood:** $325 **Good:** $300

Browning (FN) Model 1903

Bryco J-25

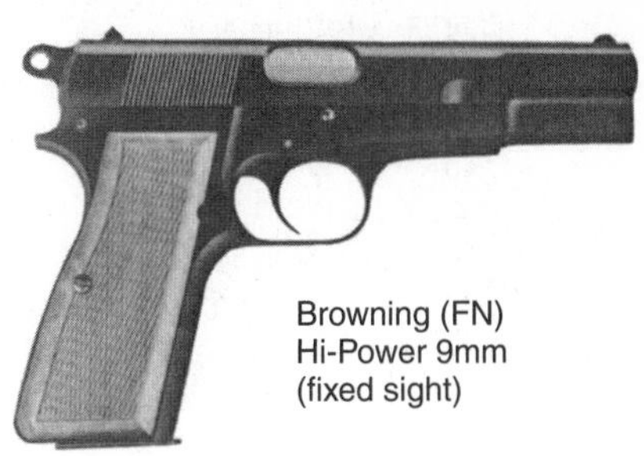
Browning (FN) Hi-Power 9mm (fixed sight)

Bryco M-38

Budischowsky TP-70

Bushmaster Carbon-15 Type 21 Pistol

BROWNING (FN) MODEL 1922

Semi-automatic; 32 ACP, 380 ACP; 9-shot magazine (32); 8-shot (380); 4-1/2-inch barrel; 7-inch overall; checkered hard rubber stocks; fixed sights; blued finish. Modified 1910 with longer barrel and slide and deeper grip to fulfill military contracts. Introduced 1922; dropped 1945. Nazi proofed pistols bring a premium.

Exc: $300 **VGood:** $275 **Good:** $250

BRYCO MODEL J-25

Semi-automatic; 25 ACP; 6-shot magazine; 2-1/2-inch barrel; 5-inch overall length; weighs 11 oz.; resin-impregnated wood stocks; fixed sights; safety locks sear and slide; satin nickel, chrome or black Teflon finish. Introduced 1988; dropped 2004. Briefly resurfaced under the name "Jimenex Arms" c. 2005.

Perf: $65 **Exc:** $55 **VGood:** $45

BRYCO MODEL M-38

Semi-automatic; 22 LR, 32 ACP, 380 ACP; 6-shot magazine; 2-13/16-inch barrel; 5-5/16-inch overall length; weighs 15 oz.; resin-impregnated wood stocks; fixed sights; safety locks sear and slide; satin nickel, chrome or black Teflon finish. Introduced 1988; dropped 2004. Briefly resurfaced under the name "Jimenez Arms" c. 2005.

Perf: $125 **Exc:** $100 **VGood:** $65

BRYCO MODEL M-48

Semi-automatic; 22 LR, 32 ACP, 380 ACP; 6-shot magazine; 4-inch barrel; 6-11/16-inch overall length; weighs 19 oz.; resin-impregnated wood stocks; fixed sights; safety locks sear and slide; satin nickel, chrome or black Teflon finish. Introduced 1988; dropped 1995.

Perf: $125 **Exc:** $100 **VGood:** $65

BRYCO MODEL 58

Semi-automatic; single action; 9mm Para.; 10-shot magazine; 4-inch barrel; 5-1/2-inch overall length; weighs 30 oz.; black composition grips; blade front sight, fixed rear; striker-fired action; manual thumb safety; polished blue finish. Made in U.S. by Jennings Firearms. Introduced 1994; dropped 1995.

Perf: $125 **Exc:** $100 **VGood:** $75

BRYCO MODEL M-59

Semi-automatic; single action; 9mm Para.; 10-shot magazine; 4-inch barrel; 6-1/2-inch overall length; weighs 33 oz.; black composition grips; blade front sight, fixed rear; striker-fired action; manual thumb safety; polished blue finish. Made in U.S. by Jennings Firearms. Introduced 1994; dropped 1995.

New: $125 **Perf:** $100 **Exc:** $65
Add $15 to above prices for 9mm chambering

BUDISCHOWSKY TP-70

Semi-automatic; double action; 22 LR, 25 ACP; 6-shot magazine; 2-7/16-inch barrel; 4-11/16-inch overall length; fixed sights; all stainless steel construction; manual, magazine safeties. Introduced 1973; dropped 1977.

Exc: $350 **VGood:** $300 **Good:** $250

BUSHMASTER CARBON-15 TYPE 21 PISTOL

Semi-automatic; 223 Rem.; tool steel side bolt operation; ultra light carbon fiber upper and lower receivers; 7-1/4-inch stainless steel barrel; quick detachable muzzle compensator; ghost ring sights; A2 pistol grip; uses standard AR-15 magazines; 40 oz. Formerly made by Professional Ordnance. Bushmaster production began 2003.

Perf: $750 **Exc:** $675 **VGood:** $600

BUSHMASTER CARBON-15 TYPE 97 PISTOL

Similar to Carbon-15 Type 21, excepot has fluted barrel; Hogue overmolded pistol grip and chrome plated bolt carrier; 46 oz. Formerly made by Professional Ordnance. Bushmaster production began 2003.

Perf: $795 **Exc:** $725 **VGood:** 625

BUTLER DERRINGER

Derringer; single shot; 22 Short; 2-1/2-inch barrel; blade front sight, no rear; smooth walnut or pearlite grips; spur trigger; blued, gold, chrome finish. Introduced 1978; dropped 1980.

Exc: $125 **VGood:** $90 **Good:** $50

CABANAS SINGLE-SHOT

Single shot; 177 pellet or round ball; 9-inch barrel; 19-inch overall length; weighs 51 oz.; smooth wood stocks, thumbrest; ramped blade front sight, open adjustable rear; automatic safety; muzzle brake. Fires pellet or ball with 22 blank cartridge. Made in Mexico. Introduced 1987; last imported by Mandall Shooting Supplies, which closed in late 2004.

Exc: $125 **VGood:** $75 **Good:** $65

CALICO MODEL M-100

Semi-automatic; single action; 22 LR; 100-shot magazine; 6-inch barrel; 17-15/16-inch overall length; weighs 3-3/4 lbs. (loaded); molded composition grip; adjustable post front sight, notch rear; aluminum alloy frame; flash suppressor; pistol grip compartment; ambidextrous safety. Uses same helical-feed magazine as M-100 Carbine. Made in U.S. by Calico. Introduced 1986 as Model 100-P; no longer in production.

Perf: $495 **Exc:** $455 **VGood:** $365

CALICO MODEL M-950

Semi-automatic; single action; 9mm Para.; 50- or 100-shot helical-feed magazine; 7-3/4-inch barrel; 14-inch overall length with 50-shot magazine; weighs 2-1/4 lbs. (empty); glass-filled polymer grip; fully-adjustable post front sight, fixed notch rear; ambidextrous safety; static cocking handle; retarded blowback action. Made in U.S. by Calico. Introduced 1989; dropped 1994.

Perf: $455 **Exc:** $410 **VGood:** $385

CAMPO-GIRO MODEL 1913

Semi-automatic; 9mm Largo (Bergmann-Bayard); 8-shot magazine; 6-1/2-inch barrel; 9-1/4-inch overall length; weighs 32 oz.; fixed sights; checkered black horn grips; blued finish. Distinguished by magazine release lever behind triggerguard. Adopted by Spanish Army in 1913, superseded by 1913-16 Model after only 1300 made.

Exc: $3000 **VGood:** $2500 **Good:** $1900

CAMPO-GIRO MODEL 1913-16

Semi-automatic; 9mm Largo; 8-shot magazine; 6-1/2-inch barrel; 9-1/4-inch overall length; weighs 35 oz.; fixed sights; checkered black horn or wood grips; blued finish. Magazine release at bottom of left grip. Total production 13,625.

Exc: $2800 **VGood:** $2250 **Good:** $1550

CARBON-15

Semi-automatic; 223, Barrel: 7.25". Weight: 46 oz. Length: 20" overall. Stock: Checkered composite. Sights: Ghost ring. Features: gas-operated, rotary bolt action. Carbon fiber upper and lower receiver; chrome-moly bolt carrier; fluted stainless match

Carbon-15

Charles Daly 1911-A1 Field EFS

Charles Daly 1911-A1 Field ECS Compact

Charles Daly Model 1873 Steel Frame

Charles Daly M-5

Charter Arms Bulldog

barrel; uses AR-15-type magazines. Introduced 1992. From Professional Ordnance, Inc.

Perf: $875 **Exc:** $795 **VGood:** $650

CENTURY FEG P9R

Semi-automatic; double action; 9mm Para.; 10-shot magazine; 4-5/8-inch barrel; 8-inch overall length; weighs 35 oz.; checkered walnut grips; blade front sight, windage drift-adjustable rear; hammer-drop safety; polished blue finish; comes with spare magazine; blue or chrome finish. Imported from Hungary by Century International Arms.

New: $300 **Perf:** $250 **Exc:** $200

Chrome finish

New: $300 **Perf:** $250 **Exc:** $200

CENTURY FEG P9RK

Same specs as the P9R except 4-1/8-inch barrel; 7-1/2-inch overall length; weighs 33-1/2 oz.; checkered walnut grips; fixed sights; 10-shot magazine. Imported from Hungary by Century International Arms, Inc. Introduced 1994.

New: $300 **Perf:** $250 **Exc:** $200

CENTURY MODEL 100

Revolver; single action; 375 Winchester, 30-30 Win., 50-70 Gov't., 444 Marlin, 45-70; 6-1/2-inch, 8-inch, 12-inch barrel; 15-inch overall length (8-inch barrel); weighs 6 lbs.; Millett adjustable square notch rear, ramp front sights; uncheckered walnut stocks; manganese bronze frame; blued cylinder, barrel; coil spring trigger mechanism. Imported by Century Gun Distributors. Introduced 1975.

Perf: $1750 **Exc:** $1400 **VGood:** $1000

CHARLES DALY M-1911-A1P

Semi-automatic; 45 ACP, 7- or 10-shot magazine. Barrel: 5-inch. Weight: 38 oz. Length: 8-3/4 inches overall. Stocks: Checkered. Sights: Blade front, rear drift adjustable for windage; three-dot system. Features: Skeletonized combat hammer and trigger; beavertail grip safety; extended slide release; oversize thumb safety; Parkerized finish. Introduced 1996. Imported from the Philippines by K.B.I., Inc.

Perf: $380 **Exc:** $330 **VGood:** $255

CHARLES DALY 1911-A1 FIELD EFS

Semi-automatic; 45 ACP, 8-shot capacity. Barrel: 5-inch. Weight: 39.5 oz. Length: 8-3/4 inches overall. Stocks: Checkered. Sights: Blade front, rear drift adjustable for windage; three-dot system. Features: Skeletonized combat hammer and trigger; beavertail grip safety; extended slide release; oversize thumb safety; matte blue finish; flared and lowered ejection port.

Perf: $400 **Exc:** $350 **VGood:** $300

CHARLES DALY 1911-A1 FIELD ECS COMPACT

Similar to 1911-A1 Field EFS but with 3.5-inch barrel, 7-1/4-inch overall length and 6-shot capacity. Values similar.

CHARLES DALY 1911-A1 EMPIRE EFS

Similar to 1911-A1 Field EFS but in stainless steel. Add 10 percent to above values.

CHARLES DALY 1911-A1 EMPIRE ECS COMPACT

Similar to 1911-A1 Field ECS Compact but in stainless steel. Values similar.

CHARLES DALY HP

Semi-automatic; 9mm Parabellum, 10-shot magazine. Barrel: 4-5/8 inches. Weight: 34.5 oz. Length: 7-3/8 inches overall. Matte blue finish. Copy of Browning Hi Power/P35.

Perf: $475 **Exc:** $395 **VGood:** $275

CHARLES DALY EMPIRE HP

Same as Charles Daly HP but in stainless steel.

CHARLES DALY M-5

Semi-automatic; 9mm Parabellum, 40 S&W, 45 ACP; 10-shot magazine; polymer frame. Based on 1911 design. Made in Israel by BUL.

CHARLES DALY MODEL 1873

Single action revolver; 357 Mag or 45 LC; 4-3/4-inch, 4-1/2-inch, or 7-1/2-inch barrel; case-hardened frame; blue finish; brass or steel backstrap and triggerguard. Importation began 2004.

Perf: $395 **Exc:** $350 **VGood:** $300

CHARLES DALY MODEL 1873 STAINLESS

Similar to Model 1873, except has matte finish, stainless construction with steel backstrap and triggerguard. Importation began 2004.

Perf: $595 **Exc:** $525 **VGood:** $450

CHARTER ARMS BONNIE & CLYDE SET

Revolvers; double action; 32 H&R Mag. (Bonnie) and 38 Spl. (Clyde); 6-shot magazine; 2-1/2-inch barrels, fully shrouded; fixed rear sight, ramp front; laminated grips; various colors; marked as "Bonnie" or "Clyde" on barrels; blued finish. Introduced 1989; dropped 1991.

Perf: $425 **Exc:** $365 **VGood:** $335

CHARTER ARMS BULLDOG

Revolver; double action; 44 Spl.; 5-shot cylinder; 2-1/2-inch, 3-inch barrel; 7-1/2-inch overall length; weighs 19 oz.; square notch fixed rear sight, Patridge-type front; checkered walnut or neoprene grips; chrome-moly steel frame; wide trigger and hammer, or spurless pocket hammer; blued or stainless finish. Introduced 1973; dropped 1996.

Perf: $400 **Exc:** $350 **VGood:** $275

Stainless Bulldog (discontinued 1991)

Perf: $400 **Exc:** $375 **VGood:** $300

CHARTER ARMS BULLDOG PUG

Same specs as Bulldog except 2-1/2-inch shrouded barrel; 7-1/4-inch overall length; weighs 19 oz.; notch rear sight, ramp front; wide trigger and hammer spur; shrouded ejector rod; blued or stainless steel finish. Introduced 1986; reintroduced 1993; dropped 1993.

Perf: $400 **Exc:** $350 **VGood:** $300

Stainless Bulldog Pug

Perf: $400 **Exc:** $350 **VGood:** $300

CHARTER ARMS CHIC LADY

Caliber: 38 Special. Double/single action or double-action-only. Five-round cylinder. Barrel: 2 inches,

Charter Arms Model 40

Charter Arms Lady On Duty

Charter Arms Pathfinder

Charter Arms Pit Bull

Charter Arms Magnum Pug

Charter Arms Mag Pug (2006)

Charter Arms 9MM Pitbull

weight is 12 oz. Two-tone pink and stainless finish. Aluminum frame.

Perf: $435 **Exc:** $365 **VGood:** $315

CHARTER ARMS COUGAR UNDERCOVER LITE

Caliber: 38 Special +P. Five-round cylinder. Barrel: 2 inches, weight is 12 oz. Two-tone pink and stainless finish with aluminum frame.

Perf: $415 **Exc:** $345 **VGood:** $295

CHARTER ARMS CRIMSON UNDERCOVER

Caliber: 38 Special +P. Five-round cylinder. Barrel: 2 inches, weight is 16 oz. Grip has Crimson Trace laser sight. Stainless finish.

Perf: $575 **Exc:** $495 **VGood:** $425

CHARTER ARMS DIXIE DERRINGER

Caliber: 22 LR, 22 Magnum or combination cylinder. Capacity is five rounds. Barrel length is 1-1/8 inches, weight is 6 ounces. Stainless finish.

Perf: $230 **Exc:** $195 **VGood:** $165

Deduct 15 percent if chambered only for one caliber

CHARTER 2000, INC. DIXIE DERRINGER

Similar to above. Single action revolver; 22 LR or 22 WMR; 5-shot; 1-1/8-inch barrel; stainless construction; spur trigger; hardwood grips; 5 oz. Introduced 2002.

Perf: $165 **Exc:** $130 **VGood:** $110

CHARTER ARMS MAG PUG (2006)

A 5-shot revolver chambered for .357 Magnum. Stainless or blue. Ported 2.2-inch barrel. 23 oz. Fixed sights, rubber grips. Stainless or black.

NIB: $325 **Exc:** $285 **VGood:** $245

CHARTER ARMS EXPLORER II

Semi-automatic; 22 LR; 8-shot magazine; 6-inch, 8-inch or 10-inch barrel; 15-1/2-inch overall length; blade front sight, open elevation-adjustable rear; serrated simulated walnut stocks; action adapted from Explorer AR-7 carbine; black, camo, gold or silver finish. Introduced 1980; discontinued 1986.

Perf: $175 **Exc:** $135 **VGood:** $100

CHARTER ARMS LADY ON DUTY

Revolver; double action; 22 LR, 22 WMR, 38 Spl.; 6-shot (22LR, 22 WMR), 5-shot (38 Spl.) cylinder; 2-inch barrel; 6-1/4-inch overall length; weighs 17 oz.; rosewood-color checkered plastic grips; ramp-style front sight, fixed rear; comes with lockable plastic case, trigger lock; choice of spur, pocket or double-action hammer; blue or nickel finish. Made in U.S. by Charco, Inc. Introduced 1995; dropped 1996.

New: $300 **Perf:** $250 **Exc:** $175

CHARTER ARMS MAGNUM PUG

Revolver; double action; 357 Mag.; 5-shot magazine; 2-1/4-inch barrel; weighs 18 oz.; Bulldog or neoprene combat grips; ramp-style front sight, fixed rear; fully shrouded barrel; pocket or spur hammer; blue finish. Made in U.S. by Charco, Inc. Introduced 1995; dropped 1996.

New: $265 **Perf:** $195 **Exc:** $165

Production resumed in 2001 by Charter 2000, Inc.

CHARTER ARMS MODEL 40

Semi-automatic; double action; 22 LR; 8-shot magazine; 3-5/16-inch barrel; weighs 2-11/2 oz.; fixed sights; stainless steel finish. Introduced 1984; discontinued 1986.

Perf: $265 **Exc:** $240 **VGood:** $220

CHARTER ARMS MODEL 79K

Semi-automatic; double action; 32 ACP, 380 ACP; 7-shot magazine; 3-5/8-inch barrel; 6-1/2-inch overall length; weighs 24-1/2 oz.; fixed sights; hammer block; firing pin, magazine safeties; stainless steel finish. Imported from West Germany. Introduced 1984; no longer imported.

Perf: $325 **Exc:** $300 **VGood:** $280

CHARTER ARMS OFF-DUTY

Revolver; double action; 22 LR, 38 Spl.; 5-shot magazine (38 Spl.); 2-inch barrel; 6-3/4-inch overall length; fixed sights; choice of smooth or checkered walnut, neoprene grips; all steel; matte black finish. Introduced 1984; reintroduced 1993; dropped 1996. Production resumed in 2002 by Charter 2000, Inc.

Perf: $275 **Exc:** $250 **VGood:** $135

Stainless Off-Duty

Perf: $295 **Exc:** $275 **VGood:** $175

CHARTER PANTHER BRONZE/ BLACK STANDARD

Caliber: 38 Special+P. Five-round cylinder. Barrel: 1-1/8 inches, weight is 6 oz. Rubber grips, fixed sights. Two-tone bronze and black finish on aluminum frame.

Perf: $415 **Exc:** $345 **VGood:** $295

CHARTER ARMS PATHFINDER

Revolver; double action; 22 LR, 22 WMR; 6-shot magazine; 2-inch, 3-inch, 6-inch barrels; 7-3/8-inch overall length; weighs 18-1/2 oz.; adjustable rear sight, ramp front; round butt; wide hammer spur and trigger; blued finish. Introduced 1971; dropped 1990. Later reintroduced. Prices shown are for reintroduced version.

NIB: $325 **Exc:** $285 **VGood:** $245

STAINLESS PATHFINDER WITH 3-1/2-INCH SHROUDED BARREL

Values shown are for Charter 2000 version.

Perf: $185 **Exc:** $165 **VGood:** $150

CHARTER ARMS PIT BULL

Revolver; double action; 9mm Federal, 38 Spl., 357 Mag.; 5-shot magazine; 2-1/2-inch, 3-1/2-inch, 4-inch barrels; 7-1/4-inch overall length; weighs 24-1/2 oz. (2-1/2-inch barrel); blade front sight, fixed rear on 2-1/2-inch, adjustable on others; checkered neoprene grips; blued finish. Introduced 1989; discontinued 1991.

Perf: $235 **Exc:** $200 **VGood:** $165

Stainless Pit Bull

Perf: $310 **Exc:** $275 **VGood:** $235

CHARTER ARMS 9 MM PITBULL RIMLESS REVOLVER

Double action/single-action, spurred hammer revolver in 9x19mm NATO with a matte stainless

Charter Arms
Target Bulldog

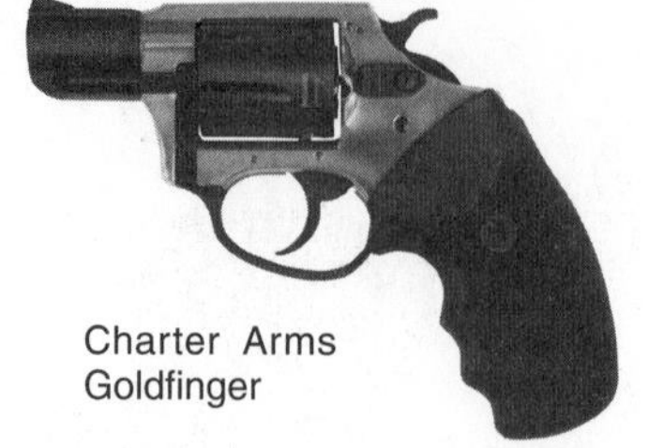

Charter Arms
Goldfinger

Charter Arms
Patriot with
Kershaw Knife

Chipmunk Silhouette Model

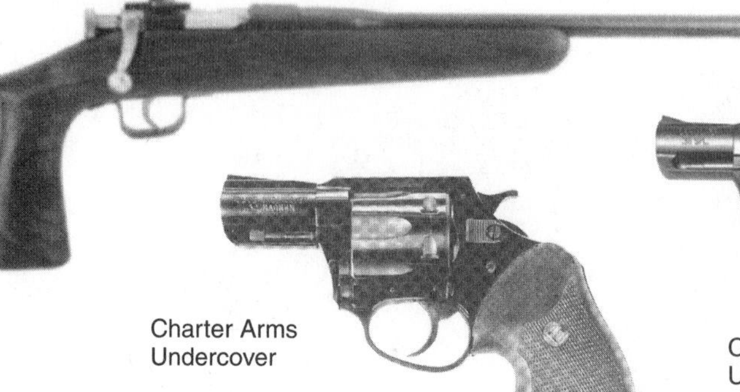

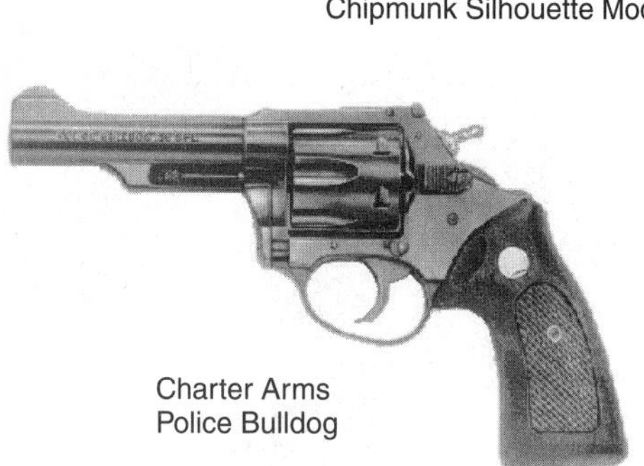

Charter Arms
Police Bulldog

Charter Arms
Undercover

Charter Arms
Undercover Lite

steel finish. Uses a rimless cartridge extractor system. 2.2 inch barrel, 6.75 inches OA and weighs 22 ounces. Black neoprene grips and fixed sights. 6 shot capacity. Introduced in 2012.

Perf: $400 **Exc:** $340 **VGood:** $300

CHARTER ARMS .40 PITBULL, MATTE STANDARD

Double action/single-action or DOA revolver in .40S&W with a matte stainless steel finish. Uses a rimless cartridge extractor system. 2.3 inch barrel, 6.75 inches long OA and weighs 20 ounces. Black rubber grips and fixed sights. 5 shot capacity. Introduced in 2011.

Perf: $400 **Exc:** $340 **VGood:** $300

CHARTER ARMS POLICE BULLDOG

Revolver; double action; 32 H&R, 38 Spl., 44 Spl.; 5-shot magazine (44) or 6-shot; 3-1/2-inch, 4-inch barrel; fixed sights; neoprene grips; square butt (44 Spl.); blued finish. Introduced 1976; dropped 1991. Production resumed in 2002 by Charter, 2000, Inc. Values shown are for original version.

Perf: $345 **Exc:** $295 **VGood:** $185

CHARTER ARMS POLICE BULLDOG STAINLESS

Same specs as Police Bulldog except also offered in 357 Mag. (5-shot); shrouded barrel; square butt; stainless finish.

Perf: $360 **Exc:** $310 **VGood:** $195

CHARTER ARMS TARGET PATHFINDER COMBO

Caliber: 22 LR/22 Mag. Six-round cylinder. Barrel is 4 inches, weight is 20 oz. Stainless finish and frame. Rubber grips, fixed sights.

Perf: $495 **Exc:** $425 **VGood:** $365

CHARTER ARMS TARGET BULLDOG

Revolver; double action; 357 Mag., 44 Spl.; 5-shot magazine; 4-inch barrel; 9-inch overall length; weighs 21 oz.; adjustable rear sight, blade front; square-butt walnut stocks; all-steel frame; shrouded barrel, ejector rod. Introduced 1986; discontinued 1988. Reintrodeuced c. 2007

Perf: $325 **Exc:** $300 **VGood:** $280

CHARTER ARMS TARGET BULLDOG STAINLESS

Same specs as Target Bulldog except also in 9mm Federal; 5-1/2-inch barrel, fully shrouded; adjustable sights; square butt target grips; stainless finish. Discontinued 1991. Reintroduced c. 2007.

Perf: $325 **Exc:** $300 **VGood:** $280

CHARTER ARMS UNDERCOVER

Revolver; double action; 22 LR, 22 WMR, 32 S&W Long, 38 Spl.; 6-shot magazine (32), 5-shot (38 Spl.); 2-inch (32), 3-inch barrels; 6 3/4-inch overall length; weighs 16 oz.; fixed rear sight, serrated ramp front; walnut standard or Bulldog grips; wide spur hammer and trigger, or pocket hammer (38 Spl.); blued. Introduced 1965; dropped 1991. Production resumed in 1998 by Charter 2000, Inc., which itself went kablooey some years later. Production resumed c. 2007.

Perf: $285 **Exc:** $250 **VGood:** $200

Stainless with 2-inch barrel only

Perf: $295 **Exc:** $260 **VGood:** $210

CHARTER ARMS UNDERCOVERETTE

Same specs as Undercover except 32 S&W Long; 6-shot magazine; 2-inch barrel; blued finish. Introduced 1969; discontinued 1981.

Perf: $285 **Exc:** $250 **VGood:** $200

CHARTER ARMS PINK LADY

Similar to Undercover Lite but with pink anodized frame. .38 Special only.

Perf: $300 **Exc:** $250 **VGood:** $200

CHARTER ARMS GOLDFINGER

Similar to above but with gold anodized frame. .38 Special only.

Perf: $300 **Exc:** $250 **VGood:** $200

CHARTER ARMS PATRIOT

Built on Bulldog frame but chambered in .327 Federal Magnum (six-shot). Rubber grips, 2.2- or 4-inch barrel. Comes with Kershaw "327" knife.

Perf: $375 **Exc:** $325 **VGood:** $275

CHARTER ARMS UNDERCOVER LITE

Caliber: 38 special +P. Five-round cylinder. Barrel is 2 inches, weight is 12 oz. Rubber grips, fixed sights. Red and black two-tone finish on aluminum frame.

Perf: $380 **Exc:** $325 **VGood:** $275

CHIAPPA M FOUR-22

Caliber: 22 LR. A scaled-down, hand-held rimfire version of AR/M4 carbine with 6-inch barrel. Magazine capacity is 28 rounds. Weight, 4.1 lbs.; length, 14.5 inches. Comes with two magazines, adjustable sights, pseudo flash hider. Red-dot sight is optional.

Perf: $410 **Exc:** $350 **VGood:** $300

Add 15 percent for red-dot optical sight.

CHIAPPA M9-22 STANDARD

Caliber: 22 LR. Based on the 9mm M9 service pistol, Barrel length is 5 inches, weight is 37 oz. Magazine capacity, 10 rounds. Fixed front sight, Novak-style rear. Tactical model has fake suppressor.

Perf: $335 **Exc:** $300 **VGood:** $250

Add 10 percent for Tactical model

CHIAPPA RHINO 60DS

Double action/single action revolver in black or hard chrome finish with dark or light wood grips, available in .357 Magnum, .40S&W and 9x21 mm. Features a 6 inch barrel, 10.5 inch OA length and weighs 2.06 pounds. Barrel aligned with bottom chamber. 6-shot capacity. Introduced 2012.

Perf: $800 **Exc:** $700 **VGood:** $625

CHIPMUNK SILHOUETTE MODEL

Bolt action; single shot; 22 LR; 14 -7/8-inch barrel; 20-inch overall length; weighs 32 oz.; American walnut stock; post ramp front sight, peep rear; meets IHMSA 22 Unlimited competition rules. Introduced 1985; dropped 1990.

Perf: $135 **Exc:** $115 **VGood:** $100

CIMARRON 1873 PEACEMAKER

Revolver; single action; 22 LR, 22 WMR, 38 Spl., 357 Mag., 44-40, 45 Colt; 3-inch, 4-inch, 4-3/4-inch, 5-1/2-inch, 7-1/2-inch barrel; 10-inch overall length (4-inch barrel); weighs 39 oz.; blade front, fixed or adjustable rear sight; walnut stocks; reproduction of original Colt design; various grades of engraving; old

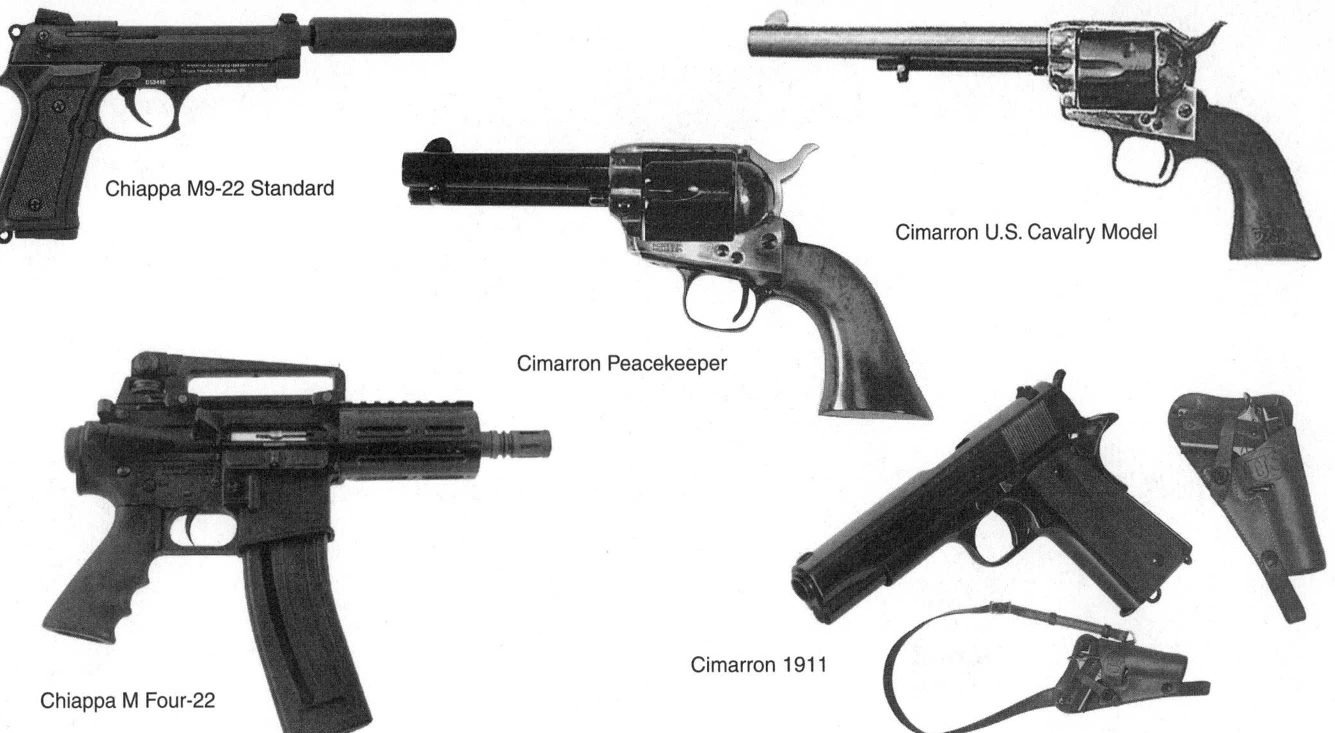
Chiappa M9-22 Standard

Cimarron U.S. Cavalry Model

Cimarron Peacekeeper

Chiappa M Four-22

Cimarron 1911

model blackpowder frame with "bullseye" ejector or New Model frame. Made in Europe. Introduced 1989; no longer imported by Cimarron Arms.

Perf: $495 **Exc:** $300 **VGood:** $250

Engraved

Perf: $800 **Exc:** $700 **VGood:** $500

CIMARRON 1873 PEACEMAKER SHERIFF'S MODEL

Same specs as 1873 Peacemaker except 44-40, 45 Colt; 3-inch, 4-inch barrels. Introduced 1989; importation dropped 1990; reintroduced 2000-2001.

Perf: $495 **Exc:** $325 **VGood:** $250

CIMARRON 1875 REMINGTON

Revolver; single action; 357 Mag., 44-40, 45 Colt; 6-shot cylinder; 7-1/2-inch barrel; 13-3/4-inch overall length; weighs 44 oz.; blade front, notch rear sight; smooth walnut stocks; replica of 1875 Remington Single Action Army model; brass triggerguard; color case-hardened frame; rest blued or nickel finished. Made in Europe. Introduced 1989; dropped 1993.

Perf: $440 **Exc:** $350 **VGood:** $225

CIMARRON 1890 REMINGTON

Revolver; single action; 357 Mag., 44-40, 45 Colt; 6-shot cylinder; 5-1/2-inch barrel; 12-1/2-inch overall length; weighs 37 oz; blade front, groove-type rear sight; American walnut stocks; replica of 1890 Remington Single Action; brass trigger guard; rest blued or nickel finished; lanyard ring. Made in Europe. Introduced 1989; dropped 1993.

Perf: $440 **Exc:** $350 **VGood:** $225

CIMARRON 1911

Single action only, hammer fired steel full-sized semi-automatic pistol with nickel or high polish blue finish, fixed sights and wood grips. Chambered in .45 ACP. 5 inch barrel and 8.25 inches OA length, weighs 2.44 pounds. 8+1 capacity. Introduced 2012.

Perf: $800 **Exc:** $720 **VGood:** $660

CIMARRON NEW THUNDERER

Revolver; single action; 357 Mag., 44 WCF, 44 Spl., 45 Colt; 6-shot; 3-1/2-inch, 4-3/4-inch barrel, with ejector; weighs 38 oz. (3-1/2-inch barrel); hand-checkered walnut grips; blade front, notch rear sight; Thunderer grip; color case-hardened frame with balance blued, or nickel finish. Imported by Cimarron Arms. Introduced 1993; still in production.

New: $430 **Perf:** $350 **Exc:** $300

Add $45 to above prices for checkered walnut grips

CIMARRON MAN WITH NO NAME

Caliber: 45 Colt. Replica of Colt Single Action used by Clint Eastwood in his Spaghetti Westerns. Barrel length, 4-3/4 inches. Weight: 42-1/2 oz. One piece walnut grip with silver rattle snake inlay. Standard blue finish with case hardened pre-war frame.

Perf: $800 **Exc:** $725 **VGood:** $650

CIMARRON PEACEKEEPER

Revolver; single action; 357 Mag., 44 WCF, 44 Spl., 45 Colt; 6-shot; 3-1/2-inch, 4-3/4-inch barrel, with ejector; weighs 38 oz. (3-1/2-inch barrel); hand-checkered walnut grips; blade front, notch rear sight; Thunderer grip; color case-hardened frame with balance blued, or nickel finish. Imported by Cimarron Arms. Introduced 1993; no longer imported.

Perf: $450 **Exc:** $350 **VGood:** $325

CIMARRON ROOSTER SHOOTER

Caliber: 357/38 Spl, 45 Colt, and 44 W.C.F. Replica of John Wayne's Colt Single Action used in many of his western films. Barrel: 4-3/4 inches, weight, 40 oz. One-piece orange finger-grooved grip, Cimarron's patented Original Finish.

Perf: $760 **Exc:** $685 **VGood:** $600

CIMARRON THUNDERSTORM

Single action only revolver in blued or stainless finish with checkered wood grips in various styles. Chambered in .45 Colt and .357 Magnum with 3.5 inch or 4.75 inch barrel lengths. Weighs 2.2 or 2.58 pounds. Wide target sights and smoothed action for competition. 6-shot capacity. Introduced 2012.

Perf: $875 **Exc:** $790 **VGood:** $700

CIMARRON U.S. ARTILLERY MODEL

Revolver; single action; 45 Colt; 5-1/2-inch barrel; 11-1/2-inch overall length; weighs 39 oz.; fixed sights; walnut stocks; Rinaldo A. Carr Commemorative Edition. Made in Europe. Introduced 1989; still imported.

Perf: $450 **Exc:** $365 **VGood:** $315

CIMARRON U.S. CAVALRY MODEL

Revolver; single action; 45 Colt; 7-1/2-inch barrel; 13-1/2-inch overall length; weighs 42 oz.; fixed sights; walnut stocks; original-type inspector and martial markings; color case-hardened frame and hammer; charcoal blued; exact copy of original. Made in Europe. Introduced 1989; still in production.

Perf: $465 **Exc:** $385 **VGood:** $335

CIMARRON 8TH ARTILLERY CASED SET

U.S. Cavalry Model in case with accessories. Discontinued 1990.

Perf: $695 **Exc:** $625 **VGood:** $550

CIMARRON ROUGH RIDER ARTILLERY MODEL SINGLE-ACTION

Similar to the U.S. Cavalry model except has 5-1/2-inch barrel, weighs 39 oz., and is 11-1/2-inch overall. U.S. markings and cartouche, case-hardened frame and hammer; 45 Colt only.

Perf: $465 **Exc:** $385 **VGood:** $335

CLARIDGE HI-TEC MODEL L-9

Semi-automatic; single action; 9mm Para., 40 S&W, 45 ACP; 18-shot magazine; 7-1/2-inch barrel; 12-3/4-inch overall length (5-inch barrel); weighs about 3 lbs.; aluminum or stainless frame; telescoping bolt; floating firing pin locked by the safety; molded composition grip; post elevation-adjustable front sight, open windage-adjustable rear. Made in U.S. by Claridge Hi-Tec, Inc. No longer produced.

Perf: $500 **Exc:** $400 **VGood:** $275

CLARIDGE HI-TEC S-9

Similar to L-9, except has 5-inch non-shrouded threaded barrel; weighs 3 lbs. 9 oz. Discontinued 1993.

Perf: $425 **Exc:** $425 **VGood:** $350

CLARIDGE HI-TEC T-9

Similar to L-9, except has 9-1/2-inch barrel. Introduced 1992; dropped 1993.

Perf: $550 **Exc:** $495 **VGood:** $375

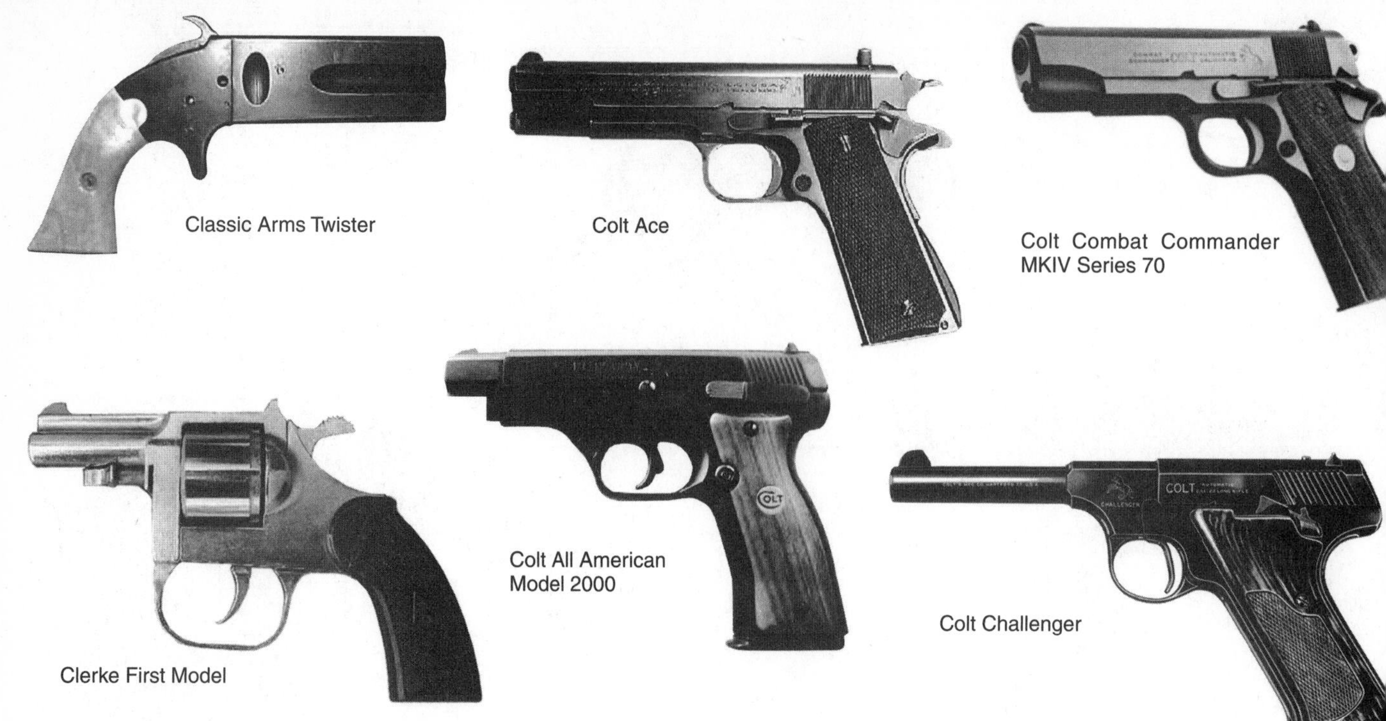
Classic Arms Twister

Colt Ace

Colt Combat Commander MKIV Series 70

Clerke First Model

Colt All American Model 2000

Colt Challenger

CLARIDGE M

Similar to L-9, except has 7-1/2-inch barrel; weighs 3 lbs. Discontinued 1991.

Perf: $550 **Exc:** $495 **VGood:** $375

CLASSIC ARMS SOUTHERN DERRINGER

Single shot; 22 LR, 41 rimfire; 2-1/2-inch barrel; 5-inch overall length; weighs 12 oz.; blade front sight; white plastic stocks; steel barrel; brass frame. Introduced 1982; dropped 1984.

Perf: $75 **Exc:** $60 **VGood:** $50

CLASSIC ARMS TWISTER

Derringer; over/under; 22 LR, 9mm rimfire; 3-1/4-inch barrel; no sights; pearlite grips; rotating barrels; spur trigger. Originally marketed by Navy Arms. Introduced 1980; dropped 1984.

Perf: $85 **Exc:** $75 **VGood:** $60

CLERKE FIRST MODEL

Revolver; double action; 32 S&W, 22 LR, 22 Long, 22 Short; 5-shot swing-out cylinder (32), 6-shot (22); 2-1/4-inch barrel; 6-1/4-inch overall length; fixed sights; checkered plastic grips; blued, nickel finish.

Perf: $50 **Exc:** $35 **VGood:** $25

COBRA SHADOW

Caliber: 38 Special +P. Five-round cylinder. Barrel length is 1-7/8 inches and weight is 15 oz. Rosewood or black rubber grips. Crimson Trace Lasergrip available. Aluminum frame. Finishes include titanium, black, red, pink, gold and blue. Double-action-only with fully enclosed hammer.

Perf: $360 **Exc:** $310 **VGood:** $265

Add 50 to 60 percent for CT Lasergrip.

COBRA TITAN

Caliber: 45 Colt/410 shotshell or 9mm. Derringer with two-round capacity. Barrel: 3-1/2 inches. Weight: 16.4 oz. Rosewood grips. Satin stainless, black stainless or brushed stainless finish.

Perf: $375 **Exc:** $325 **VGood:** $285

COLT 22 AUTOMATIC PISTOL

Semi-automatic; single action; 22 LR; 10-shot magazine; 4-1/2-inch barrel; weighs 33 oz.; 8-5/8-inch overall length; textured black polymer grip; blade front sight, rear drift-adjustable for windage; stainless steel construction; ventilated barrel rib; single-action mechanism; cocked striker indicator; push-button safety. Introduced 1994; no longer produced. Also known as Cadet.

New: $425 **Perf:** $325 **Exc:** $295

COLT 22 TARGET PISTOL

Same specs as the Colt 22 except 6-inch bull barrel; full-length sighting rib with lightening cuts and mounting rail for optical sights; fully-adjustable rear sight; removable sights for optics mounting; two-point factory adjusted trigger travel; stainless steel frame. Introduced 1995; no longer produced.

New: $450 **Perf:** $415 **Exc:** $355

COLT 70 SERIES MODEL O

A re-introduction of the 70 series. Availible in blued steel or Stainless finish. .45 caliber.
New in 2002.

Perf: $950 **Exc:** $850 **VGood:** $700

COLT 175TH ANNIVERSARY SINGLE ACTION ARMY

Caliber: 45 Colt. Barrel lengths: 4-3/4, 5-1/2,and 7-1/2 inches. Production to be limited to 175 units in each barrel length. From the Colt Custom Shop, this special edition is built on a black powder style frame with all metal surfaces polished and finished in Colt Royal Blue. The guns are embellished with Selective Gold Plating.

Perf: $1395 **Exc:** $1255 **VGood:** N/A

COLT ACE

Semi-automatic; 22 LR only, standard or high velocity; 4-3/4-inch barrel; 8-1/4-inch overall length; no floating chamber; adjustable rear, fixed front sight; target barrel; hand-honed action. Built on same frame as Government Model 45 automatic. Introduced 1931; dropped 1947.

Exc: $2400 **VGood:** $1500 **Good:** $1000

COLT ACE SERVICE MODEL

Semi-automatic; 22 LR, standard or high velocity; 10-shot magazine; identical to Colt National Match. Specially designed chamber increases recoil four-fold to approximate that of 45 auto. Introduced 1937; dropped 1945; reintroduced 1978; dropped 1982.

Old model

Exc: $3000 **VGood:** $2250 **Good:** $1500

New model

Perf: $600 **Exc:** $500 **VGood:** $450

COLT ALL AMERICAN MODEL 2000

Semi-automatic; double-action-only; 9mm Para.; 15-shot magazine; 4-1/2-inch barrel; 7-1/2-inch overall length; weighs 29 oz. (polymer frame), 33 oz. (aluminum frame); checkered polymer grips; ramped blade front sight, drift-adjustable rear; three-dot system; molded polymer or aluminum frame; blued steel slide; internal striker block safety. Made in U.S. by Colt's Mfg. Co., Inc. Introduced 1991; dropped 1993.

Polymer frame

Perf: $550 **Exc:** $450 **VGood:** $375

Aluminum frame

Perf: $850 **Exc:** $700 **VGood:** $550

COLT CHALLENGER

Semi-automatic; 22 LR; 4-1/2-inch, 6-inch barrel; 9-inch overall length (4-1/2-inch barrel); fixed sights; checkered plastic grips; blued finish. Same basic specs as third-issue Target Woodsman, with fewer features; slide does not stay open after last shot. Introduced 1950; dropped 1955.

Perf: $500 **Exc:** $375 **VGood:** $275

COLT COMBAT COMMANDER (PRE-1970)

Semi-automatic; single action; 45 ACP, 38 Super, 9mm Para.; 7-shot (45 ACP), 9-shot (38 Super, 9mm); 4-1/4-inch barrel; 7 7/8-inch overall length; weighs 35 oz.; fixed sights; thumb grip safties; steel or alloy frame; grooved trigger; walnut grips; blue or satin nickel finish. Introduced 1950; dropped 1976.

45 ACP, 38 Super

Exc: $950 **VGood:** $800 **Good:** $700

9mm

Exc: $900 **VGood:** $750 **Good:** $600

COLT COMBAT COMMANDER MKIV SERIES 70

Semi-automatic; single action; 45 ACP, 38 Super, 9mm Para.; 7-shot (45 ACP), 9-shot (38 Super, 9mm); 4-1/4-inch barrel; 7-7/8-inchoverall length; weighs 36 oz.; fixed blade front sight; square notch rear; all steel frame; grooved trigger; lanyard-style hammer; checkered walnut grips; blue or nickel finish. Introduced, 1970; dropped 1983.

Perf: $950 **Exc:** $800 **VGood:** $700

Colt 175th Anniversary Single Action Army

Colt Double Eagle Combat Commander MKII Series 90

Colt Combat Elite MKIV Series 80

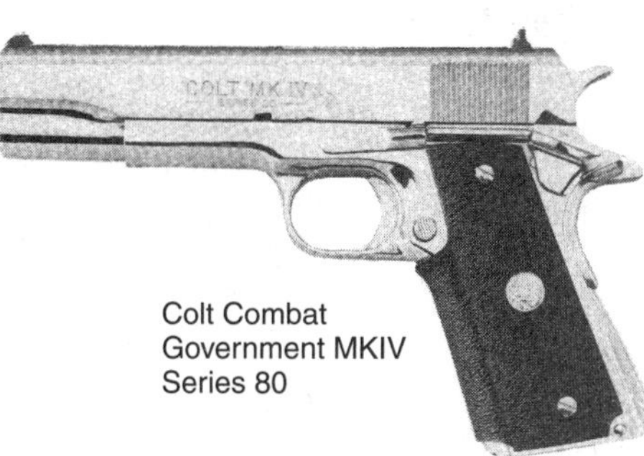
Colt Combat Government MKIV Series 80

Colt Delta Elite

Nickel finish

Perf: $1000 **Exc:** $850 **VGood:** $750

COLT COMBAT COMMANDER LIGHTWEIGHT MKIV SERIES 70

Same specs as Combat Commander MKIV Series 70 except 45 ACP; weighs 27 oz.; aluminum alloy frame; Introduced 1970; dropped 1983.

Perf: $750 **Exc:** $650 **VGood:** $500

COLT COMBAT COMMANDER MKIV SERIES 80

Semi-automatic; 45 ACP, 38 Super Auto, 9mm Para.; 7-shot (45 ACP), 9-shot (38 Super, 9mm); 4-1/4-inch barrel; 8-inch overall length; weighs 36 oz.; fixed blade front sight; grooved trigger, hammer spur; arched housing, grip and thumb safeties; steel frame; rubber combat grips; blued finish, except for satin nickel (no longer offered) and stainless steel 45 version. Introduced, 1979; called Commander until 1981; discontinued.

Perf: $750 **Exc:** $600 **VGood:** $450

Stainless steel finish

Perf: $800 **Exc:** $650 **VGood:** $500

Satin nickel finish

Perf: $850 **Exc:** $700 **VGood:** $550

COLT COMBAT ELITE MKIV SERIES 80

Semi-automatic; single action; 38 Super, 45 ACP; 7-, 8-shot magazine; 5-inch barrel; 8-1/2-inch overall length; weighs 39 oz.; high profile sights with 3-dot system; checkered rubber combat grips; stainless steel frame; ordnance steel slide, internal parts; beveled magazine well; extended grip safety. Introduced, 1986; still in production.

Perf: $750 **Exc:** $600 **VGood:** $500

COLT COMBAT GOVERNMENT MKIV SERIES 70

Semi-automatic; single action; 45 ACP; 8-shot magazine; 5-inch barrel; 8-3/8-inch overall length; weighs 40 oz. Similar to Government Model except higher undercut front sight, white outlined rear; flat mainspring housing; longer trigger; beveled magazine well; angled ejection port; Colt/Pachmayr wrap-around grips; internal firing pin safety. Introduced 1973; dropped 1983.

Perf: $950 **Exc:** $800 **VGood:** $700

COLT COMBAT GOVERNMENT MKIV SERIES 80

Semi-automatic; single action; 45 ACP; 5-shot magazine; 5-inch barrel; 8-1/2-inch overall length; weighs 39 oz. Similar to Combat Government MKIV Series 70 with higher undercut front sight, white outlined rear; flat mainspring housing; longer trigger beveled magazine well; angled ejection port; Colt/Pachmayr wrap-around grips; internal firing pin safety; 45 with blue, satin or stainless finish; 9mm, 38 blue only. Introduced 1983; dropped 1996.

Perf: $600 **Exc:** $500 **VGood:** $400

COLT COMMANDER LIGHTWEIGHT MKIV SERIES 80

Semi-automatic; 45 ACP, 38 Super, 9mm Para.; 4-1/4-inch barrel, 8-inch overall length; 7-shot magazine (45 ACP), 9-shot (38 Super, 9mm); weighs 26-1/2 oz.; basic design of Government Model auto, but of lightweight alloy, reducing weight; checkered walnut grips; fixed sights; rounded hammer spur; blued, nickel finish. Introduced 1983; dropped 1997.

Perf: $695 **Exc:** $585 **VGood:** $495

COLT DEFENDER

Semi-automatic; 45 ACP, 7-shot magazine. Barrel: 3-inch. Weight: 22-1/2 oz. Length: 6-3/4-inch overall. Stocks: Pebble-finish rubber wraparound with finger grooves. Sights: White dot front, snag-free Colt competition rear. Features: Stainless finish; aluminum frame; combat-style hammer; Hi Ride grip safety, extended manual safety, magazine disconnect safety. Introduced 1998.

Perf: $800 **Exc:** $750 **VGood:** $600

COLT DELTA ELITE

Semi-automatic; 10mm Auto; 8-shot; 5-inch barrel; 8-1/2-inch overall length; weighs 38 oz.; same general design as Government Model; 3-dot high profile combat sights; rubber combat stocks; internal firing pin safety; new recoil spring/buffer system; blued or matte stainless finish. Introduced 1987; dropped 1996. Stainless reintroduced in 2011.

Perf: $950 **Exc:** $825 **VGood:** $650

Matte stainless

Perf: $975 **Exc:** $850 **VGood:** $675

COLT DELTA GOLD CUP

Same specs as Delta Elite except Accro adjustable rear sight; adjustable trigger; wrap-around grips; stainless steel finish. Introduced 1989; dropped 1991.

Perf: $1200 **Exc:** $1050 **VGood:** $8950

COLT DOUBLE EAGLE COMBAT COMMANDER MKII SERIES 90

Semi-automatic; double action; 40 S&W, 45 ACP; 8-shot magazine; 4-1/4-inch barrel; 7-3/4-inch overall length; weighs 36 oz.; blade front sight, windage-adjustable rear; 3-dot system; Colt Accro adjustable sight optional; stainless steel; checkered, curved extended triggerguard; wide steel trigger; decocking lever; traditional magazine release; beveled magazine well; grooved frontstrap; extended grip guard; combat-type hammer. Introduced 1991; dropped 1996.

Perf: $850 **Exc:** $650 **VGood:** $500

COLT DOUBLE EAGLE MKII SERIES 90

Semi-automatic; double action; 45 ACP; 8-shot magazine; 4-1/2-inch, 5-inch barrel; 8-1/2-inch overall length; weighs 39 oz.; blade front sight, windage-adjustable rear; black checkered thermoplastic grips; stainless steel construction; matte finish; extended triggerguard; decocking lever; grooved frontstrap; beveled magazine well; rounded hammer; extended grip guard. Introduced 1989; dropped 1996.

Perf: $850 **Exc:** $650 **VGood:** $500

COLT DOUBLE EAGLE OFFICER'S MODEL MKIV SERIES 90

Semi-automatic; double action; 45 ACP; 8-shot magazine; 3-1/2-inch barrel; 7-1/4-inch overall length; weighs 35 oz.; stainless steel construction; blade front, windage-adjustable rear sight with 3-dot system; black checkered thermoplastic grips; matte finish; extended trigger guard; decocking lever; grooved frontstrap; beveled magazine well; rounded hammer; extended grip guard. Introduced 1989; dropped 1996.

Perf: $850 **Exc:** $650 **VGood:** $500

Lightweight model (25 oz.)

Perf: $900 **Exc:** $700 **VGood:** $500

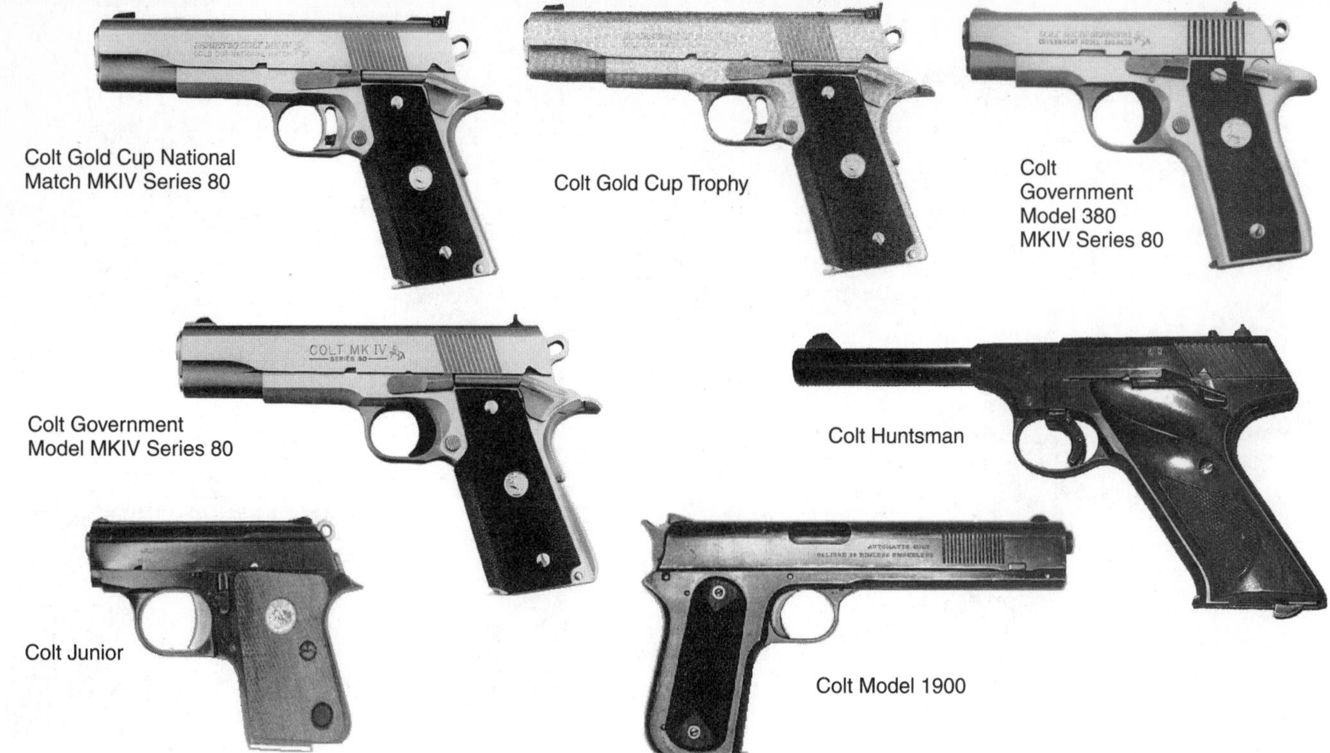
Colt Gold Cup National Match MKIV Series 80

Colt Gold Cup Trophy

Colt Government Model 380 MKIV Series 80

Colt Government Model MKIV Series 80

Colt Huntsman

Colt Junior

Colt Model 1900

COLT GOLD CUP NATIONAL MATCH MKIII

Semi-automatic; 45 ACP, 38 Spl.; 5-inch match barrel; 8-1/2-inch overall length; weighs 37 oz.; Patridge front sight, Colt Elliason adjustable rear; arched or flat housing; wide, grooved trigger with adjustable stop; ribbed top slide; hand-fitted with improved ejection port. Introduced 1959; dropped 1970.

45 ACP

Exc: $1000 **VGood:** $800 **Good:** $650

38 Spl.

Exc: $1200 **VGood:** $950 **Good:** $800

COLT GOLD CUP NATIONAL MATCH MKIV SERIES 70

Semi-automatic; 45 ACP; 7-shot magazine; 5-inch barrel; 8-3/8-inch overall length; weighs 38-1/2 oz; undercut front sight, Colt Elliason adjustable rear; match-grade barrel, bushing; long, wide grooved trigger; flat grip housing; hand-fitted slide; checkered walnut grips; blued finish. Introduced 1970; dropped 1983.

Exc: $1300 **VGood:** $995 **Good:** $700

COLT GOLD CUP NATIONAL MATCH MKIV SERIES 80

Semi-automatic; single action; 45 ACP; 8-shot magazine; 5-inch barrel; 8-1/2-inch overall length; weighs 39 oz.; Patridge front sight, Colt-Elliason adjustable rear; match-grade barrel, bushing; long, wide trigger adjustable trigger stop; flat mainspring housing; hand-fitted slide; wider ejection port; checkered walnut grips; blue, stainless, bright stainless finish. Introduced 1983; dropped 1996.

Perf: $950 **Exc:** $775 **VGood:** $600

Stainless finish

Perf: $950 **Exc:** $775 **VGood:** $600

Bright stainless

Perf: $1020 **Exc:** $850 **VGood:** $675

COLT GOLD CUP TROPHY

Semi-automatic: 45 ACP, 8-shot magazine. Barrel: 5, with new design bushing. Weight: 39 oz. Length: 8-1/2. Stocks: Checkered rubber composite with silver-plated medallion. Sights: Patridge-style front, Colt-Elliason rear adjustable for windage and elevation, sight radius 6-3/4-inch. Features: Arched or flat housing; wide, grooved trigger with adjustable stop; ribbed-top slide, hand fitted, with improved ejection port. Available only from the Colt Custom Shop.

Perf: $1250 **Exc:** $1000 **VGood:** $800

COLT GOVERNMENT MODEL MKIV SERIES 70

Semi-automatic; single action; 45 ACP, 38 Super, 9mm Para.; 7-shot magazine; 5-inch barrel; 8-3/8-inch overall length; weighs 40 oz; ramp front sight, fixed square notch rear; grip, thumb safeties; grooved trigger; accurizor barrel, bushing; blue or nickel (45 only) finish. Redesigned, redesignated Colt Model 1911A1. Introduced 1970; dropped 1983.

Perf: $925 **Exc:** $700 **VGood:** $525

Nickel finish

Perf: $1000 **Exc:** $750 **VGood:** $550

COLT GOVERNMENT MODEL MKIV SERIES 80

Semi-automatic; single action; 45 ACP, 38 Super, 9mm Para.; 7-, 8-shot magazine; 5-inch barrel; 8-1/2-inch overall length; weighs 38 oz.; ramp front sight, fixed square notch rear; grip and thumb safeties; internal firing pin safety; grooved trigger; accurizor barrel bushing; checkered walnut grips; blue, nickel, satin nickel, bright stainless, stainless steel finish. Introduced 1983; still in production.

Blue, nickel, satin nickel finish

Perf: $775 **Exc:** $650 **VGood:** $525

Stainless steel, bright stainless finish

Perf: $725 **Exc:** $600 **VGood:** $475

COLT GOVERNMENT MODEL 380 MKIV SERIES 80

Semi-automatic; 380 ACP; 7-shot magazine; 3-inch barrel; 6-inch overall length; weighs 21-3/4 oz.; checkered composition stocks; ramp front sight, fixed square-notch rear; thumb and internal firing pin safeties; blue, nickel, satin nickel or stainless steel finish. Introduced 1983; dropped 1997.

Perf: $750 **Exc:** $650 **VGood:** $495

Nickel, satin nickel finish

Perf: $795 **Exc:** $695 **VGood:** $525

Stainless steel finish

Perf: $595 **Exc:** $495 **VGood:** $425

COLT HUNTSMAN, TARGETSMAN

Semi-automatic; 22 LR; 4-1/2-inch, 6-inch barrel; 9-inch overall length; checkered plastic grips; no hold-open device; fixed sights (Huntsman), adjustable sights and 6-inch barrel only (Targetsman). Introduced 1955; dropped 1977.

Huntsman

Exc: $595 **VGood:** $495 **Good:** $350

Targetsman

Exc: $650 **VGood:** $495 **Good:** $350

COLT JUNIOR

Semi-automatic; 22 Short, 25 ACP; 6-shot magazine; 2-1/4-inch barrel; 4-3/8-inch overall length; exposed hammer with round spur; checkered walnut stocks; fixed sights; blued. Initially produced in Spain by Astra, with early versions having Spanish markings as well as Colt identity; parts were assembled in U.S., sans Spanish identification after GCA '68 import ban. Introduced 1968; dropped 1973.

Spanish model

Exc: $400 **VGood:** $325 **Good:** $275

U.S.-made model

Exc: $425 **VGood:** $375 **Good:** $250

COLT MODEL 1900

Semi-automatic; 38 ACP; 7-shot magazine; 6-inch barrel; 9-inch overall length; spur hammer; plain walnut stocks; blued finish. Dangerous to fire modern high-velocity ammo. Was made in several variations. Introduced 1900; dropped 1903. Collector value.

Standard model

Exc: $7500 **VGood:** $5650 **Good:** $4150

Altered sight safety

Exc: $10500 **VGood:** $7900 **Good:** $5100

COLT MODEL 1900 ARMY

Same specs as Model 1900. Marked U.S. on left side of triggerguard bow, with inspector markings.

Exc: $7500 **VGood:** $5500 **Good:** $450

COLT MODEL 1900 USN

Same specs as Model 1900. Marked USN and Navy serial number on left side of frame, Colt serial number on right.

Exc: $10,000 **VGood:** $8500 **Good:** $7000

Colt Model 1905

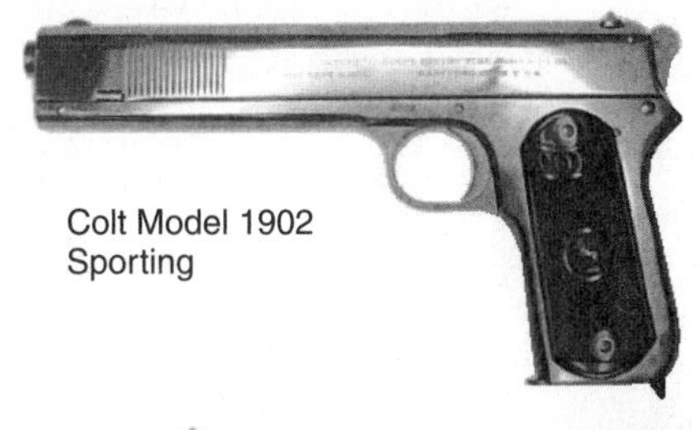

Colt Model 1902 Sporting

Colt Model 1903 Pocket Hammerless (Early Model)

Colt Model 1902 Military

Colt Model 1903 Pocket Hammerless (Fourth Issue) U.S. Property marked

Colt Vest Pocket Model 1908 Hammerless

Colt Model 1911 Military (Springfield Armory)

COLT MODEL 1902 MILITARY

Semi-automatic; 38 ACP; 8-shot magazine; 9-inch overall length; 6-inch barrel; fixed blade front, notched V rear sight; checkered hard rubber stocks; round-back hammer (changed to spur type in 1908); blued finish. Dangerous to fire modern high-velocity loads. Early production with serrations on front area of slide. U.S. Army marked pistols between serial numbers 15,001 and 15,200 have inspector stampings, slide serrations at front. Introduced 1902; dropped 1929.

Early production

Exc: $4500 **VGood:** $3750 **Good:** $2500

Standard production

Exc: $4225 **VGood:** $3500 **Good:** $2000

U.S. Army test pistols

Exc: $8500 **VGood:** $6500 **Good:** $5500

COLT MODEL 1902 SPORTING

Semi-automatic; 38 ACP; 8-shot magazine; 6-inch barrel; 9-inch overall length; sans safety; checkered hard rubber grips; blade front sight, fixed notch V rear; round hammer. Not safe with modern loads. Manufactured 1902 to 1908.

Exc: $4500 **VGood:** $3250 **Good:** $2500

COLT MODEL 1903 POCKET HAMMER

Semi-automatic; 38 ACP; 4-1/2-inch barrel; 7-1/2-inch overall length; round back hammer changed to spur type in 1908; checkered hard rubber grips; blued finish. Not safe with modern ammo. Manufactured 1903 to 1929.

Exc: $1850 **VGood:** $1550 **Good:** $850

COLT MODEL 1903 POCKET HAMMERLESS (FIRST ISSUE)

Semi-automatic; 32 ACP; 8-shot magazine; 4-inch barrel; 7-inch overall length; fixed sights; internal hammer; slidelock; grip safety; hard rubber stocks; blued or nickel finish; barrel takedown bushing. Manufactured from 1903 until 1908.

Exc: $1850 **VGood:** $1550 **Good:** $1250

COLT MODEL 1903 POCKET HAMMERLESS (SECOND ISSUE)

Same specs as First Issue except 3 3/4-inch barrel. Made from 1908 until 1910.

Exc: $800 **VGood:** $600 **Good:** $450

COLT MODEL 1903 POCKET HAMMERLESS (THIRD ISSUE)

Same specs as First Issue except no barrel bushing. Introduced 1910; dropped 1926.

Exc: $800 **VGood:** $600 **Good:** $450

COLT MODEL 1903 POCKET HAMMERLESS (FOURTH ISSUE)

Same specs as First Model except magazine safety. On all guns above serial number 468,097, safety disconnector prevents firing cartridge in chamber if magazine is removed. Manufactured from 1926 to 1945.

Exc: $775 **VGood:** $595 **Good:** $400

U.S. Property marked

Exc: $1000 **VGood:** $850 **Good:** $750

COLT MODEL 1905

Semi-automatic; single action; 45 ACP; 7-shot magazine; 5-inch barrel; snub-type and spur hammers; checkered, varnished walnut stocks; case-hardened hammer; blued finish; forerunner of the Model 1911 45 Auto; produced in standard, military test (with loaded chamber indicator, separate serial range 1-200) and shoulder-stocked models. Introduced 1905; dropped 1911.

Early production (s/n below 700)

Exc: $5500 **VGood:** $3250 **Good:** $2150

Standard production

Exc: $3500 **VGood:** $2250 **Good:** $1300

Military test model

Exc: $8500 **VGood:** $6500 **Good:** $4500

With shoulder stock

Exc: $12,500 **VGood:** $10,000 **Good:** $8500

COLT MODEL 1908 POCKET HAMMERLESS (FIRST ISSUE)

Semi-automatic; 380 ACP; 7-shot magazine; 3-3/4-inch barrel; 7-inch overall length; fixed sights; hammerless; slidelock; grip safety; hard rubber stocks; blued finish. Same general design, specs as Model 1903 Pocket Hammerless. Manufactured from 1908 to 1911.

Exc: $1000 **VGood:** $800 **Good:** $650

COLT MODEL 1908 POCKET HAMMERLESS (SECOND ISSUE)

Same specs as First Issue sans barrel bushing. Manufactured from 1911 to 1926.

Exc: $550 **VGood:** $450 **Good:** $375

COLT MODEL 1908 POCKET HAMMERLESS (THIRD ISSUE)

Same specs as Second Issue except safety disconnector installed on guns with serial numbers above 92,894. Introduced 1926; dropped 1945.

Exc: $550 **VGood:** $350 **Good:** $295

U.S. Property marked3

Exc: $1500 **VGood:** $1250 **Good:** $1000

COLT MODEL 1911 COMMERCIAL

Semi-automatic; also known as Government Model; 45 ACP; 7-shot magazine; 5-inch barrel; weighs 39 oz.; checkered walnut grips; fixed sights; blued finish; commercial variations with letter "C-inch preceding serial number. Introduced 1912; dropped 1923 to be replaced by Model 1911A1.

Early production High Polish Blue (through s/n 4500)

Exc: $12,000 **VGood:** $10,000 **Good:** $7500

Standard model

Exc: $4500 **VGood:** $3000 **Good:** $1750

COLT MODEL 1911 BRITISH 455

Same specs as standard model but carries "Calibre 455" on right side of slide and may have broad arrow British ordnance stamp; made 1915 to 1916; 11,000 manufactured.

Exc: $3500 **VGood:** $2750 **Good:** $2100

COLT MODEL 1911 MILITARY

Same specs as the civilian version except serial numbers not preceded by the letter C; produced from 1912 to 1924; bright blue finish, early production; duller blue during war. Parkerized finish indicates post-war reworking and commands lesser value than original blue finish. Navy issue marked "Model of 1911 U.S. Navy" on slide.

Standard

Exc: $2000 **VGood:** $1400 **Good:** $850

U.S. Navy marked

Exc: $6000 **VGood:** $4800 **Good:** $3600

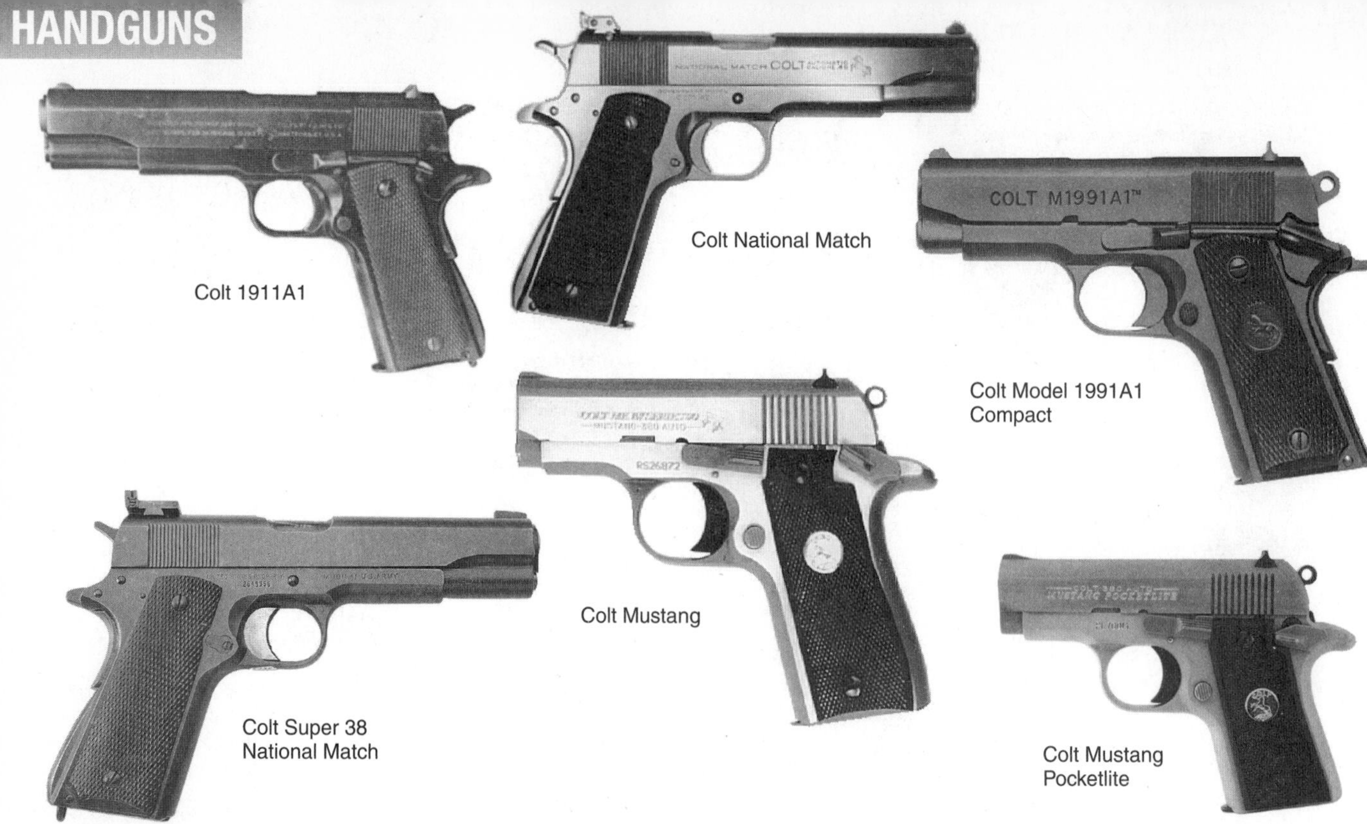

Colt 1911A1

Colt National Match

Colt Model 1991A1 Compact

Colt Mustang

Colt Super 38 National Match

Colt Mustang Pocketlite

Remington-UMC (21,676)		
Exc: $2200	**VGood:** $1700	**Good:** $950
Springfield Armory (25,767)		
Exc: $2500	**VGood:** $2000	**Good:** $950

COLT MODEL 1911 RUSSIAN

Same specs as the standard version except Russian characters ANGLOZAKAZIVAT stamped on the slide. All were in 45 ACP, carrying serial numbers C-50000 through C-85000. This is an exceedingly rare collector item.

Exc: $5000 **VGood:** $4250 **Good:** $3750

.38 SUPER (2007)

1911-style (not 1911A1-style) single-action semi-auto chambered in .38 Super. Nine-shot magazine, double-diamond walnut or checkered hard rubber stocks, fixed 3-dot sights, 5" barrel. Stainless, bright stainless or blued finish.

Exc: $900 **VGood:** $675 **Good:** $425

COLT MODEL 1911A1

Semi-automatic; single action; 45 ACP, 7-shot magazine; 5-inch barrel; 8-1/2-inch overall length; weighs 38 oz.; checkered walnut (early production) or brown composition (military version) grips; ramped blade front sight, fixed high-profile square notch rear; Parkerized finish. Same specs as Model 1911 except longer grip safety spur; arched mainspring housing; finger relief cuts in frame behind trigger; plastic grips. During WWII other firms produced the 1911A1 under Colt license, including Remington-Rand, Ithaca Gun Co., and Union Switch & Signal Co. These government models bear imprint of licensee on slide. In 1970, this model was redesigned and redesignated as Government Model MKIV Series 70; approximately 850 1911A1 guns were equipped with split-collet barrel bushing and BB prefix serial number which adds to the value. Modern version (marked "Colt M1911A1™") continues serial number range used on original GI 1911A1 guns and comes with one magazine and molded carrying case. Introduced 1923; still produced.

Commercial model (C s/n)		
Exc: $1250	**VGood:** $1000	**Good:** $850
BB s/n prefix		
Exc: $950	**VGood:** $800	**Good:** $600
Military model		
Exc: $950	**VGood:** $650	**Good:** $500
Singer Mfg. Co. (500)		
Exc: $24,000	**VGood:** $18,500	**Good:** $15,000
Union Switch & Signal (55,000)		
Exc: $2650	**VGood:** $2250	**Good:** $1750
Remington-Rand (1,000,000)		
Exc: $1200	**VGood:** $975	**Good:** $775
Ithaca Gun Co. (370,000)		
Exc: $1250	**VGood:** $1050	**Good:** $850
45/22 conversion unit		
Exc: $650	**VGood:** $550	**Good:** $400
22/45 conversion unit		
Exc: $1500	**VGood:** $1000	**Good:** $800

COLT NATIONAL MATCH

Semi-automatic; 45 ACP; 7-shot; 5-inch barrel; 8-1/2-inch overall length; weighs 37 oz.; adjustable rear, ramp front target sight; match-grade barrel; hand-honed action. Also available with fixed sights. Introduced 1933; dropped 1941.

Fixed sights		
Exc: $2750	**VGood:** $2000	**Good:** $1600
Target sights		
Exc: $3250	**VGood:** $2500	**Good:** $1850

COLT NEW FRONTIER

Caliber: 357 Magnum, 44 Special and 45 Colt. Reintroduction of Single Action Army Flattop Target Model. Barrel lengths: 4-3/4, 5-1/2, and 7-1/2 inches. Adjustable left rear, blade front sights. Walnut grips, Colt Royal Blue finish on barrel and cylinder with case colored frame.

Perf: $1300 **Exc:** $1110 **VGood:** $950

COLT SUPER 38

Semi-automatic; double action; 38 Colt Super; 9-shot magazine; fixed sights standard, adjustable rear sights available. Same frame as 1911 commercial until 1970. Introduced in 1929. In 1937, the design of the firing pin, safety, hammer, etc. were changed and the model renamed the New Style Super 38. Still in production as Government Model Mark IV/Series 80.

Exc: $1400	**VGood:** $1100	**Good:** $700
Pre-WWI		
Exc: $2500	**VGood:** $2000	**Good:** $1500

COLT SUPER 38 NATIONAL MATCH

Same specs as Colt Super 38 except hand-honed action; adjustable target sights; match-grade barrel. Manufactured from 1935 to 1941.

Exc: $4500 **VGood:** $3500 **Good:** $2500

COLT MODEL 1991A1

Semi-automatic; 45 ACP; 7-shot magazine; 5-inch barrel; 8-1/2-inch overall length; weighs 38 oz.; ramped blade front sight, fixed square notch high-profile rear; checkered black composition grips; Parkerized finish; continuation of serial number range used on original GI 1911A1 guns. Introduced 1991; still in production.

New: $700 **Perf:** $650 **Exc:** $525

COLT MODEL 1991A1 COMMANDER

Same specs as the Model 1991A1 except 4-1/4-inch barrel; Parkerized finish. Comes in molded case. Made in U.S. by Colt's Mfg. Co. Introduced 1993.

New: $700 **Perf:** $650 **Exc:** $525

COLT MODEL 1991A1 COMPACT

Same specs as the Model 1991A1 except 3-1/2-inch barrel; 7-inch overall length; 3/8-inch shorter height. Comes with one 6-shot magazine, molded case. Made in U.S. by Colt's Mfg. Co. 1993-1999.

New: $700 **Perf:** $650 **Exc:** $525

COLT MUSTANG

Semi-automatic; 380 ACP; 5-, 6-shot magazine; 2-3/4-inch barrel; 5-1/2-inch overall length; weighs 18-1/2 oz.; steel frame; stainless, blued or nickel finish. Similar to Colt Government Model 380. Introduced 1987; dropped 1997.

Perf: $550	**Exc:** $475	**VGood:** $400
Nickel finish		
Perf: $595	**Exc:** $495	**VGood:** $425
Stainless finish		
Perf: $595	**Exc:** $495	**VGood:** $425

COLT MUSTANG PLUS II

Same specs as Mustang except 7-shot magazine; weighs 20 oz.; composition grips; blued or stainless finish. Introduced 1988; dropped 1997.

Perf: $550 **Exc:** $475 **VGood:** $400

COLT MUSTANG POCKETLITE

Single-action micro-compact hammer fired pistol with aluminum alloy frame, stainless steel slide and high profile sights. Chambered in .380 ACP. 2.75 inch barrel, 5.5 inch OA length and weighs 13.7 ounces. 6+1 capacity. Reintroduced 2013.

Perf: $570 **Exc:** $500 **VGood:** $460

Colt Officer's ACP MKIV Series 80

Colt 1911 – WWI Replica

Colt Woodsman (First Issue)

Colt Pony

Colt Woodsman (Second Issue)

COLT CZ40

Semi-automatic; double action only; 40 S&W, 10-shot magazine. Barrel: 4-inch. Weight: 34 oz. Length: 7-3/4-inch overall. Stock: Textured black polymer. Sights: Dovetailed white dot front, No-Snag rear with two white dots. Features: Double-action-only mechanism; alloy frame, carbon steel slide; matte blue finish. Introduced 1998. Made under license for Colt; imported from the Czech Republic; no longer in production.

New: $795 **Perf:** $625 **Exc:** $475

COLT OFFICER'S ACP MKIV SERIES 80

Semi-automatic; single action; 45 ACP; 6-shot magazine; 3-1/2-inch barrel; 7-1/4-inch overall length; weighs 34 oz. (steel frame), 24 oz. (alloy frame); checkered walnut or rubber composite grips; blade front sight, square notch rear; 3-dot sight system; grooved trigger; flat mainspring housing; blued, matte, stainless or bright stainless finishes. Introduced 1985; discontinued 1997.

Perf: $625 **Exc:** $525 **VGood:** $435

Matte finish

Perf: $575 **Exc:** $490 **VGood:** $420

Stainless steel finish

Perf: $640 **Exc:** $525 **VGood:** $450

Bright stainless finish

Perf: $715 **Exc:** $600 **VGood:** $525

Alloy frame

Perf: $550 **Exc:** $450 **VGood:** $40

COLT PONY

Caliber: 380 ACP. Barrel: 2-3/4-inch. Weight: 19 oz. Length: 5-1/2-inch. Stocks: Black composition. Sights: Ramp front, fixed rear. Features: Stainless steel construction. Double-action-only mechanism; recoil-reducing locked breech. Produced in 1997 only.

Perf: $700 **Exc:** $625 **VGood:** $550

COLT PONY POCKETLITE LIGHTWEIGHT

Similar to Colt Pony, except has aluminum and stainless steel construction; brushed finish; 380 ACP; 13 oz. Produced from 1997 to 1999.

Perf: $700 **Exc:** $625 **VGood:** $550

COLT 1911 MARINE PISTOL

Single action only, hammer fired stainless steel full-sized semi-automatic pistol with accessory rail, ambidextrous safety, Desert Tan finish and three dot sights. Chambered in .45 ACP. 5 inch barrel and 8.25 inches OA length, weighs 2.44 pounds. 8+1 capacity. Introduced 2013.

Perf: $1125 **Exc:** $1050 **VGood:** $1000

COLT 1911 – WWI REPLICA

Single-action semi-auto chambered in .45 ACP. Faithful external reproduction of the WWI-era service pistol with original-style rollmarks, grips, sights, etc. Series 70 lockwork. 2003-2009.

NIB: $900 **Exc:** $795 **VGood:** $650

COLT CONCEALED CARRY

Chopped, lightweight 1911-style semi-auto chambered in .45 ACP. Weighs 25 oz. unloaded; overall length 6.75"; 7+1 capacity; Series 80 lockwork; black anodized aluminum frame with double-diamond wood grips.

NIB: $850 **Exc:** $775 **VGood:** $615

COLT .38 SUPER (2006)

1911-style single-action semi-auto chambered in .38 Super. Nine-shot magazine, double-diamond walnut or checkered hard rubber stocks, fixed 3-dot sights, 5" barrel. Stainless, bright stainless or blued finish.

NIB: $835 **Exc:** $695 **VGood:** $525

COLT WOODSMAN (FIRST ISSUE)

Semi-automatic; 22 LR standard velocity; 10-shot magazine; 6-1/2-inch barrel; 10-1/2-inch overall length. Designation, "The Woodsman," added after serial number 34,000; adjustable sights; checkered walnut grips. Introduced 1915; replaced 1943.

Exc: $1295 **VGood:** $995 **Good:** $650

COLT WOODSMAN (FIRST ISSUE) SPORT MODEL

Same specs as First Issue Woodsman except adjustable rear sight; adjustable or fixed front; 4-1/2-inch barrel; 8-1/2-inch overall length; fires standard- or high-velocity 22 LR ammo. Introduced 1933; dropped 1943.

Exc: $1295 **VGood:** $995 **Good:** $650

COLT WOODSMAN (FIRST ISSUE) MATCH TARGET

Same specs as Woodsman First Issue except 6-1/2-inch flat-sided barrel; 11-inch overall length; adjustable rear sight, blade front; checkered walnut one-piece extension grips; blued. Introduced 1938; dropped 1943.

Exc: $2495 **VGood:** $1895 **Good:** $1095

U.S. Property marked

Exc: $2700 **VGood:** $2200 **Good:** $1500

COLT WOODSMAN (SECOND ISSUE)

Semi-automatic; 22 LR; 10-shot magazine; 6-1/2-inch barrel; 10-1/2-inch overall length; slide stop; hold-open device; heat-treated mainspring housing for use with high-velocity cartridges; heavier barrel; push-button magazine release on top side of frame. Introduced in 1932; dropped 1948.

Exc: $895 **VGood:** $695 **Good:** $495

COLT WOODSMAN (SECOND ISSUE) SPORT MODEL

Same specs as the Second Issue Woodsman except 4-1/2-inch barrel; 9-inch overall length; plastic grips. Introduced 1947; dropped 1955.

Exc: $895 **VGood:** $695 **Good:** $495

COLT WOODSMAN (SECOND ISSUE) MATCH TARGET 4-1/2-INCH

Same specs as Second Issue Woodsman except 4-1/2-inch heavy barrel. Introduced 1947; dropped 1955.

Exc: $1295 **VGood:** $995 **Good:** $695

COLT WOODSMAN (SECOND ISSUE) MATCH TARGET 6-INCH

Same specs as Second Issue Woodsman except flat-sided 6-inch heavy barrel; 10-1/2-inch overall length; 22 LR, standard- or high-velocity; checkered walnut or plastic grips; click-adjustable rear sight, ramp front; blued. Introduced 1947; dropped 1955.

Exc: $1095 **VGood:** $895 **Good:** $600

COLT WOODSMAN (THIRD ISSUE)

Semi-automatic; 22 LR; 10-shot; 6-1/2-inch barrel; longer grip; larger thumb safety; slide stop magazine disconnector; thumbrest; plastic or walnut grips; magazine catch on bottom of grip; click-adjustable rear sight, ramp front. Introduced 1955; dropped 1977.

Exc: $750 **VGood:** $650 **Good:** $450

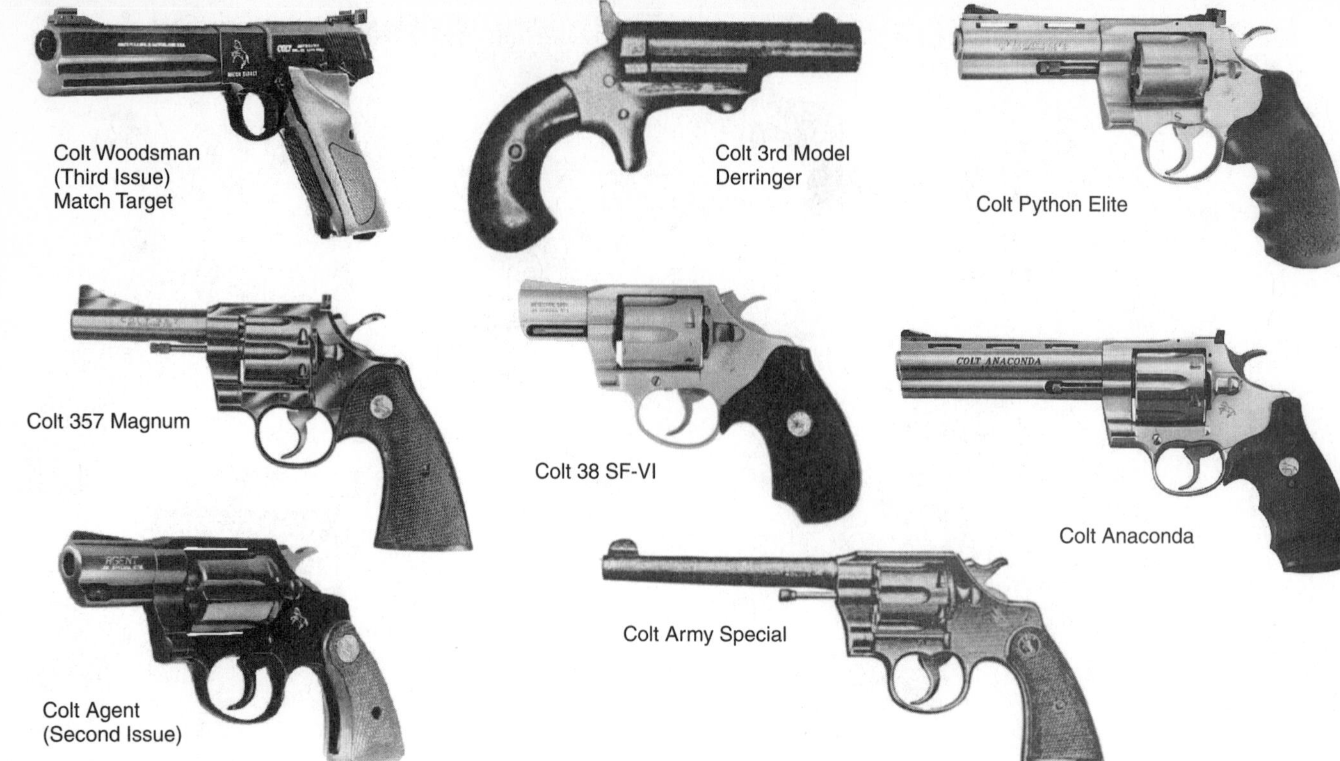
Colt Woodsman (Third Issue) Match Target
Colt 3rd Model Derringer
Colt Python Elite
Colt 357 Magnum
Colt 38 SF-VI
Colt Anaconda
Colt Army Special
Colt Agent (Second Issue)

COLT WOODSMAN (THIRD ISSUE) SPORT MODEL

Same specs as Third Issue Woodsman except 4-1/2-inch barrel. Introduced 1955; dropped 1977.

Exc: $750 **VGood:** $650 **Good:** $450

COLT WOODSMAN (THIRD ISSUE) MATCH TARGET 4-1/2-INCH

Same specs as Third Issue Woodsman except 4-1/2-inch heavy barrel. Introduced 1955; dropped 1977.

Perf: $600 **Exc:** $550 **VGood:** $500

COLT WOODSMAN (THIRD ISSUE) MATCH TARGET 6-INCH

Same specs as Third Issue Woodsman except 6-inch heavy barrel. Introduced 1955; dropped 1977.

Perf: $950 **Exc:** $850 **VGood:** $600

COLT 3RD MODEL DERRINGER

Derringer; single shot; 41 rimfire; 2-1/2-inch pivoting barrel; varnished walnut grips; bronze frame, nickel- or sliver-plated; blued or plated barrels. Introduced 1875; dropped 1912. (Note: Since 1959, Colt has produced this model intermittently in 22 caliber; it should not be confused with the 41 version.)

Exc: $1200 **VGood:** $850 **Good:** $725

S/N under 2000

Exc: $2500 **VGood:** $2000 **Good:** $1200

COLT 38 SF-VI

Revolver; double action; 38 Spl.; 6-shot cylinder; 2-inch barrel; 7-inch overall length; weighs 21 oz.; checkered black composition grips; ramp front sight, fixed rear; new (for Colt) lockwork; made of stainless steel. Made in U.S. by Colt's Mfg. Introduced 1995; dropped 1996.

New: $525 **Perf:** $400 **Exc:** $350

COLT PYTHON ELITE

Revolver; double action; 357 Magnum (handles all 38 Spec.), 6-shot. Barrel: 6-inch, with ventilated rib. Weight: 43-1/2 oz. Length: 11-1/2-inch overall. Stocks: Walnut. Sights: 1/8-inch ramp front, adjustable notch rear. Features: Ventilated rib; grooved, crisp trigger; swing-out cylinder; target hammer. Introduced 2001.

New: $1800 **Perf:** $1450 **Exc:** $1200

COLT 357 MAGNUM

Revolver; double action; 357 Mag.; 6-shot swing-out cylinder; 4-inch, 6-inch barrel; 9-1/4-inch overall length (4-inch barrel); available as service revolver or in target version; latter with wide hammer spur, target grips; checkered walnut grips; Accro rear sight, ramp front; blued finish. Introduced 1953; dropped 1961.

Perf: $625 **Exc:** $550 **VGood:** $475

Target Model

Perf: $700 **Exc:** $575 **VGood:** $4500

COLT AGENT (FIRST ISSUE)

Revolver; double action; 38 Spl.; 6-shot swing-out cylinder; 2-inch barrel; 6-3/4-inch overall length; weighs 14 oz.; minor variation of Colt Cobra with shorter stub grip for maximum concealment; Colt alloy frame, sideplate; steel cylinder, barrel; no housing around ejector rod; square butt; blued finish. Introduced 1955; dropped 1972.

Perf: $600 **Exc:** $550 **VGood:** $420

COLT AGENT (SECOND ISSUE)

Same specs as Agent First Issue except 6-5/8-inch overall length; weighs 16 oz; ramp front sight, square notch rear; checkered walnut grips; grip design extends just below bottom of frame. Introduced 1973; dropped 1981.

Perf: $495 **Exc:** $375 **VGood:** $300

COLT AGENT (THIRD ISSUE)

Same specs as Agent First Issue except shrouded ejector rod; alloy frame; Parkerized-type finish. Introduced 1982; dropped 1986.

Perf: $395 **Exc:** $325 **VGood:** $285

COLT ANACONDA

Revolver; double action; 44 Rem. Mag., 45 LC; 6-shot cylinder; 4-inch, 6-inch, 8-inch barrel; 11-5/8-inch overall length; weighs 53 oz.; red insert front sight, white-outline adjustable rear; finger-grooved black neoprene combat grips; stainless steel construction; ventilated barrel rib; offset bolt notches in cylinder; full-length ejector rod housing; wide spur hammer. Introduced 1990. Add 25 percent for camo finish; add 15 percent for factory ported barrel.

New: $1250 **Perf:** $1000 **Exc:** $900

COLT ARMY SPECIAL

Revolver; double action; 32-20, 38 Spl., 41 Colt; 6-shot cylinder; 4-inch, 4-1/2-inch, 5-inch, 6-inch barrels; 9-1/4-inch overall length (4-inch barrel); 41-caliber frame; hard rubber grips; fixed sights; blued or nickel finish. Not safe for modern 38 Special high-velocity loads in guns chambered for that caliber. Introduced 1908; dropped 1927.

Exc: $750 **VGood:** $675 **Good:** $500

COLT BANKER'S SPECIAL

Revolver; double action; 22 LR (with countersunk chambers after 1932), 38 New Police, 38 S&W; 6-shot swing-out cylinder; 2-inch barrel; 6-1/2-inch overall length; essentially the same as pre-1972 Detective Special, but with shorter cylinder of Police Positive rather than that of Police Positive Special; a few produced with Fitzgerald cutaway triggerguard; checkered hammer spur, trigger; blued or nickel finish. Low production run on 22 gives it collector value. Introduced 1926; dropped 1940.

22 blue finish

Exc: $1750 **VGood:** $1250 **Good:** $800

22 nickel finish

Exc: $2250 **VGood:** $1600 **Good:** $1000

38 blue finish

Exc: $850 **VGood:** $650 **Good:** $400

38 nickel finish

Exc: $1200 **VGood:** $800 **Good:** $500

COLT BISLEY

Revolver; single action; 455 Eley, 45, 44-40, 41, 38-40, 32-20; with trigger, hammer and grips redesigned for target shooting. Target model features target sights, flat-top frame. Bisley version of Colt SAA revolver first offered in flat-top target version in 1896 for use in target matches held at Bisley Common in England. The revolver's good performance encouraged Colt to offer it both in target and standard sighted versions until 1912. Bisley version featured a longer, more angled grip frame that placed the hand at almost a 90-degree angle to the bore. Parts, except for triggerguard, backstrap, grips, mainspring, hammer, and trigger, are totally interchangeable with standard Colt SAA. Standard

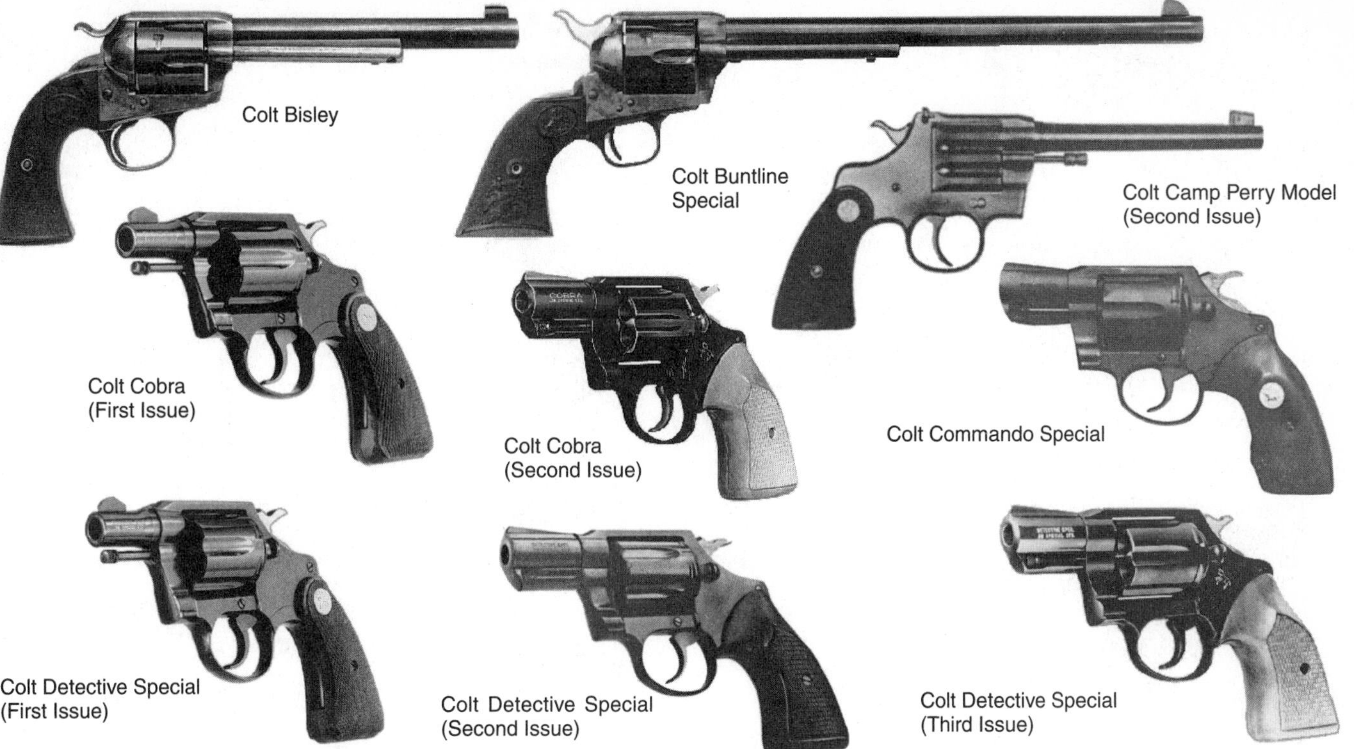
Colt Bisley
Colt Buntline Special
Colt Camp Perry Model (Second Issue)
Colt Cobra (First Issue)
Colt Cobra (Second Issue)
Colt Commando Special
Colt Detective Special (First Issue)
Colt Detective Special (Second Issue)
Colt Detective Special (Third Issue)

calibers, barrel lengths, and finishes same as 1st Generation Colt SAA. Manufactured from 1894 to 1913.

Standard model

Exc: $7000 **VGood:** $4500 **Good:** $2500

Target model

Exc: $12,000 **VGood:** $7500 **Good:** $4000

COLT BUNTLINE SPECIAL

Revolver; single action; 45 Colt; 12-inch barrel; case-hardened frame; hard rubber or walnut grips; designed after guns made as presentation pieces for author Ned Buntline. Introduced 1957; dropped 1992.

2nd Generation (1957-1975)

Perf: $1695 **Exc:** $1275 **VGood:** $1000

3rd Generation (1976-1992)

Perf: $1250 **Exc:** $850 **VGood:** $700

COLT CAMP PERRY MODEL (FIRST ISSUE)

Single shot; 22 LR, with countersunk chamber for high-velocity ammo after 1930; 10-inch barrel; 13-3/4-inch overall length; built on frame of Colt Officers Model; checkered walnut grips; hand-finished action; adjustable target sights; trigger, backstrap, hammer spur checkered; blued finish, with top, back of frame stippled to reduce glare. Chamber, barrel are single unit, pivoting to side for loading and extraction. Introduced 1926; dropped 1934.

Exc: $2000 **VGood:** $1600 **Good:** $1000

COLT CAMP PERRY MODEL (SECOND ISSUE)

Same specs as First Issue except 8-inch barrel; 12-inch overall length; shorter hammer fall. Only 440 produced. Collector value. Introduced 1934; dropped 1941.

Perf: $3000 **Exc:** $2000 **VGood:** $1500

COLT COBRA (FIRST ISSUE)

Revolver; double action; 22 LR, 32 New Police, 38 New Police, 38 Spl.; 6-shot swing-out cylinder; 2-inch, 3-inch, 4-inch, 5-inch barrels; 3-inch, 4-inch, 5-inch barrel styles special order; based on pre-1972 Detective Special, except frame, sideplate of high-tensile aluminum alloy; Coltwood plastic grips on later guns, checkered wood on early issues; square butt, early issue, replaced by round butt; optional hammer shroud; blue finish, matted on top, rear of frame; shrouded ejector rod (later issue). Introduced 1951; dropped 1972.

Perf: $445 **Exc:** $325 **VGood:** $250

Nickel finish

Perf: $475 **Exc:** $355 **VGood:** $295

22 LR

Perf: $575 **Exc:** $425 **VGood:** $300

COLT COBRA (SECOND ISSUE)

Same specs as Cobra First Issue except integral protective shroud enclosing ejector rod. Introduced 1973; dropped 1981.

Perf: $485 **Exc:** $375 **VGood:** $295

COLT COMMANDO

Revolver; double action; 38 Spl.; 6-shot cylinder; 2-inch, 4-inch, 6-inch barrels; plastic grips; sand-blasted blue finish. Government contract issue made to military specs; a downgraded version of the Colt Official Police. Introduced 1942; dropped 1945.

Exc: $450 **VGood:** $325 **Good:** $250

COLT COMMANDO SPECIAL

Revolver; 38 Spl.; 6-shot cylinder; 2-inch barrel; 6-5/8-inch overall length; weighs 22 oz.; steel frame; combat grade finish; rubber grips. Identical to Detective Special. Introduced 1984; dropped 1987.

Perf: $475 **Exc:** $375 **VGood:** $325

COLT DETECTIVE SPECIAL (FIRST ISSUE)

Revolver; double action; 38 Spl.; 6-shot swing-out cylinder; 2-inch, 3-inch barrels; 6-3/4-inch overall length; rounded butt introduced in 1934; blue or nickel finish. Introduced 1927; dropped 1936.

Exc: $850 **VGood:** $725 **Good:** $650

Nickel finish

Exc: $900 **VGood:** $800 **Good:** $725

COLT DETECTIVE SPECIAL (SECOND ISSUE)

Same specs as First Issue except 32 New Police, 38 New Police; heavier barrel; integral protective shroud enclosing ejector rod; frame, sideplate, cylinder, barrel, internal parts of high-tensile alloy steel; plastic or walnut Bulldog-type grips; fixed rear sight; notch milled in topstrap, serrated ramp front; checkered hammer spur; blue or nickel finish. Introduced 1947; dropped 1972.

Perf: $535 **Exc:** $450 **VGood:** $350

Nickel finish

Perf: $600 **Exc:** $475 **VGood:** $395

COLT DETECTIVE SPECIAL (THIRD ISSUE)

Same specs as Second Issue except 38 Spl.; shrouded ejector rod; wrap-around walnut grips. Introduced 1973; dropped 1986.

Perf: $475 **Exc:** $325 **VGood:** $275

COLT DETECTIVE SPECIAL (FOURTH ISSUE)

Same specs as Third Issue except 2-inch barrel only; weighs 22 oz.; 6-5/8-inch overall length; black composition grips; ramp front sight, fixed square notch rear; glare-proof sights; grooved trigger; Colt blue finish. Made in U.S. by Colt's Mfg. Reintroduced 1993; no longer produced.

New: $425 **Perf:** $375 **Exc:** $325

COLT DIAMONDBACK

Revolver; double action; 38 Spl., 22 LR; 6-shot swing-out cylinder; 2-1/2-inch, 4-inch (22 LR), 6-inch barrel; vent-rib barrel; scaled-down version of Python; target-type adjustable rear sight, ramp front; full checkered walnut grips; integral rounded rib beneath barrel shrouds, ejector rod; broad checkered hammer spur. Introduced 1966; dropped 1986.

Perf: $1000 **Exc:** $750 **VGood:** $475

Nickel finish

Perf: $1200 **Exc:** $850 **VGood:** $550

22 LR

Perf: $800 **Exc:** $900 **VGood:** $650

COLT FRONTIER SCOUT

Revolver; single action; 22 LR, 22 Long, 22 Short; interchangeable cylinder for 22 WMR; 4-1/2-inch barrel; 9-15/16-inch overall length; originally introduced with alloy frame; steel frame, blue finish introduced in 1959; fixed sights; plastic or wooden grips. Introduced 1958; dropped 1971.

Alloy frame

Perf: $600 **Exc:** $425 **VGood:** $325

Colt Model 1878 Frontier

Colt Model 1905 Marine Corps

Colt Lawman MKIII

Colt Frontier Scout

Colt Navy Model 1889 (First Issue)

Colt Navy Model 1892-1903 (Second Issue)

Blue finish, plastic grips

Perf: $600 **Exc:** $400 **VGood:** $300

Nickel finish, wood grips

Perf: $650 **Exc:** $475 **VGood:** $350

With 22 WMR cylinder

Perf: $650 **Exc:** $475 **VGood:** $375

COLT FRONTIER SCOUT BUNTLINE

Same specs as Frontier Scout except 9-1/2-inch barrel. Introduced 1959; dropped 1971.

Perf: $600 **Exc:** $425 **VGood:** $325

COLT KING COBRA

Revolver; double action; 357 Mag.; 6-shot cylinder; 2-1/2-inch, 4-inch, 6-inch barrels; 9-inch overall length (4-inch barrel); weighs 42 oz.; adjustable white outline rear sight, red insert ramp front; full-length contoured ejector rod housing, barrel rib; matte finish; stainless steel construction. Introduced 1986; dropped 1992.

Perf: $500 **Exc:** $425 **VGood:** $375

COLT MAGNUM CARRY REVOLVER

Caliber: 357 Mag., 6-shot. Barrel: 2-inch. Weight: 21 oz. Length: NA. Stocks: Combat-style rubber. Sights: Ramp front, fixed notch rear. Features: Stainless steel construction. Smooth combat trigger. Introduced 1998. No longer produced.

New: $525 **Perf:** $475 **Exc:** $400

COLT LAWMAN MKIII

Revolver; double action; 357 Mag.; also chambers 38 Spl.; 2-inch, 4-inch barrels; 9-3/8-inch overall length (4-inch barrel); choice of square, round butt walnut grips; fixed sights; blued, nickel finish. Introduced 1969; dropped 1983.

Perf: $400 **Exc:** $300 **VGood:** $250

Nickel finish

Perf: $425 **Exc:** $325 **VGood:** $275

COLT LAWMAN MKV

Same specs as Lawman MKIII except redesigned lockwork to reduce double-action trigger pull; faster lock time; redesigned grips; shrouded ejector rod (2-inch barrel); fixed sights; solid rib. Introduced 1984; dropped 1985.

Perf: $375 **Exc:** $275 **VGood:** $225

Nickel finish

Perf: $395 **Exc:** $295 **VGood:** $250

COLT METROPOLITAN MKIII

Revolver; double action; 38 Spl.; 6-shot swing-out cylinder; 4-inch barrel; designed for urban law enforcement; fixed sights; choice of service, target grips of checkered walnut; blued finish, standard; nickel, optional. Introduced 1969; dropped 1972.

Perf: $350 **Exc:** $300 **VGood:** $200

COLT MODEL 1877 LIGHTNING

Revolver; double action; 32 Colt, 38 Colt; 6-shot cylinder; 4-1/2-inch to 10-inch barrels with ejector; 1-1/2-inch, 2-1/2-inch, 3-1/2-inch, 4-1/2-inch, 6-inch sans ejector; fixed sights; blued or nickel finish; hard rubber grips. Manufactured 1877 to 1909.

Exc: $2000 **VGood:** $1500 **Good:** $750

COLT MODEL 1877 THUNDERER

Revolver; double action; 41 Colt; 6-shot cylinder; 4-1/2-inch to 10-inch barrels with ejector; 1-1/2-inch, 2-1/2-inch, 3-1/2-inch, 4-1/2-inch, 6-inch sans ejector; fixed sights; blued or nickel finish; hard rubber grips. Manufactured 1877 to 1909.

Exc: $2000 **VGood:** $1500 **Good:** $750

COLT MODEL 1878 FRONTIER

Revolver; double action; 32-20, 38-40, 44-40, 45 Colt, 450, 455, 476 Eley; 6-shot cylinder; 4-3/4-inch, 5-1/2-inch, 7-1/2-inch barrels with ejector; 3-1/2-inch, 4-inch without ejector; similar to Lightning model but with heavier frame; lanyard ring in butt; hard rubber grips; fixed sights; blued or nickel finish. Manufactured 1878 to 1905.

Exc: $4750 **VGood:** $2500 **Good:** $1500

COLT MODEL 1905 MARINE CORPS

Revolver; double action; 38 Spl., 38 Short, 38 Long; 6-inch barrel; round butt; double cylinder notches; shorter flutes; double locking butt. Manufactured 1905 to 1909.

Exc: $4000 **VGood:** $2000 **Good:** $1000

COLT MODEL 1917 ARMY

Revolver; double action; 6-shot swing-out cylinder; 45 Auto Rim cartridge can be fired in conventional manner; based upon New Service revolver to fire 45 ACP cartridge with steel half-moon clips; 10-13/16-inch overall length; 5-1/2-inch barrel; smooth walnut grips; fixed sights; dull finish. Should be checked for damage by corrosive primers before purchase. Introduced 1917; dropped 1925.

Exc: $1550 **VGood:** $900 **Good:** $695

COLT NAVY MODEL 1889 (FIRST ISSUE)

Revolver; double action; 38 Short Colt, 38 Long Colt, 41 Short Colt, 41 Long Colt; 6-shot left-revolving cylinder; 3-inch, 4-1/2-inch, 6-inch barrels; fixed blade front sight, V-notched rear; Colt's first solid-frame, swing-out cylinder model; hard rubber or walnut grips; blued or nickel finish. Manufactured 1889 to 1894. In demand by collectors.

Exc: $5000 **VGood:** $4000 **Good:** $2500

COLT NAVY MODEL 1892-1903 (SECOND ISSUE)

Same specs as First Issue except double cylinder notches, double locking bolt; lanyard loop on butt; added calibers; 38 Spl., 32-20; does not fire modern high-velocity loads safely. Also known as New Army, adopted by both Army and Navy. Manufactured 1892 to 1905.

Exc: $2750 **VGood:** $1500 **Good:** $600

COLT SPECIAL GOVERNMENT COMBAT

A target ready version of the Government Model. Offered in .45 auto or .38 Super. Features include tuned action, polished feed ramp, flared ejection port, extended ambidextrous safety, and more. Blue, hard chrome or satin nickel finish. Current production.

Perf: $1800 **Exc:** $1400 **VGood:** $1000

COLT XSE SERIES

These are current production versions of the Government, Commander, and Lightweight Commander. All feature front and rear slide serrations, extended ambidextrous safety, double diamond rosewood grips. Brushed stainless and blued finish available. Introduced 2001.

Perf: $950 **Exc:** $875 **VGood:** $750

COLT NEW FRONTIER

Revolver; flat-top target version of Colt Single Action Army first introduced in 1962 during 2nd Generation production and continued until 1974. Serial numbers began at 3000NF and ended in 1974 with 7288NF.

Colt New Frontier
Colt XSE Government
Colt New Police
Colt Officer's Model Match
Colt New Frontier 22
Colt New Service
Colt New Service Shooting Master

Calibers offered during 2nd Generation were 45 Colt, 44 Spl., 357 Mag., and 38 Spl. Standard barrel lengths 4-3/4-inch, 5-1/2-inch, 7-1/2-inch; a total of seventy-two 45 Colt Buntline New Frontiers manufactured with 12-inch barrels. Finish was Colt's royal blue with color case-hardened frame. Two-piece walnut grips were standard. Manufacture of New Frontiers resumed in 1978 during 3rd Generation production and continued until 1985. Serial numbers began again at 01001NF and ran to approximately 17000NF by 1985. During 3rd Generation production, calibers offered were 45 Colt, 44 Spl., and 357 Mag., with 44-40 being added in 1981. Finishes were Colt's royal blue with color case-hardened frame, with fully nickel-plated, and fully-blued being rarely-found options. Barrel lengths were the standard 4-3/4-inch, 5-1/2-inch, and 7-1/2-inch.

2nd Generation
Perf: $1500 **Exc:** $1200 **VGood:** $700

3rd Generation
Perf: $1000 **Exc:** $900 **VGood:** $695

COLT NEW FRONTIER BUNTLINE SPECIAL

Same specs as New Frontier except 45 Colt; 12-inch barrel; flat-top frame; adjustable rear sight.

2nd Generation
Perf: $2500 **Exc:** $1850 **VGood:** $1250

3rd Generation
Perf: $2000 **Exc:** $1500 **VGood:** $1000

COLT NEW FRONTIER 22

Revolver; single action; 6-shot cylinder; furnished with dual cylinders for 22 LR, 22 WMR; 4-3/8-inch, 6-inch, 7-1/2-inch barrels; 11-1/2-inch overall length (6-inch barrel); scaled-down version of New Frontier 45; target-type fully-adjustable rear sight, ramp front; checkered black plastic grips; flat topstrap; color case-hardened frame, rest blued. Introduced 1973; dropped 1975; reintroduced 1981; dropped 1982.

Perf: $600 **Exc:** $450 **VGood:** $300

7-1/2-inch barrel
Perf: $650 **Exc:** $475 **VGood:** $325

COLT NEW POCKET MODEL

Revolver; double action; 32 Colt, 32 S&W; 6-shot cylinder; 2-1/2-inch, 3-1/2-inch, 5-inch, 6-inch barrels; checkered hard rubber stocks; blued or nickel finish. Introduced 1893; dropped 1905. Collector value.

Exc: $550 **VGood:** $400 **Good:** $350

COLT NEW POLICE

Revolver; double action; 32 Colt, 32 Colt New Police; 2-1/2-inch, 4-inch, 6-inch barrels; built on New Pocket Model frame, with larger hard rubber grips; same sights as New Pocket Colt; blued or nickel finish. Manufactured 1896 to 1907.

Exc: $550 **VGood:** $425 **Good:** $350

COLT NEW POLICE TARGET

Same specs as New Police model except target sights; 6-inch barrel only. Manufactured 1896 to 1905.

Exc: $1500 **VGood:** $1250 **Good:** $750

COLT NEW SERVICE

Revolver; double action; 38 Spl., 357 Mag., 38-40, 38-44, 44 Russian, 44 Spl., 44-40, 45 Colt, 45 ACP, 450 Eley, 455 Eley, 476 Eley; 2-inch, 3-1/2-inch 4-inch, 4-1/2-inch, 5-inch, 5-1/2-inch, 6-inch, 7-1/2-inch barrels; 6-shot swing-out cylinder; large frame. Special run in 45 ACP. During WWI was designated as Model 1917 Revolver under government contract. Fixed open notch rear sight milled in topstrap, fixed front; checkered hard rubber grips on commercial New Service; lanyard loop on most variations; blued, nickel finish. Introduced 1897; dropped 1944.

Commercial model
Exc: $1675 **VGood:** $1250 **Good:** $750

Military model
Exc: $1575 **VGood:** $1350 **Good:** $850

357 Mag.
Exc: $1550 **VGood:** $1400 **Good:** $875

COLT NEW SERVICE SHOOTING MASTER

Same specs as New Service except 38 Spl., 357 Mag., 44 Spl., 45 ACP/Auto Rim, 45 Colt; 6-inch barrel; 11-1/4-inch overall length; deluxe target version; checkered walnut grips, rounded butt; windage-adjustable rear sight, elevation-adjustable front; blued. Introduced 1932; dropped 1941.

38 Special
Exc: $1750 **VGood:** $1325 **Good:** $900

44 Spl., 45 ACP, 45 Colt
Exc: $3500 **VGood:** $2500 **Good:** $1500

COLT NEW SERVICE TARGET

Same specs as standard New Service model except windage-adjustable rear sight, elevation-adjustable front; 44 Spl., 44 Russian, 45 Colt, 45 ACP, 450 Eley, 455 Eley, 476 Eley; 5-inch, 6-inch, 7-1/2-inch barrels; flat topstrap; finished action; blued finish; hand-checkered walnut grips. Introduced 1900; dropped 1940.

Exc: $2850 **VGood:** $2575 **Good:** $2100

COLT OFFICER'S MODEL TARGET (FIRST, SECOND, THIRD ISSUES)

Revolver; double action; 38 Spl. (First Issue); 32 Colt, 38 Spl. (Second Issue); 22 LR (Third Issue); 6-shot cylinder; 6-inch barrel (38 Spl.); 4-inch, 4-1/2-inch, 5-inch, 6-inch, 7-1/2-inch barrels (32 Colt, 38 Spl., 22 LR); hand-finished action; adjustable rear target, blade front sight; blued finish. First Issue manufactured 1904-1908; Second Issue, 1908-1926; Third Issue, 1927-1949.

First Issue
Exc: $1500 **VGood:** $1250 **Good:** $950

Second Issue
Exc: $1150 **VGood:** $1000 **Good:** $850

Third Issue
Exc: $825 **VGood:** $750 **Good:** $650

COLT OFFICER'S MODEL MATCH

Same specs as Officer's Model Special, which it replaced, except checkered walnut target grips; tapered heavy barrel; wide hammer spur. Introduced 1953; dropped 1970.

Perf: $425 **Exc:** $375 **VGood:** $300

COLT OFFICER'S MODEL SPECIAL

Same specs as Second Issue Officer's Model Target except heavier barrel; ramp front, Coltmaster adjustable rear sight; redesigned hammer; checkered plastic stocks; 6-inch barrel; 22 LR, 38 Spl.; blued finish. Introduced 1949; dropped 1955.

Exc: $550 **VGood:** $425 **Good:** $375

COLT OFFICIAL POLICE

Revolver; double action; 22 LR, 32-20, 38 Spl., 41 Long Colt; 6-shot cylinder; 2-inch, 6-inch heavy barrels (38 Spl. only); 4-inch, 6-inch barrels (22 LR only); 4-inch, 5-inch, 6-inch (other calibers);

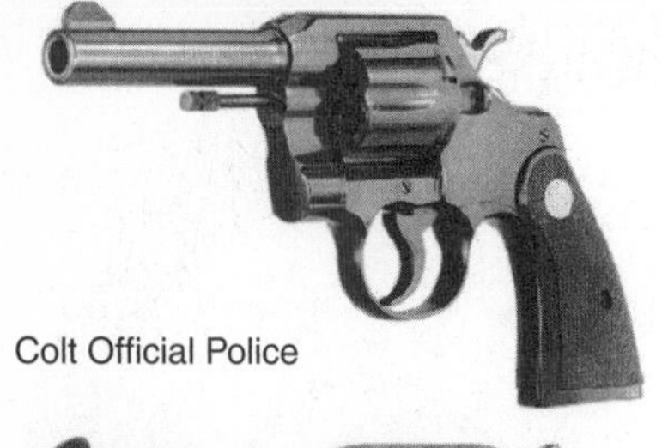
Colt Official Police

Colt Official Police MKIII

Colt Peacekeeper

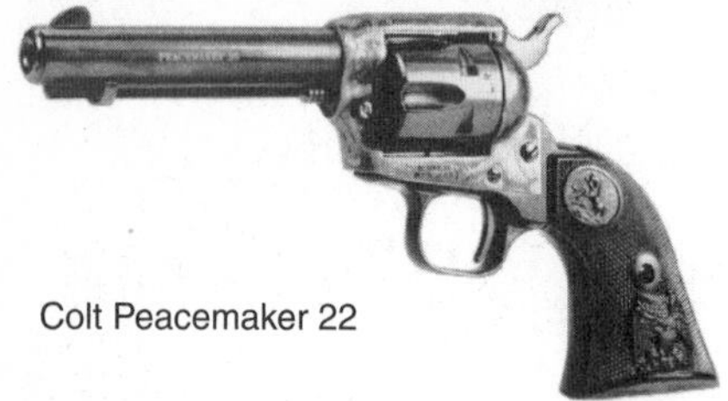
Colt Peacemaker 22

Colt Police Positive

Colt Pocket Positive

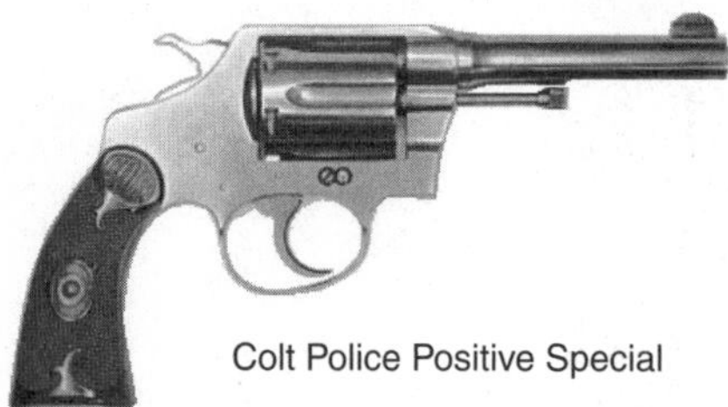
Colt Police Positive Special

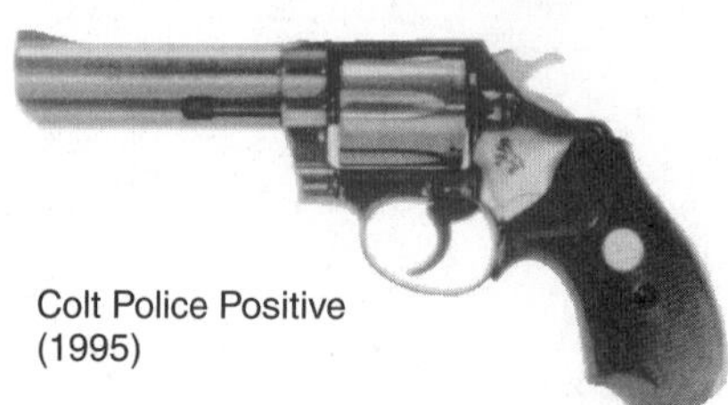
Colt Police Positive (1995)

Colt Python

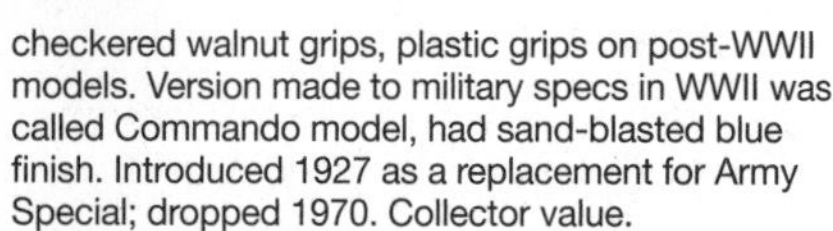

checkered walnut grips, plastic grips on post-WWII models. Version made to military specs in WWII was called Commando model, had sand-blasted blue finish. Introduced 1927 as a replacement for Army Special; dropped 1970. Collector value.

Perf: $525 **Exc:** $425 **VGood:** $350

Military model

Perf: $550 **Exc:** $460 **VGood:** $375

COLT OFFICIAL POLICE MKIII

Revolver; double action; 38 Spl.; 4-inch, 5-inch, 6-inch barrels; 9-3/8-inch overall length; an old name, but a renewed design, incorporating coil mainspring in place of leaf spring; square butt, checkered walnut grips; fixed rear sight notch milled in topstrap, fixed ramp front; grooved front surface on trigger; checkered hammer spur. Introduced 1969; dropped 1975.

Perf: $450 **Exc:** $375 **VGood:** $295

COLT PEACEKEEPER

Revolver; double action; 357 Mag.; 6-shot cylinder; 4-inch, 6-inch barrel; weighs 42 oz. (6-inch barrel); red insert ramp front sight, white outline adjustable rear; rubber round-bottom combat grips; matte blue finish. Introduced 1985; dropped 1987.

Perf: $525 **Exc:** $450 **VGood:** $300

COLT PEACEMAKER 22

Revolver; single action; dual cylinders for 22 LR, 22 WMR; 6-shot cylinder; 4-3/8-inch, 6-inch, 7-1/2-inch barrels; 11-1/4-inch overall length (6-inch barrel); scaled-down version of century-old Model 1873; rear sight notch milled into rounded topstrap; fixed blade front; color case-hardened frame, rest blued; black plastic grips. Introduced 1973; dropped 1975.

Perf: $475 **Exc:** $375 **VGood:** $300

7-1/2-inch barrel

Perf: $510 **Exc:** $425 **VGood:** $325

COLT POCKET POSITIVE

Revolver; double action; 32 Short Colt, 32 Long Colt, 32 Colt New Police (interchangeable with 32 S&W Long, S&W Short cartridges); 6-shot cylinder; 2-inch, 2-1/2-inch, 3-1/2-inch, 4-inch, 5-inch, 6-inch barrels; 7-1/2-inch overall length (3-1/2-inch barrel); rear sight groove milled in topstrap, rounded front sight; positive lock feature; hard rubber grips; blued or nickel finish. Based upon New Pocket Model dropped in 1905. Introduced 1905; dropped 1940. Subtract 5% for 32 SC and .32 LC chamberings.

Exc: $595 **VGood:** $450 **Good:** $385

Nickel finish

Exc: $650 **VGood:** $550 **Good:** $475

COLT POLICE POSITIVE

Revolver; double action; 32 Short Colt, 32 Long Colt, 32 Colt New Police, 38 S&W; 6-shot swing-out cylinder; 2-1/2-inch, 4-inch, 5-inch, 6-inch barrels; 8-1/2-inch overall length (4-inch barrel); fixed sights; checkered walnut, plastic or hard rubber grips; top of frame matted to reduce glare; blue or nickel finish; replaced New Police model. Introduced 1905; dropped 1943. Reintroduced 1995.

Exc: $450 **VGood:** $395 **Good:** $335

Nickel finish

Exc: $550 **VGood:** $450 **Good:** $375

COLT POLICE POSITIVE SPECIAL (FIRST, SECOND, THIRD ISSUES)

Same specs as standard Police Positive except lengthened frame to accommodate longer cylinder for 38 Spl., 32-20; also made in 32 and 38 Colt New Police; 4-inch, 5-inch, 6-inch barrels; 8-3/4-inch overall length (4-inch barrel); blued or nickel. Introduced 1908; dropped 1970. Reintroduced 1995; no longer produced.

Perf: $495 **Exc:** $450 **VGood:** $395

COLT POLICE POSITIVE TARGET

Same specs as standard Police Positive except 32 Short Colt, 32 Long Colt, 32 New Police, 32 S&W Short, 32 S&W Long, 22 LR. In 1932, cylinder was modified by countersinking chambers for safety with high-velocity 22 ammo; those with non-countersunk chambers should be fired only with standard-velocity 22 LR ammo. Has 6-inch barrel; 10-1/2-inch overall length, windage-adjustable rear sight, elevation-adjustable front; checkered walnut grips; blued; backstrap, hammer spur, trigger checkered. Introduced 1905; dropped 1941.

Exc: $795 **VGood:** $550 **Good:** $350

COLT PYTHON

Revolver; double action; 357 Mag., but will handle 38 Spl.; 6-shot swing-out cylinder; made first appearance in 6-inch barrel later with 2-1/2-inch, 3-inch, 4-inch, 8-inch; checkered walnut grips contoured for support for middle finger of shooting hand; vent-rib barrel; ramp front sight, fully-adjustable rear; full-length ejector rod shroud; wide-spur hammer; grooved trigger; blued, nickel finish; hand-finished action. Introduced 1955. **Discontinued.**

Perf: $1250 **Exc:** $1000 **VGood:** $850

Nickel finish

Perf: $1500 **Exc:** $1250 **VGood:** $1000

COLT PYTHON STAINLESS

Same specs as standard Python except stainless steel construction; 4-inch, 6-inch barrel lengths only. Introduced 1983.

Perf: $1150 **Exc:** $900 **VGood:** $800

COLT SINGLE ACTION ARMY

Colt Single Action Army also known as Peacemaker, or Frontier Six Shooter (44-40 caliber only). Originally introduced in 1873 and produced continuously until 1941. This production is run known as "1st Generation." The production run resumed in 1956 and stopped again in 1974 is known as "2nd Generation." Production known as "3rd Generation" began in 1976 and is still being manufactured. 1st Generation serial numbers began in 1873 with #1 and ended in 1941 with serial number 357859. The first Generation production included two frame styles: From 1873 until 1892, frames had screw angling in from front of frame to secure cylinder base pin; starting in 1892, and becoming standard by 1896, cylinder pin is secured by spring-loaded transverse catch. These frames are mistakenly called "blackpowder" and "smokeless powder" frames respectively, but it should be noted that Colt did not warranty any SAA revolvers for smokeless powder until 1900 at about serial number 192000. Rarer calibers and barrel lengths bring considerable premium over prices shown.

When 2nd Generation production began in 1956, serial numbers started at #0001SA, and continued until approximately #74000SA. 3rd Generation production started in 1976 and serial numbers resumed at #80000SA. When #99999SA was reached in 1978, the SA was made a prefix and numbers started once more at #SA00001. When #SA99999 was reached about 1993, the SA was split and numbers started once more at #S0001A. Standard barrel lengths for all three generations have been 4-3/4-inch (introduced 1879), 5-1/2-inch (introduced 1875), and 7-1/2-

Colt Python Stainless
Colt Single Action Army (1st Generation)
Colt Python (1995)
Colt Trooper
Colt Trooper MKV
Colt Single Action Army (2nd Generation)
Colt Cowboy

inch (introductory length offered in 1873). During 1st Generation production, any barrel length could be special ordered. Examples are known ranging from 2-1/2-inch to 16-inch. During 2nd and 3rd Generation production, special runs were made as Sheriff's Model with 3-inch barrels and no ejector rod housings. During 2nd and 3rd Generation, Buntline Special versions with 12-inch barrels were cataloged. A 3rd Generation Storekeeper's Model was also cataloged with 4-inch barrel and no ejector rod housing.

Standard finishes for all three generations have been color case-hardened frame with remainder blued, or fully nickel-plated. Some fully-blued SAAs have been offered by Colt from time to time. For 1st Generation, standard grips were one-piece walnut in early production and two-piece hard rubber in later production. Standard grips in 2nd Generation were hard rubber, and both hard rubber and two-piece walnut in 3rd Generation. Standard sights were groove down revolver's topstrap and blade front. However, a rare flattop target model was also offered during 1st Generation run. Caliber options for 1st Generation revolvers numbered approximately thirty, ranging from 22 rimfire to 476 Eley. However, the top five in terms of numbers produced were 45 Colt, 44-40, 38-40, 32-20 and 41 Colt. 2nd Generation calibers in order of numbers produced were 45 Colt, 357 Magnum, 38 Special, 44 Spl. 3rd Generation calibers started in 1976 with 45 Colt and 357 Mag. In 1978, 44 Spl. was added, and in 1980 44-40 was included once more. In 1993, 38-40 was made an option again. 2nd Generation Buntline and Sheriff's Models made only in 45 Colt from 1957 until 1974. 3rd Generation Buntline and Sheriff's Models made in 45 Colt, 44-40, and 44 Spl. calibers from 1980 until 1985. So-called "blackpowder frame" model with screw angling in from front of frame to secure cylinder base pin re-introduced in 1984 and offered as custom feature until early 1990s. During period 1984 to 1994, Colt SAAs could be ordered from Colt Custom Shop with almost any combination of features listed above.

1st Generation (s/n up to 357859, common models)

Exc: $8500 **VGood:** $4500 **Good:** $3000

2nd Generation (s/n #0001SA to #74000SA)

Exc: $1600 **VGood:** $1200 **Good:** $800

3rd Generation (s/n #80000SA to present)

Perf: $1200 **Exc:** $800 **VGood:** $700

COLT SINGLE ACTION (CURRENT PRODUCTION)

Revolver; single action; 32-20, .357, 38 Special, 44-40, 45 Colt, .38-40 6-shot. Barrel: 4-3/4-inch, 5-1/2-inch, 7-1/2-inch. Weight: 40 oz. (4-3/4-inch barrel). Length: 10-1/4-inch overall (4-3/4 inch barrel). Stocks: Black Eagle composite. Sights: Blade front, notch rear. Features: Available in full nickel finish with nickel grip medallions, or Royal Blue with color case-hardened frame, gold grip medallions. Reintroduced 1992.

New: $1200 **Perf:** $1000 **Exc:** $850

COLT COWBOY

Caliber: 45 Colt, 6-shot. Barrel: 5-1/2-inch. Weight: 42 oz. Stocks: Black composition, first generation style. Sights: Blade front, notch rear. Features: Dimensional replica of Colt's original Peacemaker with medium-size color case-hardened frame; transfer bar safety system; half-cock loading. Introduced 1998. Assembled in USA from parts made in Canada.

New: $675 **Perf:** $575 **Exc:** $495

COLT TROOPER

Revolver; double action; 22 LR, 38 Spl., 357 Mag.; 6-shot swing-out cylinder; ramp front sight; choice of standard hammer, service grips, wide hammer spur, target grips. Has the same specs as Officer's Match model except 4-inch barrel. Introduced 1953; dropped 1969.

Exc: $600 **VGood:** $475 **Good:** $400

Target model

Exc: $650 **VGood:** $550 **Good:** $460

Add $250 for 22 LR or 22 Mag

COLT TROOPER MKIII

Revolver; double action; 22 LR, 22 WMR, 38 Spl., 357 Mag.; 4-inch, 6-inch, 8-inch barrels; 9-1/2-inch overall length (4-inch barrel); rear sight fully-adjustable, ramp front; shrouded ejector rod; checkered walnut target grips; target hammer; wide target trigger; blued, nickel finish. Introduced 1969; dropped 1983.

Perf: $600 **Exc:** $500 **VGood:** $400

Nickel finish

Perf: $750 **Exc:** $600 **VGood:** $500

Add $250 for 22 LR or 22 Mag

COLT TROOPER MKV

Same specs as Trooper MKIII with redesigned lock work to reduce double-action trigger pull; faster lock time; redesigned grips; adjustable rear sight, red insert front; 4-inch, 6-inch, 8-inch vent-rib barrel; blued or nickel finish. Introduced 1984; dropped 1988.

Perf: $600 **Exc:** $500 **VGood:** $400

Nickel finish

Perf: $650 **Exc:** $550 **VGood:** $450

COLT VIPER

Revolver; double action; 38 Spl.; 6-shot cylinder; 4-inch barrel; 9-inch overall length; weighs 20 oz.; ramp front, fixed square-notch rear sights; checkered walnut wrap-around grips; lightweight aluminum alloy frame; blue or nickel finish. Uses Colt Cobra frame. Introduced 1977; no longer produced.

Perf: $525 **Exc:** $475 **VGood:** $425

Nickel finish

Perf: $575 **Exc:** $525 **VGood:** $475

COMANCHE I

Single-/double-action revolver chambered in .22 LR. Nine-shot cylinder, 6" barrel, adjustable sights, blued or stainless steel construction with rubber grips.

NIB: $165 **Exc:** $130 **VGood:** $90

COMANCHE II

Similar to above but in .38 Special with 2", 3" or 4" barrel.

NIB: $175 **Exc:** $140 **VGood:** $100

COMANCHE III

Similar to above but in .357 Magnum and additional 6" barrel option.

NIB: $195 **Exc:** $160 **VGood:** $120

COMANCHE SUPER COMANCHE

Single-shot break-action pistol chambered in.410/.45 Colt. Matte black finish, rubber grips.

NIB: $165 **Exc:** $140 **VGood:** $100

COMPETITION ARMS COMPETITOR

Single shot; 22 LR, 223, 7mm TCU, 7mm International, 30 Herrett, 357 Mag., 41 Mag., 454 Casull, 375 Super Mag.; other calibers on special order; 10-inch, 14-inch barrels; adjustable open rear

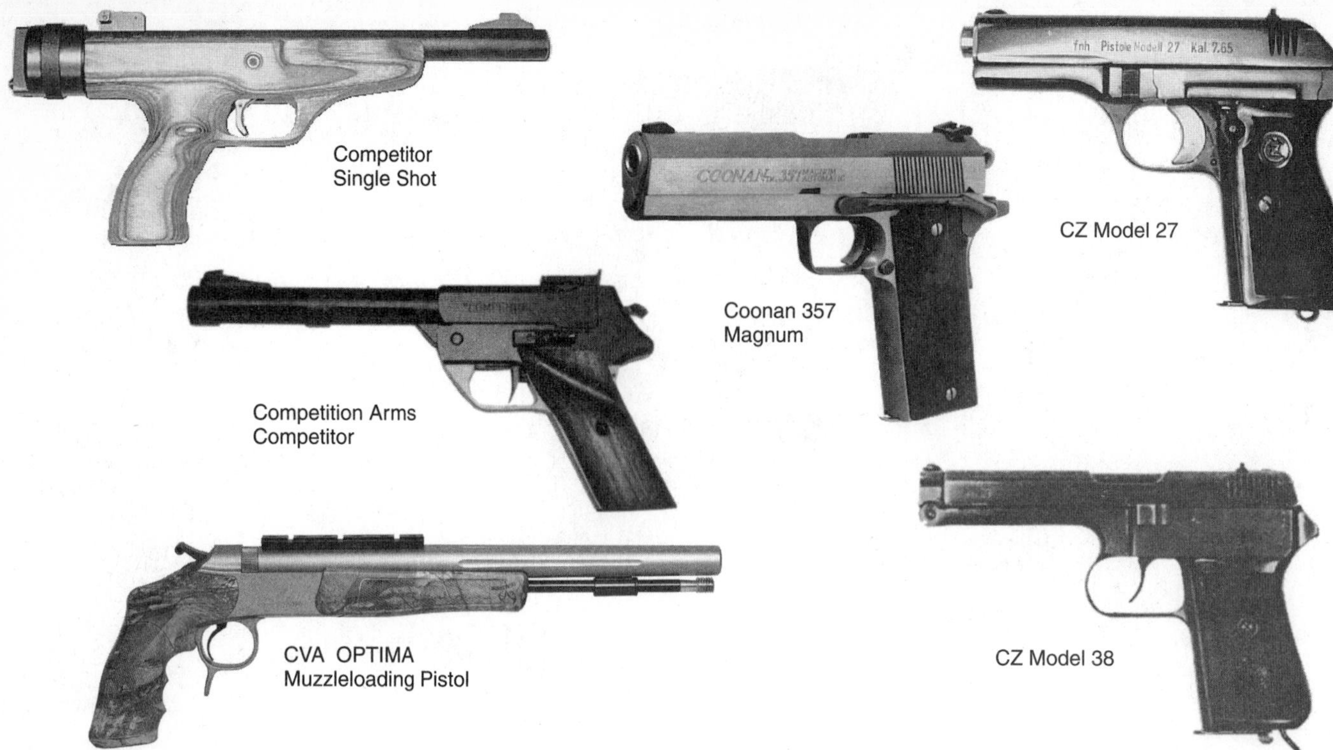
Competitor Single Shot

CZ Model 27

Coonan 357 Magnum

Competition Arms Competitor

CVA OPTIMA Muzzleloading Pistol

CZ Model 38

sight, ramp front; interchangeable barrels of blued ordnance or stainless steel; vent barrel shroud; integral scope mount. Introduced 1987; no longer in production.

Perf: $395 **Exc:** $365 **VGood:** $315

COMPETITOR SINGLE SHOT

Single shot; 22 LR through 50 Action Express, including belted magnums; 14-inch barrel (standard), 10-1/2-inch silhouette, 16-inch (optional); weights about 59 oz. (14-inch barrel); 15-1/8-inch overall length; rotary cannon-type action; ambidextrous synthetic grip (standard) or laminated or natural wood; ramp front sight, adjustable rear; actions cocks on opening; cammed ejector; interchangeable barrels, ejectors; adjustable single-stage trigger; sliding thumb safety and trigger safety; matte blue finish. Made in U.S. by Competitor Corp. Introduced 1988; still produced.

14-inch barrel, standard calibers, synthetic grips

Perf: $395 **Exc:** $365 **VGood:** $315

Extra barrels

Perf: $175 **Exc:** $165 **VGood:** $150

COONAN 357 MAGNUM

Semi-automatic; 357 Mag.; 7-shot magazine; 5-inch barrel; 8-5/16-inch overall length; weighs 42 oz.; smooth walnut stocks; open adjustable sights; barrel hood; many parts interchangeable with Colt autos; grip, hammer, half-cock safeties. Introduced 1983; dropped 1999.

New: $1500 **Perf:** $1200 **Exc:** $900

COONAN 357 MAGNUM CLASSIC

Same specs as 357 Magnum except 8-shot magazine; Teflon black two-tone or Kal-Gard finish; fully-adjustable rear sight; integral compensated barrel. Introduced 1983; dropped 1999.

New: $1550 **Perf:** $1250 **Exc:** $950

COONAN 357 MAGNUM COMPACT CADET

Semi-automatic; single action; 357 Mag.; 6-shot magazine; 3-15/16-inch barrel; weighs 39 oz.; 7-7/8-inch overall length; smooth walnut grips; interchangeable ramp front sight, windage-adjustable rear; linkless bull barrel; full-length recoil spring guide rod; extended slide latch. Introduced 1993; dropped 1999.

New: $1575 **Perf:** $1300 **Exc:** $975

COONAN 357 MAGNUM COMPENSATED MODEL

Same specs as 357 Magnum except 6-inch barrel with compensator. Introduced 1990; dropped 1999.

New: $1550 **Perf:** $1250 **Exc:** $950

CUMBERLAND MOUNTAIN ARMS THE JUDGE SINGLE SHOT

Single shot; 22 Hornet, 22 K-Hornet, 218 Bee, 7-30 Waters, 30-30; 10-inch, 16-inch barrel; walnut grip; bead on ramp front sight, open adjustable rear; break-open design; made of 17-4 stainless steel. Also available as a kit. Made in U.S. by Cumberland Mountain Arms. Introduced 1995; dropped 1999.

Perf: $395 **Exc:** $365 **VGood:** $315

CVA OPTIMA MUZZLELOADING PISTOL

Polymer frame single shot muzzle loading pistol in black and real tree cammo with stainless steel barrel and scope rail. Chambered in .50 Caliber. 14 inch barrel and 3.7 pounds total weight. Introduced 2013.

Perf: $300 **Exc:** $200 **VGood:** $175

CZ/ADCO 1911-A1

Semi-automatic; 38 Super or 45 ACP; standard size Government model; 5-inch barrel; black matte finish. Importation by ADCO began 2004.

Perf: $475 **Exc:** $425 **VGood:** $375

Add $10 to above price for 38 Super chambering

CZ MODEL 22

Semi-automatic; 380 ACP; 8-shot magazine; 3-5/16-inch barrel; 6-inch overall length; weighs 21-7/8 oz.; made under license from Mauser; external hammer; rotating barrel lock system. About 20,000 made 1921 to 1923.

Exc: $600 **VGood:** $425 **Good:** $300

CZ MODEL 24

Semi-automatic; 380 ACP; 8-shot magazine; 3-1/2-inch barrel; 6-inch overall length; weighs 24 oz.; same general design as Model 22 except addition of magazine safety; about 190,000 made. Manufactured from 1924 to 1939.

Exc: $400 **VGood:** $350 **Good:** $300

CZ MODEL 27

Semi-automatic; 32 ACP; 8-shot magazine; 3-13/16-inch barrel; 6-1/2-inch overall length; weighs 25 oz.; vertical retracting grooves on slide; fixed sights; plastic grips; blued finish. Commercial and non-commercial models made until 1939 marked on top rib and left side of frame; post-1941 omit top rib marking; post-war models made until 1951 marked on slide. Manufactured from 1927 to 1951.

Pre-war

Exc: $550 **VGood:** $450 **Good:** $350

Post-1941 — Nazi marked

Exc: $450 **VGood:** $350 **Good:** $300

Post-war

Exc: $300 **VGood:** $250 **Good:** $200

CZ MODEL 38

Semi-automatic; double-action-only; 380 ACP; 8-shot magazine; 4-5/8-inch barrel; 8 1/8-inch overall length; weighs 32 oz.; plastic grips; fixed sights; blued finish. Also listed as CZ Pistole 39(t) during German occupation. Manufactured 1939 to 1945.

Exc: $600 **VGood:** $500 **Good:** $425

CZ MODEL 50

Semi-automatic; double action; 32 ACP; 8-shot; 3-3/4-inch barrel; 6-1/2-inch overall length; weighs 24-3/4 oz.; frame mounted safety catch; loaded chamber indicator. Issued to Czech police as Model VZ50. Manufactured from 1951 to approximately 1967.

Exc: $175 **VGood:** $150 **Good:** $125

CZ MODEL 52

Semi-automatic; 7.62 Tokarev; 8-shot; 4-3/4-inch barrel; 8 1/4-inch overall length; weighs 40 oz.; complex roller locking breech system. Manufactured from 1952 to approximately 1956.

Exc: $300 **VGood:** $275 **Good:** $195

CZ MODEL 75

Semi-automatic; double action or double-action-only; 9mm Para., 40 S&W; 15-shot magazine; 4-3/4-inch barrel; 8-inch overall length; weighs 35 oz.; all-steel frame; adjustable rear sight, square

CZ 75 Shadow

CZ 75 Compact SDP

CZ Model 75

CZ 75 SP-01
Accu-Shadow

CZ Model 97 B

CZ Model 83

post front; checkered plastic; black polymer, matte or high-polish blued finish. Imported from the Czech Republic by CZ-USA.

Perf: $550 **Exc:** $475 **VGood:** $400

CZ 75 COMPACT

Same specs as Model 75 except 10-shot magazine; 3-15/16-inch barrel; weighs 32 oz.; removable front sight; non-glare ribbed slide top; squared and serrated triggerguard; combat hammer. Introduced 1993; imported from the Czech Republic by CZ-USA.

Perf: $550 **Exc:** $475 **VGood:** $400

CZ 75 COMPACT SDP

DA/SA semi-auto compact pistol with blued finish, alloy frame, aluminum grips, de-cocker safety, tritium sights, Heinie Slant Pro rear sight and competition hammer. Chambered in 9mm NATO. 3.7 inch barrel, 7.2 inch OA length and weighs 1.78 pounds. 14+1 capacity. Introduced 2013.

Perf: $1,300 **Exc:** $1,170 **VGood:** $1,000

CZ 75 SEMI-COMPACT

Same specs as Model 75 Compact with shorter slide and barrel on full-size CZ 75 frame; 10-shot magazine; 9mm Para. only. Introduced 1994; imported from the Czech Republic by CZ-USA.

Perf: $550 **Exc:** $475 **VGood:** $400

CZ 75 SHADOW

Single Action Only semi-auto pistol with a blued finish, steel frame, plastic grips, ambidextrous safety, tuned trigger with over-travel adjustment and fiber optic front sight. Chambered in 9mm NATO. 4.6 inch barrel, 8.3 inch OA length and weighs 2.2 pounds. 16+1 capacity. Introduced in 2013.

Perf: $925 **Exc:** $870 **VGood:** $790

CZ 75 SP-01 SHADOW

Chambered 9mm for IPSC "Production" Division competition. 19+1 capacity, 4.72-inch barrel. 41 oz., wood grip.

NIB: $600 **Exc:** $525 **VGood:** $425

CZ 75 SP-01 ACCU-SHADOW

DA/SA semi-auto full sized pistol with blued finish, steel frame, aluminum grips, ambidextrous safety, competition hammer, tuned trigger and adjustable fiber optic front sight and HAJO serrated target rear sight. Chambered in 9mm NATO. 4.6 inch barrel, 8.15 inch OA length and weighs 2.4 pounds. 18+1 capacity. Introduced 2013.

Perf: $1,570 **Exc:** $1,450 **VGood:** $1,270

CZ 75 STAINLESS

All steel construction, double-stack magazines, 3-dot fixed sights and chambered for 9mm. 16+1 or 10+1 capacity with 4.72-inch barrel. The first stainless from CZ. Introduced 2006.

NIB: $650 **Exc:** $550 **VGood:** $475

CZ 75 TACTICAL SPORT

Single-action for IPSC competition. Chambered in 9mm and .40 S&W. Dual tone (nickel/blued). Capacity 20+1 (9mm) or 16+1 (.40 S&W). 5.4-inch barrel; 45 oz.

NIB: $725 **Exc:** $625 **VGood:** $500

CZ 75 TS CZECHMATE

Caliber: 9mm. Custom built for IPSC Limited and Open competition with 20 or 26-round magazine. Barrel: 5.4 inches.
Weight: 48 oz. Many custom features including four-part compensator, ergonomic grip panels, C-More red dot sight and standard Tactical Sports adjustable sight.

Perf: $2650 **Exc:** $2385 **VGood:** $2150

CZ MODEL 83

Semi-automatic; double action; 32 ACP, 380 ACP; 3-13/16-inch barrel; 6-15/16-inch overall length; weighs 261/4 oz; adjustable rear, removable square post front sight; ambidextrous magazine release and safety; non-glare ribbed slide top; high-impact checkered plastic grips; blue finish. Imported from the Czech Republic by CZ-USA.

Perf: $395 **Exc:** $325 **VGood:** $275

CZ MODEL 83 9X18MM MAKAROV

Czech military surplus pistols imported recently. Same specifications as the commercial versions. Made in the 1980's & 90's.

Exc: $300 **VGood:** $250 **Good:** $200

CZ MODEL 85

Semi-automatic; double action or double-action-only; 9mm Para., 40 S&W; 15-shot magazine; 4-3/4-inch barrel; 8-inch overall length; weighs 35 oz.; all-steel frame; ambidextrous slide release and safety levers; non-glare ribbed slide top; squared, serrated trigger- guard; trigger stop to prevent overtravel; adjustable rear sight, square post front; checkered plastic; black polymer, matte or high-polish blued finish. Introduced 1986; imported from the Czech Republic by CZ-USA.

Perf: $550 **Exc:** $475 **VGood:** $400

CZ MODEL 85 COMBAT

Same specs as the Model 85 except walnut grips; round combat hammer; fully-adjustable rear sight; extended magazine release; trigger parts coated with friction-free beryllium copper. Introduced 1992; imported from the Czech Republic by CZ-USA.

Perf: $575 **Exc:** $500 **VGood:** $425

CZ 97 B

DA/SA semi-auto full sized pistol with steel frame and aluminum grips and fiber optic front sight or Tritium three dot sights. Chambered in .45 ACP and available with black polycoat or high gloss black finish. Barrel length 4.8 inches, overall length is 8.3 inches and weighs 2.54 pounds. 10+1 capacity. Introduced 2013.

Perf: $700 **Exc:** $620 **VGood:** $560

CZ 100 AUTO PISTOL

Caliber: 9mm Para., 40 S&W, 10-shot magazine. Barrel: 3.7-inch. Weight: 24 oz. Length: 6.9-inch overall. Stocks: Grooved polymer. Sights: Blade front with dot, white outline rear drift adjustable for windage. Features: Double action only with firing pin block; polymer frame, steel slide; has laser sight mount. Introduced 1996. Imported from the Czech Republic by CZ-USA.

Perf: $425 **Exc:** $365 **VGood:** $295

CZ MODEL 1945

Semi-automatic; double action; 25 ACP; 8-shot magazine; 2-inch barrel; 5-inch overall length; plastic grips; fixed sights; blued finish. Manufactured from 1945 to approximately 1960.

Exc: $300 **VGood:** $250 **Good:** $200

CZ P-07 DUTY

Calibers: 40 S&W, 9mm. Barrel is 3.8 inches, weight is 27.2 oz. and overall length, 7.3 inches. Based on CZ 75 design with improved trigger system. Polymer frame and grips. Has decocking lever installed, comes with interchangeable manual safety. Blade front sight, fixed rear.

Perf: $435 **Exc:** $375 **VGood:** $325

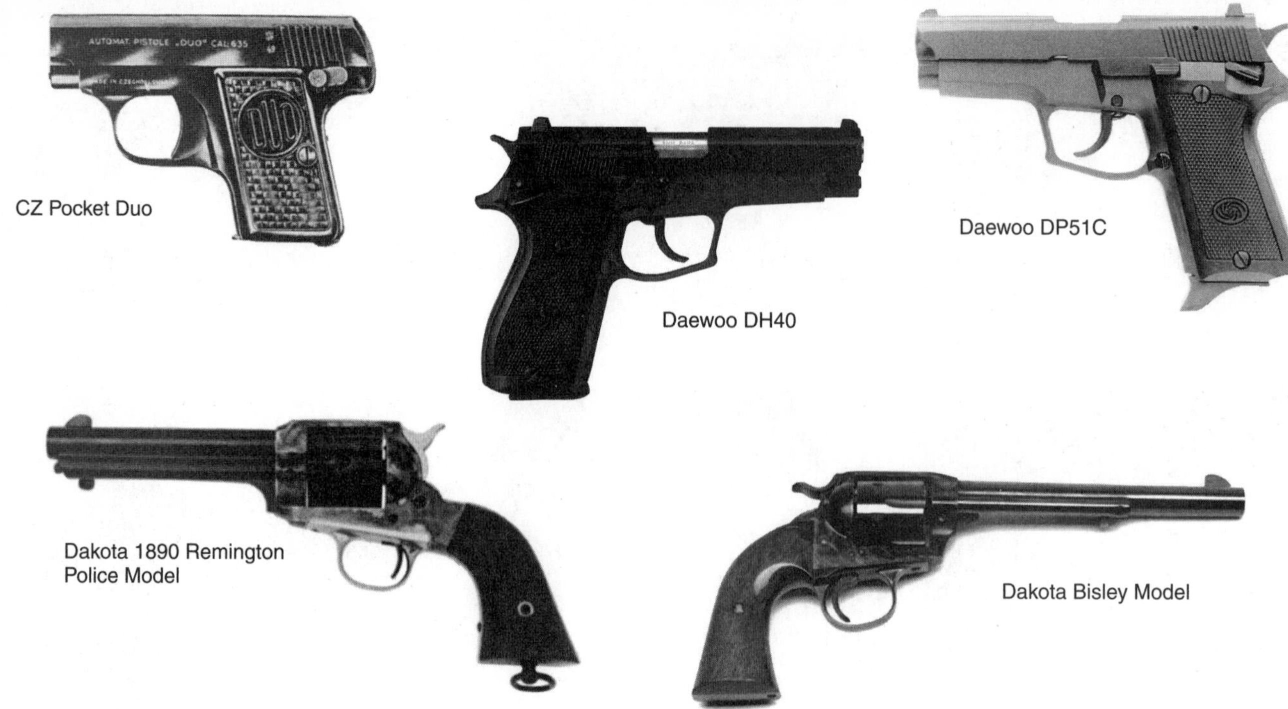
CZ Pocket Duo

Daewoo DH40

Daewoo DP51C

Dakota 1890 Remington Police Model

Dakota Bisley Model

CZ P-09 DUTY

DA/SA semi-auto full sized pistol with a polymer frame and blued finish. Chambered in .40 S&W and 9mm NATO. De-cocker or manual safety and features interchangeable back-straps. Features a 4.35 inch barrel, OA length of 8.1 inch and a weight of 1.85 pounds. 15+1 capacity in .40S&W and 19+1 capacity on 9mm. Introduced 2013.

Perf: $500 **Exc:** $425 **VGood:** $385

CZ POCKET DUO

Semi-automatic; 25 ACP; 6-shot magazine; 2-1/8-inch barrel; 4-1/2-inch overall length; fixed sights; plastic grips; manufactured in Czechoslovakia; blue or nickel finish. Manufactured 1926 to 1960.

Exc: $295 **VGood:** $240 **Good:** $170

CZ-TT

Semi-automatic; 9mm Para., 40 S&W, 45 ACP; 10-shot magazine; single/double action; polymer frame; 3.77-inch ported or unported barrel; matte finish; 26.1 oz. Importation by ADCO began 2004.

Perf: $450 **Exc:** $415 **VGood:** $375

Add $30 to above prices for ported barrel

Add $40 to above prices for ported barrel and slide serrations

Add $399 for caliber conversion kit with one magazine

CZ-T POLYMER COMPACT

Similar to CZ-TT, except has shorter barrel. Importation by ADCO began 2004.

Perf: $475 **Exc:** $425 **VGood:** $375

DAEWOO DH40

Semi-automatic; double action; 40 S&W; 10-shot magazine; 4-1/8-inch barrel; 7-1/2-inch overall length; weighs 28-1/4 oz.; checkered composition grips; 1/8-inch blade front sight, adjustable rear; three-dot system; fast-fire mechanism; ambidextrous manual safety with internal firing pin lock; no magazine safety; alloy frame; squared triggerguard; matte black finish. Formerly imported from Korea by Nationwide Sports Distributors. Introduced 1991; Now imported by Century International Arms, Inc.

Perf: $395 **Exc:** $350 **VGood:** $275

DAEWOO DH380

Semi-automatic; double action; 380 ACP; 8-shot magazine; 3-7/8-inch barrel; 6-3/4-inch overall length; weighs 23 oz.; checkered black composition thumbrest grips; 1/8-inch blade front sight, drift-adjustable rear; three-dot system; all-steel construction; blue finish; dual safety system with hammer block. Formerly imported from Korea by Kimber of America; distributed by Nationwide Sports Dist. Imported by Century International Arms, Inc. Introduced 1994.

Perf: $395 **Exc:** $350 **VGood:** $275

DAEWOO DP51

Semi-automatic; 9mm Para., 40 S&W; 12-shot (40 S&W), 13-shot (9mm) magazine; 4-1/8-inch barrel; 7-1/2-inch overall length; weighs 28-1/4 oz.; blade front, drift-adjustable square-notch rear sight; checkered composition grips; tri-action mechanism; ambidextrous manual safety, magazine catch; half-cock and firing pin block; alloy frame; matte black finish; square triggerguard. Made in Korea. Introduced 1991.

Perf: $395 **Exc:** $350 **VGood:** $275

DAEWOO DP51C

Same specs as the DP51 except 3-5/8-inch barrel; 1/4-inch shorter grip frame; flat mainspring housing; weighs 26 oz. Formerly imported from Korea by by Kimber of America, Inc.. Introduced 1995.

Perf: $395 **Exc:** $350 **VGood:** $275

DAEWOO DP51S

Same specs as the DP51 except 3-5/8-inch barrel; weighs 27 oz. Formerly imported from Korea by Kimber of America, Inc. Introduced 1995.

Perf: $395 **Exc:** $350 **VGood:** $275

DAEWOO DP52

Semi-automatic; double action; 22 LR; 10-shot magazine; 3-7/8-inch barrel; 6-3/4-inch overall length; weighs 23 oz.; checkered black composition thumbrest grips; 1/8-inch blade front sight, drift-adjustable rear; three-dot system; all-steel construction; blue finish; dual safety system with hammer block. Formerly imported from Korea by Kimber of America; distributed by Nationwide Sports Dist. Now imported and distributed by Century International Arms, Inc. Introduced 1994.

Perf: $395 **Exc:** $350 **VGood:** $275

DAKOTA 1873 PREMIER

Revolver; single action; 45 Colt; 6-shot cylinder; 4-5/8-inch, 5-1/2-inch barrel; 10-inch overall length (4-5/8-inch barrel); weighs 39 oz.; blade front, fixed rear sight; smooth walnut grips; reproduction of the 1873 Colt revolver with set-screw for the cylinder pin release; most parts said to interchange with the early Colts; blue finish, color case-hardened frame. Was imported by E.M.F.; no longer imported.

Perf: $525 **Exc:** $450 **VGood:** $275

DAKOTA 1875 REMINGTON OUTLAW MODEL

Revolver; single action; 357 Mag., 44-40, 45 Colt; 7-1/2-inch barrel; 13-1/2-inch overall length; weighs 46 oz.; blade front, fixed groove rear sight; uncheckered walnut stocks; authentic copy of 1875 Remington; color case-hardened frame; blued cylinder, barrel; steel backstrap; brass triggerguard; also made with nickel finish; factory engraving. Made in Italy. Introduced 1986; still imported by EMF.

Perf: $400 **Exc:** $350 **VGood:** $300

Nickel finish

Perf: $450 **Exc:** $400 **VGood:** $350

Engraved

Perf: $500 **Exc:** $450 **VGood:** $400

DAKOTA 1890 REMINGTON POLICE MODEL

Revolver; single action; 357 Mag., 44-40, 45 Colt; 5-1/2-inch barrel; 12-inch overall length; weighs 40 oz.; blade front, fixed groove rear sight; uncheckered walnut stocks; color case-hardened frame; blued cylinder, barrel; steel backstrap; brass trigger guard; lanyard ring in butt; also available in nickel finish, factory engraving. Made in Italy. Introduced 1986; currently imported by EMF.

Perf: $400 **Exc:** $350 **VGood:** $300

Nickel finish

Perf: $450 **Exc:** $400 **VGood:** $350

Dakota New Model Single Action

Dakota Hartford Model

Dan Wesson Elite Series Mayhem

Dan Wesson RZ-10

Dan Wesson Valor 1911

Engraved

Perf: $500 **Exc:** $450 **VGood:** $400

DAKOTA BISLEY MODEL

Revolver; single action; 22 LR, 22 WMR, 32-20, 32 H&R Mag., 357 Mag., 38-40, 44 Spl., 44-40, 45 Colt, 45 ACP; 4-3/4-inch, 5-1/2-inch, 7-1/2-inch barrels; 10-1/2-inch overall length (5-1/2-inch barrel); weighs 37 oz.; blade front, fixed groove rear sight; uncheckered walnut stocks; color case-hardened frame; blued barrel, cylinder; steel trigger guard, backstrap; Colt-type firing pin on hammer. Also available with nickel finish, factory engraving. Made in Italy. Introduced 1985; dropped 1991; reintroduced, 1993.

Perf: $400 **Exc:** $325 **VGood:** $275

Nickel finish

Perf: $425 **Exc:** $350 **VGood:** $300

Engraved

Perf: $600 **Exc:** $550 **VGood:** $500

DAKOTA HARTFORD MODEL

Revolver; single action; 22 LR, 32-20, 357 Mag., 38-40, 44 Spl., 45 Colt; 4-3/4-inch, 5-1/2-inch, 7-1/2-inch barrel; blade front, fixed rear sight; one-piece walnut stock; identical to original Colts; all major parts serial numbered with original Colt-type lettering, numbers; color case-hardened frame, hammer; various options. Made in Italy. Introduced 1990; still imported by EMF.

Perf: $400 **Exc:** $350 **VGood:** $300

Nickel plated

Perf: $500 **Exc:** $450 **VGood:** $400

Calvary or Artillery models

Perf: $400 **Exc:** $350 **VGood:** $300

Cattlebrand engraved

Perf: $500 **Exc:** $450 **VGood:** $400

Engraved nickel

Perf: $600 **Exc:** $550 **VGood:** $500

DAKOTA HARTFORD MODEL PINKERTON

Same specs as Hartford Model except 4-inch barrel; 45 Colt; bird's-head walnut grips; ejector tube. Introduced 1994; still in production.

Perf: $350 **Exc:** $300 **VGood:** $250

DAKOTA NEW MODEL SINGLE ACTION

Revolver; single action; 357 Mag., 44-40, 45 Colt; 6-shot; 4-3/4-inch, 5-1/2-inch, 7-1/2-inch barrel; blade front, fixed rear sight; one-piece walnut stock; Colt-type hammer, firing pin; nickel or color case-hardened forged frame; black nickel backstrap, triggerguard; also available in nickel finish. Made in Italy. Introduced 1991; currently imported by EMF.

Perf: $300 **Exc:** $250 **VGood:** $200

Nickel finish

Perf: $350 **Exc:** $300 **VGood:** $250

Engraved, nickel-plated

Perf: $400 **Exc:** $350 **VGood:** $300

DAKOTA OLD MODEL SINGLE ACTION

Revolver; single action; 22 LR, 32-20, 357 Mag., 38-40, 44 Spl., 44-40, 45 Colt; 6-shot cylinder; 4-5/8-inch, 5-1/2-inch, 7-1/2-inch barrel; blade front, fixed rear sight; one-piece walnut stocks; color case-hardened frame; brass grip frame, triggerguard; blued barrel cylinder; also available in nickel finish. Made in Italy. Introduced 1967; sporadic production. Was imported by EMF.

Perf: $375 **Exc:** $325 **VGood:** $250

Nickel finish

Perf: $395 **Exc:** $295 **VGood:** $225

DAKOTA SHERIFF'S MODEL

Revolver; single action; 32-20, 357 Mag., 38-40, 44 Spl., 44-40, 45 Colt; 6-shot; 3-1/2-inch barrel; blade front, fixed rear sight; one-piece walnut stock; blued finish. Made in Italy. Introduced 1994; was imported by EMF.

Perf: $415 **Exc:** $335 **VGood:** $300

DAN WESSON ELITE SERIES HAVOC

Caliber: 9mm and 38 Super, 21-round magazine capacity. Barrel: 4.25 inches. Weight: 35 oz. Length: 8 inches. Limited production competition model based on high-capacity all-steel 1911 frame.

Perf: $4100 **Exc:** $3750 **VGood:** $3250

DAN WESSON ELITE SERIES MAYHEM

Similar to Havoc model except chambered for 40 S&W with 18-shot magazine capacity, with 6-inch bull barrel. Weight: 38.7 oz. Length: 8.75 inches.

Perf: $3600 **Exc:** $3150 **VGood:** $2800

DAN WESSON ELITE SERIES TITAN

Similar to Havoc and Mayhem models. Chambered for 10mm with 21-shot magazine capacity. Barrel: 4.25 inches. Weight: 26 oz. Length: 8 inches.

Perf: $3850 **Exc:** $3500 **VGood:** $3000

DAN WESSON VALOR 1911

Caliber: 45 ACP. Full-size 1911 style pistol featuring Slim Line G10 checkered grips, Heinie Ledge Straight Eight adjustable night sights, match barrel and stainless finish.

Perf: $1375 **Exc:** $1200 **VGood:** $950

Add 20 percent for black finish

DAN WESSON VH8

.445 SuperMag revolver designed for barrel interchangeability. Also fires standard .44-caliber rounds. Stainless, 6-shot; 8-inch barrel, 4.1 lb. Single/double action. Other chamberings offered; demand for these varies.

NIB: $1300 **Exc:** $1000 **VGood:** $775

DAN WESSON RZ-10

10mm single-action semi-auto with 8+1 capacity. 5-inch barrel, 2.4 lb. Fixed sights.

NIB: $1010 **Exc:** $910 **VGood:** $785

DAVIS BIG-BORE DERRINGERS

Derringer; over/under; 22 WMR, 32 H&R Mag., 38 Spl., 9mm Para.; 2-shot; 2-3/4-inch barrels; 4-9/16-inch overall length; weighs about 14 oz.; textured black synthetic grips; fixed sights; chrome or black teflon finish. Larger than the Davis D-Series models. Formerly made in U.S. by Davis Industries. Introduced 1995; still produced by Cobra Enterprises of Salt Lake City, UT.

Perf: $125 **Exc:** $100 **VGood:** $75

Desert Industries War Eagle

Davis P-32

Desert Industries Double Deuce

Detonics Pocket 9LS

Detonics Combat Master Mark V

Detonics Scoremaster

DAVIS D-SERIES DERRINGERS

Derringer over/under; 22 WMR, 32 H&R, 38 Spl; 2-shot; 2-3/8-inch barrels; 4-inch overall length; weighs about 11-1/2 oz.; textured black synthetic grips; blade front, fixed notch rear sight; alloy frame; steel-lined barrels; steel breechblock; plunger-type safety with integral hammer block; chrome or black Teflon finish. Formerly made in U.S. by Davis Industries. Introduced 1992; still produced by Cobra Enterprises of Salt Lake City, UT.

Perf: $125 **Exc:** $100 **VGood:** $75

DAVIS LONG-BORE DERRINGERS

Derringer over/under; 22 WMR, 32 H&R Mag., 38 Spl., 9mm Para.; 2-shot; 3-1/2-inch barrels; 5-3/8-inch overall length; weighs 16 oz.; textured black synthetic grips; fixed sights; chrome or black teflon finish. Larger than the Davis D-Series models. Formerly made in U.S. by Davis Industries. Introduced 1995; still produced by Cobra Enterprises of Salt Lake City, UT.

Perf: $125 **Exc:** $100 **VGood:** $75

DAVIS P-32

Semi-automatic; double action; 32 ACP; 6-shot magazine; 2-13/16-inch barrel; 5-3/8-inch overall length; weighs 22 oz.; laminated wood stocks; fixed sights; chrome or black Teflon finish. Introduced 1986; still in production by Cobra Enterprises of Salt Lake City, UT.

Perf: $125 **Exc:** $100 **VGood:** $75

DAVIS P-380

Semi-automatic; double action; 380 ACP; 5-shot magazine; 2-13/16-inch barrel; 5-7/16-inch overall length; weighs 22 oz.; fixed sights; black composition grips; chrome or black Teflon finish. Introduced 1991; still in production by Cobra Enterprises of Salt Lake City, UT.

Perf: $125 **Exc:** $100 **VGood:** $75

DESERT INDUSTRIES DOUBLE DEUCE

Semi-automatic; double action; 22 LR; 6-shot; 2-1/2-inch barrel; 5-1/2-inch overall length; weighs 15 oz.; fixed groove sights; smooth rosewood grips; ambidextrous slide-mounted safety; stainless steel construction; matte finish. Manufactured 1991-1996.

Perf: $350 **Exc:** $295 **VGood:** $275

DESERT INDUSTRIES TWO-BIT SPECIAL

Semi-automatic; double action; 25 ACP; 5-shot; 2-1/2-inch barrel; 5-1/2-inch overall length; weighs 15 oz.; fixed groove sights; smooth rosewood grips; ambidextrous slide-mounted safety; stainless steel construction; matte finish. Introduced 1991; only about 12 prototypes were produced.

Perf: $375 **Exc:** $350 **VGood:** $295

DESERT INDUSTRIES WAR EAGLE

Semi-automatic; double action; 380 ACP, 9mm Para., 40 S&W, 10mm Auto, 45 ACP; 10-shot, 14-shot (9mm), 8-shot (380 ACP); 4-inch barrel; fixed sights; rosewood grips; stainless steel construction; matte finish. Introduced 1991. No longer produced.

Perf: $700 **Exc:** $650 **VGood:** $550

DETONICS COMBAT MASTER MARK I

Semi-automatic; 9mm Para., 38 Super, 45 ACP; 6-shot magazine (45 ACP); 3-1/2-inch barrel; 6-3/4-inch overall length; weighs 28 oz.; fixed or adjustable combat-type sights; checkered walnut stocks; throated barrel; polished feed ramp; self-adjusting cone barrel centering system; beveled magazine inlet; full-clip indicator; two-tone matte blue and stainless finish. Introduced 1977; discontinued 1992.

Perf: $850 **Exc:** $700 **VGood:** $600

DETONICS COMBAT MASTER MARK V

Same specs as Combat Master I except all matte stainless finish. Introduced 1977; discontinued 1985.

Perf: $800 **Exc:** $650 **VGood:** $600

DETONICS COMBAT MASTER MARK VI

Same specs as Combat Master Mark I except 451 Detonics Mag.; adjustable sights; polished stainless steel slide. Introduced 1977; discontinued 1989.

Perf: $995 **Exc:** $750 **VGood:** $600

DETONICS COMBAT MASTER MARK VII

Same specs as Combat Master Mark VI except no sights as special order option. Introduced 1977; discontinued 1982.

Perf: $895 **Exc:** $750 **VGood:** $650

DETONICS COMPMASTER

Semi-automatic; 45 ACP; 7-, 8-shot magazine; 5-inch, 6-inch barrel; Millet adjustable sights; checkered Pachmayr stocks; matching mainspring housing; Detonics recoil system; extended grip safety; ambidextrous safety; extended magazine release; stainless steel. Introduced 1988; discontinued 1992.

Perf: $1895 **Exc:** $1400 **VGood:** $1200

DETONICS MARK I

Semi-automatic; 45 ACP; 6-shot magazine; 3-1/2-inch barrel; 6-3/4-inch overall length; weighs 29 oz.; fixed sights; adjustable rear sights available; checkered walnut stocks; compact based on Model 1911; blued finish. Introduced 1977; discontinued 1981.

Perf: $595 **Exc:** $500 **VGood:** $450

DETONICS MARK II

Same specs as Mark I except satin nickel plated. Introduced 1977; discontinued 1979.

Perf: $675 **Exc:** $550 **VGood:** $500

DETONICS MARK III

Same specs as Mark I except hard chrome plated. Introduced 1977; discontinued 1979.

Perf: $675 **Exc:** $500 **VGood:** $425

DETONICS MARK IV

Same specs as Mark I except polished blue finish. Introduced 1977; discontinued 1981.

Perf: $695 **Exc:** $525 **VGood:** $450

DETONICS MILITARY COMBAT MC2

Semi-automatic; 38 Super, 9mm Para., 45 ACP; 6-shot magazine; 3-1/2-inch barrel; 6-3/4-inch overall length; weighs 29 oz.; fixed sights; Pachmayr grips;

D-Max Sidewinder

Dreyse Vest Pocket Model

Dreyse Model 1907 (Early model)

Diamondback DB9

Diamondback DB380

E.A.A. Big Bore Bounty Hunter

Downsizer WSP

camo pistol rug; matte finish. Introduced 1977; discontinued 1984.

Perf: $675 **Exc:** $550 **VGood:** $475

DETONICS POCKET 9

Semi-automatic; double action; 9mm Para.; 6-shot; 3-inch barrel; 5-11/16-inch overall length; weighs 26 oz.; fixed sights; black Micarta stocks; triggerguard hook; snag-free hammer; captive recoil spring; matte stainless steel finish. Introduced 1985; dropped 1986.

Perf: $400 **Exc:** $300 **VGood:** $250

DETONICS POCKET 9LS

Same specs as Pocket 9 except 4-inch barrel; weighs 28 oz. Introduced 1986; discontinued 1986.

Perf: $450 **Exc:** $375 **VGood:** $300

DETONICS POCKET 380

Same specs as Pocket 9 except in 380 ACP; weighs 23 oz. Introduced 1986; discontinued 1986.

Perf: $400 **Exc:** $350 **VGood:** $300

DETONICS POWER 9

Semi-automatic; double-action; 9mm Para.; 6-shot; 4-inch barrel; weighs 28 oz.; polished slide flats; fixed sights; black Micarta stocks; triggerguard hook; snag-free hammer; captive recoil spring; matte stainless steel finish. Introduced 1985; dropped 1986.

Perf: $525 **Exc:** $450 **VGood:** $400

DETONICS SCOREMASTER

Semi-automatic; 45 ACP, 451 Detonics Mag.; 7-, 8-shot; 5-inch, 6-inch barrel; 8-3/4-inch overall length (5-inch barrel); weighs 41 oz.; Millet adjustable sights; checkered Pachmayr stocks, matching mainspring housing; Detonics recoil system; extended grip safety; ambidextrous safety; extended magazine release; stainless steel. Introduced, 1983; discontinued, 1992.

Perf: $950 **Exc:** $800 **VGood:** $700

DETONICS SERVICEMASTER

Semi-automatic; 45 ACP; 8-shot magazine; 4-1/4-inch barrel; 7-7/8-inch overall length; weighs 39 oz.; adjustable combat sights; Pachmayr rubber stocks; extended grip safety; thumb and grip safeties; stainless steel construction; matte finish. Introduced 1977; discontinued 1986.

Perf: $875 **Exc:** $700 **VGood:** $600

DETONICS SERVICEMASTER II

Same specs as Servicemaster except polished slide flats. Introduced 1986; discontinued 1992.

Perf: $800 **Exc:** $650 **VGood:** $550

DIAMONDBACK DB380

Caliber: 380, 6+1-shot capacity. Striker-fired, double-action-only design on polymer frame. Barrel length, 2.8 inches; weight, 8.8 oz. Adjustable rear sight.

Perf: $265 **Exc:** $235 **VGood:** $200

DIAMONDBACK DB9

Similar to DB380 except in 9mm. Three-inch barrel, 6+1 capacity. Weight is 11 oz and overall length 5.6 inches.

Perf: $325 **Exc:** $275 **VGood:** $235

DOWNSIZER WSP

Single shot; 22 WMR, 32 H&R Mag., 380 ACP, 9mm Para, 357 Magnum, 40 S&W, 45 ACP. Barrel: 2.10-inch. Weight: 11 oz. Length: 3.25-inch overall. Stocks: Black polymer. Sights: None. Features: Single shot, tip-up barrel. Double action only. Stainless steel construction. Measures .900-inch thick. Introduced 1997. From Downsizer Corp.

Perf: $435 **Exc:** $350 **VGood:** $300

D-MAX SIDEWINDER

Revolver; single action; 45 Colt/410 shotshell; 6-shot cylinder; 6-1/2-inch, 7-1/2-inch barrel; 14-1/8-inch overall length (6-1/2-inch barrel); weighs 57 oz. (6-1/2-inch barrel); Hogue black rubber grips with finger grooves; blade on ramp front sight, fully-adjustable rear; stainless steel construction; removable choke for firing shotshells; grooved, wide-spur hammer; transfer bar ignition; satin finish. Made in U.S. by D-Max, Inc. Introduced 1992; still produced.

Perf: $700 **Exc:** $650 **VGood:** $600

DREYSE MODEL 1907

Semi-automatic; 32 ACP; 8-shot magazine; 3-1/2-inch barrel; 6-1/4-inch overall length; fixed sights; hard rubber checkered stocks; blued finish. Manufactured in Germany, 1907 to 1920. Very early model shown brings a premium.

Exc: $250 **VGood:** $185 **Good:** $150

DREYSE VEST POCKET MODEL

Semi-automatic; 25 ACP; 6-shot magazine; 2-inch barrel; 4-1/2-inch overall length; fixed sights; checkered hard rubber grips; blued finish. Manufactured 1909 to 1914.

Exc: $325 **VGood:** $235 **Good:** $150

DREYSE MODEL 1910

Manufactured 1912-1915; 9mm Para.; about 1,000 pieces were produced; very rare.

Perf: $6500 **Exc:** $5500 **VGood:** $4500

DWM POCKET MODEL

Semi-automatic; 32 ACP; 3-1/2-inch barrel; 6-inch overall length; hard rubber checkered stocks; blued finish. Design resembles Browning FN Model 1910. Manufactured in Germany, 1920 to 1931.

Exc: $600 **VGood:** $500 **Good:** $425

DSA B&T TP9 TACTICAL PISTOL

Swiss made recoil-operated, rotating-bolt semi-auto chambered in 9mm Parabellum. Semi-auto, civilian-legal version of B&T TP9SF select-fire submachine gun. Planned to be imported in 2007.

New.: $2200 **Exc:** $2000 **Good:** $1750

E.A.A. BIG BORE BOUNTY HUNTER

Revolver; single action; 357 Mag., 44 Mag., 45 Colt; 6-shot cylinder; 4-1/2-inch, 7-1/2-inch barrel; 11-inch overall length (4-5/8-inch barrel); weighs 2-1/2 lbs.; smooth walnut grips; blade front sight, grooved topstrap rear; transfer bar safety; three-position hammer; hammer-forged barrel; blue, nickel or case-hardened frame. Imported by European American Armory. Introduced 1992; still imported.

Blue or case-hardened frame

Perf: $315 **Exc:** $255 **VGood:** $205

Nickel finish

Perf: $345 **Exc:** $285 **VGood:** $235

E.A.A. BOUNTY HUNTER

Revolver; single action; 22 LR, 22 WMR; 6-shot cylinder; 4-3/4-inch, 6-inch, 9-inch barrel; 10-inch overall length (4-3/4-inch barrel); weighs 32 oz.; European hardwood grips; blade front sight, adjustable rear; blue finish only. From European

E.A.A. Windicator Standard Grade

E.A.A. Witness Gold Team

Ed Brown Kobra Carry LW

EntrEprise Elite P500

E.A.A. Witness

American Armory Corp. Introduced 1991; no longer available.

Perf: $160 **Exc:** $145 **VGood:** $135

4-3/4-inch, 9-inch barrel; 22 LR/22 WMR combo

Perf: $210 **Exc:** $175 **VGood:** $150

E.A.A. EA22T TARGET

Semi-automatic; 22 LR; 12-shot magazine; 6-inch barrel; 9-1/8-inch overall length; weighs 40 oz.; ramped blade front sight, fully-adjustable rear; checkered walnut grips; thumbrest; blued finish. Made in Italy. Introduced 1991; no longer imported.

Perf: $375 **Exc:** $295 **VGood:** $260

E.A.A. EUROPEAN 320

Semi-automatic; 22 LR, 32 ACP; 380 ACP, 10-shot (22), 7-shot (32 ACP, 380 ACP); 3-7/8-inch barrel; 7-3/8-inch overall length; weighs 26 oz.; fixed blade front sight, windage-adjustable rear; European hardwood grips; magazine, thumb and firing pin safeties; external hammer; safety-lever; chrome or blued finish. Made in Italy. Introduced 1991; dropped 1995. Formerly imported by European American Armory Corp.

Perf: $130 **Exc:** $110 **VGood:** $95

E.A.A. EUROPEAN 380/DA

Revolver; double action; 380 ACP; 7-shot; 3-7/8-inch barrel; 7-3/8-inch overall length; 26 oz.; double-action trigger mechanism; steel construction; blue, chrome or blue/chrome finish. From European American Armory Corp. Introduced 1992; dropped 2001. Blue finish.

Perf: $145 **Exc:** $115 **VGood:** $95

Chrome finish or blue/chrome finish

Perf: $160 **Exc:** $130 **VGood:** $110

E.A.A. EUROPEAN 380 LADIES

Same specs as European 380/DA except blue or gold finish; ivory polymer grips. From European American Armory Corp.

Perf: $200 **Exc:** $175 **VGood:** $150v

E.A.A. WINDICATOR STANDARD GRADE

Revolver; double action; 22 LR, 22 LR/22 WMR combo, 38 Spl.; 8-shot cylinder (22 LR, 22 LR/22 WMR); 6-shot cylinder (38 Spl.); 4-inch, 6-inch barrel (22); 2-inch, 4-inch barrel (38 Spl.); 8-13/16-inch overall length (4-inch barrel); weighs 38 oz. (22, 4-inch barrel); rubber grips with finger grooves; blade front sight, fixed or adjustable (22); fixed sights (32, 38 Spl. only); swing-out cylinder; hammer-block safety; blue finish. Imported from Germany by European American Armory Corp. Introduced 1991.

38 Special, 2-inch barrel

Perf: $205 **Exc:** $170 **VGood:** $145

22 LR, 6-inch barrel, 38 Special, 4-inch barrel

Perf: $140 **Exc:** $120 **VGood:** $110

22 LR/22 WMR combo, 4-inch or 6-inch barrel

Perf: $280 **Exc:** $245 **VGood:** $225

E.A.A. WINDICATOR TACTICAL GRADE

Revolver; double action; 38 Spl.; 2-inch, 4-inch barrel; fixed sights; compensator on 4-inch; bobbed hammer (DA only) on 2-inch model. Imported from Germany by European American Armory Corp. Introduced 1991; no longer imported.

2-inch barrel, bobbed hammer

Perf: $200 **Exc:** $175 **VGood:** $150

4-inch barrel, compensator

Perf: $250 **Exc:** $225 **VGood:** $200

E.A.A. WINDICATOR TARGET GRADE

Revolver; double action; 22 LR, 38 Spl., 357 Mag.; 8-shot cylinder (22 LR); 6-shot (38 Spl., 357 Mag.); 6-inch barrel; 11-13/16-inch overall length; weighs 50 oz.; walnut competition-style grips; blade front sight with three interchangeable blades, fully-adjustable rear; adjustable trigger with trigger stop and trigger shoe; frame drilled and tapped for scope mount; target hammer; comes with barrel weights, plastic carrying box. Imported from Germany by European American Armory Corp. Introduced 1991; dropped 1993.

Perf: $350 **Exc:** $300 **VGood:** $250

E.A.A. WITNESS

Semi-automatic; 9mm Para., 40 S&W, 41 AE, 45 ACP; 16-shot (9mm), 12-shot (40 S&W), 11-shot (41 AE), 10-shot (45 ACP); 4-11/16-inch barrel; 8-1/8-inch overall length; weighs 35-3/8 oz.; undercut blade front, open adjustable rear sight; squared-off triggerguard; frame mounted safety; checkered rubber grips; blue, satin chrome finish.

9mm, blue finish

Perf: $475 **Exc:** $250 **VGood:** $200

9mm, satin finis3

Perf: $485 **Exc:** $275 **VGood:** $225

40 S&W, blue finish

Perf: $495 **Exc:** $315 **VGood:** $250

40 S&W, satin finish

Perf: $500 **Exc:** $325 **VGood:** $275

45 ACP, blue finish

Perf: $500 **Exc:** $325 **VGood:** $275

45 ACP, satin finish

Perf: $525 **Exc:** $350 **VGood:** $300

41 AE

Perf: $525 **Exc:** $350 **VGood:** $300

E.A.A. WITNESS COMPACT

Same specs as Witness except 9mm, 40 S&W, 45 ACP; 10-shot (9mm), 9-shot (40 S&W), 8-shot (45 ACP); 3-5/8-inch barrel; 7-1/4-inch overall length; weighs 30 oz.; blue or hard chrome finish. Introduced 1995; still in production.

New: $300 **Perf:** $275 **Exc:** $250

45 ACP

New: $350 **Perf:** $300 **Exc:** $275

E.A.A. WITNESS GOLD TEAM

Semi-automatic; single action; 9mm Para., 9x21, 38 Super, 10mm, 40 S&W, 45 ACP; 10-shot magazine; 5-1/8-inch barrel; 9-5/8-inch overall length; weighs 41-1/2 oz.; checkered walnut competition-style grips; square post front sight, fully-adjustable rear; triple-chamber cone compensator; competition SA trigger; extended safety and magazine release; competition hammer; beveled magazine well; beavertail grip; hand-fitted major components; match-grade barrel; hard chrome finish. From E.A.A. Custom Shop. Marketed by European American Armory Corp. Introduced 1992; still offered.

Perf: $1500 **Exc:** $1225 **VGood:** $995

E.A.A. WITNESS SILVER TEAM

Semi-automatic; single action; 9mm Para., 9x21, 38 Super, 10mm, 40 S&W, 45 ACP; 10-shot magazine; 5-1/8-inch barrel; 9-5/8-inch overall length; weighs 41-1/2 oz.; black rubber grips; square post front sight, fully-adjustable rear; double-chamber compensator; competition SA trigger; extended safety; oval magazine release; competition hammer; beveled magazine well; beavertail grip; hand-fitted major components; match-grade barrel; double-dip blue finish. Comes with Super Sight and drilled and tapped for scope mount. Built for the intermediate competition shooter. From E.A.A. Custom Shop. Marketed by European American Armory Corp. Introduced 1992; still offered.

Perf: $895 **Exc:** $750 **VGood:** $655

Entréprise Tactical P500

Erma ER 773

Erma ER 777

Entréprise Boxer P500

Erma ESP-85A Target

E.A.A. WITNESS ELITE MATCH

Single action semi-auto featuring 4.5-inch polygonal rifled steel barrel, adjustable rear sights, rubber grips. Two-tone finish. Chambered for 9 mm (18+1), 10 mm (15+1), 38 Super (15+1), .40 S&W (15+1) and .45 ACP (10+1). 33 oz.

NIB: $560 **Exc:** $495 **VGood:** $375

WITNESS FCP

Novel semi-auto pistol that uses reusable tubular chambers that encase each cartridge. Chambered in .45 ACP, .38 Special, .380 ACP, 9mm Parabellum, .40 S&W, and .38 Super. Six-shot capacity. Built on EAA Witness polymer frame. Introduced 2007. As of this writing, this gun seems not to be generally available, and, like so many things in the gun business, it's unknown whether it ever will be.

New: $300 **Perf:** $275 **Exc:** $250

E.A.A. ZASTAVA EZ PISTOL

CZ75 clone. Single-/double-action pistol with four-inch (Full Size) or 3.5-inch (Compact) barrel, polymer frame. Chambered in 9mm, .40 S&W or .45 ACP. Magazine capacity varies from 7 rounds (.45 ACP) to 15 (9mm).

New: $425 **Perf:** $375 **Exc:** $300

ED BROWN KOBRA CARRY LW

Caliber: 45 ACP. Commander-style 1911 with 4.25-inch barrel, 27-oz. weight. Hogue exotic wood grips, 10-8 Performance U-notch rear sight, fixed front with white outlines. Aluminum frame with Bobtail housing, stainless slide with matte finish.

Perf: $2600 **Exc:** $2235 **VGood:** $1900

ENTRÉPRISE ELITE P500

Semi-automatic; 45 ACP, 10-shot magazine. Barrel: 5-inch. Weight: 40 oz. Length: 8-1/2-inch overall. Stocks: Black ultra-slim, double diamond, checkered synthetic. Sights: Dovetailed blade front, rear adjustable for windage; three-dot system. Features: Reinforced dust cover; lowered and flared ejection port; squared trigger guard; adjustable match trigger; bolstered front strap; high grip cut; high ride beavertail grip safety; steel flat mainspring housing; extended thumb lock; skeletonized hammer, match grade sear, disconnector; Wolff springs. Introduced 1998. Made in U.S. by Entreprise Arms. Discontinued.

Perf: $625 **Exc:** $565 **VGood:** $500

ENTRÉPRISE TACTICAL P500

Similar to the Elite model except has Tactical2 Ghost Ring sight or Novak lo-mount sight; ambidextrous thumb safety; front and rear slide serrations; full-length guide rod; throated barrel, polished ramp; tuned match extractor; fitted barrel and bushing; stainless firing pin; slide lapped to frame; dehorned. Introduced 1998. Made in U.S. by Entreprise Arms. Discontinued.

Perf: $875 **Exc:** $750 **VGood:** $650

ENTRÉPRISE MEDALIST P500

Similar to the Elite model except has adjustable Competizione "melded" rear sight with dovetailed Patridge front; machined slide parallel rails with polished breech face and barrel channel; front and rear slide serrations; lowered and flared ejection port; full-length one-piece guide rod with plug; National Match barrel and bushing; stainless firing pin; tuned match extractor; oversize firing pin stop; throated barrel and polished ramp; slide lapped to frame. Introduced 1998. Made in U.S. by Entreprise Arms. Discontinued.

Perf: $875 **Exc:** $750 **VGood:** $675

ENTRÉPRISE BOXER P500

Similar to the Medalist model except has adjustable Competizione "melded" rear sight with dovetailed Patridge front; high mass chiseled slide with sweep cut; machined slide parallel rails; polished breech face and barrel channel. Introduced 1998. Made in U.S. by Entréprise Arms. Discontinued.

Perf: $875 **Exc:** $750 **VGood:** $650

ENTRÉPRISE TOURNAMENT SHOOTER MODEL I

Semi-automatic; 45 ACP, 10-shot magazine. Barrel: 5-inch. Weight: 40 oz. Length: 8-1/2 inch overall. Stocks: Black ultra-slim double diamond checkered synthetic. Sights: Dovetailed Patridge front, adjustable Competizione "melded" rear. Features: Oversized magazine release button; flared magazine well; fully machined parallel slide rails; polished barrel channel and breech face; front and rear slide serrations; serrated top slide; stainless ramped bull barrel & fully supported chamber; full-length guide rod with plug; stainless firing pin; match extractor; polished ramp; tuned match extractor; hard chrome finish. Introduced 1998. Made in U.S. by Entreprise Arms. Discontinued.

Perf: $1850 **Exc:** $1600 **VGood:** $1450

ERMA ER 772

Revolver; double action; 22 LR; 6-shot; 6-inch shrouded barrel; 11-3/16-inch overall length; blade front, adjustable micro rear sight; sporting or adjustable match-type walnut stocks; solid rib; blued finish. Made in Germany. Introduced 1989.

Perf: $550 **Exc:** $450 **VGood:** $350

ERMA ER 773

Revolver; double action; 32 S&W Long; 6-shot; 6-inch shrouded barrel; 11-3/16-inch overall length; weighs 46 oz.; blade front, adjustable micro rear sight; sporting or adjustable match-type walnut stocks; solid rib; blued finish. Made in Germany. Introduced 1989; dropped 1995.

Perf: $1100 **Exc:** $825 **VGood:** $695

ERMA ER 777

Revolver; double action; 357 Mag.; 6-shot; 4-inch, 5-1/2-inch shrouded barrel; 9-1/2-inch overall length (4-inch barrel); weighs 44 oz.; blade front, adjustable micro rear sight; checkered sport grips; solid rear; blued finish. Made in Germany. Introduced 1989; dropped 1995.

Perf: $875 **Exc:** $775 **VGood:** $650

ERMA ESP-85A SPORTING/MATCH TARGET

Semi-automatic; single action; 22 LR, 32 S&W Long; 8-shot (22 LR), 5-shot (32 S&W Long); 6-inch barrel; 10-inch overall length; weighs 40 oz.; checkered walnut thumbrest grips; adjustable target stocks optional; interchangeable blade front sight, micrometer fully-adjustable rear; interchangeable caliber conversion kit available; adjustable trigger, trigger stop. Imported from Germany by Precision Sales Int'l. Introduced 1988; all importation ceased by 1994.

22 LR		
Perf: $1225	**Exc:** $925	**VGood:** $800
32 S&W Long		
Perf: $1225	**Exc:** $1000	**VGood:** $850
22 LR, chrome finish		
Perf: $1450	**Exc:** $1225	**VGood:** $975
22 LR conversion unit		
Perf: $1300	**Exc:** $1100	**VGood:** $975
32 S&W conversion unit		
Perf: $1300	**Exc:** $1100	**VGood:** $975

ERMA ESP-85A GOLDEN TARGET

Same specs as the ESP-85A except high-polish gold finish on the slide; adjustable match stocks with finger grooves; comes with fully

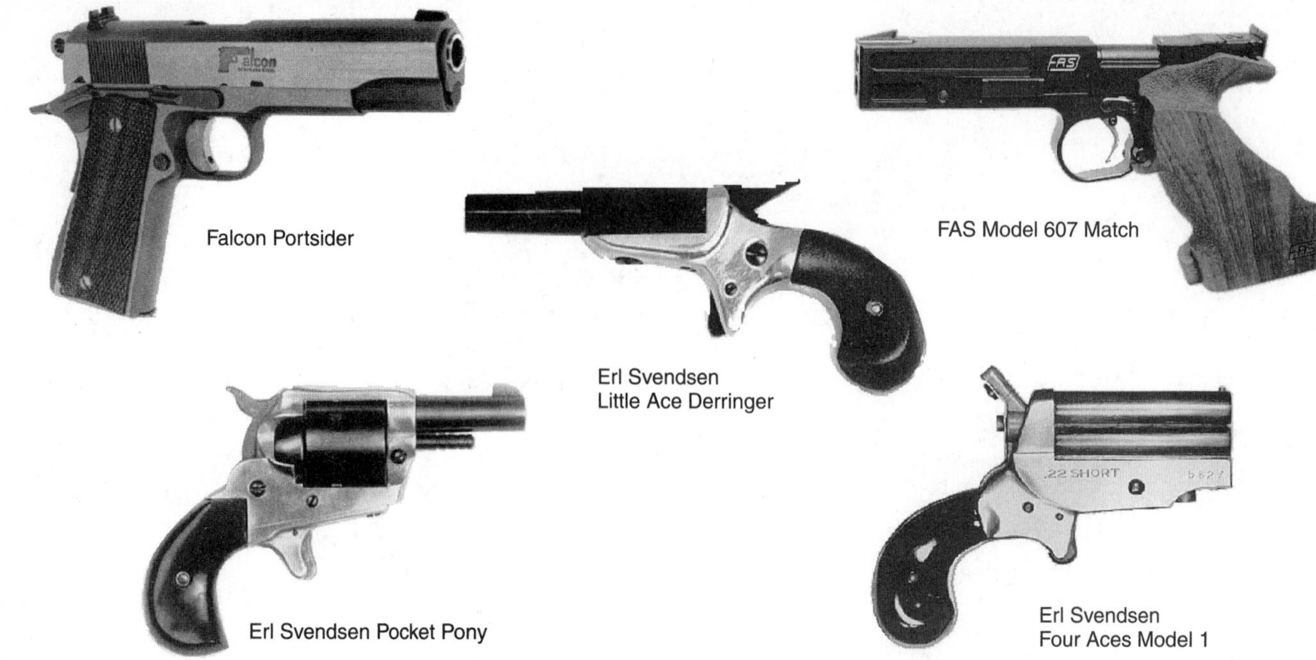
Falcon Portsider
FAS Model 607 Match
Erl Svendsen Little Ace Derringer
Erl Svendsen Pocket Pony
Erl Svendsen Four Aces Model 1

interchangeable 6-inch barrels for 22 LR and 32 S&W. Imported from Germany by Precision Sales International. Introduced 1994; no longer imported.

Perf: $1600 **Exc:** $1350 **VGood:** $1000

ERMA ESP-85A JUNIOR MATCH

Same specs as the ESP-85A except 22 LR; blue finish only; stippled non-adjustable walnut match grips (adjustable grips optional). Imported from Germany by Precision Sales International. Introduced 1995; no longer imported.

Perf: $750 **Exc:** $650 **VGood:** $600

ERMA KGP68A

Semi-automatic; 32 ACP, 380 ACP; 6-shot; 3-1/2-inch, 4-inch barrel; 6-3/4-inch overall length; weighs 20 oz.; adjustable blade front, fixed rear sight; checkered plastic or walnut grips; Luger look-alike; blued finish. Later models designated KGP32, KGP38. Introduced 1968.

Perf: $450 **Exc:** $350 **VGood:** $300

ERMA KGP69

Semi-automatic; 22 LR; 8-shot magazine; 3-3/4-inch barrel; 7-3/4-inch overall length; weighs 22 oz.; fixed sights; checkered plastic or walnut grips; Luger look-alike; blued finish. Later models designated KGP22. Introduced 1969.

Perf: $295 **Exc:** $275 **VGood:** $250

ERMA LA 22

Semi-automatic; 22 LR; 10-shot magazine; 8-3/16-inch, 11-3/4-inch barrel; adjustable target sights; checkered plastic grips; Luger look-alike; blued finish. Introduced 1964; discontinued 1967.

Exc: $350 **VGood:** $275 **Good:** $175

ERMA RX 22

Semi-automatic; double action; 22 LR; 8-shot magazine; 3-1/4-inch barrel, 5-9/16-inch overall length; fixed sights; plastic wrap-around grips; thumb safety; patented ignition safety system; polished blued finish. Assembled in USA. Introduced 1980; discontinued 1986.

Perf: $125 **Exc:** $110 **VGood:** $100

ERL SVENDSEN FOUR ACES MODEL 1

Derringer; 22 Short; 4-shot; 1-11/16-inch barrels (4); black plastic grips; round butt; post front sight; manganese bronze frame; spur trigger; barrel selector on hammer; blued steel barrels. Introduced 1973; maker ceased business 1974.

Exc: $175 **VGood:** $135 **Good:** $100

ERL SVENDSEN FOUR ACES MODEL 2

Same specs as Model 1 except square-butt frame.

Exc: $175 **VGood:** $135 **Good:** $100

ERL SVENDSEN FOUR ACES MODEL 3

Same specs as Model 2 except 2-inch barrels; 22 LR.

Exc: $160 **VGood:** $135 **Good:** $100

ERL SVENDSEN FOUR ACES MODEL 4

Same specs as Model 3 except slightly longer overall length.

Exc: $160 **VGood:** $135 **Good:** $100

ERL SVENDSEN LITTLE ACE DERRINGER

Derringer; single shot; 22 Short; 2-inch barrel; black plastic grips; no sights; manganese bronze frame; blued barrel; color case-hardened spur trigger, hammer. Introduced 1973; maker ceased business 1974.

Exc: $120 **VGood:** $95 **Good:** $80

ERL SVENDSEN POCKET PONY

Revolver; single action; 22 LR; 6-shot; 1-3/8-inch barrel; fixed sights; black plastic grips; manganese bronze frame; blued barrel; color case-hardened trigger, hammer; non-fluted cylinder. Introduced 1973; maker ceased business 1974.

Exc: $150 **VGood:** $125 **Good:** $100

FALCON PORTSIDER

Semi-automatic; 45 ACP; 7-shot magazine; 5-inch barrel; 8-1/2-inch overall length; weighs 38 oz.; fixed combat sights; checkered walnut stocks; stainless steel construction; extended safety; wide grip safety; enlarged left-hand ejection port; extended ejector. Introduced 1986; dropped about 1989. Scarce.

Perf: $595 **Exc:** $450 **VGood:** $400

Portsider Set with right and left hand models with matching serial numbers. Only 100 sets were manufactured from 1986-87.

Perf: $1300 **Exc:** $1100 **VGood:** $895

FAS MODEL 601 MATCH

Semi-automatic; 22 Short; 5-shot magazine; 5-1/2-inch barrel; 11-inch overall length; weighs 41 oz.; gas ported barrel; wrap-around adjustable walnut stocks; match blade front sight, fully-adjustable open notch rear; magazine inserts from top; adjustable, removable trigger group; single-lever take-down. Made in Italy. Introduced 1984; formerly imported by Nygord Precision Products.

Perf: $1325 **Exc:** $975 **VGood:** $695

FAS MODEL 602 MATCH

Semi-automatic; single action; 22 LR; 5-shot magazine; 5-5/8-inch barrel; 11-inch overall length; weighs 37 oz.; walnut wrap-around grips in small, medium or large, or adjustable; match blade front, open notch fully-adjustable rear sight; magazine inserted from top; adjustable and removable trigger mechanism; single-lever takedown. Formerly imported from Italy by Nygord Precision Products; no longer imported.

Perf: $1195 **Exc:** $800 **VGood:** $625

FAS MODEL 603 MATCH

Semi-automatic; single action; 32 S&W; 5-shot magazine; 5-5/8-inch barrel; 11-inch overall length; weighs 37 oz.; walnut wrap-around grips in sizes small, medium or large, or adjustable; blade front, open notch fully-adjustable rear match sight; magazine inserted from top; adjustable and removable trigger mechanism; single-lever takedown. Formerly imported from Italy by Nygord Precision Products.

Perf: $1075 **Exc:** $875 **VGood:** $755

FAS MODEL 607 MATCH

Semi-automatic; single action; 22 LR; 5-shot magazine; 5-5/8-inch barrel; 11-inch overall length; weighs 37 oz.; walnut wrap-around grips in small, medium or large, or adjustable; blade front, open notch fully-adjustable rear match sight; magazine inserted from top; adjustable and removable trigger mechanism; single-lever takedown. Formerly imported from Italy by Nygord Precision Products.

Perf: $1075 **Exc:** $875 **VGood:** $755

FEATHER GUARDIAN ANGEL

Derringer; 9mm Para., 38 Spl.; 3-inch barrel; 5-1/2-inch overall length; weighs 17 oz.; black composition stocks; fixed sights; stainless steel;

Federal Ordnance Ranger G.I. Model

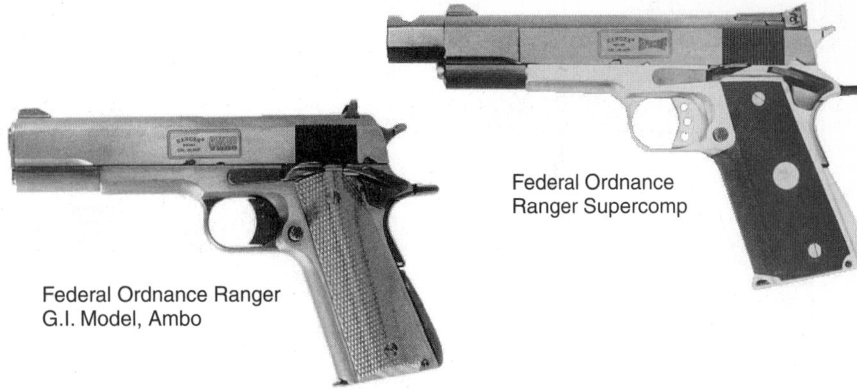

Federal Ordnance Ranger G.I. Model, Ambo

Federal Ordnance Ranger Supercomp

FEG B9R

FEG FP9

FEG GKK-45C

matte finish; two-shot drop-in magazine. Introduced 1988; dropped 1989. New 22 LR/22 WMR model introduced 1990 with 2-inch barrels; no longer in production. Was also offered for a time by Mitchell Arms.

Perf: $175 **Exc:** $125 **VGood:** $95

22 LR or 22 WMR version

Perf: $100 **Exc:** $75 **VGood:** $60

FEDERAL ORDNANCE RANGER ALPHA

Semi-automatic; single action; 38 Super, 10mm Auto, 45 ACP; 9-shot (38 Super), 8-shot (10mm Auto), 7-shot (45 ACP); 5-inch, 6-inch barrel, ported or unported; 8-1/2-inch overall length; weighs 42 oz.; wrap-around rubber grips; interchangeable front sight, fully-adjustable Peters Stahl rear; Peters Stahl linkless barrel system; polygonal rifling; extended grip safety, thumb safety, slide release, magazine release; high polish blue finish. Imported by Federal Ordnance. Introduced 1990; no longer imported.

5-inch unported barrel, 38 Super, 45 ACP

Perf: $895 **Exc:** $775 **VGood:** $675

5-inch ported barrel, 38 Super 45 ACP or unported 10mm

Perf: $920 **Exc:** $795 **VGood:** $695

5-inch, 6-inch ported barrel, 10mm, 38 Super, 45 ACP

Perf: $950 **Exc:** $750 **VGood:** $700

6-inch ported barrel, 10mm

Perf: $950 **Exc:** $750 **VGood:** $700

FEDERAL ORDNANCE RANGER G.I. MODEL

Semi-automatic; single action; 45 ACP; 7-shot magazine; 5-inch barrel; 8-1/2-inch overall length; weighs 38 oz.; checkered plastic grips; blade front sight, drift-adjustable rear; made in U.S. from 4140 steel and other high-strength alloys; barrel machined from a forged billet. From Federal Ordnance, Inc. Introduced 1988; no longer produced.

Perf: $485 **Exc:** $450 **VGood:** $410

FEDERAL ORDNANCE RANGER G.I. MODEL, AMBO

Same specs as Ranger G.I. Model except ambidextrous slide release, safety; extended grip safety, thumb safety; slide and magazine releases; weighs 40 oz. Introduced 1990; discontinued 1992.

Perf: $485 **Exc:** $450 **VGood:** $410

FEDERAL ORDNANCE RANGER G.I. MODEL, EXTENDED

Same specs as Ranger G.I. Model except extended grip safety, thumb safety; slide and magazine releases; weighs 40 oz. Introduced 1990; discontinued 1992.

Perf: $485 **Exc:** $450 **VGood:** $410

FEDERAL ORDNANCE RANGER G.I. MODEL, LITE

Same specs as Ranger G.I. Model except aluminum alloy frame; Millet fixed sights; rubber wrap-around grips; lightened speed trigger; black anodized frame; blued steel slide. Introduced 1990; discontinued 1992.

Perf: $485 **Exc:** $450 **VGood:** $410

FEDERAL ORDNANCE RANGER G.I. MODEL, TEN AUTO

Same specs as Ranger G.I. Model except 10mm Auto chambering. Introduced 1990; discontinued 1991.

Perf: $695 **Exc:** $575 **VGood:** $475

FEDERAL ORDNANCE RANGER SUPERCOMP

Semi-automatic; single action; 10mm Auto, 45 ACP; 8-shot (10mm Auto), 7-shot (45 ACP); 6-inch barrel; 9-1/2-inch overall length; weighs 42 oz.; wrap-around rubber grips; ramped blade front sight, fully-adjustable, low-profile Ranger rear; Peters Stahl linkless barrel system with polygonal rifling and integral competition compensator; lightened speed trigger; beveled magazine well; ramped and throated barrel; blued slide, electroless nickel frame. From Federal Ordnance. Introduced 1990; dropped 1991.

Perf: $895 **Exc:** $775 **VGood:** $625

FEGYVER ÉS GÉPGYÁR-BADUPEST, HUNGARY (FEG) B9R

Semi-automatic; 380 ACP; 10-shot magazine; 4-inch barrel; 7-inch overall length; weighs 25 oz.; blade front, drift-adjustable rear sight; hand-checkered walnut grips; hammer drop safety; grooved backstrap; squared trigger guard. Introduced 1993; still imported.

New: $290 **Perf:** $250 **Exc:** $200

FEG FP9

Semi-automatic; single action; 9mm Para.; 10-shot magazine; 5-inch barrel; 7-7/8-inch overall length; weighs 35 oz.; checkered walnut grips; blade front sight, windage-adjustable rear; full-length ventilated rib; polished blue finish; comes with extra magazine. Imported from Hungary by Century International Arms. Introduced 1993; still imported.

New: $225 **Perf:** $200 **Exc:** $175

FEG GKK-40C

Semi-automatic; double action; 40 S&W; 9-shot magazine; 4-1/8-inch barrel; 7-3/4-inch overall length; weighs 36 oz.; hand-checkered walnut grips; blade front sight, windage-adjustable rear; three-dot system; combat-type trigger guard; polished blue finish; comes with two magazines, cleaning rod. Imported from Hungary by K.B.I., Inc. Introduced 1995; no longer imported.

New: $300 **Perf:** $250 **Exc:** $200

FEG GKK-45C

Semi-automatic; double action; 45 ACP; 8-shot magazine; 4-1/8-inch barrel; 7-3/4-inch overall length; weighs 36 oz.; hand-checkered walnut grips; blade front sight, windage-adjustable rear; three-dot system; combat-type trigger guard; polished blue finish; comes with two magazines, cleaning rod. Imported from Hungary by K.B.I., Inc. Introduced 1995; no longer imported.

New: $300 **Perf:** $250 **Exc:** $200

FEG GKK-92C

Semi-automatic; double action; 9mm Para.; 14-shot magazine; 4-inch barrel; 7-3/8-inch overall length; weighs 34 oz.; hand-checkered walnut grips; blade front sight, windage-adjustable rear; slide-mounted safety; hooked trigger guard; finger-grooved frontstrap; polished blue finish. Imported from Hungary by K.B.I., Inc. Introduced 1992; no longer imported.

Perf: $315 **Exc:** $280 **VGood:** $250

FEG MARK II AP PISTOL

Semi-automatic; double action; 380 ACP, 7-shot magazine. Barrel: 3.9-inch. Weight: 27 oz. Length:

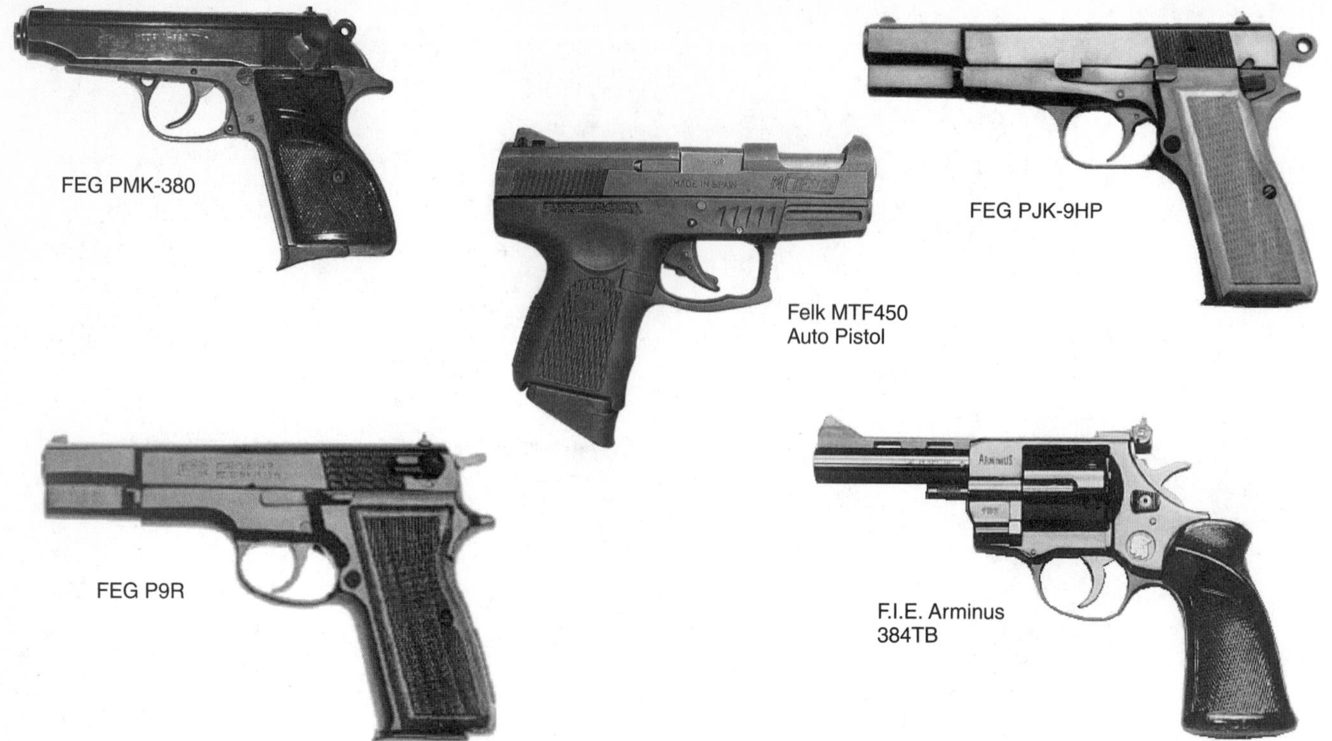
FEG PMK-380

Felk MTF450 Auto Pistol

FEG PJK-9HP

FEG P9R

F.I.E. Arminius 384TB

6.9-inch overall. Stocks: Checkered black composition. Sights: Blade front, rear adjustable for windage. Features: Double action. All-steel construction. Polished blue finish. Comes with two magazines. Introduced 1997. Imported from Hungary by Interarms. No longer imported.

Perf: $235 **Exc:** $200 **VGood:** $1755

FEG MARK II AP22 PISTOL

Semi-automatic; double action; 22 LR, 8-shot magazine. Barrel: 3.4-inch. Weight: 23 oz. Length: 6.3-inch overall. Stocks: Checkered black composition. Sights: Blade front, rear adjustable for windage. Features: Double action. All-steel construction. Polished blue finish. Introduced 1997. Formerly imported from Hungary by Interarms.

Perf: $275 **Exc:** $250 **VGood:** $225

FEG MBK-9HP

Semi-automatic; double action; 9mm Para.; 14-shot magazine; 4-5/8-inch barrel; 7-3/8-inch overall length; weighs 34 oz.; hand-checkered walnut grips; blade front sight, windage-adjustable rear; slide-mounted safety; hooked trigger guard; smooth frontstrap; polished blue finish. Imported from Hungary by K.B.I., Inc. Introduced 1992; no longer imported.

Perf: $315 **Exc:** $270 **VGood:** $250

FEG MBK-9HPC

Semi-automatic; double action; 9mm Para.; 14-shot magazine; 4-inch barrel; 7-1/4-inch overall length; weighs 34 oz.; hand-checkered walnut grips; blade front sight, windage-adjustable rear; slide-mounted safety; hooked trigger guard; smooth frontstrap; polished blue finish. Imported from Hungary by K.B.I., Inc. Introduced 1992; no longer imported.

Perf: $325 **Exc:** $275 **VGood:** $250

FEG P9R

Semi-automatic; double action; 9mm Para.; 10-shot magazine; 4-5/8-inch barrel; 7-15/16-inch overall length; weighs 35 oz.; checkered walnut grips; blade front sight, windage-adjustable rear; slide-mounted safety; all-steel construction with polished blue finish; comes with extra magazine. Imported from Hungary by Century International Arms. Introduced 1993; still imported.

New: $280 **Perf:** $235 **Exc:** $185

FEG PJK-9HP

Semi-automatic; single action; 9mm Para.; 10-shot magazine; 4-3/4-inch barrel; 8-inch overall length; weighs 32 oz.; hand-checkered walnut grips; blade front sight, windage-adjustable rear; three-dot system; polished blue or hard chrome finish; rounded combat-style serrated hammer; comes with two magazines and cleaning rod. Formerly imported from Hungary by K.B.I., Inc. Introduced 1992.

New: $300 **Perf:** $250 **Exc:** $200

FEG PMK-380

Semi-automatic; double action; 380 ACP; 7-shot magazine; 4-inch barrel; 7-inch overall length; weighs 21 oz.; checkered black nylon thumbrest grips; blade front sight, windage-adjustable rear; anodized aluminum frame; polished blue slide; comes with two magazines, cleaning rod. Imported from Hungary by K.B.I., Inc. Introduced 1992; no longer imported.

Perf: $225 **Exc:** $180 **VGood:** $160

FEG SMC-22

Semi-automatic; double action; 22 LR; 8-shot magazine; 3-1/2-inch barrel; 6-1/8-inch overall length; weighs 18-1/2 oz.; checkered composition thumbrest grips; blade front sight, windage-adjustable rear; alloy frame, steel slide; blue finish; comes with two magazines, cleaning rod. Patterned after the PPK pistol. Formerly imported from Hungary by K.B.I., Inc. Introduced 1994.

New: $250 **Perf:** $225 **Exc:** $200

FEG SMC-380

Semi-automatic; double action; 380 ACP; 6-shot magazine; 3-1/2-inch barrel; 6-1/8-inch overall length; weighs 18-1/2 oz.; checkered composition thumbrest grips; blade front sight, windage-adjustable rear; alloy frame, steel slide; blue finish; comes with two magazines, cleaning rod. Patterned after the PPK pistol. Imported from Hungary by K.B.I. Introduced 1994; no longer imported.

New: $250 **Perf:** $225 **Exc:** $200

FEG SMC-918

Semi-automatic; double action; 9x18 Makarov; 6-shot magazine; 3-1/2-inch barrel; 6-1/8-inch overall length; weighs 18-1/2 oz.; checkered composition thumbrest grips; blade front sight, rear adjustable for windage; alloy frame, steel slide; blue finish; comes with two magazines, cleaning rod. Patterned after the PPK pistol. Formerly imported from Hungary by K.B.I. Introduced 1995.

New: $250 **Perf:** $225 **Exc:** $200

FELK MTF 450 AUTO PISTOL

Semi-automatic; double action only; 9mm Para. (10-shot); 40 S&W (8-shot); 45 ACP (9-shot magazine). Barrel: 3.5-inch. Weight: 19.9 oz. Length: 6.4-inch overall. Stocks: Checkered. Sights: Blade front; adjustable rear. Features: Double-action-only trigger, striker fired; polymer frame; trigger safety, firing pin safety, trigger bar safety; adjustable trigger weight; fully interchangeable slide/barrel to change calibers. Introduced 1998. Imported from Australia by Felk Inc.

Perf: $350 **Exc:** $300 **VGood:** $250

45 ACP pistol with 9mm and 40 S&W slide/barrel assemblies

Perf: $850 **Exc:** $750 **VGood:** $650

F.I.E. ARMINIUS MODEL 222

Revolver; double action; 22 LR, 22 WMR; 8-shot; 2-inch barrel; plastic or walnut grips; swing-out cylinder; blued or chrome finish. Discontinued 1985; reintroduced as F.I.E. Arminius Model 222B 1987; discontinued 1989.

Perf: $145 **Exc:** $115 **VGood:** $100

F.I.E. ARMINIUS MODEL 232

Revolver; double action; 32 S&W; 7-shot; 2-inch barrel; fixed or adjustable sights; plastic or walnut grips; swing-out cylinder; blued finish. Discontinued 1985; reintroduced as F.I.E. Arminius Model 232B 1987; discontinued 1989.

Perf: $120 **Exc:** $105 **VGood:** $95

F.I.E. ARMINIUS MODEL 357

Revolver; double action; 357 Mag.; 6-shot; 3-inch, 4-inch, 6-inch barrel; plastic or walnut grips; blued or chrome finish. Discontinued 1990.

Perf: $200 **Exc:** $170 **VGood:** $135

Chrome finish

Perf: $235 **Exc:** $205 **VGood:** $170

F.I.E. ARMINIUS MODEL 357T

Revolver; double action; 357 Mag.; 6-shot; 2-inch barrel; plastic or walnut grips; blued or chrome finish. Discontinued 1984.

Perf: $175 **Exc:** $155 **VGood:** $135

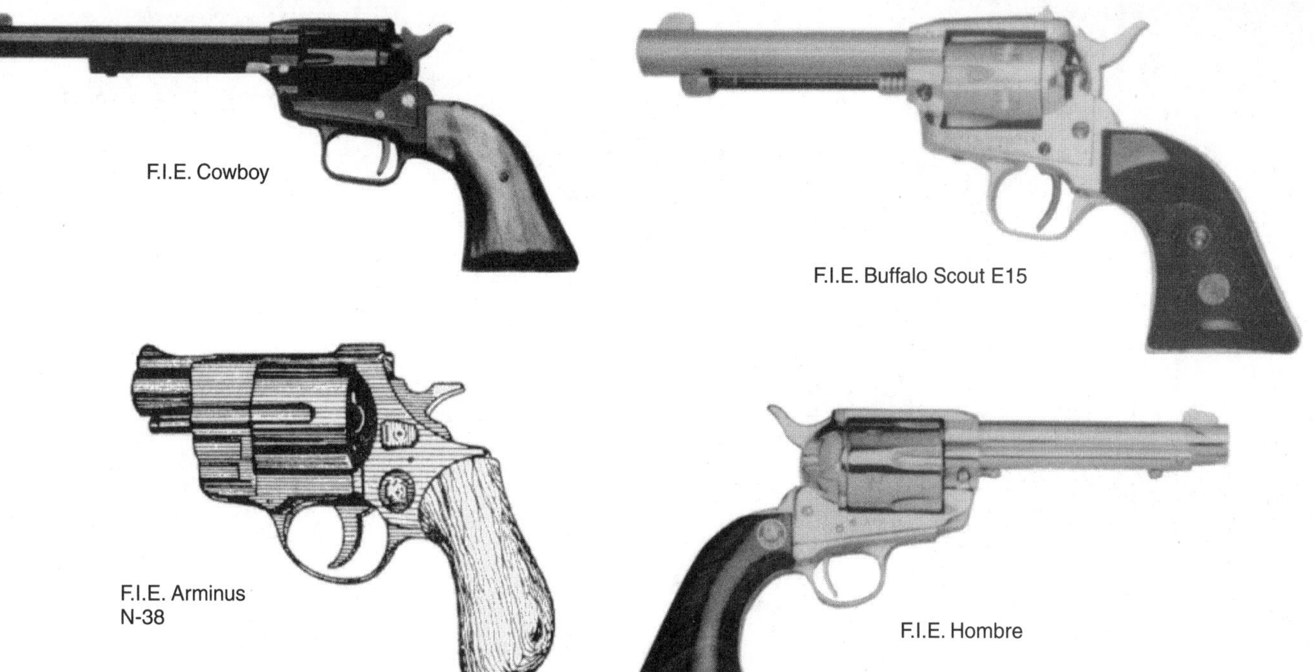
F.I.E. Cowboy

F.I.E. Buffalo Scout E15

F.I.E. Arminus N-38

F.I.E. Hombre

Chrome finish

Perf: $185 **Exc:** $175 **VGood:** $150

F.I.E. ARMINIUS MODEL 382TB

Revolver; double action; 38 Spl.; 6-shot; 2-inch barrel; plastic or walnut grips; blued or chrome finish. Discontinued 1985.

Perf: $120 **Exc:** $95 **VGood:** $85

Chrome finish

Perf: $135 **Exc:** $105 **VGood:** $95

F.I.E. ARMINIUS MODEL 384TB

Revolver; double action; 38 Spl.; 6-shot; 4-inch barrel; plastic or walnut grips; blued or chrome finish. Discontinued 1990.

Perf: $155 **Exc:** $135 **VGood:** $105

Chrome finish

Perf: $185 **Exc:** $175 **VGood:** $140

F.I.E. ARMINIUS MODEL 386TB

Revolver; double action; 38 Spl.; 6-shot; 6-inch barrel; plastic or walnut grips; blued or chrome finish. Discontinued 1990.

Perf: $150 **Exc:** $125 **VGood:** $105

Chrome finish

Perf: $175 **Exc:** $150 **VGood:** $140

F.I.E. ARMINIUS MODEL 522TB

Revolver; double action; 22 LR; 8-shot cylinder; 4-inch barrel; fixed sights; plastic or walnut grips; swing-out cylinder; blued finish. Discontinued 1990.

Perf: $135 **Exc:** $105 **VGood:** $95

F.I.E. ARMINIUS MODEL 532TB

Revolver; double action; 32 S&W; 7-shot cylinder; 4-inch barrel; adjustable sights; plastic or walnut grips; blued or chrome finish. Discontinued 1985.

Perf: $145 **Exc:** $120 **VGood:** $100

Chrome finish

Perf: $160 **Exc:** $140 **VGood:** $120

F.I.E. ARMINIUS MODEL 722

Revolver; double action; 22 LR; 8-shot cylinder; 6-inch barrel; fixed sights; plastic or walnut grips; swing-out cylinder; blued or chrome finish. Discontinued 1985.

Perf: $125 **Exc:** $100 **VGood:** $90

Chrome finish

Perf: $145 **Exc:** $125 **VGood:** $120

F.I.E. ARMINIUS MODEL 732B

Revolver; double action; 32 S&W; 7-shot cylinder; 6-inch barrel; fixed sights; blued finish. Discontinued 1988.

Perf: $130 **Exc:** $100 **VGood:** $95

F.I.E. ARMINIUS MODEL N-38

Revolver; double action; 38 Spl.; 6-shot cylinder; 2-inch, 4-inch barrel; ramp front sight, fixed rear; Bulldog-style checkered plastic or walnut grips; swing-out cylinder; one-stroke ejection; blued or chrome finish. Marketed as Titan Tiger. Introduced 1978; discontinued 1990.

Perf: $130 **Exc:** $110 **VGood:** $95

Chrome finish

Perf: $150 **Exc:** $130 **VGood:** $115

F.I.E. ARMINIUS STANDARD MODEL

Revolver; double action; 22 LR, 22 WMR, 32 H&R Mag., 38 Spl.; 8-shot cylinder (rimfire), 6-shot swing-out cylinder (centerfire); 2-inch, 4-inch barrel; 6-1/4-inch overall length (2-inch barrel); weighs 27 oz.; fixed sights; Bulldog-style checkered plastic or walnut grips; swing-out cylinder; one-stroke ejection; blued, chrome finish or gold-plated. Introduced 1989; discontinued 1990.

Perf: $100 **Exc:** $80 **VGood:** $75

Chrome finish

Perf: $120 **Exc:** $110 **VGood:** $95

Gold plated

Perf: $140 **Exc:** $130 **VGood:** $115

F.I.E. ARMINIUS ZEPHYR

Revolver; double action; 38 Spl.; 5-shot cylinder; 2-inch barrel; weighs 14 oz.; checkered grips; aluminum frame; blued finish. Introduced 1990; discontinued 1990.

Perf: $150 **Exc:** $125 **VGood:** $110

F.I.E. ARMINIUS ZEPHYR LADY

Same specs as Zephyr except polymer ivory grips with scrimshaw; gold trim; gold case. Introduced 1990; discontinued 1990.

Perf: $250 **Exc:** $210 **VGood:** $180

F.I.E. BUFFALO SCOUT E15

Revolver; single action; 22 LR, 22 WMR; 6-shot cylinder; 4-3/4-inch barrel; 10-inch overall length; adjustable sights; black checkered plastic or uncheckered red walnut grips; sliding spring ejector; blued, chromed or blue/brass finish. Introduced 1978; discontinued 1990.

Perf: $95 **Exc:** $65 **VGood:** $55

Chrome finish

Perf: $115 **Exc:** $75 **VGood:** $65

Blue/brass finish

Perf: $130 **Exc:** $115 **VGood:** $95

F.I.E. COWBOY

Revolver; single action; 22 LR, 22 WMR; 6-shot cylinder; 3-1/4-inch, 6-1/2-inch barrel; weighs 28 oz. (3-1/4-inch barrel); blade front sight, fixed rear; smooth nylon square butt grips; hammer-block safety; floating firing pin; blued finish. Introduced 1989; discontinued 1990.

Perf: $95 **Exc:** $75 **VGood:** $55

With combo cylinders

Perf: $115 **Exc:** $95 **VGood:** $65

F.I.E. GOLD RUSH

Revolver; single action; 22 LR, 22 WMR, 22 LR/22 WMR combo; 6-shot cylinder; 3-1/4-inch, 4-3/4-inch, 6-1/2-inch barrel; blade front, fixed rear sight; ivory-styled grips; gold band on barrel and cylinder; round or square butt; blue finish. Introduced 1989; discontinued 1990.

Perf: $155 **Exc:** $135 **VGood:** $125

With combo cylinders

Perf: $200 **Exc:** $175 **VGood:** $160

F.I.E. HOMBRE

Revolver; single action; 357 Mag., 44 Mag., 45 Colt; 5-1/2-inch, 6-inch, 7-1/2-inch barrels; 45 oz.; blade front, grooved backstrap rear sight; smooth walnut grips, medallion; color case-hardened frame; blue finish. Introduced 1970; discontinued 1990.

Perf: $250 **Exc:** $195 **VGood:** $150

Gold plated

Perf: $300 **Exc:** $210 **VGood:** $175

F.I.E. KG-99 PISTOL

Semi-automatic; 9mm Para.; 20-, 36-shot magazine; 3-inch, 5-inch barrel; 12-1/2-inch overall length; weighs 46 oz.; fixed sights; military-type configuration. Introduced 1982; discontinued 1984.

Perf: $400 **Exc:** $325 **VGood:** $250

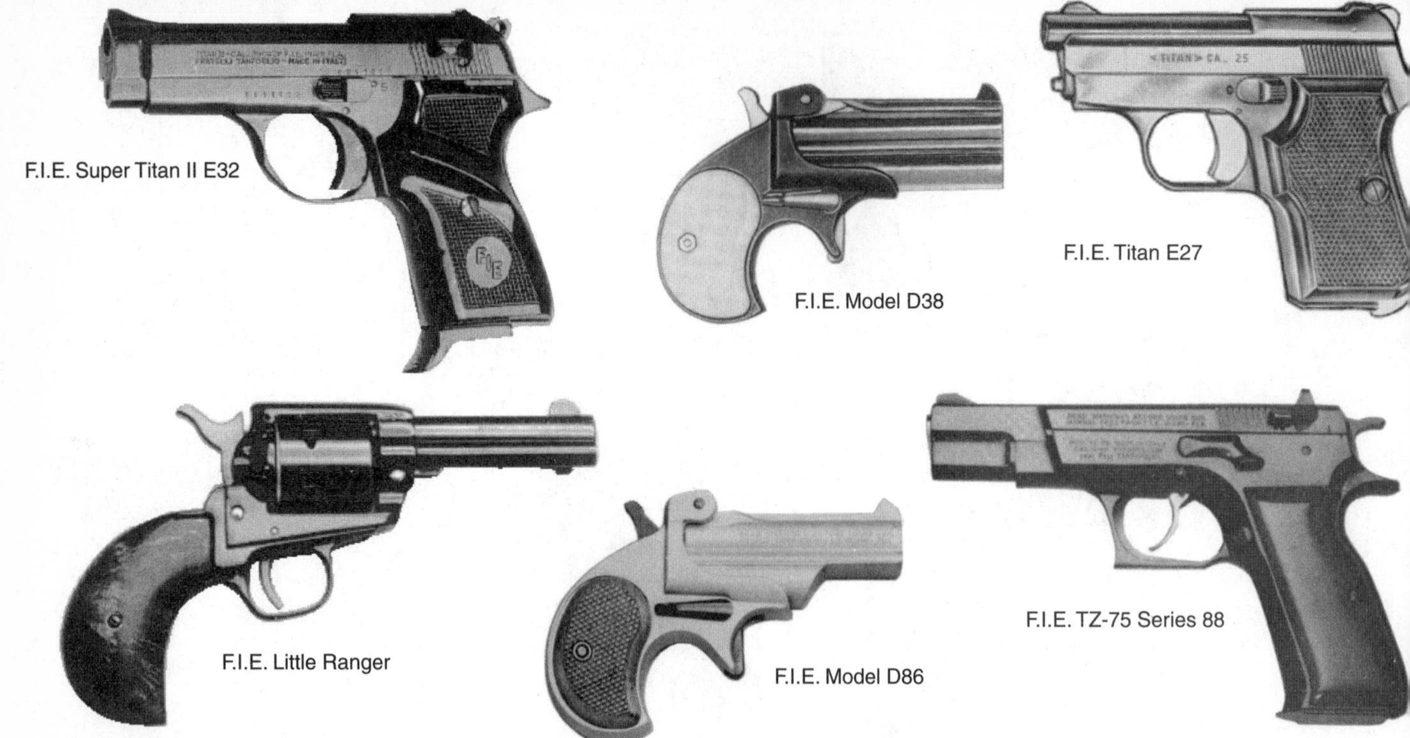
F.I.E. Super Titan II E32

F.I.E. Model D38

F.I.E. Titan E27

F.I.E. Little Ranger

F.I.E. Model D86

F.I.E. TZ-75 Series 88

F.I.E. LEGEND

Revolver; single action; 22 LR, 22 LR/22 WMR combo; 6-shot cylinder; 4-3/4-inch, 5-1/2-inch barrel; fixed sights; black checkered plastic or walnut grips; brass backstrap, trigger guard; case-hardened steel frame; blue finish. Introduced 1978; discontinued 1984.

Perf: $120 **Exc:** $100 **VGood:** $85

With combo cylinder

Perf: $140 **Exc:** $120 **VGood:** $105

F.I.E. LITTLE RANGER

Revolver; single action; 22 LR, 22LR/22WMR combo; 6-shot cylinder; 3-1/4-inch barrel; blade front, notch rear sight; American hardwood bird's-head grips; blue/black finish. Introduced 1986; discontinued 1990.

Perf: $90 **Exc:** $80 **VGood:** $70

With combo cylinders

Perf: $110 **Exc:** $95 **VGood:** $85

F.I.E. MODEL 722 TP SILHOUETTE PISTOL

Repeater; bolt action; 22 LR; 6-, 10-shot magazine; 10-inch barrel; 19-inch overall length; weighs 54 oz.; hooded front sight, micro-adjustable target rear; walnut-finished hardwood stock with stippled grip, forend; fully-adjustable match trigger; receiver grooved for scope mounting; marketed with two-piece high-base mount, both magazines. Made in Brazil. Introduced 1990; importation dropped 1990.

Perf: $220 **Exc:** $190 **VGood:** $16

F.I.E. MODEL D38

Derringer; over/under; 38 Spl.; 2-shot cylinder; 2-inch barrel; fixed sights; checkered plastic or walnut grips; spur trigger; chrome finish. Introduced 1979; discontinued 1985.

Perf: $100 **Exc:** $70 **VGood:** $55

F.I.E. MODEL D86

Derringer; single shot; 38 Spl.; 3-inch barrel; weighs 14 oz.; fixed sights; checkered black nylon or walnut grips; spur trigger; tip-up barrel; extractors; chrome or blued finish. Introduced 1986; dropped 1990.

Perf: $100 **Exc:** $75 **VGood:** $65

Chrome finish

Perf: $110 **Exc:** $85 **VGood:** $75

F.I.E. SPECTRE PISTOL

Semi-automatic; double action; 9mm Para., 45 ACP; 30-, 50-shot magazine; 6-inch barrel; weighs 76 oz.; adjustable sights; military-type configuration. Introduced 1989; discontinued 1990.

Perf: $675 **Exc:** $600 **VGood:** $525

F.I.E. SSP MODEL

Semi-automatic; single action; 32 ACP, 380 ACP; 3-1/8-inch barrel; 6-1/4-inch overall length; weighs 25 oz.; blade front, windage-adjustable rear sight; smooth European walnut grips; external hammer, magazine safety; blued, satin chrome finish. Introduced 1990; dropped 1990.

Perf: $120 **Exc:** $95 **VGood:** $85

Satin chrome finish

Perf: $140 **Exc:** $115 **VGood:** $115

F.I.E. SSP MODEL LADY

Same specs as SSP except scrimshawed polymer ivory grips; gold trimmed; gold case. Introduced 1990; discontinued 1990.

Perf: $210 **Exc:** $180 **VGood:** $155

F.I.E. SUPER TITAN II E32

Semi-automatic; single action; 32 ACP, 380 ACP; 12-shot magazine (32 ACP), 11-shot (380 ACP); 3-7/8-inch barrel; 6-3/4-inch overall length; adjustable sights; walnut grips; blue finish. Introduced 1981; discontinued 1990.

Perf: $195 **Exc:** $160 **VGood:** $135

F.I.E. TITAN A27

Semi-automatic; single action; 25 ACP; 6-shot magazine; 2-1/2-inch barrel; 4-3/8-inch overall length; fixed sights; checkered walnut stocks; all-steel construction; thumb, magazine safeties; exposed hammer; blued finish. Introduced 1978; discontinued 1988.

Perf: $125 **Exc:** $105 **VGood:** $90

F.I.E. TITAN E27

Semi-automatic; single action; 25 ACP; 6-shot magazine; 4-inch, 6-inch barrel; fixed sights; checkered walnut stocks; wide trigger; blue or chrome finish. Introduced 1977; dropped 1990.

Perf: $90 **Exc:** $70 **VGood:** $65

Chrome finish

Perf: $110 **Exc:** $80 **VGood:** $75

F.I.E. TITAN E38

Semi-automatic; single action; 25 ACP; 6-shot magazine; 4-inch, 6-inch barrel; fixed sights; checkered walnut stocks; wide trigger; blue or chrome finish. Introduced 1990; dropped 1990.

Perf: $100 **Exc:** $60 **VGood:** $45

F.I.E. TITAN II E22

Semi-automatic; single action; 22 LR; 10-shot; 3-7/8-inch barrel; 6-3/4-inch overall length; adjustable sights; walnut grips; magazine disconnector; firing pin block; standard slide safety; blued finish. Introduced 1978; discontinued 1990.

Perf: $130 **Exc:** $105 **VGood:** $90

F.I.E. TITAN II E22 LADY

Same specs as Titan II E22 except scrimshaw polymer ivory grips; blue/gold finish. Introduced 1990; discontinued 1990.

Perf: $185 **Exc:** $155 **VGood:** $130

F.I.E. TITAN II E32

Semi-automatic; single action; 32 ACP, 380 ACP; 6-shot magazine; 3-7/8-inch barrel; 6-3/4-inch overall length; adjustable sights; checkered nylon thumbrest or walnut grips; magazine disconnector; firing pin block; standard slide safety; blue or chrome finish. Introduced 1978; discontinued 1990.

Perf: $195 **Exc:** $160 **VGood:** $135

Chrome finish

Perf: $205 **Exc:** $170 **VGood:** $145

F.I.E. TZ-75

Semi-automatic; double action; 9mm Para.; 15-shot magazine; 4-3/4-inch barrel; 8-1/4-inch overall length; weighs 35 oz.; undercut blade front, windage-adjustable open rear sight; walnut stocks or rubber grips; squared-off trigger guard; rotating slide-mounted safety; steel frame, slide; blue or chrome finish. Introduced 1983; dropped 1990.

Perf: $400 **Exc:** $350 **VGood:** $275

Chrome finish

Perf: $425 **Exc:** $375 **VGood:** $300

F.I.E. TZ-75 SERIES 88

Semi-automatic; double action; 9mm Para., 41 AE; 17-shot magazine (9mm Para.), 11-shot (41 AE); 4-3/4-inch barrel; 8-1/4-inch overall length; weighs 35 oz.; undercut blade front, removable rear sight; walnut or rubber grips; re-engineered version of the TZ-75 with frame mounted safety; matte blue,

FNH FNS

FNH FNX

FNH FNX-45 Tactical

F.I.E. Texas Ranger

Firestorm 1911 MIL-SPEC Standard Government

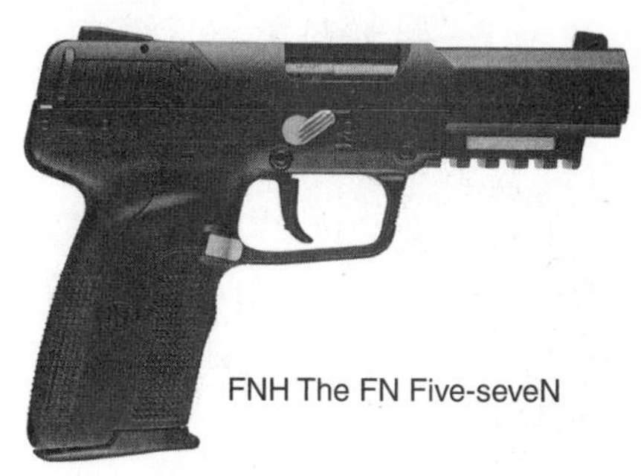
FNH The FN Five-seveN

chrome finish or with blue slide/chrome frame. Introduced 1988; discontinued 1990.

Perf: $435 **Exc:** $360 **VGood:** $330

Chrome finish

Perf: $460 **Exc:** $385 **VGood:** $355

With blue slide/chrome frame

Perf: $400 **Exc:** $375 **VGood:** $350

TZ-75 SERIES 88 COMPENSATED

Same specs as TZ-75 Series 88 except 5-3/4-inch compensated barrel; weighs 42 oz. Introduced 1990; discontinued 1990.

Perf: $700 **Exc:** $615 **VGood:** $535

Chrome finish

Perf: $750 **Exc:** $665 **VGood:** $600

With blue slide/chrome frame

Perf: $675 **Exc:** $635 **VGood:** $565

F.I.E. TZ-75 SERIES 88 GOVERNMENT MODEL

Same specs as TZ-75 Series 88 except 9mm Para.; 12-shot magazine; 3-1/2-inch barrel; 6-7/8-inch overall length; weighs 33-1/2 oz.; walnut grips; compact version of TZ-75 Series 88; blue, chrome or with blue slide/chrome frame. Introduced 1990; discontinued 1990.

Perf: $435 **Exc:** $360 **VGood:** $330

Chrome finish

Perf: $455 **Exc:** $380 **VGood:** $350

With blue slide/chrome frame

Perf: $455 **Exc:** $380 **VGood:** $350

F.I.E. TZ-75 SERIES 88 PORTED

Same specs as TZ-75 Series 88 except 5-inch barrel and slide. Introduced 1990; discontinued 1990.

Perf: $615 **Exc:** $535 **VGood:** $475

Chrome finish

Perf: $645 **Exc:** $575 **VGood:** $495

Blue slide/chrome frame finish

Perf: $645 **Exc:** $575 **VGood:** $495

F.I.E. TEXAS RANGER

Revolver; single action; 22 LR, 22 LR/22 WMR combo; 6-shot cylinder; 3-1/4-inch, 4-3/4-inch, 6-1/2-inch, 7-inch, 9-inch barrels; blade front, notch rear sight; American hardwood stocks; blue/black finish. Introduced 1983; discontinued 1990.

Perf: $100 **Exc:** $75 **VGood:** $60

With combo cylinders

Perf: $125 **Exc:** $100 **VGood:** $85

F.I.E. YELLOW ROSE

Revolver; single action; 22 LR, 22 WMR; 6-shot cylinder; 4-3/4-inch barrel; 10-inch overall length; adjustable sights; walnut grips; sliding spring ejector; 24-karat gold plated. Introduced 1986; discontinued 1990.

Perf: $150 **Exc:** $135 **VGood:** $110

With scrimshawed ivory grips and walnut case

Perf: $275 **Exc:** $225 **VGood:** $200

FIRESTORM .32

Double-action semi-auto chambered for .32 with 10+1 capacity. Blued, 3.5-inch barrel, 23 oz. Fixed sights and rubber grips.

NIB: $250 **Exc:** $200 **VGood:** $165

FIRESTORM 1911 MIL-SPEC STANDARD GOVERNMENT

1911A1-style single-action semi-auto chambered in .45 ACP; 5.125" barrel, steel frame, 7- or 8-round magazine, steel frame, plastic or wood grips, matte blue or deluxe polished blue finish.

NIB: $315 **Exc:** $275 **VGood:** $225

FNH MODEL FORTY-NINE

This pistol is built by FN Manufacturing, Inc. in Columbia, S.C. It has a polymer frame and stainless steel slide. Chambered for 9mm or .40 S&W cartridge. Barrel length is 4.25". Magazine capacity is 16 rounds for law enforcement and 10 rounds for commercial sales. It features a repeatable secure striker trigger system. Offered in stainless steel slide or black coated slide. Weight is about 26 oz. Offered primarly for sale to law enforcement agencies. Introduced in 2000.

NIB: $550 **Exc:** $495 **VGood:** $400

FNH FNS

Double action only striker fired polymer framed full-sized pistol available with black or matte silver finished slide. Ambidextrous manual safety, magazine release and slide lock. Three dot sights and night sights optional. 4 inch barrel and 7.25 inch OA length, weighs 1.57 pounds (9mm) 1.72 pounds (.40S&W). Chambered in 9mm NATO, .40S&W. Capacity is 17+1 in 9mm, 14+1 in .40 S&W. Introduced 2012.

Perf: $700 **Exc:** $620 **VGood:** $570

FNH FNX

Double action/single action hammer fired polymer framed full-sized pistol available with black or matte silver finished slide and black or FDE frame. Ambidextrous manual safety, magazine release and slide lock. 4 inch barrel and 7.4 inch OA length, weighs 1.36 pounds (9mm) 1.52 pounds (.40S&W). In .45 ACP barrel is 4.5 inches and OA length is 7.9 inches, weight is 2.07 pounds. Chambered in 9mm NATO, .40S&W and .45 ACP. Capacity is 17+1 in 9mm, 14+1 in .40 S&W and 15+1 in .45 ACP. Introduced 2012.

Perf: $700 **Exc:** $620 **VGood:** $570

FNH FNX-45 TACTICAL

Double action/single action hammer fired polymer framed full-sized pistol available in black or flat dark earth. Ambidextrous manual safety, magazine release and slide lock. Optics ready slide with high-profile combat night sights. 5.3 inch threaded barrel and 7.4 inch OA length, weighs 2.1 pounds. Chambered in .45 ACP. Capacity is 15+1. Introduced 2011.

Perf: $1,250 **Exc:** $1,150 **VGood:** $1,000

FNP-45 COMPETITION

Caliber: 45 ACP, 15-shot magazine. Barrel length is 4.5 inches, weight, 33.3 oz., length: 7.9 inches. Ambidextrous magazine controls including slide release and frame-mounted decocking lever. Single/double-action, loaded-chamber indicator, textured and checkered frame surfaces, interchangeable arched and flat backstrap inserts with lanyard holes, matte black stainless finish, accessory rail, fiber optic front and rear sights.

Perf: $850 **Exc:** $720 **VGood:** $600

FNH THE FN FIVE-SEVEN

Single Action Only semi-auto pistol available in black or FDE, polymer frame and polymer coated slide. Features ambidextrous safety and three dot sights. Chambered in 5.7x28mm. 4.8 inch barrel and 8.2 in OA length, weighs 1.3 pounds. 20+1 capacity. Introduced in 1992.

Perf: $1,250 **Exc:** $1,150 **VGood:** $1,000

FORT WORTH HSO

Semi-automatic; 22 Short: 10-shot magazine: 6-3/4-inch round tapered barrel, with stabilizer and built-in muzzlebrake; 40 oz.; 11-1/4-inch overall; checkered walnut grips with thumbrest; undercut ramp front, frame-mounted click adjustable square notch rear; drilled and tapped for scope mount; integral stabilizer with two removable weights; trigger adjustable for pull and length of travel; stippled front and backstraps; push-button barrel takedown. Introduced

Freedom Arms Model 83 Wyoming Express

Freedom Arms Model 83 Field Grade

Fraser Automatic

Freedom Arms Model 83 Premier Grade

Freedom Arms 454 Casull

1995; production ceased 2000.

Perf: $475 **Exc:** $425 **VGood:** $3500

FORT WORTH HSS

Semi-automatic; 22 LR, 10-shot magazine; 5-1/2-inch bull barrel; 45 oz.; 10.25-inch overall; checkered walnut grips; ramp front, slide-mounted square notch rear sight adjustable for windage and elevation; stainless steel construction; military grip; slide lock; smooth grip straps; push-button takedown; drilled and tapped for barrel weights. Introduced 1995; production ceased 2000.

Perf: $325 **Exc:** $275 **VGood:** $225

FORT WORTH HSSK

Semi-automatic; 22 LR; 10-shot magazine; 4-1/2-inch or 6-3/4-inch barrel; 39 oz. (with 4-1/2-inch barrel); 9-inch overall (4-1/2-inch barrel); checkered black plastic; side-mounted rear adjustable for windage; stainless steel construction; military grip; standard trigger; push-button barrel takedown. Introduced 1995; production ceased 2000.

Perf: $295 **Exc:** $265 **VGood:** $250

FORT WORTH HST TARGET PISTOL

Semi-automatic; 22 LR; 10-shot magazine; 5-1/2 bull or 7-1/4 fluted barrel; 44 oz.; 9.5-inch overall; checkered hardwood with thumbrest; undercut ramp front, frame-mounted micro-click rear sight adjustable for windage and elevation; drilled and tapped for scope mounting; gold-plated trigger; slide lock; safety-lever and magazine release; stippled front grip and backstrap; adjustable trigger and sear. Barrel weights optional. Introduced 1995; production ceased 2000.

Perf: $375 **Exc:** $325 **VGood:** $275

Left hand

Perf: $400 **Exc:** $350 **VGood:** $300

FORT WORTH HSC TARGET PISTOL

Same as the HST model except has nickel-plated trigger; slide lock; safety lever; magazine release; has slightly heavier trigger pull; stippled front-grip and backstrap; checkered walnut thumbrest grips; adjustable trigger and sear; matte finish; drilled and tapped for scope mount and barrel weight. Introduced 1995; production ceased 2000.

Perf: $375 **Exc:** $295 **VGood:** $255

FORT WORTH HSV TARGET PISTOL

Semi-automatic; 22 LR; 10-shot magazine; 4-1/2 or 5-1/2 barrel; push-button takedown; 46 oz.; 9.5-inch overall; checkered hardwood with thumbrest; undercut ramp front, micro-click rear sight adjustable for windage and elevation; also available with scope mount, rings; no sights; stainless steel construction; full-length vent rib; gold-plated trigger; slide lock; safety-lever and magazine release; stippled front grip and backstrap; polished slide; adjustable trigger and sear; barrel weight. Introduced 1995; production ceased 2000.

Perf: $455 **Exc:** $395 **VGood:** $330

With Weaver rib

Perf: $495 **Exc:** $425 **VGood:** $375

With 8-inch barrel, Weaver rib, custom grips, sights

Perf: $575 **Exc:** $525 **VGood:** $450

FORT WORTH MATCHMASTER STANDARD PISTOL

Semi-automatic; 22 LR; 3-7/8-inch, 4-1/2-inch, 5-1/2-inch, 7-1/2-inch, 10-inch; checkered walnut grips; ramp front, slide-mounted adjustable rear sights; stainless steel construction; double extractors; trigger finger magazine release button and standard button; beveled magazine well; grip angle equivalent to M1911; low-profile frame. Introduced 1997; production ceased 2000.

Perf: $395 **Exc:** $325 **VGood:** $295

FORT WORTH MATCHMASTER DELUXE PISTOL

Same as the Matchmaster Standard except comes with Weaver-style rib mount and integral adjustable rear sight system. Introduced 1997; production ceased 2000.

Perf: $475 **Exc:** $425 **VGood:** $375

FORT WORTH MATCHMASTER DOVETAIL PISTOL

Same as the Matchmaster Standard except has a dovetail-style mount and integral rear sight system. Available with 3-7/8-inch, 4-1/2-inch or 5-1/2-inch barrel only. Introduced 1997; production ceased 2000.

Perf: $435 **Exc:** $395 **VGood:** $325

FRASER AUTOMATIC

Semi-automatic; 25 ACP; 6-shot magazine; 2-1/4-inch barrel; 4-inch overall length; weighs 10 oz.; recessed fixed sights; checkered walnut or plastic pearl stocks; stainless steel construction; positive manual and magazine safeties; satin stainless, gold-plated or black QPQ finish. Introduced 1983; dropped 1986.

Exc: $195 **VGood:** $175 **Good:** $110

Gold plated

Exc: $250 **Vgood:** $235 **Good:** $200

FREEDOM ARMS MODEL 83

Revolver; single action; 357 Mag., 41 Mag., 45 LC, 454 Casull, 44 Mag., 475 Linebaugh, 50 AE; 5-shot cylinder; 4-3/4-inch, 6-inch, 7-1/2-inch, 10-inch barrel; 14-inch overall length (7-1/2-inch barrel); weighs about 59 oz.; blade front sight on ramp, fully-adjustable rear; Pachmayr rubber grips; Field Grade with matte stainless finish; Premier Grade with brushed stainless finish; impregnated hardwood grips, Premier Grade sights. Made in U.S. by Freedom Arms. Introduced 1992; still in production. Add 20% for octagonal barrel.

Field Grade

New: $1325 **Perf:** $995 **Exc:** $825

Premier Grade

New: $1500 **Perf:** $1200 **Exc:** $900

MODEL 83 .500 WYOMING EXPRESS

Similar to Model 83 but chambered in .500 Wyoming Express. Introduced 2007.

New: $2125 **Perf:** $1850 **Exc:** $1650

FREEDOM ARMS 44 MAGNUM SILHOUETTE

Same specs as the Model 83 except 10-inch barrel only; silhouette competition sights; Field Grade finish only; trigger over-travel screw; front sight hood. Made in U.S. by Freedom Arms. Introduced 1992; no longer produced.

New: $1400 **Perf:** $1100 **Exc:** $950

FREEDOM ARMS 454 CASULL

Revolver; single action; 454 Casull; 5-shot cylinder; 4-3/4-inch, 6-inch, 7-1/2-inch, 10-inch, barrels; weighs 50 oz. (7-1/2-inch barrel); impregnated hardwood stocks; blade front sight, notch or adjustable rear; stainless steel; sliding bar safety. Introduced 1983; still in production.

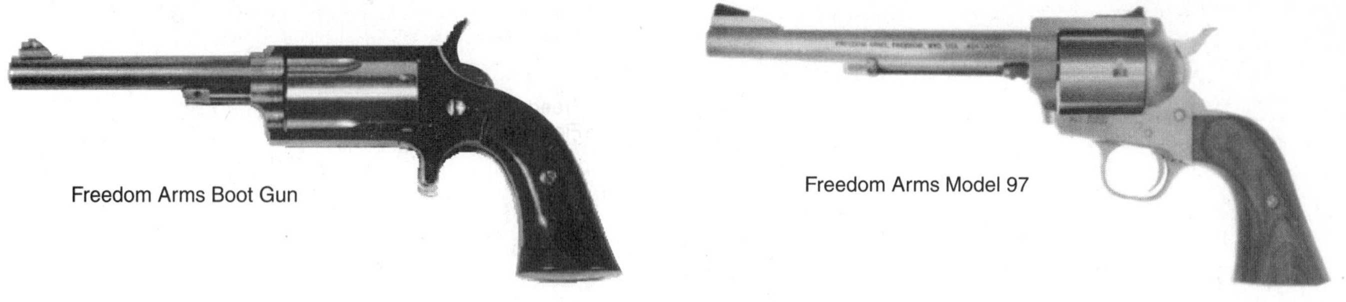
Freedom Arms Boot Gun

Freedom Arms Model 97

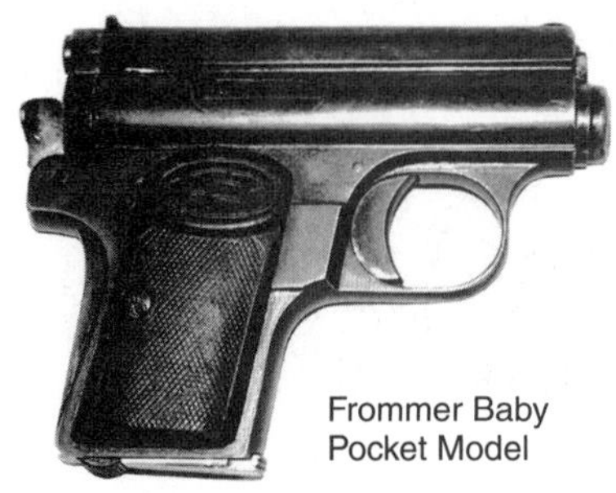
Frommer Baby Pocket Model

Frommer Liliput Pocket Model

FTL Auto Nine

Fixed sights

Perf: $1250 **Exc:** $950 **VGood:** $800

Adjustable sights

Perf: $1300 **Exc:** $1000 **VGood:** $850

FREEDOM ARMS 454 CASULL SILHOUETTE MODEL

Same specs as 454 Casull except competition sights and trigger overtravel screw.

Perf: $1350 **Exc:** $1100 **VGood:** $950

FREEDOM ARMS MODEL 83 .500 WYOMING EXPRESS

Similar to Model 83 but chambered in .500 Wyoming Express.

NIB: $2100 **Exc:** $1850 **VGood:** $1500

FREEDOM ARMS BOOT GUN

Revolver; single action; 22 LR, 22 WMR; 3-inch barrel; 5-7/8-inch overall length; weighs 5 oz.; oversize grips; floating firing pin; stainless steel construction. Introduced 1982; dropped 1990.

Perf: $335 **Exc:** $295 **VGood:** $210

22 WMR

Perf: $375 **Exc:** $315 **VGood:** $225

FREEDOM ARMS FA-S-22LR

Revolver; 22 LR; 5-shot; 1-inch, 1-3/4-inch, 3-inch barrels; blade front, notched rear sights; black ebonite grips; stainless steel construction; partial high polish finish; simulated ivory or ebony grips. No longer produced.

Perf: $295 **Exc:** $225 **VGood:** $200

FREEDOM ARMS FA-S-22M

Revolver; 22 WMR; 4-shot; 1-inch, 1-3/4-inch, 3-inch barrels; stainless steel construction; blade front, notched rear sights; simulated ivory or ebony grips. No longer produced.

Perf: $295 **Exc:** $225 **VGood:** $200

FREEDOM ARMS MINI REVOLVER

Revolver; single action; 22 LR, 22 WMR; 5-shot; 4-inch (22 WMR), 1-inch, 1-3/4-inch barrel (22 LR); 4-inch overall length; blade front sight, notched rear; black ebonite grips; stainless steel construction; marketed in presentation case. Introduced 1978; dropped 1990.

Perf: $295 **Exc:** $275 **VGood:** $210

FREEDOM ARMS MODEL 97 MID FRAME REVOLVER

Caliber: 357 Mag., 6-shot cylinder. Barrel: 5-1/2-inch, 7-1/2-inch. Weight: 40 oz. (5-1/2-inch barrel). Length: 10-3/4-inch overall (5-1/2-inch barrel). Stocks: Wine wood. Sights: Blade on ramp front, fixed or fully adjustable rear. Features: Made of stainless steel; polished cylinder, matte frame. Introduced 1997.

New: $1350 **Perf:** $1000 **Exc:** $850

FREEDOM ARMS MODEL 252 VARMINT

Same specs as Model 252 Silhouette except 7-1/2-inch barrel; weighs 59 oz.; black/green laminated hardwood grips; brass bead front sight, fully-adjustable rear; extra 22 WMR cylinder available. Introduced 1991; still produced.

Perf: $1100 **Exc:** $800 **VGood:** $700

FREEDOM ARMS MODEL 353

Revolver; single action; 5-shot; 4-3/4-inch, 6-inch, 7-1/2-inch, 9-inch barrel; 14-inch overall length (7-1/2-inch barrel); weighs about 59 oz.; blade front sight on ramp, fully-adjustable rear; Pachmayr rubber grips (Field Grade), impregnated hardwood grips (Premier Grade); Field Grade with matte stainless finish; Premier Grade with brush stainless finish. Introduced 1992; still in production.

Field Grade

New: $1200 **Perf:** $1050 **Exc:** $800

Premier Grade

New: $1600 **Perf:** $1200 **Exc:** $950

FREEDOM ARMS MODEL 353 SILHOUETTE

Same specs as Model 353 except 9-inch barrel; silhouette competition sights; Field Grade finish and grips; trigger over-travel screw; front sight hood. Introduced 1992; still in production.

New: $1100 **Perf:** $1000 **Exc:** $850

FREEDOM ARMS MODEL 555

Revolver; single action; 50 AE; 5-shot cylinder; 4-3/4-inch, 6-inch, 7-1/2-inch, 10-inch barrel; 14-inch overall length (7-1/2-inch barrel); weighs 50 oz.; removable blade front sight on ramp, adjustable rear; Pachmayr rubber grips on Field Grade; impregnated hardwood on Premier Grade; Field Grade with matte stainless finish; Premier Grade with brushed stainless finish. Introduced 1994; still produced.

Field Grade

New: $1100 **Perf:** $1000 **Exc:** $850

Premier Grade

New: $1400 **Perf:** $1250 **Exc:** $1000

FROMMER BABY POCKET MODEL

Semi-automatic; 32 ACP; 6-shot magazine; smaller version of Stop Pocket Model with 2-inch barrel; 4-3/4-inch overall length. Manufactured from 1919 to approximately 1922.

Exc: $350 **VGood:** $275 **Good:** $200

FROMMER LILIPUT POCKET MODEL

Semi-automatic; blowback action; 25 ACP; 6-shot magazine; 2-1/8-inch barrel; 4-5/16-inch overall length; hard rubber stocks; fixed sights; blued finish. Manufactured 1921 to 1924.

Exc: $400 **VGood:** $300 **Good:** $200

FROMMER STOP POCKET MODEL

Semi-automatic; 32 ACP, 380 ACP; 6-shot (380 ACP), 7-shot (32 ACP) magazine; 3-7/8-inch barrel; 6-1/2-inch overall length; external hammer; grooved wood or checkered hard rubber stocks; fixed sights; blued finish. Manufactured in Hungary, 1912 to 1920.

Exc: $325 **VGood:** $250 **Good:** $175

FTL AUTO NINE

Semi-automatic; single action; 22 LR; 8-shot magazine; 2-1/8-inch barrel; 4-5/16-inch overall length; weighs 9 1/4 oz.; blade front sight, fixed notch rear; checkered black plastic grips; manual push-button safety; alloy frame; hard chromed slide and magazine; barrel support bushing. Made by Auto Nine Corp. Marketed by FTL Marketing Corp. Introduced 1985; no longer in production.

Perf: $200 **Exc:** $160 **VGood:** $125

Galesi Model 9

Gamba SAB G91

Galesi Model 6

Gamba Trident Fast Action

Garcia/FI Model D

Girsan MC27E

FTL POCKET PARTNER

Semi-automatic; 22 LR; 8-shot magazine; 2-1/4-inch barrel; 4-3/4-inch overall length; weighs 10 oz.; internal hammer; fixed sights; checkered plastic stocks; all-steel construction; brushed blue finish. Introduced 1985; no longer in production.

Perf: $145 **Exc:** $110 **VGood:** $95

GAL COMPACT AUTO PISTOL

Semi-automatic; 45 ACP; 8-shot magazine; 4-1/4-inch barrel; 36 oz.; 7-3/4-inch overall; rubberized wrap-around grip; low profile, fixed, three-dot sight system; forged steel frame and slide; competition trigger, hammer; slide stop magazine release; beavertail grip safety; front and rear slide grooves; two-tone finish. Introduced 1996. Imported from Israel by J.O. Arms, Inc.; dropped 1997.

Perf: $425 **Exc:** $375 **VGood:** $300

GALESI MODEL 6

Semi-automatic; 25 ACP; 6-shot magazine; 2-1/2-inch barrel; 4-3/8-inch overall length; plastic stocks; slide-top groove sights; blued finish. Manufactured in Italy. Introduced 1930; no longer in production.

Exc: $175 **VGood:** $150 **Good:** $100

GALESI MODEL 9

Semi-automatic; 22 LR, 32 ACP, 380 ACP; 7-shot magazine; 3-1/4-inch barrel; plastic stocks; fixed sights; blued finish. Introduced 1930; no longer in production.

Exc: $200 **VGood:** $175 **Good:** $125

GAMBA SAB G90 STANDARD

Semi-automatic; double-action; 32 ACP, 9x18 Ultra, 9mm Para.; 15-shot magazine; 4-3/4-inch barrel; weighs 33 oz.; windage-adjustable rear sight, undercut blade front; uncheckered European walnut stocks; squared trigger guard; blue or chrome finish. Made in Italy. Introduced 1986; discontinued 1990.

Perf: $625 **Exc:** $450 **VGood:** $375

Chrome finish

Perf: $700 **Exc:** $515 **VGood:** $435

GAMBA SAB G90 COMPETITION

Same specs as SAB G90 Standard except 9mm Para. only; cocked-and-locked operation; checkered walnut grips. Introduced 1990; discontinued 1990.

Perf: $1175 **Exc:** $800 **VGood:** $600

GAMBA SAB G91 COMPACT

Semi-automatic; double action; 32 ACP, 9x18 Ultra, 9mm Para.; 12-shot magazine; 3-9/16-inch barrel; 30 oz.; windage-adjustable rear sight, undercut blade front; squared trigger guard; blued or chrome finish. Introduced 1986; discontinued 1990.

Perf: $625 **Exc:** $450 **VGood:** $375

Chrome finish

Perf: $690 **Exc:** $515 **VGood:** $435

GAMBA SAB G91 COMPETITION

Same specs as SAB G91 Compact except 9mm Para.; cocked-and-locked operation; checkered walnut grips. Introduced 1990; discontinued 1990.

Perf: $450 **Exc:** $400 **VGood:** $300

GAMBA TRIDENT FAST ACTION

Revolver; double action; 32 S&W, 38 Spl.; 6-shot; 2-1/2-inch, 3-inch barrel; 23 oz.; fixed sights; checkered walnut grips; blued finish. Discontinued 1986.

Perf: $595 **Exc:** $425 **VGood:** $365

GAMBA TRIDENT MATCH 900

Same specs as Trident Fast Action except 6-inch heavy barrel; 35 oz.; adjustable sights; checkered walnut target grips; blued finish. Discontinued 1986.

Perf: $795 **Exc:** $650 **VGood:** $595

GAMBA TRIDENT SUPER

Same specs as Trident Fast Action except 4-inch vent-rib barrel; 25 oz. Discontinued 1986.

Perf: $595 **Exc:** $425 **VGood:** $365

GARCIA REGENT

Revolver; 22 LR; 3-inch, 4-inch, 6-inch barrel; 8-shot swing-out cylinder; fixed rear sight, ramp front; checkered plastic grips; blued. Introduced 1972; dropped, 1977.

Exc: $100 **VGood:** $85 **Good:** $65

GARCIA/FI MODEL D

Semi-automatic; 380 ACP; 6-shot magazine; 3-1/8-inch barrel; 6-1/8-inch overall length; checkered American walnut stocks; windage-adjustable rear sight, blade front; blued finish; lanyard ring. Imported by Firearms International 1977 to 1979.

Perf: $300 **Exc:** $225 **VGood:** $175

GAUCHER GN1 SILHOUETTE

Single shot; bolt action; 22 LR; 10-inch barrel; 15-1/2-inch overall length; weighs 2-1/2 lbs.; blade front, open adjustable rear sight; Euopean hardwood stock; adjustable trigger. Made in France. Introduced 1990; formerly imported by Mandall Shooting Supplies.

Perf: $360 **Exc:** $325 **VGood:** $290

GAUCHER GP SILHOUETTE

Single shot; bolt action; 22 LR; 10-inch barrel; 15-1/2-inch overall length; weighs 2-1/2 lbs.; hooded ramp front, open adjustable rear sight; stained harwood grips; matte chrome barrel; blued bolt, sights. Made in France. Introduced 1991; formerly imported by Mandall Shooting Supplies.

Perf: $300 **Exc:** $275 **VGood:** $250

GAUCHER RANDALL SINGLESHOT

Bolt action; 9mm Para.; 16-1/2-inch overall length; weighs 36 oz.; bead front sight; European hardwood stock; blued finish. Made in France. Introduced 1990; discontinued 1992. Reportedly formerly imported by Mandall Shooting Supplies.

GIRSAN MC27E

Caliber: 9mm, double/single action. 15-shot magazine. Barrel, 3.9 inches; weight, 23 oz. (without magazine); 7.25 inches overall length. Black polymer grips, fixed sights, polymer frame. New for 2011.

Price: N/A

GLOCK MODEL 17

Semi-automatic; double action; 9mm Para.; 17-, 19-shot magazine; 4-1/2-inch barrel; 7-7/16-inch overall length; weighs 24 oz.; white outline adjustable rear sight, dot on front blade; polymer frame; steel slide; trigger safety; recoil-operated action; firing pin safety; drop safety. Made in Austria. Introduced, 1986; still imported.

Perf: $495 **Exc:** $425 **VGood:** $345

GLOCK MODEL 17L COMPETITION

Same specs as Model 17 except compensated 6-inch barrel; lighter trigger pull; 26 oz. Made in Austria. Introduced 1988; still imported.

Perf: $650 **Exc:** $545 **VGood:** $425

GLOCK 17 25TH ANNIVERSARY LIMITED EDITION

This special model features an emblem built into the grip signifying the 25 years Glock has been in the United States (1986 - 2011). Comes with standard features—two magazines, speed loader, cable

Gaucher GN1 Silhouette

Glock Model 24 Competition

Glock Model 20

Glock Model 22

Glock Model 23

lock, cleaning rod and brush, two interchangeable backstraps, plus a limited edition silver case and a letter of authenticity.

Perf: $765 **Exc:** $675 **VGood:** $500

GLOCK MODEL 19

Semi-automatic; double action; 9mm Para.; 15-, 17-shot magazine; 4-inch barrel; 6-7/8-inch overall length; 22 oz.; white outline adjustable rear sight, dot on front blade; polymer frame; steel slide; trigger safety; recoil-operated action; firing pin safety; drop safety. Made in Austria. Introduced 1988.

Perf: $495 **Exc:** $425 **VGood:** $345

Add $35 to above prices for Model 19C with adjustable rear sight
Add $30 for Model 19 with adjustable rear sight
Add $80 for fixed Meprolight sight
Add $105 for fixed Trijicon sight

GLOCK MODEL 20

Semi-automatic; double action; 10mm Auto; 15-shot magazine; 4-5/8-inch barrel; 28 oz.; white outline adjustable rear sight, dot on front blade; polymer frame; steel slide; trigger safety; recoil-operated action; firing pin safety; drop safety. Made in Austria. Introduced 1990; still imported.

Perf: $600 **Exc:** $525 **VGood:** $450

GLOCK 20 GEN 4

Double action only, striker fired, semi-auto full-sized pistol with a polymer frame and fixed sights. Chambered in 10mm. 4.6 inch barrel and 8.22 inch OA length, weighs 1.73 pounds. 15+1 capacity. Introduced in 2013.

Perf: $570 **Exc:** $500 **VGood:** $460

GLOCK MODEL 21

Semi-automatic; double action; 45 ACP; 13-shot magazine; 4-5/8-inch barrel; 27 oz.; white outline adjustable rear sight, dot on front blade; polymer frame; steel slide; trigger safety; recoil-operated action; firing pin safety; drop safety. Made in Austria. Introduced 1991; still imported.

Perf: $600 **Exc:** $500 **VGood:** $425

GLOCK 21 SF

Slenderized version of Model 21 with slimmer frame and ambidextrous magazine catch. Introduced 2007.

NIB: $525 **Exc:** $485 **VGood:** $400

GLOCK MODEL 22

Semi-automatic; double action; 40 S&W; 15-shot magazine; 4-1/2-inch barrel; 7-7/16-inch overall length; 24 oz.; white outline adjustable rear sight, dot on front blade; polymer frame; steel slide; trigger safety; recoil-operated action; firing pin safety; drop safety. Made in Austria. Introduced 1990; still imported.

Perf: $495 **Exc:** $425 **VGood:** $350

Add $35 to above prices for Model 22C with adjustable rear sight
Add $30 for Model 22 with adjustable rear sight
Add $80 for fixed Meprolight sight
Add $105 for fixed Trijicon sight
Add $35 for Model 22C with compensated barrel

GLOCK MODEL 23

Semi-automatic; double action; 40 S&W; 13-shot magazine; 4-inch barrel; 6-7/8-inch overall length; 22 oz.; white outline adjustable rear sight, dot on front blade; polymer frame; steel slide; trigger safety; recoil-operated action; firing pin safety; drop safety. Made in Austria. Introduced 1991; still imported.

Perf: $500 **Exc:** $450 **VGood:** $400

Add $30 to above prices for adjustable rear sight
Add $80 for fixed Meprolight sight
Add $105 for fixed Trijicon sight

GLOCK MODEL 24 COMPETITION

Semi-automatic; double action; 40 S&W; 10-shot magazine; 6-inch barrel; 8-1/2-inch overall length; weighs 29-1/2 oz.; black polymer grips; blade front sight with dot, white outline windage-adjustable rear; long-slide competition model available as compensated or non-compensated; factory-installed competition trigger; drop-free magazine. Imported from Austria by Glock, Inc. Introduced 1994; dropped 1999.

New: $665 **Perf:** $525 **Exc:** $450

Compensated barrel

New: $700 **Perf:** $575 **Exc:** $500

GLOCK 26, 27

Semi-automatic; 9mm Para (M26) 10-shot magazine; 40 S&W (M27) 9-shot magazine; 3.47-inch barrel; 21.75 oz.; 6.3-inch overall; integral stippled polymer grips; dot on front blade, fixed or fully adjustable white outline rear sight; subcompact size; polymer frame; steel slide; double-action trigger with "Safe Action" system composing three safeties; matte black Tenifer finish; hammer-forged barrel. Imported from Austria by Glock, Inc. Introduced 1996.

Perf: $500 **Exc:** $450 **VGood:** $400

Adjustable sight

Perf: $525 **Exc:** $475 **VGood:** $425

GLOCK MODEL 28

Similar to Models 26/27, except scaled down smaller size; 380 ACP; 3.46-inch barrel; 20 oz. Available to law enforcement only. Pricing unavailable.

GLOCK 29, 30

Caliber: 10mm (M29), 45 ACP (M30); 10-shot magazine; 3.78-inch barrel; 24 oz.; 6.7-inch overall; integral stippled polymer grips; dot on front, fixed or fully adjustable white outline rear sights; compact size; polymer frame; steel slide; double-recoil spring reduces recoil; Safe Action system with three safeties; Tenifer finish; two magazines supplied. Introduced 1997. Imported from Austria by Glock, Inc.

Perf: $585 **Exc:** $490 **VGood:** $425

Adjustable sight

Perf: $625 **Exc:** $530 **VGood:** $480

GLOCK 29 GEN 4

Double action only, striker fired, semi-auto compact pistol with a polymer frame and fixed sights. Chambered in 10mm. 3.77 inch barrel and 6.96 inch OA length, weighs 1.54 pounds. 10+1 capacity (15+1 optional). Introduced in 2013.

Perf: $570 **Exc:** $500 **VGood:** $460

GLOCK 30S GEN 4

Double action only, striker fired, semi-auto compact pistol with a polymer frame and fixed sights. Chambered in .45 ACP. 3.78 inch barrel and 6.77 inch OA length, weighs 1.26 pounds. 10+1 capacity. Introduced in 2013.

Perf: $570 **Exc:** $500 **VGood:** $460

GLOCK 31

Chambered for the .357 SIG cartridge this pistol is fitted with a 4.5" barrel and a magazine capacity of 10 rounds (15 rounds law enforcement). Overall length is 7.3" and the height is 5.4". Weight is about 23.3 oz. Introduced in 1998. Also available with OD green frame.

NIB.: $500 **Exc:** $450 **VGood:** $400

Grendel P-10

Grendel P-12

Grendel P-30

Great Western Frontier

Hammerli Model 33MP

GLOCK 31C

Same as the Model 31 but with an integral compensator. Also available with OD green frame.

NIB: $550 **Exc:** $500 **VGood:** $450

GLOCK 32

Similar to the Glock 31 except fitted with a 4" barrel. Overall length is 6.85" and height is 5". Magazine capacity is 10 rounds (13 rounds law enforcement). Weight is approximately 21.5 oz. Introduced in 1998. Also available with OD green frame.

NIB: $550 **Exc:** $500 **VGood:** $450

GLOCK 32C

Same as above but fitted with integral ported barrel and slide. Also available with OD green frame.

NIB: $700 **Exc:** $600 **VGood:** $500

GLOCK 33

This .357 SIG model has a 3.5" barrel and an overall length of 6.3". Height is 4.2" and weight is about 17.7 oz. Introduced in 1998. Also available with OD green frame.

NIB: $500 **Exc:** $450 **VGood:** $400

GLOCK 33 GEN 4

Double action only, striker fired, semi-auto sub-compact pistol with a polymer frame and fixed sights. Chambered in .357 Sig. 3.43 inch barrel and 6.49 inch OA length, weighs 1.23 pounds. 19+1 capacity (11/13/15/17 optional). Introduced in 2013.

Perf: $570 **Exc:** $500 **VGood:** $460

GLOCK 34

This model is chambered for the 9x19 cartridge and has a 5.3" barrel, overall length of 8.2", and a magazine capacity of 10 rounds. Empty weight is approximately 23 oz. Also available with OD green frame.

NIB: $575 **Exc:** $500 **VGood:** $450

GLOCK 35

The Glock 35 is chambered for the .40 S&W cartridge. It has the same dimensions as the Glock 34 except for weight, which is 24.5 oz. Also available with OD green frame.

NIB: $600 **Exc:** $500 **VGood:** $450

GLOCK MODEL 37

This semi-automatic pistol is chambered for the .45 G.A.P. cartridge, which is slightly shorter than the .45 ACP cartridge. This cartridge has a muzzle speed of 951 fps and muzzle energy of 405 ft. lbs. Fitted with a 4.49" barrel. Height is 5.5". Overall length is 7.3". Weight is about 26 oz. Also available with OD green frame.

NIB: $500 **Exc:** $425 **VGood:** $375

GLOCK MODEL 38

This .45 G.A.P. pistol is fitted with a 4" barrel. Height is 5" and overall length is 6.85". Magazine capacity is 8 rounds. Weight is about 24 oz. Introduced in 2005. Also available with OD green frame.

NIB: $425 **Exc:** $375 **VGood:** $350

GLOCK MODEL 39

Introduced in 2005 this sub-compact .45 G.A.P. pistol has a 3.46" barrel. Height is 4.17" and overall length is 6.3". Magazine capacity is 8 rounds. Weight is about 19.3 oz. Also available with OD green frame.

NIB: $425 **Exc:** $375 **VGood:** $350

GOLAN

Semi-automatic; 9mm Para., 40 S&W; 10-shot magazine; 3.9-inch barrel; 34 oz.; 7-inch overall; textured composition grips; fixed sights; fully ambidextrous double/single action; forged steel slide; alloy frame; matte blue finish. Introduced 1994. Imported from Israel by KSN Industries, Ltd.

Perf: $565 **Exc:** $515 **VGood:** $460

GREAT WESTERN DERRINGER

Derringer; over/under; 38 S&W, 38 S&W Special; 2-shot; 3-inch barrels; 5-inch overall length; checkered black plastic grips; fixed sights; blued finish. Replica of Remington Double Derringer. Manufactured 1953 to 1962.

Exc: $400 **VGood:** $375 **Good:** $300

GREAT WESTERN FRONTIER

Revolver; single action; 22 LR, 22 Hornet, 38 Spl., 357 Mag., 44 Spl., 44 Mag., 45 Colt; 6-shot cylinder; 4-3/4-inch, 5-1/2-inch, 7-1/2-inch barrel lengths; grooved rear sight, fixed blade front; imitation stag grips; blued finish. Was sold primarily by mail order. Manufactured 1951 to 1962. Add 10% for .44 Special. Deduct 25% for rimfire. Deduct 30% for kit guns, except if new in original kit, unassembled. Note that values shown are for unmodified factory specimens.

Exc: $595 **VGood:** $475 **Good:** $400

GRENDEL P-10

Semi-automatic; double action; 380 ACP; 10-shot magazine; 3-inch barrel; 5-5/16-inch overall length; weighs 15 oz.; checkered polycarbonate metal composite grips; fixed sights; inertia safety hammer system; magazine loads from top; matte black, electroless nickel or green finish. Made in U.S. by Grendel, Inc. Introduced 1987; discontinued 1991.

Perf: $160 **Exc:** $135 **VGood:** $125

GRENDEL P-12

Semi-automatic; double action; 380 ACP; 10-shot magazine; 3-inch barrel; 5-5/16-inch overall length; weighs 13 oz.; checkered DuPont ST-800 polymer grips; fixed sights; inertia safety hammer system; all-steel frame; grip forms magazine well and trigger guard; blue finish. Made in U.S. by Grendel, Inc. Introduced 1992; dropped 1995.

New: $155 **Perf:** $135 **Exc:** $120

Electroless nickel finish

New: $175 **Perf:** $155 **Exc:** $140

GRENDEL P-30

Semi-automatic; double action; 22 WMR; 30-shot magazine; 5-inch, 8-inch barrel; 8-1/2-inch overall length (5-inch barrel); weighs 21 oz. (5-inch barrel); checkered Zytel grips; blade front sight, fixed rear; blowback action with fluted chamber; ambidextrous safety; reversible magazine catch. Made in U.S. by Grendel, Inc. Introduced 1990; dropped 1994.

Perf: $350 **Exc:** $300 **VGood:** $250

GRENDEL P-30L

Same specs as the P-30 except 8-inch barrel only. Made in U.S. by Grendel, Inc. Introduced 1990; dropped 1994.

Perf: $350 **Exc:** $300 **VGood:** $250

GRENDEL P-30M

Same specs as the P-30 except removable muzzlebrake. Made in U.S. by Grendel, Inc. Introduced 1990; dropped 1994.

Perf: $350 **Exc:** $300 **VGood:** $250

GRENDEL P-31

Semi-automatic; 22 WMR; 30-shot magazine; 11-inch barrel; 17-1/2-inch overall length; 48 oz.; adjustable blade front, fixed rear; blowback action with fluted chamber; ambidextrous safety; muzzlebrake; scope mount optional; checkered black Zytel grip and forend; matte black finish. Made in U.S. by Grendel, Inc. Introduced 1991; dropped 1995.

Perf: $450 **Exc:** $400 **VGood:** $350

Hammerli Model 104 Match

Hammerli Model 120

Hammerli Model 120-2

Hammerli Model 106

Hammerli Model 150 Free Pistol

GUARDIAN-SS

Semi-automatic; double action; 380 ACP; 6-shot magazine; 3-1/4-inch barrel; 6-inch overall length; weighs 20 oz.; checkered walnut stocks; ramp front sight, windage-adjustable combat rear; narrow polished trigger; Pachmayr grips; blue slide; hand-fitted barrel; polished feed ramp; funneled magazine well; stainless steel. Introduced 1982; dropped 1985. Marketed by Michigan Armament, Inc.

Exc: $375 **VGood:** $295 **Good:** $225

GUNWORKS MODEL 9 DERRINGER

Derringer; over/under; 38/357 Mag., 9mm/9mm Mag.; bottom-hinged action; 3-inch barrel; weighs 15 oz.; smooth wood stocks; Millett orange bar front sight, fixed rear; all steel; half-cock, through-frame safety; dual extraction; electroless nickel finish; marketed with in-pants holster. Introduced 1984, dropped 1986.

Exc: $135 **VGood:** $120 **Good:** $105

HAMMERLI MODEL 33MP

Single shot; 22 LR; 11-1/2-inch octagonal barrel; 16-1/2-inch overall length; competition free pistol; micrometer rear sight, interchangeable front; European walnut stocks, forearm; Martini-type action; set trigger; blued finish. Manufactured in Switzerland 1933 to 1949.

Exc: $1200 **VGood:** $925 **Good:** $650

HAMMERLI MODEL 100 FREE PISTOL

Single shot; 22 LR; 11-1/2-inch octagon barrel; micrometer rear sight, interchangeable post or bead front; European walnut grips, forearm; adjustable set trigger; blued finish. Introduced 1933; discontinued 1949.

Exc: $975 **VGood:** $700 **Good:** $605

Deluxe model

Exc: $1050 **VGood:** $800 **Good:** $715

HAMMERLI MODEL 101

Single shot; 22 LR; 11-1/2-inch heavy round barrel; adjustable sights; European walnut grip, forearm; adjustable set trigger; same general specs as Model 100 Free Pistol with improved action; matte blue finish. Introduced 1956; discontinued 1960.

Exc: $1080 **VGood:** $700 **Good:** $605

HAMMERLI MODEL 102

Single shot; 22 LR; 11-1/2-inch heavy round barrel; adjustable sights; European walnut grip, forearm; adjustable set trigger; same general specs as Model 101 with high gloss blued finish. Introduced 1956; discontinued 1960.

Exc: $980 **VGood:** $660 **Good:** $605

Deluxe model

Exc: $1090 **VGood:** $770 **Good:** $715

HAMMERLI MODEL 103 FREE PISTOL

Single shot; 22 LR; 11-1/2-inch lightweight octagon barrel; adjustable sights; European walnut grip, forearm; adjustable set trigger; same general specs as Model 101 with high gloss blued finish. Introduced 1956; discontinued 1960.

Exc: $1035 **VGood:** $715 **Good:** $660

With inlaid ivory carvings

Exc: $1200 **VGood:** $900 **Good:** $690

HAMMERLI MODEL 104 MATCH

Single shot; 22 LR; 11-1/2-inch lightweight round barrel; adjustable sights; redesigned adjustable walnut grip; adjustable set trigger; action similar to Model 103; high gloss blued finish. Introduced 1961; discontinued 1965.

Exc: $860 **VGood:** $660 **Good:** $550

HAMMERLI MODEL 105 MATCH

Single shot; 22 LR; 11-1/2-inch octagon barrel; adjustable sights; redesigned adjustable walnut grip; adjustable set trigger; redesigned action; high gloss blued finish. Introduced 1962; discontinued 1965.

Exc: $1035 **VGood:** $715 **Good:** $660

HAMMERLI MODEL 106 MATCH

Single shot; 22 LR; 11-1/2-inch octagon barrel; adjustable sights; same general specs as Model 105 Match except redesigned trigger; replaced Model 104; matte blue finish. Introduced 1966; discontinued 1972.

Exc: $1010 **VGood:** $690 **Good:** $580

HAMMERLI MODEL 107

Single shot; 22 LR; 11-5/16-inch barrel; 16-3/4-inch overall length; weighs 49-1/2 oz.; octagonal barrel; adjustable five-lever set trigger. Introduced 1965; discontinued 1971.

Exc: $1090 **VGood:** $770 **Good:** $660

Deluxe model

Exc: $1400 **VGood:** $990 **Good:** $880

HAMMERLI MODEL 120

Single shot; 22 Short; 10-inch barrel; 15-3/4 inch overall length; weighs 43-1/4 oz.; side-lever operation; micrometer sight; plain butt and trigger guard.

Exc: 7600 **VGood:** $540 **Good:** $475

HAMMERLI MODEL 120-1 FREE PISTOL

Single shot; bolt action; 22 LR; 10-inch barrel; 14-3/4-inch overall length; micrometer rear sight, post front; hand-checkered walnut target grips; adjustable trigger for single- or two-stage pull; aluminum construction; blued finish. Introduced 1972; discontinued 1985.

Exc: $700 **VGood:** $540 **Good:** $475

HAMMERLI MODEL 120-2

Same specs as Model 120-1 Free Pistol except special contoured walnut hand rest; movable sights; blued finish. Introduced 1973; discontinued 1985.

Exc: $700 **VGood:** $540 **Good:** $475

HAMMERLI MODEL 120 HEAVY BARREL

Same specs as Model 120-1 Free Pistol except 5-3/4-inch bull barrel; designed to conform to existing laws governing sporting handgun sales in Great Britain. Introduced 1973; discontinued 1985.

Exc: $700 **VGood:** $540 **Good:** $475

HAMMERLI MODEL 150 FREE PISTOL

Single shot; 22 LR; 11-3/8-inch barrel; 15-3/8-inch overall length; movable front sight on collar, micrometer rear; uncheckered adjustable palm-shelf grip; Martini-type action; straight-line firing pin, no hammer; adjustable set trigger; blued finish. Introduced 1973; discontinued 1989.

Perf: $1950 **Exc:** $1495 **VGood:** $1275

Left-hand

Perf: $2065 **Exc:** $1650 **VGood:** $1425

HAMMERLI MODEL 151 FREE PISTOL

Single shot; 22 LR; 11-3/8-inch barrel; 15-3/8-inch overall length; movable front sight on collar, micrometer rear; uncheckered adjustable palm-shelf grip; Martini-type action; straight-line firing pin; no hammer; adjustable set trigger; blued finish. Replaced Model 150 Free Pistol. Introduced 1990; discontinued 1993.

Perf: $1950 **Exc:** $1495 **VGood:** $1275

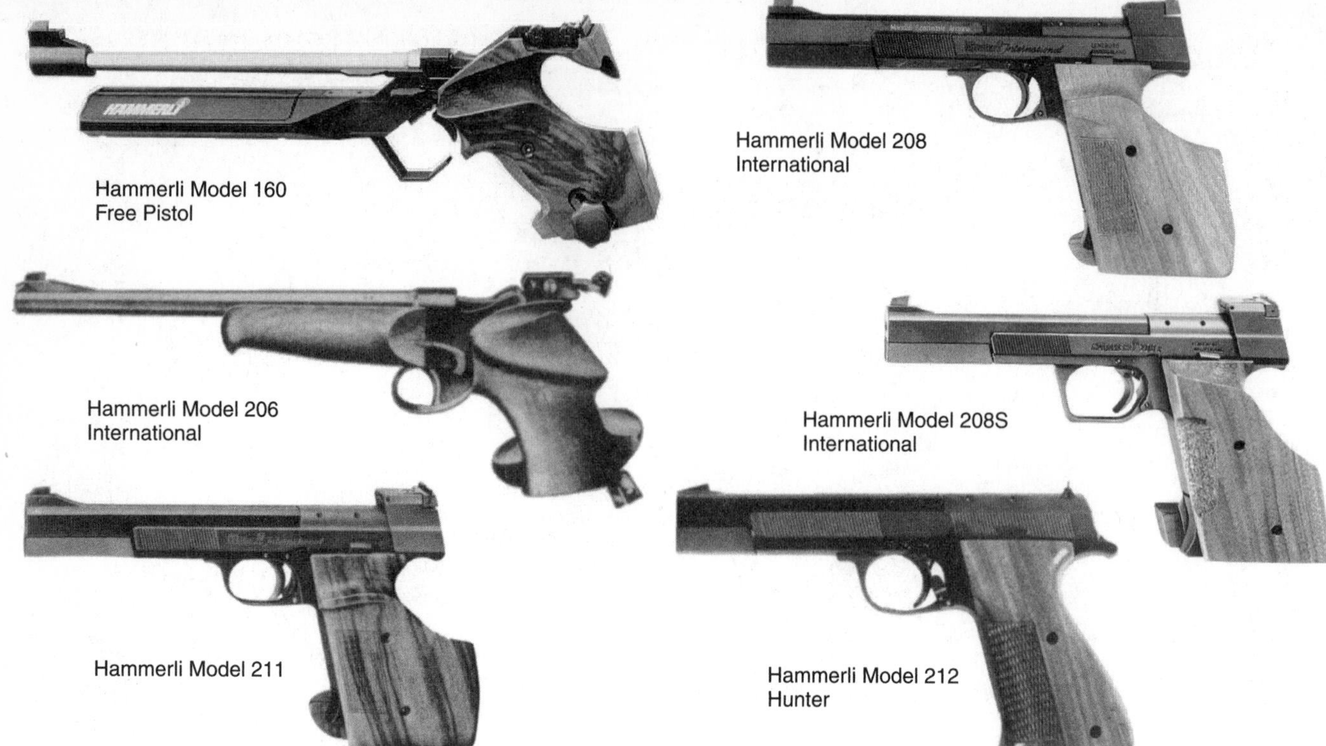
Hammerli Model 160 Free Pistol

Hammerli Model 208 International

Hammerli Model 206 International

Hammerli Model 208S International

Hammerli Model 211

Hammerli Model 212 Hunter

HAMMERLI MODEL 152 MATCH

Single shot; 22 LR; 11-5/16-inch barrel; 16-7/8-inch overall length; weighs 46-5/8 oz.; changeable post-type front sight, micrometer rear; match stocks; electronic trigger; improved Martini-style action; blued action. Introduced 1990; discontinued 1992.

Perf: $2095 **Exc:** $1600 **VGood:** $1350

Left-hand

Perf: $2060 **Exc:** $1660 **VGood:** $1410

HAMMERLI MODEL 160 FREE PISTOL

Single shot; 22 LR; 11-1/4-inch barrel; 17-1/2-inch overall length; weighs 47 oz.; walnut grip; full match-style with adjustable palm shelf, stippled surfaces; changeable blade front sight, open, fully-adjustable match rear; mechanical set trigger, fully adjustable with provision for dry firing. Imported from Switzerland by Hammerli Pistols USA. Introduced 1993; dropped 2002.

New: $1900 **Perf:** $1700 **Exc:** $1450

HAMMERLI MODEL 162 FREE PISTOL

Single shot; 22 LR; 11-1/4-inch barrel; 17-1/2-inch overall length; weighs 47 oz.; walnut grip; full match-style with adjustable palm shelf, stippled surfaces; changeable blade front sight, open, fully-adjustable match rear; electronic trigger, fully adjustable with provision for dry firing. Imported from Switzerland by Hammerli Pistols USA. Introduced 1993; dropped 2000.

New: $2250 **Perf:** $1850 **Exc:** $1500

HAMMERLI MODEL 206 INTERNATIONAL

Semi-automatic; single action; 22 LR, 22 Short; 8-shot magazine; 7-1/16-inch barrel; adjustable sights; checkered walnut thumbrest grips; muzzlebrake; slide stop; adjustable trigger; blued finish. Introduced 1964; discontinued 1967.

Exc: $775 **VGood:** $625 **Good:** $525

HAMMERLI MODEL 207 INTERNATIONAL

Semi-automatic; single action; 22 LR, 22 Short; 8-shot magazine; 7-1/16-inch barrel; adjustable sights; smooth walnut grips with adjustable grip plates; muzzlebrake; slide stop; adjustable trigger; blued finish. Introduced 1964; discontinued 1969.

Exc: $825 **VGood:** $650 **Good:** $550

HAMMERLI MODEL 208 INTERNATIONAL

Semi-automatic; single action; 22 LR; 8-shot magazine; 6-inch barrel; 10-inch overall length; weighs 37-1/2 oz.; adjustable sights; smooth walnut grips with adjustable grip plates; adjustable trigger; blued finish. Introduced 1966; discontinued 1988.

Perf: $2100 **Exc:** $1700 **VGood:** $1450

HAMMERLI MODEL 208S INTERNATIONAL

Same specs as International Model 208 except interchangeable rear sight; restyled trigger guard. Introduced 1988; dropped 2000.

New: $2550 **Perf:** $2150 **Exc:** $1750

HAMMERLI MODEL 209 INTERNATIONAL

Semi-automatic; single action; 22 Short; 5-shot magazine; 4-3/4-inch barrel; adjustable sights; walnut grips; adjustable muzzlebrake, barrel vents, gas-escape ports; lightweight bolt; blued finish. Introduced 1967; discontinued 1970.

Exc: $900 **VGood:** $690 **Good:** $635

HAMMERLI MODEL 210 INTERNATIONAL

Semi-automatic; single action; 22 Short; 5-shot magazine; 4-3/4-inch barrel; adjustable sights; adjustable walnut grip plates; adjustable muzzlebrake, barrel vents, gas-escape ports; lightweight bolt; blued finish. Introduced 1967; discontinued 1970.

Exc: $900 **VGood:** $715 **Good:** $660

HAMMERLI MODEL 211

Semi-automatic; single action; 22 LR; 9-shot magazine; 6-inch barrel; 10-inch overall length; weighs 37 oz.; walnut stocks with adjustable palm rest; fully-adjustable match sights; interchangeable front and rear blades; fully-adjustable trigger. Imported from Switzerland by Mandall Shooting Supplies, and also Beeman. Introduced 1973; discontinued 1990.

Perf: $1650 **Exc:** $1275 **VGood:** $1050

HAMMERLI MODEL 212 HUNTER

Semi-automatic; single action; 22 LR; 8-shot magazine; 5-inch barrel; 8-1/2-inch overall length; weighs 31 oz.; adjustable sights; checkered walnut stocks; adjustable trigger; blued finish. Made in Switzerland. Introduced 1984; no longer imported.

Perf: $1350 **Exc:** $1000 **VGood:** $950

HAMMERLI MODEL 215

Semi-automatic; single action; target model; 22 LR; 8-shot magazine; 5-inch barrel; adjustable sights; walnut grip with plates; adjustable trigger; blued finish. Made in Switzerland. Importation discontinued 1991.

Perf: $1495 **Exc:** $1050 **VGood:** $850

HAMMERLI MODEL 230-1

Semi-automatic; 22 Short; 5-shot magazine; 6-5/16-inch barrel; 11-5/8-inch overall length; micrometer rear sight, post front; uncheckered European walnut thumbrest grips; blued finish. Designed for rapid-fire International competition. Introduced 1970; discontinued 1983.

Exc: $800 **VGood:** $635 **Good:** $585

HAMMERLI MODEL 230-2

Same specs as Model 230-1 except partially checkered stocks; adjustable heel plate. Introduced 1970; discontinued 1983.

Exc: $835 **VGood:** $655 **Good:** $605

HAMMERLI MODEL 232-1

Semi-automatic; 22 Short; 6-shot magazine; 5-inch barrel with six exhaust ports; 10-3/8-inch overall length; weighs 44 oz.; interchangeable front, rear blades, adjustable micrometer rear sight; walnut grips; recoil-operated; adjustable trigger; blued finish. Made in Switzerland. Introduced 1984; importation discontinued 1993.

Perf: $1495 **Exc:** $1125 **VGood:** $950

HAMMERLI MODEL 232-2

Same specs as Model 232-1 except wrap-around grips. Introduced 1984; importation discontinued 1993.

Perf: $1400 **Exc:** $1150 **VGood:** $950

Hammerli Model 230-1

Hammerli Model 280 Target

Hammerli SP 20 Target

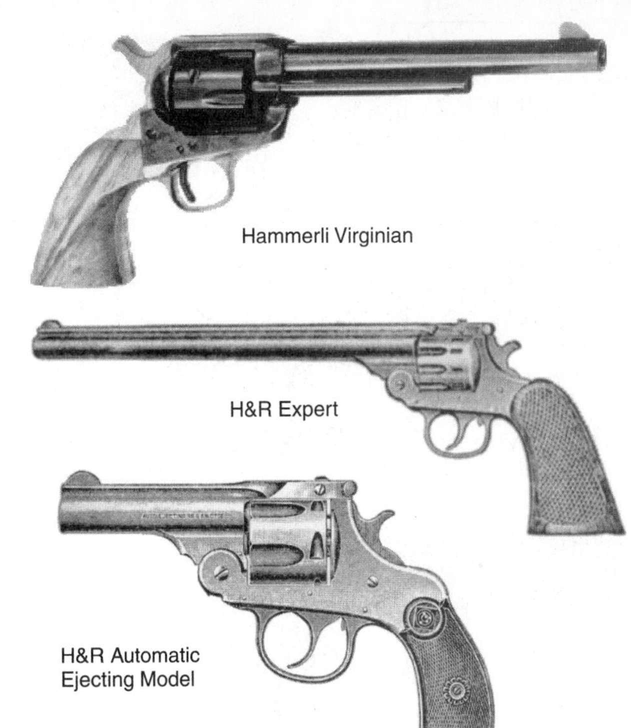
Hammerli Virginian

H&R Expert

H&R Automatic Ejecting Model

HAMMERLI MODEL 280 TARGET

Semi-automatic; 22 LR; 32 S&W Long WC; 6-shot magazine (22 LR), 5-shot (32 S&W); 4-1/2-inch barrel; 11-13/16-inch overall length; weighs 39 oz.; micro-adjustable match sights; stippled match-type walnut stocks; adjustable palm shelf carbon-reinforced synthetic frame and bolt/barrel housing; fully-adjustable, interchangeable trigger. Made in Switzerland. Introduced, 1990; importation dropped 2000.

Perf: $1550 **Exc:** $1125 **VGood:** $900

HAMMERLI SP 20 TARGET

Semi-automatic; 22 LR, 32 S&W; 4.6-inch barrel; 34.6-41.8 oz.; 11.8-inch overall; anatomically shaped synthetic Hi-Grip available in five sizes; integral front sight in three widths, adjustable rear with changeable notch widths; extremely low-level sight line; anatomically shaped trigger; adjustable JPS buffer system for different recoil characteristics; receiver available in red, blue, gold, violet or black. Introduced 1998. Imported from Switzerland by SIGARMS, Inc.

Perf: $1425 **Exc:** $1075 **VGood:** $925

HAMMERLI VIRGINIAN

Revolver; single action; 357 Mag., 45 Colt; 6-shot cylinder; 4-5/8-inch, 5-1/2-inch, 7-1/2-inch barrels; grooved rear sight, blade front; one-piece European walnut grips; case-hardened; chrome grip frame, triggerguard; blued frame cylinder; same general design as Colt SAA except for base pin safety feature. Manufactured in Europe, 1973 to 1976, for exclusive Interarms importation.

Exc: $575 **VGood:** $450 **Good:** $325

HAMMERLI-WALTHER MODEL 200 OLYMPIA

Semi-automatic; 22 LR, 22 Short; 8-shot magazine; 7-1/2-inch barrel; micrometer rear sight, ramp front; walnut thumbrest grip; muzzle brake; adjustable barrel weights; blued finish. Also known as Quickfire. Based on 1936 Olympia with some parts interchangeable. Introduced 1950. In 1958, muzzle brake was redesigned. Discontinued 1963.

Exc: $825 **VGood:** $605 **Good:** $550

HAMMERLI-WALTHER MODEL 201

Semi-automatic; 22 LR, 22 Short; 8-shot magazine; 9-1/2-inch barrel; micrometer rear sight, ramp front; adjustable custom walnut grip; muzzle brake; adjustable barrel weights; blued finish. Introduced 1955; discontinued 1957.

Exc: $750 **VGood:** $600 **Good:** $550

HAMMERLI-WALTHER MODEL 202

Semi-automatic; 22 LR, 22 Short; 8-shot magazine; 9-1/2-inch barrel; micrometer rear sight, ramp front; adjustable walnut thumbrest grip; muzzle brake; adjustable barrel weights; blued finish. Introduced 1955; discontinued 1957.

Exc: $775 **VGood:** $605 **Good:** $550

HAMMERLI-WALTHER MODEL 203

Semi-automatic; 22 LR, 22 Short; 8-shot magazine; 7-1/2-inch barrel; micrometer rear sight, ramp front; adjustable walnut thumbrest grip; optional muzzle brake (1958 model); slide stop; adjustable barrel weights; blued finish. Called the American Model. Introduced 1955; discontinued 1959.

Exc: $775 **VGood:** $605 **Good:** $550

With muzzle brake

Exc: $850 **VGood:** $660 **Good:** $605

HAMMERLI-WALTHER MODEL 204

Semi-automatic; 22 LR; 8-shot magazine; 7-1/2-inch barrel; micrometer rear sight, ramp front; walnut thumbrest grip; optional muzzle brake; slide stop; adjustable barrel weights; blued finish. Introduced 1956; discontinued 1963.

Exc: $775 **VGood:** $635 **Good:** $580

With muzzle brake

Exc: $875 **VGood:** $690 **Good:** $635

HAMMERLI-WALTHER MODEL 205

Semi-automatic; 22 LR; 8-shot magazine; 7-1/2-inch barrel; micrometer rear sight, ramp front; checkered French walnut thumbrest grip; detachable muzzle brake; slide stop; adjustable barrel weights; blued finish. Introduced 1956; discontinued 1963.

Exc: $900 **VGood:** $690 **Good:** $635

With muzzle brake

Exc: $955 **VGood:** $745 **Good:** $715

HARRINGTON & RICHARDSON 22 SPECIAL

Revolver; double action; 22 Short, 22 Long, 22 LR, 22 WMR; 9-shot cylinder; 6-inch barrel; 11-inch overall length; weighs 23 oz.; heavy hinged-frame; fixed notch rear sight, gold-plated front; checkered walnut grips; blued. Originally introduced as Model 944; later version with recessed cylinder for high-speed ammo was listed as Model 945. Introduced 1925; dropped 1941.

Exc: $165 **VGood:** $140 **Good:** $120

HARRINGTON & RICHARDSON YOUNG AMERICAN

Revolver; double action; 32 S&W Long, 32 S&W, 32 Colt New Police; 6-shot (32), 5-shot (38); 2-1/2-inch, 4-1/2-inch, 6-inch barrel; weighs 16 oz.; solid frame; fixed sights; hard rubber grips; blued, nickel finish. Introduced 1883; dropped during WWII.

Exc: $150 **VGood:** $100 **Good:** $75

HARRINGTON & RICHARDSON AUTOMATIC EJECTING MODEL

Revolver; double action; 32 S&W Long, 38 S&W; 6-shot cylinder (32), 5-shot (38); 3-1/4-inch, 4-inch, 5-inch, 6-inch barrel; weighs 16 oz.; hinged-frame; fixed sights; hard rubber or checkered walnut target grips; blued, nickel finish. Introduced 1891; dropped 1941.

Exc: $160 **VGood:** $150 **Good:** $105

HARRINGTON & RICHARDSON BOBBY MODEL

Revolver; double action; 32 S&W Long, 38 S&W; 6-shot cylinder (32), 5-shot (38); 4-inch barrel; 9-inch overall length; hinged-frame; fixed sights; checkered walnut grips; blued finish. Also listed as the Model 15. Designed for use by London police during WWII. Introduced 1941; dropped 1943. Collector value.

Exc: $200 **VGood:** $150 **Good:** $125

HARRINGTON & RICHARDSON EXPERT

Revolver; double action; 22 LR, 22 WMR; 9-shot; 10-inch barrel; heavy hinged frame; fixed rear sight; gold-plated front; checkered walnut grips; blued

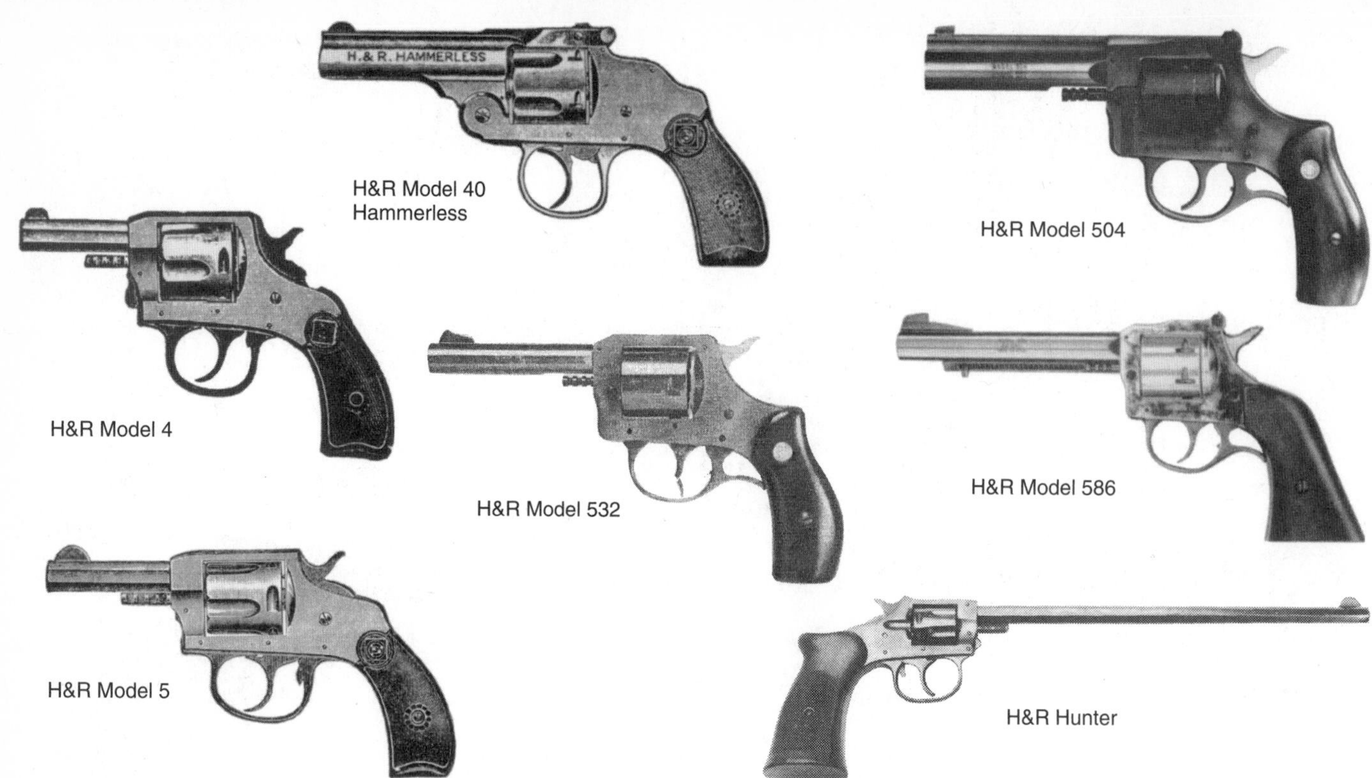
H&R Model 40 Hammerless

H&R Model 504

H&R Model 4

H&R Model 532

H&R Model 586

H&R Model 5

H&R Hunter

finish. Listed as the Model 955. Introduced 1929; dropped 1941.

Exc: $150 **VGood:** $140 **Good:** $120

HARRINGTON & RICHARDSON HUNTER MODEL

Revolver; double action; 22 LR; 9-shot cylinder; 10-inch octagon barrel; solid-frame; fixed sights; checkered walnut grips; blued finish. Introduced 1926; dropped 1941.

Exc: $200 **VGood:** $170 **Good:** $100

HARRINGTON & RICHARDSON MODEL 4

Revolver; double action; 32 S&W Long, 38 S&W, 38 Colt New Police; 6-shot cylinder (32), 5-shot (38); 21/2-inch, 41/2-inch, 6-inch barrels; solid frame; fixed sights; hard rubber grips; blued or nickel finish. Introduced 1905; dropped 1941.

Exc: $95 **VGood:** $85 **Good:** $75

HARRINGTON & RICHARDSON MODEL 5

Revolver; double action; 32 S&W Short; 5-shot cylinder; 2-1/2-inch, 4-1/2-inch, 6-inch barrels; light frame; fixed sights; hard rubber grips; blued or nickel finish. Introduced 1905; dropped 1941.

Exc: $95 **VGood:** $85 **Good:** $7

HARRINGTON & RICHARDSON MODEL 6

Revolver; double action; 22 Short, 22 Long, 22 LR; 7-shot cylinder; 2-1/2-inch, 4-1/2-inch, 6-inch barrels; solid frame; hard rubber grips; blued or nickel finish. Introduced 1906; dropped 1941.

Exc: $95 **VGood:** $85 **Good:** $70

HARRINGTON & RICHARDSON MODEL 40 HAMMERLESS

Revolver; double action; 22 LR, 32 S&W Short; 7-shot cylinder (22), 5-shot (32); 2-inch, 3-inch, 4-inch, 5-inch, 6-inch barrels; fixed sights; small hinged-frame; hard rubber stocks; blued or nickel finish. Also listed during late production as Model 45. Introduced 1899; dropped 1941.

Exc: $150 **VGood:** $85 **Good:** $65

HARRINGTON & RICHARDSON MODEL 50 HAMMERLESS

Revolver; double action; 32 S&W Long, 38 S&W; 6-shot cylinder (32), 5-shot (38); 3-1/4-inch, 4-inch, 5-inch, 6-inch barrels; fixed sights; small hinged-frame; hard rubber stocks; blued or nickel finish. Also listed during late production as Model 55. Introduced 1899; dropped 1941.

Exc: $135 **VGood:** $80 **Good:** $60

HARRINGTON & RICHARDSON MODEL 504

Revolver; 32 H&R Mag.; 5-shot cylinder; 3-inch, 4-inch, 6-inch barrel; blued finish. Introduced 1984; dropped 1985.

Perf: $300 **Exc:** $250 **VGood:** $200

HARRINGTON & RICHARDSON MODEL 532

Revolver; 32 H&R Mag.; 5-shot cylinder: 2-1/2-inch, 4-inch barrel; solid frame; round butt; wood grips; blued finish. Introduced 1984; dropped 1985.

Perf: $310 **Exc:** $275 **VGood:** $225

HARRINGTON & RICHARDSON MODEL 586

Revolver; double action; 32 H&R Mag.; 5-shot cylinder; 4-1/2-inch, 5-1/2-inch, 7-1/2-inch, 10-inch barrel; adjustable rear sight; fixed cylinder; plastic or wood grips. Introduced 1984; dropped 1985.

Perf: $375 **Exc:** $300 **VGood:** $250

HARRINGTON & RICHARDSON MODEL 603

Revolver; double action; 22 WMR; 6-shot cylinder; 6-inch flat-sided barrel; blade front sight, fully-adjustable rear; smooth walnut grips; swing-out cylinder; coil spring construction; blued finish. Introduced 1981; dropped 1983.

Exc: $200 **VGood:** $150 **Good:** $100

HARRINGTON & RICHARDSON MODEL 604

Revolver; double action; 22 WMR; 6-shot cylinder; 6-inch bull barrel with raised solid rib; blade front, fully-adjustable rear sight; smooth walnut grips; swing-out cylinder; coil spring construction; blued finish. Introduced 1981; dropped 1985.

Exc: $200 **VGood:** $150 **Good:** $100

HARRINGTON & RICHARDSON MODEL 622

Revolver; double action; 22 LR, 22 Short, 22 Long; 6-shot cylinder; 2-1/2-inch, 4-inch, 6-inch barrels; solid frame; fixed sights; checkered black plastic grips; satin blued finish. Introduced 1957; dropped 1963.

Exc: $175 **VGood:** $150 **Good:** $100

HARRINGTON & RICHARDSON MODEL 623

Revolver; double action; 22 LR, 22 Short; 6-shot cylinder; 2-1/2-inch, 4-inch, 6-inch barrels; solid frame; fixed sights; checkered plastic grips; chrome finish. Introduced 1957; dropped 1963.

Exc: $135 **VGood:** $105 **Good:** $85

HARRINGTON & RICHARDSON MODEL 632 GUARDSMAN

Revolver; double action; 32 S&W, 32 S&W Long; 6-shot cylinder; 2-1/2-inch, 4-inch barrels; weighs 20 oz.; solid frame; fixed sights; checkered Tenite grips; blued finish. Introduced 1946; dropped 1957.

Exc: $175 **VGood:** $150 **Good:** $125

HARRINGTON & RICHARDSON MODEL 633

Revolver; double action; 32 S&W, 32 S&W Long; 6-shot cylinder; 2-1/2-inch, 4-inch barrels; weighs 20 oz.; solid frame; fixed sights; checkered Tenite grips; nickel finish. Introduced 1946; dropped 1957.

Exc: $175 **VGood:** $150 **Good:** $125

HARRINGTON & RICHARDSON MODEL 649

Revolver; double action; two 6-shot cylinders; 22 LR, 22 WMR; 5-1/2-inch, 7-1/2-inch barrel; solid frame; blade front, adjustable rear sight; one-piece

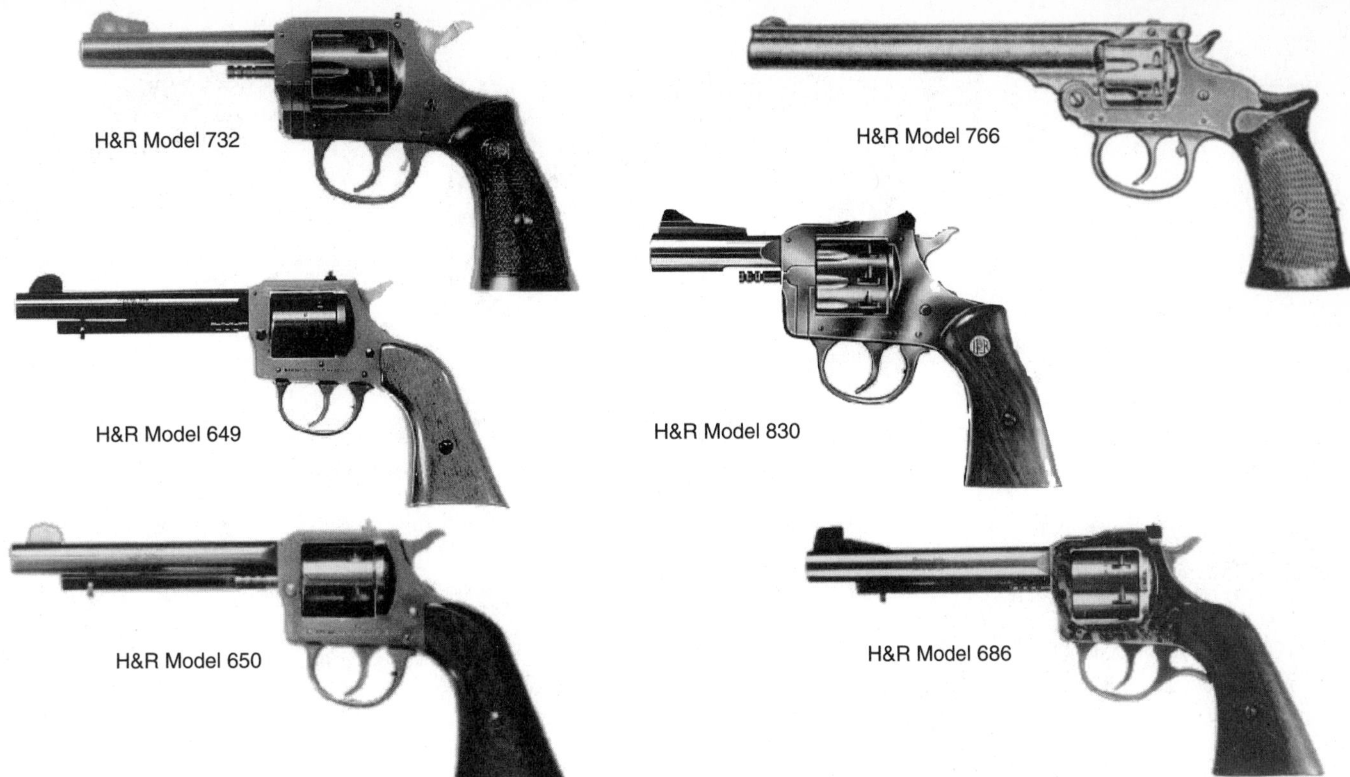
H&R Model 732

H&R Model 766

H&R Model 649

H&R Model 830

H&R Model 650

H&R Model 686

walnut grip; blued finish. Introduced in 1976; dropped 1980.

Exc: $225 **VGood:** $200 **Good:** $150

HARRINGTON & RICHARDSON MODEL 650

Revolver; double action; 22 LR, 22 WMR; 6-shot cylinder; 5-1/2-inch barrel; solid frame; blade front, adjustable rear sight; one-piece walnut grip; nickel finished. Introduced 1976; dropped 1980.

Exc: $200 **VGood:** $150 **Good:** $115

HARRINGTON & RICHARDSON MODEL 666

Revolver; double action; 22 LR, 22 WMR; two 6-shot cylinders; 6-inch barrel; solid frame; fixed sights; plastic stocks; blued finish. Introduced 1976; dropped 1980.

Exc: $225 **VGood:** $200 **Good:** $175

HARRINGTON & RICHARDSON MODEL 676

Revolver; double action; 22 LR, 22 WMR; two 6-shot cylinders; 4-1/2-inch, 5-1/2-inch, 7-1/2-inch, 12-inch barrel; solid frame; blade front, adjustable rear sight; one-piece walnut grip; color case-hardened frame; blued finish. Introduced 1976; dropped 1985.

Exc: $225 **VGood:** $200 **Good:** $175

HARRINGTON & RICHARDSON MODEL 686

Revolver; double action; 22 LR, 22 WMR; two 6-shot cylinders; 5-1/2-inch, 7-1/2-inch, 10-inch, 12-inch barrel; ramp and blade front sight, fully-adjustable rear; one-piece walnut grip; color case-hardened frame; blued finish. Introduced 1981; dropped 1985.

Exc: $225 **VGood:** $200 **Good:** $175

HARRINGTON & RICHARDSON MODEL 732

Revolver; double action; 32 S&W, 32 S&W Long, 32 H&R Mag.; 6-shot swing-out cylinder; 2-1/2-inch, 4-inch barrels; solid frame; windage-adjustable rear sight (4-inch model), fixed on shorter barrel, ramp front; black plastic checkered grips; blued finish. Introduced 1958; dropped 1985.

Exc: $150 **VGood:** $125 **Good:** $100

32 H&R Mag.

Exc: $275 **VGood:** $225 **Good:** $175

HARRINGTON & RICHARDSON MODEL 733

Revolver; double action; 32 S&W, 32 S&W Long, 32 H&R Mag.; 6-shot swing-out cylinder; 2-1/2-inch barrel; solid frame; Windage-adjustable rear sight (4-inch model), fixed on shorter barrel; ramp front; plastic checkered grips; same as Model 932 except nickel finish. Introduced 1958; dropped 1985.

Exc: $150 **VGood:** $125 **Good:** $100

32 H&R Mag.

Exc: $275 **VGood:** $225 **Good:** $175

HARRINGTON & RICHARDSON MODEL 766

Revolver; double action; 22 LR; 7-shot cylinder; 6-inch barrel; target; hinged frame; fixed sights; checkered walnut grips; blued finish. Introduced 1926; dropped 1936.

Exc: $125 **VGood:** $110 **Good:** $100

HARRINGTON & RICHARDSON MODEL 826

Revolver; double action; 22 LR, 22 WMR; 9-shot; 3-inch bull barrel; weighs 27 oz.; ramp blade front, adjustable rear sight; uncheckered American walnut stocks; recessed muzzle; swing-out cylinder; blued finish. Introduced 1982; dropped 1984.

Exc: $200 **VGood:** $175 **Good:** $125

HARRINGTON & RICHARDSON MODEL 829

Revolver; double action; 22 LR; 9-shot cylinder; 3-inch bull barrel; weighs 27 oz.; uncheckered American walnut stocks; ramp/blade front sight, adjustable rear; blued finish; recessed muzzle; swing-out cylinder. Introduced 1982; dropped 1984.

Exc: $120 **VGood:** $90 **Good:** $75

HARRINGTON & RICHARDSON MODEL 830

Revolver; double action; 22 LR, 22 WMR; 9-shot; 3-inch bull barrel; weighs 27 oz.; ramp blade front, adjustable rear sight; uncheckered American walnut stocks; recessed muzzle; swing-out cylinder; nickel finish. Introduced 1982; dropped 1984.

Exc: $120 **VGood:** $95 **Good:** $75

HARRINGTON & RICHARDSON MODEL 832

Revolver; double action; 32 S&W Long; 9-shot; 3-inch bull barrel; weighs 27 oz.; ramp blade front, adjustable rear sight; uncheckered American walnut stocks; recessed muzzle; swing-out cylinder; blued finish. Introduced 1982; dropped 1984.

Exc: $120 **VGood:** $75 **Good:** $70

HARRINGTON & RICHARDSON MODEL 833

Revolver; double action; 32 S&W Long; 9-shot; 3-inch bull barrel; weighs 27 oz.; ramp blade front, adjustable rear sight; uncheckered American walnut stocks; recessed muzzle; swing-out cylinder; nickel finish. Introduced 1982; dropped 1984.

Exc: $130 **VGood:** $95 **Good:** $75

HARRINGTON & RICHARDSON MODEL 900

Revolver; double action; 22 LR, 22 Short, 22 Long; 9-shot swing-out cylinder; 2-1/2-inch, 4-inch, 6-inch barrels; solid frame; blade front sight; high-impact black plastic grips; blued finish. Introduced 1962; dropped 1973.

Exc: $120 **VGood:** $95 **Good:** $75

HARRINGTON & RICHARDSON MODEL 901

Revolver; double action; 22 LR, 22 Short, 22 Long; 9-shot swing-out cylinder; 2-1/2-inch, 4-inch, 6-inch barrels; solid frame; fixed sights; high-impact white plastic grips; chrome finish. Introduced 1962; dropped 1963.

Exc: $150 **VGood:** $125 **Good:** $90

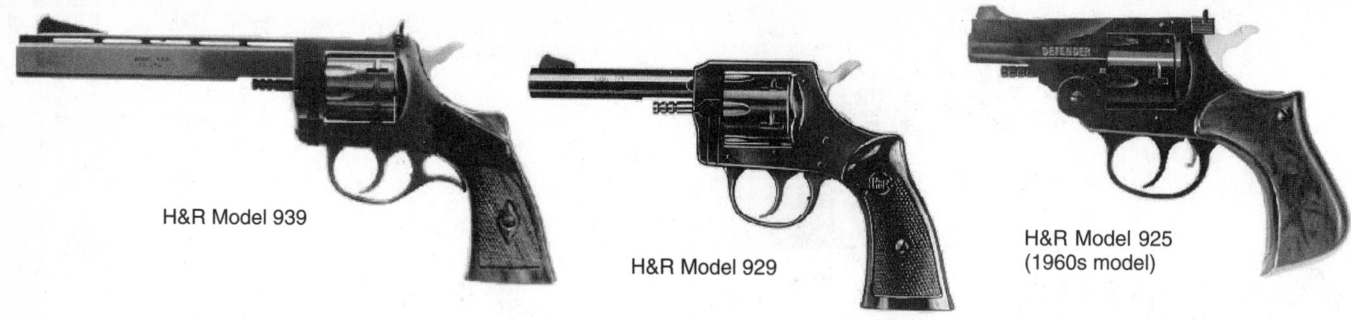

H&R Model 939

H&R Model 929

H&R Model 925 (1960s model)

H&R Model 926

H&R Model 905

H&R Model 925 (Early Model)

HARRINGTON & RICHARDSON MODEL 903

Revolver; double action; 22 LR; 9-shot cylinder; 6-inch flat-sided barrel; blade front sight, fully-adjustable rear; smooth walnut grips; swing-out cylinder; coil spring construction; blued finish. Introduced 1981; dropped 1985.

Exc: $100 **VGood:** $85 **Good:** $75

HARRINGTON & RICHARDSON MODEL 904

Revolver; double action; 22 LR; 9-shot cylinder; 6-inch bull barrel with raised solid rib; blade front, fully-adjustable rear sight; smooth walnut grips; swing-out cylinder; coil spring construction; blued finish. Introduced 1981; dropped 1985.

Exc: $150 **VGood:** $135 **Good:** $120

HARRINGTON & RICHARDSON MODEL 905

Revolver; double action; 22 LR; 9-shot cylinder; 4-inch bull barrel with raised solid rib; blade front, fully-adjustable rear sight; smooth walnut grips; swing-out cylinder; coil spring construction; H&R Hard-Guard finish. Introduced 1981; dropped 1985.

Exc: $160 **VGood:** $140 **Good:** $125

HARRINGTON & RICHARDSON MODEL 922

Revolver; double action; 22 Short, 22 Long, 22 LR; 9-shot cylinder; 4-inch, 6-inch, 10-inch barrel; 10-1/2-inch overall length (6-inch barrel); weighs 21-3/4 oz.; solid frame; fixed sights; checkered walnut or Tenite grips; blued finish. Introduced in 1919. Early production had 10-inch octagonal barrel, later dropped.

Exc: $200 **VGood:** $150 **Good:** $100

HARRINGTON & RICHARDSON MODEL 922 BANTAMWEIGHT

Same specs as Model 922 except 2-1/2-inch barrel; weighs 20 oz.; rounded butt. Introduced 1951; no longer produced.

Exc: $200 **VGood:** $150 **Good:** $100

HARRINGTON & RICHARDSON MODEL 922 CAMPER

Same specs as Model 922 except 4-inch barrel; weighs 21 oz.; special small Tenite grips. Introduced 1952.

Exc: $200 **VGood:** $150 **Good:** $100

HARRINGTON & RICHARDSON MODEL 923

Revolver; double action; 22 Short, 22 Long, 22 LR; 9-shot cylinder; 4-inch, 6-inch, 10-inch barrel; 10-1/2-inch overall length (6-inch barrel); weighs 21-3/4 oz.; solid frame; fixed sights; checkered walnut or Tenite grips; chrome finish. Introduced in 1919. Early production had 10-inch octagonal barrel, later dropped.

Exc: $200 **VGood:** $160 **Good:** $125

HARRINGTON & RICHARDSON MODEL 925

Revolver; double action; 38 S&W; 5-shot cylinder; 2-1/2-inch, 4-inch, 6-inch barrel; weighs 25 oz. (4-inch barrel); hinged frame; fixed front, adjustable rear sight; one-piece smooth or checkered plastic grip; blued finish. Advertised as the Defender Model; originally introduced as Model 25. Introduced 1964; dropped 1981.

Exc: $275 **VGood:** $200 **Good:** $150

HARRINGTON & RICHARDSON MODEL 926

Revolver; double action; 22 LR, 22 Short, 22 Long, 38 S&W; 9-shot cylinder (22), 5-shot (38 S&W); 4-inch barrel; weighs 31 oz.; hinged frame; fixed front, adjustable rear sight; checkered walnut stocks; blued finish. Introduced 1968; dropped 1980.

Exc: $250 **VGood:** $200 **Good:** $125

HARRINGTON & RICHARDSON MODEL 929

Revolver; double action; 22 LR, 22 Short, 22 Long; 9-shot cylinder; 2-1/2-inch, 4-inch, 6-inch barrels; weighs 23 oz. (2-1/2-inch barrel); solid frame; swing-out cylinder; auto extractor; fixed sights; checkered plastic grips; blued finish. Advertised as Sidekick Model. Introduced 1956; dropped 1985. Reintroduced 1996 by H&R 1871, Inc.; no longer produced.

Exc: $225 **VGood:** $175 **Good:** $125

HARRINGTON & RICHARDSON MODEL 930

Revolver; double action; 22 LR, 22 Short, 22 Long; 9-shot cylinder; 2-1/2-inch, 4-inch, 6-inch barrels; solid frame; swing-out cylinder; fixed sights; checkered plastic grips; same as Model 929 except nickel finish. Introduced 1956; dropped 1985.

Exc: $125 **VGood:** $110 **Good:** $80

HARRINGTON & RICHARDSON MODEL 939

Revolver; double action; 22 LR; 9-shot cylinder; 6-inch barrel with vent rib; solid-frame; swing-out cylinder; ramp front, adjustable rear sight; checkered walnut grips; blued finish. Advertised as the Ultra Sidekick Model. Introduced 1958; dropped 1981. Reintroduced in 1995 by H&R 1871, Inc.; no longer in production.

Exc: $200 **VGood:** $150 **Good:** $125

HARRINGTON & RICHARDSON MODEL 939 PREMIER

Revolver; double action; 22 LR; 9-shot cylinder; 6-inch heavy barrel; weighs 36 oz.; walnut-finished hardwood grips; blade front sight, fully-adjustable rear; swing-out cylinder; plunger-type ejection; solid barrel rib; high-polish blue finish; Western-style grip. Made in U.S. by H&R 1871, Inc. Introduced 1995; no longer produced.

New: $200 **Perf:** $150 **Exc:** $125

HARRINGTON & RICHARDSON MODEL 940

Revolver; double action; 22 Short, 22 Long, 22 LR; 9-shot; 6-inch barrel; vent rib; ramp front sight, adjustable rear; checkered hardwood grips; thumbrest; swingout cylinder; blued finish. Advertised as Ultra Sidekick. Introduced 1978; dropped 1982.

Exc: $200 **VGood:** $150 **Good:** $125

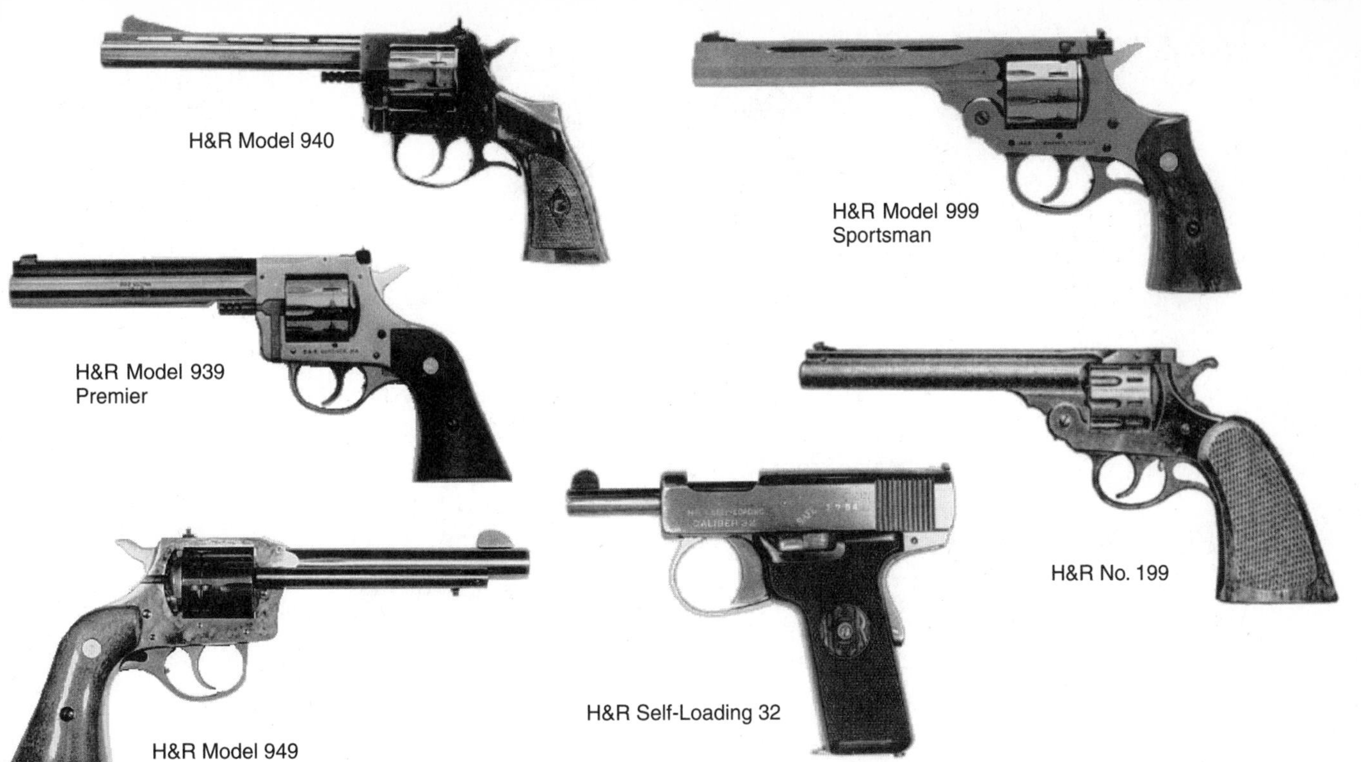
H&R Model 940

H&R Model 999 Sportsman

H&R Model 939 Premier

H&R No. 199

H&R Self-Loading 32

H&R Model 949

HARRINGTON & RICHARDSON MODEL 949

Revolver; double action; 22 LR, Long, Short; 9-shot cylinder; 5-1/2-inch barrel; solid-frame; side-loading, ejection; adjustable rear sight, blade front; one-piece plain walnut grip; blued, nickel finish. Advertised as Forty-Niner Model. Introduced in 1960; dropped, 1985.

Exc: $200 **VGood:** $160 **Good:** $125

HARRINGTON & RICHARDSON MODEL 949 WESTERN

Revolver; double action; 22 LR; 9-shot cylinder; 5-1/2-inch, 7-1/2-inch barrel; weighs 36 oz.; walnut-stained hardwood grips; blade front sight, adjustable rear; color case-hardened frame and backstrap; traditional loading gate and ejector rod. Made in U.S. by Harrington & Richardson. Introduced 1994; no longer produced.

New: $200 **Perf:** $160 **Exc:** $125

HARRINGTON & RICHARDSON MODEL 950

Revolver; double action; 22 LR, 22 Long, 22 Short; 9-shot cylinder; 5-1/2-inch barrel; solid-frame; side-loading, ejection; adjustable rear sight, blade front; one-piece plain walnut grip; nickel finish. Introduced 1960; dropped 1985.

Exc: $200 **VGood:** $175 **Good:** $150

HARRINGTON & RICHARDSON MODEL 976

Revolver; double action; 22 LR, 38 S&W; 9-shot cylinder (22 LR), 5-shot (38 S&W); 4-inch barrel; hinged frame; fixed front, adjustable rear sight; checkered walnut stocks; blued finish. Introduced 1968; dropped 1981.

Exc: $200 **VGood:** $175 **Good:** $140

HARRINGTON & RICHARDSON MODEL 999

Revolver; double action; 22 Short, 22 Long, 22 LR; 9-shot cylinder; 4-inch, 6-inch top-break barrel; weighs 34 oz.; checkered hardwood grips; elevation-adjustable front sight, windage-adjustable rear; automatic ejection; triggerguard extension; blued finish; optional engraving. Marketed as Sportsman Model. Introduced 1936; dropped 1985.

Exc: $300 **VGood:** $270 **Good:** $225

Engraved

Exc: $425 **VGood:** $375 **Good:** $300

HARRINGTON & RICHARDSON MODEL 999 SPORTSMAN

Revolver; double action; 22 LR; 9-shot cylinder; 4-inch, 6-inch barrel; 8-1/2-inch overall length; weighs 30 oz.; walnut-finished hardwood grips; elevation-adjustable blade front sight, windage-adjustable rear; top-break loading; automatic shell ejection; polished blue finish. Made in U.S. by Harrington & Richardson. Reintroduced 1992; no longer in production. Add 25% for scarce nickel variant.

Perf: $360 **Exc:** $295 **VGood:** $175

HARRINGTON & RICHARDSON NEW DEFENDER

Revolver; double action; 22 LR; 2-inch barrel; 6-1/4-inch overall length; checkered hard rubber grips; adjustable front and rear sights; automatic ejector; triggerguard extention; blued finish. Also listed as Model 299. Introduced 1936; dropped 1941.

Exc: $350 **VGood:** $300 **Good:** $225

HARRINGTON & RICHARDSON NO. 196

Revolver; 22 Short, 22 Long, 22 LR; 6-1/4-inch barrel; 11-inch overall length; weighs 32 oz.; adjustable Patridge front, adjustable rear; wide hammer; blue finish. Called the "Eureka" Sportsman.

Exc: $175 **VGood:** $150 **Good:** $100

HARRINGTON & RICHARDSON NO. 199

Revolver; single action; 22 LR; 9-shot cylinder; 6-inch barrel; 11-inch overall length; weighs 30 oz.; hinged frame; adjustable target sights; checkered walnut grips; blued finish. Single action version of the double-action Model 999 Sportsman. Introduced 1933; dropped 1951.

Exc: $300 **VGood:** $260 **Good:** $200

HARRINGTON & RICHARDSON PREMIER MODEL

Revolver; double action; hinged-frame; 22 LR, 32 S&W Short; 7-shot (22), 5-shot (32); 2-inch, 3-inch, 4-inch, 5-inch, 6-inch barrel; weighs 13 oz.; fixed sights; hard rubber grips; blued nickel finish. Introduced 1895; dropped 1941.

Exc: $275 **VGood:** $225 **Good:** $180

HARRINGTON & RICHARDSON SELF-LOADING 25

Semi-automatic; 25 ACP; 6-shot magazine; 2-inch barrel, 4-1/2-inch overall; hammerless checkered hard rubber stocks; fixed sights; blued finish. Based on Webley & Scott design. Approximately 16,000 manufactured from 1912 to 1916.

Exc: $375 **VGood:** $330 **Good:** $305

HARRINGTON & RICHARDSON SELF-LOADING 32

Semi-automatic; 32 ACP; 8-shot magazine; 3-1/2-inch barrel; 6-1/2-inch overall length; weighs 22 oz.; grip safety; magazine disconnector; hammerless; checkered hard rubber stocks; fixed sights; blued finish. Based on Webley & Scott design. Approximately 40,000 manufactured from 1916 to 1924.

Exc: $350 **VGood:** $300 **Good:** $260

HARRINGTON & RICHARDSON TRAPPER MODEL

Revolver; double action; 22 Short, 22 Long, 22 LR; 7-shot cylinder; 6-inch octagonal barrel; weighs 12-1/4 oz.; solid frame; gold front sight; checkered walnut stocks; blued finish. Introduced 1924; dropped during WWII. 15% premium for longer barrel.

Exc: $175 **VGood:** $135 **Good:** $100

HARRINGTON & RICHARDSON USRA MODEL

Single shot; 22 LR; 7-inch, 8-inch, 10-inch barrel; weighs 31 oz. (10-inch barrel); hinged frame target pistol; adjustable target sights; adjustable trigger pull; checkered walnut grips; blued finish. Introduced 1928; dropped 1943.

Exc: $650 **VGood:** $450 **Good:** $250

HARRINGTON & RICHARDSON VEST POCKET MODEL

Revolver; double action; 22 Long, 32 S&W Short; 5-shot cylinder (32), 7-shot (22); 1-1/8-inch barrel; weighs 8-1/2 oz.; solid frame; spurless hammer; no sights except for milled slot in top frame; hard rubber grips; blued or nickel finish. Introduced 1891; dropped during WWII.

Exc: $165 **VGood:** $125 **Good:** $100

HARRIS-MCMILLAN SIGNATURE JR. LONG RANGE

Bolt action; single shot or repeater; chambered for any suitable caliber; custom barrel length to customer specs.; weighs about 5 lbs.; fiberglass stock; no sights; scope rings; right- or left-hand benchrest action of titanium or stainless steel; bipod. All parts and components made in U.S. by Harris Gunworks, Inc. Introduced 1992; dropped 1995.

New: $2200 **Perf:** $1750 **Exc:** $1500

HARRIS-MCMILLAN WOLVERINE

Semi-automatic; single action; 9mm Para., 10mm Auto, 38 Wadcutter, 38 Super, 45 Italian, 45 ACP; 6-inch barrel; 9-1/2-inch overall length; weighs 45 oz.; Pachmayr rubber grips; blade front sight, fully-adjustable low profile rear; integral compensator; round burr-style hammer; extended grip safety; checkered backstrap; skeletonized aluminum match trigger. Many finish options offered. Combat or Competition Match styles. All parts and components were made in U.S. by Harris Gunworks, Inc. Introduced 1992.

New: $1600 **Perf:** $1350 **Exc:** $1200

HARTFORD TARGET AUTOMATIC

Semi-automatic; 22 LR; 10-shot magazine; 6-3/4-inch barrel; 10-3/4-inch overall length; checkered black rubber grips; target sights; blued finish. Hartford was the predecessor of High Standard. Introduced 1929; dropped 1932. Has more collector than shooter value.

Exc: $550 **VGood:** $500 **Good:** $450

HARTFORD TARGET SINGLE SHOT

Single shot; 22 LR; 5-3/4-inch barrel; 10-3/4 overall length; same general outward appearance as Hartford Target Auto; black rubber or walnut grips; target sights; color case-hardened frame; blued barrel. Introduced 1929; dropped 1932.

Exc: $550 **VGood:** $500 **Good:** $450

HASKELL JS-45

Semi-automatic; single action; 45 ACP; 7-shot magazine; 4-1/2-inch barrel; 8-inch overall length; weighs 44 oz.; checkered acetal resin grips; fixed low profile sights; internal drop-safe mechanism; all aluminum frame; matte black finish. From MKS Supply, Inc. Introduced 1991; still produced as Hi-Point JS-45.

Perf: $125 **Exc:** $110 **VGood:** $100

Brushed nickel finish

Perf: $135 **Exc:** $125 **VGood:** $110

HAWES DEPUTY MARSHAL

Revolver; single action; 22 LR, 22 WMR; 6-shot; 5-1/2-inch barrel; 11-inch overall length; blade front sight, adjustable rear; plastic or walnut grips; blued finish. Introduced 1973; dropped 1980.

Exc: $85 **VGood:** $65 **Good:** $50

HAWES DEPUTY MARSHAL, DENVER MODEL

Same specs as Deputy Marshal except brass frame. Introduced 1973; dropped 1980.

Exc: $85 **VGood:** $65 **Good:** $50

HAWES DEPUTY MARSHAL, MONTANA MODEL

Same specs as Deputy Marshal except walnut grips only; brass grip frame. Introduced 1973; dropped 1980.

Exc: $95 **VGood:** $75 **Good:** $55

HAWES DEPUTY MARSHAL, SILVER CITY MODEL

Same specs as Deputy Marshal except brass grip frame; chromed frame; blued barrel and cylinder. Introduced 1973; discontinued 1980.

Exc: $95 **VGood:** $75 **Good:** $55

HAWES DEPUTY MARSHAL, TEXAS MODEL

Same specs as Deputy Marshal except for chrome finish. Introduced 1973; discontinued 1980.

Exc: $95 **VGood:** $75 **Good:** $55

HAWES FAVORITE

Break-action single shot; 22 LR; 8-inch barrel; 12-inch overall length; tip-up action; target sights; plastic or rosewood stocks; blued barrel; chromed frame. Replica of Stevens No. 35 Target Model. Manufactured 1968 to 1976.

Exc: $195 **VGood:** $175 **Good:** $155

HAWES MARSHAL, CHIEF MODEL

Revolver; single action; 357 Mag., 9mm, 44-40, 44 Mag., 45 Colt, 45 ACP; 6-inch barrel; target-type front sight, adjustable rear; oversize rosewood stocks; available with interchangeable cylinder combos; blued finish. Manufactured in West Germany by Sauer & Sohn exclusively for Hawes. Introduced 1968; discontinued 1980.

Exc: $200 **VGood:** $165 **Good:** $135

HAWES MARSHAL, FEDERAL MODEL

Same specs as Hawes Marshal, Chief Model except color case-hardened frame; one-piece European walnut grip; brass grip frame; fixed sights. Introduced 1969; discontinued 1980.

Exc: $200 **VGood:** $165 **Good:** $135

HAWES MARSHAL, MONTANA MODEL

Same specs as Hawes Marshal, Chief Model except also 22 LR, 22 WMR chamberings; 5-inch barrel (rimfires); fixed sights; plastic stag (rimfires) or rosewood (centerfire) grips; brass stag frame. Introduced 1968; discontinued 1980.

Exc: $200 **VGood:** $165 **Good:** $135

HAWES MARSHAL, SILVER CITY MODEL

Same specs as Hawes Marshal, Chief Model except fixed sights; pearlite grips; brass frame. Introduced 1969; discontinued 1980.

Exc: $200 **VGood:** $165 **Good:** $135

HAWES MARSHAL, TEXAS MODEL

Same specs as Hawes Marshal, Chief Model except also 22 LR, 22 WMR chamberings; 5-inch barrel (rimfires); fixed sights; pearlite grips; nickel finish. Introduced 1969; discontinued 1980.

Exc: $200 **VGood:** $165 **Good:** $135

Hawes/Sig-Sauer P220
H&K HK4
Heckler & Koch Mark 23
H&K P7 M8
H&K P9S
H&K P7 M13
H&K P7 PSP
H&K P9S Competition Kit

HAWES MARSHAL, WESTERN MODEL

Same specs as Hawes Marshal, Chief Model except also 22 LR, 22 WMR chamberings; 5-inch barrel (rimfire); fixed sights; plastic stag (rimfire) or rosewood (centerfire) grips. Introduced 1968; discontinued 1980.

Exc: $200 **VGood:** $165 **Good:** $135

HAWES MEDALLION MODEL

Revolver; double action; 22 LR, 38 Spl.; 6-shot; 3-inch, 4-inch, 6-inch barrel; fixed sights; swing-out cylinder; blued finish. No longer in production.

Exc: $135 **VGood:** $125 **Good:** $100

HAWES TROPHY MODEL

Revolver; double action; 22 LR, 38 Spl.; 6-shot; 6-inch barrel; adjustable sights; swing-out cylinder; blued finish. No longer in production.

Exc: $135 **VGood:** $125 **Good:** $100

HAWES/SIG-SAUER P220

Semi-automatic; 9mm Para., 38 Super, 45 ACP; 7-shot magazine (45 ACP), 9-shot (9mm, 38); 4-3/8-inch barrel; 7-3/4-inch overall length; checkered European walnut or black plastic stocks; windage-adjustable rear sight, blade front; square combat triggerguard. Manufactured in Germany. Introduced 1977; still in production; dropped by Hawes in 1980. Also known as Browning BDA, SIG/Sauer P220.

Exc: $450 **VGood:** $400 **Good:** $350

HECKLER & KOCH HK4

Semi-automatic; double action; 22 LR, 25 ACP, 32 ACP, 380 ACP; 8-shot magazine; 3-1/2-inch barrel; 6-inch overall length; windage-adjustable rear sight, fixed front; checkered black plastic grips; blued finish. Early version available with interchangeable barrels, magazines for four calibers. Imported from Germany originally by Harrington & Richardson, then by Heckler & Koch; importation dropped 1984.

Single caliber

Exc: $375 **VGood:** $300 **Good:** $250

Four caliber set

Exc: $750 **VGood:** $650 **Good:** $500

HECKLER & KOCH MARK 23

Semi-automatic; 45 ACP; 10-shot magazine; 5.87-inch barrel; 43 oz.; 9.65-inch overall; grips integral with frame, black polymer; blade front sight; rear drift adjustable for windage, three-dot; polymer frame; double action; exposed hammer; short recoil, modified Browning action. Civilian version of the SOCOM pistol. Introduced 1996. Imported from Germany by Heckler & Koch, Inc.

Exc: $1995 **VGood:** $1750 **Good:** $1550

HECKLER & KOCH P7 K3

Semi-automatic; single action; 22 LR, 380 ACP; 8-shot magazine; 3-13/16-inch barrel; 26-1/2 oz.; fixed sights; black plastic grips; cocked by pressure on frontstrap; large triggerguard with heat shield; oil-filled buffer to decrease recoil; blue or nickel finish. Introduced 1988; no longer imported.

Exc: $1295 **VGood:** $850 **Good:** $715

22 LR conversion unit

Exc: $600 **VGood:** $500 **Good:** $400

32 ACP conversion unit

Exc: $300 **VGood:** $200 **Good:** $150

Add $85 to above prices for Tritium sights

HECKLER & KOCH P7 M8

Semi-automatic; 9mm Para.; 8-shot magazine; 4-1/8-inch barrel; 6 3/4-inch overall length; weighs 29 oz.; blade front, adjustable rear sight with three-dot system; unique squeeze-cocker system in frontstrap; gas-retarded action; squared combat-type triggerguard; stippled black plastic grips; blue finish. Imported from Germany by Heckler & Koch, Inc.

Perf: $1125 **Exc:** $950 **VGood:** $775

Add $105 to above prices for pistols fitted with Tritium sights

Add $575 for 22 LR conversion kit (barrel, slide and two magazines)

HECKLER & KOCH P7 M10

Semi-automatic; 40 S&W; 10-shot magazine; 4-1/8-inch barrel; 7-inch overall length; weighs 43 oz.; blade front, adjustable rear sight with three-dot system; unique "squeeze-cocker" system in frontstrap; gas-retarded action; squared combat-type triggerguard; stippled black plastic grips; blue finish. Imported from Germany by Heckler & Koch, Inc. Introduced 1992; no longer in production.

Perf: $1125 **Exc:** $950 **VGood:** $775

Add $85 to above prices for pistols with Tritium sights

HECKLER & KOCH P7 M13

Semi-automatic; single action; 9mm Para.; 13-shot magazine; 4-1/8-inch barrel; 6-1/2-inch overall length; 30 oz.; fixed sights; black plastic grips; cocked by pressure on frontstrap; large triggerguard with heat shield; ambidextrous magazine release; blue or nickel finish. Introduced 1986; importation discontinued 1994.

Perf: $1575 **Exc:** $1250 **VGood:** $1050

Nickel finish

Perf: $1650 **Exc:** $1350 **VGood:** $1150

Add $85 to above prices for pistols with Tritium sights

HECKLER & KOCH P7 PSP

Semi-automatic; single action; 9mm Para; 8-shot magazine; 4-1/8-inch barrel; 6-1/2-inch overall length; weighs 29 oz.; fixed sights; black plastic grips; cocked by pressure on frontstrap; squared combat triggerguard; blued finish. Imported from West Germany. Introduced 1982; discontinued 1986.

Perf: $800 **Exc:** $700 **VGood:** $600

HECKLER & KOCH P9S

Semi-automatic; double action; 9mm Para., 45 ACP; 9-shot magazine (9mm), 7-shot (45 ACP); 4-inch barrel; 5-7/16-inch overall length; fixed sights; checkered plastic grips; loaded/cocked indicators; hammer cocking lever; phosphated finish. Originally imported from Germany by Gold Rush Gun Shop in 1977, then by Heckler & Koch, Inc.; importation dropped 1984.

Exc: $900 **VGood:** $750 **Good:** $600

Add $100 for .45 ACP

HECKLER & KOCH P9S COMPETITION KIT

Same specs as P9S except 9mm Para.; additional 5-1/2-inch barrel with weight; additional slide; adjustable sights, trigger; walnut stock. Introduced 1977; discontinued 1984.

Exc: $1300 **VGood:** $950 **Good:** $750

HECKLER & KOCH P9S TARGET

Same specs as P9S except adjustable sights, trigger. Introduced 1977; discontinued 1984.

Exc: $1000 **VGood:** $800 **Good:** $650

H&K USP 9mm

H&K SP 89

H&K P30L Seies

H&K USP45 Compact

H&K VP 70Z

H&K USP Elite

H&K HK45

H&K P2000

HECKLER & KOCH P30L SERIES

Calibers: 9mm and 40 S&W with 15-shot magazines. Barrel length: 4.45 inches. Weight, 27.5 oz. and overall length, 7.56 inches. Grip frame has interchangeable panels and backstraps. Browning-type modified short recoil operation with ambidextrous controls, loaded chamber indicator, Picatinny rail. Offered in DA/SA, DAO or decocker variations.

Perf: $750 **Exc:** $635 **VGood:** $550

HECKLER & KOCH SP 89

Semi-automatic; single action; 9mm Para.; 15-, 30-shot magazine; 4-1/2-inch barrel; 12-7/8-inch overall length; weighs 4-1/2 lbs.; black high-impact plastic grip; post front sight, fully-adjustable diopter rear; design inspired by the HK94 rifle; has special flash-hider forend. Imported from Germany by Heckler & Koch, Inc. Introduced 1989; no longer imported.

Perf: $3750 **Exc:** $3400 **VGood:** $3100

HECKLER & KOCH USP

Semi-automatic; single action/double action or double-action-only; 9mm Para., 40 S&W, 45 ACP; 15-shot magazine (9mm), 13-shot (40 S&W), 12-shot (45 ACP); 4-1/4-inch barrel; 6-15/16-inch overall length; weighs 28 oz.; non-slip stippled black polymer grips; blade front sight, windage-adjustable rear; polymer frame; modified Browning action with recoil reduction system; single control lever; special "hostile environment" finish on all metal parts; available in SA/DA, DAO, left- and right-hand versions. Imported from Germany by Heckler & Koch, Inc. Introduced 1993; still imported.

Right-hand

New: $670 **Perf:** $540 **Exc:** $485

Left-hand

New: $750 **Perf:** $650 **Exc:** $560

HECKLER & KOCH USP COMPACT AUTO PISTOL

Similar to the USP except has 3.58-inch barrel, measures 6.81-inch overall, and weighs 1.60 lbs. (9mm). Available in 9mm Para. or 40 S&W with 10-shot magazine. Introduced 1996. Imported from Germany by Heckler & Koch, Inc.

Right-hand

New: $680 **Perf:** $550 **Exc:** $475

Left-hand

New: $705 **Perf:** $650 **Exc:** $550

HECKLER & KOCH USP45 COMPACT

Similar to the USP45 except has stainless slide; 8-shot magazine; modified and contoured slide and frame; extended slide release; 3.80-inch barrel, 7.09-inch overall length, weighs 1.75 lbs.; adjustable three-dot sights. Introduced 1998. Imported from Germany by Heckler & Koch, Inc.

New: $760 **Perf:** $595 **Exc:** $500

HECKLER & KOCH USP45 COMPACT TACTICAL

Blued semi-auto .45 ACP. Double-action with 4.46-inch barrel, 8-round capacity. 27.5 oz. Polymer grip.

NIB: $1050 **Exc:** $975 **VGood:** $825

HECKLER & KOCH USP45 MATCH

Semi-automatic; 45 ACP; 10-shot magazine; 6.02 barrel; 2.38 lbs.; 9.45-inch overall; textured polymer grips; high profile target front sight;, fully adjustable target rear; adjustable trigger stop; polymer frame; blue or stainless steel slide. Introduced 1997. Imported from Germany by Heckler & Koch, Inc.

Blue

New: $1275 **Perf:** $1025 **Exc:** $825

Stainless

New: $1300 **Perf:** $1100 **Exc:** $900

HECKLER & KOCH USP45 TACTICAL

Semi-automatic; 45 ACP; 10-shot magazine; 4.92-inch barrel; 2.24 lbs.; 8.64-inch overall; non-slip stippled polymer grips; blade front sight, fully adjustable target rear; has extended threaded barrel with rubber O-ring; adjustable trigger; extended magazine floorplate; adjustable trigger stop; polymer frame. Introduced 1998. Imported from Germany by Heckler & Koch, Inc.

New: $995 **Perf:** $875 **Exc:** $775

HECKLER & KOCH USP EXPERT

Similar to H&K USP but meets IPSC specifications. Add 20 percent to above values.

HECKLER & KOCH USP ELITE

Similar to H&K USP but with long (6.2-inch) barrel. Add 5 percent to above values.

HECKLER & KOCH VP 70Z

Semi-automatic; double-action-only; 9mm Para.; 18-shot magazine; 4-1/2-inch barrel; 8-inch overall length; ramp front sight, channeled rear on slide; stippled black plastic stocks; recoil-operated; only four moving parts; double-column magazine; phosphated finish. Manufactured in West Germany. Introduced 1976; importation dropped 1989.

Perf: $750 **Exc:** $675 **VGood:** $500

Add 125 percent to above prices if frame is cut for shoulder stock. Note: Such pistols are subject to provisions of the NFA.

HECKLER & KOCH P2000

Semi-automatic; 40 S&W, 357 SIG, 9mm Parabellum; 3.62-inch barrel; weight 1.5 lbs; overall length 7 inches. corrosion proof fiber-reinforced polymer frame; Polygonal bore profile for increased velocity, easier cleaning, and longer barrel life; Low profile slide and slimline, compact dimensions; Ambidextrous slide release (located on both sides of the frame); Corrosion resistant "Hostile Environment" Nitro Carburized finish.

Perf: $775 **Exc:** $700 **VGood:** $600

HECKLER & KOCH HK45

Full-size autoloader chambered in .45 ACP. Features include polygonal bore, front and rear slide serrations, integrated picatinny rail, amibi mag release levers, interchangeable backstrap panels, polymer frame, modular action design allowing for double action, singlke action or double action-only operation. Measures 7.52 inches overall length. 10+1 capacity.

New: $995 **Perf:** $875 **Exc:** $775

HECKLER & KOCH HK45 COMPACT

Similar to above but with 8-round capacity; overall length 7.2 inches.

New: $995 **Perf:** $875 **Exc:** $775

HECKLER & KOCH P30

Polymer-frame 9mm autoloader. Features include loaded chamber indicator, integral picatinny rail, oversized trigger guard, doible or single action fiurting mode with decocker, "Hostile Environment" black finish, ambidextrous, oversized controls.

New: $800 **Perf:** $700 **Exc:** $625

HELWAN 9MM

Semi-automatic; 9mm Para.; 8-shot magazine; 4-1/2-

Helwan 9mm

Heritage H25S Auto Pistol

Heritage Rough Rider

Heritage Sentry

H&K P30

H&K HK45 Compact

Hi-Point 9mm Compact with laser

inch barrel; 8 1/4-inch overall length; weighs 33 oz; blade front sight, drift-adjustable rear; grooved black plastic stocks; updated version of Beretta Model 951. Imported from Egypt by Steyr Daimler Puch of America, Navy Arms and Interarms.Introduced 1982; dropped 1983. Reintroduced recently by Century International Arms, Inc.

Exc: $285 **VGood:** $225 **Good:** $175

HERITAGE MODEL HA25

Semi-automatic; single action; 25 ACP; 6-shot magazine; 2-1/2-inch barrel; 4-5/8-inch overall length; weighs 12 oz.; smooth or checkered walnut grips; fixed sights; exposed hammer; manual safety; open-top slide; polished blue or blue/gold finish. Made in U.S. by Heritage Mfg., Inc. Introduced 1993; no longer produced.

Perf: $125 **Exc:** $95 **VGood:** $80

Blue/gold finish

Perf: $135 **Exc:** $105 **VGood:** $90

HERITAGE H25S AUTO PISTOL

Semi-automatic; 25 ACP; 6-shot magazine; 2.25-inch barrel; 13.5 oz.; 4.5-inch overall; smooth hardwood grips; fixed sights; frame-mounted trigger safety; magazine disconnect safety. Introduced 1995; dropped 1999.

New: $135 **Perf:** $95 **Exc:** $80

HERITAGE ROUGH RIDER

Revolver; single action; 22 LR, 22 LR/22 WMR combo; 6-shot cylinder; 4-3/4-inch, 6-1/2-inch, 9-inch barrel; weighs 31 to 38 oz.; Goncolo Alves grips; blade front sight, fixed rear; hammer-block safety; high polish blue or nickel finish. Made in U.S. by Heritage Mfg., Inc. Introduced 1993; still produced.

New: $130 **Perf:** $110 **Exc:** $95

2-inch, 3-inch, 4-inch, barrel, birdshead grip

New: $135 **Perf:** $110 **Exc:** $95

Steel frame series

News: $160 Perf: $125 **Exc:** $95

HERITAGE ROUGH RIDER .32

Six-shot revolver chambered for .32 H&R Magnum centerfire (interchangeably .32 S&W, .32 S&W Long). Black satin finish. Offered with 3.5-inch, 4.75-inch or 6.5-inch barrels. 35 oz. (6.5-inch bbl.). 11.785-inch LOA.) Fixed sights. Bird's head grip available.

NIB: $215 **Exc:** $180 **VGood:** $150

HERITAGE ROUGH RIDER BIG-BORE SERIES

Six-shot, steel-frame revolver chambered for .357, .44-40 or .45 Long Colt. Barrel lengths 4.75-inch, 5.5-inch or 7.5-inch. 36 oz. Fixed sights.

NIB: $375 **Exc:** $325 **VGood:** $295

HERITAGE SENTRY

Revolver; double action; 22 LR, 22 WMR, 9mm Para., 38 Spl.; 8-shot cylinder (22 LR), 6-shot (22 WMR, 9mm, 38 Spl.); 2-inch, 4-inch barrel; 6-1/4-inch overall length (2-inch barrel); weighs 23 oz.; magnum-style round butt grips of checkered plastic; ramp front sight, fixed rear; pull-pin-type ejection; serrated hammer and trigger; polished blue or nickel finish. Made in U.S. by Heritage Mfg., Inc. Introduced 1993; dropped 1997.

New: $110 **Perf:** $90 **Exc:** $75

HERITAGE STEALTH AUTO PISTOL

Semi-automatic; 9mm Para., 40 S&W; 10-shot magazine; 3.9-inch barrel; 20.2 oz.; 6.3-inch overall; black polymer integral grips; blade front sight, rear drift adjustable for windage; gas retarded blowback action; polymer frame; 17-4 stainless slide; frame mounted ambidextrous trigger safety, magazine safety. Introduced 1996. Made in U.S. by Heritage Mfg., Inc.

Blue

New: $255 **Perf:** $220 **Exc:** $190

Stainless

New: $275 **Perf:** $235 **Exc:** $220

HI-POINT FIREARMS JS-9MM

Semi-automatic; single action; 9mm Para.; 9-shot magazine; 4-1/2-inch barrel; 7-3/4-inch overall length; weighs 41 oz.; textured acetal plastic grips; fixed low profile sights; scratch-resistant, non-glare blue finish. From MKS Supply, Inc. Introduced 1990; still produced.

New: $140 **Perf:** $110 **Exc:** $95

HI-POINT FIREARMS JS-9MM COMPACT

Same specs as JS-9mm except 380 ACP, 9mm Para.; 8-shot magazine; 3-1/2-inch barrel; 6-3/4-inch overall length; weighs 35 oz.; textured acetal plastic grips; low profile, combat-style, fixed three-dot sight system; frame-mounted magazine release; scratch-resistant matte finish. From MKS Supply, Inc. Introduced 1993; still produced.

9mm Para.

New: $110 **Perf:** $90 **Exc:** $75

9mm Para, polymer frame, non-slip grips

New: $120 **Perf:** $110 **Exc:** $95

380 ACP

New: $80 **Perf:** $60 **Exc:** $50

HI-POINT FIREARMS JS-40 S&W

Semi-automatic; 40 S&W; 8-shot magazine; 4-1/2-inch barrel; 7-3/4-inch overall length; weighs 42 oz.; checkered acetal resin grips; fixed, low profile sights; optional laser sight; internal drop-safe mechansim; all aluminum frame; matte black finish. From MKS Supply, Inc. Introduced 1991; still produced.

New: $135 **Perf:** $125 **Exc:** $110

HI-POINT FIREARMS JS-45

Semi-automatic; single action; 45 ACP; 7-shot magazine; 4-1/2-inch barrel; 8-inch overall length; weighs 44 oz.; checkered acetal resin grips; fixed low profile sights; internal drop-safe mechanism; all aluminum frame. From MKS Supply, Inc. Introduced 1991; still produced.

New: $135 **Perf:** $125 **Exc:** $110

HI-POINT FIREARMS MODEL 9MM COMPACT PISTOL

Caliber: 9mm Para.; 8-shot magazine; 3.5-inch barrel; 29 oz.; 6.7-inch overall; textured acetal plastic grips; combat-style fixed three-dot sight system, low profile; single-action design; frame-mounted magazine release; polymer or alloy frame; scratch-resistant matte finish. Introduced 1993. From MKS Supply, Inc. Price: Black or chrome/black Price: $124.95 With polymer frame (29 oz.), non-slip grips.

New: $110 **Perf:** $90 **Exc:** $80

With compensator and optional laser

Perf: $250 **Exc:** $225 **VGood:** $150

HI-POINT FIREARMS MODEL 380 POLYMER PISTOL

Similar to the 9mm Compact model except chambered for 380 ACP, 8-shot magazine, adjustable three-dot sights. Weighs 29 oz. Polymer frame. Introduced 1998. Made in U.S. From MKS Supply.

New: $90 **Perf:** $70 **Exc:** $65

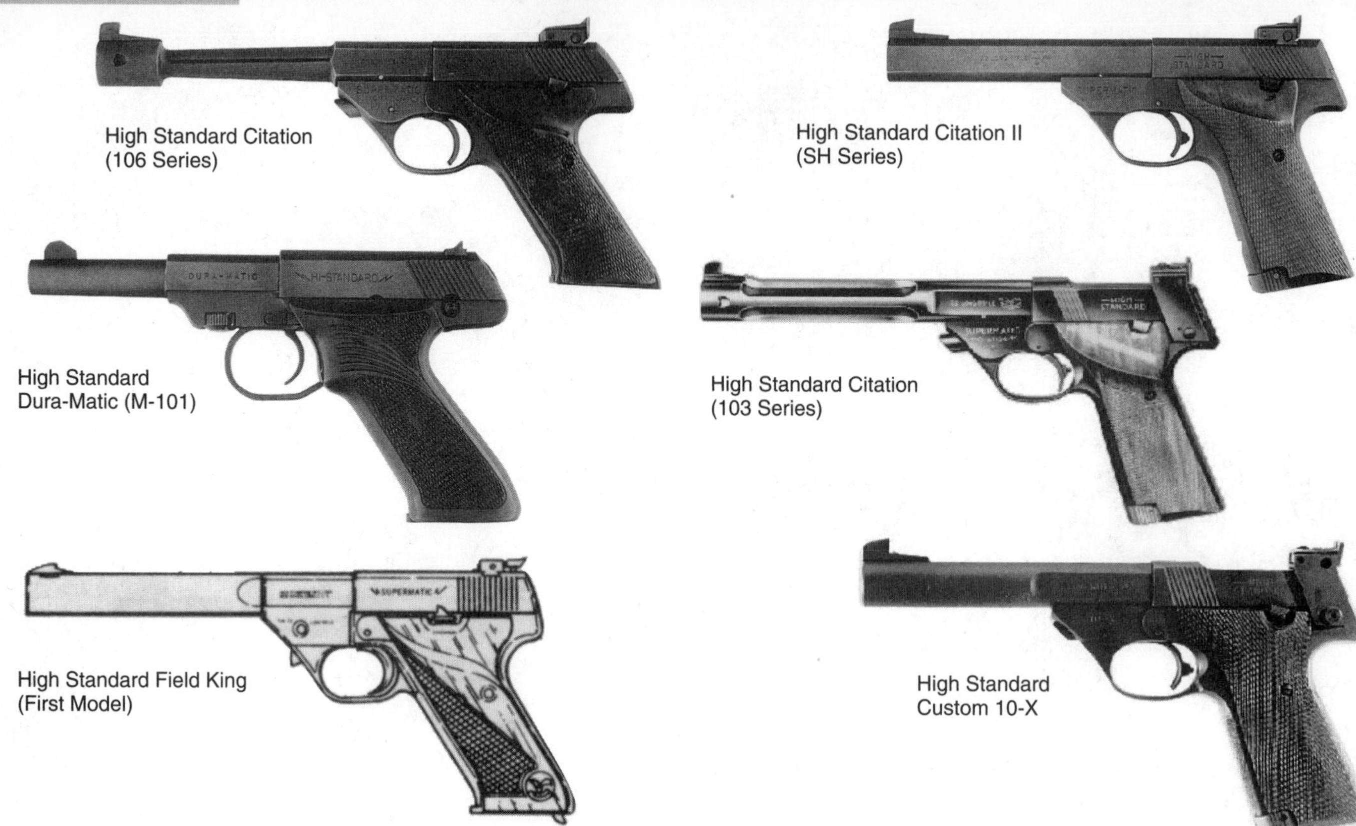

High Standard Citation (106 Series)

High Standard Citation II (SH Series)

High Standard Dura-Matic (M-101)

High Standard Citation (103 Series)

High Standard Field King (First Model)

High Standard Custom 10-X

HI-POINT .380 ACP

Compensated Semi-auto with fully-adjustable 3-dot sights, muzzle compensator, 4-inch barrel, 31 oz, polymer frame. Two magazines: one 10-round, one 8-round. Add 50 percent for laser sight.

NIB: $110 **Exc:** $95 **VGood:** $85

HIGH STANDARD SEMI-AUTOMATIC PISTOLS

HIGH STANDARD CITATION (FIRST MODEL 102 SERIES)

Semi-automatic; 22 LR; 10-shot; 6-3/4-inch, 8-inch, 10-inch interchangeable tapered barrels; hammerless; push-button takedown; ramp front, click-adjustable rear sights; trigger pull and backlash adjustment screws; new rakish-looking barrels with grooves for weight attachment and knob on end for removable stabilizer; plastic grips, walnut optional; two removable weights; blued finish. Marked "SUPERMATIC" top line; "CITATION" in smaller letters underneath on left side of frame. Introduced 1958; dropped 1963.

Two barrels

Exc: 780 **VGood:** $600 **Good:** $500

One barrel

Exc: $550 **VGood:** $450 **Good:** $375

HIGH STANDARD CITATION (103 SERIES)

Same specs as First Model except 5-1/2-inch bull barrel; tapped and notched for optional weights and stabilizer. Marked "Model 103" on right side of slide. Introduced 1962; dropped 1963.

Exc: $600 **VGood:** $500 **Good:** $400

HIGH STANDARD CITATION (104 SERIES)

Same specs as 103 Series Citation except marked "Model 104" on right side of slide. Introduced 1963; dropped 1966.

Exc: $550 **VGood:** $450 **Good:** $400

HIGH STANDARD CITATION (106 SERIES)

Same specs as 103 Series Citation except also offered in 7-1/4-inch barrel; positive magazine latch; military-style grips; stippled front, backstraps; saddle-type rear sight. Introduced 1965; dropped 1967.

Exc: $600 **VGood:** $500 **Good:** $375

HIGH STANDARD CITATION (107 SERIES)

Same specs as 106 Series Citation except marked "Model 107" on right side of slide. Introduced 1968; dropped 1968.

Exc: $500 **VGood:** $400 **Good:** $300

HIGH STANDARD CITATION (ML SERIES)

Same specs as 107 Series except "ML" prefixed serial number.

Exc: $425 **VGood:** $350 **Good:** $295

HIGH STANDARD CITATION (SEVEN NUMBER SERIES)

Same specs as 107 Series except seven-digit serial number appears alone on right side of frame.

Exc: $500 **VGood:** $425 **Good:** $325

HIGH STANDARD CITATION II (SH SERIES)

Semi-automatic; 22 LR; 10-shot magazine; 5-1/2-inch, 7-1/4-inch slab-sided bull barrel; weighs 45 oz.; adjustable sights; Allen-screw takedown; checkered walnut grips. Replaced Sharpshooter in High Standard line and early models inscribed "Sharpshooter" on frame with "Citation II" inscribed on barrel. Serial numbers prefixed with the letters "SH" Introduced 1982; dropped 1984.

Exc: $425 **VGood:** $350 **Good:** $300

HIGH STANDARD CITATION II SURVIVAL PACK

Same specs as Citation II except 5-1/2-inch barrel only; electroless nickel finish; padded canvas carry case; extra magazine. Introduced 1982; dropped 1984.

Exc: $500 **VGood:** $400 **Good:** $325

HIGH STANDARD CUSTOM 10-X

Semi-automatic; 22 LR; 10-shot magazine; 5-1/2-inch bull barrel, some with Victor barrel and vent rib with rear sight on rib; 9-3/4-inch overall length; weighs 44-1/2 oz.; black, ambidextrous, checkered walnut grips; undercut ramp front sight, frame-mounted adjustable rear; custom-made, fitted; fully-adjustable target trigger; stippled front, backstraps; slide lock; marketed with two extra magazines; non-reflective black/gray Parkerizing; stamped with maker's initials on frame under left grip. Approximately 600 produced. Introduced 1981; dropped 1984.

Perf: $2000 **Exc:** $1500 **VGood:** $1000

HIGH STANDARD CUSTOM 10-X TARGET

Semi-automatic; single action; 22 LR; 10-shot magazine; 5-1/2-inch barrel; 9-1/2-inch overall length; weighs 44 oz.; ambidextrous, checkered black epoxied walnut grips; undercut ramp front sight, fully-adjustable, micrometer-click rear; hand built with select parts; adjustable trigger and sear; push-button takedown; Parkerized finish; stippled front grip and backstrap; barrel weights optional; comes with test target. Made in U.S. by High Standard Mfg. Co., Inc. Reintroduced 1994; still produced.

New: $750 **Perf:** $650 **Exc:** $550

HIGH STANDARD DURA-MATIC

Semi-automatic; 22 LR; 4-1/2-inch, 6-1/2-inch interchangeable barrels; 10-7/8-inch overall length (6-1/2-inch barrel); hammerless; screw take-down; fixed sights; modified magazine with small rectangular recession on top left side to fit clip release; plastic grips; blued finish. Marked "DURA-MATIC" on left side of frame. Introduced 1954; dropped 1970.

Exc: $340 **VGood:** $275 **Good:** $225

HIGH STANDARD FIELD KING (FIRST MODEL)

Semi-automatic; 22 LR; 10-shot magazine; 4-1/2-inch, 6-3/4-inch medium weight barrels; 11-1/2-inch overall length (6-3/4-inch barrel); hammerless; lever take-down; fixed front, adjustable rear sights. Similar to Supermatic First Model except no notch groove for weight attachment; no raised rib atop barrel. Introduced 1951; dropped 1953.

Exc: $600 **VGood:** $500 **Good:** $375

High Standard Model B

High Standard Model G-B

High Standard Model A

High Standard Model G-D

High Standard Model G-E

High Standard Model C

High Standard Model D

HIGH STANDARD FIELD KING (101 SERIES)

Same specs as First Model except push-button takedown; optional slotted stabilizer (6-3/4-inch barrel). Marked "FK-101" on right side of slide. Introduced 1954; dropped 1957.

Exc: $550 **VGood:** $520 **Good:** $450

HIGH STANDARD FLITE KING (FIRST MODEL)

Semi-automatic; 22 Short; 10-shot magazine; 4-1/2-inch, 6-3/4-inch interchangeable lightweight barrels; hammerless; push-button takedown; aluminum alloy frame and slide; fixed sights; automatic slide lock; blue finish. Marked "LW 100" or "LW 101" on right side of frame. Introduced 1954; dropped 1960.

Two barrels
Exc: $525 **VGood:** $450 **Good:** $350

One barrel
Exc: $450 **VGood:** $375 **Good:** $300

HIGH STANDARD FLITE KING (102 SERIES)

Same specs as First Model except all-steel construction; weighs 36 oz. (6-3/4-inch barrel); improved push-button takedown; heavier weight tapered barrels. Marked "FLITE KING" in block letters on left side of frame, "Model 102" on right side. Introduced 1958; dropped 1965.

Exc: $425 **VGood:** $375 **Good:** $325

HIGH STANDARD FLITE KING (103 SERIES)

Same specs as 102 Series Flite King except marked "Model 103" on right side of frame.

Exc: $400 **VGood:** $350 **Good:** $300

HIGH STANDARD MODEL A

Semi-automatic; 22 LR; 10-shot magazine; 4-1/2-inch, 6-3/4-inch barrel; 11-1/2-inch overall length (6-3/4-inch barrel); large frame; hammerless; adjustable target-type sights; new longer grip frame with checkered walnut grips. Model A had both 1B and Type II takedowns. The new grip frame style caught Colt by surprise and prompted Colt to extend grips on the 2nd Model Woodsman. Introduced 1938; dropped 1942. Approximately 7,300 produced.

Exc: $650 **VGood:** $500 **Good:** $350

HIGH STANDARD MODEL B

Semi-automatic; 22 LR; 10-shot magazine; 4-1/2-inch, 6-3/4-inch barrels; 10-3/4-inch overall length (6-3/4-inch barrel); small frame; fixed sights; blued finish. Early Model B had checkered hard rubber grips. At S/N 31508 on Feb. 18, 1938, a new borderless grip with "HS" monogram in circle at center of grip was introduced. Approximately 65,000 produced. Introduced 1932; dropped 1942.

Exc: $600 **VGood:** $450 **Good:** $300

HIGH STANDARD MODEL C

Semi-automatic; 22 Short; 10-shot magazine; 4-1/2-inch, 6-3/4-inch barrels; 10-3/4-inch overall length (6-3/4-inch barrel); small frame; hammerless; fixed sights; checkered hard rubber grips; blued finish. Approximately 4700 produced. Introduced 1936; dropped 1942.

Exc: $800 **VGood:** $600 **Good:** $400

HIGH STANDARD MODEL D

Semi-automatic; 22 LR only; 10-shot magazine; 4-1/2-inch, 6-3/4-inch barrel; 11-1/2-inch overall length
(6-3/4-inch barrel); hammerless; adjustable target-type sights; checkered walnut grips; blued finish. The Model D had both 1B and Type II takedowns with 1B type the rarest. Introduced 1938; dropped, 1942. Approximately 2500 produced.

Exc: $900 **VGood:** $600 **Good:** $350

HIGH STANDARD MODEL E

Semi-automatic; 22 LR; 10-shot; 4-1/2-inch, 6-3/4-inch barrels; 11-1/2-inch overall length (6-3/4-inch barrel); hammerless; adjustable target-type sights; bull barrel and deluxe walnut grips with thumbrest (known as Roper grips); deluxe blued finish. Introduced 1937; dropped 1942. Approximately 2600 produced.

Exc: $950 **VGood:** $600 **Good:** $450

HIGH STANDARD MODEL G-380

Semi-automatic; 380 ACP; 5-inch barrel; visible hammer; thumb safety; first lever take-down model; fixed sights; checkered plastic grips; blued finish. Introduced 1947; dropped 1950. Approximately 7400 produced.

Exc: $600 **VGood:** $500 **Good:** $350

HIGH STANDARD MODEL G-B

Semi-automatic; 22 LR; 4-1/2-inch, 6-3/4-inch interchangeable barrels; 10-3/4-inch overall length (6-3/4-inch barrel); hammerless; small frame; fixed sights; brown checkered plastic grip with "HS" medallion; blued finish. Introduced 1949; dropped 1951.

Two barrels
Exc: $750 **VGood:** $650 **Good:** $550

One barrel
Exc: $550 **VGood:** $475 **Good:** $375

HIGH STANDARD MODEL G-D

Semi-automatic; 22 LR; 10-shot; 4-1/2-inch, 6-3/4-inch interchangeable barrels; 11-1/2-inch overall length (6-3/4-inch barrel); lever take-down; large frame; heavy barrel; adjustable target sights; checkered walnut grips; blued finish. Introduced 1949; dropped 1951. Approximately 3300 produced.

Two barrels
Exc: $1050 **VGood:** $800 **Good:** $550

One barrel
Exc: $800 **VGood:** $500 **Good:** $350

HIGH STANDARD MODEL G-E

Semi-automatic; 22 LR; 10-shot; 4-1/2-inch, 6-3/4-inch bull barrel; 11-1/2-inch overall length (6-3/4-inch barrel); large frame; lever take-down; adjustable sights; deluxe checkered walnut grips; high polish blued finish. Introduced 1949; dropped 1951. Approximately 3000 produced.

Two barrels
Exc: $1500 **VGood:** $1100 **Good:** $800

One barrel
Exc: $1250 **VGood:** $800 **Good:** $500

HIGH STANDARD MODEL H-A

Semi-automatic; 22 LR; 10-shot magazine; 4-1/2-inch, 6-3/4-inch barrels; 11-1/2-inch overall length (6-3/4-inch barrel); visible hammer; no thumb safety;

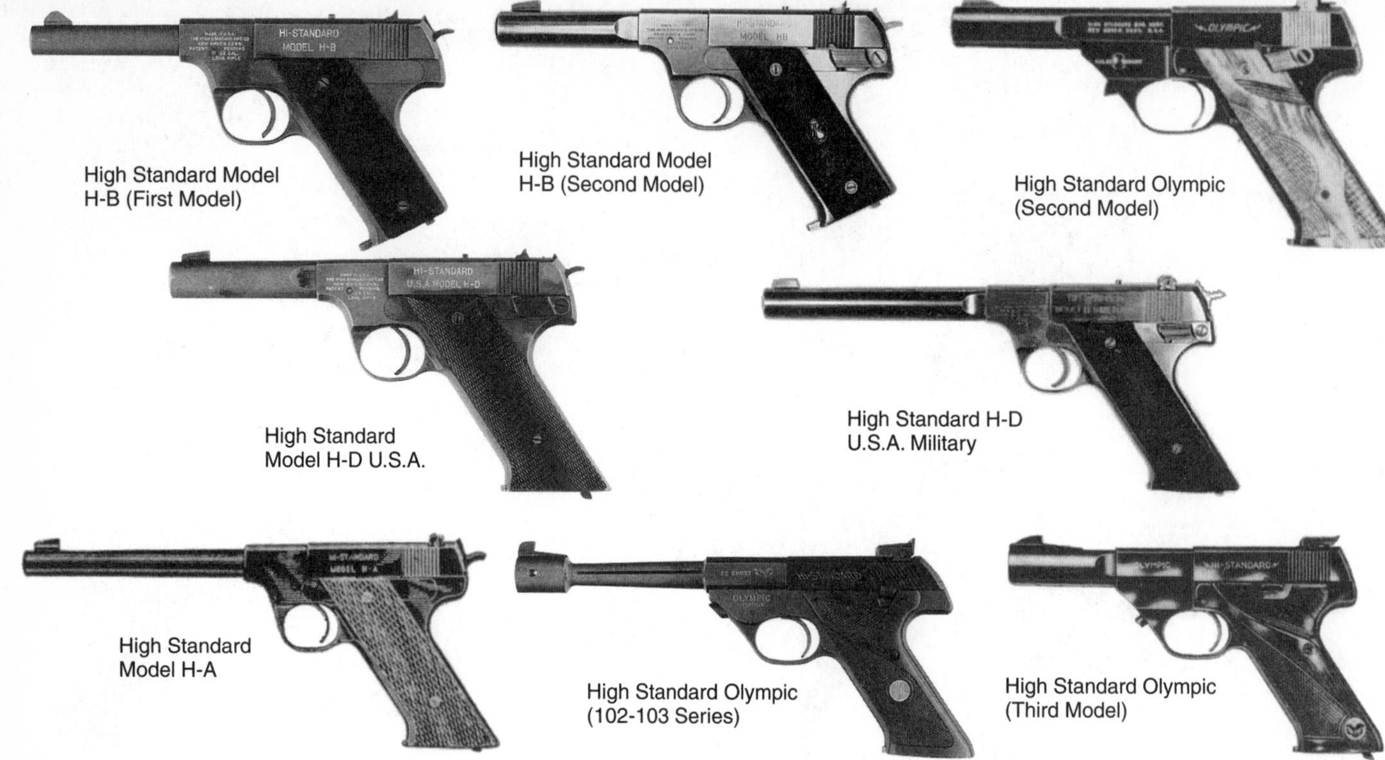

High Standard Model H-B (First Model)

High Standard Model H-B (Second Model)

High Standard Olympic (Second Model)

High Standard Model H-D U.S.A.

High Standard H-D U.S.A. Military

High Standard Model H-A

High Standard Olympic (102-103 Series)

High Standard Olympic (Third Model)

small diameter barrel; checkered walnut grips. Introduced 1940; dropped 1942. Approximately 1042 produced.

Exc: $1050 **VGood:** $750 **Good:** $500

HIGH STANDARD MODEL H-B (FIRST MODEL)

Semi-automatic; 22 LR; 10-shot magazine; 4-1/2-inch, 6-3/4-inch barrels; 10-3/4-inch overall length (6-3/4-inch barrel); fixed sights; checkered hard rubber grips. Same as Model B except visible hammer and no thumb safety. Marked "H-B." Introduced 1940; dropped 1942. Reintroduced 1949; dropped 1950. Approximately 2100 produced.

Exc: $750 **VGood:** $600 **Good:** $450

HIGH STANDARD MODEL H-B (2ND MODEL)

Same specs as Model H-B (1st Model) except presence of thumb safety. Marked "HB." Approximately 25,000 produced.

Exc: $550 **VGood:** $450 **Good:** $375

HIGH STANDARD MODEL H-D

Semi-automatic; 22 LR; 10-shot magazine; 4-1/2-inch, 6-3/4-inch barrel; 11-1/2-inch overall length (6-3/4-inch barrel); adjustable target-type sights; deluxe checkered walnut grips. Same as the Model D except visible hammer and no thumb safety. Introduced 1940; dropped 1942. Approximately 6900 produced.

Exc: $850 **VGood:** $600 **Good:** $450

HIGH STANDARD MODEL H-D U.S.A.

Semi-automatic; 22 LR; 10-shot magazine; 4-1/2-inch, 6-3/4-inch barrels; adjustable target-type sights; medium weight barrel; thumb safety; black or checkered hard rubber grips; high polish blue (early models), Parkerized finish. U.S. military training pistol. Introduced 1943; dropped 1946. Approximately 44,000 produced.

Exc: $800 **VGood:** $500 **Good:** $400

HIGH STANDARD H-D U.S.A. MILITARY

Same specs as Model H-D U.S.A. except adjustable sights. Introduced 1946; dropped 1955. Approximately 150,000 produced.

Exc: $700 **VGood:** $500 **Good:** $350

HIGH STANDARD MODEL H-E

Semi-automatic; 22 LR; 10-shot; 4-1/2-inch, 6-3/4-inch bull barrels; 11-1/2-inch overall length (6-3/4-inch barrel); large frame; adjustable target-type sights. Same specs as the Model E except visible hammer, no thumb safety, high polished blue finish and deluxe walnut grips. Introduced 1941; dropped 1942. Approximately 1006 produced.

Exc: $1800 **VGood:** $1100 **Good:** $700

HIGH STANDARD MODEL S-B

Semi-automatic; 22 shot cartridge; 6-3/4-inch barrel; 10-3/4-inch overall length; smoothbore; checkered rubber grips. Introduced 1939; dropped 1940. Only 12 produced.

Exc: $2500 **VGood:** $2000 **Good:** $1500

HIGH STANDARD OLYMPIC (FIRST MODEL)

Semi-automatic; 22 Short; 4-1/2-inch, 6-3/4-inch interchangeable bull barrels; hammerless; first use of light alloy slide; adjustable rear sight; deluxe checkered walnut grips with thumbrest; lever takedown; special banana-shaped magazine. Also known as Model G-O. Introduced 1950; dropped 1951. Approximately 1200 produced.

Two barrels

Exc: $1000 **VGood:** $1150 **Good:** $800

One barrel

Exc: $900 **VGood:** $800 **Good:** $600

HIGH STANDARD OLYMPIC (SECOND MODEL)

Same specs as First Model except medium barrel; interchangeable 2 oz. and 3 oz. weights attached by dovetail on bottom of barrel plus filler strip for dovetail when weights not in use; standard magazine with filler in front to fit 22 Short cartridges. Introduced 1951; dropped 1953.

Two barrels

Exc: $1300 **VGood:** $1100 **Good:** $850

One barrel

Exc: $1000 **VGood:** $800 **Good:** $650

HIGH STANDARD OLYMPIC (THIRD MODEL)

Same specs as First Model except push button takedown; optional slotted stabilizer for 6-3/4-inch barrel. Marked "0-101-inch on right side of slide. Introduced 1954; dropped 1958.

Exc: $800 **VGood:** $600 **Good:** $500

HIGH STANDARD OLYMPIC (102 SERIES)

Same specs as First Model except 6-3/4-inch, 8-inch, 10-inch barrel; same as Citation 102 except 22 Short with alloy slide; adjustable and removable barrel weights; removable stabilizer; aluminum slide. Marked "Model 102" on right side of slide. Introduced 1958; dropped 1965.

Exc: $1000 **VGood:** $800 **Good:** $650

HIGH STANDARD OLYMPIC (103 SERIES)

Same specs as 102 Series Olympic except plastic grips standard, walnut optional. Introduced 1963; dropped 1965.

Exc: $1000 **VGood:** $800 **Good:** $650

HIGH STANDARD OLYMPIC (104 SERIES)

Same specs as 102/103 Series Olympic except new Allen screw backlash adjustor in trigger - carried over to all future models. Introduced 1964; dropped 1972.

Exc: $900 **VGood:** $750 **Good:** $550

HIGH STANDARD OLYMPIC (106 SERIES MILITARY)

Same specs as the 104 Series except 5-1/2-inch bull barrel, 6-3/4-inch space gun barrel; new frame with military Colt 1911-style grips; fitted magazine extension foot; new magazine release. Introduced 1965; dropped 1966.

Exc: $950 **VGood:** $800 **Good:** $550

HIGH STANDARD OLYMPIC ISU (102 SERIES)

Semi-automatic; 22 Short; 10-shot magazine; ported 6-3/4-inch barrel; 11-1/2-inch overall length; larger push-button takedown; alloy slide; new rear target sight; high polished finish. Marked "Model 102" on right side of slide. Unlike Olympic 102 Series, the ISU has integral stabilizer and comes standard with checkered walnut grips.

High Standard Olympic ISU (104 Series)

High Standard Olympic ISU Standard

High Standard Olympic (104 Series)

High Standard Sport King (101 Series)

High Standard Sharpshooter

High Standard Supermatic Trophy (102 Series)

Introduced 1957; dropped 1960.

Exc: $1050 **VGood:** $850 **Good:** $700

HIGH STANDARD OLYMPIC ISU (103 SERIES)

Same specs as ISU Model 102 except 5-1/2-inch, 6-3/4-inch bull barrel. Introduced 1960; dropped 1963.

Exc: $1000 **VGood:** $800 **Good:** $650

HIGH STANDARD OLYMPIC ISU (104 SERIES)

Same specs as ISU Model 102 except bull barrel with removable stabilizer (5-1/2-inch barrel); integral stabilizer (6-3/4-inch barrel); barrel weights and new Allen screw backlash adjuster in trigger. Introduced 1964; dropped 1964.

Exc: $950 **VGood:** $800 **Good:** $650

HIGH STANDARD OLYMPIC ISU (106 SERIES MILITARY)

Same specs as the 102 Series except military Colt 1911-style grips; integral barrel stabilizer. Introduced 1965; dropped 1967.

Exc: $1050 **VGood:** $850 **Good:** $700

HIGH STANDARD OLYMPIC ISU MILITARY

Same specs as the Olympic ISU Standard model except 5-1/2-inch bull barrel with removable stabilizer; high strength aluminum slide; carbon steel frame; barrel weights; adjustable trigger and sear; overall blue finish. From High Standard Mfg. Co., Inc. Reintroduced 1994; still produced.

Perf: $500 **Exc:** $400 **VGood:** $300

HIGH STANDARD OLYMPIC ISU STANDARD

Semi-automatic; 22 Short; 5-shot magazine; 6-3/4-inch tapered barrel with intergral stabilizer; 10 3/4-inch overall length; weighs 45 oz.; push-button takedown; undercut ramp front sight, micro-click adjustable rear; checkered walnut grips; adjustable trigger and sear; stippled front grip and backstrap; comes with weights and brackets. Reintroduced 1994; still in production.

Perf: $550 **Exc:** $450 **VGood:** $375

HIGH STANDARD PLINKER

Semi-automatic; 22 LR; 10-shot magazine; interchangeable 4-1/2-inch, 6-3/4-inch barrels; 9-inch overall length (4-1/2-inch barrel); hammerless; same gun as Duramatic; grooved trigger; checkered plastic target grips; fixed square-notch rear sight, ramp front; blued finish. Introduced 1962; dropped 1973.

Exc: $350 **VGood:** $275 **Good:** $225

HIGH STANDARD SHARPSHOOTER

Semi-automatic; 22 LR; 9-shot magazine; 5-1/2-inch bull barrel; 10-1/4-inch overall length; weighs 42 oz.; push-button take-down; hammerless; scored trigger; adjustable square-notch rear, ramp front sight; slidelock; checkered laminated plastic grips with medallion or walnut with medallion; blued finish. Marked "The Sharpshooter" in block letters on barrel flat. Introduced 1972; dropped 1982.

Exc: $550 **VGood:** $450 **Good:** $300

HIGH STANDARD SPORT KING (FIRST MODEL)

Semi-automatic; 22 LR; 10-shot magazine; 4-1/2-inch, 6-3/4-inch lightweight interchangeable barrels; 11-1/2-inch overall length (6-3/4-inch barrel); lever takedown; fixed sights; optional adjustable sight; checkered thumbrest plastic grips; blue finish. Introduced 1950; dropped 1953.

Two barrels

Exc: $600 **VGood:** $500 **Good:** $400

One barrel

Exc: $400 **VGood:** $300 **Good:** $250

HIGH STANDARD SPORT KING (101 SERIES)

Same specs as First Model except push-button takedown; all-steel frame and slide. Marked "SK-100" or "SK-101" on right side of slide. Introduced 1954; dropped 1984.

Two barrels

Exc: $600 **VGood:** $500 **Good:** $400

One barrel

Exc: $400 **VGood:** $300 **Good:** $250

HIGH STANDARD SPORT KING LIGHTWEIGHT (101 SERIES)

Same specs as 101 Series Sport King except forged aluminum alloy frame; weighs 30 oz. (6-3/4-inch barrel). Marked "Lightweight" on left side of frame. Introduced 1954; dropped 1964.

Two barrels

Exc: $675 **VGood:** $575 **Good:** $525

One barrel

Exc: $500 **VGood:** $425 **Good:** $375

HIGH STANDARD SPORT KING (102 SERIES)

Same specs as 101 Series Sport King except brown plastic grips (black plastic grips on nickel-plated guns); new optional nickel-plated finish. Late Sport King 102s had "G" in front of serial number. Introduced 1958; dropped 1963.

Exc: $400 **VGood:** $350 **Good:** $300

HIGH STANDARD SPORT KING (103 SERIES)

Same specs as 102 Series Sport King except marked "Model 103" on right side of slide.

Exc: $350 **VGood:** $300 **Good:** $250

HIGH STANDARD SPORT KING (106 SERIES MILITARY MODEL)

Same specs as 102 Series Sport King except military-style grips. Introduced 1977; dropped 1983.

Exc: $300 **VGood:** $250 **Good:** $200

HIGH STANDARD SUPERMATIC (FIRST MODEL)

Semi-automatic; 22 LR; 10-shot magazine; 4-1/2-inch, 6-3/4-inch interchangeable barrels; 11-1/2-inch overall length (6-3/4-inch barrel); hammerless; lever takedown; adjustable ramp front, click-adjustable rear target sights; automatic slidelock; 2-, 3-oz. adjustable barrel weights; adjustable ramp front; click-adjustable rear; automatic slidelock; checkered plastic thumbrest grips; blue-black finish with Parkerized slide top and barrel chamber. Introduced 1951; dropped 1958.

Two barrels

Exc: $850 **VGood:** $650 **Good:** $500

One barrel

Exc: $700 **VGood:** $500 **Good:** $400

HIGH STANDARD SUPERMATIC (101 SERIES 2ND MODEL)

Same specs as First Model except push-button takedown; fixed front sight; integral stabilizer (6-3/4-inch barrel). Marked "S100" or "S101" on right side of slide. Introduced, 1954; dropped, 1958.

Exc: $800 **VGood:** $600 **Good:** $450

High Standard Supermatic Tournament (102 Series)

High Standard Victor Target Pistol

High Standard Supermatic Trophy (107 Series)

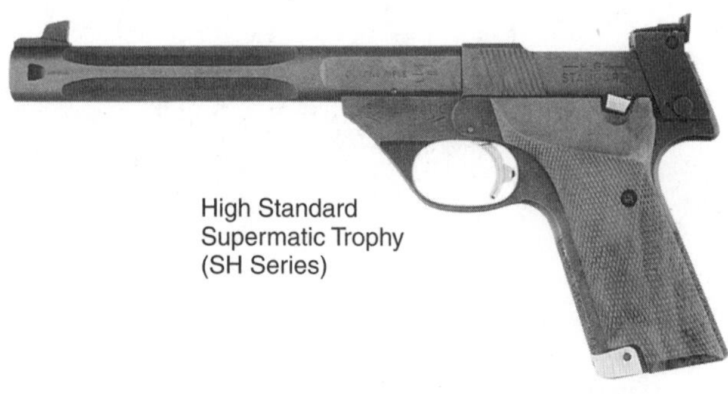
High Standard Supermatic Trophy (SH Series)

HIGH STANDARD SUPERMATIC CITATION

Semi-automatic; 22 LR; 10-shot magazine; 5-1/2-inch, 7-1/4-inch barrel; 9-1/2-inch overall length; weighs 44 oz.; under-cut ramp front, micro-click adjustable rear sight; checkered walnut grip with thumbrest; nickel-plated trigger, slidelock, safety lever, magazine release; blue finish. Reintroduced 1994; still in production.

New: $400 **Perf:** $350 **Exc:** $300

HIGH STANDARD SUPERMATIC TROPHY

Semi-automatic; single action; 22 LR; 10-shot magazine; 5-1/2-inch and 7-1/4-inch barrels are available; 9-1/2-inch overall length; weighs 44 oz.; checkered walnut with thumbrest grips; undercut ramp front sight that is fully-adjustable, micrometer-click rear; push-button takedown; removable muzzle stabilizer; gold-plated trigger, slidelock, safety-lever and magazine release; stippled front grip and backstrap; adjustable trigger and sear; drilled and tapped for scope mount; barrel weights optional. Reintroduced 1994; still produced.

New: $650 **Perf:** $500 **Exc:** $350

HIGH STANDARD SUPERMATIC TOURNAMENT

Semi-automatic; 22 LR; 10-shot magazine; 4-1/2-inch, 5-1/2-inch barrel; 8-1/2-inch overall length; weighs 43 oz.; push-button takedown; undercut ramp front, micro-click adjustable rear sight; black rubber ambidextrous grips; drilled and tapped for scope mount; blue finish. Reintroduced 1994.

New: $650 **Perf:** $500 **Exc:** $350

HIGH STANDARD SUPERMATIC TOURNAMENT (102 SERIES)

Semi-automatic; 22 LR; 10-shot magazine; 6-3/4-inch medium weight, 4-1/2-inch bull barrel; 1/4-inch high base front sight, click-adjustable rear on slide; push-button takedown; backlash adjustable screw; plastic grips; no grooving atop slide; dull black finish. Marked "SUPERMATIC" top line; "Tournament" in smaller letters underneath on left side of frame. Introduced 1958; dropped 1963.

Exc: $650 **VGood:** $525 **Good:** $400

HIGH STANDARD SUPERMATIC TOURNAMENT (103 SERIES)

Same specs as 102 Series Tournament except 5-1/2-inch bull barrel offering. Introduced 1958; dropped 1963.

Exc: $600 **VGood:** $500 **Good:** $400

HIGH STANDARD SUPERMATIC TOURNAMENT (106 SERIES MILITARY)

Same specs as 103 Series Tournament except military-style grips. Introduced 1965; dropped 1966.

Exc: $600 **VGood:** $500 **Good:** $400

HIGH STANDARD SUPERMATIC TROPHY (102 SERIES)

Semi-automatic; 22 LR; 10-shot; 6-3/4-inch, 8-inch, 10-inch tapered "space gun" barrels; push-button takedown; 2-, 3-oz. adjustable barrel weights; detachable stabilizer; trigger pull adjustment screw at rear of frame; overtravel adjustment screw on right side of frame; adjustable sights (barrel mounted on 8-inch, 10-inch); gold trigger safety; checkered walnut thumbrest grips; blue/black finish. Marked "Model 102" on right side of frame; "Supermatic Trophy" on left side. Introduced 1961; dropped 1966.

Exc: $1000 **VGood:** $700 **Good:** $600

HIGH STANDARD SUPERMATIC TROPHY (103/104 SERIES)

Same specs as the 102 Series except 5-1/2-inch, 7-1/4-inch bull barrels; recessed bore at muzzle. Marked "Supermatic Trophy" on left side of frame; "Model 103" or "Model 104" on right side of frame. Introduced 1960; dropped 1965.

Exc: $900 **VGood:** $700 **Good:** $50

HIGH STANDARD SUPERMATIC TROPHY (106/107 SERIES)

Same specs as the 102 Series except military-style grips; saddle-type rear sight; new slide with angled gripping ribs. Marked "Supermatic Trophy" and "HIGH STANDARD" on left side of slide; "Model 106" or "Model 107" above triggerguard on right side. Introduced 1965; dropped 1967.

Exc: $975 **VGood:** $850 **Good:** $700

HIGH STANDARD SUPERMATIC TROPHY (ML SERIES)

Same specs as 106/107 Series except "ML" prefixed serial number.

Exc: $700 **VGood:** $575 **Good:** $500

HIGH STANDARD SUPERMATIC TROPHY (SEVEN NUMBER SERIES)

Same specs as 106/107 Series except seven-digit serial number appears alone on right side of frame.

Exc: $800 **VGood:** $625 **Good:** $400

HIGH STANDARD SUPERMATIC TROPHY (SH SERIES)

Same specs as 106/107 Series except "SH" prefixed serial number.

Exc: $550 **VGood:** $450 **Good:** $325

HIGH STANDARD VICTOR (FIRST MODEL 107 SERIES)

Semi-automatic; 22 LR only; 10-shot magazine; 4-1/2-inch, 5-1/2-inch barrels; 8-3/4-inch overall length (4-1/2-inch barrel); 48 oz. (4-1/2-inch barrel), 52 oz. (5-1/2-inch barrel); hammerless; solid steel rib, later guns with aluminum vented rib; interchangeable barrel feature; rib-mounted click-adjustable rear sight, undercut ramp front; checkered walnut grips with thumbrest; blued finish. Marked "The Victor" on left side of barrel. Introduced 1963; dropped 1984.

Solid rib

Exc: $750 **VGood:** $650 **Good:** $450

Vent rib

Exc: $800 **VGood:** $700 **Good:** $475

HIGH STANDARD VICTOR (ML SERIES)

Same specs as standard Victor except marked "Victor" above triggerguard. Serial number prefixed with letters "ML."

Exc: $550 **VGood:** $450 **Good:** $350

HIGH STANDARD VICTOR (SEVEN NUMBER SERIES)

Same specs as Model 107 except seven-digit serial number appears alone on right side of frame.

Exc: $525 **VGood:** $325 **Good:** $300

HIGH STANDARD VICTOR (SH SERIES)

Same specs as standard Victor except Allen-screw takedown; small grip thumbrest; rib cut-out for shell ejection. Serial number prefixed with letters "SH."

Exc: $500 **VGood:** $450 **Good:** $350

High Standard Victor First Model 107 Series

High Standard Camp Gun

High Standard Crusader

High Standard Derringer

High Standard Double-Nine Convertible

HIGH STANDARD VICTOR TARGET

Semi-automatic; single action; 22 LR; 10-shot magazine; 4-1/2-inch, 5-1/2-inch barrel; 9-1/2-inch overall length; weighs 46 oz.; checkered walnut thumbrest grips; undercut ramp front sight, fully-adjustable, micrometer-click rear; push-button takedown; full-length aluminum vent rib (steel optional); gold-plated trigger, slidelock, safety-lever and magazine release; stippled front grip and backstrap; adjustable trigger and sear; comes with barrel weight; blue or Parkerized finish. Reintroduced 1994; still produced. Add 200% for Hamden-marked 4-1/2-inch barrel model with solid steel rib.

New: $650 **Perf:** $500 **Exc:** $425

HIGH STANDARD CAMP GUN

Revolver; double action; 22 LR, 22 WMR; 9-shot cylinder; 6-inch barrel; 11-1/8-inch overall length; weighs 28 oz.; steel frame; adjustable rear sight; target-type checkered walnut grips; blued finish. Introduced 1976; dropped 1979.

Exc: $200 **VGood:** $160 **Good:** $120

HIGH STANDARD CRUSADER

Revolver; double action; 357 Mag., 44 Mag., 45 Colt; 6-shot swing-out cylinder; 4-inch, 6-inch, 8-inch barrel (medium frame), 4-inch, 6-inch, 8-inch (large frame); weighs 38 oz. (med. frame), 48 oz. (large frame); unique internal gear mechanism which allows hammer to rest on frame when trigger is disengaged and brings hammer in direct line with firing pin when trigger is engaged; lack of transfer bar safety and trigger spring account for light weight; ramp front sight, adjustable rear; solid ribbed barrel; shrouded ejector rod; one-piece grip; blued finish. Introduced 1976; discontinued 1979. Limited production; slight premium for anniversary edition..

Exc: $900 **VGood:** $750 **Good:** $600

HIGH STANDARD DERRINGER

Derringer; double action; 22 LR, 22 Short, 22 WMR; 2-shot; hammerless; over/under 3-1/2-inch barrels; 5-1/8-inch overall length; weighs 11 oz.; plastic grips; fixed sights; standard model has blue, nickel finish. Early derringers marked "Hamden Conn." on barrel; later models marked "E. Hartford" on barrel. Presentation model gold-plated, introduced in 1965; dropped 1966. Presentation model has some collector value. Standard model introduced in 1963; dropped 1984.

Early model, blue finish

Exc: $250 **VGood:** $185 **Good:** $140

Early model, nickel finish

Exc: $275 **VGood:** $225 **Good:** $150

Late model, blue finish

Exc: $250 **VGood:** $185 **Good:** $140

Late model, nickel finish

Exc: $275 **VGood:** $225 **Good:** $150

Presentation model

Exc: $400 **VGood:** $350 **Good:** $300

HIGH STANDARD DOUBLE-NINE

Revolver; double action; 22 Short, 22 LR; 9-shot swing-out cylinder; 5-1/2-inch barrel; 11-inch overall length; dummy ejection rod housing; spring-loaded ejection; rebounding hammer; movable notch rear sight, blade front; plastic simulated stag, ebony or ivory grips; blued or nickel finish. Introduced 1959; dropped 1971.

Exc: $225 **VGood:** $200 **Good:** $150

Nickel finish

Exc: $240 **VGood:** $215 **Good:** $175

HIGH STANDARD DOUBLE-NINE CONVERTIBLE

Same specs as Double-Nine except two cylinders, one for 22 LR, 22 Long, 22 Short; other for 22 WMR; smooth frontier-type walnut grips; movable notched rear sight, blade front; blued, nickel finish. Introduced 1972; dropped 1984.

Exc: $200 **VGood:** $175 **Good:** $150

Nickel finish

Exc: $225 **VGood:** $220 **Good:** $175

HIGH STANDARD DURANGO

Revolver; double action; 22 LR, 22 Long, 22 Short; 4-1/2-inch, 5-1/2-inch barrels; 10-inch overall length (4-1/2-inch barrel); brass-finished triggerguard, backstrap; uncheckered walnut grips; blued only in shorter barrel length; blued, nickel (5-1/2-inch barrel). Introduced 1972; dropped 1975.

Exc: $300 **VGood:** $225 **Good:** $175

Nickel finish

Exc: $375 **VGood:** $295 **Good:** $200

HIGH STANDARD HIGH SIERRA

Revolver; double action; 22 LR, 22 WMR; 9-shot; 7-inch octagonal barrel; 12-1/2-inch overall length; blade front, adjustable rear sight; smooth walnut grips; swing-out cylinder; gold-plated backstrap, triggerguard. Introduced 1978; dropped 1984. Add 50% premium for convertible model with both cylinder assemblies.

Exc: $400 **VGood:** $300 **Good:** $195

HIGH STANDARD KIT GUN

Revolver; double action; 22 LR, 22 Long, 22 Short; 9-shot swing-out cylinder; 4-inch barrel; 9-inch overall length; micro-adjustable rear, target ramp front sight; checkered walnut grips; blued finish.

Exc: $175 **VGood:** $125 **Good:** $100

HIGH STANDARD LONGHORN

Revolver; double action; 22 LR; 4-1/2-inch, 5-1/2-inch barrels; pearl-like plastic grips; 5-1/2-inch barrel model with plastic staghorn grips; later model with walnut grips. Introduced 1961; dropped 1966.

Exc: $325 **VGood:** $250 **Good:** $200

HIGH STANDARD LONGHORN CONVERTIBLE

Same specs as standard Longhorn but with 9-1/2-inch barrel only; aluminum alloy frame; smooth walnut grips; dual cylinder to fire 22 WMR cartridge. Introduced 1971; dropped 1984.

Exc: $475 **VGood:** $400 **Good:** $275

HIGH STANDARD MARSHALL

Revolver; 22 LR; 9-shot swing-out cylinder; 5-1/2-inch barrel; fixed sights; Staglite western-style grips with gold medallion inset; blued finish; comes complete with leather holster. Introduced 1973; discontinued 1974. Limited production precludes pricing.

HIGH STANDARD NATCHEZ

Revolver; double action; 22 LR, 22 Short; 4-1/2-inch barrel; 10-inch overall length; fluted cylinder; ivory-like plastic bird's-head grips; blued. Introduced 1961; dropped 1966.

Exc: $500 **VGood:** $400 **Good:** $300

HIGH STANDARD POSSE

Revolver; double action; 22 LR; 3-1/2-inch barrel; 9-inch overall length; no ejector rod housing;

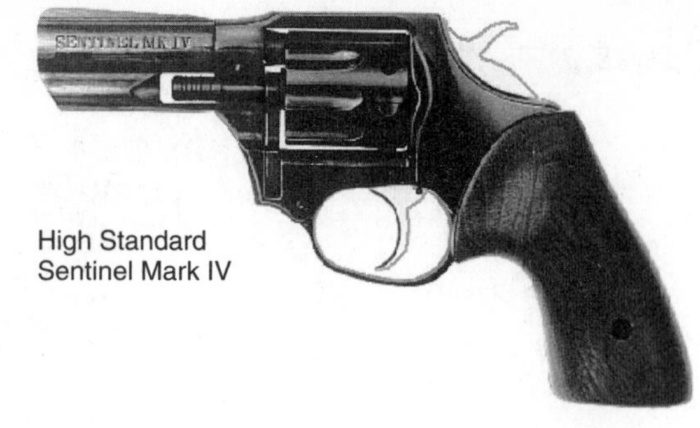

High Standard Sentinel Mark IV

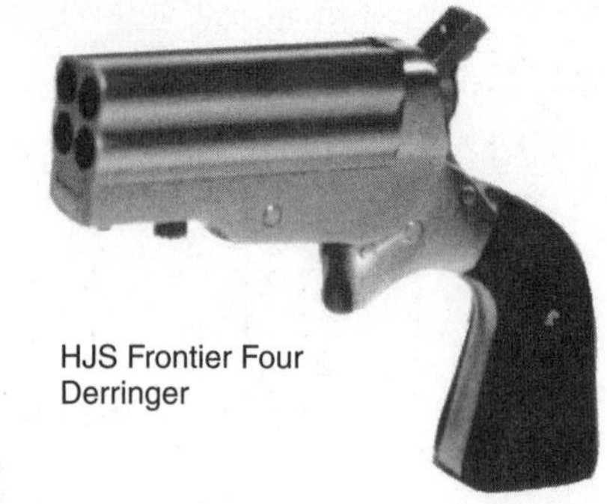
HJS Frontier Four Derringer

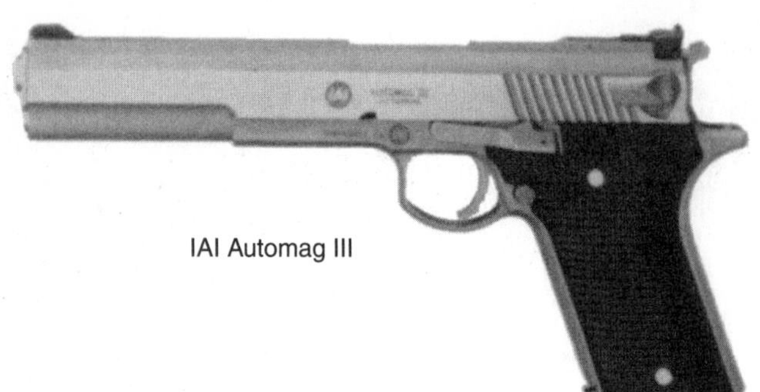
IAI Automag III

IAR Model 1873

uncheckered walnut grips; brass grip frame, triggerguard; blued. Introduced 1961; dropped 1966.

Exc: $450 **VGood:** $375 **Good:** $275

HIGH STANDARD SENTINEL

Revolver; double action; 22 Short, 22 LR; 9-shot swing-out cylinder; 3-inch, 4-inch, 6-inch barrels; 9-inch overall length (4-inch barrel); weighs 23 oz.; solid aluminum alloy frame; fixed sights; checkered plastic grips; blued or nickel finish. Introduced 1955; dropped 1974.

Exc: $275 **VGood:** $235 **Good:** $180

Nickel finish

Exc: $300 **VGood:** $250 **Good:** $200

HIGH STANDARD SENTINEL DELUXE

Same specs as the standard Sentinel except for movable rear sight; two-piece square-butt checkered walnut grips; wide triggers; 4-inch, 6-inch barrels only. Introduced 1957; dropped 1974.

Blue finish

Exc: $275 **VGood:** $250 **Good:** $200

Nickel finish

Exc: $300 **VGood:** $275 **Good:** $230

HIGH STANDARD SENTINEL IMPERIAL

Same specs as standard Sentinel model except blade ramp front sight; two-piece checkered walnut grips; onyx-black or nickel finish. Introduced 1962; dropped 1965.

Blue finish

Exc: $275 **VGood:** $250 **Good:** $200

Nickel finish

Exc: $300 **VGood:** $275 **Good:** $230

HIGH STANDARD SENTINEL MARK I

Revolver; double action; 22 LR; 9-shot cylinder; 2-inch, 3-inch, 4-inch barrel; ramp front, fixed or adjustable rear sight; uncheckered walnut stocks; blued or nickel finish. Introduced 1974; dropped 1984.

Blue finish

Exc: $200 **VGood:** $175 **Good:** $150

Nickel finish

Exc: $250 **VGood:** $225 **Good:** $190

HIGH STANDARD SENTINEL MARK II

Same specs as Sentinel Mark I except 357 Mag.; 6-shot cylinder; 2-1/2-inch, 4-inch, 6-inch barrel lengths; walnut combat grips; fixed sights; blued finish. Manufactured 1973 to 1975.

Exc: $350 **VGood:** $275 **Good:** $200

HIGH STANDARD SENTINEL MARK III

Same specs as Sentinel Mark II except ramp front sight, adjustable rear. Manufactured 1973 to 1975.

Exc: $375 **VGood:** $300 **Good:** $235

HIGH STANDARD SENTINEL MARK IV

Same specs as Sentinel Mark I except 22 WMR. Introduced 1974; dropped 1979.

Blue finish

Exc: $250 **VGood:** $225 **Good:** $200

Nickel finish

Exc: $300 **VGood:** $250 **Good:** $210

HIGH STANDARD SENTINEL SNUB

Revolver; double action; 22 LR; 9-shot swing-out cylinder; 2-3/8-inch barrel; solid aluminum alloy frame; quick draw sights and hammer; checkered bird's-head-type grips; blued or nickel finish. Introduced 1957; dropped 1974.

Blue finish

Exc: $275 **VGood:** $225 **Good:** $200

Nickel finish

Exc: $295 **VGood:** $250 **Good:** $225

HJS ANTIGUA DERRINGER

Derringer; four-shot; 22 LR; 2-inch barrels; 3-15/16-inch overall length; weighs 5-1/2 oz.; brown plastic grips; no sights; four barrel fire with rotating firing pin; blued barrels; brass frame; brass pivot pins. Made in U.S. by HJS Arms, Inc. Introduced 1994.

New: $160 **Perf:** $135 **Exc:** $125

HJS FRONTIER FOUR DERRINGER

Derringer; four-shot; 22 LR; 2-inch barrel; 3-15/16-inch overall length; weighs 5-1/2 oz.; brown plastic grips; no sights; four barrels fire with rotating firing pin; stainless steel construction. Made in U.S. by HJS Arms, Inc. Introduced 1993.

New: $135 **Perf:** $115 **Exc:** $100

HJS LONE STAR DERRINGER

Derringer; single shot; 32 S&W, 380 ACP; 2-inch barrel; 3-15/16-inch overall length; weighs 6 oz.; brown plastic grips; groove sight; stainless steel construction; beryllium copper firing pin; button-rifled barrel. Made in U.S. by HJS Arms, Inc. Introduced 1993.

New: $165 **Perf:** $135 **Exc:** $120

HUNGARIAN T-58

Semi-automatic; single action; 7.62mm, 9mm Para.; 8-shot magazine; 4-1/2-inch barrel; 7-11/16-inch overall length; weighs 31 oz.; grooved composition grips; blade front sight, windage-adjustable rear; comes with both barrels and magazines; blue finish. Imported by Century International Arms.

Perf: $160 **Exc:** $145 **VGood:** $125

IAI AUTOMAG III

Semi-automatic; single action; 30 Carbine, 9mm Win. Mag.; 8-shot magazine; 6-3/8-inch barrel; 10-1/2-inch overall length; weighs 43 oz.; blade front sight, Millett adjustable rear; wrap-around rubber grips; hammer-drop safety; sandblasted finish; stainless steel construction. Introduced 1989; discontinued 1992.

Perf: $700 **Exc:** $625 **VGood:** $550

IAI AUTOMAG IV

Semi-automatic; single-action; 45 Mag., 10mm Auto.; 7-shot magazine; 6-1/2-inch, 8-5/8-inch barrel; 10-1/2-inch overall length; weighs 46 oz; blade front sight, Millett adjustable rear; black carbon fiber grips; stainless steel construction; brushed finish. Introduced 1990; discontinued 1991.

Perf: $850 **Exc:** $700 **VGood:** $600

IAI BACKUP

Semi-automatic; 380 ACP; 5-shot magazine; 2-1/2-inch barrel; 4-1/2-inch overall length; weighs 18 oz.; fixed sights; wrap-around rubber or walnut

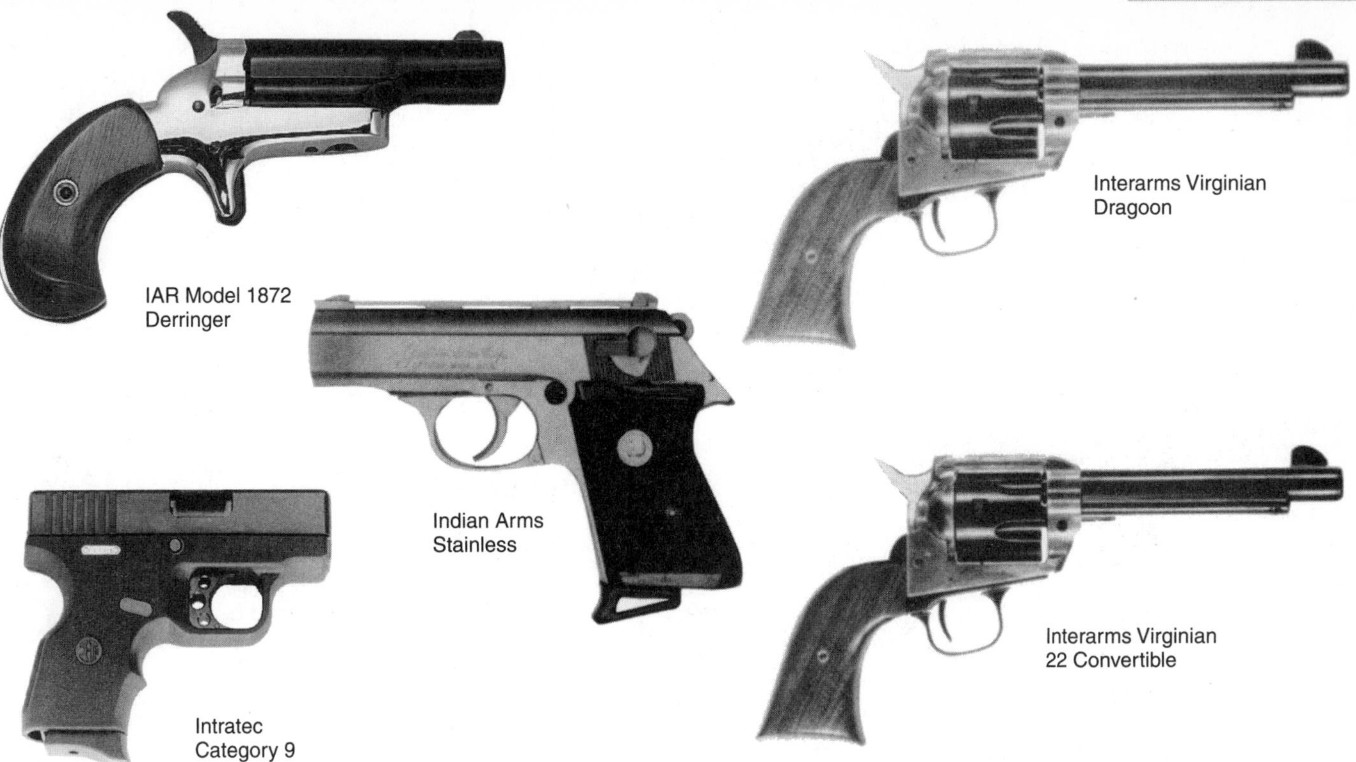
IAR Model 1872 Derringer

Interarms Virginian Dragoon

Indian Arms Stainless

Interarms Virginian 22 Convertible

Intratec Category 9

grips; stainless steel construction. Introduced 1988; discontinued 1989.

Perf: $295 **Exc:** $195 **VGood:** $135

IAI JAVELINA

Semi-automatic; 10mm Auto; 8-shot magazine; 5-inch, 7-inch barrel; 10-1/2-inch overall length; weighs 40 oz.; blade front sight, Millett adjustable rear; wrap-around rubber stocks; brushed finish; stainless steel construction. Introduced 1990; discontinued 1991.

Exc: $700 **VGood:** $595 **Good:** $375

IAR MODEL 1873

Revolver; single action; 22 LR, 22 LR/22 WMR; 4-3/4-inch barrel; 45 oz. 10-1/2-inch overall; one-piece walnut stocks with inspector's cartouche; blade front, notch rear sights; color case-hardened frame; blued barrel; black nickel-plated brass trigger guard and backstrap; bright nickel and engraved versions available. Introduced 1997. Imported from Italy by IAR, Inc.

Perf: $300 **Exc:** $250 **VGood:** $200

Nickel-plated

Perf: $350 **Exc:** $300 **VGood:** $250

22 LR/22WMR combo

Perf: $350 **Exc:** $300 **VGood:** $250

IAR MODEL 1872 DERRINGER

Single shot; 22 Short; 2-3/8-inch barrel; 7 oz.; 5-1/8-inch overall; smooth walnut grips; blade front, notch rear sights; gold or nickel frame with blue barrel. Reintroduced 1996 using original Colt designs and tooling for the Colt Model 4 Derringer. Made in U.S. by IAR, Inc.

Perf: $95 **Exc:** $75 **VGood:** $60

Single cased gun

Perf: $110 **Exc:** $85 **VGood:** $75

Double cased set

Perf: $195 **Exc:** $165 **VGood:** $135

IAR MODEL 1888 DOUBLE DERRINGER

Over under; 38 Special; 2-3/4-inch barrel; 16 oz.; smooth walnut grips; blade front, notch rear sights; all steel construction; blue barrel; color case-hardened frame. Uses original designs and tooling for the Uberti New Maverick Derringer. Introduced 1997. Made in U.S. by IAR, Inc.

Perf: $175 **Exc:** $150 **VGood:** $125

IBERIA FIREARMS JS-40 S&W

Semi-automatic; single action; 40 S&W; 8-shot magazine; 4-1/2-inch barrel; 8-inch overall length; weighs 44 oz.; checkered acetal resin grips; fixed low profile sights; internal drop-safe mechanism; all aluminum frame; matte black finish. Marketed by MKS Supply, Inc. Introduced 1991; now marketed as Hi-Point JS-40 S&W.

Perf: $115 **Exc:** $100 **VGood:** $85

Brushed nickel finish

Perf: $125 **Exc:** $110 **VGood:** $100

INDIAN ARMS STAINLESS

Semi-automatic; double action; 380 ACP; 6-shot magazine; 3-1/2-inch barrel; 6-1/16-inch overall length; checkered walnut stocks; adjustable rear sight, blade front; made of stainless steel, with natural or blued finish; optional safety lock. Introduced 1977; dropped 1978.

Exc: $395 **VGood:** $300 **Good:** $250

INTERARMS VIRGINIAN DRAGOON

Revolver; single action; 357 Mag., 44 Mag., 45 Colt; 6-shot; 6-inch, 7-1/2-inch, 8-3/8-inch barrel; 12-inch buntline on special order; ramp-type Partridge front sight, micro-adjustable target rear; smooth walnut grips; spring-loaded firing pin; color case-hardened frame; blued finish. Introduced 1977; dropped 1986.

Exc: $375 **VGood:** $325 **Good:** $250

Buntline barrel

Exc: $400 **VGood:** $350 **Good:** $275

INTERARMS VIRGINIAN DRAGOON DEPUTY MODEL

Same specs as standard model except fixed sights; 5-inch barrel (357), 6-inch (44 Mag.). Introduced 1983; dropped 1986.

Exc: $325 **VGood:** $295 **Good:** $275

INTERARMS VIRGINIAN DRAGOON ENGRAVED

Same specs as standard Dragoon except 44 Mag.; 6-inch, 7-inch barrel; fluted or unfluted cylinders; stainless or blued; hand-engraved frame, cylinder, barrel; marketed in felt-lined walnut case. Introduced 1983; dropped 1986.

Exc: $545 **VGood:** $470 **Good:** $430

INTERARMS VIRGINIAN DRAGOON SILHOUETTE

Same specs as standard model except stainless steel; 357 Mag., 41 Mag., 44 Mag.; 7-1/2-inch, 8-3/8-inch, 10-1/2-inch barrels; smooth walnut and Pachmayr rubber grips; undercut blade front sight, adjustable square notch rear; meets IHMSA standards. Made by Interarms. Introduced 1982; dropped 1986.

Exc: $365 **VGood:** $320 **Good:** $275

INTERARMS VIRGINIAN 22 CONVERTIBLE

Revolver; 22 LR, 22 WMR; 5-1/2-inch barrel; 10-3/4-inch overall length; weighs 38 oz.; smaller version of standard Dragoon; comes with both cylinders; case-hardened frame, rest blued or stainless steel. Made in Italy. Introduced 1983; dropped 1987; was imported by Interarms.

Exc: $200 **VGood:** $175 **Good:** $155

Stainless finish

Exc: $250 **VGood:** $215 **Good:** $190

INTRATEC CATEGORY 9

Semi-automatic; double action; 380 ACP, 9mm Para.; 7-shot magazine; 3-inch barrel; 5-1/2-inch overall length; weighs 21 oz.; textured black polymer grips; fixed channel sights; black polymer frame. Made in U.S. by Intratec. Introduced 1993; dropped 2000.

New: $215 **Perf:** $180 **Exc:** $155

INTRATEC CAT 45

Semi-automatic; double action; 40 S&W, 45 ACP; 6-shot magazine. Barrel: 3.25-inch. Weight: 19 oz. Length: 6.35-inch overall. Stocks: Molded composition. Sights: Fixed, channel. Features:

Iver Johnson 22 Supershot Sealed Eight (First Model)

Intratec TEC-9C

Intratec TEC-DC9

Iver Johnson 22 Supershot Sealed Eight (Second Model)

Intratec TEC-DC9M

Black polymer frame. Introduced 1996; dropped 2000.

New: $225 **Perf:** $200 **Exc:** $150

INTRATEC PROTEC-25

Semi-automatic; double-action-only; 25 ACP; 8-shot magazine; 2-1/2-inch barrel; 5-inch overall length; weighs 14 oz.; wrap-around composition grips in gray, black or driftwood color; fixed sights; choice of black, satin or Tec-Kote finishes. Introduced 1991; dropped 2000.

Black finish

Perf: $160 **Exc:** $120 **VGood:** $100

Satin or Tec-Kote finish

Perf: $175 **Exc:** $150 **VGood:** $120

INTRATEC TEC-9C

Semi-automatic; 9mm Para.; 36-shot magazine; 5-inch barrel; weighs 50 oz.; fixed sights; molded composition stocks; matte blue finish. Introduced 1987; no longer in production.

Perf: $700 **Exc:** $545 **VGood:** $325

INTRATEC TEC-22T

Semi-automatic; single action; 22 LR; 10-shot magazine; 4-inch barrel; 11-3/16-inch overall length; weighs 30 oz.; molded composition grip; protected post front, fully-adjustable front and rear sights; ambidextrous cocking knobs and safety; matte black finish; accepts any 10/22-type magazine. Made in U.S. by Intratec. Introduced 1988; no longer produced.

Perf: $300 **Exc:** $255 **VGood:** $215

INTRATEC TEC-22TK

Same specs as the TEC-22T except Tec-Kote finish. Made in U.S. by Intratec. Introduced 1988; no longer produced.

Perf: $300 **Exc:** $255 **VGood:** $215

INTRATEC TEC-DC9

Semi-automatic; single action; 9mm Para.; 10-shot magazine; 5-inch barrel; 12-1/2-inch overall length; weighs 50 oz.; molded composition grip; fixed sights; fires from closed bolt; firing pin block safety; matte blue finish. Made in U.S. by Intratec. Introduced 1985; dropped 1994.

Perf: $310 **Exc:** $265 **VGood:** $250

INTRATEC TEC-DC9S

Same specs as TEC-DC9 except stainless steel construction. Made in U.S. by Intratec. Introduced 1985; dropped 1994.

Perf: $350 **Exc:** $275 **VGood:** $200

INTRATEC TEC-DC9K

Same specs as TEC-DC9 except Tec-Kote finish. Made in U.S. by Intratec. Introduced 1985; dropped 1994.

Perf: $295 **Exc:** $250 **VGood:** $185

INTRATEC TEC-DC9M

Same specs as TEC-DC9 except 3-inch barrel; weighs 44 oz.; 20-shot magazine. Made in U.S. by Intratec. Introduced 1985; dropped 1994.

Perf: $325 **Exc:** $245 **VGood:** $185

INTRATEC TEC-DC9MK

Same specs as the TEC-DC9 except Tec-Kote finish. Made in U.S. by Intratec. Introduced 1985; dropped 1994.

Perf: $325 **Exc:** $275 **VGood:** $200

INTRATEC TEC-DC9MS

Same specs as TEC-DC9 except made of stainless steel. Made in U.S. by Intratec. Introduced 1985; dropped 1994.

Perf: $375 **Exc:** $295 **VGood:** $225

ITHACA MODEL 20

Single shot; 22 LR, 44 Mag.; 10-inch, 12-inch barrel; 15-inch overall length (10-inch barrel); weighs 3-1/4 lbs.; American walnut stock with satin finish; Ithaca Gun Raybar Deerslayer sights or drilled and tapped for scope mounting; single firing pin for RF/CF use; comes with both barrels matched to one frame; matte blue finish. Made in U.S. by Ithaca Acquisition Corp. Introduced 1994; no longer produced.

Perf: $695 **Exc:** $625 **VGood:** $550

ITHACA X-CALIBER

Single shot; 22 LR, 44 Mag.; 10-inch, 15-inch barrel; 15-inch overall length (10-inch barrel); weighs 3-1/4 lbs.; Goncalo Alves grip and forend; blade on ramp front sight, adjustable, removable target-type rear; drilled and tapped for scope mounting; dual firing pin for RF/CF use; polished blue finish. Made in U.S. by Ithaca Acquisition Corp. Made only in 1988. Deduct slightly for .22 rimfire.

Perf: $695 **Exc:** $625 **VGood:** $550

IVER JOHNSON 22 SUPERSHOT

Revolver; double action; 22 LR; 7-shot; 6-inch barrel; 10-3/4-inch overall length; weighs 24 oz.; top-break; automatic cartridge extraction; fixed sights; front sight and lettering gold-plated; one-piece saw-handle checkered walnut grips; has "Hammer the Hammer" action; blued finish. Marked 22 SUPERSHOT in script. Introduced 1928; dropped 1931.

Perf: $125 **Exc:** $100 **VGood:** $75

IVER JOHNSON 22 SUPERSHOT MODEL 90

Revolver; double action; 22 LR; 9-shot; 6-inch barrel; 10-3/4-inch overall length; weighs 24 oz.; top-break; automatic cartridge extraction; fixed sights; front sight and lettering gold-plated; one-piece saw-handle shaped checkered walnut oversize grips; has "Hammer the Hammer" action; blued finish. Marked 22 SUPERSHOT in script on left side of barrel. Pre-WWII model has adjustable finger rest. Introduced 1929; dropped 1949.

Perf: $135 **Exc:** $110 **VGood:** $85

IVER JOHNSON 22 SUPERSHOT SEALED EIGHT (FIRST MODEL)

Revolver; double action; 22 LR; 8-shot; 6-inch barrel; 10-3/4-inch overall length; weighs 24 oz.; large frame; top-break; recessed cylinder chambers; oversize target-type one-piece checkered walnut grips called Hi-Hold by the factory; has "Hammer the Hammer" action; blue finish. Three models: Model 88, fixed sights; Model 833, adjustable sights; Model 834, adjustable sights and adjustable finger rest. Marked 22 SUPERSHOT SEALED EIGHT on left side of barrel. Introduced 1932; dropped 1941.

Perf: $150 **Exc:** $125 **VGood:** $100

IVER JOHNSON 22 SUPERSHOT SEALED EIGHT (SECOND MODEL)

Same specs as First Model except weighs 28 oz.; grip frame modified for ease of manufacture.

Ithaca X-Caliber

Iver Johnson 22 Supershot Sealed Eight (Third Model 844)

Iver Johnson Bulldog

Iver Johnson Compact

Iver Johnson Cattleman Magnum

Iver Johnson Armsworth Model 855

Two models: Model 88, fixed sights; Model 833, adjustable sights. Marked 22 SUPERSHOT SEALED EIGHT on left side of barrel. Introduced 1946; dropped 1954.

Perf: $150 **Exc:** $125 **VGood:** $100

IVER JOHNSON 22 SUPERSHOT SEALED EIGHT (THIRD MODEL 844)

Same specs as First Model except 4-1/2-inch, 6-inch barrel; 9-1/4-inch (4-1/4-inch barrel), 10-3/4-inch (6-inch barrel) overall length; weighs 27 oz. (4-1/2-inch), 29 oz. (6-inch); unfluted cylinder; flat-sided barrel with full-length rib; recessed cylinder chambers with flash control front rim. Introduced 1955; dropped 1957.

Perf: $175 **Exc:** $150 **VGood:** $125

IVER JOHNSON ARMSWORTH MODEL 855

Revolver; single action; 22 LR; 6-inch barrel; 10-3/4-inch overall length; weighs 30 oz.; top-break; large frame; trigger pull factory set at 2-1/2 lbs.; recessed cylinder chambers with flash control front rim; flat-sided barrel with full-length rib; adjustable finger rest; adjustable sights; one-piece oversize target-type checkered walnut grip; does not have "Hammer the Hammer" action; blued finish. Limited production; rare. Introduced 1955; dropped 1957.

Perf: $300 **Exc:** $250 **VGood:** $225

IVER JOHNSON BULLDOG

Revolver; double action; 22 LR, 22 WMR, 38 Spl.; 6-shot (22), 5-shot (38); 2-1/2-inch, 4-inch barrel; 6-1/2-inch overall length (2-1/2-inch barrel); 9-inch overall length (4-inch barrel); weighs 26 oz. (2-1/2-inch), 30 oz. (4-inch); large solid frame; pull pin cylinder release; adjustable sights; one-piece oversize molded Tenite plastic target grips (4-inch), two-piece pocket size plastic (2-1/2-inch); full-length barrel rib; does not have "Hammer the Hammer" action; blue or nickel finish. Introduced 1974; dropped 1979.

Perf: $135 **Exc:** $110 **VGood:** $75

IVER JOHNSON CATTLEMAN MAGNUM

Revolver; single action; 357 Mag., 45 LC, 44 Mag.; 6-shot; 4-3/4-inch, 5-1/2-inch, 7-1/4-inch (357, 45); 4-3/4-inch, 6-inch, 7-1/4-inch (44) barrel; 10-1/4-inch (4-3/4-inch), 11-inch (5-1/2-inch), 11-1/2-inch (6-inch), 12-3/4-inch (7-1/4-inch) overall length; 40 oz. (4-3/4-inch), 41 oz. (5-1/2-inch), 44 oz. (7-1/4-inch); large solid frame; rod ejection; automatic hammer-block safety; fixed sights; one-piece European walnut grips; brass grip frame; color case-hardened frame; blue barrel and cylinder. A limited number chambered in 44-40 caliber; add 20 percent. Introduced 1973; dropped 1979.

Perf: $275 **Exc:** $215 **VGood:** $165

44 Magnum

Perf: $300 **Exc:** $250 **VGood:** $190

IVER JOHNSON CATTLEMAN BUCKHORN MAGNUM

Same specs as Cattleman Magnum except 5-3/4-inch, 7-1/2-inch (357, 45) barrel; 4-3/4-inch, 6-inch, 7-1/2-inch (44) barrel; 12-3/4-inch (7-1/2-inch barrel), 11-1/2-inch (6-inch barrel), 11-inch (5-3/4-inch barrel), 10-3/4-inch (4-3/4-inch barrel) overall length; 44 oz. (7-1/2-inch), 42-1/2 oz. (6-inch), 41 oz. (5-3/4-inch); 41 oz. (4-3/4-inch). A limited number manufactured with 12-inch barrel with shoulder stock lugs; add 20 percent. Introduced 1973; dropped 1979.

Perf: $250 **Exc:** $210 **VGood:** $185

IVER JOHNSON CATTLEMAN BUCKHORN BUNTLINE

Same specs as Cattleman Magnum except 18-inch barrel; 23-1/4-inch overall length; weighs 56 oz.; detachable shoulder stock; adjustable sights. Introduced 1973; dropped 1979.

Perf: $300 **Exc:** $250 **VGood:** $175

IVER JOHNSON CATTLEMAN TRAILBLAZER

Same specs as Cattleman Magnum except 22 LR, 22 WMR; 5-1/2-inch, 6-1/2-inch barrel; 10-3/4-inch (5-1/2-inch), 11-3/4-inch (6-1/2-inch) overall length; weighs 38 oz. (5-1/2-inch), 40 oz. (6-1/2-inch); adjustable sights. Introduced 1973; dropped 1979.

Perf: $175 **Exc:** $145 **VGood:** $110

IVER JOHNSON CHAMPION MODEL 822

Revolver; single-action; 22 LR; 6-inch barrel; 8-shot; 10-3/4-inch overall length; weighs 24 oz.; recessed cylinder chambers; adjustable finger rest; adjustable target-type sights; oversize one-piece target-type checkered walnut grips; does not have "Hammer the Hammer" action; blued finish. Marked CHAMPION SINGLE ACTION on left side of barrel. Cataloged several years after WWII but none manufactured after 1941. Very rare; very collectible. Introduced 1939; dropped 1941.

Perf: $300 **Exc:** $250 **VGood:** $200

IVER JOHNSON COMPACT

Semi-automatic; single action; 25 ACP; 6-shot; 3-inch barrel; 4-1/4-inch overall length; weighs 9-5/16-inch oz.; checkered composite grips; trigger block safety; matte blue frame; bright blue slide. Introduced 1991; dropped 1993.

Perf: $165 **Exc:** $135 **VGood:** $115

IVER JOHNSON COMPACT ELITE

Same specs as Compact except 24K gold finish; Ivorex grips. Introduced 1991; dropped 1993.

Perf: $550 **Exc:** $450 **VGood:** $295

IVER JOHNSON DELUXE STARTER MODEL 69

Revolver; double action; 22, 32 blanks; 8-shot (22), 5-shot (32); 2-3/4-inch solid barrel; 7-inch overall length; weighs 22 oz.; top-break; recessed cylinder chambers; built on 66S Trailsman frame; fixed sights; two-piece small pocket-size plastic grips; does not have "Hammer the Hammer" action; matte blue finish. Introduced 1964; dropped 1974.

Perf: $65 **Exc:** $45 **VGood:** $30

IVER JOHNSON ENFORCER MODEL 3000/IVER JOHNSON SUPER ENFORCER MODEL PP30

Semi-automatic; single action; 30 Carbine; 15-, 30-shot; 9-1/2-inch barrel; 17-inch overall length; weighs 4 lbs.; gas-operated; fires from closed bolt; American walnut stock; blue finish. Pistol version of Universal M1 Carbine; Iver Johnson purchased Universal in 1985. Manufactured 1986.

Perf: $550 **Exc:** $400 **VGood:** $300

Iver Johnson Hijo Quickbreak 1961

Iver Johnson Model 57 Target

Iver Johnson Model 55 Target

Iver Johnson Model 55S Cadet

Iver Johnson Model 55A

Iver Johnson Model 50 Sidewinder

Iver Johnson Model 55S-A Cadet

IVER JOHNSON HIJO QUICKBREAK 1961

Revolver; double action; 22 LR, 32 S&W, 38 S&W; 8-shot (22), 5-shot (32, 38); 7-inch overall length; weighs 25 oz.; recessed cylinder chambers; rimfire model with flash control front rim; two-piece pocket-size plastic grips; adjustable sights; does not have "Hammer the Hammer" action; nickel finish only. Same as the Model 66S made to be sold by several mail-order companies in New York City area.

Perf: $100 **Exc:** $75 **VGood:** $50

IVER JOHNSON MODEL 50 SIDEWINDER

Revolver; double action; 22 LR; 8-shot; 6-inch barrel (1961-1978/1979); 4-3/4-inch barrel (1974-1978/1979); 10-inch (4-3/4-inch barrel), 11-1/4-inch (6-inch barrel) overall length; 30 oz. (4-3/4-inch), 31 oz. (6-inch); large solid frame; rod ejection; recessed chambers with flash control front rim; 22 LR/22 WMR combo available after 1974; fixed sights; adjustable after 1974; Western-style walnut grips; stag plastic grips standard after 1968; several model numbers for different finish and sight combinations after 1974; matte blue and satin nickel finish. Introduced 1961; dropped 1979.

Perf: $110 **Exc:** $85 **VGood:** $60

IVER JOHNSON MODEL 55 TARGET

Revolver; double action; 22 LR; 8-shot; 4-1/2-inch, 6-inch barrels; 10-3/4-inch (4-1/4-inch), 9-1/4-inch (6-inch) overall length; weighs 24 oz. (4-1/2-inch), 26 oz. (6-inch); large solid frame; pull pin cylinder release with flash control front rim; recessed cylinder chambers; fixed sights; oversize molded one-piece Tenite plastic target-type grips; does not have "Hammer the Hammer" action; matte blue finish. After 1958 cylinder fluted; hard chrome lined barrel. Introduced 1955; dropped 1960.

Perf: $100 **Exc:** $70 **VGood:** $50

IVER JOHNSON MODEL 55A

Same specs as Model 55 except incorporation of loading gate; weighs 28-1/2 oz. (4-1/2-inch barrel), 30-1/2 oz. (6-inch barrel). After 1974/1975 this model called the "I J SPORTSMAN." Introduced 1961; dropped 1979.

Perf: $90 **Exc:** $70 **VGood:** $50

IVER JOHNSON MODEL 55S CADET

Same specs as Model 55 except 2-1/2-inch barrel; 7-inch overall length; weighs 27 oz.; two-piece small pocket-size grips; fluted cylinder after 1958. Introduced 1955; dropped 1960.

Perf: $145 **Exc:** $100 **VGood:** $75

IVER JOHNSON MODEL 55S-A CADET

Same specs as Model 55 except 22 LR, 32 S&W, 38 S&W; 8-shot (22), 5-shot (32, 38); 7-inch overall length; loading gate on right side of frame. After 1974/1975 this model called "I J CADET." Introduced 1961; dropped 1979.

Perf: $145 **Exc:** $100 **VGood:** $75

IVER JOHNSON MODEL 56 I J STARTER REVOLVER

Revolver; double action; 22 blank; 8-shot; 2-1/2-inch solid barrel; 6-3/4-inch overall length; weighs 10 oz.; large solid frame; pull pin cylinder release; recessed cylinder chambers; cylinder half-length; hard rubber or walnut pocket-size grips; built on Model 1900 large frame; blue finish. Introduced 1956; dropped 1960.

Perf: $75 **Exc:** $55 **VGood:** $35

IVER JOHNSON MODEL 56A I J STARTER REVOLVER

Same specs as Model 56 except 22, 32 rimfire blank; 8-shot (22), 5-shot (32); 22 oz.; plastic grips; loading gate on right side of frame; matte blue finish; built on Model 55S-A frame. Introduced 1961; dropped 1974.

Perf: $60 **Exc:** $40 **VGood:** $20

IVER JOHNSON MODEL 57 TARGET

Revolver; double action; 22 LR; 8-shot; 2-1/2-inch, 4-1/2-inch, 6-inch barrel; 7-1/2-inch (2-1/2-inch barrel), 9-1/2-inch (4-1/2-inch barrel), 10-3/4-inch (6-inch barrel) overall length; 27 oz. (2-1/2-inch), 29 oz. (4-1/2-inch), 30-1/2 oz. (6-inch); large solid frame; pull pin cylinder release; unfluted cylinder; recessed cylinder chambers with flash control front rim; scored trigger; music wire springs; checkered thumbrest; half-cock safety; adjustable front and rear sight; one-piece molded Tenite plastic target-type grips; does not have "Hammer the Hammer" action; matte blue finish. Introduced 1955; dropped 1960.

Perf: $100 **Exc:** $80 **VGood:** $55

IVER JOHNSON MODEL 57A TARGET

Same specs as Model 57 except 4-1/2-inch, 6-inch barrel only; loading gate on right side of frame; adjustable sights. After 1974 this model called "I J TARGET DELUXE." Introduced 1961; dropped 1979.

Perf: $105 **Exc:** $75 **VGood:** $55

IVER JOHNSON MODEL 1900

Revolver; double action; solid frame; pull pin cylinder release; 2-1/2-inch (standard), 4-1/2-inch, 6-inch octagon barrel; standard finish nickel, blue optional; three frame sizes. Small frame: 22 LR; 7-shot; 6-inch overall length (2-1/2-inch barrel); weighs 11 oz. Medium frame: 32 S&W; 5-shot; 6-1/8-inch overall length (2-1/2-inch barrel); weighs 12 oz. Large frame: 32 S&W Long, 38 S&W; 6-shot (32), 5-shot (38); 6-3/4-inch overall length; weighs 18 oz. Small pocket-size hard rubber grips, oversize target-type hard rubber optional. Introduced 1900; dropped 1941.

Perf: $100 **Exc:** $75 **VGood:** $50

IVER JOHNSON MODEL 1900 TARGET

Same specs as Model 1900 except blue finish only; 6-inch, 9-inch octagon barrel; 9-1/4-inch overall length (6-inch barrel), 14-3/8-inch (9-inch barrel); weighs 12-7/8 oz. (6-inch barrel), 14-3/8 oz. (9-inch barrel); built on Model 1900 small frame. Two-piece oversize walnut grips. Introduced 1925; dropped 1928. Add 20 percent for 9-inch barrel.

Perf: $135 **Exc:** $110 **VGood:** $100

IVER JOHNSON MODEL 1900 TARGET MODELS 69 & 79

Same specs as Model 1900 except blue finish only; 6-inch (Model 69), 10-inch (Model 79) octagon barrel; 9-shot; built on Model 1900 large frame; 10-3/4-inch overall length (6-inch barrel), 14-3/4-inch (10-inch barrel); weighs 24 oz. (6-inch), 27 oz. (10-inch); one-piece oversize target-type walnut grips. Introduced 1929; dropped 1941. Add 20 percent for 10-inch barrel.

Perf: $145 **Exc:** $135 **VGood:** $110

IVER JOHNSON MODEL 1908 PETITE HAMMERLESS

Revolver; double action; 22 LR; 1-1/4-inch barrel; 3-15/16-inch overall length; weighs 4-7/8 oz.; solid frame; folding trigger; pull pin cylinder release;

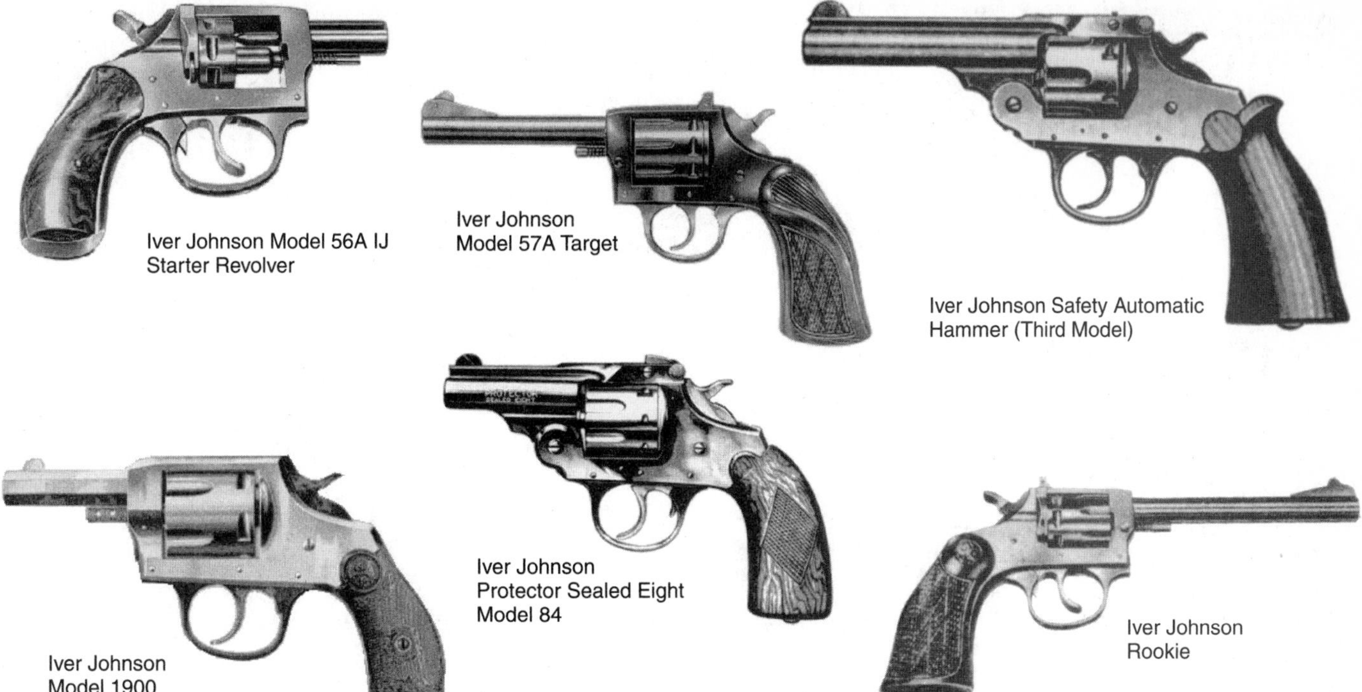
Iver Johnson Model 56A IJ Starter Revolver

Iver Johnson Model 57A Target

Iver Johnson Safety Automatic Hammer (Third Model)

Iver Johnson Model 1900

Iver Johnson Protector Sealed Eight Model 84

Iver Johnson Rookie

small pocket-size hard rubber grips. One of the smallest revolvers built in U.S. Fewer than 1000 manufactured. Manufactured 1908 only. Rare and collectible.

Perf: $450 **Exc:** $300 **VGood:** $150

IVER JOHNSON PROTECTOR SEALED EIGHT MODEL 84

Revolver; double action; 22 LR; 8-shot; 2-1/2-inch barrel; 10-3/4-inch overall length; weighs 20 oz.; large frame; top-break; automatic extraction; recessed cylinder chambers; pocket-size one-piece checkered walnut grips; fixed sights, adjustable optional; has "Hammer the Hammer" action; blue finish. Marked PROTECTOR SEALED EIGHT on left side of barrel. Rare model. Introduced 1933; dropped 1941.

Perf: $200 **Exc:** $175 **VGood:** $150

IVER JOHNSON ROOKIE

Revolver; double action; 38 Spl.; 5-shot; 4-inch barrel; 9-inch overall length; weighs 29 oz.; pull pin cylinder release; fixed sights; one-piece oversize molded Tenite plastic target-type grips; does not have "Hammer the Hammer" action; blue finish. Introduced 1974; dropped 1979.

Perf: $225 **Exc:** $160 **VGood:** $85

IVER JOHNSON SAFETY AUTOMATIC HAMMER (SECOND MODEL)

Revolver; double action; hinged frame top-break; double top post barrel latch; "Hammer the Hammer" action; flat springs; two frame sizes; standard finish, nickel; blue finish optional. Small frame: 22 LR, 32 S&W; 7-shot (22), 5-shot (32); 3-inch (standard), 4-inch, 5-inch, 6-inch barrel; 6-3/8-inch overall length; weighs 12 oz. (3-inch 22 LR), 12-1/4 oz. (32 S&W). Large frame: 38 S&W (blackpowder cartridges only); 3-1/4-inch (standard), 2-inch, 4-inch, 5-inch, 6-inch barrels; 7-3/8-inch overall length; weighs 17-1/4 oz. Fixed sights; small pocket size hard rubber grips. Introduced 1897; dropped 1908. For rimfire models add 20 percent.

Perf: $100 **Exc:** $75 **VGood:** $50

IVER JOHNSON SAFETY AUTOMATIC HAMMER (THIRD MODEL)

Same specs as Second Model except coil springs; small frame comes in 3-inch (standard), 2-inch, 4-inch, 5-inch, 6-inch barrel; large frame model in 32 S&W Long, 38 S&W for smokeless powder. Cataloged until 1948. Introduced 1909; dropped 1941. For rimfire models add 20 percent.

Perf: $125 **Exc:** $100 **VGood:** $75

IVER JOHNSON SAFETY HAMMERLESS (SECOND MODEL)

Revolver; double action; hinged frame top-break; double top post barrel latch; "Hammer the Hammer" action; flat springs; basic design comparable to Safety Hammer model; two frame sizes; standard finish, nickel; blue finish optional. Small frame: 22 LR, 32 S&W; 7-shot (22), 5-shot (32); 3-inch (standard), 2-inch, 4-inch, 5-inch, 6-inch barrel; 6-3/8-inch overall length (3-inch barrel); weighs 12-1/2 oz. (3-inch 22 LR), 13-1/2 oz. (32). Large frame: 38 S&W (blackpowder cartridges only); 5-shot (38); 3-1/4-inch (standard), 2-inch, 4-inch, 5-inch, 6-inch barrels; 7-3/8-inch overall length; weighs 18-1/4 oz. (32), 19 oz. (38). Fixed sights; small pocket size hard rubber grips. Introduced 1897; dropped 1908. For rimfire models add 20 percent.

Perf: $100 **Exc:** $75 **VGood:** $50

IVER JOHNSON SAFETY HAMMERLESS (THIRD MODEL)

Same specs as Second Model except small frame weighs 13-1/2 oz. (3-inch 22 LR), 14 oz. (32); large frame weighs 19 oz. (38 S&W); 38 S&W, 32 S&W Long (smokeless cartridge); oversize target hard rubber or walnut grips optional. Cataloged until 1948. Introduced 1909; dropped 1941. For rimfire models add 20 percent.

Perf: $125 **Exc:** $100 **VGood:** $75

IVER JOHNSON SEALED 8 SNUB MODEL 68S

Revolver; double action; 22 LR; 8-shot; 2-1/2-inch barrel; 6-3/4-inch overall length; weighs 20-1/2 oz.; large solid frame; pull pin cylinder release; recessed cylinder chambers; round barrel; small pocket-size two-piece walnut grips; does not have "Hammer the Hammer" action. Introduced 1952; dropped 1954. Rare and limited production.

Perf: $200 **Exc:** $175 **VGood:** $150

IVER JOHNSON SECRET SERVICE SPECIAL MODELS 1917 & 1923

Revolver; double action; top break; hammer and hammerless versions; two frame sizes. Small frame: 32 S&W; 5-shot; 3-inch (standard), 5-inch barrel; 6-3/8-inch overall length; weighs 12 oz. (hammer model), 13 oz. (hammerless model). Large frame: 38 S&W; 5-shot; 3-1/4-inch (standard), 5-inch barrel; 7-3/8-inch overall length; weighs 18 oz. (hammer model), 19 oz. (hammerless); blue finish, nickel optional; hard rubber pocket-size grips; oversize target grips optional. Marked on left side of barrel SECRET SERVICE SPECIAL; on top of barrel "for .32 [or .38] SMITH & WESSON CARTRIDGES." Note: Not all revolvers so marked were manufactured by Iver Johnson. The name "Secret Service Special" was owned by the Fred Biffar Co. of Chicago, IL. For models with hammer-block safety add 20 percent.

Perf: $135 **Exc:** $100 **VGood:** $50

IVER JOHNSON TARGET SEALED 8 (FIRST MODEL)

Revolver; double action; 22 LR; 8-shot; 6-inch (Model 68), 10-inch (Model 78) barrel; 10-3/4-inch (M68), 14-3/4-inch (M78) overall length; weighs 24 oz. (M68), 27 oz. (M78); large solid frame; pull pin cylinder release; recessed cylinder chambers; fixed sights, front blade gold-plated; one-piece oversized checkered walnut grips; octagon barrel; does not have "Hammer the Hammer" action. Introduced 1932; dropped 1941.

Perf: $125 **Exc:** $100 **VGood:** $75

IVER JOHNSON TARGET SEALED 8 (SECOND MODEL)

Same specs as First Model except 4-1/2-inch, 6-inch barrel; 9-1/4-inch (4-1/2-inch barrel), 10-3/4-inch (6-inch barrel) overall length; weighs 22-1/2 oz. (4-inch), 24 oz. (6-inch); round barrel. Introduced 1946; dropped 1954.

Perf: $125 **Exc:** $100 **VGood:** $75

IVER JOHNSON TP22

Semi-automatic; double action; 22 LR; 2 7/8-inch barrel; 5-3/8-inch overall length; weighs 14-1/2 oz.; hammer-block safety; no magazine safety; no slide stop; fixed sights; black plastic wrap-around grips; designed by ERMA WERKES Germany; blue and

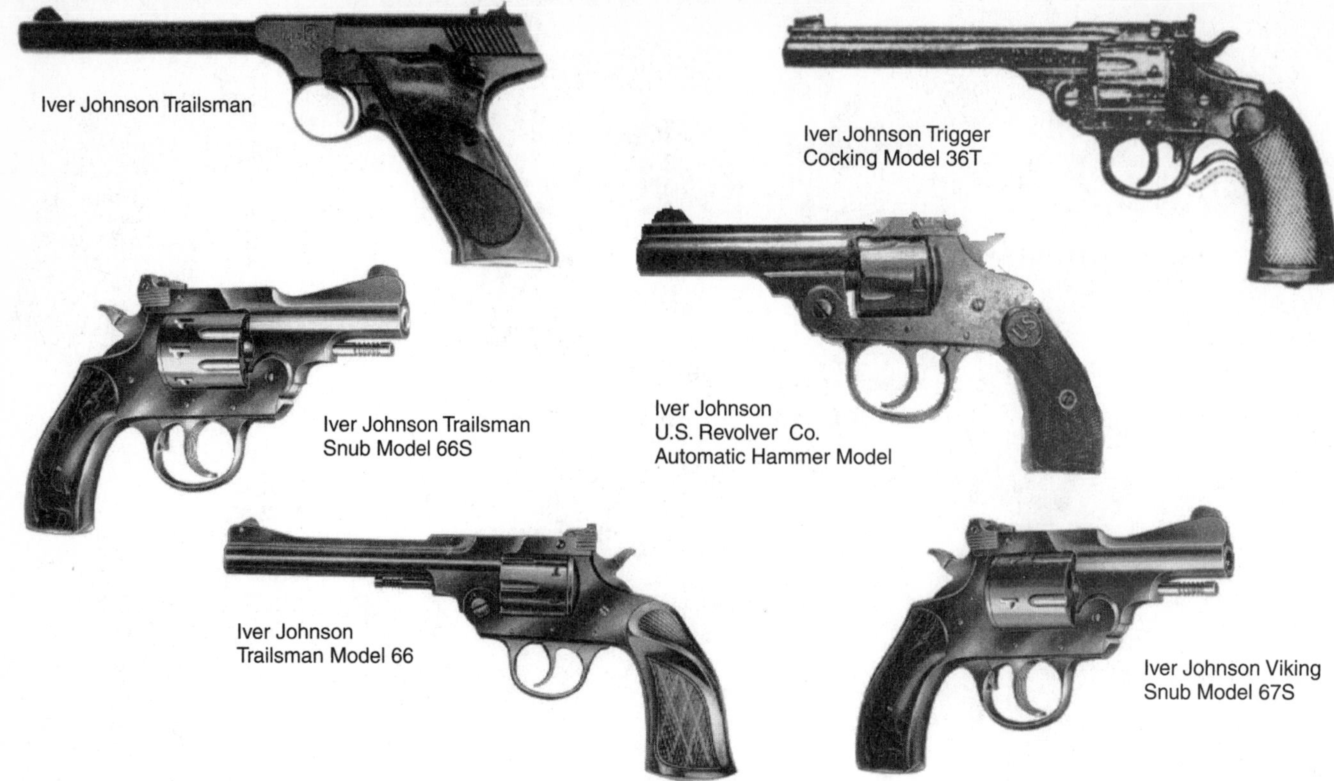
Iver Johnson Trailsman

Iver Johnson Trigger Cocking Model 36T

Iver Johnson Trailsman Snub Model 66S

Iver Johnson U.S. Revolver Co. Automatic Hammer Model

Iver Johnson Trailsman Model 66

Iver Johnson Viking Snub Model 67S

nickel finish; features patented passive firing pin block safety. Introduced 1982; dropped 1988.

Perf: $175 **Exc:** $125 **VGood:** $100

IVER JOHNSON TP25

Semi-automatic; double action; 25 ACP; 2-7/8-inch barrel; 5-3/8-inch overall length; weighs 14-1/2 oz.; hammer-block safety; no magazine safety; no slide stop; fixed sights; black plastic wrap-around grips; designed by ERMA WERKES Germany; blue finish. Introduced 1981; dropped 1988.

Perf: $175 **Exc:** $110 **VGood:** $95

IVER JOHNSON TRAILSMAN

Semi-automatic; single action; 22 LR; 4-1/2-inch, 6-inch barrel; 8-3/4-inch (4-1/2-inch barrel) overall length; weighs 46 oz. (4-1/2-inch), 64 oz. (6-inch); checkered black plastic grips; slide hold-open latch; push button magazine release; sear block safety; fixed sights; blue finish. First 500+ actually manufactured in Argentina; worth a premium. Introduced 1984; dropped 1988.

Perf: $195 **Exc:** $175 **VGood:** $145

IVER JOHNSON TRAILSMAN MODEL 66

Revolver; double action; 22 LR; 8-shot; 4-1/2-inch (added in 1962; dropped 1964), 6-inch barrel; 9-1/2-inch (4-1/2-inch barrel), 11-inch (6-inch barrel) overall length; weighs 31 oz. (4-1/2-inch), 34 oz. (6-inch); large frame; top-break; recessed cylinder chambers with flash control front rim; manual extraction; adjustable sights; one-piece molded Tenite plastic target-type grips; does not have "Hammer the Hammer" action; matte blue finish. Introduced 1958; dropped 1974.

Perf: $120 **Exc:** $95 **VGood:** $75

IVER JOHNSON TRAILSMAN SNUB MODEL 66S

Same specs as Model 66 except 22 LR, 32 S&W, 38 S&W; 8-shot (22), 5-shot (32, 38); centerfire calibers not added until 1962; 2-3/4-inch barrel; 7-inch overall length; weighs 25 oz.; two-piece pocket-size plastic grips. Introduced 1959; dropped 1963.

Perf: $110 **Exc:** $85 **VGood:** $65

IVER JOHNSON TRIGGER COCKING MODEL 36T

Revolver; single action; 22 LR; 8-shot; 6-inch barrel; 10-3/4-inch overall length; weighs 24 oz.; large frame; top-break; recessed cylinder chambers; adjustable sights; one-piece oversize target-type checkered walnut grips; adjustable finger rest; does not have "Hammer the Hammer" action; first pull of the trigger cocks the hammer; second pull releases it; blue finish. Marked "I J TRIGGER COCKING 22 SINGLE ACTION TARGET" in two lines on left side of barrel. Limited production; considered rare and collectible. Introduced 1936; dropped 1941.

Perf: $300 **Exc:** $250 **VGood:** $200

IVER JOHNSON U.S. REVOLVER CO. AUTOMATIC HAMMER MODEL

Revolver; double action; top-break; automatic cartridge extraction; two frame sizes; blue finish, nickel optional. Small frame: 22 LR, 32 S&W; 7-shot (22), 5-shot (32); 3-inch (standard), 5-inch barrel; 6-3/8-inch overall length (3-inch barrel); 12 oz. (22), 12-1/2 oz. (32). Large frame: 38 S&W; 5-shot; 7-3/8-inch overall length; weighs 17-3/4 oz.; small hard rubber pocket-size grips, oversize grips optional. Marked on barrel top rib: "U.S. REVOLVER Co." Introduced 1910; dropped 1935.

Perf: $85 **Exc:** $65 **VGood:** $45

IVER JOHNSON U.S. REVOLVER CO. AUTOMATIC HAMMERLESS MODEL

Revolver; double action; top-break; automatic cartridge extraction; two frame sizes; blue finish, nickel optional. Small frame: 32 S&W; 5-shot; 3-inch (standard), 5-inch barrel; 6-3/8-inch overall length (3-inch barrel); 12-1/2 oz. Large frame: 38 S&W; 5-shot; 7-3/8-inch overall length; weighs 18 oz.; small hard rubber pocket-size grips, two-piece oversize grips optional. Marked on barrel top rib: "U.S. REVOLVER Co." Introduced 1910; dropped 1935.

Perf: $85 **Exc:** $65 **VGood:** $45

IVER JOHNSON U.S. REVOLVER CO. DOUBLE ACTION

Revolver; double action; solid frame; pull pin cylinder release; two frame sizes; round barrel; unfluted cylinder. Small frame: 22 LR, 32 S&W; 7-shot (22), 5-shot (32); 2-1/2-inch barrel (standard), 4-1/2-inch optional; 6-inch overall length (22), 6-1/8-inch (32); weighs 10-1/2 oz. (22), 12 oz. (32). Large frame: 32 S&W Long, 38 S&W; 6-shot (32), 5-shot (38); 6-3/4-inch overall length; weighs 17 oz.; small pocket-size hard rubber grips. Marked on frame topstrap: "U.S. REVOLVER Co." Introduced 1911; dropped 1935.

Perf: $105 **Exc:** $70 **VGood:** $55

IVER JOHNSON VIKING MODEL 67

Revolver; double action; 22 LR; 8-shot; 4-1/2-inch, 6-inch barrel; 9-1/2-inch (4-1/4-inch barrel), 11-inch (6-inch barrel) overall length; weighs 31 oz. (4-1/2-inch), 34 oz. (6-inch); chrome-lined barrel; large frame; top-break; recessed cylinder chambers and flash control front rim; one-piece molded oversize target-type Tenite grip; adjustable sights; matte blue finish. Introduced 1964; dropped 1974.

Perf: $125 **Exc:** $100 **VGood:** $75

IVER JOHNSON VIKING SNUB MODEL 67S

Same specs as Model 67 except 22 LR, 32 S&W, 38 S&W; 8-shot (22), 5-shot (32, 38); centerfire calibers not added until 1962; 2-3/4-inch barrel; 7-inch overall length; weighs 25 oz.; two-piece pocket-size plastic grips. Introduced 1964; dropped 1974.

Perf: $135 **Exc:** $110 **VGood:** $85

IVER JOHNSON X300 PONY

Semi-automatic; single action; 380 ACP; 6-shot; 3-inch barrel; 6-1/4-inch overall length; weighs 20 oz.; all steel construction; inertia firing pin; loaded chamber indicator; lanyard ring; no magazine safety; adjustable rear sight; matte blue, bright blue or nickel finish. Three production periods: Middlesex, NJ 1978 to 1982; Jacksonville, AR 1983 to 1988; Jacksonville, AR by AMAC 1989 to 1991.

Perf: $225 **Exc:** $200 **VGood:** $150

Iver Johnson Viking Model 67

Kahr CW380

Kahr CM45

Jericho Model 941

Jennings Model J-25

Iver Johnson X300 Pony

Jennings/Bryco Model M-48

Jennings/Bryco Model J-22

IVER-JOHNSON FRONTIER FOUR DERRINGER

Four-barrel, stainless .22 LR single-action derringer with unique rotating firing pin. Based on old Sharps derringer. 5.5 oz.

New: $165 **Exc:** $125 **VGood:** $85

IVER-JOHNSON 1911 .45

All-steel 7+1 capacity 1911 .45 ACP with 5-inch Government or 4.5-inch Commander barrel. Adjustable white outline rear sight. Adjustable trigger. Polished blue.

New: $625 **Exc:** $565 **VGood:** $485

IVER-JOHNSON 1911 .22 LR

Aluminum slide and frame, 15+1 capacity 1911 .22 LR with 5-inch Government or 4.5-inch Commander barrel. 19 oz. Adjustable white outline rear sight. Adjustable trigger. Blued or stainless.

New: $585 **Exc:** $545 **VGood:** $475

JANA BISON

Revolver; single action; 22 LR, 22 WMR; 4-3/4-inch barrel; fixed front sight, adjustable rear: imitation stag grips; blued finish. Introduced 1978; imported from West Germany; dropped 1980.

Exc: $100 **VGood:** $85 **Good:** $60

JANZ JTL-S

Revolver; double action; 22 LR; 38 Spl./357 Mag.; 44 Mag.; 45 Win. Mag.; 454 Casull/45 LC; 6 or 7 shot; .500 S&W added 2006. unique interchangeable barrel and cylinder system allows calibers to be rapidly changed; 4 - 10-inch barrel with full lug; ergonomic stippled wood grips; target sights. Introduced in 2003. Made in Germany; limited importation.
Prices start at about $10,000 Euros.
Add $500 for 44 Magnum chambering
Add $800 for 45 Win. Mag., 45 LC or 454 Casull chambering

JENNINGS/BRYCO MODEL J-22

Semi-automatic; 22 LR; 6-shot magazine; 2-1/2-inch barrel; weighs 12 oz.; 4-15/16-inch overall length; fixed sights; walnut stocks. Introduced 1981; dropped 2004.

Perf: $125 **Exc:** $100 **VGood:** $85

JENNINGS/BRYCO MODEL J-25

Semi-automatic; 25 ACP; 6-shot magazine; 2-1/2-inch barrel; weighs 12 oz.; 4-15/16-inch overall length; fixed sights; synthetic walnut or black combat-style grips. Introduced 1981; dropped 2004.

Perf: $110 **Exc:** $90 **VGood:** $75

JENNINGS/BRYCO MODEL M-38

Semi-automatic; 22 LR, 32 ACP, 380 ACP; 2-13/16-inch barrel; weighs 16 oz.; non-ferrous alloy construction; black grips; chrome or blue finish. Production ceased in 2004 but reportedly resumed in late 2004 under the name "Jimenez Arms," a new corporate entity.

Perf: $125 **Exc:** $100 **VGood:** $80

JENNINGS MODEL M-48

Semi-automatic; 22 LR, 32 ACP, 380 ACP; 4-inch barrel; weighs 24 oz.; non-ferrous alloy construction; black grips; chrome or blue finish. dropped 1995.

Perf: $125 **Exc:** $100 **VGood:** $80

JERICHO MODEL 941

Semi-automatic; double action; 9mm Para.; 16-shot magazine; 4-3/8-inch barrel; 8-1/8-inch overall length; weighs 33 oz.; high impact black polymer grips; blade front sight, windage-adjustable rear; three tritium dots; all steel construction; polygonal rifling; ambidextrous safety. Produced in Israel by Israel Military Industries; distributed by K.B.I., Inc. Introduced 1990; dropped 1991.

Perf: $550 **Exc:** $475 **VGood:** $425

JSL SPITFIRE

Semi-automatic; double action; 9mm Para.; 15-shot magazine; 4-3/8-inch barrel; 8-7/8-inch overall length; weighs 40 oz.; textured composition grips; blade front sight, fully-adjustable rear; stainless steel construction; ambidextrous safety. Imported from England by Rogers Ltd. International. Introduced 1992; importation dropped 1993.

Perf: $1335 **Exc:** $1100 **VGood:** $925

Add $80 to above prices for adjustable rear sight

KAHR CM SERIES

Caliber: 9mm. DAO operation with stainless steel slide and polymer frame. Three-inch barrel, weight of 15.9 oz. with magazine and overall length of 5.42 inches. Mag capacity is 6+1. Textured polymer grips molded into frame.

Perf: $510 **Exc:** $435 **VGood:** $400

KAHR CM45

Double-action striker fired compact pistol with a black polymer frame and matte stainless steel slide and fixed three dot sights. Chambered in .45 ACP. 3.24 inch barrel, 5.79 inch OA length and weighs 17.3 ounces. 5+1 capacity. Introduced 2013.

Perf: $400 **Exc:** $385 **VGood:** $345

KAHR ARMS CW40

Semi-auto with textured polymer grip chambered for .40 S&W and 6+1 capacity. Double-action with 3.6-inch barrel, 16.8 oz. Adjustable rear sights.

New: $550 **Exc:** $475 **VGood:** $375

KAHR CW380

Double-action micro-compact striker fired pistol with a black polymer frame and matte stainless steel slide and fixed three dot sights. Chambered in .380 ACP. 2.58 inch barrel, 4.96 inch OA length and weighs 10.2 ounces. 6+1 capacity. Introduced 2013.

Perf: $400 **Exc:** $365 **VGood:** $325

KAHR E9

Semi-automatic; double action; 9mm Para.; economized version of the K9; matte black or duotone finish; supplied with one magazine. Produced during 1997 and 2003 only.

Perf: $450 **Exc:** $400 **VGood:** $350

KAHR K9, K40

Semi-automatic; double action; 9mm Para.; 7-shot magazine; 40 S&W; 6-shot magazine; 3-1/2-inch barrel; 6-inch overall length; weighs 25 oz.; wrap-around textured soft polymer grips; blade front sight,

Kahr K9

Kahr MK9 Micro Compact Pistol

Kareen MKII Auto Pistol

Kahr K40

Kahr TP40

KBI PSP-25

KAHR P380

windage drift-adustable rear; bar-dot combat style; passive firing pin block; made of 4140 ordnance steel; matte black finish. Made in U.S. by Kahr Arms. Many sight, finish options. Introduced 1994; dropped 2003.

New: $550 **Perf:** $475 **Exc:** $395

KAHR KS40 SMALL FRAME PISTOL

Same as standard K40 except 1/2-inch shorter grip. Comes with one 5-shot, one 6-shot magazine. Introduced 1998. Made in U.S. by Kahr Arms.

New: $550 **Perf:** $475 **Exc:** $400

With night sights $677.00

New: $600 **Perf:** $525 **Exc:** $450

KAHR MK9 MICRO-COMPACT PISTOL

Similar to the K9 except is 5.5-inch overall, 4-inch high, has a 3-inch barrel. Weighs 22 oz. Has snag-free bar-dot sights, polished feed ramp, dual recoil spring system, DA-only trigger. Comes with 6- and 7-shot magazines. Introduced 1998.

Matte stainless

New: $595 **Perf:** $495 **Exc:** $425

Matte stainless, tritium night sights

New: $650 **Perf:** $575 **Exc:** $500

Duo-Tone (stainless frame, Black-T slide) $749.00

New: $700 **Perf:** $600 **Exc:** $500

Duo-Tone with tritium night sights $$836.00

New: $775 **Perf:** $675 **Exc:** $600

KAHR MODEL 1911 STANDARD

This model features a blued finish, plastic grips with Thompson medallion and bullet logo on the slide. Seven-round magazine. Introduced in 2001.

New: $500 **Exc:** $400 **VGood:** $275

KAHR MODEL 1911C

Similar to the Standard Model but with a 4.25" barrel.

New: $500 **Exc:** $400 **VGood:** $275

KAHR MODEL 1911WGS DELUXE

This model has a blued finish, rubber wrap-around grips with Thompson medallion, high profile white dot sights, and Thompson bullet logo on the slide. Seven-round magazine. Introduced in 2001.

New: $600 **Exc:** $500 **VGood:** $275400

KAHR P45

.45 automatic. DAO operation. Stainless slide. Polymer frame. 3.6 inch barrel. 6 rd magazine. Weighs 19oz. Introduced in 2005.

Perf: $650 **Exc:** $550 **VGood:** $450

KAHR P380

.380 automatic. DAO operation. Black polymer frame. Brushed stainless or blackened slide. 2.5 inch barrel. 6rd magazine. Weighs 10oz. New 2010.

Perf: $500 **Exc:** $450 **VGood:** $400

KAHR PM 45

As above with a 3.1 inch barrel and 5rd magazine. Introduced 2007.

Perf: $650 **Exc:** $550 **VGood:** $450

KAHR ARMS TP40

Double-action-only semi-auto pistol chambered in .40 S&W. Black polymer frame, matte stainless slide, 4" barrel, textured polymer grips, 6- or 7-round capacity depending on magazine. Drift-adjustable white bar-dot sights or Novak two-dot tritium sights.

New: $650 **Exc:** $550 **VGood:** $425

KAREEN MKII AUTO PISTOL

Semi-automatic; single action; 9mm Para.; 13 (now 10)-shot magazine; 4-3/4-inch barrel; 8-inch overall length; weighs 32 oz.; blade front sight, windage-adjustable rear; checkered European walnut grips (early model), rubberized grips (later versions); blued finish, two-tone or matte black finish, optional. Made in Israel. Introduced 1969 by Century International Arms, Inc.; later imported by J.O. Arms until 1997.

Perf: $350 **Exc:** $275 **VGood:** $225

KAREEN MKII COMPACT

Same specs as MKII except 3-1/4-inch barrel; 6-1/2-inch overall length; weighs 28 oz.; rubber grips. Introduced 1995; still in production.

New: $350 **Exc:** $300 **VGood:** $275

KASSNAR M-100D

Revolver; double action; 22 LR, 22 WMR, 38 Spl.; 6-shot cylinder; 3-inch, 4-inch, 6-inch barrels; target-style checkered hardwood stocks; elevation-adjustable rear sight, ramp front; vent-rib barrel. Manufactured in the Philippines by Squires Bingham; imported by Kassnar. Introduced 1977; no longer imported.

Exc: $125 **VGood:** $110 **Good:** $100

KASSNAR MODEL M-100TC

Revolver; double action; 22 LR, 22 WMR, 38 Spl.; 6-shot cylinder; 3-inch, 4-inch, 6-inch barrels; full ejector rod shroud; target-style checkered hardwood stocks; elevation-adjustable rear sight, ramp front; vent-rib barrel. Manufactured in the Philippines by Squires Bingham; imported by Kassnar. Introduced 1977; no longer imported.

Exc: $135 **VGood:** $125 **Good:** $110

KASSNAR PJK-9HP

Semi-automatic; single action; 9mm Para.; 13-shot magazine; 4-3/4-inch barrel; 8-inch overall length; weighs 32 oz.; adjustable rear sight, ramp front; checkered European walnut stocks; with or without full-length vent rib. Made in Hungary. Introduced 1986; no longer imported.

Perf: $300 **Exc:** $250 **VGood:** $200

KBI PSP-25

Semi-automatic; single action; 25 ACP; 6-shot magazine; 2-1/8-inch barrel; 4-1/8-inch overall length; weighs 9-1/2 oz.; fixed sights; checkered black plastic grips; all-steel construction; polished blue or chrome finish. Close copy of Browning Baby 25 made under F.N. license. Introduced 1990; no longer in production.

Perf: $195 **Exc:** $175 **VGood:** $145

KEL-TEC P-11

Semi-automatic; double-action-only; 9mm Para.; 10-shot magazine; 3-1/8-inch barrel; 5-9/16-inch overall length; weighs 14 oz.; checkered black polymer grips; blade front sight, windage-adjustable rear; ordnance steel slide, aluminum frame; blue finish. Made in U.S. by Kel-Tec CNC Industries, Inc. Introduced 1995.

New: $300 **Perf:** $275 **Exc:** $250

Electroless nickel finish

New: $350 **Perf:** $300 **Exc:** $235

Gray finish

New: $280 **Perf:** $250 **Exc:** $200

KEL-TEC P-32

Semi-automatic; 32 ACP; double action only with internal hammer block safety; composite frame with steel slide; 2.68-inch barrel; blue, parkerized or hard

Kassnar M-100D

Kel-Tec P-32

Kel-Tec PLR-22

Kel-Tec P-3AT

Kassnar PJK-9HP

Kimber Classic 45 Custom

Kel-Tec P-11

Kel-Tec PMR-30

chrome finish; light blue, dark blue, grey, green or ivory finished grips; 6.6 oz.

Perf: $300 **Exc:** $250 **VGood:** $200

KEL-TEC P-3AT

Similar to the P-32. except 380 ACP; 2.76-inch barrel; 6-shot magazine; black composite frame; parkerized steel slide; 7.3 oz. Introduced 2003.

Perf: $325 **Exc:** $300 **VGood:** $250

Add $40 to above prices for parkerized finish
Add $55 for hard chrome finish

KEL-TEC P-40

Semi-automatic, 40 S&W; double action only with internal hammer block safety; composite frame; steel slide; 3.3-inch barrel; parkerized, blue, or hard chrome finish; 9 or 10-shot magazine; 15.8 oz. Introduced 1999; dropped 2001.

Perf: $275 **Exc:** $225 **VGood:** $190

KEL-TEC PF-9

9mm DAO pistol. Black polymer frame. Blued, parkerized or hard chrome slide. 3.1 inch barrel. 7 rd magazine. Weighs 13 oz. New in 2008.

Perf: $325 **Exc:** $300 **VGood:** $250

KEL-TEC PLR-16

A 5.56 mm NATO gas-operated, semi-automatic AR-15-style long-range pistol. Windage-adjustable rear sight. Picatinny rail. Muzzle threaded for muzzle-brake. 9.2-inch barrel, 51 oz. 10-round or M-16 magazine. Blued finish, polymer construction.

New: $675 **Exc:** $600 **VGood:** $550

KEL-TEC PLR-22

A 22LR semi automatic pistol. Polymer construction. Accessory rail on receiver top. 9.2 inch barrel. 26rd magazine. Weighs 2.8 lbs. New in 2008.

Perf: $400 **Exc:** $375 **VGood:** $325

KEL-TEC PMR-30

Caliber: 22 Magnum (WMR). Full-size pistol with 4.3-inch barrel, 7.9-inch overall length and weight of 13.6 oz. Double-stack magazine's capacity is 30 rounds. Operates on a hybrid blowback/locked breech system. Dovetail aluminum sights with front and rear fiber optics, Picatinny accessory rail.

Perf: $375 **Exc:** $325 **VGood:** $275

KIMBER CLASSIC 45 CUSTOM

Semi-automatic; single action; 45 ACP; 8-shot magazine; 5-inch barrel; 8-1/2-inch overall length; weighs 38 oz.; checkered hard synthetic grips; McCormick dovetailed front sight, low combat rear; Chip McCormick Corp. forged frame and slide; match barrel; extended combat thumb safety; high beavertail grip safety; skeletonized lightweight composite trigger; skeletonized Commander-type hammer; elongated Commander ejector; bead-blasted black oxide finish; flat mainspring housing; short guide rod; lowered and flared ejection port; serrated front and rear of slide; relief cut under trigger guard; Wolff spring set; beveled magazine well. Made in U.S. by Kimber of America, Inc. Introduced 1995.

New: $620 **Perf:** $550 **Exc:** $475

Custom stainless

New: $700 **Perf:** $650 **Exc:** $500

KIMBER CLASSIC 45 GOLD MATCH

Same specs as Custom except long guide rod; polished blue finish; Bo-Mar BMCS low-mount adjustable rear sight; fancy walnut grips; tighter tolerances; comes with one 10-shot and one 8-shot magazine, factory proof target. Made in U.S. by Kimber of America, Inc. Introduced 1995.

New: $1000 **Perf:** $850 **Exc:** $750

KIMBER CLASSIC 45 POLYMER FRAME

Similar to the Classic 45 Custom except has black polymer frame with stainless steel insert, hooked trigger guard, checkered front strap. Weighs 34.4 oz., overall length 8.75-inch. Introduced 1997.

New: $750 **Perf:** $675 **Exc:** $600

Polymer Stainless

New: $850 **Perf:** $675 **Exc:** $650

Polymer Target

New: $850 **Perf:** $675 **Exc:** $650

Polymer Stainless Target

New: $900 **Perf:** $800 **Exc:** $700

KIMBER CLASSIC 45 ROYAL

Same specs as the Custom model except has checkered diamond-pattern walnut grips; long guide rod; polished blue finish; comes with two 8-shot magazines. Made in U.S. by Kimber of America, Inc. Introduced 1995; still produced.

New: $750 **Perf:** $670 **Exc:** $575

KIMBER COMPACT 45 AUTO PISTOL

Similar to the Classic Custom except has 4-inch barrel fitted directly to the slide with no bushing; full-length guide rod; 7-shot magazine; grip is .400-inch shorter than full-size guns. Weighs 34 oz.; Compact Aluminum weighs 28 oz. Introduced 1998.

New: $635 **Perf:** $530 **Exc:** $435

Compact Stainless

New: $740 **Perf:** $650 **Exc:** $525

Compact Aluminum

New: $700 **Perf:** $550 **Exc:** $450

KIMBER CUSTOM TARGET AUTO PISTOL

Caliber: 45 ACP, 7-shot magazine. Barrel: 5 inches. Weight: 38 oz. Length: 8.7 inches. overall. Stocks: Black synthetic. Sights: Blade front, Kimber fully adjustable rear; dovetailed. Features: Match trigger; beveled front and rear slide serrations; lowered, flared ejection port; full-length guide rod; Wolff springs. Introduced 1996.

Custom Target

New: $675 **Perf:** $625 **Exc:** $530

Stainless Target

New: $800 **Perf:** $700 **Exc:** $625

KIMBER GOLD MATCH TARGET PISTOL

Similar to the Custom Target except has highly polished blue finish; hand-fitted stainless steel barrel, bushing, slide and frame; ambidextrous thumb safety; hand-checkered rosewood grips with double diamond pattern; and skeletonized aluminum match-grade trigger. Has 8-shot magazine. Introduced 1998.

Gold Match

New: $1050 **Perf:** $850 **Exc:** $725

Stainless Target

New: $1150 **Perf:** $985 **Exc:** $800

KIMBER KPD 40

Kimber Pro Defense double-action .40 S&W semi-auto. Comes with two 12-round magazines for 12+1 capacity. 4.1-inch barrel, 25 oz. Fixed white dot sights.

New: $545 **Exc:** $500 **VGood:** $475

KIMBER SUPER AMERICA

Billed as Kimber's ultimate top-of-the-line custom 1911. Polished/matte blue finish, scroll engraving, mammoth ivory grips, presentation case with matching sheath knife.

Kimber Master Carry Custom

Kimber Micro CDP

Kimber Warrior SOC

Kimber Pro Covert II

Kimber Solo Carry DC

Korth Semi-Automatic

New: $2300 **Exc:** $2000 **VGood:** $1750

KIMBER CUSTOM COVERT II

1911-style semiauto carry gun chambered in .45 ACP. Aluminum frame, steel slide. Frame finished in Desert Tan; slide finished in matte black. Five-inch barrel with 3-dot sights.

New: $1100 **Exc:** $975 **VGood:** $825

KIMBER PRO COVERT II

Similar to Custom Covert II but with four-inch barrel.

New: $1100 **Exc:** $975 **VGood:** $825

KIMBER ULTRA COVERT II

Similar to Pro Covert II but with three-inch barrel. Introduced 2007.

New: $1150 **Exc:** $1000 **VGood:** $850

KIMBER PRO AEGIS II

1911-style semiauto carry gun chambered in 9mm Parabellum. Aluminum frame, steel slide. Frame finished in matte aluminum; slide finished in matte black. Four-inch bull barrel with 3-dot sights.

New: $975 **Exc:** $900 **VGood:** $800

KIMBER CUSTOM AEGIS II

Full-size 1911-style semiauto carry gun chambered in 9mm Parabellum. Aluminum frame, steel slide. Frame finished in matte aluminum; slide finished in matte black. Five-inch bull barrel with 3-dot sights.

New: $995 **Exc:** $900 **VGood:** $800

KIMBER ULTRA AEGIS II

Similar to Pro Aegis II but with four-inch barrel. Introduced in 2007.

New: $975 **Exc:** $900 **VGood:** $800

KIMBER MASTER CARRY CUSTOM

Semi-automatic, 1911 style, single-action in .45 ACP. Five-inch barrel (Custom), four-inch barrel (Pro), three-inch barrel (Pro).Five-inch version has a stainless steel frame, four and three-inch barrel versions have an aluminum frame. All have stainless steel slides and barrels and a KimPro II external finish. Crimson Trace G-10 Master Series laser grips and three-dot Tactical Wedge night sights.

Perf: $1400 **Exc:** $1275 **VGood:** 1125

KIMBER MICRO CDP .380 ACP

Semi-automatic, single-action in .380 ACP. Stainless steel slide with aluminum frame. Ambidextrous thumb safety with slide lock and magazine release on left side. Lowered and flared ejection port and beveled magazine well. Steel, low-profile three-dot sights. 6+1 capacity. CDP version has Crimson Trace laser grips. Add $200 for CDP version

Perf: $600 **Exc:** $500 **VGood:** 450

KIMBER PREDATOR HUNTER

Single-shot; 221 Fireball, 223 Rem., 6mm TCU, 6x45, 7mm TCU; 15-3/4-inch barrel; weighs 88 oz.; no sights; accepts Kimber scope mount system; AA Claro walnut stock; uses Kimber Model 84 mini-Mauser action. Introduced 1987; dropped 1989.

Perf: $1500 **VGood:** $1250 **Good:** $950

KIMBER PREDATOR SUPERGRADE

Same specs as Predator Hunter except French walnut stock; ebony forend tip; 22-line hand checkering. Introduced 1987; dropped 1989.

Perf: $2200 **VGood:** $1800 **Good:** $1300

KIMBER SOLO CARRY

Caliber: 9mm. Barrel length is 2.7 inches. Weight, 17 oz., overall length is 5.5 inches. Capacity 6+1. Black synthetic, checkered or smooth grips. Fixed low-profile dovetail-mounted sights with 3-dot system. Single action striker-fired operating system with 1911-style ambidextrous thumb safety, slide release lever and magazine release button.

Perf: $675 **Exc:** $585 **VGood:** $500

KIMBER SOLO CARRY DC

Semi-automatic, striker fired 9mm. Barrel length is 2.7 inches. Weight, 17 oz., overall length 5.5 inches. Capacity 6+1. Black synthetic checkered grips or Crimson Trace Grips on the DC version. Fixed, low profile night sights. Ambidextrous thumb safety. Left side slide lock and magazine release. Add $200 for DC version

Perf: $825 **Exc:** $750 **VGood:** $680

KIMBER SUPER CARRY HD SERIES

Series of .45 ACP 1911 pattern pistols designated as HD (Heavy Duty) and with differing barrel lengths. Super Carry Ultra HD has 3-inch barrel, Carry Pro has 4-inch and Carry Custom has 5-inch barrel. All have a stainless steel slide and rounded-heel frame, premium KimPro II finish, night sights, directional slide serrations.

Perf: $1465 **Exc:** $1275 **VGood:** $1100

KIMBER ROYAL II

Caliber: 45 ACP. Standard 1911 dimensions. Solid bone-smooth grips, fixed low profile sights, charcoal blue finish, aluminum match grade trigger with factory setting of 4 to 5 pounds.

Perf: $1750 **Exc:** $1475 **VGood:** $1275

KIMBER WARRIOR SOC

1911 style semi-automatic in .45 ACP. Stainless steel frame, slide, five-inch barrel and barrel bushing. Tactical Wedge night sights, removeable Crimson Trace Rail Master laser sight. Pistol is finished in a tan/green KimPro II finish. Also fitted with ambidextrious thumb safety and a bumped and grooved grip safety.

Perf: $1500 **Exc:** $1200 **VGood:** $1050

KIMEL AP9

Semi-automatic; single action; 9mm Para.; 20-shot magazine; 5-inch barrel; 11-7/8-inch overall length; weighs 3-1/2 lbs.; checkered plastic grip; adjustable post front sight in ring, fixed open rear; matte blue/black or nickel finish; fires from closed bolt. Made in U.S. Was available from Kimel Industries. Introduced 1988; dropped 1994.

Perf: $425 **Exc:** $365 **VGood:** $325

KIMEL AP9 MINI

Same specs as the AP9 except 3-inch barrel. Made in U.S. Was available from Kimel Industries. Introduced 1988; dropped 1994.

Perf: $475 **Exc:** $425 **VGood:** $350

KIMEL AP9 TARGET

Same specs as the AP9 except 12-inch barrel; grooved forend. Made in U.S. Was available from Kimel Industries. Introduced 1988; dropped 1994.

Perf: $495 **Exc:** $462 **VGood:** $375

KLEINGUENTHER R-15

Revolver; double action; 22 LR, 22 WMR, 32 S&W; 6-shot cylinder; 6-inch barrel; 11-inch overall length; checkered thumbrest walnut stocks; adjustable

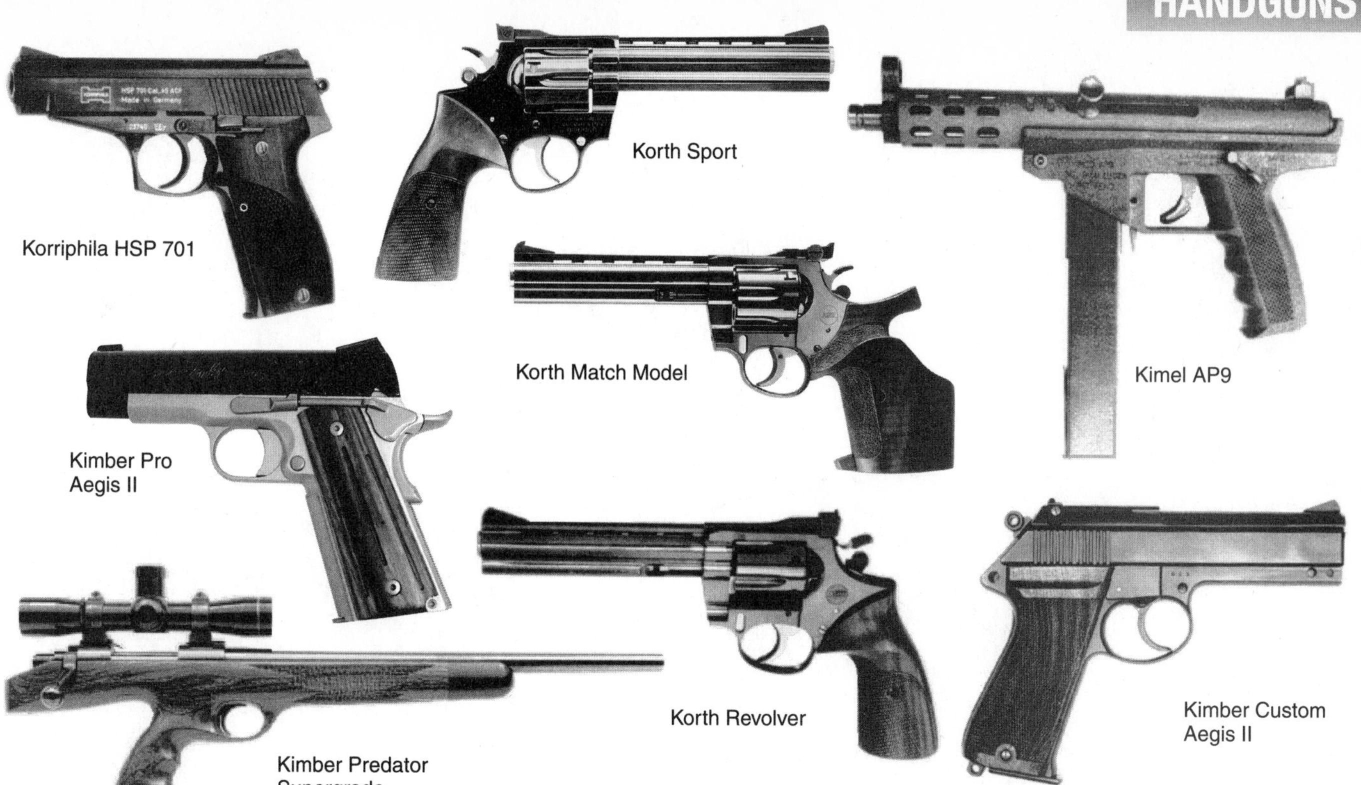
Korriphila HSP 701
Korth Sport
Kimel AP9
Korth Match Model
Kimber Pro Aegis II
Korth Revolver
Kimber Custom Aegis II
Kimber Predator Supergrade

rear sight, fixed front; full-length solid barrel rib; adjustable trigger; blued finish. Manufactured in Germany. Introduced 1976; dropped 1978.

Exc: $200 **VGood:** $175 **Good:** $150

KORRIPHILA HSP 701

Semi-automatic; double action; 9mm Para., 38 Wadcutter, 38 Super, 45 ACP; 9-shot magazine (9mm), 7-shot (45 ACP); 4-inch, 5-inch barrel; weighs 35 oz.; adjustable rear sight, ramp or target front; checkered walnut stocks; delayed roller lock action; limited production. Made in West Germany. Introduced 1986; importation dropped 1989. Importation resumed for a brief period but not currently imported.

Perf: $6500 **Exc:** $5500 **VGood:** $3700

KORRIPHILA HSP 701 ODIN'S EYE (DAMASCUS)

Similar to HSP 701, except is made entirely from one block of Damascus stainless steel; rosewood grips with Manta skin inlays. Built on custom order basis only. Not currently imported into U.S.

Perf: $12,500 **Exc:** $10,5000 **VGood:** $8500

KORTH COMBAT MODEL REVOLVER

Double action. Caliber: 357 Magnum. Barrel: 3", 4", 5-14", 6". Stocks: Checkered walnut, round butt. Sights: Baughman ramp front, fully adjustable rear. Features: Forged steel construction; trigger adjustable for slack, pull, and overtravel; hammer-forged barrel; removable cylinder. Imported from Germany by Korth U.S.A.

High polish blued finish

New: $4700 **Perf:** $4200 **Exc:** $3700

Plasma-coated matte silver finish

New: $5000 **Perf:** $4700 **Exc:** $4200

Plasma-coated high polish silver finish

New: $5700 **Perf:** $5200 **Exc:** $4400

KORTH SPORT MODEL REVOLVER

Similar to Combat model but has square-butt stocks, fully adjustable target rear sight and undercut Patridge front. Imported from Germany by Korth U.S.A.

High polish blued finish

New: $5700 **Perf:** $5500 **Exc:** $4500

Plasma-coated matte silver finish

New: $6200 **Perf:** $5700 **Exc:** $5200

Plasma-coated high polish silver finish

New: $6700 **Perf:** $6200 **Exc:** $5700

KORTH MATCH MODEL REVOLVER

Double action. Caliber: 22 LR, 32 S&W Long.. Barrel: 5-14", 6". Stocks: Adjustable stippled target match type. Sights: undercut Patridge front, fully adjustable rear with interchangeable blades. Features: Forged steel construction; trigger adjustable for slack, pull, and overtravel; hammer-forged barrel; removable cylinder. Imported from Germany by Korth U.S.A.

High polish blued finish

New: $5700 **Perf:** $5200 **Exc:** $4700

Plasma-coated matte silver finish

New: $6200 **Perf:** $6000 **Exc:** $5700

Plasma-coated high polish silver finish

New: $6700 **Perf:** $6200 **Exc:** $5700

KORTH REVOLVER

Double action. Caliber: 22 LR, 22 Mag., 32 H&R Mag., 32 S&W Long, 9mm Para., 357 Magnum. Barrel: 3", 4", 6". Stocks: Checkered walnut sport or combat grips. Sights: Blade front, fully adjustable rear. Four interchangeable cylinders available; comes with two per caliber. High polish blue; presentation models have gold trim. Formerly imported from Germany by Mandall Shooting Supplies. No longer produced.

Perf: $2700 **Exc:** $2200 **VGood:** $1900

KORTH SEMI-AUTOMATIC (OLD MODEL)

Semi-automatic; double action; 9mm Para., 9x21mm; 10-shot capacity. Barrel: 4", 5", 6". Weight: 35 oz. Features: Forged steel frame and slide, adjustable combat sights, checkered walnut grips, matte or polished blue finish. Introduced 1985, discontinued 1989. Seldom encountered.

Perf: $3000 **Perf:** $2700 **Exc:** $2200

KORTH SEMI-AUTOMATIC (NEW MODEL)

Semi-automatic; double action; 9mm Para., 40 S&W. Barrel: 4", 5". Grips: Checkered walnut. Sights: Ramp front, fully adjustable rear. Features: Forged steel construction, locked breech, recoil operated. Imported from Germany by Korth USA.

New: $6300 **Perf:** $6000 **Exc:** $5500

Plasma-coated matte silver finish

New: $7200 **Perf:** $6500 **Exc:** $6000

Plasma-coated high polish silver finish

New: $7700 **Perf:** $7200 **Exc:** $6700

LAHTI FINNISH MODEL L-35

Semi-automatic; 9mm Para.; 8-shot magazine; 4-3/4-inch barrel; fixed sights; checkered plastic stocks; blued finish. Manufactured on a limited basis in Finland from 1935 to 1954.

1st Variation serial number range 1001-3700

Perf: $2500 **Exc:** $2250 **VGood:** $1650

2nd Variation serial number range 3701-4700

Perf: $2500 **Exc:** $2250 **VGood:** $2000

3rd Variation serial number range 4701-6800

Perf: $1350 **Exc:** $1100 **VGood:** $850

4th Variation serial number range 6801-9100

Perf: $1100 **Exc:** $900 **VGood:** $850

Add $3000-$3500 to above prices for original shoulder stock

Add $1800-$2250 for more recent manufacture shoulder stock

LAHTI SWEDISH MODEL 40

Semi-automatic; 9mm Para.; 8-shot magazine; 4-3/4-inch barrel; fixed sights; checkered plastic stocks; blued finish. Manufactured in Sweden by Husqvarna. Manufactured 1942 to 1946.

Exc: $550 **VGood:** $400 **Good:** $300

L.A.R. GRIZZLY WIN. MAG. MARK I

Semi-automatic; single action; 30 Mauser, 357 Mag., 357/45 Grizzly Win. Mag., 10mm, 45 ACP, 45 Win. Mag.; 7-shot magazine; 5-1/2-inch, 6-1/2-inch barrel; 10-5/8-inch overall length; weighs 51 oz.; ramped blade front, adjustable rear sight; no-slip rubber combat grips; ambidextrous safeties; conversion units 45 to 357 Mag., 45 ACP, 10mm, 45 Win. Mag. available; phosphated finish. Introduced 1984; dropped 1999.

Perf: $1175 **Exc:** $950 **VGood:** $775

Laseraim Arms Series III

Lignose Model 3A Einhand

L.A.R. Grizzly 50 Mark V

L.A.R. Grizzly Win. Mag. Mark I

Laseraim Arms Series I

L.A.R. GRIZZLY WIN. MAG. MARK I, 8-INCH, 10-INCH

Same specs as Mark I standard except 8-inch, 10-inch barrel; lengthened slide. Introduced 1984; dropped 1999.

Perf: $1200 **Exc:** $1000 **VGood:** $900

10-inch barrel

Perf: $1250 **Exc:** $1100 **VGood:** $950

L.A.R. GRIZZLY WIN. MAG. MARK II

Same specs as the Grizzly Win. Mag. Mark I except fixed sights; standard safeties. Introduced 1986; discontinued 1986.

Perf: $1150 **Exc:** $975 **VGood:** $875

L.A.R. GRIZZLY 44 MAG. MARK IV

Semi-automatic; single action; 44 Mag.; 7-shot magazine; 5-1/2-inch, 6-1/2-inch barrel; 10-5/8-inch overall length; weighs 51 oz.; ramped blade front, adjustable rear sight; no-slip rubber combat grips; beavertail grip safety; matte blue, hard chrome, chrome or nickel finish. Introduced 1991; dropped 1999.

Perf: $1200 **Exc:** $1000 **VGood:** $900

Hand chrome, chrome or nickel finish

Perf: $1350 **Exc:** $1150 **VGood:** $1050

L.A.R. GRIZZLY 50 MARK V

Semi-automatic; single action; 50 AE; 6-shot magazine; 5-1/2-inch, 6-1/2-inch barrel; 10-5/8-inch overall length; weighs 56 oz.; ramped blade front, adjustable rear sight; no-slip rubber combat grips; ambidextrous safeties; conversion units available; phosphated finish. Made in U.S. by L.A.R. Mfg., Inc. Introduced, 1993; dropped 1999.

New: $1400 **Perf:** $1300 **Exc:** $1200

LASERAIM ARMS SERIES I

Semi-automatic; single action; 10mm Auto, 45 ACP; 8-shot magazine (10mm), 7-shot (45 ACP); 4-3/8-inch, 6-inch barrel, with compensator; 9-3/4-inch overall length (6-inch barrel); weighs 46 oz.; pebble-grained black composite grips; blade front sight, fully-adjustable rear; barrel compensator; stainless steel construction; ambidextrous safety-levers; extended slide release; integral mount for laser sight; matte black Teflon finish. Made in U.S. by Emerging Technologies, Inc. Introduced 1993; dropped 1999.

New: $500 **Perf:** $450 **Exc:** $400

With adjustable sight

New: $550 **Perf:** $500 **Exc:** $450

With fixed sight and Auto Illusion red dot sight system

New: $650 **Perf:** $600 **Exc:** $550

With fixed sight and Laseraim Laser with Hotdot

New: $750 **Perf:** $700 **Exc:** $650

LASERAIM ARMS SERIES II

Semi-automatic; single action; 10mm Auto, 45 ACP, 40 S&W; 8-shot magazine (10mm), 7-shot (45 ACP); 3-3/8-inch, 5-inch barrel without compensator; weighs 43 oz. (5-inch), 37 oz. (3-3/8-inch); pebble-grained black composite grips; blade front sight, fixed or windage-adjustable rear; stainless steel construction; ambidextrous safety-levers; extended slide release; integral mount for laser sight; matte stainless finish. Made in U.S. by Emerging Technologies, Inc. Introduced 1993; dropped 1999.

New: $550 **Perf:** $500 **Exc:** $450

With adjustable sight (5-inch barrel)

New: $575 **Perf:** $525 **Exc:** $475

With fixed sight and Auto Illusion red dot sight

New: $600 **Perf:** $525 **Exc:** $500

With fixed sight and Laseraim Laser with Hotdot

New: $650 **Perf:** $575 **Exc:** $550

LASERAIM ARMS SERIES III

Semi-automatic; single action; 10mm Auto, 45 ACP; 8-shot magazine (10mm), 7-shot (45 ACP); 5-inch barrel with dual-port compensator; 7-5/8-inch overall length; weighs 43 oz.; pebble-grained black composite grips; blade front sight, fixed or windage-adjustable rear; stainless steel construction; ambidextrous safety-levers; extended slide release; integral mount for laser sight; matte stainless finish. Made in U.S. by Emerging Technologies, Inc. Introduced 1994; dropped 1999.

With fixed sight

New: $600 **Perf:** $550 **Exc:** $500

With adjustable sight

New: $625 **Perf:** $575 **Exc:** $525

With fixed sight and Dream Team Laseraim laser sight

New: $700 **Perf:** $650 **Exc:** $600

LASERAIM ARMS SERIES IV

Semi-automatic; 45 ACP; 7-shot magazine; 3-3/8-inch, 5-inch barrel; weighs 37 oz.; full serrated slide; diamond wood grips; stainless steel construction; blade front, fully-adjustable rear sight; ambidextrous safety levers; integral mount for laser sight. Made in U.S. by Emerging Technologies, Inc. Introduced 1996; dropped 1999.

New: $675 **Perf:** $625 **Exc:** $575

LE FRANCAIS ARMY MODEL

Semi-automatic; double action; 9mm Browning Long; 8-shot magazine; 5-inch flip up barrel; 7-3/4-inch overall length; fixed sights; checkered European walnut stocks; blued finish. Manufactured 1928 to 1938.

Exc: $1500 **VGood:** $1100 **Good:** $850

Add 10 percent to above prices for finned barrel

Add 50 percent-100 percent for engraved examples, depending on amount of coverage

LE FRANCAIS POCKET MODEL

Semi-automatic; double action; 32 ACP; 7-shot magazine; 3-1/2-inch flip-up barrel; 6-inch overall length; fixed sights; checkered hard rubber stocks; blued finish. Manufactured in France. Introduced 1950; discontinued 1965. Rare in the U.S.

Exc: $750 **VGood:** $600 **Good:** $450

LE FRANCAIS POLICEMAN MODEL

Semi-automatic; double action; 25 ACP; 7-shot magazine; 2-1/2-inch, 3-1/2-inch flip up barrel; fixed sights; hard rubber stocks; blued finish. Some are marked "FRANCO." Introduced 1914; discontinued about 1960.

Exc: $375 **VGood:** $300 **Good:** $260

LES BAER 1911 .38 SUPER STINGER

Single action only, hammer fired steel compact semi-automatic pistol with blue or chrome finish, ambidextrous safety, night sights and cocobolo grips. Chambered in .38 Super.4.25 inch barrel. 8+1 capacity. Introduced 2013.

Perf: $2,350.00 **Exc:** $2,000 **VGood:** $1,850

LES BAER BAER 1911 BOSS .45

Single action only, hammer fired steel full-sized semi-automatic pistol with fiber optic front sight,

Le Francais Pocket Model

Le Francais Army Model

Les Incorporated Rogak P-18

Le Francais Policeman Model

Ljutic LJ II

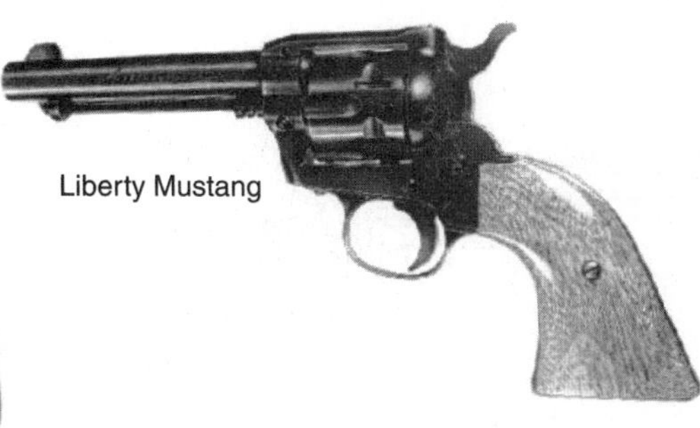
Liberty Mustang

blued slide and chrome frame and extended safety. Chambered in .45 ACP. 5 inch barrel and 8.25 inches OA length, weighs 2.44 pounds. 8+1 capacity. Introduced 2013.

Perf: $2,150.00 **Exc:** $2,000 **VGood:** $1,850

LES BAER 1911 HEMI "572"

Single action only, hammer fired steel full-sized semi-automatic pistol with double serrated slide, fiber optic adjustable sights, chrome finish, ambidextrous safety, and black grips. Chambered in .45 ACP. 5 inch barrel and 8.25 inches OA length, weighs 2.44 pounds. 8+1 capacity. Introduced 2013.

Perf: $2,320.00 **Exc:** $2,000 **VGood:** $1,850

LES BAER 1911 ULTIMATE TACTICAL CARRY 5" MODEL

Single action only, hammer fired steel full-sized semi-automatic pistol with double serrated slide, combat tritium sights, blue finish, extended safety, and slim line grips. Chambered in .45 ACP. 5 inch barrel and 8.25 inches OA length, weighs 2.44 pounds. 8+1 capacity. Introduced 2013.

Perf: $1,800 **Exc:** $1,600 **VGood:** $1,450

LES BAER CUSTOM CENTENNIAL MODEL 1911

Single action only, hammer fired steel full-sized semi-automatic pistol with charcoal blue finish, extended safety, and ivory grips. Chambered in .45 ACP. 5 inch barrel and 8.25 inches OA length, weighs 2.44 pounds. 8+1 capacity. Introduced 2011.

Perf: $3,850 **Exc:** $3,000 **VGood:** $2,850

LES INCORPORATED ROGAK P-18

Semi-automatic; double action; 9mm Para.; 18-shot magazine; 5-1/2-inch barrel; post front sight, V-notch rear, drift adjustable for windage; checkered resin stocks; stainless steel; matte or deluxe high gloss finishes. Introduced 1977; discontinued 1981.

Exc: $525 **VGood:** $400 **Good:** $300

Deluxe high gloss finish

Exc: $550 **VGood:** $425 **Good:** $325

LIBERTY MUSTANG

Revolver; single action; 22 LR, 22 WMR or combo; 8-shot cylinder; 5-inch barrel; 10-1/2-inch overall length; weighs 34 oz.; blade front, adjustable rear sight; smooth rosewood grips; side ejector rod; blued finish. Imported from Italy by Liberty. Introduced 1976; discontinued 1980.

Exc: $150 **VGood:** $135 **Good:** $110

LIGNOSE MODEL 2 POCKET

Semi-automatic; 25 ACP; 6-shot magazine; 2-inch barrel; 4-1/2-inch overall length; checkered hard rubber stocks; blued finish. Manufactured in Germany from 1920 first under Bergmann name, then Lignose to late 1920s.

Exc: $325 **VGood:** $265 **Good:** $215

LIGNOSE MODEL 2A EINHAND

Same specs as Model 2 Pocket except sliding trigger guard allows slide retraction with trigger finger.

Exc: $550 **VGood:** $450 **Good:** $325

LIGNOSE MODEL 3 POCKET

Semi-automatic; 25 ACP; 9-shot magazine; 2-inch barrel; 4-1/2-inch overall length; checkered hard rubber stocks; blued finish. Manufactured in Germany.

Exc: $250 **VGood:** $220 **Good:** $195

LIGNOSE MODEL 3A EINHAND

Same specs as Model 3 Pocket except sliding trigger guard allows slide retraction with trigger finger.

Exc: $495 **VGood:** $425 **Good:** $350

LILIPUT 4.25

Semi-automatic; 4.25mm; 6-shot; 1-13/16-inch barrel; 3-1/2-inch overall length; weighs 8 oz.; blue or nickel finish. Made by August Menz, Suhl, Germany. Introduced 1920.

Exc: $1500 **VGood:** $950 **Good:** $675

LILIPUT 25 ACP

Semi-automatic; 25 ACP; 6-shot; 2-inch barrel; 4-1/8-inch overall length; weighs 10 oz.; blue or nickel finish. Made by August Menz, Suhl Germany. Introduced 1925. Manufactured in large quantities prior to onset of World War Two. Served as the later design basis for the Lorcin line in the U.S.

Exc: $350 **VGood:** $300 **Good:** $250

LJUTIC LJ II

Derringer; double action; 22 WMR; 2-shot; 2-3/4-inch side-by-side barrels; fixed sights; checkered walnut stocks; vent rib; positive safety; stainless steel construction. Introduced 1981; dropped 1989. About 1000 produced.

Perf: $1500 **Exc:** $1200 **VGood:** $1000

LLAMA IIIA SMALL FRAME

Semi-automatic; single action; 380 ACP, 32 ACP (disc. 1993); 7-shot magazine; 3-11/16-inch barrel; 6-1/2-inch overall length; weighs 23 oz.; adjustable target sights; checkered thumbrest plastic grips; vent rib; grip safety; loaded chamber indicator; blued, chrome engraved, blue engraved or gold engraved finishes. Early versions were sans vent rib, had lanyard ring, no thumbrest on grips. Introduced 1951; no longer in production.

Blued finish

Perf: $350 **Exc:** $300 **VGood:** $250

Chrome engraved

Perf: $650 **Exc:** $550 **VGood:** $400

Blue engraved

Perf: $650 **Exc:** $500 **VGood:** $400

Gold engraved

Perf: $750 **Exc:** $600 **VGood:** $500

LLAMA VIII

Semi-automatic; 38 Super; 9-shot magazine; 5-inch barrel; 8-1/2-inch overall length; fixed sights; hand-checkered walnut grips; vent rib; grip safety; blued, chrome, chrome engraved or blued engraved finishes. Imported by Stoeger. Introduced 1952; no longer in production.

Perf: $375 **Exc:** $350 **VGood:** $325

Chrome finish

Perf: $395 **Exc:** $370 **VGood:** $270

Chrome engraved

Perf: $600 **Exc:** $500 **VGood:** $400

Blue engraved

Perf: $600 **Exc:** $500 **VGood:** $400

LLAMA IX LARGE FRAME

Semi-automatic; single action; 9mm, 38 Super, 45 ACP; 9-shot magazine (9mm, 38 Super), 7-shot (45 ACP); 5-1/8-inch barrel; 41 oz.; adjustable sights;

Llama XI
Large Frame

Llama IX-C
New Generation
Large Frame

Llama XV
Small Frame

Llama Comanche

Llama Martial

Llama Martial Deluxe

black plastic grips; blued or satin chrome finish. Introduced 1936; no longer imported.

Perf: $325 **Exc:** $275 **VGood:** $225

Satin chrome finish

Perf: $350 **Exc:** $300 **VGood:** $250

LLAMA IX-A LARGE FRAME

Semi-automatic; 45 ACP; 7-shot magazine; 5-1/8-inch barrel; 8-1/2-inch overall length; weighs 36 oz.; hand-checkered walnut grips; vent rib; fixed sights; grip safety; loaded chamber indicator; blue, chrome, chrome engraved or blue engraved finishes. Introduced 1952; no longer imported.

Perf: $375 **Exc:** $325 **VGood:** $275

Chrome finish

Perf: $400 **Exc:** $350 **VGood:** $300

Chrome engraved

Perf: $500 **Exc:** $450 **VGood:** $400

Blue engraved

Perf: $500 **Exc:** $450 **VGood:** $400

LLAMA IX-B COMPACT FRAME

Semi-automatic; single action; 45 ACP; 7-shot magazine; 4-1/4-inch barrel; 7-7/8-inch overall length; weighs 34 oz.; checkered polymer grips; blade front sight, fully-adjustable rear; scaled-down version of Llama Large Frame; locked breech mechanism; manual and grip safeties; blue or chrome finish. Formerly imported from Spain by SGS Importers Int'l., Inc. Introduced 1985.

Perf: $300 **Exc:** $250 **VGood:** $225

Chrome finish

Perf: $325 **Exc:** $275 **VGood:** $250

LLAMA IX-C NEW GENERATION LARGE FRAME

Semi-automatic; single action; 45 ACP; 13-shot magazine; 5-1/8-inch barrel; 8-1/2-inch overall length; 41 oz.; three-dot combat sights; military-style hammer; loaded chamber indicator; anatomically designed rubber grips; non-glare matte finish. Introduced 1994; Converted to 10-shot magazine 1995; no longer imported.

New: $350 **Perf:** $300 **Exc:** $250

LLAMA IX-D NEW GENERATION COMPACT FRAME

Semi-automatic; single action; 45 ACP; 13-shot; 4-1/4-inch barrel; 7-7/8-inch overall length; weighs 39 oz.; three-dot combat sights; rubber grips; non-glare matte finish. Converted to 10-shot 1995; no longer imported.

New: $350 **Perf:** $300 **Exc:** $250

LLAMA XA SMALL FRAME

Semi-automatic; 32 ACP; 7-shot magazine; 3-11/16-inch barrel; 6-1/2-inch overall length; adjustable target sights; checkered thumbrest plastic grips; grip safety; blued, chrome engraved or blue engraved finishes; successor to Llama X, which had no grip safety. Imported by Stoeger. Introduced 1951; no longer in production.

Exc: $400 **VGood:** $300 **Good:** $200

Chrome engraved

Exc: $500 **VGood:** $375 **Good:** $250

Blue engraved

Exc: $500 **VGood:** $375 **Good:** $250

LLAMA XI

Semi-automatic; 9mm Para.; 8-shot magazine; 5-inch barrel; 8-1/2-inch overall length; adjustable sights; checkered thumbrest; plastic grips; vent rib; blued, chrome, chrome engraved or blued engraved finishes. Imported by Stoeger Arms. Introduced 1954; no longer in production.

Perf: $350 **Exc:** $300 **VGood:** $250

Chrome finish

Perf: $375 **Exc:** $325 **VGood:** $275

Chrome engraved

Perf: $500 **Exc:** $400 **VGood:** $300

Blue engraved

Perf: $500 **Exc:** $400 **VGood:** $300

LLAMA XV SMALL FRAME

Semi-automatic; 22 LR; 8-shot magazine; 3-11/16-inch barrel; 6-1/2-inch overall length; weighs 23 oz.; adjustable target sights; checkered thumbrest plastic grips; vent rib; grip safety; blued, chrome engraved or blue engraved finishes. Introduced 1951; no longer in production.

Perf: $300 **Exc:** $250 **VGood:** $200

Chrome engraved

Perf: $375 **Exc:** $325 **VGood:** $275

Blue engraved

Perf: $375 **Exc:** $325 **VGood:** $275

LLAMA COMANCHE

Revolver; double action; 22 LR, 357 Mag.; 6-shot cylinder; 4-inch, 6-inch barrel; 9-1/4-inch overall length (4-inch barrel); weighs 28 oz.; blade front sight, fully-adjustable rear; checkered walnut stocks; ventilated rib; wide spur hammer; blue finish. Was imported from Spain by SGS Importers International, Inc. No longer imported.

Exc: $300 **VGood:** $250 **Good:** $200

LLAMA COMANCHE I

Revolver; double action; 22 LR; 6-shot cylinder; 6-inch barrel; 11-1/4-inch overall length; target-type sights; checkered walnut stocks; blued finish. Introduced in 1977, replacing Martial 22 model; discontinued 1982.

Exc: $300 **VGood:** $250 **Good:** $200

LLAMA COMANCHE II

Same specs as Comanche I except 38 Spl.; 4-inch barrel. Introduced 1977; discontinued 1982.

Exc: $275 **VGood:** $225 **Good:** $200

LLAMA COMANCHE III

Same specs as Comanche I except 22 LR, 357 Mag.; 4-inch, 6-inch, 8-1/2-inch barrel; 9-1/4-inch overall length; ramp front, adjustable rear sight; blued, satin chrome or gold finish. Introduced in 1977 as "Comanche"; renamed 1977; no longer in production.

Perf: $295 **Exc:** $225 **VGood:** $200

Satin chrome finish

Perf: $300 **Exc:** $250 **VGood:** $225

Gold finish

Perf: $750 **Exc:** $650 **VGood:** $500

LLAMA MARTIAL

Revolver; double action; 22 LR, 38 Spl.; 6-shot cylinder; 4-inch barrel (38 Spl.), 6-inch (22 LR); 11-1/4-inch overall length (6-inch barrel); target sights; hand-checkered walnut grips; blued finish. Imported by Stoeger. Introduced 1969; discontinued 1976.

Exc: $250 **VGood:** $205 **Good:** $180

Llama Max-I

Llama Max-I New Generation Large Frame

Llama Micromax 380

Llama Minimax Series

Llama Model 82

Llama Omni

LLAMA MARTIAL DELUXE

Same specs as Martial model except choice of satin chrome, chrome engraved, blued engraved, gold engraved finishes; simulated pearl stocks.

Satin chrome finish
Exc: $275 **VGood:** $250 **Good:** $220

Chrome engraved
Exc: $305 **VGood:** $275 **Good:** $250

Blue engraved
Exc: $290 **VGood:** $265 **Good:** $235

Gold engraved
Exc: $750 **VGood:** $600 **Good:** $500

Gold damascened
Exc: $1430 **VGood:** $880 **Good:** $660

LLAMA MAX-I

Semi-automatic; 45 ACP; 7-shot; 5-1/8-inch barrel; 36 oz.; 8-1/2-inch overall; black rubber grips; blade front, rear sight adjustable for windage, three-dot system; single-action trigger; skeletonized combat-style hammer; steel frame; extended manual and grip safeties. 1995-2006.
Price: 45 ACP, 7-shot, Government model $291.95
Price: As above, satin chrome finish $314.95

LLAMA MAX-I NEW GENERATION LARGE FRAME

Semi-automatic; single action; 9mm Para., 45 ACP; 9-shot magazine (9mm), 7-shot (45 ACP); 5-1/8-inch barrel; 8-1/2-inch overall length; weighs 36 oz.; blade front sight, windage-adjustable rear; black rubber grips; three-dot system; skeletonized combat-style hammer; steel frame; extended manual and grip safeties; blue or duo-tone finish. Formerly imported from Spain by Import Sports, Inc. 1995-2006.

New: $265 **Perf:** $220 **Exc:** $175

Duo-tone finish
New: $325 **Perf:** $300 **Exc:** $250

LLAMA MAX-I NEW GENERATION COMPACT FRAME

Same specs as the Max-I except 7-shot; 4-1/4-inch barrel; 7-7/8-inch overall length; weighs 34 oz. Imported from Spain by Import Sports, Inc. Introduced 1995; no longer imported.

New: $300 **Perf:** $275 **Exc:** $225

Duo-tone finish
New: $350 **Perf:** $325 **Exc:** $300

LLAMA MICROMAX 380

Semi-automatic; 380 ACP; 7-shot magazine; 3-11/16-inch barrel; 23 oz.; 6-1/2-inch overall; checkered grips made of high impact polymer; 3-dot combat sights; single action design; mini custom extended slide release; mini custom extended beavertail grip safety; combat-style hammer. Introduced 1997. Imported from Spain by Import Sports, Inc.

New: $260 **Perf:** $225 **Exc:** $200

Satin chrome
New: $225 **Perf:** $250 **Exc:** $225

LLAMA MINIMAX SERIES

Semi-automatic; 9mm Para., 8-shot; 40 S&W, 7-shot; 45 ACP, 6-shot magazine. Barrel: 3-1/2-inch. Weight: 35 oz. Length: 7-1/3-inch overall. Stocks: Checkered rubber. Sights: Three-dot combat. Features: Single action, skeletonized combat-style hammer, extended slide release, cone-style barrel, flared ejection port. 1996-2006.

New: $300 **Perf:** $255 **Exc:** $205

Duo-tone finish (45 only) or satin chrome
New: $320 **Perf:** $275 **Exc:** $225

LLAMA MINIMAX-II

Same as the Minimax except in 45 ACP only, with 10-shot staggered magazine. 1997-2006.

New: $300 **Perf:** $275 **Exc:** $225

Satin chrome
New: $325 **Perf:** $300 **Exc:** $250

LLAMA MODEL 82

Semi-automatic; double action; 9mm Para.; 15-shot magazine; 4-1/4-inch barrel; 8-inch overall length; weighs 39 oz.; blade-type front sight, drift-adjustable rear; 3-dot system; matte black polymer stocks; ambidextrous safety; blued finish. Made in Spain. Introduced 1987; discontinued 1993.

Perf: $650 **Exc:** $600 **VGood:** $550

LLAMA MODEL 87 COMPETITION MODEL

Semi-automatic; 9mm Para.; 14-shot magazine; 6-inch barrel; 9-1/2-inch overall length; weighs 47 oz.; Patridge-type front sight, fully-adjustable rear; Polymer composition stocks; built-in ported compensator; oversize magazine, safety releases; fixed barrel bushing; extended triggerguard; beveled magazine well. Made in Spain. Introduced 1989; discontinued 1993.

Perf: $995 **Exc:** $850 **VGood:** $750

LLAMA OMNI

Semi-automatic; double action; 9mm Para., 45 ACP; 13-shot magazine (9mm), 7-shot (45 ACP); 4-1/4-inch barrel; 7-3/4-inch overall length (45 ACP), 8-inch (9mm); weighs 40 oz.; adjustable sights; checkered plastic stocks; ball-bearing action; double sear bars; articulated firing pin; low-friction rifling; blued finish. Made in Spain. Introduced 1982; dropped 1986.

9mm version
Exc: $440 **VGood:** $380 **Good:** $330

45 ACP version
Exc: $395 **VGood:** $360 **Good:** $320

LLAMA SUPER COMANCHE IV

Revolver; double action; 44 Mag.; 6-shot cylinder; 6-inch, 8-1/2-inch barrel; adjustable sights; oversize walnut grips; wide hammer, trigger; blued finish. No longer imported.

Perf: $325 **Exc:** $275 **VGood:** $250

LLAMA SUPER COMANCHE V

Same specs as Super Comanche IV except 357 Mag. only; 4-inch barrel also available. Discontinued 1988.

Perf: $300 **Exc:** $250 **VGood:** $200

LORCIN L-9MM

Semi-automatic; single action; 9mm Para.; 10- or 13-shot magazine; 4-1/2-inch barrel; 7-1/2-inch overall length; weighs 31 oz.; grooved black composition grips; fixed sights with three-dot system; matte black finish; hooked triggerguard; grip safety. Made in U.S. by Lorcin Engineering. Introduced 1994; dropped 1999.

New: $125 **Perf:** $110 **Exc:** $90

LORCIN L-22

Semi-automatic; single action; 22 LR; 9-shot magazine; 2-1/2-inch barrel; 5-1/4-inch overall length; weighs 16 oz.; black combat, or pink or pearl grips; fixed three-dot sight system; chrome or black Teflon finish. From Lorcin Engineering. Introduced 1989; dropped 1999

Perf: $75 **Exc:** $60 **VGood:** $50

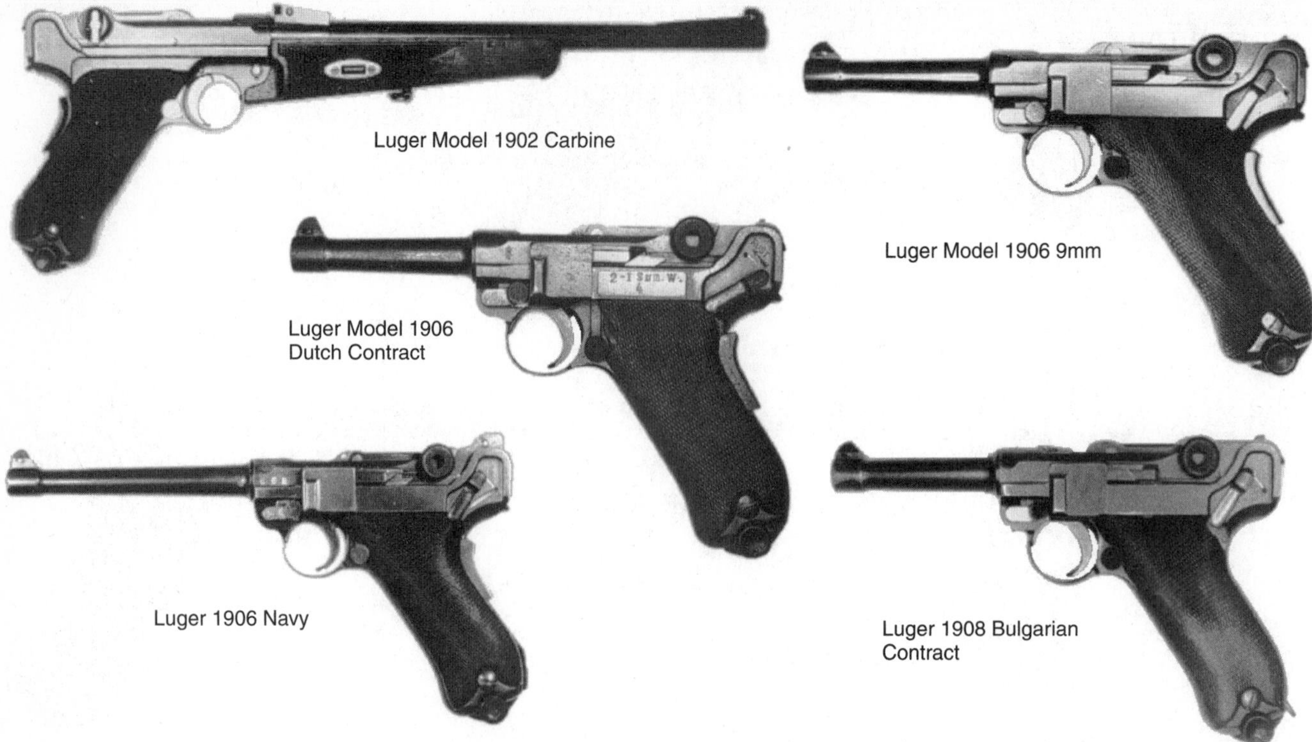
Luger Model 1902 Carbine

Luger Model 1906 9mm

Luger Model 1906 Dutch Contract

Luger 1906 Navy

Luger 1908 Bulgarian Contract

Pink grips
Perf: $80 **Exc:** $65 **VGood:** $55

LORCIN L-25

Semi-automatic; single action; 25 ACP; 7-shot magazine; 2-5/16-inch barrel; 4-5/8-inch overall length; weighs 14-1/2 oz.; fixed sights; smooth composition stocks; black/gold, chrome/satin chrome, black finish. Made in U.S. by Lorcin Engineering. Introduced 1989; dropped 1999.
Perf: $65 **Exc:** $50 **VGood:** $45

LORCIN LADY LORCIN

Same specifications as above except with pink grips. Introduced 1990; dropped 1999.
Perf: $70 **Exc:** $60 **VGood:** $50

LORCIN L-32

Semi-automatic; single action; 32 ACP; 7-shot magazine; 3-1/2-inch barrel; 6-5/8-inch overall length; weighs 23 oz.; fixed sights; grooved composition grips; black Teflon or chrome finish with black grips. Made in U.S. by Lorcin Engineering. Introduced 1992; dropped 1999.
New: $80 **Perf:** $70 **Exc:** $60

LORCIN L-380

Semi-automatic; single action; 380 ACP; 7-shot magazine; 3-1/2-inch barrel; 6 5/8-inch overall length; weighs 23 oz.; fixed sights; grooved composition grips; black Teflon or chrome finish with black grips. Made in U.S. by Lorcin Engineering. Introduced 1992; dropped 1999.
New: $85 **Perf:** $75 **Exc:** $65

LORCIN LH-380

Semi-automatic; 380 ACP; 10-shot magazine; 4-1/2-inch barrel; 7-1/2-inch overall length; weighs 31 oz.; grooved black compostion grips; fixed sights with three-dot system; matte black finish; hooked triggerguard; grip safety. Similar to Model L9MM. Made in U.S. by Lorcin Engineering. Introduced 1994; dropped 1999.
New: $125 **Perf:** $115 **Exc:** $100

LORCIN LT-25

Semi-automatic; single action; 25 ACP; 7-shot magazine; 2-1/3-inch barrel; 4-2/3-inch overall length; weighs 14-1/2 oz.; fixed sights; smooth composition grips; available in chrome, black Teflon or camouflage. Made in U.S. by Lorcin Engineering. Introduced 1989; dropped 1999.
New: $60 **Perf:** $50 **Exc:** $40

LORCIN O/U DERRINGER

Stainless steel construction, .357 Mag. Or .45 LC; 2-shot over/under 3-1/2-inch barrels; synthetic grips; rebounding hammer; fixed sights. Made in U.S. by Lorcin Engineering. Introduced 1996; dropped 1998.
New: $95 **Perf:** $80 **Exc:** $65

LUGER MODEL 1900 COMMERCIAL

Semi-automatic; 7.65mm Para.; 7-shot magazine; 4-3/4-inch barrel; 9-1/4-inch overall length; fixed sights; toggle-joint action; grip safety; checkered wood grips; blued finish. Toggle marked in script "DWM" for Deutsche Waffen und Munitionsfabrik. Distinguished by dished toggle knobs with a lock, recessed breechblock.
Exc: $3500 **VGood:** $2750 **Good:** $2000

LUGER MODEL 1900 SWISS

Same specs as Model 1900 Commercial except Swiss cross on chamber.
Exc: $4000 **VGood:** $3250 **Good:** $2500

LUGER MODEL 1900 EAGLE

Same specs as Model 1900 Commercial except American eagle on chamber.
Exc: $3500 **VGood:** $2750 **Good:** $1500

U.S. Army test guns s/n 6000-7000 distinguished by no proof marks
Exc: $5000 **VGood:** $4250 **Good:** $2750

LUGER MODEL 1902

Semi-automatic; 9mm Para.; 7-shot magazine; 4-inch fat barrel; fixed sights; toggle-joint action; grip safety; checkered walnut grips; blued finish. Made with or without American eagle. Toggle marked in script "DWM" for Deutsche Waffen und Munitionsfabrik. Distinguished by fat 9mm barrel, dished toggle knobs with a lock, recessed breechblock.
Exc: $9500 **VGood:** $7500 **Good:** $5500

LUGER MODEL 1902 CARBINE

Same specs as Model 1902 except 7.65mm Para.; 11-3/4-inch barrel with adjustable rear sight and checkered wood forend; contoured detachable wood stock.
Exc: $14,500 **VGood:** $11,000 **Good:** $7500

Without stock
Exc: $9500 **VGood:** $7000 **Good:** $5000

LUGER MODEL 1906 NAVY

Semi-automatic; 9mm Para.; 6-inch barrel; flat checkered toggle knobs; exposed breechblock with extractor that protrudes when chamber is loaded and exposes German word "GELADEN" (LOADED); adjustable rear sight on rear toggle link; coil instead of leaf recoil spring; grip safety; stock lug on rear of frame. Usually called "Model 1906 Navy" by collectors but was officially designated Model 1904 by the German navy. Note: Original 1904 Navies that have a toggle lock cut into right toggle knob like Model 1900 are very rare and valuable but beware of fakes.
Exc: $3000 **VGood:** $2500 **Good:** $1500

With proper Navy stock
Exc: $4050 **VGood:** $3550 **Good:** $2500

LUGER MODEL 1906

Semi-automatic; 7.65mm Para., 9mm Para.; 4-3/4-inch (7.65), 4-inch (9mm) barrel; flat checkered toggle knobs; exposed breechblock with extractor that protrudes when chamber is loaded and exposes German word "GELADEN" (LOADED); fixed rear sight on rear toggle link; coil instead of leaf recoil spring; no stock lug on rear frame. Note: 1906 Russian (crossed rifles on chamber) and Bulgarian (Bulgarian crest on chamber) very rare, very valuable.

With or without American Eagle, 7.65mm
Exc: $2500 **VGood:** $2000 **Good:** $1090

With or without American Eagle, 9mm
Exc: $2750 **VGood:** $2000 **Good:** $1250

With Swiss cross, 7.65mm only
Exc: $3000 **VGood:** $2500 **Good:** $1500

Portuguese contract with M2 on chamber, 7.65mm only
Exc: $2200 **VGood:** $1650 **Good:** $1050

Brazilian contract with no chamber marking, extractor marked "CARREGADA," 7.65mm only
Exc: $2500 **VGood:** $1800 **Good:** $1000

Dutch contract with safety marked "RUST" with arrow, 9mm only.
Exc: $2000 **VGood:** $1400 **Good:** $1200

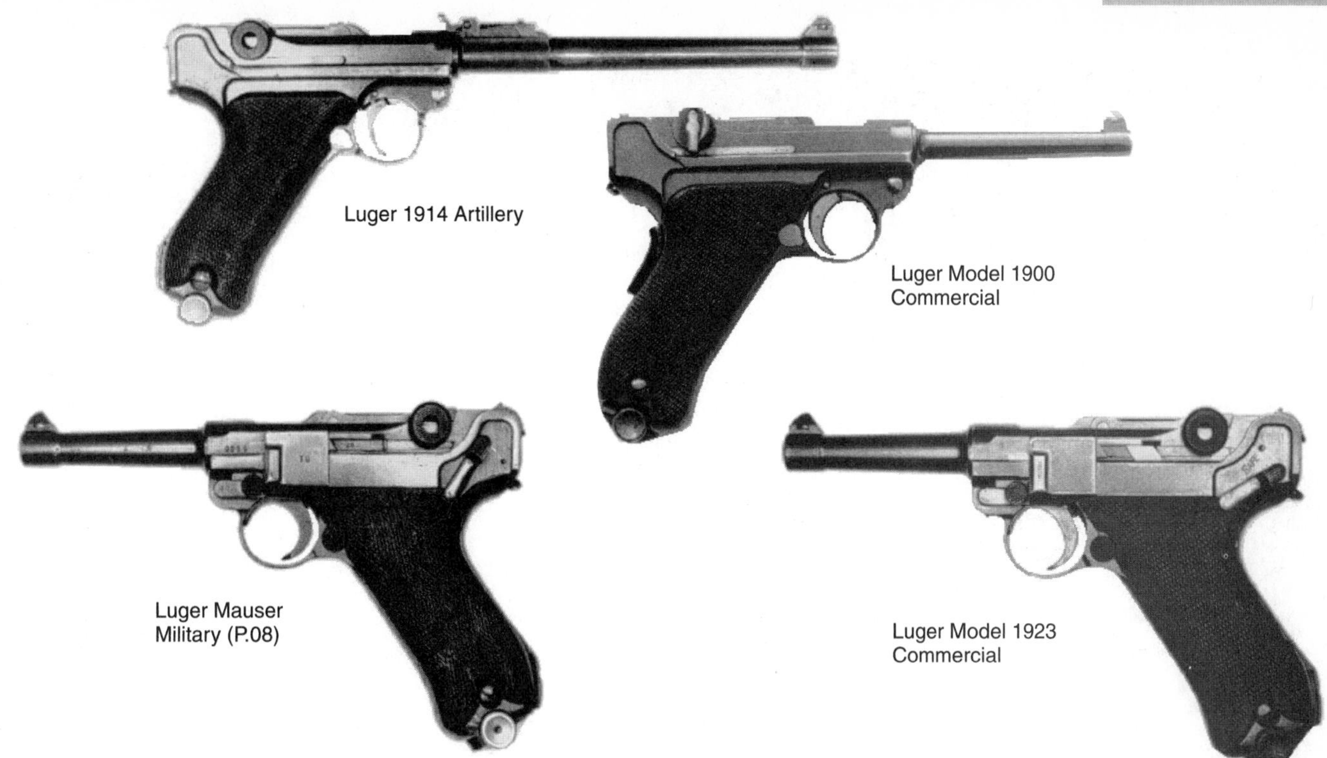
Luger 1914 Artillery

Luger Model 1900 Commercial

Luger Mauser Military (P.08)

Luger Model 1923 Commercial

Dutch Vickers made for the Dutch after WWI by Vickers in England.
Exc: $2750 **VGood:** $2200 **Good:** $1700

LUGER MODEL 1908

Semi-automatic; 9mm Para.; 4-inch barrel; flat checkered toggle knobs; no grip safety; no hold-open device on early models, added later to many 1908 militaries; fixed rear sight on rear toggle link; coil instead of leaf recoil spring; no stock lug on rear frame.

COMMERCIAL

5-digit s/n and commercial proofs
Exc: $1100 **VGood:** $850 **Good:** $600

ARMY

(Military proofs, chamber date from 1910 on, "DWM" or "Erfurt" on toggle)
Exc: $1250 **VGood:** $800 **Good:** $500

BULGARIAN CONTRACT

("DWM" over chamber, Bulgarian crest on toggle, cyrillic safety markings. Rarely found in better than Good condition.)
VGood: $1500 **Good:** $950 **Fair:** $750

NAVY

(6-inch barrel, stock lug, adjustable rear sight, no chamber date)
Exc: $2500 **VGood:** $1750 **Good:** $1250

LUGER MODEL 1914 MILITARY

Semi-automatic; 9mm Para.; 4-inch barrel; flat checkered toggle knobs; fixed rear sight; stock lug on frame; hold-open device; chamber dated 1914 to 1918.

DWM
Exc: $850 **VGood:** $600 **Good:** $350

Erfurt
Exc: $1250 **VGood:** $850 **Good:** $750

LUGER MODEL 1914 ARTILLERY

Same specs as the 1914 Military model except 8-inch barrel; adjustable sight on barrel. Add $300 for stock; $250 for holster (beware of fakes); $750 for 32-shot drum magazine.

DWM or Erfurt
Exc: $2750 **VGood:** $1900 **Good:** $1200

LUGER MODEL 1914 NAVY

Same specs as 1914 Military except 6-inch barrel; adjustable sight on rear toggle link. DWM only.
Exc: $3750 **VGood:** $2650 **Good:** $1850

LUGER MODEL 1920 MILITARY

Semi-automatic; 9mm Para.; 4-inch barrel. The Model 1914 Military Luger dated 1920, often in addition to the original date, to indicate compliance with the Treaty of Versailles for issue to the 100,000-man post-war German army.
Exc: $900 **VGood:** $700 **Good:** $600

LUGER MODEL 1920 COMMERCIAL

Same specs as Military model except 7.65mm Para. or 9mm Para. Mostly reworked wartime DWM and Erfurt handguns or made up from surplus parts in every possible variation for commercial sale outside Germany. Marked GERMANY or MADE IN GERMANY. Note: Original Stoeger or Abercrombie & Fitch markings will add $2000 to any variation.

7.65mm Para.
Exc: $900 **VGood:** $650 **Good:** $500

9mm Para.
Exc: $900 **VGood:** $650 **Good:** $500

Navy, either caliber
Exc: $2650 **VGood:** $1950 **Good:** $1250

Artillery, either caliber
Exc: $2400 **VGood:** $1950 **Good:** $1250

Carbine, either caliber
Exc: $7500 **VGood:** $6000 **Good:** $4000

LUGER MODEL 1923 COMMERCIAL

Semi-automatic; 7.65mm Para., 9mm Para.; 4-inch barrel. New manufacture by DWM and serial numbers continued from pre-war commercials starting about 73,000. Note: Original Stoeger or Abercrombie & Fitch markings will add $2000.
Exc: $900 **VGood:** $600 **Good:** $450

Marked SAFE and LOADED
Exc: $1500 **VGood:** $1075 **Good:** $875

LUGER SIMSON & CO.

Semi-automatic; 9mm Para.; 4-inch barrel. Made by Simson from surplus parts for military and limited commercial sale.

Undated
Exc: $1250 **VGood:** $1000 **Good:** $750

Dated 1925 through 1928
Exc: $2500 **VGood:** $2000 **Good:** $1500

LUGER SWISS MANUFACTURE

Semi-automatic; 7.65mm Para.; 4-3/4-inch barrel. Made at Waffenfabrik Bern for Swiss army, police and commercial sale. Model 1906 (sometimes called Model 1924) marked "Waffenfabrik Bern" with small Swiss cross on front of toggle and is mechanically same as DWM; Model 1929 has large Swiss cross in shield on front toggle; no checkering on toggle knobs; longer grip safety; other minor cosmetic differences.

Model 1906
Exc: $2375 **VGood:** $1750 **Good:** $1250

Model 1929 Commercial ("P" before s/n)
Exc: $2250 **VGood:** $1750 **Good:** $1250

Model 1929 Military
Exc: $2500 **VGood:** $1850 **Good:** $1250

LUGER MAUSER COMMERCIAL

Semi-automatic; 7.65mm Para., 9mm Para. Distinguished by Mauser banner on toggle; for commercial or contract sale outside Germany, German police issue.

4-inch barrel, 9mm
Exc: $2000 **VGood:** $1500 **Good:** $900

Nazi police proofs
Exc: $2800 **VGood:** $2150 **Good:** $1550

4-inch barrel, 7.65mm
Exc: $2250 **VGood:** $1750 **Good:** $1250

Artillery model
Exc: $3500 **VGood:** $2500 **Good:** $1750

Luger Mauser Persian (4-inch barrel)
Exc: $4000 **VGood:** $3500 **Good:** $2500

Portuguese Contract "GNR" (7.65mm, 4-3/4-inch barrel)
Exc: $2250 **VGood:** $1750 **Good:** $1250

LUGER MAUSER MILITARY (P.08)

Semi-automatic; 9mm Para.; 4-inch barrel; front toggle marked with "S/42," "42" or "byf" Nazi manufacturer's codes. Date of manufacture on

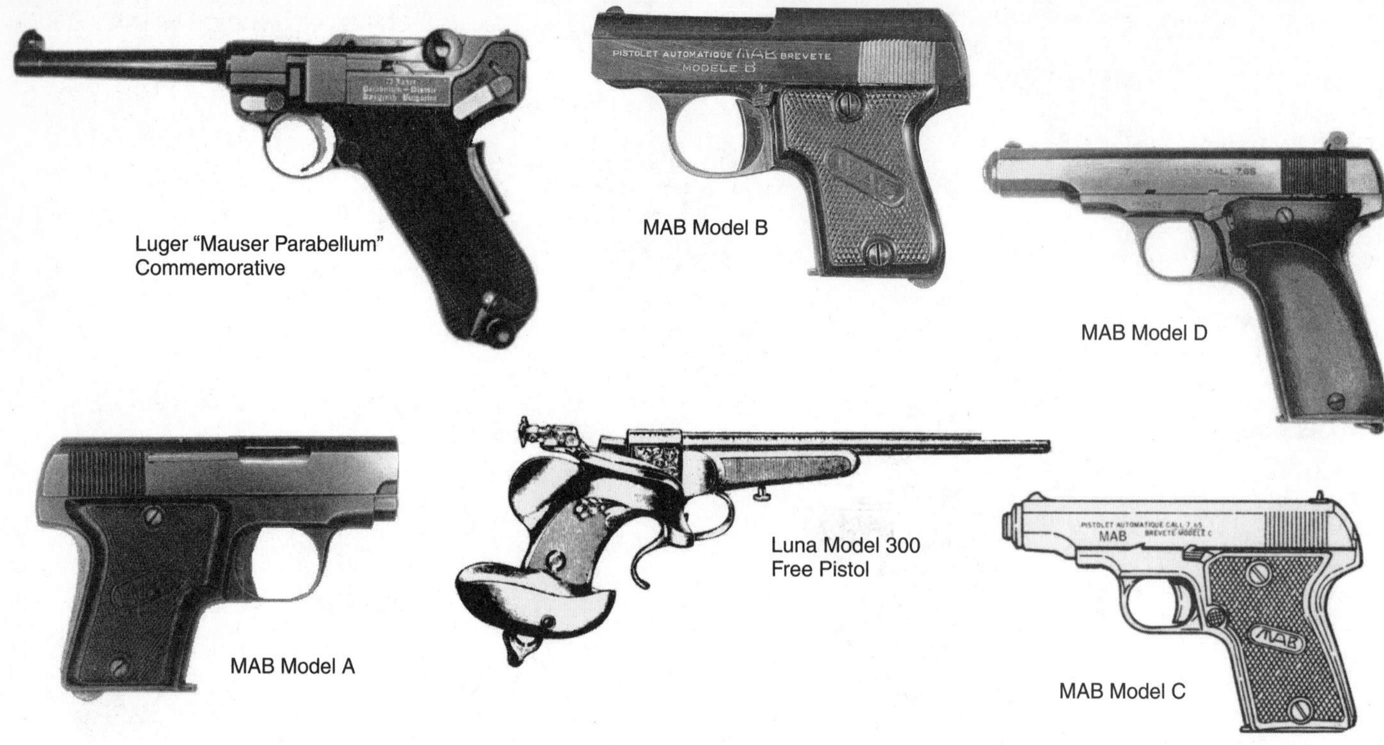
Luger "Mauser Parabellum" Commemorative

MAB Model B

MAB Model D

MAB Model A

Luna Model 300 Free Pistol

MAB Model C

chamber ("K" for 1934; "G" for 1935 or four, or later two, digits for actual year).

Exc: $1000 **VGood:** $750 **Good:** $400

"K" date

Exc: $1500 **VGood:** $1100 **Good:** $800

"G" date

Exc: $1250 **VGood:** $950 **Good:** $550

LUGER KRIEGHOFF

Semi-automatic; 9mm Para.; 4-inch barrel. Front toggle marked with anchor "HK" trademark over "KRIEGHOFF SUHL" and date of manufacture on chamber. A few from 1935 have "S" over chamber and only "SUHL."

Military

Exc: $3250 **VGood:** $2750 **Good:** $1900

Commercial, "P" before s/n, usually undated chamber

Exc: $3500 **VGood:** $2500 **Good:** $2000

LUGER MAUSER POST-WAR MANUFACTURE

In 1970 Mauser resumed limited production of the Luger using tooling purchased from the Swiss. Chambered in 7.65mm Para., 9mm Para.; 4-inch, 4-3/4-inch, 6-inch barrel; front toggle marked "Original MAUSER."

Perf: $800 **Exc:** $600 **VGood:** $500

With original box

New: $850 **Perf:** $670 **Exc:** $550

LUGER "MAUSER PARABELLUM" COMMEMORATIVES

A very limited number (250 each) of replica 1900 Swiss and Bulgarian, 1906 Russian and Navy as well as the 1902 carbine were produced by Mauser. Front toggles marked with gold inlaid "DWM" with appropriate gold inlaid inscription on side panel, cased in fitted leather case with accessories.

As new pistols

Exc: $2500

As new carbines

Exc: $4500

LUNA MODEL 200 FREE PISTOL

Single shot; falling block; 22 LR; 11-inch barrel; target sights; checkered, carved walnut stock, forearm; adjustable palm rest; set trigger; blued finish. Manufactured in Germany approximately 1929 to 1939.

Exc: $1100 **VGood:** $950 **Good:** $850

LUNA MODEL 300 FREE PISTOL

Single shot; 22 Short; 11-inch barrel; target sights; set trigger; checkered, carved walnut stock, forearm; adjustable palm rest; blued finish. Manufactured in Germany approximately 1929 to 1939.

Exc: $850 **VGood:** $750 **Good:** $500

MAB MODEL A

Semi-automatic; 25 ACP; 6-shot magazine; 2-1/2-inch barrel; 4-1/2-inch overall length; no rear sight, fixed front; checkered plastic or hard rubber grips; based on Browning design; blued finish. Introduced in 1921; production suspended in 1942; production resumed in 1945 for importation into U.S. as WAC Model A or Le Defendeur; importation dropped in 1968. Manufactured by Manufacture d'Armes de Bayonne, France.

Exc: $275 **VGood:** $225 **Good:** $180

MAB MODEL B

Semi-automatic; 25 ACP; 6-shot magazine; 2-inch barrel; 4-1/2-inch overall length; no rear sight, fixed front; hard rubber grips; blued finish. Introduced 1932; dropped 1949.

Exc: $250 **VGood:** $235 **Good:** $200

MAB MODEL C

Semi-automatic; 32 ACP, 380 ACP; 7-shot magazine (32 ACP), 6-shot (380 ACP); 3-3/4-inch barrel; 6-inch overall length; fixed sights; black checkered hard rubber grips; push-button magazine release behind trigger; blued finish. Introduced 1933; made under German supervision during WWII. Importation discontinued 1968.

Exc: $250 **VGood:** $235 **Good:** $200

MAB MODEL D

Semi-automatic; 32 ACP, 380 ACP; 9-shot magazine (32 ACP), 8-shot (380 ACP); 4-inch barrel; 7-inch overall length; fixed sights; black checkered hard rubber grips; push-button magazine release; blued finish. Introduced 1933; made under German supervision in WWII. Imported to U.S. as WAC Model D or MAB Le Gendarme. Importation discontinued 1968.

Exc: $250 **VGood:** $235 **Good:** $200

MAB MODEL E

Semi-automatic; 25 ACP; 10-shot magazine; 3-1/4-inch barrel; 6-1/8-inch overall length; fixed sights; plastic grips; blued finish. Introduced 1949; imported into U.S. as WAC Model E. Importation discontinued 1968.

Exc: $225 **VGood:** $210 **Good:** $150

MAB MODEL F

Semi-automatic; 22 LR; 10-shot magazine; 3-1/4-inch, 6-inch, 7-1/4-inch barrel; 10-3/4-inch overall length; windage-adjustable rear sight, ramp front; plastic thumbrest grips; blued finish. Introduced 1950; variation imported into U.S. as Le Chasseur. Importation discontinued 1968.

Exc: $200 **VGood:** $165 **Good:** $135

MAB MODEL PA-15

Semi-automatic; 9mm Para.; 15-shot magazine; 4-1/2-inch barrel; 8-inch overall length; fixed sights; checkered plastic grips; blued finish. Still in production; not currently imported.

Perf: $500 **Exc:** $400 **VGood:** $325

MAGNUM RESEARCH BABY EAGLE 9MM

Semi-automatic; double action; 9mm Para.; 40 S&W, 41 A.E.; 4-3/8-inch barrel; 8-1/16-inch overall length; weighs 35 oz.; high-impact polymer grips; combat sights; polygonal rifling; ambidextrous safety; matte black or chrome finish. Imported by Magnum Research. Introduced 1992.

Perf: $400 **Exc:** $350 **VGood:** $300

Chrome finish

Perf: $450 **Exc:** $400 **VGood:** $325

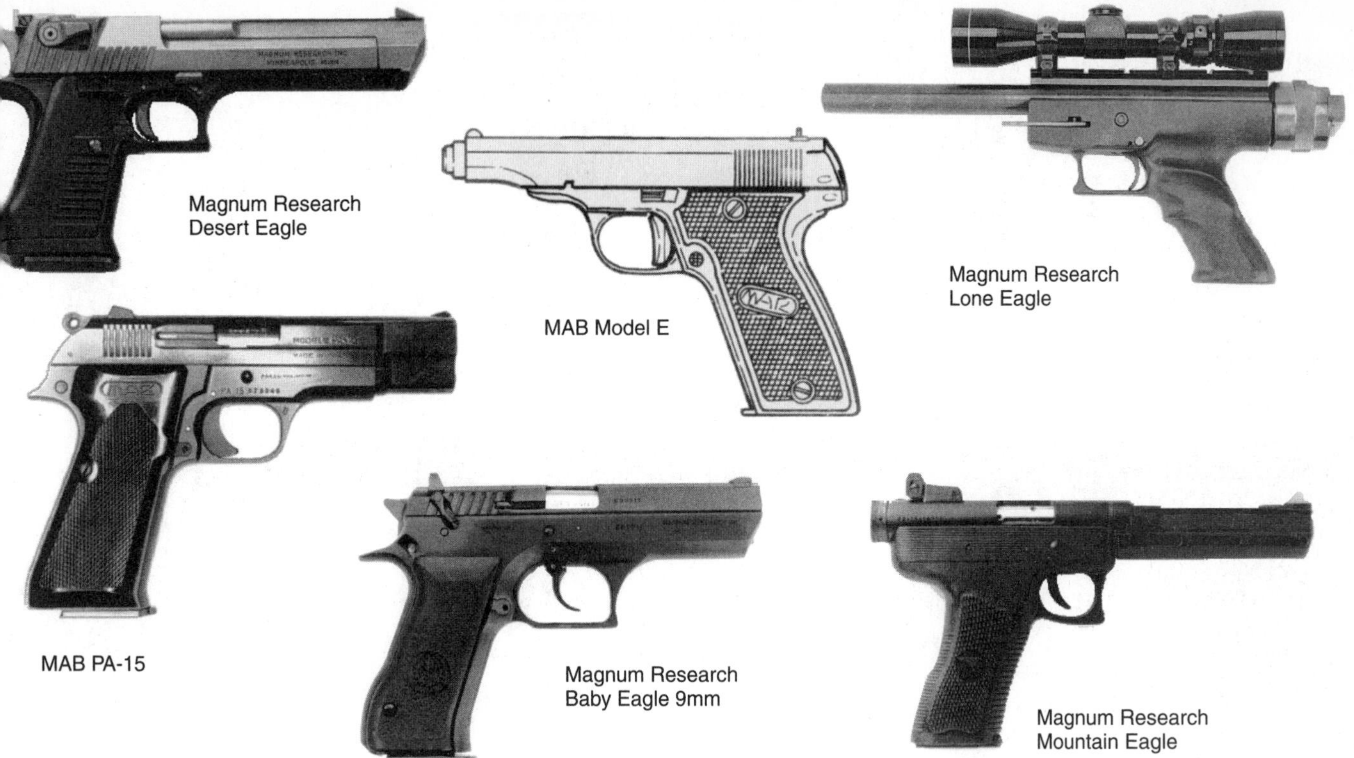
Magnum Research Desert Eagle

MAB Model E

Magnum Research Lone Eagle

MAB PA-15

Magnum Research Baby Eagle 9mm

Magnum Research Mountain Eagle

MAGNUM RESEARCH BABY EAGLE 9MM MODEL F

Same specs as the standard model except has frame-mounted safety on left side.

Perf: $425 **Exc:** $375 **VGood:** $325

MAGNUM RESEARCH BFR

Caliber: 30-30 Win., 444 Marlin, 45 Colt/.410, 45-70, 454 Casull, 460 S&W, 480 Ruger/.475 Linebaugh, 450 Marlin, 500 S&W, 50AE. Single action with five round capacity. Barrel length: 6.5, 7.5 or 10 inches. Weight: 3.6 - 5.3 lbs. Grips: Black rubber. Sights: Adjustable rear, front sights come in four heights.

Perf: $950 **Exc:** $825 **VGood:** $725

MAGNUM RESEARCH DESERT EAGLE

Semi-automatic; 357 Mag., 41 Mag., 44 Mag., 50 Mag.; 9-shot (357), 8-shot (41 Mag., 44 Mag.), 7-shot (50 Mag.); 6-inch, 10-inch, 14-inch interchangeable barrels; 10-1/4-inch overall length; weighs 62 oz. (357), 69 oz. (41,44), 72 oz. (50); wrap-around plastic stocks; blade on ramp front, combat-style rear sight; rotating three-lug bolt; ambidextrous safety; combat-style trigger guard; military epoxy finish; satin, bright nickel, hard chrome, polished and blued finishes available. Imported from Israel by Magnum Research, Inc. .50 AE 10-inch barrel discontinued in the U.S.A. 2007, reintroduced 2013.

Perf: $1200 **Exc:** $950 **VGood:** $775

50 Mag.

Perf: $1300 **Exc:** $1150 **VGood:** $950

MAGNUM RESEARCH LITTLE MAX REVOLVER

Caliber: 22 Hornet, 45 Colt, 454 Casull, 50 A.E. Barrel: 6-1/2-inch, 7-1/2-inch, 10-inch. Weight: 45 oz. Length: 13-inch overall (7-1/2-inch barrel). Stocks: Rubber. Sights: Ramp front, adjustable rear. Features: Single action; stainless steel construction. Announced 1998.

Perf: $1000 **Exc. $850** **VGood:** $600

Maxline model
(7-1/2-inch, 10-inch, 45 Colt, 45-70, 444 Marlin)

Perf: $1000 **Exc. $850** **VGood:** $600

MAGNUM RESEARCH LONE EAGLE

Single shot; 22 Hornet, 223, 22-250, 243, 7mm BR, 7mm-08, 30-30, 308, 30-06, 357 Max., 35 Rem., 358 Win., 44 Mag., 444 Marlin; 14-inch interchangeable barrel; 15-inch overall length; weighs 4 lbs. 3 oz. to 4 lbs. 7 oz.; composition thumbrest stock; no sights furnished; drilled and tapped for scope mounting and optional open sights; cannon-type rotating breech with spring-activated ejector; cross-bolt safety; external cocking lever on left side of gun; ordnance steel with matte blue finish. Made in U.S.; marketed by Magnum Research, Inc. Introduced 1991.

New: $450 **Perf:** $350 **Exc:** $300

MAGNUM RESEARCH MOUNTAIN EAGLE

Semi-automatic; single action; 22 LR; 10-shot magazine; 6-1/2-inch, 8-inch barrel; 10-5/8-inch overall length (6-1/2-inch barrel); weighs 21 oz.; serrated ramp front sight with interchangeable blades, fully-adjustable rear; one-piece impact-resistant polymer grip with checkered panels; interchangeable blades; injection molded grip frame; alloy receiver; hybrid composite barrel replicates shape of the Desert Eagle pistol; flat, smooth trigger. Made in U.S. Marketed by Magnum Research. Introduced 1992.

Perf: $200 **Excc.:** $175 **Exc:** $150

MAGNUM RESEARCH MOUNTAIN EAGLE COMPACT EDITION

Same specs as Mountain Eagle except 4-1/2-inch barrel; shorter grip; windage-adjustable rear sight; weighs 19-1/4 oz. Introduced 1995.

Perf: $200 **Excc.:** $175 **Exc:** $150

MAGNUM RESEARCH MOUNTAIN EAGLE TARGET EDITION

Same specs as the Mountain Eagle except 8-inch barrel; two-stage trigger. Made in U.S. Marketed by Magnum Research. Introduced 1992.

New: $200 **Perf:** $175 **Exc:** $150

MANDALL/CABANAS PISTOL

Caliber: 177, pellet or round ball; single shot. Barrel: 9-inch. Weight: 51 oz. Length: 19-inch overall. Stock: Smooth wood with thumbrest. Sights: Blade front on ramp, open adjustable rear. Features: Fires round ball or pellets with 22 blank cartridge. Automatic safety; muzzlebrake. Imported from Mexico by Mandall Shooting Supplies.

Perf: $125 **Exc:** $100 **VGood:** $85

MAKAROV SPECIAL EDITION PISTOL

Caliber: 9x18 Makarov, 8-shot magazine. Barrel: 3.68-inch. Weight: 24 oz. Length: 6.3-inch overall. Stocks: Textured composition. Sights: Blade front, rear drift-adjustable for windage; three-dot system. Features: Available in polished blue and brushed chrome finishes. Extended magazine floorplate. Introduced 1998. Imported from Bulgaria by Miltex, Inc.

Perf: $250 **Exc:** $200 **VGood:** $110

MANURHIN MODEL 73 CONVERTIBLE

Revolver; single action; 22 LR/38 Spl., 22 LR/32 ACP; 6-shot cylinder; 5-3/4-inch barrel (38), 6-inch (32); interchangeable blade front sight, adjustable micrometer rear; checkered walnut stocks; blued finish. Made in France. Introduced 1988 by Manurhin International.

Perf: $2000 **Exc:** $1750 **VGood:** $1250

MANURHIN MODEL 73 DEFENSE

Revolver; single action; 357 Mag./38 Spl.; 6-shot cylinder; 2-1/2-inch, 3-inch, 4-inch barrel; fixed sights; checkered walnut stocks; blued finish. Made in France. Introduced 1988 by Manurhin International.

Perf: $1100 **Exc:** $950 **VGood:** $700

MANURHIN MODEL 73 GENDARMERIE

Same specs as Model 73 Defense except also offered with 5-1/4-inch, 6-inch, 8-inch barrel; distinguished by prominent ramped front sight,

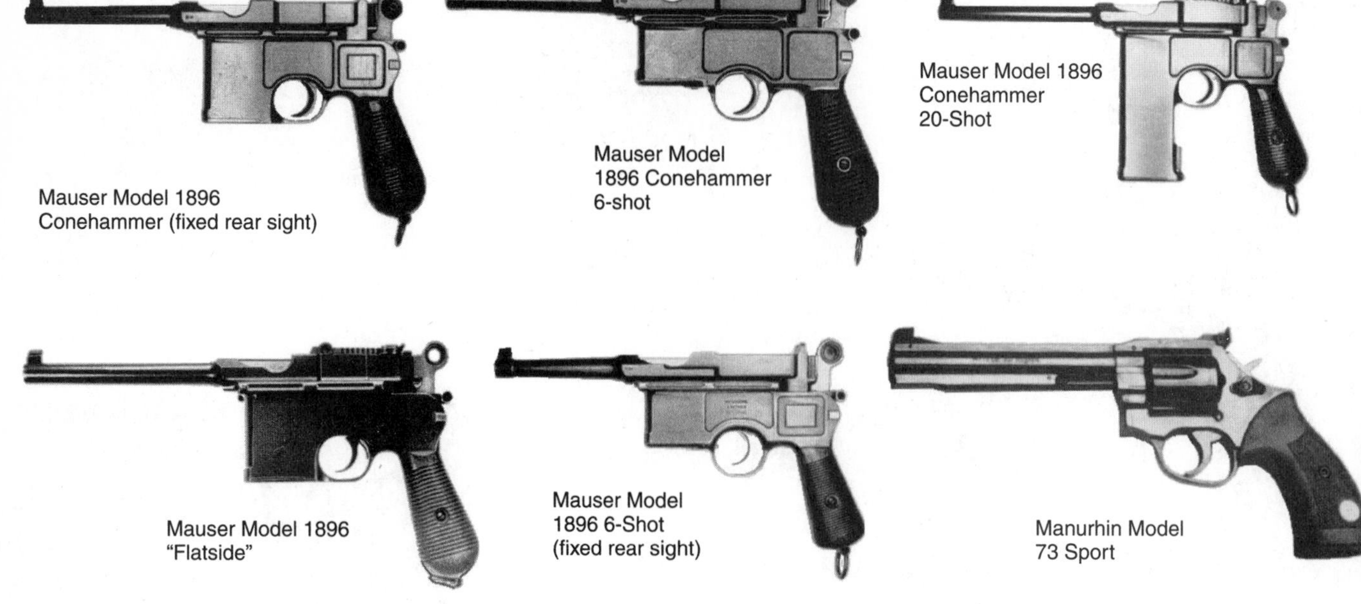
Mauser Model 1896 Conehammer (fixed rear sight)

Mauser Model 1896 Conehammer 6-shot

Mauser Model 1896 Conehammer 20-Shot

Mauser Model 1896 "Flatside"

Mauser Model 1896 6-Shot (fixed rear sight)

Manurhin Model 73 Sport

adjustable rear with rounded edge. Used by French police forces and government agencies.

Perf: $1250 **Exc:** $1000 **VGood:** $850

MANURHIN MODEL 73 SILHOUETTE

Same specs as Model 73 Defense except also offered in 22 LR; 10-inch, 10-3/4-inch heavy barrel with shroud; adjustable sights; contoured walnut stocks.

Perf: $1750 **Exc:** $1500 **VGood:** $1000

MANURHIN MODEL 73 SPORT

Same specs as Model 73 Defense except 6-inch barrel; 11-inch overall length; weighs 37 oz.; fully-adjustable rear sight; adjustable trigger; reduced hammer travel. Imported from France by Century International Arms. Introduced 1988; still in production.

Perf: $1250 **Exc:** $1000 **VGood:** $850

MANURHIN MODEL MR .32 MATCH

Revolver; 32 S&W Long; 6-shot cylinder; 6-inch barrel; 11-/4-inch overall length; weighs 42 oz.; interchangeable blade front sight, adjustable micrometer rear; anatomical target shaped but unfinished grips; externally adjustable trigger; trigger shoe. Made in France. Introduced 1984; discontinued 1986; was imported by Manurhin International.

Perf: $750 **Exc:** $600 **VGood:** $500

MANURHIN MODEL MR .38

Revolver; 38 Spl.; 6-shot cylinder; 5-3/4-inch barrel; interchangeable blade front sight, adjustable micrometer rear; anatomical target shaped but unfinished grips; externally adjustable trigger; trigger shoe. Made in France. Introduced 1984; discontinued 1986; was imported by Manurhin International.

Perf: $750 **Exc:** $600 **VGood:** $500

MANURHIN MODEL PP

Semi-automatic; double action; 22 LR, 32 ACP, 380 ACP; 10-shot magazine (22 LR), 8-shot (32 ACP), 7-shot (380 ACP); 3-7/8-inch barrel; 7-3/4-inch overall length; weighs 23 oz.; white-outline front, rear sights; checkered compostion stocks; hammer drop safety; all-steel construction; supplied with two magazines; blued finish. Made in France. 22 or 380 caliber worth 50 percent more than prices shown. Importation began in 1950s; dropped 1960s.

Perf: $300 **Exc:** $225 **VGood:** $200

MANURHIN MODEL PPK/S

Same specs as Model PP except 3-1/4-inch barrel; 6-1/8-inch overall length.

Perf: $300 **Exc:** $250 **VGood:** $225

With brushed chrome finish

Perf: $350 **Exc:** $300 **VGood:** $250

MAUSER MODEL 1896 CONEHAMMER

Semi-automatic; 7.63mm Mauser; 10-shot magazine; 5-1/2-inch barrel; 11-1/2-inch overall length; tangent rear sight; locked breech action; grooved wood or (rarely) hard rubber grips; blued finish. The first model, made from 1896-1898 and considered antique under federal law, is distinguished by a "beehive" or cone-shaped hammer (though some have a much larger open ring hammer), wide trigger and milled frame panels. Serial numbers run up to 15000. Note: First few hundred had SYSTEM MAUSER engraved on top of chamber and bring a very high premium. Add $500 for matching stock holster; $100 for engraved dealer's name.

Exc: $2000 **VGood:** $1500 **Good:** $950

Turkish contract with Turkish crest in side panel and serial/sight numbering in Cyrillic

Exc: $5000 **VGood:** $3500 **Good:** $2000

With fixed rear sight, 4-5/8-inch barrel

Exc: $2500 **VGood:** $2000 **Good:** $1500

MAUSER MODEL 1896 CONEHAMMER 6-SHOT

Same specs as standard model except shortened 6-shot magazine; may have fixed or adjustable rear sight.

Exc: $6000 **VGood:** $4000 **Good:** $2500

MAUSER MODEL 1896 CONEHAMMER 20-SHOT

Same specs as standard model except fixed 20-shot magazine extending well below trigger guard; milled out or flat frame panels. Very high collector value.

Exc: $35,000 **VGood:** $20,000 **Good:** $15,000

With original 20-shot stock holster

Exc: $40,000 **VGood:** $25,000 **Good:** $20,000

MAUSER MODEL 1896 "FLATSIDE"

Semi-automatic; 7.63mm Mauser; 10-shot magazine; 5-1/2-inch barrel; 11-1/2-inch overall length; flat frame sides; narrow trigger; large ring hammer; tangent rear sight; locked breech action; grooved wood or (rarely) hard rubber grips; blued finish. The 6-shot flatsides are very rare and very valuable.

Exc: $2000 **VGood:** $1500 **Good:** $1000

MAUSER MODEL 1899 "FLATSIDE" ITALIAN NAVY

Semi-automatic; 7.63mm Mauser; 10-shot magazine; 5-1/2-inch barrel; 11-1/2-inch overall length; flat frame sides; narrow trigger; large ring hammer; tangent rear sight; locked breech action; grooved wood grips; blued finish. 5,000 flatsides made for Italian navy and distinguished by small "DV" on chamber side and crown over "AV" under barrel; serial numbered 1 to 5000.

Exc: $2500 **VGood:** $2000 **Good:** $1000

MAUSER MODEL 1896 LARGE RING HAMMER

Semi-automatic; 7.63mm Mauser; 10-shot magazine; 5-1/2-inch barrel; 11-1/2-inch overall length; paneled frame sides like the Conehammer; narrow trigger; large ring hammer; tangent rear sight; locked breech action; grooved wood or (rarely) hard rubber grips; blued finish.

Exc: $1750 **VGood:** $1350 **Good:** $950

MAUSER MODEL 1896 PRE-WAR BOLO

Semi-automatic; 7.63mm Mauser; 10-shot magazine; 3-15/16-inch barrel; 10-inch overall length; paneled frame sides; narrow trigger; large or small ring hammer; tangent rear sight; locked breech action; small grip frame with wood or hard rubber grips; blued finish.

Exc: $2250 **VGood:** $1500 **Good:** $950

With original Bolo (short) stock-holster

Exc: $3500 **VGood:** $2750 **Good:** $1750

MAUSER MODEL 1896 6-SHOT

Semi-automatic; 7.63mm Mauser; 6-shot magazine; 3-15/16-inch barrel; large or small-ring hammer; fixed or tangent rear sight.

Exc: $4500 **VGood:** $3500 **Good:** $2000

Mauser Model 1896 "French Gendarme"

Mauser Model 1896 "Pre-War" Bolo

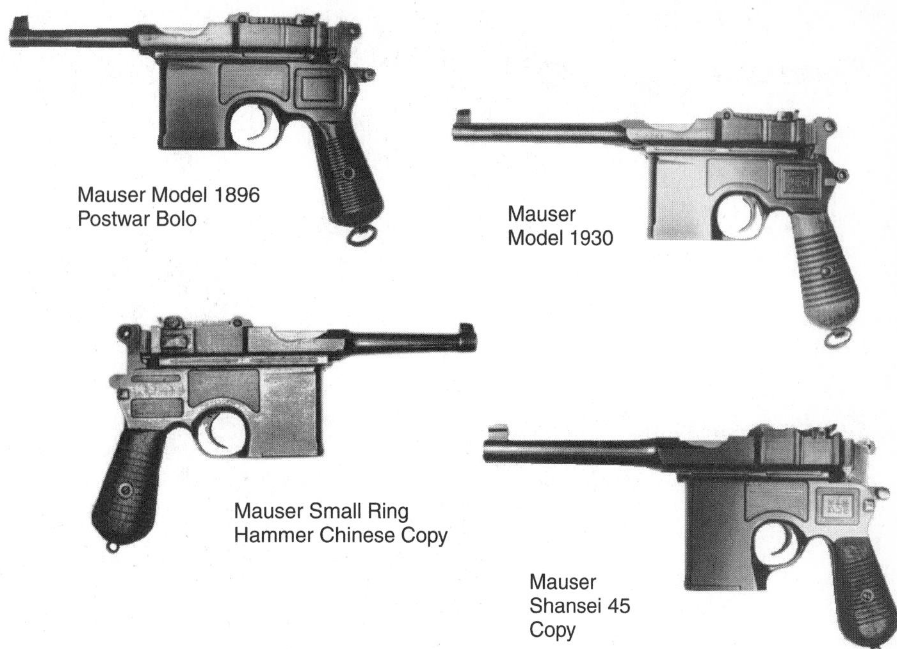

Mauser Model 1896 Postwar Bolo

Mauser Model 1930

Mauser Small Ring Hammer Chinese Copy

Mauser Shansei 45 Copy

MAUSER MODEL 1896 PRE-WAR COMMERCIAL

Semi-automatic; 7.63mm Mauser; 10-shot magazine; 5-1/2-inch barrel; 11-1/2-inch overall length; paneled frame sides like the Conehammer; narrow trigger; small ring hammer; tangent rear sight; locked breech action; grooved wood or (rarely) hard rubber grips; blued finish. Made 1905-1918. Higher serial numbered examples usually have German military proofs.

Exc: $1000 **VGood:** $850 **Good:** $500

With Mauser banner over chamber

Exc: $1500 **VGood:** $1250 **Good:** $1000

With Persian Lion crest on side s/n in 154000 range

Exc: $2750 **VGood:** $2000 **Good:** $1500

MAUSER MODEL 1896 9MM EXPORT

Semi-automatic; 9mm Mauser; 10-shot magazine; 5-1/2-inch barrel; 11 1/2-inch overall length; paneled frame sides like the Conehammer; narrow trigger; small ring hammer; tangent rear sight; locked breech action; grooved wood or (rarely) hard rubber grips; blued finish.

Exc: $1750 **VGood:** $1250 **Good:** $950

MAUSER MODEL 1896 CARBINE

Semi-automatic; 7.63mm; 10-shot; 11 3/4-inch, 16-inch barrel; take-down sporting carbine made on Mauser pistol action. Made in limited numbers from 1896 to about 1906 with paneled or smooth sides and with all three hammer styles. Very high collector value. Note: Very early cone-hammer and a few very late carbines chambered for 9mm Para. or 9mm Export bring a premium.

Exc: $15,000 **VGood:** $12,500 **Good:** $9000

MAUSER MODEL 1916 "RED 9"

Semi-automatic; 9mm Para.; 10-shot; 5-1/2-inch barrel. Made under contract for the German army. Called by collectors "Red 9" because most (but not all) have large figure "9" cut into the wood grips and painted red to distinguish them from 7.63mm pistols also in use by army.

Exc: $1350 **VGood:** $750 **Good:** $650

MAUSER MODEL 1896 WEIMAR REWORK

Many WWI Red 9 military pistols were reworked 1920-1921 to conform with the Treaty of Versailles by cutting barrels to 4-inch, replacing tangent sight with fixed rear sight. Usually identified by "1920" stamped on side.

Exc: $850 **VGood:** $600 **Good:** $500

With Weimar navy markings

Exc: $1250 **VGood:** $900 **Good:** $750

MAUSER MODEL 1896 "FRENCH GENDARME"

Semi-automatic; 7.63mm; 10-shot magazine; supposedly made for French occupation forces with 3-15/16-inch Bolo barrel but full-size grip frame; checkered hard rubber grips.

Exc: $1000 **VGood:** $850 **Good:** $600

MAUSER MODEL 1896 POSTWAR BOLO

Semi-automatic; 7.63mm; 10-shot; 3-15/16-inch barrel; small grip frame with grooved wood grips. Made about 1920 through 1930.

Exc: $950 **VGood:** $700 **Good:** $450

MAUSER MODEL 1930

Semi-automatic; 7.63mm; 10-shot; 5-1/4-inch barrel (early), 5-1/2-inch barrel. Slightly updated version of Model 1896 distinguished by small step in barrel, wide grip straps with 12-groove wood grips, high polish bright acid blue finish instead of duller rust blue. Note: A few 1930-type Mausers were made with detachable 10- or 20-shot magazines and are very rare and valuable. Beware of fakes made by welding up switch holes of a Model 1932.

Exc: $1500 **VGood:** $1250 **Good:** $500

With proper stock-holster with Mauser banner, no serial number

Exc: $2000 **VGood:** $1500 **Good:** $1100

Warning: Model 1932 (also called Model 712) pistols have a selector switch for full-auto fire as well as detachable magazine. They are illegal to own unless registered with the BATF.

MAUSER CHINESE COPIES OF THE MODEL 1896

TAKU NAVAL DOCKYARD

Semi-automatic; 7.63mm; 10-shot; 5-1/2-inch barrel; flat frame panel sides; large ring hammer; grooved wood grips. Marked "TAKU NAVAL DOCKYARD" on top of chamber.

Exc: $1250 **VGood:** $850 **Good:** $500

With unmarked chamber

Exc: $750 **VGood:** $500 **Good:** $300

MAUSER CHINESE SMALL RING HAMMER COPIES

Same specs as above except paneled frame sides; small ring hammer. Quality varies from quite good to simply awful. May be unmarked except for serial numbers with spurious Mauser markings (often misspelled) or with markings in Chinese.

Exc: $450 **VGood:** $300 **Good:** $200

MAUSER SHANSEI 45 COPY

Semi-automatic; 45 ACP; 10-shot; 6-1/4-inch barrel; 12-1/2-inch overall length; weighs 3 lbs., 7 oz. Oversize version of the Model 1896 built in the 1930s for a Chinese warlord who liked the 45 cartridge. Note: A copy of this copy, recently made in China, has been imported and sold at $1000-$1500. If the condition of a Shansei seems too good, it is.

Exc: $4500 **VGood:** $3000 **Good:** $2000

MAUSER MODEL 1910

Semi-automatic; 25 ACP; 9-shot; 3-1/8-inch barrel; 5-3/8-inch overall length; fixed sights; checkered walnut or (rarely) hard rubber wrap-around grips. Introduced 1910; dropped 1934.

Exc: $250 **VGood:** $185 **Good:** $135

Early model with takedown latch above trigger (s/n below about 60000)

Exc: $350 **VGood:** $250 **Good:** $185

MAUSER MODEL 1914

Semi-automatic; 32 ACP; 8-shot; 3-1/4-inch barrel; 6-1/8-inch overall length; fixed sights; checkered

Merrill Sportsman

Metro Arms Mac 3011 SSD

Mitchell Arms American Eagle Luger

Mitchell Arms 45 Gold Series

Medusa Model 47

walnut or (rarely) hard rubber wrap-around grip. Introduced 1914; dropped 1934.

Exc: $235 **VGood:** $185 **Good:** $135

Early model with hump on top of slide (s/n below about 3000)

Exc: $2200 **VGood:** $1800 **Good:** $1250

MAUSER MODEL 1910/1934

Semi-automatic; 25 ACP; 9-shot; 3-1/8-inch barrel; 5-3/8-inch overall length. Like the Model 1910 except for swept-back grip of walnut or plastic, bright high polish blue or nickel (rare) instead of rust blue finish.

Exc: $350 **VGood:** $250 **Good:** $175

MAUSER MODEL 1914

Semi-automatic; 32 ACP; 8-shot; 3-1/2-inch barrel; 6-1/8-inch overall length; fixed sights; swept-back grip of walnut or plastic; bright high polish blue instead of rust blue finish. Made from 1934 to 1940.

Exc: $400 **VGood:** $300 **Good:** $175

With Nazi Navy eagle over M marking

Exc: $700 **VGood:** $500 **Good:** $400

MAUSER WTP

Semi-automatic; 25 ACP; 6-shot; 2-1/2-inch barrel; 4-1/2-inch overall length; checkered wrap-around hard rubber grips; blue finish. Made from 1922 to 1938.

Exc: $275 **VGood:** $150 **Good:** $125

MAUSER WTP II

Semi-automatic; 25 ACP; 6-shot; 2-inch barrel; 4-3/16-inch overall length; checkered plastic grips; blue finish. Made from 1938 to 1944.

Exc: $350 **VGood:** $250 **Good:** $175

MAUSER HSC

Semi-automatic; double action; 32 ACP; 8-shot; 3-1/2-inch barrel; 6-1/2-inch overall length; checkered wood or plastic grips; blue finish. Made 1940 to 1946. Last production was during French occupation.

Exc: $350 **VGood:** $275 **Good:** $200

With Nazi navy eagle over M marking

Exc: $700 **VGood:** $500 **Good:** $400

Very early model with grip screws near bottom of grips

Exc: $2200 **VGood:** $1800 **Good:** $1300

MAUSER HSC POST-WAR

Same specs as above except also made in 380 ACP; 7-shot. Made from 1962 to 1976.

Exc: $300 **VGood:** $200 **Good:** $150

MAUSER HSC SUPER (GAMBA)

Semi-automatic; 32 ACP, 380; 3-1/2-inch barrel; 6-1/2-inch overall length; 13-shot magazine; checkered wood grips; double action; blue. Made for Mauser by Gamba in Italy; imported 1968-1981.

Exc: $275 **VGood:** $225 **Good:** $175

MAUSER MODEL 80

Semi-automatic; single action; 9mm Para.; 13-shot magazine; 4-11/16-inch barrel; 8-inch overall length; weighs 32 oz.; checkered beechwood grips; blade front sight, windage-adjustable rear; uses basic Hi-Power design; polished blue finish. Made in Hungary for Mauser and imported from Germany by Precision Imports, Inc. Introduced 1992; importation dropped 1993.

Perf: $450 **Exc:** $400 **VGood:** $350

MAUSER MODEL 90

Semi-automatic; double action; 9mm Para.; 14-shot magazine; 4-11/16-inch barrel; 8-inch overall length; weighs 35 oz.; checkered beechwood grips; blade front sight, windage-adjustable rear; uses basic Hi-Power design; polished blue finish. Made in Hungary for Mauser and imported from Germany by Precision Imports, Inc. Introduced 1992; importation dropped 1993.

Perf: $450 **Exc:** $400 **VGood:** $350

MAUSER MODEL 90 COMPACT

Same specs as the Model 90 except 4-1/8-inch barrel; 7-1/2-inch overall length; weighs 33-1/2-inch. Imported from Germany by Precision Imports, Inc. Introduced 1992; importation dropped 1993.

Perf: $500 **Exc:** $450 **VGood:** $400

MEDUSA MODEL 47 REVOLVER

For most 9mm, 38 and 357 caliber cartridges; 6-shot cylinder. Barrel: 2-1/2-inch, 3-inch, 4-inch, 5-inch, 6-inch; fluted. Weight: 39 oz. Length: 10-inch overall (4-inch barrel). Stocks: Gripper-style rubber. Sights: Changeable front blades, fully adjustable rear. Patented extractor allows gun to chamber, fire and extract over 25 different cartridges in the .355- to .357 range, without half-moon clips. Steel frame and cylinder; match quality barrel. Matte blue finish. Introduced 1996. Made in U.S. by Phillips & Rogers, Inc.

Perf: $950 **Exc:** $800 **VGood:** $700

METRO ARMS MAC 3011 SSD

Semi-automatic 1911 style handgun in .45 ACP. five inch barrel, 8.8 inches overall length. Weight: 40.56 ounces. Fiber optic front sight, adjustable Bomar-type rear sight. Slide and frame made of 4140 steel. Front and rear slide serrations. Beavertail grip safety. Available with blue or hard chrome finish. Manufactured in the Philippines, imported by Eagle Imports. Available / Introduced 2013.

Perf: $950 **Exc:** $800 **VGood:** $700

MERRILL SPORTSMAN

Single shot; 22 Short, 22 Long, 22 LR, 22 WMR, 22 Rem. Jet, 22 Hornet, 30 Herrett, 38 Spl. 45-70, 357 Mag., 256 Win. Mag., 45 Colt, 44 Mag., 30-30; 9-inch, 12-inch, 14-inch semi-octagon hinged barrel; adjustable rear sight, fixed front; uncheckered walnut grips with thumb, heel rest; hammerless; top rib grooved for scope mounts. Introduced 1972.

Perf: $775 **Exc:** $700 **VGood:** $550

MITCHELL ARMS 45 GOLD SERIES (HIGH STANDARD/SIGNATURE SERIES)

Semi-automatic; single action; 45 ACP; 8-, 10-shot magazine; 5-inch barrel; 8-3/4-inch overall length; weighs 39 oz.; interchangeable blade front sight, drift adjustable combat rear or fully-adjustable rear; smooth American walnut or checkered black rubber grips; bull barrel/slide lockup (no bushing design); full-length guide rod; extended ambidextrous safety; adjustable trigger; beveled magazine well; royal blue or stainless steel. Guns are marked with "High Standard" or "Signature Series" depending on date of manufacture. Made in U.S. From Mitchell Arms, Inc. Introduced 1994.

New: $550 **Perf:** $475 **Exc:** $400

Stainless finish, fixed sights.

New: $675 **Perf:** $525 **Exc:** $450

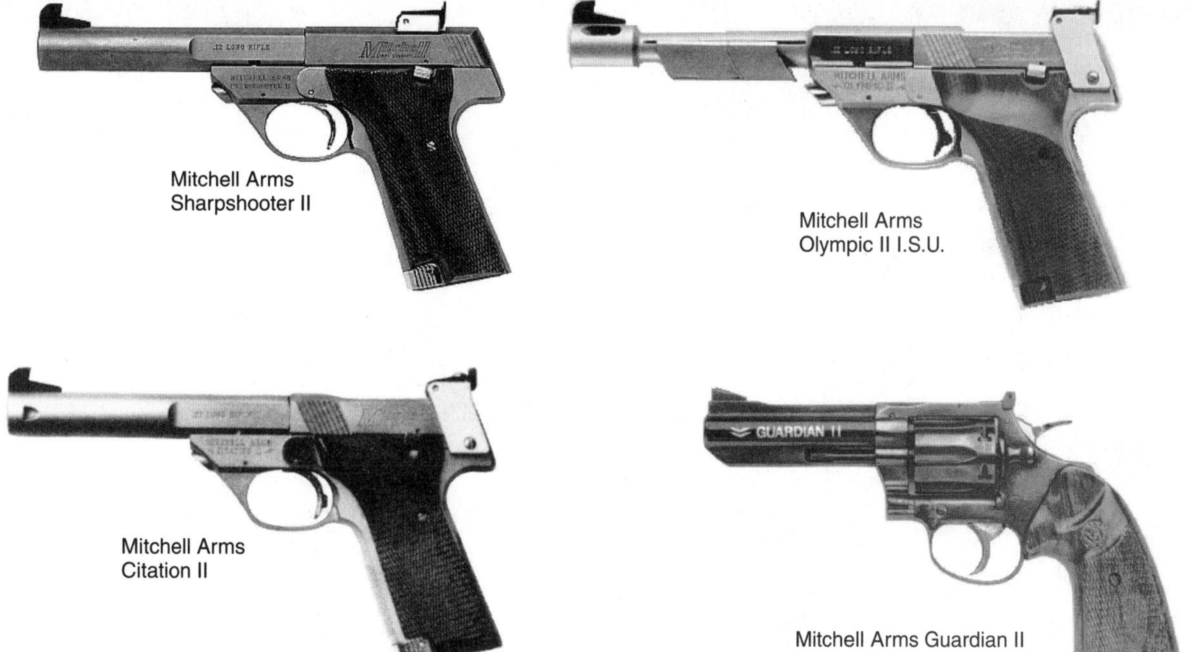

Mitchell Arms Sharpshooter II

Mitchell Arms Olympic II I.S.U.

Mitchell Arms Citation II

Mitchell Arms Guardian II

Blue finish, adjustable sights

New: $575 **Perf:** $500 **Exc:** $450

Stainless finish, adjustable sights

New: $650 **Perf:** $525 **Exc:** $475

MITCHELL ARMS 45 GOLD SERIES (HIGH-STANDARD/SIGNATURE SERIES) WIDE-BODY

Same specs as 45 Gold except 10-shot magazine (accepts 8- and 13-shot magazines); fixed combat sights; black rubber grips; blue or stainless steel. Guns are marked with "High Standard" or "Signature Series" depending on date of manufacture. Made in U.S. From Mitchell Arms, Inc. Introduced 1994.

New: $600 **Perf:** $550 **Exc:** $500

Stainless finish, fixed sights.

New: $675 **Perf:** $650 **Exc:** $500

Blue finish, fixed sights

New: $700 **Perf:** $675 **Exc:** $525

Stainless finish, adjustable sights

New: $725 **Perf:** $700 **Exc:** $575

MITCHELL ARMS AMERICAN EAGLE LUGER

Semi-automatic; single action; 9mm Para.; 7-shot magazine; 4-inch barrel; 9-5/8-inch overall length; weighs 30 oz.; blade front sight, fixed rear; checkered walnut grips; recreation of the American Eagle Parabellum pistol in stainless steel. Made in U.S. Marketed by Mitchell Arms, Inc. Introduced 1992.

New: $750 **Perf:** $600 **Exc:** $500

MITCHELL ARMS BAT MASTERSON MODEL

Revolver; single action; 45 Colt; 6-shot cylinder; 4-3/4-inch, 5-1/2-inch, 7-1/2-inch barrel; fixed sights; one-piece walnut grip; hammer-block safety; nickel-plated. Introduced 1989.

Perf: $325 **Exc:** $250 **VGood:** $175

MITCHELL ARMS CITATION II

Semi-automatic; single action; 22 LR; 10-shot magazine; 5-1/2-inch bull, 7-1/4-inch fluted barrel; weighs 44-1/2 oz. (5-1/2-inch barrel); 9-3/4-inch overall length; undercut ramp front sight, click-adjustable frame-mounted rear; checkered walnut thumbrest grips; grips duplicate feel of military 45 auto; positive action magazine latch; front- and backstraps stippled; adjustable nickel-plated trigger, safety and magazine release; silver-filled roll marks; push-button barrel takedown; made of stainless steel; satin stainless or blue finish. Guns are marked with "High Standard" depending on date of manufacture. Made in U.S. Marketed by Mitchell Arms, Inc. Introduced 1992.

New: $500 **Perf:** $400 **Exc:** $300

MITCHELL ARMS DERRINGER

Derringer; over/under; 38 Spl.; 2-shot; 2 3/4-inch barrel; 5-1/4-inch overall length; weighs 11 oz.; fixed sights; checkered walnut grips; has same basic design as original Remington except for ramp front sight; polished blue finish. Introduced 1981.

Perf: $150 **Exc:** $125 **VGood:** $100

Stainless steel

Perf: $175 **Exc:** $150 **VGood:** $125

MITCHELL ARMS GUARDIAN II

Revolver; double action; 38 Spl.; 6-shot cylinder; 3-inch, 4-inch barrel; 8-1/2-inch overall length (3-inch barrel); weighs 32 oz.; combat or target grips of checkered black rubber or walnut; blade on ramp front sight, fixed rear; target hammer; shrouded ejector rod; smooth trigger; blue finish. Made in U.S. Marketed by Mitchell Arms, Inc. Introduced 1995.

Perf: $200 **Exc:** $175 **VGood:** $135

MITCHELL ARMS GUARDIAN III

Same specs as Guardian II except 3-inch, 4-inch, 6-inch barrel; adjustable rear sight. Made in U.S. Marketed by Mitchell Arms. Introduced 1995.

Perf: $250 **Exc:** $225 **VGood:** $200

MITCHELL ARMS MODEL 57A

Semi-automatic; single action; 30 Mauser; 9-shot magazine; all-steel construction; magazine safety; hammer-block safety. Made in Yugoslavia. Introduced 1990; discontinued 1990.

Perf: $500 **Exc:** $400 **VGood:** $300

MITCHELL ARMS MODEL 70A

Semi-automatic; single action; 9mm Para.; 9-shot magazine; all-steel construction; magazine safety; hammer-block safety. Made in Yugoslavia. Introduced 1990; discontinued 1990.

Perf: $450 **Exc:** $375 **VGood:** $250

MITCHELL ARMS MODEL 1875 REMINGTON

Revolver; single action; 357 Mag., 45 Colt; 6-shot cylinder; fixed sights; walnut stock; color case-hardened frame; blued finish. Introduced 1990; discontinued 1991.

Perf: $325 **Exc:** $250 **VGood:** $225

MITCHELL ARMS OFFICERS MODEL 88A

Semi-automatic; single action; 9mm Para.; 9-shot magazine; all-steel construction; slenderized version of Model 70A; finger extension magazine. Made in Yugoslavia. Introduced 1990; discontinued 1990.

Perf: $450 **Exc:** $375 **VGood:** $250

MITCHELL ARMS OLYMPIC II I.S.U.

Semi-automatic; single action; 22 Short, 22 LR; 10-shot magazine; 6-3/4-inch round tapered barrel with stabilizer; 11-1/4-inch overall length; weighs 40 oz.; checkered walnut thumbrest grips; undercut ramp front sight, frame-mounted click-adjustable square notch rear; integral stabilizer with two removable weights; trigger adjustable for pull and over-travel; stippled front and backstraps; push-button barrel takedown; blue finish or stainless or combo. Some guns are marked with "High-Standard" depending on date of manufacture. Introduced 1992.

New: $550 **Perf:** $475 **Exc:** $400

MITCHELL ARMS ROLLING BLOCK TARGET

Single shot; 22 LR, 22 WMR, 357 Mag., 45 Colt, 223 Rem.; 9-7/8-inch half-round, half-octagon barrel; 14-inch overall length; weighs 44 oz.; walnut grip and forend; blade front sight, fully-adjustable rear; replica of the 1871 rolling block target pistol; brass trigger guard; color case-hardened frame; blue barrel. Imported from Italy by Mitchell Arms, Inc. Introduced 1992; dropped 1993.

Perf: $500 **Exc:** $400 **VGood:** $300

MITCHELL ARMS SHARPSHOOTER II

Semi-automatic; single action; 22 LR; 10-shot magazine; 5-1/2-inch bull barrel; 10-1/4-inch overall length; weighs 45 oz.; checkered walnut thumbrest

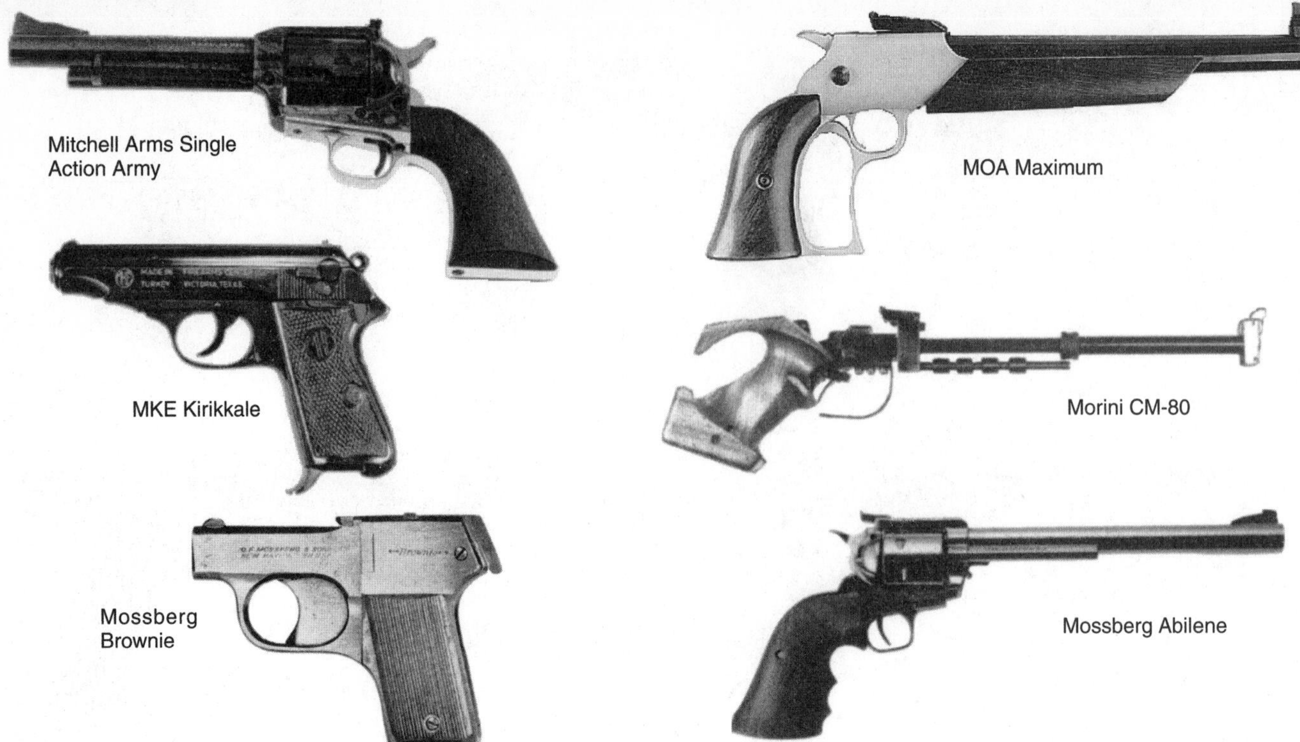
Mitchell Arms Single Action Army

MOA Maximum

MKE Kirikkale

Morini CM-80

Mossberg Brownie

Mossberg Abilene

grips; ramp front sight, slide-mounted square notch fully-adjustable rear; military grip; slide lock; smooth gripstraps; push-button takedown; drilled and tapped for barrel weights; stainless steel, blue or combo. Made in U.S. Marketed by Mitchell Arms, Inc. Introduced 1992.

New: $400 **Perf:** $300 **Exc:** $250

MITCHELL ARMS SINGLE ACTION ARMY

Revolver; single action; 22 LR, 357 Mag., 44 Mag., 45 ACP, 45 Colt; 6-shot cylinder; 4-3/4-inch, 5-1/2-inch, 6-inch, 7-1/2-inch, 10-inch, 12-inch, 18-inch barrel; ramp front, adjustable rear sight; one-piece walnut grips; brass grip frame; color case-hardened frame; hammer-block safety; blued finish. Introduced 1986.

Perf: $350 **Exc:** $300 **VGood:** $250

MITCHELL ARMS SINGLE ACTION ARMY, U.S. ARMY MODEL

Same specs as Single Action Army except 357 Mag., 45 ACP, 45 Colt; 5-1/2-inch barrel; serrated ramp front sight, fixed or adjustable rear; brass or steel backstrap/trigger guard; bright nickel-plated model and dual cylinder models available.

Perf: $375 **Exc:** $325 **VGood:** $300

Nickel finish

Perf: $400 **Exc:** $375 **VGood:** $325

With 45 Colt/45 ACP dual cylinder

Perf: $500 **Exc:** $400 **VGood:** $350

MITCHELL ARMS SINGLE ACTION ARMY, CAVALRY MODEL

Same specs as Single Action Army except 357 Mag., 45 ACP, 45 Colt; 7-1/2-inch barrel; serrated ramp front sight, fixed or adjustable rear; brass or steel backstrap/trigger guard; bright nickel-plated model and dual cylinder models available.

Perf: $350 **Exc:** $275 **VGood:** $200

Nickel finish

Perf: $375 **Exc:** $300 **VGood:** $225

With 45 Colt/45 ACP dual cylinder

Perf: $500 **Exc:** $400 **VGood:** $350

MITCHELL ARMS SINGLE ACTION ARMY, COWBOY MODEL

Same specs as Single Action Army except 357 Mag., 45 ACP, 45 Colt; 4-3/4-inch barrel; serrated ramp front sight, fixed or adjustable rear; brass or steel backstrap/trigger guard; bright nickel-plated model and dual cylinder models available.

Perf: $350 **Exc:** $275 **VGood:** $200

Nickel finish

Perf: $375 **Exc:** $300 **VGood:** $225

With 45 Colt/45 ACP dual cylinder

Perf: $425 **Exc:** $375 **VGood:** $30

MITCHELL ARMS SPORT KING II

Semi-automatic; single action; 22 LR; 10-shot magazine; 4-1/2-inch, 6-3/4-inch barrel; 9-inch overall length (4-1/2-inch barrel); weighs 39 oz.; checkered walnut or black plastic grips; blade front sight, windage-adjustable rear; military grip; standard trigger; push-button barrel takedown; stainless steel or blue. Guns are marked with "High Standard" depending on date of manufacture. Introduced 1992.

New: $250 **Perf:** $225 **Exc:** $200

MITCHELL ARMS TITAN II

Revolver; double action; 357 Mag.; 6-shot cylinder; 2-inch, 4-inch, 6-inch barrel; 7-3/4-inch overall length (2-inch barrel); weighs 38 oz.; Pachmayr black rubber grips, combat or target; blade front, fixed rear sight; crane-mounted cylinder release; shrouded ejector rod; blue or stainless steel. Introduced 1995.

New: $250 **Perf:** $225 **Exc:** $200

MITCHELL ARMS TITAN III

Same specs as the Titan II except adjustable rear sight. Made in U.S. Marketed by Mitchell Arms, Inc. Introduced 1995.

New: $325 **Perf:** $300 **Exc:** $250

MITCHELL ARMS TROPHY II

Semi-automatic; single action; 22 LR; 10-shot magazine; 5-1/2-inch bull, 7-1/4-inch fluted barrel; 9 3/4-inch overall length (5-1/2-inch barrel); weighs 44-1/2 oz.; checkered walnut thumbrest grips; undercut ramp front sight, click-adjustable frame-mounted rear; grip feel of military 45; positive action magazine latch; front and backstraps stippled; trigger adjustable for pull, over-travel; gold-filled roll marks, gold-plated trigger, safety, magazine release; push-button barrel takedown; stainless or blue finish. Made 1992 only.

New: $500 **Perf:** $400 **Exc:** $325

MITCHELL ARMS VICTOR II

Semi-automatic; single action; 22 LR; 10-shot magazine; 4-1/2-inch vent rib, 5-1/2-inch vent, dovetail or Weaver rib barrels; 9-3/4-inch overall length; weighs 44 oz.; military-type checkered walnut thumbrest or rubber grips; blade front sight, fully-adjustable rear mounted on rib; push-button takedown for barrel interchangeability; bright stainless steel combo or royal blue finish. Introduced 1994.

With 4-1/2-inch vent rib barrel

New: $500 **Perf:** $450 **Exc:** $400

With 5-1/2-inch dovetail rib barrel

New: $550 **Perf:** $500 **Exc:** $450

With 5-1/2-inch Weaver rib barrel

New: $550 **Perf:** $500 **Exc:** $450

MKE KIRIKKALE

Semi-automatic; double action; 32 ACP, 380 ACP; 8-shot magazine (32 ACP), 7-shot (380 ACP); 4-inch barrel; 6-1/2-inch overall length; adjustable notch rear sight, fixed front; checkered plastic grips; exposed hammer; safety blocks firing pin, drops hammer; chamber-loaded indicator pin; blued finish. Copy of Walther PP. Imported from Turkey by Firearms Center, Inc., then by Mandall Shooting Supplies; no longer imported.

Exc: $250 **VGood:** $200 **Good:** $175

MOA MAXIMUM

Single shot; falling block action; 28 standard chamberings from 22 to 44 caliber; 8-3/4-inch, 10-3/4-inch, 14-inch interchangeable barrel; ramp front sight, fully-adjustable open rear; drilled and tapped for scope mounts; integral grip frame/receiver; smooth walnut stocks, forend; adjustable trigger; Armaloy finish. Introduced 1983.

New: $650 **Perf:** $550 **Exc:** $475

MORINI MODEL CM-80

Single shot; 22 LR; 10-inch free-floating barrel; 21-1/4-inch overall length; weighs 30 oz.; adjustable or wrap-around stocks; adjustable match sights; adjustable grip/frame angle; adjustable barrel alignment; adjustable trigger weight, sight radius. Made in Switzerland. Introduced 1985; importation discontinued 1989.

Perf: $850 **Exc:** $750 **VGood:** $700

Nagant Model 1895 Training Model

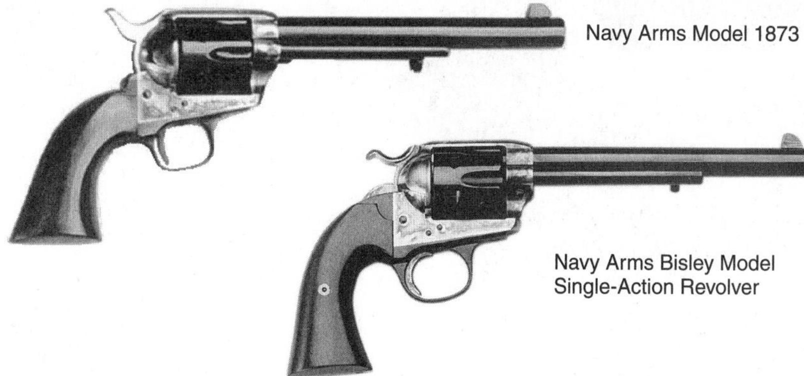

Navy Arms Model 1873

Navy Arms Bisley Model Single-Action Revolver

Nagant Model 1895

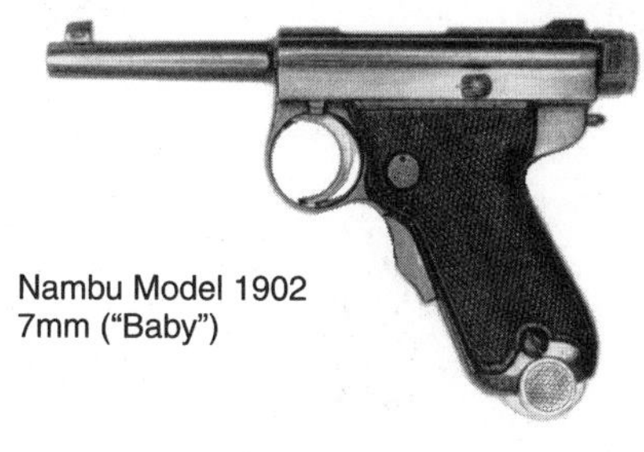

Nambu Model 1902 7mm ("Baby")

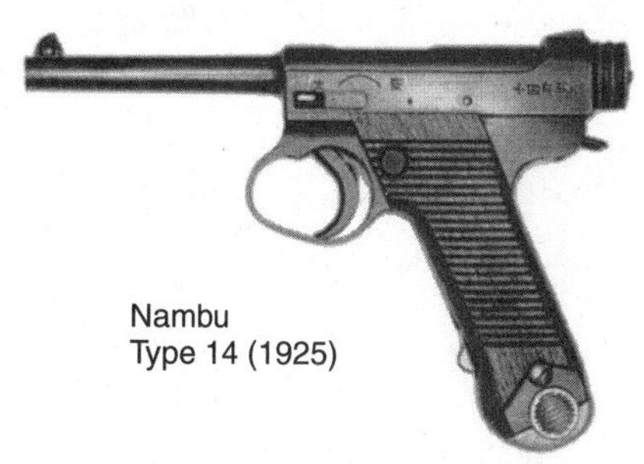

Nambu Type 14 (1925)

MORINI MODEL CM-80 SUPER COMPETITION

Same specs as Model CM-80 except deluxe finish; plexiglass front sighting system.

Perf: $1000 **Exc:** $850 **VGood:** $750

MORINI MODEL 84E FREE PISTOL

Single shot; 22 LR; 11-7/16-inch barrel; 19-1/2-inch overall length; weighs 44 oz.; adjustable match-type grip with stippled surfaces; interchangeable blade front sight, match-type fully-adjustable rear; fully-adjustable electronic trigger. Imported from Switzerland by Nygord Precision Products. Introduced 1995; still imported.

New: $1250 **Perf:** $1100 **Exc:** $1000

MOSSBERG ABILENE

Revolver; single action; 357 Mag., 44 Mag., 45 Colt; 6-shot cylinder; 4-5/8-inch, 6-inch, 7-1/2-inch barrel; serrated ramp front sight, click-adjustable rear; smooth walnut grips; wide hammer spur; transfer bar ignition; blued or Magnaloy finish. Introduced 1978 by United States Arms; taken over by Mossberg; not currently in production.

Exc: $250 **VGood:** $200 **Good:** $175

Magnaloy finish

Exc: $275 **VGood:** $225 **Good:** $200

MOSSBERG BROWNIE

Pocket pistol; top-break; double action; 22 LR, 22 Short; 4-shot; four 2-1/2-inch barrels; revolving firing pin; steel extractor. Introduced in 1919; discontinued 1932. Most found with well-worn finish; premium for VGood+ specimens.

Exc: $475 **VGood:** $370 **Good:** $300

MPA 380

Caliber: 380 ACP, DAO pistol with 5+1 magazine capacity. Barrel length, 2 inches; weight, 29 oz., overall length, 6.7 inches. Machined aluminum grips with a bead blasted finish. Fixed low-profile dovetail-mounted 3-dot sights.

Perf: $310 **Exc:** $265 **VGood:** $235

NAGANT MODEL 1895

Revolver; 7.62mm Nagant; 4-1/4-inch barrel; 9-3/16-inch overall length; 7-shot cylinder; checkered wood grips. Unique gas-seal action cams the cylinder forward to mate with end of barrel before firing. Russian military issue from 1895 to 1944.

Exc: $225 **VGood:** $195 **Good:** $150

NAGANT MODEL 1895 TRAINING MODEL

Same specs as Model 1895 except 22 LR for training purposes. Conversions from 7.62mm revolver (scarce) or arsenal manufactured in 1937 on 7.62mm frames (rare).

Exc: $600 **VGood:** $500 **Good:** $400

NAMBU MODEL 1902 FIRST TYPE ("GRANDPA")

Semi-automatic; 8mm Nambu; 8-shot magazine; 4-3/4-inch barrel; 9-inch overall lengh; adjustable rear (tangent) and front sights; blued finish; checkered wood grips and magazine bottom; grip safety; rear of frame slotted for shoulder-stock holster. Introduced 1903; discontinued 1906. Add $3500 for original (beware of reproductions!) shoulder-stock holster.

Exc: $4500 **VGood:** $3500 **Good:** $2500

NAMBU MODEL 1902 SECOND TYPE ("PAPA")

Semi-automatic; same specs as first type except not slotted (except first few hundred) for or supplied with shoulder-stock holster; aluminum bottom instead of wood bottom magazine; flexible instead of fixed lanyard ring. Introduced 1906; discontinued 1928.

Exc: $1500 **VGood:** $1000 **Good:** $700

NAMBU MODEL 1902 7MM ("BABY")

Semi-automatic; 7mm Nambu; 7-shot magazine; 3-1/4-inch barrel; 6-3/4-inch overall length; fixed rear, adjustable front sights; blued finish, checkered wood grips; grip safety. Introduced 1903; dropped 1929.

Exc: $2500 **VGood:** $1750 **Good:** $1250

NAMBU TYPE 14 (1925)

Semi-automatic; 8mm Nambu; 8-shot magazine; 4-5/8-inch barrel; 9-inch overall length; fixed rear, adjustable front sights; blued finish; grooved wood grips. Introduced 1926; discontinued 1945. Very early production brings a small premium price.

Exc: $500 **VGood:** $400 **Good:** $300

NAMBU TYPE 26 REVOLVER

Revolver; 9mm Japanese; 6-shot; 4-3/4-inch barrel; 9-inch overall length; fixed sights; blued finish; checkered or grooved (rare late production) wood grips. Introduced 1893; discontinued 1935.

Exc: $500 **VGood:** $400 **Good:** $300

NAMBU TYPE 94

Semi-automatic; 8mm Nambu; 6-shot magazine; 3-3/4-inch barrel; 7-5/16-inch overall length; fixed rear, adjustable front sights; blued finish; checkered plastic or smooth wood (late war) grips. Introduced 1935; discontinued 1945.

Exc: $500 **VGood:** $375 **Good:** $250

NAVY ARMS 1873 SINGLE-ACTION REVOLVER

Caliber: 357 Mag., 44-40, 45 Colt, 6-shot cylinder. Barrel: 3-inch, 4-3/4-inch, 5-1/2-inch, 7-1/2-inch. Weight: 36 oz. Length: 10-3/4-inch overall (5-1/2-inch barrel). Stocks: Smooth walnut. Sights: Blade front, groove in topstrap rear. Features: Blue with color case-hardened frame, or nickel. Introduced 1991. Imported by Navy Arms.

Perf: $350 **Exc:** $275 **VGood:** $200

Nickel finish

Perf: $375 **Exc:** $300 **VGood:** $225

1873 U.S. Cavalry Model (7-1/2-inch, 45 Colt, arsenal markings) or Artillery Model, 5-1/2-inch).

Perf: $350 **Exc:** $275 **VGood:** $200

NAVY ARMS BISLEY MODEL SINGLE-ACTION REVOLVER

Caliber: 44-40 or 45 Colt, 6-shot cylinder. Barrel: 4-3/4-inch, 5-1/2-inch, 7-1/2-inch Weight: 40 oz. Length: 12-1/2-inch overall (7-1/2-inch barrel). Stocks: Smooth walnut. Sights: Blade front, notch rear. Polished blue finish, color case-hardened frame. Introduced 1997. Imported by Navy Arms.

Perf: $350 **Exc:** $275 **VGood:** $200

New Advantage Derringer

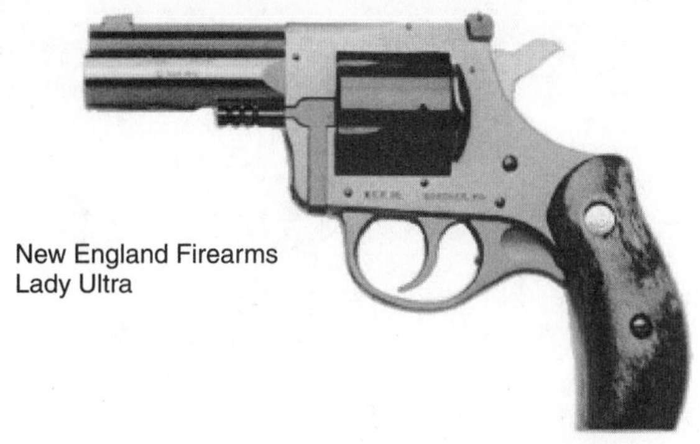
New England Firearms Lady Ultra

New England Firearms Model R92

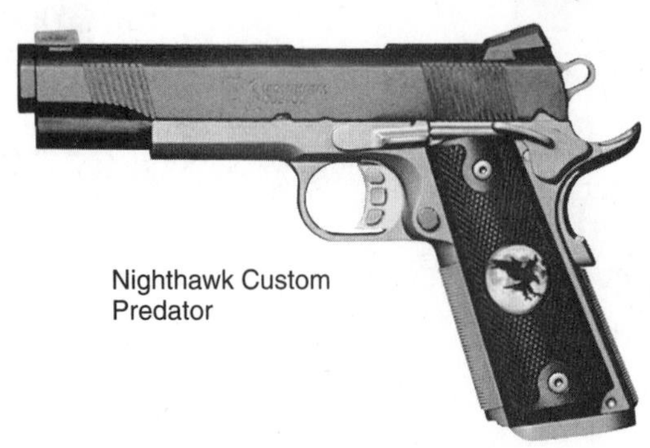
Nighthawk Custom Predator

NAVY ARMS FLAT TOP TARGET MODEL REVOLVER

Caliber: 45 Colt, 6-shot cylinder. Barrel: 7-1/2-inch. Weight: 40 oz. Length: 13-1/4-inch overall. Stocks: Smooth walnut. Sights: Spring-loaded German silver front, rear adjustable for windage. Blue with color case-hardened frame. Introduced 1997. Imported by Navy Arms.

Perf: $350 **Exc:** $275 **VGood:** $200

NAVY ARMS FRONTIER MODEL

Revolver; single action; 357 Mag., 45 Colt; 6-shot cylinder; 4-1/2-inch, 5-1/2-inch, 7-1/2-inch barrel; fixed sights; uncheckered one-piece walnut grip; brass grip frame; color case-hardened frame; blued barrel and cylinder. Manufactured in Italy. Introduced 1976; discontinued 1978.

Exc: $300 **VGood:** $225 **Good:** $175

NAVY ARMS FRONTIER, BUNTLINE MODEL

Same specs as Frontier except 16-1/2-inch barrel; detachable shoulder stock.

Exc: $450 **VGood:** $375 **Good:** $300

NAVY ARMS GRAND PRIX

Single shot; rolling block; 44 Mag., 30-30, 7mm Spl., 45-70; 13-3/4-inch barrel; weighs 64 oz.; adjustable target sights; walnut forend, thumbrest grip; adjustable aluminum barrel rib; matte blue finish. Introduced 1983; discontinued 1985.

Exc: $275 **VGood:** $225 **Good:** $185

NAVY ARMS HIGH POWER

Semi-automatic; single action; 9mm Para.; 13-shot magazine; 4-5/8-inch barrel; fixed sights; black plastic grips; similar to older FN manufacture; blued finish. Introduced 1993; no longer in production.

New: $350 **Perf:** $275 **Exc:** $200

NAVY ARMS LUGER

Semi-automatic; 22 LR; 10-shot magazine; 4-inch, 6-inch, 8-inch barrel; 9-inch overall length; weighs 44 oz.; fixed sights; checkered walnut stocks; all-steel construction; blowback toggle action; blued finish. Made in U.S. Introduced 1986; discontinued 1987.

Exc: $375 **VGood:** $300 **Good:** $200

NAVY ARMS MODEL 1873

Revolver; single action; 44-40, 45 Colt; 6-shot cylinder; 3-inch, 4-3/4-inch, 5-1/2-inch, 7-1/2-inch barrels; 10-3/4-inch overall length (5-1/2-inch barrel); weighs 47 oz.; blade front sight, grooved rear; uncheckered walnut grips; nickel or blued finish with color case-hardened frame. Made in Italy. Introduced 1991; still imported.

New: $325 **Perf:** $275 **Exc:** $225

Nickel

New: $375 **Perf:** $325 **Exc:** $275

NAVY ARMS MODEL 1873, ECONOMY MODEL

Same specs as standard Model 1873 single action except brass trigger guard, backstrap; two piece walnut grip. Introduced 1993; dropped 1996.

New: $250 **Perf:** $200 **Exc:** $175

NAVY ARMS MODEL 1875 REMINGTON

Revolver; single action; 44-40, 45 Colt; 6-shot cylinder; 7-1/2-inch barrel; 13-inch overall length; weighs 41 oz.; blade front sight, grooved rear; uncheckered walnut grips; color case-hardened frame; brass trigger guard; balance blued finish. Made in Italy. Introduced 1991; discontinued 1992; resumed 1994; discontinued 1995.

New: $350 **Perf:** $275 **Exc:** $225

NAVY ARMS MODEL 1875 SCHOFIELD WELLS FARGO MODEL

Revolver; single action; 44-40, 45 Colt; 6-shot cylinder; 5-inch barrel; 10-3/4-inch overall length; weighs 39 oz.; smooth walnut grips; blade front sight, notch rear; replica of Smith & Wesson Model 3 Schofield; top-break action with automatic ejection; polished blue finish. Imported by Navy Arms. Introduced 1994; still imported.

New: $600 **Perf:** $500 **Exc:** $400

NAVY ARMS MODEL 1875 SCHOFIELD U.S. CAVALRY MODEL

Same specs as the Wells Fargo model except 7-inch barrel; original-type military markings. Imported by Navy Arms. Introduced 1994; still imported.

New: $600 **Perf:** $500 **Exc:** $400

NAVY ARMS MODEL 1890 REMINGTON

Revolver; single action; 44-40; 6-shot cylinder; 5-1/2 inch barrel; 10-3/4-inch overall length; weighs 39 oz.; blade front, grooved rear sight; walnut grip; brass trigger guard; lanyard loop; blued finish. Made in Italy. Introduced 1991; discontinued 1992; resumed 1994; discontinued 1995.

New: $350 **Perf:** $275 **Exc:** $225

NAVY ARMS "PINCHED FRAME" SINGLE-ACTION REVOLVER

Caliber: 45 Colt. Barrel: 7-1/2-inch. Weight: 37 oz. Length: 13-inch overall. Stocks: Smooth walnut Sights: German silver blade, notch rear. Features: Replica of Colt's original Peacemaker. Color case-hardened frame, hammer, rest charcoal blued. Introduced 1997.

Perf: $350 **Exc:** $275 **VGood:** $20

NAVY ARMS ROLLING BLOCK

Single shot; 22 LR, 22 Hornet, 357 Mag.; 8-inch barrel; 12-inch overall length; adjustable sights; uncheckered walnut stocks, forearm; color case-hardened frame; brass trigger guard; blued barrel. Manufactured in Italy. Introduced 1965; Hornet chambering discontinued 1975; 22 LR discontinued 1979. No longer imported.

Exc: $350 **VGood:** $300 **Good:** $175

NAVY ARMS TT-OLYMPIA

Semi-automatic; single action; 22 LR; 4-5/8-inch barrel; 8-inch overall length; weighs 28 oz.; checkered hardwood grips; blade front sight, windage-adjustable rear; reproduction of the Walther Olympia pistol; polished blue finish. Imported by Navy Arms. Introduced 1992; no longer imported.

New: $275 **Perf:** $225 **Exc:** $175

NAVY ARMS TU-90

Semi-automatic; single action; 30 Tokarev, 9mm Para.; 8-shot magazine; 4-1/2-inch barrel; weighs 30 oz.; wrap-around synthetic grip; similar to TT-33 Tokarev. Made in China. Introduced 1992; no longer imported.

New: $305 **Perf:** $275 **Exc:** $250

NEW ENGLAND FIREARMS R92

Nighthawk Custom Talon

NEW ENGLAND FIREARMS R73

Norinco Type 54-1 Tokarev

NAVY ARMS TU-711 MAUSER

Semi-automatic; 9mm Para.; 10-, 20-shot magazine; 5-1/4-inch barrel; weighs 43 oz.; similar to Mauser 711. Introduced 1992; discontinued 1992.

Perf: $550 **Exc:** $500 **VGood:** $450

NAVY ARMS U.S. GOVERNMENT MODEL

Semi-automatic; 45 ACP; 7-shot; 5-inch barrel; fixed sights; checkered walnut grips; standard G.I. 1911 issue pistol; blue finish. Introduced 1993; no longer in production.

New: $375 **Perf:** $300 **Exc:** $250

NEW ADVANTAGE DERRINGER

Double action; 22 LR, 22 WMR; 4-shot; four 2-1/2-inch barrels; 4-1/2-inch overall length; weighs 15 oz.; fixed sights; smooth walnut stocks; revolving firing pin; rebounding hammer; polished blue finish. Reintroduced, 1989 by New Advantage Arms Corp.

Perf: $175 **Exc:** $150 **VGood:** $135

NEW DETONICS LADIES ESCORT

Semi-automatic; single action; 45 ACP; 6-shot magazine; 3-1/2-inch barrel; 4-1/2-inch overall length; weighs 26 oz.; checkered walnut grips; rubber mainspring housing; ramp front sight, adjustable rear; reduced grip frame size; color polymer finish. Made in U.S. by New Detonics Corp. Introduced 1990; dropped 1991. Very few made.

Royal Escort, iridescent purple slide, blackened stainless frame, gold-plated hammer and trigger

Perf: $750 **Exc:** $650 **VGood:** $500

Jade Escort, jade-colored slide, satin stainless frame

Perf: $750 **Exc:** $650 **VGood:** $500

Midnight Escort, black slide, satin stainless frame

Perf: $800 **Exc:** $700 **VGood:** $600

NEW ENGLAND FIREARMS LADY ULTRA

Revolver; double action; 32 H&R Mag.; 5-shot cylinder; 3-inch barrel; 7-1/4-inch overall length; weighs 31 oz.; walnut-finished hardwood grips with NEF medallion; blade front sight, fully-adjustable rear; swing-out cylinder; polished blue finish; comes with lockable storage case. From New England Firearms Co. Introduced 1992; dropped 1999.

New: $300 **Perf:** $250 **Exc:** $200

NEW ENGLAND FIREARMS MODEL R73

Revolver; double action; 32 H&R Mag.; 5-shot cylinder; 3-inch barrel; 7-1/4-inch overall length; weighs 31 oz.; walnut finished American hardwood grips with NEF medallion; fixed sights; blue or nickel finish. From New England Firearms Co. Introduced 1988; dropped 1999.

New: $300 **Perf:** $250 **Exc:** $200

NEW ENGLAND FIREARMS MODEL R92

Revolver; double action; 22 LR; 9-shot cylinder; 2-1/2-inch, 4-inch barrel; 8-1/2-inch overall length (4-inch barrel); weighs 26 oz.; walnut-finished American hardwood grips with NEF medallion; fixed sights; blue or nickel finish. From New England Firearms Co. Introduced 1988; dropped 1999.

New: $175 **Perf:** $150 **Exc:** $125

NEW ENGLAND FIREARMS SINGLE SHOT

Single shot; rotary cannon-type action; 357 Mag., 357 Rem. Maximum, 44 Mag., 223, 30-30, 7-30 Waters, 35 Rem.; 14-inch barrel; 15-1/8-inch overall length; weighs 49 oz. (synthetic stock), 70 oz. (laminated wood); ramp front sight, adjustable rear; action cocks on opening; single stage trigger; trigger and sliding thumb safeties; matte blue finish. Made by Competitor Corp. Marketed by New England Firearms. Introduced 1995; still produced.

New: $350 **Perf:** $300 **Exc:** $275

NEW ENGLAND FIREARMS ULTRA

Revolver; double action; 22 LR, 22 WMR; 9-shot (22 LR), 6-shot (22 WMR); 4-inch, 6-inch barrel; 10 5/8-inch overall length (6-inch barrel); weighs 36 oz.; walnut-finished hardwood grips with NEF medallion; blade front sight, fully-adjustable rear; bull-style barrel with recessed muzzle; high "Lustre" blue/black finish. Made in U.S. by New England Firearms. Introduced 1989; dropped 1999.

New: $175 **Perf:** $150 **Exc:** $125

NIGHTHAWK CUSTOM TALON

1911-style .45 ACP semi-auto with 5-inch or 4.25-inch barrel and fixed or adjustable sights. Several other barrel lengths/finishes available.

New: $2100 **Exc:** $1750 **VGood:** $1475

NIGHTHAWK CUSTOM PREDATOR

1911-style .45 ACP semi-auto with 5-inch barrel or 4.25-inch and fixed or adjustable sights. Several other barrel lengths/finishes available.

New: $2500 **Exc:** $2150 **VGood:** $1775

NIGHTHAWK GRP

Global Response Pistol. 1911-style .45 ACP semi-auto with 5-inch or 4.25-inch barrel and fixed or adjustable sights. Several other barrel lengths/ finishes available.

New: $2400 **Exc:** $1950 **VGood:** $1550

NORINCO MODEL 1911A1

Semi-automatic; single action; 45 ACP; 7-shot magazine; 5-inch barrel; 8-1/2-inch overall length; weighs 39 oz.; checkered wood grips; blade front sight, windage-adjustable rear; matte blue finish. Comes with two magazines. Imported from China by China Sports, Inc.; dropped 1995.

New: $400 **Perf:** $350 **Exc:** $300

NORINCO MODEL 77B

Semi-automatic; single action; 9mm Para.; 8-shot magazine; 5-inch barrel; 7-1/2-inch overall length; weighs 34 oz.; checkered wood grips; blade front sight, adjustable rear; gas-retarded recoil action; front of trigger guard able to cock the action with the trigger finger. Imported from China as the NP-20. Introduced 1989; dropped 1995; few imported.

Perf: $350 **Exc:** $275 **VGood:** $200

NORINCO TYPE 54-1 TOKAREV

Semi-automatic; single action; 7.62x25mm, 9mm Para.; 8-shot magazine; 4-1/2-inch barrel; 7-3/4-inch overall length; weighs 29 oz.; grooved black plastic

North American Arms Single-Action Revolver

Norinco Type 59 Makarov

North American Arms Guardian

North American Arms Mini-Master Black Widow

North American Arms Model 22 LR

Olympic Arms Constable

grips; fixed sights; matte blue finish. Imported from China; dropped 1995.

Perf: $300 **Exc:** $275 **VGood:** $225

NORINCO TYPE 59 MAKAROV

Semi-automatic; double action; 9x18mm, 380 ACP; 8-shot magazine; 3-1/2-inch barrel; weighs 21 oz.; 6-3/8-inch overall length; checkered plastic grips; blade front sight, adjustable rear; blue finish. Direct copy of Russian-made pistol. Imported from China. Introduced 1990; dropped 1995.

Perf: $300 **Exc:** $250 **VGood:** $200

NORTH AMERICAN ARMS GUARDIAN

Caliber: 380, 32 NAA, 32 ACP or 25 NAA, 6-shot magazine. Barrel: 2.1-inch. Weight: 13.5 oz. Length: 4.36-inch overall. Stocks: Black polymer. Sights: Fixed. Features: Doube-action-only mechanism. All stainless steel construction; snag-free. Introduced 1998. Made in U.S. by North American Arms.

Perf: $400 **Exc:** $350 **VGood:** $300

NORTH AMERICAN ARMS MINI-MASTER BLACK WIDOW

Revolver; single action; 22 LR, 22 WMR; 5-shot cylinder; 2-inch heavy vent barrel; 5-7/8-inch overall length; weighs 8-7/8 oz.; black rubber grips; Millett Low Profile fixed sights or Millett sight adjustable for elevation only; built on the 22 WMR frame; non-fluted cylinder. Made in U.S. by North American Arms. Introduced 1989; still produced.

With adjustable sight

New: $225 **Perf:** $185 **Exc:** $150

With adjustable sight, extra LR/WMR cylinder

New: $250 **Perf:** $235 **Exc:** $200

With fixed sight

New: $185 **Perf:** $175 **Exc:** $150

With fixed sight, extra LR/WMR cylinder

New: $275 **Perf:** $250 **Exc:** $200

NORTH AMERICAN ARMS MINI-MASTER TARGET

Revolver; single action; 22 LR, 22 WMR; 5-shot; heavy vent-rib 4-inch barrel; 7-3/4-inch overall length; weighs 10-3/4 oz.; blade-type front sight, elevation-adjustable white-outline rear; checkered hard black rubber stocks. Introduced 1989; still in production.

New: $235 **Perf:** $210 **Exc:** $190

NORTH AMERICAN ARMS MODEL 22 LR

Revolver; single action; 22 Short, 22 LR; 5-shot; 1-1/8-inch, 1-5/8-inch, 2-1/2-inch barrel; 3-7/8-inch overall length; weighs 4-1/2 oz.; fixed sights; plastic or rosewood grips; stainless steel construction. Introduced 1976; still in production.

New: $190 **Perf:** $175 **Exc:** $140

NORTH AMERICAN ARMS MODEL 22 MAGNUM

Revolver; single action; 22 WMR; 5-shot; 1-1/8-inch, 1-5/8-inch, 2-1/2-inch barrel; 3-7/8-inch overall length; weighs 4-1/2 oz.; fixed sights; plastic or rosewood grips; stainless steel construction. Introduced 1976; still in production.

New: $220 **Perf:** $180 **Exc:** $160

NORTH AMERICAN ARMS MODEL 22 MAGNUM CONVERTIBLE

Same specs as 22 Magnum, except supplied with extra 22 LR cylinder.

New: $250 **Perf:** $200 **Exc:** $175

NORTH AMERICAN ARMS SINGLE ACTION REVOLVER

Revolver; single action; 45 Win. Mag., 450 Mag. Express; 5-shot; 7-1/2-inch, 10-1/2-inch barrel; weighs 52 oz.; adjustable rear sight, blade front; uncheckered walnut stocks; stainless steel construction; matte finish. Introduced 1984; discontinued 1985.

Perf: $1100 **Exc:** $850 **VGood:** $750

High polish finish

Perf: $1350 **Exc:** $1000 **VGood:** $850

NORTH AMERICAN ARMS VIPER BELT BUCKLE

Revolver; single action; 22 LR; 5-shot; 1-1/8-inch, 1-5/8-inch barrel; weighs 4-1/2 oz.; fixed sights; plastic or rosewood grips; belt buckle with built-in revolver; stainless steel construction. Introduced 1976; discontinued 1990; reintroduced 1993; no longer in production.

New: $250 **Perf:** $225 **Exc:** $190

ODI VIKING

Semi-automatic; double action; 45 ACP; 7-shot; 5-inch barrel; weighs 39 oz.; fixed notched rear sight, blade front; smooth teak stocks; Seecamp double-action system; spur-type hammer; stainless steel construction; brushed satin finish. Introduced 1982; discontinued 1985.

Perf: $450 **Exc:** $400 **VGood:** $350

OLYMPIC ARMS OA-96 AR PISTOL

Caliber: 223. Barrel: 6-inch, 4140 chromemoly steel. Weight: 5 lbs. Length: 15-3/4-inch overall. Stocks: A2 stowaway pistol grip; no buttstock or receiver tube. Sights: Flat-top upper receiver, cut-down front sight base. Features: AR-15-type receivers with special bolt carrier; short aluminum hand guard; Vortex flash hider. Introduced 1996.

Perf: $850 **Exc:** $675 **VGood:** $500

OLYMPIC ARMS SCHUETZEN PISTOL WORKS BIG DEUCE

Semi-automatic; single action; 45 ACP; 7-shot magazine; 6-inch barrel; 9-1/2-inch overall length; weighs 40 oz.; smooth walnut grips; ramped blade front sight, LPA adjustable rear; stainless steel barrel; beavertail grip safety; extended thumb safety and slide release; Commander-style hammer; throated, polished and tuned; Parkerized matte black slide with satin stainless steel frame. Made in U.S. by Olympic Arms, Inc.'s specialty shop Schuetzen Pistol Works. Marked "Schuetzen Pistol Works" on the slide; "Safari Arms" on the frame. Introduced 1995; still produced.

New: $700 **Perf:** $600 **Exc:** $500

OLYMPIC ARMS SCHUETZEN PISTOL WORKS CREST SERIES

Semi-automatic; single action; 45 ACP; 6-, 7-shot magazine; 4-1/2-inch (4-star), 5-inch, 5-1/2-inch barrel; 8-1/2-inch overall length; weighs 39 oz.;

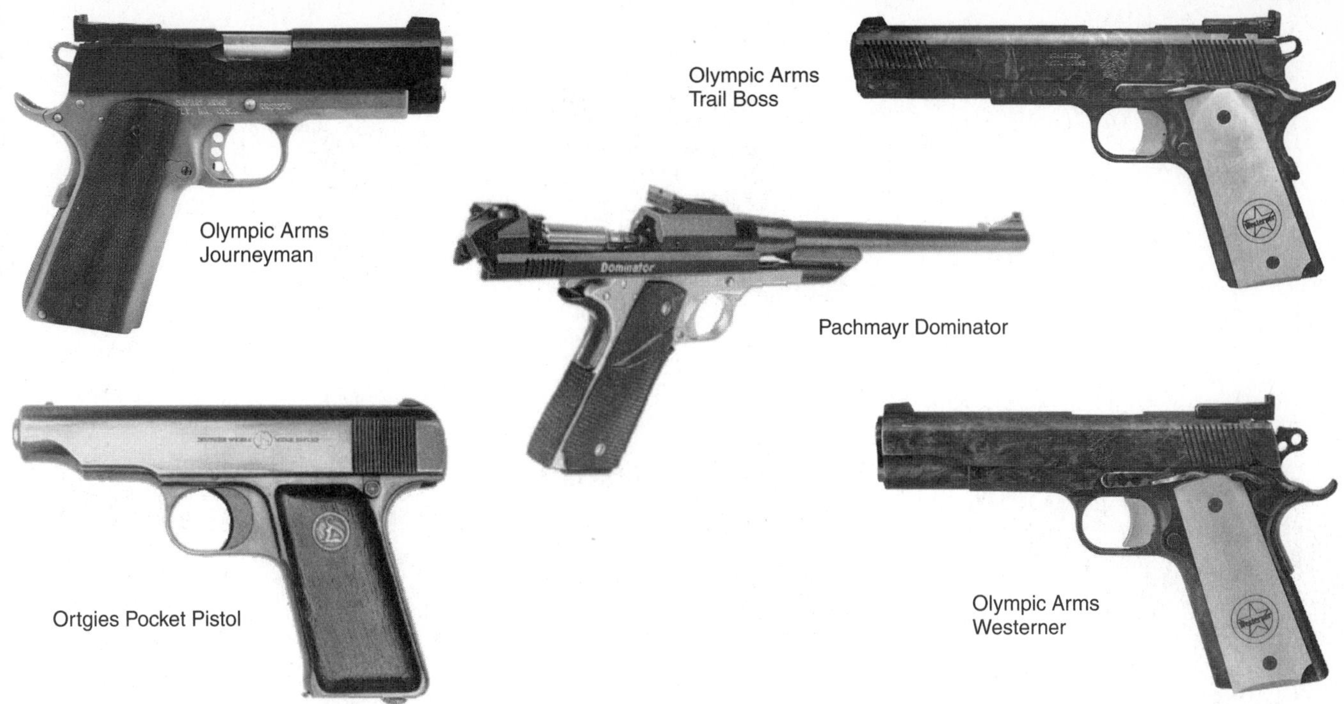
Olympic Arms Journeyman

Olympic Arms Trail Boss

Pachmayr Dominator

Ortgies Pocket Pistol

Olympic Arms Westerner

checkered walnut grips; ramped blade front sight, LPA adjustable rear; stainless steel barrel; right- or left-hand models available; long aluminum trigger; full-length recoil spring guide; throated, polished, tuned; satin stainless steel. Made in U.S. by Olympic Arms, Inc.'s specialty shop Schuetzen Pistol Works. Marked "Schuetzen Pistol Works" on the slide; "Safari Arms" on the frame. Introduced 1993; still produced.

Right-hand

Perf: $650 **Exc:** $600 **VGood:** $550

Left-hand

Perf: $750 **Exc:** $700 **VGood:** $650

OLYMPIC ARMS SCHUETZEN PISTOL WORKS GRIFFON

Semi-automatic; single action; 45 ACP; 10-shot magazine; 5-inch barrel; 8-1/2-inch overall length; smooth walnut grips; ramped blade front sight, LPA adjustable rear; stainless barrel; beavertail grip safety; long aluminum trigger; full-length recoil spring guide; Commander-style hammer; throated, polished and tuned; grip size comparable to standard 1911; satin stainless steel finish. Made in U.S. by Olympic Arms, Inc.'s specialty shop Schuetzen Pistol Works. Marked "Schuetzen Pistol Works" on the slide; "Safari Arms" on the frame. Introduced 1995; still produced.

Perf: $750 **Exc:** $625 **VGood:** $500

OLYMPIC ARMS BLACK-TAC

Semi-auto .45 ACP pistol treated with "black-tac" process – advantages of hard chrome without its drawbacks such as embrittlement.

New: $800 **Exc:** $700 **VGood:** $575

OLYMPIC ARMS CONSTABLE

Semi-auto pistol chambered for .45 ACP with 4-inch barrel, 5.75-inch sight radius, 7+1 capacity, 35 oz.

New: $900 **Exc:** $800 **VGood:** $675

OLYMPIC ARMS CUSTOM STREET DEUCE

Semi-auto chambered for .45 ACP with 5.2-inch bull barrel, 7-inch sight radius, 7+1 capacity, 38 oz. Many options.

New: $1200 **Exc:** $1100 **VGood:** $775

OLYMPIC ARMS CUSTOM JOURNEYMAN

Semi-auto chambered for .45 ACP with 4-inch bull barrel, 6-inch sight radius, 6+1 capacity, 35 oz. Many options.

New: $1200 **Exc:** $1100 **VGood:** $775

OLYMPIC ARMS TRAIL BOSS

Semi-auto pistol in the Westerner line chambered for .45 ACP. 6-inch barrel, 8-inch sight radius, 7+1 capacity, 43 oz.

New: $895 **Exc:** $775 **VGood:** $600

OLYMPIC ARMS WESTERNER

Semi-auto pistol chambered for .45 ACP with 5-inch barrel, 7-inch sight radius, 7+1 capacity, 39 oz.

New: $800 **Exc:** $675 **VGood:** $545

OLYMPIC ARMS WOLVERINE

Polymer-frame, vent-rib replica of the old "ray gun" .22 Whitney Wolverine semi-auto pistol. Cool, baby!

New: $275 **Perf:** $250 **Exc:** $225

ONE PRO .45 AUTO

Semi-automatic; double action; 45 ACP or 400 Corbon, 10-shot magazine. Barrel: 3.75-inch Weight: 31.1 oz. Length: 7.04-inch overall. Stocks: Textured composition. Sights: Blade front, drift-adjustable rear; three-dot system. Features: All-steel construction; decocking lever and automatic firing pin lock; DA or DAO operation. Introduced 1997. Imported from Switzerland by Magnum Research, Inc.

New: $550 **Perf:** $450 **Exc:** $400

Conversion kit, 45 ACP/400, 400/45 ACP

New: $200 **Perf:** $175 **Exc:** $150

ONE PRO 9 AUTO

Semi-automatic; double action; 9mm Para., 10-shot magazine. Barrel: 3.01-inch. Weight: 25.1 oz. Length: 6 inches overall. Stocks: Smooth wood. Sights: Blade front, rear adjustable for windage. Features: Rotating barrel; short slide; double recoil springs; double-action mechanism; decocking lever. Introduced 1998. Imported from Switzerland by Magnum Research. Price: NA

ORTGIES POCKET PISTOL

Semi-automatic; blowback action; 32 ACP, 380 ACP; 8-shot (32), 7-shot (380); 3-1/4-inch barrel; 6-1/2-inch overall length; fixed sights; uncheckered walnut grips; constructed without screws, uses pins and spring-loaded catches; grip safety protrudes only when firing pin is cocked; blued finish. Introduced about 1919; discontinued 1926.

Exc: $200 **VGood:** $175 **Good:** $135

Nickel finish

Exc: $300 **VGood:** $250 **Good:** $150

ORTGIES VEST POCKET PISTOL

Semi-automatic; blowback action; 25 ACP; 6-shot; 2-3/4-inch barrel; 5-3/16-inch overall length; fixed sights; uncheckered walnut grips; blued finish. Introduced 1920; discontinued 1926.

Exc: $225 **VGood:** $200 **Good:** $175

Nickel finish

Exc: $275 **VGood:** $250 **Good:** $200

PACHMAYR DOMINATOR

Single shot; bolt action on 1911A1 frame; 22 Hornet, 223, 7mm-06, 308, 35 Rem., 44 Mag.; 10-1/2-inch barrel in 44 Mag., 14-inch all other calibers; weighs 4 lbs. (14-inch barrel); 16-inch overall length; Pachmayr Signature system grips; optional adjustable sights or drilled and tapped for scope mounting. From Pachmayr. Introduced 1988; discontinued 1994.

New: $450 **Perf:** $375 **Exc:** $325

PARA-ORDNANCE P-12.45

Semi-automatic; single action; 45 ACP; 10-shot magazine (pre-1994 guns have 12-shot); 3-1/2-inch barrel; 7-1/8-inch overall length; weighs 34 oz. (steel and stainless frame), 26 oz. (alloy frame); textured composition grips; blade front sight, adjustable rear; high visibility three-dot system; matte black finish; grooved match trigger; rounded combat-style hammer; beveled magazine well; manual thumb, grip and firing pin safeties; solid barrel bushing. Made in Canada by Para-Ordnance. Introduced 1990; still produced. Steel frame, matte black

New: $650 **Perf:** $600 **Exc:** $500

Para-Ordnance P-14.45

Para-Ordnance Tac-Five

Para-Ordnance Nite-Tac .40

Para Ordnance Warthog

Para-Ordnance P-13.45

Para-Ordnance P-16.40

Alloy frame, matte black
New: $600 **Perf:** $550 **Exc:** $450
Stainless frame, stainless
New: $700 **Perf:** $650 **Exc:** $550
Stainless frame, Duotone
New: $685 **Perf:** $635 **Exc:** $575

PARA-ORDNANCE P-13.45

Semi-automatic; single action; 45 ACP; 10-shot magazine (pre-1994 guns have 13-shot); 4-1/4-inch barrel; 7-3/4-inch overall length; weighs 36 oz. (steel and stainless frame), 28 oz. (alloy frame); textured composition grips; blade front sight, adjustable rear; high visibility three-dot system; matte black finish; grooved match trigger; rounded combat-style hammer; beveled magazine well; manual thumb, grip and firing pin safeties; solid barrel bushing. Made in Canada by Para-Ordnance. Introduced 1993; still produced.

Steel frame
New: $650 **Perf:** $600 **Exc:** $500
Alloy frame
New: $600 **Perf:** $550 **Exc:** $450
Stainless frame, stainless
New: $700 **Perf:** $650 **Exc:** $550
Stainless frame, Duotone
New: $685 **Perf:** $635 **Exc:** $575

PARA-ORDNANCE P-14.40

Semi-automatic; single action; 40 S&W; 10-shot magazine; 3-1/2-inch barrel; 7-1/8-inch overall length; weighs 34 oz. (steel frame), 26 oz. (alloy frame); all the rest same as 14.45.

Steel frame
New: $600 **Perf:** $550 **Exc:** $500
Alloy frame
New: $600 **Perf:** $550 **Exc:** $450
Stainless frame, stainless
New: $625 **Perf:** $575 **Exc:** $500
Stainless frame, Duotone
New: $685 **Perf:** $635 **Exc:** $575

PARA-ORDNANCE P-14.45

Semi-automatic; single action; 45 ACP; 10-shot magazine (pre-1994 guns have 14-shot); 5-inch barrel; 8-1/2-inch overall length; weighs 40 oz. (steel frame), 31 oz. (alloy frame); textured composition grips; blade front sight, adjustable rear; high visibility three-dot system; matte black finish; grooved match trigger; rounded combat-style hammer; beveled magazine well; manual thumb, grip and firing pin safeties; solid barrel bushing. Made in Canada by Para-Ordnance. Introduced 1990; still produced.

Steel frame
New: $650 **Perf:** $600 **Exc:** $500
Alloy frame
New: $600 **Perf:** $550 **Exc:** $450
Stainless frame, stainless
New: $700 **Perf:** $650 **Exc:** $550
Stainless frame, Duotone
New: $685 **Perf:** $635 **Exc:** $575

PARA-ORDNANCE P-15.40

Semi-automatic; single action; 40 S&W; 10-shot magazine; 4-1/4-inch barrel; 7-3/4-inch overalllength; weighs 36 oz. (steel frame), 28 oz. (alloy frame); textured composition grips; blade front sight, adjustable rear; high visibility three-dot system; matte black finish; grooved match trigger; rounded combat-style hammer; beveled magazine well; manual thumb, grip and firing pin safeties; solid barrel bushing. Made in Canada by Para-Ordnance. Introduced 1990; still produced.

Steel frame
New: $650 **Perf:** $600 **Exc:** $500
Alloy frame
New: $600 **Perf:** $550 **Exc:** $450
Stainless frame, stainless
New: $700 **Perf:** $650 **Exc:** $550
Stainless frame, Duotone
New: $685 **Perf:** $635 **Exc:** $575

PARA-ORDNANCE P-16.40

Semi-automatic; single action; 40 S&W; 10-shot magazine (pre-1994 guns have 16-shot); 5-inch barrel; 8-1/2-inch overall length; weighs 40 oz. (steel frame); textured composition grips; blade front sight, windage-adjustable rear; high visibility three-dot system; matte black finish; grooved match trigger; rounded combat-style hammer; beveled magazine well; manual thumb, grip and firing pin safeties; solid barrel bushing. Made in Canada by Para-Ordnance. Introduced 1994; still produced.

Steel frame
New: $625 **Perf:** $575 **Exc:** $500
Stainless frame, stainless
New: $650 **Perf:** $600 **Exc:** $525
Stainless frame, Duotone
New: $685 **Perf:** $635 **Exc:** $575

PARA-ORDNANCE S-SERIES LIMITED PISTOLS

Similar to the P-Series pistols except with full-length recoil guide system; fully adjustable rear sight; tuned trigger with overtravel stop; beavertail grip safety; competition hammer; front and rear slide serrations; ambidextrous safety; lowered ejection port; ramped match-grade barrel; dovetailed front sight. Introduced 1998. Made in Canada by Para-Ordnance. Add 20 percent to price of comparable P-Series Model.

PARA-ORDNANCE WARTHOG

Semi-automatic; single action; 45ACP; 10+1 capacity; 3-inch barrel; weighs 24 oz.; 6.5-inch overall length; spurred hammer; 3-dot sights; Regal finish.
New: $725 **Perf:** $675 **Exc:** $600

PARA-ORDNANCE NITE HAWG

Similar to Warthog but with non-reflective black finish and tritium sights.
New: $725 **Perf:** $675 **Exc:** $600

PARA-ORDNANCE 1911 SSP

7+1 capacity .45 ACP 1911-style semi-auto with 5-inch barrel. 39 oz. Competition triggers and hammers. Fixed sights. Cocobolo grip panels.
New: $1000 **Exc:** $895 **VGood:** $725

PARA-ORDNANCE SLIM HAWG

A .45 ACP pistol with 6+1 capacity. Single-stack, single-action 1911. Barrel 3-inch, 30 oz. Stainless construction, checkered wood grips. Fixed, 3-dot sights.
New: $100 **Exc:** $895 **VGood:** $725

Para-Ordnance Slim Hawg

Para-Ordnance USA GI Expert Series "Wild Bunch"

Para-Ordnance Stainless Warthog

Para-Ordnance Nite Hawg

Para-Ordnance Todd Jarrett .45 USPSA

PARA-ORDNANCE STAINLESS WARTHOG

Stainless .45 ACP with 10+1 capacity. Single-stack, single-action 1911. Barrel 3-inch, 31 oz. Fixed, 3-dot sights and plastic grips.

New: $950 **Exc:** $850 **VGood:** $695

PARA-ORDNANCE LITE HAWG 9

Double-stack, 12+1 single-action 9mm Parabellum in non-reflective black finish. Barrel 3-inch, 31.5 oz and capacity. Fixed, 3-dot sights.

New: $1000 **Exc:** $895 **VGood:** $725

PARA-ORDNANCE MIDNIGHT BLUE P14-45

Double-stack, 14+1 single-action 45 ACP in non-reflective black. 5-inch barrel, fixed, 3-dot sights and black plastic grips.

New: $850 **Exc:** $775 **VGood:** $650

PARA-ORDNANCE TODD JARRETT .40 USPSA

A limited edition 16+1 (or 10+1) .40 S&W custom competition pistol with adjustable rear sight and fiber optic front sight. 5-inch barrel, 40 oz., covert non-reflective black or sterling.

New: $1525 **Exc:** $1395 **VGood:** $1125

PARA-ORDNANCE TODD JARRETT .45 USPSA

Limited edition 8+1 .45 ACP caliber custom competition pistol with adjustable rear sight and fiber optic front sight. 5-inch barrel, 39 oz.; covert non-reflective black or stainless finish.

New: $995 **Exc:** $895 **VGood:** $675

PARA-ORDNANCE TAC-FIVE

Light double-action 9mm with 18+1 capacity. 5-inch barrel, 37.5 oz., stainless finish, adjustable rear sight, plastic grips.

New: $1100 **Exc:** $975 **VGood:** $795

PARA-ORDNANCE NITE-TAC .40

A .40 S&W 16+1 capacity double-action duty pistol with fixed sights. 5-inch barrel, 40 oz., stainless finish.

New: $1075 **Exc:** $975 **VGood:** $800

PARA-ORDNANCE NITE-TAC 9

A 9mm 18+1 double-action duty pistol with fixed sights. 5-inch barrel, 40 oz., stainless finish.

New: $1075 **Exc:** $975 **VGood:** $800

PARA-ORDNANCE LTC

Semi-auto; single action; .45ACP; 7+1 capacity; 4.25-inch barrel; 35 oz. weight; 7.75 inches overall; 3-dot sights; steel frame; Regal finish.

New: $725 **Perf:** $675 **Exc:** $600

PARA USA GI EXPERT SERIES

Caliber: 45 ACP, basic 1911-style pistol with standard dimensions. Checkered polymer grips, fixed 3-dot sights, lowered and flared ejection port, beveled mag well, flat mainspring housing. Capacity is 8+1. LTC model has 4.25-inch barrel, fiber optic sights, spur hammer. The 100th Anniversary edition has smooth cocobolo grips, three-dot sights, special slide markings, covert black finish.

Perf: $595 **Exc:** $525 **VGood:** $450

Add 25 percent for LTC model, 50 percent for Anniversary model

PARA USA WARTHOG SERIES

Caliber: 9mm or 45 ACP, in various 1911 sizes. Single or double-stack magazines with capacity from 6 to 12 rounds. Barrel: 3 inches (3.5, Hawg 7). Weight: 24 to 31.5 oz. All have fiber optic sights, Regal or stainless finish. Prices shown are for standard Warthog with Regal finish.

Perf: $875 **Exc:** $765 **VGood:** $650

Add 10 percent for stainless finish

PARA USA PXT TACTICAL SERIES

Caliber: 45 ACP, 8+1 round capacity. Barrel: 4.25 inches; weight, 36 oz.; overall length, 7.75 inches. Checkered polymer grips, fiber-optic sights. Checkered front strap. Match grade, integral ramp 4.25-inch barrel. Double-stack 14.45 Tactical model has 5-inch barrel, 14-round magazine.

Perf: $1400 **Exc:** $1200 **VGood:** $1000

PARDINI GP RAPID FIRE MATCH

Semi-automatic; single action; 22 Short; 5-shot magazine; 4-5/8-inch barrel; 11-5/8-inch overall length; weighs 43 oz.; wrap-around stippled walnut grips; interchangeable post front sight, fully-adjustable match rear. Imported from Italy by Nygord Precision Products. Introduced 1995.

Perf: $850 **Exc:** $750 **VGood:** $650

PARDINI GP RAPID FIRE MATCH SCHUMAN

Same specs as the GP model except extended rear sight for longer sight radius. Imported from Italy by Nygord Precision Products. Introduced 1995; still imported.

New: $1500 **Perf:** $1350 **Exc:** $1100

PARDINI K50 FREE PISTOL

Single shot; 22 LR; 9-7/8-inch barrel; 18-3/4-inch overall length; weighs 35 oz.; adjustable match-type wrap-around walnut grips; interchangeable post front sight, fully-adjustable match open rear; removable, adjustable match trigger; barrel weights mount above the barrel. Imported from Italy by Nygord Precision Products. Introduced 1995; dropped 1999.

Perf: $850 **Exc:** $750 **VGood:** $650

PARDINI MODEL HP TARGET

Semi-automatic; single action; 32 S&W; 5-shot magazine; 4-3/4-inch barrel; 11-5/8-inch overall length; weighs 40 oz.; adjustable, stippled walnut, match-type grips; interchangeable blade front sight, interchangeable, fully-adjustable rear; fully-adjustable match trigger. Imported from Italy by

Phelps Heritage I

Phoenix Arms Model Raven

Plainfield Model 71

Phoenix Arms HP22

PSA-25 Auto Pocket Pistol

Nygord Precision Products. Introduced 1995; still imported.

New: $1000 **Perf:** $900 **Exc:** $800

PARDINI MODEL SP LADIES

Semi-automatic; single action; 22 LR; 5-shot magazine; 4-3/4-inch barrel; 11-5/8-inch overall length; weighs 40 oz.; adjustable, stippled walnut, small match-type grips for smaller hands; interchangeable blade front sight, interchangeable, fully-adjustable rear; fully-adjustable match trigger. Imported from Italy by Nygord Precision Products. Introduced 1986; discontinued 1990.

Perf: $850 **Exc:** $750 **VGood:** $650

PARDINI MODEL SP TARGET

Semi-automatic; single action; 22 LR; 5-shot magazine; 4-3/4-inch barrel; 11-5/8-inch overall length; weighs 40 oz.; adjustable, stippled walnut, match-type grips; interchangeable blade front sight, interchangeable, fully-adjustable rear; fully-adjustable match trigger. Imported from Italy by Nygord Precision Products. Introduced 1995; still imported.

New: $1150 **Perf:** $950 **Exc:** $650

PETERS STAHL PS-07 COMBAT COMPENSATOR

Semi-automatic; single action; 45 ACP, 10mm; 7-shot (45 ACP), 8-shot (10mm); 6-inch barrel; 10-inch overall length; weighs 45 oz.; Pachmayr Presentation rubber grips; interchangeable blade front sight, fully-adjustable Peters Stahl rear; linkless barrel with polygonal rifling and integral PS competition compensator; semi-extended PS slide stop and thumb safety; rearward extended magazine release; adjustable Videcki trigger; Wilson stainless beavertail grip safety; Pachmayr rubber mainspring housing. Imported from Germany by Federal Ordnance. Introduced 1989; dropped 1991.

45 ACP

Perf: $2200 **Exc:** $1800 **VGood:** $1350

10mm Auto

Perf: $2100 **Exc:** $1600 **VGood:** $1100

PHELPS EAGLE I

Revolver; single action; 444 Marlin; 6-shot cylinder; 8-inch barrel, others to customer specifications; 15-1/2-inch overall length (8-inch barrel); weighs 5-1/2 lbs.; smooth walnut grips; ramp front sight, adjustable rear; polished blue finish; transfer bar safety. Made in U.S. by Phelps Mfg. Co. Introduced 1978; dropped 1996.

Perf: $2000 **Exc:** $1750 **VGood:** $1500

PHELPS GRIZZLY

Revolver; single action; 50-70; 6-shot cylinder; 8-inch barrel, others to customer specifications; 15-1/2-inch overall length (8-inch barrel); weighs 5-1/2 lbs.; smooth walnut grips; ramp front sight, adjustable rear; polished blue finish; transfer bar safety. Made in U.S. by Phelps Mfg. Co. Introduced 1978; dropped 1996.

Perf: $2200 **Exc:** $1850 **VGood:** $1600

PHELPS HERITAGE I

Revolver; single action; 45-70; 6-shot cylinder; 8-inch barrel, others to customer specifications; 15-1/2-inch overall length (8-inch barrel); weighs 5-1/2 lbs.; smooth walnut grips; ramp front sight, adjustable rear; polished blue finish; transfer bar safety. Made in U.S. by Phelps Mfg. Co. Introduced 1978; dropped 1996.

Perf: $2000 **Exc:** $1750 **VGood:** $1500

PHELPS PATRIOT

Revolver; single action; 375 Win.; 6-shot; 8-inch barrel, others on special order; adjustable sights; blued finish. Introduced 1993; discontinued 1995.

New: $1850 **Perf:** $1600 **Exc:** $1350

PHOENIX ARMS HP22

Semi-automatic; single action; 22 LR; 10-shot magazine; 3-inch barrel; 5-1/2-inch overall length; weighs 20 oz.; checkered composition grips; blade front sight, adjustable rear; exposed hammer; manual hold-open; button magazine release; available in satin nickel, polished blue finish. Made in U.S. by Phoenix Arms. Introduced 1993; still produced.

New: $140 **Perf:** $100 **Exc:** $80

PHOENIX ARMS HP25

Semi-automatic; single action; 25 ACP; 10-shot magazine; 3-inch barrel; 5-1/2-inch overall length; weighs 20 oz.; checkered composition grips; blade front sight, adjustable rear; exposed hammer; manual hold-open; button magazine release; satin nickel or polished blue finish. Made in U.S. by Phoenix Arms. Introduced 1994; still produced.

New: $125 **Perf:** $100 **Exc:** $80

PHOENIX ARMS MODEL RAVEN

Semi-automatic; single action; 25 ACP; 6-shot magazine; 2-7/16-inch barrel; 4-3/4-inch overall length; weighs 15 oz.; ivory-colored or black slotted plastic grips; ramped front sight, fixed rear; available in blue, nickel or chrome finish. Made in U.S. by Phoenix Arms. Introduced 1992; no longer produced.

New: $100 **Perf:** $85 **Exc:** $70

PLAINFIELD MODEL 71

Semi-automatic; 22 LR, 25 ACP; 10-shot (22 LR), 8-shot (25 ACP); 1-inch barrel; 5-1/8-inch overall length; fixed sights; checkered walnut stocks; stainless steel slide frame. Also made with caliber conversion kit. Introduced 1970; discontinued approximately 1980.

Exc: $200 **VGood:** $165 **Good:** $125

With conversion kit

Exc: $250 **VGood:** $225 **Good:** $175

PLAINFIELD MODEL 72

Semi-automatic; 22 LR, 25 ACP; 10-shot (22 LR), 8-shot (25 ACP); 3-1/2-inch barrel; 6-inch overall length; fixed sights; checkered walnut stocks; aluminum slide. Introduced 1970; discontinued 1978.

Exc: $200 **VGood:** $175 **Good:** $125

With conversion kit

Exc: $250 **VGood:** $200 **Good:** $150

PSA-25 AUTO POCKET PISTOL

Caliber: 25 ACP, 6-shot magazine. Barrel: 2-1/8-inch. Weight: 9.5 oz. Length: 4-1/8-inch overall. Stocks: Checkered black polymer, ivory, checkered transparent carbon fiber-filled polymer. Sights: Fixed. Features: All steel construction; striker fired; single action only; magazine disconnector; cocking indicator. Introduced 1987. Made in U.S. by Precision Small Arms, Inc.

Traditional (polished black oxide) or Nouveau - Satin (brushed nickel)

Perf: $225 **Exc:** $180 **VGood:** $150

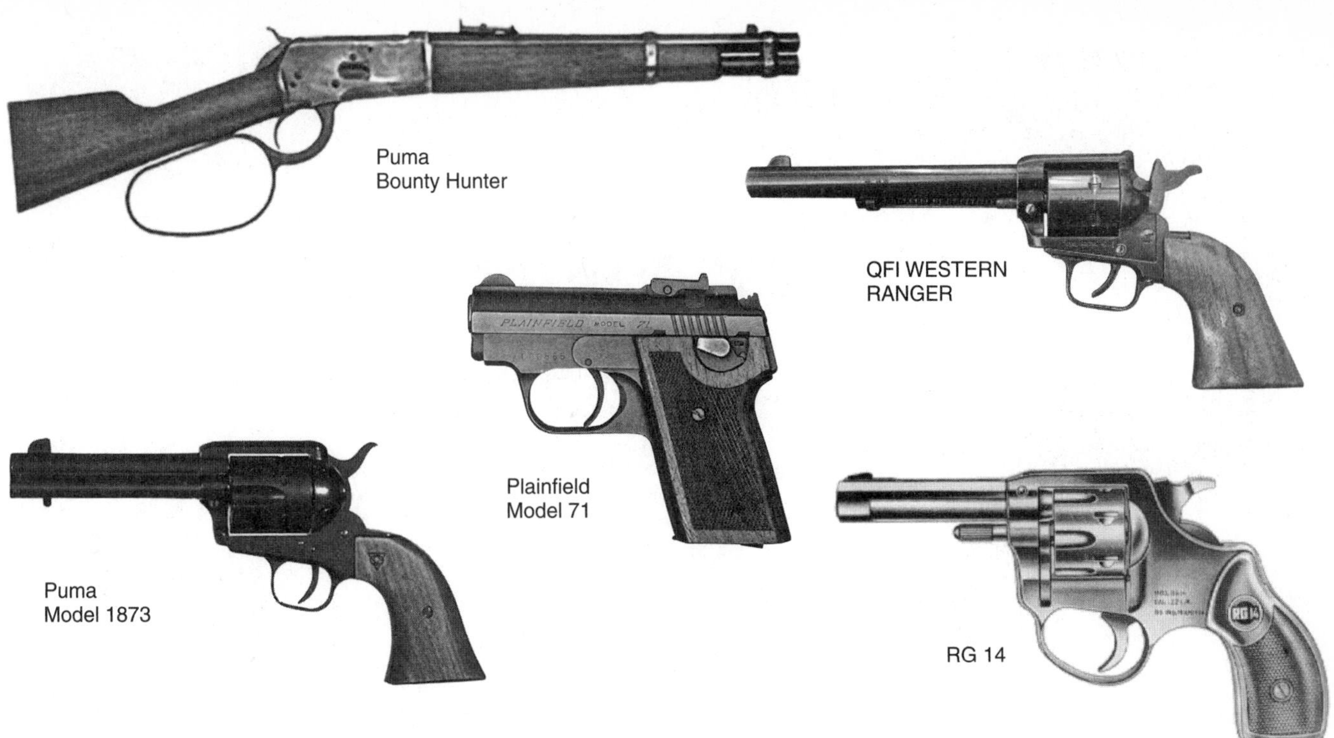
Puma Bounty Hunter

QFI WESTERN RANGER

Plainfield Model 71

Puma Model 1873

RG 14

Nouveau - Mirror (highly polished nickel)

Perf: $300 **Exc:** $250 **VGood:** $200

Featherweight (aluminum frame, nickel slide)

Perf: $325 **Exc:** $275 **VGood:** $225

Diplomat (black oxide with gold highlights, ivory grips)

Perf: $525 **Exc:** $400 **VGood:** $300

Montreaux (gold plated, ivory grips)

Perf: $550 **Exc:** $475 **VGood:** $350

Renaissance (hand engraved nickel, ivory grips)

Perf: $900 **Exc:** $750 **VGood:** $600

PUMA BOUNTY HUNTER

Lever action based on Winchester Model 92 rifle. Chambered in 44/40, 44 Mag. or 45 Colt with 6-shot magazine capacity. Replica of gun used by Steve McQueen in 1950's TV series "Wanted: Dead or Alive." Barrel length is 12 inches making it a handgun under federal law. Overall length is 24 inches and weight 4.5 pounds. Walnut stock and fore-end. Finish is case hardened and blued.

Perf: $1235 **Exc:** $1050 **VGood:** $900

PUMA MODEL 1873

Caliber: 22 LR or 22LR/22 Mag. Combo. Single Action Army replica. Barrel lengths: 4-3/4 (.22 LR only) or 5-1/2 or 7-1/2 inches. Extra .22 Mag. Cylinder included with 5-1/2 and 7-1/2 inch models. Weight: 35.2 to 38.4 oz. Wood or plastic grips. Antique or matte black finish. Prices shown are for combo models.

Perf: $300 **Exc:** $255 **VGood:** $220

Deduct 35 percent for .22LR-only model

QFI DARK HORSEMAN

Revolver; single action; 44 Mag., 45 Colt; 6-1/2-inch, 7-1/2-inch barrel; adjustable sights; black composition stocks; extended grip frame; blued finish. Introduced 1991; discontinued 1992.

Perf: $200 **Exc:** $175 **VGood:** $125

QFI HORSEMAN

Revolver; single action; 357 Mag., 44 Mag., 45 Colt; 6-1/2-inch, 7-1/2-inch barrel; weighs 45 oz. (6-1/2-inch barrel); blade front sight, grooved rear; uncheckered walnut grips; color case-hardened frame; bright blue finish. Assembled in U.S. Introduced 1991; discontinued 1992.

Perf: $250 **Exc:** $200 **VGood:** $175

QFI MODEL LA380

Semi-automatic; single action; 380 ACP; 6-shot; 3-1/8-inch barrel; 6-1/4-inch overall length; weighs 25 oz.; blade front sight, windage-adjustable rear; uncheckered European walnut grips; external hammer; magazine safety; hammer, trigger, firing pin block; blued finish. Introduced 1991; discontinued 1992.

Perf: $100 **Exc:** $90 **VGood:** $75

Chrome finish

Perf: $125 **Exc:** $110 **VGood:** $100

Stainless steel

Perf: $165 **Exc:** $145 **VGood:** $135

QFI MODEL LA380 TIGRESS

Same specs as Model LA380 except scrimshawed white polymer grips; blue frame with gold-plated slide. Introduced 1991; discontinued 1991.

Perf: $125 **Exc:** $110 **VGood:** $100

QFI MODEL SA25

Semi-automatic; single action; 25 ACP; 6-shot; 2-1/2-inch barrel; 4-5/8-inch overall length; weighs 12 oz.; fixed sights; smooth walnut or pearlite grips; external hammer; blued finish. Introduced 1991; discontinued 1991.

Perf: $60 **Exc:** $45 **VGood:** $35

QFI MODEL SA25 TIGRESS

Same specs as Model SA25 except scrimshawed white polymer grips; blue frame with gold-plated slide. Introduced 1991; discontinued 1991.

Perf: $125 **Exc:** $100 **VGood:** $85

QFI MODEL SO38

Revolver; double action; 38 Spl.; 6-shot; 2-inch solid, 4-inch vent-rib barrel; weighs 27 oz. (2-inch barrel); fixed sights; bulldog-type checkered plastic or walnut grips; one-stroke ejection. Introduced 1991; discontinued 1992.

Perf: $165 **Exc:** $145 **VGood:** $120

QFI PLAINS RIDER

Revolver; single action; 22 LR, 22 LR/22 WMR; 6-shot cylinder; 3-inch, 4-3/4-inch, 6-1/2-inch, 9-inch barrel; 11-inch overall length (6-1/2-inch barrel); weighs 35 oz. (6-1/2-inch barrel); black composition grips; blade front sight, fixed rear; blue/black finish; available with extra cylinder. From QFI. Introduced 1991; dropped 1992.

22 LR, 3-inch, 4-3/4-inch, 6-1/2-inch barrel

Perf: $110 **Exc:** $75 **VGood:** $60

22 LR, 3-inch, 4-3/4-inch, 6-1/2-inch barrel, dual cylinder

Perf: $135 **Exc:** $90 **VGood:** $85

22 LR, 9-inch barrel

Perf: $105 **Exc:** $80 **VGood:** $65

22 LR, 9-inch barrel, dual cylinder

Perf: $110 **Exc:** $100 **VGood:** $90

QFI RP SERIES

Revolver; double action; 22 LR, 22 WMR, 22 LR/WMR combo, 32 S&W, 32 S&W Long, 32 H&R Mag., 38 Spl.; 6-shot cylinder; 2-inch, 4-inch barrel; 6-1/4-inch overall length (2-inch barrel); weighs 23 oz.; magnum-style round butt grips of checkered plastic; ramp front sight, fixed square notch rear; one-piece solid frame; checkered hammer spur; serrated trigger; blue finish. Made in U.S. by QFI. Introduced 1991; dropped 1992.

Perf: $100 **Exc:** $65 **VGood:** $50

QFI WESTERN RANGER

Revolver; single action; 22 LR, 22 LR/22 WMR combo; 3-inch, 4-inch, 4-3/4-inch, 6-inch, 6-1/2-inch, 7-inch, 9-inch barrel; 10-inch overall length (4-3/4-inch barrel); weighs 31 oz.; blade front sight, notch rear; American walnut grips; blue/black finish. dropped 1992.

Perf: $100 **Exc:** $75 **VGood:** $60

RG 14

Revolver; double action; 22 LR; 6-shot; 1 3/4-inch, 3-inch barrel; 5-1/2-inch overall length (13/4 inch barrel); fixed sights; checkered plastic grips; cylinder swings out when pin removed; blued finish. Introduced 1978; discontinued 1986.

Exc: $65 **VGood:** $50 **Good:** $40

RG 16

Derringer; over/under; 22 WMR; 2-shot; 3-inch barrel; 5-inch overall length; weighs 15 oz.; fixed sights; blue or nickel finish. Introduced 1975; no longer in production.

Exc: $60 **VGood:** $50 **Good:** $35

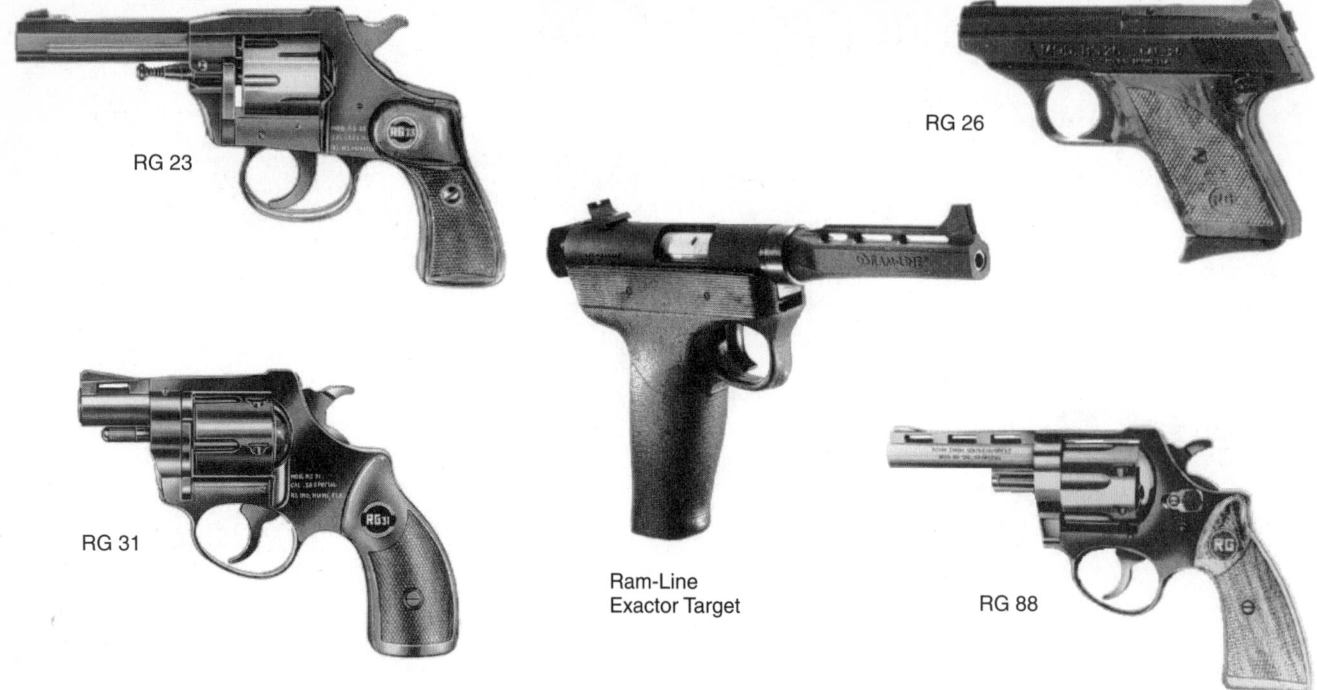
RG 23
RG 26
RG 31
Ram-Line Exactor Target
RG 88

RG 17

Derringer; over/under; 38 Spl.; 2-shot; 3-inch barrel; 5-inch overall length; weighs 15 oz.; fixed sights; blue or nickel finish. Introduced 1975; no longer in production.

Exc: $60 **VGood:** $50 **Good:** $35

RG 23

Revolver; double action; 22 LR; 6-shot; 1-3/4-inch, 3-inch barrel; 5-1/2-inch overall length (1-3/4-inch barrel); fixed sights; checkered plasticgrips; central ejector system; blued finish. Introduced 1978; discontinued 1986.

Exc: $70 **VGood:** $60 **Good:** $45

RG 25

Semi-automatic; 25 ACP; 6-shot; 2-1/2-inch barrel; 4-3/4-inch overall length; weighs 12 oz.; fixed sights; thumb safety; blue or nickel finish. Introduced 1975; no longer in production.

Exc: $75 **VGood:** $60 **Good:** $50

RG 26

Semi-automatic; single action; 25 ACP; 6-shot; 2-1/2-inch barrel; 4-3/4-inch overall length; 12 oz.; fixed sights; checkered plastic stocks; thumb safety; blued finish. Introduced 1977; discontinued 1986.

Exc: $75 **VGood:** $60 **Good:** $50

RG 30

Revolver; double action; 22 LR, 22 WMR; 6-shot swing-out cylinder; 4-inch barrel; 9-inch overall length; windage-adjustable rear sight, fixed front; checkered plastic stocks; blued finish. Introduced 1977; discontinued 1986.

Exc: $65 **VGood:** $60 **Good:** $50

Nickel finish

Exc: $70 **VGood:** $65 **Good:** $55

RG 31

Revolver; double action; 32 S&W, 38 Spl.; 6-shot (32 S&W), 5-shot (38 Spl.); 2-inch barrel; 6-3/4-inch overall length; fixed sights; checkered plastic grips; cylinder swings out when pin removed; blued finish. Introduced 1978; discontinued 1986.

Exc: $110 **VGood:** $100 **Good:** $85

RG 38S

Revolver; double action; 38 Spl.; 6-shot swing-out cylinder; 3-inch, 4-inch, 6-inch (38T) barrel; 9-1/4-inch overall length (4-inch barrel); weighs 35 oz.; windage-adjustable rear sight, fixed front; checkered plastic stocks; blued finish. Introduced 1977; discontinued 1986.

Exc: $125 **VGood:** $110 **Good:** $100

Nickel finish

Exc: $135 **VGood:** $120 **Good:** $110

RG 39

Revolver; 38 Spl., 32 S&W; 6-shot; 2-inch barrel; 7-inch overall length; weighs 21 oz.; fixed sights; American walnut grips; blue finish. Introduced 1981; no longer in production.

Exc: $125 **VGood:** $110 **Good:** $85

RG 40

Revolver; double action; 38 Spl., 32 S&W; 6-shot; 2-inch barrel; 7-inch overall length; fixed sights; checkered plastic grips; swing-out cylinder; spring ejector; blued finish. Introduced 1980; discontinued 1986.

Exc: $110 **VGood:** $100 **Good:** $75

RG 42

Semi-automatic; 25 ACP; 7-shot; 2-3/4-inch barrel; 5-5/16-inch overall length; fixed sights; thumb and magazine safety; blue finish.

Exc: $75 **VGood:** $60 **Good:** $50

RG 57

Revolver; double action; 357 Mag., 44 Mag.; 6-shot swing-out cylinder; 4-inch barrel; 9-1/2-inch overall length; fixed sights; checkered plastic stocks; steel frame; blued finish. Manufactured in Germany, imported by RG Industries. Introduced 1977; discontinued 1986.

Exc: $125 **VGood:** $110 **Good:** $85

RG 63

Revolver; double action; 22 LR; 8-shot; 5-inch barrel; 10-1/4-inch overall length; fixed sights; checkered plastic stocks; Western configuration with slide ejector rod; blued finish. Introduced 1976; discontinued 1986.

Exc: $100 **VGood:** $85 **Good:** $65

Nickel finish

Exc: $110 **VGood:** $90 **Good:** $70

RG 66

Revolver; single action; 22 LR, 22 WMR; 6-shot; 4-3/4-inch barrel; 10-inch overall length; adjustable rear sight, fixed front; checkered plastic stocks; slide ejector rod; blued finish. Introduced 1977; discontinued 1986.

Exc: $90 **VGood:** $75 **Good:** $60

Nickel finish

Exc: $95 **VGood:** $80 **Good:** $65

RG 74

Revolver; double action; 22 LR; 6-shot; 3-inch barrel; 7-3/4-inch overall length; fixed sights; checkered plastic grips; swing-out cylinder with spring ejector; blued finish. Introduced 1978; discontinued 1986.

Exc: $65 **VGood:** $50 **Good:** $40

RG 88

Revolver; double action; 38 Spl., 357 Mag.; 6-shot swing-out cylinder; 4-inch barrel; 9-inch overall length; fixed sights; checkered walnut stocks; wide spur hammer, trigger; blued finish. Introduced 1977; dropped 1986.

Exc: $135 **VGood:** $110 **Good:** $90

RADOM P-35

Semi-automatic; 9mm Para; 8-shot; 4-3/4-inch barrel; 7-3/4-inch overall length; fixed sights; checkered plastic stocks; blued finish. Design based on Colt Model 1911A1. Manufactured in Poland 1936 to 1945.

Pre-War, dated 1936 to 1939

Exc: $1500 **VGood:** $1100 **Good:** $800

Wartime manufacture

Exc: $650 **VGood:** $575 **Good:** $475

RAM-LINE EXACTOR TARGET

Semi-automatic; single action; 22 LR; 15-shot magazine; 8-inch barrel; 12-5/16-inch overall length; weighs 23 oz.; one-piece injection molded grips in conventional contour; checkered side panels; ridged front and backstraps; ramp front sight, adjustable rear; injection molded grip frame, alloy receiver; hybrid composite barrel; constant force sear spring gives 2-1/2-lb. trigger pull; Adapt-A-Barrel for mounting weights, flashlight; drilled and tapped receiver for scope mounting; jeweled bolt; comes with carrying case, test target. Made in U.S. by Ram-Line, Inc. Introduced 1990; no longer in production.

Perf: $200 **Exc:** $250 **VGood:** $175

Randall Raider/Service Model C

Raven MP-25

Remington Model 1911 R1

Remington Model 1901 Target

Remington Model 95

RAM-LINE RAM-TECH

Semi-automatic; single action; 22 LR; 15-shot magazine; 4-1/2-inch barrel; weighs 19 oz.; one-piece injection molded grips with checkered panels; ramp front sight, adjustable rear; compact frame; injection molded grip frame, alloy receiver; hybrid composite barrel; constant force sear spring gives 3-lb. trigger pull; comes with carrying case. Made in U.S. by Ram-Line, Inc. Introduced 1994; no longer produced.

Perf: $175 **Exc:** $150 **VGood:** $135

RANDALL CURTIS E. LEMAY FOUR-STAR MODEL

Semi-automatic; 9mm Para., 45 ACP; 7-shot (9mm), 6-shot (45 ACP); 4-1/4-inch barrel; 7-3/4-inch overall length; weighs 35 oz.; fixed or adjustable sights; checkered walnut stocks; squared trigger guard; stainless steel construction. Introduced 1984; discontinued 1984. Add 400% for 9mm.

Exc: $1000 **VGood:** $850 **Good:** $700

RANDALL RAIDER/SERVICE MODEL C

Semi-automatic; 9mm Para., 45 ACP; 6-shot; 4-1/4-inch barrel; 7-3/4-inch overall length; weighs 36 oz.; fixed or adjustable sights; checkered walnut stocks; squared trigger guard; extended magazine baseplate; stainless steel construction. Introduced 1983; discontinued 1984. Add 400% for 9mm.

Exc: $600 **VGood:** $500 **Good:** $450

RANDALL SERVICE MODEL

Semi-automatic; 38 Super, 9mm Para., 45 ACP; 5-inch barrel; 8-1/2-inch overall length; weighs 38 oz.; blade front sight, fixed or adjustable rear; checkered walnut stocks; round-top or ribbed slide; all stainless steel construction. Introduced 1983; discontinued 1984.

Exc: $850 **VGood:** $650 **Good:** $500

RAVEN MP-25

Semi-automatic; single action; 25 ACP; 6-shot; 2-7/16-inch barrel; 5-1/2-inch overall length; weighs 15 oz.; fixed sights; uncheckered pearlite stocks; die-cast slide serrations; blued, nickel or satin nickel finish. Manufactured in U.S. Introduced 1984; discontinued 1992.

Exc: $100 **VGood:** $75 **Good:** $60

RAVEN P-25

Semi-automatic; single action; 25 ACP; 6-shot; 2-7/16-inch barrel; 5-1/2-inch overall length; weighs 15 oz.; fixed sights; uncheckered walnut; blued, nickel or satin nickel finish. Manufactured in U.S. Introduced 1977; discontinued 1984.

Exc: $100 **VGood:** $75 **Good:** $60

RECORD-MATCH MODEL 200 FREE PISTOL

Single shot; Martini action; 22 LR; 11-inch barrel; micrometer rear sight, target-type front; carved, checkered European walnut stock, forearm, with adjustable hand base; set trigger, spur trigger guard; blued finish. Manufactured in Germany prior to WWII.

Exc: $1050 **VGood:** $950 **Good:** $600

RECORD-MATCH MODEL 210 FREE PISTOL

Single shot; Martini action; 22 LR; 11-inch barrel; micrometer rear sight, target-type front; carved, checkered deluxe European walnut stock, forearm with adjustable hand base; button release set trigger; blued finish. Manufactured in Germany prior to WWII.

Exc: $1200 **VGood:** $1050 **Good:** $700

RECORD-MATCH MODEL 210A FREE PISTOL

Same specs as Model 210 except alloy frame. Manufactured in Germany prior to WWII.

Exc: $1300 **VGood:** $1100 **Good:** $700

REISING TARGET MODEL

Semi-automatic; hinged frame; 22 LR; 12-shot; 6-1/2-inch barrel; fixed sights; hard rubber checkered stocks; external hammers; blued finish. Manufactured 1921 to 1924.

Exc: $400 **VGood:** $350 **Good:** $205

REMINGTON MODEL 51

Semi-automatic; 32 ACP, 380 ACP; 8-shot; 3-1/2-inch barrel; 6-5/8-inch overall length; weighs 21 oz.; fixed sights; hard rubber grips; blued finish. Introduced 1918; discontinued 1943. .32 is somewhat scarce; add 10 percent.

Exc: $500 **VGood:** $375 **Good:** $250

REMINGTON MODEL 95

Derringer; over/under; single action; 41 Short Rimfire; 3-inch barrels; 4-7/8-inch overall length. Introduced 1866; discontinued 1935. Prior to 1888 the model was stamped "E Remington & Sons"; from 1888 to 1910 the derringers were marked "Remington Arms Co."; from 1910 to 1935 guns were marked "Remington Arms-U.M.C. Co." The early styles have a two-armed extractor, long hammer spur. In later models a few have no extractor, majority have sliding extractor, short hammer spur. Available with all-blued finish, full nickel plate or blued barrels with nickel-plated frame; factory engraving; choice of checkered hard rubber, walnut, mother-of-pearl, ivory grips; fixed rear groove sight, front blade integral with top barrel. Values shown are for early issues. Beware of cracked barrel hinge.

Exc: $1300 **VGood:** $950 **Good:** $600

Nickel finish

Exc: $1500 **VGood:** $1150 **Good:** $750

Engraved with mother-of-pearl or ivory grips

Exc: $2300 **VGood:** $1850 **Good:** $1050

REMINGTON MODEL 1901 TARGET

Single shot; rolling block action; 22 Short, 22 LR, 25 Rimfire, 32 Centerfire, 44 S&W Russian; 10-inch barrel; 14-inch overall length; target sights; checkered walnut grips, forearm; blued finish. Manufactured 1901 to 1909.

Exc: $1500 **VGood:** $1250 **Good:** $1000

REMINGTON MODEL 1911 MILITARY

Semi-automatic; single action; 45 ACP; 8-shot; fixed sight; checkered walnut grip; Colt Model 1911 made under U.S. contract by Remington UMC; blued finish. Introduced 1918; discontinued 1919.

Exc: $1500 **VGood:** $1200 **Good:** $900

REMINGTON MODEL 1911 R1

Single-action, semi-automatic in .45 ACP. five-inch stainless steel barrel. 8.5 inches long, 38.5 ounces. Fixed front and rear dovetailed sights. Double-diamond checkered walnut grips. Carbon steel frame and slide with satin black oxide finish. Custom carry case. 7+1 capacity. Introduced 2011. Stainless steel version introduced 2013.

Perf: $640 **Exc:** $575 **VGood:** $500

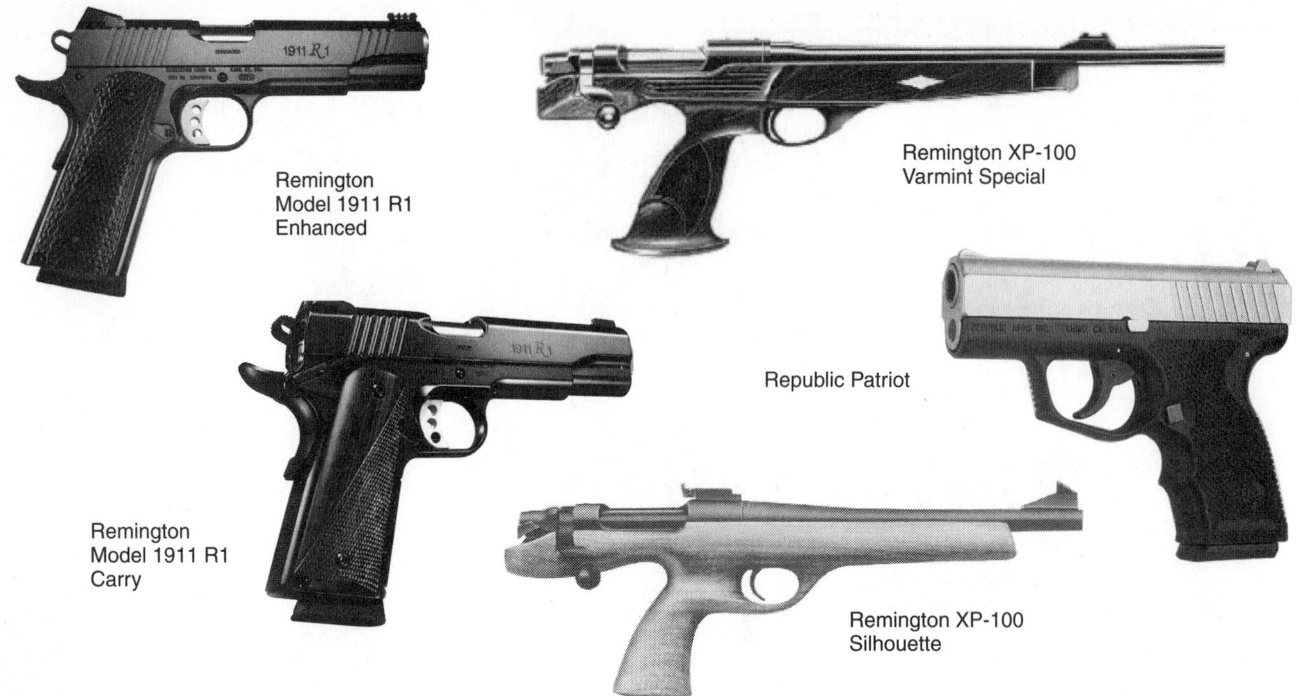
Remington Model 1911 R1 Enhanced

Remington XP-100 Varmint Special

Republic Patriot

Remington Model 1911 R1 Carry

Remington XP-100 Silhouette

REMINGTON MODEL 1911 R1 ENHANCED

Single-action, semi-automatic in .45 ACP. five-inch stainless steel barrel. 8.5 inches long, 38.5 ounces. Adjustable rear-sight, fiber optic front sight. hard wood checkered grips. Beavertail grip safety. Front and rear slide serrations with a checkered main-spring housing. Aluminum anodized trigger. Match grade barrel and bushing. Carbon steel frame and slide with satin black oxide finish. Custom carry case. 8+1 capacity. Introduced 2012. Stainless version introduced in 2013.

Perf: $875 **Exc:** $775 **VGood:** $675

REMINGTON MODEL 1911 R1 CARRY

Single-action, semi-automatic in .45 ACP. five-inch stainless steel barrel. 8.5 inches long, 38.5 ounces. Novak Tritium three-dot sights. Cocobolo checkered grips. Beavertail grip safety. Rear slide serrations with a checkered main-spring housing and front strap. All sharp edges have been dehorned. Aluminum anodized trigger. Match grade barrel and bushing. Carbon steel frame and slide with satin black oxide finish. Custom carry case. 8+1 capacity. Introduced 2013.

Perf: $1150 **Exc:** $1050 **VGood:** $975

REMINGTON XP-22R

Single shot; bolt-action; 22 LR; 5-shot; 14-1/2-inch barrel; weighs 68 oz.; no sights; drilled, tapped for scope mounts or iron sights; rear-handled stock of fiberglass-reinforced Kevlar built on Remington Model 541-7 rifle action. Available on special order from Remington Custom Shop. Introduced 1991; discontinued 1992.

Exc: $650 **VGood:** $550 **Good:** $350

REMINGTON XP-100 HUNTER PISTOL

Single shot; bolt action; 223 Rem., 7mm BR Rem., 7mm-08 Rem., 35 Rem.; 14-1/2-inch barrel; 21-1/4-inch overall length; weighs 4-1/2 lbs.; laminated wood stock with contoured grip; no sights furnished; drilled and tapped for scope mounting; mid-handle grip design with scalloped contours for right- or left-handed use; two-position safety; matte blue finish. Introduced 1993; dropped 1995.

New: $650 **Perf:** $500 **Exc:** $300

REMINGTON XP-100 CUSTOM HB LONG RANGE PISTOL

Single shot; bolt-action; 221 Rem. Fireball; 10-1/2-inch barrel; 16-3/4-inch overall length; vent rib; blade front sight, adjustable rear; receiver drilled, tapped for scope mounts; one-piece brown nylon stock; blued finish. Introduced 1963; dropped 1985.

Exc: $850 **VGood:** $700 **Good:** $575

REMINGTON XP-100 SILHOUETTE

Single shot; bolt action; 7mm BR Rem.; 10-1/2-inch barrel; 17-1/4-inch overall length; weighs 3-7/8 lbs.; American walnut stock; blade front sight, fully-adjustable square-notch rear; mid-handle grip with scalloped contours for left- or right-handed use; match-type trigger; two-position thumb safety; matte blue finish. Dropped 1995.

Perf: $600 **Exc:** $500 **VGood:** $300

REMINGTON XP-100 VARMINT SPECIAL

Single shot; bolt action; 221 Rem. Fireball, 223 Rem.; 10-1/2-inch barrel (221), 14-1/2-inch barrel (223); weighs 70 oz.; adjustable sights; drilled, tapped for scope; one-piece nylon grip; forend weights for balance; matte blue finish. Introduced 1963; discontinued 1992.

Perf: $700 **Exc:** $595 **VGood:** $350

REMINGTON XP-100R

Repeater; bolt action; 223 Rem., 22-250, 7mm-08 Rem., 250 Savage, 308, 350 Rem. Mag., 35 Rem.; blind magazine; 5-shot (7mm-08, 35), 6-shot (223 Rem.); 14-1/2-inch standard-weight barrel; weighs about 4-1/2 lbs; rear-handle, synthetic Du Pont Kevlar stock to eliminate transfer bar between forward trigger and rear trigger assembly; front and rear sling swivel studs; adjustable leaf rear sight, bead front; receiver drilled and tapped for scope mounts. From Remington Custom Shop. Introduced 1990; dropped 1995.

New: $850 **Perf:** $700 **Exc:** $600

REPUBLIC PATRIOT

Caliber: 45 ACP, 6-shot magazine. Barrel: 3-inch. Weight: 20 oz. Length: 6-inch overall. Stocks: Checkered. Sights: Blade front, drift-adjustable rear. Features: Black polymer frame, stainless steel slide; double-action-only trigger system; squared trigger guard. Introduced 1997. Made in U.S. by Republic Arms, Inc.

Perf: $275 **Exc:** $225 **VGood:** $175

REXIO PUCARA M224 REVOLVER

Caliber: 22 LR, 9-shot cylinder. Barrel: 4-inch. Weight: 33 oz. Length: 9-inch overall. Stocks: Checkered hardwood. Sights:• Blade front, square notch rear adjustable for windage. Features: Alloy frame; hammer block safety; polished blue finish. Introduced 1997. Imported from Argentina by Century International Arms.

Perf: $150 **Exc:** $125 **VGood:** $95

REXIO PUCARA M324 REVOLVER

Caliber: 32 S&W Long, 7-shot cylinder. Barrel: 4-inch. Weight: 31 oz. Length: 9-inch overall. Stocks: Checkered hardwood. Sights: Blade front, square notch rear adjustable for windage. Features: Alloy frame; polished blue finish; hammer block safety. Introduced 1997. Imported from Argentina by Century International Arms.

Perf: $150 **Exc:** $110 **VGood:** $100

REXIO PUCARA M384 REVOLVER

Caliber: 38 Spec., 6-shot. Barrel: 4-inch. Weight: 30 oz. Length: 9-inch overall. Stocks: Checkered hardwood. Sights: Blade front, rear adjustable for windage. Features: Alloy frame. Polished blue finish. Imported from Argentina by Century International Arms.

Perf: $150 **Exc:** $110 **VGood:** $100

ROCK RIVER ARMS PRO CARRY

4.25", 5" or 6" barrel and choice of Heinie or Novak tritium sights and polished finish; guaranteed to shoot 2.5" group at 50 yards with select ammunition. Other options available.

New: $1895 **Exc:** $1500 **VGood:** $1100

ROCKY MOUNTAIN ARMS 1911A1-LH

Semi-automatic; single action; 40 S&W, 45 ACP; 7-shot magazine; 5-1/4-inch barrel; 8-13/16-inch overall length; weighs 37 oz.; checkered walnut grips; red insert Patridge front sight, white outline click-adjustable rear; fully left-handed pistol; slide, frame, barrel made from stainless steel; working parts coated with Teflon-S; single-stage trigger with 3-1/2-

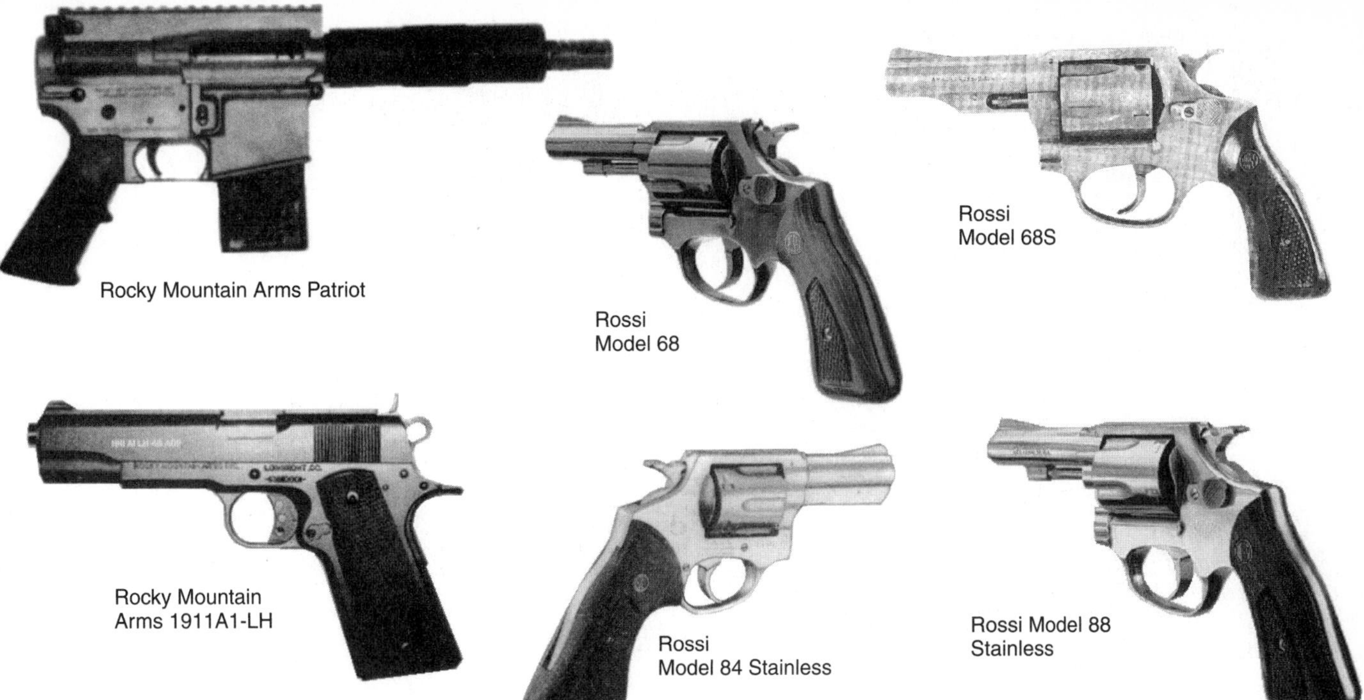
Rocky Mountain Arms Patriot
Rossi Model 68
Rossi Model 68S
Rocky Mountain Arms 1911A1-LH
Rossi Model 84 Stainless
Rossi Model 88 Stainless

lb. pull. Made in U.S. by Rocky Mountain Arms, Inc. Introduced 1993; dropped 1993.

Perf: $1200 **Exc:** $950 **VGood:** $750

ROCKY MOUNTAIN ARMS PATRIOT

Semi-automatic; single action; 223 Rem.; 10-shot magazine; 7-inch barrel with muzzlebrake; 20 1/2-inch overall length; weighs 5 lbs.; black composition grips; no sights; milled upper receiver with enhanced Weaver base; milled lower receiver from billet plate; machined aluminum National Match handguard; finished in DuPont Teflon-S matte black or NATO green; comes with black nylon case, one magazine. Made in U.S. by Rocky Mountain Arms, Inc. Introduced 1993; discontinued.

With A-2 handle top

New: $2250 **Perf:** $2000 **Exc:** $1850

Flat top model

New: $2400 **Perf:** $2200 **Exc:** $1950

ROSSI CYCLOPS REVOLVER

Caliber: 357 Magnum, 6-shot. Barrel: 6-inch, 8-inch. Weight: 44 oz. (6-inch barrel). Length: 11-3/4-inch overall (6-inch barrel). Stocks: Checkered rubber. Sights: Blade front, fully adjustable rear. Features: Extra-heavy barrel with four recessed compensator ports on each side of the muzzle. Stainless steel construction. Comes with scope mount and rings. Polished finish. Introduced 1997. Imported from Brazil by Interarms.

Exc: $400 **VGood:** $350 **Good:** $205

ROSSI LADY ROSSI

Revolver; double action; 38 Spl.; 5-shot cylinder; 2-inch, 3-inch barrel; 6-1/2-inch overall length (2-inch barrel); weighs 21 oz.; smooth rosewood grips; fixed sights; high-polish stainless steel with "Rossi" engraved on frame; comes with velvet carry bag. Imported from Brazil by Interarms. Introduced 1995; no longer imported.

New: $200 **Perf:** $160 **Exc:** $135

ROSSI MODEL 31

Revolver; double action; 38 Spl.; 5-shot; 4-inch barrel; weighs 22 oz.; ramp front sight, low-profile adjustable rear; checkered wood stocks; all-steel frame; blue or nickel finish. Introduced 1978; discontinued 1985.

Exc: $175 **VGood:** $150 **Good:** $125

ROSSI MODEL 51

Revolver; double action; 22 LR; 6-shot; 6-inch barrel; adjustable sights; checkered wood stocks; blued finish. Discontinued 1985.

Exc: $225 **VGood:** $175 **Good:** $150

ROSSI MODEL 68

Revolver; double action; 38 Spl.; 5-shot; 2-inch, 3-inch barrel; weighs 22 oz.; ramp front sight, low-profile adjustable rear; checkered rubber or wood stocks; all-steel frame; swing-out cylinder; blue or nickel finish. Made in Brazil. Introduced 1978; discontinued 1985. Reintroduced in 1993 as the Model 68S. No longer imported

Exc: $200 **VGood:** $175 **Good:** $150

ROSSI MODEL 68S

Same specs as Model 68 except weighs 23 oz.; fixed sights. Introduced 1993; no longer in production.

New: $225 **Perf:** $175 **Exc:** $160

ROSSI MODEL 69

Revolver; double action; 32 S&W; 6-shot; 3-inch barrel; ramp front sight, low-profile adjustable rear; checkered wood stocks; all-steel frame; swing-out cylinder; blue or nickel finish. Made in Brazil. Introduced 1978; discontinued 1985.

Exc: $195 **VGood:** $170 **Good:** $150

ROSSI MODEL 70

Revolver; double action; 22 LR; 6-shot; 3-inch barrel; ramp front sight, low-profile adjustable rear; checkered wood stocks; all-steel frame; swing-out cylinder; blue or nickel finish. Made in Brazil. Introduced 1978; discontinued 1985.

Exc: $195 **VGood:** $170 **Good:** $130

ROSSI MODEL 84 STAINLESS

Revolver; double action; 38 Spl.; 6-shot; 3-inch, 4-inch barrel; 8-inch overall length; weighs 271/2 oz.; fixed sights; checkered wood grips; solid raised rib; stainless steel. Made in Brazil. Introduced 1984; discontinued 1986.

Exc: $275 **VGood:** $225 **Good:** $175

ROSSI MODEL 88 STAINLESS

Revolver; double action; 38 Spl.; 5-shot; 2-inch, 3-inch barrel; 8-3/4-inch overall length; weighs 21 oz.; ramp front sight, drift-adjustable square-notch rear; checkered wood or rubber stocks; small frame; stainless steel construction; matte finish. Introduced 1993; no longer imported

New: $250 **Perf:** $200 **Exc:** $175

ROSSI MODEL 89 STAINLESS

Revolver; double action; 32 S&W; 6-shot; 3-inch barrel; 8-3/4-inch overall length; weighs 21 oz.; ramp front sight, drift-adjustable square notch rear; checkered wood or rubber stocks; stainless steel; matte finish. Introduced 1985; discontinued 1986; reintroduced 1989; no longer imported.

Exc: $200 **VGood:** $175 **Good:** $150

ROSSI MODEL 94

Revolver; double action; 38 Spl.; 6-shot; 3-inch, 4-inch barrel; 27-1/2 oz.; ramp front sight; adjustable rear; checkered wood stocks; blued finish. Introduced 1985; discontinued 1988.

Exc: $175 **VGood:** $150 **Good:** $135

ROSSI MODEL 511 SPORTSMAN

Revolver; double action; 22 LR; 6-shot; 4-inch barrel; 9-inch overall length; weighs 30 oz.; adjustable square-notch rear sight, orange-insert ramp front; checkered wood stocks; heavy barrel; integral sight rib; shrouded ejector rod; stainless steel construction. Made in Brazil. Introduced 1986; discontinued 1990.

Exc: $200 **VGood:** $175 **Good:** $150

ROSSI MODEL 515

Revolver; double action; 22 WMR; 6-shot cylinder; 4-inch barrel; 9-inch overall length; weighs 30 oz.; checkered wood and finger-groove wrap-around rubber grips; blade front sight with red insert, fully-adjustable rear; small frame; stainless steel construction; solid integral barrel rib. Imported from Brazil by Interarms. Introduced 1994; discontinued.

New: $250 **Perf:** $200 **Exc:** $175

ROSSI MODEL 518

Revolver; double action; 22 LR; 6-shot cylinder; 4-inch barrel; 9-inch overall length; weighs 30 oz.; checkered wood and finger-groove wrap-around rubber grips; blade front sight with red insert, fully-adjustable rear; small frame; stainless steel construction; solid integral barrel rib. Imported from

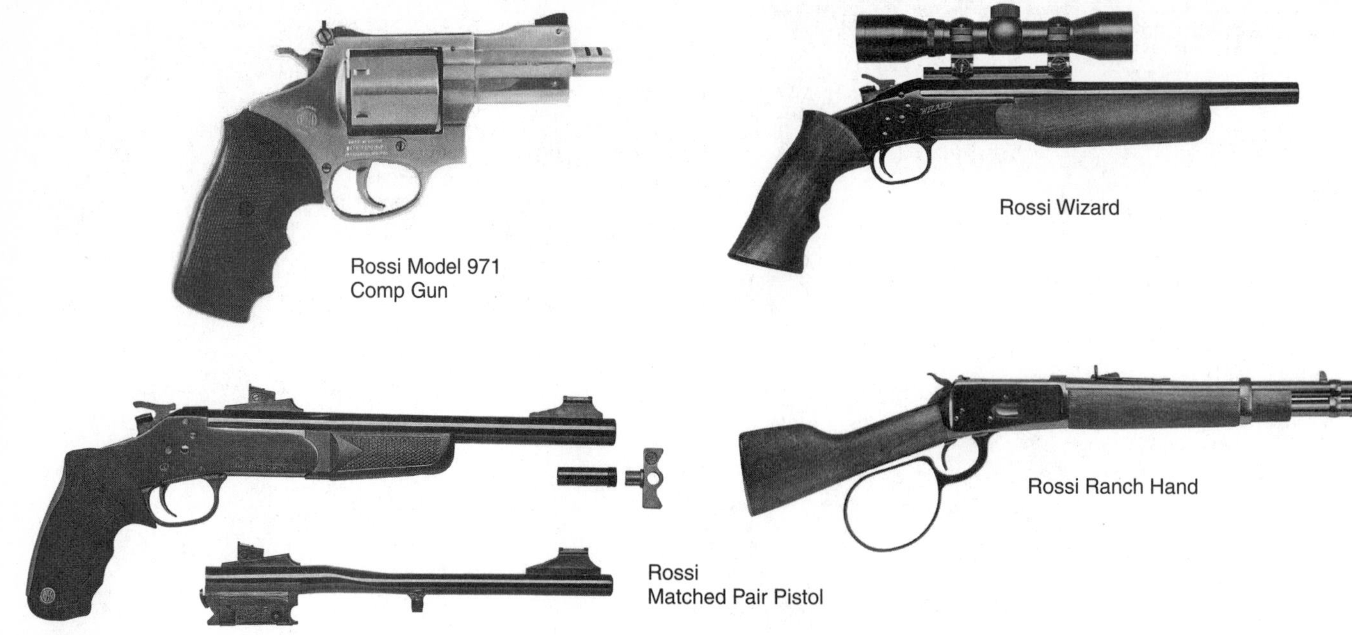
Rossi Model 971 Comp Gun

Rossi Wizard

Rossi Matched Pair Pistol

Rossi Ranch Hand

Brazil by Interarms. Introduced 1994; no longer imported.

New: $235 **Perf:** $200 **Exc:** $175

ROSSI MODEL 720

Revolver; double action; 44 Spl.; 5-shot cylinder; 3-inch barrel; 8-inch overall length; weighs 27-1/2 oz.; checkered rubber, combat-style grips; red insert front sight on ramp, fully-adjustable rear; all stainless steel construction; solid barrel rib; full ejector rod shroud. Imported from Brazil by Interarms. Introduced 1992.

New: $375 **Perf:** $315 **Exc:** $250

ROSSI MODEL 720C

Same specs as the Model 720 except spurless hammer; double-action only. Imported from Brazil by Interarms. Introduced 1992; no longer imported.

New: $375 **Perf:** $315 **Exc:** $250

ROSSI MODEL 851

Revolver; double action; 38 Spl.; 6-shot; 3-inch, 4-inch barrel; 8-inch overall length (3-inch barrel); weighs 27-1/2 oz.; red-insert blade front sight, windage-adjustable rear; checkered Brazilian hardwood grips; medium-size frame; stainless steel construction; vent rib. Introduced 1991; no longer imported.

New: $275 **Perf:** $250 **Exc:** $225

ROSSI MODEL 877 REVOLVER

Caliber: 357 Mag., 6-shot cylinder. Barrel: 2-inch. Weight: 26 oz. Length: NA. Stocks: Stippled synthetic. Sights: Blade front, fixed groove rear. Features: Stainless steel construction; fully enclosed ejector rod. Introduced 1996. no longer imported.

Perf: $275 **Exc:** $250 **VGood:** $225

ROSSI MODEL 941

Revolver; double action; 38 Spl.; 6-shot; 4-inch solid rib barrel; 9-inch overall length; weighs 30 oz.; colored insert front sight, adjustable rear; checkered hardwood combat stocks; shrouded ejector rod; blued finish. Made in Brazil. Introduced 1985; discontinued 1990.

Exc: $200 **VGood:** $175 **Good:** $150

ROSSI MODEL 951

Revolver; double action; 38 Spl.; 6-shot; 4-inch vent-rib barrel; 9-inch overall length; weighs 30 oz.; colored insert front sight, adjustable rear; checkered hardwood combat stocks; shrouded ejector rod; blued finish. Made in Brazil. Introduced 1985; discontinued 1990.

Exc: $200 **VGood:** $175 **Good:** $150

ROSSI MODEL 971

Revolver; double action; 357 Mag.; 6-shot; 2-1/2-inch, 4-inch, 6-inch heavy barrel; 9-inch overall length; weighs 36 oz.; blade front sight, fully-adjustable rear; checkered Brazilian hardwood grips; matted sight rib; target trigger; wide checkered hammer spur; full-length ejector rod shroud; blued (4-inch only) or stainless finish. Made in Brazil. Introduced 1988; no longer imported.

New: $275 **Perf:** $250 **Exc:** $225

ROSSI MODEL 971 COMP GUN

Same specs as Model 971 except stainless finish; 3-1/4-inch barrel with integral compensator; overall length 9-inch; weighs 32 oz.; red insert front sight, fully-adjustable rear; checkered, contoured rubber grips. Imported from Brazil by Interarms. Introduced 1993; no longer imported

New: $275 **Perf:** $250 **Exc:** $225

ROSSI MODEL 971 STAINLESS

Same general specs as Model 971 except 2-1/2-inch, 4-inch, 6-inch barrel; rubber grips; stainless steel construction. Introduced 1989; no longer imported.

New: $275 **Perf:** $250 **Exc:** $225

ROSSI MODEL 971 VRC REVOLVER

Similar to the Model 971 except has Rossi's 8-port Vented Rib Compensator; checkered finger-groove rubber grips; stainless steel construction. Available with 2.5-inch, 4-inch, 6-inch barrel; weighs 30 oz. with 2-5/8-inch barrel. Introduced 1996. No longer imported.

Perf: $300 **Exc:** $250 **VGood:** $225

ROSSI MODEL 972

Revolver; 6-shot polished stainless double-action .357 Magnum. Adjustable rear sight and red insert on front sight. 6-inch barrel, rubber grip, 35 oz. Uses Taurus security system.

New: $375 **Exc:** $325 **VGood:** $275

ROSSI MATCHED PAIR PISTOL

Caliber: 22LR, 45 Colt/410 bore. Single shot handgun with two interchangeable 11-inch barrels – one for .22 LR and one for either 45 Colt or 410 bore 2.5-inch shotshells. Fiber optic front sights, adjustable rear.

Perf: $300 **Exc:** $260 **VGood:** $225

ROSSI RANCH HAND

Lever action based on Winchester Model 92 rifle. Chambered in 38/.357, 45 Colt or 44 magnum, 6-shot capacity. Barrel length is 12 inches making this model a handgun under federal law. Weight: 4 lbs. Length: 24 inches overall. Brazilian hardwood stock, adjustable buckhorn rear sight. Matte blue or case hardened finish with oversized lever loop.

Perf: $550 **Exc:** $465 **VGood:** $400

ROSSI WIZARD

Caliber: 243 Win. or 22-250 Rem. Break-open single shot with interchangeable 11-inch barrel. Overall length is 20.4 inches. Fiber optic sights, blue or stainless finish, wood or synthetic stock, camo finish also available.

Perf: $285 **Exc:** $250 **VGood:** $215

Add 10 percent for stainless finish, 20 percent for fiber optic sights

ROYAL

Semi-automatic; 7.63mm Mauser; 5-1/2-inch barrel; 11-3/4-inch overall length; 10-shot magazine; grooved wood grips. Spanish copy of Mauser Model 1896 but with different internal mechanism, round bolt. Introduced 1926; dropped 1930 when the maker replaced it with the Azul, an almost identical copy of the Mauser.

Exc: $1800 **VGood:** $1250 **Good:** $850

RPM XL SINGLE SHOT

Single shot; 22 LR through 45-70; 8-inch, 10-3/4-inch, 12-inch, 14-inch barrel; weighs about 60 oz.; smooth Goncalo Alves stock with thumb and heel rest; hooded front sight with interchangeable post, ISGW fully-adjustable rear; barrel tapped and drilled for scope mount; cocking indicator; spring-loaded barrel lock; positive hammer-block safety.

New: $750 **Perf:** $600 **Exc:** $500

RPM XL HUNTER SINGLE SHOT

Same specs as RPM XL except stainless frame; 5/16-inch underlug; latch lever; positive extractor.

New: $1000 **Perf:** $850 **Exc:** $750

Royal

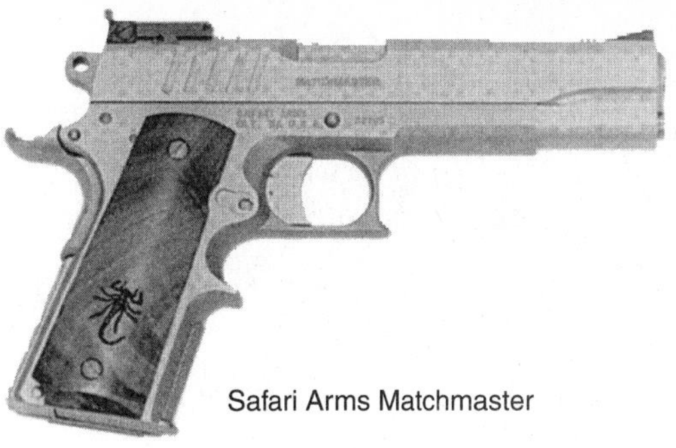
Safari Arms Matchmaster

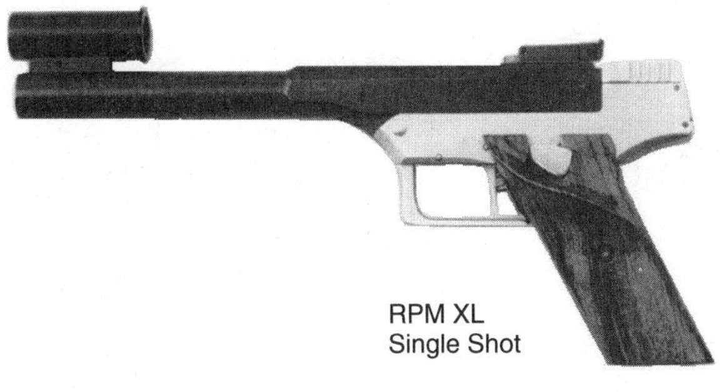
RPM XL
Single Shot

Safari Arms Enforcer

SAFARI ARMS BLACK WIDOW

Semi-automatic; 45 ACP; 6-shot; 3-3/4-inch barrel; 7-11/16-inch overall length; weighs 28 oz.; adjustable sights; scrimshawed Micarta grip with black widow ensignia; nickel finish. Discontinued 1987.

Exc: $500 **VGood:** $450 **Good:** $400

SAFARI ARMS COHORT PISTOL

Caliber: 45 ACP, 7-shot magazine. Barrel: 3.8-inch, 416 stainless. Weight: 37 oz. Length: 8.5-inch overall. Stocks: Smooth walnut with laser-etched black widow logo. Sights: Ramped blade front, LPA adjustable rear. Features: Combines the Enforcer model, slide and MatchMaster frame. Beavertail grip safety; extended thumb safety and slide release; Commander-style hammer. Throated, polished and tuned. Satin stainless finish. Introduced 1996.

New: $650 **Perf:** $600 **Exc:** $550

SAFARI ARMS ENFORCER

Semi-automatic; single action; 45 ACP; 6-shot magazine; 3-13/16-inch barrel; 7-5/16-inch overall length; weighs 36 oz.; smooth walnut grips with etched black widow spider logo; ramped blade front sight, LPA adjustable rear; stainless barrel; extended safety and slide release; Commander-style hammer; beavertail grip safety; throated, polished, tuned; Parkerized matte black or satin stainless steel finishes. In 1988 Olympic Arms bought M-S Safari Arms of Phoenix, Arizona. Some guns will be marked M-S Safari; some Safari Arms. Current production guns are still being stamped "Safari Arms." Made in U.S. by Olympic Arms, Inc.'s specialty shop Schuetzen Pistol Works. Still produced.

New: $600 **Perf:** $500 **Exc:** $450

SAFARI ARMS ENFORCER CARRYCOMP II

Same specs as the Enforcer except Wil Schueman-designed hybrid compensator system. In 1988 Olympic Arms bought M-S Safari Arms of Phoenix, Arizona. Some guns will be marked M-S Safari; some Safari Arms. Current production guns are still being stamped "Safari Arms." Made in U.S. by Olympic Arms, Inc.'s specialty shop Schuetzen Pistol Works. Introduced 1993.

New: $1100 **Perf:** $900 **Exc:** $750

SAFARI ARMS G.I. SAFARI

Semi-automatic; single action; 45 ACP; 7-shot magazine; 5-inch barrel; 8-1/2-inch overall length; weighs 40 oz.; checkered walnut grips; blade front sight, fixed rear; beavertail grip safety; extended safety and slide release; Commander-style hammer; chrome-lined 4140 steel barrel; National Match 416 stainless optional; Parkerized matte black finish. Made in U.S. by Safari Arms, Inc. Introduced 1991.

New: $450 **Perf:** $350 **Exc:** $225

SAFARI ARMS MATCHMASTER

Semi-automatic; single action; 45 ACP; 7-shot magazine; 5-inch, 6-inch barrel; 8-1/2-inch overall length; weighs 38 oz.; smooth walnut grips with etched scorpion logo; ramped blade front sight, LPA adjustable rear; stainless steel barrel; beavertail grip safety; extended safety; extended slide release; Commander-style hammer; throated, polished, tuned; Parkerized matte black or satin stainless steel. In 1988 Olympic Arms bought M-S Safari Arms of Phoenix, Arizona. Some guns will be marked M-S Safari; some Safari Arms. Current production guns are still being stamped "Safari Arms." Made in U.S. by Olympic Arms, Inc.'s specialty shop Schuetzen Pistol Works. Introduced 1995; still produced.

New: $600 **Perf:** $550 **Exc:** $475

SAFARI ARMS MATCHMASTER CARRYCOMP I

Same specs as Matchmaster except Wil Schueman-designed hybrid compensator system. Made in U.S. by Olympic Arms, Inc. Introduced 1993.

New: $1000 **Perf:** $850 **Exc:** $750

SAFARI ARMS MODEL 81

Semi-automatic; 45 ACP, 38 Spl.; 5-inch barrel; weighs 42 oz.; adjustable sights; fixed or adjustable walnut target grips; optional Aristocrat rib with extended front sight optional; nickel finish. Introduced 1983; discontinued 1987.

Exc: $750 **VGood:** $550 **Good:** $450

SAFARI ARMS MODEL 81BP

Same specs as Model 81 except contoured front grip strap; quicker slide cycle time; designed for bowling pin matches. Introduced 1983; discontinued 1987.

Exc: $850 **VGood:** $650 **Good:** $500

SAFARI ARMS MODEL 81L

Same specs as Model 81 except 6-inch barrel; long slide; weighs 45 oz. Introduced 1983; discontinued 1987.

Exc: $750 **VGood:** $550 **Good:** $400

SAFARI ARMS MODEL 81NM

Same specs as Model 81 except flat front grip strap. Introduced 1983; discontinued 1987.

Exc: $750 **VGood:** $600 **Good:** $500

SAFARI ARMS MODEL 81 SILUETA

Same specs as Model 81 except 38-45 wildcat, 45 ACP; 10-inch barrel; designed for silhouette competition. Introduced 1983; discontinued 1987.

Exc: $850 **VGood:** $650 **Good:** $500

SAFARI ARMS OA-93

Semi-automatic; single action; 223, 7.62x39mm; 20-, 30-shot magazine (223), 5-, 30-shot magazine (7.62x39mm); 6-inch, 9-inch, 14-inch 4140 steel or 416 stainless barrel; 15 oz.; 15-3/4-inch overall length (6-inch barrel); weighs 4 lbs.; A2 stowaway pistol grip; no sights; cut-off carrying handle with attached scope rail; AR-15 receiver with special bolt carrier; short slotted aluminum handguard; button-cut or broach-cut barrel; Vortex flash suppressor. Made in U.S. by Olympic Arms, Inc. Introduced 1993; dropped 1994.

New: $2500 **Perf:** $2250 **Exc:** $2000

SAFARI ARMS RELIABLE PISTOL

Caliber: 45 ACP, 7-shot magazine. Barrel: 5-inch, 416 stainless steel. Weight: 39 oz. Length: 8.5-inch overall. Stocks: Checkered walnut. Sights: Ramped blade front, LPA adjustable rear. Features: Beavertail grip safety; long aluminum trigger; full-length recoil spring guide; Commander-style hammer. Throated, polished and tuned. Satin stainless steel finish. Introduced 1996; dropped 1998.

New: $650 **Perf:** $600 **Exc:** $550

SAFARI ARMS RELIABLE 4-STAR PISTOL

Similar to the Reliable except has 4.5-inch barrel, 7.5-inch overall length, and weighs 35.7 oz. Introduced 1996.

New: $700 **Perf:** $600 **Exc:** $550

Sarsilmaz Professional

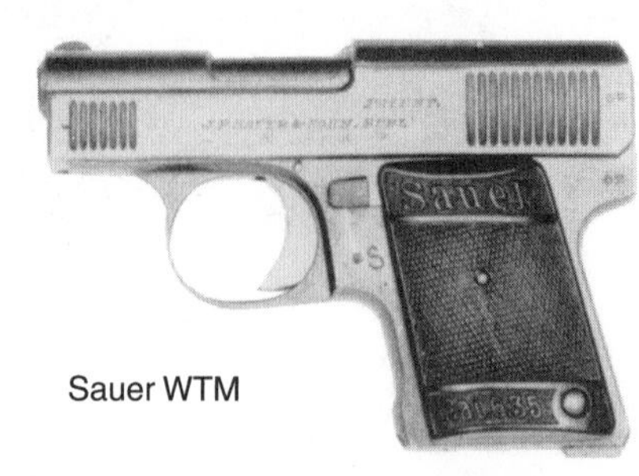
Sauer WTM

Sauer Model 38H

Sarsilmaz Hancer 2000

Sauer Model 1913

SAFARI ARMS RENEGADE

Caliber: 45 ACP, 7-shot magazine. Barrel: 5-inch, 416 stainless steel. Weight: 39 oz. Length: 8.5-inch overall. Stocks: Checkered walnut. Sights: Ramped blade, LPA adjustable rear. Features: True left-hand pistol. Beavertail grip safety; long aluminum trigger; full-length recoil spring guide; Commander-style hammer; satin stainless finish. Throated, polished and tuned. Introduced 1996; dropped 1998.

New: $950 **Perf:** $800 **Exc:** $650

SAFARI ARMS UNLIMITED

Single shot; bolt action; 308 or smaller; 14-15/16-inch barrel; 21-1/2-inch overall length; weighs 72 oz.; open iron sights; fiberglass stock; electronic trigger; black finish. Introduced 1983; discontinued 1987.

Exc: $800 **VGood:** $700 **Good:** $575

SAKO TRIACE MATCH

Semi-automatic; 22 Short, 22 LR, 32 S&W Long; 6-shot; 5-7/8-inch barrel; 11-inch overall length; weighs 44 to 48 oz.; adjustable trigger for weight of pull, free travel and sear engagement; marketed in case with tool/cleaning kit, two magazines. Made in Finland. Introduced 1988; discontinued 1989.

Exc: $1200 **VGood:** $1000 **Good:** $750

SARSILMAZ PROFESSIONAL

CZ-75-style compensated semi-auto in white chrome finish chambered for 9mm. Single-action with adjustable trigger, laser engraving. 16 or 18 round capacity. 42.3 oz.; 5.1-inch barrel.

New: $400 **Exc:** $375 **VGood:** $300

SARSILMAZ K2

CZ-75-style double-action semi-auto in white chrome or blued. Chambered for 9mm. 16 or 18 round capacity. 35.3 oz.; 4.6-inch barrel. Plastic grips.

New: $300 **Exc:** $275 **VGood:** $235

SARSILMAZ KAMA SPORT

CZ-75-style semi-auto 9mm in white chrome or blued. Double-action with 3.9-inch compensated barrel, laser engraving. 15+1 or 17+1 capacity. 35.4 oz. Plastic grips.

New: $350 **Exc:** $295 **VGood:** $250

SARSILMAZ KAMA

CZ-75-style semi-auto 9mm in white chrome or blued. Double-action with 4.3-inch compensated barrel, laser engraving. 15+1 or 17+1 capacity. 35.4 oz.; 7.7-inch. Plastic grips.

New: $350 **Exc:** $295 **VGood:** $250

SARSILMAZ KILINC 2000 MEGA

CZ-75-style semi-auto 9mm in white chrome or blued. Double-action with 4.7-inch barrel. 16 or 18 capacity. 35 oz. Plastic grips. Fixed sights.

New: $225 **Exc:** $200 **VGood:** $150

SARSILMAZ KILINC 2000 LIGHT

CZ-75-style semi-auto 9mm in white chrome, blued or camo. Double-action with 4.7-inch barrel, laser engraving. 15+1 or 17+1 capacity. 35.4 oz. Plastic grips.

New: $225 **Exc:** $200 **VGood:** $150

SARSILMAZ HANCER 2000/2000 LIGHT

CZ-75-style semi-auto 9mm in white chrome or blued. Double-action with 3.9-inch barrel, laser engraving. 13+1 capacity. 33.5 oz. (25.4 oz. Light model). Plastic grips.

New: $225 **Exc:** $200 **VGood:** $150

SARSILMAZ BERNARDELLI

CZ-75-style double-action semi-auto in 9mm. Black/white or blued finish. The 15+1 model has a 4.7-inch barrel, 27 oz., Plastic grips. The 13+1 model has a 3.9-inch barrel; 26.7 oz. Plastic grips, fixed sights.

New: $235 **Exc:** $225 **VGood:** $175

SAUER MODEL 28

Semi-automatic; 25 ACP; 6-shot; 3-inch overall length; slanted serrations on slide; top ejection; checkered black rubber grips with Sauer imprint; blued finish. Introduced about 1928; discontinued 1938.

Exc: $200 **VGood:** $165 **Good:** $135

SAUER MODEL 38H

Semi-automatic; double action; 32 ACP; 7-shot; 3-1/4-inch barrel; 6-1/4-inch overall length; fixed sights; black plastic grips; blued finish. Introduced 1938; discontinued 1944.

Exc: $500 **VGood:** $400 **Good:** $300

SAUER MODEL 1913

Semi-automatic; 32 ACP; 7-shot; 3-inch barrel; 5-7/8-inch overall length; fixed sights; checkered hard rubber black grips; blued finish. Introduced 1913; discontinued 1930.

Exc: $400 **VGood:** $300 **Good:** $200

SAUER MODEL 1913 POCKET

Same specs as Model 1913 except smaller in size; 25 ACP; 2-1/2-inch barrel; 4-1/4-inch overall length; improved grip, safety features. Introduced 1920; discontinued 1930.

Exc: $400 **VGood:** $300 **Good:** $200

SAUER MODEL 1930 (BEHORDEN MODEL)

Semi-automatic; 32 ACP; 7-shot; 3-inch barrel; fixed sights; black plastic grips; blued finish. Has grip safety on front of trigger. Introduced 1930; discontinued 1938.

Exc: $500 **VGood:** $400 **Good:** $300

SAUER WTM

Semi-automatic; 25 ACP; 6-shot; 2-1/2-inch barrel; 4-1/8-inch overall length; fixed sights; checkered hard rubber grips; top ejector; fluted slide; blued finish. Introduced 1924; discontinued 1927.

Exc: $250 **VGood:** $200 **Good:** $150

SAVAGE AUTOMATIC PISTOL

Semi-automatic; 25 ACP; 6-shot; 2-3/8-inch barrel; weighs 12 oz.; hammerless; wide or narrow slide serrations. Experimental only pre-WWI. Only 50-100 produced. Extremely rare; extremely valuable.

SAVAGE MODEL 101

Single shot; single action; 22 Short, 22 LR; 5-1/2-inch barrel integral with chamber; 9-inch overall length; adjustable slotted rear sight, blade front; compressed, plastic-impregnated wood grips; fake cylinder swings out for loading, ejection; manual ejection with spring-rod ejector;

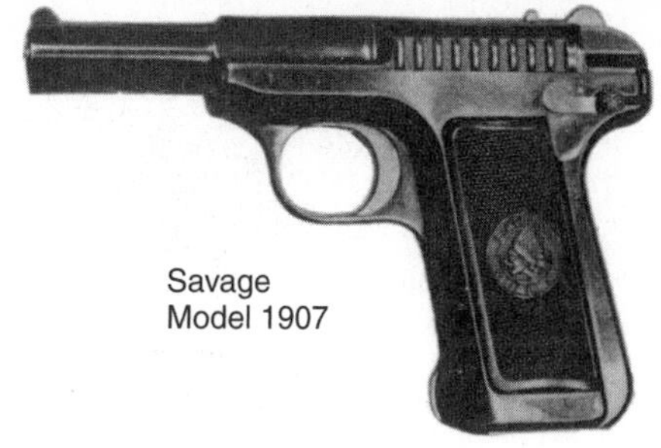
Savage Model 1907

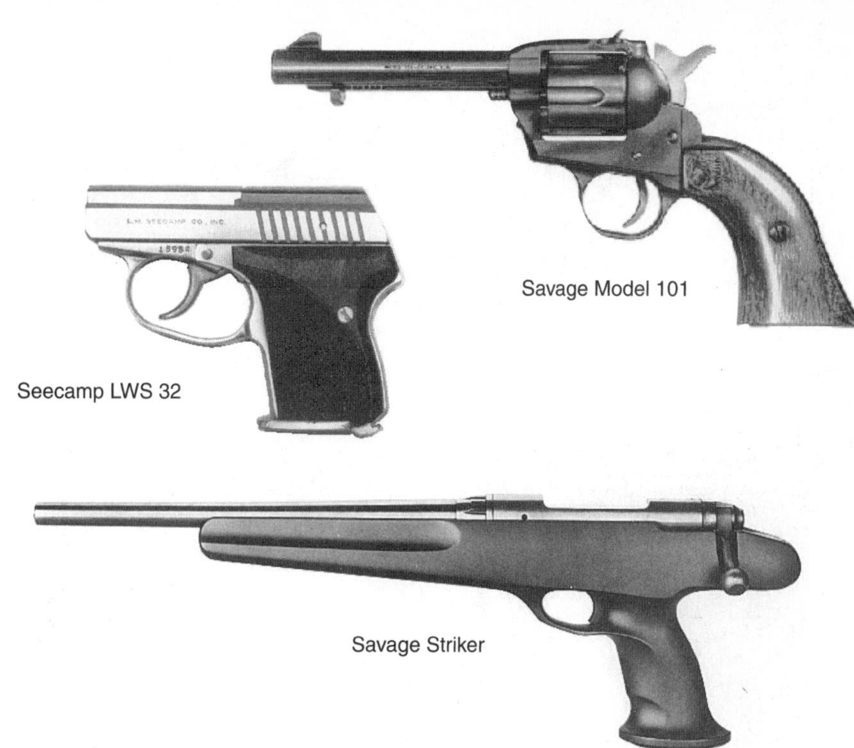
Savage Model 101

Seecamp LWS 32

Savage Striker

SCCY CPX Gen 2

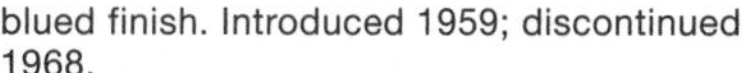

blued finish. Introduced 1959; discontinued 1968.

Exc: $295 **VGood:** $200 **Good:** $135

SAVAGE MODEL 1907

Semi-automatic; 32 ACP, 380 ACP; 10-shot (32), 9-shot (380); 3 3/4-inch barrel, 6-1/2-inch overall length (32 ACP); 4-1/2-inch barrel, 7-inch overall length (380 ACP); fixed sights; checkered hard rubber stocks; exposed hammer; blued finish. The 380-caliber serial number followed by letter "B". Manufactured 1910 to 1917.

32 ACP

Exc: $400 **VGood:** $300 **Good:** $200

380 ACP

Exc: $550 **VGood:** $400 **Good:** $300

SAVAGE MODEL 1907 U.S. ARMY TEST TRIAL

Same specs as Model 1907 except enlarged model for 45 ACP only; exposed hammer; approximately 300 made for test trials from 1907 to 1911.

Exc: $7000 **VGood:** $5500 **Good:** $3500

SAVAGE MODEL 1915 HAMMERLESS

Semi-automatic; 32 ACP, 380 ACP; 10-shot (32), 9-shot (380); 3-3/4-inch barrel, 6-1/2-inch overall length (32 ACP); 4-1/2-inch barrel, 7-inch overall (380 ACP); fixed sights; checkered hard rubber stocks; hammerless; grip safety; blued finish. Manufactured 1915 to 1917.

32 caliber

Exc: $500 **VGood:** $400 **Good:** $300

380 caliber

Exc: $600 **VGood:** $500 **Good:** $400

SAVAGE MODEL 1917

Semi-automatic; 32 ACP, 380 ACP; 10-shot (32), 9-shot (380); 3-3/4-inch barrel, 6-1/2-inch overall length (32 ACP); 4-1/2-inch barrel, 7-inch overall length (380 ACP); fixed sights; hard rubber grips; spurred hammer; blued finish. Marked "Savage Model 1917" on left side. Introduced 1920; discontinued 1928.

32 caliber

Exc: $500 **VGood:** $400 **Good:** $300

380 caliber

Exc: $600 **VGood:** $500 **Good:** $375

SAVAGE STRIKER BOLT-ACTION HUNTING HANDGUN

Caliber: 22-250, 243, 308, 2-shot magazine. Barrel: 14-inch. Weight: About 5 lbs. Length: 22-1/2-inch overall. Stock: Black composite ambidextrous mid-grip; grooved forend; "Dual Pillar" bedding. Sights: None furnished; drilled and tapped for scope mounting. Features: Short left-hand bolt with right-hand ejection; free-floated barrel; uses Savage Model 110 rifle scope rings/bases. Introduced 1998. Made in U.S. by Savage Arms, Inc.

New: $500 **Perf:** $395 **Exc:** $300

SCCY CPX GEN 2

Hammer fired double action only compact pistol with a black polymer frame and stainless steel slide and barrel with fixed three dot sights and black or matte stainless finish. Available with or without thumb safety. Chambered in 9x19 mm. Introduced in 2012.

Perf: $280 **Exc:** $250 **VGood:** $230

SECURITY INDUSTRIES MODEL PM357

Revolver; double action; 357 Mag.; 5-shot; 2-1/2-inch barrel; 7-1/2-inch overall length; fixed sights; uncheckered American walnut target stocks; stainless steel. Introduced 1973; discontinued 1977.

Exc: $225 **VGood:** $175 **Good:** $150

SECURITY INDUSTRIES MODEL PPM357

Revolver; double action; 357 Mag.; 5-shot; 2-inch barrel; 6-1/8-inch overall length; fixed sights; checkered American walnut target stocks; stainless steel. Introduced 1976 with spurless hammer, converted to conventional hammer 1977; discontinued 1977.

Exc: $225 **VGood:** $175 **Good:** $150

SECURITY INDUSTRIES MODEL PSS38

Revolver; double action; 38 Spl.; 5-shot; 2-inch barrel; 6-1/2-inch overall length; fixed sights; checkered or smooth American walnut stocks; stainless steel. Introduced 1973; discontinued 1977.

Exc: $150 **VGood:** $125 **Good:** $110

SEDCO MODEL SP-22

Semi-automatic; single action; 22 LR; 6-shot; 2-1/2-inch barrel; 5-inch overall length; weighs 11 oz.; fixed sights; simulated pearl stocks; rotary safety blocks sear, slide; chrome or black Teflon finish. Introduced 1988; discontinued 1990.

Exc: $100 **VGood:** $90 **Good:** $70

SEDGELY BABY HAMMERLESS MODEL

Revolver; double action; 22 LR; 6-shot; 4-inch overall length; solid frame; hard rubber stocks; fixed sights; folding trigger; blued or nickel finish. Manufactured 1930 to 1939.

Exc: $275 **VGood:** $200 **Good:** $150

SEECAMP LWS 25 ACP MODEL

Semi-automatic; double action; 25 ACP; 7-shot; 2-inch barrel; 4-1/8-inch overall length; weighs 12 oz.; fixed sights; plastic grips; stainless steel; matte finish. Introduced 1982; discontinued 1985.

Exc: $400 **VGood:** $300 **Good:** $225

SEECAMP LWS 32

Semi-automatic; double-action-only; 32 ACP Win. Silvertip; 6-shot magazine; 2-inch barrel; 4-1/8-inch overall length; weighs 10-1/2 oz.; glass-filled nylon grips; smooth, no-snag, contoured slide and barrel top serve as sights; aircraft quality 17-4 PH stainless steel; inertia-operated firing pin; magazine safety disconnector; polished stainless. Made in U.S. by L.W. Seecamp. Introduced 1985.

New: $500 **Perf:** $450 **Exc:** $400

SHERIDAN KNOCABOUT

Single shot; tip-up action; 22 Short, 22 LR; 5-inch barrel; 8-3/4-inch overall length; fixed sights; checkered plastic grips; blued finish. Introduced 1953; discontinued 1960. Note that the correct spelling is "Knocabout" (without the "k"). It was also referred to by the factory as the Model D.

Exc: $295 **VGood:** $225 **Good:** $175

SIGARMS P220R SAO

SIGARMS P220 Platinum Elite

SIGARMS P220R Carry Equinox

SIGARMS P220 ELITE

SIG Arms MPX9

SIG Sauer P220 "American"

SIG P210-2

Semi-automatic; single action; 9mm Para., 7.65mm Luger; 8-shot; 4-3/4-inch barrel; 8-1/2-inch overall length; weighs 32 oz.; fixed sights; black plastic grips; standard-issue Swiss army sidearm; blued finish. Manufactured in Switzerland. Introduced 1947; still in production.

Exc: $1600 **VGood:** $1250 **Good:** $900

SIG P210-1

Same specs as P210-2 except; walnut grips; polished blued finish. Discontinued 1986.

Exc: $2250 **VGood:** $2000 **Good:** $1750

SIG P210-5

Same specs as P210-2 except 6-inch barrel; micrometer sights; target trigger special hammer; hard rubber grips; matte finish.

Exc: $2250 **VGood:** $1950 **Good:** $1500

SIG P210-6

Same specs as P210-2 except fixed rear sight, target front; target trigger. Still in production.

New: $2000 **Perf:** $1750 **Exc:** $1500

SIG-HAMMERLI MODEL P240

Semi-automatic; single action; 32 S&W Long, 38 Spl.; 5-shot; 6-inch barrel; 10-inch overall length; micrometer rear sight, post front; uncheckered European walnut stocks with target thumbrest; adjustable triggers; blued finish. Manufactured in Switzerland. Introduced 1975; discontinued 1988.

Exc: $1350 **VGood:** $1000 **Good:** $850

SIG SAUER P210 LEGEND

Caliber: 9mm, 8-shot magazine. Single-action. Barrel length, 4.7 inches; overall length, 8.5 inches; weight, 37.4 oz. Custom wood grips. Fixed or adjustable target sights. Carbon steel slide and frame with Nitron coating, improved beavertail and manual safety.

Perf: $1975 **Exc:** $1710 **VGood:** $1450

Add 10 percent for adjustable sights

SIG SAUER P220 "AMERICAN"

Semi-automatic; double action; 38 Super, 45 ACP; 9-shot (38 Super), 7-shot (45 ACP) magazine; 4-3/8-inch barrel; 7-3/4-inch overall length; weighs 28-1/4 oz. (9mm); checkered black plastic grips; blade front sight, drift-adjustable rear; squared combat-type trigger guard; side-button magazine release. Imported from Germany by SIGARMS, Inc. Still imported but only in 45 ACP.

New: $850 **Perf:** $700 **Exc:** $550

With Siglite night sights

New: $950 **Perf:** $700 **Exc:** $550

With K-Kote finish

New: $875 **Perf:** $725 **Exc:** $575

With K-Kote finish, Siglite night sights

New: $975 **Perf:** $900 **Exc:** $700

SIGARMS MPX 9

Select-fire (semi/full) automatic, short-stroke gas piston SMG. Semi-automatic version (MPX-C) is available for civilian purchase. 9mm, .40 S&W and .357 Sig. AR styled lower receiver with monolithic, modular upper receiver. Several variants with barrel lengths ranging from 4.5 to 16 inches. Functions with frangible, sub-sonic, standard or high velocity ammunition. Capacity: 10, 20 or 30 rounds. Full-auto version rate of fire: 850 rpm. Introduced 2013.

Perf: $2000 **Exc:** $1800 **VGood:** $1650

SIGARMS P220R SAO

An 8+1 or 10+1 capacity single-action semi-auto chambered for .45 ACP. Polymer grip and Nitron finish, 4.4-inch barrel, 30.4 oz., 5-lb. trigger. Picatinny rail.

New: $800 **Exc:** $725 **VGood:** $625

SIGARMS P220R DAK

Semi-auto with 8+1 or 10+1 capacity chambered for .45 ACP. Polymer grip and Nitron finish, 4.4-inch barrel, 30.4 oz., 7.5-lb. trigger. Picatinny rail.

New: $800 **Exc:** $725 **VGood:** $625

SIGARMS P220 SAS

An 8+1 capacity double-action semi-auto chambered for .45 ACP. Fixed sights, wood grips, 4.4-inch barrel, 30.4 oz., 6.5-lb. trigger.

New: $1000 **Exc:** $900 **VGood:** $750

SIGARMS P220 CARRY SAS

An 8+1 capacity double-action semi-auto chambered for .45 ACP. Fixed sights, wood grips, 3.9-inch barrel, 30.4 oz., 6.5-lb. trigger.

New: $1000 **Exc:** $900 **VGood:** $750

SIGARMS P220 CARRY

An 8+1 or 10+1 capacity single/double-action semi-auto chambered for .45 ACP. Fixed sights, polymer grips, 3.9-inch barrel, 30.4 oz.

New: $950 **Exc:** $750 **VGood:** $650

SIGARMS P220R EQUINOX

An 8+1 or 10+1 capacity single/double-action semi-auto chambered for .45 ACP. Fixed sights, wood grips, 4.4-inch barrel, 30.4 oz.

New: $1100 **Exc:**950 **VGood:** $750

SIGARMS P220R CARRY EQUINOX

An 8+1 or 10+1 capacity single/double-action semi-auto chambered for .45 ACP. Fixed sights, wood grips, 3.9-inch barrel, 30.4 oz.

New: $1200 **Exc:** $1000 **VGood:** $850

SIGARMS P220 COMBAT

Similar to P220 but with sand-colored alloy slide and steel frame. Capacity 8+1 or 10+1. Designed for SOCOM sidearm trials.

New: $1000 **Exc:** $900 **VGood:** $700

SIGARMS P220 MATCH

Similar to P220 but with 5-inch barrel and adjustable sights.

New: $1250 **Exc:** $1000 **VGood:** $800

SIGARMS P220 SUPER MATCH

Super-accurized version of P220 Match with single-action-only trigger and custom wood grips. Limited edition.

New: $1795 **Exc:** $1200 **VGood:** $975

SIGARMS P220 COMPACT

Similar to P220 but with 3.9-inch barrel and 6+1 capacity. Single-action-only or single-/double-action. Various finish, grip and sight options.

New: $1000 **Exc:** $875 **VGood:** $700

SIGARMS P220 ELITE

Similar to P220 but with SIG's new Short Reset Trigger or SRT. Beavertail safety, front cocking serrations, front strap checkering, SIGLITE® Night Sights and custom wood grips. Introduced in 2008. Also available in single action-only model.

New: $1140 **Exc:** $925 **VGood:** $700

SIGARMS P226 Elite

SIGARMS P226 SCT

SIGARMS P226 Platinum Elite

SIGARMS P226 Elite Stainless

SIGARMS P226 SAO

SIGARMS P227

SIGARMS P220 ELITE STAINLESS

Similar to above but in stainless. Introduced 2008.

New: $1240 **Exc:** $1000 **VGood:** $800

SIGARMS P220 CARRY ELITE STAINLESS

Compact version of above with 3.9-inch barrel; chambered in .45 ACP with 8-round capacity. Introduced 2008.

New: $1250 **Exc:** $1050 **VGood:** $850

SIGARMS P220 PLATINUM ELITE

Fine-tuned, enhanced version of P220 Elite with front cocking serrations, front strap checkering, SIGLITE® Adjustable Combat Night Sights and custom aluminum grips.

New: $1400 **Exc:** $1200 **VGood:** $1000

SIG SAUER P225

Semi-automatic; double action, DA-only; 9mm Para.; 8-shot; 3-7/8-inch barrel; 7-3/32-inch overall length; weighs 26 oz.; blade-type front sight, windage-adjustable rear; checkered black plastic stocks; squared combat-type trigger guard; shorter, lighter version of P220; blued finish. Made in Germany. Introduced 1985, dropped 1998.

New: $600 **Perf:** $550 **Exc:** $450

K-Kote finish

New: $650 **Perf:** $600 **Exc:** $500

Nickel finish

New: $650 **Perf:** $600 **Exc:** $500

Siglite night sights

New: $700 **Perf:** $650 **Exc:** $525

SIG SAUER P226

Semi-automatic; double action, DA-only; 9mm Para.; 15-, 20-shot; 4-3/8-inch barrel; weighs 26-1/2 oz.; high contrast sights; black plastic checkered stocks; blued finish. Made in Germany. Introduced 1983; still imported.

New: $900 **Perf:** $750 **Exc:** $600

K-Kote finish

New: $950 **Perf:** $750 **Exc:** $600

Nickel finish

New: $950 **Perf:** $750 **Exc:** $600

Siglite night sights

New: $1000 **Perf:** $875 **Exc:** $700

SIGARMS P226 SAS

Double-action semi-auto with 12+1 capacity chambered for .40 S&W. Fixed sights, wood grips, 4.4-inch barrel, 34 oz., 6.5-lb. trigger.

New: $1000 **Exc:** $900 **VGood:** $750

SIGARMS P 226 SAO

Semi-automatic, 9mm handgun. Single action only (SAO) trigger mechanism. 7.7 inches long, 32.6 ounces. 15+1 capacity. Alloy frame, stainless steel slide with Nitron finish. Plastic checkered stocks. Made in Germany. Introduced 2013.

Perf: $1150 **Exc:** $1075 **VGood:** $950

SIGARMS P226R EQUINOX

An 10+1 or 12+1 capacity single/double-action semi-auto chambered for .40 S&W. Fixed sights, wood grips, 4.4-inch barrel, 34 oz.

New: $1200 **Exc:** $975 **VGood:** $750

SIGARMS P226 SCT

An all black, Nitron® finished P226 featuring front cocking serrations, a SIGLITE® rear night sight, a TRUGLO® tritium fiber optic front sight and comes with four newly designed 20-round magazines for the 9mm version or four 15-round magazines for the .40S&W version.

New: $1100 **Exc:** $900 **VGood:** $650

SIGARMS P226 ELITE

Introduced 2008. Similar to P226 but with redesigned shoprt-reset trigger and improved ergonomics. Chambered in 9mm, .40 S&W and .357 SIG.

New: $1100 **Exc:** $900 **VGood:** $650

SIGARMS P226 ELITE STAINLESS

Similar to above but in stainless steel.

New: $1200 **Exc:** $900 **VGood:** $700

SIGARMS P226 PLATINUM ELITE

Fine-tuned, enhanced version of P226 Elite with front cocking serrations, front strap checkering, SIGLITE® Adjustable Combat Night Sights and custom aluminum grips.

New: $1275 **Exc:** $950 **VGood:** $750

SIGARMS P 227

Semi-automatic, .45 ACP handgun. Double-action (DA) / Single-action (SA) trigger mechanism. 7.7 inches long, 32.0 ounces. 10+1 capacity or 14+1 with extended magazine. Alloy frame, stainless steel slide with Nitron finish. SIG-Lite night sights. One-piece ergonomic grips. Made in Germany. Introduced 2013.

Perf: $950 **Exc:** $825 **VGood:** $715

SIG SAUER P228

Semi-automatic; double action, DA-only; 9mm Para.; 10-shot; 3-7/8-inch barrel; 7-inch overall length; weighs 29 oz.; three-dot sights; black plastic grips; blued finish. Made in Germany. Introduced 1989; dropped 1997.

New: $650 **Perf:** $550 **Exc:** $475

K-Kote finish

New: $700 **Perf:** $600 **Exc:** $500

Nickel finish

New: $700 **Perf:** $600 **Exc:** $500

Siglite night sights

New: $750 **Perf:** $650 **Exc:** $550

SIG SAUER P229

Semi-automatic; double action, DA-only; 9mm Para., 40 S&W, 357 SIG; 12-shot; 3-7/8-inch barrel; 7-inch overall length; 30-1/2 oz.; three-dot sights; checkered black plastic grips; aluminum alloy frame; blued slide. Made in Germany. Introduced 1991; still produced.

New: $700 **Perf:** $600 **Exc:** $500

Siglite night sights

New: $800 **Perf:** $700 **Exc:** $575

Nickel

New: $850 **Perf:** $750 **Exc:** $650

SIG SAUER P229 S AUTO PISTOL

Similar to the P229 except available in 357 SIG only; 4.8-inch heavy barrel; 8.6-inch overall length; weighs 40.6 oz.; vented compensator; adjustable target sights; rubber grips; extended slide latch and magazine release. Made of stainless steel. Introduced 1998.

New: $1100 **Perf:** $950 **Exc:** $750

SIGARMS P229 ELITE

The P229 Elite features an ergonomic beavertail grip, front cocking serrations, front strap checkering,

SIGARMS P229 Elite

SIG Sauer P238 Extreme

SIGARMS P229 Platinuim Elite

SIG Sauer P230

SIGARMS P250 Compact

SIGLITE Night Sights, custom wood grips and the new Short Reset Trigger or SRT. Available in 9mm and .40 S&W.

New: $1100 **Perf:** $950 **Exc:** $750

SIGARMS P229 PLATINUM ELITE

Fine-tuned, enhanced version of P229 Elite with front cocking serrations, front strap checkering, SIGLITE® Adjustable Combat Night Sights and custom aluminum grips.

New: $1200 **Perf:** $950 **Exc:** $750

SIGARMS 1911 C3

!911-style 6+1 autoloader in .45 ACP. 4-2/4-inch barrel, alloy frame. Introduced in 2008.

New: $1100 **Perf:** $950 **Exc:** $750

SIGARMS 1911 PLATINUM ELITE

!911-style 8+1 autoloader in .45 ACP. 5-inch barrel, Nitron frame, aluminum grips. Introduced in 2008.

New: $1200 **Perf:** $950 **Exc:** $750

SIGARMS 1911 PLATINUM ELITE CARRY

Compact version of the above with 4.5-inch barrel. Introduced in 2008.

New: $1200 **Perf:** $950 **Exc:** $750

SIG SAUER P230

Semi-automatic; double action; 22 LR, 32 ACP, 380 ACP, 9mm Ultra; 10-shot (22 LR), 8-shot (32 ACP), 7-shot (380 ACP, 9mm); 3-3/4-inch barrel; 6-1/2-inch overall length; weighs 16 oz.; fixed sights; checkered black plastic stocks; blued finish. Introduced 1977; dropped 1996. Manufactured in Germany.

New: $425 **Exc:** $375 **Exc:** $350

SIG SAUER P230 SL STAINLESS

Same specs as P230 except stainless steel; 22 oz.

New: $450 **Exc:** $400 **Exc:** $350

SIG SAUER P232 PERSONAL SIZE PISTOL

Semi-automatic; double action. Improved version of P230; 32 ACP, 380 ACP, 8-shot (32 ACP), 7-shot (380 ACP); 3-3/4-inch barrel; 6-1/2-inch overall length; weighs 16 oz.; fixed sights; checkered black plastic stocks; blued finish. Introduced 1997. Imported from Germany by SIGARMS, Inc.

New: $500 **Exc:** $600 **Exc:** $500

SIG SAUER P238/P238 EXTREME

Caliber: 380 ACP, 6 or 7-shot magazine. Similar to Colt Mustang. Barrel length, 2.7 inches; weight, 15.4 oz., overall length 5.5 inches. Hogue G-10 or Rosewood grips. Contrast / SIGLITE night sights. Blued or two-tone finish. Extreme model has extended grip

Perf: $520 **Exc:** $450 **VGood:** $395

Add 15 percent for rosewood grips or Extreme model

SIG SAUER P-238 EQUINOX

As above with two tone nitron finish. Truglo front sight and Siglite rear sight.

Perf: $600 **Exc:** $525 **VGood:** $475

SIG SAUER P-238 STAINLESS

As above, made from stainless steel.

Perf: $625 **Exc:** $550 **VGood:** $475

SIG SAUER P239 PISTOL

Semi-automatic; double action; 9mm Para., 8-shot, 357 SIG, 40 S&W, 7-shot magazine. Barrel: 3.6-inch Weight: 25.2 oz. Length: 6.6-inch overall. Stocks: Checkered black composite. Sights: Blade front, rear adjustable for windage. Optional Siglite night sights. Features: SA/DA or DAO; blackened stainless steel slide, aluminum alloy frame. Introduced 1996.

New: $600 **Exc:** $500 **Exc:** $450

With Siglite night sights

New: $675 **Exc:** $550 **Exc:** $500

SIGARMS P250 COMPACT

Introduced in 2008. A 9mm semiauto pistol of so-called "modular design" that enables the shooter to quickly remove the functional mechanism and place it into the polymer grip of his choice. This allows an immediate change in caliber and size;(subcompact, compact and full). And after any change the pistol delivers both outstanding accuracy and reliable functionality. Its modularity not only provides incredible ease of maintenance, but also provides a solution for accommodating different hand sizes - there are 6 different ergonomic combinations for each size, accomplished by changes in grip circumference and trigger style. Matte or duotone finish.

New: $650 **Exc:** $550 **Exc:** $450

SIG SAUER P290

Caliber: 9mm, 6 or 8-shot magazine. Barrel: 2.9 inches. Weight: 20.5 oz. Length: 5.5 inches. Polymer grips, Contrast / SIGLITE night sights, or laser sight. Stainless or Nitro finish. Interchangeable grip panels.

Perf: $375 **Exc:** $325 **VGood:** $275

Add 10 percent for laser sight

SIG SAUER MOSQUITO

22LR semi automatic pistol. SA/DA, decocker operation. 3.9" barrel. Steel slide in matte black or nickel. Polymer frame available in black, blue, pink or digital camo. Accessory rail on lower frame. 10rd magazine. Weighs 25oz. Introduced in 2005.

Perf: $375 **Exc:** $325 **VGood:** $275

SIG SAUER P522

A .22LR version of the P556. 10.6" barrel. Single accessory rail on top. 25rd polymer magazine. New in 2010

Perf: $525 **Exc:** $475 **VGood:** $400

SIG SAUER P522 SWAT

As above with a quad rail forend.

Perf: $575 **Exc:** $525 **VGood:** $450

SIG SAUER P556

A pistol version of the Sig 556 carbine. Caliber 5.56mm/.223. 10 inch barrel. Picatinny rail on top. Accepts standard M-16/AR-15 magazines. Weighs 6.3 lbs. New in 2009.

Perf: $1750 **Exc:** $1400 **VGood:** $1150

SIG SAUER P556 SWAT

As above with a quad rail forend

Perf: $1850 **Exc:** $1550 **VGood:** $1250

SIGARMS REVOLUTION

All-stainless frames and slides in four configurations. Novak Night Sights, Roswood- or DiamondWood custom grips. Stainless or Nitron

SIGARMS Revolution TTT

Smith & Wesson 22 Straight Line

SIG Sauer P522 SWAT

SIGARMS Custom Compact RCS

finish. 8+1 capacity, 45 ACP, single-action, 5-inch barrel, 40.3 oz.

New: $1000 **Exc:** $900 **VGood:** $750

SIGARMS REVOLUTION CUSTOM STX

Single-action .45 ACP stainless semi-auto with 8+1 capacity. Adjustable combat night sights and custom wood grip panels, 5-inch barrel, 40.6 oz.

New: $1250 **Exc:** $1100 **VGood:** $800

SIGARMS REVOLUTION TTT

Stainless semi-auto with 8+1 capacity. Single-action .45 ACP. Adjustable combat night sights and custom wood grip panels, 5-inch barrel, 40.3 oz.

New: $1250 **Exc:** $1100 **VGood:** $800

SIGARMS REVOLUTION XO

Single-action .45 ACP stainless semi-auto with 8+1 capacity. Polymer grip panels. 8.65-inch LOA, 5-inch barrel, 40.3 oz.

New: $850 **Exc:** $795 **VGood:** $650

SIGARMS REVOLUTION TARGET

Single-action .45 ACP stainless semi-auto with 8+1 capacity. Adjustable target night sights. Custom wood grip panels, 5-inch barrel, 40.3 oz. Stainless or Nitron finish.

New: $1050 **Exc:** $950 **VGood:** $825

SIGARMS REVOLUTION CARRY

Single-action .45 ACP stainless semi-auto with 8+1 capacity. Fixed sights. Custom wood grip panels, 4-inch barrel, 35.4 oz. Stainless or Nitron finish.

New: $1000 **Exc:** $900 **VGood:** $750

SIGARMS REVOLUTION COMPACT

Stainless semi-auto single-action .45 ACP with 6+1 capacity. Fixed sights. Custom wood grip panels, 4-inch barrel, 30.3 oz. Stainless or Nitron finish.

New:$1000 **Exc:** $900 **VGood:** $750

SIGARMS REVOLUTION COMPACT SAS

Dehorned version of Revolution Compact. "SAS" stands for "SIG Anti Snag."

New: $1000 **Exc:** $900 **VGood:** $750

SIGARMS REVOLUTION CUSTOM COMPACT RCS

Stainless semi-auto single-action .45 ACP with 6+1 capacity. Fixed sights. Custom wood grip panels, 4-inch barrel, 30.3 oz. Stainless or Nitron finish.

New: $1000 **Exc:** $900 **VGood:** $750

SIGARMS REVOLUTION COMPACT C3

Similar to Revolution Compact but with black anodized alloy frame and stainless or Nitron-finished slide.

New: $900 **Exc:** $850 **VGood:** $725

SMITH & WESSON 22 STRAIGHT LINE

Single shot; 22 LR; 10-inch barrel; pivoted frame; has the appearance of a single-action semi-automatic; smooth walnut grips; target sights; blued finish only; came in green felt-lined blued steel case with cleaning rod and screwdriver. Manufactured 1925 to 1936 with a total of 1870 produced.

Exc: $1200 **VGood:** $850 **Good:** $500

With case

Exc: $1600 **VGood:** $1100 **Good:** $700

SMITH & WESSON 32 DOUBLE ACTION

Revolver; double action; 32 S&W; 5-shot cylinder; 3-inch, 3-1/2-inch, 6-inch, 8-inch, 10-inch barrels; hard rubber stocks; fixed sights; blued or nickel finish. Manufactured 1880 to 1919. Early serial numbers have great collector significance, with numbers through 50 bringing as high as $6500.

Exc: $350 **VGood:** $225 **Good:** $150

SMITH & WESSON 32 SAFETY HAMMERLESS

Revolver; double action; 32 S&W; 5-shot; 2-inch, 3-inch, 3-1/2-inch, 6-inch barrels; black, hard rubber or walnut grips; blue or nickel finish. Numbered in separate serial number series. The 2-inch barrel models called "Bicycle Model" and demand premium prices. 249,981 produced. Manufactured from 1887 to 1937.

Exc: $400 **VGood:** $325 **Good:** $200

2-inch barrel Bicycle Model

Exc: $450 **VGood:** $300 **Good:** $175

SMITH & WESSON 38 DOUBLE ACTION

Revolver; double action; 38 S&W; 5-shot cylinder; 4-inch, 4-1/2-inch, 5-inch, 6-inch, 8-inch, 10-inch barrel; hinged frame; hard rubber checkered stocks; fixed sights; blued or nickel finish. Several design variations. Manufactured 1880 to 1911; some collector value.

S/N through 4000

Exc: $800 **VGood:** $650 **Good:** $375

S/N over 4000

Exc: $325 **VGood:** $225 **Good:** $150

8-inch, 10-inch barrels

Exc: $2500 **VGood:** $1750 **Good:** $1200

SMITH & WESSON 38 DOUBLE ACTION PERFECTED MODEL

Revolver; double action; 38 S&W; 5-shot; 3-1/4-inch to 6-inch barrels; hard black rubber grips; blue or nickel finish. Distinguishing features include: manufactured on a modified 32 Hand Ejector frame; incorporates both a top barrel latch and frame-mounted side latch. The last top-break revolver introduced by S&W, the Perfected model was introduced in 1909 and produced until 1920 with a total production run of 59,400.

Exc: $500 **VGood:** $300 **Good:** $200

SMITH & WESSON 38 SAFETY HAMMERLESS (NEW DEPARTURE)

Revolver; double action; 38 S&W; 5-shot; 3-1/4-inch, 4-inch, 5-inch, 6-inch barrel; checkered hard rubber or walnut grips; blue or nickel finish. Numbered in separate serial number series. Total production run of 261,493. Manufactured from 1887 to 1937.

Exc: $450 **VGood:** $275 **Good:** $200

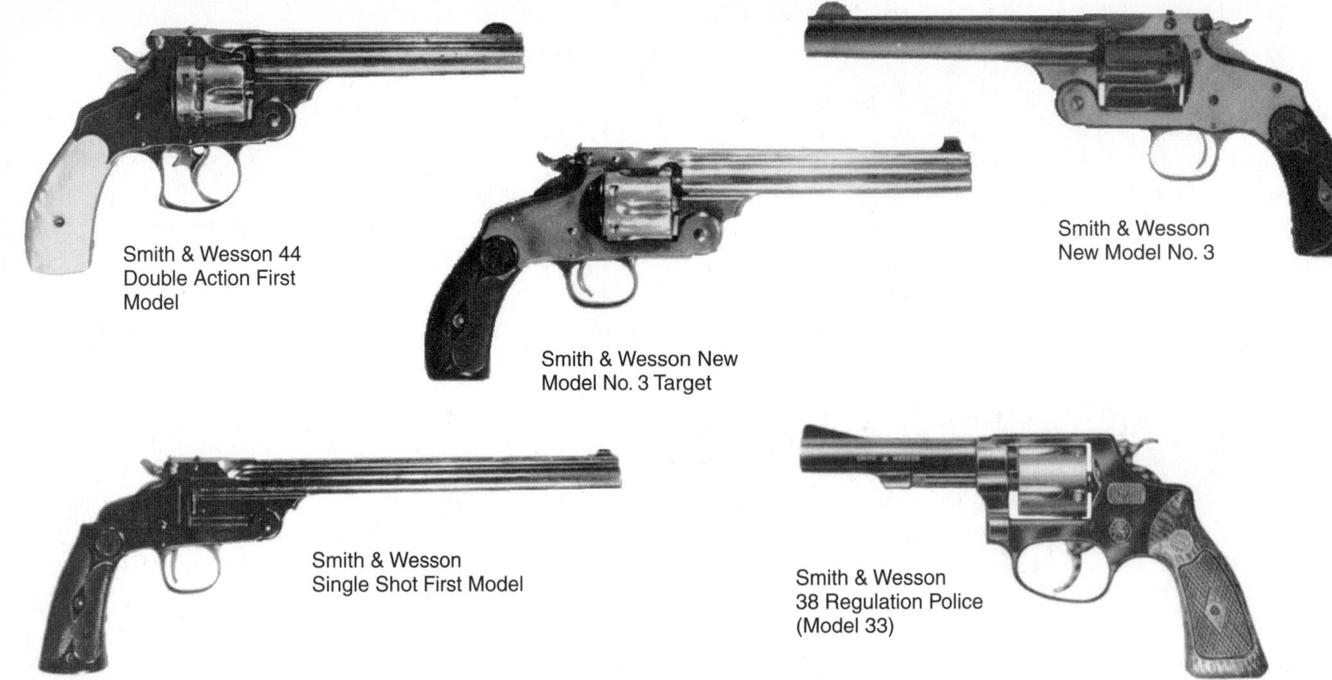
Smith & Wesson 44 Double Action First Model

Smith & Wesson New Model No. 3 Target

Smith & Wesson New Model No. 3

Smith & Wesson Single Shot First Model

Smith & Wesson 38 Regulation Police (Model 33)

SMITH & WESSON 38 SINGLE ACTION THIRD MODEL (MODEL 1891)

Revolver; single action; 38 S&W; 5-shot; 3-1/4-inch, 4-inch, 5-inch, 6-inch barrel; fixed sights; checkered hard rubber or walnut grips; blued or nickel finish. A special variation was manufactured with a spur trigger assembly inserted in place of the standard trigger and trigger guard. This was called the Mexican Model (100 percent premium) and is very rare; beware of fakes.

Conventional trigger guard

Exc: $1600 **VGood:** $1250 **Good:** $750

SMITH & WESSON 44 DOUBLE ACTION FIRST MODEL

Revolver; double action; 44 Russian, 38-40; 6-shot cylinder; 4, 5, 6, & 6-1/2-inch barrel; hard rubber or walnut grips; fixed sights; blued or nickel finish. Manufactured 1881 to 1913. 53,668 manufactured.

Exc: $1800 **VGood:** $950 **Good:** $700

SMITH & WESSON 44 DOUBLE ACTION FAVORITE

Same specs as the First Model except 5-inch barrel. Approximately 1000 manufactured between 1882 to 1883.

Exc: $6000 **VGood:** $4000 **Good:** $2500

SMITH & WESSON NEW MODEL NO. 3

Revolver; single action; hinged frame; 44 Russian; 3-1/2-inch, 4-inch, 5-inch, 6-inch, 6-1/2-inch, 7-inch, 7-1/2-inch, 8-inch barrel; rounded hard rubber or walnut stocks; fixed or target sights; blued or nickel finish; manufactured 1878 to 1908; broad collector value.

Exc: $2200 **VGood:** $1800 **Good:** $1000

SMITH & WESSON NEW MODEL NO. 3 FRONTIER

Same specs as New Model No. 3 except 44-40 Win.; 4-inch, 5-inch, 6-3/4-inch barrel; longer 19/16-inch cylinder. Manufactured 1885 to 1908; great collector interest.

Exc: $3000 **VGood:** $2250 **Good:** $1600

SMITH & WESSON NEW MODEL NO. 3 TARGET

Same specs as New Model No. 3 except 32-44 S&W, 38-44 S&W; 6-inch, 61/2-inch barrel; adjustable sights. Manufactured 1887 to 1910; collector interest.

Exc: $2250 **VGood:** $1600 **Good:** $1000

SMITH & WESSON NEW MODEL NO. 3 WINCHESTER

Same specs as New Model No. 3 Frontier except 38-40. Manufactured 1900 to 1907; extremely rare; only 74 manufactured.

Exc: $10,000 **VGood:** $7500 **Good:** $4000

SMITH & WESSON SINGLE SHOT FIRST MODEL

Single shot; 22 LR, 32 S&W, 38 S&W; 6-inch, 8-inch, 10-inch barrels; target sights; square-butt, hard rubber grips; blued or nickel finish; built on same frame as 38 Single Action Third Model. Also furnished with 38 S&W barrel, cylinder to convert to single action. 1200 manufactured between 1893 and 1905; collector interest.

22 LR

Exc: $1500 **VGood:** $1700 **Good:** $950

32 S&W

Exc: $2000 **VGood:** $1500 **Good:** $1000

38 S&W

Exc: $2500 **VGood:** $2000 **Good:** $1500

SMITH & WESSON SINGLE SHOT SECOND MODEL

Same specs as First Model except 22 LR only; 10-inch barrel; cannot be converted to revolver configuration; serial numbered in separate series.

Exc: $950 **VGood:** $800 **Good:** $700

SMITH & WESSON SINGLE SHOT THIRD MODEL (PERFECTED SINGLE SHOT)

Same specs as First Model except 22 LR; hinged frame; target model; redesigned to incorporate new frame design developed for the 38 Double Action Perfected Model; checkered walnut target grips. Manufactured from 1909 to 1923. A special group featuring a short chamber was manufactured in 1910 and called the Olympic Model; the 22 LR cartridge must be forced into the rifling.

Perfected Single Shot

Exc: $1200 **VGood:** $850 **Good:** $700

SMITH & WESSON 22 WMR SERVICE KIT GUN (MODEL 650)

Revolver; double action; 22 WMR; 6-shot cylinder; 3-inch heavy barrel; 7-1/4-inch overall length; weighs 23 oz.; stainless steel construction; fixed 1/10-inch serrated front ramp, micro-click adjustable rear; checkered walnut round butt stocks with medallion; satin finish. Introduced 1983; dropped 1987.

Exc: $500 **VGood:** $425 **Good:** $350

SMITH & WESSON 22/32 KIT GUN

Revolver; 22 LR; 6-shot; 4-inch barrel; 8-inch overall length; weighs 21 oz.; 1/10-inch Patridge or pocket revolver front sight, with rear sight adjustable for elevation and windage; checkered round-butt Circassian walnut or hard rubber stocks; (small or special oversized target square-butt stocks were offered on special order); blued or nickel finish; a compact outdoorsman's revolver based on the 22/32 Target. Introduced in 1935; replaced in 1953 by the Model 34.

Exc: $750 **VGood:** $500 **Good:** $400

SMITH & WESSON 22/32 KIT GUN (MODEL 34)

Revolver; 22 LR; 6-shot; 2-inch, 4-inch barrels; 8-inch overall length (4-inch barrel); weighs 22-1/2 oz.; fixed 1/10-inch serrated front ramp sight, micro-click adjustable rear; checkered walnut round or square-butt grips with medallion; blued finish. Originally introduced in 1936; pre-war variations feature round barrel and bring premium prices. Discontinued in 1991.

Exc: $550 **VGood:** $450 **Good:** $350

SMITH & WESSON 22/32 TARGET

Revolver; 22 LR; 6-shot; 6-inch barrel; 10-1/2-inch overall length; sights, 1/10-inch or 1/8-inch Patridge front, fully-adjustable square notch rear sight; stocks, special, oversize, square-butt pattern in checkered Circassian walnut with S&W monogram; chambers countersunk at the heads around 1935 for the higher-

Smith & Wesson Single Shot Third Model

Smith & Wesson 32 Hand Ejector First Model (Model of 1896)

Smith & Wesson 22/32 Kit Gun (Model 34)

Smith & Wesson 32 Hand Ejector (Model 30)

Smith & Wesson 1977 22/32 Kit Gun M.R.F. (Model 63)

velocity cartridges; blued finish only. A forerunner of the Model 35. Introduced in 1911; superseded by the Model 35 in 1953.

Exc: $800 **VGood:** $650 **Good:** $400

SMITH & WESSON 32 HAND EJECTOR FIRST MODEL (MODEL OF 1896)

Revolver; double action, hand ejector; 32 S&W Long; 3-1/4-inch, 4-1/4-inch, 6-inch barrel; fixed sights; hard rubber stocks; blued or nickel finish. First S&W solid-frame revolver with swing-out cylinder. Company name and patent dates marked on cylinder rather than barrel. Total production run of 19,712. Manufactured 1896 to 1903. Significant premium for factory-0engraved presentation models.

Exc: $600 **VGood:** $450 **Good:** $225

SMITH & WESSON 32 HAND EJECTOR (MODEL 30)

Revolver; double action; 32 S&W Long; will accept 32 S&W and 32 S&W Long wadcutter; 6-shot; 2-inch, 3-inch, 4-inch barrels; 6-inch available at one time; 8-inch overall length (4-inch barrel); weighs 18 oz.; checkered walnut grips with medallion; formerly hard rubber; serrated ramp front and square notch rear; blue or nickel finish. Introduced 1908; dropped 1972. Values are for later production.

Exc: $550 **VGood:** $450 **Good:** $350

SMITH & WESSON 38 REGULATION POLICE (MODEL 31)

Revolver; 32 S&W Long; accepts 32 S&W, 32 Colt New Police; 6-shot; 2-inch, 3-inch, 3-1/4-inch, 4-inch, 4-1/4-inch, 6-inch barrels; 8-1/2-inch overall length (4-inch barrel); weighs 18-3/4 oz.; fixed sights with 1/10-inch serrated ramp front and square notch rear; checkered walnut stocks with medallion; blue or nickel finish. Introducted 1917; dropped 1991.

Exc: $450 **VGood:** $350 **Good:** $290

SMITH & WESSON 38 REGULATION POLICE TARGET MODEL

Same specs as Model 31 except target model with 6-inch barrel; 10-1/4-inch overall length; weighs 20 oz.; adjustable target sights. Introduced 1917; dropped 1941.

Exc: $800 **VGood:** $650 **Good:** $500

SMITH & WESSON 38 REGULATION POLICE (MODEL 33)

Revolver; 38 S&W; accepts 38 Colt New Police; 5-shot; 4-inch barrel; 8-1/2-inch overall length; weighs 18 oz.; fixed sights, with 1/10-inch serrated ramp front and square notch rear; checkered walnut stocks with medallion; blue or nickel finish. Introduced in 1917; dropped 1974.

Exc: $500 **VGood:** $425 **Good:** $350

SMITH & WESSON 1960 22/32 KIT GUN WMR (MODEL 51)

Revolver; 22 WMR; 3-1/2-inch barrel; 8-inch overall length; weighs 24 oz.; all steel frame and cylinder; fixed 1/10-inch serrated front ramp, micro-click adjustable rear; checkered walnut, round or square-butt stocks; blue or nickel finish. Introduced 1960; dropped 1974.

Exc: $550 **VGood:** $475 **Good:** $350

Nickel finish

Exc: $650 **VGood:** $550 **Good:** $475

SMITH & WESSON 1977 22/32 KIT GUN WMR (MODEL 63)

Revolver; 22 LR; 6-shot; 2-inch, 4-inch barrel; 8-inch overall length (4-inch barrel); weighs 24-1/4 oz.; stainless steel construction; fixed 1/10-inch serrated front ramp sight, micro-click adjustable rear; round butt soft rubber or checkered walnut square-butt stocks with medallion; satin finish. 1977-1998.

New: $550 **Exc:** $475 **V.G.:** $400

SMITH & WESSON AIRWEIGHT KIT GUN (MODEL 43)

Revolver; 22 LR; 3-1/2-inch barrel; 8-inch overall length; weighs 14-1/4-inch oz.; alloy aluminum frame and cylinder; fixed 1/10-inch serrated front ramp, micro-click adjustable rear; checkered walnut, round or square-butt stocks; blue or nickel finish. Introduced 1955; dropped 1974.

Exc: $550 **VGood:** $475 **Good:** $400

SMITH & WESSON BODYGUARD 380

Caliber: 380 Auto, 6+1 round capacity. Double-action-only operation with second strike capability. Barrel: 2.75 inches. Weight: 11.85 oz. Length: 5.25 inches. Polymer frame with integral grips. Integrated laser sight plus with stainless steel front, drift adjustable rear.

Perf: $465 **Exc:** $400 **VGood:** $350

SMITH & WESSON BODYGUARD (MODEL 49)

Revolver; double action; 38 Spl.; 5-shot; 2-inch barrel; 6-5/16-inch overall length; steel construction; weighs 20-1/2 oz.; fixed 1/10-inch serrated front ramp, square notch rear; blue or nickel finish; features shrouded hammer that can be cocked manually for single-action firing. Introduced 1955; dropped 1996. Later reintroduced.

Perf: $460 **Exc:** $395 **VGood:** $325

SMITH & WESSON BODYGUARD (MODEL 649)

Revolver; double action; 38 Spl.; 5-shot; 2-inch barrel; 6-5/16-inch overall length; weighs 20 1/2 oz.; stainless steel construction; fixed 1/10-inch serrated front ramp, square notch rear; satin finish; features shrouded hammer that can be cocked manually for single-action firing. Introduced 1955; still in production.

Perf: $550 **Exc:** $475 **VGood:** $400

SMITH & WESSON BODYGUARD AIRWEIGHT (MODEL 38)

Revolver; double action; 38 Spl.; 5-shot; 2-inch barrel; 6 5/16-inch overall length; weighs 14-1/2 oz.; fixed 1/10-inch serrated front ramp, square notch rear; blue or nickel finish; features shrouded hammer that can be cocked manually for single-action firing. Introduced 1955; dropped 1998.

Perf: $550 **Exc:** $475 **VGood:** $400

SMITH & WESSON CENTENNIAL (MODEL 40)

Revolver; double action; 38 Spl; 5-shot; 2-inch barrel; 6-1/2-inch overall length; weighs 19 oz.; concealed

Smith & Wesson Centennial (Model 640)

Smith & Wesson Centennial Airweight (Model 442)

Smith & Wesson Chief's Special Airweight (Model 37)

Smith & Wesson Centennial Airweight (Model 642)

Smith & Wesson Chief's Special (Model 36)

Smith & Wesson Model 642 PowerPort Pro Series

hammer; fixed 1/10-inch serrated front ramp, square notch rear. Swing-out version of earlier top-break design with grip safety. Introduced 1953; dropped 1974. Collector value.

Exc: $600 **VGood:** $500 **Good:** $400

SMITH & WESSON CENTENNIAL (MODEL 640)

Revolver; double action; 38 Spl.; 5-shot; 2-inch, 3-inch barrel; 6-5/16-inch overall length; weighs 20 oz.; serrated ramp front, fixed notch rear sight; Goncalo Alves round-butt grips; stainless steel version of the Model 40 sans grip safety; concealed hammer; smoothed edges. Introduced 1990; still in production.

Perf: $550 **Exc:** $475 **VGood.:** $400

SMITH & WESSON CENTENNIAL (MODEL 940)

Revolver; double action; 9mm Para.; 5-shot; 2-inch, 3-inch barrel; 6-5/16-inch overall length; weighs 20 oz.; serrated ramp front, fixed notch rear sight; rubber grips; stainless steel version of the Model 40 sans grip safety; concealed hammer; smoothed edges. Introduced 1990; dropped 1998.

New: $600 **Perf:** $500 **Exc:** $400

SMITH & WESSON CENTENNIAL AIRWEIGHT (MODEL 42)

Revolver; double action; 38 Spl; 5-shot; 2-inch barrel; 6-1/2-inch overall length; concealed hammer; aluminum alloy frame and cylinder; fixed 1/10-inch serrated front ramp, square notch rear. Lightweight version of Model 40. Introduced 1953; dropped 1974. Collector value.

Blue

Exc: $600 **VGood:** $500 **Good:** $400

Nickel

Exc: $850 **VGood:** $700 **Good:** $550

SMITH & WESSON CENTENNIAL AIRWEIGHT (MODEL 442)

Revolver; double action; 38 Spl.; 5-shot cylinder; 2-inch barrel; weighs 15-3/4 oz.; 6-5/8-inch overall length; Uncle Mike's Custom Grade Santoprene grips; serrated ramp front sight, fixed notch rear; alloy frame; carbon steel barrel and cylinder; concealed hammer. Made in U.S. by Smith & Wesson. Introduced 1993; still produced.

Perf: $550 **Exc:** $500 **VGood.:** $450

Nickel finish

Perf: $575 **Exc..:** $525 **VGood.:** $475

SMITH & WESSON CENTENNIAL AIRWEIGHT (MODEL 642)

Revolver; double action; 38 Spl.; 5-shot; 2-inch carbon steel barrel; 6-5/16-inch overall length; anodized alloy frame; weighs 16 oz.; serrated ramp front, fixed notch rear sight; Uncle Mike's Custom Grade Santoprene grips; same as the Model 40 sans grip safety; concealed hammer; smoothed edges. Introduced 1990; still in production.

Perf: $550 **Exc:** $475 **VGood:** $400

SMITH & WESSON MODEL 642 POWERPORT PRO SERIES

Similar to Model 642 buit with gray aluminum frame and black stainless ported barrel. Dealer sets pricing. Introduced 2008.

New: $695 **Perf:** $525 **Exc:** $375

SMITH & WESSON CHIEF'S SPECIAL (MODEL 36)

Revolver; double action; 38 Spl.; 5-shot; 2-inch, 3-inch barrel; 7-3/8-inch overall length (3-inch barrel); weighs 21-1/2 oz.; fixed 1/10-inch serrated front ramp, square notch rear; all steel frame and cylinder; checkered round butt soft rubber grips most common; square-butt available; blue or nickel finish. Dropped 1999.

New: $550 **Perf:** $475 **Exc:** $400

SMITH & WESSON CHIEF'S SPECIAL AIRWEIGHT (MODEL 37)

Revolver; double action; 38 Spl.; 5-shot; 2-inch barrel; 6-1/2-inch overall length; weighs 19-1/2 oz.; lightweight version of Model 36, incorporating aluminum alloy frame; weighs 14-1/2 oz.; fixed 1/10-inch serrated front ramp, square notch rear; all steel frame and cylinder; checkered round butt grips most common; square-butt available; blue or nickel finish. Discontinued in 1995.

New: $550 **Perf:** $475 **Exc:** $400

SMITH & WESSON MODEL 637 AIRWEIGHT REVOLVER

Similar to the Model 37 Airweight except has alloy frame, stainless steel barrel, cylinder and yoke; rated for 38 Spec. +P; Uncle Mike's Boot Grip. Weighs 15 oz. Introduced 1996.

New: $550 **Perf:** $500 **Exc:** $450

SMITH & WESSON CHIEF'S SPECIAL STAINLESS (MODEL 60)

Revolver; double action; 38 Spl.; 5-shot; 2-inch barrel; 6-1/2-inch overall length; weighs 19 oz.; stainless steel construction; fixed 1/10-inch serrated front ramp, square notch rear; checkered walnut round butt grips. Dropped 1996.

New: $500 **Perf:** $475 **Exc:** $425

SMITH & WESSON MODEL 60 .357 MAGNUM CHIEFS SPECIAL

Similar to the Model 60 in 38 Special except is 357 Magnum; 2-1/8-inch or 3-inch barrel. Weighs 24 oz.; 7-1/2-inch overall length (3-inch barrel). Has Uncle Mike's Combat grips.

New: $600 **Perf:** $550 **Exc:** $450

SMITH & WESSON MODEL 60 PRO SERIES

Similar to Model 60 but in .38/.357 with night front sights, "high-hold" enforcing walnut grips, 3-inch battel and matte stainless finish. Introduced 2008.

New: $750 **Perf:** $550 **Exc:** $475

SMITH & WESSON LADYSMITH (MODEL 36-LS)

Revolver; double action; 38 Spl.; 5-shot; 2-inch barrel; 6-5/16-inch overall length; weighs 20 oz.; carbon steel construction; serrated front ramp, square notch rear; rosewood laminate grips; comes in fitted carry/storage case; blue finish. Introduced 1989; still in production.

New: $550 **Perf:** $500 **Exc:** $450

SMITH & WESSON LADYSMITH (MODEL 60-LS)

Revolver; double action; 38 Spl.; 5-shot; 2-inch barrel; 6-5/16-inch overall length; weighs 20 oz.; stainless steel construction; serrated front ramp, square notch rear; rosewood laminate grips;

Smith & Wesson Model 637 Airweight Revolver

Smith & Wesson Ladysmith (Model 36-LS)

Smith & Wesson Model 60 .357 Magnum Chiefs Special

Smith & Wesson Ladysmith (Model 60-LS)

Smith & Wesson Model 60 3 inch Full Lug

Smith & Wesson Target Model 1953 (Model 35)

Smith & Wesson Model 651

Smith & Wesson Model 60 Pro Series

stainless satin finish. Introduced 1989; still in production.

New: $550 **Perf:** $500 **Exc:** $450

SMITH & WESSON MODEL 60 3-INCH FULL LUG

Revolver; double action; 38 Spl.; 5-shot; 3-inch full lug barrel; 7-1/2-inch overall length; weighs 24-1/2 oz.; stainless steel construction; fixed pinned black ramp front sight, adjustable black blade rear; rubber combat grips. Introduced 1991; Still in production.

New: $550 **Perf:** $500 **Exc:** $450

SMITH & WESSON MODEL 651

Revolver; double action; 22 WMR; 6-shot cylinder; 4-inch heavy barrel; 8-11/16-inch overall length; weighs 24-1/2 oz.; stainless steel construction; ramp front, adjustable micrometer-click rear; semi-target hammer; combat trigger; soft rubber or checkered walnut square-butt stocks with medallion; satin finish. Introduced 1983; dropped 1998.

Exc: $300 **VGood:** $250 **Good:** $150

SMITH & WESSON TARGET MODEL 1953 (MODEL 35)

Revolver; 22 LR; 6-shot; 6-inch barrel; 10-1/2-inch overall length; weighs 25 oz.; ribbed barrel; micrometer rear sight; Magna-type stocks; flattened cylinder latch; blue finish. A redesign of the 22/32 Target model. Introduced 1953; dropped 1974.

Exc: $650 **VGood:** $550 **Good:** $450

SMITH & WESSON TERRIER (MODEL 32)

Revolver; 38 S&W, 38 Colt New Police; 5-shot; 2-inch barrel; 6-1/4-inch overall length; weighs 17 oz.; fixed sights with 1/10-inch serrated ramp front, square notch rear; round butt checkered walnut stocks with medallion; blue or nickel finish. Introduced 1936; dropped 1974.

Exc: $500 **VGood:** $450 **Good:** $375

SMITH & WESSON K AND L MEDIUM FRAME REVOLVERS

Smith & Wesson's original medium-frame revolver was the "K" frame introduced in 1899. In 1980, S&W offered an improved medium frame revolver for the 357 Magnum cartridge and this new frame was called the "L" frame.

SMITH & WESSON 32-20 HAND EJECTOR

Revolver; 32 Winchester; 6-shot; 4-inch, 5-inch, 6-inch, 6-1/2-inch barrels; fixed or adjustable sights (rare); hard black rubber round or checkered walnut square-butt grips; caliber marking on early models, 32 Winchester; late models, 32 W.C.F., marked 32/20.

Exc: $600 **VGood:** $500 **Good:** $400

SMITH & WESSON 38 MILITARY & POLICE

Revolver; double action; 38 Spl.; 6-shot; 4-inch, 5-inch, 6-inch, 6-1/2-inch barrels; hard rubber round butt (early models) or checkered walnut square-butt grips; blue or nickel finish. The first S&W K-frame was the 38 Hand Ejector which later became known as the 38 Military & Police. This model was introduced in 1899 and has been in continuous production. During the last 96 years, S&W has produced over 5 million of these revolvers, resulting in numerous variations which affect values only slightly. The most collectable of these, the 38 Hand Ejector First Model, can be easily recognized by the lack of a locking lug located on the underside of the barrel and the serial number 1 through 20,975. Between 1899 and 1940 this model was available with both fixed sights and an adjustable target sight. The target model, referred to as the 38 Military and Police Target Model, brings a premium price and was the predecessor to all K-frame target models.

38 Hand Ejector First Model

Exc: $450 **VGood:** $300 **Good:** $150

Standard models

Exc: $300 **VGood:** $225 **Good:** $135

SMITH & WESSON 38 MILITARY & POLICE VICTORY MODEL

Revolver; 38 Spl., 38 S&W; 2-inch, 4-inch, 5-inch barrels; smooth walnut grips; midnight black finish. The Victory Model is the WWII production variation of the 38 Military & Police Model. Its name was derived from the serial number prefix "V," a symbol for "Victory." The revolvers provided the U.S. government were in 38 Special; those provided to the U.S. Allied Forces in 38 S&W. At the end of WWII the "V" serial number prefix was changed to "S," which was continued to 1948 when the series again reached 1,000,000. Add 50 percent for U.S. military markings (beware of fakes!).

Exc: $500 **VGood:** $375 **Good:** $250

SMITH & WESSON K-22 OUTDOORSMAN

Revolver; 22 LR; 6-shot; 6-inch round barrel; adjustable rear sight; square-butt checkered walnut grips; blue finish. Also known as the K-22 First Model, this was the first in a long line of K-frame 22 rimfire target revolvers. Introduced 1931.

Exc: $575 **VGood:** $475 **Good:** $350

SMITH & WESSON K-22 SECOND MODEL

Revolver; 22 LR; 6-shot; 6-inch round barrel; checkered walnut square-butt grips; blue finish. This revolver was the first to be called the "Masterpiece." It was introduced in 1940 and, because of the factory shift to wartime production, it was manufactured for only a limited time. Total production was 1067 revolvers in serial number range 682,420 to 696,952 without a letter prefix.

Exc: $1000 **VGood:** $850 **Good:** $500

SMITH & WESSON K-32 FIRST MODEL

Revolver; 32 S&W Long; 6-inch round barrel; checkered walnut square-butt grips; blue finish. The K-32 First Model was a companion model to both the 38 M&P and K-22 Outdoorsman. It was introduced in 1938 and only produced until 1940 with approximately 125 handguns manufactured. It is the rarest of the early target models.

Exc: $3000 **VGood:** $2500 **Good:** $1800

SMITH & WESSON MODEL 10 MILITARY & POLICE

Revolver; double action; 38 Spl.; 6-shot; 2-inch, 3-inch, 4-inch, 5-inch, 6-1/2-inch barrel; 11-1/8-inch overall length with square butt, 1/4-inch less for round butt; weighs 31 oz.; 1/10-inch service-type front sight and square notch non-adjustable rear; square-butt checkered walnut stocks, round butt pattern with choice of hard rubber or checkered walnut; blued or nickel finish. In 1957 a 4-inch heavy barrel became available and is the 4-inch barrel configuration still available. The 38 M&P has been the true workhorse of the Smith & Wesson line of revolvers. The basic frame is termed S&'s K-frame, the derivative source of

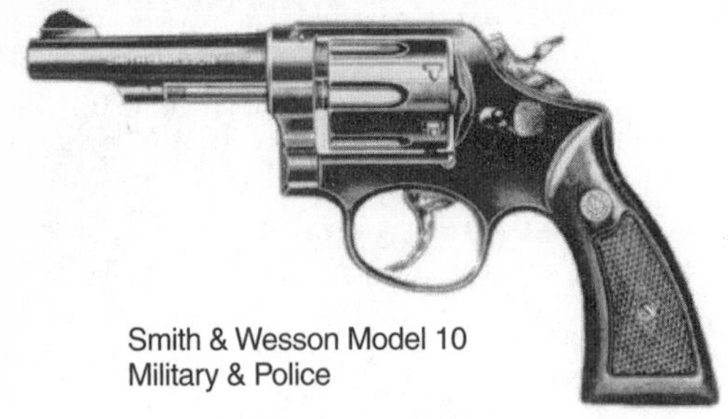
Smith & Wesson Model 10 Military & Police

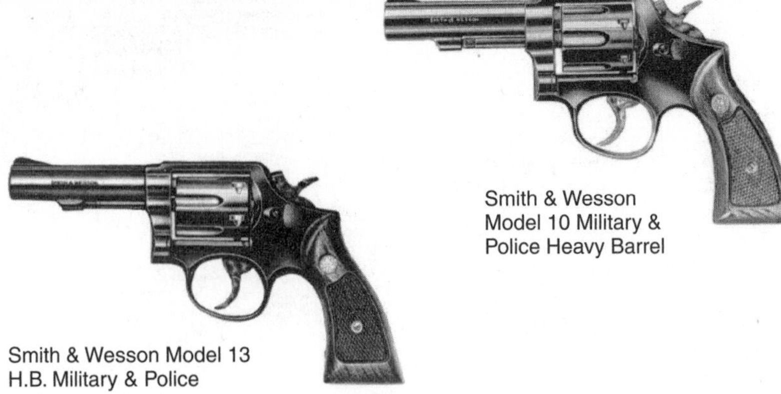
Smith & Wesson Model 13 H.B. Military & Police

Smith & Wesson Model 10 Military & Police Heavy Barrel

Smith & Wesson Model 10 Military & Police (1995 model)

Smith & Wesson Model 14 K-38 Masterpiece

the K-38, et al. It is, quite possibly, the most popular, widely accepted police duty revolver ever made. Introduced about 1902. Reintroduced 1995.

Perf: $400 **Exc:** $375 **VGood:** $350

Nickel finish

Perf: $450 **Exc:** $400 **VGood:** $375

SMITH & WESSON MODEL 10 MILITARY & POLICE HEAVY BARREL

Same specs as standard Model 10 except 4-inch heavy ribbed barrel; ramp front sight, square notch rear; square-butt; blued or nickel finish. Introduced 1957.

Perf: $450 **Exc:** $400 **VGood:** $350

SMITH & WESSON MODEL 12 MILITARY & POLICE AIRWEIGHT

Revolver; double action; 38 Spl.; 6-shot; 2-inch, 4-inch barrel; overall length, 6-7/8-inch (2-inch, round butt); weighs 18 oz.; aluminum alloy frame; fixed 1/8-inch serrated ramp front sight, square-notch rear; checkered walnut Magna-type, round or square-butt. Introduced about 1952; dropped 1986.

Exc: $350 **VGood:** $300 **Good:** $250

SMITH & WESSON MODEL 13 H.B. MILITARY & POLICE

Revolver; double action; 357 Mag.; 6-shot cylinder; 3-inch, 4-inch heavy barrel; 9-5/16-inch overall length (4-inch barrel); weighs 34 oz.; serrated ramp front sight, fixed square notch rear; square or round butt; blued finish. Introduced 1974; dropped 1998.

Exc: $500 **VGood:** $450 **Good:** $375

SMITH & WESSON MODEL 14 K-38 MASTERPIECE

Revolver; double action; 38 Spl.; 6-shot; 6-inch, 8-3/8-inch barrel; 11-1/8-inch overall length (6-inch barrel); swing-out cylinder; micrometer rear sight, 1/8-inch Patridge-type front; hand-checkered service-type walnut grips; blued. Introduced 1947; dropped 1983.

Exc: $600 **VGood:** $365 **Good:** $270

SMITH & WESSON MODEL 14 K-38 MASTERPIECE FULL LUG

Same specs as standard Model 14 except 6-inch full-lug barrel; weighs 47 oz.; pinned Patridge-type front sight, micrometer click-adjustable rear; square-butt combat grips; combat trigger, hammer; polished blue finish. 1991-1999.

Exc: $550 **VGood:** $475 **Good:** $400

SMITH & WESSON MODEL 14 K-38 MASTERPIECE SINGLE ACTION

Same specs as standard Model 14 except 6-inch barrel only; single-action only; target hammer; target trigger.

Exc: $550 **VGood:** $475 **Good:** $400

SMITH & WESSON MODEL 15 38 COMBAT MASTERPIECE

Revolver; double action; 38 Spl.; 6-shot; 2-inch, 4-inch, 6-inch, 8-3/8-inch barrel; 9-1/8-inch overall length; weighs 34 oz.; blue or nickel finish. It took some years after WWII to re-establish commercial production and begin catching up with civilian demands at S&W. By the early '50s the situation was bright enough to warrant introducing a 4-inch version of the K-38, which was designated the 38 Combat Masterpiece. Its only nominal companion was the 22 Combat Masterpiece and no attempt was made to match loaded weights, as in the K-series-the 38 weighing 34 oz. empty, compared to 36-1/2 oz. for the 22 version. Barrel ribs were narrower than the K-series and front sights were of the Baughman, quick-draw ramp pattern, replacing the vertical surface of the K-series Patridge-type. No longer in production.

Exc: $550 **VGood:** $500 **Good:** $450

Nickel finish

Exc: $650 **VGood:** $550 **Good:** $475

SMITH & WESSON MODEL 16 K-32 MASTERPIECE

Revolver; double action; 32 S&W Long; 6-shot; 6-inch barrel; target hammer; target trigger; red-insert front sight, white-outline rear; optional Patridge or Baughman front sights; walnut, Magna-pattern stocks with medallions standard; optional factory target stocks in exotic woods; blued finish. Originated as target version of the hand-ejector in 32 S&W Long about 1935, and dropped at the beginning of WWII. Appeared in its present form in the late '40s and designated the K-32 as a companion to the K-22 and K-38. Introduced 1947; dropped 1983.

Exc: $2000 **VGood:** $900 **Good:** $675

SMITH & WESSON MODEL 16 K-32 MASTERPIECE FULL LUG

Same specs as standard Model 16 except 32 Mag.; 4-inch, 6-inch, 8-3/8-inch full-lug barrel; Patridge-type front sight, click-adjustable micrometer rear; combat-style Goncalo Alves grips; polished blue finish. Introduced 1990; dropped 1992.

Semi-target 4-inch barrel

Perf: $900 **Exc:** $650 **VGood:** $450

Target 6-inch barrel

Perf: $1000 **Exc:** $725 **VGood:** $495

Target 8-3/8-inch barrel

Perf: $1050 **Exc:** $800 **VGood:** $525

SMITH & WESSON MODEL 17 K-22 MASTERPIECE

Revolver; double action; 22 LR; 6-shot; 6-inch barrel standard, 8-3/8-inch available; 11-1/8-inch overall length (6-inch barrel); weighs 38-1/2 oz. (6-inch), 42-1/2 oz. (8-3/8-inch) loaded; blue finish. Redesigned version of Model 16. Postwar production added the refinement of a broad barrel rib, intended to compensate for weight variations between the three Masterpiece models. Likewise added were the redesigned hammer with its broad spur and thumb tip relief notch, an adjustable anti-backlash stop for the trigger and the Magna-type grips developed in the mid-'30s to help cushion the recoil of the 357 Magnum. Introduced around 1947; dropped 1998.

6-inch barrel

Perf: $550 **Exc:** $500 **VGood:** $450

8-3/8-inch barrel

Perf: $500 **Exc:** $400 **VGood:** $325

SMITH & WESSON MODEL 17 K-22 MASTERPIECE FULL LUG

Same specs as standard Model 17 except 4-inch, 6-inch, 8-3/8-inch barrel; Patridge-type front sight on two longer barrel lengths (serrated type on 4-inch version), S&W click-adjustable micrometer rear; grooved tang; polished blue finish. Introduced 1990; dropped 1998.

4-inch, 6-inch barrel

Perf: $550 **Exc:** $500 **VGood:** $450

8-3/8-inch barrel

Perf: $800 **Exc:** $650 **VGood:** $525

Smith & Wesson Model 15 38 Combat Masterpiece

Smith & Wesson Model 16 K-32 Masterpiece Full Lug

Smith & Wesson Model 17 K-22 Masterpiece

Smith & Wesson Model 14 K-38 Masterpiece Single Action

Smith & Wesson Model 48 K-22 Masterpiece WMR

Smith & Wesson Model 18 22 Combat Masterpiece

Smith & Wesson Model 19 Combat Magnum

Smith & Wesson Model 53 (22 Magnum)

SMITH & WESSON MODEL 18 22 COMBAT MASTERPIECE

Revolver; double action; 22 LR, 22 Long, 22 Short; 6-shot; 4-inch barrel; 9-1/8-inch overall length; weighs 36-1/2 oz. (loaded); Baughman 1/8-inch quick-draw front sight on plain ramp, fully-adjustable S&W micrometer-click rear; checkered walnut, Magna-type grips with S&W medallion; options include broad-spur target hammer, wide target trigger, hand-filling target stocks, red front sight insert and white outlined rear sight notch; finish, blue only. Dropped 1985.

Exc: $550 **VGood:** $500 **Good:** $450

SMITH & WESSON MODEL 19 COMBAT MAGNUM

Revolver; double action; 357 Mag.; 6-shot; 2-1/2-inch, 4-inch, 6-inch barrel; available with 4-inch barrel; 9-1/2-inch overall length; weighs 35 oz.; 1/8-inch Baughman quick-draw front plain ramp, fully-adjustable S&W micrometer-click rear; checkered Goncalo Alves grips with S&W medallion; S&W bright blue or nickel finish; built on the lighter S&W K-frame as used on the K-38, et al., rather than on the heavier N-frame used for the Model 27 and 28. Introduced about 1956; dropped 1999.

Perf: $550 **Exc..:** $500 **VGood:** $450

SMITH & WESSON MODEL 48 K-22 MASTERPIECE WMR

Revolver; double action; 22 WMR; 4-inch, 6-inch, 8-3/8-inch barrel; weighs 39 oz. (6-inch barrel). A modification of the K-22 Model 17 without being distinctly designated as a Combat Masterpiece in 4-inch barrel configuration; auxiliary cylinder offered to permit the use with 22 LR cartridge with 1969 quoted price of $35.50. Dropped 1986.

Exc: $550 **VGood:** $500 **Good:** $450

With 22 LR and 22 WMR cylinder

Exc: $650 **VGood:** $600 **Good:** $550

SMITH & WESSON MODEL 53

Revolver; double action; 22 Jet; 6-shot; 4-inch, 6-inch, 8-3/8-inch barrel; 11-1/4-inch overall length (6-inch barrel); weighs 40 oz.; 1/8-inch Baughman ramp front, adjustable S&W micrometer-click rear; checkered walnut grips with S&W medallion; blued finish only. Starting in the late '50s, there was considerable interest in converting K-22s to centerfire wildcat (i.e., nonstandard cartridge) configurations usually being chambered for a shortened version of the 22 Hornet, known as the 22 Harvey K-Chuck. With the intent of capitalizing on this interest, S&W introduced the 22 Remington CFM or centerfire magnum cartridge – also termed the 22 Jet – and the Model 53 chambered for it. The 22 Jet was a necked-down 357 case, designed to use a bullet of .222-inch to .223-inch diameter. The Model 53 was supplied with six chamber bushings, adapting it for firing 22 rimfire ammo, by means of repositioning the striker on the hammer. Alternatively, a standard 22 LR cylinder was offered as a factory-fitted accessory at about $35.30 for interchanging with the 22 Jet cylinder. Introduced 1960; dropped 1974.

Exc: $650 **VGood:** $500 **Good:** $400

With chamber inserts

Exc: $900 **VGood:** $750 **Good:** $600

With 22 LR cylinder

Exc: $1000 **VGood:** $850 **Good:** $700

With 8-3/8-inch barrel.

Exc: $950 **VGood:** $750 **Good:** $650

SMITH & WESSON MODEL 64

Revolver; double action; 38 Spl.; 6-shot cylinder; 4-inch barrel; 9-1/2-inch overall length; weighs 30-1/2 oz.; Military & Police design; stainless steel construction; fixed, serrated front ramp sight, square-notch rear; service-style checkered American walnut square-butt stocks; satin finish. Introduced 1981.

Perf: $450 **Exc:** $375 **VGood:** $300

SMITH & WESSON MODEL 65

Revolver; double action; 357 Mag.; 6-shot cylinder; 3-inch, 4-inch heavy barrel; 9-5/16-inch overall length (4-inch barrel); weighs 34 oz.; stainless steel construction; serrated ramp front sight, fixed square notch rear; square or round butt; blued finish. Introduced 1974; still in production.

Perf: $450 **Exc:** $375 **VGood:** $300

SMITH & WESSON MODEL 65LS LADYSMITH

Same specs as the Model 65 except 3-inch barrel; weighs 31 oz.; rosewood round-butt grips; stainless steel construction with frosted finish; smooth combat trigger; service hammer; shrouded ejector rod; comes with soft case. Made in U.S. by Smith & Wesson. Introduced 1992.

Perf: $550 **Exc:** $450 **VGood:** $350

SMITH & WESSON MODEL 66 COMBAT MAGNUM

Revolver; double action; 357 Mag., 38 Spl.; 6-shot cylinder; 2-1/2-inch, 4-inch, 6-inch barrel; 9-1/2-inch overall length (4-inch barrel); weighs 36 oz.; stainless steel construction; checkered Goncalo Alves target stocks; Baughman Quick Draw front sight on plain ramp, micro-click adjustable rear; grooved trigger, adjustable stop; satin finish. Introduced 1971.

Perf: $550 **Exc:** $450 **VGood:** $350

SMITH & WESSON MODEL 67 K-38 COMBAT MASTERPIECE

Revolver; double action; 38 Spl.; 6-shot cylinder; 4-inch barrel; 9-1/2-inch overall length; weighs 32 oz.; stainless steel construction; marketed as Combat Masterpiece; soft rubber or service-style checkered American walnut stocks; Baughman Quick Draw front sight on ramp, micro-click adjustable rear; square-butt with grooved tangs; grooved trigger, adjustable stop. Introduced 1972; reintroduced 1994.

Perf: $550 **Exc:** $475 **VGood:** $400

SMITH & WESSON MODEL 547

Revolver; double action; 9mm Para.; 3-inch, 4-inch heavy barrel; 9-1/8-inch overall length (4-inch barrel); half-spur hammer; special extractor system; serrated ramp front sight, fixed square notch rear; checkered square-butt Magna Service stocks with 4-inch barrel; checkered round butt target stocks with 3-inch; blued finish. Introduced 1981; dropped 1985.

Exc: $825 **VGood:** $525 **Good:** $375

SMITH & WESSON MODEL 317 AIRLITE, 317 LADYSMITH

Revolver; single action; 22 LR, 8-shot. Barrel: 1-7/8-inch. Weight: 9.9 oz. Length: 6-3/16-inch overall. Stocks: Dymondwood Boot or Uncle Mike's Boot. Sights: Serrated ramp front, fixed notch rear. Features: Aluminum alloy, carbon and stainless steels, and titanium construction. Short spur hammer, smooth combat trigger. Clear Cote finish. Introduced 1997.

New: $575 **Perf:** $500 **Exc:** $400

Smith & Wesson 640 Centennial

Smith & Wesson Model 657

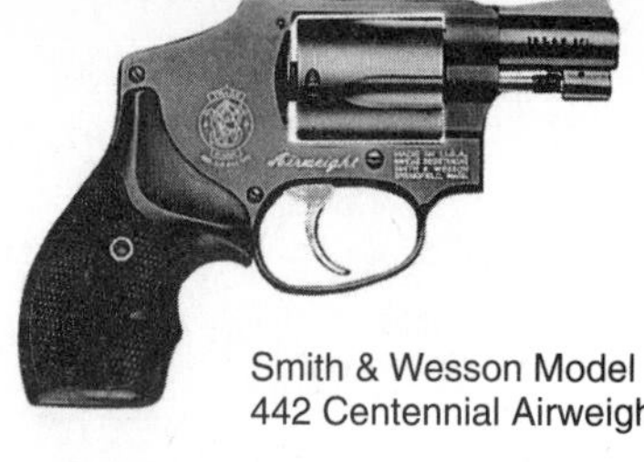

Smith & Wesson Model 442 Centennial Airweight

Smith & Wesson Model 642 Airweight

Smith & Wesson Model 686

Smith & Wesson 642LS LadySmith

Smith & Wesson Model 686 Magnum PLUS

Model 317 LadySmith (DymondWood only, comes with display case).

New: $550 **Perf:** $475 **Exc:** $400

SMITH & WESSON MODEL 317 AIRLITE KIT GUN

Similar to the Model 317 Airlite except has 3-inch barrel, pinned black front sight, micro-click rear adjustable for windage and elevation. Weighs 11 oz. Introduced 1998.

New: $575 **Perf:** $475 **Exc:** $400

SMITH & WESSON MODEL 586 DISTINGUISHED COMBAT MAGNUM

Revolver; double action; 357 Mag.; 4-inch, 6-inch heavy barrel; weighs 46 oz. (6-inch barrel), 41 oz. (4-inch barrel); L-frame design; ejector rod shroud; combat-type trigger; semi-target hammer; Baughman red ramp front sight, micrometer-click rear; soft rubber or Goncalo Alves target stocks; blued or nickel finish. Introduced 1981; dropped 1999.

Perf: $475 **Exc..:** $425 **VGood:** $350

SMITH & WESSON MODEL 610 CLASSIC HUNTER REVOLVER

Revolver; double action; 10mm, 6-shot cylinder. Barrel: 6-1/2-inch full lug. Weight: 52 oz. Length: 12-inch overall. Stocks: Hogue rubber combat. Sights: Interchangeable blade front, micro-click rear adjustable for windage and elevation. Features: Stainless steel construction; target hammer, target trigger; unfluted cylinder; drilled and tapped for scope mounting. 1998-2009.

Perf: $750 **Exc:** $650 **VGood:** $550

SMITH & WESSON MODEL 617 K-22 MASTERPIECE FULL LUG

Revolver; double action; 22 LR; 6-shot; 4-inch, 6-inch, 8-3/8-inch barrel; weighs 42 oz. (4-inch barrel); Patridge-type front sight on two longer barrel lengths, serrated type on 4-inch version, S&W click-adjustable micrometer rear; grooved tang; polished blue finish. Has same general specs as Model 17 Full Lug version except made of stainless steel; semi-target hammer (4-inch barrel); smooth combat trigger standard; smooth or serrated trigger or target hammer (6-inch barrel) optional; target hammer, serrated trigger (8-3/8-inch barrel). Introduced 1990; still in production.

4-inch barrel

New: $600 **Perf:** $525 **Exc:** $450

8-3/8-inch barrel with target hammer, trigger

New: $660 **Perf:** $550 **Exc:** $475

SMITH & WESSON MODEL 651

Revolver; double action; 22 WMR, 6-shot cylinder. Barrel: 4-inch. Weight: 24-1/2 oz. Length: 8-11/16-inch overall. Stocks: Soft rubber; wood optional. Sights: Red ramp front, adjustable micrometer click rear. Features: Stainless steel construction with semi-target hammer, smooth combat trigger. 1983-1987 and 1991-1998.

Exc: $550 **VGood:** $475 **Good:** $400

SMITH & WESSON MODEL 657

Revolver; double action; 41 Mag., 6-shot. Barrel: 6-inch. Weight: 48 oz. Length: 11-3/8-inch overall. Stocks: Soft rubber; wood optional. Sights: Pinned 1/8-inch red ramp front, micro-click rear adjustable for windage and elevation. Features: Stainless steel construction. 1986-2008.

New: $800 **Perf:** $725 **Exc:** $650

SMITH & WESSON MODEL 696

Revolver; double action; 44 Spec., 5-shot. Barrel: 3-inch. Weight: 35.5 oz. Length: 8-1/4-inch overall. Stocks: Uncle Mike's Combat. Sights: Red ramp front, click adjustable white outline rear. Features: Stainless steel construction; round butt frame; satin finish. 1997-2002.

New: $650 **Perf:** $575 **Exc:** $500

MODEL 396 NIGHT GUARD

A 2-1/2-inch snubbie chambered for .44 Special. 5-shot cylinder. Tritium sights, scandium alloy frame, matte black finish overll. Neoprene grips. 2008-2009.

New: $750 **Perf:** $625 **Exc:** $500

SMITH & WESSON MODEL 640 CENTENNIAL

Revolver; double action; 357 Mag., 38 Spec., 5-shot. Barrel: 1-7/8-inch (38 Spec.), 2-1/8-inch (357 Magnum). Weight: 25 oz. Length: 6-3/4-inch overall. Stocks: Uncle Mike's Boot Grip. Sights: Serrated ramp front, fixed notch rear. Features: Stainless steel version of the original Model 40 but without the grip safety. Fully concealed hammer, snag-proof smooth edges. Introduced 1995 in 357 Magnum.

New: $550 **Perf:** $475 **Exc:** $400

Model 940 (9mm Para.)

New: $575 **Perf:** $500 **Exc:** $425

SMITH & WESSON MODEL 442 CENTENNIAL AIRWEIGHT

Similar to the Model 640 Centennial except has alloy frame giving weight of 15.8 oz. Chambered for 38 Special, 2-inch carbon steel barrel; carbon steel cylinder; concealed hammer; Uncle Mike's Custom Grade Santoprene grips. Fixed square notch rear sight, serrated ramp front. Introduced 1993.

New: $500 **Perf:** $475 **Exc:** $425

SMITH & WESSON MODEL 642 AIRWEIGHT

Similar to the Model 442 Centennial Airweight except has stainless steel barrel, cylinder and yoke with matte finish; Uncle Mike's Boot Grip; weights 15.8 oz. Introduced 1996.

New: $500 **Perf:** $450 **Exc:** $400

SMITH & WESSON MODEL 642LS LADYSMITH

Same as the Model 642 except has smooth combat wood grips, and comes with case; aluminum alloy frame, stainless cylinder, barrel and yoke; frosted matte finish. Weighs 15.8 oz. Introduced 1996.

New: $525 **Perf:** $475 **Exc:** $400

SMITH & WESSON MODEL 648 K-22 MASTERPIECE WMR

Revolver; double action; 22 WMR; 6-shot; 6-inch full lug barrel; 11-1/8-inch overall length; weighs 38-1/2 oz. loaded; stainless steel construction; combat trigger; semi-target hammer; square-butt combat-style grips; satin finish. Introduced 1991; dropped 1994.

Exc: $575 **VGood:** $500 **Good:** $400

SMITH & WESSON MODEL 681

Revolver; double action; 357 Mag.; 4-inch, 6-inch heavy barrels; L-frame design; stainless steel construction; ejector rod shroud; combat-type trigger; semi-target hammer; fixed sights; Goncalo Alves target stocks; satin finish. Introduced 1981.

Perf: $450 **Exc:** $400 **VGood:** $350

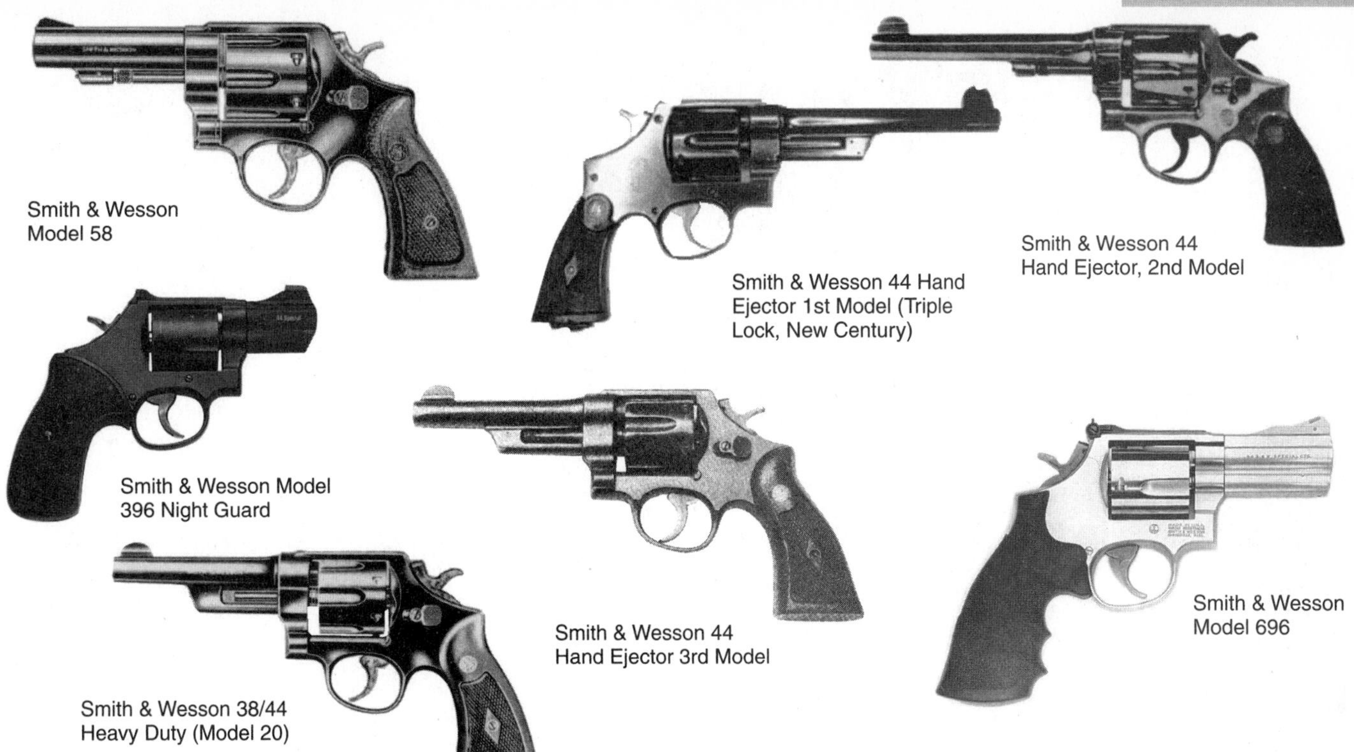
Smith & Wesson Model 58

Smith & Wesson 44 Hand Ejector 1st Model (Triple Lock, New Century)

Smith & Wesson 44 Hand Ejector, 2nd Model

Smith & Wesson Model 396 Night Guard

Smith & Wesson 44 Hand Ejector 3rd Model

Smith & Wesson Model 696

Smith & Wesson 38/44 Heavy Duty (Model 20)

SMITH & WESSON MODEL 686

Revolver; double action; 357 Mag.; 2-1/2-inch, 4-inch, 6-inch heavy barrels; weighs 46 oz. (6-inch barrel); L-frame design; stainless steel construction; ejector rod shroud; combat-type trigger; semi-target hammer; Baughman red ramp front sight, micrometer-click rear; soft rubber or Goncalo Alves target stocks; satin finish. Introduced 1981.

Perf: $550 **Exc:** $475 **VGood:** $400

SMITH & WESSON MODEL 686 MAGNUM PLUS

Similar to the Model 686 except has 7-shot cylinder, 2-1/2-inch, 4-inch or 6-inch barrel. Weighs 34-1/2 oz., overall length 7-1/2-inch (2-1/2-inch barrel). Hogue rubber grips. Introduced 1996.

New: $650 **Perf:** $600 **Exc:** $500

SMITH & WESSON MODEL 686 MIDNIGHT BLACK

Same specs as Model 686 except black finish; semi-target hammer; red ramp front sight, plain or white-outline micro rear; speedloader cut-out; full lug barrel; Goncalo Alves target stocks. Introduced 1989; no longer in production.

Exc: $600 **VGood:** $550 **Good:** $450

SMITH & WESSON 38/44 HEAVY DUTY (MODEL 20)

Revolver; 38 Spl.; 6-shot; 4-inch, 5-inch, 6-1/2-inch barrel; 10-3/8-inch overall length (5-inch barrel); weighs 40 oz.; built on the S&W 44 frame, often termed N-frame, hence the 38/44 designation; designed to handle high-velocity 38 Special ammunition; fixed sights, with 1/10-inch service-type (semi-circle) front and square notch rear; checkered walnut Magna-type grips with S&W medallion; blued or nickel finish. Introduced 1930; discontinued 1967.

Pre-War

Exc: $1000 **VGood:** $750 **Good:** $450

Post-War

Exc: $775 **VGood:** $525 **Good:** $375

SMITH & WESSON 38/44 OUTDOORSMAN (MODEL 23)

Revolver; 38 Spl.; 6-shot; 6-1/2-inch barrel; 11-3/4-inch overall length; weighs, 41-3/4 oz.; plain Patridge 1/8-inch front sight, S&W micro-adjustable rear; blue finish. Introduced in 1930 as a companion to the Model 20; reintroduced about 1950 with ribbed barrel and Magna-type stocks. Discontinued 1967.

Pre-War

Exc: $1000 **VGood:** $800 **Good:** $600

Post-War

Exc: $950 **VGood:** $675 **Good:** $500

SMITH & WESSON MODEL 57

Revolver; 41 Mag.; 6-shot; 4-inch, 6-inch, 8-3/8-inch barrel; 11-3/8-inch overall length (6-inch barrel); weighs 48 oz.; wide, grooved target trigger and broad-spur target hammer; 1/8-inch red ramp front, S&W micro-adjustable rear with white-outline notch; special oversize target-type of Goncalo Alves grips with S&W medallion; bright blue or nickel finish. Introduced as a deluxe companion to the Model 58, both being chambered for a new cartridge developed especially for them at that time, carrying a bullet of .410-inch diameter. The old 41 Long Colt cartridge cannot be fired in guns chambered for the 41 Magnum, nor can any other standard cartridge. Introduced 1964; dropped 1993.

4-inch and 6-inch barrels

Perf: $675 **Exc:** $600 **VGood:** $550

8-3/8-inch barrel

Perf: $675 **Exc:** $600 **VGood:** $550

SMITH & WESSON MODEL 58

Revolver; 41 Mag.; 6-shot; 4-inch barrel; 9-1/4-inch overall length; weighs 41 oz.; 1/8-inch serrated ramp front, square notch rear sight; checkered Magna-type walnut grips with S&W medallion; blue or nickel finish. Also known as the 41 Military & Police, this is a fixed-sight version of the Model 57. No longer in production.

Perf: $850 **Exc:** $650 **VGood:** $450

Nickel finish

Perf: $900 **Exc:** $675 **VGood:** $475

SMITH & WESSON 44 HAND EJECTOR 1ST MODEL (TRIPLE LOCK, NEW CENTURY)

Revolver; 44 S&W Spl., 44 S&W Russian, 44-40, 45 Colt, 45 S&W Spl., 450 Eley, 455 Mark II; 6-shot cylinder; 4-inch, 5-inch, 6-1/2-inch, 7-1/2-inch barrel; also known as 44 Triple Lock and 44 New Century; square-butt checkered walnut grips; fixed or factory-fitted target sights. Introduced 1908; dropped 1915.

44 Russian, 44-40, 45 Colt, 45 S&W Spl., 450 Eley

Exc: $1900 **VGood:** $1200 **Good:** $800

44 S&W Special

Exc: $1950 **VGood:** $1250 **Good:** $850

455 Mark II

Exc: $1000 **VGood:** $700 **Good:** $400

SMITH & WESSON 44 HAND EJECTOR 2ND MODEL

Revolver; 44 S&W Special, 38-40, 44-40, 45 Colt; 4-inch, 5-inch, 6-inch, 6-1/2-inch barrel; internal changes; on exterior, heavy barrel lug was dropped; cylinder size and frame cut enlarged; fixed or factory target sights. Introduced 1915; dropped 1937. Collector value.

44 S&W Special

Exc: $1100 **VGood:** $750 **Good:** $495

Other calibers

Exc: $1500 **VGood:** $1200 **Good:** $600

SMITH & WESSON 44 HAND EJECTOR 3RD MODEL

Revolver; 44 S&W, 44-40, 45 LC; 6-shot cylinder; 4-inch, 5-inch, 6-1/2-inch barrel; also known as Model 1926; fixed or factory target sights; checkered walnut square-butt grips; blue or nickel finish. Introduced 1925; dropped 1949.

44 S&W Special

Exc: $1250 **VGood:** $1050 **Good:** $675

Other calibers

Exc: $1700 **VGood:** $1200 **Good:** $950

SMITH & WESSON 44 MAGNUM (MODEL 29)

Revolver; 44 Mag.; also handles 44 Spl., 44 Russian; 6-shot; 4-inch, 5-inch, 6-1/2-inch, 8-3/8-inch; 11-7/8-inch overall length (6-1/2-inch barrel); weighs 43 oz. (4-inch barrel), 47 oz. (6-1/2-inch barrel), 51-1/2 oz. (8-3/8-inch barrel); 1/8-inch red ramp front sight, S&W micro-adjustable rear; target-type Goncalo Alves grips with S&W medallion; broad, grooved target trigger; wide-spur target hammer; bright blue or nickel finish.

Smith & Wesson 357 Magnum (Pre-War Registered)

Smith & Wesson 1950 44 Military (Model 21)

Smith & Wesson 1950 Army (Model 22)

Smith & Wesson 357 Magnum (Post-war Model 27)

Smith & Wesson 1950/1955 45 Target (Model 25 and 26)

As with the Model 27, the Model 29 was developed to take a new cartridge developed by lengthening the 44 Special case by 0.125-inch to prevent use of 44 Magnum ammo in guns chambered for the 44 Special. The 44 Magnum is loaded to pressures approximately twice that of the 44 Special. Introduced in 1956. Premium of 30 percent for 1956 production; 75 percent premium for Model 29-2.

Exc: $750 **VGood:** $675 **Good:** $500

SMITH & WESSON 44 MAGNUM MODEL 29 CLASSIC

Same specs as standard model except 5", 6-1/2", 8-3/8" barrel; chamfered cylinder front; interchangeable red ramp front, adjustable white outline rear sights; Hogue square-butt Santoprene grips; D&T for scope mount. Introduced 1990; no longer in production.

Exc: $650 **VGood:** $550 **Good:** $500

SMITH & WESSON 44 MAGNUM MODEL 29 CLASSIC DX

Same specs as Model 29 Classic except 6-1/2", 8-3/8" barrel with full-length lug; Morado combat-type grips. Five different front sight options and Hogue combat-style square butt conversion grip. Introduced 1991; no longer in production.

Exc: $650 **VGood:** $550 **Good:** $500

SMITH & WESSON 44 MAGNUM MODEL 29 SILHOUETTE

Same specs as Model 29 except 10-5/8"; oversize target-type checkered Goncalo Alves grips; four click-adjustable front sight positions. Introduced 1983; dropped 1991. Not successful; a scarce model.

Exc: $675 **VGood:** $575 **Good:** $500

SMITH & WESSON 44 MAGNUM MODEL 629

Same specs as Model 29 except in stainless steel.

Exc: $650 **VGood:** $575 **Good:** $500

SMITH & WESSON 44 MAGNUM MODEL 629 CLASSIC

Same specs as Model 29 Classic except in stainless steel.

Exc: $650 **VGood:** $575 **Good:** $500

SMITH & WESSON 44 MAGNUM MODEL 629 CLASSIC DX

Same specs as Model 29 Classic DX except in stainless steel.

Exc: $650 **VGood:** $575 **Good:** $375

SMITH & WESSON 357 MAGNUM (PRE-WAR REGISTERED)

Revolver; 357 Magnum; 3-1/2", 5", 6", 6-1/2", and 8-3/8" barrel with custom lengths up to 8-3/8" available; variety of optional target sights; 3-1/2" version ("FBI model") usually had Baughman quick-draw sight on a King ramp; finely-checkered topstrap and barrel rib; bright blue or nickel finish; square or Magna walnut grips. Introduced 1935 for the new 357 S&W Magnum cartridge. Guns made 1935-1938 were registered to original owner (approximately 6,000). Later reintroduced as Model 27-8.

Exc: $4750 **VGood:** $1900 **Good:** $1200

1938-1941 (Unregistered)

Exc: $1200 **VGood:** $800 **Good:** $500

SMITH & WESSON 357 MAGNUM (POST-WAR/MODEL 27)

Revolver, .357 Magnum. Similar to pre-war unregistered model except for short action (post-1950) and minor differences. Known as Model 27 after 1957. Nickeled examples increasingly command a premium.

Exc: $650 **VGood:** $550 **Good:** $450

SMITH & WESSON 1950 44 MILITARY (MODEL 21)

Revolver; 44 Special; 5-1/2" barrel; 10-1/2" overall length; semi-circular front sight and fixed groove rear. Blued or nickel finish; checkered walnut Magna grips. Post-WWII version of the Model of 1926 with new short action, and other improvements. Remained in the S&W lineup until 1967. A Target version with adjustable sights was also available.

Exc: $1200 **VGood:** $750 **Good:** $550

SMITH & WESSON MODEL 27 (1991 REINTRODUCTION)

Same specs as Model 27 but with 3-1/2" or 5" barrel lengths only. Reintroduced in 1991 in limited edition; dropped 1992.

Exc: $550 **VGood:** $450 **Good:** $400

MODEL 627 PRO SERIES

Introduced in 2008. This is an eight-shot .357 revolver with stainless steel frame, adjustable sights, 4-inch barrel and various accurizing refinements.

Exc: $950 **VGood:** $750 **Good:** $550

SMITH & WESSON 455 HAND EJECTOR 1ST MODEL

Revolver; .455 Mark II cartridge (British); 6-1/2" barrel; fized sights; checkered walnut square-butt grips; blue finish. Designed in 1914 for the British war effort in 1916. Discontinued 1918. Usually have British proof marks. As war surplus, many were rechambered to 45 Colt (deduct 30 percent).

Exc: $750 **VGood:** $575 **Good:** $375

SMITH & WESSON 455 HAND EJECTOR 2ND MODEL

Similar to 455 Hand Ejector First Model but lacks ejector rod housing/barrel lug. Introduced 1915; discontinued 1916. Usually have British proof marks. As war surplus, many were rechambered to 45 Colt (deduct 30 percent).

Exc: $700 **VGood:** $550 **Good:** $375

SMITH & WESSON 1950 ARMY (MODEL 22)

Revolver; 45 ACP, 45 Auto Rim; 5-1/2" barrel; 10-1/2" overall length; semi-circular front sight and fixed groove rear. Post-WWII version of the Model of 1917 with redesigned grips, short action, and other improvements. Remained in the S&W lineup until 1967. A Target version with adjustable sights was also available.

44 S&W Special

Exc: $1050 **VGood:** $750 **Good:** $600

Smith & Wesson Highway Patrolman (Model 28)

Smith & Wesson Military Model of 1917

Smith & Wesson Model 624

Smith & Wesson Model 625-2

Smith & Wesson Model 1926 44 Military

Other calibers

Exc: $1000 **VGood:** $725 **Good:** $575

SMITH & WESSON 1950 44 TARGET (MODEL 24)

Revolver; 44 Special; 6-shot; 4", 6" barrel. Introduced in 1950 as an updated version of the Model 1926 Target Model. Post-1957 models known as Model 24. Patridge-type front sight with perpendicular leading edge, S&W Micro rear sights. 4" version had Baughman quick-draw front sight on serrated ramp. Blued or nickel finish. 4" versions command 20 percent premium; nickel finish add 25 percent.

Exc: $1500 **VGood:** $1200 **Good:** $800

SMITH & WESSON MODEL 24 TARGET (1983 REINTRODUCTION)

Same specs as earlier Model 24 except offered in 4" and 6-1/2" barrel lengths; grooved topstrap; barrel rib. 7500 produced in 1983.

Exc: $750 **VGood:** $600 **Good:** $500

SMITH & WESSON 1950/1955 45 TARGET (MODEL 25 & 26)

Revolver; 45 ACP, 45 Auto Rim; 6-1/2" barrel; 11-7/8" overall length. Sights: Patridge front and S&W Micro rear. Checkered walnut grips. Blued finish. Introduced in 1950 as a companion to the Model 1950 44 Target. Redesigned in 1955 and released as the Model of 1955, known post-1957 as the Model 25, while the 1950 Model became known as the Model 26.

1950/Model 26

Exc: $1100 **VGood:** $750 **Good:** $500

1955/Model 25

Exc: $1050 **VGood:** $700 **Good:** $500

SMITH & WESSON HIGHWAY PATROLMAN (MODEL 28)

Similar to Model 27 except offered in 4" and 6" barrel lengths only; has uncheckered topstrap and matte finish overall. Known as Model 28 after 1957. Introduced 1954. Once a dog on the market; now increasingly desirable.

Exc: $575 **VGood:** $500 **Good:** $425

SMITH & WESSON MILITARY MODEL OF 1917

Revolver; 45 ACP, 45 Auto Rim. Entry of the U.S. into WWI found facilities unable to produce sufficient quantities of the recently adopted Colt Government Model auto pistol, so approximately 175,000 Smith & Wesson revolvers were manufactured, being chambered to fire the 45 ACP cartridge by means of the two 3-shot steel clips; also fires the 45 Auto Rim round. The wartime units had a duller blued finish and smooth walnut grips, with 5-1/2-inch barrel; overall length, 10-1/4-inch; weighs 36-1/4 oz. with lanyard ring in the butt. A commercial version remained in production after the end of WWI to the start of WWII, distinguished by a bright blue finish and checkered walnut stocks.

Military model

Exc: $750 **VGood:** $595 **Good:** $450

Commercial model

Exc: $1000 **VGood:** $700 **Good:** $495

SMITH & WESSON MODEL 25

Revolver; double action; 45 Colt; 6-shot cylinder; 4-inch, 6-inch, 8-3/8-inch barrel; 11-3/8-inch overall length (6-inch barrel); weighs about 46 oz.; target-type checkered Goncalo Alves grips; S&W red ramp front sight, S&W micrometer-click rear with white outline; available in bright blue or nickel finish; target trigger; target hammer. Dropped 1994. Model 25-2 chambered in 45 ACP.

4-inch or 6-inch barrel, blue

Perf: $650 **Exc:** $575 **VGood:** $500

8-3/8-inch barrel, blue or nickel

Perf: $650 **Exc:** $575 **VGood:** $500

SMITH & WESSON MODEL 625

Revolver; double action; 45 ACP, 6-shot. Barrel: 5-inch. Weight: 46 oz. Length: 11-3/8-inch overall. Stocks: Soft rubber; wood optional. Sights: Patridge front on ramp, S&W micrometer click rear adjustable for windage and elevation. Features: Stainless steel construction with .400-inch semi-target hammer, .312-inch smooth combat trigger; full lug barrel. Introduced 1989.

New: $650 **Perf:** $575 **Exc:** $500

SMITH & WESSON MODEL 25-5

Revolver; 45 Colt; 6-shot; 4-inch, 6-inch, 8-3/8-inch barrel; adjustable sights; square-butt, checkered, target-type Goncalo Alves grips; blue or nickel finish. Introduced in 1978 and called the 25-5 to distinguish it from the Model 25-2 in 45 ACP. Available with presentation case. Discontinued 1987.

Exc: $650 **VGood:** $550 **Good:** $475

SMITH & WESSON MODEL 610

Revolver; 10mm; 5-inch, 6-1/2-inch barrel; .500-inch target hammer; .400-inch smooth combat trigger; round-butt frame with smooth Goncalo Alves finger groove grips; stainless steel construction; satin finish. Introduced April 1990.

Perf: $650 **Exc:** $550 **VGood:** $475

SMITH & WESSON MODEL 624

Revolver; 44 Spl.; 6-shot cylinder; 4-inch, 6-inch barrel; 9-1/2-inch overall length (4-inch barrel); weighs 41-1/2 oz.; target-type checkered Goncalo Alves stocks; black ramp front sight, adjustable micrometer-click rear; stainless steel version of Model 24. Dropped 1986.

Exc: $700 **VGood:** $625 **Good:** $550

SMITH & WESSON MODEL 625-2

Revolver; double-action; 45 ACP; 3-inch full-lug barrel; same general specs as S&W Model 25, but is made of stainless steel; black pinned ramp front sight, micrometer rear; semi-target hammer; combat trigger; full lug barrel; round butt Pachmayr stocks. Introduced 1989.

New: $650 **Perf:** $575 **Exc:** $500

SMITH & WESSON MODEL 1926 44 MILITARY

Revolver; primarily produced in 44 Spl., sometimes encountered in 45 Colt, 455 Webley or 455 Eley; 6-shot; 4-inch, 5-inch, 6-1/2-inch barrel; 11-3/4-inch overall length (6-1/2-inch barrel); weighs 39-1/2 oz.; 1/10-inch service-type front sight, fixed square-notch rear; checkered walnut, square or Magna-type grips

Smith & Wesson M&P340CT

Smith & Wesson Model 386 SC/S

Smith & Wesson M&P340

Smith & Wesson M&P360

Smith & Wesson Model 686 Plus

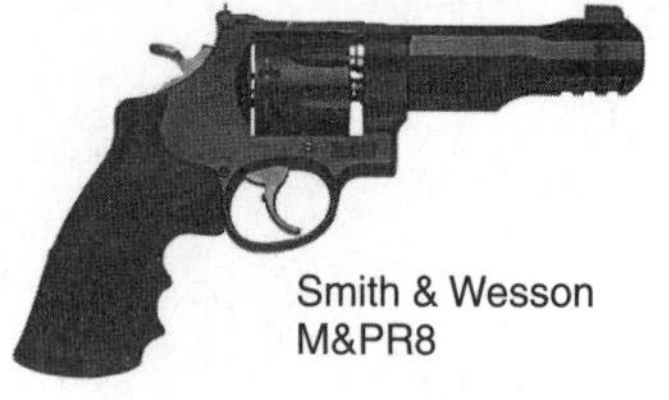

Smith & Wesson M&PR8

Smith & Wesson Model 36 Classic

Smith & Wesson Model 21 Classic

with S&W medallion; blued or nickel finish. Modified version of S&W's earlier 44 Hand Ejector First Model, minus the triple-lock feature, but retaining the heavy shroud around the ejector rod. Discontinued at the start of WWII; replaced after the war by the 1950 model.

Exc: $900 **VGood:** $700 **Good:** $400

Nickel finish

Exc: $800 **VGood:** $600 **Good:** $350

SMITH & WESSON MODEL 1926 44 TARGET

Same specs as 1926 44 Military except target version with rear sight adjustable for windage and elevation; produced from 1926 to the beginning of WWII; replaced after the war by the 1950 Target Model 24.

Exc: $1100 **VGood:** $950 **Good:** $700

SMITH & WESSON MODEL 500

Monstrous extra-large-frame (X frame) single/double action revolver chambered in .500 S&W. Stainless finish, sorbothane grips. Adjustable sights, 5-shot cylinder.

Exc: $1000 **VGood:** $895 **Good:** $700

SMITH & WESSON MODEL 460V

X-frame double-action trigger and 5-inch barrel in .460 S&W Magnum caliber. Also accepts .454 Casull and .45 Colt. Sorbothane recoil-reducing grip, interchangeable muzzle compensator. 5-shot, stainless with satin finish. 62.5 oz. Introduced in 2005.

New: $1100 **Exc:** $975 **VGood:** $800

SMITH & WESSON MODEL 22 - THUNDER RANCH .45 ACP

Limited edition six-shot single/double-action chambered for .45 ACP. Blued with 4-inch tapered barrel, 37.5 oz. Cocobolo grips engraved with Thunder Ranch insignia. Fixed sights. SNs begin with TRR0000.

New: $725 **Exc:** $625 **VGood:** $500

SMITH & WESSON FIFTIETH ANNIVERSARY MODEL 29

A commemorative edition of the classic .44 Magnum. Carbon steel with polished blue finish. Double-action 6-shot. LOA 12-inch, 6.5-inch barrel, 48.5 oz. Cocobolo wood grips with 24kt gold anniversary logo.

New: $1050 **Exc:** $875 **VGood:** $695

SMITH & WESSON M&P340

Double-action-only revolver built on Centennial (hammerless J) frame. .357 Magnum/.38 Special; five-shot cylinder; 1.87" barrel with fixed night sights. Matte black finish on scandium/alloy frame.

New: $675 **Exc:** $600 **VGood:** $525

SMITH & WESSON MODEL 325 NIGHT GUARD

A 2-1/2-inch snubbie chambered for .45 ACP. Tritium sights, scandium alloy frame, matte black finish overll. Neoprene grips. Introduced 2008.

New: $1050 **Exc:** $895 **VGood:** $600

SMITH & WESSON MODEL 327 NIGHT GUARD

A 2-1/2-inch snubbie chambered for .357 Magnum. 8-shot cylinder. Tritium sights, scandium alloy frame, matte black finish overll. Neoprene grips. Introduced 2008.

New: $1050 **Exc:** $895 **VGood:** $600

SMITH & WESSON MODEL 329 NIGHT GUARD

A 2-1/2-inch snuibbie chambered for .44 Magnum. Scandium frame, fixed sights, matte black finish overall. Introduced 2008.

New: $1050 **Exc:** $895 **VGood:** $600

SMITH & WESSON M&P340CT

Similar to above but with Crimson Trace lasergrips.

New: $725 **Exc:** $650 **VGood:** $575

SMITH & WESSON M&P360

Double-action-only revolver built on Chief's Special (hammered J) frame. .357 Magnum/.38 Special; five-shot cylinder; 1.87" barrel with fixed night sights. Matte black finish on scandium/alloy frame.

New: $795 **Exc:** $725 **VGood:** $595

SMITH & WESSON MODEL 315 NIGHT GUARD .38

Scandium-framed, 5-shot .38 snubbie with 2.5-inch barrel. Finished overall in matte black. Tritium sights. Introduced 2008.

New: $795 **Exc:** $725 **VGood:** $595

SMITH & WESSON MODEL 637 POWER PORT PRO SERIES

Aluminum J-frame 5-shot revolver with stainless steel cylinder chambered for .38 Special (5 shots). 2-1/8-inch ported black stainless barrel. Introduced 2008.

New: $795 **Exc:** $725 **VGood:** $595

SMITH & WESSON M&PR8

Double-action-only revolver built on large (N) frame. .357 Magnum/.38 Special; eight-shot cylinder; 5" barrel with adjustable Patridge sights with interchangeable inserts. Matte black finish on scandium/alloy frame.

New: $1250 **Exc:** $1150 **VGood:** $1025

SMITH & WESSON MODEL 60 WITH HI-VIZ SIGHT

Similar to Model 60 but with light-gathering HI-VIZ red dot front sight and adjustable rear sight.

New: $650 **Exc:** $595 **VGood:** $435

SMITH & WESSON MODEL 386 SC/S

Single-/double-action L-frame revolver in .38/.357 Magnum. 7-shot cylinder, 2.5" barrel, Patridge front sight, adjustable rear, scandium/alloy frame, matte black finish, rubber grips.

New: $800 **Exc:** $725 **VGood:** $635

SMITH & WESSON MODEL 686 PLUS

Single-/double-action L-frame revolver in .38/.357 Magnum. 7-shot cylinder, 3" barrel, Patridge front sight, adjustable rear, stainless finish, rubber grips. Introduced 2007.

New: $600 **Exc:** $525 **VGood:** $400

SMITH & WESSON MODEL 36 CLASSIC

Replica of vintage Model 36 Chief's Special in .38 Special. Five-shot cylinder. Carbon steel frame, 1-7/8" or 3" barrel, fixed sights. Blued, case colored, or nickel finish with Altamont wood grips.

New: $625 **Exc:** $550 **VGood:** $425

ith & Wesson 35

Smith & Wesson Model 39 9mm Auto

Smith & Wesson Model 59 9mm Auto

Smith & Wesson 38 Target Auto (Model 52)

Smith & Wesson Model 457

Smith & Wesson Model 469

SMITH & WESSON MODEL 21 CLASSIC

Replica of vintage Model 21 N-frame revolver in .44 Special. Six-shot cylinder. Carbon steel frame, 4" barrel, fixed sights. Blued, case colored, or nickel finish with Altamont wood grips.

New: $950 **Exc:** $825 **VGood:** $500

SMITH & WESSON MODEL 22 CLASSIC

Replica of vintage Model 22 N-frame revolver in .45 ACP. Six-shot cylinder. Carbon steel frame, 4" barrel, fixed sights. Blued, case colored, or nickel finish with Altamont wood grips.

New: $950 **Exc:** $825 **VGood:** $500

SMITH & WESSON MODEL 22 OF 1917 CLASSIC

Similar to Model 22 Classic but without ejector rod shroud and with lanyard ring on butt. Replica of U.S. Army WWI-era revolver.

New: $950 **Exc:** $825 **VGood:** $500

SMITH & WESSON MODEL 29 CLASSIC

Replica of original (1956) Model 29 N-frame revolver in .44 Magnum. Six-shot cylinder. Carbon steel frame, 6.5" barrel, fixed sights. Blued or nickel finish with or without engraving. Altamont wood grips.

New: $975 **Exc:** $850 **VGood:** $575

SMITH & WESSON MODEL 32 AUTO

Semi-automatic; 32 ACP, 7.65mm; 8-shot; 4-inch barrel; 7-inch overall length; weighs 28 oz.; unusual grip safety just below the trigger guard; successor to S&W's original auto pistol; walnut, uncheckered grips; blue or nickel finish. Introduced 1924; discontinued 1937. Collector interest.

Exc: $2500 **VGood:** $2000 **Good:** $1500

SMITH & WESSON MODEL 35

Semi-automatic; 35 S&W Auto; 7-shot magazine; 3-1/2-inch barrel; 6-1/2-inch overall length; uncheckered walnut stocks; fixed sights; blued or nickel finish. Manufactured 1913 to 1921. Collector interest.

Exc: $700 **VGood:** $375 **Good:** $250

SMITH & WESSON 38 TARGET AUTO (MODEL 52)

Semi-automatic; 38 Spl.; 5-shot; 5-inch barrel; 8-5/8-inch overall length; weighs 41 oz.; Patridge-type front on ramp, S&W micro-adjustable rear; checkered walnut grips with S&W medallion; blue finish only. Designed to fire a mid-range loading of the 38 Special, requiring a wadcutter bullet seated flush with the case mouth; action is straight blowback, thus not suited for firing of high-velocity 38 Special ammo. Introduced 1961. Considerable premium for early issues.

Exc: $900 **VGood:** $800 **Good:** $650

SMITH & WESSON MODEL 39 9MM AUTO

Semi-automatic; 9mm; 8-shot magazine; 4-inch barrel; 7-7/16-inch overall length; weighs 26-1/2 oz. sans magazine; 1/8-inch serrated ramp front, windage-adjustable square notch rear; checkered walnut grips with S&W medallion; bright blue or nickel finish. During the first dozen years of production, a limited number were made with steel frames rather than the standard aluminum alloy and command premium price. Introduced 1954. Collector value.

Exc: $500 **VGood:** $450 **Good:** $375

Nickel finis3

Exc: $550 **VGood:** $475 **Good:** $400

Steel frame model

Exc: $1100 **VGood:** $850 **Good:** $750

SMITH & WESSON MODEL 59 9MM AUTO

Semi-automatic; 9mm; 14-shot staggered column magazine; 4-inch barrel; 7-7/16-inch overall length; weighs 27-1/2 oz. sans magazine; 1/8-inch serrated ramp front, windage-adjustable square notch rear; checkered high-impact molded nylon; bright blue or nickel finish. Similar to the Model 39. Like the Model 39, the 59 offers the option of carrying a round in the chamber, with hammer down, available for firing via a double-action pull of the trigger. Introduced 1971; dropped 1981.

Exc: $475 **VGood:** $375 **Good:** $325

Nickel finish

Exc: $575 **VGood:** $425 **Good:** $315

SMITH & WESSON MODEL 439

Semi-automatic; double-action; 9mm Para.; 8-shot magazine; 4-inch barrel; 7-7/16-inch overall length; weighs 27-1/2 oz. sans magazine; same specs as Model 39 except new trigger-actuated firing pin lock; magazine disconnector; new extractor design; 1/8-inch serrated ramp front, windage-adjustable square notch rear and protective shield on both sides of blade; checkered high-impact molded nylon; bright blue or nickel finish. Introduced 1980; dropped 1988.

Exc: $375 **VGood:** $350 **Good:** $300

Nickel finish

Exc: $400 **VGood:** $375 **Good:** $325

SMITH & WESSON MODEL 457

Semi-automatic; double-action; 45 ACP, 7-shot magazine. Barrel: 3-3/4-inch. Weight: 29 oz. Length: 7-1/4-inch overall. Stocks: One-piece Xenoy, wrap-around with straight backstrap. Sights: Post front, fixed rear, three-dot system. Features: Aluminum alloy frame, matte blue carbon steel slide; bobbed hammer; smooth trigger. 1996-2008.

New: $500 **Perf:** $425 **Exc:** $400

SMITH & WESSON MODEL 459

Semi-automatic; double-action; 9mm Para.; 14-shot magazine; 4-inch barrel; 7-7/16-inch overall length; weighs 27-1/2 oz. sans magazine; has same general specs as Model 439, except for increased magazine capacity, straighter, longer grip frame; blued or nickel finish. Introduced 1980; dropped 1989.

Blue finish

Exc: $400 **VGood:** $350 **Good:** $300

Nickel finish

Exc: $450 **VGood:** $400 **Good:** $350

SMITH & WESSON MODEL 469

Semi-automatic; 9mm Para.; 3-1/2-inch barrel; 12-shot magazine; accepts 14-shot 459 magazine; 6-7/8-inch overall length; weighs 26 oz.; cut-down version of Model 459; cross-hatching on front of trigger guard, backstrap; plastic pebble-grain grips; curved finger-extension magazine; bobbed hammer; sandblasted blued finish. Introduced 1983; dropped 1988.

Exc: $350 **VGood:** $300 **Good:** $275

Smith & Wesson Model 908

Smith & Wesson Model 745

Smith & Wesson Model 410 DA

Smith & Wesson Model 915

Smith & Wesson Model 909

Smith & Wesson Model 910

SMITH & WESSON MODEL 539

Semi-automatic; double action; 9mm Para.; 8-shot magazine; 4-inch barrel; 7-7/16-inch overall length; weighs 36 oz.; carbon steel construction; trigger-actuated firing pin lock; magazine disconnector; 1/8-inch serrated ramp front, windage-adjustable square notch rear and protective shield on both sides of blade; checkered high-impact molded nylon; bright blue or nickel finish. Approximately 10,000 manufactured. Introduced 1981; dropped 1984.

Exc: $450 **VGood:** $350 **Good:** $300

SMITH & WESSON MODEL 559

Semi-automatic; double action; 9mm Para.; 14-shot magazine; 4-inch barrel; 7-7/16-inch overall length; weighs 40 oz. sans magazine; has same general specs as Model 459, except carbon steel construction; blue or nickel finish. Approximately 10,000 manufactured. Introduced 1981; dropped 1984.

Exc: $450 **VGood:** $400 **Good:** $350

SMITH & WESSON MODEL 639

Semi-automatic; double action; 9mm Para.; 8-shot magazine; 4-inch barrel; 7-7/16-inch overall length; weighs 27-1/2 oz. sans magazine; stainless steel construction; trigger-actuated firing pin lock; magazine disconnector; 1/8-inch serrated ramp front, windage-adjustable square notch rear with protective shield on both sides of blade; checkered high-impact molded nylon; bright blue or nickel finish. Introduced 1981; dropped 1988.

Exc: $400 **VGood:** $350 **Good:** $300

SMITH & WESSON MODEL 645

Semi-automatic; double action; 45 ACP; 8-shot magazine; 5-inch barrel; 8-3/4-inch overall length; weighs 37-5/8 oz.; red ramp front sight, drift-adjustable rear; checkered nylon stocks; stainless steel construction; cross-hatch knurling on recurved front trigger guard, backstrap; beveled magazine well. Introduced 1985; dropped 1988.

Exc: $500 **VGood:** $425 **Good:** $350

SMITH & WESSON MODEL 659

Semi-automatic; double action; 9mm Para.; 14-shot magazine; 4-inch barrel; 7-7/16-inch overall length; weighs 27-1/2 oz. sans magazine; has same general specs as Model 439, except stainless steel construction. Introduced 1981; dropped 1988.

Exc: $400 **VGood:** $350 **Good:** $300

SMITH & WESSON MODEL 669

Semi-automatic; 9mm Para.; 3-1/2-inch barrel; 12-shot magazine; accepts 14-shot 459 magazine; 6-7/8-inch overall length; weighs 26 oz.; same specs as Model 469 except slide and barrel manufactured of stainless steel; aluminum alloy frame finished in natural finish. Introduced 1985; dropped 1988.

Exc: $400 **VGood:** $350 **Good:** $300

SMITH & WESSON MODEL 745

Semi-automatic; 45 ACP; 8-shot magazine; 5-inch barrel; 8-5/8-inch overall length; weighs 38-3/4 oz.; fixed Novak rear sight, serrated ramp front; blued slide, trigger, hammer, sights. Marketed with two magazines. Introduced 1987; dropped 1990.

Exc: $500 **VGood:** $450 **Good:** $400

SMITH & WESSON MODEL 356 TSW LIMITED

Semi-automatic; single action; 356 TSW; 15-shot magazine; 5-inch barrel; weighs 44 oz.; 8-1/2-inch overall length; checkered black composition grips; blade front sight drift adjustable for windage, fully-adjustable Bo-Mar rear; stainless steel frame and slide; hand-fitted titanium-coated stainless steel bushing; match grade barrel; extended magazine well and oversize release; magazine pads; extended safety. Checkered front strap. Made in U.S. by Smith & Wesson; available through Lew Horton Dist. Introduced 1993; no longer in production.

Exc: $1200 **VGood:** $850 **Good:** $750

SMITH & WESSON MODEL 356 TSW COMPACT

Same specs as the 356 TSW Limited except has 3-1/2-inch barrel; 12-shot magazine; Novak LoMount combat sights; 7-inch overall length; weighs 37 oz. Made in U.S. by Smith & Wesson; available from Lew Horton Dist. Introduced 1993; no longer in production.

Exc: $850 **VGood:** $725 **Good:** $550

SMITH & WESSON MODEL 410 DA

Semi-automatic; double action; 40 S&W, 10-shot magazine. Barrel: 4-inch. Weight: 28.5 oz. Length: 7.5 oz. Stocks: One-piece Xenoy, wrap-around with straight backstrap. Sights: Post front, fixed rear; three-dot system. Features: Aluminum alloy frame; blued carbon steel slide; traditional double action with left-side slide-mountd decocking lever. Introduced 1996; discontinued 2007.

New: $475 **Perf:** $400 **Exc:** $375

SMITH & WESSON MODEL 411

Semi-automatic; double action; 40 S&W; 10-shot magazine; 4-inch barrel; weighs 28 oz.; 7-3/8-inch overall length; one-piece Xenoy wrap-around grips with straight backstrap; post front sight with white dot, fixed two-dot rear; alloy frame, blue carbon steel slide; slide-mounted decocking lever. Made in U.S. by Smith & Wesson. 1993-1995.

New: $450 **Perf:** $400 **Exc:** $325

SMITH & WESSON MODEL 908

Caliber: 9mm Para., 8-shot magazine. Barrel: 3-1/2-inch. Weight: 26 oz. Length: 6-13/16-inch. Stocks: One-piece Xenoy, wrap-around with straight backstrap. Sights: Post front, fixed rear, three-dot system. Features: Aluminum alloy frame, matte blue carbon steel slide; bobbed hammer; smooth trigger. 1996-2007.

New: $425 **Perf:** $375 **Exc:** $300

SMITH & WESSON MODEL 909

Semi-automatic; double action; 9mm Para.; 9-shot magazine; 4-inch barrel; weighs 27 oz.; 7-3/8-inch overall length; one-piece Xenoy wrap-around grips with curved backstrap; post front sight with white dot, fixed two-dot rear; alloy frame, blue carbon steel slide; slide mounted decocking lever. Made in U.S.

Smith & Wesson Model 1066

Smith & Wesson Model 1086

Smith & Wesson Model 3904

Smith & Wesson Model 1006

Smith & Wesson Model 1026

Smith & Wesson Model 3906

Smith & Wesson Model 3913

Smith & Wesson Model 3913 LadySmith

by Smith & Wesson. Introduced 1994; discontinued 1996.

New: $375 **Perf:** $325 **Exc:** $275

SMITH & WESSON MODEL 910

Semi-automatic; double action; 9mm Para.; 10-shot magazine; 4-inch barrel; weighs 27 oz.; 7-3/8-inch overall length; one-piece Xenoy wrap-around grips with curved backstrap; post front sight with white dot, fixed two-dot rear; alloy frame, blue carbon steel slide; slide mounted decocking lever. Introduced 1995; discontinued 2007.

New: $375 **Perf:** $325 **Exc:** $275

SMITH & WESSON MODEL 915

Semi-automatic; double action; 9mm Para.; 15-shot magazine; 4-inch barrel; 7-1/2-inch overall length; weighs 28-1/2 oz.; one-piece Xenoy wrap-around grips with straight backstrap; post front sight with white dot, fixed rear; alloy frame, blue carbon steel slide; slide-mounted decocking lever. Made in U.S. by Smith & Wesson. Introduced 1992; dropped 1995.

New: $375 **Perf:** $325 **Exc:** $275

SMITH & WESSON MODEL 1006

Semi-automatic; double action; 10mm auto; 9-shot magazine; 5-inch barrel; weighs 38 oz.; one-piece Xenoy wrap-around grips with straight backstrap; rounded trigger guard; choice of Novak LoMount Carry fixed rear sight with two white dots or adjustable micro-click rear with two white dots; stainless steel construction; satin stainless finish. Introduced 1990; dropped 1993.

Perf: $750 **Exc:** $575 **VGood:** $450

SMITH & WESSON MODEL 1026

Semi-automatic; double action; 10mm auto; 9-shot magazine; 5-inch barrel; weighs 38 oz.; frame mounted decocking lever, fixed sights; one-piece Delrin grips; rounded trigger guard. Introduced 1990; dropped 1992.

Exc: $700 **VGood:** $550 **Good:** $420

SMITH & WESSON MODEL 1046

Semi-automatic; double-action-only; 10mm auto; 9-shot magazine; 5-inch barrel; weighs 38 oz.; rounded trigger guard; fixed sights; wrap-around grips with straight backstrap; stainless steel with satin finish. Introduced 1990; dropped 1992.

Exc: $700 **VGood:** $495 **Good:** $375

SMITH & WESSON MODEL 1066

Semi-automatic; double action; 10mm auto; 9-shot magazine; 4-1/4-inch barrel; fixed sights; wrap-around grips with straight backstrap; ambidextrous safety. Introduced 1990; dropped 1992.

Exc: $725 **VGood:** $550 **Good:** $375

SMITH & WESSON MODEL 1066-NS

Same specs as Model 1066 except Tritium night sights.

Exc: $750 **VGood:** $600 **Good:** $400

SMITH & WESSON MODEL 1076

Semi-automatic; double action; 10mm auto; 9-shot magazine; 4-1/4-inch barrel; frame mounted decocking lever; wrap-around grips with straight backstrap; fixed sights. Introduced 1990; dropped 1993.

Exc: $700 **VGood:** $600 **Good:** $395

SMITH & WESSON MODEL 1086

Semi-automatic; double-action-only; 10mm auto; 9-shot magazine; 4-1/4-inch barrel; wrap-around grips with straight backstrap; fixed sights; ambidextrous safety. Introduced 1990; dropped 1993.

Perf: $700 **Exc:** $600 **VGood:** $450

SMITH & WESSON MODEL 3904

Semi-automatic; double action; 9mm Para.; 8-shot magazine; 4-inch barrel; 7-1/2-inch overall length; weighs 28 oz.; one-piece wrap-around Delrin stocks; post front sight with white dot, fixed or fully-adjustable two-dot rear; blued finish; smooth trigger; serrated hammer. Introduced 1989; dropped 1991.

Exc: $400 **VGood:** $350 **Good:** $300

SMITH & WESSON MODEL 3906

Semi-automatic; double action; 9mm Para.; 8-shot magazine; 4-inch barrel; 7-5/8-inch overall length; weighs 28 oz.; stainless steel construction; one-piece wrap-around Delrin stocks; post front sight with white dot, fixed or fully-adjustable two-dot rear; blued finish; smooth trigger; serrated hammer. Introduced 1989; dropped 1991.

Exc: $450 **VGood:** $400 **Good:** $350

SMITH & WESSON MODEL 3913

Semi-automatic; double action; 9mm Para.; 8-shot magazine; 3-1/2-inch barrel; 6-13/16-inch overall length; weighs 26 oz.; post white-dot front sight, two-dot windage-adjustable Novak LoMount Carry rear; aluminum alloy frame; stainless steel slide; bobbed hammer; no half-cock notch; smooth trigger; straight backstrap. Introduced 1990; dropped 1999.

New: $500 **Perf:** $450 **Exc:** $350

SMITH & WESSON MODEL 3913 LADYSMITH

Semi-automatic; double action; 9mm Para.; 8-shot magazine; 3-1/2-inch barrel; 6-13/16-inch overall length; weighs 26 oz.; post white-dot front sight, two-dot windage-adjustable Novak LoMount Carry rear; upswept frame at front; rounded trigger guard; frosted stainless steel finish; gray ergonomic grips designed for smaller hands. Introduced 1990; discontinued 2006.

New: $575 **Perf:** $500 **Exc:** $400

SMITH & WESSON MODEL 3913-NL

Same specs as Model 3913 except without LadySmith logo; slightly modified frame design; right-hand safety only; stainless slide in alloy frame. Introduced 1990; dropped 1994.

Perf: $450 **Exc:** $350 **VGood:** $275

Smith & Wesson Model 3954

Smith & Wesson Model 4006

Smith & Wesson Model 4013

Smith & Wesson Model 3914

Smith & Wesson Model 3914 LadySmith

Smith & Wesson Model 4014

Smith & Wesson Model 4046

Smith & Wesson Model 4053

SMITH & WESSON MODEL 3913TSW/3953TSW AUTO PISTOLS

Similar to the Model 3913 and 3953 except TSW guns have tighter tolerances, ambidextrous manual safety/decocking lever, flush-fit magazine, delayed-unlock firing system. DAO Model 3953 has magazine disconnector. Compact alloy frame, stainless steel slide. Straight backstrap. Introduced 1998.

New: $600 **Perf:** $525 **Exc:** $450

SMITH & WESSON MODEL 3914

Semi-automatic; double action; 9mm Para.; 8-shot magazine; 3-1/2-inch barrel; 6-13/16-inch overall length; weighs 26 oz.; post white-dot front sight, two-dot windage-adjustable Novak LoMount Carry rear; aluminum alloy frame; blued steel slide; bobbed hammer; no half-cock notch; smooth trigger straight backstrap. Introduced 1990; dropped 1995.

New: $400 **Perf:** $325 **Exc:** $250

SMITH & WESSON MODEL 3914 LADYSMITH

Semi-automatic; double action; 9mm Para.; 8-shot magazine; 3-1/2-inch barrel; 6-13/16-inch overall length; weighs 26 oz.; post white-dot front sight, two-dot windage-adjustable Novak LoMount Carry rear; same specs as standard 3913, except slide is of blued steel. Introduced 1990; dropped 1992.

Perf: $450 **Exc:** $375 **VGood:** $275

SMITH & WESSON MODEL 3914-NL

Same specs as 3914 except without LadySmith logo; slightly modified frame design; right-hand safety only; blued finish, black grips. Introduced 1990; dropped 1991.

Perf: $400 **Exc:** $300 **VGood:** $250

SMITH & WESSON MODEL 3953

Semi-automatic; double-action-only; 9mm Para.; 8-shot magazine; 3-1/2-inch barrel; 7-inch overall length; weighs 25-1/2 oz.; post white-dot front sight, two-dot windage-adjustable Novak LoMount Carry rear; aluminum alloy frame; stainless steel slide; bobbed hammer; no half-cock notch; smooth trigger straight backstrap. Introduced 1990; dropped 1999.

New: $500 **Perf:** $450 **Exc:** $350

SMITH & WESSON MODEL 3954

Semi-automatic; double-action-only; 9mm Para.; 8-shot magazine; 3-1/2-inch barrel; 7-inch overall length; weighs 25-1/2 oz.; post white-dot front sight, two-dot windage-adjustable Novak LoMount Carry rear; aluminum alloy frame; blued steel slide; alloy frame; bobbed hammer; no half-cock notch; smooth trigger straight backstrap. Introduced 1990; dropped 1992.

Perf: $400 **Exc:** $350 **VGood:** $275

SMITH & WESSON MODEL 4006

Semi-automatic; 40 S&W; 11-shot magazine; 4-inch barrel; 7-1/2-inch overall length; weighs 38 oz.; replaceable white-dot post front sight, Novak two-dot fixed rear or two-dot micro-click adjustable rear; Xenoy wrap-around grips, checkered panels; straight backstrap; made of stainless steel; non-reflective finish. Introduced 1991; discontinued 1999.

New: $650 **Perf:** $600 **Exc:** $500

Tritium night sights

New: $725 **Perf:** $675 **Exc:** $575

SMITH & WESSON MODEL 4043

Similar to the Model 4006 except is double-action-only. Has a semi-bobbed hammer, smooth trigger, 4-inch barrel; Novak LoMount Carry rear sight, post front with white dot. Overall length is 7-1/2-inch, weighs 28 oz. Alloy frame. Extra magazine included. Introduced 1991; dropped 1999.

New: $700 **Perf:** $600 **Exc:** $500

SMITH & WESSON MODEL 4013

Semi-automatic; double action; 40 S&W; 7-shot magazine; 3-1/2-inch barrel; 7-inch overall length; weighs 26 oz.; white-dot post front sight, two-dot Novak LoMount Carry rear; one-piece Xenoy wrap-around grip; straight backstrap; alloy frame; stainless steel slide. Introduced 1991; dropped 1996.

New: $550 **Perf:** $475 **Exc:** $425

SMITH & WESSON MODEL 4053 TSW

Semi-automatic; double action; 40 S&W, 9-shot magazine. Barrel: 3-1/2-inch. Weight: 26.4 oz. Length: 6-7/8-inch overall. Stocks: Checkered black polymer. Sights: Novak three-dot system. Features: double-action only system; stainless slide, alloy frame; fixed barrel bushing; ambidextrous decocker; reversible magazine catch. Introduced 1997.

New: $725 **Perf:** $625 **Exc:** $550

SMITH & WESSON MODEL 4014

Semi-automatic; double action; 40 S&W; 7-shot magazine; 3-1/2-inch barrel; 7-inch overall length; weighs 26 oz.; blued steel slide; white-dot post front sight, two-dot Novak LoMount Carry rear; one-piece Xenoy wrap-around grip; straight backstrap; alloy frame; stainless steel slide. Introduced 1991; dropped 1993

Perf: $500 **Exc:** $450 **VGood:** $350

SMITH & WESSON MODEL 4046

Semi-automatic; double-action-only; 40 S&W; 11-shot; 4-inch barrel; 7-1/2-inch overall length; weighs 38 oz.; smooth trigger; semi-bobbed hammer; post white-dot front sight, Novak LoMount Carry rear. Introduced 1991; dropped 1999.

Perf: $550 **Exc:** $475 **VGood:** $350

SMITH & WESSON MODEL 4053

Semi-automatic; double-action-only; 40 S&W; 7-shot magazine; 3-1/2-inch barrel; 7-inch overall length; weighs 26 oz.; white-dot post front sight, two-dot Novak LoMount Carry rear; one-piece Xenoy wrap-around grip; straight backstrap; alloy frame; stainless steel slide. Introduced 1991; dropped 1997.

New: $600 **Perf:** $550 **Exc:** $450

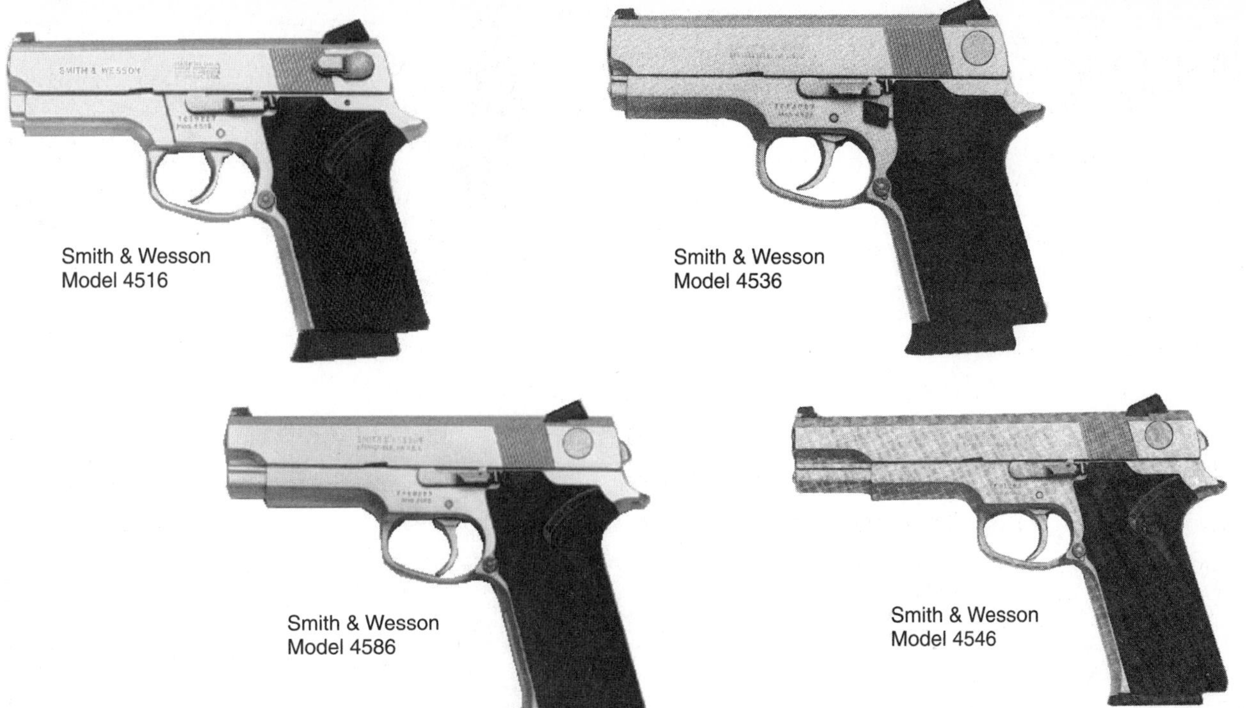
Smith & Wesson Model 4516

Smith & Wesson Model 4536

Smith & Wesson Model 4586

Smith & Wesson Model 4546

SMITH & WESSON MODEL 4054

Semi-automatic; double-action-only; 40 S&W; 7-shot magazine; 3-1/2-inch barrel; 7-inch overall length; weighs 26 oz.; blued steel slide; white-dot post front sight, two-dot Novak LoMount Carry rear; one-piece Xenoy wrap-around grip; straight backstrap; alloy frame; stainless steel slide. Introduced 1991; dropped 1992.

Perf: $475 **Exc:** $400 **VGood:** $300

SMITH & WESSON MODEL 4505

Semi-automatic; 45 ACP; 8-shot magazine; 5-inch barrel; one-piece wrap-around Delrin stock; arched or straight backstrap; post front sight with white dot, fixed or adjustable rear; blued finish. Introduced 1990; dropped 1991.

Perf: $500 **Exc:** $400 **VGood:** $295

SMITH & WESSON MODEL 4506

Semi-automatic; 45 ACP; 8-shot magazine; 5-inch barrel; one-piece, wrap-around Xenoy stocks; arched or straight backstrap; post front sight with white dot, fixed or adjustable Novak LoMount Carry rear; serrated hammer spur; stainless steel construction. Introduced 1989; dropped 1999.

Perf: $500 **Exc:** $400 **VGood:** $295

SMITH & WESSON MODEL 4513TSW/4553TSW

Semi-automatic; double action; 45 ACP, 6-shot magazine. Barrel: 3-3/4-inch. Weight: 28 oz. (M4513TSW). Length: 6-7/8 overall. Stocks: Checkered Xenoy; straight backstrap. Sights: White dot front, Novak Lo Mount Carry 2-Dot rear. Features: Model 4513TSW is traditional double action, Model 4553TSW is double action only. TSW series has tighter tolerances, ambidextrous manual safety/decocking lever, flush-fit magazine, delayed-unlock firing system. DAO has magazine disconnector. Compact alloy frame, stainless steel slide. Introduced 1998.

Model 4513TSW

Perf: $500 **Exc:** $400 **VGood:** $295

Model 4553TSW

Perf: $500 **Exc:** $400 **VGood:** $295

SMITH & WESSON MODEL 4516

Semi-automatic; 45 ACP; 7-shot magazine; 3-3/4-inch barrel; one-piece wrap-around Xenoy stock; straight backstrap; post front sight with white dot; fixed Novak rear sight; bobbed hammer. Introduced 1989; dropped 1997.

Perf: $500 **Exc:** $400 **VGood:** $295

SMITH & WESSON MODEL 4526

Semi-automatic; 45 ACP; 8-shot magazine; 5-inch barrel; decocking lever; one-piece wrap-around Delrin stock; arched or straight backstrap; post front sight with white dot, fixed or adjustable rear; serrated hammer spur; stainless steel construction. Introduced 1991; dropped 1993.

Perf: $500 **Exc:** $400 **VGood:** $295

SMITH & WESSON MODEL 4536

Semi-automatic; 45 ACP; 8-shot magazine; 3-3/4-inch barrel; decocking lever; one-piece wrap-around Delrin stock; arched or straight backstrap; post front sight with white dot, fixed or adjustable rear; serrated hammer spur; stainless steel construction. Introduced 1990; dropped 1991.

Perf: $500 **Exc:** $400 **VGood:** $295

SMITH & WESSON MODEL 4546

Semi-automatic; double-action-only; 45 ACP; 8-shot magazine; 5-inch barrel; decocking lever; stainless steel construction; one-piece wrap-around Delrin stock; arched or straight backstrap; post front sight with white dot, fixed or adjustable rear; serrated hammer spur; stainless steel construction. Introduced 1990; dropped 1991.

Perf: $500 **Exc:** $400 **VGood:** $295

SMITH & WESSON MODEL 4556

Semi-automatic; double-action-only; 45 ACP; 8-shot magazine; 3-3/4-inch barrel; decocking lever; stainless steel construction; one-piece wrap-around Delrin stock; arched or straight backstrap; post front sight with white dot, fixed or adjustable rear; serrated hammer spur; stainless steel construction. Introduced 1990; dropped 1991.

Perf: $500 **Exc:** $400 **VGood:** $295

SMITH & WESSON MODEL 4566

Semi-automatic; double-action-only; 45 ACP; 8-shot magazine; 4-1/4-inch barrel; ambidextrous safety; decocking lever; stainless steel construction; one-piece wrap-around Delrin stocks; arched or straight backstrap; fixed sights; serrated hammer spur; stainless steel construction. Introduced 1990; dropped 1999.

Perf: $500 **Exc:** $400 **VGood:** $295

SMITH & WESSON MODEL 4567-NS

Semi-automatic; 45 ACP; 4-1/4-inch barrel; stainless steel slide; blued steel frame; bobbed hammer; one-piece wrap-around grip; straight, blued backstrap; rounded edges; Novak sights with tritium inserts. Introduced 1991; dropped 1991.

Perf: $550 **Exc:** $450 **VGood:** $350

SMITH & WESSON MODEL 4576

Semi-automatic; double action; 45 ACP; 8-shot magazine; 4-1/4-inch barrel; ambidextrous safety; decocking lever; stainless steel construction; one-piece wrap-around Delrin stocks; arched or straight backstrap; fixed sights; serrated hammer spur made of stainless steel. Introduced 1990; no longer produced.

Perf: $500 **Exc:** $400 **VGood:** $295

SMITH & WESSON MODEL 4586

Semi-automatic; double-action-only; 45 ACP; 8-shot magazine; 4-1/4-inch barrel; ambidextrous safety;

Smith & Wesson Model 5906

Smith & Wesson Model 5926

Smith & Wesson Model 5946

Smith & Wesson Model 5903

Smith & Wesson Model 6906

Smith & Wesson Model 5904

decocking lever; stainless steel construction; one-piece wrap-around Xenoy stock; arched or straight backstrap; fixed sights; serrated hammer spur. Introduced 1990; dropped 1999.

Perf: $500 **Exc:** $400 **VGood:** $295

SMITH & WESSON MODEL 5903

Semi-automatic; double action; 9mm Para.; 14-, 10-shot magazine; 4-inch barrel; 7-1/2-inch overall length; weighs 28-37 oz.; stainless steel alloy frame; ambidextrous safety; one-piece wrap-around Xenoy stocks; fixed sights; blued finish; smooth trigger; serrated hammer. Introduced 1989; dropped 1997.

New: $550 **Perf:** $500 **Exc:** $425

SMITH & WESSON MODEL 5904

Semi-automatic; double action; 9mm Para.; 14-, 10-shot magazine; 4-inch barrel; 7-1/2-inch overall length; weighs 28 to 37 oz.; one-piece wrap-around Xenoy stocks; fixed or adjustable sights; blued finish; smooth trigger; serrated hammer. Introduced 1989; dropped 1998.

New: $550 **Perf:** $500 **Exc:** $400

SMITH & WESSON MODEL 5905

Semi-automatic; double action; 9mm Para.; 14-shot magazine; 4-inch barrel; 7-5/8-inch overall length; weighs 30 oz.; blued frame, slide; ambidextrous safety; one-piece wrap-around Delrin stocks; adjustable sights; blued finish; smooth trigger; serrated hammer. Introduced 1989; dropped 1992.

Perf: $650 **Exc:** $600 **VGood:** $550

SMITH & WESSON MODEL 5906

Semi-automatic; double action; 9mm Para.; 14-, 10-shot magazine; 4-inch barrel; 7-1/2-inch overall length; weighs 28-38 oz.; stainless steel construction; ambidextrous safety; one-piece wrap-around Xenoy stock; fixed or adjustable sights; blued finish; smooth trigger; serrated hammer. Introduced 1989; dropped 1999.

New: $600 **Perf:** $525 **Exc:** $425

SMITH & WESSON MODEL 5924

Semi-automatic; double action; 9mm Para.; 14-shot magazine; 4-inch barrel; 7-1/2-inch overall length; weighs 30 oz.; blue frame; frame mounted decocking lever; ambidextrous safety; one-piece wrap-around Delrin stocks; fixed sights; blued finish; smooth trigger; serrated hammer. Introduced 1989; dropped 1992.

Perf: $450 **Exc:** $350 **VGood:** $300

SMITH & WESSON MODEL 5926

Semi-automatic; double action; 9mm Para.; 14-shot magazine; 4-inch barrel; 7-1/2-inch overall length; weighs 30 oz.; stainless steel construction; frame mounted decocking lever; ambidextrous safety; one-piece wrap-around Delrin stocks; fixed sights; blued finish; smooth trigger; serrated hammer. Introduced 1989; dropped 1992.

Perf: $550 **Exc:** $450 **VGood:** $375

SMITH & WESSON MODEL 5943

Semi-automatic; double-action-only; 9mm Para.; 14-shot magazine; 4-inch barrel; 7-1/2-inch overall length; weighs 30 oz.; stainless alloy frame; frame mounted decocking lever; ambidextrous safety; one-piece wrap-around Delrin stocks; fixed sights; blued finish; smooth trigger; serrated hammer. Introduced 1989; dropped 1992.

Perf: $500 **Exc:** $450 **VGood:** $350

SMITH & WESSON MODEL 5943-SSV

Same specs as 5943 except 3-1/2-inch barrel; bobbed hammer; short slide; double-action-only; alloy frame; blued slide, slide stop, magazine release, trigger, hammer; black post front sight, Novak fixed rear tritium inserts; black curved backstrap grips. Introduced 1990; dropped 1992.

Perf: $525 **Exc:** $475 **VGood:** $350

SMITH & WESSON MODEL 5944

Semi-automatic; double-action-only; 9mm Para.; 14-shot magazine; 4-inch barrel; 7-1/2-inch overall length; weighs 30 oz.; blue alloy frame; frame mounted decocking lever; ambidextrous safety; one-piece wrap-around Delrin stocks; fixed sights; blued finish; smooth trigger; serrated hammer. Introduced 1989; dropped 1992.

Perf: $450 **Exc:** $400 **VGood:** $325

SMITH & WESSON MODEL 5946

Semi-automatic; double-action-only; 9mm Para.; 14-shot magazine; 4-inch barrel; 7-5/8-inch overall length; weighs 30 oz.; stainless steel construction; frame mounted decocking lever; ambidextrous safety; one-piece wrap-around Delrin stocks; fixed sights; blued finish; smooth trigger; serrated hammer. Introduced 1989; dropped 1999.

New: $500 **Perf:** $450 **Exc:** $450

SMITH & WESSON MODEL 6904

Semi-automatic; double action; 9mm Para.; 12-, 10-shot magazine; 3-1/2-inch barrel; weighs 26-1/2 oz.; fixed rear sight; .260-inch bobbed hammer; blue finish. Introduced 1989; dropped 1997.

New: $500 **Perf:** $450 **Exc:** $375

SMITH & WESSON MODEL 6906

Semi-automatic; double action; 9mm Para.; 12-, 10-shot magazine; 3-1/2-inch barrel; weighs 26-1/2 oz.; stainless steel construction; fixed rear sight; .260-inch bobbed hammer. Introduced 1989; dropped 1999.

New: $500 **Perf:** $400 **Exc:** $350

With night sights

New: $600 **Perf:** $500 **Exc:** $450

SMITH & WESSON MODEL 6926

Semi-automatic; double action; 9mm Para.; 12-shot magazine; 3-1/2-inch barrel; weighs 26-1/2 oz.; aluminum alloy frame; stainless slide; decocking lever; fixed sights; bobbed hammer. Introduced 1990; dropped 1992.

Perf: $400 **Exc:** $350 **VGood:** $300

SMITH & WESSON MODEL 6944

Semi-automatic; double-action-only; 9mm Para.; 12-shot magazine; 3-1/2-inch barrel; weighs 26-1/2 oz.;

Smith & Wesson
Model 6904

Smith & Wesson
Sigma SW40F

Smith & Wesson 22
Auto Match (Model 41)

Smith & Wesson
Model 422

Smith & Wesson
Model 6946

aluminum alloy frame; blued steel slide; decocking lever; fixed sights; bobbed hammer. Introduced 1990; dropped 1992.

Perf: $450 **Exc:** $400 **VGood:** $300

SMITH & WESSON MODEL 6946

Semi-automatic; double-action-only; 9mm Para.; 12-, 10-shot magazine; 3-1/2-inch barrel; weighs 26-1/2 oz.; aluminum alloy frame; stainless steel slide; decocking lever; fixed sights or night sights; .260-inch bobbed hammer. Introduced 1990; dropped 1999.

New: $400 **Perf:** $300 **Exc:** $295

With night sights

New: $550 **Perf:** $500 **Exc:** $400

SMITH & WESSON SIGMA SW9F

Semi-automatic; double action; 9mm Para.; 10-shot magazine; 4-1/2-inch barrel; 7-1/2-inch overall length; weighs 26 oz.; integral polymer grips; post front sight with white dot, fixed rear with two dots; tritium night sights optional; ergonomic polymer frame; internal striker firing system; corrosion-resistant slide; Teflon-filled, electroless-nickel coated magazine. Introduced 1994; dropped 1996.

New: $400 **Perf:** $350 **Exc:** $300

With fixed tritium night sights

New: $425 **Perf:** $375 **Exc:** $425

SMITH & WESSON SIGMA SW9C

Same specs as the SW9F except 4-inch barrel; weighs 24-1/2 oz. Introduced 1995; dropped 1998.

New: $400 **Perf:** $350 **Exc:** $300

With fixed tritium night sights

New: $425 **Perf:** $375 **Exc:** $425

SMITH & WESSON SIGMA SW40F

Semi-automatic; double action; 40 S&W; 10-shot magazine; 4-1/2-inch barrel; weighs 26 oz.; 7-1/2-inch overall length; integral polymer grips; post front sight with white dot, fixed rear with two dots; tritium night sights optional; ergonomic polymer frame; internal striker firing system; corrosion-resistant slide; Teflon-filled, electroless-nickel coated magazine. Made in U.S. by Smith & Wesson. Introduced 1994; dropped 1998.

New: $400 **Perf:** $350 **Exc:** $300

With fixed tritium night sights

New: $425 **Perf:** $375 **Exc:** $425

SMITH & WESSON SIGMA SW40C

Same specs as the SW40F except 4-inch barrel; weighs 24-1/2 oz. Introduced 1995; dropped 1998.

New: $400 **Perf:** $350 **Exc:** $300

With fixed tritium night sights

New: $425 **Perf:** $375 **Exc:** $425

SMITH & WESSON SIGMA SW380

Semi-automatic; double-action-only; 380 ACP; 6-shot magazine; 3-inch barrel; 5-13/16-inch overall length; weighs 14 oz.; integral polymer grips; fixed groove in the slide sights; polymer frame; grooved/serrated front and rear grip straps; two passive safeties. Introduced 1995; dropped 1996.

New: $350 **Perf:** $300 **Exc:** $275

SMITH & WESSON 22 AUTO TARGET (MODEL 41)

Semi-automatic; 22 LR; 10-shot clip magazine; 5-inch, 7-3/8-inch barrel; 12-inch overall length (7 3/8-inch barrel); weighs 43-1/2 oz.; 3/8-inch wide trigger, grooved, with adjustable stop; detachable muzzle brake supplied with 7-3/8-inch barrel only (muzzle brake recently dropped); 1/8-inch undercut Patridge-type front sight, fully-adjustable S&W micrometer-click rear; checkered walnut grips with modified thumbrest for right- or left-handed shooters; S&W bright blue finish. The Model 41 was at one time also available in 22 Short for international competition. Introduced about 1957; still in production.

New: $900 **Perf:** $775 **Exc:** $650

SMITH & WESSON 22 AUTO MATCH (MODEL 41)

Same specs as Model 41 except 5-1/2-inch heavy barrel; 9-inch overall length; weighs 44-1/2 oz.; checkered walnut stocks; modified thumbrest; 1/8-inch Patridge front sight on ramp base, S&W micro-click adjustable rear; grooved trigger; adjustable trigger stop; bright blued finish; matted top area. Extension front sight added 1965. Introduced 1963; dropped 1989.

Exc: $700 **VGood:** $600 **Good:** $500

SMITH & WESSON MODEL 41 FIFTIETH ANNIVERSARY EDITION

Similar to original Model 41 but machine-engraved with Class A+ coverage, gold plated borders, and glass-topped presentation case. Introduced 2008. Serial Number Range: FYA0001 - FYA0500.

New: $1350 **Perf:** $1100 **Exc:** $650

SMITH & WESSON 22 AUTO TARGET (MODEL 46)

Semi-automatic; 22 LR; 10-shot; 5-inch, 5-1/2-inch, 7-inch heavy barrel; same as the Model 41 except with or without extendable front sight; less elaborate; molded nylon stocks. Approximately 4000 manufactured.

Exc: $675 **VGood:** $550 **Good:** $450

SMITH & WESSON ESCORT MODEL 61

Semi-automatic; 22 LR; 5-shot magazine; 2-1/4-inch barrel; 4-13/16-inch overall length; hammerless; thumb safety on left side of grip; fixed sights; cocking indicator; checkered plastic grips; blued or nickel finish. Introduced in 1970; dropped 1973. Collector value.

Exc: $225 **VGood:** $175 **Good:** $135

Nickel finish

Exc: $250 **VGood:** $200 **Good:** $150

SMITH & WESSON MODEL 422

Semi-automatic; 22 LR; 10-shot magazine; 4-1/2-inch, 6-inch barrel; 7-1/2-inch overall length (4-1/2-inch barrel); weighs 22 oz.; serrated ramp front, fixed rear field sights; serrated ramp front, adjustable rear target sights; checkered plastic stocks on field model, checkered walnut on target version; aluminum frame, steel slide; brushed blued finish; internal hammer. Introduced 1987.

Adjustable sights

Perf: $250 **Exc:** $200 **VGood:** $175

Fixed sights

New: $225 **Perf:** $175 **Exc:** $150

SMITH & WESSON MODEL 622

Semi-automatic; 22 LR; 10-shot magazine; 4-1/2-inch, 6-inch barrel; 7-1/2-inch overall length (4-1/2-inch barrel); weighs 22 oz.; serrated ramp front, fixed rear field sight or serrated ramp front, adjustable rear target sights; checkered plastic stocks on field model, checkered walnut on target version; stainless steel construction; satin finish; internal hammer. Introduced 1990; dropped 1996.

Adjustable sights

Perf: $250 **Exc:** $225 **VGood:** $175

Fixed sights

Perf: $225 **Exc:** $175 **VGood:** $150

SMITH & WESSON MODEL 2206

Semi-automatic; single action; 22 LR; 10-shot magazine; 4-1/2-inch, 6-inch barrel; weighs 35 oz. (4-1/2-inch barrel); fixed or adjustable sights; checkered black plastic stocks; stainless steel construction with non-reflective finish; internal hammer. Introduced 1990; dropped 1996.

Adjustable sights

New: $300 **Perf:** $250 **Exc:** $200

Fixed sights

New: $275 **Perf:** $225 **Exc:** $175

SMITH & WESSON MODEL 2206 TARGET

Same specs as Model 2206 except 6-inch barrel; Millett Series adjustable sight system; Patridge front sight; Herett walnut target grips with thumbrest; serrated trigger with adjustable stop; bead blasted sight plane; drilled, tapped for scope mounts. Introduced 1994; dropped 1996.

New: $375 **Perf:** $300 **Exc:** $250

SMITH & WESSON MODEL 2213

Semi-automatic; 22 LR; 8-shot magazine; 3-inch barrel 6-1/8-inch overall length; weighs 18 oz.; dovetailed Patridge front sight with white dot, two-dot fixed rear; black composition grips with checkered panels; stainless steel slide and alloy frame with satin stainless finish. Comes with holster and softside carry case. Introduced 1990; dropped 1999.

Perf: $250 **Exc:** $200 **VGood:** $175

SMITH & WESSON MODEL 2214 SPORTSMAN

Semi-automatic; 22 LR; 8-shot magazine; 3-inch barrel; 6-1/4-inch overall length; weighs 18 oz.; dovetail Patridge front sight with white dot, two-dot fixed rear; black composition grips with checkered panels; matte blue finish. Introduced 1990; dropped 1999.

Adjustable sights

New: $225 **Perf:** $175 **Exc:** $150

SMITH & WESSON MODEL 22A SPORT

Semi-automatic; 22 LR, 10-shot magazine. Barrel: 4-inch, 5-1/2-inch, 7-inch. Weight: 29 oz. Length: 8-inch overall. Stocks: Two-piece polymer. Sights: Patridge front, fully adjustable rear. Features: Comes with a sight bridge with Weaver-style integral optics mount; alloy frame; .312-inch serrated trigger; stainless steel slide and barrel with matte blue finish. Introduced 1997.

New: $250 **Perf:** $200 **Exc:** $175

7-inch barrel

New: $260 **Perf:** $210 **Exc:** $185

SMITH & WESSON MODEL 22S SPORT

Similar to the Model 22A Sport except with stainless steel frame. Available only with 5-1/2-inch or 7-inch barrel. Introduced 1997; discontinued 2007.

New: $250 **Perf:** $225 **Exc:** $175

5-1/2-inch bull barrel, wood target stocks with thumbrest

New: $300 **Perf:** $275 **Exc:** $250

5-1/2-inch bull barrel, two-piece target stocks with thumbrest

New: $275 **Perf:** $250 **Exc:** $200

SMITH & WESSON MODEL 22A TARGET

Semi-automatic; 22 LR, 10-shot magazine. Barrel: 5-1/2 bull. Weight: 38.5 oz. Length: 9-1/2 overall. Stocks: Dymondwood with ambidextrous thumbrests and flared bottom. Sights: Patridge front, fully adjustable rear. Features: Sight bridge with Weaver-style integral optics mount; alloy frame, stainless barrel and slide; matte blue finish. Introduced 1997.

New: $275 **Perf:** $250 **Exc:** $200

SMITH & WESSON MODEL 22S TARGET PISTOL

Similar to the Model 22A except has stainless steel frame. Introduced 1997.

New: $300 **Perf:** $275 **Exc:** $225

SMITH & WESSON GOVERNOR

Caliber: 410 shotshell, 45 ACP, 45 Colt. Six-round cylinder capable of handling 45 Colt, 45 ACP and 410 gauge 2-1/2 inch shotshells, interchangeably. Barrel length is 2.75 inches; weight, 29.6 oz. and overall length, 7.5 inches. Grip: Synthetic or Crimson Trace Lasergrips. Sights: Front: Tritium Night Sight (Dovetailed), Rear: fixed. Matte Black finish.

Perf: $615 **Exc:** $550 **VGood:** $475

Add 30 percent for Crimson Trace Laser Grip

SMITH & WESSON M&P 9

Full-size Military and Police semi-auto chambered in 9mm. Capacity 17+1, 4.25-inch barrel, 6 1/2 lb. trigger, 24.25 oz. Picatinny rail and polymer frame. Optional tritium low-light sights.

New: $675 **Exc:** $615 **VGood:** $525

SMITH & WESSON MODEL M&P9-JG

Similar to above but with interchangeable palmswell grip panels, including two pink ones. Dealer sets pricing. Inroduced 2008.

New: $675 **Exc:** $615 **VGood:** $525

SMITH & WESSON MODEL M&P9 PRO SERIES

Similar to M&P9 but with green fiber optic sights and interchangeable palmswell grip panels. Black Melonite finish. Introduced 2008.

New: $675 **Exc:** $615 **VGood:** $525

SMITH & WESSON MODEL M&P9L

Similar to M&P9 but with 5-inch barrel. Introduced 2008.

New: $675 **Exc:** $615 **VGood:** $525

SMITH & WESSON M&P 40

Full-size semi-auto chambered in .40 S&W; this is the first of the new Military and Police series. Capacity 15+1, 4.25-inch barrel, .5 lb. trigger, 24.25 oz. Polymer frame and Picatinny rail. Optional tritium low-light sights.

New: $675 **Exc:** $600 **VGood:** $500

Smith & Wesson SW9VE

Smith & Wesson SW40VE

Smith & Wesson SW1911 Rolling Thunder Commemorative

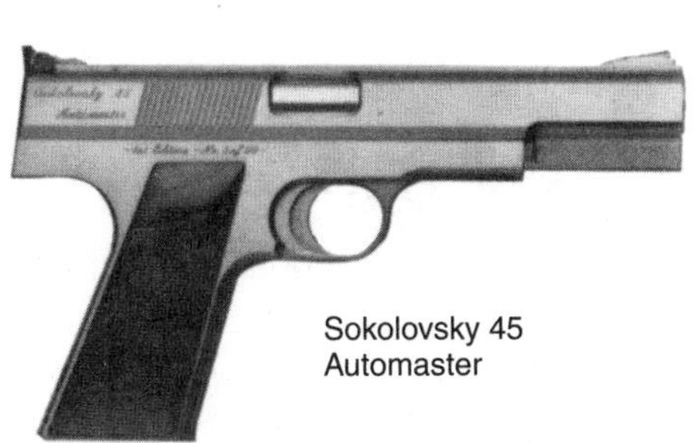
Sokolovsky 45 Automaster

Smith & Wesson Model SW1911 Pro Series

Smith & Wesson SW1911 PD Gunsite Commemorative

SMITH & WESSON M&P .357 SIG

Full-size Military and Police semi-auto chambered in .357 SIG. Capacity 15+1, 4.25-inch barrel, 6.5 lb. trigger, 24.25 oz. Polymer frame and Picatinny rail. Optional tritium low-light sights.

New: $685 **Exc:** $600 **VGood:** $500

SMITH & WESSON M&P45

Semi-auto; similar to M&P40 but in .45 ACP. Black or Dark Earth Brown finish.

New: $685 **Exc:** $600 **VGood:** $500

SMITH & WESSON M&P9C

Semi-auto; compact model; similar to M&P9 but with 3.5" barrel, short grip frameM&P and 10+1 or 12+1 capacity. Black Melonite finish.

New: $685 **Exc:** $625 **VGood:** $500

SMITH & WESSON M&P40C

Semi-auto; compact model; similar to M&P9C but in .40 S&W. Black Melonite finish.

New: $685 **Exc:** $625 **VGood:** $500

SMITH & WESSON M&P357C

Semi-auto; compact model; similar to M&P40c but in .357 SIG. Black Melonite finish.

New: $685 **Exc:** $625 **VGood:** $500

SMITH & WESSON SW9VE ALLIED FORCES

Similar to SW9VE but with black Melonite slide. Adopted by Afghanistan internal security and border forces. Add 75 percent for "Disaster Ready Kit" (case and emergency supplies).

New: $400 **Exc:** $350 **VGood:** $295

SMITH & WESSON SW40VE ALLIED FORCES

Similar to SW9VE Allied Forces but in .40 S&W. Add 75 percent for "Disaster Ready Kit" (case and emergency supplies).

New: $400 **Exc:** $350 **VGood:** $295

SMITH & WESSON MODEL SW1911

1911-style semiauto pistol in .45 ACP. 5" barrel; blued, stainless, or two-tone finish; carbon steel frame and slide with polished flats on slide; standard GI recoil guide; external extractor; laminated double diamond walnut grips with silver S&W medallions, adjustable target sight. Introduced 2003.

New: $900 **Exc:** $795 **VGood:** $650

SMITH & WESSON MODEL SW1911 PD

Part of Tactical Rail Series developed for SWAT Teams and tactical operations. Picatinny rail. Scandium alloy, single-action .45 ACP with 5-inch barrel and 8+1 capacity. Fixed sights. 32 oz.

New: $1100 **Exc:** $950 **VGood:** $695

SMITH & WESSON MODEL SW1911 PD GUNSITE COMMEMORATIVE

Honors Lt. Col. Jeff Cooper's Gunsite Training Academy. Scandium alloy, single-action .45 ACP with 4.25-inch barrel and 8+1 capacity. Fixed sights. 28 oz.

New: $1150 **Exc:** $1000 **VGood:** $725

SMITH & WESSON SW1911 TACTICAL RAIL

One of Tactical Rail Series for SWAT Teams and tactical applications. Picatinny rail and fixed sights. Blued or stainless, single-action .45 ACP with 5-inch barrel and 8+1 capacity. 39 oz.

New: $1000 **Exc:** $895 **VGood:** $700

SMITH & WESSON MODEL SW1911 – ROLLING THUNDER COMMEMORATIVE

Limited edition commemorating American POW-MIAs. Rolling Thunder and POW-MIA logos in imitation bonded ivory grips. Chambered for .45 ACP. Blued, 8+1 capacity, 5-inch barrel, 38.5 oz.

New: $1550 **Exc:** $1200 **VGood:** $875

SMITH & WESSON MODEL SW1911 PRO SERIES

Similar to Model SW1911 but with Novak fiber optic sights, skeletonized trigger and various tactical/performance enhancements. Introduced 2008.

New: $975 **Exc:** $825 **VGood:** $650

SMITH & WESSON SD9

Caliber: 40 S&W or 9mm, available in 10, 14 and 16-round magazine capacities. Barrel: 4 inches. Weight: 39 oz. Length: 8.7 inches. Wood or rubber grips. Tritium Night Sight, rear, fixed 2-dot, front. Picatinny rail, slim ergonomic textured grip.

Perf: 420 **Exc:** $350 **VGood:** $300

SOKOLOVSKY 45 AUTOMASTER

Semi-automatic; single action; 45 ACP; 6-shot; 6-inch barrel; 9-1/2-inch overall length; weighs 55 oz.; ramp front sight, Millett adjustable rear; smooth walnut stocks; semi-custom built with precise tolerances for target shooting; special safety trigger; primarily stainless steel. Introduced 1985; dropped 1990.

Exc: $2500 **VGood:** $2000 **Good:** $1750

SPECIALIZED WEAPONS SPECTRE FIVE

Revolver; double action; 45 Colt/410 2-inch, 3-inch shotshell; 5-shot; 2-inch barrel; 9-inch overall length; weighs 48 oz.; fixed sights; Pachmayr checkered rubber grips; ambidextrous hammer-block safety; draw bar safety; squared triggerguard; steel construction; matte blue finish. Introduced 1991; discontinued 1992. Limited production; lack of information precludes pricing.

SPHINX AT-380

Semi-automatic; double-action-only; 380 ACP; 10-shot magazine; 3-1/4-inch barrel; 6-inch overall length; weighs 25 oz.; checkered plastic grips; fixed sights; chamber loaded indicator; ambidextrous magazine release and slide latch; blued slide, bright Palladium frame, or bright Palladium finish overall. Imported from Switzerland by Sphinx U.S.A., Inc. Introduced 1993; discontinued 1996.

New: $450 **Perf:** $350 **Exc:** $300

SPHINX AT-2000S

Semi-automatic; double action; 9mm Para., 9x21mm, 40 S&W; 10-shot magazine; 4-1/2-inch barrel; 8-inch overall length; weighs 36 oz.; checkered neoprene grips; blade front sight, fixed rear; three-dot system; double-action mechanism changeable to double-action-only; stainless frame, blued slide; ambidextrous safety, magazine release, slide latch. Imported from Switzerland by Sphinx U.S.A., Inc. Introduced 1993; discontinued 2002.

9mm, two-tone finish

New: $900 **Perf:** $850 **Exc:** $750

Sphinx 3000

Sportarms Model HS21S

Sphinx AT-2000PS

Sportarms Tokarev Model 213

Sportarms Model HS38S

Springfield Armory Model 1911-A1

Springfield Amory Model 1911-A1 Basic Competition

9mm, Palladium finish		
New: $1000	**Perf:** $900	**Exc:** $800
40 S&W, two-tone finish		
New: $1000	**Perf:** $900	**Exc:** $800
40 S&W, Palladium finish		
New: $1100	**Perf:** $1000	**Exc:** $900

SPHINX AT-2000C COMPETITOR

Same specs as AT-2000S except 5-5/16-inch barrel; 9-7/8-inch overall length; weighs 40-1/2 oz.; fully-adjustable Bo-Mar open sights or Tasco Pro-Point dot sight in Sphinx mount; extended magazine release; competition slide with dual-port compensated barrel; two-tone finish only. Imported from Switzerland by Sphinx U.S.A., Inc. Introduced 1993.

With Bo-Mar sights		
New: $1750	**Perf:** $1200	**Exc:** $850
With Tasco Pro-Point and mount		
New: $1900	**Perf:** $1450	**Exc:** $1250

SPHINX AT-2000GM GRAND MASTER

Same specs as the AT-2000S except single-action-only trigger mechanism; squared triggerguard; extended beavertail grip, safety and magazine release; notched competition slide for easier cocking; two-tone finish; dual-port compensated barrel; fully-adjustable Bo-Mar open sights or Tasco Pro-Point and Sphinx mount. Imported from Switzerland by Sphinx U.S.A., Inc. Introduced 1993.

With Bo-Mar sights		
New: $2500	**Perf:** $1750	**Exc:** $1250
With Tasco Pro-Point and mount		
New: $2650	**Perf:** $1850	**Exc:** $1350

SPHINX AT-2000H

Same specs as the AT-2000S except shorter slide with 3-1/2-inch barrel; shorter frame; 7-inch overall length; weighs 32 oz. Imported from Switzerland by Sphinx U.S.A., Inc. Introduced 1993.

9mm, two-tone finish		
New: $800	**Perf:** $750	**Exc:** $650
9mm, Palladium finish		
New: $850	**Perf:** $800	**Exc:** $700
40 S&W, two-tone finish		
New: $850	**Perf:** $800	**Exc:** $700
40 S&W, Palladium finish		
New: $900	**Perf:** $850	**Exc:** $750

SPHINX AT-2000P

Same specs as AT-2000S except 13-shot magazine; 3-3/4-inch barrel; 7-1/4-inch overall length; weighs 34 oz.; double-action mechanism changeable to double-action-only; stainless steel frame, blued slide, or bright Paladium overall finish; ambidextrous safety magazine release and slide latch. Imported from Switzerland by Sphinx U.S.A., Inc. Introduced 1993.

9mm, two-tone finish		
New: $800	**Perf:** $750	**Exc:** $650
9mm, Paladium finish		
New: $850	**Perf:** $800	**Exc:** $700
40 S&W, two-tone finish		
New: $850	**Perf:** $800	**Exc:** $700
40 S&W, Paladium finish		
New: $900	**Perf:** $850	**Exc:** $750

SPHINX AT-2000PS

Same specs as the AT-2000S except 3-3/4-inch barrel; 7-1/4-inch overall length; full-size frame; weighs 34 oz. Imported from Switzerland by Sphinx U.S.A., Inc. Introduced 1993.

9mm, two-tone finish		
New: $800	**Perf:** $750	**Exc:** $650
9mm, Palladium finish		
New: $850	**Perf:** $800	**Exc:** $700
40 S&W, two-tone finish		
New: $850	**Perf:** $800	**Exc:** $700
40 S&W, Palladium finish		
New: $900	**Perf:** $850	**Exc:** $750

SPHINX 3000

16+1 autoloader chambered in 9mm or .45 ACP. Stainless steel frame and slide, manual safety, single/double/decocking action, weight 40.56 oz. Also available in compact version.

New: $1800	**Perf:** $1350	**Exc:** $850

SPORTARMS MODEL HS21S

Revolver; single action; 22 LR, 22 LR/22 WMR combo; 6-shot cylinder; 5-1/2-inch barrel; 11-inch overall length; weighs 33-1/2 oz.; smooth hardwood or imitation stag grips; blade front sight, windage-adjustable rear; blue finish. Made in Germany by Herbert Schmidt; imported by Sportarms of Florida. Dropped 1994.

22 LR, blue, stag grips		
Perf: $125	**Exc:** $110	**VGood:** $100
22 LR/22 WMR combo, blue, wood grips		
Perf: $150	**Exc:** $135	**VGood:** $125

SPORTARMS MODEL HS38S

Revolver; double action; 38 Spl.; 6-shot cylinder; 3-inch, 4-inch barrel; 8-inch overall length (3-inch barrel); weighs 31 oz.; checkered hardwood grips, round butt on 3-inch model, target-style on 4-inch; blade front sight, adjustable rear; polished blue finish; ventilated rib on 4-inch barrel. Made in Germany by Herbert Schmidt; imported by Sportarms of Florida. Dropped 1994.

Perf: $135	**Exc:** $100	**VGood:** $85

SPORTARMS TOKAREV MODEL 213

Semi-automatic; single action; 9mm Para.; 8-shot magazine; 4-1/2-inch barrel; 7-1/2-inch overall length; weighs 31 oz.; grooved plastic grips; fixed sights; blue finish, hard chrome optional; 9mm version of the famous Russian Tokarev pistol. Made in China by Norinco. Imported by Sportarms of Florida. Introduced 1988; dropped 1994.

Perf: $275	**Exc:** $225	**VGood:** $175

SPRINGFIELD ARMORY M6

Single shot; 22 rimfire/45 Colt; 16-inch barrel; weighs 3 lbs.; rubberized wrap-around grips; blade front sight, adjustable rear; pistol version of the M6 rifle; matte blue/black finish. From Springfield Armory; now Springfield, Inc. Introduced 1991; dropped 1992.

Perf: $450	**Exc:** $400	**VGood:** $350

SPRINGFIELD ARMORY MODEL 1911-A1

Semi-automatic; 38 Super, 9mm Para., 10mm Auto, 45 ACP; 10-shot (38 Super, 9mm), 9-shot (10mm), 8-shot (45 ACP); 4-inch, 5-inch barrel; 8-1/2-inch overall length (5-inch barrel); weighs 35-1/2 oz.; blade front, windage drift-adjustable rear; walnut grips; reproduction of original Colt model; all new forged parts; phosphated finish. Introduced 1985; replaced by '90s Edition, 1990.

Perf: $500	**Exc:** $425	**VGood:** $350
Blued finish		
Perf: $525	**Exc:** $450	**VGood:** $375
Duotone finish		
Perf: $500	**Exc:** $425	**VGood:** $350

Springfield Armory Model 1911-A1 Bullseye Wadcutter

Springfield Armory Model 1911-A1 Champion

Springfield Armory Model 1911-A1 Combat Commander

Springfield Amory Model 1911-A1 Compact

Springfield Armory Model 1911-A1 Compact V10 Ultra

Springfield Amory Model 1911-A1 Custom Carry

SPRINGFIELD ARMORY MODEL 1911-A1 BASIC COMPETITION

Same specs as the standard 1911-A1 except low-mounted Bo-Mar adjustable rear sight, undercut blade front; match throated barrel and bushing; polished feed ramp; lowered and flared ejection port; fitted Videcki speed trigger with tuned 3-1/2-lb. pull; fitted slide to frame; recoil buffer system; Pachmayr mainspring housing; Pachmayr grips; comes with two magazines with slam pads, plastic carrying case. From Springfield, Inc. Introduced 1992; still produced.

New: $1200 **Perf:** $1000 **Exc:** $850

SPRINGFIELD ARMORY MODEL 1911-A1 BULLSEYE WADCUTTER

Same specs as Model 1911-A1 except 45 ACP; 7-shot magazine; weighs 45 oz.; checkered walnut grips; Bo-Mar rib with undercut blade front sight, fully-adjustable rear; built for wadcutter loads only; full-length recoil spring guide rod; fitted Videcki speed trigger with 3-1/2-lb. pull; match Commander hammer and sear; beavertail grip safety; lowered and flared ejection port; tuned extractor; fitted slide to frame; recoil buffer system; beveled and polished magazine well; checkered frontstrap and steel mainspring housing (flat housing standard); polished and throated National Match barrel and bushing. From Springfield, Inc. Introduced 1992.

Perf: $1250 **Exc:** $1000 **VGood:** $850

SPRINGFIELD ARMORY MODEL 1911-A1 WADCUTTER ENTRY LEVEL

Same specs as the 1911-A1 Bullseye Wadcutter except low-mounted Bo-Mar adjustable rear sight, undercut blade front; match throated barrel and bushing; polished feed ramp; lowered and flared ejection port; fitted Videcki speed trigger with tuned 3-1/2-lb. pull; fitted slide to frame; Shok Buff; Pachmayr mainspring housing; Pachmayr grips; comes with two magazines with slam pads, plastic carrying case, test target. From Springfield, Inc. Introduced 1992; dropped 1993.

Perf: $800 **Exc:** $700 **VGood:** $600

SPRINGFIELD ARMORY MODEL 1911-A1 CHAMPION

Same specs as the standard 1911-A1 except 4-1/4-inch slide; low-profile three-dot sight system; skeletonized hammer; walnut stocks; available in 45 ACP only; blue or stainless. From Springfield, Inc. Introduced 1992; discontinued 2002.

Blue finish
New: $550 **Perf:** $475 **Exc:** $375

Stainless steel
New: $575 **Perf:** $500 **Exc:** $400

Blue, with compensator
New: $700 **Perf:** $600 **Exc:** $500

SPRINGFIELD ARMORY MODEL 1911A1 DEFENDER PISTOL

Similar to the 1911A1 Champion except has tapered cone dual-port compensator system, rubberized grips. Has reverse recoil plug, full-length recoil spring guide, serrated frontstrap, extended thumb safety, skeletonized hammer with modified grip safety to match and a Videki speed trigger. Bi-Tone finish. Introduced 1991; discontinued 1998.

New: $600 **Perf:** $500 **Exc:** $400

SPRINGFIELD ARMORY MODEL 1911-A1 COMMANDER

Same general specs as Model 1911-A1 except 45 ACP only; 3-5/8-inch barrel; shortened slide; Commander hammer; three-dot sight system; walnut stocks; phosphated finish. Introduced 1989; discontinued 1990.

Perf: $550 **Exc:** $475 **VGood:** $400

Blued finish
Perf: $550 **Exc:** $475 **VGood:** $400

Duotone finish
Perf: $550 **Exc:** $475 **VGood:** $400

SPRINGFIELD ARMORY MODEL 1911-A1 COMBAT COMMANDER

Same general as Model 1911-A1 except 45 ACP only; 4-1/2-inch barrel; bobbed hammer; walnut grips. Introduced 1988; discontinued 1989.

Perf: $475 **Exc:** $400 **VGood:** $350

Blued finish
Perf: $475 **Exc:** $400 **VGood:** $350

SPRINGFIELD ARMORY MODEL 1911-A1 COMPACT

Same general specs as Model 1911-A1 except 45 ACP only; 6-shot; 4-1/2-inch barrel, 7-1/4-inch overall length; three-dot sight system; checkered walnut stocks. Introduced 1989; discontinued 1990.

Perf: $450 **Exc:** $400 **VGood:** $350

Blued finish
Perf: $450 **Exc:** $400 **VGood:** $350

Duotone finish
Perf: $450 **Exc:** $400 **VGood:** $350

SPRINGFIELD ARMORY MODEL 1911-A1 COMPACT V10 ULTRA

Same specs as the 1911-A1 Compact except recoil reducing compensator built into the barrel and slide; beavertail grip safety; beveled magazine well; "hi-viz" combat sights; Videcki speed trigger; flared ejection port; stainless steel frame, blued slide; match-grade barrel; walnut grips. From Springfield, Inc. Introduced 1995; still produced.

New: $500 **Perf:** $450 **Exc:** $375

Without compensator
New: $450 **Perf:** $375 **Exc:** $300

SPRINGFIELD ARMORY MODEL 1911-A1 COMPETITION

Same specs as Model 1911-A1 except low-mounted Bo-Mar adjustable rear, brazed serrated improved ramp front sight; extended ambidextrous thumb safety; match Commander hammer and sear; serrated rear slide; Pachmayr flat mainspring housing; extended magazine release; beavertail grip safety; full-length recoil spring guide; Pachmayr wrap-around grips; 45 ACP; blue finish; comes with two magazines with slam pads, plastic carrying case. From Springfield, Inc. Introduced 1992; still produced.

New: $1250 **Perf:** $1000 **Exc:** $850

SPRINGFIELD ARMORY MODEL 1911-A1 CUSTOM CARRY

Same specs as the standard 1911-A1 except fixed, three-dot low profile sights; Videcki speed trigger; match barrel and bushing; extended thumb and beavertail grip safeties; beveled, polished magazine well; polished feed ramp; throated barrel; match Commander hammer and sear; tuned extractor; lowered and flared ejection port; recoil buffer system; full-length spring guide rod; walnut grips; comes with two magazines with slam pads, plastic carrying case. Available in all popular calibers. From Springfield, Inc. Introduced 1992.

New: $800 **Perf:** $650 **Exc:** $500

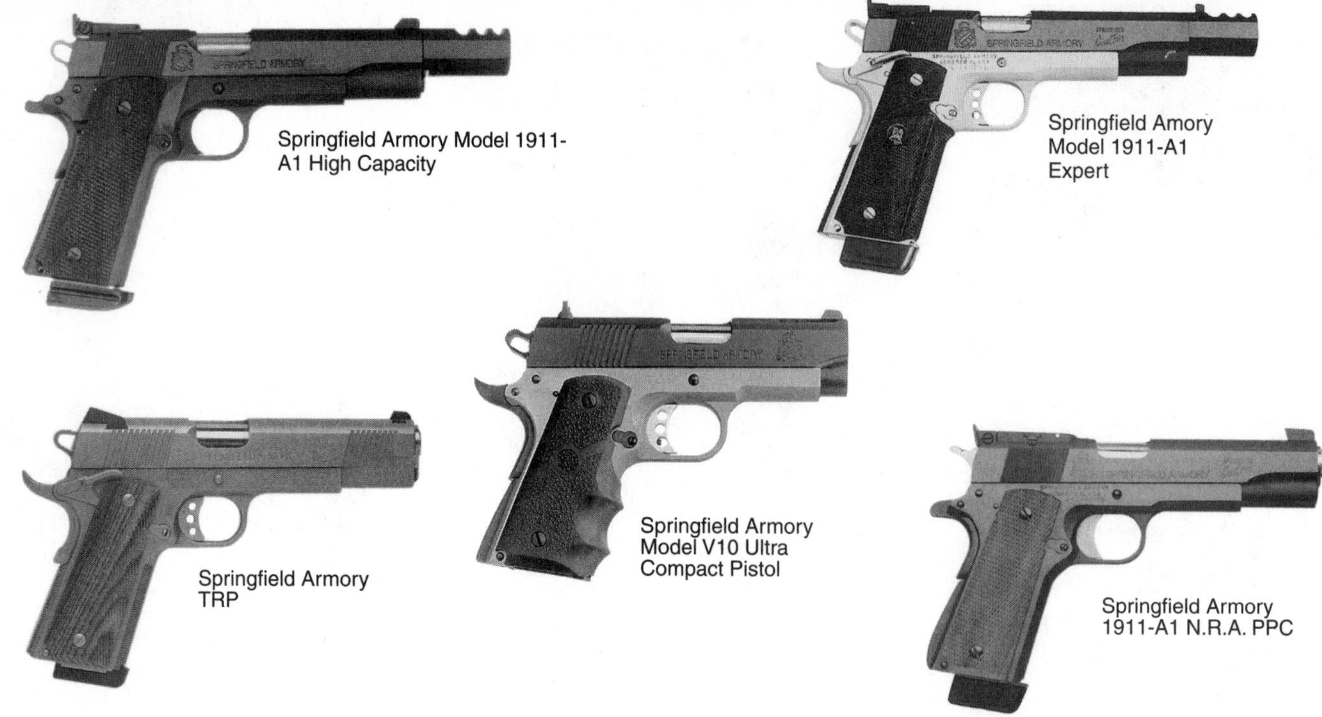

Springfield Armory Model 1911-A1 High Capacity

Springfield Amory Model 1911-A1 Expert

Springfield Armory Model V10 Ultra Compact Pistol

Springfield Armory TRP

Springfield Armory 1911-A1 N.R.A. PPC

SPRINGFIELD ARMORY MODEL 1911-A1 CUSTOM COMPACT

Same specs as Model 1911-A1 except 45 ACP; 4-inch barrel with compensator; Videcki speed trigger; match barrel and bushing; extended thumb and beavertail grip safeties; beveled, polished magazine well; polished feed ramp; throated barrel; match Commander hammer and sear; tuned extractor; lowered and flared ejection port; recoil buffer system; full-length spring guide rod; shortened slide; fixed three-dot sights; walnut grips; blued finish. Introduced 1991; no longer in production.

Perf: $1400 **Exc:** $1100 **VGood:** $850

SPRINGFIELD ARMORY MODEL 1911-A1 DISTINGUISHED

Same specs as the 1911-A1 except full-house pistol with match barrel with compensator; Bo-Mar low-mounted adjustable rear sight; full-length recoil spring guide rod and recoil spring retainer; beveled and polished magazine well; walnut grips; hard chrome finish; 45 ACP; comes with two magazines with slam pads, plastic carrying case. From Springfield, Inc. Introduced 1992.

New: $2200 **Perf:** $1850 **Exc:** $1500

SPRINGFIELD ARMORY MODEL 1911-A1 EXPERT PISTOL

Same specs as Model 1911-A1 except triple-chamber tapered cone compensator on match barrel with dovetailed front sight; lowered and flared ejection port; fully tuned for reliability; bobbed hammer; match trigger; Duotone finish; comes with two magazines, plastic carrying case. From Springfield, Inc. Introduced 1992.

New: $1600 **Perf:** $1250 **Exc:** $1000

SPRINGFIELD ARMORY MODEL 1911-A1 FACTORY COMP

Same specs as the standard 1911-A1 except bushing-type dual-port compensator; adjustable rear sight; extended thumb safety; Videcki speed trigger; beveled magazine well; checkered walnut grips standard. Available in 38 Super or 45 ACP, blue only. From Springfield, Inc. Introduced 1992.

New: $750 **Perf:** $650 **Exc:** $500

SPRINGFIELD ARMORY MODEL 1911-A1 HIGH CAPACITY

Same specs as the Model 1911-A1 except 45 ACP, 9mm; 10-shot magazine; Commander-style hammer; walnut grips; ambidextrous thumb safety; beveled magazine well; plastic carrying case. From Springfield, Inc. Introduced 1993; still produced.

45 ACP		
New: $600	**Perf:** $500	**Exc:** $350
9mm Para.		
New: $500	**Perf:** $450	**Exc:** $375
45 ACP Factory Comp		
New: $700	**Perf:** $600	**Exc:** $500
45 ACP Comp Lightweight, matte finish		
New: $700	**Perf:** $600	**Exc:** $500
45 ACP Compact, blued		
New: $550	**Perf:** $475	**Exc:** $350
45 ACP Compact, stainless steel		
New: $650	**Perf:** $550	**Exc:** $450

SPRINGFIELD ARMORY MODEL V10 ULTRA COMPACT PISTOL

Similar to the 1911A1 Compact except has shorter slide, 3.5-inch barrel, recoil reducing compensator built into the barrel and slide. Beavertail grip safety, beveled magazine well, "hi-viz" combat sights, Videcki speed trigger, flared ejection port, stainless steel frame, blued slide, match grade barrel, walnut grips. Introduced 1996. From Springfield, Inc.

New: $550 **Perf:** $475 **Exc:** $400

SPRINGFIELD ARMORY TRP PISTOLS

Similar to the 1911A1 except 45 ACP only; has checkered front strap and mainspring housing; Novak combat rear sight and matching dovetailed front sight; tuned, polished extractor; oversize barrel link; lightweight speed trigger and combat action job; match barrel and bushing; extended thumb safety and fitted beavertail grip safety; carry bevel on entire pistol; checkered cocobolo wood grips; comes with two Wilson 8-shot magazines. Frame is engraved "Tactical," both sides of frame "TRP." Introduced 1998.

Standard with Armory Kote finish		
New: $1200	**Perf:** $950	**Exc:** $750
Standard, stainless steel		
New: $1250	**Perf:** $1000	**Exc:** $800
Price: Champion, Armory Kote		
New: $1100	**Perf:** $950	**Exc:** $800

SPRINGFIELD ARMORY MODEL 1911-A1 N.M. HARDBALL

Same specs as Model 1911-A1 except Bo-Mar adjustable rear sight with undercut front blade; fitted match Videcki trigger with 4-lb. pull; fitted slide to frame; throated National Match barrel and bushing; polished feed ramp; recoil buffer system; tuned extractor; Herrett walnut grips; comes with two magazines, plastic carrying case, test target. From Springfield, Inc. Introduced 1992.

New: $1000 **Perf:** $850 **Exc:** $650

SPRINGFIELD ARMORY MODEL 1911-A1 N.R.A. PPC

Specifically designed to comply with NRA rules for PPC competition; custom slide-to-frame fit; polished feed ramp; throated barrel; total internal honing; tuned extractor; recoil buffer system; fully checkered walnut grips; two fitted magazines; factory test target; custom carrying case. From Springfield, Inc. Introduced 1995; still produced.

New: $1350 **Perf:** $1100 **Exc:** $900

SPRINGFIELD ARMORY MODEL 1911-A1 PRODUCT IMPROVED DEFENDER

Same specs as Model 1911-A1 except 4-1/4-inch slide; low-profile three-dot sight system; tapered cone dual-port compensator system; rubberized grips; reverse recoil plug; full-length recoil spring guide; serrated frontstrap; extended thumb safety; skeletonized hammer with modified grip safety to match; Videcki speed trigger; Bi-Tone finish. From Springfield, Inc. Introduced 1991.

New: $800 **Perf:** $700 **Exc:** $600

SPRINGFIELD ARMORY MODEL 1911-A1 TROPHY MASTER COMPETITION PISTOL

Same specs as Model 1911-A1 except combat-type sights; Pachmayr wrap-around grips; ambidextrous safety; match trigger; bobbed hammer. Introduced 1988; discontinued 1990.

Perf: $1450 **Exc:** $1200 **VGood:** $950

Springfield Armory Model 1911-A1 '90s Edition

Springfield Armory 1911-A2 S.A.S.S.

Springfield Armory Bobcat

Springfield Armory Firecat

Springfield Armory Model P9

SPRINGFIELD ARMORY MODEL 1911-A1 TROPHY MASTER COMPETITION EXPERT PISTOL

Same specs as Model 1911-A1 except match barrel with compensator; wrap-around Pachmayer grips; ambidextrous thumb safety; lowered, flared ejection port; blued finish. Introduced 1988; discontinued 1990.

Perf: $1600 **Exc:** $1350 **VGood:** $1000

SPRINGFIELD ARMORY MODEL 1911-A1 TROPHY MATCH

Same specs as Model 1911-A1 except factory accurized; 4- to 5-1/2-lb. trigger pull; click-adjustable rear sight; match-grade barrel and bushing; checkered walnut grips. From Springfield, Inc. Introduced 1994; still produced.

Blue finish

New: $800 **Perf:** $700 **Exc:** $600

Stainless steel

New: $825 **Perf:** $725 **Exc:** $650

High Capacity
(stainless steel, 10-shot magazine, front slide serrations, checkered slide serrations)

New: $950 **Perf:** $800 **Exc:** $700

SPRINGFIELD ARMORY MODEL 1911-A1 '90S EDITION

Semi-automatic; single action; 38 Super, 9mm Para., 10mm Auto, 40 S&W, 45 ACP; 10-shot (38 Super), 9-shot (9mm, 10mm), 8-shot (40 S&W, 45 ACP); 5-inch barrel; 8-1/2-inch overall length; weighs 36 oz.; fixed low-profile combat sights; checkered walnut grips; beveled magazine well; linkless operation; all parts forged; phosphated finish. Introduced 1990; still in production.

Perf: $600 **Exc:** $500 **VGood:** $400

SPRINGFIELD ARMORY MODEL 1911-A1 '90S EDITION CHAMPION COMP

Same specs as Model 1911-A1 '90s Edition except 45 ACP only; 4-inch barrel with compensator; three-dot sights; blued finish. Introduced 1993.

New: $750 **Perf:** $650 **Exc:** $550

SPRINGFIELD ARMORY MODEL 1911-A1 '90S EDITION CHAMPION XM4 HIGH CAPACITY

Same specs as Model 1911-A1 '90s Edition except 9mm, 45 ACP only; high-capacity variant. Introduced 1994; discontinued 1994.

Perf: $575 **Exc:** $500 **VGood:** $425

SPRINGFIELD ARMORY MODEL 1911-A1 '90S EDITION COMBAT COMMANDER

Same specs as Model 1911-A1 '90s Edition except 45 ACP only; 4-1/2-inch barrel; walnut grips; bobbed hammer. Introduced 1991; discontinued 1991.

Perf: $400 **Exc:** $350 **VGood:** $300

SPRINGFIELD ARMORY MODEL 1911-A1 '90S EDITION COMMANDER

Same specs as Model 1911-A1 '90s Edition except 45 ACP only; 3-5/8-inch barrel; shortened slide; three-dot sights; walnut grips; commander hammer. Introduced 1991; discontinued 1992.

Perf: $500 **Exc:** $425 **VGood:** $350

SPRINGFIELD ARMORY MODEL 1911-A1 '90S EDITION COMPACT

Same specs as Model 1911-A1 '90s Edition except 45 ACP only; 7-shot; 4-inch barrel; shortened slide; three-dot sights; combat hammer; standard or lightweight alloy frame; phosphated finish. Introduced 1991.

New: $350 **Perf:** $300 **Exc:** $275

Blued finish

New: $400 **Perf:** $350 **Exc:** $250

Stainless steel finish

New: $475 **Perf:** $425 **Exc:** $375

SPRINGFIELD ARMORY MODEL 1911-A1 '90S EDITION COMPACT COMP

Same specs as Model 1911-A1 '90s Edition except 45 ACP only; 7-shot; 4-inch barrel with compensator; shortened slide; three-dot sights; combat hammer; standard or lightweight alloy frame; duotone finish. Introduced 1993.

Perf: $750 **Exc:** $650 **VGood:** $500

SPRINGFIELD ARMORY MODEL 1911-A1 '90S EDITION STAINLESS

Same specs as Model 1911-A1 '90s Edition except 9mm Para., 45 ACP only; 8-shot; rubber grips; stainless steel construction. Introduced 1991; still in production.

New: $500 **Perf:** $400 **Exc:** $350

SPRINGFIELD ARMORY MODEL 1911-A2 S.A.S.S.

Single shot; break-open action; 22 LR, 223, 7mm BR, 7mm-08, 308, 357 Mag., 358 Win., 44 Mag.; 10-3/4-inch, 14-15/16-inch barrel; 17-1/4-inch overall length (14-15/16-inch barrel); weighs 66 oz.; ramped blade front sight, fully adjustable open rear; drilled, tapped for scope mounts; rubberized wrap-around stock; built on standard 1911-A1 frame. Introduced 1989; discontinued 1992.

Perf: $600 **Exc:** $500 **VGood:** $400

SPRINGFIELD ARMORY BOBCAT

Semi-automatic; 380 ACP; 13-shot magazine; 3-1/2-inch barrel; 6-1/2-inch overall length; weighs 22 oz.; blade front sight, windage-adjustable rear; textured composition stocks; slide-mounted ambidextrous decocker; frame-mounted slide stop; button magazine release; Commander hammer; matte blue finish. Announced 1991; never manufactured.

SPRINGFIELD ARMORY FIRECAT

Semi-automatic; single action; 9mm Para., 40 S&W; 8-shot (9mm), 7-shot (40 S&W) magazine; 3-1/2-inch barrel; 6-1/2-inch overall length; weighs 25-3/4 oz.; checkered walnut grips; low profile blade front sight, fixed rear; three-dot system; all-steel construction; firing pin block safety and frame-mounted thumb safety; frame-mounted slide stop; button magazine release; checkered front and rear straps; checkered and squared triggerguard; Commander hammer; matte blue only. From Springfield, Inc. Introduced 1991; dropped 1993.

Perf: $450 **Exc:** $350 **VGood:** $30

SPRINGFIELD ARMORY LYNX

Semi-automatic; 25 ACP; 7-shot magazine; 2-1/4-inch barrel; 4-3/8-inch overall length; weighs 10-1/2 oz.; blade front sight, windage-adjustable rear with three-dot system; all steel construction; frame-mounted thumb safety/ slide stop; Commander hammer; magazine safety; matte blue finish. Announced 1991; never manufactured.

SPRINGFIELD ARMORY MODEL P9

Semi-automatic; double action; 9mm Para., 9x21mm, 40 S&W, 45 ACP; 15-shot (9mm, 9x21), 11-shot

Springfield Armory Model P9 Factory Comp

Springfield Armory Enhanced Micro Pistol (EMP)

Star Firestar

Springfield Armory XD 45ACP

(40 S&W, 45 ACP); 4-3/4-inch barrel; 8-inch overall length; weighs 35.3 oz.; blade front sight; three-dot windage-adjustable sight system; checkered walnut stocks; based upon CZ-75 design; firing pin safety block; thumb safety on frame; interchangeable magazine catch; Commander hammer; blued finish. Introduced 1990; dropped 1993.

Perf: $450 **Exc:** $375 **VGood:** $300

Phosphated finish

Perf: $475 **Exc:** $400 **VGood:** $300

Stainless steel

Perf: $550 **Exc:** $475 **VGood:** $400

SPRINGFIELD ARMORY MODEL P9 COMPACT

Same specs as Model P9 except 9mm Para., 40 S&W; 13-shot (9mm), 10-shot (40 S&W); 3-7/8-inch barrel; 7-1/4-inch overall length; weighs 32 oz.; compact slide frame; round triggerguard. Introduced 1990; discontinued 1992.

Perf: $500 **Exc:** $425 **VGood:** $375

SPRINGFIELD ARMORY MODEL P9 FACTORY COMP

Same specs as the standard P9 except comes with dual-port compensator system; extended sear safety; extended magazine release; fully-adjustable rear sight; extra-slim competition wood grips; stainless or bi-tone (stainless and blue) finish; overall length is 9-1/2-inch with 5-1/2-inch barrel; weighs 34 oz. From Springfield, Inc. Introduced 1992; dropped 1993.

9mm Para., bi-tone finish or stainless

Perf: $650 **Exc:** $550 **VGood:** $450

40 S&W, bi-tone finish

Perf: $675 **Exc:** $575 **VGood:** $475

40 S&W, stainless, 45 ACP bi-tone finish

Perf: $600 **Exc:** $550 **VGood:** $475

45 ACP, stainless

Perf: $700 **Exc:** $600 **VGood:** $500

SPRINGFIELD ARMORY MODEL P9 SUBCOMPACT

Same specs as Model P9 except 9mm Para., 40 S&W; 12-shot (9mm), 9-shot (40 S&W); 3-1/2-inch barrel; weighs 32 oz.; compact slide frame; squared triggerguard; extended magazine floorplate. Introduced 1990; discontinued 1992.

Perf: $350 **Exc:** $300 **VGood:** $250

SPRINGFIELD ARMORY MODEL P9 ULTRA LSP

Same specs as Model P9 except 5-inch barrel; 8-3/8-inch overall length; weighs 34-1/4 oz.; long slide ported; rubber or walnut stocks; blued, Parkerized or blue/stainless finish. Introduced 1991; discontinued 1993.

Perf: $550 **Exc:** $450 **VGood:** $350

Phosphated finish

Perf: $575 **Exc:** $475 **VGood:** $375

Stainless steel

Perf: $600 **Exc:** $500 **VGood:** $450

Stainless frame/matte black slide

Perf: $600 **Exc:** $525 **VGood:** $450

SPRINGFIELD ARMORY OMEGA

Semi-automatic; single action; 38 Super, 10mm, 40 S&W, 45 ACP; 5-shot (10mm, 40 S&W), 7-shot (45 ACP), 9-shot (38 Super) magazine; 5-inch, 6-inch barrel; weighs 46 oz.; polygonal rifling; rubberized wrap-around grips; removable ramp front sight, fully-adjustable rear. Convertible between calibers; double serrated slide; built on 1911-A1 frame. Made in U.S. by Springfield Armory; now Springfield, Inc. Introduced 1987; discontinued 1990.

Exc: $650 **VGood:** $500 **Good:** $350

SPRINGFIELD ARMORY OMEGA MATCH

Same specs as Omega except adjustable breech face; new extractor system; low profile combat sights; double serrated slide. Introduced 1991; discontinued 1992.

Perf: $750 **Exc:** $650 **VGood:** $500

SPRINGFIELD ARMORY PANTHER

Semi-automatic; double action; 9mm Para., 40 S&W, 45 ACP; 15-shot (9mm Para.), 11-shot (40 S&W), 9-shot (45 ACP); 40 S&W, 11-shot; 45 ACP, 9-shot magazine; 3-3/4-inch barrel; 7-inch overall length; weighs 29 oz.; narrow profile checkered walnut grips; low profile blade front sight, windage-adjustable rear; three-dot system; hammer drop and firing pin safeties; serrated front and rear straps; serrated slide top; Commander hammer; frame-mounted slide stop; button magazine release; matte blue finish. From Springfield Armory; now Springfield, Inc. Introduced 1991; dropped 1992.

Perf: $500 **Exc:** $400 **VGood:** $350

SPRINGFIELD ARMORY XD 45ACP

Polymer semi-auto in black, green or bi-tone holds 13+1 .45 ACP. Imported from Croatia. Fixed sights. Service model: 4-inch barrel, 30 oz. Tactical model: 5-inch barrel, 32 oz. Picatinny rail. Introduced 2006.

New: $600 **Exc:** $495 **VGood:** $395

SPRINGFIELD ARMORY LIGHTWEIGHT OPERATOR

Blued, semi-auto .45 ACP with 5-inch bull barrel. Fixed sights, 5-6-lb. trigger pull, Cocobolo grips, 31 oz. Picatinny rail.

New: $995 **Exc:** $875 **VGood:** $550

SPRINGFIELD ARMORY LIGHTWEIGHT CHAMPION OPERATOR

Similar to above but with 4-inch bull barrel.

New: $995 **Exc:** $875 **VGood:** $550

SPRINGFIELD ARMORY ENHANCED MICRO PISTOL (EMP)

Tiny little 1911-style semi-auto chambered in 9mm Parabellum or .40 S&W. Short-action single-action design, 7-shot capacity, 3" bull barrel, fixed sights, stainless frame that is 1/8" shorter than the company's Compact models.

New: $1050 **Exc:** $950 **VGood:** $675

SPRINGFIELD ARMORY XD(M)

Polymer-framed 16+1 autoloader chambered in .40 S&W. Features include easy-access magazine release, "minimal error disassembly" design, interchangeable backstraps. Introduced 2008.

New: $650 **Exc:** $495 **VGood:** $395

STAR FIRESTAR

Semi-automatic; single action; 9mm Para., 40 S&W; 7-shot (9mm), 6-shot (40 S&W); 3-3/8-inch barrel; 6-1/2-inch overall length; weighs 30 oz.; blade front

Star Megastar

Star Model B

Star Model A

Star Model 30M

Star Model CO Pocket

Star Model 28

sight, fully-adjustable three-dot rear; ambidextrous safety; blued or Starvel finish. Introduced 1990. Dropped 1993.

New: $350 **Perf:** $275 **Exc:** $250

STAR FIRESTAR M45

Same specs as Firestar except 45 ACP; 6-shot magazine; 3-1/2-inch barrel; 6-13/16-inch overall length; weighs 35 oz.; reverse-taper Acculine barrel. Imported from Spain by Interarms. Introduced 1992. Production ended when Star went out of business in 1997.

Blue finish

New: $350 **Perf:** $275 **Exc:** $250

Starvel finish

New: $375 **Perf:** $300 **Exc:** $250

STAR FIRESTAR PLUS

Same specs as Firestar except 10-shot (9mm) magazine; also available in 40 S&W and 45 ACP. Imported from Spain by Interarms. Introduced 1994. Production ended 1997.

Blue finish, 9mm

New: $300 **Perf:** $250 **Exc:** $200

Starvel finish, 9mm

New: $325 **Perf:** $275 **Exc:** $225

Blue finish, 40 S&W

New: $350 **Perf:** $300 **Exc:** $250

Starvel finish, 40 S&W

New: $375 **Perf:** $325 **Exc:** $300

Blue finish, 45 ACP

New: $375 **Perf:** $325 **Exc:** $300

Starvel finish, 45 ACP

New: $400 **Perf:** $350 **Exc:** $375

STAR MEGASTAR

Semi-automatic; double action; 10mm, 45 ACP; 14-shot (10mm), 12-shot (45 ACP) magazine; 4-9/16-inch barrel; 8-1/2-inch overall length; weighs 47-1/2 oz.; checkered composition grips; blade front sight, adjustable rear; steel frame and slide; reverse-taper Acculine barrel. Imported from Spain by Interarms. Introduced 1992. Production ended 1997.

Blue finish, 10mm, 45 ACP

Perf: $475 **Exc:** $400 **VGood:** $350

Starvel finish, 10mm, 45 ACP

Perf: $475 **Exc:** $425 **VGood:** $350

STAR MODEL 28

Semi-automatic; double action; 9mm Para.; 15-shot; 4-1/4-inch barrel; 8-inch overall length; weighs 40 oz.; square blade front sight, square-notch click-adjustable rear; grooved triggerguard face, front and backstraps; checkered black plastic stocks; ambidextrous safety; blued finish. Introduced 1983; discontinued 1984; replaced by Model 30M.

Exc: $400 **VGood:** $350 **Good:** $300

STAR MODEL 30M

Semi-automatic; double action; 9mm Para.; 15-shot; 4-5/16-inch barrel; 8-inch overall length; weighs 40 oz.; square blade front sight, click-adjustable rear; grooved front, backstraps, triggerguard face; checkered black plastic stocks; ambidextrous safety; steel frame; blued finish. Introduced 1985; discontinued 1991.

Perf: $400 **Exc:** $350 **VGood:** $300

STAR MODEL 31P

Semi-automatic; double action; 9mm Para.; 15-shot magazine; 3-7/8-inch barrel; 7-5/8-inch overall length; weighs 30 oz.; checkered black plastic grips; square blade front sight, square notch click-adjustable rear; grooved front- and backstraps and triggerguard face; ambidextrous safety cams firing pin forward; removable backstrap houses the firing mechanism. Imported from Spain by Interarms. Introduced 1984; last imported 1991.

9mm or 40 S&W, blue finish

Perf: $375 **Exc:** $325 **VGood:** $300

9mm or 40 S&W, Starvel finish

Perf: $400 **Exc:** $375 **VGood:** $300

STAR MODEL 31PK

Same specs as the Model 31P except alloy frame with blue finish. Imported from Spain by Interarms. Introduced 1984; last imported 1991.

Perf: $400 **Exc:** $350 **VGood:** $300

STAR MODEL A

Semi-automatic; 7.63 Mauser, 9mm Largo, 38 Super, 45 ACP; 8-shot; 5-inch barrel; 8-1/2-inch overall length; fixed or adjustable sights; checkered walnut grips; modified version of Colt 1911; blued finish. Introduced 1921; no longer produced.

Exc: $550 **VGood:** $400 **Good:** $250

STAR MODEL B

Semi-automatic; 9mm Para.; 9-shot; 4-1/8-inch, 4-3/16-inch, 6-5/16-inch barrel; fixed sights; checkered walnut grips; blued finish. Introduced 1928; no longer produced.

Exc: $400 **VGood:** $300 **Good:** $250

STAR MODEL BKM

Semi-automatic; single action; 9mm Para.; 8-shot; 4-inch barrel; weighs 25 oz.; fixed sights; checkered walnut or plastic grips; lightweight duraluminum frame; blued finish. Introduced 1976; importation discontinued 1991.

Perf: $300 **Exc:** $275 **VGood:** $250

STAR MODEL BKS STARLIGHT

Semi-automatic; 9mm Para.; 8-shot; 4-1/4-inch barrel; fixed sights; checkered plastic grips; magazine, manual safeties; blued, chrome finish. Introduced in 1970; discontinued 1981.

Exc: $300 **VGood:** $275 **Good:** $250

STAR MODEL BM

Semi-automatic; single action; 9mm Para.; 8-shot; 4-inch barrel; 25 oz.; fixed sights; checkered walnut or plastic grips; blued or Starvel finish. Importation discontinued 1991.

Perf: $275 **Exc:** $225 **VGood:** $200

Starvel or Chrome finish

Perf: $300 **Exc:** $275 **VGood:** $225

STAR MODEL CO POCKET

Semi-automatic; 25 ACP; 6-shot; 2-3/4-inch barrel; 4-1/2-inch overall length; fixed sights; checkered plastic grips; blued finish. Introduced 1934; discontinued 1957.

Exc: $300 **VGood:** $225 **Good:** $175

STAR MODEL CU STARLET

Semi-automatic; 25 ACP; 5-shot; 2 3/8-inch barrel; fixed sights; plastic grips; aluminum alloy frame; blue, chrome slide; number of color finish options. Introduced 1957; discontinued 1968.

Exc: $350 **VGood:** $225 **Good:** $190

STAR MODEL DK

Semi-automatic; 380 ACP; 3-1/8-inch barrel; 5-11/16-inch overall length; fixed sights; plastic stocks; aluminum alloy frame; blue, chrome slide; number color finish options. Introduced 1957;

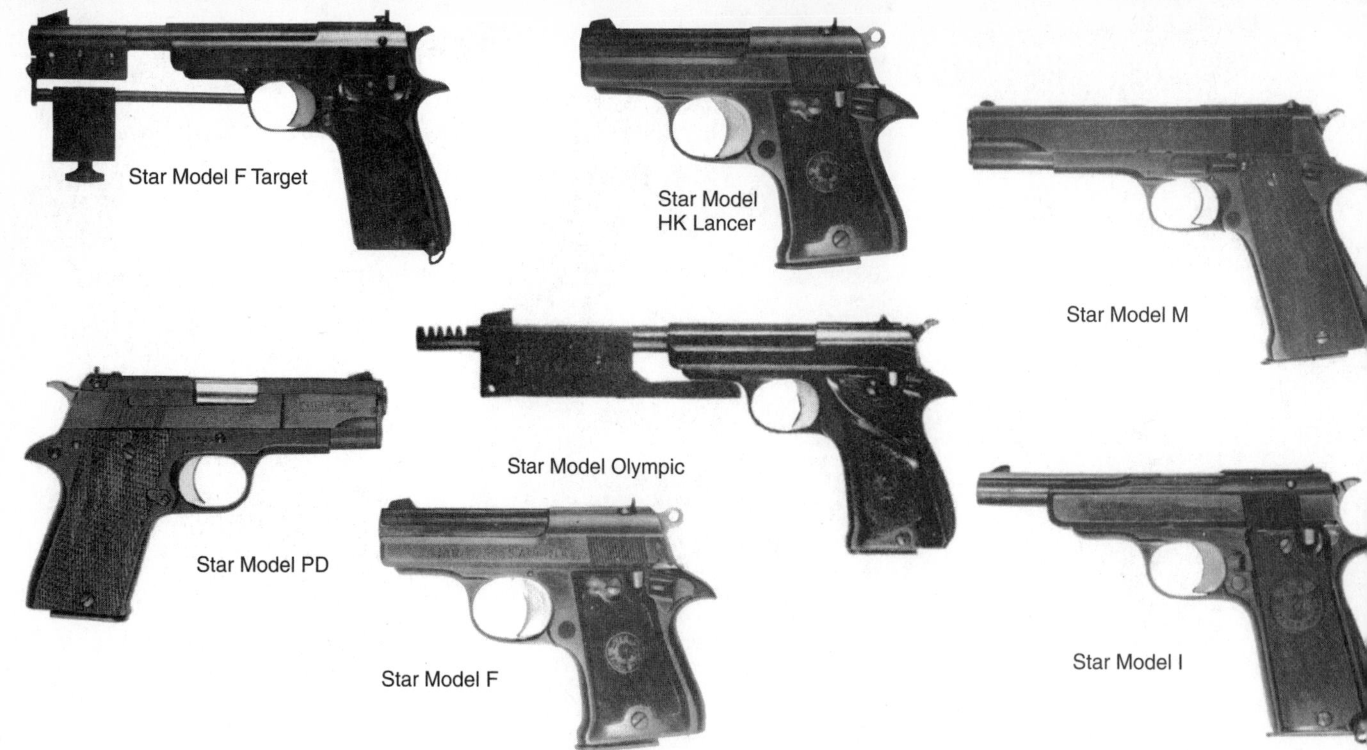
Star Model F Target

Star Model HK Lancer

Star Model M

Star Model Olympic

Star Model PD

Star Model F

Star Model I

discontinued 1968.

Exc: $400 **VGood:** $325 **Good:** $250

STAR MODEL F

Semi-automatic; 22 LR; 10-shot; 4-inch barrel; 7-1/4-inch overall length; fixed sights; checkered thumbrest plastic grips; blued finish. Introduced 1942; discontinued 1969.

Exc: $325 **VGood:** $250 **Good:** $175

STAR MODEL F SPORT

Same specs as Model F except 6-inch barrel; adjustable target-type rear sight. Introduced 1942; dropped 1969.

Exc: $325 **VGood:** $250 **Good:** $185

STAR MODEL F TARGET

Same specs as Model F except adjustable target sights; 7-inch barrel; weights. Introduced 1942; dropped 1969.

Exc: $325 **VGood:** $250 **Good:** $185

STAR MODEL FM

Semi-automatic; 22 LR; 10-shot; 4-1/2-inch barrel; adjustable sights; checkered plastic grips; heavy frame; triggerguard web; blued frame. Introduced 1972; no longer in production.

Perf: $250 **Exc:** $200 **VGood:** $165

STAR MODEL FR

Semi-automatic; 22 LR; 10-shot; 4-inch barrel; adjustable sights; checkered plastic grips; slide stop; blued finish. Introduced 1967; discontinued 1972.

Exc: $225 **VGood:** $200 **Good:** $175

STAR MODEL FRS

Semi-automatic; 22 LR; 10-shot; 6-inch barrel; adjustable sights; checkered plastic grips; blued or chrome finish. Introduced 1967; no longer in production.

Perf: $225 **Exc:** $200 **VGood:** $175

STAR MODEL FS

Semi-automatic; 22 LR; 10-shot; 6-inch barrel; adjustable sights; checkered plastic grips; blued finish. Introduced 1942; discontinued 1967.

Exc: $225 **VGood:** $175 **Good:** $165

STAR MODEL H

Semi-automatic; 32 ACP; 7-shot; 2-3/4-inch barrel; fixed sights; plastic grips; blued finish. Introduced 1934; discontinued 1941.

Exc: $300 **VGood:** $250 **Good:** $200

STAR MODEL HK LANCER

Semi-automatic; 22 LR; 10-shot; 3-1/8-inch barrel; fixed sights; plastic grips; blued finish. Introduced 1955; discontinued 1968.

Exc: $250 **VGood:** $225 **Good:** $200

STAR MODEL HN

Semi-automatic; 380 ACP; 6-shot; 2-3/4-inch barrel; fixed sights; plastic grips; blued finish. Introduced 1934; discontinued 1941.

Exc: $350 **VGood:** $300 **Good:** $250

STAR MODEL I

Semi-automatic; 32 ACP; 9-shot; 4-3/4-inch barrel; 7-1/2-inch overall length; fixed sights; checkered plastic grips: blued finish. Introduced 1934; discontinued 1945.

Exc: $350 **VGood:** $300 **Good:** $250

STAR MODEL IN

Semi-automatic; 380 ACP; 8-shot; 4-3/4-inch barrel; 7-1/2-inch overall length; fixed sights; checkered plastic grips; blued finish. Introduced 1934; discontinued 1945.

Exc: $225 **VGood:** $185 **Good:** $165

STAR MODEL M

Semi-automatic; 9mm Bergman, 9mm Para., 38 Super, 45 ACP; 8-shot (9mm, 38), 7-shot (45 ACP); 5-inch barrel; 8-1/2-inch overall length; fixed sights; checkered walnut grips; blued finish. Not imported into U.S. Introduced 1935.

Exc: $375 **VGood:** $325 **Good:** $250

STAR MODEL OLYMPIC

Semi-automatic; 22 Short; 9-shot; 7-inch barrel; 11-1/16-inch overall length; adjustable rear target sight; checkered plastic grips; alloy slide; muzzle brake; blued finish. Introduced 1942; discontinued 1967.

Exc: $350 **VGood:** $300 **Good:** $200

STAR MODEL P

Semi-automatic; 45 ACP; 7-shot; 5-inch barrel; 8-1/2-inch overall length; fixed sights; checkered walnut grips; blued finish. Introduced 1934; discontinued 1975.

Exc: $450 **VGood:** $350 **Good:** $300

STAR MODEL PD

Semi-automatic; single action; 45 ACP; 6-shot; 4-inch barrel; 7-inch overall length; weighs 25 oz.; adjustable rear sight, ramp front; checkered walnut stocks; blued finish. Introduced 1975; discontinued 1991.

Exc: $450 **VGood:** $350 **Good:** $300

STAR MODEL S

Semi-automatic; 380 ACP; 9-shot; 4-inch barrel; 6-1/2-inch overall length; fixed sights; checkered plastic grips; no grip safety; blued finish. Scaled-down modification of Colt 1911. Introduced 1941; discontinued 1965.

Exc: $275 **VGood:** $225 **Good:** $200

Starvel finish

Exc: $275 **VGood:** $225 **Good:** $200

STAR MODEL SI

Semi-automatic; 32 ACP; 8-shot; 4-inch barrel; 6-1/2-inch overall length; fixed sights; checkered plastic grips; no grip safety; blued finish. Scaled-down modification of Colt 1911. Introduced 1941; discontinued 1965.

Exc: $300 **VGood:** $250 **Good:** $200

STAR MODEL SUPER A

Semi-automatic; 38 Super; 8-shot; 5-inch barrel; luminous sights; checkered plastic grips; magazine safety; disarming bolt; loaded chamber indicator; blued finish. Introduced 1946; discontinued 1989.

Exc: $300 **VGood:** $250 **Good:** $200

STAR MODEL SUPER B

Semi-automatic; 9mm Para.; 8-shot; 5-inch barrel; luminous sights; checkered walnut grips; magazine safety; disarming bolt; loaded chamber indicator; blued finish. Discontinued 1990.

Exc: $200 **VGood:** $175 **Good:** $150

Starvel finish

Exc: $225 **VGood:** $200 **Good:** $175

STAR MODEL SUPER M

Semi-automatic; 9mm Bergman, 9mm Para., 38 Super, 45 ACP; 8-shot (9mm, 38), 7-shot (45); 5-inch barrel; luminous sights; checkered walnut grips; magazine safety; disarming bolt; loaded chamber indicator; blued finish. Introduced 1946; discontinued 1989.

Exc: $375 **VGood:** $275 **Good:** $200

Star Ultrastar

Star Model Super P

Sterling Model 286

Sterling Model 284

Sterling Model 400

Sterling Model 300

Star Super SM

Sterling Model 302

STAR MODEL SUPER P

Semi-automatic; 45 ACP; 7-shot; 5-inch barrel; luminous sights; checkered walnut grips; magazine safety; disarming bolt; loaded chamber indicator; blued finish. Introduced 1946; discontinued 1989.

Exc: $650 **VGood:** $550 **Good:** $450

STAR MODEL SUPER S

Semi-automatic; 380 ACP; 9-shot; 4-inch barrel; 6-1/2-inch overall length; luminous sights; checkered plastic grips; magazine safety; disarming bolt; loaded chamber indicator; blued finish. Introduced 1946; discontinued 1972.

Exc: $350 **VGood:** $300 **Good:** $250

STAR MODEL SUPER SI

Semi-automatic; 32 ACP; 8-shot; 4-inch barrel; 6-1/2-inch overall length; luminous sights; checkered plastic grips; magazine safety; disarming bolt; loaded chamber indicator; blued finish. Introduced 1946; discontinued 1972.

Exc: $300 **VGood:** $250 **Good:** $200

STAR SUPER SM

Semi-automatic; 380 ACP; 9-shot; 4-inch barrel; 6-5/8-inch overall length; adjustable luminous sights; walnut grips; magazine safety; disarming bolt; loaded chamber indicator; blued finish. Introduced 1973; discontinued 1981.

Exc: $350 **VGood:** $275 **Good:** $250

STAR MODEL SUPER TARGET

Semi-automatic; 9mm Para., 38 Super, 45 ACP; 8-shot (9mm, 38), 7-shot (45); 5-inch barrel; adjustable target sights; wood grips; blue finish. Introduced 1942; discontinued 1954.

Exc: $450 **VGood:** $350 **Good:** $275

STAR ULTRASTAR

Semi-automatic; double action; 9mm Para.; 9-shot magazine; 3-1/2-inch barrel; 7-inch overall length; weighs 26 oz.; checkered black polymer grips; blade front sight, windage-adjustable rear; three-dot system; polymer frame with inside steel slide rails; ambidextrous two-position safety (Safe and Decock). Imported from Spain by Interarms. Introduced 1994. Production ended 1997.

New: $300 **Perf:** $250 **Exc:** $200

STERLING MODEL 283

Semi-automatic; 22 LR; 10-shot; 4-1/2-inch, 6-inch, 8-inch barrel; 9-inch overall length (4-1/2-inch barrel); micrometer rear sight, blade front; checkered plastic grips; external hammer; adjustable trigger; all-steel construction; blued finish. Also designated Model 300 Target. Introduced 1970; discontinued 1972.

Exc: $175 **VGood:** $150 **Good:** $135

STERLING MODEL 284

Semi-automatic; 22 LR; 10-shot; 4-1/2-inch, 6-inch tapered barrel; 9-inch overall length (4-1/2-inch barrel); micrometer rear sight, blade front; checkered plastic grips; adjustable trigger; all-steel construction; blued finish. Also designated Model 300L Target. Introduced 1970; discontinued 1972.

Exc: $185 **VGood:** $165 **Good:** $135

STERLING MODEL 285

Semi-automatic; 22 LR; 10-shot; 4-1/2-inch barrel; 9-inch overall length; fixed sights; checkered plastic grips; external hammer; adjustable trigger; all-steel construction; blued finish. Also designated Husky. Introduced 1970; discontinued 1971.

Exc: $165 **VGood:** $135 **Good:** $110

STERLING MODEL 286

Semi-automatic; 22 LR; 10-shot; 4-1/2-inch, 6-inch tapered barrel; 9-inch overall length (4-1/2-inch barrel); fixed rear sight, serrated ramp front; checkered plastic grips; external hammer; target-type trigger; all-steel construction; blued finish. Also designated Trapper. Introduced 1970; discontinued 1972.

Exc: $165 **VGood:** $135 **Good:** $110

STERLING MODEL 295

Semi-automatic; 22 LR; 10-shot; 4-1/2-inch heavy barrel; 9-inch overall length; fixed rear sight, serrated ramp front; checkered plastic grips; external hammer; target-type trigger; all-steel construction; blued finish. Also designated Husky Heavy Barrel. Introduced 1970; discontinued 1972.

Exc: $175 **VGood:** $150 **Good:** $135

STERLING MODEL 300

Semi-automatic; blowback action; 25 ACP; 6-shot; 2-1/2-inch barrel; 4-1/2-inch overall length; no sights; black, white plastic grips; all-steel construction; blued finish. Introduced 1971; discontinued 1984.

Exc: $125 **VGood:** $100 **Good:** $85

Satin nickel finish

Exc: $135 **VGood:** $110 **Good:** $85

Stainless steel

Exc: $135 **VGood:** $110 **Good:** $100

STERLING MODEL 302

Semi-automatic; blowback action; 22 LR; 6-shot; 2-1/2-inch barrel; 4-1/2-inch overall length; no sights; black plastic grips; all-steel construction; blued finish. Introduced 1972; discontinued 1984.

Exc: $125 **VGood:** $110 **Good:** $100

Satin nickel finish

Exc: $135 **VGood:** $115 **Good:** $100

Stainless steel

Exc: $135 **VGood:** $115 **Good:** $100

STERLING MODEL 400

Semi-automatic; double action; 380 ACP; 3-1/2-inch barrel; 6-1/2-inch overall length; micrometer rear sight, fixed ramp front; checkered rosewood grips; thumb-roll safety; all-steel construction; blued finish. Introduced 1973; discontinued 1984.

Exc: $225 **VGood:** $200 **Good:** $175

Satin nickel finish

Exc: $175 **VGood:** $150 **Good:** $125

Stainless steel

Exc: $175 **VGood:** $165 **Good:** $135

STERLING MODEL 402

Semi-automatic; double action; 22 LR; 3-1/2-inch barrel; 6-1/2-inch overall length; micrometer rear sight, fixed ramp front; checkered rosewood grips; thumb-roll safety; all-steel construction; blued finish. Introduced 1973; discontinued 1974.

Exc: $125 **VGood:** $115 **Good:** $100

Satin nickel finish

Exc: $135 **VGood:** $125 **Good:** $115

Stainless steel

Exc: $150 **VGood:** $135 **Good:** $125

STERLING X-CALIBER

Single shot; 22 LR, 22 WMR, 357 Mag., 44 Mag.; interchangeable 8-inch, 10-inch barrel; 13-inch overall length (8-inch barrel); Patridge front sight, fully-adjustable rear; drilled/tapped for scope mounts; Goncalo Alves stocks; notched hammer for easy cocking; finger-grooved grips. Introduced 1980; discontinued 1984.

Exc: 325 **VGood:** $250 **Good:** $215

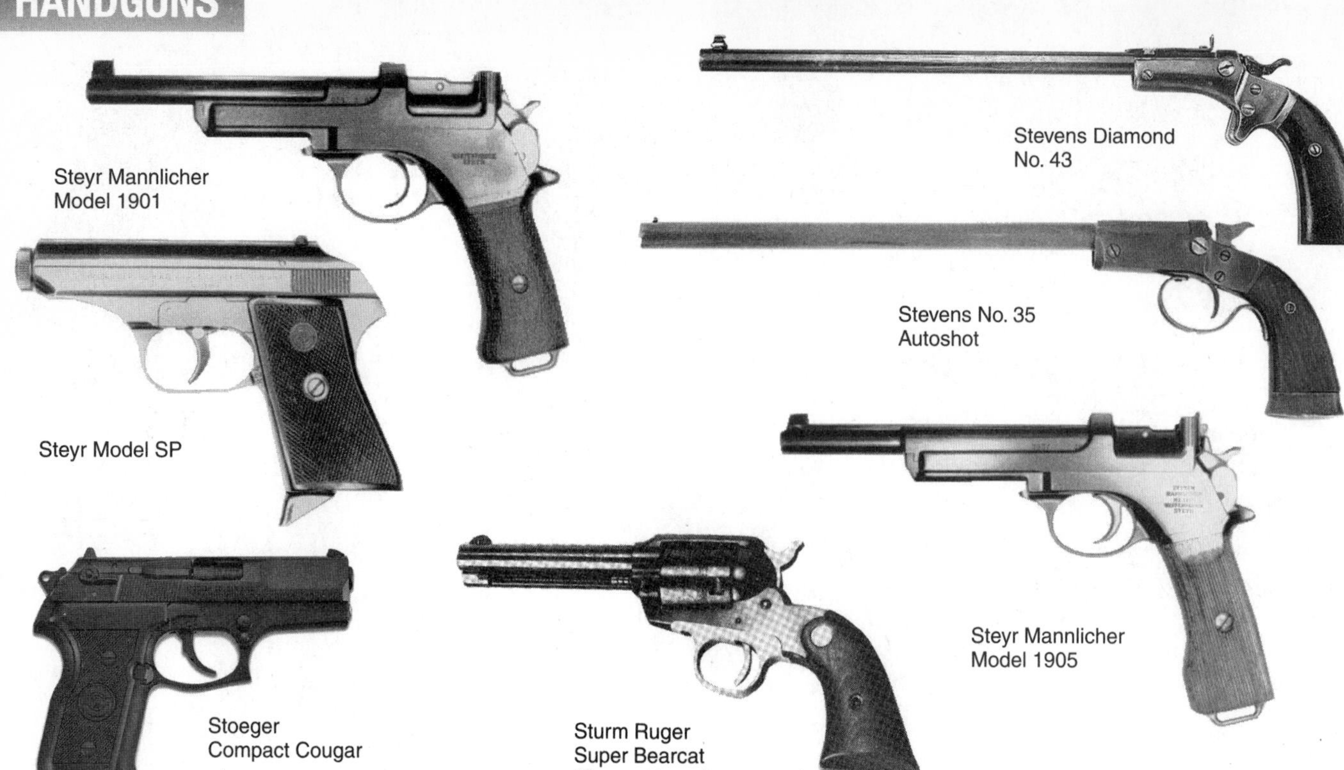

Steyr Mannlicher Model 1901

Stevens Diamond No. 43

Stevens No. 35 Autoshot

Steyr Model SP

Steyr Mannlicher Model 1905

Stoeger Compact Cougar

Sturm Ruger Super Bearcat (Second issue)

STEVENS CONLIN NO. 38

Single shot; 22 Short, 22 LR, 22 WMR, 25 Stevens, 32 Long, 32 Short Colt; finger-rest grip; tip-down barrel; conventional trigger and guard with spur; peep rear, globe front sight. Manufactured from 1884 to 1903.

Exc: $750 **VGood:** $600 **Good:** $450

STEVENS DIAMOND NO. 43

Single shot; 22 Short, 22 LR; 6-inch, 10-inch barrel; weighs 10 oz. (6-inch barrel), 12 oz. (10-inch barrel); round barrel; octagon breech; plain walnut grips; open or peep rear, globe front sights; spur trigger; nickel-plated finish. Manufactured from 1886 to early 1900s.

Exc: $250 **VGood:** $175 **Good:** $125

STEVENS GOULD NO. 37

Single shot; 22 Short, 22 LR, 22 WMR, 25 Stevens, 32 Long, 32 Short Colt; tip-down barrel; conventional trigger and guard without spur; peep rear, globe front sight. Manufactured from 1889 to 1903.

Exc: $800 **VGood:** $600 **Good:** $400

STEVENS LORD NO. 36

Single shot; 22 Short, 22 LR, 22 WMR, 25 Stevens, 32 Short Colt, 38 Long Colt, 44 Russian Centerfire; 10-inch heavy tip-down barrel; weighs 2-3/4 lbs. (10-inch barrel); octagon breech; triggerguard with spur; sporting rear and bead front sights; checkered walnut grips; nickel-plated finish. Manufactured from 1880 to 1911.

Exc: $850 **VGood:** $700 **Good:** $500

STEVENS NO. 10

Single shot; tip-up action; 22 LR; 8-inch barrel; 11-1/2-inch overall length; target sights; hard rubber stocks; blued finish. Manufactured 1919 to 1933.

Exc: $300 **VGood:** $225 **Good:** $175

STEVENS NO. 35 OFF-HAND TARGET

Single shot; tip-up action; 22 LR; 6-inch, 8-inch, 10-inch barrel; weighs 27-1/2 oz.; external hammer; triggerguard without spur; target sights; walnut grips; nickel-plated, case-hardened or blued finish. Introduced 1907; discontinued 1939.

Exc: $300 **VGood:** $250 **Good:** $150

STEVENS NO. 35 AUTOSHOT

Single shot; tip-up action; 410 shotshell; 8-inch, 12-1/4-inch barrel; walnut grips; blued finish. Manufactured from 1929 to 1934. Illegal unless registered with BATF.

Exc: $300 **VGood:** $250 **Good:** $150

STEVENS TIP-UP NO. 41

Single shot; 22 Short, 30 Short; 3-1/2-inch barrel; weighs 7 oz.; round barrel; octagon breech; open sights; plain walnut grips; nickel-plated finish. Early manufacture with brass frame; later with iron. Manufactured from 1886 to 1916.

Exc: $225 **VGood:** $175 **Good:** $125

STEYR C-A1

Double action only, striker fired, semi-auto compact pistol with a polymer frame and triangular or three dot fixed sights. Chambered in 9x19mm. 3.6 inch barrel and 6.7 inch OA length, weighs 1.6 pounds. 17+1 capacity. Introduced in 2012.

Perf: $600 **Exc:** $525 **VGood:** $480

STEYR GB

Semi-automatic; double action; 9mm Para.; 18-shot; 5-1/4-inch barrel; 8-3/8-inch overall length; weighs 53 oz.; post front sight, fixed rear; checkered European walnut stocks; matte finish. Imported from Germany by Gun South, Inc. Introduced 1981; discontinued 1988.

Exc: $550 **VGood:** $450 **Good:** $300

STEYR M-A1

Double action only, striker fired, semi-auto full-sized pistol with a polymer frame and triangular fixed sights. Chambered in 9mm and .40S&W. 4 inch barrel and 7.2 inch OA length, weighs 1.7 pounds. 15+1 capacity (9mm) and 12+1 capacity (.40S&W). Introduced in 2012.

Perf: $600 **Exc:** $525 **VGood:** $480

STEYR MODEL SP

Semi-automatic; double action; 32 ACP; 7-shot; adjustable rear sight, fixed front; checkered black plastic grips; revolver-type trigger; blued finish. Very few made; collector value. Introduced 1957; discontinued 1959.

Exc: $900 **VGood:** $750 **Good:** $500

STEYR SSP

Semi-automatic; single action; 9mm Para.; 15- or 30-shot magazine; 5-15/16-inch barrel; 12-3/4-inch overall length; weighs 42 oz.; grooved synthetic grips; post elevation-adjustable front sight, open windage-adjustable rear; delayed blowback, rotating barrel operating system; synthetic upper and lower receivers; drop and cross-bolt safeties; rail mount for optics. Imported from Austria by GSI, Inc. Introduced 1993; dropped 1994.

Perf: $700 **Exc:** $600 **VGood:** $500

STEYR MANNLICHER MODEL 1901

Semi-automatic; 7.63mm Mannlicher; 5-1/2 inch barrel; 8-3/4-inch overall length; 8-shot; fine checkered wood or hard rubber (rare) grips; marked WAFFENFABRIK STEYR and SYSTEM MANNLICHER on sides.

Exc: $2400 **VGood:** $1850 **Good:** $1100

STEYR MANNLICHER MODEL 1905

Semi-automatic; 7.63mm Mannlicher; 6-inch barrel; 9-1/2-inch overall length; 10-shot; grooved wood grips; Marked WAFFENFABRIK STEYR and SYSTEM MANNLICHER on sides. Also marked "Md. 1905" on side.

Exc: $1750 **VGood:** $1100 **Good:** $700

STEYR 1907 (ROTH STEYR)

Semi-automatic; 8mm Roth Steyr; 5-1/8-inch barrel; 8-13/16-inch overall length; grooved wood grips. Slight premium for Budapest manufacture.

Exc: $1000 **VGood:** $800 **Good:** $450

STEYR 1911 (STEYR HAHN)

Semi-automatic; 9mm Steyr; 5-1/8-inch barrel; 8-5/8-inch overall length; checkered wood grips.

Exc: $600 **VGood:** $500 **Good:** $400

STI EAGLE 5.1 PISTOL

Semi-automatic. 9mm Para., 38 Super, 40 S&W, 45 ACP, 10-ACP, 10-shot magazine. Barrel:5, bull. Weight: 34 oz. Length: 8.62 overall. Stocks: Checkered polymer. Sights: Bo-Mar blade front, Bo-Mar fully adjustable rear. Features: Modular frame design; adjustable match trigger; skeletonized

Steyr 1907 (Roth Steyr)

STI Eagle 5.1

STI GP6

STI Sentinel Premier

Sturm Ruger 22/45 Lite

STI Trubor

Steyr 1911 (Steyr Hahn)

hammer; extended grip safety with locator pad; match-grade fit of all parts. Many options available. Introduced 1994.

New: $1400 **Perf:** $1200 **Exc:** $1000

STI TRUSIGHT

Chambered for 9mm, .40 S&W, .45 ACP double-stack. Steel frame, GFN grips and 4.15-inch slide/barrel. Dawson fiber optic front sight, adjustable rear sight. LOA 8.6-inch and 36.1 oz. Blue with multiple options. IPSC, USPSA approved.

New: $1875 **Exc:** $1750 **VGood:** $1350

STI DUTY CT

1911 steel frame single-stack with integral tactical rail and rosewood grips. 5-inch slide/barrel, fixed 2-dot tritium rear sight. LOA 7.75-inch and 36.6 oz. Also available in 4.15-inch commander size. Blue.

New: $1575 **Exc:** $1450 **VGood:** $1000

STI LEGACY

Chambered for .45 ACP single-stack. 5-inch slide/barrel, LOA 8.5-inch, 38 oz. with adjustable rear sight. Cocobola smooth grips. IDPA, USPSA approved.

New: $1875 **Exc:** $1750 **VGood:** $1350

STI RANGEMASTER II

Single-stack blued variation of Rangemaster. Chambered for 9mm, .40 S&W, .45 ACP. 5-inch slide/barrel, LOA 8.5-inch, 37 oz.

New: $1295 **Exc:** $1100 **VGood:** $895

STI GP6

Polymer-framed single/double action pistol with ambidextrous safeties and fized three-dot sight system. Chambered in 9mm Parabellum.

New: $675 **Exc:** $595 **VGood:** $395

STI SENTINEL PREMIER

Top-of-the-line ISPC and IDPAcompetition 1911 with Dawson Precision/STI "Perfect Impact" style white outline tritium adjustable sights and the STI Tritium competition front; forged steel, government length, standard-width frame; and many other refinements. The Sentinel Premier comes standard with case, owner's manual, and one Wilson Combat ® Elite Tactical magazine.

New: $2295 **Exc:** $1925 **VGood:** $1375

STI STEELMASTER

Caliber: 9mm. Barrel is 4.15 inches, weight is 38.9 oz. Length: 9.5 inches overall. Built on STI's patented modular steel frame with polymer grip. Mounted with a C-More red-dot scope, STI's Spur hammer and Recoil Master guide-rod system, checkered front strap and mainspring housing.

Perf: $2650 **Exc:** $2300 **VGood:** $2000

STI TRUBOR

Caliber: 9mm, 9x23, 38 Super. Five-inch barrel with integrated compensator. Weight: 41.3 oz. including scope and mount. Length: 10.5 inches. Other features similar to Steelmaster, including mounted C-More Railway sight.

Perf: $2600 **Exc:** $2250 **VGood:** $1950

STOEGER AMERICAN EAGLE LUGER

Semi-automatic; single action; 9mm Para.; 7-shot magazine; 4-inch barrel; 9-5/8-inch overall length; weighs 32 oz.; checkered walnut grips; blade front sight, fixed rear; recreation of the American Eagle Luger pistol in stainless steel; chamber loaded indicator. Made in U.S. From Stoeger Industries. Introduced 1994.

New: $750 **Perf:** $600 **Exc:** $500

With matte black finish $789.00

New: $550 **Perf:** $475 **Exc:** $400

STOEGER AMERICAN EAGLE LUGER NAVY MODEL

Same general specs as the American Eagle except has 6-inch barrel. Made in U.S. From Stoeger Industries. Introduced 1994.

New: $550 **Perf:** $475 **Exc:** $425

STOEGER COMPACT COUGAR

Caliber: 9mm, 13-round magazine capacity. Barrel: 3.6 inches. Weight: 32 oz. Length: 7 inches. Wood or rubber grips. Three-dot sights. Double/single action with ambidextrous safety and decocking lever. Bruniton Matte black finish.

Perf: $410 **Exc:** $350 **VGood:** $300

STOEGER LUGER

Semi-automatic; 22 LR; 11-shot; 4-1/2-inch, 5-1/2-inch barrel; blade front sight, fixed rear; checkered or smooth wooden grips; blued finish. Based on original Luger design. Introduced 1970; discontinued 1978; all-steel model reintroduced 1980; discontinued 1985.

Exc: $250 **VGood:** $225 **Good:** $200

STOEGER LUGER TARGET

Same general specs as Stoeger Luger, except target sights; checkered hardwood stocks. Introduced 1975; all-steel model reintroduced 1980; discontinued 1985.

Exc: $260 **VGood:** $240 **Good:** $205

STRUM RUGER 22/45 LITE

Semi-automatic, single-action in .22 LR. Grip angle and shape designed to mimic feel of 1911 pistol. 4.4 inch threaded barrel. Zytel polymer grip frame with replaceable black laminate stocks. Fixed front sight and adjustable rear sight. 8.5 inches long, weight: 23 ounces. Introduced 2013.

Perf: $450 **Exc:** $400 **VGood:** 350

STURM RUGER BEARCAT (FIRST ISSUE)

Revolver; single action; 22 LR, 22 Long, 22 Short; 6-shot cylinder; 4-inch barrel; 8-7/8-inch overall length; weighs 17 oz.; non-fluted cylinder; fixed Patridge front, square notch rear sights; alloy solid frame; uncheckered walnut grips; blued. Introduced 1958; dropped 1973.

Exc: $450 **VGood:** $400 **Good:** $325

STURM RUGER BEARCAT (SECOND ISSUE) SUPER BEARCAT

Revolver; single action; 22 LR, 22 Long, 22 Short; improved version of Bearcat except all-steel construction; weighs 22-1/2 oz.; music wire coil springs; non-fluted engraved cylinder. Introduced 1971; dropped 1975.

Exc: $450 **VGood:** $400 **Good:** $350

Sturm Ruger Bearcat (Third Issue)
New Super Bearcat

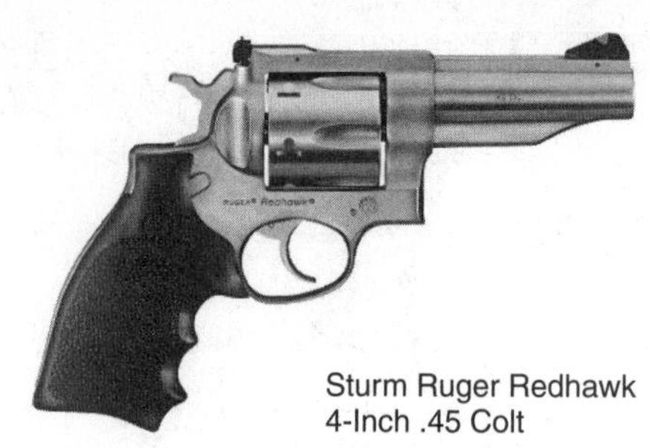

Sturm Ruger Redhawk
4-Inch .45 Colt

Sturm Ruger LCR

Sturm Ruger Blackhawk

Sturm Ruger Blackhawk
Flat-Top 44 Magnum

STURM RUGER BEARCAT (THIRD ISSUE) NEW SUPER BEARCAT

Revolver; single action; 22 LR/22 WMR; 6-shot cylinder; 4-inch barrel; weighs 23 oz.; 8-7/8-inch overall length; smooth rosewood grips with Ruger medallion; blade front sight, fixed notch rear; reintroduction of the Ruger Super Bearcat with slightly lengthened frame; Ruger patented transfer bar safety system; comes with two cylinders; available in blue or stainless steel. Made in U.S. by Sturm, Ruger & Co. Introduced 1993; still produced.

New: $450 **Perf:** $400 **Exc:** $350

Stainless

New: $475 **Perf:** $425 **Exc:** $375

STURM RUGER BISLEY

Revolver; single action; 22, 32 H&R Mag., 357, 41 Mag., 44 Mag., 45 Colt; 7-1/2-inch barrel; 13-inch overall length; flat-top frame; low hammer with deeply checkered wide spur; wide, smooth trigger; longer grip frame; unfluted cylinder; roll engraved with Bisley marksman, trophy. Introduced 1985.

New: $475 **Perf:** $425 **Exc:** $350

STURM RUGER BISLEY SMALL FRAME

Same specs as Bisley except 22 LR, 32 H&R; 6-1/2-inch barrel; weighs 41 oz.; 11-1/2-inch overall length; American walnut grips; front sight base accepts interchangeable square blades of various heights and fully-adjustable dovetailed rear; large oval trigger guard. Made in U.S. by Sturm, Ruger. Introduced 1985; still produced.

New: $350 **Perf:** $325 **Exc:** $225

STURM RUGER BLACKHAWK

Revolver; single action; 357 Mag., 41 Mag., 45 LC; 6-shot; 4-5/8-inch, 6-1/2-inch (357, 41 Mag.) barrel; 12-inch overall length (6-1/2-inch barrel); large frame; checkered hard rubber or uncheckered walnut grips; hooded adjustable rear sight, ramp front; blued. Introduced 1956; dropped 1972.

Exc: $550 **VGood:** $475 **Good:** $350

STURM RUGER BLACKHAWK CONVERTIBLE

Same specs as standard Blackhawk except interchangeable cylinders for 9mm Para., 357 Mag. or 45 Colt/45 ACP. Introduced 1967; dropped 1985.

Exc: $600 **VGood:** $525 **Good:** $450

STURM RUGER BLACKHAWK FLAT-TOP

Revolver; single action; 357 Mag.; 6-shot; 4-5/8-inch, 6-1/2-inch, 10-inch barrel; 12-inch overall length (6-1/2-inch barrel); checkered hard rubber or unchecкered walnut grips; click-adjustable rear sight, ramp front; blued. Introduced 1955; dropped 1963.

Exc: $900 **VGood:** $600 **Good:** $400

6-1/2-inch barrel

Exc: $975 **VGood:** $650 **Good:** $475

10-inch barrel

Exc: $1500 **VGood:** $1275 **Good:** $800

STURM RUGER BLACKHAWK FLAT-TOP 44 MAGNUM

Same specs as Blackhawk Flat-Top except 44 Mag.; 6-1/2-inch, 7-1/2-inch, 10-inch barrel; 121/8-inch overall length; uncheckered walnut grips; blued. Introduced 1956; dropped 1963.

Exc: $1675 **VGood:** $1050 **Good:** $775

7-1/2-inch, 10-inch barrel

Exc: $1700 **VGood:** $1075 **Good:** $800

STURM RUGER BLACKHAWK NEW MODEL

Revolver; single action; 30 Carbine, 357 Mag./38 Spl., 41 Mag., 45 LC; 6-shot cylinder; 4-5/8-inch, 6-1/2-inch barrel; 7-1/2-inch barrel (30 Carbine, 45 LC); 12-1/2-inch overall length (6-1/2-inch barrel); weighs 42 oz.; new Ruger interlocked mechanism; transfer bar ignition; hardened chrome-moly steel frame; wide trigger music wire springs; independent firing pin; blue, stainless or high-gloss stainless finish. Introduced 1973; still in production. As of 2005

New: $500 **Perf:** $400 **Exc:** $300

Stainless finish

New: $550 **Perf:** $450 **Exc:** $350

High-gloss stainless finish

New: $560 **Perf:** $475 **Exc:** $400

STURM RUGER BLACKHAWK NEW MODEL 357 MAXIMUM

Same specs as Blackhawk New Model except 357 Maximum; 7-1/2-inch, 10-inch bull barrel; 16-7/8-inch overall length (10-1/2-inch barrel). Introduced 1983; dropped 1984.

Exc: $800 **VGood:** $700 **Good:** $550

STURM RUGER BLACKHAWK NEW MODEL CONVERTIBLE

Same specs as Blackhawk New Model except interchangeable cylinders for 357 Mag./9mm, 44 Mag./44-40, 45 LC/45 ACP; 4-5/8-inch, 6-1/2-inch barrel. Add 10 percent to above pricing.

STURM RUGER FIFTIETH ANNIVERSARY .44 MAGNUM FLATTOP NEW MODEL BLACKHAWK

Six-shot, single-action .44 Magnum (also accepts .44 Special) with 6.5-inch barrel and adjustable rear sight, 47 oz. Recreation of original .44 Flat-Top Blackhawk. Blued with checkered rubber grips. Gold, color-filled rollmark on top of barrel. Introduced 2006.

New: $600 **Exc:** $525 **VGood:** $425

STURM RUGER GP-100

Revolver; double action; 357 Mag., 38 Spl.; 6-shot cylinder; 3-inch, 4-inch, 6-inch standard or heavy barrel; weighs 40 oz.; fully-adjustable rear sight, interchangeable blade front; Ruger cushioned grip with Goncalo Alves inserts; new design action, frame; full-length ejector shroud; satin blue finish or stainless steel. Introduced 1986; still in production.

New: $500 **Perf:** $425 **Exc:** $375

STURM RUGER HAWKEYE

Single shot; single action; 256 Mag.; 8-1/2-inch barrel; 14-1/2-inch overall length; standard frame with cylinder replaced with rotating breech block; uncheckered walnut grips; click-adjustable rear sight, ramp front; barrel drilled, tapped for scope mounts; blued. Introduced 1963; dropped 1964.

Exc: $1600 **VGood:** $1100 **Good:** $900

STRUM RUGER LCR (LIGHTWEIGHT COMPACT REVOLVER)

Polymer framed, double-action only revolver. 1.8 inch barrel, 6.5 inches long. Weight varies depending on chambering between 13 and 17 ounces. U-notch integral rear sight, fixed front sight - XS Big Dot sight version available (LCR-XS). Some versions available with Crimson Trace laser grips. Introduced 2012. .22 LR introduced 2013. Add $200 for Crimson Trace laser grips, $50 for XS sight.

Perf: $500 **Exc:** $425 **VGood:** 375

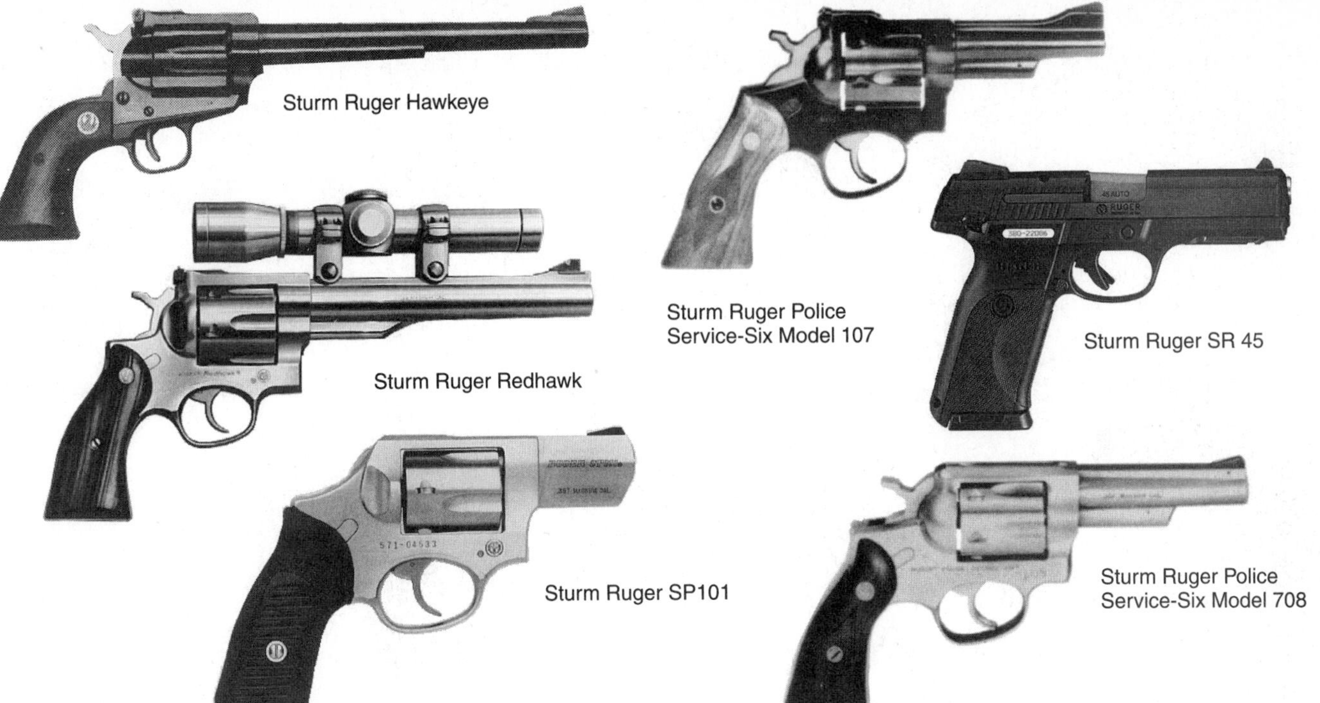

Sturm Ruger Hawkeye

Sturm Ruger Police Service-Six Model 107

Sturm Ruger SR 45

Sturm Ruger Redhawk

Sturm Ruger SP101

Sturm Ruger Police Service-Six Model 708

STURM RUGER POLICE SERVICE-SIX MODEL 107

Revolver; double action; 357 Mag.; 6-shot cylinder; 2-3/4-inch, 4-inch, 6-inch barrel; 6-inch barrel dropped in 1973; 9-1/4-inch overall length (4-inch barrel); integral ejector rod shroud and sight rib; fixed sights; semi-target-type checkered walnut grips; blued. Introduced 1972; dropped 1987.

Exc: $350 **VGood:** $275 **Good:** $235

STURM RUGER POLICE SERVICE-SIX MODEL 108

Same specs as Model 107 except 38 Spl.; 4-inch barrel. Introduced 1972; dropped 1987.

Exc: $300 **VGood:** $250 **Good:** $200

STURM RUGER POLICE SERVICE-SIX MODEL 109

Same specs as Model 107 except 9mm Para.; 4-inch barrel. Introduced 1976; dropped 1984.

Exc: $500 **VGood:** $400 **Good:** $295

STURM RUGER POLICE SERVICE-SIX MODEL 707

Same specs as Model 107 except 357 Mag.; stainless steel construction; 4-inch standard or heavy barrel. Introduced 1973; dropped 1987.

Exc: $300 **VGood:** $285 **Good:** $265

STURM RUGER POLICE SERVICE-SIX MODEL 708

Same specs as Model 107 except 38 Spl.; stainless steel construction; 4-inch standard or heavy barrel; square butt grips. Introduced 1973; dropped 1987.

Exc: $300 **VGood:** $250 **Good:** $200

STURM RUGER REDHAWK

Revolver; double action; 357 Mag., 41 Mag., 44 Mag.; 6-shot; 5-1/2-inch, 7-1/2-inch barrel; 5-1/2-inch barrel added 1984; 13-inch overall length (7-1/2-inch barrel); weighs 54 oz.; stainless steel brushed satin or blued finish; Patridge-type front sight, fully-adjustable rear; square-butt Goncalo Alves grips. Introduced 1979; still in production. Add 15 percent for .357, 20 percent for .41. Four-inch barrel introduced 2007. .45 Colt introduced 2008.

Blue		
New: $525	**Perf:** $400	**Exc:** $350
Stainless		
New: $550	**Perf:** $475	**Exc:** $400

STURM RUGER REDHAWK 4-INCH .45 COLT

Similar to original stainless Redhawk but in .45 Colt only and with a 4-inch barrel. Hogue molded grips.

New: $600 **Perf:** $525 **Exc:** $425

STURM RUGER S ECURITY-SIX MODEL 117

Revolver; double action; 357 Mag.; 6-shot cylinder; 2 -/4-inch, 4-inch, 6-inch barrel; 9-1/4-inch overall length (4-inch barrel); hand-checkered semi-target walnut grips; adjustable rear sight, Patridge type front on ramp; music wire coil springs throughout. Introduced 1974; dropped 1985.

Exc: $400 **VGood:** $350 **Good:** $300

STURM RUGER SECURITY-SIX MODEL 717

Same specs as Model 117 except 357 Mag.; all metal parts except sights of stainless steel; black alloy sights for visibility. Introduced 1974; dropped 1985.

Exc: $400 **VGood:** $350 **Good:** $300

STURM RUGER SINGLE-SIX

Revolver; single action; 22 LR, 22 WMR; 6-shot; 4-5/8-inch, 5-1/2-inch, 6-1/2-inch, 9-1/2-inch barrel; 10-inch overall length (4-inch barrel); checkered hard rubber grips on early production, uncheckered walnut on later versions; windage-adjustable rear sight; blued. Introduced 1953; dropped 1972.

Exc: $475 **VGood:** $400 **Good:** $325

STURM RUGER SINGLE-SIX CONVERTIBLE

Same general specs as standard Single-Six except interchangeable cylinders, 22 LR, Long, Short/22 WRM; 5-1/2-inch, 6-1/2-inch, 91/2-inch barrel. Introduced 1962; dropped 1972.

Exc: $550 **VGood:** $475 **Good:** $400

STURM RUGER SUPER SINGLE SIX

Same specs as Single Six except Ruger "Interlocked" mechanism, transfer bar ignition; gate-controlled loading; hardened chrome-moly steel frame; wide trigger; music wire springs; independent firing pin. Introduced 1973; still in production.

New: $425 **Perf:** $375 **Exc:** $325

STURM RUGER SINGLE SIX SSM

Same specs as Super Single Six except 32 H&R Mag. Introduced 1985; discontinued.

New: $700 **Perf:** $625 **Exc:** $550

STURM RUGER SP101

Revolver; double action; 22 LR, 32 H&R Mag., 9mm Para., 38 Spl. +P, 357 Mag.; 6-shot (22 LR, 32 H&R Mag.), 5-shot (9mm, 38 Spl. +P, 357 Mag.); 2-1/4-inch, 3-1/16-inch, 4-inch barrel; weighs 25 oz. (2-1/4-inch), 27 oz. (3-1/16-inch); adjustable sights (22, 32), fixed (others); Ruger Santoprene cushioned grips with Xenoy inserts; incorporates improvements and features found in the GP-100 revolvers into a compact, small frame, double-action revolver; full-length ejector shroud; stainless steel only; available with high-polish finish. Introduced 1988; still in production. .327 Federal added in 2008.

New: $500 **Perf:** $400 **Exc:** $300

STURM RUGER SP101 DOUBLE-ACTION-ONLY REVOLVER

Similar to the standard SP101 except is double-action-only with no single-action sear notch. Has spurless hammer for snag-free handling, floating firing pin and Ruger's patented transfer bar safety system. Available with 2-1/4-inch barrel in 38 Special +P and 357 Magnum only. Weighs 25-1/2 oz., overall length 7.06-inch. Natural brushed satin or high-polish stainless steel. Introduced 1993.

New: $500 **Perf:** $400 **Exc:** $300

STRUM RUGER SR 22

Semi-automatic, striker fired, polymer framed pistol in .22 LR. Adjustable sights, 6.4 inches long weighing 17.5 ounces. Ambidextrous thumb safety, de-cocking lever and magazine release. Interchangeable slip-on grips and Picatinny accessory rail under barrel. Introduced in 2012. Version with silver anodized slide and version with threaded barrel introduced in 2013.

Perf: $390 **Exc:** $340 **VGood:** 310

STRUM RUGER SR 45

Striker fired, semi-automatic in .45 ACP. Stainless steel with brushed stainless or black Nitride finish. 4.5 inch barrel, 8.0 inches long and a weight of 30.15 ounces. Polymer frame with checkered grip surface. Three-dot sights with adjustable rear sight. Interchangeable grip back-strap. 10+1 capacity. Introduced 2012.

Perf: $500 **Exc:** $430 **VGood:** $390

Sturm Ruger Bisley Vaquero

Sturm Ruger Vaquero

Sturm Ruger P85 Mark II

Sturm Ruger Super Blackhawk Hunter

Sturm Ruger SR1911 Commander

Sturm Ruger 22/45 KP4 Mark II

STRUM RUGER SR1911 COMMANDER

Semi-automatic, single-action, 1911 style in .45 ACP. Stainless steel frame, slide, 4.25 inch barrel and bushing. 7.75 inches long with a weight of 36.4 ounces. Windage adjustable Novak style three-dot sights. Double-diamond checkered hardwood grips with checkered back-strap. Slide lock, thumb safety and grip safety have a black Nitride finish. Introduced 2012.

Perf: $800 **Exc:** $725 **VGood:** $675

STURM RUGER SUPER BLACKHAWK

Revolver; 44 Mag.; 5-1/2-inch, 7-1/2-inch, 10-1/2-inch barrel; 13-3/8-inch overall length (7-1/2-inch barrel); weighs 48 oz.; 1/8-inch ramp front, micro-click fully-adjustable rear; American walnut grips; interlock mechanism; non-fluted cylinder; steel grip and cylinder frame; square back trigger guard; wide serrated trigger; wide spur hammer.

New: $550 **Perf:** $450 **Exc:** $350

Stainless

New: $575 **Perf:** $475 **Exc:** $400

STURM RUGER SUPER BLACKHAWK HUNTER

Same specs as Super Blackhawk except stainless finish; 7-1/2-inch; scope rings. Introduced 1992; still in prduction.

New: $700 **Perf:** $575 **Exc:** $400

STURM RUGER SUPER REDHAWK

Revolver; double action; 44 Mag.; 6-shot; 7-1/2-inch, 9-1/2-inch barrel; 13-inch overall length (7-1/2-inch barrel); weighs 54 oz.; heavy extended frame with Ruger Integral Scope Mounting System; wide topstrap; ramp front with interchangeable sight blades, adjustable rear; Santoprene grips with Goncalo Alves panels; satin polished stainless steel finish. Introduced 1987; still in production. 480 Ruger version discontinued in 2011, reintroduced in 2013.

New: $750 **Perf:** $650 **Exc:** $500

STURM RUGER SUPER REDHAWK ALASKAN

Snubby version of Super Redhawk with 2-1/2-inch barrel.. Chambered in .480 Ruger (discontinued), .454 Casual/.45 Colt, and .44 Magnum. 480 Ruger version discontinued in 2011, reintroduced in 2013.

New: $800 **Perf:** $700 **Exc:** $600

STURM RUGER VAQUERO

Revolver; single action; 44-40, 44 Mag., 45 Colt; 6-shot; 4-5/8-inch, 5-1/2-inch, 7-1/2-inch barrel; 13-3/8-inch overall length (7-1/2-inch barrel); weighs 41 oz.; blade front, fixed notch rear sight; transfer bar safety system; loading gate interlock; color case-hardened frame on blue model; blue or high-polish stainless finish. Introduced 1993; still in production. with new, smaller frame.

New: $525 **Perf:** $450 **Exc:** $400

STURM RUGER BISLEY VAQUERO

Similar to the Vaquero except has Bisley-style hammer, grip and trigger and is available in 44 Magnum and 45 Colt only, with 5-1/2-inch barrel. Has smooth rosewood grips with Ruger medallion. Introduced 1997. Discontinued.

Color case-hardened frame, blue grip frame, barrel and cylinder

New: $600 **Perf:** $525 **Exc:** $450

High-gloss stainless steel

New: $600 **Perf:** $500 **Exc:** $425

STURM RUGER "COWBOY PAIR"

Matched pair of engraved and consecutively serial-numbered New Vaquero revolvers in .45 Colt. Includes lined wood collector case. Production limited to 500 sets.

New: $3700 **Exc:** $2000 **VGood:** $995

STURM RUGER 50TH ANNIVERSARY MATCHED SET .357 AND .44 MAGNUM

Matched pair of Ruger New Blackhawks, one in .44 and the other in .357, commemorating 50th anniversary of Ruger Blackhawk revolver. Gold-filled rollmarked 6-1/2" and 4-5/8" barrels, respectively. Includes presentation case. Limited production.

New: $1250 **Exc:** $975 **VGood:** $575

STURM RUGER 22/45 KP4 MARK II

Semi-automatic; single action; 22 LR; 10-shot magazine; 4-3/4-inch stainless steel barrel; 8-7/8-inch overall length; weighs 28 oz.; Zytel grip frame matches angle and magazine latch of Model 1911 45 ACP pistol; Patridge front sight, square notch windage-adjustable rear; brushed stainless steel. Introduced 1992; still produced.

New: $345 **Perf:** $315 **Exc:** $275

STURM RUGER 22/45 KP512 MARK II

Same specs as P4 except 5-1/2-inch stainless steel bull barrel; weighs 35 oz. Made in U.S. by Sturm, Ruger & Company. Introduced 1992; still produced

New: $345 **Perf:** $315 **Exc:** $275

STURM RUGER 22/45 P512 BULL BARREL MARK II

Same specs as P4 except 5-1/2-inch steel bull barrel; 9-5/8-inch overall length; weighs 36 oz.; fully-adjustable rear sight; brushed satin blue finish. Introduced 1995; still produced.

New: $345 **Perf:** $315 **Exc:** $275

STURM RUGER MARK I STANDARD MODEL

Semi-automatic; 22 LR only; 9-shot magazine 4-3/4-inch, 6-inch barrel (4-3/4-inch barrel), 8-3/4-inch overall length (6-inch barrel); checkered hard rubber grips walnut optional; windage-adjustable square-notch rear, fixed wide blade front sight; blued. Introduced 1949; dropped 1982 in favor of Mark II. Until 1951 featured red eagle insignia in grips; changed to black upon death of Alex Sturm. This type has considerable collector value.

Exc: $250 **VGood:** $225 **Good:** $195

Red eagle model (pre-1951)

Exc: $650 **VGood:** $300 **Good:** $250

STURM RUGER MARK I TARGET MODEL

Same specs as Standard Model except 5-1/2-inch heavy barrel, 5-3/4-inch tapered barrel, 6-7/8-inch heavy tapered barrel; adjustable rear, target front sight. Introduced 1951; dropped 1982.

Exc: $345 **VGood:** $315 **Good:** $275

STURM RUGER MARK II STANDARD MODEL

Semi-automatic; 22 LR; 10-shot magazine; 4-3/4-inch, 6-inch barrel; checkered hard rubber stocks; fixed blade front sight, square-notch

Sturm Ruger 22/45 KP512 Mark II

Sturm Ruger 22/45 Mark III Hunter

Sturm Ruger Mark II Standard Model

Sturm Ruger MK-4B Compact

Sturm Ruger Mark I Standard Model

Sturm Ruger Mark II Government Model Target

Sturm Ruger Cowboy Pair

windage-adjustable rear; new bolt hold-open device, magazine catch; new receiver contours; stainless steel or blued. Introduced 1982; still in production.

Exc: $250 **VGood:** $200 **Good:** $160

Stainless steel finish

Exc: $275 **VGood:** $225 **Good:** $200

STURM RUGER MARK II BULL BARREL

Same specs as standard model except 5-1/2-inch, 10-inch heavy barrel. Introduced 1982; still in production.

Perf: $275 **Exc:** $225 **VGood:** $200

Stainless finish

Exc: $300 **VGood:** $275 **Good:** $225

STURM RUGER MARK II GOVERNMENT MODEL TARGET

Same specs as Mark II Standard except 6-7/8-inch bull barrel; adjustable rear sight; black plastic grips; roll-stamped "Government Target Model" on right side of receiver; blued finish. Introduced 1987; discontinued 2004.

New: $350 **Perf:** $300 **Exc:** $250

STURM RUGER MARK II GOVERNMENT MODEL STAINLESS

Same specs as Model Target except 6 -7/8-inch slab-sided barrel; receiver drilled, tapped for Ruger scope base adaptor; checkered walnut grip panels; right-hand thumb rest; blued open sights. Marketed with 1-inch stainless scope rings, integral base. Introduced 1992; discontinued 2004.

New: $400 **Perf:** $350 **Exc:** $275

STURM RUGER MARK II TARGET

Same specs as standard model except 5-1/4-inch, 6-7/8-inch barrel; 11-1/8-inch overall length; weighs 42 oz.; .125-inch blade front sight, adjustable micro-click rear; sight radius 9-3/8-inch. Introduced 1982; discontinued 2004.

New: $275 **Perf:** $235 **Exc:** $200

Stainless steel finish

New: $325 **Perf:** $275 **Exc:** $225

STURM RUGER MK-4B COMPACT

Similar to the Mark II Standard pistol except has 4-inch bull barrel, Patridge-type front sight, fully adjustable rear, and smooth laminated hardwood thumbrest stocks. Weighs 38 oz., overall length of 8-3/16-inch. Comes with extra magazine, plastic case, lock. Introduced 1996.

New: $300 **Perf:** $250 **Exc:** $200

STURM RUGER MARK III STANDARD MODEL

Introduced in 2005 this .22 caliber pistol is fitted with a 4.75" or 6" barrel. Fixed rear sight. Blued finish. Magazine capacity is 10 rounds. Black checkered grips. Weight is about 35 oz. depending on barrel length.

New: $325 **Perf:** $250 **Exc:** $200

STURM RUGER MARK III HUNTER

This .22 caliber pistol is fitted with a 6.88" target crowned fluted stainless steel barrel. Adjustable rear sight with Hi-Viz front sight. Checkered Cocobolo grips. Drilled and tapped for scope mount. Supplied with green case, scope base adapter, and 6 interchangeable LitePipes for front sight. Weight is about 41 oz. Introduced in 2005. Add 50 percent for Crimson Trace lasergrips (limited edition for 2008).

New: $375 **Perf:** $325 **Exc:** $275

STURM RUGER MARK III COMPETITION

This .22 caliber model features a 6.88" flat sided heavy barrel with adjustable rear sight and Patridge front sight. Stainless steel finish. Checkered wood grips. Weight is about 45 oz. Introduced in 2005.

New: $425 **Perf:** $350 **Exc:** $295

STURM RUGER MARK III 512 PISTOL

This .22 LR pistol has a 5.5" bull barrel and adjustable rear sight. Steel frame is blued. Checkered black synthetic grips. Weaver-style scope base adapter included. Magazine capacity is 10 rounds. Weight is about 41 oz.

New: $375 **Perf:** $225 **Exc:** $200

STURM RUGER 22/45 MARK III HUNTER

Similar to 22/45 .22 pistol but with Mark III-style improvements. 6-7/8" or 4-1/2" fluted barrel, HiViz front sight with six interchangeable inserts. Blued or stainless finish. Pricing is for stainless model. Introduced in 2007.

New: $425 **Perf:** $300 **Exc:** $275

STURM RUGER CHARGER

Introduced in 2008. A 10-inch-barrel pistol version of the 10/22 .22 LR rifle. Black matte finish, black laminated stock, bipod, and Weaver-style mounts. Include one 10-round magazine.

New: $350 **Perf:** $300 **Exc:** $250

STURM RUGER P85 MARK II

Semi-automatic; double action, DAO; 9mm Para.; 15-shot magazine; 4-1/2-inch barrel; 7-13/16-inch overall length; weighs 32 oz.; windage-adjustable square-notch rear sight, square post front; ambidextrous slide-mounted safety levers; 4140 chome-moly steel slide; aluminum alloy frame; grooved Xenoy composition stocks; ambidextrous magazine release; blue or stainless finish. Decocker version also available. Introduced 1986; dropped 1992.

Exc: $325 **VGood:** $300 **Good:** $250

Stainless finish

New: $375 **Perf:** $325 **Exc:** $275

STURM RUGER P89

Semi-automatic; double action; 9mm Para., 10-shot magazine. Barrel: 4.50-inch. Weight: 32 oz. Length: 7.84-inch overall. Stocks: Grooved black Xenoy composition. Sights: Square post front, square notch rear adjustable for windage, both with white dot inserts. Features: Double action with ambidextrous slide-mounted safety-levers. Slide is 4140 chrome-moly steel or 400-series stainless steel, frame is a lightweight aluminum alloy. Ambidextrous magazine release. Blue or stainless steel. Introduced 1986; discontinued 2007.

Exc: $325 **VGood:** $300 **Good:** $250

Stainless finish

Exc: $375 **VGood:** $325 **Good:** $275

STURM RUGER P89D DECOCKER

Similar to the standard P89 except has ambidextrous decocking levers in place of the regular slide-mounted safety. The decocking levers move the firing pin inside the slide where the hammer can not reach it, while simultaneously blocking the firing pin from forward movement-allows shooter to decock a cocked pistol without manipulating the trigger. Conventional thumb decocking procedures are

Sturm Ruger SR9

Sturm Ruger P94

Sturm Ruger P93 Compact Decocker Model

Sundance Laser 25

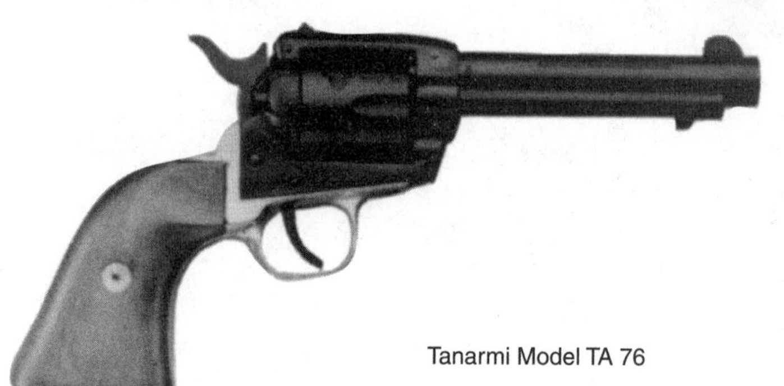
Tanarmi Model TA 76

therefore unnecessary. Blue or stainless steel. Introduced 1990.

New: $325 **Perf:** $300 **Exc:** $250

Stainless finish

New: $375 **Perf:** $325 **Exc:** $275

STURM RUGER P89/DAO

Semi-automatic; double action, double-action-only; 9mm Para.; 15-shot magazine; 4-1/2-inch barrel; 7-13/16-inch overall length; weighs 32 oz.; improved version of P85 Mark II; windage-adjustable square-notch rear sight, square post front; internal safety; bobbed, spurless hammer; gripping grooves on rear of slide; stainless steel construction. Decocker model also available at no extra cost; blue or stainless
(DAO) finish. Marketed with plastic case, extra magazine, loading tool. Introduced 1991; still in production.

New: $325 **Perf:** $300 **Exc:** $250

Stainless

New: $400 **Perf:** $350 **Exc:** $300

STURM RUGER P90

Semi-automatic; double action; 45 ACP; 7-shot magazine; 4-1/2-inch barrel; 7-15/16-inch overall length; weighs 33-1/2 oz.; aluminum frame; stainless steel slide; ambidextrous slide-mounted safety levers; square post front, square notch windage-adjustable rear; stainless steel only. Decocker model also available at no extra cost. Introduced 1991; still in production.

New: $400 **Perf:** $350 **Exc:** $300

STURM RUGER P91 DC DECOCKER

Semi-automatic; double action, double-action-only; 40 S&W; 11-shot magazine; 4-1/2-inch barrel; 7-15/16-inch overall length; weighs 33 oz.; ambidextrous slide-mounted safety levers; square post front, windage-adjustable square notch rear with white dot inserts; grooved black Xenoy composition grips; stainless finish. Marketed with plastic case, extra magazine, loading tool. Introduced 1991; dropped 1994.

New: $400 **Perf:** $350 **Exc:** $300

STURM RUGER P93 COMPACT

Semi-automatic; double action; 9mm Para.; 10-shot magazine; 3-15/16-inch barrel; 7 5/16-inch overall length; weighs 31 oz.; grooved black Xenoy composition grips; square post front sight, square notch windage-adjustable rear with white dot inserts; forward third of the slide tapered and polished to the muzzle; front of the slide crowned with a convex curve; seven finger grooves on slide; 400-series stainless steel slide; lightweight alloy frame. Available as decocker-only or double-action-only. Introduced 1993; discontinued 2004.

New: $425 **Perf:** $375 **Exc:** $325

STURM RUGER P94

Semi-automatic; double-action-only, decock only, or manual safety; 9mm Para., 40 S&W; 10-shot magazine; 4-1/4-inch barrel; 7-1/2-inch overall length; weighs 33 oz.; grooved Xenoy grips; square post front sight, windage-adjustable rear; three-dot system; slide gripping grooves roll over top of slide; ambidextrous safety-levers; ambidextrous decocking levers; matte finish stainless slide and barrel, alloy frame; frame size between full-size P-Series and compact P93. Introduced 1994; discontinued 2004.

New: $350 **Perf:** $300 **Exc:** $275

STURM RUGER P94L

Same specs as the KP94 except laser sight mounts in housing cast integrally with frame; Allen-head screws control windage and elevation adjustments. Made in U.S. by Sturm, Ruger. Introduced 1994; still produced for law enforcement only.

STURM RUGER KP94

Sized midway between the full-size P-Series and the compact P93. Has 4.25-inch barrel, 7.5-inch overall length and weighs about 33 oz. KP94 is manual safety model; KP94DAO is double-action-only (both 9mm Para., 10-shot magazine); KP94D is decocker-only in 40-caliber with 10-shot magazine. Slide gripping grooves roll over top of slide. KP94 has ambidextrous safety-levers; KP94DAO has no external safety, full-cock hammer position or decocking lever; KP94D has ambidextrous decocking levers. Matte finish stainless slide, barrel, alloy frame. Also available in blue. Introduced 1994; discontinued 2004.

New: $450 **Perf:** $375 **Exc:** $275

STURM RUGER P95 SEMI-AUTO PISTOL

Semi-automatic; double action; 9mm Para., 10-shot magazine. Barrel: 3.9-inch. Weight: 27 oz. Length: 7.3-inch overall. Stocks: Grooved; integral with frame. Sights: Blade front, rear drift adjustable for windage; three-dot system. Features: Molded polymer grip frame, stainless steel or chrome-moly slide. Suitable for +P+ ammunition. Decocker or DAO. Introduced 1996.

New: $400 **Perf:** $325 **Exc:** $275

Stainless finish

New: $425 **Perf:** $350 **Exc:** $300

STURM RUGER SR9

Introduced in 2008. Ruger's first striker-fired semi-auto pistol. Chambered in 9mm Parabellum. Double-action only with 4.14-inch barrel, 17+1 capacity. Available in three finish cofigurations: stainless steel slide with matte black frame; blackened stainless slide with matte black frame; and blackened stainless slide with matte black frame. Note: Ruger recalled all early-production SR9 pistols with a "330" serial number prefix because of a potential safety issue.

New: $575 **Perf:** $500 **Exc:** $425

RUGER LC9

Caliber: 9mm, 7+1 capacity. Barrel, 3.12 inches; weight, 17.1 oz. Adjustable 3-dot sights. Double-action-only, hammer-fired, locked-breech action.

Perf: $400 **Exc:** $325 **VGood:** $275

STURM RUGER LCP (LIGHTWEIGHT COMPACT PISTOL)

Introduced in 2008. Ruger's first true pocket pistol. Chambered in .380 (6+1 capacity) with a 2.75-inchc barrel. Double action only. Glass-filled nylon frame with steel barrel. Black matte finish.

New: $350 **Perf:** $300 **Exc:** $250

RUGER LCR

.38 special, 5 shot. Hammerless DAO. 1 7/8" barrel. Black stainless cylinder. Polymer frame housing. Weighs 14 oz. New 2010

Perf: $500 **Exc:** $450 **VGood:** $375

SUNDANCE MODEL A-25

Semi-automatic; 25 ACP; 7-shot; 2-1/2-inch barrel; 4-7/8-inch overall length; weighs 16 oz.; fixed sights; grooved black plastic or smooth simulated pearl stocks; rotary safety blocks rear; bright chrome or black Teflon finish. Introduced 1989.

New: $60 **Perf:** $50 **Exc:** $40

Sundance Model BOA

Sturm Ruger LCP

Sturm Ruger LC9

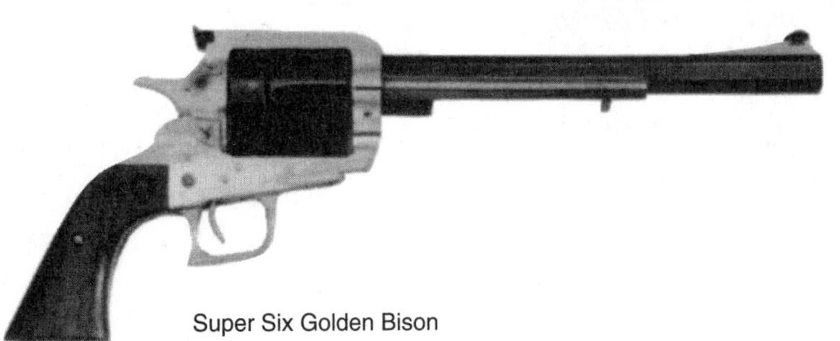
Super Six Golden Bison

Sundance Point Blank

SUNDANCE MODEL BOA

Semi-automatic; 25 ACP; 7-shot; 2-1/2-inch barrel; 4-7/8-inch overall length; weighs 16 oz.; fixed sights; grooved ABS or simulated pearl grips; patented grip safety; manual rotary safety; button magazine release; bright chrome or black Teflon finish. Introduced 1991.

New: $75 **Perf:** $60 **Exc:** $50

SUNDANCE LASER 25

Semi-automatic; 25 ACP, 7-shot magazine. Barrel: 2-1/2-inch. Weight: 18 oz. Length: 4-7/8-inch overall. Stocks: Grooved black ABS. Sights: Class IIIa laser, 670 NM, 5mW, and fixed open. Features: Factory installed and sighted laser sight activated by squeezing the grip safety; manual rotary safety; button magazine release. Bright chrome or black finish. Introduced 1995.

New: $175 **Perf:** $150 **Exc:** $135

SUNDANCE POINT BLANK

Derringer; two-shot; 22 LR; 3-inch barrel; 4-5/8-inch overall length; weighs 8 oz.; grooved composition grips; blade front sight, fixed notch rear; double action trigger; push-bar safety; automatic chamber selection; fully enclosed hammer; matte black finish. Made in U.S. by Sundance Industries. Introduced 1994. Kind of a clone of the old High Standard derringer.

New: $75 **Perf:** $60 **Exc:** $50

SUPER SIX GOLDEN BISON

Revolver; single action; 45-70; 6-shot; 8-inch, 10-1/2-inch octagon barrel; 15-inch overall length (8-inch barrel); weighs 92 oz.; adjustable Millett rear sight, blaze orange blade on ramp front; walnut grips; manganese bronze used in cylinder frame, grip frame; coil springs; half-cock, cross-bolt traveling safeties; antique brown or blued finish. Marketed in fitted walnut presentation case. Discontinued 1992.

Perf: $1500 **Exc:** $1300 **VGood:** $1000

SUPER-SIX LTD. BISON BULL

Massive single-action .45-70 revolver with blued carbon steel (Bison Bull) or engraved molybdenum bronze (Golden Bison Bull) frame. Adjustable sights, 10.5" barrel, 17.5" overall length, weight 6 lbs. Value shown is for blued version. Add 350 percent for engraved version.

New: $995 **Exc:** $800 **VGood:** $675

TANARMI MODEL BTA 90

Semi-automatic; double action; 9mm Para.; 12-shot; 3-1/2-inch barrel; weighs 30 oz.; blade front sight, white outline rear; checkered neoprene stocks; blued finish. Imported from Italy by Excam. Introduced 1987; discontinued 1990.

Perf: $350 **Exc:** $300 **VGood:** $250

Matte chrome finish

Perf: $375 **Exc:** $325 **VGood:** $275

TANARMI MODEL TA 22

Revolver; single action; 22 Short, 22 LR, 22 LR/22 WMR combo; 6-shot; 4-3/4-inch barrel; 10-inch overall length; blade front sight, drift-adjustable rear; checkered nylon grips, walnut optional; manual hammer-block safety frame; blued finish. Imported from Italy by Excam. Introduced 1978; discontinued 1991.

Perf: $100 **Exc:** $80 **VGood:** $60

TANARMI MODEL TA 38 OVER/UNDER DERRINGER

Single shot; tip-up action; 38 Spl.; 3-inch barrel; 4-3/4-inch overall length; weighs 14 oz.; fixed sights; checkered white nylon stocks; blued finish. Assembled in U.S. by Excam. Discontinued 1988.

Exc: $75 **VGood:** $60 **Good:** $50

TANARMI MODEL TA 41

Semi-automatic; double action; 41 AE; 11-shot; 4-3/4-inch barrel; combat sights; black neoprene grips; matte blue finish. Imported from Italy by Excam; discontinued 1990.

Exc: $400 **VGood:** $350 **Good:** $275

Matte chrome finish

Exc: $425 **VGood:** $375 **Good:** $275

TANARMI MODEL TA 41 SS

Same general specs as Model TA 41 except 5-inch compensated barrel; competition sights; blue/chrome finish. Introduced 1989; discontinued 1990.

Exc: $450 **VGood:** $400 **Good:** $350

TANARMI MODEL TA 76

Revolver; single action; 22 LR, 22 LR/22 WMR combo; 6-shot; 4-3/4-inch barrel; 10-inch overall length; weighs 32 oz.; adjustable rear sight, blade front; uncheckered walnut stocks; color case-hardened frame; brass backstrap, trigger guard; manual hammer-block safety; blued finish. Imported from Italy by Excam. Introduced 1987; discontinued 1991.

Exc: $110 **VGood:** $90 **Good:** $75

TANARMI MODEL TA 90

Semi-automatic; double action; 9mm Para.; 15-shot; 4-3/4-inch barrel; 8-1/4-inch overall length; weighs 38 oz.; blade front sight, white-outline rear; checkered neoprene stocks; chromed barrel, trigger; extended slide release lever; blued finish. Imported from Italy by Excam. Introduced 1987; discontinued 1990.

Perf: $350 **Exc:** $295 **VGood:** $200

TANARMI MODEL TA 90 SS

Same specs as Model TA 90 except 5-inch compensated barrel; competition sights; blue/chrome finish. Imported from Italy by Excam. Introduced 1989; discontinued 1990.

Perf: $425 **Exc:** $375 **VGood:** $325

TARGA MODEL GT 22

Semi-automatic; single action; 22 LR; 10-shot; 3-7/8-inch barrel; weighs 26 oz.; blade ramp front sight, windage-adjustable rear; checkered walnut stocks; finger-rest magazine; steel frame; blued finish. Imported from Italy by Excam. Discontinued 1990.

Perf: $150 **Exc:** $125 **VGood:** $110

Chrome finish

Perf: $165 **Exc:** $135 **VGood:** $115

TARGA MODEL GT 22 TARGET

Same specs as Model GT 22 except 6-inch barrel; 12-shot; weighs 30 oz. Introduced 1988; discontinued 1990.

Perf: $175 **Exc:** $135 **VGood:** $125

TARGA MODEL GT 26

Semi-automatic; single action; 25 ACP; 6-shot; 2-1/2-inch barrel; weighs 13 oz.; fixed sights; wooden grips; blued finish. Imported from Italy by Excam. Discontinued 1990.

Exc: $90 **VGood:** $75 **Good:** $50

(GT 26S) With steel frame

Exc: $115 **VGood:** $100 **Good:** $75

TARGA MODEL GT 27

Semi-automatic; single action; 25 ACP; 6-shot; 2-1/2-inch barrel; 4-5/8-inch overall length; fixed sights; checkered nylon stocks; external hammer with half-cock feature; safety lever takedown; blued

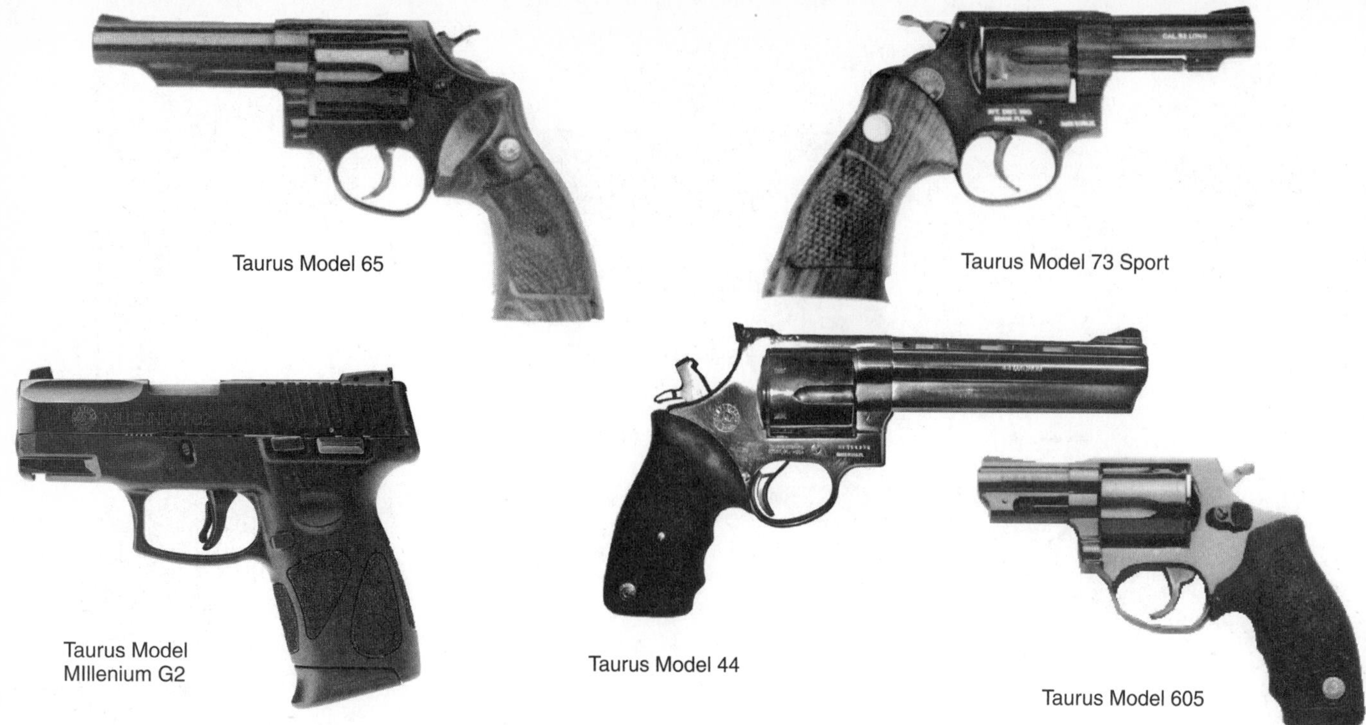
Taurus Model 65

Taurus Model 73 Sport

Taurus Model Mlllenium G2

Taurus Model 44

Taurus Model 605

finish. Imported from Italy by Excam. Introduced 1977; discontinued 1990.

Exc: $100 **VGood:** $80 **Good:** $60

TARGA MODEL GT 32

Semi-automatic; single action; 32 ACP; 7-shot; 3-7/8-inch barrel; 7-3/8-inch overall length; weighs 26 oz.; windage-adjustable rear sight, blade front; optional checkered nylon thumbrest or walnut stocks; external hammer; blued finish. Imported from Italy by Excam. Introduced 1977; discontinued 1990.

Exc: $150 **VGood:** $125 **Good:** $100

TARGA MODEL GT 32 XE

Same general specs as Model GT 32 except 12-shot; blue finish. Introduced 1980; discontinued 1985.

Exc: $175 **VGood:** $150 **Good:** $125

TARGA MODEL GT 380

Semi-automatic; single action; 380 ACP; 6-shot; 3-7/8-inch barrel; weighs 26 oz.; windage-adjustable rear sight, blade front; optional checkered nylon thumbrest or walnut stocks; blued finish. Introduced 1977; discontinued 1990.

Blue or chrome finish

Perf: $150 **Exc:** $135 **VGood:** $110

Light alloy frame

Perf: $125 **Exc:** $100 **VGood:** $85

TARGA MODEL GT 380 XE

Same specs as Model GT 380 except 12-shot; blue finish. Introduced 1980; discontinued 1990.

Perf: $175 **Exc:** $150 **VGood:** $125

TAURUS MILLENNIUM G2

Single action/double action hammer fired polymer framed compact pistol with high profile three dot sights. Chambered in 9mm (PT 111) and .40S&W (PT 140). 3.2 inch barrel and 6.2 inches OA length, weighs 1.37 pounds. 12+1 capacity (9mm) and 10+1 capacity (.40S&W). Introduced 2013.

Perf: $315 **Exc:** $290 **VGood:** $260

TAURUS MODEL 44

Revolver; double action; 44 Mag.; 6-shot cylinder; 4-inch, 6-1/2-inch, 8-3/8-inch barrel; weighs 44-3/4-inch oz. (4-inch barrel); checkered Brazilian hardwood grips; serrated ramp front sight, micro-click fully-adjustable rear; heavy solid rib (4-inch), vent rib (6-1/2-inch, 8-3/8-inch barrel); compensated barrel; blued model with color case-hardened hammer and trigger. Imported by Taurus International. Introduced 1994; discontinued 2004.

Blue finish, 4-inch barrel

New: $375 **Perf:** $325 **Exc:** $275

Blue finish, 6-1/2-inch or 8-3/8-inch barrel

New: $400 **Perf:** $350 **Exc:** $325

Stainless steel, 4-inch barrel

New: $450 **Perf:** $400 **Exc:** $350

Stainless steel, 6-1/2-inch or 8-3/8-inch barrel

New: $475 **Perf:** $425 **Exc:** $375

TAURUS MODEL 65

Revolver; double action; 357 Mag.; 6-shot; 2-1/2-inch, 4-inch barrel; weighs 34 oz.; fixed sights; round butt grip; checkered wood grips; blue, satin nickel or stainless steel finish. Introduced 1978; still imported.

New: $350 **Perf:** $300 **Exc:** $235

Satin nickel finish

New: $350 **Perf:** $300 **Exc:** $235

Stainless steel

New: $375 **Perf:** $320 **Exc:** $250

TAURUS MODEL 66

Revolver; double action; 357 Mag.; 6-shot; 2-1/2-inch, 4-inch, 6-inch barrel; weighs 35 oz. (4-inch barrel); serrated ramp front sight, micro-click fully-adjustable rear; checkered wood grips; wide target hammer spur; floating firing pin; heavy barrel; shrouded ejector rod; blue, satin nickel or stainless steel finish. Introduced 1978; still imported.

New: $350 **Perf:** $300 **Exc:** $250

Stainless steel

New: $375 **Perf:** $300 **Exc:** $275

TAURUS MODEL 73 SPORT

Revolver; double action; 32 S&W Long; 6-shot; 3-inch heavy barrel; 8-1/4-inch overall length; weighs 20 oz.; target-type wood grips; ramp front sight, notch rear; blue or satin nickel finish. Introduced 1979; discontinued 1992.

Perf: $300 **Exc:** $275 **VGood:** $250

Satin nickel finish

Perf: $300 **Exc:** $275 **VGood:** $250

TAURUS MODEL 74 SPORT

Revolver; double action; 32 S&W Long; 6-shot; 3-inch barrel; 8-1/4-inch overall length; adjustable rear sight, ramp front; hand-checkered walnut stocks; blued finish. Introduced 1971; discontinued 1978.

Exc: $300 **VGood:** $275 **Good:** $250

Nickel finish

Exc: $300 **VGood:** $275 **Good:** $250

TAURUS MODEL 76

Revolver; double action; 32 H&R Mag.; 6-shot; 6-inch heavy barrel with solid rib; weighs 34 oz.; Patridge-type front sight, fully-adjustable micro-click rear; checkered Brazilian hardwood grips; adjustable trigger; target hammer; blued finish. Introduced 1991; dropped 1994.

New: $300 **Perf:** $275 **Exc:** $250

TAURUS MODEL 80

Revolver; double action; 38 Spl.; 6-shot; 3-inch, 4-inch barrel; 9-1/4-inch overall length; weighs 30 oz.; fixed sights; hand-checkered Brazilian hardwood stocks; blue, satin nickel or stainless steel finish. Introduced 1971; discontinued 1996.

New: $275 **Perf:** $190 **Exc:** $150

Satin nickel finish

New: $250 **Perf:** $190 **Exc:** $150

Stainless steel

New: $275 **Perf:** $225 **Exc:** $200

TAURUS MODEL 82

Revolver; double action; 38 Spl.; 6-shot; 3-inch, 4-inch heavy barrel; 9-1/4-inch overall length; weighs 34 oz.; fixed sights; checkered Brazilian hardwood grips; blue, satin nickel or stainless steel finish. Introduced 1971; still in production.

New: $250 **Perf:** $200 **Exc:** $175

Satin nickel finish

New: $265 **Perf:** $190 **Exc:** $175

Stainless steel

New: $275 **Perf:** $225 **Exc:** $200

TAURUS MODEL 83

Revolver; double action; 38 Spl.; 6-shot; 4-inch heavy barrel; 9-1/2-inch overall length; weighs 34 oz.; adjustable rear sight, ramp front; hand-checkered oversize Brazilian hardwood grips; blue or stainless steel finish. Introduced 1977; discontinued 1983.

New: $225 **Perf:** $180 **Exc:** $150

Stainless steel

New: $250 **Perf:** $200 **Exc:** $175

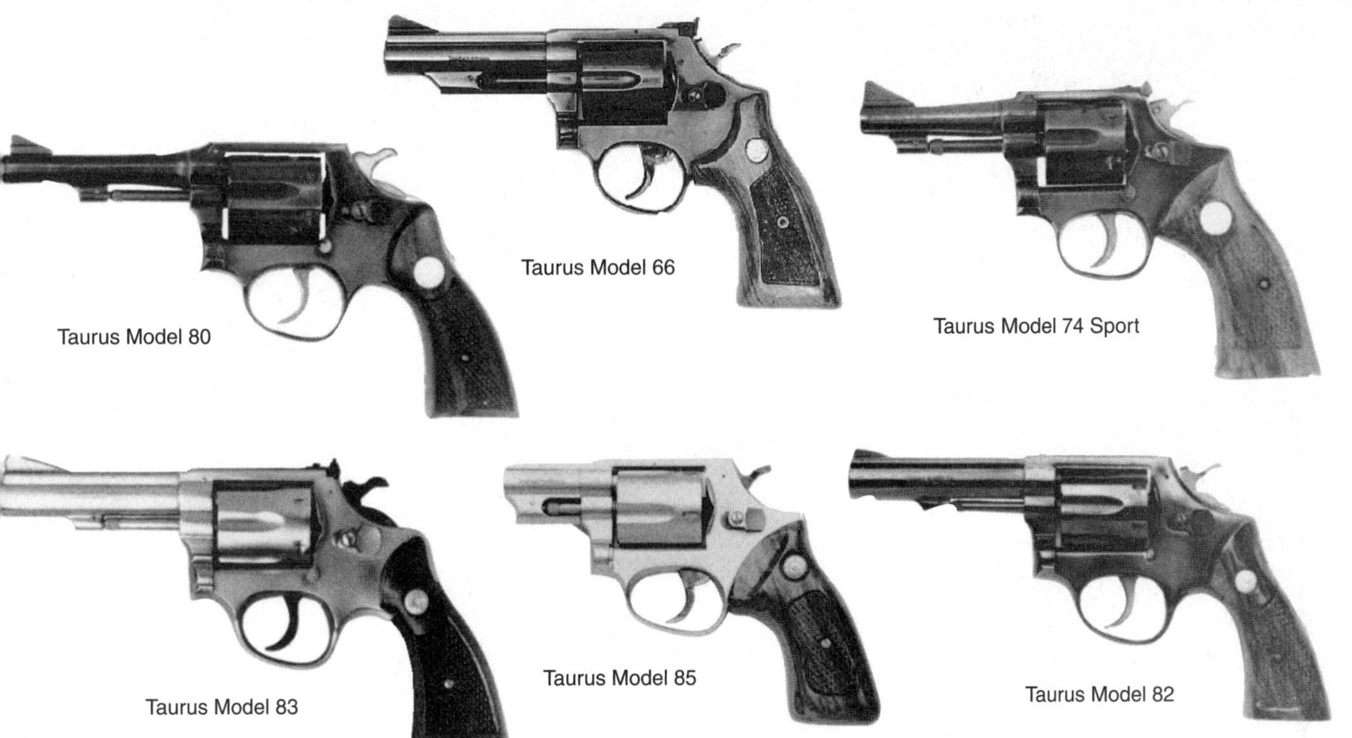
Taurus Model 80

Taurus Model 66

Taurus Model 74 Sport

Taurus Model 83

Taurus Model 85

Taurus Model 82

TAURUS MODEL 84

Revolver; double action; 38 Spl.; 6-shot; 4-inch barrel; 9-1/2-inch overall length; adjustable rear sight, ramp front; checkered wood grips; blued finish. Introduced 1971; discontinued 1978.

Exc: $200 **VGood:** $180 **Good:** $150

TAURUS MODEL 85

Revolver; double action; 38 Spl.; 5-shot; 2-inch, 3-inch barrel; weighs 21 oz.; ramp front sight, square-notch rear; checkered Brazilian hardwood grips; blued, satin nickel or stainless finish. Introduced 1980; still imported.

New: $375 **Perf:** $325 **Exc:** $275

Satin nickel finish

New: $390 **Perf:** $325 **Exc:** $300

Stainless steel

New: $335 **Perf:** $300 **Exc:** $245

TAURUS MODEL 85CH

Same specs as Model 85 except 2-inch barrel; weighs 21 oz.; smooth Brazilian hardwood grips; concealed hammer. Introduced 1992; discontinued 2004.

Blue

New: $315 **Perf:** $285 **Exc:** $225

Stainless Steel

New: $325 **Perf:** $295 **Exc:** $235

TAURUS MODEL 85 HY-LITE MAGNESIUM

Similar to Model 85 but weighs only 13.8 oz. Gray alloy frame. Introduced 2007.

New: $450 **Perf:** $350 **Exc:** $295

MODEL 850 CIA

Similar to Model 85 but with lightweight alloy frame. Chamberd for .38 Special +P or .357. Concealed hammer. Introduced 2007.

New: $375 **Perf:** $300 **Exc:** $265

TAURUS MODEL 86 TARGET MASTER

Revolver; double action; 38 Spl.; 6-shot cylinder; 6-inch barrel; 11-1/4-inch overall length; weighs 34 oz.; oversize target-type grips of checkered Brazilian hardwood; Patridge front sight, micro-click fully-adjustable rear; blue finish with non-reflective finish on barrel. Imported from Brazil by Taurus International. Dropped 1994.

Perf: $275 **Exc:** $225 **VGood:** $200

TAURUS MODEL 94

Revolver; double action; 22 LR; 9-shot; 3-inch, 4-inch barrel; weighs 25 oz.; serrated ramp front sight, click-adjustable rear; checkered Brazilian hardwood stocks; color case-hardened hammer, trigger; floating firing pin; blued or stainless finish. Introduced 1988; still imported.

New: $300 **Perf:** $270 **Exc:** $200

Stainless steel

New: $350 **Perf:** $300 **Exc:** $250

TAURUS MODEL 94 UL

Revolver, double action; 22 LR, 9-shot cylinder. Barrel: 2-inch, 4-inch, 5-inch. Weight: 25 oz. Stocks: Soft black rubber. Sights: Serrated ramp front, click-adjustable rear for windage and elevation. Floating firing pin, color case-hardened hammer and trigger. Introduced 1989. Imported by Taurus International.

New: $300 **Perf:** $275 **Exc:** $200

Stainless finish

New: $350 **Perf:** $300 **Exc:** $250

TAURUS MODEL 96 SCOUT MASTER

Revolver; double action; 22 LR; 6-shot; 6-inch barrel; weighs 34 oz.; heavy solid barrel rib; adjustable target trigger; Patridge type front, micrometer click-adjustable rear; checkered Brazilian hardwood grips; blued finish. Introduced 1971; discontinued 1988.

New: $300 **Perf:** $250 **Exc:** $200

TAURUS MODEL 431

Revolver; double action; 44 Spl.; 5-shot; 3-inch, 4-inch, 6-inch barrel; weighs 40-1/2 oz. (6-inch barrel); checkered Brazilian hardwood grips; serrated ramp front sight, fixed rear; heavy barrel with solid rib and full-length ejector shroud; blue or stainless finish. Imported by Taurus International. Introduced 1993; discontinued 1997.

Blue finish

New: $395 **Perf:** $355 **Exc:** $300

Stainless steel

New: $425 **Perf:** $395 **Exc:** $345

TAURUS MODEL 441

Revolver; double action; 44 Spl.; 5-shot cylinder; 3-inch, 4-inch, 6-inch barrel; weighs 40-1/2 oz. (6-inch barrel); checkered Brazilian hardwood grips; serrated ramp front sight, micrometer click fully-adjustable rear; heavy barrel with solid rib and full-length ejector shroud; blue or stainless finish. Imported by Taurus International. Introduced 1993; discontinued 1997.

Blue finish

New: $395 **Perf:** $355 **Exc:** $300

Stainless steel

New: $425 **Perf:** $395 **Exc:** $345

TAURUS MODEL 445, 445CH

Revolver; double action; 44 Special, 5-shot. Barrel: 2-inch. Weight: 28.25 oz. Length: 6-3/4-inch overall. Stocks: Soft black rubber. Sights: Serrated ramp front, notch rear. Features: Blue or stainless steel. Standard or concealed hammer. Introduced 1997; discontinued 2003.

Blue finish

New: $395 **Perf:** $355 **Exc:** $300

Stainless steel

New: $425 **Perf:** $395 **Exc:** $345

TAURUS MODEL RAGING BULL

Revolver; double action; 454 Casull or 480 Ruger, 5-shot. Barrel: 5-inch, 6-1/2-inch, 8-3/8-inch. Weight: 53 oz. (6-1/2-inch barrel). Length: 12-inch overall (6-1/2-inch barrel). Stocks: Soft black rubber. Sights: Patridge front, micrometer click adjustable rear. Features: Ventilated rib; integral compensating system. Introduced 1997. Imported by Taurus International.

Blue finish

New: $650 **Perf:** $550 **Exc:** $450

Stainless steel

New: $725 **Perf:** $650 **Exc:** $550

TAURUS RAGING BULL 500 S&W

Similar to Raging Bull 454 Casull stainless version but chambered in 500 S&W.

New: $725 **Perf:** $650 **Exc:** $550

TAURUS MODEL 605

Revolver; double action; 357 Mag.; 5-shot; 2-1/4-inch barrel; weighs 24-1/2 oz.; finger-groove Santoprene I grips; serrated ramp front sight, fixed notch rear; heavy, solid rib barrel; floating firing pin; blue or stainless finish. Imported by Taurus International. Introduced 1995; still imported.

Blue finish

New: $300 **Perf:** $250 **Exc:** $200

Taurus Model 689

Taurus Model 741

Taurus Model 669

Taurus Model PT 58

Taurus Model 827

Taurus Model 941

Taurus Gaucho S/A-45-B12

Stainless steel

New: $325 **Perf:** $275 **Exc:** $250

TAURUS MODEL 607

Revolver; double action; 357 Mag.; 7-shot; 4-inch, 6-1/2-inch barrel; weighs 44 oz.; Santoprene I grips with finger grooves; serrated ramp front sight, fully-adjustable rear; ventilated rib with built-in compensator (6-1/2-inch barrel). Imported by Taurus International. Introduced 1995; discontinued 1997.

Blue finish, 4-inch barrel

New: $350 **Perf:** $300 **Exc:** $250

Blue finish, 6-1/2-inch barrel

New: $350 **Perf:** $300 **Exc:** $250

Stainless steel, 4-inch barrel

New: $400 **Perf:** $350 **Exc:** $300

Stainless steel, 6-1/2-inch barrel

New: $425 **Perf:** $375 **Exc:** $325

TAURUS MODEL 608

Revolver; double action; 357 Mag., 8-shot. Barrel: 4-inch, 6-1/2-inch, 8-3/8. Weight: 44 oz. Length: NA. Stocks: Soft black rubber. Sights: Serrated ramp front, fully adjustable rear. Features: Ventilated rib with built-in compensator on 6-1/2-inch barrel. Available in blue or stainless. Introduced 1996; discontinued 2004.

Blue finish, 4-inch

New: $375 **Perf:** $300 **Exc:** $250

Stainless steel, 4-inch

New: $425 **Perf:** $350 **Exc:** $275

Blue finish, 6-1/2-inch, 8-3/8-inch

New: $400 **Perf:** $325 **Exc:** $275

Stainless steel, 6-1/2-inch, 8-3/8-inch

New: $450 **Perf:** $375 **Exc:** $300

TAURUS MODEL 617, 606CH

Revolver; double action; 357 Magnum, 7-shot. Barrel: 2-inch. Weight: 29 oz. Length: 6-3/4-inch overall. Stocks: Soft black rubber. Sights: Serrated ramp front, notch rear. Features: Heavy, solid barrel rib, ejector shroud. Available with porting, concealed hammer. Introduced 1998. Imported by Taurus International.

Blue finish

New: $350 **Perf:** $300 **Exc:** $250

Stainless steel

New: $390 **Perf:** $325 **Exc:** $275

TAURUS MODEL 669

Revolver; double action; 357 Mag.; 6-shot; 4-inch, 6-inch barrel; weighs 37 oz. (4-inch barrel); serrated ramp front sight, click-adjustable rear; checkered target-type Brazilian hardwood stocks; floating firing pin; full-length barrel shroud; target-type trigger; blued finish. Introduced 1988; discontinued 1998.

Blue

New: $250 **Perf:** $200 **Exc:** $175

Stainless steel

New: $350 **Perf:** $300 **Exc:** $250

With compensated barrel, blue

New: $275 **Perf:** $225 **Exc:** $200

With compensated barrel, stainless

New: $375 **Perf:** $325 **Exc:** $275

TAURUS MODEL 689

Revolver; double action; 357 Mag.; 6-shot cylinder; 4-inch, 6-inch barrel; weighs 37 oz. (4-inch barrel); checkered Brazilian walnut grips; serrated ramp front sight, fully-adjustable rear; wide target-type hammer; floating firing pin; full-length barrel shroud; full-length ventilated barrel rib. Introduced 1988; discontinued 1998.

Blue finish

New: $275 **Perf:** $225 **Exc:** $175

Stainless steel

New: $325 **Perf:** $275 **Exc:** $200

TAURUS MODEL 709 G2 SLIM

Caliber: 9mm double/single action pistol with 9+1-shot magazine. Barrel: 3 inches. Weight: 19 oz. Length: 6.24 inches overall. Polymer frame with black finish. Grips: Black. Low profile fixed sights.

Perf: $435 **Exc:** $385 **VGood:** $325

TAURUS MODEL 740 G2 SLIM

Caliber: 40 S&W caliber, double/single action operation, 6+1 and 8+1-shot magazines. Barrel: 4 inches. Weight: 19 oz. Length: 6.24 inches overall. Polymer frame.

Perf: $435 **Exc:** $385 **VGood:** $325

TAURUS MODEL 741

Revolver; double action; 32 H&R Mag.; 6-shot cylinder; 3-inch, 4-inch heavy barrel; weighs 32 oz. (4-inch barrel); checkered Brazilian hardwood grips; serrated ramp; target hammer; adjustable trigger. Imported by Taurus International. Introduced 1991; dropped 1995.

Blue finish

Perf: $350 **Exc:** $300 **VGood:** $250

Stainless steel

Perf: $375 **Exc:** $340 **VGood:** $300

TAURUS MODEL 761

Revolver; double action; 32 H&R Magnum; 6-shot cylinder; 6-inch heavy barrel with solid rib; weighs 34 oz.; checkered Brazilian hardwood grips; Patridge-type front sight, micro-click fully-adjustable rear; target hammer, adjustable target trigger; blue only. Imported by Taurus International. Introduced 1991; dropped 1995.

Perf: $350 **Exc:** $300 **VGood:** $250

TAURUS MODEL 809 COMPACT

Caliber: 9mm, 357 SIG or 40 S&W. 12+1 round capacity. Barrel: 3 inches. Polymer frame. Compact version of 809 series.

Perf: $500 **Exc:** $425 **VGood:** $360

TAURUS MODEL 827

Revolver; double action; 38 Special, 7-shot. Barrel: 4-inch. Weight: 36 oz. Length: NA. Stocks: Finger-groove Santoprene. Sights: Serrated ramp front, notch rear. Features: Solid rib; shrouded ejector rod. Introduced 1998.

Blue finish

New: $250 **Perf:** $200 **Exc:** $175

Stainless steel

New: $300 **Perf:** $250 **Exc:** $200

TAURUS MODEL 941

Revolver; double action; 22 WMR; 8-shot; 3-inch, 4-inch barrel; weighs 27-1/2 oz. (4-inch barrel); checkered Brazilian hardwood grips; serrated ramp front sight, fully-adjustable rear; solid rib heavy barrel with full-length ejector rod shroud. Imported by Taurus International. Introduced 1992; still imported.

Blue finish

New: $350 **Perf:** $300 **Exc:** $250

Stainless steel

New: $375 **Perf:** $300 **Exc:** $275

Taurus Judge
Taurus Model 740 G2 Slim
Taurus Model 709 G2 Slim
Taurus Model PT 22
Taurus Model PT 92AF
Taurus Gaucho S/A-357-B
Taurus Tracker 10mm 10TSS4

TAURUS TRACKER 10MM 10TSS4

Matte stainless 10mm single/double action revolver with 4-inch barrel and fixed sights. 5-shot, 34.8 oz, rubber grip.

New: $495 **Exc:** $450 **VGood:** $395

TAURUS TRACKER 10SS8

10mm 6-shot matte stainless with either 6.5-inch (54.5 oz.) or 8.375-inch (59.5 oz.) barrel. Fixed sights and rubber grips.

New: $500 **Exc:** $460 **VGood:** $400

TAURUS TRACKER .45

Similar to other Tracker models but chambered in .45 ACP (via full-moon clips) with 5-shot cylinder. Four-inch ported barrel .

New: $500 **Exc:** $460 **VGood:** $400

TAURUS MODEL 917

Lightweight, compact version of Model 92 chambered in 9mm Parabellum. Matte blue or stainless finish, 19+1 capacity.

New: $400 **Exc:** $365 **VGood:** $295

TAURUS JUDGE

Stainless steel- or lightweight alloy-frame version of Tracker Model 4410. Chambered in 3" .410/.45 Colt (4510TKR-3MAG) or 2.5" .410/.45 Colt (4510TKR-3UL) with 3" (3" Magnum) or 2.5" barrel (2.5").

New: $475 **Exc:** $415 **VGood:** $350

TAURUS TRACKER .45

Similar to other Tracker models but chambered in .45 ACP (via full-moon clips) with 5-shot cylinder. Four-inch barrel with Picatinny rail. Stainless steel frame and cylinder.

New: $495 **Exc:** $450 **VGood:** $395

TAURUS TRACKER 4410 10TKR2SS

Shoots 2.5-inch .410 bore shells or .45 Colt. Holds 5 shots. Stainless or blued, 2.25-inch or 6.5-inch barrel, rubber grip. Single/double action, 32 oz., 9.1-inch LOA. Later version had 3-inch chamber.

New: $450 **Exc:** $400 **VGood:** $315

TAURUS GAUCHO S/A-357-B, S/SM, S/S, CHSA

Single action 6-shot chambered for .357/.38 caliber. Barrel lengths 4.75-inch (36.2 oz.), 5.5-inch (36.7 oz.), 7.5-inch (37.7 oz.). Fixed sights. Blued, matte stainless, polished stainless or blued/case hardened receiver.

New: $415 **Exc:** $325 **VGood:** $295

TAURUS GAUCHO S/A-44-40B, S/SM, S/S, CHSA

Single action 6-shot chambered for .44-40 caliber. Barrel lengths 4.75-inch (36.2 oz.), 5.5-inch (36.7 oz.), 7.5-inch (37.7 oz.). Fixed sights. Blued, matte stainless, polished stainless or blued/case hardened receiver.

New: $415 **Exc:** $325 **VGood:** $295

TAURUS GAUCHO S/A-45-B12, S/SM12, S/S12, CHSA12

Single action Buntline-style 6-shot revolver chambered for .45 Colt. Barrel length 12-inch (41.5 oz.). Fixed sights. Blued, matte stainless, polished stainless or blued/case hardened receiver.

New: $415 **Exc:** $325 **VGood:** $295

TAURUS MODEL PT 22

Semi-automatic; double action; 22 LR; 9-shot magazine; 2-3/4-inch barrel; 5-1/4-inch overall length; weighs 12-1/2 oz.; smooth Brazilian hardwood grips; blade front sight, fixed rear; tip-up barrel for loading, cleaning. Made in U.S. by Taurus International. Introduced 1992; still produced.

Blue finish

New: $165 **Perf:** $135 **Exc:** $110

Stainless steel

New: $175 **Perf:** $150 **Exc:** $135

TAURUS MODEL PT 25

Semi-automatic; double action; 25 ACP; 8-shot magazine; 2-3/4-inch barrel; 5-1/4-inch overall length; weighs 12-1/2 oz.; smooth Brazilian hardwood grips; blade front sight, fixed rear; tip-up barrel for loading, cleaning. Made in U.S. by Taurus International. Introduced 1992; still produced.

Blue finish

New: $150 **Perf:** $125 **Exc:** $110

Stainless steel

New: $175 **Perf:** $150 **Exc:** $135

TAURUS MODEL PT 58

Semi-automatic; double action; 380 ACP; 12-, 10-shot; 4-inch barrel; weighs 30 oz.; integral blade front sight, notch rear with three-dot system; Brazilian hardwood stocks; exposed hammer; inertia firing pin; blued finish. Introduced 1988; discontinued 1996.

New: $325 **Perf:** $300 **Exc:** $250

Stainless steel

New: $400 **Perf:** $350 **Exc:** $300

TAURUS MODEL PT 91AF

Semi-automatic; double action; 41 AE; 10-shot; 5-inch barrel; weighs 34 oz.; fixed sights; smooth wood grips; exposed hammer; blued finish. Introduced 1990; discontinued 1991.

Perf: $350 **Exc:** $300 **VGood:** $250

Satin nickel finish

Perf: $375 **Exc:** $325 **VGood:** $275

TAURUS MODEL PT 92AF

Semi-automatic; double action; 9mm Para.; 15-, 10-shot; 5-inch barrel; 8-1/2-inch overall length; weighs 34 oz.; fixed sights; black plastic stocks; exposed hammer; chamber loaded indicator; inertia firing pin; blued, nickel or stainless finish. Introduced 1983; discontinued 2004.

Blue, nickel finish

New: $450 **Perf:** $375 **Exc:** $325

Stainless steel (PT 92SS)

New: $475 **Perf:** $425 **Exc:** $375

TAURUS MODEL PT 92AFC

Same specs as PT 92AF except 4-inch barrel; 13-, 10-shot; 7-1/2-inch overall length; weighs 31 oz. Introduced 1991; discontinued 1996.

New: $350 **Perf:** $325 **Exc:** $275

Stainless steel

New: $400 **Perf:** $350 **Exc:** $300

TAURUS MODEL PT 99AF

Semi-automatic; double action; 9mm Para.; 15-, 10-shot; 5-inch barrel; 8-1/2-inch overall length; adjustable sights; uncheckered Brazilian walnut stocks; exposed hammer; chamber-loaded

Taurus Model PT 101

Texas Longhorn Grover's Improved No. 5

Texas Longhorn Jezebel

Taurus Model PT-911

Texas Longhorn Texas Border Special

indicator; inertia firing pin; blue, satin nickel or stainless steel finish. Introduced 1983; still in production.

Blue

New: $500 **Perf:** $400 **Exc:** $325

Stainless steel

New: $525 **Perf:** $425 **Exc:** $350

TAURUS MODEL PT 100

Semi-automatic; double action; 40 S&W; 11-, 10-shot; 5-inch barrel; weighs 34 oz.; fixed sights; three-dot combat system; uncheckered Brazilian hardwood grips; ambidextrous hammer-drop safety; exposed hammer; chamber-loaded indicator; inertia firing pin; blue or stainless steel finish. Introduced 1991; still imported.

Blue

New: $450 **Perf:** $400 **Exc:** $325

Stainless steel

New: $475 **Perf:** $425 **Exc:** $375

TAURUS MODEL PT 101

Semi-automatic; double action; 40 S&W; 11-, 10-shot; 5-inch barrel; 34 oz.; adjustable sights; uncheckered Brazilian hardwood grips; ambidextrous hammer-drop safety; exposed hammer; chamber-loaded indicator; inertia firing pin; blue or stainless steel finish. Introduced 1992; still imported.

Blue

New: $450 **Perf:** $375 **Exc:** $300

Stainless steel

New: $475 **Perf:** $425 **Exc:** $375

TAURUS MODEL PT-111 MILLENNIUM

Semi-automatic; double action only; 9mm Para., 10-shot magazine. Barrel: 3.30-inch. Weight: 19 oz. Length: 6 inches overall. Stocks: Polymer. Sights: Fixed. Low profile, three-dot combat. Features: Double action only. Firing pin lock; polymer frame; striker fired; push-button magazine release. Introduced 1998; discontinued 2004.

Blue finish

New: $275 **Perf:** $225 **Exc:** $185

Stainless steel

New: $300 **Perf:** $250 **Exc:** $200

TAURUS MODEL PT 908

Semi-automatic; double action; 9mm Para.; 8-shot magazine; 3-13/16-inch barrel; 7-inch overall length; weighs 30 oz.; checkered black composition grips; drift-adjustable front and rear sights, three-dot combat; exposed hammer; manual ambidextrous hammer-drop; inertia firing pin; chamber loaded indicator; blue or stainless steel finish. Imported by Taurus International. Introduced 1993; discontinued 1997.

Blue

New: $325 **Perf:** $300 **Exc:** $250

Stainless steel

New: $375 **Perf:** $350 **Exc:** $300

TAURUS MODEL PT-911

Semi-automatic; double action; 9mm Para., 10-shot magazine. Barrel: 3.85-inch. Weight: 28.2 oz. Length: 7.05-inch overall. Stocks: Black rubber. Sights: Fixed. Low profile, three-dot combat. Features: Double action, exposed hammer; ambidextrous hammer drop; chamber loaded indicator. Introduced 1997. Imported by Taurus International.

Blue finish

New: $375 **Perf:** $325 **Exc:** $275

Stainless steel

New: $400 **Perf:** $350 **Exc:** $325

TAURUS MODEL PT-938

Semi-automatic; double action only; 380 ACP, 10-shot magazine. Barrel: 3.72-inch. Weight: 27 oz. Length: 6.75-inch overall. Stocks: Black rubber. Sights: Fixed. Low profile, three-dot combat. Features: Double action only. Chamber loaded indicator; firing pin block; ambidextrous hammer drop. Introduced 1997; discontinued 2005.

Blue finish

New: $350 **Perf:** $300 **Exc:** $225

Stainless steel

New: $375 **Perf:** $325 **Exc:** $250

TAURUS 800 SERIES

Double-action semi-auto chambered in 9mm Parabellum (17+1), .40 S&W (15+1) and .45 ACP (12+1). Four-inch barrel; blued or stainless frame slide on polymer frame with integral grips. External hammer with "Strike Two" (trigger reset) feature. Model 809-B is a civilian version of the 24/7OSS. Introduced 2007.

New: $575 **Perf:** $495 **Exc:** $350

TAURUS MODEL PT-940

Semi-automatic; double action; 40 S&W, 10-shot magazine. Barrel: 3.35-inch. Weight: 28.2 oz. Length: 7.05-inch overall. Stocks: Black rubber. Sights: Drift-adjustable front and rear; three-dot combat. Features: Double action, exposed hammer; manual ambidextrous hammer-drop; inertia firing pin; chamber loaded indicator. Introduced 1996. Imported by Taurus International.

Blue finish

New: $475 **Perf:** $400 **Exc:** $325

Stainless steel

New: $500 **Perf:** $425 **Exc:** $350

TAURUS MODEL PT-945

Semi-automatic; double action; 45 ACP, 8-shot magazine. Barrel: 4.25. Weight: 29.5 oz. Length: 7.48 overall. Stocks: Black rubber. Sights: Drift-adjustable front and rear; three-dot system. Features: Double-action, manual ambidextrous hammer drop safety, intercept notch, firing pin block, chamber loaded indicator, last-shot hold-open. Introduced 1995. Imported by Taurus International.

Blue finish

New: $525 **Perf:** $450 **Exc:** $350

Stainless steel

New: $540 **Perf:** $450 **Exc:** $350

Blue finish, ported

New: $450 **Perf:** $375 **Exc:** $325

Stainless steel

New: $475 **Perf:** $425 **Exc:** $375

TAURUS PT24/7LS-9SS-17

Full-size stainless semi-auto chambered for 9mm. Long grip, long slide. Capacity 17+1. Single/double action. 5-inch barrel, 27.2 oz. Fixed, 2-dot rear sight. Also in short grip 10+1 capacity. Introduced 2006.

New: $455 **Exc:** $395 **VGood:** $325

TAURUS PT24/79SSC-17

Compact stainless semi-auto chambered for 9mm, short grip, short slide. Capacity 15+1. Single/double action. 5-inch barrel, 27.2 oz. Fixed, 2-dot rear sight. Also in short grip 10+1 capacity.

New: $455 **Exc:** $395 **VGood:** $325

Taurus Model PT 908

Taurus Model PT-940

Taurus Model PT 945

Taurus Model PT-938

Taurus 24/7OSS

Taurus Model PT24/7PLS-9SSPTI-17

TAURUS PT24/7PLS-9SSPTI-17

Full-size semi-auto chambered for 9mm. Capacity 17+1 or 10+1. Single/double action. Titanium slide, 4-inch barrel, 27.2 oz.

New: $515 **Exc:** $465 **VGood:** $395

TAURUS PT24/7PLS-9SSCTI-17

Compact semi-auto chambered for 9mm. Capacity 17+1. Single/double action. Titanium slide, 3.3-inch barrel, 25.4 oz.

New: $515 **Exc:** $465 **VGood:** $395

TAURUS PT1911B

Blued or stainless 1911-style single action in .45 ACP. 8+1 capacity. LOA 8.5-inch, 32 oz., 5-inch barrel, fixed Heinie two-dot straight-eight sight. Numerous options. Add 10 percent for stainless. Introduced 2005.

New: $600 **Exc:** $525 **VGood:** $425

TAURUS PT-745GB

Blued semi-auto in .45 GAP with 7+1 capacity. 3.25-inch barrel, fixed sights, 22 oz., polymer grip plates.

New: $455 **Exc:**400 **VGood:** $335

TAURUS PT745B/SS-LS

Blued or stainless semi-auto in .45 ACP. 4.25-inch barrel, 23.3 oz. 7+1 capacity, polymer grip plates.

New: $455 **Exc:** $400 **VGood:** $335

TAURUS PT917 B20

9mm blued or stainless semi-auto with 20+1 capacity. Fixed sights, 4-inch barrel, 31.8 oz.

New: $510 **Exc:** $465 **VGood:** $355

TAURUS PT609TI-13

This 9mm semi-auto has a titanium finish plus 13+1 capacity, 3.25-inch barrel. Fixed sights, 19.2 oz.

New: $525 **Exc:** $460 **VGood:** $375

TAURUS PT59B/SS-15

Blued or stainless semi-auto in .380 ACP with 15+1 capacity. Fixed sights, 5-inch barrel, 32.8 oz.

New: $525 **Exc:** $460 **VGood:** $375

TAURUS 24/7OSS

Available in .45 ACP, .40 S&W and 9mm Parabellum. 12+ 1 capacity (.45), single-/double-action. Ambidextrous decock and safety, match grade barrel, polymer frame with steel upper. Claimed to exceed all requirements set by United States Special

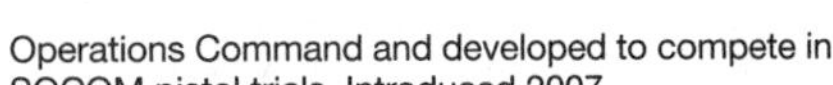

Operations Command and developed to compete in SOCOM pistol trials. Introduced 2007.

New: $595 **Exc:** $515 **VGood:** $395

TEXAS ARMORY DEFENDER

Derringer; 9mm Para., 357 Mag., 44 Mag., 45 ACP, 45 Colt/410; 2-shot; 3-inch barrel; 5-inch overall length; weighs 21 oz.; smooth wood grips; blade front sight, fixed rear; interchangeable barrels; retracting firing pins; rebounding hammer; cross-bolt safety; removable trigger guard; automatic extractor; blasted stainless steel finish. Made in U.S. by Texas Armory. Introduced 1993.

New: $250 **Perf:** $200 **Exc:** $175

TEXAS LONGHORN GROVER'S IMPROVED NO. 5

Revolver; single action; 44 Mag., 45 Colt; 6-shot; 5-1/2-inch barrel; weighs 44 oz.; square blade ramped front sight, fully-adjustable rear; fancy walnut stocks; double locking bolt; music wire coil springs; Elmer Keith design; polished blue finish. Introduced 1988; only 1200 made.

New: $1500 **Perf:** $1150 **Exc:** $850

TEXAS LONGHORN JEZEBEL

Single shot; top-break action; 22 LR, 22 WMR; 6-inch half-round, half-octagon; barrel; 8-inch overall length; weighs 15 oz.; automatic hammer-block safety; fixed rear sight, bead front; one-piece walnut grip; all stainless steel construction. Introduced 1986; discontinued 1992.

New: $500 **Perf:** $175 **Exc:** $135

TEXAS LONGHORN SOUTH TEXAS ARMY

Revolver; single action; 357 Mag., 44 Spl., 45 Colt; 4-3/4-inch barrel; blade front sight, grooved topstrap rear; one-piece fancy walnut grips; loading gate and ejector on left side of gun; cylinder rotates to left; all steel; color case-hardened frame; music wire coil springs; high-polish blue finish. Only 1000 made. Introduced 1984; no longer made.

New: $1250 **Perf:** $1000 **Exc:** $850

TEXAS LONGHORN TEXAS BORDER SPECIAL

Revolver; single action; 44 Spl., 45 Colt; 3-1/2-inch, 4-inch barrel; grooved topstrap rear sight, blade front; one-piece fancy walnut bird's-head-style stocks; loading gate, ejector housing on left side; cylinder rotates to left; color case-hardened frame; music wire coil springs; high-polish blue finish. Introduced 1984; 1000 made.

New: $1250 **Perf:** $1000 **Exc:** $850

TEXAS LONGHORN WEST TEXAS FLATTOP TARGET

Revolver; single action; 32-20, 357 Mag., 44 Spl./44 Mag., 45 Colt; 7-1/2-inch barrel; standard rear sight, contoured ramp front; one-piece walnut stock; flat-top style frame; polished blue finish. Introduced 1984; 1000 made.

New: $1250 **Perf:** $1000 **Exc:** $850

THOMAS 45

Semi-automatic; double action; 45 ACP; 6-shot magazine; 3-1/2-inch barrel; 6-1/2-inch overall length; checkered plastic stocks; windage-adjustable rear sight, blade front; blued finish; matte sighting surface; blowback action. Introduced 1977; dropped 1978. Only about 600 ever made. Collector value.

Exc: $750 **VGood:** $450 **Good:** $375

THOMPSON/CENTER CONTENDER

Single shot; break-open action; chambered for 29 calibers; 8-3/4-inch, 10-inch, 14-inch round, heavy, octagon barrel; adjustable sights; checkered walnut grip, forearm; interchangeable barrels; detachable choke for shot cartridges; blued finish. Introduced 1967; discontinued 2000.

New: $550 **Perf:** $395 **Exc:** $325

THOMPSON/CENTER CONTENDER BULL BARREL ARMOUR ALLOY II

Same specs as Contender except chambered for 7 calibers; 10-inch round barrel; extra-hard satin finish. Introduced 1986; discontinued 1989.

Perf: $500 **Exc:** $350 **VGood:** $300

THOMPSON/CENTER CONTENDER STAINLESS

Same specs as Contender except stainless steel construction with blued sights; black Rynite forend; ambidextrous finger-groove grip with built-in rubber recoil cushion with sealed-in air pocket; receiver with different cougar etching; 10-inch bull barrel in 22 LR, 22 LR Match, 22 Hornet,

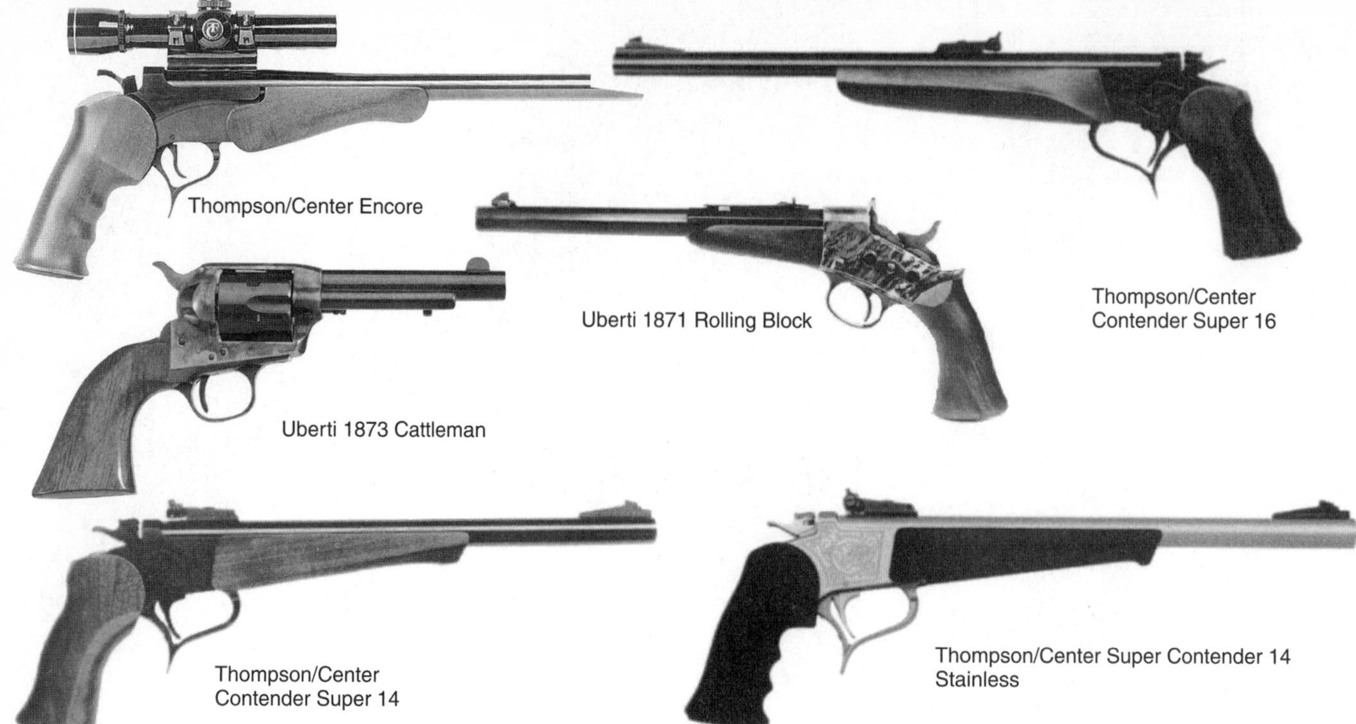
Thompson/Center Encore

Uberti 1871 Rolling Block

Thompson/Center Contender Super 16

Uberti 1873 Cattleman

Thompson/Center Contender Super 14

Thompson/Center Super Contender 14 Stainless

223 Rem., 30-30 Win., 357 Mag., 44 Mag., 45 Colt/410. Made in U.S. by Thompson/Center. Introduced 1993.

New: $500 **Perf:** $350 **Exc:** $300

THOMPSON/CENTER CONTENDER VENT RIB BARREL

Same specs as Contender except 357 Mag., 44 Mag., 45 Colt/410; 10-inch vent rib barrel.

Perf: $465 **Exc:** $350 **VGood:** $325

THOMPSON/CENTER CONTENDER VENT RIB BARREL ARMOUR ALLOY II

Same specs as Contender except 45 Colt/410 only; 10-inch vent rib barrel; extra hard satin finish. Introduced 1986; dropped 1997.

Perf: $465 **Exc:** $350 **VGood:** $325

THOMPSON/CENTER CONTENDER HUNTER

Single shot; break-open action; chambered for 8 calibers; 12-inch, 14-inch, barrel with muzzlebrake; 2-1/2x scope with illuminated reticle; walnut grips with rubber insert; interchangeable barrels; sling with studs and swivels; carrying case; blued finish. Introduced 1990; still in production.

New: $650 **Perf:** $575 **Exc:** $525

THOMPSON/CENTER ENCORE

Single shot, break-open action; 22-250, 223, 260 Rem., 7mmBR, 7mm-08, 243, 7.62x39, 308, 270, 30-06, 44 Mag., 444 Marlin single shot. Barrel: 10-inch, 15-inch, tapered round. Weight: NA. Length: 19-inch overall with 10-inch barrel. Stocks: American walnut with finger grooves, walnut forend. Sights: Blade on ramp front, adjustable rear, or none. Features: Interchangeable barrels; action opens by squeezing the trigger guard; drilled and tapped for scope mounting; blue finish. Announced 1996.

New: $575 **Perf:** $400 **Exc:** $325

THOMPSON/CENTER SUPER CONTENDER SUPER 14, SUPER 16

Single shot; break-open action; chambered for 13 calibers; 14-inch, 16-1/4-inch bull barrel; adjustable sights; walnut grips; beavertail forearm; interchangeable barrels; detachable choke for shot cartridges; blued finish. Introduced 1978;.

New: $550 **Perf:** $400 **Exc:** $335

45 Colt/410

New: $565 **Perf:** $415 **Exc:** $350

THOMPSON/CENTER SUPER CONTENDER ARMOUR ALLOY II

Same specs as Super Contender except chambered for only 5 calibers; extra-hard satin finish. Introduced 1986; discontinued 1989.

New: $565 **Perf:** $415 **Exc:** $350

THOMPSON/CENTER CONTENDER SUPER 14, SUPER 16 STAINLESS

Same specs as the standard Super Contender except stainless steel construction; blued sights; black Rynite forend and finger-groove; ambidextrous grip with built-in rubber recoil cushion with sealed-in air pocket; different cougar etching on receiver. Introduced 1993.

With bull barrel

New: $565 **Perf:** $415 **Exc:** $350

45 Colt/410, 14-inch barrel

New: $565 **Perf:** $415 **Exc:** $350

THOMPSON/CENTER SUPER CONTENDER VENT RIB BARREL

Same specs as Super Contender except 45 Colt/410 only; 14-inch, 16-1/4-inch vent rib barrel.

New: $565 **Perf:** $415 **Exc:** $350

THUNDER FIVE

Revolver; double action; 45 Colt/410 shotshell, 2-inch, 3-inch; 5-shot cylinder; 2-inch barrel; 9-inch overall length; weighs 48 oz.; Pachmayr checkered rubber grips; fixed sights; ambidextrous hammer-block safety; squared triggerguard; internal draw bar safety; made of chrome moly steel; matte blue finish. Made in U.S. Marketed by Holston Ent., Dragun Ent. Introduced 1991.

Perf: $400 **Exc:** $350 **VGood:** $300

THUNDER FIVE T-70

Same specs as the Thunder Five except chambered for 45-70 cartridge. Marketed by Dragun Ent.

Perf: $450 **Exc:** $400 **VGood:** $350

TISAS FATIH 13

Beretta-style semi-auto clone chambered in .32 ACP.

New: $300 **Exc:** $250 **VGood:** $195

TISAS KANUNI 16

Single-/double-action autopistol chambered in 9mm Parabellum with 15- or 17-shot capacity. Black, chrome or chrome/gold finish.

New: $325 **Exc:** $275 **VGood:** $195

TISAS KANUNI S

Lightweight version of Kanuni 16. Black, chrome or chrome/black finish.

New: $325 **Exc:** $275 **VGood:** $195

TISAS ZIGANA M16

Single-/double-action autopistol chambered in 9mm Parabellum with 15- or 17-shot capacity and 5" barrel.

New: $375 **Exc:** $325 **VGood:** $250

TISAS ZIGANA K

Compact version of Zigana M16 with 4" barrel.

New: $375 **Exc:** $325 **VGood:** $250

TISAS ZIGANA T

Longer (5.5") barrel version of Zigana M16.

New: $375 **Exc:** $325 **VGood:** $250

TISAS ZIGANA SPORT

Compensated version of Zigana K with 4.5" barrel.

New: $375 **Exc:** $325 **VGood:** $250

TISAS ZIGANA C45

Similar to Zigana M16 but chambered in .45 ACP with 4.75" barrel.

New: $395 **Exc:** $350 **VGood:** $275

TISAS ZIGANA F

"Meltdown" version of Zigana M16 with radiused edges and improved ergonomics.

New: $395 **Exc:** $350 **VGood:** $275

TMI SINGLE SHOT

Single shot; 22 LR, 223, 7mm TCU, 7mm Int., 30 Herrett, 357 Maximum, 41 Mag., 44 Mag., 454 Casull, 375 Super Mag., others on special order; 10-1/2-inch, 14-inch barrel; smooth walnut grips with thumbrest; ramp front sight, open adjustable rear; interchangeable barrels of blue ordnance or bright

Tisas Kanuni S

Tisas Kanuni 16

Tokarev TT-1930

Tisas Fatih 13

Tisas Zigana T

Tisas Zigana M16

Tisas Zigana Sport

stainless steel; ventilated barrel shroud; receiver has integral scope mount. From TMI Products. Introduced 1987; no longer produced.

Exc: $450 **VGood:** $375 **Good:** $275

TOKAREV TT-1930

Semi-automatic; 7.62mm Tokarev (comparable to 7.63mm Mauser); 8-shot; 4-7/16-inch barrel; 7-3/4-inch overall length; grooved plastic grips. TT-30 is rare first model with separate block in rear of frame for hammer mechanism, dated 1933, 1934 or 1935.

Exc: $750 **VGood:** $500 **Good:** $350

TOKAREV TT-33

Same as TT-30 except simplified mechanism, dates 1936-1945.

Exc: $500 **VGood:** $400 **Good:** $300

TOKAREV POST-WAR

Same as TT-33, except made in various countries including China. Some countries and dates have some collector value, but recent China imports have sold new for under $100.

New: $350 **Perf:** $250 **Exc:** $175

TRADITIONS 1873

Revolver; single action; 22 LR, 357 Mag., 44-40, 45 Colt, 6-shot cylinder. Barrel: 4-3/4-inch, 5-1/2-inch, 7-1/2-inch. Weight: 44 oz. Length: 10-3/4-inch overall (5-1/2-inch barrel). Stocks: Walnut. Sights: Blade front, groove in topstrap rear. Features: Blued barrel, cylinder, color case-hardened frame, blue or brass trigger guard. Nickel-plated frame with polished brass trigger guard available in 357 Mag., 44-40, 45 Colt. Introduced 1998.

New: $300 **Perf:** $250 **Exc:** $185

TRADITIONS 1894 BISLEY

Similar to the 1873 except has special tight-curl grip frame, modified trigger guard, wide-spur hammer. Available in 45 Colt only with 4-3/4-inch barrel. Introduced 1998.

New: $325 **Perf:** $275 **Exc:** $200

TRADITIONS THUNDERER REVOLVER

Similar to the 1873 single-action revolver except has special birds-head grip with spur, and smooth or checkered walnut grips. Introduced 1998.

Smooth grips

New: $300 **Perf:** $250 **Exc:** $185

Checkered grips

New: $350 **Perf:** $300 **Exc:** $250

TRADITIONS 1875 SCHOFIELD

Revolver; single action; 44-40, 45 Schofield, 45 Colt, 6-shot cylinder. Barrel: 5-1/2-inch. Weight: 40 oz. Length: 11-1/4-inch overall. Stocks: Walnut. Sights: Blade front, notch rear. Features: Blue finish, case-hardened frame, hammer, trigger. Introduced 1998.

New: $750 **Perf:** $650 **Exc:** $525

TRADITIONS 1851 NAVY CONVERSION

Revolver; single action; 38 Spec. Barrel: 7-1/2-inch. Weight: 40 oz. Length: 14-1/2-inch overall. Stocks: Smooth walnut. Sights: Post front, hammer-notch rear. Features: Steel frame, brass trigger guard. Introduced 1998.

New: $425 **Perf:** $395 **Exc:** $335

TURNBULL MODEL 1911 CENTENNIAL

Faithful limited-edition replica of WWI version of the U.S. military .45 auto with appropriate shape and styling of slide, sights, barrel contour, safety, hammer, lanyard and other features. Forged slide has early 1913 patent markings including United States Property. U.S. Army, U.S. Navy and U.S. Marine Corps variations available. Carbonia Charcoal bluing on all parts, hand polished in same manner as early production guns.

Perf: $3700 **Exc:** $3500 **VGood:** $3200

UBERTI 1871 ROLLING BLOCK

Single shot; 22 LR, 22 WMR, 22 Hornet, 357 Mag., 45 Colt; 9-1/2-inch barrel; 14-inch overall length; weighs 44 oz.; fully-adjustable rear sight, blade front; walnut grip, forend; brass trigger guard; color case-hardened frame; blued barrel. Introduced 1987.

New: $350 **Perf:** $300 **Exc:** $250

UBERTI 1873 CATTLEMAN

Revolver; single action; 22 LR, 22 WMR, 38 Spl., 357 Mag., 38-40, 44 Spl., 44-40, 45 Colt; 6-shot; 4-3/4-inch, 5-1/2-inch, 7-1/2-inch barrel; 10-3/4-inch overall length (5-1/2-inch barrel); weighs 38 oz.; fixed or adjustable sights; wood grips; blued finish. Made in Italy, still imported.

Brass backstrap

New: $375 **Perf:** $300 **Exc:** $250

Steel backstrap

New: $425 **Perf:** $360 **Exc:** $275

UBERTI 1873 BUCKHORN

A slightly larger version of the Cattleman revolver. Available in 44 Magnum or 44 Magnum/44-40 convertible, otherwise has same specs.

New: $375 **Perf:** $325 **Exc:** $275

UBERTI 1873 CATTLEMAN, SHERIFF'S MODEL

Same specs as Cattleman except 44-40, 45 Colt only; 3-inch barrel; brass backstrap. Made in Italy, no longer imported.

Perf: $375 **Exc:** $300 **VGood:** $250

UBERTI 1873 CATTLEMAN, TARGET

Same specs as Cattleman except adjustable rear sight; brass backstrap. Discontinued 1990.

Perf: $300 **Exc:** $250 **VGood:** $200

Stainless steel

Perf: $325 **Exc:** $275 **VGood:** $225

UBERTI 1873 CATTLEMAN, BUNTLINE

Same specs as Cattleman except 357 Mag., 44-40, 45 Colt; 18-inch barrel; wood grips; steel backstrap cut for shoulder stock. Made in Italy. Importation discontinued 1989; reintroduced 1993; discontinued 2004.

Perf: $375 **Exc:** $325 **VGood:** $275

UBERTI 1873 COLT STALLION

Revolver; single action; 22 LR/22 WMR combo; 4-3/4-inch, 5-1/2-inch, 6-1/2-inch barrel; 10-3/4-inch overall length; weighs 36 oz.; grooved or adjustable rear sight, blade front; one-piece uncheckered European walnut stocks; brass triggerguard, backstrap; blued finish. Made in Italy. Introduced 1986; discontinued 1989.

Perf: $300 **Exc:** $250 **VGood:** $200

Stainless steel construction

Perf: $350 **Exc:** $275 **VGood:** $250

UBERTI 1875 REMINGTON OUTLAW

Revolver; single action; 357 Mag., 44-40, 45 Colt, 45 ACP; 6-shot; 7-1/2-inch barrel; 13 3/4-inch overall length; weighs 44 oz; notch rear sight, blade front; uncheckered European walnut stocks; brass triggerguard, color case-hardened frame; blued

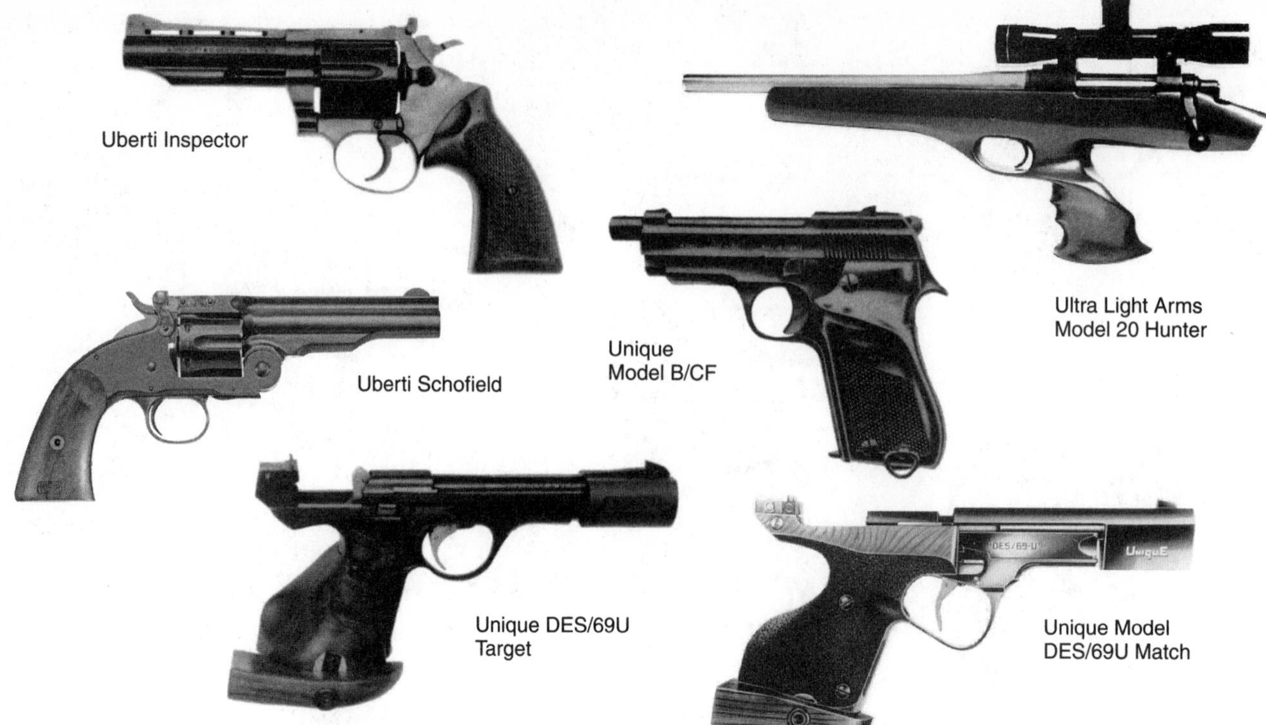

Uberti Inspector

Ultra Light Arms Model 20 Hunter

Unique Model B/CF

Uberti Schofield

Unique DES/69U Target

Unique Model DES/69U Match

finish. Replica of 1875 Remington SAA. Made in Italy. Introduced 1987.

New: $350 **Perf:** $275 **Exc:** $225

UBERTI 1890 ARMY OUTLAW

Revolver; single action; 357 Mag., 44-40, 45 Colt, 45 Colt/45 ACP convertible, 6-shot. Barrel: 5-1/2-inch, 7-1/2-inch. Weight: 37 oz. Length: 12-1/2-inch overall. Stocks: American walnut. Sights: Blade front, groove rear. Features: Replica of the 1890 Remington single-action. Brass trigger guard, rest is blued. Imported by Uberti U.S.A.

New: $435 **Perf:** $400 **Exc:** $350

UBERTI BUCKHORN

Revolver; single action; 44-40, 44 Spl., 44 Mag.; 6-shot; 4-3/4-inch, 5-1/2-inch, 7-1/2-inch barrel; wood grips; brass or steel backstrap; blued finish. Made in Italy. Importation discontinued 1989; reintroduced 1992; discontinued 2002.

New: $375 **Perf:** $300 **Exc:** $275

UBERTI INSPECTOR

Revolver; double action; 32 S&W Long, 38 Spl.; 6-shot; 3-inch, 4-inch, 6-inch barrel; 8-inch overall length (3-inch barrel); weighs 24 oz.; fixed or adjustable rear sight, blade ramp front; checkered walnut stocks; blued finish. Made in Italy. Introduced 1986; discontinued 1990.

Perf: $350 **Exc:** $300 **VGood:** $275

Chrome finish

Perf: $375 **Exc:** $325 **VGood:** $300

UBERTI PHANTOM SILHOUETTE MODEL

Single shot; 357 Mag., 44 Mag.; 10-1/2-inch barrel; adjustable rear sight, blade ramp front; target-style walnut stocks; hooked trigger guard; blue finish. Made in Italy. Introduced 1986; discontinued 1989.

Perf: $375 **Exc:** $300 **VGood:** $250

UBERTI SCHOFIELD

Revolver; single action; 38 special, 44-40, 45 45 Colt, 6-shot cylinder. Barrel: 3-1/2, 5, and 7 inches. Weight: 40 oz. Stocks: Walnut. Sights: Blade front, notch rear. Features: Blue finish, case-hardened frame, hammer, trigger. Introduced 2000; discontinued 2002.

New: $750 **Perf:** $600 **Exc:** $500

ULTRA LIGHT ARMS MODEL 20 HUNTER

Bolt action; 22-250 through 308 Win., most silhouette calibers on request; 5-shot; 14-inch barrel; weighs 64 oz.; Kevlar/graphite reinforced stock in four colors; two-position safety; Timney adjustable trigger; matte or bright stock, metal finish; left- or right-hand action. Introduced 1987; discontinued 1989.

Perf: $1250 **Exc:** $1000 **VGood:** $850

ULTRA LIGHT ARMS MODEL 20 RIMFIRE

Same specs as Model 20 except includes hard case. Introduced 1994; still in production.

New: $1350 **Perf:** $1250 **Exc:** $1000

UNIQUE KRIEGSMODELL

Semi-automatic; 32 ACP; 9-shot; 3-7/16-inch barrel; 5-13/16-inch overall length; fixed sights; grooved plastic stocks; blued finish. Manufactured in France 1940 to 1945 during WWII German occupation.

Exc: $450 **VGood:** $350 **Good:** $250

UNIQUE MODEL 2000-U MATCH

Semi-automatic; single action; 22 Short; 5-shot; 5-15/16-inch barrel; 11-3/8-inch overall length; weighs 43 oz.; anatomically shaped, adjustable, stippled French walnut grips; blade front sight, fully-adjustable rear; light alloy frame, steel slide and shock absorber; five barrel vents reduce recoil, three can be blocked; trigger adjustable for position and pull weight; comes with 340-gram weight housing, 160-gram available. Imported from France by Nygord Precision Products. Introduced 1984; dropped 1993.

Perf: $1250 **Exc:** $1000 **VGood:** $800

UNIQUE MODEL B/CF

Semi-automatic; 32 ACP, 380 ACP; 9-shot (32 ACP), 8-shot (380 ACP); 4-inch barrel; 6 5/8-inch overall length; fixed sights; thumbrest plastic stocks; blued finish. Manufactured in France. Introduced 1954; still in production, but not imported.

Exc: $200 **VGood:** $175 **Good:** $150

UNIQUE MODEL D2

Semi-automatic; 22 LR; 10-shot; 4-1/2-inch barrel; 7-1/2-inch overall length; adjustable sights; thumbrest plastic stocks; blued finish. Introduced 1954; still in production, but not imported.

Perf: $275 **Exc:** $225 **VGood:** $185

UNIQUE MODEL D6

Semi-automatic; 22 LR; 10-shot; 6-inch barrel; 9-1/4-inch overall length; adjustable sights; thumbrest plastic stocks; blued finish. Introduced 1954; still in production, but not imported.

Perf: $275 **Exc:** $225 **VGood:** $185

UNIQUE DES/32U TARGET

Caliber: 32 S&W Long wadcutter. Barrel: 5.9. Weight: 40.2 oz. Stocks: Anatomically shaped, adjustable stippled French walnut. Sights: Blade front, micrometer click rear. Features: Trigger adjustable for weight and position; dry firing mechanism; slide stop catch. Optional sleeve weights. Introduced 1990. Imported from France by Nygord Precision Products.
Price: Right-hand, about $1,350
Price: Left-hand, about $1,380

UNIQUE MODEL DES/32U

Semi-automatic; single action; 32 S&W Long wadcutter; 5-, 6-shot; 5-15/16-inch barrel; weighs 40 oz.; blade front sight, micrometer click rear; adjustable, stippled French walnut stocks; position-, weight-adjustable trigger; slide-stop catch; dry firing mechanism; optional sleeve weights of 120, 220, 320 grams. Made in France. Introduced 1990; still imported.

New: $1100 **Perf:** $900 **Exc:** $750

UNIQUE DES/69U TARGET

Semi-automatic; 22 LR, 5-shot magazine. Barrel: 5.91-inch. Weight: 35.3 oz. Length: 10.5-inch overall. Stocks: French walnut right- or left-hand target-style with thumbrest and adjustable shelf; hand-checkered panels. Sights: Ramp front, micro. adjustable rear mounted on frame; 8.66-inch sight radius. Features: Meets U.I.T. standards. Comes with 260-gram barrel weight; 100-, 150-, 350-gram weights available. Fully adjustable match trigger; dry-firing safety device. Imported from France by Nygord Precision Products.

New: $1100 **Perf:** $900 **Exc:** $750

UNIQUE MODEL DES/69U MATCH

Semi-automatic; 22 LR; 5-shot; 5-7/8-inch barrel; 10-1/2-inch overall length; click-adjustable rear sight mounted on frame, ramp front; checkered walnut thumbrest stocks; adjustable handrest; blued finish. Introduced 1969; still in production.

New: $1000 **Perf:** $850 **Exc:** $650

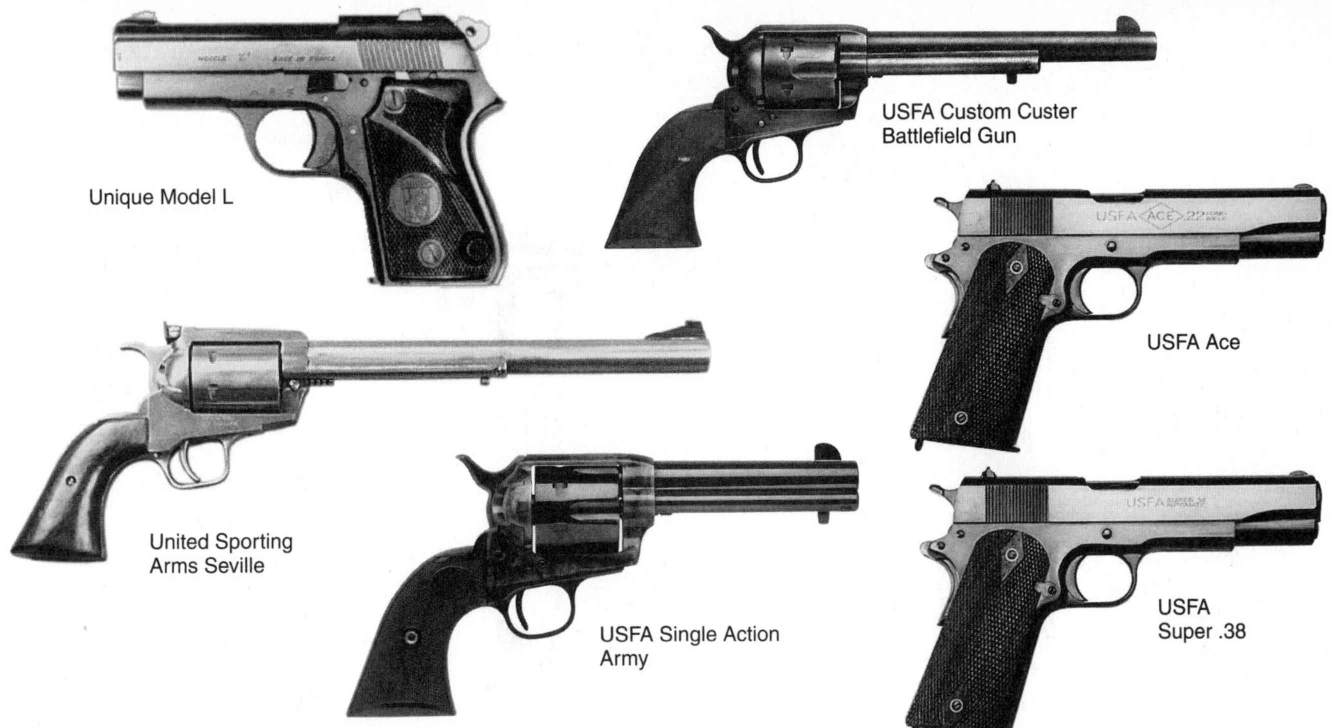
Unique Model L

USFA Custom Custer Battlefield Gun

USFA Ace

United Sporting Arms Seville

USFA Single Action Army

USFA Super .38

UNIQUE MODEL 96U TARGET

Semi-automatic; 22 LR, 5- or 6-shot magazine. Barrel: 5.9. Weight: 40.2 oz. Length: 11.2 overall. Stocks: French walnut. Target style with thumbrest and adjustable shelf. Sights: Blade front, micrometer rear mounted on frame. Features: Designed for Sport Pistol and Standard U.I.T. shooting. External hammer; fully adjustable and movable trigger; dry-firing device. Introduced 1997. Imported from France by Nygord Precision Products.

New: $1100 **Perf:** $850 **Exc:** $700

UNIQUE MODEL DES/823-U RAPID FIRE MATCH

Semi-automatic; 22 Short; 5-shot; 5-7/8-inch barrel; 10-7/16-inch overall length; adjustable rear sight, blade front; hand-checkered walnut thumbrest stocks; adjustable handrest; adjustable trigger; blued finish. Introduced 1974; importation dropped 1988.

Perf: $1000 **Exc:** $850 **VGood:** $700

UNIQUE MODEL L

Semi-automatic; 22 LR, 32 ACP, 380 ACP; 10-shot (22 LR), 7-shot (32 ACP), 6-shot (380 ACP); 3-5/16-inch barrel; 5-13/16-inch overall length; fixed sights; checkered plastic stocks; steel or alloy frame; blued finish. Introduced 1955; still in production but not imported.

Exc: $175 **VGood:** $150 **Good:** $135

UNIQUE MODEL MIKROS POCKET

Semi-automatic; 22 Short, 22 LR; 6-shot; 2-1/4-inch barrel; 4-7/16-inch overall length; fixed sights; checkered plastic stocks; alloy or steel frame; blued finish. Introduced 1957; still in production, but not imported.

Exc: $175 **VGood:** $150 **Good:** $125

UNIQUE MODEL RR

Semi-automatic; 32 ACP; 9-shot; 3-7/16-inch barrel; 5-13/16-inch overall length; fixed sights; grooved plastic stock; commercial version of Kriegsmodell with improved blued finish. No longer in production.

Exc: $175 **VGood:** $150 **Good:** $125

UNITED SPORTING ARMS SEVILLE

Revolver; single action; 357 Mag., 41 Mag., 44 Mag., 45 Colt; 6-shot; 4-5/8-inch, 5-1/2-inch, 6-1/2-inch, 7-1/2-inch barrel; ramp front sight with red insert, fully-adjustable rear; smooth walnut, Pachmayr or thumbrest stocks; blued finish. Introduced 1981; discontinued 1986.

Exc: $675 **VGood:** $475 **Good:** $300

UNITED SPORTING ARMS SEVILLE SHERIFF'S MODEL

Revolver; single action; 357 Mag., 38 Spl., 44 Spl., 44 Mag., 45 Colt; 6-shot; 3-1/2-inch barrel; ramp or blade front sight, adjustable or fixed rear; square-butt or bird's-head smooth walnut grips; blued finish. Made in U.S. Introduced 1983; discontinued 1986.

Exc: $525 **VGood:** $375 **Good:** $275

UNITED SPORTING ARMS SEVILLE SILHOUETTE

Revolver; single action; 357 Mag., 41 Mag., 44 Mag.; 6-shot; 10-1/2-inch barrel; weighs 55 oz.; undercut Patridge-style front sight, adjustable rear; smooth walnut thumbrest or Pachmayr stocks; stainless steel frame with blued barrel.

Exc: $700 **VGood:** $500 **Good:** $325

UNITED STATES FIRE ARMS CUSTOM CUSTER BATTLEFIELD GUN

Replica of 1873 revolver used during height of Indian Wars, including Custer's Last Stand. Limited edition with cartouche of Ordnance Sub-inspector Orville W. Ainsworth; serial range 200-14,343. 7.5-inch barrel, six shot. Antique patina-aged blue. One-piece walnut stock.

New: $1395 **Exc:** $1100 **VGood:** $875

UNITED STATES FIRE ARMS ACE

Recreation of 1911-style Colt Ace. .22 LR with 10+1 capacity. Walnut grips.

New: $1875 **Exc:** $1725 **VGood:** $1300

UNITED STATES FIRE ARMS SUPER .38

1911-style semi-auto. Blued finish; chambered for .38 Super Auto with 9+1 capacity. Walnut grips.

New: $1875 **Exc:** $1725 **VGood:** $1300

UNITED STATES FIRE ARMS SINGLE ACTION ARMY

Revolver; single action; 22 LR, 22 WMR, 357 Mag., 44 Russian, 38-40, 44-40, 45 Colt, 6-shot cylinder. Barrel: 3, 4, 4-3/4, 5-1/2, 7-1/2, or 10-inch. Weight: 37 oz. Length: NA. Stocks: Smooth walnut. Sights: Blade front, notch rear. Features: Recreation of original guns; 3 & 4-inch have no ejector. Available with all-blue, blue with color case-hardening, or full nickel-plate finish. Made in USA; early production was assembled and finished in USA from components manufactured in Italy. Available from United States Patent Fire-Arms Mfg. Co.

New: $1250 **Perf:** $1050 **Exc:** $900

UNITED STATES FIRE ARMS BISLEY

Revolver; single action; 45 Colt, 32WCF, 38S&W, 44S&W, 41 Colt, 38WCF, 44WCF. 6-shot cylinder. Barrel: 4-3/4-inch, 5-1/2-inch, 7-1/2-inch, 10-inch. Weight: 38 oz. (5-1/2-inch barrel). Length: NA. Stocks: Smooth walnut. Sights: Blade front, notch rear. Features: Available in all-blue, blue with color case-hardening, or full nickel plate finish.

New: $1100 **Perf:** $850 **Exc:** $500

UNITED STATES FIRE ARMS FLATTOP TARGET REVOLVER

Similar to the Single Action Army except 4-3/4, 5-1/2, or 7-1/2-inch barrel, two-piece hard rubber stocks, flat top frame, adjustable rear sight.

New: $1100 **Perf:** $1000 **Exc:** $850

UNITED STATES FIRE ARMS NETTLETON CAVALRY REVOLVER

Similar to the single Action Army, except in 45 Colt only, with 7-1/2-inch barrel, color case-hardened/ blue finish, and has old-style hand numbering, exact cartouche branding and correct inspector hand-stamp markings. Made in Italy, available from United States Patent Fire-Arms Mfg. Co.

New: $1395 **Exc:** $1100 **VGood:** $875

UNITED STATES FIRE ARMS BIRD'S HEAD MODEL REVOLVER

Similar to the Single Action Army except has bird's-head grip and comes with 3-1/2-inch, 4-inch or 4-1/2-inch barrel.

New: $1250 **Perf:** $1050 **Exc:** $900

UNITED STATES FIRE ARMS RODEO/RODEO II

Entry-level but very high-quality 1873 clone. Rodeo has matte blue finish; Rodeo II has matte nickel finish. Add 10% for Rodeo II. No longer in production.

New: $750 **Exc:** $675 **VGood:** $545

Voere VEC-RG Repeater

Walther Model 2

Walther Model 3

Walther Model 4

Walther Model 5

Walther Model 6

Walther Model 7

UNIVERSAL FIREARMS ENFORCER PISTOL, MODEL 3000

A pistol version of the M-1 Carbine. Cal. .30M-1. 11 ¼" barrel. Blue, parkerized or nickel finish. 5-15-30 rd magazines. 1964-1983.

Exc: $550 **VGood:** $450 **Good:** $375

USELTON ARMS ULTRA COMPACT CLASSIC

1911-style semi-auto .45 with fixed sights. 4.25-inch barrel, 34 oz. 3-4 lb. trigger pull, 7+1 capacity. Rosewood or imitation ivory grips. Various finishes.

New: $2000 **Exc:** $1750 **VGood:** $1300

UZI EAGLE AUTO PISTOL

Caliber: 9mm Para., 40 S&W, 45 ACP, 10-shot magazine. Barrel: 4.4. Weight: 35 oz. Length: 8.1 overall. Stocks: Textured, high-impact polymer. Sights: Three-dot tritium night sights. Features: Double-action mechanism with decocker; polygonal rifling; matte blue/black finish. Introduced 1997; dropped 1998. Imported from Israel by Uzi America, Inc.

New: $950 **Perf:** $800 **Exc:** $650

VEGA STAINLESS 45

Semi-automatic; 45 ACP; 7-shot; 5-inch barrel; 8-3/8-inch overall length; stainless steel construction; almost exact copy of 1911-A1 Colt; fixed sights or adjustable sights; polished slide, frame flats, balance sand-blasted. Introduced 1980 by Pacific International Merchandising; dropped about 1984.

Exc: $525 **VGood:** $475 **Good:** $425

VOERE VEC-95CG

Bolt action; single shot; 5.56mm, 6mm UCC caseless; 12-inch, 14-inch barrel; weighs 3 lbs.; black synthetic, center-grip stock; no sights furnished; fires caseless ammunition via electronic ignition; two batteries in the grip last about 500 shots; two forward locking lugs; tang safety; drilled and tapped for scope mounting. Imported from Austria by JagerSport, Ltd. Introduced 1995; still imported.

New: $2000 **Perf:** $1700 **Exc:** $1350

VOERE VEC-RG REPEATER

Bolt action; 5.56mm, 6mm UCC caseless; 5-shot; 12-inch, 14-inch barrel; weighs 3 lbs.; black synthetic, rear-grip stock; no sights furnished; fires caseless ammunition via electronic ignition; two batteries in the grip last about 500 shots; two forward locking lugs; tang safety; drilled and tapped for scope mounting. Imported from Austria by JagerSport, Ltd. Introduced 1995; still imported.

New: $2000 **Perf:** $1700 **Exc:** $1350

WALTHER MODEL 1

Semi-automatic; 25 ACP; 6-shot magazine; 2-inch barrel; 4-7/16-inch overall length; checkered hard rubber stocks; fixed sights; blued finish. Manufactured in Germany 1908 to 1918; collector value.

Exc: $550 **VGood:** $375 **Good:** $300

WALTHER MODEL 2

Semi-automatic; 25 ACP; 6-shot magazine; 2-inch barrel; 4-7/16-inch overall length; checkered hard rubber stocks; fixed sights; blued finish. Same general internal design as Model 1 but has a knurled takedown nut at the muzzle. Manufactured 1909 to 1918; collector value.

Exc: $350 **VGood:** $300 **Good:** $250

WALTHER MODEL 3

Semi-automatic; 32 ACP; 8-shot magazine; 2-5/8-inch barrel; 5-inch overall length; checkered hard rubber stocks; fixed sights; blued finish. Manufactured 1909 to 1918. Rare; collector value.

Exc: $950 **VGood:** $750 **Good:** $550

WALTHER MODEL 4

Semi-automatic; 32 ACP; 8-shot magazine; 3-1/2-inch barrel; 5-7/8-inch overall length; checkered hard rubber stocks; fixed sights; blued finish. Manufactured 1910 to 1920.

Exc: $250 **VGood:** $150 **Good:** $100

WALTHER MODEL 5

Semi-automatic; 25 ACP; 6-shot magazine; 2-inch barrel; 4-7/16-inch overall length; checkered hard rubber stocks; fixed sights; blued finish. Same specs as Model 2 except better workmanship; improved finish. Manufactured 1913 to 1918; collector value.

Exc: $350 **VGood:** $250 **Good:** $200

WALTHER MODEL 6

Semi-automatic; 9mm Para.; 8-shot magazine; 4-3/4-inch barrel; 8-1/4-inch overall length; checkered hard rubber stocks; fixed sights; blued finish. Manufactured 1915 to 1917. Rare.

Exc: $4500 **VGood:** $3500 **Good:** $2750

WALTHER MODEL 7

Semi-automatic; 25 ACP; 8-shot magazine; 3-inch barrel; 5-5/16-inch overall length; checkered hard rubber stocks; fixed sights; blued finish. Manufactured 1917 to 1918.

Exc: $500 **VGood:** $425 **Good:** $350

WALTHER MODEL 8

Semi-automatic; 25 ACP; 8-shot magazine; 2-7/8-inch barrel; 5-1/8-inch overall length; fixed sights; checkered plastic grips; blued. Manufactured by Waffenfabrik Walther, Zella-Mehlis, Germany. Introduced 1920; dropped 1945.

Exc: $400 **VGood:** $325 **Good:** $275

WALTHER MODEL 8 LIGHTWEIGHT

Same specs as Model 8, except aluminum alloy. Introduced 1927; dropped about 1935.

Exc: $1000 **VGood:** $750 **Good:** $600

WALTHER MODEL 9

Semi-automatic; 25 ACP; 6-shot magazine; 2-inch barrel; 3-15/16-inch overall length; checkered plastic grips; fixed sights; blued. Introduced 1921; dropped 1945.

Exc: $450 **VGood:** $375 **Good:** $325

WALTHER MODEL HP

Semi-automatic; 9mm, 7.65mm Para. (very rare); 10-shot magazine; 5-inch barrel; 8-3/8-inch overall length; checkered (early) or grooved plastic or checkered wood (rare) grips; fixed sights; blued. Early examples have rectangular firing pin. Introduced 1939; dropped 1945.

Rectangular firing pin

Exc: $2250 **VGood:** $1850 **Good:** $1200

Round firing pin

Exc: $1500 **VGood:** $950 **Good:** $700

WALTHER MODEL PP

Semi-automatic; 22 LR, 25 ACP, 32 ACP, 380 ACP; 8-shot magazine; 3-7/8-inch barrel; 6-5/16-inch overall length; designed as law-enforcement model; fixed sights; checkered plastic grips; blued. WWII production has less value because of poorer

Walther Model 8

Walther Model 9

Walther Model HP

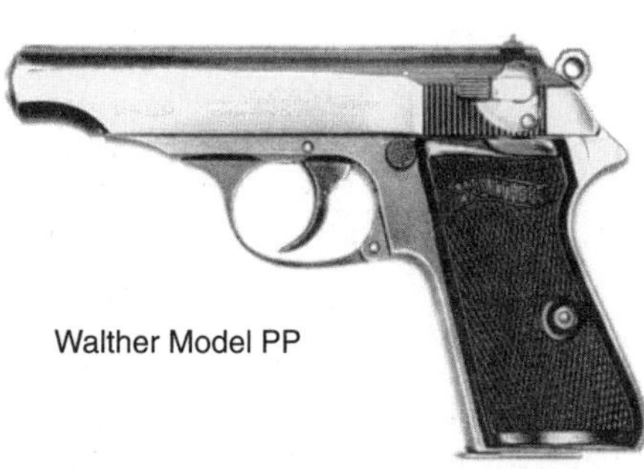
Walther Model PP

Walther Model PPK

Walther Model PPK/S

workmanship. Introduced 1929; dropped 1945. RZM, PDM and other special markings bring a premium.

Wartime models
Exc: $500 **VGood:** $400 **Good:** $300

32 caliber
Exc: $400 **VGood:** $300 **Good:** $225

380 caliber
Exc: $1000 **VGood:** $750 **Good:** $500

22 caliber
Exc: $850 **VGood:** $650 **Good:** $450

25 caliber
Exc: $3000 **VGood:** $2500 **Good:** $2000

WALTHER MODEL PP LIGHTWEIGHT

Same specs as Model PP except aluminum alloy frame. Introduced 1929; dropped 1945.

32 caliber
Exc: $750 **VGood:** $450 **Good:** $375

380 caliber
Exc: $1200 **VGood:** $950 **Good:** $700

WALTHER MODEL PP MARK II

Same specs as pre-WWII model. Currently manufactured in France by Manufacture De Machines Du Haut-Rhin. Introduced 1953; still in production, but not imported.

Exc: $250 **VGood:** $200 **Good:** $175

WALTHER MODEL PP POST-WWII

Same specs as pre-war except not made in 25-caliber. Currently manufactured by Carl Walther Waffenfabrik, Ulm/Donau, West Germany. Still in production. Imported by Interarms.

Exc: $375 **VGood:** $300 **Good:** $250

WALTHER MODEL PPK

Semi-automatic; 22 LR, 25 ACP, 32 ACP, 380 ACP; 7-shot magazine; 3-1/4-inch barrel; 5-7/8-inch overall length; the Kurz (short) version of the PP; checkered plastic grips; fixed sights; blued finish. WWII production has less value due to poorer workmanship. Introduced 1931; dropped 1945. RZM, PDM and other special markings bring a premium.

Wartime models
Exc: $600 **VGood:** $500 **Good:** $375

32 caliber
Exc: $550 **VGood:** $475 **Good:** $350

380 caliber
Exc: $1250 **VGood:** $950 **Good:** $650

22 caliber
Exc: $900 **VGood:** $700 **Good:** $500

25 caliber
Exc: $4500 **VGood:** $4000 **Good:** $3500

WALTHER MODEL PPK AMERICAN

Same specs as PPK except 6-shot magazine; 3-7/8-inch barrel; 6-5/16-inch overall length; weighs 21 oz.; 380 ACP only; blued or stainless finish. Made in U.S. Introduced 1986; still marketed by Interarms.

New: $575 **Perf:** $500 **Exc:** $400

WALTHER MODEL PPK LIGHTWEIGHT

Same specs as standard model except for incorporation of aluminum alloys. Introduced 1933; dropped 1945.

32 caliber
Exc: $800 **VGood:** $650 **Good:** $500

380 caliber
Exc: $1600 **VGood:** $1350 **Good:** $1000

22 caliber
Exc: $1250 **VGood:** $950 **Good:** $800

WALTHER MODEL PPK MARK II

Same specs as pre-WWII PPK. Was manufactured in France by Manufacture De Machines Du Haut-Rhin. Introduced 1953; dropped 1960s.

Exc: $450 **VGood:** $375 **Good:** $300

WALTHER MODEL PPK MARK II LIGHTWEIGHT

Same specs as standard model except receiver of Dural; 22 LR, 32 ACP only. Introduced 1953; still in production, but not imported.

Exc: $600 **VGood:** $300 **Good:** $250

WALTHER MODEL PPK POST-WWII

Same specs as pre-war model except steel or aluminum alloy construction. Currently manufactured in Germany by Carl Walther Waffenfabrik. Still in production, although U.S. importation was dropped in 1968.

32 ACP
Exc: $500 **VGood:** $375 **Good:** $300

22 LR
Exc: $575 **VGood:** $500 **Good:** $400

380 ACP
Exc: $525 **VGood:** $450 **Good:** $375

WALTHER MODEL PPK/S (GERMAN)

Semi-automatic; 22 LR, 32 ACP, 380 ACP; 9-shot magazine; 3-1/4-inch barrel; 6-1/8-inch overall length; fixed sights; checkered plastic grips; blued. Same general specs as Walther PP except grip frame 1/2-inch longer and one shot larger magazine capacity to meet GCA '68 factoring system. Made in Germany. Introduced 1968; dropped 1982.

22 LR
Exc: $550 **VGood:** $450 **Good:** $375

32 ACP, 380 ACP
Exc: $475 **VGood:** $425 **Good:** $375

WALTHER MODEL PPK/S (AMERICAN)

Same specs as German-made PPK/S except made entirely in U.S. by Interarms. Made only in 380 ACP in blue ordnance steel or stainless. Introduced 1980; still in production.

New: $550 **Perf:** $500 **Exc:** $400

WALTHER PPK/S (ENGRAVED)

Caliber: 380 ACP, 8-round capacity. Barrel: 3.3 inches. Weight: 22.4 oz. Length: 6.1 inches. Machine-engraved receiver and wooden grips. Stainless frame, slide and barrel. Mahogany presentation case included.

Perf: $800 **Exc:** $700 **VGood:** $600

WALTHER MODEL TPH

Semi-automatic; 22 LR, 25 ACP; 6-shot magazine; 2-1/4-inch barrel; 5-3/8-inch overall length; weighs 14 oz.; drift-adjustable rear sight, blade front; constructed of stainless steel; scaled-down version of PP/PPK series. Made in U.S. by Interarms. Introduced 1987; still in production.

New: $600 **Perf:** $525 **Exc:** $450

WALTHER MODEL TP

Semi-automatic; 22 LR, 25 ACP; 6-shot magazine; 2-1/2-inch barrel; 5-1/8-inch overall length; checkered plastic grips; fixed front sight only; blued. Updated version of Model 9 with safety lever in center of slide. Introduced 1962; dropped 1968.

Exc: $600 **VGood:** $400 **Good:** $300

Walther Olympia Sport Model

Walther P-38 (480 code marking)

Walther Sport Model 1926

Walther OSP Rapid-Fire

Walther GSP Match

Walther Free Pistol

Walther P-38 Military Model

WALTHER SPORT MODEL 1926

Semi-automatic; 22 LR; 6-inch, 9-inch barrels; 9-7/8-inch overall length (6-inch barrel); checkered one-piece walnut grip; adjustable target sights; blued. Introduced 1926; dropped 1936.

Exc: $800 **VGood:** $650 **Good:** $500

WALTHER OLYMPIA SPORT MODEL

Semi-automatic; 22 LR; 7-3/8-inch barrel; 10-11/16-inch overall length; checkered wood grips; adjustable target sights; blued. Available with set of four detachable weights. Introduced 1936; dropped during WWII.

Exc: $1000 **VGood:** $850 **Good:** $700

WALTHER OLYMPIA FUNKAMPF MODEL

Same specs as Sport model except 9-5/8-inch barrel; 13-inch overall length; set of four detachable weights. Introduced 1937; dropped during WWII.

Exc: $1350 **VGood:** $1000 **Good:** $800

WALTHER OLYMPIA HUNTING MODEL

Same specs as Sport Model except 4-inch barrel. Introduced 1936; dropped during WWII.

Exc: $950 **VGood:** $750 **Good:** $600

WALTHER OLYMPIA RAPID FIRE MODEL

Same specs as Sport model except 22 Short; detachable muzzle weight. Introduced 1936; dropped during WWII.

Exc: $1250 **VGood:** $950 **Good:** $700

WALTHER OSP RAPID-FIRE

Semi-automatic; single action; 22 Short; 5-shot; 5-3/4-inch barrel; 11-13/16-inch overall length; weighs 45 oz.; walnut, special adjustable free-style grip with hand rest; fixed front sight, fully-adjustable rear; available with either 2.2-lb. (1000 gm) or 3-lb. (1360 gm) trigger; spare mag., barrel weight, tools supplied in Match Pistol Kit. Imported from Germany by Interarms. Importation dropped 1992.

Perf: $1350 **Exc:** $1000 **VGood:** $800

WALTHER FREE PISTOL

Single shot; 22 LR; 11-11/16-inch barrel; 17-3/16-inch overall length; weighs 48 oz.; fully-adjustable match sights; hand-fitting walnut stocks; electronic trigger; matte blue finish. Made in Germany. Imported by Interarms; importation dropped 1991.

Perf: $1400 **Exc:** $1000 **VGood:** $850

WALTHER GSP MATCH

Semi-automatic; single action; 22 LR; 5-shot; 5-3/4-inch barrel; 11-13/16-inch overall length; weighs 45 oz.; walnut, special hand-fitting design grip; fixed front sight, fully-adjustable rear; available with either 2.2-lb. (1000 gm) or 3-lb. (1360 gm) trigger; spare mag., barrel weight, tools supplied in Match Pistol Kit. Imported from Germany by Interarms. Still imported.

New: $1250 **Perf:** $1000 **Exc:** $850

WALTHER GSP-C MATCH

Same specs as GSP except 32 S&W Long wadcutter cartridge; weighs 49-1/2 oz.; comes with case. Imported from Germany by Interarms. Still imported.

New: $1500 **Perf:** $1350 **Exc:** $1000

WALTHER P-5

Semi-automatic; 9mm Para.; 3-1/2-inch barrel; 7-inch overall length; same basic double-action mechanism as P-38 but differs externally. Introduced 1978; still imported from Germany by Interarms.

New: $700 **Perf:** $600 **Exc:** $500

WALTHER P22

.22LR pistol. SA/DA operation. 3.4" barrel. Steel slide with black, nickel or chrome finish. Polymer frame available in black or military green color. Weighs 15oz. 10rd magazine. Introduced in 2001.

Perf: $350 **Exc:** $300 **VGood:** $250

WALTHER P22 TARGET

As above with a 5" barrel and extended frame. Weighs 18 oz.

Perf: $400 **Exc:** $350 **VGood:** $300

WALTHER MODEL P-38

Semi-automatic; 9mm Para.; 10-shot magazine; 5-inch barrel; 8-3/8-inch overall length; checkered (early) or grooved plastic grips; fixed sights; blued. Walther Model HP as adopted by German military in 1939 and produced by various makers (identified by code markings on slide) through 1945. Early Walther (-inchac code-inch) manufacture with high polish finish brings considerable premium from collectors; first few thousand had rectangular firing pin.

Walther banner, rectangular firing pin

Exc: $4500 **VGood:** $3500 **Good:** $2200

Walther banner marked, round firing pin

Exc: $1750 **VGood:** $1250 **Good:** $800

480 code marking

Exc: $3500 **VGood:** $1500 **Good:** $1000

ac Code, no date, with high polish finish

Exc: $3000 **VGood:** $2000 **Good:** $600

ac Code, dated 40, and 41, high polish finish

Exc: $1250 **VGood:** $750 **Good:** $400

Letter codes, dated 42 to 45

Exc: $600 **VGood:** $500 **Good:** $400

WALTHER P-38 POST-WAR

Same specs as WWII military model except improved workmanship; alloy frame.

New: $600 **Perf:** $450 **Exc:** $350

WALTHER P-1 POST-WAR

Same specs as WWII military model; manufactured for German police market until late 1960s. Alloy frame., blued finish. Deduct 20 percent for Manufrance manufacture. These pistols have been imported in great numbers and are not scarce. alloy frame.

New: $375 **Perf:** $325 **Exc:** $275

WALTHER P-38IV

Same specs as P-38 post-war except 4-1/2-inch barrel; 8-inch overall length. Introduced 1977; imported by Interarms.

Exc: $475 **VGood:** $375 **Good:** $275

WALTHER P-38K

Same specs as P-38 except streamlined version of original with 2-1/4-inch barrel; 6-1/2-inch overall length; strengthened slide; no dust cover; windage-adjustable rear sight; hammer decocking lever; non-reflective matte finish. Imported from Germany by Interarms 1976; dropped 1980.

Exc: $800 **VGood:** $650 **Good:** $450

Walther PP Super

Walther P22

Walther SP22-M1

Walther Model P-88 Compact

Walther P-38 (banner, round firing pin) Zero Series

Walther Model SP22-M2

Walther P99

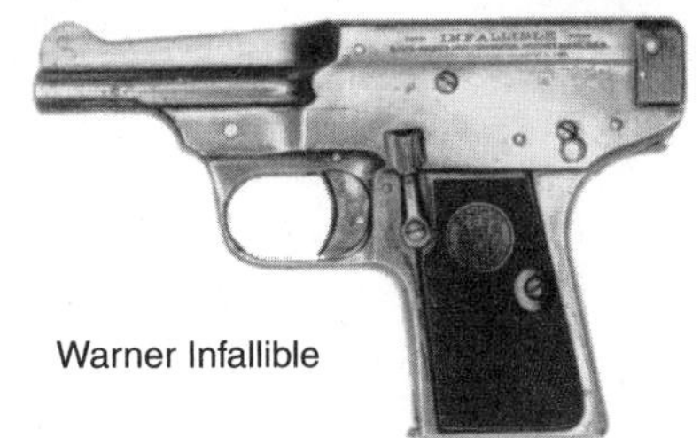
Warner Infallible

Walther 75th Anniversary PPK

WALTHER P-88 COMPACT

Semi-automatic; double action; 9mm Para., 14-shot; 4-inch barrel; 7-3/8-inch overall length; weighs 31-1/2 oz.; checkered black composition grips; blade front sight, fully-adjustable rear; ambidextrous decocking lever and magazine release; alloy frame; loaded chamber indicator; matte finish. Imported from Germany by Interarms. Introduced 1987; importation dropped 1994.

Perf: $800 **Exc:** $700 **VGood:** $550

WALTHER PP SUPER

Semi-automatic; 9mm Ultra, 380 ACP; 7-shot magazine; 3-5/8-inch barrel; 6-15/16-inch overall length; weighs 29 oz. loaded; utilizes P-38 mechanism; introduced for West German police in 1972 in 9mm Ultra. Several hundred 9mm Ultra models were imported in used condition, plus 1000 new guns in 380 ACP in 1984-85 by Interarms. Some collector value.

9mm Ultra

Exc: $500 **VGood:** $400 **Good:** $300

380 ACP

Exc: $600 **VGood:** $500 **Good:** $400

WALTHER P99

Semi-automatic; double action; 9mm Para., 10-shot magazine. Barrel: 4. Weight: 25 oz. Length: 7 overall. Stocks: Textured polymer. Sights: Blade front (comes with three interchangeable blades for elevation adjustment), micrometer rear adjustable for windage. Features: Double-action mechanism with trigger safety, decock safety, internal striker safety; chamber loaded indicator; ambidextrous magazine release levers; polymer frame with interchangeable backstrap inserts. Comes with two magazines. Introduced 1997. Imported from Germany by Interarms.

Exc: $600 **VGood:** $500 **Good:** $40

WALTHER 75TH ANNIVERSARY PPK

Blued with wood grips, machine engraving and available in .380 ACP with 6+1 capacity. Special SN beginning with 0000PPK, shipped with glass-top display case. Single/double-action, 3.3-inch barrel, 20.8 oz. Windage-adjustable rear sight.

New: $700 **Exc:** $595 **VGood:** $395

WALTHER MODEL SP22-M1

.22 LR autoloader with aluminum frame and 4-inch barrel.

Exc: $400 **VGood:** $300 **Good:** $225

WALTHER MODEL SP22-M2

Similar to above but with a 6-inch barrel.

Exc: $425 **VGood:** $325 **Good:** $250

WALTHER MODEL SP22-M3

Similar to above but with match-grade barrel and adjustable trigger.

Exc: $475 **VGood:** $375 **Good:** $275

WALTHER MODEL SP22-M4

Similar to above but with wooden free-style grip assembly.

Exc: $750 **VGood:** $600 **Good:** $425

WARNER INFALLIBLE

Semi-automatic; 32 ACP; 7-shot; 3-inch barrel; 6-1/2-inch overall length; checkered hard rubber stocks; fixed sights; blued finish. Manufactured 1917 to 1919.

Exc: $300 **VGood:** $200 **Good:** $150

WEATHERBY MARK IV SILHOUETTE

Single shot; bolt action; 22, 250, 308; 15-inch barrel; globe front sight with inserts, target-type rear peep; thumbhole Claro walnut stock; rosewood forend tip with grip cap; modified Mark V Varmintmaster action; drilled and tapped for scope. Introduced 1980; dropped 1981.

Exc: $3250 **VGood:** $2500 **Good:** $2000

WEATHERBY MARK V CFP PISTOL

Single shot; bolt action; 22-250, 243, 7mm-08, 308. Barrel: 15-inch fluted stainless. Weight: NA. Length: NA. Stock: Brown laminate with ambidextrous rear grip. Sights: None furnished; drilled and tapped for scope mounting. Features: Uses Mark V lightweight receiver of chrome moly steel, matte blue finish. Introduced 1998.

Exc: $700 **VGood:** $500 **Good:** $350

WEBLEY-FOSBERY AUTOMATIC REVOLVER

Revolver; 455 Webley, 38 Colt Auto; 6-shot cylinder
(455), 8-shot (38 Colt Auto); hinged frame; 6-inch barrel; 12-inch overall length; hand-checkered walnut stocks; fixed sights; blued finish. Recoil revolves cylinder, cocking hammer, leading to automatic terminology. Flat-top model was submitted for U.S. Army trials. Manufactured 1901 to 1924. Both calibers have collector value.

455 Webley

Exc: $5000 **VGood:** $4000 **Good:** $3200

38 Colt Auto

Exc: $7500 **VGood:** $5500 **Good:** $4500

WEBLEY GOVERNMENT MODEL

Revolver; 450 to 476; 6-shot; 4-inch to 7-1/2-inch barrels; hinged frame; Vulcanite or wood grips; bird's-head or square-butt grip configuration; fixed or target sights; bright blue or nickel finish. Standard Webley markings. Manufactured from 1886 to 1915.

Exc: $800 **VGood:** $550 **Good:** $400

WEBLEY MARK I, II, III, IV, V REVOLVERS

Revolver; 455 Webley; 6-shot; 4-inch barrel; hinged frame; Vulcanite grips; brush blue finish. Standard proofs with Webley MKI through Webley MKV marks. Some models have commercial counterparts available in 450 through 476 calibers. Manufactured from 1887 to 1915. Deduct 25 percent if cylinder shortened for 45 Auto Rim cartridge.

Exc: $850 **VGood:** $625 **Good:** $325

WEBLEY MARK III POLICE MODEL

Revolver; double action; 32 S&W, 320 S&W, 38 S&W; 6-shot cylinder: 3-inch, 4-inch barrel; 9-1/2-inch

Webley Mark III Police Model

Webley Model 1911

Webley-Fosbery Automatic Revolver

Webley Mark IV Police Model

Webley Mark VI

Webley R.I.C. (Royal Irish Constabulary)

overall length; hinged frame; fixed sights; checkered Vulcanite or walnut grips; blued finish. Introduced 1897; dropped 1945. Beware of Indian/Pakistani copies.

Exc: $575 **VGood:** $450 **Good:** $300

WEBLEY MARK III POLICE MODEL TARGET

Revolver; double action; 38 S&W; 6-shot cylinder: 3-inch, 4-inch, 6-inch, 10-inch barrel; 9-1/2-inch overall length; hinged frame; adjustable sights; checkered Vulcanite or walnut grips; blued finish. Introduced 1897; dropped 1945.

Exc: $725 **VGood:** $550 **Good:** $400

WEBLEY MARK IV POLICE MODEL

Revolver; double action; hinged frame; 38 S&W; 6-shot cylinder: 3-inch, 4-inch, 5-inch, 6-inch barrel; 9-1/8-inch overall length (5-inch barrel); fixed or target sights; checkered plastic grips; lanyard ring; blued finish. Introduced 1929; dropped 1968.

Exc: $650 **VGood:** $450 **Good:** $400

WEBLEY MARK IV WAR MODEL

Same specs as the Police Model. Built during WWII, it usually has poor blueing over unpolished surfaces. To protect the corporate reputation, most were stamped "WAR FINISH." Deduct 15 percent for near-identical Enfield-manufactured model with bobbed hammer ("Tanker").

Exc: $475 **VGood:** $315 **Good:** $225

WEBLEY MARK IV TARGET MODEL

Same specs as Police Model except 22 LR; adjustable rear sight. Built in small quantities; virtually a custom-produced handgun. Introduced 1931; dropped 1968.

Exc: $550 **VGood:** $375 **Good:** $275

WEBLEY MARK IV 32 POLICE

Same specs as Police Model except 32 S&W. Introduced 1929; dropped 1968.

Exc: $675 **VGood:** $450 **Good:** $300

WEBLEY MARK IV MILITARY REVOLVER

Revolver; 455 Webley; 6-shot; 4-inch, 6-inch barrel; hinged frame; Vulcanite grips; brush blue finish. Manufactured at Webley from 1915 to 1923 and at Enfield Arsenal from 1921 to 1926. Standard proofs: Webley Mark IV and date or Enfield MkVI and date. Manufactured from 1915 to 1926. Deduct 25 percent if cylinder shortend for 45 Auto Rim cartridge.

Webley 6-inch barrel

Exc: $725 **VGood:** $575 **Good:** $450

Webley 4-inch barrel

Exc: $725 **VGood:** $575 **Good:** $450

Enfield

Exc: $575 **VGood:** $425 **Good:** $375

WEBLEY MARK VI

Revolver; top-break; 6-shot double/single action. Caliber: 38/200 British WWII service cartridge, aka 38 S&W. Barrel: 4". Finish: Bright blue or matte "WAR FINISH. (see above). Very similar to the Enfield service revolver but generally commands a premium. Discontinued in the late 1960's. Commercial models in Excellent condition command as much as a 100 percent premium.

Exc: $550 **VGood:** $350 **Good:** $275

WEBLEY 1905 POCKET 32

Semi-automatic; 32 ACP; 3-1/2-inch barrel; 6-1/4-inch overall length; 8-shot magazine; external hammer; checkered hard rubber grips; blue finish. Introduced 1905; extensively redesigned in 1908; dropped 1940.

Exc: $550 **VGood:** $345 **Good:** $300

WEBLEY MODEL 1907 HAMMER MODEL

Semi-automatic; 25 ACP only; 2-1/8-inch barrel; 4-1/4-inch overall length; 6-shot magazine; checkered wood (early) or hard rubber grips. Introduced 1907; dropped 1940.

Exc: $550 **VGood:** $345 **Good:** $300

WEBLEY MODEL 1909

Semi-automatic; 9mm Browning Long; 8-shot magazine; 5-inch barrel; 8-inch overall length; external hammer; checkered hard rubber or wood grips; blue finish; only 1694 made. Introduced 1909; dropped 1914.

Exc: $1400 **VGood:** $950 **Good:** $700

WEBLEY MODEL 1909 TARGET PISTOL

Single shot; tip-up action; 22, 32 S&W, 38 S&W; 9-7/8-inch barrel; blade front sight; plastic thumbrest target grips; late versions had ballast chamber in butt to permit weight adjustment; rebounding hammer; matte-finish barrel; blued. Introduced 1909; dropped 1965.

Exc: $650 **VGood:** $500 **Good:** $350

WEBLEY MODEL 1910

Semi-automatic; 380 ACP; 7-shot; 3-1/2-inch barrel; 6-1/4-inch overall length; exposed hammer; checkered hard rubber grips. Revised Model 1905 built for 380 cartridge. Introduced 1910; dropped 1932.

Exc: $950 **VGood:** $625 **Good:** $475

WEBLEY MODEL 1910 HIGH VELOCITY

Semi-automatic; 38 ACP; 8-shot magazine; 5-inch barrel 8-1/2-inch overall length; internal hammer. Only about 1000 made. Introduced 1910; dropped 1911.

Exc: $1950 **VGood:** $1350 **Good:** $850

WEBLEY MODEL 1911

Semi-automatic; single shot; 22 Long; 4-1/2-inch, 9-inch barrel; 6-1/2-inch overall length (4-1/2-inch barrel); external hammer; checkered hard rubber grips; blue finish. Built on revised 1905-32 ACP pistol frame for police practice; upon firing, action blows open to eject and be ready for reloading. Total production 1500. Introduced 1911; dropped 1932.

Exc: $700 **VGood:** $500 **Good:** $250

WEBLEY MODEL 1913 (NAVY MODEL 455)

Semi-automatic; 455 Webley Self-Loading Pistol; 5-inch barrel; 8-1/2-inch overall length; external hammer; checkered hard rubber or wood grips; blue finish. About 1200 made for commercial sale; 7600 for the Royal Navy, and under 500 were "Royal Horse Artillery" models cut for shoulder stock and with adjustable rear sight. Introduced 1912; dropped 1933. Note: Serial numbers of all commercial Webley auto pistols were in a single series so do not reflect

Webley Model 1907
Hammer Model

Webley Model 1913
(Navy Model 455)

Webley Mark IV
Target Model

Webley
Model 1912
Hammerless

Webley Model 1910

Webley No.2
British Bulldog

quantity actually produced of any model. Military 455 autos had their own series, from 1 through 8050.

Commercial production

Exc: $1700 **VGood:** $1200 **Good:** $1000

Navy production

Exc: $1750 **VGood:** $1000 **Good:** $850

Royal Horse Artillery

Exc: $3750 **VGood:** $3000 **Good:** $2575

WEBLEY MODEL 1912 HAMMERLESS

Semi-automatic; 25 ACP only; 6-shot; 2-1/8-inch barrel; 4-1/4-inch overall length; striker fired; hard rubber grips. Introduced 1912; dropped 1938.

Exc: $550 **VGood:** $345 **Good:** $300

WEBLEY MODEL 1922

Semi-automatic; 9mm Browning Long; 8-shot; 5-inch barrel; 8-3/8-inch overall length; external hammer; checkered or plain wood grips; blued finish. Redesign of Model 1909 for possible military sale; of the 2000 made, 1000 were actually delivered to South African Defense Forces and 330 to Latvia. Introduced 1924; dropped 1932.

Exc: $1800 **VGood:** $1150 **Good:** $900

WEBLEY NO. 2 BRITISH BULLDOG

Revolver; 320, 380, 450; 5-shot; 2-inch, 3-inch barrel; fluted or round cylinders; solid frame; wood grips; bright blue or nickel finish. Marked "Webley No. 2" and caliber; topstrap marked THE BRITISH BULLDOG or with name of British retailer. Many No. 2s are marked with name of California retailer since the Bulldog was very popular in the American West. Manufactured from 1878 to 1915.

Exc: $600 **VGood:** $450 **Good:** $375

With American retailer or broad arrow marking

Exc: $650 **VGood:** $500 **Good:** $42

WEBLEY R.I.C. (ROYAL IRISH CONSTABULARY)

Revolver; 320 through 476; 5-, 6-shot cylinder; 2-inch, 6-inch barrels; solid frame; wood grips; bright blue or nickel finish. Early models had straighter grips and many had unfluted cylinders. Standard proofs with "Webley R.I.C." and caliber. Manufactured from 1868 to 1932.

Exc: $650 **VGood:** $450 **Good:** $375

WEBLEY WP WEBLEY POCKET

Revolver; double action; hinged frame; 32 S&W only; 6-shot; 2-inch, 3-inch barrel; 6-inch overall length (2-inch); checkered plastic grips; fixed sights; blued finish. Introduced 1908; dropped 1940.

Exc: $650 **VGood:** $395 **Good:** $300

WESSON FIREARMS 45 PIN GUN

Revolver; double action; 45 ACP; 6-shot; 5-inch barrel; 12-1/2-inch overall length; weighs 54 oz.; 1:14-inch twist; Taylor two-stage forcing cone; compensated shroud; finger-groove Hogue Monogrip grips; pin front sight, fully-adjustable rear; based on 44 Magnum frame; polished blue or brushed stainless steel; uses half-moon clips with 45 ACP, or 45 Auto Rim ammunition. Made in U.S. by Wesson Firearms Co., Inc. Introduced 1994; dropped 1995.

Blue finish, regular vent barrel shroud

Perf: $550 **Exc:** $500 **VGood:** $400

Stainless steel, regular vent barrel shroud

Perf: $600 **Exc:** $575 **VGood:** $500

Stainless steel vent heavy barrel shroud

Perf: $675 **Exc:** $600 **VGood:** $550

WESSON FIREARMS ACTION CUP/PPC

Revolver; double action; 38 Spl., 357 Mag.; 6-shot; extra heavy 6-inch barrel with bull shroud, removable underweight; weighs 4-1/2 lbs.; Pachmayr Gripper grips; Tasco Pro Point II sight; competition tuned with narrow trigger; chamfered cylinder chambers; stainless steel only. Made in U.S. by Wesson Firearms. Introduced 1989; dropped 1995.

Perf: $700 **Exc:** $625 **VGood:** $550

WESSON FIREARMS FB14-2

Revolver; double action; 357 Mag.; 2-1/2-inch, 4-inch fixed barrel; 8-1/4-inch overall length; weighs 36 oz. (2-1/2-inch barrel); service-style rubber grips; blade front sight, fixed rear; satin blue or stainless finish. Introduced 1993; dropped 1995.

New: $250 **Perf:** $200 **Exc:** $175

WESSON FIREARMS FB15, FB715

Revolver; double action; 357 Mag.; 6-shot; 3-inch, 4-inch, 5-inch, 6-inch fixed barrel; 8-3/4-inch overall length; weighs 37 oz. (3-inch barrel); Hogue rubber grips; blade front sight, adjustable rear; polished blue or stainless finish. FB715 is Service Model, with 2-1/2-inch or 4-inch barrel. Introduced 1993; dropped 1995.

New: $275 **Perf:** $275 **Exc:** $235

WESSON FIREARMS FB44

Revolver; double action; 44 Mag.; 6-shot; 4-inch, 5-inch, 6-inch, 8-inch barrel; 9-3/4-inch overall length (4-inch barrel); weighs 50 oz.; Hogue finger-groove rubber grips; interchangeable blade front sight, fully-adjustable rear; fixed, non-vented heavy barrel shrouds; polished blue finish. Introduced 1994; dropped 1995.

New: $350 **Perf:** $300 **Exc:** $275

WESSON FIREARMS FB744

Revolver; double action; 44 Mag.; 6-shot; 4-inch, 5-inch, 6-inch, 8-inch barrel; 9-3/4-inch overall length (4-inch barrel); weighs 50 oz.; Hogue finger-groove rubber grips; interchangeable blade front sight, fully-adjustable rear; fixed, non-vented heavy barrel shrouds; brushed stainless steel. Introduced 1994; dropped 1995.

New: $400 **Perf:** $350 **Exc:** $325

WESSON FIREARMS HUNTER SERIES

Revolver; double action; 357 Supermag, 41 Mag., 44 Mag., 445 Supermag; 6-shot cylinder; 6-inch, 7-1/2-inch fixed barrel; 14-inch overall length; weighs 64 oz.; Hogue finger-groove rubber or wood presentation grips; blade front sight, dovetailed Iron Sight Gunworks rear; 1:18-3/4-inch twist barrel; Alan Taylor two-stage forcing cone; non-fluted cylinder; bright blue or satin stainless. Introduced 1994; dropped 1995.

7-1/2-inch barrel, blue finish

New: $700 **Perf:** $650 **Exc:** $600

7-1/2-inch barrel, stainless steel

New: $750 **Perf:** $700 **Exc:** $650

6-inch compensated barrel, 7-inch shroud, blue finish

New: $725 **Perf:** $675 **Exc:** $625

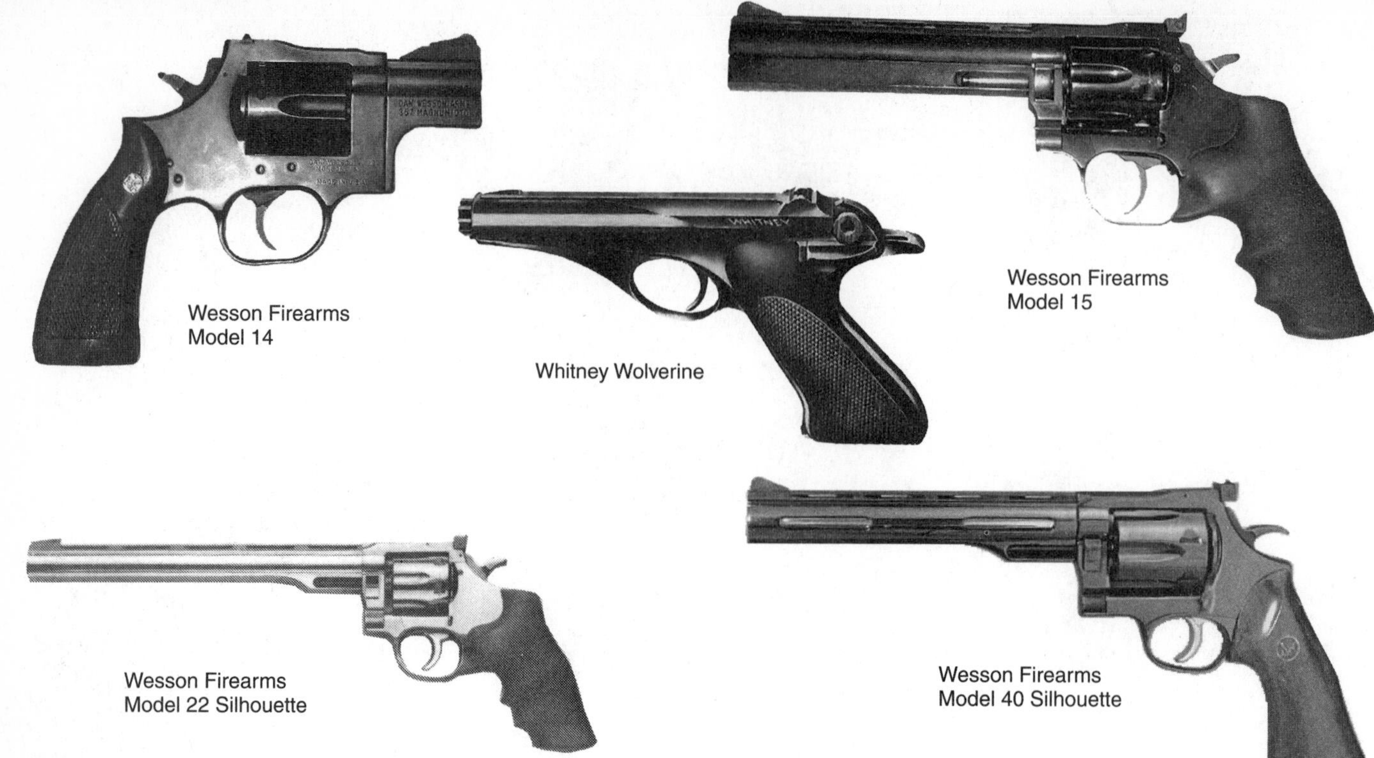
Wesson Firearms Model 14

Whitney Wolverine

Wesson Firearms Model 15

Wesson Firearms Model 22 Silhouette

Wesson Firearms Model 40 Silhouette

6-inch compensated barrel, 7-inch shroud), stainless steel

New: $775 **Perf:** $725 **Exc:** $675

6-inch compensated barrel, 7-inch shroud, scope rings on shroud, blue finish

New: $775 **Perf:** $725 **Exc:** $625

6-inch compensated barrel, 7-inch shroud, scope rings on shroud, stainless steel

New: $800 **Perf:** $750 **Exc:** $700

WESSON FIREARMS MODEL 8-2

Revolver; double-action; 38 Spl.; 6-shot; 2-1/2-inch, 4-inch, 6-inch interchangeable barrels; 9 1/4-inch overall length (4-inch barrel); weighs 30 oz.; serrated front, fixed rear sight; checkered grips; stainless or bright blue finish. Introduced 1975; dropped 1995.

Perf: $200 **Exc:** $175 **VGood:** $150

WESSON FIREARMS MODEL 9-2H

Revolver; double action; 38 Spl.; 2-inch-15-inch barrel; ramp front, adjustable rear sight; heavy barrel options; blue or nickel finish. Introduced, 1975; dropped 1995, reintroduced 1997.

Perf: $250 **Exc:** $200 **VGood:** $175

WESSON FIREARMS MODEL 9-2V

Same specs as Model 9-2H except standard vent-rib barrel. Introduced 1975; discontinued 1995, reintroduced 1997.

Perf: $275 **Exc:** $225 **VGood:** $200

WESSON FIREARMS MODEL 9-2HV

Same specs as Model 9-2 except heavy vent-rib barrel; 38 Spl. only. Introduced 1975; discontinued 1995, reintroduced 1997.

Perf: $325 **Exc:** $275 **VGood:** $225

WESSON FIREARMS MODEL 11

Revolver; double action; 357 Mag.; 6-shot; 2-1/2-inch, 4-inch, 6-inch interchangeable barrel; 9-1/4-inch overall length (4-inch barrel); interchangeable grips; adjustable dovetail rear sight, serrated ramp front. Marketed with tools for changing barrels, grips; non-recessed barrel nut, blued. Introduced 1969; dropped 1974.

Perf: $200 **Exc:** $175 **VGood:** $150

WESSON FIREARMS MODEL 12

Revolver; 357 Mag.; 6-shot; 2-1/2-inch, 3-3/4-inch, 5-3/4-inch interchangeable barrels and grips; adjustable target-type rear sight, serrated ramp front. Marketed with tools for changing barrels, grips; blued. Introduced 1969; dropped 1974.

Perf: $200 **Exc:** $175 **VGood:** $150

WESSON FIREARMS MODEL 14

Revolver; double-action; 357 Mag.; 6-shot; 2-1/4-inch, 3-3/4-inch, 5-3/4-inch interchangeable barrel; 9-inch overall length (3-3/4-inch barrel); interchangeable walnut grips; fixed dovetail rear sight, serrated ramp front; wide trigger with adjustable over-travel stop; wide spur hammer; recessed barrel nut; blued, nickel, matte nickel finish. Introduced 1971; dropped 1975. Replaced by Model 14-2.

Perf: $225 **Exc:** $175 **VGood:** $150

WESSON FIREARMS MODEL 14-2

Same general specs as Model 14, except 2-1/2-inch, 4-inch Quickshift interchangeable barrels; Quickshift grips interchangeable with three other styles. Introduced 1976; dropped 1995.

New: $400 **Perf:** $300 **Exc:** $250

WESSON FIREARMS MODEL 15

Revolver; double action; 357 Mag.; 6-shot; 2-1/4-inch, 3-3/4-inch, 5-3/4-inch interchangeable barrel; fully-adjustable rear sight; wide trigger with adjustable over-travel stop; wide spur hammer; recessed barrel nut; blued, nickel, matte nickel finish. Introduced in 1971; dropped, 1975. Replaced by Model 15-2.

Perf: $275 **Exc:** $225 **VGood:** $175

WESSON FIREARMS MODEL 15-1

Same specs as Model 15 except reduced size of rear sight. Introduced, 1973; dropped, 1975.

Perf: $250 **Exc:** $200 **VGood:** $175

WESSON FIREARMS MODEL 15-2

Same specs as Model 15-1 except no barrel shroud. Introduced 1973; dropped, then reintroduced 1997.

Perf: $300 **Exc:** $200 **VGood:** $175

WESSON FIREARMS MODEL 15-2H

Same specs as the Model 15-2, except heavy barrel options. Introduced 1975; dropped 1995.

Perf: $300 **Exc:** $200 **VGood:** $175

WESSON FIREARMS MODEL 15-2HV

Same specs as Model 15-2 except heavy vent-rib barrel, ranging from 2-inch to 15-inch. Introduced 1975; dropped 1995.

Perf: $325 **Exc:** $275 **VGood:** $225

WESSON FIREARMS MODEL 15 GOLD SERIES

Same specs as Model 15 except smoother tuned action; 6-inch or 8-inch vent heavy slotted barrel shroud; blued barrel; rosewood stocks; orange dot Patridge-type front sight, white triangle on rear blade; stamped "Gold Series" with gold-filled Dan Wesson signature. Introduced 1989; dropped 1994.

Perf: $400 **Exc:** $325 **VGood:** $275

WESSON FIREARMS MODEL 715VH

Same specs as Model 15-2 except stainless steel construction with compensated barrel. Discontinued 2005. (NOTE: In mid-2005, the assets of Wesson Firearms were acquired by CZ-USA. Future production of Dan Wesson revolvers is uncertain.)

Perf: $700 **Exc:** $550 **VGood:** $375

WESSON FIREARMS MODEL 22

Revolver; double action; 22 LR, 22 WMR; 6-shot cylinder; 2-1/2-inch, 4-inch, 6-inch, 8-inch, 10-inch interchangeable barrel; checkered, undercover, service or target stocks of American walnut; serrated, interchangeable front sight; adjustable white outline rear; blued or stainless steel; wide trigger; over-travel trigger adjustment; wide hammer spur. Introduced 1982; dropped, then reintroduced 1997.

Perf: $300 **Exc:** $200 **VGood:** $175

WESSON FIREARMS MODEL 22 SILHOUETTE

Revolver; single action; 22 LR; 6-shot; 10-inch regular vent or vent heavy barrel; weighs 53 oz.; combat-style grips; Patridge-style front sight, .080-inch rear. From Wesson Firearms Co., Inc. Introduced 1989; dropped 1995.

Blue finish, regular vent barrel

New: $400 **Perf:** $350 **Exc:** $325

Blue finish, vent heavy barrel

New: $425 **Perf:** $375 **Exc:** $350

Stainless steel, regular vent barrel

New: $450 **Perf:** $400 **Exc:** $375

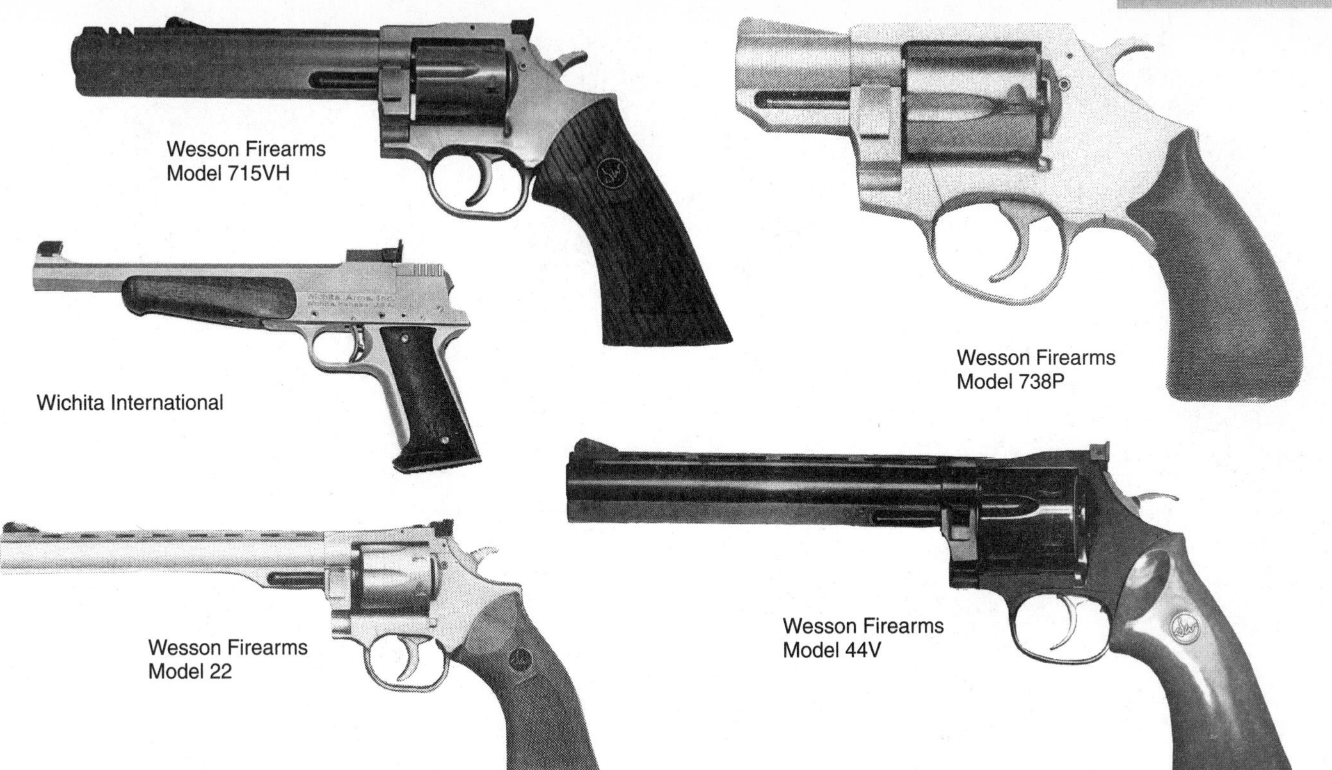
Wesson Firearms Model 715VH

Wesson Firearms Model 738P

Wichita International

Wesson Firearms Model 22

Wesson Firearms Model 44V

Stainless steel, vent heavy barrel

New: $475 **Perf:** $425 **Exc:** $410

WESSON FIREARMS MODEL 32M

Revolver; 32 H&R Mag.; 6-shot; 2-1/2-inch, 3-3/4-inch, 5-3/4-inch barrel; adjustable rear sight, ramp front; blued or stainless steel. Introduced 1984.

Perf: $300 **Exc:** $200 **VGood:** $175

WESSON FIREARMS MODEL 40 SILHOUETTE

Revolver; 357 Maximum; 6-shot cylinder; 6-inch, 8-inch, 10-inch barrel; 14-5/16-inch overall length (8-inch barrel); weighs 64 oz.; adjustable rear sight, serrated front; blued or stainless steel; meets IHMSA competition criteria. Introduced 1986; dropped 1995.

Perf: $600 **Exc:** $525 **VGood:** $375

WESSON FIREARMS MODEL 41V

Revolver; double action; 41 Mag.; 6-shot cylinder; 4-inch, 6-inch, 8-inch, 10-inch interchangeable barrel; smooth walnut stocks; serrated front sight, adjustable white-outline rear; wide trigger; adjustable trigger over-travel feature; wide hammer spur; blued or stainless steel. Introduced 1982; dropped 1995.

Perf: $350 **Exc:** $300 **VGood:** $250

WESSON FIREARMS MODEL 44V

Revolver; double action; 44 Mag.; 6-shot; 4, 6, 8 or 10-inch interchangeable barrel; walnut stocks; serrated front sight; adjustable rear; wide trigger with adjustable over-travel feature; wide hammer spur; blued or stainless finish. Introduced 1982; dropped 1995.

Perf: $375 **Exc:** $325 **VGood:** $275

WESSON FIREARMS MODEL 45V

Revolver; double action; 41 Mag., 44 Mag., 45 Colt; 6-shot cylinder; 4-inch, 6-inch, 8-inch, 10-inch interchangeable barrel; 12-inch overall length (6-inch barrel); weighs 48 oz. (4-inch barrel); smooth wood grips; 1/8-inch serrated front sight, fully-adjustable white outline rear; smooth, wide trigger with adjustable over-travel; wide hammer spur. Made in U.S. by Wesson Firearms. Introduced 1993; dropped 1995.

Blue finish

New: $400 **Perf:** $350 **Exc:** $300

Stainless steel

New: $450 **Perf:** $400 **Exc:** $375

WESSON FIREARMS MODEL 322

Revolver; double action; 32-20; 6-shot cylinder; 2-1/2-inch, 4-inch, 6-inch, 8-inch barrel, standard, vent, vent heavy; 11-1/4-inch overall length; weighs 43 oz. (6-inch barrel); checkered walnut grips; red ramp interchangeable front sight, fully-adjustable rear; blue or stainless finish. Made in U.S. by Wesson Firearms Co., Inc. Introduced 1991; dropped 1995, reintroduced 1997. Longer barrels bring a premium.

New: $300 **Perf:** $250 **Exc:** $200

WESSON FIREARMS MODEL 738P

Revolver; double action; 38 Spl. +P; 5-shot cylinder; 2-inch barrel; 6-1/2-inch overall length; weighs 24-1/2 oz.; Pauferro wood or rubber grips; blade front sight, fixed notch rear; designed for +P ammunition; stainless steel construction. Made in U.S. by Wesson Firearms Co., Inc. Introduced 1992; dropped 1995. Reintroduced 1997.

New: $300 **Perf:** $250 **Exc:** $200

WESSON FIREARMS MODEL 7322

Revolver; double action; 32-20; 6-shot cylinder; 2-1/2-inch, 4-inch, 6-inch, 8-inch barrel, standard, vent, vent heavy; 11 1/4-inch overall length; weighs 43 oz. (6-inch barrel); checkered walnut grips; red ramp interchangeable front sight, fully-adjustable rear; stainless steel. Made in U.S. by Wesson Firearms Co., Inc. Introduced 1991; dropped 1995.

New: $375 **Perf:** $325 **Exc:** $300

WESSON FIREARMS .455 SUPERMAG

Revolver; has same general specs as Model 40 series; chambered for the .455 Supermag cartridge; blued or stainless steel; 4-inch, 6-inch, 8-inch, 10-inch barrel. Introduced, 1989; dropped, then reintroduced in 1997.

Perf: $675 **Exc:** $575 **VGood:** $500

WESSON FIREARMS PPC

Revolver; double action; 38 Spl., 357 Mag.; 6-shot cylinder; 6-inch extra heavy barrel with bull shroud, removable underweight; weighs 4 lbs., 7 oz.; Pachmayr Gripper grips; Aristocrat sights with three-postion rear; competition tuned with narrow trigger; chamfered cylinder chambers; bright blue finish or stainless steel. Made in U.S. by Wesson Firearms. Introduced 1989; dropped 1995.

Perf: $550 **Exc:** $500 **VGood:** $450

WHITNEY WOLVERINE

Semi-automatic; 22 LR; 4-1/2-inch barrel; 9-inch overall length; aluminum alloy frame; windage-adjustable rear; 1/8-inch Patridge-type front; top of slide serrated to reduce reflection; checkered plastic grips; blued or nickel finish. Introduced 1956; dropped 1963. Reintroduced in polymer-frame version by Olympic Arms in 2005. Deduct 30 percent for Olympic production.

Exc: $550 **VGood:** $395 **Good:** $300

Nickel finish

Exc: $1000 **VGood:** $800 **Good:** $500

WICHITA CLASSIC SILHOUETTE

Bolt action; all standard calibers to 2.80-inch; 11-1/14-inch barrel; weighs 4 lbs.; hooded post front sight; open adjustable rear; AAA American walnut stock with checkered pistol grip; three locking lug bolts; three gas ports; adjustable trigger. From Wichita Arms. Introduced 1981; still in production.

Perf: $3200 **Exc:** $2400 **VGood:** $1900

WICHITA INTERNATIONAL

Single shot; 22 LR, 22 WMR, 32 H&R Mag., 357 Super Mag., 357 Mag., 7R, 7mm Super Mag., 7-30 Waters, 30-30 Win.; 10-inch, 10-1/2-inch, 14-inch barrel; weighs 3 lbs. 2 oz. (10-inch barrel); walnut grip and forend; Patridge front sight, adjustable rear; Wichita Multi-Range sight system optional; made of stainless steel; break-open action; grip dimensions same as Colt 45 Auto; drilled and tapped for furnished see-thru rings; extra barrels are factory fitted. Available from Wichita Arms. Introduced 1983; dropped 1994.

New: $750 **Perf:** $650 **Exc:** $550

WICHITA MASTER

Bolt action; 6mm BR, 7mm BR, 243, 7mm-08, 22-250, 308; 3-shot magazine; 13-inch, 14-7/8-inch barrel; weighs 4-1/2 lbs. (13-inch barrel); American walnut stock with oil finish; glass bedded; hooded post front sight, open adjustable rear; left-hand

Wichita Silhouette

Wildey Automatic Pistol

Wildey Hunter

Wilkinson Diane

Wildey Jaws Viper

Wildey Pin Gun

action with right-hand grip; round receiver and barrel; Wichita adjustable trigger. Made in U.S. by Wichita Arms. Introduced 1991; dropped 1994.

Perf: $1275 **Exc:** $850 **VGood:** $600

WICHITA SILHOUETTE PISTOL

Bolt action; 308 Win., 7mm IHSMA, 7mm-08; 14-15/16-inch barrel; 21-3/8-inch overall length; weighs 4-1/2 lbs.; Wichita Multi-Range sight system; American walnut glass-bedded stock; round barrel; fluted bolt with flat bolt handle; adjustable trigger. From Wichita Arms. Introduced 1979; still in production.

Perf: $1500 **Exc:** $1200 **VGood:** $950

WILDEY AUTOMATIC PISTOL

Semi-automatic; 10mm Wildey Mag., 11mm Wildey Mag., 357 Peterbuilt, 45 Win. Mag.; 7-shot; 5-inch, 6-inch, 7-inch, 8-inch, 10-inch, 12-inch, 14-inch (45 Win. Mag.); 8-inch, 10-inch, 12-inch, 15-inch (other calibers) interchangeable barrel; 11-inch overall length (7-inch barrel); weighs 64 oz. (5-inch barrel); ramp front sight, fully-adjustable rear; hardwood grips; stainless steel construction; three lug rotary belt; double or single action; polished and matte finish.

Perf: $1400 **Exc:** $1150 **VGood:** $900

WILDEY HUNTER

Semi-automatic; 44 Magnum, 45 Win. Mag.; 7-shot; 5-inch, 6-inch, 7-inch, 8-inch, 10-inch, 12-inch, 14-inch length; weighs 64 oz. (5-inch barrel); ramp front sight, fully-adjustable rear; hardwood grips; stainless steel construction; three lug rotary belt; double or single action; polished and matte finish.

Perf: $1400 **Exc:** $1150 **VGood:** $900

WILDEY PIN GUN

Gas-operated auto-loading pistol in polished or matte stainless for competition shooting. With muzzle brake; variety of calibers and barrel lengths (7-inch, 8-inch, 10-inch, 12-inch, 14-inch). 4.09 lb. (8-inch barrel).

New: $1550 **Exc:** $1475 **VGood:** $1195

WILDEY JAWS VIPER

Jordanian Arms & Weapons System manufactured in Jordan. Semi-auto chambered for 9mm, .40 S&W, 45 ACP. Barrels: 4.4-inch and 5-inch. 10-round magazine. Stainless finish with rubberized grip.

New: $695 **Exc:** $625 **VGood:** $495

WILKINSON DIANE

Semi-automatic; 22 LR, 25 ACP; 8-shot magazine; 2-1/8-inch barrel; 4-1/2-inch overall length; internal hammer; separate ejector; checkered styrene stocks; fixed sights integral with slide; matte blued finish. Introduced 1977; no longer in production.

Exc: $250 **VGood:** $175 **Good:** $125

WILKINSON LINDA

Semi-automatic; 9mm Para.; 31-shot magazine; 8-5/16-inch barrel; 12-1/4-inch overall length; weighs 5 lbs.; protected blade front sight, Wiliams adjustable rear; maple forend; checkered black plastic stocks; blowback action; crossbolt safety. Introduced 1982.

New: $725 **Perf:** $600 **Exc:** $425

WILKINSON SHERRY

Semi-automatic; 22 LR; 8-shot magazine; 2-1/8-inch barrel; 4-3/4-inch overall length; weighs 9-1/4 oz.; no sights; checkered black plastic stocks; crossbolt safety; blue finish or gold-plated frame; blued slide, trigger. Introduced 1985.

New: $595 **Perf:** $495 **Exc:** $395

WILSON COMBAT ADP 9MM

Wilson's first production pistol. 11-round capacity, polymer frame. 19.5 oz. 6.3-inch overall length, 3.75-inch barrel.

New: $579 **Exc:** $515 **VGood:** $400

WILSON COMBAT COMPACTS

1911 style, single action only, hammer fired, steel frame and slide, compact semi-automatic pistol. Available in .45 ACP. 3.6 inch barrel, 7.2 inches long, weight: 26 - 36 ounces. Sight and other options available / variations exist.

Sentinel

Perf: $3,300 **Exc:** $3,000 **VGood:** $2,750

WILSON COMBAT KZ 9MM

Polymer-frame 1911 chambered for 9mm. Full size is 16+1 capacity with 5-inch barrel at 33 oz. Compact size is 14+1 capacity with 4.1-inch barrel at 31 oz.

New: $1300 **Exc:** $1195 **VGood:** $895

WILSON COMBAT SENTINELS

1911 style, single action only, hammer fired, steel frame and slide, compact semi-automatic pistol. Available in 9mm Luger. 3.6 inch barrel, 7.2 inches long, weight: 31.7 ounces. Full length guide rod, battle-sight with fiber optic front sight, Armor-Tuff finish. 8+1 capacity. Other variations include the Super Sentinel (.38 Super), Ms. Sentinel (9mm), Ultralight Carry Sentinel (9mm).

Sentinel

Perf: $2,950 **Exc:** $2,600 **VGood:** $2,400

Super Sentinel, Ms. Sentinel, Ultralight Carry Sentinel

Perf: $3,350 **Exc:** $3,000 **VGood:** $2,800

WILSON COMBAT SUPERGRADES

1911 style, single action only, hammer fired, steel frame and slide, semi-automatic pistol. Available in 9mm Luger, .38 Super, .40 S&W, 10mm & .45 ACP. 5.0 inch barrel, 8.7 inches long, weight: 36.6 ounces. Ambidextrous safety, 30 LPI Checkering and Low-Mount adjustable rear sight. Variations exist.

Sentinel

Perf: $4,850 **Exc:** $4,000 **VGood:** $3,750

WILSON COMBAT X-TAC

1911 style, single action only, hammer fired, steel frame and slide, semi-automatic pistol. Available in .45 ACP. 5.0 inch barrel, 8.7 inches long, weight: 38.1 ounces. X-Tac checkering on front strap, back strap and rear of slide. Contoured magazine well. Battle-sight with fiber optic front sight. Parkerized finish. Variations exist.

Sentinel

Perf: $2,450 **Exc:** $2,100 **VGood:** $1,750

WYOMING ARMS PARKER AUTO

Semi-automatic; single action; 10mm Auto, 40 S&W, 45 ACP; 8-shot (10mm, 40 S&W), 7-shot (45 ACP); 3-3/8-inch, 5-inch, 7-inch barrel; 6-3/8-inch overall length; weighs 29 oz. to 44 oz.; grooved composition grips; fixed or Millett adjustable sights; made of stainless steel. Made in the U.S. by Wyoming Arms Mfg. Corp. Introduced 1990; dropped 1992.

3-3/8-inch, 5-inch barrel, fixed sights

Perf: $425 **Exc:** $375 **VGood:** $350

7-inch barrel, adjustable sights

Perf: $450 **Exc:** $350 **VGood:** $300

MODERN GUN VALUES

RIFLES

Directory of Manufacturers

A.A. ARMS 266
AAO..................... 266
ACKLEY.................. 266
ACTION ARMS 266
ALPHA 266
ALPINE.................. 266
AMAC 266
AMERICAN ARMS........... 267
AMERICAN FIREARMS....... 267
AMT 267
ANSCHUTZ................ 267
ARMALITE 273
ARMSCOR 274
ARMSPORT 275
ARNOLD ARMS 275
A-SQUARE 276
AUTO-ORDNANCE 276
BALLARD 276
BARRETT 277
BAYARD 277
BEEMAN/HW 277
Benelli 277
BENTON & BROWN 278
BERETTA 278
BERNARDELLI 279
BIG HORN 279
BLASER 279
BORTMESS 280
BRNO 280
BRONCO..................281
Ed Brown 282
BROWN................... 282
BROWNING 282
BSA..................... 288
BUSHMASTER 289
CABANAS 290
CABELA'S 290
CALICO..................291
CARL GUSTAF 291
CENTURY 292
CHAPUIS 292
CHIPMUNK................ 292
Christensen Arms........ 293
CHURCHILL 293
CIMARRON................ 293
CITADEL 294
CLARIDGE 294
CLAYCO 294
CLERKE 294
COLT.................... 294
COMMANDO arms 296
COOPER ARMS 296
CUMBERLAND MOUNTAIN ARMS 297
CVA..................... 297
CZ...................... 298
D-MAX................... 300
DAEWOO 300
DAISY 300
DAKOTA 301
CHARLES DALY 302
DAN WESSON 302
DIANA................... 302
DIXIE................... 303
DPMS 303
DSA..................... 304
DuBIEL.................. 304
DUMOULIN................ 304
E.A.A................... 305
EAGLE ARMS 306
E.M.F................... 307
ERMA 307
FAJEN................... 308
FEATHER 308
FEDERAL ENGINEERING.... 308
FEDERAL ORDNANCE 308
FEG..................... 308
FEINWERKBAU............. 309
FERLACH 309
F.I.E................... 309
FINNISH LION 310
F.N. 310
FNH-USA 311
Forbes..................311
FOX.....................311
FRANCOTTE...............311
GALIL 312
GAMBA 312
GARBI...................312
GARCIA..................312
GARRETT ARMS 312
GEVARM 312
GOLDEN EAGLE............312
GREIFELT................313
GRENDEL.................313
HAENEL 313
HAMMERLI 313
HAMMERLI-TANNER 313
HARRINGTON & RICHARDSON..........313
HARRIS-McMILLAN 317
HECKLER & KOCH 319
HENRY 320
HEYM 321
HEYM-RUGER 323
HI-POINT 323
HI-STANDARD 323
HOENIG 324
HOLLAND & HOLLAND 324
Howa 324
Huldra Arms 325
HUSQVARNA 326
IAI..................... 327
IAR 327
IBUS 327
INTERARMS............... 327
ISSC.................... 328
ITHACA.................. 328
IVER JOHNSON 328
JAEGER 330
KBI 330
KDF..................... 330
KEL TEC................. 330
KIMBER 331
KIMEL................... 334
KINTREK................. 334
KLEINGUENTHER 334
KODIAK.................. 334
KRICO................... 334
KRIEGHOFF 336
LAKEFIELD ARMS 337
L.A.R. 338
LEBEAU-COURALLY......... 338
LEGACY SPORTS INTERNATIONAL 338
LES BAER................ 339
LJUTIC 339
MAGNUM RESEARCH 339
MAGTECH 339
MANNLICHER-SCHOENAUER 340
MAPIZ....................341
MARATHON 341
MARCEL...................341
MARLIN 341
MAUSER.................. 353
McMILLAN 356
MERKEL 358
MIDLAND 359
MITCHELL 359
MONTANA ARMORY 360
Mossberg 361
MOUNTAIN EAGLE 369
M-S SAFARI ARMS 369
MUSGRAVE 370
NAVY ARMS 370
NEW ENGLAND FIREARMS .. 373
New Ultra Light Arms.... 373
NEWTON 374
NOBLE 374
NORINCO................. 374
NORRAHAMMAR 375
Nosler.................. 375
NS FIREARMS 375
OLYMPIC ARMS 375
OMEGA III............... 377
PARKER-HALE 377
PEDERSEN................ 378
PERUGINI-VISINI 379
PHILLIPS & RODGERS...... 379
PLAINFIELD 379
PROFESSIONAL ORDNANCE 379
PUMA 379
PURDEY 379
QUALITY PARTS/ BUSHMASTER 379
Remington 380
RIGBY................... 394
RIZZINI................. 394
ROSS 394
ROSSI................... 394
SAKO 395
SAUER 398
SAVAGE 399
SCHULTZ & LARSEN 412
SEDGELY 412
SERRIFLE.................412
C. SHARPS ARMS 412
SHILEN...................413
SHILOH...................413
SIGARMS 414
SMITH & WESSON 414
SOVEREIGN 415
SPRINGFIELD INC. 415
SQUIRES BINGHAM 416
Stag Arms.................417
STEVENS 417
STEYR 421
STI 423
STONER.................. 423
STEYR 424
Strum Ruger............. 424
SURVIVAL ARMS 430
SWISS................... 430
TANNER 430
TAURUS 430
THOMPSON/CENTER 431
TIKKA 432
TRADEWINDS.............. 450
TRADITIONS.............. 450
TRISTAR................. 450
TYROL 451
UBERTI....................451
ULTIMATE ACCURACY 451
ULTRA-HI 451
UNIQUE 452
UNIVERSAL 452
VALMET 452
VARNER 452
VEKTOR 453
VICKERS.................. 453
VOERE 453
WALTHER 454
WEATHERBY................ 456
WEIHRAUCH.................461
WESSON & HARRINGTON 461
WESTLEY RICHARDS.........461
WHITWORTH 461
WICHITA...................461
WICKLIFFE.................461
WILKINSON 462
WINCHESTER............... 462
WINSLOW.................. 479
ZOLI 479

A.A. ARMS AR9

Semi-automatic; 9mm Para.; 20-shot magazine; 16-1/4-inch barrel; 33-inch overall length; weighs 6-1/2 lbs.; folding buttstock, checkered plastic grip; adjustable post front sight in ring, fixed open rear; fires from closed bolt; lever safety blocks trigger and sear; vented barrel shroud; matte blue/black or nickel finish. Made in U.S. Marketed by Kimel Industries, later by A. A. Arms. Introduced 1991; no longer produced.

Exc: $850 **VGood:** $600 **Good:** $450

AAO MODEL 2000 50 CALIBER

Bolt action; 50 BMG; 5-shot magazine; 30-inch barrel, 1:15-inch twist; weighs 24 lbs.; muzzlebrake; cast alloy stock with gray anodized finish; Kick-Ease recoil pad; no sights; drilled and tapped for scope base; controlled feeding via rotating enclosed claw extractor; 90-degree bolt rotation; cone bolt face and barrel; trigger-mounted safety blocks sear; fully-adjustable, detachable tripod. Made in U.S. by American Arms & Ordnance. Introduced 1994.

New: $3750 **Perf:** $2995 **Exc:** $1995

ACKLEY OLYMPUS GRADE

Bolt action; 22-250, 25-06, 257 Roberts, 270, 7x57, 30-06, 7mm Rem. Mag., 300 Win. Mag.; 4-shot magazine (standard calibers), 3-shot (magnums); 24-inch barrel; no sights; drilled, tapped for scope mounts; hand-checkered select American walnut stock; rubber buttpad; swivel studs; Ackley barrel; hinged floorplate; fully-adjustable trigger; Mark X Mauser action. Introduced 1971; discontinued 1975.

Perf: $900 **Exc:** $725 **VGood:** $550

ACKLEY OLYMPUS GRADE II

Same specs as Olympus Grade except finely hand-checkered select American walnut stock; rubber recoil pad. Custom offering only; precludes pricing.

ACKLEY STANDARD MODEL

Bolt action; 22-250, 25-06, 257 Roberts, 270, 7x57, 30-06, 7mm Rem. Mag., 300 Win. Mag.; 4-shot magazine (standard calibers), 3-shot (magnums); 24-inch barrel; engraved receiver; no sights, drilled, tapped for scope mounts; hand-checkered American walnut stock; rubber recoil pad, swivel studs; Ackley barrel; hinged floorplate; fully-adjustable trigger; Mark X Mauser action. Introduced 1971; discontinued 1975.

Perf: $700 **Exc:** $650 **VGood:** $450

ACKLEY VARMINT SPECIAL

Bolt action; 22-250, 220 Swift, 25-06, 257 Roberts, 270, 7x57, 30-06, 7mm Rem. Mag., 300 Win. Mag.; 4-shot magazine (standard calibers), 3-shot (magnums); 26-inch barrel; no sights; drilled tapped for scope mounts; hand-checkered American walnut stock; varmint forend; rubber recoil pad; swivel studs. Introduced 1971; discontinued 1975.

Perf: $700 **Exc:** $600 **VGood:** $450

ACTION ARMS TIMBERWOLF

Slide action; 38 Spl./357 Mag., 44 Mag.; 10-shot magazine; 18-1/2-inch barrel; 36-1/2-inch overall length; weighs 5-1/2 lbs.; blade front sight, adjustable rear; plain walnut stock; grooved slide handle; push-button safety on trigger guard; takedown; integral scope mount; blued or chrome finish. Was imported by Action Arms Ltd. (357 only) and Springfield Armory (357 Mag. and 44 Mag.). Made in Israel. Introduced 1989; no longer imported.

Exc: $650 **VGood:** $495 **Good:** $290

Chrome finish

Exc: $665 **VGood:** $510 **Good:** $305

ALPHA ALASKAN

Bolt action; 308 Win., 350 Rem. Mag., 358 Win., 458 Win. Mag.; 4-shot magazine; 20- to 24-inch barrel; weighs 6-3/4 to 7-1/2 lbs.; no sights; drilled tapped for scope mounts; Alphawood stock; Neidner-style grip cap; barrel band swivel stud; right- or left-hand models; stainless steel construction. Introduced 1985; discontinued 1987.

Exc: $1400 **VGood:** $1100 **Good:** $825

Ackley Olympus Grade II

Action Arms Timberwolf

Alpha Alaskan

Alpha Custom Model

Alpha Jaguar Grade I

ALPHA BIG-FIVE

Bolt action; 300 H&H to 458 Win. Mag.; 4-shot magazine; 20-inch-24-inch Douglas barrel; no sights; drilled tapped for scope mounts; satin-finish American walnut reinforced stock; three-position safety; honed action and trigger; lightened action; swivel studs; decelerator recoil pad. Introduced 1987; discontinued 1987.

Exc: $1500 **VGood:** $1200 **Good:** $875

ALPHA CUSTOM MODEL

Bolt action; 17 Rem., 222, 223, 22-250, 338-284, 25-06, 35 Whelen, 257 Weatherby, 338 Win. Mag.; other calibers available in short, medium, long actions; 20- to 24-inch barrel; 40- to 43-inch overall length; weighs 6 to 7 lbs.; no sights; drilled, tapped for scope mounts; hand-checkered classic-style California Claro walnut stock; hand-rubbed oil finish; ebony forend tip; custom steel grip cap; solid buttpad; inletted swivel studs; three-lug locking system; three-position safety; left- or right-hand models; satin blue finish. Introduced 1984; discontinued 1987.

Exc: $1250 **VGood:** $1100 **Good:** $875

ALPHA GRAND SLAM

Bolt action; 17 Rem., 222, 223, 22-250, 338-284, 25-06, 35 Whelen, 257 Weatherby, 338 Win. Mag.; other calibers available in short, medium, long actions; 20- to 24-inch barrel; 40- to 43-inch overall length; weighs 6-1/2 lbs.; no sights; drilled, tapped for scope mounts; hand-checkered classic-style California Claro walnut or laminated stock; hand-rubbed oil finish; ebony forend tip; custom steel grip cap; solid buttpad; inletted swivel studs; three-lug locking system; three-position safety; fluted bolt; left- or right-hand models; matte blue finish. Introduced 1984; discontinued 1987.

Exc: $1250 **VGood:** $975 **Good:** $750

ALPHA JAGUAR GRADE I

Bolt action; from 222 to 338 Win. Mag.; 4-shot magazine; 20- to 24-inch round tapered barrel; 39-1/2-inch overall length; weighs 6 lbs.; no sights; drilled, tapped for scope mounts; satin-finish American walnut Monte Carlo stock; rubber buttpad; swivel studs; medium-length Mauser-type action; slide safety; cocking indicator; aluminum bedding block; Teflon-coated trigger guard, floorplate assembly. Introduced 1987; discontinued 1987.

Exc: $975 **VGood:** $875 **Good:** $700

ALPHA JAGUAR GRADE II

Same specs as Grade I except Douglas premium barrel.

Exc: $970 **VGood:** $790 **Good:** $600

ALPHA JAGUAR GRADE III

Same specs as Grade I except Douglas barrel; three-position safety; honed action and trigger.

Exc: $1225 **VGood:** $1100 **Good:** $875

ALPHA JAGUAR GRADE IV

Same specs as Grade I except Douglas barrel; three-position safety; honed action and trigger; lightened action; swivel studs.

Exc: $1300 **VGood:** $1150 **Good:** $900

ALPINE SPORTER

Bolt action; 22-250, 243 Win., 264 Win., 270, 30-06, 308, 308 Norma Mag., 7mm Rem. Mag., 8mm, 300 Win. Mag.; 5-shot magazine (standard calibers), 3-shot (magnums); 23-inch barrel (standard calibers), 24-inch (magnums); ramp front sight, open adjustable rear; checkered pistol-grip Monte Carlo stock of European walnut; recoil pad; sling swivels. Imported from England by Mandall Shooting Supplies. Introduced 1978; no longer imported.

Perf: $450 **Exc:** $400 **VGood:** $270

AMAC TARGETMASTER

Slide-action; 22 Short, 22 Long, 22 LR; 19-shot magazine (22 Short), 15-shot (22 Long), 12-shot (22 LR); 18-1/2-inch barrel; 36-1/2-inch overall length; weighs 5-3/4 lbs.; hooded ramp front sight, open adjustable rear; receiver grooved for scope mounts; walnut-finished hardwood stock; polished blued finish. Made in standard and youth models. Introduced 1985 by Iver Johnson; dropped 1990.

Exc: $245 **VGood:** $195 **Good:** $175

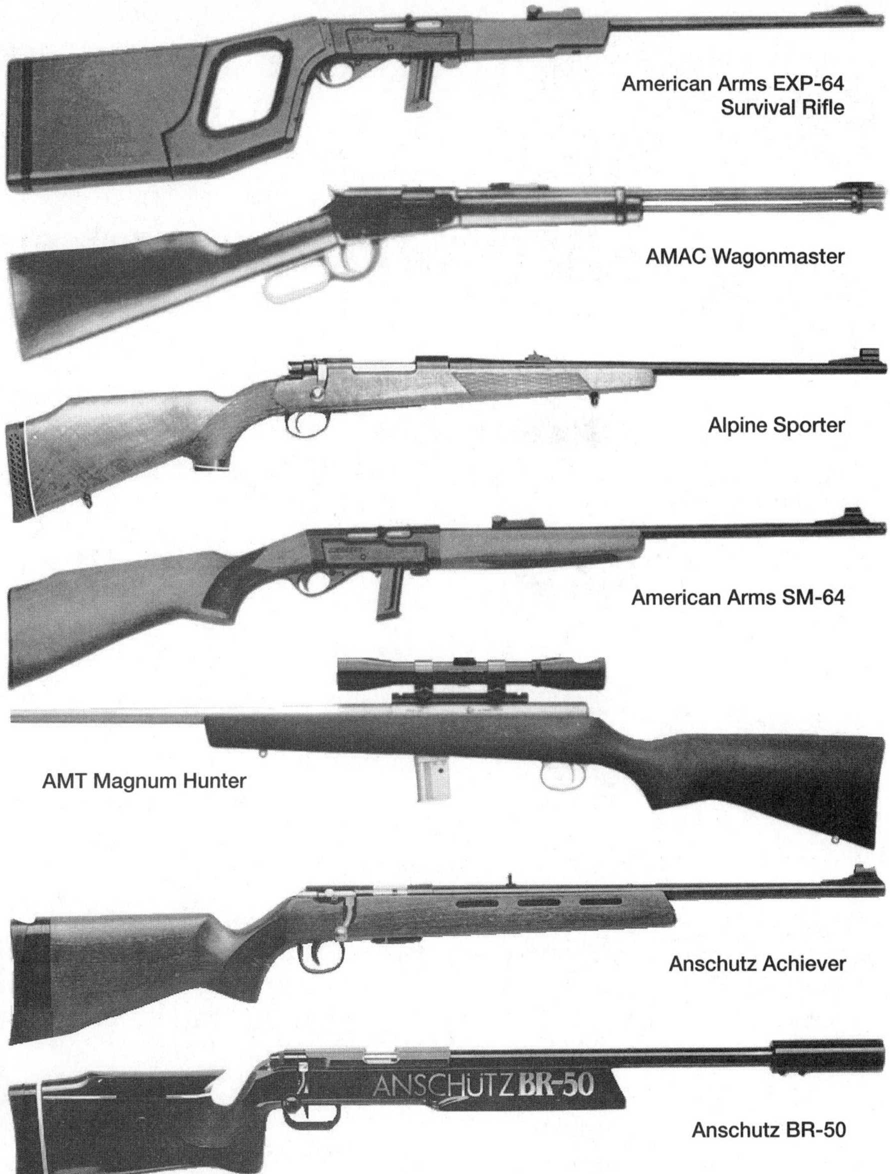
American Arms EXP-64 Survival Rifle

AMAC Wagonmaster

Alpine Sporter

American Arms SM-64

AMT Magnum Hunter

Anschutz Achiever

Anschutz BR-50

AMAC WAGONMASTER

Lever action; 22 Short, 22 Long, 22 LR, 22 WMR; 21-shot magazine (22 Short), 17-shot (22 Long), 15-shot (22 LR), 12-shot (22 WMR); 18-inch barrel; 36-1/2-inch overall length; weighs 5-3/4 lbs.; hooded ramp front sight, open adjustable rear; receiver grooved for scope mount; walnut-finished stock, forend; polished blued finish. Add $20 for 22 WMR version. Introduced 1985 by Iver Johnson; dropped 1990.

Exc: $225 **VGood:** $175 **Good:** $150

AMERICAN ARMS AKY 39

Semi-automatic; 7.62x39mm; 30-shot magazine; 19-1/2-inch barrel; 40-1/2-inch overall length; weighs 9 lbs.; hooded post front sight, open adjustable rear; flip-up tritium sights; teakwood stock. Manufactured in Yugoslavia. Introduced 1988; discontinued 1989.

Perf: $950 **Exc:** $800 **VGood:** $600

Folding stock model

Perf: $1000 **Exc:** $850 **VGood:** $700

AMERICAN ARMS EXP-64 SURVIVAL RIFLE

Semi-automatic; 22 LR; 10-shot magazine; 21-inch barrel; 40-inch overall length; weighs 7 lbs.; blade front sight, adjustable rear; receiver grooved for scope mounts; synthetic stock with storage compartment; takedown feature; crossbolt safety. Made in Italy. Introduced 1989; discontinued 1990.

Exc: $200 **VGood:** $160 **Good:** $125

AMERICAN ARMS MINI-MAX

Semi-automatic; 22 LR; 10-shot magazine; 18-3/4-inch barrel; 36-1/2-inch overall length; weighs 4-1/2 lbs.; blade front sight, adjustable open rear; black synthetic or wood stock; trigger-block safety on trigger guard; receiver grooved for scope mounts. Introduced 1990; discontinued 1990.

Perf: $125 **Exc:** $100 **VGood:** $75

AMERICAN ARMS RS COMBO

Combination gun; over/under box lock; 222 or 308/12-ga. 3-inch; 24-inch barrel; weighs 7 lbs. 14 oz.; Full-choke tube; vent rib; blade front sight, folding rear; grooved for scope mounts; European walnut Monte Carlo stock; checkered pistol grip, forend; double triggers; extractors; silver finish, engraving; barrel connectors allow for windage/elevation adjustment of rifle barrel. Made in Italy. Introduced 1989; discontinued 1989.

Perf: $795 **Exc:** $695 **VGood:** $525

AMERICAN ARMS SM-64

Semi-automatic; 22 LR; 10-shot magazine; 21-inch barrel; 40-inch overall length; weighs 7 lbs.; hooded front sight, adjustable rear; checkered hardwood stock, forend; takedown feature. Made in Italy. Introduced 1989; discontinued 1990.

Exc: $160 **VGood:** $135 **Good:** $110

AMERICAN FIREARMS STAINLESS MODEL

Bolt action; 22-250, 243, 6mm Rem., 6mm Win. Mag., 25-06, 257 Win. Mag., 264 Win. Mag., 6.5mm Rem. Mag., 6.5x55, 270 Win. Mag., 284 Win., 7x57, 7mm Rem. Mag., 7.62x39, 308 Win., 30-06, 300 Win. Mag., 338 Win. Mag., 458 Mag.; 16-1/2-inch, 18-inch, 20-inch, 22-inch, 24-inch, 26-inch, 28-inch barrel; no sights; drilled, tapped for scope mounts; hand-checkered walnut or maple stock; side safety; hinged floorplate; adjustable trigger; made of blued or satin stainless steel. Manufactured in four grades. Introduced 1972; dropped 1974.

Grade I, Presentation

Perf: $1495 **Exc:** $1095 **VGood:** $895

Grade II, Deluxe

Perf: $1095 **Exc:** $895 **VGood:** $650

Grade III, Standard

Perf: $895 **Exc:** $695 **VGood:** $495

Grade IV, 338 & 458 Standard

Perf: $995 **Exc:** $795 **VGood:** $595

AMT LIGHTNING 25/22

Semi-automatic; 22 LR; 25 or 30-shot magazine; 17-1/2-inch tapered barrel; 26-1/2-inch overall length (folded), 37-inch (open); weighs 6 lbs.; folding stainless steel stock; ramp front sight, fixed rear; made of stainless steel with matte finish; receiver dovetailed for scope mounting; extended magazine release; adjustable rear sight optionally available; youth stock available. Made in U.S. by AMT. Introduced 1984; dropped 1994.

Perf: $325 **Exc:** $275 **VGood:** $195

AMT LIGHTNING SMALL-GAME HUNTING RIFLE (HUNTER) II

Same specs as Lightning 25/22 except conventional stock of black fiberglass-filled nylon, checkered at the grip and forend, and fitted with Uncle Mike's swivel studs; removable recoil pad for ammo storage, cleaning rod and survival knife; no sights, receiver grooved for scope mounting; 22-inch full-floating target weight barrel; 40-1/2-inch overall length; weighs 6 lbs.; 10-shot rotary magazine. Made in U.S. by AMT. Introduced 1987; 22 WMR introduced 1992; dropped 1994.

Perf: $325 **Exc:** $275 **VGood:** $195

AMT MAGNUM HUNTER

Semi-automatic; 22 WMR; 10-shot magazine; 22-inch barrel; 40-1/2-inch overall length; weighs 6 lbs.; black fiberglass-filled nylon stock with checkered grip and forend; no sights; drilled and tapped for Weaver mount; stainless steel construction; free-floating target-weight barrel. Made in U.S. by AMT. Introduced 1992; dropped 1994.

Exc: $375 **VGood:** $295 **Good:** $195

ANSCHUTZ ACHIEVER

Bolt action; single shot; 22 LR; 5-shot magazine; 19-1/2-inch barrel; spacers allow 35-1/2-inch to 36-1/2-inch overall length; weighs 5 lbs.; fully-adjustable open rear sight, hooded front; walnut-finished European hardwood stock; Mark 2000-type action; adjustable two-stage trigger; grooved for scope mounts. Made in Germany. Introduced 1993.

Perf: $440 **Exc:** $365 **VGood:** $220

ANSCHUTZ ACHIEVER ST SUPER TARGET

Same specs as Achiever except single shot, 22-inch barrel with 3/4-inch diameter; accepts optional micrometer target sights; 38-3/4-inch to 39-3/4-inch overall length; weighs about 6-1/2 lbs.; 13-1/2-inch accessory rail on forend; designed for the advanced junior shooter with adjustable length of pull from 13-1/4-inch to 14-1/4-inch via removable butt spacers. Imported from Germany. Introduced 1994.

Perf: $415 **Exc:** $370 **VGood:** $280

ANSCHUTZ BR-50

Bolt action; 22 LR; single shot; 19-3/4-inch barrel (without 11-oz. muzzle weight); 37-3/4-inch to 42-1/2-inch overall length; weighs about 11 lbs.; benchrest-style stock of European hardwood with stippled grip; cheekpiece vertically adjustable to

1 inch; stock length adjustable via spacers and buttplate; glossy blue-black paint finish; no sights; receiver grooved for mounts; barrel drilled and tapped for target mounts; uses the Anschutz 2013 target action with #5018 two-stage adjustable target trigger. Imported from Germany. Introduced 1994.

Perf: $2695 **Exc:** $1995 **VGood:** $1125

ANSCHUTZ KADETT

Bolt action; 22 LR; 5-shot clip; 22-inch barrel; 40-inch overall length; weighs 5-1/2 lbs.; Lyman adjustable folding leaf rear sight, hooded bead on ramp front; checkered walnut-finish European hardwood stock; Mark 2000 target action; single-stage trigger; grooved for scope mount. Made in Germany. Introduced 1987; discontinued 1988.

Perf: $335 **Exc:** $300 **VGood:** $260

ANSCHUTZ MARK 525 DELUXE AUTO

Semi-automatic; 22 LR; 10-shot clip magazine; 24-inch barrel; 43-inch overall length; weighs 6-1/2 lbs.; European hardwood stock with checkered pistol grip, Monte Carlo comb, beavertail forend; hooded ramp front sight, folding leaf rear; rotary safety; empty shell deflector; single stage trigger; receiver grooved for scope mounting. Imported from Germany. Introduced 1984; no longer imported.

Perf: $560 **Exc:** $475 **VGood:** $390

ANSCHUTZ MARK 525 CARBINE

Same specs as Mark 525 except 20-inch barrel, handguard, adjustable peep sight. Discontinued 1985.

Perf: $500 **Exc:** $425 **VGood:** $295

ANSCHUTZ MARK 2000

Bolt action; single shot; 22 LR; heavy 26-inch barrel; 43-inch overall length; weighs 7-1/2 lbs.; globe insert front sight, micro-click peep rear; walnut-finish hardwood stock; thumb groove in stock; pistol grip swell. Made in Germany. Introduced 1980; importation discontinued 1988. Marketed in U. S. as Savage/Anschutz Mark 12.

Perf: $440 **Exc:** $390 **VGood:** $320

ANSCHUTZ MODEL 54.18MS

Bolt action; single shot; uses Super Match 54 action; for metallic silhouette shooting. 22 LR; 20, 22-1/2-inch barrel; 41-3/8-inch overall length; weighs 9 lbs. 4 oz.; no sights; stippled walnut stock, pistol grip, forearm; two-stage trigger. Introduced 1981.

Right-hand action

Perf: $1400 **Exc:** $1075 **VGood:** $800

Left-hand action

Perf: $1450 **Exc:** $1125 **VGood:** $825

ANSCHUTZ MODEL 54.18MS ED

Same specs as Model 54.18MS except 19-1/4-inch barrel; 14-1/4-inch extension tube; three removable muzzle weights. Introduced 1984; discontinued 1988.

Right-hand action

Perf: $1100 **Exc:** $875 **VGood:** $625

Left-hand action

Perf: $1200 **Exc:** $975 **VGood:** $700

ANSCHUTZ MODEL 54.18MS FORTNER SILHOUETTE RIFLE

Same specs as the 54.18MS except Anschutz/Fortner system straight-pull bolt action; 21-inch barrel, 3/4-inch-diameter; McMillan Fibergrain fiberglass silhouette stock; two-stage #5020 trigger adjustable from 3-1/2 oz. to 2 lbs.; extremely fast lock time. Imported from Germany. Introduced 1995.

Right-hand

Perf: $3250 **Exc:** $2795 **VGood:** $1995

Left-hand

Perf: $3500 **Exc:** $2995 **VGood:** $2125

ANSCHUTZ MODEL 54.18MS REP

Same specs as Model 54.18MS except repeater with 5-shot magazine; 22- to 30-inch barrel; weighs 7-3/4 lbs.; thumbhole wood or synthetic stock with vented forearm; Super Match 54 action. Introduced 1989.

Perf: $1700 **Exc:** $1300 **VGood:** $900

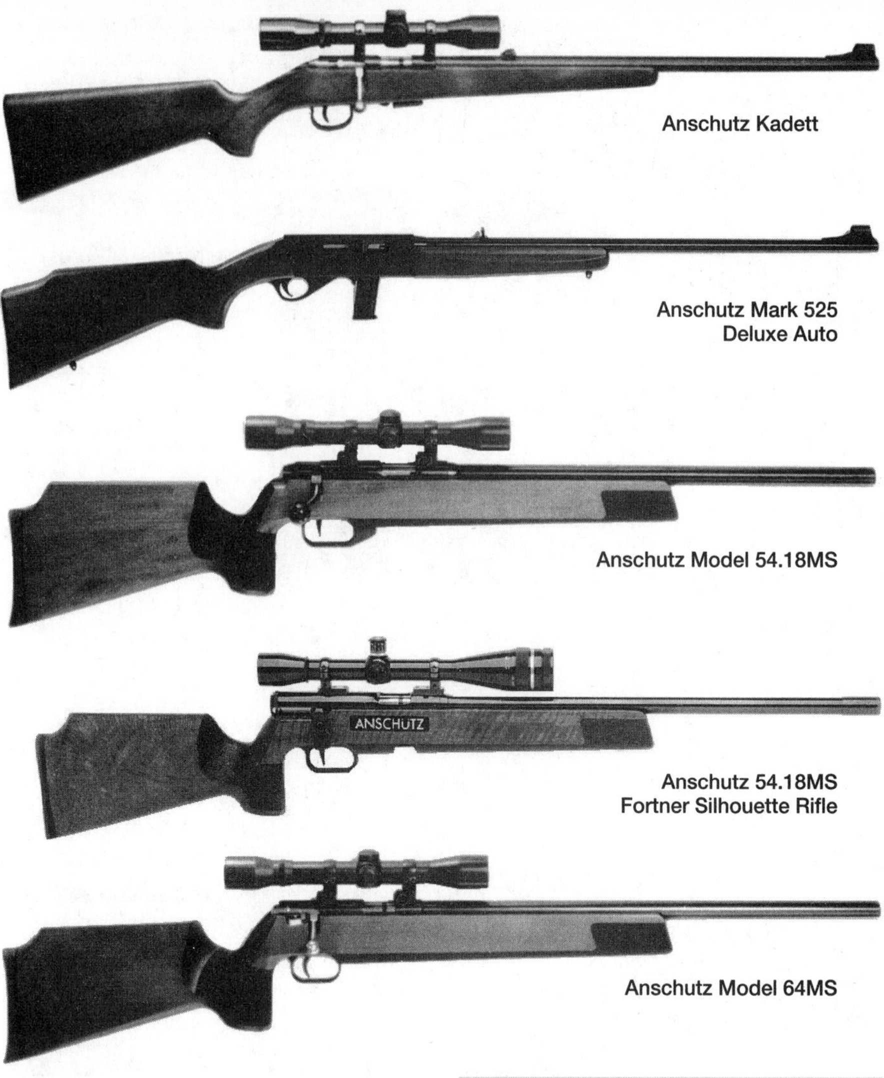

Anschutz Kadett

Anschutz Mark 525 Deluxe Auto

Anschutz Model 54.18MS

Anschutz 54.18MS Fortner Silhouette Rifle

Anschutz Model 64MS

ANSCHUTZ MODEL 54.18MS REP DELUXE

Same specs as Model 54.18 REP except Fibergrain McMillan thumbhole stock with stippling. Introduced 1990.

Perf: $1700 **Exc:** $1100 **VGood:** $900

ANSCHUTZ MODEL 64

Bolt action; single shot; 22 LR; 26-inch barrel, 11/16-inch diameter; 44-inch overall length; weighs 7-3/4 lbs.; no sights; scope blocks receiver grooved for Anschutz sights; walnut-finish hardwood stock; cheekpiece; hand-checkered pistol grip, beavertail forearm; adjustable buttplate; adjustable single-stage trigger; sliding side safety; forward sling swivel for competition sling. Marketed in U.S. as Savage/Anschutz Model 64. Introduced 1963; discontinued 1981.

Right-hand model

Perf: $500 **Exc:** $400 **VGood:** $300

Left-hand model

Perf: $600 **Exc:** $500 **VGood:** $400

ANSCHUTZ MODEL 64MS

Bolt action; single shot; 22 LR; 21-1/4-inch barrel; 39-1/2-inch overall length; weighs 8 lbs.; no sights; drilled, tapped for scope mounts; stippled thumbhole wood stock with pistol grip; adjustable two-stage trigger; Match 64 action. Introduced 1981; still imported.

Right-hand model

Perf: $800 **Exc:** $700 **VGood:** $500

Left-hand model

Perf: $850 **Exc:** $750 **VGood:** $550

ANSCHUTZ MODEL 64MS-FWT

Same specs as Model 64MS except weighs 6-1/4 lbs.; single-stage trigger. Introduced 1985; discontinued 1988.

Perf: $595 **Exc:** $525 **VGood:** $375

ANSCHUTZ MODEL 64MS LEFT-HAND SILHOUETTE

Same specs as Model 64MS except left-hand model. Imported from Germany. Introduced 1980; still imported.

Perf: $895 **Exc:** $775 **VGood:** $550

ANSCHUTZ 64-MSR SILHOUETTE RIFLE

Bolt action; 22 LR, 5-shot magazine. 21-1/2-inch barrel, medium heavy; 7/8-inch diameter; weighs 8 lbs. 39-1/2-inch overall. Walnut-finished hardwood stock, silhouette-type. Uses Match 64 action. Repeater designed for metallic silhouette competition. Stock has stippled checkering, contoured thumb groove with Wundhammer swell. Two-stage #5098 trigger. Slide safety locks sear and bolt. Imported from Germany by AcuSport Corp., Accuracy International, Gunsmithing, Inc.

Perf: $800 **Exc:** $700 **VGood:** $500

ANSCHUTZ MODEL 64S

Bolt action; single shot; 22 LR; 26-inch barrel; 44-inch overall length; target sights; walnut-finish hardwood stock; cheekpiece; hand-checkered pistol grip; beavertail forearm; adjustable buttplate; adjustable single-stage trigger; sliding side safety;

Anschutz Model 54.18MS REP

Anschutz Model 1403B Biathlon

Anschutz Model 1407

Anschutz Model 1403D Match

Anschutz Model 1408ED

Anschutz Model 1411

Anschutz Model 1413

forward sling swivel for competition sling. Marketed in U.S. as Savage/Anschutz Model 64S. Introduced 1963; discontinued 1981.

Right-hand model
Perf: $595 **Exc:** $525 **VGood:** $350

Left-hand model
Perf: $625 **Exc:** $550 **VGood:** $375

ANSCHUTZ MODEL 520/61

Semi-automatic; 22 LR; 10-shot clip magazine; 24-inch barrel; 43-inch overall length; weighs 6-1/2 lbs.; folding adjustable rear sight, hooded ramp front; receiver grooved for scope mounts; European Monte Carlo walnut stock, forend; hand checkering; rotary-style safety; single-stage trigger; swivel studs. Made in Germany. Introduced 1982; discontinued 1983.

Perf: $375 **Exc:** $300 **VGood:** $165

ANSCHUTZ MODEL 1403B BIATHLON

Bolt action; 22 LR; 5-shot magazine; 21-1/2-inch barrel; 42-1/2-inch overall length; weighs 8-1/2 lbs.; blonde-finish European hardwood stock; stippled pistol grip; globe front sight with snow cap and muzzle cover, optional micrometer peep rear with spring-hinged snow cap; uses Match 64 Target action with three-way adjustable two-stage trigger; slide safety; comes with five magazines; adjustable buttplate. Imported from Germany. Introduced 1991; no longer imported.

Perf: $950 **Exc:** $800 **VGood:** $525

ANSCHUTZ MODEL 1403D MATCH

Bolt action; single shot; 22 LR; 25-1/4-inch barrel; 43-1/4-inch overall length; weighs 8.6 lbs.; no sights; receiver grooved for scope mounts; walnut-finished hardwood stock cheekpiece; checkered pistol grip, beavertail forend; adjustable buttplate; slide safety; #5053 adjustable single-stage trigger. Made in Germany. Introduced 1980; importation discontinued 1990.

Right-hand model
Perf: $750 **Exc:** $650 **VGood:** $450

Left-hand model
Perf: $775 **Exc:** $675 **VGood:** $475

ANSCHUTZ MODEL 1407

Bolt action; single shot; 22 LR; 26-inch barrel; 44-1/2-inch overall length; weighs 10 lbs.; weight conforms to ISU competition requirements, also suitable for NRA matches; no sights; receiver grooved for Anschutz sights; scope blocks; French walnut prone-style stock; Monte Carlo, cast-off cheekpiece; hand-stippled pistol grip, forearm; swivel rail, adjustable swivel; adjustable rubber buttplate; single-stage trigger; wing safety. Marketed in U.S. by Savage. Introduced in 1967; no longer in production.

Right-hand model
Perf: $475 **Exc:** $425 **VGood:** $275

Left-hand model
Perf: $495 **Exc:** $440 **VGood:** $290

ANSCHUTZ MODEL 1408

Bolt action; 22 LR; 5-, 10-shot magazine; 26-inch heavy barrel; weighs 10 lbs.; receiver grooved for micrometer sights; hooded ramp front sight; European walnut stock; checkered pistol grip, forearm; adjustable cheek-piece. Marketed in the U.S. by Savage. Introduced 1967; no longer in production.

Perf: $375 **Exc:** $325 **VGood:** $275

ANSCHUTZ MODEL 1408ED

Same specs as Model 1908 except 23-inch barrel; European walnut thumbhole stock; adjustable comb and buttplate; single-stage trigger; oversize bolt knob. Introduced in 1976; no longer in production.

Perf: $550 **Exc:** $500 **VGood:** $400

ANSCHUTZ MODEL 1411

Bolt action; single shot; 22 LR; 27-1/2-inch barrel; 46-inch overall length; weighs 11 lbs.; no sights; receiver grooved for Anschutz sights; scope blocks; French walnut prone-style stock; Monte Carlo, cast-off cheekpiece; hand-stippled pistol grip, forearm; swivel rail, adjustable swivel; adjustable rubber buttplate; single-stage trigger; wing safety. Marketed in U.S. by Savage. Introduced 1965; no longer in production.

Perf: $450 **Exc:** $400 **VGood:** $250

ANSCHUTZ MODEL 1413

Bolt action; single shot; heavy match rifle; 22 LR; 27-1/2-inch barrel; 50-inch overall length; weighs 15-1/2 lbs; no sights; receiver grooved for Anschutz sights; scope blocks; International-type French walnut stock; adjustable aluminum Schuetzen hook buttplate; adjustable cheekpiece; new yoke-type adjustable palm rest; single-stage trigger; wing safety. Marketed in the U.S. by Savage. Introduced 1967; no longer in production.

Perf: $650 **Exc:** $580 **VGood:** $400

ANSCHUTZ MODEL 1416D KL CLASSIC

Bolt action; 22 LR; 5-shot clip; 22-1/2-inch or 23-inch barrel; 41-inch overall length; weighs 5-1/2 to 6 lbs.; classic-style European walnut stock with straight comb, checkered pistol grip and forend; hooded ramp front sight, folding leaf rear; uses Match 64 action; adjustable single stage trigger; receiver grooved for scope mounting. Imported from Germany by Precision Sales International, later AcuSport.

Perf: $700 **Exc:** $600 **VGood:** $400

Left-hand
Perf: $725 **Exc:** $620 **VGood:** $415

ANSCHUTZ MODEL 1416D CUSTOM

Same specs as Model 1416 Classic except European walnut stock with roll-over Monte Carlo cheekpiece; slim forend with schnabel tip; fine cut checkering on grip and forend. Imported from Germany by Precision Sales International, later AcuSport. Introduced 1988.

Perf: $750 **Exc:** $650 **VGood:** $450

ANSCHUTZ MODEL 1416D DELUXE

Same specs as Model 1416 except European walnut Monte Carlo stock with cheekpiece; schnabel forend; Model 1403 target rifle action. Imported from Germany by Precision Sales International. No longer imported.

Perf: $750 **Exc:** $675 **VGood:** $450

ANSCHUTZ MODEL 1416D FIBERGLASS

Same specs as Model 1416D except 40-1/4-inch overall length; weighs 5-1/4 lbs.; McMillan fiberglass Monte Carlo stock with roll-over cheekpiece; Wundhammer grip swell; adjustable trigger; slide safety; 10-shot magazine and single shot adaptor optional. Imported from Germany by Precision Sales International, Inc. Introduced 1991; no longer imported.

Perf: $925 **Exc:** $795 **VGood:** $495

ANSCHUTZ MODEL 1418D

Bolt action; 22 LR; 5-shot clip; 19-3/4-inch barrel; weighs 5-1/2 lbs.; European walnut Mannlicher-style stock with mahogany schnabel tip, checkered pistol grip and forend; hooded ramp front sight, folding leaf rear; uses Model 1403 target rifle action; adjustable single-stage trigger; receiver grooved for scope mounting. Imported from Germany by Precision Sales International, later AcuSport. Still imported.

Perf: $975 **Exc:** $800 **VGood:** $650

ANSCHUTZ MODEL 1422D CLASSIC

Bolt action; 22 LR; 5-shot clip; 24-inch barrel; 43-inch overall length; weighs 7-1/4 lbs.; hooded ramp front sight, folding leaf rear; drilled, tapped for scope mounting; select European walnut stock; checkered pistol grip, forend; adjustable single-stage trigger. Made in Germany. Introduced 1982; importation discontinued 1988.

Perf: $995 **Exc:** $850 **VGood:** $695

ANSCHUTZ MODEL 1422D CUSTOM

Same specs as Model 1422D Classic except weighs 6-1/2 lbs.; Monte Carlo stock with roll-over cheekpiece; slim forend; schnabel tip; palm swell on pistol grip; rosewood grip cap, diamond insert; skip-line checkering. Made in Germany. Introduced 1982; importation discontinued 1988.

Perf: $1195 **Exc:** $995 **VGood:** $695

ANSCHUTZ MODEL 1432 CLASSIC

Bolt action; 22 Hornet; 5-shot box magazine; 23-1/2-inch barrel; 42-1/2-inch overall length; weighs 7-3/4 lbs.; receiver grooved for scope mounting; folding leaf rear sight, hooded ramp front; European walnut Monte Carlo-type stock; hand-checkered pistol grip, forearm; cheekpiece. Introduced 1976; no longer in production.

Perf: $1195 **Exc:** $1095 **VGood:** $850

ANSCHUTZ MODEL 1432 CUSTOM

Same specs as Model 1432 except 24-inch barrel; 43-inch overall length; weighs 6-1/2 lbs.; Monte Carlo stock with roll-over cheekpiece; palm swell on pistol grip; rosewood grip cap; diamond insert. No longer in production.

Perf: $1395 **Exc:** $1125 **VGood:** $895

ANSCHUTZ MODEL 1433D

Bolt action; 22 Hornet; European walnut Mannlicher-type stock; 4-shot clip magazine; 19-3/4-inch barrel; 39-inch overall length; weighs 6-1/4 lbs.; receiver grooved for scope mounting; folding leaf rear sight, hooded ramp front; hand-checkered pistol grip, forearm; cheekpiece; Match 54 target action; single-stage or double-set trigger. Introduced 1976; discontinued 1986.

Perf: $1000 **Exc:** $800 **VGood:** $550

Anschutz Model 1416D Custom

Anschutz Model 1418D

Anschutz Model 1422D Classic

Anschutz Model 1432 Custom

Anschutz Model 1433D

Anschutz Model 1449 Youth

Anschutz Model 1451D KL Classic

ANSCHUTZ MODEL 1449 YOUTH

Bolt action; 22 LR; 5-shot clip; 16-1/4-inch barrel; 32-1/2-inch overall length; weighs 3-1/2 lbs.; hooded ramp front sight, open adjustable rear; grooved for scope mounts; walnut-finished European hardwood stock; built on Anschutz Mark 2000 action; single-shot clip adaptor and 10-shot magazine available. Made in Germany. Introduced 1990; discontinued 1991.

Perf: $300 **Exc:** $270 **VGood:** $130

ANSCHUTZ MODEL 1450B BIATHLON

Bolt action; single shot; 22 LR; 19-1/2-inch barrel; 36-inch overall length; weighs 5 lbs.; aperture sights; European hardwood stock with ventilated forend and adjustable buttplate; Mark 2000 action. Introduced 1993; discontinued 1993.

Perf: $695 **Exc:** $625 **VGood:** $460

ANSCHUTZ MODEL 1451D KL CLASSIC

Bolt action; 22LR; bbl. 22.5-inch; 5-shot magazine weighs 5.5 lbs.; overall length 41-inch folding leaf rear, ramp front sight, with hood; hardwood stock with checkered pistol grip and forearm; single-stage trigger. Introduced 1998. Imported from Germany.

Perf: $400 **Exc:** $350 **VGood:** $200

ANSCHUTZ MODEL 1451D KL MONTE CARLO CLASSIC

Same specs as 1451D KL Classic, but with walnut Monte Carlo stock with schnabel forearm, 1-inch sling swivels.

Perf: $500 **Exc:** $450 **VGood:** $300

Anschutz Model 1451R Sporter Target

Anschutz Model 1502 D HB Classic

Anschutz Model 1518D

Anschutz Model 1700D Bavarian

Anschutz Model 1700D Custom

ANSCHUTZ MODEL 1451R SPORTER TARGET

Same specs as 1451D KL, but designed as smallbore target and varmint rifle; stippled hardwood target stock, adjustable horizontally and vertically at butt, length can be extended with spacers; aluminum accessory rail; 22-inch heavy target barrel, grooved for target front sight; receiver grooved for target rear sight or scope mounting; weighs 6.3 lbs; 10-shot magazine; 2-stage trigger. Introduced 1998.

Perf: $560 **Exc:** $550 **VGood:** $400

ANSCHUTZ MODEL 1451ST R

Same specs as 1451D KL, but heavy-barrel repeater with multi-purpose beavertail hardwood stock; 22-inch bbl; grooved for sights or scope mounting; 5-shot magazine; 2-stage trigger; weighs 6.6 lbs.

Perf: $600 **Exc:** $550 **VGood:** $400

ANSCHUTZ MODEL 1502 D HB CLASSIC

Similar to Model 1702 D HB but with single-stage trigger, fewer refinements. Add 10 percent for beavertail forend.

NIB: $495 **Exc. $400** **VGood:** $300

ANSCHUTZ MODEL 1516D CLASSIC

Bolt action; 22 WMR; 4-shot clip; 22-1/2-inch barrel; 41-inch overall length; weighs 6 lbs.; classic-style European walnut stock with straight comb; checkered pistol grip and forend; hooded ramp front sight, folding leaf rear; uses Match 64 action; adjustable single-stage trigger; receiver grooved for scope mounting. Imported from Germany by Precision Sales International, later AcuSport.

Perf: $695 **Exc:** $525 **VGood:** $460

ANSCHUTZ MODEL 1516D CUSTOM

Same specs as Model 1516D Classic except European walnut stock with roll-over Monte Carlo cheekpiece; slim forend with schnabel tip; fine cut checkering on grip and forend. Imported from Germany. Introduced 1988.

Perf: $700 **Exc:** $560 **VGood:** $340

ANSCHUTZ MODEL 1516D DELUXE

Same specs as Model 1516D Classic except European walnut Monte Carlo stock with cheekpiece; schnabel forend; Model 1403 target rifle action. Imported from Germany by Precision Sales International. No longer imported.

Perf: $800 **Exc:** $660 **VGood:** $450

ANSCHUTZ MODEL 1518D

Bolt action; 22 WMR; 4-shot clip; 19-3/4-inch barrel; 38-inch overall length; weighs 5-1/2 lbs.; European walnut Mannlicher-style stock with mahogany schnabel tip; checkered pistol grip and forend; hooded ramp front sight, folding leaf rear; set trigger. Introduced 1976; still in production.

Perf: $850 **Exc:** $740 **VGood:** $500

ANSCHUTZ MODEL 1518D DELUXE

Same specs as Model 1518D except Model 1403 target rifle action; adjustable single stage trigger; receiver grooved for scope mounting. Imported from Germany. No longer imported.

Perf: $795 **Exc:** $695 **VGood:** $470

ANSCHUTZ 1518D LUXUS BOLT-ACTION RIFLE

Bolt action, caliber: 22 WMR, 4-shot magazine. Barrel: 19-3/4-inch. Weight: 5-1/2 lbs. Length: 37-1/2-inch overall. Stock: European walnut. Sights: Blade on ramp front, folding leaf rear. Features: Receiver grooved for scope mounting; single stage trigger; skip-line checkering; rosewood forend tip; sling swivels. Imported from Germany by AcuSport Corp.

Perf: $975 **Exc:** $850 **VGood:** $700

ANSCHUTZ MODEL 1522D CLASSIC

Bolt action; 22 WMR; 5-shot clip; 24-inch barrel; 43-inch overall length; weighs 7-1/4 lbs.; hooded ramp front sight, folding leaf rear; drilled, tapped for scope mount; select European walnut stock; checkered pistol grip, forend; adjustable single-stage trigger. Made in Germany. Introduced 1982; importation discontinued 1988.

Perf: $1050 **Exc:** $950 **VGood:** $695

ANSCHUTZ MODEL 1522D CUSTOM

Same specs as Model 1522D except Monte Carlo cheekpiece; slim forend; schnabel tip; palm swell on pistol grip; rosewood grip cap, diamond insert; skip-line checkering. Introduced 1982; importation discontinued 1988.

Perf: $1050 **Exc:** $895 **VGood:** $595

ANSCHUTZ MODEL 1533D

Bolt action; 222 Rem.; 3-shot box magazine; 19-3/4-inch barrel; receiver grooved for scope mount; folding leaf rear sight, hooded ramp front; European walnut Mannlicher-style stock; hand-checkered pistol grip, forend; cheekpiece; single-stage or double-set trigger. Introduced 1976; no longer in production.

Perf: $1050 **Exc:** $950 **VGood:** $695

ANSCHUTZ MODEL 1700D BAVARIAN

Bolt action; 22 LR, 22 Hornet, 222 Rem.; 5-shot clip (22 Hornet); 24-inch barrel; 43-inch overall length; weighs 7-1/2 lbs.; European Monte Carlo walnut stock with Bavarian cheek rest; checkered pistol grip and forend; hooded ramp front sight, folding leaf rear; improved 1700 Match 54 action with adjustable #5096 trigger; drilled and tapped for scope mounting. Imported from Germany. Introduced 1988; still imported.

Rimfire

Perf: $995 **Exc:** $895 **VGood:** $500

Centerfire

Perf: $1100 **Exc:** $975 **VGood:** $700

ANSCHUTZ MODEL 1700D BAVARIAN MEISTERGRADE

Same specs as Model 1700D Bavarian except select European walnut stock; gold engraved trigger guard. Introduced 1988.

Rimfire

Perf: $1100 **Exc:** $975 **VGood:** $720

Centerfire

Perf: $1250 **Exc:** $1050 **VGood:** $725

ANSCHUTZ MODEL 1700D CLASSIC

Same specs as Model 1700D Bavarian except 22 LR; weighs 6-3/4 lbs.; #5095 trigger; select European walnut stock with checkered pistol grip and forend. Imported from Germany. Introduced 1988; importation dropped 1994.

Perf: $1100 **Exc:** $950 **VGood:** $600

ANSCHUTZ MODEL 1700D CLASSIC MEISTERGRADE

Same specs as 1700D Classic except better grade of wood; gold engraved trigger guard. Introduced 1988; importation dropped 1994.

Perf: $1150 **Exc:** $1000 **VGood:** $775

ANSCHUTZ MODEL 1700D CUSTOM

Same specs as Model 1700D Bavarian except European walnut stock with roll-over Monte Carlo cheekpiece; slim forend; schnabel tip; palm swell on pistol grip; skip-line checkering. Made in Germany. Introduced 1988; discontinued 1991.

Perf: $1200 **Exc:** $950 **VGood:** $675

ANSCHUTZ MODEL 1700D CUSTOM GRAPHITE

Same specs as Model 1700D Custom except 22 LR; 22-inch barrel; 41-inch overall length; weighs 7-1/2 lbs.; McMillan graphite-reinforced stock, roll-over cheekpiece; quick-detach sling swivels; embroidered sling. Introduced 1991; still imported.

Perf: $1150 **Exc:** $975 **VGood:** $695

ANSCHUTZ MODEL 1700D CUSTOM MEISTERGRADE

Same specs as Model 1700D Custom except select European walnut stock; gold, engraved trigger guard. Introduced 1988; discontinued 1991.

Perf: $1100 **Exc:** $900 **VGood:** $550

ANSCHUTZ MODEL 1700D FEATHERWEIGHT

Same specs as Model 1700D Bavarian except 22 LR; 22-inch barrel; 41-inch overall length; weighs 6-1/4 lbs.; matte black McMillan fiberglass stock; single-stage #5096 trigger. Introduced 1989; dropped about 1996.

Perf: $1100 **Exc:** $950 **VGood:** $715

ANSCHUTZ MODEL 1700D FEATHERWEIGHT DELUXE

Same specs as Model 1700D Featherweight except Fibergrain synthetic stock with simulated wood grain and skip-line checkering. Introduced 1990; no longer imported.

Perf: $1150 **Exc:** $1000 **VGood:** $750

ANSCHUTZ MODEL 1700D GRAPHITE HORNET

Same specs as Model 1700D Custom except 22 Hornet; 22-inch barrel; 41-inch overall length; weighs 7-1/2 lbs.; McMillan graphite-reinforced fiberglass stock with roll-over cheekpiece; built on Anschutz sporter action; fitted with Anschutz logo sling and quick-release swivels. Imported from Germany by Precision Sales International. Introduced 1995; still imported.

Perf: $1150 **Exc:** $975 **VGood:** $725

ANSCHUTZ MODEL 1702 D HB CLASSIC

Chambered in .17 Mach 2. Features include finely-tuned double-stage trigger, walnut stock, 23-inch blued heavy sightless barrel, 5-shot magazine.

NIB: $950 **Exc:** $795 **VGood:** $600

ANSCHUTZ MODEL 1710D CUSTOM RIFLE

Bolt action; 22 LR, 5-shot clip. 24-1/4-inch barrel; weighs 7-3/8 lbs. 42-1/2-inch overall. Select European walnut stock. Sights: Hooded ramp front, folding leaf rear; drilled and tapped for scope mounting. Match 54 action with adjustable single-stage trigger; roll-over Monte Carlo cheekpiece, slim forend with schnabel tip, wundhammer palm swell on pistol grip, rosewood gripcap with white diamond insert; skip-line checkering on grip and forend. Imported from Germany by AcuSport Corp.

Perf: $1100 **Exc:** $950 **VGood:** $700

ANSCHUTZ MODEL 1712 SILHOUETTE SPORTER

Chambered in .22 LR. Features include two-stage trigger, deluxe walnut stock with schnabel, 21.6-inch blued sightless barrel, 5-shot magazine.

NIB: $1375 **Exc:** $1200 **VGood:** $900

ANSCHUTZ MODEL 1733D MANNLICHER

Bolt action; 22 Hornet; 5-shot clip; 19-3/4-inch barrel; 39-inch overall length; weighs 6-1/4 lbs.; full-length Mannlicher-style stock; hooded ramp front sight, Lyman folding rear; improved Match 54 action with #5096 single-stage trigger with 2-1/2-lb. adjustable pull weight; sling swivels. Imported from Germany. Introduced 1993.

Perf: $1250 **Exc:** $975 **VGood:** $600

ANSCHUTZ MODEL 1740 CUSTOM RIFLE

Bolt action; caliber: 22 Hornet, 5-shot clip; 222 Rem., 3-shot clip. Barrel: 24-inch. Weighs 6-1/2 lbs. 43-1/4-inch overall length. Select European walnut stock. Sights: Hooded ramp front, folding leaf rear; drilled and tapped for scope mounting. Uses match 54 action. Adjustable single stage trigger. Stock has roll-over Monte Carlo cheekpiece, slim forend with schnabel tip, Wundhammer palm swell on grip, rosewood gripcap with white diamond insert. Skip-line checkering on grip and forend. Introduced 1997. Imported from Germany by AcuSport Corp.

Perf: $1100 **Exc:** $950 **VGood:** $700

Anschutz Model 1700D Meister Grade

Anschutz Model 1702 D HB Classic

Anschutz Model 1733D Mannlicher

Anschutz Model 1808ED Super

Anschutz Model 1907 Match

ANSCHUTZ MODEL 1743D BOLT-ACTION RIFLE

Bolt action; caliber: 222 Rem., 3-shot magazine. 19.7-inch barrel. weighs 6.4 lbs; 39-inch overall length. Stock: European walnut, Mannlicher-style. Sights: Hooded blade front, folding leaf rear. Receiver grooved for scope mounting; single stage trigger; claw extractor; sling safety; sling swivels. Imported from Germany by AcuSport Corp.

Perf: $1350 **Exc:** $1050 **VGood:** $700

ANSCHUTZ MODEL 1803D

Bolt action; single shot; 22 LR; 25-1/2-inch heavy barrel; 43-3/4-inch overall length; weighs 8-3/8 lbs.; no sights; blonde or walnut-finished European hardwood target stock; adjustable cheekpiece; stippled grip, forend; built on Anschutz Match 64 action; #5091 two-stage trigger; right- or left-hand models. Made in Germany. Introduced 1987; discontinued 1993.

Perf: $900 **Exc:** $825 **VGood:** $585

ANSCHUTZ MODEL 1808D RT

Bolt action; single shot; 22 LR; 32-1/2-inch barrel; 50-1/2-inch overall length; weighs 9-3/8 lbs.; no sights furnished; grooved for scope mount; European walnut stock, heavy beavertail forend; adjustable cheekpiece, buttplate; stippled grip, forend; nine-way adjustable single-stage trigger; slide safety; right- or left-hand. Made in Germany. Introduced 1991.

Perf: $1500 **Exc:** $1400 **VGood:** $900

ANSCHUTZ MODEL 1808ED SUPER

Bolt action; single shot; designed for Running Target competition; 22 LR; 23-1/2-inch heavy barrel; 42-inch overall length; 9-1/4 lbs.; no sights; receiver grooved for scope mount; European hardwood stock; adjustable cheekpiece; beavertail forend; stippled pistol grip, forend; removable barrel weights; adjustable trigger; Special order only. Made in Germany. Introduced 1982; importation discontinued 1990.

Right-hand version

Perf: $1595 **Exc:** $1395 **VGood:** $995

Left-hand version

Perf: $1600 **Exc:** $1400 **VGood:** $1000

ANSCHUTZ MODEL 1827B BIATHLON

Bolt action; 22 LR; 5-shot magazine; 21-1/2-inch barrel; 42-1/2-inch overall length; weighs 8-1/2 lbs.; special Biathlon globe front sight, micrometer rear with snow cap; adjustable trigger; adjustable wooden buttplate; adjustable handstop rail; Biathlon butthook. Made in Germany. Introduced 1982.

Right-hand version

Perf: $1995 **Exc:** $1595 **VGood:** $1100

Left-hand version

Perf: $2100 **Exc:** $1675 **VGood:** $1150

ANSCHUTZ MODEL 1827BT FORTNER BIATHLON

Same specs as the Anschutz 1827B Biathlon rifle except Anschutz/Fortner system straight-pull bolt action. Imported from Germany. Introduced 1982.

Perf: $2995 **Exc:** $2195 **VGood:** $1600

Left-hand

Perf: $3050 **Exc:** $2250 **VGood:** $1650

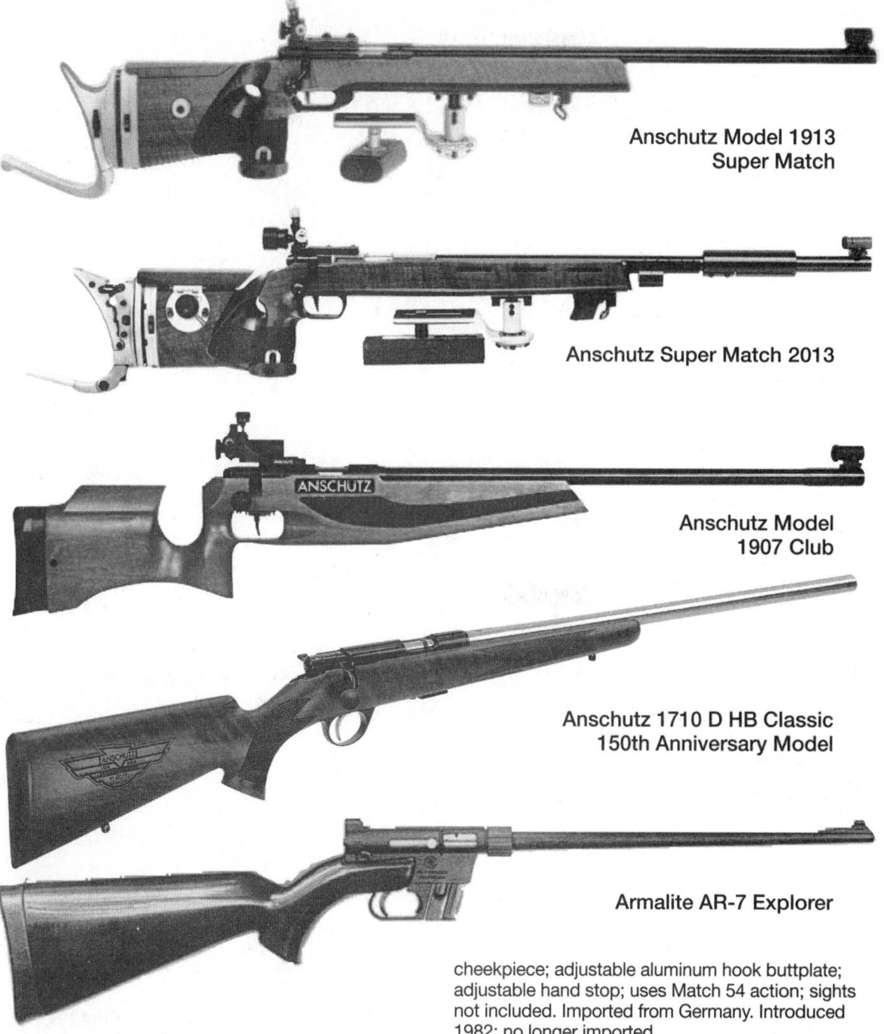
Anschutz Model 1913 Super Match

Anschutz Super Match 2013

Anschutz Model 1907 Club

Anschutz 1710 D HB Classic 150th Anniversary Model

Armalite AR-7 Explorer

ANSCHUTZ MODEL 1903 MATCH

Bolt action; single shot; 22 LR; 25-inch barrel, 3/4-inch diameter; 43-3/4-inch overall length; weighs 8-1/2 lbs.; walnut-finished hardwood stock with adjustable cheekpiece; stippled grip and forend; no sights; accepts #6825 sight set; Anschutz Match 64 action; #5098 two-stage trigger; designed for intermediate and advanced Junior Match competition. Imported from Germany. Introduced 1987.

Right-hand

Perf: $900 **Exc:** $800 **VGood:** $525

Left-hand

Perf: $950 **Exc:** $850 **VGood:** $575

ANSCHUTZ MODEL 1907 MATCH

Bolt action; single shot; 22 LR; 26-inch barrel with 7/8-inch diameter barrel; 44-1/2-inch overall length; weighs 10 lbs.; blonde-finished European hardwood target stock with vented forend; stippled pistol grip and forend; no sights; designed for ISU requirements; suitable for NRA matches. Imported from Germany.

Perf: $1695 **Exc:** $1350 **VGood:** $895

ANSCHUTZ MODEL 1907-L MATCH

Same specs as Model 1907 Match except true left-hand action and stock. Imported from Germany.

Perf: $1750 **Exc:** $1400 **VGood:** $950

ANSCHUTZ MODEL 1910 SUPER MATCH II

Bolt action; single shot; 22 LR; 27-1/4-inch barrel; 46-inch overall length; weighs about 14 lbs.; European walnut International-type stock with adjustable cheekpiece; adjustable aluminum hook buttplate; adjustable hand stop; uses Match 54 action; sights not included. Imported from Germany. Introduced 1982; no longer imported.

Right-hand

Perf: $2400 **Exc:** $1995 **VGood:** $1300

Left-hand

Perf: $2500 **Exc:** $2100 **VGood:** $1400

ANSCHUTZ MODEL 1911 PRONE MATCH

Bolt action; 22 LR; single shot; 27-1/4-inch barrel; 46-inch overall length; weighs 12 lbs.; walnut-finished European hardwood stock of American prone style with Monte Carlo, cast-off cheekpiece; checkered pistol grip; beavertail forend with swivel rail and adjustable swivel; adjustable rubber buttplate; no sights; receiver grooved for Anschutz sights; scope blocks included; two-stage #5018 adjustable trigger. Imported from Germany.

Perf: $1850 **Exc:** $1350 **VGood:** $950

ANSCHUTZ 1912 SPORT RIFLE

Bolt action; 22 LR, single shot. 25.9-inch barrel; weighs about 11.4 lbs. Length: 41.7 to 42.9-inch. European walnut or aluminum stock; no sights; Lightweight sport rifle version. Uses the 54 match action of the 1913 but weighs 1.5 pounds less. Stainless or blue barrel. Introduced 1997.

Perf:$1800 **Exc:** $1500 **VGood:** $1100

ANSCHUTZ MODEL 1913 SUPER MATCH

Bolt action; single shot; 22 LR; 27-1/4-inch barrel; 46-inch overall length; weighs 15-1/2 lbs.; international diopter sights; match-grade European walnut International-type stock with adjustable cheekpiece, aluminum hook buttplate; fully-adjustable hand stop. Introduced 1988; still in production.

Right-hand action

Perf: $2700 **Exc:** $2000 **VGood:** $1100

Left-hand action

Perf: $2800 **Exc:** $2100 **VGood:** $1200

ANSCHUTZ SUPER MATCH 2007 ISU STANDARD

Bolt action; 22 LR; single shot; 19-3/4-inch barrel; 43-1/2-inch to 44-1/2-inch overall length; weighs about 11 lbs.; ISU Standard design stock of European walnut or blonde hardwood; no sights; uses improved Super Match 54 action, #5018 trigger; micro-honed barrel. Imported from Germany. Introduced 1992.

Right-hand

Perf: $2100 **Exc:** $1500 **VGood:** $950

Left-hand

Perf: $2200 **Exc:** $1600 **VGood:** $1050

ANSCHUTZ 2012 SPORT RIFLE

Bolt action; 22 LR. Barrel: 22.4-inch to 25.9-inch match; detachable muzzle tube; weighs 7.9 to 13 lbs. European walnut stock, thumbhole design. No sights; Uses Anschutz 54.18 barreled action with two-stage match trigger. Introduced 1997. Imported from Germany by AcuSport Corp.

Perf: $2100 **Exc:** $1600 **VGood:** $1000

ANSCHUTZ SUPER MATCH 2013

Bolt action; single shot; 22 LR; 19-3/4-inch barrel (26-inch with tube installed); 43-1/2-inch to 45-1/2-inch overall length; weighs 15-1/2 lbs.; target adjustable European walnut stock; no sights; #7020/20 sight set optional; improved Super Match 54 action; #5018 trigger; micro-honed barrel; two-stage, nine-point adjustment trigger; slide safety. Imported from Germany. Introduced 1992.

Right-hand

Perf: $2995 **Exc:** $2495 **VGood:** $1500

Left-hand

Perf: $3100 **Exc:** $2600 **VGood:** $1600

ANSCHUTZ WOODCHUCKER

Bolt action; 22 LR; 5-shot clip; 16-1/4-inch barrel; 32-1/4-inch overall length; weighs 3-1/2 lbs.; bead front sight, U-notched rear; receiver grooved for scope mounting; walnut finished European hardwood stock; dual opposing extractors; built on Anschutz Mark 2000 action. Made in Germany. Introduced 1985; discontinued 1990.

Perf: $375 **Exc:** $275 **VGood:** $150

ANSCHUTZ MODEL 1907 CLUB

Single-shot economy target rifle chambered in .22 LR. Features include target trigger, short lock time, 26-inch blued barrel, micrometer rear peep and hood front sights, ambidextrous removable cheekpiece and walnut buttstock with rubber buttplate and stock spacers. Weighs 9.7 lbs. Introduced 2006.

NIB: $1300 **Exc:** N/A **VGood:** N/A

ANSCHUTZ MODEL 1710 D HB CLASSIC 150 YEARS ANNIVERSARY VERSION

Similar to Model 1710 D HB Classic but with heavy stainless barrel and stock laser-engraved with 150th anniversary and 1901 "Germania" logos. Introduced in 2007.

NIB: $2150 **Exc:** N/A **VGood:** N/A

ARMALITE AR-7 CUSTOM

Semi-automatic; 22 LR; 8-shot box magazine; 16-inch cast aluminum barrel with steel liner; 33-1/2-inch overall length; peep rear sight, blade front; walnut stock; pistol grip; cheekpiece; variation of the AR-7 Explorer survival rifle, but not designed to float. Introduced 1964; discontinued 1970.

Perf: $300 **Exc:** $225 **VGood:** $175

ARMALITE AR-7 EXPLORER

Semi-automatic; 22 LR; takedown survival rifle with 8-shot box magazine; 16-inch aluminum barrel with steel liner; rear peep sight; weighs 2-3/4 lbs; length assembled 34-1/2-inch, stowed in stock, 16-1/2-inch; moulded Fiberglas, later Cycolac plastic stock, hollow for storing action, barrel, magazine; designed to float; snap-on rubber buttcap; modification of survival rifle designed for Air Force. Introduced in 1959 by Armalite; made by Charter Arms from 1973 to 1990; reintroduced 1992 by Survival Arms; discontinued 1995. Reintroduced 1997 by AR-7 Arms LLD.

Perf: $275 **Exc:** $200 **VGood:** $150

ARMALITE AR-10 (T) RIFLE

Semi-automatic, caliber: 308, 10-shot magazine; 24-inch target-weight custom barrel; weighs 10.4 lbs. Length: 43.5-inch overall. Green or black composition stock; N.M.fiberglass handguard tube. Detachable handle, front sight, or scope mount available. Comes with international-style flattop receiver with Picatinny rail. National Match two-stage trigger. Forged upper receiver. Receivers hard-coat anodized. Introduced 1995. Made in U.S.A. by ArmaLite, Inc.

Perf: $1700 **Exc:** $1400 **VGood:** $1000

AR-10 (T) Carbine; Lighter 16-inch barrel, single stage trigger, weighs 8.8 lbs.

Perf: $1750 **Exc:** $1500 **VGood:** $1000

ARMALITE AR-10A4 SPECIAL PURPOSE RIFLE

Semi-automatic; 308 Win., 243 Win., 10-shot magazine. 20-inch chrome-lined barrel, 1:12-inch twist; weighs 9.6 lbs. Length: 41-inch overall; Green or black composition stock; Detachable handle, front sight, or scope mount available; comes with international style flattop receiver with Picatinny rail. Proprietary recoil check. Forged upper receiver with case deflector. Receivers are hard-coat anodized. Introduced 1995. Made in U.S.A. by ArmaLite, Inc.

Perf: $1200 **Exc:** $1000 **VGood:** $800

AR-10A4 Carbine: Same specs except 16-inch barrel.

Perf: $1200 **Exc:** $1000 **VGood:** $800

ARMALITE M15A2 CARBINE

Semi-automatic; 223, 7-shot magazine; 16-inch heavy chrome lined barrel; 1:9 twist; weighs 7 lbs. 35-11/16-inch overall. Green or black composition stock. Standard A2 sights. Upper and lower receivers have push-type pivot pin; hard coat anodized; A2-style forward assist; M16A2- type raised fence around magazine release button. Made in U.S.A. by ArmaLite, Inc., still in production.

Perf: $1000 **Exc:** $750 **VGood:** $600

M15A2 Carbine; Same specs except 16-inch barrel.

Perf: $1000 **Exc:** $750 **VGood:** $600

ARMALITE M15A4

Semi-automatic; 223, 7-shot magazine. 20-inch heavy stainless barrel; 1:9-inch twist; weighs 9 lbs. 40-1/2-inch overall. Green or black plastic stock; N.M. fiberglass handguard tube. One-piece international-style flattop receiver with Weaver-type rail. Detachable carry handle, front sight and scope mount available. National Match two-stage trigger group; Picatinny rail; upper and lower receivers have push-type pivot pin; hard coat anodized finish. Made in U.S.A. by ArmaLite, Inc., still produced.

Perf: $1300 **Exc:** $1050 **VGood:** $700

ARMALITE M15A4(T)

Semi-automatic, 223, 7-shot magazine. 24-inch heavy stainless barrel; 1:8-inch twist. weighs 9.2 lbs. 42-3/8-inch overall. Green or black buttstock; N.M. fiberglass handguard tube. One-piece international-style flattop receiver with Weaver-type rail, including case deflector. Detachable carry handle, front sight and scope mount (30mm or 1-inch) available. Upper and lower receivers have push-type pivot pin, hard coat anodized. Made in U.S.A. by ArmaLite, Inc., still produced.

Perf: $1200 **Exc:** $900 **VGood:** $700

ARMSCOR MODEL 14D

Bolt action; 22 LR; 10-shot magazine; 23-inch barrel; 41-1/2-inch overall length; weighs 6-1/2 lbs.; fully-adjustable rear sight, bead ramp front; grooved for scope mounts; checkered walnut-finished mahogany stock; blued finish. Made in Philippines. Introduced 1987.

Armalite M15A2 Carbine

Armscor Model 14D

Armscor Model 20C

Armscor Model 50S

Exc: $100 **VGood:** $75 **Good:** $55

ARMSCOR MODEL 14P

Same specs as Model 14D except hooded bead ramp front sight; plain uncheckered stock. Made in the Philippines. Introduced 1987.

Exc: $90 **VGood:** $70 **Good:** $50

ARMSCOR MODEL 20C

Semi-automatic; 22 LR; 10-shot or 15-shot magazine; 18-1/4-inch barrel; 38-inch overall length; weighs 6-1/4 lbs.; fully-adjustable rear sight, bead ramp front; receiver grooved for scope mounts; walnut finished Philippine mahogany; carbine-style stock; steel barrel band, buttplate; blued finish. Introduced 1990.

Exc: $110 **VGood:** $85 **Good:** $60

ARMSCOR MODEL 20P

Same specs as Model 20C except 20-3/4-inch barrel; 40-1/2-inch overall length; hooded bead ramp front sight; elevation-adjustable rear; no barrel band. Made in the Philippines. Introduced 1987.

Exc: $90 **VGood:** $70 **Good:** $50

ARMSCOR MODEL 50S

Semi-automatic; 22 LR; 25-, 30-shot magazine; 18-1/4-inch ventilated barrel shroud; 38-inch overall length; weighs 6-1/2 lbs.; bead ramp front sight, open U-notch fully-adjustable rear; mahogany stock; blued finish. Introduced 1990. Reseembles Soviet PPSh.

Perf: $275 **Exc:** $240 **VGood:** $200

ARMSCOR MODEL 1400SC (SUPER CLASSIC)

Bolt action; 22 LR; 6-shot or 10-shot magazine; 22-1/2-inch barrel; 41-1/4-inch overall length; weighs 6-3/4 lbs.; hand-checkered American walnut Monte Carlo stock with cheekpiece; contrasting wood forend tip and grip cap; red recoil pad; engine-turned bolt; bead ramp front sight, fully-adjustable open rear; grooved for scope mount; blue finish. Imported from the Philippines by Ruko Products. Introduced 1990; dropped 1994, reintroduced.

Perf: $230 **Exc:** $190 **VGood:** $130

ARMSCOR MODEL 1400LW

Same specs as 1400SC except weighs 6 lbs.; schnabel forend; hard rubber recoil pad; blued finish. Made in Philippines. Introduced 1990; discontinued 1992.

Perf: $175 **Exc:** $145 **VGood:** $105

ARMSCOR MODEL 1500S

Bolt action; 22 WMR; 5-shot magazine; 23-inch barrel; 41-inch overall length; weighs 6-1/2 lbs.; fixed sights; receiver grooved for scope mounts; double-lug bolt; plain mahogany stock; blued finish. Made in the Philippines. Introduced 1987.

Perf: $160 **Exc:** $135 **VGood:** $95

ARMSCOR MODEL 1500LW

Same specs as Model 1500S except lightweight European-style checkered walnut stock with recoil pad. Introduced 1990; discontinued 1992.

Perf: $180 **Exc:** $145 **VGood:** $105

ARMSCOR MODEL 1500SC (SUPER CLASSIC)

Same specs as Model 1500S except 41-1/4-inch overall length; hand-checkered Monte Carlo stock of American walnut; contrasting wood forend tip, grip cap; red rubber recoil pad; lathe-turned bolt. Introduced 1990; no longer in production.

Perf: $225 **Exc:** $175 **VGood:** $125

ARMSCOR MODEL 1600

Semi-automatic; 22 LR; military styling; 15-shot magazine; 19-1/2-inch barrel; 38-1/2-inch overall length; weighs 6 lbs.; peep rear sight, post front; black ebony wood stock; matte black finish; resembles Colt AR-15. Made in the Philippines. Introduced 1987.

Perf: $200 **Exc:** $150 **VGood:** $125

Armscor Model 1600

Armscor Model AK22

Armsport 1866 Sharps Carbine

Arnold Arms Alaskan Guide Rifle

Arnold Arms Grand Alaskan Rifle

Arnold Arms Alaskan Trophy Rifle

ARMSCOR MODEL 1600R

Same specs as Model 1600 except with stainless-steel retractable buttstock; weighs 7 lbs.; ventilated forend.

Perf: $200 **Exc:** $165 **VGood:** $125

ARMSCOR MODEL 2000SC (SUPER CLASSIC)

Semi-automatic; 22 LR; 15-shot magazine; 20-3/4-inch barrel; 40-1/2-inch overall length; weighs 6-1/4 lbs.; fully-adjustable open U-notch rear, bead ramp front sight; receiver grooved for scope mounts; checkered American walnut Monte Carlo sporter stock with cheekpiece; rubber recoil pad; blued finish. Made in Philippines. Introduced 1987.

Perf: $110 **Exc:** $75 **VGood:** $55

ARMSCOR MODEL AK22

Semi-automatic; 22 LR; military styling; 10-, 15-, 30-shot magazine; 18-1/4-inch barrel; 36-inch overall length; weighs 7 lbs.; plain mahogany stock; post front sight, open U-notch fully-adjustable rear; matte black finish; resembles the AK-47. Imported from the Philippines by Ruko Products. later KBI, Inc. Introduced 1987.

Perf: $265 **Exc:** $225 **VGood:** $110

With folding steel stock

Perf: $295 **Exc:** $250 **VGood:** $120

ARMSPORT 1866 SHARPS RIFLE

Single shot; 45-70; 28-inch round or octagonal barrel; 46-inch overall length; weighs 8 lbs.; walnut stock and forend; blade front sight, folding adjustable rear; tang sight set optionally available; replica of the 1866 Sharps; color case-hardened frame, rest blued.

Perf: $650 **Exc:** $495 **VGood:** $395

With octagonal barrel

Perf: $675 **Exc:** $525 **VGood:** $425

ARMSPORT 1866 SHARPS CARBINE

Same specs as the 1866 Rifle except 22-inch round barrel.

Perf: $650 **Exc:** $495 **VGood:** $395

ARMSPORT 2800 SERIES

Bolt action; 30-06 (2801), 308 (2802), 270 Win. (2803), 243 Win. (2804), 7mm Rem. Mag. (2805), 300 Win. Mag. (2806); 24-inch barrel; weighs 8 lbs.; open adjustable rear, ramp front sight; checkered European walnut Monte Carlo stock; blued finish, Made in Italy. Introduced 1986; discontinued 1986.

Perf: $595 **Exc:** $495 **VGood:** $375

ARMSPORT 4000 SERIES

Double rifle; 243, 270, 284, 7.65mm, 308, 30-06, 7mm Rem. Mag., 9.3mm, 300 H&H, 375 H&H; interchangeable 16-, 20-ga. shotgun barrels; blade front sight with bead, windage-adjustable leaf rear; engraved receiver, sideplates; marketed in hand-fitted leather case. Introduced 1978; discontinued 1985.

Armsport 4010 (side-by-side version)

Perf: $15,000 **Exc:** $11,995 **VGood:** $8995

Armsport 401

Perf: $11,995 **Exc:** $8995 **VGood:** $6995

Armsport 4012

Perf: $25,000 **Exc:** $19,995 **VGood:** $15,000

Armsport 4013

Perf: $22,000 **Exc:** $16,500 **VGood:** $12,000

Armsport 4020

Perf: $3600 **Exc:** $2700 **VGood:** $2100

Armsport 4021

Perf: $3300 **Exc:** $2400 **VGood:** $1800

Armsport 4022

Perf: $3350 **Exc:** $2500 **VGood:** $1850

Armsport 4023

Perf: $2900 **Exc:** $2200 **VGood:** $1750

ARMSPORT 4500 SERIES

Lever action; 20-inch barrel (carbine), 24-inch barrel (standard); adjustable rear, blade front sight; engraved sideplates; walnut stock; black chromed barrels; replica of Winchester 1873. Discontinued 1986.

Armsport 4500 Standard, 44-40

Perf: $1050 **Exc:** $850 **VGood:** $650

Armsport 4501 Standard, 357 Mag.

Perf: $1000 **Exc:** $800 **VGood:** $600

Armsport 4502 Carbine, 44-40

Perf: $1050 **Exc:** $850 **VGood:** $650

Armsport 4503 Carbine, 357 Mag.

Perf: $1000 **Exc:** $800 **VGood:** $600

Armsport 4504 Carbine, 357 Mag.

Perf: $500 **Exc:** $410 **VGood:** $320

ARMSPORT TIKKA 4600 SERIES

Bolt action; 30-06 (4601), 308 Win. (4602), 270 Win. (4603), 243 Win. (4604), 7mm Rem. (4605), 300 Win. Mag. (4606), 222 Rem. (4607); adjustable rear, blade front sight; walnut stock; rubber recoil pad; blued finish. Discontinued 1984.

Perf: $595 **Exc:** $410 **VGood:** $380

ARNOLD ARMS ALASKAN RIFLE

Bolt action, calibers 300 Win. Magnum to 458 Arnold; 22-inch to 26-inch barrel. Synthetic stock; black, woodland or arctic camouflage; drilled and tapped for scope mounting. Uses Apollo, Remington or Winchester action with controlled round feed or push feed; chrome- moly steel or stainless; one-piece bolt, handle, knob; cone head bolt and breech; three-position safety; fully adjustable trigger. Introduced 1996. Made in U.S.A. by Arnold Arms Co.

Perf: $2300 **Exc:** $1700 **VGood:** $1300

ARNOLD ARMS ALASKAN GUIDE RIFLE

Similar to the Alaskan rifle except chambered for 257 to 338 Magnum; choice of A-grade English walnut or synthetic stock; three-position safety; scope mount only. Introduced 1996. Made in U.S.A. by Arnold Arms Co.

Perf: $1800 **Exc:** $1550 **VGood:** $1100

ARNOLD ARMS GRAND ALASKAN RIFLE

Similar to the Alaskan rifle except has AAA fancy select or exhibition-grade English walnut; barrel band swivel; comes with iron sights and scope mount; 24-inch to 26-inch barrel; 300 Magnum to 458 Win. Mag. Introduced 1996. Made in U.S.A. by Arnold Arms Co.

Perf: $2800 **Exc:** $2250 **VGood:** 1200

ARNOLD ARMS ALASKAN TROPHY RIFLE

Similar to the Alaskan rifle except chambered for 300 Magnum to 458 Win. Mag.; 24-inch to 26-inch barrel; black synthetic or laminated stock; comes with barrel band on 375 H&H and larger; scope mount; iron sights. Introduced 1996. Made in U.S.A. by Arnold Arms Co.

Perf: $2400 **Exc:** $1800 **VGood:** $1100

ARNOLD ARMS SAFARI RIFLE

Bolt action, calibers 300 Win. Mag. to 458 Win. Mag. 22-inch to 26-inch barrel; Grade A and AA Fancy English walnut stock; drilled and tapped for scope mounting. Uses Apollo, Remington or Winchester action with controlled or push round feed; one-piece bolt, handle, knob; cone head bolt and breech; three-position safety; fully adjustable trigger; chrome-moly steel in matte blue, polished, or bead blasted stainless. Introduced 1996. Made in U.S.A. by Arnold Arms Co.

Perf: $2200 **Exc:** $1600 **VGood:** $1100

ARNOLD ARMS AFRICAN TROPHY RIFLE

Similar to the Safari rifle except has AAA Extra Fancy English walnut stock with wrap-around checkering; matte blue chrome-moly or polished or bead blasted stainless steel; scope mount standard or optional Express sights. Introduced 1996. Made in U.S.A. by Arnold Arms Co.

Perf: $6100 **Exc:** $5000 **VGood:** $4000

ARNOLD ARMS GRAND AFRICAN RIFLE

Similar to the Safari rifle except has Exhibition Grade stock; polished blue chrome-moly steel or bead-blasted or Teflon-coated stainless; barrel band; scope mount, express sights; calibers 338 Magnum to 458 Win. Mag.; 24-inch to 26-inch barrel. Introduced 1996. Made in U.S.A. by Arnold Arms Co.

Perf: $7500 **Exc:** $6000 **VGood:** $5000

A-SQUARE CAESAR

Bolt action; numerous calibers; 20-inch to 26-inch barrel; weighs 8-1/2 to 11 lbs.; three-leaf express sights or scope; Claro walnut hand-rubbed oil-finish or synthetic stock; Coil-Chek recoil reducer; flush detachable swivels; double cross-bolts; claw extractor; right- or left-hand models; built on M700 receiver; matte blue finish. Introduced about 1985.

Perf: $3500 **Exc:** $2700 **VGood:** $1500

A-SQUARE GENGHIS KHAN

Similar to Hamilcar, but chambered for varmint calibers, 243 to 264 Win Mag.

Perf: $3500 **Exc:** $2700 **VGood:** $1500

A-SQUARE HAMILCAR "SMALL BORE" RIFLE

Bolt action; 25-06, 6.5x55, 270 Win., 7x57, 280 Rem., 30-06, 338-06, 9.3x62, 257 Wea. Mag., 264 Win. Mag., 270 Wea. Mag., 7mm Rem. Mag., 7mm Wea. Mag., 7mm STW, 300 Win. Mag., 300 Wea. Mag.; 4- or 6-shot magazine, depending upon caliber; custom barrel lengths to customer specifications; weighs 8-8-1/2 lbs.; oil-finished Claro walnut stock with A-Square Coil-Chek, recoil pad; choice of three-leaf express, forward or normal-mount scope; matte blue finish; Mauser-style claw extractor; two-position safety; three-way target trigger. From A-Square Co., Inc. Introduced 1994; still produced.

Perf: $3200 **Exc:** $2200 **VGood:** $1400

A-SQUARE HANNIBAL "BIG BORE" RIFLE

Bolt action; numerous calibers, up to and including 577 Tyrannosaur; 20-inch to 26-inch barrel; weighs 9 to 11-3/4 lbs.; three-leaf express sights or scope; Claro walnut hand-rubbed oil-finish or synthetic stock; Coil-Chek recoil reducer; double cross-bolts; claw extractor; two-position safety; three-way target trigger; built on P-17 Enfield receiver. Introduced about 1985.

Perf: $4400 **Exc:** $3200 **VGood:** $1400

AUTO-ORDNANCE 1927 A1 THOMPSON

Semi-automatic; 45 ACP; 30-shot magazine; 16-inch barrel; 42-inch overall length; weighs about 12 lbs.; walnut stock and vertical forend; blade front sight, open windage-adjustable rear; recreation of Thompson Model 1927; semi-auto only; finned barrel. Made in U.S. by Auto-Ordnance Corp. Add 20 percent for Auto-Ordnance (pre-Kahr) manufacture.

Perf: $1200 **Exc:** $900 **VGood:** $675

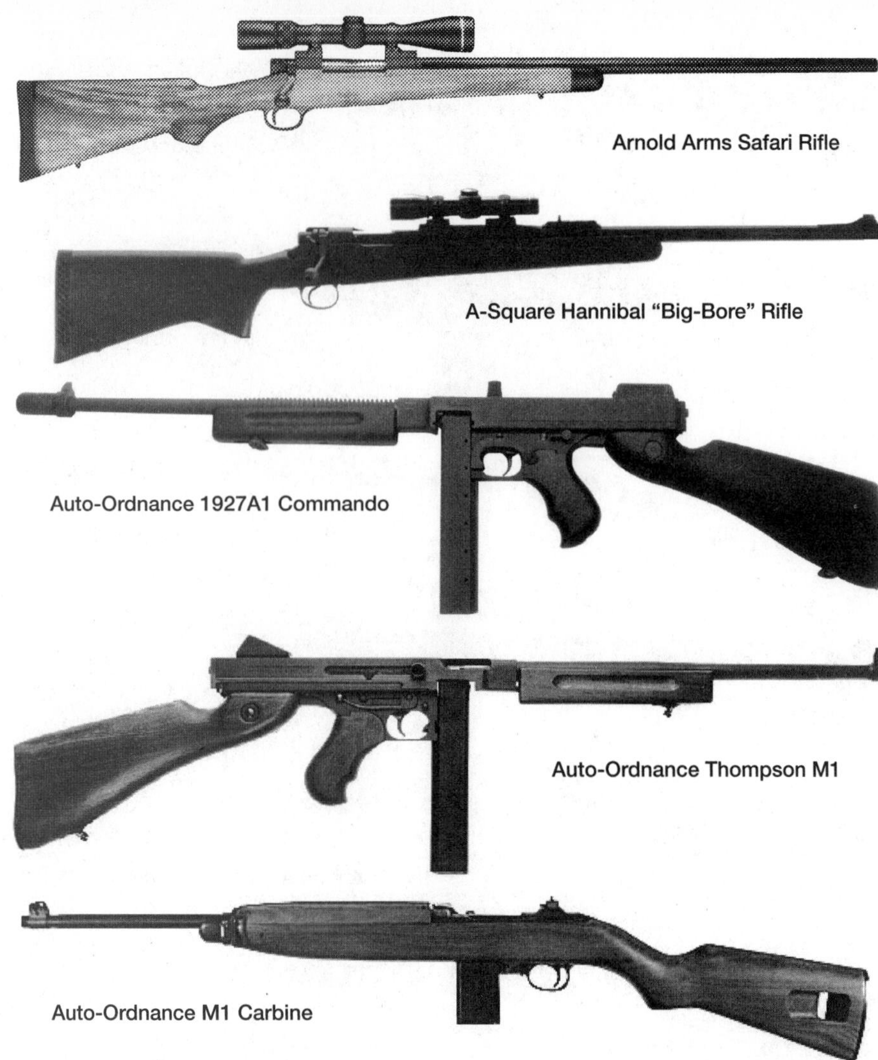

Arnold Arms Safari Rifle

A-Square Hannibal "Big-Bore" Rifle

Auto-Ordnance 1927A1 Commando

Auto-Ordnance Thompson M1

Auto-Ordnance M1 Carbine

AUTO-ORDNANCE 1927 A1C THOMPSON

Same specs as 1927 A1, except lightweight aluminum receiver, weighs 9-1/2 lbs. Add 20 percent for Auto-Ordnance (pre-Kahr) manufacture.

Perf: $1200 **Exc:** $900 **VGood:** $675

AUTO-ORDNANCE 1927A1 COMMANDO

Similar to the 1927A1 except has Parkerized finish, black-finish wood butt, pistol grip, horizontal forend. Comes with black nylon sling. Introduced 1998. Made in U.S.A. by Auto-Ordnance Corp. Add 20 percent for Auto-Ordnance (pre-Kahr) manufacture.

Perf: $1100 **Exc:** $750 **VGood:** $600

AUTO-ORDNANCE 1927A3

Semi-automatic; 22 LR; 10-, 30- or 50-shot magazine; 16-inch finned barrel; weighs about 7 lbs; walnut stock and forend; blade front sight, open fully-adjustable rear; recreation of the Thompson Model 1927; alloy receiver. Made in U.S. by Auto-Ordnance. No longer produced. Add 20% if drum magazine present.

Perf: $1800 **Exc:** $1600 **VGood:** $975

AUTO-ORDNANCE THOMPSON M1

Semi-automatic; 45 ACP; 30-shot magazine; 16-inch barrel; 42-inch overall length; weighs 11-1/2 lbs.; walnut stock and horizontal forend; blade front sight, fixed rear; side cocking knob; smooth unfinned barrel; sling swivels on butt and forend. Made in U.S. by Auto-Ordnance Corp. Introduced 1985. Add 20 percent for Auto-Ordnance (pre-Kahr) manufacture.

Perf: $1100 **Exc:** $750 **VGood:** $600

AUTO-ORDNANCE M1 CARBINE

Newly-manufactured replica of military M1 carbine chambered in .30 Carbine. Introduced 2005. Birch stock, parkerized finish. (Add 5 percent for walnut stock.)

NIB: $675 **Exc:** $625 **VGood:** $495

BALLARD NO. 1-3/4 FAR WEST

Single shot, calibers 22 LR, 32-40, 38-55, 40-65, 40-70, 45-70, 45-110, 50-70, 50-90. 30-inch std. or heavyweight barrel; weighs 10-1/2 lbs. (std.) or 11-3/4 lbs. (heavyweight bbl.) Walnut stock. Blade front, Rocky Mountain rear sights. Single or double-set triggers, S-lever or ring-style lever; color case-hardened finish; hand polished and lapped Badger barrel. Made in U.S.A. by Ballard Rifle & Cartridge Co.

Perf: $2600 **Exc:** $2300 **VGood:** $1995

BALLARD NO. 4 PERFECTION

Single shot, calibers 22 LR, 32-40, 38-55, 40-65, 40-70, 45-70, 45-90, 45-110, 50-70, 50-90. Barrel: 30-inch or 32-inch octagon, standard or heavyweight; weighs 10-1/2 lbs. (std.) or 11-3/4 lbs. (heavy bbl.) Smooth walnut stock. Blade front, Rocky Mountain rear sights. Rifle or shotgun-style buttstock, straight grip action, single or double-set trigger, "S" or right lever, hand polished and lapped Badger barrel. Made in U.S.A. by Ballard Rifle & Cartridge Co.

Perf: $2700 **Exc:** $2500 **VGood:** $2200

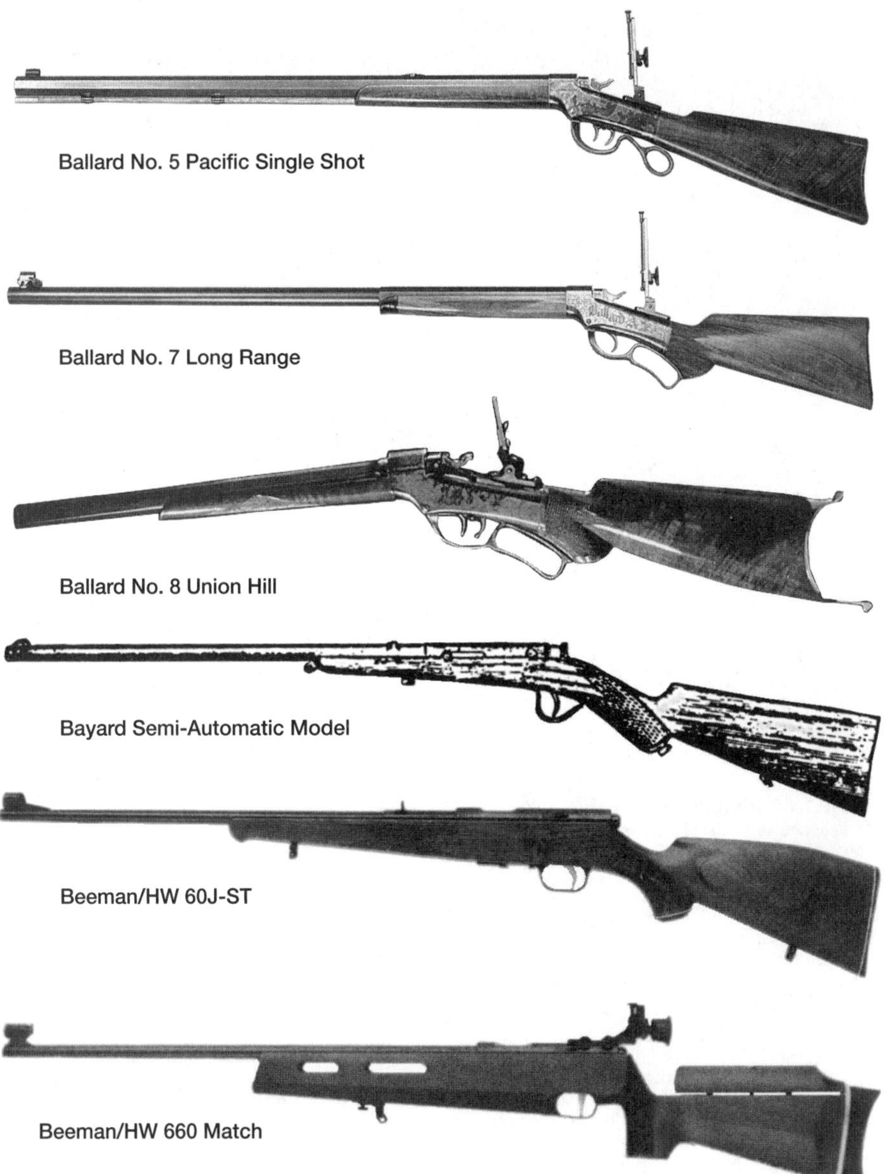

Ballard No. 5 Pacific Single Shot

Ballard No. 7 Long Range

Ballard No. 8 Union Hill

Bayard Semi-Automatic Model

Beeman/HW 60J-ST

Beeman/HW 660 Match

BALLARD NO. 5 PACIFIC SINGLE-SHOT

Single shot; calibers 32-40, 38-55, 40-65, 40-90, 40-70 SS, 45-70 Govt., 45-110 SS, 50- 70 Govt., 50-90. 30-inch, or 32-inch octagonal barrel; weighs 10-1/2 lbs. High-grade walnut stock; rifle or shotgun style. Blade front, Rocky Mountain rear sights; Standard or heavy barrel; double-set triggers; under-barrel wiping rod; ring lever. Introduced 1999. Made in U.S.A. by Ballard Rifle & Cartridge Co.

Perf: $2350 **Exc:** $1950 **VGood:** $1650

BALLARD NO. 7 LONG RANGE

Single shot; 32-40, 38-55, 40-65, 40-70 SS, 45-70 Govt., 45-90, 45-110. Barrel: 32-inch, 34-inch half-octagon; weighs 11-3/4 lbs. Walnut stock; checkered pistol grip shotgun butt, ebony forend cap. Globe front sight. Designed for shooting up to 1000 yards. Standard or heavy barrel; single or double-set trigger; hard rubber or steel buttplate. Introduced 1999. Made in U.S.A. by Ballard Rifle & Cartridge Co.

Perf: $2350 **Exc:** $1850 **VGood:** $1350

BALLARD NO. 8 UNION HILL

Single shot; calibers 22 LR, 32-40, 38-55, 40-65 Win., 40-70. Barrel: 30-inch half-octagon; weighs about 10-1/2 lbs. Walnut stock; pistol grip butt with cheekpiece. Globe front sight; Designed for 200- yard offhand shooting. Standard or heavy barrel; double-set triggers; full loop lever; hook Schuetzen buttplate. Introduced 1999. Made in U.S.A. by Ballard Rifle & Cartridge Co.

Perf: $2600 **Exc:** $2100 **VGood:** $1600

BALLARD MODEL 1885 HIGH WALL SINGLE SHOT

Single shot; calibers 17 Bee, 22 Hornet, 218 Bee, 219 Don Wasp, 219 Zipper, 22 Hi- Power, 225 Win., 25-20 WCF, 25-35 WCF, 25 Krag, 7mmx57R, 30-30, 30- 40 Krag, 303 British, 33 WCF, 348 WCF, 35 WCF, 35-30/30, 9.3x74R, 405 WCF, 50-110 WCF, 500 Express, 577 Express; barrel Lengths to 34-inch. Straight-grain American walnut stock; buckhorn or flat top rear sight, blade front. Faithful copy of original Model 1885 High Wall; parts interchange with original rifles; variety of options available. Introduced 2000. Made in U.S.A. by Ballard Rifle & Cartridge Co.

Perf: $2000 **Exc:** $1895 **VGood:** $1600

BARRETT MODEL 82A-1

Semi-automatic; 50 BMG; 10-shot detachable box magazine; 29-inch barrel; 57-inch overall length; weighs 28-1/2 lbs.; composition stock with Sorbothane recoil pad; no sights, scope optional; recoil operated with recoiling barrel; three-lug locking bolt; muzzlebrake; self-leveling bipod; fires same 50-caliber ammunition as the Browning machinegun. From Barrett Firearms. Introduced 1982; still produced.

Perf: $9500 **Exc:** $8000 **VGood:** $7000

BARRETT MODEL 90

Bolt action; 50 BMG; bullpup design; 5-shot magazine; 29-inch barrel; 45-inch overall length; weighs 22 lbs.; Sorbothane recoil pad on stock; no sights, scope optional; extendable bipod legs; match-grade barrel; high efficiency muzzlebrake. Made in U.S. by Barrett Firearms Mfg., Inc. Introduced 1990; dropped 1994.

Perf: $4500 **Exc:** $3500 **VGood:** $2000

BARRETT MODEL 95

Bolt action; 50 BMG; bullpup design; 5-shot magazine; 29-inch barrel; 45-inch overall length; weighs 22 lbs.; Sorbothane recoil pad on butt; no sights, scope optional; updated version of the Model 90; extendable bipod legs; match-grade barrel; high efficiency muzzlebrake. Made in U.S. by Barrett Firearms Mfg., Inc. Introduced 1995; still produced.

Perf: $5700 **Exc:** $4100 **VGood:** $2700

BARRETT MODEL 99 SINGLE SHOT

Bolt action, 50 BMG. 33-inch barrel; weighs 25 lbs. 50.4-inch overall. Anodized aluminum stock with energy-absorbing recoil pad; no sights; integral M1913 scope rail; detachable bipod; match-grade barrel with high-efficiency muzzle brake. Introduced 1999. Made in U.S.A. by Barrett Firearms.

Perf: $3800 **Exc:** $2900 **VGood:** $2000

BAYARD SEMI-AUTOMATIC MODEL

Single shot; 22 Short, 22 Long; 19-inch barrel; 39-inch overall length; weighs 3-3/4 lbs.; fixed sights; loads cartridge when release stud is activated; American walnut stock. Originally priced at $4.50. Introduced 1908; discontinued 1914.

Perf: $350 **Exc:** $300 **VGood:** $190

BEEMAN/HW 60

Bolt action; single shot; 22 LR; 26-7/8-inch barrel; 45-3/4-inch overall length; weighs 11 lbs.; walnut target stock with adjustable buttplate; stippled pistol grip and forend; accessory rail with adjustable swivel; hooded ramp front sight, match-type aperture rear; adjustable match trigger with push-button safety. Imported from Germany by Beeman. Introduced 1981; no longer imported.

Right-hand

Perf: $595 **Exc:** $450 **VGood:** $375

Left-hand

Perf: $795 **Exc:** $595 **VGood:** $425

BEEMAN/HW 60J-ST

Bolt action; 22 LR; 22 7/8-inch barrel; 41-3/4-inch overall length; weighs 6-1/2 lbs.; walnut stock with cheekpiece; cut checkered pistol grip and forend; hooded blade front, open rear sight; polished blue finish; oil-finished walnut. Imported from Germany by Beeman. Introduced 1988; dropped 1992.

Perf: $525 **Exc:** $395 **VGood:** $295

222 Rem. caliber

Perf: $795 **Exc:** $650 **VGood:** $495

BEEMAN/HW 660 MATCH

Bolt action; single shot; 22 LR; 26-inch barrel; weighs 10-3/4 lbs.; 45-5/16-inch overall length; match-type walnut stock with adjustable cheekpiece and buttplate; globe front sight, match aperture rear; adjustable match trigger; stippled pistol grip and forend; forend accessory rail. Imported from Germany by Beeman. Introduced 1988; no longer imported.

Perf: $725 **Exc:** $550 **VGood:** $400

BENELLI R1

Semi-auto rifle chambered in .270 WSM, .300 WSM, .308 Win., .30-06, or .300 WSM. Interchangeable barrels. Blued finish with walnut, synthetic or ComforTech stock. Add 20 percent for ComforTech.

NIB: $925 **Exc:** $875 **VGood:** $725

BENTON & BROWN MODEL 93

Bolt action; 243, 6mm Rem., 25-06, 270, 280 Rem., 308, 30-06 (standard calibers); 257 Wea. Mag., 264 Win. Mag., 7mm Rem. Mag., 300 Wea. Mag., 300 Win. Mag., 338 Win. Mag., 340 Wea. Mag., 375 H&H (magnum calibers); 22-inch barrel (standard calibers), 24-inch (magnum calibers); 41-inch overall length (22-inch barrel); weighs about 8-1/2 lbs.; two-piece stock design of fancy walnut or fiberglass; oil finish; 20 lpi borderless checkering; sights optional; short-throw bolt action with 60° bolt throw; takedown design; interchangeable barrels and bolt assemblies; left-hand models available; safety locks firing pin and bolt. Made in U.S. by Benton & Brown Firearms, Inc. Introduced 1995.

Perf: $1750 **Exc:** $1300 **VGood:** $1000

Fiberglass stock model

Perf: $1550 **Exc:** $1100 **VGood:** $800

BERETTA AR-70

Semi-automatic; 223; 5-, 8-, 30-shot magazine; 17-3/4-inch barrel; weighs 8-1/4 lbs.; medium action; diopter adjustable sights; military-like epoxy resin finish. Offered with two magazines, cleaning kit and military-style carrying strap. Introduced 1984; discontinued 1989.

Perf: $2200 **Exc:** $1935 **VGood:** $1700

BERETTA MATO DELUXE

Bolt action; 270, 280 Rem., 30-06, 7mm Rem. Mag., 300 Win. Mag., 338 Win. Mag., 375 H&H. 23.6-inch barrel; weighs 7.9 lbs. 44-1/2-inch overall length. XXX claro walnut stock with ebony forend tip, hand-rubbed oil finish. Bead on ramp front, open fully adjustable rear sights; drilled and tapped for scope mounting. Mauser-style action with claw extractor; three-position safety; removable box magazine; 375 H&H has muzzle brake; premium for 375 caliber. Introduced 1997, dropped 2003. From Beretta U.S.A.

Perf: $1000 **Exc:** $800 **VGood:** $725

BERETTA MATO SYNTHETIC

Similar to the Mato except has fiberglass/Kevlar/carbon-fiber stock in classic American style with shadow line cheekpiece, aluminum bedding block and checkering. Introduced 1998, dropped 2003. From Beretta U.S.A. Premium for 375 caliber.

Perf: $1050 **Exc:** $850 **VGood:** $675

BERETTA MODEL 455

Double rifle; side-by-side; sidelock action; 375 H&H, 416 Rigby, 458 Win. Mag., 470 NE, 500 NE 3-inch; 23-1/2-inch, 25-1/2-inch barrels; weighs 11 lbs.; blade front sight, folding leaf V-notch rear; hand-checkered European walnut stock; removable sideplates; double triggers; recoil pad; color case-hardened finish. Made in Italy. Introduced, 1990; no longer imported.

Perf: $46,000 **Exc:** $38,000 **VGood:** $26,000

Model 455EELL with select walnut, engraving,

Perf: $58,000 **Exc:** $49,000 **VGood:** $39,000

BERETTA MODEL 500

Bolt action (short action); 222 Rem., 223 Rem.; 5-shot; 24-inch barrel; weighs 6-1/2-7 lbs.; short action; hood front sight, fully-adjustable rear; European walnut stock; oil-finished, hand-checkered; rubber buttpad. Made in Italy. Introduced 1984; importation discontinued 1990.

Perf: $600 **Exc:** $510 **VGood:** $420

BERETTA MODEL 500 S

Same specs as Model 500 except with iron sights.

Perf: $625 **Exc:** $550 **VGood:** $440

BERETTA MODEL 500 DL

Same specs as Model 500 except with select walnut, engraving, grip cap.

Perf: $1300 **Exc:** $1100 **VGood:** $900

BERETTA MODEL 500 DLS

Same specs as Model 500 except with iron sights, select walnut, engraving.

Perf: $1400 **Exc:** $1200 **VGood:** $1000

Beretta Mato Deluxe

Beretta Model 500

Beretta 455EELL

Beretta Model 501

BERETTA MODEL 500 EELL

Same specs as Model 500 except with fine walnut, more engraving.

Perf: $1500 **Exc:** $1300 **VGood:** $1100

BERETTA MODEL 500 EELLS

Same specs as Model 500 except with iron sights, fine walnut, more engraving.

Perf: $1600 **Exc:** $1400 **VGood:** $1200

BERETTA MODEL 501 (MEDIUM-LENGTH ACTION)

Bolt action; 243, 308; 5-shot magazine; 23-inch barrel; weighs 7 to 7-1/2 lbs.; hood front sight, fully-adjustable rear; checkered burled walnut stock; full pistol grip cap and palm swell; engraved receiver, trigger guard, magazine floorplate; rubber buttpad. Made in Italy. Introduced 1984; discontinued 1986.

Perf: $595 **Exc:** $510 **VGood:** $420

BERETTA MODEL 501 S

Same specs as Model 501 except with iron sights.

Perf: $625 **Exc:** $560 **VGood:** $475

BERETTA MODEL 501 DL

Same specs as Model 501 except with select walnut, engraving.

Perf: $1285 **Exc:** $1070 **VGood:** $900

BERETTA MODEL 501 DLS

Same specs as Model 501 except with iron sights, select walnut, engraving.

Perf: $1400 **Exc:** $1200 **VGood:** $1000

BERETTA MODEL 501 EELL

Same specs as Model 501 except with fine walnut, more engraving.

Perf: $1550 **Exc:** $1300 **VGood:** $1100

BERETTA MODEL 501 EELLS

Same specs as Model 501 except with iron sights, fine walnut, more engraving.

Perf: $1575 **Exc:** $1400 **VGood:** $1200

BERETTA MODEL 502 (LONG ACTION)

Bolt action; 6.5x55, 7mm Rem. Mag., 270, 7x64, 30-06, 300 Win. Mag., 375 H&H; 4-, 5-shot magazine; 24-1/2-inch barrel; weighs 8 to 8-1/2 lbs.; no sights; checkered walnut stock; schnabel forend; sling swivels; rubber buttpad. Made in Italy. Introduced, 1984; discontinued, 1986.

Perf: $640 **Exc:** $530 **VGood:** $480

BERETTA MODEL 502 DL

Same specs as Model 502 except with select walnut, engraving.

Perf: $1450 **Exc:** $1175 **VGood:** $950

BERETTA MODEL 502 DLS

Same specs as Model 502 except with iron sights, select walnut, engraving.

Perf: $1425 **Exc:** $1195 **VGood:** $975

BERETTA MODEL 502 EELL

Same specs as Model 502 except with fine walnut, more engraving.

Perf: $1595 **Exc:** $1295 **VGood:** $1050

BERETTA MODEL 502 EELLS

Same specs as Model 502 except with iron sights, fine walnut, more engraving

Perf: $1595 **Exc:** $1295 **VGood:** $1050

BERETTA MODEL 502 S

Same specs as Model 502 except with iron sights.

Perf: $675 **Exc:** $550 **VGood:** $495

BERETTA MODEL S689

Double rifle; over/under boxlock; 9.3x74R, 30-06; 23-inch barrel; weighs 7-3/4 lbs.; open V-notch rear sight, blade front on ramp; European walnut stock; checkered grip, forend; silvered, lightly engraved receiver; double triggers; ejectors; solid buttplate. Made in Italy. Introduced 1984; importation discontinued 1990.

Perf: $3695 **Exc:** $2995 **VGood:** $2200

BERETTA MODEL S689E

Same specs as Model S689 except auto ejectors.

Perf: $3995 **Exc:** $3250 **VGood:** $2250

BERETTA SPORTING CARBINE

Bolt action/semi-automatic; 22 LR; 4-, 8-, 20-shot magazine; 20-1/2-inch barrel; three-leaf folding rear sight, Patridge-type front; European walnut

Beretta Storm CX4 Carbine

Bernardelli Express VB

Big Horn Custom

stock; sling swivels; hand-checkered pistol-grip. When bolt handle is dropped, acts as more-or-less conventional bolt-action; with bolt handle raised fires semi-auto. Produced in Italy following World War II.

Perf: $370 **Exc:** $300 **VGood:** $230

BERETTA SSO EXPRESS

Double rifle; over/under sidelock; 9.3x74R, 375 H&H, 458 Win. Mag.; 23-, 25-1/2-inch barrels; weighs 11 lbs.; blade front sight on ramp, open V-notch rear; hand-checkered European walnut stock; color case-hardened receiver, trigger, trigger guard; double triggers, ejectors; recoil pad. Made in Italy. Introduced 1984; discontinued 1990.

Perf: $14,500 **Exc:** $11,000 **VGood:** $8500

BERETTA SSO5 EXPRESS

Same specs as Model SSO except with select walnut, engraving

Perf: $17,000 **Exc:** $14,000 **VGood:** $12,000

BERETTA SSO6 EXPRESS CUSTOM

Double rifle; over/under sidelock; 9.3x74R, 375 H&H, 458 Win. Mag.; individually built to buyer's specifications; 25-1/2-inch barrel; weighs 11 lbs.; blade front sight on ramp; open V-notch rear; hand-checkered European walnut stock; color case-hardened receiver; double triggers, ejectors; recoil pad. Made in Italy. Introduced 1990.

Perf: $34,500 **Exc:** $28,500 **VGood:** $22,900

With gold engraving

Perf: $39,500 **Exc:** $33,500 **VGood:** $27,500

BERETTA STORM CX4 CARBINE

Semi-automatic; 9mm, 40 S&W, 45 ACP; 8 to 15-round magazines, 20 round 9mm magazines available as an option; 16.6-inch barrel; 29.7-inch overall length; weighs 5-3/4 lbs; black polymer stock with rubber recoil pad; aperture rear sight, adjustable post front sight. Introduced 2003, still produced.

Perf: $685 **Exc:** $550 **VGood:** $450

BERNARDELLI CARBINE

Semi-automatic; 22 LR; 5-, 10-shot magazine; 21-inch barrel; 40-inch overall length; weighs 5-3/8 lbs.; checkered Monte Carlo-style European walnut stock; steel receiver; hooded front sight, fully-adjustable rear; push-button safety; blued/black finish. Made in Italy. Introduced 1986; importation discontinued 1991.

Perf: $550 **Exc:** $500 **VGood:** $390

BERNARDELLI EXPRESS VB

Double rifle; 9.3x74R, 8x57 JRS, 7x65R, 30-06, 375 H&H; 25-1/2-inch barrels; weighs about 8 lbs.; select walnut stock with cheekpiece; long beavertail-schnabel forend; hand-checkered grip and forend; pistol grip or straight English; bead on ramp front sight, quarter-rib with leaf rear; coin-finished or color case-hardened boxlock action with automatic ejectors; double trigger; hand-cut rib. Imported from Italy by Magnum Research. Introduced 1990; no longer imported.

Perf: $10,000 **Exc:** $7400 **VGood:** $3000

With single trigger

Perf: $12,000 **Exc:** $8800 **VGood:** $3100

BERNARDELLI MINERVA

Double rifle, side-by-side, similar to Express, but with outside hammers; 9.3x74R only.

Perf: $9000 **Exc:** $7500 **VGood:** $6500

BERNARDELLI MODEL 120

Combination gun; over/under boxlock; 12-ga. over 22 Hornet, 222 Rem., 5.6x50R Mag., 243, 6.5x57R, 270, 7x57R, 308, 30-06, 6.5x55, 7x65R, 8x57JRS, 9.3x74R; iron sights; checkered walnut stock, forearm; double trigger; automatic ejectors or extractors; ventilated recoil pad; engraved action. Made in Italy. No longer in production.

Perf: $3295 **Exc:** $2275 **VGood:** $1400

BERNARDELLI MODEL 190

Combination gun; over/under boxlock; 12-, 16-, 20-ga. over 222, 243, 30-06, 308, 5.6x50R Mag. 5.6x57R, 6.5x55, 6.5x57R, 7x57R, 7x65R, 8x57JRS, 9.3x74R; iron sights; checkered walnut stock, forearm; double trigger; extractors. Made in Italy. Introduced 1989; discontinued 1989.

Perf: $3295 **Exc:** $2275 **VGood:** $1400

BERNARDELLI MODEL 2000

Combination gun; over/under boxlock action; 12-, 16-, 20-ga. over/under 22 Hornet, 222 Rem., 5.6x50R Mag., 243, 6.5x55, 6.5x57R, 270, 7x57R, 308, 30-06, 8x57JRS, 9.3x74R; 23-1/2-inch barrels; weighs 6-3/4 lbs.; blade front sight, open rear with quarter-rib for rail-type scope mount; hand-checkered, oil-finished select European walnut stock with Bavarian-type cheekpiece; double set triggers; auto ejectors; silvered, engraved action. Made in Italy. Introduced 1990; dropped 1991.

Perf: $3295 **Exc:** $2275 **VGood:** $1400

With extra set of barrels

Perf: $4200 **Exc:** $3300 **VGood:** $2000

BIG HORN CUSTOM

Bolt action; chambered to customer's specs; 22-250 through all magnums; furnished with two barrels to customer specs; weighs about 6-3/4 lbs.; no sights; drilled, tapped for scope mounts; Mauser action; classic-style Claro walnut stock; Pachmayr flush swivel sockets; adjustable trigger; recoil pad. Introduced 1983; discontinued 1984.

Perf: $1900 **Exc:** $1500 **VGood:** $1000

BLASER K77A

Single-shot, break-open; 22-250, 243, 6.5x55, 270, 280, 7x57R, 7x65R, 30-06, 7mm Rem. Mag., 300 Win. Mag., 300 Weatherby Mag.; 23-inch, 24-inch barrel; 39-1/2-inch overall length (23-inch barrel); weighs 5-1/2 lbs.; no sights; marketed with Blaser scope mount; checkered two-piece Turkish walnut stock; solid buttpad; three-piece take-down; tang-mounted sliding safety; interchangeable barrels. Made in Germany. Introduced 1988; dropped 1990.

Perf: $2800 **Exc:** $2700 **VGood:** $2300

Magnum calibers

Perf: $2850 **Exc:** $2750 **VGood:** $2400

With interchangeable barrels

Perf: $3300 **Exc:** $3200 **VGood:** $3100

BLASER K95

Single-shot, breakopen; 243, 270, 7x57, 30-06, 308, 7mm Rem Mag, 300 Win Mag, 300 Weatherby Mag; 20-, 24-, 26-inch barrels, 37-1/2 to 42-inch overall length, weighs about 5.8 lbs., Turkish walnut stock and forearm; locking block secures barrel into receiver.

Perf: $4250 **Exc:** $3850 **VGood:** $2600

BLASER R84

Bolt action; 22-250, 243, 6mm Rem., 25-06, 270, 280, 30-06 (standard calibers); 257 Wea., 264 Win. Mag., 7mm Rem. Mag., 300 Win. Mag., 300 Wea., 338 Win. Mag., 375 H&H; 23-inch barrel (standard calibers), 24-inch (magnum calibers); 41-inch overall length (23-inch barrel); weighs 7 to 7-1/4 lbs.; two-piece Turkish walnut stock and forend; solid black buttpad; no sights; comes with low-profile Blaser scope mounts; interchangeable barrels and magnum/standard caliber bolt assemblies; left-hand models available in all calibers. No longer imported.

Perf: $2400 **Exc:** $2000 **VGood:** $1400

Left-hand

Perf: $2700 **Exc:** $2200 **VGood:** $1500

BLASER R93

Bolt action, straight pull; 222, 243, 6.5x55, 270, 7x57, 308, 30-06, 7mm Rem. Mag., 300 Win. Mag., 300 Wea. Mag., 338 Win. Mag., 375 H&H, 416 Rem. Mag.; 3-shot magazine; 22-inch barrel (standard calibers), 24-inch (magnum calibers); 40-inch overall length (22-inch barrel); weighs 6-1/2 to 7-1/2 lbs.; two-piece European walnut stock; blade front sight on ramp, open rear, or no sights; thumb-activated safety slide/cocking mechanism; interchangeable barrels and bolt heads. Imported from Germany by Autumn Sales, later Sigarms. Introduced 1994. Add 10 percent-25 percent for premium grades, depending on degree of ornamentation.

Perf: $4000 **Exc:** $3850 **VGood:** $3300

BLASER R93 LONG RANGE RIFLE

Bolt action, straight pull; 308 Win., 10-shot detachable box magazine; 24-inch barrel; weighs 10.4 lbs. 44-inch overall; aluminum stock with synthetic lining, adjustable cheeckpiece and butt, folding bipod; no sights furnished; accepts detachable scope mount; adjustable trigger; fully adjustable stock; quick takedown; corrosion resistant finish. Introduced 1998. Imported from Germany by Sigarms.

Perf: $3700 **Exc:** $2900 **VGood:** $2500

BLASER R93 SAFARI

Same specs as the R93 except 375 H&H, 416 Rem. Mag.; 24-inch barrel; weighs 9.5 lbs.; open sights; broad forend. Imported from Germany by Autumn Sales, Inc. Introduced 1994; no longer imported.

Perf: $3900 **Exc:** $3100 **VGood:** $2200

BLASER R93 SYNTHETIC

Same specs as R93 except one-piece black synthetic stock.

Perf: $3050 **Exc:** $2700 **VGood:** $2100

BLASER ULTIMATE BOLT ACTION

Bolt action; 60 degree bolt throw; bolt lugs lock into rear of barrel; 22-250, 243, 25-06, 270, 308, 30-06, 7x57, 7x64, 264 Win. Mag., 7mm Rem. Mag., 300 Win. Mag., 338 Win. Mag., 375 H&H; 22-inch, 24-inch barrel; interchangeable capability; weighs 6-3/4 lbs.; select checkered walnut stock, forearm; aluminum receiver with engraving;. Introduced 1985; discontinued 1989.

Perf: $2900 **Exc:** $2250 **VGood:** $1850

BORTMESS BIG HORN

Bolt action; calibers from 22-250 through 458 Win.; 24-inch, 25-inch barrel; no sights; drilled, tapped for scope mounts; Monte Carlo stock of American walnut; roll-over cheekpiece; half-curl pistol grip; rosewood cap; tapering forend; rosewood forend cap; high-gloss finish; steel buttplate or recoil pad; built on Ranger Arms action. Introduced 1974; discontinued 1977.

Perf: $695 **Exc:** $595 **VGood:** $435

B0RTMESS CLASSIC MODEL

Bolt action; calibers from 22-250 through 458 Win.; 24-inch, 25-inch barrel; no sights; drilled, tapped for scope mounts; hand-checkered American walnut stock; plastic pistol grip cap, forend tip; built on Ranger Arms action; Pachmayr solid rubber recoil pad. Introduced 1974; discontinued 1977.

Perf: $695 **Exc:** $595 **VGood:** $450

BORTMESS OMEGA

Bolt action; calibers from 22-250 through 358 Norma; 24-inch, 25-inch barrel; no sights; drilled, tapped for scope mounts; American walnut stock; high-gloss finish. Introduced 1974; discontinued 1977.

Perf: $895 **Exc:** $695 **VGood:** $550

BRNO 500 COMBINATION GUN

Combination gun, breakopen; 12 gauge (2-3/4-inch chamber) over 5.6x52R, 5.6x50R, 222 Rem., 243, 6.x55, 308, 7x57R, 7x65R, 30-06. 23.6-inch barrel; weighs 7.6 lbs. 40-1/2-inch overall length. European walnut stock. Bead front, V-notch rear sights; grooved for scope mounting. hammerless boxlock action; double set trigger; blue finish with etched engraving; also available as double rifle. Announced 1998. Imported from the Czech Republic by Euro-Imports.

Perf: $1700 **Exc:** $1350 **VGood:** $850

BRNO CZ 98 HUNTER CLASSIC

Bolt action, Mauser-type; 243, 6.5x55, 270, 7x57, 7x64, 308, 30-06, 7.92x57, 7mm Rem. Mag., 300 Win. Mag.; 24-inch barrel; 45-inch overall length; weighs 7-5/8 lbs.; walnut or synthetic stock; optional sights; integral Weaver-type base; controlled round feeding; fixed ejector; hinged floorplate; adjustable trigger; swivel studs. Imported from the Czech Republic by Springfield, Inc., later by Euro-Imports; Introduced 1995.

Perf: $500 **Exc:** $330 **VGood:** $280

Blaser R93 Long Range Rifle

Blaser R93 Synthetic

Bortmess Big Horn

Bortmess Omega

Bortmess Classic Model

Brno 500 Combination Gun

With synthetic stock

Perf: $415 **Exc:** $300 **VGood:** $260

BRNO CZ 99 PRECISION 22

Bolt action; 22 LR; 5-shot magazine; 20-inch barrel; 41-inch overall length; weighs 6 lbs.; hooded bead on ramp front sight, fully-adjustable rear; receiver grooved for scope mount; checkered European hardwood stock; sliding safety; polished blue finish. Made in Yugoslavia. Introduced 1990; discontinued 1991.

Perf: $300 **Exc:** $270 **VGood:** $220

BRNO CZ 537 SPORTER

Bolt action; 270, 30-06 (internal 5-shot magazine), 243, 308 (detachable 5-shot magazine); 23 5/8-inch barrel; 44-3/4-inch overall length; weighs 7 lbs. 9 oz.; checkered walnut stock; hooded ramp front sight, adjustable folding leaf rear; improved standard-size Mauser-style action with non-rotating claw extractor; externally adjustable trigger; American-style safety; streamlined bolt shroud with cocking indicator. Imported from the Czech Republic by Magnum Research. Introduced 1992.

Perf: $550 **Exc:** $475 **VGood:** $375

With full stock, 308, 30-06

Perf: $650 **Exc:** $575 **VGood:** $475

BRNO CZ 550

Bolt action; 243, 308 (4-shot detachable magazine), 7x57, 270, 30-06, 7mm Rem. Mag., 300 Win. Mag. (5-shot internal magazine); 23-5/8-inch barrel; 44-3/4-inch overall length; weighs 7-1/4 lbs.; walnut stock with high comb; checkered grip and forend; no sights; drilled and tapped for Remington 700-style bases; polished blue finish. Imported from the Czech Republic by Magnum Research. Introduced 1995.

Perf: $550 **Exc:** $450 **VGood:** $375

BRNO ZH 300 COMBINATION GUN

Combination gun, breakopen; 22 Hornet, 5.6x50R Mag., 5.6x52R, 7x57R, 7x65R, 8x57JRS over 12, 16 (2-3/4-inch chamber); 23.6-inch barrel; weighs 7.9 lbs. 40-1/2-inch overall length. European walnut stock; Blade front, open adjustable rear sights. Boxlock action; double triggers; automatic safety; introduced 1986. Also available as double rifles. Imported from the Czech Republic by Pragotrade, later by Euro-Imports.

Perf: $2995 **Exc:** $2395 **VGood:** $1795

Brno CZ 99 Precision 22

Brno CZ 537 Sporter

Brno ZH Series 300

BRNO HORNET

Bolt action; 22 Hornet; 5-shot box magazine; 23-inch barrel; three-leaf rear sight, hooded ramp front; double-set trigger; sling swivels; hand-checkered pistol grip, forearm. Manufactured in Czechoslovakia from 1949 to 1973.

Exc: $1000 **VGood:** $900 **Good:** $800

BRNO MODEL 1

Bolt action; 22 LR; 5-shot magazine; 23-inch barrel; weighs 6 lbs.; three-leaf rear sight, hooded ramp front; sporting stock; hand-checkered pistol grip; sling swivels. Introduced 1947; discontinued 1957.

Exc: $450 **VGood:** $350 **Good:** $300

BRNO MODEL 2

Bolt action; 22 LR; 5-shot magazine; 23-inch barrel; weighs 6 lbs.; three-leaf rear sight, hooded ramp front; deluxe walnut sporting stock; hand-checkered pistol grip; sling swivels. Introduced 1946; discontinued 1957.

Exc: $470 **VGood:** $380 **Good:** $310

BRNO MODEL 3

Bolt action; 22 LR; 5-shot magazine; 27-1/2-inch heavy barrel; weighs 9-1/2 lbs.; click-adjustable target sights; smooth target stock; sling swivels. Introduced 1949; discontinued 1956.

Exc: $515 **VGood:** $430 **Good:** $325

BRNO MODEL 4

Bolt action; 22 LR; 5-shot magazine; 27-1/2-inch heavy barrel; weighs 9-1/2 lbs.; click-adjustable target sights; smooth target stock; sling swivels; improved safety, trigger. Introduced 1957; discontinued 1962.

Exc: $635 **VGood:** $513 **Good:** $440

BRNO MODEL 5

Bolt action; 22 LR; 5-shot magazine; 23-inch barrel; weighs 6 lbs.; three-leaf rear sight, hooded ramp front; sporting stock; hand-checkered pistol grip; sling swivels. Introduced 1957; discontinued 1973.

Exc: $575 **VGood:** $495 **Good:** $400

BRNO MODEL 21H

Bolt action; 6.5x55, 7x57, 7x64, 8x57mm; 5-shot box magazine; 20-1/2-inch, 23-inch barrel; Mauser-type; two-leaf rear sight, ramp front; half-length sporting stock; hand-checkered pistol grip, forearm; sling swivels; double-set trigger. Introduced 1946; discontinued 1955.

Exc: $900 **VGood:** $700 **Good:** $500

BRNO MODEL 22F

Bolt action; 6.5x55, 7x57, 7x64, 8x57mm; 5-shot box magazine; 20-1/2-inch, 23-inch barrel; Mauser-type; two-leaf rear sight, ramp front; Mannlicher-type stock; sling swivels; double-set trigger. Introduced 1946; discontinued 1955.

Perf: $1100 **Exc:** $850 **VGood:** $600

BRNO MODEL ZG-47

Bolt action; 270, 30-06, 7x57, 7x64, 8x64S, 8x57, 9.3x62, 10.75x68; 23-1/2-inch barrel; checkered walnut stock, pistol grip; schnabel forend; hinged floorplate; single trigger. Made in Czechoslovakia. Introduced 1956; discontinued 1962.

Perf: $995 **Exc:** $875 **VGood:** $700

BRNO MODEL ZKM-456

Bolt action; 22 LR; 5-, 10-shot magazine; 24-1/2-inch barrel; weighs 6-1/2 lbs.; folding rear sight, fixed front; Beechwood stock; pistol grip; blued finish. Introduced 1992; no longer imported.

Perf: $330 **Exc:** $270 **VGood:** $230

BRNO MODEL ZKM-456 L TARGET

Same specs as Model ZKM-456 except 27-1/2-inch barrel; adjustable front and rear sights; weighs 10 lbs. Introduced 1992; no longer imported.

Perf: $330 **Exc:** $270 **VGood:** $230

BRNO MODEL ZKM-456 MATCH

Same specs as Model ZKM-456 except single shot; 27-1/2-inch barrel; aperture sights; adjustable buttplate, cheekpiece; weighs 10 lbs. Introduced 1992; no longer imported.

Perf: $375 **Exc:** $300 **VGood:** $250

BRNO SUPER EXPRESS

Double rifle; over/under sidelock; 7x65R, 9.3x74R, 375 H&H, 458 Win. Mag.; 23-1/2-inch barrel; 40-inch overall length; weighs about 8-1/2 lbs.; quarter-rib with open rear sight, bead on ramp front; checkered European walnut stock; engraved sideplates; double-set triggers; selective auto ejectors; rubber recoil pad. Made in Czechoslovakia. Introduced 1986; discontinued 1992.

Perf: $3450 **Exc:** $2875 **VGood:** $1800

BRNO SUPER SAFARI

Double rifle; over/under sidelock; 7x64R, 375 H&H Mag., 9.3x74R; 23-1/2-inch barrel; weighs 9 lbs.; open sights; checkered walnut stock, forearm; double trigger with set trigger; ventilated recoil pad. Introduced 1992; no longer imported.

Perf: $2295 **Exc:** $1895 **VGood:** $1350

BRNO ZBK 110 SINGLE SHOT RIFLE

Single shot; 222 Rem., 5.6x52R, 22 Hornet, 5.6x50 Mag., 6.5x57R, 7x57R, 8x57JRS; 23.6-inch barrel; weighs 5.9 lbs. 40.1-inch overall. European walnut stock; no sights; drilled and tapped for scope mounting. Top tang opening lever; cross-bolt safety; polished blue finish. Announced 1998.

Perf: $230 **Exc:** $190 **VGood:** $150

BRNO ZKB 527 FOX

Bolt action; 22 Hornet, 222 Rem., 223 Rem.; 5-shot detachable magazine; 23-1/2-inch barrel, standard or heavy; 42-1/2-inch overall length; weighs 6 lbs. 1 oz.; European walnut Monte Carlo stock; hooded front sight, open adjustable rear; improved mini-Mauser action with non-rotating claw extractor; grooved receiver.

Perf: $595 **Exc:** $515 **VGood:** $415

BRNO ZKB 680 FOX

Bolt action; 22 Hornet, 222 Rem.; 5-shot detachable box magazine; 23-1/2-inch barrel; 42-1/2-inch overall length; weighs 5 lbs. 12 oz.; Turkish walnut Monte Carlo stock; hooded front sight, open adjustable rear; adjustable double-set triggers. Imported from Czechoslovakia by T.D. Arms. No longer imported.

Perf: $445 **Exc:** $380 **VGood:** $315

BRNO ZKK 600

Bolt action (medium-length action); 30-06, 270, 7x57, 7x64; 5-shot magazine; 23-1/2-inch barrel; 43-inch overall length; weighs 7-1/4 lbs.; open folding adjustable rear sight, hooded ramp front; synthetic or checkered walnut stock; improved Mauser action with controlled feed, claw extractor; adjustable set trigger; easy-release sling swivels. Made in Czechoslovakia. Introduced 1986.

Perf: $500 **Exc:** $425 **VGood:** $375

BRNO ZKK 601

Bolt action (short action); 223 Rem., 243 Win., 308 Win.; 5-shot magazine; 23-1/2-inch barrel; 43' overall length; 7-1/4 lbs.; open folding adjustable rear sight, hooded ramp front; synthetic or checkered walnut stock; improved Mauser action with controlled feed, claw extractor; adjustable set trigger; easy-release sling swivels. Made in Czechoslovakia. Introduced 1986.

Perf:. $500 **Exc:** $425 **VGood:** $370

BRNO ZKK 602

Bolt action (long action); 300 Win. Mag., 375 H&H, 8x68, 416 Rigby, 458 Win. Mag.; 5-shot magazine; 25-inch barrel; 9-5/8 lbs.; three-leaf express rear sight, hooded ramp front; synthetic or checkered walnut stock; adjustable set trigger; easy-release sling swivels. Made in Czechoslovakia. Introduced 1986.

Perf: $650 **Exc:** $575 **VGood:** $495

BRNO ZKM 452 STANDARD

Bolt action; 22 LR; 5-, 10-shot magazine; 25-inch barrel; 43-1/2-inch overall length; weighs 6 lbs. 9 oz.; beechwood stock; hooded bead front sight, open elevation-adjustable rear; blue finish; oiled stock; grooved receiver. Imported from Czechoslovakia by Action Arms, later Bauska. No longer imported.

Perf: $285 **Exc:** $225 **VGood:** $195

BRNO ZKM 452 DELUXE

Same specs as ZKM 452 except 23-5/8-inch barrel; 42-1/2-inch overall length; checkered walnut stock; sling swivels. Introduced 1992; no longer imported.

Perf: $350 **Exc:** $265 **VGood:** $210

BRNO ZKM 611

Semi-automatic; 22 WMR; 6-shot magazine; 20-inch barrel; 37-inch overall length; weighs 6 lbs. 2 oz.; European walnut stock with checkered grip and forend; blade front sight, open rear; removable box magazine; polished blue finish; grooved receiver for scope mounting; sling swivels; thumbscrew takedown. Discontinued.

Perf: $860 **Exc:** $800 **VGood:** $730

BRONCO

Single shot; 22 Short, 22 Long, 22 LR; 16-1/2-inch barrel; barrel pivots to side to load; weighs 3 lbs.; adjustable rear sight, blade front;

early version solid construction, later, instant takedown; skeletonized crackle-finished alloy stock; cross-bolt safety. Introduced 1967; offered first by Firearms International, later by Garcia; discontinued 1978. Found in four versions: .22 LR single-shot, .22 Magnum single-shot, .410 single-shot, and .22/.410 O/U. Add 15% for .22/.410.

Perf: $395 **Exc:** $350 **VGood:** $190

ED BROWN SAVANNAH

Bolt-action medium-weight centerfire rifle. Chambered in a variety of short- and long-action standard and magnum chamberings. Fluted bolt, McMillan stock, optional muzzlebrake, blackened stainless barrel.

NIB: $3250 **Exc:** $2995 **VGood:** $2100

ED BROWN DAMARA

Similar to Savannah but in a lightweight configuration with natural-finish stainless barrel.

NIB: $3250 **Exc:** $2995 **VGood:** $2100

ED BROWN COMPACT VARMINT

Similar to Damara but with shorter barrel, beavertail forend.

NIB: $3250 **Exc:** $2995 **VGood:** $2100

BROWN MODEL ONE

Single shot; 22 LR, 357 Mag., 44 Mag., 7-30 Waters, 30-30 Win., 375 Win., 45-70; custom chamberings from 17 Rem. through 45-caliber available; 22-inch or custom length barrel, bull or tapered; weighs about 6 lbs.; smooth walnut stock; custom takedown design by Woodsmith; palm swell for right- or left-hand; rubber buttpad; sights optional; drilled and tapped for scope mounting; rigid barrel/receiver; falling-block action with short lock time, automatic case ejection; air-gauged barrels by Wilson and Douglas; muzzle has 11-degree target crown; matte black oxide finish standard, polished and electroless nickel optional. Made in U.S. by E.A. Brown Mfg. Introduced 1988.

Per.f: $1050 **Exc:** $975 **VGood:** $550

BROWN MODEL 97D

Single shot, falling block; 17 Ackley through 45-70; barrels up to 26-inch; air-gauged match grade; weighs about 5 lbs., 11 oz.; sporter stock with pistol grip, cheekpiece and schnabel forearm; no sights furnished; drilled and tapped for scope mounting; polished blue-black finish; hand-fitted action; many options; Made in U. S. by E. Arthur Brown Co. Introduced about 1998.

Per.f: $1050 **Exc:** $975 **VGood:** $550

BROWNING A-BOLT HUNTER

Bolt action; 25-06, 270, 30-06, 280, 7mm Rem. Mag., 300 Win. Mag., 338 Win. Mag., 375 H&H (long action); 22-250, 243 Win., 257 Roberts, 22-250, 7mm-08, 308 Win., also 223 WSSM, 243 WSSM, 270 WSM, 7mm WSM, 300 WSM (short action); 22-inch, 24-inch, 26-inch barrel; 44-3/4-inch overall length; weighs 6-1/2 to 7-1/2 lbs.; recessed muzzle; magnum and standard action; classic-style American walnut stock; recoil pad on magnum calibers; short throw fluted bolt; three locking lugs; plunger-type ejector; adjustable, grooved gold-plated trigger; hinged floorplate; detachable box magazine; slide tang safety; rosewood grip, forend caps. Made in Japan. Introduced 1985; redesigned in 1994 as A-Bolt II.

Perf: $600 **Exc:** $575 **VGood:** $395

BROWNING A-BOLT HUNTER, LEFT-HAND

Similar to A-Bolt Hunter but in left-hand version.

Perf: $650 **Exc:** $625 **VGood:** $420

BROWNING A-BOLT CAMO STALKER

Same specs as A-Bolt Hunter except camo-stained laminated wood stock; cut checkering; non-glare finish on metal; 270, 30-06, 7mm Rem. Mag. Made in Japan. Introduced 1987; dropped 1989.

Perf: $525 **Exc:** $495 **VGood:** $375

Ed Brown Savannah

Ed Brown Damara

Ed Brown Compact Varmint

Browning A-Bolt II Hunter

Browning A-Bolt Hunter, Left-Hand

BROWNING A-BOLT COMPOSITE STALKER

Same specs as the A-Bolt Hunter except checkered black composite stock. Imported from Japan by Browning. Introduced 1985.

Perf: $595 **Exc:** $560 **VGood:** $420

BROWNING A-BOLT EURO-BOLT

Same specs as the A-Bolt Hunter except satin-finished walnut stock with Continental-style cheekpiece; palm swell grip and schnabel forend; rounded bolt shroud and Mannlicher-style flattened bolt handle; 30-06, 270 (22-inch barrel), 7mm Rem. Mag. (26-inch barrel); weighs about 6 lbs., 11 oz. Imported from Japan by Browning. Introduced 1993. Now known as Euro-Bolt II.

Perf: $775 **Exc:** $575 **VGood:** $450

BROWNING A-BOLT GOLD MEDALLION

Same specs as A-Bolt Hunter except select walnut stock; gold-filled inscription on barrel; engraved receiver; brass spacers between rubber recoil pad, rosewood grip cap, forend tip; palm swell pistol grip; Monte Carlo-style comb; double-border 22 lpi checkering; 270, 30-06, 300 Win. Mag., 7mm Rem. Mag. Made in Japan. Introduced 1988.

Perf: $950 **Exc:** $900 **VGood:** $700

BROWNING A-BOLT MEDALLION

Same specs as A-Bolt Hunter except 375 H&H Mag.; 1-inch deluxe sling swivels; rosewood pistol grip, forend cap; slide tang safety; with or without sights; glossy stock finish; high polish blue. Imported from Japan by Browning. Introduced 1985.

Perf: $750 **Exc:** $700 **VGood:** $595

375 H&H, with sights

Perf: $800 **Exc:** $750 **VGood:** $645

BROWNING A-BOLT MEDALLION LEFT-HAND

Same specs as the Medallion except left-hand action; 270, 30-06, 7mm Rem. Mag., 375 H&H. Imported from Japan by Browning. Introduced 1987.

Perf: $800 **Exc:** $750 **VGood:** $625

BROWNING A-BOLT MICRO MEDALLION

Same specs as A-Bolt Hunter except scaled-down version with 20-inch barrel; shortened, 13 5/16-inch length of pull; 3-shot magazine; weighs 6 lbs., 1 oz.; 243, 308, 7mm-08, 257 Roberts, 223, 22-250; no sights. Imported from Japan by Browning. Introduced 1988. Add 100% for .284.

Perf: $695 **Exc:** $650 **VGood:** $495

BROWNING A-BOLT STAINLESS STALKER

Same specs as A-Bolt Hunter except stainless steel receiver; matte silver-gray finish; graphite-fiberglass composite textured stock; no sights; 270, 30-06, 7mm Rem. Mag, 375 H&H. Made in Japan. Imported from Japan by Browning. Introduced 1987.

Perf: $750 **Exc:** $700 **VGood:** $495

Left-hand

Perf: $775 **Exc:** $725 **VGood:** $520

375 H&H caliber

Perf: $950 **Exc:** $900 **VGood:** $695

BROWNING A-BOLT 22

Bolt action; 22 LR, 22 WMR; 5-, 15-shot magazine; 22-inch barrel; 40-1/4-inch overall length; weighs 5 lbs. 9 oz.; walnut stock with cut checkering;

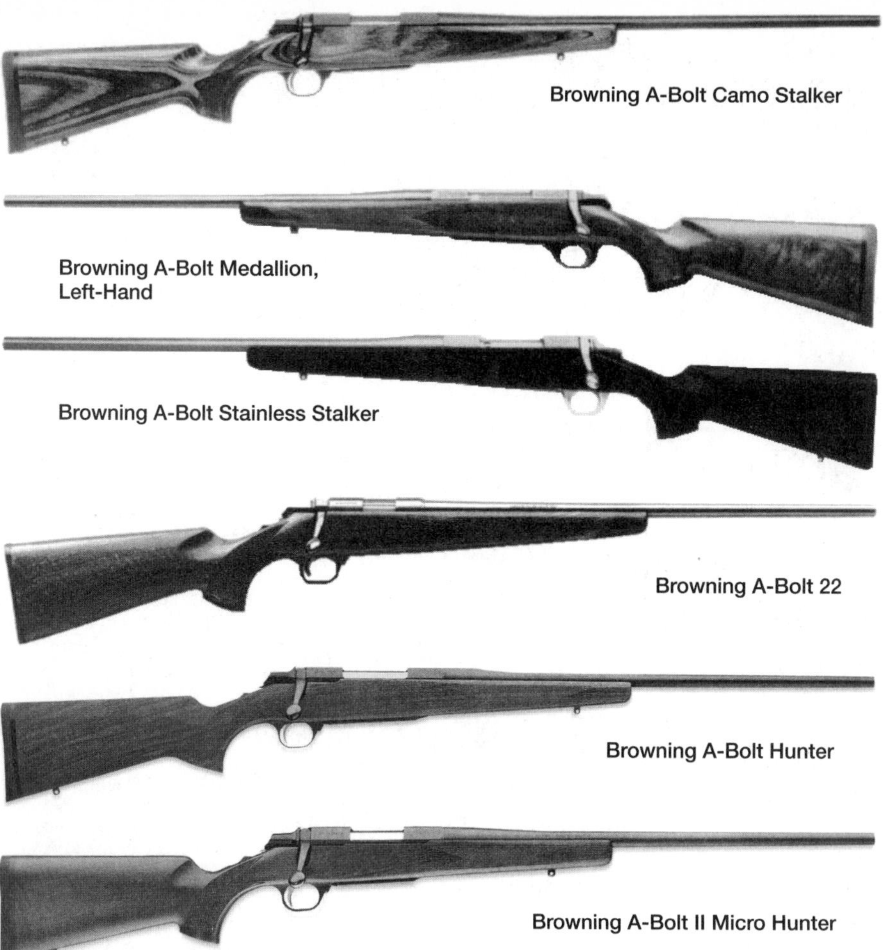
Browning A-Bolt Camo Stalker

Browning A-Bolt Medallion, Left-Hand

Browning A-Bolt Stainless Stalker

Browning A-Bolt 22

Browning A-Bolt Hunter

Browning A-Bolt II Micro Hunter

rosewood grip cap and forend tip; with or without open sights; open sight model with ramp front and adjustable folding leaf rear; short 60°; bolt throw; top tang safety; grooved for 22 scope mount; drilled and tapped for full-size scope mounts; detachable magazine; gold-colored trigger. Imported from Japan by Browning. Introduced 1986; no longer imported.

22 LR

Perf: $750 **Exc:** $650 **VGood:** $525

22 WMR

Perf: $775 **Exc:** $675 **VGood:** $550

BROWNING A-BOLT 22 GOLD MEDALLION

Same specs as A-Bolt 22 except high-grade walnut stock with brass spacers between stock and rubber recoil pad, and rosewood grip cap and forend; Medallion-style engraving on receiver flats; "Gold Medallion" engraved and gold filled on right side of barrel; high-gloss stock finish; no sights. Imported from Japan by Browning. Introduced 1988; no longer imported.

Perf: $800 **Exc:** $750 **VGood:** $700

BROWNING A-BOLT II HUNTER

Bolt action; 223, 223 WSSM, 22-250, 243, 243 WSSM, 25-06, 270, 270 WSM, 280, 7mm-08, 7mm Rem. Mag., 308, 30-06, 300 Win. Mag., 300 WSM, 325 WSM, 338 Win. Mag., 375 H&H Mag.; 4-shot (standard calibers), 3-shot (magnum calibers) detachable box magazine; 22-inch medium sporter weight barrel with recessed muzzle; 26-inch on magnum calibers; 44-3/4-inch overall length, 41-3/4-inch (short action); weighs 6-1/2 to 7-1/2 lbs.; classic-style American walnut stock; recoil pad standard on magnum calibers; short-throw (60-degree) fluted bolt; three locking lugs; plunger-type ejector; grooved and gold-plated adjustable trigger; hinged floorplate; slide tang safety; glossy stock finish, rosewood grip and forend cap; high polish blue; BOSS barrel vibration modulator and muzzlebrake system not available in 375 H&H. Imported from Japan by Browning. Introduced 1994; still imported.

Perf: $750 **Exc:** $550 **VGood:** $450

With open sights

Perf: $700 **Exc:** $550 **VGood:** $480

With BOSS

Perf: $740 **Exc:** $580 **VGood:** $500

BROWNING A-BOLT II MICRO HUNTER

Similar to the A-Bolt II Hunter except has shorter barrel and stock, 13-5/16-inch length of pull, 20-inch barrel, and comes in 260 Rem., 243, 308, 7mm-08, 223, 22-250, 22 Hornet, also 270 WSM, 7mm WSM, 300 WSM. Weighs 6 lbs., 1 oz. Introduced 1999. Imported by Browning.

Perf: $700 **Exc:** $550 **VGood:** $500

BROWNING A-BOLT II COMPOSITE STALKER

Same specs as A-Bolt II Hunter except black graphite fiberglass stock with textured finish; matte blue finish on metal; .223 WSSM, .243 WSSM, .25 WSSM, .223, .243, .7mm-08, .270 WSM, 7mm WSM, .300 WSM, .325 WSM, .25-06, .270, .280, .30-06, 7mm RM, .300 WM, .338 WM. Add 10 percent for BOSS or left-hand version..; no sights; BOSS barrel vibration modulator and muzzlebrake system offered in all calibers. Imported from Japan by Browning. Introduced 1994; still imported.

Perf: $650 **Exc:** $500 **VGood:** $450

With BOSS

Perf: $740 **Exc:** $580 **VGood:** $500

BROWNING EURO-BOLT II

Same specs as A-Bolt II Hunter except satin-finished walnut stock with Continental-style cheekpiece; palm-swell grip and schnabel forend; rounded bolt shroud and Mannlicher-style flattened bolt handle; 30-06, 270 (22-inch barrel), 7mm Rem. Mag. (26-inch barrel); weighs about 6 lbs., 11 oz.; BOSS barrel vibration modulator and muzzlebrake system optional. Imported from Japan by Browning. Introduced 1993.

Perf: $750 **Exc:** $590 **VGood:** $450

With BOSS

Perf: $825 **Exc:** $700 **VGood:** $550

BROWNING A-BOLT II GOLD MEDALLION

Same specs as A-Bolt II Hunter except select walnut stock with brass spacers between rubber recoil pad, and rosewood grip cap and forend tip; gold-filled barrel inscription; palm swell pistol grip; Monte Carlo comb; 22 lpi checkering with double borders; engraved receiver flats; 270, 30-06, 7mm Rem. Mag. only. Imported from Japan by Browning. Introduced 1988.

Perf: $700 **Exc:** $590 **VGood:** $500

With BOSS

Perf: $770 **Exc:** $665 **VGood:** $550

BROWNING A-BOLT II HUNTER SHORT ACTION

Same specs as the standard A-Bolt II Hunter except short action for 223, 22-250, 243, 257 Roberts, 7mm-08, 284 Win., 308, new short magnum chamberings; weighs 6-1/2 lbs.; BOSS barrel vibration modulator and muzzlebrake system optional. Imported from Japan by Browning. Introduced 1994.

Perf: $700 **Exc:** $600 **VGood:** $500

With sights

Perf: $750 **Exc:** $650 **VGood:** $550

With BOSS

Perf: $795 **Exc:** $695 **VGood:** $595

BROWNING A-BOLT II MEDALLION

Same specs as A-Bolt II Hunter except .223 WSSM, .243 WSSM, .25 WSSM, .223, .243, .7mm-08, .270 WSM, 7mm WSM, .300 WSM, .325 WSM, .25-06, .270, .280, .30-06, 7mm RM, .300 WM, .338 WM. Add 10 percent for BOSS or left-hand version.istol grip, forend cap; slide tang safety; glossy stock finish; high polish blue. Imported from Japan by Browning. Introduced 1984; still imported.

Perf: $725 **Exc:** $650 **VGood:** $500

With BOSS

Perf: $775 **Exc:** $700 **VGood:** $575

375 H&H

Perf: $900 **Exc:** $825 **VGood:** $675

WSSM version, chambered for 223 WSSM and 243 WSSM, introduced 2003.

Perf: $725 **Exc:** $650 **VGood:** $500

223 WSSM, 243 WSSM, 25 WSSM chambering

Perf: $725 **Exc:** $650 **VGood:** $500

BROWNING A-BOLT II MEDALLION SHORT ACTION

Same specs as the standard A-Bolt II Medallion except short action for 223, 22-250, 243, 257 Roberts, 7mm-08, 284 Win., 308; weighs 6-1/2 lbs. BOSS barrel vibration modulator and muzzlebrake system optional. Imported from Japan by Browning. Introduced 1994.

Perf: $725 **Exc:** $650 **VGood:** $500

BROWNING A-BOLT II MICRO MEDALLION

Same specs as A-Bolt II Medallion except scaled-down version with 20-inch barrel; shortened length of pull (13-5/16-inch); 3-shot magazine; weighs 6 lbs. 1 oz.; 22 Hornet, 243, 308, 7mm-08, 257 Roberts, 223, 22-250; BOSS feature not available. Imported from Japan by Browning. Introduced 1994; no longer imported.

Perf: $640 **Exc:** $580 **VGood:** $500

BROWNING A-BOLT II STAINLESS STALKER

Bolt-action rifle. Calibers: .223 WSSM, .243 WSSM, .25 WSSM, .223, .243, .7mm-08, .270 WSM, 7mm WSM, .300 WSM, .325 WSM, .25-06, .270, .280,

.30-06, 7mm RM, .300 WM, .338 WM, .375 H&H. Barrel: 22-inch, 23-inch, 24-inch, 26-inch stainless steel, sightless (except for .375 H&H). Magazine: Detachable box. Stock: Black composite. Add 10 percent for BOSS system and left-hand version.

Perf: $745 **Exc:** $695 **VGood:** $550

With BOSS

Perf:. $800 **Exc:** $750 **VGood:** $600

375 H&H, with sights

Perf: $715 **Exc:** $670 **VGood:** $550

Left-hand, with BOSS

Perf: $950 **Exc:** $900 **VGood:** $750

BROWNING A-BOLT II VARMINT

Same specs as A-Bolt II Hunter except heavy varmint/target barrel; laminated wood stock with special dimensions; flat forend and palm swell grip; 223, 22-250, 308; comes with BOSS barrel vibration modulator and muzzlebrake system. Imported from Japan by Browning. Introduced 1994; no longer imported.

Perf: $695 **Exc:** $600 **VGood:** $500

BROWNING NRA A-BOLT WILDLIFE CONSERVATION COLLECTION

Commemorates NRA's Environment Conservation and Hunting Outreach Program. Caliber: .243 Win. Barrel: 22-inch blued sightless. Stock: Satin-finish walnut with NRA Heritage logo lasered on buttstock.

NIB: $750 **Exc:** $695 **VGood:** $545

BROWNING A-BOLT SPECIAL HUNTER RMEF

Similar to A-Bolt Hunter but honors Rocky Mountain Elk Foundation. Chambered in .325 WSM. Satin finish. Introduced 2007.

NIB: $825 **Exc:** $775 **VGood:** $650

BROWNING A-BOLT WHITE GOLD RMEF

Similar to A-Bolt Special Hunter RMEF but with stainless barrel and receiver and glossy finish. Introduced 2007.

NIB: $1200 **Exc:** $1100 **VGood:** $895

BROWNING X-BOLT COMPOSITE STALKER

Features include steel receiver with matte blue finish, free-flaotinmg crowned barrel, matte black composite stock with palm swell, Inflex recoil pad. Various barrel lengths depending on chambering, which include both medium and long cartridges ranging from .243 Winchester to .338 Winchester Magnum. Introduced in 2008.

NIB: $800 **Exc:** $700 **VGood:** $575

BROWNING X-BOLT STAINLESS STALKER

Similar to above but with stainless steel receiver and barrel. Various barrel lengths depending on chambering, which include both medium and long cartridges ranging from .243 Winchester to .375 H&H Magnum. Introduced in 2008.

NIB: $800 **Exc:** $700 **VGood:** $575

BROWNING X-BOLT HUNTER

Similar to above but with sculpted, satin-finished walnut stock with cut checkering and low-luster blued barrel and receiver. Various barrel lengths depending on chambering, which include both medium and long cartridges ranging from .243 Winchester to .338 Winchester Magnum. Introduced in 2008.

NIB: $800 **Exc:** $700 **VGood:** $575

BROWNING X-BOLT MEDALLION

Similar to above but with high-gloss finish and engraved, blued barrel and receiver. Various barrel lengths depending on chambering, which include both medium and long cartridges ranging from .243 Winchester to .375 H&H Magnum. Introduced in 2008.

NIB: $1000 **Exc:** $850 **VGood:** $675

Browning A-Bolt II Varmint

Browning NRA A-Bolt, Wildlife Conservation Collection

Browning A-Bolt Special Hunter RMEF

Browning A-Bolt White Gold RMEF

Browning Acera Straight Pull

BROWNING X-BOLT MICRO MIDAS

Calibers offered are 243 Win., 7mm-08 Rem., 308 Win., 22-250 Rem. **Barrel length is 20 inches, weight 6 pounds. Satin finished checkered walnut stock with 12.5-inch length-of-pull designed for smaller-framed shooters.** Hooded front and adjustable rear sights.

Perf: $725 **Exc:** $625 **VGood:** $525

BROWNING ACERA STRAIGHT-PULL

Bolt action, straight pull; 30-06, 300 Win. Mag.; barrel length 22-inch; 24-inch for magnums; weighs 6 lbs., 9 oz. 41-1/4-inch overall. American walnut stock with high gloss finish. Optional blade on ramp front, open adjustable rear sights. Straight-pull action; detachable box magazine; Teflon coated breechblock; drilled and tapped for scope mounting. Introduced about 1999. No longer imported. Increasingly collectible.

Perf: $900 **Exc:** $850 **VGood:** $700

BROWNING BBR

Bolt action; 25-06, 270, 30-06, 7mm Rem. Mag., 300 Win. Mag., 338 Win. Mag. (long action), 22-250, 243 Win., 257 Roberts, 7mm-08 Rem., 308 Win. (short action); 4-shot (std. calibers), 3-shot (magnum calibers); 22 & 24-inch sporter barrel; recessed muzzle; American walnut Monte Carlo stock; high cheek-piece; full/ checkered pistol grip, forend; recoil pad on magnums; grooved, gold-plated adjustable trigger; detachable box magazine; tang slide safety; low-profile swing swivels. Made in Japan by Miroku. Introduced 1978; dropped 1984. Add $250 for 243 caliber.

Perf:. $570 **Exc:** $490 **VGood:** $375

BROWNING MODEL 52

Bolt action; 22 LR; 5-shot magazine; 24-inch barrel; weighs 7 lbs.; high-grade walnut stock with oil-like finish; cut-checkered grip and forend; metal grip cap, rosewood forend tip; no sights furnished; drilled and tapped for scope mounting or iron sights; recreation of the Winchester Model 52C Sporter with minor safety improvements; duplicates the adjustable Micro-Motion trigger system; button release magazine. Only 5000 made. Imported from Japan by Browning. Introduced 1991; dropped 1992.

Perf: $750 **Exc:** $595 **VGood:** $475

BROWNING (FN) HIGH-POWER SAFARI

Bolt action; 243, 257 Roberts, 264 Win Mag, 270, 284, 30-06, 7mm Rem Mag, 300 Win Mag, 308 Norma Mag., 300 H&H, 338 Win. Mag., 375 H&H Mag., 458 Win. Mag.; 4-shot magazine (magnum cartridges), 6-shot (standard calibers); 24-inch barrel (magnum calibers), 22-inch (standard calibers); European walnut stock; hand-checkered pistol grip, forearm; Monte Carlo cheekpiece; recoil pad on magnum models; folding leaf rear sight, hooded ramp front; quick-detachable sling swivels. Introduced 1960; dropped 1974. Premium for rare calibers.

Standard calibers

Exc: $895 **VGood:** $675 **Good:** $550

Magnum calibers

Exc: $995 **VGood:** $750 **Good:** $650

BROWNING (FN) HIGH-POWER SAFARI-GRADE MEDIUM-ACTION

Same specs as standard grade Safari except action length; 22-250, 243 Win., 284 Win., 308 Win.; 22-inch lightweight barrel standard, but available in 22-250, 243 with 24-inch heavy barrel. Dropped 1974.

Exc: $895 **VGood:** $795 **Good:** $550

BROWNING (FN) HIGH-POWER SAFARI-GRADE SHORT-ACTION

Same specs as standard Safari except short action; 222 Rem., 222 Rem. Mag.; 22-inch lightweight, 24-inch heavy barrel. Dropped 1974.

Exc: $895 **VGood:** $795 **Good:** $550

BROWNING (FN) HIGH-POWER SAFARI MEDALLION-GRADE

Same specs as standard Safari grade except scroll-engraved receiver, barrel; engraved ram's head on floorplate; select European walnut stock

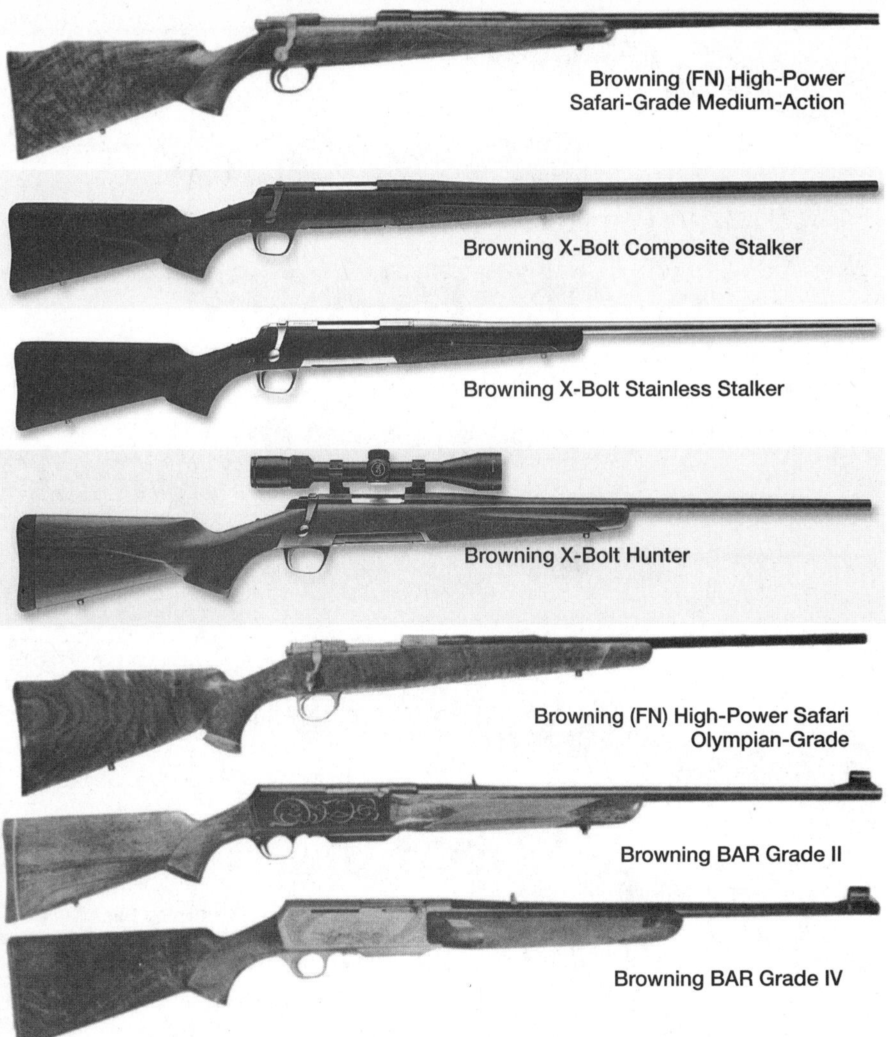
Browning (FN) High-Power Safari-Grade Medium-Action

Browning X-Bolt Composite Stalker

Browning X-Bolt Stainless Stalker

Browning X-Bolt Hunter

Browning (FN) High-Power Safari Olympian-Grade

Browning BAR Grade II

Browning BAR Grade IV

with rosewood grip cap, forearm tip. Dropped 1974.

Exc: $1600 **VGood:** $1200 **Good:** $750

BROWNING (FN) HIGH-POWER SAFARI OLYMPIAN-GRADE

Same specs as Safari grade except engraving on barrel; chrome-plated floorplate, trigger guard, receiver, all engraved with game scenes; figured European walnut stock; 32 lpi checkering; rosewood forearm tip, grip cap; grip cap inlaid with 18-karat gold medallion. Discontinued 1974. Premium for rare cals.

Exc: $3500 **VGood:** $2450 **Good:** $1595

BROWNING T-BOLT MODEL T-1

Bolt action; straight-pull; 22 LR; 5-shot clip magazine; 22-inch or 24-inch barrel; weighs 5-1/2 lbs.; uncheckered walnut pistol grip stock; peep rear sight, ramp blade front; left- or right-hand models available. Introduced 1965. Premium for left-hand model.

Perf: $675 **Exc:** $625 **VGood:** $585

BROWNING T-BOLT MODEL T-2

Same specs as Model T-1 except figured, hand-checkered walnut stock. 24-inch barrel. Not regularly imported. Last run T-2 was with plain stock.

Perf: $650 **Exc:** $600 **VGood:** $530

Late production model

Perf: $600 **Exc:** $550 **VGood:** $480

BROWNING T-BOLT (2006)

Reintroduction of classic and collectible T-bolt straight-pull .22 rifle but now with 10-shot rotary magazine. Introduced 2006. Add 5-10 percent for target/varmint version.

NIB: $525 **Exc:** $475 **VGood:** $350

BROWNING T-BOLT TARGET/ VARMINT STAINLESS

Similar to above but with stainless steel receiver and barrel. Introduced 2008.

Perf: $850 **Exc:** $725 **VGood:** $600

BROWNING T-BOLT COMPOSITE HUNTER

Sporter version of the new T-Bolt with black composite Monte Carlo stock and glossy blue barrel and receiver. Cham,bered in .17 HMR, .22 WMR or .22 LR. Scope not included. Introduced 2008.

Perf: $675 **Exc:** $575 **VGood:** $425

BROWNING T-BOLT COMPOSITE TARGET/VARMINT

Sporter version of the new T-Bolt Target/Varmint with black composite Monte Carlo stock and glossy blue barrel and receiver. Cham,bered in .17 HMR, .22 WMR or .22 LR. SCope not included. Introduced 2008.

Perf: $700 **Exc:** $550 **VGood:** $450

BROWNING T-BOLT SPORTER

Sporter version of the new T-Bolt with satin walnut stock and bright blue barrel and receiver. Scope not included. Introduced 2008.

Perf: $700 **Exc:** $550 **VGood:** $450

BROWNING AUTO 22 GRADE I

Semi-automatic; 22 LR, 22 Short; 11-shot (22 LR), 16-shot (22 Short); 19-1/4-inch barrel (22 LR), 22-1/4-inch barrel (22 Short); weighs 4-3/4 lbs.; buttstock tube magazine; select European walnut stock; hand-checkered pistol grip, semi-beaver tail forearm; open rear sight, bead front; engraved receiver, grooved for tip-off scope mount; cross-bolt safety. Introduced in 1958. Manufactured in Belgium until 1972; production transferred to Miroku in Japan; still in production.

Belgian manufacture

Perf: $805 **Exc:** $420 **VGood:** $360

Japanese manufacture

Perf: $510 **Exc:** $470 **VGood:** $310

BROWNING AUTO 22 GRADE II

Same specs as Grade I except gold-plated trigger; small game animal scenes engraved on receiver. No longer in production.

Belgian manufacture

Perf: $1200 **Exc:** $1000 **VGood:** $800

Japanese manufacture

Perf: $500 **Exc:** $400 **VGood:** $300

BROWNING AUTO 22 GRADE III

Same specs as Grade I except gold-plated trigger; extra-fancy walnut stock forearm; skip checkering on pistol grip, forearm; satin chrome-plated receiver; hand-carved, engraved scrolls, leaves, dog/game bird scenes; 22 LR only. No longer in production.

Belgian manufacture

Perf: $3000 **Exc:** $2600 **VGood:** $1900

Japanese manufacture

Perf: $800 **Exc:** $625 **VGood:** $495

BROWNING AUTO 22 GRADE VI

Same specs as Grade I except grayed or blued receiver; extensive engraving; gold-plated animals; stock forend of high-grade walnut with double-border cut checkering. Made in Japan. Introduced 1987.

Perf: $715 **Exc:** $645 **VGood:** $510

BROWNING BAR

Semi-automatic; 243 Win., 308 Win., 270 Win., 280 Rem., 30-06, 7mm Rem. Mag., 300 Win. Mag., 338 Win. Mag., also 270 WSM, 7mmWSM, 300 WSM; 22-inch barrel; 4-shot detachable box magazine (standard calibers), 3-shot (magnum calibers); adjustable folding leaf rear sight, gold bead hooded ramp front; receiver tapped for scope mounts; checkered walnut pistol-grip stock forearm. weighs 7-1/2 to 8-1/2 lbs. Not to be confused with the military Browning fully-automatic rifle. Grades I, II introduced in 1967; several grades still in production. Grades vary according to amount of checkering, carving, engraving, inlay work. Premium for Belgian marked.

Grade I

Perf: $800 **Exc:** $725 **VGood:** $400

Grade I Magnum

Perf: $910 **Exc:** $835 **VGood:** $550

Grade II

Perf: $1000 **Exc:** $920 **VGood:** $650

Grade II Magnum

Perf: $1100 **Exc:** $1050 **VGood:** $750

Grade III

Perf: $1300 **Exc:** $1250 **VGood:** $950

Grade III Magnum

Perf: $1400 **Exc:** $1350 **VGood:** $1050

Grade IV

Perf: $1500 **Exc:** $1450 **VGood:** $1150

Grade IV Magnum

Perf: $1600 **Exc:** $1550 **VGood:** $1250

Grade V

Perf: $3000 **Exc:** $2600 **VGood:** $2100

Grade V Magnum

Perf: $3300 **Exc:** $2900 **VGood:** $2300

BROWNING BAR-22

Semi-automatic; 22 LR; 15-shot, tubular magazine; 20-1/4-inch barrel; weighs 5 lbs. 2 oz.; receiver grooved for scope mount; folding leaf rear sight, gold bead ramp front; French walnut stock hand-checkered pistol grip, forearm. Introduced 1977; dropped 1986. Manufactured in Japan.

Grade I

Perf: $495 **Exc:** $425 **VGood:** $350

Grade II

Perf: $595 **Exc:** $525 **VGood:** $450

BROWNING BAR MARK II SAFARI

Semi-automatic; 243, 25-06, 270, 270 WSM, 7mm WSM, 300 WSM, 30-06, 308; 4-shot detachable magazine; 22-inch round tapered barrel; 43-inch overall length; weighs 7-3/8 lbs.; hand-checkered French walnut stock and forend; gold bead on hooded ramp front sight, click-adjustable rear, or no sights; updated version with new bolt release lever; removable trigger assembly with larger trigger guard; redesigned gas and buffer systems; scroll-engraved receiver tapped for scope mounting. BOSS barrel vibration modulator and muzzlebrake system available on models without sights. Imported from Belgium by Browning. Introduced 1993; still imported.

Perf: $730 **Exc:** $610 **VGood:** $530

BROWNING BAR MARK II LIGHTWEIGHT

Similar to the Mark II Safari except has lighter alloy receiver and 20-inch barrel. Available in 243, 308, 270, 30-06, 7mm Rem. Mag., 300 Win. Mag., 338 Win. Mag. Weighs 7 lbs., 2 oz.; overall length 41-inch. Has dovetailed, gold bead front sight on hooded ramp, open rear click adjustable for windage and elevation. Introduced 1997. Still imported by Browning. Premium for magnum calibers.

Perf: $750 **Exc:** $650 **VGood:** $500

BROWNING BAR MARK II SAFARI MAGNUM

Same specs as the standard caliber model except weighs 8-3/8 lbs.; 45-inch overall length; 24-inch barrel; 3-round magazine; calibers 7mm Mag., 300 Win. Mag., 338 Win. Mag.; BOSS barrel vibration modulator and muzzlebrake system available only on models without sights. Imported from Belgium by Browning. Introduced 1993; still imported.

With sights		
Perf: $775	**Exc:** $660	**VGood:** $560
No sights		
Perf: $725	**Exc:** $645	**VGood:** $545
With BOSS, no sights		
Perf: $825	**Exc:** $725	**VGood:** $595

BROWNING BAR STALKER

Semi-automatic; 243, 308, 270, 270 WSM, 7mm WSM, 30-06, 7mm Rem. Mag., 300 Win. Mag., 338 Win. Mag. Barrel: 20-inch, 22-inch and 24-inch; weighs 6 lbs., 12 oz. (243) to 8 lbs., 2 oz. (magnum cals.); 41-inch to 45-inch overall length. Black composite stock and forearm. Sights: Hooded front and adjustable rear or none. Optional BOSS (no sights); gas-operated action with seven-lug rotary bolt; dual action bars; 3- or 4-shot magazine (depending on caliber). Introduced 2001. Still imported by Browning. Premium for magnum calibers.

Perf: $775 **Exc:** $650 **VGood:** $600

BROWNING BAR SHORTTRAC

A streamlined version of the BAR with walnut stock, blued barrel and receiver, and short-action design. Very similar to the Winchester SXR. Chambered for a variety of short-action calibers from .243 Winchester to 7mm WSM. Available in left-hand version and various synthetic and camo finishes.

NIB: $925 **Exc:** $865 **VGood:** $695

BROWNING BAR LONGTRAC

Similar to BAR ShortTrac but chambered in a variety of long-action calibers ranging from .270 Winchester to .300 Winchester Magnum. Available in left-hand version and various synthetic and camo finishes.

NIB: $925 **Exc:** $865 **VGood:** $695

BROWNING BAR SHORTTRAC STALKER

Similar to BAR ShortTrac but with matte blue barrel and composite stock. Introduced 2006.

NIB: $900 **Exc:** $840 **VGood:** $695

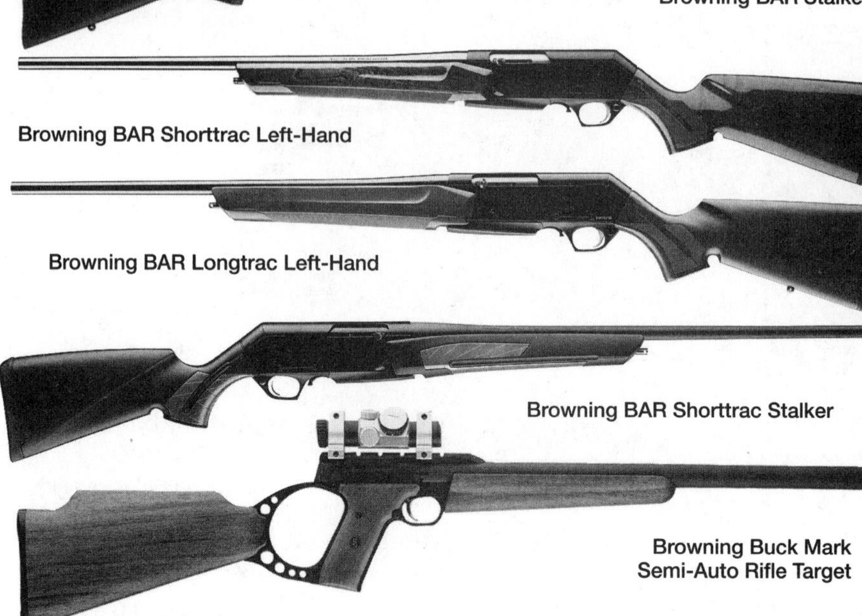

Browning BAR Mark II Safari

Browning BAR Mark II Lightweight

Browning BAR Stalker

Browning BAR Shorttrac Left-Hand

Browning BAR Longtrac Left-Hand

Browning BAR Shorttrac Stalker

Browning Buck Mark Semi-Auto Rifle Target

BROWNING BAR LONGTRAC STALKER

Long-action version of the BAR ShortTrac Stalker.

NIB: $900 **Exc:** $840 **VGood:** $695

BROWNING BUCK MARK SEMI-AUTO RIFLE

Semi-automatic; 22 LR, 10-shot magazine. 18-inch tapered barrel (Sporter) or heavy bull barrel (Target); weighs 4 lbs., 2 oz. (Sporter) or 5 lbs., 4 oz. (Target). 34-inch overall. Walnut stock and forearm with full pistol grip. Hi-Viz adjustable sights (Sporter); rifle version of the Buck Mark Pistol; straight blowback action; machined aluminum receiver with integral rail scope mount; recessed muzzle crown; manual thumb safety. Introduced 2001.

Sporter		
Perf: $500	**Exc:** $400	**VGood:** $350
Target, heavy bull barrel		
Perf: $500	**Exc:** $400	**VGood:** $350
FLD Target, bull barrel, gray laminated stock		
Perf: $540	**Exc:** $425	**VGood:** $375
FLD Carbon Rifle, light carbon composite barrel, introduced 2003		
Perf: $610	**Exc:** $475	**VGood:** $400

BROWNING B-92 CARBINE

Lever-action; 357 Mag., 44 Mag.; 11-shot magazine; 20-inch round barrel; post front sight, classic rear with notched elevation ramp; straight-grip European walnut stock; high-gloss finish; steel buttplate; tubular magazine. Designed from original Model 92 lever-action. Manufactured in Japan. Introduced 1978; dropped 1988. Premium for .357.

Perf: $750 **Exc:** $650 **VGood:** $495

BROWNING BL-22

Lever-action; 22 LR, 22 Long, 22 Short; 22-shot magazine (22 Short), 17-shot (22 Long), 15-shot (22 LR); 20-inch barrel; 36-3/4-inch overall length; weighs 5 lbs.; folding leaf rear sight, bead post front; two-piece uncheckered Western-style walnut stock, forearm; barrel band; half-cock safety; receiver grooved for tip-off mounts. Grade II with engraved receiver, checkered grip, forearm. Produced by Miroku Firearms. Introduced 1970; still in production.

Grade I		
Perf: $400	**Exc:** $345	**VGood:** $290
Grade II		
Perf: $475	**Exc:** $420	**VGood:** $320

BROWNING BL-22 NRA GRADE 1

Similar to BL-22 but with NRA logo lasered on buttstock.

NIB: $475 **Exc:** $415 **VGood:** $365

BROWNING BL-22 GRAY LAMINATE STAINLESS

Similar to BL-22 but with gray laminated stock, nickeled receiver and stainless steel barrel.

NIB: $675 **Exc:** $625 **VGood:** $500

BROWNING MODEL 53

Lever action; 32-20; 7-shot magazine; 22-inch round tapered barrel; 39-1/2-inch overall length; weighs 6 lbs. 8 oz.; full pistol grip stock of select walnut with semi-beavertail forend; high gloss finish; cut checkering on grip and forend; metal grip cap; post bead front sight, adjustable open rear; blue finish, including trigger. Based on the Model 92 Winchester with half-length magazine. Limited to 5000 guns. Imported from Japan by Browning. Made only in 1990.

Perf: $900 **Exc:** $750 **VGood:** $600

Browning Buck Mark FLD Carbon

Browning B-92 Carbine

Browning Model 81 BLR Long Action

Browning BLR Lightweight Takedown

Browning BLR Lightweight 81 Stainless Takedown

Browning Model 1895

Browning Model 1885 High Wall

BROWNING MODEL 65 GRADE I

Lever action; 218 Bee; 7-shot magazine; 24-inch round tapered barrel; 41-3/4-inch overall length; weighs 6 lbs.; select walnut pistol-grip stock, semi-beavertail forend; hooded ramp front sight, adjustable buckhorn-type rear; blued finish. Limited edition reproduction of Winchester Model 65; half-length magazine. Made in Japan. Only 3500 manufactured. Introduced 1989; dropped 1990.

Perf: 1000 **Exc:** $900 **VGood:** $750

BROWNING MODEL 65 HIGH GRADE

Same specs as Grade I except better wood; cut checkering; high-gloss finish; receiver with grayed finish, scroll engraving, game scenes. Made in Japan. Only 1500 made. Introduced 1989; dropped 1990.

Perf: $1300 **Exc:** $1200 **VGood:** $1050

BROWNING MODEL 71 RIFLE AND CARBINE

Lever action; 348 Win.; 4-shot magazine; 20-inch, 24-inch barrel; 45-inch overall length; weighs 8 lb. 2 oz.; pistol-grip stock; classic-style forend; metal buttplate; reproduction of Winchester Model 71; half-length magazine; High Grade has blued barrel and magazine, grayed lever and receiver with scroll engraving, gold-plated game scene. Grade I production limited to 3000 rifles, 4000 carbines. Made in Japan. Introduced 1987; dropped 1989.

Grade I

Perf: $1000 **Exc:** $900 **VGood:** $795

High Grade

Perf: $1300 **Exc:** $1195 **VGood:** $950

BROWNING MODEL 81 BLR

Lever action; 223, 22-250, 243, 257 Roberts, 284 Win., 7mm-08, 308 Win., 358 Win.; 4-shot detachable box magazine; 20-inch round, tapered barrel; 39-3/4-inch overall length; weighs 7 lbs.; gold bead front sight, hooded ramp, square-notch adjustable rear; drilled, tapped for scope mounts; oil-finished, checkered, straight-grip walnut stock; recoil pad; half-cock hammer safety; wide, grooved trigger. Introduced 1971; made only in Japan after 1972; still imported by Browning.

Belgian manufacture

Perf: $700 **Exc:** $650 **VGood:** $500

Japanese manufacture

Perf: $600 **Exc:** $550 **VGood:** $400

BROWNING MODEL 81 BLR LONG ACTION

Same specs as Model 81 BLR except long action; 270, 30-06, 7mm Rem. Mag., 300 Win. Mag.; 22-inch, 24-inch barrel; weighs 8-1/2 lbs.; six-lug fluted, rotary bolt. Made in Japan. Introduced 1991.

Perf: $700 **Exc:** $650 **VGood:** $530

BROWNING BLR LIGHTWEIGHT TAKEDOWN

Similar to BLR Model 81 long- and short-action but with takedown feature.

NIB: $850 **Exc:** $800 **VGood:** $695

BROWNING BLR LIGHT WEIGHT 81 STAINLESS TAKEDOWN

Similar to above but with stainless steel barrel and receiver. Introduced 2008.

NIB: $975 **Exc:** $850 **VGood:** $695

BROWNING MODEL 1886 RIFLE AND CARBINE

Lever action; 45-70; 8-shot magazine; 22-inch barrel; 40-3/4-inch overall length; weighs 8 lbs. 3 oz.; satin-finished select walnut stock with metal crescent buttplate; blade front sight, open adjustable rear; full-length magazine; classic-style forend with barrel band, saddle ring; polished blue finish. Recreation of original John M. Browning-designed Winchester 1886. Limited to 7000 guns. Imported from Japan by Browning. Introduced 1992; dropped 1993.

Carbine

Perf: $1000 **Exc:** $900 **VGood:** $600

Rifle

Perf: $1175 **Exc:** $975 **VGood:** $695

BROWNING MODEL 1886 RIFLE AND CARBINE, HIGH GRADE

Same specs as Model 1886 Rifle and Carbine except high grade walnut with cut-checkered grip and forend and gloss finish; grayed steel receiver and lever; scroll engraved receiver with game scenes highlighted by a special gold-plating and engraving process. Limited to 3000 guns. Introduced 1992; dropped 1993.

Rifle

Perf: $1500 **Exc:** $1100 **VGood:** $900

Carbine

Perf: $1395 **Exc:** $995 **VGood:** $795

BROWNING MODEL 1895

Lever action; 30-06, 30-40 Krag, 405 Winchester; 4-shot non-detachable box magazine; 24-inch round barrel; 42-inch overall length; weighs 8 lbs.; straight-grip walnut stock forend; matte finish; buckhorn rear sight with elevator, gold bead front on ramp; replica of John M. Browning's first box-magazine lever action; top loading magazine; half-cock hammer safety; High Grade Model with gold-plated moose, grizzly on gray engraved receiver. Made in Japan. Limited edition. Introduced 1985. 405 brings premium.

Grade I

Perf: $1000 **Exc:** $750 **VGood:** $550

High Grade (2000 made)

Perf: $1400 **Exc:** $1150 **VGood:** $895

BROWNING MODEL 1885 HIGH WALL

Single shot; falling block; 223, 22-250, 30-06, 270, 7mm Rem. Mag., 45-70; 28-inch octagon barrel with recessed muzzle; 43-1/2-inch overall length; weighs about 8-1/2 lbs.; walnut stock with straight grip; schnabel forend; no sights furnished; drilled and tapped for scope mounting; replica of John M. Browning's high-wall falling block rifle. Imported from Japan by Browning. Introduced 1985.

Perf: $925 **Exc:** $750 **VGood:** $595

BROWNING MODEL 1885 BPCR (BLACK POWDER CARTRIDGE RIFLE)

Similar to the 1885 High Wall rifle except the ejector system and shell deflector have been removed; chambered only for 40-65 and 45-70; color case-hardened full-tang receiver, lever, buttplate and gripcap; matte blue 30-inch part octagon, part round barrel. The Vernier tang sight has indexed elevation, is screw adjustable windage, and has three peep diameters. The hooded front sight has a built-in spirit level and comes with sight interchangeable inserts. Adjustable trigger. Overall length 46-1/8-inch, weighs about 11 lbs. Introduced 1996. Imported from Japan.

Perf: $1700 **Exc:** $1400 **VGood:** $1100

BROWNING MODEL 1885 LOW WALL

Same specs as the Model 1885 High Wall except trimmer receiver; thinner 24-inch octagonal barrel; forend mounted to receiver; adjustable trigger; walnut pistol grip stock; trim schnabel forend with high-gloss finish; 22 Hornet, 223 Rem., 243 Win.; 39-1/2-inch overall length; weighs 6 lbs. 4 oz.; polished blue finish. Rifling twist rates: 1:16-inch (22 Hornet); 1:12-inch (223); 1:10-inch (243). Imported from Japan by Browning. Introduced 1995.

Perf: $895 **Exc:** $700 **VGood:** $575

BROWNING MODEL 1885 LOW WALL TRADITIONAL HUNTER

Similar to the Model 1885 Low Wall except chambered for 357 Mag., 44 Mag. and 45 Colt; steel crescent buttplate; 1/16-inch gold bead front sight, adjustable buckhorn rear, and tang-mounted peep sight with barrel-type elevation adjuster and knob-type windage adjustments. Barrel is drilled and tapped for a Browning scope base. Oil-finished select walnut stock with swivel studs. Introduced 1997.

Perf: $900 **Exc:** $800 **VGood:** $695

BROWNING MODEL 78

Single shot, falling block; 30-06, 25-06, 6mm Rem., 243, 22-250, 7mm Rem. Mag.; 26-inch tapered octagon or heavy round barrel; hand-rubbed, hand-checkered select walnut stock; rubber recoil pad; no sights; furnished with scope mounts and rings; falling-block action; exposed hammer; adjustable trigger; automatic ejector. Based on John M. Browning's first patent. Made in Japan. Introduced about 1974; dropped about 1983.

Perf: $900 **Exc:** $850 **VGood:** $695

BROWNING MODEL B-78

Same specs as Model 78 except 45-70; 24-inch heavy octagon barrel; blade front sight, step adjustable rear; drilled, tapped for scope mounts; straight-grip hand-checkered walnut stock; semi-schnabel forend; sling swivels; curved, blued steel buttplate. Introduced about 1978; dropped about 1983.

Perf: $900 **Exc:** $800 **VGood:** $725

BROWNING BPR

Pump-action; 243, 308 (short action); 270, 30-06, 7mm Rem. Mag., 300 Win. Mag., 4-shot magazine (3 for magnums); 22-inch barrel; 24-inch for magnum calibers; weighs 7 lbs., 3 oz. 43-inch overall (22-inch barrel). Select walnut stock with full pistol grip, high gloss finish. Gold bead on hooded ramp front sight, open click adjustable rear. Slide-action mechanism cams forend down away from the barrel on the rearward stroke. Seven-lug rotary bolt; cross-bolt safety behind trigger; removable magazine; alloy receiver. Introduced 1997. Imported from Belgium by Browning; no longer imported.

Perf: $875 **Exc:** $750 **VGood:** $600

BROWNING BPR-22

Pump-action; 22 LR, 22 WMR; 11-shot (22 WMR), 15-shot (22 LR) tube magazine; 20-1/2-inch barrel; hammerless. Grade II with engraved action; select walnut stocks. Made in Japan. Introduced in 1977; 22 LR dropped, 1982; 22 WMR dropped 1986.

22 LR

Perf: $525 **Exc:** $450 **VGood:** $325

22 WMR

Perf: $600 **Exc:** $495 **VGood:** $350

Grade II

Perf: $650 **Exc:** $595 **VGood:** $500

BROWNING CONTINENTAL

Double rifle, superposed breakopen; 270 Win., 30-06, 9.3x74R; interchangeable 20-ga. barrels; 24-inch rifle barrels; 26-1/2-inch shotgun barrels; flat face gold bead front sight on matted ramp, folding leaf rear; straight-grip, oil-finished American walnut stock hand checkered; schnabel forend; action built on re-engineered Superposed 20-ga. frame; single selective inertia trigger; manual top tang safety barrel selector. Marketed in fitted case. Made in Belgium. Introduced 1979; dropped 1987.

Perf: $11000 **Exc:** $5700 **VGood:** $3750

BROWNING EXPRESS

Double rifle, superposed breakopen; 270, 30-06; 24-inch barrels; 41-inch overall length; weighs 7 lbs.; gold bead on ramp front sight, adjustable folding leaf rear; straight grip, oil-finished select European walnut stock; schnabel forend; hand checkered; reinforced breech face; single selective trigger; selective ejectors; manual safety; hand-engraved receiver; marketed in fitted case. Made in Belgium. Introduced 1981; dropped 1987.

Perf: $8000 **Exc:** $6500 **VGood:** $4650

BSA CENTURION

Single shot; Martini action; 22 LR; 24-inch match barrel; BSA No. 30 rear sight, No. 20 front; uncheckered walnut target stock; cheekpiece; pistol grip; long semi-beavertail forend. Discontinued 1932.

Exc: $595 **VGood:** $485 **Good:** $300

Browning Model 78

Browning BPR

Browning Continental

BSA CF-2 Varminter

BSA Majestic Deluxe Featherweight

BSA CF-2 CARBINE

Bolt action; 222 Rem., 22-250, 243, 6.5x55, 7mm Mauser, 7x64, 270, 308, 30-06, 7mm Rem. Mag., 300 Win. Mag.; 20-inch barrel; open adjustable rear sight, hooded ramp front; roll-over Monte Carlo stock of European walnut; high-gloss finish; pistol grip, skip-line checkering; adjustable single trigger or optional double-set trigger. Manufactured in England. Discontinued 1985.

Exc: $450 **VGood:** $375 **Good:** $250

BSA CF-2 HEAVY BARREL

Same specs as CF-2 except 222 Rem., 22-250, 243; 23- to 26-inch heavy barrel; weighs 9 lbs.; no sights. No longer in production.

Exc: $475 **VGood:** $400 **Good:** $270

BSA CF-2 SPORTER/CLASSIC

Same specs as CF-2 except 23- to 26-inch barrel; oil finished walnut stock. Manufactured in England. Introduced 1980; discontinued 1985.

Exc: $420 **VGood:** $350 **Good:** $24

BSA CF-2 STUTZEN

Same specs as CF-2 except 222 Rem., 22-250, 243, 6.5x55, 7mm Mauser, 7x64, 270, 308, 30-06; 20-1/2-inch barrel; full-length Stutzen-style stock, contrasting schnabel forend tip, grip cap; improved bolt guide. Manufactured in England. Introduced 1982; discontinued 1985.

Exc: $570 **VGood:** $470 **Good:** $270

BSA CF-2 VARMINTER

Same specs as CF-2 except 222 Rem., 22-250, 243; 23- to 26-inch heavy barrel; matte finish; sling swivels. Introduced 1986; discontinued 1986.

Exc: $350 **VGood:** $280 **Good:** $255

BSA CFT TARGET

Bolt action; single shot; 308; 26-1/2-inch barrel; weighs 11 lbs.; globe front sight, aperture rear; European walnut stock. Introduced 1987. Discontinued 1987.

Exc: $700 **VGood:** $595 **Good:** $475

BSA IMPERIAL

Bolt action; 270 Win., 308 Win., 30-06 (lightweight model), 22 Hornet, 222 Rem., 243 Win., 257 Roberts, 7x57mm, 300 Savage, 30-06 (standard weight); 22-inch barrel; recoil reducer cut into muzzle; European walnut cheekpiece stock; hand-checkered pistol grip, schnabel forend; black buttplate; pistol grip cap with white spacers; drilled, tapped for scope mounts; fully-adjustable trigger. Introduced 1959; discontinued 1964.

Exc: $475 **VGood:** $380 **Good:** $300

BSA MAJESTIC DELUXE

Bolt action; 22 Hornet, 222 Rem., 243 Win., 308 Win., 30-06, 7x57mm; 4-shot magazine; 22-inch heavy barrel; weighs 6-1/4 lbs.; folding leaf rear, hooded ramp front sight; European walnut stock; checkered pistol grip, forend; cheekpiece; schnabel forend; sling swivels. Introduced 1959; discontinued 1965.

Exc: $350 **VGood:** $300 **Good:** $250

BSA MAJESTIC DELUXE FEATHERWEIGHT

Same specs as Majestic Deluxe except recoil pad; lightweight 22-inch barrel; recoil reducer; 243, 270, 308, 30-06, 458. Premium for 458 chambering.

Exc: $400 **VGood:** $300 **Good:** $230

BSA MARTINI INTERNATIONAL ISU MATCH

Single shot; 22 LR; 28-inch barrel; 43-inch-44-inch overall length; weighs 10-3/4 lbs.; Martini action; modified PH-1 Parker-Hale tunnel front sight, PH-25 aperture rear; match-type French butt and forend; flat cheekpiece; fully-adjustable trigger; designed for ISU specs. Introduced 1968; discontinued 1986.

Exc: $700 **VGood:** $500 **Good:** $380

BSA MARTINI INTERNATIONAL MATCH

Single shot; 22 LR; 29-inch heavy barrel; Martini action; match sights; uncheckered two-piece target stock; full cheekpiece; pistol grip; broad beavertail forend; hand stop; swivels; right- or left-hand styles. Introduced 1950; discontinued 1953.

Exc: $575 **VGood:** $375 **Good:** $300

BSA MARTINI INTERNATIONAL MATCH LIGHT

Same specs as Martini International Match except lightweight 26-inch barrel. Introduced 1950; discontinued 1953.

Exc: $575 **VGood:** $375 **Good:** $300

BSA Model 12/15

BSA Model 13

BSA Model 15

BSA Monarch Deluxe

BSA MARTINI INTERNATIONAL MATCH MARK II

Same specs as Martini International Match except choice of light (26-inch), heavy (29-inch) barrel; weighs 14 lbs. (29-inch barrel), 11 lbs. (26-inch barrel); redesigned stock forearm, trigger mechanism, ejection system; Introduced in 1953; discontinued 1959.

Exc: $600 **VGood:** $400 **Good:** $320

BSA MARTINI INTERNATIONAL MATCH MARK III

Same specs as International Match Mark II heavy barrel model plus redesigned stock forend; free-floating barrel; longer frame with alloy strut to attach forend. Introduced 1959; discontinued 1967.

Exc: $650 **VGood:** $450 **Good:** $375

BSA MARTINI INTERNATIONAL MATCH MARK V

Same specs as International Match except 28-inch heavy barrel; weighs 12-1/4 lbs. Introduced 1976; no longer produced.

Exc: $650 **VGood:** $550 **Good:** $450

BSA MODEL 12/15 MATCH

Single shot; 22 LR; 29-inch barrel; Martini action; Parker-Hale PH-7A rear, PH-22 front sight; walnut target stock with high comb, cheekpiece, beavertail forend; forward sling swivel. Introduced 1938; production suspended during WWII; discontinued 1950.

Exc: $450 **VGood:** $350 **Good:** $300

BSA MODEL 12/15

Same as 12/15 Match except heavy barrel. This was designation given rifle when reintroduced following WWII. Dropped 1950.

Exc: $450 **VGood:** $350 **Good:** $300

BSA MODEL 13

Single shot; 22 LR; 25-inch barrel; Martini action; Parker-Hale No. 7 rear, hooded front sight; straight-grip walnut stock; hand-checkered forearm; lightweight version of BSA No. 12. Introduced 1913; discontinued 1929.

Exc: $400 **VGood:** $350 **Good:** $300

BSA MODEL 13 SPORTER

Same specs as Model 13 except Parker-Hale Sportarget rear sight, bead front. Also available in 22 Hornet. discontinued 1932.

Exc: $475 **VGood:** $325 **Good:** $275

22 Hornet

Exc: $525 **VGood:** $375 **Good:** $325

BSA MODEL 15

Single shot; 22 LR; 29-inch barrel; Martini action; BSA No. 30 rear, No. 20 front sight; uncheckered walnut target stock; cheekpiece, pistol grip, long semi-beavertail forend. Introduced 1915; discontinued 1932.

Exc: $395 **VGood:** $300 **Good:** $250

BSA MONARCH DELUXE

Bolt action; 22 Hornet, 222 Rem., 243 Win., 270 Win., 7mm Rem. Mag., 308 Win., 30-06; 22-inch barrel; weighs 6-1/4 lbs.; Mauser-type; fully-adjustable trigger; bolt head encloses cartridge and in turn enclosed by barrel extension; gas-proof cocking piece; hinged floorplate; silent safety with cocking indicator; folding leaf rear sight, hooded ramp front; checkered American-style stock; hardwood forend tip, grip cap; recoil pad. Introduced 1965; discontinued 1974.

Exc: $395 **VGood:** $340 **Good:** $260

BSA MONARCH DELUXE VARMINT

Same specs as Monarch Deluxe except 222 Rem., 243 Win; 24-inch heavy barrel. Introduced 1965; discontinued 1977.

Perf: $395 **Exc:** $350 **VGood:** $300

BSA NO. 12

Single shot; 22 LR; 29-inch barrel; Martini action; Parker-Hale No. 7 rear, hooded front sight; straight-grip walnut stock; hand-checkered forearm. Introduced 1912; discontinued 1929.

Exc: $450 **VGood:** $300 **Good:** $200

BUSHMASTER 308 HUNTER

AR-pattern semiauto chambered for 308 Win /7.62 NATO with 5-round magazine, 20 inch barrel. Weight is 8-1/2 lbs. Standard A2 stock with Hogue rubberized pistol grip. Sights: Two mini-risers (3/4 inch) for optics mounting.

Perf: $1375 **Exc:** $1175 **VGood:** $1000

BUSHMASTER ACR SERIES

Advanced Combat Rifle is a modular semiauto in 5.56mm (.223) or 6.8mm Rem. Thirty-round polymer magazine. Barrel choices are 10.5, 14.5, 16.5 and 18 inches. Average weight 7 pounds. Composite A-frame stock with rubber butt pad and sling mounts (ORC & A-TACS). Tool-less, quick-change barrel system available in multiple calibers. Multi-caliber bolt carrier assembly changes from 223 to 6.8mm.

Perf: $2100 **Exc:** $1800 **VGood:** $1500

Add 10 percent for A-TACS with Magpul MBUS flip-up sights

BUSHMASTER ACR ENHANCED

Semi-auto in 5.56 NATO. 10.5" SBR with M4 contour barrel with AAC Blackout 51T ratchet mount flash hider. Cold hammer forged 1-7" twist barrel, 3 rail aluminum enhanced hand guard and a 7-position folding / telescoping stock. Ships with one 30 round Magpul PMAG. Introduced in 2013.

Perf: $2450 **Exc:** $2200 **VGood:** $1900

BUSHMASTER M17S BULLPUP RIFLE

Semi-automatic; 223, 10-shot magazine. 21.5-inch barrel, chrome lined; 1:9-inch twist; weighs 8.2 lbs. 30-inch overall. Fiberglass-filled nylon stock. Designed for optics-carrying handle; incorporates scope mount rail for Weaver-type rings; also includes 25-meter open iron sights. Gas-operated, short-stroke piston system; ambidextrous magazine release. Introduced 1993. Made in U.S.A. by Bushmaster Firearms, Inc./Quality Parts Co.

Perf: $1000 **Exc:** $900 **VGood:** $775

BUSHMASTER SHORTY XM15 E2S CARBINE

Semi-automatic, 223,10-shot magazine. 16-inch barrel, heavy; 1:9-inch twist; weighs 7.2 lbs. 34.75-inch overall. A2 type stock; fixed black composition. Fully adjustable M16A2 sight system; patterned after Colt M-16A2. Chrome-lined barrel with manganese phosphate finish. "Shorty"handguard. Has forged aluminum receivers with push-pin. Made in U.S.A. by Bushmaster Firearms Inc.

Perf: $900 **Exc:** $750 **VGood:** $600

BUSHMASTER XM15 E2S DISSIPATOR CARBINE

Similar to the XM15 E2S Shorty carbine except has full-length "Dissipator" handguard, longer sight radius; Weighs 7.6 lbs.; 34-3/4-inch overall length; forged aluminum receivers with push-pin style takedown. Made in U.S.A. by Bushmaster Firearms, Inc.

Perf: $900 **Exc:** $750 **VGood:** $600

BUSHMASTER XM15 E25 AK SHORTY CARBINE

Similar to the XM15 E2S Shorty except has 14.5-inch barrel with an AK muzzle brake permanently attached giving 16-inch barrel length. Weighs 7.3 lbs. Introduced 1999. Made in U.S.A. by Bushmaster Firearms, Inc.

Perf: $900 **Exc:** $750 **VGood:** $600

BUSHMASTER XM15 E2S TARGET MODEL RIFLE

Semi-automatic; 223. 20-inch, 24-inch, 26-inch; 1:9-inch twist heavy barrel; weighs 8.3 lbs. 38.25-inch overall (20-inch barrel). Black composition stock; A2 type. Adjustable post front, adjustable aperture rear sights. Patterned after Colt M-16A2. Chrome-lined barrel with manganese phosphate exterior. Forged aluminum receivers with push-pin takedown. Made in U.S.A. by Bushmaster Firearms Co./Quality Parts Co.

Perf: $900 **Exc:** $750 **VGood:** $600

BUSHMASTER DCM COMPETITION RIFLE

Similar to the XM15 E2S Target Model except designed for DCM/CMP competition; has 20-inch extra-heavy (1-inch diameter) barrel with 1.8-inch twist for heavier competition bullets. Weighs about 12 lbs. with balance weights. Has special competition rear sight with interchangeable apertures, extra-fine 1/2- or 1/4-MOA windage and elevation adjustments; specially ground front sight post in choice of three widths. Full-length handguards over free-floating barrel tube. Introduced 1998. Comes in case with accessoriea. Made in U.S.A. by Bushmaster Firearms, Inc.

Perf: $1300 **Exc:** $1200 **VGood:** $1000

BUSHMASTER XM15 E2S V-MATCH RIFLE

Semi-automatic; 223. 20- or 24-inch, 1:9 twist heavy barrel; weighs 8.1 lbs. 38-1/4-inch overall (20-inch barrel). Black composition stock, A2 type; upper receiver has integral scope mount base. Chrome-lined .950-inch heavy barrel with counter-bored crown, manganese phosphate finish, free-floating aluminum handguard, forged aluminum receivers with push-pin takedown, hard anodized mil-spec finish. Competition trigger optional. Made in U.S.A. by Bushmaster Firearms, Inc.

Perf: $950 **Exc:** $800 **VGood:** $695

BUSHMASTER VARMINTER RIFLE

Semi-automatic; 223 Rem., 5-shot. 24-inch barrel, 1:9-inch twist, fluted, heavy; weighs 8-3/4 lbs. 42-1/4-inch length. Stock has rubberized pistol grip. no sights; 1/2-inch scope risers. 2 stage trigger, slotted free floater forend, lockable hard case.

Perf: $1000 **Exc:** $900 **VGood:** $825

BUSHMASTER CARBON 15 9MM CARBINE

Semi-auto carbine chambered in 9mm Parabellum. Carbon fiber frame, 16-inch steel barrel, six-position telescoping stock, 30-rd. detachable magazine.

NIB: $850 **Exc:** $800 **VGood:** $715

BUSHMASTER CARBON 15 QUAD RAIL FLAT TOP

Semi-auto (AR15) in 5.56 NATO. 16.5" M4 contour barrel with A2 flash hider, fixed front sight bases and bayonet lug. Flat top upper receiver and a Mission First Tactical polymer quad rail with four rail covers and a 6-position adjustable stock. New in 2013.

Perf: $800 **Exc:** $700 **VGood:** $600

BUSHMASTER CARBON 15 TOP LOADING RIFLE

Semi-auto rifle chambered in .223. Carbon fiber frame, 16-inch steel barrel, retractable stock, Picatinny rail, 10-rd. fixed magazine. Based on AR-15.

NIB: $850 **Exc:** $800 **VGood:** $715

BUSHMASTER PREDATOR

Semi-auto rifle chambered in .223. 20-inch DCM-type barrel, fixed composite buttstock, 2-stage competition trigger, Picatinny rail, 1/2-inch scope risers. Based on AR-15.

NIB: $1200 **Exc:** $1100 **VGood:** $895

BUSHMASTER CARBON 15 .22 RIMFIRE RIFLE

Similar to Shorty carbine but chambered in .22 LR. Blowback; 10-rd. magazine.

NIB: $675 **Exc:** $615 **VGood:** $525

BUSHMASTER BA50 .50 BMG RIFLE

A bolt-action, 10-round repeater intended for long-range target shooting. 30-inch barrel, muzzle brake.

NIB: $5000 **Exc:** $4250 **VGood:** $3300

BUSHMASTER BA50 .50 BMG CARBINE

Similar to above but with 22-inch barrel.

NIB: $5000 **Exc:** $4250 **VGood:** $3300

CABANAS ESPRONCEDA

Bolt action, single shot; 177 pellet with 22 Blank cartridge; 18-3/4-inch barrel; 40-inch overall length; weighs 5-1/2 lbs.; open fully-adjustable rear sight, blade front; full sporter stock. Made in Mexico. Introduced 1986.

Perf: $125 **Exc:** $90 **VGood:** $65

CABANAS LASER RIFLE

Bolt action, single shot; 177 pellet with 22 Blank cartridge; 19-inch barrel; weighs 6 lbs., 12 oz. 42-inch overall. Target-type thumbhole stock; Blade front, open fully adjustable rear sights; Fires round ball or pellet with 22 blank cartridge. Imported from Mexico by Mandall Shooting Supplies.

Perf: $145 **Exc:** $110 **VGood:** $70

Bushmaster XM15 E2S V-Match Rifle

Bushmaster BA50 .50 BMG Rifle

Bushmaster BA50 .50 BMG Carbine

CABANAS LEYRE

Bolt action; single shot; 177 pellet with 22 Blank cartridge; 19-1/2-inch barrel; 44-inch overall length; weighs 8 lbs.; adjustable rear, blade front sight; sport/target walnut stock. Made in Mexico. Introduced 1984.

Perf: $140 **Exc:** $115 **VGood:** $100

CABANAS MASTER

Bolt action; single shot; 177 pellet with 22 Blank cartridge; 19-1/2-inch barrel; 45-1/2-inch overall length; weighs 8 lbs.; adjustable rear sight, blade front; Monte Carlo target-type walnut stock. Made in Mexico. Introduced 1984.

Perf: $150 **Exc:** $120 **VGood:** $90

CABANAS MINI-82 YOUTH PONY

Bolt action; single shot; 177 pellet with 22 Blank cartridge; 16-1/2-inch barrel; 34-inch overall length; weighs 3-1/8 lbs.; adjustable rear, blade front sight; youth-sized stock. Made in Mexico. Introduced 1984.

Perf: $65 **Exc:** $55 **VGood:** $50

CABANAS PHASER

Bolt action; single shot; 177 pellet with 22 Blank cartridge; 19-inch barrel; 42-inch overall length; weighs 6-3/4 lbs.; open fully-adjustable rear sight, blade front; target-type thumbhole stock. Made in Mexico. Introduced 1991; no longer imported.

Perf: $150 **Exc:** $120 **VGood:** $80

CABANAS R83

Bolt action; single shot; 177 pellet with 22 Blank cartridge; 17-inch barrel; 40-inch overall length; adjustable rear, blade front sight; large youth-sized hardwood stock. Made in Mexico. Introduced 1984.

Perf: $75 **Exc:** $70 **VGood:** $60

CABANAS TASER

Bolt action; single shot; 177 pellet with 22 Blank cartridge; 19-inch barrel; 42-inch overall length; weighs 6-3/4 lbs.; target-type thumbhole stock; blade front sight, open fully-adjustable rear; fires round ball or pellets with 22-caliber blank cartridge. Imported from Mexico by Mandall Shooting Supplies.

Perf: $150 **Exc:** $120 **VGood:** $80

CABANAS VARMINT

Bolt action; single shot; 177 pellet with 22 Blank cartridge; 21-1/2-inch barrel; 41-inch overall length; weighs 4-1/2 lbs.; adjustable rear, blade front sight; varmint-type walnut stock. Made in Mexico. Introduced 1984.

Perf: $110 **Exc:** $90 **VGood:** $75

CABELA'S 1858 HENRY REPLICA

Lever action; 44-40; 13-shot magazine; 24-1/4-inch barrel; 43-inch overall length; weighs 9-1/2 lbs.; European walnut stock; bead front sight, open adjustable rear; brass receiver and buttplate; uses original Henry loading system; faithful to the original Henry rifle. Imported by Cabela's. Introduced 1994.

Perf: $900 **Exc:** $825 **VGood:** $695

CABELA'S 1866 WINCHESTER REPLICA

Lever action; 44-40; 13-shot magazine; 24-1/4-inch barrel; 43-inch overall length; weighs 9 lbs.; European walnut stock; bead front sight, open adjustable rear; solid brass receiver, buttplate, forend cap; octagonal barrel. Faithful to the original Winchester '66 rifle. Imported by Cabela's. Introduced 1994.

Perf: $750 **Exc:** $650 **VGood:** $495

CABELA'S 1873 WINCHESTER REPLICA

Lever action; 44-40, 45 Colt; 13-shot magazine; 24-1/4-inch, 30-inch barrel; 43-1/4-inch overall length; weighs 8-1/2 lbs.; European walnut stock; bead front sight, open adjustable rear, or globe front, tang rear; color case-hardened steel receiver. Faithful to the original Model 1873 rifle. Imported by Cabela's. Introduced 1994.

Perf: $825 **Exc:** $695 **VGood:** $425

With tang sight, globe front

Perf: $900 **Exc:** $725 **VGood:** $495

CABELA'S 1873 WINCHESTER REPLICA SPORTING MODEL

Same specs as 1873 Winchester except 30-inch barrel. Imported by Cabela's. Introduced 1994.

Perf: $740 **Exc:** $595 **VGood:** $550

With half-round/half-octagon barrel, half magazine

Perf: $750 **Exc:** $650 **VGood:** $550

CABELA'S CATTLEMAN'S CARBINE

Revolver; 44-40; 6-shot cylinder; 18-inch barrel; 34-inch overall length; weighs 4 lbs.; European walnut

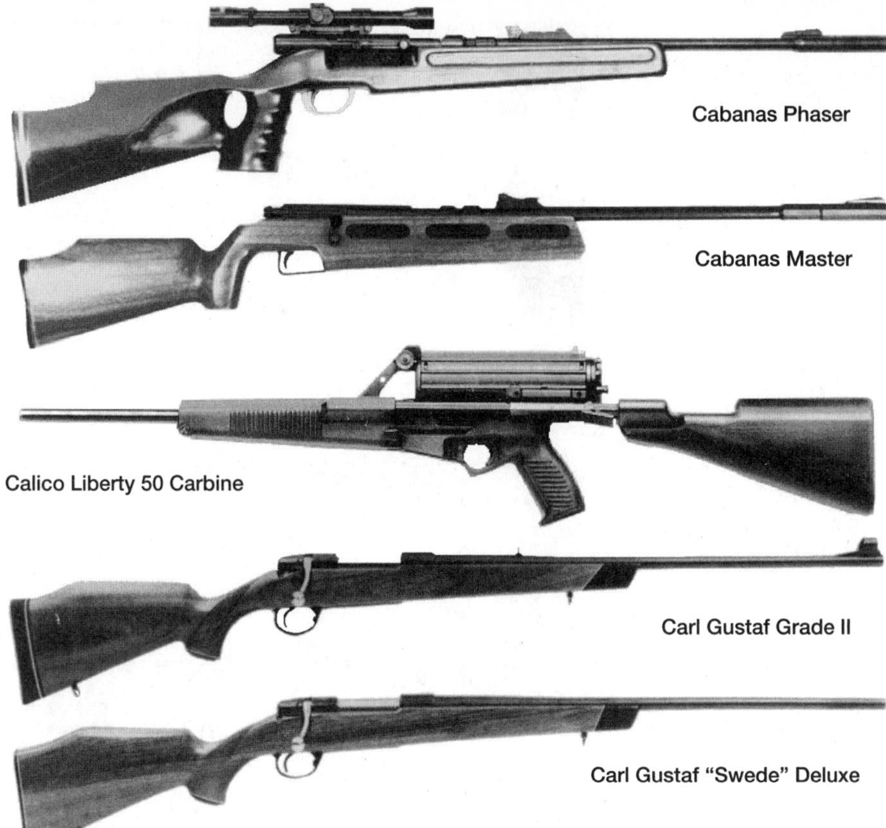
Cabanas Phaser

Cabanas Master

Calico Liberty 50 Carbine

Carl Gustaf Grade II

Carl Gustaf "Swede" Deluxe

stock; blade front sight, notch rear; color case-hardened frame, rest blued. Imported by Cabela's. Introduced 1994.

Perf: $460 **Exc:** $395 **VGood:** $325

CABELA'S SHARPS SPORTING RIFLE

Single shot; 45-70; 32-inch tapered octagon barrel; 47-1/4-inch overall length; weighs 9 lbs.; checkered walnut stock; blade front sight, open adjustable rear; color case-hardened receiver and hammer, rest blued. Imported by Cabela's. Introduced 1995.

Perf: $750 **Exc:** $695 **VGood:** $550

CALICO LIBERTY 50 CARBINE

Semi-automatic; 9mm Para.; 50-shot magazine; 16-1/8-inch barrel; 34-1/2-inch overall length; weighs 7 lbs.; glass-filled, impact resistant polymer stock; adjustable post front sight, fixed notch and aperture flip rear; helical feed magazine; ambidextrous, rotating sear/striker block safety; static cocking handle; retarded blowback action; aluminum alloy receiver. Made in U.S. by Calico. Introduced 1995.

Perf: $650 **Exc:** $560 **VGood:** $470

CALICO LIBERTY 100 CARBINE

Semi-automatic; 9mm Para.; 100-shot magazine; 16-1/8-inch barrel; 34-1/2-inch overall length; weighs 7 lbs.; glass-filled, impact resistant polymer stock; adjustable post front sight, fixed notch and aperture flip rear; helical feed magazine; ambidextrous, rotating sear/striker block safety; static cocking handle; retarded blowback action; aluminum alloy receiver. Made in U.S. by Calico. Introduced 1995.

Perf: $750 **Exc:** $760 **VGood:** $590

CALICO MODEL M-100 CARBINE

Semi-automatic; 22 LR; 100-shot magazine; 16-inch barrel; 35 7/8-inch overall length with stock extended; weighs 5-3/4 lbs. (loaded); folding steel stock; post front sight elevation-adjustable, notch windage-adjustable rear; alloy frame and helical-feed magazine; ambidextrous safety; removable barrel assembly; pistol grip compartment; flash suppressor; bolt stop. Made in U.S. From Calico. Introduced 1986; dropped 1995.

Perf: $625 **Exc:** $535 **VGood:** $450

CALICO M-100FS CARBINE

Semi-automatic; 22 LR.; 16.25-inch barrel; weighs 5 lbs. 36-inch overall. Glass-filled, impact-resistant polymer stock. Adjustable post front, notch rear sights. Has helical-feed magazine; aluminum receiver; ambidextrous safety. Made in U.S.A. by Calico. Introduced 1996, after federal magazine ban.

Perf: $450 **Exc:** $375 **VGood:** $250

CALICO MODEL M-105 SPORTER

Semi-automatic; 22 LR; 100-shot magazine; 16-inch barrel; 35 7/8-inch overall length; weighs 4-3/4 lbs. (empty); hand-rubbed wood buttstock and forend; post front sight elevation-adjustable, notch windage-adjustable rear; alloy frame and helical-feed magazine; ambidextrous safety; removable barrel assembly; pistol grip compartment; flash suppressor; bolt stop. Made in U.S. From Calico. Introduced 1987; dropped 1995.

Perf: $350 **Exc:** $300 **VGood:** $250

CALICO MODEL M-900 CARBINE

Semi-automatic; 9mm Para.; 50-, 100-shot magazine; 16-1/8-inch barrel; 28-1/2-inch overall length with stock collapsed; weighs 3-3/4 lbs (empty); sliding steel buttstock; post front sight fully-adjustable, fixed notch rear; helical feed magazine; ambidextrous safety; static cocking handle; retarded blowback action; glass-filled polymer grip. Made in U.S. by Calico. Introduced 1989; dropped 1995.

Perf: $660 **Exc:** $575 **VGood:** $480

CALICO MODEL M-951 TACTICAL CARBINE

Semi-automatic; 9mm Para.; 50-, 100-shot magazine; 16-1/8-inch barrel with long compensator; 28-3/4-inch overall length with stock collapsed; weighs 3-3/4 lbs. (empty); sliding steel buttstock, adjustable forward grip; fully-adjustable post front sight, fixed notch rear; helical feed magazine; ambidextrous safety; static cocking handle; retarded blowback action; glass-filled polymer grip. Made in U.S. by Calico. Introduced 1990; dropped 1995.

Perf: $750 **Exc:** $760 **VGood:** $590

CALICO MODEL M-951S TACTICAL CARBINE

Same specs as the M-951 except fixed stock. Made in U.S. by Calico. Introduced 1989; dropped 1995.

Perf: $750 **Exc:** $760 **VGood:** $590

CARL GUSTAF 2000

Bolt action; 243, 6.5x55, 7x64, 270, 308, 30-06, 7mm Rem. Mag., 300 Win. Mag., 9.3x62; 4-shot detachable magazine; 24-inch barrel; 44-inch overall length; weighs about 7-1/2 lbs.; sights optional; receiver drilled and tapped for scope mounting; select European walnut stock with hand-rubbed oil finish; Monte Carlo cheekpiece; Wundhammar swell pistol grip; 18 lpi checkering; three-way adjustable single-stage, roller bearing trigger; three-position safety; triple front locking lugs; 60-degree bolt rotation; free-floating barrel; swivel studs. Imported from Sweden by Precision Sales International. Introduced 1991; discontinued 1993.

Perf: $900 **Exc:** $750 **VGood:** $500

Magnum calibers

Perf: $1000 **Exc:** $850 **VGood:** $600

CARL GUSTAF GRADE II

Bolt action; 22-250, 243, 25-06, 6.5x55, 270, 308, 30-06; 5-shot magazine; 23-1/2-inch barrel; folding leaf rear, hooded ramp front sight; walnut Monte Carlo stock with cheekpiece; rosewood forearm tip, grip cap. Available as left-hand model in 25-06, 6.5x55, 270, 30-06. Made in Sweden. Introduced 1970; discontinued 1977.

Perf: $795 **Exc:** $595 **VGood:** $450

CARL GUSTAF GRADE II, MAGNUM MODEL

Same specs as Grade II except 7mm Rem. Mag., 300 Win. Mag.; 3-shot magazine; rubber recoil pad. Introduced 1970; discontinued 1977.

Perf: $825 **Exc:** $675 **VGood:** $475

CARL GUSTAF GRADE III

Bolt action; 22-250, 243, 25-06, 6.5x55, 270, 308, 30-06; 5-shot magazine; 23-1/2-inch barrel; 44-inch overall length; weighs 7-1/8 lbs.; no sights; deluxe high-gloss French walnut stock with additional checkering, rosewood forend tip; jeweled bolt; engraved floorplate; detachable swivels. Introduced 1970; discontinued 1977.

Perf: $850 **Exc:** $750 **VGood:** $595

CARL GUSTAF GRADE III, MAGNUM MODEL

Same specs as Grade III except 7mm Rem. Mag., 300 Win. Mag.; 3-shot magazine; recoil pad. Introduced 1970; discontinued 1977.

Perf: $900 **Exc:** $750 **VGood:** $625

CARL GUSTAF GRAND PRIX

Single shot; 22 LR; 26-3/4-inch barrel; adjustable weight; no sights; uncheckered French walnut target-style stock; adjustable cork buttplate; single-stage adjustable trigger. Introduced 1970; no longer in production.

Perf: $700 **Exc:** $600 **VGood:** $475

CARL GUSTAF "SWEDE" STANDARD

Bolt action; 22-250, 243, 25-06, 6.5x55, 270, 308, 30-06; 5-shot magazine; 23-1/2-inch barrel; folding leaf rear, hooded ramp front sight; Classic-style French walnut Monte Carlo or sloping comb with schnabel forend stock; hand-checkered pistol grip, forearm; sling swivels. Available as left-hand model. Made in Sweden. Introduced 1970; discontinued 1977.

Perf: $600 **Exc:** $500 **VGood:** $275

CARL GUSTAF "SWEDE" DELUXE

Same specs as "Swede" Standard except no sights; deluxe high-gloss walnut Monte Carlo stock;

rosewood schnabel forend tip; jeweled bolt; engraved floorplate. Introduced 1970; discontinued 1977.

Perf: $675 **Exc:** $550 **VGood:** $325

CARL GUSTAF "SWEDE" STANDARD, MONTE CARLO MODEL

Same specs as "Swede" Standard except also 7mm Rem. Mag.; Monte Carlo-style stock with cheekpiece. Introduced 1970; discontinued 1977.

Perf: $600 **Exc:** $500 **VGood:** $300

CARL GUSTAF VARMINT TARGET MODEL

Bolt action; 222 Rem., 22-250, 243 Win., 6.5x55mm; 26-3/4-inch barrel; no sights; target-style stock, French walnut; adjustable trigger. Introduced 1970; no longer in production.

Perf: $800 **Exc:** $700 **VGood:** $500

CENTURY CENTURION P14 SPORTER

Bolt action; 303 British, 7mm Rem. Mag., 300 Win. Mag.; 5-shot magazine; 24-inch barrel; 43-5/8-inch overall length; no sights; drilled, tapped for scope mounts; checkered Monte Carlo European beechwood stock; uses modified Pattern 14 Enfield action; blued finish. Introduced 1987; no longer available.

Perf: $350 **Exc:** $275 **VGood:** $160

CENTURY CUSTOM SPORTING RIFLE

Bolt action; 308, 7.62x39mm; 5-shot magazine; new 22-inch barrel; 43-3/4-inch overall length; weighs 6-3/4 lbs.; walnut-finished hardwood stock; no sights; two-piece Weaver-type base; uses small ring Model 98 action; low-swing safety; blue finish. From Century International Arms. Introduced 1994; no longer produced.

Perf: $295 **Exc:** $225 **VGood:** $120

CENTURY DELUXE CUSTOM SPORTER

Bolt action; 243, 270, 308, 30-06; 5-shot magazine; 24-inch barrel; 44-inch overall length; black synthetic stock; no sights, but scope base installed; Mauser 98 action; bent bolt handle for scope use; low-swing safety; matte black finish; blind magazine. From Century International Arms. Introduced 1992; no longer produced.

Perf: $230 **Exc:** $180 **VGood:** $140

CENTURY ENFIELD SPORTER NO.4

Bolt action; 303 British; 10-shot magazine; 25-1/4-inch barrel; 44-1/2-inch overall length; adjustable aperture rear sight, blade front; checkered beechwood Monte Carlo stock; built on Lee-Enfield No. 4 action; blued finish. Introduced 1987; no longer available.

Perf: $225 **Exc:** $190 **VGood:** $115

CENTURY INTERNATIONAL FAL SPORTER

Semi-automatic; 308 Win.; 20-3/4-inch barrel; 41-1/8-inch overall length; weighs 9 lbs., 13 oz.; Bell & Carlson thumbhole sporter stock; protected post front sight, adjustable aperture rear; matte blue finish; rubber buttpad. From Century International Arms. No longer produced.

Perf: $700 **Exc:** $575 **VGood:** $400

CENTURY INTERNATIONAL M-14

Semi-automatic; 308 Win.; 10-shot magazine; 22-inch barrel; 40-7/8-inch overall length; weighs 8-1/4 lbs.; walnut stock with rubber recoil pad; protected blade front sight, fully-adjustable aperture rear; gas-operated; forged receiver; Parkerized finish. Imported from China by Century International Arms. No longer imported.

Perf: $950 **Exc:** $850 **VGood:** $705

CENTURY MAUSER 98 SPORTER

Bolt action; 243, 270, 308, 30-06; 24-inch barrel; 44-inch overall length; black synthetic stock; no sights; scope base installed; Mauser 98 action; bent bolt handle for scope use; low-swing safety; matte black

Carl Gustaf Varmint Target Model

Century Centurion P14 Sporter

Century Custom Sporting Rifle

Century Swedish Sporter #38

Century Tiger Dragunov

finish; blind magazine. From Century International Arms. Introduced 1992; no longer produced.

Perf: $300 **Exc:** $250 **VGood:** $140

CENTURY SWEDISH SPORTER #38

Bolt action; 6.5x55 Swede; 5-shot magazine; 24-inch barrel; 44-inch overall length; adjustable rear sight, blade front; checkered European hardwood Monte Carlo stock; marketed with Holden Ironsighter see-through scope mount; made on Model 38 Swedish Mauser action. Introduced 1987; no longer available.

Perf: $250 **Exc:** $200 **VGood:** $175

CENTURY TIGER DRAGUNOV

Semi-automatic; 7.62x54R; 5-shot magazine; 20-7/8-inch barrel; 42-15/16-inch overall length; weighs 8-1/2 lbs.; thumbhole stock of laminated European hardwood, black composition forend; blade front sight, open elevation-adjustable rear; 4x rangefinding scope with sunshade, lighted reticle; new manufacture of shortened version of Russian SVD sniper rifle; blued metal; quick-detachable scope mount; comes with sling, cleaning kit, gas regulator tool, case. Imported from Russia by Century International Arms. No longer imported. Deduct 25% for currently-imported Romanian model.

Perf: $1100 **Exc:** $1000 **VGood:** $850

CENTURY WEEKENDER

Bolt action; 22 LR; 5-shot magazine; 23-1/2-inch barrel; 42-inch overall length; open adjustable rear sight, hooded blade front; sling swivels; blued finish. Made in Europe. Introduced 1987; discontinued 1989.

Perf: $175 **Exc:** $140 **VGood:** $100

CHAPUIS AGEX EXPRESS SERIES

Double rifle; side-by-side boxlock; 375 H&H, 416 R Chapuis, 470 NE; 25-5/8-inch barrels; various grades of engraving; French walnut stock. Made in France. No longer imported.

Africa model

Perf: $17,995 **Exc:** $15,995 **VGood:** $12,500

Brousse model

Perf: $9,995 **Exc:** $7350 **VGood:** $5250

Jungle model

Perf: $15,950 **Exc:** $10,995 **VGood:** $5750

Safari model

Perf: $28,000 **Exc:** $24,900 **VGood:** $17,995

Savanna model

Perf: $36,900 **Exc:** $31,000 **VGood:** $18,995

CHAPUIS BOXLOCK DOUBLE RIFLE

Double rifle; side-by-side; 7x65R, 8x57 JRS, 9.3x74R, 375 H&H; 23 5/8-inch barrels; 40-5/16-inch overall length; weighs 8-3/8 lbs.; ramp bead front sight, adjustable express rear on quarter rib; oil-finished French walnut pistol-grip stock; engraved, coin-finished receiver; double-hook barrels, double triggers; automatic ejectors. Made in France. Introduced 1989; no longer imported.

Perf: $6500 **Exc:** $4850 **VGood:** $3650

CHAPUIS OURAL EXEL

Single shot; boxlock; 270, 300 Win. Mag., 7mm Rem. Mag.; 23-5/8-inch barrel; various grades of engraving; French walnut stocking. Made in France. No longer imported.

Perf: $5995 **Exc:** $4450 **VGood:** $3750

CHAPUIS RGEX EXPRESS

Double rifle; 30-06, 7x65R, 8x57 JRS, 9.3x74R; 23-5/8-inch barrel; weighs 8 to 9 lbs.; deluxe walnut stock with Monte Carlo comb, oil finish; bead on ramp front sight, adjustable express rear on quarter-rib; boxlock action with long trigger guard; automatic ejectors; double hook Blitz system action with coil springs; coin metal finish; trap grip cap for extra front sight. Imported from France by Armes de Chasse. No longer imported.

Perf: $7100 **Exc:** $5300 **VGood:** $4900

CHIPMUNK SINGLE SHOT

Bolt action; single-shot; 22 Short, 22 Long, 22 LR, also 22 WMR, 17 HMR, 17 Mach 2; 16-1/8-inch barrel; 30-inch overall length; weighs 2-1/2 lbs.; post on ramp front sight, adjustable peep rear; drilled, tapped for scope mounting; American walnut stock. Introduced 1982; offered by Chipmunk Manufacturing, Oregon Arms, then Rogue Rifle Co.; still in production. 17 and 22 WMR bring a premium.

Perf: $170 **Exc:** $135 **VGood:** $110

Deluxe model with hand checkering

Perf: $225 **Exc:** $190 **VGood:** $140

Chipmunk Single Shot

Chapuis Boxlock Double Rifle

Christensen Arms Carbon One Bolt-Action Rifle

Churchill Highlander

CHIPMUNK TM (TARGET MODEL)

Bolt action, single shot; 22 LR.; heavier 18-inch barrel; weighs 5 lbs.; Length: 33-inch. Walnut stock with target accessory rail in forearm; 1/4-minute micrometer adjustable rear sight; Manually cocking single shot bolt action, blue receiver, adjustable butt plate and butt pad. Introduced 2002.

Perf: $300 **Exc:** $245 **VGood:** $190

CHRISTENSEN ARMS CARBON ONE HUNTER

Semi-custom bolt action rifle built around choice of receivers; steel barrel encased in carbon alloy shroud; synthetic stock. All popular calibers. Weight: 6.5 – 7 lbs.

NIB: $1550 **Exc:** $1475 **VGood:** $1050

CHRISTENSEN ARMS CARBON RANGER REPEATER

Semi-custom bolt-action rifle chambered in .50 BMG. Five-shot magazine; steel Pac-Nor barrel encased in carbon alloy. Muzzle brake. Weight: 20 lbs.

NIB: $5250 **Exc:** $4900 **VGood:** $3500

CHRISTENSEN ARMS CARBON RANGER SINGLE SHOT

Similar to Christensen Carbon Ranger Repeater but single shot.

NIB: $4675 **Exc:** $1000 **VGood:** $3250

CHRISTENSEN ARMS CARBON ONE BOLT-ACTION RIFLE

Bolt action; 22-250 to 375 H&H calibers; barrel lengths up to 28-inch. Weight: 5-1/2 to 7-1/4 lbs. Synthetic or wood stock; No sights furnished. Choice of Remington, Browning or Winchester action with free-floated Christensen graphite/epoxy/steel barrel, trigger pull tuned to 3 to 3-1/2 lbs. Made in U.S.A. by Christensen Arms. Prices will vary with custom features.

Carbon One Custom

Perf: $2500 **Exc:** $2000 **VGood:** $1750

Carbon Lite, weighs about 5 lbs.

Perf: $2550 **Exc:** $2100 **VGood:** $1800

Carbon Cannon (for belted magnum cartridges)

Perf: $2550 **Exc:** $2100 **VGood:** $1800

CHURCHILL HIGHLANDER

Bolt action; 243, 25-06, 300 Win. Mag., 270, 308, 30-06, 7mm Rem. Mag.; 3-, 4-shot magazine, depending on caliber; 22-inch, 24-inch barrel; 42-1/2-inch overall length (22-inch barrel); weighs 7-1/2 to 8 lbs.; no sights or optional fully-adjustable rear sight, gold bead on ramp front; checkered classic-style European walnut stock; oil-finish wood; swivel posts; recoil pad; positive safety. Made in Europe. Introduced 1986; importation discontinued 1989.

Perf: $495 **Exc:** $450 **VGood:** $350

With optional sights

Perf: $525 **Exc:** $480 **VGood:** $390

CHURCHILL REGENT

Bolt action; 243, 25-06, 300 Win. Mag., 270, 308, 30-06, 7mm Rem. Mag.; 3-, 4-shot magazine, depending on caliber; 22-inch, 24-inch barrel; 42-1/2-inch overall length (22-inch barrel); weighs 7-1/2 to 8 lbs.; no sights or optional fully-adjustable rear sight, gold bead on ramp front; Monte Carlo stock with deluxe checkering; swivel posts; recoil pad; positive safety. Made in Europe. Introduced 1986; discontinued 1988.

Perf: $540 **Exc:** $490 **VGood:** $420

With optional sights

Perf: $590 **Exc:** $500 **VGood:** $430

CHURCHILL REGENT COMBO

Combination gun; over/under; 3-inch 12-ga. over 222, 223, 243, 270, 308, 30-06; 25-inch barrels; 42-inch overall length; weighs 8 lbs.; open rear sight, blade on ramp front; hand-checkered, oil-finished European walnut Monte Carlo stock; dovetail scope mount; double triggers; silvered engraved receiver. Made in Europe. Introduced 1985; importation discontinued 1989.

Perf: $900 **Exc:** $700 **VGood:** $600

CIMARRON 1860 HENRY REPLICA

Lever action; 44-40, 44 Spl., 45 Colt; 13-shot tubular magazine; 22-inch carbine, 24-1/2-inch rifle barrel; 43-inch overall length (24-1/2-inch barrel); weighs 9-1/2 lbs.; bead front sight, open adjustable rear; original Henry loading system; brass receiver, buttplate. Made in Italy. Introduced 1991; still imported.

Perf: $900 **Exc:** $800 **VGood:** $700

Steel-frame version

Perf: $940 **Exc:** $840 **VGood:** $740

CIMARRON 1866 WINCHESTER REPLICA

Lever action; 22 LR, 22 WMR, 44-40, 45 Colt; 24-1/4-inch octagonal barrel; 43-inch overall length; weighs 9 lbs.; bead front sight, open adjustable rear; European walnut stock; brass receiver, buttplate, forend cap. Made in Italy. Introduced 1991; still imported.

Perf: $800 **Exc:** $650 **VGood:** $500

CIMARRON 1866 WINCHESTER REPLICA CARBINE

Lever action; 22 LR, 22 WMR, 38 Spl., 44-40, 45 Colt; 19-inch round barrel; bead front, open adjustable rear; smooth walnut stock, forearm; brass receiver, buttplate, forend cap. Made in Italy. Introduced 1991; still imported.

Perf: $800 **Exc:** $650 **VGood:** $500

CIMARRON 1866 WINCHESTER REPLICA CARBINE, INDIAN MODEL

Same specs as 1866 Replica Carbine except engraved brass frame. Discontinued 1989.

Perf: $625 **Exc:** $525 **VGood:** $405

CIMARRON 1866 WINCHESTER REPLICA CARBINE, TRAPPER MODEL

Same specs as 1866 Replica Carbine except 44-40 only; 16-inch round barrel. Discontinued 1990, reintroduced, still imported.

Perf: $725 **Exc:** $585 **VGood:** $415

CIMARRON 1873 SADDLE SHORTY

Lever action repeating carbine rifle with blued finish and hard wood walnut straight stock and adjustable sights. Chambered in .357/.38 Special, .44 and .45 LC. Barrel's length 18 inches, and weight is 7.5 pounds. Capacity is 10 plus 1. Introduced 2013.

Perf: $1,000 **Exc:** $875 **VGood:** $750

CIMARRON 1873 WINCHESTER REPLICA SPORTING RIFLE

Lever action; 44-40, 45 Colt; 24-inch octagon barrel; 43-inch overall length; 8 lbs.; adjustable semi-buckhorn rear sight, fixed front; walnut stock, forend; color case-hardened receiver. Introduced 1989.

Perf: $865 **Exc:** $675 **VGood:** $625

CIMARRON 1873 WINCHESTER REPLICA, LONG RANGE MODEL

Same specs as 1873 Winchester except 22 LR, 22 WMR, 357 Mag., 38-40, 44-40, 45 Colt; 30-inch octagon barrel marked "Kings Improved"; 48-inch overall length; weighs 8-1/2 lbs. Introduced 1989.

Perf: $950 **Exc:** $750 **VGood:** $650

CIMARRON 1873 WINCHESTER REPLICA, SADDLE RING CARBINE

Same specs as 1873 Winchester except 19-inch round barrel; blued receiver; saddle ring. Introduced 1989; still imported.

Perf: $950 **Exc:** $675 **VGood:** $595

CIMARRON 1873 WINCHESTER REPLICA, SHORT MODEL

Same specs as 1873 Winchester except 22 LR, 22 WMR, 357 Mag., 44-40, 45 Colt; 20-inch octagon barrel; 39-inch overall length; weighs 7-1/2 lbs. Introduced 1989; still imported.

Perf: $865 **Exc:** $675 **VGood:** $595

CIMARRON 1873 WINCHESTER REPLICA, TRAPPER CARBINE

Same specs as 1873 Winchester except 357 Mag., 44-40, 45 Colt; 16-inch barrel; blued finish. Introduced 1989; discontinued 1990; reintroduced, still imported.

Perf: $800 **Exc:** $595 **VGood:** $495

CIMARRON BILLY DIXON 1874 SHARPS SPORTING RIFLE

Single shot, falling block; 40-90, 45-70; 32-inch tapered octagonal barrel. European walnut stock; Blade front, Creedmoor rear sights; color case-hardened frame, blued barrel. Hand-checkered grip and forend; hand-rubbed oil finish. Introduced

1999. Made by Pedersoli, imported by Cimarron F.A. Co.

Perf: $1400 **Exc:** $1200 **VGood:** $1000

CIMARRON QUIGLEY MODEL 1874 SHARPS SPORTING RIFLE

Single shot, falling block; 45-70, 45-90, 45-120. Barrel: 34-inch octagonal. Checkered walnut stock; Blade front, adjustable rear sights; Blued finish; double set triggers. Replica of rifle used in movie, *Quigley Down Under*. Made by Pedersoli, imported by Cimarron F.A. Co. Introduced 1995, still available.

Perf: $1550 **Exc:** $1200 **VGood:** $1000

CIMARRON SILHOUETTE MODEL 1874 SHARPS SPORTING RIFLE

Single shot, falling block; 45-70. 32-inch octagonal barrel; Blade front, adjustable rear sights; Pistol-grip walnut stock with shotgun-style butt plate; cut-rifled barrel; imported by Cimarron F.A. Co., still available.

Perf: $1000 **Exc:** $925 **VGood:** $840

CIMARRON MODEL 86/71 LEVER ACTION

Lever action repeating rifle with blued finish and hard wood walnut stock, pistol grip and adjustable sights. Chambered in .45-70 and .444 Marlin. Barrel's length 19 to 24 inches, and OA length 38.5 inches to 42.5 inches. Weight is 7.49 to 7.71 pounds. Capacity is 5 plus 1. Introduced 2013.

Perf: $1,700 **Exc:** $1,500 **VGood:** $1,200

CIMARRON MODEL 1885 HIGH WALL RIFLE

Single shot, falling block; 38-55, 40-65, 45-70, 45-90, 45-120. 30-inch octagonal barrel; European walnut stock; Bead front, semi-buckhorn rear sights; Replica of the Winchester 1885 High Wall rifle. Color case-hardened receiver and lever, blued barrel. Curved buttplate. Optional double set triggers. Introduced 1999. Imported by Cimarron F.A. Co., still available.

Perf: $900 **Exc:** $775 **VGood:** $650

CITADEL M-1 CARBINE

Rimfire (22 LR) version of famous M-1 military carbine. 10-round magazine. Barrel is 18 inches, weight 4.8 pounds and overall length 35 inches. Built to the exacting specifications of the G.I. model used in both WWII theaters of battle and in Korea. Add $40 for threaded barrel.

Perf: $280 **Exc:** $230 **VGood:** $200

CLARIDGE HI-TEC C CARBINE

Semi-automatic; 9mm Para., 40 S&W, 45 ACP; 18-shot magazine; 16-1/8-inch barrel; 31-3/4-inch overall length; weighs 4 lbs. 9 oz.; walnut stock; adjustable post in ring front sight, open windage-adjustable rear; aluminum or stainless frame; telescoping bolt, floating firing pin; safety locks the firing pin; sight radius of 20-1/8-inch; accepts same magazines as Claridge Hi-Tec pistols. Can be equipped with scope or Aimpoint sight. Made in U.S. From Claridge Hi-Tec, Inc. Introduced 1991; dropped 1993.

Perf: $595 **Exc:** $495 **VGood:** $395

CLARIDGE HI-TEC MODEL LEC-9 CARBINE

Semi-automatic; 9mm Para., 40 S&W, 45 ACP; 18-shot magazine; 16-1/8-inch barrel; 31-3/4-inch overall length; weighs 4 lbs. 9 oz.; graphite composite stock; adjustable post in ring front sight, open windage-adjustable rear; aluminum or stainless frame; telescoping bolt, floating firing pin; safety locks the firing pin; sight radius of 20-1/8-inch; accepts same magazines as Claridge Hi-Tec pistols. Can be equipped with scope or Aimpoint sight. Made in U.S. From Claridge Hi-Tec, Inc. Made only in 1992.

Perf: $650 **Exc:** $575 **VGood:** $485

Cimarron Quigley Model 1874 Sharps Sporting Rifle

Cimarron Silhouette Model 1874 Sharps Sporting Rifle

Cimarron Model 1885 High Wall Rifle

Clayco Model 4

Clerke Hi-Wall

Citadel M-1 Carbine

CLARIDGE HI-TEC MODEL ZLEC-9 CARBINE

Same specs as the LEC-9 except laser sight system. Made in U.S. by Claridge Hi-Tec, Inc. Made only in 1992.

Perf: $995 **Exc:** $895 **VGood:** $795

CLAYCO MODEL 4

Bolt action; 22 LR; 5-shot clip; 24-inch barrel; 42-inch overall length; weighs 5-3/4 lbs.; adjustable open rear sight, ramp front with bead; walnut-finished hardwood stock; wing-type safety; black composition buttplate; pistol-grip cap; receiver grooved for tip-off scope. Made in China. Introduced 1983 by Clayco Sports; discontinued 1985.

Perf: $130 **Exc:** $100 **VGood:** $80

CLERKE HI-WALL

Single shot; falling block; 223, 22-250, 243, 6mm Rem., 250 Savage, 257 Roberts, 25-06, 264 Win., 270, 7mm Rem. Mag., 30-30, 30-06, 300 Win., 375 H&H, 458 Win., 45-70; 26-inch barrel; no sights; drilled, tapped for scope mounts; walnut pistol-grip stock, forearm; no checkering; black buttplate; exposed hammer; schnabel forearm; curved finger lever. Introduced about 1970; discontinued about 1975.

Perf: $800 **Exc:** $650 **VGood:** $500

CLERKE HI-WALL DELUXE

Same specs as standard model except half-octagon barrel; adjustable trigger; checkered pistol grip, forearm, cheekpiece; plain or optional double-set trigger.

Perf: $900 **Exc:** $750 **VGood:** $600

With double-set trigger

Perf: $950 **Exc:** $800 **VGood:** $650

COLT 57

Bolt action; 243, 30-06; adjustable sights; checkered American walnut Monte Carlo stock; FN Mauser action; 5000 manufactured by Jefferson Manufacturing Co. Introduced 1957; discontinued 1957.

Exc: $575 **VGood:** $485 **Good:** $350

Deluxe stock

Exc: $600 **VGood:** $500 **Good:** $370

COLT AR-15A2 CARBINE

Semi-automatic; 223 Rem.; 5-shot magazine; 16-inch barrel; 5-13/16 lbs.; post front, adjustable rear sight; aluminum stock with collapsible butt; sling swivels. Introduced 1985; discontinued 1989.

Perf: $1800 **Exc:** $1500 **VGood:** $1000

COLT AR-15A2 RIFLE

Same specs as AR-15A2 Carbine except 20-inch barrel; 39-inch overall length; 7-1/2 lbs.; black composition stock, grip, forend; military matte black finish. Introduced 1985; discontinued 1989.

Perf: $1700 **Exc:** $1200 **VGood:** $850

COLT COLTEER

Semi-automatic; 22 LR; 19-3/8-inch barrel; 15-shot tube magazine; weighs 4-3/4 lbs.; open rear sight, hooded ramp front; uncheckered straight Western-style carbine stock; barrel band; alloy receiver. Introduced 1964; discontinued 1975.

Exc: $375 **VGood:** $300 **Good:** $170

COLT COLTEER 1-22

Bolt action; single shot; 22 Short, 22 Long, 22 LR, 22 WMR; 20-inch, 22-inch barrel; open rear sight, ramp front; uncheckered walnut pistol grip; Monte Carlo stock. Introduced 1957; discontinued 1967.

Exc: $320 **VGood:** $270 **Good:** $130

COLT COLTSMAN STANDARD

Bolt action; 223, 243, 264, 308, 30-06, 300 H&H Mag.; 5-, 6-shot box magazine; 22-inch, 24-inch barrel; weighs 6-1/2 to 7-1/2 lbs.; FN Mauser action; folding

Colt Colteer

Colt Colteer 1-22

Colt Coltsman Sako Custom

Colt Courier

Colt Light Rifle

Colt Lightning

leaf rear sight, hooded post front; hand-checkered pistol-grip American walnut stock; Monte Carlo comb and cheekpiece; quick-detachable sling swivels. Introduced 1957; replaced in 1962 by Sako action model.

Exc: $575 **VGood:** $500 **Good:** $440

COLT COLTSMAN CUSTOM

Same specs as Coltsman except 23-3/4-inch, 23-inch, 24-1/2-inch barrel; fancy select French walnut stock; rosewood forearm, pistol grip; Monte Carlo comb, cheekpiece, engraved floorplate; recoil pad; sling swivels. Introduced 1957; replaced in 1962 by Sako action.

Exc: $695 **VGood:** $595 **Good:** $470

COLT COLTSMAN DELUXE

Same specs as Coltsman except better checkering, wood; adjustable rear sight, ramp front. Introduced 1957; discontinued 1962.

Exc: $695 **VGood:** $595 **Good:** $495

COLT COLTSMAN LONG-ACTION SAKO CUSTOM

Same specs as Coltsman Standard except Sako action; fancy Monte Carlo stock; recoil pad; dark wood forend tip and pistol-grip cap; skip-line checkering. Introduced 1962; dropped 1965.

Exc: $695 **VGood:** $595 **Good:** $495

300, 375 H&H calibers

Exc: $750 **VGood:** $650 **Good:** $525

COLT COLTSMAN LONG-ACTION SAKO STANDARD

Same specs as Coltsman Standard except Sako long action; 264 Win., 270 Win., 30-06, 300 H&H, 375 H&H; hinged floorplate; hand-checkered walnut stock; standard sling swivels; bead front sight on hooded ramp, folding leaf rear; sliding safety. Introduced 1962; dropped 1965.

Exc: $695 **VGood:** $595 **Good:** $495

300, 375 magnum calibers

Exc: $850 **VGood:** $750 **Good:** $625

COLT COLTSMAN MEDIUM-ACTION SAKO CUSTOM

Same specs as Coltsman Standard except Sako medium action; fancy Monte Carlo stock; recoil pad; dark wood forend tip; pistol-grip cap; skip-line checkering. Introduced 1962; discontinued 1965.

Exc: $695 **VGood:** $595 **Good:** $495

COLT COLTSMAN MEDIUM-ACTION SAKO STANDARD

Same specs as Coltsman Standard except Sako medium action; hinged floorplate; hand-checkered walnut stock; standard sling swivels; bead front sight on hooded ramp, folding leaf rear; sliding safety; 243 Win., 308 Win. Introduced 1962; dropped 1965.

Exc: $595 **VGood:** $495 **Good:** $395

COLT COLTSMAN SHORT-ACTION SAKO CUSTOM

Same specs as Coltsman Standard except Sako short action; 243, 308 Win. Introduced 1963; discontinued 1965.

Exc: $595 **VGood:** $495 **Good:** $395

COLT COLTSMAN SHORT-ACTION SAKO DELUXE

Same specs as Coltsman Standard except Sako short action; 243, 308 Win.; action with integral scope blocks. Introduced 1963; discontinued 1965.

Exc: $695 **VGood:** $595 **Good:** $495

COLT COURIER

Semi-automatic; 22 LR; 15-shot tubular magazine; 19-3/8-inch barrel; weighs 4-3/4 lbs.; receiver grooved for tip-off scope mount; American walnut stock forend; pistol grip. Introduced 1970; discontinued 1976.

Exc: $375 **VGood:** $290 **Good:** $170

COLT LIGHT RIFLE

Bolt action; 243, 7x57, 7mm-08, 308 (short action); 25-06, 270, 280, 7mm Rem., Mag., 30-06, 300 Win. Mag. 24-inch barrel; weighs 5.4 to 6 lbs. Black synthetic stock; no sights furnished; low, medium, high scope mounts. Matte black finish; three-position safety. Introduced 1999, dropped 2002. Made in U.S.A. From Colt's Mfg., Inc.

Perf: $750 **Exc:** $700 **VGood:** $600

COLT LIGHTNING

Slide action; 22 LR, 32-20, 38-40, 44-40, 38-56, 50-96; 15-shot tubular magazine; 26-inch round or octagon barrel; open rear, blade front sight; American walnut stock, forend. Introduced 1884; discontinued 1902.

Small frame

Exc: $2250 **VGood:** $900 **Good:** $650

Medium frame

Exc: $2500 **VGood:** $1395 **Good:** $850

Large frame

Exc: $4750 **VGood:** $2795 **Good:** $1650

COLT LIGHTNING BABY CARBINE

Same specs as Colt Lightning except 10-shot tubular magazine; 15-inch, 16-inch barrel; weighs 5-1/4 lbs. Introduced 1884; discontinued 1902.

Medium frame

Exc: $5850 **VGood:** $3450 **Good:** $1950

Large frame

Exc: $10,000 **VGood:** $6950 **Good:** $5350

COLT LIGHTNING CARBINE

Same specs as Colt Lightning except 20-inch, 22-inch barrel; weighs 6-1/4 lbs. Introduced 1884; discontinued 1902.

Medium frame

Exc: $2700 **VGood:** $1000 **Good:** $600

Large frame

Exc: $8500 **VGood:** $6995 **Good:** $3950

COLT LIGHTNING SMALL FRAME

Same specs as Colt Lightning except 22 Short, 22 Long; 24-inch round or octagon barrel; 16-shot (22 Short), 15-shot (22 Long); bead front sight. Collector value. Manufactured 1887 to 1904.

Exc: $1900 **VGood:** $900 **Good:** $650

COLT MATCH TARGET RIFLE

Semi-automatic; 223 Rem., 5-shot magazine. 16.1-inch or 20-inch barrel; weighs 7.1 to 8-1/2 lbs. 34-1/2-inch to 39-inch overall length; composition stock, grip, forend. Post front sight, rear sight adjustable for windage and elevation. 5-round detachable box magazine, flash suppressor, sling swivels. Forward bolt assist included. Introduced 1991. Made in U.S.A. by Colt's Manufacturing Co. Inc.

Perf: $1100 **Exc:** $900 **VGood:** $725

COLT ACCURIZED RIFLE

Similar to the Colt Match Target Model except has 24-inch stainless steel heavy barrel with 1:9-inch rifling, flattop receiver with scope mount and 1-inch rings, weighs 9.25 lbs. Introduced 1998, still in production. Made in U.S.A. by Colt's Mfg. Co., Inc.

Perf: $1200 **Exc:** 995 **VGood:** $750

COLT MATCH TARGET HBAR RIFLE

Similar to the Target Model except has heavy barrel, 800-meter rear sight adjustable for windage and elevation. Introduced 1991, still in production.

Perf: $1100 **Exc:** $900 **VGood:** $725

COLT SPORTER TARGET

Semi-automatic; 223 Rem.; 5-shot detachable box magazine; 20-inch barrel; 39-inch overall length; weighs 7-1/2 lbs.; composition stock, grip, forend; post front sight, aperture fully-adjustable rear; standard-weight barrel; flash suppressor; sling swivels; forward bolt assist; military matte black finish. Made in U.S. by Colt. Introduced 1991.

Perf: $1100 **Exc:** $800 **VGood:** $650

COLT SPORTER COMPETITION HBAR

Same specs as Sporter Target except flat-top receiver with integral Weaver-type base for scope mounting; counter-bored muzzle; 1:9-inch rifling twist. Made in U.S. by Colt. Introduced 1991.

Perf: $1100 **Exc:** $900 **VGood:** $725

COLT SPORTER COMPETITION HBAR RANGE SELECTED

Same specs as Sporter Competition HBAR except range selected for accuracy; 3-9x rubber armored scope, scope mount; carrying handle with iron sights; Cordura nylon carrying case. Made in U.S. by Colt. Introduced 1992; dropped 1994.

Perf: $1450 **Exc:** $1050 **VGood:** $850

COLT SPORTER LIGHTWEIGHT

Same specs as Sporter Target except 9mm Para., 223 Rem., 7.62x39mm; 16-inch barrel; 34-1/2-inch overall length; weighs 6-3/4 lbs. (223 Rem.), 7-1/8 lbs. (9mm Para.). Made in U.S. by Colt. Introduced 1991; no longer produced.

Perf: $1000 **Exc:** $800 **VGood:** $600

COLT SPORTER MATCH DELTA HBAR

Same specs as the Sporter Target except standard stock; heavy barrel; refined and inspected by the Colt Custom Shop; 3-9x rubber armored scope; removable cheekpiece; adjustable scope mount; black leather military-style sling; cleaning kit; hard carrying case; pistol grip with Delta medallion. Made in U.S. by Colt. Introduced 1987; dropped 1991.

Perf: $1500 **Exc:** $1150 **VGood:** $895

COLT SPORTER MATCH HBAR

Same specs as the Sporter Match Delta HBAR except with heavy barrel; 800-meter M-16A2 fully-adjustable rear sight. Made in U.S. by Colt. Introduced 1991; no longer produced.

Perf: $1500 **Exc:** $1000 **VGood:** $700

COLT SPORTER MATCH TARGET COMPETITION HBAR II

Same specs as the Sporter Match HBAR except 16-1/8-inch barrel; weighs 7-1/8 lbs.; 34-1/2-inch overall length; 1:9-inch twist barrel. Made in U.S. by Colt. Introduced 1995; still produced.

Perf: $1275 **Exc:** $1000 **VGood:** $800

COLT STAGECOACH

Semi automatic; 22 LR; 13-shot magazine; 16-1/2-inch barrel; 33-3/4-inch overall length; weighs 4-3/4 lbs.; deluxe American black walnut straight Western-style carbine stock with saddle ring; adjustable rear sight; engraved receiver. Introduced 1965; discontinued 1975.

Exc: $400 **VGood:** $300 **Good:** $210

COLT-SAUER SPORTER

Bolt action; 22-250, 243, 308, 25-06, 270, 30-06, 7mm Rem. Mag., 300 Win. Mag., 300 Weatherby Mag.; 375 H&H Mag., 458 Win. Mag.; 3-, 4-shot detachable box magazine; 24-inch barrel; 43-3/4-inch overall length; weighs 8 lbs.; no sights; hand-checkered American walnut pistol-grip stock; rosewood pistol grip, forend caps; recoil pad; quick-detachable sling swivels. Introduced 1971; discontinued 1986.

Long action

Exc: $1050 **VGood:** $895 **Good:** $695

Short action

Exc: $1050 **VGood:** $895 **Good:** $695

Magnum action

Exc: $1150 **VGood:** $995 **Good:** $795

Grand Alaskan model

Exc: $1400 **VGood:** $1195 **Good:** $895

Colt Match Target Competition HBAR

Colt Sporter Lightweight

Colt Sporter Match HBAR

Colt-Sauer Sporter

Grand African model

Exc: $1450 **VGood:** $1295 **Good:** $995

COLT-SHARPS FALLING BLOCK

Single shot; falling block; 17 Bee, 22-250, 243, 25-06, 7mm Rem. Mag., 30-06, 375 H&H Mag.; iron sights; checkered walnut stock, forearm; blued finish. Introduced 1970; discontinued 1977.

Perf: $2900 **Exc:** $2000 **VGood:** $1200

COMMANDO ARMS MARK 9

Semi-automatic; 9mm Para.; 5-, 15-, 30-, 90-shot magazine; 16-1/2-inch barrel; weighs 8 lbs.; peep-type rear sight, blade front; walnut stock, forearm; choice of vertical or horizontal foregrip; muzzlebrake; cooling sleeve. Introduced 1969 by Volunteer Enterprises.

Perf: $495 **Exc:** $425 **VGood:** $230

COMMANDO ARMS MARK 45

Semi-automatic; 45 ACP; 5-, 15-, 30-, 90-shot magazine; 16-1/2-inch barrel; weighs 8 lbs.; peep-type rear sight, blade front; walnut stock and forearm; available with choice of vertical or horizontal foregrip; muzzlebrake, cooling sleeve. Introduced 1969 by Volunteer Enterprises.

Perf: $600 **Exc:** $440 **VGood:** $350

COOPER ARMS MODEL 21 VARMINT EXTREME

Bolt action; single shot; 17 Rem., 17 Mach IV, 221 Fireball, 222, 222 Rem. Mag., 223, 22 PPC, 6x47; 23-3/4-inch stainless steel barrel with competition step crown; free-floated; AAA Claro walnut stock with flared oval forend, ambidextrous palm swell; 22 lpi checkering; oil finish; Pachmayr buttpad; weighs 8 lbs.; no sights; drilled and tapped for scope mounting; three mid-bolt locking lugs; adjustable trigger; glass bedded; swivel studs. Made in U.S. by Cooper Arms. Introduced 1994.

Perf: $1500 **Exc:** $1200 **VGood:** $900

COOPER ARMS MODEL 21 BENCHREST

Same specs as the Model 21 Varmint Extreme except 22 PPC, 223 Rem.; McMillan Benchrest composition stock; 24-inch, 1-inch straight taper stainless barrel with competition step crown, match chamber; Jewell two-stage, 1-oz. fully-adjustable trigger; weighs 7-1/4 lbs. Made in U.S. by Cooper Arms. Introduced 1994.

Perf: $2000 **Exc:** $1700 **VGood:** $1400

COOPER ARMS MODEL 22 PRO VARMINT EXTREME

Bolt action; single shot; 22-250, 220 Swift, 243, 25-06, 6mm PPC, 308; 26-inch stainless steel match-grade barrel with straight taper; free-floated; AAA Claro walnut stock with oil finish; 22 lpi wrap-around borderless ribbon checkering; beaded cheekpiece; steel grip cap; flared varminter forend; Pachmayr pad; no sights; drilled and tapped for scope mounting; three front locking lug system; available with sterling silver inlaid medallion, skeleton grip cap, and French walnut. Made in U.S. by Cooper Arms. Introduced 1995; still produced.

Perf: $1650 **Exc:** $1500 **VGood:** $1200

Black Jack model with McMillan synthetic stock

Perf: $1750 **Exc:** $1600 **VGood:** $1300

COOPER ARMS MODEL 22 BENCHREST

Same specs as the Model 22 Pro Varmint Extreme except 6mm PPC, 243, 308; McMillan Benchrest composition stock; 1-inch straight taper stainless steel barrel; competition step muzzle crown; match chamber. Made in U.S. by Cooper Arms. Introduced 1995; still produced.

Perf: $2000 **Exc:** $1700 **VGood:** $1300

COOPER ARMS MODEL 36 CENTERFIRE SPORTER

Bolt action; 17 CCM, 22 CCM, 22 Hornet; 5-shot magazine; 23-inch barrel; 42-1/2-inch overall length; weighs 7 lbs.; AA Claro walnut stock with 22 lpi checkering, oil finish (standard grade); AAA Claro or AA French walnut (custom grade); no sights; three mid-bolt locking lugs, 45° bolt rotation; fully-adjustable trigger; swivel studs; Pachmayr buttpad. Made in U.S. by Cooper Arms. Introduced 1994; no longer made.

Perf: $1395 **Exc:** $995 **VGood:** $795

Cooper Arms Model 22 Pro Varmint Extreme

Cooper Arms Model BR-50

Cooper Arms Model TRP-1 ISU Standard

Cumberland Mountain Arms Plateau

CVA Accura MR

CVA Optima V2

COOPER ARMS MODEL 36 RIMFIRE SPORTER

Bolt action; 22 LR; 5-shot magazine; 22-3/4-inch barrel; 42-1/2-inch overall length; weighs 7 lbs.; hand-checkered AAA Claro walnut stock (standard grade); AA fancy French walnut or AAA Claro walnut with beaded Monte Carlo cheekpiece (Custom grade); sights optional; three front locking lugs, 45-degree bolt rotation; fully-adjustable single stage trigger; Wiseman/McMillan competition barrel; swivel studs; Pachmayr buttpad; oil-finished wood. Made in U.S. by Cooper Arms. Introduced 1991.

Perf: $1395 **Exc:** $995 **VGood:** $795

Custom grade

Perf: $1495 **Exc:** $1100 **VGood:** $895

COOPER ARMS MODEL 36 RF CUSTOM CLASSIC

Same specs as the Model 36RF grade except ebony forend tip; steel grip cap; Brownell No. 1 checkering pattern. Made in U.S. by Cooper Arms. Introduced 1991; no longer made.

Perf: $1500 **Exc:** $1000 **VGood:** $700

COOPER ARMS MODEL 36 RF FEATHERWEIGHT

Same specs as the Model 36RF except custom stock shape with black textured finish. Made in U.S. by Cooper Arms. Introduced 1991; no longer made.

Perf: $1400 **Exc:** $950 **VGood:** $650

COOPER ARMS MODEL 38 CENTERFIRE SPORTER

Bolt action; 17 CCM, 22 CCM; 3-shot magazine; 23-3/4-inch Shilen match barrel; 42-1/2-inch overall length; weighs 8 lbs.; AA Claro walnut stock with 22 lpi checkering, oil finish (standard grade); AAA Claro or AA French walnut, beaded Monte Carlo cheekpiece (custom grade); no sights; three front locking lugs, 45-degree bolt rotation; fully-adjustable single stage match trigger; swivel studs. Pachmayr buttpad. Made in U.S. by Cooper Arms. Introduced 1991; no longer produced.

Perf: $995 **Exc:** $895 **VGood:** $795

Custom grade

Perf: $1295 **Exc:** $1095 **VGood:** $895

COOPER ARMS MODEL 40 CENTERFIRE SPORTER

Bolt action; 17 CCM, 17 Ackley Hornet, 22 CCM, 22 Hornet, 22 K-Hornet; 5-shot magazine; 23-inch barrel; 42-1/2-inch overall length; weighs 7 lbs.; AAA Claro walnut stock with 22 lpi borderless wrap-around ribbon checkering; oil finish; steel grip cap; Pachmayr pad; no sights; three mid-bolt locking lugs; 45-degree bolt rotation; fully-adjustable trigger; swivel studs. Made in U.S. by Cooper Arms. Introduced 1994.

Perf: $1700 **Exc:** $1400 **VGood:** $1100

COOPER ARMS MODEL 40 CUSTOM CLASSIC

Same specs as Model 40 except AAA Claro walnut; Monte Carlo beaded cheekpiece; oil finish. Made in U.S. by Cooper Arms. Introduced 1994.

Perf: $1800 **Exc:** $1500 **VGood:** $1200

COOPER ARMS MODEL 40 CLASSIC VARMINTER

Same specs as the Model 40 except AAA Claro walnut; wrap-around ribbon checkering; beaded cheekpiece; steel grip cap; flared varminter forend. Made in U.S. by Cooper Arms. Introduced 1994.

Perf: $1490 **Exc:** $1195 **VGood:** $995

COOPER MODEL 56

Calibers are 257 Weatherby Mag., 264 Win. Mag., 270 Weatherby, 7mm Remington, 7mm Weatherby, 7mm Shooting Times Westerner, 300 H&H, 300 Win Mag., 300 Weatherby, 308 Norma Mag., 8mm Rem. Mag., 338 Win. Mag., 340 Weatherby. Barrel lengths, 22 to 26 inches. Weight is 7.75 to 8 lbs. AA-AAA select claro walnut stock with 20 line-per-inch checkering. Fully adjustable single-stage trigger.

Perf: $725 **Exc:** $625 **VGood:** $525

COOPER ARMS MODEL 57-M BOLT-ACTION RIFLE

Bolt action; 22 LR, 22 WMR, 17 HMR. 23-3/4-inch stainless steel or 41-40 match grade barrel; weighs 6.6 lbs.; Claro walnut stock, 22 lpi hand checkering; no sights furnished. Three rear locking lug, repeating bolt-action with 5-shot mag. Fully adjustable trigger. Many options can affect price. Introduced 2002; Made in U.S.A. by Cooper Firearms of Montana, Inc.

Perf: $1000 **Exc:** $900 **VGood:** $800

COOPER ARMS MODEL BR-50

Bolt action; single shot; 22 LR; 22-inch barrel, .860-inch straight; 40-1/2-inch overall length; weighs 6-13/16 lbs.; McMillan Benchrest stock; no sights; three mid-bolt locking lugs; fully-adjustable match-grade trigger; stainless barrel. Made in U.S. by Cooper Arms. Introduced 1994.

Perf: $1700 **Exc:** $1400 **VGood:** $1100

COOPER ARMS MODEL TRP-1 ISU STANDARD

Bolt action; single shot; 22 LR; 22-inch barrel; 40-1/2-inch overall length; weighs 10 lbs.; walnut competition-style stock with adjustable cheekpiece and buttpad; no sights; accepts Anschutz sight packages; three front locking lugs, 45-degree bolt rotation; fully-adjustable single stage trigger; hand-lapped match-grade Shilen stainless barrel. Made in U.S. by Cooper Arms. Introduced 1991; no longer produced.

Perf: $1450 **Exc:** $1150 **VGood:** $895

With benchrest-style stock

Perf: $1350 **Exc:** $1050 **VGood:** $795

CUMBERLAND MOUNTAIN ARMS ELK RIVER

Single shot, falling block; 22 through 300 Win. Mag.; 32-40, 40-65, 45-70 single shot; 24-inch, 26-inch, 28-inch, round or octagon barrel; 44-inch overall length (28-inch barrel); weighs about 6-1/4 lbs.; American walnut stock; Marble's bead front sight, Marble's adjustable open rear; falling block action with underlever; blued barrel and receiver. Made in U.S. by Cumberland Mountain Arms, Inc. Introduced 1993; no longer produced.

Perf: $895 **Exc:** $795 **VGood:** $695

CUMBERLAND MOUNTAIN ARMS PLATEAU

Single shot, falling block; 40-65, 45-70, other calibers on special order; barrel length up to 32-inch, round; 48-inch overall length; weighs about 10-1/2 lbs. (32-inch barrel); American walnut stock; Marble's bead front sight, Marble's open rear; falling block action with underlever; blued barrel and receiver; lacquer finish stock; crescent buttplate. Made in U.S. by Cumberland Mountain Arms, Inc. Introduced 1995.

Perf: $950 **Exc:** $800 **VGood:** $675

CVA ACCURA MR

Break-action muzzleloading rifle with weather guard finish, adjustable trigger, quick release breech plug, 416 stainless steel barrel and camouflage polymer stock. Chambered in .50 Caliber. 25 inch barrel with 40 inch OA length and weighs 6.18 pounds. Single Shot. Introduced 2012.

Perf: $525 **Exc:** $450 **VGood:** $400

CVA OPTIMA V2

Break-action muzzleloading rifle with black or real tree cammo finish, quick release breech plug, 416 stainless steel barrel and polymer stock. Chambered in .50 Caliber. 26 inch barrel with 41 inch OA length and weighs 6.65 pounds. Single Shot. Introduced 2012.

Perf: $360 **Exc:** $300 **VGood:** $270

CZ MODEL 3

Bolt action; 270 WSM, 7mm WSM, 300 WSM, 3-shot magazine; left or right hand action, blue or stainless steel, Mauser-style claw extractor; 3-position safety; adjustable trigger; introduced in 2004, still available.

Perf: $800 **Exc:** $750 **VGood:** $600

CZ 452 AMERICAN CLASSIC BOLT-ACTION RIFLE

Bolt action; 22 LR, 22 WMR, 17 HMR, 17 Mach 2; 5-shot or 10-shot detachable magazine, weighs 6.6 lbs.; has classic-style stock of Circassian walnut; 22-1/2-inch free-floating barrel with recessed target crown; receiver dovetail for scope mounting. No open sights furnished. Introduced 1999. Imported from the Czech Republic by CZ-USA, still available.

Perf: $350 **Exc:** $275 **VGood:** $225

CZ 452 FS

Bolt action; 22 LR, 22 WMR, 17 HMR; similar to 452 LUX, but with full-length Mannlicher-type stock; introduced 2004, still available.

Perf: $420 **Exc:** $320 **VGood:** $300

CZ 452 LUX BOLT-ACTION RIFLE

Bolt action; 22 LR, 22 WMR, 5-shot or 10-shot detachable magazine. 24.8-inch barrel; weighs 6.6 lbs. Length: 42.63-inch overall. Walnut stock with checkered pistol grip. Sights: Hooded front, fully adjustable tangent rear. All-steel construction, adjustable trigger, polished blue finish. Imported from the Czech Republic by CZ-USA, still available.

Perf: $350 **Exc:** $280 **VGood:** $220

CZ 452 SCOUT

Similar to 452 LUX, but has short stock with 12-inch pull for young shooters; 16.2-inch barrel; equipped with single-shot adapter; introduced 2000, still available.

Perf: $210 **Exc:** $160 **VGood:** $140

CZ 452 SILHOUETTE

Similar to 452 LUX, but with black synthetic stock; no sights furnished; 22 LR only.

Perf: $375 **Exc:** $275 **VGood:** $200

CZ 452 STYLE

Similar to 452 Silhouette, but with matte nickel finish on all metal surfaces; 22LR only.

Perf: $375 **Exc:** $275 **VGood:** $200

CZ 452 TRAINING RIFLE

Similar to 452 LUX, but with beechwood stock; comes with 5-round magazine; 22 LR only.

Perf: $250 **Exc:** $200 **VGood:** $180

CZ 452 VARMINT RIFLE

Similar to the 452 American Classic model except has heavy 20.8-inch barrel; stock has beavertail forend; weighs 7 lbs.; no sights furnished. Available in 22 LR, 22 WMR, 17 HMR, 17 Mach 2. Imported from the Czech Republic by CZ-USA, still available.

Perf: $375 **Exc:** $300 **VGood:** $250

CZ-USA 455 AMERICAN

Bolt action rim-fire rifle with a blued finish, interchangeable barrel system, adjustable trigger, synthetic or walnut stock. Available Combo Package with .22LR and a .17 HMR barrels. Chambered in .22 LR or .17 HMR. 20.5 inch barrel and 38.2 inch OA length it weighs 6.1 pounds. 5 round capacity and detachable magazine. Introduced 2013.

Perf: $400 **Exc:** $370 **VGood:** $330

CZ-USA 455 VARMINT TACTICOOL

Bolt action rim-fire rifle with a blued finish, adjustable target trigger, ergonomic black laminate stock with ambidextrous palm swells, pistol grip, Monte Carlo

CZ Model 3

CZ-USA 455 American

CZ-USA 455 Varmint Tacticool

CZ 452 Varmint Rifle

CZ-USA 455 Varmint Thumbhole SST Fluted

CZ-USA 527 American

comb, and beavertail forend. Cambered in .22 LR. 20.5 inch barrel and 38.75 inch OA length it weighs 7.4 pounds. 5 round capacity and detachable magazine. Introduced 2013.

Perf: $500 **Exc:** $440 **VGood:** $400

CZ-USA 455 VARMINT THUMBHOLE SST FLUTED

Bolt action rim-fire rifle with a blued finish, vented thumbhole forest camo laminate stock, fluted barrel and single set trigger. Chambered in .22 LR or .17 HMR. 20.5 inch barrel and 38.75 inch OA length it weighs 7 pounds. 5 round capacity and detachable magazine. Introduced 2013.

Perf: $580 **Exc:** $530 **VGood:** $480

CZ 511 AUTO RIFLE

Semi-automatic; 22 LR, 8-shot magazine. 22.2-inch barrel. weighs 5.39 lbs. 38.6-inch overall. Walnut stock with checkered pistol grip. Sights: Hooded front, adjustable rear. Features: Polished blue finish; detachable magazine; sling swivel studs. Imported from the Czech Republic by CZ-USA, still available.

Perf: $325 **Exc:** $275 **VGood:** $225

CZ MODEL 512 RIFLE

Caliber: 22 LR/22 WMR, 5-round magazines. Barrel: 20.6 inches. Weight: 5.9 lbs. Length: 39.3 inches. Stock: Beech. The action consists of aluminum alloy upper receiver that secures the barrel, bolt assembly and polymer lower half that houses trigger mechanism and detachable magazine.

Perf: $385 **Exc:** $325 **VGood:** $275

CZ 513 BASIC

Similar to CZ 452, but simplified; uncheckered beechwood stock and non-adjustable trigger; 22 LR only. Introduced 2004, still available.

Perf: $210 **Exc:** $165 **VGood:** $140

CZ-USA 527 AMERICAN

Bolt action center-fire rifle with a blued finish, Turkish walnut stock, light weight barrel, a single set trigger and recessed target crown. Optics ready and equipped with 1 inch rigs. Chambered in .17 Hornet, .204 Ruger, .221 Fireball, .222 Rem, .223 Rem, and .22 Hornet. 21.9 inch barrel and 40.4 inch OA length it weighs 6.34 pounds. 5 round capacity and detachable magazine. Introduced 2013.

Perf: $680 **Exc:** $610 **VGood:** $525

CZ 527 CARBINE

Bolt action; 223, 7.62x39; detachable 5-shot magazine; 18.5-inch bbl.; walnut stock; 5.8 lbs.; introduced 2000, still made.

Perf: $525 **Exc:** $450 **VGood:** $375

CZ-USA 527 VARMINT

Bolt action center-fire rifle with a blued finish, Turkish walnut stock or laminate stock with palm swell, heavy weight barrel, a single set trigger and recessed target crown. Optics ready with integrated scope mount. Chambered in .17 Rem, .204 Ruger and .223 Rem. 24 inch barrel and 41.5 inch OA length it weighs 7.5

pounds. 5 round capacity and detachable magazine. Introduced 2013.

Perf: $650 **Exc:** $570 **VGood:** $520

CZ 527 LUX BOLT-ACTION RIFLE

Bolt action; 22 Hornet, 222 Rem., 223 Rem., detachable 5-shot magazine. 23-1/2-inch standard or heavy barrel. weighs 6 lbs., 1 oz.; 42-1/2-inch overall. Stock of European walnut with Monte Carlo. Hooded front, open adjustable rear sights. Improved mini-Mauser action with non-rotating claw extractor; single set trigger; grooved receiver. Imported from the Czech Republic by CZ-USA.

Perf: $550 **Exc:** $550 **VGood:** $350

CZ 527 FS

Similar to 527 LUX, but with full-length Mannlicher-type stock, steel muzzle cap; 20.5-inch bbl.; weighs 6.2 lbs.

Perf: $650 **Exc:** $500 **VGood:** $400

CZ 527 VARMINT KEVLAR

Bolt action; 223; 527 action, 24-inch bbl.; Kevlar varmint stock.

Perf: $740 **Exc:** $600 **VGood:** $520

CZ 527 VARMINT LAMINATE

Bolt action; 223; similar to 527 Varmint Kevlar, but with laminated wood stock.

Perf: $640 **Exc:** $500 **VGood:** $420

CZ 527 VARMINT WALNUT

Bolt action; 17 Rem., 204 Ruger; 527 series Varmint rifle with 24-inch bbl. and walnut stock.

Perf: $540 **Exc:** $400 **VGood:** $320

CZ 527 PRESTIGE

Bolt action; 22 Hornet, 223; 21-inch barrel; prestige version of 527 series.

Perf: $830 **Exc:** $700 **VGood:** $600

CZ 550 AMERICAN CLASSIC BOLT-ACTION RIFLE

Bolt action; 22-250, 243, 6.5x55, 270, 308, 30-06, 9.3x62; Similar to CZ 550 Lux except has American classic-style stock with 18 lpi checkering; free-floating barrel; recessed target crown. Has 25.6-inch barrel; weighs 7.48 lbs. No sights furnished. Introduced 1999. Imported from the Czech Republic by CZ-USA. Still available.

Perf: $550 **Exc:** $500 **VGood:** $450

CZ 550 LUX BOLT-ACTION RIFLE

Bolt action; 22-250, 243, 6.5x55, 7x57, 7x64, 308 Win., 9.3x62, 270 Win., 30-06. 20.47 barrel-inch; weighs 7.5 lbs. 44.68-inch overall length. Stock of Turkish walnut in Bavarian style or FS (Mannlicher). Hooded front sight, adjustable rear. Improved Mauser-style action with claw extractor, fixed ejector, square bridge dovetailed receiver; single set trigger. Imported from the Czech Republic by CZ-USA.

Perf: $550 **Exc:** $450 **VGood:** $400

CZ 550 FS

Similar to 550 LUX, but with full-length Mannlicher-type stock, 20.5-inch bbl. Imported by CZ-USA; still made.

Perf: $650 **Exc:** $550 **VGood:** $500

CZ 550 MAGNUM (AMERICAN SAFARI MAGNUM)

Bolt action, 375 H&H, 416 Rigby, 458 Win. Mag., 458 Lott; 25-inch bbl., weighs 9.9 lbs.; introduced 2004, still made.

Perf: $875 **Exc:** $640 **VGood:** $600

CZ 550 MAGNUM (MEDIUM MAGNUM)

Similar to the CZ 550 Lux except chambered for the 300 Win. Mag. and 7mm Rem. Mag.; 5-shot magazine. Adjustable iron sights, hammer-forged barrel, single-set trigger, Turkish walnut stock. Weighs 7.5 lbs. Introduced 2001. Still available. Imported from the Czech Republic by CZ USA.

Perf: $600 **Exc:** $500 **VGood:** $400

CZ 550 MAGNUM (SAFARI MAGNUM)

Similar to CZ 550 Lux and CZ 550 American Safari Magnum except has long action for 300 Win. Mag., 375 H&H, 416 Rigby, 458 Win. Mag. Overall length is 46.45 inches; barrel length 25 inches; weighs 9.24 lbs. Hooded front sight, express rear with one standing, two folding leaves. Imported from the Czech Republic by CZ-USA. Still available.

Perf: $830 **Exc:** $650 **VGood:** $600

CZ 550 VARMINT KEVLAR

Bolt action; 22-250, 308; 25.6-inch bbl.; heavy varmint rifle with Kevlar stock. Introduced 2004, still made.

Perf: $700 **Exc:** $600 **VGood:** $500

CZ 550 VARMINT LAMINATE

Bolt action; 22-250, 308; 25.6-inch bbl.; similar to Kevlar-stocked varmint rifle, but with laminated wood stock. Introduced 2002, still made.

Perf: $620 **Exc:** $500 **VGood:** $450

CZ 550 VARMINT WALNUT

Similar to Varmint Laminate rifle, but in 308 caliber only, with walnut stock.

Perf: $600 **Exc:** $500 **VGood:** $450

CZ 550 ULTIMATE HUNTING RIFLE

Similar to CZ550 American Safari Magnum but chambered for .300 WM only and with custom select wood. 23.6-inch barrel. Accuracy guaranteed at one MOA to 1000 yards. Introduced 2006.

NIB: $2300 **Exc:** $1995 **VGood:** $1575

CZ 700 M1 SNIPER RIFLE

Bolt action; 308 Winchester, 10-shot magazine. 25.6-inch barrel; weighs 11.9 lbs. Length: 45 inches overall. Laminated wood thumbhole stock with adjustable buttplate and cheekpiece; permanently attached Weaver rail for scope mounting. 60-degree bolt throw; oversized trigger guard and bolt handle for use with gloves; full-length equipment rail on forend; fully adjustable trigger. Introduced 2001. Imported from the Czech Republic by CZ USA. No longer available.

Perf: $1900 **Exc:** $1700 **VGood:** $1500

CZ 750 SNIPER

Bolt-action rifle; .308 Win. 10-shot detachable magazine, 26-inch blued barrel, two scope mount systems, polymer stock, weighs 12 lbs. Replaces CZ 700 M1 sniper rifle. Introduced 2006.

NIB: $1925 **Exc:** $1825 **VGood:** $1575

CZ 584 SOLO COMBINATION GUN

Combination gun; 7x57R; 12, 2-3/4-inch chamber. 24.4-inch barrels; weighs 7.37 lbs. 45-1/4 inches overall. Circassian walnut stock. Blade front sight, open rear adjustable for windage. Kersten-style double lump locking system; double-trigger Blitz-type mechanism with drop safety and adjustable set trigger for the rifle barrel; auto safety, dual extractors; receiver dovetailed for scope mounting. Imported from the Czech Republic by CZ-USA. Still available.

Per.f: $800 **Exc:** $675 **VGood:** $590

CZ 589 STOPPER OVER/UNDER GUN

Double rifle, over/under; 458 Win. Magnum. 21.7-inch barrels. weighs 9.3 lbs. Length: 37-1/2 inches overall. Turkish walnut stock with sling swivels. Blade front, fixed rear sights. Kersten-style action; Blitz-type double trigger; hammer-forged, blued barrels; satin-nickel, engraved receiver. Introduced 2001, no longer available; Imported from the Czech Republic by CZ USA.

Perf: $2700 **Exc:** $2500 **VGood:** $2200

D-MAX AUTO CARBINE

Semi-automatic; 9mm Para., 10mm Auto, 40 S&W, 45 ACP; 30-shot magazine; 16-1/4-inch barrel; 38-1/2-inch overall length; weighs about 7-3/4 lbs.; walnut butt, grip, forend; post front sight, open fully-adjustable rear; aperture rear optional; blowback operation, fires from closed bolt; trigger-block safety; side-feed magazine; integral optical sight base; Max-Coat finish. Made in U.S. by D-Max Industries. No longer produced.

Perf: $650 **Exc:** $550 **VGood:** $400

DAEWOO DR200 VARMINT

Semi-automatic; 223 Rem.; 6-shot magazine; 18-3/8-inch barrel; 39-1/4-inch overall length; weighs 9 lbs.; synthetic thumbhole-style stock with rubber buttpad; post front sight in ring, aperture fully-adjustable rear; forged aluminum receiver; bolt, bolt carrier, firing pin, piston and recoil spring contained in one assembly; rotating bolt locking; uses AR-15 magazines. Imported from Korea by Kimber of America, Inc.; distributed by Nationwide Sports Dist. Introduced 1995; no longer imported.

Perf: $650 **Exc:** $525 **VGood:** $450

DAISY LEGACY MODEL 2201/2211

Bolt action; single shot; 22 LR; 19-inch barrel with octagonal shroud; weighs 6-1/2 lbs.; ramp blade front sight, fully-adjustable removable notch rear; moulded copolymer stock (Model 2201) or walnut stock (Model 2211); adjustable-length stock; removable bolt/trigger assembly; adjustable trigger; dovetailed for scope mounting; barrel interchanges with smoothbore. Introduced 1988; discontinued 1990.

Model 2201

Perf: $160 **Exc:** $125 **VGood:** $100

Daewoo DR200 Varmint

Daisy Legacy Model 2201/2211

Daisy Legacy Model 2202/2212

Daisy Legacy Model 2203/2213

Daisy V/L Presentation

Dakota 10 Single Shot

Dakota 76 African

Dakota 76 Classic

Model 2211

Perf: $175 **Exc:** $140 **VGood:** $120

DAISY LEGACY MODEL 2202/2212

Bolt action; 22 LR; 10-shot rotary magazine; 19-inch barrel with octagon shroud; weighs 6-1/2 lbs.; moulded copolymer stock (Model 2202) or walnut stock (Model 2212); ramp blade front sight, fully-adjustable removable rear; receiver dovetailed for scope mounting; adjustable butt length; removable bolt/trigger assembly; barrel interchanges with smoothbore. Introduced 1988; discontinued 1990.

Model 2202

Perf: $160 **Exc:** $125 **VGood:** $100

Model 2212

Perf: $175 **Exc:** $125 **VGood:** $100

DAISY LEGACY MODEL 2203/2213

Semi-automatic; 22 LR; 7-shot clip; 19-inch barrel; 34-3/4-inch overall length; weighs 6-1/2 lbs.; blade on ramp front sight, fully-adjustable, removable notch rear; moulded copolymer stock (Model 2203) or American hardwood stock (Model 2213); receiver dovetailed for scope mount; removable trigger assembly. Introduced 1988; discontinued 1991.

Model 2203

Perf: $160 **Exc:** $130 **VGood:** $100

Model 2213

Perf: $160 **Exc:** $130 **VGood:** $100

DAISY V/L

Single shot; underlever; 22 V/L caseless cartridge; 18-inch barrel; adjustable open rear sight, ramp blade front; stock of wood-grained Lustran plastic. Introduced 1968; discontinued 1969; only 19,000 manufactured. Values are for gun with ammo.

Perf: $300 **Exc:** $225 **VGood:** $175

DAISY V/L COLLECTOR KIT

Same specs as V/L except American walnut stock; gold-plate engraved with owner's name, gun's serial number; gun case; brass wall hangers; 300 rounds of V/L ammo. Introduced 1968; discontinued 1969; only 1000 produced.

Perf: $375 **Exc:** $250 **VGood:** $200

DAKOTA 76 TRAVELER TAKEDOWN RIFLE

Bolt-action takedown rifle; 257 Roberts, 25-06, 7x57, 270, 280, 30-06, 338-06, 35 Whelen (standard length); 7mm Rem. Mag., 300 Win. Mag., 338 Win. Mag., 416 Taylor, 458 Win. Mag. (short magnums); 7mm, 300, 330, 375 Dakota Magnums. Other calibers available. 23-inch barrel; weighs 7-1/2 lbs. 43-1/2-inch overall. Medium fancy- grade walnut stock in classic style. Checkered grip and forend; solid butt pad; drilled and tapped for scope mounts. Threadless disassembly. Uses modified Model 76 design with many features of the Model 70 Winchester. Left-hand model also available. Introduced 1989, still available. Made in U.S.A. by Dakota Arms, Inc.

Classic,

Perf: $4200 **Exc:** $3200 **VGood:** $2700

Safari

Perf: $5000 **Exc:** $4000 **VGood:** $3200

DAKOTA 76 VARMINT

Bolt action; single shot; 17 Rem., 22 BR, 222 Rem., 22-250, 220 Swift, 223, 6mm BR, 6mm PPC; heavy barrel contour; special stock dimensions for varmint shooting. Made in U.S. by Dakota Arms, Inc. Introduced 1994; dropped 1998.

Perf: $2200 **Exc:** $1800 **VGood:** $1300

DAKOTA LIMITED EDITION .30-06 MODEL 76

Ultra-decked-out version of Model 76; commemorates 100th anniversary of .30-06 cartridge; production limited to 101 units.

NIB: $8500 **Exc:** N/A **VGood:** N/A

DAKOTA LIMITED EDITION .30-06 MODEL 10

Ultra-decked-out version of Model 76; commemorates 100th anniversary of .30-06 cartridge; production limited to 101 units.

NIB: $8000 **Exc:** N/A **VGood:** $775

DAISY V/L PRESENTATION

Same specs as V/L except American walnut stock. Introduced 1968; discontinued 1969; only 4000 manufactured.

Perf: $375 **Exc:** $250 **VGood:** $200

DAKOTA 10 SINGLE SHOT

Lever action; chambered for most rimmed and rimless commercial cartridges; 23-inch barrel; 39-1/2-inch overall length; weighs 6 lbs.; falling block; no sights; drilled, tapped for scope mounts; medium-fancy classic-style walnut stock; checkered grip, forend; top tang safety; removable trigger plate. Made in U.S. Introduced 1993; still in production. Most Model 10 rifles have custom features, and prices vary widely.

Perf: $3500 **Exc:** $2750 **VGood:** $2000

DAKOTA 22 SPORTER

Bolt action; 22 LR, 22 Hornet; 5-shot magazine; 22-inch Premium barrel; 42-1/2-inch overall length; weighs about 6-1/2 lbs.; Claro or English walnut stock in classic design; 13-1/2-inch length of pull; point panel hand checkering; swivel studs; black buttpad; no sights; comes with mount bases; combines features of Winchester 52 and Dakota 76 rifles; full-sized receiver; rear locking lugs and bolt machined from bar stock; trigger and striker-blocking safety; adjustable trigger. Made in U.S. by Dakota Arms, Inc. Introduced 1992; out of production in 1998, reintroduced 2003. Premium for 22 Hornet chambering.

Perf: $2000 **Exc:** $1500 **VGood:** $1000

DAKOTA 76 AFRICAN

Bolt action; 338 Lapua Magnum, 404 Jeffery, 416 Rigby, 416 Dakota, 416 Remington, 450 Dakota; 4-shot magazine; 24-inch barrel; weighs 9 to 10 lbs.; select wood; two stock cross-bolts; ramp front sight, standing leaf rear. Made in U.S. by Dakota Arms, Inc. Introduced 1989; still produced.

Perf: $4800 **Exc:** $3700 **VGood:** $2900

DAKOTA 76 ALPINE

Bolt action; 22-250, 243, 6mm Rem., 250-3000, 7mm-08, 308, 358; 4-shot magazine; 21-inch, 23-inch barrel; weighs 6-1/2 lbs.; slim checkered walnut stock; blind magazine. Introduced 1989; discontinued 1992.

Perf: $1795 **Exc:** $1495 **VGood:** $1200

DAKOTA 76 CLASSIC

Bolt action; 22-250, 243, 6mm Rem., 250-3000, 7mm-08, 308, 358, 257 Roberts, 270, 280, 30-06, 7mm Rem. Mag., 338 Win. Mag., 300 Win. Mag., 375 H&H, 458 Win. Mag.; 4-shot magazine; 21-inch, 23-inch barrel; weighs 7-1/2 lbs.; no sights; drilled, tapped for scope mounts; composite or classic-style medium-fancy walnut stock; one-piece rail trigger guard assembly; solid buttpad; steel grip cap; adjustable trigger. Based on original Winchester Model 70 design. Right- or left-handed. Introduced 1988; still in production.

Perf: $3400 **Exc:** $2750 **VGood:** $1400

DAKOTA 76 CLASSIC SHORT ACTION

Same specs as Model 76 Classic except 22-250, 243, 6mm Rem., 250-3000, 7mm-08, 308; 21-inch barrel. Introduced 1989.

Perf: $2095 **Exc:** $1595 **VGood:** $1195

DAKOTA 76 SAFARI

Bolt action; 300 Win. Mag., 338 Win. Mag., 375 H&H, 458 Win. Mag.; 23-inch barrel; weighs 8-1/2 lbs.; ramp front sight, standing leaf rear; checkered plastic composite or English walnut stock; shadowline cheekpiece; barrel band front swivel, inletted rear. Introduced 1988; still in production.

Perf: $4200 **Exc:** $3200 **VGood:** $2200

With composite stock

Perf: $2750 **Exc:** $1995 **VGood:** $1495

DAKOTA 97 LIGHTWEIGHT HUNTER

Bolt action; 22-250 to 330 Dakota Magnum. 22-inch, 24-inch barrel; weighs 6.1 to 6.5 lbs. 43-inch overall length. Lightweight Fiberglass stock. Sights are optional. Matte blue finish, black stock. Right-hand action only. Introduced 1998. Made in U.S.A. by Dakota Arms, Inc.

Perf: $1800 **Exc:** $1400 **VGood:** $1000

DAKOTA 97 LONG RANGE HUNTER RIFLE

Bolt action; 25-06, 257 Roberts, 270 Win., 280 Rem., 7mm Rem. Mag., 7mm Dakota Mag., 30-06, 300 Win. Mag., 300 Dakota Mag., 338 Win. Mag., 330 Dakota Mag., 375 H&H Mag., 375 Dakota Mag. 24-inch, 26-inch match-quality; free-floating barrel; weighs 7.7 lbs. 45-inch to 47-inch overall length. H-S Precision black synthetic stock, with one-piece bedding block system. Drilled and tapped for scope mounting. Cylindrical machined receiver controlled round feed; Mauser-style extractor; three-position striker blocking safety; fully adjustable match trigger. Right-hand action only. Introduced 1997, still available. Made in U.S.A. by Dakota Arms, Inc.

Perf: $1800 **Exc:** $1300 **VGood:** $1000

DAKOTA DOUBLE RIFLE

Double rifle, breakopen; 7x57R, 30-30, 9.3x74R, 375 H&H Flanged, 45-70, 470 Nitro Express, 500 Nitro Express. 25-inch barrel; Exhibition-grade walnut stock; Express sights; Round action; selective ejectors; engraving extra; recoil pad; Americase. From Dakota Arms Inc. Still available.

Perf: $25,000 **Exc:** $22,000 **VGood:** $20,000

DAKOTA LONGBOW TACTICAL E.R. RIFLE

Bolt action; 300 Dakota Magnum, 330 Dakota Magnum, 338 Lapua Magnum. 28-inch barrel, .950-inch at muzzle; weighs 13.7 lbs. 50-inch to

52-inch overall length. Ambidextrous McMillan A-2 fiberglass stock, black or olive green color; adjustable cheekpiece and buttplate. Comes with Picatinny one-piece optical rail. Uses the Dakota 76 action with controlled-round feed; three-position firing pin block safety, claw extractor; Model 70-style trigger. Comes with bipod, case, tool kit. Introduced 1997. Made in U.S.A. by Dakota Arms, Inc.

Perf: $4200 **Exc:** $3200 **VGood:** $2750

CHARLES DALY BOLT ACTION (EARLY)

Bolt action; 22 Hornet; 5-shot box magazine; 24-inch barrel; miniaturized Mauser; leaf rear, ramp front sight; walnut stock; hand-checkered pistol-grip forearm; hinged floorplate. Introduced 1931; discontinued 1939. Imported by Charles Daly; manufactured by Franz Jaeger Co. of Germany. Note: Same model was imported by A.F. Stoeger and sold as Herold Rifle.

Perf: $1000 **Exc:** $750 **VGood:** $650

CHARLES DALY BOLT-ACTION CENTERFIRE RIFLE, FIELD GRADE

Bolt action; 22-250, 30-06, 22-inch bbl., 5-shot magazine, 43-inch OAL, walnut-finished hardwood stock, or black polymer stock, Mauser action.

Perf: $530 **Exc:** $470 **VGood:** $430

CHARLES DALY BOLT-ACTION CENTERFIRE RIFLE, FIELD GRADE, MAGNUM

Like the Field Grade, but chambered for 7mm Rem Mag, 300 Win Mag; 24-inch barrel, 44-5/8-inch OAL, weighs 7-1/4 lbs.

Perf: $550 **Exc:** $490 **VGood:** $450

CHARLES DALY BOLT-ACTION CENTERFIRE RIFLE, SUPERIOR GRADE

Like the Field Grade, but highly-polished blued barreled action with gold-plated trigger, hand-checkered European walnut stock with Monte Carlo comb, rollover cheekpiece.; open rear and ramp front sights, or none, for scope mounting. Introduced 1996, imported by KBI.

Perf: $570 **Exc:** $525 **VGood:** $460

CHARLES DALY BOLT-ACTION CENTERFIRE RIFLE, SUPERIOR GRADE, MAGNUM

Like the Superior grade, but calibers 7mm Rem Mag through 458 Win Mag; 24-inch, 26-inch barrels, weighs about 8-1/4 lbs.

Perf: $650 **Exc:** $600 **VGood:** $550

CHARLES DALY BOLT-ACTION CENTERFIRE RIFLE, EMPIRE GRADE

Like the Superior Grade, but has oil-finished American walnut stock with 18 lpi hand checkering; black gripcap and forearm tip, highly-polished barreled action, jeweled bolt, recoil pad, and swivel studs. Imported by KBI, no longer available.

Perf: $650 **Exc:** $600 **VGood:** $550

CHARLES DALY BOLT-ACTION CENTERFIRE RIFLE, EMPIRE GRADE, MAGNUM

Like the Empire Grade, but for magnum calibers. Imported by KBI; no longer available.

Perf: $700 **Exc:** $650 **VGood:** $600

CHARLES DALY BOLT-ACTION 22-CALIBER RIFLE, FIELD GRADE

Bolt action; 22 LR, 6- or 10-shot magazine; 22-5/8-inch barrel, 6-1/8 lbs. walnut-finished hardwood stock; bead front, adjustable rear sights; receiver grooved for scope mounting. Introduced 1998 by KBI.

Perf: $260 **Exc:** $240 **VGood:** $220

Charles Daly Bolt Action

Charles Daly Bolt-Action 22-Caliber Rifle, Field Grade

Charles Daly Bolt-Action 22-Caliber Rifle, Superior Grade

Dan Wesson Coyote Classic Bolt-Action Rimfire

CHARLES DALY BOLT-ACTION 22-CALIBER RIFLE, SUPERIOR GRADE

Like the Field Grade, but high polished barreled action, checkered Monte Carlo walnut stock; 22 LR, 22 WMR or 22 Hornet; premium for 22 Hornet.

Perf: $310 **Exc:** $280 **VGood:** $250

CHARLES DALY BOLT-ACTION 22-CALIBER RIFLE, EMPIRE GRADE

Like the Superior Grade, but Monte Carlo stock of California walnut, 20 lpi hand checkering, black grip cap and forearm cap, damascened bolt.

Perf: $480 **Exc:** $430 **VGood:** $360

CHARLES DALY SUPERIOR COMBINATION GUN

Combination gun; 12 ga. over 22 Hornet, 223 Rem., 22-250, 243 Win., 270 Win., 308 Win., 30-06. 23.5-inch barrels, shotgun choked Imp. Cyl.; weighs about 7.5 lbs. Checkered walnut pistol grip buttstock and semi- beavertail forend. Silvered, engraved receiver; chrome-moly steel barrels; double triggers; extractors; sling swivels; gold bead front sight. Introduced 1997. Imported from Italy by K.B.I. Inc., still available.

Perf: $1250 **Exc:** $1100 **VGood:** $1000

CHARLES DALY EMPIRE COMBINATION GUN

Same as the Superior grade except has deluxe wood with European-style comb and cheekpiece; slim forend. Introduced 1997, still available. Imported from Italy by K.B.I., Inc.

Perf: $1650 **Exc:** $1500 **VGood:** 1200

CHARLES DALY FIELD GRADE AUTO RIFLE

Semi-automatic; 22 LR, 10-shot magazine. 20-3/4-inch barrel; weighs 6.5 lbs. 40-1/2-inch overall. Walnut-finished hardwood stock with Monte Carlo; hooded front sight, adjustable open rear. Receiver grooved for scope mounting; blue finish; shell deflector. Introduced 1998. Imported by K.B.I.

Perf: $120 **Exc:** $100 **VGood:** $80

CHARLES DALY EMPIRE GRADE AUTO RIFLE

Similar to the Field Grade except has select California walnut stock with 24 lpi hand checkering, contrasting forend and gripcaps, damascened bolt, high-polish blue. Introduced 1998. Imported by K.B.I.; no longer available.

Perf: $170 **Exc:** $130 **VGood:** $100

CHARLES DALY TRUE YOUTH BOLT-ACTION RIFLE

Bolt action; 22 LR, single shot. 16-1/4-inch barrel; weighs about 3 lbs. 32-inch overall. Walnut-finished hardwood stock; blade front, adjustable rear sights; Scaled-down stock for small shooters. Blue finish. Introduced 1998. Imported by K.B.I., Inc.

Perf: $115 **Exc:** $90 **VGood:** $65

DAN WESSON COYOTE CLASSIC BOLT-ACTION RIMFIRE RIFLE

Bolt action; 22 LR or 22 WMR. 5-shot magazine (10-shot optional magazine). 22-3/4-inch barrel; Laminated wood or exotic hardwood stock; fully adjustable V-notch rear sight, brass bead ramp front. Receiver drilled and tapped for scope mount; checkered pistol grip and fore end with DW medallion end cap; recessed target crown; sling swivel studs. Introduced 2001, dropped 2003. From Dan Wesson Firearms.

Perf: $210 **Exc:** $170 **VGood:** $120

DAN WESSON COYOTE TARGET BOLT-ACTION RIMFIRE RIFLE

Bolt action; 22 LR or 22 WMR, 5-shot magazine (10-shot optional magazine). 18-3/8-inch heavy barrel; laminated wood or exotic hardwood stock. Receiver drilled and tapped for scope mount; target-crowned muzzle; high comb, smooth pistol grip and rubber butt plate. Introduced 2001, dropped 2003. From Dan Wesson Firearms.

Perf: $250 **Exc:** $200 **VGood:** $150

DIANA MODEL 820F MATCH

Bolt action; single shot; 22 LR; 27-1/8-inch barrel; 44-1/2-inch overall length; weighs 15-1/2 lbs.; walnut target stock; tunnel front sight, fully-

Dan Wesson Coyote Target Bolt-Action Rimfire

Diana Model 820L

Dixie Model 1873 Rifle

Dixie 1874 Sharps Blackpowder Silhouette

DPMS Panther Arms A-15 Rifle

DPMS Panther Race Gun

adjustable match rear; designed for free rifle events; adjustable hook buttplate, adjustable cheekpiece, hand stop; stock stabilizer and palm rest optional; trigger adjustable from 1.4 to 8.8 oz. Imported from Germany by Dynamit Nobel-RWS, Inc. Introduced 1990; discontinued 1992.

Perf: $1695 **Exc:** $1395 **VGood:** $995

DIANA MODEL 820K

Same specs as Model 820F except 24-inch barrel; 41-inch overall length; weighs 9-1 /2 lbs.; no sights; detachable 3-piece barrel weight; designed for running boar events; European walnut stock. Made in Germany. Discontinued 1986.

Perf: $895 **Exc:** $750 **VGood:** $550

DIANA MODEL 820L

Same specs as Model 820F except 24-inch, 26-inch barrel; weighs 10-1/2 lbs; designed for three-position match shooting. Made in Germany. Introduced 1990; discontinued 1992.

Perf: $1195 **Exc:** $895 **VGood:** $650

DIANA MODEL 820S

Same specs as Model 820L except 24-inch barrel; 41-inch overall length; weighs 10 5/16 lbs.; Model 82 or 75 aperture rear sight. Made in Germany. Introduced 1990; discontinued 1992.

Perf: $995 **Exc:** $795 **VGood:** $595

DIANA MODEL 820SF

Same specs as Model 820F except 41-inch overall length; weighs 11 lbs.; heavy barrel; Model 82 or 75 aperture rear sight. Made in Germany. Introduced 1990; discontinued 1992.

Perf: $1095 **Exc:** $895 **VGood:** $595

DIXIE MODEL 1873 RIFLE

Lever action; 44-40; 11-shot tubular magazine; 24-1/2-inch octagonal barrel; leaf rear sight, blade front; walnut stock forearm, receiver color case-hardened. Replica of Winchester '73. Introduced 1975.

Perf: $795 **Exc:** $695 **VGood:** $595

Engraved Model 1873 Rifle

Perf: $1200 **Exc:** $1000 **VGood:** $700

DIXIE MODEL 1873 CARBINE

Same specs as Model 1873 except 20-inch barrel, carbine bands.

Perf: $695 **Exc:** $595 **VGood:** $495

DIXIE 1874 SHARPS BLACKPOWDER SILHOUETTE

Single shot; falling block; 45-70; 30-inch tapered octagon barrel with 1:18-inch twist; 47-1/2-inch overall length; weighs 10-5/16 lbs.; oiled walnut shotgun-style butt with checkered metal buttplate; blade front sight, ladder-type hunting rear; replica of the Sharps #1 Sporter; color case-hardened receiver, hammer, lever and buttplate; blued barrel; tang drilled and tapped for tang sight; double-set triggers. Meets standards for NRA blackpowder cartridge matches. Imported from Italy by Dixie Gun Works. Introduced 1995; still imported.

Perf: $1100 **Exc:** $1000 **VGood:** $895

DIXIE 1874 SHARPS LIGHTWEIGHT HUNTER/TARGET

Same specs as Dixie 1874 Sharps Blackpowder Silhouette except straight-grip buttstock with military-style buttplate. Based on the 1874 military model. Imported from Italy by Dixie Gun Works. Introduced 1995.

Perf: $1100 **Exc:** $1000 **VGood:** $895

DIXIE REMINGTON CREEDMORE LONG RANGE

Rolling block; 45-70; 30-inch octagon barrel; weighs 13 lbs.; Creedmore sights; checkered wood stock; blued barrel; color case-hardening or exposed metal. No longer in production.

Perf: $950 **Exc:** $795 **VGood:** $695

DPMS 6.8 HUNTER

Semi-auto (AR15) in 6.8 Remington SPC. 20" stainless, teflon fluted barrel and carbon fiber free float tube. New for 2013.

Perf: $1100 **Exc:** $950 **VGood:** 800

DPMS 3G2

Semi-auto (AR15) in .223 Remington. 16" stainless lightweight barrel, M111 Hand guards, Ergo Grip and Magpul STR Stock, DPMS 2 Stage trigger. Introduced new in 2013.

Perf: $1250 **Exc:** $1000 **VGood:** $900

DPMS 300 AAC BLK PERSONAL DEFENSE WEAPON

Semi-auto (AR15) in .300 Blackout. Compact, SBR with 7.5" Barrel and AAC Blackout flash hider. PDW 4 rail handguard and SOG vertical grip with Magpul flip up sights. New for 2013.

Perf: $1250 **Exc:** $1100 **VGood:** $950

DPMS PANTHER ARMS A-15 RIFLES

Semi-automatic; 223 Rem., 7.62x39. Barrel: 16-inch to 24-inch weighs 7-3/4 to 11-3/4 lbs. 34-1/2 to 42-1/4-inch overall. Black Zytel composite stock; Square front post, adjustable A2 rear sights; Steel or stainless steel heavy or bull barrel; hard-coat anodized receiver; aluminum free-float tube handguard; many options. From DPMS Panther Arms.

Panther Bull A-15 (20-inch stainless bull barrel)

Perf: $875 **Exc:** $700 **VGood:** $575

Panther Bull Twenty-Four (24-inch stainless bull barrel)

Perf: $920 **Exc:** $760 **VGood:** $610

Bulldog (20-inch stainless fluted barrel, flat top receiver)

Perf: $1150 **Exc:** $975 **VGood:** $850

Panther Bull Sweet Sixteen (16-inch stainless bull barrel)

Perf: $840 **Exc:** $710 **VGood:** $600

Panther DCM (20-inch stainless heavy bbl., national match sights.

Perf: $1000 **Exc:** $780 **VGood:** $630

Panther 7.62x39 (20-inch steel heavy barrel)

Perf: $800 **Exc:** $700 **VGood:** $575

DPMS PANTHER RACE GUN

Similar to Panther Bull but with 24-inch fluted bull barrel. Sights: JP Micro adjustable rear, JP front sight adjustable for height. Includes Lyman globe and Shaver inserts.

NIB: $1600 **Exc:** $1475 **VGood:** $1150

DPMS PANTHER TUBER

Similar to Panther Bull 24 but with 16-inch barrel with cylindrical aluminum shroud.

NIB: $1600 **Exc:** $1475 **VGood:** $1150

DPMS SINGLE SHOT RIFLE

AR-15-style single-shot rifle with manually-operated bolt, no magazine.

NIB: $775 **Exc:** $725 **VGood:** $595

DPMS PANTHERA PARDUS

Similar to Panther Post-ban but with 16-inch bull barrel, telescoping buttstock and tan Teflon finish. Introduced 2006.

NIB: $1600 **Exc:** $1475 **VGood:** $1150

DPMS PANTHER 20TH ANNIVERSARY RIFLE

Similar to Panther Post-ban but with 20-inch bull barrel and engraved, chrome-plated lower receiver.

NIB: $2600 **Exc:** $2475 **VGood:** $1950

DPMS PANTHER MARK 12

Similar to Panther but with flash hider and other refinements.

NIB: $1400 **Exc:** $1325 **VGood:** $1075

DPMS PANTHER SDM-R

Similar to Panther but with stainless steel barrel and Harris bipod.

NIB: $1300 **Exc:** $1225 **VGood:** $1000

DPMS LRT-SASS

Semi-automatic rifle based on AR-15 design. Chambered in .308 Win. With 18-inch stainless steel barrel with flash hider, collapsible Vitor Clubfoot carbine stock and 19-rd. detachable magazine.

NIB: $1800 **Exc:** $1655 **VGood:** $1250

DPMS LR-260

Similar to LRT-SASS but with 24-inch stainless steel barrel and chambered in .260 Remington. Also available with 20-inch chrome-moly barrel as LR-260H. Introduced 2006.

NIB: $1200 **Exc:** $1155 **VGood:** $975

DPMS LR-243

Similar to LR-260 but with 20-inch chrome-moly barrel and chambered in .243 Win. Introduced 2006.

NIB: $1200 **Exc:** $1155 **VGood:** $975

DPMS LR-204

Similar to LRT-260 but chambered in .204 Ruger. Introduced 2006.

NIB: $1200 **Exc:** $1155 **VGood:** $975

DSA SA58 CARBINE

Semi-automatic; 308 Win., limited 243 and 260; 16-1/4-inch barrel with integrally machined muzzle brake; weighs 8-3/4 lbs. Fiberglass stock with reinforced synthetic handguard. Adjustable post front, adjustable rear peep sights; Gas-operated semi-auto with fully adjustable gas system, high grade steel or 416 stainless upper receiver. In variety of camo finishes. Made in U.S.A. by DSA, Inc.

Perf: $1250 **Exc:** $1100 **VGood:** $900

DSA SA58 MEDIUM CONTOUR

Semi-automatic; 308 Win., limited 243 and 260; 21-inch barrel with integrally machined muzzle brake; weighs 9.75 lbs. 43-inch length; fiberglass reinforced stock with synthetic handguard. Adjustable post front sight with match rear peep. Gas-operated semi-auto with fully adjustable gas system, high grade steel or 416 stainless upper receiver. In variety of camo finishes. Made in U.S.A. by DSA, Inc.

Perf: $1400 **Exc:** $1250 **VGood:** $1000

DSA SA58 MEDIUM CONTOUR TACTICAL

Semi-automatic: 308 Win.; Fluted barrel, 16.25-inch; weighs 8 lbs.; 38-1/4-inch length. Fiberglass reinforced stock, short synthetic handguard. Adjustable post front sight, adjustable rear peep. Gas-operated semi-auto with fully adjustable gas system, high grade steel upper receiver. In variety of camo finishes. Made in U.S.A. by DSA, Inc.

Perf: $1400 **Exc:** $1250 **VGood:** $1000

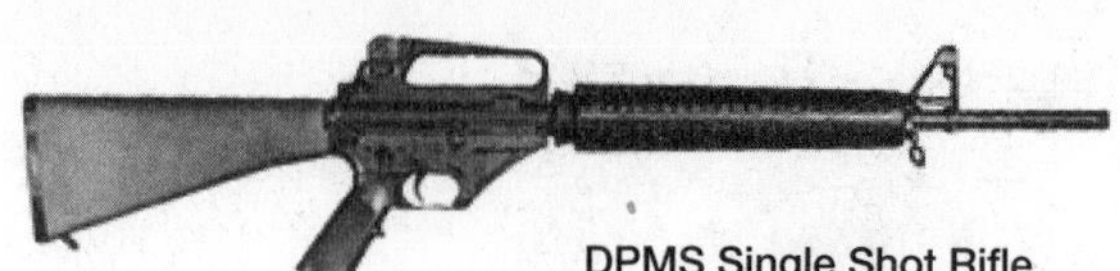

DPMS Single Shot Rifle

DPMS Panther Tuber

DPMS Panther Mark 12

DPMS Panther SDM-R

DSA SA58 STANDARD

Semi-automatic; 308 Win.; 21-inch barrel with integrally machined muzzle brake; weighs 8-3/4 lbs.; 43-inch length; Fiberglass reinforced stock, synthetic handguard. Adjustable post front sight, adjustable rear peep. Gas-operated semi-auto with fully adjustable gas system, high grade steel upper receiver. In variety of camo finishes. Made in U.S.A. by DSA, Inc.

Perf: $1250 **Exc:** $1100 **VGood:** $900

DSA SA58 T48 TACTICAL

Semi-automatic; 308 Win.; 21-inch chrome-moly barrel with Browning flashhider; weighs 9.68 lbs.; 45-inch overall length; Field grade finish wood stock; Adjustable post front sight, adjustable rear peep. 10- or 20- round fixed magazine with stripper clip top cover. Gas operated semi-auto with fully adjustable gas system. Made in U.S.A. by DSA, Inc.

Perf: $1650 **Exc:** $1400 **VGood:** $1200

DSA SA58 BULL BARREL

Semi-automatic; 308 Win.; 21-inch or 24-inch bull barrel; weighs 11.1 or 11.5 lbs.; 41.5-inch and 44.5-inch lengths; Stock with free floating handguard. Elevation adjustable protected post front sight, match rear peep. Gas-operated semi-auto with fully adjustable gas system, high grade steel or stainless upper receiver. Extra for stainless barrel. Made in U.S.A. by DSA, Inc.

Perf: $1700 **Exc:** $1400 **VGood:** $1100

DUBIEL CUSTOM

Bolt action; 22-250 through 458 Win. Mag., selected wildcats; barrel weights, lengths depend upon caliber; Douglas Premium barrel; no sights; integral scope mount bases; walnut, maple or laminate stocks; hand-checkered; left- or right-hand models; 5-lug locking mechanism; 36-degree bolt rotation; adjustable Canjar trigger; oil or epoxy stock finish; slide-type safety; floorplate release; jeweled, chromed bolt; sling swivel studs; recoil pad. Introduced 1978; discontinued 1990.

Perf: $2200 **Exc:** $1900 **VGood:** $1500

DUMOULIN AMAZONE

Bolt action; various calibers from 270 to 458; 20-inch barrel; classic two-leaf rear sight, hooded blade on ramp front; full-length, hand-checkered, oil-finished European walnut stock; built on Mauser 98 action; adjustable trigger; Model 70-type safety. Made in Belgium. Introduced 1986; discontinued 1987.

Perf: $1695 **Exc:** $1495 **VGood:** $900

DUMOULIN BAVARIA DELUXE

Bolt action; various calibers from 222 to 458; 21-inch, 24-inch, 25-1/2-inch octagonal barrel; weighs about 7 lbs.; classic two-leaf rear sight, hooded blade on ramp front; hand-checkered, oil-finished

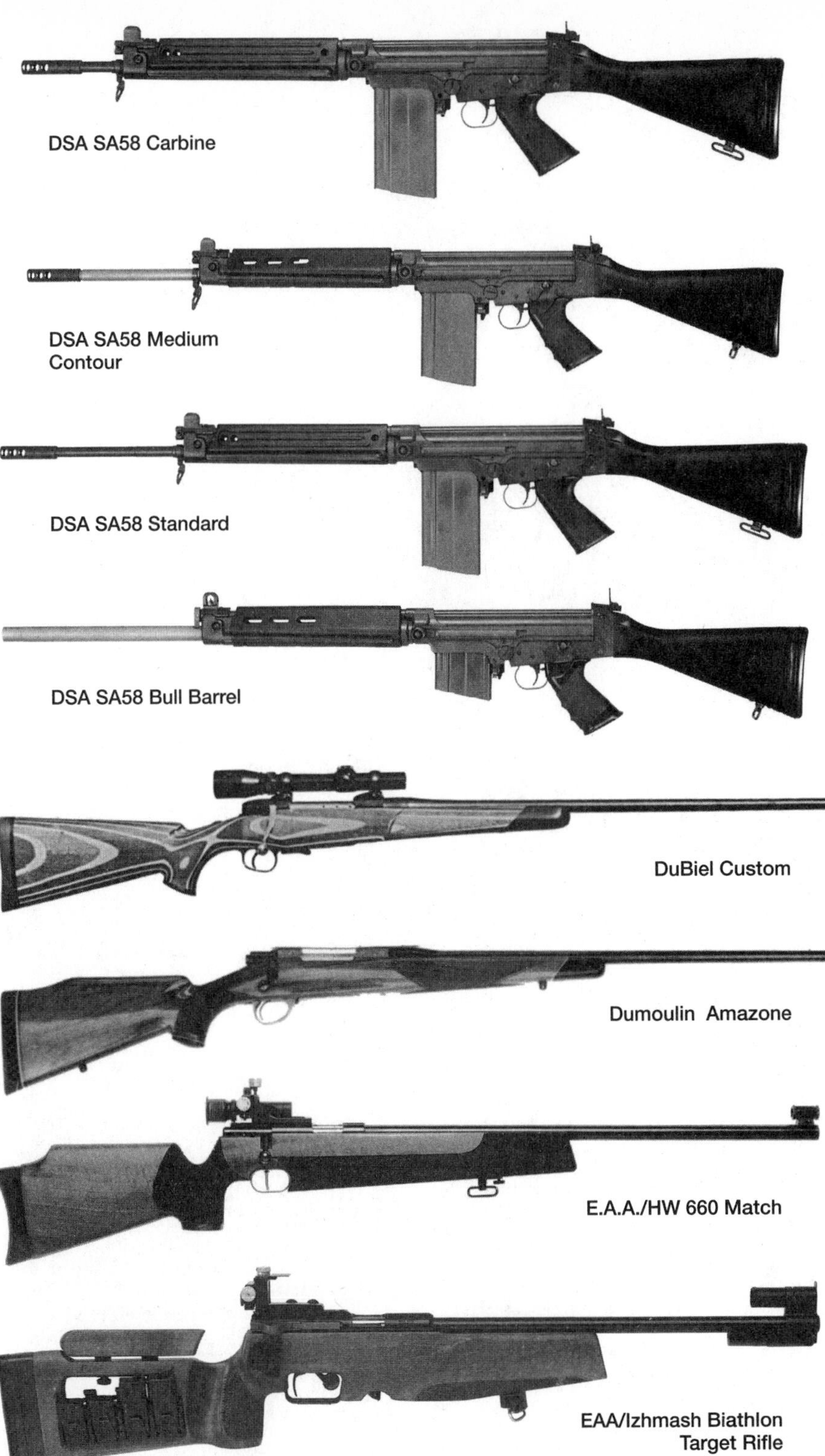
DSA SA58 Carbine

DSA SA58 Medium Contour

DSA SA58 Standard

DSA SA58 Bull Barrel

DuBiel Custom

Dumoulin Amazone

E.A.A./HW 660 Match

EAA/Izhmash Biathlon Target Rifle

select European walnut stock; built on Mauser or Sako action; adjustable trigger; Model 70-type safety; quick-detachable sling swivels; solid buttpad; deluxe engraving. Made in Belgium. Imported by Midwest Gun Sport. Introduced 1986; discontinued 1987.

Perf: $1800 **Exc:** $1400 **VGood:** $1000

DUMOULIN CENTURION

Bolt action; various calibers from 270 to 458; 21-1/2-inch, 24-inch, 25-inch barrel; no sights; hand-checkered, oil-finished select European walnut stock; built on Mauser or Sako action. Made in Belgium. Introduced 1986; discontinued 1987.

Perf: $795 **Exc:** $595 **VGood:** $495

DUMOULIN CENTURION CLASSIC

Same specs as Centurion except Mauser 98 action only; higher grade of wood stock. Introduced 1986; discontinued 1987.

Perf: $950 **Exc:** $795 **VGood:** $600

DUMOULIN DIANE

Bolt action; various calibers from 270 to 458; 22-inch barrel; classic two-leaf rear sight, hooded blade on ramp front; hand-checkered, oil-finished European walnut stock; built on Mauser 98 action; adjustable trigger; Model 70-type safety. Made in Belgium. Introduced 1986; discontinued 1987.

Perf: $1450 **Exc:** $1200 **VGood:** $800

DUMOULIN PIONEER EXPRESS

Double rifle; various calibers from 22 Hornet-600 Nitro Express; 24-inch, 26-inch barrel; 45-inch overall length (24-inch barrel); weighs 9-1/2 lbs.; two-leaf rear sight on quarter-rib, bead on ramp front; boxlock triple-lock system; Greener crossbolt; H&H type ejectors; articulated front trigger; various grades of engraving effect price. Made in Belgium. Introduced 1987; no longer imported. Prices range from $6500 to $12,000.

DUMOULIN SAFARI

Bolt action; magnum calibers up to 458; 24-inch to 26-inch barrel; 44-inch overall length (24-inch barrel); weighs 8-1/2 to 9 lbs.; two-leaf rear sight, hooded front on banded ramp; built on modified Sako or Mauser Oberndorf action; classic English-style deluxe European walnut stock; oil finish; buffalo horn grip cap; rubber buttpad; Model 70-type or side safety. Custom built in Belgium. Introduced 1986; discontinued 1987.

Perf: $2400 **Exc:** $1900 **VGood:** $1500

DUMOULIN SIDELOCK PRESTIGE

Double rifle; sidelock; traditional chopper lump or classic Ernest Dumoulin barrel system; 22-inch, 24-inch barrel, depending on caliber; deluxe European walnut stock; internal parts are gold-plated; Purdey lock system; ten grades, built to customer specs; differing engraving styles. Made in Belgium. Introduced 1986; no longer imported.

Perf: $17,900 **Exc:** $14,950 **VGood:** $9995

E.A.A./ANTONIO ZOLI EXPRESS RIFLE

Double rifle; boxlock; 7.65R, 30-06, 9.3x74R; 25-1/2-inch barrels; 40-1/2-inch overall length; weighs about 8 lbs.; fancy European walnut stock with raised cheekpiece, fine-line checkering; bead front sight, adjustable express rear on quarter-rib; engraved coin-finish frame; double-set triggers; selective automatic ejectors; rubber recoil pad; sling swivels. Imported from Italy by European American Armory. Importation dropped 1993.

Perf: $3695 **Exc:** $2995 **VGood:** $2195

Express Model E, better engraving, ejectors

Perf: $4295 **Exc:** $3495 **VGood:** $2495

Express Model EM, elaborate engraving, extra-fancy wood

Perf: $4795 **Exc:** $3995 **VGood:** $2995

E.A.A./BAIKAL IZH-94 COMBINATION GUN

Combination gun; 12 gauge, 3-inch chamber; 222 Rem., 223, 5.6x50R, 5.6x55E, 7x57R, 7x65R, 7.62x39, 7.62x51, 308, 7.62x53R, 7.62x54R, 30-06; 24-inch or 26-inch barrels; imp., mod. and full choke tubes. weighs 7.28 lbs. Walnut stock; rubber butt pad. Express style sights. Hammer-forged barrels with chrome- lined bores; machined receiver; single-selective or double triggers. Imported by European American Armory.

Perf: $600 **Exc:** $545 **VGood:** $375

E.A.A./HW 660 MATCH

Bolt action; single shot; 22 LR; 26-inch barrel; 45-3/8-inch overall length; weighs 10-3/4 lbs.; match-type walnut stock with adjustable cheekpiece and buttplate; stippled pistol grip and forend; globe front sight, match aperture rear; adjustable match trigger; forend accessory rail. Imported from Germany by European American Armory. Introduced 1988; dropped 1994. Reintroduced, no longer available.

Perf: $750 **Exc:** $550 **VGood:** $425

E.A.A./IZHMASH BIATHLON TARGET RIFLE

Bolt Action; 22 LR; biathlon rifle with snow covers for barrel and sights, stock holding extra magazines, round trigger block. Unique bolt utilizes toggle action. Designed to compete in 40 meter biathlon event. 19.5-inch bbl.

Perf: $900 **Exc:** $800 **VGood:** $700

E.A.A./IZHMASH BIATHALON BASIC TARGET RIFLE

Same action as Biathlon but designed for plinking or fun. Beech stock, heavy barrel with Weaver rail for scope mount. 22 LR, 19.5-inch bbl.

Perf: $300 **Exc:** $200 **VGood:** $100

E.A.A./SABATTI MODEL 1822

Semi-automatic; 22 LR; 10-shot magazine; 18-1/2-inch round tapered barrel; 37-inch overall length; weighs 5-1/4 lbs.; stained hardwood stock; bead front sight, folding leaf elevation-adjustable rear; cross-bolt safety; blue finish. Imported from Italy by European American Armory. Introduced 1993; no longer imported.

Perf: $180 **Exc:** $150 **VGood:** $100

Heavy model, bull barrel, no sights

Perf: $250 **Exc:** $200 **VGood:** $150

Thumbhole model, heavy, bull barrel, no sights, one-piece stock

Perf: $300 **Exc:** $250 **VGood:** $200

E.A.A./SABATTI ROVER 870

Bolt action; 22-250, 243, 25-06, 270, 30-06, 308, 7mm Rem. Mag., 300 Win. Mag., 338 Win. Mag.; 23-inch barrel; 42-1/2-inch overall length; weighs about 7 lbs.; gold bead on ramp front sight, open adjustable rear; walnut stock with straight comb, cut checkering on grip and forend; positive safety locks trigger; blue finish. Imported by E.A.A. Introduced 1986; importation dropped 1987.

Perf: $595 **Exc:** $495 **VGood:** $395

E.A.A./SAIGA SEMI-AUTO RIFLE

Semi-automatic; 7.62x39, 308, 223. Barrel: 20.5-inch, 22-inch, 16.3-inch; weighs 7 to 8-1/2 lbs; 43-inch length; synthetic or wood stock; adjustable sights, sight base. Based on AK Combat rifle by Kalashnikov. Imported from Russia by EAA Corp.

Perf: $250 **Exc:** $210 **VGood:** $180

E.A.A./WEIHRAUCH HW 60

Bolt action; single shot; 22 LR; 26-7/8-inch barrel; 45-3/4-inch overall length; weighs 11 lbs.; walnut target stock with adjustable buttplate, stippled pistol grip and forend; forend rail with adjustable swivel; hooded ramp front sight, match-type aperture rear; adjustable match trigger with push-button safety. Imported from Germany by European American Armory. Introduced 1981; no longer imported.

Perf: $595 **Exc:** $450 **VGood:** $375

Left-hand model

Perf: $795 **Exc:** $595 **VGood:** $425

EAGLE ARMS EA-15

Semi-automatic; 223 Rem.; 30-shot magazine; 20-inch barrel; 39-inch overall length; weighs about 7 lbs.; black composition stock, trapdoor-style; post front sight, fully-adjustable rear; push-type receiver pivot pin for easy takedown; receivers hard coat anodized; E2-style forward assist mechanism; integral raised M-16A2-type fence around magazine release button. Made in U.S. by Eagle Arms, Inc. Introduced 1989; discontinued 1993.

Perf: $750 **Exc:** $650 **VGood:** $495

EAGLE ARMS EA-15 ACTION MASTER

Same specs as EA-15 except no sights, one-piece international-style upper receiver for scope mounting; solid aluminum handguard tube; free-floating 20-inch premium barrel; muzzle compensator; NM trigger group; weighs about 8-3/4 lbs. Renamed the 15A3 Action Master. Made in U.S. by Eagle Arms, Inc. Introduced 1991.

Perf: $800 **Exc:** $700 **VGood:** $500

EAGLE ARMS EA-15 EAGLE SPIRIT

Same specs as EA-15 rifle except 16-inch premium air-gauged barrel; weighs 8 lbs.; full-length tubular aluminum handguard; match accessories. Introduced 1993.

Perf: $800 **Exc:** $700 **VGood:** $500

EAA/Izhmash Biathalon Basic Target Rifle

Eagle Arms EA-15 Golden Eagle

Eagle Arms M15A3 Post-Ban Predator

E.M.F. Sharps Carbine

E.M.F. Sharps Rifle

EAGLE ARMS EA-15 GOLDEN EAGLE

Same specs as EA-15 except E2-style National Match rear sight with 1/2-MOA adjustments, elevation-adjustable NM front sight with set screw; 20-inch Douglas Premium extra-heavy match barrel with 1:9-inch twist; NM trigger group and bolt carrier group; weighs about 12-3/4 lbs. Made in U.S. by Eagle Arms, Inc. Introduced 1991.

Perf: $800 **Exc:** $700 **VGood:** $500

EAGLE ARMS EA-15A2 POST-BAN HEAVY BARREL

Same specs as EA-15 except 10-shot magazine; elevation-adjustable front sight; A2-style forward assist mechanism. Introduced 1995; no longer in production.

Perf: $795 **Exc:** $695 **VGood:** $595

EAGLE ARMS EA-15E2 CARBINE

Same specs as EA-15 except collapsible carbine-type buttstock; 16-inch heavy carbine barrel; M177-type flash supressor; weighs about 7-1/4 lbs. Made in U.S. by Eagle Arms, Inc. Introduced 1989; no longer in production.

Perf: $795 **Exc:** $695 **VGood:** $595

EAGLE ARMS EA-15E2 H-BAR

Same specs as EA-15 except 20-inch, slightly lighter and smaller heavy match barrel with 1:9-inch twist; weighs about 9 lbs. Made in U.S. by Eagle Arms, Inc. Introduced 1989; no longer in production.

Perf: $895 **Exc:** $795 **VGood:** $600

With NM sights

Perf: $1195 **Exc:** $995 **VGood:** $725

EAGLE ARMS M15A3 POST-BAN PREDATOR

Semi-automatic; 223; 10-shot magazine; 18-inch, 1-1/4-inch diameter, stainless barrel with 1:8-inch twist; 34-3/8-inch overall length; weighs 9-1/4 lbs.; sights optional; one-piece international-style upper receiver; NM trigger; free-floating barrel; receiver hard-coat anodized; black composition stock; integral raised M16A2-type fence around magazine release button; A2-style forward assist. Made in U.S. by Eagle Arms, Inc. Introduced 1995.

Perf: $800 **Exc:** $700 **VGood:** $500

EAGLE ARMS EA-15A3 EAGLE EYE

Same specs as EA-15 except 24-inch, 1-1/4-inch diameter, stainless, air-gauged, free-floating heavy match barrel; weighted buttstock to counterbalance barrel; match-type hand-stop on handguard; 42-1/2-inch overall length; weighs about 13 lbs. Match sights available on special order. Made in U.S. by Eagle Arms, Inc. Introduced 1994; no longer in production.

Perf: $800 **Exc:** $700 **VGood:** $500

EAGLE ARMS M15A3 S.P.R.

Same specs as M15A3 Predator except 18-inch barrel with 1:9-inch twist and front sight housing. Detachable carry handle. Made in U.S. by Eagle Arms, Inc. Introduced 1995; no longer produced.

Perf: $1100 **Exc:** $850 **VGood:** $595

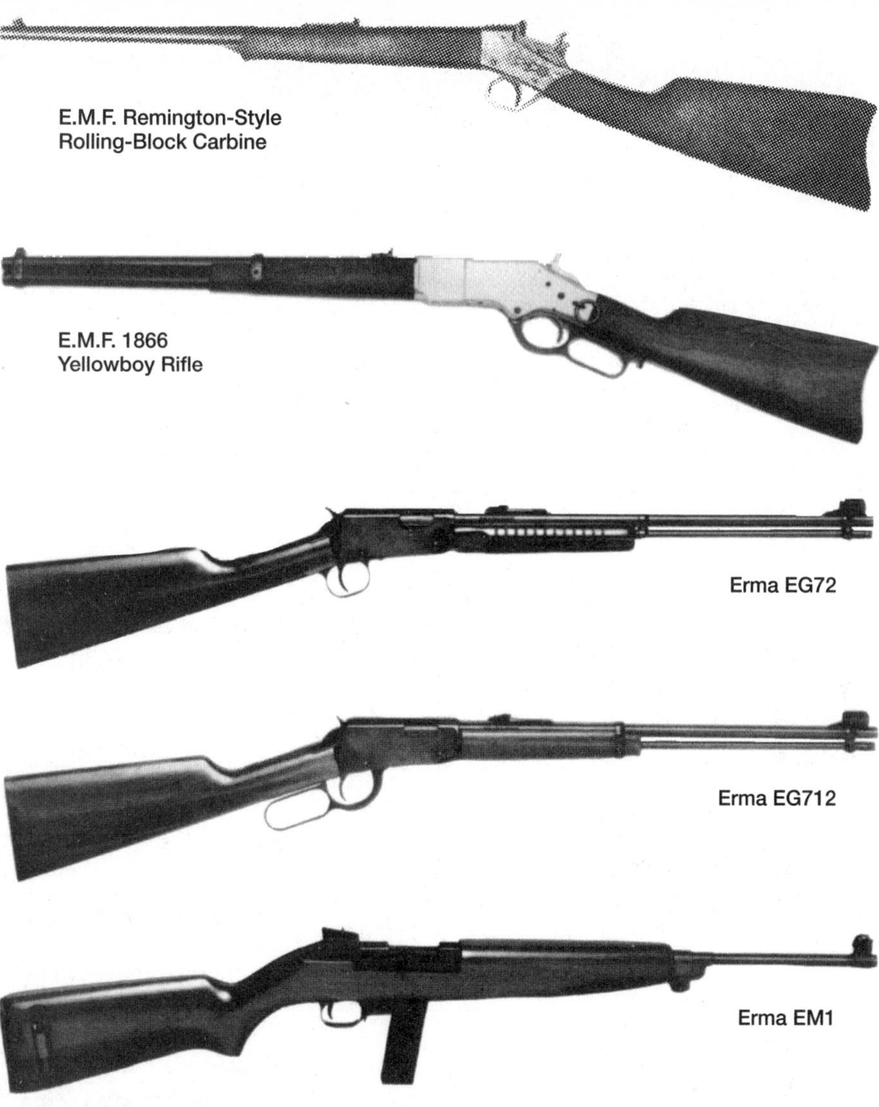
E.M.F. Remington-Style Rolling-Block Carbine

E.M.F. 1866 Yellowboy Rifle

Erma EG72

Erma EG712

Erma EM1

E.M.F. 1860 HENRY

Lever action; 44-40, 44 rimfire; 24-1/4-inch barrel; 43-3/4-inch overall length; weighs about 9 lbs.; blade front sight, elevation-adjustable rear; oil-stained American walnut stock; reproduction of the original Henry rifle with brass frame and buttplate, rest blued. Imported by E.M.F.

Perf: $895 **Exc:** $695 **VGood:** $595

E.M.F. 1866 YELLOWBOY RIFLE

Lever action; 38 Spl., 44-40; 24-inch barrel; 43-inch overall length; weighs 9 lbs.; bead front sight, open adjustable rear; European walnut stock; solid brass frame; blued barrel, lever, hammer, buttplate. Imported from Italy by E.M.F.

Perf: $795 **Exc:** $695 **VGood:** $495

E.M.F. 1866 YELLOW BOY CARBINE

Same specs as 1866 Yellow Boy Rifle except 19-inch barrel; 38-inch overall length. Imported from Italy by E.M.F.

Perf: $795 **Exc:** $695 **VGood:** $495

E.M.F. MODEL 1873 RIFLE

Lever action; 357 Mag., 44-40, 45 Colt; 24-inch barrel; 43-1/4-inch overall length; weighs 8 lbs.; bead front sight, fully-adjustable rear; European walnut stock; color case-hardened frame. Imported by E.M.F.

Perf: $950 **Exc:** $850 **VGood:** $695

E.M.F. MODEL 1873 CARBINE

Same specs as Model 1873 Rifle except 19-inch barrel; blued frame. Imported by E.M.F.

Perf: $950 **Exc:** $850 **VGood:** $695

E.M.F. PREMIER MODEL 1873 CARBINE/RIFLE

Lever action; 45 Colt; 19-inch barrel (carbine), 24-1/2-inch barrel (rifle); 43-1/4-inch overall length; bead front, adjustable rear sight; uncheckered walnut stock, forearm; color case-hardened frame (rifle) or blued frame (carbine). Introduced 1988; discontinued 1989.

Rifle

Perf: $1000 **Exc:** $950 **VGood:** $695

Carbine

Perf: $1000 **Exc:** $950 **VGood:** $695

E.M.F. MODEL 1892 RIFLE

Lever action; 45 Colt, 44 Mag, 44-40, 357 Mag; 24-inch barrel, blued, round or octagon; case-colored frame. Introduced 1998.

Perf: $500 **Exc:** $425 **VGood:** $375

E.M.F MODEL 1892 CARBINE

Similar to Model 1892 rifle, except 20-inch barrel, carbine bands.

Perf: $500 **Exc:** $425 **VGood:** $375

E.M.F. REMINGTON-STYLE ROLLING-BLOCK RIFLE

Single shot; rolling block; 45-70; 30-inch octagon barrel; 46-1/2-inch OAL; weighs 11-3/4 lbs.; blade front, adjustable rear sights; walnut stock and forearm; color case-hardened receiver, brass trigger guard, buttplate and barrel band; blued barrel. Imported from Italy by E.M.F., still imported.

Perf: $575 **Exc:** $450 **VGood:** $350

E.M.F. REMINGTON-STYLE ROLLING-BLOCK CARBINE

Similar to Rolling-block rifle, except carbine with 26-inch barrel.

Perf: $500 **Exc:** $400 **VGood:** $300

E.M.F. SHARPS RIFLE

Single shot; falling block; 45-70; 28-inch octagonal barrel; weighs 10-3/4 lbs.; blade front sight, flip-up open rear; oiled walnut stock; color case-hardened lock; double-set trigger; blue finish. Replica of the 1874 Sharps Sporting rifle. Imported by E.M.F.

Perf: $950 **Exc:** $795 **VGood:** $695

With browned finish

Perf: $975 **Exc:** $825 **VGood:** $715

E.M.F. SHARPS CARBINE

Same specs as Sharps Rifle except has 22-inch round barrel; barrel band. Imported by E.M.F.

Perf: $895 **Exc:** $695 **VGood:** $595

E.M.F. TEXAS REMINGTON REVOLVING CARBINE

Single action; 22 LR; 6-shot cylinder; 21-inch barrel; 36-inch overall length; blade front sight, windage-adjustable rear; smooth walnut stock; brass frame, buttplate, trigger guard; blued cylinder, barrel. Made in Italy. Introduced 1991; no longer imported.

Perf: $300 **Exc:** $375 **VGood:** $250

ERMA EG72

Slide action; 22 LR; 15-shot magazine; 18-1/2-inch barrel; open rear sight, hooded ramp front; receiver grooved for scope mounts; straight hardwood stock; grooved slide handle; visible hammer. Made in Germany. Introduced 1970; discontinued 1976.

Perf: $150 **Exc:** $110 **VGood:** $90

ERMA EG73

Lever action; 22 WMR; 12-shot tube magazine; 18-1/2-inch barrel; open rear sight, hooded ramp front; receiver grooved for scope mount; European hardwood stock, forearm. Originally made in Germany. Introduced 1973; no longer in production.

Perf: $200 **Exc:** $160 **VGood:** $130

ERMA EG712

Lever action; 22 Short, 22 Long, 22 LR.; 21-shot (22 Short), 17-shot (22 Long), 15-shot (22 LR) tubular magazine; 18-1/2-inch barrel; open rear sight, hooded ramp front; carbine-style stock forearm of European hardwood, barrel band; receiver grooved for scope mount; near replica of Model 94 Winchester. Introduced 1976; no longer in production.

Perf: $200 **Exc:** $175 **VGood:** $150

ERMA MODEL EG712 L

Same specs as EG712 except European walnut stock; heavy octagon barrel; engraved, nickel silver finished receiver. Introduced 1978; no longer imported.

Perf: $300 **Exc:** $250 **VGood:** $200

ERMA EGM1

Semi-automatic; 22 LR; 5-shot magazine; 18-inch barrel; M-1-type sights with ramp front; receiver grooved for scope mounts; European walnut M-1 carbine-type stock; sling swivels; patterned after U.S. Cal. 30 M-1 Carbine. Introduced 1970; no longer imported.

Perf: $190 **Exc:** $160 **VGood:** $120

ERMA EM1

Semi-automatic; 22 LR; 10-, 15-shot magazine; 18-inch barrel; M1-type sights; receiver grooved for scope mounts; European walnut M1 Carbine-type stock; sling swivel in barrel band, oiler slot in stock; patterned after U.S. Cal. 30 M-1 Carbine. Introduced 1966; no longer imported.

Perf: $265 **Exc:** $245 **VGood:** $165

ERMA ESG22 CARBINE

Semi-automatic; 22 WMR; 5-, 12-shot magazine; 19-inch barrel; 38-inch overall length; military post front sight, adjustable peep rear; walnut stained beechwood stock; receiver grooved for scope mounts; gas-operated; styled after M-1 carbine. Made in Germany. Introduced 1978; no longer imported.

Perf: $275 **Exc:** $225 **VGood:** $175

FAJEN ACRA M-18

Bolt action; 270, 30-06, 243, 308, 284, 22-250, 6mm, 25-06, 7x57, 257 Roberts; 18-inch barrel; no sights; full-length Mannlicher-style stock; glass-bedded stock; rosewood pistol grip cap, forend tip; Santa Barbara Mauser action; recoil pad; blued finish. Introduced 1969; discontinued 1973.

Perf: $595 **Exc:** $495 **VGood:** $395

FAJEN ACRA RA

Bolt action; 270, 30-06, 243, 308, 284, 22-250, 6mm, 25-06, 7x57, 257 Roberts; 24-inch barrel; no sights; Monte Carlo stock of American walnut; glass-bedded stock; tenite buttplate, pistol-grip cap, forend tip; recoil pad; blued finish.

Perf: $495 **Exc:** $395 **VGood:** $325

FAJEN ACRA S-24

Bolt action; 270, 30-06, 243, 308, 284, 22-250, 6mm, 25-06, 7x57, 257 Roberts, 7mm Rem. Mag., 308 Norma Mag., 300 Win. Mag., 264 Win. Mag.; 24-inch barrel; no sights; checkered Monte Carlo stock of American walnut; recoil pad; glass-bedded stock; Santa Barbara Mauser action; blued finish; rosewood pistol-grip cap, forend tip. Introduced 1969; discontinued 1973.

Perf: $495 **Exc:** $420 **VGood:** $330

FAJEN ACRA VARMINT

Bolt action; 270, 30-06, 243, 308, 284, 22-250, 6mm, 25-06, 7x57, 257 Roberts, 7mm Rem. Mag., 308 Norma Mag., 300 Win. Mag., 264 Win. Mag.; 26-inch heavy barrel; no sights; checkered Monte Carlo stock of American walnut; glass-bedded stock; rosewood pistol grip cap, forend tip; recoil pad; blued finish. Introduced 1969; discontinued 1973.

Perf: $495 **Exc:** $395 **VGood:** $295

FEATHER AT-9 CARBINE

Semi-automatic; 9mm Para.; 17-inch barrel; 35-inch overall length (stock extended), 26-1/2-inch (stock closed); weighs 5 lbs.; hooded post front sight, adjustable aperture rear; telescoping wire stock, composition pistol grip; matte black finish. Made in U.S. by Feather Industries. Introduced 1988; no longer produced.

Perf: $325 **Exc:** $265 **VGood:** $200

FEATHER AT-22 CARBINE

Semi-automatic; 22 LR; 20-shot magazine; 17-inch barrel; 35-inch overall (stock extended), 26-inch (folded); weighs 3-1/4 lbs.; protected post front sight, adjustable aperture rear; telescoping wire stock, composition pistol grip; removable barrel; matte black finish. Made in U.S. by Feather Industries. Introduced 1986; still produced.

Perf: $210 **Exc:** $175 **VGood:** $130

FEATHER MODEL F2 CARBINE

Semi-automatic; 22 LR; 20-shot magazine; 17-inch barrel; 35-inch overall (stock extended); weighs 3-1/4 lbs.; protected post front sight, adjustable aperture rear; composition stock and pistol grip; removable barrel; matte black finish. Made in U.S. by Feather Industries. Introduced 1986; no longer produced.

Perf: $240 **Exc:** $200 **VGood:** $150

FEATHER MODEL F9 CARBINE

Semi-automatic; 9mm Para.; 17-inch barrel; 35-inch overall length; weighs 5 lbs.; hooded post front sight, adjustable aperture rear; composition stock and pistol grip; matte black finish. Made in U.S. by Feather Industries. Introduced 1988; no longer produced.

Perf: $525 **Exc:** $450 **VGood:** $325

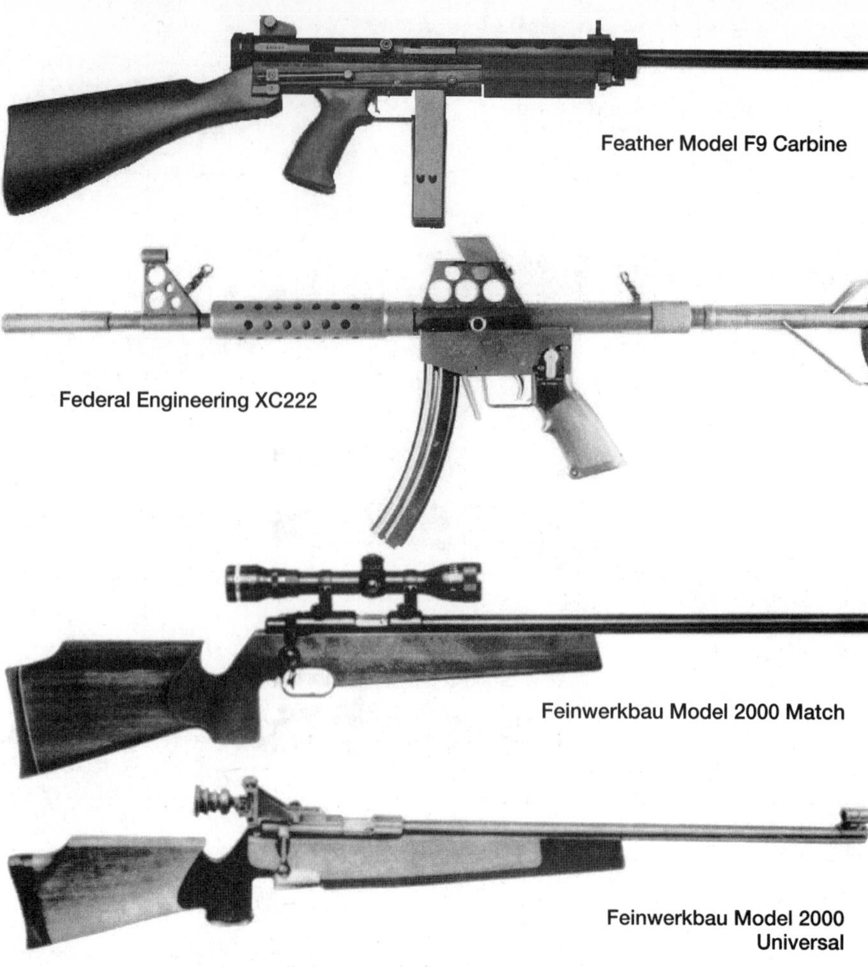

Feather Model F9 Carbine

Federal Engineering XC222

Feinwerkbau Model 2000 Match

Feinwerkbau Model 2000 Universal

FEDERAL ENGINEERING XC222

Semi-automatic; 22 LR; 30-shot magazine; 16-1/2-inch barrel with flash hider; 34-1/2-inch overall length; weighs 7-1/4 lbs.; hooded post front sight, Williams adjustable rear; sight bridge grooved for scope mounting; quick-detachable tube steel stock; quick takedown; all-steel Heli-arc welded construction; internal parts industrial hard chromed. Made in U.S. by Federal Engineering Corp. Introduced 1993; no longer produced.

Perf: $380 **Exc:** $320 **VGood:** $250

FEDERAL ENGINEERING XC450

Semi-automatic; 45 ACP; 16-shot magazine; 16-1/2-inch barrel with flash hider; 34-1/2-inch overall length; weighs 8 lbs.; hooded post front sight, Williams adjustable rear; sight bridge grooved for scope mounting; quick-detachable tube steel stock; quick takedown; all-steel Heli-arc welded construction; internal parts industrial hard chromed. Made in U.S. by Federal Engineering Corp. Introduced 1984; dropped 1994.

Perf: $650 **Exc:** $535 **VGood:** $450

FEDERAL ENGINEERING XC900

Semi-automatic; 9mm Para.; 32-shot magazine; 16-1/2-inch barrel with flash hider; 34-1/2-inch overall length; weighs 8 lbs.; hooded post front sight, Williams adjustable rear; sight bridge grooved for scope mounting; quick-detachable tube steel stock; quick takedown; all-steel Heli-arc welded construction; internal parts industrial hard chromed. Made in U.S. by Federal Engineering Corp. Introduced 1984; dropped 1994.

Perf: $550 **Exc:** $435 **VGood:** $350

FEDERAL ORDNANCE M14SA TARGET

Semi-automatic; 7.62mm NATO; 20-shot magazine; 22-inch barrel; 48-inch overall length; weighs 9-1/2 lbs.; fully-adjustable G.I.-issue sights; fiberglass or wood stock; Parkerized metal finish. Civilian version of the M-14 service rifle. From Federal Ordnance. Introduced 1988; dropped 1992.

With fiberglass or black textured stock

Perf: $1050 **Exc:** $825 **VGood:** $650

With walnut stock, forend

Perf: $1200 **Exc:** $975 **VGood:** $795

FEDERAL ORDNANCE MODEL 713 MAUSER CARBINE, DELUXE GRADE

Semi-automatic; 7.63 Mauser, 9mm Para.; 10-, 20-shot detachable magazine; 16-inch barrel; weighs 5 lbs.; adjustable sights; deluxe walnut detachable stock. Introduced 1986; discontinued 1992.

Perf: $1695 **Exc:** $1250 **VGood:** $950

FEDERAL ORDNANCE MODEL 713 MAUSER CARBINE, FIELD GRADE

Same specs as Model 713 Mauser Carbine except 10-shot fixed magazine; walnut fixed stock. Introduced, 1987; discontinued 1992.

Perf: $1050 **Exc:** $795 **VGood:** $595

FEG SA-85M

Semi-automatic; AK STYLE; 7.62x39mm; 6-shot magazine; 16-3/8-inch barrel; 34-3/4-inch overall length; weighs 7-5/8 lbs.; hardwood handguard and thumbhole buttstock; cylindrical post front sight, fully-adjustable tangent rear; matte finish; chrome-

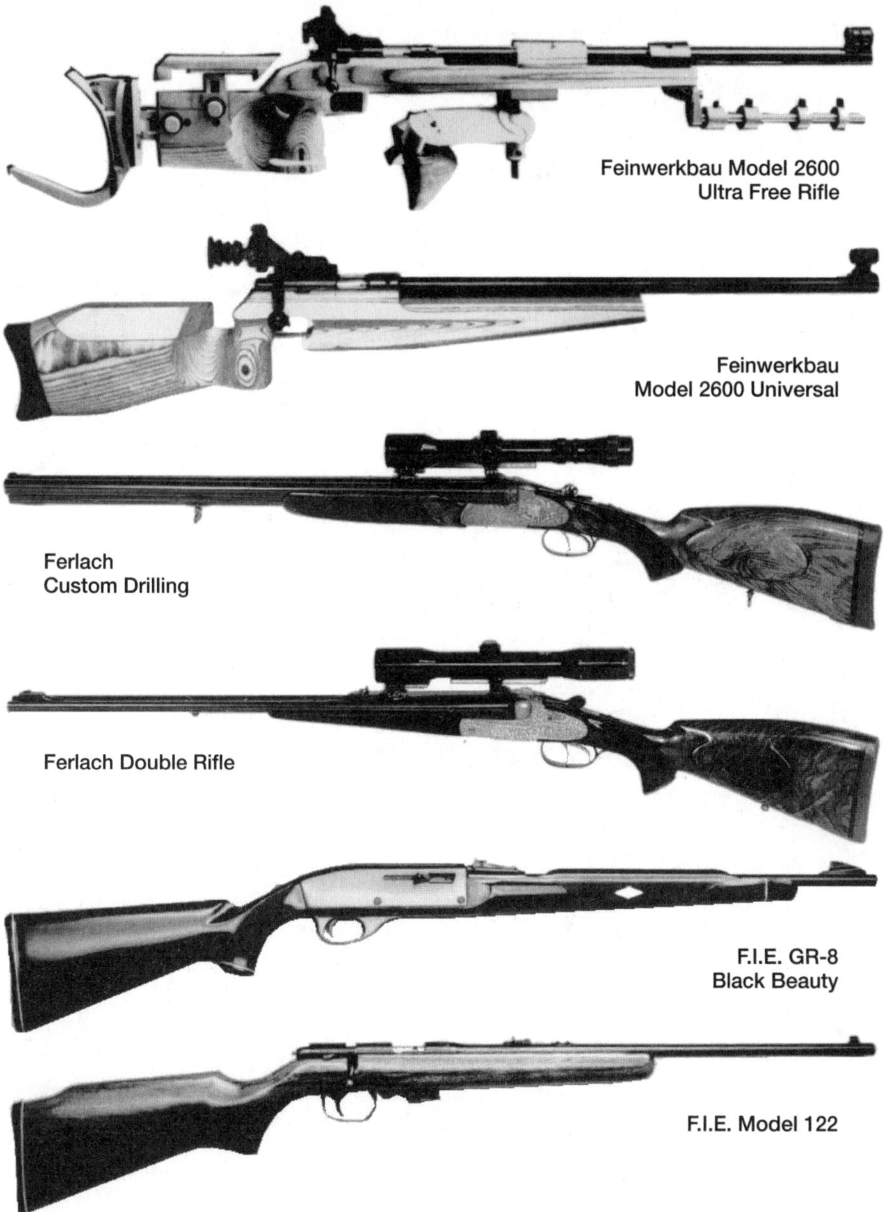
Feinwerkbau Model 2600 Ultra Free Rifle

Feinwerkbau Model 2600 Universal

Ferlach Custom Drilling

Ferlach Double Rifle

F.I.E. GR-8 Black Beauty

F.I.E. Model 122

lined barrel. Imported from Hungary by K.B.I., Inc. No longer imported.

Perf: $775 **Exc:** $600 **VGood:** $550

FEINWERKBAU MODEL 2000 MATCH

Bolt action; single shot; 22 LR; 26-1/4-inch barrel; 43-3/4-inch overall length; weighs 8-3/4 lbs.; micrometer match aperture rear sight, globe front with interchangeable inserts; standard walnut match stock; stippled pistol grip, forend; electronic or mechanical trigger. Made in Germany. Introduced 1979; discontinued 1988.

Perf: $995 **Exc:** $895 **VGood:** $695

With electronic trigger

Perf: $1250 **Exc:** $1095 **VGood:** $895

Left-hand version

Perf: $1095 **Exc:** $995 **VGood:** $795

FEINWERKBAU MODEL 2000 METALLIC SILHOUETTE

Bolt action; single-shot; 22 LR; 21-13/16-inch barrel; 39-inch overall length; weighs 6-1/2 lbs.; no sights; grooved for standard mounts; thumbhole walnut match stock; stippled pistol grip; fully-adjustable match trigger; heavy bull barrel. Made in Germany. Introduced 1985; no longer imported.

Perf: $695 **Exc:** $595 **VGood:** $450

Left-hand version

Perf: $725 **Exc:** $615 **VGood:** $450

FEINWERKBAU MODEL 2000 MINI-MATCH

Bolt action; single shot; 22 LR; 22-inch barrel; walnut-stained birchwood match stock; stippled pistol grip; micrometer match aperture rear sight, globe front with interchangeable inserts; electronic or mechanical trigger. Made in Germany. Introduced 1979; discontinued 1988.

Perf: $1000 **Exc:** $750 **VGood:** $595

With electronic trigger

Perf: $1350 **Exc:** $995 **VGood:** $695

Left-hand version

Perf: $1150 **Exc:** $795 **VGood:** $595

FEINWERKBAU MODEL 2000 UNIVERSAL

Bolt action; single shot; 22 LR; 26-3/8-inch barrel; weighs 9-3/4 lbs.; standard walnut stock; stippled pistol grip, forend; micrometer match aperture rear sight, globe front with interchangeable inserts; electronic or mechanical trigger. Made in Germany. Introduced 1979; discontinued 1988.

Perf: $1250 **Exc:** $995 **VGood:** $795

With electronic trigger

Perf: $1400 **Exc:** $1195 **VGood:** $1000

Left-hand version

Perf: $1300 **Exc:** $1100 **VGood:** $900

FEINWERKBAU MODEL 2600 ULTRA FREE RIFLE

Bolt action; single-shot; 22 LR; 26-inch barrel; 40-7/16-inch overall length; weighs 14 lbs.; micrometer match aperture rear sight, globe front with interchangeable inserts; laminated wood thumbhole stock; electronic or mechanical trigger; accessory rails for movable weights; adjustable cheekpiece; hooked buttplate; right- or left-hand styles. Made in Germany. Introduced 1983; discontinued 1988.

Perf: $1795 **Exc:** $1295 **VGood:** $795

With electronic trigger

Perf: $1995 **Exc:** $1395 **VGood:** $1895

Left-hand version

Perf: $1795 **Exc:** $1395 **VGood:** $800

FEINWERKBAU MODEL 2600 UNIVERSAL

Single shot; 22 LR; 26-5/16-inch barrel; 43-3/4-inch overall length; weighs 10-1/2 lbs.; identical smallbore companion to the Model 600 air rifle; micrometer match aperture rear sight, globe front with interchangeable inserts; laminated European hardwood stock; free-floating barrel; match trigger with fingertip weight adjustment dial. Made in Germany. Introduced 1986; no longer imported.

Perf: $1395 **Exc:** $995 **VGood:** $750

Left-hand version

Perf: $1495 **Exc:** $995 **VGood:** $795

FERLACH CUSTOM DRILLING

Combination gun, drilling; Blitz action; various calibers/gauges; custom-built as to barrel length, sights, stock dimensions, wood; Greener crossbolt. Manufactured in Ferlach, Austria. Introduced 1976; no longer imported by Adler Arms of Pittsburgh. Because of the variety of grades and features, it is impossible to attribute used values. Have the rifle appraised by someone experienced and aware of quality in craftsmanship.

FERLACH DOUBLE RIFLE

Side-by-side or over/under; boxlock or sidelock; various calibers; any sighting combo desired; custom stocked; auto ejection. Introduced 1980; no longer imported by Adler Arms of Pittsburgh. Because of the variety of grades and features, it is impossible to attribute used values. Have the rifle appraised by someone experienced and aware of quality in craftsmanship.

F.I.E. GR-8 BLACK BEAUTY

Semi-automatic; 22 LR; 14-shot magazine; 19-1/2-inch barrel; 39-1/2-inch overall length; weighs 4 lbs.; adjustable open rear sight, band on ramp front; molded black nylon stock; checkered pistol grip, forend; top tang safety; receiver grooved for tip-off scope mounts. Similar to Remington Nylon 66 rifle. Made in Brazil. Introduced 1984; discontinued 1988.

Perf: $190 **Exc:** $170 **VGood:** $160

F.I.E. MODEL 122

Bolt action; 22 Short, 22 Long, 22 LR; 6- or 10-shot magazine; 21-inch barrel; 39-inch overall length; weighs 5-1/2 lbs.; fully-adjustable open rear sight, blade front; receiver grooved for scope mounts; Monte Carlo walnut stock; sliding wing safety lever; double extractors; red cocking indicator. Made in Brazil. Introduced 1986; discontinued 1988.

Perf: $100 **Exc:** $75 **VGood:** $65

F.I.E. MODEL 322

Bolt action; 22 Short, 22 Long, 22 LR; 6-, 10-shot magazine; 26-1/2-inch barrel; weighs 7 lbs.; adjustable sights; checkered wood stock; adjustable trigger. Introduced 1990; discontinued 1990.

Perf: $475 **Exc:** $350 **VGood:** $265

F.I.E. MODEL 422

Bolt action; 22 Short, 22 Long, 22 LR; 6-, 10-shot magazine; 26-1/2-inch heavy barrel; weighs 9 lbs.; adjustable sights; checkered wood stock; adjustable trigger. Introduced 1990; discontinued 1990.

Perf: $475 **Exc:** $375 **VGood:** $285

F.I.E./FRANCHI PARA CARBINE

Semi-automatic; 22 LR; 11-shot magazine; 19-inch barrel; 39-1/4-inch overall length; weighs 4-3/4 lbs.; open adjustable rear sight, hooded front; takedown; receiver grooved for scope mounts; magazine feeds through skeleton stock. Marketed in fitted carrying case. Made in Italy. Introduced 1986; discontinued 1988.

Perf: $210 **Exc:** $170 **VGood:** $120

FINNISH LION CHAMPION MODEL

Bolt action; single shot; 22 LR; 28-3/4-inch barrel; free rifle design; extension-type rear peep sight, aperture front; European walnut stock; full pistol grip; beavertail forearm; thumbhole, palm rest, hand stop; hooked buttplate. Introduced 1965; discontinued 1972.

Perf: $700 **Exc:** $600 **VGood:** $500

FINNISH LION ISU TARGET MODEL

Bolt action; single shot; 22 LR; 27-1/2-inch barrel; extension-type rear peep sight, aperture front; European walnut target-design stock; hand-checkered beavertail forearm; full pistol grip; adjustable buttplate; swivel. Manufactured in Finland. Introduced 1966; discontinued 1977.

Perf: $400 **Exc:** $300 **VGood:** $250

FINNISH LION MATCH MODEL

Bolt action; single shot; 22 LR; 29-inch barrel; weight 14.3 lbs; extension-type rear peep sight, aperture front; European walnut free rifle-type stock; full pistol grip; beavertail forearm; thumbhole, palm rest, hand stop; hooked buttplate, swivel. Introduced 1937; discontinued 1972.

Perf: $595 **Exc:** $495 **VGood:** $395

FINNISH LION STANDARD TARGET MODEL

Bolt action; single shot; 22 LR; 27-5/8-inch barrel; 44-9/16-inch overall length; weighs 10-1/2 lbs.; aperture sights; French walnut target stock; adjustable trigger; many accessories available. Made in Finland. Introduced 1978; imported by Mandall Shooting Supplies.

Perf: $675 **Exc:** $575 **VGood:** $410

F.N. DELUXE MAUSER

Bolt action; 220 Swift, 243 Win., 244 Rem., 257 Roberts, 250-3000, 270 Win., 7mm, 300 Savage, 308 Win., 30-06, 8mm, 9.3x62, 9.5x57, 10.75x68; 5-shot box magazine; 24-inch barrel; Tri-range rear, hooded ramp front sight; hand-checkered European walnut stock, pistol-grip; cheekpiece; sling swivels. Manufactured in Belgium. Introduced 1947; discontinued 1963.

Exc: $700 **VGood:** $500 **Good:** $400

F.N. DELUXE MAUSER, PRESENTATION GRADE

Same specs as Deluxe Mauser except engraved receiver, trigger guard, barrel breech, floorplate; select walnut stock. Introduced 1947; discontinued 1963.

Exc: $995 **VGood:** $875 **Good:** $650

F.N. SUPREME MAUSER

Bolt action; 243 Win., 270 Win., 7mm, 308 Win., 30-06; 5-shot magazine, 4-shot (243 and 308); 22-inch barrel; Tri-range rear, hooded ramp front sight; hand-checkered European walnut stock; pistol grip; Monte Carlo cheekpiece, sling swivels. Introduced 1957; discontinued 1975.

Exc: $750 **VGood:** $650 **Good:** $520

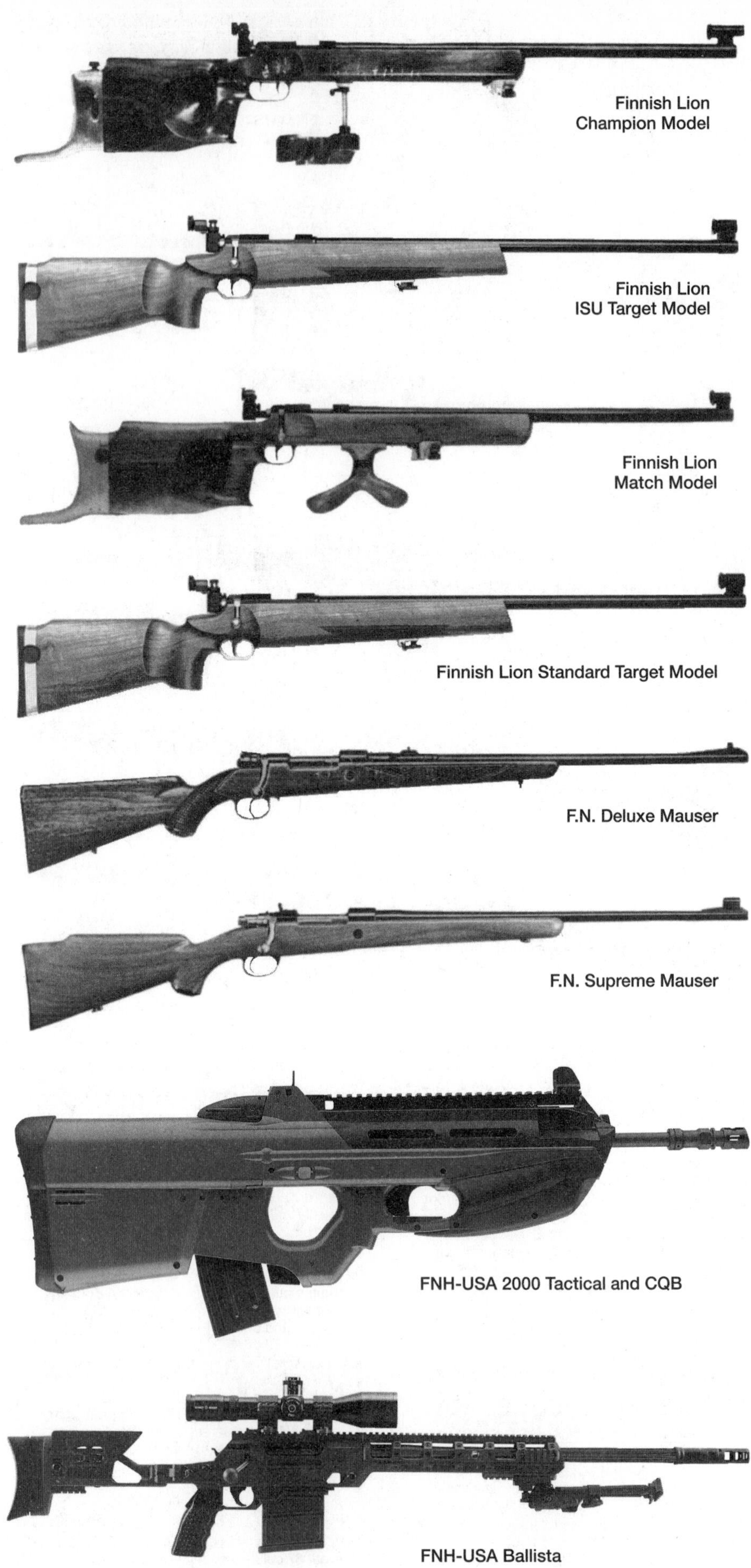

Finnish Lion Champion Model

Finnish Lion ISU Target Model

Finnish Lion Match Model

Finnish Lion Standard Target Model

F.N. Deluxe Mauser

F.N. Supreme Mauser

FNH-USA 2000 Tactical and CQB

FNH-USA Ballista

FNH-USA AR Standard and Heavy

FNH-USA PS90

FNH-USA SCAR 16S and 17S

FNH-USA SPR A1, A1A, A3G and A5M

FNH-USA TSR XP and TSR XP USA

Fox Model FB-1

F.N. SUPREME MAUSER, MAGNUM MODEL

Same specs as Supreme Mauser except 264 Win. Mag., 7mm Rem. Mag., 300 Win. Mag.; 3-shot magazine. Introduced 1957; discontinued 1973.

Perf: $800 **Exc:** $695 **VGood:** $575

FNH-USA 2000 TACTICAL AND CQB

Semi-automatic bull-pup center-fire rifle with a black or OD polymer thumbhole stock, folding sights and optics rail, and ambidextrous operating controls. Chambered in 5.56x45mm NATO/223 Remington. 17.44 inch barrel, 29.29 OA length and weighs 7.58 pounds. 10 and 30 round capacity magazine. Introduced 2001.

Perf: $2,779

FNH-USA AR STANDARD AND HEAVY

Semi-automatic center-fire rifle with a blued finish, aluminum alloy receiver, synthetic tactical stock, fluted barrel and optics rail. Chambered in .308 Winchester/7.62x51mm NATO. Barrel length from 16 to 20 inches, OA length 37.5 to 41.5 inches, and weighs 8.125 pounds. 10 and 20 round capacity detachable box magazine. Introduced 2008.

Perf: $1,500 **Exc:** $1,300 **VGood:** $1,100

FNH-USA BALLISTA

Modular, multi-caliber bolt-action rifle with aluminum alloy receiver, adjustable trigger, fluted barrel, ambidextrous folding stock and optics rail. Chambered in .338 Lapua Mag., .300 Win. Mag. and .308 Win. Barrel length from 24 to 26 inches, OA length 37 collapsed to 40 inches extended, and weighs 15 pounds. 5-15 round capacity box magazine. Introduced 2012.

Perf: $6,250 **Exc:** $5,700 **VGood:** $5,000

FNH-USA PS90

Semi-automatic bull-pup center-fire rifle with a black or OD polymer thumbhole stock, fixed sights and optics rail, and ambidextrous operating controls. Chambered in 5.7x28mm. 16.04 inch barrel, 26.23 OA length and weighs 6.28 to 8 pounds. 10 and 30 round capacity magazine. Introduced 1990.

Perf: $1,449

FNH-USA SCAR 16S AND 17S

Semi-automatic center-fire rifle with a black or FDE finish, hard anodized aluminum receiver, telescoping side-folding polymer stock, integrated optics rail, and ambidextrous operating controls. Chambered in .223 Remngton/5.56x45mm NATO and .308 Winchester/7.62x51mm NATO. 16.25 inch barrel, 27.5 to 38.5 OA length and weighs 7.25 to 8 pounds. 10 and 30 round capacity box magazine. Introduced 2009.

Perf: $3,000 **Exc:** $2,300 **VGood:** $1,950

FNH-USA SPR A1, A1A, A3G AND A5M

Bolt action center-fire rifle with a blued finish, McMillan fiberglass tactical stocks and standard optics rail. Standard and fluted barrels. Chambered in .308 Winchester and .300 WSM (SPR A5M). Barrel length from 20 to 24 inches, OA length 40 to 44 inches, and weight from 11.5 to 11.875 pounds. 4 round capacity with detachable box magazine, 5 round capacity with hinged floorplate. Introduced 2002.

Perf: $3,000 **Exc:** $2,600 **VGood:** $2,200

(SPR A5M)

Perf: $1,850 **Exc:** $1,600 **VGood:** $1,400

FNH-USA TSR XP AND TSR XP USA

Bolt action center-fire rifle with a blued finish, FN/Hogue synthetic stock, standard optics rail and fluted barrel. Chambered in .223 Remington (USA Model) .308 Winchester and .300 WSM. Barrel length from 20 to 24 inches, OA length 40.5 to 44.5 inches, and weight from 8.7 to 10.1 pounds. 6 round capacity in .223 Rem with hinged floorplate, 4 round capacity with detachable box magazine, 3 round capacity (.300 WSM) with hinged floorplate. Introduced 2009.

Perf: $1,150 **Exc:** $1,050 **VGood:** $950

FORBES RIFLE MODEL 24B

Bolt action; .25-06 Rem., .270 Win., .30-06 Sprg. Production version of the New Ultra Light Arms model 24 with a 24"; button-rifled, chrome-moly barrel, Timney Trigger, blind box magazine, two-position three-function safety, hand-laid, Kevlar/carbon fiber stock with a LOP of 13.50. Length 43.75", weight 5.25 lbs. Matte metal finish with Talley 1-piece scope mounts. RH or LH. Stainless steel an option. New for 2012. Add $100 for stainless steel and / or left hand

Perf: $1350 **Exc:** $1200 **VGood:** $1100

FOX MODEL FB-1

Bolt action; 22 LR; 5-shot clip; 24-inch barrel; 43-inch overall length; hooded ramp front, adjustable open rear sight; select walnut stock; palm swell grip, roll-over cheekpiece; rosewood pistol grip cap, forend tip; receiver grooved for tipoff scope mount; also drilled, tapped; double extractors. Marketed by Savage Arms. Introduced 1981; discontinued 1983.

Perf: $250 **Exc:** $175 **VGood:** $130

FRANCOTTE, AUGUSTE

Francotte rifles are custom made to the customer's specifications. Because of the individuality of rifles encountered used, values will fluctuate greatly within models. Options such as engraving, inlays, sights, wood and caliber will determine each rifle's worth. An individual expert appraisal is recommended. Priced new from $15,000 to

$40,000. Used values range from 50 percent to 75 percent of new pricing.

FRANCOTTE BOXLOCK DOUBLE

Side-by-side; 243, 270, 30-06, 7x64, 7x65R, 8x57JRS, 9.3x74R, 375 H&H, 470 N.E.; 23-1/2-inch-26-inch barrel lengths; bead front sight on ramp, quarter-rib with fixed V rear; primarily custom-built gun; oil-finished European walnut stock; checkered butt; double triggers; manual safety; floating firing pins; gas-vent safety screws; coin finish or color case-hardening; English scroll engraving; numerous options. Made in Belgium. Still imported by Armes de Chasse.

FRANCOTTE CARPATHE MOUNTAIN

Single shot; 243, 270, 308, 30-06, 7x65R, 7x57R, 5.6x52R, 5.6x57R, 6.5x57R. 6.5x68R, 7mm Rem. Mag., 300 Win. Mag.; 23-1/2-inch-26-inch barrel; no sights furnished; scope mount extra; deluxe walnut stock to customer specs; oil finish, fine checkering; boxlock or sidelock action with third fastener, extractor, manual safety; splinter forend. Many options available. Imported from Belgium by Armes de Chasse. No longer imported.

FRANCOTTE RIMAG

Bolt action; 358 Norma Mag., 375 H&H, 378 Wea. Mag., 404 Jeffery, 416 Rigby, 450 Watts, 460 Wea. Mag., 458 Win. Mag., 505 Gibbs, others on request; heavy round barrel, 23-5/8-inch to 26-inch; weighs 9 to 10 lbs.; ring-mounted front sight blade, fixed leaf rear; deluxe European walnut stock to customer specifications, oil finish, steel grip cap; A. Francotte Rimag action with three-position safety, round or square bridge. Imported from Belgium by Armes de Chasse. No longer imported.

FRANCOTTE SIDELOCK DOUBLE

Side-by-side; 243, 7x64, 7x65R, 8x57JRS, 270, 30-06, 9.3x74R, 375 H&H, 470 N.E.; 23-1/2-inch to 26-inch barrel lengths; weighs 7-5/8 lbs. (medium calibers), 11 lbs. (magnums); bead front sight on ramp, leaf rear on quarter-rib; hand-checkered, oil-finished European walnut stock; back-action sidelocks; double trigger, with hinged front trigger; auto or free safety; numerous options; largely a custom-built gun. Made in Belgium. Still imported by Armes de Chasse.

GALIL SPORTER

Semi-automatic; 223, 308; 5-shot magazine; 16-1/8-inch barrel (223), 18-1/2-inch (308); 40-1/2-inch overall length (223); weighs 8-3/4 lbs.; hardwood thumbhole stock; hooded post front, flip-type adjustable rear sight; black-finished wood and metal. Imported by Action Arms Ltd. Introduced 1991; discontinued 1993.

Perf: $1000 **Exc:** $850 **VGood:** $710

GAMBA BAYERN 88

Combo; boxlock over/under; 2-3/4-inch 12 ga. over 5.6x50R, 5.6x57R, 6.5x57R, 7x57R, 7x65R, 222 Rem. Mag., 243, 270, 30-06; 24-1/2-inch barrels; modified choke; weighs 7-1/2 lbs.; folding leaf rear sight, bead front on ramp; checkered European walnut stock; double-set trigger; case-hardened receiver; game, floral scene engraving; extractors; solid barrel rib. Made in Italy. Introduced 1987; no longer imported.

Perf: $1395 **Exc:** $995 **VGood:** $795

GAMBA MUSTANG

Single shot; sidelock; 5.6x50, 5.6x57R, 6.5x57R, 7x65R, 222 Rem. Mag., 243, 270, 30-06; 25-1/2-inch barrel; weighs 6-1/4 lbs.; leaf rear sight, bead on ramp front; hand-checkered, oil-finished figured European walnut stock; double-set trigger; silvered receiver; Renaissance engraving signed by engraver; claw-type scope mounts. Made in Italy. Introduced 1987; no longer in production.

Perf: $10,500 **Exc:** $8950 **VGood:** $6500

Garcia Musketeer

Golden Eagle Model 7000 Grade 1

Grendel R-31 Carbine

Hammerli Model 45 Match

Hammerli Model 503 Free Rifle

GAMBA RGZ 1000

Bolt action; 270, 7x64, 7mm Rem. Mag., 300 Win. Mag.; 20-1/2-inch barrel; weighs 7 lbs.; open notch ramp rear sight bead front; Monte Carlo-style European walnut stock; modified 98K Mauser action; single trigger. Introduced 1987; discontinued 1988.

Perf: $1100 **Exc:** $900 **VGood:** $720

GAMBA RGZ 1000 GAME

Same specs as RGZ 1000 except 23-3/4-inch barrel; 7-3/4 lbs.; double-set trigger.

Perf: $1195 **Exc:** $995 **VGood:** $795

GAMBA SAFARI EXPRESS

Double rifle; boxlock side-by-side; 7x65R, 9.3x74R, 375 H&H Mag.; 25-inch barrels; weighs about 10 lbs.; leaf rear sight, bead on ramp front; checkered select European walnut stock; cheekpiece; rubber recoil pad; triple Greener locking system; auto ejectors; double-set triggers; engraved floral, game scenes. Made in Italy. Introduced 1987; no longer imported.

Perf: $5500 **Exc:** $4250 **VGood:** $2595

GARBI EXPRESS DOUBLE RIFLE

Double rifle; 7x65R, 9.3x74R, 375 H&H. 24-3/4-inch barrel; weighs 7-3/4 to 8-1/2 lbs. 41-1/2-inch overall. Turkish walnut stock. Quarter-rib with express sight. Side-by-side double; H&H-pattern sidelock ejector with reinforced action, chopper lump barrels of Boehler steel; double triggers; fine scroll and rosette engraving, or full coverage ornamental; coin-finished action. Introduced 1997. Imported from Spain by Wm. Larkin Moore.

Perf: $19,000 **Exc:** $16,000 **VGood:** $12,000

GARCIA MUSKETEER

Bolt action; 243, 264, 270, 30-06, 308 Win., 308 Norma Mag., 7mm Rem. Mag., 300 Win. Mag.; 3-shot magazine (magnums), 5-shot (standard calibers); 44-1/2-inch overall length; Williams Guide open rear, hooded ramp front sight; checkered walnut Monte Carlo stock, pistol grip; FN Mauser Supreme action; adjustable trigger; sliding thumb safety; hinged floorplate. Introduced 1970; discontinued 1972.

Perf: $595 **Exc:** $495 **VGood:** $375

GARRETT ARMS ROLLING BLOCK

Single shot; 45-70; 30-inch octagon barrel; 48-inch overall length; weighs 9 lbs.; ladder-type tang sight, open folding rear on barrel, hooded globe front; European walnut stock; reproduction of Remington rolling block long-range sporter. Made in Italy. Introduced 1987; no longer imported.

Perf: $595 **Exc:** $475 **VGood:** $350

GEVARM E-1 AUTOLOADING

Semi-automatic; blowback; 22 LR; 10-shot magazine; 19-inch barrel; open sights; walnut stock, pistol grip; blued finish. No longer in production.

Exc: $450 **VGood:** $340 **Good:** $275

GEVARM MODEL A2

Semi-automatic; blowback; 22 LR; 8-shot clip magazine; 21-1/2-inch barrel; takedown; tangent rear, hooded globe front sight; uncheckered walnut stock; schnabel forearm; no firing pin (as such) or extractor; fires from open bolt; ridge on bolt face offers twin ignition. Imported by Tradewinds, Inc. Introduced 1958; discontinued 1963.

Exc: $550 **VGood:** $495 **Good:** $375

GOLDEN EAGLE MODEL 7000 GRADE I

Bolt action; 22-250, 243 Win., 25-06, 270 Win., 270 Weatherby Mag., 7mm Rem. Mag., 30-06, 300 Weatherby Mag., 300 Win. Mag., 338 Win. Mag.; 3-shot magazine, 4-shot (22-250); 24-inch, 26-inch barrel; no sights; checkered American

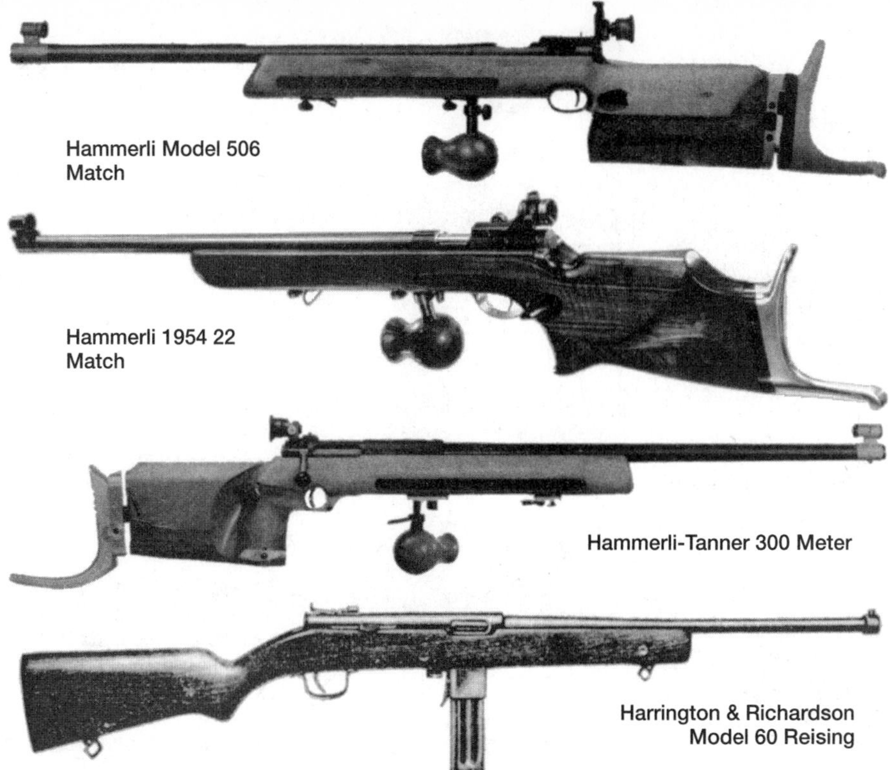
Hammerli Model 506 Match

Hammerli 1954 22 Match

Hammerli-Tanner 300 Meter

Harrington & Richardson Model 60 Reising

walnut stock; contrasting grip cap; forend tip; golden eagle head inset in grip cap; recoil pad. Made in Japan. Introduced 1976; discontinued 1979.

Perf: $610 **Exc:** $495 **VGood:** $385

GOLDEN EAGLE MODEL 7000 GRADE I, AFRICAN

Same specs as Model 7000 Grade I except 375 H&H Mag., 458 Win. Mag.; open sights. Introduced 1976; discontinued 1979.

Perf: $670 **Exc:** $565 **VGood:** $450

GOLDEN EAGLE MODEL 7000 GRADE II

Bolt action; 22-250, 243 Win., 25-06, 270 Win., 270 Weatherby Mag., 300 Win. Mag., 338 Win. Mag.; 3-shot magazine, 4-shot (22-250); 24-inch, 26-inch barrel; no sights; best grade checkered American walnut stock, contrasting grip cap, forend tip, golden eagle head inset in grip cap; recoil pad; carrying case. Made in Japan. Introduced 1976; discontinued 1979.

Perf: $695 **Exc:** $595 **VGood:** $425

GREIFELT DRILLING

Combination gun; drilling; 12-, 16-, 20-, 28-ga., .410 over any standard rifle caliber; 24-inch, 26-inch barrels; folding rear sight; matted rib; auto or non-auto ejectors. Manufactured prior to WWII.

Exc: $3400 **VGood:** $2500 **Good:** $2000

Obsolete calibers

Exc: $2500 **VGood:** $2200 **Good:** $1800

GREIFELT SPORT MODEL

Bolt action; 22 Hornet; 5-shot box magazine; 22-inch barrel; two-leaf rear, ramp front sight; hand-checkered European walnut stock; pistol grip. Made in Germany prior to World War II.

Perf: $495 **Exc:** $395 **VGood:** $295

GRENDEL R-31 CARBINE

Semi-automatic; 22 WMR; 30-shot magazine; 16-inch barrel; 23-1/2-inch overall length (stock collapsed); weighs 4 lbs.; fully-adjustable post front sight, aperture rear; telescoping tube stock, Zytel forend; blowback action with fluted chamber; ambidextrous safety; steel receiver; matte black finish; muzzlebrake. Scope mount optional. Made in U.S. by Grendel, Inc. Introduced 1991; discontinued 1994.

Perf: $295 **Exc:** $220 **VGood:** $180

GRENDEL SRT-20F COMPACT RIFLE

Bolt action; 243, 308 Win.; 9-shot magazine; 20-inch, fluted, unfluted barrel; weighs 6 5/8 lbs.; no sights; integral scope bases; muzzlebrake; folding fiberglass-reinforced Zytel stock; built on Sako A-2 action. Introduced 1987; discontinued 1990.

Perf: $535 **Exc:** $455 **VGood:** $350

With 24-inch barrel (SRT -24)

Perf: $570 **Exc:** $475 **VGood:** $375

HAENEL '88 MAUSER SPORTER

Bolt action; 7x57, 8x57, 9x57mm; 5-shot Mauser box magazine; 22-inch, 24-inch barrel, half or full octagon; leaf open rear, ramp front sight; hand-checkered European walnut sporting stock, cheekpiece, schnabel tip, pistol grip; raised matted rib; action based on Model '88 Mauser; double-set trigger; sling swivels. Manufactured in Germany prior to WWII.

Perf: $800 **Exc:** $675 **VGood:** $400

HAENEL MAUSER MANNLICHER

Bolt action; 7x57, 8x57, 9x57mm; 5-shot Mannlicher-type box magazine; 22-inch, 24-inch barrel, half or full octagon; leaf open rear sight, ramp front; hand-checkered European walnut sporting stock, cheekpiece, schnabel tip, pistol grip; raised matted rib; action based on Model '88 Mauser; double-set trigger; sling swivels. Manufactured in Germany prior to WWII.

Perf: $800 **Exc:** $675 **VGood:** $400

HAENEL MODEL 900 MATCH

Bolt action; single shot; 22 LR; 25-15/16-inch barrel; 44-1/2-inch overall length; weighs 10-1/2 lbs.; match-type globe front sight, fully-adjustable aperture rear; sight radius adjustable from 31-inch to 32-1/2-inch; match-type beech stock with stippled grip and forend; adjustable comb and buttpad; adjustable trigger; polished blue finish. Imported from Germany by GSI, Inc. Introduced 1992; discontinued 1993.

Perf: $695 **Exc:** $550 **VGood:** $425

HAMMERLI MODEL 45 MATCH

Bolt action; single shot; 22 LR; 27-1/2-inch barrel; micrometer peep rear sight, blade front; free-rifle stock with full pistol grip, thumbhole, cheekpiece; palm rest, beavertail forearm; Swiss-type buttplate; sling swivels. Introduced 1945; discontinued 1957.

Exc: $725 **VGood:** $610 **Good:** $500

HAMMERLI MODEL 54 MATCH

Bolt action; single shot; 22 LR; 27-1/2-inch barrel; micrometer peep rear, globe front sight; European walnut free-rifle stock; cheekpiece; adjustable hook buttplate; palm rest; thumbhole; swivel. Introduced 1954; discontinued 1957.

Exc: $760 **VGood:** $640 **Good:** $550

HAMMERLI MODEL 503 FREE RIFLE

Bolt action; single shot; 22 LR; 27-1/2-inch barrel; micrometer rear, globe front sight; European walnut free-rifle stock; cheekpiece; adjustable hook buttplate; palm rest; thumbhole; swivel. Introduced 1957; discontinued 1962.

Exc: $700 **VGood:** $580 **Good:** $510

HAMMERLI MODEL 505 MATCH

Bolt action; single shot; 22 LR; 27-1/2-inch barrel; aperture rear, globe front sight; European walnut free-rifle stock; cheekpiece; palm rest; thumbhole. Introduced 1957; discontinued 1962.

Exc: $695 **VGood:** $550 **Good:** $450

HAMMERLI MODEL 506 MATCH

Bolt action; single shot; 22 LR; 26-3/4-inch barrel; micrometer peep rear, globe front sight; European walnut free-rifle stock; cheekpiece; adjustable hook buttplate; palm rest; thumbhole; swivel. Introduced 1963; discontinued 1966.

Exc: $695 **VGood:** $600 **Good:** $550

HAMMERLI MODEL 1954 22 MATCH

Bolt action; single shot; 22 LR; 27-1/2-inch barrel; weighs 15 lbs.; double locking lugs; adjustable trigger, 5 to 16 oz.; hooded front sight, micrometer peep rear; sling; palm rest; Swiss buttplate. Imported by H. Grieder.

Exc: $695 **VGood:** $575 **Good:** $480

HAMMERLI MODEL OLYMPIA

Bolt action; single shot; 6.5x55 and 7.5mm (Europe), 30-06 and 300 H&H Mag. (U.S.); other calibers on special order; 29-1/2-inch heavy barrel; designed for 300-meter event; micrometer peep rear, hooded front sight; double-pull or double-set trigger; free-type rifle stock with full pistol grip, thumbhole; cheekpiece; palm rest; beavertail forearm; swivels; Swiss-type buttplate. Imported by H. Grieder. Introduced 1949; discontinued 1962.

Exc: $895 **VGood:** $750 **Good:** $595

HAMMERLI-TANNER 300 METER

Bolt action; single shot; 7.5mm Swiss and other centerfires on request; 29-1/2-inch barrel; micrometer peep rear, globe front sight; uncheckered European walnut free-rifle stock; cheekpiece; adjustable hook buttplate; thumbhole; palm rest; swivel. Manufactured in Switzerland. Introduced 1962; no longer in production.

Exc: $895 **VGood:** $795 **Good:** $630

HARRINGTON & RICHARDSON MODEL 60 REISING

Semi-automatic; 45 ACP; 12-, 20-shot detachable box magazine; 18-1/4-inch barrel; open rear, blade front sight; uncheckered hardwood pistol-grip stock.

Introduced 1944; discontinued 1946. Some collector value.

Exc: $1900 **VGood:** $1600 **Good:** $1100

HARRINGTON & RICHARDSON MODEL 65

Semi-automatic; 22 LR; 10-shot detachable box magazine; 23-inch barrel; rear peep, blade front sight; uncheckered hardwood pistol-grip stock; used as training rifle by the Marine Corps in WWII; same general dimensions as M-1 Garand. Introduced 1944; discontinued 1946.

Exc: $475 **VGood:** $350 **Good:** $250

HARRINGTON & RICHARDSON MODEL 150

Semi-automatic; 22 LR; 5-shot detachable box magazine; 22-inch barrel; 42-inch overall length; weighs 7-1/4 lbs.; marble open rear, blade front sight on ramp; oil-finished uncheckered pistol-grip stock; cocking lever under forend; side safety; clip ejector. Introduced 1949; discontinued 1953.

Exc: $150 **VGood:** $125 **Good:** $100

HARRINGTON & RICHARDSON MODEL 151

Semi-automatic; 22 LR; 5-shot detachable box magazine; 22-inch barrel; 42-inch-inch overall length; weighs 7-1/4 lbs.; Redfield No. 70 peep rear sight. Introduced 1949; discontinued 1953.

Exc: $150 **VGood:** $125 **Good:** $100

HARRINGTON & RICHARDSON MODEL 165

Semi-automatic; 22 LR; 10-shot detachable box magazine; 23-inch barrel; Redfield No. 70 rear peep sight, blade front on ramp; uncheckered hardwood pistol-grip stock; sling swivels; web sling. Called the Leatherneck Model, it was a variation of Model 65 military autoloader used to train Marines in basic marksmanship during WWII. Introduced 1945; discontinued 1961.

Exc: $500 **VGood:** $350 **Good:** $250

HARRINGTON & RICHARDSON MODEL 360

Semi-automatic; gas operated; 243 Win., 308 Win.; 3-shot detachable box magazine; 22-inch barrel; 43-1/2-inch overall length; weighs 7-1/2 lbs.; open adjustable rear, gold bead front sight; one-piece American walnut hand-checkered stock; roll-over cheekpiece, full pistol grip; exotic wood pistol-grip cap, forearm tip; sling swivels. Introduced 1967; discontinued 1973.

Exc: $365 **VGood:** $310 **Good:** $240

HARRINGTON & RICHARDSON MODEL 361

Semi-automatic; gas operated; 243 Win., 308 Win.; 3-shot detachable box magazine; 22-inch barrel; open adjustable rear, gold bead front sight; hand-checkered walnut stock; full roll-over cheekpiece, full pistol grip; exotic wood pistol-grip cap, forearm tip; sling swivels. Introduced 1970; discontinued 1973.

Exc: $400 **VGood:** $340 **Good:** $280

HARRINGTON & RICHARDSON MODEL 700

Semi-automatic; 22 WMR; 5-, 10-shot magazine; 22-inch barrel; 43-1/4-inch overall length; weighs 6-1/2 lbs.; folding leaf rear, blade front sight on ramp; American walnut Monte Carlo stock with full pistol grip; composition buttplate. Introduced 1977; discontinued 1985.

Exc: $315 **VGood:** $265 **Good:** $180

HARRINGTON & RICHARDSON MODEL 700 DELUXE

Same specs as Model 700 except walnut stock with cheekpiece; checkered grip, forend; rubber recoil pad; no sights; marketed with H&R Model 432 4X scope, base and rings. Introduced 1979; discontinued 1985.

Exc: $345 **VGood:** $300 **Good:** $190

Harrington & Richardson Model 361

Harrington & Richardson Model 700 Deluxe

Harrington & Richardson Model 800

Harrington & Richardson Model 158 Topper Jet

Harrington & Richardson Model 171 Deluxe

HARRINGTON & RICHARDSON MODEL 755

"Semi-automatic"; single shot with automatic ejection; 22 LR, 22 Long, 22 Short; 22-inch barrel; open rear, military front sight; hardwood Mannlicher-type stock. Advertised as the Sahara Model. Introduced 1963; discontinued 1971. Some collector interest.

Exc: $170 **VGood:** $140 **Good:** $100

HARRINGTON & RICHARDSON MODEL 760

"Semi-automatic"; Single shot with automatic ejection; 22 LR, 22 Long, 22 Short; 22-inch barrel; open rear, military front sight; hardwood sporter stock. Introduced 1965; discontinued 1970.

Exc: $100 **VGood:** $90 **Good:** $70

HARRINGTON & RICHARDSON MODEL 800

Semi-automatic; 22 LR; 5-, 10-shot clip-type magazine; 22-inch barrel; open rear, bead ramp front sight; uncheckered walnut pistol-grip stock; solid frame; side thumb safety. Introduced 1958; discontinued 1960.

Exc: $150 **VGood:** $125 **Good:** $160

HARRINGTON & RICHARDSON MODEL 058

Single shot; 30-30, 22 Hornet; 22-inch barrel; 37-1/2-inch overall length; weighs 6 lbs.; blade front sight, folding leaf rear; walnut finished hardwood stock; rubber buttplate.

Exc: $195 **VGood:** $145 **Good:** $110

HARRINGTON & RICHARDSON MODEL 155 SHIKARI

Single shot; 44 Rem. Mag., 45-70; 24-inch (44, 45-70), 28-inch (45-70) barrel; 39-inch (24-inch barrel), 43-inch (28-inch barrel) overall length; weighs 7 lbs. (24-inch); adjustable folding leaf rear, blade front sight; uncheckered straight-grip walnut-finished hardwood stock forearm; blue-black finish with color case-hardened frame; barrel band; built on Model 158 action; brass cleaning rod. Introduced 1972; discontinued 1982.

Exc: $325 **VGood:** $295 **Good:** $215

HARRINGTON & RICHARDSON MODEL 157

Single shot; 22 Hornet; 30-30; 22-inch barrel; 37-inch overall length; weighs 6-1/2 lbs.; adjustable folding leaf rear, ramp-mounted blade front sight; uncheckered walnut-finished hardwood pistol-grip buttstock; full-length forearm; drilled and tapped for scope mounts; sling swivels; built on Model 158 action. Introduced 1976; discontinued 1985.

Exc: $275 **VGood:** $175 **Good:** $140

HARRINGTON & RICHARDSON MODEL 158 TOPPER

Single shot; 22 Jet, 22 Hornet, 30-30, 357 Mag., 44 Mag.; 22-inch interchangeable barrels; 37-1/2-inch overall length; weighs 5-1/4 lbs.; shotgun-type action; Lyman folding adjustable open rear sight, ramp front; visible hammer; side lever; automatic ejector; uncheckered walnut pistol-grip stock, forearm; recoil pad. Introduced 1963; no longer in production.

Exc: $195 **VGood:** $150 **Good:** $100

HARRINGTON & RICHARDSON MODEL 158 MUSTANG

Same specs as Model 158 Topper except 30-30 only; fitted with 26-inch 20-ga. barrel as accessory. Introduced 1968; discontinued 1985.

Exc: $210 **VGood:** $195 **Good:** $110

HARRINGTON & RICHARDSON MODEL 158 TOPPER JET

Same specs as Model 158 Topper except 22 Rem. Jet; interchangeable with 20-ga., 410-bore, 30-30 barrels. Introduced 1963; discontinued 1967.

Exc: $260 **VGood:** $240 **Good:** $200

30-30 barrel, combo

Exc: $275 **VGood:** $255 **Good:** $215

20-ga. barrel, combo

Exc: $275 **VGood:** $255 **Good:** $215

Harrington & Richardson Model 258 Handy Gun II

Harrington & Richardson Model 422

Harrington & Richardson Model 424

Harrington & Richardson Ultra Varmint

Harringtron & Richardson Ultra Comp Rifle

Harrington & Richardson Buffalo Classic

410 barrel, combo

Exc: $275 **VGood:** $255 **Good:** $215

HARRINGTON & RICHARDSON MODEL 163

Single shot; break open action; 22 Hornet, 30-30, 357 Mag., 44 Mag.; 22-inch barrel; visible hammer; side lever; automatic ejector; straight-grip stock, contoured forearm; gold-plated hammer, trigger. Introduced 1964; discontinued 1967.

Exc: $195 **VGood:** $150 **Good:** $100

HARRINGTON & RICHARDSON MODEL 164

Single shot; break open action; 22 Hornet, 30-30, 357 Mag., 44 Mag.; 22-inch barrel; visible hammer; side lever; automatic ejector; straight-grip unchecked walnut stock; contoured forearm; gold-plated hammer, trigger. Introduced 1964; discontinued 1967.

Exc: $195 **VGood:** $150 **Good:** $100

HARRINGTON & RICHARDSON MODEL 171

Single shot; trap door action; 45-70; 22-inch barrel; 41-inch overall length; weighs 7 lbs.; open fully-adjustable rear, blade front sight; uncheckered American walnut stock. Replica of Model 1873 Springfield cavalry carbine. Introduced 1972; discontinued 1985.

Exc: $525 **VGood:** $475 **Good:** $395

HARRINGTON & RICHARDSON MODEL 171 DELUXE

Same specs as Model 171 except folding leaf rear sight; engraved breechblock, side lock, hammer. Introduced 1972; discontinued 1985.

Exc: $675 **VGood:** $575 **Good:** $495

HARRINGTON & RICHARDSON MODEL 172

Single shot; trapdoor action; 45-70; 22-inch barrel; 41-inch overall length; weighs 7 lbs.; tang-mounted aperture sight; fancy checkered walnut stock; silver-plated hardware. Introduced 1972; discontinued 1977.

Exc: $695 **VGood:** $595 **Good:** $475

HARRINGTON & RICHARDSON MODEL 173

Single shot; trapdoor action; 45-70; 26-inch barrel; 44-inch overall length; weighs 8 lbs.; Vernier tang rear, blade front sight; engraved breechblock receiver, hammer, barrel band, lock, buttplate; checkered walnut stock; ramrod. Replica of Model 1873 Springfield Officers Model. Introduced 1972; discontinued 1977.

Exc: $695 **VGood:** $595 **Good:** $495

HARRINGTON & RICHARDSON MODEL 178

Single shot; trapdoor action; 45-70; 32-inch barrel; 52-inch overall length; weighs 8 5/8 lbs.; leaf rear, blade front sight; uncheckered full-length walnut stock; barrel bands, sling swivels, ramrod. Replica of Model 1873 Springfield Infantry Rifle. Introduced 1973; discontinued 1975.

Exc: $350 **VGood:** $250 **Good:** $205

HARRINGTON & RICHARDSON MODEL 258 HANDY GUN II

Single shot; 22 Hornet, 30-30, 357 Mag., 357 Maximum, 44 Mag., 20-ga. 3-inch; 22-inch barrel; 37-inch overall length; weighs 6-1/2 lbs.; interchangeable rifle/shotgun barrels; ramp blade front, adjustable folding leaf rear sight; bead front sight on shotgun barrel; walnut-finished American hardwood stock; electroless matte nickel finish. Introduced 1982; discontinued 1985.

Exc: $180 **VGood:** $150 **Good:** $120

HARRINGTON & RICHARDSON MODEL 422

Slide-action; 22 LR, 22 Long, 22 Short; 24-inch barrel; 15-shot (22 LR), 17-shot (22 Long), 21-shot (22 Short) tube magazine; open rear, ramp front sight; uncheckered walnut pistol-grip stock; grooved slide handle. Introduced 1952; discontinued 1958.

Exc: $125 **VGood:** $100 **Good:** $70

HARRINGTON & RICHARDSON MODEL 424

Single shot; 22 Short, 22 Long, 22 LR; 24-inch barrel; open rear, blade front sight; manual cocking action; uncheckered American walnut stock. Introduced 1960; discontinued 1961. Some collector value.

Exc: $100 **VGood:** $75 **Good:** $45

HARRINGTON & RICHARDSON MODEL 749

Pump action; 22 Short, 22 Long, 22 LR; 18-shot (22 Short), 15-shot (22 Long), 13-shot (22 LR) tube magazine; 19-inch barrel; 35-1/2-inch overall length; weighs 4 5/8 lbs.; dovetail blade front, adjustable rear sight; positive ejection; walnut-finished American hardwood stock, contoured forend. Introduced 1971; discontinued 1971.

Exc: $150 **VGood:** $125 **Good:** $90

HARRINGTON & RICHARDSON ULTRA HEAVY BARREL 22 MAG RIFLE

Single shot, breakopen; 22 WMR. 22-inch bull barrel. Cinnamon laminated wood stock with Monte Carlo cheekpiece; no sights furnished; scope mount rail included. Hand-checkered stock and forend; deep-crown rifling; tuned trigger; trigger locking system; hammer extension. Introduced 2001. From H&R 1871 LLC.

Perf: $200 **Exc:** $150 **VGood:** $120

HARRINGTON & RICHARDSON ULTRA HUNTER

Single shot; 223, 243, 25-06, 270, 308 Win., 450 Marlin; 26-inch (25-06), 24-inch (223 and 243), 22-inch (308 and 450 Marlin) barrel; weighs about 7-1/2 lbs.; no sights furnished; drilled, tapped for scope mounting; cinnamon-colored laminate stock and forend; hand-checkered grip and forend; break-open action with side-lever release; positive ejection; comes with scope mount; swivel studs; blued receiver and barrel. From H&R 1971, Inc. Introduced 1995; still produced. Premium for 450 Marlin.

Perf: $200 **Exc:** $150 **VGood:** $110

HARRINGTON & RICHARDSON ULTRA VARMINT

Single shot; 204 Ruger, 223 Rem., 22-250; 22-inch heavy barrel; weighs about 7-1/2 lbs.; no sights; drilled, tapped for scope mounting; hand-checkered laminated birch stock with Monte Carlo comb; break-open action with side-lever release; positive ejection; comes with scope mount; swivel studs; blued receiver and barrel. From H&R 1971, Inc. Introduced 1993.

Perf: $210 **Exc:** $150 **VGood:** $110

HARRINGTON & RICHARDSON ULTRA COMP RIFLE

Similar to Ultra Varmint except chambered for 270 or 30-06; compensator to reduce recoil; camo-laminate stock and forend; blued, highly polished frame; scope mount. Made in U.S.A. by H&R 1871, LLC, no longer offered.

Perf: $300 **Exc:** $260 **VGood:** $210

HARRINGTON & RICHARDSON BUFFALO CLASSIC

This model, chambered in .38-55 Winchester or .45-70, employs a 28" heavy target barrel and original style rifling for consistent accuracy. It has a Williams receiver sight, and a Lyman target front sight with eight aperture inserts. Premium for special edition.

Perf: $395 **Exc:** $350 **VGood:** $310

HARRINGTON & RICHARDSON CR CARBINE

Single-shot rifle based on the Handi-Rifle design. Two-piece checkered walnut stock with schnabel forend. Marble's front and rear sights, crescent steel buttplate. Chambered in .45 Colt.

NIB: $400 **Exc:** $365 **VGood:** $300

HARRINGTON & RICHARDSON SYNTHETIC HANDI-RIFLE

Basic Handi-Rifle design but with synthetic buttstock and forend (eather grooved or beavertail). Available with iron sights or picatinny rail for mounting optics.

NIB: $375 **Exc:** $300 **VGood:** $215

HARRINGTON & RICHARDSON STAINLESS HANDI-RIFLE

Similar to above but with stainless barrel. Chambered in .223, .270 or .30-06.

NIB: $385 **Exc:** $315 **VGood:** $225

HARRINGTON & RICHARDSON SYNTHETIC HANDI-RIFLE/SLUG GUN COMBO

Similar to above but with extra slug barrel. Available in .44 Mag/12 ga. and .357 Magnum/20 ga. Introduced in 2008.

NIB: $375 **Exc:** $300 **VGood:** $215

HARRINGTON & RICHARDSON SUPERLITE HANDI-RIFLE COMPACT

Similar to Synthetic Handi-Rifle but weighs only 5.5 lbs. Chambered in .223 and .243. Alao available with optional scope. Values shown are for scoped model.

NIB: $395 **Exc:** $325 **VGood:** $225

HARRINGTON & RICHARDSON SPORTSTER

A .22 LR or .22 WMR version of the Handi-Rifle with black polymer stock, sculpted forend and iron sights. Overall length 36-1/4 inches.

NIB: $175 **Exc:** $145 **VGood:** $100

HARRINGTON & RICHARDSON MODEL 250

Bolt action; 22 LR; 5-, 10-shot detachable box magazine; 23-inch barrel; 40-inch overall length; weighs 6-1/2 lbs.; open rear sight, blade front on ramp; uncheckered oil-finished walnut pistol-grip stock. Advertised as the Sportster Model. Introduced 1948; discontinued 1961.

Exc: $175 **VGood:** $150 **Good:** $120

HARRINGTON & RICHARDSON MODEL 251

Bolt action; 22 LR; 5-shot detachable box magazine; 22-inch barrel; Lyman No. 55H rear sight, blade front on ramp; uncheckered hardwood pistol-grip stock. Introduced 1948; discontinued 1961.

Exc: $250 **VGood:** $200 **Good:** $175

HARRINGTON & RICHARDSON MODEL 265

Bolt action; 22 LR; 5-, 10-shot detachable box magazine; 22-inch barrel; 40-inch overall length; weighs 6-3/4 lbs.; Lyman No. 17A rear peep sight, blade front on ramp; uncheckered hardwood pistol-grip stock; spring-type bolt release; thumb-operated safety. Called the Reg'lar Model in advertising. Introduced 1946; discontinued 1949.

Exc: $150 **VGood:** $125 **Good:** $100

HARRINGTON & RICHARDSON MODEL 265 TARGETEER JR.

Same specs as Model 265 except 20-inch barrel; 36-3/4-inch overall length; weighs 7 lbs.; Redfield No. 70 rear peep sight, Lyman No. 17A front; shorter youth uncheckered walnut pistol-grip stock; sling swivels; web sling. Introduced 1948; discontinued 1951.

Exc: $300 **VGood:** $225 **Good:** $175

HARRINGTON & RICHARDSON MODEL 300 ULTRA

Bolt action; 22-250, 243 Win., 270 Win., 30-06, 308 Win., 300 Win. Mag., 7mm Rem. Mag.; 3-shot magazine (magnums), 5-shot (others); 22-inch, 24-inch barrel; FN Mauser action; with or without open rear sight, ramp front; hand-checkered American walnut stock; cheekpiece, full pistol grip; pistol-grip cap, forearm tip of contrasting exotic wood; rubber buttplate, sling swivels. Introduced 1965; discontinued 1978.

H&R Synthetic Handi-Rifle

H&R Synthetic Handi-Rifle with Iron Sights

H&R Superlite Synthetic Handi-Rifle/Slug Gun Combo

H&R Sportster

Superlite Handi-Rifle with Scope

Exc: $370 **VGood:** $295 **Good:** $250

HARRINGTON & RICHARDSON MODEL 301 ULTRA

Bolt action; 243 Win., 270 Win., 30-06, 308 Win., 300 Win. Mag., 7mm Rem. Mag.; 3-shot magazine (magnums), 5-shot (others); 18-inch barrel; FN Mauser action; with or without open rear sight, ramp front; Mannlicher-style stock; cheekpiece; full pistol grip; pistol-grip cap; metal forearm tip; rubber buttplate, sling swivels. Introduced 1978; discontinued 1978.

Exc: $375 **VGood:** $300 **Good:** $250

HARRINGTON & RICHARDSON MODEL 317 ULTRA

Bolt action; 17 Rem., 222 Rem., 223 Rem., 17/223 handloads; 6-shot magazine; 20-inch tapered barrel; no sights; receiver dovetailed for scope mounts. Advertised as the Ultra Wildcat. Introduced 1966; discontinued 1976.

Exc: $430 **VGood:** $350 **Good:** $290

HARRINGTON & RICHARDSON MODEL 317P ULTRA

Same specs as Ultra Model 317 except better grade of walnut; basketweave checkering. Discontinued 1976.

Exc: $495 **VGood:** $395 **Good:** $320

HARRINGTON & RICHARDSON MODEL 330

Bolt action; 243, 270, 30-06, 308, 7mm Rem., 300 Win.; 22-inch tapered round barrel; 42-1/2-inch overall length; 7-1/8 lbs.; gold bead on ramp front sight, fully-adjustable rear; walnut hand-checkered stock with Monte Carlo; hinged floorplate; adjustable trigger; sliding side safety; receiver tapped for scope mounts. Introduced 1972; no longer in production.

Exc: $395 **VGood:** $295 **Good:** $200

HARRINGTON & RICHARDSON MODEL 333

Bolt action; 30-06, 7mm Rem. Mag.; 22-inch barrel; 42-1/2-inch overall length; weighs 7-3/4 lbs.; no sights; walnut finished hardwood stock; adjustable trigger; Sako barrel and action; sliding thumb safety.

Exc: $280 **VGood:** $210 **Good:** $180

HARRINGTON & RICHARDSON MODEL 340

Bolt action; 243, 7x57, 308, 270, 30-06; 5-shot; 22-inch barrel; 43-inch overall length; weighs 7-1/4 lbs.; no sights; drilled and tapped for scope mounts; American walnut stock; hand-checkered pistol grip, forend; carved, beaded cheekpiece; grip cap; recoil pad; Mauser-design action; hinged steel floorplate; adjustable trigger; high-luster blued finish. Introduced 1983; discontinued 1984.

Exc: $395 **VGood:** $350 **Good:** $300

HARRINGTON & RICHARDSON MODEL 365

Bolt action; single shot; 22 LR; 22-inch barrel; Lyman No. 55 rear peep sight, blade front on ramp; uncheckered hardwood pistol-grip stock. Called the Ace in advertising. Introduced 1946; discontinued 1947.

Perf: $225 **Exc:** $175 **VGood:** $150

HARRINGTON & RICHARDSON MODEL 370 ULTRA

Bolt action; 22-250, 243 Win., 6mm Rem.; 24-inch heavy target/varmint barrel; built on Sako action; no sights; tapped for open sights and/or scope mounts; uncheckered, oil-finished walnut stock; roll-over comb; adjustable trigger; recoil pad; sling swivels. Advertised as Ultra Medalist. Introduced 1967; discontinued 1974.

Exc: $375 **VGood:** $325 **Good:** $275

HARRINGTON & RICHARDSON MODEL 450

Bolt action; 22 LR; 5-, 10-shot detachable box magazine; 26-inch barrel; no sights; uncheckered American walnut target stock with full pistol grip,

Harrington & Richardson Model 300 Ultra

Harrington & Richardson Model 317 Ultra

Harrington & Richardson Model 317P Ultra

Harrington & Richardson Model 340

Harrington & Richardson Model 465

Harris-McMillan M-86 Sniper

thick forend; scope bases; sling swivels, sling. Introduced 1948; discontinued 1961.

Exc: $150 **VGood:** $125 **Good:** $100

HARRINGTON & RICHARDSON MODEL 451

Bolt action; 22 LR; 5-, 10-shot detachable box magazine; 26-inch barrel; Lyman 524F extension rear sight, Lyman No. 77 front sight; crowned muzzle; uncheckered American walnut target stock with full pistol grip, thick forend; scope bases; sling swivels; sling. Introduced 1948; discontinued 1961.

Exc: $225 **VGood:** $175 **Good:** $150

HARRINGTON & RICHARDSON MODEL 465

Bolt action; 22 LR; 10-shot detachable box magazine; 25-inch barrel; Lyman No. 57 rear peep sight, blade front on ramp; uncheckered walnut pistol-grip stock; sling swivels; web sling. Advertised as Targeteer Special. Introduced 1946; discontinued 1947.

Exc: $250 **VGood:** $200 **Good:** $175

HARRINGTON & RICHARDSON MODEL 750

Bolt action; single shot; 22 LR, 22 Long, 22 Short; 22-inch (early), 24-inch barrel; 39-inch overall length; weighs 5 lbs.; open rear, blade front sight; double extractors; uncheckered walnut finished Monte Carlo hardwood stock with pistol grip; feed ramp. Introduced 1954; no longer in production.

Exc: $125 **VGood:** $100 **Good:** $90

HARRINGTON & RICHARDSON MODEL 751

Bolt action; single shot; 22 LR, 22 Long, 22 Short; 24-inch barrel; open rear, bead front sight; double extractors; Mannlicher stock; feed ramp. Introduced 1971; discontinued 1971.

Exc: $125 **VGood:** $100 **Good:** $70

HARRINGTON & RICHARDSON MODEL 765

Bolt action; single shot; 22 LR, 22 Long, 22 Short; 24-inch barrel; 41-inch overall length; adjustable open rear sight, Red Devil hooded bead front; uncheckered oil-finished walnut or hardwood pistol-grip stock. Introduced 1948; discontinued 1954.

Exc: $95 **VGood:** $70 **Good:** $50

HARRINGTON & RICHARDSON MODEL 852

Bolt action; 22 LR, 22 Long, 22 Short; 24-inch barrel; 15-shot (22 LR), 17-shot (22 Long), 21-shot (22 Short) tube magazine; open rear, bead front sight; uncheckered pistol-grip hardwood stock. Introduced 1952; discontinued 1953.

Exc: $150 **VGood:** $125 **Good:** $100

HARRINGTON & RICHARDSON MODEL 865

Bolt action; 22 Short, 22 Long, 22 LR; 5-shot clip magazine; 24-inch (early), 22-inch round tapered barrel; 40-1/2-inch overall length; weighs 5 lbs.; "Cottontail" bead (early), blade front, step-adjustable open rear sight; receiver grooved for tip-off scope mounts; oil-finish walnut (early), walnut-finished American hardwood stock with Monte Carlo pistol grip; sliding side safety; cocking indicator. Introduced 1949; discontinued 1985.

Exc: $150 **VGood:** $125 **Good:** $100

HARRINGTON & RICHARDSON MODEL 866

Bolt action; 22 Short, 22 Long, 22 LR; 5-shot clip magazine; 22-inch round tapered barrel; 39-inch overall length; weighs 5 lbs.; blade front, step-adjustable open rear sight; receiver grooved for tip-off scope mounts; Mannlicher stock with Monte Carlo pistol grip; sliding side safety; cocking indicator. Introduced 1971; discontinued 1971.

Exc: $250 **VGood:** $175 **Good:** $150

HARRINGTON & RICHARDSON MODEL 5200 SPORTER

Bolt action; single shot; 22 LR; 24-inch barrel; 42-inch overall length; weighs 6-1/2 lbs.; hooded ramp front sight; fully-adjustable Lyman peep rear; classic American walnut stock with hand cut checkering; rubber buttplate; adjustable trigger; drilled and tapped for scope mounts.

Exc: $325 **VGood:** $270 **Good:** $210

HARRINGTON & RICHARDSON MODEL 5200 MATCH

Same specs as Model 5200 Sporter except 28-inch barrel; 46-inch overall length; weighs 11 lbs.; drilled, tapped for sights, scope; target-style American walnut stock; full-length accessory rail; rubber buttpad, palm stop; fully-adjustable trigger; dual extractors; polished blue-black metal finish. Introduced 1981; discontinued 1985.

Exc: $420 **VGood:** $375 **Good:** $315

HARRIS-MCMILLAN ANTIETAM SHARPS

Falling block; single shot; 40-65, 45-75; 30-inch, 32-inch octagon or round barrel; 47-inch overall length; weighs 11-1/4 lbs.; hand-lapped stainless or chrome-moly barrel; Montana Vintage Arms #111 Low Profile Spirit Level front sight, #108 mid-range tang rear with windage adjustments; choice of straight grip, pistol grip or Creedmoor-style stock; schnabel forend; pewter tip optional; standard A Fancy wood, higher grades available; recreation of the 1874 Sharps sidehammer; action color case-hardened; barrel satin black; chrome-moly barrel optionally blued; optional sights include #112 Spirit Level Globe front with windage, #107 Long Range rear with windage. All parts and components made in U.S. by Harris Gunworks, Inc. Introduced 1994.

Perf: $2300 **Exc:** $2000 **VGood:** $1450

HARRIS-MCMILLAN LONG RANGE RIFLE

Bolt action; single shot; 300 Win. Mag., 7mm Rem. Mag., 300 Phoenix, 338 Lapua; 26-inch stainless steel match-grade barrel; 46-1/2-inch overall length; weighs 14 lbs.; barrel band and Tompkins front sight; no rear sight furnished; fiberglass stock with adjustable buttplate and cheekpiece; adjustable for length of pull, drop, cant and cast-off; solid bottom single shot action and Canjar trigger; barrel twist of 1:12-inch. All parts and components made in U.S. by Harris Gunworks, Inc. Introduced 1989.

Perf: $3200 **Exc:** $2750 **VGood:** $1600

HARRIS-MCMILLAN M-86 SNIPER

Bolt action; 308, 30-06, 300 Win. Mag.; 4-shot (308, 30-06), 3-shot (300 Win. Mag.) magazine; 24-inch McMillan match-grade barrel in heavy contour; 43-1/2-inch overall length; weighs 11-1/4 lbs. (308), 11-1/2 lbs. (30-06, 300); no sights; specially designed fiberglass stock with textured grip and forend, recoil pad; repeating action; comes with bipod; matte black finish; sling swivels. All parts and components made in U.S. by Harris Gunworks, Inc. Introduced 1989.

Perf: $2500 **Exc:** $2100 **VGood:** $1850

Takedown model

Perf: $2200 **Exc:** $1900 **VGood:** $1350

HARRIS-MCMILLAN M-87

Bolt action; single shot; 50 BMG; 29-inch barrel, with muzzlebrake; 53-inch overall length; weighs 21-1/2 lbs.; no sights; fiberglass stock; stainless steel receiver; chrome-moly barrel with 1:15-inch twist. All parts and components made in U.S. by Harris Gunworks, Inc. Introduced 1987; still in production.

Perf: $3250 **Exc:** $2800 **VGood:** $2000

HARRIS-MCMILLAN M-87R

Same specs as M-87 except 5-shot repeater. All parts and components made in U.S. by Harris Gunworks, Inc. Introduced 1990; still produced.

Perf: $3795 **Exc:** $3100 **VGood:** $2230

HARRIS-MCMILLAN M-89 SNIPER

Bolt action; 308 Win.; 5-shot magazine; 28-inch barrel with suppressor; weighs 15-1/4 lbs.; no sights; fiberglass stock adjustable for length; recoil pad; drilled and tapped for scope mounting; repeating action; comes with bipod. All parts and components made in U.S. by Harris Gunworks, Inc. Introduced 1990.

Perf: $2700 **Exc:** $2100 **VGood:** $1650

HARRIS-MCMILLAN M-92 BULLPUP

Bolt action; single shot; 50 BMG; bullpup barrel, with muzzlebrake; no sights; fiberglass bullpup stock; stainless steel receiver; chrome-moly barrel with 1:15-inch twist as on M87. All parts and components made in U.S. by Harris Gunworks, Inc. Introduced 1993.

Perf: $4000 **Exc:** $3200 **VGood:** $2100

HARRIS-MCMILLAN M-93

Bolt action; 50 BMG; 5-, 10-shot magazine; 29-inch barrel, with muzzlebrake; 53-inch overall length; weighs about 21-1/2 lbs.; no sights; folding fiberglass stock; right-handed stainless steel receiver; chrome-moly barrel with 1:15-inch twist. All parts and components made in U.S. by Harris Gunworks, Inc. Introduced 1987.

Perf: $3995 **Exc:** $3450 **VGood:** $2350

HARRIS-MCMILLAN NATIONAL MATCH

Bolt action; 7mm-08, 308; 5-shot magazine; 24-inch stainless steel barrel; 43-inch overall length; weighs about 11 lbs.; barrel band and Tompkins front sight, no rear sight; modified ISU fiberglass stock with adjustable buttplate; McMillan repeating action with clip slot, Canjar trigger; match-grade barrel. Fibergrain stock, sight installation, special machining and triggers optional. All parts and components made in U.S. by Harris Gunworks, Inc. Introduced 1989.

Perf: $3200 **Exc:** $2700 **VGood:** $2000

HARRIS-MCMILLAN SIGNATURE CLASSIC SPORTER

Bolt action; 22-250, 243, 6mm Rem., 7mm-08, 284, 308 (short action); 25-06, 270, 280 Rem., 30-06, 7mm Rem. Mag., 300 Win. Mag., 300 Wea. (long action); 338 Win. Mag., 340 Wea., 375 H&H (magnum); 4-shot magazine (standard calibers), 3-shot (magnums); 22-inch, 24-inch, 26-inch barrel; weighs about 7 lbs. (short action); no sights; fiberglass stock in green, beige, brown or black; recoil pad and 1-inch swivels installed; length of pull up to 14-1/4-inch; comes with 1-inch rings and bases; right- or left-hand action with matte black finish; aluminum floorplate. Fibergrain and wood stocks optional. All parts and components made in U.S. by Harris Gunworks, Inc. Introduced 1987; still produced.

Perf: $2500 **Exc:** $2150 **VGood:** $1500

HARRIS-MCMILLAN SIGNATURE ALASKAN

Same specs as Classic Sporter except 270, 280 Rem., 30-06, 7mm Rem. Mag., 300 Win. Mag., 300 Wea., 358 Win., 340 Wea., 375 H&H; match-grade barrel with single leaf rear sight, barrel band front; 1-inch detachable rings and mounts; steel floorplate; electroless nickel finish; wood Monte Carlo stock with cheekpiece; palm swell grip; solid buttpad. All parts and components made in U.S. by Harris Gunworks, Inc. Introduced 1989.

Perf: $3525 **Exc:** $3000 **VGood:** $2100

Harris-McMillan Signature Alaskan

Harris-McMillan Signature Titanium Mountain

Harris-McMillan Signature Varminter

Harris-McMillan Talon Safari

Heckler & Koch HK91 A-2

HARRIS-MCMILLAN SIGNATURE CLASSIC STAINLESS SPORTER

Same specs as Classic Sporter except addition of 416 Rem. Mag.; barrel and action made of stainless steel; fiberglass stock; right- or left-hand action in natural stainless, glass bead or black chrome sulfide finishes. All parts and components made in U.S. by Harris Gunworks, Inc. Introduced 1990; still produced.

Perf: $2700 **Exc:** $2250 **VGood:** $1600

HARRIS-MCMILLAN SIGNATURE SUPER VARMINTER

Same specs as Classic Sporter except 223, 22-250, 220 Swift, 243, 6mm Rem., 25-06, 7mm-08, 7mm BR, 308, 350 Rem. Mag.; heavy-contour barrel; adjustable trigger; field bipod and special hand-bedded fiberglass stock; comes with 1-inch rings and bases. Fibergrain optional. All parts and components made in U.S. by Harris Gunworks, Inc. Introduced 1989.

Perf: $2495 **Exc:** $1995 **VGood:** $1395

HARRIS-MCMILLAN SIGNATURE TITANIUM MOUNTAIN RIFLE

Same specs as Classic Sporter except 270, 280 Rem., 30-06, 7mm Rem. Mag., 300 Win. Mag.; weighs 5-1/2 lbs.; action of titanium alloy; barrel of chrome-moly steel; graphite reinforced fiberglass stock. Fibergrain stock optional. All parts and components made in U.S. by Harris Gunworks, Inc. Introduced 1989; still produced. Premium for graphite-steel composite light weight barrel.

Perf: $3000 **Exc:** $2450 **VGood:** $1795

HARRIS GUNWORKS SIGNATURE VARMINTER

Similar to Signature Classic Sporter except has heavy contoured barrel, adjustable trigger, field bipod and special hand-bedded fiberglass stock. Chambered for 223, 22-250, 220 Swift, 243, 6mm Rem., 25-06, 7mm-08, 7mm BR, 308, 350 Rem. Mag. Comes with 1-inch rings and bases. Introduced 1989.

Perf: $2500 **Exc:** $2000 **VGood:** $1400

HARRIS-MCMILLAN TALON SAFARI

Bolt action; 300 Win. Mag., 300 Wea. Mag., 300 Phoenix, 338 Win. Mag., 30-378, 338 Lapua, 300 H&H, 340 Wea. Mag., 375 H&H, 404 Jeffery, 416 Rem. Mag., 458 Win. Mag. (Safari Magnum); 378 Wea. Mag., 416 Rigby, 416 Wea. Mag., 460 Wea. Mag. (Safari Super Magnum); 24-inch match grade barrel; 43-inch overall length; weighs about 9-10 lbs.; barrel band front ramp sight, multi-leaf express rear; McMillan Safari action; fiberglass Safari stock; quick-detachable 1-inch scope mounts; positive locking steel floorplate; barrel band sling swivel; matte black finish standard. All parts and components made in U.S. by Harris Gunworks, Inc. Introduced 1989.

Perf: $3200 **Exc:** $2600 **VGood:** $2100

Talon Safari Super Magnum

Perf: $3700 **Exc:** $3200 **VGood:** $2600

HARRIS-MCMILLAN TALON SPORTER

Bolt action; 22-250, 243, 6mm Rem., 6mm BR, 7mm BR, 7mm-08, 25-06, 270, 280 Rem., 284, 308, 30-06, 350 Rem. Mag. (Long Action); 7mm Rem. Mag., 7mm STW, 300 Win. Mag., 300 Wea. Mag., 300 H&H, 338 Win. Mag., 340 Wea. Mag., 375 H&H, 416 Rem. Mag.; 24-inch barrel; no sights; weighs about 7-1/2 lbs.; choice of walnut or fiberglass stock; comes with rings and bases; uses pre-'64 Model 70-type action with cone breech, controlled feed, claw extractor and three-position safety; barrel and action of stainless steel; open sights optional and chrome-moly optional. All parts and components made in U.S. by Harris Gunworks, Inc. Introduced 1991.

Perf: $2700 **Exc:** $2295 **VGood:** $1710

Heckler & Koch HK93 A-2

Heckler & Koch HK94 A-2

Heckler & Koch HK300

Heckler & Koch HK770

Heckler & Koch PSG-1 Marksman

Heckler & Koch SLB 2000

Heckler & Koch MR556A1

HECKLER & KOCH HK91 A-2

Semi-automatic; 308 Win.; 5-, 20-shot detachable box magazine; 17-3/4-inch barrel; weighs 9-3/4 lbs.; V and aperture rear sight, post front; plastic buttstock forearm; delayed roller-lock blowback action. Introduced 1976; discontinued 1989. Imported for law enforcement sales only.

Perf: $2700 **Exc:** $2300 **VGood:** $1900

HECKLER & KOCH HK91 A-3

Same specs as HK91 A-2 except collapsible metal buttstock. Introduced 1976; discontinued 1989. Imported for law enforcement sales only.

Perf: $3000 **Exc:** $2600 **VGood:** $2100

HECKLER & KOCH HK93 A-2

Semi-automatic; 223 Rem.; 25-shot magazine; 16-1/8-inch barrel; weighs 8 lbs.; V and aperture rear sight, post front; plastic buttstock, forearm; delayed roller-lock blowback action. Introduced 1976; discontinued 1989. Imported for law enforcement sales only.

Perf: $2950 **Exc:** $2500 **VGood:** $2100

HECKLER & KOCH HK93 A-3

Same specs as HK93 A-2 except collapsible metal buttstock. Introduced 1976; discontinued 1989. Imported for law enforcement sales only.

Perf: $3100 **Exc:** $2650 **VGood:** $2250

HECKLER & KOCH HK94 A-2

Semi-automatic; 9mm Para.; 15-shot magazine; 16-inch barrel; 34-3/4-inch overall length; weighs 6-1/2 lbs. (fixed stock); hooded post front sight, fully-adjustable aperture rear; high-impact plastic butt and forend or retractable metal stock; delayed roller-locked action; accepts H&K quick-detachable scope mount. Imported from Germany by Heckler & Koch, Inc. Introduced 1983; discontinued 1994.

Perf: $3800 **Exc:** $3500 **VGood:** $3100

HECKLER & KOCH HK94 A-3

Same specs as HK94 A-2 except retractable metal stock. Imported from Germany by Heckler & Koch, Inc. Introduced 1983; discontinued 1994.

Perf: $4100 **Exc:** $3800 **VGood:** $3400

HECKLER & KOCH HK270

Semi-automatic; 22 LR; 5-, 20-shot magazine; 19-3/4-inch barrel; 38-1/4-inch overall length; weighs 5-3/4 lbs.; post front sight, fully-adjustable diopter rear; uncheckered European walnut cheekpiece stock; integral H&K scope mounts. Manufactured in Germany. Introduced 1977; discontinued 1985.

Perf: $570 **Exc:** $480 **VGood:** $410

HECKLER & KOCH HK300

Semi-automatic; 22 WMR; 5-, 15-shot detachable box magazine; 19-3/4-inch barrel; post windage-adjustable front, adjustable V-notch rear; hand-checkered European walnut Monte Carlo stock with cheekpiece; checkered pistol grip and schnabel forend integral H&K scope mounts. Manufactured in Germany. Introduced 1977; discontinued 1989.

Perf: $1000 **Exc:** $775 **VGood:** $650

HECKLER & KOCH HK630

Semi-automatic; 223; 4-, 10-shot magazine; 17-3/4-inch barrel; weighs 7 lbs.; V-notch rear, ramp front sight; European walnut stock with checkered forend, pistol grip; magazine catch at front of trigger guard; receiver dovetailed to accept clamp-type scope. Discontinued 1986.

Perf: $1000 **Exc:** $850 **VGood:** $650

HECKLER & KOCH HK770

Semi-automatic; 308 Win.; 3-, 10-shot magazine; 19-1/2-inch barrel; weighs 8 lbs.; vertically-adjustable blade front, open fold-down windage-adjustable rear sight; checkered European walnut pistol-grip stock; polygonal rifling; delayed roller-locked bolt system; receiver top dovetailed for clamp-type scope mount. Imported from Germany. Introduced 1976; discontinued 1986.

Perf: $1450 **Exc:** $1200 **VGood:** $800

HECKLER & KOCH HK940

Semi-automatic; 30-06; 3-, 10-shot magazine; 21-1/2-inch barrel; weighs 8-3/8 lbs.; vertically-adjustable blade front, open fold-down windage-adjustable rear sight; checkered European walnut pistol-grip stock; polygonal rifling; delayed roller-locked bolt system; receiver top dovetailed for clamp-type scope mount. Imported from Germany. Discontinued 1986.

Perf: $1450 **Exc:** $1200 **VGood:** $800

HECKLER & KOCH HK940K

Same specs as HK940 except 16-inch barrel; fuller cheekpiece. Introduced 1984; discontinued 1984.

Perf: $1400 **Exc:** $1100 **VGood:** $900

HECKLER & KOCH MR556A1

Descendent of the HK416 in 5.56/.223 caliber with 16.5-inch barrel. Weight, 8.9 lbs., overall length from 33.9 to 37.7 inches. Black synthetic adjustable stock. Hand guard system allows all current accessories, sights, lights, and aimers used on M4/M16-type weapons to be fitted to the MR rifles.

Perf: $2700 **Exc:** $2300 **VGood:** $2000

HECKLER & KOCH PSG-1 MARKSMAN

Semi-automatic; 308 Win.; 5-, 20-shot magazines; 25-1/2-inch heavy barrel; 47-1/2-inch overall length; weighs 17-1/2 lbs.; no iron sights; 6x42 Hensoldt scope; matte black high-impact plastic stock adjustable for length; pivoting buttcap; adjustable cheekpiece; target-type pistol grip, palm shelf; built on H&K 91 action; T-way rail for tripod, sling swivel. Made in Germany. Introduced 1986; no longer imported.

Perf: $6250 **Exc:** $5750 **VGood:** $4000

HECKLER & KOCH SLB 2000 RIFLE

Semi-automatic; 30-06; 2-, 5- and 10-shot magazines. 19.7-inch barrel; weighs 8 lb.; 41.3-inch long; Oil-finished, checkered walnut stock; Ramp front, Patridge notch rear sights; Short-stroke, piston-actuated gas operation; modular steel and polymer construction; free-floating barrel; pistol grip angled for natural feel. Introduced 2001. From H&K.

Perf: $900 **Exc:** $800 **VGood:** $650

HECKLER & KOCH SL6

Semi-automatic; 223 Rem.; 4-shot magazine; 17-1/2-inch barrel; weighs 8-3/8 lbs.; adjustable aperture rear, hooded post-front sight; oil-finished European walnut stock; polygonal rifling; delayed roller-locked action; dovetailed for quick-detachable scope mount. Made in Germany. Introduced 1983; discontinued 1986.

Perf: $1300 **Exc:** $1200 **VGood:** $950

HECKLER & KOCH SL7

Semi-automatic; 308 Win.; 3-shot magazine; 17-1/2-inch barrel; 39-3/4-inch overall length; weighs 8-3/8 lbs.; adjustable aperture rear, hooded post-front sight; oil-finished European walnut stock; polygon rifling; delayed roller-locked action; dovetailed for H&K quick-detachable scope mount. Made in Germany. Introduced 1983; no longer imported by H&K.

Perf: $1300 **Exc:** $1200 **VGood:** $950

HECKLER & KOCH SL8-1

Semi-automatic; 223; 10-shot magazine. 17.7-inch barrel; weighs 8.6 lbs.; 38.6-inch overall length; Polymer thumbhole stock; Blade front sight with integral hood; fully adjustable rear diopter. Picatinny rail. Based on German military G36 rifle. Uses short-stroke piston-actuated gas operation; almost entirely constructed of carbon fiber-reinforced polymer. Free-floating heavy target barrel. Introduced 2000, no longer available from H&K.

Perf: $1800 **Exc:** $1450 **VGood:** $1100

HECKLER & KOCH SR9

Semi-automatic; 308 Win.; 5-shot magazine; 19-3/4-inch bull barrel with polygonal rifling; 42-7/16-inch overall length; weighs 11 lbs.; post-front sight, fully-adjustable aperture rear; Kevlar reinforced fiberglass thumbhole stock with woodgrain finish; redesigned version of the HK91 rifle. Imported from Germany by Heckler & Koch, Inc. Introduced 1990; discontinued 1994.

Perf: $3900 **Exc:** $2600 **VGood:** $1900

HECKLER & KOCH SR9 (T) TARGET

Same specs as SR9 except MSG90 adjustable buttstock; trigger group from the PSG1 Marksman's Rifle; and the PSG1 contoured pistol grip with palm shelf. Imported from Germany by Heckler & Koch, Inc. Introduced 1992; discontinued 1994.

Perf: $5000 **Exc:** $4800 **VGood:** $3900

HECKLER & KOCH SR9 (TC) TARGET

Same specs as SR9 except PSG1 adjustable buttstock; target/competition version of the SR9 rifle; trigger group and contoured grip. Imported from Germany by Heckler & Koch, Inc. Introduced 1993; discontinued 1994.

Perf: $4000 **Exc:** $3700 **VGood:** $3200

HECKLER & KOCH USC CARBINE

Semi-automatic; 45 ACP, 10-shot magazine. 16-inch barrel; weighs 8.6 lb.; 35.4-inch overall length; Skeletonized polymer thumbhole. Blade front sight with integral hood, fully adjustable diopter rear. Based on German UMP submachine gun. Blowback operation; almost entirely constructed of carbon fiber-reinforced polymer. Free-floating heavy target barrel. Introduced 2000. Discontinued.

Perf: $1600 **Exc:** $1400 **VGood:** $1050

HENRY LEVER-ACTION 22

Lever action; 22 Long Rifle (15-shot); 18-1/4-inch round barrel; weighs 5-1/2 lbs.; 34-inch overall length. Walnut stock. Hooded blade front, open adjustable rear sights; Polished blue finish; full-length tubular magazine; side ejection; receiver grooved for scope mounting. Introduced 1997. Made in U.S.A. by Henry Repeating Arms Co.

Perf: $245 **Exc:** $180 **VGood:** $135

22 WMR; 11-shot, 19-1/4-inch bbl.

Perf: $345 **Exc:** $280 **VGood:** $235

17 HMR; 11-shot, 20-inch bbl.

Perf: $345 **Exc:** $280 **VGood:** $235

HENRY LEVER-ACTION FRONTIER

Similar to Henry Lever Action but with 20-inch octagon barrel. Chambered in .22 WMR and .17HMR.

NIB: $300 **Exc:** $275 **VGood:** $225

HENRY BIG BOY LEVER-ACTION RIFLE

Lever action; 44 Mag., 45 Colt, .357 Magnum; 10-shot tubular magazine; 20-inch octogon bbl.; 38-1/2-inch long; weighs 8.6 pounds; solid-top brass receiver; straight-grip American walnut stock and forend; Marble semi-buckhorn rear sight and brass bead front sight.

Perf: $650 **Exc:** $595 **VGood:** 495

HENRY BIG BOY DELUXE ENGRAVED .44 MAGNUM

Similar to Henry Big Boy but with deluxe deep-cut German-style engraving on receiver. Introduced 2006.

NIB: $1350 **Exc:** N/A **VGood:** N/A

HENRY BIG BOY .44 MAGNUM "WILDLIFE EDITION"

Similar to Big Boy .44 Magnum but with forend and buttstock laser-engraved with whitetail deer scenes.

NIB: $1000 **Exc:** $950 **VGood:** $775

HENRY BIG BOY .45 COLT "COWBOY EDITION"

Similar to Big Boy .45 Colt but with forend and buttstock laser-engraved with Old West scenes.

NIB: $1000 **Exc:** $950 **VGood:** $775

Heckler & Koch SL7

Heckler & Koch SL8-1

Heckler & Koch SR9

Heckler & Koch USC Carbine

Henry Lever-Action 22

Henry Lever-Action Frontier

Henry Big Boy Deluxe Engraved .44 Magnum

Henry Big Boy .44 Magnum "Wildlife Edition"

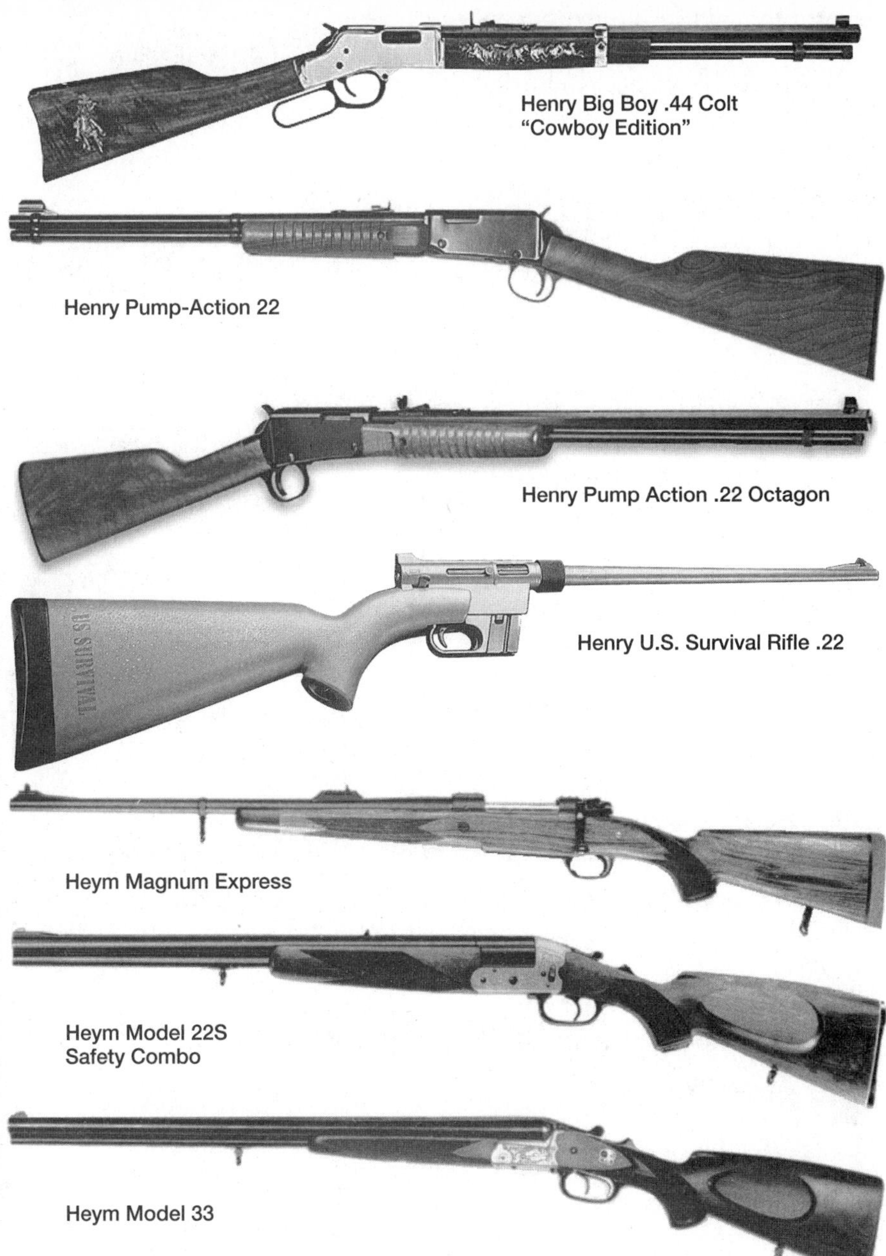
Henry Big Boy .44 Colt "Cowboy Edition"

Henry Pump-Action 22

Henry Pump Action .22 Octagon

Henry U.S. Survival Rifle .22

Heym Magnum Express

Heym Model 22S Safety Combo

Heym Model 33

HENRY GOLDEN BOY 22 LEVER-ACTION

Lever action; 22 LR, 22 Magnum, 17 HRM; 16-shot. 20-inch octagonal barrel; weighs 6.25 lbs.; 38-inch overall length; American walnut stock; Blade front, open rear sights. Brasslite receiver, brass buttplate, blued barrel and lever. Introduced 1998. Made in U.S.A.; from Henry Repeating Arms Co.

Perf: $375 **Exc:** $300 **VGood:** $210

22 WMR

Perf: $425 **Exc:** $350 **VGood:** $250

17 HMR

Perf: $430 **Exc:** $360 **VGood:** N/A

Deluxe

Perf: $1000 **Exc:** $900 **VGood:** N/A

HENRY DELUXE ENGRAVED GOLDEN BOY MAGNUM

Similar to Golden Boy Deluxe but chambered in .22 WMR. Features deluxe deep-cut German-style engraving on receiver. Discontinued.

NIB: $1100 **Exc:** 950 **VGood:** N/A

HENRY "MINI" BOLT 22

Bolt action; single shot; 22 LR.; 16-inch stainless barrel, 8-groove rifling; weighs 3.25 lbs.; 30-inch length; LOP 11-1/2-inch. Synthetic stock, pistol grip, wraparound checkering and beavertail forearm. Williams Fire sights. One piece bolt configuration, manually operated safety. Designed for beginners or ladies.

Perf: $165 **Exc:** $125 **VGood:** $100

HENRY PUMP-ACTION 22

Pump action; 22 LR, 15-shot; 18-1/4-inch barrel; weighs 5.5 lbs. American walnut stock. Bead on ramp front, open adjustable rear sights. Polished blue finish; receiver grooved for scope mount; grooved slide handle; two barrel bands. Introduced 1998. Made in U.S.A., from Henry Repeating Arms Co.

Perf: $260 **Exc:** $210 **VGood:** $170

HENRY PUMP ACTION .22 OCTAGON

Similar to Henry Pump-Action Rifle but with 20-inch octagon barrel. Introduced 2006. Add 10 percent for .22 WMR.

NIB: $400 **Exc:** $365 **VGood:** $300

HENRY U.S. SURVIVAL RIFLE .22

Semi-automatic; 22 LR, 8-shot magazine; 16-inch steel lined barrel; weighs 2.5 lbs. ABS plastic stock; Blade front sight on ramp, aperture rear. Takedown design stores barrel and action in hollow stock. Light enough to float. Silver, black or camo finish. Comes with two magazines. Introduced 1998. From Henry Repeating Arms Co.

Perf: $175 **Exc:** $145 **VGood:** $100

HEYM MODEL 55SS

Double rifle; over/under; 7x65R, 308, 30-06, 8x57JRS, 9.3x74R; 25-inch barrels; 42-inch overall length; weighs about 8 lbs.; silver bead ramp front, open V-type rear sight; dark European walnut stock with hand-checkered pistol grip and forend, oil finish; full sidelock action; Kersten double cross-bolt; cocking indicators; hand-engraved hunting scenes. Options include interchangeable barrels, Zeiss scopes in claw mounts, deluxe engravings and stock carving, etc. and increase values. Imported from Germany by Heckler & Koch, Inc. No longer imported.

Exc: $8700 **VGood:** $8300 **Good:** $7200

HEYM MAGNUM EXPRESS

Bolt action; 338 Lapua Mag., 375 H&H, 378 Wea. Mag., 416 Rigby, 500 Nitro Express 3-inch 460 Wea. Mag., 500 A-Square, 450 Ackley, 600 N.E.; 5-shot magazine (416 Rigby); 24-inch barrel; 45-1/4-inch overall length; weighs about 10 lbs.; adjustable post front sight on ramp, three-leaf express rear; classic English stock of AAA-grade European walnut with cheekpiece; solid rubber buttpad; steel grip cap; modified magnum Mauser action with double square bridge; Timney single trigger; special hinged floorplate; barrel-mounted quick detachable swivel, quick detachable rear; vertical double recoil lug in rear of stock; three-position safety. Imported from Germany by JagerSport, Ltd. Introduced 1989; no longer imported.

Exc: $5750 **VGood:** $4495 **Good:** $3250

600 Nitro Express caliber

Exc: $9995 **VGood:** $7995 **Good:** $5150

HEYM MODEL 22S SAFETY COMBO

Combination gun; 16- or 20-ga. (2-3/4-inch, 3-inch), 12-ga. (2-3/4-inch) over 22 Hornet, 22 WMR, 222 Rem., 222 Rem Mag, 223, 22-250, 243 Win., 5.6x50R, 5.6x52R, 6.5x55, 6.5x57R, 7x57R, 8x57 JRS; 24-inch barrel with solid rib; weighs about 5-1/2 lbs.; silver bead ramp front, folding leaf rear sight; dark European walnut stock with hand-checkered pistol grip and forend; oil finish; tang-mounted cocking slide; floating rifle barrel; single-set trigger; base supplied for quick-detachable scope mounts; patented rocker-weight system automatically uncocks gun if accidentally dropped or bumped hard. Imported from Germany by Heckler & Koch, Inc. No longer imported.

Exc: $3000 **VGood:** $2295 **Good:** $1895

HEYM MODEL 33

Drilling; side-by-side shotgun barrels with rifle barrel below; 5.6x50R Mag., 5.6x52R, 6.5x55, 6.5x57R, 7x57R, 7x65R, 8x57JRS, 9.3x74R, 222, 243, 270, 308, 30-06; 16x16 (2-3/4-inch), 20x20 (3-inch); 25-inch (Full & Mod.) barrels; 42-inch overall length; weighs about 6-1/2 lbs.; silver bead front, folding leaf rear sight; dark European walnut stock with checkered pistol grip and forend; oil finish; automatic sight positioner; boxlock action with Greener-type cross-bolt and safety, double under lugs; double-set triggers; plastic or steel trigger guard. Imported from Germany by Heckler and Koch, Inc. No longer imported.

Exc: $6000 **VGood:** $5000 **Good:** $4350

HEYM MODEL 33 DELUXE

Same specs as Model 33 except extensive hunting scene engraving. Imported from Germany by Heckler & Koch, Inc. No longer imported.

Exc: $7695 **VGood:** $6150 **Good:** $4595

HEYM MODEL 37B DOUBLE RIFLE DRILLING

Drilling; side-by-side rifle barrels with shotgun barrel below; 7x65R, 30-06, 8x57JRS, 9.3x74R; 20-ga. (3-inch); 25-inch barrels choked Full or Mod.; 42-inch overall length; weighs about 8-1/2 lbs.; silver bead front, folding leaf rear sight; dark European walnut stock with hand-checkered pistol grip and forend; oil finish; full sidelock construction; Greener-type cross-bolt; double under lugs; cocking indicators. Imported from Germany by Heckler & Koch, Inc. No longer imported.

Exc: $12,995 **VGood:** $10,000 **Good:** $7995

HEYM MODEL 37B DELUXE

Same specs as Model 37B except extensive hunting scene engraving. Imported from Germany by Heckler & Koch, Inc. No longer imported.

Exc: $15,500 **VGood:** $12,000 **Good:** $8995

HEYM MODEL 37 SIDELOCK DRILLING

Same specs as Model 37B except 12x12, 16x16 or 20x20 over 5.6x50R Mag., 5.6x52R, 6.5x55, 6.5x57R, 7x57R, 7x65R, 8x57JRS, 9.3x74R, 243, 308, 30-06; rifle barrel manually cocked and uncocked. Imported from Germany by Heckler & Koch, Inc. No longer imported.

Perf: $11,995 **Exc:** $8995 **VGood:** $6995

HEYM MODEL 55B

Double rifle; over/under; 7x65R, 308, 30-06, 8x57JRS, 8x75 RS, 9.3x74R, 375 H&H, 458 Win. Mag., 470 N.E.; 25-inch barrels; 42-inch overall length; weighs about 8 lbs., depending upon caliber; silver bead ramp front, open V-type rear sight; dark European walnut stock with hand-checkered pistol grip and forend; oil finish; boxlock or full sidelock action; Kersten double cross-bolt; cocking indicators; hand-engraved hunting scenes. Options include interchangeable barrels, Swarovski scopes in claw mounts, deluxe engravings and stock carving, etc. Imported from Germany by JagerSport, Ltd. No longer imported.

Exc: $5000 **VGood:** $4500 **Good:** $4000

HEYM MODEL 55BF O/U COMBO

Same specs as Model 55B O/U rifle except 12-, 16-, 20-ga. (2-3/4-inch or 3-inch) over 5.6x50R, 222 Rem., 223 Rem., 5.6x52R, 243, 6.5x57R, 270, 7x57R, 7x65R, 308, 30-06, 8x57JRS, 9.3x74R; solid rib barrel. Available with interchangeable shotgun and rifle barrels. No longer imported.

Exc: $5000 **VGood:** $4500 **Good:** $4000

HEYM MODEL 55BW

Same specs as Model 55B except solid rib barrel. Available with interchangeable shotgun and rifle barrels. No longer imported.

Exc: $9295 **VGood:** $7725 **Good:** $5495

HEYM MODEL 55FW O/U COMBO

Same specs as Model 55B O/U rifle except 12-, 16-, 20-ga. (2-3/4-inch or 3-inch) over 7x65R, 308, 30-06, 8x57JRS, 8x75 RS, 9.3x74R, 375 H&H, 458 Win. Mag., 470 N.E.; solid rib barrel. Available with interchangeable shotgun and rifle barrels. No longer imported.

Exc: $10,995 **VGood:** $8995 **Good:** $6995

HEYM MODEL 77B

Double rifle; over/under boxlock; 9.3x74R, 375 H&H, 458 Win. Mag.; 25-inch, 28-inch barrels; weighs 8-1/2 lbs.; silver bead front, folding leaf rear sight; dark oil-finished European walnut stock; hand-checkered pistol grip, forend; fine engraving; Greener-type crossbolt; double under lugs. Introduced 1980; discontinued 1986.

Exc: $5250 **VGood:** $4695 **Good:** $3395

HEYM MODEL 77BF

Same specs as Model 77B except over/under combo; boxlock or sidelock; 12-, 16-, 20-ga. over 5.6x50R, 222 Rem., 5.6x57R, 243, 6.5x57R, 270, 7x57R, 7x65R, 308, 30-06, 8x57 JRS, 9.3x74R, 375 H&H; solid rib barrel. Introduced 1986.

Boxlock (77BF)

Exc: $5495 **VGood:** $4895 **Good:** $3695

Sidelock (77BFSS)

Exc: $9500 **VGood:** $8250 **Good:** $5250

Heym Model 33 Deluxe

Heym Model 55B

Heym Model 55BF O/U Combo

Heym Model 88B

Heym Model 88B Safari

Heym Model SR20 Trophy

HEYM MODEL 88B

Side-by-side double rifle; 30-06, 300 Win Mag, 8x57JRS, 9.3x74R, 375 H&H; 25-inch Krupp steel barrels; 42-inch overall length; weighs 7-3/4 lbs. (standard calibers), 8-1/2 lbs. (magnums); silver bead post on ramp front sight, fixed or three-leaf express rear; fancy French walnut stock of classic North American design; Monte Carlo cheekpiece; hand-checkered forend; pistol grip; action with complete coverage hunting scene engraving; Anson-type boxlock action; Greener-type cross-bolt; double under-locking lugs; recoil pad. Imported from Germany by JagerSport, Ltd. No longer imported.

Exc: $9600 **VGood:** $8795 **Good:** $7000

HEYM MODEL 88B SAFARI

Same specs as Model 88B except 375 H&H, 458 Win. Mag., 470 NE, 500 NE; weighs about 10 lbs.; large frame; ejectors. Imported from Germany by JagerSport, Ltd. No longer imported.

Exc: $13,995 **VGood:** $10,995 **Good:** $8995

HEYM MODEL 88BSS

Same specs as Model 88B except quick detachable sidelocks. Imported from Germany by JagerSport, Ltd. No longer imported.

Perf: $13,995 **Exc:** $10,195 **VGood:** $8995

HEYM MODEL SR20 TROPHY

Bolt action; 243, 7x57, 270, 308, 30-06, 7mm Rem. Mag., 338 Win. Mag., 375 H&H, other calibers on request; 22-inch barrel (standard calibers), 24-inch (magnums); weighs about 7 lbs.; German silver bead ramp front sight, open rear on quarter-rib; drilled and tapped for scope mounting; AAA-grade European walnut stock with cheekpiece; solid rubber buttpad; checkered grip and forend; oil finish; rosewood grip cap; octagonal barrel; barrel-mounted quick detachable swivel, standard quick detachable rear swivel. Imported from Germany by Heckler & Koch, Inc. No longer imported.

Perf: $2495 **Exc:** $1995 **VGood:** $1195

HEYM MODEL SR20 ALPINE

Same specs as SR20 Trophy except 243, 270, 7x57, 308, 30-06, 6.5x55, 7x64, 8x57JS; 20-inch barrel; open sights; full-length “Mountain Rifle” stock with steel forend cap, steel grip cap. Imported from Germany by Heckler & Koch, Inc. Introduced 1989; no longer imported.

Perf: $2400 **Exc:** $2000 **VGood:** $1600

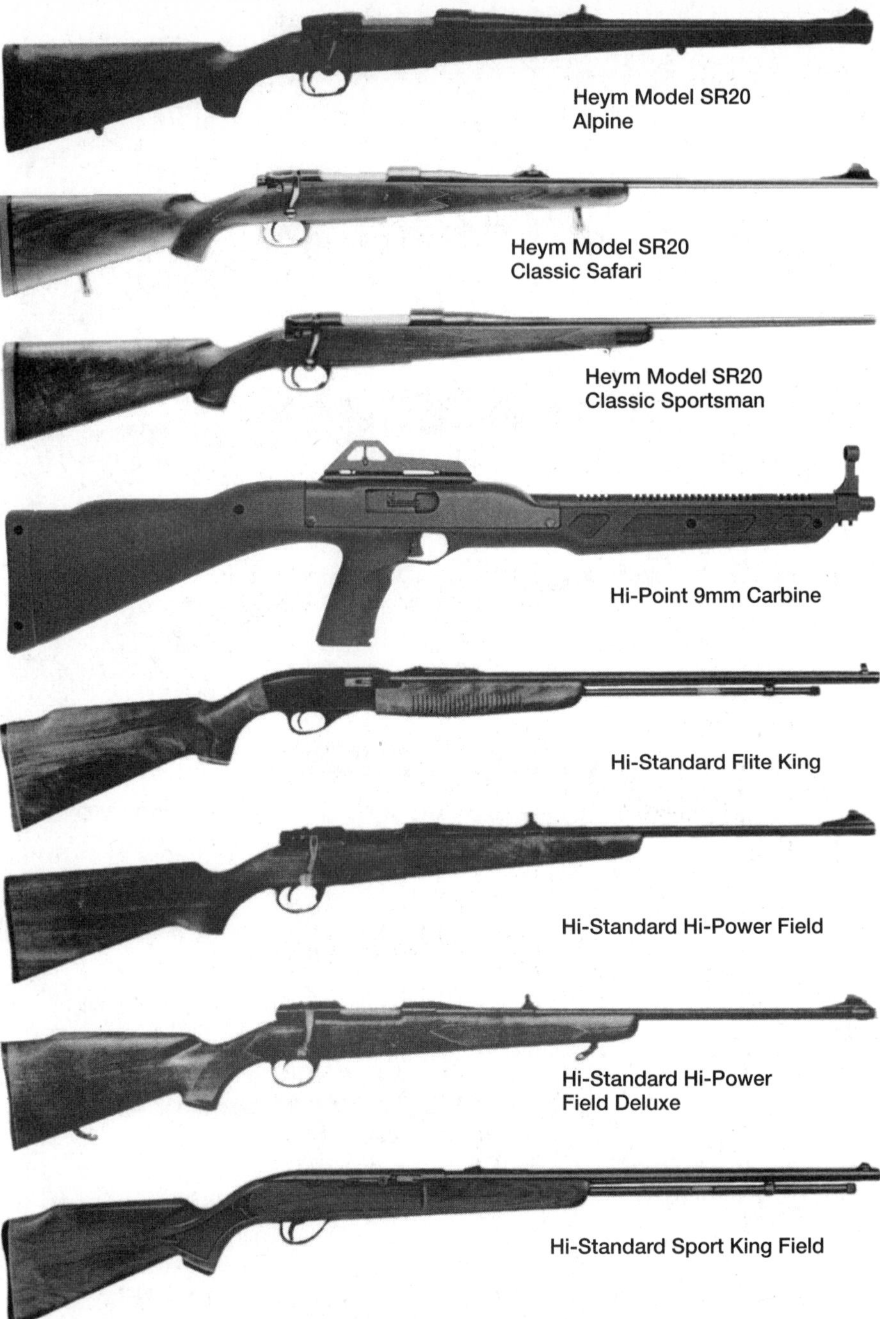
Heym Model SR20 Alpine

Heym Model SR20 Classic Safari

Heym Model SR20 Classic Sportsman

Hi-Point 9mm Carbine

Hi-Standard Flite King

Hi-Standard Hi-Power Field

Hi-Standard Hi-Power Field Deluxe

Hi-Standard Sport King Field

HEYM MODEL SR20 CLASSIC SAFARI

Same specs as SR20 Trophy except 404 Jeffery, 425 Express, 458 Win. Mag.; 24-inch barrel; large post front, three-leaf express rear sight; barrel-mounted ring-type front quick detachable swivel, quick detachable rear; double-lug recoil bolt in stock. Imported from Germany by Heckler & Koch, Inc. Introduced 1989; no longer imported.

Perf: $3375 **Exc:** $2895 **VGood:** $2495

HEYM MODEL SR20 CLASSIC SPORTSMAN

Same specs as SR20 Trophy except round barrel without sights. Imported from Germany by Heckler & Koch, Inc. Introduced 1989; no longer imported.

Perf: $1695 **Exc:** $1395 **VGood:** $995

Magnum calibers

Perf: $1795 **Exc:** $1495 **VGood:** $1095

HEYM MODEL SR40

Bolt action, short action; 222, 222 Rem Mag, 223, 22-250, 5.6x50 Mag.; 24-inch barrel; 44-inch overall length; weighs 6-1/4 lbs.; silver bead ramp front, adjustable folding leaf rear sight; carbine-length Mannlicher-style stock; recoil pad; hinged floorplate; three-position safety. Made in Germany. Introduced 1984; discontinued 1988.

Perf: $895 **Exc:** $695 **VGood:** $495

Left-hand model

Perf: $995 **Exc:** $795 **VGood:** $595

HEYM-RUGER MODEL HR30

Single shot; 243, 6.5x57R, 7x64, 7x65R, 270, 308, 30-06; 24-inch round barrel; weighs 6-3/8 lbs.; bead ramp front, leaf rear sight; hand-checkered European walnut Mannlicher or sporter stock; oil finish; recoil pad; Ruger No. 1 action. Custom-made gun, many options available. Introduced 1978; discontinued 1987.

Sporter stock

Exc: $3000 **VGood:** $2700 **Good:** $2100

Mannlicher stock

Exc: $3100 **VGood:** $2800 **Good:** $2200

HEYM-RUGER MODEL HR30G

Same specs as HR30 except 6.5x68R, 300 Win. Mag., 8x68S, 9.3x74R; 25-inch barrel.

Sporter stock

Exc: $3100 **VGood:** $2800 **Good:** $2200

Mannlicher stock

Exc: $3200 **VGood:** $2900 **Good:** $2300

HEYM-RUGER MODEL HR38

Single shot; 243, 6.5x57R, 7x64, 7x65R, 270, 308, 30-06; 24-inch octagon barrel; weighs 6-3/8 lbs.; bead ramp front, leaf rear sight; hand-checkered European walnut Mannlicher or sporter stock; oil finished; recoil pad; Ruger No. 1 action. Custom-made gun, many options available. Introduced 1978; discontinued 1987.

Sporter stock

Exc: $3200 **VGood:** $2900 **Good:** $2300

Mannlicher stock

Exc: $3300 **VGood:** $3000 **Good:** $2400

HEYM-RUGER MODEL HR38G

Same specs as HR38 except 6.5x68R, 300 Win. Mag., 8x68S.

Sporter stock

Exc: $3300 **VGood:** $3000 **Good:** $2400

Mannlicher stock

Exc: $3400 **VGood:** $3100 **Good:** $2500

HI-POINT 9MM CARBINE

Caliber: 9mm Para., 40 S&W, 10-shot magazine; 16-1/2 barrel-inch (17-1/2-inch for 40 S&W); weighs 4-1/2 lbs.; 31-1/2-inch overall; Black polymer stock; Protected post front, aperture rear sights. Scope mount, sling and swivels furnished. Grip-mounted magazine release. Black or chrome finish. Sling swivels. Introduced 1996, still available. Made in U.S.A. by MKS Supply, Inc.

Perf: $255 **Exc:** $225 **VGood:** $195

HI-POINT .40 S&W CARBINE

Similar to Hi-Point 9mm carbine but in .40 S&W. Features include all-weather, black, polymer stock, 10 shot maazine, 17.5-inch barrel, sling swivels, grip mounted clip release, quick on & off thumb safety, rear peep sight, 32.5-inch OAL and a scope mount.

NIB: $255 **Exc:** $225 **VGood:** $195

HI-STANDARD FLITE KING

Pump-action; hammerless; 22 LR, 22 Long, 22 Short; 17-shot (22 LR), 19-shot (22 Long), 24-shot (22 Short) tubular magazine; 24-inch barrel; 41-3/4-inch overall length; weighs 5-1/2 lbs.; Patridge-type rear sight, bead front; checkered hardwood Monte Carlo pistol-grip stock; grooved slide handle. Introduced 1962; discontinued 1975.

Exc: $250 **VGood:** $175 **Good:** $125

HI-STANDARD HI-POWER FIELD

Bolt action; 270, 30-06; 4-shot magazine; 22-inch barrel; 42-3/4-inch overall length; weighs 7 lbs.; built on Mauser-type action; folding leaf open rear sight, ramp front; uncheckered walnut field-style pistol-grip stock; sliding safety; quick-detachable sling swivels. Introduced 1962; discontinued 1966.

Exc: $340 **VGood:** $290 **Good:** $240

HI-STANDARD HI-POWER FIELD DELUXE

Same specs as Hi-Power Field except impressed checkering on Monte Carlo stock; sling swivels. Introduced 1962; discontinued 1966.

Exc: $375 **VGood:** $320 **Good:** $265

HI-STANDARD SPORT KING FIELD

Semi-automatic; 22 LR, 22 Long, 22 Short; 22-1/4-inch tapered barrel; 15-shot (22 LR), 17-shot (22 Long), 21-shot (22 Short) tubular magazine; open rear, bead post front sight; uncheckered pistol-grip stock. Introduced 1960; dropped 1966.

Exc: $150 **VGood:** $125 **Good:** $100

HI-STANDARD SPORT KING CARBINE

Same specs as Sport King except 12-shot (22 LR), 14-shot (22 Long), 17-shot (22 Short) tubular magazine; 18-inch barrel; 38-1/2-inch overall length; weighs 5-1/2 lbs.; open rear, bead post front sight; receiver grooved for scope mounts; straight-grip stock; brass buttplate; sling swivels; golden trigger guard, trigger, safety. Introduced 1964; discontinued 1973.

Exc: $140 **VGood:** $120 **Good:** $100

HI-STANDARD SPORT KING DELUXE

Same specs as Sport King Field except impressed checkering on stock. Introduced 1966; dropped 1975.

Exc: $160 **VGood:** $140 **Good:** $110

HI-STANDARD SPORT KING SPECIAL

Same specs as Sport King Field except Monte Carlo stock; semi-beavertail forearm. Introduced 1960; discontinued 1966.

Exc: $120 **VGood:** $100 **Good:** $90

HOENIG ROTARY ROUND ACTION DOUBLE RIFLE

Unique round action; Most popular calibers from 225 Win. to 9.3x74R.; 22-inch-26-inch barrel; English Walnut stock; to customer specs. Swivel hood front sight with button release (extra bead stored in trap door gripcap), express-style rear on quarter-rib adjustable for windage and elevation; scope mount. Round action opens by rotating barrels, pulling forward. Inertia extractor system; rotary safety blocks strikers. Single lever quick-detachable scope mount. Simple takedown without removing forend. Introduced 1997. Made in U.S.A. by George Hoenig.

Perf: $24,000 **Exc:** $22,000 **VGood:** $20,000

HOENIG ROTARY ROUND ACTION COMBINATION

Like double rifle, but with a 28-gauge shotgun barrel in combination with a rifle barrel; barrels 26-inch; weighs 7 lbs.; English Walnut stock to customer specs. Front ramp sight with button release blades. Foldable aperture tang sight windage and elevation adjustable. Quarter rib with scope mount. Round action opens by rotating barrels, pulling forward. Inertia extractor; rotary safety blocks strikers. Simple takedown without removing forend. Made in U.S.A. by George Hoenig.

Perf: $24,000 **Exc:** $22,000 **VGood:** $20,000

HOLLAND & HOLLAND BEST QUALITY

Bolt action; 240 Apex, 300 H&H Mag., 375 H&H Mag.; 4-shot box magazine; 24-inch barrel; built on Mauser or Enfield action; folding leaf rear, hooded ramp front; cheekpiece stock of European walnut; hand-checkered pistol grip, forearm; sling swivels, recoil pad; not imported to U.S. Prices can go higher than $30,000, depending on features.

HOLLAND & HOLLAND DELUXE

Bolt action; 240 Apex, 300 H&H Mag., 375 H&H Mag.; 4-shot box magazine; 24-inch barrel; built on Mauser or Enfield action; folding leaf rear, hooded ramp front sight; exhibition-grade European walnut cheekpiece stock; hand-checkered pistol grip, forearm; sling swivels; recoil pad. Introduced following World War II; not imported to U.S. Prices vary based on features.

HOLLAND & HOLLAND NO. 2 MODEL

Double rifle; sidelock; side-by-side; 240 Apex, 7mm H&H Mag., 300 H&H Mag., 375 H&H Mag., 458 Win. Mag., 465 H&H Mag., 577 H&H Mag.; 24-inch, 26-inch, 28-inch barrels; folding leaf rear, ramp front sight; two-piece European stock; hand-checkered pistol grip, forearm; swivels; not imported to U.S.

Exc: $40,000 **VGood:** $28,500 **Good:** $12,000

Hoenig Rotary Round Action Double Rifle

Hoenig Rotary Round Action Combination

Holland & Holland Best Quality

Holland & Holland Royal

Howa Lightning

Howa M-1500 Ultralight

Howa Classic Laminate Thumbhole Varminter

HOLLAND & HOLLAND ROYAL

Double rifle; hammerless sidelock; 240 Apex, 7mm H&H Mag., 300 H&H Mag., 375 H&H Mag., 458 Win., 465 H&H; 24-inch, 26-inch, 28-inch barrels; folding leaf rear, ramp front sight; two-piece choice European stock; hand-checkered pistol grip, forearm; swivels; custom-engraved receiver. Special-order rifle in the realm of semi-production, with original buyer's options available; not imported to U.S. Prices range from $20,000 to over $100,000 based on features.

HOLLAND & HOLLAND ROYAL DELUXE

Same specs as Royal Model except more ornate engraving; better grade European walnut stock; better fitting. Still in production; not imported to U.S. Prices vary based on features.

HOWA CLASSIC LAMINATE THUMBHOLE VARMINTER

Bolt action; .223 Rem., .204 Ruger, .22-250 Rem., .308 Win., .243 Win. Laminated hardwood stock in grey or nutmeg, 24 inch # 6 contour barrel, dual swivel studs, detachable magazine conversion kit available as aftermarket accessory. Add $50 for detachable magazine

Perf: $750 **Exc:** $600 **VGood:** $500

HOWA HEAVY BARREL VARMINT

Bolt action; 223, 22-250, 308; 24-inch heavy barrel; 42-inch overall length; weighs 7-1/2-7-3/4 lbs.; no sights; drilled and tapped for scope mounts; American walnut stock with Monte Carlo comb and cheekpiece; 18 lpi checkering on pistol grip and forend; single unit trigger guard and magazine box with hinged floorplate; Parkerized finish; quick detachable swivel studs; composition non-slip buttplate with white spacer. Imported from Japan by Interarms. Introduced 1989; discontinued 1992.

Perf: $475 **Exc:** $375 **VGood:** $300

HOWA LIGHTNING

Bolt action; 223, 22-250, 243, 270, 308, 30-06, 7mm Rem. Mag., 300 Win. Mag., 338 Win. Mag.; 22-inch barrel (standard calibers), 24-inch (magnums); 42-inch overall length (22-inch barrel); weighs 7-1/2 lbs.; no sights; drilled and tapped for scope mounting; black Bell & Carlson Carbelite composite stock with Monte Carlo comb; checkered grip and forend; sliding thumb safety; hinged floorplate; polished blue/black finish. From Interarms. Introduced 1993; still imported. Premium for magnum calibers.

Perf: $425 **Exc:** $335 **VGood:** $300

Howa M-1500 Varminter

Howa Model 1500 Hunter

Husqvarna Hi-Power

Husqvarna Model 456

Huldra Arms Carbine 5.45

Huldra Arms Carbine 5.56

Huldra Arms Tactical Elite

HOWA LIGHTNING WOODGRAIN

Same specs as Lightning except 243, 270, 30-06, 308, 7mm Rem. Mag.; 5-shot magazine; lightweight Carbelite synthetic stock with simulated woodgrain. Introduced 1994; no longer in production.

Perf: $495 **Exc:** $350 **VGood:** $320

HOWA M-1500 ULTRALIGHT

Similar to Howa M-1500 Lightning except receiver milled to reduce weight, tapered 22-inch barrel; 1-10-inch twist. Chambered for 243 Win. Stocks are black texture-finished hardwood. Weighs 6.4 lbs. Length 40-inch overall.

Perf: $475 **Exc:** $375 **VGood:** $300

HOWA M-1500 VARMINTER AND VARMINTER SUPREME RIFLES

Similar to M-1500 Lightning except has heavy 24-inch hammer-forged barrel. Chambered for 223, 22-250, 380. Weighs 9.3 lbs.; overall length 44-1/2-inch. Introduced 1999. Imported from Japan by Interarms/Howa. Varminter Supreme has heavy barrel, target crown muzzle. Heavy 24-inch barrel, laminated wood with raised comb stocks, rollover cheekpiece, vented beavertail forearm; available in 223 Rem., 22-250 Rem., 308 Win. Weighs 9.9 lbs. Introduced 2001. Imported from Japan by Legacy Sports International. Still available.

Perf: $525 **Exc:** $425 **VGood:** $300

HOWA MODEL 1500 HUNTER

Bolt action; 22-250, 223, 243, 270, 308, 30-06, 300 Win. Mag., 7mm Rem. Mag.; 3-, 5-shot magazine; 22-inch, 24-inch barrel; weighs 7-1/2 lbs.; ramped gold bead front, adjustable open rear sight; Monte-Carlo-type walnut stock; checkered pistol grip, forend; swivels; adjustable trigger. Made in Japan. Introduced 1988; discontinued 1988. Premium for magnum calibers.

Perf: $475 **Exc:** $325 **VGood:** $29

HOWA MODEL 1500 TROPHY

Bolt action; 223, 22-250, 243, 270, 30-06, 308, 7mm Rem. Mag., 300 Win. Mag., 338 Win. Mag.; 22-inch barrel (standard calibers), 24-inch (magnums); 42-inch overall length; weighs 7-1/2 to 7-3/4 lbs.; hooded ramp gold bead front sight, open round-notch fully-adjustable rear; drilled and tapped for scope mounts; American walnut stock with Monte Carlo comb and cheekpiece; 18 lpi checkering on pistol grip and forend; single unit trigger guard and magazine box with hinged floorplate; quick detachable swivel studs; composition non-slip buttplate with white spacer; magnum models with rubber recoil pad. Imported from Japan by Interarms. Introduced 1979; discontinued 1992.

Perf: $495 **Exc:** $395 **VGood:** $280

HOWA REALTREE CAMO

Bolt action; 270, 30-06; 5-shot magazine; 22-inch barrel; 42-1/4-inch overall length; weighs 8 lbs.; no sights; drilled and tapped for scope mounting; Bell & Carlson Carbelite composite stock with straight comb, checkered grip and forend; completely covered with Realtree camo finish, except bolt; sliding thumb safety; hinged floorplate; sling swivel studs; recoil pad. Imported from Japan by Interarms. Introduced 1993; discontinued 1994.

Perf: $495 **Exc:** $395 **VGood:** $320

HULDRA ARMS CARBINE

AR 15 style Semi-automatic in 5.45x39mm and 5.56 x 45mm. 16 inch M4 contour barrel with Melonite coating and A2 style flash hider. M4 handguards. Single stage trigger. MIL SPEC 6-position stock. 35 9/16 inches overall length. Weight: 6.16 pounds. Introduced 2011.

Perf: $925 **Exc:** $850 **VGood:** $780

HULDRA ARMS TACTICAL ELITE

AR 15 style Semi-automatic in 5.56 x 45mm. 16 inch Government contour barrel with Melonite coating and mid-length gas system and A2 style flash hider. Free-float extended quad rail handguard. JP 4.5 pound single stage trigger. 6-position stock. 35.5 inches overall length. Weight: 7.2 pounds. Introduced 2012.

Perf: $1400 **Exc:** $1250 **VGood:** $1100

HULDRA ARMS TACTICAL EVO

AR 15 style Semi-automatic in 5.56 x 45mm. 14.5 barrel with Melonite with permanently affixed flash hider. Free-float aluminum handguard. Single stage trigger. 6-position stock. 34 1/3 inches overall length. Weight: 6.6 pounds. Introduced 2012.

Perf: $1250 **Exc:** $1100 **VGood:** $975

Huldra Arms Tactical EVO

HULDRA ARMS TACTICAL EVO FLUTED BARREL

AR 15 style Semi-automatic in 5.56 x 45mm. 16 inch medium contour fluted stainless steel barrel. Free-float monolithic rail with mid-length gas system. JP 4.5 pound single stage trigger. 6-position stock. 36 1/8 inches overall length. Weight: 7.2 pounds. Introduced 2012.

Perf: $1850 **Exc:** $1600 **VGood:** $1450

Huldra Arms Tactical EVO Fluted Barrel

HUSQVARNA HI-POWER

Bolt action; 220 Swift, 270 Win., 30-06, 6.5x55, 8x57, 9.3x57; 23-3/4-inch barrel; 5-shot box magazine; Mauser-type action; open rear, hooded ramp front sight; hand-checkered pistol-grip beech stock; sling swivels. Introduced 1946; discontinued 1959.

Exc: $545 **VGood:** $490 **Good:** $460

Husqvarna Series 1100

HUSQVARNA MODEL 456

Bolt action; 243, 270, 30-06, 308, 7mm Rem. Mag.; 5-shot box magazine; 20-1/2-inch barrel; Husqvarna improved Mauser action; open adjustable rear, hooded ramp front sight; full-length European walnut stock; slope-away cheekpiece; metal forearm cap; sling swivels. Introduced 1959; discontinued 1970.

Exc: $425 **VGood:** $330 **Good:** $270

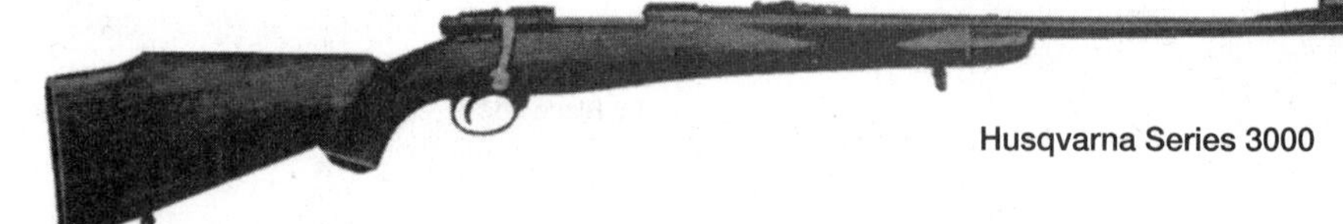

Husqvarna Series 3000

HUSQVARNA MODEL 1950

Bolt action; 220 Swift, 270 Win., 30-06; 5-shot box magazine; 23-3/4-inch barrel; Mauser-type action; open rear, hooded ramp front sight; hand-checkered pistol-grip beech stock; sling swivels. Introduced 1950; discontinued 1952.

Exc: $425 **VGood:** $350 **Good:** $280

HUSQVARNA MODEL 1951

Bolt action; 220 Swift, 30-06; 5-shot box magazine; 23-3/4-inch barrel; Mauser-type action; open rear, hooded ramp front sight; hand-checkered pistol-grip beech stock with high-comb, low safety. Introduced 1951; discontinued 1951.

Exc: $425 **VGood:** $365 **Good:** $300

Husqvarna Series 3100

HUSQVARNA MODEL 8000

Bolt action; 270 Win., 30-06, 300 Win. Mag., 7mm Rem. Mag.; 5-shot box magazine; 23-3/4-inch barrel; improved Husqvarna action; no sights; hand-checkered deluxe French walnut stock; Monte Carlo cheekpiece; rosewood forearm tip; pistol-grip cap; adjustable trigger; jeweled bolt; hinged engraved floorplate. Introduced 1971; discontinued 1972.

Exc: $695 **VGood:** $595 **Good:** $475

Husqvarna Series 4000

HUSQVARNA MODEL 9000

Bolt action; 270 Win., 30-06, 300 Win. Mag., 7mm Rem. Mag.; 5-shot box magazine; 23-3/4-inch barrel; improved Husqvarna action; folding leaf rear, hooded ramp front sight; Monte Carlo cheekpiece stock; adjustable trigger. Introduced 1971; discontinued 1972.

Exc: $495 **VGood:** $430 **Good:** $360

HUSQVARNA SERIES 1000

Bolt action; 220 Swift, 270, 30-06; 5-shot box magazine; 23-3/4-inch barrel; Mauser-type action; open rear, hooded ramp front sight; European walnut stock, with cheekpiece; Monte Carlo comb. Introduced 1952; discontinued 1956.

Exc: $450 **VGood:** $395 **Good:** $315

HUSQVARNA SERIES 1100

Bolt action; 220 Swift, 270, 30-06, 6.5x55, 8x57, 9.3x57; 5-shot box magazine; 23-1/2-inch barrel; Mauser-type action; open rear, hooded ramp front sight; European walnut Monte Carlo stock; jeweled bolt. Introduced 1952; discontinued 1956.

Exc: $475 **VGood:** $425 **Good:** $340

HUSQVARNA SERIES 3000

Bolt action; 243, 270, 30-06, 308, 7mm Rem. Mag.; 5-shot box magazine; 23-3/4-inch barrel; Husqvarna improved Mauser action; open rear, hooded ramp front sight; European walnut Monte Carlo-style stock; sling swivels. Introduced 1954; discontinued 1976.

Exc: $450 **VGood:** $395 **Good:** $320

HUSQVARNA SERIES 3100

Bolt action; 243 Win., 270 Win., 7mm Rem. Mag., 30-06, 308 Win.; 5-shot box magazine; 23-3/4-inch barrel; Husqvarna improved Mauser action; open rear, hooded ramp front sight; hand-checkered European walnut pistol-grip stock; cheekpiece; black forearm tip; pistol-grip cap; sling swivels. Introduced 1954; discontinued 1976.

Exc: $550 **VGood:** $430 **Good:** $360

HUSQVARNA SERIES 4000

Bolt action; 243 Win., 270 Win., 30-06, 308 Win., 7mm Rem. Mag.; 5-shot box magazine; 20-1/2-inch barrel; Husqvarna improved Mauser action; no rear sight, hooded ramp front; drilled, tapped for scope mounts; European walnut Monte Carlo stock; hand-checkered pistol grip, forearm; sling swivels. Introduced 1954; discontinued 1976.

Exc: $495 **VGood:** $430 **Good:** $360

HUSQVARNA SERIES 4100

Bolt action; 243 Win., 270 Win., 30-06, 308 Win., 7mm Rem. Mag.; 5-shot box magazine; 20-1/2-inch

Husqvarna Series 4100

Husqvarna Series 7000

Ibus M17S 223 Bullpup

Interarms Mark X Cavalier

barrel; Husqvarna improved action; adjustable open rear, hooded ramp front sight; lightweight European walnut stock with cheekpiece; sling swivels. Introduced 1954; discontinued 1976.

Exc: $575 **VGood:** $460 **Good:** $350

HUSQVARNA SERIES 6000

Bolt action; 243 Win., 270 Win., 30-06, 308 Win., 7mm Rem. Mag.; 5-shot box magazine; 23-3/4-inch barrel; three-leaf folding rear, hooded ramp front sight; fancy walnut stock; adjustable trigger; sling swivels. Introduced 1968; discontinued 1970.

Exc: $595 **VGood:** $495 **Good:** $385

HUSQVARNA SERIES 7000

Bolt action; 243 Win., 270 Win., 30-06, 308 Win.; 5-shot box magazine; 20-1/2-inch barrel; three-leaf folding rear, hooded ramp front sight; lightweight fancy walnut stock; adjustable trigger; sling swivels. Introduced 1968; discontinued 1970.

Exc: $595 **VGood:** $495 **Good:** $395

HUSQVARNA SERIES P-3000

Bolt action; 243 Win., 270 Win., 30-06, 7mm Rem. Mag.; 5-shot box magazine; 23-3/4-inch barrel; Husqvarna improved action; open rear, hooded ramp front sight; top-grade walnut stock; engraved action; adjustable trigger; sling swivels. Introduced 1968; discontinued 1970.

Perf: $795 **Exc:** $650 **VGood:** $495

IAI M-333 M1 GARAND

Semi-automatic; 30-06, 8-shot clip; 24-inch barrel; weighs 9-1/2 lbs.; 43.6-inch overall length; Hardwood stock; Blade front, aperture adjustable rear sights; Parkerized finish; gas-operated semi-automatic; remanufactured to military specifications. From IAI.

Perf: $900 **Exc:** $810 **VGood:** $650

IAI M-888 M1 CARBINE SEMI-AUTOMATIC RIFLE

Semi-automatic; 30 Carbine. 18-inch-20-inch barrel; weighs 5-1/2 lbs.; 35-inch- 37-inch overall length; Laminate, walnut or birch stock; Blade front, adjustable rear sights; gas-operated, air cooled, manufactured to military specifications. 10/15/30 round. magazines; scope available. From IAI.

Perf: $600 **Exc:** $500 **VGood:** $400

IAR MODEL 1873 REVOLVING CARBINE

Revolver, 357 Mag., 45 Colt. 18-inch barrel; weighs 4 lbs., 8 oz.; 34-inch overall length; One-piece walnut stock; Blade front, notch rear sights. Color case-hardened frame, blue barrel, backstrap and trigger guard. Introduced 1998. Imported from Italy by IAR, Inc.

Perf: $500 **Exc:** $425 **VGood:** $350

IBUS M17S 223 BULLPUP

Semi-automatic; 223 Remington; 10-shot magazine; 21-1/2" barrel; 30" overall length; no sights, but comes with scope mount for Weaver-type rings; Zytel glass-filled bullpup-style nylon stock; gas-operated; short-stroke piston action; ambidextrous magazine release. Made in USA by Bushmaster Firearms. Introduced 1993.

Perf: $900 **Exc:** $800 **VGood:** $695

INTERARMS MARK X ALASKAN

Bolt action; 375 H&H Mag., 458 Win. Mag.; 3-shot magazine; 24-inch barrel; 44-3/4-inch overall length; weighs 8-1/4 lbs.; adjustable folding leaf rear, ramp front sight with removable hood; select walnut Monte Carlo-style stock with crossbolt; hand-checkered pistol grip, forend; sling swivels; heavy-duty recoil pad. Introduced 1976; discontinued 1985.

Exc: $750 **VGood:** $495 **Good:** $295

INTERARMS MARK X AMERICAN FIELD

Bolt action; 22-250, 243, 25-06, 270, 7x57, 7mm Rem. Mag., 308 Win., 30-06, 300 Win. Mag.; 24-inch barrel; 45-inch overall length; weighs 7 lbs.; Mauser-system action; ramp front sight with removable hood, open fully-adjustable rear; drilled and tapped for scope mounts and receiver sight; hand-checkered walnut stock; 1-inch sling swivels; one-piece trigger guard with hinged floorplate; adjustable trigger; hammer-forged chrome vanadium steel barrel. Imported from Yugoslavia by Interarms. Discontinued 1994.

Exc: $495 **VGood:** $350 **Good:** $295

INTERARMS MARK X CAVALIER

Bolt action; 22-250, 243, 25-06, 270, 7x57, 7mm Rem. Mag., 30-06, 300 Win. Mag., 308 Win.; 3-, 5-shot magazine; 24-inch barrel; 44-inch overall length; weighs 7-1/2 lbs.; adjustable folding leaf rear, ramp front sight with removable hood; drilled, tapped for receiver sights, scope mounts; checkered walnut stock with roll-over cheekpiece; rosewood grip cap and forend tip; recoil pad; adjustable trigger. Introduced 1974; discontinued 1983.

Exc: $450 **VGood:** $300 **Good:** $270

INTERARMS MARK X CONTINENTAL CARBINE

Bolt action; 243, 270, 308, 30-06, 7x57; 3-, 5-shot magazine; 20-inch barrel; 40-inch overall length; weighs 7-1/2 lbs.; adjustable folding leaf rear, ramp front sight with removable hood; hand-checkered European walnut full-length stock with roll-over cheekpiece; recoil pad; double-set trigger; button-release hinged floorplate. Introduced 1976; discontinued 1983.

Exc: $495 **VGood:** $295 **Good:** $240

INTERARMS MARK X LIGHTWEIGHT

Bolt action; 22-250, 270, 30-06, 7mm Rem. Mag.; 3-, 5-shot magazine; 20-inch barrel; adjustable folding leaf rear, ramp front sight with removable hood; lightweight Carbolite synthetic stock; adjustable trigger. Introduced 1988; discontinued 1990; reintroduced 1994; no longer in production.

Exc: $450 **VGood:** $290 **Good:** $245

INTERARMS MARK X MARQUIS

Bolt action; 243, 270 Win., 308, 30-06, 7x57mm; 3-, 5-shot magazine; 20-inch barrel; 40-inch overall length; weighs 7-1/2 lbs.; adjustable folding leaf rear, ramp front sight with removable hood; hand-checkered European walnut full-length stock; adjustable trigger; quick-detachable sling swivels; blue steel forend cap; Mark X action; white line spacers buttplate, pistol grip cap. Discontinued 1984.

Exc: $475 **VGood:** $400 **Good:** $330

INTERARMS MARK X MINI

Bolt action; 223 Rem., 7.62x39mm; 20-inch barrel; 39-3/4-inch overall length; weighs 6-3/8 lbs.; blade on ramp front sight, open adjustable rear; drilled and tapped for scope mounting; checkered European hardwood stock; adjustable trigger; miniature M98 Mauser action. Imported from Yugoslavia by Interarms. Introduced 1987; importation dropped 1994.

Exc: $425 **VGood:** $375 **Good:** $350

INTERARMS MARK X REALTREE

Bolt action; 270, 30-06; 3-, 5-shot magazine; 22-inch barrel; 42-1/4-inch overall length; weighs 8 lbs.; adjustable folding leaf rear, ramp front sight with removable hood; Realtree camo stock; adjustable trigger; sliding thumb safety; hinged floorplate; mono-block receiver. Introduced 1994; no longer imported.

Exc: $480 **VGood:** $320 **Good:** $290

INTERARMS MARK X VISCOUNT

Bolt action; 22-250, 243, 25-06, 270, 7x57, 308, 30-06, 7mm Rem. Mag., 300 Win. Mag.; 24-inch barrel; 44-inch overall length; weighs about 7 lbs.; blade on ramp front sight, open fully-adjustable rear; drilled and tapped for scope mounting; European hardwood stock with Monte Carlo comb; checkered grip and forend; polished blue finish; uses Mauser system action with sliding thumb safety, hinged floorplate, adjustable trigger. Imported from Yugoslavia by Interarms. Reintroduced 1987; discontinued 1994. Marked "Manchester England."

Exc: $495 **VGood:** $330 **Good:** $290

INTERARMS MARK X WHITWORTH

Bolt action; 22-250, 243, 25-06, 270, 7x57, 308, 30-06, 7mm Rem. Mag., 300 Win. Mag.; 5-shot magazine, 3-shot (300 Win. Mag.); 24-

inch barrel; 44-inch overall length; weighs 7 lbs.; hooded blade on ramp front sight, open fully-adjustable rear; select grade European walnut stock with checkered grip and forend, straight comb; Mauser system action with sliding thumb safety, hinged floorplate, adjustable trigger; polished blue finish; swivel studs. Imported from Yugoslavia by Interarms. Introduced 1984; discontinued 1994. Marked "Manchester England."

Perf: $475 **Exc:** $395 **VGood:** $310

INTERARMS WHITWORTH EXPRESS

Bolt action; 375 H&H, 458 Win. Mag.; 24-inch barrel; 44-3/4-inch overall length; weighs about 8-1/4 to 8-1/2 lbs.; ramp front sight with removable hood, three-leaf open rear calibrated for 100, 200, 300 yards, on 1/4-rib; solid rubber recoil pad; classic English Express rifle design of hand-checkered, select European walnut; barrel-mounted sling swivel; adjustable trigger; hinged floorplate; solid steel recoil cross-bolt. From Interarms. Introduced 1974; no longer produced.

Perf: $695 **Exc:** $595 **VGood:** $475

INTERARMS WHITWORTH MANNLICHER-STYLE CARBINE

Bolt action; 243, 270, 308, 30-06, 7x57; 5-shot magazine; 20-inch barrel; 40-inch overall length; weighs 7 lbs.; hooded ramp front sight, fully-adjustable rear; full-length checkered European walnut stock with cheekpiece; sling swivels; rubber buttplate. Introduced 1984; discontinued 1987.

Perf: $595 **Exc:** $475 **VGood:** $350

ISSC SPA STRAIGHT PULL ACTION RIFLE

Bolt action; .22 LR, .22 Mag., .17 HMR, Wood or synthetic sporter stock or synthetic target stock. 10-round detachable magazine. Imported from Austria. Add $50 for synthetic stock. Add $100 for synthetic target stock

Perf: $450 **Exc:** $400 **VGood:** $370

ITHACA MODEL LSA-55

Bolt action; 22-250, 222 Rem., 6mm Rem., 243, 25-06, 270 Win., 30-06; 3-shot detachable box magazine; 23-inch free-floating barrel; 41-1/2-inch overall length; weighs 6-1/2 lbs.; adjustable rear, hooded ramp front sight; drilled, tapped for scope mounts; checkered European walnut pistol-grip Monte Carlo stock; adjustable trigger. Introduced 1972; discontinued 1976.

Exc: $500 **VGood:** $450 **Good:** $350

ITHACA MODEL LSA-55 DELUXE

Same specs as LSA-55 except no sights; scope mounts; roll-over cheekpiece; rosewood forearm tip, grip cap; white spacers; sling swivel.

Exc: $550 **VGood:** $475 **Good:** $395

ITHACA MODEL LSA-55 HEAVY BARREL

Same specs as LSA-55 except 22-250, 22 Rem.; 23-inch heavy barrel; no sights; redesigned stock; beavertail forearm. Introduced 1974; discontinued 1976.

Exc: $600 **VGood:** $525 **Good:** $495

ITHACA MODEL LSA-55 TURKEY GUN

Over/under rifle/shotgun combo; 12-ga./222 Rem.; 24-1/2-inch ribbed barrel; folding leaf rear sight, bead front; plain extractor; single trigger; exposed hammer. Imported from Finland. Introduced 1970; discontinued 1979.

Exc: $900 **VGood:** $625 **Good:** $405

ITHACA MODEL LSA-65

Bolt action; 25-06, 270, 30-06; 4-shot magazine; 23-inch barrel; 41-1/2-inch overall length; weighs 6-1/2 lbs.; adjustable rear, hooded ramp front sight; drilled, tapped for scope mounts; checkered European walnut pistol-grip Monte Carlo stock; adjustable trigger. Introduced 1969; discontinued 1976.

Exc: $550 **VGood:** $475 **Good:** $395

Ithaca Model LSA-55

Ithaca Model 49 Saddlegun

Ithaca Model 49 Presentation

Ithaca Model 49 Saddlegun Repeater

ITHACA MODEL LSA-65 DELUXE

Same specs as LSA-65 except no sights; scope mounts; roll-over cheekpiece; rosewood grip cap, forend tip. Introduced 1969; discontinued 1976.

Exc: $600 **VGood:** $525 **Good:** $495

ITHACA MODEL 49 SADDLEGUN

Lever action; single shot; 22 Short, 22 Long, 22 LR, 22 WMR; 18-inch barrel; 34-1/2-inch overall length; weighs 5-1/2 lbs.; blank tube magazine for appearance only; open adjustable rear, bead post front sight; straight uncheckered two-piece Western-style carbine stock; barrel band on forearm; Martini-type action. Introduced 1961; discontinued 1976. Add 20 percent for 22 WMR.

Exc: $165 **VGood:** $145 **Good:** $115

ITHACA MODEL 49 DELUXE

Same specs as Model 49 Saddlegun except figured walnut stock; gold-plated hammer, trigger, sling swivels. Introduced 1962; discontinued 1975.

Exc: $295 **VGood:** $250 **Good:** $150

ITHACA MODEL 49 PRESENTATION

Same specs as Model 49 Saddlegun except fancy figured walnut stock; gold nameplate inlay; gold trigger, hammer; engraved receiver. Introduced 1962; discontinued 1974.

Exc: $295 **VGood:** $250 **Good:** $150

ITHACA MODEL 49 SADDLEGUN REPEATER

Same specs as Model 49 Saddlegun except tubular magazine; 20-inch barrel; open rear, bead front sight; checkered grip. Introduced 1968; discontinued 1971.

Exc: $210 **VGood:** $170 **Good:** $120

ITHACA MODEL 49 SADDLEGUN YOUTH

Same specs as Model 49 Saddlegun except shorter stock. Introduced 1961; discontinued 1976.

Exc: $130 **VGood:** $100 **Good:** $80

ITHACA MODEL 72 SADDLEGUN

Lever action; 22 Short, 22 Long, 22 LR, 22 WMR; 11-, 15-shot tube magazine; 18-1/2-inch barrel; weighs 5 lbs.; step-adjustable open rear sight, hooded ramp front; grooved for scope mounts; uncheckered Western-style straight American walnut stock; barrel band on forearm; half-cock safety. Introduced 1972; discontinued 1977.

Exc: $280 **VGood:** $210 **Good:** $160

ITHACA MODEL 72 SADDLEGUN DELUXE

Same specs as Model 72 Saddlegun except engraved, silver-finished receiver; octagon barrel; semi-fancy European walnut stock, forearm. Introduced 1974; discontinued 1976.

Exc: $295 **VGood:** $230 **Good:** $180

ITHACA MODEL X5-C

Semi-automatic; 22 LR; 7-shot clip magazine; 22-inch barrel; 40-1/2-inch overall length; weighs 6 lbs.; open rear, Raybar front sight; uncheckered hardwood pistol-grip stock; grooved forearm. Introduced 1958; discontinued 1964.

Perf: $350 **Exc:** $220 **VGood:** $130

ITHACA MODEL X5-T

Same specs as Model X5-C except 16-shot tube magazine; smooth forearm. Introduced 1959; discontinued 1963.

Perf: $360 **Exc:** $210 **VGood:** $140

ITHACA MODEL X15

Semi-automatic; 22 LR; 7-shot clip magazine; 22-inch barrel; 40-1/2-inch overall length; weighs 6 lbs.; open rear, Raybar front sight; uncheckered walnut pistol-grip stock; beavertail forend. Introduced 1964; discontinued 1967.

Perf: $380 **Exc:** $220 **VGood:** $150

IVER JOHNSON 22 CARBINE MODEL EWHBA

Semi-automatic; 22 LR, 22 WMR; 15-shot; 18-1/2-inch barrel; 38-inch overall length; weighs 5-3/4 lbs.; 22 WMR gas-operated; military-style front sight protected by wings, fully-adjustable peep-style rear; sling swivels; walnut finished hardwood stock

Ithaca Model X5-T

Iver Johnson 22 Carbine Model EWHBA

Iver Johnson Model 2-X

Iver Johnson Plainfield M1 Carbine

Iver Johnson Survival Carbine

and front hand guard; blue finish. Imported from Germany. Introduced 1985; dropped 1988.

Exc: $250 **VGood:** $225 **Good:** $195

IVER JOHNSON LI'L CHAMP

Bolt action; single shot; 22 Short, 22 Long, 22 LR; 16-1/4-inch barrel; 32-1/2-inch overall length; weighs 3-1/8 lbs.; front ramp sight, step-adjustable rear; black moulded stock; nickeled bolt; blue receiver and barrel; stock designed for young shooters. Introduced 1986; dropped 1988.

Exc: $125 **VGood:** $100 **Good:** $75

IVER JOHNSON MODEL 2-X

Bolt action; single shot; 22 Short, 22 Long, 22 LR; 24-inch round tapered barrel; 41-inch overall length; weighs 4-1/2 lbs.; thumb-screw takedown; drop at comb 1-3/8-inch; drop at heel 2-3/8-inch; length of pull 14-inch; patented automatic safety; adjustable rear sight, blade front; steel buttplate; checkered full pistol grip; grooves in forend; chromium-plated bolt and trigger. Introduced 1930; dropped 1957.

Exc: $200 **VGood:** $190 **Good:** $150

IVER JOHNSON MODEL 2-XA

Same specs as 2-X except Lyman #55 adjustable rear sight, Lyman #3 ivory 1/16-inch bead front; sling swivels; leather sling strap. Introduced 1930; dropped 1941.

Exc: $220 **VGood:** $200 **Good:** $170

IVER JOHNSON MODEL 1003 UNIVERSAL CARBINE

Semi-automatic; 30 Carbine; 5-, 15-, 30-shot detachable magazine; 18-inch barrel; 35-3/4-inch overall length; weighs 5-1/2 lbs.; twin guide springs; drilled and tapped for scope mounting; hardwood stock with sling swivels; stainless or blue finish. Not made to military specifications. Manufactured 1986 only.

Exc: $400 **VGood:** $350 **Good:** $300

IVER JOHNSON MODEL 1256 UNIVERSAL CARBINE

Semi-automatic; 256 Win. Mag.; 5-shot detachable magazine; 18-inch barrel; 35-3/4-inch overall length; weighs 5-1/2 lbs.; twin guide springs; drilled and tapped for scope mounting; hardwood stock with sling swivels; stainless or blue finish. Not made to military specifications. Manufactured 1986 only.

Perf: $435 **Exc:** $375 **VGood:** $315

IVER JOHNSON MODEL 5100 SPECIAL APPLICATION RIFLE

Bolt action; single shot; 338/416, 50 BMG; 29-inch free-floating fluted barrel; 51-1/2-inch overall length; weighs 36 lbs.; sniper rifle; marketed with Leupold Ultra M1 20x scope; adjustable composition stock; adjustable trigger; limited production in both calibers.

Exc: $5000 **VGood:** $3950 **Good:** $2995

IVER JOHNSON MODEL X (EARLY MODEL)

Bolt action; single shot; 22 Short, 22 Long, 22 LR; 22-inch round tapered barrel; 39-1/4-inch overall length; weighs 4 lbs.; thumb-screw takedown; drop at comb 1-3/8-inch; drop at heel 2-5/8-inch; length of pull 13-1/4-inch; patented automatic safety; fixed open rear sight, blade front; steel buttplate; stock with large knob at front of forend; solid walnut stock. Introduced 1928; dropped 1932.

Exc: $150 **VGood:** $95 **Good:** $50

IVER JOHNSON MODEL X (LATE MODEL)

Same specs as Early Model except 24-inch barrel; weighs 4-1/2 lbs.; larger, heavier stock; drop at heel 2-3/8-inch; length of pull 14-inch; overall length 41-inch; finger grooves in forend. Model X-A with adjustable sights. Introduced 1933; dropped 1941.

Exc: $160 **VGood:** $100 **Good:** $60

IVER JOHNSON PLAINFIELD MODEL M1 CARBINE

Semi-automatic; 30 Carbine, 5.7mm MMJ, 9mm; 15-shot detachable magazine; 18-inch barrel; 35-1/2-inch overall length; weighs 6-1/2 lbs.; exact copy of WWII U.S. military carbine and manufactured to military specifications; American walnut or hardwood stock; blue or stainless finish; model names and numbers changed several times; M-2 full-automatic model available in early 1980s; Paratrooper Model with folding stock also available; 5.7mm MMJ caliber dropped early; 9mm caliber added in 1986. Introduced 1978; dropped 1992.

Exc: $450 **VGood:** $375 **Good:** $300

IVER JOHNSON SURVIVAL CARBINE

Semi-automatic; 30 Carbine, 5.7mm MMJ; 15-shot detachable magazine; 18-1/2-inch barrel; 35-1/2-inch overall length; weighs 6-1/2 lbs.; exact copy of U.S. WWII military carbine and manufactured to military specifications; Zytel plastic stock with pistol grip standard; folding stock available; stainless steel or blue finish. Introduced 1983; dropped 1985. Add 15 percent for 5.7.

Exc: $575 **VGood:** $475 **Good:** $400

IVER JOHNSON TARGETMASTER EW22HBP

Pump action; 22 Short, 22 Long, 22 LR; 19-shot (22 Short), 15-shot (22 Long), 12-shot (22 LR); 18-1/2-inch barrel; 36-1/2-inch overall length; weighs 5-3/4 lbs.; tubular magazine under barrel; hooded front sight, step-adjustable rear; walnut finished hardwood buttstock and forearm; plastic buttplate; blue finish. Imported from Germany. Introduced 1985; dropped 1988.

Exc: $190 **VGood:** $130 **Good:** $115

IVER JOHNSON TRAILBLAZER MODEL IJ22HBA

Semi-automatic; 22 LR; 10-shot magazine; 18-1/2-inch barrel; 38-inch overall length; weighs 5-3/4 lbs.; blade front sight, rear step-adjustable for elevation; Monte Carlo-styled checkered hardwood stock; plastic buttplate; blue finish. Imported from Canada. Introduced 1984; dropped 1986.

Exc: $130 **VGood:** $95 **Good:** $70

IVER JOHNSON WAGONMASTER EW22HBL

Lever action; 22 LR, 22 Short, 22 Long, 22 WMR; 21-shot (22 Short), 17-shot (22 Long), 15-shot (22 LR), 12-shot (22 WMR); 18-1/2-inch barrel; 36-1/2-inch overall length; weighs 5-3/4 lbs.; tubular magazine under barrel; hooded front sight, step-adjustable rear; walnut finished hardwood buttstock and forearm; plastic buttplate; blue finish. Imported from Germany. Introduced 1985; dropped 1988.

Exc: $190 **VGood:** $140 **Good:** $110

IVER JOHNSON WAGONMASTER JUNIOR MODEL EW22HBLY

Same specs as Wagonmaster except 22 Short, 22 Long, 22 LR; 18-shot (22 Short), 15-shot (22 Long); 14-shot (22 LR); 16-1/4-inch barrel; 33-inch overall length; weighs 5-1/4 lbs. Imported from Germany. Introduced 1985; dropped 1988.

Exc: $190 **VGood:** $140 **Good:** $110

IVER JOHNSON UNIVERSAL PARATROOPER

Semi-automatic; 30 Carbine; 5-, 15-, 30-shot detachable magazine; 18-inch barrel; 36-inch overall length (stock open), 27-inch overall length (stock folded); twin action guide springs; drilled and tapped for scope mounting; folding Schmeisser-type stock. Not manufactured to military specifications. Manufactured 1986 only.

Exc: $400 **VGood:** $330 **Good:** $250

JAEGER AFRICAN MODEL

Bolt action; 375 H&H Mag., 416 Taylor, 458 Win. Mag.; 3-shot magazine; 22-inch, 24-inch barrel; weighs 9 lbs.; V-notch rear, hooded ramp front sight; deluxe black fiberglass stock with graphite-reinforcing; swivel studs; recoil pad; single-stage adjustable trigger; hinged floorplate; Mauser-type action; blue/black finish. Introduced 1989; discontinued 1990.

Perf: $795 **Exc:** $675 **VGood:** $495

JAEGER ALASKAN MODEL

Bolt action; 7mm Rem. Mag., 300 Win. Mag., 338 Win. Mag.; 4-shot magazine; 22-inch, 24-inch barrel; weighs 8 lbs.; Williams open rear, silver bead ramp front sight; black fiberglass stock; integral sling; rubber recoil pad; checkered pistol-grip, forend; single-stage trigger; hinged floorplate; Mauser-type action; black wrinkle finish. Introduced 1989; discontinued 1990.

Perf: $595 **Exc:** $495 **VGood:** $395

JAEGER HUNTER MODEL

Bolt action; 243, 257 Roberts, 25-06, 7x57, 7mm-08, 280, 308, 30-06; 4-shot magazine; 22-inch, 24-inch barrel; weighs 7 lbs.; no sights; drilled, tapped for scope mounts; black fiberglass stock; integral sling; rubber recoil pad; checkered pistol grip, forend; single-stage adjustable trigger; hinged floorplate; Mauser-type action; black wrinkle finish. Introduced 1989; discontinued 1990.

Perf: $595 **Exc:** $495 **VGood:** $395

Laminated wood stock

Perf: $550 **Exc:** $495 **VGood:** $375

KBI SA-85M SEMI-AUTO RIFLE

Semi-automatic; 7.62x39mm; 6-shot magazine; 16-3/8-inch barrel; 34-3/4-inch overall length; weighs 7-1/2 lbs.; European hardwood thumbhole stock; post front sight, open adjustable rear; BATF-approved version of the gas-operated Kalashnikov rifle; black phosphate finish; comes with one magazine, cleaning rod, cleaning/tool kit. Imported from Hungary by K.B.I., Inc. Introduced 1995; dropped 1995.

Perf: $695 **Exc:** $625 **VGood:** $475

KDF K15

Bolt action; 25-06, 257 Wea. Mag., 270, 270 Wea. Mag., 7mm Rem. Mag., 30-06, 300 Win. Mag., 300 Wea. Mag., 338 Win. Mag., 340 Wea. Mag., 375 H&H, 411 KDF Mag., 416 Rem. Mag., 458 Win. Mag.; 4-shot magazine (standard calibers), 3-shot (Magnums); 22-inch barrel (standard calibers), 24-inch optional; 44-inch overall (24-inch barrel); weighs about 8 lbs.; sights optional; drilled and tapped for scope mounting; laminated stock standard; Kevlar composite or AAA walnut in Monte Carlo, classic, schnabel or thumbhole styles optional; three-lug locking design with 60° bolt lift; ultra-fast lock time; fully-adjustable trigger. Imported from Germany by KDF, Inc. Introduced 1976; no longer imported.

Perf: $1495 **Exc:** $1000 **VGood:** $750

KDF K15 DANGEROUS GAME MODEL

Same specs as K15 except 411 KDF Mag.; choice of iron sights or scope mounts; oil-finished deluxe walnut stock; gloss blue, matte blue, Parkerized or electroless nickel finish; hinged floorplate. Introduced 1986; discontinued 1988.

Perf: $1695 **Exc:** $1395 **VGood:** $895

KDF K15 FIBERSTOCK PRO-HUNTER MODEL

Same specs as K15 except Brown Precision fiberglass stock in black, green, brown or camo with wrinkle finish; Parkerized, matte blue or electroless finish; recoil arrestor. Introduced 1986; discontinued 1988.

Perf: $1650 **Exc:** $1350 **VGood:** $875

KDF K15 IMPROVED MODEL

Same specs as K15 except 243, 25-06, 270, 7x57, 308, 30-06, 257 Weatherby, 270 Weatherby, 308 Norma Mag., 375 H&H Mag.; hand-checkered, oil-finished featherweight European walnut stock with schnabel or Monte Carlo style. Introduced 1987; discontinued 1988.

Perf: $1695 **Exc:** $1395 **VGood:** $895

KDF K15 SWAT MODEL

Same specs as K15 except 308; 24-inch, 26-inch barrel; weighs 10 lbs.; oil-finished walnut target stock; Parkerized metal. Introduced 1986; discontinued 1988.

Perf: $1550 **Exc:** $1495 **VGood:** $795

KDF K22

Bolt action; 22 LR, 22 WMR; 5-, 6-shot magazine; 21-1/2-inch barrel; 40-inch overall length; weighs 6-1/2 lbs.; no sights; receiver grooved for scope mounts; hand-checkered, oil-finished European walnut Monte Carlo stock; front-locking lugs on bolt; pillar bedding system. Made in Germany. Introduced 1984; discontinued 1988.

Perf: $345 **Exc:** $270 **VGood:** $220

KDF K22 DELUXE

Same specs as K22 except 22 LR only; quick-detachable swivels; rosewood forend tip; rubber recoil pad. Introduced 1984; discontinued 1988.

Perf: $425 **Exc:** $340 **VGood:** $280

Jaeger Alaskan Model

Jaeger Hunter Model

KDF K15

KDF K15 Improved Model

KDF K22

Kel-Tec RFB Hunter

Kel-Tec SU-16B Lightweight

KEL TEC RFB HUNTER

Short-stroke gas piston operated semi-automatic bull-pup rifle with polymer stock and detachable magazine. Chambered in 7.62 NATO Caliber. 24 inch barrel with 31 inch OA length and weighs 9.8 pounds. 20 round magazine capacity. Introduced 2012.

Perf: $2,000 **Exc:** $1,500 **VGood:** $1,200

KEL-TEC SU-16

Semi-automatic; 223; 18.5-inch bbl.; uses M-16 type locking and feeding system; polymer stock holds extra 5-round magazines, polymer forend opens to provide bipod; Picatinny rail on receiver; produced in black, NATO Green or Desert Beige colors. Variations: U-16A, 18.5-inch barrel; SU-16B, 16-inch lightweight barrel; SU-16C, 16-inch barrel, folding stock; SU-16CA, 16-inch standard barrel and standard stock.

Perf: $500 **Exc:** $400 **VGood:** $350

Kel-Tec SUB2000 Carbine

Kel-Tec RFB

Kimber 22

Kimber 22 SuperAmerica

Kimber 22 SVT

Kimber 22 HS Hunter Silhouette

Kimber Model 82

Kimber Model 82, Government Target Model

KEL-TEC SU-16B LIGHTWEIGHT

Similar to Kel-Tec SU-16, but lightweight version with 16-inch bbl.

Perf: $500 **Exc:** $400 **VGood:** $350

KEL-TEC SU-16C CARBINE

Similar to Kel-Tec SU-16, but 16-inch bbl.; polymer stock folds forward for carrying; length open 35.5-inch, length folded 25.5-inch; weighs 4.7 lbs.

Perf: $500 **Exc:** $400 **VGood:** $350

KEL-TEC SUB2000 CARBINE

Semi-automatic; 9mm, 40 S&W; 16.1-inch bbl., weighs 4 lbs.; different polymer housings accept S&W, Glock, Beretta, SIG or Kel-Tec magazines; folds to provide compact storage, overall length 30 inches, folded 16.1 inches. Blued, with black grip and forend; parkerized and chrome versions also made. Introduced 1996 by Kel-Tec CNC Industries, still in production.

Perf: $375 **Exc:** $ 350 **VGood:** $280

KEL-TEC RFB RIFLE

Bullpup semi-auto rifle with 32", 24" or 18" barrel, black laminated stock, third swivel for bipod. Forward ejection; takes FAL-type magazines. Chambered in .308 Winchester. Introduced in 2007. Price shown is for sporter.

NIB: $2300 **Exc:** N/A **VGood:** N/A

KIMBER 22

Bolt action; 22 LR, 5-shot magazine. 18-inch, 22-inch, 24-inch match grade barrel; 11-degree target crown; weighs 5-8 lbs.; 35-inch to 43-inch length; Classic Claro walnut stock, hand-cut checkering, steel gripcap, swivel studs. Sights: None, drilled and tapped. All-new action with Mauser-style full-length claw extractor, two-position wing safety, match trigger, pillar-bedded action with recoil lug. Introduced 1999. Made in U.S.A. by Kimber Mfg., Inc.

Perf: $950 **Exc:** $850 **VGood:** $750

KIMBER 22 SUPERAMERICA

Similar to 22 Classic except has AAA Claro walnut stock with wrap- around 22 lpi hand-cut checkering, ebony forend tip, beaded cheekpiece. Introduced 1999. Made in U.S.A. by Kimber Mfg., Inc.

Perf: $1550 **Exc:** $1300 **VGood:** $1100

KIMBER 22 SVT (SHORT VARMINT/TARGET)

Similar to 22 Classic except has 18-inch stainless steel, fluted bull barrel, gray laminated, high-comb target-style stock with deep pistol grip, high comb, beavertail forend with bipod stud. Weighs 7.5 lbs., overall length 36-1/2 inches. Matte finish on action. Introduced 1999. Made in U.S.A. by Kimber Mfg., Inc.

Perf: $900 **Exc:** $800 **VGood:** $700

KIMBER 22 HS (HUNTER SILHOUETTE)

Similar to 22 Classic except 24-inch medium sporter match-grade barrel with half-fluting; high comb, walnut, Monte Carlo target stock with 18 lpi checkering; matte blue metal finish. Introduced 1999. Made in U.S.A. by Kimber Mfg., Inc.

Perf: $775 **Exc:** $675 **VGood:** $575

KIMBER MODEL 82

Bolt action; 22 Short, 22 Long, 22 LR, 22 WMR, 22 Hornet; 5-shot magazine (22 Short, 22 Long, 22 LR), 4-shot (22 WMR), 3-shot (22 Hornet); 22-inch, 24-inch barrel; weighs 6-1/2 lbs.; blade front sight on ramp, open adjustable rear; receiver grooved for special Kimber scope mounts; classic-style or Cascade-design select walnut stock; hand-checkered pistol grip, forend; rocker-type silent safety; checkered steel buttplate; steel grip cap; all-steel construction; blued finish. Classic model. Introduced 1980; discontinued 1988.

Perf: $1100 **Exc:** $1000 **VGood:** $795

KIMBER MODEL 82 ALL-AMERICAN MATCH

Same specs as Model 82 except 22 LR; 25-inch target barrel; weighs 9 lbs.; fully-adjustable stock; palm swell, thumb dent pistol grip; step-crowned .9-inch diameter free-floating barrel; forend inletted for weights; adjustable trigger. Introduced 1990; discontinued 1991.

Perf: $950 **Exc:** $835 **VGood:** $695

KIMBER MODEL 82 CONTINENTAL

Same specs as Model 82 except deluxe full-length walnut stock. Introduced 1987; discontinued 1988.

Perf: $1000 **Exc:** $900 **VGood:** $695

KIMBER MODEL 82 GOVERNMENT TARGET

Same specs as Model 82 except 22 LR; 25-inch heavy target barrel; 43-1/2-inch overall length; weighs 10-3/4 lbs.; oversize target-type Claro walnut stock; single-stage adjustable trigger;

designed as U.S. Army trainers. Introduced 1987; discontinued 1991.

Perf: $900 **Exc:** $800 **VGood:** $695

KIMBER MODEL 82 HUNTER

Same specs as Model 82 except 22 LR; 22-inch barrel; laminated stock; rubber recoil pad; matte finish. Introduced 1990; discontinued 1990.

Perf: $750 **Exc:** $635 **VGood:** $495

KIMBER MODEL 82 MINI CLASSIC

Same specs as Model 82 except 22 LR; 18-inch barrel; sling swivels. Introduced 1988; discontinued 1988.

Perf: $795 **Exc:** $695 **VGood:** $595

KIMBER MODEL 82 SPORTER

Same specs as Model 82 except 22 LR; 22-inch barrel; 4-shot magazine; round-top receiver. Introduced 1991; discontinued 1991.

Perf: $895 **Exc:** $795 **VGood:** $595

KIMBER MODEL 82 SUPERAMERICA

Same specs as Model 82 except checkered top quality California Claro walnut stock; beaded cheekpiece; ebony forend tip; detachable scope mounts. Introduced 1982; discontinued 1988; reintroduced 1990; discontinued 1991.

Perf: $1500 **Exc:** $1400 **VGood:** $1300

KIMBER MODEL 82 VARMINTER

Same specs as Model 82 except 22 LR; 5-, 10-shot magazine; 25-inch heavy barrel; weighs 8-1/4 lbs.; laminated stock; rubber recoil pad. Introduced 1990; discontinued 1991.

Perf: $895 **Exc:** $795 **VGood:** $695

KIMBER MODEL 82C CLASSIC

Bolt action; 22 LR; 4-shot magazine; 21-inch premium air-gauged barrel; 40-1/2-inch overall length; weighs 6-1/2 lbs.; no sights; drilled and tapped for Warne scope mounts optionally available from factory; classic-style stock of Claro walnut; 13-1/2-inch length of pull; hand-checkered; red rubber buttpad; polished steel grip cap; action with aluminum pillar bedding for consistent accuracy; single-set fully-adjustable trigger with 2-1/2-lb. pull. Made in U.S. by Kimber of America, Inc. Reintroduced 1994; no longer produced.

Perf: $795 **Exc:** $695 **VGood:** $595

KIMBER MODEL 82C CUSTOM MATCH

Same specs as Model 82C Classic except high-grade stock French walnut stock with black ebony forend tip; full coverage 22 lpi borderless checkering; steel Neidner (uncheckered) buttplate; satin rust blue finish. Made in U.S. by Kimber of America, Inc. Reintroduced 1995; no longer produced.

Perf: $1650 **Exc:** $1475 **VGood:** $995

KIMBER MODEL 82C SUPERAMERICA

Same specs as Model 82C except AAA fancy grade Claro walnut with beaded cheekpiece; ebony forend cap; hand-checkered 22 lpi patterns with wrap-around coverage; black rubber buttpad. Made in U.S. by Kimber of America, Inc. Reintroduced 1994; no longer produced.

Perf: $1500 **Exc:** $1400 **VGood:** $1050

KIMBER MODEL 82C SUPERAMERICA CUSTOM

Same specs as SuperAmerica except Neidner-style buttplate. Available options include: steel skeleton grip cap and buttplate; quarter-rib and open express sights; jewelled bolt; checkered bolt knob; special length of pull; rust blue finish. Made in U.S. by Kimber of America, Inc. Reintroduced 1994; still produced.

Perf: $1600 **Exc:** $1500 **VGood:** $1150

Kimber Model 82 Varminter Model

Kimber Model 82C Classic

Kimber Model 82C SuperAmerica

Kimber Model 84 SuperAmerica

Kimber Model 84 Ultra Varminter

KIMBER MODEL 82C SUPERCLASSIC

Same specs as Model 82C except AAA Claro walnut stock with black rubber buttpad, as used on the SuperAmerica. Made in U.S. by Kimber of America, Inc. Introduced 1995; no longer produced.

Perf: $1500 **Exc:** $1400 **VGood:** $1050

KIMBER MODEL 82C VARMINT

Same specs as Model 82C except slightly larger forend to accommodate the medium/heavy barrel profile; fluted, stainless steel match-grade barrel; weighs about 7-1/2 lbs. Made in U.S. by Kimber of America, Inc. Introduced 1995; no longer produced.

Perf: $995 **Exc:** $895 **VGood:** $795

KIMBER MODEL 84

Bolt action; 17 Rem., 17 Mach IV, 6x47, 5.6x50, 221 Rem. Fireball, 222 Rem. Mag., 222 Rem., 223 Rem.; 5-shot magazine; 22-inch barrel; 40-1/2-inch overall length; weighs 6-1/4 lbs.; hooded ramp front sight with bead, folding leaf rear are optional; grooved for scope mounts; Claro walnut plain straight comb stock with hand-cut borderless checkering; steel grip cap; checkered steel buttplate; new Mauser-type head locking action; steel trigger guard; three-position safety (new in '87); hinged floorplate; Mauser-type extractor; fully-adjustable trigger. Introduced 1984; discontinued 1989.

Perf: $1050 **Exc:** $995 **VGood:** $795

KIMBER MODEL 84 CONTINENTAL MODEL

Same specs as Model 84 except 221 Fireball, 222 Rem., 223 Rem.; 22-inch barrel; full-length deluxe checkered walnut stock. Introduced 1987; discontinued 1988.

Perf: $1250 **Exc:** $1095 **VGood:** $895

KIMBER MODEL 84 CUSTOM CLASSIC MODEL

Same specs as Model 84 except select-grade Claro walnut stock with ebony forend tip, Neidner-style buttplate. Introduced 1984; discontinued 1988.

Perf: $995 **Exc:** $895 **VGood:** $695

KIMBER MODEL 84 HUNTER MODEL

Same specs as Model 84 except 17 Rem., 222 Rem., 223 Rem.; 22-inch barrel; laminated stock; matte finish. Introduced 1990; discontinued 1990.

Perf: $825 **Exc:** $750 **VGood:** $595

KIMBER MODEL 84 SPORTER MODEL

Same specs as Model 84 except 17 Rem., 22 Hornet, 222 Rem., 22-250, 223 Rem., 250 Savage, 35 Rem.; 4-shot magazine; hand-checkered Claro walnut. Introduced 1991; discontinued 1991.

Perf: $950 **Exc:** $795 **VGood:** $695

KIMBER MODEL 84 SUPERAMERICA

Same specs as Model 84 except 17 Rem., 221 Rem., 22 Hornet, 22-250, 222 Rem., 223 Rem., 250 Savage, 35 Rem.; 4-shot magazine; 22-inch barrel; detachable scope mounts; top-quality stock; right- or left-hand versions. Introduced 1985; discontinued 1988; reintroduced 1990; discontinued 1991.

Perf: $1525 **Exc:** $1195 **VGood:** $995

KIMBER MODEL 84 SUPER GRADE

Same specs as Model 84 except 17 Rem., 222 Rem., 223 Rem.; Mauser bolt action; 22-inch barrel; grade

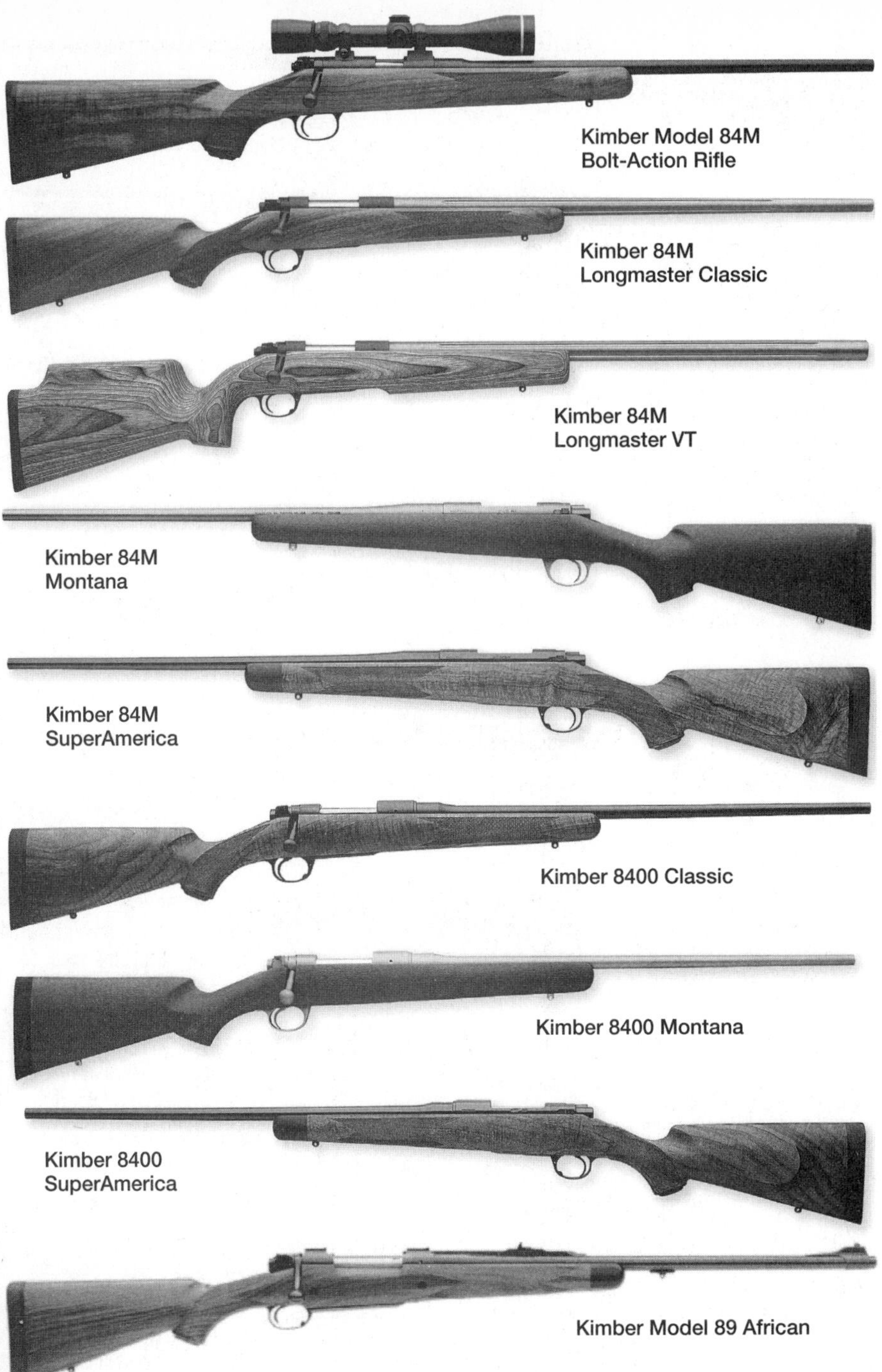
Kimber Model 84M Bolt-Action Rifle

Kimber 84M Longmaster Classic

Kimber 84M Longmaster VT

Kimber 84M Montana

Kimber 84M SuperAmerica

Kimber 8400 Classic

Kimber 8400 Montana

Kimber 8400 SuperAmerica

Kimber Model 89 African

AAA walnut stock. Introduced 1989; discontinued 1989.

Perf: $1600 **Exc:** $1250 **VGood:** $1050

KIMBER MODEL 84 ULTRA VARMINTER

Same specs as Model 84 except 17 Rem., 22 Hornet, 221 Rem., 222 Rem., 22-250, 223 Rem.; 24-inch barrel; weighs 7-3/4 lbs.; laminated birchwood stock. Introduced 1989; discontinued 1991.

Perf: $1295 **Exc:** $995 **VGood:** $795

KIMBER MODEL 84M

Bolt action; 22-250, 243, 260 Rem., 7mm-08, 308, 5-shot. Barrel: 22-inch, 24-inch, 26-inch; weighs 5 lbs., 10 oz. to 10 lbs.; 41-inch to 45-inch length; Claro walnut stock, checkered with steel grip cap or gray laminate; drilled and tapped for bases. Mauser claw extractor, two-position wing safety, action bedded on aluminum pillars, free-floated barrel, match-grade trigger set at 4 lbs., matte blue finish. Introduced 2001. Made in U.S.A. by Kimber Mfg. Inc.

Kimber Model 84M Classic; 22-250, 243, 260, 7mm-08, 308; 22-inch barrel.

Perf: $900 **Exc:** $800 **VGood:** $700

Kimber Model 84M Longmaster Classic; 223, 243, 308; 24-inch fluted stainless-steel bbl., introduced 2002.

Perf: $950 **Exc:** $850 **VGood:** $760

Kimber Model 84M LongMaster VT; 22-250, heavy varmint rifle, 24-inch or 26-inch stainless-steel bbl., laminated target stock.

Perf: $1100 **Exc:** $900 **VGood:** $800

Kimber Model 84M Montana; 243, 260, 7mm-08, 308; stainless steel, synthetic stock, introduced 2003.

Perf: 1040 **Exc:** $950 **VGood:** $890

Kimber Model 84M Varmint; 22-250; 26-inch bbl.

Perf: $950 **Exc:** $840 **VGood:** $750

Kimber Model 84M Pro Varmint; 204 Ruger, 22-250, 223, 308; introduced 2004.

Perf: $1030 **Exc:** $ 945 **VGood:** $850

Kimber Model 84M SuperAmerica; 223, 243, 260, 7mm-08, 308; has high-grade wood, checkering, ebony forend tip; introduced 2003.

Perf: $1690 **Exc:** $1430 **VGood:** $1250

KIMBER MODEL 84M LPT TACTICAL

Based on Model 84 action but with 24" mediumweight fluted match barrel, black laminated stock, third swivel for bipod. Chambered in .308 Winchester.

NIB: $1100 **Exc:** $1000 **VGood:** $875

KIMBER MODEL 8400 SERIES

This series was introduced in 2003 and features the smallest action size compatible with the WSM family of cartridges.

KIMBER MODEL 8400 CLASSIC

This model is fitted with a select walnut stock with 20 lpi checkering. Chambered for the WSM calibers: .270, 7mm, .300, and .325. Barrel length is 24" with no sights. Magazine capacity is 3 rounds. Weight is about 6.6 lbs.

NIB: $1100 **Exc:** $1000 **VGood:** $875

KIMBER MODEL 8400 MONTANA

This model features a 24" stainless steel barrel with no sights. Stock is black synthetic with no checkering. Same calibers as the Classic. Weight is about 6.25 lbs.

NIB: $1100 **Exc:** $1000 **VGood:** $875

KIMBER MODEL 8400 SUPERAMERICA

This model is fitted with a AAA walnut stock with 24 lpi checkering. Cheekpiece and ebony forend tip are standard. Barrel length is 24" with no sights and chambered for the same calibers as the Classic. Weight is about 6.6 lbs.

NIB: $2100 **Exc:** $1875 **VGood:** $1350

KIMBER 8400 CLASSIC SELECT GRADE

Similar to 8400 Classic but with hand-rubbed, oil-finished select stock of Claro or French walnut.

NIB: $1550 **Exc:** $1350 **VGood:** $995

KIMBER MODEL 8400 TACTICAL

Based on Model 8400 action (oversized bolt handle and knob, etc.) but with 24" heavyweight match barrel, stippled black McMillan stock, third swivel for bipod. Chambered in .308 Winchester.

NIB: $1550 **Exc:** $1475 **VGood:** $1250

KIMBER MODEL 8400 ADVANCED TACTICAL

Similar to Model 8400 Tactical but with KimPro II Dark Earth finish, fully-adjustable stock and hard case. Introduced in 2007.

NIB: $2100 **Exc:** $1950 **VGood:** $1695

KIMBER MODEL 89

Bolt action; 257 Roberts, 25-06, 7x57, 270, 280, 7mm Rem. Mag., 30-06, 300 Win. Mag., 300 H&H, 35 Whelen, 338 Win. Mag., 375 H&H Mag.; 3-, 5-shot magazine; 22-inch, 24-inch barrel; 42-inch overall length (22-inch barrel); weighs 7-3/4 lbs.; no sights; Claro or English walnut stock in Classic, Custom Classic design; Model 70-type trigger, ejector design; Mauser-type extractor; three-position safety. Introduced 1988; discontinued 1991.

Perf: $900 **Exc:** $800 **VGood:** $700

KIMBER MODEL 89 AFRICAN

Same specs as Model 89 except 375 H&H Mag., 404 Jeffery, 416 Rigby, 460 Weatherby Mag., 505

Gibbs; 5-shot magazine (375 H&H Mag.), 4-shot (404 Jeffery, 416 Rigby), 3-shot (460 Weatherby, 505 Gibbs); 26-inch heavy barrel; 47-inch overall length; weighs 10-1/2 lbs.; ramped blade front, express rear sight; English walnut stock with cheekpiece; rubber buttpad; double crossbolts. Introduced 1990; discontinued 1991.

Perf: $4000 **Exc:** $3595 **VGood:** $2495

KIMBER MODEL 89 FEATHERWEIGHT DELUXE

Same specs as Model 89 except 257 Roberts, 25-06, 7x57, 270, 280, 30-06; 5-shot magazine; 22-inch light barrel; weighs 7-1/2 lbs.; deluxe walnut stock. Introduced 1989; discontinued 1990.

Perf: $1295 **Exc:** $1095 **VGood:** $895

KIMBER MODEL 89 HEAVYWEIGHT DELUXE

Same specs as Model 89 except 375 H&H Mag., 458 Win. Mag.; 3-shot magazine; 24-inch heavy barrel; weighs 9 lbs. Introduced 1989; discontinued 1990.

Perf: $1500 **Exc:** $1300 **VGood:** $1000

KIMBER MODEL 89 HUNTER

Same specs as Model 89 except 270, 30-06, 300 Win. Mag., 338 Win. Mag., 7mm Rem. Mag.; 22-inch barrel; laminated stock; matte finish. Introduced 1990; discontinued 1991.

Perf: $1195 **Exc:** $995 **VGood:** $750

KIMBER MODEL 89 MEDIUM WEIGHT DELUXE

Same specs as Model 89 except 300 Win. Mag., 300 H&H Mag., 300 Weatherby, 338 Win. Mag., 35 Whelen, 7mm Rem. Mag.; 3-shot magazine; 24-inch barrel; weighs 8 lbs. Introduced 1989; discontinued 1990.

Perf: $1595 **Exc:** $1095 **VGood:** $795

KIMBER MODEL 89 SUPER GRADE

Same specs as Model 89 except 22-inch barrel; grade AAA walnut stock; square receiver. Introduced 1989; discontinued 1989.

Perf: $1595 **Exc:** $1295 **VGood:** $995

KIMEL AR9

Semi-automatic; 9mm Para.; 20-shot magazine; 16-1/4-inch barrel; 33-inch overall length; weighs 6-1/2 lbs.; adjustable post front sight in ring, fixed open rear; folding buttstock, checkered plastic grip; fires from closed bolt; lever safety blocks trigger and sear; vented barrel shroud; matte blue/black or nickel finish. Made in U.S. Marketed by Kimel Industries. Introduced 1991; no longer produced.

Perf: $510 **Exc:** $450 **VGood:** $300

KINTREK MODEL KBP-1

Semi-automatic; 22 LR; 17-shot magazine; 25-inch barrel; 31-1/2-inch overall length; weighs 5-1/2 lbs.; post front sight, fully-adjustable aperture rear; drilled and tapped for scope mount; solid black synthetic bullpup stock with smooth pebble finish; grip safety and trigger-blocking safeties; ejects empties out through bottom of stock; bolt hold-open operated by grip safety; matte black finish. Made in U.S. by Kintrek, Inc. Introduced 1991; discontinued 1992.

Perf: $175 **Exc:** $150 **VGood:** $130

KLEINGUENTHER K-15

Bolt action; 243, 25-06, 270, 30-06, 308 Win., 7x57, 308 Norma Mag., 300 Weatherby Mag., 7mm Rem. Mag., 375 H&H, 257 Winchester, 270 Weatherby Mag., 300 Weatherby Mag.; 24-inch barrel (standard calibers); 26-inch (Magnums); no sights; drilled, tapped for scope mounts; hand-checkered Monte Carlo stock of European walnut; rosewood grip cap; high-luster or satin finish; recoil pad; many optional features available on special order. Manufactured in Germany. Imported and assembled by Kleinguenther; discontinued 1985.

Perf: $1295 **Exc:** $995 **VGood:** $750

KLEINGUENTHER K-22

Bolt action; 22 LR, 22 WMR; 5-shot magazine; 21-1/2-inch barrel; 40-inch overall length; weighs 6-1/2 lbs.; no sights; drilled, tapped for scope mounts; walnut-stained beechwood Monte Carlo stock; hand-cut checkering; sling swivels; no sights; two forward locking lugs; adjustable trigger; optional set trigger; silent safety. Made in Germany. Introduced 1984; discontinued 1985.

Kimber Model 89 Medium Weight Deluxe

Kleinguenther K-15

Kleinguenther K-22

Kodiak Mk. IV Double Rifle

Krico Model 260

Krico Model 302

Perf: $350 **Exc:** $290 **VGood:** $200

With double-set trigger

Perf: $395 **Exc:** $320 **VGood:** $220

KODIAK MK. IV DOUBLE RIFLE

Double rifle; 45-70; 24-inch barrels; 42-1/2-inch overall length; weighs 10 lbs.; ramp front sight with bead, adjustable two-leaf rear; European walnut stock with semi-pistol grip; exposed hammers; color case-hardened locks; rubber recoil pad. Imported from Italy by Trail Guns Armory. Manufactured in Italy by Pedersoli. Introduced 1988; discontinued 1994.

Exc: $2000 **VGood:** $1500 **Good:** $895

KRICO CARBINE

Bolt action; 22 Hornet, 222 Rem; 4-shot clip magazine; 20-inch, 22-inch barrel; open rear, hooded ramp front sight; hand-checkered European walnut full-length stock; miniature Mauser-type action; single- or double-set trigger; sling swivels. Made in Germany. Introduced 1956; discontinued 1962.

Exc: $695 **VGood:** $575 **Good:** $450

KRICO MODEL 120M

Bolt action; 22 LR; 5-shot magazine; 19-1/2-inch barrel; 46-inch overall length; weighs 6 lbs.; military trainer; tangent elevation-adjustable rear, hooded blade front; receiver grooved for scope mounts; European hardwood stock; blued finish; adjustable trigger. Made in Germany. No longer imported.

Perf: $350 **Exc:** $290 **VGood:** $220

KRICO MODEL 260

Semi-automatic; 22 LR; 5-shot magazine; 19-1/2-inch barrel; 39-inch overall length; weighs 6-3/8 lbs.; ramp blade front sight, open adjustable rear; receiver grooved for scope mounting; beechwood stock; sliding safety. Made in Germany. Introduced 1989.

Perf: $495 **Exc:** $395 **VGood:** $285

KRICO MODEL 300

Bolt action; 22 LR, 22 WMR, 22 Hornet; 19-1/2-inch, 23-1/2-inch barrel; weighs 6 lbs.; ramp blade front sight, open adjustable rear; walnut-stained beech stock; double triggers; sliding safety; checkered grip, forend. Made in Germany. Introduced 1989.

Perf: $600 **Exc:** $485 **VGood:** $375

KRICO MODEL 300 DELUXE

Same specs as Model 300 except European walnut stock; better checkering. Introduced 1989.

Perf: $625 **Exc:** $495 **VGood:** $395

KRICO MODEL 300 SA

Same specs as Model 300 except Monte Carlo-style walnut stock. Introduced 1989.

Perf: $575 **Exc:** $450 **VGood:** $350

KRICO MODEL 300 STUTZEN

Same specs as Model 300 except full-length Stutzen-type walnut stock. Introduced 1989.

Perf: $595 **Exc:** $495 **VGood:** $395

KRICO MODEL 302

Bolt action; 22 LR; 5-, 10-shot magazine; 24-inch barrel; 43-inch overall length; weighs 6-1/2 lbs.; hooded post front, windage-adjustable rear sight; European walnut stock; checkered pistol

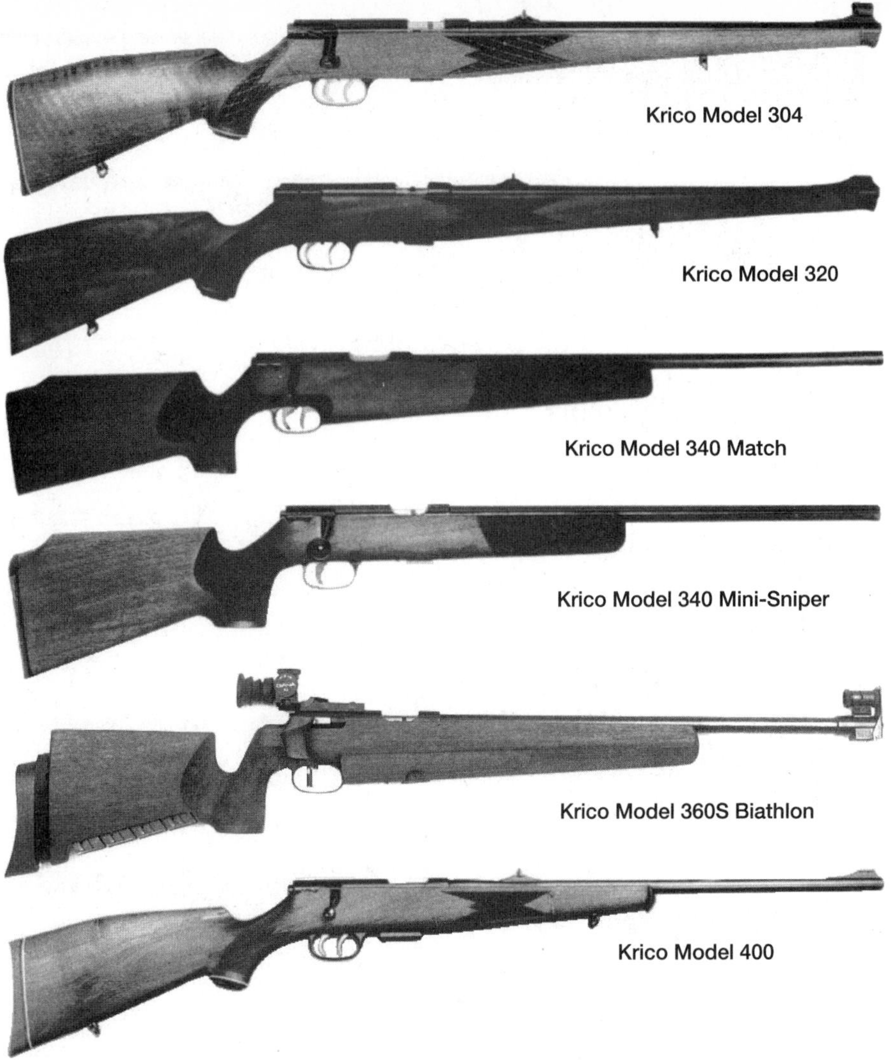
Krico Model 304

Krico Model 320

Krico Model 340 Match

Krico Model 340 Mini-Sniper

Krico Model 360S Biathlon

Krico Model 400

grip, forend; single- or double-set trigger. Made in Germany. Introduced 1982; discontinued 1984.

Exc: $575 **VGood:** $450 **Good:** $350

With double-set trigger

Exc: $675 **VGood:** $495 **Good:** $395

KRICO MODEL 302DR C

Same specs as Model 302 except 22 LR, 22 WMR; classic-style European walnut stock. Introduced 1983; discontinued 1984.

Exc: $595 **VGood:** $495 **Good:** $395

KRICO MODEL 302E

Same specs as Model 302 except straight forend; walnut-finished hardwood stock; single trigger. Introduced 1982; discontinued 1983.

Exc: $625 **VGood:** $495 **Good:** $395

KRICO MODEL 304

Bolt action; 22 LR; 5-, 10-shot magazine; 20-inch barrel; weighs 6-1/4 lbs.; hooded ramp front, windage-adjustable rear sight; full-length Mannlicher-type stock; single- or double-set trigger. Made in Germany. Introduced 1982; discontinued 1984.

Exc: $615 **VGood:** $525 **Good:** $395

KRICO MODEL 311

Bolt action; 22 LR; 5-, 10-shot clip magazine; 22-inch barrel; open rear sight, hooded ramp front; hand-checkered European walnut stock, pistol grip, cheekpiece; single- or double-set trigger; sling swivels. Also available with 2-1/2X scope. Introduced 1958; discontinued 1962.

Exc: $340 **VGood:** $300 **Good:** $225

With scope

Exc: $440 **VGood:** $380 **Good:** $290

KRICO MODEL 320

Bolt action; 22 LR; 5-shot magazine; 19-1/2-inch barrel; 38-1/2-inch overall length; weighs 6 lbs.; windage-adjustable open rear sight, blade front on ramp; Mannlicher-style select European walnut stock; cut-checkered grip, forend; blued steel forend cap; detachable box magazine; single- or double-set triggers. Made in Germany. Introduced 1986; discontinued 1988.

Exc: $650 **VGood:** $570 **Good:** $480

KRICO MODEL 330S MATCH

Single shot; 22 LR; 25-1/2-inch heavy barrel; hooded front sight with interchangeable inserts, diopter match rear, rubber eye-cup; walnut-finished beechwood match stock; built-in hand stop; adjustable recoil pad; factory-set match trigger; stippled pistol grip. Introduced 1981; no longer imported.

Exc: $705 **VGood:** $595 **Good:** $450

KRICO MODEL 340

Bolt action; 22 LR; 5-shot clip magazine; 21-inch match barrel; 39-1/2-inch overall length; weighs 7-1/2 lbs.; no sights; receiver grooved for tip-off mounts; European walnut match-style stock; stippled grip, forend; free-floating barrel; adjustable two-stage match trigger or double-set trigger; meets NRA MS rules. Made in Germany. Introduced 1983; discontinued 1988.

Exc: $715 **VGood:** $605 **Good:** $480

KRICO MODEL 340 KRICOTRONIC

Same specs as Model 340 except electronic ignition system, replacing firing pin; fast lock time. Made in Germany. Introduced 1985; discontinued 1988.

Exc: $1200 **VGood:** $900 **Good:** $750

KRICO MODEL 340 MINI-SNIPER

Same specs as Model 340 except weighs 8 lbs.; 40 overall length; high comb; palm swell, stippled ventilated forend; receiver grooved for scope mounts; free-floating bull barrel; muzzlebrake; large bolt knob; match-quality single trigger; sandblasted barrel, receiver. Made in Germany. Introduced 1984; discontinued 1986.

Exc: $995 **VGood:** $795 **Good:** $575

KRICO MODEL 352E

Bolt action; 22 WMR; 24-inch barrel; 43-inch overall length; weighs 6-1/2 lbs.; hooded post front, windage-adjustable rear sight; walnut finished hard stock; wood straight forend; no white line spaces. Introduced 1982; discontinued 1984.

Exc: $375 **VGood:** $325 **Good:** $235

KRICO MODEL 360S BIATHLON

Bolt action; 22 LR; 5-shot magazine; 21-1/4-inch barrel; 40-1/2-inch overall length; weighs 9-1/4 lbs.; globe front, fully-adjustable Diana 62 match peep rear sight; high-comb European walnut stock; adjustable buttplate; muzzle/sight snow cap; straight-pull action; match trigger. Marketed with five magazines, four stored in stock. Made in Germany. Introduced 1991.

Perf: $1600 **Exc:** $1300 **VGood:** $800

KRICO MODEL 360S2 BIATHLON

Same specs as Model 360S except weighs 9 lbs.; biathlon stock design of black epoxy-finished walnut with pistol grip; pistol-grip-activated action. Imported from Germany by Mandall Shooting Supplies. Introduced 1991; no longer imported.

Perf: $1450 **Exc:** $1150 **VGood:** $750

KRICO MODEL 400

Bolt action; 22 LR, 22 Hornet; 5-shot detachable magazine; 23-1/2-inch barrel; 41-inch overall length; weighs 8-1/2 lbs.; hooded post front, windage-adjustable open rear sight; hand-checkered deluxe European walnut stock; schnabel forend; solid rubber recoil pad; rear locking lugs; twin extractors; sling swivels; single- or double-set triggers. Introduced 1983; discontinued 1989.

Exc: $765 **VGood:** $625 **Good:** $535

KRICO MODEL 400E

Same specs as Model 400 except straight forend; walnut-finished beech stock; no forend tip; hard rubber buttplate; single- or double-set trigger. Introduced 1982; discontinued 1983.

Perf: $595 **Exc:** $495 **VGood:** $375

KRICO MODEL 400L

Same specs as Model 400 except select French walnut stock; no schnabel. Introduced 1982; discontinued 1983.

Perf: $795 **Exc:** $695 **VGood:** $585

KRICO MODEL 400 MATCH

Same specs as Model 400 except single shot; 22 LR; 23-1/2-inch heavy barrel; no sights; match-type stock. Introduced Still in production.

Perf: $850 **Exc:** $705 **VGood:** $595

KRICO MODEL 420L

Bolt action; 22 Hornet; 5-shot magazine; 20-inch barrel; weighs 6-1/2 lbs.; hooded post front, windage-adjustable open rear sight; full-length walnut stock; solid rubber buttpad; rear locking lugs; twin extractors; sling swivels; single- or double-set trigger. Introduced 1982; discontinued 1983.

Exc: $850 **VGood:** $725 **Good:** $575

KRICO MODEL 500 KRICOTRONIC MATCH

Bolt action; single shot; 22 LR; 23-1/2-inch barrel; 45-1/5-inch overall length; weighs 9-1/5 lbs.; globe front, match-type rear sight; match-type European walnut stock; adjustable butt; electronic ignition system; adjustable trigger. Made in Germany.

Perf: $3700 **Exc:** $2695 **VGood:** $1695

KRICO MODEL 600

Bolt action; 17 Rem., 22-250, 222, 222 Rem. Mag., 223, 243, 308, 5.6x50 Mag.; 3-, 4-shot magazine; 23-1/2-inch barrel; 43-3/4-inch overall length; weighs 8 lbs.; hooded ramp front, fixed rear sight; tangent rear sight optional; hand-checkered European walnut Monte Carlo stock; schnabel forend; classic American-style stock also available; adjustable single- or double-set trigger, silent safety; double front locking lugs. Introduced 1983; no longer imported.

Exc: $995 **VGood:** $850 **Good:** $750

KRICO MODEL 600 EAC

Same specs as Model 600 except American-style classic stock; sling swivels. Introduced 1983; discontinued 1984.

Exc: $995 **VGood:** $795 **Good:** $595

KRICO MODEL 600 DELUXE

Same specs as Model 600 except traditional European-style select fancy walnut stock; rosewood schnabel forend tip; Bavarian cheekpiece; fine checkering; front sling swivel attaches to barrel; butterknife bolt handle; gold-plated single-set trigger. Introduced 1983; discontinued 1984.

Exc: $1095 **VGood:** $795 **Good:** $625

KRICO MODEL 600 MATCH

Same specs as Model 600 except no sights; drilled, tapped for scope mounts; cheekpiece match stock; vented forend; rubber recoil pad. Introduced 1983.

Perf: $1150 **Exc:** $895 **VGood:** $750

KRICO MODEL 600 SINGLE SHOT

Same specs as Model 600 except match barrel; no sights; drilled, tapped for scope mounts; adjustable buttplate; match-type stock; flash hider; Parkerized finish; large bolt knob; wide trigger shoe. Made in Germany. Introduced 1983.

Perf: $1150 **Exc:** $895 **VGood:** $750

KRICO MODEL 600 SNIPER

Same specs as Model 600 except match barrel; no sights; drilled, tapped for scope mounts; adjustable buttplate; flash hider; Parkerized finish; large bolt knob; wide trigger shoe. Made in Germany. Introduced 1983.

Perf: $2550 **Exc:** $2000 **VGood:** $1795

KRICO MODEL 620

Bolt action; 222 Rem., 223 Rem., 22-250, 243, 308, 5.6x50 Mag.; 3-shot magazine; 20-3/4-inch barrel; weighs 6-3/4 lbs.; hooded ramp front, fixed rear sight; tangent rear sight optional; drilled, tapped for scope mounts; full-length walnut stock; double-set trigger. Introduced 1988; discontinued 1988.

Perf: $1165 **Exc:** $880 **VGood:** $790

KRICO MODEL 640S

Bolt action; 222, 223, 22-250, 308; 5-shot magazine; 20-inch semi-bull barrel; no sights; pistol-grip stock of French walnut; ventilated forend; single- or double-set triggers. Introduced 1981; discontinued 1988.

Exc: $1295 **VGood:** $995 **Good:** $750

KRICO MODEL 640 VARMINT

Bolt action; 22-250, 222 Rem., 223 Rem.; 4-shot magazine; 23-3/4-inch barrel; weighs 9-3/8 lbs.; no sights; drilled, tapped for scope mounts; cut-checkered select European walnut stock; high Monte Carlo comb; Wundhammer palm swell; rosewood forend tip. Made in Germany. Importation discontinued 1988.

Exc: $1125 **VGood:** $995 **Good:** $895

KRICO MODEL 650S

Bolt action; 222, 223, 308; 3-shot magazine; 23-inch bull barrel; muzzlebrake/flash hider; no sights; drilled, tapped for scope mounts; oil-finished select European walnut stock; adjustable cheekpiece, recoil pad; match trigger; single- or double-set trigger available; all metal; matte blue finish. Introduced 1981; discontinued 1988.

Exc: $1395 **VGood:** $995 **Good:** $795

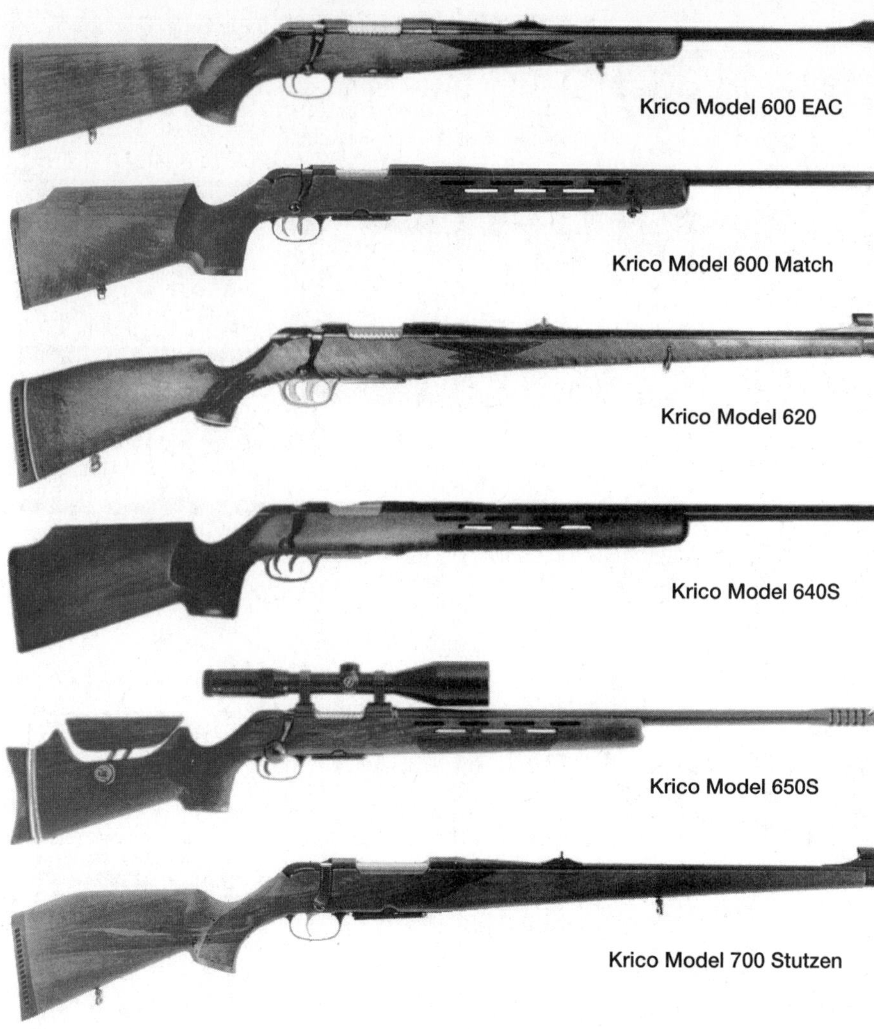

Krico Model 600 EAC

Krico Model 600 Match

Krico Model 620

Krico Model 640S

Krico Model 650S

Krico Model 700 Stutzen

KRICO MODEL 650S2

Same specs as Model 650 except special benchrest stock of French walnut. Introduced 1981; discontinued 1983.

Exc: $1395 **VGood:** $1095 **Good:** $825

KRICO MODEL 650 SUPER SNIPER

Same specs as Model 650 except 223, 308; 26-inch bull barrel. Made in Germany. Introduced 1981; discontinued 1988.

Exc: $1495 **VGood:** $1095 **Good:** $825

KRICO MODEL 700

Bolt action; 17 Rem., 222, 222 Rem. Mag., 223, 5.6x50 Mag., 243, 308, 5.6x57 RWS, 22-250, 6.5x55, 6.5x57, 7x57, 270, 7x64, 30-06, 9.3x62, 6.5x68, 7mm Rem. Mag., 300 Win. Mag., 8x68S, 7.5 Swiss, 9.3x64, 6x62 Freres; 23-1/2-inch barrel (standard calibers), 25-1/2-inch (magnums); 43-3/8-inch overall length (23-1/2-inch barrel); weighs about 7 lbs.; blade on ramp front sight, open adjustable rear; drilled, tapped for scope mounting; European walnut stock with Bavarian cheekpiece; removable box magazine; sliding safety. Imported from Germany by Mandall Shooting Supplies.

Exc: $1000 **VGood:** $795 **Good:** $680

KRICO MODEL 700 DELUXE

Same specs as Model 700 except better grade of wood, checkering. Imported from Germany by Mandall Shooting Supplies.

Exc: $1050 **VGood:** $875 **Good:** $725

KRICO MODEL 700 STUTZEN

Same specs as Model 700 except full-length stock. Imported from Germany by Mandall Shooting Supplies.

Exc: $1195 **VGood:** $895 **Good:** $695

KRICO MODEL 720

Bolt action; 17 Rem., 222, 222 Rem. Mag., 223, 5.6x50 Mag., 243, 308, 5.6x57 RWS, 22-250, 6.5x55, 6.5x57, 7x57, 270, 7x64, 30-06, 9.3x62, 6.5x68, 7mm Rem. Mag., 300 Win. Mag., 8x68S, 7.5 Swiss, 9.3x64, 6x62 Freres; 3-shot magazine; 20-3/4-inch barrel; weighs 6-3/4 lbs.; hooded ramp front, fixed rear sight; tangent rear sight optional; drilled, tapped for scope mounting; full-length walnut stock; double-set trigger. Introduced 1983; discontinued 1990.

Exc: $1095 **VGood:** $925 **Good:** $695

KRICO SPORTER

Bolt action; 22 Hornet, 222 Rem.; 4-shot clip magazine; 22-inch, 24-inch, 26-inch barrel; open rear, hooded ramp front sight; hand-checkered European walnut stock, cheekpiece, pistol grip, forend tip; miniature Mauser-type action; single- or double-set trigger; sling swivels. Made in Germany. Introduced 1956; discontinued 1962.

Exc: $645 **VGood:** $525 **Good:** $400

KRICO VARMINT MODEL

Bolt action; 222 Rem.; 4-shot magazine; 22-inch, 24-inch, 26-inch heavy barrel; no sights. Made in Germany. Introduced 1956; discontinued 1962.

Exc: $665 **VGood:** $575 **Good:** $435

KRIEGHOFF CLASSIC DOUBLE RIFLE

Double rifle; 7x65R, 308 Win., 30-06, 8x57 JRS, 8x75RS, 9.3x74R; 23.5-inch barrel; weighs 7.3 to 8 lbs. High grade European walnut stock. Standard has conventional rounded cheekpiece, Bavaria has Bavarian-style cheekpiece. Bead front sight with removable, adjustable wedge (375 H&H and below), standing leaf rear on quarter-rib. Boxlock action; double triggers; short opening angle for fast loading;

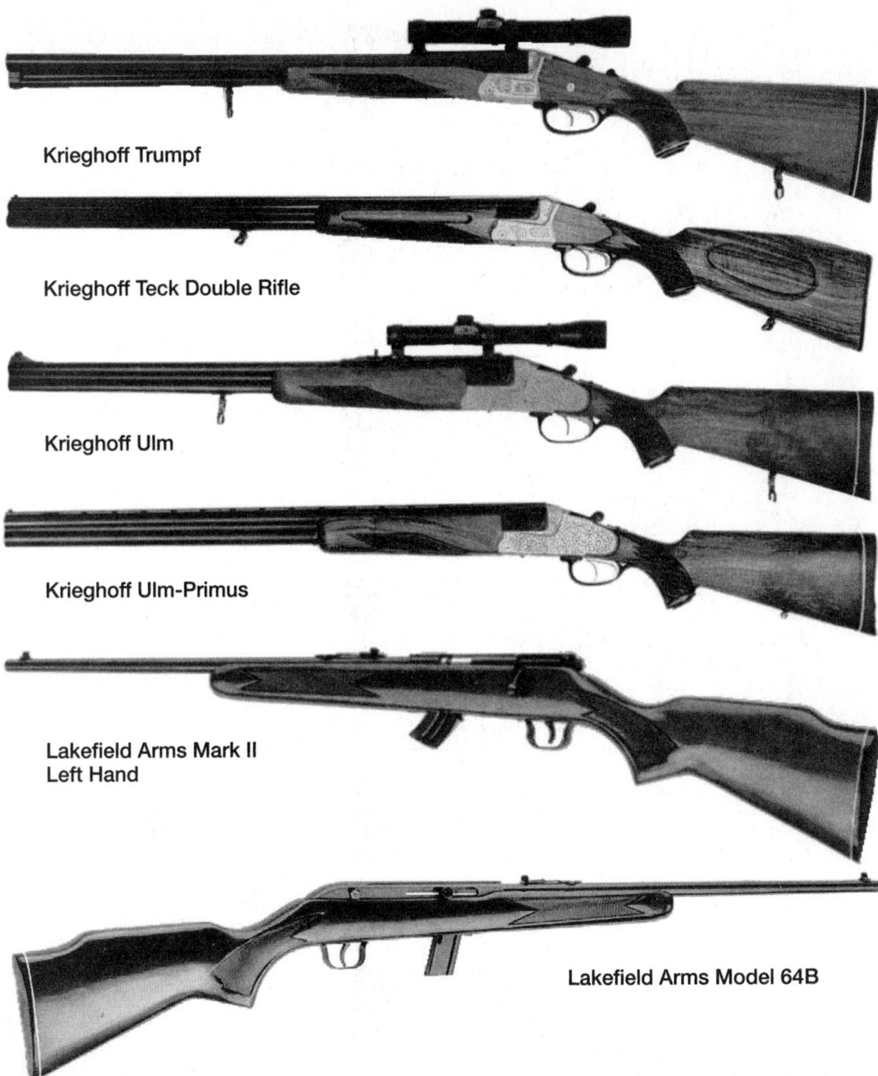
Krieghoff Trumpf

Krieghoff Teck Double Rifle

Krieghoff Ulm

Krieghoff Ulm-Primus

Lakefield Arms Mark II Left Hand

Lakefield Arms Model 64B

quiet extractors; sliding, self-adjusting wedge for secure bolting; Purdey-style barrel extension; horizontal firing pin placement. Many options available. Introduced 1997. Imported from Germany by Krieghoff International.

Perf: $9700 **VGood:** $7500 **Good:** $5500

KRIEGHOFF CLASSIC BIG FIVE DOUBLE RIFLE

Similar to the standard Classic except available in 375 Flanged Mag. N.E., 500/416 N.E., 470 N.E., 500 N.E. 3-inch, 375 H&H, 416 Rigby, 458. Double trigger; has hinged front trigger, non- removable muzzle wedge (larger than 375-caliber), Universal Trigger System, Combi Cocking Device, steel trigger guard, specially weighted stock bolt for weight and balance. Many options available. Introduced 1997. Imported from Germany by Krieghoff International.

Perf: $14500 **Exc:** $11500 **VGood:** $7000

KRIEGHOFF HUBERTUS SINGLE-SHOT RIFLE

Single shot; 222, 243, 270, 308, 30-06, 5.6x50R Mag., 5.6x52R, 6x62R Freres, 6.5x57R, 6.5x65R, 7x57R, 7x65R, 8x57JRS, 8x75RS, 7mm Rem. Mag., 300 Win. Mag.; 23-1/2-inch barrel; weighs 6-1/2 lbs. High-grade walnut stock; Blade front, open rear sights. Break-loading with manual cocking lever on top tang; take-down; extractor; schnabel forearm; many options. Imported from Germany by Krieghoff International Inc.

Perf: $5700 **Exc:** $4900 **VGood:** $3800

KRIEGHOFF NEPTUN

Drilling; 12-, 16-, 20-ga./22 Hornet, 222 Rem., 243, 270, 30-06, 308; standard European calibers also available up to 9.3x74R; 25-inch barrels; shot barrels choked Imp. Mod. & Full; optional free-floating rifle barrel available; weighs about 7-1/2 lbs.; bead front sight, automatic pop-up open rear; hand-checkered European walnut stock with German-style grip and cheekpiece, oil finish; full sidelock action with double or optional single trigger, top tang shotgun safety; fine, light scroll engraving. Imported from Germany by Krieghoff International, Inc. No longer imported.

Perf: $17000 **Exc:** $13000 **VGood:** $9100

KRIEGHOFF TECK COMBO

Combination gun; over/under; 12-, 16-, 20-ga./22 Hornet, 222, 243, 270, 30-06, 308 and standard European calibers; O/U rifle also available in 458 Win. on special order; 25-inch barrels on double rifle combo, 28-inch on O/U shotgun; optional free-floating rifle barrel; weighs about 7 to 7-1/2 lbs.; white bead front sight on shotgun, open or folding on rifle or combo; hand-checkered European walnut stock with German-style grip and cheekpiece; boxlock action with non-selective single trigger or optional single/double trigger; Greener cross-bolt; ejectors standard on all but O/U rifle; top tang safety; light scroll engraving. Imported from Germany by Krieghoff International, Inc. No longer imported. Premium for 458 Win Mag caliber.

Perf: $9700 **Exc:** $7000 **VGood:** $5000

KRIEGHOFF TECK DOUBLE RIFLE

Double rifle; boxlock; over/under; 7x57R, 7x64, 7x65R, 308 Win., 30-06, 300 Win. Mag., 8x57JRS, 9.3x74R, 375 H&H Mag., 458 Win. Mag.; 25-inch barrel; Express rear, ramp front sight; hand-checkered European walnut stock, forearm; double crossbolt; double underlugs. Introduced 1967; No longer imported. Premium for 458.

Perf: $10,000 **Exc:** $8000 **VGood:** $6000

KRIEGHOFF TRUMPF

Drilling; 12-, 16-, 20-ga./22 Hornet, 222 Rem., 243, 270, 30-06, 308; standard European calibers also available, up to 9.3x74R; 25-inch barrels; shot barrels choked Imp. Mod. & Full; optional free-floating rifle barrel; weighs about 7-1/2 lbs.; bead front sight, automatic pop-up open rear; hand-checkered European walnut stock with German-style grip and cheekpiece; oil finish; boxlock action with double or optional single trigger; top tang shotgun safety; fine, light scroll engraving. Imported from Germany by Krieghoff International, Inc. No longer imported.

Perf: $10,000 **Exc:** $8000 **VGood:** $6000

KRIEGHOFF ULM COMBO

Combination gun; over/under; 12-, 16-, 20-ga./22 Hornet, 222, 243, 270, 30-06, 308 and standard European calibers; O/U rifle also available in 458 Win. on special order; 25-inch barrels (double rifle combo), 28-inch (O/U shotgun); optional free-floating rifle barrel; weighs about 7-7-1/2 lbs.; white bead front sight on shotgun, open or folding on rifle or combo; hand-checkered European walnut stock with German-style grip and cheekpiece; full sidelock action with non-selective single trigger or optional single/double trigger; Greener cross-bolt; ejectors standard on all but O/U rifle; top tang safety; light scroll engraving. Imported from Germany by Krieghoff International, Inc. No longer imported.

Perf: $14,500 **Exc:** $12,000 **VGood:** $8950

KRIEGHOFF ULM DOUBLE RIFLE

Double rifle; boxlock; over/under; 7x57R, 7x64, 7x65R, 308 Win., 30-06, 300 Win. Mag., 8x57JRS, 9.3x74R, 375 H&H Mag., 458 Win. Mag.; 25-inch barrel; express rear, ramp front sight; hand-checkered European walnut stock, forearm; double cross-bolt; double underlugs; leaf arabesque engraving. Introduced 1963; still imported.

Perf: $16,800 **Exc:** $14,500 **VGood:** $11,000

KRIEGHOFF ULM-PRIMUS

Same specs as Ulm except deluxe modifications including higher grade of engraving, wood; detachable side locks. Introduced 1963; discontinued 1983.

Perf: $24,500 **Exc:** $20,500 **VGood:** $16,000

LAKEFIELD ARMS MARK I

Bolt action; single shot; 22 LR; 20-1/2-inch barrel; 39-1/2-inch overall length; weighs 5-1/2 lbs.; bead front, open adjustable rear sight; receiver grooved for scope mounts; checkered Monte Carlo-type stock of walnut-finished hardwood; thumb-activated rotating safety; right-, left-hand variations; youth model available with smaller dimensions; blued finish. Made in Canada. Introduced 1990.

Perf: $100 **Exc:** $75 **VGood:** $60

LAKEFIELD ARMS MARK II

Bolt action; 22 LR; 10-shot magazine; 20-1/2-inch barrel; 39-1/2-inch overall length; weighs 5-1/2 lbs.; bead front, open adjustable rear sight; receiver grooved for scope mounts; checkered Monte Carlo-type stock of walnut-finished hardwood; thumb-activated rotary safety; right-, left-hand variations; youth model available with smaller dimensions; blued finish. Made in Canada. Introduced 1990.

Perf: $110 **Exc:** $80 **VGood:** $65

LAKEFIELD ARMS MODEL 64B

Semi-automatic; 22 LR; 10-shot magazine; 20-inch barrel; 40-inch overall length; weighs 5-1/2 lbs.; bead front, open adjustable rear sight; checkered Monte Carlo-type walnut stained hardwood stock; side ejection; bolt hold-open device; thumb-activated rotary safety; blued finish. Made in Canada. Introduced 1990.

Perf: $110 **Exc:** $90 **VGood:** $80

LAKEFIELD ARMS MODEL 90 BIATHLON

Bolt action; 22 LR; 5-shot magazine; 21-inch barrel; 39-1/2-inch overall length; weighs 8-1/4 lbs.; target front sight with inserts, adjustable peep rear; natural-finish hardwood stock; clip holder; carrying, shooting rails; hand stop; butthook; snow-cap muzzle protector; right-, left-hand versions. Marketed with five magazines. Made in Canada. Introduced 1991; discontinued 1995.

Perf: $400 **Exc:** $360 **VGood:** $290

LAKEFIELD ARMS MODEL 91T

Bolt action; single shot; 22 LR; 25-inch barrel; 43-1/2-inch overall length; weighs 8 lbs.; target front sight with inserts; click-adjustable peep rear; target-type walnut-finished hardwood stock; shooting rail; hand stop. Made in Canada. Introduced 1991; discontinued 1995.

Perf: $330 **Exc:** $290 **VGood:** $220

LAKEFIELD ARMS MODEL 91TR

Same specs as Model 91T except repeater with 5-shot magazine. Made in Canada. Introduced 1991; discontinued 1995.

Perf: $350 **Exc:** $300 **VGood:** $230

LAKEFIELD ARMS MODEL 92S SILHOUETTE

Bolt action; 22 LR; 5-shot magazine; 21-inch barrel; 39-1/2-inch overall length; weighs 8 lbs.; no sights; receiver drilled, tapped for scope base; high-comb target-type stock of walnut-finished hardwood; right-, left-hand versions. Made in Canada by Lakefield Arms. Introduced 1992; discontinued 1995.

Perf: $300 **Exc:** $270 **VGood:** $200

Left-hand model

Perf: $320 **Exc:** $280 **VGood:** $210

LAKEFIELD ARMS MODEL 93M

Bolt action; 22 WMR; 5-shot magazine; 20-3/4-inch barrel; 39-1/2-inch overall length; weighs 5-3/4 lbs.; bead front sight, adjustable open rear; receiver grooved for scope mount; walnut-finished hardwood stock with Monte Carlo-type comb; checkered grip and forend; thumb-operated rotary safety; blue finish. Made in Canada by Lakefield Arms Ltd. Introduced 1994.

Perf: $130 **Exc:** $100 **VGood:** $90

L.A.R. GRIZZLY 50 BIG BOAR

Bolt action; single shot; 50 BMG; 36-inch barrel; 45-1/2-inch overall length; weighs 28-1/2 lbs.; no sights; scope mount; integral stock; ventilated rubber recoil pad; bullpup design; thumb safety; all-steel construction. Made in U.S. by L.A.R. Mfg., Inc. Introduced 1994; still produced.

Perf: $2150 **Exc:** $2000 **VGood:** $1800

LEBEAU-COURALLY BOXLOCK

Double rifle; 8x57JRS, 9.3x74R; 23-1/2-inch to 26-inch chopper lump barrels; made to customer specs; weighs 8 lbs.; Express rear sight on quarter-rib, bead on ramp front; French walnut stock; pistol grip with cheekpiece, splinter or beavertail forend; steel grip cap; ejectors; several engraving patterns. Made in Belgium. Introduced 1987; no longer imported.

Perf: $16,995 **Exc:** $14,950 **VGood:** $9995

LEBEAU-COURALLY EXPRESS RIFLE SXS

Double rifle; 7x65R, 8x57JRS, 9.3x74R, 375 H&H, 470 N.E.; 24-inch to 26-inch barrels; weighs 7-3/4 to 10-1/2 lbs.; Fancy French walnut stock with cheekpiece; Bead on ramp front sight, standing express rear on quarter-rib. Holland & Holland-type sidelock with automatic ejectors; double triggers. Built to order only. Imported from Belgium by Wm. Larkin Moore.

Perf: $38,000 **Exc:** $30,000 **VGood:** $20,000

Lakefield Arms Model 90 Biathlon

Lakefield Arms Model 91T

Lakefield Arms Model 92S Silhouette

Lakefield Arms Model 93M

L.A.R. Grizzly 50 Big Boar

Lebeau-Courally Sidelock

Legacy Sports International M-1500 Custom

LEBEAU-COURALLY SIDELOCK

Double rifle; 8x57 JRS, 9.3x74R, 375 H&H, 458 Win. Mag., 470 NE, 577 NE; 23-1/2-inch to 26-inch chopper lump barrels; weighs 8 lbs.; made to customer specs; Express rear sight on quarter-rib, bead on ramp front; French walnut stock; pistol grip with cheekpiece, splinter or beavertail forend; steel grip cap; ejectors; reinforced action; several engraving patterns. Made in Belgium. Introduced 1987; no longer imported.

Perf: $34,000 **Exc:** $28,000 **VGood:** $19,000

LEGACY SPORTS INTERNATIONAL M-1500 CUSTOM RIFLES

Bolt action; 300 WSM, 300 Win. Mag.; 3 plus 1 in chamber; weighs 7.6 to 8.3 lbs.; 42-1/2-inch overall length. Black polymer or laminated wood stock; Built on Howa M-1500 stainless steel short-action, 3-position thumb safety, hinged floorplate, drilled and tapped for standard scope mounts. 300 WSM has stainless steel short action, 22-inch barrel. 300 Win. Mag. has blued long action, 24-inch bbl. with integral ported muzzle brake by Bill Wiseman. Introduced 2001 by Legacy Sports International.

Polymer stock

Perf: $850 **Exc:** $750 **VGood:** $650

Laminated wood stock

Perf: $900 **Exc:** $800 **VGood:** $700

LEGACY SPORTS INTERNATIONAL TEXAS SAFARI RIFLES

Bolt action; 270 Win., 300 Win. Mag. 270 Win.: 5 plus 1 in chamber; 300 Mag., 3 plus 1 in chamber; weighs 7.8 lbs; 42-1/2-inch overall length; 44-1/2 inches in 300 Win. Mag.; Brown/black laminated wood stock. Built on Howa M-1500 action customized by Bill Wiseman, College Station, TX; Wiseman-designed 3-position thumb safety and bolt-release, hinged floorplate, drilled and tapped for standard scope mounts. Action glass-bedded, Farrell free floated. 300 Win. Mag. has integral muzzle brake. Introduced 2001 by Legacy Sports International.

Perf: $1495 **Exc:** $1375 **VGood:** $1265

Legacy Sports International Mauser 98

Les Baer Ultimate AR 223 Super Varmint

Les Baer Ultimate AR 223 M4 Flattop

Les Baer Ultimate AR 223 IPSC

Magnum Research MagnumLite Graphite Rifle

Magnum Research MagnumLite MLR-1722 .22 WMR Graphite Rifle

300 Win. Mag.

Perf: $1600 **Exc:** $1550 **VGood:** $1450

LEGACY SPORTS INTERNATIONAL MAUSER 98 RIFLE

Bolt action; 300 Win. Mag.; 24-inch barrel, 1-10-inch twist; weighs 8.4 lbs.; 45-inch overall length; Premium American walnut stock. Square-bridge Mauser 98 action dovetailed for ring mounts (scope and rings not included). 3-position thumb safety, hinged floorplate, adjustable trigger. Introduced 2001. Imported from Italy by Legacy Sports International.

Perf: $875 **Exc:** $775 **VGood:** $650

LES BAER CUSTOM ULTIMATE AR 223 RIFLE

Semi-automatic; 223. 18-inch barrel, 20-inch, 22-inch, 24-inch; weighs 7-3/4 to 9-3/4 lb.; Black synthetic stock; Picatinny-style flat top rail for scope mounting. Forged receiver; Ultra single-stage trigger (Jewell two-stage trigger optional); titanium firing pin; Versa-Pod bipod; chromed National Match carrier; stainless steel, hand-lapped and cryo-treated barrel; guaranteed to shoot 1/2 or 3/4 MOA, depending on model. Made in U.S.A. by Les Bear Custom Inc.

Super Varmint Model

Perf: $2000 **Exc:** $1700 **VGood:** $1400

M4 Flattop or IPSC Action Model

Perf: $2200 **Exc:** $1900 **VGood:** $1600

LES BAER LBC CUSTOM SPECIAL TACTICAL RIFLE

Semi-automatic center-fire rifle with a black finish, hard anodized aluminum receiver, optional flash hider and a collapsible stock, Geisselle trigger, and 416R stainless steel barrel. Chambered in .223 Remngton/5.56x45mm NATO. 16 inch barrel, and weighs 7.37 pounds. 30 round capacity box magazine. Introduced 2012.

Perf: $2,000 **Exc:** $1,850 **VGood:** $1,600

LES BAER MID-LENGTH MONOLITH .308 SWAT MODEL

Semi-automatic center-fire rifle with a black finish, hard anodized aluminum receiver, one piece upper rail system, Geissele two-stage trigger, 416R stainless steel barrel and Magpul PRS stock. Chambered in .308 Winchester/7.62x51mm NATO. 16 inch barrel. 20 round capacity box magazine. Introduced 2012.

Perf: $3,500 **Exc:** $3,000 **VGood:** $2,600

LJUTIC SPACE GUN

Single shot; 22-250, 30-30, 30-06, 308; 24-inch barrel; 44-inch overall length; iron sights or scope mounts; American walnut stock grip, forend; anti-recoil mechanism; twist-bolt action. Introduced 1981; discontinued 1988.

Perf: $3000 **Exc:** $2795 **VGood:** $2495

MAGNUM RESEARCH MAGNUMLITE TACTICAL RIFLE

Bolt action; 223 Rem., 22-250, 308 Win., 300 Win. Mag., 300 WSM.; 26-inch Magnum Lite graphite barrel; weighs 8.3 lbs. H-S Precision tactical black synthetic stock; drilled and tapped for scope mount. Accurized Remington 700 action; adjustable trigger; adjustable comb height. Tuned to shoot 1/2-inch MOA or better. Introduced 2001. From Magnum Research Inc.

Perf: $2250 **Exc:** $2000 **VGood:** $1600

MAGNUM RESEARCH MAGNUMLITE GRAPHITE RIFLE

Bolt action rifle built on Remington or Sako action with H-S Precsion or Hogue stock. Chambered in .22-250, .223, 7mm Rem. Mag., .280, or .30-06.

NIB: $2300 **Exc:** $1900 **VGood:** $1200

MAGNUM RESEARCH MAGNUMLITE MLR-1722 RIFLE

Semi-auto rimfire rifle with graphite barrel and black Hogue overmolded stock. 10-shot rotary magazine.

NIB: $600 **Exc:** $500 **VGood:** $350

MAGNUM RESEARCH MAGNUMLITE MLR-1722 .17 MACH-2 RIFLE

Similar to above but chambered in .17 Mach-2.

NIB: $600 **Exc:** $500 **VGood:** $350

MAGNUM RESEARCH MAGNUMLITE MLR-1722 .22 WMR GRAPHITE RIFLE

Semi-auto rimfire rifle with graphite barrel and skeletonized laminated stock with thumbhole in a variety of laminate colors. Chambered in .22 WMR.

NIB: $700 **Exc:** $550 **VGood:** $395

MAGNUM RESEARCH MAGNUMLITE MLR-1722 .17 HMR GRAPHITE RIFLE

Similar to above but with conventional Hogue overmolded stock. Chamberd in 17 HMR.

NIB: $700 **Exc:** $550 **VGood:** $395

MAGNUM RESEARCH MAGNUMLITE MLR-1722 .17 HMR STAINLESS STEEL RIFLE

Similar to above but with stainless steel receiver and barrel.

NIB: $700 **Exc:** $550 **VGood:** $395

MAGTECH MODEL 122.2R

Bolt action; 22 Short, 22 Long, 22 LR; 6-, 10-shot magazines; 24-inch six-groove barrel; 43-inch overall length; weighs 6-1/2 lbs.; blade front sight, open fully-adjustable rear; receiver grooved for scope mount; Brazilian hardwood stock; sliding safety; double extractors. Imported from Brazil by Magtech Recreational Products, Inc. Introduced 1994; no longer imported.

Exc: $100 **VGood:** $80 **Good:** $60

MAGTECH MODEL 122.2S

Same specs as Model 122.2R except no sights; receiver grooved for scope mounting. Imported from Brazil by Magtech Recreational Products, Inc. Introduced 1994; no longer imported.

Exc: $90 **VGood:** $70 **Good:** $50

MAGTECH MODEL 122.2T

Same specs as Model 122.2R except ramp front sight, micrometer-adjustable open rear; receiver grooved for scope mounting. Imported from Brazil by Magtech Recreational Products, Inc. Introduced 1994; no longer imported.

Exc: $110 **VGood:** $100 **Good:** $80

MAGTECH MODEL MT-122C

Bolt action; 22 Short, 22 Long, 22 LR; 6-, 10-shot detachable magazines; 21-inch six-groove barrel; 39-inch overall length; weighs 5-3/4 lbs.; blade front sight, fully-adjustable open rear; receiver grooved for scope mount; Brazilian hardwood stock; sliding wing-type safety; double extractors; red cocking indicator. Imported from Brazil by Magtech Recreational Products, Inc. Introduced 1991; discontinued 1993.

Exc: $90 **VGood:** $80 **Good:** $60

MAGTECH MODEL MT-122T

Same specs as MT-22C except 15-shot tubular magazine. Imported from Brazil by Magtech Recreational Products, Inc. Introduced 1991; discontinued 1993.

Exc: $150 **VGood:** $120 **Good:** $90

MAGTECH MODEL MT-52-T TARGET

Bolt action; 22 LR; 6-, 10-shot magazine; 26-1/4-inch eight-groove barrel; 43-3/8-inch overall length; weighs about 9 lbs.; globe front sight with inserts, match-type aperture rear; receiver grooved for scope mounting; Brazilian hardwood stock with stippled grip; fully-adjustable rubber buttplate; aluminum forend rail with sling support; fully-adjustable trigger; free-floating barrel. Imported from Brazil by Magtech Recreational Products, Inc. Introduced 1991; discontinued 1993.

Exc: $150 **VGood:** $120 **Good:** $90

MAGTECH MODEL MT-66

Semi-automatic; 22 LR; 14-shot tubular magazine; 19 5/8-inch six-groove barrel; 38-1/2-inch overall length; weighs 4-1/2 lbs.; blade front sight, open adjustable rear; receiver grooved for scope mounts; moulded black nylon stock with checkered pistol grip and forend; tube magazine loads through buttplate; top tang safety. Imported from Brazil by Magtech Recreational Products, Inc. Introduced 1991; discontinued 1993.

Exc: $90 **VGood:** $80 **Good:** $70

MAGTECH MT 7022 AUTO RIFLE

Semi-automatic; 22 LR, 10-shot magazine. 18-inch barrel; weighs 4.8 lbs.; 37-inch overall length; Brazilian hardwood stock; Hooded blade front, fully adjustable open rear sights. Cross-bolt safety; last-shot bolt hold-open; alloy receiver is drilled and tapped for scope mounting. Introduced 1998. No longer offered. Imported from Brazil by Magtech Ammunition Co.

Perf: $95 **Exc:** $85 **VGood:** $75

With synthetic stock, as Model 7022 S

Perf: $95 **Exc:** $85 **VGood:** $75

MANNLICHER-SCHOENAUER HIGH VELOCITY

Bolt action; 30-06, 7x64 Brenneke, 8x60 Mag., 9.3x62, 10.75x57mm; 5-shot rotary magazine; 23-1/2-inch barrel; British-type three-leaf open rear sight, ramp front; hand-checkered traditional sporting stock of European walnut; cheekpiece, pistol grip; sling swivels. Introduced 1922; discontinued 1937.

Exc: $2600 **VGood:** $2200 **Good:** $1725

MANNLICHER-SCHOENAUER MODEL 1903 CARBINE

Bolt action; 6.5x53mm; 5-shot rotary magazine; 17-1/2-inch barrel; two-leaf rear, ramp front sight; full-length uncheckered European walnut stock; metal forearm cap; pistol grip; cartridge trap in buttplate; double-set trigger; flat bolt handle; sling swivels. Introduced 1903; discontinued 1937.

Exc: $1400 **VGood:** $1100 **Good:** $875

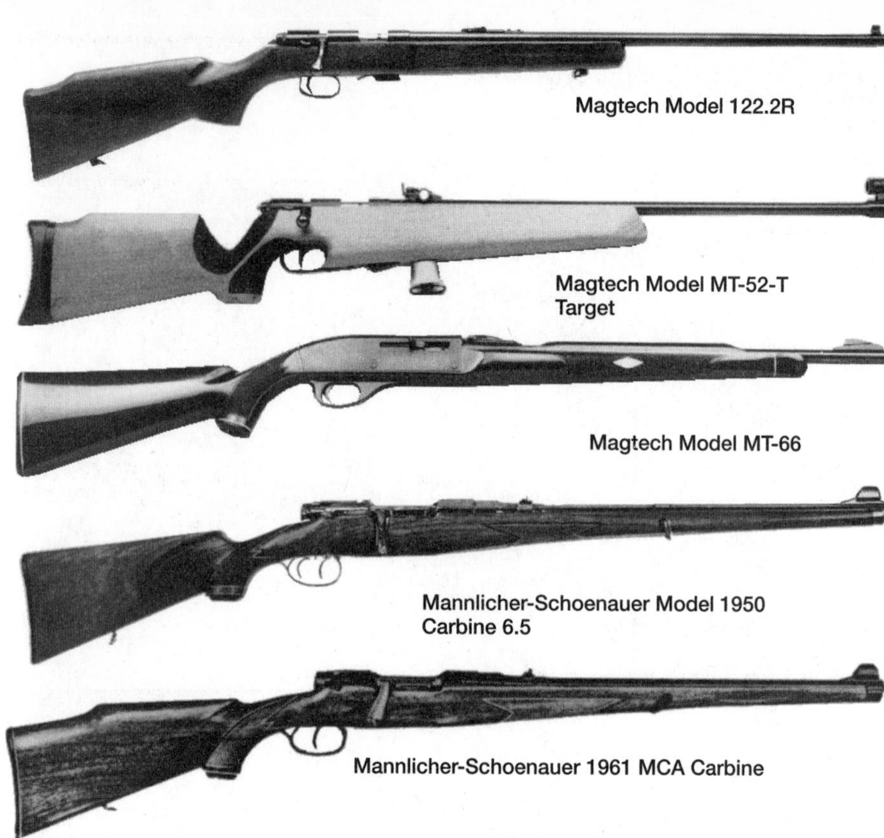

Magtech Model 122.2R

Magtech Model MT-52-T Target

Magtech Model MT-66

Mannlicher-Schoenauer Model 1950 Carbine 6.5

Mannlicher-Schoenauer 1961 MCA Carbine

MANNLICHER-SCHOENAUER MODEL 1905 CARBINE

Bolt action; 9x56mm; 5-shot rotary magazine; 19-1/2-inch barrel; two-leaf rear, ramp front sight; full-length uncheckered European walnut stock; metal forearm cap; pistol grip; cartridge trap in buttplate; double-set trigger; flat bolt handle; sling swivels. Introduced 1905; discontinued 1937.

Exc: $1600 **VGood:** $1300 **Good:** $975

MANNLICHER-SCHOENAUER MODEL 1908 CARBINE

Bolt action; 7x57mm, 8x56mm; 5-shot rotary magazine; 19-1/2-inch barrel; two-leaf rear, ramp front sight; full-length uncheckered European walnut stock; metal forearm cap; pistol grip; cartridge trap in buttplate; double-set trigger; flat bolt handle; sling swivels. Introduced 1908; discontinued 1947.

Exc: $1600 **VGood:** $1300 **Good:** $975

MANNLICHER-SCHOENAUER MODEL 1910 CARBINE

Bolt action; 9x56, 9.5x57, 375 Express; 5-shot rotary magazine; 19-1/2-inch barrel; two-leaf rear, ramp front sight; full-length uncheckered European walnut stock; metal forearm cap; pistol grip; cartridge trap in buttplate; double-set trigger; flat bolt handle; sling swivels. Introduced 1910; discontinued 1937.

Exc: $1500 **VGood:** $1200 **Good:** $875

MANNLICHER-SCHOENAUER MODEL 1924 CARBINE

Bolt action; 30-06; 5-shot rotary magazine; 19-1/2-inch barrel; two-leaf rear, ramp front sight; full-length uncheckered European walnut stock; metal forearm cap; pistol grip; cartridge trap in buttplate; double-set trigger; flat bolt handle; sling swivels. Introduced 1924; discontinued 1937.

Exc: $2400 **VGood:** $1975 **Good:** $1425

MANNLICHER-SCHOENAUER MODEL 1950

Bolt action; 244, 257 Roberts, 270, 280, 30-06, 358 Win. Mag., 6.5x54, 7x57, 8x57, 9.3x62; 5-shot rotary magazine; 23-1/2-inch barrel; weighs 7-1/2 lbs.; folding leaf open rear sight, hooded ramp front; standard hand-checkered European walnut half-stock; pistol grip, cheekpiece; ebony forend tip; single- or double-set trigger; flat bolt handle; shotgun-type safety; sling swivels. Original price: $179. Introduced 1950; discontinued 1952.

Exc: $1550 **VGood:** $1300 **Good:** $1000

MANNLICHER-SCHOENAUER MODEL 1950 CARBINE

Same specs as Model 1950 rifle except weighs 7 lbs.; full-length walnut stock; metal forend cap; 20-inch barrel. Introduced 1950; discontinued 1952.

Exc: $1500 **VGood:** $1250 **Good:** $950

MANNLICHER-SCHOENAUER MODEL 1950 CARBINE 6.5

Same specs as Model 1950 except 6.5x54; 18-1/4-inch barrel; full-length walnut stock. Introduced 1950; discontinued 1952.

Exc: $1400 **VGood:** $1100 **Good:** $950

MANNLICHER-SCHOENAUER MODEL 1952 IMPROVED

Bolt action; 244, 257 Roberts, 270, 280, 30-06, 358 Win. Mag., 6.5x54, 7x57, 8x57, 9.3x62; 5-shot rotary magazine; 24-inch barrel; weighs 7-1/4 lbs.; folding leaf open rear sight, hooded ramp front; improved hand-checkered European walnut half-stock; pistol grip; deluxe hand-carved cheekpiece; ebony forend tip; single- or double-set trigger; swept-back bolt handle; shotgun-type safety; sling swivels. Introduced 1952; discontinued 1956.

Exc: $1500 **VGood:** $1200 **Good:** $1000

MANNLICHER-SCHOENAUER MODEL 1952 IMPROVED CARBINE

Same specs as Model 1952 Improved except 257 Roberts, 270, 30-06; 20-inch, 24-inch barrel; weighs 7 lbs.; improved full-length walnut stock design; swept back bolt handle. Introduced 1952; discontinued 1956.

Exc: $1500 **VGood:** $1200 **Good:** $1000

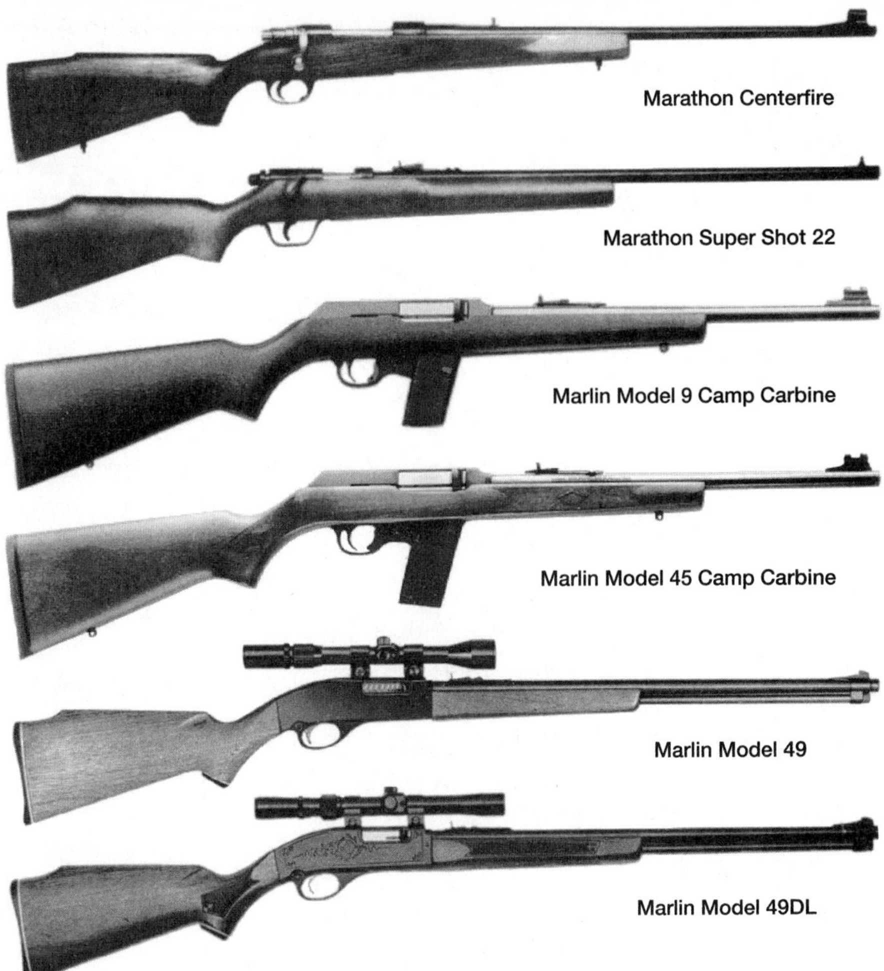
Marathon Centerfire

Marathon Super Shot 22

Marlin Model 9 Camp Carbine

Marlin Model 45 Camp Carbine

Marlin Model 49

Marlin Model 49DL

MANNLICHER-SCHOENAUER MODEL 1952 IMPROVED CARBINE 6.5

Same specs Model 1952 Improved except 6.5x53; 18-1/4-inch barrel; weighs 6-3/4 lbs.; improved full-length walnut stock. Introduced 1952; discontinued 1956.

Exc: $1450 **VGood:** $1150 **Good:** $950

MANNLICHER-SCHOENAUER MODEL 1956

Bolt action; 243 Win., 30-06; 5-shot rotary magazine; 22-inch barrel; folding leaf open rear sight, hooded ramp front; high-comb improved walnut half-stock; pistol grip; cheekpiece; ebony forend tip; single- or double-set trigger; swept-back bolt handle; shotgun-type safety; sling swivels. Introduced 1956; discontinued 1960.

Exc: $1200 **VGood:** $1000 **Good:** $800

MANNLICHER-SCHOENAUER MODEL 1956 CARBINE

Same specs as Model 1956 except 243, 257 Roberts, 270, 30-06, 308, 6.5x53, 7mm; 20-inch barrel; redesigned high-comb walnut full-length stock. Introduced 1956; discontinued 1960.

Exc: $1350 **VGood:** $1100 **Good:** $900

MANNLICHER-SCHOENAUER MODEL 1956 MAGNUM

Same specs as Model 1956 except 257 Weatherby Mag., 6.5x68, 8x68, 458 Win. Mag. Introduced 1956; discontinued 1960.

Exc: $1400 **VGood:** $1200 **Good:** $975

MANNLICHER-SCHOENAUER MODEL 1961 MCA

Bolt action; 243 Win., 270 Win., 30-06; 5-shot rotary magazine; 22-inch barrel; folding leaf open rear sight, hooded ramp front; Monte Carlo walnut half-stock; pistol grip; cheekpiece; ebony forend tip; single- or double-set trigger; swept-back bolt handle; shotgun-type safety; sling swivels. Introduced 1961; discontinued 1971.

Exc: $1300 **VGood:** $1135 **Good:** $950

MANNLICHER-SCHOENAUER 1961 MCA CARBINE

Same specs as Model 1956 except 243 Win., 270 Win., 30-06, 308 Win., 6.5x53; 20-inch barrel; Monte Carlo-style walnut full-length stock. Introduced 1961; discontinued 1971.

Exc: $1350 **VGood:** $1180 **Good:** $995

MAPIZ ZANARDINI OXFORD

Double rifle; boxlock side-by-side; 444 Marlin, 7x65R, 6.5x57R, 9.3x74R, 375 H&H Mag., 458 Win. Mag., 465 N.E., 470 N.E., 577 N.E., 600 N.E., 375 Flanged N.E.; 24-inch, 25-inch, 25-1/2-inch barrel; oil-finished European walnut stock; rubber or hard buttplate; automatic ejectors; double triggers; heavy engraving. Made in Italy. Introduced 1989; discontinued 1990.

Perf: $7900 **Exc:** $6100 **VGood:** $4100

MARATHON CENTERFIRE

Bolt action; 243, 308, 7x57, 30-06, 270, 7mm Rem. Mag., 300 Win. Mag.; 5-shot magazine; 24-inch barrel; 45-inch overall length; weighs 8 lbs.; open adjustable rear sight, bead front on ramp; select walnut Monte Carlo stock; rubber recoil pad; Santa Barbara Mauser action; triple thumb locking safety; blued finish. Made in Spain. Introduced 1984; discontinued 1986.

Exc: $310 **VGood:** $270 **Good:** $200

MARATHON SUPER SHOT 22

Bolt action; single shot; 22 LR; 24-inch barrel; 41-1/2-inch overall length; weighs 5 lbs.; step-adjustable open rear sight, bead front; receiver grooved for scope mounts; select hardwood stock; blued finish. Made in Spain. Introduced 1984; discontinued 1986.

Exc: $65 **VGood:** $55 **Good:** $40

MARCEL THYS KING ROYAL

Double rifle; sidelock side-by-side; 22 LR, 22 Hornet, 30-06, 375 H&H Mag., 450 #2, 458 Win. Mag., 470 Nitro, 500-3-inch, 577, 600 Nitro; 24-inch to 27-inch chopper lump barrels; weighs 6 to 14 lbs. depending on caliber, accessories; bead on ramp front sight, one standing leaf, two folding leaves on quarter-rib; oil-finished European walnut stock; hand-detachable locks; reinforced top tang extension; reinforced Holland-type frame; full-coverage game scene engraving with gold inlay; coin finish or color case-hardened action. Made in Belgium. Introduced 1990; discontinued 1992.

Exc: $16,000 **VGood:** $13,900 **Good:** $11,500

MARCEL THYS LIEGE ROYAL LUX

Double rifle; sidelock side-by-side; 22 LR, 22 Hornet, 30-06, 375 H&H Mag., 450 #2, 458 Win. Mag., 470 Nitro, 500-3-inch, 577, 600 Nitro; 24-inch-27-inch chopper lump barrels; weighs 6-14 lbs. depending on caliber, accessories; bead on ramp front sight, one standing leaf, two folding leaves on quarter-rib; oil-finished dark European walnut stock; hand-detachable locks; reinforced top tang extension; reinforced Holland-type frame; full-coverage game scene engraving; coin finish or color case-hardened action. Made in Belgium. Introduced 1990; discontinued 1992.

Exc: $14,500 **VGood:** $12,500 **Good:** $9950

MARLIN MODEL 9 CAMP CARBINE

Semi-automatic; 9mm Para.; 12-shot magazine; 16-1/2-inch barrel; 35-1/2-inch overall length; weighs 6-3/4 lbs.; adjustable open rear sight, ramp front with bead, hood; drilled, tapped for scope mount; wood stock; rubber buttpad; manual hold-open; Garand-type safety; magazine safety; loaded chamber indicator. Introduced 1985; discontinued 2000.

Perf: $550 **Exc:** $510 **VGood:** $425

MARLIN MODEL 9N

Same specs as Model 9 except nickel finish. Introduced 1991. No longer in production.

Perf: $450 **Exc:** $375 **VGood:** $300

MARLIN MODEL 45 CAMP CARBINE

Semi-automatic; 45 ACP; 7-shot magazine; 16-1/2-inch barrel; 35-1/2-inch overall length; weighs 6-3/4 lbs.; ramp front, open adjustable rear sight; walnut-finished hardwood stock; rubber buttpad; sling swivels. Introduced 1986, discontinued 2000.

Perf: $850 **Exc:** $750 **VGood:** $645

MARLIN MODEL 49

Semi-automatic; 22 LR; 19-shot tubular magazine; 22-inch barrel; 40-1/4-inch overall length; weighs 5-1/2 lbs.; open rear, hooded ramp front sight; two-piece checkered or uncheckered hardwood stock; same as Model 99C except solid top receiver; manual bolt hold-open. Introduced 1968; discontinued 1971.

Exc: $150 **VGood:** $125 **Good:** $110

MARLIN MODEL 49DL

Same specs as Model 49 except capped pistol grip; checkered forearm and pistol grip; gold trigger; scroll-engraved receiver; grooved for tip-off scope mounts. Introduced 1970; no longer produced.

Exc: $160 **VGood:** $135 **Good:** $120

MARLIN MODEL 50

Semi-automatic; 22 LR; 6-shot detachable box magazine; 22-inch barrel; take-down action; open adjustable rear sight, bead front; uncheckered pistol-grip walnut stock, grooved forearm. Introduced 1931; discontinued 1934.

Exc: $230 **VGood:** $175 **Good:** $150

MARLIN MODEL 50E

Same specs as Model 50 except hooded front sight, peep rear.

Exc: $250 **VGood:** $175 **Good:** $150

MARLIN MODEL 60

Semi-automatic; 22 LR; 14-shot tubular magazine; 22-inch round tapered barrel; 40-1/2-inch overall length; weighs 5-1/2 lbs.; ramp front sight, open adjustable rear; matted receiver; grooved for tip-off mounts; walnut-finished Monte Carlo hardwood stock; auto last-shot bolt hold-open. Originally marketed as Marlin Glenfield Model 60. Introduced 1982; still in production, with variations in stock and finish options. Older, unremarkable examples frequently sell for less than $100.

Perf: $175 **Exc:** $150 **VGood:** $125

MARLIN MODEL 60SS

Same specs as Model 60 except breech bolt, barrel and outer magazine tube of stainless steel construction; most other parts either nickel-plated or coated to match the stainless finish; black/gray Maine birch laminate Monte Carlo stock; nickel-plated swivel studs; rubber buttpad. Made in U.S. by Marlin. Introduced 1993; still produced.

Perf: $190 **Exc:** $150 **VGood:** $130

Model 60SSK (black fiberglass-filled stock)

Perf: $160 **Exc:** $110 **VGood:** $80

Model 60SB (walnut-finished birch stock)

Perf: $130 **Exc:** $90 **VGood:** $70

MARLIN MODEL 60SN

Similar to Model 60SS but with black synthetic stock with molded checkering and swivel studs. Introduced in 2007. Available with factory-mounted 3x9 scope. Add 10 percent for scope package.

Perf: $265 **Exc:** $215 **VGood:** $150

MODEL 60S-CF

Similar to Model 60SN but with carbon fiber-dippedd black synthetic stock, giving it a – quote – "racy, high tech look."

Perf: $265 **Exc:** $215 **VGood:** $150

MARLIN MODEL 70HC

Semi-automatic; 22 LR; 7-, 15-shot clip magazine; 18-inch barrel; 36-3/4-inch overall length; weighs 5-1/2 lbs.; ramp front sight, adjustable open rear; receiver grooved for scope mount; Monte Carlo-type walnut-finished hardwood stock; cross-bolt safety; manual bolt hold-open. Introduced 1988; no longer in production.

Perf: $160 **Exc:** $140 **VGood:** $100

MARLIN MODEL 70P PAPOOSE

Same specs as Model 70HC except takedown model with easily removable barrel; 16-1/4-inch Micro-Groove barrel; walnut-finished hardwood stock; 35-1/4-inch overall length; weighs 3-1/4 lbs. Comes with zippered case. Made in U.S. by Marlin. Introduced 1986; discontinued 1995.

Perf: $180 **Exc:** $150 **VGood:** $120

MARLIN MODEL 70PSS

Same specs as Model 70P except stainless-steel barrel, other parts finished to match, fiberglass-filled synthetic stock; take-down model. Introduced 1986; still in production.

Perf: $210 **Exc:** $170 **VGood:** $140

MARLIN MODEL 75C

Semi-automatic; 22 LR; 13-shot tubular magazine; 18-inch barrel; 36-1/2-inch overall length; weighs 5 lbs.; ramp front, adjustable open rear sight; receiver grooved for scope mounts; walnut-finished Monte Carlo hardwood stock; cross-bolt safety; auto last-shot bolt hold-open. Introduced 1982; no longer in production.

Perf: $150 **Exc:** $125 **VGood:** $100

Marlin Model 50

Marlin Model 60

Marlin Model 60SN

Marlin Model 60S-CF

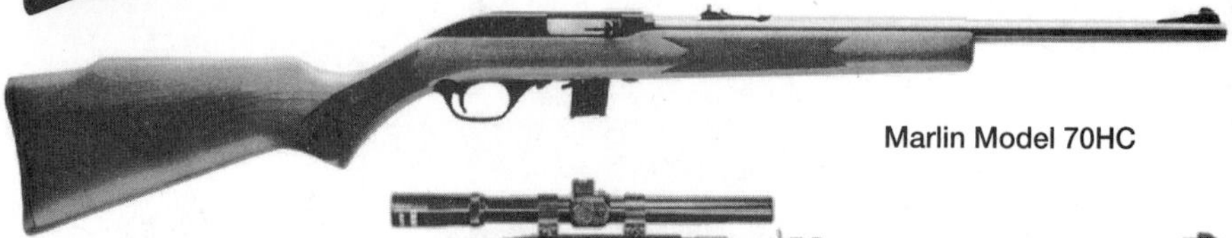

Marlin Model 70HC

Marlin Model 70P Papoose

Marlin Model 70PSS

Marlin Model 75C

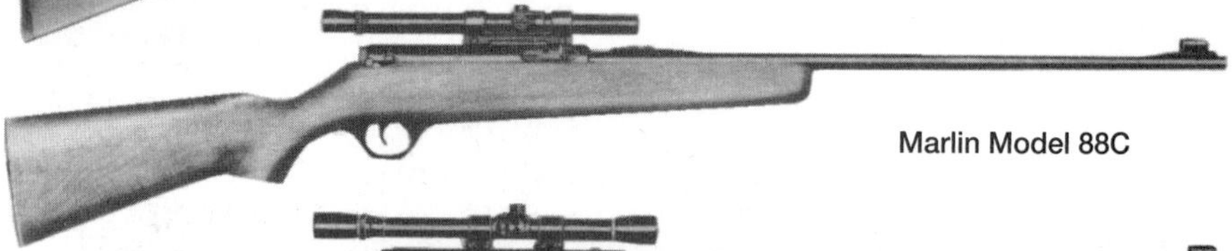

Marlin Model 88C

Marlin Model 98

MARLIN MODEL 88C

Semi-automatic; 22 LR; 15-shot; 24-inch barrel; 45-inch overall length; weighs 6-3/4 lbs.; tube magazine in buttstock; open rear, hooded front sight; chrome-plated cocking handle; safety button; positive sear lock safety; black walnut uncheckered pistol-grip stock. Introduced 1948; discontinued 1956.

Exc: $150 **VGood:** $125 **Good:** $100

MARLIN MODEL 88DL

Same specs as Model 88C except hand-checkered stock; sling swivels; receiver peep sight in rear. Introduced 1953; discontinued 1956.

Exc: $150 **VGood:** $125 **Good:** $100

MARLIN MODEL 89C

Semi-automatic; 22 LR; 5-shot clip magazine (early model), 12-shot (late model); 24-inch barrel; 45-inch overall length; weighs 6-1/2 lbs.; hooded front, open rear sight; uncheckered pistol-grip stock. Introduced 1948; discontinued 1961.

Exc: $150 **VGood:** $125 **Good:** $100

MARLIN MODEL 89DL

Same specs as Model 89C except sling swivels; receiver peep sight.

Exc: $150 **VGood:** $125 **Good:** $100

MARLIN MODEL 98

Semi-automatic; 22 LR; 15-shot buttstock tube magazine; 22-inch barrel; 42-inch overall length; weighs 6-1/2 lbs.; fully-adjustable peep rear, hooded ramp front sight; solid frame; Bishop-

Marlin Model 99M1 Carbine

Marlin Model 922 Magnum

Marlin Model 989M2 Carbine

Marlin Model 990L

Marlin Model 995

Marlin Model 995SS

Marlin Model 795

style uncheckered Monte Carlo walnut stock, cheekpiece. Introduced 1957; discontinued 1959.

Exc: $150 **VGood:** $125 **Good:** $100

MARLIN MODEL 99

Semi-automatic; 22 LR; 18-shot tube magazine; 22-inch barrel; 42-inch overall length; weighs 5-1/2 lbs.; open rear, hooded ramp front sight; uncheckered walnut pistol-grip stock. Introduced 1959; discontinued 1961.

Exc: $150 **VGood:** $125 **Good:** $100

MARLIN MODEL 99C

Same specs as Model 99 except uncheckered walnut pistol-grip stock with fluted comb; grooved receiver for tip-off scope mounts; gold-plated trigger. Later production features checkering on pistol grip, forearm. Introduced 1962; discontinued 1978.

Exc: $150 **VGood:** $125 **Good:** $100

MARLIN MODEL 99DL

Same specs as Model 99 except for uncheckered black walnut Monte Carlo stock; jeweled bolt; gold-plated trigger; sling, sling swivels. Introduced 1960; discontinued 1965.

Exc: $150 **VGood:** $125 **Good:** $100

MARLIN MODEL 99G

Same specs as Model 99C except plainer stock; bead front sight. Introduced 1960; discontinued 1965.

Exc: $150 **VGood:** $125 **Good:** $100

MARLIN MODEL 99M1 CARBINE

Same specs as Model 99C except designed after U.S. 30M1 carbine; 18-inch barrel; 37-inch overall length; weighs 4-3/4 lbs.; 10-shot tube magazine; uncheckered pistol grip carbine stock; hand guard with barrel band; open rear, military-type ramp front sight; drilled, tapped for receiver sights; grooved for tip-off mount; gold-plated trigger; sling swivels. Introduced 1964; discontinued 1978.

Exc: $225 **VGood:** $200 **Good:** $150

MARLIN MODEL 922 MAGNUM

Semi-automatic; 22 WMR; 7-shot magazine; 20-1/2-inch barrel; 39-3/4-inch overall length; weighs 6-1/2 lbs.; ramp front sight with bead and removable Wide-Scan hood, adjustable folding semi-buckhorn rear; action based on the centerfire Model 9 Carbine; receiver drilled and tapped for scope mounting; checkered American black walnut stock with Monte Carlo comb; swivel studs; rubber buttpad; automatic last-shot bolt hold-open; magazine safety. Made in U.S. by Marlin Firearms Co. Introduced 1993; no longer in production.

Perf: $400 **Exc:** $355 **VGood:** $295

MARLIN MODEL 989M2 CARBINE

Semi-automatic; 22 LR; 7-shot detachable clip magazine; 18-inch barrel; 37-inch overall length; weighs 4-3/4 lbs.; open rear sight, military-type ramp front; uncheckered pistol-grip carbine walnut stock and handguard; barrel band; sling swivels; gold-plated trigger. Introduced 1965; discontinued 1978.

Exc: $250 **VGood:** $225 **Good:** $195

MARLIN MODEL 990

Semi-automatic; 22 LR; 18-shot tubular magazine; 22-inch barrel; 40-3/4-inch overall length; weighs 5-1/2 lbs.; ramp bead hooded front, adjustable folding semi-buckhorn rear sight; American walnut Monte Carlo stock; checkered fluted comb; full pistol grip; cross-bolt safety; receiver grooved for tip-off mount. Introduced 1979; discontinued 1988.

Exc: $135 **VGood:** $115 **Good:** $100

MARLIN MODEL 990L

Same specs as Model 990 except 14-shot magazine; 40-1/2-inch overall length; weighs about 5-3/4 lbs.; laminated hardwood stock with black rubber rifle buttpad and swivel studs; gold-plated trigger; manual bolt hold-open; automatic last-shot bolt hold-open. Made in U.S. by Marlin Firearms Co. Introduced 1992; dropped 1994.

Exc: $110 **VGood:** $100 **Good:** $90

MARLIN MODEL 995

Semi-automatic; 22 LR; 7-shot clip magazine; 18-inch Micro-Groove barrel; 36-3/4-inch overall length; weighs 5 lbs.; ramp bead front sight with Wide-Scan hood, adjustable folding semi-buckhorn rear; receiver grooved for scope mount; American black walnut stock with Monte Carlo; full pistol grip; checkered grip and forend; white buttplate spacer; Mar-Shield finish; bolt hold-open device; cross-bolt safety. Introduced 1979; dropped 1994.

Exc: $125 **VGood:** $110 **Good:** $90

MARLIN MODEL 995SS

Same specs as Model 995 except stainless steel 18-inch barrel; ramp front sight with orange post and cut-away Wide-Scan hood, screw-adjustable open rear; black fiberglass-filled synthetic stock with nickel-plated swivel studs, moulded-in checkering; stainless steel breechbolt. Introduced 1979; no longer produced.

Perf: $160 **Exc:** $140 **VGood:** $110

MARLIN MODEL 7000 AUTO RIFLE

Semi-automatic; 22 LR, 10-shot box magazine; 18-inch heavy target barrel with 16-groove Micro-Groove rifling, recessed muzzle; weighs 5-1/2 lbs.; 37-inch overall length; Black fiberglass-filled synthetic stock with Monte Carlo comb, swivel studs, moulded-in checkering; comes with ring mounts. Automatic last-shot bolt hold-open, manual bolt hold-open; cross-bolt safety; steel charging handle; blue finish, nickel-plated magazine. Introduced 1997, still offered. Made in U.S.A. by Marlin Firearms Co.

Perf: $200 **Exc:** $150 **VGood:** $125

MARLIN MODEL 795 AUTO RIFLE

Similar to Model 7000 except standard-weight 18-inch barrel with 16-groove Micro-Groove rifling. Ramp front sight with brass bead, screw adjustable open rear. Receiver grooved for scope mount. Introduced 1997, still offered. Made in U.S.A. by Marlin Firearms Co.

Perf: $175 **Exc:** $125 **VGood:** $90

MARLIN MODEL 795SS AUTO RIFLE

Similar to Model 795 except stainless steel barrel. Most other parts nickel- plated. Adjustable folding semi-buckhorn rear sights, ramp front high-visibility post and removable cutaway wide scan hood. Still available.

Perf: $200 **Exc:** $175 **VGood:** $140

Marlin Model A-1

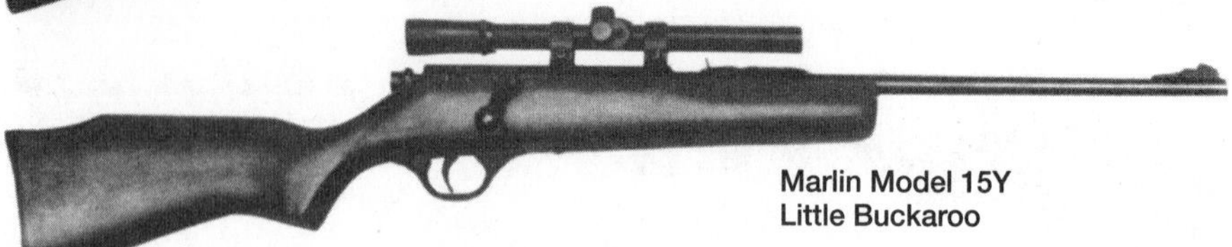

Marlin Model 15Y Little Buckaroo

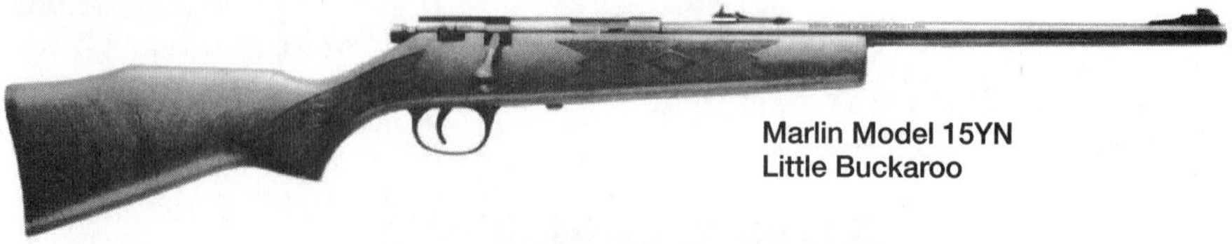

Marlin Model 15YN Little Buckaroo

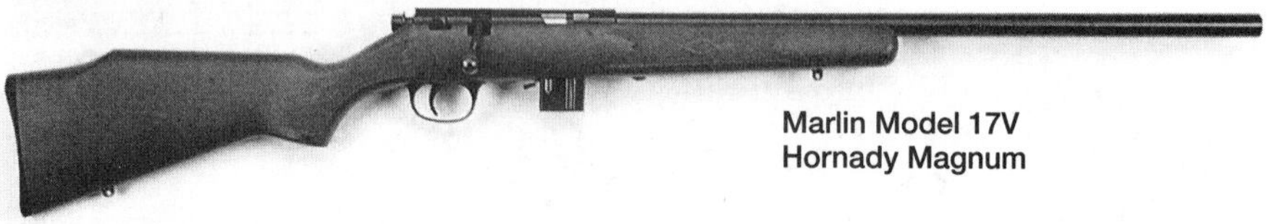

Marlin Model 17V Hornady Magnum

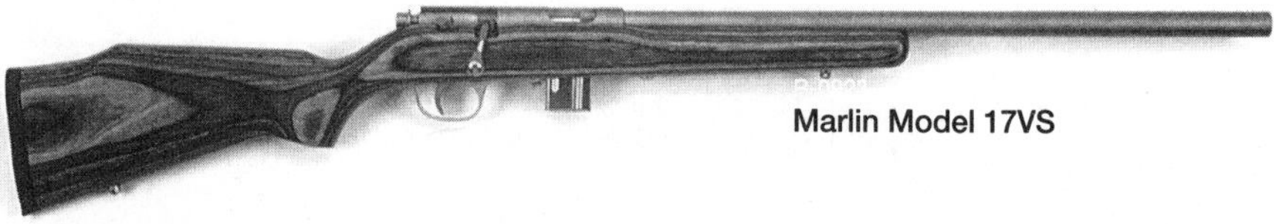

Marlin Model 17VS

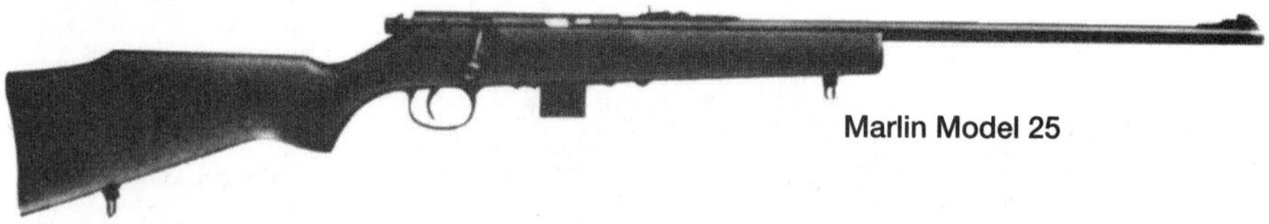

Marlin Model 25

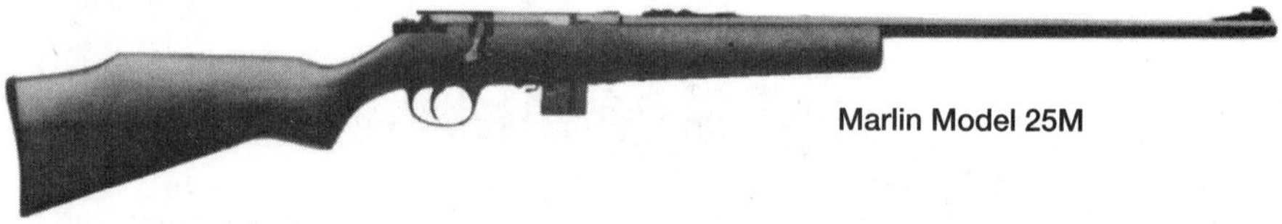

Marlin Model 25M

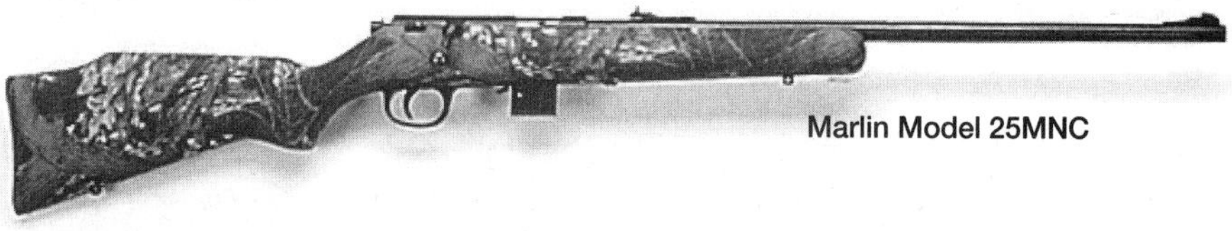

Marlin Model 25MNC

Marlin Model 25NC

MARLIN MODEL A-1

Semi-automatic; 22 LR; 6-shot detachable box magazine; 24-inch barrel; open rear sight, bead front; uncheckered walnut pistol-grip stock. Introduced 1935; discontinued 1946.

Exc: $200 **VGood:** $150 **Good:** $125

MARLIN MODEL A-1C

Same specs as Model A-1 except off/on safety; military-style one-piece buttstock with fluted comb and semi-beavertail forearm. Introduced 1940; discontinued 1946.

Exc: $200 **VGood:** $170 **Good:** $140

MARLIN MODEL A-1DL

Same specs as Model A-1C except sling swivels; hooded front sight, peep rear.

Exc: $195 **VGood:** $150 **Good:** $125

MARLIN MODEL A-1E

Same specs as Model A-1 except hooded front sight, peep rear.

Exc: $195 **VGood:** $150 **Good:** $125

MARLIN MODEL 15

Bolt Action; 22 Short, 22 Long, 22 LR; 22-inch barrel; 41-inch overall length; weighs 5-1/2 lbs.; ramp front sight, adjustable open rear; walnut finished hardwood Monte Carlo stock with full pistol grip; receiver grooved for tip-off scope mount; thumb safety; cocking indicator.

Exc: $100 **VGood:** $80 **Good:** $65

MARLIN MODEL 15Y LITTLE BUCKAROO

Bolt action; single shot; 22 Short, 22 Long, 22 LR; 16-1/4-inch barrel; 33-1/4-inch overall length; weighs 4-1/4 lbs.; adjustable open rear sight, ramp front; marketed with 4x15 scope, mount; walnut-finished hardwood stock. Introduced 1984; discontinued 1986.

Perf: $120 **Exc:** $100 **VGood:** $80

MARLIN MODEL 15YN LITTLE BUCKAROO

Same specs as Model 15Y except without scope. Reintroduced 1989; still produced as Model 915Y.

Perf: $165 **Exc:** $125 **VGood:** $75

MARLIN MODEL 15YS

Stainless steel with fire sights.

Perf: $175 **Exc:** $135 **VGood:** $85

MARLIN MODEL 17V HORNADY MAGNUM

Bolt action; 17 HMR; 7-shot. 22-inch barrel; weighs 6 lbs., stainless; 41-inch overall length; Checkered walnut Monte Carlo stock, laminated black/grey. No sights but receiver grooved. Swivel studs, positive thumb safety, red cocking indicator, 1-inch scope rings, safety lock. Still offered as Model 917V.

Perf: $240 **Exc:** $200 **VGood:** $180

MARLIN MODEL 17VS

Same as Model 17V, but with stainless-steel barrel and action, laminated stock.

Perf: $375 **Exc:** $320 **VGood:** $ 290

MARLIN MODEL 25

Bolt action; 22 Short, 22 Long, 22 LR; 7-shot box magazine; 22-inch barrel; 41-inch overall length; weighs 5 lbs.; ramp front, open rear sight; walnut-finished hardwood pistol-grip stock. Introduced 1982; still produced as Model 925.

Perf: $150 **Exc:** $125 **VGood:** $90

MARLIN MODEL 25M

Same specs as Model 25 except 22 WMR.

Perf: $165 **Exc:** $140 **VGood:** $110

MARLIN MODEL 25MB MIDGET MAGNUM

Same specs as Model 25 except 22 WMR; 16-1/4-inch barrel; 35-1/4-inch overall length; weighs

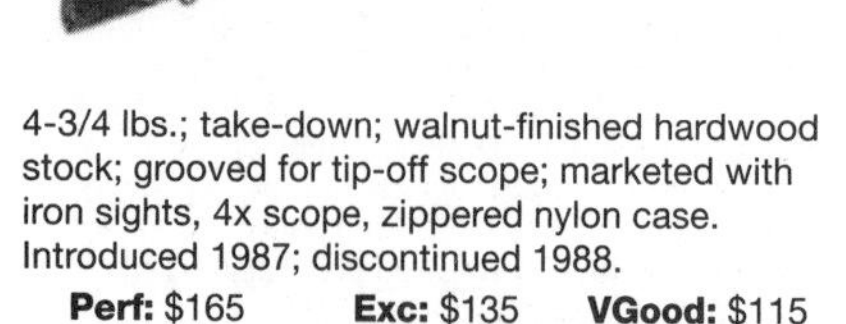

4-3/4 lbs.; take-down; walnut-finished hardwood stock; grooved for tip-off scope; marketed with iron sights, 4x scope, zippered nylon case. Introduced 1987; discontinued 1988.

Perf: $165 **Exc:** $135 **VGood:** $115

MARLIN MODEL 25MN

Same specs as Model 25 except 22 WMR; weighs 6 lbs.; walnut-finished Maine birch pistol-grip Monte Carlo stock; ramp front sight, adjustable open rear. Introduced 1989; still in production as Model 915M.

Perf: $150 **Exc:** $125 **VGood:** $90

MARLIN MODEL 25MNC

Same specs as Model 25MN but with camo stock.

Perf: $170 **Exc:** $140 **VGood:** $120

MARLIN MODEL 25N

Same specs as Model 25 except 22 LR; adjustable open rear sight; receiver grooved for scope mounting. Introduced 1989; still in production as Model 925.

Perf: $150 **Exc:** $125 **VGood:** $95

MARLIN MODEL 25NC

Same specs as Model 25N but with camo stock.

Perf: $155 **Exc:** $130 **VGood:** $100

Marlin Model 80C

Marlin Model 83TS

Marlin Model 100

Marlin Model 101

Marlin Model 122

Marlin Model 322

Marlin Model 455

MARLIN MODEL 65

Bolt action; single shot; 22 Short, 22 Long, 22 LR; 24-inch barrel; open rear, bead front sight; uncheckered walnut pistol-grip stock, grooved forearm. Introduced 1935; discontinued 1937.

Exc: $100 **VGood:** $90 **Good:** $70

MARLIN MODEL 65E

Same specs as Model 65 except equipped with hooded front sight, peep rear.

Exc: $125 **VGood:** $115 **Good:** $85

MARLIN MODEL 80

Bolt action; 22 Short, 22 Long, 22 LR; 8-shot detachable box magazine; 24-inch barrel; open rear, bead front sight; uncheckered walnut pistol-grip stock; black buttplate. Introduced 1934; discontinued 1939.

Exc: $125 **VGood:** $115 **Good:** $85

MARLIN MODEL 80C

Same specs as Model 80 except one-piece military-style buttstock with fluted comb and semi-beavertail forearm; off/on safety. Model 80-C replaced standard Model 80 in 1940; discontinued 1970.

Exc: $135 **VGood:** $125 **Good:** $95

MARLIN MODEL 80DL

Same specs as Model 80C except peep rear, hooded front sight; sling swivels. Introduced 1940; discontinued 1965.

Exc: $145 **VGood:** $135 **Good:** $105

MARLIN MODEL 80E

Same specs as Model 80 except peep rear sight, hooded front.

Exc: $155 **VGood:** $145 **Good:** $115

MARLIN MODEL 81

Bolt action; 22 Short, 22 Long, 22 LR; 18-shot tubular magazine (22 LR), 20-shot (22 Long), 25-shot (22 Short); 24-inch round tapered barrel; 42-1/2-inch overall length; weighs 6-1/2 lbs.; open rear, silver bead front sight; uncheckered pistol-grip stock. Introduced 1937; discontinued 1965.

Exc: $150 **VGood:** $125 **Good:** $100

MARLIN MODEL 81C

Same specs as Model 81 except improved military-type one-piece buttstock with fluted comb and semi-beavertail forearm. Introduced 1940; discontinued 1971.

Exc: $150 **VGood:** $125 **Good:** $100

MARLIN MODEL 81DL

Same specs as Model 81C except hooded front, peep rear sight; sling swivels. Introduced 1940; discontinued 1965.

Exc: $155 **VGood:** $145 **Good:** $115

MARLIN MODEL 81E

Same specs as Model 81 except hooded front, peep rear sight.

Exc: $155 **VGood:** $145 **Good:** $115

MARLIN MODEL 83TS BOLT-ACTION RIFLE

Bolt action; 22 LR, 12-shot tubular magazine, black Monte Carlo fiberglass-filled synthetic stock with sling swivel studs. Weighs 6 lbs., length 41-inch overall. Introduced 2001, still offered. Made in U.S.A. by Marlin Firearms Co.

Perf: $200 **Exc:** $175 **VGood:** $100

MARLIN MODEL 100

Bolt action; take-down single shot; 22 Short, 22 Long, 22 LR; 24-inch barrel; weighs 4-1/2 lbs.; open adjustable rear sight, bead front; uncheckered walnut pistol-grip stock. Introduced 1936; discontinued 1941.

Exc: $70 **VGood:** $60 **Good:** $50

MARLIN MODEL 100S

Same specs as Model 100 except sling; peep rear, hooded front sight. It is known as the Tom Mix Special, allegedly because Tom Mix used such a rifle in his vaudeville act in the '30s. Manufactured 1937 only. Value is based largely upon rarity.

Exc: $300 **VGood:** $270 **Good:** $220

MARLIN MODEL 100SB

Same specs as Model 100 except smoothbore for use with 22 shot cartridge; shotgun sight. Actually, this may well have been the version used by Tom Mix in his act, as he used shot cartridges for breaking glass balls and other on-stage targets. Introduced 1936; discontinued 1941.

Exc: $150 **VGood:** $110 **Good:** $80

MARLIN MODEL 101

Bolt action; single shot; 22 Short, 22 Long, 22 LR; 22-inch barrel; 40-inch overall length; weighs 4-1/2 lbs.; fully-adjustable semi-buckhorn rear sight, hooded Wide-Scan front; black plastic trigger guard; ring or T-shaped cocking piece; uncheckered walnut stock with beavertail forearm; receiver grooved for tip-off scope mount. Improved version of Model 100 with improved bolt, redesigned stock. Introduced 1941; discontinued 1976.

Exc: $80 **VGood:** $60 **Good:** $50

MARLIN MODEL 101DL

Same specs as Model 101 except 24-inch barrel; 42-1/2-inch overall length; weighs 5 lbs.; peep rear, hooded front sight; sling swivels. Introduced 1941; discontinued 1945.

Exc: $90 **VGood:** $75 **Good:** $55

MARLIN MODEL 122

Bolt action; single shot; 22 Short, 22 Long, 22 LR; 22-inch barrel; 40-inch overall length; weighs 5 lbs.; open rear, hooded ramp front sight; drilled, tapped for receiver sights, tip-off scope mount; junior target model with shortened uncheckered stock; walnut Monte Carlo pistol-grip stock. Introduced 1962; discontinued 1965.

Exc: $80 **VGood:** $70 **Good:** $50

MARLIN MODEL 322

Bolt action; 222 Rem.; 3-shot clip-type magazine; 24-inch medium weight barrel; 42-inch overall length; weighs 7-1/2 lbs.; short Sako Mauser-type action; two-position peep sight rear, hooded ramp front with hunting bead; checkered walnut stock, forearm; sling swivels. Introduced 1954; discontinued 1958.

Exc: $525 **VGood:** $485 **Good:** $350

MARLIN MODEL 455

Bolt action; 270, 308, 30-06; 5-shot box magazine; 24-inch medium-weight stainless steel barrel; 42-1/2-inch overall length; weighs 7-3/4 lbs.; Lyman No. 48 receiver sight, hooded ramp front; FN Mauser action; Sako trigger; checkered walnut Monte Carlo stock with cheekpiece; checkered forearm; receiver drilled, tapped for scope mounts. Introduced 1956; discontinued 1959.

Exc: $525 **VGood:** $485 **Good:** $350

MARLIN MODEL XL7

Introduced in 2008, this is a centerfire bolt-action rifle with adjustable Pro-Fire trigger system. 4+1 capacity. Chambered in .25-06, .270 and .30-06 with a crowned, precision-rifled 22-inch barrel that is joined to the receiver with a pressure nut. Black synthetic stock and Soft-Tech recoil pad. No sights; drilled and tapped for mounts.

NIB: $300 **Exc:** $275 **VGood:** $225

MODEL XL7C

Similar to above but with RealTree APG HD camo finish.

NIB: $345 **Exc:** $300 **VGood:** $350

MARLIN MODEL 780

Bolt action; 22 Short, 22 Long, 22 LR; 7-shot clip magazine; 22-inch barrel; 40-1/2-inch overall length; weighs 5-1/2 lbs.; open rear, ramp front sight; receiver grooved for scope mounts; Monte Carlo American walnut stock; checkered pistol grip, forearm; gold-plated trigger. Introduced 1971; discontinued 1988.

Exc: $100 **VGood:** $80 **Good:** $65

MARLIN MODEL 781

Bolt action; 22 Short, 22 Long, 22 LR; 17-shot tubular magazine; 22-inch barrel; weighs 6 lbs.; open rear, ramp front sight; receiver grooved for scope mounts; American walnut Monte Carlo stock; checkered pistol-grip, forearm. Introduced 1971; discontinued 1988.

Exc: $150 **VGood:** $130 **Good:** $100

MARLIN MODEL 782

Bolt action; 22 WMR; 7-shot clip magazine; 22-inch barrel; 41-inch overall length; weighs 6 lbs.; open rear, ramp front sight; receiver grooved for scope mounts; American walnut Monte Carlo stock; checkered pistol grip, forearm; sling swivels; leather sling. Introduced 1971; discontinued 1988.

Exc: $175 **VGood:** $150 **Good:** $110

MARLIN MODEL 783

Bolt action; 22 WMR; 13-shot tubular magazine; 22-inch barrel; 41-inch overall length; weighs 6 lbs.; open rear, ramp front sight; receiver grooved for scope mounts; select American walnut Monte Carlo stock; checkered pistol grip, forearm; white line spacer; gold-plated trigger; sling swivels; leather sling. Introduced 1971; discontinued 1988.

Exc: $175 **VGood:** $150 **Good:** $110

MARLIN MODEL 880

Bolt action; 22 LR; 7-shot clip magazine; 22-inch Micro Groove barrel; 41-inch overall length; weighs 5-1/2 lbs.; ramp front, adjustable semi-buckhorn rear sight; receiver grooved for tip-off scope mount; black walnut Monte Carlo stock; checkered pistol grip, forend; swivel studs; rubber buttpad. Mar-Shield finish. Replaces Model 780. Introduced 1989; no longer in production; replaced by Model 980.

Perf: $170 **Exc:** $140 **VGood:** $120

MARLIN MODEL 880SS

Same specs as Model 880 except barrel, receiver, front breech bolt, striker knob, trigger stud, cartridge lifter stud and outer magazine tube made of stainless steel; most other parts nickel-plated to match stainless finish; black fiberglass-filled AKZO synthetic stock with moulded-in checkering; stainless steel swivel studs. Made in U.S. by Marlin Firearms Co. Introduced 1994; no longer in production.

Perf: $220 **Exc:** $170 **VGood:** $120

MARLIN MODEL 880SQ SQUIRREL RIFLE

Similar to Model 880SS except uses heavy target barrel of Marlin's Model 2000L target rifle. Black synthetic stock with moulded-in checkering, double bedding screws, matte blue finish. Without sights, no dovetail or filler screws; receiver grooved for scope mount. Weighs 7 lbs. Introduced 1996, no longer offered. Made in U.S.A. by Marlin.

Perf: $285 **Exc:** $225 **VGood:** $210

Marlin Model XL7

Marlin Model XL7C

Marlin Model XL7C with Scope

Marlin Model 780

Marlin Model 781

Marlin Model 783

Marlin Model 880

Marlin Model 880SQ Squirrel Rifle

Marlin Model 882

Marlin Model 882SS

MARLIN MODEL 881

Bolt action; 22 LR, 22 Short, 22 Long; 17-shot (22 LR), 19-shot (22 Long), 25-shot (22 Short) tubular magazine; 22-inch Micro Groove barrel; 41-inch overall length; weighs 6 lbs.; ramp front, adjustable semi-buckhorn rear sight; receiver grooved for tip-off scope mount; black walnut Monte Carlo stock; checkered pistol grip, forend; swivel studs; rubber buttpad. Mar-Shield finish. Replaced Model 781. Introduced 1989; no longer in production; replaced by Model 981.

Perf: $180 **Exc:** $150 **VGood:** $125

MARLIN MODEL 882

Bolt action; 22 WMR; 7-shot clip magazine; 22-inch Micro Groove barrel; 41-inch overall length; weighs 5-1/2 lbs.; ramp front, adjustable semi-buckhorn rear sight; receiver grooved for tip-off scope mount; black walnut Monte Carlo stock; checkered pistol grip, forend; swivel studs; rubber buttpad. Mar-Shield finish. Replaces Model 782. Introduced 1989; no longer in production; replaced by Model 982.

Perf: $150 **Exc:** $120 **VGood:** $100

MARLIN MODEL 882L

Same specs as Model 882 except laminated hardwood stock. No longer in production.

Perf: $180 **Exc:** $160 **VGood:** $120

MARLIN MODEL 882SS

Same specs as Model 882 except stainless steel front breech bolt, barrel, receiver and bolt knob; other parts either stainless steel or nickel-plated; black Monte Carlo stock of fiberglass-filled polycarbonate with moulded-in checkering; nickel-plated swivel studs. Made in U.S. by Marlin Firearms Co. Introduced 1995; no longer produced.

Perf: $180 **Exc:** $160 **VGood:** $130

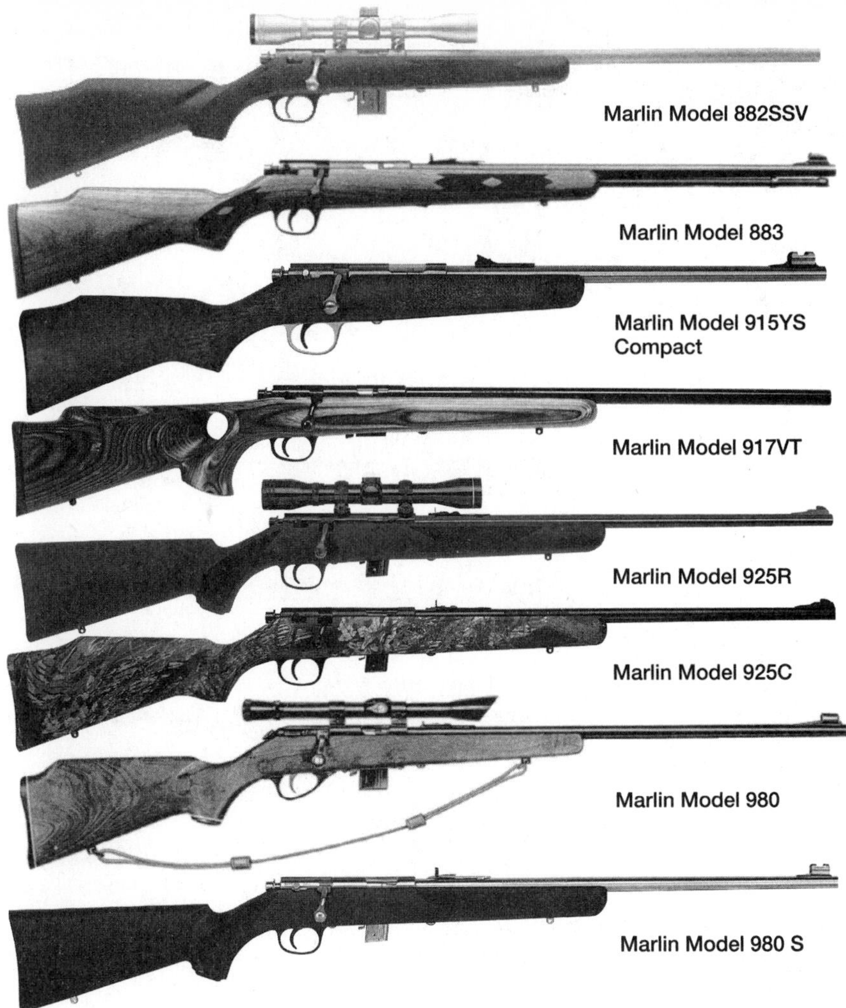

MARLIN MODEL 882SSV
Similar to the Model 882SS except chambered for 22 WMR, has selected heavy 22-inch stainless steel barrel with recessed muzzle, and comes without sights; receiver is grooved for scope mount and 1-inch ring mounts are included. Weighs 7 lbs. Introduced 1997, no longer in production. Made in U.S.A. by Marlin Firearms Co.

Perf: $240 **Exc:** $180 **VGood:** $120

MARLIN MODEL 883
Bolt action; 22 WMR; 12-shot tubular magazine; 22-inch Micro Groove barrel; 41-inch overall length; weighs 5-1/2 lbs.; ramp front, adjustable semi-buckhorn rear sight; receiver grooved for tip-off scope mount; black walnut Monte Carlo stock; checkered pistol grip, forend; swivel studs; rubber buttpad. Mar-Shield finish. Replaces Model 783. Introduced 1989; no longer in production; replaced by Model 983.

Perf: $190 **Exc:** $150 **VGood:** $100

MARLIN MODEL 883SS
Same specs as Model 883 except front breech bolt, striker knob, trigger stud, cartridge lifter stud, outer magazine tube of stainless steel; other parts nickel-plated; two-tone brown laminated Monte Carlo stock with swivel studs; rubber buttpad. Made in U.S. by Marlin Firearms Co. Introduced 1993; no longer in production; replaced by Model 983S.

Perf: $200 **Exc:** $150 **VGood:** $110

MARLIN MODEL 915Y COMPACT
Single shot .22 rimfire rifle with 16-1/4-inch barrel, hardwood stock with impressed checkering and iron sights.

NIB: $225 **Exc:** $150 **VGood:** $110

MARLIN MODEL 915YS COMPACT
Similar to above but with stainless steel receiver and barrel, no checkering and fiber optic sights.

NIB: $225 **Exc:** $150 **VGood:** $110

MARLIN MODEL 917
Bolt-action rifle chambered in 17 Hornady Mag. Rimfire or .17 Mach 2; 7-shot clip magazine; fiberglass-filled synthetic stock with full pistol grip; swivel studs and molded-in checkering. Adjustable open rear sight, ramp front. 22-inch barrel. Introduced 2006.

NIB: $275 **Exc:** $235 **VGood:** $195

MARLIN MODEL 917VT
Similar to above but with laminated brown thumbhole stock. Introduced 2008.

NIB: $410 **Exc:** $350 **VGood:** $265

MARLIN MODEL 917VST
Similar to above but with laminated gray/black thumbhole stock. Introduced 2008.

NIB: $410 **Exc:** $350 **VGood:** $265

MARLIN MODEL 925
This model is chambered for the .22 LR cartridge and fitted with a 22" standard weight barrel with adjustable sights. Monte Carlo hardwood stock with full pistol grip. Seven-round magazine. Weight is about 5.5 lbs.

NIB: $275 **Exc:** $235 **VGood:** $190

MARLIN MODEL 925R
As above but with factory-mounted 3x9 scope.

NIB: $300 **Exc:** $250 **VGood:** $190

MARLIN MODEL 925C
As above but with Monte Carlo hardwood stock with Mossy Oak Break-up camo pattern. Adjustable sights.

NIB: $325 **Exc:** $275 **VGood:** $215

MARLIN MODEL 980
Bolt action; 22 WMR; 8-shot clip-type magazine; 24-inch barrel; 43-inch overall length; weighs 6 lbs.; open adjustable rear sight, hooded ramp front; uncheckered walnut Monte Carlo-style stock with white spacers at pistol grip and buttplate; sling; sling swivels. Introduced 1966; discontinued 1971.

Exc: $150 **VGood:** $130 **Good:** $100

MARLIN MODEL 980S
As above but with standard weight 22" barrel and 7-round nickel plated magazine and stainless steel barrel and receiver. Adjustable sights. Weight is about 6 lbs.

NIB: $250 **Exc:** $200 **VGood:** $165

MARLIN MODEL 980S-CF
As above but with carbon fiber stock. Introduced in 2007.

NIB: $275 **Exc:** $225 **VGood:** $195

MARLIN MODEL 981T
This model is chambered to handle interchangeably the .22 Short, Long, or LR cartridges in a tubular magazine. Black Monte Carlo fiberglass stock with full pistol grip. Adjustable sights. Fitted with a standard weight 22" barrel. Weight is about 6 lbs.

NIB: $275 **Exc:** $225 **VGood:** $195

MARLIN MODEL 982VS
As above but with black fiberglass Monte Carlo stock. Heavy 22" stainless steel barrel. Nickel plated 7-round magazine. No sights. Weight is about 7 lbs.

NIB: $345 **Exc:** $295 **VGood:** $200

MARLIN MODEL 982VS-CF
As above but with synthetic stock with dipped carbon-fiber textured finish.

NIB: $345 **Exc:** $295 **VGood:** $200

MARLIN MODEL 983
This .22 WMR model features a Monte Carlo stock of American black walnut with full pistol grip and checkering.

NIB: $345 **Exc:** $300 **VGood:** $225

MARLIN MODEL 983T
Chambered for the .22 WMR cartridge and fitted with a 22" barrel. Monte Carlo black fiberglass stock with checkering. Adjustable sights. Tubular 12-round magazine. Weight is about 6 lbs.

NIB: $275 **Exc:** $235 **VGood:** $195

MARLIN MODEL 983S
As above but with laminated two-tone stock.

NIB: $365 **Exc:** $300 **VGood:** $200

MARLIN MODEL 2000
Bolt action; single shot; 22 LR; 22-inch heavy barrel; 41-inch overall length; weighs 8 lbs.; hooded Lyman front sight, fully-adjustable Lyman target peep rear; high-comb, blue-enameled fiberglass/Kevlar stock; stippled grid forend; adjustable buttplate; aluminum forend rail; quick-detachable swivel; two-stage target trigger; red cocking indicator. Marketed with seven front sight inserts. Current models with Williams sights. Introduced 1991; no longer produced.

Perf: $395 **Exc:** $350 **VGood:** $295

MARLIN MODEL 2000A
Same specs as Model 2000 except adjustable comb; ambidextrous pistol grip; Marlin logo moulded into the blue Carbelite stock. Weighs 8-1/2 lbs. Made in U.S. by Marlin Firearms Co. Introduced 1994; discontinued 1995.

Perf: $425 **Exc:** $375 **VGood:** $310

MARLIN MODEL 2000L
Bolt action; 22 LR, single shot. 22-inch heavy barrel, Micro-Groove rifling, match chamber, recessed muzzle; weighs 8 lbs; 41-inch overall length. Laminated black/gray stock with ambidextrous pistol

grip. Hooded front sight with ten aperture inserts, fully adjustable target rear peep. Buttplate adjustable for length of pull, height and angle. Aluminum forend rail with stop and quick-detachable swivel. Two-stage target trigger; red cocking indicator. Introduced 1991, discontinued 2003.

Perf: $425 **Exc:** $375 **VGood:** $310

MARLIN MODEL 18

Slide action; 22 Short, 22 Long, 22 LR; tube magazine; 20-inch round or octagonal barrel; exposed hammer; open rear sight, bead front; solid frame; uncheckered straight stock, slide handle. Deluxe special-order models available. Introduced 1906; discontinued 1909. Some collector value.

Exc: $400 **VGood:** $320 **Good:** $200

MARLIN MODEL 20

Slide action; 22 Short, 22 Long, 22 LR; 18-shot (22 LR) full-length tubular magazine, 10-shot (22 LR) half-length magazine; 24-inch octagonal barrel; open rear sight, bead front; uncheckered straight grip stock. Later versions designated as 20S and 20A. Introduced 1907; discontinued 1922. Some collector value.

Exc: $400 **VGood:** $310 **Good:** $200

MARLIN MODEL 25

Slide action; 22 Short; 15-shot tubular magazine; 23-inch barrel; exposed hammer; open rear sight, bead front; uncheckered straight grip stock, slide handle. Introduced 1909; discontinued 1910. Some collector value.

Exc: $400 **VGood:** $300 **Good:** $200

MARLIN MODEL 27

Slide action; 25-20, 32-20; 7-shot tubular magazine; 24-inch octagonal barrel; open rear, bead front sight; uncheckered straight-grip stock; grooved slide handle. Introduced 1910; discontinued 1916. Some collector value.

Exc: $650 **VGood:** $500 **Good:** $375

MARLIN MODEL 27S

Same specs as Model 27 except available in caliber 25 Stevens RF; round barrel. Introduced 1920; discontinued 1932.

Exc: $500 **VGood:** $400 **Good:** $325

MARLIN MODEL 30AS

Lever action; 30-30; 6-shot tube magazine; 20-inch barrel; 38-1/2-inch overall length; weighs 7 lbs.; adjustable rear sight, bead front; walnut-finished Maine birch pistol grip stock; hammer-block safety. Introduced 1985; later in production as Model 336AS.

Perf: $300 **Exc:** $275 **VGood:** $250

MARLIN MODEL 32

Slide action; 22 Short, 22 Long, 22 LR; 10-shot short tubular magazine, 18-shot full-length magazine; 24-inch octagonal barrel; open rear, bead front sight; uncheckered pistol-grip stock, grooved slide handle. Marlin's first hammerless slide action rifle, some collector value. Introduced 1914; discontinued 1915.

Exc: $475 **VGood:** $420 **Good:** $300

MARLIN MODEL 36 RIFLE AND CARBINE

Lever action; 30-30, 32 Spl., 6-shot tube magazine, 20-inch (carbine), 24-inch (rifle) barrel. open rear sight, bead front; uncheckered walnut pistol grip stock, semibeavertail forearm. Introduced in 1936, designation changed to Model 36 in 1937. Discontinued 1948.

Exc: $500 **VGood:** $400 **Good:** $350

MARLIN MODEL 36-DL DELUXE RIFLE

Lever action; 32 Spl., 30-30; 6-shot tubular magazine; 24-inch barrel; 42-inch overall length; weighs 6-3/4 lbs.; "Huntsmen" hooded ramp front sight with silver bead, flat-top rear; checkered American black walnut pistol-grip stock; semi-beavertail forearm; case-hardened receiver, lever; visible hammer; drilled, tapped for tang peep sight; detachable swivels; 1-inch leather sling. Introduced 1938; discontinued 1947.

Exc: $600 **VGood:** $450 **Good:** $325

Marlin Model 2000 Target

Marlin Model 2000A

Marlin Model 2000L Target

Marlin Model 18

Marlin Model 20

Marlin Model 27

Marlin Model 39A Mountie

MARLIN MODEL 36-DL CARBINE

Same specs as Model 36A except 20-inch barrel; 38-inch overall length; no checkering, swivels, sling.

Exc: $600 **VGood:** $450 **Good:** $325

MARLIN MODEL 36RC

Same specs as Model 36 Carbine except "Huntsman" ramp front sight with silver bead and hood. Introduced 1938; discontinued 1947.

Exc: $600 **VGood:** $450 **VGood:** $325

MARLIN MODEL 38

Slide action; 22 Short, 22 Long, 22 LR; 10-shot tube magazine (22 LR), 12-shot (22 Long), 15-shot (22 Short); 24-inch octagon barrel; hammerless takedown; open rear, bead front sight; uncheckered pistol-grip walnut stock; grooved slide handle. Introduced 1920; discontinued 1930.

Exc: $490 **VGood:** $360 **Good:** $290

MARLIN MODEL 39

Lever action; 22 Short, 22 Long, 22 LR; 18-shot (22 LR), 20-shot (22 Long), 25-shot (22 Short); 24-inch octagon barrel with tube magazine; open rear, bead front sight; uncheckered pistol-grip walnut stock, forearm. Introduced 1922; discontinued 1938.

Perf: $1295 **Exc:** $995 **VGood:** $450

MARLIN MODEL 39A

Same specs as Model 39 except heavier stock; semi-beavertail forearm; semi-heavy round barrel. Introduced 1939; a version still remains in production. Early variations, better condition bring a premium.

Exc: $450 **VGood:** $375 **Good:** $300

MARLIN MODEL 39A GOLDEN

Same specs as Model 39 except gold-plated trigger, other refinements. Introduced 1960. No longer in production.

Perf: $450 **Exc:** $375 **VGood:** $300

MARLIN MODEL 39A MOUNTIE

Same specs as Model 39A except 15-shot tubular magazine (22 LR), 16-shot (22 Long), 21-shot (22 Short); American black walnut straight-grip stock; slim forearm; 20-inch barrel; 36-inch overall length; weighs 6 lbs. Designation changed in 1972 to Model 39M. Introduced 1953; discontinued 1969.

Exc: $550 **VGood:** $450 **Good:** $350

MARLIN MODEL 39A MOUNTIE CARBINE

Same specs as Model 39A Mountie except weighs 5-1/4 lbs.; shorter tube magazine; 18-shot (22 Short, 14-shot (22 Long), 12-shot (22 LR).

Exc: $550 **VGood:** $450 **Good:** $350

MARLIN MODEL 39D

Same specs as Model 39 except 20-1/2-inch barrel; 36-1/2-inch overall length; weighs 5-3/4 lbs.; 21-shot (22 Short), 16-shot (22 Long), 15-shot (22 LR); adjustable rear, target front sight; grip cap; white line spacers; offset hammer spur. Introduced 1971; discontinued 1973.

Exc: $550 **VGood:** $450 **Good:** $350

MARLIN MODEL 39M

Same specs as Model 39 except 20-inch barrel; 36-inch overall length; weighs 6 lbs.; 21-shot (22 Short), 16-shot (22 Long), 15-shot (22 LR); straight-grip stock. Introduced 1963; discontinued 1987.

Exc: $550 **VGood:** $450 **Good:** $350

Marlin Model 39AS Golden

Marlin Model 56 Levermatic

Marlin Model 57 Levermatic

Marlin Model 62 Levermatic

Marlin Model 93

Marlin Model 94

MARLIN MODEL 39M OCTAGON

Same specs as Model 39M except octagon barrel; bead front sight; hard rubber buttplate; squared lever. Introduced 1973.

Exc: $650 **VGood:** $500 **Good:** $400

MARLIN MODEL 39TDS CARBINE

Same specs as Model 39A except 16-shot magazine (22 Short), 12-shot (22 Long), 10-shot (22 LR); 16-1/2-inch Micro-Groove barrel; 32-5/8-inch overall length; weighs 5-1/4 lbs.; hooded ramp front sight, adjustable semi-buckhorn rear; straight-grip American black walnut stock; hammer-block safety; rebounding hammer; gold-plated trigger; take-down style; blued finish. Marketed with case. Introduced 1988; discontinued 1996.

Perf: $500 **Exc:** $425 **VGood:** $350

MARLIN MODEL 39AS GOLDEN

Lever action; 22 Short, 22 Long, 22 LR; 26-shot tubular magazine (22 Short), 21-shot (22 Long), 19-shot (22 LR); 24-inch Micro-Groove barrel; 40-inch overall length; weighs 6-1/2 lbs.; takedown action; bead on ramp front sight with detachable Wide-Scan hood, folding fully-adjustable semi-buckhorn rear; receiver tapped for scope mount (supplied); checkered American black walnut stock with white line spacers at pistol-grip cap and buttplate; Mar-Shield finish; swivel studs; rubber buttpad; hammer-block safety; rebounding hammer; offset hammer spur; gold-plated steel trigger. Made in U.S. by Marlin. Introduced 1988; no longer in production.

Exc: $450 **VGood:** $375 **Good:** $300

MARLIN MODEL 56 LEVERMATIC

Lever action, short-throw lever; 22 Short, 22 Long, 22 LR; 7-shot clip magazine; 24-inch (early), 22-inch barrel; 41-inch overall length; weighs 6-1/4 lbs.; open rear, ramp front sight; one-piece Bishop-style uncheckered walnut Monte Carlo-type pistol-grip stock. Introduced 1955; discontinued 1964.

Exc: $275 **VGood:** $250 **Good:** $175

MARLIN MODEL 56 CLIPPER KING LEVERMATIC

Special version of the Model 56. Came with mounted 4X scope, had special package and accessories, 10-shot magazine. Made in 1959 only, 152 specimens made, some collector value.

Exc: $325 **VGood:** $290 **Good:** $250

MARLIN MODEL 57 LEVERMATIC

Lever action, short-throw lever; 22 Short, 22 Long, 22 LR; 25-shot tubular magazine (22 Short), 20-shot (22 Long), 18-shot (22 LR); 22-inch barrel; 41-inch overall length; weighs 6-1/4 lbs.; open rear sight, hooded ramp front; one-piece Bishop-style uncheckered walnut Monte Carlo-type pistol-grip stock. Introduced 1959; discontinued 1965.

Exc: $275 **VGood:** $250 **Good:** $175

MARLIN MODEL 57M LEVERMATIC

Same specs as Model 57 except 22WMR, 24-inch barrel; 43-inch overall length; weighs 6-1/2 lbs.; 15-shot magazine; 25-degree lever throw. Introduced 1959; discontinued 1969.

Exc: $295 **VGood:** $270 **Good:** $195

MARLIN MODEL 62 LEVERMATIC

Lever action, short-throw lever; 256 Mag., 22 Jet, 30 Carbine; 4-shot clip magazine; 24-inch barrel; 43-inch overall length; weighs 7 lbs.; open windage-adjustable rear sight, hooded ramp front; swivels; sling; uncheckered American black walnut Monte Carlo-type pistol-grip stock. The 256 Mag. was introduced in 1963; discontinued 1969. Premium for 22 Jet.

256 Magnum

Exc: $420 **VGood:** $365 **Good:** $325

30 Carbine

Exc: $425 **VGood:** $385 **Good:** $335

MARLIN MODEL 92

Lever action; 22 Short, 22 Long, 22 LR, 32 Short, 32 LR, 32 Centerfire (with interchangeable firing pin); 16-inch, 24-inch, 26-inch, 28-inch barrel; tubular magazine; open rear, blade front sight; uncheckered straight-grip stock, forearm. Originally marketed as Model 1892. Introduced 1892; discontinued 1915. Collector value.

22 Caliber

Exc: $1350 **VGood:** $1095 **Good:** $600

32 Caliber

Exc: $1225 **VGood:** $995 **Good:** $500

MARLIN MODEL 93

Lever action; 25-36 Marlin, 30-30, 32 Spl., 32-40, 38-55; 10-shot tubular magazine; 26-inch, 28-inch, 30-inch, 32-inch round or octagonal barrel; solid frame or take-down; open rear, bead front sight; uncheckered straight-grip stock, forearm. Originally marketed as Model 1893. Introduced 1893; discontinued 1935. Collector value.

Exc: $1500 **VGood:** $1025 **Good:** $795

MARLIN MODEL 93 CARBINE

Same specs as Model 93 except 20-inch barrel; 7-shot magazine; 30-30, 32 Spl.; carbine sights. Collector value.

Exc: $1500 **VGood:** $1025 **Good:** $795

MARLIN MODEL 93SC

Same specs as Model 93 Carbine except shorter 5-shot magazine. Designated Sports Carbine. Collector value.

Exc: $1500 **VGood:** $1025 **Good:** $795

MARLIN MODEL 94

Lever action; 25-20, 32-20, 38-40, 44-40; 10-shot magazine; 24-inch (standard), 15-inch, 20-inch, 26-inch, 28-inch, 30-inch, 32-inch round or octagonal barrel; solid frame or takedown; open rear, bead front sight; uncheckered pistol grip or straight stock, forearm. Originally marketed as Model 1894. Introduced 1894; discontinued 1933. Collector value.

Exc: $1400 **VGood:** $895 **Good:** $695

MARLIN MODEL 95

Lever action; 33 WCF, 38-56, 40-65, 40-70, 40-82, 45-70; 9-shot tubular magazine; 24-inch round or octagonal barrel, other lengths on special order; open rear, bead front sight; uncheckered straight or pistol-grip stock, forearm. Originally marketed as Model 1895. Introduced 1895; discontinued 1915. Collector value.

Exc: $2895 **VGood:** $2495 **Good:** $1700

MARLIN MODEL 97

Lever action; 22 Short, 22 Long, 22 LR; tubular magazine; 16-inch, 24-inch, 26-inch, 28-inch barrel; open rear, bead front sight; uncheckered straight or pistol grip stock, forearm. Originally marketed as Model 1897. Introduced 1897; discontinued 1916. Collector value.

Exc: $1500 **VGood:** $1025 **Good:** $795

MARLIN MODEL 336C

Lever-action; 30-30, 35 Rem., 32 Spl.; 6-shot tubular magazine; 20-inch barrel; 38-1/2-inch overall length; weighs 7 lbs.; updated version of Model 36 carbine; semi-buckhorn adjustable folding rear sight, ramp front with Wide-Scan hood; receiver tapped for scope mounts; round breech bolt; gold-plated trigger; offset hammer spur; top of receiver sandblasted to reduce glare. Introduced 1948; discontinued 1983; updated version still in production.

Exc: $395 **VGood:** $350 **Good:** $295

MARLIN MODEL 336 COWBOY

Similar to the Model 336C except chambered for 30-30 and 38-55 Win., 24-inch tapered octagon barrel with deep-cut Ballard-type rifling; straight-grip walnut stock with hard rubber buttplate; blued steel forend cap; weighs 7-1/2 lbs.; 42-1/2-inch overall. Introduced 1999, no longer in production. Made in U.S.A. by Marlin. Add $100 to all prices if marked "JM."

Perf: $650 **Exc:** $525 **VGood:** $410

MARLIN MODEL 336A

Same as the Marlin 336C except 20-inch barrel; has cut-checkered, walnut-finished hardwood pistol grip stock with swivel studs, 30-30 only, 6-shot. Hammer- block safety. Adjustable rear sight, brass bead front. Add 30 percent for 1/2 magazine tube version.

Exc: $350 **VGood:** $325 **Good:** $300

MARLIN MODEL 336A-DL

Same specs as Model 336A except sling; swivels; hand-checkered stock, forearm. Discontinued 1962.

Exc: $395 **VGood:** $350 **Good:** $295

MARLIN MODEL 336CC

Same as the Marlin 336A except has Mossy Oak Break-Up camouflage stock and forearm. 30-30 only, 6-shot; receiver tapped for scope mount or receiver sight. Introduced 2001, still in production. Made in U.S.A. by Marlin.

Perf: $465 **Exc:** $410 **VGood:** $375

MARLIN MODEL 336CS

Same specs as Model 336A except 30-30, 35 Rem.; 6-shot two-thirds tube magazine; 20-inch barrel; 38-1/2-inch overall length; weighs 7 lbs.; select black walnut stock; capped pistol grip; hammer-block safety; tapped for scope mounts; offset hammer spur. Introduced 1984; discontinued 2001.

Exc: $395 **VGood:** $350 **Good:** $295

MARLIN MODEL 336 ER (EXTRA-RANGE)

Same specs as Model 336A except 307 Win. (advertised), 356 Win.(produced); 4-shot tubular magazine; new hammer-block safety; rubber buttpad; marketed with detachable sling swivels, branded leather sling. Introduced 1983; discontinued 1986.

Exc: $850 **VGood:** $700 **Good:** $450

MARLIN MODEL 336SS

Same as the 336C except receiver, barrel and other major parts are machined from stainless steel. 30-30 only, 6-shot; receiver tapped for scope. Still offered.

Perf: $475 **Exc:** $425 **VGood:** $250

MARLIN MODEL 336W

Similar to the Model 336CS except has walnut-finished, cut-checkered Maine birch stock; blued steel barrel band has integral sling swivel; no front sight hood; comes with padded nylon sling; hard rubber butt plate. Introduced 1998, still offered. Made in U.S.A. by Marlin.

Perf: $310 **Exc:** $230 **VGood:** $170

MARLIN MODEL 336 MARAUDER

Same specs as Model 336A except 30-30, 35 Rem.; 16-1/4-inch barrel. Introduced 1963; discontinued 1964.

Exc: $410 **VGood:** $330 **Good:** $230

Marlin Model 336C

Marlin Model 336 Cowboy

Marlin Model 336A

Marlin Model 336CC

Marlin Model 336T Texan

Marlin Model 336XLR

MARLIN MODEL 336 OCTAGON

Same specs as Model 336A except octagon barrel. Introduced 1973.

Exc: $430 **VGood:** $390 **Good:** $310

MARLIN MODEL 336 SPORT CARBINE

Same specs as Model 336A rifle except 20-inch barrel; weighs 7 lbs.; two-thirds 6-shot magazine. Introduced 1948; discontinued 1963.

Exc: $350 **VGood:** $300 **Good:** $250

MARLIN MODEL 336SC ZIPPER

Same specs as Model 336 Sport Carbine except chambered only for 219 Zipper; 20-inch heavy barrel; weighs 7-3/4 lbs. Introduced 1955; discontinued 1960.

Exc: $800 **VGood:** $675 **Good:** $425

MARLIN MODEL 336SD

Same specs as Model 336A except 20-inch barrel; checkered pistol grip, forend; 38-1/2-inch overall length; weighs 7-1/2 lbs.; leather sling; deluxe sports carbine. Introduced 1954; discontinued 1962.

Exc: $550 **VGood:** $325 **Good:** $220

MARLIN MODEL 336T TEXAN

Same specs as Model 336A except 18-1/2-inch (1953), 20-inch barrel; straight-grip uncheckered walnut stock; squared lever. Called the Texan Model. Introduced in 1953; discontinued 1983. Originally chambered in 30-30, 35 Rem.; chambered in 44 Mag. from 1963 to 1967. Deluxe 336TDL version manufactured 1962-1963. No longer in production.

Exc: $425 **VGood:** $375 **Good:** $325

Deluxe 336TDL

Exc: $425 **VGood:** $325 **Good:** $300

MARLIN MODEL 336TS TEXAN

Same specs as Model 336CS except 30-30; 18-1/2-inch barrel; straight grip-stock; cross-bolt safety. Introduced 1984; discontinued 1987.

Exc: $425 **VGood:** $325 **Good:** $275

MARLIN MODEL 336Y

Similar to Model 336C, but with 16-1/2-inch barrel, short stock with 12-1/2-inch length of pull; designed for young or smaller-stature hunters; 30-30 only.

Perf: $500 **Exc:** $400 **VGood:** N/A

MARLIN MODEL 336XLR

Lever-action chambered in .30/30, with 5-shot tubular magazine, 24-inch stainless steel barrel, along with stainless steel receiver, trigger, trigger guard plate, magazine tube, loading gate, and lever. Full pistol grip, swivel studs, and Ballard-

Marlin Model 375

Marlin Model 444 Sporter

Marlin Model 444P Outfitter

Marlin Model 1894C

Marlin Model 1894CL Classic

Marlin Model 1894CS Carbine

Marlin Model 1894P/1894CP Carbine

type rifling precision fluted bolt. Features solid top receiver with side-ejection, adjustable folding semi-buckhorn rear sight, ramp front sight, tapped for scope mount. Designed for Hornady LEVERevolution cartridges.

NIB: $650 **Exc:** $595 **VGood:** $475

MARLIN MODEL 375

Lever action; 375 Win.; 5-shot tube magazine; 20-inch barrel; 38-1/2-inch overall length; weighs 6-3/4 lbs.; hooded ramp front, adjustable semi-buckhorn folding rear sight; checkered American black walnut stocks; quick-detachable swivels; leather sling. Introduced 1980; discontinued 1983.

Exc: $550 **VGood:** $475 **Good:** $350

MARLIN MODEL 444

Lever action; 444 Marlin; 5-shot tube magazine; 24-inch (early), 22-inch barrel; 42-1/2-inch overall length; weighs 7-1/2 lbs.; open elevation-adjustable rear sight, hooded ramp front; action is strengthened version of Model 336; straight-grip Monte Carlo stock of uncheckered American walnut; recoil pad; carbine forearm; barrel band; sling; sling swivels. Introduced 1965; discontinued 1972.

Exc: $425 **VGood:** $390 **Good:** $345

MARLIN MODEL 444 SPORTER

Same specs as Model 444 Rifle except 22-inch barrel, 40-1/2-inch overall length; folding rear, brass bead front sight; Model 336A-type pistol-grip stock, forearm; recoil pad; detachable swivels; sling. Introduced 1972; discontinued 1983; updated version still offered.

Exc: $445 **VGood:** $390 **Good:** $345

MARLIN MODEL 444P OUTFITTER

Similar to the 444 with 18-1/2-inch ported barrel; weighs 6-3/4 lbs.; overall length 37-inch. Available only in 444 Marlin. Introduced 1999, dropped 2003.

Perf: $475 **Exc:** $425 **VGood:** $400

MARLIN MODEL 444SS

Same specs as Model 444 Sporter except 22-inch barrel with deep-cut Ballard-type rifling; fully-adjustable folding semi-buckhorn rear sight; hammer-block safety; offset hammer spur; Mar-Shield finish. Introduced 1984; dropped 2001.

Perf: $450 **Exc:** $425 **VGood:** $395

MARLIN MODEL 1894

Lever action; 41 Mag., 44 Mag., 45 Colt; 10-shot tube magazine; 20-inch carbine barrel; 37-1/2-inch overall length; weighs 6 lbs.; hooded ramp front sight, semi-buckhorn adjustable rear; uncheckered straight grip black walnut stock, forearm; gold-plated trigger; receiver tapped for scope mount; offset hammer spur; solid top receiver sand blasted to reduce glare. 41 Mag. produced 1985-1988; 45 Colt produced 1989-1990. Introduced 1969; later production as Model 1894S. Add $400 for guns marked "New Haven, CT" and/or "JM."

Perf: $550 **Exc:** $475 **VGood:** $375

MARLIN MODEL 1894C

Same specs as Model 1894 except 357 Mag.; 9-shot tube magazine; 18-1/2-inch barrel; 35-1/2-inch overall length; weighs 6 lbs. Introduced 1979; discontinued 1985. Improved version still offered. Add $400 for guns marked "New Haven, CT" and/or "JM."

Perf: $550 **Exc:** $475 **VGood:** $400

MARLIN MODEL 1894CL CLASSIC

Same specs as 1894CL except 218 Bee, 25-20, 32-20; brass bead front sight, adjustable semi-buckhorn folding rear; hammer-block safety; rubber rifle buttpad; swivel studs. Introduced 1988; discontinued 1994. Later reintroduced in .32-20; add 15% for earlier .25-20/.218 production. Add $400 for guns marked "New Haven, CT" and/or "JM."

Perf: $600 **Exc:** $500 **VGood:** $395

MARLIN MODEL 1894CS CARBINE

Same specs Model 1894 except 38 Spl., 357 Mag.; 18-1/2-inch barrel; 9-shot magazine; brass bead front sight; hammer-block safety. Introduced 1985; dropped 2001. Add $400 for guns marked "New Haven, CT" and/or "JM."

Perf: $495 **Exc:** $395 **VGood:** $320

MARLIN MODEL 1894FG

Similar to Model 1894, but current production chambered for 41 Magnum cartridge only; 20-inch barrel. Add $400 for guns marked "New Haven, CT" and/or "JM."

Perf: $515 **Exc:** $475 **VGood:** 400

MARLIN MODEL 1894M

Same specs as Model 1894 except 22 WMR; 11-shot magazine; no gold-plated trigger; receiver tapped for scope mount or receiver sight. Introduced 1982; discontinued 1986. Add $400 for guns marked "New Haven, CT" and/or "JM."

Exc: $400 **VGood:** $365 **Good:** $290

MARLIN MODEL 1894P/1894CP CARBINE

Similar to the Model 1894 except has ported 16-1/4-inch barrel with 8-shot magazine. Overall length 33-1/4-inch, weighs 5-3/4 lbs. Discontinued 2003. Add $400 for guns marked "New Haven, CT" and/or "JM."

Model 1894P (44 Spec./44 Mag.)

Perf: $530 **Exc:** $450 **VGood:** $370

Model 1894CP (38 Spec./357 Mag.)

Perf: $530 **Exc:** $450 **VGood:** $350

MARLIN MODEL 1894 COWBOY

Lever action; 357 Mag., 44 Mag., 45 Colt, 10-shot magazine. 24-inch tapered octagon barrel, deep cut rifling; weighs 7-1/2 lbs.; 41-1/2-inch overall length; straight grip American black walnut stock, hard rubber buttplate, Marble carbine front, adjustable Marble semi- buckhorn rear sights. Squared finger lever; straight grip stock; blued steel fore-end tip. Designed for Cowboy Action shooting events. Introduced 1996. Add $400 for guns marked "New Haven, CT" and/or "JM."

Perf: $600 **Exc:** $480 **VGood:** $370

MARLIN MODEL 1894 COWBOY COMPETITION RIFLE

Similar to Model 1894 except 38 Spl. or 45 Colt only; 20-inch barrel, 37-1/2-inch long, weighs only 6 lbs., antique finish on receiver, lever and bolt. Factory-tuned for competitive cowboy action shooting. Add $400 for guns marked "New Haven, CT" and/or "JM."

Perf: $790 **Exc:** $680 **VGood:** $575

MARLIN MODEL 1894 OCTAGON

Same specs as Model 1894CS Carbine except octagon barrel; bead front sight. Introduced 1973. No longer produced. Add $400 for guns marked "New Haven, CT" and/or "JM."

Exc: $500 **VGood:** $450 **Good:** $375

MARLIN MODEL 1894 SPORTER

Same specs as Model 1894CS Carbine except 22-inch barrel, 6-shot magazine. Introduced 1973. Add $400 for guns marked "New Haven, CT" and/or "JM."

Exc: $500 **VGood:** $450 **Good:** $375

MARLIN MODEL 1894S

Same specs as Model 1894 except 41 Mag., 44 Spl., 44 Mag.; buttpad; swivel studs; hammer-block safety; offset hammer spur. Discontinued 2001, reintroduced as updated Model 1894 (without letter suffix). Add $400 for guns marked "New Haven, CT" and/or "JM."

Perf: $550 **Exc:** $475 **VGood:** $375

MARLIN MODEL 1894SS

Similar to Model 1894 except has stainless steel barrel, receiver, lever, guard plate, magazine tube and loading plate. Nickel-plated swivel studs. Add $400 for guns marked "New Haven, CT" and/or "JM."

Perf: $615 **Exc:** $580 **VGood:** $500

MARLIN MODEL 1895

Lever action; 45-70; 4-shot tube magazine; 22-inch round barrel; 40-1/2-inch overall length; weighs 7 lbs.; offset hammer spur; adjustable semi-buckhorn folding rear sight, bead front; solid receiver tapped for scope mounts, receiver sights; two-piece uncheckered straight grip American walnut stock, forearm of black walnut; rubber buttplate; blued steel forend cap. Meant to be a recreation of the original Model 1895 discontinued in 1915. Actually built on action of Marlin Model 444. Introduced 1972; discontinued 1979. Updated version still in production.

Exc: $495 **VGood:** $400 **Good:** $395

MARLIN MODEL 1895 COWBOY

Similar to Model 1895 except has 26-inch tapered octagon barrel with Ballard-type rifling, Marble carbine front sight and Marble adjustable semi-buckhorn rear sight. Receiver tapped for scope or receiver sight. Overall length is 44-1/2-inch, weighs about 8 lbs. Introduced 2001. Made in U.S.A. by Marlin.

Perf: $700 **Exc:** $650 **VGood:** $500

MARLIN MODEL 1895G GUIDE GUN

Similar to Model 1895 with deep-cut Ballard-type rifling; 18-1/2-inch ported barrel; straight-grip walnut stock. Overall length is 37 inches, weight 7 lbs. Introduced 1998. Discontinued.

Perf: $450 **Exc:** $350 **VGood:** $275

MARLIN MODEL 1895GS GUIDE GUN

Similar to Model 1895G except receiver, barrel and most metal parts are machined from stainless steel. Chambered for 45-70, 4-shot, 18-1/2-inch barrel.

Marlin Model 1894 Cowboy

Marlin Model 1894 Cowboy Competition Rifle

Marlin Model 1894SS

Marlin Model 1895

Marlin Model 1895 Cowboy

Marlin Model 1895G Guide Gun

Marlin Model 1895GS Guide Gun

Marlin Model 1895XLR

Overall length is 37 inches, weight 7 lbs. Introduced 2001. Current production features non-ported barrel.

Perf: $700 **Exc:** $575 **VGood:** $500

MARLIN MODEL 1895M

Similar to Model 1895 except has an 18-1/2-inch ported barrel with Ballard-type cut rifling. Chambered for 450 Marlin. Introduced 2000, still offered without ported barrel.

Perf: $550 **Exc:** $500 **VGood:** $425

MARLIN MODEL 1895S

Same specs as Model 1895 except full pistol-grip stock; straight buttpad. Introduced 1980; discontinued 1983.

Exc: $425 **VGood:** $365 **Good:** $315

MARLIN MODEL 1895SS

Same specs as Model 1895 except full pistol-grip stock; hammer-block safety. Introduced 1984; discontinued 2001.

Exc: $450 **VGood:** $365 **Good:** $315

MARLIN MODEL 1895XLR

Lever-action chambered in .45-70 Government or .450 Marlin with a 4-shot tubular magazine, 24-inch stainless steel barrel, along with stainless steel receiver, trigger, trigger guard plate, magazine tube, loading gate, and lever. Full pistol grip, swivel studs, and Ballard-type rifling precision fluted bolt. Features solid top receiver with side-ejection, adjustable folding semi-buckhorn rear sight, ramp front sight, tapped for scope mount. Designed for Hornady LEVERevolution cartridges.

NIB: $650 **Exc:** $595 **VGood:** $475

MARLIN MODEL 444XLR

Similar to Model 1895XLR but chambered in .444 Marlin.

NIB: $650 **Exc:** $595 **VGood:** $475

MARLIN MODEL 1897 COWBOY

Lever Action; 22 S,L,LR; 24-inch octagon barrel; 40-inch OAL; American walnut stock and forearm with cut checkering; Marble semibuckhorn rear, gold bead front sights; introduced 1999, discontinued 2002.

Perf: $575 **Exc:** $500 **VGood:** 425

MARLIN MODEL 1897T

Lever action 22, S (21), L (16), LR (14), tubular mag. 20-inch tapered octagon barrel. Marble semi-buckhorn rear, Marble front brass bead sights.

Marlin Model 1897 Cowboy

Marlin Model 1897T

Mauser Model 10 Varminter

Mauser Model 66 Magnum

Mauser Model 66SP Match

Hammer block safety, solid top receiver tapped, base for scope rings. Introduced 2002, no longer offered.

Perf: $525 **Exc:** $450 **VGood:** $375

MARLIN-GLENFIELD MODEL 15

Bolt action; single shot; 22 Short, 22 Long, 22 LR; 22-inch barrel; 41-inch overall length; weighs 5-1/2 lbs.; ramp front, adjustable open rear sight; receiver grooved for tip-off scope mount; Monte Carlo walnut-finished hardwood stock; checkered full pistol grip; red cocking indicator; thumb safety. Introduced 1979; discontinued 1983.

Exc: $75 **VGood:** $60 **Good:** $50

MARLIN-GLENFIELD MODEL 20

Bolt action; 22 Short, 22 Long, 22 LR; 8-shot clip magazine; 22-inch barrel; bead front sight; walnut finished stock.

Exc: $75 **VGood:** $65 **Good:** $55

MARLIN-GLENFIELD MODEL 30

Lever action; 30-30, some made in 35 Rem.; 4-shot tubular magazine; 20-inch barrel; 38-1/2-inch overall length; weighs 7 lbs.; adjustable rear sight, bead front; receiver tapped for scope mounts; walnut finished hardwood stock with semi-beavertail forend; round breech bolt; offset hammer spur; top of receiver sandblasted to reduce glare; blued forearm cap. Introduced 1966; discontinued 1972.

Exc: $225 **VGood:** $195 **Good:** $150

MARLIN-GLENFIELD MODEL 30A

Same specs as Model 30 except impressed checkering on stock, forearm. Introduced 1969; still in production as Marlin Model 30AS.

Exc: $225 **VGood:** $195 **Good:** $150

MARLIN-GLENFIELD MODEL 30GT

Same specs as Marlin-Glenfield Model 30 except 18-1/2-inch barrel; brass bead front, adjustable rear sight; straight grip walnut-finished hardwood stock; receiver sandblasted. Introduced 1979; discontinued 1981.

Exc: $210 **VGood:** $180 **Good:** $135

MARLIN-GLENFIELD MODEL 60

Semi-automatic; 22 LR; 14-, 18-shot tubular magazine; 22-inch tapered, round barrel; 40-1/2-inch overall length; weighs 5-1/2 lbs.; ramp front, fully-adjustable rear sight; press-checkered, walnut-finished Maine birch stock with Monte Carlo full pistol grip; manual bolt hold-open; Mar-Shield finish. Introduced 1966; still in production as Marlin Model 60.

Exc: $125 **VGood:** $95 **Good:** $75

MARLIN-GLENFIELD MODEL 70

Semi-automatic; 22 LR; 7-shot detachable clip magazine; 18-inch barrel; 36-1/2-inch overall length; weighs 4-1/2 lbs.; open adjustable rear, ramp front sight; chrome-plated trigger; cross-bolt safety; bolt hold-open; chrome-plated magazine; sling swivels; walnut-finished hardwood stock. Introduced 1967; discontinued 1994.

Exc: $125 **VGood:** $95 **Good:** $75

MARLIN-GLENFIELD MODEL 75C

Semi-automatic; 22 LR; 14-shot magazine; 18-inch barrel; 36-3/4-inch overall length; weighs 5 lbs.; ramp front, open adjustable rear sight; walnut finished hardwood Monte Carlo stock with full pistol grip; bolt hold-open; cross-bolt safety; receiver grooved for scope mounts. Introduced 1980. No longer in production.

Exc: $125 **VGood:** $95 **Good:** $75

MARLIN-GLENFIELD MODEL 81G

Bolt action; 22 Short, 22 Long, 22 LR; 18-shot (22 LR), 20-shot (22 Long), 24-shot (22 Short) tube magazine; open rear, bead front sight; standard uncheckered pistol-grip stock; chrome-plated trigger. Introduced 1937; discontinued 1971.

Exc: $110 **VGood:** $95 **Good:** $70

MARLIN-GLENFIELD MODEL 101G

Bolt action; single shot; 22 Short, 22 Long, 22 LR; 22-inch barrel; semi-buckhorn fully-adjustable rear sight, hooded wide-scan front; black plastic trigger guard; T-shaped cocking piece; uncheckered hardwood stock with beavertail forearm; receiver grooved for tip-off scope mount. Introduced 1960; discontinued 1965.

Exc: $110 **VGood:** $95 **Good:** $70

MARLIN-GLENFIELD MODEL 989G

Semi-automatic; 22 LR; 7-shot clip detachable magazine; 18-inch barrel; bead front, open rear sight; plain stock. Same as Marlin Model 989M2. Introduced 1962; discontinued 1964.

Exc: $175 **VGood:** $150 **Good:** $115

MARLIN MODEL XT-17

Clip-fed bolt-action repeater chambered for 17 HMR. Barrel choice is heavy varmint, fluted bull or bull profile, all 22 inches. Blue or stainless finish. Synthetic, wood, laminated or laminated/thumbhole stock. One 4-shot and one 7-shot magazine. Also available with factory-mounted and boresighted 3-9x32mm scope. Prices shown are for blue finish, synthetic stock and heavy varmint barrel.

Perf: $230 **Exc:** $200 **VGood:** $175

Add 10 percent for scope, 20 percent for stainless finish, 50 percent for laminated stock

MARLIN MODEL XT-22 SERIES

Similar to XT-17 except chambered for 22 S/L/LR, or for 22 WMR. Barrel options are sporting, bull or heavy varmint. Clip or tubular magazine; synthetic, wood or laminated stocks; blue or stainless finish. Also available with 3-9x32mm scope. Youth model has 16.5-inch barrel, shorter stock. Prices shown are for 22 LR, hardwood stock, blue finish, standard sporter barrel.

Perf: $200 **Exc:** $175 **VGood:** $150

Add 10 percent for scope or for 22 WMR, 20 percent for stainless finish, 50 percent for laminated stock.

MAUSER MODEL 10 VARMINTER

Bolt action; 22-250; 5-shot box magazine; 24-inch heavy barrel; no sights; drilled, tapped for scope mounts; hand-checkered European walnut Monte Carlo pistol-grip stock; externally adjustable trigger; hammer-forged Krupp Special Ordnance steel barrel. Introduced 1973; discontinued 1975.

Exc: $595 **VGood:** $540 **Good:** $400

MAUSER MODEL 66

Bolt action; 243, 270, 308, 30-06, 5.6x57, 6.5x57, 7x64, 9.3x62, 7mm Rem. Mag., 300 Wea. Mag., 300 Win. Mag., 6.5x68, 8x68S, 9.3x64; 3-shot magazine; 24-inch barrel (standard calibers), 26-inch (magnum caliber); 39-inch overall length (standard calibers); weighs 7-1/2 to 9-3/8 lbs.; blade front sight on ramp, fully-adjustable open rear; hand-checkered European walnut stock with Monte Carlo comb; hand-rubbed oil finish; rosewood forend and grip caps; telescoping short-stroke action; interchangeable, free-floated, medium-heavy barrels; mini-claw extractor; adjustable single-stage trigger; internal magazine. Imported from Germany by Precision Imports, Inc. Introduced 1989; discontinued 1994.

Perf: $1400 **Exc:** $1200 **VGood:** $795

Magnum calibers

Perf: $1500 **Exc:** $1300 **VGood:** $900

MAUSER MODEL 66 SAFARI

Same specs as Model 66 except 375 H&H, 458 Win. Mag.; weighs 9-3/8 lbs. Imported from Germany by Precision Imports, Inc. Introduced 1989; discontinued 1994.

Perf: $2000 **Exc:** $1600 **VGood:** $1200

MAUSER MODEL 66 STUTZEN

Same specs as Model 66 except 21-inch barrel; full-length Stutzen stock. Imported from Germany by Precision Imports, Inc. Introduced 1989; discontinued 1994.

Perf: $1500 **Exc:** $1250 **VGood:** $1000

MAUSER MODEL 66SP MATCH

Bolt action; 308 Win.; 3-shot magazine; 27-1/2-inch barrel, muzzle brake; no sights; scope supplied; match-design European walnut stock; thumbhole pistol grip; spring-loaded cheekpiece; Morgan adjustable recoil pad; adjustable match trigger. Introduced 1976; discontinued 1990.

Perf: $2200 **Exc:** $1800 **VGood:** $1600

MAUSER MODEL 77

Bolt action; 243, 270, 6.5x57, 7x64, 308, 30-06; 3-shot detachable magazine; 24-inch barrel; weighs 7-1/4 lbs.; ramp front sight, open adjustable rear; oil-finished European walnut stock; rosewood grip cap; forend tip; palm-swell pistol grip; Bavarian cheekpiece; recoil pad; interchangeable double-set or single trigger. Introduced 1981; no longer imported.

Perf: $1150 **Exc:** $910 **VGood:** $750

MAUSER MODEL 77 BIG GAME

Same specs as Model 77 except 375 H&H, 458 Win. Mag.; 26-inch barrel; weighs 8-1/2 lbs. Introduced 1981; no longer imported.

Perf: $1295 **Exc:** $995 **VGood:** $810

MAUSER MODEL 77 MAGNUM

Same specs as Model 77 except 7mm Rem. Mag., 6.5x68, 300 Win. Mag., 300 Weatherby Mag., 9.3x62, 9.3x64, 8x68S; 26-inch barrel; weighs 8-1/8 lbs. Introduced 1981; no longer imported.

Perf: $1365 **Exc:** $1100 **VGood:** $895

MAUSER MODEL 77 MANNLICHER

Same specs as Model 77 except 20-inch barrel; 7-3/4 lbs.; European walnut full-stock; set trigger. Introduced 1981; no longer imported.

Perf: $1195 **Exc:** $995 **VGood:** $750

MAUSER MODEL 77 SPORTSMAN

Same specs as Model 77 except 243, 308; weighs 9 lbs.; no sights; set trigger. No longer imported.

Perf: $1395 **Exc:** $995 **VGood:** $750

MAUSER MODEL 77 ULTRA

Same specs as Model 77 except 6.5x57, 7x64, 30-06; 20-inch barrel; weighs 7-3/4 lbs. Introduced 1981; no longer imported.

Perf: $1250 **Exc:** $995 **VGood:** $725

MAUSER MODEL 83

Bolt action; 308; 10-shot magazine; 26-inch barrel; European walnut match stock; adjustable buttplate comb; match trigger. No longer imported.

Perf: $2195 **Exc:** $1695 **VGood:** $1345

MAUSER MODEL 83 SINGLE SHOT

Same specs as Model 83 except single shot action. No longer imported.

Perf: $1995 **Exc:** $1495 **VGood:** $995

MAUSER MODEL 83 MATCH UIT

Same specs as Model 83 except single shot action; free rifle designed for UIT competition. No longer imported.

Perf: $2250 **Exc:** $1795 **VGood:** $1375

MAUSER MODEL 86-SR SPECIALTY RIFLE

Bolt action; 308 Win.; 9-shot detachable magazine; 25-5/8-inch fluted barrel with 1:12-inch twist; 47-3/4-inch overall length; weighs about 11 lbs.; no sights; competition metallic sights or scope mount optional; laminated wood, fiberglass, or special match thumbhole wood stock with rail in forend and adjustable recoil pad; match barrel with muzzle brake; action with two front bolt locking lugs and bedded in stock with free-floated barrel; match trigger adjustable as single or two-stage, fully-adjustable for weight, slack, and position; silent safety locks bolt, firing pin. Imported from Germany by Precision Imports, Inc. Introduced 1989; discontinued 1994.

With fiberglass stock

Perf: $3395 **Exc:** $2500 **VGood:** $2150

With match thumbhole stock

Perf: $3595 **Exc:** $3295 **VGood:** $2500

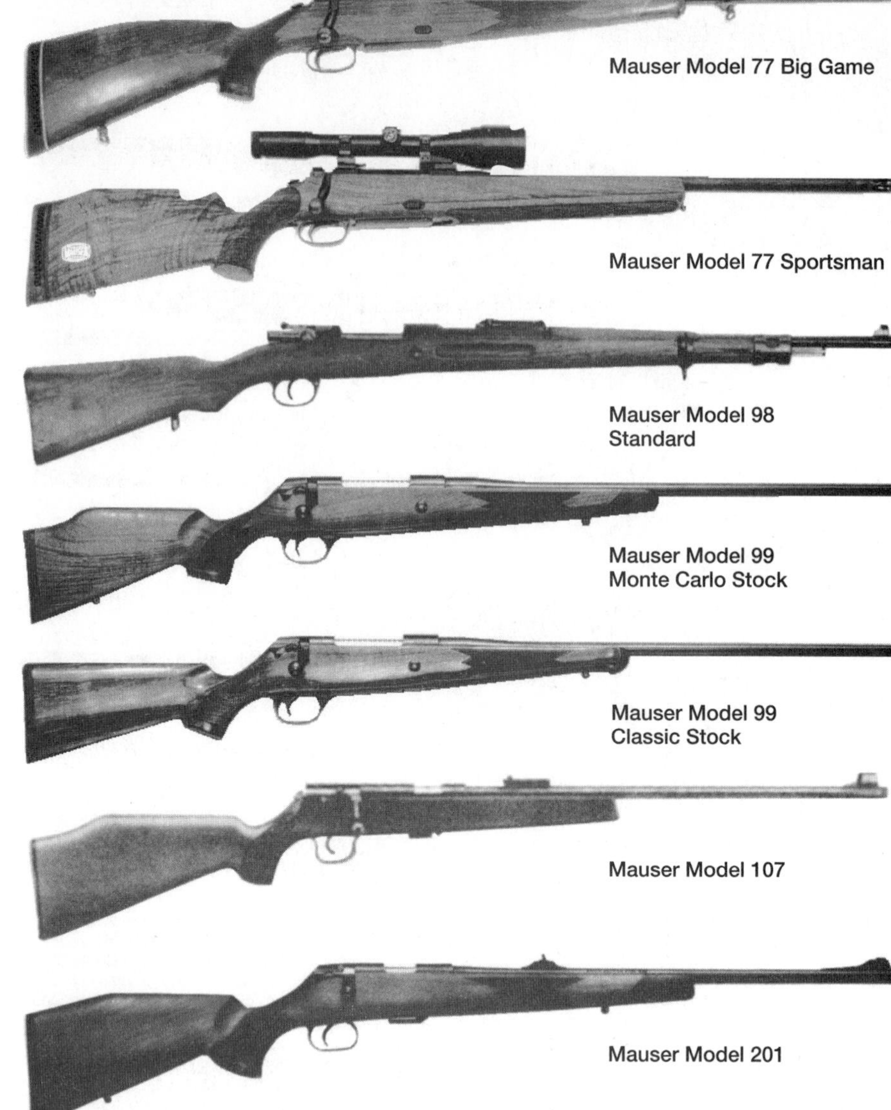

Mauser Model 77 Big Game

Mauser Model 77 Sportsman

Mauser Model 98 Standard

Mauser Model 99 Monte Carlo Stock

Mauser Model 99 Classic Stock

Mauser Model 107

Mauser Model 201

MAUSER MODEL 98 STANDARD

Bolt action; 7mm Mauser, 7.9mm (8mm) Mauser; 5-shot box magazine; 23-1/2-inch barrel; adjustable rear, blade front sight; military-style uncheckered European walnut stock; straight military-type bolt handle; Mauser trademark on receiver ring; commercial version of German military rifle. Introduced post-WWI; discontinued 1938.

Exc: $795 **VGood:** $525 **Good:** $375

MAUSER MODEL 99

Bolt action; 243, 25-06, 270, 308, 30-06, 5.6x57, 6.5x57, 7x57, 7x64 (standard calibers); 7mm Rem. Mag., 257 Wea. Mag., 270 Wea. Mag., 300 Wea. Mag., 300 Win. Mag., 338 Win. Mag., 375 H&H, 8x68S, 9.3x64 (magnum calibers); removable 4-shot magazine (standard calibers), 3-shot (magnums); 24-inch barrel (standard calibers), 26-inch (magnums); 44-inch overall length (standard calibers); weighs about 8 lbs.; no sights; drilled and tapped for scope mounting; hand-checkered European walnut stock with rosewood grip cap; accuracy bedding with free-floated barrel, three front-locking bolt lugs, 60-degree bolt lift; adjustable single-stage trigger; silent safety locks bolt, sear, trigger. Imported from Germany by Precision Imports, Inc. Introduced 1989; discontinued 1994.

Classic stock, oil finish

Perf: $900 **Exc:** $700 **VGood:** $600

Classic stock, high luster finish

Perf: $900 **Exc:** $725 **VGood:** $600

Monte Carlo stock, oil finish

Perf: $925 **Exc:** $710 **VGood:** $610

Monte Carlo stock, high luster finish

Perf: $915 **Exc:** $700 **VGood:** $600

MAUSER MODEL 107

Bolt action; 22 LR; 5-shot magazine; 21-1/2-inch barrel; 40-inch overall length; weighs about 5 lbs.; hooded blade front sight, adjustable open rear; grooved receiver for scope mounting; walnut-stained beechwood stock with Monte Carlo comb; checkered grip and forend; sling swivels; dual extractors; 60-degree bolt throw; steel trigger guard and floorplate; satin blue finish. Imported from Germany by Precision Imports, Inc. Introduced 1992; discontinued 1994.

Perf: $250 **Exc:** $215 **VGood:** $190

MAUSER MODEL 201

Bolt action; 22 LR, 22 WMR; 5-shot magazine; 21-inch barrel; 40-inch overall length; weighs about 6-1/2 lbs.; sold with or without sights; receiver accepts rail mounts and drilled, tapped for scope mounting; walnut-stained beechwood stock with Monte Carlo comb and cheekpiece; checkered grip and forend; hammer forged medium-heavy, free-floated barrel; bolt with two front locking lugs, dual extractors; adjustable trigger; safety locks bolt, sear and trigger. Imported from Germany by Precision Imports, Inc. Introduced 1989; discontinued 1994.

22 LR

Perf: $400 **Exc:** $325 **VGood:** $250

Mauser Model 225

Mauser Model 660

Mauser Model 660 Safari

Mauser Model 3000

Mauser Model 4000 Varmint

Mauser Model KKW

22 WMR
Perf: $425 **Exc:** $350 **VGood:** $300

MAUSER MODEL 201 LUXUS

Same specs as Model 201 except walnut stock with rosewood forend tip. Imported from Germany by Precision Imports, Inc. Introduced 1989; discontinued 1994.

22 LR
Perf: $550 **Exc:** $475 **VGood:** $400

22 WMR
Perf: $600 **Exc:** $500 **VGood:** $425

MAUSER MODEL 225

Bolt action; 243, 25-06, 270, 7x57, 308, 30-06, 257 Weatherby, 270 Weatherby, 7mm Rem. Mag., 300 Win. Mag., 300 Weatherby, 308 Norma Mag., 375 H&H Mag.; 3-shot magazine (magnums), 4-shot (standard); 24-inch barrel (standard), 26-inch (magnums); 44-1/2-inch overall length with longer barrel; weighs 8 lbs.; no sights; drilled, tapped for scope mounts; hand-checkered, oil-finished European Monte Carlo stock; recoil pad; swivel studs. Made in Germany. Introduced 1988; discontinued 1989.

Standard calibers
Perf: $1350 **Exc:** $1200 **VGood:** $950

Magnum calibers
Perf: $1450 **Exc:** $1300 **VGood:** $1000

MAUSER MODEL 660

Bolt action; 243 Win., 25-06, 270 Win., 308 Win., 30-06, 7x57, 7mm Rem. Mag.; 24-inch barrel; no sights; drilled, tapped for scope mounts; checkered European Monte Carlo walnut stock; white line pistol-grip cap, recoil pad; adjustable single-stage trigger; push-button safety. Introduced 1973; discontinued 1975.

Exc: $895 **VGood:** $795 **Good:** $595

MAUSER MODEL 660 SAFARI

Same specs as Model 660 except only 458 Win. Mag., 375 H&H Mag., 338 Win. Mag., 7mm Rem. Mag.; 28-inch barrel; express rear sight, fixed ramp front. Introduced 1973; discontinued 1975.

Exc: $995 **VGood:** $795 **Good:** $595

MAUSER MODEL 660 ULTRA

Same specs Model 660 except 21-inch barrel. Introduced 1965; discontinued 1975.

Exc: $795 **VGood:** $695 **Good:** $495

MAUSER MODEL 660P TARGET

Same specs as Model 660 except 308 Win., other calibers on special order; 3-shot magazine; 26-1/2-inch heavy barrel, muzzle brake; dovetail rib for scope mounting; European walnut target stock with full pistol-grip, thumbhole, adjustable cheekpiece, adjustable rubber buttplate. Not imported.

Exc: $1295 **VGood:** $895 **Good:** $695

MAUSER MODEL 660S DELUXE

Same specs as Model 660 except 21-inch barrel; carbine version; engraving; gold/silver inlay work; heavy carving on select walnut stock. Special order only; no longer imported. Prices vary depending on special order features. $2500+

MAUSER MODEL 660SH

Same specs as Model 660 except 6.5x68, 7mm Rem. Mag., 7mm SE v. Hoff, 300 Win. Mag., 8x68S, 9.3x64. Introduced 1965; discontinued 1975.

Exc: $995 **VGood:** $795 **Good:** $595

MAUSER MODEL 660T CARBINE

Same specs as Model 660 except 21-inch barrel; full-length stock. Introduced 1965; discontinued 1975.

Exc: $1050 **VGood:** $875 **Good:** $695

MAUSER MODEL 2000

Bolt action; 270 Win., 308 Win., 30-06; 5-shot magazine; 24-inch barrel; folding leaf rear sight, hooded ramp front; hand-checkered European walnut stock; Monte Carlo comb; cheekpiece; forend tip; sling swivels. Introduced 1969; discontinued 1971.

Exc: $350 **VGood:** $300 **Good:** $270

MAUSER MODEL 3000

Bolt action; 243 Win., 270 Win., 308 Win., 30-06, 375 H&H Mag., 7mm Rem. Mag.; 3-shot magazine (magnum), 4-shot (standard); 22-inch barrel (standard calibers), 26-inch (magnums); no sights; drilled, tapped for scope mounts; hand-checkered European walnut Monte Carlo stock; white line spacer on pistol-grip cap; recoil pad; sliding safety; fully-adjustable trigger; detachable sling swivels. Left-hand action available. Introduced 1971; discontinued 1975.

Exc: $495 **VGood:** $450 **Good:** $400

Left-hand model
Exc: $550 **VGood:** $500 **Good:** $460

Magnum calibers
Exc: $535 **VGood:** $480 **Good:** $440

Left-hand model
Exc: $625 **VGood:** $575 **Good:** $500

MAUSER MODEL 4000 VARMINT

Bolt action; 222 Rem., 223 Rem.; 4-shot magazine; 22-inch barrel; folding leaf rear sight, hooded ramp front; hand-checkered European walnut Monte Carlo stock; rubber buttplate. Introduced 1971; discontinued 1975.

Exc: $425 **VGood:** $365 **Good:** $310

MAUSER MODEL DSM34

Bolt action; single shot; 22 LR; 26-inch barrel; tangent curve open rear sight, barleycorn front; Model 98 Mauser military-type stock; no checkering; sling swivels. Introduced 1934; discontinued 1939.

Exc: $800 **VGood:** $650 **Good:** $500

MAUSER MODEL EL320

Bolt action; single shot; 22 LR; 23-1/2-inch barrel; adjustable open rear sight, bead front; sporting-style European walnut stock; hand-checkered pistol grip, forearm; grip cap; sling swivels. Introduced 1927; discontinued 1935.

Exc: $450 **VGood:** $375 **Good:** $300

MAUSER MODEL EN310

Bolt action; single shot; 22 LR; 19-3/4-inch barrel; fixed open rear sight, blade front; uncheckered European walnut pistol-grip stock. Introduced post-WWI; discontinued 1935.

Exc: $400 **VGood:** $325 **Good:** $275

MAUSER MODEL ES340

Bolt action; single shot; 22 LR; 25-1/2-inch barrel; tangent curve rear sight, ramp front; European walnut sporting stock; hand-checkered pistol grip; grooved forearm; sling swivels. Introduced 1923; discontinued 1935.

Exc: $450 **VGood:** $350 **Good:** $300

MAUSER MODEL ES340B

Same specs as Model ES340 except 26-3/4-inch barrel; uncheckered pistol-grip stock. Introduced 1935; discontinued 1939.

Exc: $450 **VGood:** $350 **Good:** $300

MAUSER MODEL ES350

Bolt action; repeater; 22 LR; 27-1/2-inch barrel; open micrometer rear sight, ramp front; target-style walnut stock; hand-checkered pistol grip, forend; grip cap. Introduced 1925; discontinued 1935.

Exc: $550 **VGood:** $450 **Good:** $400

MAUSER MODEL ES350B

Same specs as Model ES350 except single shot; 26-3/4-inch barrel; receiver grooved for scope mount. Introduced 1935; discontinued 1938.

Exc: $375 **VGood:** $315 **Good:** $260

MAUSER MODEL KKW

Bolt action; single shot; 22 LR; 26-inch barrel; tangent curve open rear sight, barleycorn front; Model 98 Mauser military-type walnut stock; no checkering; sling swivels; used in training German troops in WWII. Introduced 1935; discontinued 1939.

Exc: $800 **VGood:** $650 **Good:** $500

MAUSER MODEL MM410

Bolt action; 22 LR; 5-shot detachable box magazine; 23-1/2-inch barrel; tangent curve open rear sight, ramp front; European walnut sporting stock; hand-checkered pistol grip; sling swivels. Introduced 1926; discontinued 1935.

Exc: $650 **VGood:** $500 **Good:** $375

MAUSER MODEL MM410B

Same specs as MM410 except lightweight sporting stock. Introduced 1935; discontinued 1939.

Exc: $650 **VGood:** $500 **Good:** $375

MAUSER MODEL MS350B

Bolt action; 22 LR; 5-shot detachable box magazine; 26-3/4-inch barrel; micrometer open rear sight, ramp front; barrel grooved for detachable rear sight/scope; target stock of European walnut; hand-checkered pistol grip, forearm; sling swivels. Replaced Model ES350. Introduced 1935; discontinued 1939.

Exc: $650 **VGood:** $500 **Good:** $375

MAUSER MODEL MS420

Bolt action; 22 LR; 5-shot detachable box magazine; 25-1/2-inch barrel; tangent curve open rear sight, ramp front; European walnut sporting stock; hand-checkered pistol grip; grooved forearm; sling swivels. Introduced 1925; discontinued 1935.

Exc: $650 **VGood:** $500 **Good:** $375

MAUSER MODEL MS420B

Same specs as Model MS420 except 25-3/4-inch barrel; better stock wood. Introduced 1935; discontinued 1939.

Exc: $425 **VGood:** $340 **Good:** $300

MAUSER SPORTER (EARLY)

Bolt action; 6.5x55, 6.5x58, 7x57, 9x57, 9.3x62, 10.75x68; 5-shot box magazine; 23-1/2-inch barrel; tangent-curve rear sight, ramp front; uncheckered European walnut stock, pistol grip; schnabel-tipped forearm; sling swivels; double-set trigger. Made in Germany prior to World War I.

Exc: $1250 **VGood:** $995 **Good:** $700

MAUSER SPORTER CARBINE

Same specs Sporter except only 6.5x54, 6.5x58, 7x57, 8x57, 9x57; 19-3/4-inch barrel. Manufactured prior to WWI.

Perf: $1395 **Exc:** $1095 **VGood:** $750

MAUSER SPORTER, MILITARY MODEL

Same specs as Sporter except 7x57, 8x57, 9x57; military front sight; Model 98-type barrel; two-stage trigger. Manufactured prior to WWI.

Exc: $600 **VGood:** $500 **Good:** $450

MAUSER SPORTER, SHORT MODEL

Same specs as Sporter except only 6.5x54, 8x58; 19-3/4-inch barrel. Manufactured prior to WWI.

Exc: $3295 **VGood:** $2995 **Good:** $2195

MAUSER SPECIAL BRITISH MODEL TYPE A

Bolt action; 7x57, 8x60, 9x57, 9.3x62mm, 30-06; 5-shot box magazine; 23-1/2-inch barrel; express rear sight, hooded ramp front; hand-checkered pistol grip; Circassian walnut sporting stock; buffalo horn grip cap, forearm tip; military-type trigger; detachable sling swivels. Introduced before WWI; discontinued 1938.

Exc: $2995 **VGood:** $2395 **Good:** $1695

MAUSER SPECIAL BRITISH MODEL TYPE A MAGNUM

Same specs as Type A except magnum action; 10.75x68mm, 280 Ross, 318 Westley Richards Express, 404 Jeffery. Introduced before WWI; discontinued 1939.

Exc: $3995 **VGood:** $3750 **Good:** $3225

MAUSER SPECIAL BRITISH MODEL TYPE A SHORT

Same specs as Type A except short action; 6.5x54, 8x51mm, 250-3000; 21-1/2-inch barrel. Introduced before WWI; discontinued 1938.

Exc: $3900 **VGood:** $3395 **Good:** $2995

Mauser Model MS420B

Mauser Special British Model Type A

Mauser Special British Model Type A Magnum

Mauser Type B

McMillan 300 Phoenix Long Range Rifle

McMillan M-86 Sniper

MAUSER TYPE B

Bolt action; 7x57, 8x57, 8x60, 9x57, 9.3x62, 10.75x68mm, 30-06; 5-shot box magazine; 23-1/2-inch barrel; three-leaf rear sight, ramp front; hand-checkered walnut pistol-grip stock; schnabel forearm tip; grip cap; double-set triggers; sling swivels. Introduced before WWI; discontinued 1938.

Exc: $4000 **VGood:** $3600 **Good:** $3000

MCMILLAN 300 PHOENIX LONG RANGE RIFLE

Bolt action; 300 Phoenix; 28-inch barrel; weighs 12-1/2 lbs.; no sights furnished; fiberglass stock with adjustable cheekpiece, adjustable buttplate; comes with rings and bases; matte black finish; textured stock. All parts and components made in U.S. by Harris Gunworks. Introduced 1992; no longer produced.

Perf: $2600 **Exc:** $2100 **VGood:** $1300

MCMILLAN M-40 SNIPER MODEL

Bolt action; 308 Win.; 4-shot magazine; 24-inch, 26-inch match-grade heavy contour barrel; weighs 9 lbs.; no sights; fiberglass stock; recoil pad. Introduced 1990; no longer in production.

Perf: $1800 **Exc:** $1450 **VGood:** $995

MCMILLAN M-86 SNIPER

Bolt action; 308, 30-06, 300 Win. Mag.; 4-shot (308, 30-06), 3-shot (300 Win. Mag.); 24-inch heavy match-grade barrel; 43-1/2-inch overall length; weighs 11-1/4 lbs. (308), 11-1/2 lbs. (30-06, 300); McHale fiberglass stock with textured grip and forend; recoil pad; no sights; bipod; sling swivels; matte black finish. Introduced 1989; no longer in production.

Perf: $1800 **Exc:** $1100 **VGood:** $850

MCMILLAN M-87

Bolt action; 50 BMG; single shot; 29-inch barrel, with muzzle brake; 53-inch overall length; weighs about 21-1/2 lbs.; no sights furnished; McMillan fiberglass stock; right-handed McMillan stainless steel receiver, chrome-moly barrel with 1:15-inch twist. All parts and components made in U.S. by Harris Gunworks. Introduced 1987; still produced.

Perf: $2950 **Exc:** $2400 **VGood:** $1900

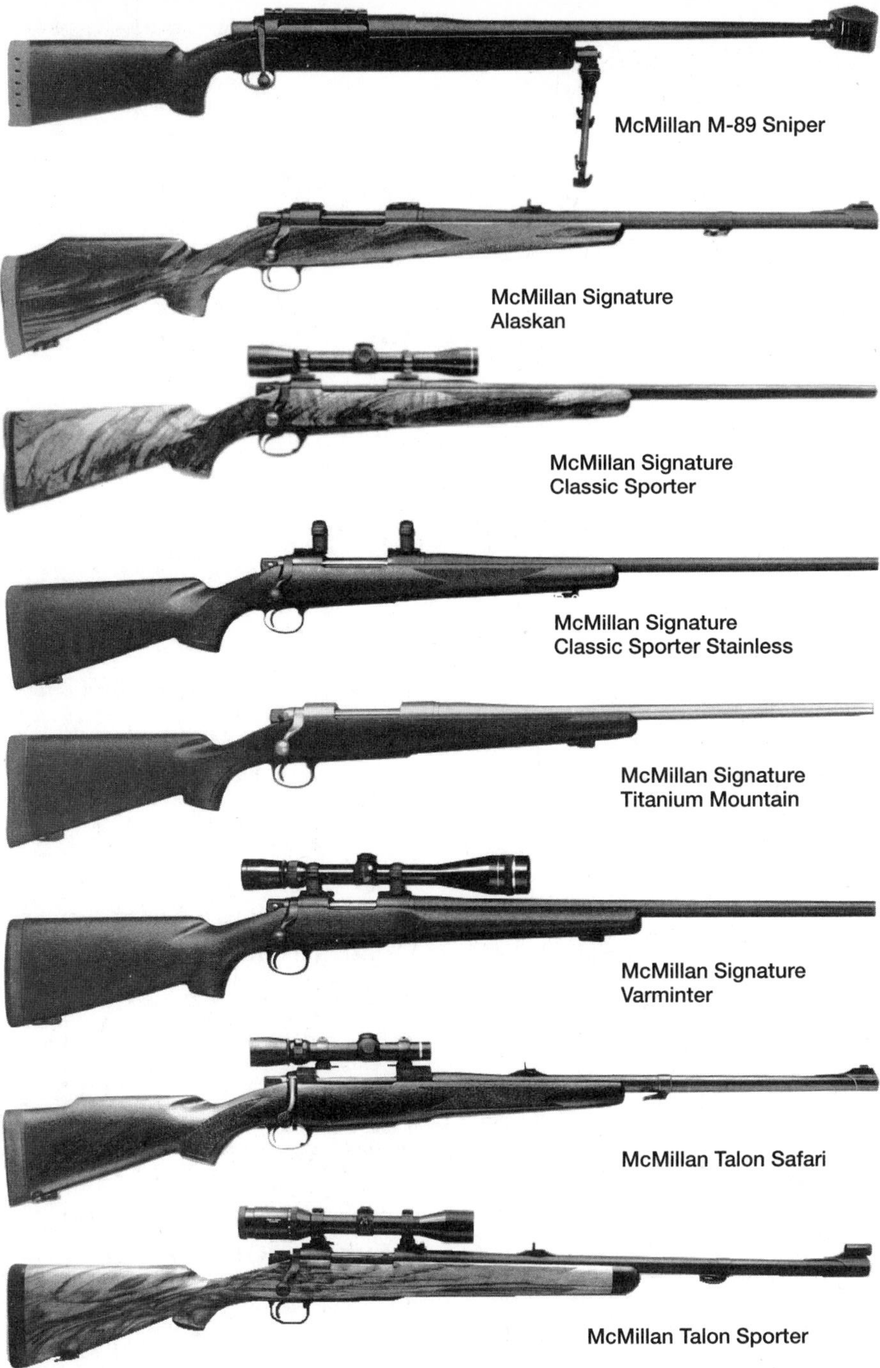
McMillan M-89 Sniper

McMillan Signature Alaskan

McMillan Signature Classic Sporter

McMillan Signature Classic Sporter Stainless

McMillan Signature Titanium Mountain

McMillan Signature Varminter

McMillan Talon Safari

McMillan Talon Sporter

MCMILLAN M-87R
Same specs as M-87 except 5-shot repeater. All parts and components made in U.S. by Harris Gunworks. Introduced 1987; still produced.

Perf: $3795 **Exc:** $3100 **VGood:** $2230

MCMILLAN M-89 SNIPER
Bolt action; 308 Win.; 5-shot magazine; 28-inch barrel with optional suppressor; weighs 15-1/4 lbs.; drilled, tapped for scope mounts; length-adjustable McMillan fiberglass stock; bipod. Introduced 1990.

Perf: $2700 **Exc:** $2100 **VGood:** $1650

MCMILLAN M-92 BULLPUP
Bolt action; single shot; 50 BMG; 24-inch, 26-inch barrel; no sights; fiberglass bullpup-style stock; recoil pad. Introduced 1995; still in production.

Perf: $4000 **Exc:** $3200 **VGood:** $2100

MCMILLAN M-93
Bolt action; 50 BMG; 5-, 10-shot detachable magazine; 29-inch chrome-moly with muzzle brake; 53-inch overall length; 21-1/2 lbs.; no sights; folding fiberglass stock. Introduced 1995.

Perf: $3975 **Exc:** $3550 **VGood:** $2595

MCMILLAN NATIONAL MATCH
Bolt action; 308; 5-shot magazine; 24-inch stainless steel barrel; 43-inch overall length; weighs 11 lbs.; barrel band-type Tomkins front sight, no rear sight; modified ISU fiberglass stock; adjustable buttplate; Canjar trigger; right-hand only. Options include Fibergrain stock, sights. Introduced 1989; still in production.

Perf: $3200 **Exc:** $2700 **VGood:** $2000

MCMILLAN SIGNATURE ALASKAN
Bolt action; 270, 280 Rem., 30-06, 7mm Rem. Mag., 300 Win. Mag., 300 Weatherby, 358 Win. Mag., 340 Weatherby, 375 H&H Mag.; 3-shot magazine (magnums), 4-shot (standard calibers); 22-inch, 24-inch, 26-inch match-grade barrel; single-leaf rear sight, barrel band front; Monte Carlo walnut stock, cheekpiece, palm-swell grip; steel floorplate; Teflon or electroless nickel finish. Introduced 1989; still in production.

Perf: $3125 **Exc:** $2800 **VGood:** $2100

MCMILLAN SIGNATURE CLASSIC SPORTER
Bolt action; 22-250, 243, 6mm Rem., 7mm-08, 284, 308, 25-06, 270, 280 Rem., 30-06, 7mm Rem. Mag., 300 Win. Mag., 300 Weatherby, 338 Win. Mag., 340 Weatherby Mag., 375 H&H Mag.; 3-shot magazine (magnum), 4-shot (standard); 22-inch, 24-inch, 26-inch barrel; weighs 7 lbs. (magnums); no sights; 1-inch rings, bases furnished; McMillan fiberglass stock; recoil pad; sling swivels; matte-black McMillan right- or left-hand action; aluminum floorplate; Fibergrain, wood stocks optional. Introduced 1987.

Perf: $2100 **Exc:** $1695 **VGood:** $1095

MCMILLAN SIGNATURE CLASSIC SPORTER STAINLESS
Same specs as Classic Sporter except barrel and action made of stainless steel; same calibers in addition to 416 Rem. Mag.; fiberglass stock; right- or left-hand action; natural stainless, glass bead or black chrome sulfide finishes. All parts and components made in U.S. by Harris Gunworks. Introduced 1990; still produced.

Perf: $2300 **Exc:** $2150 **VGood:** $1300

MCMILLAN SIGNATURE TITANIUM MOUNTAIN
Bolt action; 270, 280, 30-06, 300 Win. Mag., 338 Win. Mag., 7mm Rem. Mag; 3-shot magazine (magnum), 4-shot (standard); 22-inch, 24-inch, 26-inch barrel; chrome-moly steel or titanium match-grade barrel; weighs 6-1/2 lbs.; graphite-reinforced fiberglass stock; titanium-alloy action. Introduced 1989; still in production.

Steel barrel

Perf: $2695 **Exc:** $2250 **VGood:** $1795

Titatium barrel

Perf: $2995 **Exc:** $2395 **VGood:** $1895

MCMILLAN SIGNATURE VARMINTER
Bolt action; 223, 22-250, 220 Swift, 243, 6mm Rem., 25-06, 7mm-08, 308; 4-shot magazine; 22-inch, 24-inch, 26-inch barrel; weighs 7 lbs.; heavy contoured barrel; hand-bedded fiberglass or Fibergrain stock; adjustable trigger; field bipod; marketed with rings, bases. Introduced 1989.

Perf: $2495 **Exc:** $1995 **VGood:** $1395

MCMILLAN STANDARD SPORTER
Bolt action; 6.5x55, 7mm-08, 308, 270, 280 Rem., 30-06, 7mm Rem. Mag., 300 Win. Mag., 338 Win. Mag.; 24-inch barrel; weighs 7-1/2 lbs.; no sights; drilled, tapped for scope mounts; American walnut or painted fiberglass stock; chrome-moly action; button rifled barrel; Shilen trigger; hinged floorplate. Introduced 1991; discontinued 1992.

Perf: $995 **Exc:** $795 **VGood:** $695

MCMILLAN TALON SAFARI
Bolt action; 300 Win. Mag., 300 Weatherby, 338 Win. Mag., 340 Weatherby, 375 Weatherby, 375 H&H Mag., 378 Weatherby, 416 Taylor, 416 Rigby, 458 Win. Mag.; 4-shot magazine; 24-inch stainless barrel; 43-inch overall length; weighs 10 lbs.; barrel-band ramp front sight, multi-leaf express rear; fiberglass stock; barrel-band sling swivels; 1-inch scope mounts; steel floorplate; matte black finish. Introduced 1989; still in production.

Perf: $3300 **Exc:** $2800 **VGood:** $2100

MCMILLAN TALON SAFARI SUPER MAG
Same specs as Talon Safari except 338 Lapua, 378 Wea. Mag., 416 Rigby, 460 Weatherby, 416 Weatherby, 300 Phoenix, 30-378. Still in production.

Perf: $3700 **Exc:** $3200 **VGood:** $2600

MCMILLAN TALON SPORTER

Bolt action; 25-06, 270, 280 Rem., 30-06, 7mm Rem. Mag., 300 Win. Mag., 300 Weatherby Mag., 300 H&H, 338 Win. Mag., 340 Weatherby Mag., 375 H&H Mag., 416 Rem. Mag.; 24-inch barrel; weighs 7-1/2 lbs.; no sights; drilled, tapped for scope mounts; American walnut or McMillan fiberglass stock; built on pre-'64 Model 70-type action; cone breech; controlled feed; claw extractor; three-position safety; stainless steel barrel, action; chrome-moly optional. Introduced 1991.

Perf: $2600 **Exc:** $2200 **VGood:** $1710

MERKEL MODEL 90S DRILLING

Drilling; 12-, 20-ga., 3-inch chambers, 16-ga., 2-3/4-inch chambers; 22 Hornet, 5.6x50R Mag., 5.6x52R, 222 Rem., 243 Win., 6.5x55, 6.5x57R, 7x57R, 7x65R, 308, 30-06, 8x57JRS, 9.3x74R, 375 H&H; 25-5/8-inch barrels; weighs 8 to 8-1/2 lbs. depending upon caliber; blade front sight, fixed rear; oil-finished walnut stock with pistol-grip; cheekpiece on 12-, 16-gauge; selective sear safety; double barrel locking lug with Greener cross-bolt; scroll-engraved, case-hardened receiver; automatic trigger safety; Blitz action; double triggers. Imported from Germany by GSI. No longer imported.

Perf: $5500 **Exc:** $4995 **VGood:** $3495

MERKEL MODEL 90K DRILLING

Same specs as Model 90S Drilling except manually cocked rifle system. Imported from Germany by GSI. No longer imported.

Perf: $5995 **Exc:** $5250 **VGood:** $3995

MERKEL MODEL 95S DRILLING

Drilling; 12, 20, 3-inch chambers, 16, 2-3/4-inch chambers; 22 Hornet, 5.6x50R Mag., 5.6x52R, 222 Rem., 243 Win., 6.5x55, 6.5x57R, 7x57R, 7x65R, 308, 30-06, 8x57JRS, 9.3x74R, 375 H&H; 25-5/8-inch barrels; weighs 8 to 8-1/2 lbs., depending upon caliber; blade front sight, fixed rear; oil-finished walnut stock with pistol grip; cheekpiece on 12-, 16-gauge; double barrel locking lug with Greener cross-bolt; scroll-engraved, case-hardened receiver; selective sear safety; Blitz action; double triggers. Imported from Germany by GSI; no longer imported.

Perf: $6995 **Exc:** $5995 **VGood:** $4995

MERKEL MODEL 95K DRILLING

Same specs as Model 95S Drilling except manually cocked rifle system. Imported from Germany by GSI. Still imported.

Perf: $7950 **Exc:** $6650 **VGood:** $4995

MERKEL MODEL 96K DRILLING

Drilling; 23.6-inch barrels; 12 or 20 gauge over 22 Hornet, 243, 308, 30-06. Greener cross bolt; case-hardened receiver with scroll engraving; automatic safety; Rifle system manually cocked from tang slide; double triggers; fitted baggage case furnished with gun. Imported by GSI.

Perf: $6700 **Exc:** $5000 **VGood:** $4150

MERKEL MODEL 140-1 DOUBLE RIFLE

Double rifle; side-by-side; 22 Hornet, 5.6x50R Mag., 5.6x52R, 222 Rem., 243 Win., 6.5x55, 6.5x57R, 7x57R, 7x65R, 308, 30-06, 8x57JRS, 9.3x74R, 375 H&H; 25-5/8-inch barrels; weighs about 7-3/4 lbs., depending upon caliber; blade front sight on ramp, fixed rear; oil-finished walnut stock with pistol grip, cheekpiece; Anson & Deeley boxlock action with cocking indicators, double triggers; engraved color case-hardened receiver. Imported from Germany by GSI. Still imported.

Perf: $5900 **Exc:** $4770 **VGood:** $3795

MERKEL MODEL 140-1.1 DOUBLE RIFLE

Same as Model 140-1 Double Rifle except engraved; silver-gray receiver. Imported from Germany by GSI. Still imported.

Perf: $6800 **Exc:** $5795 **VGood:** $3995

Merkel Model 96K Drilling

Merkel Model 140-1

Merkel Model 140-1.1

Merkel Model 210E Combination Gun

MERKEL MODEL 150-1 DOUBLE RIFLE

Double rifle; side-by-side; 22 Hornet, 5.6x50R Mag., 5.6x52R, 222 Rem., 243 Win., 6.5x55, 6.5x57R, 7x57R, 7x65R, 308, 30-06, 8x57JRS, 9.3x74R, 375 H&H; 25-5/8-inch barrels; weighs about 7-3/4 lbs., depending upon caliber; blade front sight on ramp, fixed rear; oil-finished walnut stock with pistol grip, cheekpiece; Anson & Deeley boxlock action with cocking indicators, double triggers, false sideplates; silver-gray receiver with Arabesque engraving. Imported from Germany by GSI. No longer imported.

Perf: $7500 **Exc:** $5695 **VGood:** $4495

MERKEL MODEL 150-1.1 DOUBLE RIFLE

Same specs as Model 150-1 Double Rifle except English Arabesque engraving. Imported from Germany by GSI. No longer imported.

Perf: $8500 **Exc:** $7250 **VGood:** $5295

MERKEL MODEL 160 DOUBLE RIFLE

Double rifle; side-by-side; 22 Hornet, 5.6x50R Mag., 5.6x52R, 222 Rem., 243 Win., 6.5x55, 6.5x57R, 7x57R, 7x65R, 308, 30-06, 8x57JRS, 9.3x74R, 375 H&H; 25-5/8-inch barrels; weighs about 7-3/4 lbs., depending upon caliber; blade front sight on ramp, fixed rear; oil-finished walnut stock with pistol grip, cheekpiece; sidelock action; double barrel locking lug with Greener cross-bolt; fine engraved hunting scenes on sideplates; Holland & Holland ejectors; double triggers. Imported from Germany by GSI. No longer imported.

Perf: $12,875 **Exc:** $10,875 **VGood:** $7995

MERKEL MODEL 210E COMBINATION GUN

Combination gun; over/under; 12-, 16-, 20-ga. (2-3/4-inch chamber) over 22 Hornet, 5.6x50R, 5.6x52R, 222 Rem., 243 Win., 6.5x55, 6.5x57R, 7x57R, 7x65R, 308 Win., 30-06, 8x57JRS, 9.3x74R, 375 H&H; 25-5/8-inch barrels; weighs about 7-1/2 lbs.; bead front sight, fixed rear; oil-finished walnut stock with pistol grip, cheekpiece; Kersten double cross-bolt lock; scroll-engraved, color case-hardened receiver; Blitz action; double triggers. Imported from Germany by GSI. No longer imported.

Perf: $5780 **Exc:** $4395 **VGood:** $3550

MERKEL MODEL 211E COMBINATION GUN

Combination gun; over/under; 12-, 16-, 20-ga. (2-3/4-inch chamber) over 22 Hornet, 5.6x50R, 5.6x52R, 222 Rem., 243 Win., 6.5x55, 6.5x57R, 7x57R, 7x65R, 308 Win., 30-06, 8x57JRS, 9.3x74R, 375 H&H; 25-5/8-inch barrels; weighs about 7-1/2 lbs.; bead front sight, fixed rear; oil-finished walnut stock with pistol grip, cheekpiece; Kersten double cross-bolt lock; silver-grayed receiver with fine hunting scene engraving; Blitz action; double triggers. Imported from Germany by GSI. No longer imported.

Perf: $6700 **Exc:** $4995 **VGood:** $3995

MERKEL MODEL 213E COMBINATION GUN

Combination gun; over/under; 12-, 16-, 20-ga. (2-3/4-inch chamber) over 22 Hornet, 5.6x50R, 5.6x52R, 222 Rem., 243 Win., 6.5x55, 6.5x57R, 7x57R, 7x65R, 308 Win., 30-06, 8x57JRS, 9.3x74R, 375 H&H; 25-5/8-inch barrels; weighs about 7-1/2 lbs.; bead front sight, fixed rear; oil-finished walnut stock with pistol grip, cheekpiece; Kersten double cross-bolt lock; English-style, large scroll Arabesque engraving; sidelock action; double triggers. Imported from Germany by GSI. No longer imported.

Perf: $11,995 **Exc:** $9995 **VGood:** $6995

MERKEL MODEL 220E DOUBLE RIFLE

Double rifle; over/under; boxlock; 22 Hornet, 5.6x50R Mag., 5.6x52R, 222 Rem., 243 Win., 6.5x55, 6.5x57R, 7x57R, 7x65R, 308, 30-06, 8x57JRS, 9.3x74R; 25-5/8-inch barrels; weighs about 7-3/4 lbs., depending upon caliber; blade front sight, fixed rear; oil-finished walnut stock with pistol grip, cheekpiece; Kersten double cross-bolt lock; scroll-engraved, case-hardened receiver; Blitz action with double triggers. Imported from Germany by GSI. No longer imported.

Perf: $9295 **Exc:** $7195 **VGood:** $5495

MERKEL MODEL 221E DOUBLE RIFLE

Double rifle; over/under; boxlock; 22 Hornet, 5.6x50R Mag., 5.6x52R, 222 Rem., 243 Win., 6.5x55, 6.5x57R, 7x57R, 7x65R, 308, 30-06, 8x57JRS, 9.3x74R; 25-5/8-inch barrels; weighs about 7-3/4 lbs, depending upon caliber; blade front sight, fixed rear; oil-finished walnut stock with pistol grip, cheekpiece; Kersten double cross-bolt lock; silver-grayed receiver with hunting scene engraving; Blitz action with double triggers. Imported from Germany by GSI. No longer imported.

Perf: $9900 **Exc:** $7995 **VGood:** $5995

Mitchell 1858 Henry Replica

Mitchell 1873 Winchester Replica

Mitchell AK-22

Mitchell CAR-15/22

Mitchell Galil/22

MERKEL MODEL 223E DOUBLE RIFLE

Double rifle; over/under; sidelock; 22 Hornet, 5.6x50R Mag., 5.6x52R, 222 Rem., 243 Win., 6.5x55, 6.5x57R, 7x57R, 7x65R, 308, 30-06, 8x57JRS, 9.3x74R; 25-5/8-inch barrels; weighs about 7-3/4 lbs, depending upon caliber; blade front sight, fixed rear; oil-finished walnut stock with pistol grip, cheekpiece; sidelock action; English-style large-scroll Arabesque engraving; Blitz action with double triggers. Imported from Germany by GSI. No longer imported.

Perf: $14,995 **Exc:** $12,500 **VGood:** $9500

MERKEL MODEL 313E COMBINATION GUN

Combination gun; over/under; 12-, 16-, 20-ga. (2-3/4-inch chamber) over 22 Hornet, 5.6x50R, 5.6x52R, 222 Rem., 243 Win., 6.5x55, 6.5x57R, 7x57R, 7x65R, 308 Win., 30-06, 8x57JRS, 9.3x74R, 375 H&H; 25-5/8-inch barrels; weighs about 7-1/2 lbs.; bead front sight, fixed rear; oil-finished walnut stock with pistol grip, cheekpiece; Kersten double cross-bolt lock; medium-scroll engraving on receiver; sidelock action; double triggers. Imported from Germany by GSI. No longer imported.

Perf: $13,950 **Exc:** $10,995 **VGood:** $9250

MERKEL MODEL 323E DOUBLE RIFLE

Double rifle; over/under; sidelock; 22 Hornet, 5.6x50R Mag., 5.6x52R, 222 Rem., 243 Win., 6.5x55, 6.5x57R, 7x57R, 7x65R, 308, 30-06, 8x57JRS, 9.3x74R; 25-5/8-inch barrels; weighs about 7-3/4 lbs., depending upon caliber; blade front sight, fixed rear; oil-finished walnut stock with pistol grip, cheekpiece; medium-scroll engraving on action; Blitz action with double triggers. Imported from Germany by GSI. No longer imported.

Perf: $20,000 **Exc:** $17,500 **VGood:** $13,500

MERKEL MODEL K-1 LIGHTWEIGHT STALKING RIFLE

Single shot, breakopen; 243 Win., 270 Win., 7x57R, 308 Win., 30-06, 7mm Rem. Mag., 300 Win. Mag., 9.3x74R; 23.6-inch barrels; weighs 5.6 lbs. unscoped; Satin-finished walnut stock, fluted and checkered; sling-swivel studs; scope base furnished. Franz Jager single-shot break- open action, cocking/uncocking slide-type safety, matte silver receiver, selectable trigger pull weights, integrated, quick detach 1-inch or 30mm optic mounts. Imported from Germany by GSI. Still imported.

Standard, simple border engraving

Perf: $3800 **Exc:** $3200 **VGood:** $2600

Premium, light arabesque scroll

Perf: $4300 **Exc:** $3500 **VGood:** $2900

Jagd, fine engraved hunting scenes

Perf: $4700 **Exc:** $3900 **VGood:** $3200

MIDLAND 1500S SURVIVOR

Bolt action; 308 Win.; 5-shot magazine; 22-inch barrel; 43-inch overall length; weighs 7 lbs.; hooded ramp front sight, open adjustable rear; black composite stock with recoil pad; Monte Carlo cheekpiece; stainless steel barreled action with satin chromed bolt. Made by Gibbs Rifle Co. Introduced 1993; discontinued 1994.

Perf: $650 **Exc:** $550 **VGood:** $450

MIDLAND MODEL 1500C SURVIVOR

Same specs as Model 1500S Survivor except detachable clip magazine. Made by Gibbs Rifle Co. Introduced 1993; discontinued 1994.

Perf: $600 **Exc:** $500 **VGood:** $400

MITCHELL 1858 HENRY REPLICA

Lever action; 44-40; 13-shot magazine; 24-1/4-inch barrel; 43-inch overall length; weighs 9-1/2 lbs.; bead front sight, open adjustable rear; European walnut stock; brass receiver and buttplate; uses original Henry loading system; faithful to the original rifle. Imported by Mitchell Arms, Inc. Introduced 1990; discontinued 1993.

Perf: $800 **Exc:** $630 **VGood:** $500

MITCHELL 1866 WINCHESTER REPLICA

Lever action; 44-40; 13-shot magazine; 24-1/4-inch barrel; 43-inch overall length; weighs 9 lbs.; bead front sight, open adjustable rear; European walnut stock; solid brass receiver, buttplate, forend cap; octagonal barrel; faithful to the original Winchester '66 rifle. Imported by Mitchell Arms, Inc. Introduced 1990; discontinued 1993.

Perf: $700 **Exc:** $530 **VGood:** $430

MITCHELL 1873 WINCHESTER REPLICA

Lever action; 45 Colt; 13-shot magazine; 24-1/4-inch barrel; 43-inch overall length; weighs 9-1/2 lbs.; bead front sight, open adjustable rear; European walnut stock; color case-hardened steel receiver; faithful to the original Model 1873 rifle. Imported by Mitchell Arms, Inc. Introduced 1990; discontinued 1993.

Perf: $750 **Exc:** $625 **VGood:** $495

MITCHELL AK-22

Semi-automatic; 22 LR, 22 WMR; 20-shot magazine (22 LR), 10-shot (22 WMR); 18-inch barrel; 36-inch overall length; weighs 6-1/2 lbs.; post front sight, open adjustable rear; European walnut stock; 22-caliber rimfire replica of the AK-47 rifle; wide magazine to maintain appearance. Imported from Italy by Mitchell Arms, Inc. Introduced 1985; discontinued 1993.

Perf: $375 **Exc:** $300 **VGood:** $250

MITCHELL CAR-15/22

Semi-automatic; 22 LR; 15-shot magazine; 16-3/4-inch barrel; telescoping butt; 32-inch overall length when collapsed; adjustable post front sight, adjustable aperture rear. Scope mount available. Replica of the CAR-15 rifle. Imported by Mitchell Arms, Inc. Introduced 1990; discontinued 1993.

Perf: $400 **Exc:** $325 **VGood:** $300

MITCHELL GALIL/22

Semi-automatic; 22 LR, 22 WMR; 20-shot magazine (22 LR), 10-shot (22 WMR); 18-inch barrel; 36-inch overall length; weighs 6-1/2 lbs.; elevation-adjustable post front sight, windage-adjustable rear; European walnut grip and forend with metal folding or wood fixed stock; replica of the Israeli Galil rifle. Imported by Mitchell Arms, Inc. Introduced 1987; discontinued 1993.

Perf: $375 **Exc:** $300 **VGood:** $250

MITCHELL HIGH STANDARD 15/22

Semi-automatic; 22 LR; 15-shot magazine, 30-shot available; 20-1/2-inch barrel; 37-1/2-inch overall length; weighs 6-1/4 lbs.; blade on ramp front sight, open adjustable rear; American walnut stock; polished blue finish; barrel band on forend. Imported from Philippines by Mitchell Arms, Inc. Introduced 1994; discontinued 1995.

Perf: $130 **Exc:** $110 **VGood:** $80

MITCHELL HIGH STANDARD 15/22D

Same specs as Mitchell High Standard 15/22 except fancy walnut stock with checkering; rosewood grip and forend caps. Imported from the Philippines by Mitchell Arms, Inc. Introduced 1994; discontinued 1995.

Perf: $140 **Exc:** $120 **VGood:** $90

MITCHELL HIGH STANDARD 20/22

Semi-automatic; 22 LR; 10-shot magazine; 20-1/2-inch barrel; 37-1/2-inch overall length; weighs 6-1/4 lbs.; blade on ramp front sight, open adjustable rear; American walnut stock; polished blue finish; barrel band on forend. Imported from Philippines by Mitchell Arms, Inc. Introduced 1994; discontinued 1995.

Perf: $125 **Exc:** $100 **VGood:** $75

MITCHELL HIGH STANDARD 20/22D

Same specs as Mitchell High Standard 20/22 except fancy walnut stock with checkering; rosewood grip and forend caps. Imported from the Philippines by Mitchell Arms, Inc. Introduced 1994; discontinued 1995.

Perf: $150 **Exc:** $120 **VGood:** $90

MITCHELL HIGH STANDARD 20/22 SPECIAL

Same specs as Mitchell High Standard 20/22 except heavy barrel. Imported from the Philippines by Mitchell Arms, Inc. Introduced 1994; discontinued 1995.

Perf: $150 **Exc:** $120 **VGood:** $90

MITCHELL HIGH STANDARD 9301

Bolt action; 22 LR; 10-shot magazine; 22-1/2-inch barrel; 40-3/4-inch overall length; weighs about 6-1/2 lbs.; bead on ramp front sight, open adjustable rear; American walnut with rosewood grip and forend caps; checkering; polished blue finish. Imported from the Philippines by Mitchell Arms, Inc. Introduced 1994; discontinued 1995.

Perf: $200 **Exc:** $160 **VGood:** $110

MITCHELL HIGH STANDARD 9302

Bolt action; 22 WMR; 5-shot magazine; 22-1/2-inch barrel; 40-3/4-inch overall length; weighs about 6-1/2 lbs.; bead on ramp front sight, open adjustable rear; American walnut stock with rosewood grip and forend caps; checkering; polished blue finish. Imported from the Philippines by Mitchell Arms, Inc. Introduced 1994; discontinued 1995.

Perf: $250 **Exc:** $200 **VGood:** $150

MITCHELL HIGH STANDARD 9303

Bolt action; 22 LR; 10-shot magazine; 22-1/2-inch barrel; 40-3/4-inch overall length; weighs about 6-1/2 lbs.; bead on ramp front sight, open adjustable rear; American walnut stock; polished blue finish. Imported from the Philippines by Mitchell Arms, Inc. Introduced 1994; discontinued 1995.

Perf: $200 **Exc:** $150 **VGood:** $110

MITCHELL HIGH STANDARD 9304

Bolt action; 22 WMR; 5-shot magazine; 22-1/2-inch barrel; 40-3/4-inch overall length; weighs about 6-1/2 lbs.; bead on ramp front sight, open adjustable rear; American walnut stock; rosewood grip and forend caps; checkering; polished blue finish. Imported from the Philippines by Mitchell Arms, Inc. Introduced 1994; discontinued 1995.

Perf: $220 **Exc:** $165 **VGood:** $120

MITCHELL HIGH STANDARD 9305

Bolt action; 22 LR; 10-shot magazine; 22-1/2-inch heavy barrel; 40-3/4-inch overall length; weighs about 7 lbs.; bead on ramp front sight, open adjustable rear; American walnut stock; polished blue finish. Imported from the Philippines by Mitchell Arms, Inc. Introduced 1994; discontinued 1995.

Perf: $250 **Exc:** $175 **VGood:** $130

MITCHELL M-16A1

Semi-automatic; 22 LR; 15-shot magazine; 20-1/2-inch barrel; 38-1/2-inch overall length; weighs 7 lbs.; adjustable post front sight, adjustable aperture rear; full width magazine; black composition stock; comes with military-type sling. 22 rimfire replica of the AR-15 rifle. Imported by Mitchell Arms, Inc. Introduced 1990; discontinued 1994.

Perf: $350 **Exc:** $300 **VGood:** $250

Mitchell High Standard 20/22

Mitchell High Standard 9302

Mitchell M-16A1

Mitchell MAS/22

Mitchell PPS/50

Mossberg 464 SPC .22 LR

Mossberg 464 SPX .30-30

MITCHELL MAS/22

Semi-automatic; 22 LR; 20-shot magazine; 18-inch barrel; 28-1/2-inch overall length; weighs 7-1/2 lbs.; adjustable post front sight, flip-type aperture rear; walnut butt, grip and forend; top cocking lever; flash hider; bullpup design resembles French armed forces rifle. Imported by Mitchell Arms, Inc. Introduced 1987; discontinued 1993.

Perf: $500 **Exc:** $425 **VGood:** $350

MITCHELL PPS/50

Semi-automatic; 22 LR; 20- or 50-shot magazine; styled after Russian PPSh submachinegun; 16-1/2-inch barrel; 33-1/2-inch overall length; weighs 5-1/2 lbs.; blade front sight, adjustable rear; walnut stock; full-length perforated barrel shroud; matte finish. Imported by Mitchell Arms, Inc. Introduced 1989; discontinued 1993.

20-shot

Perf: $325 **Exc:** $295 **VGood:** $250

50-shot

Perf: $350 **Exc:** $320 **VGood:** $275

MONTANA ARMORY MODEL 1885 HIGH WALL

Single shot, falling block; 30-40, 32-40, 38-55, 40-65, 45-70; 26-inch barrel (30-40), 28-inch other calibers; Douglas premium tapered octagon barrel; American black walnut stock. Marble's ivory bead front, number 66 rear sights; recreation of early High Wall, with coil-spring action. Tang drilled and tapped for tang sight; color case hardened receiver, lever, hammer and breechblock. Introduced 1991, no longer in production.

Perf: $1200 **Exc:** $1050 **VGood:** $925

Mossberg ATR Night Train

Mossberg MMR Hunter

Mossberg Model 26B

Mossberg Model 35

Mossberg Model L42A

MOSSBERG 464 SPC .22 LR

Lever action rifle in .22LR with 18.5 inch. Synthetic six-position adjustable stock, Tri-rail Picatinny forearm. 6 pounds, 33.5 inches long. 14 +1 capacity, shipped with rail covers and rifle sights.

Perf: $425 **Exc:** $380 **VGood:** $330

MOSSBERG 464 SPX .30-30

Lever action rifle in .30-30 Winchester with 16 7/8 inch threaded barrel with flash hider. Synthetic, six-position adjustable stock, Tri-rail Picatinny forearm. 7 pounds, 34 inches long. 5+1 capacity, shipped with rail covers and three-dot fiber optic sights.

Perf: $500 **Exc:** $425 **VGood:** $390

MOSSBERG ATR NIGHT TRAIN

Center-fire bolt action rifle in .308 Winchester. 22 inch fluted barrel, synthetic stock in either green or camo. 8.5 pounds, 42 inches. Ships as a package with Picatinny one-piece scope rail, 4-16X 50 or 6-24X50 riflescope and bi-pod. LBA trigger and blind magazine box.

Perf: $520 **Exc:** $480 **VGood:** $440

MOSSBERG MMR HUNTER

AR 15 style semi-automatic carbine in 5.56 with 20 inch, free-floated barrel. 7.0 pounds, 39.0 inches long. Features include; Start SE-1 pistol grip with battery compartment, fixed A-2 style stock, round aluminum handguard, flat top receiver and no sights. Available in black, Mossy Oak Brush Camo or Mossy Oak Treestand Camo.

Perf: $885 **Exc:** $790 **VGood:** $700

MOSSBERG MMR TACTICAL

AR 15 style semi-automatic carbine in 5.56 with 16.5 inch barrel. 7.5 pounds, 32.5 inches long. Features include; Start SE-1 pistol grip with battery compartment, 6-position adjustable stock, Picatinny quad-rail handguard, flat top receiver and adjustable sights. Variations exist.

Perf: $885 **Exc:** $790 **VGood:** $700

MOSSBERG MODEL 10

Bolt action; single shot; 22 Short, 22 Long, 22 LR; 22-inch barrel; take-down; open rear sight, bead front; uncheckered walnut pistol-grip stock; swivels, sling. Introduced 1933; discontinued 1935.

Exc: $150 **VGood:** $120 **Good:** $90

MOSSBERG MODEL 14

Bolt action; single shot; 22 Short, 22 Long, 22 LR; 24-inch barrel; take down; rear peep sight, hooded ramp front; uncheckered pistol-grip stock; semi-beavertail forearm; sling swivels. Introduced 1934; discontinued 1935.

Exc: $150 **VGood:** $125 **Good:** $90

MOSSBERG MODEL 20

Bolt action; single shot; 22 Short, 22 Long, 22 LR; 24-inch barrel; take down; open rear sight, bead front; uncheckered pistol-grip stock; forearm with finger grooves. Introduced 1933; discontinued 1935.

Exc: $150 **VGood:** $120 **Good:** $90

MOSSBERG MODEL 21

Bolt action; single shot; 22 Short, 22 Long, 22 LR; 24-inch barrel; take down. Similar to Model 20. Introduced 1934; discontinued 1935.

Exc: $150 **VGood:** $120 **Good:** $90

MOSSBERG MODEL 25

Bolt action; single shot; 22 Short, 22 Long, 22 LR; 24-inch barrel; take down; rear peep sight, hooded ramp front; uncheckered pistol-grip stock; semi-beavertail forearm; sling swivels. Introduced 1935; discontinued 1936.

Exc: $170 **VGood:** $125 **Good:** $100

MOSSBERG MODEL 25A

Same specs as Model 25 except with master action; better wood and finish. Introduced 1937; discontinued 1938.

Exc: $200 **VGood:** $140 **Good:** $100

MOSSBERG MODEL 26B

Bolt action; single shot; 22 Short, 22 Long, 22 LR; 26-inch tapered barrel; 41-3/4-inch overall length; weighs 5-1/2 lbs.; No.2A open sporting or No.4 micrometer peep rear sight, hooded ramp front; uncheckered pistol-grip stock; sling swivels. Manufactured 1938 to 1941.

Exc: $175 **VGood:** $125 **Good:** $100

MOSSBERG MODEL 26C

Same specs as Model 26B except open sights; no sling swivels.

Exc: $155 **VGood:** $115 **Good:** $80

MOSSBERG MODEL 26T TARGO RIFLE/SHOTGUN

Bolt action; single shot; Targo 22 smoothbore with smoothbore and rifled screw-on adapters. Fewer than 1000 manufactured. Introduced 1940; discontinued 1942. Add 15 percent premium for target thrower and clay birds.

Exc: $550 **VGood:** $400 **Good:** $250

MOSSBERG MODEL 30

Bolt action; single shot; 22 Short, 22 Long, 22 LR; 24-inch barrel; takedown; rear peep sight, hooded ramp bead front; uncheckered pistol-grip stock; grooved forearm. Introduced 1933; discontinued 1935.

Exc: $150 **VGood:** $125 **Good:** $100

MOSSBERG MODEL 34

Bolt action; single shot; 22 Short, 22 Long, 22 LR; 24-inch barrel; takedown; rear peep sight, hooded ramp bead front; uncheckered pistol-grip stock with semi-beavertail forearm. Introduced 1934; discontinued 1935.

Exc: $150 **VGood:** $125 **Good:** $100

MOSSBERG MODEL 35

Bolt action; single shot; 22 LR; 26-inch barrel, target grade; micrometer rear peep sight; hooded ramp front; target stock with full pistol grip, beavertail forearm; sling swivels. Introduced 1935; discontinued 1937.

Exc: $295 **VGood:** $250 **Good:** $135

MOSSBERG MODEL 35A

Same specs as Model 35 except heavy barrel; new Master action; uncheckered target stock with cheekpiece, full pistol grip. Introduced 1937; discontinued 1938.

Exc: $295 **VGood:** $250 **Good:** $135

MOSSBERG MODEL 35A-LS

Same specs as Model 35A except Lyman 17A front, Lyman No. 57 rear sight.

Exc: $310 **VGood:** $260 **Good:** $150

MOSSBERG MODEL 40

Bolt action; 22 Short, 22 Long, 22 LR; 16-shot tube magazine (22 LR), 18-shot (22 Long), 22-shot (22 Short); takedown repeater. Introduced 1933; discontinued 1935.

Exc: $250 **VGood:** $200 **Good:** $125

MOSSBERG MODEL 42

Bolt action; 22 Short, 22 Long, 22 LR; 7-shot detachable box magazine; 24-inch barrel; takedown; receiver peep sight, open rear sight, hooded ramp front; uncheckered walnut pistol-grip stock; sling swivels. Introduced 1935; discontinued 1937.

Exc: $275 **VGood:** $220 **Good:** $150

MOSSBERG MODEL 42A

Same specs as Model 42 with Master action, minor upgrading. Introduced 1937 to replace dropped Model 42; discontinued 1938.

Exc: $275 **VGood:** $225 **Good:** $150

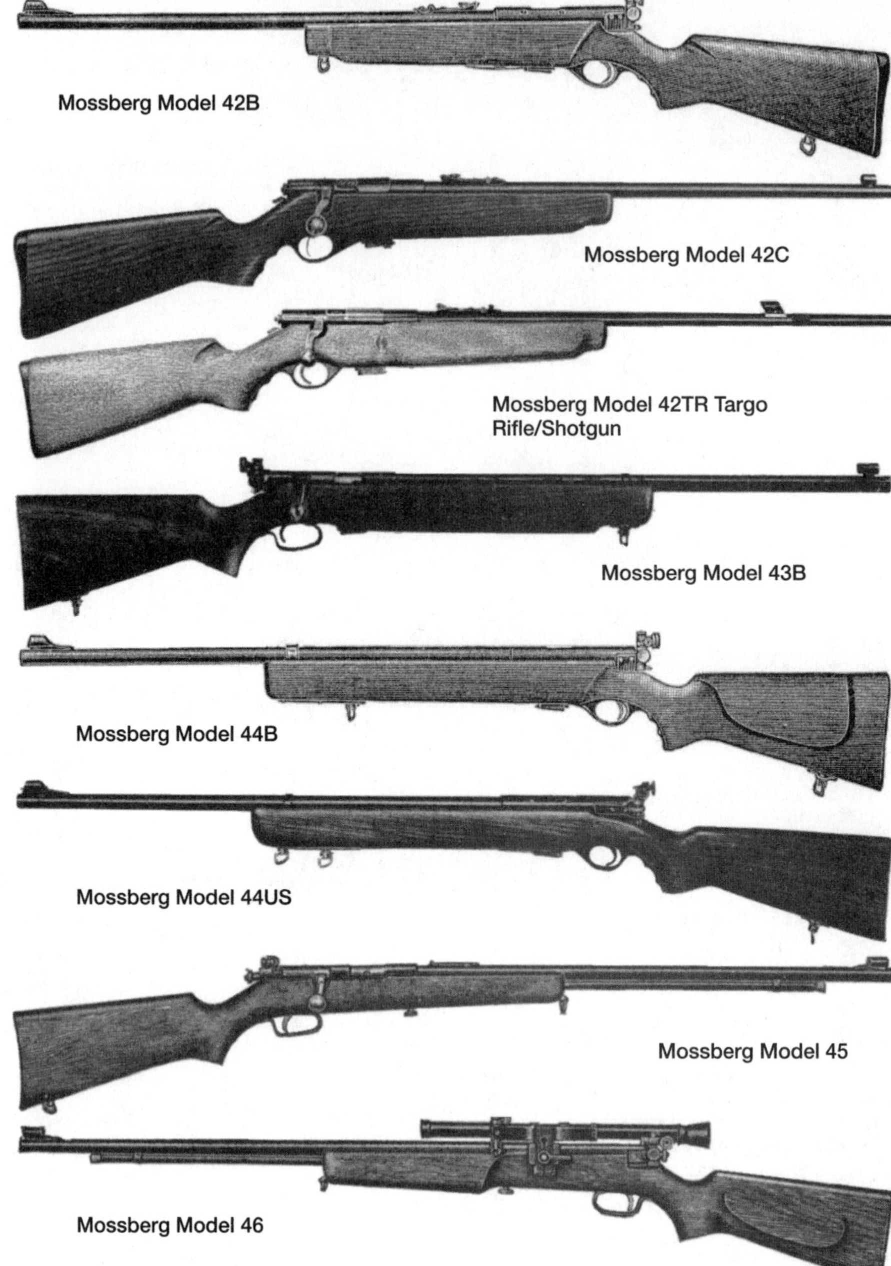

MOSSBERG MODEL L42A
Same specs as Model 42A except left-handed action. Introduced 1938; discontinued 1941.

Exc: $300 **VGood:** $225 **Good:** $150

MOSSBERG MODEL 42B
Same specs as Model 42A except design improvements; replaced the Model 42A; micrometer peep sight in addition to open rear; 5-shot detachable box magazine. Introduced 1938; discontinued 1941.

Exc: $300 **VGood:** $225 **Good:** $150

MOSSBERG MODEL 42C
Same specs as Model 42B except no rear peep sight.

Exc: $235 **VGood:** $165 **Good:** $115

MOSSBERG MODEL 42M
Same specs as Model 42 except 23-inch tapered barrel; 40-inch overall length; weighs 6-3/4 lbs.; two-piece Mannlicher-type long stock with pistol grip, cheekpiece; micrometer receiver peep sight, open rear sight, hooded ramp front. Introduced 1940; discontinued 1950.

Exc: $275 **VGood:** $200 **Good:** $150

MOSSBERG MODEL 42M (A), 42M (B), 42M (C)
Same specs as Model 42M except minor changes in extractors and sights. No military markings. Introduced 1944; discontinued 1950.

Exc: $250 **VGood:** $200 **Good:** $150

MOSSBERG MODEL 42MB
Same same specs as Model 42M except no cheekpiece; approximately 50,000 made for U.S. and Great Britain; U.S. Property and British proofmarks. Produced only during World War II. Some collector value.

U.S. Property marked

Exc: $400 **VGood:** $350 **Good:** $300

British proof marks

Exc: $390 **VGood:** $335 **Good:** $265

MOSSBERG MODEL 42TR TARGO RIFLE/SHOTGUN
Bolt action; 22 Short; Long, Long Rifle, 22 Long Rifle Shot, 7-shot box magazine; smoothbore and rifled screw-on adapters; no sling swivels. Introduced commercially 1940; discontinued 1942.

Exc: $500 **VGood:** $400 **Good:** $325

MOSSBERG MODEL 42T TARGO RIFLE/SHOTGUN
Same specs as Model 42TR except not provided with rifled adapter; front sight hood or rear sight, which were available separately. Introduced commercially 1940; discontinued 1942.

Exc: $500 **VGood:** $400 **Good:** $325

MOSSBERG MODEL 43
Bolt action; 22 LR; 7-shot detachable box magazine; 26-inch barrel; Lyman No. 57 rear sight, selective aperture front; adjustable trigger, speed lock; target stock with cheekpiece, full pistol grip; beavertail forend; adjustable front swivel. Introduced 1937; discontinued 1938.

Exc: $275 **VGood:** $225 **Good:** $170

MOSSBERG MODEL L43
Same specs as Model 43 except left-hand action.

Exc: $300 **VGood:** $225 **Good:** $200

MOSSBERG MODEL 43B
Bolt action; 22 LR; 7-shot detachable magazine; 26-inch heavy barrel; Lyman No. 57 receiver sight, Lyman No. 17A front sight; walnut target stock with cheekpiece, full pistol-grip; beavertail forearm; not styled after standard Model 43. Introduced 1938; discontinued 1939.

Exc: $350 **VGood:** $275 **Good:** $175

MOSSBERG MODEL 44B
Bolt action; target configuration; 22 LR; 7-shot clip magazine; 26-inch heavy barrel; 43-inch overall length; weighs 8-1/2 lbs.; micrometer receiver peep sight, hooded front; speed lock; thumb safety; grooved adjustable trigger; walnut target stock with cheekpiece, full pistol grip; beavertail forearm; adjustable sling swivels. Introduced 1938; discontinued 1943.

Exc: $350 **VGood:** $280 **Good:** $175

MOSSBERG MODEL 44US
Bolt action; 22 LR; 7-shot detachable box magazine; 26-inch heavy barrel; 43-inch overall length; weighs 8-1/2 lbs.; same specs as Model 44B except designed primarily for teaching marksmanship to Armed Forces during World War II; uncheckered walnut target stock; sling swivels. Introduced 1943; discontinued 1948. Collector value.

Exc: $310 **VGood:** $260 **Good:** $150

U.S. Property marked

Exc: $400 **VGood:** $350 **Good:** $300

MOSSBERG MODEL 44US(A), 44US(B), 44US(C), 44US(D)
Same specs as Model 44US except minor changes in sights and extractors.

Exc: $310 **VGood:** $260 **Good:** $150

U.S. Property marked

Exc: $400 **VGood:** $350 **Good:** $300

MOSSBERG MODEL 45
Bolt action; 22 Short, 22 Long, 22 LR; 15-shot tube magazine (22 LR), 18-shot (22 Long), 22-shot (22 Short); 24-inch heavy barrel; 42-1/2-inch overall length; weighs 6-3/4 lbs.; take-down, repeater; receiver peep sight, open rear, hooded ramp front; uncheckered pistol-grip stock; sling swivels. Introduced 1935; discontinued 1937.

Exc: $250 **VGood:** $200 **Good:** $150

MOSSBERG MODEL 45A
Same specs as Model 45 except improved version of discontinued Model 45 with Master action, minor design variations. Introduced 1937; discontinued 1938.

Exc: $250 **VGood:** $200 **Good:** $150

MOSSBERG MODEL 45AC
Same specs as Model 45A except without receiver peep sight.

Exc: $225 **VGood:** $175 **Good:** $150

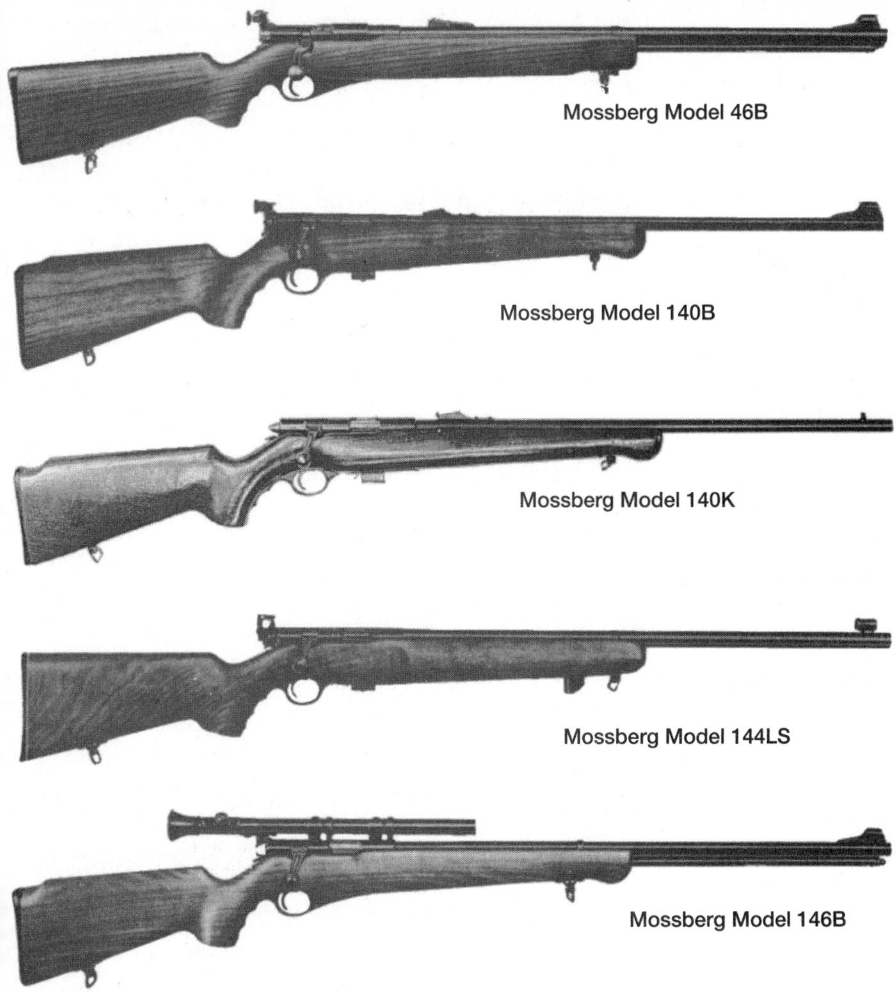
Mossberg Model 46B

Mossberg Model 140B

Mossberg Model 140K

Mossberg Model 144LS

Mossberg Model 146B

MOSSBERG MODEL 45B
Same specs as Model 45A except open rear sight. Introduced 1938; discontinued 1940.
Exc: $225 **VGood:** $175 **Good:** $150

MOSSBERG MODEL 45C
Same specs as Model 45 except no sights; designed for use only with scope sight.
Exc: $225 **VGood:** $175 **Good:** $150

MOSSBERG MODEL L45A
Same specs as Model 45A except left-hand action. Introduced 1937; discontinued 1938.
Exc: $275 **VGood:** $200 **Good:** $150

MOSSBERG MODEL 46
Bolt action; 22 Short, 22 Long, 22 LR; 15-shot (22 LR), 18-shot (22 Long), 22-shot (22 Short) tube magazine; 26-inch barrel; 44-1/2-inch overall length; weighs 7-1/2 lbs.; takedown repeater; micrometer rear peep sight; hooded ramp front; uncheckered walnut pistol-grip stock with cheekpiece; beavertail forearm; sling swivels. Introduced 1935; discontinued 1937.
Exc: $275 **VGood:** $200 **Good:** $150

MOSSBERG MODEL 46A
Same specs as discontinued Model 46 with Master action and minor design improvements; detachable sling swivels. Introduced 1937; discontinued 1938.
Exc: $275 **VGood:** $200 **Good:** $150

MOSSBERG MODEL 46AC
Same specs as Model 46A except open rear sight instead of micrometer peep sight.
Exc: $275 **VGood:** $200 **Good:** $150

MOSSBERG MODEL 46A-LS
Same specs as Model 46A except equipped with factory-supplied Lyman No. 57 receiver sight.
Exc: $300 **VGood:** $250 **Good:** $175

MOSSBERG MODEL 46B
Same specs as Model 46A except receiver peep and open rear sights. Introduced 1938; discontinued 1940.
Exc: $275 **VGood:** $200 **Good:** $150

MOSSBERG MODEL 46BT
Same specs as Model 46B except heavier barrel; target-styled stock. Introduced 1938; discontinued 1939.
Exc: $275 **VGood:** $200 **Good:** $150

MOSSBERG MODEL 46C
Same specs as Model 46 except heavier barrel.
Exc: $275 **VGood:** $200 **Good:** $150

MOSSBERG MODEL 46M
Same specs as Model 46 except 23-inch barrel; 40-inch overall length; weighs 7 lbs.; micrometer receiver peep sight, open rear, hooded ramp front; two-piece Mannlicher-type stock with pistol grip, cheekpiece; sling swivels. Introduced 1940; discontinued 1952.
Exc: $275 **VGood:** $200 **Good:** $150

MOSSBERG MODEL 46M(A), 46M(B)
Same specs as Model 46M except minor sight changes.
Exc: $275 **VGood:** $200 **Good:** $150

MOSSBERG MODEL 46T
Same specs as Model 46 except heavier barrel and stock; target version. Introduced 1936; discontinued 1937.
Exc: $275 **VGood:** $200 **Good:** $150

MOSSBERG MODEL L46A-LS
Same specs as Model 46A-LS except left-hand action.
Exc: $325 **VGood:** $275 **Good:** $200

MOSSBERG MODEL 140B
Bolt action; 22 Short, 22 Long, 22 LR; 7-shot clip magazine; 24-1/2-inch barrel; 42-inch overall length; weighs 5-3/4 lbs.; target/sporter version of Model 140K; peep rear sight, ramp front. Introduced 1957; discontinued 1958
Exc: $150 **VGood:** $125 **Good:** $100

MOSSBERG MODEL 140K
Same specs as Model 140B except uncheckered walnut pistol-grip stock; Monte Carlo with cheekpiece; open rear sight, bead front; sling swivels. Introduced 1955; discontinued 1958.
Exc: $150 **VGood:** $125 **Good:** $100

MOSSBERG MODEL 142
Bolt action; 22 Short, 22 Long, 22 LR; 7-shot removable box magazine; 18-inch tapered barrel; 36-inch overall length; weighs 5 lbs.; rear fully-adjustable peep sight, military-style ramp front; walnut Monte Carlo pistol-grip stock; as with Model 152, sling swivels, sling mount on left side of stock; forearm hinges down to act as handgrip. Some barrels marked 142A. Introduced 1949; discontinued 1957.
Exc: $245 **VGood:** $175 **Good:** $125

MOSSBERG MODEL 142K
Same specs as Model 142 except peep sight is replaced by open rear sight. Introduced 1953; discontinued 1957.
Exc: $225 **VGood:** $165 **Good:** $95

MOSSBERG MODEL 144
Bolt action; 22 LR; 26-inch heavy barrel; 7-shot detachable clip magazine; 43-inch overall length; weighs 8 lbs.; target model; micrometer receiver peep sight, hooded front; pistol-grip target stock; grooved trigger; grooved receiver for Mossberg No. 4M4 scope; thumb safety; T-shaped bolt handle; adjustable hand stop; beavertail forearm; sling swivels. Introduced 1949; discontinued 1954.
Exc: $275 **VGood:** $215 **Good:** $200

MOSSBERG MODEL 144LS
Same specs as Model 144 except Lyman No. 57MS receiver peep sight, Lyman No. 17A front. Introduced 1954; discontinued 1960.
Exc: $300 **VGood:** $250 **Good:** $200

MOSSBERG MODEL 144LS-A
Same specs as Model 144LS except Mossberg 330 rear peep sight. Introduced 1960; discontinued 1978.
Exc: $300 **VGood:** $160 **Good:** $120

MOSSBERG MODEL 144LS-B (TARGET)
Same specs as Model 144 except 27-inch round barrel; Lyman 17A hooded front sight with inserts, Mossberg 5331 receiver peep sight; target-style American walnut stock; adjustable forend hand stop. Introduced 1978; discontinued 1985.
Exc: $300 **VGood:** $260 **Good:** $200

MOSSBERG MODEL 146B
Bolt action; 22 Short, 22 Long, 22 LR; 20-shot (22 LR), 23-shot (22 Long), 30-shot (22 Short) tube magazine; 26-inch barrel; 43-1/4-inch overall length; weighs 7 lbs.; takedown repeater; micrometer fully-adjustable peep rear sight on receiver, hooded front sight, open fully-adjustable rear; uncheckered walnut pistol-grip Monte Carlo-type stock with cheekpiece; adjustable trigger; moulded finger-groove trigger guard; schnabel forearm; sling swivels. Introduced 1949; discontinued 1954.
Exc: $275 **VGood:** $200 **Good:** $125

MOSSBERG MODEL 146B-A
Same specs as Model 146B except different sights. Introduced 1954; discontinued 1958.
Exc: $275 **VGood:** $200 **Good:** $125

MOSSBERG MODEL 320B
Bolt action; single shot; 22 LR, 22 Short, 22 Long; 24-inch tapered barrel; 43-1/2-inch overall length; weighs 5-3/4 lbs.; hooded ramp front, rear target precision peep sight; automatic safety; hammerless; walnut pistol-grip Monte Carlo stock; sling swivels.

Designated by manufacturer as a Boy Scout target model. Introduced 1960; discontinued 1971.

Exc: $125 **VGood:** $90 **Good:** $70

MOSSBERG MODEL 320K

Same specs as Model 320B except open sights; no sling swivels; drop-in loading platform; automatic safety. Introduced 1958; discontinued 1960.

Exc: $125 **VGood:** $100 **Good:** $75

MOSSBERG MODEL 320K-A

Same specs as Model 320K.

Exc: $125 **VGood:** $100 **Good:** $75

MOSSBERG MODEL 320TR TARGO RIFLE/SHOTGUN

Bolt action; single shot; 22 Short, 22 Long, 22 LR; smoothbore with interchangeable rifled and smoothbore barrel adapters; adjustable open rear sight, blade front; sold with Model 1A hand trap thrower. Introduced 1961; discontinued 1962.

Exc: $500 **VGood:** $400 **Good:** $300

MOSSBERG MODEL 321B

Bolt action; single shot; 22 Short, 22 Long, 22 LR; 24-inch barrel; 43-1/2-inch overall length; weighs 6-1/2 lbs.; S330 peep sight with 1/4-minute click adjustments; hardwood stock with walnut finish; cheekpiece; checkered pistol grip, forearm; hammerless bolt-action with drop-in loading platform; automatic safety. Discontinued 1976.

Exc: $125 **VGood:** $100 **VGood:** $75

MOSSBERG MODEL 321K

Same specs as Model 321B except adjustable open rear sight, ramp front. Introduced 1972; no longer in production.

Exc: $125 **VGood:** $100 **VGood:** $75

MOSSBERG MODEL 340B, 340B-A

Bolt action; 22 Short, 22 Long, 22 LR; 7-shot box magazine; 24-inch barrel; 43-1/2-inch overall length; weighs 6-1/2 lbs.; hammerless; rear precision target peep sight, hooded ramp front; walnut Monte Carlo stock with cheekpiece, pistol-grip; buttplate white line spacer. Introduced 1958; no longer in production.

Exc: $125 **VGood:** $90 **VGood:** $60

MOSSBERG MODEL 340K, 340K-A

Same specs as Model 340B except for open rear sight, bead front. Introduced 1958; discontinued 1971.

Exc: $100 **VGood:** $80 **Good:** $50

MOSSBERG MODEL 340M

Same specs as Model 340K except for 18-1/2-inch barrel; 38-1/2-inch overall length; weighs 5-1/4 lbs.; one-piece Mannlicher-style Monte Carlo pistol-grip stock; sling; sling swivels. Introduced 1970; discontinued 1971.

Exc: $230 **VGood:** $180 **Good:** $130

MOSSBERG MODEL 340TR TARGO RIFLE/SHOTGUN

Bolt action; 22 Short, 22 Long, 22 LR; 22LR-shot; smoothbore; rifled and choke adapters screw into muzzle for shooting bullets or shot. Smoothbore was designed for short-range trap shooting; the special Mossberg trap could be fastened to the barrel to allow the shooter to throw his own miniature targets. Introduced 1961; discontinued 1962.

Exc: $300 **VGood:** $175 **Good:** $275

MOSSBERG MODEL 341

Bolt action; 22 Short, 22 Long, 22 LR; 7-shot clip magazine; 24-inch barrel; 43-1/2-inch overall length; weighs 6-1/2 lbs.; fully-adjustable open rear sight, bead post ramp front; walnut Monte Carlo stock with cheekpiece; checkered pistol grip, forearm; plastic buttplate with white line spacer; sliding side safety; sling swivels. Introduced 1972; discontinued 1976.

Exc: $150 **VGood:** $125 **Good:** $100

MOSSBERG MODEL 342

Bolt action; 22 Short, 22 Long, 22 LR; 7-shot clip magazine; 18-inch tapered barrel; hammerless action; peep rear sight, bead front; receiver grooved for scope mounts; uncheckered walnut Monte Carlo pistol-grip stock; two-position forearm that folds down for rest or handgrip; thumb safety; sling swivels; web sling. Introduced 1957; discontinued 1959.

Exc: $175 **VGood:** $125 **VGood:** $100

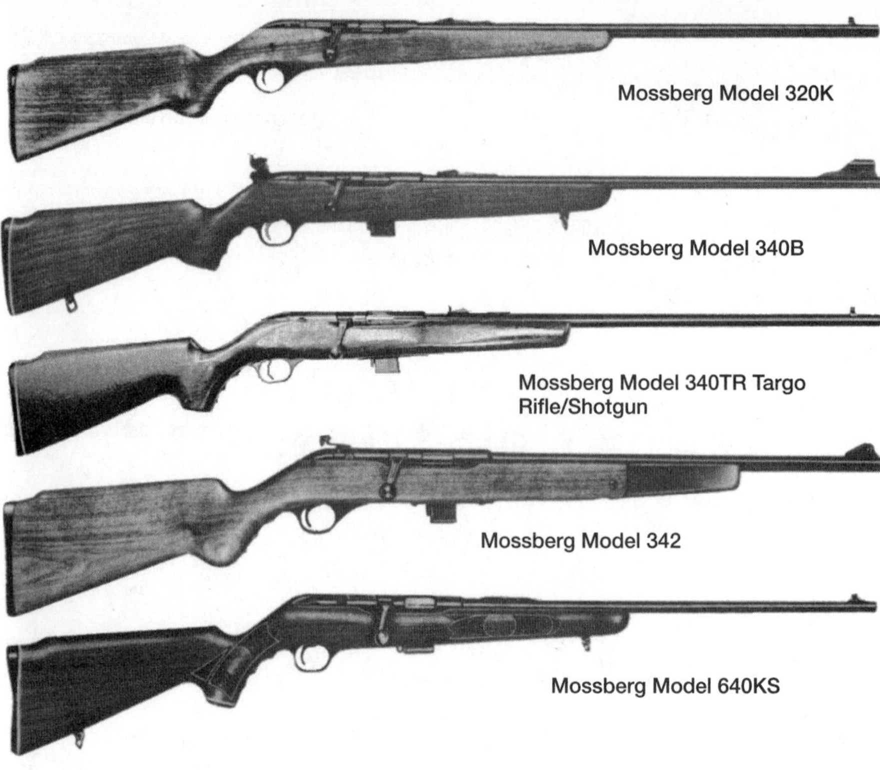

Mossberg Model 320K

Mossberg Model 340B

Mossberg Model 340TR Targo Rifle/Shotgun

Mossberg Model 342

Mossberg Model 640KS

MOSSBERG MODEL 342K, 342K-A

Same specs as Model 342 except with open rear sight. Introduced 1958; discontinued 1971.

Exc: $175 **VGood:** $125 **Good:** $100

MOSSBERG MODEL 344

Bolt action; 22 LR; 7-shot clip magazine; walnut finished, checkered stock. Introduced 1985.

Exc: $150 **VGood:** $125 **Good:** $100

MOSSBERG MODEL 344K

Same specs as Model 344 except carbine length.

Exc: $150 **VGood:** $125 **Good:** $100

MOSSBERG MODEL 346B

Bolt action; 22 Short, 22 Long, 22 LR; 18-shot tube magazine (22 LR), 20-shot (22 Long), 25-shot (22 Short); 24-inch barrel; hammerless action; triple sight combination; hooded ramp front, receiver peep with open rear sight; uncheckered walnut stock with pistol grip; Monte Carlo comb; cheekpiece; quick-detachable sling swivels. Introduced 1958; discontinued 1967.

Exc: $175 **VGood:** $150 **Good:** $100

MOSSBERG MODEL 346K, 346K-A

Same specs as Model 346B except open rear sight, bead front. Introduced 1958; discontinued 1971.

Exc: $150 **VGood:** $125 **Good:** $100

MOSSBERG MODEL 620K, 620K-A

Bolt action; single shot; 22 WMR; 24-inch barrel; 44-3/4-inch overall length; weighs 6 lbs.; fully-adjustable open rear sight, bead front; extra heavy duty receiver and bolt; grooved trigger; thumb safety; receiver grooved for scope mounts; hammerless action; walnut Monte Carlo pistol-grip stock with cheekpiece; sling swivels; impressed checkering on pistol-grip, forearm. Introduced 1958; discontinued 1974.

Exc: $150 **VGood:** $125 **Good:** $100

MOSSBERG MODEL 640K

Bolt action; 22 WMR; 5-shot detachable box magazine; 24-inch barrel; 44-3/4-inch overall length; weighs 6 lbs.; hammerless action; fully-adjustable open rear sight, bead front; receiver grooved for scope mounts; extra heavy duty receiver and bolt; grooved trigger; thumb safety; walnut Monte Carlo pistol-grip stock with cheekpiece; open rear sight, bead front; sling swivels; impressed checkering on pistol grip, forearm. Called the "Chuckster". Introduced 1959; no longer in production.

Exc: $175 **VGood:** $125 **Good:** $100

MOSSBERG MODEL 640KS

Same specs as Model 640K except select walnut stock, checkered pistol grip, forearm; gold-plated front sight, rear sight elevator and trigger. Discontinued 1974.

Exc: $200 **VGood:** $150 **VGood:** $125

MOSSBERG MODEL 640M

Same specs as Model 640K except full-length checkered Monte Carlo Mannlicher stock; 20-inch barrel; heavy receiver; jeweled bolt. Manufactured 1971.

Exc: $275 **VGood:** $200 **Good:** $150

MOSSBERG MODEL 642K

Bolt action; 22 WMR; 5-shot box magazine; 18-inch barrel; 38-1/4-inch overall length; weighs 5 lbs.; bead front sight, fully-adjustable open rear; fold-down forend; walnut Monte Carlo pistol-grip stock; grip cap and buttplate white line spacers; web sling. Introduced 1960; discontinued 1968.

Exc: $275 **VGood:** $200 **Good:** $150

MOSSBERG MODEL 800

Bolt action; 222 Rem., 22-250, 243 Win., 308 Win.; 4-shot magazine, 3-shot (22-250); 22-inch barrel; 42-inch overall length; weighs 6-1/2 lbs.; folding-leaf rear sight, ramp front; checkered pistol-grip Monte Carlo stock, forearm; recessed bolt head with six locking lugs; top tang safety; hinged floorplate with button release; cheekpiece; sling swivels. Manufactured 1967; discontinued 1980.

Exc: $350 **VGood:** $300 **Good:** $250

MOSSBERG MODEL 800D SUPER GRADE

Same specs as Model 800 except 22-250, 243 Win., 308 Win.; Monte Carlo stock with roll-over comb,

Mossberg Model 800

Mossberg Model 800M

Mossberg Model 800VT

Mossberg Model 810

Mossberg Model 1500 Mountaineer Deluxe

Mossberg Model RM-7A

cheekpiece; rosewood forend tip, pistol-grip cap; hand-Damascened bolt. Manufactured 1970 to 1973.

Exc: $375 **VGood:** $325 **Good:** $250

MOSSBERG MODEL 800M

Same specs as Model 800 except 20-inch barrel; 40-inch overall length; 22-250, 243 Win., 308 Win.; full-length Mannlicher-type stock; flat bolt handle. Manufactured 1969 to 1972.

Exc: $350 **VGood:** $300 **Good:** $250

MOSSBERG MODEL 800SM

Same specs as Model 800 except weighs 7-1/2 lbs.; equipped with Mossberg Model 84 4x scope.

Exc: $350 **VGood:** $300 **Good:** $250

MOSSBERG MODEL 800VT

Same specs as Model 800 except varmint/target model; 222 Rem., 22-250, 243 Win.; 24-inch heavy barrel; weighs 9-1/2 lbs.; 44-inch overall length; no sights; Marksman-style stock; scope mount blocks. Manufactured 1968 to 1980.

Exc: $350 **VGood:** $300 **Good:** $250

MOSSBERG MODEL 810, 810A

Bolt action; 270 Win., 30-06, 7mm Rem. Mag., 338 Win. Mag.; 4-shot (standard calibers), 3-shot (magnum calibers) detachable or internal magazine; 22-inch barrel (standard calibers), 24-inch (magnum calibers); 42-inch overall length; weighs 7-1/2-8 lbs.; folding leaf rear sight, ramp front with gold bead, fully-adjustable folding leaf middle sight; receiver drilled, tapped for peep or scope; hinged floorplate; checkered pistol-grip walnut stock, forearm; Monte Carlo comb, cheekpiece; pistol-grip cap; recoil pad with white liners; sling swivels. Manufactured 1970 to 1980.

Standard calibers

Exc: $350 **VGood:** $275 **Good:** $250

Magnum calibers

Exc: $375 **VGood:** $300 **Good:** $250

MOSSBERG MODEL 810ASM

Same Specs as Model 810 except 30-06; no sights; comes fitted with Mossberg Model 84 4x scope. Introduced 1972.

Exc: $350 **VGood:** $300 **Good:** $250

MOSSBERG MODEL 810B

Same specs as Model 810 except 24-inch barrel; 44-inch overall length. Introduced 1972.

Exc: $350 **VGood:** $300 **Good:** $250

MOSSBERG MODEL 810BSM

Same specs as Model 810B except 7mm Rem. Mag.; no sights; comes fitted with Mossberg Model 84 4x scope. Introduced 1972.

Exc: $350 **VGood:** $300 **Good:** $215

MOSSBERG MODEL 810C

Same specs as Model 810 except 270 Win. Introduced 1973.

Exc: $350 **VGood:** $300 **Good:** $215

MOSSBERG MODEL 810D

Same specs as Model 810 except 338 Win. Mag. Introduced 1973.

Exc: $350 **VGood:** $300 **Good:** $215

MOSSBERG MODEL 1500 MOUNTAINEER

Bolt action; 222, 223, 22-250, 243, 25-06, 270, 30-06, 308, 7mm Rem. Mag., 300 Win. Mag., 338 Win. Mag., 22-inch, 24-inch barrel; weighs 7-1/2 lbs.; open round-notch adjustable rear sight, hooded ramp gold bead front; American walnut stock; Monte Carlo comb, cheekpiece; cut checkering; single-unit triggerguard/magazine box; hinged floorplate; swivel studs; composition buttplate; magnums with rubber recoil pad. Made in Japan by Howa. Originally marketed by S&W. Introduced 1979; discontinued 1987.

Standard calibers

Exc: $300 **VGood:** $250 **Good:** $220

Magnum calibers

Exc: $350 **VGood:** $310 **Good:** $270

MOSSBERG MODEL 1500 MOUNTAINEER DELUXE

Same specs as Model 1500 except sans sights; engine-turned bolt; decorated floorplate with scrollwork; skip-line checkering; sling, swivels, swivel posts included; magnum models with vent, recoil pad.

Standard calibers

Exc: $350 **VGood:** $300 **Good:** $250

Magnum calibers

Exc: $370 **VGood:** $320 **Good:** $270

MOSSBERG MODEL 1500 MOUNTAINEER VARMINT DELUXE

Same specs as Model 1500 except 222, 22-250, 223, 308; 24-inch heavy barrel; no sights; fully-adjustable trigger; skip-line checkering; quick-detachable swivels. Originally marketed by S&W. Introduced 1986; discontinued by Mossberg, 1987.

Exc: $370 **VGood:** $310 **Good:** $280

MOSSBERG MODEL 1550

Bolt action; 243, 270, 30-06; box magazine; 22-inch, 24-inch barrel; weighs 7-1/2 lbs.; with or without sights; American walnut stock; Monte Carlo comb, cheekpiece; cut checkering; swivel studs; composition buttplate; magnums with rubber recoil pad. Made in Japan by Howa. Introduced 1986; discontinued 1987.

Exc: $330 **VGood:** $280 **Good:** $250

MOSSBERG MODEL 1700LS

Bolt action; 243, 270, 30-06; 22-inch barrel; 4-shot removable box magazine; classic-style stock; tapered forend; schnabel tip; hand-checkering; black rubber buttpad; flush-mounted sling swivels; jeweled bolt body. Marketed as Classic Hunter. Made in Japan. Originally marketed by S&W. Introduced 1986; discontinued 1987.

Exc: $400 **VGood:** $350 **Good:** $275

MOSSBERG MODEL B

Bolt action; single shot; 22 Short, 22 Long, 22 LR; 22-inch barrel; take-down; uncheckered pistol-grip walnut stock. Introduced 1930; discontinued 1932.

Exc: $125 **VGood:** $100 **Good:** $75

MOSSBERG MODEL C

Bolt action; single shot; 22 Short, 22 Long, 22 LR; 24-inch barrel; ivory bead front sight, open sporting rear. Introduced 1931; discontinued 1932.

Exc: $125 **VGood:** $100 **Good:** $75

MOSSBERG MODEL C-1

Same specs as Model C except Lyman front and rear sights; leather sling, swivels.

Exc: $150 **VGood:** $125 **Good:** $100

MOSSBERG MODEL R

Bolt action; 22 Short, 22 Long, 22 LR; 24-inch barrel; tube magazine; take-down; open rear sight, bead front; uncheckered pistol-grip stock. Introduced 1930; discontinued 1932.

Exc: $200 **VGood:** $150 **Good:** $125

MOSSBERG MODEL RM-7A

Bolt action; 30-06; 22-inch barrel; 5-shot magazine; gold bead front sight on ramp, adjustable folding leaf rear; drilled, tapped for scope mounts; classic-style checkered pistol-grip stock of American walnut; rotary magazine; three-position bolt safety; sling swivel studs. Introduced 1978; discontinued 1981. Few made.

Perf: $500 **Exc:** $400 **VGood:** $300

MOSSBERG MODEL RM-7B
Same specs as Model RM-7A except 7mm Rem. Mag.; 4-shot magazine; 24-inch barrel; 45-1/4-inch overall length. Introduced 1978; discontinued 1981. Very rare.

Perf: $550 **Exc:** $450 **VGood:** $350

MOSSBERG MODEL 50
Semi-automatic; 22 LR; 24-inch barrel; 15-shot tube magazine in buttstock; 43-3/4-inch overall length; weighs 6-3/4 lbs.; takedown; open rear sight, hooded ramp front; uncheckered walnut pistol-grip stock; finger grooves in grip; no sling swivels. Introduced 1939; discontinued 1942.

Exc: $200 **VGood:** $150 **VGood:** $125

MOSSBERG MODEL 51
Semi-automatic; 22 LR; 15-shot tube magazine; 24-inch barrel; 43-3/4-inch overall length; weighs 7-1/4 lbs.; receiver peep sight; sling swivels; cheekpiece stock; heavy beavertail forearm. Made only in 1939.

Exc: $200 **VGood:** $150 **Good:** $125

MOSSBERG MODEL 51M
Same specs as Model 51 except 20-inch round tapered barrel; 40-inch overall length; weighs 7 lbs.; two-piece Mannlicher-style stock. Introduced 1939; discontinued 1946.

Exc: $275 **VGood:** $200 **Good:** $150

MOSSBERG MODEL 151K
Semi-automatic; 22LR; 24-inch tapered barrel; 44-inch overall length; weighs 6 lbs.; no peep sight; sling swivels; uncheckered sporting stock; Monte Carlo comb; cheekpiece; schnabel forearm. Introduced 1950; discontinued 1951.

Exc: $275 **VGood:** $200 **VGood:** $150

MOSSBERG MODEL 151M
Semi-automatic; 22 LR; 15-shot tube magazine; 20-inch barrel; 40-inch overall length; weighs 7 lbs.; No. S101 hooded ramp front, No. S107 open sporting rear or No. S130 micro-click adjustable rear; two-piece Mannlicher stock; sling swivels; steel buttplate. Introduced 1946; discontinued 1958.

Exc: $275 **VGood:** $200 **VGood:** $150

MOSSBERG MODEL 151M(A), 151M(B), 151M(C)
Same specs as Model 151M except minor changes in sights and buttplate. Introduced 1947; discontinued 1958.

Exc: $275 **VGood:** $200 **VGood:** $150

MOSSBERG MODEL 152
Semi-automatic; 22 LR; 7-shot detachable box magazine; 18-inch barrel; 38-inch overall length; weighs 5 lbs.; rear peep sight, military-type ramp front; walnut Monte Carlo pistol-grip stock; hinged forearm swings down to act as forward handgrip; sling swivels and adjustable sling mounted on left side. Introduced 1948; discontinued 1957.

Exc: $250 **VGood:** $175 **VGood:** $125

MOSSBERG MODEL 152K
Same specs as Model 152 except open rear sight. Introduced 1950; discontinued 1957.

Exc: $225 **VGood:** $175 **VGood:** $125

MOSSBERG MODEL 333
Semi-automatic; 22 LR; 15-shot tubular magazine; 20-inch barrel; 39-1/2-inch overall length; weighs 6-1/4 lbs.; fully-adjustable open rear sight, beaded ramp front; checkered pistol-grip Monte Carlo American walnut stock, forearm; buttplate, pistol grip white line spacers; automatic bolt hold-open; tang safety; gold-plated, grooved trigger; Damascened bolt; receiver grooved for scope mounts; barrel band; sling swivels. Manufactured 1972 to 1973.

Exc: $175 **VGood:** $150 **Good:** $120

MOSSBERG MODEL 350K, 350K-A
Semi-automatic; 22 high-speed Short, 22 Long, 22 LR; 7-shot clip magazine; 23-1/2-inch barrel; 43-1/2-inch overall length; weighs 6 lbs.; fully-adjustable open rear sight with U-notch, bead front; receiver grooved for scope mount; walnut Monte Carlo pistol-grip stock. Introduced 1958; discontinued 1971.

Exc: $175 **VGood:** $150 **Good:** $120

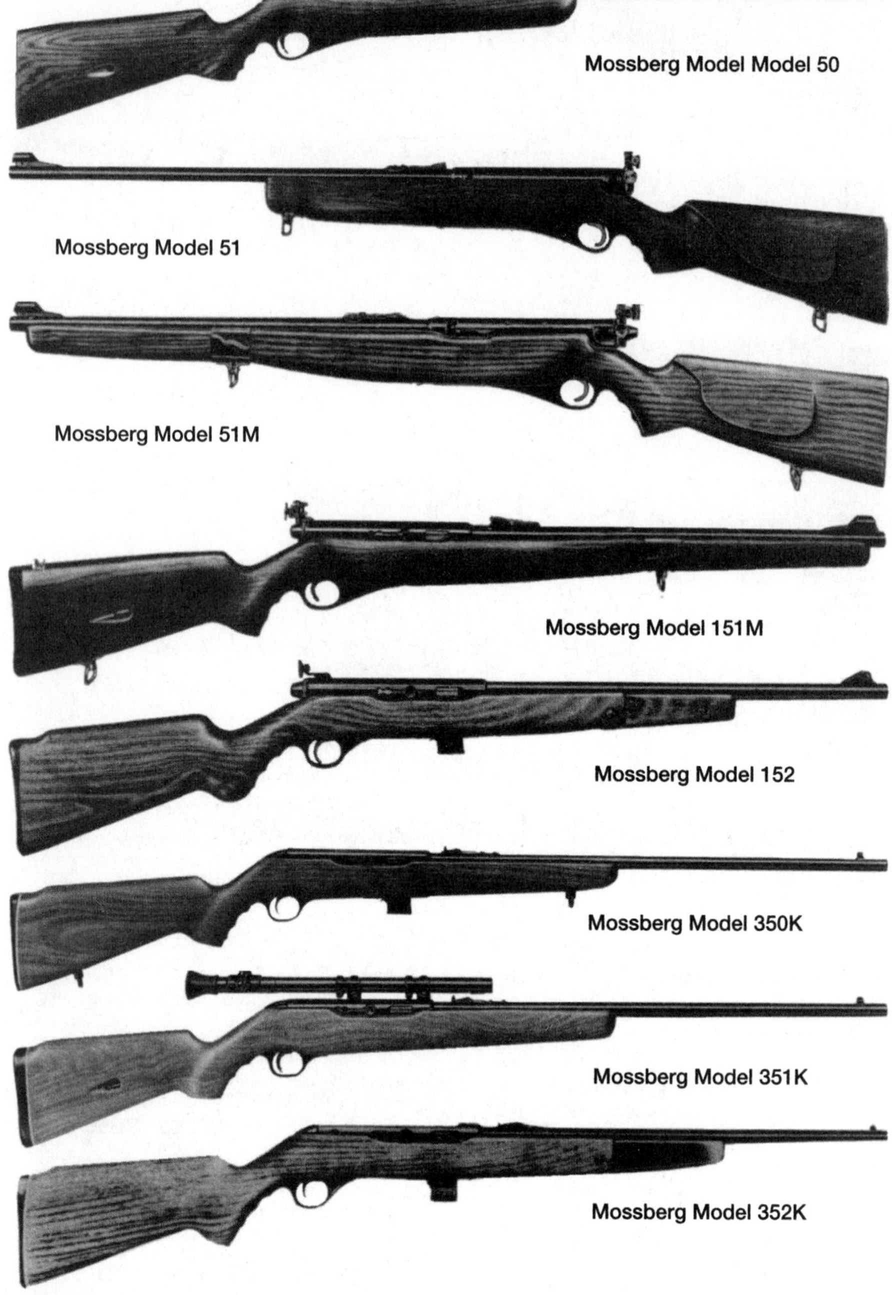

Mossberg Model Model 50

Mossberg Model 51

Mossberg Model 51M

Mossberg Model 151M

Mossberg Model 152

Mossberg Model 350K

Mossberg Model 351K

Mossberg Model 352K

MOSSBERG MODEL 351K, 351K-A
Semi-automatic; 22 LR; 15-shot tube magazine in buttstock; 24-inch barrel; 43-inch overall length; weighs 6 lbs.; fully-adjustable open rear sight with U-notch, bead front; receiver grooved for scope mount; walnut Monte Carlo pistol-grip stock. Introduced 1960; discontinued 1971.

Exc: $175 **VGood:** $150 **Good:** $120

MOSSBERG MODEL 351C
Same specs as Model 351K except 18-1/2-inch barrel; 38-1/2-inch overall length; weighs 5-1/2 lbs.; straight Western-type carbine stock with barrel band; sling swivels. Called the "Jack Rabbit Special." Introduced 1965; discontinued 1971.

Exc: $175 **VGood:** $150 **Good:** $120

MOSSBERG MODEL 352
Semi-automatic; 22 Short, 22 Long, 22 LR; 7-shot detachable box magazine; 18-inch barrel; 38-inch overall length; weighs 5 lbs.; peep rear sight, bead front; uncheckered walnut Monte Carlo pistol-grip stock; two-position Tenite forearm extension folds down for rest or hand grip; sling swivels; web sling. Introduced 1958; discontinued 1971.

Exc: $175 **VGood:** $150 **Good:** $120

MOSSBERG MODEL 352K, 352K-A, 352K-B
Same specs as Model 352 except with fully-adjustable open rear sight. Introduced 1960; discontinued 1971.

Perf: $175 **Exc:** $150 **VGood:** $120

MOSSBERG MODEL 353
Semi-automatic; 22 LR; 7-shot detachable box magazine; 18-inch barrel; 38-inch overall length; weighs 5 lbs.; fully-adjustable open rear sight, ramp front with bead; American walnut Monte Carlo Pistol-grip stock; black Tenite fold down forend extension; checkered pistol grip, forend; receiver grooved for scope mount; sling swivels, web strap on left side of stock. Introduced 1972.

Exc: $175 **VGood:** $150 **Good:** $120

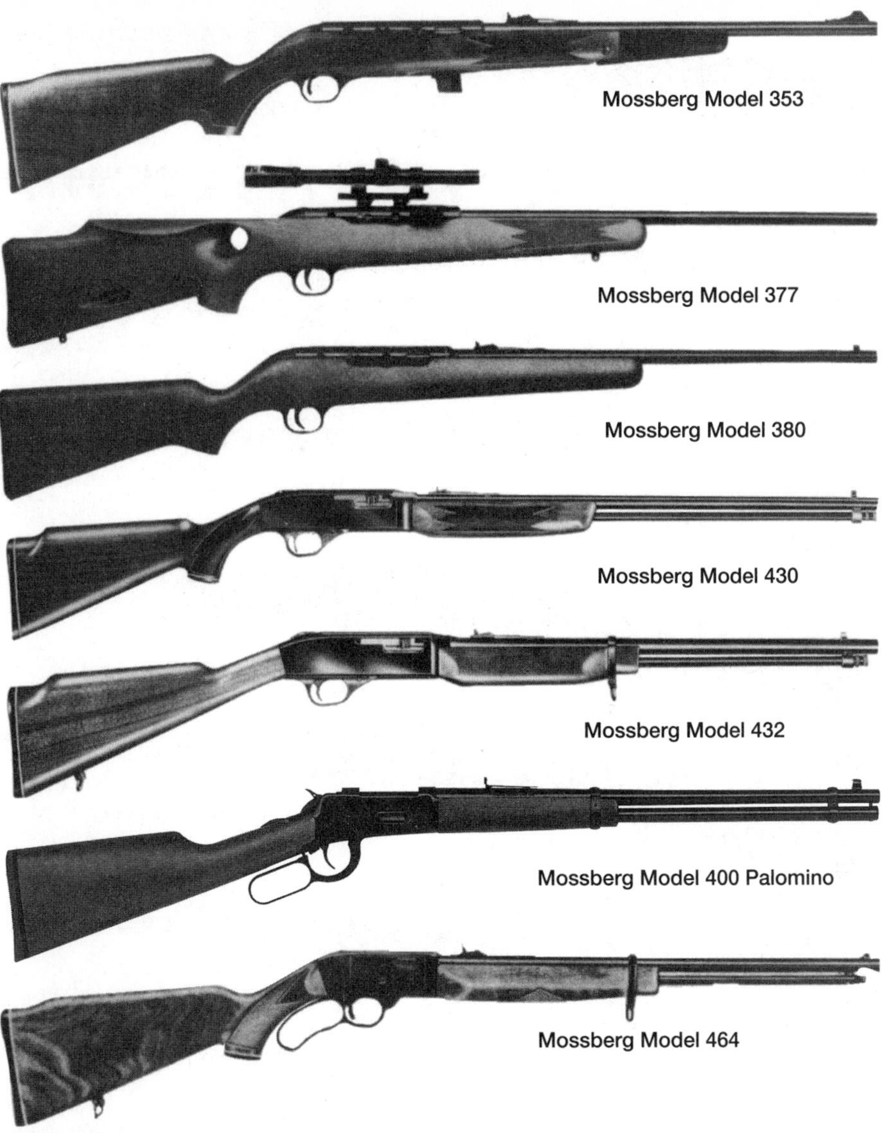
Mossberg Model 353

Mossberg Model 377

Mossberg Model 380

Mossberg Model 430

Mossberg Model 432

Mossberg Model 400 Palomino

Mossberg Model 464

MOSSBERG MODEL 377

Semi-automatic; 22 LR; 15-shot tubular magazine; 20-inch barrel; 40-inch overall length; weighs 6-1/4 lbs.; no open sights; 4x scope mounted; moulded polystyrene straight-line thumbhole stock; roll-over cheekpiece; Monte Carlo comb; checkered forearm. Advertised as the Plinkster. Introduced 1977; discontinued 1985.

Exc: $175 **VGood:** $150 **Good:** $120

MOSSBERG MODEL 380, 380S

Semi-automatic; 22 LR; 15-shot tubular magazine in stock; 20-inch tapered barrel; weighs about 5-1/2 lbs.; bead front sight, adjustable open rear; receiver grooved for scope mounting; walnut-finished hardwood stock; black plastic buttplate. Introduced 1981; discontinued 1985.

Exc: $175 **VGood:** $150 **Good:** $120

MOSSBERG MODEL 430

Semi-automatic; 22 LR; 18-shot tube magazine; 24-inch barrel; 43-1/2-inch overall length; weighs 6-1/4 lbs.; open rear sight, gold bead front; two-piece walnut Monte Carlo stock; checkered pistol grip, forearm; gold-plated, grooved trigger; Damascened bolt; buttplate, pistol grip cap white line spacers; top tang safety; hammerless action. Introduced 1970; discontinued 1971.

Exc: $175 **VGood:** $150 **Good:** $120

MOSSBERG MODEL 432

Semi-automatic; 22 LR; 15-shot magazine; 20-inch barrel; 39-1/2-inch overall length; weighs 6 lbs.; gold-plated, grooved trigger; Damascened bolt; buttplate, pistol grip white line spacers; top tang safety; hammerless action; carbine; uncheckered straight-grip carbine stock, forearm; barrel band; sling swivels. Introduced 1970; discontinued 1971.

Exc: $175 **VGood:** $150 **Good:** $120

MOSSBERG MODEL 400 PALOMINO

Lever action; 22 Short, 22 Long, 22 LR; 15-shot (22 LR), 17-shot (22 Long), 20-shot (22 Short) tube magazine; 24-inch barrel; 41-inch overall length; weighs 5-1/2 lbs.; fully-adjustable open notch rear sight, bead front; walnut Monte Carlo stock; moulded pistol-grip cap and buttplate; beavertail forearm; hammerless action; lightweight high-tensile alloy receiver; removable sideplate; grooved trigger; cross-bolt safety; blued finish; receiver grooved for scope. Introduced 1959; discontinued 1963.

Exc: $300 **VGood:** $225 **Good:** $150

MOSSBERG MODEL 402 PALOMINO

Same specs as Model 400 except 18-1/2-inch, 20-inch barrel; 36-1/2-inch overall length; weighs 4-3/4 lbs.; barrel band on forearm, sling swivels; magazine holds two fewer rounds in 22 Long, 22 LR lengths. Manufactured 1961 to 1971.

Exc: $300 **VGood:** $225 **VGood:** $150

MOSSBERG MODEL 472 CARBINE

Lever action; 30-30, 35 Rem.; 6-shot tubular magazine; 20-inch barrel; adjustable buckhorn rear sight, ramp front; with gold bead; barrel tapped for scope mounting; off-set hammer spur; side-ejecting; pistol-grip or straight stock; barrel band on forearm; sling swivels on pistol-grip style, removable saddle ring on straight-stock model. Manufactured 1972 to 1980.

Exc: $350 **VGood:** $300 **Good:** $230

MOSSBERG MODEL 472 BRUSH GUN

Same specs as Model 472 Carbine except 18-inch barrel; 30-30; 5-shot magazine; straight stock. Manufactured 1974 to 1976.

Exc: $375 **VGood:** $325 **Good:** $295

MOSSBERG MODEL 472 RIFLE

Same specs as Model 472 Carbine except 24-inch barrel; 5-shot magazine; pistol-grip stock only. Manufactured 1974 to 1976.

Exc: $350 **VGood:** $300 **Good:** $230

MOSSBERG MODEL 472 "1 OF 5000"

Same specs as Model 472 Brush Gun except etched Native American frontier scenes on receiver; gold-plated trigger; brass saddle ring, buttplate, barrel bands; select walnut stock forearm; limited edition, numbered 1 through 5000. Manufactured 1974.

Exc: $430 **VGood:** $255 **Good:** $200

MOSSBERG MODEL 479PC

Lever action; 30-30, 35 Rem.; 6-shot tube magazine; 20-inch barrel; 38-1/2-inch overall length; weighs 6-3/4-7 lbs.; ramp front sight, elevation-adjustable rear; American walnut stock with pistol grip and fluted comb; composition buttplate; pistol-grip cap; hammer-block safety; side ejection. Introduced 1978; discontinued 1981.

Exc: $325 **VGood:** $300 **Good:** $250

MOSSBERG MODEL 479PCA

Same specs as Model 479PC except 30-30 only; bead on ramp front sight, adjustable open rear; walnut-finished hardwood stock; rebounding hammer; trigger built into cocking lever; blued finish. Reintroduced 1983; no longer in production.

Exc: $325 **VGood:** $300 **Good:** $250

MOSSBERG MODEL 479RR ROY ROGERS

Same specs as Model 479PCA except 5-shot magazine; 18-inch barrel; 36-1/2-inch overall length; gold bead on ramp front sight, adjustable semi-buckhorn rear; American walnut stock; gold-finished trigger; barrel bands; Rogers' signature, American eagle, stars and stripes etched in receiver. 5000 guns produced only in 1983.

Perf: $375 **Exc:** $275 **VGood:** $225

MOSSBERG MODEL 479SC

Same specs as Model 479PC except straight grip stock. Introduced 1978; discontinued 1981.

Exc: $325 **VGood:** $300 **Good:** $250

MOSSBERG MODEL 464 LEVER ACTION CENTERFIRE RIFLE

Side-loading, top-ejecting lever rifle with button-rifled 20-inch barrel, blued finish and hardwood stock. Tang-mounted thumb safety. Chambered in .30-30.

NIB: $375 **Exc:** $275 **VGood:** $225

MOSSBERG MODEL 464 LEVER ACTION RIMFIRE RIFLE

A .22 LR version of the above with 18-inch barrel. 14-round tubular magazine.

NIB: $465 **Exc:** $365 **VGood:** $265

MOSSBERG MODEL K

Slide action; 22 Short, 22 Long, 22 LR; 14-shot (22 LR), 16-shot (22 Long), 20-shot (22 Short) tube magazine; 22-inch barrel; take-down; hammerless; open rear sight, bead front; uncheckered straight-grip walnut stock; grooved slide handle. Introduced 1922; discontinued 1931.

Exc: $350 **VGood:** $275 **Good:** $200

MOSSBERG MODEL L

Lever action, single shot, falling block; 22 Short, 22 Long, 22 LR; 24-inch barrel; take-down; Martini-design falling-block lever-action; open rear sight, bead front; uncheckered walnut pistol-grip stock, forearm. Introduced 1929; discontinued 1932. This is a very scarce Mossberg and would be the foundation or the finishing touch to any Mossberg collection.

Exc: $550 **VGood:** $450 **Good:** $325

MOSSBERG MODEL L-1

Same specs as Model L except target version with Lyman 2A tang sight; factory sling. Introduced about 1930; discontinued about 1931.

Exc: $575 **VGood:** $475 **Good:** $350

MOSSBERG MODEL M

Slide action; 22 Short, 22 Long, 22 LR; 14-shot (22 LR), 16-shot (22 Long), 20-shot (22 Short) tube magazine; 24-inch octagonal barrel; take-down; hammerless; open rear sight, bead front; uncheckered pistol-grip stock; grooved slide handle. Introduced 1928; discontinued 1931.

Exc: $350 **VGood:** $275 **Good:** $200

MOSSBERG MODEL S

Slide action; 22 Short, 22 Long, 22 LR; 19-3/4-inch barrel; similar to Model K except shorter magazine tube. Introduced 1927; dropped 1931.

Exc: $350 **VGood:** $275 **Good:** $200

MOSSBERG/NEW HAVEN MODEL 220K

Bolt action; single shot; 22 Short, 22 Long, 22 LR; 24-inch barrel with crowned muzzzle; weighs 5-3/4 lbs.; open adjustable rear sight, bead front; walnut finished Monte Carlo pistol-grip stock; hand-rubbed oil finish; automatic safety. Introduced 1961.

Exc: $125 **VGood:** $100 **Good:** $75

MOSSBERG/NEW HAVEN MODEL 240K

Bolt action; 22 Short, 22 Long, 22 LR; 24-inch barrel with crowned muzzle; fully-adjustable open rear sight, bead front; walnut finished Monte Carlo pistol-grip stock; hammerless; takedown; grooved trigger; thumb safety. Lower-priced version of the Mossberg Model 340K. Introduced 1961.

Exc: $125 **VGood:** $100 **Good:** $75

MOSSBERG/NEW HAVEN MODEL 246K

Bolt action; 22 Short, 22 Long, 22 LR; 25-shot (22 Short), 20-shot (22 Long), 18-shot (22 LR); 24-inch round tapered barrel with crowned muzzle; 43-1/4 overall length; weighs 6-1/4 lbs.; fully-adjustable open rear sight, sporting front; receiver grooved for scope mounts; tapped and drilled for Mossberg No. S-330 peep; hammerless; takedown; grooved trigger; thumb safety. A lower-priced version of the Mossberg Model 346K. Introduced 1961.

Exc: $150 **VGood:** $125 **Good:** $100

MOSSBERG/NEW HAVEN MODEL 250K

Semi-automatic; 22 LR; 7-shot detachable box magazine; 24-inch round tapered barrel; 44-inch overall length; weighs 5-1/2 lbs.; open adjustable rear sight, bead front; American walnut Monte Carlo stock with tapered forend; hand-rubbed oil finish; receiver grooved for scope mounting. A lower-priced version of the Mossberg Model 350K. Introduced 1960.

Exc: $150 **VGood:** $125 **Good:** $100

MOSSBERG/NEW HAVEN MODEL 250KB

Same specs as Model 250K except 22 Long, 22 LR; weighs 6 lbs.; Ac-Kro-Gruv rifling; fully-adjustable rear peep sight. Introduced 1961.

Exc: $150 **VGood:** $125 **Good:** $100

Mossberg Model 472 Carbine

Mossberg Model 479PC

Mossberg Model K

Mossberg Model L

Mossberg Model 702 Plinkster

Mossberg Model 817 Plinkster

Mossberg MVP Flex 7.62

Mossberg MVP Flex 5.56

Mossberg MVP Patrol

MOSSBERG MODEL 702 PLINKSTER

Semi-auto chambered for .22 LR. Black synthetic stock with schnabel forend; silver-finished barrel and receiver. Ten-shot magazine. Also available as scope package (add 10 percent) and with tiger maple or carbon fiber stock and chromed barrel and receiver.

NIB: $160 **Exc:** $125 **VGood:** $100

MOSSBERG MODEL 802 PLINKSTER BOLT ACTION

Bolt-action rifle chambered in .22 LR with 18-inch steel barrel and black synthetic stock with schnabel. Also available with 4X scope package (add 10 percent).

NIB: $160 **Exc:** $125 **VGood:** $100

MOSSBERG MODEL 817 PLINKSTER

Similar to Model 802 Plinkster but chambered in .17 HMR.

NIB: $175 **Exc:** $150 **VGood:** $125

MODEL 817 VARMINT

Introduced in 2008, this offering by Mossberg International features a 21-inch free-floating blued or brushed chrome barrel, hardwood or black synthetic stock, factory Weaver mounts, detachable box magazine and .17 HMR chambering.

NIB: $235 **Exc:** $175 **VGood:** $115

MOSSBERG MVP FLEX

Bolt-action centerfire rifle in 5.56 & 7.62 NATO. 18.5 or 20 inch barrel with or without threaded muzzle

Mossberg MVP Predator 5.56

Mossberg MVP Predator 7.62

Mossberg MVP Varmint 5.56

Mossberg MVP Thunder Ranch

Mossberg SSi-One

Mossberg Model 100 ATR

M-S Safari Arms 1000-Yard Match Model

M-S Safari Arms Silhouette Model

and flash hider on 18.5 inch barrel. Synthetic FLEX system stock, 6.5 pounds, 35.75 to 38.5 inches. Feeds from any capacity AR 15 style magazines (5.56 NATO) or AR 10 / M14 magazines (7.62 NATO). Spiral fluted bolt, LBA trigger, no sights, one-piece scope rail included. Variations exist.

Perf: $850 **Exc:** $700 **VGood:** $625

MOSSBERG MVP PATROL

Bolt-action centerfire rifle in 5.56 & 7.62 NATO and .300 Blackout. 16.25 inch barrel with or without threaded muzzle and flash hider. Synthetic stock, 7 pounds, .35.25 inches. Feeds from any capacity AR 15 style magazines (5.56 NATO / .300 Blackout) or AR 10 / M14 magazines (7.62 NATO). Spiral fluted bolt, adjustable fiber optic sights and one-piece scope rail included.

Perf: $600 **Exc:** $525 **VGood:** $480

MOSSBERG MVP PREDATOR/ VARMINT

Bolt-action centerfire rifle in 5.56 or 7.62 NATO. 18.5 or 20 inch barrel (7.62 NATO), 18.5, 20, or 24 inch barrel (5.56 NATO). Varmint version in 5.56 NATO has a target style laminated stock. Predator versions in both 5.56 NATO or 7.62 NATO have sporter style laminated stocks. Measurements; 8.0 pounds, 37.5 to 39.0 inches (Predator version), 9.25 pounds, 43 inches (Varmint 5.56 NATO version.) Feeds from any capacity AR 15 style magazine (5.56 NATO) or AR 10 / M14 magazine (7.62 NATO). Spiral fluted bolt, LBA trigger, no sights, two-piece scope bases included.

Perf: $770 **Exc:** $690 **VGood:** $620

MOSSBERG MVP THUNDER RANCH SERIES

Bolt-action centerfire rifle in 5.56 NATO. 18.5 inch fluted, threaded barrel with protector. Measurements; 8.25 pounds, 37.5 inches. Feeds from any capacity AR 15 style magazine. Spiral fluted bolt, LBA trigger, no sights, one-piece scope base, green synthetic stock with Thunder Ranch logo.

Perf: $875 **Exc:** $800 **VGood:** $725

MOSSBERG SSI-ONE

Lever action, single shot, breakopen; 223 Rem., 22-250 Rem., 243 Win., 270 Win., 308 Rem., 30-06; 24-inch barrel; weighs 8 lbs.; 40-inch long; Satin-finished walnut stock, fluted and checkered; sling-swivel studs. no sights (scope base furnished); Frame accepts interchangeable barrels, including 12- gauge, fully rifled slug barrel and 12 ga., 3-1/2-inch chambered barrel with Ulti- Full Turkey choke tube. Lever-opening, break-action design; single-stage trigger; ambidextrous, top-tang safety; internal eject/extract selector. Introduced 2000, no longer in production.

SSi-One Sporter (standard barrel)

Perf: $450 **Exc:** $350 **VGood:** $250

SSi-One Varmint (bull barrel, 22-250 Rem. only.

Perf: $475 **Exc:** $375 **VGood:** $270

MOSSBERG MODEL 100 ATR (ALL TERRAIN RIFLE)

Bolt-action rifle chambered in .243 Win, .270 Win, .30-06, or .308 Win. 22" free-floated barrel, matte blue or Marinecote, wood, black synth, Durawood synthetic or 100 percent Mossy Oak Break Up camo coverage stock with recoil pad, three-shot top loading magazine. Weight around 7 lbs. Also available as 3X9 scope package (add 10 percent).

NIB: $300 **Exc:** $260 **VGood:** $190

MOSSBERG 100 ATR SUPER BANTAM

Similar to Model 100 ATR but chambered only in .243 and .308. No sights. Synthetic black stock adjustable for length of pull.

NIB: $275 **Exc:** $230 **VGood:** $175

MOSSBERG 4X4 RIFLE

Bolt-action centerfire rifle chambered in .25-06, .270, .30-06, 7mm Rem Mag, .300 Win Mag, .338 Win Mag. Barrel length 22" (iron sight) or 24" (sightless). Detachable box magazine, two-position safety. Walnut, laminated or black synthetic stock with lightening cutouts in butt and forend. Scope package also available.

NIB: $450 **Exc:** $395 **VGood:** $275

MOUNTAIN EAGLE MAGNUM LITE RIFLE

Bolt action; 22-250, 223 Rem. (Varmint); 280, 30-06 (long action); 7mm Rem. Mag., 300 Win. Mag., (magnum action); 24-inch, 26-inch, free floating barrel; weighs 7 lbs., 13 oz.; 44-inch overall length (24-inch barrel); Kevlar-graphite stock with aluminum bedding block, high comb, recoil pad, swivel studs; made by H-S Precision; no sights; accepts any Remington 700-type base. Special Sako action with one-piece forged bolt, hinged steel floorplate, lengthened receiver ring; adjustable trigger. Krieger cut-rifled benchrest barrel. Introduced 1996. From Magnum Research, Inc.

Perf: $2000 **Exc:** $1500 **VGood:** $900

Later rifles with Remington actions

Perf: $1650 **Exc:** $1200 **VGood:** $650

M-S SAFARI ARMS 1000-YARD MATCH MODEL

Bolt action; single shot; 28-inch heavy barrel; no sights; drilled/tapped for scope mount; sleeved stainless steel action; electronic trigger; custom-painted fully-adjustable fiberglass stock; custom-built to buyer's specs. Introduced 1982; discontinued 1985.

Exc: $1385 **VGood:** $995 **Good:** $750

M-S SAFARI ARMS SILHOUETTE MODEL

Bolt action; single shot; 22 LR, all standard centerfires; 23-inch barrel (22 LR), 24-inch (centerfires); no sights; drilled/tapped for scope mounts; custom-painted fiberglass silhouette stock; stainless steel action; electronic trigger; custom built to buyer's specs. Introduced 1982; discontinued 1985.

Exc: $700 **VGood:** $600 **Good:** $450

M-S SAFARI ARMS VARMINT MODEL

Bolt action; single shot; any standard centerfire chambering; 24-inch stainless steel barrel; no sights; drilled, tapped for scope mounts; custom-painted thumbhole or pistol-grip fiberglass stock; stainless steel action; electronic trigger; custom built to buyer's specs. Introduced 1983; discontinued 1985.

Exc: $925 **VGood:** $700 **Good:** $525

MUSGRAVE PREMIER NR5

Bolt action; 243 Win., 270 Win., 30-06, 308 Win., 7mm Rem. Mag.; 5-shot magazine; 25-1/2-inch barrel; no sights; European walnut Monte Carlo stock; cheekpiece; hand-checkered pistol-grip, forearm; pistol-grip cap, forend tip; recoil pad; sling swivel studs. Introduced 1972; discontinued 1973.

Exc: $400 **VGood:** $300 **Good:** $220

MUSGRAVE RSA SINGLE SHOT NR1

Bolt action; 308 Win.; 26-inch barrel; target aperture rear sight, tunnel front; European walnut target stock with handguard; barrel band; rubber buttplate; sling swivels. Introduced 1972; discontinued 1973.

Exc: $450 **VGood:** $325 **Good:** $240

MUSGRAVE VALIANT NR6

Bolt action; 243 Win., 270 Win., 30-06, 308 Win., 7mm Rem. Mag; 5-shot magazine; 24-inch barrel; removable leaf rear sight, hooded ramp front; straight-comb stock; skip-line checkering; sans grip cap, forend tip. Introduced 1972; discontinued.

Exc: $365 **VGood:** $250 **Good:** $200

NAVY ARMS 45-70 MAUSER RIFLE

Bolt action; 45-70 Government; 3-shot magazine; 24-inch, 26-inch barrel; open rear sight, ramp front; hand-checkered Monte Carlo stock; built on Siamese Mauser action. Introduced 1973; no longer in production.

Exc: $395 **VGood:** $350 **Good:** $295

NAVY ARMS 45-70 MAUSER CARBINE

Same specs as 45-70 Mauser except 18-inch barrel; straight walnut stock.

Exc: $375 **VGood:** $330 **Good:** $275

NAVY ARMS 1860 HENRY RIFLE

Lever action; 44-40, 45 Colt. 24-1/4-inch octagonal barrel, 1:16-inch twist; weighs 9.26 lbs.; 43-3/4-inch overall length; Walnut stock; Blade front, adjustable folding rear sights; Steel color-case hardened or brass receiver; 13-shot magazine. Introduced 2001. Imported from Uberti by Navy Arms.

Steel color-case hardened receiver

Perf: $900 **Exc:** $700 **VGood:** $620

Brass receiver

Perf: $925 **Exc:** $725 **VGood:** $655

NAVY ARMS 1860 HENRY MILITARY RIFLE

Lever action; 44-40, 44 Rem.; 13-shot magazine; 24-1/4-inch barrel; weighs 9-1/4 lbs.; blade front sight, elevation-adjustable rear; oil-stained American walnut stock; brass frame, buttplate; sling swivels; no forend; blued barrel; optional engraving. Recreation of the model used by cavalry units in the Civil War. Introduced 1985; still in production.

Perf: $895 **Exc:** $725 **VGood:** $600

NAVY ARMS 1860 HENRY CARBINE

Same specs as Henry except 22-inch barrel; 41-inch overall length; weighs 8-3/4 lbs.; no sling swivels. Imported from Italy by Navy Arms. Introduced 1992; no longer imported.

Perf: $795 **Exc:** $695 **VGood:** $595

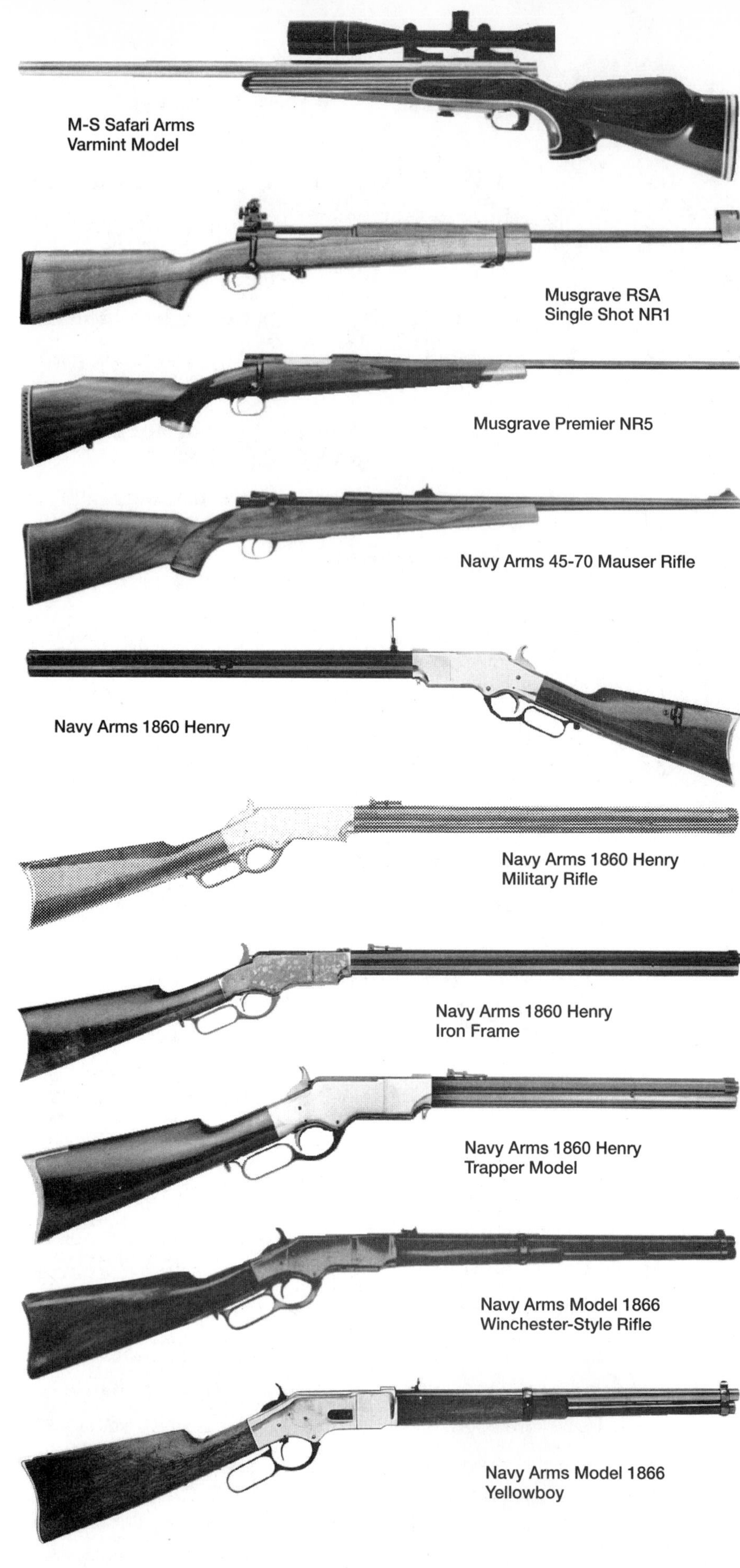

M-S Safari Arms Varmint Model

Musgrave RSA Single Shot NR1

Musgrave Premier NR5

Navy Arms 45-70 Mauser Rifle

Navy Arms 1860 Henry

Navy Arms 1860 Henry Military Rifle

Navy Arms 1860 Henry Iron Frame

Navy Arms 1860 Henry Trapper Model

Navy Arms Model 1866 Winchester-Style Rifle

Navy Arms Model 1866 Yellowboy

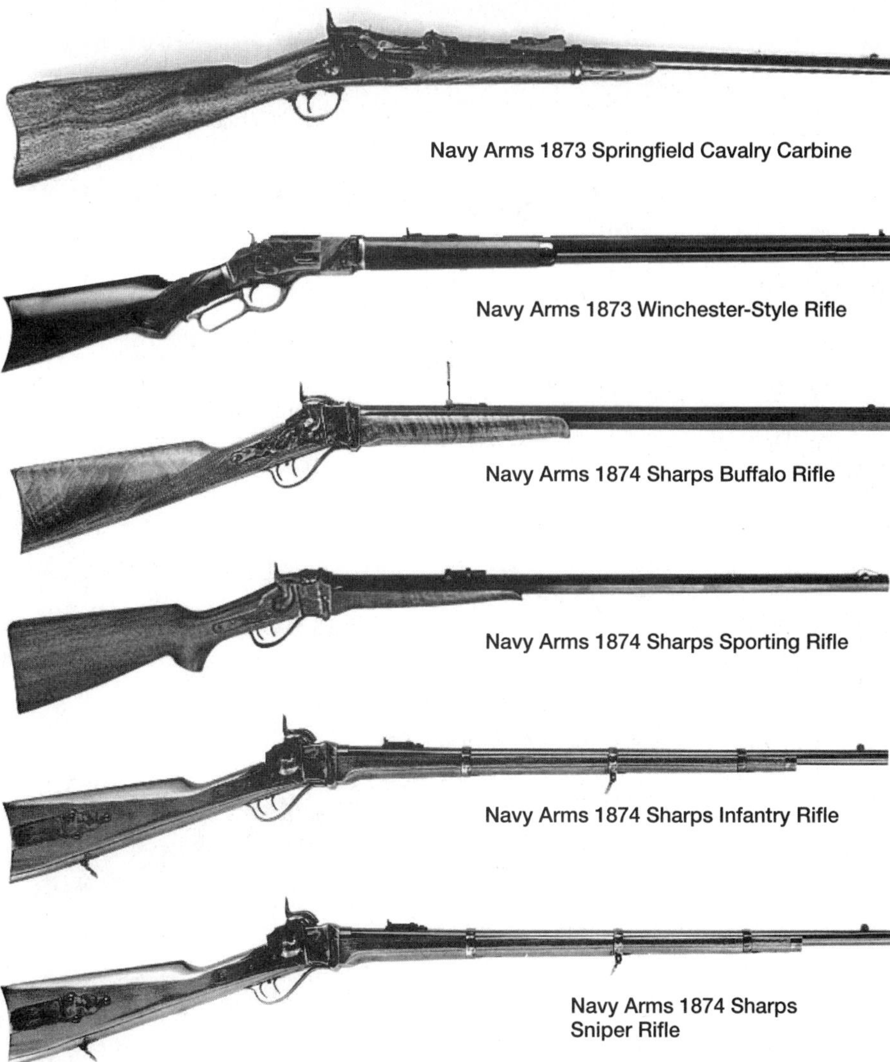
Navy Arms 1873 Springfield Cavalry Carbine

Navy Arms 1873 Winchester-Style Rifle

Navy Arms 1874 Sharps Buffalo Rifle

Navy Arms 1874 Sharps Sporting Rifle

Navy Arms 1874 Sharps Infantry Rifle

Navy Arms 1874 Sharps Sniper Rifle

NAVY ARMS 1860 HENRY IRON FRAME

Same specs as Henry except receiver of blued or color case-hardened steel. Made in Italy. Introduced 1991.

Perf: $925 **Exc:** $750 **VGood:** $650

NAVY ARMS 1860 HENRY TRAPPER MODEL

Same specs as Henry except 8-shot magazine; 16-1/2-inch barrel; weighs 7-1/2 lbs.; brass frame, buttplate; blued barrel. Made in Italy. Introduced, 1991.

Perf: $795 **Exc:** $675 **VGood:** $575

NAVY ARMS MODEL 1866 WINCHESTER-STYLE RIFLE

Lever action; 38 Spl., 357 Mag., 44-40, 45 Colt; full-length tube magazine; 24-inch octagon barrel; 39-1/2-inch overall length; weighs 9-1/4 lbs.; open leaf rear sight, fixed blade front; walnut straight grip stock, forearm; barrel band; polished brass frame, buttplate; other parts blued. Introduced in 1966; similar model still imported.

Perf: $695 **Exc:** $595 **VGood:** $495

NAVY ARMS MODEL 1866 CARBINE

Same specs as Model 1866 except 10-shot magazine; 19-inch barrel; carbine forearm, barrel band. Introduced 1967; no longer in production.

Perf: $695 **Exc:** $595 **VGood:** $495

NAVY ARMS MODEL 1866 TRAPPER

Same specs as Model 1866 except 22 LR; 8-shot magazine; 16-1/2-inch barrel.

Perf: $695 **Exc:** $595 **VGood:** $495

NAVY ARMS MODEL 1866 YELLOWBOY

Same specs as Model 1866 except 44-40; 12-shot tubular magazine; 24-inch full-octagon barrel; 42-1/2-inch overall length; weighs 8-1/2 lbs.; ladder-type adjustable rear sight; European walnut stock; brass forend tip; blued barrel, hammer, lever. Made in Italy. Introduced 1991; still imported.

Perf: $675 **Exc:** $525 **VGood:** $385

NAVY ARMS MODEL 1866 YELLOWBOY CARBINE

Same specs as Model 1866 Yellowboy except 10-shot magazine; 19-inch barrel. Made in Italy. Introduced 1991.

Perf: $770 **Exc:** $620 **VGood:** $565

NAVY ARMS 1873 SPRINGFIELD INFANTRY RIFLE

Single shot, trapdoor; 45-70; 32.5-inch barrel; weighs about 8 lbs.; walnut stock; blade front, long-range military ladder-type rear sights; blued lockplate and barrel; case-hardened breechblock; cleaning rod under barrel; replica of standard military rifle used by U.S. after 1873. Imported by Navy Arms.

Perf: $975 **Exc:** $800 **VGood:** $600

NAVY ARMS 1873 SPRINGFIELD CAVALRY CARBINE

Single shot, trapdoor; 45-70. 22-inch barrel; weighs 7 lbs.; 40-1/2-inch overall length; Walnut stock; Blade front, military ladder rear sights; Blued lockplate and barrel; color case-hardened breechblock; saddle ring with bar. Replica of 7th Cavalry gun. Imported by Navy Arms.

Perf: $875 **Exc:** $700 **VGood:** $550

NAVY ARMS 1873 WINCHESTER-STYLE RIFLE

Lever action; 44-40, 45 Colt; 12-shot magazine; 24-inch barrel; 43-inch overall length; weighs 8-1/4 lbs.; blade front sight, buckhorn rear; European walnut stock and forend; color case-hardened frame, rest blued; full-octagon barrel. Imported by Navy Arms. Introduced 1991; still imported.

Perf: $795 **Exc:** $695 **VGood:** $550

NAVY ARMS 1873 WINCHESTER-STYLE SPORTING RIFLE

Same specs as 1873 Winchester-Style rifle except checkered pistol-grip stock; 30-inch octagonal barrel (24-inch available). Imported by Navy Arms. Introduced 1992; still imported.

Perf: $870 **Exc:** $775 **VGood:** $695

NAVY ARMS 1873 WINCHESTER-STYLE CARBINE

Same specs as 1873 Winchester-Style Rifle except 19-inch barrel. Imported by Navy Arms. Introduced 1991; still imported.

Perf: $795 **Exc:** $650 **VGood:** $500

NAVY ARMS 1874 SHARPS CAVALRY CARBINE

Falling block; single shot; 45-70; 22-inch barrel; 39-inch overall length; weighs 7-3/4 lbs.; blade front sight, military ladder-type rear; walnut stock; color case-hardened receiver and furniture. Replica of the 1874 Sharps miltary carbine. Imported by Navy Arms. Introduced 1991.

Perf: $995 **Exc:** $795 **VGood:** $595

NAVY ARMS 1874 SHARPS BUFFALO RIFLE

Caliber: 45-70, 45-90. 28-inch heavy octagon barrel; weighs 10 lbs., 10 oz.; 46-inch overall length; Walnut stock; checkered grip and forend; Blade front, ladder rear sights; tang sight optional. Color case-hardened receiver, blued barrel; double-set triggers.

Perf: $1100 **Exc:** $950 **VGood:** $765

NAVY ARMS SHARPS PLAINS RIFLE

Similar to Sharps Buffalo rifle except 45-70 only, 32-inch medium-weight barrel, weighs 9 lbs., 8 oz., and is 49-inch overall. Imported by Navy Arms.

Perf: $1100 **Exc:** $950 **VGood:** $765

NAVY ARMS SHARPS SPORTING RIFLE

Same as the Navy Arms Sharps Plains Rifle except has pistol grip stock. Introduced 1997. Imported by Navy Arms.

Perf: $1050 **Exc:** $925 **VGood:** $745

NAVY ARMS 1874 SHARPS INFANTRY RIFLE

Same specs as 1874 Sharps Calvary Carbine except 30-inch barrel; double-set triggers; weighs 8-1/2 lbs.; 46-3/4-inch overall length; three-band model. Imported by Navy Arms. Introduced 1984; still imported.

Perf: $1100 **Exc:** $950 **VGood:** $765

NAVY ARMS 1874 SHARPS SNIPER RIFLE

Same specs as Navy Arms 1874 Sharps Carbine except 30-inch barrel; double-set triggers; weighs 8-1/2 lbs.; 46-3/4-inch overall length. Imported by Navy Arms. Introduced 1984; still imported.

Perf: $1200 **Exc:** $1050 **VGood:** $865

NAVY ARMS 1885 HIGH WALL RIFLE

Single shot, falling block; 45-70; others available on special order; 28-inch round, 30-inch octagonal barrel; weighs 9.5 lbs.; 45-1/2-inch overall length (30-

inch barrel); walnut stock; blade front sight, vernier tang-mounted peep rear. Replica of Winchester's High Wall designed by Browning. Color case-hardened receiver, blued barrel. Introduced 1998. Imported by Navy Arms.

Perf: $900 **Exc:** $700 **VGood:** $600

NAVY ARMS 1892 RIFLE

Lever action; 357 Mag., 44-40, 45 Colt. 24-1/4-inch octagonal barrel; weighs 7 lbs.; 42-inch overall length; American walnut stock; Blade front sight, semi- buckhorn rear. Replica of Winchester's early Model 1892 with octagonal barrel, forend cap and crescent buttplate. Blued or color case- hardened receiver. Introduced 1998. Imported by Navy Arms.

Perf: $520 **Exc:** $425 **VGood:** $350

NAVY ARMS 1892 STAINLESS CARBINE

Similar to the 1892 Rifle except stainless steel, has 20-inch round barrel, weighs 5-3/4 lbs., and is 37-1/2-inch overall. Introduced 1998. Imported by Navy Arms.

Perf: $530 **Exc:** $445 **VGood:** $360

NAVY ARMS 1892 SHORT RIFLE

Similar to the 1892 Rifle except has 20-inch octagonal barrel, weighs 6-1/4 lbs., and is 37-3/4-inch overall. Replica of the rare, special order 1892 Winchester nicknamed the "Texas Special." Blued or color case-hardened receiver and furniture. Introduced 1998.

Perf: $520 **Exc:** $420 **VGood:** $355

NAVY ARMS 1892 STAINLESS RIFLE

Lever action; 357 Mag., 44-40, 45 Colt; 24-1/4-inch octagonal barrel; weighs 7 lbs.; 42-inch length; American walnut stock; brass bead front sight, semi-buckhorn rear; designed for the Cowboy Action shooter. Stainless steel barrel, receiver and furniture. Introduced 2000.

Perf: $530 **Exc:** $445 **VGood:** $360

NAVY ARMS EM-331

Bolt action; 7.62x39mm; 5-shot detachable magazine; 21-inch barrel; 42-inch overall length; weighs 7-1/2 lbs.; hooded ramp front sight, open adjustable rear; receiver dovetailed for scope rings; Monte Carlo style stock with sling swivels, rubber recoil pad, contrasting forend tip; polished blue finish. Imported by Navy Arms. Introduced 1994; discontinued 1994.

Perf: $300 **Exc:** $265 **VGood:** $225

NAVY ARMS MARTINI

Single shot; 444 Marlin, 45-70; 26-inch, 30-inch half or full octagon barrel; Creedmore tang peep sight, open middle sight, blade front; checkered pistol-grip stock; schnabel forend; cheekpiece. Introduced 1972; discontinued 1984.

Perf: $495 **Exc:** $420 **VGood:** $350

NAVY ARMS REVOLVING CARBINE

Carbine; 357 Mag., 44-40, 45 Colt; 6-shot cylinder; 20-inch barrel; 38-inch overall length; weighs 5 lbs.; open rear sight, blade front; straight-grip stock; brass buttplate, triggerguard. Action based on Remington Model 1874 revolver. Manufactured in Italy. Introduced, 1968; discontinued 1984.

Perf: $575 **Exc:** $450 **VGood:** $360

NAVY ARMS ROLLING BLOCK BABY CARBINE

Single shot; 22 LR, 22 Hornet, 357 Mag., 44-40; 20-inch octagon barrel, 22-inch round barrel; open rear sight; blade front; uncheckered straight-grip stock forearm; case-hardened frame; brass triggerguard; brass buttplate. Introduced, 1968; discontinued 1984.

Perf: $500 **Exc:** $400 **VGood:** $300

NAVY ARMS ROLLING BLOCK BUFFALO RIFLE

Single shot, rolling block; 45-70; 26-inch, 30-inch half or full octagonal barrel; brass barrel band; open rear sight, blade front. Introduced 1971; still in production.

Perf: $670 **Exc:** $595 **VGood:** $425

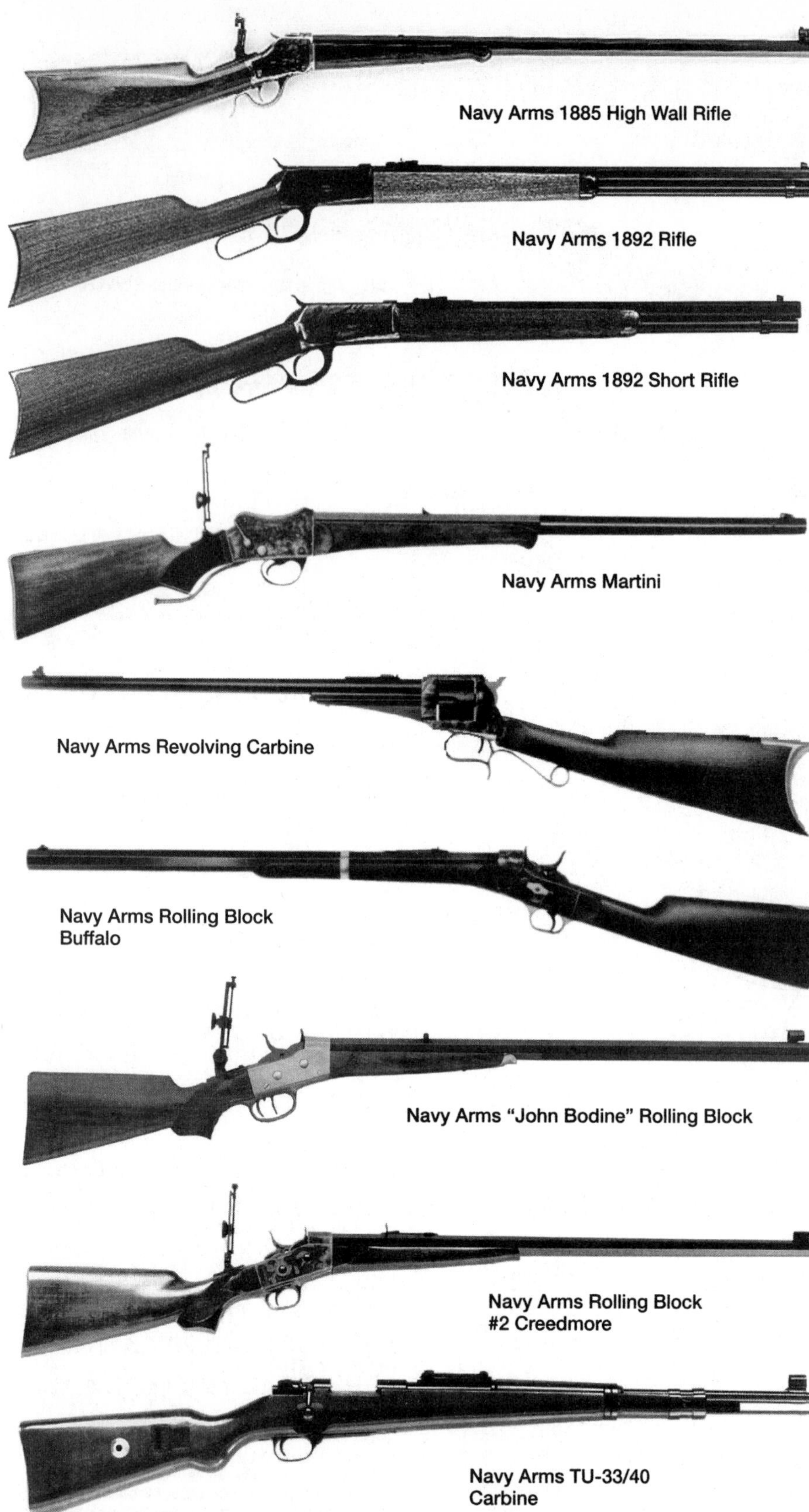

Navy Arms 1885 High Wall Rifle

Navy Arms 1892 Rifle

Navy Arms 1892 Short Rifle

Navy Arms Martini

Navy Arms Revolving Carbine

Navy Arms Rolling Block Buffalo

Navy Arms "John Bodine" Rolling Block

Navy Arms Rolling Block #2 Creedmore

Navy Arms TU-33/40 Carbine

NAVY ARMS ROLLING BLOCK BUFFALO CARBINE

Same specs as Rolling Block Buffalo except 18-inch barrel. Introduced 1971; discontinued 1985.

Perf: $650 **Exc:** $395 **VGood:** $420

NAVY ARMS ROLLING BLOCK RIFLE

Single shot, rolling block; 45-70. 26-inch, 30-inch barrel; Walnut stock; Blade front sight, adjustable rear. Reproduction of classic rolling block action. Available with full-octagon or half-octagon-half-round barrel. Color case- hardened action, steel fittings.

Perf: $700 **Exc:** $600 **VGood:** $500

Navy Arms TU-KKW Sniper Trainer

New England Firearms Handi-Rifle

New England Firearms Super Light

New England Firearms Sportster Single-Shot Rifle

New England Firearms Survivor Rifle

NAVY ARMS "JOHN BODINE" ROLLING BLOCK RIFLE

Single shot, rolling block; 45-70; 30-inch heavy octagonal barrel; Walnut stock; Globe front sight, Soule tang rear. Double set triggers.

Perf: $1300 **Exc:** $1100 **VGood:** $900

NAVY ARMS ROLLING BLOCK #2 CREEDMORE

Single shot; 45-70, 45-90; 26-inch, 28-inch, 30-inch heavy half or full octagon barrel; Creedmore tang peep sight; checkered walnut stock; color case-hardened receiver. Still in production.

Perf: $875 **Exc:** $695 **VGood:** $600

NAVY ARMS SHARPS NO. 3 LONG RANGE RIFLE

Single shot, falling block; 45-70, 45-90; 34-inch octagon barrel; weighs 10 lbs., 12 oz.; 51-1/2-inch length; Deluxe walnut stock; Globe target front and match grade rear tang sights; Shotgun buttplate, German silver forend cap, color case hardenend receiver.

Perf: $1700 **Exc:** $1300 **VGood:** $950

NAVY ARMS SHARPS PLAINS RIFLE

Single shot; falling block; 45-70; 28-1/2-inch barrel; 45-3/4-inch overall length; weighs 8 lbs., 10 oz.; blade front sight, open windage-adjustable rear; checkered walnut butt and forend; color case-hardened action, rest blued. Imported by Navy Arms. Introduced 1991; no longer imported.

Perf: $795 **Exc:** $625 **VGood:** $520

NAVY ARMS TU-33/40 CARBINE

Bolt action; 22 LR; 5-shot magazine; 20-3/4-inch barrel; 38-inch overall length; weighs 6-1/2 lbs.; hooded barleycorn front sight, military V-notch adjustable rear; miniature Mauser-style action; hardwood stock; comes with leather sling. Based on Mauser G.33/40 carbine. Imported by Navy Arms. Introduced 1992; discontinued 1994.

Exc: $300 **VGood:** $250 **Good:** $200

NAVY ARMS TU-KKW SNIPER TRAINER

Bolt action; 22 LR; 5-shot magazine; 20-3/4-inch barrel; 38-inch overall length; weighs 7-3/8 lbs.; hooded barleycorn front sight, military V-notch adjustable rear; Type 89 2-3/4x scope with quick detachable mount system; hardwood stock; miniature Mauser-style action; comes with leather sling; cleaning rod. Based on Mauser G.33/40 carbine. Imported by Navy Arms. Introduced 1992; discontinued 1994.

Exc: $350 **VGood:** $300 **Good:** $250

NEW ENGLAND FIREARMS HANDI-RIFLE

Break-open; single shot; 204 Ruger, 22 Hornet, 223, 22-250, 243, 25-06, 270, 280, 30-30, 44 Mag., 45-70; 22-inch barrel; weighs 7 lbs.; ramp front sight, folding rear; drilled, tapped for scope mounts; walnut-finished hardwood stock; break-open action; side-lever release; blued finish or stainless steel. Introduced 1989; still in production.

Perf: $200 **Exc:** $170 **VGood:** $140

NEW ENGLAND FIREARMS SUPER LIGHT RIFLE

Similar to Handi-Rifle except different barrel taper, shorter 20-inch barrel with recessed muzzle, special lightweight synthetic stock and forend. No sights furnished on 223 and 243 versions, but have factory-mounted scope base and offset hammer spur; Monte Carlo stock; 22 Hornet has ramp front, fully adjustable open rear. Overall length 36-inch, weighs about 5.5 lbs. Introduced 1997. Made in U.S.A. by New England Firearms.

Perf: $175 **Exc:** $125 **VGood:** $100

NEW ENGLAND FIREARMS SPORTSTER SINGLE-SHOT RIFLE

Single shot, breakopen; 22 LR, 22 WMR, 17 HMR, 17 Mach 2; 20-inch barrel; weighs 5-1/2 lbs.; 36-1/4-inch overall length; Black polymer stock; no sights; scope mount included; Break open, side-lever release; automatic ejection; recoil pad; sling swivel studs; trigger locking system. Introduced 2001.

Perf: $105 **Exc:** $95 **VGood:** $80

Youth model. 20-inch bbl., shorter stock, 33-inch overall

Perf: $105 **Exc:** $95 **VGood:** $85

17-caliber

Perf: $140 **Exc:** $115 **VGood:** N/A

NEW ENGLAND FIREARMS SURVIVOR RIFLE

Single shot, breakopen; 223, 357 Mag., 308 Win., 45 Colt/410; 22-inch barrel; weighs 6 lbs.; 36-inch overall length; Black polymer stock, thumbhole design; no sights; scope mount provided. Receiver drilled and tapped for scope mounting. Stock and forend have storage compartments for ammo, etc.; comes with integral swivels and black nylon sling. Introduced 1996. Made in U.S.A. by New England Firearms.

Perf: $200 **Exc:** $180 **VGood:** $150

NEW ULTRA LIGHT ARMS MODEL 20

NOTES: Leave text as is with following exceptions: delete ."17 Rem., .222 Rem., .223 Rem., .22 Hornet." change "Company name changed to New Ultra Light Arms LLC in 2002." to "Formerly Ultra Light Arms. Name changed in 2002. Add $50 for Left Hand"

Perf: $3000 **Exc:** $2400 **VGood:** $1900

NEW ULTRA LIGHT ARMS MODEL 20 SHORT

Bolt action (ultra short); .17 Rem., .222 Rem., .223 Rem., .22 Hornet, .22-250 Rem., 6.8 SPC, 7mm BR, .30 Rem AR. (other cartridges on request) Barrel length and stock length of pull to customer order with a nominal weight of 4.5 pounds. Light weight scope mounts included. Stock is hand laid Kevlar and carbon fiber painted to customer choice. Two-positing, three-function safety, Shipped in hard case and left or right hand options available. Introduced in 1986. Company name changed from Ultra Light Arms in 2002. Add $50 for Left Hand

Perf: $3000 **Exc:** $2400 **VGood:** $1900

NEW ULTRA LIGHT ARMS MODEL 20 RIMFIRE

NOTES: Leave text as is with following exception: change "Made in U.S. by New Ultra Light Arms." to "Formerly Ultra Light Arms. Name changed in 2002. Add $50 for Left Hand. Add $100 for repeater."

Perf: $1600 **Exc:** $1100 **VGood:** $900

NEW ULTRA LIGHT ARMS MODEL 24

NOTES: Leave test as is but add, "Formerly Ultra Light Arms. Name changed in 2002. Add $50 for Left Hand."

Perf: $3000 **Exc:** $2400 **VGood:** $1900

NEW ULTRA LIGHT ARMS MODEL 28

NOTES: Leave text as is with following exception: change "Made in U.S. by New Ultra Light Arms." to "Formerly Ultra Light Arms. Name changed in 2002. Add $50 for Left Hand."

Perf: $3000 **Exc:** $2400 **VGood:** $1900

NEW ULTRA LIGHT ARMS MODEL 40 MAGNUM

NOTES: Leave text as is with following exception: change "Made in U.S. by New Ultra Light Arms." to

"Formerly Ultra Light Arms. Name changed in 2002. Add $50 for Left Hand."

Perf: $3100 **Exc:** $2500 **VGood:** $1900

NEWTON BUFFALO SPORTER

Bolt action; 256, 30, 35 Newton, 30-06; 5-shot box magazine; 24-inch barrel; open rear sight, ramp front; hand-checkered pistol-grip stock; reversed set-trigger; Enfield-designed bolt handle. Introduced 1922; discontinued 1924. Collector value.

Exc: $1700 **VGood:** $950 **Good:** $650

NEWTON-MAUSER SPORTER

Bolt action; 256 Newton; 5-shot box magazine; 24-inch barrel; open rear sight, ramp front; checkered American walnut pistol-grip stock; double-set triggers; hinged floorplate. Introduced 1914; discontinued 1915.

Exc: $1975 **VGood:** $1350 **VGood:** $825

NEWTON STANDARD SPORTER (TYPE I)

Bolt action; 22, 256, 280, 30, 33, 35 Newton, 30-06; 24-inch barrel; open rear sight, ramp front; hand-checkered pistol-grip stock; double-set triggers. Introduced 1916; discontinued 1918. Collector value.

Exc: $1680 **VGood:** $950 **Good:** $750

NEWTON STANDARD SPORTER (TYPE II)

Same specs as Sporter Type I except improved bolt-action design; 256, 30, 35 Newton, 30-06; 5-shot box magazine; reversed set-trigger; Enfield-design bolt handle. Collector value. Introduced 1921; discontinued 1922.

Exc: $1650 **VGood:** $950 **Good:** $670

NOBLE MODEL 10

Bolt action; single shot; 22 Short, 22 Long, 22 LR; 24-inch barrel; open rear sight, bead front; uncheckered hardwood pistol-grip stock. Introduced 1955; discontinued 1958.

Exc: $95 **VGood:** $80 **Good:** $50

NOBLE MODEL 20

Bolt action; single shot; 22 Short, 22 Long, 22 LR; 22-inch barrel; weighs 5 lbs.; open rear sight, bead front; uncheckered walnut pistol-grip stock. Introduced 1958; discontinued 1963.

Exc: $95 **VGood:** $80 **Good:** $50

NOBLE MODEL 33

Slide action; 22 Short, 22 Long, 22 LR; 21-shot (22 Short), 17-shot (22 Long), 15-shot (22 LR) tube magazine; 24-inch barrel; 41-3/4-inch overall length; weighs 6 lbs.; hammerless; open rear sight, bead front; Tenite stock; grooved wood slide handle. Introduced 1949; discontinued 1953.

Exc: $185 **VGood:** $145 **Good:** $95

NOBLE MODEL 33A

Same specs as Model 33 except hardwood stock and slide handle. Introduced 1953, as replacement for Model 33; discontinued 1955.

Exc: $175 **VGood:** $135 **Good:** $85

NOBLE MODEL 222

Bolt action; single shot; 22 Short, 22 Long, 22 LR; 22-inch barrel; 38-inch overall length; weighs 5 lbs.; barrel, receiver milled as integral unit; interchangeable peep and V-notch rear sight, ramp front; scope mounting base; uncheckered hardwood pistol-grip stock. Introduced 1958; discontinued 1971.

Exc: $95 **VGood:** $80 **Good:** $50

NOBLE MODEL 235

Slide-action; 22 Short, 22 Long, 22 LR; 21-shot (22 Short), 17-shot (22 Long), 15-shot (22 LR) tube magazine; 24-inch barrel; hammerless; open rear sight, ramp front; hardwood pistol-grip stock; grooved wood slide handle. Introduced 1951; discontinued 1973.

Exc: $185 **VGood:** $150 **Good:** $135

Noble Model 10

Noble Model 20

Noble Model 222

Noble Model 235

Norinco Model ATD

Norinco Model EM-321

NOBLE MODEL 275

Lever action; 22 Short, 22 Long, 22 LR; 21-shot (22 Short), 17-shot (22 Long), 15-shot (22 LR) tube magazine; 24-inch barrel; 42-inch overall length; weighs 5-1/2 lbs.; hammerless; open rear sight, ramp front; receiver grooved for tip-off scope mount; uncheckered one-piece hardwood full pistol-grip stock. Introduced 1958; discontinued 1971. Funny, dopey little rifle.

Exc: $165 **VGood:** $135 **Good:** $95

NOBLE MODEL 285

Semi-automatic; 22 LR; 15-shot tube magazine; 22-inch barrel; 40-inch overall length; weighs 5-1/2 lbs.; ramp front sight, adjustable open rear; top thumb safety; receiver grooved for tip-off mount; walnut finished pistol-grip stock.

Exc: $150 **VGood:** $125 **Good:** $95

NORINCO MAK 90

Semi-automatic, AK-47 type action; 7.62x39, 223; 5-shot magazine; 16-1/4-inch barrel; 35-1/2-inch overall length; weighs 8 lbs.; adjustable post front sight, open adjustable rear; walnut-finished thumbhole stock with recoil pad; chrome-lined barrel; forged receiver; black oxide finish. Comes with extra magazine, oil bottle, cleaning kit, sling. Imported from China by Century International Arms. No longer imported. Add 25 percent for milled receiver side panels. NOTE: Add 10% for MAK-91 heavy-barrel National Match.

Perf: $650 **Exc:** $550 **VGood:** $450

NORINCO MODEL ATD

Semi-automatic; 22 LR; modeled after Browning 22 rifle; 11-shot magazine; 19-3/8-inch barrel; 36 5/8-inch overall length; weighs 4-3/8 lbs.; blade front sight, open adjustable rear; checkered hardwood stock; Browning-type take-down action; tube magazine loads through buttplate; cross-bolt safety; blued finish; engraved receiver. Made in China. Introduced 1987; no longer imported.

Perf: $170 **Exc:** $140 **VGood:** $120

NORINCO MODEL EM-321

Slide action; 22 LR; 9-shot tubular magazine; 19-1/2-inch barrel; 37-inch overall length; weighs 6 lbs.; blade front sight, open folding rear; hardwood stock; blue finish; grooved slide handle. Imported from China by China Sports, Inc. No longer imported.

Perf: $150 **Exc:** $125 **VGood:** $100

NORINCO MODEL JW-14

Semi-automatic; 22 LR; 10-shot magazine, 20-inch barrel, 40-inch OAL, post front sight with ears, Mauser-style military rear sight to 200M; walnut-finished hardwood stock. Imported from China by Interstate Arms Corp. No longer imported.

Perf: $250 **Exc:** $200 **VGood:** $150

NORINCO MODEL JW-15

Bolt action; 22 LR; 5-shot detachable magazine; 24-inch barrel; 41-3/4-inch overall length; weighs 5-3/4 lbs.; hooded blade front sight, windage-adjustable open rear; walnut-stained hardwood stock; sling swivels; wing-type safety. Made in China. No longer imported.

Perf: $200 **Exc:** $150 **VGood:** $100

NORINCO MODEL JW-27

Bolt action; 22 LR; 5-shot magazine; 22-3/4-inch barrel; 41-3/4-inch overall length; weighs 5-3/4 lbs.; dovetailed bead on blade front sight, fully-adjustable rear; receiver grooved for scope mounting; walnut-finished hardwood stock with checkered grip and forend; blued finish. Imported from China by Century International Arms. Introduced 1992; no longer imported.

Perf: $150 **Exc:** $125 **VGood:** $100

Norinco Model JW-27

Norrahammar Model N-900

Nosler Custom Model 48 Varmint

NS Firearms Model 522

Olympic Arms CAR-97

Olympic Arms International Match

NORINCO TYPE EM-332

Bolt action; 22 LR; 5-shot magazine; 18-1/2-inch barrel; 41-1/2-inch overall length; weighs 4-1/2 lbs.; blade front sight on ramp, open adjustable rear; hardwood stock; magazine holder on right side of butt for two extra magazines; blue finish. Imported from China by China Sports, Inc. Introduced 1990; no longer imported.

Perf: $150 **Exc:** $125 **VGood:** $100

NORRAHAMMAR MODEL N-900

Bolt action; 243 Win., 270 Win., 308 Win., 30-06; 20-1/4-inch barrel; hooded front sight, adjustable rear; hand-checkered European walnut pistol-grip stock, forearm; single-stage trigger; ebony grip cap; buttplate; side safety; hinged floorplate; sling swivels. Made in Sweden. Introduced 1957; discontinued 1967.

Exc:. $325 **VGood:** $270 **Good:** $210

NOSLER CUSTOM MODEL 48 SPORTER

Bolt-action centerfire rifle chambered in .270 Winchester Short Magnum. 24" barrel, round top receiver, onyx gray composite stock. Introduced 2007. Price includes scope.

NIB: $2200 **Exc:** $1800 **VGood:** $1500

NOSLER MODEL 48 VARMINT RIFLE

Calibers: 204 Ruger, 223 Rem., 22-250 Remington. Heavy 24-inch barrel, 4-shot capacity. Weight: 7.25 lbs. Coyote tan or Onyx black Kevlar and carbon fiber stock. Built on same action as Nosler Custom rifle with proprietary push-feed action, two-position safety and adjustable trigger.

Perf: $2700 **Exc:** $2300 **VGood:** $1950

NS FIREARMS MODEL 522

Bolt action; 22 LR; 5-shot magazine; 21-inch barrel; 39-1/2-inch overall length; weighs 7-3/4 lbs.; no sights; receiver grooved for scope mount; walnut stock with cut-checkered grip and forend; satin finish; free-floated hammer-forged heavy barrel; forged receiver and bolt with two locking lugs, dual extractors; safety locks bolt and trigger. Imported by Keng's Firearms Specialty. Introduced 1993; discontinued 1994.

Exc: $170 **VGood:** $220 **VGood:** $95

OLYMPIC ARMS AR-15 MATCH

Semi-automatic; 223; 20- or 30-shot magazine; 20-inch stainless steel barrel; 39-1/2-inch overall length; weighs 8-3/4 lbs.; post front sight, fully-adjustable aperture rear; cut-off carrying handle with scope rail attached; button-rifled 4140 ordnance steel or stainless barrel with 1:9-inch twist standard, 1:7, 1:12, 1:14 twists optional; weighs 8-1/2 lbs. Made in U.S. by Olympic Arms, Inc. Introduced 1993; discontinued 1994.

Perf: $750 **Exc:** $700 **VGood:** $600

OLYMPIC ARMS CAR-97 RIFLES

Semi-automatic; 223, 7-shot; 9mm Para., 45 ACP, 40 S&W, 10mm, 10-shot; 16-inch barrel; weighs 7 lbs.; 34.75-inch overall length; A2 stowaway grip stock, telescoping-look butt; post front sight, fully adjustable aperature rear. Based on AR-15 rifle. Post-ban version of the CAR-15. Made in U.S.A. by Olympic Arms, Inc.

Perf: $850 **Exc:** $750 **VGood:** $650

OLYMPIC ARMS INTERCONTINENTAL MATCH

Semi-automatic; 223; 5-shot magazine; 20-inch stainless steel barrel; 39-1/2-inch overall length; weighs about 10 lbs.; no sights; cut-off carrying handle with scope rail attached; synthetic woodgrain thumbhole buttstock; broach-cut, free-floating barrel with 1:10 or 1:8.5 twist; magazine well floorplate; fluting optional. Made in U.S. by Olympic Arms, Inc. Introduced 1992; discontinued 1994.

Perf: $1595 **Exc:** $1195 **VGood:** $950

OLYMPIC ARMS INTERNATIONAL MATCH

Semi-automatic; 223; 20- or 30-shot magazine; 20-inch or 24-inch stainless steel barrel; 39-1/2-inch overall length (20-inch barrel); weighs 10 lbs.; standard AR-15-type post front sight, adjustable target peep rear; cut-off carrying handle with scope rail attached; black composition A2 stow-away butt and grip; broach-cut, free-floating barrel with 1:10 or 1:8.5 twist; fluting optional. Based on the AR-15 rifle. Made in U.S. by Olympic Arms, Inc. Introduced 1985; no longer made.

Perf: $1395 **Exc:** $995 **VGood:** $825

OLYMPIC ARMS UM-1P

Premium-grade gas-operated .223 semi-auto target rifle based on AR-15 chassis. Features include 24-inch stainless steel bull barrel, anodized finish, pistol grip with bottom swell, Picatinny rail, Harris bipod, and competition trigger.

NIB: $1600 **Exc:** $1200 **VGood:** $900

OLYMPIC ARMS UM-1

Plain-jane variant of UM-1P but with 20-inch stainless steel bull barrel, standard pistol grip, no bipod.

NIB: $1100 **Exc:** $1000 **VGood:** $800

OLYMPIC ARMS SM-1P

Tricked-out AR-15 in .223 with 20-inch stainless steel barrel, free-floating sleeve handguard, carry handle upper or Picatinny rail flattop, pneumatic recoil buffer, Bob Jones interchangeable sight system, competition trigger, and Maxhard receivers.

NIB: $1600 **Exc:** $1200 **VGood:** $900

OLYMPIC ARMS SM-1

Plain-jane variant of SM-1P but with standard receivers, trigger and sights. No pneumatic recoil buffer.

NIB: $1100 **Exc:** $800 **VGood:** $600

OLYMPIC ARMS ML-1

Similar to SM-1 but with 16-inch barrel with flash hider, 6-position collapsible buttstock and free-floating aluminum tube handguard.

NIB: $1000 **Exc:** $800 **VGood:** $600

OLYMPIC ARMS ML-2

Similar to ML-1 but with flat-top upper receiver with Picatinny rails, standard buttstock and bull barrel.

NIB: $1000 **Exc:** $800 **VGood:** $600

OLYMPIC ARMS MODEL K8
Similar to ML-2 but with 20-inch barrel and extended aluminum tube handguard.
NIB: $1000 **Exc:** $800 **VGood:** $600

OLYMPIC ARMS MODEL K8-MAG
Similar to K8 but with 24-inch bull barrel and chambered in .223 WSM, .243 WSM or .25 WSM.
NIB: $1250 **Exc:** $900 **VGood:** $750

OLYMPIC ARMS K3B
Features include 16-inch chrome-moly barrel with flash-hidefully adjustable rear sight, 6-position collapsible buttstock and carbine-length handguard.
NIB: $850 **Exc:** $750 **VGood:** $600

OLYMPIC ARMS K3B-M4
Similar to K3B but with M4S fiberite handguard with heatshield and 32.25-inch overall length.
NIB: $850 **Exc:** $750 **VGood:** $600

OLYMPIC ARMS K3B-CAR
Similar to K3B but with 30.5-inch overall length.
NIB: $850 **Exc:** $750 **VGood:** $600

OLYMPIC ARMS K3B-FAR
Similar to K3B but with featherweight barrel and weight of 5.84 lbs.
NIB: $825 **Exc:** $750 **VGood:** $600

OLYMPIC ARMS K4B
Similar to K3B but with 20-inch barrel and rifle-length fiberite handguard.
NIB: $800 **Exc:** $750 **VGood:** $600

OLYMPIC ARMS K4B-A4
Similar to K4B but with ventilated FIRSH rifle-length handguard.
NIB: $905 **Exc:** $750 **VGood:** $600

OLYMPIC ARMS LTF
Features include 16-inch chrome-molybdenum barrel, free-floating FIRSH handguard with Picatinny rails, ACE FX skeleton stock, ERGO pistol grip and multiple-aperture flipup sight system.
NIB: $1225 **Exc:** $750 **VGood:** $600

OLYMPIC ARMS LT-M4
Similar to LTF but with 16-inch stainless steel barrel.
NIB: $1150 **Exc:** $900 **VGood:** $600

OLYMPIC ARMS K16
Similar to K8 but with 16-inch bull chrome-moly barrel.
NIB: $850 **Exc:** $700 **VGood:** $600

OLYMPIC ARMS GI-16
Basic military AR-15-inspired semi-auto rifle chambered in .223. 16-inch chrome-moly barrel with flash-hider, 6-position collapsible buttstock, carbine-length handguard and rear sight adjustable for windage only.
NIB: $750 **Exc:** $700 **VGood:** $650

OLYMPIC ARMS K30
Similar to GI-16 but chambered in .30 Carbine. Includes mag well insert to accept military-spec magazines.
NIB: $900 **Exc:** N/A **VGood:** N/A

OLYMPIC ARMS K9/K10/K40/K45
Similar to K30 but chambered, respectively, for 9mm Parabellum, 10mm, .40 S&W and .45ACP. Models use converted surplus military magazines.
NIB: $950 **Exc:** $750 **VGood:** $600

OLYMPIC ARMS K9-GL/K40-GL
Similar to K9 and K40 but accept standard Glock pistol magazines.
NIB: $925 **Exc:** $750 **VGood:** $600

OLYMPIC ARMS PLINKER PLUS
Similar to GI-16 but with standard buttstock.
NIB: $750 **Exc:** $650 **VGood:** $600

Olympic Arms PCR-1

Olympic Arms PCR-2

Olympic Arms PCR-5

Olympic Arms Service Match

OLYMPIC ARMS PLINKER PLUS 20
Similar to Plinker Plus but with 20-inch barrel and rifle-length handguard.
NIB: $750 **Exc:** $650 **VGood:** $600

OLYMPIC ARMS K7 ELIMINATOR
Similar to K4 but with 16-inch barrel with extended handguard and sight radius of 20-inch-barreled models.
NIB: $845 **Exc:** $700 **VGood:** $600

OLYMPIC ARMS K-4 AR-15
Semi-automatic; 223; 30-shot magazine; 20-inch barrel; 39-inch overall length; weighs about 8 lbs.; post elevation-adjustable front sight, peep-style windage-adjustable rear; E-2-style sight system optionally available; full-length M-16-style black composition stock; heavy match-grade barrel; trapdoor in buttstock; A-2 stow-away pistol grip. Made in U.S. by Olympic Arms, Inc. Introduced 1975; no longer produced.
Perf: $950 **Exc:** $800 **VGood:** $650

OLYMPIC ARMS MULTIMATCH
Semi-automatic; 223; 30-shot magazine; 16-inch free-floating, broach-cut, stainless steel barrel with 1:10-inch or 1:8-1/2-inch twist; 36-inch overall length; weighs 7-1/2 lbs.; E2 fully adjustable or International Match upper receiver for scope mounting; telescoping stock or collapsible aluminum buttstock; cut-off carrying handle with scope rail attached (ML2); based on the AR-15 rifle. Made in U.S. by Olympic Arms, Inc. Introduced 1991; still produced.
Perf: $800 **Exc:** $750 **VGood:** $600

OLYMPIC ARMS PCR-1
Semi-automatic; 223; 10-shot magazine; 20-inch barrel of 416 stainless steel; 38-1/4-inch overall length; weighs about 10 lbs.; no sights; flat-top upper receiver, cut-down front sight base; black composition A2 stowaway grip and trapdoor butt; broach-cut, free-floating barrel with 1:8.5 or 1:10 twist; no bayonet lug; crowned barrel; fluting available. Based on the AR-15 rifle. Made in U.S. by Olympic Arms, Inc. Introduced 1994; discontinued 1995. Reintroduced.
Perf: $1095 **Exc:** $950 **VGood:** $800

OLYMPIC ARMS PCR-2
Same specs as PCR-1 except 16-inch barrel; weighs about 8 lbs.; post front sight, fully-adjustable aperture rear. Made in U.S. by Olympic Arms, Inc. Introduced 1994; discontinued 1995. Reintroduced.
Perf: $925 **Exc:** $825 **VGood:** $650

OLYMPIC ARMS PCR-3
Same specs as PCR-1 except 16-inch barrel; flat-top upper receiver, cut-down front sight base. Made in U.S. by Olympic Arms, Inc. Introduced 1994; dropped 1995. Reintroduced.
Perf: $975 **Exc:** $825 **VGood:** $650

Olympic Arms Ultramatch

Omega III

Parker-Hale Model 81 Classic African

Parker-Hale Model 85 Sniper

Parker-Hale Model 87 Target

OLYMPIC ARMS PCR-4

Same specs as PCR-1 except 16-inch barrel, weighs 8-1/2 lbs.; post front sight, A1 windage-adjustable rear; button-rifled 1:7, 1:9, 1:12 or 1:14 twist barrel. Made in U.S. by Olympic Arms, Inc. Introduced 1994; discontinued 1995. Reintroduced.

Perf: $850 **Exc:** $700 **VGood:** $600

OLYMPIC ARMS PCR-5

Same specs as PCR-1 except 9mm Para., 40 S&W, 45 ACP, 223; 16-inch barrel; 34-3/4-inch overall length; weighs 7 lbs.; post front sight, A1 windage-adjustable rear. Based on the CAR-15. Made in U.S. by Olympic Arms, Inc. Introduced 1994; discontinued 1995, reintroduced; still produced as K-series pistol-caliber carbines.

Perf: $850 **Exc:** $700 **VGood:** $600

OLYMPIC ARMS PCR-6

Same specs as PCR-1 except 7.62x39mm; 16-inch barrel; 34-3/4-inch overall length; weighs 7 lbs.; post front sight, A1 windage-adjustable rear. Based on the CAR-15. Made in U.S. by Olympic Arms, Inc. Introduced 1994; discontinued 1995. Reintroduced, then discontinued again.

Perf: $900 **Exc:** $800 **VGood:** $600

OLYMPIC ARMS PCR-9

Same specs as PCR-5 except 9mm Para; 16-inch barrel; 34-inch overall length (stock extended); weighs 7 lbs.; post elevation-adjustable front sight, windage-adjustable rear; telescoping buttstock. Made in U.S. by Olympic Arms, Inc. Introduced 1982; still produced as K3B-9.

Perf: $850 **Exc:** $750 **VGood:** $650

OLYMPIC ARMS PCR-10

Same specs as PCR-5 except 16-inch barrel; 34-inch overall length (stock extended); weighs 7 lbs.; post elevation-adjustable front sight, windage-adjustable rear; telescoping buttstock. Based on the AR-15 rifle. Made in U.S. by Olympic Arms, Inc. Introduced 1982.

Perf: $1095 **Exc:** $995 **VGood:** $895

OLYMPIC ARMS PCR-40

Same specs as PCR-1 except 40 S&W; 16-inch barrel; 34-inch overall length (stock extended); weighs 7 lbs.; post elevation-adjustable front sight, windage-adjustable rear; telescoping buttstock. Made in U.S. by Olympic Arms, Inc. Introduced 1982; still made as K3B-40.

Perf: $995 **Exc:** $895 **VGood:** $795

OLYMPIC ARMS PCR-45

Same specs as PCR-1 except 45 ACP; 16-inch barrel; 34-inch overall length (stock extended); weighs 7 lbs.; post elevation-adjustable front sight, windage-adjustable rear; telescoping buttstock. Made in U.S. by Olympic Arms, Inc. Introduced 1982; still made as K3B-45.

Perf: $995 **Exc:** $895 **VGood:** $795

OLYMPIC ARMS SERVICE MATCH

Semi-automatic; 223; 20-, 30-shot magazine; 20-inch stainless steel barrel; 39-1/2-inch overall length; weighs 8-3/4 lbs.; post front sight, fully-adjustable aperture rear; black composition A2 standard stock; barrel broach-cut and free-floating with 1:10 or 1:8.5 twist; fluting optional. Based on the AR-15 rifle. Conforms to all DCM standards. Made in U.S. by Olympic Arms, Inc. Introduced 1989; reintroduced as PCR-SM.

Perf: $900 **Exc:** $800 **VGood:** $700

OLYMPIC ARMS ULTRAMATCH

Semi-automatic; 223; 20-, 30-shot magazine; 20-inch or 24-inch stainless steel barrel; 39-1/2-inch overall length (20-inch barrel); weighs about 10 lbs.; no sights; cut-off carrying handle with scope rail attached; black composition A2 stowaway butt and grip; broach-cut, free-floating barrel with 1:10 or 1:8.5 twist; fluting optional. Based on the AR-15 rifle. Made in U.S. by Olympic Arms, Inc. Introduced 1985; discontinued 2002.

Perf: $1550 **Exc:** $1250 **VGood:** $925

OMEGA III

Bolt action; 25-06, 270, 30-06, 7mm Rem. Mag., 300 Win. Mag., 338 Win. Mag., 358 Norma Mag.; 4-shot (belted), 5-shot (standard) rotary magazine; 22-inch, 24-inch barrel; no sights; choice of Monte Carlo, Classic or thumbhole varminter; Claro walnut English laminated or laminated walnut/maple; right- or left-hand action; octagonal bolt; square locking system, enclosed bolt face; fully-adjustable trigger. Introduced 1973; discontinued 1976.

Exc: $695 **VGood:** $550 **Good:** $425

PARKER-HALE MODEL 81 CLASSIC

Bolt action; 22-250, 243, 6mm Rem., 270, 6.5x55, 7x57, 7x64, 308, 30-06, 300 Win. Mag., 7mm Rem. Mag.; 4-shot magazine; 24-inch barrel; 44-1/2-inch overall length; weighs 7-3/4 lbs.; Mauser-style action; one-piece steel Oberndorf-style triggerguard with hinged floorplate; drilled and tapped for open sights and scope mounting; scope bases included; rubber buttpad; quick-detachable sling swivels. Introduced 1985; no longer produced.

Exc: $750 **VGood:** $600 **Good:** $485

PARKER-HALE MODEL 81 CLASSIC AFRICAN

Same specs as Model 81 Classic except 375 H&H, 9.3x62; African express rear sight; adjustable trigger; barrel band front swivel; engraved receiver; classic-style stock with solid buttpad; checkered pistol grip and forend. Introduced 1986; no longer produced.

Exc: $1200 **VGood:** $970 **Good:** $625

PARKER-HALE MODEL 85 SNIPER RIFLE

Bolt action; 308 Win.; 10-shot magazine; 24-1/4-inch barrel; 45-inch overall length; weighs 12-1/2 lbs. (with scope); post front windage-adjustable sight, fold-down elevation-adjustable rear; McMillan fiberglass stock with several color patterns available; quick-detachable bipod; palm stop with rail; sling swivels; matte finish. No longer made.

Exc: $2695 **VGood:** $2350 **Good:** $1200

PARKER-HALE MODEL 87 TARGET

Bolt action; 308 Win., 243, 6.5x55, 308, 30-06, 300 Win. Mag. (other calibers on request); 5-shot detachable box magazine; 26-inch heavy barrel; 45-inch overall length; weighs about 10 lbs.; no sights; walnut target-style stock adjustable for length of pull; solid buttpad; accessory rail with hand-stop; deeply stippled grip and forend; receiver dovetailed for Parker-Hale "Roll-Off" scope mounts; Mauser-style action with large bolt knob; Parkerized finish. Made by Gibbs Rifle Co. Introduced 1987; no longer made.

Exc: $1200 **VGood:** $950 **Good:** $750

PARKER-HALE MODEL 1000

Bolt action; 22-250, 243, 6mm, 270, 6.5x55, 7x57, 7x64, 308, 30-06, 7mm Rem. Mag.; 4-shot magazine; 22-inch barrel, 24-inch (22-250); 42-1/2-inch overall length; weighs 7-1/4 lbs.; no sights; drilled and tapped for scope mounting; walnut Monte Carlo stock with checkered palm swell pistol grip and forend; rosewood grip cap; Mauser-style action; one-piece steel Oberndorf-style trigger guard with hinged floorplate. Introduced 1992; no longer made.

Exc: $450 **VGood:** $350 **Good:** $300

PARKER-HALE MODEL 1000 CLIP

Same specs as Model 1000 except detachable box magazine. Introduced 1992; no longer made.

Exc: $450 **VGood:** $340 **Good:** $300

PARKER-HALE MODEL 1100 LIGHTWEIGHT

Bolt action; 22-250, 243, 6mm Rem., 270, 6.5x55, 7x57, 7x64, 308, 30-06, 300 Win. Mag., 7mm Rem. Mag.; 4-shot magazine; 24-inch barrel; 44-1/2-inch overall length; weighs 7-3/4 lbs.; no sights; drilled, tapped for open sights or scope mounting; classic-style European walnut stock with hand-cut checkering; palm swell; rosewood grip cap; Mauser-style action; Oberndort-style triggerguard; buttpad; sling swivels. Imported from England by Precision Sports. Introduced 1984; no longer imported.

Exc: $450 **VGood:** $350 **Good:** $300

PARKER-HALE MODEL 1100M AFRICAN

Same specs as Model 1100 except 375 H&H Mag., 458 Win. Mag; 46-inch overall length; weighs 9-1/2 lbs.; hooded post front sight; V-notch rear; heavily reinforced, glass-beaded, weighted stock; vent recoil pad. Introduced 1984; no longer imported.

Exc: $625 **VGood:** $490 **Good:** $400

PARKER-HALE MODEL 1200 SUPER

Bolt action; 22-250, 243, 6mm, 270, 6.5x55, 7x57, 7x64, 308, 30-06, 300 Win. Mag., 7mm Rem. Mag.; 22-inch barrel; 43-inch overall length; weighs about 7 lbs.; Mauser-type action with twin locking lugs; hinged floorplate; adjustable single stage trigger; silent side safety; hooded post front, flip-up rear sight; European walnut stock; cut-checkered pistol grip and forend; sling swivels. Introduced 1984; no longer produced.

Exc: $525 **VGood:** $450 **Good:** $375

PARKER-HALE MODEL 1200P PRESENTATION

Same specs as Model 1200 Super except 243, 30-06; no sights; engraved action, floorplate, triggerguard; detachable sling swivels. Introduced 1969; discontinued 1975.

Exc: $495 **VGood:** $450 **Good:** $395

PARKER-HALE MODEL 1200V VARMINTER

Same specs as Model 1200 Super except 22-250, 6mm Rem., 25-06, 243; 24-inch barrel; no sights. Introduced 1969; discontinued 1983.

Exc: $510 **VGood:** $450 **Good:** $380

PARKER-HALE MODEL 1300C SCOUT

Bolt action; 243, 308; 10-shot magazine; 20-inch barrel; 41-inch overall length; weighs 8-1/2 lbs.; no sights; drilled and tapped for scope mounting; checkered laminated birch stock; detachable magazine; muzzle brake; polished blue finish. Introduced 1992; no longer made.

Exc: $650 **VGood:** $540 **Good:** $400

PARKER-HALE MODEL 2100 MIDLAND

Bolt action; 22-250, 243, 6mm, 270, 6.5x55, 7x57, 7x64, 308, 30-06; 22-inch barrel; 43-inch overall length; weighs about 7 lbs.; hooded post front, flip-up open rear; Mauser-type action has twin front locking lugs; rear safety lug, claw extractor; hinged floorpate; adjustable single stage trigger; silent slide safety. Imported from England by Precision Sports, Inc. Introduced 1984; discontinued 1989.

Exc: $300 **VGood:** $250 **Good:** $200

Parker-Hale Model 1000

Parker-Hale Model 1100M African Magnum

Parker-Hale Model 1200 Super

Parker-Hale Model 2100 Midland

Pedersen Model 3000

PARKER-HALE MODEL 2600 MIDLAND

Bolt action; 22-250, 243, 6mm, 270, 6.5x55, 7x57, 7x64, 308, 30-06, 300 Win. Mag., 7mm Rem. Mag.; 22-inch barrel; 43-inch overall length; weighs about 7 lbs.; hooded post front sight, flip-up open rear; European hardwood stock with cut-checkered pistol grip and forend; sling swivels; Mauser-type action with twin front locking lugs, rear safety lug, and claw extractor; hinged floorplate; adjustable single-stage trigger; silent side safety. Introduced 1984; no longer produced.

Exc: $375 **VGood:** $300 **Good:** $250

PARKER-HALE MODEL 2700 LIGHTWEIGHT MIDLAND

Bolt action; 22-250, 243, 6mm, 270, 6.5x55, 7x57, 7x64, 308, 30-06, 7mm Rem. Mag.; 22-inch light barrel; 43-inch overall length; weighs about 6-1/2 lbs.; hooded post front sight, flip-up open rear; receiver drilled and tapped for scope mounting; lightweight European walnut stock with checkered pistol grip and forend; sling swivels. Introduced 1992; no longer made.

Exc: $350 **VGood:** $300 **Good:** $240

PARKER-HALE MODEL 2800 MIDLAND

Bolt action; 22-250, 243, 6mm, 270, 6.5x55, 7x57, 7x64, 308, 30-06, 300 Win. Mag., 7mm Rem. Mag.; 22-inch barrel; 43-inch overall length; weighs about 7 lbs.; hooded post front sight, flip-up open rear; laminated birch Monte Carlo stock with cut-checkered pistol grip and forend; sling swivels; Mauser-type action with twin front locking lugs, rear safety lug, and claw extractor; hinged floorplate; adjustable single-stage trigger; silent side safety. No longer produced.

Exc: $375 **VGood:** $325 **Good:** $300

PEDERSEN MODEL 3000

Bolt action; 270, 30-06, 7mm Rem. Mag., 338 Win. Mag.; 3-shot magazine; 22-inch barrel (270, 30-06), 24-inch (magnums); no sights; drilled, tapped for scope mount; American walnut stock, roll-over cheekpiece; hand-checkered pistol-grip, forearm; Mossberg Model 800 action; adjustable trigger; sling swivels. Grades differ in amount of engraving and quality of stock wood. Introduced 1972; discontinued 1975. Pedersen was a upper-shelf Mossberg name brand.

Grade I

Exc: $950 **VGood:** $750 **Good:** $550

Grade II

Exc: $650 **VGood:** $550 **Good:** $450

Grade III

Exc: $550 **VGood:** $450 **Good:** $385

PEDERSEN MODEL 3500

Bolt action; 270 Win., 30-06, 7mm Rem. Mag.; 22-inch barrel (standard calibers), 24-inch (7mm Mag.); 3-shot magazine; drilled, tapped for scope mounts; hand-checkered black walnut stock, forearm; rosewood pistol-grip cap, forearm tip; hinged steel floorplate; Damascened bolt; adjustable trigger. Introduced 1973; discontinued 1975.

Exc: $550 **VGood:** $480 **Good:** $420

PEDERSEN MODEL 4700

Lever action; 30-30, 35 Rem.; 5-shot tubular magazine; 24-inch barrel; open rear sight, hooded ramp front; black walnut stock beavertail forearm; Mossberg Model 472 action; barrel

Plainfield M-1 Carbine, Commando Model

Professional Ordnance Carbon 15 (Type 97S)

Quality Parts/Bushmaster V Match

band swivels. Introduced 1975; discontinued 1975.

Exc: $360 **VGood:** $330 **Good:** $290

PERUGINI-VISINI BOXLOCK EXPRESS

Double rifle; side-by-side; 9.3x74R, 444 Marlin; 25-inch barrel; 41-1/2-inch overall length; bead on ramp front sight, express rear on rib; oil-finished European walnut stock; hand-checkered pistol grip, forend; cheekpiece; non-ejector action; double triggers; color case-hardened receiver; rubber recoil pad; marketed in trunk-type case. Made in Italy. Introduced 1983; discontinued 1989.

Perf: $2995 **Exc:** $2675 **VGood:** $1900

PERUGINI-VISINI BOXLOCK MAGNUM

Double rifle; over/under; 7mm Rem. Mag., 7x65R, 9.3x74R, 270 Win., 338 Win. Mag., 375 H&H Mag., 458 Win. Mag.; 24-inch barrels; 40-1/2-inch overall length; bead on ramp front sight, express rear on rib; oil-finished European walnut stock; cheekpiece; hand-checkered pistol grip, forend; ejectors; silvered receiver, other metal parts blued; marketed in trunk-type case. Made in Italy. Introduced 1983; discontinued 1989.

Perf: $5495 **Exc:** $4895 **VGood:** $3695

PERUGINI-VISINI EAGLE

Single shot; boxlock; 17 Rem., 222, 22-250, 243, 270, 30-06, 7mm Rem. Mag., 300 Win. Mag., 5.6x50R, 5.6x57R, 6.5x68R, 7x57R, 9.3x74R, 10.3x60R; 24-inch, 26-inch barrel; no sights; claw-type scope mounts; oil-finished European walnut stock; adjustable set trigger ejector; engraved, case-hardened receiver. Made in Italy. Introduced 1986; discontinued 1989.

Perf: $4995 **Exc:** $4250 **VGood:** $2995

PERUGINI-VISINI MODEL SELOUS

Double rifle; 30-06, 7mm Rem. Mag., 7x65R, 9.3x74R, 270 Win., 300 H&H, 338 Win., 375 H&H, 458 Win. Mag., 470 Nitro; 22-inch-26-inch barrels; 41-inch overall length (24-inch barrels); weighs 7-1/4 to 10-1/2 lbs.; bead on ramp front sight, express rear on quarter-rib; oil-finished walnut stock with checkered grip and forend, cheekpiece; true sidelock action with ejectors; sideplates hand detachable; comes with leather trunk case. Imported from Italy by Wm. Larkin Moore. Introduced 1983; discontinued 1992.

Perf: $21,995 **Exc:** $17,995 **VGood:** $10,975

PERUGINI-VISINI PROFESSIONAL

Bolt action; 222 Rem. through 458 Win. Mag.; 24-inch, 26-inch barrel; no sights; oil-finished European walnut stock; modified Mauser 98k bolt action; single or double-set triggers. Made in Italy. Introduced 1986; discontinued 1987.

Perf: $3495 **Exc:** $2995 **VGood:** $1995

PERUGINI-VISINI PROFESSIONAL DELUXE

Same specs as Professional except open sights; checkered oil-finished European walnut stock; knurled bolt handle. Made in Italy. Introduced 1986; discontinued 1987.

Perf: $3495 **Exc:** $2995 **VGood:** $1995

PERUGINI-VISINI SIDELOCK EXPRESS

Double rifle; side-by-side; various up to 470 Nitro Express; 22-inch, 26-inch barrels; bead on ramp front sight, express rear on rib; oil-finished walnut stock; hand-checkered grip, forend; cheekpiece; ejectors; hand-detachable side plates; marketed in trunk-type case. Made in Italy. Introduced 1983; discontinued 1989.

Perf: $10,000 **Exc:** $7995 **VGood:** $6495

PERUGINI-VISINI VICTORIA

Double rifle; 30-06, 7x65R, 9.3x74R, 375 H&H, 458 Win. Mag., 470 Nitro; 22-inch-26-inch barrels; 41-inch overall length (24-inch barrels); weighs 7-1/4 to 10-1/2 lbs.; bead on ramp front sight, express rear on quarter-rib; oil-finished walnut stock with checkered grip and forend, cheekpiece; true sidelock action with automatic ejectors; sideplates hand detachable; double triggers; comes with leather trunk case. Imported from Italy by Wm. Larkin Moore. Introduced 1983; discontinued 1992.

Perf: $10500 **Exc:** $5490 **VGood:** $3700

PHILLIPS & RODGERS WILDERNESS EXPLORER

Bolt action; 22 Hornet, 218 Bee, 44 Mag, 50 AE (interchangeable barrels). 18-inch barrel; weighs 5.5 lbs.; 38-1/2-inch OAL; quick-change bolt faces and barrels allow using four different cartridges. Introduced 1997, discontinued 1997. Few made.

Perf: $900 **Exc:** $700 **VGood:** N/A

PLAINFIELD M-1 CARBINE

Semi-automatic; 5.7mm, 30 Carbine, 256 Ferret; 15-shot magazine; 18-inch barrel; weighs 5-1/2 lbs.; open sights; military-style wood stock; early models with standard military fittings, some from surplus parts; later models with ventilated metal hand guard, no bayonet lug. Introduced 1960; discontinued 1976.

30 Carbine

Exc: $475 **VGood:** $350 **Good:** $275

256 Ferret

Perf: $400 **Exc:** $375 **VGood:** $315

PLAINFIELD M-1 CARBINE, COMMANDO OR PARATROOPER MODEL

Same specs as M-1 Carbine except telescoping wire stock; pistol-grips front and rear.

Exc: $500 **VGood:** $425 **Good:** $375

PLAINFIELD M-1 CARBINE, DELUXE SPORTER

Same specs as M-1 Carbine except Monte Carlo sporting stock. Introduced 1960; discontinued 1973.

Exc: $425 **VGood:** $350 **Good:** $275

PLAINFIELD M-1 CARBINE, MILITARY SPORTER

Same specs as M-1 Carbine except unslotted buttstock; wood handguard.

Exc: $475 **VGood:** $350 **Good:** $275

PROFESSIONAL ORDNANCE CARBON 15 (TYPE 97)

Semi-automatic; 223; 16-inch barrel, weighs 3.9 lbs., 35-inch OAL; carbon fiber buttstock and forearm, with rubberized pistol grip; no sights, base for optics. Carbon fiber upper and lower carriers; QD compensator. Made in US by Professional Ordnance.

Perf: $1000 **Exc:** $800 **VGood:** $600

PROFESSIONAL ORDNANCE CARBON 15 TYPE 97S (INSULATED FOREND, OTHER IMPROVEMENTS)

Perf: $1200 **Exc:** $900 **VGood:** $700

PUMA BOUNTY HUNTER

Lever action based on Winchester Model 92 rifle. Chambered in 44/40, 44 Mag. or 45 Colt with 6-shot magazine capacity. Based on gun used by Steve McQueen in 1950's TV series "Wanted: Dead or Alive." Barrel length is 12 inches making it a handgun under Federal law. Overall length is 24 inches and weight 4.5 pounds. Walnut stock and fore-end. Finish is case hardened and blued.

Perf: $1235 **Exc:** $1050 **VGood:** $900

PURDEY BIG GAME SPORTER

Bolt action; 7x57, 300 H&H Mag., 375 H&H Mag., 404 Jeffery, 10.75x73; 3-shot magazine; 24-inch barrel; Mauser-design; folding leaf rear sight, hooded ramp front; hand-checkered European walnut pistol-grip stock. Introduced post World War I; not imported.

Exc: $6995 **VGood:** $5695 **Good:** $4295

PURDEY DOUBLE RIFLE

Double rifle; sidelock; 300 H&H Mag., 375 H&H Mag., 375 Flanged Nitro Express, 500-465 Nitro Express, 470 Nitro Express, 577 Nitro Express, 600 Nitro Express; 25-1/2-inch barrel; hammerless; folding leaf rear sight, hooded ramp front; hand-checkered European cheekpiece stock; ejectors; sling swivels; recoil pad. Introduced prior to World War I; not imported. Prices range from $25,000 to $85,000.

QUALITY PARTS/ BUSHMASTER V MATCH

Semi-automatic; 223; 10-shot magazine; 20-inch, 24-inch, 26-inch barrel with 1:9-inch twist; 38-1/4-inch overall length (20-inch barrel); weighs 8-1/4 lbs.; .950-inch barrel diameter with counter-bored crown, integral flash suppressor; no sights; comes with scope mount base installed; black composition stock; hand-built match gun with E2 lower receiver, push-pin-style takedown; upper receiver with brass deflector; free-floating steel handguard accepts laser sight, flashlight, bipod. Made in U.S. by Quality Parts Co./Bushmaster Firearms Co.

Perf: $920 **Exc:** $800 **VGood:** $695

Remington Model R15CS VTR Predator Carbine

Remington Model 597 TVP

Remington Model 597 Blaze Camo

Remington Model 597 Pink Camo

REMINGTON MODEL 7400D PEERLESS

Same specs as Model 7400 except fine checkered fancy walnut stock; engraving.

Perf: $2495 **Exc:** $1995 **VGood:** $1395

REMINGTON MODEL 7400F PREMIER

Same specs as Model 7400 except best-grade fine checkered walnut stock; extensive engraving.

Perf: $5295 **Exc:** $4495 **VGood:** $2695

REMINGTON MODEL 7400F PREMIER GOLD

Same specs as Model 7400 except best-grade fine checkered walnut stock; extensive engraving with gold inlays.

Perf: $7995 **Exc:** $6450 **VGood:** $2995

REMINGTON MODEL 7400 SPECIAL PURPOSE

Same specs as Model 7400 except 270, 30-06; non-glare finish on the American walnut stock; all exposed metal with non-reflective matte black finish; quick-detachable sling swivels; camo-pattern Cordura carrying sling. Made in U.S. by Remington. Introduced 1993; discontinued 1994.

Perf: $430 **Exc:** $350 **VGood:** $290

REMINGTON MODEL 750 WOODSMASTER

Wood-stocked, traditionally-styled, updated version of Model 7400 semi-auto. Reminiscent of the old M740 semi-auto. Rifle version has 22-inch barrel; carbine has 18.5-inch barrel. Introduced 2006.

NIB: $625 **Exc:** $565 **VGood:** $400

REMINGTON MODEL 750 SYNTHETIC

Similar to Model 750 Woodsmaster but with black synthetic stock and forend. Introduced in 2007.

NIB: $675 **Exc:** $625 **VGood:** $475

REMINGTON MODEL R15 VTR PREDATOR RIFLE

AR-style rifle chambered for .223 Remington or .204 Ruger. Supplied with one 5-shot magazine but accepts AR-style higher-cap magazines. 22-inch fluted barrel; fixed stock. Finish: Advantage MAX-12 HD overall.

Perf: $1145 **Exc:** $950 **VGood:** $795

REMINGTON MODEL R15 VTR PREDATOR CARBINE

Similar to above but with 18-inch barrel.

Perf: $1145 **Exc:** $950 **VGood:** $795

REMINGTON MODEL R15CS VTR PREDATOR CARBINE

Similar to above but with collapsible buttstock.

Perf: $1145 **Exc:** $950 **VGood:** $795

REMINGTON "NYLON" SERIES .22 RIFLES

These rifles are becoming increasingly collectible. Buyers should note that the Hohawk Brown rifles are the most common, followed in order by the "Apache Black" and "Seneca Green". Values shown are for Mohawk Brown. Increase given values by 100 percent for Apache Black and 175 percent for Seneca Green.

REMINGTON NYLON 10

Single-shot bolt action. Add 40% for rare 24" barrel version.,

Exc: $600 **VGood:** $475 **Good:** $350

REMINGTON NYLON 10-C

Semi-automatic, 22 LR; succeeded and virtually identical to Nylon 77. Introduced 1971; discontinued 1978.

Exc: $200 **VGood:** $175 **Good:** $150

REMINGTON NYLON 11

Bolt action; 22 Short, 22 Long, 22 LR; 6-, 10-shot detachable box magazines; 19 5/8-inch barrel; 38-1/2-inch overall length; weighs 4-1/2 lbs.; blade front sight, thumb-screw adjustable rear; Mohawk brown nylon stock with diamond inlay; checkered pistol grip, forearm grip cap, buttplate with white line spacers. Introduced 1962; discontinued 1964.

Exc: $400 **VGood:** $275 **Good:** $175

REMINGTON NYLON 12

Bolt action; 22 Short, 22 Long, 22 LR; 22-shot (22 Short), 17-shot (22 Long), 15-shot (22 LR) tube magazine; 19-5/8-inch barrel; 38-1/2-inch overall length; weighs 4-1/2 lbs.; blade front sight, thumb-screw adjustable rear; Mohawk brown nylon stock with diamond inlay; checkered pistol grip, forearm grip cap, buttplate with white line spacers. Introduced 1962; discontinued 1964.

Exc: $400 **VGood:** $275 **Good:** $200

REMINGTON NYLON 66

Semi-automatic; 22 LR; 14-shot tube magazine in buttstock; 19-1/2-inch barrel; 38-1/2-inch overall length; weighs 4 lbs.; blade front sight, fully-adjustable open rear; receiver grooved for tip-off mounts; moulded nylon stock with checkered pistol grip, forearm; white diamond forend inlay; black pistol-grip cap.Introduced 1959; discontinued 1988.

Exc: $285 **VGood:** $225 **Good:** $175

REMINGTON NYLON 76

Lever-action; 22 LR; 14-shot tube magazine in buttstock; 19-1/2-inch barrel; weighs 4-1/2 lbs.; blade front sight, open rear; receiver grooved for tip-off mounts; moulded nylon stock with checkered pistol grip, forearm; available in two stock colors: Mohawk brown and Apache black; latter has chrome-plated receiver. Introduced 1962; discontinued 1964. Values shown are for Mohawk Brown. Add as much as 300% for Apache Black.

Exc: $700 **VGood:** $525 **Good:** $350

REMINGTON NYLON 77

Semi-automatic; 22 LR; 5-shot detachable box magazine; 19-1/2-inch barrel; 38-1/2-inch overall length; weighs 4 lbs.; blade front sight, open rear; receiver grooved for tip-off mounts; moulded nylon stock with checkered pistol grip, forearm. Available in same colors as Nylon 66. Introduced 1970; discontinued 1971.

Exc: $300 **VGood:** $250 **Good:** $200

REMINGTON NYLON 77 APACHE

Same specs as Nylon 77 except red-green speckled nylon stock; 10-shot detachable box magazine; made for K-Mart. Introduced 1987; discontinued 1987.

Exc: $300 **VGood:** $250 **Good:** $200

MODEL 597 TVP (TARGET/VARMINT/PLINKER)

Ultra-funky .22 LR autoloader built on the Model 597 chassis. Features include bolt-guidance system with twin, tool-steel guide rails; laminated, skeletonized wood stock; non-glare matte finish; 10-shot metal detachable magazine; and last-shot hold-open bolt for added safety. Scope rail. Introduced in 2008.

Exc: $530 **VGood:** $425 **Good:** $250

REMINGTON MODEL 597 YELLOW JACKET

Similar to above but with yellow and black laminated stock.

Exc: $505 **VGood:** $415 **Good:** $235

REMINGTON MODEL 597 BLAZE CAMO

A Model 597 with synthetic stock molded in screamin' blaze orange and black.

Exc: $250 **VGood:** $225 **Good:** $150

REMINGTON MODEL 597 PINK CAMO

Similar to above but with a pink – yes, pink – and black camo-pattern stock.

Exc: $250 **VGood:** $225 **Good:** $150

REMINGTON BOLT-ACTION RIFLES REMINGTON MODEL 30A

Bolt action; 25, 30, 32, 35 Rem., 7mm Mauser, 30-06; 5-shot box magazine; early models with 24-inch barrel; military-type double-stage trigger; schnabel forearm tip; later versions with 22-inch barrel, checkered walnut stock forearm; uncheckered on earlier version with finger groove in forearm; pistol grip; bead front sight, open rear; modified commercial version of 1917 Enfield action. Introduced 1921; discontinued 1940.

Exc: $695 **VGood:** $575 **Good:** $390

REMINGTON MODEL 30R CARBINE

Same specs as Model 30A except 20-inch barrel; plain stock.

Exc: $695 **VGood:** $575 **Good:** $390

REMINGTON MODEL 30S SPORTING

Same specs as Model 30A except 25 Rem., 257 Roberts, 7mm Mauser, 30-06; 5-shot box magazine, 24-inch barrel; bead front sight, No. 48 Lyman receiver sight; long full forearm, high-comb checkered stock. Introduced 1930; discontinued 1940. Add 25 percent for 25 Remington.

Exc: $695 **VGood:** $575 **Good:** $390

REMINGTON MODEL 33

Bolt action; single shot; 22 Short, 22 Long, 22 LR; 24-inch barrel; takedown; bead front sight, open rear; uncheckered pistol-grip stock; grooved forearm. Introduced 1931; discontinued 1936.

Exc: $200 **VGood:** $150 **Good:** $75

REMINGTON MODEL 33 NRA JUNIOR

Same specs as Model 33 except Patridge front sight, Lyman peep-style rear; 7/8-inch sling; swivels.

Exc: $250 **VGood:** $195 **Good:** $125

REMINGTON MODEL 34

Bolt action; 22 Short, 22 Long, 22 LR; 22-shot (22 Short), 17-shot (22 Long), 15-shot (22 LR) tube magazine; 24-inch barrel; takedown; bead front sight, open rear; uncheckered hardwood pistol-grip stock; grooved forearm. Introduced 1932; discontinued 1936.

Exc: $250 **VGood:** $175 **Good:** $125

REMINGTON MODEL 34 NRA

Same specs as Model 34 except Patridge front sight, Lyman peep rear; swivels; 7/8-inch sling.

Exc: $300 **VGood:** $250 **Good:** $175

REMINGTON MODEL 37 RANGEMASTER

Bolt action; 22 LR; 5-shot box magazine; single shot adapter supplied as standard; 28-inch heavy barrel; 46-1/2-inch overall length; weighs 12 lbs.; Remington peep rear sight, hooded front; models available with Wittek Vaver or Marble-Goss receiver sight; scope bases; uncheckered target stock with or without sling; swivels. When introduced, barrel band held forward section of stock to barrel; with modification of forearm, barrel band eliminated in 1938. Introduced 1937; original version discontinued 1940.

Exc: $750 **VGood:** $600 **Good:** $500

REMINGTON MODEL 37 OF 1940

Same specs as Model 37 except Miracle trigger mechanism; high-comb stock; beavertail forearm. Introduced 1940; discontinued 1954.

Exc: $775 **VGood:** $625 **Good:** $500

REMINGTON MODEL 40X

Bolt action; single shot; 22 LR; 28-inch standard or heavy barrel; 46-3/4-inch overall length; weighs 12-3/4 lbs. (heavy barrel); Redfield Olympic sights optional; scope bases; American walnut, high comb target stock; built-in adjustable bedding device; adjustable swivel; rubber buttplate; action similar to Model 722; adjustable trigger. Introduced 1955; discontinued 1964.

Exc: $1050 **VGood:** $895 **Good:** $595

With sights

Exc: $1250 **VGood:** $995 **Good:** $650

REMINGTON MODEL 40X CENTERFIRE

Same specs as Model 40X except only 222 Rem., 222 Rem. Mag., 30-06, 308, other calibers on special request at additional cost. Introduced 1961; discontinued 1964.

Exc: $1400 **VGood:** $950 **Good:** $650

With sights

Exc: $1500 **VGood:** $1050 **Good:** $730

REMINGTON MODEL 40X STANDARD

Same specs as Model 40X except lighter standard-weight 28-inch barrel; weighs 10-3/4 lbs.

Exc: $1000 **VGood:** $900 **Good:** $750

With sights

Exc: $1100 **VGood:** $1000 **Good:** $850

REMINGTON MODEL 40-XB RANGEMASTER RIMFIRE

Bolt action; single shot; 22 LR; 28-inch barrel, standard or heavyweight; 47-inch overall length; weighs 10-3/4 lbs. (standard barrel); no sights; American walnut target stock, with palm rest; adjustable swivel block on guide rail; adjustable trigger; rubber buttplate. Replaced Model 40X. Introduced 1964; discontinued 1974.

Exc: $500 **VGood:** $400 **Good:** $350

REMINGTON MODEL 40-XB RANGEMASTER CENTERFIRE

Same specs as Model 40-XB Rangemaster except 222 Rem., 222 Rem. Mag., 223 Rem., 6mm, 7.62mm, 220 Swift, 243, 25-06, 7mm BR, 7mm Rem. Mag., 30-338, 300 Win. Mag., 30-06, 6mmx47, 6.5x55, 22-250, 244, 30-06, 308; stainless steel 27-1/4-inch barrel, standard or heavyweight; 47-inch overall length; weighs 11-1/4 lbs.; no sights; target stock; adjustable swivel block on guide rail; rubber buttplate. Introduced 1964; still in production.

Exc: $1400 **VGood:** $1125 **Good:** $950

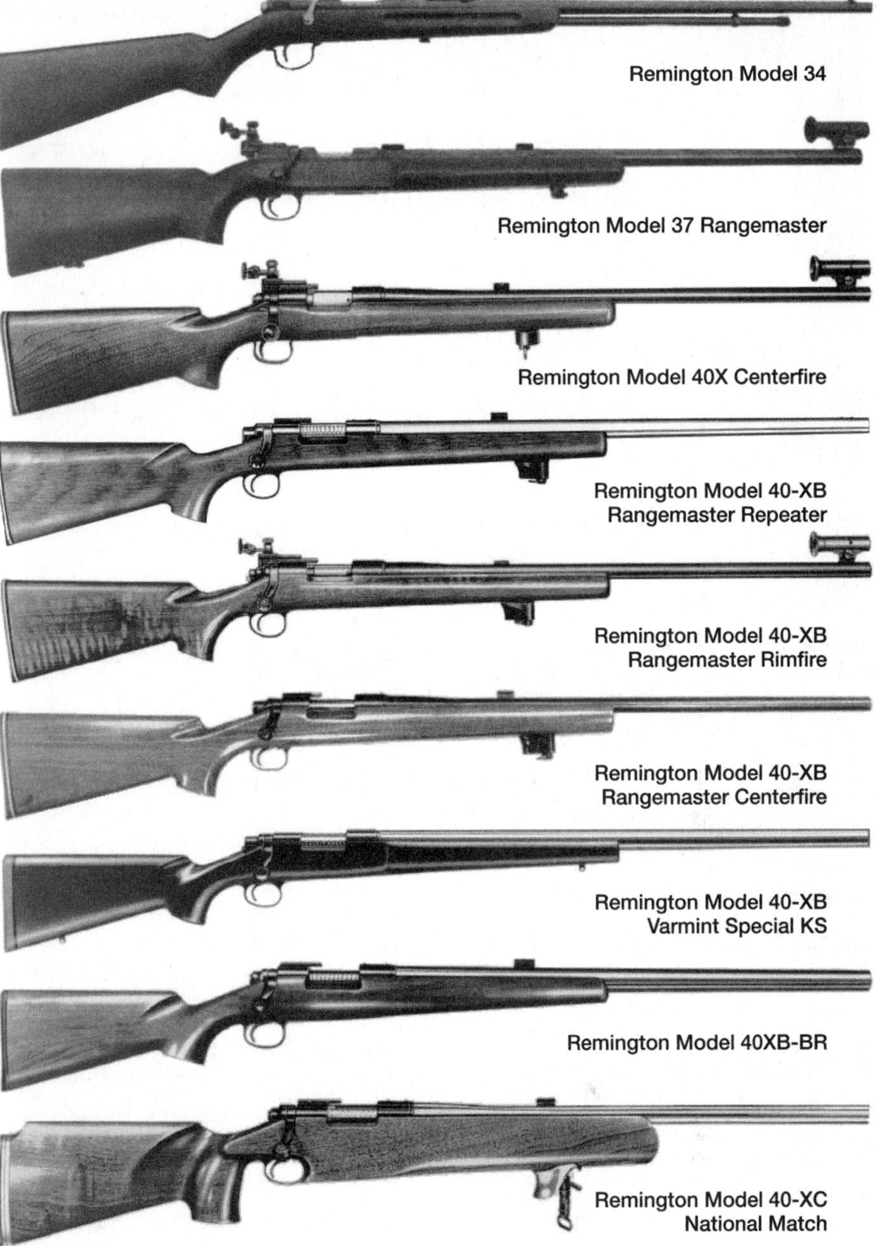

Remington Model 34

Remington Model 37 Rangemaster

Remington Model 40X Centerfire

Remington Model 40-XB Rangemaster Repeater

Remington Model 40-XB Rangemaster Rimfire

Remington Model 40-XB Rangemaster Centerfire

Remington Model 40-XB Varmint Special KS

Remington Model 40XB-BR

Remington Model 40-XC National Match

REMINGTON MODEL 40-XB RANGEMASTER REPEATER

Same specs as Model 40-XB Rangemaster except repeater with 5-shot magazine. No longer in production.

Exc: $1300 **VGood:** $1025 **Good:** $850

REMINGTON MODEL 40-XB RANGEMASTER VARMINT SPECIAL KS

Same specs as Model 40-XB except single shot or repeater; 220 Swift; 27-1/4-inch stainless steel barrel; 45-3/4-inch overall length; weighs 9-3/4 lbs.; no sights; Kevlar aramid fiber stock; straight comb; cheekpiece; palm swell grip; black recoil pad; removable swivel studs; custom-built to order. Introduced 1987; discontinued 1990.

Perf: $1395 **Exc:** $1095 **VGood:** $930

REMINGTON MODEL 40-XB-BR

Bolt action; single shot; 22 BR Rem., 222, 222 Rem. Mag., 223, 6mmx47, 6mm BR Rem., 7.62 NATO; stainless steel 20-inch light varmint, 26-inch heavy varmint barrel; 38-inch overall length (20-inch barrel); weighs 9-1/4 lbs.; no sights; supplied with scope blocks; select walnut stock; wide squared-off forend; adjustable trigger. Introduced 1978; discontinued 1989.

Perf: $995 **Exc:** $795 **VGood:** $650

REMINGTON MODEL 40-XB-BR KS

Same specs as Model 40XB-BR except Kevlar stock. Introduced 1989; still in production.

Perf: $1195 **Exc:** $895 **VGood:** $730

REMINGTON MODEL 40-XC NATIONAL MATCH

Bolt action; 7.62 NATO (308 Win); 5-shot magazine; receiver has clip-slot for top-loading; 24-inch stainless steel barrel; 43-1/2-inch overall length; weighs 11 lbs.; no sights; position-style American walnut stock; palm swell; adjustable buttplate; adjustable trigger to meet all ISU Army Rifle specs. Introduced 1978; later production made with Kevlar stock as 40-XC KS.

Perf: $1195 **Exc:** $895 **VGood:** $730

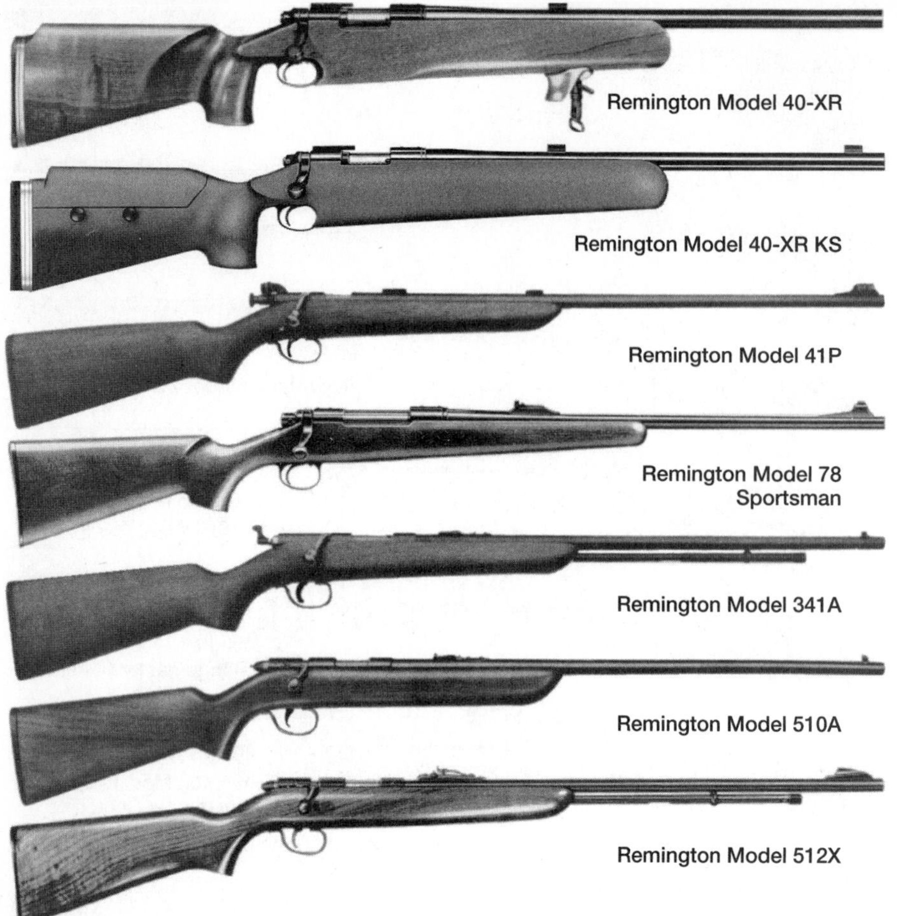

REMINGTON MODEL 40-XC KS NATIONAL MATCH

Same specs as Model 40-XC except Kevlar stock. Introduced 1992.

Perf: $1250 **Exc:** $995 **VGood:** $795

REMINGTON MODEL 40-XR

Bolt-action; single-shot; 22 LR; 24-inch heavy target barrel; 42-1/2-inch overall length; weighs 9-1/4 lbs.; no sights; drilled, tapped, furnished with scope blocks; American walnut position-style stock, with front swivel block, forend guide rail; adjustable buttplate; adjustable trigger. Meets ISU specs. Introduced 1975; discontinued 1991.

Exc: $995 **VGood:** $850 **Good:** $695

REMINGTON MODEL 40-XR CUSTOM SPORTER

Same specs as Model 40-XR except Custom Shop model; available in four grades. Duplicates Model 700 Centerfire rifle. Introduced 1986; discontinued 1991. Premium for higher grades.

Perf: $1100 **Exc:** $925 **VGood:** $795

REMINGTON MODEL 40-XR KS

Same specs as Model 40-XR except 43-1/2-inch overall length; weighs 10-1/2 lbs.; Kevlar stock. Introduced 1989.

Exc: $1150 **VGood:** $895 **Good:** $695

REMINGTON MODEL 40-XR KS SPORTER

Same specs as Model 40-XR except match chamber; Kevlar stock; special order only. Introduced 1994.

Exc: $925 **VGood:** $680 **Good:** $535

REMINGTON MODEL 41A TARGETMASTER

Bolt action; single shot; 22 Short, 22 Long, 22 LR; 27-inch barrel; takedown; bead front sight, open rear; uncheckered pistol-grip stock. Introduced 1936; discontinued 1940.

Exc: $175 **VGood:** $150 **Good:** $125

REMINGTON MODEL 41AS

Same specs as Model 41A Targetmaster except 22 Remington Special (22WRF) cartridge.

Exc: $250 **Vgood:** $200 **Good:** $175

REMINGTON MODEL 41P

Same specs as Model 41A Targetmaster except hooded front sight, peep-type rear.

Exc: $175 **VGood:** $150 **Good:** $125

REMINGTON MODEL 41SB

Same specs as Model 41A Targetmaster except smoothbore barrel for 22 shot cartridges.

Exc: $350 **VGood:** $300 **Good:** $250

REMINGTON MODEL 78 SPORTSMAN

Bolt action; 223, 243, 308, 270, 30-06; 4-shot magazine; 22-inch barrel; 42-1/2-inch overall length; weighs 7-1/2 lbs.; open adjustable sights; straight-comb walnut-finished hardwood stock; cartridge head inset on receiver bottom denotes caliber; positive cross-bolt safety; tapped for scope mount. Introduced 1984; discontinued 1989.

Exc: $400 **VGood:** $350 **Good:** $300

REMINGTON MODEL 341A

Bolt action; 22 Short, 22 Long, 22 LR; 22-shot (22 Short), 17-shot (22 Long), 15-shot (22 LR) tube magazine; 27-inch barrel; takedown; bead front sight, open rear; uncheckered hardwood pistol-grip stock. Introduced 1936; discontinued 1940.

Exc: $275 **VGood:** $225 **Good:** $150

REMINGTON MODEL 341P

Same specs as Model 341A except hooded front sight, peep rear.

Exc: $275 **VGood:** $225 **Good:** $150

REMINGTON MODEL 341SB

Same specs as Model 341A except smoothbore barrel for 22 shot cartridges.

Exc: $450 **VGood:** $350 **Good:** $250

REMINGTON MODEL 510A

Bolt action; single shot; 22 Short, 22 Long, 22 LR; 25-inch barrel; 43-inch overall length; 5-3/4 lbs.; takedown; bead front sight, open rear; uncheckered American walnut pistol-grip stock; shotgun-style checkered buttplate; semi-beavertail forend; grooved trigger; double locking lugs, extractors; thumb safety; auto ejector. Introduced 1939; discontinued 1963.

Exc: $175 **VGood:** $125 **Good:** $100

REMINGTON MODEL 510P

Same specs as Model 510A except Patridge-design front sight on ramp,"Point-crometer" peep rear.

Exc: $175 **VGood:** $150 **Good:** $125

REMINGTON MODEL 510SB

Same specs as Model 510A except smoothbore barrel for 22 shot cartridge; shotgun bead front sight, no rear sight.

Exc: $250 **VGood:** $200 **Good:** $175

REMINGTON MODEL 510X

Same specs as Model 510A except redesigned fully-adjustable rear sight, ramped front sight. Introduced 1964; discontinued 1966.

Exc: $175 **VGood:** $150 **Good:** $100

REMINGTON 510X-SB

Same specs as Model 510X except smoothbore barrel for use with 22-shot cartridge.

Exc: $275 **VGood:** $225 **Good:** $175

REMINGTON MODEL 511A

Bolt action; 22 Short, 22 Long, 22 LR; 6-shot detachable box magazine; 25-inch barrel; 43-inch overall length; weighs 5-3/4 lbs.; takedown; white metal bead front sight, step-adjustable rear; uncheckered pistol-grip stock; grooved trigger; thumb safety. Introduced 1939; discontinued 1962.

Exc: $175 **VGood:** $150 **Good:** $125

REMINGTON MODEL 511P

Same specs as Model 511A except "Point-crometer" peep sight on rear of receiver; Patridge-type ramp blade front.

Exc: $175 **VGood:** $150 **Good:** $125

REMINGTON MODEL 511SB

Same specs as Model 511A except smoothbore for use with 22 shot cartridge; open sights.

Exc: $275 **VGood:** $200 **Good:** $150

REMINGTON MODEL 511X

Same specs as Model 511A except box or clip-type magazine; improved sights. Introduced 1965; discontinued 1966.

Exc: $175 **VGood:** $150 **Good:** $125

REMINGTON MODEL 512A

Bolt action; 22 Short, 22 Long, 22 LR; 22-shot (22 Short), 17-shot (22 Long), 15-shot (22 LR) tube magazine; 25-inch barrel; 43-inch overall length; weighs 6 lbs.; takedown; double extractors, locking lugs; automatic ejector; thumb safety; white metal bead front sight, open rear; uncheckered pistol-grip stock; semi-beavertail forearm. Introduced 1940; discontinued 1963.

Exc: $200 **VGood:** $160 **Good:** $135

REMINGTON MODEL 512P

Same specs as Model 512A except Patridge-type blade front sight on ramp, "Point-crometer" peep rear.

Exc: $200 **VGood:** $165 **Good:** $135

REMINGTON MODEL 512SB

Same specs as Model 512 except smoothbore for use with 22-shot cartridge; open sights.

Exc: $275 **VGood:** $225 **Good:** $175

REMINGTON MODEL 512X

Same specs as Model 512A except one cartridge shorter magazine; improved sights. Introduced 1964; discontinued 1966.

Exc: $175 **VGood:** $150 **Good:** $125

REMINGTON MODEL 513S SPORTER

Bolt action; 22 LR; 6-shot detachable box magazine; 27-inch barrel; 45-inch overall length; weighs 6-3/4 lbs.; Patridge-type ramp front sight, Marble open rear; receiver drilled, tapped for Redfield No. 75 micrometer sight; adjustable trigger stop; double extractors, locking lugs; side-lever safety; checkered American walnut sporter-style stock; checkered steel buttplate; sling swivels. Introduced 1940; discontinued 1956.

Exc: $550 **VGood:** $450 **Good:** $360

REMINGTON MODEL 513TR MATCHMASTER

Same specs as Model 513TR except weighs 9 lbs.; Redfield globe front sight, Redfield No. 75 peep-type rear; uncheckered target-style stock; 1-1/4-inch government-style leather sling; adjustable trigger stop; double extractors, locking lugs; side-lever safety. Introduced 1940; discontinued 1969.

Exc: $450 **VGood:** $375 **Good:** $300

REMINGTON MODEL 514

Bolt action; single shot; 22 Short, 22 Long, 22 LR; 24-3/4-inch barrel; 42-inch overall length; weighs 5-1/4 lbs.; flat integral bead front sight, step-adjustable rear; uncheckered pistol-grip stock; black plastic buttplate. Introduced 1948; discontinued 1971. Add 5 percent for short-stocked, short-barrelled youth model (514 Boy's Rifle).

Exc: $175 **VGood:** $150 **Good:** $125

REMINGTON MODEL 514P

Same specs as Model 514 except for ramp front sight, peep-type rear.

Exc: $195 **VGood:** $170 **Good:** $145

REMINGTON MODEL 514SB

Same specs as Model 514 except smoothbore barrel for 22 shot cartridge.

Perf: $275 **Exc:** $215 **VGood:** $150

REMINGTON MODEL 521T

Bolt action; 22 LR; 6-shot detachable box magazine; 25-inch barrel; 43-inch overall length; weighs 7 lbs.; takedown; Patridge-type blade front sight, Lyman 57RS peep-type rear; double locking lugs, extractors; firing indicator; side-lever safety; uncheckered American walnut target stock; black Bakelite buttplate; sling; swivels. Named "The Junior Special." Introduced 1947; discontinued 1969.

Exc: $350 **VGood:** $275 **Good:** $180

REMINGTON MODEL 540X

Bolt action; single shot; 22 LR; 26-inch heavy barrel; 43-1/2-inch-47-inch overall length; weighs 8 lbs.; no sights; drilled, tapped for scope blocks; fitted with front sight base; target-style stock with Monte Carlo comb and thumb rest groove; full-length guide rail; adjustable buttplate. Introduced 1969; discontinued 1974.

Exc: $400 **VGood:** $350 **Good:** $275

REMINGTON MODEL 540XR

Bolt action; single shot; 22 LR; 26-inch medium-weight barrel; 43-1/2-inch to 46-3/4-inch overall length; weighs 8-7/8 lbs.; no sights; drilled, tapped for scope blocks; fitted with front sight base; Monte Carlo position-style stock; thumb groove, cheekpiece; adjustable buttplate; full-length guide rail; adjustable match trigger. Introduced 1974; discontinued 1983.

Exc: $425 **VGood:** $365 **Good:** $280

REMINGTON MODEL 540XR JR

Same specs as Model 540XR except 1-3/4-inch shorter stock to fit junior shooter; adjustable length of pull. Introduced 1974; discontinued 1983.

Exc: $350 **VGood:** $300 **Good:** $275

REMINGTON MODEL 541S

Bolt action; 22 Short, 22 Long, 22 LR; 5-shot clip magazine; 24-inch barrel; 42-5/8-inch overall length; weighs 5-1/2 lbs.; no sights; drilled, tapped for scope mounts, receiver sights; American walnut Monte Carlo stock; checkered pistol grip, forearm; rosewood colored forend tip, pistol grip cap; checkered buttplate; thumb safety; engraved receiver, trigger guard. Introduced 1972; discontinued 1983.

Exc: $395 **VGood:** $350 **Good:** $275

Remington Model 513TR Matchmaster

Remington Model 514

Remington Model 521T

Remington Model 541S

Remington Model 541T

Remington Model XR-100 Rangemaster

Remington Model 580

Remington Model 581

REMINGTON MODEL 541T

Same specs as Model 541S except drilled, tapped for scope mounts only; satin finish; no engraving. Introduced 1986.

Perf: $350 **Exc:** $275 **VGood:** $240

REMINGTON MODEL 541T HB

Same specs as Model 541T except weighs about 6-1/2 lbs; heavy target-type barrel without sights; receiver drilled and tapped for scope mounting; American walnut stock with straight comb, satin finish, cut checkering, black checkered buttplate, black grip cap and forend tip. Made in U.S. by Remington. Introduced 1993.

Perf: $375 **Exc:** $320 **VGood:** $280

REMINGTON MODEL XR-100 RANGEMASTER

Single-shot target rifle built on Model Seven/XP-100 action and chambered in .204 Ruger, .223 Remington, and .22-250. Laminated thumbhole stock with cutouts in forend and 26" heavy varmint barrel.

NIB: $850 **Exc:** $700 **VGood:** $575

REMINGTON MODEL 580

Bolt action; single shot; 22 Short, 22 Long, 22 LR; 24-inch tapered barrel; 42-3/8-inch overall length; weighs 5 lbs.; screw-lock adjustable rear sight, bead post front; hardwood stock with Monte Carlo comb, pistol grip; black composition buttplate; side safety; integral loading platform; receiver grooved for tipoff mounts. Introduced 1957; discontinued 1976.

Exc: $175 **VGood:** $150 **Good:** $125

REMINGTON MODEL 580BR "BOYS' RIFLE"

Same specs as Model 580 except youth model with stock 1-inch shorter. Introduced 1971; discontinued 1978.

Exc: $200 **VGood:** $175 **Good:** $150

REMINGTON MODEL 580SB

Same specs as Model 580 except smoothbore barrel for 22 shot cartridges.

Exc: $200 **VGood:** $175 **Good:** $150

REMINGTON MODEL 581

Bolt action; 22 Short, 22 Long, 22 LR; 5-shot box magazine; 24-inch round barrel; 42-3/8-inch overall length; weighs 5-1/4 lbs.; screw-adjustable open rear sight, bead on post front; hardwood Monte Carlo pistol-grip stock; side safety; wide trigger;

Remington Model 582

Remington Model 591

Remington Model 592

Remington Model 547

Remington Model Five

Remington Model 600

receiver grooved for tip-off mounts. Introduced 1967; discontinued 1984.

Exc: $275 **VGood:** $225 **Good:** $175

REMINGTON MODEL 581 SPORTSMAN

Same specs as Model 581 except with single-shot adapter. Reintroduced 1986.

Exc: $275 **VGood:** $225 **Good:** $175

REMINGTON MODEL 582

Bolt action; 22 Short, 22 Long, 22 LR; 20-shot (22 Short), 15-shot (22 Long), 14-shot (22 LR) tube magazine; 24-inch round barrel; 42-3/8-inch overall length; weighs 5-1/4 lbs.; screw-adjustable open rear sight, bead on post front; hardwood Monte Carlo pistol-grip stock; side safety; wide trigger; receiver grooved for tip-off mounts. Introduced 1967; discontinued 1983.

Exc: $275 **VGood:** $225 **Good:** $175

REMINGTON MODEL 591

Bolt action; 5mm Rem. Mag. caliber; 4-shot box magazine; 24-inch barrel; 42-3/8-inch overall length; weighs 5 lbs.; screw-adjustable open rear sight, bead post front; uncheckered hardwood stock, with Monte Carlo comb; black composition pistol-grip cap, buttplate; side safety; wide trigger; receiver grooved for tip-off scope mounts. Introduced 1970; discontinued 1974.

Perf: $400 **Exc:** $325 **VGood:** $250

REMINGTON MODEL 592

Bolt action; 5mm Rem. rimfire; 10-shot tube magazine; 24-inch barrel; 42-3/8-inch overall length; weighs 5-1/2 lbs.; screw-adjustable open rear sight, bead post front; uncheckered hardwood stock, with Monte Carlo comb; black composition pistol-grip cap, buttplate; side safety; wide trigger; receiver grooved for tip-off scope mounts. Introduced 1970; discontinued 1974.

Perf: $400 **Exc:** $325 **VGood:** $250

REMINGTON MODEL 504

.22 rimfire bolt-action sporter. Calibers: .22 LR, .22 WMR, .17 Mach 2, .17 HMR; five-shot detachable magazine. Barrel: 22-inch blued with iron sights; receiver blued for scope mounts. Stock: laminated walnut with QD swivels. Add 20 percent for target version.

NIB: $550 **Exc:** $495 **VGood:** $375

REMINGTON MODEL 547

High-quality magazine-fed bolt-action .17 or .22 rimfire sporter with walnut stock, crowned muzzle, tuned trigger and other goodies. A dealer exclusive for 2007.

NIB: $975 **Exc:** $225 **VGood:** $175

REMINGTON MODEL FIVE

A more economical, Serbian-made version of the discontinued Model 504. Chambered for .22 LR.

NIB: $350 **Exc:** $300 **VGood:** $265

REMINGTON MODEL 600

Bolt action; 222 Rem., 6mm Rem., 243, 308, 35 Rem.; 5-, 6-shot (222 Rem. only) magazine; 18-1/2-inch round barrel with ventilated nylon rib; 37-1/4-inch overall length; weighs 5-1/2 lbs.; blade ramp front sight, fully-adjustable open rear; drilled, tapped for scope mounts; checkered walnut Monte Carlo pistol-grip stock. Introduced 1964; discontinued 1967. Add $200 for .35 Remington.

Exc: $650 **VGood:** $525 **Good:** $425

223 Rem. (Rare)

Exc: $750 **VGood:** $600 **Good:** $500

REMINGTON MODEL 600 MAGNUM

Same specs as Model 600 except 6.5mm Rem. Mag., 350 Rem. Mag.; 4-shot box magazine; heavy Magnum-type barrel; weighs 6-1/2 lbs.; laminated walnut/beech stock; recoil pad; swivels; sling. Introduced 1965; discontinued 1967.

Exc: $900 **VGood:** $700 **Good:** $500

REMINGTON MODEL 600 MOHAWK

Same specs as Model 600 except 222 Rem., 6mm Rem., 243, 308; 18-1/2-inch barrel with no rib; promotional model. Introduced 1971; discontinued 1980.

Exc: $500 **VGood:** 425 **Good:** $350

REMINGTON MODEL 660

Bolt action; 222 Rem., 6mm Rem., 243, 308; 5-, 6-shot (222 Rem. only) magazine; 20-inch barrel; 38-3/4-inch overall length; weighs 6-1/2 lbs.; brass bead front sight on ramp, open adjustable rear; checkered Monte Carlo stock; black pistol-grip cap, forearm tip. Introduced 1968; discontinued 1971.

Exc: $525 **VGood:** $450 **Good:** $350

REMINGTON MODEL 660 MAGNUM

Same specs as Model 660 except 6.5mm Rem. Mag., 350 Rem. Mag.; 4-shot magazine; laminated walnut/beech stock for added strength; quick-detachable sling swivels, sling; recoil pad. Introduced 1968; discontinued 1971.

Exc: $850 **VGood:** $670 **Good:** $550

REMINGTON MODEL 673

Bolt action, 6.5 Rem. Mag., 308, 300 Rem. SAUM, 350 Rem. Mag.; 3-shot magazine; 22-inch bbl., 41-3/16-inch long; weighs 7-1/2 lbs.; laminated stock; ventilated rib on blued barrel; adjustable open sights. Introduced 2003, considered a modern replacement for the discontinued Model 600 and 660 Magnum rifles.

Perf: $600 **Exc:** $525 **VGood:** $395

REMINGTON MODEL 700 ADL

Bolt action; 222, 222 Rem. Mag., 22-250, 243, 25-06, 264 Win. Mag., 6mm Rem., 270, 280, 7mm Rem. Mag., 308, 30-06; 4-shot (264, 7mm), 6-shot (222, 222 Rem. Mag.), 5-shot (others); 20-inch, 22-inch, 24-inch round tapered barrel; 39-1/2-inch overall length (222, 222 Rem. Mag., 243 Win.); removable, adjustable rear sight with windage screw, gold bead ramp front; tapped for scope mounts; walnut Monte Carlo stock, with pistol grip; originally introduced with hand-checkered pistol grip, forearm; made for several years with RKW finish, impressed checkering; more recent models with computerized cut checkering. Introduced 1962; still in production.

Perf: $400 **Exc:** $320 **VGood:** $285

With optional laminated stock

Perf: $420 **Exc:** $350 **VGood:** $300

REMINGTON MODEL 700 ADL SYNTHETIC

Similar to the 700 ADL except has a fiberglass-reinforced synthetic stock with straight comb, raised cheekpiece, positive checkering, and black rubber butt pad. Metal has matte finish. Available in 22-250, 223, 243, 270, 308, 30-06 with 22-inch barrel, 300 Win. Mag., 7mm Rem. Mag. with 24-inch barrel. Introduced 1996. Still offered.

Perf: $350 **Exc:** $300 **VGood:** $260

REMINGTON MODEL 700 ADL SYNTHETIC YOUTH

Similar to the Model 700 ADL Synthetic except has 1-inch shorter stock, 20-inch barrel. Chambered for 243, 308. Introduced 1998.

Perf: $375 **Exc:** $315 **VGood:** $265

REMINGTON MODEL 700 APR AFRICAN PLAINS RIFLE

Bolt action; 7mm Rem. Mag., 300 Win. Mag., 300 Wea. Mag., 338 Win. Mag., 375 H&H, 375 Rem Ultra Mag; 26-inch Custom Shop barrel with satin finish; Magnum receiver; laminated wood stock with raised cheekpiece; satin finish; black buttpad; 20 lpi cut checkering. Made in U.S. by Remington. Introduced 1994; still produced as a custom shop item.

Perf: $1450 **Exc:** $1350 **VGood:** $950

REMINGTON MODEL 700 AS

Bolt action; 22-250, 243, 270, 280, 30-06, 308, 7mm Rem. Mag., 300 Weatherby Mag.; 4-shot magazine, 3-shot (7mm, 300 Wea. Mag.); 22-inch, 24-inch (22-250, 7mm Rem. Mag., 300 Wea. Mag.) barrel; weighs 6-1/2 to 7 lbs.; no sights; Arylon thermoplastic resin stock; black, lightly textured finish; hinged floorplate; solid buttpad; right-hand only. Introduced 1989; discontinued 1991.

Perf: $450 **Exc:** $400 **VGood:** $330

REMINGTON MODEL 700 AWR ALASKAN WILDERNESS RIFLE

Bolt action; 7mm Rem. Mag., 300 Win. Mag., 300 Weatherby Mag., 338 Win. Mag., 375 H&H; 24-inch Custom Shop barrel profile; stainless barreled action with satin blue finish; matte gray stock of fiberglass and graphite, reinforced with DuPont Kevlar; straight comb with raised cheekpiece; Magnum-grade black rubber recoil pad. Made in U.S. by Remington. Introduced 1994; still produced as a custom shop rifle.

Perf: $1200 **Exc:** $950 **VGood:** $750

REMINGTON MODEL 700 BDL

Bolt action; 17 Rem., 22-250, 222 Rem., 222 Rem. Mag., 243, 25-06, 264 Win. Mag., 270, 280, 300 Savage, 30-06, 308, 35 Whelen, 6mm Rem., 7mm Rem. Mag., 7mm-08, 300 Win. Mag., 338 Win. Mag., 8mm Mag.; 4-shot magazine; 20-inch, 22-inch, 24-inch barrel; stainless barrel (7mm Rem. Mag., 264, 300 Win. Mag.); with or without sights; select walnut, hand-checkered Monte Carlo stock; black forearm tip, pistol-grip cap, skip-line checkering; matted receiver top; quick-release floorplate; quick-detachable swivels, sling.

Perf: $465 **Exc:** $400 **VGood:** $325

Left-hand model

Perf: $545 **Exc:** $470 **VGood:** $370

Remington Model 660

Remington Model 700ADL Synthetic Youth

Remington Model 700APR African Plains Rifle

Remington Model 700AWR Alaskan Wilderness Rifle

Remington Model 700 BDL

Remington Model 700 BDL Limited Classic

REMINGTON MODEL 700 BDL 50TH ANNIVERSARY EDITION

Bolt Action in 7mm Rem. Mag. 24" barrel with adjustable rear and hooded ramp front sight, satin-finished "B" grade walnut stock with Fleur-Di-Lis cut checkering, satin bluing, 50-year commemorative laser-engraved hinged floorplate and X-Mark Pro trigger. Introduced in 2012 for one year only. Limited edition - unknown quantity offered.

Perf: $1500 **Exc:** $1100 **VGood:** $850

REMINGTON MODEL 700 LSS

Similar to 700 BDL except stainless steel barreled action, gray laminated wood stock with Monte Carlo comb and cheekpiece. No sights furnished. Available in 7mm Rem. Mag., 7mm Rem. Ultra Mag., 375 Rem. Ultra Mag., LH 7mm Rem. Ultra Mag., 300 Rem. Ultra Mag., 300 Win. Mag., and 338 Rem. Ultra Mag. in right-hand, and 30-06, 300 Rem. Ultra Mag., 338 Rem. Ultra Mag. in left-hand model; premium for left-hand. Introduced 1996.

Perf: $600 **Exc:** $485 **VGood:** $410

REMINGTON MODEL 700 BDL DM

Same specs as Model 700BDL except right-hand action calibers: 6mm, 243, 25-06, 270, 280, 7mm-08, 30-06, 308, 7mm Rem. Mag., 300 Win. Mag., 338 Win. Mag.; left-hand calibers: 243, 270, 7mm-08, 30-06, 7mm Rem. Mag., 300 Win. Mag.; 3-shot (Magnums), 4-shot (standard) detachable box magazine; glossy stock finish; open sights; recoil pad; sling swivels. Made in U.S. by Remington. Introduced 1995.

Right-hand, standard calibers

Perf: $500 **Exc:** $450 **VGood:** $380

Left-hand, standard calibers, right-hand Magnums

Perf: $525 **Exc:** $475 **VGood:** $400

Left-hand, Magnum calibers

Perf: $550 **Exc:** $485 **VGood:** $425

REMINGTON MODEL 700 BDL EUROPEAN

Same specs as Model 700BDL except 243, 270, 7mm-08, 280 Rem., 30-06 (22-inch barrel), 7mm Rem. Mag. (24-inch barrel); oil-finished walnut stock. Made in U.S. by Remington. Introduced 1993.

Standard calibers

Perf: $440 **Exc:** $385 **VGood:** $325

7mm Rem. Mag.

Perf: $465 **Exc:** $425 **VGood:** $375

REMINGTON MODEL 700 BDL LIMITED CLASSIC

Same specs as Model 700BDL except made in classic style, with a different single chambering for each year; In sequence, from 1981 through 2005, the calibers were: 1981: 7x57, 1982: 257 Roberts., 1983: 300 H&H, 1984: 250-3000, 1985: 350 Rem Mag, 1986: 264 Win Mag, 1987: 338 Win Mag, 1988: 35 Whelen, 1989: 300 Wby Mag, 1990: 25-06, 1991: 7mm Wby Mag, 1992: 220 Swift, 1993: 222, 1994: 6.5x55, 1995: 300 Win Mag, 1996: 375 H&H, 1997: 280, 1998: 8mm Rem Mag, 1999: 17 Rem, 2000: 223, 2001: 7mm-08, 2002: 221 Fireball, 2003: 300 Savage, 2004: 8x57, 2005: 308; classic-style, hand-checkered walnut straight stock; black forearm tip, pistol-grip cap; high gloss blued finish. New caliber announced annually and produced for that year only. Introduced 1981; still in production.

Perf: $635 **Exc:** $480 **VGood:** $385

REMINGTON MODEL 700 BDL MOUNTAIN RIFLE

Same specs as Model 700BDL except 243, 25-06, 257 Roberts, 270, 7mm-08, 280, 30-06, 308, 7x57; 22-inch tapered barrel; checkered American walnut stock with cheekpiece; ebony forend tip. Introduced 1986; no longer in production.

Perf: $435 **Exc:** $375 **VGood:** $325

REMINGTON MODEL 700 BDL MOUNTAIN CUSTOM KS WOOD GRAINED

Same specs as Model 700BDL Mountain except 375 H&H Mag., 416 Rem. Mag., 458 Win. Mag.; wood-grained Kevlar stock. Introduced 1992; discontinued 1993.

Perf: $900 **Exc:** $795 **VGood:** $625

REMINGTON MODEL 700BDL MOUNTAIN STAINLESS

Same specs as Model 700BDL Mountain except 25-06, 270, 280, 30-06; 22-inch stainless barrel;

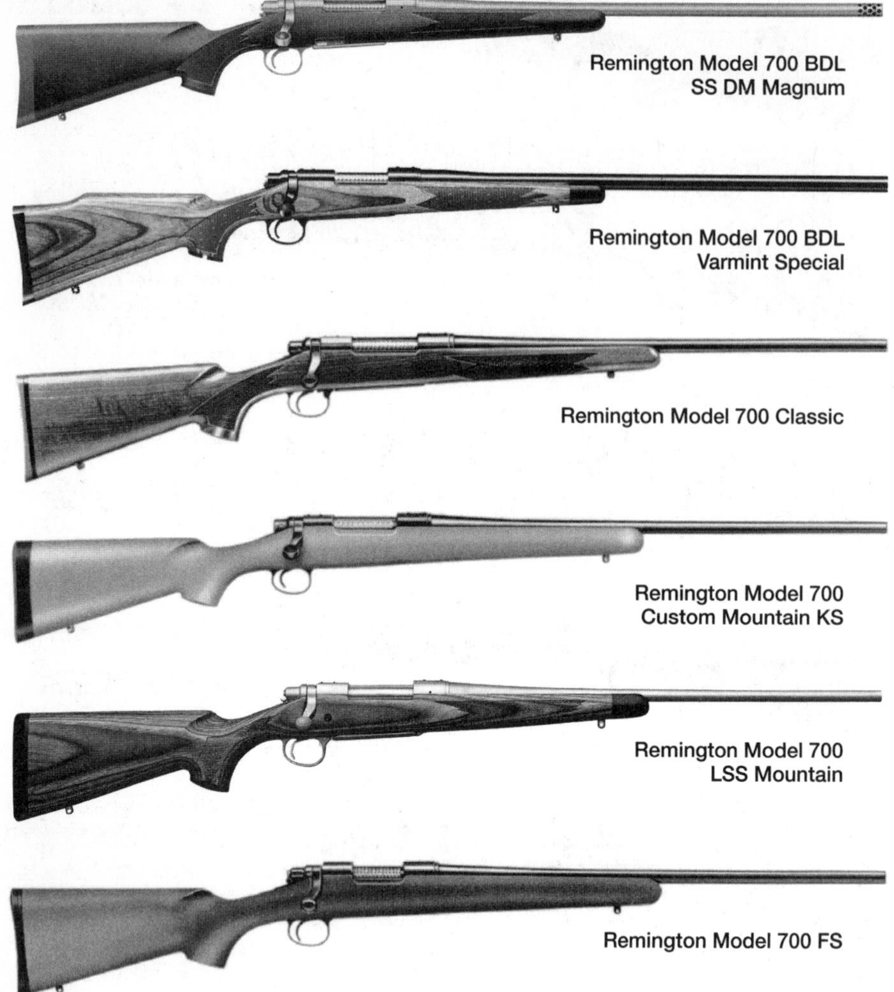
Remington Model 700 BDL SS DM Magnum

Remington Model 700 BDL Varmint Special

Remington Model 700 Classic

Remington Model 700 Custom Mountain KS

Remington Model 700 LSS Mountain

Remington Model 700 FS

weighs 7-1/4 lbs.; black synthetic stock with checkering. Introduced 1993; discontinued 1993.

Perf: $460 **Exc:** $400 **VGood:** $375

REMINGTON MODEL 700 BDL SAFARI

Same specs as Model 700BDL except 375 H&H Mag., 8mm Rem. Mag., 416 Rem. Mag., 458 Win. Mag.; 3-shot magazine; 24-inch, 26-inch barrel; 46-3/8-inch overall length; weighs 9 lbs.; no sights; Classic or Monte Carlo hand-checkered walnut stock; recoil pad. Introduced 1962; still in production.

Perf: $875 **Exc:** $695 **VGood:** $530

Left-hand model

Perf: $925 **Exc:** $750 **VGood:** $565

REMINGTON MODEL 700 BDL SAFARI CUSTOM KS

Same specs as Model 700BDL Safari except 8mm Rem. Mag., 375 H&H Mag., 416 Rem. Mag., 458 Win. Mag.; lightweight Kevlar straight-line classic stock; comb; no cheekpiece. Introduced 1989; still in production.

Perf: $1100 **Exc:** $925 **VGood:** $700

Left-hand model

Perf: $1150 **Exc:** $950 **VGood:** $725

REMINGTON MODEL 700 BDL SAFARI CUSTOM KS STAINLESS

Same specs as Model 700BDL Safari except 375 H&H Mag., 416 Rem. Mag., 458 Win. Mag.; Kevlar stock; stainless barrel and action. Introduced 1993; still in production.

Perf: $1200 **Exc:** $950 **VGood:** $750

REMINGTON MODEL 700 BDL SS

Same specs as Model 700BDL Safari Custom KS Stainless rifle except 223, 243, 6mm Rem., 7mm-08 Rem., 308 (short action), 25-06, 270, 280 Rem., 30-06, 7mm Rem. Mag., 7mm Weatherby Mag., 300 Win. Mag., 300 Weatherby Mag., 338 Win. Mag. (standard long action); 24-inch barrel; Magnum-contour barrel (Magnums); weighs 6-3/4 to 7 lbs; corrosion-resistant follower and fire control; stainless #416 BDL-style barreled action with fine matte finish; synthetic stock with straight comb and cheekpiece, textured finish, positive checkering, plated swivel studs. Made in U.S. by Remington. Introduced 1993; still produced.

Standard calibers

Perf: $500 **Exc:** $450 **VGood:** $400

Magnum calibers

Perf: $535 **Exc:** $465 **VGood:** $410

REMINGTON MODEL 700 BDL SS DM

Same specs as Model 700BDL SS except 6mm, 243, 25-06, 270, 280, 7mm-08, 7mm Rem. Mag., 300 Win. Mag., 300 Weatherby Mag.; detachable box magazine; black synthetic stock. Made in U.S. by Remington. Introduced 1995; still produced.

Standard calibers

Perf: $520 **Exc:** $450 **VGood:** $400

Magnum calibers

Perf: $545 **Exc:** $475 **VGood:** $425

REMINGTON MODEL 700 BDL VARMINT SPECIAL

Same specs as Model 700BDL except 24-inch heavy barrel; 43-1/2-inch overall length; weighs 9 lbs.; no sights; 222, 223, 22-250, 25-06, 6mm Rem., 243, 7mm-08 Rem., 308; 5-, 6-shot magazine. Introduced 1967.

Perf: $470 **Exc:** $400 **VGood:** $325

REMINGTON MODEL 700 BDL VARMINT SYNTHETIC

Same specs as Model 700BDL Varmint except 220 Swift, 22-250, 223 Rem., 308; black/gray synthetic stock; aluminum bedding block; matte metal finish. Introduced 1992; still in production.

Perf: $540 **Exc:** $420 **VGood:** $350

REMINGTON MODEL 700 C

Bolt action; 17 Rem., 22-250, 222 Rem., 222 Rem. Mag., 223 Rem., 243, 25-06, 264 Mag., 270, 280, 300 Savage, 30-06, 308, 35 Whelen, 6mm Rem., 6.5mm Rem. Mag., 7mm Rem. Mag., 7mm-08, 300 Win. Mag., 338 Win. Mag., 350 Rem. Mag., 8mm Mag.; 4-shot magazine; 20-inch, 22-inch, 24-inch barrel; with or without sights; select walnut, hand-checkered stock; rosewood forearm tip, grip cap; hand-lapped barrel; hinged floorplate; Custom Shop rifle. Introduced 1964; discontinued 1983.

Perf: $895 **Exc:** $795 **VGood:** $650

REMINGTON MODEL 700D PEERLESS

Same specs as Model 700C except best-grade wood; scroll engraving.

Perf: $1695 **Exc:** $1295 **VGood:** $995

REMINGTON MODEL 700F PREMIER

Same specs as Model C except best-grade wood; extensive engraving.

Perf: $3125 **Exc:** $2625 **VGood:** $2100

REMINGTON MODEL 700 CAMO SYNTHETIC RIFLE

Bolt action; 22-250, 243, 7mm-08, 270, 280, 30-06, 308, 7mm Rem. Mag., 300 Weatherby Mag.; 4-shot, 3-shot (7mm, 300 Wea. Mag.) magazine; open adjustable sights; synthetic stock, stock and metal (except bolt and sights) fully camouflaged in Mossy Oak Bottomland camo; swivel studs. Made in U.S. by Remington. Introduced 1992; discontinued 1994.

Perf: $450 **Exc:** $375 **VGood:** $330

REMINGTON 700 CDL CLASSIC DELUXE

Calibers are 223, 243, 25-06, 270 Win., 7mm-08 Rem., 280, 7mm Rem. Mag., 7mm Rem. Ultra Mag., 30-06, 300 Rem. Ultra Mag., 300 Win. Mag., 35 Whelen. Barrel: 24 or 26 inches. Weight approximately 7.5 pounds. Straight-comb checkered American walnut stock with satin finish, cheek piece, black fore-end tip and grip cap, sling swivel studs. CDL SF (stainless fluted) chambered for 260 Rem., 257 Wby., 270 Win., 270 WSM, 7mm-08 Rem., 7mm Rem., 30-06, 300 WSM.

Perf: $865 **Exc:** $735 **VGood:** $625

Add 15 percent for CDL SF

REMINGTON MODEL 700 CLASSIC

Bolt action; 22-250, 6mm Rem., 243, 270, 7mm Mauser, 30-06, 7mm Rem. Mag., 350 Rem. Mag., 375 H&H, 300 Win. Mag.; 24-inch barrel; 44-1/2-inch overall length; weighs 7-3/4 lbs.; no sights; drilled and tapped for scope mounting; American walnut straight-comb stock with 20 lpi checkered pistol grip, forend; rubber recoil pad; sling swivel studs; hinged floorplate. Introduced 1978. Considreable premium for scarce chamberings such as .264 WM.

Perf: $500 **Exc:** $450 **VGood:** $400

REMINGTON MODEL 700 CUSTOM MOUNTAIN KS

Bolt action; 270, 280, 300 Win. Mag., 300 Weatherby Mag., 30-06, 338 Win. Mag., 35 Whelen, 7mm Rem. Mag., 8mm Rem. Mag., 375 H&H Mag. 375 Rem Ultra Mag.; 4-shot magazine; 22-inch barrel; 42-1/2-inch overall length; weighs 6-3/8 lbs.; no sights; Kevlar reinforced resin stock; left- and right-hand versions; Custom Shop rifle. Introduced 1986; still in production.

Perf: $995 **Exc:** $895 **VGood:** $650

Left-hand model

Perf: $1025 **Exc:** $925 **VGood:** $675

REMINGTON MODEL 700 MOUNTAIN

Same specs as Model 700 Custom Mountain KS except walnut stock with satin finish, fine-line checkering. Introduced 1986; no longer in production.

Perf: $450 **Exc:** $375 **VGood:** $300

REMINGTON MODEL 700 LSS MOUNTAIN RIFLE

Similar to Model 700 Custom KS Mountain Rifle except stainless steel 22-inch barrel and two-tone laminated stock. Chambered in 260 Rem., 7mm-08, 270 Winchester and 30-06. Overall length 42-1/2-inch, weighs 6-5/8 oz. Introduced 1999.

Perf: $675 **Exc:** $550 **VGood:** $450

REMINGTON MODEL 700 FS

Bolt action; 243, 270, 30-06, 308, 7mm Rem. Mag.; 4-shot magazine; 22-inch, 24-inch (7mm) barrel; weighs 6-1/4 to 6-3/4 lbs.; classic-style gray or gray camo fiberglass stock reinforced with Kevlar; black Old English-type rubber recoil pad; right- or left-hand actions. Introduced 1987; discontinued 1988.

Perf: $635 **Exc:** $565 **VGood:** $400

REMINGTON MODEL 700LS

Bolt action; 243, 270, 30-06, 7mm Rem. Mag.; 5-shot, 4-shot (7mm); 22-inch, 24-inch barrel (7mm); weighs 7-1/4 lbs.; open sights; laminated light/dark wood Monte Carlo pistol-grip stock with cut checkering; sling swivels. Introduced 1990; no longer in production.

Perf: $450 **Exc:** $385 **VGood:** $310

REMINGTON MODEL 700 MTN DM

Bolt action; 243, 260 Rem., 270 Win., 7mm-08, 25-06, 280 Rem., 30-06; 4-shot detachable box magazine; 22-inch barrel; 42-1/2-inch overall length; weighs 6-3/4 lbs.; no sights; drilled, tapped for scope mounting; redesigned pistol grip; straight comb; contoured cheekpiece; hand-rubbed oil satin finish; two position thumb safety. Introduced 1986; still in production.

Perf: $450 **Exc:** $400 **VGood:** $335

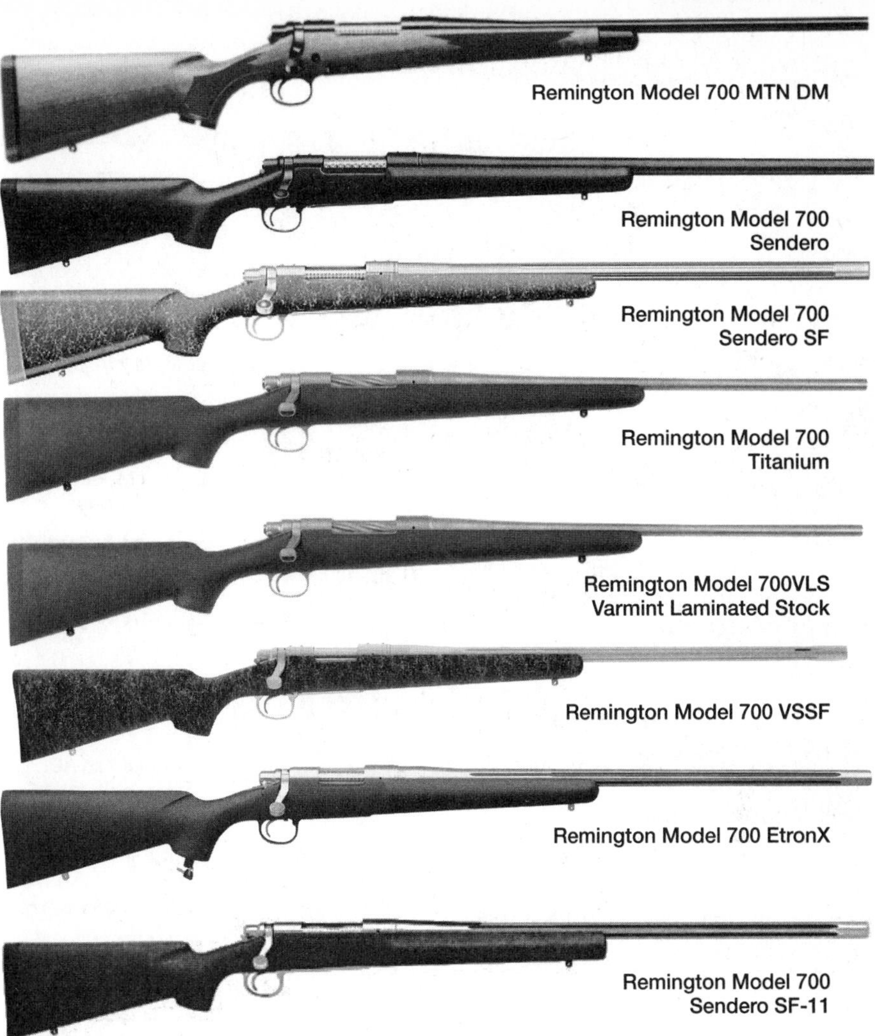

Remington Model 700 MTN DM

Remington Model 700 Sendero

Remington Model 700 Sendero SF

Remington Model 700 Titanium

Remington Model 700VLS Varmint Laminated Stock

Remington Model 700 VSSF

Remington Model 700 EtronX

Remington Model 700 Sendero SF-11

REMINGTON MODEL 700 MTRSS

Bolt action; 25-06, 270, 280 Rem., 30-06; weighs 6-3/4 lbs.; 22-inch barrel; stainless steel barreled action; textured black Rynite synthetic stock with positive checkering; straight comb and cheekpiece. Made in U.S. by Remington. Introduced 1993; discontinued 1994.

Perf: $510 **Exc:** $420 **VGood:** $360

REMINGTON MODEL 700 RS

Bolt action; 270, 280, 30-06; 4-shot magazine; 22-inch barrel; weighs 7-1/4 lbs.; open sights; glass-reinforced Rynite synthetic thermoplastic resin stock; textured gray or camouflage finish; solid buttpad; hinged floorplate. Introduced 1987; discontinued 1989.

Perf: $500 **Exc:** $425 **VGood:** $380

REMINGTON MODEL 700 SENDERO

Bolt action; 25-06, 270, 7mm Rem. Mag., 300 Win. Mag.; 26-inch heavy barrel with spherical concave crown; long action for Magnum calibers; composite stock. Made in U.S. by Remington. Introduced 1994; still produced.

Perf: $585 **Exc:** $475 **VGood:** $400

REMINGTON MODEL 700 SPS TACTICAL (16 INCH)

Bolt action; .223 Rem., .300 Black Out, .308 Win. Threaded muzzle with 16 ½" heavy barrel - 1/2 x 28 on 223 Rem., 5/8 x 24 on 300 Black Out and 308 Win. Hogue Ghillie Green Overmolded Stock and X-Mark Pro trigger. Introduced in 2013.

Perf: $700 **Exc:** $625 **VGood:** $550

REMINGTON MODEL 700 SPS WOOD TECH

Bolt Action; .270 Win., 7mm Rem. Mag., .30-06 Sprg., .300 Win. Mag. 22" or 24" inch barrel in a wood grain finished synthetic stock with X-Mark Pro trigger and Super Cell recoil pad. Introduced 2013.

Perf: $730 **Exc:** $600 **VGood:** $500

REMINGTON MODEL 700 SENDERO SF

Similar to 700 Sendero except stainless-steel action and 26-inch stainless-steel fluted barrel. Weighs 8-1/2 lbs. Chambered for 25-06, 7mm Rem. Mag., 7mm Rem. Ultra Mag., 7mm STW, 300 Win. Mag., 300 Rem. Ultra Mag., 338 Rem. Ultra Mag., Introduced 1996. Still offered.

Perf: $850 **Exc:** $715 **VGood:** $600

REMINGTON MODEL 700 TITANIUM

Similar to 700 BDL except has titanium receiver, spiral-cut fluted bolt, skeletonized bolt handle and carbon-fiber and aramid fiber reinforced stock with sling swivel studs. Barrel 22-inch; weighs 5-1/4 lbs. (short action) or 5-1/2 lbs. (long action). Satin stainless finish. 260 Rem., 270 Win., 7mm-08, 30-06, 308 Win. Introduced 2001.

Perf: $1000 **Exc:** $800 **VGood:** $700

REMINGTON MODEL 700 VLS (VARMINT LAMINATED STOCK)

Bolt action; 222 Rem., 223 Rem., 22-250, 243, 308; 26-inch heavy barrel; no sights; brown laminated stock with forend tip, grip cap, rubber buttpad; polished blue finish. Made in U.S. by Remington. Introduced 1995; still produced.

Perf: $580 **Exc:** $475 **VGood:** $380

REMINGTON MODEL 700 VS (VARMINT SYNTHETIC)

Similar to 700 BDL Varmint Laminated except composite stock reinforced with aramid fiber reinforced, fiberglass and graphite. Aluminum bedding block that runs full length of receiver. Free-floating 26-inch barrel. Metal has black matte finish; stock has textured black and gray finish and swivel studs. Available in 223, 22-250, 308. Right- and left-hand. Introduced 1992, still offered.

Perf: $580 **Exc:** $445 **VGood:** $410

REMINGTON MODEL 700 VSSF

Bolt action; 223, 220 Swift, 22-250, 243, 308; 26-inch fluted barrel; satin-finish stainless barreled action; spherical concave muzzle crown. Made in U.S. by Remington. Introduced 1994; still produced.

Perf: $750 **Exc:** $565 **VGood:** $465

REMINGTON MODEL 700 ETRONX (ELECTRONIC IGNITION RIFLE)

Similar to Model 700 VS SF except features battery-powered ignition system for near-zero lock time and electronic trigger mechanism. Requires ammunition with EtronX electrically fired primers. Aluminum-bedded 26-inch heavy, stainless steel, fluted barrel; overall length 45-7/8-inch; weight 8 lbs., 14 oz. Black, Kevlar-reinforced composite stock. Light-emitting diode display on grip top indicates fire or safe mode, loaded or unloaded chamber, battery condition. Available in 220 Swift, 22-250 or 243 Win. Introduced 2000.

Perf: $1700 **Exc:** $1500 **VGood:** $1200

Remington Model 700 CDL SF Limited

Remington Model 700 VTR

Remington Model 770 Youth

Remington Model 715 Sportsman

Remington Model 721A Magnum

Remington Model 725 ADL

REMINGTON MODEL 700 RMEF

Bolt action; 7mm Rem. Ultra Mag., 300 Rem. Ultra Mag.; 26-inch barrel; weighs 7-5/8 lbs.; 46.5-inch overall length; Synthetic stock, Realtree hardwood finish; no sights, drilled and tapped. Special Edition (sold one year only), Rocky Mountain Elk Foundation rifle, 416 stainless bolt, varrel, receiver. Portion of proceeds to RMEF.

Perf: $780 **Exc:** $585 **VGood:** $470

REMINGTON MODEL 700 SENDERO SF-II

Similar to Sendero SF but with HS Precision synthetic stock. Chambered in .264 WM, 7mm RM, 7mm RUM, .300 WM, and .300 RUM.

NIB: $925 **Exc:** $865 **VGood:** $695

REMINGTON MODEL 700 CDL

Similar to Model 700 Classic with straight-comb, oil-finished walnut stock with ebony tip, satin blue receiver and barrel (24" standard calibers, 26" magnum) and fine-cut checkering. Available in a variety of standard, magnum, and short magnum chamberings. Add 25 percent for .30-06 commemorative version.

NIB: $525 **Exc:** $485 **VGood:** $395

REMINGTON MODEL 700 CDL SF LIMITED

Similar to Model 700 CDL but with engraved floorplate and stainless, fluted barrel. Chambered in .30-06 and .17 Remington Fireball. 2006 "Centennial" model commemorates the centennial of the .30-06 cartridge and was introduced in 2006 for one year only. Reintroduced in .260 Remington in 2008. .300 Win. Mag. introduced in 2013

NIB: $995 **Exc:** $895 **VGood:** $695

REMINGTON MODEL 700 VTR (VARMINT TACTICAL)

Similar to Model 700 but with green stock with black overmold grips (similar to XCR models); tactical-style 1 in 9" twist (223 caliber) or tactical-style 1 in 12" twist (308 caliber):22" barrel with integrated muzzle brake design and triangular barrel contour to enhance accuracy. Chambered in .204, .223, .22-250 and .308. Introduced in 2008.

NIB: $900 **Exc:** $800 **VGood:** $675

REMINGTON 700 XCR II

Bolt action chambered in 25-06 Remington, 270 Win, 280 Remington, 7mm Remington Mag., 7mm Remington Ultra Mag., 300 WSM, 300 Win Mag., 300 Remington Ultra Mag, 338 Win. Mag., 338 Remington Ultra Mag, 375 H&H, 375 Remington Ultra Mag., 30-06 Springfield. Black TriNyte coated stainless steel barrel and receiver; olive drab green Hogue overmolded synthetic stock; SuperCell recoil pad; X-Mark Pro Trigger System.

Perf: $875 **Exc:** $750 **VGood:** $635

REMINGTON MODEL 700 XCR II RMEF LIMITED EDITION

Bolt Action in .257 Weatherby Magnum. 26" barrel with Black TriNyte finish on 416 Stainless, Nickel Plate, and PVD. Realtree AP-HD Stock with Hogue Overmolded Grip Panels, X-Mark Pro externally adjustable trigger and a SuperCell recoil pad. Introduced in 2013.

Perf: $1075 **Exc:** $950 **VGood:** $800

REMINGTON MODEL 710

Bolt action; 270 Win., 30-06, 7mm Rem. Mag., 300 Win. Mag.; 22-inch barrel; weighs 7-1/8 lbs.; 42-1/2-inch overall length; Gray synthetic stock; Bushnell Sharpshooter 3-9x scope mounted and bore-sighted. Unique action locks bolt directly into barrel; 60-degree bolt throw; 4-shot dual-stack magazine; key-operated Integrated Security System locks bolt open. Introduced 2001. Discontinued.

Perf: $ 295 **Exc:** $250 **VGood:** $175

REMINGTON MODEL 770 YOUTH

Similar to Model 710 but with shorter barrel and stock. Introduced 2006. Discontinued.

NIB: $375 **Exc:** $325 **VGood:** $265

REMINGTON MODEL 715 SPORTSMAN

Similar to Model 710. A dealer exclusive for 2007.

NIB: $325 **Exc:** $295 **VGood:** $250

REMINGTON MODEL 720A

Bolt action; 257 Roberts, 270, 30-06; 5-shot detachable box magazine; 22-inch barrel; 42-1/2-inch overall length; weighs 8 lbs.; bead front sight on ramp, open rear; models available with Redfield No. 70RST micrometer or Lyman No. 48 receiver sights; checkered American walnut pistol-grip stock; modified Model 1917 Enfield action. Made only in 1941 as factory facilities were afterwards converted to wartime production. Note: Most 720s were made in 30-06; few in 270; and only a handful in 257 Roberts. Add premium for rarer calibers.

Exc: $1250 **VGood:** $1000 **Good:** $700

REMINGTON MODEL 720R

Same specs as Model 720A except 20-inch barrel; models available with Redfield No. 70RST micrometer or Lyman No. 48 receiver sights.

Exc: $1250 **VGood:** $1000 **Good:** $700

REMINGTON MODEL 720S

Same specs as Model 720A except 24-inch barrel; models available with Redfield No. 70RST micrometer or Lyman No. 48 receiver sights.

Exc: $1250 **VGood:** $1000 **Good:** $700

REMINGTON MODEL 721A

Bolt action; 270, 280, 30-06; 4-shot box magazine; 24-inch barrel; 44-1/4-inch overall length; weighs 7-1/4 lbs.; white metal bead front sight on ramp, step-adjustable sporting rear; uncheckered American walnut sporter stock with pistol grip; semi-beavertail forend; checkered shotgun-style buttplate; thumb safety; receiver drilled, tapped for scope mounts, micrometer sights. Introduced 1948; discontinued 1962.

Exc: $400 **VGood:** $335 **Good:** $275

REMINGTON MODEL 721A MAGNUM

Same specs as Model 721A except only 264 Win. Mag., 300 H&H Mag.; 3-shot magazine; heavy 26-inch barrel; 46-1/4-inch overall length; weighs 8-1/4 lbs.; recoil pad. Values shown are for .264; deduct 15% for .300.

Exc: $675 **VGood:** $550 **Good:** $340

REMINGTON MODEL 721 ADL

Same specs as Model 721A except deluxe checkered walnut sporter stock, forearm. Introduced 1948; discontinued 1962.

Exc: $425 **VGood:** $375 **Good:** $295

REMINGTON MODEL 721 ADL MAGNUM

Same specs as Model 721ADL except 264 Win. Mag., 300 H&H Mag.; 3-shot magazine; 26-inch barrel; recoil pad. Values shown are for .264; deduct 15% for .300.

Exc: $625 **VGood:** $500 **Good:** $300

REMINGTON MODEL 721 BDL

Bolt action; 270, 280, 30-06; 4-shot magazine; 24-inch barrel; bead front sight on ramp, open rear; select checkered walnut sporter stock, forearm. Introduced 1948; discontinued 1962.

Exc: $415 **VGood:** $365 **Good:** $310

REMINGTON MODEL 721 BDL MAGNUM

Same specs as Model 721BDL except 264 Win. Mag., 300 H&H Mag.; 3-shot magazine; 26-inch barrel; recoil pad.

Exc: $625 **VGood:** $500 **Good:** $300

REMINGTON MODEL 722A

Bolt action, short action version of Model 721; 222 Rem., 222 Rem. Mag., 243 Win., 244 Rem., 257 Roberts, 300 Savage, 308; 4-, 5-shot (222 Rem.) magazine; 24-inch, 26-inch (222 Rem., 244 Rem.) barrel; 43-1/4-inch overall length; weighs 7 lbs.; shorter action than Model 721A; white metal bead front sight on ramp, step-adjustable sporting rear; receiver drilled, tapped for scope mounts or micrometer sights; uncheckered walnut sporter stock. Introduced 1948; discontinued 1962.

Exc: $415 **VGood:** $365 **Good:** $310

REMINGTON MODEL 722 ADL

Same specs as Model 722A except deluxe checkered walnut sporter stock.

Exc: $425 **VGood:** $375 **Good:** $325

REMINGTON MODEL 722 BDL

Same specs as Model 722A except select checkered walnut sporter stock.

Exc: $450 **VGood:** $350 **Good:** $250

REMINGTON MODEL 725 ADL

Bolt action; 222 Rem., 243, 244, 270, 280, 30-06; 4-, 5-shot (222 Rem.) box magazine; 22-inch, 24-inch (222 Rem.) barrel; 42-1/2-inch, 43-1/2-inch (222) overall length; weighs 7 lbs.; removable hood ramp front sight, adjustable open rear; Monte Carlo comb, walnut stock; hand-checkered pistol grip, forearm; hinged floorplate; swivels. Some calibers bring premium. Introduced 1958; discontinued 1961.

Exc: $385 **VGood:** $290 **Good:** $210

REMINGTON MODEL 725 ADL KODIAK MAGNUM

Same specs as Model 725ADL except 375 H&H Mag., 458 Win. Mag.; 3-shot box magazine; 26-inch barrel; reinforced deluxe Monte Carlo stock; recoil pad; special recoil reduction device built into barrel; black forearm tip; sling, swivels. Made only in 1962.

Exc: $950 **VGood:** $850 **Good:** $700

REMINGTON MODEL 783

Bolt action; .270 Win., 7mm Rem. Mag., .308 Win., .30-06 Sprg. Cylindrical receiver with barrel attached via external nut, injection modeled synthetic stock, pillar bedded action, detachable box magazine, recoil pad and Crossfire trigger. New for 2013.

Perf: $410 **Exc:** $380 **VGood:** $325

REMINGTON MODEL 788

Bolt action; 222, 22-250, 223, 6mm Rem., 243, 7mm-08, 308, 30-30, 44 Mag.; 3-, 4-shot (222) detachable box magazine; 22-inch, 24-inch (222, 22-250) barrel; 41-inch to 43-5/8-inch overall length; weighs 7-7-1/2 lbs.; open fully-adjustable rear sight, blade ramp front; receiver tapped for scope mounts; American walnut or walnut-finished hardwood pistol-grip stock, uncheckered with Monte Carlo comb; thumb safety; artillery-type bolt. Introduced 1967; discontinued 1983.

Exc: $360 **VGood:** $305 **Good:** $270

44 Mag., 7mm-08

Exc: $600 **VGood:** $500 **Good:** $395

REMINGTON MODEL 788 CARBINE

Same specs as Model 788 except 18-1/2-inch barrel.

Exc: $370 **VGood:** $315 **Good:** $280

REMINGTON MODEL 788 LEFT-HAND

Same specs as Model 788 except 6mm, 308; left-hand version. Introduced 1969.

Exc: $375 **VGood:** $310 **Good:** $260

REMINGTON MODEL INTERNATIONAL FREE RIFLE

Bolt action; single shot; used 40XB action; 22 LR; 222 Rem., 222 Rem. Mag., 223 Rem., 7.62 NATO, 30-06; 27-1/4-inch barrel; 47-inch overall length; weighs 15 lbs.; no sights; hand-finished stock; adjustable buttplate and hook; movable front sling swivel; adjustable palm rest; 2-oz. adjustable trigger. Introduced 1964; discontinued 1974.

Perf: $1900 **Exc:** $1600 **VGood:** $1300

REMINGTON MODEL INTERNATIONAL MATCH FREE RIFLE

Bolt action; single shot; 22 LR, 222 Rem., 222 Rem. Mag., 30-06, 7.62mm NATO, others on special order; 28-inch barrel; no sights; freestyle hand-finished stock with thumbhole; interchangeable, adjustable rubber buttplate and hook-type buttplate; adjustable palm rest; adjustable sling swivel; 2-oz. adjustable trigger. Introduced 1961; discontinued 1964.

Perf: $2000 **Exc:** $1700 **VGood:** $1400

Remington Model 783

Remington Model 788

Remington International Match Free Rifle

Remington Model Seven

Remington Model Seven Custom KS

Remington Model Seven FS

Remington Model Seven LS

REMINGTON MODEL SEVEN

Bolt action; 17 Rem., 222 Rem., 223 Rem., 243, 7mm-08, 6mm, 308; 4-shot magazine, 5-shot (222 only); 18-1/2-inch barrel; 37-1/2-inch overall length; weighs 6-1/4 lbs.; ramp front sight, adjustable open rear; American walnut stock; modified schnabel forend; machine-cut checkering; short action; silent side safety; free-floated barrel. Introduced 1983.

Perf: $450 **Exc:** $370 **VGood:** $320

REMINGTON MODEL SEVEN CUSTOM KS

Same specs as Model Seven except 223 Rem., 7mm BR, 7mm-08, 308, 35 Rem., 350 Rem. Mag.; 20-inch barrel; weighs 5-3/4 lbs.; Kevlar aramid fiber stock; iron sights; drilled, tapped for scope mounts. Special order through Remington Custom Shop. Introduced 1987.

Perf: $950 **Exc:** $750 **VGood:** $600

REMINGTON MODEL SEVEN CUSTOM MS

Same specs as Model Seven except 222 Rem., 223, 22-250, 243, 6mm Rem., 7mm-08 Rem., 308, 350 Rem. Mag.; 20-inch barrel; weighs 6-3/4 lbs.; full-length Mannlicher-style stock of laminated wood with straight comb, solid black recoil pad, black steel forend tip, cut checkering, gloss finish; polished blue finish; calibers 250 Savage, 257 Roberts, 35 Rem. available on special order. From Remington Custom Shop. Introduced 1993; no longer produced.

Perf: $910 **Exc:** $710 **VGood:** $650

REMINGTON MODEL SEVEN FS

Same specs as Model Seven except 243, 7mm-08, 308; weighs 5-1/4 lbs.; fiberglass/Kevlar classic-style stock gray or camo; rubber buttpad. Introduced 1987; discontinued 1989.

Perf: $550 **Exc:** $475 **VGood:** $400

REMINGTON MODEL SEVEN LS

Similar to Model Seven except has satin-finished, brown laminated stock with 20-inch carbon steel barrel. 223, 243 Win., 7mm-08, 300 Win. Introduced 2000, still produced.

Perf: $600 **Exc:** $500 **VGood:** $400

REMINGTON MODEL SEVEN SS

Same specs as Model Seven except 243, 260, 7mm-08, 308, also 7mm Rem SA Ultra Mag, 300 Rem SA Ultra Mag; 20-inch or 22-inch barrel; stainless steel barreled action; black synthetic stock. Made in U.S. by Remington. Introduced 1994; still produced.

Perf: $475 **Exc:** $430 **VGood:** $390

7mm Rem.SAUM, 300 Rem. SAUM, 22-inch bbl.

Perf: $500 **Exc:** $450 **VGood:** $400

REMINGTON MODEL SEVEN LSS

Bolt action; 22-250, 7mm-08; 20-inch barrel; weighs 6-1/2 lbs.; 39-1/4-inch overall length; Brown laminated stock; Cut checkering. Short-action design; silent side safety; free-floated barrel except for single pressure point at forend tip. Stainless barreled action. Introduced 1983.

Perf: $690 **Exc:** $580 **VGood:** $450

REMINGTON MODEL SEVEN YOUTH

Same specs as Model Seven except 6mm Rem., 243, 7mm-08; hardwood stock with 12-3/16-inch length of pull. Made in U.S. by Remington. Introduced 1993; still produced.

Perf: $450 **Exc:** $400 **VGood:** $325

Model Seven Youth Synthetic, short gray synthetic stock

Perf: $425 **Exc:** $375 **VGood:** $300

REMINGTON MODEL SEVEN CDL

Similar to Model Seven but with satin walnut.satin blue finish, sightless barrel, and Limbsaver recoil pad.

NIB: $650 **Exc:** $595 **VGood:** $450

REMINGTON MODEL SEVEN XCR CAMO

Similar to Model Seven LSS but with camo stock, fluted barrel and weather-resistant coating. Chambered in .243, 7mm-08, .308, .270 WSM and .300 WSM. Introduced in 2007.

NIB: $850 **Exc:** $700 **VGood:** $575

REMINGTON MODEL SEVEN 25TH ANNIVERSARY VERSION

Similar to Model Seven but in 7mm-08 only with 25th anniversary medallion inset at the pistol grip cap area, high-sheen blued finish on the receiver, bolt and 22" standard-contour barrel, X-Mark Pro Trigger and SuperCell recoil pad. Introduced 2008.

NIB: $950 **Exc:** $825 **VGood:** $675

MODEL SEVEN PREDATOR

Similar to Model Seven but with full coverage in Mossy Oak® Brush® camo; fluted, magnum contour 22" barrel, synthetic stock as on Model Seven XCR; X-Mark Pro Trigger. Chambered in .17 Remington Fireball, .204, .223, .22-250 and .243.

NIB: $800 **Exc:** $650 **VGood:** $525

REMINGTON MODEL 770

Package rifle similar to Model 710 but with redesigned bolt assembly and magazine catch. Chambered in .243, .270, 7mm-08, .308, .30-06, and .300 WM. Also available in Youth model chambered in .243 only. Introduced in 2007. In 2008 a version with stainless steel barrel and receiver and full camo finish was introduced.

NIB: $400 **Exc:** $350 **VGood:** $250

REMINGTON MODEL 798

Long-action sporting rifle built on reworked 98 Mauser action. Calibers: .243, .308, .30-06, .270, .300 WM, .375 H&H, .458 WM. Barrel: 22-inch or 24-inch blued sightless. Stock: Brown laminated with recoil pad. Claw extractor, 2-position safety, hinged floorplate. Add 10 percent for Magnum chamberings; add 40 percent for .375 and .458.

NIB: $550 **Exc:** $495 **VGood:** $365

REMINGTON MODEL 798 STAINLESS LAMINATE

Similar to Model 798 but with laminated stock and stainless barrel. Chambered in .243, .25-06, .270, .30-06, 7mm Mag, .300 WM, .375 H&H Mag and .458 Win Mag. Add 30 percent for .458.

NIB: $695 **Exc:** $625 **VGood:** $495

MODEL 798 SPS

Similar to Model 798 but with blued barrel and black synthetic stock. Introduced 2008.

NIB: $525 **Exc:** $425 **VGood:** $300

MODEL 798 SAFARI

Similar to Model 798 but chambered in .375 H&H or .458 Winchester Magnum. Introduced 2008.

NIB: $1150 **Exc:** $900 **VGood:** $675

REMINGTON MODEL 799

Similar to Model 798 but short-action without recoil pad. Calibers: .22 Hornet, .222 Remington, .22-250, .223, 762X39.

NIB: $525 **Exc:** $470 **VGood:** $340

REMINGTON-LEE SPORTER

Bolt action; 6mm USN, 30-30, 30-40, 303 British, 7mm Mauser, 7.65 Mauser, 32 Spl., 32-40, 35 Spl., 38-55, 38-72, 405 Win., 43 Spanish, 45-70, 45-90; 5-shot detachable box magazine; 24-inch, 26-inch barrel; open rear sight, bead front; hand-checkered American walnut pistol-grip stock. Collector value. Introduced 1886; discontinued 1906.

Exc: $1550 **VGood:** $965 **Good:** $595

REMINGTON-LEE SPORTER DELUXE

Same specs as Remington-Lee Sporter except half-octagon barrel; Lyman sights; deluxe walnut stock. Collector value. Introduced 1886; discontinued 1906.

Exc: $1795 **VGood:** $995 **Good:** $695

REMINGTON MODEL SIX

Slide action; 6mm Rem., 243, 270, 308 Win., 308 Accelerator, 30-06, 30-06 Accelerator; 4-shot detachable clip magazine; 22-inch round tapered barrel; 42-inch overall length; weighs 7-1/2 lbs.; gold bead front sight on matted ramp, open adjustable sliding ramp rear; cut-checkered Monte Carlo walnut stock with full cheekpiece; cross-bolt safety; tapped for scope mount; cartridge head medallion on receiver bottom to denote caliber. Special version of Model 760. Introduced 1981; discontinued 1988.

Perf: $395 **Exc:** $350 **VGood:** $300

D Peerless Grade

Perf: $1995 **Exc:** $1795 **VGood:** $1095

F Premier Grade

Perf: $4195 **Exc:** $3795 **VGood:** $2695

F Premier Gold Grade

Perf: $6495 **Exc:** $5195 **VGood:** $3995

REMINGTON MODEL 12, 12A

Slide action; 22 Short, 22 Long, 22 LR; 15-shot (22 Short), 12-shot (22 Long), 10-shot (22 LR) tube magazine; 22-inch barrel; hammerless takedown; bead front sight, open rear; uncheckered straight stock; grooved slide handle. Introduced 1909; discontinued 1936.

Exc: $450 **VGood:** $350 **Good:** $300

REMINGTON MODEL 12B

Same specs as Model 12A except 22 Short only; octagonal barrel.

Exc: $475 **VGood:** $350 **Good:** $300

REMINGTON MODEL 12C

Same specs as Model 12A except 24-inch octagonal barrel; pistol-grip stock.

Exc: $460 **VGood:** $385 **Good:** $315

REMINGTON MODEL 12CS

Same specs as Model 12A except 22 Rem. Spl. (22 WRF); 12-shot magazine; 14-inch octagonal barrel; pistol-grip stock.

Exc: $460 **VGood:** $360 **Good:** $310

REMINGTON MODEL 14, 14A

Slide action; 25, 30, 32, 35 Rem.; 5-shot tube magazine; 22-inch barrel; hammerless; takedown; bead front sight, open rear; uncheckered walnut straight stock; grooved slide handle. Introduced 1912; discontinued 1935. Add 25 percent for 25 Remington.

Exc: $550 **VGood:** $450 **Good:** $320

REMINGTON MODEL 14R CARBINE

Same specs as Model 14 except 18-inch barrel.

Exc: $625 **VGood:** $495 **Good:** $345

REMINGTON MODEL 14-1/2

Slide action; 38-40, 44-40; 11-shot tube magazine; 22-1/2-inch barrel; hammerless; takedown; bead front sight, open rear; uncheckered walnut straight stock; grooved slide handle. Introduced 1912; discontinued 1925.

Exc: $830 **VGood:** $560 **Good:** $470

REMINGTON MODEL 14-1/2 CARBINE

Same specs as Model 14-1/2 except 9-shot full-length tube magazine; 18-1/2-inch barrel. Introduced 1912; discontinued 1925.

Exc: $860 **VGood:** $580 **Good:** $490

REMINGTON MODEL 25, 25A

Slide action; 25-20, 32-20; 10-shot tube magazine; 24-inch barrel; hammerless; takedown; blade front sight, open rear; uncheckered walnut pistol-grip stock; grooved slide handle. Introduced 1923; discontinued 1936.

Exc: $650 **VGood:** $495 **Good:** $365

REMINGTON MODEL 25R CARBINE

Same specs as Model 25A except 6-shot magazine; 18-inch barrel; straight stock.

Exc: $675 **VGood:** $525 **Good:** $390

REMINGTON MODEL 76 SPORTSMAN

Slide action; 30-06; 4-shot magazine; 22-inch barrel; 42-inch overall length; weighs 7-1/2 lbs.; open adjustable sights; walnut-finished hardwood stock, forend; cartridge head inset on receiver bottom denotes caliber; cross-bolt safety; tapped

Remington Model Six

Remington Model 14-½

Remington Model 25A

Remington Model 121A Fieldmaster

Remington Model 141A Gamemaster

Remington Model 572A Fieldmaster

Remington Model 572 BDL Deluxe

for scope mounts. Introduced 1984; discontinued 1987.

Perf: $300 **Exc:** $270 **VGood:** $225

REMINGTON MODEL 121A FIELDMASTER

Slide action; 22 Short, 22 Long, 22 LR; 20-shot (22 Short), 15-shot (22 Long), 14-shot (22 LR); 24-inch round barrel; weighs 6 lbs.; hammerless; takedown; white metal bead ramp front sights, step-adjustable rear; uncheckered pistol-grip stock; grooved semi-beavertail slide handle. Introduced 1936; discontinued 1954.

Exc: $375 **VGood:** $325 **Good:** $250

REMINGTON MODEL 121S

Same specs as Model 121A except 22 Rem. Spl.; 12-shot magazine.

Exc: $520 **VGood:** $430 **Good:** $335

REMINGTON MODEL 121SB

Same specs as Model 121A except smoothbore barrel for 22 shot cartridge.

Exc: $600 **VGood:** $500 **Good:** $400

REMINGTON MODEL 141, 141A GAMEMASTER

Slide action; 30, 32, 35 Rem.; 5-shot tube magazine; 24-inch barrel; 42-3/4-inch overall length; weighs 7-3/4 lbs.; hammerless; takedown; white metal bead ramp front sight, step-adjustable rear; uncheckered American walnut half-pistol-grip stock; grooved slide handle. Introduced 1936; discontinued 1950.

Exc: $470 **VGood:** $325 **Good:** $270

REMINGTON MODEL 141R CARBINE

Same specs as Model 141 except 30, 32 Rem., 18-1/2-inch barrel.

Exc: $490 **VGood:** $350 **Good:** $285

REMINGTON MODEL 572A FIELDMASTER

Slide action; 22 Short, 22 Long, 22 LR; 20-shot (22 Short), 17-shot (22 Long), 15-shot (22 LR) tube magazine; 25-inch barrel; weighs 5-1/2 lbs.; hammerless; ramp front sight, open rear; uncheckered hardwood pistol-grip stock, grooved forearm. Introduced 1955; discontinued 1988.

Perf: $250 **Exc:** $225 **VGood:** $190

REMINGTON MODEL 572 FIELDMASTER

Same specs as Model 572A except 23-inch barrel; weighs 4 lbs.; "Sun-Grain" stock, forend in Buckskin tan or Crow-Wing black colors; chrome-plated magazine tube, trigger, floorplate. Add 20 percent for Crow Wing black.

Perf: $450 **Exc:** $425 **VGood:** $325

REMINGTON MODEL 572 BDL DELUXE

Same specs as Model 572A except pistol-grip cap; RKW wood finish; checkered grip, slide handle; adjustable rear sight, ramp front. Still in production.

Perf: $365 **Exc:** $335 **VGood:** $275

REMINGTON MODEL 572 SB

Same specs as Model 572A except smoothbore barrel for 22 shot cartridge. No longer produced.

Perf: $395 **Exc:** $230 **VGood:** $160

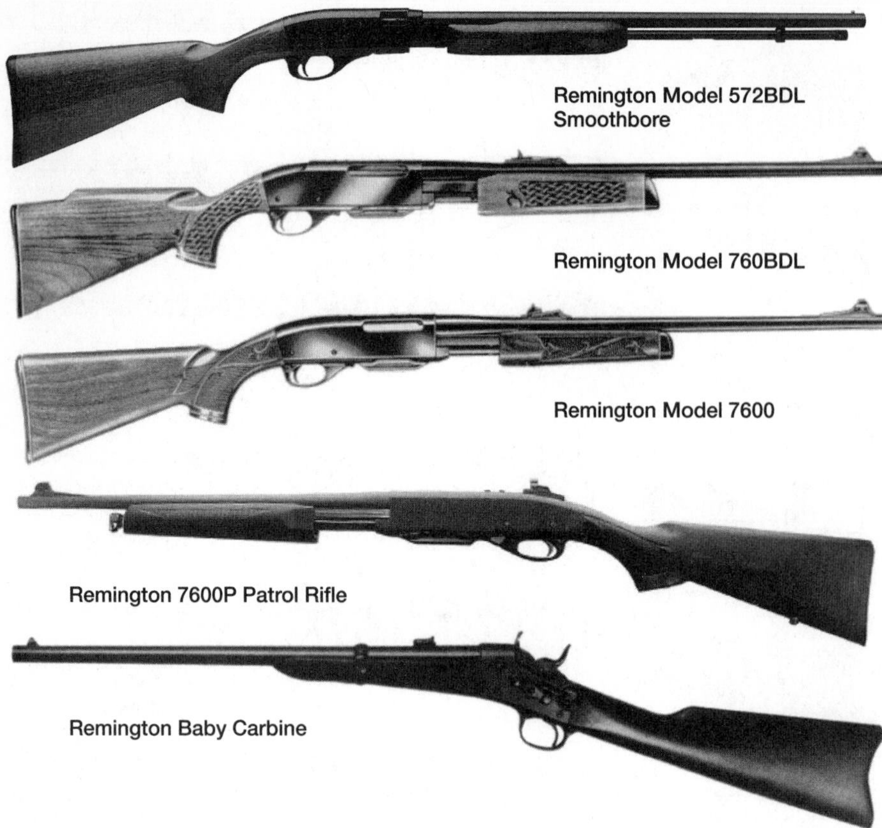

Remington Model 572BDL Smoothbore

Remington Model 760BDL

Remington Model 7600

Remington 7600P Patrol Rifle

Remington Baby Carbine

REMINGTON MODEL 572 BDL SMOOTHBORE (2007)

Similar to Model 572 but with unrifled barrel for use with shot cartridges. Introduced in 2007.

NIB: $550 **Exc:** $475 **VGood:** $315

REMINGTON MODEL 760

Slide action; 222 Rem., 223 Rem., 6mm Rem., 243 Win., 244 Rem., 257 Roberts, 270 Win., 280 Rem., 30-06, 300 Savage, 308 Win., 35 Rem.; 4-shot magazine; 22-inch barrel; 42-1/4-inch overall length; weighs 7-1/2 lbs.; hammerless; white metal bead front sight on ramp, step-adjustable, semi-buckhorn rear. Models from mid-'60s to early '70s with impressed checkering; others hand-checkered on pistol grip, slide handle; early versions with grooved slide handle, no checkering on stock. Introduced 1952; discontinued 1980.

Perf: $325 **Exc:** $220 **VGood:** $180

222 Rem., 223 Rem.

Perf: $1195 **Exc:** $895 **VGood:** $695

257 Roberts

Perf: $710 **Exc:** $570 **VGood:** $375

REMINGTON MODEL 760 ADL

Same specs as Model 760 except deluxe checkered stock, forend; grip cap; sling swivels; standard or high comb. Introduced 1953; discontinued 1963.

Perf: $335 **Exc:** $240 **VGood:** $200

REMINGTON MODEL 760 BDL

Same specs as Model 760 except 270, 30-06, 308; basketweave checkering on pistol grip, forearm; black forearm tip; early versions in right- or left-hand styles.

Perf: $350 **Exc:** $250 **VGood:** $220

REMINGTON MODEL 760 CARBINE

Same specs as Model 760 except 270, 280, 30-06, 308, 35 Rem.; 18-1/2-inch barrel; 38-1/2-inch overall length; weighs 6-1/2 lbs.

Perf: $410 **Exc:** $300 **VGood:** $260

REMINGTON MODEL 760 CDL

Same specs as Model 760 Carbine except checkered stock, forend; decorated receiver.

Perf: $435 **Exc:** $375 **VGood:** $310

REMINGTON MODEL 760D PEERLESS

Same specs as Model 760 except fine checkered fancy stock; engraving.

Perf: $1000 **Exc:** $850 **VGood:** $650

REMINGTON MODEL 760F PREMIER

Same specs as Model 760 except figured American walnut best-grade stock; fine checkered stock, forend; extensive engraved game scenes.

Perf: $2420 **Exc:** $1910 **VGood:** $1500

REMINGTON MODEL 760F PREMIER GOLD

Same specs as Model 760 except best-grade fine checkered fancy stock; extensive engraving with gold inlay.

Perf: $5000 **Exc:** $4000 **VGood:** $3000

REMINGTON MODEL 7600

Slide action; 6mm Rem., 243, 270, 280, 30-06, 308, 35 Whelen; 4-shot detachable magazine; 22-inch barrel; 42-inch overall length; weighs 7-1/2 lbs.; removable gold bead ramp front, windage-adjustable sliding ramp rear sight; tapped for scope mount; impressed checkered American walnut pistol-grip stock; positive cross-bolt safety. Introduced 1981; still in production in a number of variations.

Perf: $425 **Exc:** $350 **VGood:** $275

REMINGTON MODEL 7600 CARBINE

Same specs as Model 7600 except 30-06 only; 18-1/2-inch barrel; weighs 7-1/4 lbs.

Perf: $425 **Exc:** $350 **VGood:** $275

REMINGTON 7600 SPECIAL PURPOSE

Same specs as Model 7600 except 270, 30-06; non-glare finished American walnut stock; all exposed metal with non-reflective matte black finish; quick-detachable sling swivels; camo-pattern Cordura carrying sling. Made in U.S. by Remington. Introduced 1993; discontinued 1994.

Perf: $400 **Exc:** $360 **VGood:** $280

REMINGTON 7600D PEERLESS

Same specs as Model 7600 except fine checkered fancy walnut stock; engraving.

Perf: $2100 **Exc:** $1600 **VGood:** $1200

REMINGTON 7600F PREMIER

Same specs as Model 7600 except best-grade fine checkered walnut stock; extensive engraving.

Perf: $4600 **Exc:** $4000 **VGood:** $2600

REMINGTON 7600F PREMIER GOLD

Same specs as Model 7600 except best-grade fine checkered walnut stock; extensive engraving with gold inlays.

Perf: $7000 **Exc:** $5100 **VGood:** $3400

REMINGTON 7600P PATROL RIFLE

Same specs as Model 7600, except 308 only, 16.5-inch barrel, 4-shot magazine; parkerized metal, black synthetic stock and forend, with sling swivel studs; weighs 7 lbs. Wilson Combat ghost-ring rear sight. Introduced 2002.

Perf: $460 **Exc:** $375 **VGood:** $285

REMINGTON MODEL 7615 TACTICAL PUMP CARBINE

Pump-action rifle based on Model 7600 action and chambered in .223 Remington with 16-1/2" barrel. Folding synthetic stock. Introduced in 2007.

Perf: $700 **Exc:** $575 **VGood:** N/A

REMINGTON MODEL 7615 SPECIAL PURPOSE SYNTHETIC

Similar to Model 7615 Tactical but with fixed stock and picatinny rail. A dealer exclusive for 2007.

Perf: $535 **Exc:** $475 **VGood:** $400

REMINGTON MODEL 7615 CAMO HUNTER

Similar to Model 7615 Tactical but with fixed buttstock and entirely camo-finished except for action parts and trigger guard assembly. Introduced in 2007.

Perf: $535 **Exc:** $475 **VGood:** $400

REMINGTON MODEL 7615 RANCH CARBINE

Similar to Model 7615 Tactical but with fixed buttstock, walnut buttstock and forend, and 18-1/2" barrel. No iron sights but drilled and tapped for scope mounts. Introduced in 2007.

Perf: $535 **Exc:** $475 **VGood:** $400

REMINGTON BABY CARBINE

Single shot; rolling block; 44 Win.; 20-inch barrel; open rear sight, blade front; uncheckered American walnut carbine-style straight stock, forearm; barrel band. Introduced 1902; discontinued 1902.

Exc: $3000 **VGood:** $2500 **Good:** $1500

REMINGTON NO. 1 ROLLING BLOCK MID-RANGE SPORTER

Single shot, modern-production rolling block; 45-70, later 30-30, 444 Marlin; 30-inch round barrel; weighs 8-3/4 lbs.; 46-1/2-inch overall length; American walnut stock with checkered pistol grip and forend; Beaded blade front sight, adjustable center-notch buckhorn rear. Recreation of the original Remington rolling block, made new in U.S.A. by Remington. Reintroduced in 1998. Discontinued.

Perf: $1200 **Exc:** $900 **VGood:** $700

REMINGTON NO. 2

Single shot; rolling block; 22, 25, 32, 38, 44 rimfire or centerfire; 24-inch, 26-inch, 28-inch, 30-inch barrel; open rear sight, bead front; American walnut straight-grip stock, schnabel forearm. Collector value. Introduced 1873; discontinued 1910.

Exc: N/A **VGood:** $950 **Good:** $500

REMINGTON NO. 3

Single shot; falling block side-lever; 22 WCF, 22 Extra Long, 25-20 Stevens, 25-21 Stevens, 25-25 Stevens, 32 WCF, 32 Ballard & Marlin, 32-40 Rem., 38 WCF, 38-40 Rem., 38-50 Rem., 38-55 Ballard & Marlin, 40-60 Ballard & Marlin, 40-60 WCF, 45-60 Rem., 40-82 WCF, 45-70 Govt., 45-90 WCF; 28-inch, 30-inch half- or full-octagon barrel; open rear sight, blade front; hand-checkered pistol-grip stock. Collector value. Introduced 1880; discontinued 1911.

VGood: $1100 **Good:** $800

REMINGTON NO. 3 HIGH POWER

Same specs as Model No. 3 except 30-30, 30-40, 32 Spl., 32-40, 38-55, 38-72; open rear sight, bead front; hand-checkered pistol-grip stock, forearm. Introduced 1893; discontinued 1907. Collector value.

VGood: $1150 **Good:** $850

REMINGTON NO. 4

Single shot; rolling block; 22 Short, 22 Long, 22 LR, 25 Stevens rimfire, 32 Short, 32 Long, 32 Rimfire; 22-1/2-inch, 24-inch (32 Rimfire) octagonal barrel; blade front sight, open rear; plain walnut stock, forearm; solid-frame and takedown models. 1890 to 1901, solid frame; 1901 to 1926 first takedown with lever on right side; 1926 to 1933, second takedown with large screw head. Some collector value. Introduced 1890; discontinued 1933.

VGood: $625 **Good:** $300

REMINGTON NO. 4-S MILITARY

Same specs as No. 4 except 22 Short, 22 Long, 22 LR; 26-inch barrel; military stock, including stacking swivel, sling; bayonet stud on barrel; bayonet, scabbard originally included. Early production was marked "American Boy Scout"; later production was marked "Military Model." This rifle was never the officially adopted arm of the Boy Scouts of America; the reasons behind the early production markings are still unknown. Collector value. Introduced 1913; discontinued 1923.

VGood: $1895 **Good:** $875

REMINGTON NO. 5

Single shot; rolling block; 7mm Mauser, 30-30, 30-40 Krag, 303 British, 32-40, 32 Spl., 38-55; 24-inch, 26-inch, 28-inch barrel; open sporting rear sight, blade front; uncheckered straight-grip stock. Some collector value. Introduced 1897; discontinued 1905.

VGood: $1595 **Good:** $695

REMINGTON NO. 5 MILITARY

Same specs as No. 5 except only 8mm Lebel, 7mm Mauser, 7.62 Russian, 30 U.S.; 30-inch barrel. Also known as Model 1902.

VGood: $1595 **Good:** $695

REMINGTON NO. 6

Single shot; rolling block; 22 Short, 22 Long, 22 LR, 32 Rimfire Short, 32 Rimfire Long; 20-inch barrel; takedown; open front, rear sights; tang peep sight optional; plain straight stock, forearm. Introduced 1901; discontinued 1933.

VGood: $425 **Good:** $350

REMINGTON NO. 7

Single shot; 22 Short, 22 Long, 22 LR, 22 Stevens RF; other calibers on special order; 24-inch, 26-inch, 28-inch half-octagon barrel; Lyman combination rear sight, Beach combination front; rear tang sight on projection from curved pistol-grip tang; hand-checkered American walnut stock, forearm. About 1000 made, collector value. Introduced 1903; discontinued 1911.

VGood: $4195 **Good:** $1995

REMINGTON MODEL SPR18

An imported (Baikal) break-action rifle with silvertone receiver and fluted barrel. Formerly branded as "Remington Spartan." Calibers: .223, .243, .270, .30-06, .308. Weight: 6-3/4 lbs. Introduced 2005.

NIB: $350 **Exc:** $300 **VGood:** $225

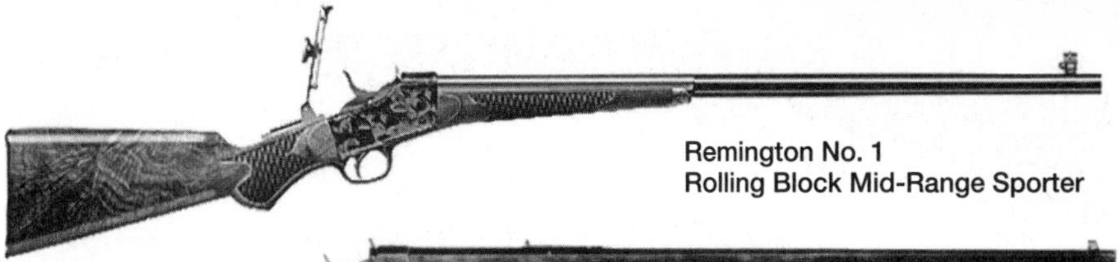

Remington No. 1
Rolling Block Mid-Range Sporter

Remington No. 2

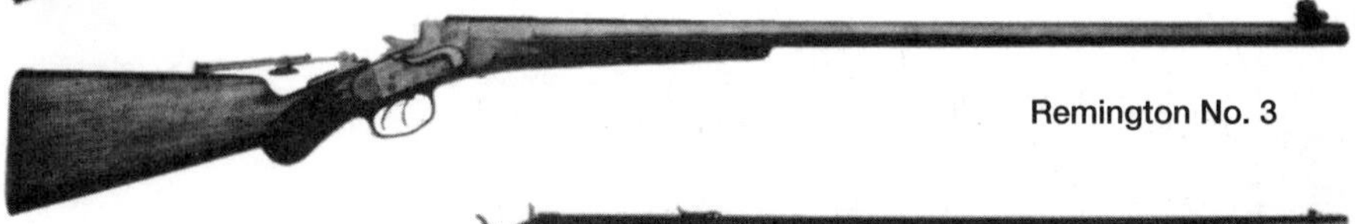

Remington No. 3

Remington No. 4

Remington No. 4-S Military

Remington No. 5

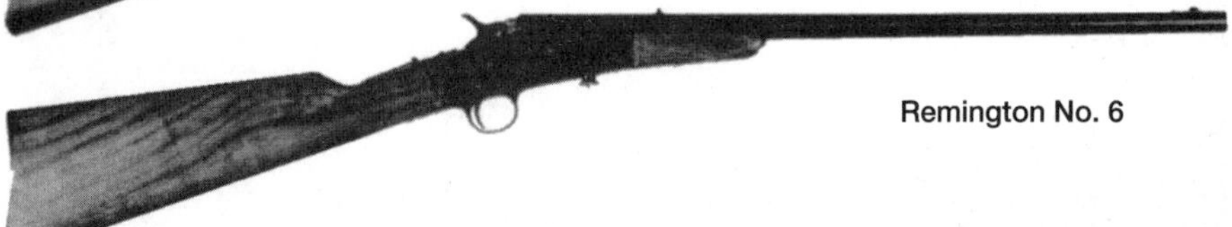

Remington No. 6

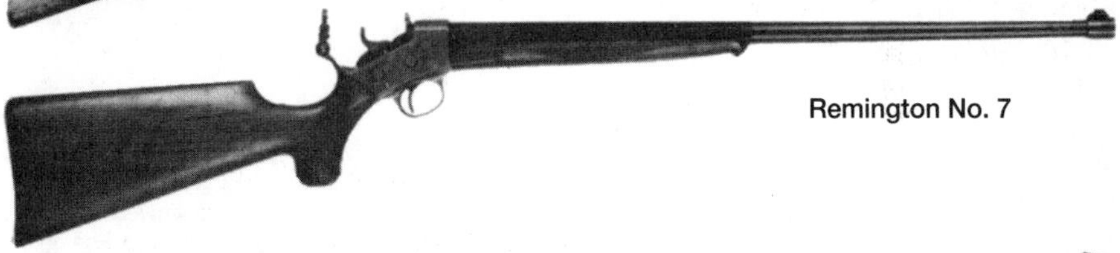

Remington No. 7

Remington Model
SPR18

Remington Model 412

REMINGTON MODEL SPR94 COMBO GUN

Over/under rifle shotgun. Combinations: .410/.22 rimfire, .410/.17HMR, .41o/.22WMR, 12-ga./.223, 12-ga./.30-06, 12-ga./.308. Double triggers, tang safety. Imported; formerly branded as "Remington Spartan."

NIB: $575 **Exc:** $500 **VGood:** $395

REMINGTON MODEL 412

Compact single-shot chambered for .22 LR. 19.5-inch blued barrel, hardwood stock.

NIB: $135 **Exc:** $110 **VGood:** $75

REMINGTON R15 MOE

Semi-Auto (AR15) with AAC 51 Tooth Brakeout flash hider, Magpul Grip and Trigger Guard,

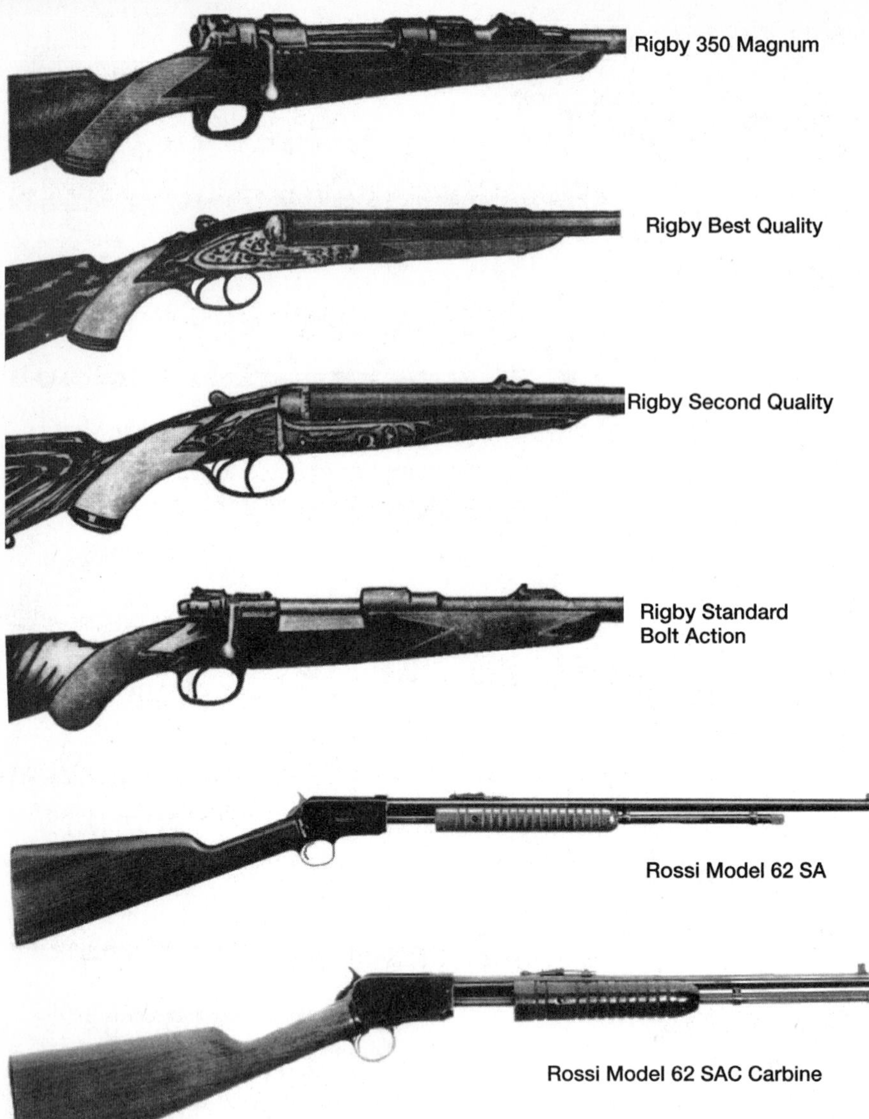
Rigby 350 Magnum

Rigby Best Quality

Rigby Second Quality

Rigby Standard Bolt Action

Rossi Model 62 SA

Rossi Model 62 SAC Carbine

Competition two-stage trigger, finished in Mossy Oak Brush camo. 16" carbine with collapsible stock and mid-length fore end, 18" carbine with fixed stock and Dissipator fore end, 18" carbine with collapsible stock and Dissipator fore end, 22" Rifle with fixed stock and Dissipator fore end. Introduced 2013.

Perf: $1300 **Exc:** $1000 **VGood:** $850

RIGBY NOTE: RIFLES SHOULD BE INDIVIDUALLY APPRAISED AS CALIBER AND OPTIONS CAN AFFECT VALUES.

RIGBY 350 MAGNUM

Bolt action; 350 Mag.; 24-inch barrel; 5-shot box magazine; high-quality walnut stock with checkered full pistol grip, forearm; folding leaf rear sight, bead front. No longer in production.

Perf: $3995 **Exc:** $3400 **VGood:** $2600

RIGBY 416 MAGNUM

Bolt action; 375 H&H, 404, 416 Rigby, 416 Rem. Mag., 458 Win. Mag., 505; 24-inch barrel; 4-shot box magazine; walnut sporting stock with checkered pistol grip, forearm; folding leaf rear sight, bead front.

Perf: $9250 **Exc:** $7995 **VGood:** $5495

RIGBY BEST QUALITY

Double rifle; sidelock; 22 LR, 275 Mag., 350 Mag., 416 Rigby, 458 Win. Mag., 465, 470 NE, 577 NE, 600 NE; 24-inch-28-inch barrel; hammerless ejector; folding leaf rear sight, bead front; hand-checkered walnut stock; pistol-grip forearm; engraved receiver.

Perf: $40,000 **Exc:** $32,500 **VGood:** $25,000

RIGBY BIG GAME BOLT ACTION

Bolt action; 350 Mag., 375 H&H Mag., 404, 416 Rigby, 416 Rem. Mag., 458 Win. Mag., 505; 4-, 5-shot magazine; 21-inch-24-inch barrel; folding leaf rear sight, bead front; high-quality walnut sporting stock with checkered pistol grip, forearm.

Perf: $8500 **Exc:** $7600 **VGood:** $4900

RIGBY SECOND QUALITY

Double rifle; boxlock; 22 LR, 275 Mag., 350 Mag., 416 Rigby, 458 Win. Mag., 465, 470 NE, 577 NE, 600 NE; 22-inch-26-inch barrel; hammerless ejector; folding leaf rear sight, bead front; hand-checkered walnut stock; pistol grip, forearm; engraved receiver.

Perf: $16,500 **Exc:** $12,995 **VGood:** $9995

RIGBY STANDARD BOLT ACTION

Bolt action; 243, 270, 275 Rigby, 7x57, 30-06, 300 H&H Mag., 300 Win. Mag., 308, 7mm Rem. Mag., 375 H&H Mag., 404 Rigby, 458 Win. Mag.; 3-, 4-, 5-shot magazine; 20- to 25-inch barrel; folding leaf rear sight, bead front; walnut sporting stock with hand-checkered half pistol grip, forearm.

Perf: $7995 **Exc:** $5500 **VGood:** $3250

Magnum calibers

Perf: $8500 **Exc:** $5995 **VGood:** $3650

RIGBY STANDARD LIGHTWEIGHT

Same specs as Standard Bolt Action except 24-inch barrel; lighter weight.

Perf: $7995 **Exc:** $5500 **VGood:** $3250

Magnum calibers

Perf: $8500 **Exc:** $5995 **VGood:** $3650

RIGBY THIRD QUALITY

Double rifle; boxlock; 22 LR, 275 Mag., 350 Mag., 416 Rigby, 458 Win. Mag., 465, 470 NE, 577 NE, 600 NE; 22-inch-26-inch barrel; hammerless ejector; folding leaf rear sight, bead front; checkered walnut stock; engraved receiver. No longer in production.

Perf: $12,000 **Exc:** $10,000 **VGood:** $7500

RIZZINI EXPRESS 90L DOUBLE RIFLE

Double rifle, over/under; 30-06, 7x65R, 9.3x74R; 24-inch barrel; weighs 7-1/2 lbs; 40-inch overall length; Select European walnut stock with satin oil finish; English- style cheekpiece. Ramp front sight, quarter-rib with express sight. Color case-hardened boxlock action; automatic ejectors; single selective trigger; polished blue barrels. Extra 20-gauge shotshell barrels available. Comes with case. Imported for Italy by Wm. Larkin Moore.

Perf: $4100 **Exc:** $3200 **VGood:** $2500

ROSS MODEL 1905 MARK II

Bolt action; 303 British; 4-shot magazine; 28-inch barrel; two-leaf open rear sight, bead front; hand-checkered American walnut sporting stock; straight-pull action. Introduced prior to WWI; no longer in production.

Exc: $600 **VGood:** $495 **Good:** $395

ROSS MODEL 1910 MARK III

Bolt action; 280 Ross, 303 British; 4- or 5-shot magazine; 22-inch, 24-inch, 26-inch barrel; two-leaf open rear sight, bead front; hand-checkered American walnut sporting stock. Made in Canada. Some collector value. Some may be unsafe to fire. Introduced 1910; discontinued 1918.

Exc: $600 **VGood:** $495 **Good:** $395

ROSSI MATCHED PAIR CENTERFIRE RIFLE/ SHOTGUN

Single shot, breakopen, 12 or 20 ga. shotgun barrel with interchangeable rifle barrel in 243, 270, 308, 30-06; weighs 5 to 7 lbs, depending on variant. Adjustable rifle sights, bead front on shotgun; internal transfer-bar mechanism, manual safety, trigger-block system.

Perf: $190 **Exc:** $160 **VGood:** $120

ROSSI MATCHED PAIR RIMFIRE RIFLE/SHOTGUN

Single shot, breakopen; 22 LR or 22 Mag. or 17 HMR; 18-1/2-inch or 23-inch barrel; weighs 6 lbs.; Hardwood stock (brown or black finish); Fully adjustable front and rear sights; Break-open action, transfer-bar manual safety, includes matched 410-, 20- or 12-gauge shotgun barrel with bead front sight. Introduced 2001. Imported by BrazTech/ Taurus.

Perf: $110 **Exc:** $90 **VGood:** $80

ROSSI MODEL 59 SA

Slide action; 22 WMR; 23-inch round or octagonal barrel; 39-1/4-inch overall length; weighs 5-3/4 lbs.; takedown; blade front sight, adjustable rear; walnut stock with straight grip, grooved forend; blue finish. Imported from Brazil by Interarms. Introduced by Interarms 1978; no longer imported.

Exc: $275 **VGood:** $225 **Good:** $175

ROSSI MODEL 62 SA

Slide action; 22 Short, 22 Long, 22 LR; 20-shot (22 Short), 16-shot (22 Long), 14-shot (22 LR) tube magazine; 23-inch round or octagon barrel; 39-1/4-inch overall length; weighs 5-3/4 lbs.; takedown; blade front sight, adjustable rear; walnut stock with straight grip, grooved forend; blued or nickel finish. Imported from Brazil. Introduced by Interarms 1978.

Exc: $275 **VGood:** $235 **Good:** $150

Nickel finish

Exc: $295 **VGood:** $250 **Good:** $155

Blue, with octagonal barrel

Exc: $295 **VGood:** $250 **Good:** $155

ROSSI MODEL 62 SAC CARBINE

Same specs as Model 62 SA except 16-1/4-inch barrel. Introduced 1975.

Exc: $225 **VGood:** $190 **Good:** $165

ROSSI MODEL 62 SA STAINLESS

Same specs as Model 62 SA except stainless steel barrel and action. Introduced 1986; discontinued 1986.

Exc: $295 **VGood:** $250 **Good:** $200

ROSSI MODEL 65 SRC

Lever action; 44 Spl./44 Mag., 44-40; 10-shot tube magazine; 20-inch barrel; weighs 5-3/4 lbs.; blade front sight, buckhorn rear; uncheckered walnut stock; saddle ring. Introduced 1989.

Exc: $450 **VGood:** $350 **Good:** $300

ROSSI MODEL 92 SRC

Lever action; 38 Spl., 357 Mag., 44-40, 44 Mag.; 9-shot (38 Spl.), 8-shot (other calibers); 20-inch barrel; blade front sight, buckhorn rear; uncheckered walnut stock. Made in Brazil. Introduced 1978.

Exc: $450 **VGood:** $350 **Good:** $300

Engraved model

Exc: $475 **VGood:** $400 **Good:** $350

ROSSI MODEL 92 SRS PUMA SHORT CARBINE

Same specs as Model 92 except 38-357; 16-inch barrel; 33-inch overall length. Early production with Puma medallion on side of receiver. Imported from Brazil by Interarms. Introduced 1986.

Exc: $450 **VGood:** $375 **Good:** $300

ROSSI SINGLE SHOT CENTERFIRE RIFLE

Single shot, breakopen; 308 Win., 270 Win., 30-06 Spfld., 223 Rem., 243 Win.; 23-inch barrel; weighs 6-6.5 lbs.; Monte carlo stock, exotic woods, walnut finish & swivels with white line space and recoil pad. Scope rails and hammer extension included. Break Open, positive ejection, internal transfer bar mechanism and manual external safety. Trigger block system included.

Perf: $200 **Exc:** $175 **VGood:** $150

SAKO CLASSIC

Bolt action; 243, 270, 30-06, 7mm Rem. Mag.; 21-3/4-inch barrel; weighs 6 lbs.; classic-style stock with straight comb; matte finish wood. Imported from Finland by Stoeger. Introduced 1993.

Exc: $700 **VGood:** $560 **Good:** $440

SAKO FIBERGLASS

Bolt action; 22-250, 243, 308, 7mm-08, 25-06, 270, 30-06, 7mm Rem. Mag., 300 Win. Mag., 338 Win. Mag., 375 H&H Mag.; 4-shot (Magnums), 5-shot magazine (standard calibers); 23-inch barrel; no sights; marketed with scope mounts; black fiberglass stock; wrinkle finish; rubber buttpad. Made in Finland. Introduced 1985.

Perf: $1050 **Exc:** $800 **VGood:** $600

Left-hand model

Perf: $1100 **Exc:** $1000 **VGood:** $800

SAKO FIBERGLASS CARBINE

Same specs as Fiberglass except 18-1/2-inch barrel; 243, 308, 25-06, 270, 30-06, 7mm Rem. Mag., 300 Win. Mag., 375 H&H Mag. Introduced 1986; discontinued 1991.

Perf: $1050 **Exc:** $800 **VGood:** $600

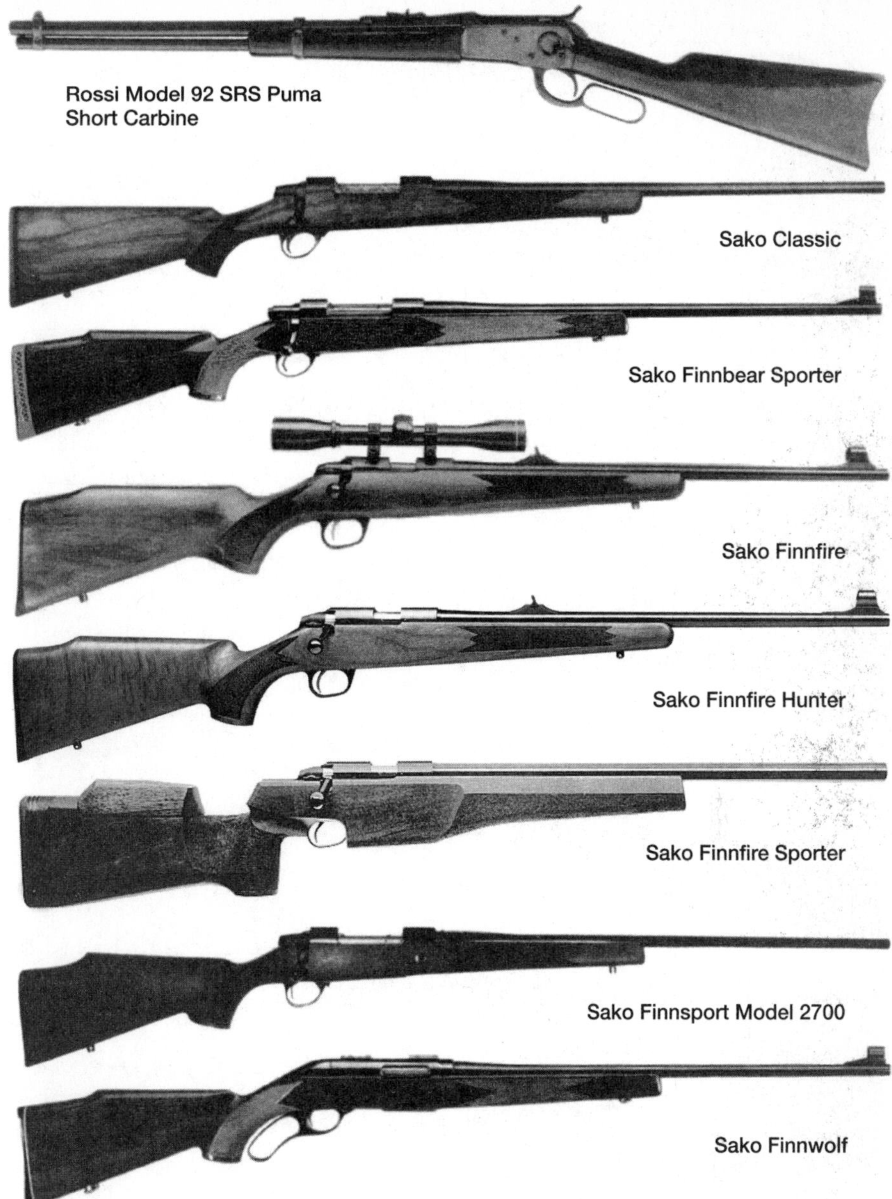

Rossi Model 92 SRS Puma Short Carbine

Sako Classic

Sako Finnbear Sporter

Sako Finnfire

Sako Finnfire Hunter

Sako Finnfire Sporter

Sako Finnsport Model 2700

Sako Finnwolf

SAKO FINNBEAR SPORTER

Bolt action; 25-06, 264 Win. Mag., 270, 30-06, 300 Win. Mag., 338 Mag., 7mm Rem. Mag., 375 H&H Mag.; 4-shot (Magnums), 5-shot magazine (standard calibers); 24-inch barrel; no rear sight, hooded ramp front; drilled, tapped for scope mounts; hand-checkered European walnut, Monte Carlo, pistol-grip stock; recoil pad; sling swivels. Introduced 1961; discontinued 1971.

Exc: $795 **VGood:** $650 **Good:** $550

SAKO FINNFIRE

Bolt action; 22 LR; 5-shot magazine; 22-inch barrel; 40-inch overall length; weighs 5-1/4 lbs.; hooded blade front sight, open adjustable rear; European walnut stock with checkered grip and forend; adjustable single-stage trigger; 50-degree bolt lift. Imported from Finland by Stoeger Industries. Introduced 1994.

Exc: $670 **VGood:** $490 **Good:** $410

SAKO FINNFIRE HUNTER

Bolt action; 22 LR, 5-shot magazine; 22-inch barrel; weighs 5.75 lbs.; 39-1/2-inch overall length; European walnut stock with checkered grip and forend; Hooded blade front sight, open adjustable rear; Adjustable single-stage trigger; has 50-degree bolt lift. Introduced 1994. Imported from Finland by Beretta USA.

Perf: $820 **Exc:** $700 **VGood:** $600

SAKO FINNFIRE SPORTER

Bolt action; 22 LR. 22-inch barrel; heavy, free-floating; Match style stock of European walnut; adjustable cheekpiece and buttplate; stippled pistol grip and forend; no sights; has 11mm integral dovetail scope mount. Based on the Sako P94S action with two bolt locking lugs, 50-degree bolt lift and 30mm throw; adjustable trigger. Introduced 1999. Imported from Finland by Beretta USA.

Perf: $890 **Exc:** $770 **VGood:** $660

SAKO FINNSPORT MODEL 2700

Bolt action; 270, 300 Win. Mag.; 4-shot magazine; 21-inch, 22-inch barrel; no sights; scope mounts; Monte Carlo stock design. Introduced 1983; no longer in production.

Perf: $795 **Exc:** $675 **VGood:** $550

SAKO FINNWOLF

Lever action; 243 Win., 308 Win.; 3-, 4-shot magazine (early models); 23-inch barrel; hammerless; no rear

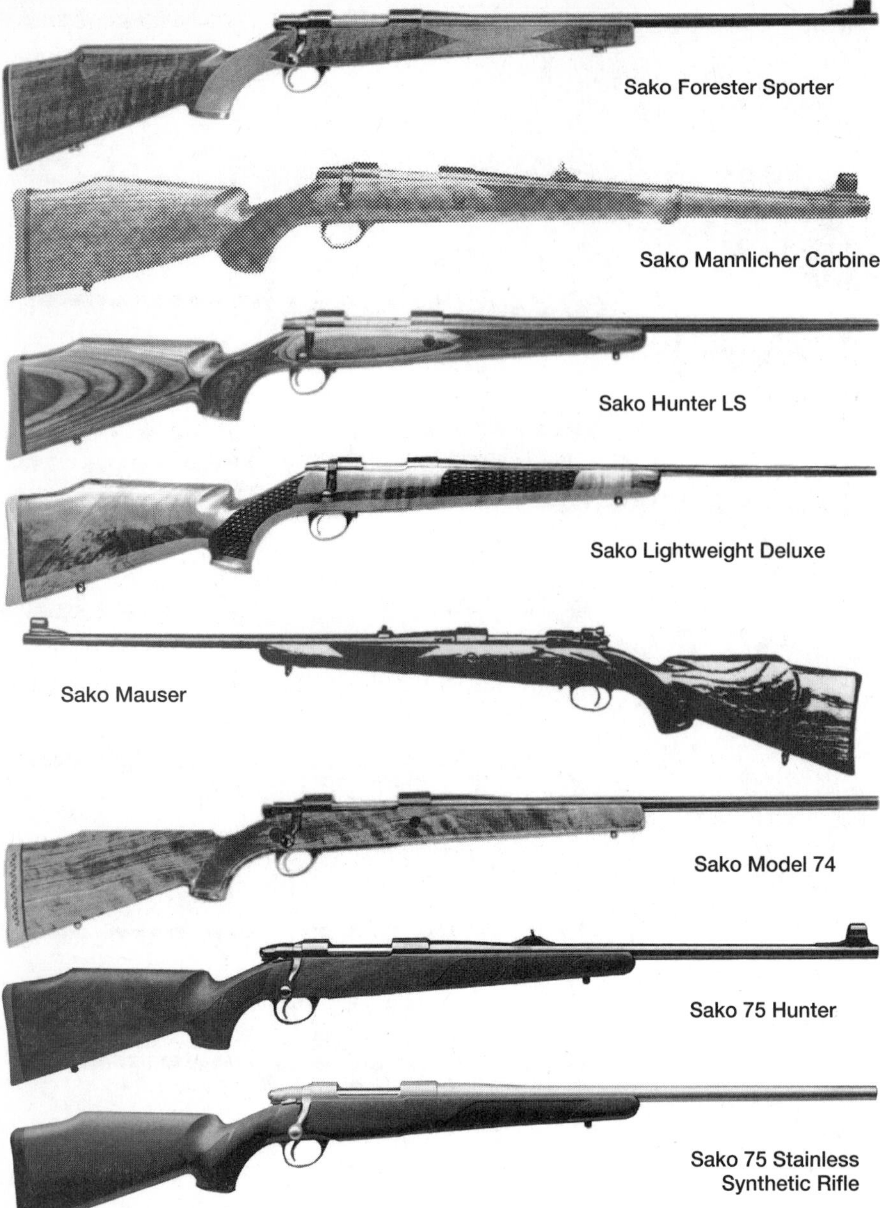
Sako Forester Sporter

Sako Mannlicher Carbine

Sako Hunter LS

Sako Lightweight Deluxe

Sako Mauser

Sako Model 74

Sako 75 Hunter

Sako 75 Stainless Synthetic Rifle

sight, hooded ramp front; drilled, tapped for scope mounts; hand-checkered European walnut Monte Carlo stock in left- or right-hand styling; sling swivels. Introduced 1964; discontinued 1972.

Exc: $1700 **VGood:** $1300 **Good:** $995

SAKO FORESTER SPORTER

Bolt action; 22-250, 243 Win., 308 Win.; 5-shot magazine; 23-inch barrel; no rear sight, hooded ramp front; drilled, tapped for scope mounts; hand-checkered walnut Monte Carlo pistol-grip stock; sling swivel studs. Introduced 1957; discontinued 1971.

Exc: $775 **VGood:** $600 **Good:** $500

SAKO FORESTER SPORTER CARBINE

Same specs as Forester Sporter except 20-inch barrel; Mannlicher-type stock.

Exc: $925 **VGood:** $695 **Good:** $600

SAKO FORESTER SPORTER HEAVY BARREL

Same specs as Forester Sporter except 24-inch heavy barrel.

Exc: $800 **VGood:** $625 **Good:** $525

SAKO HUNTER

Bolt action; 17 Rem., 222 Rem., 223 Rem., 22-250, 243, 308, 7mm-08, 25-06, 270, 280, 30-06, 7mm Rem. Mag., 300 Win. Mag., 300 Weatherby Mag., 338 Win. Mag., 375 H&H Mag., 416 Rem. Mag.; 4-shot (Magnums), 5-shot magazine (standard calibers); 21-1/4-inch, 21-3/4-inch, 22-inch barrel; no sights; scope mounts; checkered classic-style French walnut stock; sling swivels. Made in Finland. Introduced 1986.

Exc: $675 **VGood:** $495 **Good:** $410

Left-hand model

Exc: $750 **VGood:** $575 **Good:** $440

SAKO HUNTER CARBINE

Same specs as Hunter except 22-250, 243, 7mm-08, 308, 300 Win. Mag., 25-06, 6.5x55, 270, 7x64, 30-06, 7mm Rem. Mag., 375 H&H Mag.; 18-1/2-inch barrel; oil-finished stock. Introduced 1986; discontinued 1991.

Exc: $650 **VGood:** $450 **Good:** $400

SAKO HUNTER LS

Same specs as Hunter except laminated stock with dull finish. Introduced 1987.

Perf: $975 **Exc:** $795 **VGood:** $595

Left-hand model

Perf: $995 **Exc:** $825 **VGood:** $595

SAKO LIGHTWEIGHT DELUXE

Bolt action; 17 Rem., 222, 223, 22-250, 243, 308, 7mm-08, 25-06, 270, 280 Rem., 30-06, 7mm Rem. Mag., 300 Win. Mag., 338 Win. Mag., 300 Wea., 375 H&H, 416 Rem. Mag.; 21-inch, 22-inch barrel; select wood with skip-line checkering; rosewood grip cap and forend tip; ventilated recoil pad; fine checkering on top surfaces of integral dovetail bases, bolt sleeve, bolt handle root and bolt knob; mirror finish bluing. Imported from Finland by Stoeger Industries.

Standard calibers

Perf: $1125 **Exc:** $925 **VGood:** $675

Magnum calibers

Perf: $1175 **Exc:** $950 **VGood:** $695

SAKO MANNLICHER CARBINE

Bolt action; 17 Rem., 222, 223, 243, 25-06, 270, 308, 30-06, 7mm Rem. Mag., 300 Win. Mag., 375 H&H Mag.; 4-shot (Magnums), 5-shot magazine (standard calibers); 18-1/2-inch barrel; open sights; full Mannlicher-style stock. Made in Finland. Introduced 1977.

Perf: $895 **Exc:** $695 **VGood:** $495

Magnum calibers

Perf: $950 **Exc:** $750 **VGood:** $550

SAKO MAUSER

Bolt action; 270, 30-06; 5-shot magazine; 24-inch barrel; open leaf rear sight, Patridge front; hand-checkered European walnut, Monte Carlo cheekpiece stock; sling swivel studs. Introduced 1946; discontinued 1961.

Exc: $550 **VGood:** $500 **Good:** $420

SAKO MAUSER MAGNUM

Same specs as Mauser except 8x60S, 8,2x57, 300 H&H Mag., 375 H&H Mag.; recoil pad. Discontinued 1961.

Exc: $650 **VGood:** $560 **Good:** $450

SAKO MODEL 72

Bolt action; 222 Rem., 223 Rem., 22-250, 243 Win., 25-06, 270 Win., 30-06, 308, 7mm Rem. Mag., 300 Win. Mag., 338 Win. Mag., 375 H&H Mag.; 23-inch, 24-inch barrel; adjustable rear sight, hooded front; hand-checkered European walnut stock; adjustable trigger; hinged floorplate. Introduced 1973; discontinued 1976.

Exc: $530 **VGood:** $470 **Good:** $400

SAKO MODEL 73

Lever action; 243 Win., 308 Win.; 3-shot clip magazine; 23-inch barrel; no rear sight, hooded ramp front; drilled, tapped for scope mounts; hand-checkered European walnut Monte Carlo stock; sling swivels; flush floorplate. Introduced 1973; discontinued 1975.

Exc: $495 **VGood:** $420 **Good:** $330

SAKO MODEL 74

Bolt action; 222 Rem., 223 Rem., 220 Swift, 22-250, 243, 25-06, 270, 7mm Rem. Mag., 30-06, 300 Win. Mag., 338 Win. Mag., 375 H&H Mag.; 4-shot (Magnums), 5-shot (standard calibers) magazine; 23-1/2-inch, 24-inch standard or heavy barrel; no sights; hand-checkered European walnut Monte Carlo stock; Mauser-type action; detachable sling swivels. Introduced 1974; no longer in production.

Exc: $575 **VGood:** $450 **Good:** $380

SAKO MODEL 74 CARBINE

Same specs as Model 74 except only 30-06; 20-inch barrel; Mannlicher-design full-length stock. Introduced 1974; no longer in production.

Exc: $595 **VGood:** $495 **Good:** $400

SAKO 75 HUNTER

Bolt action; 17 Rem., 222, 223, 22-250, 243, 260, 7mm-08, 308 Win., 25-06, 270, 6.5x55, 280, 30-06;

270 Wea. Mag., 7mm WSM, 7mm Rem. Mag., 7mm STW, 7mm Wea. Mag., 300 Win. Mag., 300 Wea. Mag., 338 Win. Mag., 340 Wea. Mag., 375 H&H, 416 Rem. Mag.; 22-inch barrel, standard calibers; 24-inch, 26-inch magnum calibers. weighs about 6 lbs.; European walnut stock with matte lacquer finish; no sights; dovetail scope mount rails. New design with three locking lugs and a mechanical ejector, key locks firing pin and bolt, cold hammer-forged barrel is free-floating, 2- position safety, hinged floorplate or detachable magazine that can be loaded from the top, short 70 degree bolt lift. Five action lengths. Introduced 1997. Imported from Finland by Beretta USA.

Perf: $1010 **VGood:** $800 **Good:** $660

SAKO 75 HUNTER LEFT-HAND

Similar to Sako 75 Hunter, but true left-hand action, 25-06, 270, 30-06.

Perf: $1200 **Exc:** $1000 **VGood:** N/A

SAKO 75 HUNTER STAINLESS

Similar to Sako 75 Hunter except all metal is stainless steel. Walnut stock with matte lacquer finish, rubber butt pad. Introduced 1999. Imported from Finland by Beretta USA. Still available.

Perf: $1100 **Exc:** $880 **VGood:** $700

SAKO 75 DELUXE

Similar to 75 Hunter except select wood rosewood gripcap and forend tip. Available in 17 Rem., 222, 223, 243, 260, 7mm-08, 7mm WSM, 308, 25-06, 270, 280, 30-06; 270 Wea. Mag., 7mm Rem. Mag., 7mm STW, 7mm Wea. Mag., 300 Win. Mag., 300 Wea. Mag., 338 Win. Mag., 340 Wea. Mag., 375 H&H, 416 Rem. Mag. Introduced 1997. Imported from Finland by Beretta USA.

Perf: $1550 **Exc:** $1200 **VGood:** $900

SAKO 75 FINNLIGHT

Similar to Sako 75 Hunter, but stainless-steel metal parts and synthetic stock; calibers 243 Win., 7mm-08 Rem., 308 Win., 25-06 Rem., 270 Win., 280 Rem, 30-06 Spfld, 6.5x55, 7mm Rem. Mag., 300 Win. Mag.; 20-inch, 22-inch barrel, weighs 6-1/2 lbs.; no sights; introduced 2001, still imported from Finland by Beretta USA.

Perf: $1300 **Exc:** $1000 **VGood:** 800

SAKO 75 SINGLE SHOT CUSTOM

Similar to Sako 75 Hunter, but single-shot only, 308, heavy 23.6-inch fluted stainless-steel barrel; laminated stock with beavertail forend; single set trigger; weighs 9 lbs.; introduced 2004.

Perf: $2800 **Exc:** $2100 **VGood:** $1600

SAKO 75 STAINLESS SYNTHETIC

Similar to 75 Hunter except all metal is stainless steel, synthetic stock has soft composite panels moulded into forend and pistol grip. Available in 22-250, 243, 308 Win., 25-06, 270, 30-06 with 22-inch barrel, 7mm Rem. Mag., 7mm STW, 300 Win. Mag., 338 Win. Mag. and 375 H&H Mag. with 24-inch barrel and 300 Wea. Mag., 300 Rem.Ultra Mag. with 26-inch barrel. Introduced 1997. Imported from Finland by Beretta USA.

Perf: $1100 **VGood:** $900 **Good:** $700

SAKO 75 VARMINT

Similar to Model 75 Hunter except chambered only for 17 Rem., 204 Ruger, 222 Rem., 223 Rem., 22-250 Rem., 22 PPC, 243, 260, 6mm PPC, 308, 24-inch heavy barrel with recessed crown, beavertail forend. Introduced 1998. Imported from Finland by Beretta USA.

Perf: $1200 **Exc:** $980 **VGood:** $770

SAKO 75 VARMINT STAINLESS LAMINATED

Similar to Sako 75 Hunter except chambered only for 204 Ruger, 222, 223, 22-250, 22 PPC USA, 6mm PPC, 243, 260, 308, heavy 24-inch barrel with recessed crown, all metal is stainless steel, laminated wood stock with beavertail forend. Introduced 1999. Imported from Finland by Beretta USA.

Perf: $1350 **Exc:** $1100 **VGood:** $900

Sako 75 Deluxe

Sako 75 Finnlight

Sako 75 Single Shot Custom

Sako 75 Varmint

Sako 75 Varmint Stainless Laminated Rifle

Sako Model 78

Sako Standard Sporter

SAKO MODEL 78

Bolt action; 22 WMR, 22 LR, 22 Hornet; 4-shot (22 Hornet), 5-shot magazine; 22-1/2-inch barrel; no sights; hand-checkered European walnut Monte Carlo stock. Introduced 1977; discontinued 1986.

Rimfire:

Exc: $420 **VGood:** $400 **Good:** $350

22 Hornet:

Exc: $480 **VGood:** $420 **Good:** $400

SAKO 85 HUNTER

Bolt-action centerfire rifle chambered in short and long calibers ranging from .223 Remington to .375 H&H Mag. Controlled round feeding, checkered walnut stock, satin blued sightless 22-7/16", 22-7/8", or 24-3/8" barrel.

NIB: $1250 **Exc:** $1150 **VGood:** $875

SAKO 85 STAINLESS SYNTHETIC

Similar to Sako 85 Hunter but with stainless steel receiver and barrel.

NIB: $1300 **Exc:** $1200 **VGood:** $900

SAKO 85 FINNLIGHT

Similar to Sako 85 Stainless Synthetic but with recoil pad and ultra-lightweight synthetic stock. Chambered in long and short cartridges ranging from .243 to .300 Win Mag.

NIB: $1200 **Exc:** $1100 **VGood:** $850

SAKO 85 VARMINT

Similar to Sako 85 Hunter but with recoil pad and 7.5-oz. set trigger. Chambered in .204 Ruger, .243, .22-250 or .308.

NIB: $1350 **Exc:** $1250 **VGood:** $950

SAKO 85 LAMINATED SS VARMINT

Similar to Sako 85 Varmint but with laminated stock and stainless steel barrel. Introduced 2007.

NIB: $1500 **Exc:** $1400 **VGood:** $1100

SAKO QUAD

Bolt-action rimfire rifle with four interchangeable barrels for .22 LR, .22 Magnum, .17 Mach 2 and .17 HMR. Available with satin walnut or grey synthetic stock. Four- and two-barrel combos available. Pricing is for four-barrel Hunter version (walnut stock).

NIB: $1500 **Exc:** $1400 **VGood:** $1050

SAKO PPC MODEL

Bolt action; single shot; 22 PPC, 6mm PPC; 5-shot magazine; 21-3/4-inch, 23-3/4-inch (Benchrest) barrel; weighs 8-1/2 lbs. (heavy barrel); checkered walnut stock; beavertail forend; rosewood pistol grip, forearm (Deluxe). Introduced 1989; no longer in production.

Hunter model

Perf: $1100 **Exc:** $900 **VGood:** $650

Deluxe model

Perf: $1350 **Exc:** $1050 **VGood:** $900

Benchrest model

Perf: $995 **Exc:** $895 **VGood:** $695

SAKO SAFARI GRADE

Bolt action; 338 Win. Mag., 375 H&H Mag., 416 Rem. Mag.; 4-shot magazine; 22-inch barrel; quarter-rib "express" rear sight, hooded ramp front; French walnut stock; checkered 20 lpi, solid rubber buttpad; grip cap and forend tip; front sling swivel band-mounted on barrel. Imported from Finland by Stoeger Industries.

Exc: $1750 **VGood:** $1100 **Good:** $700

SAKO STANDARD SPORTER

Bolt action; 17 Rem., 222, 223 (short action); 22-250, 220 Swift, 243, 308 (medium action); 25-06, 270, 30-06, 7mm Rem. Mag., 300 Win. Mag., 338 Win. Mag., 375 Mag., 375 H&H Mag. (long action); 23-inch,

24-inch barrel; no sights; hand-checkered European walnut pistol-grip stock; hinged floorplate; adjustable trigger. Imported from Finland. Introduced 1978; no longer imported.

Short action		
Exc: $670	**VGood:** $550	**Good:** $450
Medium action		
Exc: $670	**VGood:** $550	**Good:** $450
Long action		
Exc: $670	**VGood:** $550	**Good:** $450

SAKO STANDARD SPORTER CARBINE

Same specs as Standard Sporter except 222, 243, 270, 30-06; 20-inch barrel; full Mannlicher-type stock. Introduced 1977; no longer imported.

Exc: $675 **VGood:** $565 **Good:** $460

SAKO STANDARD SPORTER CLASSIC

Same specs as Standard Sporter except 243, 270, 30-06, 7mm Rem. Mag.; receiver drilled, tapped for scope mounts; straight-comb stock with oil finish; solid rubber recoil pad; recoil lug. Introduced 1980; no longer imported.

Exc: $675 **VGood:** $545 **Good:** $450

SAKO STANDARD SPORTER DELUXE

Same specs as Standard Sporter except select wood; rosewood pistol-grip cap, forend tip; metal checkering on dovetail bases, bolt sleeve, bolt handle; ventilated recoil pad; skip-line checkering. No longer imported.

Exc: $865 **VGood:** $725 **Good:** $600

SAKO STANDARD SPORTER HEAVY BARREL

Same specs as Standard Sporter except beavertail forend; made with short, medium actions only.

Exc: $695 **VGood:** $595 **Good:** $450

SAKO STANDARD SPORTER SAFARI

Same specs as Standard Sporter except long action; 7mm Rem. Mag., 300 Win. Mag., 338 Win Mag., 375 H&H Mag.; quarter-rib express rear sights, hooded ramp front; hand-checkered European walnut stock, solid rubber recoil pad; pistol-grip cap, forend tip; front sling swivel mounted on barrel. No longer imported.

Exc: $1900 **VGood:** $1125 **Good:** $800

SAKO STANDARD SPORTER SUPER DELUXE

Same specs as Standard Sporter Deluxe except select European walnut stock with deep-cut oak leaf carving; rosewood pistol-grip cap, forend tip; high-gloss finish; metal checkering on dovetail bases, bolt sleeve, bolt handle; metal has super-high polish. No longer imported.

Perf: $2500 **Exc:** $1800 **VGood:** $1000

SAKO STANDARD SPORTER VARMINT HEAVY BARREL

Same specs as Standard Sporter Super Deluxe except 17 Rem., 222, 223 (short action), 22-250, 243, 308, 7mm-08 (medium action); 5-shot magazine; weighs from 8-1/4 to 8-1/2 lbs.; beavertail forend. Imported from Finland by Stoeger Industries.

Perf: $900 **Exc:** $750 **VGood:** $600

SAKO TRG-21

Bolt action; 308 Win.; 10-shot magazine; free-floating 25-3/4-inch heavy stainless barrel; 46-1/2-inch overall length; weighs 10-1/2 lbs.; no sights; optional quick-detachable, one-piece scope mount base, 1-inch or 30mm rings; reinforced polyurethane stock with fully-adjustable cheekpiece and buttplate; resistance-free bolt; 60-degree bolt lift; two-stage trigger adjustable for length, pull, horizontal or vertical pitch. Imported from Finland by Stoeger. Introduced 1993.

Perf: $3200 **Exc:** $2600 **VGood:** $1800

SAKO TRG-22

Bolt action; 308 Win., 10-shot magazine; 26-inch barrel; weighs 10-1/4 lbs.; 45-1/4-inch overall length; Reinforced polyurethane stock with fully adjustable cheekpiece and buttplate; no sights; Optional quick- detachable, one-piece scope mount base, 1-inch or 30mm rings. Resistance-free bolt, free-floating heavy stainless barrel, 60-degree bolt lift. Two-stage trigger adjustable for length, pull, horizontal or vertical pitch. Introduced 2000.

Perf: $2500 **Exc:** $2000 **VGood:** $1700

SAKO TRG-S

Bolt action; 243, 7mm-08, 270, 30-06, 7mm Rem. Mag., 300 Win. Mag., 338 Win. Mag., 375 H&H, 416 Rem. Mag.; 5-shot magazine (4-shot for 375 H&H); 22-inch, 24-inch (Magnum calibers) barrel; 45-1/2-inch overall length; weighs 7-3/4 lbs.; no sights; reinforced polyurethane stock with Monte Carlo comb; resistance-free bolt with 60-degree lift; recoil pad adjustable for length; free-floating barrel; detachable magazine; fully-adjustable trigger; matte blue metal. Imported from Finland by Stoeger. Introduced 1993.

Perf: $720 **Exc:** $650 **VGood:** $475

SAKO TRG-42 BOLT-ACTION RIFLE

Similar to TRG-S except 5-shot magazine, fully adjustable stock and competition trigger. Offered in 338 Lapua Mag. and 300 Win. Mag. Still imported from Finland by Beretta USA.

Perf: $2950 **Exc:** $2100 **VGood:** $1700

SAKO VIXEN SPORTER

Bolt action (short action); 218 Bee, 22 Hornet, 222 Rem., 222 Rem. Mag., 223; 5-shot magazine; 23-1/2-inch barrel; no rear sight, hooded ramp front; drilled, tapped for scope mounts; checkered European walnut, Monte Carlo, pistol-grip stock; cheekpiece; sling swivels. Introduced 1946; discontinued 1976.

Exc: $795 **VGood:** $650 **Good:** $500

SAKO VIXEN SPORTER CARBINE

Same specs as Vixen Sporter except 20-inch barrel; Mannlicher-type stock.

Exc: $895 **VGood:** $695 **Good:** $550

SAKO VIXEN SPORTER HEAVY BARREL

Same specs as Vixen Sporter except only 222 Rem., 222 Rem. Mag., 223; heavy barrel; target-style stock; beavertail forearm.

Exc: $1050 **VGood:** $795 **Good:** $550

SAUER DRILLING

Drilling; side-by-side; 12-gauge, 2-3/4-inch chambers/243, 6.5x57R, 7x57R, 7x65R, 30-06,

9.3x74R; 16-gauge, 2-3/4-inch chambers/6.5x57R, 7x57R, 7x65R, 30-06; 25-inch barrel; 46-inch overall length; weighs 7-1/2 lbs.; bead front sight, automatic pop-up rifle rear; fancy French walnut stock with checkered grip and forend, hog-back comb, sculptured cheekpiece, hand-rubbed oil finish; Greener boxlock cross-bolt action with double underlugs; Greener side safety; separate rifle cartridge extractor; nitride-coated, hand-engraved receiver available with English Arabesque or relief game animal scene engraving; Lux Model with profuse relief-engraved game scenes, extra-fancy stump wood. Was imported from Germany by Paul Co.

Standard

Perf: $3795 **Exc:** $3050 **VGood:** $2495

Lux

Perf: $5295 **Exc:** $4495 **VGood:** $3750

SAUER MAUSER SPORTER

Bolt action; 7x57, 8x57, 30-06; other calibers on special order; 5-shot box magazine; 22-inch, 24-inch half-octagon barrels, matted raised rib; three-leaf open rear sight, ramp front; hand-checkered pistol-grip European walnut stock; raised side panels; schnabel tip; double-set triggers; sling swivels; also manufactured with full-length Mannlicher-style stock, 20-inch barrel. Manufactured prior to WWII.

Exc: $695 **VGood:** $595 **Good:** $495

Full-length stock

Exc: $795 **VGood:** $695 **Good:** $550

SAUER MODEL 90

Bolt action; 222, 22-250, 243, 308, 25-06, 270, 30-06, 7mm Rem. Mag., 300 Win. Mag., 300 Weatherby Mag., 338 Win. Mag., 375 H&H Mag., 458 Win. Mag.; 3-shot (Magnums), 4-shot detachable box magazine (standard calibers); 22-1/2-inch, 26-inch barrel; windage-adjustable open rear sight, post front on ramp; oil-finished European walnut stock; recoil pad; rear bolt-locking lugs; front sling swivel on barrel band. Made in Germany. Introduced 1986; discontinued 1989.

Exc: $895 **VGood:** $650 **Good:** $600

SAUER MODEL 90 LUX

Same specs as Model 90 except only 300 Win. Mag., 300 Weatherby Mag., 338 Win. Mag., 375 H&H Mag.; deluxe oil-finished European walnut stock; rosewood forearm tip, pistol-grip cap; gold trigger.

Exc: $1395 **VGood:** $995 **Good:** $660

SAUER MODEL 90 SAFARI

Same specs as Model 90 except 458 Win. Mag.; 23-2/3-inch barrel. Introduced 1986; discontinued 1988.

Perf: $1295 **Exc:** $995 **VGood:** $795

SAUER MODEL 90 SAFARI LUX

Same specs as Model 90 except 458 Win. Mag.; 23-2/3-inch barrel; Williams sights; rosewood forearm, pistol-grip cap; gold trigger.

Exc: $1400 **VGood:** $1100 **Good:** $900

SAUER MODEL 90 STUTZEN

Same specs as Model 90 except 222, 22-250, 243, 308, 25-06, 270, 30-06; Mannlicher-style full stock. Introduced 1986; discontinued 1989.

Exc: $800 **VGood:** $700 **Good:** $600

SAUER MODEL 90 STUTZEN LUX

Same specs as Model 90 Lux except Mannlicher-style stock.

Exc: $1195 **VGood:** $895 **Good:** $795

SAUER MODEL 90 SUPREME

Same specs as Model 90 except 25-06, 270, 30-06, 300 Win. Mag., 300 Weatherby Mag., 7mm Rem. Mag., 338 Win. Mag., 375 H&H Mag.; high-gloss European walnut stock; jeweled bolt; gold trigger. Introduced 1987; still in production.

Grade I engraving

Perf: $1295 **Exc:** $995 **VGood:** $875

Grade II engraving

Perf: $2595 **Exc:** $1995 **VGood:** $1195

Grade III engraving

Perf: $2895 **Exc:** $2295 **VGood:** $1395

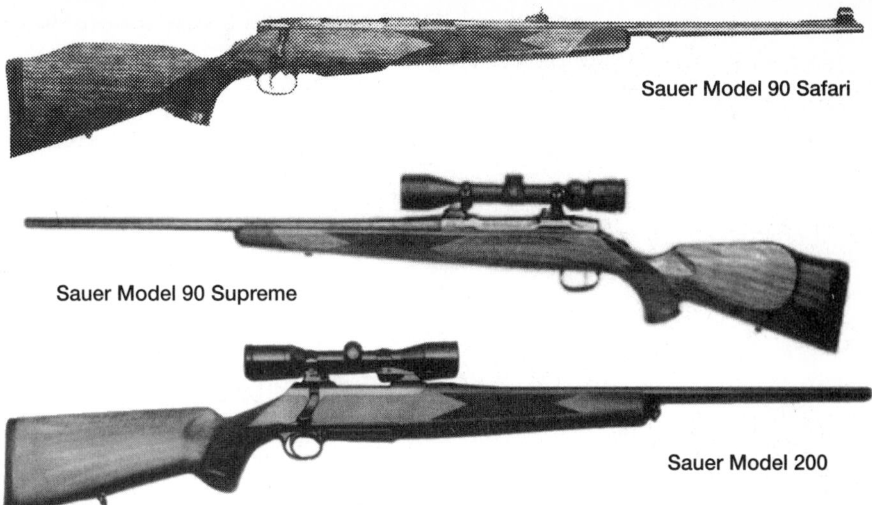

Sauer Model 90 Safari

Sauer Model 90 Supreme

Sauer Model 200

Grade IV engraving

Perf: $3495 **Exc:** $2995 **VGood:** $1995

SAUER MODEL 200

Bolt action; various calibers from 243 to 375 H&H Mag.; 3-shot (Magnums), 4-shot detachable box magazine (standard calibers); 24-inch interchangeable barrels; 44-inch overall length; no sights; drilled, tapped for iron sights or scope mounts; checkered European walnut pistol-grip stock; left-hand model available; steel or alloy versions. Made in Germany. Introduced 1986; discontinued 1993.

Exc: $795 **VGood:** $595 **Good:** $500

Left-hand model

Exc: $850 **VGood:** $650 **Good:** $550

SAUER MODEL 200 CARBON FIBER

Same specs as Model 200 except carbon fiber stock. Introduced 1986; discontinued 1988.

Exc: $800 **VGood:** $725 **Good:** $660

SAUER MODEL 200 LUX

Same specs as Model 200 except deluxe walnut stock; rosewood forearm tip, pistol-grip cap; gold trigger. Introduced 1986; discontinued 1988.

Exc: $765 **VGood:** $645 **Good:** $550

Left-hand model

Exc: $860 **VGood:** $750 **Good:** $600

SAUER MODEL 202

Bolt action; 22 LR, 243, 6.5x55, 6.5x57, 25-06, 270, 280, 7x64, 308, 30-06, 9,3x62 (standard calibers); 6.5x68, 8x68S, 7mm Rem. Mag., 300 Win. Mag., 300 Wea. Mag., 338 Win. Mag., 375 H&H (Magnum calibers); interchangeable 24-inch barrel (standard calibers), 26-inch (Magnum calibers); weighs 7-1/2 lbs. (steel), 6-1/2 lbs. (alloy); sights optional; drilled, tapped for scope mounting; modular receiver accepts interchangeable barrels; steel or alloy receiver; standard stock of fancy Claro walnut, two-piece, with Monte Carlo comb, palm swell grip, semi-schnabel forend tip; Super Grade with extra-fancy Claro walnut with rosewood grip cap, forend tip, high-gloss epoxy finish; French walnut Eurostock with oil finish available; right- or left-hand bolt; tang safety; fully-adjustable trigger; cocking indicator; detachable magazine. Was imported from Germany by Paul Co., now by Sigarms. Introduced 1994.

Exc: $855 **VGood:** $755 **Good:** $625

Super Grade

Exc: $895 **VGood:** $795 **Good:** $675

375 H&H Magnum

Exc: $950 **VGood:** $795 **Good:** $695

375 H&H Magnum Super Grade

Exc: $1050 **VGood:** $895 **Good:** $750

SAUER MODEL 202 ALASKA

Same specs as Model 202 except 300 Wea. Mag. or 300 Win. Mag.; 26-inch barrel; weighs 8-1/4 lbs.; laminated brown stock; metal coated with "Ilaflon" for protection. Accepts any Model 202 Magnum barrel. Was imported from Germany by Paul Co. Introduced 1994.

Perf: $1095 **Exc:** $925 **VGood:** $750

SAUER MODEL 202 HUNTER MATCH

Same specs as Model 202 except 6.5x55, 308; 28-inch match barrel; French walnut sporter stock; matte black finish. Introduced 1994.

Perf: $1295 **Exc:** $995 **VGood:** $795

SAUER 202 TR TARGET

Bolt action; 6.5x55mm, 308 Win.; 5-shot magazine; 26-inch, 28-1/2-inch heavy match target barrel; 44-1/2-inch overall length; weighs 12 lbs.; globe front sight, Sauer-Busk 200-600m diopter rear; drilled, tapped for scope mounting; one-piece true target-type stock of laminated beechwood/ epoxy; adjustable buttplate and cheekpiece; interchangeable free-floating, hammer-forged barrel; two-stage adjustable trigger; vertical slide safety; 3 millisecond lock time; rail for swivel, bipod; right- or left-hand; converts to 22 rimfire. Was imported from Germany by Paul Co. Introduced 1994.

Exc: $1500 **VGood:** $1100 **Good:** $800

SAUER MODEL SSG 2000

Bolt action; 223, 308, 7.5 Swiss, 300 Weatherby Mag.; 4-shot detachable box magazine; 24-inch, 26-inch barrel; weighs 13-1/5 lbs.; no sights; scope mounts; thumbhole walnut stock; adjustable comb, buttplate, forend rail; stippled grip, forend; right- or left-hand models; flash hider/muzzlebrake; double-set triggers; sliding safety. Made in Germany. Introduced 1985; discontinued 1986.

Exc: $4495 **VGood:** $2595 **Good:** $1750

SAVAGE AXIS SERIES

Formerly known as Savage Edge series. Calibers: 223, 22-250, 243, 7mm-08, 308, 25-06, 270 Win., 30-06. Barrel, 22 inches. Weight is 6.5 lbs. and overall length 43.9 inches. Black synthetic stock or camo. Detachable box magazine with four-round capacity.

Perf: $320 **Exc:** $275 **VGood:** $240

Add 10 percent for camo stock, 25 percent for XP stainless camo.

SAVAGE CUB

Bolt action, single shot; 22LR, 17 Mach 2; 16-1/8-inch barrel; weighs 3.3 lbs; rear peep, post front sights; uses Mark I bolt action in scaled-down junior-size rifle; blued barrel and action; walnut-finished hardwood stock. Made in Canada, from Savage Arms; Introduced 2003, still in production.

Perf: $135 **Exc:** 100 **VGood:** $75

SAVAGE MODEL CUB-T

Similar to Model CUB but with laminated thumbhole stock.

NIB: $235 **Exc:** $200 **VGood:** $175

SAVAGE MARK I

Bolt action; 22 LR, single shot, 22 LR Shot version also available; 20-3/4-inch barrel; weighs 5-1/2 lbs.; 39-1/2-inch overall length; Walnut-finished hardwood stock with Monte Carlo-type comb, checkered grip and forend, synthetic stock also available; Bead front sight, open adjustable rear. Receiver grooved for scope mounting. Thumb-operated rotating safety. Blue finish. Youth models with camo or color-laminate stocks also produced. Introduced 1990. Made in Canada, from Savage Arms Inc.

Perf: $115 **Exc:** $95 **VGood:** $70

SAVAGE MARK II

Bolt action; 22 LR, 17 Mach 2; repeater with 10-shot detachable box magazine; 20-1/2-inch barrel; weighs 5-1/2 lbs.; 39-1/2-inch overall length; Walnut-finished hardwood stock with Monte Carlo-type comb, checkered grip and forend, synthetic stock also available; Bead front sight, open adjustable rear. Receiver grooved for scope mounting. Thumb- operated rotating safety; left-hand version also available. Blue finish. Introduced 1990. Made in Canada, from Savage Arms, Inc.

Mark II standard model

Perf: $125 **Exc:** $100 **VGood:** $80

Mark II (youth), 19-inch barrel, 37-inch overall, 5 lbs.

Perf: $125 **Exc:** $100 **VGood:** $80

SAVAGE MARK II-LV HEAVY BARREL

Similar to Mark II-G except heavy 21-inch barrel with recessed target-style crown, laminated hardwood stock with cut checkering. No sights furnished, has dovetailed receiver for scope mounting. Overall length is 39-3/4-inch, weighs 6-1/2 lbs. Comes with 10-shot detachable box magazine. Introduced 1997. Imported from Canada by Savage Arms, Inc.

Perf: $170 **Exc:** $150 **VGood:** $120

With black synthetic stock

Perf: $160 **Exc:** $140 **VGood:** $110

SAVAGE MODEL MARK II CLASSIC

Similar to Mark II but with sporter-weight barrel and oil-finished premium walnut stock. AccuTrigger.

NIB: $415 **Exc:** $375 **VGood:** $300

SAVAGE MODEL 3

Bolt action; single shot; 22 Short, 22 Long, 22 LR; 26-inch barrel (pre-WWII), 24-inch (post-WWII); 43-inch overall length; weighs 5 lbs.; takedown; chromium-plated bolt, trigger; adjustable flat-top rear sight, gold bead front; receiver drilled. tapped for scope mounting; uncheckered American walnut one-piece pistol-grip stock; early forearm with finger grooves; checkered hard rubber or steel buttplate. Introduced 1933; discontinued 1952.

Exc: $90 **VGood:** $80 **Good:** $60

SAVAGE MODEL 3S

Same specs as Model 3 except rear peep sight, hooded front sight with three inserts. Introduced 1933; discontinued 1942.

Exc: $100 **VGood:** $90 **Good:** $70

SAVAGE MODEL 3ST

Same specs as Model 3S except rear peep sight, hooded front sight; swivels, sling. Introduced 1933; discontinued 1942.

Exc: $110 **VGood:** $90 **Good:** $80

SAVAGE MODEL 4

Bolt action; 22 Short, 22 Long, 22 LR; 5-shot detachable box magazine; 24-inch barrel; weighs 5-1/2 lbs.; takedown; chromium-plated bolt, trigger; pre-WWII version with open rear sight, bead front; checkered pistol grip; American walnut stock, grooved forearm; post-WWII model with uncheckered stock; rubber buttplate. Introduced 1933; discontinued 1965.

Pre-WWII model

Exc: $110 **VGood:** $95 **Good:** $80

Post-WWII model

Exc: $115 **VGood:** $100 **Good:** $90

SAVAGE MODEL 4M

Same specs as post-war Model 4 except 22 WMR; gold-plated trigger. Introduced 1961; discontinued 1965.

Exc: $120 **VGood:** $95 **Good:** $80

SAVAGE MODEL 4S

Same specs as Model 4 except fully-adjustable rear peep sight, hooded front with three inserts. Introduced 1933; discontinued 1942.

Exc: $120 **VGood:** $100 **Good:** $90

SAVAGE MODEL 5

Bolt action; 22 Short, 22 Long, 22 LR; 21-shot (22 Short), 17-shot (22 Long), 15-shot (22 LR) tubular magazine; 24-inch tapered barrel with crowned muzzle; weighs 6 lbs.; takedown; chromium-plated bolt, trigger; fully-adjustable sporting rear sight, gold bead front; redesigned American walnut stock, bolt handle, trigger guard; hard rubber buttplate. Introduced 1936; discontinued 1961.

Exc: $120 **VGood:** $105 **Good:** $90

SAVAGE MODEL 5S

Same specs as Model 5 except No. 15 Micro peep rear sight, hooded No. 150 front. Introduced 1936; discontinued 1942.

Exc: $125 **VGood:** $110 **Good:** $90

SAVAGE MODEL 10FM SIERRA ULTRA LIGHT

Bolt action; 223, 243, 308. 20-inch barrel; weighs 6 lbs.; 41-1/2-inch overall length; "Dual Pillar" bedding in black synthetic stock with silver medallion in gripcap; no sights; drilled and tapped for scope mounting. True short action. Comes with sling and quick-detachable swivels. Introduced 1998, still offered. Made in U.S.A. by Savage Arms, Inc.

Perf: $390 **Exc:** $290 **VGood:** $220

SAVAGE MODEL 10FCM SCOUT ULTRA LIGHT

Bolt action; 7mm-08 Rem., 308 Win. 20-inch barrel; weighs 6.25 lbs.; 39.75-inch overall length; Synthetic stock with checkering, dual pillar bed. Ghost ring rear sight, gold bead front. Blued, detachable 4-shot box magazine, Savage shooting sling/carry strap. Quick detachable swivels. Introduced 1999, discontinued after two years; reintroduced 2007.

Perf: $525 **Exc:** $460 **VGood:** $310

SAVAGE MODEL 19

Bolt action; 22 LR; 5-shot detachable box magazine; 25-inch barrel; weighs 8 lbs.; early model with adjustable rear peep sight, blade front; later model with hooded front sight, Savage No. 15

fully-adjustable aperture extension rear; target-type uncheckered one-piece walnut stock; full pistol grip, 2-inch wide beavertail forearm; checkered buttplate; receiver drilled for scope blocks; 1-1/4-inch sling; sling swivels. Introduced 1933; discontinued 1946.

Exc: $230 **VGood:** $190 **Good:** $150

SAVAGE MODEL 19H

Same specs as Model 19 except chambered for 22 Hornet. Introduced 1933; discontinued 1942.

Exc: $495 **VGood:** $440 **Good:** $300

SAVAGE MODEL 19L

Same specs as Model 19 except Lyman 48Y receiver sight, No. 17A front sight. Introduced 1933; discontinued 1942.

Exc: $325 **VGood:** $265 **Good:** $200

SAVAGE MODEL 19M

Same specs as Model 19 except heavy 28-inch barrel; scope bases. Introduced 1933; discontinued 1942.

Exc: $350 **VGood:** $290 **Good:** $220

SAVAGE MODEL 19 NRA

Same specs as Model 19 except adjustable rear sight, blade front; American walnut military-type full stock, pistol grip; uncheckered. Introduced 1919; discontinued 1933.

Exc: $230 **VGood:** $190 **Good:** $150

SAVAGE MODEL 23A

Bolt action; 22 LR; 5-shot detachable box magazine; 23-inch barrel; open rear sight, blade or bead front; uncheckered American walnut pistol-grip stock, thin forearm, schnabel tip. Introduced 1923; discontinued 1933.

Exc: $220 **VGood:** $180 **Good:** $130

SAVAGE MODEL 23AA

Same specs as Model 23A except 22 Short, 22 Long, 22 LR; checkered stock; swivel studs; speed lock; receiver tapped for No. 10 Savage aperture rear sight. Introduced 1933; discontinued 1942.

Exc: $270 **VGood:** $220 **Good:** $170

SAVAGE MODEL 23B

Same specs as Model 23A except 25-20; 25-inch barrel; weighs 6-1/2 lbs.; swivel studs; no schnabel tip. Introduced 1923; discontinued 1942.

Exc: $400 **VGood:** $325 **Good:** $250

SAVAGE MODEL 23C

Same specs as Model 23B except 32-20; 25-inch barrel; swivel studs; no schnabel tip. Introduced 1923; discontinued 1942.

Exc: $400 **VGood:** $325 **Good:** $250

SAVAGE MODEL 23D

Same specs as Model 23B except 22 Hornet; 25-inch barrel; weighs 6-1/2 lbs.; swivel studs; no schnabel tip; flat-top adjustable rear sight, gold bead front. Introduced 1923; discontinued 1947.

Exc: $450 **VGood:** $350 **Good:** $300

SAVAGE MODEL 30 STEVENS FAVORITE

Single shot, falling block; 22 LR, 22WMR, 17 HMR; 20-1/2-inch barrel; weighs 4.25 lbs.; 36.75-inch overall length; Walnut stock, straight grip, schnabel forend; Adjustable rear sight, bead post front. Lever action falling block, inertia firing pin system, half octagonal or full octagonal bbl. Add $20 for camo finish.

Perf: $200 **Exc:** $170 **VGood:** $140

SAVAGE MODEL 34

Bolt action; 22 Short, 22 Long, 22 LR; 5-shot magazine; 20-inch barrel; open rear sight, blade front; uncheckered hardwood pistol grip or checkered Monte Carlo stock. Introduced 1969; discontinued 1973.

Exc: $150 **VGood:** $125 **Good:** $100

Savage Model 19

Savage Model 10FCM Scout

Savage Model 19 NRA

Savage Model 23AA

Savage Model 23D

Savage Model 30 Stevens Favorite

Savage Model 40

Savage Model 40 Varmint Hunter

SAVAGE MODEL 34M

Same specs as Model 34 except 22 WMR. Introduced 1969; discontinued 1973.

Exc: $175 **VGood:** $140 **Good:** $100

SAVAGE MODEL 35

Bolt action; 22 LR; 5-shot magazine; 22-inch barrel; 41-inch overall length; ramp front sight, step-adjustable open rear; walnut-finished hardwood Monte Carlo stock; checkered pistol grip, forend; receiver grooved for scope mount. Introduced 1982; discontinued 1985.

Exc: $150 **VGood:** $125 **Good:** $100

SAVAGE MODEL 35M

Same specs as Model 35 except 22 WMR. Introduced 1982; discontinued 1985.

Exc: $150 **VGood:** $125 **Good:** $100

SAVAGE MODEL 36

Bolt action; single shot; 22 LR; 22-inch barrel; 41-inch overall length; ramp front sight, step-adjustable rear; walnut-finished hardwood Monte Carlo stock; checkered pistol grip, forend; receiver grooved for scope mount. Introduced 1982; discontinued 1985.

Exc: $125 **VGood:** $100 **Good:** $75

SAVAGE MODEL 40

Bolt action; 250-3000, 30-30, 300 Savage, 30-06; 4-shot detachable box magazine; 22-inch, 24-inch barrel (300 Savage, 30-06); weighs 7-1/2 lbs.; semi-buckhorn rear sight, white metal bead front on ramp; uncheckered American walnut pistol-grip stock; tapered forearm; schnabel tip; steel buttplate. Introduced 1928; discontinued 1940.

Exc: $500 **VGood:** $400 **Good:** $300

SAVAGE MODEL 40 VARMINT HUNTER

Bolt action, single shot; 22 Hornet, 223; 24-inch heavy barrel; new Model 40 action with AccuTrigger; heavy laminated stock with beavertail forend; no sights. 223 chambering was dropped shortly after introduction, will bring a premium. Introduced 2004, still produced.

Perf: $375 **Exc:** $300 **VGood:** $225

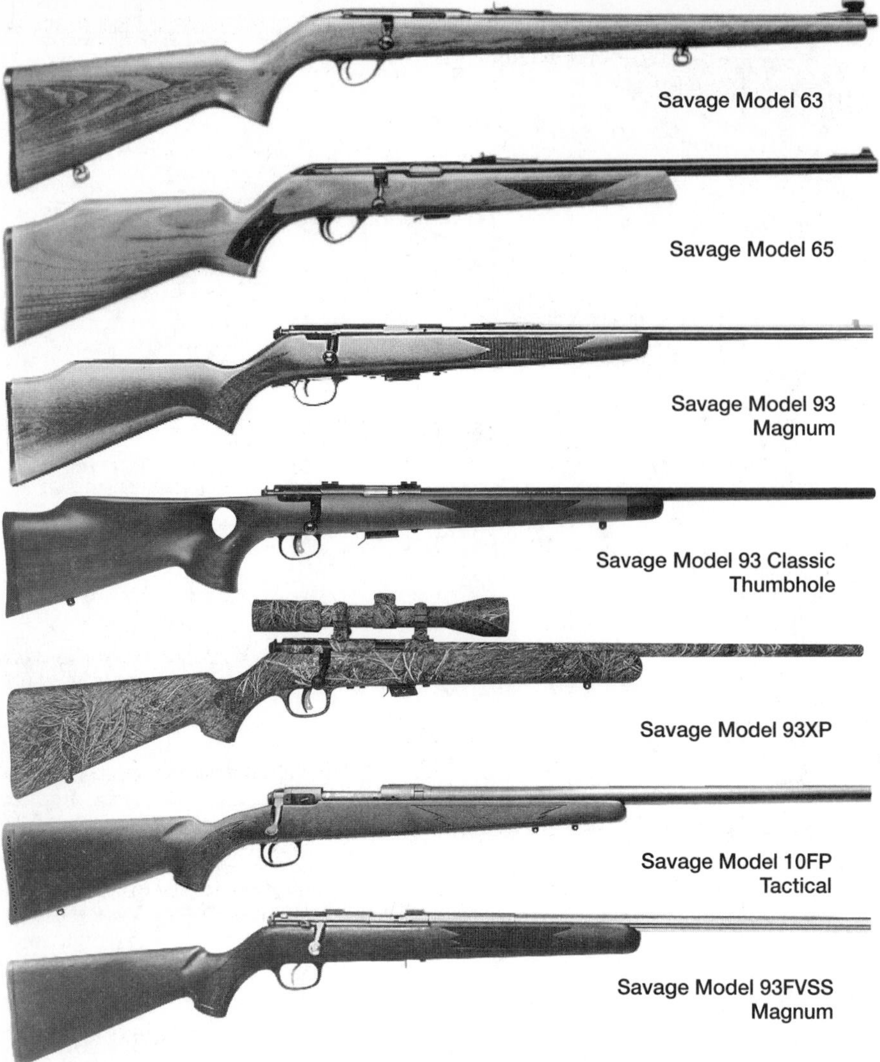

SAVAGE MODEL 45

Bolt action; 250-3000, 30-30, 300 Savage, 30-06; 4-shot detachable box magazine; 22-inch (250-3000, 30-30), 24-inch barrel; Deluse version of Model 40 rifle. Lyman receiver sight, bead front on ramp; hand-checkered pistol-grip stock, forearm, schnabel tip. Introduced 1928; discontinued 1940.

Exc: $550 **VGood:** $450 **Good:** $350

SAVAGE MODEL 46

Bolt action; 22 Short, 22 Long, 22 LR; 20-shot (22 Short), 17-shot (22 Long), 15-shot (22 LR) tubular magazine; open rear sight, blade front; uncheckered hardwood pistol grip or checkered Monte Carlo stock. Introduced 1969; discontinued 1973.

Exc: $125 **VGood:** $100 **Good:** $75

SAVAGE MODEL 63

Bolt action; single shot; 22 Short, 22 Long, 22 LR; 18-inch barrel; 36-inch overall length; weighs 4 lbs.; open rear sight, hooded ramp front; one-piece full-length walnut-finished hardwood pistol-grip stock; sling swivels; furnished with key to lock trigger. Introduced 1970; discontinued 1972.

Exc: $110 **VGood:** $90 **Good:** $75

SAVAGE MODEL 63M

Same specs as Model 63K except only 22 WMR. Introduced 1970; discontinued 1972.

Exc: $120 **VGood:** $100 **Good:** $90

SAVAGE MODEL 65

Bolt action; 22 LR; 5-shot detachable clip magazine; 20-inch lightweight tapered barrel; 39-inch overall length; weighs 4-3/4 lbs.; gold bead ramp front sight, open rear with elevator; receiver grooved for scope mounting; select walnut Monte Carlo pistol-grip stock; buttplate with white line spacer; raised fluted comb; thumb safety; double extractors. Introduced 1965; discontinued 1974.

Exc: $125 **VGood:** $100 **Good:** $75

SAVAGE MODEL 65M

Same specs as Model 65 except 22 WMR. Introduced 1966; discontinued 1981.

Exc: $150 **VGood:** $125 **Good:** $100

SAVAGE MODEL 93 MAGNUM

Bolt action; 22 WMR, 17 HMR; 5-shot magazine. 20-3/4-inch barrel; weighs 5-3/4 lbs.; 39-1/2-inch overall length; Walnut-finished hardwood stock with Monte Carlo-type comb, checkered grip and forend. Bead front sight, adjustable open rear. Receiver grooved for scope mount. Thumb-operated rotary safety. Blue finish. Introduced 1994. Made in Canada, from Savage Arms.

Perf: $140 **Exc:** $120 **VGood:** $100

With black synthetic stock

Perf: $130 **Exc:** $110 **VGood:** $90

SAVAGE MODEL 93 CLASSIC THUMBHOLE

Similar to above but with thumbhole stock.

NIB: $350 **Exc:** $295 **VGood:** $250

SAVAGE MODEL 93XP

.22 WMR package gun with 22-inch barrel and factory-mounted 3x9 scope. Finished overall with Mossy Oak Brush stock.

NIB: $375 **Exc:** $295 **VGood:** $250

SAVAGE MODEL 93FSS MAGNUM

Similar to Model 93G except stainless steel barreled action and black synthetic stock with positive checkering. Weighs 5-1/2 lbs. Introduced 1997. Imported from Canada by Savage Arms, Inc.

Perf: $190 **Exc:** $150 **VGood:** $100

SAVAGE MODEL 93FVSS MAGNUM

Similar to Model 93FSS Magnum except 21-inch heavy barrel with recessed target-style crown, satin-finished stainless barreled action, black graphite/fiberglass stock. Drilled and tapped for scope mounting; comes with Weaver-style bases. Introduced 1998. Made in Canada by Savage Arms, Inc.

Perf: $200 **Exc:** $160 **VGood:** $120

SAVAGE MODEL 93BTVS

Similar to Model 93FVSS but with laminated thumbhole stock.

NIB: $390 **Exc:** $335 **VGood:** $290

SAVAGE MODEL 93R17 CLASSIC

Similar to Model 93 but in .17HMR only with sporter-weight barrel and oil-finished premium walnut stock. AccuTrigger. Introduced in 2007.

NIB: $450 **Exc:** $395 **VGood:** $295

SAVAGE MODEL 10 PREDATOR HUNTER

Similar to Model 110FC but with overall camo finish, 22" medium-contour barrel, and AccuTrigger. Chambered in .204 Ruger, .22-250 and .223.

NIB: $575 **Exc:** $525 **VGood:** $400

SAVAGE MODEL 10FP TACTICAL RIFLE

Similar to the Model 110FP except has true short action, chambered for 223, 308; black synthetic stock with Pillar bedding. Introduced 1998. Made in U.S.A. by Savage Arms, Inc.

Perf: $500 **Exc:** $400 **VGood:** $320

SAVAGE MODEL 10FCP-HS PRECISION

Similar to Model 110FP but with one-piece HS Precision synthetic target stock and detachable box magazine. Introduced in 2007.

NIB: $795 **Exc:** $725 **VGood:** $595

SAVAGE MODEL 10FCP CHOATE

Similar to Model 10FP but with Choate synthetic stock.

NIB: $650 **Exc:** $600 **VGood:** $495

SAVAGE MODEL 10FCP MCMILLAN

Similar to Model 10FP but with synthetic McMillan precision stock.

NIB: $725 **Exc:** $685 **VGood:** $595

SAVAGE MODEL 110

Bolt action; 243, 270, 308, 30-06; 4-shot box magazine; 22-inch medium-weight barrel; 43-inch overall length; weighs 6-3/4 lbs.; step-adjustable rear sight, gold bead ramp front; hand-checkered American walnut pistol-grip stock; aluminum buttplate; pistol-grip cap. Introduced 1958; discontinued 1963.

Exc: $375 **VGood:** $325 **Good:** $250

SAVAGE MODEL 110B

Same specs as Model 110 except 243, 270, 30-06; 4-shot internal magazine; checkered American walnut Monte Carlo pistol-grip stock, forearm. Introduced 1977; discontinued 1979.

Perf: $375 **Exc:** $325 **VGood:** $300

Left-hand model

Exc: $375 **VGood:** $325 **Good:** $300

SAVAGE MODEL 110B LAMINATE

Same specs as Model 110 except 300 Win. Mag., 338 Win. Mag.; 3-shot internal magazine; 24-inch barrel; brown laminated hardwood Monte

Carlo pistol-grip stock, forearm. Introduced 1989; discontinued 1991.

Exc: $400 **VGood:** $350 **Good:** $300

SAVAGE MODEL 110C

Same specs as Model 110 except 22-250, 243 Win., 25-06, 270 Win., 30-06, 308 Win., 7mm Rem. Mag., 300 Win. Mag.; 3-shot (Magnums), 4-shot detachable box magazine; 22-inch, 24-inch (22-250, Magnums) barrel; open folding leaf rear sight, gold bead ramp front; hand-checkered Monte Carlo American walnut pistol-grip stock; recoil pad (Magnums). Introduced 1966.

Exc: $375 **VGood:** $325 **Good:** $250

Left-hand model

Exc: $375 **VGood:** $325 **Good:** $250

SAVAGE MODEL 110CY LADIES/ YOUTH

Same specs as Model 110 except 223, 243, 270, 300 Sav., 308; 5-shot magazine; ramp front sight, fully-adjustable rear; drilled and tapped for scope mounting; walnut-stained hardwood stock with high comb, cut checkering; 12-1/2-inch length of pull; red rubber buttpad. Made in U.S. by Savage. Introduced 1991.

Perf: $375 **Exc:** $325 **VGood:** $250

SAVAGE MODEL 110D

Same specs as Model 110 except 22-250, 223 Rem., 243, 25-06, 270, 308, 30-06, 7mm Rem. Mag., 264, 300 Win. Mag., 338 Win. Mag.; 3-shot (Magnums), 4-shot magazine; 22-inch, 24-inch (22-250) barrel; 42-1/2 to 45-inch overall length; weighs 6-3/4 to 8 lbs. (22-250); semi-buckhorn step-adjustable folding rear sight; hinged floorplate; aluminum buttplate or hard rubber (22-250) recoil pad. Introduced 1966; discontinued 1988.

Exc: $375 **VGood:** $325 **Good:** $275

Left-hand model

Exc: $375 **VGood:** $325 **Good:** $275

SAVAGE MODEL 110E

Same specs as Model 110 except 22-250, 223, 243 Win., 30-06, 270, 7mm Rem. Mag., 308; 3-shot (Magnum), 4-shot box magazine; 20-inch, 24-inch (7mm, stainless) barrel; 40-1/2-inch overall length (20-inch barrel), 45-1/2-inch (24-inch); weighs 6-3/4 lbs.; uncheckered Monte Carlo stock (early versions); checkered pistol grip, forearm (later models); recoil pad (Magnum). Introduced 1963; discontinued 1989.

Exc: $375 **VGood:** $325 **Good:** $275

Left-hand model

Exc: $375 **VGood:** $325 **Good:** $275

SAVAGE MODEL 110ES

Same specs as Model 110E except 30-06, 243, 308 Win.; comes with 4x scope and mount. Introduced 1983.

Exc: $375 **VGood:** $325 **Good:** $275

SAVAGE 110F

Same as Model 110 except 22-250, 223 Rem., 243 Win., 250 Savage, 25-06, 308 Win., 30-06, 270 Win., 7mm Rem Mag., 300 Savage, 300 Win. Mag., 7mm-08, 338 Win. Mag.; removable open sights; black Du Pont Rynite stock with black buttpad, swivel studs; right-hand only. Made in U.S. by Savage. Introduced 1988; discontinued 1994.

Exc: $380 **VGood:** $300 **Good:** $270

SAVAGE 110FNS

Same specs as Model 110F except no sights; black composite stock. Made in U.S. by Savage. No longer made.

Exc: $320 **VGood:** $240 **Good:** $190

SAVAGE MODEL 110FP

Composite stock and 24" heavy barrel. In 2003 the Savage AccuTrigger was added to this model. Discontinued.

Exc: $285 **VGood:** $250 **Good:** $175

SAVAGE MODEL 110FP POLICE

Same specs as Model 110F except 223, 308, 30-06, 300 Win. Mag., 7mm Rem. Mag., 25-06; 4-shot internal magazine; 24-inch heavy barrel; 45-1/2-inch

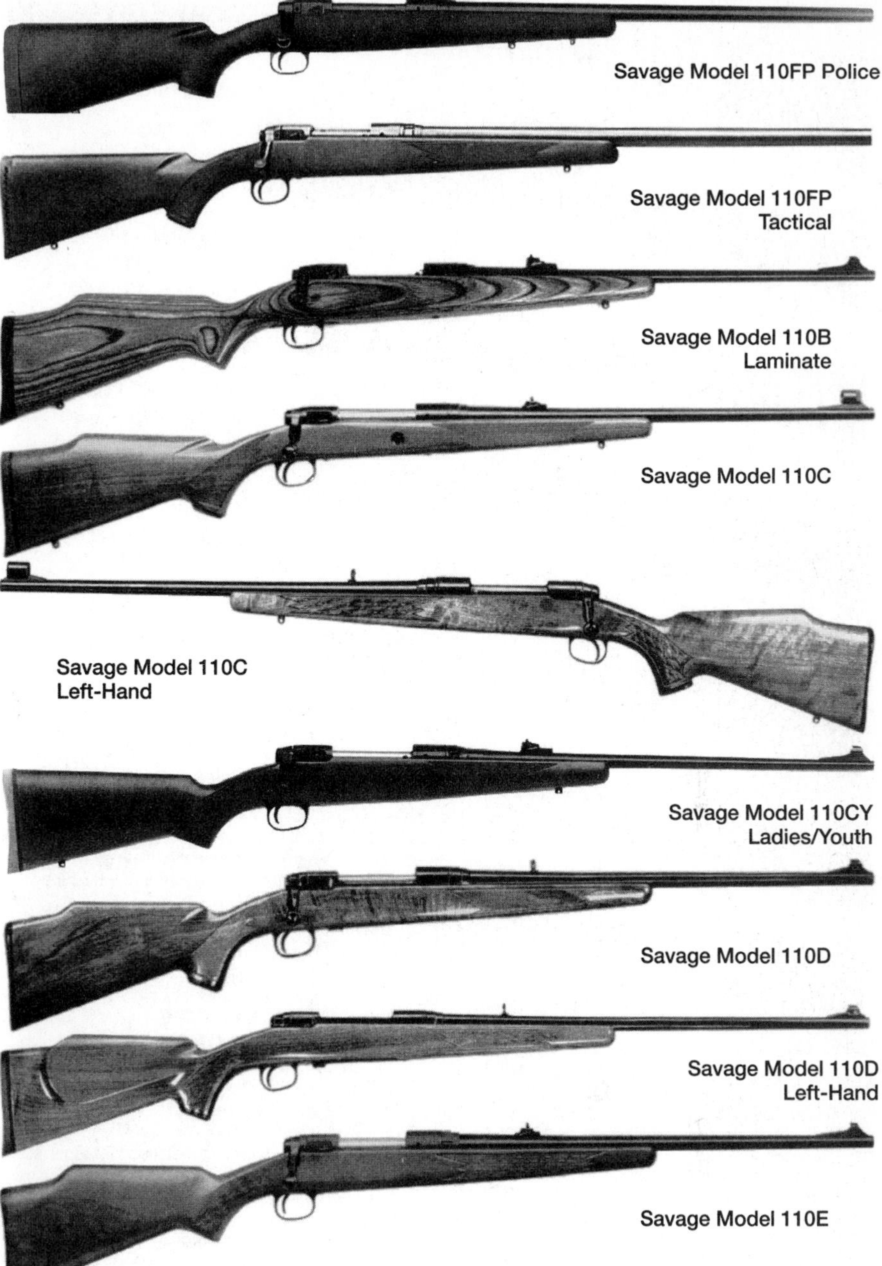

Savage Model 110FP Police

Savage Model 110FP Tactical

Savage Model 110B Laminate

Savage Model 110C

Savage Model 110C Left-Hand

Savage Model 110CY Ladies/Youth

Savage Model 110D

Savage Model 110D Left-Hand

Savage Model 110E

overall length; weighs 8-1/2 lbs.; no sights; drilled, tapped for scope mounts; black graphite/fiberglass composition stock; double swivel studs on forend for swivels or bipod; matte finish on all metal parts. Introduced 1990; still in production.

Exc: $400 **VGood:** $330 **Good:** $280

SAVAGE MODEL 110FP TACTICAL

Bolt action, long action; 223, 25-06, 308, 30-06, 300 Win. Mag., 7mm Rem. Mag., 4-shot magazine; 24-inch heavy barrel; recessed target muzzle crown; weighs 8-1/2 lbs.; 45-1/2-inch overall length; Black graphite/fiberglass composition stock; positive checkering; no sights; receiver drilled and tapped for scope mounting; pillar-bedded stock; black matte finish on all metal parts. Double swivel studs on the forend for sling and/or bipod mount. Right or left-hand. Introduced 1990. From Savage Arms, Inc.

Perf: $500 **Exc:** $400 **VGood:** $320

SAVAGE MODEL 110G

Same specs as Model 110 except 22-250, 223 Rem., 250 Savage, 25-06, 270 Win., 300 Savage, 308 Win., 30-06, 243 Win., 7mm-08, 7mm Rem. Mag., 300 Win. Mag.; 5-shot (standard calibers), 4-shot (Magnums); 22-inch 24-inch round tapered barrels; 42-inch overall length (22-inch barrel); checkered walnut-finished Monte Carlo hardwood stock; hard rubber buttplate; ramp front sight, step-adjustable rear; top tang safety; tapped for scope mounts; floating barrel; adjustable trigger. Introduced, 1989.

Exc: $375 **VGood:** $325 **Good:** $275

Left-hand model (110GL)

Exc: $375 **VGood:** $325 **Good:** $275

SAVAGE 110GC

Same specs as Model 110G except 30-06, 270, 7mm Rem. Mag., 300 Win. Mag.; detachable box magazine. Made in U.S. by Savage. No longer made.

Perf: $375 **Exc:** $325 **VGood:** $275

SAVAGE MODEL 110GCXP3 PACKAGE

Same specs as Model 110G except 270, 30-06, 7mm Rem. Mag., 300 Win. Mag.; detachable box magazine; factory-mounted and bore-sighted 3-9x32 scope, rings and bases; quick-detachable swivels; sling; Monte Carlo-style hardwood stock with walnut finish; left-hand models available in all calibers. Made in U.S. by Savage Arms, Inc. Introduced 1994

Exc: $410 **VGood:** $370 **Good:** $320

Savage Model 110S

Savage Model 110 50th Anniversary

Savage Model 111G Classic Hunter

Savage Model 11BTH

SAVAGE 110GLNS
Same specs as Model 110G except 30-06, 270, 7mm Rem. Mag.; true left-hand action; no sights. Made in U.S. by Savage. No longer made.

Exc: $375 **VGood:** $325 **Good:** $275

SAVAGE 110GNS
Same specs as Model 110G except no sights. Made in U.S. by Savage. No longer made.

Exc: $375 **VGood:** $325 **Good:** $275

SAVAGE 110GV VARMINT
Same as Model 110G except 22-250, 223; no sights; receiver drilled and tapped for scope mounting; medium-weight varmint barrel. Made in U.S. by Savage. Introduced 1989; discontinued 1993.

Exc: $400 **VGood:** $350 **Good:** $300

SAVAGE MODEL 110GXP3 PACKAGE
Same specs as Model 110G except package with scope and sling; 223, 22-250, 243, 250 Savage, 25-06, 270, 300 Sav., 30-06, 308, 7mm Rem. Mag., 7mm-08, 300 Win. Mag.; factory mounted bore-sighted 3-9x32 scope, rings and bases; quick-detachable swivels; sling; Monte Carlo-style hardwood stock with walnut finish; left-hand models available in all calibers. Made in U.S. by Savage Arms, Inc. Introduced 1991; still produced.

Exc: $450 **VGood:** $375 **Good:** $300

SAVAGE MODEL 110K
Same specs as Model 110 except laminated camouflage stock; 243, 270, 30-06, 7mm Rem. Mag., 338 Win. Mag.; Introduced 1986; discontinued 1988.

Exc: $375 **VGood:** $325 **Good:** $275

SAVAGE MODEL 110M
Same specs as Model 110 except 264 Win. Mag., 300 Win. Mag., 7mm Rem. Mag., 338 Win. Mag.; 3-shot magazine; 24-inch stainless steel barrel; 45-inch overall length; weighs 8 lbs. (338); hand-checkered American walnut pistol-grip Monte Carlo stock; recoil pad. Introduced 1963; discontinued 1969.

Exc: $400 **VGood:** $350 **Good:** $300

Left-hand model (110ML)

Exc: $375 **VGood:** $325 **Good:** $275

SAVAGE MODEL 110MC
Same specs as Model 110 except 22-250; 24-inch barrel; hand-checkered American walnut pistol-grip Monte Carlo stock. Introduced 1959; discontinued 1969.

Exc: $370 **VGood:** $330 **Good:** $270

Left-hand model (110MC-L)

Exc: $390 **VGood:** $340 **Good:** $300

SAVAGE MODEL 110P PREMIER GRADE
Same specs as Model 110 except 243 Win., 30-06, 7mm Rem. Mag.; 3-shot (Magnum), 4-shot magazine; 22-inch, 24-inch (7mm, stainless) barrel; 43-inch-45-inch overall length; weighs 7-7-3/4 lbs.; recessed bolt head; double front locking lugs; top tang safety; aluminum buttplate; skip-checkered Monte Carlo select French walnut stock; hand-carved roll-over cheekpiece; rosewood pistol-grip cap, forearm tip with white inlay; recoil pad (Magnum); left- or right-hand action. Introduced 1964; discontinued 1970.

Exc: $440 **VGood:** $330 **Good:** $310

7mm Rem. Mag. model

Exc: $460 **VGood:** $350 **Good:** $330

SAVAGE MODEL 110PE PRESENTATION GRADE
Same specs as Model 110 except 243 Win., 30-06, 7mm Rem. Mag.; 3-shot (Magnum), 4-shot magazine; 22-inch, 24-inch (Magnum) barrel; skip-checkered Monte Carlo fancy French walnut stock; rosewood pistol-grip cap, forearm tip; recoil pad (Magnum); right-, or left-hand action; engraved receiver, trigger guard, floorplate. Introduced 1958; discontinued 1970.

Exc: $695 **VGood:** $595 **Good:** $495

7mm Rem. Mag. model

Exc: $725 **VGood:** $625 **Good:** $525

SAVAGE MODEL 110S
Same specs as Model 110 except 308, 7mm-08; 5-shot magazine; 22-inch heavy tapered barrel; weighs 8-1/2 lbs.; no sights; drilled, tapped for scope mounts; special silhouette stock with Wundhammer swell stippled pistol grip, forend; rubber recoil pad. Introduced 1978; discontinued 1985.

Exc: $350 **VGood:** $300 **Good:** $275

SAVAGE MODEL 110V
Same specs as Model 110 except 22-250, 223; 5-shot magazine; 26-inch heavy barrel; no sights; checkered American walnut varmint stock. Introduced 1983; discontinued 1989.

Exc: $375 **VGood:** $325 **Good:** $275

SAVAGE 110WLE LIMITED EDITION ONE OF ONE THOUSAND
Same specs as Model 110 except 7x57mm Mauser, 250-3000 Savage, 300 Savage; high-luster #2 fancy-grade American walnut stock with cut checkering; swivel studs, and recoil pad; highly polished barrel; the bolt with laser-etched Savage logo. Sold with gun lock, ear plugs, sight-in target and shooting glasses. Made in U.S. by Savage. Introduced 1992; no longer made.

Exc: $460 **VGood:** $400 **Good:** $360

SAVAGE MODEL 110 - FIFTIETH ANNIVERSARY
Short-action rifle commemorating the 50th anniversary of the Model 10. Chambered in .300 Savage with 22-inch barrel. 1000 numbered rifles, high-luster blued barrel and action, unique checkering pattern on select walnut stock, high-grade hinged floorplate, Scroll pattern on receiver, 24-karat gold plated double barrel bands, 24-karat gold plated AccuTrigger, embossed recoil pad.

NIB: $700 **Exc:** $525 **VGood:** $375

SAVAGE MODEL 111 CHIEFTAIN
Bolt action; 243 Win., 270 Win., 7x57, 7mm Rem. Mag., 30-06; 3-shot (Magnum), 4-shot detachable clip magazine; 22-inch, 24-inch (Magnum, stainless) barrel; 43- to 45-inch overall length; 7-1/2 to 8-1/4 lbs.; leaf rear sight, hooded ramp front; select checkered American walnut pistol-grip stock; Monte Carlo comb; cheekpiece; pistol-grip cap; hard rubber or recoil pad (Magnum) with white line spacer; detachable swivels; sling. Introduced 1974; discontinued 1978.

Exc: $370 **VGood:** $330 **Good:** $280

SAVAGE MODEL 111 HUNTER
Bolt action; 25-06, 270, 30-06, 7mm Rem. Mag., 300 Win. Mag., 338 Win. Mag., 300 Rem. Ultra Mag., 7mm WSM, 300 Rem. Ultra Mag., 7mm Rem. Ultra Mag., 270 WSM, 300 Win. Short Mag., 7mm Rem. Short Ultra Mag. Barrel: 22-inch, 24-inch (magnum calibers). Weight: 6.3 to 7 lbs. Length: 43-1/2 inches overall (22-inch barrel). Stock: Walnut-finished hardwood or synthetic. Sights: Ramp front, open fully adjustable rear; drilled and tapped for scope mounting. Three-position top tang safety, double front locking lugs, free-floated button-rifled barrel. Introduced 1994, still produced. Made in U.S.A. by Savage Arms, Inc.

Perf: $340 **Exc:** $320 **VGood:** $270

SAVAGE MODEL 11 HUNTER
Similar to the Model 111 except has true short action, chambered for 223, 22-250, 243, 308; black synthetic or walnut-finished hardwood stock. Introduced 1998, still produced. Made in U.S.A. by Savage Arms, Inc.

Perf: $320 **Exc:** $300 **VGood:** $250

SAVAGE MODEL 11FYCAK
Short-action youth model chambered in .243, 7mm-08, and .308. Barrel: 22-inch blued with muzzlebrake, no sights. Stock: Black composite. Weight 6.5 lbs.; 41.5-inch overall length.

NIB: $495 **Exc:** $460 **VGood:** $355

SAVAGE MODEL 111FYCAK
Similar to Model 11FYCAK but long-action chambered for .25-06, .270 and .30-06.

NIB: $495 **Exc:** $460 **VGood:** $355

SAVAGE MODEL 11BTH
Laminated, thumbhole-stock version of the Model 11 chambered in .204, .223, .22-250 and .22 Hornet. 22-inch blued barrel.

Exc: $460 **VGood:** $400 **Good:** $360

SAVAGE MODEL 111F CLASSIC HUNTER
Same specs as Model 111 except calibers from 25-06 to 338 Win. Mag.; top-loading magazine; graphite/fiberglass filled classic-style stock with non-glare finish; positive checkering; black recoil pad; swivel studs. Right- or left-hand action. Made in U.S. by Savage Arms, Inc. Model number reintroduced 1994; still produced.

With sights

Exc: $350 **VGood:** $300 **Good:** $250

Without sights as Model 111FNS

Exc: $290 **VGood:** $250 **Good:** $210

With detachable magazine as Model 111FC

Exc: $300 **VGood:** $270 **Good:** $230

SAVAGE MODEL 111G CLASSIC HUNTER

Same specs as Model 111 except 223, 22-250, 243, 250 Sav., 25-06, 270, 300 Sav., 30-06, 308, 7mm Rem. Mag., 7mm-08, 300 Win. Mag.; weighs about 6-1/2 lbs.; ramp front sight, open fully-adjustable rear (or no sights); receiver drilled, tapped for scope mounting; classic-style, walnut-finished hardwood stock with straight comb, ventilated red rubber recoil pad; three-position top tang safety; double front locking lugs; free-floated button-rifled barrel; trigger lock, target, ear puffs. Right- or left-hand action. Made in U.S. by Savage Arms, Inc. Model number reintroduced 1994; still produced.

With sights

Perf: $325 **Exc:** $300 **VGood:** $250

Without sights as Model 111GNS

Perf: $300 **Exc:** $275 **VGood:** $225

With detachable magazine as Model 111GC

Perf: $300 **Exc:** $270 **VGood:** $230

SAVAGE MODEL 12 LONG RANGE

Similar to the Model 112 Long Range except with true short action, chambered for 223, 22-250, 308; black synthetic stock or brown laminated stock; fluted stainless barrel. Introduced 1998. Made in U.S.A. by Savage Arms, Inc.

Perf: $440 **Exc:** $390 **VGood:** $340

SAVAGE MODEL 12 LONG RANGE PRECISION VARMINTER (LRPV)

Single-shot bolt action chambered in .204 Ruger, .223 or .22-250. Features include AccuTrigger and oversized bolt handle. Composite stock, sightless stainless steel fluted barrel. Weight: 11.25 lbs.

NIB: $875 **Exc:** $825 **VGood:** $675

SAVAGE MODEL 12VSS VARMINTER RIFLE

Similar to other Model 12s except blue/stainless steel action, fluted stainless barrel, Choate full pistol-grip, adjustable synthetic stock, Sharp Shooter trigger. Overall length 47-1/2 inches, weighs appx. 15 lbs. No sights; drilled and tapped for scope mounts. Chambered in 223, 22-250, 308 Win. Made in U.S.A. by Savage Arms Inc.

Perf: $640 **Exc:** $500 **VGood:** $400

SAVAGE MODEL 12BTCSS

Similar to Model 12VSS but with laminated thumbhole MonteCarlo stock with short action and detachable box magazine.

NIB: $725 **Exc:** $595 **VGood:** $350

SAVAGE MODEL 12 F/TR F-CLASS TARGET RIFLE

International-class target rifle chambered in .6.5x284 Norma. Ventilated forend, laminated "underhold" target stock, oversize bolt knob, AccuTrigger, 30" stainless barrel. Also available in Model 12F/TR version with conventional buttstock and elevated cheekpiece.

NIB: $1100 **Exc:** $995 **VGood:** $850

SAVAGE MODEL 112 LONG RANGE

Bolt action; 25-06, 30-06, 7mm Rem Mag, 300 Win Mag; 5-shot magazine; 26-inch heavy barrel; weighs 8.8 lbs.; 47-1/2-inch overall length; Black graphite/fiberglass filled composite stock with positive checkering. no sights; drilled and tapped for scope mounting; pillar-bedded stock; Blued barrel with recessed target-style muzzle crown; double front swivel studs for attaching bipod. Introduced 1991. Made in U.S.A. by Savage Arms, Inc.

Perf: $450 **Exc:** $400 **VGood:** $350

SAVAGE MODEL 112BV

Bolt action; 22-250, 223 Rem.; 4-shot magazine; 26-inch barrel; no sights; drilled, tapped for scope mounts; brown laminate stock, Wundhammer pistol grip; alloy steel construction. Introduced 1993; discontinued 1993.

Exc: $475 **VGood:** $430 **Good:** $365

Savage Model 114CU Classic Ultra

Savage Model 12BTCSS

Savage Model 112V

Savage Model 116FSS Weather Warrior

SAVAGE MODEL 112BT COMPETITION GRADE

Same specs as Model 112BV except 223, 300 Win. Mag., 308 Win.; 5-shot (223, 308 Win.) magazine; single shot (300 Win.); stainless barrel with black finish; laminated wood stock with straight comb, adjustable cheek rest, Wundhammer palm swell, ventilated forend; recoil pad adjustable for length of pull; matte black alloy receiver; bolt with black titanium nitride coating, large handle ball; alloy accessory rail on forend. Sold with safety gun lock, target and ear puffs. Made in U.S. by Savage Arms, Inc. Introduced 1994.

Perf: $910 **Exc:** $800 **VGood:** $675

SAVAGE MODEL 112FV VARMINT

Same specs as Model 112BV except 220 Swift (single shot), 22-250, 223 (4-shot magazine); weighs 8-1/2 lbs.; blued, heavy 26-inch barrel with recessed target-style muzzle; black graphite/fiberglass filled composite stock with positive checkering; double front swivel studs for attaching bipod. Made in U.S. by Savage Arms, Inc. Introduced 1991; no longer produced.

Exc: $360 **VGood:** $300 **Good:** $240

SAVAGE MODEL 112FVSS

Same specs as Model 112BV except 223, 22-250, 25-06, 7mm Rem. Mag., 300 Win. Mag.; heavy 26-inch barrel with recessed target-style muzzle; stainless fluted steel barrel, bolt handle, trigger guard; black graphite/fiberglass filled composite stock with positive checkering; double front swivel studs for attaching bipod. Made in U.S. by Savage Arms, Inc. Introduced 1991; no longer produced.

Perf: $470 **Exc:** $400 **VGood:** $345

SAVAGE MODEL 112FVSS-S

Same specs as Model 112BV except solid bottom single shot action; 223, 22-250, 220 Swift; ; heavy 26-inch barrel with recessed target-style muzzle; fluted stainless steel barrel, bolt handle, trigger guard; black graphite/fiberglass filled composite stock with positive checkering; double front swivel studs for attaching bipod. Made in U.S. by Savage Arms, Inc. Introduced 1991; no longer produced.

Perf: $450 **Exc:** $380 **VGood:** $320

SAVAGE MODEL 112R

Same specs as Model 112BV except 22-250, 243, 25-06; 5-shot magazine; 26-inch tapered free-floating barrel; no sights; drilled, tapped for scope mounts; American walnut stock; fluted comb, Wundhammer swell at pistol grip; top tang safety. Introduced 1979; discontinued 1980.

Exc: $330 **VGood:** $280 **Good:** $240

SAVAGE MODEL 112V

Same specs as Model 112BV except 220 Swift, 222 Rem., 223 Rem., 225 Win., 22-250 Rem., 243 Win., 25-06 Rem; 26-inch heavy barrel; 47-inch overall length; weighs 9-1/4 lbs.; scope bases; select American walnut varminter stock; high comb; checkered pistol grip; detachable sling swivels; recoil pad with white line spacer. Introduced 1975; discontinued 1979.

Exc: $340 **VGood:** $290 **Good:** $250

SAVAGE MODEL 112 VARMINT LOW PROFILE

Long-action bolt rifle chambered for .25-06 (4) and .300 WM (3). Stock: Brown laminated with recoil pad. Barrel: 26-inch sightless stainless steel bull. Weight: 11.25 lbs.

NIB: $675 **Exc:** $625 **VGood:** $495

SAVAGE MODEL 14 CLASSIC

Short-action bolt-action rifle chambered for .22-250, .243, .270 WSM, 7mm-08, .300 WSM and .308. Barrel: 22-inch or 24-inch polished blue without sights. Stock: Select lacquered walnut with contrasting forend.

NIB: $540 **Exc:** $495 **VGood:** $375

SAVAGE MODEL 14 EURO CLASSIC

Similar to Model 14 Classic but with iron sights.

NIB: $540 **Exc:** $495 **VGood:** $375

SAVAGE MODEL 114 CLASSIC

Similar to Model 14 Classic but long-action chambered for .270, 7mm RM and .300 WM.

NIB: $540 **Exc:** $495 **VGood:** $375

SAVAGE MODEL 114U ULTRA RIFLE

Similar to the Model 114C except has high-luster blued finish, high-gloss walnut stock with custom cut checkering, ebony tip. No sights; drilled and tapped for scope. Chambered for 270, 30-06, 7mm Rem. Mag., 7mm STW and 300 Win. Mag.

Exc: $400 **VGood:** $300 **Good:** $250

SAVAGE MODEL 114CU CLASSIC ULTRA

Bolt action; 270, 30-06, 7mm Rem. Mag., 300 Win. Mag.; 4-shot (Magnums), 5-shot removable box magazine; 22-inch, 24-inch (Magnums) barrel; weighs 7-1/8 lbs.; ramp front sight, step-adjustable rear; tapped for scope mounts; checkered, high-gloss straight American walnut stock; grip cap; recoil pad; cut checkering; tang safety. Introduced 1991.

Exc: $460 **VGood:** $410 **Good:** $350

SAVAGE MODEL 114 EURO CLASSIC

Similar to Model 114 Classic but with iron sights.

NIB: $540 **Exc:** $495 **VGood:** $375

SAVAGE MODEL 116FSS WEATHER WARRIOR

Bolt action; 223, 243, 270, 30-06, 308, 7mm Rem. Mag., 300 Win. Mag., 338 Win. Mag.; free-

floated 22-inch barrel (standard calibers), 24-inch (Magnums); weighs 6-3/4 lbs.; no sights; drilled, tapped for scope mounting; graphite/ fiberglass filled black composite stock; stainless steel barreled action; right- or left-hand action. Made in U.S. by Savage Arms, Inc. Introduced 1991; still produced as a long action rifle only.

Perf: $420 **Exc:** $380 **VGood:** $320

With detachable magazine as Model 116FCS

Perf: $430 **Exc:** $385 **VGood:** $340

SAVAGE MODEL 116FHSS

Similar to Model 116FSS but with hinged floorplate.

NIB: $550 **Exc:** $500 **VGood:** $395

SAVAGE MODEL 116FSAK

Same specs as Model 116FSS except 270, 30-06, 7mm Rem. Mag., 338 Win. Mag.; Savage "Adjustable Muzzle Brake" with fluted barrel. Made in U.S. by Savage Arms, Inc. Introduced 1994.

Perf: $510 **Exc:** $445 **VGood:** $380

With detachable magazine as Model 116FCSAK

Perf: $500 **Exc:** $440 **VGood:** $370

SAVAGE MODEL 116FSK

Same specs as Model 116FSS except 270, 30-06, 7mm-Rem. Mag., 338 Win. Mag.; 22-inch "Shock-Suppressor" barrel; fixed muzzle brake. Made in U.S. by Savage Arms, Inc. Introduced 1993; no longer produced.

Exc: $500 **VGood:** $430 **Good:** $370

SAVAGE MODEL 116FHSAK

Similar to 116FSAK but with hinged floorplate.

NIB: $550 **Exc:** $500 **VGood:** $395

SAVAGE MODEL 16FHSAK

Similar to Model 116FHSAK but short-action only.

NIB: $550 **Exc:** $500 **VGood:** $395

SAVAGE MODEL 116SE SAFARI EXPRESS

Bolt action; 300 Win. Mag., 338 Win. Mag., 425 Express, 458 Win. Mag.; 3-shot magazine; 24-inch barrel; 45-1/2-inch overall length; weighs 8-1/2 lbs.; bead on ramp front sight, three-leaf rear; select grade classic-style American walnut stock with ebony forend tip; cut-checkered grip and forend; two stainless steel cross-bolts; internally vented recoil pad; 400 series stainless steel barreled action; controlled round feeding; adjustable muzzlebrake; barrel band-mounted front swivel stud. Made in U.S. by Savage Arms, Inc. Introduced 1994.

Exc: $795 **VGood:** $675 **Good:** $580

SAVAGE MODEL 16FSS

Similar to Model 116FSS except true short action, chambered for 204, 223, 22-250, 243, 270 WSM, 7-08, 7mm WSR, 300 WSM; 22-inch free-floated barrel; black graphite/fiberglass stock with "Dual Pillar" bedding. Also left-hand. Introduced 1998, still available. Made in U.S.A. by Savage Arms, Inc.

Perf: $420 **Exc:** $380 **VGood:** $320

SAVAGE MODEL 16 FHSS

Similar to Model 16FSS but with hinged floorplate. Introduced 2006.

NIB: $550 **Exc:** $500 **VGood:** $395

SAVAGE MODEL 16 FLHSS WEATHER WARRIOR

Similar to Model 16 FSS but in left-hand version.

NIB: $475 **Exc:** $425 **VGood:** $325

SAVAGE MODEL 116US ULTRA STAINLESS RIFLE

Same specs as Model 116SE except 270, 30-06, 7mm Rem. Mag., 300 Win. Mag.; stock has high-gloss finish; no open sights; stainless steel barreled action with satin finish. Made in U.S. by Savage Arms, Inc. Introduced 1995; no longer produced.

Perf: $600 **Exc:** $500 **VGood:** $400

SAVAGE MODEL 25 LIGHTWEIGHT VARMINTER

Short-action rifle chambered in .204 and .223. Medium-contour fluted barrel with recessed target crown, free-floating sleved barrel, dual pillar bedding, three locking lugs, 60-degree bolt lift, AccuTrigger adjustable from 2.5 to 3.25 lbs., detachable box magazine. Weight 8.25 lbs.

NIB: $700 **Exc:** $550 **VGood:** $395

SAVAGE MODEL 25 LIGHTWEIGHT VARMINTER THUMBHOLE

Similar to above but with thumbhole stock.

NIB: $725 **Exc:** $575 **VGood:** $415

SAVAGE MODEL 25 CLASSIC SPORTER

Short-action rifle chambered in .204 and .223. Free-floating sleeved barrel, Dual pillar bedding, three locking lugs, 60-degree bolt lift, AccuTrigger adjustable from 2.5 to 3.25 lbs., Detachable box magazine. Satin lacquer American walnut stock with contrasting forend tip and wraparound checkering.

NIB: $700 **Exc:** $550 **VGood:** $395

SAVAGE MODEL 340

Bolt action; 22 Hornet, 222 Rem., 30-30; 3-, 4-shot detachable box magazine; 20-inch, 22-inch, 24-inch medium-weight barrel; 40-inch overall length (20-inch barrel); weighs 6-3/4 lbs.; click-adjustable middle sight, ramp front; uncheckered one-piece American walnut pistol-grip stock; thumb safety at right rear of receiver. Introduced 1950; discontinued 1986.

Exc: $300 **VGood:** $275 **Good:** $250

SAVAGE MODEL 340C

Same specs as Model 340 except 30-30; 3-shot detachable box magazine; 18-1/2-inch medium-weight barrel; 36-1/2-inch overall length; weighs 6-1/4 lbs.; checkered American walnut pistol-grip stock; pistol grip, buttplate white line spacer; sling swivels. Introduced 1962; discontinued 1965.

Exc: $275 **VGood:** $250 **Good:** $225

SAVAGE MODEL 340S DELUXE

Same specs as Model 340 Savage No. 175 except peep rear sight, hooded gold bead front; 3-shot magazine (30-30) hand-checkered American walnut pistol-grip stock; swivel studs. Introduced 1952; discontinued 1960.

Exc: $300 **VGood:** $275 **Good:** $250

SAVAGE MODEL 340V

Same specs as Model 340 except 225 Win.; 24-inch barrel; American walnut varmint-style stock. Introduced 1967; no longer in production.

Exc: $425 **VGood:** $400 **Good:** $375

SAVAGE MODEL 342

Bolt action; 22 Hornet; 4-shot detachable box magazine; 22-inch, 24-inch barrel; 40-inch overall length; weighs 6-3/4 lbs.; click-adjustable middle sight, ramp front; tapped for Weaver scope side mounts; uncheckered one-piece American walnut pistol-grip stock; after 1953 was incorporated into Model 340 line. Introduced 1950; discontinued 1953.

Exc: $300 **VGood:** $275 **Good:** $250

SAVAGE MODEL 342S DELUXE

Same specs as Model 340 except Savage No. 175 peep rear sight, hooded ramp front with gold bead; hand-checkered American walnut pistol-grip stock; swivel studs; after 1953 was incorporated into Model 340 line.

Exc: $325 **VGood:** $295 **Good:** $275

SAVAGE MODEL 1904

Bolt action; single shot; 22 Short, 22 Long, 22 LR; 18-inch barrel; takedown; open rear sight, bead front; uncheckered one-piece straight stock. Introduced 1904; discontinued 1917.

Exc: $150 **VGood:** $100 **Good:** $75

SAVAGE MODEL 1905

Bolt action; single shot; 22 Short, 22 Long, 22 LR; 22-inch barrel; takedown; open rear sight, bead front; uncheckered one-piece straight stock. Introduced 1905; discontinued 1918.

Exc: $150 **VGood:** $100 **Good:** $75

SAVAGE MODEL 1920

Bolt action; 250-3000, 300 Savage; 5-shot box magazine; 22-inch (250-3000), 24-inch (300 Savage) barrel; Mauser-type action; open rear sight, bead front; hand-checkered American walnut pistol-grip stock; slender schnabel forearm. Introduced 1920; discontinued 1926.

Exc: $400 **VGood:** $360 **Good:** $300

SAVAGE MODEL 1920 (1926 VERSION)

Bolt action; 250-3000, 300 Savage; 5-shot box magazine; 24-inch barrel; Mauser-type action; Lyman No. 54 rear peep sight; redesigned stock. Introduced 1926; discontinued 1929.

Exc: $410 **VGood:** $375 **Good:** $310

SAVAGE MODEL 25

Slide action; 22 Short, 22 Long, 22 LR; 20-shot (22 Short), 17-shot (22 Long), 15-shot (22 LR) tube magazine; 24-inch octagon barrel; hammerless; takedown; open rear sight, blade front; uncheckered American walnut pistol-grip stock; grooved slide handle. Introduced 1925; discontinued 1929.

Exc: $290 **VGood:** $250 **Good:** $210

SAVAGE MODEL 29

Slide action; 22 Short, 22 Long, 22 LR; 20-shot (22 Short), 17-shot (22 Long), 15-shot (22 LR) tube magazine; hammerless; takedown; 21-inch overall length; weighs 5-3/4 lbs.; push-button safety rear of trigger guard; flat-top sporting rear sight, gold beat front; open rear sight, blade front; pre-WWII model with 24-inch octagon barrel, hand-checkered walnut pistol-grip stock, slide handle; post-WWII model with 24-inch round barrel, uncheckered stock. Introduced 1929; discontinued 1967.

Pre-WWII model

Exc: $295 **VGood:** $250 **Good:** $200

Post-WWII model

Exc: $235 **VGood:** $200 **Good:** $160

SAVAGE MODEL 29-G

Same specs as Model 29 post-WWII except shorter magazine, 16-shot (22 Long), 14-shot (22 LR); short 1-1/4-inch slide action. Introduced 1955.

Exc: $235 **VGood:** $200 **Good:** $160

SAVAGE MODEL 99 (MODEL 1899, ORIGINAL VERSION)

Lever action; 25-35, 30-30, 303 Savage, 32-40, 38-55,; 5-shot rotary magazine; 22-inch (round), 26-inch (half, full octagon) barrel; hammerless; open rear sight, bead front; uncheckered walnut straight-grip stock, tapered forearm. Introduced, 1899; discontinued 1922.

Exc: $1200 **VGood:** $900 **Good:** $695

SAVAGE MODEL 99-358

Same specs as Model 99 except only 358 Win. caliber; grooved forend; recoil pad. Introduced 1977; discontinued 1980.

Exc: $695 **VGood:** $550 **Good:** $400

SAVAGE MODEL 99-375

Same specs as Model 99 except only 375 Win. caliber; recoil pad. Introduced 1980; discontinued 1980.

Exc: $650 **VGood:** $505 **Good:** $355

SAVAGE MODEL 99A (EARLY MODEL)

Same specs as Model 99 except 30-30, 300 Savage, 303 Savage; 24-inch or 26-inch barrel. Introduced 1920; discontinued 1936.

Exc: $950 **VGood:** $700 **Good:** $500

SAVAGE MODEL 99A (LATE MODEL)

Same specs as Model 99 except 243, 250 Savage, 300 Savage, 308, 375 Win.; 20-inch, 22-inch barrel; 39-3/4-inch (20-inch barrel) overall length; weighs 7 lbs.; grooved trigger; straight walnut stock with schnabel forend. Introduced 1971; discontinued 1981.

Exc: $475 **VGood:** $375 **Good:** $300

SAVAGE MODEL 99B

Same specs as original Model 99 except takedown design. Introduced 1922; discontinued 1936.

Exc: $925 **VGood:** $595 **Good:** $475

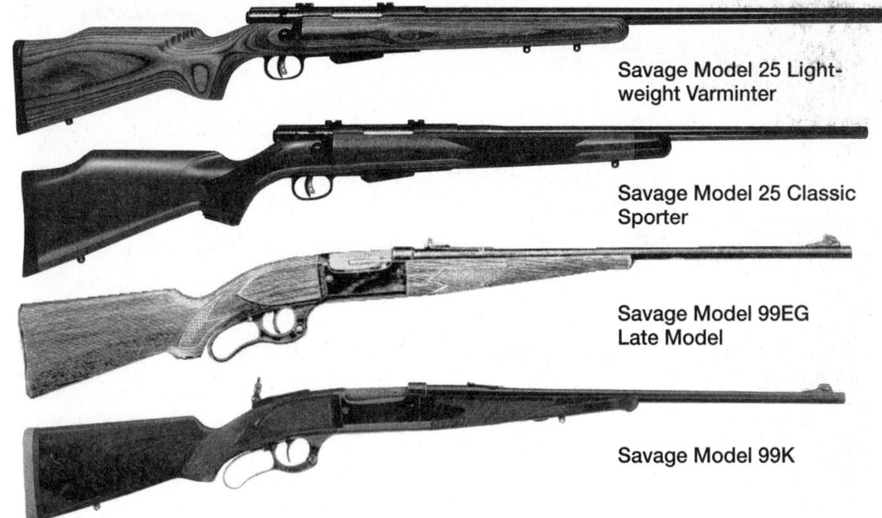

Savage Model 25 Lightweight Varminter

Savage Model 25 Classic Sporter

Savage Model 99EG Late Model

Savage Model 99K

SAVAGE MODEL 99C

Same specs as late-production Model 99 except detachable clip magazine replaces rotary type; 22-250, 243 Win., 284 Win., 308 Win. (284 dropped in 1974); 4-shot detachable magazine, 3-shot (284); 22-inch barrel; 41-3/4-inch overall length; weighs 6-3/4 lbs.; hammerlass; solid breech; Damascened bolt; case-hardened lever; blue receiver; gold-plated trigger; top tang safety; hooded gold bead ramp front, adjustable folding ramp rear sight; receiver tapped for scope mounts; walnut stock with checkered pistol grip, forend; Monte Carlo comb; swivel studs. Introduced in 1965; last variation of the Model 99; production discontinued 1998.

Exc: $520 **VGood:** $430 **Good:** $370

SAVAGE MODEL 99CD

Same specs as Model 99C except 22-250, 243, 284 Win., 7mm-08, 308; white line recoil pad, pistol-grip cap; quick-detachable swivels, sling. Introduced 1976; discontinued 1980.

Exc: $530 **VGood:** $430 **Good:** $370

SAVAGE MODEL 99DE CITATION

Same specs as Model 99 except 243, 284 Win., 308; 22-inch barrel; checkered American walnut Monte Carlo pistol-grip stock, forearm; engraved, receiver, tang, lever; quick detachable swivels. Introduced 1968; discontinued 1970.

Exc: $1050 **VGood:** $795 **Good:** $650

SAVAGE MODEL 99DL

Same specs as Model 99 except 243, 250-3000, 284, 300 Savage, 308, 358 Win.; 24-inch, 22-inch barrel; 43-3/4-inch overall length; 6-3/4 lbs.; hammerless; solid breach; Damascened bolt; case-hardened laver; blued receiver; gold-plated trigger; top tang safety; high comb, checkered; walnut Monte Carlo pistol-grip stock; step adjustable, rear sight, gold bead front; semi-buckhorn; sling swivels; deluxe model. Introduced 1960; discontinued 1974.

Exc: $450 **VGood:** $385 **Good:** $345

SAVAGE MODEL 99E (EARLY MODEL)

Same specs as Model 99 except 22 Hi-Power, 250-3000, 30-30, 300 Savage, 303 Savage; 22-inch 24-inch (300 Savage) barrel; solid frame. Introduced 1920; discontinued 1936. Add 20 percent for 22 Hi-Power.

Exc: $800 **VGood:** $550 **Good:** $480

SAVAGE MODEL 99E (LATE MODEL)

Same specs as Model 99 except 243, 250 Savage, 300 Savage, 308; 20-inch, 22-inch, 24-inch medium-weight barrel; weighs 7-1/4 lbs.; hardwood pistol-grip stock; trigger guard safety. Introduced 1960 as "economy" version; discontinued 1982.

Exc: $425 **VGood:** $395 **Good:** $300

SAVAGE MODEL 99EG (EARLY MODEL)

Same specs as Model 99 except 22 Hi-Power, 250-3000, 30-30, 300 Savage, 303 Savage; 22-inch, 24-inch (300 Savage) barrel; solid frame model; no checkering. Introduced 1936; discontinued 1941.

Exc: $695 **VGood:** $395 **Good:** $260

SAVAGE MODEL 99EG (LATE MODEL)

Same specs as Model 99 except 243, 250-3000, 250 Savage, 300 Savage, 308, 358 Win.; 24-inch barrel; 43-1/4 overall length; weighs 7-1/4 lbs.; checkered pistol-grip stock. Introduced 1946; discontinued 1960. 20 percent premium for .358.

Exc: $425 **VGood:** $395 **Good:** $300

SAVAGE MODEL 99F CARBINE

Lever action, early-production carbine; 303, 30-30, 25-35, 32-40, 38-55; produced before 1919 and below serial number 200,000; some made with barrel bands or saddle rings.

Exc: $890 **VGood:** $680 **Good:** $410

SAVAGE MODEL 99F FEATHERWEIGHT (EARLY MODEL)

Same specs as Model 99 except 22 Hi-Power, 250-3000, 30-30, 300 Savage, 303 Savage; 22-inch, 24-inch (300 Savage) barrel; lightweight takedown model. Introduced 1920; discontinued 1942. Add 20 percent for 22 Hi-Power.

Exc: $695 **VGood:** $475 **Good:** $210

SAVAGE MODEL 99F FEATHERWEIGHT (LATE MODEL)

Same specs as Model 99 except 243, 250-3000, 284 Win., 300 Savage, 308, 358 Win.; 22-inch lightweight barrel; 41-1/4-inch overall length; weighs 6-1/2 lbs.; solid breech; polished Damascened finish bolt; case-hardened lever; blued receiver; grooved trigger; checkered walnut pistol-grip stock; featherweight solid frame model. Introduced 1955; discontinued 1972. 20 percent premium for .358; 10 percent premium for 284 Win.

Exc: $595 **VGood:** $420 **Good:** $310

SAVAGE MODEL 99G

Same specs as Model 99 except 22 Hi-Power, 250-3000, 30-30, 300 Savage, 308, 303 Savage; 5-shot rotary box-type magazine; 22-inch, 24-inch (300 Savage) medium-weight barrel; weighs 7-3/4 lbs.; takedown; hand-checkered full pistol grip, tapered forearm; shotgun butt. Introduced 1920; discontinued 1942.

Exc: $595 **VGood:** $475 **Good:** $270

SAVAGE MODEL 99H

Same specs as Model 99 except 250-3000, 30-30, 303 Savage; 20-inch barrel; solid frame; carbine stock with barrel band. Introduced 1931; discontinued 1942.

Exc: $795 **VGood:** $575 **Good:** $280

SAVAGE MODEL 99K

Same specs as Model 99 except 22 Hi-Power, 250-3000, 30-30, 300 Savage, 303 Savage; 22-inch 24-

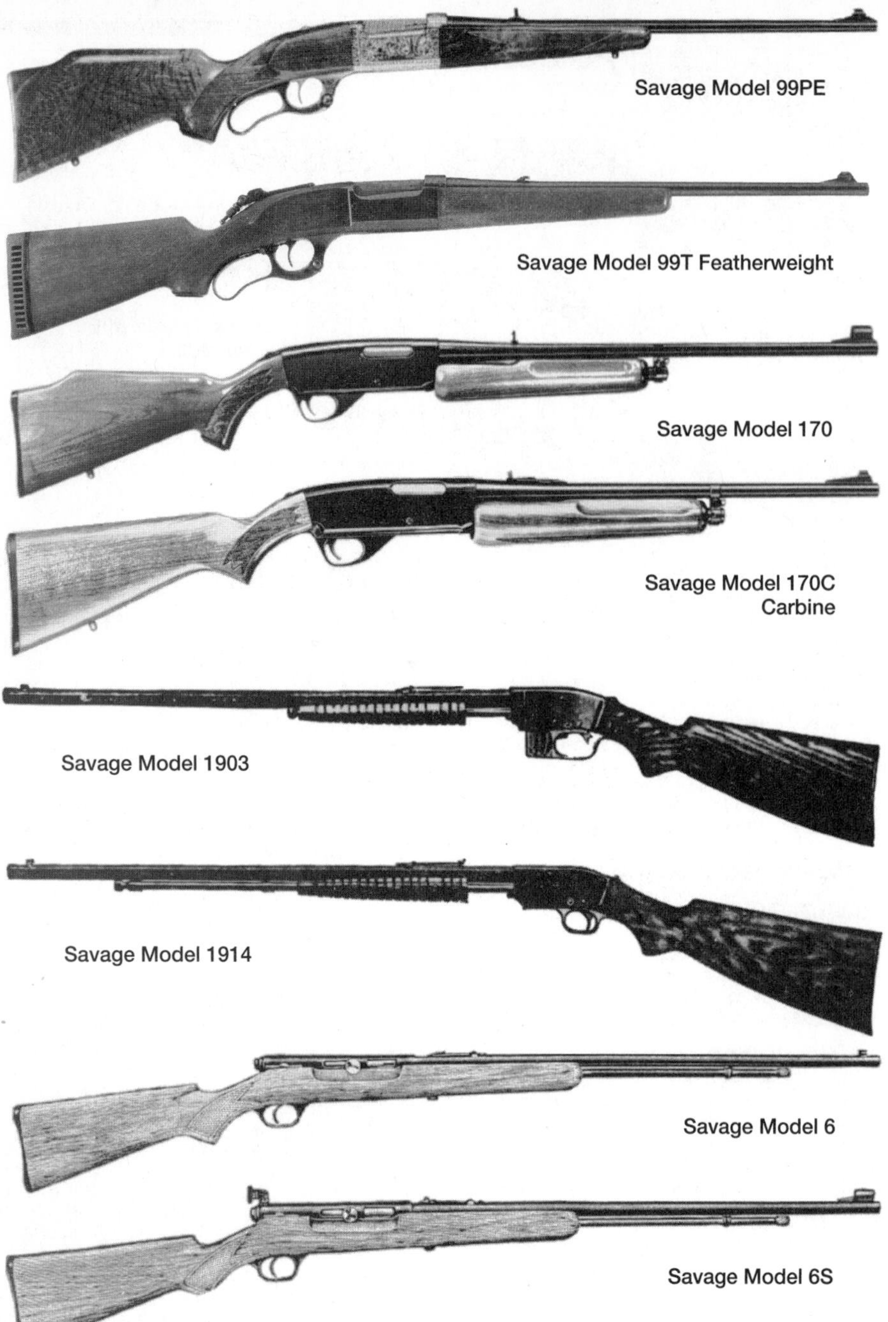

Savage Model 99PE

Savage Model 99T Featherweight

Savage Model 170

Savage Model 170C Carbine

Savage Model 1903

Savage Model 1914

Savage Model 6

Savage Model 6S

inch (300 Savage) barrel; takedown; Lyman peep rear sight, folding middle sight; fancy grade checkered walnut pistol-grip stock, forearm; engraved receiver, barrel. Introduced 1931; discontinued 1942. Add 15 percent for 22 Hi-Power.

Exc: $1995 **VGood:** $1495 **Good:** $860

SAVAGE MODEL 99PE

Same specs as Model 99 except 243, 284 Win., 308; 22-inch barrel; 41-3/4-inch overall length; weighs 6-3/4 lbs.; Damascened bolt; gold-plated trigger; case-hardened lever; hand-checkered fancy American walnut Monte Carlo pistol-grip stock, forearm; game scene engraved on receiver sides; engraved tang, lever; quick-detachable swivels. Introduced 1966; discontinued 1970. Add 10 percent for 284 Win.

Exc: $1175 **VGood:** $925 **Good:** $570

SAVAGE MODEL 99R (EARLY MODEL)

Same specs as Model 99 except 250-3000, 300 Savage; 22-inch (250-3000), 24-inch (300 Savage) tapered medium-weight barrel; weighs 7-1/4 lbs.; hand-checkered American walnut oversize pistol-grip stock, forearm; solid frame model; semi-buckhorn rear sight, raised ramp gold bead front. Introduced 1936; discontinued 1942.

Exc: $695 **VGood:** $450 **Good:** $230

SAVAGE MODEL 99R (LATE MODEL)

Same specs as Model 99 except 243, 250-3000, 300 Savage, 308, 358 Win.; 24-inch barrel; 43-3/4-inch overall length; weighs 7-1/2 lbs.; tapped for Weaver scope mount; hand-checkered American walnut oversize pistol-grip stock, semi-beavertail forearm; sling swivel studs. Introduced 1946; discontinued 1960.

Exc: $640 **VGood:** $390 **Good:** $220

SAVAGE MODEL 99RS (EARLY MODEL)

Same specs as Model 99 except 250-3000, 300 Savage; 22-inch, 24-inch (300 Savage) tapered medium-weight barrel; weighs 7-1/2 lbs.; Lyman rear peep sight, gold bead front; hand-checkered American walnut oversize pistol-grip stock, forearm; sling, swivels; solid frame model. Introduced 1936; discontinued 1942.

Exc: $795 **VGood:** $495 **Good:** $240

SAVAGE MODEL 99RS (LATE MODEL)

Same specs as Model 99 except 243, 250 Savage, 300 Savage, 308, 358 Win.; 24-inch barrel; weighs 7-1/2 lbs.; Redfield 70LH adjustable receiver sight; milled slot for a middle sight; No. 34 Lyman gold bead front; hand-checkered American walnut oversize pistol-grip stock, forearm; quick-release sling swivel; leather sling. Introduced 1946; discontinued 1958. Add 20 percent for 358.

Exc: $550 **VGood:** $450 **Good:** $350

SAVAGE MODEL 99T FEATHERWEIGHT

Same specs as Model 99 except 22 Hi-Power, 30-30, 300 Savage, 303 Savage; 20-inch 22-inch (300 Savage) barrel; hand-checkered walnut pistol-grip stock; beavertail forend; solid frame model. Introduced 1936; discontinued 1942. Add 15 percent for 22 Hi-Power.

Exc: $575 **VGood:** $475 **Good:** $310

SAVAGE MODEL 170

Slide action; 30-30, 35 Rem.; 3-shot tubular magazine; 22-inch barrel; 41-1/2-inch overall length; weighs 6-3/4 lbs.; folding leaf rear sight, gold bead ramp front; receiver drilled, tapped for scope mount; select checkered American walnut pistol-grip stock; Monte Carlo comb, grooved slide handle; hard rubber buttplate. Introduced 1970; discontinued 1981. Deduct 10 percent for 30-30.

Exc: $375 **VGood:** $325 **Good:** $295

SAVAGE MODEL 170C CARBINE

Same specs as Model 170 except 30-30; 18-1/2-inch barrel; weighs 6 lbs.; straight-comb stock. Introduced 1974; discontinued 1981.

Exc: $350 **VGood:** $325 **Good:** $275

SAVAGE MODEL 1903

Slide action; 22 Short, 22 Long, 22 LR; hammerless; takedown; detachable box magazine; 24-inch octagonal barrel; open rear sight, bead front; checkered one-piece pistol grip or straight stock. Introduced 1903; discontinued 1921.

Exc: $270 **VGood:** $220 **Good:** $160

SAVAGE MODEL 1909

Slide action; 22 Short, 22 Long, 22 LR; detachable box magazine; 20-inch round barrel; open rear sight, bead front; uncheckered one-piece pistol grip or straight stock. Introduced 1909; discontinued 1915.

Exc: $200 **VGood:** $165 **Good:** $130

SAVAGE MODEL 1914

Slide action; 22 Short, 22 Long, 22 LR; 17-shot (22 LR) tubular magazine; 24-inch octagonal barrel; hammerless; takedown; open rear sight, bead front; uncheckered pistol-grip stock, grooved slide handle. Introduced 1914; discontinued 1924.

Exc: $190 **VGood:** $150 **Good:** $100

SAVAGE MODEL 6

Semi-automatic; 22 Short, 22 Long, 22 LR; 21-shot (22 Short), 17-shot (22 Long), 15-shot (22 LR) tube magazine; 24-inch tapered barrel with crowned muzzle; weighs 6 lbs.; takedown; open fully-adjustable sporting rear sight, gold bead front; receiver tapped for Weaver scope; pre-WWII version has checkered pistol-grip walnut stock; post-WWII model has uncheckered stock; receiver, triggerguard with silver-gray finish. Introduced 1938; discontinued 1968.

Pre-WWII model

Exc: $150 **VGood:** $130 **Good:** $110

Post-WWII model

Exc: $140 **VGood:** $120 **Good:** $100

SAVAGE MODEL 6P
Same specs as Model 6 except checkered pistol grip, forend; rosewood forend tip come with 0420 scope and mount. Introduced 1965.

Exc: $175 **VGood:** $150 **Good:** $110

SAVAGE MODEL 6S
Same specs as Model 6 except fully-adjustable peep rear sight with two discs, hooded front with three inserts. Introduced 1938; discontinued 1942.

Exc: $160 **VGood:** $140 **Good:** $100

SAVAGE MODEL 7
Semi-automatic; 22 Short, 22 Long, 22 LR; 5-shot detachable clip magazine; 24-inch tapered barrel with crowned muzzle; weighs 6 lbs.; takedown; fully-adjustable sporting rear sight, gold bead front; takedown; pre-WWII model with checkered pistol-grip walnut stock; post-WWII model with uncheckered stock; hard rubber buttplate. Introduced 1939; discontinued 1951.

Pre-WWII model

Exc: $140 **VGood:** $120 **Good:** $100

Post-WWII model

Exc: $150 **VGood:** $130 **Good:** $100

SAVAGE MODEL 7S
Same specs as Model 7 except fully-adjustable peep rear sight with two discs, hooded front with three inserts. Introduced 1938; discontinued 1942.

Exc: $150 **VGood:** $130 **Good:** $100

SAVAGE MODEL 24
Over/under combo; 22 LR, 22 Short, 22 Long/410-3-inch or 2-1/2-inch; 24-inch barrels; 40-1/2-inch overall length; weighs 7 lbs.; takedown; barrel selection slide button on right side of receiver; full choke shotgun barrel; top-lever break-open; ramp front sight, elevation-adjustable rear; uncheckered walnut pistol-grip stock; visible hammer; single trigger; barrel selector on frame, later on hammer. Introduced 1950; discontinued 1965.

Exc: $350 **VGood:** $300 **Good:** $250

SAVAGE MODEL 24C CAMPER'S COMPANION
Same specs as Model 24 except 22 LR/20-ga.; 20-inch barrel; Cylinder bore; weighs 5-3/4 lbs.; straight walnut stock; storage in buttstock for ten 22 LR cartridges and one 20-ga. shell; some with nickel finish. Introduced 1972; discontinued 1988.

Exc: $500 **VGood:** $400 **Good:** $250

SAVAGE MODEL 24D
Same specs as Model 24 except 22 LR, 22 WMR/20-ga., 410; black or color case-hardened frame with engraving; checkered walnut pistol-grip stock. Introduced 1981; no longer in production.

Exc: $400 **VGood:** $300 **Good:** $225

SAVAGE MODEL 24DL
Same specs as Model 24 except 22/20-ga., 410; checkered walnut Monte Carlo pistol-grip stock; checkered forend; top lever; scope dovetails; satin chrome frame with game scenes; pistol grip cap; pistol grip, buttplate white line spacer. Introduced 1962; discontinued 1969.

Exc: $425 **VGood:** $325 **Good:** $250

SAVAGE MODEL 24F
Same specs as Model 24 except 22 LR, 22 Hornet, 223, 30-30/12-, 20-ga.; black Rynite composition or walnut stock; removable buttcap for storage; removable grip cap with integral compass, screwdriver. Introduced 1989; still in production.

Exc: $540 **VGood:** $475 **Good:** $320

SAVAGE MODEL 24F-12T TURKEY GUN
Same specs as Model 24F except 22 Hornet, 223 over 12-gauge with 3-inch chamber; camouflage Rynite stock and Full, Imp. Cyl., Mod. choke tubes. Made in U.S. by Savage. Introduced 1989.

Exc: $560 **VGood:** $475 **Good:** $350

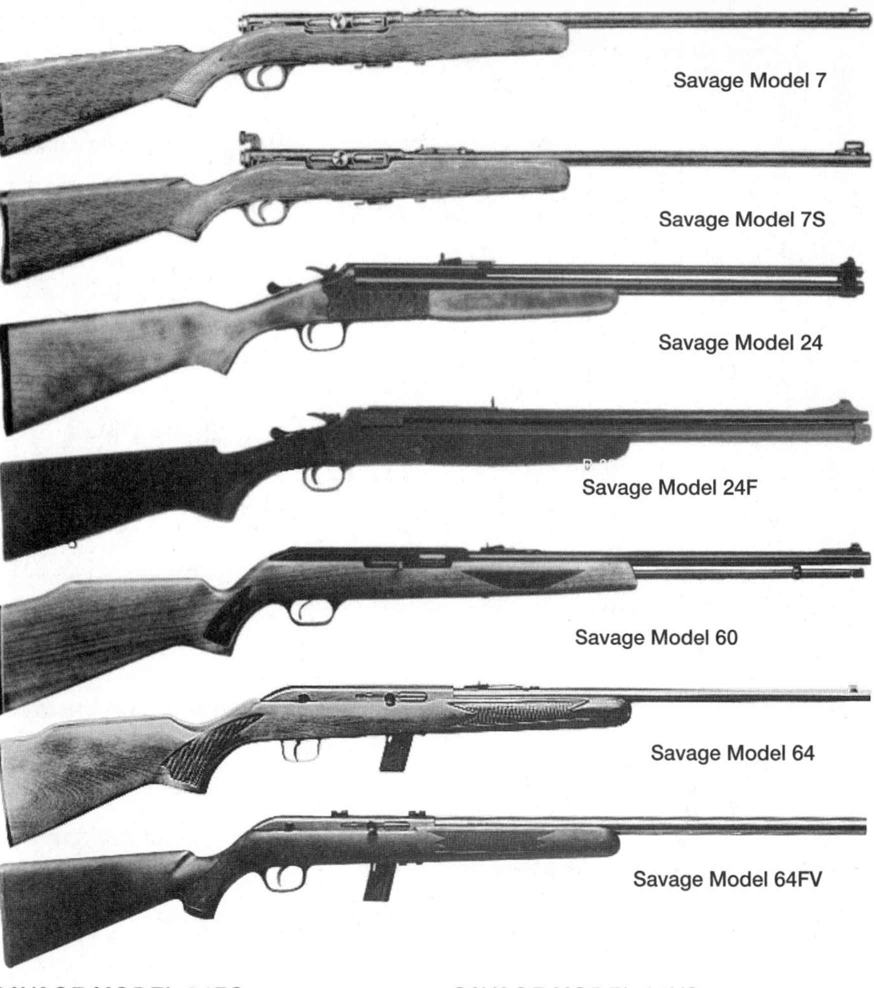
Savage Model 7

Savage Model 7S

Savage Model 24

Savage Model 24F

Savage Model 60

Savage Model 64

Savage Model 64FV

SAVAGE MODEL 24FG
Same specs as Model 24 except 22 LR/20-ga., 410; top lever; scope dovetails; color case-hardened frame; walnut finish hardwood straight stock; no checkering. Introduced 1972; no longer in production.

Exc: $400 **VGood:** $350 **Good:** $265

SAVAGE MODEL 24 FIELD
Same specs as Model 24 except 22 LR, 22 WMR/20-ga., 410; weighs 6-3/4 lbs.; lightweight field model. Discontinued 1989.

Exc: $400 **VGood:** $310 **Good:** $260

SAVAGE MODEL 24MDL
Same specs as Model 24 except 22 WMR/20-ga., 410; checkered walnut pistol-grip stock; top lever; scope dovetails; satin chrome frame. Introduced 1965; discontinued 1969.

Exc: $425 **VGood:** $395 **Good:** $350

SAVAGE MODEL 24MS
Same specs as Model 24 except 22 WMR/20-ga., 410; sidelever; scope dovetails. Introduced 1962; discontinued 1971.

Exc: $425 **VGood:** $395 **Good:** $350

SAVAGE MODEL 24S
Same specs as Model 24 except 22 LR/20-ga., 410; sidelever; scope dovetails. Introduced 1965; discontinued 1971.

Exc: $400 **VGood:** $375 **Good:** $325

SAVAGE MODEL 24V
Same specs as Model 24 except 22 Hornet, 222, 223, 30-30, 357 Mag., 357 Max./20-ga. 3-inch; stronger receiver; color case-hardened frame; scope dovetails; walnut finished hardwood stock. Introduced 1971; discontinued 1989. Add 20 percent for 357 Mag or Max.

Exc: $550 **VGood:** $495 **Good:** $425

SAVAGE MODEL 24VS
Same specs as Model 24 except 357 Mag./20-ga.; 20-inch barrel; cylinder bore; pistol-grip walnut stock; nickel finish. No longer in production.

Exc: $625 **VGood:** $595 **Good:** $475

SAVAGE MODEL 60
Semi-automatic; 22 LR; 15-shot tubular magazine; 20-inch barrel; 40-1/2-inch overall length; weighs 6 lbs.; open rear sight, gold bead ramp front; tang slide safety; American walnut Monte Carlo stock; checkered pistol-grip, forearm; Wundhammer swell pistol grip; beavertail forend; buttplate white line spacer. Introduced 1969; discontinued 1972.

Exc: $100 **VGood:** $75 **Good:** $70

SAVAGE MODEL 64
Semi-automatic; 22 LR, 10-shot magazine; 20-inch, 21-inch barrel; weighs 5-1/2 lbs.; 40-inch, 41-inch overall length; Walnut-finished hardwood stock with Monte Carlo-type comb, checkered grip and forend. Bead front, open adjustable rear sights. Receiver grooved for scope mounting. Thumb-operated rotating safety. Blue finish. Side ejection, bolt hold-open device. Introduced 1990. Made in Canada, from Savage Arms.

Perf: $120 **Exc:** $90 **VGood:** $70

Model 64FSS, stainless

Perf: $160 **Exc:** $140 **VGood:** $110

Model 64F, black synthetic stock

Perf: $130 **Exc:** $110 **VGood:** $100

SAVAGE MODEL 64FV
Similar to the Model 64F except has heavy 21-inch barrel with recessed crown; no sights provided-comes with Weaver-style bases. Introduced 1998. Imported from Canada by Savage Arms, Inc.

Perf: $150 **Exc:** $130 **VGood:** $100

Savage Model 64FVSS

Savage Model 64 BTV

Savage Model 88

Savage Model 90 Carbine

Savage Model 219

Savage Model 219L

Savage Model 221

Savage Model 1912

Savage/Anschutz Mark 10D

SAVAGE MODEL 64FVSS

Like Model 64, but with stainless-steel action and barrel; Introduced 2002, still offered.

Perf: $200 **Exc:** $170 **VGood:** $130

SAVAGE MODEL 64 BTV

Similar to Model 64 but with laminated thumbhole stock.

Perf: $175 **Exc:** $145 **VGood:** $100

SAVAGE MODEL 88

Semi-automatic; 22 LR; 15-shot tubular magazine; 20-inch barrel; open rear sight, bead front; checkered American walnut pistol-grip stock; side safety. Introduced 1969; discontinued 1972.

Exc: $100 **VGood:** $90 **Good:** $75

SAVAGE MODEL 90 CARBINE

Semi-automatic; 22 LR; 10-shot tubular magazine; 16-1/2-inch barrel; 37-1/2-inch overall length; weighs 5-3/4 lbs.; satin blued receiver; tang slide safety; folding leaf rear sight, gold bead front; uncheckered walnut carbine stock; barrel band; sling swivels. Introduced 1969; discontinued 1972.

Exc: $100 **VGood:** $90 **Good:** $75

SAVAGE MODEL 219

Single shot; 22 Hornet, 25-20, 30-30, 32-20; 26-inch tapered medium-weight barrel; weighs 6 lbs.; hammerless; takedown; break-open; top tang safety; adjustable flat-top rear sight, bead front on ramp; uncheckered walnut pistol-grip stock, forearm; top lever. Introduced 1938; discontinued 1965. Add 20 percent for 22 Hornet, 25-20 or 32-20. Barrels alone $150-$200.

Exc: $425 **VGood:** $395 **Good:** $325

SAVAGE MODEL 219L

Same specs as Model 219 except sidelever action. Introduced 1965; discontinued 1967.

Exc: $400 **VGood:** $370 **Good:** $300

SAVAGE MODEL 221

Single shot; 30-30; 26-inch barrel; takedown; hammerless; break-open; open rear sight, bead front on ramp; uncheckered walnut pistol-grip stock, forearm; top lever; interchangeable 30-inch 12-ga. shotgun barrel. Introduced 1939; discontinued 1960.

Exc: $325 **VGood:** $295 **Good:** $245

SAVAGE MODEL 222

Single shot; 30-30; 26-inch barrel; takedown; hammerless; break-open; open rear sight, bead front on ramp; uncheckered walnut pistol-grip stock, forearm; top lever; interchangeable 28-inch 16-ga. shotgun barrel.

Exc: $295 **VGood:** $265 **Good:** $225

SAVAGE MODEL 223

Single shot; 30-30; 26-inch barrel; takedown; hammerless; break-open; open rear sight, bead front on ramp; uncheckered walnut pistol-grip stock, forearm; top lever; interchangeable 28-inch 20-ga. shotgun barrel.

Exc: $325 **VGood:** $295 **Good:** $245

SAVAGE MODEL 227

Single shot; 22 Hornet; 26-inch barrel; takedown; hammerless; break-open; open rear sight, bead front on ramp; uncheckered walnut pistol-grip stock, forearm; top lever; interchangeable 30-inch 12-ga. shotgun barrel.

Exc: $325 **VGood:** $295 **Good:** $245

SAVAGE MODEL 228

Single shot; 22 Hornet; 26-inch barrel; takedown; hammerless; break-open; open rear sight, bead front on ramp; uncheckered walnut pistol-grip stock, forearm; top lever; interchangeable 28-inch 16-ga. shotgun barrel.

Exc: $325 **VGood:** $295 **Good:** $245

SAVAGE MODEL 229

Single shot; 22 Hornet; 26-inch barrel; takedown; hammerless; break-open; open rear sight, bead front on ramp; uncheckered walnut pistol-grip stock, forearm; top lever; interchangeable 28-inch 20-ga. shotgun barrel.

Exc: $325 **VGood:** $295 **Good:** $245

SAVAGE MODEL 389

Over/under combo; 12-ga./222, 308; 25-3/4-inch barrels; hammerless; floating front mount for windage, elevation adjustment; blade front sight, folding leaf rear; oil-finished walnut stock; recoil pad; checkered grip, forend; matte finish; double triggers; swivel studs. Introduced 1988; discontinued 1990. Manufactured in Finland by Valmet.

Exc: $650 **VGood:** $550 **Good:** $400

SAVAGE MODEL 980DL

Semi-automatic; 22 LR; 15-shot tube magazine; 20-inch barrel; 40-1/2-inch overall length; weighs 6 lbs.; solid steel receiver; receiver grooved for scope mounting; hooded ramp front sight, folding leaf adjustable rear; checkered walnut Monte Carlo stock, pistol grip, forend. Introduced 1981.

Exc: $120 **VGood:** $90 **Good:** $60

SAVAGE MODEL 1912

Semi-automatic; 22 LR; 7-shot detachable box magazine; takedown; open rear sight, bead front; uncheckered straight stock. Introduced 1912; discontinued 1916.

Exc: $310 **VGood:** $225 **Good:** $185

SAVAGE-ANSCHUTZ MARK 10

Bolt action; single shot; 22 LR; 26-inch barrel; 44-inch overall length; weighs 8-1/2 lbs.; micrometer click-adjustable rear sight, globe front; European walnut pistol-grip target stock; cheekpiece; adjustable hand stop; adjustable single-stage trigger; sling swivels. Imported from Germany. Introduced 1967; discontinued 1972.

Exc: $320 **VGood:** $270 **Good:** $150

SAVAGE-ANSCHUTZ MARK 10D

Same specs as Mark 10 except different rear sight; Monte Carlo stock. Imported 1972 only.

Exc: $330 **VGood:** $280 **Good:** $150

SAVAGE-ANSCHUTZ MARK 12

Bolt action; single shot; 22 LR; 26-inch heavy barrel; 43-inch overall length; weighs 8 lbs.; globe front sight, micro-click peep rear; walnut-finished hardwood target stock; thumb groove, Wundhammer pistol-grip swell, adjustable hand stop; sling swivels. Imported from Germany. Introduced 1978; discontinued 1981.

Exc: $350 **VGood:** $300 **Good:** $150

SAVAGE-ANSCHUTZ MODEL 54

Bolt action; 22 LR; 5-shot clip magazine; 22-1/2-inch barrel; 42-inch overall length; weighs 6-3/4 lbs.; folding leaf sight, hooded ramp gold bead front; receiver grooved for tip-off mount, tapped for scope blocks; French walnut stock with Monte Carlo roll-over comb; schnabel forearm tip; hand-checkered pistol grip, forearm; adjustable single-stage trigger; wing safety. Introduced 1966; discontinued 1981.

Exc: $595 **VGood:** $495 **Good:** $270

SAVAGE-ANSCHUTZ MODEL 54M

Same specs as Model 54 except 22 WMR. Introduced 1973; discontinued 1981.

Exc: $625 **VGood:** $525 **Good:** $300

SAVAGE-ANSCHUTZ MODEL 141

Bolt action; 22 LR; 5-shot clip magazine; 22-inch barrel; 40-3/4-inch overall length; weighs 5-1/2 lbs.; right side slide safety; adjustable single-stage trigger; gold bead hooded ramp front sight, folding leaf rear; receiver grooved for scope mount, tapped for aperture sight; French walnut Monte Carlo stock with cheekpiece; skip-line hand-checkered pistol grip, forend; rosewood forend tip with white inlay; buttplate with white-line spacer; sling swivel studs. Introduced 1966.

Exc: $125 **VGood:** $100 **Good:** $90

SAVAGE-ANSCHUTZ MODEL 153

Bolt action; 222 Rem.; 24-inch barrel; 43-inch overall length; weighs 6-3/4 lbs.; recessed bolt head with double locking lugs; wing-type safety; adjustable single-stage trigger; folding leaf open rear sight, hooded ramp front; skip-checkered high grade French walnut stock; hand-carved roll-over cheekpiece; rosewood grip cap, forearm tip with white inlay; sling swivels. Introduced 1964; discontinued 1967.

Exc: $540 **VGood:** $430 **Good:** $240

SAVAGE-ANSCHUTZ MODEL 164

Bolt action; 22 LR; 5-shot detachable clip magazine; 24-inch barrel; 40-3/4-inch overall length; weighs 6 lbs.; receiver grooved for tip-off mount; hooded ramp gold bead front, folding leaf rear; European walnut stock; hand-checkered pistol grip, forearm; Monte Carlo comb, cheekpiece; sliding side safety; schnabel forearm; fully-adjustable single-stage trigger. Introduced 1966; discontinued 1981.

Exc: $350 **VGood:** $300 **Good:** $180

SAVAGE-ANSCHUTZ MODEL 164M

Same specs as Model 164 except 22 WMR; 4-shot magazine.

Exc: $380 **VGood:** $330 **Good:** $190

SAVAGE-ANSCHUTZ MODEL 184

Bolt action; 22 LR; 5-shot detachable clip magazine; 21-1/2-inch barrel; folding leaf rear sight, hooded ramp front; receiver grooved for scope mounts; European walnut stock with Monte Carlo comb, schnabel forearm; hand-checkered pistol grip, forearm. Introduced 1966; discontinued 1974.

Exc: $350 **VGood:** $300 **Good:** $160

SAVAGE-ANSCHUTZ MODEL 1410

Bolt action; single shot; 22 LR; 27-1/2-inch barrel; 50-inch overall length; weighs 15-1/2 lbs.; no sights; receiver grooved for Anschutz sights; scope blocks;

Savage/Anschutz Mark 12

Savage/Anschutz Model 54

Savage/Anschutz Model 164M

Savage/Anschutz Model 184

Savage-Stevens Model 80

Savage-Stevens Model 88

International-type stock with thumb hole, aluminum hook buttplate; vertically adjustable buttplate. Introduced 1968.

Exc: $350 **VGood:** $300 **Good:** $140

SAVAGE-ANSCHUTZ MODEL 1418 SPORTER

Bolt action; 22 LR; 5-shot detachable clip magazine; 24-inch barrel; receiver grooved for tip-off mount; European Mannlicher stock, inlays, skip-line hand-checkering; double-set or single-stage trigger. Made in Germany. Introduced 1981; discontinued 1981.

Exc: $595 **VGood:** $495 **Good:** $260

SAVAGE-ANSCHUTZ MODEL 1518 SPORTER

Bolt action; 22 WMR; 5-shot detachable clip magazine; 24-inch barrel; receiver grooved for tip-off mount; European Mannlicher stock, inlays, skip-line hand-checkering; double-set or single-stage trigger. Made in Germany. Introduced 1981; discontinued 1981.

Exc: $645 **VGood:** $535 **Good:** $280

SAVAGE-STEVENS MODEL 35

Bolt action; 22 LR; 5-shot clip magazine; 22-inch barrel; 41-inch overall length; weighs 4-3/4 lbs.; ramp front sight, step-adjustable rear; walnut finished hardwood stock; checkered pistol grip, forend; receiver grooved for scope mounts. Introduced 1982; discontinued 1985.

Exc: $80 **VGood:** $55 **Good:** $40

SAVAGE-STEVENS MODEL 35M

Same specs as Model 35 except 22 WMR.

Exc: $90 **VGood:** $70 **Good:** $50

SAVAGE-STEVENS MODEL 36

Bolt action; single shot; 22 LR; 22-inch barrel; 41-inch overall length; 4-3/4 lbs.; ramp front sight, step-adjustable open rear; walnut-finished hardwood stock; checkered pistol grip, forend; receiver grooved for scope mounts. Introduced 1983.

Exc: $80 **VGood:** $60 **Good:** $40

SAVAGE-STEVENS MODEL 72 CRACKSHOT

Lever action; single shot; 22 Short, 22 Long, 22 LR; 22-inch octagonal barrel; falling block; open rear sight, bead front; uncheckered American walnut straight-grip stock, forearm; color case-hardened frame. Introduced 1972; discontinued 1987.

Exc: $175 **VGood:** $150 **Good:** $125

SAVAGE-STEVENS MODEL 73

Bolt action; single shot; 22 Short, 22 Long, 22 LR; 20-inch barrel; 38-inch overall length; weighs 4-1/2 lbs.; plated trigger; takedown screw; cocking knob; open rear sight, blade front; receiver grooved for scope mounting; one-piece uncheckered hardwood pistol grip stock. Introduced 1965; discontinued 1980.

Exc: $120 **VGood:** $90 **Good:** $70

SAVAGE-STEVENS MODEL 73Y

Same specs as Model 73 except 18-inch barrel; 35-inch overall length; weighs 4 lbs.; shorter buttstock. Introduced 1965; discontinued 1980.

Exc: $120 **VGood:** $90 **Good:** $70

SAVAGE-STEVENS MODEL 74

Lever action; single shot; 22 Short, 22 Long, 22 LR; 22-inch round barrel; hardwood stock; black-finished frame. Introduced 1972; discontinued 1974.

Exc: $135 **VGood:** $110 **Good:** $85

SAVAGE-STEVENS MODEL 80

Semi-automatic; 22 LR; 15-shot tube magazine; 20-inch barrel; 40-inch overall length; weighs 6 lbs.; blade front sight, fully-adjustable open rear; select walnut Monte Carlo stock with checkered forens, pistol grip; buttplate, pistol grip white line spacers; receiver grooved for scope mounting. Introduced 1977; no longer in production.

Exc: $125 **VGood:** $110 **Good:** $90

SAVAGE-STEVENS MODEL 88

Semi-automatic; 22 LR; 15-shot tube magazine; 20-inch barrel; 40-1/2-inch overall length; weighs 5-3/4 lbs.; open rear sight, ramp gold bead front;

Savage-Stevens Model 125

Sedgely Springfield Sporter

Serrifle Schuetzen Model

C. Sharps Arms New Model 1875 Carbine

C. Sharps Arms New Model 1875 Rifle

C. Sharps Arms New Model 1875 Classic

checkered hardwood straight stock with pistol grip; slide safety on tang. Introduced 1969; discontinued 1972.

Exc: $125 **VGood:** $100 **Good:** $75

SAVAGE-STEVENS MODEL 89 CRACKSHOT

Lever action; single shot; 22 LR; 18-1/2-inch barrel; 35-inch overall length; weighs 5 lbs.; sporting front sight, open rear; walnut finished hardwood straight stock; hammer cocked by hand; automatic ejection; hard rubber buttplate black satin finish. Introduced 1977; discontinued 1985.

Exc: $175 **VGood:** $150 **Good:** $100

SAVAGE-STEVENS MODEL 120

Bolt action; single shot; 22 Short, 22 Long, 22 LR; tubular magazine; 20-inch round, tapered barrel; action cocks on opening of bolt; sporting front/rear sights; grooved for scope mounts; walnut-finished hardwood stock; pistol-grip; thumb safety; double extractors; recessed bolt face. Introduced 1979; discontinued 1983.

Exc: $125 **VGood:** $100 **Good:** $70

SAVAGE-STEVENS MODEL 125

Bolt action; single shot; 22-inch barrel; 39-inch overall length; sporting front sight, open rear with elevator; walnut-finished stock; manual cocking; blued finish. Introduced 1981; no longer made.

Exc: $125 **VGood:** $100 **Good:** $70

SCHULTZ & LARSEN MODEL 47

Bolt action; single shot; 22 LR; 28-1/2-inch barrel; micrometer receiver sight, globe front; free-rifle style European walnut stock; cheekpiece; thumbhole; buttplate; palm rest; sling swivels; set trigger. Made in Germany. No longer in production.

Exc: $695 **VGood:** $610 **Good:** $495

SCHULTZ & LARSEN MODEL 54

Bolt action; single shot; 6.5x55mm, American calibers available on special order; 27-1/2-inch barrel; micrometer receiver sight, globe front; free-rifle style European walnut stock; adjustable buttplate; cheekpiece; palm rest; sling swivels. No longer in production.

Exc: $895 **VGood:** $795 **Good:** $625

SCHULTZ & LARSEN MODEL 54J

Bolt action; 270 Win., 30-06, 7x61 Sharpe & Hart; 3-shot magazine; 24-inch, 26-inch barrels; no sights; hand-checkered European walnut sporter stock; Monte Carlo comb, cheekpiece.

Exc: $725 **VGood:** $615 **Good:** $535

SCHULTZ & LARSEN MODEL 61

Bolt action; single shot; 22 LR; 28-1/2-inch barrel; micrometer receiver sight, globe front; free-rifle style European walnut stock; cheekpiece; buttplate; palm rest; sling swivels; set trigger. No longer in production.

Exc: $895 **VGood:** $795 **Good:** $685

SCHULTZ & LARSEN MODEL 62

Bolt action; single shot; various calibers; 28-1/2-inch barrel; micrometer receiver sight, globe front; free-rifle style European walnut stock; cheekpiece; buttplate; palm rest; sling swivels; set trigger. No longer in production.

Exc: $1025 **VGood:** $895 **Good:** $710

SCHULTZ & LARSEN MODEL 68

Bolt action; 22-250, 243, 6mm Rem., 264 Win. Mag., 270, 30-06, 308, 7x61 Sharpe & Hart, 7mm Rem. Mag., 8x57JS, 300 Win. Mag., 308 Norma Mag., 338 Win. Mag., 358 Norma Mag., 458 Win. Mag.; 24-inch barrel; no sights; select French walnut sporting stock; adjustable trigger. No longer in production.

Exc: $795 **VGood:** $695 **Good:** $595

SEDGELY SPRINGFIELD SPORTER

Bolt action; 218 Bee, 22-3000, 220 Swift, 22-4000, 22 Hornet, 25-35, 250-3000, 257 Roberts, 270 Win., 30-06, 7mm; 24-inch barrel; Lyman No. 48 rear sight, bead front on matted ramp; hand-checkered walnut stock; sling swivels, grip cap; many variations. Introduced 1928; discontinued 1941.

Perf: $1295 **Exc:** $1125 **VGood:** $895

Left-hand model

Perf: $1495 **Exc:** $1295 **VGood:** $995

SEDGELY SPRINGFIELD SPORTER CARBINE

Same specs as Springfield Sporter except 20-inch barrel; full-length walnut stock.

Perf: $1495 **Exc:** $1295 **VGood:** $995

SERRIFLE SCHUETZEN MODEL

Single shot, falling block; 22, 32, 38, 41, 44, 45; octagon, half-octagon or round barrel to 32-inch at customer's preference; no sights; furnished with scope blocks; fancy Helm-pattern walnut stock; Niedner-type firing pin; coil spring striker based on Winchester Hi-Wall action. Introduced 1984; discontinued 1986.

Perf: $1295 **Exc:** $1050 **VGood:** $895

C. SHARPS ARMS MODEL 1874 SPORTING

Single shot; 40, 45, 50; 30-inch octagon barrel; weighs 9-1/2 lbs.; Lawrence-type open rear sight, blade front; American walnut stock; color case-hardened receiver, buttplate, barrel bands; blued barrel; recreation of original Sharps models in several variations. Introduced 1985; discontinued 1987.

Sporting Rifle No. 1

Exc: $1400 **VGood:** $1200 **Good:** $895

Sporting Rifle No. 3

Exc: $1400 **VGood:** $1200 **Good:** $895

Long Range Express Rifle

Exc: $1500 **VGood:** $1300 **Good:** $995

Military Rifle

Exc: $1200 **VGood:** $1100 **Good:** $795

Carbine

Exc: $1100 **VGood:** $1000 **Good:** $695

Business Rifle

Exc: $1400 **VGood:** $1200 **Good:** $995

C. SHARPS ARMS NEW MODEL 1874 OLD RELIABLE

Single shot; 40-50, 40-70, 40-90, 45-70, 45-90, 45-100, 45-110, 45-120, 50-70, 50-90, 50-140; 26-inch, 28-inch, 30-inch tapered, octagon barrel; weighs 10 lbs.; blade front sight, buckhorn rear; drilled, tapped for tang sight installation; straight-grip American black walnut stock; shotgun butt; heavy forend with schnabel tip; recreation of original C. Sharps design; double-set triggers. Manufactured by Shiloh Products. Reintroduced 1991.

Exc: $2000 **VGood:** $1895 **Good:** $1695

C. SHARPS ARMS NEW MODEL 1875 RIFLE

Single shot, falling block; 22 LR, 32-40 Ballard, 38-55 Ballard, 38-56 WCF, 40-65 WCF, 40-90-3-1/4-inch, 40-90-2-5/8-inch, 40-70-2-1/10-inch, 40-70-2-1/4-inch, 40-7- 2-1/2-inch, 40-50-1-11/16-inch, 40-50-1-7/8-inch, 45-90, 40-70, 45-100, 45-110, 45-120, 50-70, 50-90, 50-140; 24-inch, 26-inch, 28-inch, 30-inch, 32-inch, 34-inch barrel; weighs 8 to 12 lbs; buckhorn rear sight, blade front; straight-grip walnut stock; case-colored receiver; reproduction of 1875 Sharps rifle. Manufactured by Shiloh Rifle Mfg. Co. Introduced 1986.

Carbine model

Exc: $2000 **VGood:** $1800 **Good:** $1495

Saddle Rifle

Exc: $2100 **VGood:** $1900 **Good:** $1610

Sporting model

Exc: $2000 **VGood:** $1800 **Good:** $1595

Business model

Exc: $2200 **VGood:** $1975 **Good:** $1495

C. SHARPS ARMS NEW MODEL 1875 CLASSIC

Same specs as New Model 1875 except 30-inch full octagon barrel; weighs 10 lbs.; Rocky Mountain buckhorn rear sight; crescent buttplate with toe plate; Hartford-style forend with German silver nose cap. Introduced 1987.

Exc: $1895 **VGood:** $1795 **Good:** $1150

C. SHARPS ARMS NEW MODEL 1875 TARGET & LONG RANGE

Same specs as New Model 1875 except available in all listed calibers except 22 LR; 34-inch tapered octagon barrel; globe with post front sight, Long Range Vernier tang sight with windage adjustments; pistol-grip stock with cheek rest; checkered steel buttplate. Made in U.S. by C. Sharps Arms Co., distributed by Montana Armory, Inc. Introduced 1991.

Exc: $1995 **VGood:** $1895 **Good:** $1250

C. SHARPS ARMS NEW MODEL 1885 HIGH WALL

Single shot; 22 LR, 22 Hornet, 219 Zipper, 30-40 Krag, 32-40, 38-55, 40-65 WCF, 45-70; 26-inch, 28-inch, 30-inch Douglas Premium tapered octagon barrels; Marble's ivory bead front sight, #66 long-blade, flat-top rear with reversible notch, elevator; American black walnut stock; recreation of original octagon-top High Wall; coil-spring action; tang drilled for tang sight; color case-hardened finish on most external parts. Introduced 1991; no longer in production.

Exc: $1400 **VGood:** $1150 **Good:** $975

SHILEN DGA SPORTER

Bolt action; 17 Rem., 222, 223, 22-250, 220 Swift, 6mm Rem., 243 Win., 250 Savage, 257 Roberts, 284 Win., 308 Win., 358 Win.; 3-shot magazine; 24-inch barrel; no sights; uncheckered Monte Carlo walnut or fiberglass stock; cheekpiece; pistol-grip; sling swivels. Introduced 1976; discontinued 1987.

Exc: $650 **VGood:** $550 **Good:** $450

SHILEN DGA BENCHREST

Same specs as DGA Model except single shot; 26-inch medium or heavy barrel; classic or thumbhole walnut or fiberglass stock. Introduced 1977; no longer in production.

Exc: $700 **VGood:** $600 **Good:** $500

SHILEN DGA SILHOUETTE

Same specs as DGA Model except 308 Win.; 25-inch heavy barrel. No longer in production.

Exc: $700 **VGood:** $600 **Good:** $500

SHILEN DGA VARMINTER

Same specs as DGA Model except 25-inch heavy barrel. Introduced 1976; discontinued 1987.

Exc: $650 **VGood:** $550 **Good:** $500

SHILOH SHARPS MODEL 1874 BUSINESS RIFLE

Single shot; 40-50 BN, 40-70 BN, 40-90 BN, 45-70 ST, 45-90 ST, 50-70 ST, 50-100 ST, 32-40, 38-55; 28-inch heavy round barrel; blade front sight, buckhorn rear; straight-grip steel buttplate; double-set trigger. Introduced 1986; still in production.

Exc: $2200 **VGood:** $1975 **Good:** $1495

SHILOH SHARPS MODEL 1874 CARBINE

Same specs as other Model 1874 series rifles except 24-inch round barrel; single trigger. Introduced 1986; no longer in production.

Exc: $1900 **VGood:** $1675 **Good:** $1195

SHILOH SHARPS MODEL 1874 JAEGER

Same specs as other Model 1874 series rifles except 30-40, 30-30, 307 Win., 45-70; 26-inch half-octagon lightweight barrel; standard supreme black walnut stock; shotgun, pistol grip or military-style butt. Introduced 1986; no longer in production.

Exc: $2200 **VGood:** $1975 **Good:** $1495

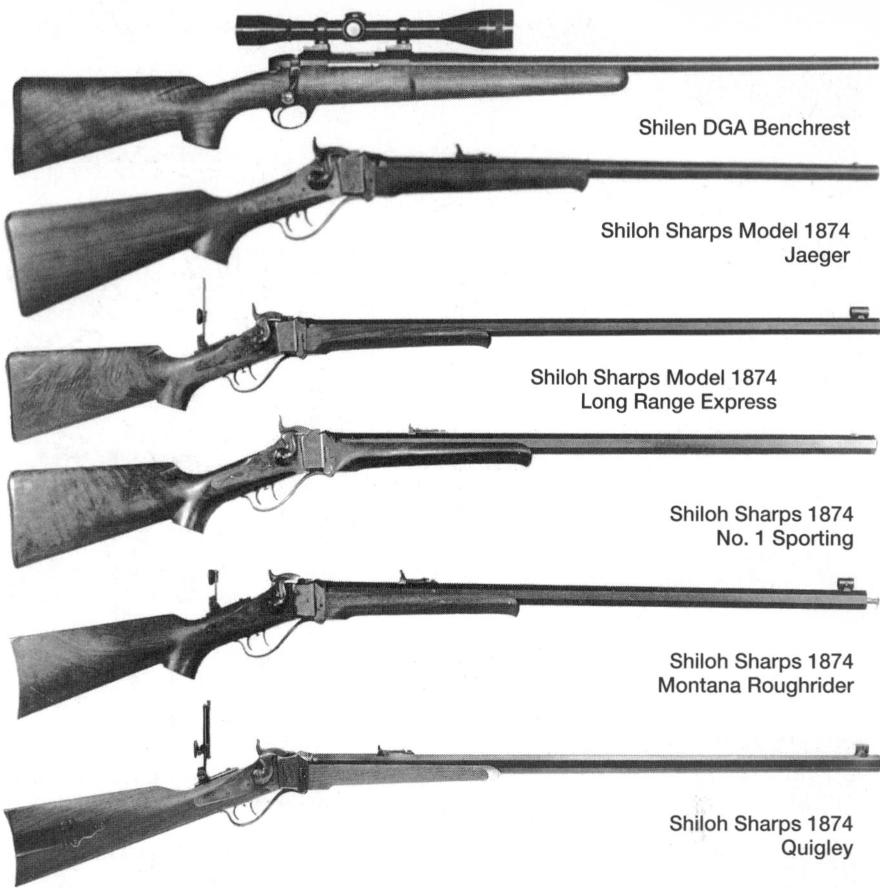

Shilen DGA Benchrest

Shiloh Sharps Model 1874 Jaeger

Shiloh Sharps Model 1874 Long Range Express

Shiloh Sharps 1874 No. 1 Sporting

Shiloh Sharps 1874 Montana Roughrider

Shiloh Sharps 1874 Quigley

SHILOH SHARPS MODEL 1874 LONG RANGE EXPRESS

Same specs as other Model 1874 series rifles except 34-inch tapered octagon barrel; sporting tang rear sight, globe front; semi-fancy, oil-finished pistol-grip walnut stock; shotgun-type buttplate; schnabel forend. Introduced 1985; still in production.

Exc: $2200 **VGood:** $1975 **Good:** $1495

SHILOH SHARPS MODEL 1874 MILITARY

Same specs as other Model 1874 series rifles except 30-inch round barrel; Lawrence-style rear ladder sight, iron block front; military buttstock with steel buttplate and patchbox; long forend with three barrel bands; sling swivels; single trigger. Introduced 1985; no longer in production.

PExc: $2000 **VGood:** $1775 **Good:** $1295

SHILOH SHARPS MODEL 1874 MILITARY CARBINE

Same specs as other Model 1874 series rifles except 40-70 BN, 45-70, 50-70; 22-inch round barrel; blade-type front sight, ladder-type rear; oil-finished military-type buttstock with steel buttplate; carbine forend with barrel band; saddle bar and ring; single trigger; Introduced 1989; no longer in production.

Perf: $1300 **Exc:** $1100 **VGood:** $975

SHILOH SHARPS MODEL 1874 MONTANA ROUGHRIDER

Same specs as other Model 1874 series rifles except 30-40, 30-30, 40-50x1-11/16 BN, 40-70x2-1/10, 45-70x2-1/10 ST; 24-inch, 26-inch, 28-inch, 30-inch, 34-inch half-octagon or full-octagon barrel; globe front and tang sight optional; standard supreme or semi-fancy oil-finished pistol-grip walnut stock; shotgun, pistol grip or military-style butt; schnabel forend. Introduced 1985; still in production.

Exc: $2200 **VGood:** $1975 **Good:** $1495

SHILOH SHARPS MODEL 1874 NO. 1 SPORTING

Same specs as other Model 1874 rifles except 40-50 BN, 40-90 BN, 45-70 ST, 45-110 ST, 50-70 ST, 50-90 ST, 50-110 ST, 32-40, 38-55, 40-70 ST, 40-90 ST; 30-inch octagon barrel; semi-fancy, oil-finished pistol-grip walnut stock; shotgun-type buttplate; schnabel forend. Introduced 1985; still in production.

Exc: $2200 **VGood:** $1975 **Good:** $1495

SHILOH SHARPS MODEL 1874 NO. 2 SPORTING

Same specs as other Model 1874 rifles except 45-70, 45-90, 45-120, 50-90, 50-140; 30-inch octagon barrel; semi-fancy, oil-finished pistol-grip walnut stock; shotgun-type buttplate; schnabel forend. No longer in production.

Exc: $2200 **VGood:** $1975 **Good:** $1495

SHILOH SHARPS MODEL 1874 NO. 3 SPORTING

Same specs as other Model 1874 rifles except 40-50 BN, 40-90 BN, 45-70 ST, 45-110 ST, 50-70 ST, 50-90 ST, 50-110 ST, 32-40, 38-55, 40-70 ST, 40-90 ST; 30-inch octagon barrel; oil-finished straight-grip stock standard wood; shotgun-type buttplate. Introduced 1985; still in production.

Exc: $2200 **VGood:** $1975 **Good:** $1495

SHILOH SHARPS MODEL 1874 SADDLE RIFLE

Same specs as other Model 1874 rifles except 26-inch octagon barrel; semi-fancy shotgun-type butt. Introduced 1986; still in production.

Perf: $1400 **Exc:** $1100 **VGood:** $900

SHILOH SHARPS 1874 QUIGLEY

Single shot, falling block; 45-70, 45-110. 34-inch heavy octagon barrel; Military-style stock with

Shiloh Sharps 1874 Creedmoor Target

Sigarms SHR 970

Sigarms SIG 556

SIGARMS Sauer SSG 3000

Smith & Wesson Model 125

Smith & Wesson Model 1500

Smith & Wesson Model 1500 Deluxe

SIGARMS M400 Predator Varminter

SIGARMS 716 Patrol

patch box, standard grade American walnut; Semi buckhorn rear sight, interchangeable front and midrange vernier tang sight with windage; replica of rifle used in the motion picture, "Quigley Down Under." Gold inlay initials, pewter tip, hartford collar, case color or antique finish. Double set triggers.

Perf: $2800 **Exc:** $2500 **VGood:** $2000

SHILOH SHARPS 1874 CREEDMOOR TARGET

Single shot, falling block; 38-55, 40-50 BN, 40-65 Win., 40-70 BN, 40-70 ST, 40-90 BN, 40- 90 ST, 44-77 BN, 44-90 BN, 45-70 ST, 45-90 ST, 45-100 ST, 45-110 ST, 45-120 ST, 50-70 ST, 50-90 ST; 32-inch barrel, half round-half octagon. Extra fancy American walnut shotgun style stock with pistol grip. Single trigger, AA finish on stock, polished barrel and screws, pewter tip.

Exc: $2200 **VGood:** $1975 **Good:** $1495

SIGARMS M400 PREDATOR VARMINTER

Semi-automatic, AR 15 style rifle in 5.56 NATO with a match grade heavy barrel with 1 in 9 twist. Two-stage Geissele trigger. Houge pistol grip and free-floating handguard. Varminter version has 22 inch barrel (8.1 pounds / 38.25 inches long), Predator version has an 18 inch barrel (7.6 pounds / 36.25 inches long). Flat top upper receiver.

Perf: $1290 **Exc:** $1100 **VGood:** $950

SIGARMS 716 PATROL

Semi-automatic, AR 10 style rifle in 7.62 NATO with an 18 inch match grade heavy barrel with 1 in 10 twist. Two-stage Geissele trigger. Magpul MIAD grip and UBR stock with and free-floating quad-rail handguard and flip-up iron sights. Flat top upper receiver.

Perf: $2400 **Exc:** $2000 **VGood:** $1800

SIGARMS SHR 970

Bolt action; 25-06, 270, 280, 308, 30-06. 22-inch barrel; weighs 7.2 lbs.; 41.9-inch overall length; black fiberglass or walnut stock; drilled and tapped for scope mounting. Quick takedown; interchangeable barrels; removable box magazine; cocking indicator; three-position safety. Introduced 1998. Imported by Sigarms, Inc.

Perf: $720 **Exc:** $660 **VGood:** $500

SIGARMS SIG 556

Generally similar to the Swiss-made SIG 556 tactical rifle but made in the USA. Chambered in 5.56 NATO. Collapsible stock, 16" mil-spec barrel, picatinny rail and all the trendy tactical goodies.

NIB: $1275 **Exc:** $1175 **VGood:** $1050

SIGARMS SIG 556 HOLO

Similar to above but with holographic sight.

NIB: $1575 **Exc:** $1375 **VGood:** $11250

SIGARMS SIG 556 DMR

A sniper version of the SIG 556 SWATwith bipod and other accurizing features.

NIB Exc V.G. Good Fair Poor

NIB: $2100 **Exc:** $1775 **VGood:** $1250

SIGARMS SAUER SSG 3000

Imported by SIGARMS. A 5-round bolt action sniper rifle chambered in .308 Winchester. The heavy-contoured, hammer forged barrel is fitted with a flash suppressor/muzzle brake to provide greater accuracy with reduced muzzle signature. Both the barrel and the receiver feature a black oxide finish to eliminate glare. The short, smooth 60 degree bolt throw allows for rapid operation and, like the safety release, the bolt action is quiet. A massive six-lug lockup system is used to give the SSG 3000 greater strength and accuracy. Pistol grip and fully adjustable stock to give the shooter a custom fit. The trigger is adjustable for trigger position, trigger take up, let-off point, and trigger pull weight. The receiver on the SSG 3000 features a dovetail that will accept a wide range of sighting systems, including a factory available M1913 rail.

NIB: $3000 **Exc:** $2600 **VGood:** $2200

SIGARMS SSG 3000 PATROL RIFLE

Bolt-action in 7.62 NATO with a 24 inch tapered heavy barrel with a 1 in 11 twist. Barrel is threaded 5/8 x 24 to accept flash hider, muzzle break or suppressor. New for 2013 fully adjustable precision stock. 60-degree bolt throw and integral zero M 1913 rail. Adjustable two-stage match trigger. Feeds from a single-stock detachable box magazine. Weight: 12 poounds.

Perf: $1400 **Exc:** $1300 **VGood:** $1200

SMITH & WESSON MODEL 125

Bolt action; 270 Win., 30-06; 5-shot magazine; 24-inch barrel; step-adjustable rear sight, hooded ramp front; action drilled, tapped for scope mounts; thumb safety; standard grade with hand-checkered stock of European walnut; deluxe grade adds rosewood forearm tip, pistol-grip cap. Introduced 1973; discontinued 1973.

Standard grade

Exc: $450 **VGood:** $400 **Good:** $280

Deluxe grade

Exc: $500 **VGood:** $450 **Good:** $290

SMITH & WESSON MODEL 1500

Bolt action; 22-250, 222, 223, 25-06, 243, 270, 30-06, 308, 7mm Rem. Mag., 300 Win. Mag., 338

Win. Mag.; 5-shot box magazine; 22-inch, 24-inch (magnum) barrel; hooded gold bead front sight, open round-notch fully-adjustable rear; checkered American walnut stock; single-set trigger; one-piece trigger guard; hinged floorplate; quick-detachable swivel studs; composition non-slip buttplate; rubber recoil pad (magnums). Introduced 1979; discontinued 1984.

Exc: $425 **VGood:** $400 **Good:** $300

SMITH & WESSON MODEL 1500 DELUXE

Same specs as Model 1500 except no sights; decorative scrollwork on floorplate; skip-line checkering; pistol-grip cap with S&W seal; sling, swivels. Introduced 1980; discontinued 1984.

Exc: $450 **VGood:** $425 **Good:** $325

SMITH & WESSON MODEL 1500 MOUNTAINEER

Same specs as Model 1500 except 22-inch, 24-inch barrel; no sights; drilled, tapped for scope mounts; satin-finished, checkered American walnut stock; recoil pad (magnum). Introduced 1983; discontinued 1984.

Exc: $450 **VGood:** $425 **Good:** $325

SMITH & WESSON MODEL 1500 VARMINT DELUXE

Same specs as Model 1500 except 222, 22-250, 223; 22-inch heavy barrel; oil-finished stock; quick-detachable swivels; fully-adjustable trigger; blued or Parkerized finish. Introduced 1982; discontinued 1984.

Exc: $450 **VGood:** $425 **Good:** $325

SMITH & WESSON MODEL 1700LS CLASSIC HUNTER

Bolt action; 243, 270, 30-06; 5-shot removable magazine; hooded globe bead front sight, open round-notch fully-adjustable rear; checkered American classic walnut stock, tapered forend, schnabel tip; ribbon checkering pattern; black rubber buttpad; flush-mounted sling swivels; jeweled bolt body; knurled bolt knob. Introduced 1983; discontinued 1984.

Exc: $550 **VGood:** $425 **Good:** $325

SMITH & WESSON MODEL A

Bolt action; 22-250, 243 Win., 270 Win., 308 Win., 30-06, 7mm Rem. Mag., 300 Win. Mag.; 3-shot (magnum), 5-shot magazine; 23-3/4-inch barrel; folding leaf rear sight, hooded ramp front; hand-checkered European walnut stock; Monte Carlo, rosewood pistol-grip cap, forend tip; sling swivels. Manufactured in Sweden by Husqvarna. Introduced 1969; discontinued 1972.

Exc: $475 **VGood:** $450 **Good:** $350

SMITH & WESSON MODEL B

Same specs as Model A except 243 Win., 270 Win., 30-06, 308; 23-3/4-inch light barrel; three-leaf folding rear sight, hooded German silver bead front; Monte Carlo stock; schnabel forend tip. Introduced 1969; discontinued 1972.

Exc: $475 **VGood:** $450 **Good:** $350

SMITH & WESSON MODEL C

Same specs as Model A except 243 Win., 270 Win., 30-06, 308; 23-3/4-inch light barrel; open sporting rear sight, hooded German silver bead front; straight-comb stock; cheekpiece, schnabel forend tip. Introduced 1969; discontinued 1972.

Exc: $475 **VGood:** $450 **Good:** $350

SMITH & WESSON MODEL D

Same specs as Model A except 243 Win., 270 Win., 30-06, 308; 20-3/4-inch light barrel; straight comb full-length Mannlicher-type stock; cheekpiece; open sporting rear sight, hooded German silver bead front. Introduced 1969; discontinued 1972.

Exc: $475 **VGood:** $450 **Good:** $350

SMITH & WESSON MODEL E

Same specs as Model A except 243 Win., 270 Win., 30-06, 308; 20-3/4-inch light barrel; full-length Mannlicher-type Monte Carlo stock; schnabel forend tip; open sporting rear sight, hooded German silver bead front. Introduced 1969; discontinued 1972.

Exc: $475 **VGood:** $450 **Good:** $350

SIGARMS SSG 3000 Patrol Rifle

Smith & Wesson Model 1500 Mountaineer

Smith & Wesson Model 1700LS Classic Hunter

Smith & Wesson Model B

Smith & Wesson Model C

Smith & Wesson Model D

Smith & Wesson M&P15 PC

SMITH & WESSON M&P15 MILITARY AND POLICE TACTICAL RIFLE

Gas-operated semi-auto built along lines of AR-15. Caliber: 5.56mm NATO. Magazine capacity: 30. Barrel: 16-inch 1:9. Stock: Six-position telescoping composite. Weight: 6.74 lbs. unloaded. Sights: Adjustable front and rear. Variants: M&P15A & M&P15T (no carry handle; folding battle sight).

NIB: $1150 **Exc:** $1075 **VGood:** $950

SMITH & WESSON M&P 15 PC

Generally similar to the M&P rifle but with accurized tubular floated barrel, 2-stage match trigger, 20" matte stainless barrel. No sights.

NIB: $1375 **Exc:** $1295 **VGood:** $1100

SOVEREIGN TD 22

Semi-automatic; 22 LR; 10-shot clip; 21-inch barrel; 41-inch overall length; weighs 6-1/2 lbs.; takedown; fully-adjustable open rear sight, hooded ramp front; walnut-finished hardwood stock; blued finish. Introduced 1986; no longer in production.

Exc: $125 **VGood:** $100 **Good:** $75

SPRINGFIELD INC. BM-59 (ITALIAN MODEL)

Semi-automatic; 7.62mm NATO (308 Win.); 20-shot box magazine; 19-3/8-inch barrel; 43-3/4-inch overall length; weighs 9-1/4 lbs.; military square-blade front sight, click-adjustable peep rear; walnut stock with trapped rubber buttpad; full military-dress Italian service rifle with winter trigger, grenade launcher and sights, tri-compensator, bipod. Refined version of the M-1 Garand. Made in Italy, assembled by Springfield Armory, Inc. Introduced 1981; no longer available.

Exc: $1495 **VGood:** $1195 **Good:** $880

SPRINGFIELD INC. BM-59 ALPINE PARATROOPER

Same specs as BM-59 Italian Model except Beretta-made folding metal buttstock with pistol grip. Made in Italy, assembled in U.S. by Springfield Armory, Inc. Introduced 1981; no longer available.

Exc: $1695 **VGood:** $1295 **Good:** $900

SPRINGFIELD INC. BM-59 NIGERIAN MODEL

Same specs as BM-59 Italian Model except Beretta-made vertical pistol grip stock. Made in Italy, assembled in U.S. by Springfield Armory, Inc. Introduced 1981; no longer available.

Exc: $1695 **VGood:** $1350 **Good:** $900

SPRINGFIELD INC. M-1 GARAND

Semi-automatic; 30-06, 308 Win., 270 Win., 8-shot. 24-inch barrel; weighs 9.5 lbs.; 43.6-inch overall length; American walnut stock. Military square post front, military aperture, MOA adjustable rear sights.

Springfield, Inc. M-1 Garand

Springfield, Inc. M1A

Springfield, Inc. M1A /M21 Tactical

Springfield, Inc. M-6 Scout Rifle/Shotgun

Squires Bingham Model 14D

Limited production, certificate of authenticity, all new receiver, barrel and stock with remaining parts USGI mil-spec. 2-stage military trigger; discontinued 1990; reintroduced in 2002 in 30-06 and 308 only, still in production; premium for 270 caliber.

Exc: $1200 **VGood:** $995 **Good:** $695

SPRINGFIELD INC. M1A

Semi-automatic; gas-operated; 308 Win. (7.62 NATO), 243 Win., 7mm-08; 5-, 10-, 20-shot box magazine; 22-inch barrel, flash suppressor; adjustable aperture rear sight, blade front; walnut, birch or fiberglass stock; fiberglass hand guard; sling swivels, sling. Same general specs as military M14 but without full-auto capability. Maker is private Illinois firm, not a U.S. government facility. Introduced 1974; still in production.

Exc: $1200 **VGood:** $995 **Good:** $695

Fiberglass stock

Perf: $1050 **Exc:** $950 **VGood:** $750

SPRINGFIELD INC. M1A MATCH

Same specs as M1A except National Match grade barrel, sights; glass-bedded American walnut or fiberglass stock; better trigger pull; modified gas system, mainspring guide. Still in production.

Perf: $1550 **Exc:** $1200 **VGood:** $955

SPRINGFIELD INC. M1A SCOUT SQUAD RIFLE

Same specs as M1A except 18-inch barrel with muzzle brake, 308, weighs 9.3 pounds, 10 or 20 round magazine.

Perf: $1525 **Exc:** $1100 **VGood:** $800

SPRINGFIELD INC. M1A SOCOM RIFLE

Same specs as M1A except 16.25-inch barrel with muzzle brake, forward-positioned scope mount, fiberglass stock; 308, weighs 8.9 pounds, 10 or 20 round magazine. Introduced 2004, still in production.

Perf: $1675 **Exc:** $1250 **VGood:** $900

SPRINGFIELD ARMORY M1A SOCOM 16

Similar to SOCOM but with walnut stock and 16-inch barrel.

NIB: $1550 **Exc:** $1450 **VGood:** $1195

SPRINGFIELD INC. M1A SUPER MATCH

Same specs as M1A except heavier, premium-grade barrel; National Match sights; glass-bedded oversize American walnut or fiberglass stock; better trigger pull; modified gas system, mainspring guide. Still in production.

Perf: $2100 **Exc:** $1695 **VGood:** $1100

SPRINGFIELD INC. M1A/M21 TACTICAL

Same specs as M1A Super Match except Douglas Premium match barrel and special sniper stock with adjustable cheekpiece; weighs 11-1/4 lbs. From Springfield, Inc.

Perf: $2000 **Exc:** $1400 **VGood:** $1100

SPRINGFIELD INC. M1A/M21 LAW ENFORCEMENT

Semi-automatic; 243, 7mm-08, 308 Win.; 20-shot magazine; air-gauged 22-inch Douglas heavy barrel; 44-1/4-inch overall length; weighs 11-7/8 lbs.; National Match front and rear sights; glass-bedded heavy walnut stock with adjustable comb, ventilated recoil pad. Refinement of the standard M1A rifle with specially knurled shoulder for figure-eight operating rod guide. From Springfield Armory, Inc. Introduced 1987; no longer made.

Perf: $2000 **Exc:** $1400 **VGood:** $1100

SPRINGFIELD INC. M1A/M21 SNIPER

Semi-automatic; 308 Win.; 20-shot box magazine; 22-inch heavy barrel; 44-1/4-inch overall length; weighs 15-1/4 lbs. with bipod, scope mount; National Match sights; heavy American walnut stock with adjustable comb, ventilated recoil pad; based on M1A rifle; folding, removable bipod; leather military sling. Introduced 1987; discontinued 1992.

Perf: $2100 **Exc:** $1500 **VGood:** $1200

SPRINGFIELD INC. M1A/M25 CARLOS HATHCOCK MODEL

Same specs as M1A/M21 except synthetic stock with adjustable comb, 308, 22-inch barrel, 12.75 pounds; Picatinny rail for optical sights only, no provision for iron sights; Harris bipod. Special model in honor of U.S. Marine Gunnery Sergeant Carlos N. Hathcock; rifle bears a facsimile of his signature. Introduced in 2001, still in production. Top dollar for unfired, absolutely mint specimens.

Perf: $3700 **Exc:** $2700 **VGood:** $ 1700

SPRINGFIELD INC. M-6 SCOUT RIFLE/SHOTGUN

Combination gun; 22 LR, 22 WMR, 22 Hornet over 410-bore; 18-1/4-inch barrel; 32-inch overall length; weighs 4-1/2 lbs.; blade front sight, military aperture for 22, V-notch for 410; folding steel stock with storage for fifteen 22 LR, four 410 shells; all-metal construction; designed for quick disassembly and minimum maintenance; folds for compact storage. Early examples made in U.S. by Springfield, Inc., later guns imported from the Czech Republic. Introduced 1982; reintroduced 1995, no longer in production. Pricing shown is for later CZ production; 100 percent premium for marked USA production.

Perf: $250 **Exc:** $225 **VGood:** $185

Stainless steel version

Perf: $275 **Exc:** $250 **VGood:** $210

SPRINGFIELD INC. MODEL 700 BASR

Bolt action; 308 Win.; 5-shot magazine; 26-inch heavy Douglas Premium barrel; 46-1/4-inch overall length; weighs 13-1/2 lbs.; no sights; synthetic fiber stock; rubber recoil pad; marketed with military leather sling; adjustable, folding Parker-Hale bipod. Introduced 1987; discontinued 1988.

Exc: $695 **VGood:** $595 **Good:** $440

SPRINGFIELD INC. SAR-8 SPORTER

Semi-automatic; 308 Win.; 20-shot magazine; 18-inch barrel; 40-3/8-inch overall length; weighs 8-3/4 lbs.; protected post front sight, rotary-style adjustble rear; black or green composition forend; wood thumbhole butt; delayed roller-lock action; fluted chamber; matte black finish. From Springfield Inc. Introduced 1990; discontinued; reintroduced 1995, no longer in production.

Perf: $2200 **Exc:** $1900 **VGood:** $1500

SPRINGFIELD INC. SAR-4800

Semi-automatic; 5.56, 7.62 NATO (308 Win.); 10-shot magazine; 21-inch barrel; 43-3/8-inch overall length; weighs 9-1/2 lbs.; protected post front sight, adjustable peep rear; fiberglass forend; wood thumbhole butt. New production. From Springfield Inc. Reintroduced 1995, no longer in production.

Perf: $2100 **Exc:** $1800 **VGood:** $1400

SPRINGFIELD INC. SAR-4800 22

Same specs as SAR-4800 except 22 LR. No longer in production.

Perf: $1100 **Exc:** $950 **VGood:** $695

SPRINGFIELD INC. SAR-4800 BUSH

Same specs as SAR-4800 except 18-inch barrel. No longer in production.

Perf: $2100 **Exc:** $1800 **VGood:** $1400

SQUIRES BINGHAM MODEL 14D

Bolt action; 22 LR; 5-shot box magazine; 24-inch barrel; V-notch rear sight, hooded ramp front; grooved receiver for scope mounts; exotic hand-checkered wood stock, contrasting forend tip, pistol-grip cap. Made in the Philippines. No longer in production.

Exc: $70 **VGood:** $50 **Good:** $45

SQUIRES BINGHAM MODEL 15

Bolt action; 22 WMR; 5-shot box magazine; 24-inch barrel; V-notch rear sight, hooded ramp front; grooved receiver for scope mounts; exotic hand-checkered wood stock, contrasting forend tip; pistol-grip cap. Made in the Philippines. No longer in production.

Exc: $80 **VGood:** $60 **Good:** $50

SQUIRES BINGHAM MODEL M16

Semi-automatic; 22 LR; 15-shot detachable box magazine; 19-1/2-inch barrel; muzzlebrake/flash hider; integral rear sight, ramped post front; black painted mahogany buttstock, forearm; similar to military M16. No longer imported.

Exc: $200 **VGood:** $165 **Good:** $115

SQUIRES BINGHAM MODEL M20D

Semi-automatic; 22 LR; 15-shot detachable box magazine; 19-1/2-inch barrel; muzzlebrake/flash hider; V-notch rear sight, blade front; grooved receiver for scope mount; hand-checkered exotic wood stock; contrasting pistol-grip cap, forend tip. No longer imported.

Exc: $125 **VGood:** $100 **Good:** $75

STAG ARMS STAG-15 MODEL 1 PRE-BAN

Basic M-4 Carbine pattern. Cal. 5.56mm/.223. 16-inch M-4 barrel with flash hider and bayonet lug. A2 upper receiver with adjustable rear sight. Six-position collapsible buttstock.

New: $950 **Exc:** $825 **VGood:** $695

STAG ARMS STAG-15 MODEL 2 PRE-BAN

As above but with a flat top upper receiver. Includes MI ERS flip type rear sight assembly.

New: $975 **Exc:** $850 **VGood:** $715

STAG ARMS STAG-15 MODEL 2 T

As above but with a A.R.M.S. sight system and Samson MRFS-C four sided hand guard.

New: $1125 **Exc:** $995 **VGood:** $750

STAG ARMS STAG-15 MODEL 3 PRE-BAN

M-4 type carbine featuring a flat top receiver and gas block with picatinny rails. Six position collapsible buttstock.

New: $900 **Exc:** $800 **VGood:** $675

STAG ARMS STAG-15 MODEL 4 PRE-BAN

An A-2 type rifle featuring a 20-inch barrel. Flash hider and bayonet lug.

New: $1000 **Exc:** $900 **VGood:** $700

STAG ARMS STAG 6.8 MODEL 5 PRE-BAN

Cal. 6.8 SPC. 16-inch barrel. Flat top receiver with picitinny rail. Six position collapsible buttstock. 25-round magazine.

New: $1050 **Exc:** $950 **VGood:** $750

STAG ARMS STAG-15 MODEL 6 PRE-BAN SUPER VARMINTER

24-inch heavy barrel. No flash hider. Flat top receiver with picitinny rail. Two stage trigger. Free float round hand guard. A2 type fixed stock.

New: $1075 **Exc:** $975 **VGood:** $775

STAG ARMS MODEL 3

AR-style chambered for 5.56/223 with 16-inch chrome-lined barrel. Six-position collapsible stock, A3 forged aluminum upper, black anodized finish.

Stag Arms Stag-15 Model 2 Pre-Ban

Stag Arms Stag-15 Model 3 Pre-Ban

Stag Arms Stag 6.8 Model 5 Pre-Ban

Stag Arms Stag-15 Model 6 Pre-Ban Super Varminter

Stevens Buckhorn Model 056

Diamondhead Versa Rail system with rails at top, bottom and sides. Available in LH version.

Perf: $825 **Exc:** $700 **VGood:** $600

STAG ARMS MODEL 8T & 8TL

Semi-auto (AR15) in .223 Rem. / 5.56 NATO. M4 profiled, 16 inch Chrome-Lined, 1 in 9 twist barrel with an overall length of 32.50 - 35.75 inches and a weight of 7.0 pounds. Synthetic pistol grip and Diamondhead VRS-T aluminum handguard and Diamondhead flip-up front and rear sights. Adjustable gas piston action with all metal hard coat anodized. Shipped with one 20 round magazine. Left hand version (model 8TL) available. New in 2012.

Perf: $1175 **Exc:** $1050 **VGood:** $900

STANDARD ARMS MODEL G

Semi-automatic; 25 Rem., 30 Rem., 35 Rem.; 4-shot (35 Rem.), 5-shot magazine; 22-3/8-inch barrel; gas operated; hammerless; takedown; open rear sight, ivory bead front; American walnut buttstock; slide handle-type forearm; gas port, when closed, could be used as a manual slide action. Introduced 1912. Notorious for malfunctioning!

VGood: $650 **Good:** $395 **Fair:** $250

STANDARD ARMS MODEL M

Slide action; 25 Rem., 30 Rem., 35 Rem.; 4-shot (35 Rem.), 5-shot magazine; 22-3/8-inch barrel; hammerless; takedown; open rear sight, ivory bead front; American walnut buttstock, slide handle-type forearm. Introduced 1912. Some collector value.

VGood: $675 **Good:** $420 **Fair:** $275

STEVENS BUCKHORN MODEL 053

Bolt action; single shot; 25 Stevens, 22 Short, 22 Long, 22 LR, 22 WMR; 24-inch barrel; 41-1/4-inch overall length; weighs 5-1/2 lbs.; takedown; receiver peep sight, open folding middle sight, hooded ramp front with three inserts, removable hood; uncheckered walnut stock; pistol grip; black forearm tip. Introduced 1935; discontinued 1948.

Exc: $150 **VGood:** $130 **Good:** $95

STEVENS BUCKHORN MODEL 53

Same specs as Buckhorn Model 053 except open rear sight, gold bead front.

Exc: $150 **VGood:** $130 **Good:** $95

STEVENS BUCKHORN MODEL 056

Bolt action; 22 Short, 22 Long, 22 LR; 5-shot detachable box magazine; 24-inch barrel; 43-1/2-inch overall length; weighs 6 lbs.; takedown; receiver peep sight, open middle sight, hooded front; uncheckered walnut sporter-type stock; pistol grip, black forearm tip; rubber buttplate. Introduced 1935; discontinued 1948.

Exc: $175 **VGood:** $155 **Good:** $120

STEVENS BUCKHORN MODEL 56

Same specs as Buckhorn Model 056 except open rear sight, gold bead front.

Exc: $175 **VGood:** $155 **Good:** $120

Stevens Buckhorn Model 066
Stevens Buckhorn Model 66
Stevens Buckhorn No. 076
Stevens Model 15Y
Stevens Model 84
Stevens Model 84S
Stevens Model 86S
Stevens Model 87

STEVENS BUCKHORN MODEL 066

Bolt action; 22 Short, 22 Long, 22 LR; 21-shot (22 Short), 17-shot (22 Long), 15-shot (22 LR) tube magazine; 24-inch barrel; 43-1/2-inch overall length; weighs 6 lbs.; receiver peep sight, folding sporting middle sight, hooded front; uncheckered walnut sporting stock; pistol grip, black forearm tip; rubber buttplate. Introduced 1935; discontinued 1948.

Exc: $150 **VGood:** $130 **Good:** $95

STEVENS BUCKHORN MODEL 66

Same specs as Model 066 except fully-adjustable sporting rear sight, gold bead front.

Exc: $150 **VGood:** $130 **Good:** $95

STEVENS BUCKHORN NO. 057

Semi-automatic; 22 LR; 5-shot detachable box magazine; 24-inch barrel; takedown; peep receiver sight, hooded front; uncheckered sporter-style stock; black forearm tip. Introduced 1939; discontinued 1948.

Exc: $150 **VGood:** $125 **Good:** $100

STEVENS BUCKHORN NO. 57

Same specs as Buckhorn No. 057 except open rear sight, plain bead front.

Exc: $150 **VGood:** $125 **Good:** $100

STEVENS BUCKHORN NO. 076

Semi-automatic; 22 LR; 15-shot tube magazine; 24-inch barrel; weighs 6 lbs.; takedown; cross-bolt locks for use as single shot with 22 Short, 22 Long, 22 LR; peep rear receiver sight, folding flat-top middle sight, hooded front; uncheckered sporter-style stock; black forearm tip; rubber buttplate. Introduced 1938; discontinued 1948.

Exc: $150 **VGood:** $130 **Good:** $115

STEVENS BUCKHORN NO. 76

Same specs as Buckhorn No. 076 except open rear sight; gold bead front.

Exc: $150 **VGood:** $130 **Good:** $115

STEVENS MODEL 15

Bolt action; single shot; 22 Short, 22 Long, 22 LR; 22-inch, 24-inch barrel; 43-inch overall length; weighs 4 lbs.; elevation-adjustable open rear sight, gold bead front; uncheckered walnut pistol-grip stock. Introduced 1948; discontinued 1965.

Exc: $100 **VGood:** $75 **Good:** $55

STEVENS MODEL 15Y

Same specs as Model 15 except 21-inch barrel; 35-1/4-inch overall length; shorter youth-size buttstock. Introduced 1958; discontinued 1965.

Exc: $100 **VGood:** $75 **Good:** $55

STEVENS MODEL 66

Bolt action; 22 Short, 22 Long, 22 LR; 19-shot (22 Short), 15-shot (22 Long), 13-shot (22 LR) tube magazine; 24-inch barrel; takedown; open rear sight, bead front; uncheckered walnut pistol-grip stock; grooved forearm. Introduced 1931; discontinued 1935.

Exc: $100 **VGood:** $75 **Good:** $55

STEVENS MODEL 76

Semi-automatic; usable as repeater or single shot; 22 LR (semi-auto), 22 Short, 22 Long, 22 LR (repeater or single shot); 15-shot tubular magazine; 24-inch tapered barrel with crowned muzzle; weighs 6 lbs.; hammer release mechanism for single shot operation; open rear sight, gold bead front; American walnut full pistol-grip stock; hard rubber buttplate. Introduced 1947.

Exc: $150 **VGood:** $130 **Good:** $115

STEVENS MODEL 84

Bolt action; 22 Short, 22 Long, 22 LR; 15-shot (22 LR), 17-shot (22 Long), 21-shot (22 Short) tube magazine; 24-inch barrel; 43-inch overall length; weighs 6 lbs.; cross-bolt locks for single shot operation; takedown; elevation-adjustable micro peep rear sight, gold bead front; uncheckered walnut military-style full pistol-grip stock; plated bolt, trigger. Introduced 1949; discontinued 1965.

Exc: $150 **VGood:** $125 **Good:** $100

STEVENS MODEL 84S

Same specs as Model 84 except No. 150 micro peep rear sight, No. 150 hooded front. Introduced 1948; discontinued 1952.

Exc: $100 **VGood:** $125 **Good:** $100

STEVENS MODEL 85

Semi-automatic; 22 LR; 5-shot detachable box magazine; 24-inch barrel; 44-inch overall length; weighs 6 lbs.; takedown; cross-bolt locks for repeater or single shot operation; open rear sight, bead front; uncheckered American walnut full pistol-grip stock; black forearm tip; hard rubber buttplate. Introduced 1948; discontinued 1976.

Exc: $150 **VGood:** $125 **Good:** $100

STEVENS MODEL 85K

Same specs as Model 85 except 20-inch barrel; 40-inch overall length; weighs 53/4 lbs. Introduced 1959.

Exc: $150 **VGood:** $125 **Good:** $100

STEVENS MODEL 85S

Same specs as Model 85 except peep rear sight, hooded front. Introduced 1948; discontinued 1976.

Exc: $150 **VGood:** $125 **Good:** $100

STEVENS MODEL 86

Bolt action; 22 Short, 22 Long, 22 LR; 21-shot (22 Short), 17-shot (22 Long), 15-shot (22 LR) tube magazine; 24-inch barrel; 43-1/2-inch overall length; weighs 6 lbs.; takedown; sporting elevation-adjustable rear sight, gold bead front; uncheckered walnut military-style full pistol-grip stock; plated bolt, trigger. Introduced 1935; discontinued 1948.

Exc: $150 **VGood:** $125 **Good:** $100

STEVENS MODEL 86S

Same specs as Model 86 except No. 150 peep rear sight, hooded front. Introduced 1948; discontinued 1952.

Exc: $150 **VGood:** $125 **Good:** $100

STEVENS MODEL 87, 87A

Semi-automatic; 22 LR; can also be used as repeater or single shot; 15-shot tube magazine; 24-inch barrel (until late '60s), 20-inch barrel (later version); weighs 6 lbs.; takedown; cross-bolt locks for single shot operation; open rear sight, bead front; uncheckered American walnut full pistol-grip stock; black forearm tip; hard rubber buttplate. Marketed as Springfield Model 87 from 1938 to 1948, when trade name dropped. Introduced as the Stevens Model 87 in 1948; discontinued 1976.

Exc: $150 **VGood:** $125 **Good:** $100

STEVENS MODEL 87K

Same specs as Model 87 except 20-inch barrel; 40-inch overall length; weighs 5-3/4 lbs. Introduced 1959.

Exc: $150 **VGood:** $125 **Good:** $100

STEVENS MODEL 87S

Same specs as Model 87 except peep rear sight, hooded front. Introduced with Stevens name in 1948; discontinued 1953.

Exc: $150 **VGood:** $125 **Good:** $100

Stevens Model 110ES

Stevens Model 325

Stevens No. 419 Junior Target

Stevens Favorite No. 17

Stevens Ideal No. 44

STEVENS MODEL 110E

Bolt action; 243, 308, 30-06; 4-shot magazine; 22-inch round tapered barrel; removable bead ramp front sight, step-adjustable rear; drilled, tapped for peep sight or scope mounts; walnut-finished hardwood Monte Carlo stock; checkered pistol grip, forend; hard rubber buttplate; top tang safety. Introduced 1978; discontinued 1984.

Exc: $350 **VGood:** $275 **Good:** $225

STEVENS MODEL 110ES

Same specs as Model 110E except 5-shot magazine; free-floating barrel; marketed with 4x scope, mounts. Introduced 1981; discontinued 1985.

Exc: $350 **VGood:** $300 **Good:** $250

STEVENS MODEL 120

Bolt action; single shot; 22 Short, 22 Long, 22 LR; 20-inch round tapered barrel; sporting front/rear sights; grooved for scope mounts; walnut-finished hardwood stock; pistol grip; action cocks on opening of bolt; thumb safety; double extractors; recessed bolt face. Introduced 1979; discontinued 1983.

Exc: $80 **VGood:** $70 **Good:** $50

STEVENS MODEL 125

Bolt action; single shot; 22 Short, 22 Long, 22 LR; 22-inch barrel; 39-inch overall length; sporting front sight, open rear with elevator; walnut-finished stock; manual cocking; blued finish. Introduced 1981; no longer made.

Exc: $100 **VGood:** $75 **Good:** $55

STEVENS MODEL 322

Bolt action; 22 Hornet; 4-shot detachable box magazine; 21-inch barrel; open rear sight, ramp front; uncheckered walnut pistol grip stock. Introduced 1947; discontinued 1950.

Exc: $300 **VGood:** $250 **Good:** $200

STEVENS MODEL 322S

Same specs as Model 322 except peep rear sight. Introduced 1947; discontinued 1950.

Exc: $300 **VGood:** $250 **Good:** $200

STEVENS MODEL 325

Bolt action; 30-30; 4-shot detachable box magazine; 21-inch barrel; open rear sight, bead front; uncheckered pistol-grip stock; flat bolt handle; Introduced 1947; discontinued 1950.

Exc: $240 **VGood:** $200 **Good:** $170

STEVENS MODEL 325S

Same specs as Model 325 except peep rear sight. Introduced 1947; discontinued 1950.

Exc: $250 **VGood:** $210 **Good:** $190

STEVENS MODEL 416-2

Bolt action; 22 LR; 5-shot detachable box magazine; 26-inch heavy barrel; weighs 9-1/2 lbs.; No. 106 receiver peep sight, No. 25 hooded front; uncheckered American walnut target-type stock; checkered steel buttplate; sling swivels, 1-1/4-inch sling. Introduced 1937; discontinued 1949.

Exc: $325 **VGood:** $230 **Good:** $150

With U.S. Property markings

Exc: $395 **VGood:** $300 **Good:** $200

STEVENS NO. 419 JUNIOR TARGET

Bolt action; single shot; 22 LR; 26-inch barrel; takedown; Lyman No. 55 peep rear sight, blade front; uncheckered walnut junior target stock; pistol grip; sling; swivels. Introduced 1932; discontinued 1936.

Exc: $275 **VGood:** $200 **Good:** $150

STEVENS FAVORITE NO. 17

Lever action; single shot; 22 LR, 25 rimfire, 32 rimfire; 24-inch barrel, other lengths available on special order; takedown; open rear sight, Rocky Mountain front; uncheckered walnut straight-grip stock; tapered forearm. Introduced 1894; discontinued 1935. Collector value.

Exc: $270 **VGood:** $200 **Good:** $165

STEVENS FAVORITE NO. 18

Lever action; single shot; 22 LR, 25 rimfire, 32 rimfire; 24-inch barrel, other lengths available on special order; takedown; Vernier peep rear sight, Beach combination front, leaf middle sight; uncheckered walnut straight-grip stock, tapered forearm. Introduced 1894; discontinued 1917. Collector value.

Exc: $290 **VGood:** $230 **Good:** $180

STEVENS FAVORITE NO. 19

Lever action; single shot; 22 LR, 25 rimfire, 32 rimfire; 24-inch barrel, other lengths available on special order; takedown; Lyman combination rear sight, Lyman front, leaf middle sight; uncheckered walnut straight-grip stock, tapered forearm. Introduced 1895; discontinued 1917. Collector value.

Exc: $290 **VGood:** $230 **Good:** $170

STEVENS FAVORITE NO. 20

Lever action; single shot; 22 rimfire, 32 rimfire only; smoothbore barrel; takedown; open rear sight, Rocky Mountain front; uncheckered walnut straight-grip stock; tapered forearm. Introduced 1895; discontinued 1935. Collector value.

Exc: $290 **VGood:** $240 **Good:** $170

STEVENS FAVORITE NO. 26 CRACKSHOT

Lever action; single shot; 22 LR, 32 rimfire; 18-inch, 22-inch barrel; takedown; open rear sight, blade front; uncheckered straight-grip walnut stock, tapered forearm. Introduced 1913; discontinued 1939. Collector value.

Exc: $220 **VGood:** $180 **Good:** $145

STEVENS FAVORITE NO. 26-1/2 CRACKSHOT

Same specs as No. 26 Crackshot except smoothbore barrel for 22, 32 rimfire shot cartridges. Introduced 1914; discontinued 1939. Collector value.

Exc: $240 **VGood:** $175 **Good:** $135

STEVENS FAVORITE NO. 27

Lever action; single shot; 22 LR, 25 rimfire, 32 rimfire; 24-inch octagon barrel, other lengths available on special order; takedown; open rear sight, Rocky Mountain front; uncheckered walnut straight-grip stock; tapered forearm. Introduced 1912; discontinued 1939. Collector value.

Exc: $210 **VGood:** $170 **Good:** $140

STEVENS FAVORITE NO. 28

Lever action; single shot; 22 LR, 25 rimfire, 32 rimfire; 24-inch octagon barrel, other lengths available on special order; takedown; Vernier peep sight, Beach combination front, leaf middle sight; uncheckered walnut straight-grip stock, tapered forearm. Introduced 1896; discontinued 1935. Collector value.

Exc: $280 **VGood:** $190 **Good:** $160

STEVENS FAVORITE NO. 29

Lever action; single shot; 22 LR, 25 rimfire, 32 rimfire; 24-inch octagon barrel, other lengths available on special order; takedown; Lyman combination rear sight, Lyman front, leaf middle sight; uncheckered walnut straight-grip stock, tapered forearm. Introduced 1896; discontinued 1935. Collector value.

Exc: $290 **VGood:** $190 **Good:** $165

STEVENS FAVORITE MODEL 30

Lever action, single shot; modern recreation of older Stevens Favorite series of rifles, still in production; 22 LR, 22 WMR, 17 HMR; 21-inch half-octagon barrel; weighs 4 ¼ pounds; open sights.

Perf: $190 **Exc:** $170 **VGood:** $140

Takedown version

Perf: $210 **Exc:** $190 **VGood:** $160

STEVENS IDEAL NO. 44

Lever action; single shot; 22 LR, 25 rimfire, 32 rimfire, 25-20, 32-20, 32-40, 38-40, 38-55, 44-40; 24-inch, 26-inch round, full- or half-octagon barrel; rolling block; takedown; open rear sight, Rocky Mountain front; uncheckered straight-grip walnut stock, forearm. Introduced 1894; discontinued 1932. Primarily of collector interest.

Exc: $685 **VGood:** $550 **Good:** $465

STEVENS IDEAL NO. 44-1/2

Same specs as Ideal No. 44 except improved falling block, lever action. Introduced 1903; discontinued 1916. Collector interest.

Exc: $980 **VGood:** $790 **Good:** $585

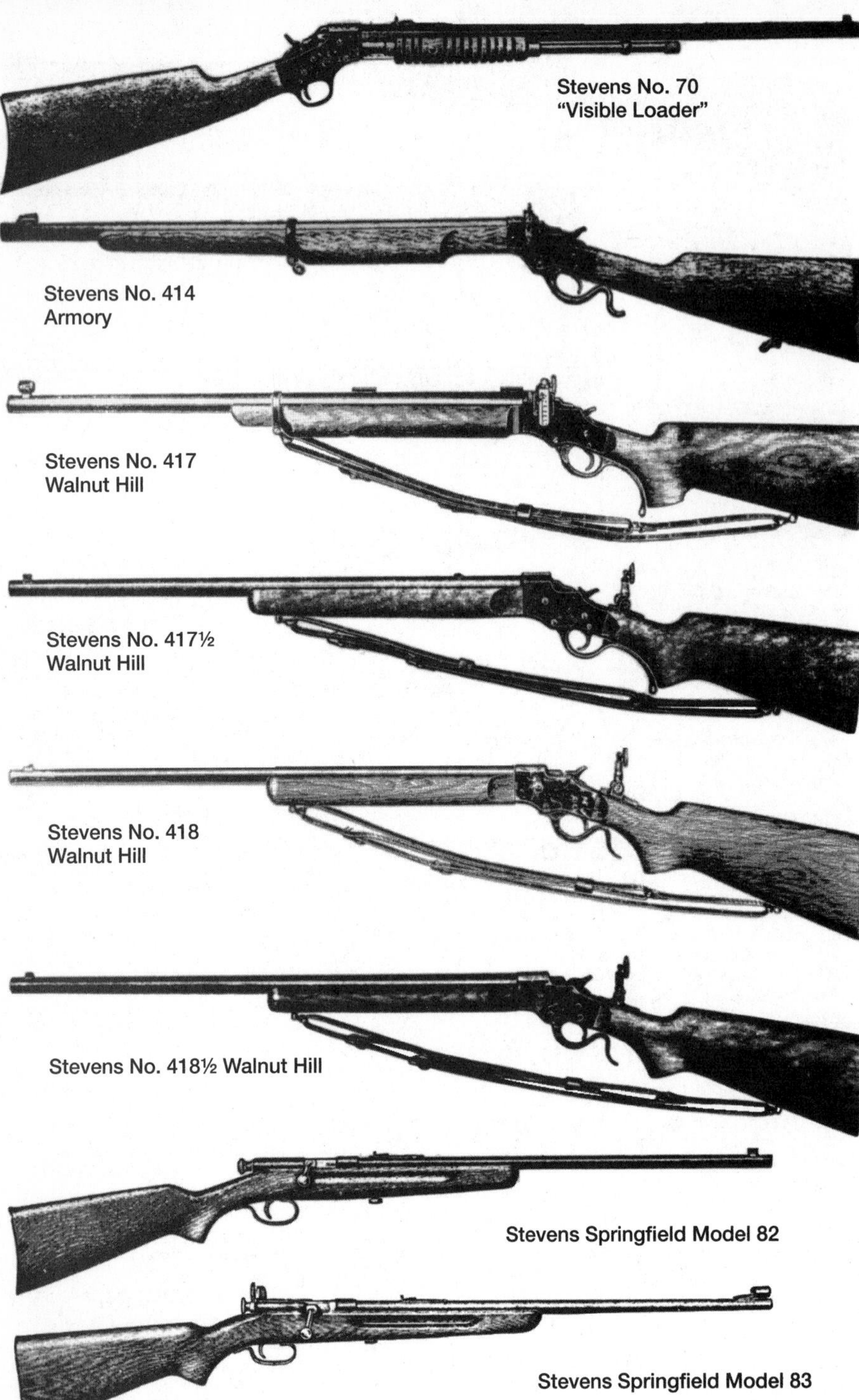

Stevens No. 70 "Visible Loader"

Stevens No. 414 Armory

Stevens No. 417 Walnut Hill

Stevens No. 417½ Walnut Hill

Stevens No. 418 Walnut Hill

Stevens No. 418½ Walnut Hill

Stevens Springfield Model 82

Stevens Springfield Model 83

STEVENS IDEAL NOS. 45 THROUGH 56

Lever actions; rolling and falling block; 22 LR, 25 rimfire, 32 rimfire, 25-20, 32-20, 32-40, 38-40, 38-55, 44-40; 24-inch, 26-inch round, full-, half-octagon barrel; other lengths available on special order; various sights available; various walnut stock options; similar to Ideal No. 44 with numerous updated improvements. Introduced 1896; discontinued 1916. Because of special order features, triggers, barrel makers, stocks and engraving, these models require separate evaluation. Higher grades and Schuetzens are very collectible and desirable.

STEVENS NO. 70 VISIBLE LOADER

Slide action; 22 Short, 22 Long, 22 LR; 15-shot (22 Short), 13-shot (22 Long), 11-shot (22 LR) tube magazine; 22-inch barrel; open rear sight, bead front; uncheckered straight-grip stock; grooved slide handle. Introduced 1907; discontinued 1934. Collector value.

Exc: $360 **VGood:** $280 **Good:** $210

STEVENS NO. 414 ARMORY

Lever action; single shot; 22 Short, 22 LR; 26-inch barrel; rolling block; Lyman receiver peep sight, blade front; checkered straight-grip walnut stock; military-style forearm; sling swivels. Introduced 1912; discontinued 1932.

Exc: $700 **VGood:** $500 **Good:** $400

STEVENS NO. 417 WALNUT HILL

Lever action; single shot; 22 Short, 22 LR, 22 Hornet; 28-inch heavy, 29-inch extra heavy barrel; Lyman No. 52L extension rear sight, No. 17A front; uncheckered walnut target stock; full pistol grip, beavertail forearm; sling swivels; barrel band; sling. Introduced 1932; discontinued 1947.

Exc: $1200 **VGood:** $1000 **Good:** $750

STEVENS NO. 417-1 WALNUT HILL

Same specs as No. 417 Walnut Hill except Lyman No. 48L receiver sight. Introduced 1932; discontinued 1947.

Exc: $1200 **VGood:** $900 **Good:** $700

STEVENS NO. 417-2 WALNUT HILL

Same specs as No. 417 Walnut Hill except Lyman No. 1441 tang sight. Introduced 1932; discontinued 1947.

Exc: $1200 **VGood:** $900 **Good:** $700

STEVENS NO. 417-3 WALNUT HILL

Same specs as No. 417 Walnut Hill except no sights. Introduced 1932; discontinued 1947.

Exc: $1150 **VGood:** $800 **Good:** $650

STEVENS NO. 417-1/2 WALNUT HILL

Same specs as No. 417 Walnut Hill except 22 Hornet, 25 rimfire, 22 WRF, 22 LR; 28-inch barrel; Lyman No. 144 tang peep sight, folding middle sight, bead front; uncheckered walnut sporting-style stock; pistol grip; semi-beavertail forearm. Introduced 1932; discontinued 1940.

Exc: $1200 **VGood:** $1000 **Good:** $800

STEVENS NO. 418 WALNUT HILL

Lever action; single shot; 22 Short, 22 LR; 26-inch barrel; takedown; Lyman No. 144 tang peep sight, blade front; uncheckered walnut stock; pistol grip, semi-beavertail forearm; sling swivels, sling. Introduced 1932; discontinued 1940.

Exc: $775 **VGood:** $595 **Good:** $300

STEVENS NO. 418-1/2 WALNUT HILL

Same specs as No. 418 Walnut Hill except 22 Short, 22 LR, 22 WRF, 25 Stevens; Lyman No. 2A tang peep sight, bead front. Introduced 1932; discontinued 1940.

Exc: $795 **VGood:** $595 **Good:** $300

STEVENS SPRINGFIELD MODEL 15

Bolt action; single shot; 22 Short, 22 Long, 22 LR; 22-inch barrel; 37-inch overall length; weighs 4 lbs.; takedown; elevation-adjustable sporting rear sight, gold bead front; uncheckered walnut-finished pistol-grip stock. Introduced 1937; discontinued 1948.

Exc: $110 **VGood:** $90 **Good:** $75

NOTE: Springfield was used as a brand name from 1935 until 1948, with the designation being dropped at that time. It should not be confused with Springfield Armory, although the name may have been registered with such mistaken identity in mind. After the Springfield brand name was dropped, rifles were known strictly by the Stevens name.

STEVENS SPRINGFIELD MODEL 82

Bolt action; single shot; 22 Short, 22 Long, 22 LR; 22-inch barrel; takedown; open rear sight, bead front; uncheckered walnut pistol-grip stock; grooved forearm. Introduced 1935; discontinued 1939.

Exc: $110 **VGood:** $90 **Good:** $75

STEVENS SPRINGFIELD MODEL 83

Bolt action; single shot; 25 Stevens, 22 WRF, 22 Short, 22 Long, 22 LR; 24-inch barrel; takedown; open rear sight, bead front; uncheckered walnut pistol-grip stock; grooved forearm. Introduced 1935; discontinued 1939.

Exc: $115 **VGood:** $90 **Good:** $75

STEVENS SPRINGFIELD MODEL 084

Bolt action; 22 Short, 22 Long, 22 LR; 5-shot detachable clip magazine; 24-inch barrel; 43-1/2-inch overall length; weighs 6 lbs.; takedown; rear peep sight, hooded front; uncheckered walnut pistol-grip stock; black forearm tip; plated bolt, trigger. Introduced 1935; discontinued 1948.

Exc: $150 **VGood:** $125 **Good:** $90

STEVENS SPRINGFIELD MODEL 84

Same specs Model 084 except open sights. Introduced 1935; discontinued 1948.

Exc: $150 **VGood:** $125 **Good:** $90

STEVENS SPRINGFIELD MODEL 085

Semi-automatic; 22 LR; 5-shot detachable box magazine; 24-inch barrel; takedown; peep rear sight, hooded front; uncheckered pistol-grip stock; black forend tip. Introduced 1939; discontinued 1948.

Exc: $150 **VGood:** $125 **Good:** $100

STEVENS SPRINGFIELD MODEL 85

Same specs as Model 085 except open sights. Introduced 1939; discontinued 1948.

Exc: $150 **VGood:** $125 **Good:** $100

STEVENS SPRINGFIELD MODEL 086

Bolt action; 22 Short, 22 Long, 22 LR; 21-shot (22 Short), 17-shot (22 Long), 15-shot (22 LR) tube magazine; 24-inch barrel; 41-1/2-inch overall length; weighs 5-1/2 lbs.; chromium-plated bolt, trigger; takedown; peep rear sight, folding sporting middle, hooded front; uncheckered walnut pistol-grip stock; black forearm tip; plated bolt, trigger. Introduced 1935; discontinued 1948.

Exc: $125 **VGood:** $100 **Good:** $75

STEVENS SPRINGFIELD MODEL 86

Same specs as Model 086 except open sights. Introduced 1935; discontinued 1948.

Exc: $125 **VGood:** $100 **Good:** $75

STEVENS SPRINGFIELD MODEL 087

Semi-automatic; 22 LR; 24-inch barrel; takedown; peep rear sight, hooded front; uncheckered pistol-grip stock; black forearm tip. Introduced 1938; discontinued 1948.

Exc: $150 **VGood:** $125 **Good:** $100

STEVENS SPRINGFIELD MODEL 87

Same specs as Model 087 except open rear sight, bead front. Introduced 1938; discontinued 1948.

Exc: $150 **VGood:** $125 **Good:** $100

NOTE: In 2005 Savage reintroduced the Stevens brand to designate a new series of entry-level rimfire and centerfire rifles.

STEVENS MODEL 200

Long- or short-action bolt rifle chambered in .223, .22-250, .243, 7MM-08, .308, .25-06, .270, .30-06, 7mm RM, or .300 WM. Gray checkered synthetic stock and 22-inch (short-action) or 24-inch (long-action) blued sightless barrel.

NIB: $300 **Exc:** $265 **VGood:** $195

STEVENS CADET MINI-YOUTH

Single-shot bolt-action .22 with hardwood stock. Similar to Savage Cub .22 rimfire. Introduced 2006.

NIB: $150 **Exc:** $120 **VGood:** $75

STEVENS MODEL 315 YOUTH

Similar to Cadet Mini-Youth but with sightless barrel.

NIB: $155 **Exc:** $130 **VGood:** $95

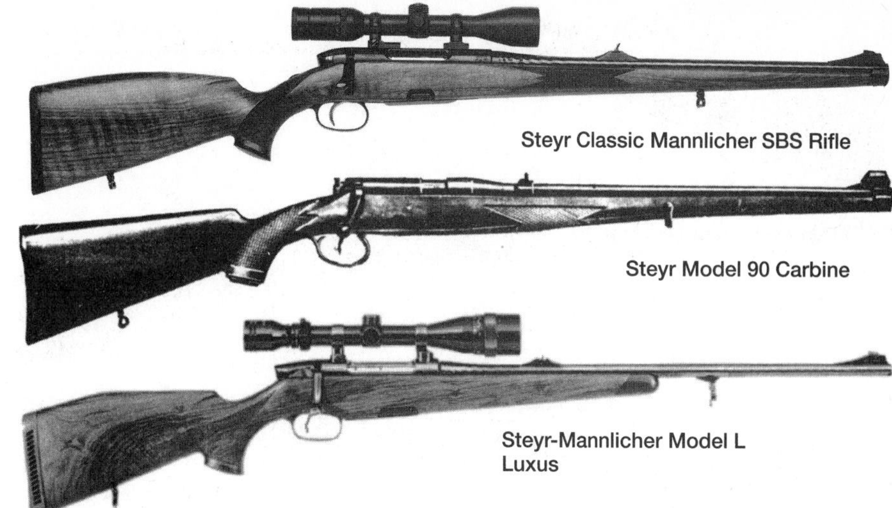

Steyr Classic Mannlicher SBS Rifle

Steyr Model 90 Carbine

Steyr-Mannlicher Model L Luxus

STEVENS MODEL 310

Five-shot bolt-action repeater chambered for .17 HMR. Detachable box magazine, synthetic stock, blued 20.75-inch sightless barrel.

NIB: $199 **Exc:** $165 **VGood:** $100

STEVENS MODEL 310 HEAVY BARREL

Similar to Stevens Model 310 but with 21-inch bull barrel.

NIB: $225 **Exc:** $200 **VGood:** $155

STEVENS MODEL 300

Clip-fed bolt-action repeater chambered for .22 rimfire. Gray synthetic stock and 20.75-inch blued barrel. Also available with scope package (add 10 percent).

NIB: $155 **Exc:** $125 **VGood:** $85

STEVENS MODEL 305

Similar to Stevens Model 310 but chambered in .22 WMR.

NIB: $189 **Exc:** $165 **VGood:** $115

STEYR A.U.G.-SA

Semi-automatic; 223 Rem.; 30- or 42-shot magazine; 20-inch barrel; 31-inch overall length; weighs 8-1/2 lbs.; synthetic green stock; one-piece molding houses receiver group, hammer mechanism and magazine; integral 1.5x scope; scope and mount form the carrying handle; gas-operated action; conversion to suit right- or left-handed shooters, including ejection port; folding vertical front grip. Imported from Austria by Gun South, Inc. Introduced 1983; no longer imported. Values were greatly affected by 1994 import ban, can still fluctuate widely.

Perf: $3500 **Exc:** $2700 **VGood:** $2400

STEYR CLASSIC MANNLICHER SBS RIFLE

Bolt action; 243, 25-06, 308, 6.5x55, 6.5x57, 270, 7x64 Brenneke, 7mm-08, 7.5x55, 30-06, 9.3x62, 6.5x68, 7mm Rem. Mag., 300 Win. Mag., 8x685, 4-shot magazine. Barrel: 23.6-inch standard; 26-inch magnum; 20-inch full stock standard calibers. Weighs 7 lbs.; 40.1-inch overall length. Stock: Hand-checkered fancy European oiled walnut with standard forend. Sights: Ramp front adjustable for elevation, V-notch rear adjustable for windage. Single adjustable trigger; 3-position roller safety with "safe-bolt" setting; drilled and tapped for Steyr factory scope mounts. Introduced 1997. Imported from Austria by GSI, Inc.

Perf: $1200 **Exc:** $1000 **VGood:** $800

STEYR MODEL 90 CARBINE

Bolt action; 22 LR; 5-shot detachable box magazine; 19-inch barrel; leaf rear sight, hooded bead front; hand-checkered European walnut Mannlicher-type stock; sling swivels. Manufactured in Austria. Introduced 1953; discontinued 1967.

Perf: $1195 **Exc:** $995 **VGood:** $725

STEYR MODEL 95

Bolt action; 8x50R Mannlicher; 30-inch barrel; straight pull; adjustable leaf rear sight, hooded bead front; military walnut Mannlicher-style stock; sling swivels. No longer produced.

Perf: $165 **Exc:** $115 **VGood:** $85

STEYR-MANNLICHER JAGD MATCH

Bolt action; 222 Rem., 243 Win., 308 Win.; 23-1/2-inch heavy barrel; Mannlicher sights; checkered laminate half-stock. Still in production.

Perf: $1595 **Exc:** $1295 **VGood:** $895

STEYR-MANNLICHER MATCH SPG-UIT

Bolt action; 308 Win.; 25-1/2-inch barrel; 44-inch overall length; weighs 10 lbs.; Steyr globe front sight, Steyr peep rear; laminated and ventilated stock of special UIT Match design; double-pull trigger adjustable for let-off point, slack, weight of first-stage pull, release force and length; buttplate adjustable for height and length. Meets UIT specifications. Imported from Austria by GSI, Inc. Introduced 1992.

Perf: $3495 **Exc:** $2995 **VGood:** $2395

STEYR-MANNLICHER MODEL L

Bolt action; 22-250, 5.6x57mm, 243 Win., 6mm Rem., 308 Win.; 5-shot detachable rotary magazine; 23-5/8-inch barrel; 42-1/2-inch overall length; open rear sight, hooded ramp front; European walnut half-stock; Monte Carlo comb, cheekpiece; skip-checkered pistol grip, forearm; double-set triggers; detachable sling-swivels; buttpad. Introduced 1968.

Perf: $1750 **Exc:** $1380 **VGood:** $850

STEYR-MANNLICHER MODEL L CARBINE

Same specs as Model L except 20-inch barrel; 39-inch overall length; full-length checkered European walnut stock. Introduced 1968.

Perf: $1790 **Exc:** $1410 **VGood:** $900

STEYR-MANNLICHER MODEL L LUXUS

Same specs as Model L except only 5.6x57, 6mm Rem., 22-250, 243, 308; 3-shot detachable steel magazine; single set trigger; rear tang slide safety; European walnut full- or half-stock.

Perf: $2100 **Exc:** $1495 **VGood:** $1190

With full stock

Perf: $2400 **Exc:** $1595 **VGood:** $1290

Steyr-Mannlicher Model L Varmint

Steyr-Mannlicher Model M

Steyr-Mannlicher Model M Luxus

Steyr-Mannlicher Model MIII Professional

Steyr-Mannlicher Model S

Steyr SBS Forester Rifle

Steyr SBS Prohunter Rifle with camo stock

Steyr Scout

STEYR-MANNLICHER MODEL L LUXUS CARBINE

Same specs as Model L except 5.6x57, 6mm Rem., 22-250, 243, 308; 3-shot magazine; 20-inch barrel; European walnut full-stock.

Perf: $2450 **Exc:** $1595 **VGood:** $1295

STEYR-MANNLICHER MODEL L VARMINT

Same specs as Model L except 22-250, 243 Win.; 26-inch heavy barrel; no sights; ventilated square forearm. Introduced 1969.

Perf: $1775 **Exc:** $1100 **VGood:** $890

STEYR-MANNLICHER MODEL M

Bolt action; 6.5x57mm, 7x57mm, 7x64mm, 25-06, 270 Win., 30-06, 8x57JS, 9.3x62; 5-shot detachable rotary magazine; 23-1/2-inch barrel; open rear sight, hooded ramp front; European walnut full- or half-stock; forend tip, recoil pad; detachable sling swivels. Also left-hand model, with 6.5x55, 7.5mm Swiss as additional calibers. Standard version introduced, 1969; left-hand version, 1977.

Perf: $1900 **Exc:** $1295 **VGood:** $895

Left-hand model

Perf: $2100 **Exc:** $1495 **VGood:** $995

STEYR-MANNLICHER MODEL M CARBINE

Same specs as Model M except 20-inch barrel; full-length stock. Introduced 1977.

Perf: $1950 **Exc:** $1350 **VGood:** $995

Left-hand model

Perf: $2200 **Exc:** $1550 **VGood:** $1050

STEYR-MANNLICHER MODEL M LUXUS

Same specs as Model M except 6.5x57, 270, 7x64, 30-06, 9.3x62, 7.5 Swiss; 3-shot detachable, in-line steel magazine; single set trigger; rear tang slide safety; full or half-stock. Imported from Austria by GSI, Inc.

Perf: $2000 **Exc:** $1295 **VGood:** $895

With full stock

Perf: $2300 **Exc:** $1595 **VGood:** $1095

STEYR-MANNLICHER MODEL M LUXUS CARBINE

Same specs as Model M except only 6.5x55, 6.5x57, 7x64, 7.5 Swiss, 270, 30-06; 3-shot magazine; 20-inch barrel; European walnut full-stock.

Perf: $2300 **Exc:** $1595 **VGood:** $1095

STEYR-MANNLICHER MODEL M PROFESSIONAL

Same specs as Model M except 270, 7x57, 7x64, 30-06, 9.3x62; 20-inch , 23-2/3-inch barrel; Cycolac synthetic stock; Parkerized finish. Introduced 1977; discontinued 1993.

Perf: $1475 **Exc:** $995 **VGood:** $795

STEYR-MANNLICHER MODEL MIII PROFESSIONAL

Same specs as the Model M except 6.5x57, 270, 30-06, 7x64, 9.3x62; 23-1/2-inch barrel; weighs about 7-1/2 lbs.; no sights; black ABS Cycolac or stippled, checkered European wood half-stock; single or optional double-set trigger. Imported from Austria by GSI, Inc. Reintroduced 1994.

Perf: $895 **Exc:** $695 **VGood:** $595

STEYR-MANNLICHER MODEL M72 L/M

Bolt action; 22-250, 5.6x57mm, 6mm Rem., 243 Win., 6.5x57mm, 270 Win., 7x57mm, 7x64mm, 308 Win., 30-06; 23-2/3-inch barrel; 5-shot rotary magazine; open rear sight, hooded ramp front; European walnut half-stock; hand-checkered pistol-grip forearm, rosewood forend tip; recoil pad; interchangeable single- or double-set trigger; detachable sling swivels; front locking bolt. Introduced 1972; no longer in production.

Exc: $995 **VGood:** $795 **Good:** $595

STEYR-MANNLICHER MODEL M72 MODEL L/M CARBINE

Same specs as Model M72 L/M except 20-inch barrel; full-length stock. Introduced 1972; no longer in production.

Exc: $1100 **VGood:** $850 **Good:** $650

STEYR-MANNLICHER MODEL S

Bolt action; 6.5x68mm, 257 Weatherby Mag., 264 Win. Mag., 7mm Rem. Mag., 300 Win. Mag., 300 H&H Mag., 308 Norma Mag., 8x68S, 338 Win. Mag., 9.3x64mm, 375 H&H Mag., 458 Win. Mag.; 5-shot detachable rotary magazine; 26-inch barrel; open rear sight, hooded ramp front; European walnut half-stock; Monte Carlo comb, cheekpiece; skip-checkered pistol grip, forearm; forend tip; recoil pad. Introduced 1969.

Perf: $1725 **Exc:** $1195 **VGood:** $950

STEYR SBS FORESTER

Caliber: 243, 25-06, 270, 7mm-08, 308 Win., 30-06, 7mm Rem. Mag., 300 Win. Mag. Detachable 4-shot magazine. 23.6-inch barrel, standard calibers; 25.6-inch, magnum calibers; weighs 7-1/2 lbs.; 44-1/2-inch overall length (23.6-inch barrel); oil-finished American walnut stock with Monte Carlo cheekpiece. Pachmayr 1-inch swivels; no sights; drilled and tapped for Browning A-Bolt mounts; Steyr Safe Bolt system, three-position ambidextrous roller tang safety, for Safe, Loading, Fire. Matte finish on barrel and receiver; adjustable trigger. Rotary cold-hammer forged barrel. Introduced 1997. Imported by GSI, Inc.

Standard calibers

Perf: $650 **Exc:** $600 **VGood:** $500

Magnum calibers

Perf: $700 **Exc:** $650 **VGood:** $550

STEYR SBS PROHUNTER

Similar to the SBS Forester except has ABS synthetic stock with adjustable butt spacers, straight comb without cheekpiece, palm swell, Pachmayr 1-inch swivels. Special 10-round magazine conversion kit available. Introduced 1997. Imported by GSI.

Standard calibers

Perf: $650 **Exc:** $580 **VGood:** $475

Magnum calibers

Perf: $700 **Exc:** $625 **VGood:** $500

STEYR SCOUT

Bolt action; 308 Win., 376 Steyr; 5-shot magazine. 19-inch barrel, fluted; Gray Zytel stock; Pop-up front & rear sights; Leupold M8 2.5x28 IER scope on Picatinny optic rail with Steyr mounts. offered with luggage case, scout sling, two stock spacers, two magazines. Introduced 1998. Imported by GSI. Add 10 percent for Jeff Cooper memorial version.

Perf: $1750 **Exc:** $1500 **VGood:** $1200

STEYR SSG 08

Bolt action center-fire rifle with a blued finish, fully adjustable aluminum folding stock and pistol grip, Versa-Pod, optics rail and muzzle brake. Chambered in .308 Winchester and .300 Win. Mag. and .338 Lapua. Barrel length from 20 to 23.6 inches, OA length 34.25 to 46.53 inches, and weight from 12.12 to 12.56 pounds. Capacity 10 rounds (.308 Win.), 8 rounds (.300 Win. Mag.), 6 rounds (.338 Lapua) with detachable box magazine. Introduced 2012.

Perf: $6,200 **Exc:** $5,700 **VGood:** $4,900

STEYR-MANNLICHER MODEL SL

Bolt action; 5.6x50, 22-250, 222 Rem., 222 Rem. Mag., 223 Rem.; 5-shot detachable rotary Makrolon magazine; 23-5/8-inch barrel; 42-1/2-inch overall length; open rear sight, hooded ramp front with .080 gold bead; European walnut half-stock; Monte Carlo comb, cheekpiece; skip-checkered pistol-grip, forearm; interchangeable single- or double-set triggers; detachable sling swivels; buttpad. Introduced 1968.

Perf: $1700 **Exc:** $1495 **VGood:** $895

STEYR-MANNLICHER MODEL SL CARBINE

Same specs as Model SL except 20-inch barrel; 39-inch overall length; full-length stock. Introduced 1968.

Perf: $1800 **Exc:** $1595 **VGood:** $995

STEYR-MANNLICHER MODEL SL VARMINT

Same specs as Model SL except only 22-250, 222 Rem., 222 Rem. Mag., 223; 26-inch barrel; no sights; vent. square forearm. Introduced 1969.

Perf: $1900 **Exc:** $1695 **VGood:** $1100

STEYR-MANNLICHER MODEL SSG

Bolt action; 308 Win.; 5- or 10-shot magazine; 25-1/2-inch heavy barrel; 44-1/2-inch overall length; weighs 8-3/8 lbs.; micrometer peep rear sight, globe front; European walnut or synthetic target stock; full pistol grip; wide forearm; swivel rail; adjustable buttplate; single trigger; single shot plug; also made with high-impact ABS Cycolac plastic stock. Introduced 1969.

Perf: $1550 **Exc:** $1200 **VGood:** $1000

With plastic stock

Perf: $1500 **Exc:** $1150 **VGood:** $950

STEYR-MANNLICHER MODEL SSG MATCH

Same specs as Model SSG except 26-inch heavy barrel; weighs 11 lbs.; Walther target peep sights; brown synthetic or walnut stock; adjustable rail in forend; match bolt. Introduced 1981; discontinued 1991.

Synthetic stock

Perf: $2500 **Exc:** $2000 **VGood:** $1400

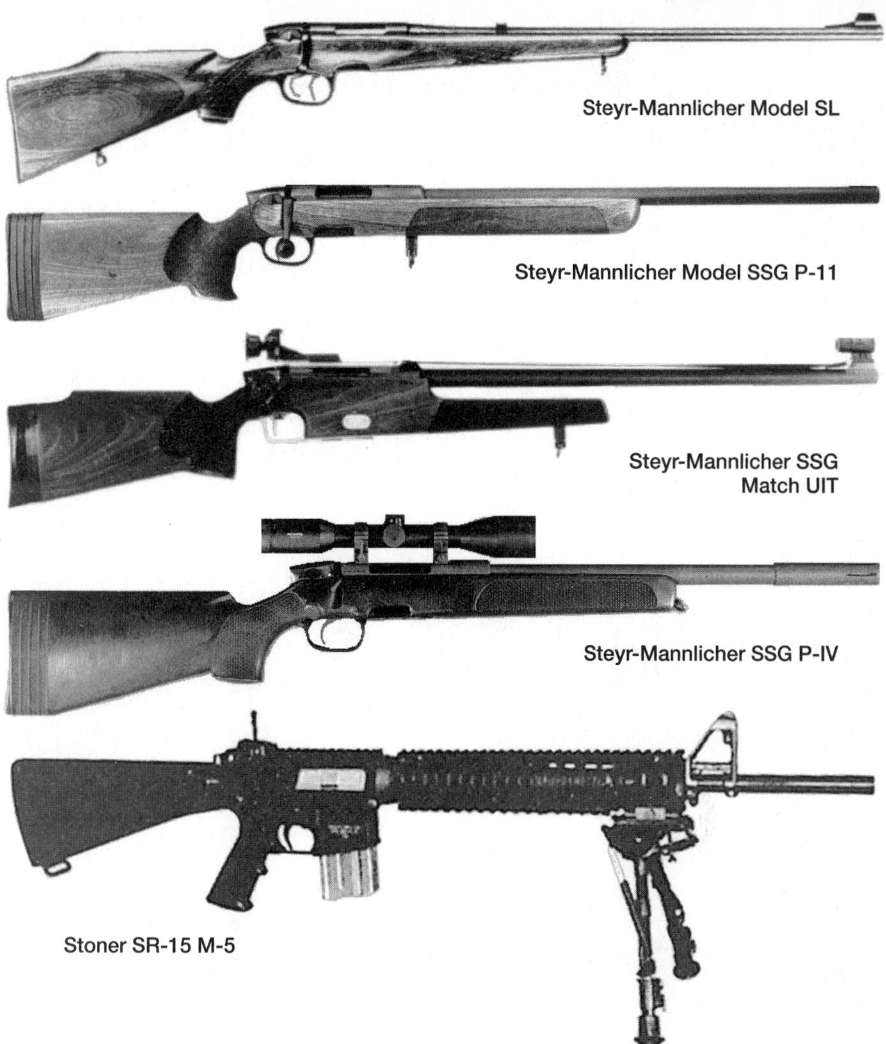

Steyr-Mannlicher Model SL

Steyr-Mannlicher Model SSG P-11

Steyr-Mannlicher SSG Match UIT

Steyr-Mannlicher SSG P-IV

Stoner SR-15 M-5

Walnut stock

Perf: $2600 **Exc:** $2100 **VGood:** $1500

STEYR-MANNLICHER MODEL SSG MATCH UIT

Same specs as Model SSG except 243, 308; weighs 11 lbs.; 10-shot magazine; Walther rear peep sight, globe front; UIT Match walnut stock; stippled grip, forend; adjustable double-pull trigger; adjustable buttplate. Introduced 1984; still in production.

Perf: $3375 **Exc:** $3000 **VGood:** $2000

STEYR-MANNLICHER SSG P-II

Same specs as Model SSG except 243, 308; large modified bolt handle; no sights; forend rail. Still in production.

Perf: $1650 **Exc:** $1350 **VGood:** $995

STEYR-MANNLICHER SSG P-IIK

Same specs as Model SSG P-II except 20-inch heavy barrel.

Perf: $1650 **Exc:** $1350 **VGood:** $995

STEYR-MANNLICHER SSG P-III

Same specs as Model SSG except 26-inch heavy barrel; diopter match sight bases; H-S Precision Pro-Series stock (black only). Imported from Austria by GSI, Inc. Introduced 1992; discontinued 1993.

Perf: $2025 **Exc:** $1695 **VGood:** $995

STEYR-MANNLICHER SSG P-IV

Same specs as Model SSG except 16-3/4-inch heavy barrel with flash hider; ABS Cycolac synthetic stock in green or black. Imported from Austria by GSI, Inc. Introduced 1992.

Perf: $2300 **Exc:** $1800 **VGood:** $1200

STEYR-MANNLICHER MODEL S/T

Bolt action; 9.3x64, 375 H&H Mag., 458 Win. Mag.; 5-shot detachable rotary magazine; 26-inch heavy barrel; open rear sight, hooded ramp front; European walnut half-stock; Monte Carlo comb, cheekpiece; skip-checkered pistol grip, forearm; forend tip; recoil pad. Introduced 1975.

Perf: $2050 **Exc:** $1695 **VGood:** $1200

STEYR-MANNLICHER MODEL S LUXUS

Same specs as the Model S/T except 6.5x68, 7mm Rem. Mag., 300 Win. Mag., 8x68S; 3-shot detachable steel, in-line magazine; single set trigger; rear tang slide safety; half-stock only. Imported from Austria by GSI, Inc.

Perf: $2300 **Exc:** $1900 **VGood:** $995

STI SPORTING COMPETITION

AR-style semiauto rifle chambered in 5.56 NATO. Features include 16-inch 410 stainless, 1:8-twist barrel; mid-length gas system; Nordic Tactical Compensator and JP Trigger group; custom STI Valkyrie handguard and gas block; flat-top design with Picatinny rail; anodized finish with black Teflon coating. Also available in Tactical configuration.

Perf: $1200 **Exc:** $1025 **VGood:** $865

STONER SR-15 M-5 RIFLE

Semi-automatic; 223; 20-inch barrel; weighs 7.6 lbs.; 38-inch overall length; Black synthetic stock; Post front sight, fully adjustable rear (300-meter sight); Modular weapon system; two-stage trigger. Black finish. Introduced 1998. Made in U.S.A.

Stoner SR-15 Match

Stoner SR-25 Match

Stoner SR-25 Match Lightweight

Stoner SR-25 Sporter

Stoner SR-25 Carbine

Sturm Ruger Deerfield 99/44 Carbine

Sturm Ruger American Compact

by Knight's Mfg. Add 100 percent for "1 of 100" edition.

Perf: $2200 **Exc:** $1900 **VGood:** $1500

STONER SR-15 MATCH RIFLE

Semi-automatic; 223; 20-inch barrel; weighs 7.9 lbs.; 38-inch overall length; Black synthetic stock; no sights furnished; flat-top upper receiver for scope mounting; Short Picatinny rail, two-stage match trigger. Introduced 1998. Made in U.S.A. by Knight's Mfg.Co.

Perf: $2300 **Exc:** $2000 **VGood:** $1600

STONER SR-25 MATCH

Semi-automatic; 7.62 NATO; (308); 10-shot steel magazine, 5-shot optional; 24-inch heavy match barrel with 1:11.25-inch twist; 44-inch overall length; weighs 10-3/4 lbs.; no sights; black synthetic stock of AR-15A2 design; full floating forend of Mil-spec synthetic attaches to upper receiver at a single point; integral Weaver-style rail; rings and iron sights optional; improved AR-15 trigger; AR-15-style seven-lug rotating bolt; gas block rail mounts detachable front sight. Made in U.S. by Knight's Mfg. Co. Introduced 1993.

Perf: $3100 **Exc:** $2200 **VGood:** $1500

STONER SR-25 MATCH LIGHTWEIGHT

Same specs as SR-25 Match except 20-inch medium match target contour barrel; 40-inch overall length; weighs 9-1/2 lbs.

Perf: $2995 **Exc:** $2100 **VGood:** $1500

STONER SR-25 SPORTER

Same specs as SR-25 Match except 20-inch barrel; 40-inch overall length; weighs 83/4 lbs.; AR-15A2-style elevation-adjustable front sight, detachable windage-adjustable rear; upper and lower receivers made of lightweight aircraft aluminum alloy; quick-detachable carrying handle/rear sight assembly; two-stage target trigger, shell deflector, bore guide, scope rings optional. Made in U.S. by Knight's Mfg. Co. Introduced 1993.

Perf: $2695 **Exc:** $1995 **VGood:** $1200

STONER SR-25 CARBINE

Same as the SR-25 Sporter except 16-inch light/hunting contour barrel; 36-inch overall length; weighs 7-3/4 lbs.; no sights; integral Weaver-style rail; scope rings; iron sights optional. Made in U.S. by Knight's Mfg. Co. Introduced 1995.

Perf: $2995 **Exc:** $2100 **VGood:** $1400

STEYR SSG08

Calibers are 7.62x51mm NATO (.308Win) or 7.62x63B (.300 Win Mag). Ten-shot magazine capacity. Barrel length is 20 or 23.6 inches (magnum). Weight: 12.1 to 12.6 pounds. Black Dural aluminium folding stock black with various Picatinny-rails. High-grade alumnium folding stock, adjustable cheek piece and butt plate.

Perf: $4425 **Exc:** $3750 **VGood:** $3200

STRUM RUGER AMERICAN

Bolt action; .22-250 Rem., .243 Win., .270 Win., 7mm-08 Rem., .308 Win., .30-06 Sprg. Matte finished alloy steel action and 22 inch barrel, synthetic stock, tang safety, adjustable trigger and detachable rotary magazine. No sights and drilled and tapped for scope bases. uses a three-lug bolt with a 70 degree throw. Weight: 6.25 pounds. Length: 42 inches. Introduced in 2012.

Perf: $400 **Exc:** $340 **VGood:** $290

STRUM RUGER AMERICAN COMPACT

Bolt action; 243 Win., 7mm-08 Rem. Matte finished alloy steel action and 18 inch barrel, synthetic stock, tang safety, adjustable trigger and detachable rotary magazine. No sights and drilled and tapped for scope bases. Uses a three-lug bolt with a 70 degree throw. Weight: 6 pounds. Length: 36.75 inches. Introduced in 2013.

Perf: $400 **Exc:** $340 **VGood:** $290

STURM RUGER DEERFIELD 99/44 CARBINE

Semi-automatic; 44 Mag., 4-shot rotary magazine; 18-1/2-inch barrel; weighs 6-1/4 lbs.; 36-7/8-inch overall length; Hardwood stock; Gold bead front, folding adjustable aperture rear sights; Semi-automatic action; dual front-locking lugs lock directly into receiver; integral scope mount; push-button safety; marketed with 1-inch rings and gun lock. Introduced 2000. Made in U.S.A. by Sturm, Ruger & Co.

Perf: $700 **Exc:** $600 **VGood:** $550

STRUM RUGER GUIDE GUN

Bolt action built on model 77 Mark II action; .338 RCM, .338 Win. Mag., .375 Ruger. Three position safety, laminated hard wood stock, stainless steel, 20 inch barrel, fixed sights, 42.5 inches and 8.5 pounds. This rifle is fitted with a muzzle break, a barrel band and an adjustable length of pull. Magazine capacity is three rounds and the rifle is shipped with Ruger 1 inch stainless scope rings. Introduced in 2013.

Perf: $1130 **Exc:** $950 **VGood:** $800

STURM RUGER GUNSITE SCOUT

In 308 Winchester with 16.5-inch barrel, 10-shot magazine capacity. Weight is 7 lbs., overall length 38 inches. Black laminated stock. Front post sight and adjustable ghost-ring rear. Forward mounted Picatinny rail. Stainless steel version introduced in 2013. Add $50 for stainless steel.

Perf: $900 **Exc:** $765 **VGood:** $650

STURM RUGER MINI-14

Semi-automatic; 223 Rem., 222 Rem.; 5-shot detachable box magazine; 18-1/2-inch barrel; weighs 6-1/2 lbs.; gas-operated, fixed-piston carbine; uncheckered, reinforced American hardwood carbine-type stock (early versions with walnut); positive primary extraction; fully-adjustable rear sight, gold bead front. Introduced 1973.

Perf: $600 **Exc:** $475 **VGood:** $400

STURM RUGER MINI-14 RANCH

Same specs as Mini-14 except 222 (1984 only), 223; steel-reinforced hardwood stock; ramp-type front sight; marketed with Sturm Ruger S100R scope rings; 20-shot magazine available; blued or stainless steel.

Perf: $600 **Exc:** $475 **VGood:** $400

STURM RUGER MINI-14 STAINLESS

Same specs as Mini-14 except barrel, action built of stainless steel. Introduced 1978.

Perf: $650 **Exc:** $525 **VGood:** $450

STURM RUGER MINI-14 WITH FOLDING STOCK

Same specs as Mini-14 Ranch Rifle except metal folding stock; checkered plastic vertical pistol grip; 47-3/4-inch overall length with stock extended, 27-1/2-inch with stock closed; weighs 7-3/4 lbs.; blued or stainless steel; no longer in production.

Perf: $850 **Exc:** $650 **VGood:** $500

STURM RUGER MINI 14/5

Same as Mini 14 but with five-round magazine; hardwood stock, 18-1/2-inch barrel, blued or stainless metal.

Perf: $480 **Exc:** $420 **VGood:** $375

STURM RUGER MINI-14 TARGET RIFLE

Acccurized version of the Mini-14 but with matte stainless barrel and receiver, black laminated thumbhole stock, adjustable harmonic dampener. No sights.

NIB: $825 **Exc:** $765 **VGood:** $595

STURM RUGER NRA MINI-14

Ruger NRA Mini-14 Rifle with two 20-round magazines, gold-tone medallion in grip cap, and special serial number sequence (NRA8XXXXX). Produced in 2008 only. Also available with 5-round magazines.

Perf: $900 **Exc:** $695 **VGood:** $450

Sturm Ruger Guide Gun

Sturm Ruger Mini-14

Sturm Ruger Mini-14 Ranch

Sturm Ruger Mini-14 Folding Stock

Sturm Ruger Mini-14/5

Sturm Ruger NRA Mini-14

Sturm Ruger Model 10/22 Carbine Stainless Steel

Sturm Ruger Model 10/22 Deluxe Sporter

STURM RUGER MINI THIRTY

Semi-automatic; 7.62x39mm Russian or 6.8 Remington; 5-shot detachable staggered box magazine; 18-1/2-inch barrel; weighs 7-1/4 lbs.; six-groove barrel; Sturm Ruger integral scope mount bases; folding peep sight; blued or stainless finish. Introduced 1987; still in production.

Perf: $575 **Exc:** $500 **VGood:** $450

Stainless finish

Perf: $650 **Exc:** $550 **VGood:** $475

STURM RUGER MODEL 10/22 CARBINE

Semi-automatic; 22 LR; 10-shot detachable rotary magazine; 18-1/2-inch barrel; uncheckered walnut carbine stock on early versions; as of 1980, standard models with birch stocks; barrel band; receiver tapped for scope blocks or tip-off mount; adjustable folding leaf rear sight, gold bead front; blue or stainless finish. Introduced 1964; still in production.

Perf: $200 **Exc:** $150 **VGood:** $125

Uncheckered walnut stock

Perf: $250 **Exc:** $200 **VGood:** $150

Stainless steel finish

Perf: $250 **Exc:** $200 **VGood:** $175

STURM RUGER MODEL 10/22 DELUXE SPORTER

Same specs as Model 10/22 except checkered walnut stock; flat buttplate; sling swivels; no barrel band. Introduced 1971, still in production.

Perf: $215 **Exc:** $185 **VGood:** $140

STURM RUGER MODEL 10/22 INTERNATIONAL

Same specs as Model 10/22 except full-length Mannlicher-type walnut stock (early

manufacture); birch full-length Mannlicher stock (1994); sling swivels. Introduced 1964; discontinued 1971. Reintroduced 1994. Premium for early production.

Perf: $250 **Exc:** $200 **VGood:** $175

Checkered stock

Perf: $300 **Exc:** $250 **VGood:** $200

STURM RUGER 10/22 RIFLE

Same specs as 10/22 Carbine except 20-inch barrel, rifle stock with flat butt, no barrel band.

Perf: $240 **Exc:** $ 180 **VGood:** $120

STURM RUGER MODEL 10/22 SPORTER

Same specs as Model 10/22 except Monte Carlo stock with grooved forearm; grip cap; sling swivels. Dropped in 1971, but reintroduced in 1973, with hand-checkered walnut pistol-grip stock. Dropped 1975. Reintroduced, still in production. Premium for early model.

Exc: $300 **VGood:** $270 **Good:** $190

STURM RUGER 10/22T TARGET RIFLE

Similar to the 10/22 except has 20-inch heavy, hammer-forged barrel with tight chamber dimensions, improved trigger pull, laminated hardwood stock dimensioned for optical sights; no iron sights supplied; weighs 7-1/4 lbs. Introduced 1996; still offered.

Perf: $420 **Exc:** $350 **VGood:** $280

STURM RUGER 10/22 ALL-WEATHER RIFLE

Similar to the stainless 10/22 except has black composite stock of thermoplastic polyester resin reinforced with fiberglass; checkered grip and forend. Brushed satin, natural metal finish with clear hardcoat finish. Weighs 5 lbs., measures 36-3/4-inch overall. Introduced 1997, still in production.

Perf: $230 **Exc:** $200 **VGood:** $150

STURM RUGER 10/22 CRR COMPACT RIFLE

Similar to 10/22 standard rifle but with 16.25-inch blued barrel, shorter hardwood stock, fiber optic sights and 34.5-inch overall length.

NIB: $250 **Exc:** $205 **VGood:** $175

STURM RUGER K10/22T RUGER 10/22 TARGET STAINLESS

Similar to 10/22 Target but with stainless steel barrel and laminated stock.

NIB: $375 **Exc:** $335 **VGood:** $295

STURM RUGER 10/22-T

Similar to 100/22 Target Stainless but with blued steel barrel and blued receiver.

NIB: $295 **Exc:** $245 **VGood:** $180

STRUM RUGER 10-22 TAKEDOWN

Semi-auto in .22 LR with synthetic stock, alloy steel, fixed front sight with adjustable, folding rear sight, threaded muzzle with flash suppressor, 10-shot detachable magazine. overall length is 36.75 inches and the rifle weighs 4.67 pounds. This is a takedown rifle where the barrel and forearm separates from the action and stock. Comes with a nylon carry bag.

Perf: $380 **Exc:** $310 **VGood:** $270

STURM RUGER 10/22 MAGNUM AUTOLOADING CARBINE

Semi-automatic; 22 WMR, 9-shot rotary magazine; 18-1/2-inch barrel; weighs 6 lbs.; 37-1/4-inch overall length; Birch stock; Gold bead front, folding rear sights. All-steel receiver has integral Ruger scope bases for the included 1-inch rings. Introduced 1999. Discontinued.

Perf: $700 **Exc:** $595 **VGood:** $400

STURM RUGER MODEL 44 CARBINE

Semi-automatic; 44 Mag.; 4-shot tubular magazine; 18-1/2-inch barrel; magazine release button incorporated in 1967; uncheckered walnut pistol-grip carbine stock; barrel band; receiver tapped for scope mount; folding leaf rear sight, gold bead front. Introduced 1961; dropped 1985. Premium for 1961-1962 specimens marked "Deerstalker."

Exc: $600 **VGood:** $500 **Good:** $400

STURM RUGER MODEL 44 INTERNATIONAL

Same specs as Model 44 except full-length Mannlicher-type walnut stock; sling swivels. Dropped 1971.

Exc: $795 **VGood:** $625 **Good:** $395

STURM RUGER MODEL 44RS

Same specs as Model 44 except sling swivels; built-in peep sight.

Exc: $600 **VGood:** $500 **Good:** $400

STURM RUGER MODEL 44 SPORTER

Same specs as Model 44 except sling swivels; Monte Carlo sporter stock; grooved forearm; grip cap; flat buttplate. Dropped 1971.

Exc: $600 **VGood:** $500 **Good:** $400

STRUM RUGER 77/357

Bolt action in .357 Magnum. Will also fire .38 Special ammunition. 4-shot rotary magazine, 18.5 inch barrel, fixed front sight and adjustable folding rear sight. 6 pounds, 38 1/4 inches. Synthetic stock and stainless steel. Ships with medium height, 1 inch, stainless steel scope rings. Three position safety. Introduced in 2011.

Perf: $500 **Exc:** $410 **VGood:** $340

STURM RUGER MODEL 77R

Bolt-action; 22-250, 220 Swift, 243 Win., 7mm-08, 6.5 Rem. Mag., 280 Rem., 284 Win., 308

Win., 300 Win. Mag., 338 Win. Mag., 350 Rem. Mag., 25-06, 257 Roberts, 250-3000, 6mm Rem., 270 Win., 7x57mm, 7mm Rem. Mag., 30-06; 3-, 5-shot magazine, depending upon caliber; 22-inch tapered barrel; hinged floorplate; adjustable trigger; hand-checkered American walnut stock; pistol-grip cap; sling swivel studs; recoil pad; integral scope mount base; optional folding leaf adjustable rear sight, gold bead ramp front. Introduced in 1968; no longer in production. Replaced by the Model M77 Mark II.

Perf: $420 **Exc:** $350 **VGood:** $320

350 Rem. Mag. caliber

Perf: $470 **Exc:** $390 **VGood:** $360

STURM RUGER MODEL 77RL ULTRA LIGHT

Same specs as Model 77R except 243, 308, 270, 30-06, 257, 22-250, 250-3000; 20-inch light barrel; Sturm Ruger 1-inch scope rings. Introduced 1983.

Perf: $420 **Exc:** $350 **VGood:** $300

STURM RUGER MODEL 77RS

Same specs as Model 77R except magnum-size action; 257 Roberts, 25-06, 270 Win., 30-06, 7mm Rem. Mag., 300 Win. Mag., 338 Win. Mag.; 3-, 5-shot, depending upon caliber; 22-inch barrel (270, 30-06, 7x57, 280 Rem.); 24-inch barrel (all others).

Perf: $510 **Exc:** $450 **VGood:** $400

STURM RUGER MODEL 77RS TROPICAL

Same specs as Model 77RS except 458 Win. Mag.; 24-inch barrel; steel triggerguard, floorplate; weighs 8-3/4 lbs.; open sights; 1-inch scope rings. Introduced 1990; dropped 1991.

Perf: $550 **Exc:** $480 **VGood:** $400

STURM RUGER MODEL 77 ROUND TOP MAGNUM

Same specs as Model 77R except round top action; drilled, tapped for standard scope mounts, open sights; 25-06, 270 Win., 7mm Rem. Mag., 30-06, 300 Win. Mag., 338 Win. Mag. Introduced 1971; dropped 1985.

Perf: $390 **Exc:** $350 **VGood:** $300

STURM RUGER MODEL 77V VARMINT

Same specs as Model 77R except 22-250, 220 Swift, 243 Win., 25-06, 308; 24-inch heavy straight tapered barrel, 26-inch (220 Swift); drilled, tapped for target scope mounts or integral scope mount bases on receiver; checkered American walnut stock. Introduced 1970; dropped 1992. Replaced by Model 77V Mark II in 1992.

Perf: $430 **Exc:** $380 **VGood:** $340

STURM RUGER MODEL 77 RSI INTERNATIONAL

Same specs as Model 77R except 18-1/2-inch barrel; full-length Mannlicher-style stock; steel forend cap; loop-type sling swivels; open sights; Sturm Ruger steel scope rings; improved front sight; 22-250, 250-3000, 243, 308, 270, 30-06; weighs 7 lbs; 38-3/8-inch overall length. Introduced 1986.

Perf: $495 **Exc:** $410 **VGood:** $350

STURM RUGER MODEL 77 RLS ULTRA LIGHT CARBINE

Same specs as Model 77R except 18-1/2-inch barrel; Sturm Ruger scope mounting system; iron sights; hinged floorplate; 270, 30-06, 243, 308; 38-7/8-inch overall length; weighs 6 lbs. Introduced 1987; no longer in production.

Perf: $430 **Exc:** $370 **VGood:** $310

STURM RUGER MODEL 77R MARK II

Bolt-action; 223, 22-250, 243 Win., 25-06, 257 Roberts, 270 Roberts, 270 Win., 280 Rem., 6mm Rem., 6.5x55, 7x57, 30-06, 308 Win. Mag., 7mm Rem. Mag., 300 Win. Mag., 338 Win. Mag.; 4-shot magazine; 20-inch barrel; 39-1/2-inch overall length; weighs 6-1/2 lbs.; American walnut stock; no sights; Ruger integral scope mount base; marketed with 1-inch scope rings; new three-position wing safety; redesigned trigger; short action. Introduced 1989; still in production.

Perf: $590 **Exc:** $450 **VGood:** $340

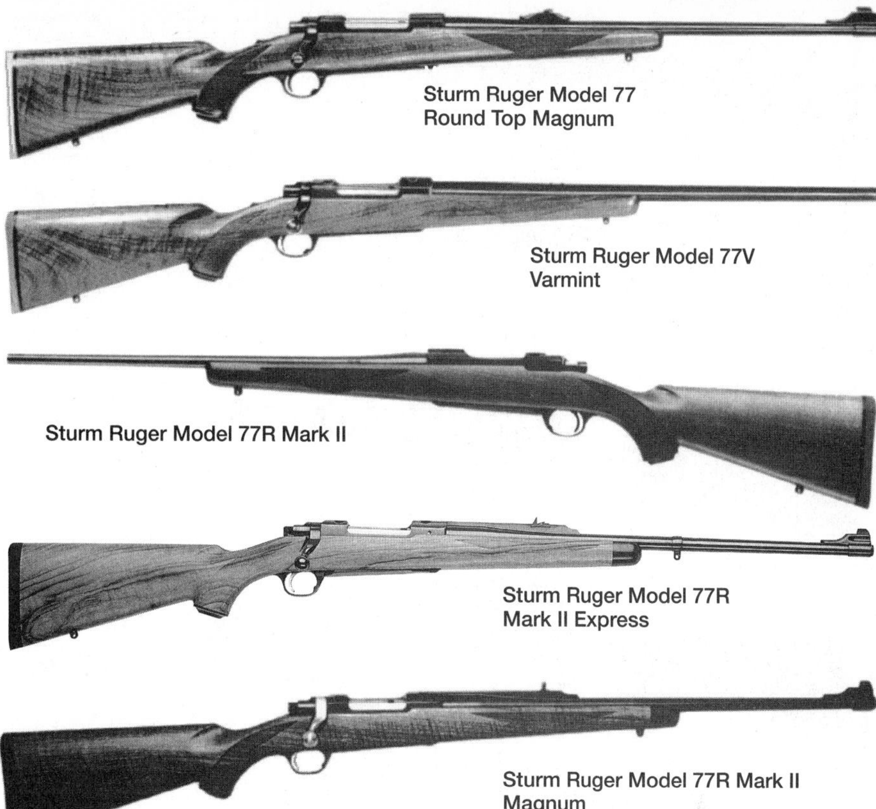

Sturm Ruger Model 77 Round Top Magnum

Sturm Ruger Model 77V Varmint

Sturm Ruger Model 77R Mark II

Sturm Ruger Model 77R Mark II Express

Sturm Ruger Model 77R Mark II Magnum

STURM RUGER MODEL 77R MARK II EXPRESS

Same specs as Model 77R Mark II except 270, 30-06, 7mm Rem. Mag., 300 Win. Mag., 338 Win. Mag., 375 H&H, 416 Rigby, 458 Lott; 4-shot magazine (3-shot for magnums); 22-inch barrel with integral sight rib; checkered French walnut stock; live-rubber recoil pad; steel grip cap; rear swivel stud, barrel-mounted front swivel stud; blade front sight, adjustable V-notch folding-leaf express rear sight with one standing leaf, one folding; three-position safety; Mauser-type extractor; controlled feeding. Introduced 1991.

Perf: $1250 **Exc:** $900 **VGood:** $650

STURM RUGER MODEL 77R MARK II MAGNUM

Same specs as Model 77R Mark II except 7/16-inch longer receiver with increased locking area and lengthened front; 375 H&H, 404 Jeffery, 416 Rigby, 458 Lott; 4-shot magazine (375, 404, 458), 3-shot (416) magazine; 22-inch barrel with integral sight rib; ramp front, three-leaf express sight; high-grade Circassian walnut stock with checkered grip and forend; black live-rubber recoil pad; steel floorplate and triggerguard. Introduced 1989, still in production.

Perf: $1495 **Exc:** $1100 **VGood:** $795

STURM RUGER MODEL 77 MARK II ALL-WEATHER STAINLESS

Same specs as Model 77R Mark II except all metal parts of stainless steel; fiberglass-reinforced Zytel stock; 223, 243, 270, 308, 30-06, 7mm Rem. Mag, 300 Win Mag, 338 Win Mag; fixed blade-type ejector; new triggerguard; patented floorplate latch; three-position safety; integral scope base, 1-inch Sturm Ruger scope rings; built-in swivel loops. Introduced 1990, still in production.

Perf: $595 **Exc:** $480 **VGood:** $400

STURM RUGER M77VT MARK II TARGET RIFLE

Bolt action; 22-250, 220 Swift, 223, 243, 25-06, 308; 26-inch heavy stainless steel barrel with target gray finish; weighs 9-3/4 lbs.; Approx. 44-inch overall length; Laminated American hardwood stock with beavertail forend, steel swivel studs; no checkering or gripcap; Integral scope mount bases in receiver. Ruger diagonal bedding system. Ruger steel 1-inch scope rings supplied. Fully adjustable trigger. Steel floorplate and trigger guard. New version introduced 1992.

Perf: $650 **Exc:** $500 **VGood:** $370

STURM RUGER M77 MKII FRONTIER RIFLE

Bolt-action rifle based on M77 MkII chassis but configured for scout-style scope mount system. Chambered in .243, .308, 7mm-08, .300 WSM, .325 WSM. Gray laminated stock, 16.5-inch blued or stainless barrel (add 15 percent for stainless). Introduced 2005; stainless model introduced 2006 (add 10 percent).

NIB: $585 **Exc:** $510 **VGood:** $425

STURM RUGER HM77R HAWKEYE

Slimmed-down version of the M77. American walnut stock, blued barrel, Mauser-style controlled feed extractor, soft red rubber recoil pad, stainless steel bolt, new LC6 trigger, engraved solid steel floorplate. Chambered in 7mm-08, 7mm Magnum, .308, .30-06, .300 Win Mag, .338 Win Mag. Left-hand version available.

NIB: $550 **Exc:** $765 **VGood:** $595

STURM RUGER HK77RFP HAWKEYE

All-weather version of the HM77R Hawkeye but with synthetic stock and stainless barrel. Same chamberings as HM77R but with .338 Federal and .358 Winchester as well.

NIB: $1000 **Exc:** $790 **VGood:** $620

Sturm Ruger HK77RFP Hawkeye

Sturm Ruger Hawkeye African

Sturm Ruger Model 77/22

Sturm Ruger Model 77/22RMP

Sturm Ruger Model 77/22RSP

Sturm Ruger Model 96/22

STURM RUGER HM77RSPHAB HAWKEYE ALASKAN

Similar to HK77RFP but with iron sights, Diamondblack finish and Hogue stock. Chambered in .375 Ruger. Add 5% for left-hand model.

NIB: $1075 **Exc:** $995 **VGood:** $850

STURM RUGER HKM77PRCM HAWKEYE COMPACT MAGNUM

Similar to Hawkeye but with 1/2-inch shorter synthetic stock and stainless steel barrel and receiver. Chambered for .300 and .338 RCM (Ruger Compact Magnum). Introduced 2008.

NIB: $1000 **Exc:** $790 **VGood:** $620

STURM RUGER HKM77RCM HAWKEYE COMPACT MAGNUM

Similar to above but with blued barrel and walnut stock. Introduced 2008.

NIB: $1000 **Exc:** $790 **VGood:** $620

STURM RUGER HM77RSPHAB HAWKEYE AFRICAN

Similar to HK77RFP but with checkered walnut stock and express-style sights. Chambered in .375 Ruger. Chambered in .375 Ruger. Introduced in 2007. A left-hand version was introduced in 2008. .416 Rem. added in 2013.

NIB: $1175 **Exc:** $825 **VGood:** $695

STURM RUGER MODEL 77/17

Bolt action; 17 HMR, 17 Mach 2; 9-shot detachable rotary magazine (17 HMR) or 10-shot (17 Mach 2); similar to earlier Model 77/22 rifles chambered for 22 WMR and 22 LR, but for the new 17 HMR and 17 Mach 2 cartridges; several variations; introduced 2002, still in production.

For 17 HMR versions, 22-inch barrel

Perf: $520 **Exc:** $410 **VGood:** $350

For 17 Mach 2 versions, 20-inch barrel

Perf: $620 **Exc:** $510 **VGood:** $450

STURM RUGER MODEL 77/22

Bolt action; 22 LR; 10-shot rotary magazine; 20-inch barrel; 39-3/4-inch overall length; weighs 5-3/4 lb.; checkered American walnut or nylon-reinforced Zytel stock; gold bead front sight, adjustable folding leaf rear; 1-inch Sturm Ruger rings optional; Mauser-type action; three-position safety simplified bolt stop; 10/22 dual screw barrel attachment system. Blued model introduced 1983; stainless steel and blued models with synthetic stock introduced 1989; still in production.

Perf: $480 **Exc:** $390 **VGood:** $290

With synthetic stock

Perf: $480 **Exc:** $390 **VGood:** $290

STURM RUGER MODEL 77/22 HORNET

Same specs as Model 77/22 except 22 Hornet; 6-shot rotary magazine; weighs about 6 lbs.; checkered American walnut stock; black rubber buttpad; brass bead front sight, open adjustable rear; slightly lengthened receiver; comes with 1-inch Sturm Ruger scope rings. Made in U.S. by Sturm Ruger & Co. Introduced 1994; still produced.

Perf: $490 **Exc:** $400 **VGood:** $370

STURM RUGER MODEL 77/22MP

Same specs as Model 77/22 except 22 WMR; stainless steel; synthetic stock. Introduced 1989.

Perf: $450 **Exc:** $390 **VGood:** $290

STURM RUGER MODEL 77/22RM

Same specs as Model 77/22 except 22 WMR.; blued metal; walnut stock. Introduced 1989; still produced.

Perf: $460 **Exc:** $400 **VGood:** $300

STURM RUGER MODEL 77/22RMP

Same specs as Ruger Model 77/22 RM except stainless finish; synthetic stock. Still in production.

Perf: $460 **Exc:** $400 **VGood:** $300

STURM RUGER MODEL 77/22RP

Same specs as Model 77/22 except synthetic stock; no iron sights; comes with scope rings. Made in U.S. by Sturm, Ruger & Co. Introduced 1989; still in production.

Perf: $445 **Exc:** $390 **VGood:** $260

STURM RUGER MODEL 77/22RS

Same specs as the Model 77/22 except blade front sight, fully-adjustable open rear; comes with scope rings. Made in U.S. by Sturm, Ruger & Co. Still produced.

Perf: $370 **Exc:** $250 **VGood:** $230

STURM RUGER MODEL 77/22RSH HORNET

Same as the 77/22 except 22 Hornet; blade front sight, fully-adjustable open rear adjustable. Made in U.S. by Sturm, Ruger & Co. Introduced 1994.

Perf: $420 **Exc:** $320 **VGood:** $290

STURM RUGER MODEL 77/22RSM

Same specs as the Model 77/22R except 22 WMR; blade front sight, fully-adjustable open rear; blue finish; checkered walnut stock. Made in U.S. by Sturm Ruger & Co. Still produced.

Perf: $400 **Exc:** $260 **VGood:** $230

STURM RUGER MODEL 77/22 RSMP

Same specs as Model 77/22 RSM except stainless finish; synthetic stock.

Perf: $390 **Exc:** $260 **VGood:** $230

STURM RUGER MODEL 77/22 RSP

Same specs as Model 77/22 except stainless finish; synthetic stock.

Perf: $390 **Exc:** $260 **VGood:** $230

STURM RUGER MODEL 77/22 VH

Same specs as Model 77/22 except 22 Hornet; laminated stock. Still in production.

Perf: $500 **Exc:** $425 **VGood:** $290

STURM RUGER MODEL 77/44 BOLT-ACTION RIFLE

Bolt action; 44 Magnum, 4-shot magazine; 18-1/2-inch barrel; seighs 6 lbs.; 38-1/4-inch overall length; American walnut stock with rubber butt pad and swivel studs, or black polymer (stainless only). Gold bead front, folding leaf rear sights; Comes with Ruger 1-inch scope rings. Uses same action as the Ruger 77/22. Short bolt stroke; rotary magazine; three-position safety. Introduced 1997.

Perf: $520 **Exc:** $440 **VGood:** $360

STURM RUGER MODEL 96/22

Lever action, short-throw lever; 22LR; 10-round rotary magazine; 18-1/2-inch barrel; weighs 5-1/4 lbs. 37-1/4-inch OAL; hardwood stock; gold bead front,folding leaf rear sights; cross-button safety; visible cocking indicator. Introduced 1996, still in production.

Perf: $320 **Exc:** $265 **VGood:** $210

STURM RUGER MODEL 96/17

Like Model 96/22, but chambered for 17 HRM cartridge, 9-round magazine. Introduced 2003, still in production.

Perf: $350 **Exc:** $275 **VGood:** $230

STURM RUGER MODEL 96/22M

Like Model 96/22, but chambered for 22 WMR cartridge, 9-round magazine.

Perf: $350 **Exc:** $275 **VGood:** $230

STURM RUGER MODEL 96/44M

Like Model 96/22, but chambered for 44 Mag. cartridge; 4-round magazine.

Perf: $500 **Exc:** $400 **VGood:** $315

STURM RUGER NO. 1B STANDARD SINGLE SHOT

Single-shot; 204 Ruger, 218 Bee, 22 Hornet, 22-250, 220 Swift, 243 Win., 223, 257 Roberts, 280, 6mm Rem., 25-06, 270 Win., 308, 30-06, 7mm Rem. Mag., 300 Win. Mag., 338 Mag., 270 Weatherby, 300 Weatherby; 26-inch barrel with quarter rib; American walnut, two-piece stock; hand-checkered pistol grip, forearm; open sights or integral scope mounts; hammerless falling-block design; automatic ejector; top-tang safety. Introduced 1967; still in production.

Perf: $670 **Exc:** $580 **VGood:** $385

STURM RUGER NO. 1A LIGHT SPORTER

Same specs as No. 1B except 22-inch barrel; Alex Henry-style forearm; iron sights; 204 Ruger, 243 Win., 270 Win., 30-06, 7x57mm. Introduced 1968; still in production. .222 Rem. added in 2013.

Perf: $665 **Exc:** $580 **VGood:** $385

STURM RUGER NO. 1S MEDIUM SPORTER

Same specs as No. 1A Light Sporter except 7mm Rem. Mag., 300 Win. Mag., 338 Win. Mag., 45-70; 26-inch barrel, 22-inch (45-70) barrel. Introduced 1968; still in production.

Perf: $770 **Exc:** $530 **VGood:** $420

STURM RUGER NO. 1H TROPICAL

Same specs as No. 1S Medium Sporter except 375 H&H Mag., 405 Win., 416 Rigby, 458 Win. Mag., 458 Lott; 24-inch heavy barrel; open sights. Introduced 1968; still in production.

Perf: $790 **Exc:** $630 **VGood:** $470

STURM RUGER NO. 1 RSI INTERNATIONAL

Same specs as No. 1B, except full-length Mannlicher-style stock of American walnut, 20-inch barrel; 243, 30-06, 7x57, 270. Introduced 1983; still in production.

Perf: $780 **Exc:** $580 **VGood:** $410

STURM RUGER NO. 1V SPECIAL VARMINTER

Same specs as No. 1B except 24-inch heavy barrel; 22-250, 220 Swift, 223, 25-06, 6mm; supplied with target scope bases. Introduced 1970; still in production. 6.5-284 added in 2013.

Perf: $760 **Exc:** $620 **VGood:** $475

Sturm Ruger Model 96/44

Sturm Ruger No. 1B

Sturm Ruger No. 1A Light Sporter

Sturm Ruger No. 1S Medium Sporter

Sturm Ruger No. 1H Tropical

Sturm Ruger No. 1 RSI International

Sturm Ruger No. 1 Light Standard 1-AB

Sturm Ruger No. 3

Sturm Ruger PC9 Carbine

RUGER NO. 1 LIGHT STANDARD 1-AB

Similar to Light Sporter 1-A but with 22-inch sightless blued barrel. Chambered in .204 Ruger only; introduced 2006.

NIB: $725 **Exc:** $665 **VGood:** $525

STURM RUGER NO. 3

Single-shot; 22 Hornet, 223, 30-40 Krag, 375 Win., 44 Mag., 45-70; 22-inch barrel; same action as Sturm Ruger No. 1, except for different lever; uncheckered American walnut, two-piece carbine-type stock; folding leaf rear sight, gold bead front; adjustable trigger; barrel band on forearm; automatic ejector. Introduced 1969; 30-40 chambering dropped 1978; model discontinued 1986. Premium for 30-40.

Perf: $650 **Exc:** $595 **VGood:** $475

223, 44 Mag. calibers

Perf: $615 **Exc:** $560 **VGood:** $440

STURM RUGER PC4 CARBINE

Semi-automatic; 40 S&W cal., 10-shot magazine; 16.25-inch barrel; weighs 6 lbs., 4 oz.; 34.75-inch overall length; Black high impact synthetic stock with checkered grip and forend; blade front, open

Strum Ruger SR22

Strum Ruger SR556

Swiss K-31 Target Model

Tanner 300-Meter Free Rifle

Taurus Model 62

Taurus CT G2 Carbine

adjustable rear sights or ghost ring peep sights; integral Ruger scope mounts; delayed blowback action; manual push-button cross bolt safety and internal firing pin block safety automatic slide lock. Introduced 1997. Discontinued.

Perf: $550 **Exc:** $475 **VGood:** $400

STURM RUGER PC9 CARBINE

Like PC4 Carbine, but chambered for 9mm cartridge, 10- or 15-shot magazine. Introduced 1997. Discontinued.

Perf: $550 **Exc:** $475 **VGood:** $400

STURM RUGER SR 22

Semi-auto in .22 LR. This rifle is built around the Ruger 10-22 action with accessories to make it resemble an AR 15 style rifle. 6.9 pounds with 33 to 36 inch over all length, dependant on position of adjustable stock. Flash suppressor, flip-up adjustable sights, ventilated hand guard and flat top upper receiver. Compliant models available. Introduced in 2009.

Perf: $575 **Exc:** $450 **VGood:** $390

STURM RUGER SR 556

Semi-auto (AR15) in .223 Rem. / .556 NATO. Two stage gas piston upper on MIL SPEC lower. Standard and Carbine version have a 16 inch barrel, Varmint version (introduced in 2013) has a 20 inch barrel. Standard and Carbine versions have flip-up adjustable sights mounted on a full length upper rail. Varmint version has no sights. All versions but the Varmint model have adjustable stocks. The Varmint version has an A2 style stock. The E-Model is a less expensive version of this model and all versions are available with fixed stocks in a compliant variation. Original Standard model introduced 2009.

Standard, Carbine and Varmint Target Model

Perf: $1750 **Exc:** $1500 **VGood:** $1320

E-Model

Perf: $1300 **Exc:** $1200 **VGood:** $1000

SURVIVAL ARMS AR-7 EXPLORER

Semi-automatic; 22 LR; 8-shot magazine; 16-inch barrel; 34-1/2-inch overall length with barrel mounted, 16-1/2-inch stowed; weighs 2-1/2 lbs.; square blade front sight, aperture elevation-adjustable rear; moulded Cycolac stock with snap-on buttcap; takedown design stores barrel and action in hollow stock; black, silvertone or camouflage finish. Light enough to float. Survival Arms took over manufacture of the AR-7 from Charter Arms. Reintroduced 1992; discontinued 1995.

Perf: $130 **Exc:** $115 **VGood:** $90

SURVIVAL ARMS AR-7 SPORTER

Same specs as AR-7 Explorer except 25-shot magazine; black finish with telescoping stock. Made in U.S. by Survival Arms, Inc. Introduced 1992; discontinued 1995.

Perf: $180 **Exc:** $150 **VGood:** $125

SURVIVAL ARMS AR-7 WILDCAT

Same specs as AR-7 Explorer except black finish and wood stock. Made in U.S. by Survival Arms, Inc. Introduced 1992; discontinued 1995.

Perf: $165 **Exc:** $130 **VGood:** $110

SWISS K-31 TARGET MODEL

Bolt action; 308; 6-shot magazine; 26-inch barrel; 44-inch overall length; straight pull; protected blade front sight, ladder-type adjustable rear; European walnut stock; sling, muzzle cap; based on straight-pull Schmidt-Rubin design. Made in Switzerland. Introduced 1982; no longer in production.

Perf: $395 **Exc:** $350 **VGood:** $300

TANNER 50-METER FREE RIFLE

Bolt action; single shot; 22 LR; 27-2/3-inch barrel; 43-2/5-inch overall length; weighs 14 lbs.; micrometer-diopter rear sight, globe front with interchangeable inserts; nutwood stock with palm rest; accessory rail; adjustable hook buttplate; adjustable set trigger. Made in Switzerland. Introduced 1984; dropped 1988.

Perf: $2995 **Exc:** $2495 **VGood:** $1895

TANNER 300-METER FREE RIFLE

Bolt action; single shot; 308, 7.5 Swiss; 28-5/8-inch barrel; 45-5/16-inch overall length; weighs 15 lbs.; Tanner micrometer-diopter rear sight, globe front with interchangeable inserts; walnut stock; accessory rail; palm rest; adjustable hook buttplate; three-lug revolving bolt design; adjustable set trigger. Made in Switzerland. Introduced 1984; discontinued 1988.

Perf: $4750 **Exc:** $3700 **VGood:** $2800

TANNER 300-METER UIT STANDARD FREE RIFLE

Same specs as 300-Meter Free Rifle except repeater with 10-shot magazine; 24-13/16-inch barrel; 40-5/8-inch overall length; weighs 10-1/2 lbs.; no palm rest; no adjustable buttplate. Made in Switzerland. Introduced 1984; discontinued 1988.

Perf: $4800 **Exc:** $3900 **VGood:** $3000

TAURUS CT G2 CARBINE

Chambered for 40 S&W, 9 mm or 45 ACP, capacity is 34+1 for 9mm, 15+1 for 40 S&W and 10+1 for 45. Barrel length is 16 inches, weight from 8.4 to 9.2 pounds. Overall length is 35.7 inches. Composite stock of aluminum and polymer. Full-length Picatinny rail.

Perf: $575 **Exc:** $500 **VGood:** $435

TAURUS MODEL 62 PUMP RIFLE

Slide action; 22 LR, 17 Mach 2; 12- or 13-shot magazine; 16-1/2-inch or 23-inch round barrel; weighs 5.9 lbs.; 39-inch overall length; premium hardwood stock; adjustable rear sight, bead blade front, optional tang sight; blue, case-hardened or stainless finishes; bolt-mounted safety, pump action, manual firing pin block, integral security lock system. Imported from Brazil by Taurus International, still available.

Perf: $250 **Exc:** $200 **VGood:** $150

TAURUS MODEL 62LAR LEVER RIFLE

Lever-action rifle based on Model 62 pump action and chambered in .22 LR. 23-inch blued barrel, walnut-finish hardwood stock. Introduced 2006. Add 10 percent for stainless steel.

NIB: $265 **Exc:** $225 **VGood:** $175

TAURUS MODEL 72 PUMP RIFLE

Same as Model 62 except chambered in 22 WMR, 17 HMR; 16-1/2-inch bbl. holds 10 shots, 23-inch bbl. holds 11 shots. Weighs 108.8 oz. Introduced 2001, still in production. Imported from Brazil by Taurus International, still available.

Perf: $260 **Exc:** $210 **VGood:** $160

TAURUS THUNDERBOLT

Clone of old Colt Lightning Magazine Rifle. Chambered in .45 Colt and .38/.357 with 14-round tubular magazine. Blued finish with hardwood buttstock and forend. Add 15 percent for stainless steel.

NIB: $550 **Exc:** $450 **VGood:** $365

TAURUS MODEL 63 SEMI-AUTOMATIC RIFLE

Semi-automatic; 22 LR; 10-shot tube magazine in buttstock; 23-inch round barrel; blued metal; walnut-finished hardwood stock and forearm; Based on the Winshester Model 63 rifle. Introduced 2002, still in production.

Perf: $270 **Exc:** $220 **VGood:** $170

THOMPSON/CENTER CONTENDER CARBINE

Single shot, breakopen; 17 HMR, 17 Mach 2, 204 Ruger, 22 LR, 22 Hornet, 223 Rem., 6.8 Rem., 7mm TCU, 7-30 Waters, 30-30, 357 Rem. Max., 35 Rem., 375 JDJ, 44 Mag., 410; 21-inch barrel; 35-inch overall length; weighs 5-1/8 lbs.; open adjustable rear sight, blade front; drilled, tapped for scope mounts; checkered American walnut stock; rubber buttpad; built on T/C Contender action; interchangeable barrels. Introduced 1985; still in production with new G2 frame.

Perf: $400 **Exc:** $325 **VGood:** $270

THOMPSON/CENTER CONTENDER CARBINE RYNITE

Same specs as Contender Carbine except Rynite stock, forend. Introduced 1990; discontinued 1993.

Perf: $390 **Exc:** $280 **VGood:** $230

THOMPSON/CENTER CONTENDER CARBINE STAINLESS

Same specs as Contender Carbine except stainless steel with blued sights; walnut or Rynite stock, forend. Made in U.S. by Thompson/Center. Introduced 1993; no longer produced.

Perf: $420 **Exc:** $330 **VGood:** $280

THOMPSON/CENTER CONTENDER CARBINE SURVIVAL SYSTEM

Same specs as Contender Carbine except Rynite stock; two 16-1/4-inch barrels, 223 Rem., 45 Colt/410. Marketed in Cordura nylon case. Introduced 1991; no longer in production.

Perf: $470 **Exc:** $410 **VGood:** $340

THOMPSON/CENTER CONTENDER CARBINE YOUTH MODEL

Same specs as Contender Carbine except 22 LR, 22 WMR, 223, 7-30 Waters, 30-30, 35 Rem., 44 Mag.; 16-1/4-inch barrel; 29-inch overall length; fully-adjustable open sights; shorter buttstock; also available with rifled vent rib barrel chambered for 45/410. Introduced 1987.

Perf: $350 **Exc:** $300 **VGood:** $250

THOMPSON/CENTER CUSTOM SHOP TCR '87

Single shot, breakopen; 22 Hornet, 222 Rem., 22-250, 243 Win., 270, 308, 7mm-08, 30-06, 32-40 Win., 12-ga. slug, 10-ga. and 12-ga. field barrels; 23-inch (standard), 25-7/8-inch (heavy) barrel; 39-1/2-inch overall length; weighs about 6-3/4 lbs.; break-open; no sights; checkered American black walnut stock, forend; interchangeable barrels; single-stage trigger; cross-bolt safety. Made in U.S. by T/C. Available only through the T/C custom shop. Introduced 1987; no longer offered. Values shown are for complete rifle.

Perf: $800 **Exc:** $600 **VGood:** $375

THOMPSON/CENTER ENCORE

Single shot, breakopen; 204 Ruger, 22 Hornet, 22-250, 223, 243, 260, 25-06, 270, 7mm-08, 280, 308, 30-06, 7mm Rem. Mag., 300 Win. Mag., 405 Win., 45-70; 24-inch, 26-inch barrel; weighs 6 lbs., 12 oz. (24-inch barrel); 38-1/2-inch overall length (24-inch barrel); American walnut stock, Monte Carlo style, with schnabel forend, or black composite stock; Ramp-style white bead front, fully adjustable leaf-type rear sights; Interchangeable barrels; action opens by squeezing trigger guard; drilled and tapped for T/C scope mounts; polished blue finish. Introduced 1996, still in production.

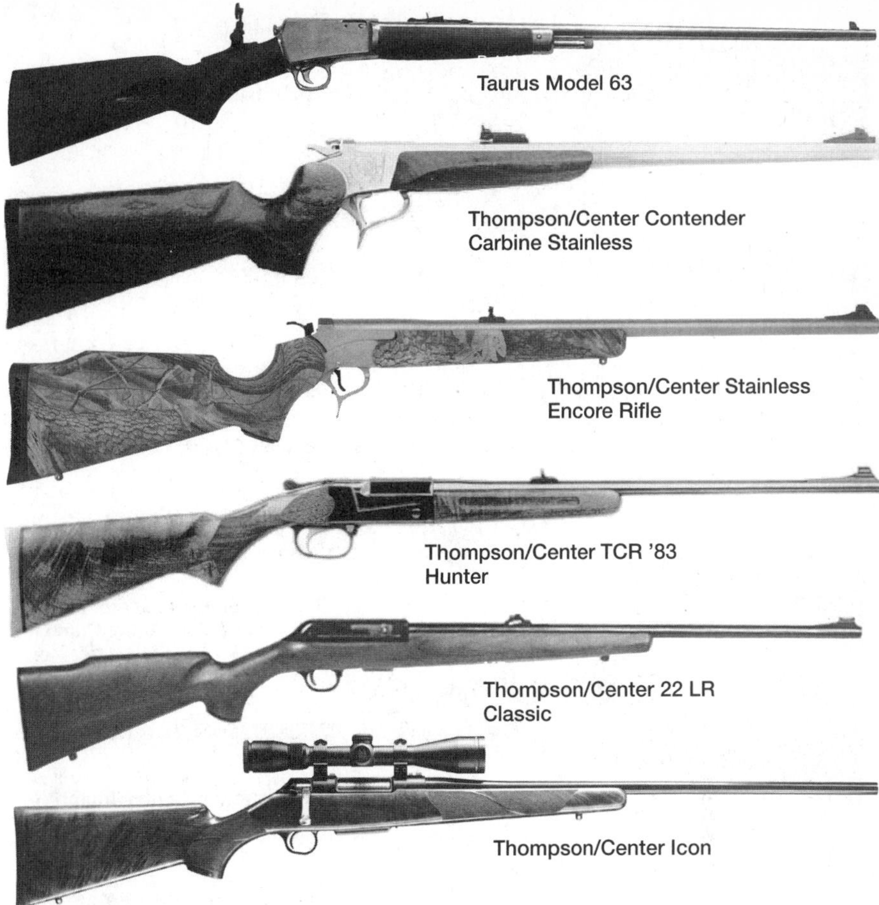

Taurus Model 63

Thompson/Center Contender Carbine Stainless

Thompson/Center Stainless Encore Rifle

Thompson/Center TCR '83 Hunter

Thompson/Center 22 LR Classic

Thompson/Center Icon

Perf: $570 **Exc:** $450 **VGood:** $410

With black composite stock and forend

Perf: $530 **Exc:** $400 **VGood:** $350

THOMPSON/CENTER STAINLESS ENCORE RIFLE

Similar to blued Encore except stainless steel with blued sights, black composite stock and forend or camp composite stock and forend. Available in 22-250, 223, 7mm-08, 30-06, 308. Introduced 1999, still available. Made in U.S.A. by Thompson/Center Arms.

Perf: $590 **Exc:** $470 **VGood:** $420

THOMPSON/CENTER TCR '83 HUNTER

Single shot, breakopen, hammerless; 223, 22-250, 243 Win., 7mm Rem. Mag., 30-06; 23-inch barrel; 39-1/2-inch overall length; weighs 6-7/8 lbs.; blade on ramp front sight, windage-adjustable open rear; American black walnut stock; cut-checkering on pistol-grip, forend; interchangeable barrels; cross-bolt safety; single-stage or double-set trigger. Introduced 1983; discontinued 1986.

Perf: $580 **Exc:** $525 **VGood:** $450

THOMPSON/CENTER TCR '87 HUNTER

Single shot, breakopen, hammerless; 22 Hornet, 222 Rem., 223 Rem., 22-250, 243 Win., 270, 308, 7mm-08, 30-06, 32-40 Win., 375 H&H, 416 Rem. Mag.; 12-gauge slug; 23-inch (standard), 25 7/8-inch heavy barrel; no sights; checkered American black walnut stock; interchangeable barrels; single-stage trigger; cross-bolt safety. Introduced 1987; discontinued 1992.

Perf: $600 **Exc:** $550 **VGood:** $475

THOMPSON/CENTER 22 CLASSIC

Semi-automatic; 22 LR, 8-shot magazine; 22-inch match-grade barrel; weighs 5-1/2 pounds; 39-1/2-inch overall length; Satin-finished American walnut stock with Monte Carlo-type comb and pistol grip cap, swivel studs; Ramp-style front sight and fully adjustable rear, both with fiber optics; All-steel receiver drilled and tapped for scope mounting; barrel threaded to receiver; thumb-operated safety. Introduced 2000, still offered.

Perf: $290 **Exc:** $220 **VGood:** $180

THOMPSON/CENTER 22 BENCHMARK

Similar to 22 Classic, but has 18-inch heavy target barrel, laminated stock; no sights, drilled and tapped for scope base; weighs 6.8 pounds; 10-round detachable magazine. Introduced in 2003, still produced.

Perf: $430 **Exc:** $360 **VGood:** $300

THOMPSON/CENTER SILVER LYNX

Similar to 22 Classic, but stainless steel, with 20-inch match-grade barrel, black composite stock; adjustable open sights; trap in buttplate holds extra 5- or 10-shot magazine. Introduced in 2004, still produced.

Perf: $385 **Exc:** $260 **VGood:** $220

THOMPSON/CENTER ICON

Bolt-action centerfire rifle chambered in .22-250, .243, .308 and .30 Thompson-Center. Premium checkered walnut stock. Barrel length 22" (iron sight) or 24" (sightless). Detachable box magazine.

NIB: $695 **Exc:** $550 **VGood:** $400

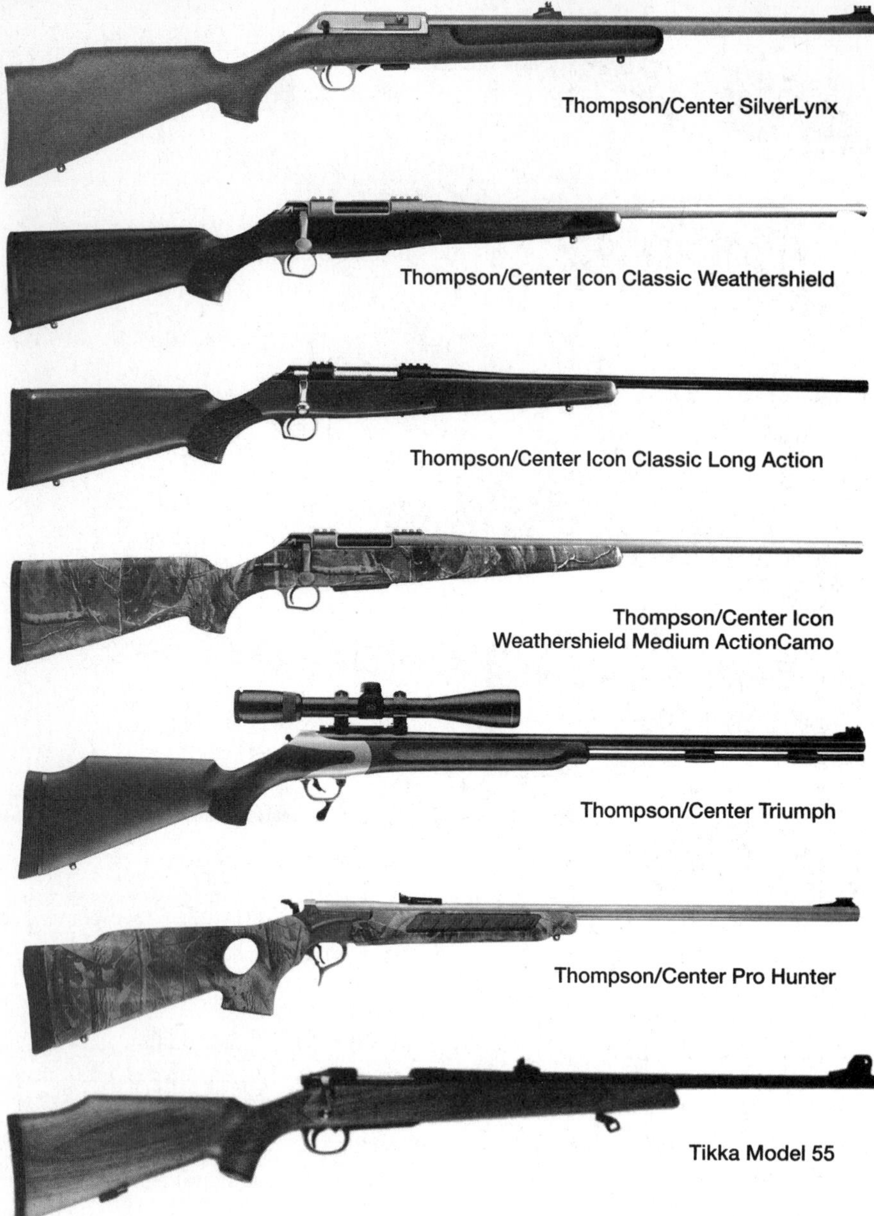
Thompson/Center SilverLynx

Thompson/Center Icon Classic Weathershield

Thompson/Center Icon Classic Long Action

Thompson/Center Icon Weathershield Medium ActionCamo

Thompson/Center Triumph

Thompson/Center Pro Hunter

Tikka Model 55

THOMPSON/CENTER ICON CLASSIC LONG ACTION
Similar to Icon but with long-action design and chambered for .270, .30-06, .300 Winchester Magnum and 7mm Remington Magnum.

NIB: $750 **Exc:** 650 **VGood:** 475

THOMPSON/CENTER ICON WEATHERSHIELD MEDIUM ACTION
Similar to Icon but with stainless steel barrel and receiver and black synthetic or RealTree AP Camo stock. Add 5% for camo.

NIB: $750 **Exc:** 650 **VGood:** 475

THOMPSON/CENTER TRIUMPH
Fifty-caliber toggle-breech inline muzzleloader with only four moving parts. Blued/synthetic, Weathershield/synthetic, or Weathershield/stainless finish.

NIB: $395 **Exc:** $335 **VGood:** $250

THOMPSON/CENTER PRO HUNTER
Similar to Encore rifle but with plain or fluted barrel and various finish and stock options. Barrels interchange with standard Encore barrels. Muzzleloading and pistol versions available. Introduced 2007.

NIB: $775 **Exc:** $695 **VGood:** $550

TIKKA MODEL 07
Over/under combination gun; 222, 5.6x52R, 5.6x50R Mag., beneath 12-ga. barrel; 22-3/4-inch barrels; bead front sight, open windage-adjustable rear; Monte Carlo stock of European walnut; palm swell with pistol grip; exposed hammer, sling swivels; vent rib, rosewood pistol-grip cap. Introduced 1979; discontinued 1982.

Exc: $595 **VGood:** $495 **Good:** $395

TIKKA MODEL 55
Bolt action; 17 Rem., 222, 22-250, 6mm Rem., 243, 308; 3-shot detachable magazine; 23-inch barrel; bead ramped front sight, fully-adjustable rear; drilled, tapped for scope mounts; hand-checkered Monte Carlo stock of European walnut; palm swell on pistol grip. Introduced 1979; discontinued 1981.

Exc: $370 **VGood:** $300 **Good:** $250

TIKKA MODEL 55 DELUXE
Same specs as Model 55 except roll-over cheekpiece; forend tip; grip cap of rosewood. Introduced 1979; discontinued 1981.

Exc: $430 **VGood:** $370 **Good:** $300

TIKKA MODEL 55 SPORTER
Same specs as Model 55 except 222, 22-250, 243, 308; 5-, 10-shot magazine; 23-inch heavy barrel; no sights; varmint-type stock; oil-finish. Introduced 1979; discontinued 1981.

Exc: $390 **VGood:** $330 **Good:** $260

TIKKA MODEL 65
Bolt action; 25-06, 6.5x55, 7x57, 7x64, 270, 308, 30-06, 7mm Rem. Mag., 300 Win. Mag.; 5-shot magazine; 22-inch barrel; bead ramped front sight, fully-adjustable rear; drilled, tapped for scope mounts; hand-checkered Monte Carlo stock of European walnut; palm swell on pistol grip; adjustable trigger. Introduced 1979; discontinued 1981.

Exc: $420 **VGood:** $370 **Good:** $300

TIKKA MODEL 65 DELUXE
Same specs as Model 65 except roll-over cheekpiece; forend tip; rosewood grip cap. Introduced 1979; discontinued 1981.

Exc: $430 **VGood:** $370 **Good:** $300

TIKKA MODEL 65 TARGET
Same specs as Model 65 except 25-06, 6.5x55, 270, 308, 30-06; 22-inch heavy barrel; no sights; target-type walnut stock; stock designed to meet ISU requirements, with stippled forend, palm swell. Introduced 1969; discontinued 1981.

Exc: $500 **VGood:** $430 **Good:** $360

TIKKA MODEL 77K
Combo; over/under; 222, 5.6x52R, 6.5x55, 7x57R, 7x65R, 308 beneath 12-ga. barrel; 22-3/4-inch barrel; hammerless; bead front sight, open windage-adjustable rear; Monte Carlo stock of European walnut; palm swell with pistol-grip; sling swivels; ventilated rib; rosewood pistol-grip cap. Introduced 1979; discontinued 1982.

Exc: $795 **VGood:** $625 **Good:** $475

TIKKA MODEL 412S DOUBLE RIFLE
Double rifle; 9.3x74R; 24-inch barrel; weighs 8-5/8 lbs.; ramp front sight, adjustable open rear; American walnut stock with Monte Carlo-style comb; barrel selector mounted in trigger; cocking indicators in tang; recoil pad; ejectors. Imported from Italy by Stoeger. Introduced 1980; no longer imported.

Perf: $1700 **Exc:** $1400 **VGood:** $1050

TIKKA MODEL 512S COMBINATION GUN
Combination gun, over/under; replaced Model 412S; 12 gauge over 222, 308; 24-inch barrels, shotgun barrel choked Imp. Mod.; weighs 7-5/8 lbs.; blade front sight, flip-up-type open rear; American walnut stock with recoil pad, Monte Carlo comb; barrel selector on trigger; hand-checkered stock and forend; barrels are screw-adjustable to change point of bullet impact; interchangeable barrels. Imported from Italy by Stoeger. Introduced 1980, no longer imported.

Perf: $1100 **Exc:** $920 **VGood:** $710

TIKKA MODEL 512S DOUBLE RIFLE
Double rifle; 9.3x74R; 24-inch barrel; weighs 8-5/8 lbs.; ramp front sight, adjustable open rear; American walnut stock with Monte Carlo-style comb; barrel selector mounted in trigger; cocking indicators in tang; recoil pad; ejectors. Imported from Italy by Stoeger. Introduced 1980; no longer imported.

Perf: $1700 **Exc:** $1400 **VGood:** $1050

TIKKA PREMIUM GRADE
Bolt action; 22-250, 223, 243, 270, 30-06, 7mm Rem. Mag., 300 Win. Mag., 338 Win. Mag.; 3-, 5-shot magazine; 22-inch (standard), 24-inch (magnum) barrel; 43-inch overall length; weighs 7-1/4 lbs.; no sights; Monte Carlo select walnut stock with roll-over cheekpiece; rosewood grip, forend caps; hand-checkered grip, forend; polished, blued barrel. Made in Finland. Introduced 1990; no longer in production.

Exc: $680 **VGood:** $520 **Good:** $400

Today's GUNS for Tomorrow's COLLECTOR

COLT NEW AGENT

The Colt New Agent is a compact, big-bore semi-auto designed for deep—and we do mean deep—concealment. Despite being chambered in a sledgehammer of a cartridge (.45 ACP), it has a teensy little three-inch, bushing-less barrel. You can yank it from your pants quick-like, due to its smooth top slide and trench-style sights.

Modern Gun Values has traditionally split its coverage between guns having more recently come on the market and those that, in some cases, are now more than 100 years old! While this book addresses a wide variety of interests—everything from home-defense and waterfowling guns to those for elk, squirrels, and long-range target competition—it's the collector who tends to gain the most from such a comprehensive reference. But think about this: Today's collectibles were once "modern," "hip," and "gotta have 'ems." That means today's modern, hip, and gotta have 'em firearms are tomorrow's treasures! To that end, we thought we'd highlight just a few of the hundreds of new firearms introduced each year by the likes of Colt's, Browning, SIG, and others leading the way in cutting-edge technology and design. Enjoy, then do a little shopping—50 years from now, we think you'll be glad you did.

BERETTA 92FS/90-TWO

It took quite a gun to displace the venerable Colt 1911A1 Government as the military's primary sidearm. But the 9mm Beretta 92FS (above) did just that, unseating the single-action .45 ACP, in 1985. The slightly modified version, the Model 90-Two, saw improved fit, function, and form over the original, including a subtle restyling effort, weight reduction, interchangeable wrap-around grips, and a MIL-STD-1913 accessory rail and rail cover..

TAURUS PT-22 PLY

Long a favorite of concealed carry practitioners, the tip-up barrel PT-22 from Taurus got a makeover with a polymer frame and fish-scale texturized slide in the PT-22 PLY model. The DAO gun, with is also available in the .25 ACP PT-25 PLY variant, holds eight rounds in the magazine, which has a nicely angled floor plate for more finger purchase on the grip.

SIG SAUER MOSQUITO

The hot pink Mosquito from SIG Sauer is chambered in .22 LR and scaled to fit smaller hands. While the screaming fuchsia variant is certainly marketed toward the fairer gender, it's an excellent choice for getting both women and young adults started in the shooting sports (and, if you can't dig the pink, then the Multi-Cam version covers the other end of the aesthetic spectrum). SIG Sauer's Mosquito is a 90-percent scale version of the original, full-size 9mm P226. Standard equipment includes the integrated rail on the frame's underside for accessory mounting, as well as multiple safety features.

NORTH AMERICAN ARMS 1860 HOGLEG

The North American Arms 1860 Hogleg is a five-shot, single-action, mini-revolver chambered in .22 Magnum. The pistol features a half-way notch cylinder that allows the hammer to rest on a loaded chamber without fear of accidental discharge. It has a fixed bead front sight and rosewood grips.

RUGER BEARCAT

The Ruger Bearcat is a single-action .22 LR revolver with a one-piece, six-shot cylinder frame. Compact and light, it was designed to be an easy to carry trail gun for general use in the outdoors—think snakes and other small, generally disagreeable creatures you might come across as you wander the the fields and mountains. It comes in a blued or satin stainless finish.

SMITH & WESSON CLASSIC MODEL 586

The Smith & Wesson Classic Model 586 is a retro-styled revolver modeled after the old school Model 586, a handgun favored by decades of law enforcement officers. Chambered for .357 Magnum and, of course, its shorter .38 Special brother, the double-action revolver has a carbon steel frame and cylinder with a blue finish. It is available with 4- or 6-inch barrels.

ROSSI MODEL R46202

Did you know Rossi's been making firearms for more than a century? Revolvers like the forged steel Model R46202 are as strong as any other on the market, yet usually are priced significantly lower than comparable guns from other makers. This particular model is chambered in .357 Magnum and, with its low-profile front sight and short barrel, it makes an excellent carry gun. Especially beneficial is the shape of the forward-push cylinder release tab, which is angled on the backside and serrated to easily engage the thumb.

Today's GUNS for Tomorrow's COLLE

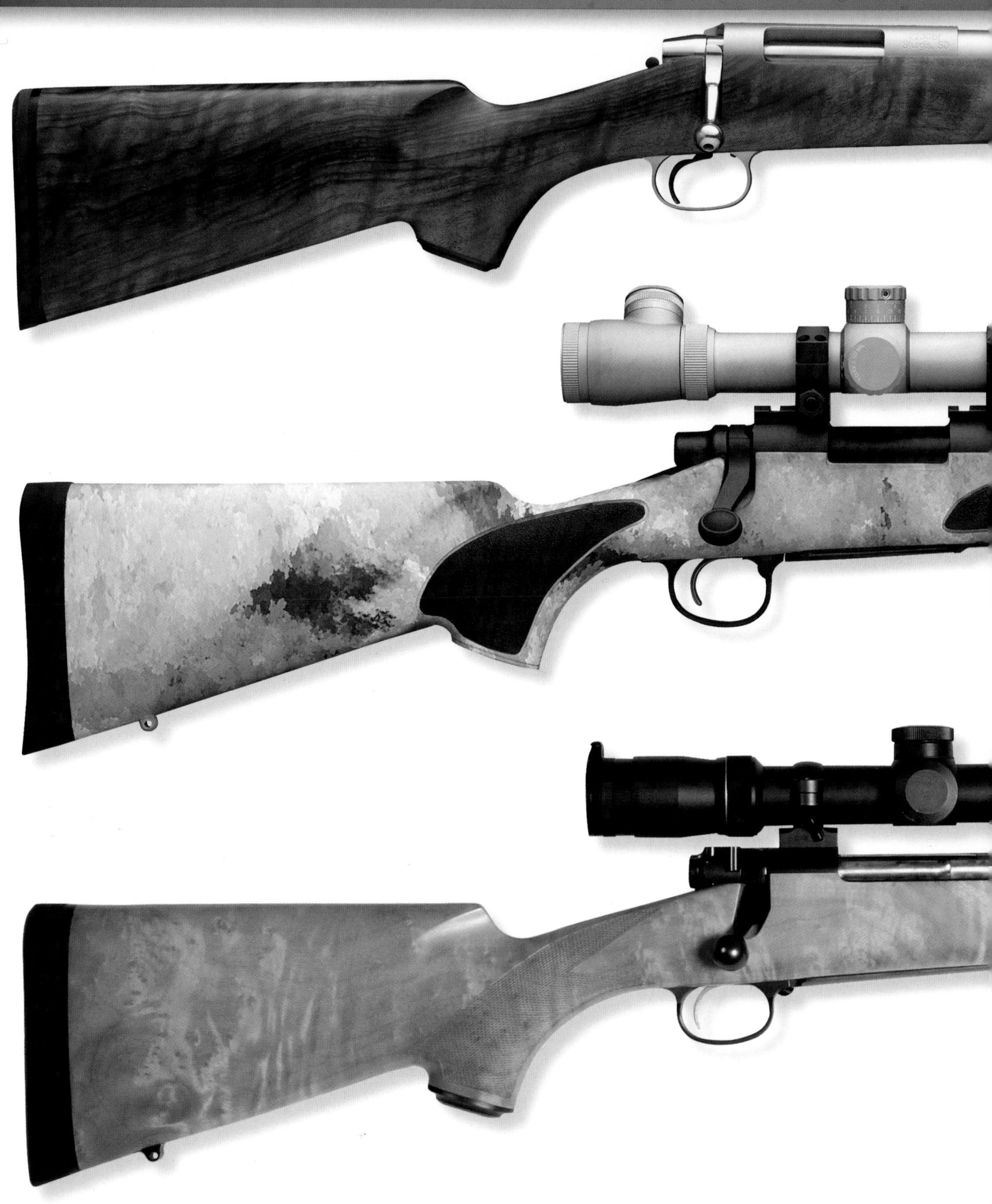

DAKOTA ARMS HEAVY VARMINTER

Most of today's prairie dog and coyotes guns you wouldn't call pretty. But Dakota Arms' Heavy Varminter in a Claro walnut stock gets high marks for good looks that are exceeded only by its accuracy.

REMINGTON 700 VTR A-TACS

True or false: barrels are round. Answer? False, at least if it's the barrel on Remington's VTR (Varmint-Tactical Rifle) A-TACS. Here the barrel is triangular, a design that speeds heat dissipation. The A-TACs is a digitized camo that performs with a chameleon effect, perfect for aiding concealment from sharp-eyed varmints like coyotes.

MONTANA RIFLE COMPANY SAFARI SUPREME

For the plains of Africa, the highly figured AAA Myrtle wood stock on the Montana Safari Supreme bolt-action rifle will do anything but give you away to sharp-eyed game.

MAGNUM RESEARCH MAGNUMLITE

Magnum Research's MagnumLite .22 LR rifle is definitely a head-turner. And, as if looks weren't enough, this rifle has a graphite barrel—that's right, graphite—with claims of super accuracy and faster cooling over steel barrels.

THOMPSON/CENTER VENTURE

The elements won't give you a slippery grip, when you're using one of Thompson/Center's Venture bolt-action rifles. Available in a wide variety of readily available cartridges, these synthetic-stocked rifles feature raised traction panels at the pistol grip and forearm, to make sure you've got a steady hold when you need it most.

TIKKA T3 HUNTER

Tikka's T3 Hunter is simply beautiful, with a high-gloss blued barrel, burled wood, and ergonomic checkering at the hand points. It also has a free-floating, match-grade barrel and an adjustable trigger, to make every shot count.

BROWNING CITORI TRAP LEFT-HAND

Browning's Citori XT Trap 12-gauge comes with 30- or 32-inch tubes, HIVIZ ProComp fiber optics, and stretched forcing cones. Now, left-handed shooters have a version cast just for them. Straight runs of 25 are nothing but a walk in the park.

REMINGTON 1187 SURESHOT CANTILEVER

Love slugs for deer hunting? Remington's 11-87 Sportsman Shurshot Camo Cantilever is prime for mounting a low-powered scope, and the thumbhole stock ensures a dead-on hold when the big one walks up.

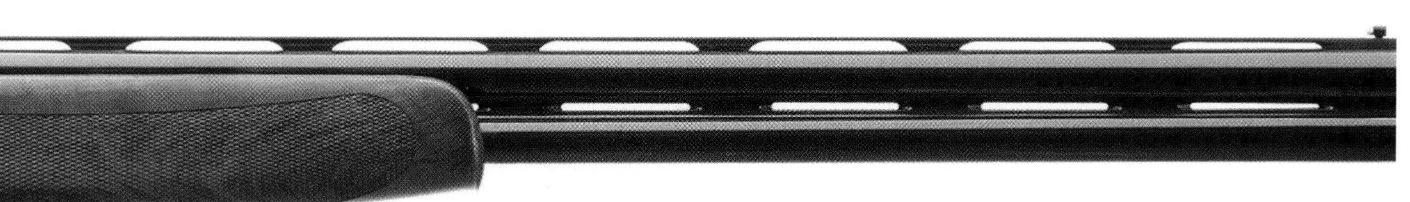

BENELLI VELOCE

The Veloce SP 20-gauge over/under from Benelli is a classy, gorgeous example of its Italian heritage and, at just 5½ pounds, is a beautifully swinging choice for quail, woodcock, and grouse.

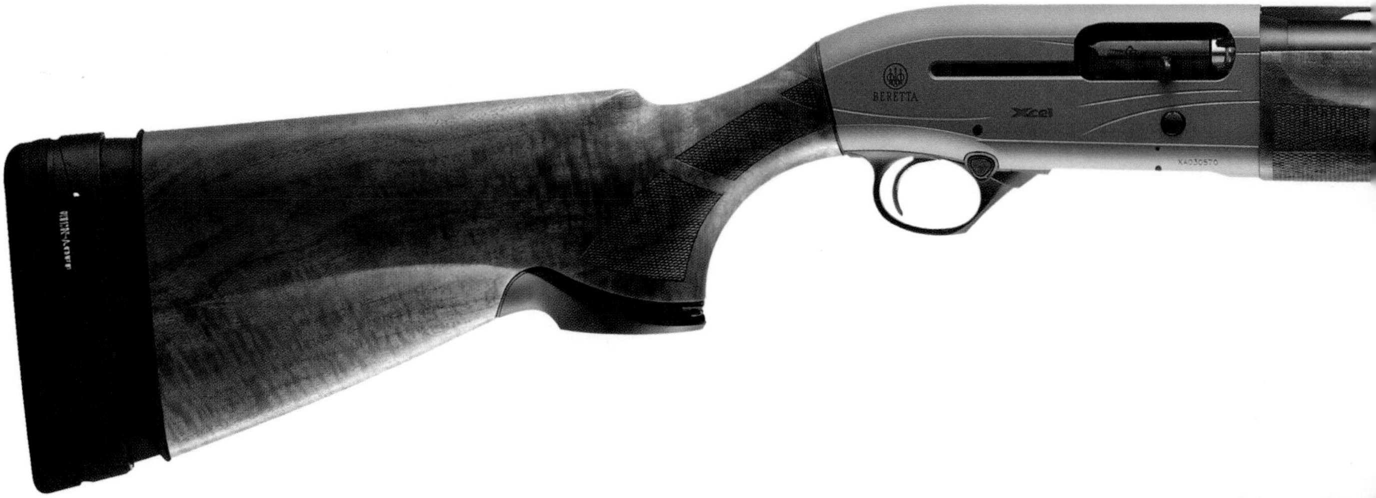

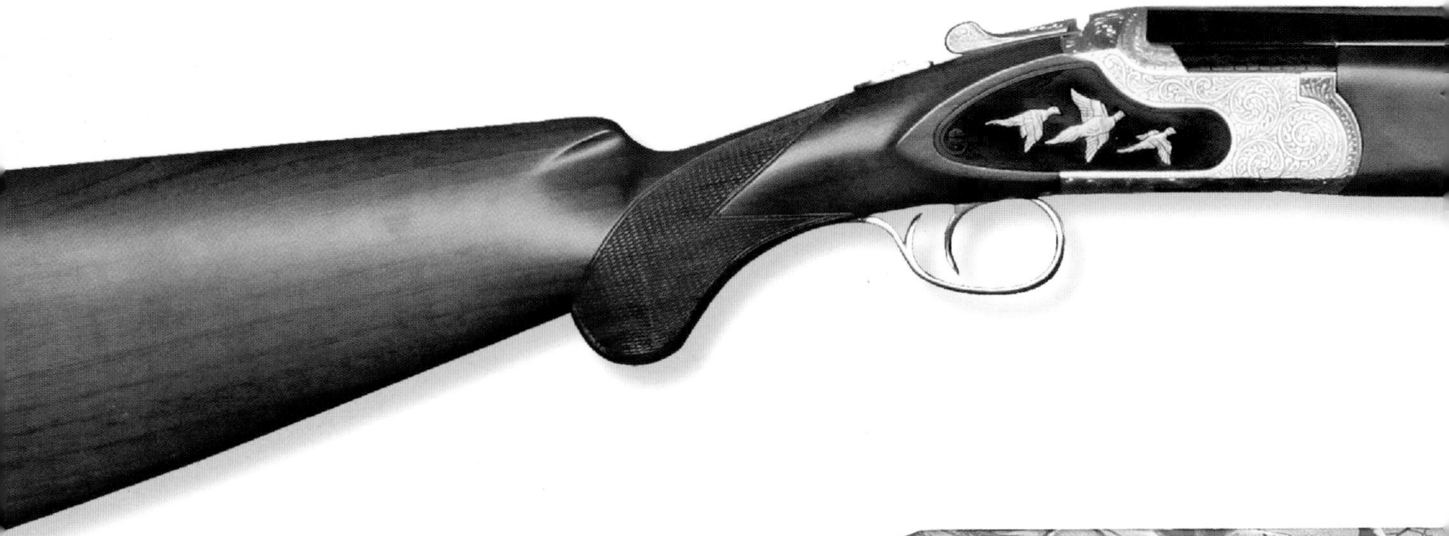

BERETTA A400 X-CEL SPORTING

Benchrest shooters are those most notorious for being picky about their ammunition, but there are definitely a number of shotgunners out there who rival the BR practitioners' level of tweakiness. For those scattergun lovers who can't stop fooling with a tenth of a grain of powder here and there, Beretta offers up its A400 Xcel Sporting. The turquoise receiver houses Beretta's revolutionary GunPod system that digitally reads out ambient air temperature, cartridge pressure, and numbers of rounds fired.

CZ WINGSHOOTER

An eye-catching twist on engraving really brings the CZ Wingshooter to life. A striking contrast of blue, gold, and stainless is both unique and attractive. We especially like that CZ builds this gun in a traditional, non-ejector .410-bore that has fixed chokes in Improved and Modified. For 12-gauge and 20-gauge shooters, the gun chambers 3-inch shells and comes with the American preferred auto-ejectors.

STOEGER P350

You can run any 12-gauge shell you wan from standard 2¾-inch through the magnum 3½-inchers through Stoeger's P350 pump. The Steady Grip version, complete with full-coverage camo, is made specifically for turkey hunting.

ARMALITE AR-10A4 ▲

This hard-hitting carbine from Armalite, chambered in 7.62 NATO (.308 Win.), is compact and powerful with a 16-inch barrel and collapsible buttstock. The AR-10A4 features a clamping gas block, which allows the removable front sight to be rotated to zero. This assures that the rear sight is centered, giving full left and right windage movement for enhanced accuracy tuning in strong winds. As part of Armalite's "A" family of rifles, this newer offering also accepts third-party magazines from Magpul (PMAGS), Knight's Armament, and DPMS, in addition to the traditional style "waffle" mags.

▼ARMALITE AR-10A SUPERSASS

Armalite's AR10A SuperSASS is a suppressor-ready 7.62 rifle that has an adjustable gas system to fine-tune performance with a variety of ammunition and suppressors. Its 20-inch, stainless steel, match grade barrel and two-stage match trigger group—first stage 2½ pounds, second stage 4½ to 5 pounds—ensure pinpoint accuracy. With a quad Picatinny rail handguard and adjustable Magpul buttstock, it is highly customizable. The rifle weights 11.84 pounds and shoots 1 MOA from the factory.

DPMS ARCTIC PANTHER

You can shoot just about anything you want to with the Arctic Panther from DPMS, but this white-garbed AR is a particularly sweet choice for winter coyotes. Clad in a hard coat anodized Mil Spec white on the A3 flattop receiver and fore-end, this .223 has a 20-inch fluted and Teflon-coated barrel. An optics-only rifle (i.e., DPMS did away with the iron sights you wouldn't use anyway), it weighs a totally tote-able nine pounds when empty.

DMPS PANTHER 6.5 CREEDMOOR

Hi-power match rifles shooting .223 and .308 are a dime a dozen. Be different and shoot a DPMS Panther 6.5 Creedmoor! Introduced by Hornady, in 2007, the cartridge mimics the .300 Win. Mag.'s flight, but with less recoil and a high ballistic coefficient, both of which can be a huge bonus in long, drawn-out matches.

TIKKA SPORTER RIFLE

Bolt action; 223, 22-250, 308, detachable 5-shot magazine; 23-1/2-inch heavy barrel; weighs 9 lbs.; 43-5/8-inch overall length; European walnut stock with adjustable comb, adjustable buttplate; stippled grip and forend; no sights; drilled and tapped for scope mounting. Buttplate adjustable for length, angle, height and pitch, adjustable trigger, free-floating barrel. Introduced 1998. Imported from Finland by Beretta USA.

Perf: $900 **Exc:** $750 **Good:** $650

TIKKA STANDARD

Bolt action; 22-250, 223, 243, 270, 30-06, 7mm Rem. Mag., 300 Win. Mag., 338 Win. Mag.; 3-, 5-shot magazine; 22-inch barrel (standard), 24-inch (magnums); 43-inch overall length; weighs 7-1/4 lbs.; no sights; Monte Carlo European walnut stock; checkered grip, forend; rubber buttplate; receiver dovetailed for scope mounts. Made in Finland. Introduced 1988; no longer in production.

Exc: $595 **VGood:** $475 **Good:** $350

TIKKA T3 HUNTER

Bolt action; 223, 22-250, 243, 308, 25-06, 270, 6.5x55, 270 WSM, 7mm Rem Mag, 30-06, 300 WSM, 300 Win Mag, 338 Win Mag; 22-7/16-inch barrel (24-3/8-inch magnum calibers) 6-3/4 lbs.; no sights; walnut stock with rubber butt pad; introduced 2003, still imported by Beretta USA.

Perf: $600 **Exc:** $500 **VGood:** $400

TIKKA T3 LAMINATED STAINLESS

Similar to T3 Hunter, but with laminated stock and barrel and action of stainless steel.

Perf: $800 **Exc:** $750 **VGood:** $600

TIKKA T3 LITE

Similar to T3 Hunter, but with synthetic stock; weighs 6 lbs, 3 oz; introduced 2003, still imported by Beretta USA.

Perf: $550 **Exc:** $450 **VGood:** $400

TIKKA T3 LITE STAINLESS

Similar to T3 Lite, but barrel and action of stainless steel.

Perf: $600 **Exc:** $475 **VGood:** $400

TIKKA T3 TACTICAL

Similar to T3 Hunter, but tactical rifle for law enforcement; 223, 308; 20-inch barrel; black phosphate finish, synthetic stock with adjustable comb; 5-shot detachable magazine; Picatinny rail on action; fitted for muzzle brake and bipod. Imported by Beretta USA.

Perf: $1300 **Exc:** $1100 **VGood:** $900

TIKKA T3 VARMINT

Similar to T3 Hunter, but with bull barrel, synthetic stock, adjustable trigger; 223, 22-250, 308, 5-shot detachable magazine. Imported by Beretta USA.

Perf: $750 **Exc:** $690 **VGood:** $600

TIKKA T3 VARMINT STAINLESS

Similar to T3 Varmint, but barrel and action of stainless steel. Imported by Beretta USA.

Perf: $800 **Exc:** $750 **VGood:** N/A

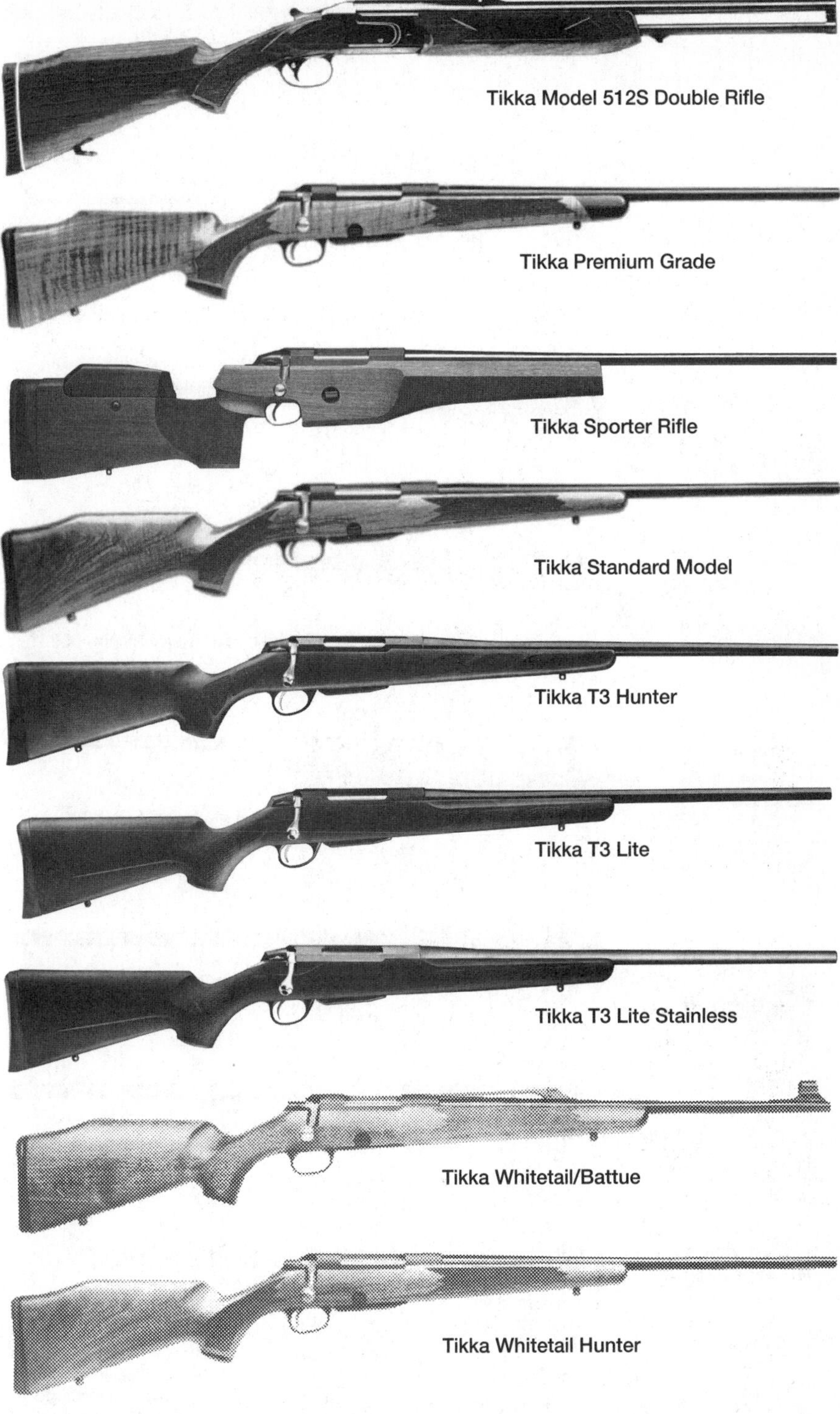

Tikka Model 512S Double Rifle

Tikka Premium Grade

Tikka Sporter Rifle

Tikka Standard Model

Tikka T3 Hunter

Tikka T3 Lite

Tikka T3 Lite Stainless

Tikka Whitetail/Battue

Tikka Whitetail Hunter

TIKKA WHITETAIL/BATTUE

Bolt action; 270, 308, 30-06, 7mm Rem. Mag., 300 Win. Mag., 338 Win. Mag.; 3-, 5-shot magazine; 20-1/2-inch barrel; raised quarter-rib; V-shaped rear sight, blade front; Monte Carlo European walnut stock; checkered pistol grip, forend; rubber buttplate; receiver dovetailed for scope mounts. Made in Finland. Introduced 1991; no longer in production.

Perf: $530 **Exc:** $440 **VGood:** $370

TIKKA WHITETAIL HUNTER BOLT-ACTION RIFLE

Bolt action; 22-250, 223, 243, 7mm-08, 25-06, 270, 308, 30-06, 7mm Rem. Mag., 300 Win. Mag., 338 Win. Mag; 22-1/2-inch barrel (std. cals.), 24-1/2-inch (magnum cals.); weighs 7-1/8 lbs.; 43-inch overall length (std. cals.); European walnut stock with Monte Carlo comb, rubber butt pad, checkered grip and forend; Detachable four-shot magazine (standard calibers), three-shot in magnums. Receiver dovetailed for scope mounting. Reintroduced 1996. Imported from Finland by Beretta USA.

Standard calibers

Perf: $620 **Exc:** $500 **VGood:** $400

Magnum calibers

Perf: $650 **Exc:** $520 **VGood:** $430

Left-hand

Perf: $660 **Exc:** $540 **VGood:** $440

TIKKA CONTINENTAL VARMINT RIFLE

Similar to the standard Tikka rifle except has 26-inch heavy barrel, extra-wide forend. Chambered for 17 Rem., 22-250, 223, 308. Reintroduced 1996. Made in Finland by Sako. Imported by Beretta USA.

Perf: $690 **Exc:** $550 **VGood:** $490

TIKKA WHITETAIL HUNTER DELUXE

Similar to the Whitetail Hunter except has select walnut stock with rollover Monte Carlo comb, rosewood grip cap and forend tip. Has adjustable trigger, detachable magazine, free-floating barrel. Same calibers as the Hunter. Introduced 1999. Imported from Finland by Beretta USA.

Standard calibers

Perf: $720 **Exc:** $600 **VGood:** $500

Magnum calibers

Perf: $775 **Exc:** $625 **VGood:** $525

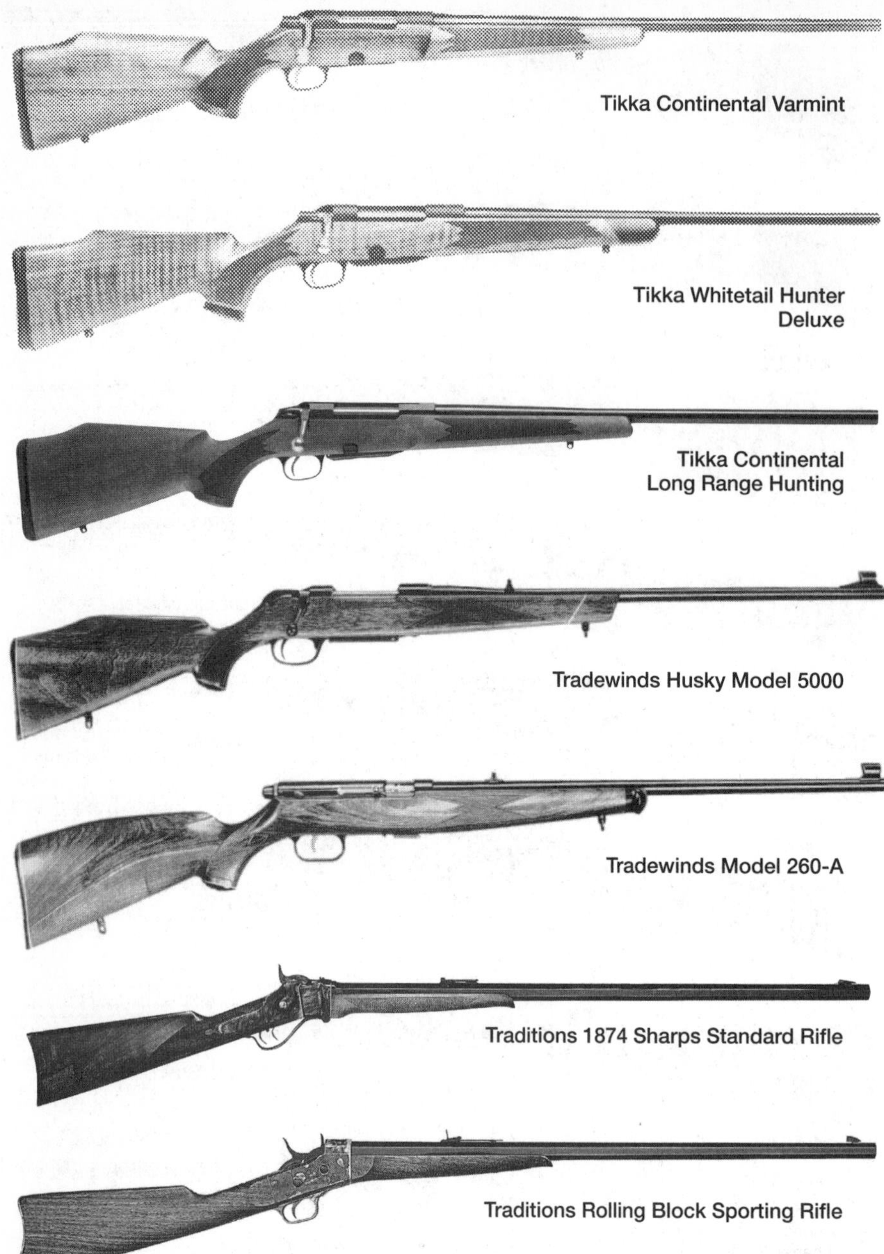
Tikka Continental Varmint

Tikka Whitetail Hunter Deluxe

Tikka Continental Long Range Hunting

Tradewinds Husky Model 5000

Tradewinds Model 260-A

Traditions 1874 Sharps Standard Rifle

Traditions Rolling Block Sporting Rifle

TIKKA WHITETAIL HUNTER SYNTHETIC RIFLE

Similar to the Whitetail Hunter except has black synthetic stock; calibers 223, 22-250, 243, 7mm-08, 25-06, 270 Win., 30-06, 7mm Rem. Mag., 300 Win. Mag., 338 Win. Mag. Introduced 1996. Imported from Finland by Beretta USA.

Perf: $600 **Exc:** $500 **VGood:** $400

TIKKA CONTINENTAL LONG RANGE HUNTING

Similar to the Whitetail Hunter except has 26-inch heavy barrel. Available in 25-06, 270 Win., 7mm Rem. Mag., 300 Win. Mag. Introduced 1996. Imported from Finland by Beretta USA.

Perf: 680 **Exc:** $550 **VGood:** 480

TIKKA WHITETAIL HUNTER STAINLESS SYNTHETIC

Similar to the Whitetail Hunter except all metal is of stainless steel, and it has a black synthetic stock. Available in 22-250, 223, 243, 7mm-08, 25- 06, 270, 308, 30-06, 7mm Rem. Mag., 300 Win. Mag., 338 Win. Mag. Introduced 1997. Imported from Finland by Beretta USA.

Perf: $600 **Exc:** $500 **VGood:** $410

TRADEWINDS HUSKY MODEL 5000

Bolt action; 22-250, 243, 270, 30-06, 308; removable 4-shot magazine; 23-3/4-inch barrel; fixed hooded front sight, adjustable rear; hand-checkered Monte Carlo stock of European walnut; white-line spacers on pistol-grip cap, forend tip, buttplate; recessed bolt head; adjustable trigger. Imported from Europe. Introduced 1973; discontinued 1983.

Exc: $350 **VGood:** $320 **Good:** $290

TRADEWINDS MODEL 260-A

Semi-automatic; 22 LR; 5-shot magazine; 22-1/2-inch barrel; 41-1/2-inch overall length; hooded ramp front sight, three-leaf folding rear; walnut stock; hand-checkered pistol grip, forend; double extractors; sliding safety; sling swivels; receiver grooved for scope mount. Made in Japan. Introduced 1975; discontinued 1989.

Exc: $200 **VGood:** $170 **Good:** $130

TRADEWINDS MODEL 311-A

Bolt action; 22 LR; 5-shot magazine; 22-1/2-inch barrel; 41-1/4-inch overall length; hooded ramp front sight, folding leaf rear; receiver grooved for scope mount; Monte Carlo walnut stock; hand-checkered pistol grip, forend; sliding safety. Made in Europe. Introduced 1976; no longer in production.

Exc: $180 **VGood:** $150 **Good:** $110

TRADITIONS 1874 SHARPS DELUXE RIFLE

Single shot; falling block; 45-70; 32-inch octagonal barrel with 1:18-inch twist; weighs 11.67 lbs.; 48.8-inch overall length; Checkered walnut stock with German silver nose cap and steel butt plate. Globe front sight, adjustable creedmore rear with 12 inserts. Color-case hardened receiver; double-set triggers. Introduced 2001. Imported from Pedersoli by Traditions.

Perf: $900 **Exc:** $700 **VGood:** $550

TRADITIONS 1874 SHARPS SPORTING DELUXE RIFLE

Similar to Sharps Deluxe but custom silver engraved receiver, European walnut stock and forend, satin finish, set trigger, fully adjustable.

Perf: $1600 **Exc:** $1200 **VGood:** $1000

TRADITIONS 1874 SHARPS STANDARD RIFLE

Similar to 1874 Sharps Deluxe Rifle, except has blade front and adjustable buckhorn-style rear sight. Weighs 10.67 pounds. Introduced 2001. Imported from Pedersoli by Traditions.

Perf: $1100 **Exc:** $975 **VGood:** $800

TRADITIONS ROLLING BLOCK SPORTING RIFLE

Single shot, rolling block; 45-70; 30-inch octagonal barrel with 1:18-inch twist; 46.7-inch overall length; weighs 11.67 lbs.; walnut stock; blade front, adjustable rear sights; Antique silver, color-case hardened receiver, drilled and tapped for tang/globe sights; brass butt plate and trigger guard. Introduced 2001. Imported from Pedersoli by Traditions.

Perf: $900 **Exc:** $775 **VGood:** $650

TRISTAR 1860 HENRY RIFLE

Lever action; 44-40, 45 Colt; 24-1/4-inch barrel, half-octagon; weighs 9.2 lbs.; 43-3/4-inch overall length; American walnut stock; blade front sight, rear adjustable for elevation. Frame, elevator, magazine follower, buttplate are brass, balance blue. Made by Uberti. Imported by Tristar Sporting Arms Ltd. Arms, Inc.

Perf: $890 **Exc:** $700 **VGood:** $540

TRISTAR 1860 HENRY TRAPPER CARBINE

Similar to the 1860 Henry Rifle except has 18-1/2-inch barrel, overall measurement 37- 3/4-inches, and weighs 8 lbs. Rifle was introduced 1999. Imported from Uberti of Italy by Tristar Sporting Arms Ltd.

Perf: $860 **Exc:** $700 **VGood:** $540

TRISTAR 1874 SHARPS SPORTING RIFLE

Single shot, falling block; 45-70; 28-inch, 32-inch, 34-inch octagonal barrel; 44.5-inch overall length; weighs 9.75 lbs.; Walnut stock; Dovetail front, adjustable rear sights. Cut checkering, case colored frame finish.

Perf: $1150 **Exc:** $1000 **VGood:** $850

TRISTAR 1885 SINGLE SHOT

Single shot, falling block; 45-70; 28-inch barrel; 44.5-inch overall length; weighs 8.75 lbs.; European walnut stock; bead on blade front sight, open step-adjustable rear; Recreation of the 1885 Winchester by Uberti. Color case-hardened receiver and lever, blued barrel. Introduced 1998. Imported from Italy by Tristar Sporting Arms Ltd.

Perf: $680 **Exc:** $560 **VGood:** $400

TYROL CUSTOM CRAFTED MODEL

Bolt action; 243, 25-06, 30-06, 308, 7mm, 300 Win.; 23-3/4-inch barrel; hooded ramp front sight, adjustable rear; drilled, tapped for scope mounts; hand-checkered Monte Carlo stock of European walnut; adjustable trigger; shotgun-type tang safety. Manufactured in Austria. Introduced 1973; discontinued 1975.

Exc: $400 **VGood:** $320 **Good:** $210

UBERTI HENRY RIFLE

Lever action; 44-40; 24-1/2-inch half-octagon barrel; 43-3/4-inch overall length; weighs 9 lbs.; elevation-adjustable rear sight, blade front; uncheckered walnut stock; brass buttplate, frame, elevator, magazine follower; rest charcoal blued or of polished steel. Made in Italy. Introduced 1987.

Perf: $850 **Exc:** $720 **VGood:** $510

UBERTI HENRY CARBINE

Same specs as Henry Rifle except 22-1/4-inch barrel. Improted by Uberti USA; still in production.

Perf: $850 **Exc:** $720 **VGood:** $510

UBERTI HENRY TRAPPER

Same specs as Henry Rifle except 16-inch or 18-inch barrel. Imported by Uberti USA; still in production.

Perf: $850 **Exc:** $720 **VGood:** $510

UBERTI MODEL 1866 SPORTING RIFLE

Lever action; 22 LR, 22 WMR, 38 Spl., 44-40; 24-1/2-inch octagonal barrel; 43-1/4-inch overall length; weighs 8 lbs.; elevation-adjustable rear sight, windage-adjustable blade front; polished brass frame, buttplate, forend cap; rest charcoal blued. Made in Italy. Introduced 1987.

Perf: $710 **Exc:** $570 **VGood:** $440

UBERTI MODEL 1866 YELLOWBOY CARBINE

Same specs as Model 1866 except 19-inch round barrel, carbine bands; 38-1/4-inch overall length; weighs 7 7/16 lbs. Introduced 1987; still in production.

Perf: $710 **Exc:** $570 **VGood:** $440

UBERTI MODEL 1866 TRAPPER CARBINE

Same specs as Model 1866 except 22 LR, 38 Spl., 44-40; 16-1/8-inch barrel. Introduced 1987; discontinued 1989.

Perf: $710 **Exc:** $570 **VGood:** $440

UBERTI MODEL 1873 BUCKHORN

Revolving carbine; 44 Mag., 44 Spl., 44-40; 6-shot cylinder; 18-inch barrel; 34-inch overall length; weighs 4-1/2 lbs.; grooved or target rear sight, blade front; carbine version of single-action revolver; color case-hardened frame; blued cylinder, barrel; brass buttplate. Introduced 1987; discontinued 1989.

Perf: $410 **Exc:** $350 **VGood:** $290

With target sights

Perf: $440 **Exc:** $380 **VGood:** $320

UBERTI MODEL 1873 CATTLEMAN

Revolving carbine; 22 LR/22 WMR, 38 Spl., 357 Mag., 44-40, 45 Colt; 6-shot cylinder; 18-inch barrel; 34-inch overall length; weighs 4-1/2 lbs.; grooved or target rear sight, blade front; carbine version of single-action revolver; case hardened frame; blued cylinder, barrel; brass buttplate. Made in Italy. Introduced 1987; discontinued 1989, reintroduced.

Perf: $400 **Exc:** $330 **VGood:** $270

With target sights

Perf: $425 **Exc:** $350 **VGood:** $280

UBERTI MODEL 1873 SPORTING RIFLE

Lever action; 22 LR, 22 WMR, 38 Spl., 357 Mag., 44-40, 45 Colt; 24-1/4-inch, 30-inch octagonal barrel; 43-1/4-inch overall length; weighs 8 lbs.; elevation-adjustable rear sight, windage-adjustable blade front; uncheckered walnut stock; brass elevator; color case-hardened frame; blued barrel, hammer, lever, buttplate. Reproduction of 1873 Winchester, made in Italy. Introduced 1987; still in production.

Perf: $820 **Exc:** $675 **VGood:** $540

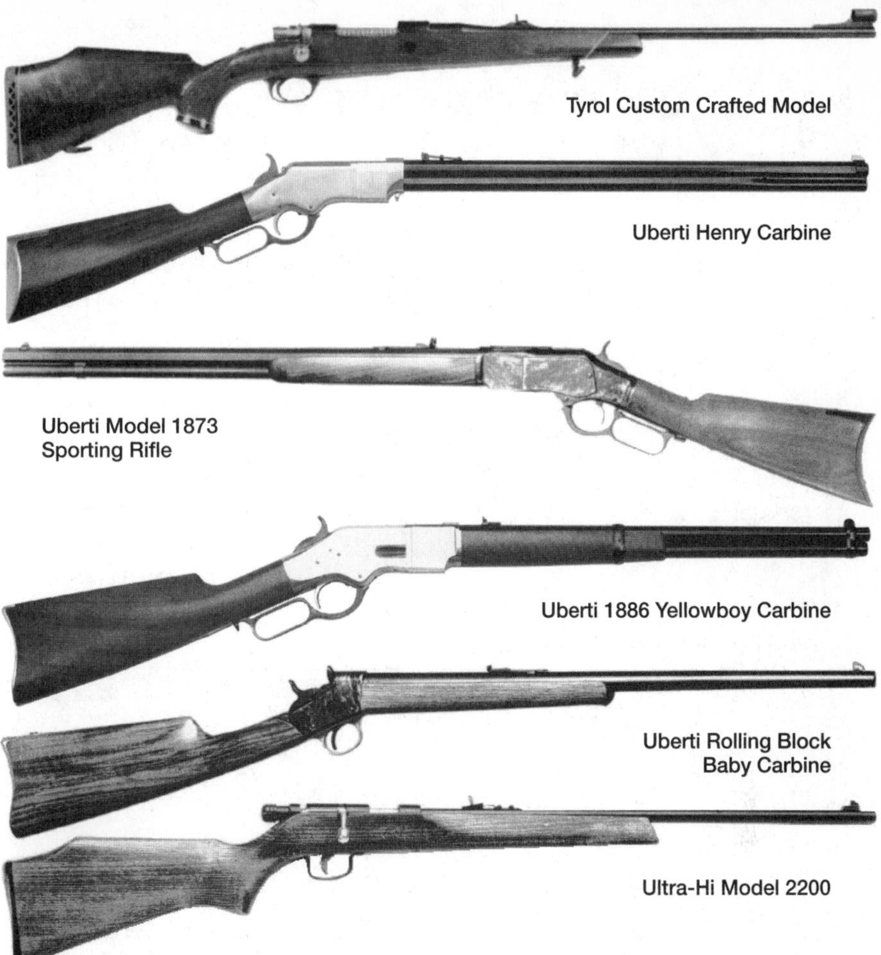

Tyrol Custom Crafted Model

Uberti Henry Carbine

Uberti Model 1873 Sporting Rifle

Uberti 1886 Yellowboy Carbine

Uberti Rolling Block Baby Carbine

Ultra-Hi Model 2200

UBERTI MODEL 1873 SPORTING CARBINE

Same specs as Model 1873 Sporting except 19-inch round barrel; 38-1/4-inch overall length; weighs 7-1/4 lbs.; available with nickel plating. Introduced 1987; still in production.

Perf: $790 **Exc:** $625 **VGood:** $500

Nickel finish

Perf: $820 **Exc:** $645 **VGood:** $525

UBERTI MODEL 1873 SPORTING CARBINE, TRAPPER MODEL

Same specs as Model 1873 Sporting except 357 Mag., 44-40, 45 Colt; 16-inch barrel. Discontinued 1990.

Perf: $800 **Exc:** $630 **VGood:** $500

UBERTI MODEL 1875 ARMY TARGET

Revolving carbine; 357 Mag., 44-40, 45 Colt; 6-shot cylinder; 18-inch barrel; 37-inch overall length; weighs 4-1/2 lbs.; carbine version of 1875 single-action revolver; elevation-adjustable rear sight, ramp front; uncheckered walnut stock; polished brass buttplate, triggerguard; case-hardened frame; blued or nickel-plated cylinder, barrel. Made in Italy. Introduced 1987; discontinued 1989.

Blued finish

Perf: $400 **Exc:** $325 **VGood:** $260

Nickel finish

Perf: $430 **Exc:** $350 **VGood:** $285

UBERTI ROLLING BLOCK BABY CARBINE

Single shot; 22 LR, 22 WMR, 22 Hornet, 357 Mag.; 22-inch barrel; 35-1/2-inch overall length; weighs 4-13/16 lbs.; copy of Remington New Model No. 4 carbine; brass buttplate, triggerguard; blued barrel; color case-hardened frame. Introduced 1986, still available.

Perf: $375 **Exc:** $300 **VGood:** $270

Rifle version, 26-inch bbl.

Perf: $500 **Exc:** $400 **VGood:** $375

ULTIMATE ACCURACY MODEL 5100A1 LONG-RANGE RIFLE

Bolt action; 50 BMG; 5-shot magazine; 29-inch fully fluted, free-floating barrel; 51-1/2-inch overall length; weighs 36 lbs.; no sights; optional Leupold Ultra M1-16x scope; composition buttstock with comb adjustment for drop; adjustable trigger; breaks down for transport, storage. Made in U.S. by Ultimate Accuracy. Introduced 1994; no longer in production.

Perf: $2995 **Exc:** $2495 **VGood:** $1995

ULTIMATE ACCURACY MODEL 5100A1 IMPROVED MODEL

Same specs as Model 5100A1 except receiver is drilled and tapped for scope mount; manual safety; one-piece muzzle brake. Made in U.S. by Ultimate Accuracy. No longer in production.

Perf: $2995 **Exc:** $2495 **VGood:** $1995

ULTRA-HI MODEL 2200

Bolt action; single shot; 22 Short, 22 Long, 22 LR; 23-inch barrel; weighs 5 lbs.; blade front sight, open rear; pistol-grip Monte Carlo hardwood stock. Made in Japan. Introduced 1977; no longer in production.

Perf: $60 **Exc:** $50 **VGood:** $40

Unique Model T.66 Match

Universal Model 1000

Valmet Hunter Model

Valmet 412 Double Rifle

UNIQUE MODEL G.21

Semi-automatic; 22 LR; 5-, 10-shot magazine; 18-inch barrel; 33-1/2-inch overall length; weighs 6 lbs.; adjustable rear peep sight; French walnut stock; magazine and manual safeties. Was imported by Nygord Precision Products; no longer imported.

Perf: $300 **Exc:** $280 **VGood:** $250

UNIQUE MODEL T AUDAX

Bolt action; 22 LR, 22 Short; 5-shot (22 Short), 10-shot magazine; 21-1/2-inch barrel; 39-1/4-inch overall length; weighs 6-1/2 lbs.; adjustable rear sight; dovetailed grooves on receiver for scope or target sight; lateral safety; French walnut stock. Was imported by Nygord Precision Products; no longer imported.

Perf: $545 **Exc:** $500 **VGood:** $400

UNIQUE MODEL T DIOPTRA

Bolt action; 22 LR, 22 WMR; 5-shot (22 WMR), 10-shot (22 LR) magazine; 23-1/2-inch barrel; 41-inch overall length; weighs 6-1/2 lbs.; adjustable rear sight; dovetailed grooves on receiver for scope or target sight; lateral safety; French Monte Carlo walnut stock. Was imported by Nygord Precision Products; no longer imported.

Perf: $750 **Exc:** $620 **VGood:** $510

UNIQUE MODEL T/SM

Bolt action; 22 LR, 22 WMR; 5-shot (22 WMR), 10-shot (22 LR) magazine; 20-1/2-inch barrel; 38-1/2-inch overall length; weighs 6-1/2 lbs.; adjustable rear sight; adjustable trigger; dovetailed grooves on receiver for scope or target sight; French Monte Carlo walnut stock; left-handed stock available. Was imported by Nygord Precision Products; no longer imported.

Perf: $770 **Exc:** $630 **VGood:** $525

UNIQUE MODEL T/SM BIATHALON JUNIOR

Same specs as Model T/SM except metallic grooves on stock for sling and harness mounting. Was imported by Nygord Precision Products; no longer imported.

Perf: $725 **Exc:** $595 **VGood:** $495

UNIQUE MODEL T/SM MATCH JUNIOR

Same specs as Model T/SM except adjustable buttplate; metallic grooves on stock for sling and harness mounting. Was imported by Nygord Precision Products; no longer imported.

Perf: $725 **Exc:** $595 **VGood:** $495

UNIQUE MODEL T.66 MATCH

Bolt action; single shot; 22 LR; 25-1/2-inch barrel; 44-1/8-inch overall length; weighs 10 7/8 lbs.; interchangeable globe front sight, Micro-Match rear; French walnut stock; stippled forend, pistol-grip; left-hand model available; meets NRA, UIT standards. Imported from France. Introduced 1980; no longer in production.

Perf: $450 **Exc:** $410 **VGood:** $360

UNIQUE MODEL T.791 BIATHLON

Bolt action; 22 LR; 5-shot magazine; 22-1/2-inch barrel; 40-1/4-inch overall length; weighs 10 lbs.; interchangeable globe front sight, MIcro-Match rear; French walnut stock; stippled forend, pistol grip; left-hand model available; meets NRA, UIT standards. Imported from France. Introduced 1980; no longer in production.

Perf: $750 **Exc:** $695 **VGood:** $475

UNIQUE MODEL X51 BIS

Semi-automatic; 22 LR; 5-, 10-shot magazine; 23-1/2-inch barrel; 40-1/2-inch overall length; weighs 6 lbs.; adjustable rear sight; French walnut stock; magazine and manual safeties. Was imported by Nygord Precision Products; no longer imported.

Perf: $350 **Exc:** $290 **VGood:** $240

UNIVERSAL MODEL 1000

Semi-automatic; 30 Carbine; 5-shot magazine; 18-inch barrel; 35-1/4-inch overall length; weighs 6 lbs.; military iron sights; receiver tapped for scope mount; birchwood stock; copy of G.I. version of M1 Carbine with bayonet lug. Introduced about 1965. No longer in production.

Exc: $475 **VGood:** $450 **Good:** $275

UNIVERSAL MODEL 1002

Same specs as Model 1003 except military type, but with metal handguard.

Exc: $400 **VGood:** $325 **Good:** $250

UNIVERSAL MODEL 1003

Semi-automatic; 30 carbine; 5-shot magazine; 18-inch barrel (other lengths have been reported); 35-1/2-inch overall length; weighs 5-1/2 lbs.; military iron sights; receiver tapped for scope mount; birchwood stock; similar to 30 M1 Carbine without bayonet lug. No longer in production.

Exc: $475 **VGood:** $450 **Good:** $275

UNIVERSAL MODEL 1005 DELUXE

Same specs as Model 1003 except polished super-mirror blue finish; Monte Carlo walnut stock; weighs 6-1/2 lbs. No longer in production.

Exc: $500 **VGood:** $475 **Good:** $450

UNIVERSAL MODEL 1010

Same specs as Model 1003 except nickel-plated.

Exc: $500 **VGood:** $475 **Good:** $450

UNIVERSAL MODEL 1015

Same specs as Model 1003 except gold-plated finish.

Exc: $575 **VGood:** $495 **Good:** $295

UNIVERSAL MODEL 1020

Same specs as Model 1003 except black DuPont teflon coated.

Exc: $500 **VGood:** $475 **Good:** $450

UNIVERSAL MODEL 1025

Same specs as Model 1003 except camouflage olive DuPont teflon coated.

Exc: $500 **VGood:** $475 **Good:** $450

UNIVERSAL MODEL 1256 FERRET

Semi-automatic; 256 Win. Mag.; 5-shot magazine; 18-inch barrel; no sights; 4x Universal scope; birchwood stock; M1 Carbine action; satin blue finish. No longer in production.

Exc: $500 **VGood:** $475 **Good:** $450

VALMET HUNTER MODEL

Semi-automatic; 223, 243, 308; 5-, 9-, 20-shot magazine; 20-1/2-inch barrel; 42-inch overall length; weighs 8 lbs.; open rear sight, blade front; American walnut butt, forend; checkered palm swell pistol grip, forend; Kalashnikov-type action. Made in Finland. Introduced 1986; discontinued 1989.

Perf: $1400 **Exc:** $1195 **VGood:** $795

VALMET MODEL 412 DOUBLE RIFLE

Double rifle; 243, 308, 30-06, 375 Win, 9.3x74R; 24-inch barrels; weighs 8-5/8 lbs.; ramp front sight, adjustable open rear; barrel selector mounted on trigger; hand-checkered Monte Carlo stock of American walnut; recoil pad. Importation began 1980; no longer imported from Finland by Valmet.

Perf: $1300 **Exc:** $1200 **VGood:** $1000

VALMET MODEL 412S COMBO GUN

Combination gun; 12 ga. over 222, 223, 243, 308, 30-06; 24-inch barrel (Imp. & Mod.); weighs 7-5/8 lbs.; blade front, flip-up-type open rear; hand-checkered American walnut stock, forend; recoil pad. Importation began 1980; no longer imported from Finland by Valmet.

Perf: $1150 **Exc:** $910 **VGood:** $705

VARNER FAVORITE HUNTER

Single shot; 22 LR; 21-1/2-inch half-round/half-octagon barrel; weighs 5 lbs.; takedown; blade front sight, open step-adjustable rear and peep; checkered American walnut stock; recreation of Stevens

Favorite rifle with takedown barrel. Introduced 1988; discontinued 1990.

Perf: $375 **Exc:** $300 **VGood:** $230

VARNER FAVORITE SCHEUTZEN

Same specs as Favorite Hunter except 24-inch half-round/half-octagon target-grade barrel; ladder-type tang-mounted peep sight, globe-type front with six inserts; checkered AAA fancy walnut pistol-grip perch-belly stock, extended forend; scroll-engraved color case-hardened frame, lever; recreation of the Stevens Ladies Favorite Scheutzen, originally produced 1910 to 1916. Reintroduced 1989; discontinued 1990.

Perf: $995 **Exc:** $825 **VGood:** $685

VEKTOR H5 SLIDE-ACTION RIFLE

Slide action; 223 Rem., 5-shot magazine; 18-inch, 22-inch barrel; 42-1/2-inch overall length (22-inch barrel); weighs 9 lbs., 15 oz.; walnut thumbhole stock; comes with 1-inch 4x32 scope with low-light reticle. AR-15 type rotating bolt mechanism. Matte black finish. Introduced 1999. Imported from South Africa by Vektor USA; no longer imported.

Perf: $800 **Exc:** $700 **VGood:** $560

VEKTOR BUSHVELD BOLT-ACTION RIFLE

Bolt action; 243, 308, 7x57, 7x64 Brenneke, 270 Win., 30-06, 300 Win. Mag., 300 H&H, 9.3x62. 22- to 26-inch barrel; Turkish walnut stock with wrap-around hand checkering; blade on ramp front, fixed standing leaf rear sights. Controlled-round feed; Mauser-type extractor; no cut-away through the bolt locking lug; M70-type three-position safety; Timney-type adjustable trigger. Introduced 1999. Imported from South Africa by Vektor USA; no longer imported.

Perf: $1400 **Exc:** $1100 **VGood:** $900

VEKTOR MODEL 98

Bolt action; 243, 308, 7x57, 7x64 Brenneke, 270 Win., 30-06, 300 Win. Mag., 300 H&H, 375 H&H, 9.3x62; 22- to 26-inch barrel; Turkish walnut stock with hand-checkered grip and forend; no sights furnished; drilled and tapped for scope mounting. Bolt has guide rib; non- rotating, long extractor enhances positive feeding; polished blue finish. Updated Mauser 98 action. Introduced 1999. Imported from South Africa by Vektor USA; no longer imported.

Perf: $980 **Exc:** $840 **VGood:** $670

VICKERS EMPIRE MODEL

Single shot; 22 LR; 27-inch, 30-inch barrel; Martini-type action; perfection rear peep sight, Parker-Hale No. 2 front; straight-grip walnut stock. Manufactured prior to WWII.

Exc: $475 **VGood:** $350 **Good:** $275

VICKERS JUBILEE MODEL

Single-shot; 22 LR; 28-inch heavy barrel; Martini-type action; Perfection rear peep sight, Parker-Hale No. 2 front; single-piece European walnut target stock; full pistol grip; forearm. Manufactured prior to World War II.

Exc: $470 **VGood:** $380 **Good:** $310

VOERE MODEL 1007

Bolt action; 22 LR; 18-inch barrel; weighs 5-1/2 lbs.; open adjustable rear sight, hooded front; military-type oil-finished beech stock; single-stage trigger; sling swivels; convertible to single-shot; Biathlon model. Made in Austria. Introduced 1984; discontinued 1991.

Perf: $230 **Exc:** $180 **VGood:** $150

VOERE MODEL 1013

Bolt action; 22 WMR; 5-, 8-shot magazine; 18-inch barrel; weighs 5-1/2 lbs.; open adjustable rear sight, hooded front; military-type oil-finished stock; double-set trigger; sling swivels. Made in Austria. Introduced 1984; discontinued 1991.

Perf: $280 **Exc:** $230 **VGood:** $190

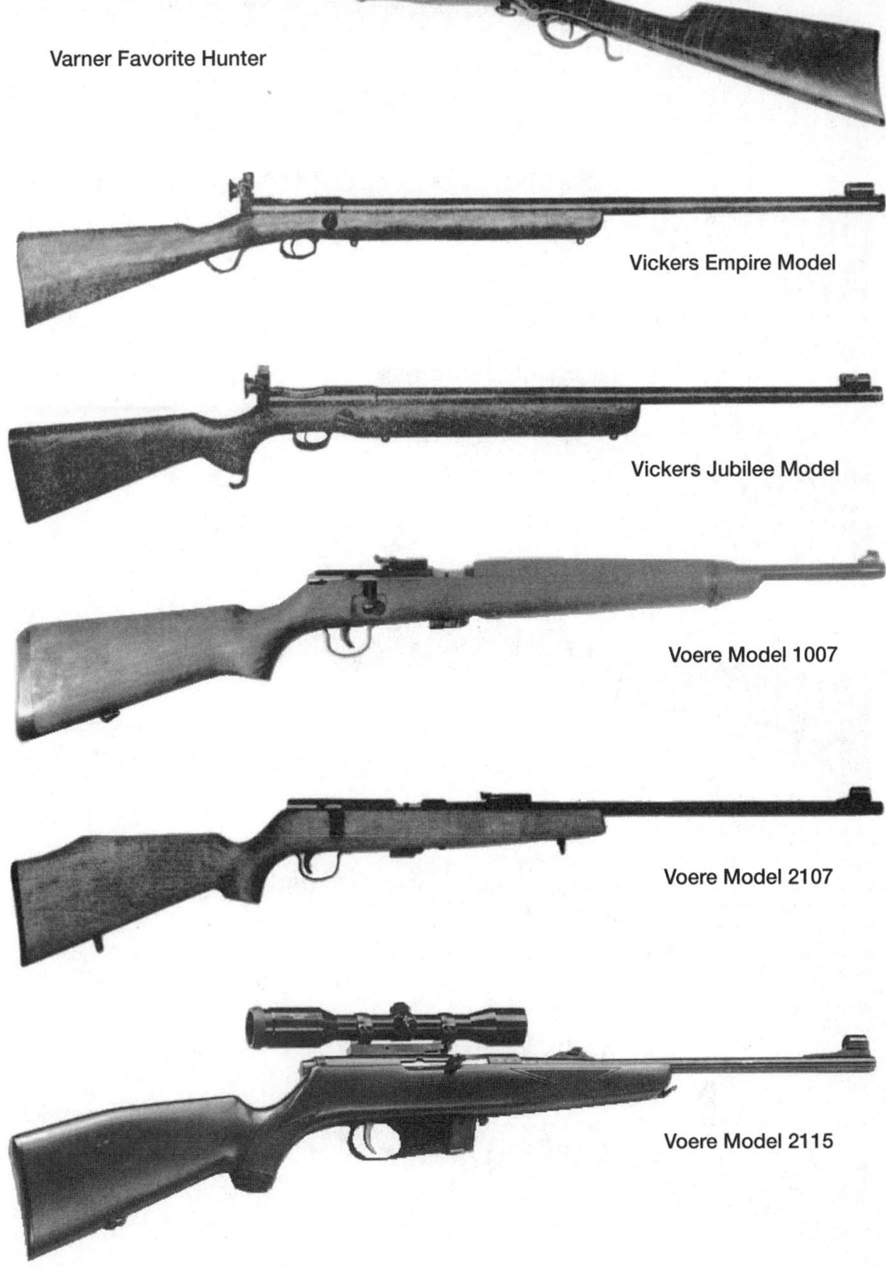

Varner Favorite Hunter

Vickers Empire Model

Vickers Jubilee Model

Voere Model 1007

Voere Model 2107

Voere Model 2115

VOERE MODEL 2107

Bolt action; 22 LR; 5-, 8-shot magazine; 19-1/2-inch barrel; 41-inch overall length; weighs 6 lbs.; fully adjustable open rear sight, hooded front; European hardwood Monte Carlo stock; swivel studs; buttpad. Made in Germany. Introduced 1986; discontinued 1988.

Perf: $325 **Exc:** $290 **VGood:** $230

VOERE MODEL 2107 DELUXE

Same specs as Model 2107 except checkered stock; raised cheekpiece. Introduced 1986; discontinued 1988.

Perf: $350 **Exc:** $280 **VGood:** $230

VOERE MODEL 2114S

Semi-automatic; 22 LR; 8-, 15-shot clip magazine; 18-inch barrel; 37-2/3-inch overall length; weighs 5-3/4 lbs.; leaf rear sight, hooded ramp front; walnut-finished beechwood stock, pistol grip, forend; single-stage trigger; wing-type safety. Made in Austria. Introduced 1984; no longer in production.

Perf: $265 **Exc:** $210 **VGood:** $170

VOERE MODEL 2115

Semi-automatic; 22 LR; 8-, 10-, 15-shot clip magazine; 18-inch barrel; 37-3/4-inch overall length; weighs 5-3/4 lbs.; leaf rear sight, hooded ramp front; walnut-finished beechwood stock; checkered pistol grip, forend; cheekpiece; single-stage trigger wing type safety. Made in Austria. Introduced 1984; discontinued 1995.

Perf: $300 **Exc:** $260 **VGood:** $230

VOERE MODEL 2150

Bolt action; 22-250, 243, 270, 7x57, 7x64, 308, 30-06 (standard), 7mm Rem. Mag., 300 Win. Mag., 9.3x64, 338 Win. Mag. (375 H&H, 458 Win. Mag. on special order); 22-inch barrel, 24-inch (magnums); weighs about 8 lbs.; ramp front sight, adjustable open rear; walnut stock with hand-rubbed oil finish, hand-checkered grip and forend; barrel-mounted front sling swivel; K-98 Mauser action with hinged floorplate; Was imported from Austria; importation dropped 1995.

Perf: $800 **Exc:** $675 **VGood:** $520

VOERE MODEL 2155

Bolt action; 270, 243, 30-06 (standard), 308, 22-250, 7x64, 5.6x57, 6.5x55, 8x57 JRS, 7mm Rem. Mag., 300 Win. Mag., 8x68S, 9.3x62, 9.3x64, 6.5x68; 5-shot non-detachable box magazine; 22-inch (standard), 24-inch barrel; Mauser-type action; fixed post front sight, fully adjustable rear sight; drilled, tapped for scope mount; European walnut stock; checkered pistol grip, forend; single- or double-set trigger. Made in Austria. Introduced 1984; importation dropped 1995.

Perf: $800 **Exc:** $650 **VGood:** $530

VOERE MODEL 2165

Bolt action; 22-250, 243, 270, 7x57, 7x64, 308, 30-06 (standard), 7mm Rem. Mag., 300 Win. Mag., 9.3x64 (magnum); 5-shot magazine (standard calibers), 3-shot (magnums); 22-inch barrel (standard calibers), 24-inch (magnums); 44-1/2-inch overall length (22-inch barrel); weighs 7 to 7-1/2 lbs.; ramp front sight, open adjustable rear; European walnut stock with Bavarian cheekpiece, schnabel forend tip, rosewood grip cap; built on Mauser 98-type action; tang safety; detachable box magazine; comes with extra magazine. No longer imported.

Perf: $850 **Exc:** $690 **VGood:** $550

VOERE MODEL 2185

Semi-automatic; 7x64, 308, 30-06; 2-shot detachable magazine; 20-inch barrel; 43-1/2-inch overall length; weighs 7-3/4 lbs.; blade on ramp front sight, open adjustable rear; receiver drilled, tapped for scope mounts; European walnut stock with checkered grip and forend; ventilated rubber recoil pad; oil finish; gas-operated action with three forward locking lugs; hammer-forged free-floating barrel; two-stage trigger; cocking indicator inside trigger guard. Importation dropped 1994.

Perf: $1700 **Exc:** $1350 **VGood:** $900

With Mannlicher-style full stock

Perf: $1750 **Exc:** $1400 **VGood:** $975

VOERE MODEL 2185 MATCH

Same specs as Model 2185 except 5-shot magazine; hooded post front sight, aperture rear; laminated match-type stock with glass bedding; adjustable cheekpiece and buttplate. Introduced 1992; discontinued 1994.

Perf: $2900 **Exc:** $2300 **VGood:** $1600

VOERE TITAN

Bolt action; 243, 25-06, 270, 7x57, 308, 30-06, 257 Weatherby, 270 Weatherby, 7mm Rem. Mag., 300 Win. Mag., 300 Weatherby, 308 Norma Mag., 375 H&H; 3-, 4-shot magazine, depending on caliber; 24-inch, 26-inch barrel; 44-1/2-inch overall length (24-inch barrel); weighs 8 lbs.; no sights; drilled, tapped for scope mounts; hand-checkered, oil-finished European walnut Monte Carlo stock; recoil pad; swivel studs; three-lug, front-locking action. Made in Austria. Introduced 1986; discontinued 1988.

Perf: $800 **Exc:** $675 **VGood:** $535

VOERE TITAN MENOR

Bolt action; 222 Rem., 223 Rem.; 3-shot magazine; 23-1/2-inch barrel; 42-inch overall length; weighs 6 lbs.; no sights; drilled, tapped for scope mounts; hand-checkered, oil-finished European walnut Monte Carlo stock; rosewood grip cap, forend tip. Made in Austria. Introduced 1986; discontinued 1988.

Perf: $600 **Exc:** $500 **VGood:** $400

VOERE VEC-91 LIGHTNING

Bolt action, electronic ignition; 5.56 UCC (223-cal.), 6mm UCC caseless ammunition; 5-shot magazine; 20-inch barrel; 39-inch overall length; weighs 6 lbs.; blade on ramp front sight, open adjustable rear; drilled, tapped for scope mounts; European walnut stock with cheekpiece; checkered grip and schnabel forend; top tang safety; fires caseless ammunition via electric ignition; two batteries housed in pistol grip last about 5000 shots; trigger adjustable from 5 oz. to 7 lbs.; twin forward locking lugs. Imported from Austria. Introduced 1991. Without ammunition, this gun is a paperweight – buyer beware!

Perf: $850 **Exc:** $700 **VGood:** $575

VOERE VEC-91BR

Same specs as VEC-91 except single shot; heavy 20-inch barrel; synthetic benchrest stock. Imported from Austria. Introduced 1995. Deduct 50 percent if no ammunition.

Perf: $1700 **Exc:** $1400 **VGood:** $900

VOERE VEC-91HB VARMINT SPECIAL

Same specs as VEC-91 except 22-inch heavy sporter barrel; black synthetic or laminated wood stock. Imported from Austria. Introduced 1995. Deduct 50 percent if no ammunition.

Perf: $1350 **Exc:** $1000 **VGood:** $720

VOERE VEC-91SS

Same specs as VEC-91 except no sights; synthetic stock with straight comb, matte-finished metal. Imported from Austria. Introduced 1995. Deduct 50 percent if no ammunition.

Perf: $1200 **Exc:** $930 **VGood:** $700

WALTHER MODEL 1

Semi-automatic; 22 LR; 5-, 9-shot detachable box magazine; 20-inch barrel; tangent curve rear sight, ramp front; hand-checkered European walnut sporting stock; pistol grip; grooved forend; sling swivels; with bolt-action feature makes it possible to fire as semi-automatic, single-shot or as bolt-operated repeater. Manufactured prior to WWII.

Exc: $600 **VGood:** $525 **Good:** $350

WALTHER MODEL 2

Semi-automatic; 22 LR; 5-, 9-shot detachable box magazine; 24-1/2-inch barrel; tangent curve rear sight, ramp front; hand-checkered European walnut sporting stock; pistol grip; grooved forend; sling swivels; bolt-action feature makes it possible to fire as semi-automatic, single-shot or as bolt-operated repeater. Manufactured prior to WWII.

Exc: $590 **VGood:** $490 **Good:** $365

WALTHER MODEL 2 LIGHTWEIGHT

Same specs as Model 2 except 20-inch barrel; lightweight stock.

Exc: $590 **VGood:** $490 **Good:** $365

WALTHER MODEL G22

Semi-automatic, bullpup design, 22 LR; polymer frame and stock; 10-shot detachable box magazine, stock holds spare magazine; 20-inch barrel; 29-1/2-inch overall length; weighs 5.9 pounds; adjustable sights, rails will mount optical or laser sights, combination packages offered; introduced 2004, still available from Walther USA.

Perf: $390 **Exc:** $300 **VGood:** $275

WALTHER MODEL GX-1 MATCH

Bolt action; single shot; 22 LR; 25-1/2-inch heavy barrel; micrometer aperture rear sight, globe front; European walnut thumbhole stock; adjustable cheekpiece, buttplate; removable butthook; accessory rail; hand stop; palm rest; counterweight; sling swivels; free rifle design. No longer in production.

Perf: $1875 **Exc:** $1375 **VGood:** $1100

WALTHER MODEL KK/MS METALLIC SILHOUETTE

Bolt action; single shot; 22 LR; 25-1/2-inch barrel; 44-3/4-inch overall length; weighs 8-3/4 lbs.; no sights; receiver grooved for scope mounts; thumbhole European walnut stock; stippled grip, forend; adjustable trigger; oversize bolt knob; rubber buttpad. Made in Germany. Introduced 1989; discontinued 1991.

Exc: $1230 **VGood:** $1000 **Good:** $800

WALTHER MODEL KKJ

Bolt action; 22 LR; 5-shot box magazine; 22-1/2-inch medium-heavy target barrel; open rear sight, ramp front; checkered European walnut pistol-grip stock forearm; high tapered comb; sling swivels. Introduced in 1957; no longer imported.

Exc: $700 **VGood:** $575 **Good:** $420

WALTHER MODEL KKJ-HO

Same specs as Model KKJ except chambered for 22 Hornet.

Exc: $800 **VGood:** $680 **Good:** $550

WALTHER MODEL KKJ-MA

Same specs as Model KKJ except 22 WMR.

Exc: $760 **VGood:** $600 **Good:** $420

WALTHER MODEL KKM MATCH

Bolt action; single shot; 22 LR; 26-inch barrel; micrometer rear sight, Olympic front with post, aperture inserts; European walnut stock with adjustable hook buttplate, hand shelf, ball-type offset yoke palm rest; fully-adjustable match trigger. Imported from Germany. Introduced 1957; no longer in production.

Exc: $1400 **VGood:** $1100 **Good:** $800

WALTHER MODEL KKM-S

Same specs as Model KKM except adjustable cheekpiece.

Exc: $1500 **VGood:** $1175 **Good:** $900

WALTHER MODEL KKW

Bolt action; single shot; 22 LR; tangent curve rear sight, ramp front; walnut military-style stock. Manufactured prior to WWII.

Exc: $695 **Vgood:** $575 **Good:** $390

WALTHER MODEL PRONE 400

Bolt action; single shot; 22 LR; 25-1/2-inch barrel; micrometer rear sight, interchangeable post or aperture front; European walnut stock with adjustable length, drop; cheekpiece; forearm guide rail for sling or palm rest; fully-adjustable trigger; especially designed for prone shooting. Introduced 1972; no longer in production.

Exc: $750 **VGood:** $630 **Good:** $510

Walther Model 2

Walther G22

Walther Model KKJ

Walther Model KKM Match

Walther Model Prone 400

Walther Model SSV Varmint Rifle

Walther MovingTarget Model

WALTHER MODEL SSV VARMINT RIFLE

Bolt action; single shot; 22 LR, 22 Hornet; 25-1/2-inch barrel; no sights; European walnut Monte Carlo stock; high cheekpiece; full pistol grip, forend. No longer in production.

Exc: $600 **VGood:** $520 **Good:** $420

22 Hornet model

Exc: $700 **VGood:** $620 **Good:** $510

WALTHER MODEL V

Bolt action; single shot; 22 LR; 26-inch barrel; open rear sight, ramp front; uncheckered European walnut pistol-grip sporting stock, grooved forend; sling swivels. Manufactured prior to World War II.

Exc: $400 **VGood:** $375 **Good:** $300

WALTHER MODEL V MEISTERBUSCHE

Same specs as Model V except micrometer open rear sight; checkered pistol grip.

Exc: $480 **VGood:** $440 **Good:** $340

WALTHER MOVING TARGET MODEL

Bolt action; single shot; 22 LR; 23-1/2-inch barrel; micrometer rear sight, globe front; receiver grooved for dovetail scope mounts; European walnut thumbhole stock; stippled forearm, pistol grip; adjustable cheekpiece, buttplate; especially designed for running boar competition. Imported from Germany. Introduced 1972; no longer in production.

Exc: $1295 **VGood:** $1095 **Good:** $850

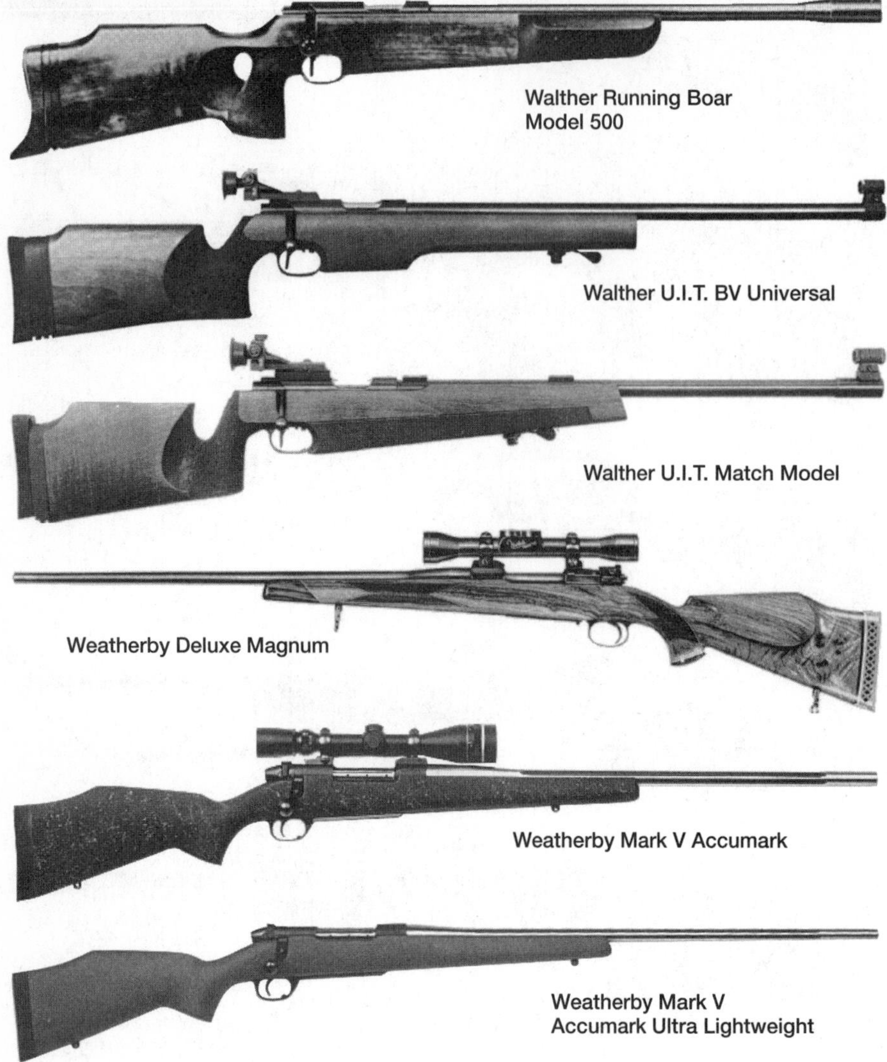
Walther Running Boar Model 500

Walther U.I.T. BV Universal

Walther U.I.T. Match Model

Weatherby Deluxe Magnum

Weatherby Mark V Accumark

Weatherby Mark V Accumark Ultra Lightweight

WALTHER OLYMPIC MODEL

Bolt action; single shot; 22 LR; 26-inch heavy barrel; extension micrometer rear sight, interchangeable front; hand-checkered pistol-grip target stock of European walnut; full rubber-covered beavertail forend; thumbhole; palm rest; adjustable buttplate; sling swivels. Manufactured in Germany prior to WWII.

Exc: $950 **VGood:** $850 **Good:** $695

WALTHER RUNNING BOAR MODEL 500

Bolt action; single shot; 22 LR; 23-1/2-inch barrel; no sights; receiver grooved for dovetail scope mounts; European walnut thumbhole stock; stippled pistol grip; forend; adjustable cheekpiece, buttplate; left-hand stock available. Introduced 1975; discontinued 1990.

Exc: $1200 **VGood:** $1000 **Good:** $800

WALTHER U.I.T. BV UNIVERSAL

Bolt action; single shot; 22 LR; 25-1/2-inch barrel; 44-3/4-inch overall length; weighs about 10 lbs.; globe-type front sight, fully-adjustable aperture rear; European walnut stock, adjustable for length, drop; forend rail; meets NRA, UIT requirements; fully-adjustable trigger. Made in Germany. Introduced 1988; discontinued 1990.

Exc: $1450 **VGood:** $1300 **Good:** $1050

WALTHER U.I.T. MATCH MODEL

Same specs as U.I.T. BV except new tapered forend profile; scope mount bases; fully stippled forend. Imported from Germany by Interarms. Introduced 1966; no longer imported.

Exc: $1300 **VGood:** $1000 **Good:** $775

WALTHER U.I.T.-E MATCH MODEL

Same specs as U.I.T. BV except state-of-the-art electronic trigger. Introduced 1984; no longer imported.

Exc: $1350 **VGood:** $1050 **Good:** $875

WEATHERBY CLASSICMARK I

Bolt action; 240 through 460 Wea. Mag.; 22-inch, 26-inch barrel; straight comb stock of hand-selected American Claro walnut with oil finish; 18 lpi panel point checkering; 1-inch Presentation recoil pad; all metal satin finished; Mark V action. Available in right- or left-hand versions. Imported from Japan by Weatherby. Introduced 1992; discontinued 1993.

Perf: $1050 **Exc:** $825 **VGood:** $700

Calibers 300, 340 Wea. Mag., 378 Wea. Mag., 416 Wea. Mag., 460 Wea. Mag.

Perf: $1125 **Exc:** $895 **VGood:** $695

WEATHERBY CLASSICMARK II

Same as the Classicmark I except stock of deluxe hand-selected American walnut with shadow-line cheekpiece, rounded forend; 22 lpi wrap-around point checkering, oil finish; steel grip cap; Old English recoil pad; satin-finished metal; uses Mark V action. Available in right-hand version only. Imported from Japan by Weatherby. Made only in 1992.

Perf: $1400 **Exc:** $1175 **VGood:** $985

Calibers 300, 340 Wea. Mag., 378 Wea. Mag.

Perf: $1500 **Exc:** $1275 **VGood:** $1075

Calibers 416 Wea. Mag., 460 Wea. Mag.

Perf: $1800 **Exc:** $1475 **VGood:** $1275

WEATHERBY CLASSICMARK II SAFARI CLASSIC

Same specs as Classicmark II except 375 H&H; 24-inch barrel; engraved floorplate; ramp front sight, quarter-rib express rear; barrel band front sling swivel. Made in 1992 only.

Perf: $2200 **Exc:** $1850 **VGood:** $1450

WEATHERBY DELUXE (EARLY)

Bolt action; 270, 30-06; 24-inch barrel; no sights; Monte Carlo stock with cheekpiece; hand-checkered pistol-grip, forearm; black grip cap, forearm tip; quick-detachable sling swivels; Mauser action built to Weatherby specs by FN; some Springfield actions were used. Introduced 1948; discontinued 1955.

Exc: $1695 **VGood:** $1495 **Good:** $975

WEATHERBY DELUXE MAGNUM (EARLY)

Same specs as Deluxe except 220 Rocket, 257 Weatherby Mag., 7mm Weatherby Mag., 300 Weatherby Mag., 375 Weatherby Mag., 378 Weatherby Mag.; 24-inch, 26-inch barrel. Introduced 1948; discontinued 1955.

Exc: $1895 **VGood:** $1695 **Good:** $1175

WEATHERBY MARK V ACCUMARK

Bolt action; 223, 22-250, 243, 25-06, 240 Wea Mag, 257, 270, 7mm, 300, 340 Wea. Mags., 338-378 Wea. Mag., 30-378 Wea. Mag., 7mm STW, 7mm Rem. Mag., 300 Win. Mag.; 26-inch, 28-inch barrel; weighs 8-1/2 lbs.; 46-5/8-inch overall length; Bell & Carlson stock with full length aluminum bedding block. Drilled and tapped for scope mounting. Uses Mark V action with heavy-contour fluted stainless barrel with black oxidized flutes, muzzle diameter of .705-inch. Introduced 1996; still offered. Made in U.S.A. From Weatherby. Left Hand add $50.

Perf: $1900 **Exc:** $1500 **VGood:** $1300

WEATHERBY MARK V ACCUMARK RC

Bot action; .240 Wby. Mag., .257 Wby Mag., .270 Win., .270 Wby Mag., 7mm Rem. Mag., 7mm Wby. mag., .308 Win., .30-06 Sprg., .300 Win. Mag., .300 Wby. Mag., .30-378 Wby. Mag., .338-378 Wby. Mag., .340 Wby. Mag., .338 Lapua. 26-inch stainless steel barrel, .28-inch barrel .30-378, .338-378, .338 Lapua. Muzzle break on .338-378 and .338 Lapua. Hand laminated composite stock, Tuned and adjustable trigger, button-rifled, free floated, fluted barrel with target crown, full length T-6 bedding block, engraved floor plate, Pachmayr recoil pad. Range Certified (RC) to deliver three-shot, sub one-inch groups with Weatherby ammo. Introduced 2013.

Perf: $2100 **Exc:** $1500 **VGood:** $1250

WEATHERBY MARK V ACCUMARK ULTRA LIGHTWEIGHT

Similar to the Mark V Accumark except weighs 5-3/4 lbs.; 24-inch, 26-inch fluted barrel with recessed target crown; hand-laminated stock with CNC- machined aluminum bedding plate and faint gray "spider web" finish. Available in 257, 270, 7mm, 300 Wea. Mags., (26-inch); 243, 240 Wea. Mag., 25-06, 270 Win., 280 Rem., 7mm-08, 7mm Rem. Mag., 30-06, 338-06 A- Square, 308, 300 Win. Mag. (24-inch). Introduced 1998. Made in U.S.A. by Weatherby. Left Hand add $50.

Perf: $1850 **Exc:** $1400 **VGood:** $1200

WEATHERBY MARK V OUTFITTER (CUSTOM)

Bolt action; .257 Wby. Mag., .270 Wby. Mag., 7mm Rem. Mag., 7mm Wby. Mag., .300 Win. Mag., .300 Wby. Mag. Composite carbon fiber and Kevlar stock in desert camo. 24" or 26" barrel, CNC bedding block, Hand honed action LH available. Introduced in 2008. Left Hand add $100

Perf: $2700 **Exc:** $1700 **VGood:** $1550

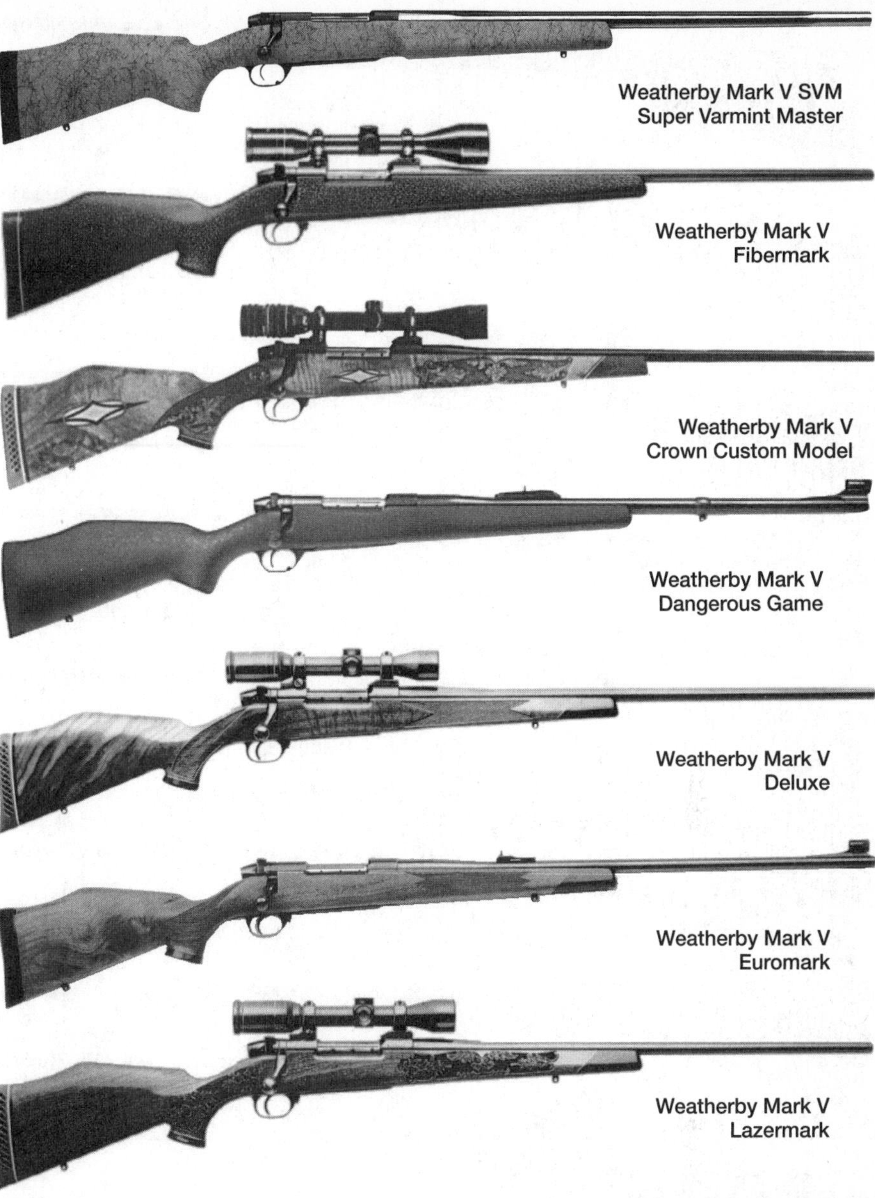

Weatherby Mark V SVM Super Varmint Master

Weatherby Mark V Fibermark

Weatherby Mark V Crown Custom Model

Weatherby Mark V Dangerous Game

Weatherby Mark V Deluxe

Weatherby Mark V Euromark

Weatherby Mark V Lazermark

WEATHERBY MARK V SVM SUPER VARMINT MASTER

Similar to the Mark V Accumark except has 26-inch fluted Krieger barrel, spiderweb-pattern tan laminated synthetic stock; fully adjustable trigger. Chambered for 223, 22-250, 220 Swift, 243; 220 Swift made as a single-shot rifle. Made in U.S.A. by Weatherby, introduced in 2000, still in production.

Perf: $1380 **Exc:** $1100 **VGood:** $900

WEATHERBY MARK V FIBERMARK

Similar to other Mark V models except has black Kevlar and fiberglass composite stock and bead-blast blue or stainless finish. Chambered for 19 standard and magnum calibers. Introduced 1983; reintroduced 2001; still offered. Made in U.S.A. by Weatherby. Left Hand add $50.

Perf: $1300 **Exc:** $900 **VGood:** $800

WEATHERBY MARK V FIBERMARK ALASKAN

Same specs as Fibermark except 270 Weatherby Mag., 7mm Weatherby Mag., 300 Weatherby Mag., 340 Weatherby Mag.; all metal parts plated with electroless nickel for corrosion protection. Introduced 1991; discontinued 1994.

Perf: $1150 **Exc:** $995 **VGood:** $895

WEATHERBY MARK V CROWN CUSTOM MODEL

Bolt action; 240 Weatherby Mag., 257 Weatherby Mag., 7mm Weatherby Mag., 300 Weatherby Mag., 30-06, 340 Weatherby Mag.; 3-, 5-shot magazine; 24-inch, 26-inch barrel; optional sights; super-fancy walnut stock with carving, inlays; utilizes hand-honed, engraved Mark V barreled action; fully checkered bolt knob; engraved floorplate; damascened bolt, follower; gold monogramed name or initials; right-hand only. Introduced 1989; still offered by Weatherby Custom Shop.

Perf: $5695 **Exc:** $4995 **VGood:** $2900

WEATHERBY MARK V CUSTOM MODEL

Bolt action; 22-250, 30-06, 224 Weatherby Varmintmaster (standard action), 240, 257, 270, 7mm, 300, 340, 378, 460 (magnum action); 2-, 5-shot box magazine, depending on caliber; 24-inch, 26-inch barrel; available in right- or left-hand model; scope mounts; super deluxe stock with buttstock inlay, two forend inlays; gold monogram inlay; engraved with name or initials; stock carving with stained background; fully checkered bolt knob; damascened bolt and follower; hand-honed action; engraved floorplate.

Perf: $2995 **Exc:** $2485 **VGood:** $1775

WEATHERBY MARK V DANGEROUS GAME

Bolt action; 375 H&H, 375 Wea. Mag., 378 Wea. Mag., 416 Rem. Mag., 416 Wea. Mag., 458 Win. Mag., 458 Lott, 460 Wea. Mag. 300 Win. Mag., 300 Wby., Mag., 338 Win. Mag., 340 Wby. Mag.; 24-inch or 26-inch barrel; weighs 8-3/4 to 9-1/2 lbs.; 44-5/8-inch to 46-5/8-inch overall length; Kevlar and fiberglass composite stock; Barrel-band hooded front sight with large gold bead, adjustable ramp/shallow V rear. Designed for dangerous-game hunting. Black oxide matte finish on all metalwork; Pachmayr Decelerator recoil pad, short-throw Mark V action. Introduced 2001, still produced. Made in U.S.A. by Weatherby.

Perf: $3100 **Exc:** $1900 **VGood:** $1750

WEATHERBY MARK V DELUXE

Bolt action; 22-250, 30-06, 224 Weatherby Varmintmaster (standard action), 240, 257, 270, 7mm, 300, 340, 378, 416, 460 Weatherby Magnums (magnum action); 2-, 5-shot box magazine, depending on caliber; 24-inch, 26-inch barrel; available in right- or left-hand model; some actions made by Sauer in Germany to Weatherby specs; no sights; drilled, tapped for scope mounts; Monte Carlo stock with cheekpiece; skip checkering on pistol grip, forearm; forearm tip, pistol grip cap, recoil pad; quick-detachable sling swivels. Introduced in 1958; made in U.S. from 1958 to 1960, then production transferred to Germany, later to Japan; still in production.

Standard calibers, German-made

Exc: $1395 **VGood:** $1185 **Good:** $920

Standard calibers, Japan-made

Exc: $1095 **VGood:** $990 **Good:** $850

Magnum calibers, German-made

Exc: $1745 **VGood:** $1435 **Good:** $1240

Magnum calibers, Japanese-made

Exc: $1345 **VGood:** $1240 **Good:** $1100

WEATHERBY MARK V EUROMARK

Bolt action; chambered for all Weatherby calibers except 224, 22-250; 24-inch, 26-inch round tapered barrel; 44-1/4-inch overall length (24-inch barrel); weighs 6-1/2 to 10-1/2 lbs.; open sights optional; walnut Monte Carlo stock with extended tail, fine-line hand checkering; satin oil finish; ebony forend tip and grip cap with maple diamond; solid buttpad; cocking indicator; adjustable trigger; hinged floorplate; thumb safety; quick-detachable sling swivels. Uses Mark V action. Introduced 1986.

Perf: $1600 **Exc:** $1250 **VGood:** $1050

Calibers 378 Wea. Mag., 416 Wea. Mag., 460 Wea. Mag.

Perf: $1900 **Exc:** $1550 **VGood:** $1350

WEATHERBY MARK V EUROSPORT

Bolt action; 22-250, 30-06, 224 Weatherby Varmintmaster (standard action), 240, 257, 270, 7mm, 300, 340, 378, 460 Wby. Mag. (magnum action); 2-, 5-shot box magazine, depending on caliber; 24-inch barrel; Mark V action; available in right-hand only; no sights; drilled, tapped for scope mounts; raised-comb Monte Carlo stock with hand-rubbed satin oil finish; no grip cap, forend tip; recoil pad; quick-detachable sling swivels. Introduced 1995.

Perf: $775 **Exc:** $660 **VGood:** $580

375 caliber

Perf: $825 **Exc:** $690 **VGood:** $610

WEATHERBY MARK V LAZERMARK

Bolt action; 240, 257, 270, 7mm Wea. Mag., 300, 340, 378 WM, 416 WM, 460 WM, 300 WM; 3-, 5-shot magazine; 24-inch, 26-inch round tapered barrel; checkered pistol-grip American walnut stock; rosewood forearm, pistol grip; lazer-carved stock, forend. Introduced 1981; still in production. (Add $250 for 416 WM & 460 WM calibers.)

Perf: $2200 **Exc:** $1750 **VGood:** $1550

Weatherby Mark V Royal Custom

Weatherby Mark V Safari Grade Custom

Weatherby Mark V Sporter

Weatherby Mark V SLS Stainless Laminate Sporter

Weatherby Mark V Super Big Game Master Deer Rifle

Weatherby Mark V Synthetic

Weatherby Mark V Deluxe

Weatherby Mark XXII Clip

WEATHERBY MARK V ROYAL CUSTOM

Bolt action; 257, 270, 7mm, 300, 340 all Wby. Mags. Other calibers available upon request. Barrel: 26-inch. Stock: Monte Carlo hand-checkered claro walnut with high gloss finish. Bolt and follower are damascened with checkered knob. Engraved receiver, bolt sleeve and floorplate sport scroll pattern. Animal images on floorplate optional. High gloss blue, 24-karat gold and nickel-plating. Made in U.S.A., still offered by Weatherby Custom Shop.

Perf: $5200 **Exc:** $4300 **VGood:** $3100

WEATHERBY MARK V SAFARI GRADE CUSTOM

Bolt action; 300 WM, 340 WM, 378 WM, 416 WM, 460 WM; 24-inch barrel; satin oil-finished European walnut stock; ebony forend tip, pistol grip cap; black recoil pad; fine-line checkering; matte blue finish; barrel band front sling swivel; quarter-rib rear sight, hooded ramp front with brass bead; engraved floorplate; custom-built rifle; Introduced, 1989; still offered by Weatherby Custom Shop. (Add $200 for 378 WM and larger calibers.)

Perf: $5100 **Exc:** $3965 **VGood:** $2800

WEATHERBY MARK V TRR CUSTOM MAGNUM & TRR RC VERSION

Bolt action; .300 Win. Mag., .300 Wby. Mag., .30-378 Wby. Mag., .338 Lapua Mag., .338-378 Wby. Mag. Fully adjustable composite stock, free floated barrel with recessed target crown, hand tuned fully adjustable trigger and Accubrake muzzle break (.30-378, .338-378 and .338 Lapua only) TRR RC version has a 26" Krieger # 3 contour free floated barrel, hand tuned trigger, honed action, drop box magazine, hand laminated stock with aluminum bedding block and slide for bi-pod attachment. Guaranteed to shoot sub MOA three-shot groups at 100 yards with Weatherby ammo.

TRR Custom Magna

Perf: $2650 **Exc:** $2000 **VGood:** $1850

TRR RC

Perf: $3850 **Exc:** $2800 **VGood:** $2500

WEATHERBY MARK V SPORTER

Bolt action; 257, 270, 7mm, 300, 340 Wea. Mag., 7mm Rem Mag., 300 Win Mag., 338 Win. Mag., 375 H&H; 24-inch, 26-inch barrel; Mark V action; low-luster blue metal; Monte Claro walnut stock with high-gloss epoxy finish; Monte Carlo comb, recoil pad. Introduced 1993; still produced.

Perf: $1150 **Exc:** $950 **VGood:** $850

WEATHERBY MARK V STAINLESS

Bolt action; 22-250, 30-06, 224 Weatherby Varmintmaster (standard action), 240, 257, 270, 7mm, 300, 340, 378, 460 (magnum action); 2-, 5-shot box magazine, depending on caliber; 24-inch, 26-inch barrel; available in right-hand only; 400 series stainless steel construction; lightweight injection-moulded synthetic stock with raised Monte Carlo comb; checkered grip and forend; custom floorplate release. Made in U.S. From Weatherby. Introduced 1995.

Perf: $885 **Exc:** $695 **VGood:** $585

375 H&H

Perf: $995 **Exc:** $795 **VGood:** $700

WEATHERBY MARK V SLS STAINLESS LAMINATE SPORTER

Similar to the Mark V Stainless except all metalwork is 400 series stainless with a corrosion-resistant black oxide bead-blast matte finish. Action is hand-bedded in a laminated stock with a 1-inch recoil pad. Weighs 8-1/2 lbs. Introduced 1997, no longer offered. Made in U.S.A. From Weatherby.

Perf: $1100 **Exc:** $970 **VGood:** $800

WEATHERBY MARK V SUPER BIG GAME MASTER DEER RIFLE

Bolt action; 240 Wby. Mag., 25-06 Rem., 270 Win., 280 Rem., 30-06 Spfld., 257 Wby. Mag., 270 Wby. Mag., 7mm Rem., Mag., 7mm Wby. Mag., 338- 06 A- Square, 300 Win. Mag., 300 Wby. Mag.; 26-inch barrel with target crown; weighs 5-3/4 lbs., (6-3/4 lbs. Magnum); raised comb Monte Carlo composite stock; fluted barrel, aluminum bedding block, Pachmayr decelerator, 54-degree bolt lift, adj. trigger.

Perf: $1100 **Exc:** $970 **VGood:** $850

WEATHERBY MARK V SYNTHETIC

Bolt action; 7mm Rem Mag, 300 Win Mag, 338 Win Mag, 375 H&H Mag.; 24-inch barrel; weighs 7-1/2 lbs.; synthetic stock with raised Monte Carlo comb, dual-taper checkered forend; low-luster blued metal; uses Mark V action. Right-hand only. Made in U.S. From Weatherby. Introduced 1995; still produced.

Perf: $750 **Exc:** $540 **VGood:** $475

WEATHERBY MARK XXII CLIP

Semi-automatic; 22 LR; 5-, 10-shot clip magazine; 24-inch barrel; folding leaf open rear sight, ramp front; Monte Carlo stock cheekpiece; skip checkering on pistol grip, forearm; forearm tip, grip cap, quick-detachable sling swivels. Introduced 1963; discontinued 1989. Made in Italy. Deduct 5 percent for Japanese manufacture.

Perf: $700 **Exc:** $600 **VGood:** $375

WEATHERBY MARK XXII TUBULAR

Same specs as Mark XXII Clip except 15-shot tube magazine. Introduced 1973; discontinued 1989.

Perf: $700 **Exc:** $600 **VGood:** $375

WEATHERBY MARK XXII BOLT ACTION RIFLE (2007)

Bolt action rifle chambered in 22 LR and 17 HMR. Checkered walnut Monte Carlo stock, 23-inch barrel, rubber rifle buttpad, blued receiver and barrel, magazine capacity 4+1 (17) or 5+1 (22). Introduced 2007.

Perf: $775 **Exc:** 550 **VGood:** 395

WEATHERBY THREAT RESPONSE RIFLES (TRR) SERIES

Bolt action; 223 Rem., 308 Win., 300 Win. Mag., 300 Wby. Mag., 30-378 Wby. Mag., 338-378 Wby. Mag.

22-inch or 26-inch barrel, target crown. Laminated composite stock. Adjustable trigger, aluminum bedding block, beavertail forearms dual tapered, flat-bottomed. "Rocker Arm" lockdown scope mounting. 54-degree bolt lift. Pachmayr decelerator pad. Made in U.S.A., still in production.

Standard calibers

Perf: $1400 **Exc:** $1200 **VGood:** $950

Magnum calibers

Perf: $1500 **Exc:** $1300 **VGood:** $1000

WEATHERBY ULTRAMARK

Bolt action; 240 Wea. Mag., 257 Wea. Mag., 270 Wea. Mag., 30-06, 7mm Wea. Mag., 300 Wea. Mag., 378 Wea. Mag., 416 Wea. Mag.; 3-, 5-shot magazine; 24-inch, 26-inch barrel; fancy American walnut stock, basketweave checkering; hand-honed jeweled action; engraved floorplate; right- or left-hand models. Introduced 1989; discontinued 1990.

Perf: $995 **Exc:** $895 **VGood:** $795

378 Wea. Mag.

Perf: $1250 **Exc:** $1100 **VGood:** $950

416 Wea. Mag.

Perf: $1350 **Exc:** $1200 **VGood:** $1050

WEATHERBY VANGUARD

Bolt action; 25-06, 243, 270, 30-06, 308, 264, 7mm Rem. Mag., 300 Win. Mag.; 3-, 5-shot magazine, depending on caliber: 24-inch hammer-forged barrel; 44-1/2-inch overall length; weighs 7-7/8 lbs.; no sights; receiver drilled, tapped for scope mounts; American walnut stock; pistol-grip cap; forearm tip; hand checkered forearm, pistol grip; adjustable trigger; hinged floorplate. Introduced 1970; discontinued 1983; reintroduced as Vanguard Sporter, still in production.

Perf: $480 **Exc:** $385 **VGood:** $325

WEATHERBY VANGUARD ALASKAN

Same as the Vanguard except 223, 243, 7mm-08, 270 Win., 7mm Rem. Mag., 308, 30-06; forest green or black wrinkle-finished synthetic stock; all metal finished with electroless nickel; right-hand only. Introduced 1992; discontinued 1993.

Perf: $650 **Exc:** $550 **VGood:** $475

WEATHERBY VANGUARD BACK COUNTRY SERIES 2

Bolt action. Pillar bedded composite stock. Guaranteed sub MOA out of box and comes with a "creep free" 2-stage trigger. .240 Wby. Mag., .270 Win., .257 Wby. mag., .30-06 Sprg., .300 Win. Mag., .300 Wby. Mag. 24 " barrel, Cerakote finish, 6.75 pounds. Introduced in 2013.

Perf: $1250 **Exc:** $1050 **VGood:** $950

WEATHERBY VANGUARD CLASSIC I

Same specs as Vanguard except 223, 243, 270, 7mm-08, 7mm Rem. Mag., 30-06, 308; 24-inch barrel; classic-style stock without Monte Carlo comb, no forend tip; distinctive Weatherby grip cap; satin finish on stock. Introduced 1989; discontinued 1993.

Perf: $475 **Exc:** $400 **VGood:** $335

WEATHERBY VANGUARD CLASSIC II

Same specs as Vanguard except 22-250, 243, 270, 7mm Rem. Mag., 30-06, 300 Win. Mag., 338 Win. Mag., 270 Wea. Mag., 300 Wea. Mag.; rounded forend with black tip, black grip cap with walnut diamond inlay, 20 lpi checkering; solid black recoil pad; oil-finished stock. Introduced 1989; discontinued 1993.

Perf: $625 **Exc:** $510 **VGood:** $410

WEATHERBY VANGUARD FIBERGUARD

Same specs as Vanguard except 223, 243, 308, 270, 7mm Rem. Mag., 30-06; 20-inch barrel; weighs 6-1/2 lbs.; forest green wrinkle-finished fiberglass stock; matte blued metal. Made in Japan. Introduced 1985; discontinued 1988.

Perf: $475 **Exc:** $395 **VGood:** $350

WEATHERBY VANGUARD SERIES 2 CARBINE

Bolt action; .223 Rem., .22-250 Rem., .243 Win., 7mm-08 Rem., .308 Win. Two-stage trigger, composite Griptonite stock, matte bead blasted finish, 20" # 1 contour barrel, three position safety, seven pounds. Introduced in 2013.

Perf: $650 **Exc:** $550 **VGood:** $500

WEATHERBY VANGUARD SERIES 2 DELUXE

Bolt action; .257 Wby. Mag., .270 Win., .30-06 Sprg., .300 Win. Mag., .300 Wby. Mag., .338 Win. Mag. Two-stage trigger, Monte-Carlo high grade claro walnut stock with high gloss finish, rosewood forend with fine-line checkering, blued metal work with high lustre finish, three position safety. Introduced in 2013.

Perf: $1150 **Exc:** $1050 **VGood:** $950

WEATHERBY VANGUARD SERIES 2 SPORTER & SPORTER DBM

Bolt action; .223 Rem., .22-250 Rem., .243 Win., .25-06 Rem., .257 Wby. Mag., .270 Win., 7mm-08 Rem., 7mm Rem. Mag., .308 Win., .30-06 Sprg., .300 Win. Mag., .300 Wby. Mag., .338 Win. Mag. Two-stage trigger, Monte-Carlo grade A Turkish walnut stock, rosewood forend with diamond point checkering, matte bead blasted finish, three position safety. Introduced in 2013. Add $50 for Detachable Box Magazine (DBM) Version in .25-06, .270 & .30-06.

Perf: $850 **Exc:** $700 **VGood:** $600

WEATHERBY VANGUARD SERIES 2 STAINLESS SYNTHETIC

Bolt action; .223 Rem., .243 Win., .270 Win., .308 Win., .30-06 Sprg., .257 Wby. Mag., 7mm Rem. Mag., .300 Win. Mag., .300 Wby. Mag. 400 stainless steel matte finish steel, two-stage trigger, composite Griptonite stock, 24" barrel, three position safety. Introduced in 2013.

Perf: $750 **Exc:** $650 **VGood:** $550

WEATHERBY VANGUARD SERIES 2 SYNTHETIC

Bolt action; .223 Rem., .22-250 Rem., .240 Wby Mag., .243 Win., .25-06 Rem., .270 Win., .7mm-08 Rem., .308 Win., .30-06 Sprg., .257 Wby. Mag., 7mm Rem. Mag., .300 Win. Mag., .300 Wby. .338 Win. Mag.Two-stage trigger, composite Griptonite stock, matte bead blasted finish, 24" barrel, three position safety. Introduced in 2013.

Perf: $650 **Exc:** $550 **VGood:** $500

WEATHERBY VANGUARD SERIES 2 SYNTHETIC DBM

Bolt action; .25-06 Rem., .270 Win., .30-06 Sprg. Two-stage trigger, composite Griptonite stock, detachable three-round box magazine, matte bead blasted finish, 24" barrel, three position safety, seven pounds. Introduced in 2013.

Perf: $750 **Exc:** $700 **VGood:** $600

WEATHERBY VANGUARD SERIES 2 SYNTHETIC YOUTH

Bolt action; .223 Rem., .22-250 Rem., .243 Win., 7mm-08 Rem., .308 Win. Two-stage trigger, injection molded composite stock with adjustable length of pull, matte bead blasted finish, 20" # 1 contour barrel, three position safety, seven pounds. Introduced in 2013.

Perf: $600 **Exc:** $500 **VGood:** $450

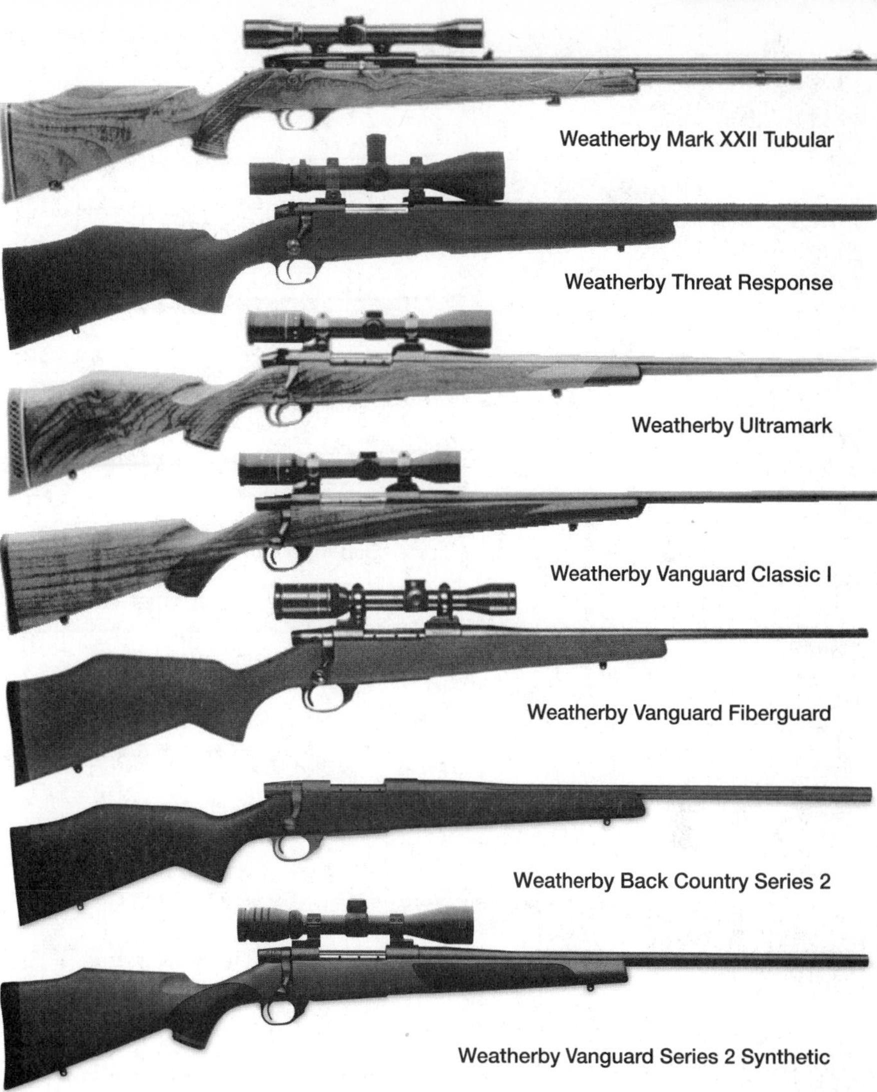

Weatherby Mark XXII Tubular

Weatherby Threat Response

Weatherby Ultramark

Weatherby Vanguard Classic I

Weatherby Vanguard Fiberguard

Weatherby Back Country Series 2

Weatherby Vanguard Series 2 Synthetic

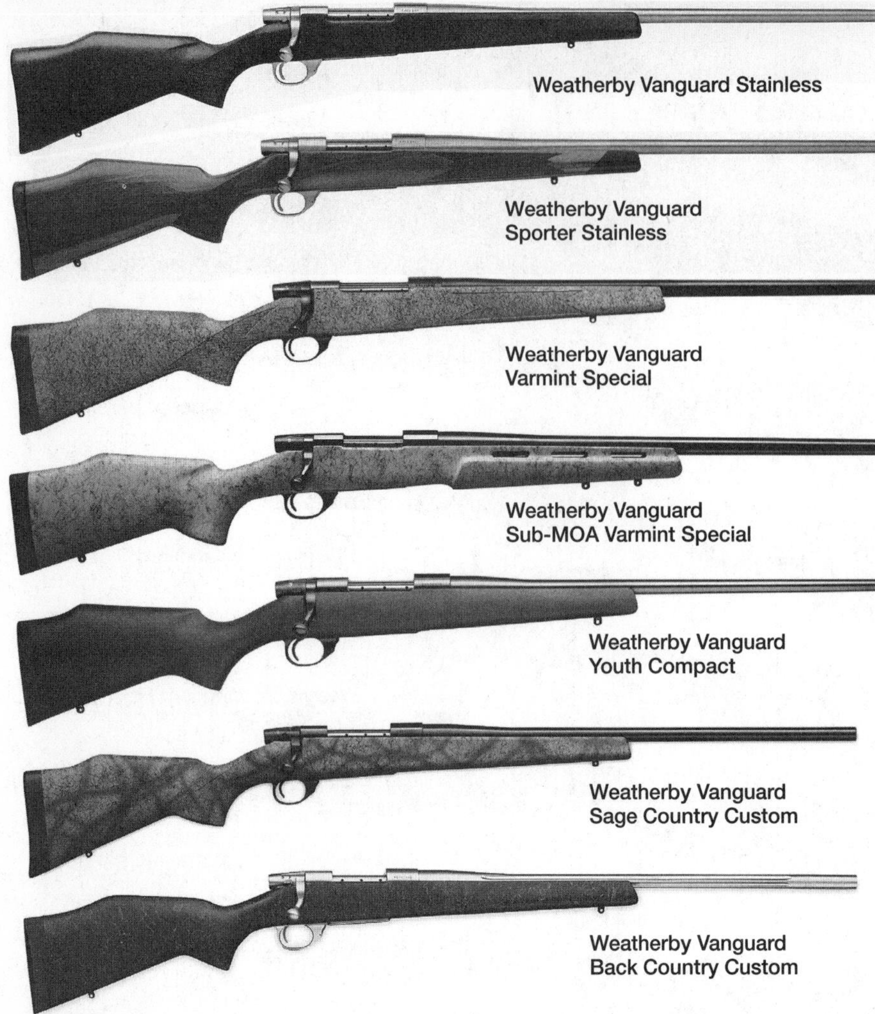
Weatherby Vanguard Stainless

Weatherby Vanguard Sporter Stainless

Weatherby Vanguard Varmint Special

Weatherby Vanguard Sub-MOA Varmint Special

Weatherby Vanguard Youth Compact

Weatherby Vanguard Sage Country Custom

Weatherby Vanguard Back Country Custom

WEATHERBY VANGUARD SERIES 2 VARMINT SPECIAL

Bolt action; .223 Rem., .22-250 Rem., .308 Win. Two-stage trigger, composite Griptonite stock, matte bead blasted finish, 22" # 3 contour barrel, three position safety, recessed target crown. Introduced in 2013

Perf: $850 **Exc:** $750 **VGood:** $600

WEATHERBY VANGUARD STAINLESS

Similar to Vanguard, but matte-finish stainless-steel parts, synthetic stock; 223, 22-250, 243, 257 Wby. Mag., 270, 270 WSM, 270, 7mm Rem. Mag., 308, 300 Win. Mag., 300 WSM, 300 Win. Mag., 300 Wby. Mag., 338 Win. Mag.

Perf: $500 **Exc:** $400 **VGood:** $300

WEATHERBY VANGUARD SYNTHETIC

Similar to Vanguard, but black synthetic stock, metal parts have matte black finish; same cartridge chamberings as Vanguard Stainless.

Perf: $475 **Exc:** $375 **VGood:** $245

WEATHERBY VANGUARD TRR RC & SERIES 2 TRR RC

Bolt action; .223 Rem., .308 Win. Guaranteed to shoot three-shot sub MOA groups with Weatherby ammo. Hand laid composite stock with aluminum bedding plate and beaver tail forearm, dual swivel studs. 22" # 3 contour barrel with recessed target crown. Series 2 version has a match quality two stage trigger. Series 2 introduced in 2013. Add $50 for Series 2 version.

Perf: $1050 **Exc:** $850 **VGood:** $750

WEATHERBY VANGUARD VGL LIGHTWEIGHT RIFLE

Same specs as Vanguard except 223, 243, 270, 30-06, 7mm Rem. Mag., 308; 5-, 6-shot magazine; 20-inch barrel; non-glare blued finish; satin-finished stock; hand checkering; black buttpad, spacer. Made in Japan. Introduced 1984; discontinued 1988.

Perf: $415 **Exc:** $360 **VGood:** $300

WEATHERBY VANGUARD VGS

Same specs as Vanguard except 222-250, 25-06, 243, 270, 30-06, 7 mm Rem. Mag., 300 Win. Mag.; side safety. Made in Japan. Introduced 1984; discontinued 1988.

Perf: $415 **Exc:** $360 **VGood:** $300

WEATHERBY VANGUARD VGX

Same specs as Vanguard except 22-250, 243, 270, 270 Wea. Mag., 7mm Rem. Mag., 30-06, 300 Win. Mag., 300 Wea. Mag., 338 Win. Mag.; 24-inch No. 2 contour barrel; walnut stock with high luster finish; rosewood grip cap and forend tip. Imported from Japan by Weatherby. Introduced 1984; discontinued 1993.

Perf: $500 **Exc:** $415 **VGood:** $360

WEATHERBY VANGUARD WEATHERGUARD

Same specs as Vanguard except 223, 243, 308, 270, 7mm-08, 7mm Rem. Mag., 30-06; 24-inch barrel; 44-1/2-inch overall length; weighs 7-1/2 lbs.; accepts same scope mount bases as Mark V action; forest green or black wrinkle-finished synthetic stock; all metal is matte blue. Right-hand only. Introduced 1989; discontinued 1993.

Perf: $400 **Exc:** $350 **VGood:** $300

WEATHERBY VANGUARD SPORTER STAINLESS

Similar to Vanguard but with sporter-style stock, stainless steel barrel and receiver.

NIB: $750 **Exc:** $695 **VGood:** $600

WEATHERBY VANGUARD VARMINT SPECIAL

Chambered in .223, .22-250, or .308. 22-inch blued #3 contour heavy crowned barrel, adjustable trigger, synthetic tan composite stock with black spiderweb pattern. Introduced 2006.

NIB: $575 **Exc:** $525 **VGood:** $450

WEATHERBY VANGUARD SUB-MOA VARMINT SPECIAL

Similar to Vanguard Varmint Special but with ventilated beavertail forend and other accuracy refinements.

NIB: $825 **Exc:** $750 **VGood:** $625

WEATHERBY VANGUARD SUB-MOA MATTE OR STAINLESS

Introduced in 2005 this model features a guarantee to shoot .99" at 100 yards. Calibers from .223 Rem. to .338 Win. Mag. Barrel length is 24" with Monte Carlo Fiberguard stock. Adjustable trigger. Weight is about 7.75 lbs. Also available in stainless steel. Add 15% for stainless steel.

NIB: $825 **Exc:** $750 **VGood:** $625

WEATHERBY VANGUARD DELUXE

Similar to Vanguard but features 24-inch polished blued barrel, glossy select Monte Carlo walnut stock with rosewood forend, adjustable trigger. Chambered in .270, .30-06, .257 Weatherby Mag., and .300 Weatherby Mag. Introduced 2006.

NIB: $725 **Exc:** $655 **VGood:** $525

WEATHERBY VANGUARD COMPACT

This model, chambered for the ..223, 22-250, .243, or .308, is fitted with a 20" barrel and scaled-down hardwood stock with shorter length of pull. Also included is a full size composite stock. Weight is about 6.75 lbs. Introduced in 2005.

Perf: $550 **Exc:** $500 **VGood:** $425

WEATHERBY VANGUARD YOUTH COMPACT

Similar to above but with synthetic stock. Introduced 2008.

Perf: $550 **Exc:** $500 **VGood:** $425

WEATHERBY VANGUARD SAGE COUNTRY CUSTOM

Introduced in 2008, this is similar to the Vanguard Synthetic but with injection-molded Desert Camo stock. Available in a variety of chamberings from ..223 to .338 Winchester Magnum.

Perf: $950 **Exc:** $795 **VGood:** $525

WEATHERBY VANGUARD BACK COUNTRY CUSTOM

Introduced in 2008, this is a lightweight version of the Vanguard Synthetic with a fluted barrel, textured stock and overall weight of 6-3/4 lbs. Available in a variety of chamberings from ..257 Weatherby Magnum to .300 Weatherby Magnum.

Perf: $950 **Exc:** $795 **VGood:** $525

WEATHERBY WEATHERMARK

Bolt action; 240, 257, 270, 7mm, 300, 340 Wea. Mags, 7mm Rem. Mag., 270 Win., 30-06; 22-inch, 24-inch barrel; weighs 7-1/2 lbs.; impregnated-color black composite stock with raised point checkering; Mark V action; right-hand only. Introduced 1992; no longer made.

Perf: $800 **Exc:** $675 **VGood:** $425

375 H&H

Perf: $900 **Exc:** $775 **VGood:** $500

WEATHERBY WEATHERMARK ALASKAN

Same specs as Weathermark except all metal plated with electroless nickel. Available in right-hand only. Introduced 1992; no longer produced.

Perf: $750 **Exc:** $615 **VGood:** $515

375 H&H

Perf: $800 **Exc:** $720 **VGood:** $545

WEIHRAUCH MODEL HW 60

Single shot; 22 LR; 26-3/4-inch barrel; hooded ramp front sight, match-type aperture rear; European walnut stock with stippled pistol-grip, forend; adjustable buttplate; rail with adjustable swivel; adjustable trigger; push-button safety. Introduced 1981; no longer imported from Germany.

Perf: $670 **Exc:** $550 **VGood:** $430

WEIHRAUCH MODEL HW 60J

Same specs as Model HW 60 except 22 LR, 222; checkered walnut sporter-style stock. Discontinued 1992.

Perf: $535 **Exc:** $420 **VGood:** $375

222 caliber

Perf: $725 **Exc:** $625 **VGood:** $595

WEIHRAUCH MODEL HW 66

Bolt action; 22 Hornet, 222; 22-3/4-inch barrel; 41-3/4-inch overall length; weighs 6-1/2 lbs.; hooded blade ramp front sight, open rear; oil-finished walnut stock with cheekpiece; checkered pistol grip, forend. Introduced 1988; discontinued 1990.

Perf: $625 **Exc:** $515 **VGood:** $400

Double-set trigger

Perf: $665 **Exc:** $560 **VGood:** $460

WEIHRAUCH MODEL HW 660 MATCH

Bolt action; 22 LR; 26-inch barrel; 45-1/3-inch overall length; weighs 10-3/4 lbs.; globe front sight, match aperture rear; match-type walnut stock with adjustable cheekpiece, buttplate; checkered pistol grip, forend; forend accessory rail; adjustable match trigger. Introduced 1990; no longer in production.

Perf: $735 **Exc:** $660 **VGood:** $560

WESSON & HARRINGTON BUFFALO CLASSIC

Single shot; 45-70; 32-inch heavy barrel; 52-inch overall length; weighs 9 lbs.; no sights; drilled and tapped for peep sight; American black walnut stock and forend; barrel dovetailed for front sight; color case-hardened Handi-Rifle action with exposed hammer; color case-hardened crescent buttplate; 19th century checkering pattern. Made in U.S. by H&R 1871, Inc. Introduced 1995; still produced.

Perf: $400 **Exc:** $335 **VGood:** $250

WESSON & HARRINGTON 38-55 TARGET CLASSIC RIFLE

Similar to the Buffalo Classic rifle except chambered for 38-55 Win., has 28-inch barrel; barrel and steel furniture, including steel trigger guard and forend spacer, are highly polished and blued. Color case-hardened receiver and buttplate. Barrel is dovetailed for a front sight, and drilled and tapped for receiver sight or scope mount. Introduced 1998. Made in U.S.A. by H&R 1871, Inc.

Perf: $400 **Exc:** $335 **VGood:** $250

WESTLEY RICHARDS DOUBLE

Double rifle; boxlock; 30-06, 318 Accelerated Express, 375 Mag., 425 Mag. Express, 465 Nitro Express, 470 Nitro Express; 25-inch barrels; hammerless; leaf rear sight, hooded front; French walnut stock; hand-checkered pistol-grip, forearm; cheekpiece; horn forearm tip; sling swivels; ejectors. Favored for African big game. Values vary according to caliber and engraving; range $16,000 to $45,000.

WESTLEY RICHARDS MAGAZINE MODEL

Bolt action; 30-06, 7mm high velocity, 318 Accelerated Express, 375 Mag., 404 Nitro Express, 425 Mag.; 22-inch barrel (7mm High Velocity), 25-inch (425 Mag.) 24-inch other calibers; leaf rear sight, hooded front; sporting stock of French walnut; hand-checkered pistol grip, forearm; cheekpiece; horn forearm tip; sling swivels.

Perf: $7700 **Exc:** $6800 **VGood:** $5600

WHITWORTH EXPRESS

Bolt action; 22-250, 243, 25-06, 270, 7x57, 308, 30-06, 300 Win. Mag., 7mm Rem. Mag., 375 H&H, 458 Win. Mag.; 24-inch barrel; 44-inch overall length; 3-leaf open sight (magnums); open sights (others); classic European walnut English Express stock; hand checkering; adjustable trigger; hinged floorplate; steel recoil crossbolt; solid recoil pad; barrel-mounted sling swivel. Made originally in England; barreled actions later produced in Yugoslavia. Introduced 1974; no longer imported. Add 20 percent for African chamberings.

Exc: $650 **VGood:** $425 **Good:** $300

Westley Richards Magazine Model

Whitworth Express

Wichita Classic Model

Wichita Silhouette Model

Wichita Stainless Magnum

WHITWORTH EXPRESS CARBINE

Same specs as Safari Express except 243, 270, 308, 7x57, 30-06; 20-inch barrel; Mannlicher-style stock. Introduced 1986; discontinued 1988.

Exc: $500 **VGood:** $430 **Good:** $340

WHITWORTH SAFARI EXPRESS

Bolt action; 375 H&H, 458 Win. Mag.; 24-inch barrel; 44-inch overall length; weighs 7-1/2 to 8 lbs.; ramp front sight with removable hood, three-leaf open rear calibrated for 100, 200, 300 yards on 1/4-rib; classic English Express rifle stock design of hand checkered, select European walnut; solid rubber recoil pad; barrel-mounted sling swivel; adjustable trigger; hinged floorplate; solid steel recoil crossbolt. From Interarms. No longer imported.

Exc: $700 **VGood:** $500 **Good:** $375

WICHITA CLASSIC MODEL

Bolt action; single shot; calibers 17 through 308 Win.; 21-1/8-inch octagon barrel; no sights; drilled, tapped for scope mounts; hand-checkered American walnut pistol-grip stock; steel grip cap; Pachmayr rubber recoil pad; right-, left-hand action; Canjar trigger; checkered bolt handle; jeweled bolt; non-glare blue finish. Introduced 1978.

Perf: $1700 **Exc:** $1200 **VGood:** $900

Left-hand model

Perf: $1800 **Exc:** $1300 **VGood:** $925

WICHITA SILHOUETTE MODEL

Bolt action; single shot; all standard calibers; 24-inch free-floated barrel; no sights; drilled/tapped for scope mounts; metallic gray fiberthane stock; vent rubber recoil pad; 2-oz. Canjar trigger; fluted bolt; left- or right-hand; marketed in hard case. Introduced 1983; no longer in production.

Perf: $1900 **Exc:** $1600 **VGood:** $1200

Left-hand model

Perf: $2000 **Exc:** $1700 **VGood:** $1300

WICHITA STAINLESS MAGNUM

Bolt action; calibers 270 Win. through 458 Win. Mag.; single shot or with blind magazine; 22-inch, 24-inch target-grade barrel; no sights; drilled, tapped for Burris scope mounts; hand-inletted, glass-bedded fancy American walnut stock; hand-checkered; steel pistol-grip cap; Pachmayr rubber recoil pad; fully-adjustable trigger; stainless steel barrel, action. Introduced 1980; no longer in production.

Perf: $1725 **Exc:** $1350 **VGood:** $1000

WICHITA VARMINT MODEL

Bolt action; calibers 17 Rem. through 308 Win.; 3-shot magazine; 21-1/8-inch Atkinson chrome-moly barrel; no sights; drilled, tapped for scope mounts; hand inletted, hand-rubbed, hand-checkered American walnut pistol-grip stock; steel grip cap; Pachmayr rubber recoil pad; right- or left-hand action; checkered bolt handle; jeweled bolt; non-glare blued finish. Introduced 1978.

Perf: $1725 **Exc:** $1350 **VGood:** $1000

WICKLIFFE MODEL 76

Single shot; 22 Hornet, 223 Rem., 22-250, 243 Win., 25-06, 308 Win., 30-06, 45-70; 22-inch lightweight, 26-inch heavy sporter barrel; falling block; no sights; American walnut Monte Carlo stock; cheekpiece, pistol grip, semi-beavertail forend. Introduced 1976; discontinued 1979.

Exc: $900 **VGood:** $650 **Good:** $500

WICKLIFFE MODEL 76 DELUXE

Same specs as Model 76 except 30-06; 22-inch barrel; high-luster blue finish; nickel-silver grip

Wilkinson Terry Carbine

Winchester Lee Sporter

Winchester Model 43

Winchester Model 43 Special Grade

Winchester Model 47

Winchester Model 52A Heavy Barrel

cap, better wood. Introduced 1976; discontinued 1979.

Exc: $975 **VGood:** $725 **Good:** $575

WICKLIFFE STINGER

Single shot; 22 Hornet, 223 Rem.; 22-inch barrel; falling block; no sights; American walnut Monte Carlo stock, Continental-type forend; etched receiver logo; quick-detachable sling swivels. Introduced 1979; discontinued 1980.

Exc: $900 **VGood:** $650 **Good:** $500

WICKLIFFE STINGER DELUXE

Same specs as Stinger except 22-inch lightweight barrel; high-luster blue finish; nickel-silver grip cap; better wood. Introduced 1979; discontinued 1980.

Exc: $975 **VGood:** $725 **Good:** $575

WICKLIFFE TRADITIONALIST

Single shot; 30-06, 45-70; 24-inch chrome-moly barrel; falling block; open sights; American walnut classic-style buttstock; hand-cut checkering; sling; sling swivels. Introduced 1979; discontinued 1980.

Exc: $975 **VGood:** $725 **Good:** $575

WILKINSON LINDA CARBINE

Semi-automatic; 9mm Para.; 16-3/16-inch barrel; weighs 7 lbs.; fixed tubular stock with wood pad. Aperture rear sight. Aluminum receiver, pre-ban configuration, vent. barrel shroud, small wooden forearm, 18 or 31 shot mag. Pre-ban receivers made into carbines by Northwest Arms.

Perf: $1000 **Exc:** $770 **VGood:** $560

WILKINSON TERRY CARBINE

Semi-automatic; 9mm Para.; 30-shot magazine; 16-3/16-inch barrel; 30-inch overall length; weighs about 6 lbs.; protected post front sight, aperture rear; dovetailed receiver for scope mounting; uncheckered maple or black synthetic stock forend; bolt-type safety; ejection port has automatic trap door; blowback action; fires from closed bolt. Introduced 1975.

Exc: $425 **VGood:** $325 **Good:** $275

WINCHESTER LEE MUSKET

Bolt action; 6mm (236 USN); 5-shot box magazine; 28-inch barrel; folding leaf rear sight, post front; military semi-pistol-grip stock; blued finish. Commercial version of Lee Navy Model 1895 rifle. Introduced 1897; discontinued 1905. Collector value.

Exc: $2300 **VGood:** $2000 **Good:** $1770

WINCHESTER LEE SPORTER

Same specs as Lee Musket except 24-inch barrel; open rear sight, bead front; sporter-style walnut stock. Introduced 1897; discontinued 1905. Collector value.

Exc: $2350 **VGood:** $2050 **Good:** $1820

WINCHESTER MODEL 43

Bolt action; 218 Bee, 22 Hornet, 25-20, 32-20; 3-shot box magazine, 2-shot (32-20); 24-inch barrel; 42-1/2-inch overall length; weighs 6 lbs.; open rear sight, No. 103 bead front on hooded ramp; uncheckered American walnut pistol-grip stock; swivels. Introduced 1950; discontinued 1957.

Exc: $600 **VGood:** $500 **Good:** $400

WINCHESTER MODEL 43 SPECIAL GRADE

Same specs as Model 43 except for grip cap; checkered pistol grip, forearm; Lyman 59A micrometer rear sight.

Exc: $680 **VGood:** $570 **Good:** $485

WINCHESTER MODEL 47

Bolt action; single shot; 22 Short, 22 Long, 22 LR; 25-inch barrel; peep or open rear sight, No. 97 bead front on ramp with detachable sight-cover or No. 95 bead; uncheckered American walnut pistol grip stock. Introduced 1949; discontinued 1954.

Exc: $380 **VGood:** $310 **Good:** $240

WINCHESTER MODEL 52 (EARLY PRODUCTION)

Bolt action; 22 Short, 22 LR; 5-shot box magazine; 28-inch barrel; folding leaf peep rear sight, blade front; scope bases; semi-military stock; pistol grip; grooves on forearm. Later versions had higher comb, semi-beavertail forearm; slow lock model was replaced in 1929 by speed lock. Last arms of this model bore serial numbers followed by the letter "A." Introduced 1919; discontinued 1937.

Exc: $1050 **VGood:** $815 **Good:** $625

WINCHESTER MODEL 52 SPORTER

Same specs as Model 52 except for 24-inch lightweight barrel; weighs 7-1/4 lbs.; Lyman No. 48F receiver sight, Redfield gold bead on hooded ramp at front; deluxe walnut sporting stock with cheekpiece; checkered forend, pistol grip; black forend tip; leather sling. Beware of fakes. Introduced 1934; discontinued 1958.

Exc: $3500 **VGood:** $3000 **Good:** $1900

WINCHESTER MODEL 52A

Bolt action; 22 Short, 22 LR; 5-shot box magazine; 28-inch barrel; folding leaf peep rear sight, blade front; scope bases; semi-military stock; pistol grip; grooves on forearm; speedlock action. Introduced 1929; discontinued 1939.

Exc: $975 **VGood:** $825 **Good:** $675

WINCHESTER MODEL 52A HEAVY BARREL

Same specs as Model 52A except 28-inch heavy barrel; Lyman 17G front sight. Discontinued 1939.

Exc: 1100 **VGood:** $900 **Good:** $700

WINCHESTER MODEL 52A SPORTER

Same specs as Model 52A except 24-inch lightweight barrel; Lyman No. 48 receiver sight, gold bead on hooded ramp front; deluxe walnut sporting stock, checkered; black forend tip; cheekpiece. Introduced 1937; discontinued 1939.

Exc: $4500 **VGood:** $4000 **Good:** $2500

WINCHESTER MODEL 52B

Bolt action; 22 Short, 22 LR; 5-shot box magazine; 28-inch barrel; various sighting options; target or Marksman pistol-grip stock with high comb, beavertail forearm; round-top receiver; redesigned Model 52A action. Introduced 1940; discontinued 1947.

Exc: $900 **VGood:** $720 **Good:** $585

WINCHESTER MODEL 52B BULL GUN

Same specs as Model 52B except 28-inch extra-heavy barrel; Marksman pistol-grip stock; Vaver No. 35 Mielt extension receiver sight, Vaver WIIAT front.

Exc: $1000 **VGood:** $820 **Good:** $695

WINCHESTER MODEL 52B HEAVY BARREL

Same specs as Model 52B except 28-inch heavy barrel; Lyman No. 48FH rear sight, Lyman No. 77 front.

Exc: $1195 **VGood:** $900 **Good:** $600

WINCHESTER MODEL 52B SPORTER

Same specs as Model 52 except 5-shot detachable box magazine; 24-inch lightweight barrel; Lyman No. 48 receiver sight, gold bead on hooded ramp front; deluxe walnut sporting stock, checkered; black forend tip; cheekpiece; sling swivels; single shot adapter.

Exc: $3500 **VGood:** $2900 **Good:** $2000

WINCHESTER MODEL 52B SPORTER (1993)

Same specs as Model 52B except no sights; drilled, tapped for scope mounting; Remake of early Model 52 Sporter; Model 52C mechanism with stock configuration of the Model 52B; Micro-Motion trigger. Production limited to 6000 rifles. Introduced 1993; discontinued 1993.

Perf: $700 **Exc:** $575 **VGood:** $390

WINCHESTER MODEL 52C

Bolt action; 22 Short, 22 LR; 5-, 10-shot box magazine; 28-inch barrel; various sighting systems; Marksman pistol-grip stock with high comb, beavertail forearm; Micro-Motion trigger; single shot adapter. Introduced 1947; discontinued 1961.

Exc: $1125 **VGood:** $920 **Good:** $680

WINCHESTER MODEL 52C BULL GUN

Same specs as Model 52C except 28-inch extra-heavy bull barrel; weighs 12 lbs.

Exc: $1200 **VGood:** $1000 **Good:** $795

WINCHESTER MODEL 52C HEAVY BARREL

Same specs as Model 52C except 28-inch heavy barrel.

Exc: $1120 **VGood:** $940 **Good:** $670

WINCHESTER MODEL 52C SPORTER

Same specs as Model 52C except 24-inch lightweight barrel; Lyman No. 48 receiver sight, gold bead on hooded ramp front; deluxe walnut sporting stock, checkered; black forend tip; cheekpiece; sling swivels; single shot adapter; Micro-Motion trigger.

Exc: $3400 **VGood:** $2900 **Good:** $2000

WINCHESTER MODEL 52D

Bolt action; single shot; 22 LR; 28-inch free-floating standard or heavy barrel; 46-inch overall length; weighs 9-3/4 lbs. (standard barrel), 11 lbs. (heavy barrel); no sights; scope blocks for standard target scopes; redesigned Marksman stock; rubber buttplate; accessory channel in stock with forend stop. Introduced 1961; discontinued 1980.

Exc: $1100 **VGood:** $920 **Good:** $750

WINCHESTER MODEL 52D INTERNATIONAL MATCH

Same specs as Model 52D except laminated international-style stock with aluminum forend assembly; hook butt plate; adjustable palm rest; ISU or Kenyon trigger. Introduced 1969; discontinued 1980.

ISU trigger

Exc: $1960 **Vgood:** $1850 **Good:** $1740

Kenyon trigger

Exc: $2000 **VGood:** $1900 **Good:** $1800

WINCHESTER MODEL 52D INTERNATIONAL PRONE

Same specs as Model 52D International Match except stock designed for prone shooting only; no hook butt plate or palm rest; oil-finished stock with removable roll-over cheekpiece for easy bore cleaning. Introduced 1975; discontinued 1980.

Exc: $1000 **VGood:** $900 **Good:** $700

WINCHESTER MODEL 54

Bolt action; 270, 7x57mm, 30-30, 30-06, 7.65x53mm, 9x57mm; 5-shot box magazine; 24-inch barrel; open rear sight, bead front; checkered pistol-grip stock; two-piece firing pin; steel buttplate (checkered from 1930 on). Introduced 1925; discontinued 1930.

Exc: $775 **VGood:** $675 **Good:** $525

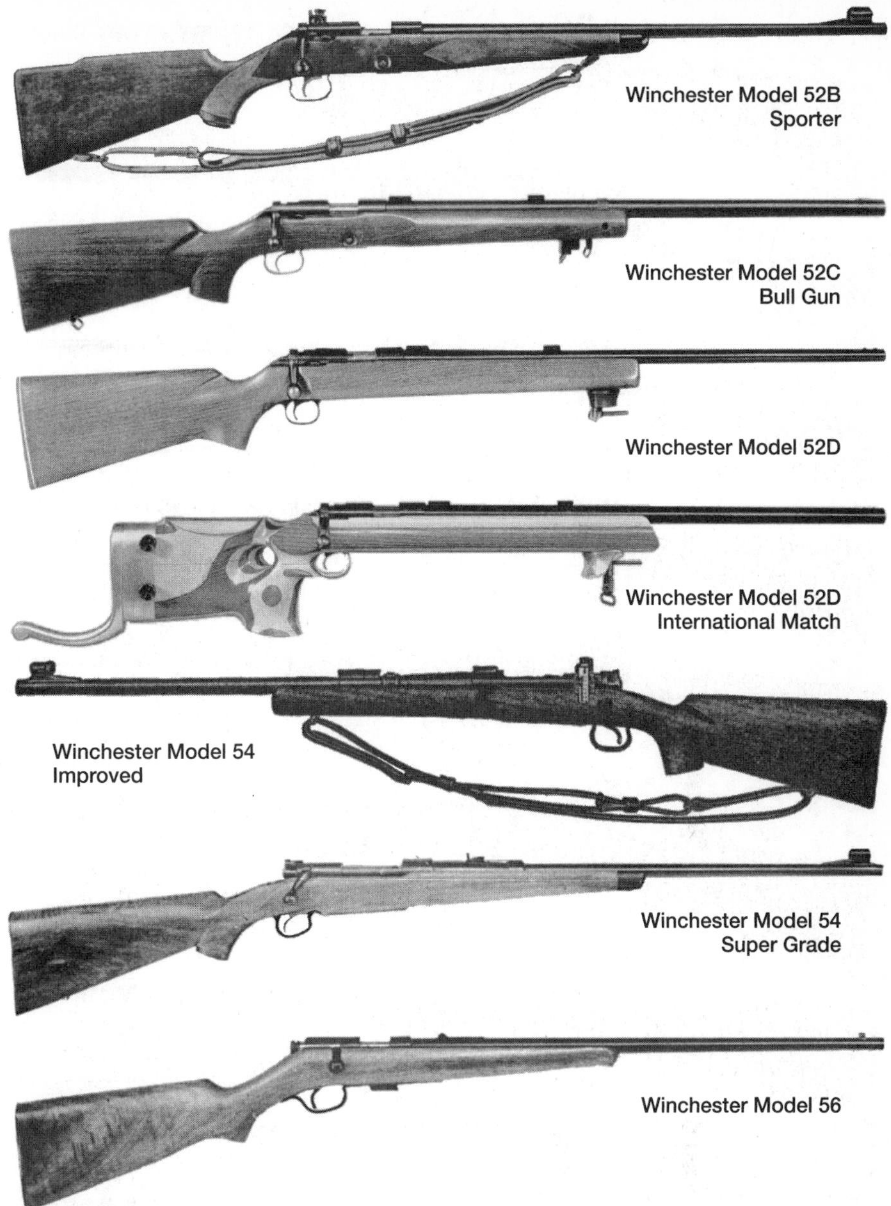

Winchester Model 52B Sporter

Winchester Model 52C Bull Gun

Winchester Model 52D

Winchester Model 52D International Match

Winchester Model 54 Improved

Winchester Model 54 Super Grade

Winchester Model 56

WINCHESTER MODEL 54 CARBINE

Same specs as Model 54 except 20-inch barrel; plain pistol-grip stock; grooves on forearm. Introduced 1927; discontinued 1930.

Exc: $850 **VGood:** $775 **Good:** $550

WINCHESTER MODEL 54 IMPROVED

Same specs as Model 54 except with mechanical improvements; 22 Hornet, 220 Swift, 250-3000, 257 Roberts, 270, 7x57mm, 30-06; 24-inch, 26-inch (220 Swift) barrel; NRA-type stock; checkered pistol-grip, forearm; one-piece firing pin; speed lock. Introduced 1930; discontinued 1936.

Exc: $775 **VGood:** $700 **Good:** $545

WINCHESTER MODEL 54 IMPROVED CARBINE

Same specs as Model 54 except 22 Hornet, 220 Swift, 250-3000, 257 Roberts, 270, 7x57mm, 30-06; 20-inch barrel; lightweight or NRA-type stock; checkered pistol-grip, forearm; one-piece firing pin; speed lock. Introduced 1930; discontinued 1936.

Exc: $800 **VGood:** $750 **Good:** $575

WINCHESTER MODEL 54 NATIONAL MATCH

Same specs as Model 54 except Lyman sights; Marksman target stock; scope bases. Introduced 1935; no longer in production.

Exc: $995 **VGood:** $890 **Good:** $695

WINCHESTER MODEL 54 SNIPER'S RIFLE

Same specs as Model 54 except 30-06; heavy 26-inch barrel; Lyman No. 48 rear peep sight, blade front sight; semi-military type stock.

Exc: $1095 **VGood:** $995 **Good:** $795

WINCHESTER MODEL 54 SUPER GRADE

Same specs as Model 54 except deluxe stock with pistol grip cap, cheekpiece, black forend tip; quick-detachable sling swivels; 1-inch leather sling. Introduced 1934; discontinued 1935.

Exc: $1100 **VGood:** $950 **Good:** $800

WINCHESTER MODEL 56

Bolt action; 22 Short, 22 LR; 5-, 10-shot magazine; 22-inch barrel; open rear sight, bead front; unchecked pistol-grip stock; schnabel-type forearm. Introduced 1926; discontinued 1929. Premium for 22 Short chambering.

Exc: $1145 **VGood:** $795 **Good:** $550

Deluxe model with checkering

Exc: $1595 **VGood:** $995 **Good:** $795

WINCHESTER MODEL 57

Bolt action; 22 Short, 22 LR; 5-, 10-shot magazine; 22-inch barrel; Lyman peep sight, blade front; drilled, tapped receiver; semi-military-type pistol-grip target

Winchester Model 57

Winchester Model 58

Winchester Model 59

Winchester Model 60

Winchester Model 60A

Winchester Model 67 Junior (Boy's Rifle)

Winchester Model 68

Winchester Model 69

Winchester Model 70 (1936-1963)

stock; swivels; web sling; barrel band. Introduced 1927; discontinued 1936. Premium for 22 Short chambering.

Exc: $650 **VGood:** $495 **Good:** $385

WINCHESTER MODEL 58

Bolt action; single shot; 22 Short, 22 Long, 22 LR; 18-inch barrel; open rear sight, blade front sight; uncheckered straight-grip hardwood stock; takedown; manual cocking. Introduced 1928; discontinued 1931.

Exc: $420 **VGood:** $320 **Good:** $270

WINCHESTER MODEL 59

Bolt action; single shot; 22 Short, 22 Long, 22 LR; 23-inch barrel; open rear sight, blade front; pistol grip, uncheckered one-piece hardwood stock; buttplate; takedown; manual cocking. Introduced 1930; discontinued 1931.

Exc: $600 **VGood:** $500 **Good:** $370

WINCHESTER MODEL 60

Bolt action; single shot; 22 Short, 22 Long, 22 LR; 23-inch barrel (until 1933), 27-inch thereafter; open rear sight, blade front; uncheckered pistol-grip hardwood stock; buttplate; takedown; manual cocking. Introduced 1931; discontinued 1934.

Exc: $325 **VGood:** $200 **Good:** $160

WINCHESTER MODEL 60A

Same specs as Model 60 except 27-inch barrel; Lyman rear peep sight, square-top front; heavy semi-military target stock; web sling. Introduced 1933; discontinued 1939.

Exc: $495 **VGood:** $295 **Good:** $200

WINCHESTER MODEL 67

Bolt action; single shot; 22 Short, 22 Long, 22 LR, 22 WMR, 22-shot cartridge; 24-inch rifled, 27-inch rifled or smoothbore barrel; takedown; open rear sight, bead front; uncheckered pistol-grip stock; grooved forearm (early models); manual cocking. Introduced 1934; discontinued 1963.

Exc: $190 **VGood:** $150 **Good:** $125

WINCHESTER MODEL 67 JUNIOR (BOY'S RIFLE)

Same specs as Model 67 except 20-inch barrel; shorter stock.

Exc: $240 **VGood:** $200 **Good:** $130

WINCHESTER MODEL 68

Bolt action; single shot; 22 Short, 22 Long, 22 LR, 22 WMR; 24-inch, 27-inch; takedown; adjustable rear peep sight, ramp front; uncheckered walnut pistol-grip stock; grooved forearm (early models); manual cocking. Introduced 1934; discontinued 1946.

Exc: $285 **VGood:** $205 **Good:** $145

WINCHESTER MODEL 69, 69A

Bolt action; 22 Short, 22 Long, 22 LR; 5-, 10-shot detachable box magazine; 25-inch barrel; takedown; open rear sight, bead ramp front; uncheckered pistol-grip stock. Introduced 1935; discontinued 1963.

Exc: $315 **VGood:** $230 **Good:** $190

WINCHESTER MODEL 69 MATCH

Same specs as Model 69 except Lyman No. 57EW receiver sight, Winchester No. 101 front; Army-type leather sling.

Exc: $335 **VGood:** $245 **Good:** $210

WINCHESTER MODEL 69 TARGET

Same specs as Model 69 except rear peep sight, Winchester No. 93 blade front sight; sling swivels; Army-type leather sling.

Exc: $325 **VGood:** $240 **Good:** $200

WINCHESTER MODEL 70

This bolt action, centerfire repeating rifle is a versatile longarm, having been produced in more variations and configurations than any other of the manufacturer's firearms. The rifle is divided into roughly three historical categories, the original variations having been made from 1936 to 1963; at that time, the rifle was redesigned to a large degree, actually downgraded in an effort to meet rising costs, but to hold the retail price. This series of variations was produced from 1964 until 1972, at which time the rifle was upgraded and the retail price increased. Additional changes have been made in years since. The venerable Winchester Model 70 was discontinued in 2006.

WINCHESTER MODEL 70 (1936-1963)

Bolt action; 22 Hornet, 220 Swift, 243, 250-3000, 7mm, 257 Roberts, 264 Win. Mag., 270, 7x57mm, 300 Savage, 300 H&H Mag., 300 Win. Mag., 30-06, 308, 338 Win. Mag., 35 Rem., 358 Win., 375 H&H Mag., (other calibers on special order such as 9x57mm and 7.65mm); 4-shot box magazine (magnums); 5-shot (other calibers); 20-inch, 24-inch, 25-inch, 26-inch barrel; claw extractor; hooded ramp front sight, open rear; hand-checkered walnut pistol-grip stock; Monte Carlo comb on later productions. Introduced 1936; discontinued 1963. In many cases, the value depends largely on the caliber of the rifle. Note: 300 Savage, 35 Rem., 7.65mm, 9x57mm very rare; see appraiser.

PRE-WWII (1936-1945)

Standard calibers

Exc: $1100 **VGood:** $850 **Good:** $650

220 Swift, 257 Roberts, 300 H&H Mag.

Exc: $1400 **VGood:** $900 **Good:** $700

375 H&H Mag., 7x57mm, 250-3000

Exc: $1800 **VGood:** $1100 **Good:** $900

POST-WWII (1946-1963)

Standard calibers

Exc: $1000 **VGood:** $800 **Good:** $600

220 Swift, 243, 257 Roberts

Exc: $1300 **VGood:** $900 **Good:** $650

22 Hornet, 300 H&H Mag.,

Exc: $1700 **VGood:** $1300 **Good:** $1100

300 Win. Mag., 338 Win. Mag., 375 H&H Mag.

Exc: $1700 **VGood:** $1200 **Good:** $1000

Note: 250-3000, 300 Savage, 358, 35 Rem., 7x57mm Very rare; see appraiser.

WINCHESTER MODEL 70 ALASKAN

Same specs as Model 70 (1936-1963) except 300 Win. Mag., 338 Win. Mag., 375 H&H Mag.; 3-, 4-shot (375 H&H Mag.) magazine; 24-inch barrel (300 Win. Mag.), 25-inch barrel; 45-5/8-inch overall length; weighs 8 to 8-3/4 lbs.; bead front, sight, folding leaf rear; tapped for scope mounts, receiver sights; Monte Carlo stock; recoil pad. Introduced 1960; discontinued 1963.

Exc: $1900 **VGood:** $1400 **Good:** $995

WINCHESTER MODEL 70 BULL GUN

Same specs as Model 70 (1936-1963) except 30-06, 300 H&H Mag.; 28-inch extra heavy barrel; scope bases; walnut target Marksman stock; Lyman No. 77 front sight, Lyman No. 48WH rear; Army-type leather sling strap. Discontinued 1963.

Exc: $2300 **VGood:** $1700 **Good:** $1295

WINCHESTER MODEL 70 CARBINE

Same specs as Model 70 (1936-1963) except 22 Hornet, 250-3000, 257 Roberts, 270, 7x57mm, 30-06; 20-inch barrel. The 250-3000, 7x57mm are rare; see appraiser. Introduced 1936; discontinued 1946.

Calibers 270, 30-06

Exc: $1695 **VGood:** $1195 **Good:** $895

22 Hornet, 257 Roberts

Exc: $2695 **VGood:** $1995 **Good:** $1295

WINCHESTER MODEL 70 FEATHERWEIGHT

Same specs as Model 70 (1936-1963) except 243, 264 Win. Mag., 270, 308, 30-06, 358 Win.; 22-inch lightweight barrel, 24-inch (special order); weighs 6-1/2 lbs.; lightweight American walnut Monte Carlo or straight comb stock; checkered pistol grip, forend; aluminum triggerguard, checkered buttplate, floorplate; 1-inch swivels. Introduced 1952; discontinued 1963.

Calibers 243, 270, 30-06, 308

Exc: $1050 **VGood:** $800 **Good:** $650

264 Win. Mag., 358 Win.

Exc: $1600 **VGood:** $1300 **Good:** $1000

WINCHESTER MODEL 70 NATIONAL MATCH

Same specs as Model 70 (1936-1963) except 30-06; 24-inch barrel; Lyman No. 77 front ramp sight, Lyman No. 48WH rear; Army-type leather sling strap; scope bases; checkered walnut Marksman target stock. Discontinued 1960.

Exc: $1775 **VGood:** $1200 **Good:** $850

WINCHESTER MODEL 70 SUPER GRADE

Same specs as Model 70 (1936-1963) except 24-inch, 25-inch, 26-inch barrel; Winchester 22G open sporting rear sight; deluxe stock, cheekpiece; black forearm tip; sling; quick-detachable sling swivels; grip cap. Introduced 1936; discontinued 1960.

Exc: $1950 **VGood:** $1300 **Good:** $1000

375 H&H Mag.

Exc: $3000 **VGood:** $2300 **Good:** $1600

WINCHESTER MODEL 70 SUPER GRADE AFRICAN

Same specs as Model 70 (1936-1963) except 458 Win. Mag.; 3-shot magazine; 25-inch barrel; weighs 9-1/2 lbs.; Monte Carlo checkered walnut pistol-grip stock; cheekpiece; recoil pad; stock crossbolts; front sling swivel stud mounted on barrel. Introduced 1956; discontinued 1963.

Exc: $3700 **VGood:** $3000 **Good:** $2300

WINCHESTER MODEL 70 SUPER GRADE FEATHERWEIGHT

Same specs as Model 70 (1936-1963) except 243, 270, 30-06, 308; 22-inch barrel; lightweight deluxe Monte Carlo stock, cheekpiece; black pistol-grip cap, forearm tip; aluminum buttplate, triggerguard, floorplate; sling; quick-detachable swivels. Discontinued 1960.

Exc: $3050 **VGood:** $1995 **Good:** $1095

WINCHESTER MODEL 70 TARGET

Same specs as Model 70 (1936-1963) except 24-inch, 26-inch medium-weight barrel; scope bases; walnut target Marksman stock; Lyman No. 77 front sight, Lyman No. 48WH rear, Army-type leather sling strap.

Exc: $1995 **VGood:** $1100 **Good:** $795

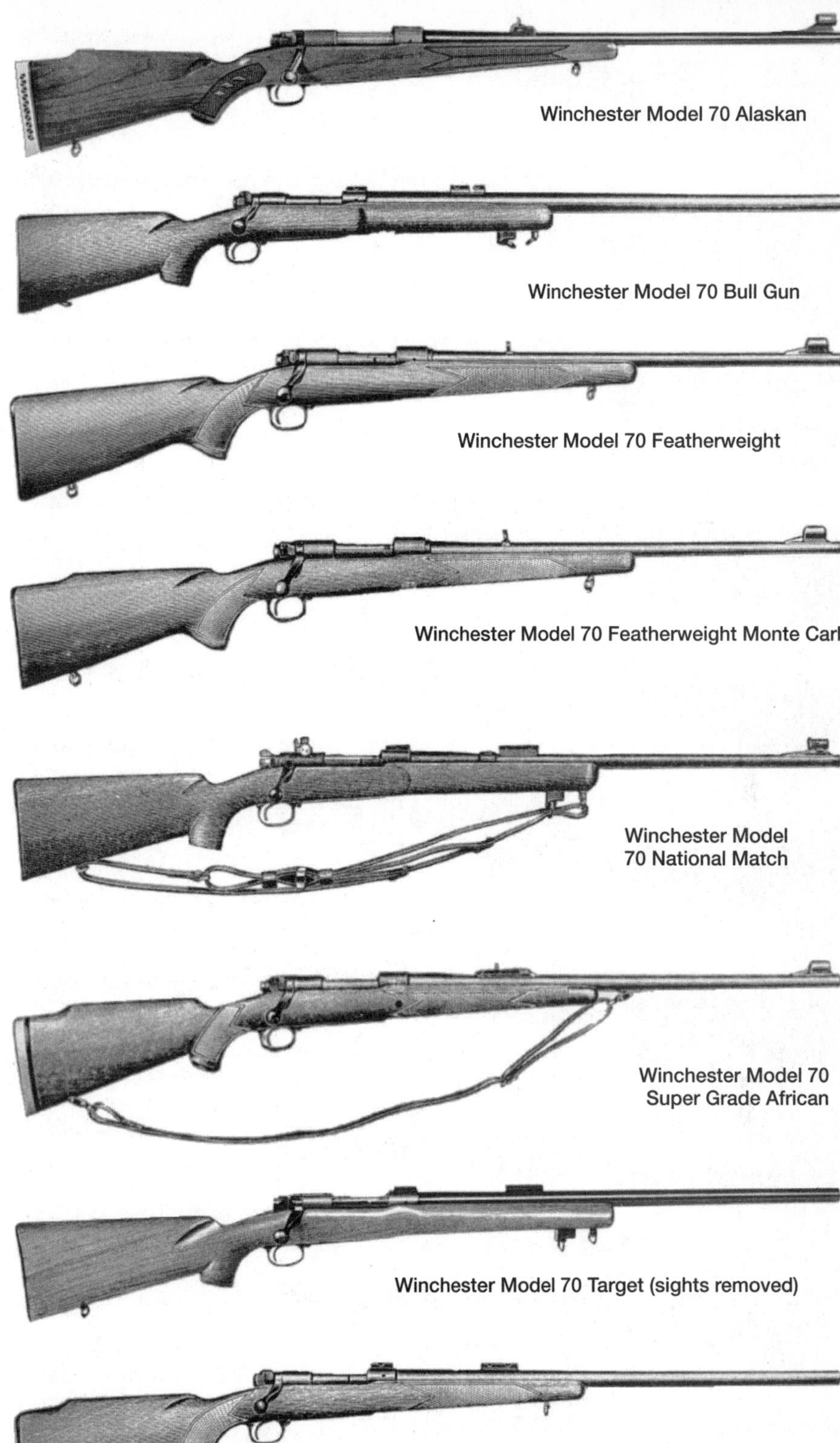

WINCHESTER MODEL 70 VARMINT

Same specs as Model 70 (1936-1963) except 220 Swift, 243 Win.; 26-inch stainless heavy barrel; weighs 9-3/4 lbs. scope bases; checkered walnut varminter stock. Introduced 1956; discontinued 1963.

Exc: $1195 **VGood:** $895 **Good:** $750

WINCHESTER MODEL 70 (1964-1971)

Bolt action; 22-250, 222, 225, 243, 270, 308, 30-06, (standard calibers); 5-shot box magazine; 22-inch heavy barrel; 42-1/2-inch overall length; weighs 7

lbs.; plunger-type extractor; hooded ramp front sight, adjustable open rear; checkered walnut Monte Carlo stock, cheekpiece; sling swivels. Introduced 1964; discontinued 1971.

Exc: $395 **VGood:** $325 **Good:** $300

WINCHESTER MODEL 70 AFRICAN

Same specs as Model 70 (1964-1971) except 375 H&H Mag., 458 Win. Mag.; 22-inch barrel (375 H&H Mag.), 24-inch (458 Win. Mag.); 42-1/2-inch overall length; weighs 8-1/2 lbs.; special sights; hand-checkered Monte Carlo stock; ebony forearm tip; recoil pad; quick-detachable swivels; sling; twin crossbolts. Introduced 1964; discontinued 1971.

Perf: $795 **Exc:** $525 **VGood:** $450

WINCHESTER MODEL 70 DELUXE

Same specs as Model 70 (1964-1971) except 243, 270 Win., 30-06, 300 Win. Mag.; 3-shot magazine (magnum), 5-shot (other calibers); 22-inch, 24-inch barrel (magnum); hand-checkered walnut Monte Carlo stock, forearm; ebony forearm tip; recoil pad (magnum). Introduced 1964; discontinued 1971.

Perf: $550 **Exc:** $300 **VGood:** $250

WINCHESTER MODEL 70 INTERNATIONAL ARMY MATCH

Same specs as Model 70 (1964-1971) except 308; 5-shot box magazine; 24-inch heavy barrel; optional sights; International Shooting Union stock; forearm rail for accessories; adjustable buttplate; externally adjustable trigger. Introduced 1971; discontinued 1971.

Perf: $850 **Exc:** $650 **VGood:** $500

WINCHESTER MODEL 70 MAGNUM

Same specs as Model 70 (1964-1971) except 264 Win. Mag., 7mm Rem. Mag., 300 H&H Mag., 300 Win. Mag., 338 Win. Mag., 375 H&H Mag.; 3-shot magazine; 24-inch barrel; 441/2-inch overall length; weighs 7-1/4 lbs.

Perf: $550 **Exc:** $395 **VGood:** $260

WINCHESTER MODEL 70 MANNLICHER

Same specs as Model 70 (1964-1971) except 243, 220, 30-06, 308; 19-inch barrel; checkered Mannlicher stock with Monte Carlo comb, cheekpiece; steel forearm cap. Introduced 1969; discontinued 1972.

Perf: $815 **Exc:** $595 **VGood:** $495

WINCHESTER MODEL 70 TARGET

Same specs as Model 70 (1964-1971) except 30-06, 308; 5-shot box magazine; 24-inch heavy barrel; 44-1/2-inch overall length; weighs 10-1/4 lbs.; no sights; target scope blocks; checkered heavy high-comb Marksman stock; aluminum hand stop. Introduced 1964; discontinued 1971.

Perf: $750 **Exc:** $500 **VGood:** $400

WINCHESTER MODEL 70 (1972 TO PRESENT)

Bolt action; 22-250, 222, 25-06, 243, 270, 308, 30-06; 5-shot box magazine; 22-inch swaged, floating barrel; removable hooded ramp bead front sight, open rear; tapped for scope mounts; walnut Monte Carlo stock; cut checkering on pistol grip, forearm; forend tip; hinged floorplate; steel grip cap; sling swivels. Introduced 1972; discontinued 1980.

Perf: $460 **Exc:** $300 **VGood:** $220

WINCHESTER MODEL 70 BLACK SHADOW

Bolt action; 270, 30-06, 7mm Rem Mag, 300 Win Mag; 22-inch or 24-inch barrel; black composite stock, matte blue barrel and action. Push-feed bolt design; hinged floorplate. Made in U.S.A. by U.S. Repeating Arms Co. Introduced in 2000.

Perf: $475 **Exc:** $350 **VGood:** $300

WINCHESTER MODEL 70 CLASSIC CUSTOM GRADE

Same specs as Model 70 (1972 to present) except 270, 30-06, 7mm Rem. Mag., 300 Win. Mag., 338 Win. Mag.; 3-shot (magnum), 5-shot magazine; 24-inch, 26-inch barrel; fancy satin-finished walnut stock; hand-honed and fitted parts; Introduced 1990; discontinued 1994.

Perf: $1350 **Exc:** $995 **VGood:** $695

WINCHESTER MODEL 70 CLASSIC CUSTOM GRADE FEATHERWEIGHT

Same specs as Model 70 (1972 to present) except 22-250, 223, 243, 270, 280, 30-06, 308, 7mm-08 Rem.; no sights; checkered, satin-finished, high-grade American walnut stock, schnabel forend; rubber buttpad; high polish blued finish; controlled round feeding. Introduced 1992; no longer in production.

Perf: $950 **Exc:** $650 **VGood:** $500

WINCHESTER MODEL 70 CLASSIC CUSTOM GRADE SHARPSHOOTER

Same specs as Model 70 (1972 to present) except 223, 22-250, 308 Win., 300 Win. Mag.; 24-inch (308), 26-inch (223, 22-250, 300 Win. Mag.) barrel; 44-1/2-inch overall length (24-inch barrel); weighs 11 lbs.;

no sights; scope bases and rings; glass-bedded McMillan A-2 target style stock with recoil pad, swivel studs; controlled round feeding; hand-honed and fitted action; Schneider barrel; matte blue finish. Introduced 1992; discontinued 1994.

Perf: $1795 **Exc:** $1395 **VGood:** $795

WINCHESTER MODEL 70 CLASSIC CUSTOM GRADE SPORTING SHARPSHOOTER

Same specs as Model 70 (1972 to present) except 220 Swift, 270, 7mm STW, 300 Win. Mag.; 24-inch (270), 26-inch stainless steel Schneider barrel, glass-bedded with natural finish; 44-1/2-inch overall length (24-inch barrel); no sights; scope bases and rings; McMillan sporter-style, gray-finished composite stock; blued receiver; pre-'64-style action with controlled round feeding. Introduced 1994; discontinued 1994.

Perf: $1650 **Exc:** $1195 **VGood:** $895

WINCHESTER MODEL 70 CLASSIC DBM (DETACHABLE BOX MAGAZINE)

Same specs as Model 70 (1972 to present) except 22-250, 243, 308, 284 Win., 270, 30-06, 7mm Rem. Mag., 300 Win. Mag.; 3-shot detachable box magazine; 24-inch, 26-inch barrel; with or without sights; scope bases and rings; pre-'64-type action with controlled round feeding. Introduced 1994; discontinued 1995.

Perf: $485 **Exc:** $395 **VGood:** $330

WINCHESTER MODEL 70 CLASSIC DBM-S

Same specs as Model 70 (1972 to present) except 270, 30-06, 7mm Rem. Mag., 300 Win. Mag.; 3-shot detachable box magazine; 24-inch barrel; with or without sights; scope bases and rings; black fiberglass/graphite composite stock; pre-'64-type controlled round feeding. Introduced 1994; discontinued 1994.

Perf: $560 **Exc:** $390 **VGood:** $330

WINCHESTER MODEL 70 CLASSIC FEATHERWEIGHT

Same specs as Model 70 (1972 to present) except 22-250, 223, 243, 270, 280, 30-06, 308, 7mm-08; no sights; scope bases and rings; standard-grade walnut stock; claw extractor; controlled-round feeding system. Introduced 1992.

Perf: $590 **Exc:** $510 **VGood:** $330

WINCHESTER MODEL 70 CLASSIC FEATHERWEIGHT COMPACT

Similar to Classic Featherweight except scaled down for smaller shooters. 20-inch barrel, 12-1/2-inch length of pull. Pre-'64-type action. Available in 243, 308 or 7mm-08. Introduced 1998. Made in U.S.A. by U. S. Repeating Arms Co.

Perf: $650 **Exc:** $560 **VGood:** $385

WINCHESTER MODEL 70 CLASSIC SAFARI EXPRESS

Bolt action; 375 H&H Mag., 416 Rem. Mag., 458 Win. Mag., 3-shot magazine; 24-inch barrel; weighs 8-1/4 to 8-1/2 lbs. American walnut stock with Monte Carlo cheekpiece. Wrap-around checkering and finish. Sights: Hooded ramp front, open rear. Controlled round feeding. Two steel cross bolts in stock for added strength. Front sling swivel stud mounted on barrel. Contoured rubber butt pad. From U.S. Repeating Arms Co. Introduced 1999.

Perf: $925 **Exc:** $750 **VGood:** $670

WINCHESTER MODEL 70 CLASSIC SM

Same specs as Model 70 (1972 to present) except black composite, graphite-impregnated stock; black matte-finished metal; pre-'64-type action with controlled feeding; 264 Win. Mag., 270, 30-06, 7mm Rem. Mag., 300 Win. Mag., 300 Weatherby Mag., 338 Win. Mag., 375 H&H Mag.; 3-shot magazine (magnum), 5-shot (others); 24-inch, 26-inch barrel; weighs 7-3/4 lbs.; with or without sights; scope bases and rings; BOSS barrel vibration modulator and muzzle brake system optional. Introduced 1994.

Perf: $495 **Exc:** $410 **VGood:** $360

Winchester Model 70 Classic Safari Express

Winchester Model 70 Classic Sporter LT

Winchester Model 70 Classic Stainless

Winchester Model 70 Classic Super Grade

Winchester Model 70 Coyote

375 H&H

Perf: $560 **Exc:** $460 **VGood:** $390

With BOSS (270, 30-06, 7mm Rem. Mag., 300 Win. Mag., 338 Win. Mag.)

Perf: $600 **Exc:** $510 **VGood:** $440

WINCHESTER MODEL 70 CLASSIC SPORTER

Same specs as Model 70 (1972 to present) except 25-06, 264 Win. Mag., 270, 270 Win. Mag., 30-06, 300 Win. Mag., 300 Weatherby Mag., 338 Win. Mag., 7mm Rem. Mag.; 3-shot magazine (magnum), 5-shot (others); 24-inch, 26-inch barrel; controlled round feeding. Introduced 1994.

Perf: $705 **Exc:** $610 **VGood:** $560

WINCHESTER MODEL 70 CLASSIC SPORTER LT

Bolt action; 25-06, 270 Win., 30-06, 7mm STW, 7mm Rem. Mag., 300 Win. Mag., 338 Win. Mag., 3-shot magazine; 5-shot for 25-06, 270 Win., 30-06; 24-inch barrel, 26-inch for magnums; weighs 7-3/4 to 8 lbs.; 46-3/4-inch overall length (26-inch bbl.); American walnut stock with cut checkering and satin finish, classic style with straight comb. Drilled and tapped for scope mounting. Uses pre-64-type action with controlled round feeding. Three-position safety, stainless steel magazine follower; rubber butt pad; epoxy bedded receiver recoil lug. From U.S. Repeating Arms Co. Introduced 1999; premium for left-hand action.

Perf: $610 **Exc:** $510 **VGood:** $400

WINCHESTER MODEL 70 CLASSIC STAINLESS

Same specs as Model 70 (1972 to present) except 22-250, 243, 308, 270, 30-06, 7mm Rem. Mag., 300 Win. Mag., 300 WSM, 300 Weatherby Mag., 338 Win. Mag., 375 H&H Mag.; 3-shot magazine (magnum), 5-shot (others); 22-inch, 24-inch, 26-inch stainless steel barrel; weighs 6-3/4 lbs.; no sights; drilled, tapped for scope mounts; black fiberglass/graphite composite stock; matte gray finish; stainless steel pre-'64-type action with controlled feeding; BOSS barrel vibration modulator and muzzlebrake system optional. Introduced 1994.

Perf: $625 **Exc:** $420 **VGood:** $360

375 H&H Mag., with sights

Perf: $875 **Exc:** $670 **VGood:** $610

With BOSS (all except 300 Wea. Mag., 375 H&H Mag.)

Perf: $700 **Exc:** $535 **VGood:** $430

WINCHESTER MODEL 70 CLASSIC SUPER GRADE

Same specs as Model 70 (1972 to present) except 270, 30-06, 7mm Rem. Mag., 300 Win. Mag., 338 Win. Mag.; 3-shot magazine (magnum), 5-shot (others); 24-inch barrel; no sights; scope bases and rings; straight-comb walnut stock with sculptured cheekpiece, tapered forend; wraparound cut checkering; solid buttpad; stainless steel claw extractor, magazine follower, bolt guide rail; three-position safety; hinged floorplate; pre-'64-type action with controlled round feeding; BOSS barrel vibration modulator and muzzlebrake system optional. Introduced 1994.

Perf: $1050 **Exc:** $975 **VGood:** $795

With BOSS system

Perf: $1100 **Exc:** $1025 **VGood:** $975

WINCHESTER MODEL 70 CLASSIC SUPER EXPRESS MAGNUM

Same specs as Model 70 (1972 to present) except 375 H&H, 375 JRS, 7mm STW, 416 Rem. Mag., 458 Win. Mag., 470 Capstick; 3-shot magazine; 22-inch barrel (458 Win. Mag.), 24-inch (others); weighs 8-1/2 lbs.; three-leaf express rear sight; deluxe checkered, satin-finished walnut stock; controlled round feed action; two steel crossbolts; barrel mounted front swivel stud. Introduced 1990.

Perf: $1500 **Exc:** $1200 **VGood:** $975

WINCHESTER MODEL 70 COYOTE

Similar to Model 70 Black Shadow except laminated wood stock, 24-inch medium-heavy stainless steel barrel. 223, 223 WSSM, 22-250, 243, 243 WSSM, 25 WSSM, 270, 270 WSM, 7mm WSM, 300 WSM, 325 WSM. Introduced 2000. Add 15 percent for short magnum chamberings.

Perf: $680 **Exc:** $500 **VGood:** $430

WINCHESTER MODEL 70 CUSTOM SHARPSHOOTER

Same specs as Model 70 (1972 to present) except 223, 22-250, 308 Win., 300 Win. Mag.; 24-inch barrel (308), 26-inch (others); weighs 11 lbs.; no sights;

Winchester Model 70 Heavy Varmint

Winchester Model 70 Lightweight

Winchester Model 70 Lightweight Carbine

Winchester Model 70 Ranger

Winchester Model 70 Ranger Youth/Ladies

Winchester Model 70 Stealth

Winchester Model 70 Target

scope bases and rings; McMillan A-2 target-style stock, glass bedded; hand-honed and fitted action; Schneider barrel; matte blue finish. Introduced 1992; discontinued 1994.

Perf: $1300 **Exc:** $950 **VGood:** $750

WINCHESTER MODEL 70 DBM

Same specs as Model 70 (1972 to present) except 22-250, 223, 243, 270, 30-06, 308, 7mm Rem. Mag., 300 Win. Mag.; 3-shot detachable box magazine; 24-inch, 26-inch barrel; with or without sights; scope bases and rings. Introduced 1992; discontinued 1994.

Perf: $780 **Exc:** $695 **VGood:** $525

WINCHESTER MODEL 70 FEATHERWEIGHT WINTUFF

Same specs as Model 70 (1972 to present) except 22-250, 223, 243, 270, 30-06, 308; no sights; scope bases and rings; brown laminated checkered pistol-grip stock; schnabel forend. Introduced 1988; discontinued 1990.

Perf: $750 **Exc:** $675 **VGood:** $510

WINCHESTER MODEL 70 HEAVY BARREL VARMINT

Same specs as Model 70 (1972 to present) except 22-250, 223, 243, 308; heavy 26-inch barrel with counter-bored muzzle; 46-inch overall length; weighs 9 lbs.; no sights; drilled, tapped for scope mounts; sporter-style stock; rubber buttpad. Introduced 1989; discontinued 1994.

Perf: $650 **Exc:** $500 **VGood:** $420

WINCHESTER MODEL 70 HEAVY VARMINT

Same specs as Model 70 (1972 to present) except 220 Swift, 22-250, 223, 243, 308; weighs 10-3/4 lbs.; heavy 26-inch stainless barrel with counter-bored muzzle; no sights; black synthetic stock with full-length Pillar Plus AccuBlock, beavertail forend; rubber buttpad. Introduced 1989; discontinued 1994.

Perf: $685 **Exc:** $610 **VGood:** $530

WINCHESTER MODEL 70 LIGHTWEIGHT

Same specs as Model 70 (1972 to present) except 22-250, 223 Rem., 243 Win., 270 Win., 280, 308 Win., 30-06; 5-shot magazine, 6-shot (223 Rem.); 22-inch barrel; no sights; drilled, tapped for scope mounts; satin-finished American walnut stock; machine-cut checkering; three-position safety; stainless steel magazine follower; hinged floorplate. Introduced 1984.

Perf: $520 **Exc:** $430 **VGood:** $400

WINCHESTER MODEL 70 LIGHTWEIGHT CARBINE

Same specs as Model 70 (1972 to present) except 22-250, 222, 223, 243, 250 Savage, 270, 308, 30-06; 5-shot magazine, 6-shot (223); 20-inch barrel; drilled, tapped for scope mounts; satin-finished American walnut stock; cut checkering; stainless steel magazine follower; three-position safety; hinged floorplate. Introduced 1984; discontinued 1986.

Perf: $520 **Exc:** $410 **VGood:** $380

WINCHESTER MODEL 70 RANGER

Bolt action; 223, 243, 270, 30-06, 7mm Rem. Mag.; 3-shot magazine (7mm Rem. Mag.), 4-shot (others); 22-inch, 24-inch barrel; weighs 7-1/8 lbs.; economy version of Winchester Model 70; American hardwood stock; no checkering; composition buttplate; matte blue finish. Introduced 1985.

Perf: $370 **Exc:** $320 **VGood:** $235

WINCHESTER MODEL 70 RANGER YOUTH/LADIES RIFLE

Same specs as Ranger; 223, 243, 308; 7mm-08; 4-shot magazine; 20-inch, 22-inch barrel; weighs 5-3/4 lbs.; scaled-down American hardwood stock with 1-inch shorter length of pull; no checkering; composition buttplate; matte blue finish. Introduced 1985.

Perf: $370 **Exc:** $320 **VGood:** $220

WINCHESTER MODEL 70 SHB (SYNTHETIC HEAVY BARREL)

Same specs as Model 70 (1972 to present) except 308; heavy 26-inch barrel with counter-bored muzzle; weighs 9 lbs.; black synthetic stock with checkering; matte blue finish. Introduced 1992; discontinued 1992.

Perf: $460 **Exc:** $400 **VGood:** $340

WINCHESTER MODEL 70 SPORTER SSM

Same specs as Model 70 (1972 to present) except 223, 22-250, 243, 270, 308, 30-06, 7mm Rem. Mag., 300 Win. Mag., 338 Win. Mag., 375 H&H Mag.; 3-shot magazine (magnum), 5-shot (others); 24-inch, 26-inch barrel; weighs 7-3/4 lbs.; no sights; scope bases and rings; black composite, graphite-impregnated stock; matte finish metal. Introduced 1992; discontinued 1993.

Perf: $450 **Exc:** $360 **VGood:** $310

WINCHESTER MODEL 70 SPORTER WINTUFF

Same specs as Model 70 (1972 to present) except 270, 30-06, 7mm Rem. Mag., 300 Win. Mag., 300 Weatherby Mag., 338 Win. Mag.; 3-shot magazine (magnum), 5-shot (others); 24-inch barrel; bases and rings for scope mounts; checkered brown laminated stock; rubber recoil pad. Introduced 1992; discontinued 1992.

Perf: $560 **Exc:** $470 **VGood:** $420

WINCHESTER MODEL 70 STEALTH

Bolt action; 223, 223 WSSM, 22-250, 243 WSSM, 25 WSSM, 308 Win.; 26-inch barrel; weighs 10-3/4 lbs.; 46-inch overall length; Kevlar/fiberglass/graphite stock, Pillar Plus Accu-Block with full-length aluminum bedding block. Push-feed bolt design; matte finish. Introduced 1999. Made in U.S.A. by U.S. Repeating Arms Co

Perf: $820 **Exc:** $650 **VGood:** $560

WINCHESTER MODEL 70 SYNTHETIC HEAVY VARMINT

Same specs as Model 70 (1972 to present) except 223, 22-250, 243, 308; 26-inch heavy stainless steel barrel; weighs 10-3/4 lbs.; fiberglass/graphite stock; full-length Pillar Plus AccuBlock stock bedding system. Introduced 1993.

Perf: $625 **Exc:** $495 **VGood:** $410

WINCHESTER MODEL 70 TARGET

Same specs as Model 70 (1972 to present) except 30-06, 308; 26-inch heavy barrel; contoured aluminum hand stop for either left- or right-handed shooter; high-comb target stock; tapped for micrometer sights. No longer in production.

Perf: $710 **Exc:** $520 **VGood:** $480

WINCHESTER MODEL 70 VARMINT

Same specs as Model 70 (1972 to present) except 22-250, 223, 225, 243, 308; 24-inch heavy barrel; no sights; black serrated buttplate; black forend tip;

high-luster finish on walnut stock. Introduced 1972; designated XTR 1978; designation dropped 1989; discontinued 1993.

Perf: $560 **Exc:** $500 **VGood:** $440

WINCHESTER MODEL 70 WINLITE

Same specs as Model 70 (1972 to present) except 25-06, 270, 280, 30-06, 7mm Rem. Mag., 300 Win. Mag., 300 Weatherby Mag., 338 Win. Mag.; 3-, 4-shot magazine; 22-inch, 24-inch (magnum) barrel; McMillan brown fiberglass stock. Introduced 1986; discontinued 1990.

Perf: $470 **Exc:** $400 **VGood:** $350

WINCHESTER MODEL 70 XTR

Same specs as Model 70 (1972 to present) except 222, 22-250, 25-06, 243, 270, 308, 30-06, 264 Win. Mag., 7mm Rem. Mag., 300 Win. Mag., 338 Win. Mag.; 3-shot magazine (magnum), 5-shot (others); 22-inch, 24-inch (magnum) barrel; satin-finished stock. Introduced 1978; discontinued 1989.

Perf: $495 **Exc:** $440 **VGood:** $400

WINCHESTER MODEL 70 XTR FEATHERWEIGHT

Same specs as Model 70 (1972 to present) except 22-250, 223, 243, 25-06, 257 Roberts, 270, 280, 7x57, 6.5x55 Swedish, 30-06, 308, 7mm-08, 7mm Rem. Mag., 300 Win. Mag.; 22-inch, 24-inch (300 Win. Mag.) tapered barrel; optional sights; checkered satin-finished American walnut stock, schnabel forend; red rubber buttpad; high-polish blued finish on metal; optional blade front sight, adjustable folding rear. Introduced 1981; XTR designation dropped 1989; no longer in production. Add 10 percent for 257, 6.5 chamberings.

Perf: $510 **Exc:** $450 **VGood:** $400

With sights

Perf: $530 **Exc:** $460 **VGood:** $400

WINCHESTER MODEL 70 XTR FEATHERWEIGHT EUROPEAN

Same specs as Model 70 (1972 to present) except 6.5x55 Swedish chambering; weighs 6-3/4 lbs. Introduced 1986; discontinued 1986.

Perf: $570 **Exc:** $530 **VGood:** $490

WINCHESTER MODEL 70 XTR SPORTER

Same specs as Model 70 (1972 to present) except 22-250, 223, 243, 25-06, 264 Win. Mag., 270, 270 Weatherby Mag., 30-06, 300 Win. Mag., 300 Weatherby Mag., 300 H&H, 308, 7mm Rem. Mag., 338 Win. Mag.; 3-shot magazine (magnum), 5-shot (others); 24-inch barrel; three-position safety; stainless steel magazine follower; rubber buttpad. Introduced 1980; XTR designation dropped 1989; no longer in production.

Perf: $395 **Exc:** $330 **VGood:** $300

WINCHESTER MODEL 70 XTR SUPER EXPRESS MAGNUM

Same specs as Model 70 (1972 to present) except 375 H&H Mag., 458 Win Mag.; 3-shot magazine; 22-inch, 24-inch barrel; steel crossbolts; contoured rubber buttpad. Introduced 1981; discontinued 1989.

Perf: $1100 **Exc:** $1000 **VGood:** $850

WINCHESTER MODEL 70 SHADOW ELITE STAINLESS

Bolt-action rifle. Calibers: .22-250, .243, .308, .270, .30-06, .300 WM, .338 WM, .375 H&H, .270 WSM, 7mm WSM, .300 WSM, .325 WSM. Barrel: Stainless steel, 24-inch or 26-inch (.300, .338 WM). Stock: Overmolded composite. Weight: 6-1/2 – 7-3/4 lbs. Magazine capacity: 3 or 5 (.22-250, .243, .308, .270, .30-06).

NIB: $700 **Exc:** $620 **VGood:** $495

WINCHESTER MODEL 70 SHADOW ELITE CAMO STAINLESS

Similar to Shadow Elite Stainless but with Mossy Oak New Break Up camo synthetic stock.

NIB: $775 **Exc:** $675 **VGood:** $495

Winchester Model 70 Winlite

Winchester Model 70 XTR Featherweight

Winchester Model 70 Featherweight Deluxe (2008 Production)

Winchester Model 70 Sporter Deluxe (2008 Production)

Winchester Model 70 Extreme Weather SS (2008 Production)

Winchester Model 70A

WINCHESTER MODEL 70 PRO SHADOW BLUED

Bolt-action rifle. Calibers: .22-250, .243, .308, .270, .30-06, 7mm RM, .300 WM, .270 WSM, 7mm WSM, .300 WSM, .325 WSM. Barrel: Blued steel, 22-inch (standard) or 24-inch (magnum). Stock: Overmolded composite. Weight: 6-1/2 – 7 lbs. Magazine capacity: 3 (magnum) or 5 (standard).

NIB: $550 **Exc:** $495 **VGood:** $375

WINCHESTER MODEL 70 PRO SHADOW STAINLESS

Similar to Pro Shadow blued but with stainless steel barrel and .338 WM and .375 H&H chamberings.

NIB: $650 **Exc:** $595 **VGood:** $495

WINCHESTER MODEL 70 LAMINATED COYOTE OUTBACK STAINLESS

Similar to Model 70 Coyote Lite but with skeletonized laminated stock and stainless steel only. Calibers: .22-250, .243, .308, .270, .30-06, 7mm RM, .300 WM, .270 WSM, 7mm WSM, .300 WSM, .325 WSM. Weight: 7-3/4 lbs.

NIB: $975 **Exc:** $895 **VGood:** $625

WINCHESTER MODEL 70 LAMINATED COYOTE GRAY OR BROWN STAINLESS

Similar to Model 70 Laminated Coyote Outback but with non-fluted barrel and choice of brown or gray laminated stock.

NIB: $675 **Exc:** $600 **VGood:** $475

WINCHESTER MODEL 70 FEATHERWEIGHT DELUXE (2008 PRODUCTION)

Pre-64 action, three-position safety, jewelled bolt, knurled bolt handle, walnut stock with slight schnabel, cut checkering, Pachmayr Decelerator recoil pad., 22- or 24-inch barrel depending on caliber. Chambered for a variety of cartridges from .243 to .325 Winchester Short Magnum. Weight 6.5 to 7 lbs.

New: $1100 **Exc:** $890 **VGood:** $650

WINCHESTER MODEL 70 SPORTER DELUXE (2008 PRODUCTION)

Similar to above but with non-schnabel forend and cheekpiece.

New: $1000 **Exc:** $790 **VGood:** $550

WINCHESTER NEW MODEL 70 SUPER GRADE SPECIAL LIMITED EDITION

Very fancy version of the Model 70 featuring post-'64 action, ultra-premium walnut, gold-filled engraving, black forend cap, steel grip cap, and shadowline cheekpiece. Only 250 produced in 2008. Chambered in .300 Winchester Magnum only.

New: $2400 **Exc:** $1775 **VGood:** $1200

WINCHESTER MODEL 70 EXTREME WEATHER SS (2008 PRODUCTION)

Post-'64 styule action with 22-, 24- or 26-inch barrel depending on chambering. Three-position safety, fluted stainless barrel and Bell and Carlson composite stock. Chambered for a variety of cartridges from .308 to .325 Winchester Short Magnum.

New: $1100 **Exc:** $890 **VGood:** $650

WINCHESTER MODEL 70A

Bolt action; 222 Rem., 22-250, 243 Win., 25-06, 264 Win. Mag., 270 Win., 30-06, 308 Win., 7mm Rem. Mag., 300 Win. Mag.; 22-inch, 24-inch barrel;

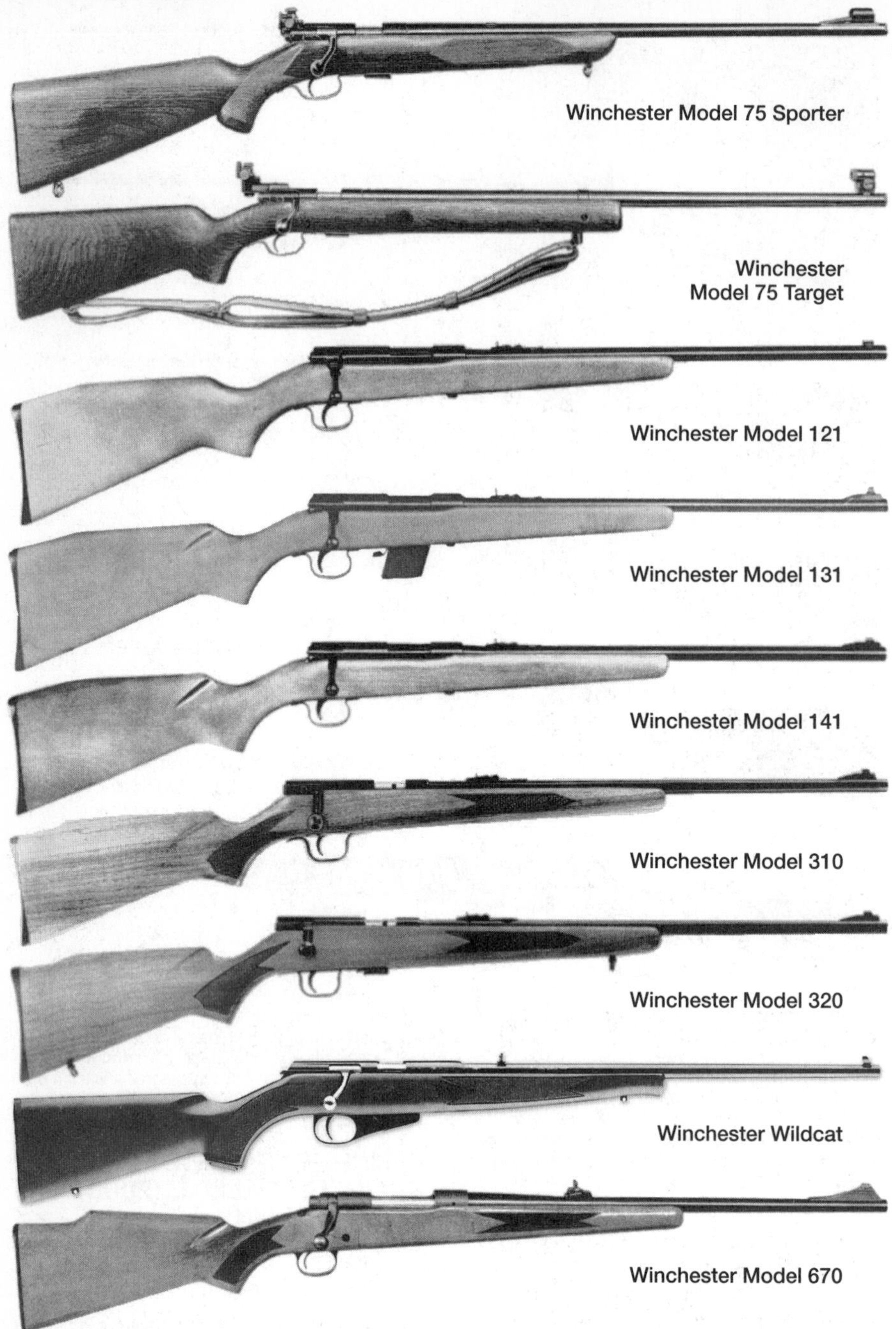
Winchester Model 75 Sporter

Winchester Model 75 Target

Winchester Model 121

Winchester Model 131

Winchester Model 141

Winchester Model 310

Winchester Model 320

Winchester Wildcat

Winchester Model 670

adjustable leaf rear sight with white diamond for quick sighting, hooded ramp front; dark American walnut with high-comb Monte Carlo, undercut cheekpiece; three-position safety. Introduced 1972 as replacement for Model 770, more closely following style of Model 70; discontinued 1978.

Perf: $320 **Exc:** $290 **VGood:** $240

WINCHESTER MODEL 72

Bolt action; 22 Short, 22 Long, 22 LR; 22-shot tubular magazine (22 Short), 16-shot (22 Long), 15-shot (22 LR); 25-inch barrel; takedown; peep or open rear sight, bead front; uncheckered pistol-grip stock. Introduced 1938; discontinued 1959.

Exc: $390 **VGood:** $280 **Good:** $245

WINCHESTER MODEL 72 GALLERY

Same specs as Model 72 except 22 Short only. Introduced 1939; discontinued 1942.

Perf: $465 **Exc:** $295 **VGood:** $260

WINCHESTER MODEL 72 TARGET

Same specs as Model 72 except rear peep sight, blade front; sling swivels.

Exc: $415 **VGood:** $290 **Good:** $250

WINCHESTER MODEL 75 SPORTER

Bolt action; 22 LR; 5-, 10-shot clip magazine; 24-inch barrel; weighs 5-1/2 lbs.; open rear sight, hooded ramp blade front; checkered select walnut stock, pistol grip; hard rubber grip cap; swivels; checkered steel buttplate; cocked with opening movement of bolt. Introduced 1939; discontinued 1958.

Exc: $750 **VGood:** $625 **Good:** $525

WINCHESTER MODEL 75 TARGET

Same specs as Model 75 except 28-inch barrel; 44-3/4-inch overall length; weighs 8-5/8 lbs.; target scope or variety of sights; uncheckered walnut stock, semi-beavertail forearm, pistol grip; 1-inch Army-type leather sling. Introduced 1938; discontinued 1958.

Exc: $570 **VGood:** $440 **Good:** $300

WINCHESTER MODEL 99 THUMB TRIGGER

Bolt action; single shot; 22 Short, 22 Long, 22 Extra Long; 18-inch round barrel; takedown; open rear sight, blade front; straight-grip one-piece American walnut stock; thumb button at rear of cocking piece serves as trigger. Introduced 1904; discontinued 1923. Some collector interest.

Exc: $1995 **VGood:** $995 **Good:** $695

WINCHESTER MODEL 121

Bolt action; single shot; 22 Short, 22 Long, 22 LR; 20-3/4-inch barrel; weighs 5 lbs.; standard post bead front sight, adjustable V rear; one-piece American hardwood pistol-grip stock with modified Monte Carlo profile; grooved for tip-off scope mounts. Introduced 1967; discontinued 1973.

Exc: $200 **VGood:** $175 **Good:** $150

Winchester Model 121Y Youth with shortened stock

Exc: $185 **VGood:** $160 **Good:** $135

Winchester Model 121 Deluxe with ramp front sight, swivels

Exc: $225 **VGood:** $200 **Good:** $175

WINCHESTER MODEL 131

Bolt action; 22 Short, 22 Long, 22 LR; 7-shot clip magazine; 20-inch barrel; weighs 5 lbs.; ramped bead post front sight, adjustable rear; receiver grooved for telescopic sight mounts; one-piece American hardwood stock with fluted comb, modified Monte Carlo profile; red safety; red cocking indicator. Introduced 1967; discontinued 1973.

Exc: $200 **VGood:** $175 **Good:** $150

WINCHESTER MODEL 141

Bolt action; 22 Short, 22 Long, 22 LR; 19-shot tube magazine (22 Short), 15-shot (22 Long), 13-shot (22 LR); 20-3/4-inch barrel; weighs 5 lbs.; ramped bead post front, adjustable rear sight; American hardwood stock with fluted comb, modified Monte Carlo; red cocking indicator; red-marked safety. Introduced 1967; discontinued 1973.

Exc: $200 **VGood:** $175 **Good:** $150

WINCHESTER MODEL 310

Bolt action; single shot; 22 Short, 22 Long, 22 LR; 22-inch barrel; 39-inch overall length; weighs 5-5/8 lbs.; ramped bead post front sight, adjustable rear; grooved for scope sight; drilled, tapped for micrometer rear sight; checkered American walnut Monte Carlo pistol-grip stock, forearm; serrated trigger; positive safety lever; swivels. Introduced 1971; discontinued 1974.

Exc: $180 **VGood:** $150 **Good:** $115

WINCHESTER MODEL 320

Bolt action; 22 Short, 22 Long, 22 LR; 5-shot magazine; 22-inch barrel; 30-1/2-inch overall length; weighs 5-5/8 lbs.; ramped bead post front sight, adjustable rear; grooved for scope mounts; drilled, tapped for micrometer rear sight; American walnut Monte Carlo pistol-grip stock, forearm; sling swivels; serrated trigger; positive safety. Introduced 1971; discontinued 1974.

Exc: $310 **VGood:** $250 **Good:** $1390

WINCHESTER WILDCAT

Bolt-action repeater styled after Mosin-Nagant military sporter. Caliber: .22 LR. Magazine: 5- and 10-round detachable. Stock: checkered walnut with Schnabel. Barrel: 21-inch blued. Weight:4.5 lbs. Imported.

NIB: $275 **Exc:** $225 **VGood:** $175

WINCHESTER MODEL 670

Bolt action; Introduced in 1967 as economy version of Model 70; 225, 243, 270, 308, 30-06; 4-shot magazine; 19-inch, 24-inch barrel; ramp bead front sight, adjustable rear; sights easily detached for scope mounting; hardwood Monte Carlo pistol-grip stock; 2-position safety; discontinued 1973.

Exc: $375 **VGood:** $265 **Good:** $200

WINCHESTER MODEL 670 MAGNUM

Same specs as Model 670 except 264 Win. Mag., 7mm Rem. Mag., 300 Win. Mag.; 3-shot magazine. Introduced 1967; discontinued 1970.

Exc: $400 **VGood:** $300 **Good:** $275

WINCHESTER MODEL 677

Bolt action; single shot; scoped version of Model 67; 22 Short, 22 Long, 22 LR, 22 WRF; 24-inch barrel; takedown; no sights; scope mounts mounted on barrel, Winchester 5A scope provided; uncheckered pistol-grip stock, grooved forearm. Enjoyed little success due to poor scope-mounting system. Introduced 1937; discontinued 1939. Only 2239 produced. Some collector value with original scope. Premium for 22 WMRFchambering.

Exc: $895 **VGood:** $595 **Good:** $395

WINCHESTER MODEL 697

Bolt action; repeater; scoped version of Model 69; 22 Short, 22 Long, 22 LR; 5-, 10-shot detachable box magazine; 25-inch barrel; no sights; scope bases attached to barrel; choice of 2-3/4x or 5x Winchester scope. Introduced 1937; discontinued 1941. Collector interest with original scope.

Exc: $995 **VGood:** $695 **Good:** $425

WINCHESTER MODEL 770

Bolt action; 222 Rem., 22-250, 243 Win., 270 Win., 308 Win., 30-06; 22-inch barrel; weighs 7-1/2 lbs.; hooded ramp front sight, adjustable rear; checkered walnut Monte Carlo pistol-grip stock, cheekpiece, forearm; composition buttplate; red cocking indicator. This rifle was designed as a lower-echelon Model 70 but failed to meet acceptance, and was dropped after only four years and replaced by Model 70A. Introduced 1969; discontinued 1972.

Exc: $330 **VGood:** $300 **Good:** $250

WINCHESTER MODEL 770 MAGNUM

Same specs as Model 770 except 264 Win. Mag., 7mm Rem. Mag., 300 Win. Mag.; 3-shot magazine; 24-inch barrel; rubber recoil pad. Introduced 1969; discontinued 1972. Replaced by Model 70A.

Exc: $350 **VGood:** $320 **Good:** $270

WINCHESTER MODEL 1900

Bolt action; single shot; 22 Short, 22 Long; 18-inch round barrel; takedown; open rear sight, blade front; straight-grip one-piece American walnut stock. Introduced 1899; discontinued 1902. Some collector interest.

VGood: $450 **Good:** $325 **Fair:** $220

WINCHESTER MODEL 1902

Bolt action; single shot; 22 Short, 22 Long, 22 Extra Long; 18-inch round barrel; takedown; open rear sight, blade front; straight-grip one-piece American walnut stock; enlarged trigger guard forms pistol grip. Introduced 1902; discontinued 1931.

VGood: $275 **Good:** $175 **Fair:** $125

WINCHESTER MODEL 1904

Bolt action; single shot; 22 Short, 22 Long, 22 Extra Long, 22 LR; 21-inch round barrel; takedown; open rear sight, blade front; straight-grip one-piece American walnut stock; enlarged trigger guard forms pistol grip. Introduced 1904; discontinued 1931. Some collector interest.

VGood: $300 **Good:** $200 **Fair:** $160

WINCHESTER MODEL 1904/1899 THUMB TRIGGER

Similar to basic Model 1904 but has no traditional trigger. Trigger is loctaed on upper tang and is operated with thumb. A John Browning design (who else)?

VGood: $550 **Good:** $2450 **Fair:** $275

WINCHESTER MODEL 1904-A

Same specs as Model 1904 except 22 LR. Introduced 1927; discontinued 1931.

VGood: $300 **Good:** $200 **Fair:** $160

WINCHESTER MODEL 53

Lever action; 25-20, 32-20, 44-40; 6-shot half-magazine; 22-inch barrel; open rear sight, bead front; walnut pistol-grip or straight-grip stock; blued finish; based on the Model 92 design. Introduced 1924; discontinued 1932.

Exc: $2295 **VGood:** $1295 **Good:** $795

Winchester Model 770

Winchester Model 1900 (sights removed)

Winchester Model 1902

Winchester Model 1904

Winchester Model 55 Centerfire

Winchester Model 64 (Early Production)

Winchester Model 64 Deer Rifle

Takedown model

Exc: $2495 **VGood:** $1495 **Good:** $995

(Premium for .44-40 Cal)

WINCHESTER MODEL 55 CENTERFIRE

Lever action; 25-35, 30-30, 32 Spl.; 3-shot tubular magazine; 24-inch round barrel; open rear sight, bead front; uncheckered American walnut straight grip stock, forend. Based on Model 94 design. Collector value. Introduced 1924; discontinued 1932.

Exc: $1495 **VGood:** $895 **Good:** $595

Takedown model

Exc: $1595 **VGood:** $995 **Good:** $650

WINCHESTER MODEL 64 (EARLY PRODUCTION)

Lever action; 219 Zipper, 25-35, 30-30, 32 Spl.; 20-inch, 24-inch barrel; weighs 7 lbs.; Winchester No. 22H open sporting or Lyman No. 56 (20-inch barrel) open rear sight, hooded ramp bead front; uncheckered American walnut pistol-grip stock, forend. Originally manufactured 1933 to 1957. Collector value on original production. Premium for .219 Zipp[er.

Exc: $1295 **VGood:** $895 **Good:** $540

WINCHESTER MODEL 64 (LATE PRODUCTION)

Lever action; 30-30; 5-shot tube magazine; 24-inch barrel; open rear sight, ramped bead front; uncheckered American walnut pistol-grip stock, forend. Introduced 1972; discontinued 1973.

Exc: $395 **VGood:** $300 **Good:** $250

WINCHESTER MODEL 64 DEER RIFLE

Same specs as Model 64 except 30-30, 32 Spl.; weighs 7-3/4 lbs.; hand-checkered pistol-grip stock, forend; 1-inch sling swivels; sling; checkered steel buttplate; discontinued 1957.

Exc: $1320 **VGood:** $950 **Good:** $650

Winchester Model 65

Winchester Model 71 Deluxe

Winchester Model 88

Winchester Model 88 Carbine

Winchester Model 94 Antique

Winchester Model 94 Classic

Winchester Model 94 Legacy

Winchester Model 94 Limited Edition Centennial Grade 1

WINCHESTER MODEL 64 ZIPPER

Same specs as Model 64 except chambered for 219 Zipper; 26-inch barrel; weighs 7 lbs.; Winchester No. 98A peep rear sight. Introduced 1938; discontinued 1941. Collector value.

Exc: $1695 **VGood:** $1295 **Good:** $995

WINCHESTER MODEL 65

Lever action; 218 Bee, 25-20, 32-20; 7-shot tube half-magazine; 22-inch, 24-inch (218 Bee) barrel; based on the Model 92 design; weighs 6-1/2 lbs.; open or peep rear sight, Lyman gold bead front on ramp base; plain pistol-grip stock, forearm; shotgun-type butt with checkered steel buttplate. Introduced 1933; discontinued 1947.

Exc: $2795 **VGood:** $1995 **Good:** $1050

WINCHESTER MODEL 71

Lever action; 348 Win.; 4-shot tube magazine; 24-inch barrel; weighs 8 lbs.; open rear sight, bead front on ramp with hood; plain walnut pistol-grip stock, beavertail forend; blued finish; action is improved version of Model 1886. Introduced 1936; discontinued 1957. Premium for pre-war/long-tang models.

Exc: $2100 **VGood:** $1395 **Good:** $825

WINCHESTER MODEL 71 CARBINE

Same specs as Model 71 except 20-inch barrel. Introduced 1936; discontinued 1938.

Exc: $2500 **VGood:** $1750 **Good:** $1350

WINCHESTER MODEL 71 DELUXE

Same specs as Model 71 except No. 98A rear peep sight; checkered stock, forearm, grip cap; quick-detachable sling swivels; leather sling.

Exc: $1795 **VGood:** $995 **Good:** $750

WINCHESTER MODEL 88

Lever action; 243 Win., 284 Win., 308 Win., 358 Win.; 5-shot detachable box magazine; 22-inch barrel; 39-1/2-inch overall length; weighs 6-1/2 lbs.; hammerless; hooded white metal bead front sight, Lyman folding leaf middle sight; one-piece checkered walnut stock with steel-capped pistol grip, fluted comb, sling swivels; three-lug bolt; crossbolt safety; side ejection. Introduced 1955; discontinued 1974. Add 10 percent for 358.

308 Win.

Exc: $695 **VGood:** $650 **Good:** $390

243 Win. (pre-1964)

Exc: $715 **VGood:** $600 **Good:** $410

243 Win. (post-1964)

Exc: $595 **VGood:** $450 **Good:** $390

284 Win. (pre-1964)

Exc: $1575 **VGood:** $1150 **Good:** $650

284 Win. (post-1964)

Exc: $995 **VGood:** $695 **Good:** $430

358 Win.

Exc: $1350 **VGood:** $920 **Good:** $740

WINCHESTER MODEL 88 CARBINE

Same specs as Model 88 except 243, 284, 308; 19-inch barrel; barrel band. Introduced 1968; discontinued 1973.

Perf: $1200 **Exc:** $1090 **VGood:** $710

Note: The Winchester Model 94 was discontinued in 2006. Values fluctuate wildly.

WINCHESTER MODEL 94 (POST-1964 PRODUCTION)

Lever action; 30-30, 32 Spl., 7-30 Waters, 44 Mag.; 6-tube magazine; 20-inch, 24-inch barrel; weighs 6-1/4 lbs.; open rear sight, ramp front; plain American walnut straight-grip stock; barrel band on forearm; saddle ring; side or angle ejection (post-1982); blued finish. Introduced 1964; modified variations still in production. Premium for 7-30.

Exc: $540 **VGood:** $480 **Good:** $350

Side or Angle Eject Model

Exc: $550 **VGood:** $495 **Good:** $360

WINCHESTER MODEL 94 ANTIQUE

Same specs as Model 94 except 20-inch barrel; case-hardened receiver with scrollwork; gold-colored saddle ring. Introduced 1964; discontinued 1983.

Exc: $530 **VGood:** $500 **Good:** $380

WINCHESTER MODEL 94 CLASSIC

Same specs as Model 94 except 30-30; 20-inch, 26-inch octagonal barrel; semi-fancy American walnut stock, forearm; steel buttplate; scrollwork on receiver. Introduced 1967; discontinued 1970.

Exc: $610 **VGood:** $550 **Good:** $400

WINCHESTER MODEL 94 DELUXE

Same specs as Model 94 except 30-30; checkered walnut stock, forearm. Introduced 1988; later in production as Model 94 Traditional.

Exc: $650 **VGood:** $605 **Good:** $480

WINCHESTER MODEL 94 LEGACY

Same specs as Model 94 except half-pistol-grip walnut stock; checkered grip and forend. 30-30, 357 Mag., 38-55, 44 Mag., 45 Colt. Introduced 1995.

Perf: $575 **Exc:** $425 **VGood:** $360

WINCHESTER MODEL 94 LIMITED EDITION CENTENNIAL GRADE I

Same specs as Model 94 except made to commemorate the 100th anniversary of the Model 94; 30-30; 26-inch half-octagon barrel; tube half-magazine; drilled, tapped for tang sight; close reproduction of the turn-of-the-century #9 factory engraving; diamond-style "H" checkering pattern on the pistol-grip stock, forend; engraving on receiver sides shows whitetail deer profiles. Introduced 1994; discontinued 1994.

Perf: $1000 **Exc:** $950 **VGood:** $795

WINCHESTER MODEL 94 LIMITED EDITION CENTENNIAL HIGH GRADE RIFLE

Same specs as Model 94 except high-grade rifle made to commemorate the 100th anniversary of the Model 94; 30-30; 26-inch half-octagon barrel; tube half-magazine; Lyman No. 2 tang sight; spade-pattern checkering on pistol-grip stock; blued receiver with gold inlays and #6-style engraving pattern showing a gold deer on the right, gold mountain sheep on the left. Only 3,000 produced. Introduced 1994; discontinued 1994.

Perf: $1350 **Exc:** $1050 **VGood:** $795

WINCHESTER MODEL 94 LIMITED EDITION CENTENNIAL HIGH GRADE CUSTOM

Same specs as Model 94 except highest grade rifle made to commemorate the 100th anniversary of the Model 94; 30-30; 26-inch half-octagon barrel; tube half-magazine; Lyman No. 2 tang sight; spade-pattern checkering on pistol-grip stock; top ejection; hand-engraved, grayed action with inking in #5 style with gold inlaid ovals containing a pair of pronghorns on the right, caribou on the left; crescent buttplate. Only 94 produced. Introduced 1994; discontinued 1994.

Perf: $6995 **Exc:** $5995 **VGood:** $3550

WINCHESTER MODEL 94 RANGER

Same specs as Model 94 except economy version; 30-30 only; 5-shot or 6-shot magazine; 20-inch barrel; uncheckered hardwood stock, forearm. Introduced 1985.

Perf: $475 **Exc:** $400 **VGood:** $365

WINCHESTER MODEL 94 RANGER COMPACT

Similar to the Model 94 Ranger except has shorter 16-inch barrel and 12-1/2-inch length of pull, rubber recoil pad, post front sight. 30-30, 357 Mag; Introduced 1998. Made in U.S.A. by U.S. Repeating Arms Co., Inc.

Perf: $475 **Exc:** $400 **VGood:** $365

WINCHESTER MODEL 94 SADDLE RING CARBINE

Same specs as Model 94 except saddle ring; 44 Mag.; 20-inch barrel; top ejection. Introduced 1967; discontinued 1972.

Perf: $775 **Exc:** $625 **VGood:** $560

WINCHESTER MODEL 94 TIMBER CARBINE

Similar to the Model 94 Big Bore and XTR Big Bore rifles. Chambered for 444 Marlin, later 450 Marlin; 18-inch ported barrel; half-pistol grip stock with butt pad; checkered walnut grip and forend. Introduced 1999; still offered. Made in U.S.A. by U.S. Repeating Arms Co., Inc.

Perf: $750 **Exc:** $625 **VGood:** $560

Winchester Model 94 Ranger

Winchester Model 94 Ranger Compact

Winchester Model 94 Traditional

Winchester Model 94 Trails End

Winchester Model 94 Trapper

Winchester Model 94 Wrangler II

Winchester Model 94 XTR Side Eject

WINCHESTER MODEL 94 TRADITIONAL

Lever action; 30-30 Win., 6-shot; 44 Mag., 11-shot tubular magazine; 20-inch barrel; weighs 6-1/2 lbs.; 37-3/4-inch overall length; Straight grip checkered walnut stock and forend; Hooded blade front, semi-buckhorn rear. Drilled and tapped for scope mount; forged steel receiver; side ejection, exposed rebounding hammer with automatic trigger-activated transfer bar. Introduced 1984.

Perf: $600 **Exc:** $550 **VGood:** $490

WINCHESTER MODEL 94 TRAILS END

Similar to the Model 94 except chambered only for 357 Mag., 44- 40, 44 Mag., 45 Colt, 25-35, 30-30; 11-shot magazine. Walnut stock and forearm; saddle ring. Introduced 1997. From U.S. Repeating Arms Co., Inc.. Add 20 percent for 25-35.

Perf: $950 **Exc:** $825 **VGood:** $650

WINCHESTER MODEL 94 TRAPPER

Same specs as Model 94 except short 16-inch barrel; 30-30 (standard), 357 Mag., 44 Mag./44 Spl., 45 Colt; 5-shot tube magazine in 30-30, 9 shots in other calibers; side ejection. Introduced 1985.

Perf: $650 **Exc:** $540 **VGood:** $500

WINCHESTER MODEL 94 WIN-TUFF

Same specs as Model 94 except 30-30; drilled, tapped for scope mounts; checkered hardwood stock, forearm. Introduced 1987.

Perf: $650 **Exc:** $540 **VGood:** $500

WINCHESTER MODEL 94 WRANGLER

Same specs as Model 94 except 32 Spl.; 16-inch barrel; top ejection; roll-engraved Western scene on receiver. Introduced 1983; no longer in production.

Exc: $610 **VGood:** $475 **Good:** $390

WINCHESTER MODEL 94 WRANGLER II

Same specs as Model 94 except 32 Spl., 38-55; 16-inch barrel; angle ejection; loop-type finger lever; roll-engraved Western scenes on receiver. Introduced 1983; discontinued 1986.

Exc: $740 **VGood:** $650 **Good:** $510

WINCHESTER MODEL 94 WRANGLER LARGE LOOP

Same specs as Model 94 except 30-30, 44 Mag.; 16-inch barrel; extra-large loop lever. Introduced 1992.

Exc: $640 **VGood:** $550 **Good:** $390

Side or Angle Eject Model

Exc: $650 **VGood:** $560 **Good:** $400

WINCHESTER MODEL 94 XTR

Same specs as Model 94 except higher-grade version; 30-30, 7-30 Waters; 20-inch, 24-inch barrel (7-30 Waters); hooded front sight; select checkered walnut straight-grip stock. Introduced 1978; discontinued 1988.

Exc: $650 **VGood:** $575 **Good:** $350

7-30 Waters

Exc: $800 **VGood:** $750 **Good:** $575

WINCHESTER MODEL 94 XTR BIG BORE

Same specs as Model 94 XTR except 307 Win., 356 Win., 375 Win.; 6-shot tube magazine; 20-inch barrel; cut-checkered satin-finish American walnut stock, rubber recoil pad. XTR designation dropped 1989. Introduced 1978. Deduct 10 percent for 375.

Exc: $800 **VGood:** $650 **Good:** $575

Side or Angle Eject model

Exc: $825 **VGood:** $675 **Good:** $600

Winchester Model 94 XTR Big Bore

Winchester Model 150

Winchester Model 250

Winchester Model 250 Deluxe

Winchester Model 255

Winchester Model 1873

Winchester Model 1873 Carbine

WINCHESTER MODEL 94 XTR DELUXE

Same specs as Model 94 XTR except 30-30; 20-inch barrel; deluxe checkered walnut straight-grip stock, long forearm; rubber buttplate. Introduced 1987; discontinued 1988.

Exc: $670 **VGood:** $610 **Good:** $550

WINCHESTER MODEL 150

Lever action; 22 Short, 22 Long, 22 LR; 21-shot tube magazine (22 Short), 17-shot (22 Long), 15-shot (22 LR); 20-1/2-inch barrel; weighs 5 lbs.; aluminum alloy receiver grooved for scope sight; walnut-finished American hardwood stock; forearm has frontier-style barrel band; straight grip; no checkering. Introduced 1967; discontinued 1974.

Exc: $150 **VGood:** $100 **Good:** $85

WINCHESTER MODEL 250

Lever action; 22 Short, 22 Long, 22 LR; 21-shot tube magazine (22 Short), 17-shot (22 Long), 15-shot (22 LR); 20-1/2-inch barrel; 39-inch overall length; weighs 5 lbs.; hammerless; ramped square post front sight, adjustable square notch rear; aluminum alloy receiver grooved for tip-off scope mounts; walnut-finished hardwood stock; crossbolt safety on front of trigger guard. Introduced 1963; discontinued 1973.

Exc: $175 **VGood:** $110 **Good:** $90

WINCHESTER MODEL 250 DELUXE

Same specs as Model 250 except select walnut stock, fluted comb, cheekpiece; basketweave checkering; white spacer between buttplate and stock; sling swivels. Introduced 1965; discontinued 1971.

Exc: $215 **VGood:** $150 **Good:** $100

WINCHESTER MODEL 255

Lever action; 22 WMR; 11-shot tube magazine; 20-1/2-inch barrel; 39-inch overall length; weighs 5 lbs.; hammerless; ramped square post front sight, adjustable square notch rear; aluminum alloy receiver grooved for scope mounts; walnut-finish hardwood pistol-grip stock; crossbolt safety. Introduced 1964; discontinued 1970.

Exc: $215 **VGood:** $150 **Good:** $100

WINCHESTER MODEL 255 DELUXE

Same specs as Model 255 except high-gloss Monte Carlo select walnut stock, fluted comb, cheekpiece; basketweave checkering; white spacer between butt-plate and stock; sling swivels. Introduced 1965; discontinued 1971.

Exc: $250 **VGood:** $230 **Good:** $175

WINCHESTER MODEL 1873

Lever action; 32-20, 38-40, 44-40; 6-, 12-, 15- or 17-shot tubular magazine; 24-inch barrel standard, other lengths made; open rear sight, bead or blade front; uncheckered American walnut straight-grip stock, forend; blued finish. Introduced 1873; discontinued 1924. 1 of 1000, and 1 of 100 are extremely rare. Appraisal recommended. Beware of fakes. Collector value.

Exc: $4000 to $11000
VGood: $2500 to $6000
Good: $900 to $4000

WINCHESTER MODEL 1873 CARBINE

Same specs as Model 1873 except 20-inch barrel; 12-shot magazine; two barrel bands. Collector value.

Exc: $5000 to $14000
VGood: $2900 to $10000
Good: $1000 to $5000

WINCHESTER MODEL 1873 MUSKET

Same specs as Model 1873 except 30-inch barrel; extra capacity tube magazine; three barrel bands. Values from $1000 to $7000.

WINCHESTER MODEL 1873 RIMFIRE

Same specs as Model 1873 except 22 Short, 22 Long, 22 Extra Long. Introduced 1884; discontinued 1904. Collector value.

Exc: $10,000 **VGood:** $6750 **Good:** $2500

WINCHESTER MODEL 1873 SPECIAL

Same specs as Model 1873 except octagon barrel only; color case-hardened receiver; select American walnut pistol-grip stock. Case-hardened receivers brings substantial premium. Need appraisal. Collector value.

WINCHESTER MODEL 1876

Lever action; 40-60, 45-60, 45-75, 50-95; tube magazine; 26-inch, 28-inch barrel; open rear sight, bead or blade front; uncheckered American walnut straight-grip stock, forend; blued finish. Model 1876 values to over $6000. 1 of 1000 and 1 of 100 Model values to $75,000, an appraiser is needed. Introduced 1876; discontinued 1897.

WINCHESTER MODEL 1876 CARBINE

Same specs as Model 1876 except 22-inch barrel; full-length forearm; one barrel band. Values to $7500.

WINCHESTER MODEL 1876 MUSKET

Same specs as Model 1876 except 32-inch barrel; carbine-like forend tip; one barrel band. Values to $8000.

Model 1885 Note: All Model 1885 Single Shot rifles were available in many calibers and barrel contours. Each example merits expert appraisal.

WINCHESTER MODEL 1885 HIGH WALL

Lever action; single shot; 22 RF through 50; 30-inch barrel of various weights; open rear sight, blade front; uncheckered American walnut straight-grip stock, forend; solid frame. Introduced 1885; discontinued 1920. Collector value.

Color case-hardened (pre-1901)

Exc: $3495 **VGood:** $2995 **Good:** $1995

Blued finish (post-1901)

Exc: $2695 **VGood:** $2195 **Good:** $1650

WINCHESTER MODEL 1885 HIGH WALL DELUXE GRADE

Same specs as Model 1885 High Wall except better wood; hand-checkered stock, forend. Collector value.

Exc: $4995 **VGood:** $4250 **Good:** $3295

WINCHESTER MODEL 1885 HIGH WALL SCHUETZEN

Same specs as Model 1885 High Wall except 30-inch octagonal barrel; Vernier rear tang peep sight wind-gauge front; European walnut Schuetzen-type stock; hand-checkered forend, pistol grip; Schuetzen buttplate, adjustable palm rest; spur finger lever; double-set trigger. Collector value.

Exc: $8995 **VGood:** $6995 **Good:** $4250

Takedown model

Exc: $9995 **VGood:** $7995 **Good:** $5250

WINCHESTER MODEL 1885 LOW WALL SPORTER

Lever action; single shot; 22 RF; 28-inch round, octagonal barrel; solid frame; open rear sight, blade front; uncheckered American walnut straight stock, forend. Introduced 1885; discontinued 1920. Collector value. Premium for optional features and for rifles made before 1898.

Exc: $1295 **VGood:** $995 **Good:** $795

WINCHESTER MODEL 1885 LOW WALL RIMFIRE (RECENT MANUFACTURE)

Single shot, falling block; 22 LR, later 17 HMR, with 17 Mach 2 introduced in 2005; 24-1/2-inch barrel, half-octagon; 41-inch overall length; weighs 8 lbs; Walnut stock; Blade front, semi-buckhorn rear sights; Drilled and tapped for scope mount or tang sight; target chamber. Introduced 1999; Limited production. From U.S. Repeating Arms Co.

Grade I (2,400 made)

Perf: $750 **Exc:** $600 **VGood:** $515

High Grade (1,100 made; engraved/gold inlaid)

Perf: $1100 **Exc:** $900 **VGood:** $700

WINCHESTER MODEL 1885 LOW WALL WINDER MUSKET

Same specs as Model 1885 Low Wall except 22 Short, 22 LR; 28-inch round barrel; solid frame or takedown; musket-type rear sight, blade front; straight-grip military-type stock, forend. Collector value.

Exc: $2100 **VGood:** $1450 **Good:** $695

WINCHESTER MODEL 1885 HIGH WALL HUNTER

Single shot; patterned after original Model 1885 designed by John Browning. Calibers: .223, .22-250, .270 WSM, 7mm WSM, .300 WSM, .325 WSM. Stock: Checkered walnut. Barrel: 28-inch blued, sightless octagon with Pachmayr pad. Weight: 8-1/2 lbs.

NIB: $800 **Exc:** $725 **VGood:** $625

WINCHESTER MODEL 1885 .30-06 CENTENNIAL HIGH WALL HUNTER

Similar to Model 1885 High Wall Hunter but with premium wood and gold inlay on receiver. Commemorates centennial of .30-06 cartridge.

NIB: $1500 **Exc:** $1375 **VGood:** $1095

WINCHESTER MODEL 1885 LOW WALL 17 MACH 2

Similar to Model 1885 High Wall but with low-profile receiver, crescent buttplate, and 24-inch barrel. Chambered for 17 Mach 2 rimfire cartridge. Introduced 2006.

NIB: $995 **Exc:** $820 **VGood:** $695

WINCHESTER MODEL 1886

Lever action; 33 WCF, 45-70, 45-90, 40-82, 40-65, 38-56, 40-70, 38-70, 50-100-450, 50-110 Express; 8-shot tube magazine or 4-shot half-magazine; 26-inch round, half-octagonal, octagonal barrel; open rear sight, bead or blade front; plain straight stock, forearm; color case-hardened (pre-1901) or blued (post-1901) finish. Premiums for many features and calibers. Appraisal necessary. Introduced 1886; discontinued 1935. Collector value.

Exc: $9000 **VGood:** $6000 **Good:** $4500

With deluxe checkered stock

Exc: $15000 **VGood:** $9995 **Good:** $5250

WINCHESTER MODEL 1886 CARBINE

Same specs as Model 1886 except 22-inch round barrel. Rare.

Exc: $13950 **VGood:** $9450 **Good:** $5995

Winchester Model 1885 Low Wall Rimfire

Winchester Model 1886

Winchester Model 1892

Winchester Model 1895

Winchester Model 1895 Limited Edition Grade I

Winchester Model 1885 High Wall Hunter

Winchester Model 1885 Centennial High Wall Hunter

WINCHESTER MODEL 1886 LIGHTWEIGHT

Same specs as Model 1886 except lightened; 33 WCF, 45-70; 22-inch, 24-inch round barrel; rubber buttplate; blued finish.

Exc: $3995 **VGood:** $2850 **Good:** $1495

WINCHESTER MODEL 1886 MUSKET

Same specs as Model 1886 except 30-inch round barrel; one barrel band.

Exc: $18995 **VGood:** $9995 **Good:** $6700

WINCHESTER MODEL 1886 TAKEDOWN

Same specs as Model 1886 except 24-inch round barrel; takedown feature.

Exc: $7495 **VGood:** $4500 **Good:** $2450

WINCHESTER MODEL 1886 LEVER-ACTION RIFLE (RECENT MANUFACTURE)

Lever action; 45-70, 4-shot magazine; 22-inch round tapered barrel; 40-1/2-inch overall length; weighs 7-1/4 lbs.; Smooth walnut stock; Bead front sight, ramp-adjustable buckhorn-style rear. Recreation of the Model 1886 lightweight rifle. Polished blue finish; crescent metal butt plate; metal forend cap; pistol grip stock. Reintroduced 1998. From U.S. Repeating Arms Co., Inc. Add 10% for takedown version.

Grade I

Perf: $1200 **Exc:** $900 **VGood:** $650

High Grade

Perf: $1450 **Exc:** $1200 **VGood:** $900

WINCHESTER MODEL 1892

Lever action; 218 Bee (rare), 25-20, 32-20, 38-40, 44-40; 13-shot tube magazine, 7-shot half-magazine, 10-shot two-thirds magazine; 24-inch round or octagonal barrel; open rear sight, bead front; plain, straight stock, forearm; blued finish. Introduced 1892; discontinued 1941.

Exc: $2745 **VGood:** $1495 **Good:** $875

With takedown feature

Exc: $3105 **VGood:** $1995 **Good:** $1250

WINCHESTER MODEL 1892 CARBINE

Same specs as Model 1892 except 5-, 11-shot magazine; 20-inch barrel; two barrel bands.

Exc: $2995 **VGood:** $1995 **Good:** $1250

WINCHESTER MODEL 1892 MUSKET

Same specs as Model 1892 except 30-inch barrel; three barrel bands; buttplate.

Exc: $8995 **VGood:** $5350 **Good:** $3450

Winchester Model 1895 Saddle Ring Carbine

Winchester Model 9417

Winchester Model 9422

Winchester Model 9422 High Grade

Winchester Model 9422 Legacy

Winchester Model 9422 XTR Classic

WINCHESTER MODEL 1892 TRAPPER'S CARBINE

Same specs as Model 1892 except 12-inch, 14-inch, 15-inch, 16-inch, 18-inch barrel; shortened tube magazine; two barrel bands; browned finish.

Exc: $9995 **VGood:** $5995 **Good:** $2550

WINCHESTER MODEL 1894

Lever action; 25-35, 30-30, 32-40, 32 Spl., 38-55; 4-, 6-shot tube magazine; 22-inch, 26-inch barrel; open rear sight, blade or ramp (post-1931) front; plain American walnut straight-grip stock; blued finish. Introduced 1894; discontinued 1936. Premium for those made before 1898.

Exc: $2495 **VGood:** $1295 **Good:** $695

Takedown model

Exc: $2995 **VGood:** $1895 **Good:** $895

WINCHESTER MODEL 1894 CARBINE

Same specs as Model 1894 except 20-inch barrel. Premium for original saddle ring.

Exc: $2495 **VGood:** $1370 **Good:** $700

WINCHESTER MODEL 1894 TRAPPER CARBINE

Same specs as Model 1894 except 14-inch, 15-inch, 16-inch, 17-inch, 18-inch barrel. No longer in production.

Exc: $5550 **VGood:** $3500 **Good:** $1570

WINCHESTER MODEL 1895

Lever action; 30-40 Krag, 30 Govt.'03 (30-03), 30 Govt.'06 (30-06), 303 British, 7.62mm Russian, 35 Win., 38-72, 405 Win., 40-72; 4-, 5-shot (30-40, 303 British) box magazine; 24-inch, 28-inch barrel; open rear sight, bead or blade front; uncheckered American walnut straight-grip stock, forend; blued finish. Introduced 1895; discontinued 1931. Collector value. Premium for .405.

Exc: $4000 **VGood:** $2500 **Good:** $1400

Takedown model

Exc: $4400 **VGood:** $2800 **Good:** $1600

WINCHESTER MODEL 1895 CARBINE

Same specs as Model 1895 except 30-40 Krag, 30-03, 30-06, 303 British; 22-inch barrel; one barrel band; carbine stock; solid frame. Collector value.

Exc: $2900 **VGood:** $2000 **Good:** $1000

With U.S. Government markings

Exc: $4000 **VGood:** $3300 **Good:** $1800

WINCHESTER MODEL 1895 LIMITED EDITION (RECENT PRODUCTION)

Lever action; 30-06, 270, 405 Win, 4-shot non-datachable box magazine; 24-inch round barrel; 42-inch overall length; weighs 8 lbs.; American walnut stock; Gold bead front sight, buckhorn rear adjustable for elevation. Recreation of the original Model 1895 for its 100th anniversary. Polished blue finish with Nimschke-style scroll engraving on receiver. Scalloped receiver, two-piece cocking lever, schnabel forend, straight-grip stock. Introduced 1995; standard version no longer in production.

Grade 1

Perf: $900 **Exc:** $800 **VGood:** $695

High Grade, extensive engraving, 4000 rifles made.

Perf: $1600 **Exc:** $1400 **VGood:** $995

405 caliber, Grade I, Introduced 2000, discontinued 2003.

Perf: $1425 **Exc:** $1125 **VGood:** $900

405 High Grade

Perf: $1700 **Exc:** $1300 **VGood:** $950

WINCHESTER MODEL 1895 MUSKET

Same specs as Model 1895 except 30-40 Krag, 30 Govt'03, 30 Govt'06; 28-inch, 30-inch barrel; two-barrel bands; handguard over barrel.

Exc: $2000 **VGood:** $1495 **Good:** $1095

With U.S. Government markings

Exc: $2995 **VGood:** $1650 **Good:** $1295

WINCHESTER MODEL 1895 NRA MUSKET

Same specs as Model 1895 except 24-inch barrel; meets NRA specs for competition.

Exc: $4500 **VGood:** $1900 **Good:** $1400

WINCHESTER MODEL 1895 SADDLE RING CARBINE (RECENT MFR.)

Patterned after original Model 1895 carbine. Features include blued 22-inch barrel, ladder style rear sight; D&T for Lyman side mount; saddle ring on left side of receiver; .30-'06. Chambered in .30-06 only; commemorates centennial of .30-06 cartridge.

NIB: $1275 **Exc:** $1050 **VGood:** $875

WINCHESTER MODEL 9417

Lever action; 17 HMR; 11-shot tube magazine; 20-1/2-inch or 22-1/2-inch barrel; weighs 6 lbs; adjustable rear, ramp front sights; grooved for scope mounting; introduced 2003 as 17-caliber variant of Model 9422.

Perf: $1000 **Exc:** $800 **VGood:** $570

WINCHESTER MODEL 9422

Lever action; 22 Short, 22 Long, 22 LR; 21-shot tube magazine (22 Short), 17-shot (22 Long), 15-shot (22 LR); 20-1/2-inch barrel; weighs 6-1/2 lbs.; hooded ramp bead front sight, adjustable semi-buckhorn rear; grooved for scope mounts; checkered American walnut straight-grip stock, forearm. Introduced 1972; designated XTR 1978; XTR designation dropped 1989; still in production.

Perf: $740 **Exc:** $670 **VGood:** $515

WINCHESTER MODEL 9422 HIGH GRADE

Same specs as Model 9422 except 22 LR; high grade walnut with gloss finish; blued and engraved receiver with coonhound on right side, racoon profile on left, both framed with detailed Nimschke-style scrollwork. Introduced 1995.

Perf: $900 **Exc:** $795 **VGood:** $495

WINCHESTER MODEL 9422 LEGACY

Like Model 9422, but checkered pistol-grip walnut stock and forearm; longer 22-1/2-inch barrel; adjustable rear, ramp front sights; receiver grooved for scope mounting; hammer extension; 22 LR or 22WMR; still in production.

Perf: $1000 **Exc:** $900 **VGood:** $780

WINCHESTER MODEL 9422 MAGNUM

Same specs as Model 9422 except 22 WMR; 11-shot tube magazine. Introduced 1972.

Perf: $950 **Exc:** $825 **VGood:** $525

WINCHESTER MODEL 9422 WIN-CAM

Same specs as Model 9422 except 22 WMR only; 11-shot tube magazine; checkered green laminated hardwood stock, forearm. Introduced 1987.

Perf: $1050 **Exc:** $950 **VGood:** $830

WINCHESTER MODEL 9422 WIN-TUFF

Same specs as Model 9422 except 22 LR, 22 WMR; checkered brown laminated hardwood stock, forearm. Introduced 1988.

Perf: $1050 **Exc:** $950 **VGood:** $830

WINCHESTER MODEL 9422 XTR CLASSIC

Same specs as Model 9422 except 22-1/2-inch barrel; 39-1/8-inch overall length; satin-finished walnut stock fluted comb; no checkering; crescent steel buttplate; curved finger lever; capped pistol grip. Introduced 1985; discontinued 1988.

Perf: $1050 **Exc:** $950 **VGood:** $830

WINCHESTER MODEL 55 RIMFIRE

Single shot, "semi-automatic;" 22 Short, 22 Long, 22 LR; 22-inch barrel; weighs 5-1/2 lbs.; action automatically ejects the fired case, recocks, and remains open for loading after each shot; top loading; open rear sight, bead front; one-piece uncheckered walnut stock. Introduced 1958; discontinued 1961.

Exc: $210 **VGood:** $170 **Good:** $100

WINCHESTER MODEL 63 (1933-1958)

Semi-automatic; 22 LR Super Speed or Super-X; 10-shot tube magazine in buttstock; 20-inch barrel (early series), 23-inch (later series); takedown; open rear sight, bead front; uncheckered walnut pistol-grip stock and forearm. Introduced 1933; discontinued 1958.

20-inch barrel

Exc: $800 **VGood:** $700 **Good:** $575

23-inch barrel

Exc: $900 **VGood:** $775 **Good:** $595

WINCHESTER MODEL 63 (1997-1998)

Semi-automatic; 22 LR; 10-shot tube magazine; 23-inch barrel; 39-inch overall length; weighs 6-1/4 lbs.; Recreation of the original Model 63. Magazine tube loads through a port in the buttstock. Reintroduced 1997. From U. S. Repeating Arms Co.

Grade I

Perf: $700 **Exc:** $650 **VGood:** $570

High grade, select walnut, cut checkering, engraved scenes,

Perf: $950 **Exc:** $825 **VGood:** $700

WINCHESTER MODEL 74

Semi-automatic; 22 Short or 22 LR; 20-shot tube magazine in buttstock (22 Short), 14-shot (22 LR); 24-inch barrel; takedown; open rear sight, bead front; uncheckered one-piece pistol-grip stock; safety on top of receiver. Introduced 1939; discontinued 1955. Premium for 22 Short (Gallery) model.

Exc: $295 **VGood:** $195 **Good:** $180

WINCHESTER MODEL 77 CLIP

Semi-automatic; 22 LR; 8-shot clip magazine; 22-inch barrel; weighs 5-1/2 lbs.; #75C bead front sight, #32B open rear; plain, American walnut one-piece stock; pistol grip; beavertail forend; rotary thumb safety; black composition buttplate. Introduced 1955; discontinued 1963.

Exc: $230 **VGood:** $190 **Good:** $150

WINCHESTER MODEL 77 TUBE

Same specs as Model 77 Clip except for 15-shot tube magazine.

Exc: $280 **VGood:** $240 **Good:** $180

WINCHESTER MODEL 100

Semi-automatic; gas-operated; 243 Win., 284 Win., 308 Win.; 3-shot magazine (284 Win.), 4-shot (others); 22-inch barrel; 42-1/2-inch overall length; weighs 7-1/2 lbs.; hooded bead front sight, folding leaf rear; tapped for receiver sights, scope mounts; one-piece walnut with checkered pistol-grip stock, forearm; sling swivels. Introduced 1960; discontinued 1974. Add $400 for .284 chambering.

Pre-1964 Model

Exc: $725 **VGood:** $650 **Good:** $560

Post-1964 Model

Exc: $675 **VGood:** $500 **Good:** $415

WINCHESTER MODEL 100 CARBINE

Same specs as Model 100 except 19-inch barrel; no checkering; barrel band. Introduced 1967; discontinued 1973.

Exc: $750 **VGood:** $675 **Good:** $500

WINCHESTER MODEL 190

Semi-automatic; 22 Short, 22 Long, 22 LR; 21-shot tube magazine (22 Short), 17-shot (22 Long), 15-shot (22 LR); 20-1/2-inch, 24-inch barrel with 1:16-inch twist; 39-inch overall length; weighs 5 lbs; bead post front sight, adjustable V rear; aluminum alloy receiver grooved for scope mounts; American hardwood stock with plain, uncheckered pistol-grip, forearm; Introduced 1967; discontinued 1980.

Exc: $175 **VGood:** $140 **Good:** $70

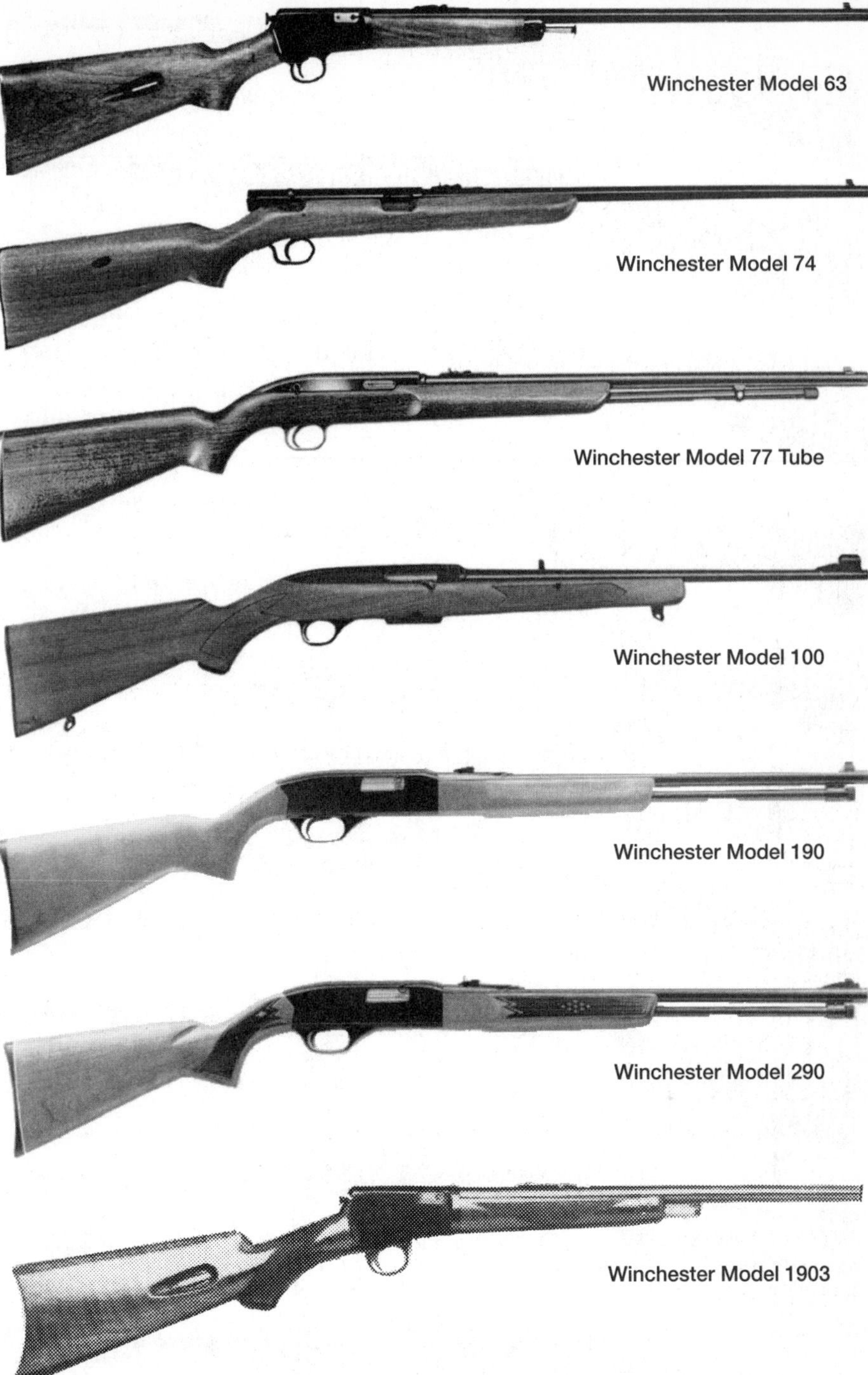

Winchester Model 63

Winchester Model 74

Winchester Model 77 Tube

Winchester Model 100

Winchester Model 190

Winchester Model 290

Winchester Model 1903

WINCHESTER MODEL 290

Semi-automatic; 22 Short, 22 Long, 22 LR; 21-shot tube magazine (22 Short), 17-shot (22 Long), 15-shot (22 LR); 20-1/2-inch barrel; 39-inch overall length; weighs 5 lbs.; open rear sight, ramp front; uncheckered or impress-checkered hardwood pistol-grip stock, forend. Introduced 1963; discontinued 1977.

Exc: $185 **VGood:** $150 **Good:** $90

WINCHESTER MODEL 290 DELUXE

Same specs as Model 290 except fancy American walnut Monte Carlo stock, forend. Introduced 1965; discontinued 1977.

Exc: $190 **VGood:** $155 **Good:** $95

WINCHESTER MODEL 490

Semi-automatic; 22 LR; 5-shot detachable box magazine; 22-inch barrel; folding leaf rear sight, hooded ramp front; one-piece checkered American walnut pistol-grip stock, resembles Model 100 centerfire rifle. Introduced 1975; discontinued 1978.

Exc: $185 **VGood:** $150 **Good:** $90

NOTE: For The Following Winchester Self-loading Rifles (Models 1903, 1905, 1907 And 1910), A Considerable Premium Can Be Expected For 98% Or Better And For Special-order Examples.

WINCHESTER MODEL 1903

Semi-automatic; 22 Winchester Automatic RF cartridge; 10-shot tube magazine in butt; 20-inch barrel; takedown; open rear sight, bead front; uncheckered straight-grip stock, forend; special wood and factory checkering bring a premium. Introduced 1903; discontinued 1932. Collector value.

Exc: $985 **VGood:** $815 **Good:** $645

Winchester Model 1905

Winchester Model 1907

Winchester Model 1910

Winchester Model SXR Super X

Winchester Combination Gun Super Grade

Winchester Double Express

Winchester Model 61

Winchester Model 62

Winchester Model 270

Deluxe rifle with checkered pistol-grip stock and forearm

Exc: $1200 **VGood:** $730 **Good:** $560

WINCHESTER MODEL 1905

Semi-automatic; 32 Win. Self-Loading, 35 Win. Self-loading; 5-, 10-shot box magazine; 22-inch barrel; takedown; open rear sight, bead front; uncheckered American walnut pistol-grip stock, forend. Introduced 1905; discontinued 1920. Collector value.

Exc: $645 **VGood:** $525 **Good:** $445

WINCHESTER MODEL 1907

Semi-automatic; 351 Win. Self-Loading; 5-, 10-shot box magazine; 20-inch barrel; takedown; open rear sight, bead front; uncheckered walnut pistol-grip stock, forend. Introduced 1907; discontinued 1957. Collector value.

Exc: $700 **VGood:** $585 **Good:** $375

WINCHESTER MODEL 1910

Semi-automatic; 401 Win. Self-Loading; 4-shot box magazine; 20-inch barrel; takedown; open rear sight, bead front; uncheckered walnut pistol-grip stock, forend. Introduced 1910; discontinued 1936. Collector value. Add 15 percent for high grade.

Exc: $700 **VGood:** $585 **Good:** $375

WINCHESTER MODEL SXR SUPER X RIFLE

Gas-operated semi-automatic patterned after Browning BAR ShortTrac and LongTrac. Calibers: .30-06, .300WM, .270 WSM, .300 WSM. Barrel: 22-inch (.30-06), 24-inch. Weight: 7-1/4 lbs. Stock: Two-piece checkered walnut.

NIB: $850 **Exc:** $775 **VGood:** $625

WINCHESTER COMBINATION GUN SUPER GRADE

Over/under; 30-06/12-ga.; 25-inch Winchoke shot barrel; 41-1/4-inch overall length; bead front sight, folding leaf rear; fancy American walnut stock; hand-checkered pistol grip, forend; full-length top barrel rib; silvered, engraved receiver; blued barrels; integral scope bases; single selective mechanical trigger. Made in Japan. Introduced 1982; discontinued 1985.

Exc: $2400 **VGood:** $1700 **Good:** $1400

WINCHESTER DOUBLE EXPRESS RIFLE

Double rifle; over/under; 30-06, 9.3x74R, 6.5mm, 270, 7.65R, 257 Roberts; 23-1/2-inch barrel; 39-5/8-inch overall length; bead on ramp front sight, folding leaf rear on quarter-rib; integral scope bases; fancy American walnut stock; hand-checkered pistol grip, forend; uses Model 101 shotgun action; silvered, engraved receiver; blued barrels; quick-detachable sling swivels; marketed in hard case. Made in Japan. Introduced 1982; discontinued 1985.

Exc: $3100 **VGood:** $2495 **Good:** $2195

WINCHESTER MODEL 61

Slide action; 22 Short, 22 Long, 22 LR; 20-shot tube magazine (22 Short), 16-shot (22 Long), 14-shot (22 LR); 24-inch round or octagon barrel; hammerless; takedown; open rear sight, bead front; uncheckered pistol-grip stock; grooved semi-beavertail slide handle. Introduced 1932; discontinued 1963. Premium for early examples.

Exc: $850 **VGood:** $650 **Good:** $465

Octagon barrel model

Exc: $1095 **VGood:** $795 **Good:** $495

WINCHESTER MODEL 61 MAGNUM

Same specs as Model 61 except 22 WMR; 12-shot tube magazine. Introduced 1960; discontinued 1963.

Exc: $1000 **VGood:** $750 **Good:** $575

WINCHESTER MODEL 62

Slide action; 22 Short, 22 Long, 22 LR; 20-shot tube magazine (20 Short), 16-shot (22 Long), 14-shot (22 LR); 23-inch barrel; visible hammer; bead front sight, open rear; plain, straight-grip stock; grooved semi-beavertail slide handle; also available in gallery model in 22 Short only. Introduced 1932; discontinued 1959.

Exc: $645 **VGood:** $465 **Good:** $350

WINCHESTER MODEL 270

Slide action; 22 Short, 22 Long, 22 LR; 21-shot tube magazine (22 Short), 17-shot (22 Long), 15-shot (22 LR); 20-1/2-inch barrel; 39-inch overall length; weighs 5 lbs.; ramped square post front sight, adjustable square notch rear; aluminum alloy receiver grooved for tip-off scope mounts; walnut-finished hardwood, or black or brown cycolac plastic pistol-grip stock; crossbolt safety. Introduced 1963; discontinued 1973.

Walnut stock

Exc: $185 **VGood:** $140 **Good:** $90

Plastic stock

Exc: $165 **Vgood:** $125 **Good:** $70

WINCHESTER MODEL 270 DELUXE

Same specs as Model 270 except high-gloss Monte Carlo select walnut stock, fluted comb, cheekpiece; basketweave checkering; white buttspacer. Introduced 1965; discontinued 1973.

Exc: $190 **VGood:** $145 **Good:** $95

WINCHESTER MODEL 275

Slide action; similar to Model 270, but chambered for 22 WMR; 11-shot tube magazine; 20-1/2-

inch barrel; 39-inch overall length; weighs 5 lbs.; ramped square post front sight, adjustable square notch rear; aluminum alloy receiver grooved for tip-off scope mounts; walnut-finished hardwood pistol-grip stock; crossbolt safety. Introduced 1964; discontinued 1971.

Exc: $290 **VGood:** $215 **Good:** $145

WINCHESTER MODEL 275 DELUXE

Same specs as Model 275 except Monte Carlo select American walnut stock, fluted comb, cheekpiece; basketweave checkering; white buttspacer. Introduced 1965; discontinued 1971.

Exc: $300 **VGood:** $225 **Good:** $155

WINCHESTER MODEL 1890

Slide action; 22 Short, 22 Long, (not interchangeable), 22 WRF, (22 LR was added after 1919); 15-shot tube magazine (22 Short), 12-shot (22 Long), 11-shot (22 LR), 10-shot (22 WRF); 24-inch octagonal barrel; open rear, bead front sight; plain, straight stock, grooved slide handle; visible hammer; originally solid-frame design; after serial No. 15,552, all were takedowns; color case-hardened (pre-1901) or blued (post-1901) finish. Collector value. Because of production variations, expert appraisal is recommended. Introduced 1890; discontinued 1934.

Color case-hardened model

Exc: $4500 **VGood:** $3600 **Good:** $2100

Blued finish

Exc: $1000 **VGood:** $750 **Good:** $500

WINCHESTER MODEL 1906

Slide action; 22 Short, 22 Long, 22 LR; 15-shot tube magazine (22 Short), 12-shot (22 Long), 11-shot (22 LR); takedown; open rear sight, bead front; straight-grip uncheckered gumwood or walnut stock, grooved forend; visible hammer; shotgun buttplate. Originally offered as low-cost variant of the Model 1890; first rifles for 22 Short only; in 1908 a new version handled Short, Long and Long Rifle cartridges interchangeably; Introduced 1906; discontinued 1932. Collector value. Because of production variations, expert appraisal is recommended.

Exc: $700 **VGood:** $575 **Good:** $475

WINCHESTER MODEL 1906 EXPERT

Same specs as Model 1906 except pistol-grip stock, redesigned forend; blue/nickel or nickel finish. Introduced 1918; discontinued 1924.

Exc: $1695 **VGood:** $950 **Good:** $620

WINCHESTER CUSTOM SHOP MODEL 70 CUSTOM 100TH ANNIVERSARY .30-06

Semi-fancy walnut Featherweight stock with single steel crossbolt, one-piece engraved floorplate, high-lustre blued and engraved 22-inch barrel. Commemorates centennial of .30-06 cartridge. Only 100 manufactured.

NIB: $2600 **Exc:** $2000 **VGood:** $1450

WINCHESTER CUSTOM SHOP MODEL 70 CUSTOM SPECIAL "70 YEARS OF THE MODEL 70"

Calibers: .270, .30-06 Springfield, .300 WM. Barrel: 24-inch or 26-inch (.300 WM) blued sightless. Engraved floorplate and barrel. Stock: semi-fancy checkered walnut. Introduced 2006, only 70 manufactured per caliber.

NIB: 3000 **Exc:** N/A **VGood:** N/A

WINCHESTER CUSTOM SHOP MODEL 70 CUSTOM MAPLE

Calibers: .284, .270, .308, .30-06. Barrel: 24-inch blued. Weight: 7-3/4 lbs. Stocked in fiddleback maple with pre-'64 pattern checkering. Quantities "very limited." Introduced 2006.

NIB: 4300 **Exc:** N/A **VGood:** N/A

Winchester Model 275

Winchester Model 1890

Winchester Model 1906

Winslow Bolt-Action Sporter

A. Zoli AZ-1900 Classic

WINCHESTER CUSTOM SHOP MODEL 70 CUSTOM CONTINENTAL HUNTER

Calibers: .284, .270, .308, .30-06. Barrel: 22-inch blued or stainless Krieger. Stock: glossy claro walnut, round knob pistol grip, schnabel forend.

NIB: $5200 **Exc:** N/A **VGood:** N/A

WINCHESTER CUSTOM SHOP MODEL 70 CUSTOM STAINLESS LAMINATE

Calibers: .270 WSM, 7mm WSM, .300 WSM, .325 WSM. Barrel: 24-inch stainless sporter. Stock: black/gray or brown Featherweight laminated with Schnabel and Pachmayr pad.

NIB: $2300 **Exc:** N/A **VGood:** N/A

WINSLOW BOLT-ACTION SPORTER

Bolt action; all popular standard and magnum centerfire calibers; 3-, 4-shot magazine; 24-inch barrel, 26-inch (magnums); two stock styles: slim pistol grip with beavertail forearm or hooked pistol grip with wide flat forearm; Monte Carlo stock with cheekpiece in walnut, maple or myrtle; rosewood pistol grip, forend tip; custom rifle in eight grades. Introduced 1963; discontinued 1978.

Commander Grade

Exc: $495 **VGood:** $430 **Good:** $350

Regal Grade

Exc: $595 **VGood:** $530 **Good:** $450

Regent Grade

Exc: $750 **Vgood:** $650 **Good:** $550

Regimental Grade

Exc: $950 **VGood:** $825 **Good:** $635

Crown Grade

Exc: $1395 **VGood:** $1195 **Good:** $930

Royal Grade

Exc: $1595 **VGood:** $1295 **Good:** $1100

Imperial Grade

Exc: $3495 **VGood:** $2895 **Good:** $2000

Emperor Grade

Exc: $6100 **Vgood:** $4695 **Good:** $4000

ZOLI COMBINATO

Combination gun; over/under; boxlock; 222, 243/12. ga.; 24-inch barrels; blade front sight, flip-up rear; checkered European walnut stock; double triggers. From Antonio Zoli in Italy. Introduced 1980; discontinued 1993.

Perf: $1695 **Exc:** $1295 **VGood:** $935

ZOLI MODEL AZ-1900 CLASSIC

Bolt action; 243, 6.5x55, 270, 308, 30-06, 7mm Rem. Mag, 300 Win. Mag.; 21-inch barrel (24-inch on 7mm Rem. Mag., 300 Win. Mag.); 41-3/4-inch overall length with 21-inch barrel; weighs 7-1/4 lbs.; open sights were supplied with gun but not mounted; drilled, tapped for scope mounts; checkered Turkish circassian walnut stock; polished blue finish; oil-finished stock; engine-turned bolt. Made by Angelo Zoli; Imported from Italy by European American Armory. Introduced 1989; discontinued 1993.

Perf: $800 **Exc:** $670 **VGood:** $500

ZOLI MODEL AZ-1900M

Same specs as Model AZ-1900 except Bell & Carlson composite stock. Made by Angelo Zoli. Imported from Italy by European American Armory. Imported only in 1991.

Perf: $695 **Exc:** $495 **VGood:** $425

ZOLI SAVANA DOUBLE RIFLE

Double rifle; 7x65R, 30-06, 9.3x74R; 25-1/2-inch barrels; gold bead front sight, fixed V-notch rear in quarter-rib; premium grade French walnut stock with full pistol grip, cheekpiece; Anson & Deeley boxlock action with choice of single or double triggers; bushed firing pins; cocking indicators; silvered, engraved frame. Made by Angelo Zoli. Imported from Italy by European American Armory. Introduced 1989; discontinued 1991.

Perf: $6095 **Exc:** $5000 **VGood:** $3895

MODERN GUN VALUES

SHOTGUNS

Directory of Manufacturers

AMERICAN ARMS .481
APOLLO 482
ARIZAGA 482
ARMALITE 482
ARMSCOR 483
ARMSPORT 483
ARRIETA 486
ASTRA 487
AYA 487
BAIKAL 489
BAKER 490
BEEMAN .491
BENELLI .491
BERETTA 496
BERNARDELLI 508
BLASER .512
BOSS .512
BREDA .512
BRETTON .512
BRI .512
BRNO .512
BRNO .512
BROWNING .513
CAESAR GUERINI 525
CAPRINUS 525
CARLO CASARTELLI 526
CENTURION ORDNANCE 526
CENTURY 526
CHAPUIS 526
CHARLES DALY 526
CHIPMUNK 530
CHURCHILL, E.J., 530
CHURCHILL .531
CITADEL 533
CLAYCO 533
COGSWELL & HARRISON 533
COLT 533
CONNECTICUT SHOTGUN MANUFACTURING CO. 534
CONNECTICUT VALLEY CLASSIC 534
COSMI 534
CROSSFIRE 534
CRUCELEGUI HERMANOS 534
CZ 534
DAKOTA 534
DARNE 534
DAVIDSON 535
DESERT INDUSTRIES 535
DIAMOND 535
DUMOULIN 535
EAA/BAIKAL 535
E.A.A./SABATTI 536
EAA/SAIGA 536
E.M.F. 536
ERA 536
ERBI 537
ESCORT 537
EXEL 537
FABARM 538
FAUSTI 540
FERLACH 540
FERLIB 540
FIAS 540
F.I.E. 540
FOX .541
STEVENS/FOX .541
A.H. FOX .541
FRANCHI 543
FRANCOTTE 550
GALEF .551
GAMBA 552
GARBI 554
GARCIA 555
GOLDEN EAGLE 555
GOROSABEL 555
GREENER 555
GREIFELT 556
BILL HANUS 556
HARRINGTON & RICHARDSON 556
HATFIELD 560
HEYM 560
HHF .561
HI-STANDARD .561
HOENIG 564
HOLLAND & HOLLAND 564
HUNTER 565
IGA 565
INDUSTRIAS 566
ITHACA 566
IVER JOHNSON 573
KASSNAR 575
KAWAGUCHIYA 575
KDF 575
KEL-TEC 576
KEMEN 576
KESSLER 576
KIMBER 576
KOLAR 576
KRIEGHOFF 576
LANBER 579
MIGUEL LARRANAGA 579
LAURONA 579
LEBEAU-COURALLY 580
LEFEVER ARMS 580
D.M. LEFEVER 582
LJUTIC 582
LUGER 583
MAGTECH 584
MANUFRANCE 584
MARLIN 584
MAROCCHI 588
MAUSER 589
MAVERICK 590
MERCURY 590
MERKEL 590
MIIDA 593
MITCHELL 594
MONTE CARLO 595
MOSSBERG 595
NAVY ARMS 600
NEW ENGLAND FIREARMS .601
NEW HAVEN 602
NOBLE 603
NORINCO 605
OMEGA 605
PARKER 605
PARKER REPRODUCTIONS 606
PARKER-HALE 606
PARQUEMY 607
PEDERSEN 607
PERAZZI 608
PERUGINI-VISINI .614
PIOTTI .614
PRECISION SPORTS .615
PREMIER .616
PURDEY .616
REMINGTON .617
RHODE ISLAND ARMS 630
RICHLAND 630
RIGBY .631
RIZZINI .631
ROSSI 632
ROTTWEIL 632
ROYAL ARMS 633
SAE 633
SAN MARCO 633
SARASQUETA 633
SARRIUGARTE 634
SARSILMAZ 634
SAUER 634
SAUER/FRANCHI 635
SAVAGE 635
SCATTERGUN TECHNOLOGIES 638
W&C SCOTT (GUNMAKERS) LTD. 638
W&C SCOTT & SON 639
SECOLO 639
SENATOR 639
SIGARMS 639
SILE 640
SILMA 640
SKB 640
S&M 10-GAUGE 645
L.C. SMITH 645
SMITH & WESSON 648
SPORTING ARMS 648
STEVENS 648
STOEGER 650
STURM RUGER 652
TAR-HUNT 652
TECHNI-MEC 653
THOMPSON/CENTER 653
TIKKA 653
TOLEDO ARMAS 654
TRADEWINDS 654
TRADITIONS 654
TRIDENT 655
TRISTAR 655
UGARTECHEA 657
UNION ARMERA 657
UNION ARMERA 657
UNIVERSAL FIREARMS 657
URBIOLA 658
VALMET 658
VENTURA AVANTI 658
VENTURA 658
VERONA 659
WEATHERBY 659
WESSON & HARRINGTON 663
WESTERN ARMS 663
WESTLEY RICHARDS 663
WINCHESTER 663
WOODWARD 674
ZABALA 674
PIETRO ZANOLETTI 674
ZOLI 674

AMERICAN ARMS BRISTOL

Over/under; boxlock; 12-, 20-ga.; 3-inch chambers; 24-inch, 26-inch, 28-inch barrels; standard choke combos or choke tubes; front bead sight; glossy hand-checkered walnut stock; ejectors; single set trigger; engraved dummy sideplates; silver-finished frame; gold trigger. Made in Spain. Introduced 1987; discontinued 1988.

Fixed chokes

Perf: $625 **Exc:** $500 **VGood:** $425

Choke tubes

Perf: $685 **Exc:** $550 **VGood:** $470

AMERICAN ARMS BRITTANY

Side-by-side; boxlock ejectors; 12-, 20-ga; 3-inch chambers; 27-inch barrel (12-ga.), 25-inch barrel (20-ga.); weighs 6-1/2 lbs.; Imp. Cyl., Mod., Full choke tubes; straight English-style hand-checkered European walnut stock; semi-beavertail forend; engraving; single selective trigger; automatic safety; rubber recoil pad; case-color finish. Made in Spain. Introduced 1989; dropped 2000.

Perf: $725 **Exc:** $575 **VGood:** $485

AMERICAN ARMS DERBY

Side-by-side; sidelock; 12-, 20-, 28-ga., .410; 3-inch chambers, 2-3/4-inch (28-ga.); 26-inch, 28-inch barrel; weighs 6-1/2 to 6-3/4 lbs.; standard chokes; chromed bores; metal bead front sight; hand-checkered European walnut straight-grip stock, splinter forend; single selective trigger; hand rubbed oil finish; chromed receiver. Made in Spain. Introduced 1987; dropped 1994.

Perf: $1150 **Exc:** $975 **VGood:** $850

Add 10 percent to above prices for 28 gauge or .410 bore

AMERICAN ARMS EXCELSIOR

Over/under; sidelock; 12-, 20-ga.; 3-inch chambers; 26-inch, 28-inch barrels; standard choke combos or choke tubes; metal middle bead sight, glow worm front; hand-checkered European walnut stock, forend; auto selective ejectors; single non-selective trigger; manual safety; raised relief hand-engraved, gold-plated hunting scenes on sideplates. Made in Spain. Introduced 1987; discontinued 1987.

Fixed chokes

Perf: $1725 **Exc:** $1510 **VGood:** $1250

Choke tubes

Perf: $1795 **Exc:** $1580 **VGood:** $1320

AMERICAN ARMS FS200 COMPETITION

Over/under; boxlock; 12-ga.; 2-3/4-inch chambers; 26-inch, 32-inch barrels; Skeet/Skeet, Improved/Full; weighs 7-3/4 lbs.; hand-checkered, oil-finished European walnut stock; palm swell; ventilated recoil pad; selective auto ejectors; single selective trigger; black or satin chrome-finished frame. Made in Spain. Introduced 1987; discontinued 1987.

Perf: $685 **Exc:** $550 **VGood:** $470

AMERICAN ARMS FS300 COMPETITION

Same specs as FS200 Competition except 26-inch, 30-inch, 32-inch barrels; engraved false sideplates; satin chrome-finished receiver. Introduced 1986; discontinued 1986.

Perf: $785 **Exc:** $625 **VGood:** $530

AMERICAN ARMS FS400 COMPETITION

Same specs as FS200 Competition except sidelock; 26-inch, 30-inch, 32-inch barrels; single trigger; engraved chrome-finished receiver. Introduced 1986; discontinued 1986.

Perf: $1125 **Exc:** $900 **VGood:** $765

AMERICAN ARMS FS500 COMPETITION

Same specs as FS200 Competition except sidelock; 26-inch, 30-inch, 32-inch barrels; single trigger; engraved chrome-finished receiver. Introduced 1985; discontinued 1985.

Perf: $1125 **Exc:** $895 **VGood:** $775

American Arms Bristol

American Arms Brittany

American Arms Derby

American Arms Gentry

American Arms Grulla #2

American Arms Silver I

American Arms Silver II

AMERICAN ARMS GENTRY

Side-by-side; boxlock; 12-, 20-, 28-ga., .410; 3-inch chambers, 2-3/4-inch (28-ga.); 26-inch, 28-inch barrel; weighs about 6-1/4 to 6-3/4 lbs.; standard chokes; chromed bores; metal bead front sight; hand-checkered European walnut stock with semi-gloss finish; English-type scroll engraving; extractors; floating firing pin; silver finish on receiver. Introduced 1987; dropped 2000.

Perf: $675 **Exc:** $475 **VGood:** $375

Add $50 to above prices for 28 gauge or .410 bore

AMERICAN ARMS GRULLA #2

Side-by-side; sidelock; 12-, 20-, 28-ga., .410; 26-inch, 28-inch barrel; weighs about 6 lbs.; standard choke combos; select European walnut straight English stock; splinter forend; hand-rubbed oil finish; checkered grip, forend, butt; double triggers; detachable locks; automatic selective ejectors; cocking indicators; gas escape valves; English-style concave rib; color case-hardened receiver; scroll engraving. Made in Spain. Introduced 1989.

Perf: $2575 **Exc:** $2050 **VGood:** $1750

AMERICAN ARMS LINCE

Over/under; boxlock ejector; 12-, 20-ga., .410; 3-inch chambers; weighs 6-3/4 lbs.; metal bead front sight; standard choke combinations; checkered European walnut stock; single selective trigger; manual safety; rubber recoil pad; chrome-lined barrels; scroll engraving; blue or silver finish. Introduced 1986; discontinued 1986.

Perf: $510 **Exc:** $400 **VGood:** $380

.410

Perf: $555 **Exc:** $450 **VGood:** $420

Add $75 to above prices for choke tubes

AMERICAN ARMS ROYAL

Over/under; sidelock; 12-, 20-ga.; 3-inch chambers; 26-inch, 28-inch barrels; weighs 7-1/4 lbs.; standard choke combos or choke tubes; metal middle bead sight, glow worm front; hand-checkered European walnut stock, forend; auto selective ejectors; single non-selective trigger; manual safety; silvered sideplates; English-style hand-engraved scrollwork. Made in Spain. Introduced 1987; discontinued 1987.

Fixed chokes

Perf: $1595 **Exc:** $1310 **VGood:** $1080

Choke tubes

Perf: $1660 **Exc:** $1385 **VGood:** $1140

AMERICAN ARMS SHOTGUN

Side-by-side; boxlock ejector; 10-ga.; 3-1/2-inch chambers; double triggers; English-style hand-engraved scrollwork; chrome-finished receiver. Introduced 1986; discontinued 1986.

Perf: $450 **Exc:** $335 **VGood:** $295

AMERICAN ARMS SILVER I

Over/under; boxlock; 12-, 20-, 28-ga., .410; 2-3/4-inch chamber (28-ga.), 3-inch chamber (others); 26-inch, 28-inch barrels; standard choke combinations; weighs 6-3/4 lbs.; checkered European walnut stock with cast-off; single selective trigger; extractors; manual safety; rubber recoil pad; chrome-lined barrels; scroll engraving; metal bead front sight; silver finish. Made in Europe. Introduced 1987; dropped 2000.

Perf: $535 **Exc:** $430 **VGood:** $350

Add $40 to above prices for 28 gauge or .410 bore

AMERICAN ARMS SILVER II

Same specs as Silver I except 26-inch, 28-inch barrels in 12-ga., 26-inch (others); choke tubes. Also available in two-barrel set in 28/.410. Introduced 1987; still in production.

Perf: $660 **Exc:** $560 **VGood:** $475

Add $50 to above prices for 28 gauge or .410 bore (fixed chokes only)

American Arms Silver Sporting

American Arms Silver WS/OU 12

American Arms WS/SS 10

American Arms York

Apollo TR 30 Field

Arizaga Model 31

Armalite AR-17 Golden Gun

AMERICAN ARMS SILVER II UPLAND LIGHT

Same specs as Silver II except 12-, 20-ga.; 26-inch barrels; Franchoke tubes; weighs 6-1/4 lbs. (12-ga.), 5-3/4 lbs. (20-ga.); ejectors; ventilated rib; engraved frame with antique silver finish. Made in Spain. Introduced 1994; dropped 1998.

Perf: $800 **Exc:** $625 **VGood:** $550

AMERICAN ARMS SILVER SPORTING

Over/under; boxlock; 12-, 20-ga.; 2-3/4-inch (12-ga.), 3-inch (20-ga.) chambers; 28-inch (20-ga.), 30-inch barrels; weighs 7-3/8 lbs.; wide vent rib; Franchoke choke tubes; figured walnut stock with cut checkering; elongated forcing cones; ported barrels; pistol-grip stock with palm swell; radiused recoil pad; tapered target rib; target bead sights; mechanical single selective trigger; nickel finish. Introduced 1990; dropped 2000.

Perf: $835 **Exc:** $680 **VGood:** $550

AMERICAN ARMS SILVER SPORTING SKEET

Same specs as Silver Sporting except 26-inch ported barrels with elongated forcing cones; weighs 7-3/8 lbs.; stock dimensions of 14-3/8-inch by 1-3/8-inch by 2-3/8-inch; target-type ventilated rib with two bead sights; Skeet, Skeet, Imp. Cyl., Mod. choke tubes. Introduced 1992; no longer in production.

Perf: $790 **Exc:** $685 **VGood:** $575

AMERICAN ARMS SILVER SPORTING TRAP

Same specs as Silver Sporting except 30-inch ported barrels with elongated forcing cones; weighs 7-3/4 lbs.; stock dimensions of 14 3/8-inchx 1-1/2-inch by 1-5/8-inch; Mod., Imp. Mod., Full, Full choke tubes; target-type ventilated rib with two sight beads. Introduced 1992; dropped 1993.

Perf: $790 **Exc:** $685 **VGood:** $575

AMERICAN ARMS SILVER WS/OU 12

Over/under; boxlock ejector; 12-ga.; 3-1/2-inch chambers; 28-inch barrels; 46-inch overall length; weighs 7 lbs., 2 oz.; cut-checkered European walnut stock; black vented recoil pad; single selective trigger; chromed bores; matte metal finish. Made in Italy. Introduced 1988; dropped 2000.

Perf: $675 **Exc:** $365 **VGood:** $300

AMERICAN ARMS SILVER WT/OU 10

Over/under; boxlock; 10-ga.; 3-1/2-inch chambers; 26-inch barrels; Full/Full choke tubes; weighs 9-3/8 lbs.; extractors; chromed bores; non-reflective wood stock; dull metal finish; recoil pad; single trigger; ventilated rib; top tang safety. Introduced 1988; discontinued 2000.

Perf: $775 **Exc:** $750 **VGood:** $650

AMERICAN ARMS TS/OU 12

Over/under; boxlock ejector; 12-ga.; 3-1/2-inch chambers; 24-inch barrels; 46-inch overall length; weighs 6 lbs., 14 oz.; cut-checkered European walnut stock; black vented recoil pad; single selective trigger; chromed bores; matte metal finish. Made in Italy. Introduced 1988; no longer in production.

Perf: $685 **Exc:** $545 **VGood:** $475

AMERICAN ARMS TS/SS 12 DOUBLE

Side-by-side; boxlock; 12-ga.; 3-1/2-inch chambers; 26-inch barrels; choke tubes; extractors; single selective trigger; camouflage sling, sling swivels; recoil pad; chromed bores; raised matted rib; wood and metal matte finish. Made in Spain. Introduced 1988; dropped 2000.

Perf: $665 **Exc:** $550 **VGood:** $450

AMERICAN ARMS TS/SS 10 DOUBLE

Same specs as TS/SS 12 except 10-ga.; weighs about 11 lbs.; double triggers; AAI choke tubes Full/Full. Made in Spain. Introduced 1988; DISC. 2000.

Perf: $665 **Exc:** $550 **VGood:** $450

AMERICAN ARMS WS/SS 10

Side-by-side; boxlock; 10-ga.; 3-1/2-inch chambers; 32-inch barrels choked Full & Full; weighs 11-1/4 lbs.; flat rib; hand-checkered European walnut stock with beavertail forend; full pistol grip; dull finish; rubber recoil pad; double triggers; extractors; camouflaged sling; sling swivels. All metal with Parkerized finish. Introduced 1987; no longer produced.

Perf: $775 **Exc:** $650 **VGood:** $550

AMERICAN ARMS YORK

Side-by-side; boxlock; 12-, 20-, 28-ga., .410; 3-inch chambers; 25-inch, 28-inch barrels; standard choke combos; weighs 7-1/4 lbs.; gold bead front sight; gloss-finished, hand-checkered European walnut stock; beavertail forend; pistol grip; double triggers; extractors; manual safety; independent floating firing pins. Made in Spain. Introduced 1987; discontinued 1988.

Perf: $625 **Exc:** $475 **VGood:** $375

Optional single selective trigger

Perf: $650 **Exc:** $500 **VGood:** $400

Add $50 to above prices for 28 gauge or .410 bore

APOLLO TR AND TT SHOTGUNS

Gauge: 12, 20 and .410, 3" chambers; 28 ga. 2-3/4" chambers. Barrels: 26", 28", 20" or 32". Weight: 6 to 7-1/4 lbs. Stock: Oil-finished European walnut. Features include bioxlock action, chromed bores, automatic ejectors, single selective trigger, choke tubes (12and 20 ga. only). Introduced 2000 by SIGarms.

TR30 Field (color case-hardened sideplates).

Perf: $1800 **Exc:** $1550 **VGood:** $1100

TR40 Gold (with gold inlay over engraving)

Perf: $2200 **Exc:** $1750 **VGood:** $1300

TT25 Competition (wide vent rib with mid-bead)

Perf: $1750 **Exc:** $1400 **VGood:** $1100

ARIZAGA MODEL 31

Side-by-side; boxlock; 12-, 16-. 20-, 28-ga., .410; 26-inch, 28-inch barrels; standard choke combos; 45-inch overall length; weighs 6-5/8 lbs; European walnut; English-style straight or pistol-grip stock; double triggers; engraved receiver; blued finish. Made in Spain. Introduced 1986; still in production.

Perf: $475 **Exc:** $395 **VGood:** $340

ARMALITE AR-17 GOLDEN GUN

Semi-auto; 12-ga.; 2-shot; 28-inch barrel; recoil operated; interchangeable choke tubes for Improved, Modified, Full chokes; polycarbonate stock, forearm;

barrel, receiver housing of aluminum alloy; recoil pad; gold-anodized finish; also with black anodized finish. Introduced 1964; discontinued 1965. Only 2000 made.

Exc: $750 **VGood:** $575 **Good:** $475

ARMSCOR MODEL 30D

Slide-action; 12-ga.; 5-shot magazine; 26-inch Modified, 30-inch Full barrel; 47-inch overall length; weighs 7-1/4 lbs.; metal bead front sight; Philippine plain mahogany stock; checkered double slidebars; blued finish. Made in the Philippines. Introduced 1990; discontinued 1991.

Perf: $195 **Exc:** $160 **VGood:** $135

ARMSCOR MODEL 30D/IC

Same specs as Model 30D except interchangeable choke tubes; checkered stock. No longer imported.

Perf: $220 **Exc:** $185 **VGood:** $160

ARMSCOR MODEL 30DG

Same specs as Model 30D except 20-inch plain barrel; rifle sights; 6-, 8-shot; plain pistol grip and grooved forend. Introduced 1987; discontinued 1991; reintroduced 2001.

Perf: $185 **Exc:** $150 **VGood:** $130

ARMSCOR MODEL 30FS

Same specs as Model 30D except black folding stock, pistol grip. Introduced 1990; discontinued 1991.

Perf: $240 **Exc:** $215 **VGood:** $190

ARMSCOR MODEL 30K

Same specs as Model 30D except 7-shot magazine; 21-inch barrel; olive green butt, forend. Introduced 1990; discontinued 1991.

Perf: $215 **Exc:** $190 **VGood:** $165

ARMSCOR MODEL 30P

Same specs as Model 30D except 11-1/2-inch barrel; 3-, 5-shot; bolo-type short stock; 22-1/2-inch overall length; weighs 5-1/2 lbs. For law enforcement. No longer imported.

Perf: $250 **Exc:** $225 **VGood:** $200

ARMSCOR MODEL 30R

Same specs as Model 30D except 6-, 8-shot; 20-inch Cylinder-bore barrel; 39-inch overall length; weighs 6-3/4 lbs.; bead front sight; smooth pistol-grip stock and grooved forend. No longer imported.

Perf: $175 **Exc:** $150 **VGood:** $125

ARMSCOR MODEL 30RP

Same specs as Model 30D except 18-inch barrel; 27-inch overall length; weighs 6-1/8 lbs.; black wood butt, forend. For law enforcement. Introduced 1987; discontinued 1991; reintroduced 2001.

Perf: $210 **Exc:** $175 **VGood:** $145

ARMSCOR M-30F FIELD PUMP SHOTGUN

Gauge: 12, 3-inch chamber. Barrel: 28-inch fixed Mod., or with Mod. and Full choke tubes; weighs: 7.6 lbs.; walnut-finished hardwood; double action slide bars; blued steel receiver; damascened bolt. Introduced 1996. Imported from the Philippines by K.B.I., Inc.

Perf: $175 **Exc:** $170 **VGood:** $160

ARMSPORT MODEL 1032 GOOSE GUN

Side-by-side; 10-ga.; 3-1/2-inch chambers: 32-inch barrels; weighs 11 lbs.; solid matted rib; engraved; checkered pistol-grip European walnut stock, forend; double triggers; vent rubber recoil pad with white spacer. Made in Spain. Introduced 1979; no longer imported.

Perf: $365 **Exc:** $310 **VGood:** $275

ARMSPORT MODEL 1040

Side-by-side; 12-ga.; 26-inch barrel; Imp./Mod.; oil-finished walnut stock and forend; hand-engraved receiver. No longer imported.

Perf: $375 **Exc:** $335 **VGood:** $295

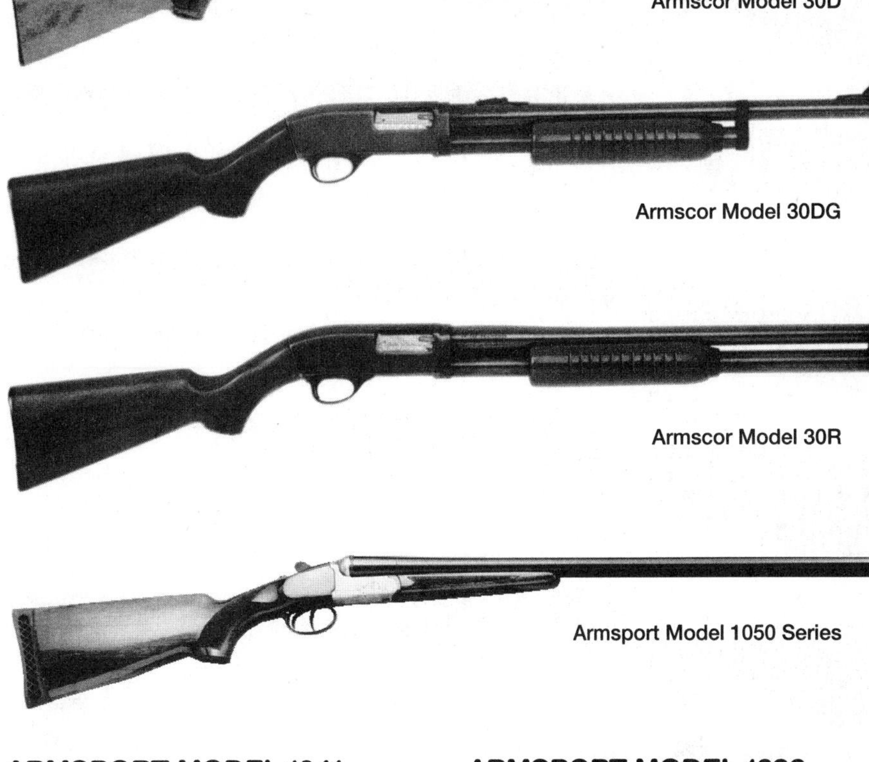

Armscor Model 30D

Armscor Model 30DG

Armscor Model 30R

Armsport Model 1050 Series

ARMSPORT MODEL 1041

Side-by-side; 12-ga.; 28-inch barrel; Mod./Full; oil-finished walnut stock and forend; hand-engraved receiver. No longer imported.

Perf: $375 **Exc:** $335 **VGood:** $295

ARMSPORT MODEL 1042

Side-by-side; 20-ga.; 26-inch barrel; Imp./Mod.; oil-finished walnut stock and forend; hand-engraved receiver. No longer imported.

Perf: $380 **Exc:** $345 **VGood:** $295

ARMSPORT MODEL 1043

Side-by-side; 20-ga.; 28-inch barrel; Mod./Full; oil-finished walnut stock and forend; hand-engraved receiver. No longer imported.

Perf: $375 **Exc:** $335 **VGood:** $295

ARMSPORT MODEL 1050 SERIES

Side-by-side; boxlock; 12-, 20-, 28-ga., .410; 3-inch chambers; 26-inch, 28-inch barrels; weighs 6-3/4 lbs.; chrome-lined barrels; European walnut stock; double triggers; extractors; silvered, engraved receiver. Made in Italy. Introduced 1986; no longer imported.

Model 1050 (12-ga.)

Perf: $595 **Exc:** $475 **VGood:** $395

Model 1053 (20-ga.)

Perf: $610 **Exc:** $485 **VGood:** $400

Model 1054 (.410)

Perf: $635 **Exc:** $520 **VGood:** $425

Model 1055 (28-ga.)

Perf: $635 **Exc:** $520 **VGood:** $425

ARMSPORT MODEL 1212 WESTERN

Side-by-side; 12-ga.; 3-inch chambers; 20-inch barrels; weighs 6-1/2 lbs.; checkered pistol-grip stock of European walnut, beavertail forend; metal front bead on matted solid rib; exposed hammers. Made in Spain. Introduced 1979; no longer imported.

Perf: $350 **Exc:** $275 **VGood:** $240

ARMSPORT MODEL 1626

Over/under; boxlock; 12-ga.; 3-inch chambers; 26-inch barrels; Improved/Modified; non-ejector; single selective trigger; vent rib; hand-checkered European walnut stock, forend; recoil pad; engraved. Made in Italy. No longer imported.

Perf: $565 **Exc:** $365 **VGood:** $300

ARMSPORT MODEL 1628

Over/under; boxlock; 12-ga.; 3-inch chambers; 28-inch barrels; Modified/Full; non-ejector; single selective trigger; vent rib; hand-checkered European walnut stock, forend; recoil pad; engraved. Made in Italy. No longer imported.

Perf: $565 **Exc:** $365 **VGood:** $300

ARMSPORT MODEL 1726

Over/under; boxlock; 20-ga.; 3-inch chambers; 26-inch barrels; Improved/Modified; non-ejector; single selective trigger; vent rib; hand-checkered European walnut stock, forend; recoil pad; engraved. Made in Italy. No longer imported.

Perf: $565 **Exc:** $365 **VGood:** $300

ARMSPORT MODEL 1728

Over/under; boxlock; 20-ga.; 3-inch chambers; 28-inch barrels; Modified/Full; non-ejector; single selective trigger; vent rib; hand-checkered European walnut stock, forend; recoil pad; engraved. Made in Italy. No longer imported.

Perf: $575 **Exc:** $375 **VGood:** $300

ARMSPORT MODEL 1810

Over/under; .410-bore; 3-inch chambers; 26-inch barrels; Full/Full chokes; blued receiver and barrels. No longer imported.

Perf: $575 **Exc:** $375 **VGood:** $300

ARMSPORT MODEL 2526

Over/under; 12-ga.; 26-inch barrels; Imp./Mod.; vent rib; hand-checkered European walnut pistol-grip stock; single selective trigger; auto ejectors; engraved receiver. Manufactured in Europe. Introduced 1979; no longer imported.

Perf: $585 **Exc:** $375 **VGood:** $300

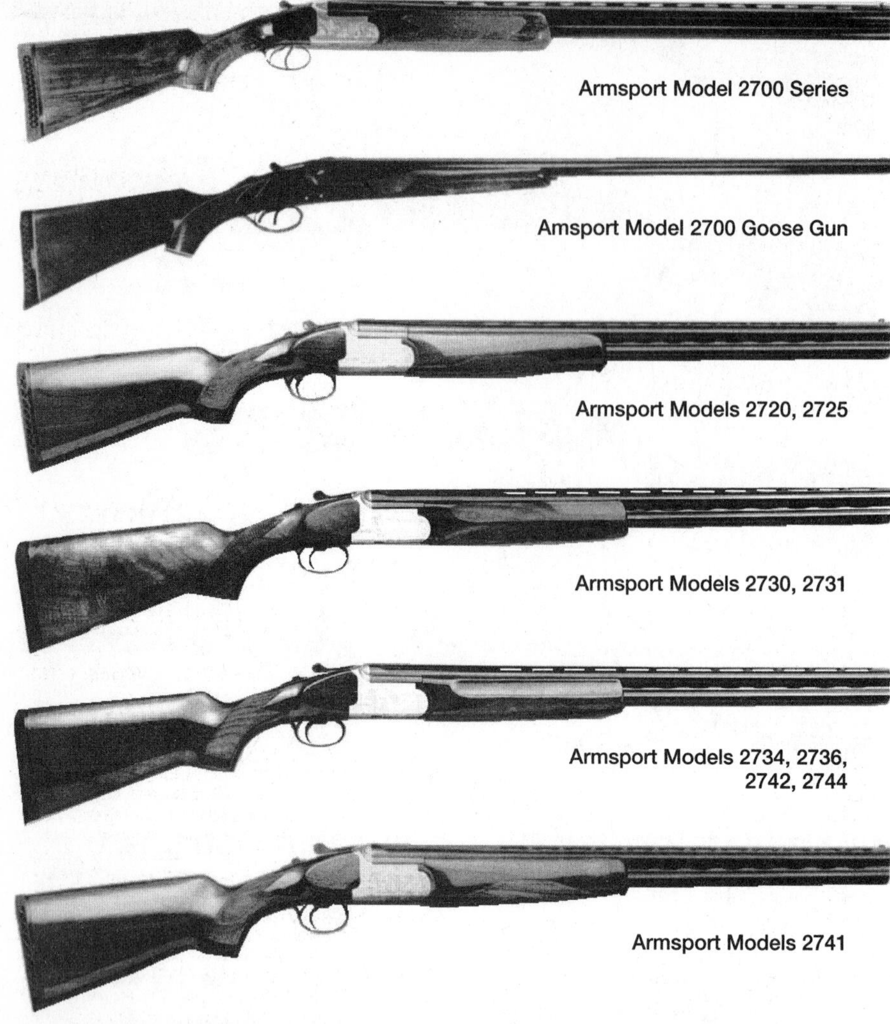

Armsport Model 2700 Series

Amsport Model 2700 Goose Gun

Armsport Models 2720, 2725

Armsport Models 2730, 2731

Armsport Models 2734, 2736, 2742, 2744

Armsport Models 2741

ARMSPORT MODEL 2528

Over/under; 12-ga.; 28-inch barrels; Modified/Full; vent rib; hand-checkered European walnut pistol-grip stock; single selective trigger; auto ejectors; engraved receiver. Manufactured in Europe. Introduced 1979; no longer imported.

Perf: $585 **Exc:** $375 **VGood:** $300

ARMSPORT MODEL 2626

Over/under; boxlock; 20-ga.; 26-inch barrels; Imp./Mod.; automatic ejectors; vent rib; single selective trigger; walnut stock and forend; recoil pad; engraved. No longer imported.

Perf: $595 **Exc:** $395 **VGood:** $330

ARMSPORT MODEL 2628

Over/under; boxlock; 20-ga.; 28-inch barrels; Mod./Full; automatic ejectors; vent rib; single selective trigger; walnut stock and forend; recoil pad; engraved. No longer imported.

Perf: $585 **Exc:** $375 **VGood:** $330

ARMSPORT MODEL 2697

Over/under; boxlock; 10-ga. Magnum; 3-1/2-inch chambers; 28-inch chrome-lined barrels; choke tubes; engraved silver finished receiver; wide vent rib; hand-checkered walnut forend and stock. No longer imported.

Perf: $925 **Exc:** $700 **VGood:** $600

ARMSPORT MODEL 2698

Over/under; boxlock; 10-ga. Magnum; 3-1/2-inch chambers; 32-inch chrome-lined barrels; choke tubes; engraved silver finished receiver; wide vent rib; hand-checkered walnut forend and stock. No longer imported.

Perf: $925 **Exc:** $700 **VGood:** $600

ARMSPORT MODEL 2699

Over/under; boxlock; 10-ga. Magnum; 3-1/2-inch chambers; 28-inch chrome-lined barrels; Full/Improved-Modified chokes; engraved silver finished receiver; wide vent rib; hand-checkered walnut forend and stock. No longer imported.

Perf: $995 **Exc:** $605 **VGood:** $565

ARMSPORT MODEL 2700 GOOSE GUN

Over/under; 10-ga; 3-1/2-inch chambers; 28-inch Full/Imp. Mod., 32-inch Full/Full barrels; weighs 9-1/2 lbs.; Boss-type action; European walnut stock; double triggers; extractors. Made in Italy. Introduced 1986; still in production.

Perf: $875 **Exc:** $605 **VGood:** $565

ARMSPORT MODEL 2700 SERIES

Over/under; boxlock; 10-ga. Mag.; 3-1/2-inch chambers; 32-inch chrome-lined barrels; Full/Full chokes; engraved silver finished receiver; extractors; wide vent rib; hand-checkered walnut forend and stock. No longer imported.

Perf: $875 **Exc:** $615 **VGood:** $565

ARMSPORT MODEL 2701, 2702

Same specs as 2700 except 12-ga.; 3-inch Mag. chambers; 28-inch barrels; Modified/Full. No longer imported by Armsport.

Perf: $450 **Exc:** $355 **VGood:** $290

ARMSPORT MODEL 2703, 2704

Same specs as 2700 except 20-ga.; 3-inch Mag. chambers; Improved/Modified chokes. No longer imported by Armsport.

Perf: $475 **Exc:** $355 **VGood:** $290

ARMSPORT MODEL 2705

Same specs as 2700 except .410; 26-inch barrels; Modified/Full chokes. Made in Italy. No longer imported.

Perf: $625 **Exc:** $425 **VGood:** $355

ARMSPORT MODEL 2706 COMMANDER

Same specs as 2700 except 12-ga.; 20-inch barrels; double triggers; extractors. No longer imported by Armsport.

Perf: $300 **Exc:** $250 **VGood:** $225

ARMSPORT MODEL 2707

Same specs as 2700 except 28-ga.; Improved/Modified; double trigger. No longer imported by Armsport.

Perf: $625 **Exc:** $425 **VGood:** $355

ARMSPORT MODEL 2708 SLUG GUN

Same specs as 2700 except 12-ga.; 20-inch or 23-inch barrels; double or single trigger. No longer imported by Armsport.

Perf: $575 **Exc:** $450 **VGood:** $390

ARMSPORT MODEL 27 16, 2717

Same specs as 2700 except 12-ga.; 3-inch Mag. chambers; 28-inch barrels; Modified/Full chokes; single selective trigger; extractors. No longer imported.

Perf: $600 **Exc:** $475 **VGood:** $390

ARMSPORT MODEL 2718, 2719

Same specs as 2700 except 20-ga.; 3-inch Mag. chambers; 26-inch barrels; Improved/Modified chokes; single selective trigger; extractors. No longer imported.

Perf: $600 **Exc:** $475 **VGood:** $390

ARMSPORT MODEL 2720

Same specs as 2700 except .410; 26-inch barrels; Modified/Full chokes; single selective trigger; extractors. No longer imported.

Perf: $640 **Exc:** $515 **VGood:** $430

ARMSPORT MODEL 2725

Same specs as 2700 except 28-ga.; 26-inch barrels; Improved/Modified choke tubes. No longer imported.

Perf: $640 **Exc:** $515 **VGood:** $430

ARMSPORT MODEL 2730

Same specs as 2700 except 12-ga.; 28-inch barrels; Skeet set with choke tubes; single trigger; ejectors. No longer imported.

Perf: $740 **Exc:** $525 **VGood:** $475

ARMSPORT MODEL 2731

Same specs as 2700 except 20-ga.; 26-inch barrels; Skeet set with choke tubes; single trigger; ejectors. No longer imported.

Perf: $740 **Exc:** $525 **VGood:** $475

ARMSPORT MODEL 2733

Same specs as 2700 except 12-ga.; 28-inch barrels; Modified/Full; Boss-type action; extractors; single selective trigger. No longer imported.

Perf: $685 **Exc:** $460 **VGood:** $370

ARMSPORT MODEL 2734

Same specs as 2700 except 12-ga.; 28-inch barrels; choke tubes; extractors; single selective trigger. No longer imported.

Perf: $720 **Exc:** $505 **VGood:** $455

ARMSPORT MODEL 2735

Same specs as 2700 except 20-ga.; 26-inch barrels; Improved/Modified; Boss-type action; extractors; single selective trigger. No longer imported.

Perf: $685 **Exc:** $460 **VGood:** $370

ARMSPORT MODEL 2736

Same specs as 2700 except 20-ga.; 26-inch barrels; choke tubes; Boss-type action; extractors; single selective trigger. No longer imported.

Perf: $600 **Exc:** $475 **VGood:** $425

ARMSPORT MODEL 2741

Same specs as 2700 except 12-ga.; 28-inch barrels; Modified/Full; Boss-type action; ejectors; single selective trigger. No longer imported.

Perf: $640 **Exc:** $440 **VGood:** $375

ARMSPORT MODEL 2742 SPORTING CLAYS

Same specs as 2700 except 12-ga.; 28-inch barrels; choke tubes; single selective trigger. No longer imported.

Perf: $600 **Exc:** $450 **VGood:** $390

ARMSPORT MODEL 2744 SPORTING CLAYS

Same specs as 2700 except 20-ga.; 26-inch barrels; choke tubes; ejectors; single selective trigger. No longer imported.

Perf: $625 **Exc:** $450 **VGood:** $390

ARMSPORT MODEL 2746

Same specs as 2700 except 12-ga. Mag.; 3-1/2-inch chambers; 28-inch barrels; choke tubes. No longer imported.

Perf: $695 **Exc:** $425 **VGood:** $390

ARMSPORT MODEL 2747

Same specs as 2700 except 12-ga. Mag.; 3-1/2-inch chambers; 32-inch barrels; choke tubes. No longer imported.

Perf: $695 **Exc:** $425 **VGood:** $390

ARMSPORT MODEL 2750 SPORTING CLAYS

Same specs as 2700 except 12-ga.; 28-inch barrels; choke tubes; single selective trigger; ejectors; equipped with decorative sideplates. No longer imported.

Perf: $725 **Exc:** $575 **VGood:** $525

ARMSPORT MODEL 2751 SPORTING CLAY

Same specs as 2700 except 20-ga.; 26-inch barrels; choke tubes; single selective trigger; ejectors; equipped with decorative sideplates. No longer imported.

Perf: $925 **Exc:** $575 **VGood:** $525

ARMSPORT MODEL 2751

Semi-automatic; 12-ga.; 3-inch chamber; 28-inch Modified, 30-inch Full (2751A) choke barrels; weighs 7 lbs.; choke tube version available; European walnut stock; rubber recoil pad; blued or silvered receiver with engraving. Made in Italy. Introduced 1986; no longer imported.

Perf: $400 **Exc:** $320 **VGood:** $275

With choke tubes

Perf: $420 **Exc:** $340 **VGood:** $285

Silvered receiver

Perf: $420 **Exc:** $340 **VGood:** $285

ARMSPORT MODEL 2755

Pump-action; 12-ga.; 3-inch chamber; 28-inch Modified, 30-inch Full (2755A) barrel; weighs 7 lbs.; choke tubes available; vent rib; European walnut stock; rubber recoil pad; blued finish. Made in Italy. Introduced 1986; no longer imported.

Perf: $320 **Exc:** $225 **VGood:** $165

With choke tubes

Perf: $335 **Exc:** $245 **VGood:** $195

ARMSPORT MODEL 2900 TRI-BARREL

Over/under; 12-ga.; 3-inch chambers; 28-inch barrels; weighs 7-3/4 lbs.; choked Improved/Modified/Full; standard choke combos; European walnut stock; double triggers; top-tang barrel selector; silvered, engraved frame. Made in Italy. Introduced 1986; no longer imported.

Perf: $2675 **Exc:** $2150 **VGood:** $1700

ARMSPORT MODEL 2901 TRI-BARREL

Same specs as 2900 Tri-Barrel except 12-ga.; 3-inch Mag. chambers; choked Modified/Full/Full. No longer imported.

Perf: $2675 **Exc:** $2150 **VGood:** $1700

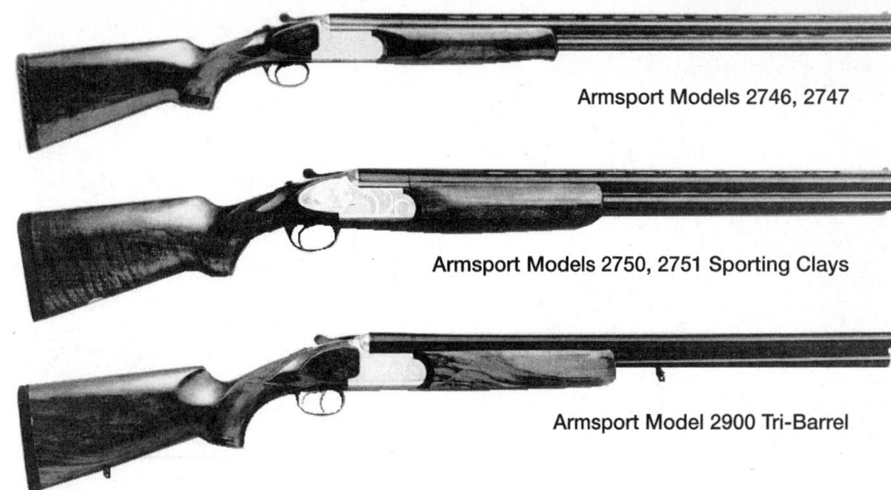

Armsport Models 2746, 2747

Armsport Models 2750, 2751 Sporting Clays

Armsport Model 2900 Tri-Barrel

ARMSPORT MODEL 3030 DELUXE GRADE TRAP

Over/under; 12-ga.; 32-inch barrels; wide ventilated rib; ventilated lateral rib; single selective trigger; automatic ejectors; fluorescent bead front sight; checkered walnut stock; beavertail forend; Greener-type cross-bolt; engraved sideplates. No longer imported.

Perf: $625 **Exc:** $475 **VGood:** $375

ARMSPORT MODEL 3032 DELUXE GRADE TRAP

Over/under; 12-ga.; 30-inch barrels; wide ventilated rib; ventilated lateral rib; single selective trigger; automatic ejectors; fluorescent bead front sight; checkered walnut stock; beavertail forend; Greener-type cross-bolt; engraved sideplates. No longer imported.

Perf: $645 **Exc:** $495 **VGood:** $385

ARMSPORT MODEL 3101 DELUXE MONO TRAP

Single or over/under; 12-ga.; 30-inch (O/U), 32-inch (single) barrels; single selective trigger; automatic ejectors; highly grained walnut stock, forend with high-lustre finish; choice of mono trap or as a combo set should be 30 percent higher with over/under barrels. No longer imported.

Perf: $650 **Exc:** $500 **VGood:** $400

ARMSPORT MODEL 3102 DELUXE MONO TRAP SET

Single or over/under; 12-ga.; 32-inch (O/U), 34-inch (single) barrels; single selective trigger; automatic ejectors; highly grained walnut stock, forend with high lustre finish; choice of mono trap or as a set; combo set should be 30 percent higher with over/under barrels. No longer imported.

Perf: $1100 **Exc:** $895 **VGood:** $700

ARMSPORT MODEL 3103 DELUXE MONO TRAP

Single shot; 12-ga.; 32-inch barrels; single selective trigger; automatic ejectors; highly grained walnut stock, forend with high lustre finish; choice of mono trap or as a set; combo set should be 30 percent higher with over/under barrels. No longer imported.

Perf: $700 **Exc:** $575 **VGood:** $400

ARMSPORT MODEL 3104 DELUXE MONO TRAP

Single shot; 12-ga.; 34-inch barrels; single selective trigger; automatic ejectors; highly grained walnut stock, forend with high lustre finish; choice of mono trap or as a set; combo set should be 30 percent higher with over/under barrels. No longer imported.

Perf: $700 **Exc:** $575 **VGood:** $400

ARMSPORT MODEL 4000 EMPEROR OVER/UNDER

Over/under; 12-, 16-, 20-ga.; any barrel length; any choke; handcrafted barrels, action, root walnut stock, forend; hand engraved receiver, sideplate; custom made to order; luggage-type case. No longer imported.

Perf: $1200 **Exc:** $975 **VGood:** $725

ARMSPORT MODEL 4010 EMPEROR SIDE-BY-SIDE

Side-by-side; sidelock; 12- 16-, 20-ga.; any barrel length; any choke; handcrafted barrels, action, root walnut stock, forend; engraved receiver, sideplate; luggage-type case; custom made. No longer imported.

Perf: $1750 **Exc:** $1425 **VGood:** $1200

ARMSPORT MODEL 4031

Side-by-side; sidelock; 12-, 20-ga. 26-inch, 28-inch barrels; Improved/Modified or Modified/Full chokes; English-style straight walnut stock; hand detachable locks; silver finish hand-engraved receiver; highly polished steel barrels. Made in Italy. No longer imported.

Perf: $3800 **Exc:** $2500 **VGood:** $1950

ARMSPORT MODEL 4032 MONO TRAP

Single shot; 12-ga.; 32-inch barrel; vent rib; single trigger; walnut stock with pistol grip; recoil pad; automatic ejector; premier grade; hand engraved. No longer imported.

Perf: $1750 **Exc:** $1300 **VGood:** $1100

ARMSPORT MODEL 4033 MONO TRAP

Single shot; 12-ga.; 34-inch barrel; vent rib; single trigger; walnut stock with pistol grip; recoil pad; automatic ejector; premier grade; hand engraved. No longer imported.

Perf: $1750 **Exc:** $1300 **VGood:** $1100

ARMSPORT MODEL 4034 MONO TRAP SET

Single shot; 12-ga.; 32-inch barrel; vent rib; single trigger; walnut stock with pistol grip; recoil pad; automatic ejector; premier grade; hand engraved. Additional set of 30-inch O/U barrels. No longer imported.

Perf: $2500 **Exc:** $1900 **VGood:** $1000

ARMSPORT MODEL 4034 O/U TRAP SET

Single shot; 12-ga.; 30-inch barrels; vent rib; single trigger; walnut stock with pistol grip; recoil pad; automatic ejector; premier grade; hand engraved. Additional set of 30-inch O/U barrels. No longer imported.

Perf: $2500 **Exc:** $1900 **VGood:** $1650

Arrieta Model 557

Arrieta Model 570

Arrieta Model 578

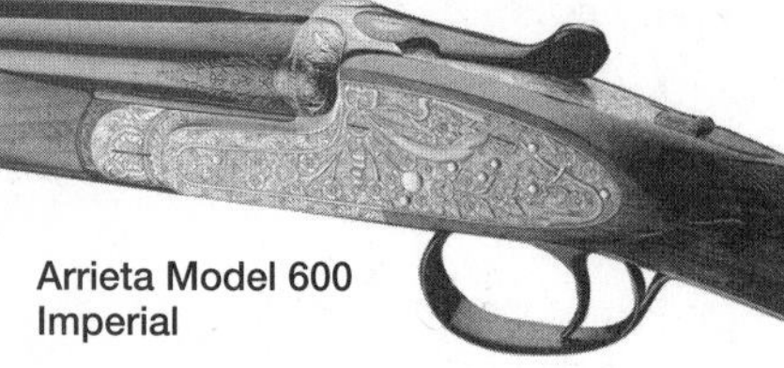
Arrieta Model 600 Imperial

Arrieta Model 600 Imperial Tiro

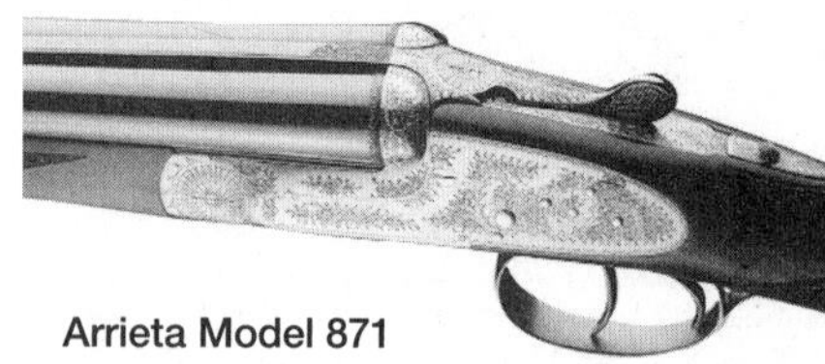
Arrieta Model 871

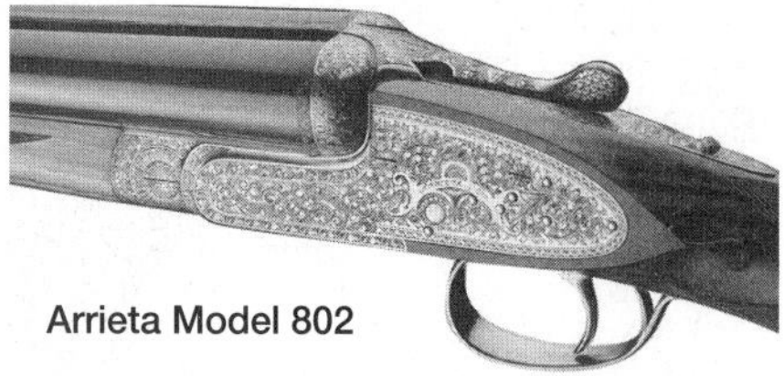
Arrieta Model 802

Arrieta Model 803

Arrieta Model 874

Arrieta Model 872

Arrieta Model 873

Arrieta Model 875

ARMSPORT MODEL 4035 MONO TRAP SET

Single shot; 12-ga.; 34-inch barrel; vent rib; single trigger; walnut stock with pistol grip; recoil pad; ejector; premier grade; hand engraved. Additional set of 32-inch O/U barrels. No longer imported.

Perf: $2500 **Exc:** $1900 **VGood:** $1650

ARMSPORT MODEL 4035 O/U TRAP SET

Single shot; 12-ga.; 32-inch barrels; vent rib; single trigger; walnut stock with pistol grip; recoil pad; automatic ejectors; premier grade; hand engraved. Additional set of 32-inch O/U barrels. No longer imported.

Perf: $2500 **Exc:** $1900 **VGood:** $1650

ARMSPORT MODEL 4040 PREMIER SLUG

Side-by-side; 12-ga.; 23-inch barrels; Cyl./Imp. Cyl.; rib with leaf rear sight, blade front; hand-checkered walnut stock with half pistol grip and beavertail forend; hand relief engraved receiver. No longer imported.

Perf: $1250 **Exc:** $800 **VGood:** $700

ARMSPORT MODEL 4041 PREMIER SLUG

Side-by-side; 12-ga.; 23-inch, 28-inch barrels; Cyl./Imp. Cyl. (23-inch), Mod./Full (28-inch); rib with leaf rear sight, blade front; hand-checkered walnut stock with half pistol grip and beavertail forend; hand relief-engraved receiver. No longer imported.

Perf: $1250 **Exc:** $800 **VGood:** $700

ARMSPORT MODEL 4046 MONO TRAP

Single shot; 12-ga.; 34-inch barrel; specially reinforced receiver carved from a solid block of gun steel; unique coil spring trigger assembly; handcrafted Italian leather fitted case. No longer imported.

Perf: $2750 **Exc:** $2150 **VGood:** $1800

ARMSPORT MODEL 4047 MONO TRAP

Single shot; 12-ga.; 32-inch barrel; specially reinforced receiver carved from a solid block of gun steel; unique coil spring trigger assembly; handcrafted Italian leather fitted case. No longer imported.

Perf: $2750 **Exc:** $2150 **VGood:** $1800

ARMSPORT MODEL 4048 MONO TRAP SET

Single shot; 12-ga.; 32-inch (over/under), 34-inch (mono) barrel; specially reinforced receiver carved from a solid block of gun steel; unique coil spring trigger assembly; comes with extra trigger assembly; handcrafted Italian leather fitted case. No longer imported.

Perf: $1100 **Exc:** $875 **VGood:** $700

ARMSPORT MODEL 4049 MONO TRAP SET

Single shot; 12-ga.; 30-inch (over/under), 32-inch (mono) barrel; specially reinforced receiver carved from a solid block of gun steel; unique coil spring trigger assembly; comes with extra trigger assembly; handcrafted Italian leather fitted case. No longer imported.

Perf: $1100 **Exc:** $875 **VGood:** $700

ARMSPORT SINGLE

Single-shot; 12-, 20-ga.; 3-inch chamber; 26-inch, 28-inch barrel; weighs 6-1/2 lbs.; oil-finished hardwood stock; chrome-lined barrel; cocking indicator opening lever behind trigger guard; manual safety. Made in Europe. Introduced 1987; no longer imported.

Perf: $85 **Exc:** $55 **VGood:** $45

Model 1125 (12-ga., Modified)

Perf: $85 **Exc:** $55 **VGood:** $45

Model 1126 (12-ga., Full)

Perf: $85 **Exc:** $55 **VGood:** $45

Model 1127 (20-ga., Modified)

Perf: $85 **Exc:** $55 **VGood:** $45

ARRIETA SIDELOCK DOUBLE SHOTGUNS

Side-by-side; sidelock; 12-, 16-, 20-, 28-ga., .410; barrel length and chokes to customer specs.; select European walnut stock with oil finish, straight English grip, checkered butt (standard), or pistol-grip; essentially a custom gun with myriad options; Holland & Holland-pattern hand-detachable sidelocks, selective automatic ejectors, double triggers (hinged front) standard. Some have self-opening action. Finish and engraving to customer specs. Imported from Spain by importers including Wingshooting Adventures, Orvis, Griffin & Howe, New England Arms Corp. and Quality Arms.

Model 557, detachable engraved sidelocks, auto ejectors

Perf: $3000 **Exc:** $2100 **VGood:** $1600

Model 570, non-detachable sidelocks, auto ejectors

Perf: $3475 **Exc:** $2450 **VGood:** $1825

Model 578, scrollwork engraved, auto ejectors

Perf: $4050 **Exc:** $2800 **VGood:** $1975

Model 600 Imperial, lightly engraved, self-opening

Perf: $5275 **Exc:** $4150 **VGood:** $3300

Model 601 Imperial Tiro, nickel-plated action, self-opening

Perf: $6600 **Exc:** $4250 **VGood:** $3500

Model 801, detachable sidelocks, fine engraving, self-opening

Perf: $8175 **Exc:** $7200 **VGood:** $6325

Model 802, non-detachable sidelocks, finely engraved

Perf: $8135 **Exc:** $7200 **VGood:** $6300

Model 803, detachable sidelocks, finely engraved, self-opening

Perf: $6175 **Exc:** $5300 **VGood:** $4175

Model 871, auto ejectors, scroll engraved, rounded frame action

Perf: $4400 **Exc:** $3425 **VGood:** $2750

Model 872, self-opening, rounded frame action, finely engraved

Perf: $11,000 **Exc:** $9500 **VGood:** $8200

Model 873, self-opening, automatic ejectors, engraved with game scene

Perf: $7525 **Exc:** $5500 **VGood:** $4325

Model 874, self-opening, gold engraved

Perf: $8225 **Exc:** $7200 **VGood:** $6200

Model 875, self-opening, custom-made only

Perf: $13,000 **Exc :** $10,650 **VGood:** $9450

Model 931, self-opening, all gauges, elaborate engraving, H&H selective ejectors

Perf: 23,500 **Exc:** $15,000 **VGood:** $10,000

ASTRA MODEL 650

Over/under; 12-ga; 28-inch, 30-inch barrels; standard chokes; vent rib; hand-checkered European walnut stock; double triggers; ejectors or extractors; scroll-engraved receiver. Was imported from Spain. Introduced 1980; discontinued 1987.

Perf: $450 **Exc:** $375 **VGood:** $300

Extractors

Perf: $410 **Exc:** $335 **VGood:** $260

Trap and Skeet models

Perf: $460 **Exc:** $375 **VGood:** $300

ASTRA MODEL 750

Over/under; 12-ga.; 28-inch, 30-inch barrels; vent rib; hand-checkered European walnut stock; single selective trigger; ejectors or extractors; scroll-engraved receiver. Introduced 1980; discontinued 1987.

Perf: $440 **Exc:** $365 **VGood:** $290

Extractors only

Perf: $410 **Exc:** $335 **VGood:** $275

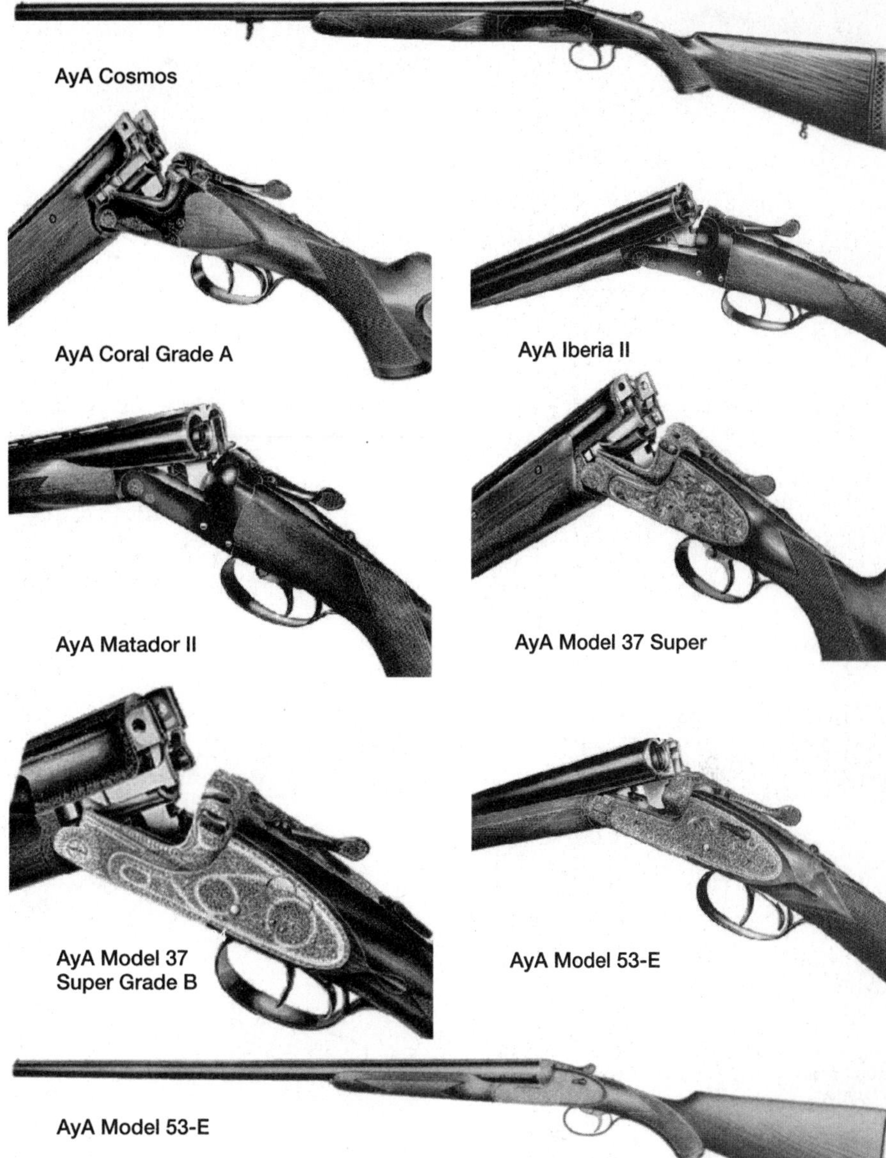

AyA Cosmos

AyA Coral Grade A

AyA Iberia II

AyA Matador II

AyA Model 37 Super

AyA Model 37 Super Grade B

AyA Model 53-E

AyA Model 53-E

AyA AUGUSTA

Over/under; sidelock; 12-ga.; vent rib; single or double trigger; high-grade scroll engraving; fancy walnut; Kersten cross bolts. A deluxe gun modeled after the Merkel.

Perf: $20,000 **Exc:** $15,000 **VGood:** $14,000

AyA BOLERO

Side-by-side; boxlock; extractors; 12-, 16-, 20-, 28-ga., .410; single non-selective trigger. Imported as Model 400 by Firearms International. Introduced 1955; discontinued 1963.

Perf: $350 **Exc:** $275 **VGood:** $225

AyA CORAL

Over/under; boxlock; 12-, 16-ga.; 26-inch, 28-inch, 30-inch barrels; 2-3/4-inch chambers; any choke desired; Kersten crossbolt; ejectors; pistol-grip stock; single or double trigger; two grades of engraving. No longer imported; discontinued 1985.

Perf: $1300 **Exc:** $1000 **VGood:** $800

AyA COSMOS

Single barrel; single shot; 12 Mag., 12-, 16-, 20-, 24-, 28-ga., .410; ejector; hammer; top lever; pistol-grip walnut stock; buttpad; sling swivels; interchangeable barrels. No longer imported.

Perf: $345 **Exc:** $295 **VGood:** $250

AyA IBERIA

Side-by-side; boxlock; 12-ga.; 2-3/4-inch chambers; 28-inch barrels; straight, half or full pistol-grip stock; hand checkered walnut; minimal engraving; extractors; double trigger. No longer imported; discontinued 1984.

Perf: $545 **Exc:** $395 **VGood:** $359

AyA IBERIA/E

Same specs as Iberia except ejectors. No longer imported.

Perf: $575 **Exc:** $425 **VGood:** $395

AyA IBERIA II

Same specs as Iberia except 12-, 16-ga.; no engraving; earlier version had straight receiver-to-wood joint; newer Iberia has a single scallop. No longer imported.

Perf: $520 **Exc:** $360 **VGood:** $310

AyA MATADOR

Side-by-side; boxlock; ejectors; 10-, 12-, 16-, 20-, 28-ga., .410; 2-3/4-inch, 3-inch (20-ga.), 3-1/2-inch (10-ga.) chambers; 26-inch, 28-inch, 30-inch barrels; any standard choke combo; European walnut stock; checkered pistol grip; beavertail forearm; single-selective trigger. Imported as Model 400E by Firearms International. Introduced 1955; discontinued 1963.

Exc: $350 **VGood:** $300 **Good:** $220

AyA MATADOR II

Same specs as Matador except 12-, 20-ga.; better wood. Manufactured 1964 to 1969.

Exc: $350 **VGood:** $315 **Good:** $265

AyA MODEL 4 DELUXE

Side-by-side; boxlock; 12-, 16-, 20-, 28-ga., .410; 26-inch, 27-inch, 28-inch barrels, depending upon gauge; weighs 5 to 7 lbs.; select European walnut stock and forend; Anson & Deeley system with double locking lugs; chopper lump barrels; bushed firing pins; automatic safety and ejectors; articulated front trigger. Still imported.

Perf:: $2750 **Exc:** $2575 **VGood:** $1095

AyA MODEL 37 SUPER

Over/under; sidelock; 12-, 16-, 20-ga.; 26-inch, 30-inch barrels; any standard choke combo; vent rib; single selective or double trigger(s); automatic ejectors; hand-checkered stock, forearm; heavily engraved pistol-grip or straight stock. Introduced 1963; no longer in production.

Perf: $2000 **Exc:** $1600 **VGood:** $1350

AyA MODEL 53-E

Side-by-side; sidelock ejector; 12-, 16-, 20-ga.; 2-3/4-inch chambers, 3-inch Mag. (available in 20-ga.); 26-inch, 28-inch, 30-inch barrels; any choke; finely hand-engraved with full coverage; hand-detachable

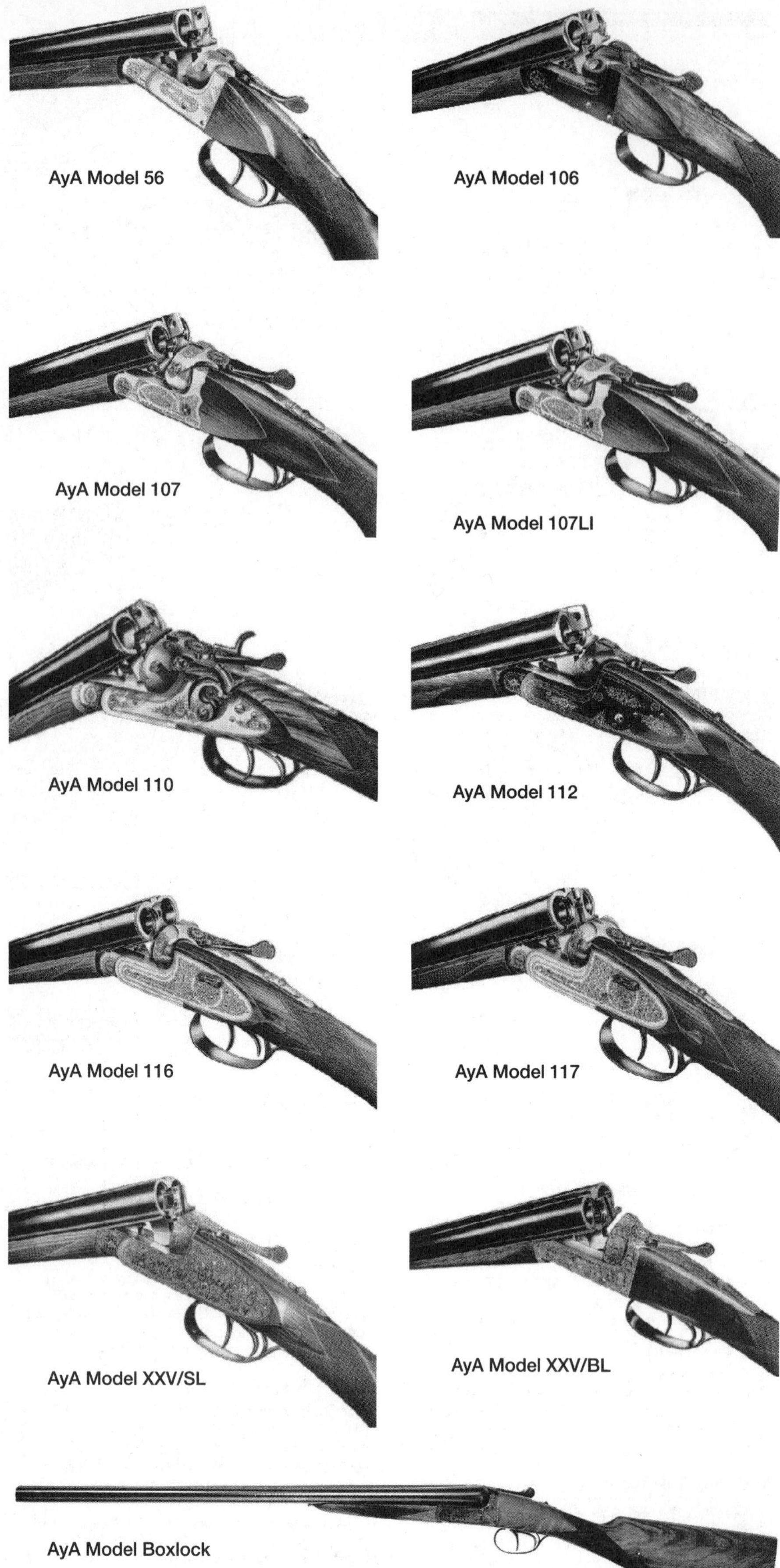
AyA Model 56

AyA Model 106

AyA Model 107

AyA Model 107LI

AyA Model 110

AyA Model 112

AyA Model 116

AyA Model 117

AyA Model XXV/SL

AyA Model XXV/BL

AyA Model Boxlock

locks; side clips; third locking bite; gas vents; single or double trigger; straight grip; half or full pistol grip on request; stock made to measure on request; plain or vent rib. Still imported.

Perf: $3750 **Exc:** $1850 **VGood:** $1250

AyA MODEL 56

Side-by-side; sidelock ejectors; triple-bolting; 12-, 16-, 20-ga.; barrel length, chokes to customers specs; European walnut stock to customer's specs; semi-custom manufacture; matted rib, vent rib available; automatic safety; cocking indicators; gas escape valves; folding front trigger; highly engraved receiver. Introduced 1972. 12-, 20-ga. still imported by Armes de Chasse.

Perf: $6500 **Exc:** $2900 **VGood:** $2350

AyA MODEL 106

Side-by-side; boxlock; 12-, 16-, 20-ga.; 2-3/4-inch chambers; 28-inch barrels; half or full pistol-grip with or without cheekpiece; almost no engraving; Greener-type cross bolt. No longer imported; discontinued 1985.

Perf: $570 **Exc:** $460 **VGood:** $420

AyA MODEL 107

Side-by-side; boxlock; 12-, 16-, 20-ga.; 2-3/4-inch chambers; 26-inch, 28-inch, 30-inch barrels; Modified/Full; cross bolt; brightly-finished receiver or color case-hardened; extractors; double trigger; checkered wood. No longer imported.

Perf: $570 **Exc:** $450 **VGood:** $390

AyA MODEL 107LI

Same specs as Model 107 except 12-, 16-ga.; Half/Full choke; side clips; scalloped receiver; modest engraving. No longer imported.

Perf: $695 **Exc:** $565 **VGood:** $525

AyA MODEL 110

Side-by-side; hammer gun; sidelock; 12-, 16-ga.; 2-3/4-inch chambers; 28-inch, 30-inch barrels; cross bolt and double underlugs; hand-checkered walnut; extractors. No longer imported.

Perf: $750 **Exc:** $550 **VGood:** $450

AyA MODEL 112

Side-by-side; sidelock; 12-, 16-, 20-ga.; 2-3/4-inch chambers; 28-inch, 30-inch barrels; hand-checkered walnut stock and forend; sideclips; cross bolt; extractors; modest engraving; double triggers; straight, semi- or full pistol grip. No longer imported.

Perf: $695 **Exc:** $525 **VGood:** $450

AyA MODEL 116

Side-by-side; sidelock; 12-, 16-, 20-ga.; 2-3/4-inch chambers; 27-inch, 28-inch, 30-inch barrels; hand-detachable locks; double trigger; third bite; hand-checkered walnut stock, forend; extractors. No longer imported.

Perf: $1000 **Exc:** $845 **VGood:** $795

AyA MODEL 117

Side-by-side; sidelock ejector; 12-, 16-, 20-ga.; 2-3/4-inch chambers; 26-inch, 27-inch, 28-inch, 30-inch barrels; standard choke combos; hand-checkered European walnut stock; beavertail forend; straight, half or full pistol grip; Holland & Holland design hand-detachable locks; double or selective single trigger. Was imported by Precision Sports. No longer in production.

Perf: $850 **Exc:** $715 **VGood:** $660

AyA MODEL 931

Over/under; boxlock; 12-, 16-, 20-, 28-ga., .410; 26-inch, 27-inch, 28-inch barrels; weighs 5 to 7 lbs; self-opening; Anson & Deeley system with double locking lugs; chopper lump barrels; bushed firing pins; automatic safety, ejectors; articulated front trigger. Imported by Armes de Chasse. Still in production.

Perf: $1000 **Exc:** $750 **VGood:** $555

AyA MODEL XXV/SL

Side-by-side; boxlock; 12-, 20-ga.; 26-inch, 27-inch, 28-inch, 29-inch barrels, depending upon gauge; weighs 5 to 7 lbs.; European walnut stock and forend; Holland & Holland system with double locking lugs; chopper lump barrels; bushed firing pins; automatic safety and ejectors; articulated front trigger. Still imported.

Perf: $2850 **Exc:** $1850 **VGood:** $1550

AyA MODEL XXV/BL

Side-by-side; boxlock ejector; 12- or 20-ga.; 2-1/2-inch chambers; 2-3/4-inch chambers on request; 25-inch barrels; standard chokes; straight-grip European walnut stock; half or full pistol grip on request; checkered butt; fine hand engraving; double triggers; Churchill-type narrow rib; color case-hardened or coin-finished receiver. Made in Spain. Introduced 1981; still imported by Armes de Chasse.

Perf: $2000 **Exc:** $1225 **VGood:** $995

AyA NO. 1

Side-by-side; sidelock; 12-, 20-ga.; 26-inch, 27-inch, 28-inch, 29-inch barrels; weighs 5-7 lbs.; double triggers; articulated front trigger; automatic safety; selective automatic ejectors; cocking indicators; bushed firing pins; replaceable hinge pins and chopper lump barrels; hand-cut checkered walnut stocks with oil finish; metal oval on buttstock for engraved initials; concave rib; straight hand; double triggers; engraved. Still imported by Armes de Chasse.

Perf: $6325 **Exc:** $2350 **VGood:** $1850

AyA NO. 2

Side-by-side; sidelock; 12-, 16-, 20-, 28-ga., .410; 3-inch chambers; 28-inch barrels; standard choke combos; weighs 7 lbs.; silver bead front sight; English-style oil-finished walnut stock, splinter forend; checkered butt; single selective or double triggers; engraved sideplates; auto safety; gas escape valves. Made in Spain. Introduced 1987; discontinued 1988. Now imported by Armes de Chasse.

12-, 20-ga., double triggers

Perf: $2775 **Exc:** $1150 **VGood:** $900

12-, 20-ga., single trigger

Perf: $2825 **Exc:** $1200 **VGood:** $950

28-ga., .410, double triggers

Perf: $2850 **Exc:** $1350 **VGood:** $1000

28-ga., .410, single trigger

Perf: $2875 **Exc:** $1275 **VGood:** $1000

AyA MODEL 3-A

Side-by-side; boxlock; 12-, 16-, 20-, 28-ga., .410; 26-inch, 28-inch, 30-inch barrels; 3-inch chambers (12-ga.); standard chokes; straight, half or full pistol grip; double triggers; border-engraved only; Spanish walnut stock; hand-checkered; chopper lump barrels; double underlug lock only. Discontinued 1985.

Perf: $645 **Exc:** $545 **VGood:** $495

AyA NO. 4

Side-by-side; boxlock; 12-, 16-, 20-, 28-ga., .410; 26-inch, 28-inch, 30-inch barrels; standard chokes; hand-checkered straight-grip European walnut stock; other stock types made to order; checkered butt; classic forend; automatic ejectors, safety; double or single triggers; color case-hardened receiver. Made in Spain. Introduced 1981; still imported by Armes de Chasse.

12-, 16-ga.

Perf: $1400 **Exc:** $625 **VGood:** $525

20-ga.

Perf: $1400 **Exc:** $625 **VGood:** $525

28-ga., .410

Perf: $1450 **Exc:** $675 **VGood:** $575

AyA YEOMAN

Side-by-side; boxlock; 12-ga.; ejectors; very plain gun with no engraving; color-hardened receiver; hand-checkered walnut stock. No longer imported.

Perf: $495 **Exc:** $395 **VGood:** $355

BAIKAL 66 COACH GUN

Side-by-side; exposed hammers; 12-ga.; 2-3/4-inch chambers; 20-inch Improved/Modified, 28-inch Modified/ Full barrels; weighs 6-1/4 lbs. (20-inch), 7-1/4 lbs. (28-inch); hand-checkered European hardwood pistol-grip stock, beavertail forearm; chromed bores, chambers; hand engraved receiver; extractors. Also known as the TOZ-66/54. Made in Russia. No longer imported.

Perf: $175 **Exc:** $140 **VGood:** $125

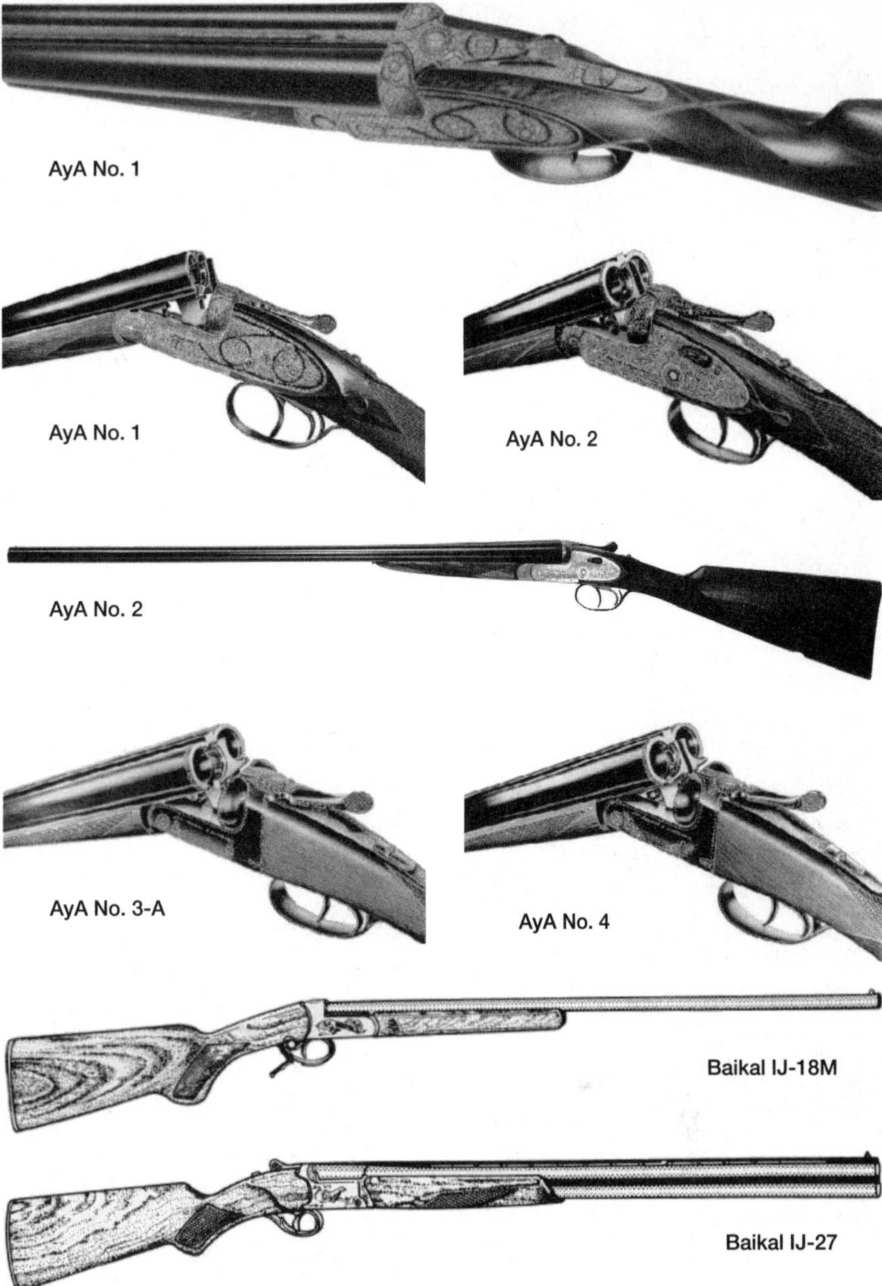

AyA No. 1

AyA No. 1

AyA No. 2

AyA No. 2

AyA No. 3-A

AyA No. 4

Baikal IJ-18M

Baikal IJ-27

BAIKAL IJ-18

Single shot; single barrel; 12-, 16-, 20-ga., .410; 2-3/4-inch chamber; 26-inch Modified, 28-inch Modified, 30-inch Full choke barrel; 44-1/2-inch overall length; weighs 6 lbs.; hand-checkered European walnut pistol-grip stock, forearm; white spacers at pistol grip, plastic buttplate; chrome-lined bore, chamber; extractor; cocking indicator; crossbolt safety. Made in Russia. Introduced 1973; still in production.

Perf: $75 **Exc:** $65 **VGood:** $55

BAIKAL IJ-18EM

Same specs as IJ-18 except automatic ejector. Imported from Russia by Century International Arms. Still imported.

Perf: $80 **Exc:** $65 **VGood:** $55

BAIKAL IJ-18M

Same specs as IJ-18 except 12-, 16-, 20-ga., .410; 2-3/4-inch chamber (12, 16), 3-inch chamber (20, .410); 26-inch, 28-inch barrel; choked Improved Cylinder, Full, Modified; trigger block safety; engraved, blued receiver. Imported from Russia by K.B.I., Inc. Reintroduced 1994; still imported.

Perf: $65 **Exc:** $55 **VGood:** $45

BAIKAL IJ-25

Over/under; 12-ga; 2-3/4-inch chambers; 26-inch Skeet/ Skeet, 28-inch Modified/Full, 30-inch Improved/Full barrels; vent rib; hand-checkered European walnut pistol-grip stock, ventilated forearm; white spacers at pistol-grip cap, recoil pad; single non-selective trigger; chrome-lined barrels, chambers, internal parts; hand-engraved, silver inlaid receiver, forearm latch, triggerguard. Made in Russia. Introduced 1973; discontinued 1978.

Perf: $305 **Exc:** $225 **VGood:** $175

BAIKAL IJ-27

Over/under; 12- (2-3/4-inch), 20-ga. (3-inch); 26-inch Skeet/Skeet, 28-inch Modified/Full barrels; hand-fitted ventilated rib; hand-checkered European walnut pistol-grip stock, ventilated forend; white spacers at pistol-grip cap, rubber recoil pad; double triggers; automatic safety; extractors; chrome-lined barrels, chambers, internal parts; hand-engraved, silver inlaid

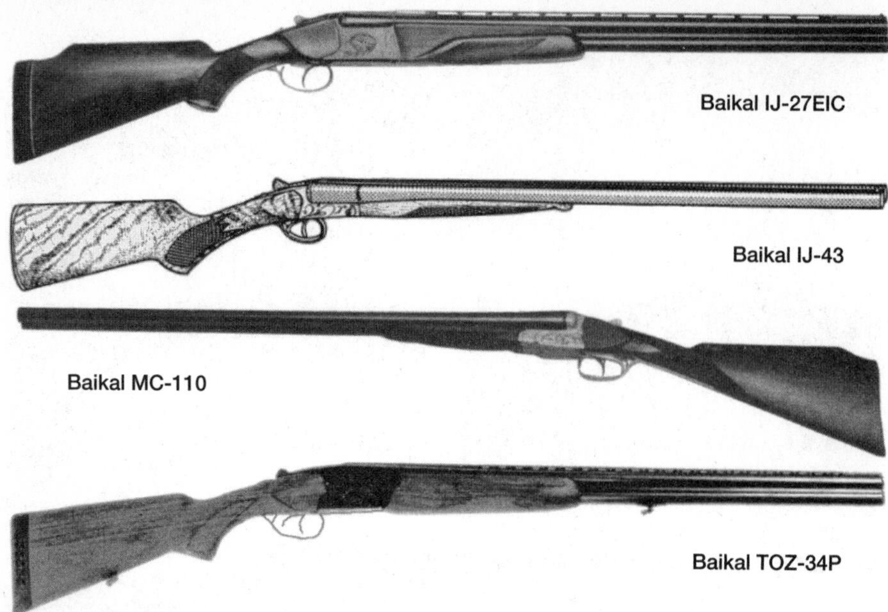
Baikal IJ-27EIC

Baikal IJ-43

Baikal MC-110

Baikal TOZ-34P

receiver, forearm latch, triggerguard. Made in Russia. Introduced 1973; dropped 1996.

Perf: $330 **Exc:** $275 **VGood:** $250

BAIKAL IJ-27EIC

Same specs as IJ-27 except automatic ejectors; single trigger; dropped 1996. M

Perf: $370 **Exc:** $315 **VGood:** $290

BAIKAL IJ-27EM

Same specs as IJ-27 except 12-ga.; 2-3/4-inch chambers; 28-1/2-inch chrome-lined barrels; weighs 7-1/2 lbs.; European hardwood stock; double triggers; selective automatic ejectors. Imported from Russia by Century International Arms. Still imported.

Perf: $330 **Exc:** $260 **VGood:** $215

BAIKAL IJ-27M

Same specs as IJ-27 except 12-ga.; 2-3/4-inch chambers; 28-1/2-inch chrome-lined barrels; European hardwood stock; double triggers; extractors; sling swivels. Imported from Russia by Century International Arms; still imported.

Perf: $350 **Exc:** $325 **VGood:** $295

BAIKAL IJ-43

Side-by-side; boxlock; 12-ga.; 2-3/4-inch chambers; 20-inch Cylinder/Cylinder, 28-inch Modified/Full barrels; weighs 6-3/4 lbs.; checkered walnut stock, forend; double triggers; extractors; blued, engraved receiver. Imported from Russia by K.B.I., Inc. Reintroduced 1994; dropped 1996.

Perf: $235 **Exc:** $200 **VGood:** $130

BAIKAL IJ-43EM

Same specs as IJ-43 except 28-1/2-inch chrome-lined barrels; European hardwood stock; automatic ejectors. Imported from Russia by Century International Arms. Still imported.

Perf: $250 **Exc:** $190 **VGood:** $150

BAIKAL IJ-43M

Same specs as IJ-43 except 28-1/2-inch chrome-lined barrels; European hardwood stock; automatic safety. Imported from Russia by Century International Arms. Still imported.

Perf: $250 **Exc:** $200 **VGood:** $165

BAIKAL IJ-58M

Side-by-side; hammerless; 12-ga.; 2-3/4-inch chambers; 26-inch Improved/Modified, 28-inch Modified/Full barrels; hand-checkered European walnut pistol-grip stock, beavertail forend; hinged front double trigger; chrome-lined barrels, chambers; hand-engraved receiver; hammer interceptors; recoil pad; extractors. Made in Russia. Introduced 1973; discontinued 1982.

Perf: $235 **Exc:** $185 **VGood:** $145

BAIKAL MC-5

Over/under; 12-, 20-ga.; 2-3/4-inch chambers; 26-inch Improved/Modified, Skeet/Skeet barrels; weighs 5-3/4 lbs.; hand-fitted solid rib; fancy hand-checkered walnut stock; straight or pistol grip, with or without cheekpiece; non-removable forend; double triggers; extractors; hammer interceptors; silver-finished, fully engraved receiver; chrome-lined barrels, chambers, internal parts; marketed with case. Made in Russia. Introduced 1973; discontinued 1982.

Perf: $325 **Exc:** $350 **VGood:** $295

BAIKAL MC-6

Over/under; 12-ga.; 2-3/4-inch chambers; 26-inch Skeet/ Skeet, Improved Cylinder/Modified barrels; hand-fitted solid raised rib; fancy hand-checkered walnut stock; pistol grip or straight stock, with or without cheekpiece; non-removable forend; single non-selective or double triggers, extractors; hammer interceptors; silver-finished, fully engraved receiver; chrome-lined barrels, chambers, internal parts; marketed with case. Made in Russia. Introduced 1973; discontinued 1982.

Perf: $495 **Exc:** $395 **VGood:** $300

BAIKAL MC-7

Over/under; 12-, 20-ga.; 2-3/4-inch chambers; 26-inch Improved/Modified, 28-inch Modified/Full barrels; solid raised rib; hand-checkered fancy walnut straight or pistol-grip stock, beavertail forend; ejectors; double triggers; optional single selective trigger; hand-chiseled, engraved receiver; chrome-lined barrels, chambers, internal parts; marketed with case. Made in Russia. Introduced 1973; discontinued 1982.

Perf: $900 **Exc:** $750 **VGood:** $625

BAIKAL MC-8

Over/under; 12-ga.; 2-3/4-inch chambers; 2-barrel set of 26-inch Skeet/Skeet, 28-inch Modified/Full; hand-fitted vent rib; weighs 7-3/4 lbs.; hand-checkered fancy European walnut Monte Carlo pistol-grip stock, non-removable beavertail forend; double triggers; extractors; optional single selective trigger, selective ejectors; hand-engraved, blued receiver; chrome-lined barrels, chambers, internal parts; marketed with case. Made in Russia. Introduced 1973; discontinued 1982.

Perf: $875 **Exc:** $700 **VGood:** $595

With single selective trigger, selective ejectors

Perf: $925 **Exc:** $750 **VGood:** $625

BAIKAL MC-10

Side-by-side; hammerless; 12-, 20-ga.; 2-3/4-inch chambers; 26-inch Improved/Modified, 28-inch Modified/Full barrels; raised solid rib; hand-checkered fancy European walnut stock, semi-beavertail forearm; straight or pistol grip; chrome-lined barrels, chambers, internal parts; double triggers; auto safety; extractors or selective ejectors; receiver engraved with animal, bird scenes; engraved trigger guard, tang. Made in Russia. Introduced 1973; discontinued 1978.

Perf: $375 **Exc:** $310 **VGood:** $275

BAIKAL MC-21

Autoloader; takedown; 12-ga; 5-shot magazine; 26-inch Improved, 28-inch Modified, 30-inch Full choke barrel; vent rib; hand-rubbed, hand-checkered European walnut cheekpiece stock, grooved forearm; white spacers at pistol grip, buttplate; chrome-lined barrel, chamber; reversible safety; target-grade trigger. Made in Russia. Introduced 1973; discontinued 1978.

Perf: $275 **Exc:** $200 **VGood:** $175

BAIKAL MC-109

Over/under; hand-detachable sidelock; 12-ga.; 2-3/4-inch chambers; 28-inch barrels; raised rib; weighs 7-1/4 lbs.; hand-carved, checkered fancy walnut stock, beavertail forend; straight or pistol grip with or without cheekpiece; single selective trigger; chromed barrels, chambers, internal parts; hand-chiseled scenes on receiver to customer specs; marketed with case. Made in Russia. Introduced 1975; discontinued 1982.

Perf: $925 **Exc:** $700 **VGood:** $595

BAIKAL MC-110

Side-by-side; 12-, 20-ga.; 2-3/4-inch chambers; 26-inch Improved Cylinder/Modified (20-ga.), 28-inch Modified/Full (12-ga.) barrels; raised solid rib; weighs 6 lbs. (20-ga.), 6-3/4 lbs. (12-ga.); hand-checkered fancy walnut straight or pistol-grip stock, semi-beavertail forend; double triggers; chromed barrels, chambers, internal parts; hammer interceptors; extractors; auto safety; fully engraved receiver, triggerguard, tang; marketed in case. Made in Russia. Introduced 1975; discontinued 1982.

Perf: $500 **Exc:** $400 **VGood:** $300

BAIKAL MC-111

Side-by-side; hand-detachable sidelock; 12-ga.; 2-3/4-inch chambers; barrel lengths, chokes to customer's specifications; hand-checkered European walnut straight or pistol-grip stock, semi-beavertail forend; single selective trigger; hammer interceptors; cocking indicators; gold, silver inlays in butt; hand-chiseled bird, animal scenes on receiver; chromed barrels, chambers, internal parts; marketed with case. Made in Russia. Introduced 1975; discontinued 1982.

Perf: $975 **Exc:** $750 **VGood:** $625

BAIKAL TOZ-34P

Over/under; boxlock; 12-ga.; 2-3/4-inch chambers; 28-inch Full/ Improved Cylinder barrels; vent rib; 44-inch overall length; weighs 7-1/2 lbs.; European walnut stock, forend; extractors; optional ejectors; cocking indicator; double triggers; engraved, blued receiver; ventilated rubber buttpad. Imported from Russia by Century International Arms. Still imported.

Perf: $350 **Exc:** $280 **VGood:** $210

With ejectors

Perf: $375 **Exc:** $300 **VGood:** $235

BAIKAL TOZ-66

Side-by-side; exposed hammers; 12-ga.; 2-3/4-inch chambers; 20-inch Improved/Modified, 28-inch Modified/Full barrels; hand-checkered European hardwood pistol-grip stock, beavertail forearm; chrome-lined barrels, chambers; hand-engraved receiver; extractors. Made in Russia. Introduced 1973; discontinued 1978.

Perf: $225 **Exc:** $150 **VGood:** $100

BAKER BATAVIA EJECTOR

Side-by-side; sidelock; hammerless; 12-, 16-, 20-ga.; 26-inch to 32-inch Damascus or forged steel barrels; any standard choke combo; best-grade hand-checkered American walnut pistol-grip stock, forearm; auto ejectors. Introduced 1921; discontinued 1930.

Exc: $880 **VGood:** $770 **Good:** $745

Damascus

Exc: $500 **VGood:** $400 **Good:** $305

BAKER BATAVIA LEADER

Same specs as Batavia Ejector except forged steel barrels; extractors or auto ejectors; less expensive finish. Discontinued around 1930.

Extractors

Exc: $500 **VGood:** $425 **Good:** $375

Auto ejectors

Exc: $595 **VGood:** $510 **Good:** $470

BAKER BATAVIA SPECIAL

Same specs as Batavia Ejector except forged steel barrels; extractors; less expensive finish. Discontinued around 1930.

Exc: $495 **VGood:** $405 **Good:** $375

BAKER BLACK BEAUTY SPECIAL

Side-by-side; sidelock; hammerless; 12-, 16-, 20-ga.; 26-inch to 32-inch barrels; any standard choke combination; ejectors or extractors; hand-checkered American walnut pistol-grip stock, forearm; engraved. Introduced 1921; discontinued 1930.

Extractors

Exc: $745 **VGood:** $650 **Good:** $615

Auto ejectors

Exc: $855 **VGood:** $760 **Good:** $725

BAKER GRADE R

Side-by-side; sidelock; hammerless; 12-, 16-, 20-ga.; 26-inch, 28-inch, 30-inch, 32-inch Damascus or Krupp steel barrels; select hand-checkered European walnut pistol-grip stock, forend; extractors or auto ejectors; extensive engraving with game scenes. Introduced 1915; discontinued 1933.

Extractors

Exc: $1000 **VGood:** $925 **Good:** $800

Auto ejectors

Exc: $1200 **VGood:** $1125 **Good:** $1000

Paragon Grade, extractors

Exc: $1300 **VGood:** $1125 **Good:** $1000

Paragon Grade, auto ejectors

Exc: $1500 **VGood:** $1275 **Good:** $1000

Expert Grade, ejectors, select finish

Exc: $1975 **VGood:** $1350 **Good:** $1100

Deluxe Grade, best-grade finish

Exc: $3250 **VGood:** $2650 **Good:** $2000

BAKER GRADE S

Side-by-side; sidelock; hammerless; 12-, 16-, 20-ga.; 26-inch, 28-inch, 30-inch, 32-inch fluid-tempered steel barrels; select hand-checkered European walnut pistol-grip stock, forend; scroll, line engraving; extractors or auto ejectors. Introduced 1915; discontinued 1933.

Extractors

Exc: $880 **VGood:** $775 **Good:** $745

Auto ejectors

Exc: $1100 **VGood:** $990 **Good:** $965

BEEMAN FABARM

Over/under; boxlock; 12-ga.; 2-3/4-inch chambers; 26-1/2-inch Skeet/Skeet, 29-inch Full/Modified barrels; weighs about 7-1/2 lbs.; red bead front sight, white bead middle; select cut-checkered walnut stock, schnabel forend; single selective trigger; auto ejectors; chrome-lined bores, chambers; silvered, engraved receiver; Skeet/Trap combo with interchangeable barrels cased. Made in Italy. Introduced 1984; discontinued 1984.

Field Grade

Perf: $650 **Exc:** $525 **VGood:** $410

Trap/Skeet

Perf: $750 **Exc:** $625 **VGood:** $500

Combo

Perf: $1100 **Exc:** $860 **VGood:** $750

Baker Batavia Leader

Baker Batavia Special

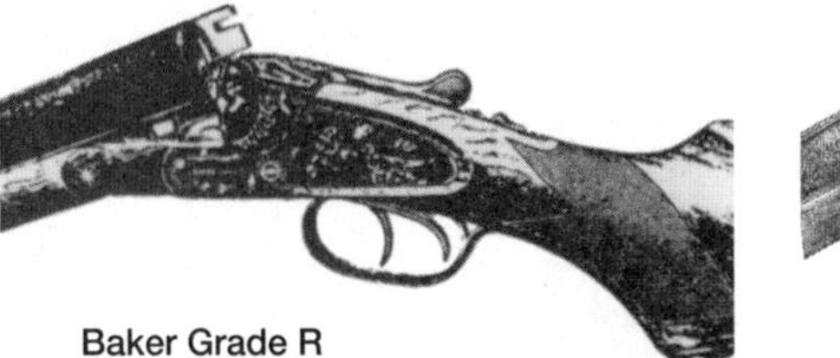

Baker Grade R

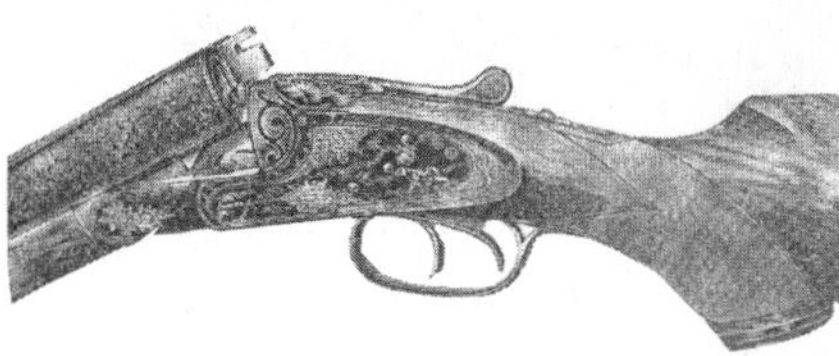

Baker Paragon Grade

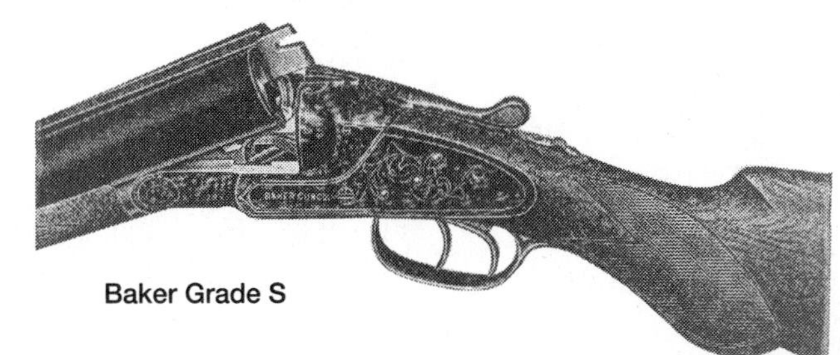

Baker Grade S

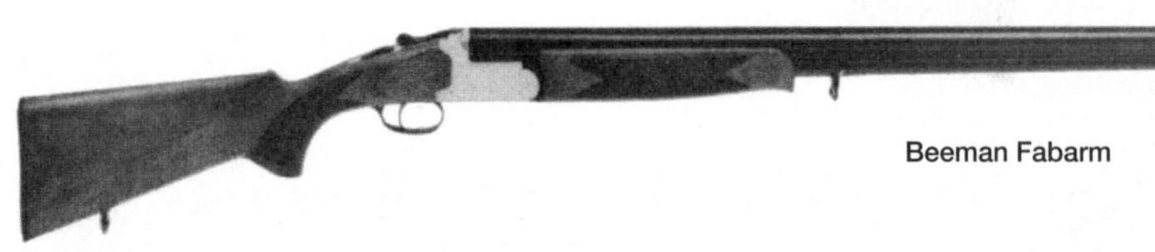

Beeman Fabarm

Benelli Cordoba

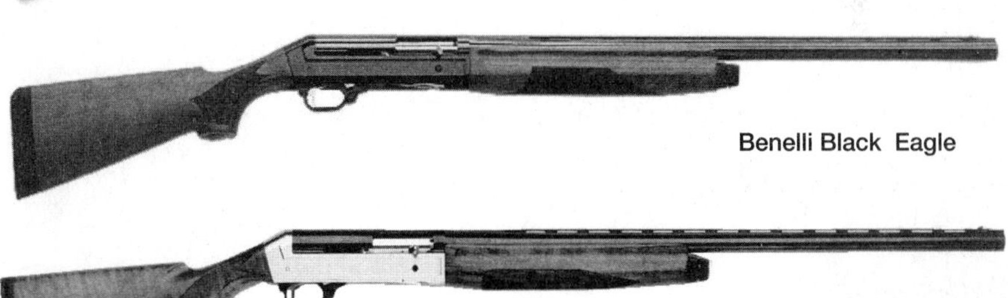

Benelli Black Eagle

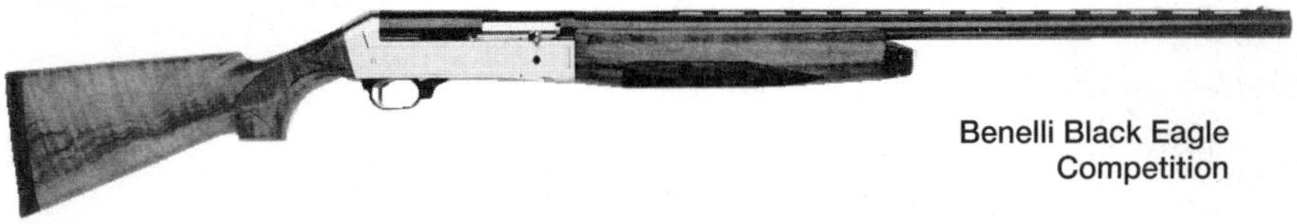

Benelli Black Eagle Competition

BENELLI CORDOBA

Autoloader; black synthetic stock; 12- or 20-ga., 2-3/4- and 3-inch chamber; 28- and 30-inch barrels with 4 extended choke tubes; red bar sights; 7.2 to 7.3 lbs. overall weight.

Perf: $1510 **Exc:** $1210 **VGood:** $975

BENELLI BLACK EAGLE

Autoloader; Montefeltro recoil action; 12-ga.; 3-inch chambers; 5-shot magazine; 21-inch, 24-inch, 26-inch, 28-inch vent-rib barrels; choke tubes; weighs 7-3/8 lbs.; high-gloss European walnut stock; marketed with drop adjustment kit; two-piece steel/aluminum receiver; silver finish on lower receiver, blued upper. Made in Italy. Introduced 1989; discontinued 1991.

Perf: $825 **Exc:** $675 **VGood:** $550

BENELLI BLACK EAGLE COMPETITION

Same specs as Black Eagle except 26-inch, 28-inch barrel; mid-bead sight; competition stock; two-piece etched aluminum receiver. Made in Italy. Introduced 1989; dropped 1997.

Perf: $1025 **Exc:** $795 **VGood:** $675

BENELLI BLACK EAGLE COMPETITION "LIMITED EDITION"

Same specs as Black Eagle except gold inlays; fancy wood; special serial numbers.

Perf: $1850 **Exc:** $1500 **VGood:** $1225

BENELLI BLACK EAGLE SLUG GUN

Same specs as Black Eagle except 24-inch rifled barrel; no rib; weighs 7-1/8 lbs.; two-piece steel/alloy receiver; drilled, tapped for scope mount; marketed

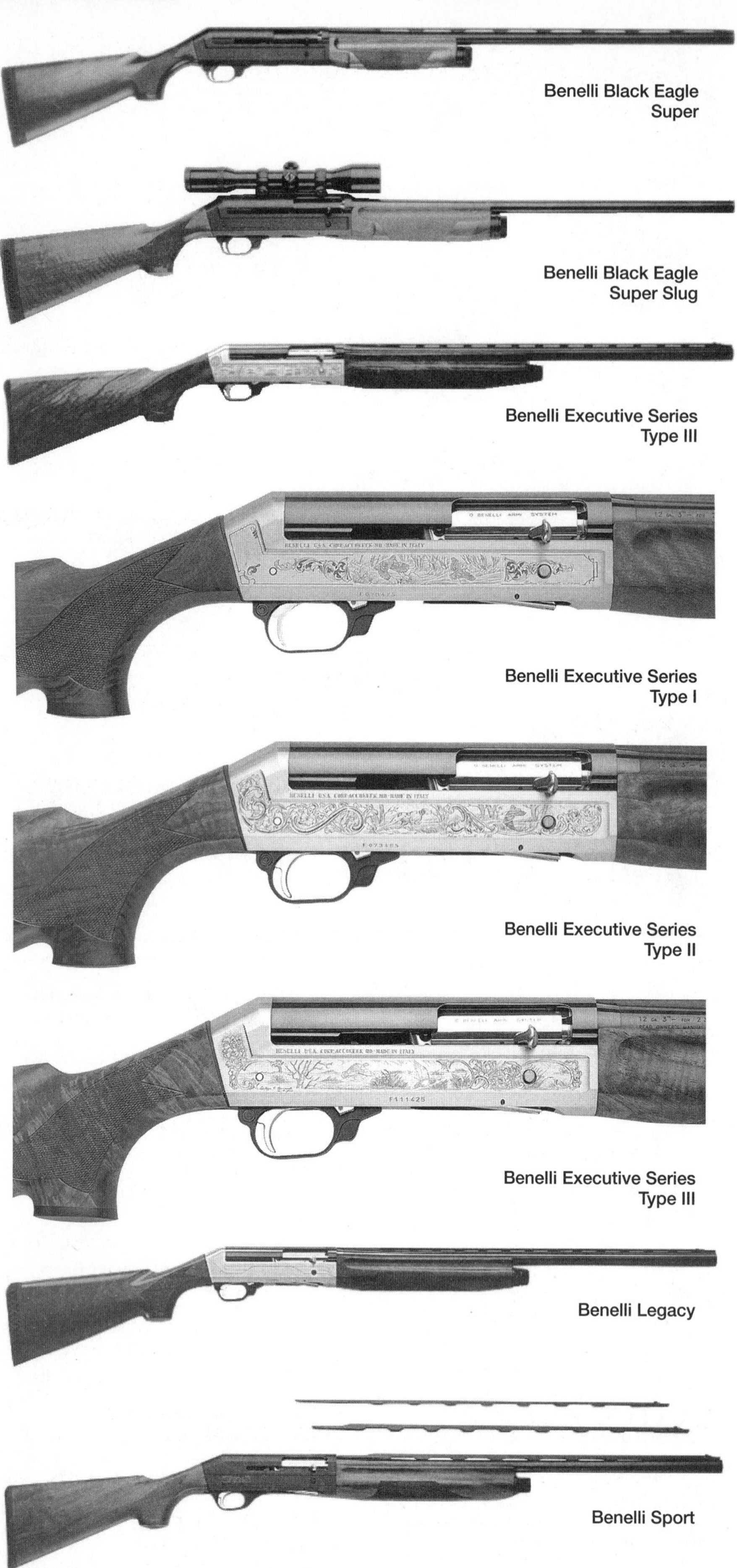
Benelli Black Eagle Super

Benelli Black Eagle Super Slug

Benelli Executive Series Type III

Benelli Executive Series Type I

Benelli Executive Series Type II

Benelli Executive Series Type III

Benelli Legacy

Benelli Sport

with scope mount. Made in Italy. Introduced 1989; discontinued 1991; reintroduced 1992; dropped 2003.

Perf: $1110 **Exc:** $910 **VGood:** $775

BENELLI BLACK EAGLE SUPER

Same specs as Black Eagle except 3-1/2-inch chamber; 24-inch, 26-inch, 28-inch barrels; 49-3/8-inch overall length (28-inch barrel); weighs 7-1/2 lbs.; bead front sight; European walnut stock adjustable for drop; satin or gloss finish. Introduced 1991; still imported.

Perf: $1075 **Exc:** $895 **VGood:** $775

Timber HD Camo 24-inch, 26-inch, 28-inch barrel

With 24-inch, 26-inch and 28-inch barrel, polymer stock

Left-hand, 24-inch, 26-inch, 28-inch, polymer stock

Perf: $1200 **Exc:** $995 **VGood:** $875

Left-hand, 24-inch, 26-inch, 28-inch, camo stock

Perf: $1275 **Exc:** $1025 **VGood:** $925

BENELLI BLACK EAGLE SUPER SLUG

Same specs as Benelli Black Eagle except 3-1/2-inch chamber; 24-inch E.R. Shaw Custom rifled barrel; 45-1/2-inch overall length; weighs 7-1/2 lbs.; scope mount base; matte-finish receiver; wood or polymer stocks available. Imported from Italy by Heckler & Koch, Inc. Introduced 1992.

With wood stock

Perf: $1120 **Exc:** $920 **VGood:** $785

With polymer stock

Perf: $1110 **Exc:** $910 **VGood:** $775

24-inch barrel, Timber HD Camo

Perf: $1235 **Exc:** $1035 **VGood:** $900

BENELLI EXECUTIVE SERIES

Autoloader; Montefeltro recoil action; 12-ga.; 3-inch chamber; 5-shot magazine; 21-inch, 24-inch, 26-inch, 28-inch barrel; choke tubes; weighs 7-3/8 lbs.; highest grade of walnut stock with drop adjustment kit; two-piece steel/aluminum receiver; grayed steel lower receiver; hand-engraved and gold inlaid (Type III). Special order only. Made in Italy. Introduced 1995.

Type I (about two-thirds engraving coverage)

Perf: $4825 **Exc:** $3775 **VGood:** $2550

Type II (full coverage engraving)

Perf: $5375 **Exc:** $4175 **VGood:** $3075

Type III (full coverage, gold inlays)

Perf: $6200 **Exc:** $4600 **VGood:** $3500

BENELLI EXTRALUXE

Autoloader; inertial action; 12-ga.; 2-3/4-inch chamber; 5-shot magazine; 26-inch, 28-inch barrel; vent rib; weighs 6-3/4 lbs.; hand-checkered walnut stock; crossbolt safety; interchangeable barrels; similar to SL-121 but with extra-fancy wood; fine hand engraving; gold trigger; carrying case. No longer imported.

Perf: $295 **Exc:** $250 **VGood:** $220

BENELLI LEGACY

Gauge: 12, 20; 2-3/4-inch and 3-inch chamber; 24-inch, 26-inch, 28-inch barrel (Full, Mod., Imp. Cyl., Imp. Mod., cylinder choke tubes); mid-bead sight; weighs 5.8 to 7.6 lbs.; 49-5/8-inch overall (28-inch barrel); select European walnut with satin finish. Uses the rotating bolt inertia recoil operating system with a two-piece steel/aluminum etched receiver (bright on lower, blue upper). Drop adjustment kit allows the stock to be custom fitted without modifying the stock. Introduced 1998. Imported from Italy by Benelli USA, Corp.

Perf: $1175 **Exc:** $935 **VGood:** $785

BENELLI SPORT

Similar to the Legacy model except has matte blue receiver, two carbon fiber interchangeable ventilated ribs, adjustable butt pad, adjustable buttstock, and functions with ultra-light target loads. Walnut stock with satin finish. Introduced 1997. Imported from Italy.

Perf: $1125 **Exc:** $895 **VGood:** $750

BENELLI M1 FIELD

Gauge: 20-ga., 2-3/4- and 3-inch chamber; 24- and 26-inch barrel; weighs 5.7 to 5.8 lbs.; black or camo synthetic stock; stepped ventilated rib with red bar sights. Comes with set of five choke tubes. Imported from Italy.

Black synthetic stock version

Perf: $800 **Exc:** $675 **VGood:** $575

Camo stock version

Perf: $815 **Exc:** $690 **VGood:** $590

BENELLI M2 FIELD

Autoloader; 12-ga., 2-3/4- and 3-inch chamber; 21-inch, 24-inch, 26-inch, 28-inch barrel; weighs 6.9 to 7.2 lbs.; high impact polymer stock; wood on 26-inch, 28-inch; red bar sights; ventilated rib; blue finish. Available with or without ComforTech stock. Uses the rotating Montefeltro bolt system. Comes with set of five choke tubes. Imported from Italy. Add 5% for SteadyGrip.

Black synthetic stock version

Perf: $1000 **Exc:** $875 **VGood:** $575

Walnut stock version

Perf: $1075 **Exc:** $925 **VGood:** $590

Camo stock

Perf: $1100 **Exc:** $950 **VGood:** $610

BENELLI M2 TACTICAL

Inertia-operated semi-auto; 12 ga., 2-3/4" and 3"; 5+1 capacity. 18-1/2" barrel, pistol grip synthetic ComforTech stock, ghost ring aperture rear sight and bead front sight with tritium inserts. Standard stock model available. Introduced 2005 by Benelli USA.

New: $1065 **Exc:** $800 **VGood:** $650

BENELLI M2 PRACTICAL

Similar to M2 Tactical but with 26-inch barrel, 9-shot capacity, and oversized controls.

Exc: $1000 **VGood:** $925 **Good:** $800

BENELLI M1 SUPER 90

Autoloader; rotating Montefeltro bolt system; 12-ga; 3-inch chamber; 3-shot magazine; extended magazine available with 26-inch, 28-inch barrels; 21-inch, 24-inch, 26-inch, 28-inch barrels; choke tubes; vent rib; weighs 7-1/2 lbs.; metal bead front sight; wood or polymer stock, forearm; blued finish. Made in Italy. Introduced 1987; still imported.

Perf: $865 **Exc:** $685 **VGood:** $600

BENELLI M1 SUPER 90 DEFENSE

Same specs as M1 Super 90 except 5-shot magazine; 18-1/2-inch Cylinder barrel; open or aperture (ghost ring) rifle-type sights; polymer pistol-grip stock; matte black finish. Introduced 1993; dropped 1998.

Perf: $685 **Exc:** $525 **VGood:** $395

Add $45 to above prices for ghost ring sighting system

BENELLI M1 SUPER 90 ENTRY

Same specs as M1 Super 90 except 5-shot magazine; 14-inch Cylinder barrel; open or aperture (ghost ring) rifle-type sights; polymer straight or pistol-grip stock; matte black finish. Introduced 1992; still imported.

Perf: $810 **Exc:** $675 **VGood:** $585

Add $15 to above prices for synthetic pistol grip stock Add $65 for ghost ring sights

Note: Ownership of this model requires special registration under the National Firearms Act due to its short barrel.

BENELLI M1 SUPER 90 MONTEFELTRO

Same specs as M1 Super 90 except 12- or 20-ga.; 4-shot magazine; checkered European walnut drop-adjustable stock with satin finish; matte blue metal finish. Made in Italy. Introduced 1987; still imported.

Perf: $865 **Exc:** $725 **VGood:** $600

Timber HD Camo, 21-inch, 24-inch barrel

Perf: $920 **Exc:** $780 **VGood:** $685

20 ga., 24-inch, 26-inch bbl. syn.

Perf: $850 **Exc:** $700 **VGood:** $525

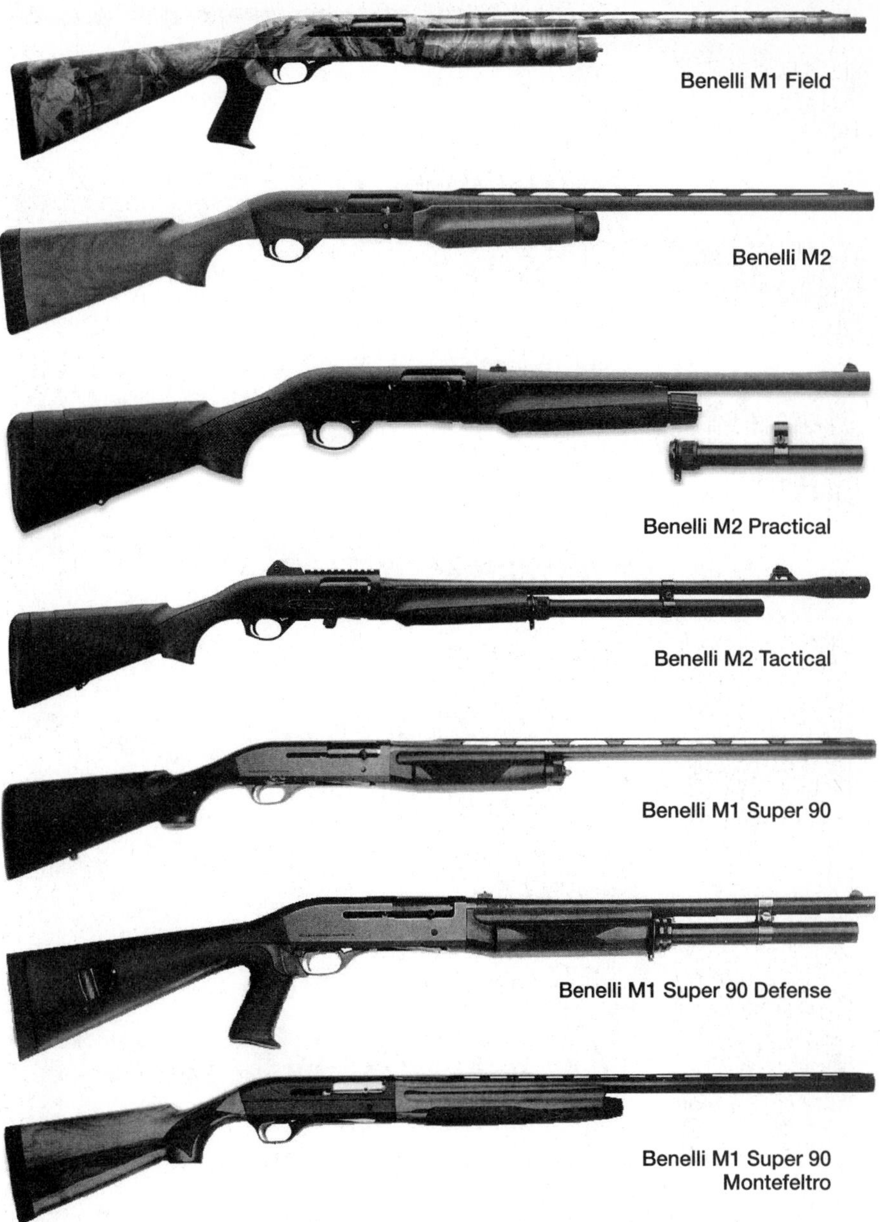

Benelli M1 Field

Benelli M2

Benelli M2 Practical

Benelli M2 Tactical

Benelli M1 Super 90

Benelli M1 Super 90 Defense

Benelli M1 Super 90 Montefeltro

BENELLI M1 SUPER 90 MONTEFELTRO 20-GAUGE LIMITED EDITION

Same specs as M1 Super 90 except 20-ga.; 3-inch chamber; 4-shot magazine; 26-inch barrel; weighs 5-3/4 lbs.; checkered European walnut drop-adjustable stock with satin finish; special nickel-plated and engraved receiver inlaid with gold. Made in Italy. Introduced 1993; still imported.

Perf: $1700 **Exc:** $1250 **VGood:** $900

BENELLI M1 SUPER 90 MONTEFELTRO, LEFT-HAND

Same specs as M1 Super 90 except left-hand action; 12- or 20-ga.; 4-shot magazine; checkered European walnut drop-adjustable stock with satin finish; matte blue metal finish. Made in Italy. Introduced 1987; still imported.

Perf: $750 **Exc:** $470 **VGood:** $410

BENELLI M1 SUPER 90 MONTEFELTRO UPLANDER

Same specs as M1 Super 90 except 12-, 20-ga.; 4-shot magazine; 21-inch, 24-inch barrels; checkered European walnut drop-adjustable stock with satin finish. Made in Italy. Introduced 1987; discontinued 1992.

Perf: $600 **Exc:** $350 **VGood:** $300

BENELLI M1 SUPER 90 MONTEFELTRO SLUG

Same specs as M1 Super 90 except 12-ga.; 3-inch chamber; 4-shot magazine; 24-inch barrel; Cylinder choke; 45-1/2-inch overall length; weighs 7 lbs.; checkered European walnut drop-adjustable stock with satin finish; matte blue metal finish. Made in Italy. Introduced, 1988; discontinued, 1992.

Perf: $590 **Exc:** $340 **VGood:** $290

BENELLI M1 SUPER 90 SLUG

Same specs as M1 Super 90 except 5-shot magazine; 18-1/2-inch Cylinder barrel; open or aperture (ghost ring) rifle-type sights; polymer straight stock; matte black finish. Introduced 1986; still imported.

Perf: $615 **Exc:** $310 **VGood:** $280

BENELLI M1 SUPER 90 SPORTING SPECIAL

Same specs as M1 Super 90 except 18-1/2-inch barrel; Improved Cylinder, Modified, Full choke tubes; 39-3/4-inch overall length; weighs 6-1/2 lbs.; ghost ring sight; sporting-style polymer stock with drop adjustment; matte black finish receiver. Made in Italy. Introduced 1993; still imported.

Perf: $680 **Exc:** $410 **VGood:** $375

Benelli M1 Super 90 Tactical

Benelli M1 Practical

Benelli M2 Field with ComforTech

Benelli M2 Field w/o ComforTech

Benelli M3 Convertible Standard Stock and ghost ring sights

Benelli M3 Convertible with folding stock

Benelli M3 pistolgrip stock ghost ring sights

Benelli M4

BENELLI M1 SUPER 90 TACTICAL

Same specs as M1 Super 90 except 5-shot magazine; 18-1/2-inch Improved Cylinder, Modified, Full barrel; open or aperture (ghost ring) rifle-type sights; polymer straight or pistol-grip stock; matte black finish. Numerous law enforcement and military options. Introduced 1993; still imported.

Perf: $810 **Exc:** $675 **VGood:** $575

BENELLI M1 TACTICAL

Gauge: 12; 2-3/4-inch, 3-inch chambers; 5-shot magazine; 18.5-inch barrel, IC, M, F choke tubes; weighs 6.7 lbs.; 39.75-inch overall; black polymer stock; rifle type sights with ghost ring system, tritium night sights optional; semi-auto inertia recoil action; cross-bolt safety; bolt release button; matte-finish metal. Introduced 1993. Imported from Italy.

With rifle sights, standard stock

Perf: $900 **Exc:** $700 **VGood:** $600

With ghost ring rifle sights, standard stock

Perf: $795 **Exc:** $595 **VGood:** $435

With ghost ring sights, pistol grip stock

Perf: $810 **Exc:** $610 **VGood:** $450

With rifle sights, pistol grip stock

Perf: $810 **Exc:** $610 **VGood:** $450

BENELLI M1 PRACTICAL

Similar to M1 Field Shotgun, Picatinny receiver rail for scope mounting, nine-round magazine, 26-inch compensated barrel and ghost ring sights. Designed for IPSC competition.

Perf: $1055 **Exc:** $875 **VGood:** $750

BENELLI MONTEFELTRO SHOTGUN

Gauge: 12-, 20-ga., 2-3/4-inch and 3-inch chamber. Barrel: 24-inch, 26-inch, 28-inch with 5 choke tubes. Stock: Satin walnut. Sights: Red bar. Features: Lightweight, one-piece receiver.

12-, 20-ga.

Perf: $865 **Exc:** $725 **VGood:** $600

Left-hand 26-inch, 28-inch, 12 ga.

Perf: $855 **Exc:** $720 **VGood:** $600

20 ga. short stock

Perf: $860 **Exc:** $715 **VGood:** $615

BENELLI M2 FIELD WITH COMFORTECH

In 12 gauge, this model is offered with a 21", 24", 26" or 28" barrel with a black matte synthetic finish or Max-4, Timber or APG camo. The 20 gauge has a 24" or 26" barrel in black, Timber or APG. Average 12 gauge weight is 7 lbs.; average 20 gauge weight is 5.8 lbs. Add $120 for camo.

NIB: $995 **Exc:** $820 **VGood:** $695

BENELLI M2 FIELD WITHOUT COMFORTECH

Same features as above without ComforTech features. Available only in satin walnut with 26" or 28" barrel.

NIB: $900 **Exc:** $725 **VGood:** $600

BENELLI M3 CONVERTIBLE

Combination pump/auto action; 12-ga., 2-3/4-inch, 3-inch chambers; 5-shot magazine; 19-3/4-inch barrel (Cyl.); weighs 7 lbs., 4oz.; 41-inch overall; high-impact polymer stock with sling loop in side of butt; rubberized pistol grip on stock; open rifle sights, fully adjustable; ghost ring and rifle type; alloy receiver with inertia recoil rotating locking lug bolt; matte finish; automatic shell release lever. Introduced 1989. Imported from Italy.

With standard stock, open rifle sights

Perf: $955 **Exc:** $745 **VGood:** $630

With ghost ring sight system, standard stock

Perf: $1010 **Exc:** $795 **VGood:** $685

With ghost ring sights, pistol-grip stock

Perf: $1010 **Exc:** $805 **VGood:** $695

With folding stock

Perf: $2200 **Exc:** $1500 **VGood:** $1000

BENELLI M4

Proprietary ARGO system semi-auto; 12-ga., 2-3/4" and 3", 5+1 capacity. 18-1/2" barrel, pistol grip synthetic ComforTech stock or optional standard or folding stock. Ghost ring aperture rear sight and bead front sight with tritium inserts. Picatinny rail for optics mounting. Civilian version of military M1014. Introduced 2005 by Benelli USA.

New: $1529 **Perf:** $1100 **VGood:** $900

BENELLI NOVA PUMP

Gauge: 12-, 20-ga., 2-3/4-inch, 3-inch chamber (3-1/2-inch 12-ga. only) 24-inch, 26-inch, 28-inch barrel; synthetic stock, X-tra Brown 12 ga., Timber HD 20-ga.; red bar sights. Montefeltro rotating bolt design with dual action bars, magazine cut-off, synthetic trigger assembly, 4-shot magazine. Introduced 1999. Imported from Italy.

Black stock, 12-ga.

Perf: $295 **Exc:** $265 **VGood:** $235

X-tra Brown, 12-ga.

Perf: $360 **Exc:** $330 **VGood:** $300

Black stock, 20-ga.

Perf: $295 **Exc:** $265 **VGood:** $235

Timber HD, 20-ga.

Perf: $360 **Exc:** $330 **VGood:** $300

Add $15 to above prices for Youth Model with 13-inch length of pull

Add $55 for 2- or 4-shot magazine extension

Add $70 for 24-inch barrel with full Timber HD camo coverage (Turkey Model)

Add $42 for recoil reducer (10 oz.) or mercury (14 oz.) installed in stock

BENELLI NOVA PUMP SLUG GUN

Similar to the Nova except has 18.5-inch barrel with adjustable rifle-type or ghost ring sights; weighs 7.2 lbs.; black synthetic stock. Introduced 1999. Imported from Italy.

With rifle sights

With ghost-ring sight

Perf: $425 **Exc:** $385 **VGood:** $350

Add $75 to above prices for Advantage Timber HD camo

BENELLI NOVA PUMP RIFLED SLUG GUN

Similar to Nova Pump Slug Gun except has 24-inch barrel and rifled bore; open rifle sights; synthetic stock; weighs 8.1 pounds.

Perf: $425 **Exc:** $385 **VGood:** $350

BENELLI SUPER VINCI

In-line Inertia Driven 12-gauge semi-auto. Handles all loads from 2-3/4"/3-dram/1-1/8 oz. to 3-1/2 inch magnums. Barrel lengths, 26 or 28 inches with red bar front sight, metal bead middle sight, Crio Choke system with five choke tubes. Weight is 7 pounds (28" bbl.). Black synthetic or Realtree camo stock. Receiver drilled and tapped for scope.

Perf: $1500 **Exc:** $1350 **VGood:** $1125

BENELLI VINCI

Gas-operated semi-automatic 12-gauge. Similar design and features of Super Vinci except chambered to handle all 12-gauge ammo from light 2¾-inch loads to 3½-inch magnums. Modular assembly with synthetic contoured stocks. Black, Realtree MAX-4 or APG camo finish.

Perf: $1200 **Exc:** $1000 **VGood:** $800

BENELLI SUPERNOVA

Introduced in 2006, the Supernova incorporates Benelli's ComforTech stock system into the Nova pump shotgun. Available in 24-inch, 26-inch and 28-inch barrel lengths in matte black synthetic, 24-inch and 26-inch barrel lengths in Advantage Timber camo, and 26-inch and 28-inch barrel lengths in Max-4 camo. Weight is about 8 lbs. with 28-inch barrel. All versions are chambered for 3.5-inch shells. Three choke tubes. Add 15 percent for camo versions.

NIB: $395 **Exc:** $350 **VGood:** $295

BENELLI SUPERNOVA STEADYGRIP

As above but with extended pistol grip in 24-inch barrel only. Matte black synthetic or Advantage Timber stock. Add 15 percent for camo model.

NIB: $405 **Exc:** $360 **VGood:** $300

BENELLI SUPERNOVA TACTICAL

Matte black synthetic stock with 18-inch barrel. Available with ComforTech or pistol grip stock. Fixed cylinder bore. Open rifle sights. Ghost ring sights optional.

NIB: $400 **Exc:** $355 **VGood:** $295

Benelli Nova Pump Shotgun

Benelli Nova Turkey

Benelli Nova Pump Slug Gun

Benelli Nova Pump Rifled Slug Gun

Benelli Supernova

Benelli Super Vinci

Benelli Supernova Tactical

Benelli SL-121

Benelli SL-121 Slug

Benelli SL-123

BENELLI SL-121

Autoloader; 12-ga.; 2-3/4-inch chamber; 5-shot magazine; 26-inch, 28-inch barrel; plain or vent rib (SL-121V); 6-3/4 lbs.; metal bead front sight; hand-checkered European walnut pistol-grip stock; crossbolt safety; quick-interchangeable barrels; optional engraving; slug model available. Made in Italy. Introduced 1977; dropped 1985.

Perf: $385 **Exc:** $360 **VGood:** $325

Engraved model

Perf: $420 **Exc:** $375 **VGood:** $295

Slug model

Perf: $400 **Exc:** $360 **VGood:** $325

BENELLI SL-123

Autoloader; 12-ga; 2-3/4-inch chamber; 5-shot magazine; 26-inch, 28-inch barrels; plain or vent rib (SL-123V); weighs 6-3/4 lbs.; metal bead front sight; fancy hand-checkered European walnut pistol-grip stock; crossbolt safety; quick-interchangeable barrels; optional engraving; slug model available. Made in Italy. Introduced 1977; dropped 1985.

Perf: $420 **Exc:** $365 **VGood:** $350

Engraved model

Perf: $495 **Exc:** $395 **VGood:** $315

Slug model

Perf: $400 **Exc:** $365 **VGood:** $320

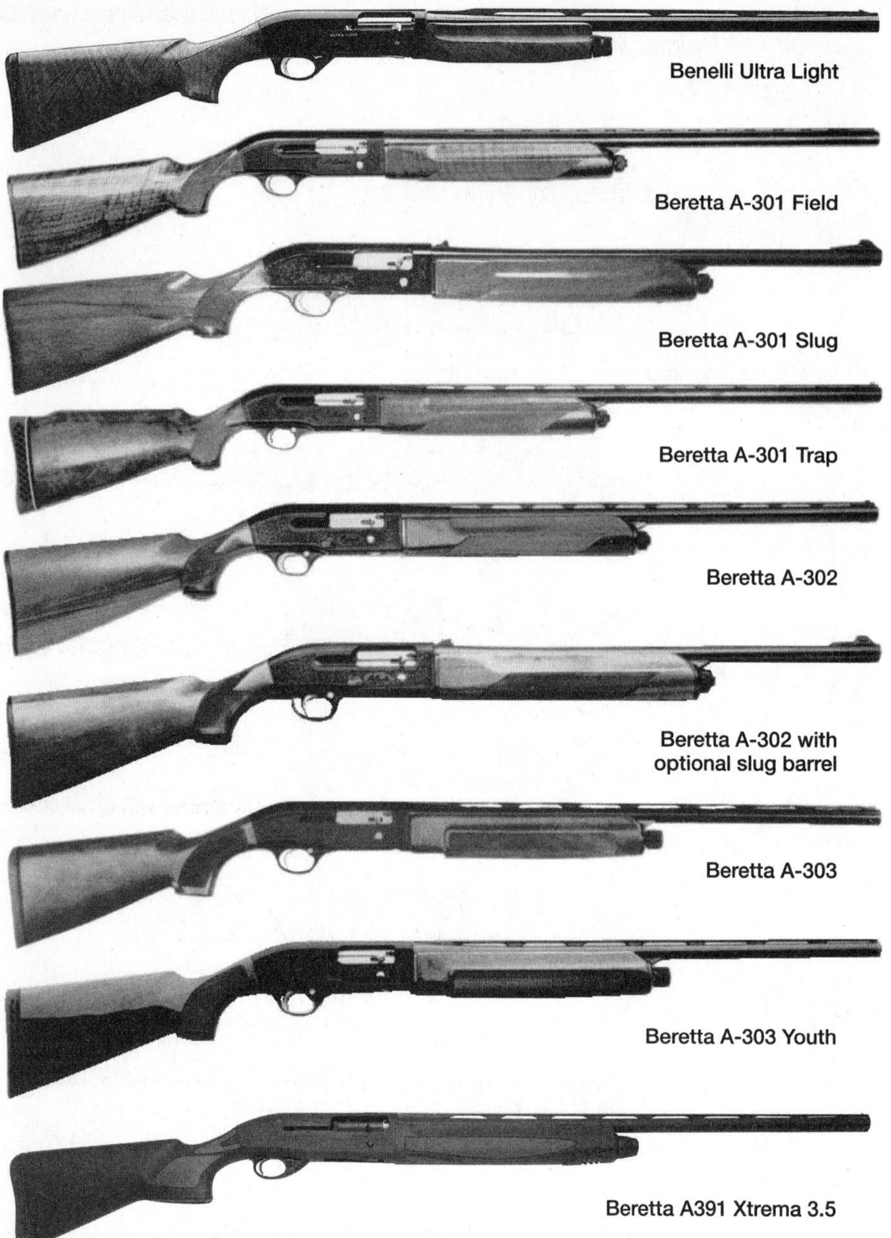
Benelli Ultra Light

Beretta A-301 Field

Beretta A-301 Slug

Beretta A-301 Trap

Beretta A-302

Beretta A-302 with optional slug barrel

Beretta A-303

Beretta A-303 Youth

Beretta A391 Xtrema 3.5

BENELLI SL-201

Autoloader; 20-ga.; 4-shot magazine; 26-inch barrel; vent rib; weighs 5-3/4 lbs.; hand-checkered walnut stock; crossbolt safety; quick-interchangeable barrels; similar to SL-121. No longer imported.

Perf: $350 **Exc:** $250 **VGood:** $200

BENELLI ULTRA LIGHT

Inertia-driven 12 gauge semi-auto features an alloy receiver, carbon fiber rib and small proportions to bring weight down to about 6 lbs. Walnut stock with Weathercoat finish. Chambered for 3-inch shells. Offered in 24-inch barrel only with 5 Crio chokes. Introduced 2006.

NIB: $1175 **Exc:** $1050 **VGood:** $900

BERETTA (DR. FRANCO) ARIETE STANDARD

Autoloader, gas-operated; 12 gauge; 2-3/4-inch, 3-inch chamber; various barrel lengths with or without choke tubes; aluminum receiver; checkered stock and forearm; weighs 6.9 lbs. Imported during 1993 only.

Perf: $995 **Exc:** $795 **VGood:** $525

BERETTA (DR. FRANCO) ARIETE

Slide-action; 12-ga.; 3-inch chamber; various barrel lengths without ventilated rib; twice action bars; matte finish; recoil pad. Imported during 1993 only.

Perf: $780 **Exc:** $695 **VGood:** $550

BERETTA AUTOLOADING SHOTGUNS

BERETTA A-301 FIELD

Gas-operated autoloader; 12- (2-3/4-inch), 20-ga. (3-inch); 3-shot magazine; 26-inch Improved, 28-inch Full, Modified barrels; vent rib; checkered European walnut pistol-grip stock, forend. Introduced 1977; discontinued 1982.

Perf: $395 **Exc:** $360 **VGood:** $330

BERETTA A-301 MAGNUM

Same specs as A-301 Field except 12-ga.; 3-inch chamber; 30-inch Full choke barrel; recoil pad. Introduced 1977; discontinued 1982.

Perf: $425 **Exc:** $385 **VGood:** $330

BERETTA A-301 SKEET

Same specs as A-301 Field except 26-inch Skeet barrel; checkered European walnut Skeet-style stock; gold-plated trigger. Introduced 1977; discontinued 1982.

Perf: $400 **Exc:** $360 **VGood:** $330

BERETTA A-301 SLUG

Same specs as A-301 Field except 22-inch barrel; Slug choke; no rib; rifle sights. Introduced 1977; discontinued 1982.

Perf: $395 **Exc:** $360 **VGood:** $330

BERETTA A-301 TRAP

Same specs as A-310 Field except 30-inch Full choke barrel; checkered European walnut Monte Carlo stock; recoil pad; gold-plated trigger. Introduced 1977; discontinued 1982.

Perf: $390 **Exc:** $350 **VGood:** $295

BERETTA A-302

Gas-operated autoloader; 12-, 20-ga.; 2-3/4-inch, 3-inch chamber; 3-shot magazine; 22-inch Slug, 26-inch Improved or Skeet, 28-inch Modified or Full, 30-inch (12-ga. only) Full or Full Trap barrel; optional Mobilchokes; cut-checkered European walnut pistol-grip stock, forend; scroll-engraved alloy receiver; push-button safety. Made in Italy. Introduced 1983; discontinued 1987. Optional, cylinder-bore slug barrel with sights.

Standard chokes

Perf: $400 **Exc:** $350 **VGood:** $340

Mobilchokes

Perf: $430 **Exc:** $380 **VGood:** $370

BERETTA A-303

Gas-operated autoloader; 12-, 20-ga.; 2-3/4-inch, 3-inch chamber; 3-shot magazine; 22-inch, 24-inch, 26-inch, 28-inch, 30-inch, 32-inch barrel; optional Mobilchokes; weighs 6 lbs. (20-ga.), 7 lbs. (12-ga.); hand-checkered American walnut stock; alloy receiver; magazine cut-off; push-button safety. Made in Italy. Introduced 1983; 20-ga. still imported.

Standard chokes

Perf: $600 **Exc:** $340 **VGood:** $300

Mobilchokes

Perf: $650 **Exc:** $390 **VGood:** $340

BERETTA A-303 MATTE FINISH

Same specs as A-303 except 3-inch chamber; 24-inch, 26-inch, 28-inch, 30-inch barrel; Mobilchoke tubes; non-reflective finish on all wood, metal surfaces; studs, sling swivels. Introduced 1991; discontinued 1992.

Perf: $650 **Exc:** $390 **VGood:** $340

BERETTA A-303 SPORTING CLAYS

Same specs as A-303 except 12-, 20-ga.; 2-3/4-inch chamber; 28-inch barrel; Mobilchoke tubes; wide competition-style vent rib; slightly different stock dimensions; special rubber buttpad. Made in Italy. Introduced 1989; still imported.

Perf: $670 **Exc:** $450 **VGood:** $380

BERETTA A-303 UPLAND MODEL

Same specs as A-303 except 12-, 20-ga.; 2-3/4-inch, 3-inch chamber; 24-inch vent rib barrel; Mobilchoke tubes; straight English-style stock. Made in Italy. Introduced 1989; still imported.

Perf: $600 **Exc:** $360 **VGood:** $330

BERETTA A-303 YOUTH

Same specs as A-303 except shorter length of pull; weighs 6 lbs. Introduced 1991; dropped 1996.

Perf: $500 **Exc:** $360 **VGood:** $300

BERETTA A391 XTREMA 3.5

Gauge: 12-ga. 3-1/2-inch chamber. Barrel: 24-inch, 26-inch, 28-inch. Weight: 7.8 lbs. Stock: Synthetic. Features: Semi-auto goes with two-lug rotating bolt and self-compensating gas valve, extended tang, cross bolt safety, self-cleaning, with case.

Synthetic; MSR

Perf: $950 **Exc:** $825 **VGood:** $750

Realtree Hardwood HD Camo

Perf: $1075 **Exc:** $900 **VGood:** $825

Add $135 to above prices for 24-inch barrel in Hardwoods Camo

BERETTA A391 XTREMA2

An upgraded version of the Xtrema with additional recoil-reducing features was introduced in 2005. Available with 24-inch, 26-inch or 28-inch barrels with black, Max-4 HD or Hardwoods HD synthetic stock. Optima-Bore five choke system. Optional Kick Off recoil reduction feature available. Add 10 percent for camo finish. Add 30 percent for Kick Off option.

Perf: $1215 **Exc:** $1100 **VGood:** $925
Add 20 percent for Kick-Off system

BERETTA A391 XTREMA2 SLUG GUN

24-inch rifled barrel version of Xtrema2. Black synthetic only. Add 10 percent for Kick Off option.

NIB: $1000 **Exc:** $900 **VGood:** $800

BERETTA A400 XPLOR LIGHT

Gas-operated 12-gauge designed for 2-3/4 and 3-inch loads. Blink operating system. Barrel is 26 or 28 inches with vent rib, Optima-Choke tubes. Oil-finished stock of walnut/polymer combination, adjustable for drop. Also available with Kick-Off recoil damper system.

Perf: $1400 **Exc:** $1250 **VGood:** $1050
Add 20 percent for Kick-Off system

BERETTA AL-2

Gas-operated autoloader; 12-, 20-ga.; 3-shot magazine; 2-3/4-inch, 3-inch chamber; 26-inch, 28-inch, 30-inch interchangeable barrel; Full, Modified, Improved Cylinder, Skeet chokes; vent rib; medium front bead sight; diamond-point hand-checkered European walnut pistol-grip stock, forend. Introduced 1969; discontinued 1975.

Standard grade
Perf: $330 **Exc:** $305 **VGood:** $275

Trap/Skeet model
Perf: $380 **Exc:** $320 **VGood:** $290

Magnum model
Perf: $415 **Exc:** $385 **VGood:** $330

BERETTA AL-3

Gas-operated autoloader; 12-, 20-ga.; 3-shot magazine; 2-3/4-inch, 3-inch chamber; 26-inch, 28-inch, 30-inch interchangeable barrel; Full, Modified, Improved Cylinder, Skeet chokes; vent rib; medium front bead sight; diamond-point hand-checkered select European walnut pistol-grip stock, forend; hand-engraved receiver. Introduced 1969; discontinued 1975.

Standard grade
Perf: $380 **Exc:** $350 **VGood:** $295

Trap/Skeet model
Perf: $390 **Exc:** $350 **VGood:** $295

Magnum model
Perf: $425 **Exc:** $385 **VGood:** $330

BERETTA GOLD LARK

Gas-operated autoloader; takedown; 12-ga.; 26-inch, 28-inch, 30-inch, 32-inch vent-rib barrels; Improved Cylinder, Modified, Full choke; hand-checkered European walnut pistol-grip stock, beavertail forearm; push-button safety in triggerguard; all parts hand polished; fine engraving. Introduced 1960; discontinued 1967.

Exc: $480 **VGood:** $400 **Good:** $325

BERETTA MODEL 390 FIELD GRADE

Gas-operated autoloader; 12-ga.; 3-inch chamber; 3-shot magazine; 22-inch, 24-inch, 26-inch, 28-inch, 30-inch barrel; Mobilchoke tubes; floating vent rib; weighs 7 lbs.; select walnut stock adjustable for drop and cast; self-compensating valve allows action to shoot all loads without adjustment; alloy receiver; reversible safety; chrome-plated bore. Made in Italy. Introduced 1992; still imported.

Perf: $680 **Exc:** $420 **VGood:** $360

BERETTA MODEL 390 FIELD GRADE GOLD MALLARD

Same specs as Model 390 Field Grade except highly select walnut stock; receiver with gold engraved animals. Introduced 1992; still imported.

Perf: $850 **Exc:** $575 **VGood:** $460

Beretta A391 Xtrema 2

Beretta AL-2

Beretta Model 390 Field Grade

Beretta Model 390 Competition Skeet Sport

Beretta Model 390 Competition Trap Sport

Beretta AL391 Urika

BERETTA MODEL 390 FIELD GRADE SILVER MALLARD

Same specs as Model 390 Field Grade except select walnut stock with gloss or matte finish; medium or thin rubber buttpad. Introduced 1992; dropped 1997.

Perf: $680 **Exc:** $520 **VGood:** $415

BERETTA MODEL 390 FIELD GRADE SILVER SLUG

Same specs as Model 390 Field Grade except 22-inch slug barrel; no rib; weighs 7 1/4 lbs.; grooved receiver for scope mount; blade front sight, adjustable rear; swivels. Introduced 1992; dropped 1997.

Perf: $680 **Exc:** $420 **VGood:** $360

BERETTA MODEL 390 COMPETITION SKEET SPORT

Gas-operated autoloader; 12-ga.; 3-inch chamber; 3-shot magazine; 26-inch, 28-inch Skeet-choke barrel; vent rib; select walnut Skeet-style stock, forearm; self-compensating valve allows action to shoot all loads without adjustment; reversible safety; chrome-plated bore; lower-contour, rounded alloy receiver; recoil pad; ported barrel available. Made in Italy. Introduced 1995; still imported.

Perf: $680 **Exc:** $420 **VGood:** $360

With ported barrel
Perf: $750 **Exc:** $520 **VGood:** $460

BERETTA MODEL 390 COMPETITION SKEET SPORT SUPER

Same specs as Model 390 Competition Skeet Sport except 28-inch Skeet-choke ported barrel; wide ventilated rib with orange front sight; select walnut Skeet-style stock; adjustable comb and length of pull. Made in Italy. Introduced 1993; still imported.

Perf: $900 **Exc:** $600 **VGood:** $500

BERETTA MODEL 390 COMPETITION SPORTING

Same specs as Model 390 Competition Skeet Sport except 28-inch, 30-inch vent-rib barrel; Full, Modified, Improved Cylinder, Skeet choke tubes; select walnut Monte Carlo stock. Made in Italy. Introduced 1995; still imported.

Perf: $650 **Exc:** $380 **VGood:** $300

With ported barrel
Perf: $680 **Exc:** $.410 **VGood:** $330

BERETTA MODEL 390 COMPETITION TRAP SPORT

Same specs as Model 390 Competition Skeet Sport except 30-inch, 32-inch step-tapered vent-rib barrel; Full, Improved Modified, Modified choke tubes; white front bead; select walnut trap-style stock. Made in Italy. Introduced 1995; still imported.

Perf: $680 **Exc:** $375 **VGood:** $340

With ported barrel
Perf: $750 **Exc:** $475 **VGood:** $440

BERETTA MODEL 390 COMPETITION TRAP SUPER

Same specs as 390 Competition Skeet Sport except 30-inch, 32-inch ported barrel; Mobilchoke tubes; wide ventilated rib with orange front sight; select walnut trap-style stock; adjustable comb and length of pull. Made in Italy. Introduced 1993; still imported.

Perf: $1000 **Exc:** $620 **VGood:** $580

BERETTA AL391 URIKA

Gauge: 12-, 20-gauge; 3" chamber. Barrel: 22", 24", 26", 28", 30"; five Mobilchoke choke tubes. Weight: 5.95 to 7.28 lbs. Length: Varies by model. Stock: Walnut, black or camo synthetic; shims, spacers and interchangeable recoil pads allow custom fit. Features: self-compensating gas operation handles full range of loads; recoil reducer in receiver; enlarged trigger guard; reduced-weight receiver, barrel and

Beretta AL391 Urika Trap

Beretta AL391 Urika Gold Sporting

Beretta AL391 Urika Parallel Target RL

Beretta AL391 Teknys

Beretta AL391 Teknys Gold

Beretta 3901 Target RL

Beretta Model 1200F

Beretta Model 1201FP3

forend; hard-chromed bore. Introduced 2000. Imported from Italy by Beretta USA.

Urika (12-ga., 26", 28", 30" barrels)

Perf: $835 **Exc:** $700 **VGood:** $600

Urika (20-ga., 24", 26", 28" barrels)

Perf: $835 **Exc:** $700 **VGood:** $600

Urika Synthetic (12-ga., 24", 26", 28", 30" barrels)

Perf: $835 **Exc:** $700 **VGood:** $600

Urika Camo. (12-ga., Realtree Hardwoods or Advantage Wetlands)

Perf: $925 **Exc:** $795 **VGood:** $675

BERETTA AL391 URIKA GOLD AND GOLD SPORTING AUTO SHOTGUNS

Similar to AL391 Urika except features deluxe wood, jeweled bolt and carrier, gold-inlaid receiver with black or silver finish. Introduced 2000. Imported from Italy.

Urika Gold (12- or 20-ga., black receiver)

Perf: $995 **Exc:** $700 **VGood:** $540

Urika Gold (silver, lightweight receiver)

Perf: $1035 **Exc:** $741 **VGood:** $581

Urika Gold Sporting (12 or 20, black receiver, engraving)

Perf: $995 **Exc:** $700 **VGood:** $540

Urika Gold Sporting (12-ga., silver receiver, engraving)

Perf: $1035 **Exc:** $741 **VGood:** $581

BERETTA AL391 URIKA SPORTING AUTO SHOTGUNS

Similar to AL391 Urika except has competition sporting stock with rounded rubber recoil pad, wide ventilated rib with white front and mid-rib beads, satin-black receiver with silver markings. Available in 12- and 20-gauge. Introduced 2000. Imported from Italy by Beretta USA.

Perf: $880 **Exc:** $650 **VGood:** $525

BERETTA AL391 URIKA TRAP AND GOLD TRAP AUTO SHOTGUNS

Similar to AL391 Urika except in 12-ga. only, has wide ventilated rib with white front and mid-rib beads, Monte Carlo stock and special trap recoil pad. Gold Trap features highly figured walnut stock and forend, gold-filled Beretta logo and signature on receiver. Introduced 2000. Imported from Italy.

Urika Trap

Perf: $995 **Exc:** $700 **VGood:** $540

Urika Gold Trap

Perf: $995 **Exc:** $700 **VGood:** $540

BERETTA AL391 URIKA PARALLEL TARGET RL AND SL AUTO SHOTGUNS

Similar to AL391 Urika except has parallel-comb, Monte Carlo stock with tighter grip radius to reduce trigger reach and stepped ventilated rib. SL model has same features but with 13.5-inch length of pull stock. Introduced 2000. Imported from Italy by Beretta USA.

Urika Parallel Target RL; $1027

Perf: $880 **Exc:** $650 **VGood:** $525

Urika Parallel Target SL

Perf: $880 **Exc:** $650 **VGood:** $525

BERETTA AL391 URIKA YOUTH SHOTGUN

Similar to AL391 except has a 24-inch or 26-inch barrel with 13.5-inch stock for youth and smaller shooters. Introduced 2000. From Beretta USA.

Perf: $835 **Exc:** $700 **VGood:** $600

BERETTA AL391 TEKNYS

This model features a nickel receiver with polished sides and anti-glare top. Offered in 12 or 20 gauge with 26" or 28" vent rib barrel. X-wood stock with Gel-Tek recoil. Weight is about 7.2 lbs. for 12 gauge and 5.9 lbs. for the 20 gauge. Introduced in 2003.

Perf: $935 **Exc:** $800 **VGood:** $675

BERETTA AL391 TEKNYS GOLD

As above, but with engraved hunting scene on the receiver, gold plated trigger, jeweled breech bolt and carrier. Select walnut checkered stock with oil finish. Introduced in 2003.

Perf: $1035 **Exc:** $900 **VGood:** $775

BERETTA AL391 TEKNYS GOLD TARGET

Similar to AL391 Teknys Gold but with adjustable comb, 8.5 oz. recoil reducer and additional stepped rib for trap shooting. 30-inch barrel.

NIB: $1700 **Exc:** $1595 **VGood:** $11

BERETTA 3901 TARGET RL

Gas-operated semi-auto chambered in 3-inch 12-gauge. Specifically designed for smaller-stature shooters with adjustable length of pull from 12 to 13 inches. Stock is adjustable for cast on or cast off. Adjustable comb and Sporting style flat rib. Available in 12 gauge only with 26-inch or 28-inch barrel.

NIB: $800 **Exc:** $750 **VGood:** $625

BERETTA MODEL 1200F

Recoil-operated autoloader; 12-ga.; 2-3/4-inch chamber; 4-shot magazine; 26-inch, 28-inch vent-rib barrel; Mobilchokes; weighs 7-1/8 lbs.; checkered European walnut or matte-black finished polymer stock, forend; recoil pad. Left-handed model available. Made in Italy. Introduced 1984; discontinued 1990.

Perf: $500 **Exc:** $415 **VGood:** $350

BERETTA MODEL 1200FP

Same specs as Model 1200F except 6-shot magazine; 20-inch Cylinder barrel; no vent rib; adjustable rifle-type sights; designed for law enforcement. Made in Italy. Introduced 1988; discontinued 1990.

Perf: $725 **Exc:** $595 **VGood:** $500

BERETTA MODEL 1201F

Recoil-operated autoloader; 12-ga.; 3-inch chamber; 4-shot magazine; 24-inch, 26-inch, 28-inch vent-rib barrel; Mobilchokes; weighs 7-1/4 lbs.; matte-black finished polymer stock, forend; adjustable butt, recoil pad. Made in Italy. Introduced 1988; discontinued 1994.

Perf: $725 **Exc:** $595 **VGood:** $500

BERETTA MODEL 1201FP

Same specs as Model 1201F except 6-shot magazine; 20-inch Cylinder barrel; no vent rib; adjustable rifle-type sights; designed for law enforcement. Made in Italy. Introduced 1991; still imported.

Perf: $725 **Exc:** $595 **VGood:** $500

BERETTA MODEL 1201FP3

Same specs as Model 1201F except 20-inch Cylinder barrel; fixed rifle type sight; 6-shot magazine. Introduced 1988; still in production.

Perf: $475 **Exc:** $300 **VGood:** $225

BERETTA MODEL 1201FP GHOST RING AUTO SHOTGUN

Gauge: 12, 3-inch chamber; 18-inch barel (Cyl.); weighs 6.3 lbs.; special strengthened technopolymer stock; matte black finish; 5-shot magazine. Adjustable Ghost Ring rear sight, tritium front. Introduced 1988. Imported from Italy.

Perf: $695 **Exc:** $515 **VGood:** $385

BERETTA PINTAIL

Recoil-operated autoloader; 12-ga.; 3-inch chamber; 24-inch rifled Slug choke, 24-inch, 26-inch Mobilchoke barrels; weighs 7 lbs.; metal bead front sight; select checkered hardwood stock, forend with matte finish; recoil pad; crossbolt safety; matte-black receiver. Slug version has rifle sights, sling swivels. Imported from Italy. Introduced 1993; dropped 2001; reintroduced 2003.

Perf: $575 **Exc:** $475 **VGood:** $425

BERETTA RUBY LARK

Gas-operated autoloader; takedown; 12-ga.; 26-inch, 28-inch, 30-inch, 32-inch vent-rib stainless barrels; Improved Cylinder, Modified, Full choke; hand-checkered European walnut pistol-grip stock, beavertail forearm; push-button safety in triggerguard; all parts hand-polished; extensive engraving. Introduced 1960; discontinued 1967.

Exc: $675 **VGood:** $550 **Good:** $475

BERETTA SILVER LARK

Gas-operated autoloader; takedown; 12-ga.; 26-inch, 28-inch, 30-inch, 32-inch barrels; Improved Cylinder, Modified, Full choke; hand-checkered European walnut pistol-grip stock, beavertail forearm; push-button safety in trigger guard; all parts hand polished. Introduced 1960; discontinued 1967.

Exc: $295 **VGood:** $260 **Good:** $240

BERETTA TX4 STORM

Gas-operated semiauto in 12 gauge only. Three-inch chamber, 18-inch barrel, overall length of 39.2 inches, and weight is 6.4 pounds. Synthetic stock with black rubber overlays is adjustable for length of pull. Capacity is 5+1. Receiver is mounted with Picatinny rail.

Perf: $1275 **Exc:** $1075 **VGood:** $925

BERETTA AL391 URIKA 2

Introduced in 2007, the Urika 2 is an enhanced version of the original AL391 Urika semi-auto. Improvements include the addition of a spinning, self-cleaning action for faster cycling and longer functioning periods between cleanings.

NIB: $975 **Exc:** $895 **VGood:** $775

BERETTA AL391 URIKA 2 X-TRA GRAIN

This series features Beretta's wood-enhancement treatment to highlight the color contrast of the wood. Offered in 3" 12 and 20 gauge with 26" and 28" barrels. A 20 gauge youth model with shorter stock and 24" barrel is also offered.

NIB: $1125 **Exc:** $1075 **VGood:** $895

BERETTA AL391 URIKA 2 GOLD

Select oil-finished wood stock and forend with gold-filled game bird inlays on the receiver. The 12 gauge has a 28" barrel and the 20 gauge has a 26" barrel.

NIB: $1225 **Exc:** $1175 **VGood:** $995

BERETTA AL391 URIKA 2 KICK-OFF

These waterfowl models feature Beretta's Kick-Off recoil reduction system. Matte black synthetic, Max-4 or Realtree AP finish with 26" or 28" barrel. Deduct 30 percent for models without Kick-Off. Add 10 percent for camo finish.

NIB: $1125 **Exc:** $1075 **VGood:** $895

Beretta Silver Lark

Beretta AL391 Urika 2 X-tra Grain

Beretta AL391 Urika 2 Gold

Beretta ASE 90 Gold Trap

Beretta BL-1

Beretta BL-2/S

BERETTA AL391 URIKA 2 GOLD SPORTING

Enhanced wood with gold inlays and floral motif engraving on receiver in 12 gauge with 28" or 30" barrel.

NIB: $1375 **Exc:** $1200 **VGood:** $900

BERETTA AL391 URIKA 2 PARALLEL TARGET X-TRA GRAIN

Target model in 12 gauge with 28", 30" or 32" barrel.

NIB: $1150 **Exc:** $1100 **VGood:** $925

BERETTA AL391 URIKA 2 GOLD PARALLEL TARGET

Enhanced wood with gold inlays and floral motif engraving on receiver in 12 gauge with 30" or 32" barrel.

NIB: $1225 **Exc:** $1175 **VGood:** $1050

BERETTA OVER/UNDER SHOTGUNS

BERETTA ASE 90 PIGEON

Over/Under; 12-ga.; 2-3/4-inch chambers; 3-shot magazine; 28-inch Improved Modified/Full barrels; vent rib; weighs about 8 lbs.; high-grade checkered walnut stock, forend; drop-out trigger assembly; recoil pad; silver-finished or blued receiver; gold etching; hard-chrome bores; comes with hard case. Made in Italy. Introduced 1992; discontinued 1994.

Perf: $7100 **Exc:** $5000 **VGood:** $4000

BERETTA ASE 90 GOLD SKEET

Same specs as ASE 90 Gold Pigeon except 28-inch Skeet/Skeet barrels; high-grade checkered walnut Skeet-style stock, forend. Made in Italy. Introduced 1992; still imported.

Perf: $7500 **Exc:** $5000 **VGood:** $4000

BERETTA ASE 90 GOLD SPORTING CLAYS

Same specs as ASE 90 Gold Pigeon except 28-inch, 30-inch vent-rib barrel; Mobilchoke tubes; high-grade checkered walnut Monte Carlo stock, forend. Introduced 1992; still imported.

Perf: $7550 **Exc:** $5000 **VGood:** $4000

BERETTA ASE 90 GOLD TRAP

Same specs as ASE 90 Gold Pigeon except 30-inch vent-rib barrel; fixed chokes or Mobilchokes; high-grade checkered walnut trap-style stock, forend; extra trigger group. Introduced 1992; still imported.

Perf: $7550 **Exc:** $5000 **VGood:** $4000

BERETTA ASE 90 GOLD TRAP COMBO

Same specs as ASE 90 Gold Pigeon except two-barrel set with 30-inch vent-rib over/under and 32-inch or 34-inch single over barrel; fixed chokes or Mobilchokes; high-grade checkered walnut trap-style stock, forend; extra trigger group. Introduced 1992; still imported.

Perf: $9500 **Exc:** $7000 **VGood:** $5000

BERETTA ASEL

Over/under; boxlock; 12-, 20-ga.; 26-inch, 28-inch, 30-inch barrels; Improved/Modified, Modified/Full chokes; hand-checkered pistol-grip stock, forend; single nonselective trigger; selective automatic ejectors. Introduced 1947; discontinued 1964.

12-ga.

Exc: $2750 **VGood:** $2375 **Good:** $1975

20-ga.

Exc: $4650 **VGood:** $3950 **Good:** $3500

BERETTA BL-1

Over/under; boxlock; 12-ga.; 2-3/4-inch chambers; 26-inch, 28-inch, 30-inch chrome-moly steel barrels; Improved/Modified, Modified/Full chokes; ramp front sight with fluorescent inserts; hand-checkered European walnut pistol-grip stock, forearm; double triggers; extractors; automatic safety; Monoblock design. Introduced 1969; discontinued 1972.

Exc: $395 **VGood:** $350 **Good:** $285

BERETTA BL-2

Over/under; boxlock; 12-ga.; 2-3/4-inch chambers; 26-inch, 28-inch, 30-inch chrome-moly steel barrels; Improved/Modified, Modified/Full chokes; ramp

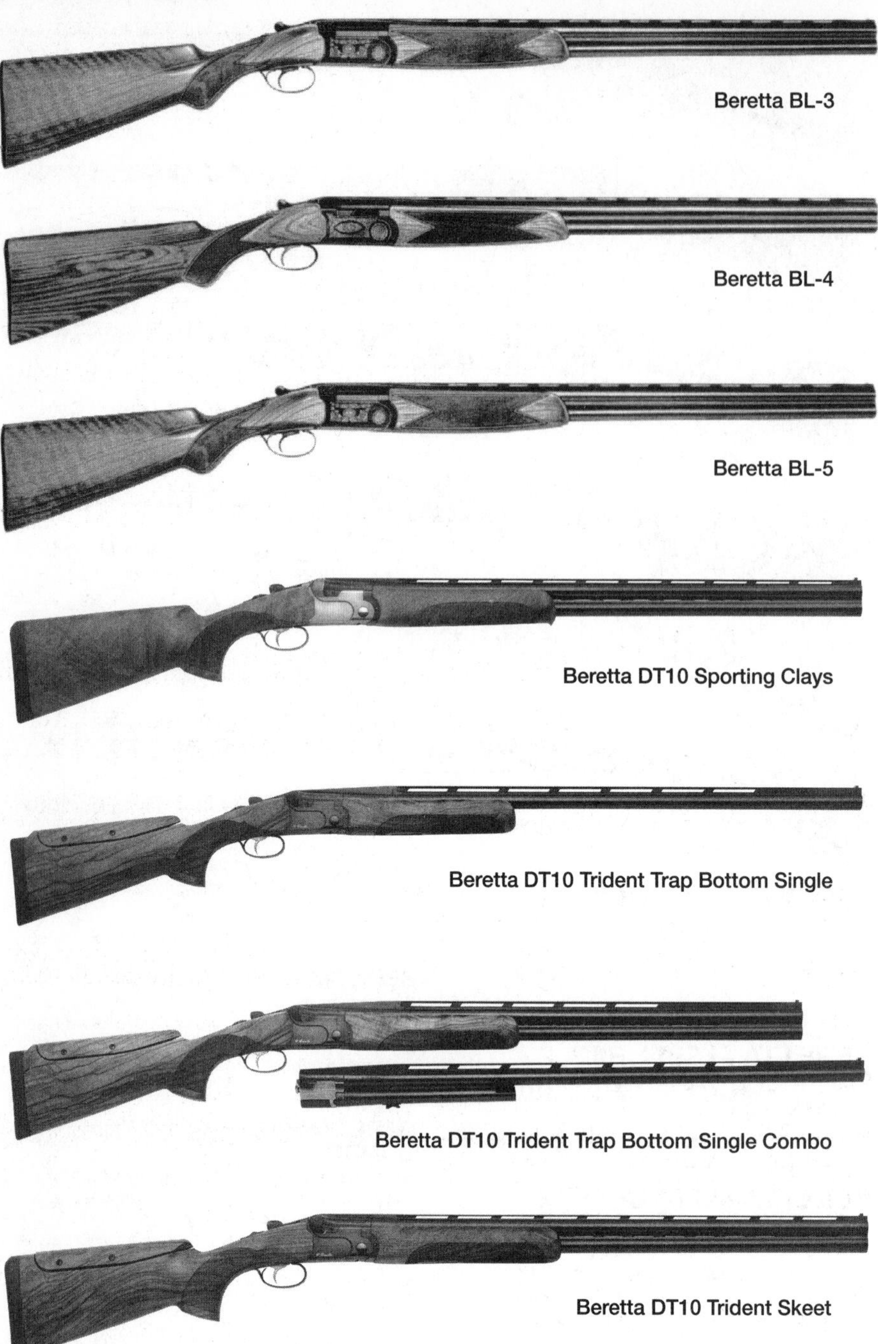

Beretta BL-3

Beretta BL-4

Beretta BL-5

Beretta DT10 Sporting Clays

Beretta DT10 Trident Trap Bottom Single

Beretta DT10 Trident Trap Bottom Single Combo

Beretta DT10 Trident Skeet

front sight with fluorescent inserts; hand-checkered European walnut pistol-grip stock, forearm; single selective triggers; extractors; automatic safety; Monoblock design; engraving. Introduced 1969; discontinued 1972.

Exc: $450 **VGood:** $395 **Good:** $350

BERETTA BL-2/S

Same specs as BL-2 except 2-3/4-inch, 3-inch chambers; vent rib. Introduced 1974; discontinued 1976.

Perf: $475 **Exc:** $425 **VGood:** $365

BERETTA BL-3

Over/under; boxlock; 12-, 20-ga; 2-3/4-inch, 3-inch chambers; 26-inch, 28-inch, 30-inch chrome-moly steel barrels; vent rib; Improved/Modified, Modified/Full chokes; ramp front sight with fluorescent inserts; hand-checkered European walnut pistol-grip stock, forearm; single selective triggers; ejectors; automatic safety; Monoblock design; engraved receiver. Introduced 1968; discontinued 1976.

Perf: $600 **Exc:** $550 **VGood:** $525

Add 50 percent to above prices for 20 gauge in at least 90 percent condition.

BERETTA BL-4

Over/under; boxlock; 12-, 20-, 28-ga; 2-3/4-inch, 3-inch chambers; 26-inch, 28-inch, 30-inch chrome-moly steel barrels; vent rib; Improved/Modified, Modified/Full chokes; ramp front sight with fluorescent inserts; hand-checkered select European walnut pistol-grip stock, forearm; single selective triggers; ejectors; automatic safety; Monoblock design; heavily engraved receiver. Introduced 1968; discontinued 1976.

Perf: $900 **Exc:** $800 **VGood:** $725

Add 20 percent to above price for 20 gauge

Add 50 percent for 28 gauge

BERETTA BL-5

Over/under; boxlock; 12-, 20-ga; 2-3/4-inch, 3-inch chambers; 26-inch, 28-inch, 30-inch chrome-moly steel barrels; vent rib; Improved/Modified, Modified/Full chokes; ramp front sight with fluorescent inserts; hand-checkered fancy European walnut pistol-grip stock, forearm; single selective triggers; ejectors; automatic safety; Monoblock design; heavily engraved receiver. Introduced 1968; discontinued 1976.

Perf: $1050 **Exc:** $900 **VGood:** $825

BERETTA BL-6

Over/under; boxlock; 12-, 20-ga; 2-3/4-inch, 3-inch chambers; 26-inch, 28-inch, 30-inch chrome-moly steel barrels; vent rib; Improved/Modified, Modified/Full chokes; ramp front sight with fluorescent inserts; best-grade hand-checkered fancy European walnut pistol-grip stock, forearm; single selective triggers; ejectors; automatic safety; Monoblock design; false sideplates; extensive engraving. Introduced 1973; discontinued 1976.

Perf: $1400 **Exc:** $1100 **VGood:** $1000

Add 20 percent to above prices for 20 gauge.

BERETTA DT10 TRIDENT

Gauge: 12, 2-3/4-inch, 3-inch chambers; 28-inch, 30-inch, 32-inch, 34-inch barrel; competition-style vent rib; fixed or Optima Choke tubes; weighs 7.9 to 9 lbs.; High-grade walnut stock with oil finish; hand-checkered grip and forend, adjustable stocks available; detachable, adjustable trigger group; raised and thickened receiver; forend iron has replaceable nut to guarantee wood-to-metal fit; Optima Bore to improve shot pattern and reduce felt recoil. Introduced 2000. Imported from Italy.

Trident Trap (selective, lockable single trigger, adjustable stock)

Perf: $6850 **Exc:** $5650 **VGood:** $4950

Trident Trap Combo (single and O/U barrels)

Perf: $9250 **Exc:** $7750 **VGood:** $6500

Trident Trap Bottom Single Combo (adj. point of impact rib on single bbl.)

Perf: $9500 **Exc:** $7875 **VGood:** $6600

Trident Skeet (skeet stock with rounded recoil pad, tapered rib)

Perf: $7200 **Exc:** $6500 **VGood:** $5200

Trident Sporting (sporting clays stock with rounded recoil pad)

Perf: $6850 **Exc:** $5650 **VGood:** $4950

BERETTA GOLDEN SNIPE

Over/under; boxlock; 12-, 20-ga.; 2-3/4-inch, 3-inch chambers; 26-inch, 28-inch, 30-inch barrels; Improved/Modified, Modified/Full, Full/Full chokes; vent rib; hand-checkered European walnut pistol-grip stock, forearm; non-selective, selective trigger; auto ejectors; nickel steel receiver. Introduced 1955; discontinued 1975.

Nonselective trigger

Exc: $995 **VGood:** $875 **Good:** $775

Selective trigger

Exc: $995 **VGood:** $875 **Good:** $775

BERETTA GOLDEN SNIPE DELUXE

Same specs as Golden Snipe except finer engraving; better walnut. Available in Skeet, Trap models. Introduced 1955; discontinued 1975.

Exc: $1140 **VGood:** $1000 **Good:** $890

BERETTA GRADE 100

Over/under; sidelock; 12-ga.; 26-inch, 28-inch, 30-inch barrel; any standard choke combination; hand-checkered straight or pistol-grip European walnut stock, forend; double triggers; automatic ejectors. Introduced post-World War II; discontinued 1960s.

Exc: $1500 **VGood:** $1000 **Good:** $775

BERETTA GRADE 200

Over/under; sidelock; 12-ga.; 26-inch, 28-inch, 30-inch barrel; any standard choke combination; hand-checkered select European walnut straight or pistol-grip stock, forend; double triggers; automatic ejectors; chrome-plated bores, action; engraving. Introduced post-World War II; discontinued 1960s.

Exc: $1750 **VGood:** $1400 **Good:** $1000

BERETTA MODEL 57E

Over/under; boxlock; 12-, 20-ga.; 2-3/4-inch, 3-inch chambers; 26-inch, 28-inch, 30-inch vent-rib barrel; hand-checkered European walnut pistol-grip stock, beavertail forend; automatic ejectors; single non-selective trigger; optional single selective trigger; similar to Golden Snipe model but overall quality is higher. Introduced 1955; discontinued 1967.

Exc: $825 **VGood:** $770 **Good:** $660

Single selective trigger

Exc: $850 **VGood:** $800 **Good:** $690

BERETTA SERIES 682 GOLD E SKEET, TRAP, SPORTING OVER/UNDERS

Gauge: 12, 2-3/4-inch chambers; Skeet-28-inch barrel, trap-30-inch and 32-inch; Imp., Mod. & Full and Mobilchoke; trap mono shotguns-32-inch and 34-inch Mobilchoke; trap top single guns-32-inch and 34-inch full and Mobilchoke; trap combo sets from 30-inch barrel O/U, to 32-inch O/U, 34-inch top single; close-grained walnut, hand checkered; white Bradley bead front sight and center bead; Greystone gunmetal gray finish receiver with gold accents. Trap Monte Carlo stock has deluxe trap recoil pad. Various grades available. Imported from Italy.

S682 Gold E Skeet, adjustable stock

Perf: $2575 **Exc:** $2250 **VGood:** $2125

S682 Gold E Trap Top Combo

Perf: $2950 **Exc:** $2350 **VGood:** $1900

S682 Gold E Trap with adjustable stock

Perf: $2700 **Exc:** $2200 **VGood:** $1800

S692 Gold E Sporting

Perf: $2950 **Exc:** $2400 **VGood:** $1975

S687 EELL Diamond Pigeon Skeet; discontinued 2002

Perf: $4155 **Exc:** $3075 **VGood:** $2550

S687 EELL Diamond Pigeon Skeet, adjustable stock

Perf: $5295 **Exc:** $4675 **VGood:** $4125

S687 EELL Diamond Pigeon Sporting

Perf: $3850 **Exc:** $3175 **VGood:** $2475

BERETTA MODEL 682 COMPETITION GOLD SKEET

Over/under; low-profile, improved boxlock; 12-, 20-, 28-ga., .410; 26-inch, 28-inch Skeet/Skeet barrels; weighs 7-1/2 lbs.; white bead front sight; highly select hand-checkered European walnut Skeet-type stock, beavertail forearm with matte finish; manual safety; single selective trigger with adjustable length of pull; recoil pad; gray-finished receiver. Introduced 1991; still in production.

Perf: $2200 **Exc:** $1350 **VGood:** $1000

Four-barrel set in all four gauges

Perf: $4895 **Exc:** $3000 **VGood:** $2700

Beretta S682 Gold E Skeet

Beretta S682 Gold E Trap Combo

Beretta S682 Gold E Trap

Beretta S692 Gold E Sporting

Beretta S687 EELL Diamond Pigeon Skeet

Beretta S687 EELL Diamond Pigeon Skeet w/adjustable stock

Beretta S687 EELL Diamond Pigeon Sporting

Beretta Model 682 Competition Gold Skeet

Beretta Model 682 Competition Gold Trap Super

BERETTA MODEL 682 COMPETITION GOLD SKEET SUPER

Same specs as Model 682 Competition Gold Skeet except adjustable comb and buttpads; ported barrel. Introduced 1991; still imported.

Perf: $2650 **Exc:** $1720 **VGood:** $1500

BERETTA MODEL 682 COMPETITION GOLD SPORTING

Same specs as Model 682 Competition Gold Skeet except 12-ga.; 2-3/4-inch chamber; 28-inch, 30-inch barrels; Mobilchokes; 1/2-inch wide ventilated rib; weighs 7-3/8 lbs.; highly select hand-checkered European walnut Sporting stock, schnabel forend with matte finish. Made in Italy. Still imported.

Perf: $2750 **Exc:** $2500 **VGood:** $2300

BERETTA MODEL 682 COMPETITION GOLD SPORTING PORTED

Same specs as Model 682 Competition Gold Skeet except 12-ga.; 2-3/4-inch chamber; 28-inch, 30-inch ported barrels; Mobilchokes; 1/2-inch wide ventilated rib; weighs 7-3/8 lbs.; highly select hand-checkered European walnut Sporting stock, schnabel forend with matte finish. Made in Italy. Still imported.

Perf: $2300 **Exc:** $1350 **VGood:** $1000

BERETTA MODEL 682 COMPETITION GOLD SPORTING SUPER

Same specs as Model 682 Competition Gold Skeet except 12-ga.; 2-3/4-inch chamber; 28-inch, 30-inch ported barrels; Mobilchokes; 1/2-inch wide ventilated tapered rib; weighs 7-3/8 lbs.; adjustable highly select hand-checkered European walnut Sporting stock, schnabel forend with matte finish. Made in Italy. Still imported.

Perf: $2600 **Exc:** $1750 **VGood:** $1000

BERETTA MODEL 682 COMPETITION GOLD TRAP SUPER

Same specs as Model 682 Competition Gold Skeet except 12-ga.; 2-3/4-inch chamber; 30-inch, 32-inch barrel; Mobilchokes; stepped, tapered rib; highly select hand-checkered European walnut Monte Carlo stock. Made in Italy. Introduced 1987; still imported.

Perf: $2500 **Exc:** $1700 **VGood:** $1200

Combo with extra single 32-inch, 34-inch over barrel

Perf: $3000 **Exc:** $2100 **VGood:** $1500

BERETTA MODEL 682 COMPETITION GOLD TRAP LIVE BIRD

Same specs as Model 682 Competition Gold Skeet except 12-ga.; 2-3/4-inch chamber; 30-inch barrel; Mobilchokes; Strada or flat tapered rib; highly select hand-checkered European walnut trap-style stock, beavertail forend with matte finish. Still in production.

Perf: $2200 **Exc:** $1500 **VGood:** $1000

BERETTA MODEL 682 COMPETITION GOLD TRAP MONO

Same specs as Model 682 Competition Gold Skeet except 12-ga.; 2-3/4-inch chambers; single 32-inch,

Beretta Model 685

Beretta Model 686 Competition Sporting Onyx

Beretta Model 686 Competetion Sporting Silver Perdiz

Beretta Silver Pigeon

Beretta Model 686 Field EL Gold Perdiz

Beretta Model 686 Field Essential

34-inch over barrel; Multichokes; vent rib; highly select hand-checkered European walnut Monte Carlo stock. Made in Italy. Introduced 1987; still imported.

Perf: $2300 **Exc:** $1500 **VGood:** $1000

BERETTA MODEL 682 COMPETITION GOLD TRAP MONO SUPER

Same specs as Model 682 Competition Skeet except 12-ga.; 2-3/4-inch chambers; single 32-inch, 34-inch over barrel; fixed or Mobilchokes; vent rib; highly select hand-checkered European walnut Monte Carlo stock. Made in Italy. Introduced 1991; still imported.

Perf: $2500 **Exc:** $1650 **VGood:** $1000

BERETTA MODEL 682 COMPETITION GOLD TRAP SUPER

Same specs as Model 682 Competition Gold Skeet except 12-ga.; 2-3/4-inch chamber; 30-inch, 32-inch ported barrels; Mobilchokes; stepped, tapered rib; adjustable highly select hand-checkered European walnut Monte Carlo stock with matte finish; silver sideplates with hand engraved game scenes. Introduced 1991; still imported.

Perf: $2500 **Exc:** $1650 **VGood:** $1000

Combo with extra single 32-inch, 34-inch over barrel

Perf: $3000 **Exc:** $2000 **VGood:** $1400

BERETTA MODEL 682 COMPETITION SPORTING CONTINENTAL COURSE

Same specs as Model 682 Competition Gold Skeet except 12-ga.; 2-3/4-inch chambers; 28-inch, 30-inch Mobilchoke barrel; reverse tapered rib; Highly select hand-checkered European walnut stock, schnabel forend with matte finish; palm swell; black receiver; made for English Sporting Clays competition. Introduced 1994; still in production.

Perf: $2400 **Exc:** $1500 **VGood:** $1000

BERETTA MODEL 685

Over/under; boxlock; 12-, 20-ga.; 2-3/4-inch or 3-inch chambers; 26-inch, 28-inch, 30-inch barrels; standard chokes; hand-checkered walnut stock; steel receiver; single trigger; extractors; light engraving. Discontinued 1986.

Perf: $620 **Exc:** $490 **VGood:** $400

BERETTA MODEL 686 COMPETITION SKEET SILVER PERDIZ

Over/under; low-profile, improved boxlock; 12-ga.; 2-3/4-inch chambers; 28-inch Skeet/Skeet barrels; tapered rib; weighs 7-5/8 lbs.; white front bead sight; select checkered walnut stock, beavertail forend with matte finish; manual safety; single trigger; recoil pad; silver receiver with scroll engraving. Made in Italy. Introduced 1994; still imported.

Perf: $1150 **Exc:** $890 **VGood:** $690

BERETTA MODEL 686 COMPETITION SPORTING COLLECTION SPORT

Same specs as Model 686 Competition Skeet Silver Perdiz except 12-ga.; 3-inch chambers; 28-inch Strada-rib barrel; Mobilchokes; select checkered multi-colored walnut stock, beavertail forend with matte finish; single selective trigger; multi-colored receiver. Made in Italy. Introduced 1996; still imported.

Perf: $1200 **Exc:** $850 **VGood:** $700

BERETTA MODEL 686 COMPETITION SPORTING ONYX

Same specs as Model 686 Competition Skeet Silver Perdiz except 12-ga.; 3-inch chambers; 28-inch, 30-inch Strada-rib barrels; Mobilchokes; single selective trigger; semi-matte black receiver with gold lettering. Made in Italy. Introduced 1994; still imported.

Perf: $1150 **Exc:** $950 **VGood:** $850

BERETTA MODEL 686 COMPETITION SPORTING ONYX ENGLISH COURSE

Same specs as Model 686 Competition Skeet Silver Perdiz except 12-ga.; 3-inch chamber; 28-inch vent-rib barrels; Mobilchokes; semi-matte black receiver; designed for English Sporting Clays competition. Made in Italy. Introduced 1991; discontinued 1992.

Perf: $1700 **Exc:** $1100 **VGood:** $950

BERETTA MODEL 686 COMPETITION SPORTING SILVER PERDIZ

Same specs as Model 686 Competition Skeet Silver Perdiz except 12-, 20-ga.; 3-inch chamber; 28-inch, 30-inch barrels; Mobilchokes; Strada rib (12-ga.), flat rib (20-ga.); weighs 7-3/4 lbs.; checkered select walnut stock, semi-beavertail forend with matte finish. Made in Italy. Introduced 1994; discontinued 1996.

Perf: $1200 **Exc:** $775 **VGood:** $500

Combo with two-barrel set

Perf: $1800 **Exc:** $1300 **VGood:** $1100

BERETTA MODEL 686 COMPETITION SPORTING SILVER PIGEON

Same specs as Model 686 Competition Skeet Silver Perdiz except 12-, 20-ga.; 3-inch chamber; 28-inch, 30-inch barrels; Mobilchokes; Strada rib (12-ga.), flat rib (20-ga.); weighs 7-3/4 lbs.; checkered select walnut stock, schnabel forend with matte finish; single selective trigger. Made in Italy. Introduced 1996; still imported.

Perf: $1250 **Exc:** $900 **VGood:** $600

BERETTA MODEL 686 COMPETITION TRAP INTERNATIONAL

Same specs as Model 686 Competition Skeet Silver Perdiz except 30-inch Improved Modified/Full barrels; vent rib; select checkered walnut trap-style stock, forearm. Made in Italy. Introduced, 1994; discontinued 1995.

Perf: $1000 **Exc:** $600 **VGood:** $525

BERETTA MODEL 686 FIELD EL GOLD PERDIZ

Over/under; low-profile, improved boxlock; 12-, 20-ga.; 3-inch chamber; 26-inch, 28-inch vent-rib barrels; Mobilchokes; weighs 6-7/8 lbs.; highly select checkered walnut stock, beavertail forend with gloss finish; auto safety; single selective trigger; rubber recoil pad; silver receiver with full sideplates and floral scroll engraving. Made in Italy. Introduced 1994; still imported.

Perf: $1800 **Exc:** $1120 **VGood:** $910

BERETTA MODEL 686 FIELD ESSENTIAL

Same specs as Model 686 Field EL Gold Perdiz except 12-ga.; 3-inch chamber; weighs 6-3/4 lbs.; matte black plain receiver. Made in Italy. Introduced 1994; still imported.

Perf: $910 **Exc:** $590 **VGood:** $510

BERETTA MODEL 686 FIELD ONYX

Same specs as Model 686 Field EL Gold Perdiz except 12-, 20-ga.; 3-inch, 3-1/2-inch chambers; weighs 6-7/8 lbs.; checkered select walnut straight English-style or pistol-grip stock, semi-beavertail forend (schnabel forend for English stock) with matte finish; semi-matte black receiver; ventilated rib. Imported from Italy by Beretta U.S.A. Introduced 1988; still imported.

Perf: $1100 **Exc:** $650 **VGood:** $540

BERETTA MODEL 686 FIELD ONYX MAGNUM

Same specs as Model 686 Field EL Gold Perdiz except 12-ga.; 3-1/2-inch chambers; checkered select walnut straight English-style or pistol-grip stock, semi-beavertail forend (schnabel forend for English stock) with matte finish; matte black plain receiver. Made in Italy. Introduced 1990; discontinued 1993.

Perf: $1175 **Exc:** $700 **VGood:** $600

BERETTA MODEL 686 FIELD SILVER PERDIZ

Same specs as Model 686 Field EL Gold Perdiz except 12-, 20-, 28-ga.; 2-3/4-inch, 3-inch chambers; checkered select walnut straight English-style or pistol-grip stock, semi-beavertail forend (schnabel forend for English stock) with gloss finish; silver receiver with floral scroll engraving. Made in Italy. Introduced 1994; discontinued 1996.

Perf: $1100 **Exc:** $750 **VGood:** $650

Combo with two-barrel set for 20-, 28-ga.

Perf: $1475 **Exc:** $1250 **VGood:** $1100

BERETTA MODEL 686 FIELD SILVER PIGEON

Same specs as Model 686 Field EL Gold Perdiz except 12-, 20-, 28-ga.; 2-3/4-inch, 3-inch chambers; highly select checkered walnut stock, schnabel forend with gloss finish; silver receiver with floral scroll engraving. Made in Italy. Introduced 1996; still imported.

Perf: $1225 **Exc:** $825 **VGood:** $575

BERETTA MODEL 686 FIELD ULTRALIGHT

Same specs as Model 686 Field EL Gold Perdiz except 12-ga.; 2-3/4-inch chamber; weighs 5-3/4 lbs.; checkered select walnut stock, schnabel forend with matte finish; aluminum alloy receiver with titanium plate; game scene engraving. Made in Italy. Introduced 1994; still imported.

Perf: $1450 **Exc:** $1000 **VGood:** $750

BERETTA MODEL S686 WHITEWING AND BLACKWING

Gauge: 12, 3-inch chambers; 26-inch, 28-inch barrel; Mobilchoke tubes (Imp. Cyl., Mod., Full); weighs 6.7 lbs.; 45.7-inch overall (28-inch barrels); 14.5-inch by 2.2-inch by 1.4-inch dimensioned American walnut stock with radiused black buttplate; matte chrome finish on receiver; matte blue barrels; hard-chrome bores; low- profile receiver with dual conical locking lugs; single selective trigger; ejectors. Imported from Italy.

Whitewing

Perf: $1155 **Exc:** $995 **VGood:** $875

Blackwing (Rugged Blue, schnabel forend)

Perf: $1155 **Exc:** $995 **VGood:** $875

BERETTA S686 ONYX

Gauge: 12, 3-inch chambers; 28-inch, 30-inch barrel (Mobilchoke tubes); weighs 7.7 lbs.; checkered American walnut; wide, vented 12.5mm target rib; radiused recoil pad; polished black finish on receiver and barrels. Intended for the beginning Sporting Clays shooter. Introduced 1993. Imported from Italy.

Perf: $1375 **Exc:** $1100 **VGood:** $900

With X-Tra Wood (highly figured)

Perf: $1439 **Exc:** $1109 **VGood:** $919

BERETTA S686 SILVER PIGEON O/U SHOTGUN

Gauge: 12, 20, 28; 3-inch chambers (2-3/4-inch 28-ga.); 26-inch, 28-inch barrel; weighs 6.8 lbs.; checkered walnut; interchangeable barrels (20- and 28-ga.); single selective gold-plated trigger; boxlock action; auto safety; schnabel forend.

Perf: $1565 **Exc:** $1150 **VGood:** $950

20 ga. and 28 ga.

Perf: $1877 **Exc:** $1462 **VGood:** $1262

BERETTA MODEL 687 COMPETITION SKEET EELL DIAMOND PIGEON

Over/under; low-profile, improved boxlock; 12-ga.; 2-3/4-inch chambers; 28-inch Skeet/Skeet barrels; tapered rib; weighs 7-1/2 lbs.; white front bead sight; highly select checkered walnut stock, beavertail forend with matte finish; rubber recoil pad; manual safety; single selective trigger; silver receiver with full sideplates; hand-engraved game scenes; comes with a case. Made in Italy. Introduced 1994; still imported.

Perf: $4775 **Exc:** $4000 **VGood:** $3550

Four-barrel set in 12-, 20-, 28-ga., .410

Perf: $6750 **Exc:** $4900 **VGood:** $4000

BERETTA MODEL 687 COMPETITION SPORTING EELL DIAMOND PIGEON

Same specs as Model 687 Competition Skeet EELL Diamond Pigeon except 12-ga.; 2-3/4-inch, 3-inch chambers; 28-inch, 30-inch Strada-rib barrels; Mobilchokes; highly select checkered walnut stock, schnabel forend with matte finish; stock oval plate. Made in Italy. Introduced 1994; still imported.

Perf: $4350 **Exc:** $2700 **VGood:** $2000

BERETTA MODEL 687 COMPETITION SPORTING EL GOLD PIGEON

Same specs as Model 687 Competition Skeet EELL Diamond Pigeon except 12-ga.; 3-inch chambers; 28-inch, 30-inch Strada-rib barrels; Mobilchokes; weighs 7-1/4 lbs.; highly select checkered walnut stock, schnabel forend with matte finish; stock oval plate; silver receiver with full sideplates; gold engraved animals. Made in Italy. Introduced 1994; still imported.

Perf: $2800 **Exc:** $1500 **VGood:** $1100

BERETTA MODEL 687 COMPETITION SPORTING L SILVER PIGEON

Same specs as Model 687 Competition Skeet EELL Diamond Pigeon except 12-, 20-ga.; 3-inch chambers; 28-inch, 30-inch barrel; Mobilchokes; Strada rib (12-ga.), flat rib (20-ga.); weighs 7-1/4 lbs.; select checkered walnut stock, schnabel forend with matte finish; stock oval plate. Made in Italy. Introduced 1994; still imported.

Perf: $2150 **Exc:** $1600 **VGood:** $1200

BERETTA MODEL 687 COMPETITION SPORTING SILVER PERDIZ ENGLISH COURSE

Same specs as Model 687 Competition Skeet EELL Diamond Pigeon except 28-inch vent-rib barrels; Mobilchokes; designed for English Sporting Clays competition. Made in Italy. Introduced 1991; discontinued 1992.

Perf: $2350 **Exc:** $1400 **VGood:** $1125

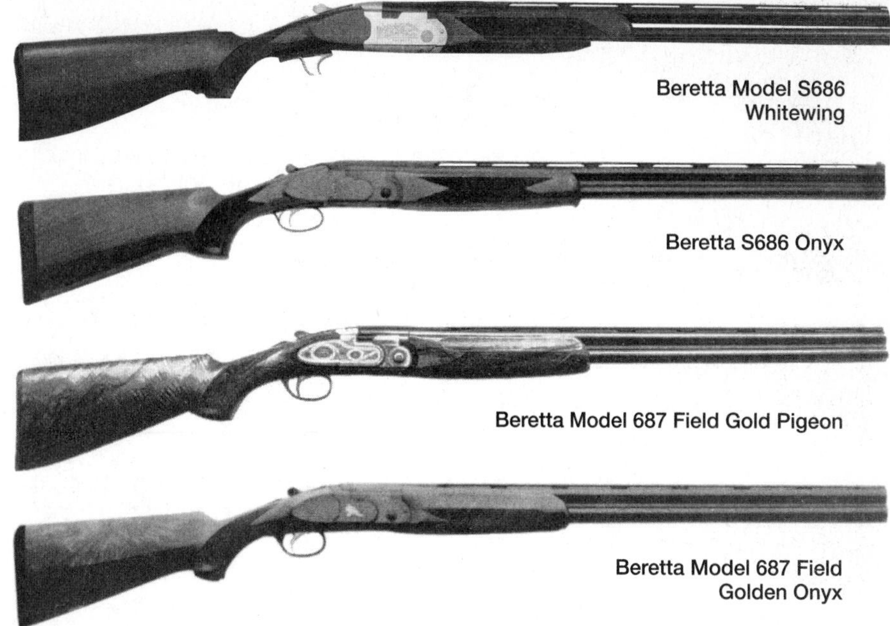

Beretta Model S686 Whitewing

Beretta S686 Onyx

Beretta Model 687 Field Gold Pigeon

Beretta Model 687 Field Golden Onyx

BERETTA MODEL 687 COMPETITION TRAP EELL DIAMOND PIGEON

Same specs as Model 687 Competition Skeet EELL Diamond Pigeon except 30-inch barrel; Mobilchokes; stepped, tapered rib; weighs 8-7/8 lbs.; highly select checkered walnut Monte Carlo stock, beavertail forend with matte finish; single adjustable trigger. Made in Italy. Introduced 1994; still imported.

Perf: $4250 **Exc:** $2700 **VGood:** $2200

BERETTA MODEL 687 COMPETITION TRAP EELL DIAMOND PIGEON COMBO

Same specs as Model 687 Competition Skeet EELL Diamond Pigeon except two-barrel set with 32-inch over/under and single 34-inch over; Mobilchokes; stepped, tapered rib; weighs 8-7/8 lbs.; highly select checkered walnut Monte Carlo stock, beavertail forend with matte finish; single adjustable trigger. Made in Italy. Introduced 1994; still imported.

Perf: $5000 **Exc:** $3500 **VGood:** $3000

BERETTA MODEL 687 COMPETITION TRAP EELL DIAMOND PIGEON MONO

Same specs as Model 687 Competition Skeet EELL Diamond Pigeon except 32-inch, 34-inch barrel; Full or Mobilchokes; stepped, tapered rib; weighs 8-1/8 lbs.; highly select checkered walnut Monte Carlo stock, beavertail forend with gloss finish; single adjustable trigger. Made in Italy. Introduced 1994; still imported.

Perf: $3250 **Exc:** $2600 **VGood:** $2300

BERETTA MODEL 687 FIELD EELL DIAMOND PIGEON

Over/under; low-profile, improved boxlock; 12-, 20-, 28-ga.; 2-3/4-inch, 3-inch chambers; 26-inch, 28-inch vent-rib barrels; Mobilchokes; weighs 6-7/8 lbs.; metal front bead sight; highly select checkered walnut stock, schnabel forend with gloss finish; rubber recoil pad; stock oval plate; auto safety; single selective trigger; silver receiver with full sideplates; hand-engraved game scenes; comes with case. Made in Italy. Introduced 1994; still imported.

Perf: $4775 **Exc:** $4000 **VGood:** $3550

BERETTA MODEL 687 FIELD EL GOLD PIGEON

Same specs as Model 687 Field EELL Diamond Pigeon except 12-, 20-, 28-ga., .410; 2-3/4-inch, 3-inch chambers; silver receiver with full sideplates;

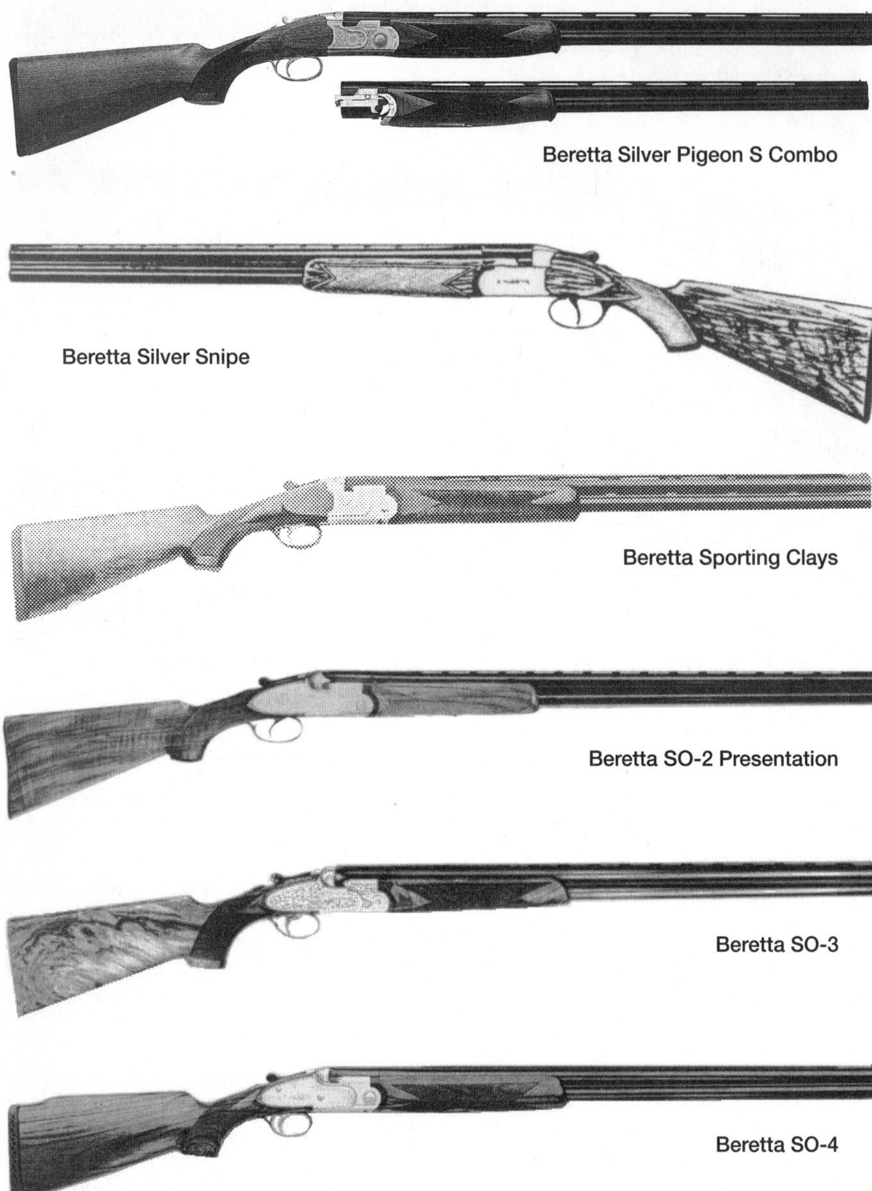
Beretta Silver Pigeon S Combo

Beretta Silver Snipe

Beretta Sporting Clays

Beretta SO-2 Presentation

Beretta SO-3

Beretta SO-4

gold engraved animals. Made in Italy. Introduced 1994; still imported.

Perf: $2925 **Exc:** $1975 **VGood:** $1700

Combo (28 and .410)

Perf: $4775 **Exc:** $4075 **VGood:** $3425

BERETTA MODEL 687 FIELD EL ONYX

Same specs as Model 687 Field EELL Diamond Pigeon except 12-, 20-ga.; 3-inch chambers; black receiver with dummy sideplates; engraving. Made in Italy. Introduced 1990; discontinued 1991.

Perf: $2350 **Exc:** $1775 **VGood:** $1520

BERETTA MODEL 687 FIELD GOLDEN ONYX

Same specs as Model 687 Field EELL Diamond Pigeon except 12-, 20-ga.; 3-inch chambers; black receiver; gold engraving. Made in Italy. Introduced 1988; discontinued 1989.

Perf: $1400 **Exc:** $900 **VGood:** $795

BERETTA MODEL 687 FIELD L ONYX

Same specs as Model 687 Field EELL Diamond Pigeon except 12-, 20-ga.; 3-inch chambers; black receiver; engraved game scenes. Made in Italy. Introduced 1990; discontinued 1991.

Perf: $1300 **Exc:** $860 **VGood:** $720

BERETTA MODEL 687 FIELD L SILVER PIGEON

Same specs as Model 687 Field EELL Diamond Pigeon except 12-, 20-ga.; 3-inch chambers; silver receiver with game scenes. Made in Italy. Introduced 1994; still imported.

Perf: $1625 **Exc:** $950 **VGood:** $800

BERETTA SILVER PIGEON S

New in 2007, the Silver Pigeon S Series features scroll and floral engraving on a satin nickel-alloy finished receiver. It is available in 12, 20 and 28 gauge with 26" or 28" barrels, and .410 bore with 28" barrels. All come with five chokes. Weight is about 6.8 lbs.

NIB: $1875 **Exc:** $1725 **VGood:** $1500

BERETTA SILVER PIGEON S COMBO

Combo model comes with 26" 20 gauge barrels and 28" 28 gauge barrels.

NIB: $2250 **Exc:** $2050 **VGood:** $1700

BERETTA 687 SILVER PIGEON V

This is the top-of-the-line model in the Silver Pigeon Series. Available in 12, 20 and 28 gauges with 26-inch and 28-inch barrels and .410-bore (added in 2006). Pistol-grip stock of richly figured walnut with oil finish. Color case-hardened receiver with gold-filled game bird inlays. English stocked versions of the 20 and 28 gauges and .410 bore were added in 2006.

NIB: $3150 **Exc:** $2900 **VGood:** $2375

BERETTA S-55B

Over/under; boxlock; 12-, 20-ga.; 2-3/4-inch, 3-inch chambers; 26-inch, 28-inch, 30-inch vent-rib barrels; standard choke combos; checkered European walnut pistol-grip stock, forend; selective single trigger; extractors. Introduced 1977; no longer in production.

Perf: $565 **Exc:** $455 **VGood:** $390

BERETTA S-56E

Over/under; boxlock; 12-, 20-ga.; 2-3/4-inch, 3-inch chambers; 26-inch, 28-inch, 30-inch vent-rib barrels; standard choke combos; checkered European walnut pistol-grip stock, forend; selective single trigger; ejectors; scroll engraved. Introduced 1977; no longer in production.

Perf: $620 **Exc:** $525 **VGood:** $480

BERETTA S-58 SKEET

Over/under; boxlock; 12-, 20-ga.; 2-3/4-inch, 3-inch chambers; 26-inch Skeet/Skeet barrels; vent rib; checkered European walnut Skeet-style stock, forend; recoil pad; selective single trigger; ejectors; scroll engraved. Introduced 1977; no longer in production.

Perf: $750 **Exc:** $620 **VGood:** $500

BERETTA S-58 TRAP

Same specs as S-58 Skeet except 30-inch Improved Modified/Full; checkered European walnut Monte Carlo stock, forend. Introduced 1977; no longer in production.

Perf: $680 **Exc:** $520 **VGood:** $450

BERETTA SILVER SNIPE

Over/under; boxlock; 12-, 20-ga.; 2-3/4-inch, 3-inch chambers; 26-inch, 28-inch, 30-inch barrels; Improved/Modified, Modified/Full, Full/Full chokes; plain or vent rib; hand-checkered European walnut pistol-grip stock, forearm; nonselective, selective trigger; extractors; nickel steel receiver. Introduced 1955; discontinued 1967.

Nonselective trigger

Exc: $725 **VGood:** $650 **Good:** $595

Selective trigger

Exc: $775 **VGood:** $695 **Good:** $650

BERETTA SPORTING CLAYS

Over/under; 12-, 20-ga.; 2-3/4-inch, 3-inch chambers; 28-inch, 30-inch, 32-inch barrel Mobilchoke; close-grained walnut; Beretta Mobilchoke flush-mounted screw-in choke tube system; wide 12.5mm top rib with 2.5mm center groove; 686 Silver Pigeon has silver receiver with scroll engraving; 687 Silver Pigeon Sporting has silver receiver, highly figured walnut; 687 EL Pigeon Sporting has game scene engraving with gold inlaid animals on full sideplate. Introduced 1994. Imported from Italy by Beretta USA.

Perf: $1795 **Exc:** $1550 **VGood:** $1325

BERETTA SO-2 PRESENTATION

Over/under; sidelock; 12-ga.; 26-inch Improved/Modified, 28-inch Modified/Full Boehler anti-rust barrels; vent rib; hand-checkered European walnut straight or pistol-grip stock; chrome-nickel receiver; all interior parts chromed; checkered trigger, safety, top lever; scroll engraving; silver pigeon inlaid in top lever. Made in Field, Skeet, Trap models. Made in Italy. Introduced 1965; no longer in production.

Perf: $3995 **Exc:** $2950 **VGood:** $2350

BERETTA SO-3

Over/under; sidelock; 12-ga.; 26-inch Improved/Modified, 28-inch Modified/Full Boehler anti-rust barrels; vent rib; fancy hand-checkered European walnut straight or pistol-grip stock; chrome-nickel receiver; all interior parts chromed; checkered trigger, safety, top lever; profuse scroll and relief engraving;

silver pigeon inlaid in top lever. Made in Field, Skeet, Trap models. Made in Italy. Introduced 1965; no longer in production.

Perf: $6500 **Exc:** $4800 **VGood:** $4300

BERETTA SO-4

Over/under; hand-detachable sidelock; 12-ga.; 26-inch Improved/Modified, 28-inch Modified/Full Boehler anti-rust barrels; vent rib; fancy hand-checkered European full-grain walnut straight or pistol-grip stock; chrome-nickel receiver; all interior parts chromed; checkered trigger, safety, top lever; elaborate scroll and relief engraving; silver pigeon inlaid in top lever. Made in Field, Skeet, Trap models. Made in Italy. Introduced 1965; no longer in production.

Perf: $7500 **Exc:** $6000 **VGood:** $5500

BERETTA SO-5

Over/under; hand-detachable sidelock; 12-ga.; handmade gun built to customer specs; fancy hand-checkered European full-grain walnut straight or pistol-grip stock; chrome-nickel receiver; all interior parts chromed; checkered trigger, safety, top lever; elaborate scroll and relief engraving; Crown Grade symbol inlaid in top lever. Made in Field, Skeet, Trap models. Made in Italy. Still in production on special-order basis.

Perf: $15,500 **Exc:** $9500 **VGood:** $7750

BERETTA SO-6

Over/under or side-by-side; hand-detachable sidelock; 12-ga.; handmade gun built to customer specs; fancy hand-checkered European full-grain walnut straight or pistol-grip stock; chrome-nickel receiver; all interior parts chromed; checkered trigger, safety, top lever; elaborate scroll and relief engraving; Crown Grade symbol inlaid in top lever. Made in Skeet, Trap, Sporting models. Made in Italy. Still in production on special-order basis.

Perf: $16,650 **Exc:** $13,500 **VGood:** $10,750

BERETTA SO-6 EELL

Same specs as SO-6 except produced on custom order to buyer's specs; special engraving and inlays. Made in Italy. Introduced 1989; still imported.

Perf: $27,500 **Exc:** $21,500 **VGood:** $16,750

BERETTA SO-7

Side-by-side; sidelock; 12-ga.; 26-inch Improved/Modified, 28-inch Modified/Full Boehler anti-rust barrels; vent rib; fancy hand-checkered European full-grain walnut straight or pistol-grip stock; chrome-nickel receiver; all interior parts chromed; checkered trigger, safety, top lever; elaborate scroll and relief engraving; silver pigeon inlaid in top lever. Made in Field model. Made in Italy. Introduced 1948; no longer in production.

Perf: $9000 **Exc:** $8300 **VGood:** $7500

BERETTA SO-9

Over/under; hand-detachable sidelock; 12-, 20-, 28-ga., .410; handmade gun built to customer specs; Boehler anti-rust steel barrels; fixed or screw-in Mobilchoke system; fancy hand-checkered European full-grain walnut straight or pistol-grip stock; chrome-nickel receiver; all interior parts chromed; checkered trigger, safety, top lever; highly decorated, engraved. Made in Skeet, Trap, Sporting models. Made in Italy. Introduced 1989; still imported.

Perf: $35,000 **Exc:** $27,500 **VGood:** $20,500

BERETTA ULTRALIGHT

Gauge: 12, 2-3/4-inch chambers; 26-inch, 28-inch barrel, Mobilchoke choke tubes; weighs about 5 lbs., 13 oz.; select American walnut with checkered grip and forend; low-profile aluminum alloy receiver with titanium breech face insert; game scene engraving; single selective trigger; automatic safety. Introduced 1992. Imported from Italy.

Perf: $1600 **Exc:** $1195 **VGood:** $895

BERETTA ULTRALIGHT DELUXE

Similar to the Ultralight except has matte electroless nickel finish receiver with gold game scene

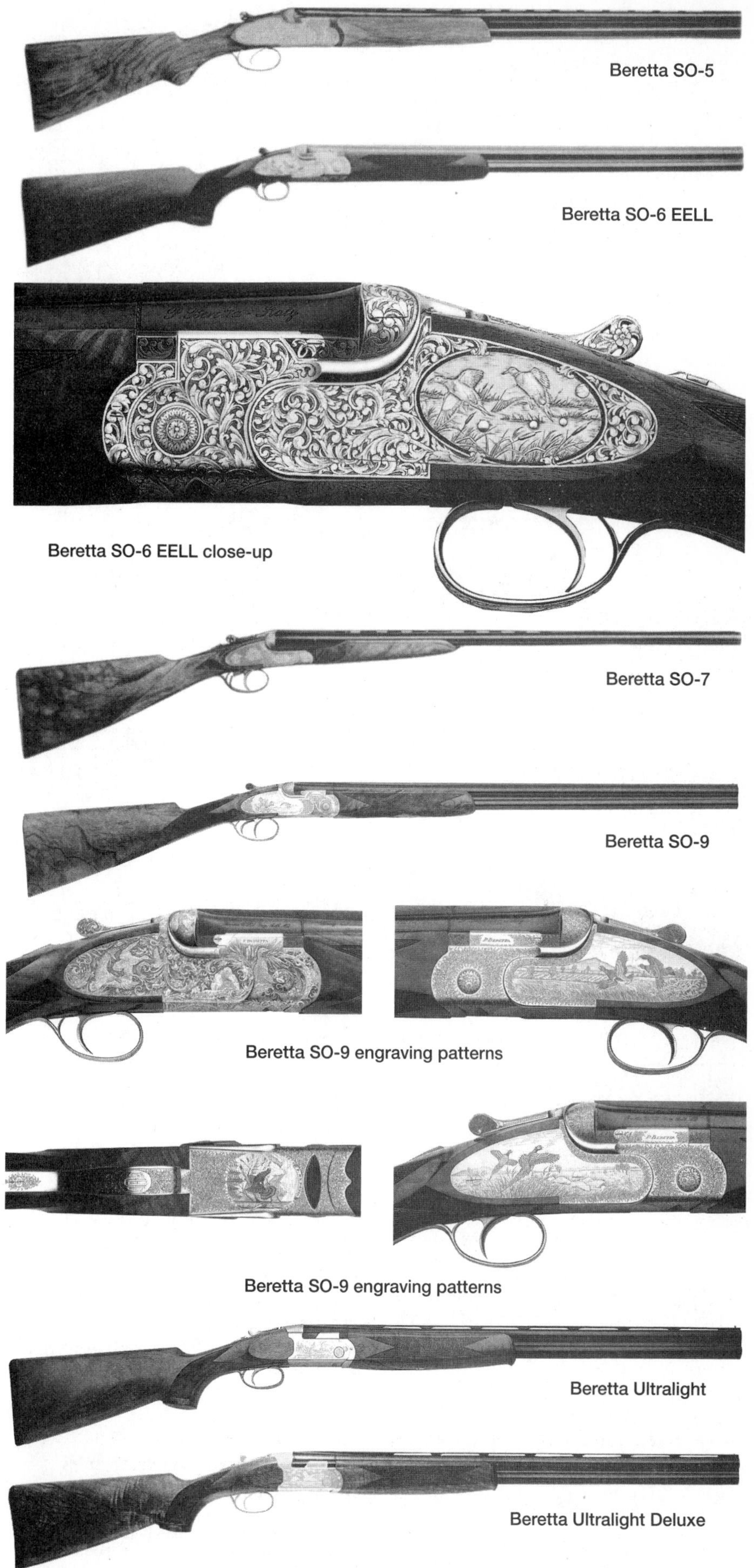

Beretta SO-5

Beretta SO-6 EELL

Beretta SO-6 EELL close-up

Beretta SO-7

Beretta SO-9

Beretta SO-9 engraving patterns

Beretta SO-9 engraving patterns

Beretta Ultralight

Beretta Ultralight Deluxe

Beretta GR-2

Beretta GR-3

Beretta GR-4

Beretta Model 409PB

Beretta Model 410E

Beretta Model 424

Beretta Model 452 EELL

engraving; matte oil-finished, select walnut stock and forend. Imported from Italy.

Perf: $1875 **Exc:** $1550 **VGood:** $1250

BERETTA OVER/UNDER FIELD SHOTGUNS

Gauge: 12-, 20-, 28-ga., .410, 2-3/4-inch, 3-inch and 3-1/2-inch chambers; 26-inch and 28-inch barrel (Mobilchoke tubes); close-grained, highly-figured, American walnut stocks and forends; unique, weather-resistant finish on barrels. Silver designates standard 686, 687 models with silver receivers; 686 Silver Pigeon has enhanced engraving pattern, schnabel forend; 686 Silver Essential has matte chrome finish; Gold indicates higher grade 686EL, 687EL models with full sideplates; Diamond is for 687EELL models with highest grade wood, engraving. Case provided with Gold and Diamond grades. Imported from Italy by Beretta U.S.A.

S686 Silver Pigeon two-bbl. set

Perf: $2125 **Exc:** $1575 **VGood:** $1300

S686 Silver Pigeon

Perf: $1565 **Exc:** $1150 **VGood:** $950

S687 Silver Pigeon II Sporting

Perf: $1825 **Exc:** $1600 **VGood:** $1450

Combo 29-inch and 30-inch

Perf: $2500 **Exc.; $2200** **VGood:** $1900

S687EL Gold Pigeon (gold inlays, sideplates)

Perf: $3335 **Exc:** $2475 **VGood:** $1950

S687EL Gold Pigeon, .410, 26-inch; 28 ga., 28-inch

Perf: $4395 **Exc:** $3475 **VGood:** $2950

S687 EL Gold Pigeon II (deep relief engraving)

Perf: $3700 **Exc:** $3300 **VGood:** $2900

S687 EL Gold Pigeon II Sporting (d.r. engraving)

Perf: $3950 **Exc:** $3500 **VGood:** $3100

BERETTA GR-2

Side-by-side; boxlock; 12-(2-3/4-inch), 20-ga. (3-inch); 26-inch, 28-inch 30-inch barrels; standard choke combos; checkered European walnut pistol-grip stock, forend; plain extractors; double triggers. Introduced 1968; discontinued 1976.

Perf: $670 **Exc:** $560 **VGood:** $520

BERETTA GR-3

Side-by-side; boxlock; 12-, 20-ga.; 3-inch chambers; 26-inch, 28-inch 30-inch barrels; standard choke combos; checkered European walnut pistol-grip stock, forend; plain extractors; single selective trigger; recoil pad. Introduced 1968; discontinued 1976.

Perf: $780 **Exc:** $660 **VGood:** $575

BERETTA GR-4

Side-by-side; boxlock; 12-ga.; 2-3/4-inch chambers; 26-inch, 28-inch 30-inch barrel; standard choke combos; checkered select European walnut pistol-grip stock, forend; auto ejectors; single selective trigger; engraving. Introduced 1968; discontinued 1976.

Perf: $1500 **Exc:** $1215 **VGood:** $1075

BERETTA MODEL 409PB

Side-by-side; boxlock; hammerless; 12-, 16-, 20-, 28-ga.; 27-1/2-inch, 28-1/2-inch, 30-inch barrels; Improved/Modified, Modified/Full chokes; hand-checkered European walnut straight or pistol-grip stock, beavertail forearm; double triggers; plain extractors; engraved action. Introduced 1934; discontinued 1964.

Exc: $775 **VGood:** $675 **Good:** $600

Add 25 percent to above prices for 20 gauge

Add 50 percent for 28 gauge

BERETTA MODEL 410

Side-by-side; boxlock; hammerless; 10-ga.; 3-1/2-inch chambers; 27-1/2-inch, 28-1/2-inch, 30-inch barrels; Improved/Modified, Modified/Full chokes; hand-checkered European walnut straight stock; recoil pad; plain extractors; double triggers. Introduced 1934; discontinued 1963.

Exc: $1200 **VGood:** $995 **Good:** $880

BERETTA MODEL 410E

Same specs as Model 410 except 12-, 16-, 20-, 28-ga.; hand-checkered European walnut straight or pistol-grip stock, beavertail forend; double triggers; automatic ejectors; engraved action. Introduced 1934; discontinued 1964.

12 Gauge

Exc: $1275 **VGood:** $1000 **Good:** $895

20 Gauge

Exc: $1750 **VGood:** $1550 **Good:** $1275

28 Gauge

Exc: $3775 **VGood:** $3300 **Good:** $2800

BERETTA MODEL 411E

Side-by-side; boxlock; hammerless; 12-, 16-, 20-, 28-ga.; 27-1/2-inch, 28-1/2-inch, 30-inch barrels; Improved/Modified, Modified/Full chokes; hand-checkered European walnut straight or pistol-grip stock; beavertail forend; sideplates; engraved action; automatic ejectors; double triggers. Introduced 1934; discontinued 1964.

12 Gauge

Exc: $2000 **VGood:** $1750 **Good:** $1350

20 Gauge

Exc: $2750 **VGood:** $2325 **Good:** $1750

28 Gauge

Exc: $4250 **VGood:** $3775 **Good:** $3300

BERETTA MODEL 424

Side-by-side; boxlock; hammerless; 12-, 20-ga.; 26-inch Improved/Modified, 28-inch Modified/Full barrels; checkered European walnut straight-grip stock, forend; plain extractors; border engraving on action. Introduced 1977; discontinued 1984. Redesignated as Model 625.

Perf: $1475 **Exc:** $1175 **VGood:** $975

Add 50 percent to above prices for 20 gauge

BERETTA MODEL 426

Side-by-side; boxlock; hammerless; 12-, 20-ga.; 26-inch Improved/Modified, 28-inch Modified/Full barrels; high-grade checkered European walnut straight-grip stock, forend; ejectors; finely engraved action; silver pigeon inlaid on top lever. Introduced 1977; discontinued 1984. Redesignated as Model 626.

Perf: $1575 **Exc:** $1275 **VGood:** $1075

BERETTA MODEL 452 CUSTOM

Side-by-side; detachable sidelock; 12-ga; 26-inch, 28-inch, 30-inch barrels; choked to customer specs; weighs 6-3/4 lbs.; highly figured European walnut stock; double bolting; ejectors; double triggers; optional single non-selective trigger; manual safety; coin-finished frame. Essentially custom built. Made in Italy. Introduced 1990; still in production.

Perf: $28,750 **Exc:** $20,500 **VGood:** $15,750

BERETTA MODEL 452 EELL
Same specs as Model 452 except walnut briar stock; full engraving. Introduced 1992; still imported.
Perf: $38,950 **Exc:** $27,750 **VGood:** $21,000

BERETTA MODEL 626
Side-by-side; boxlock; 12-, 20-ga.; 2-3/4-inch chambers; 26-inch, 28-inch barrels; standard choke combos; concave matted rib; hand-checkered European walnut straight or pistol-grip stock, forearm; coil springs; double underlugs, bolts; double triggers; auto safety; ejectors. Made in Italy. Introduced 1985; discontinued 1988. Formerly designated as Beretta 426.
Perf: $1450 **Exc:** $1050 **VGood:** $875

BERETTA MODEL 626 ONYX
Same specs as Model 626 except 12-, 20-ga.; 3-1/2-inch, 3-inch chambers; choke tubes; select hand-checkered European walnut stock, forearm. Introduced 1988; discontinued 1993.
Perf: $1650 **Exc:** $1250 **VGood:** $1000

BERETTA MODEL 627 EL
Side-by-side; boxlock; 12-, 20-ga.; 2-3/4-inch, 3-inch chambers; 26-inch, 28-inch barrels; fixed or Mobilchokes; front , center bead sights; concave matted barrel rib; fine-quality hand-checkered European walnut straight or pistol-grip stock, forend; coil springs; double underlugs, bolts; single trigger; auto safety ejectors; fine engraving; gold inlays on dummy sideplates; comes with case. Made in Italy. Introduced 1985; discontinued 1993.
Perf: $2700 **Exc:** $1600 **VGood:** $1400
Add 25 percent to above prices for 20 gauge
Subtract 5 percent from above prices for fixed choke and 2 ¾-inch chambers

BERETTA MODEL 627 EELL
Same specs as 627 EL except profuse engraving on dummy sideplates. Made in Italy. Introduced 1985; discontinued 1993.
Perf: $4500 **Exc:** $3000 **VGood:** $2700

BERETTA MODEL 470 SILVER HAWK
Side-by-side; boxlock; 12-, 20-ga.; 3-inch chambers; 26-inch (Imp. Cyl. & Imp. Mod.), 28-inch (Mod. & Full) barrel; weighs 5.9 lbs. (20-gauge); select European walnut stock; straight English grip; single selective trigger; selector provides automatic ejection or extraction; silver-chrome action and forend iron with fine engraving; top lever highlighted with gold inlaid hawk's head. ABS case. Imported from Italy.
Perf: $1950 **Exc:** $1700 **VGood:** $1475
Add 15 percent to above prices for 20 gauge
Add $130 for multi-chokes

BERETTA SILVER HAWK FEATHERWEIGHT
Side-by-side; boxlock; 12-, 16-, 20-, 28-ga.; 26-inch to 32-inch barrels; all standard choke combos; matted rib; hand-checkered European walnut stock, beavertail forearm; plain extractors; double or nonselective single trigger. Introduced 1954; discontinued 1967.

Single trigger
Exc: $495 **VGood:** $440 **Good:** $413

Double triggers
Exc: $550 **VGood:** $495 **Good:** $440

BERETTA SILVER HAWK MAGNUM
Same specs as Silver Hawk Featherweight except 10- (3-1/2-inch), 12-ga. (3-inch); 30-inch, 32-inch barrels; chrome-plated bores; raised rib; recoil pad. Introduced 1954; discontinued 1967.

Single trigger
Exc: $495 **VGood:** $.450 **Good:** $395

Double triggers
Exc: $530 **VGood:** $500 **Good:** $450

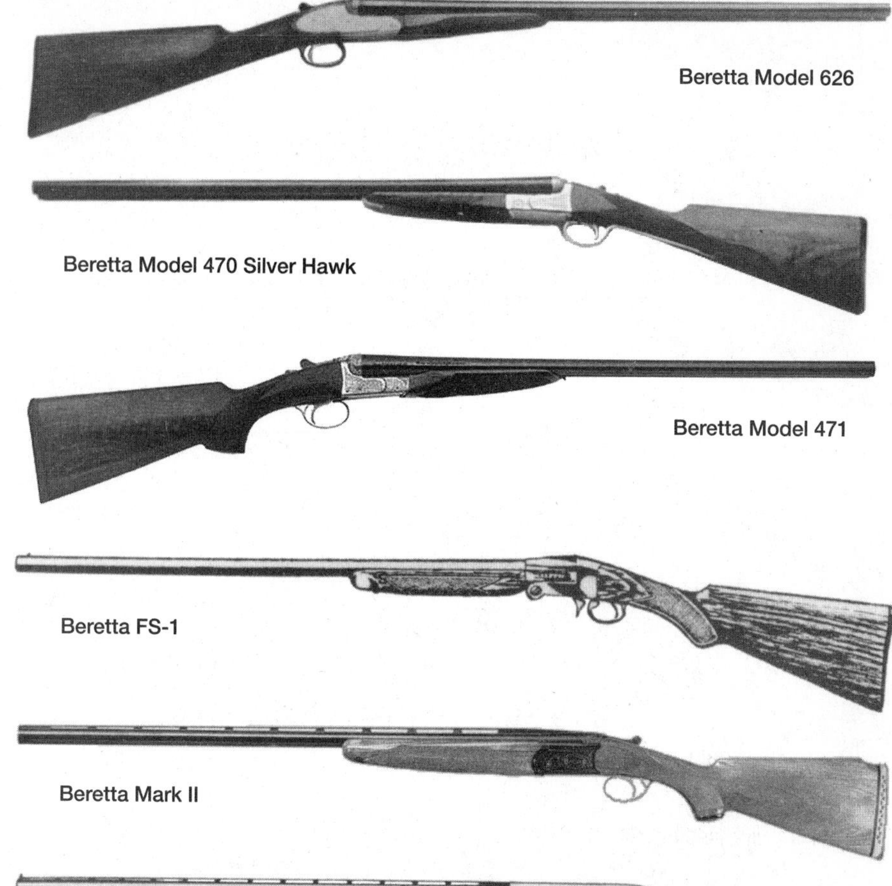
Beretta Model 626

Beretta Model 470 Silver Hawk

Beretta Model 471

Beretta FS-1

Beretta Mark II

Beretta Silver Pigeon

BERETTA MODEL 471
Side-by-side double in 12- or 20-gauge with 26 or 28-inch barrels, 3-inch chambers, MobilChoke or Optima choke tubes. Selective single trigger, lever on fore-end allows setting action to automatic ejectors or extractors. Pistol grip or straight grip stock with beavertail or splinter fore-end. Manufactured in Italy and imported 2003 to 2012.
Perf: $3500 **Exc:** $2700 **VGood:** $1900

BERETTA DT 10 TRIDENT TRAP TOP SINGLE SHOTGUN
Gauge: 12, 3-inch chamber; 34-inch barrel; five Optima Choke tubes (Full, Full Imp., Modified, Mod. and Imp. Cyl.); weighs 8.8 lbs.; high-grade walnut; adjustable stock;.detachable, adjustable trigger group; Optima Bore for improved shot pattern and reduced recoil; slim Optima Choke tubes; raised and thickened receiver for long life. Introduced 2000. Imported from Italy.
Perf: $7550 **Exc:** $6500 **VGood:** $5750

BERETTA FS-1
Single barrel; single shot; hammerless under-lever; 12-, 16-, 20-, 28-ga., .410; 26-inch (28-ga., .410), 28-inch (16-, 20-ga.), 30-inch barrel (12-ga.); Full choke; hand-checkered pistol-grip stock, forearm; folds to length of barrel; barrel release ahead of trigger guard. Advertised as the Companion. Introduced 1959; no longer in production.
Exc: $175 **VGood:** $150 **Good:** $125

BERETTA GOLD PIGEON
Slide action; 12-ga.; 5-shot magazine; 26-inch, 30-inch, 32-inch vent-rib barrels; standard chokes; hand-checkered walnut pistol-grip stock, beavertail forearm; hand-polished, engine-turned bolt; gold trigger; moderate engraving; inlaid gold pigeon. Introduced 1959; discontinued 1966.
Exc: $475 **VGood:** $375 **Good:** $310

BERETTA MARK II
Single shot; boxlock; 12-ga.; 32-inch, 34-inch barrel; wide vent rib; weighs about 8-3/8 lbs.; checkered European walnut Monte Carlo pistol-grip stock, beavertail forend; ejector; recoil pad. Introduced 1972; discontinued 1976.
Perf: $550 **Exc:** $450 **VGood:** $400

BERETTA MODEL 680 COMPETITION MONO TRAP
Single shot; boxlock; 12-ga.; 2-3/4-inch chamber; 32-inch, 34-inch barrel; ventilated rib; weighs about 8 lbs.; luminous front sight, center bead; hand-checkered European walnut Monte Carlo stock, forearm; automatic ejector; single trigger; deluxe trap recoil pad; silver finish. Introduced 1979; no longer in production.
Perf: $1050 **Exc:** $700 **VGood:** $650

BERETTA MODEL 680 COMPETITION TRAP
Same specs as Model 680 Competition Mono Trap except over/under; 29-1/2-inch Improved Modified/Full barrels. No longer imported.
Perf: $1150 **Exc:** $800 **VGood:** $710

BERETTA MODEL 680 COMPETITION TRAP COMBO
Same specs as Model 680 Competition Mono Trap except over/under; two-barrel set with 29-1/2-inch Improved Modified/Full over/under and 32-inch or 34-inch single over barrels. No longer in production.
Perf: $1150 **Exc:** $800 **VGood:** $700

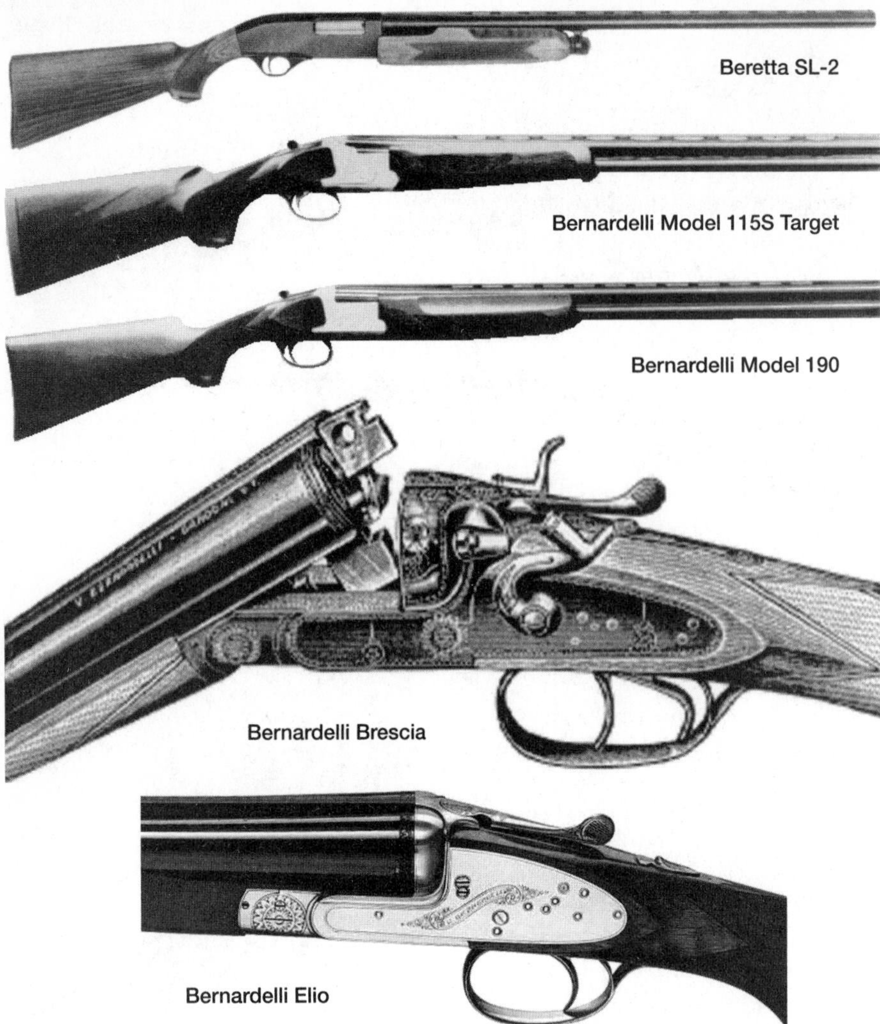
Beretta SL-2

Bernardelli Model 115S Target

Bernardelli Model 190

Bernardelli Brescia

Bernardelli Elio

BERETTA MODEL 680 COMPETITION SKEET

Same specs as Model 680 Competition Mono Trap except over/under; 28-inch Skeet/Skeet barrels; smooth recoil pad. No longer in production.

Perf: $1150 **Exc:** $800 **VGood:** $700

BERETTA RUBY PIGEON

Slide action; 12-ga.; 5-shot magazine; 26-inch, 30-inch, 32-inch vent-rib barrels; standard chokes; hand-checkered walnut pistol-grip stock, beavertail forearm; hand-polished, engine-turned bolt; gold trigger; elaborate engraving; inlaid gold pigeon with ruby eye. Introduced 1959; discontinued 1966.

Exc: $600 **VGood:** $475 **Good:** $395

BERETTA SILVER PIGEON

Slide action; 12-ga.; 5-shot magazine; 26-inch, 30-inch, 32-inch barrels; standard chokes; hand-checkered walnut pistol-grip stock, beavertail forearm; hand-polished, engine-turned bolt; chromed trigger; light engraving; inlaid silver pigeon. Introduced 1959; discontinued 1966.

Exc: $250 **VGood:** $200 **Good:** $175

BERETTA SL-2

Slide action; 12-ga.; 3-shot magazine; 26-inch Improved, 28-inch Full or Modified, 30-inch Full barrels; vent rib; checkered European walnut stock, forend. Introduced 1968; discontinued 1971.

Exc: $225 **VGood:** $175 **Good:** $150

BERETTA TR-1

Single shot; underlever; 12-ga.; 32-inch vent-rib barrel; checkered European walnut Monte Carlo pistol-grip stock, beavertail forend; engraved frame; recoil pad. Introduced 1968; discontinued 1971.

Exc: $250 **VGood:** $165 **Good:** $110

BERETTA TR-2

Single shot; underlever; 12-ga.; 32-inch extended vent-rib barrel; checkered European walnut Monte Carlo pistol-grip stock, beavertail forend; engraved frame; recoil pad. Introduced 1968; discontinued 1972.

Exc: $250 **VGood:** $165 **Good:** $110

BERNARDELLI OVER/UNDER SHOTGUNS

BERNARDELLI MODEL 115

Over/under; boxlock; 12-ga.; 2-3/4-inch chambers; 25-1/2-inch, 26-3/4-inch, 29-1/2-inch barrels; Multichokes or standard chokes; concave top rib, vented middle rib; specially designed anatomical grip stock for competition; schnabel forend; leather-faced recoil pad; inclined-plane locking; ejectors; selective or non-selective trigger. Made in Italy. Introduced 1989; discontinued 1991.

Perf: $1770 **Exc:** $1175 **VGood:** $950

BERNARDELLI MODEL 115E

Same specs as Model 115 except sideplates; engraving; silver finish.

Perf: $4500 **Exc:** $3525 **VGood:** $3000

BERNARDELLI MODEL 115L

Same specs as Model 115 except engraving; silver finish.

Perf: $2600 **Exc:** $2375 **VGood:** $2050

BERNARDELLI MODEL 115S

Same specs as Model 115 except engraving.

Perf: $2150 **Exc:** $1925 **VGood:** $1745

BERNARDELLI MODEL 115 TARGET

Same specs as Model 115 except configured for trap shooting. Introduced 1989; discontinued 1991.

Perf: $1800 **Exc:** $1595 **VGood:** $1375

BERNARDELLI MODEL 115E TARGET

Same specs as Model 115 Target except sideplates; engraving; silver finish.

Perf: $5950 **Exc:** $4800 **VGood:** $4125

BERNARDELLI MODEL 115L TARGET

Same specs as Model 115 Target except engraving; silver finish.

Perf: $3700 **Exc:** $2995 **VGood:** $2600

BERNARDELLI MODEL 115S TARGET

Same specs as Model 115 Target except engraving.

Perf: $3275 **Exc:** $2425 **VGood:** $1825

BERNARDELLI MODEL 115S TARGET MONOTRAP

Same specs as Model 115 Target except single barrel.

Perf: $1550 **Exc:** $1100 **VGood:** $900

BERNARDELLI MODEL 190

Over/under; 12-ga.; various barrel lengths; checkered walnut English straight or pistol-grip stock, forearm; ejectors; single selective trigger; silver finished receiver; engraving. Introduced 1986; discontinued 1989.

Perf: $1400 **Exc:** $900 **VGood:** $750

BERNARDELLI MODEL 190MC

Same specs as Model 190 except Monte Carlo stock.

Perf: $1000 **Exc:** $825 **VGood:** $700

BERNARDELLI MODEL 190 SPECIAL

Same specs as Model 190 except select walnut; elaborate engraving.

Perf: $1335 **Exc:** $1000 **VGood:** $895

BERNARDELLI MODEL 190 SPECIAL MS

Same specs as Model 190 except select walnut stock; single trigger; elaborate engraving.

Perf: $1300 **Exc:** $850 **VGood:** $750

BERNARDELLI MODEL 192

Over/under; boxlock; 12-ga.; 2-3/4-inch chambers; 25-1/2-inch, 26-3/4-inch, 28-inch, 29-1/2-inch barrels; standard choke combos or multichoke tubes; weighs 7 lbs.; hand-checkered European walnut English straight or pistol-grip stock; ejectors; single selective trigger silvered, engraved action. Made in Italy. Introduced 1989; still imported.

Perf: $1175 **Exc:** $895 **VGood:** $750

Add $65 to above prices for single trigger
Add $200 for choke tubes
Add $350 for Model 192 Special (includes double triggers and ejectors)

BERNARDELLI MODEL 192MS MC

Same specs as Model 192 except 3-inch chambers; five choke tubes. Introduced 1989; still imported.

Perf: $1750 **Exc:** $1200 **VGood:** $900

BERNARDELLI MODEL 192MS MC WF

Same specs as Model 192 except 3-1/2-inch chambers; three choke tubes. Introduced 1989; still imported.

Perf: $1275 **Exc:** $950 **VGood:** $875

BERNARDELLI MODEL 220MS

Over/under; boxlock; 12-, 20-ga.; 25-1/2-inch, 26-3/4-inch, 28-inch, 29-1/2-inch barrels; standard choke combos or multichoke tubes; hand-checkered walnut English straight or pistol-grip stock; ejectors; double triggers; silver-gray receiver with engraving. Made in Italy. Introduced 1989; still in production.

Perf: $1350 **Exc:** $995 **VGood:** $850

With selective trigger

Perf: $1410 **Exc:** $1050 **VGood:** $920

BERNARDELLI 9MM GARDEN GUN

Autoloader; rimfire 9mm Flobert shot cartridge; 3-shot magazine; 24-2/5-inch barrel; uncheckered walnut stock, forearm. Introduced 1987.

Perf: $500 **Exc:** $465 **VGood:** $325

BERNARDELLI BRESCIA

Side-by-side; sidelock; exposed hammer; 12-, 16-, 20-ga.; 2-3/4-inch, 3-inch chambers; 25-1/2-inch Cylinder/Modified or Improved Cylinder/Improved Modified, 26-3/4-inch Improved Cylinder/Improved Modified or Modified/Full, 29-1/2-inch Improved Modified/Full barrels; weighs about 7 lbs.; checkered European walnut English straight-grip stock; extractors; double triggers; color case-hardened action. Made in Italy. Introduced 1960; no longer imported.

Perf: $2050 **Exc:** $1795 **VGood:** $1600

BERNARDELLI ELIO

Side-by-side; boxlock; hammerless; 12-ga.; 25-inch Improved/Modified, 28-inch Modified/Full barrels; hand-checkered European walnut straight stock; double triggers; extractors; silver-finished receiver; English-style scroll engraving; lightweight game model. Introduced 1970; no longer imported.

Perf: $1200 **Exc:** $900 **VGood:** $750

Elio E with ejectors

Perf: $1250 **Exc:** $950 **VGood:** $800

Elio M with single trigger

Perf: $1250 **Exc:** $950 **VGood:** $800

Elio EM

Perf: $1300 **Exc:** $1000 **VGood:** $850

BERNARDELLI GAMECOCK

Side-by-side; boxlock; hammerless; 12-, 16-, 20-, 28-ga.; 25-inch Improved/Modified, 28-inch Modified/Full barrels; hand-checkered European walnut straight stock; extractors; double triggers. Introduced 1970; no longer imported.

Perf: $900 **Exc:** $620 **VGood:** $580

With ejectors

Perf: $1050 **Exc:** $770 **VGood:** $620

With Deluxe engraving

Perf: $1250 **Exc:** $950 **VGood:** $800

BERNARDELLI HEMINGWAY

Side-by-side; boxlock; 12-, 16-, 20-, 28-ga; 2-3/4-inch, 3-inch chambers; 23-1/2-inch to 28-inch barrels; weighs 6-1/4 lbs.; European walnut stock; ejectors; front trigger folds on double-trigger; silvered, engraved action. Introduced 1990; dropped 1997.

Perf: $2050 **Exc:** $1500 **VGood:** $1050

With single trigger

Perf: $2120 **Exc:** $1570 **VGood:** $1120

With single selective trigger

Perf: $2170 **Exc:** $1620 **VGood:** $1170

BERNARDELLI HEMINGWAY DELUXE

Same specs as Hemingway except sideplates; select wood; elaborate engraving.

Perf: $2350 **Exc:** $1750 **VGood:** $1150

With single trigger

Perf: $2475 **Exc:** $1875 **VGood:** $1275

BERNARDELLI HOLLAND VB

Side-by-side; Holland & Holland-design sidelock; 12-ga.; 26-inch to 32-inch barrels; all standard choke combos; hand-checkered European walnut straight or pistol-grip stock, forearm; double triggers; automatic ejectors. Introduced 1946; discontinued 1992.

Liscio Model

Perf: $10,350 **Exc:** $5300 **VGood:** $4450

Inciso Model with engraving

Perf: $10,700 **Exc:** $7000 **VGood:** $5500

Lusso Model with engraving, select walnut

Perf: $9000 **Exc:** $7900 **VGood:** $6500

Extra Model with deluxe engraving, select wood

Perf: $13,250 **Exc:** $9700 **VGood:** $7450

Add $625 to above prices for single trigger
Add $1035 for engraving pattern No. 4
Add $4550 for engraving pattern No. 12
Add $9000 for engraving pattern No. 20

Gold Model

Perf: $47,500 **Exc:** $32,500 **VGood:** $24,000

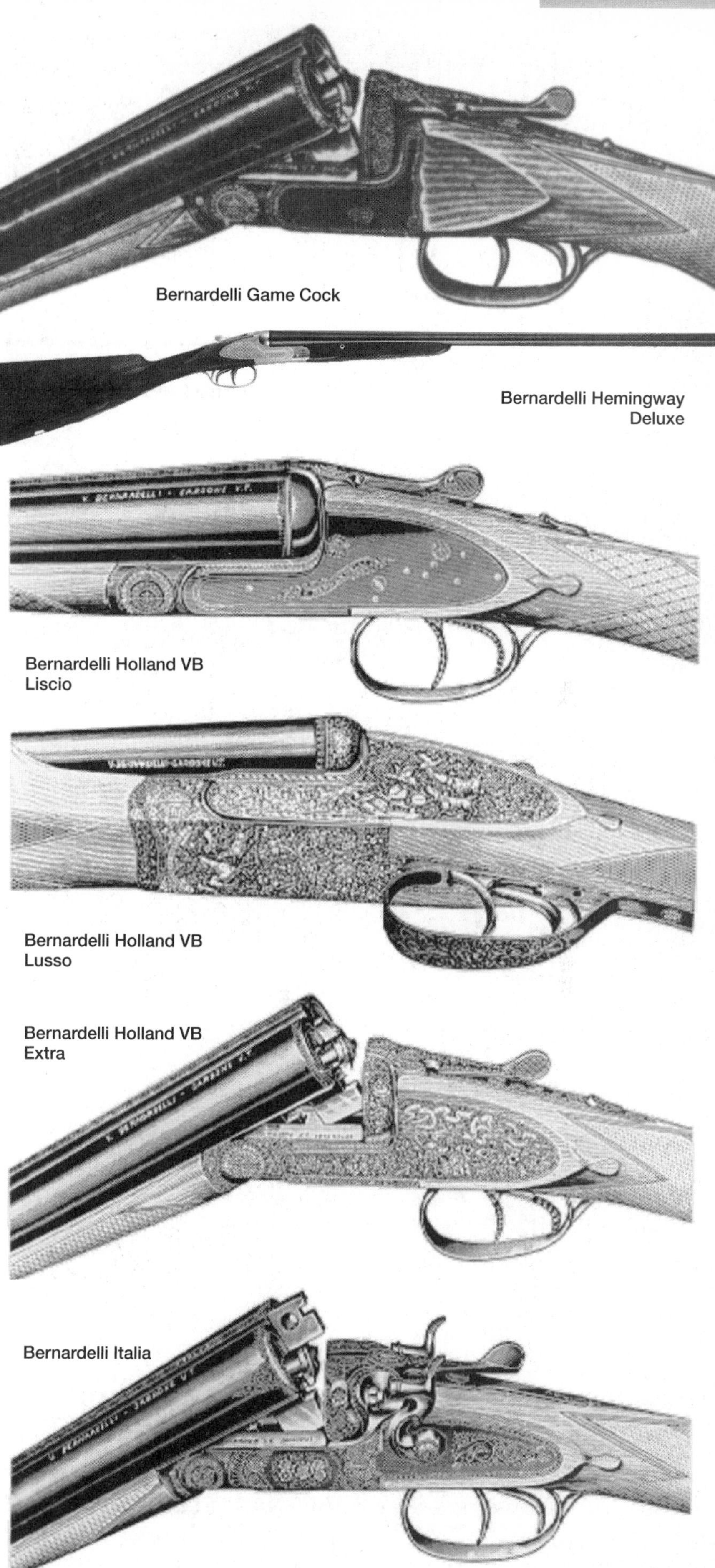

Bernardelli Game Cock

Bernardelli Hemingway Deluxe

Bernardelli Holland VB Liscio

Bernardelli Holland VB Lusso

Bernardelli Holland VB Extra

Bernardelli Italia

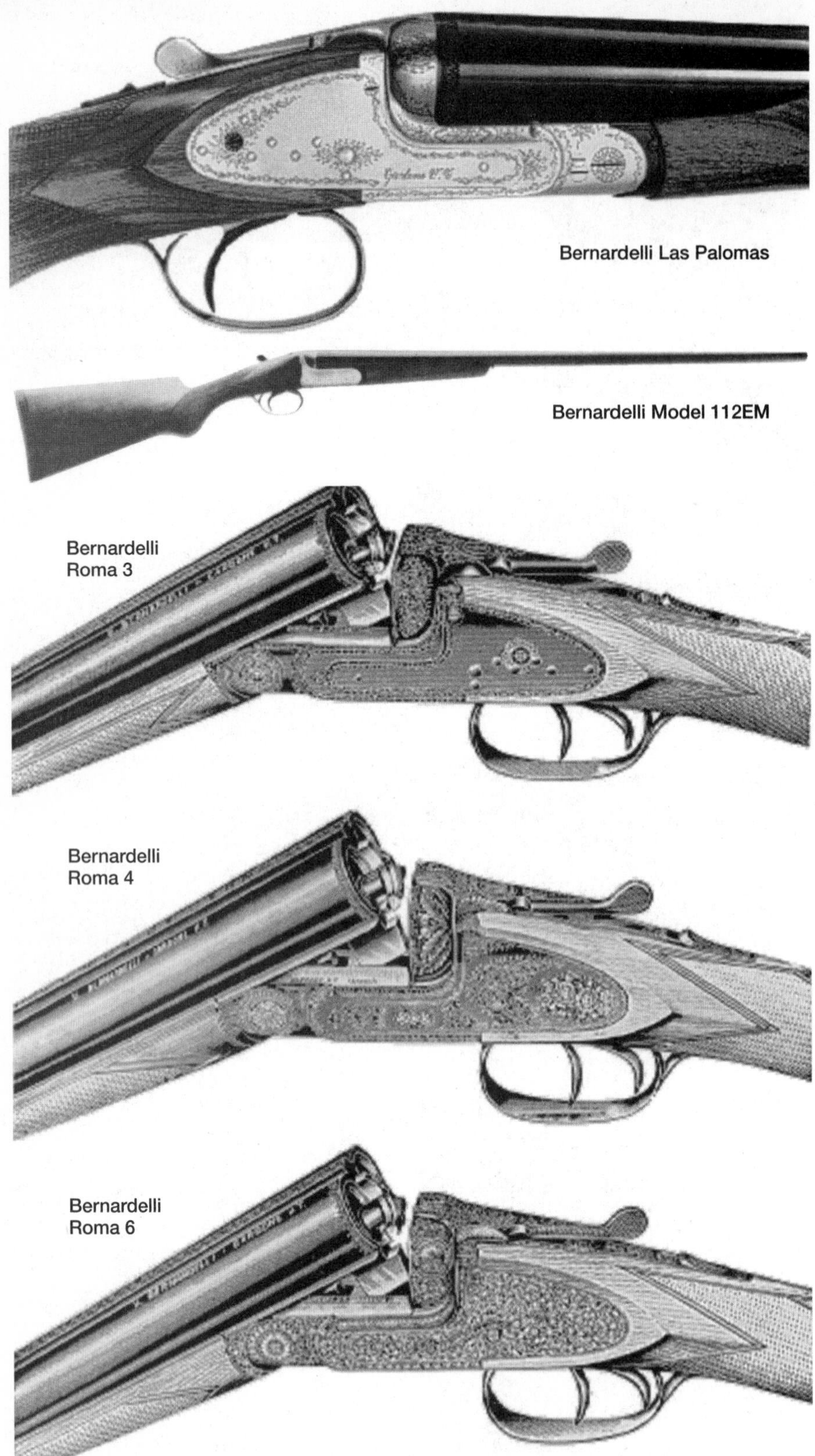

Bernardelli Las Palomas

Bernardelli Model 112EM

Bernardelli Roma 3

Bernardelli Roma 4

Bernardelli Roma 6

BERNARDELLI ITALIA

Side-by-side; sidelock; exposed hammer; 12-, 16-, 20-ga.; 2-3/4-inch, 3-inch chambers; 25-1/2-inch Cylinder/Modified or Improved Cylinder/Improved Modified, 26-3/4-inch Improved Cylinder/Improved Modified or Modified/Full, 29-1/2-inch Improved Modified/Full barrels; weighs about 7 lbs.; checkered high-grade European walnut English straight-grip stock; profuse engraving. Made in Italy. Introduced 1990; no longer imported.

Perf: $2275 **Exc:** $1200 **VGood:** $900

BERNARDELLI ITALIA EXTRA

Same specs as Italia except highest grade of engraving and wood. Made in Italy. Introduced 1990; no longer imported.

Perf: $6400 **Exc:** $3150 **VGood:** $2200

BERNARDELLI LAS PALOMAS

Side-by-side; Anson & Deeley boxlock; 12-ga.; 2-3/4-inch chambers; 28-inch barrels bored for pigeon shooting; select European walnut stock; Australian pistol grip with shaped heel, palm swell; double or single trigger; special trigger guard; manual safety; auto safety optional; vent recoil pad; optional features. Made in Italy. Introduced 1984; dropped 1997.

Perf: $3000 **Exc:** $1850 **VGood:** $1600

Las Palomas M with single trigger

Perf: $3600 **Exc:** $2400 **VGood:** $2150

BERNARDELLI MODEL 112

Side-by-side; 12-ga.; Anson & Deeley boxlock; 12-ga.; 2-3/4-inch chambers; 25-5/8-inch, 26-3/4-inch, 28-inch, 29-1/8-inch barrels; Modified/Full; European walnut stock; extractors; double triggers. Made in Italy. Introduced 1989; discontinued 1989.

Perf: $850 **Exc:** $750 **VGood:** $675

Model 112E with engraving

Perf: $995 **Exc:** $850 **VGood:** $775

Model 112M with single trigger

Perf: $925 **Exc:** $825 **VGood:** $750

BERNARDELLI MODEL 112EM

Same specs as Model 112 except engraving; single trigger. Introduced 1989; dropped 1997.

Perf: $1200 **Exc:** $800 **VGood:** $650

BERNARDELLI MODEL 112EM MC

Same specs as Model 112EM except 3-inch chamber; 5 choke tubes; engraving; single trigger. Introduced 1990; discontinued 1992.

Perf: $1600 **Exc:** $1000 **VGood:** $850

BERNARDELLI MODEL 112EM MC WF

Same specs as Model 112EM except 3-1/2-inch chamber; 3 choke tubes; engraving; single trigger. Introduced 1990; discontinued 1991.

Perf: $1275 **Exc:** $975 **VGood:** $850

BERNARDELLI ROMA 3

Side-by-side; Anson & Deeley boxlock; false sideplates; hammerless; 12-, 16-, 20-, 28-ga.; 27-1/2-inch, 29-1/2-inch barrels; Modified/Full chokes; hand-checkered European walnut straight or pistol-grip stock, forearm; extractors; double triggers; color case-hardened receiver. Introduced 1946; dropped 1997.

Perf: $1425 **Exc:** $1200 **VGood:** $895

BERNARDELLI ROMA 3E

Same specs as Roma 3 except ejectors; dropped 1997.

Perf: $1600 **Exc:** $1325 **VGood:** $1050

BERNARDELLI ROMA 3EM

Same specs as Roma 3 except ejectors; single trigger. No longer in production.

Perf: $1700 **Exc:** $1400 **VGood:** $1125

BERNARDELLI ROMA 3M

Same specs as Roma 3 except single trigger. No longer in production.

Perf: $1450 **Exc:** $900 **VGood:** $775

BERNARDELLI ROMA 4

Side-by-side; Anson & Deeley boxlock; false sideplates; hammerless; 12-, 16-, 20-, 28-ga.; 27-1/2-inch, 29-1/2-inch barrels; Modified/Full chokes; hand-checkered European walnut straight or pistol-grip stock, forearm; extractors; double triggers; scroll engraving; silver finish; dropped 1989.

Perf: $1550 **Exc:** $900 **VGood:** $695

BERNARDELLI ROMA 4E

Same specs as Roma 4 except ejectors. Still in production.

Perf: $1775 **Exc:** $1475 **VGood:** $1150

BERNARDELLI ROMA 4EM

Same specs as Roma 4 except ejectors; single trigger. No longer in production.

Perf: $1850 **Exc:** $1550 **VGood:** $1250

BERNARDELLI ROMA 4M

Same specs as Roma 4 except single trigger; dropped 1989.

Perf: $1650 **Exc:** $1100 **VGood:** $975

BERNARDELLI ROMA 6

Side-by-side; Anson & Deeley boxlock; hammerless; 12-, 16-, 20-, 28-ga.; 27-1/2-inch, 29-1/2-inch barrels; Modified/Full chokes; select hand-checkered European walnut straight or pistol-grip stock, forearm; extractors; double triggers; elaborate engraved sideplates; silver finish. Importation dropped 1989.

Perf: $1700 **Exc:** $1100 **VGood:** $900

BERNARDELLI ROMA 6E

Same specs as Roma 6 except ejectors. Importation discontinued 1997.

Perf: $2400 **Exc:** $1825 **VGood:** $1475

BERNARDELLI ROMA 6EM

Same specs as Roma 6 except ejectors; single trigger. No longer in production.

Perf: $2475 **Exc:** $2000 **VGood:** $1550

BERNARDELLI ROMA 6M

Same specs as Roma 6 except single trigger. Importation discontinued 1989.

Perf: $1850 **Exc:** $1295 **VGood:** $1150

BERNARDELLI ROMA 7

Side-by-side; Anson & Deeley boxlock; hammerless; 12-ga.; 27-1/2-inch, 29-1/2-inch barrels; Modified/ Full chokes; fancy hand-checkered European walnut straight or pistol-grip stock, forearm; ejectors; double triggers; elaborately engraved, silver-finished sideplates. Introduced 1994; dropped 1997.

Perf: $3200 **Exc:** $2200 **VGood:** $1675

BERNARDELLI ROMA 8

Side-by-side; Anson & Deeley boxlock; hammerless; 12-ga.; 27-1/2-inch, 29-1/2-inch barrels; Modified/ Full chokes; fancy select hand-checkered European walnut straight or pistol-grip stock, forearm; ejectors; double triggers; elaborately engraved, silver-finished sideplates. Introduced 1994; dropped 1997.

Perf: $3700 **Exc:** $2700 **VGood:** $1950

BERNARDELLI ROMA 9

Side-by-side; Anson & Deeley boxlock; hammerless; 12-ga.; 27-1/2-inch, 29 1/2-inch barrels; Modified/ Full chokes; best-grade hand-checkered European walnut straight or pistol-grip stock, forearm; ejectors; double triggers; very elaborately engraved, silver-finished sideplates. Introduced 1994; dropped 1997.

Perf: $4550 **Exc:** $3200 **VGood:** $2500

BERNARDELLI S. UBERTO 1

Side-by-side; Anson & Deeley-style boxlock; Purdey locks; 12-, 16-, 20-, 28-ga.; 2-3/4-inch, 3-inch chambers; 25-5/8-inch, 26-3/4-inch, 28-inch, 29-1/8-inch barrels; Modified/Full; select hand-checkered European walnut stock; extractors; double triggers; color case-hardened receiver. Made in Italy. Introduced 1946; discontinued 1990.

Perf: $1050 **Exc:** $950 **VGood:** $800

BERNARDELLI S UBERTO 1E

Same specs as S. Uberto 1 except ejectors. No longer in production.

Perf: $1175 **Exc:** $950 **VGood:** $850

BERNARDELLI S. UBERTO 1EM

Same specs as S. Uberto 1 except ejectors; single trigger. No longer in production.

Perf: $1225 **Exc:** $1020 **VGood:** $920

BERNARDELLI S. UBERTO 1M

Same specs as S. Uberto 1 except single trigger. No longer in production.

Perf: $1050 **Exc:** $800 **VGood:** $650

BERNARDELLI S. UBERTO 2

Side-by-side; Anson & Deeley-style boxlock; Purdey locks; 12-, 16-, 20-, 28-ga.; 2-3/4-inch, 3-inch chambers; 25-5/8-inch, 26-3/4-inch, 28-inch, 29-1/8-inch barrels; Modified/Full; select hand-checkered European walnut stock; extractors; double triggers; engraved, silver-finished receiver. Made in Italy. Introduced 1946; dropped 1997.

Perf: $1375 **Exc:** $1150 **VGood:** $875

BERNARDELLI S UBERTO 2E

Same specs as S. Uberto 2 except ejectors. No longer in production.

Perf: $1525 **Exc:** $1300 **VGood:** $1050

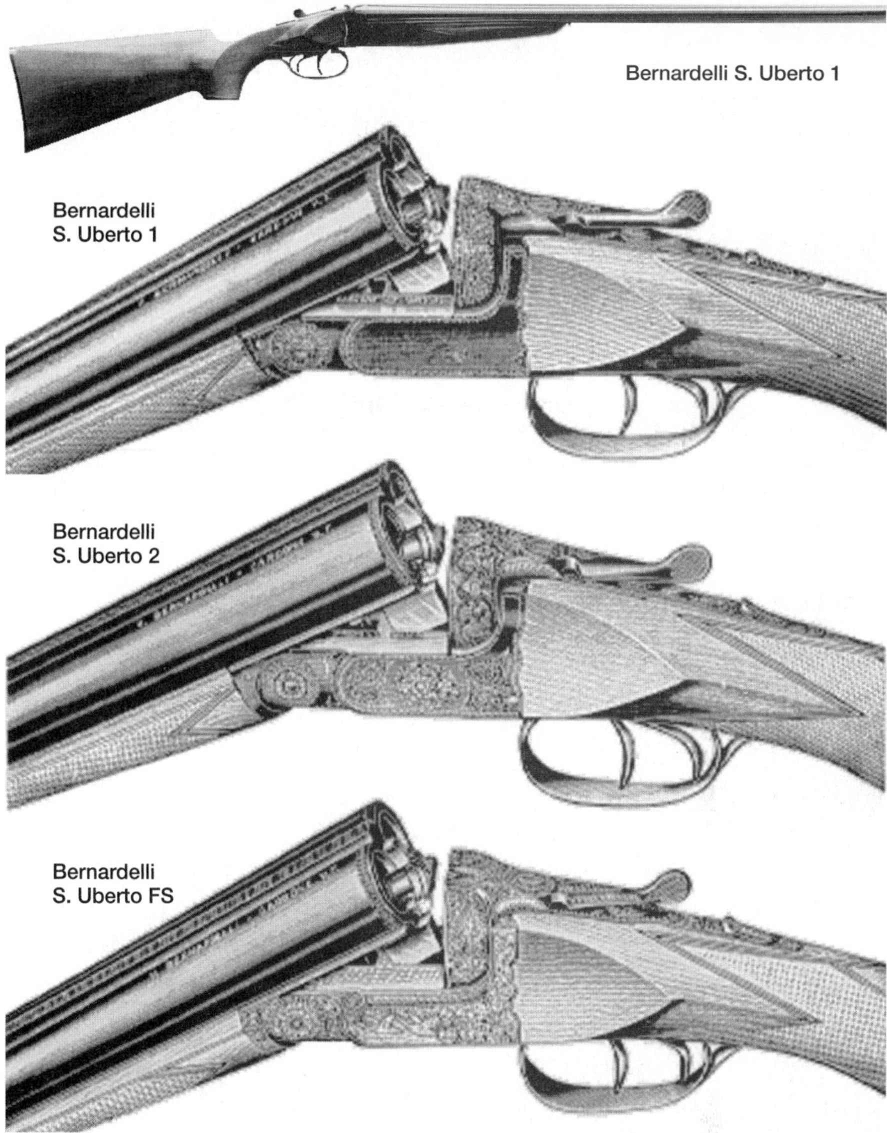

Bernardelli S. Uberto 1

Bernardelli S. Uberto 1

Bernardelli S. Uberto 2

Bernardelli S. Uberto FS

BERNARDELLI S. UBERTO 2EM

Same specs as S. Uberto 2 except ejectors; single trigger. No longer in production.

Perf: $1600 **Exc:** $1375 **VGood:** $1125

BERNARDELLI S. UBERTO 2M

Same specs as S. Uberto 2 except single trigger. No longer in production.

Perf: $1410 **Exc:** $1110 **VGood:** $910

BERNARDELLI S. UBERTO FS

Side-by-side; Anson & Deeley-style boxlock; Purdey locks; 12-, 16-, 20-, 28-ga.; 2- 3/4-inch, 3-inch chambers; 25-5/8-inch, 26-3/4-inch, 28-inch, 29-1/8-inch barrels; Modified/Full; select hand-checkered European walnut stock; extractors; double triggers; elaborately engraved, silver-finished receiver. Made in Italy. Introduced 1987; no longer in production.

Perf: $1695 **Exc:** $1450 **VGood:** $1125

BERNARDELLI S UBERTO FSE

Same specs as S. Uberto FS except ejectors. Still in production.

Perf: $1400 **Exc:** $1100 **VGood:** $975

BERNARDELLI S. UBERTO FSEM

Same specs as S. Uberto FS except ejectors; single trigger. No longer in production.

Perf: $1500 **Exc:** $1165 **VGood:** $1025

BERNARDELLI S. UBERTO FSM

Same specs as S. Uberto FS except single trigger. No longer in production.

Perf: $1760 **Exc:** $1510 **VGood:** $1185

BERNARDELLI SLUG GUN

Side-by-side; Anson & Deeley boxlock; 12-ga.; 23-3/4-inch barrels; slug bores; walnut English straight or pistol-grip stock, forearm; extractors; double trigger; silver finished receiver; engraving. Discontinued 1990.

Perf: $1325 **Exc:** $1000 **VGood:** $895

BERNARDELLI SLUG LUSSO

Same specs as Slug Gun except ejectors; sideplates; elaborate engraving. Discontinued 1992.

Perf: $2325 **Exc:** $1550 **VGood:** $1200

BERNARDELLI SLUG LUSSO M

Same specs as Slug Gun single trigger; ejectors; sideplates; elaborate engraving. No longer in production.

Perf: $2400 **Exc:** $1625 **VGood:** $1265

BERNARDELLI SLUG M GUN

Same specs as Slug Gun except single trigger. No longer in production.

Perf: $1495 **Exc:** $1065 **VGood:** $970

BERNARDELLI XXVSL

Side-by-side; Holland & Holland-type sidelock; 12-ga.; 25-inch demi-block barrels; standard chokes; custom-fitted European walnut stock, classic or beavertail forend; selective ejectors; manual or auto safety; double sears; fitted luggage case. Made in Italy. Introduced 1982; discontinued 1984.

Perf: $1700 **Exc:** $1200 **VGood:** $800

Boss Over/Under

Breda Pegaso Hunter

Bretton Baby

Brno CZ-581

BLASER F3 SUPERSPORT

O/U 12 gauge with 3-inch chambers and 32-inch free-floating chrome-plated barrels. Designed primarily for sporting clays competition. Adjustable semi-custom stock of grade 4 Turkish walnut. Weight is 9 pounds. Comes with Briley Spectrum-5 choke tubes, competition trigger.

Perf: $5850 **Exc:** $5000 **VGood:** $4500

BOSS SIDE-BY-SIDE

Side-by-side; sidelock; 12-, 16-, 20-, 28-ga., .410; 26-inch, 28-inch, 30-inch, 32-inch barrels; any desired choke combo; hand-checkered European walnut stock, forearm; straight or pistol-grip stock; automatic ejectors; double or non-selective single trigger; selective single trigger extra; round or flat action sides. Made to order. Introduced 1880; still in production.

12-ga.

Perf: $40,000 **Exc:** $30,000 **VGood:** $20,000

Smaller gauges

Perf: $45,000 **Exc:** $35,000 **VGood:** $25,000

BOSS OVER/UNDER

Over/under; sidelock; 12-, 16-, 20-, 28-ga., .410; 26-inch, 28-inch, 30-inch, 34-inch barrels; any desired choke combo; matted or vent rib; hand-checkered European walnut stock, forearm; recoil pad; automatic ejectors; double or non-selective single trigger; selective single trigger extra. Made to order. Introduced 1909; still in production.

12-ga.

Perf: $60,000 **Exc:** $40,000 **VGood:** $30,000

Smaller gauges

Perf: $65,000 **Exc:** $45,000 **VGood:** $35,000

BREDA AUTOLOADER

Autoloader; takedown; 12-, 20-ga.; 4-shot tube magazine; 25-1/2-inch, 27-1/2-inch barrels; chrome bore; plain or with matted rib; hand-checkered European walnut straight or pistol-grip stock, forearm; available in 3 grades with chromed receivers, engraving. Grade, value depends upon amount of engraving, quality of wood. Made in Italy. Introduced 1946; no longer imported.

Standard

Exc: $300 **VGood:** $275 **Good:** $255

Grade I

Exc: $575 **VGood:** $530 **Good:** $485

Grade II

Exc: $685 **VGood:** $620 **Good:** $560

Grade III

Exc: $850 **VGood:** $790 **Good:** $700

BREDA AUTOLOADER MAGNUM 12

Same specs as Autoloader except 12-ga.; 3-inch chamber. Introduced 1950; no longer imported.

Plain barrel

Exc: $470 **VGood:** $375 **Good:** $380

Matte rib

Exc: $495 **VGood:** $355 **Good:** $395

BREDA VEGA SPECIAL

Over/under; box lock action; 12-, 20-ga.; 26-inch, 28-inch barrels; single trigger; ejectors; blue finish.

Exc: $575 **VGood:** $495 **Good:** $460

BREDA VEGA SPECIAL TRAP

Over/under; boxlock action; 12 ga.; trigger and lock designed for competition shooting; 30-inch, 32-inch barrels; single trigger; ejectors; blue finish. Still imported.

Exc: $885 **VGood:** $820 **Good:** $760

BREDA VEGA LUSSO

Over/under; scalloped boxlock action; 12 ga.; 3-inch chambers; SST; ejectors; 26-inch, 28-inch barrels; vent rib; coin finished receiver with light perimeter engraving; checkered Circassian walnut stock and forearm. Introduced 2001; dropped 2002.

Exc: $1695 **VGood:** $820 **Good:** $760

BREDA SIRIO STANDARD

Over/under; box lock action; 12-, 20-ga.; 26-inch, 28-inch barrels; single trigger; ejectors; action extensively engraved; blue finish. Also available in skeet configuration (28-inch barrels).

Exc: $2000 **VGood:** $1850 **Good:** $1630

BREDA PEGASO HUNTER

Over/under; boxlock action; 12-, 20-ga.; 3-inch chambers; 26-inch, 28-inch (12 ga. Only), 30-inch (Sporting Clays only); vent rib barrels with 7mm (Hunter) or 11mm (sporting Clays) rib; 5 interchangable chokes; removable trigger group; engraved silver steel (Hunter Model) or blue finished (Sporting Clays), inertia SST; oil finished deluxe walnut stock and forearm; weighs 7 – 7-1/2 lbs.. Importation began 2004.

Exc: $2739 **VGood:** $2400 **Good:** $2050

BREDA PEGASO SPORTING CLAYS

Similar to Pegaso Hunter, except 12 ga. Only; upgraded wood; Breda logos in 24 Kt. Gold; supplied with ABS fitted case. Importation began 2004.

Exc: $3300 **VGood:** $2875 **Good:** $2400

BREDA ANDROMEDA SPECIAL

Side-by-side; 12 ga. Only; single trigger; ejectors; select checkered walnut; satin finished receiver with elaborate engraving.

Exc: $640 **VGood:** $550 **Good:** $480

BRETTON BABY

Over/under; 12-, 20-ga.; 2-3/4-inch chambers; 27-1/2-inch barrels; standard choke tubes; weighs 5 lbs.; oil-finished checkered European walnut stock; receiver slides open on guide rods, locks with thumblever; extractors. Made in France. Introduced 1986; still in production.

Perf: $995 **Exc:** $885 **VGood:** $700

BRETTON BABY DELUXE

Same specs as Bretton Baby except 12-, 16-, 20-ga.; double triggers; silvered engraved receiver. Discontinued 1994.

Perf: $1050 **Exc:** $925 **VGood:** $800

BRETTON SPRINT DELUXE

Over/under; sliding breech; 12-, 16 (disc.), 20-ga.; engraved coin finished receiver; 27-1/2-inch separated barrels; deluxe checkered walnut stock and forearm; weighs 4.8 lbs.; Importation discontinued 1994.

Perf: $895 **Exc:** $725 **VGood:** $625

BRETTON FAIR PLAY

Similar to Sprint deluxe, except that action pivots like a normal O/U; 12-, 20 ga.; 27-1/2-inch separated barrels; weighs 4.8 lbs.; No longer imported.

Perf: $966 **Exc:** $850 **VGood:** $675

BRI SPECIAL MODEL

Slide action; 12-ga.; 3-inch chamber; 24-inch rifled Cylinder barrel; 44-inch overall length; weighs 7-1/2 lbs.; no sights; scope mount on barrel; high, straight comb walnut stock; rubber recoil pad; built on Mossberg Model 500 Trophy Slugster action. Made by Ballistic Research Industries. Introduced, 1988; discontinued, 1990.

Perf: $300 **Exc:** $225 **VGood:** $180

BRNO CZ-581

Over/under; boxlock; 12-ga.; 2-3/4-inch chambers; 28-inch barrels; vent rib; 45-1/2-inch overall length; weighs 7-1/3 lbs.; Turkish walnut stock; raised cheekpiece; auto safety; sling swivels; selective ejectors; double triggers. Made in Czechoslovakia. Introduced 1986; discontinued 1991.

Perf: $550 **Exc:** $425 **VGood:** $350

BRNO MODEL 500

Over/under; boxlock; 2-3/4-inch chambers; 27-inch Full/Modified barrels; weighs 7 lbs.; European walnut raised cheekpiece stock; ejectors; double triggers; acid-etched engraving. Made in Czechoslovakia. Introduced 1987; discontinued 1991.

Perf: $845 **Exc:** $725 **VGood:** $625

Add $50 to above prices for single trigger (disc. 1999)

BRNO SUPER

Over/under; sidelock; 12-ga.; 2-3/4-inch chambers; 27-1/2-inch Full/Modified barrels; weighs 7-1/4 lbs.; European walnut raised cheekpiece stock; double safety interceptor sears; selective ejectors; double or single triggers; engraved sideplates. Made in Czechoslovakia. Introduced 1987; discontinued 1991.

Perf: $800 **Exc:** $700 **VGood:** $640

BRNO ZBK 100 SINGLE BARREL SHOTGUN

Gauge: 12 or 20. Barrel: 27.5-inch. Weight: 5.5 lbs. Length: 44-inch overall. Stock: Beech. Features:

Polished blue finish; sling swivels. Announced 1998. Imported from The Czech Republic by Euro-Imports.

Perf: $180 **Exc:** $160 **VGood:** $140

BRNO ZH-301 SERIES

Over/under; boxlock; 12-ga.; 2-3/4-inch chambers; 27-1/2-inch barrels; Modified/Full; weighs 7 lbs.; European walnut stock; double triggers; acid-etched engraving. Made in Czechoslovakia. Introduced 1987; discontinued 1991.

Brno ZH-301 Field

Perf: $600 **Exc:** $475 **VGood:** $375

Brno ZH-302 Skeet with 26-inch Skeet/Skeet barrels

Perf: $650 **Exc:** $515 **VGood:** $375

Brno ZH-303 Trap with 30-inch barrels

Perf: $600 **Exc:** $450 **VGood:** $350

BRNO ZH 300 OVER/UNDER SHOTGUN

Gauge: 12, 2-3/4-inch chambers. Barrel: 26-inch, 27-1/2-inch, 29-inch (Skeet, Imp. Cyl., Mod., Full). Weight: 7 lbs. Length: 44.4-inch overall. Stock: European walnut. Features: Double triggers; automatic safety; polished blue finish engraved receiver. Announced 1998. Imported from the Czech Republic by Euro-Imports.

ZH 301, Field

Perf: $600 **Exc:** $475 **VGood:** $395

ZH 302, Skeet

Perf: $650 **Exc:** $515 **VGood:** $375

ZH 303, 12 ga. Trap

Perf: $650 **Exc:** $515 **VGood:** $375

ZH 321, 16 ga.

Perf: $600 **Exc:** $475 **VGood:** $375

Add $20 to above prices for Monte Carlo stock

BRNO ZP-49

Side-by-side; sidelock; 12-ga.; 2-3/4-inch chambers; 28-1/2-inch Full/Modified barrels; Turkish or Yugoslavian walnut straight or pistol-grip stock; barrel indicators; ejectors; double triggers; auto safety; sling swivels. Introduced 1986; discontinued 1994.

Perf: $535 **Exc:** $.460 **VGood:** $420

BRNO ZP-149

Side-by-side; sidelock; 12-ga.; 2-3/4-inch chambers; 28-1/2-inch Full/Modified barrels; weighs 7-1/4 lbs.; Turkish or Yugoslavian walnut straight or pistol-grip stock; raised cheekpiece; barrel indicators; ejectors; double triggers; auto safety; engraving available. Made in Czechoslovakia. Introduced 1986; discontinued 1991.

Perf: $575 **Exc:** $495 **VGood:** $425

With engraving

Perf: $550 **Exc:** $450 **VGood:** $350

Add $25 to above prices for pistol grip stock

BRNO ZP-349

Side-by-side; sidelock; 12-ga.; 2-3/4-inch chambers; 28-1/2-inch Full/Modified barrels; weighs 7-1/4 lbs.; Turkish or Yugoslavian walnut straight or pistol-grip stock, beavertail forearm; raised cheekpiece; barrel indicators; extractors; double triggers; auto safety; engraving available. Made in Czechoslovakia. Introduced 1986; discontinued 1991.

Perf: $450 **Exc:** $390 **VGood:** $360

With engraving

Perf: $470 **Exc:** $410 **VGood:** $380

BRNO 501.2 OVER/UNDER SHOTGUN

Gauge: 12, 2-3/4-inch chambers. Barrel: 27.5-inch (Full & Mod.). Weight: 7 lbs. Length: 44-inch overall. Stock: European walnut. Features: Boxlock action with double triggers, ejectors; automatic safety; hand-cut checkering. Announced 1998. Imported from The Czech Republic by Euro-Imports.

Perf: $845 **Exc:** $725 **VGood:** $625

BROWNING A-500G

Gas-operated autoloader; 12-ga.; 3-inch chamber; 26-inch, 28-inch, 30-inch interchangeable barrel with Invector choke tubes; ventilated rib; weighs

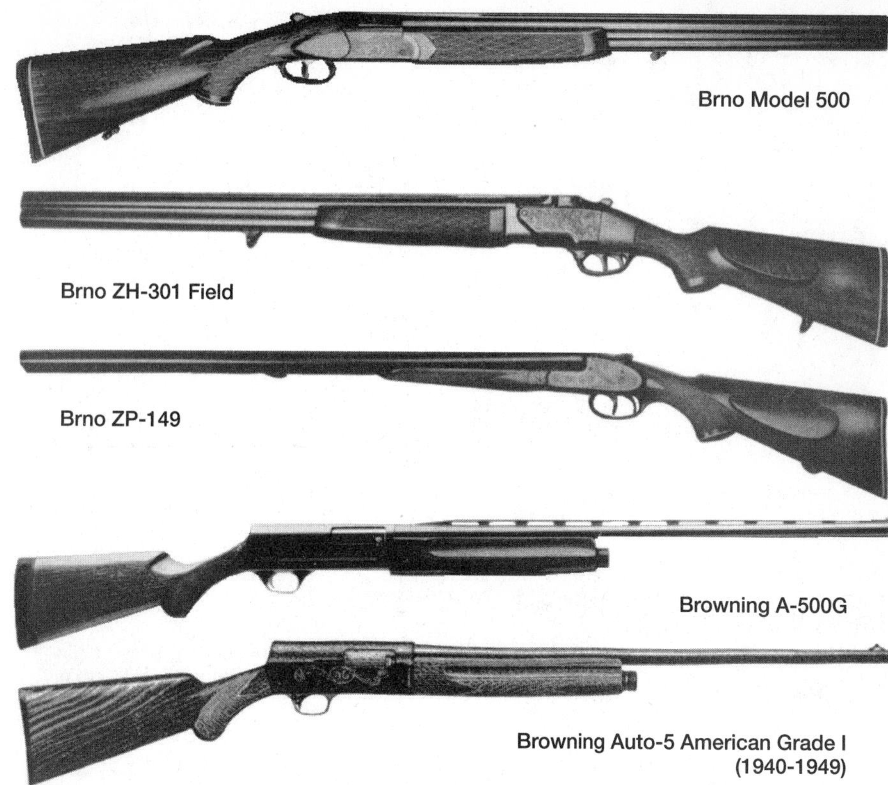

Brno Model 500

Brno ZH-301 Field

Brno ZP-149

Browning A-500G

Browning Auto-5 American Grade I (1940-1949)

7-3/4 lbs.; 47-1/2-inch overall length; select walnut rounded pistol-grip stock with gloss finish; recoil pad; four-lug rotary bolt; crossbolt safety; patented gas metering system to handle all loads; built-in buffering system to absorb recoil, reduce stress on internal parts; high-polish blue finish with light engraving on receiver and "A-500G" in gold color. Made in Japan. Introduced 1990; discontinued 1993.

Perf: $555 **Exc:** $425 **VGood:** $375

BROWNING A-500G BUCK SPECIAL

Same specs as A-500G except 24-inch barrel; 45-1/2-inch overall length; weighs 7-3/4 lbs.; screw adjustable rear sight, countoured ramp front with gold bead. Made in Japan. Introduced 1990; discontinued 1992.

Perf: $540 **Exc:** $395 **VGood:** $350

BROWNING A-500G SPORTING CLAYS

Same specs as A-500G except 28-inch, 30-inch Invector choke barrel; receiver has semi-gloss finish with "Sporting Clays" in gold lettering. Made in Japan. Introduced 1992; discontinued 1993.

Perf: $555 **Exc:** $425 **VGood:** $375

BROWNING A-500R

Short-recoil autoloader; 12-ga.; 3-inch chamber; 26-inch, 28-inch, 30-inch barrel; Invector choke tubes; weighs about 7-1/2 lbs.; select walnut pistol-grip stock, forend with gloss finish; black ventilated recoil pad; four-lug rotary bolt; composite and coil spring buffering system; shoots all loads without adjustment; magazine cut-off. Made in Belgium. Introduced 1987; discontinued 1993.

Perf: $475 **Exc:** $425 **VGood:** $375

BROWNING A-500R BUCK SPECIAL

Same specs as A-500R except 24-inch barrel; ramp front sight, open adjustable rear. Made in Belgium. Introduced 1987; discontinued 1993.

Perf: $510 **Exc:** $460 **VGood:** $410

BROWNING AUTO-5 (1900-1940)

Recoil-operated autoloader; takedown; 12-, 16-ga.; 3- (pre-WWII), 4-shot magazine; 26-inch to 32-inch barrels; various chokes; plain barrel, vent or raised matted rib; hand-checkered European walnut pistol-grip stock, forearm. Made by FN. Introduced 1900; has been made in a wide variety of configurations grades and gauges; redesignated as Grade I in 1940. Deduct 25 percent for "suicide safety" inset into the front end of the trigger guard.

With plain barrel

Exc: $675 **VGood:** $575 **Good:** $475

With raised rib

Exc: $750 **VGood:** $675 **Good:** $575

With ventilated rib

Exc: $825 **VGood:** $725 **Good:** $650

BROWNING AUTO-5 (1900-1940) GRADE III

Same specs as Auto-5 (1900-1940) except better wood, checkering and more engraving. Discontinued 1940.

Exc: $2350 **VGood:** $2100 **Good:** $1900

With raised matted rib

Exc: $2500 **VGood:** $2250 **Good:** $2050

With ventilated rib

Exc: $2795 **VGood:** $2475 **Good:** $2225

BROWNING AUTO-5 (1900-1940) GRADE IV

Same specs as Auto-5 (1900-1940) except better wood, checkering and engraving; profuse inlays of green, yellow gold. Sometimes called Midas Grade. Discontinued 1940.

Exc: $3655 **VGood:** $3300 **Good:** $2995

With raised matted rib

Exc: $3995 **VGood:** $3655 **Good:** $3300

BROWNING AUTO-5 AMERICAN GRADE I (1940-1949)

Autoloader; 12-, 16-, 20-ga.; 2-3/4-inch chamber; 3-, 5-shot tube magazine; 26-inch, 28-inch, 30-inch, 32-inch barrel; standard chokes; no rib; weighs 6-7/8 lbs. (20-ga.), 7-1/4 lbs. (16-ga.), 8 lbs. (12-ga.); hand-checkered American walnut pistol-grip stock, forend; identical to the Remington Model 11A; manufactured by Remington for Browning. Introduced 1940; discontinued 1949.

Exc: $495 **VGood:** $395 **Good:** $350

Add 10 percent to above prices for vent. Rib or 20 ga.

Browning Auto-5 American Utility Field Model (1940-1949)

Browning Auto-5 Belgium Standard (1947-1953)

Browning Auto-5 Classic

Browning Auto-5 Classic Gold

Browning Auto-5 Light Buck Special (Miroku)

Browning Auto-5 Light Sweet 16 (FN)

BROWNING AUTO-5 AMERICAN SPECIAL (1940-1949)

Same specs as Auto-5 American Grade I (1940-1949) except either ventilated rib or matted raised rib. Introduced 1940; discontinued 1949.

With ventilated rib		
Exc: $375	**VGood:** $320	**Good:** $290
With raised rib		
Exc: $360	**VGood:** $300	**Good:** $280

BROWNING AUTO-5 AMERICAN SPECIAL SKEET (1940-1949)

Same specs as Auto-5 American Grade I (1940-1949) except 26-inch barrel; ventilated rib; Cutts Compensator. Introduced 1940; discontinued 1949.

Exc: $375 **VGood:** $325 **Good:** $295

BROWNING AUTO-5 AMERICAN UTILITY FIELD MODEL (1940-1949)

Same specs as Auto-5 American Grade I (1940-1949) except 28-inch barrel; PolyChoke. Introduced 1940; discontinued 1949.

Exc: $395 **VGood:** $255 **Good:** $220

BROWNING AUTO-5 BELGIUM STANDARD (1947-1953)

Autoloader; 12-, 16-ga.; 3-, 5-shot magazine; 2-3/4-inch chambers; 26-inch, 28-inch, 30-inch, 32-inch barrel; standard choke tubes; plain, matted or ventilated rib; weighs 8 lbs.; hand-checkered French walnut stock with high-gloss finish; hand-engraved receiver. Introduced 1947; discontinued 1953.

With plain barrel		
Exc: $595	**VGood:** $425	**Good:** $375
With hollow matted rib		
Exc: $680	**VGood:** $335	**Good:** $315
With ventilated rib		
Exc: $695	**VGood:** $550	**Good:** $500

BROWNING AUTO-5 CLASSIC

Autoloader; 12-ga.; 2-3/4-inch chamber; 5-shot magazine with 3-shot plug furnished; 28-inch Modified barrel; select figured walnut stock; special checkering; hunting, wildlife scenes engraved in satin gray receiver; engraved portrait of John M. Browning; engraved legend, "Browning Classic. One of Five Thousand." Only 5000 manufactured. Introduced 1984; discontinued 1984.

Exc: $1195 **VGood:** $945 **Good:** $725

BROWNING AUTO-5 CLASSIC GOLD

Same specs as Auto-5 Classic except engraved scenes are inlaid with gold animals portrait; engraved with "Browning Gold Classic One of Five Hundred." Only 500 made. Introduced 1984; discontinued 1984.

Perf: $4195 **Exc:** $3495 **VGood:** $2495

BROWNING AUTO-5 LIGHT (FN)

Autoloader; 12-, 20-ga.; 2-3/4-inch chamber; 5-shot magazine with 3-shot plug furnished; 26-inch, 28-inch, 30-inch barrel; standard chokes; checkered walnut pistol-grip stock, forend; hand-engraved receiver; gold-plated trigger; double extractors; interchangeable barrels; with or without ventilated rib. Made by FN Belgium. Introduced 1952; discontinued 1976.

Without rib		
Perf: $650	**Exc:** $550	**VGood:** $450
With ventilated rib		
Perf: $950	**Exc:** $795	**VGood:** $645

BROWNING AUTO-5 LIGHT (MIROKU)

Same specs as Auto-5 Light (FN) except ventilated rib; Invector choke tubes. Made by Miroku of Japan. Introduced 1976.

Perf: $775 **Exc:** $595 **VGood:** $525

BROWNING AUTO-5 LIGHT BUCK SPECIAL (MIROKU)

Same specs as Auto-5 Light (FN) except 24-inch barrel; choked for slugs; vent rib; adjustable rear sight, gold bead front on contoured ramp; detachable swivels, sling optional on current model. Made by Miroku of Japan. Introduced 1976; discontinued 1985; reintroduced 1989.

Perf: $700 **Exc:** $400 **VGood:** $350

BROWNING AUTO-5 LIGHT SKEET (FN)

Same specs as the Auto-5 Light (FN) except for 26-inch, 28-inch Skeet/Skeet barrel; plain barrel or vent rib (late models). Made by FN Belgium. Introduced 1952; discontinued 1976.

Perf: $675 **Exc:** $575 **VGood:** $400

BROWNING AUTO-5 LIGHT SKEET (MIROKU)

Same specs as the Auto-5 Light (FN) except for 26-inch, 28-inch Skeet/Skeet barrel; vent rib. Made by Miroku of Japan. Introduced 1976; discontinued 1983.

Perf: $650 **Exc:** $585 **VGood:** $400

BROWNING AUTO-5 LIGHT STALKER

Same specs as Auto-5 Light (FN) except 12-ga.; 2-3/4-inch chamber; 26-inch, 28-inch vent-rib barrel; Invector choke tubes; weighs 8 lbs. (26-inch); black graphite-fiberglass stock, forend with checkered panels; matte blue metal finish. Made by Miroku of Japan. Introduced 1992.

Perf: $650 **Exc:** $595 **VGood:** $425

BROWNING AUTO-5 SWEET 16 (FN)

Same specs as Auto-5 (FN) except 16-ga.; 2-9/16-inch, 2-3/4-inch chamber; weighs 6-3/4 lbs. (without rib); gold-plated trigger, safety, safety latch. Introduced 1937; discontinued 1976. Deduct 10 percent for suicide safety.

Without rib		
Exc: $860	**VGood:** $660	**Good:** $600
With hollow matted rib		
Exc: $1295	**VGood:** $995	**Good:** $825
With ventilated rib		
Exc: $1595	**VGood:** $1295	**Good:** $950

BROWNING AUTO-5 SWEET 16 (MIROKU)

Same specs as Auto-5 (FN) except 16-ga.; 2-3/4-inch chamber; Invector chokes; vent rib; weighs 7-1/4 lbs. Made by Miroku of Japan. Introduced 1987; discontinued 1992.

Perf: $1295 **Exc:** $925 **VGood:** $850

BROWNING AUTO-5 TRAP (FN)

Same specs as Auto-5 Light (FN) except 12-ga.; 30-inch Full barrel; vent rib; weighs 8-1/4 lbs.; trap stock. Made by FN Belgium. Discontinued 1971.

Exc: $850 **VGood:** $665 **Good:** $625

BROWNING AUTO-5 MAGNUM (FN)

Autoloader; 12-, 20-ga.; 3-inch chamber; 26-inch, 28-inch, 30-inch, 32-inch barrels; Full, Modified, Improved Cylinder chokes; plain or vent-rib; checkered walnut pistol-grip stock, forend; recoil pad. Made by FN Belgium. Introduced 1958; discontinued 1976.

With plain barrel		
Perf: $725	**Exc:** $650	**VGood:** $550
With ventilated rib		
Perf: $825	**Exc:** $795	**VGood:** $695

BROWNING AUTO-5 MAGNUM (MIROKU)

Same specs as Auto-5 Magnum (FN) except 26-inch, 28-inch barrel; Invector choke tubes. Made by Miroku of Japan. Introduced 1976.

Perf: $825 **Exc:** $650 **VGood:** $595

BROWNING AUTO-5 MAGNUM STALKER
Same specs as the Auto-5 Magnum (FN) except 26-inch, 28-inch back-bored vent-rib barrel; Invector choke tubes; weighs 8-3/4 lbs. (28-inch); black graphite-fiberglass stock, forend with checkered panels; matte blue metal finish. Made by Miroku of Japan. Introduced 1992.

Perf: $750 **Exc:** $650 **VGood:** $400

BROWNING A5 HUNTER
Semi-auto 12-gauge with 3-inch chamber, 26, 28, or 30-inch vent-rib barrel with Invector DS choke tubes. Kinematic Drive recoil operating system with fixed barrel. Squared receiver is similar in appearance to original Auto-5 models, but the design is totally different. Introduced in 2012.

Perf: $1250 **Exc:** $1000 **VGood:** $850

BROWNING B-80
Autoloader; 12-, 20-ga.; 2-3/4-inch, 3-inch chamber; 5-shot magazine; 22-inch slug barrel, 26-inch Improved Cylinder, Cylinder, Cylinder Skeet, Full, Modified, 28-inch Full, Modified, 30-inch Full, 32-inch Full choke barrels; ventilated rib; hand-checkered French walnut stock; solid black recoil pad; steel receiver; interchangeable barrels. Made in Belgium. Introduced 1981; discontinued 1989.

Perf: $425 **Exc:** $300 **VGood:** $275

BROWNING B-80 UPLAND SPECIAL
Same specs as B-80 except 2-3/4-inch chamber; 22-inch barrel; hand-checkered French walnut straight-grip stock. Made in Belgium. Introduced 1986; discontinued 1989.

Perf: $450 **Exc:** $320 **VGood:** $290

BROWNING B-2000
Autoloader; 12-, 20-ga.; 2-3/4-inch chamber; 4-shot magazine; 26-inch, 28-inch, 30-inch barrel; choice of standard chokes; vent rib or plain matted barrel; checkered pistol-grip stock of European walnut. Manufactured in Belgium, assembled in Portugal. Introduced 1974; discontinued 1982.

Perf: $345 **Exc:** $280 **VGood:** $240

BROWNING B-2000 BUCK SPECIAL
Same specs as B-2000 except 12- (2-3/4-inch), 20-ga. (3-inch); 24-inch slug barrel; no rib; open rear sight, front ramp. Introduced 1974; discontinued 1982.

Perf: $350 **Exc:** $280 **VGood:** $250

BROWNING B-2000 MAGNUM
Same specs as B-2000 except 3-inch chamber; 3-shot magazine; 26-inch, 28-inch, 30-inch, 32-inch barrel; vent rib. Introduced 1974; discontinued 1982.

Perf: $350 **Exc:** $300 **VGood:** $275

BROWNING B-2000 SKEET
Same specs as B-2000 except 26-inch Skeet-choke barrel; Skeet stock; recoil pad. Introduced 1974; discontinued 1982.

Perf: $350 **Exc:** $290 **VGood:** $260

BROWNING B-2000 TRAP
Same specs as B-2000 except 12-ga.; 2-3/4-inch chamber; 30-inch, 32-inch barrel; high post vent rib; Modified, Improved, Full chokes; Monte Carlo-style stock; recoil pad. Introduced 1974; discontinued 1982.

Perf: $350 **Exc:** $290 **VGood:** $260

BROWNING DOUBLE AUTO
Short-recoil autoloader; takedown; 12-ga.; 2-shot magazine; 26-inch, 28-inch, 30-inch barrel; any standard choke; plain or recessed rib barrel; weighs about 7-3/4 lbs; hand-checkered European walnut pistol-grip stock, forearm; steel receiver; conservative engraving. Introduced 1955; discontinued 1961.

Exc: $650 **VGood:** $525 **Good:** $450

With ventilated rib

Exc: $750 **VGood:** $550 **Good:** $475

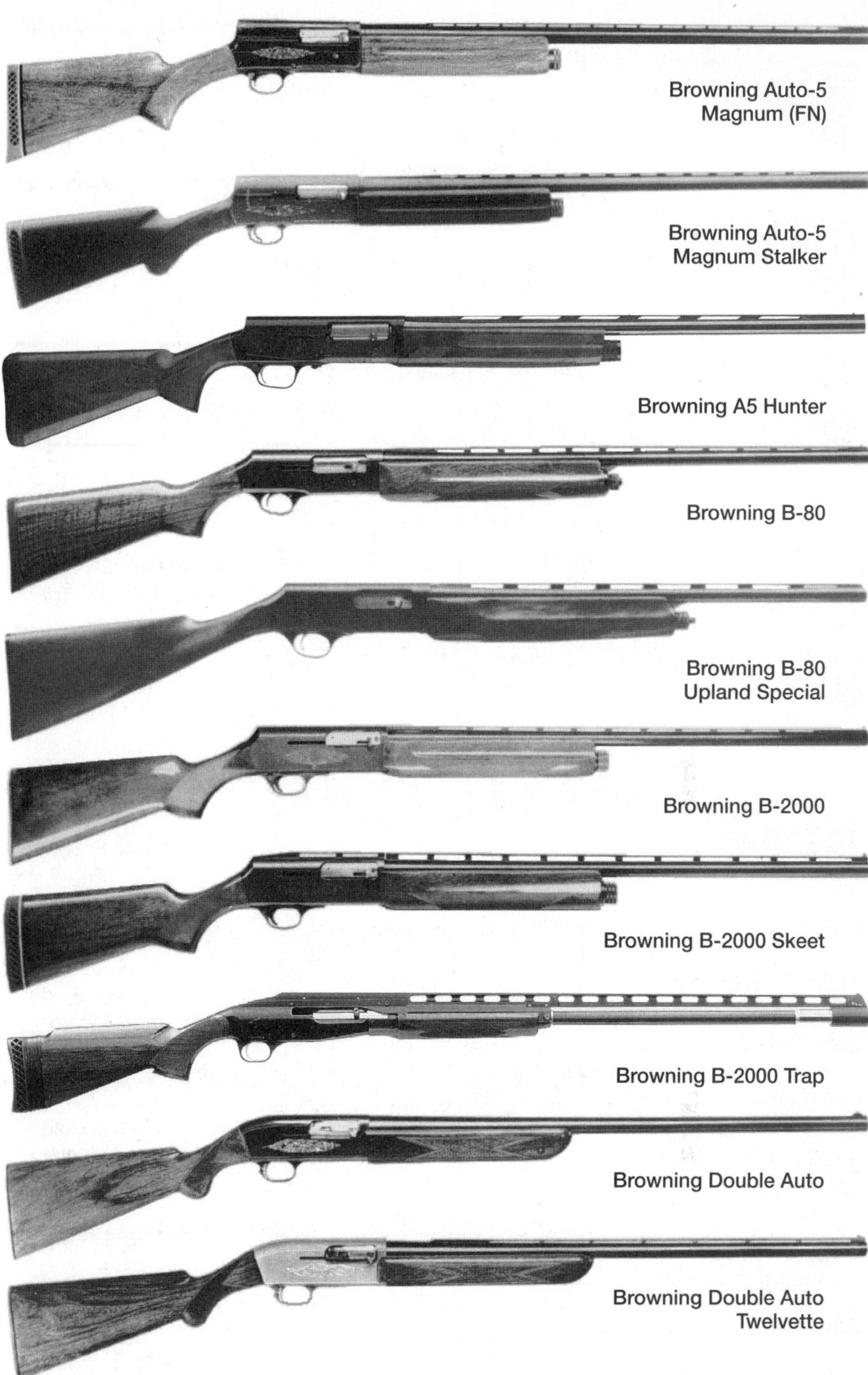

Browning Auto-5 Magnum (FN)

Browning Auto-5 Magnum Stalker

Browning A5 Hunter

Browning B-80

Browning B-80 Upland Special

Browning B-2000

Browning B-2000 Skeet

Browning B-2000 Trap

Browning Double Auto

Browning Double Auto Twelvette

BROWNING DOUBLE AUTO TWELVETTE
Same specs as Double Auto except aluminum receiver; barrel with plain matted top or vent rib; black anodized receiver with gold-wiped engraving; some receivers anodized in brown, gray or green with silver-wiped engraving; weighs about a pound less than standard model. Introduced 1955; discontinued 1971.

Exc: $650 **VGood:** $525 **Good:** $450

With ventilated rib

Exc: $750 **VGood:** $650 **Good:** $575

BROWNING DOUBLE AUTO TWENTYWEIGHT
Same specs as Double Auto except 26-1/2-inch barrel; weighs almost 2 lbs. less, largely due to thinner stock. Introduced 1956; discontinued 1971.

Exc: $650 **VGood:** $525 **Good:** $450

With ventilated rib

Exc: $825 **VGood:** $735 **Good:** $625

BROWNING GOLD
Gas-operated autoloader; 12-, 20-ga; 3-inch chamber; 4-shot magazine; 26-inch, 28-inch, 30-inch back-bored (12-ga.) or 26-inch, 30-inch (20-ga.) barrel; Invector choke tubes; weighs about 7-5/8 lbs. (12-ga.); cut-checkered select walnut stock, palm swell grip with gloss finish; self-regulating, self-cleaning gas system shoots all loads; lightweight receiver with special non-glare deep black finish; large reversible safety button; large rounded trigger guard, gold trigger; crossbolt safety; recoil pad. Made in Japan. Introduced 1994; still imported.

Perf: $660 **Exc:** $340 **VGood:** $300

Price: 12 ga., 3-1/2-inch chamber

Perf: $895 **Exc:** $725 **VGood:** $625

BROWNING GOLD RIFLED DEER HUNTER
Similar to the Gold Hunter except 12- or 20-gauge, 22-inch rifled barrel with cantilever scope mount, walnut stock with extra-thick recoil pad. Weighs

Browning Gold

Browning Gold Deer Stalker

Browning Gold Sporting Clays

Browning Gold Ladies/Youth Sporting Clays

Browning Gold Micro

Browning Gold Stalker

Browning Gold Mossy Oak Break-Up

Browning Gold Classic Hunter

Browning Gold Classic Stalker

7 lbs., 12 oz., overall length 42-1/2-inch. Sling swivel studs fitted on the magazine cap and butt. Introduced 1997. Imported by Browning.

12-gauge

Perf: $860 **Exc:** $625 **VGood:** $525

With Mossy Oak Break-up camouflage

Perf: $945 **Exc:** $745 **VGood:** $610

20-gauge (satin-finish walnut stock, 3-inch chamber)

Perf: $875 **Exc:** $695 **VGood:** $600

BROWNING GOLD DEER STALKER

Similar to the Gold Deer Hunter except has black composite stock and forend, fully rifled 12-gauge barrel, cantilever scope mount. Introduced 1999. Imported by Browning.

Perf: $755 **Exc:** $550 **VGood:** $450

BROWNING GOLD SPORTING CLAYS

Similar to the Gold Hunter except 12-gauge only with 28-inch or 30-inch barrel; front Hi-Viz Pro-Comp and center bead on tapered ventilated rib; ported and back-bored Invector Plus barrel; 2-3/4-inch chamber; satin-finished stock with solid, radiused recoil pad with hard heel insert; non-glare black alloy receiver has "Sporting Clays" inscribed in gold. Introduced 1996. Imported from Japan.

Perf: $825 **Exc:** $570 **VGood:** $460

BROWNING GOLD SPORTING GOLDEN CLAYS

Similar to the Sporting Clays except has silvered receiver with gold engraving, high-grade wood. Introduced 1999. Imported by Browning.

Perf: $1275 **Exc:** $1025 **VGood:** $840

BROWNING GOLD LADIES/YOUTH SPORTING CLAYS

Similar to the Gold Sporting Clays except has stock dimensions of 14-1/4-inch by 1-3/4-inch by 2-inch for women and younger shooters. Introduced 1999. Imported by Browning.

Perf: $780 **Exc:** $550 **VGood:** $455

BROWNING GOLD MICRO

Similar to the Gold Hunter except has a 26-inch barrel, 13-7/8-inch pull length and smaller pistol grip for youths and other small shooters. Weighs 6 lbs., 10 oz. Introduced 2001.

Perf: $780 **Exc:** $550 **VGood:** $435

BROWNING GOLD STALKER

Similar to the Gold Hunter except has black composite stock and forend. Choice of 3-inch or 3-1/2-inch chamber.

12 ga. with 3-inch chamber

Perf: $755 **Exc:** $550 **VGood:** $430

With 3-1/2-inch chamber

Perf: $765 **Exc:** $565 **VGood:** $950

BROWNING GOLD MOSSY OAK® SHADOW GRASS

Similar to the Gold Hunter except 12-gauge only, completely covered with Mossy Oak Shadow Grass camouflage. Choice of 3-inch or 3-1/2-inch chamber and 26-inch or 28-inch barrel. Introduced 1999. Imported by Browning.

12 ga. 3-inch chamber

Perf: $1035 **Exc:** $800 **VGood:** $675

12 ga., 3-1/2-inch chamber

Perf: $1075 **Exc:** $870 **VGood:** $750

BROWNING GOLD MOSSY OAK® BREAK-UP

Similar to the Gold Hunter except 12-gauge only, completely covered with Mossy Oak Break-Up camouflage. Imported by Browning.

3-inch chamber

Perf: $855 **Exc:** $585 **VGood:** $475

3-1/2-inch chamber

Perf: $875 **Exc:** $635 **VGood:** $500

NWTF model, 3-inch chamber, 24-inch bbl. with Hi-Viz sight

Perf: $885 **Exc:** $610 **VGood:** $495

NWTF model, 3-1/2-inch chamber, 24-inch bbl. with Hi-Viz sight.

Perf: $950 **Exc:** $700 **VGood:** $600

Gold Rifled Deer (22-inch rifled bbl., cantilever scope mount)

Perf: $795 **Exc:** $565 **VGood:** $455

BROWNING GOLD CLASSIC HUNTER

Similar to the Gold Hunter 3-inch except has semi-hump back receiver, magazine cut-off, adjustable comb, and satin-finish wood. Introduced 1999. Imported by Browning.

12 or 20 gauge

Perf: $780 **Exc:** $550 **VGood:** $435

Classic High Grade (silvered, gold engraved receiver, high-grade wood)

Perf: $1575 **Exc:** $1250 **VGood:** $1050

BROWNING GOLD CLASSIC STALKER

Similar to the Gold Classic Hunter except has adjustable composite stock and forend. Introduced 1999. Imported by Browning.

Perf: $725 **Exc:** $530 **VGood:** $430

BROWNING GOLD FUSION

Similar to the Gold Hunter except is 1/2 lb. lighter, has a new-style vent rib, adjustable comb system, Hi-Viz Pro-Comp front sight and five choke tubes. Offered with 26-inch, 28-inch or 30-inch barrel, 12-gauge, 3-inch chamber only. Includes hard case. Introduced 2001. Imported by Browning.

Perf: $865 **Exc:** $600 **VGood:** $475

BROWNING NWTF GOLD TURKEY STALKER

Similar to the Gold Hunter except 12-ga., 3-inch chamber only, has 24-inch barrel with Hi-Viz front sight and National Wild Turkey Federation logo on stock. Imported by Browning.

Perf: $710 **Exc:** $525 **VGood:** $425

BROWNING GOLD TURKEY/ WATERFOWL CAMO

Similar to the Gold Turkey/Waterfowl Hunter except 12-gauge only, 3-inch or 3-1/2-inch chamber, 24-inch barrel with extra-full turkey choke tube, Hi-Viz front sight. Completely covered with Mossy Oak Break-Up camouflage. Introduced 1999. Imported by Browning.

Perf: $715 **Exc:** $500 **VGood:** $400

Turkey/Waterfowl Stalker (black stock and metal)

Perf: $875 **Exc:** $695 **VGood:** $600

BROWNING GOLD NWTF TURKEY SERIES CAMO

Similar to the Gold Turkey/Waterfowl model except 10- or 12-gauge (3-inch or 3-1/2-inch chamber), 24-inch barrel with extra-full choke tube, Hi-Viz fiber-optic sights and complete gun coverage in Mossy Oak Break-Up camouflage with National Wild Turkey Federation logo on stock. Introduced 2001.

10 gauge

Perf: $1075 **Exc:** $875 **VGood:** $775

12 gauge, 3-1/2-inch chamber

Perf: $1075 **Exc:** $875 **VGood:** $775

12 gauge, 3-inch chamber

Perf: $635 **Exc:** $475 **VGood:** $415

BROWNING GOLD UPLAND SPECIAL

Similar to the Gold Classic Hunter except has straight-grip walnut stock, 12- or 20-gauge, 3-inch chamber. Introduced 2001.

12-gauge (24-inch bbl., weighs 7 lbs.)

Perf: $750 **Exc:** $535 **VGood:** $425

20-gauge (26-inch bbl., weighs 6 lbs., 12 oz.)

Perf: $750 **Exc:** $535 **VGood:** $425

BROWNING GOLD SUPERLITE HUNTER

Introduced in 2006, this gun uses an aluminum alloy receiver and alloy magazine tube to reduce weight to about 7 lbs. in 12 gauge. Gloss finish walnut stock. Available with 3-inch or 3.5-inch chamber and 26-inch or 28-inch barrel. Magazine cut-off feature on 3.5-inch model. A 6.5 lb. 20 gauge with 3-inch chamber and 26-inch or 28-inch barrel is also offered. Three choke tubes. Add 15 percent for 3.5-inch chamber.

NIB: $950 **Exc:** $875 **VGood:** $725

BROWNING GOLD SUPERLITE FIELD HUNTER

Similar to Gold Superlite Hunter but with semi-humpback style receiver and satin finish walnut stock and 3-inch chamber only. Magazine cut-off on 12 gauge models. Adjustable shim system and three choke tubes.

NIB: $950 **Exc:** $875 **VGood:** $725

BROWNING GOLD SUPERLITE MICRO

Similar to Gold Superlite Hunter but with compact dimensions for smaller shooters. Only in 20 gauge with 26-inch barrel. Weighs about 6.25 pounds. Three choke tubes.

NIB: $945 **Exc:** $870 **VGood:** $720

BROWNING GOLD 10

Same specs as Gold except 10-ga.; 3-1/2-inch chamber; 26-inch, 28-inch, 30-inch barrel; Invector tubes choked Improved Cylinder, Modified, Full; weighs about 10-1/2 lbs.; forged steel receiver with polished blue finish. Made in Japan. Introduced 1993; still imported.

Perf: $820 **Exc:** $550 **VGood:** $480

BROWNING GOLD 10-GAUGE AUTO COMBO

Similar to the Gold 10 except comes with 24-inch and 26-inch barrels with Imp. Cyl., Mod., Full Invector choke tubes. Introduced 1999. Imported by Browning.

Perf: $880 **Exc:** $764 **VGood:** $633

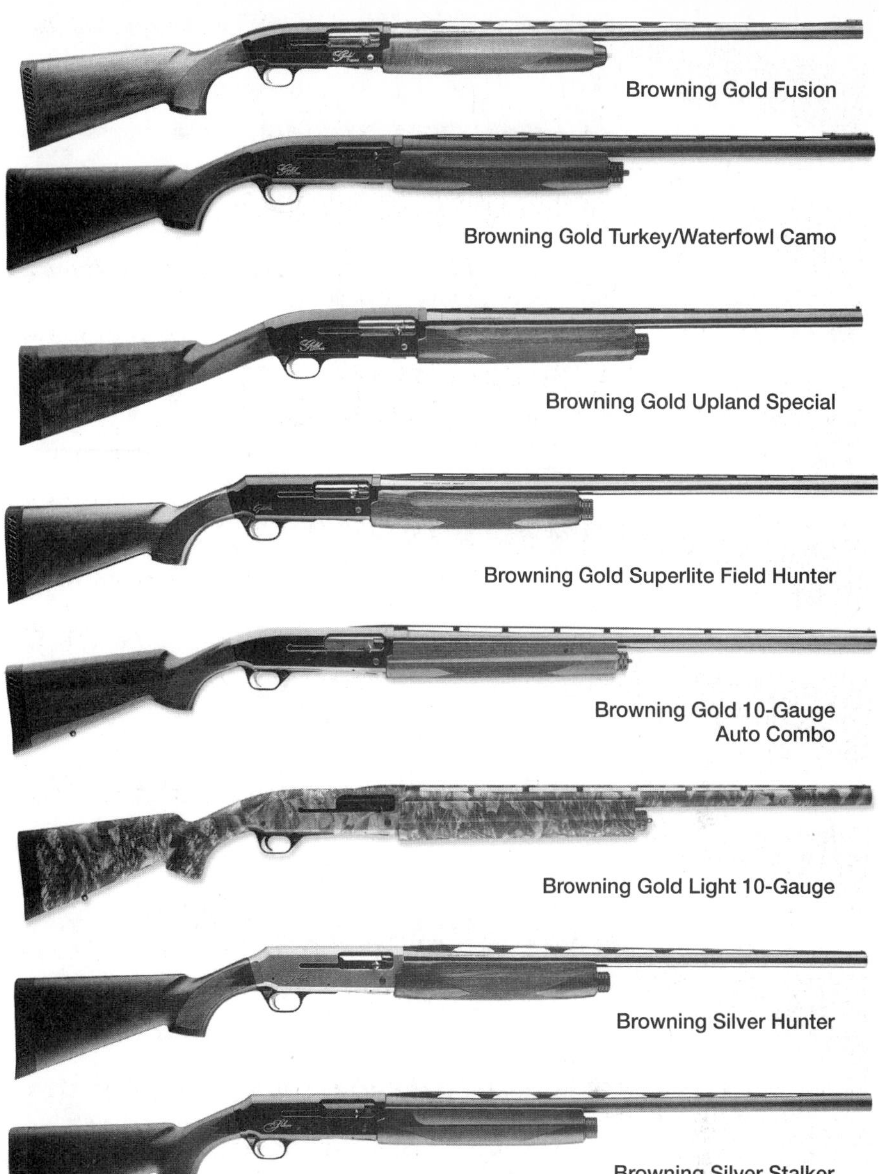

Browning Gold Fusion

Browning Gold Turkey/Waterfowl Camo

Browning Gold Upland Special

Browning Gold Superlite Field Hunter

Browning Gold 10-Gauge Auto Combo

Browning Gold Light 10-Gauge

Browning Silver Hunter

Browning Silver Stalker

BROWNING GOLD LIGHT 10-GAUGE

Similar to the Browning Gold 10, except has an alloy receiver that is 1 lb. lighter than standard model. Offered in 26-inch or 28-inch bbls. With Mossy Oak Break-Up or Shadow Grass coverage; 5-shot magazine. Weighs 9 lbs., 10 oz. (28-inch bbl.). Introduced 2001. Imported by Browning.

Perf: $1025 **Exc:** $800 **VGood:** $695

Stalker (black composite stock and forearm)

Perf: $1127 **Exc:** $880 **VGood:** $764

BROWNING GOLD 10 STALKER

Same specs as Gold except 10-ga.; 3-1/2-inch chamber; 26-inch, 28-inch, 30-inch barrel; Invector tubes choked Improved Cylinder, Modified, Full; weighs about 10-1/2 lbs.; checkered black graphite-fiberglass composite stock with dull finish; non-glare metal finish. Made in Japan. Introduced 1993; still imported.

Perf: $820 **Exc:** $550 **VGood:** $480

BROWNING SILVER HUNTER

This semi-auto features a satin finish walnut stock and forend. It is available with a 3-inch chamber in 26-inch, 28-inch and 30-inch barrel lengths or with a 3.5-inch chamber in 26-inch or 28-inch barrel length. Add 15 percent for 3.5-inch chamber.

NIB: $800 **Exc:** $725 **VGood:** $600

BROWNING SILVER STALKER

Similar to Silver Hunter but with matte black composite stock and forend. Sling swivel studs. 3.5-inch chamber only.

NIB: $775 **Exc:** $710 **VGood:** $575

BROWNING SILVER MOSSY OAK

Similar to Silver Stalker but in choice of Mossy Oak New Break-Up with 26-inch barrel or Mossy Oak New Shadow Grass with 26-inch or 28-inch barrel.

NIB: $975 **Exc:** $895 **VGood:** $675

BROWNING SILVER MICRO

This is a 20 gauge with a 26" barrel and shorter stock dimensions for smaller shooters.

NIB: $825 **Exc:** $750 **VGood:** $625

BROWNING SILVER SPORTING MICRO

This 2.75" 12 gauge includes adjustment spacers for changing stock length. Barrel is 28". Three choke tubes included. Weight is about 7 lbs.

NIB: $825 **Exc:** $750 **VGood:** $625

BROWNING SILVER NWTF

New in 2008, this 3" 12 gauge turkey gun is fully camouflaged with Mossy Oak's New Break-Up pattern. The 24" barrel is outfitted with fiber-optic rifle sights. Weight is about 7 lbs. Add 10% for 3.5" chamber.

NIB: $1100 **Exc:** $900 **VGood:** $725

BROWNING SILVER RIFLED DEER

New in 2008, this 3" 12 gauge slug gun features a rifled barrel with cantilever scope mount. Finishes include satin walnut, black composite and Mossy Oak New Break-Up camo. Add 10% for camo finish.

NIB: $1100 **Exc:** $900 **VGood:** $725

BROWNING BSS

Side-by-side; boxlock; hammerless; 12-, 20-ga.; 3-inch chambers; 26-inch, 28-inch, 30-inch barrel; standard choke combos; checkered walnut pistol grip stock, beavertail forend; non-selective single trigger. Made in Japan. Introduced 1972; discontinued 1987.

Perf: $925 **Exc:** $750 **VGood:** $550

Add 50 percent to above prices for 20 gauge in 95+ percent condition Subtract 20 percent from above prices for early guns with single, non-selective trigger

BROWNING BSS SPORTER

Same specs as BSS except 20-ga.; 26-inch, 28-inch barrel; walnut straight stock, forend; selective trigger. Made in Japan. Introduced 1977; discontinued 1987.

Perf: $1150 **Exc:** $950 **VGood:** $800

BROWNING B-SS SPORTER GRADE II

Similar to Sporter, except has satin grey finished receiver with an engraved pheasant, duck, quail and dogs. Discontinued 1983.

Perf: $1750 **Exc:** $1475 **VGood:** $1100

Add 50 percent to above prices for 20 ga. In 95 percent + condition

BROWNING BSS SIDELOCK

Side-by-side; sidelock; 12-, 20-ga.; 26-inch, 28-inch, barrel; straight-grip French walnut stock; checkered butt; double triggers; auto safety; cocking indicator; receiver, forend iron, trigger guard, top lever, tang are satin gray with rosettes, scrollwork. Made in Japan. Introduced 1984; discontinued 1987.

12-Gauge

Perf: $3500 **Exc:** $3100 **VGood:** $2600

20-Gauge

Perf: $4750 **Exc:** $4100 **VGood:** $3500

BROWNING CITORI (HUNTING) MODELS

Over/under; boxlock; 12-, 16-, 20-, 28-ga., .410; 3-inch, 3-1/2-inch chambers; 26-inch, 28-inch, 30-inch barrel; Improved/Modified, Modified/Full, Full/Full chokes or Invector choke tubes; checkered pistol-grip stock, semi-beavertail forearm; automatic ejectors; selective single trigger; recoil pad. Various grades available with price dependent on type of engraving. Made in Japan. Introduced 1973; dropped 2001.

Grade I

Perf: $750 **Exc:** $675 **VGood:** $575

Grade I, 12-ga., 3-1/2-inch

Perf: $950 **Exc:** $720 **VGood:** $600

Grade I, Hunter (discontinued 2001); Invector, 12 and 20

Grade I, Lightning; Invector Plus; 12, 20

Grade I, Lightning; 28 and .410; Invector

Grade II

Perf: $995 **Exc:** $810 **VGood:** $740

Grade III, grayed steel receiver, light engraving. Lightning; Invector Plus; 12, 20

Lightning; 28 and .410; Invector Plus

Perf: $1350 **Exc:** $800 **VGood:** $700

Grade V, extensive engraving

Perf: $1450 **Exc:** $1000 **VGood:** $950

Grade VI, blue or grayed receiver, extensive engraving and inlays. Grade VI, Lightning, Invector Plus; 12, 20

Grade VI, Lightning; 28-ga. and .410; Invector

Perf: $2000 **Exc:** $1200 **VGood:** $1000

Gran Lightning; 26-inch, 28-inch, Invector Plus; 12, 20

Perf: $1825 **Exc:** $1300 **VGood:** $1050

Gran Lightning; 28-ga., .410

Perf: $1948 **Exc:** $1423 **VGood:** $1173

Micro Lightning, 20-ga., 24-inch bbl.; discontinued 2001

Perf: $1250 **Exc:** $945 **VGood:** $785

White Lightning (silver nitride receiver w/engraving, 12- or 20-ga., 26-inch, 28-inch)

Perf: $1265 **Exc:** $960 **VGood:** $800

White Lightning, 28-ga. or .410-bore

Perf: $1337 **Exc:** $1032 **VGood:** $872

BROWNING CITORI SATIN HUNTER

12-ga., satin-finished wood, matte-finished bbls and receiver, 3-1/2-inch chambers. Discontinued 2001.

Perf: $1150 **Exc:** $825 **VGood:** $650

BROWNING CITORI LIGHTNING (HUNTING)

Same specs as Citori Hunting except Invector choke tubes; hand-checkered French walnut pistol-grip stock, slim forearm; ivory bead sights. Introduced 1988; still in production.

Grade I

Perf: $950 **Exc:** $520 **VGood:** $480

Grade III, grayed steel receiver, light engraving

Perf: $1850 **Exc:** $1350 **VGood:** $1035

Grade VI, blue or grayed receiver, extensive engraving and inlays

Perf: $2825 **Exc:** $2100 **VGood:** $1475

BROWNING CITORI GRAN LIGHTNING (HUNTING)

Same specs as Citori Hunting except 3-inch chambers; 26-inch, 28-inch barrels; Invector choke tubes; high-grade walnut stock; satin-oil finish. Introduced 1990; still in production.

Perf: $1400 **Exc:** $800 **VGood:** $650

BROWNING CITORI LIGHTNING MICRO (HUNTING)

Same specs as Citori Hunting except scaled down for smaller shooters; 24-inch barrels; Invector choke system; weighs 6-1/8 lbs. Introduced 1991; discontinued 2001.

Grade I

Perf: $1250 **Exc:** $945 **VGood:** $785

BROWNING CITORI HUNTING SPORTER

Same specs as Citori Hunting except 3-inch chamber; 26-inch barrel; walnut straight-grip stock, schnabel forend with satin oil finish. Introduced 1978; no longer in production.

Grade I

Perf: $800 **Exc:** $550 **VGood:** $500

Grade II

Perf: $1150 **Exc:** $980 **VGood:** $850

Grade V

Perf: $1450 **Exc:** $1150 **VGood:** $1000

BROWNING CITORI SPORTING HUNTER

Similar to the Citori Hunting I except has Sporting Clays stock dimensions, a Superposed-style forend, and Sporting Clays butt pad. Available in 12-gauge with 3-inch chambers, back-bored 26-inch, 28-

inch and 30-inch, all with Invector Plus choke tube system. Introduced 1998; discontinued 2001. Imported from Japan by Browning.

12-gauge, 3-1/2-inch

Perf: $1352 **Exc:** $997 **VGood:** $827

12-, 20-gauge, 3-inch

Perf: $1250 **Exc:** $895 **VGood:** $725

BROWNING CITORI HUNTING SUPERLIGHT

Same specs as Citori Hunting except 12-, 20-, 28-ga., .410; 2-3/4-inch chambers; 24-inch, 26-inch, 28-inch barrels; straight-grip stock; schnabel forend. Made in Japan. Introduced 1982; all but Superlight Feather discontinued 2001.

Grade I

Perf: $950 **Exc:** $575 **VGood:** $480

Grade III, grayed steel receiver, light engraving

Perf: $1750 **Exc:** $1275 **VGood:** $975

Subtract 10 percent from above prices if without Invector choke tubes

Add $275 to above prices for 28 ga. Or .410 bore

Grade VI, blue or grayed receiver, extensive engraving and inlays

Perf: $1950 **Exc:** $1175 **VGood:** $1000

Grade I, 28 or .410, Invector

Perf: $1325 **Exc:** $925 **VGood:** $775

Grade III, Invector, 12-ga.

Perf: $1750 **Exc:** $1275 **VGood:** $975

Grade VI, Invector, 12 or 20, gray or blue

Perf: $2625 **Exc:** $1875 **VGood:** $1425

Grade VI, 28 or .410, Invector, gray or blue

Perf: $2895 **Exc:** $2145 **VGood:** $1695

Grade I Invector, 12 or 20

Perf: $1175 **Exc:** $875 **VGood:** $675

Grade I Invector, White Upland Special (24-inch bbls.); 12 or 20

Perf: $1175 **Exc:** $875 **VGood:** $675

Citori Superlight Feather (12 ga., alloy receiver)

Perf: $1415 **Exc.** $1025 **VGood:** $800

BROWNING CITORI LIGHTNING FEATHER

Similar to the 12 gauge Citori Grade I except has 2-3/4-inch chambers, rounded pistol grip, Lightning-style forend, and lighweight alloy receiver. Weighs 6 lbs. 15 oz. with 26-inch barrels (12-ga.); 6 lbs., 2 oz. (20-ga., 26-inch bbl.). Silvered, engraved receiver. Introduced 1999. Imported by Browning.

12- or 20-ga., 26-inch or 28-inch barrels

Perf: $1385 **Exc:** $1000 **VGood:** $785

Lightning Feather Combo (20- and 28-ga. bbls., 27-inch each)

Perf: $2475 **Exc:** $2025 **VGood:** $1850

BROWNING CITORI SKEET, SPECIAL SKEET, ULTRA XS SKEET, XS SKEET

Over/under; boxlock; 12-, 20-, 28-ga., .410; 26-inch, 28-inch barrels; Skeet/Skeet fixed choke of Invector choke tubes; ventilated rib or target high-post wide rib; checkered walnut pistol-grip Skeet-style stock, forearm; single selective trigger; ejectors; recoil pad. Various grades available with price dependent on type of engraving. Made in Japan. Introduced 1974; still in production as XS Skeet.

Grade I

Perf: $1150 **Exc:** $700 **VGood:** $550

Grade I with 3-barrel set

Perf: $2400 **Exc:** $1750 **VGood:** $1350

Grade III

Perf: $1500 **Exc:** $820 **VGood:** $700

Grade III with 4-barrel set

Perf: $4500 **Exc:** $2650 **VGood:** $2100

Grade III with 3-barrel set

Perf: $3000 **Exc:** $2000 **VGood:** $1400

Grade VI

Perf: $1950 **Exc:** $1500 **VGood:** $1100

Grade VI with 3-barrel set

Perf: $3100 **Exc:** $1850 **VGood:** $1650

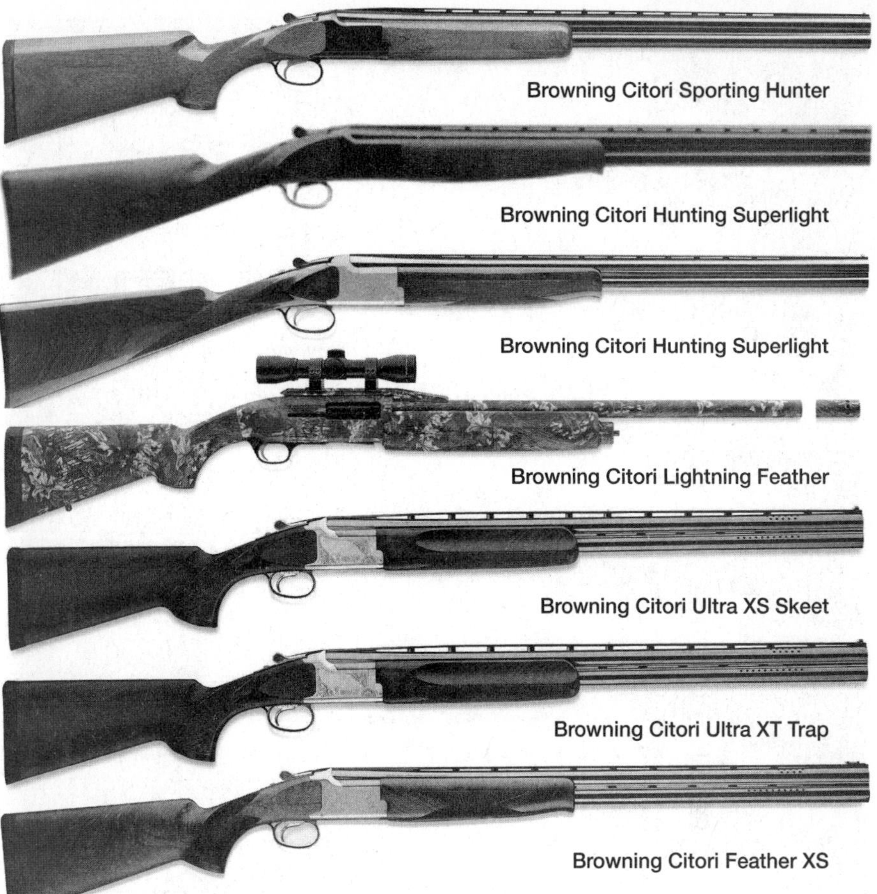

Browning Citori Sporting Hunter

Browning Citori Hunting Superlight

Browning Citori Hunting Superlight

Browning Citori Lightning Feather

Browning Citori Ultra XS Skeet

Browning Citori Ultra XT Trap

Browning Citori Feather XS

Grade VI with 4-barrel set

Perf: $4450 **Exc:** $2650 **VGood:** $2100

Golden Clays

Perf: $2300 **Exc:** $1500 **VGood:** $1100

Golden Clays with 3-barrel set

Perf: $4000 **Exc:** $2750 **VGood:** $2000

Golden Clays with 4-barrel set

Perf: $5400 **Exc:** $3250 **VGood:** $2500

BROWNING CITORI ULTRA XS SKEET

Similar to other Citori Ultra models except features a semi-beavertail forearm with deep finger grooves, ported barrels and triple system. Adjustable comb is optional. Introduced 2000.

Price: 12- and 20-ga.; 28-inch or 30-inch barrel

Perf: $1825 **Exc:** $1350 **VGood:** $1025

Adjustable comb model; 12- or 20-ga.

Perf: $2056 **Exc:** $1581 **VGood:** $1256

BROWNING CITORI ULTRA XT TRAP

Similar to other Citori Ultra models except offered in 12-ga. only with 30-inch or 32-inch ported barrel, high-post rib, ventilated side ribs, Triple Trigger System and silver nitride receiver. Includes Full, Modified and Imp. Cyl. choke tubes. From Browning.

Price: 30-inch or 32-inch barrel

Perf: $1700 **Exc:** $1250 **VGood:** $950

Adjustable-comb model

Perf: $1978 **Exc:** $1528 **VGood:** $1228

BROWNING CITORI ULTRA XS SPORTING

Similar to other Citori Ultra XS models except offered in 12-, 20-, 28-ga., and .410-bore. Silver nitride receiver, schnabel forearm, ventilated side rib. Imported by Browning.

.410 or 28-ga.

Perf: $1901 **Exc:** $1426 **VGood:** $1226

12- or 20-ga.

Perf: $1825 **Exc:** $1350 **VGood:** $1150

BROWNING CITORI FEATHER XS

Similar to the standard Citori except has lightweight alloy receiver, silver nitrade Nitex receiver, 28-inch or 30-inch barrel, schnabel forearm, ventilated side rib and Hi-Viz Comp fiber optics sight. Available in 12-, 20-, 28-ga., and .410-bore. Introduced 2000; discontinued 2001. Add 10 percent for .410 and 28.

Perf: $1800 **Exc:** $1375 **VGood:** $1150

BROWNING CITORI HIGH GRADE

Similar to standard Citori except has full sideplates with engraved hunting scenes and gold inlays, high-grade, hand-oiled walnut stock and forearm. Introduced 2000. From Browning.

Citori Privilege (fully embellished sideplates), 12- or 20-ga.

Perf: $4775 **Exc:** $4075 **VGood:** $3450

Citori BG VI Lightning (gold inlays of ducks and pheasants); 28-inch or 30-inch barrel

Perf: $2775 **Exc:** $1975 **VGood:** $1475

Citori BG III Superlight (scroll engraving on grayed receiver, gold inlays)

Perf: $1415 **Exc:** $1025 **VGood:** $800

Citori 425 Golden Clays (engraving of game bird-clay bird transition, gold accents); 12- or 20-ga.

Perf: $3150 **Exc:** $2275 **VGood:** $1675

BROWNING CITORI XS SPORTING CLAYS

Similar to the Citori Grade I except has silver nitride receiver with gold accents, stock dimensions of 14-3/4-inch by 1-1/2-inch by 2-1/4-inch with satin finish, right- hand palm swell, schnabel forend. Comes with Modified, Imp. Cyl. and Skeet Invector-Plus choke tubes. Back-bored barrels; vented side ribs. Introduced 1999. Imported by Browning.

12-, 20-ga.

Perf: $1825 **Exc:** $1350 **VGood:** $1025

28-ga., .410-bore

Perf: $1825 **Exc:** $1350 **VGood:** $1025

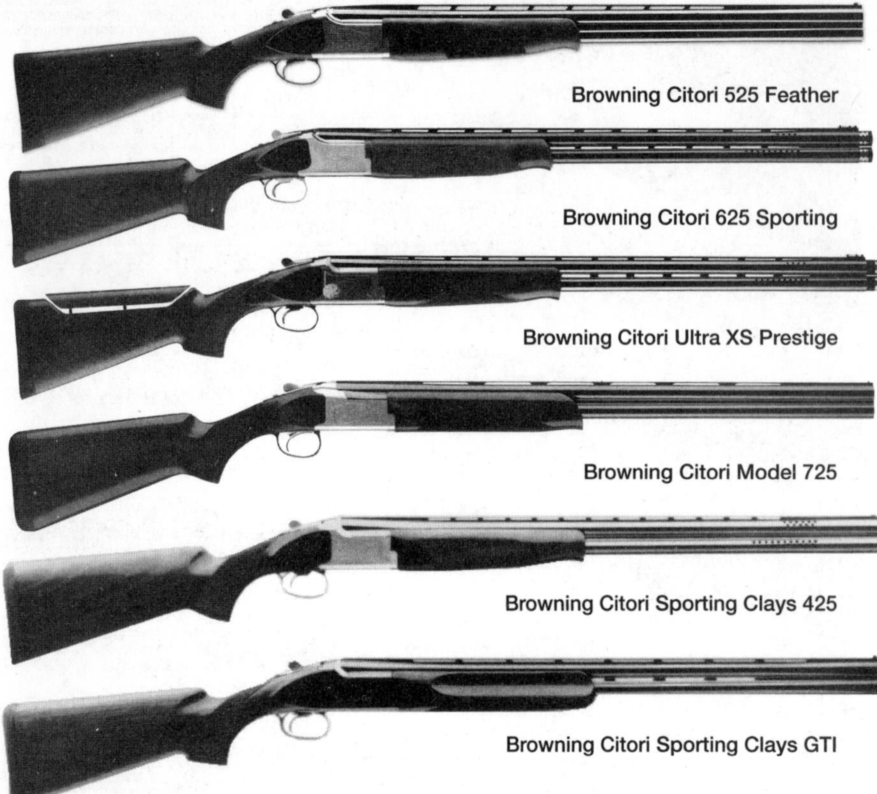

CITORI 525 FEATHER

This lightweight Citori features an alloy receiver with a steel breech face and high-relief engraving. The stock and Schnabel forend are Grade II/III oil finished walnut. Available in 12, 20 and 28 gauges and .410 bore with 26" or 28" barrels. All but 28 gauge have 3" chambers. Weight is about 6.9 lbs. in12 gauge and 5.5 to 5.7 lbs. in others. Three choke tubes.

Perf: $2275 **Exc:** $1875 **VGood:** $1500

CITORI 625 SPORTING

Introduced in 2008, this 2.75" 12 gauge has 28", 30" or 32" ported barrels with Browning's Vector Pro lengthened forcing cones system. The stock and Schnabel forend are Grade III/IV walnut. The steel receiver has a silver nitride finish with high-relief engraving and gold embellishment. Five choke tubes included. Weight is 7.9 to 8.2 lbs. Add 5% for adjustable comb stock.

Perf: $3300 **Exc:** $2875 **VGood:** $2250

CITORI 625 FIELD

This 3" 12 gauge has 26" or 28" barrels and a gloss oil finish Grade II/III walnut stock and schnabel forend. Steel receiver with silver nitride finish and high-relief engraving. Three choke tubes. Weight is about 7.8 lbs.

Perf: $2275 **Exc:** $1875 **VGood:** $1500

CITORI MODEL 725

Over/under 12-gauge only with 26 or 28-inch barrels, Invector choke tubes. New low-profile action. Single selective trigger, automatic ejectors, checkered walnut stock with gloss finish and recoil pad. Introduced in 2012

Perf: $2400 **Exc:** $1700 **VGood:** $1200

CITORI ULTRA XS PRESTIGE

New in 2008, this 12 gauge sporting clays model features an adjustable comb and Grade III/IV walnut stock with right hand palm swell. Ported barrels are 28", 30" or 32". Gold accented, high relief Ultra XS Special engraving on the steel/silver nitride finish receiver. Weight is about 8 lbs.

Perf: $4500 **Exc:** $3875 **VGood:** $3250

BROWNING SPECIAL SPORTING CLAYS

Similar to the Citori Ultra Sporter except has full pistol grip stock with palm swell, gloss finish, 28-inch, 30-inch or 32-inch barrels with back-bored Invector Plus chokes (ported or non-ported); high post tapered rib. Also available as 28-inch and 30-inch two-barrel set. Introduced 1989; discontinued 2001.

With ported barrels

Perf: $1300 **Exc:** $925 **VGood:** $775

As above, adjustable comb

Perf: $1520 **Exc:** $1145 **VGood:** $995

BROWNING LIGHTNING SPORTING CLAYS

Similar to the Citori Lightning with rounded pistol grip and classic forend. Has high post tapered rib or lower hunting-style rib with 30-inch back-bored Invector Plus barrels, ported or non-ported, 3-inch chambers. Gloss stock finish, radiused recoil pad. Has "Lightning Sporting Clays Edition" engraved and gold filled on receiver. Introduced 1989.

Low-rib, ported

Perf: $1425 **Exc:** $1025 **VGood:** $875

High-rib, ported

Perf: $1506 **Exc:** $1106 **VGood:** $956

BROWNING LIGHT SPORTING 802 ES O/U

Gauge: 12, 2-3/4-inch chambers. Barrel: 28-inch, back-bored Invector Plus. Comes with flush-mounted Imp. Cyl. and Skeet; 2-inch extended Imp. Cyl. and Mod.; and 4-inch extended Imp. Cyl. and Mod. tubes. Weight: 7 lbs., 5 oz. Length: 45-inch overall. Stock: 14-3/8-inch by 1/8-inch by 1-9/16-inch by 1-3/4-inch. Select walnut with radiused solid recoil pad, schnabel-type forend. Features: Trigger adjustable for length of pull; narrow 6.2mm ventilated rib; ventilated barrel side rib; blued receiver. Introduced 1996; discontinued 2001. Imported from Japan.

Perf: $1700 **Exc:** $1175 **VGood:** $975

BROWNING CITORI SPORTING CLAYS 325

Over/under; boxlock; 12-, 20-ga.; 2-3/4-inch chambers; back-bored 28-inch, 30-inch, 32-inch vent-rib barrels; barrels are ported on 12-gauge guns; Invector Plus choke tubes; weighs about 7-3/4 lbs.; select cut-checkered walnut stock, schnabel forend with gloss finish; three interchangeable trigger shoes to adjust length of pull; grayed receiver with engraving; blued barrels. Made in Japan. Introduced 1993; discontinued 1994.

Perf: $1250 **Exc:** $800 **VGood:** $700

BROWNING CITORI SPORTING CLAYS 325 GOLDEN CLAYS

Same specs as Citori Sporting Clays 325 except high-grade walnut; grayed receiver highlighted with 24-karat gold. Made in Japan. Introduced 1993; discontinued 1994.

Perf: $2250 **Exc:** $1350 **VGood:** $1050

BROWNING CITORI SPORTING CLAYS 425

Over/under; 12-, 20-ga.; 2-3/4-inch chambers; back-bored 28-inch, 30-inch, 32-inch vent-rib barrels; barrels are ported on 12-ga. guns; Invector Plus choke tubes; weighs about 7-3/4 lbs.; select cut-checkered walnut stock, schnabel forend with gloss finish; three interchangeable trigger shoes to adjust length of pull; grayed receiver with engraving, blued barrels. Made in Japan. Introduced 1993; still imported.

Perf: $1380 **Exc:** $800 **VGood:** $700

Grade I, 12-, 20-ga., Invector Plus

Perf: $1665 **Exc:** $1150 **VGood:** $935

Golden Clays, 12-, 20-ga., Invector Plus

Perf: $3150 **Exc:** $2275 **VGood:** $1675

BROWNING CITORI SPORTING CLAYS 425 GOLDEN CLAYS

Same specs as Sporting Clays 425 except high-grade walnut; grayed receiver highlighted with 24-karat gold. Made in Japan. Introduced 1995; discontinued 2001.

Perf: $2500 **Exc:** $1350 **VGood:** $1000

BROWNING CITORI SPORTING CLAYS 425 WSSF

Same specs as Sporting Clays 425 except 12-ga.; stock dimensions specifically tailored to women shooters; top lever and takedown lever are easier to operate; stock and forend have teal-colored finish with WSSF logo. Made in Japan. Introduced 1995; discontinued.

Perf: $1400 **Exc:** $800 **VGood:** $700

BROWNING CITORI SPORTING CLAYS GTI

Over/under; boxlock; 12-ga.; 28-inch, 30-inch vent-rib barrels (ported or non-ported); Invector Plus choke tubes; ventilated side ribs; checkered walnut semi-pistol grip stock, grooved semi-beavertail forend with satin finish; radiused rubber buttpad; three interchangeable trigger shoes for three length of pull adjustments. Made in Japan. Introduced 1989; discontinued 1994.

Grade I, non-ported barrels

Perf: $1100 **Exc:** $550 **VGood:** $450

Grade I, ported barrels

Perf: $1200 **Exc:** $650 **VGood:** $550

Golden Clays, ported barrels

Perf: $2200 **Exc:** $1350 **VGood:** $1000

BROWNING CITORI SPORTING CLAYS LIGHTNING

Over/under; boxlock; 12-ga.; back-bored 30-inch Invector Plus barrels (ported or non-ported); high-post tapered rib or hunting-type rib; checkered walnut pistol-grip stock, forend with gloss stock finish; adjustable comb, recoil pad; engraved, gold-filled receiver. Made in Japan. Introduced, 1989; still imported.

Grade I, non-ported

Perf: $1100 **Exc:** $625 **VGood:** $490

Grade I, ported

Perf: $1150 **Exc:** $700 **VGood:** $550

Pigeon Grade, ported

Perf: $1250 **Exc:** $800 **VGood:** $650

Golden Clays, ported

Perf: $2200 **Exc:** $1350 **VGood:** $1000

BROWNING CITORI SPECIAL SPORTING CLAYS

Over/under; boxlock; 12-ga.; back-bored 28-inch, 30-inch, 32-inch barrels (ported or non-ported); Invector Plus choke tubes; high-post tapered rib; checkered walnut pistol-grip stock, forend with gloss finish; palm swell. Also available as 28-inch, 30-inch two-barrel set. Made in Japan. Introduced 1989; discontinued.

Grade I, non-ported
Perf: $1050 **Exc:** $900 **VGood:** $700

Grade I, ported
Perf: $1100 **Exc:** $950 **VGood:** $750

Grade I, two-barrel set
Perf: $1900 **Exc:** $1700 **VGood:** $1500

Golden Clays, ported
Perf: $3100 **Exc:** $2800 **VGood:** $2200

BROWNING CITORI SPORTING CLAYS ULTRA SPORTER

Over/under; boxlock; 12-ga.; back-bored 28-inch or 30-inch barrels (ported or non-ported); Invector Plus choke tubes; ventilated side ribs; checkered walnut pistol-grip stock, grooved semi-beavertail forend with satin finish; radiused rubber buttpad; three interchangeable trigger shoes for three length of pull adjustments. Made in Japan. Introduced 1995; discontinued 1999.

Grade I, non-ported
Perf: $1500 **Exc:** $1250 **VGood:** $1000

Grade I, ported
Perf: $1595 **Exc:** $1300 **VGood:** $1100

Golden Clays
Perf: $3300 **Exc:** $2850 **VGood:** $2200

BROWNING CITORI TRAP, SPECIAL TRAP, ULTRA XT AND XT

Over/under; boxlock; 12-ga.; 30-inch, 32-inch ported or non-ported barrels; Full/Full, Improved Modified/Full, Modified/Full, or Invector Plus choke tubes; vent rib or high-post target wide vent rib; fitted with trap-style recoil pad; checkered walnut Monte Carlo cheekpiece stock, beavertail forearm. Introduced 1974; still in production.

Grade I, Invector Plus, ported
Perf: $1500 **Exc:** $1250 **VGood:** $1000

Grade I Combo, with extra 34-inch single barrel, Invector Plus, ported
Perf: $1800 **Exc:** $1500 **VGood:** $1300

Grade III, Invector Plus, ported
Perf: $1500 **Exc:** $1250 **VGood:** $1000

Grade V, Invector Plus, ported
Perf: $2650 **Exc:** $2200 **VGood:** $1950

Grade VI, Invector Plus, ported
Perf: $2100 **Exc:** $1800 **VGood:** $1650

Golden Clays, satin-gray receiver with engraving, inlays
Perf: $3000 **Exc:** $2750 **VGood:** $2400

Pigeon Grade, deluxe wood, inlays
Perf: $3200 **Exc:** $2950 **VGood:** $2650

Singature Painted, red and black painted stock
Perf: $1475 **Exc:** $1175 **VGood:** $950

BROWNING CITORI TRAP PLUS

Same specs as Citori Trap except back-bored 30-inch, 32-inch barrels; .745-inch over-bore; Invector Plus choke tubes with Full, Improved Modified and Modified; high post, ventilated, tapered, target rib adjustable for impact from 3-inch to 12-inch above point of aim; with or without ported barrels; select walnut Monte Carlo stock, modified beavertail forend with high-gloss finish; fully adjustable for length of pull, drop at comb, drop at Monte Carlo; Browning Recoil Reduction System. Made in Japan. Introduced 1989; no longer imported.

Grade I, Invector Plus, ported
Perf: $1500 **Exc:** $900 **VGood:** $750

Grade I Combo with extra 34-inch single barrel, Invector Plus, ported
Perf: $2600 **Exc:** $1900 **VGood:** $1700

Browning Citori Sporting Clays Ultra Sporter

Browning Citori Trap

Browning Citori Trap Plus

Browning Liege

Browning ST-100

Browning Superposed Broadway Trap

Golden Clays, satin-gray receiver with engraving, inlays
Perf: $4300 **Exc:** $2650 **VGood:** $2100

Pigeon Grade, deluxe wood, inlays
Perf: $1650 **Exc:** $850 **VGood:** $700

BROWNING CITORI XT TRAP OVER/UNDER

Similar to the Citori Special Trap except has engraved silver nitride receiver with gold highlights, vented side barrel rib. Available in 12-gauge with 30-inch or 32-inch barrels, Invector-Plus choke tubes. Introduced 1999. Imported by Browning.

Perf: $1715 **Exc:** $1250 **VGood:** $950

With adjustable-comb stock
Perf: $1935 **Exc:** $1470 **VGood:** $1170

BROWNING LIEGE

Over/under; boxlock; 12-ga.; 2-3/4-inch, 3-inch chamber; 26-1/2-inch, 28-inch, 30-inch barrels; standard choke combos; vent rib; checkered walnut pistol-grip stock, forearm; automatic ejectors; non-selective single trigger. Introduced 1973; discontinued 1975.

Perf: $720 **Exc:** $550 **VGood:** $490

BROWNING ST-100

Over/under; 12-ga.; 30-inch barrels; floating Broadway rib; five-position impact adjustment; hand-checkered select walnut stock, semi-beavertail forend with high-gloss finish; selective auto ejectors; single selective mechanical trigger; manual top tang safety. Introduced 1979; discontinued 1982.

Perf: $2200 **Exc:** $1650 **VGood:** $1400

BROWNING SUPERPOSED

Over/under; 12-, 20-, 28-ga., .410; 26-1/2-inch, 28-inch, 30-inch, 32-inch (discontinued WWII) barrels; gun is made in a wide spectrum of variations, grades, choke combinations; early models and pre-WWII had double triggers, twin single triggers or non-selective single trigger (pre-WWII production ended when Belgium was invaded); hand-checkered French walnut pistol-grip or straight stock, forearm. Standard Grade is listed as Grade I, with raised matted rib or vent rib. Introduced 1928; no longer in production.

Exc: $950 **VGood:** $800 **Good:** $575

BROWNING SUPERPOSED BROADWAY TRAP

Same specs as Superposed except 30-inch, 32-inch barrel; 5/8-inch-wide Broadway vent rib. No longer in production.

Exc: $850 **VGood:** $720 **Good:** $500

BROWNING SUPERPOSED DIANA GRADE

Same specs as Superposed except raised matted rib or vent rib before WWII; post-war models have only vent rib; better wood, more extensive engraving; redesignated as Grade V after WWII; improved general quality. No longer in production.

Perf: $4700 **Exc:** $2700 **VGood:** $2100

BROWNING SUPERPOSED GRADE I LIGHTNING MODEL

Same specs as Superposed except matted barrel; no rib before WWII; post-war models have vent rib. Other specs generally the same as Standard Superposed model. No longer in production.

Perf: $1550 **Exc:** $1275 **VGood:** $995

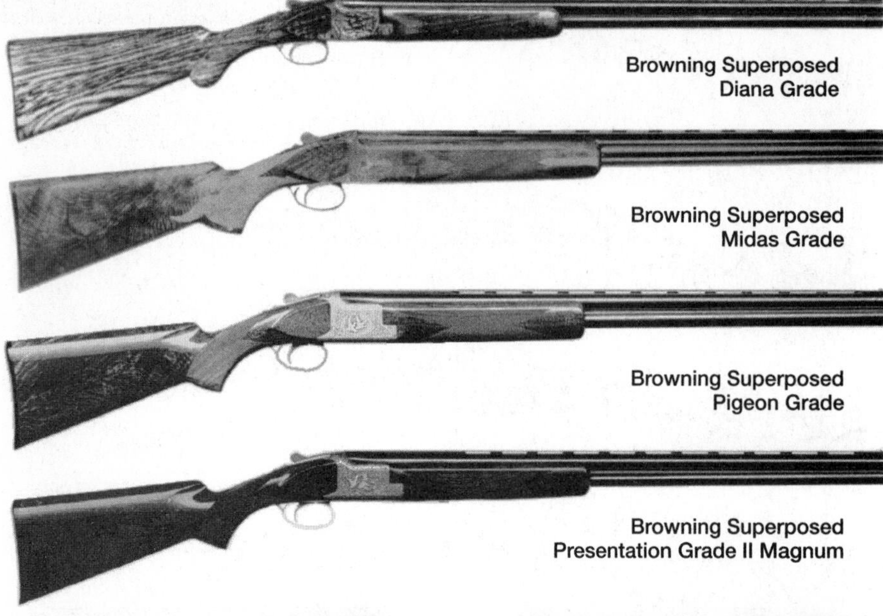

Browning Superposed Diana Grade

Browning Superposed Midas Grade

Browning Superposed Pigeon Grade

Browning Superposed Presentation Grade II Magnum

Browning Superposed Presentation Grade II Magnum

Browning Superposed Presentation Grade II Magnum

Browning Superposed Presentation Grade II Magnum

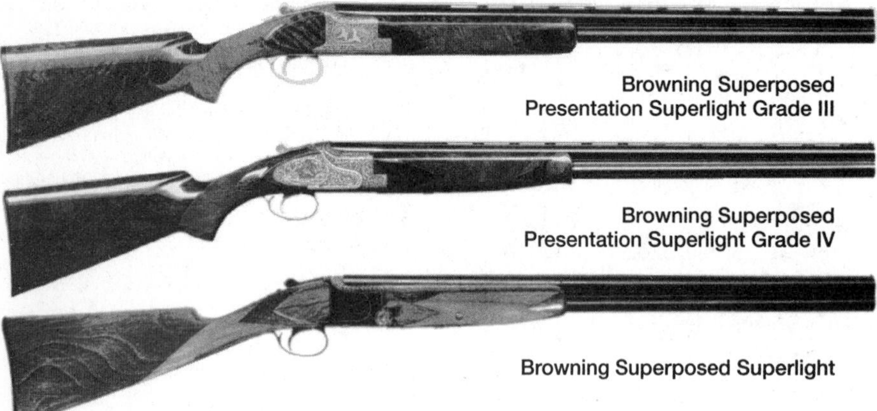

Browning Superposed Presentation Superlight Grade III

Browning Superposed Presentation Superlight Grade IV

Browning Superposed Superlight

BROWNING SUPERPOSED MAGNUM

Same specs as Superposed except 12-ga.; 3-inch chamber; 30-inch vent-rib barrel; choked Full/Full or Full/Mod.; recoil pad. No longer in production.

Perf: $1350 **Exc:** $875 **VGood:** $800

BROWNING SUPERPOSED MIDAS GRADE

Same specs as Superposed except heavily engraved, gold inlaid; pre-war versions with raised matted rib or vent rib; later versions have only wide vent rib. No longer in production.

Perf: $6950 **Exc:** $6000 **VGood:** $4950

BROWNING SUPERPOSED PIGEON GRADE

Same specs as Superposed except better wood, finer checkering, more engraving than Standard Superposed model; raised matted rib or vent rib. Was redesignated as Grade II after WWII. No longer in production.

Perf: $4000 **Exc:** $3400 **VGood:** $2150

BROWNING SUPERPOSED SKEET

Same specs as Superposed except 12-, 20-, 28-ga., .410; 26-1/2-inch, 28-inch barrel; choked Skeet/Skeet. No longer in production.

Exc: $900 **VGood:** $750 **Good:** $560

BROWNING SUPERPOSED PRESENTATION SUPERLIGHT

Over/under; boxlock; 12-, 20-ga; 26-1/2-inch barrel; solid or vent rib; hand-checkered straight-grip stock of select walnut; top lever single selective trigger barrel selector combined with manual tang safety. Options too numerous to mention; available in 4 grades. Introduced 1977; no longer imported.

Grade I

Perf: $2800 **Exc:** $1900 **VGood:** $1680

Grade II

Perf: $3300 **Exc:** $2200 **VGood:** $2000

Grade III

Perf: $5500 **Exc:** $4000 **VGood:** $3500

Grade IV

Perf: $6500 **Exc:** $4500 **VGood:** $3900

BROWNING SUPERPOSED PRESENTATION SUPERLIGHT BROADWAY TRAP

Same specs as Superposed Presentation Superlight except 30-inch, 32-inch barrel; wide vent rib; different stock measurements. Discontinued 1984.

Grade I

Perf: $2500 **Exc:** $1650 **VGood:** $1500

Grade II

Perf: $3000 **Exc:** $1900 **VGood:** $1750

Grade III

Perf: $5000 **Exc:** $3600 **VGood:** $3200

Grade IV

Perf: $6000 **Exc:** $4000 **VGood:** $3500

BROWNING SUPERPOSED PRESENTATION SUPERLIGHT LIGHTNING SKEET

Same specs as Superposed Presentation Superlight except 12-, 20-, 28-ga., .410; center and front ivory bead sights; special Skeet stock, forend. Introduced 1977; discontinued 1982.

Grade I

Perf: $2500 **Exc:** $1650 **VGood:** $1500

Grade II

Perf: $3000 **Exc:** $1900 **VGood:** $1750

Grade III

Perf: $5000 **Exc:** $3600 **VGood:** $3200

Grade IV

Perf: $6000 **Exc:** $4000 **VGood:** $3500

BROWNING SUPERPOSED PRESENTATION SUPERLIGHT LIGHTNING TRAP

Same specs as Superposed Presentation Superlight except 30-inch barrels; trap stock, semi-beavertail forend. Discontinued 1984.

Grade I

Perf: $2500 **Exc:** $1650 **VGood:** $1500

Grade II

Perf: $3000 **Exc:** $1900 **VGood:** $1750

Grade III

Perf: $5000 **Exc:** $3600 **VGood:** $3200

Grade IV

Perf: $6000 **Exc:** $4000 **VGood:** $3500

BROWNING SUPERPOSED PRESENTATION SUPERLIGHT MAGNUM

Same specs as Superposed Presentation Superlight except 3-inch chambers; 30-inch barrels; factory fitted recoil pad. Discontinued 1984.

Grade I

Perf: $2500 **Exc:** $1650 **VGood:** $1500

Grade II

Perf: $3000 **Exc:** $1900 **VGood:** $1750

Grade III

Perf: $5000 **Exc:** $3600 **VGood:** $3200

Grade IV

Perf: $6000 **Exc:** $4000 **VGood:** $3500

BROWNING SUPERPOSED SUPERLIGHT

Over/under; boxlock; 12-, 20-ga.; 2-3/4-inch chambers; 26-1/2-inch vent-rib barrels; choked Modified/Full or Improved/Modified; hand-checkered select walnut straight-grip stock, forearm; top lever; barrel selector combined with manual tang safety; single selective trigger; engraved receiver. Introduced 1967; discontinued 1976.

12-ga.

Perf: $1650 **Exc:** $1150 **VGood:** $1000

20-ga.

Perf: $2300 **Exc:** $1400 **VGood:** $1200

BROWNING CYNERGY CLASSIC FIELD

This more traditionally styled 12 gauge was added to the Cynergy line in 2006. It features a steel receiver with silver nitride finish and game bird scenes on each side. Satin finish walnut stock and schnabel style forend. Three choke tubes. Available in barrel lengths of 26-inch and 28-inch with an average weight of 7.75 lbs.

NIB: $1875 **Exc:** $1775 **VGood:** $1500

BROWNING CYNERGY CLASSIC SPORTING

New for 2006, this traditionally styled version of the Cynergy Sporting is available in 12 gauge with 28-inch, 30-inch or 32-inch ported barrels. Oil finish walnut stock with Schnabel forend and Browning logo on steel receiver with silver nitride finish. Three Invector-Plus Midas Grade choke tubes. Average weight 7.75 lbs.

NIB: $2825 **Exc:** $2695 **VGood:** $2000

BROWNING CYNERGY SPORTING, ADJUSTABLE COMB

Similar to Cynergy Sporting but with a comb adjustable for cast and drop. Average weight 8.2 lbs.

NIB: $2900 **Exc:** $2725 **VGood:** $2375

BROWNING CYNERGY FEATHER

This lightweight Cynergy 12 gauge was introduced in 2006, followed by 20 and 28 gauge and .410 bore versions in 2008. Satin finish walnut stock. Weight is about 6.5 lbs. in 12 gauge and about 5 lbs. in others.

NIB: $2400 **Exc:** $2195 **VGood:** $1700

CYNERGY FEATHER COMPOSITE

As above but with synthetic stock and forend in 12 gauge only.

NIB: $2400 **Exc:** $2195 **VGood:** $1700

BROWNING CYNERGY EURO SPORTING

Sporting clays and skeet version comes in 2.75" 12 and 20 gauge with 28", 30" or 32" barrels. Stock is oil finish Grade III/IV walnut. Three choke tubes. Weight is about 8 lbs. in 12 gauge and 6.5 lbs. in 20 gauge.

NIB: $3500 **Exc:** $3000 **VGood:** $2700

BROWNING CYNERGY CLASSIC TRAP UNSINGLE COMBO

Trap shotgun in 12 gauge comes with a double barrel set in 32/34", 32/32", 30/34" or 30/32". Gloss finish Monte Carlo Grade III/IV walnut stock with right hand palm swell and adjustable comb. Weight is about 8.9 lbs. Four choke tubes. Aluminum fitted carrying case.

NIB: $5000 **Exc:** $4195 **VGood:** $3500

BROWNING A-BOLT HUNTER

Bolt action; 12-ga.; 3-inch chamber; 2-shot detachable magazine; 22-inch fully rifled barrel or 23-inch barrel with 5-inch Invector choke tube; weighs 7-1/8 lbs.; 44-3/4-inch overall length; blade front sight with red insert, open adjustable rear, or no sights; drilled and tapped for scope mount; walnut stock with satin finish; A-Bolt rifle action with 60° bolt throw; front-locking bolt with claw extractor; hinged floorplate; swivel studs; matte finish on barrel, receiver. Imported by Browning. Introduced 1995.

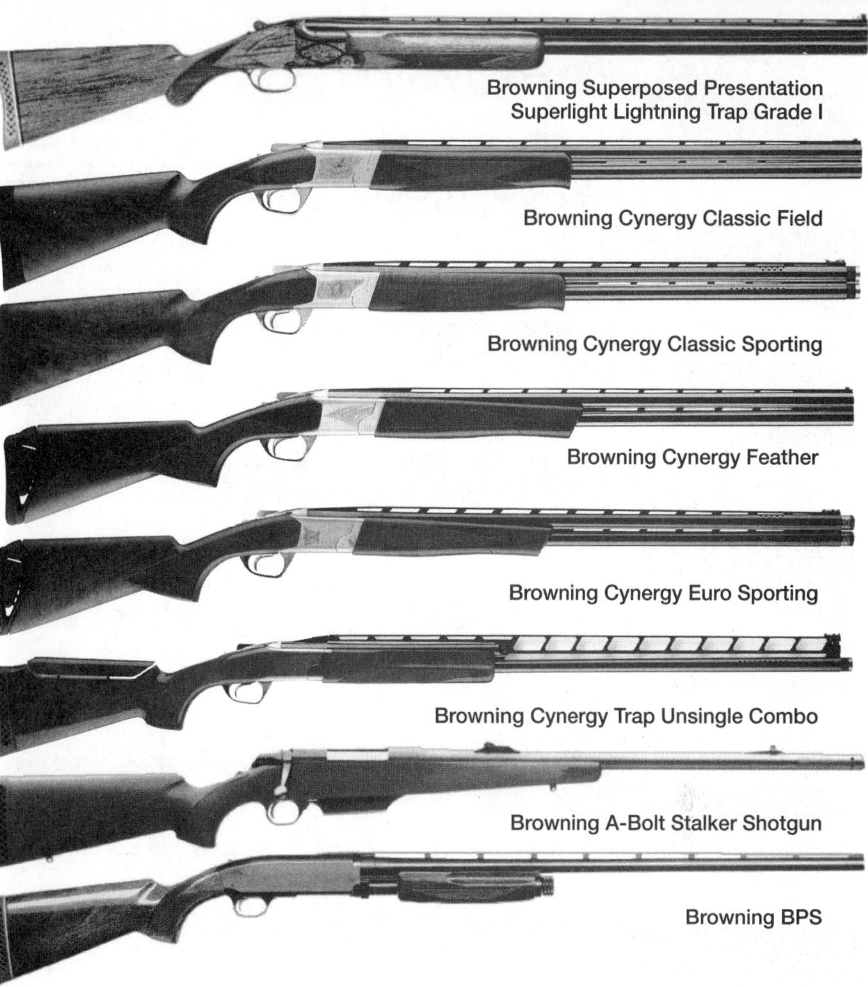

Browning Superposed Presentation Superlight Lightning Trap Grade I

Browning Cynergy Classic Field

Browning Cynergy Classic Sporting

Browning Cynergy Feather

Browning Cynergy Euro Sporting

Browning Cynergy Trap Unsingle Combo

Browning A-Bolt Stalker Shotgun

Browning BPS

Rifled barrel

Perf: $1085 **Exc:** 925 **VGood:** 785

Invector barrel

Perf: $1100 **Exc:** $925 **VGood:** $750

BROWNING A-BOLT STALKER

Same specs as A-Bolt Hunter except black, non-glare composite pistol-grip stock, forend. Imported by Browning. Introduced 1995.

Rifled barrel

Perf: $900 **Exc:** $800 **VGood:** $650

Invector barrel

Perf: $950 **Exc:** $850 **VGood:** $750

BROWNING BPS

Slide action; 10-, 12-, 20-, 28-ga.; 3-inch, 3-1/2-inch chamber; 4-, 5-shot magazine; 24-inch, 26-inch, 28-inch, 30-inch barrel; Invector chokes; high-post vent rib; 48-3/4-inch overall length; weighs 7-1/2 lbs.; select walnut pistol-grip stock, semi-beavertail forend; bottom feeding, ejection; receiver top safety. Made in Japan. Introduced 1977; still imported by Browning.

Perf: $400 **Exc:** $325 **VGood:** $290

10-ga., Hunter, Invector

Perf: $445 **Exc:** $380 **VGood:** $335

12-ga., 3-1/2-inch Magnum Hunter, Invector Plus

Perf: $540 **Exc:** $495 **VGood:** $.410

12-ga., 3-1/2-inch Magnum Stalker (black syn. stock)

Perf: $465 **Exc:** $400 **VGood:** $355

12-, 20-ga., Hunter, Invector Plus

Perf: $445 **Exc:** $380 **VGood:** $335

12-ga. Deer Hunter (22-inch rifled bbl., cantilever mount)

Perf: $460 **Exc:** $385 **VGood:** $310

28-ga., Hunter, Invector

Perf: $423 **Exc:** $343 **VGood:** $298

.410 bore, Hunter, Invector

Perf: $423 **Exc:** $343 **VGood:** $298

BROWNING BPS ALL WEATHER HIGH CAPACITY

Slide-action 12 gauge with 3-inch chamber. Barrel is 20 inches with fixed cylinder choke. Stainless steel, matte finish. Weight is 7.5 lbs., length 40.75 inches. Black composite stock with matte finish. Action has bottom ejection with dual steel action bars. HiViz Tactical fiber-optic front sight. Capacity 5+1.

Perf: $625 **Exc:** $535 **VGood:** $450

BROWNING BPS BUCK SPECIAL

Same specs as BPS except 24-inch Cylinder barrel; no Invector choke tubes. Introduced 1977; reintroduced 1989; still in production.

Perf: $375 **Exc:** $240 **VGood:** $200

10-ga.

Perf: $525 **Exc:** $375 **VGood:** $340

BROWNING BPS GAME GUN DEER SPECIAL

Same specs as BPS except 12-ga.; 3-inch chamber; heavy 20-1/2-inch barrel with rifled choke tube; rifle-type sights with adjustable rear; solid receiver scope mount; "rifle" stock dimensions for scope or open sights; gloss or matte finished wood with checkering; newly designed receiver/magazine tube/ barrel mounting system to eliminate play; sling swivel studs; polished blue metal. Made by Miroku in Japan. Introduced 1992.

Perf: $430 **Exc:** $240 **VGood:** $200

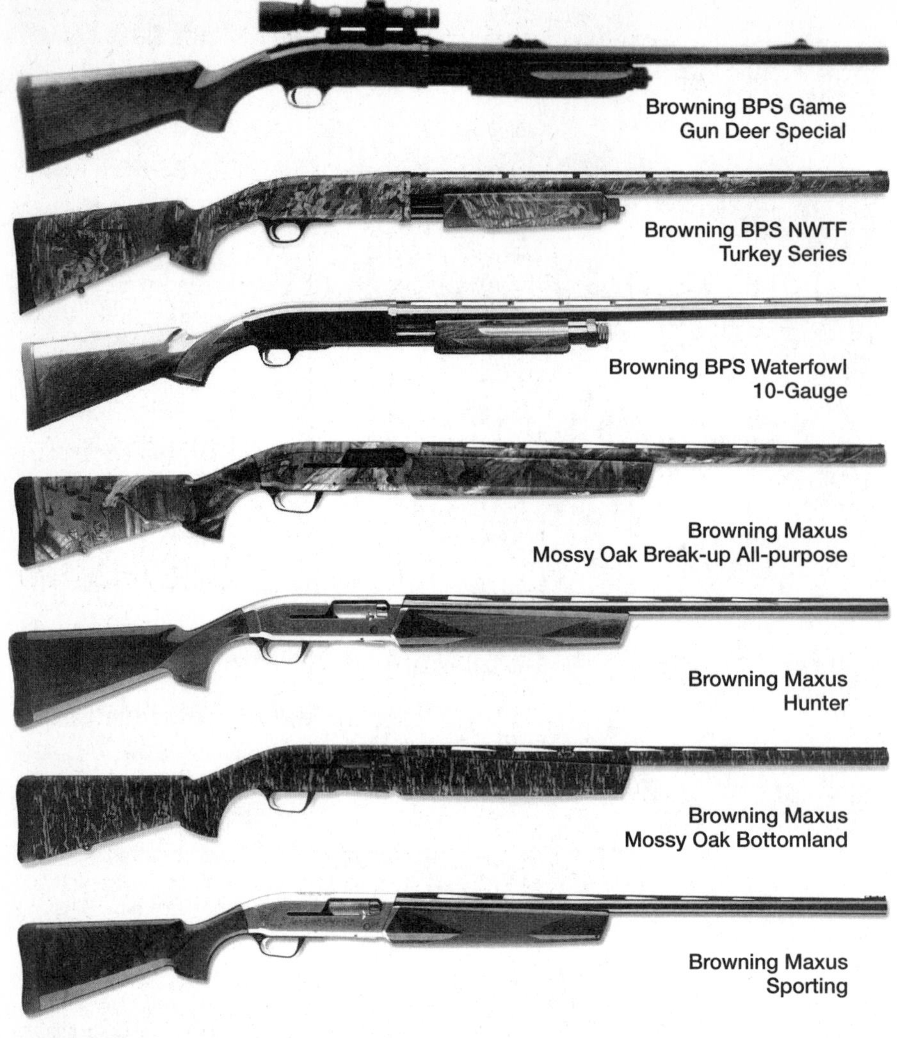
Browning BPS Game Gun Deer Special

Browning BPS NWTF Turkey Series

Browning BPS Waterfowl 10-Gauge

Browning Maxus Mossy Oak Break-up All-purpose

Browning Maxus Hunter

Browning Maxus Mossy Oak Bottomland

Browning Maxus Sporting

BROWNING BPS GAME GUN TURKEY SPECIAL

Same specs as BPS except 12-ga.; 3-inch chamber; light 20-1/2-inch barrel; Extra-Full Invector choke tube; drilled and tapped for scope mounting; rifle-style satin-finished walnut stock; swivel studs; dull-finished barrel, receiver. Made in Japan by Miroku. Introduced 1992.

Perf: $400 **Exc:** $275 **VGood:** $240

BROWNING BPS LADIES & YOUTH MODEL

Same specs as BPS except 20-ga.; 22-inch barrel; shortened walnut pistol-grip stock; recoil pad. Made in Japan. Introduced 1986.

Perf: $380 **Exc:** $220 **VGood:** $195

BROWNING BPS PIGEON GRADE

Same specs as BPS except 12-ga.; 3-inch chamber; 26-inch, 28-inch vent-rib barrels; select high grade walnut stock, forend; gold-trimmed receiver. Made in Japan. Introduced 1992; still imported.

Perf: $500 **Exc:** $420 **VGood:** $345

BROWNING BPS STALKER

Same specs as BPS except 10-, 12-ga.; 3-inch, 3-1/2-inch chamber; 24-inch, 26-inch, 28-inch, 30-inch barrel; black-finished synthetic stock, forearm; matte blued finish on metal; black recoil pad. Made in Japan. Introduced 1987; still imported.

Perf: $445 **Exc:** $380 **VGood:** $335

BROWNING BPS NWTF TURKEY SERIES

Similar to the BPS Stalker except has full coverage Mossy Oak Break- Up camo finish on synthetic stock, forearm and exposed metal parts. Offered in 10 and 12 gauge, 3-inch or 3-1/2-inch chamber; 24-inch bbl. has extra-full choke tube and Hi-Viz fiber optic sights. Introduced 2001.

10-ga., 3-1/2-inch chamber

Perf: $400 **Exc:** $340 **VGood:** $275

12-ga., 3-1/2-inch chamber

Perf: $400 **Exc:** $340 **VGood:** $275

12-ga., 3-inch chamber

Perf: $400 **Exc:** $340 **VGood:** $275

BROWNING BPS UPLAND SPECIAL

Same specs as BPS except 12-, 20-ga.; 22-inch barrel; walnut straight-grip stock, forearm. Made in Japan. Introduced 1989.

Perf: $575 **Exc:** $440 **VGood:** $300

BROWNING BPS MICRO

Same as BPS Upland Special except 20-ga. only, 22-inch Invector barrel, stock has pistol grip with recoil pad. Length of pull is 13-1/4-inch; weighs 6 lbs., 12 oz. Introduced 1986.

Perf: $395 **Exc:** $310 **VGood:** $265

BROWNING BPS WATERFOWL 10-GAUGE

Same specs as BPS except 10-ga.; 3 1/2-inch chamber; 28-inch, 30-inch vent-rib barrel; high grade stock; gold-trimmed receiver. Made in Japan. Introduced 1993.

Perf: $625 **Exc:** $430 **VGood:** $375

BROWNING BPS WATERFOWL CAMO

Similar to the BPS Hunter except completely covered with Mossy Oak Shadow Grass camouflage. Available in 12-gauge, with 24-inch, 26-inch or 28-inch barrel, 3-inch chamber. Introduced 1999.

Perf: $460 **Exc:** $385 **VGood:** $340

BROWNING BPS 10 GAUGE SHOTGUNS

Chambered for the 10-gauge, 3-1/2-inch load. Offered in 24-inch, 26-inch and 28-inch barrels. Offered with walnut, black composite (Stalker models) or camouflage stock and forend. Introduced 1999. Imported.

Hunter (walnut)

Perf: $460 **Exc:** $395 **VGood:** $350

Stalker (composite)

Perf: $465 **Exc:** $400 **VGood:** $355

Mossy Oak Shadow Grass or Break-Up Camo

Perf: $540 **Exc:** $495 **VGood:** $.410

BROWNING BPS 10-GAUGE CAMO PUMP

Similar to the BPS 10-gauge Hunter except completely covered with Mossy Oak Shadow Grass camouflage. Available with 24-inch, 26-inch, 28-inch barrel. Introduced 1999. Imported.

Perf: $540 **Exc:** $495 **VGood:** $410

BROWNING MAXUS ALL-PURPOSE

Gas-operated 12 gauge with 3-1/2 inch chamber. Light-profile 26-inch barrel with flat ventilated rib. Comes with four Invector Plus choke tubes. Composite stock adjustable for length of pull, cast and drop. Mossy Oak Break-Up camo finish. HiViz 4-in-1 fiber optic sight included.

Perf: $1450 **Exc:** $1225 **VGood:** $1100

BROWNING MAXUS HUNTER

Gas-operated 12 gauge with 3 or 3-1/2 inch chamber. Barrel lengths are 26, 28 or 30 inches with flat ventilated rib, three Invector Plus choke tubes. Aluminum alloy receiver with satin nickel finish. Gloss finished, checkered walnut stock adjustable for length of pull, cast and drop.

Perf: $1285 **Exc:** $1085 **VGood:** $925

Add 10 percent for 3-1/2-inch chamber

BROWNING MAXUS MOSSY OAK BOTTOMLAND

Gas-operated 12 gauge with 3-1/2 inch chamber, 28-inch barrel. Same features as Maxus Hunter. Stock has Mossy Oak Bottomland finish. Weight is 6.9 pounds.

Perf: $1385 **Exc:** $1175 **VGood:** $995

BROWNING MAXUS MOSSY OAK DUCK BLIND

Gas-operated 12 gauge with 3 or 3-1/2 chamber. Barrel lengths, 26 or 28 inches. Other features similar to Maxus Mossy Oak Bottomland except with Mossy Oak Duck Blind camo finish.

Perf: $1225 **Exc:** $1050 **VGood:** $900

Add 10 percent for 3-1/2 inch chamber

BROWNING MAXUS SPORTING

Gas-operated 12 gauge with 3-inch chamber, choice of 28 or 30-inch barrel. Features similar to other Maxus models except has high-grade walnut stock with high gloss finish, generous checkering. Alloy receiver decorated with laser engraved game birds. HiViz Tri-comp fiber optic front sight with ivory mid-rib sight. Invector Plus chokes, Inflex recoil pad.

Perf: $1500 **Exc:** $1300 **VGood:** $1100

BROWNING MAXUS SPORTING CARBON FIBER

Same features as Maxus Sporting model except has composite stock with Dura-Touch Armor coating and Carbon Fiber finish on receiver and barrel.

Perf: $1275 **Exc:** $1075 **VGood:** $900

BROWNING MAXUS RIFLED DEER STALKER

Similar features to other Maxus models except has 22-inch, thick-walled fully rifled barrel designed for slug ammunition only. Chambered for 3-inch 12-gauge loads. Matte black finish with Dura-Touch

Armor coating. Cantilevered scope mount, composite stock.

Perf: $1295 **Exc:** $1095 **VGood:** $925

BROWNING MODEL 12

Slide action; 20-, 28-ga.; 2-3/4-inch chamber; 26-inch Modified barrel; high post floating rib with grooved sighting plane; weighs about 7 lbs.; cut-checkered select walnut stock, forearm with semi-gloss finish; Grade V has high-grade walnut; crossbolt safety in trigger guard; polished blue finish. Made in Japan. Reproduction of the Winchester Model 12. The 20-ga. was limited to 8000 guns; introduced 1988, discontinued 1990. The 28-ga. was limited to 8500 Grade I and 4000 Grade V guns; introduced 1991, discontinued 1992.

Grade I

Perf: $450 **Exc:** $320 **VGood:** $280

Grade V

Perf: $795 **Exc:** $600 **VGood:** $450

BROWNING MODEL 42

Slide action; .410; 3-inch chamber; 26-inch Full barrel; high post floating rib with grooved sighting plane; weighs about 6-3/4 lbs.; cut-checkered select walnut stock, forearm with semi-gloss finish; Grade V has high-grade walnut; crossbolt safety in trigger guard; polished blue finish. Made in Japan. Reproduction of the Winchester Model 42. Limited to 6000 Grade I and 6000 Grade V guns. Introduced 1991; discontinued 1993.

Grade I

Perf: $500 **Exc:** $370 **VGood:** $300

Grade V

Perf: $795 **Exc:** $625 **VGood:** $500

BROWNING RECOILLESS TRAP

Bolt action; single shot; 12-ga.; 2-3/4-inch chamber; back-bored 30-inch barrel; Invector Plus tubes; ventilated rib adjusts to move point of impact; weighs about 9 lbs.; cut-checkered select walnut stock, forearm with high gloss finish; adjustable for drop at comb and length of pull; bolt action eliminates up to 72 percent of recoil; forend is used to cock action when the action is forward. Made in Japan. Introduced 1993.

Perf: $825 **Exc:** $790 **VGood:** $680

BROWNING RECOILLESS TRAP MICRO

Same specs as Recoilless Trap except 27-inch barrel; weighs 8-5/8 lbs.; stock length of pull is adjustable from 13-inch to 13-3/4-inch. Made in Japan. Introduced 1993; still imported.

Perf: $825 **Exc:** $790 **VGood:** $680

BROWNING SINGLE SHOT SHOTGUNS

BROWNING BT-99 MAX

Single shot; boxlock; 12-ga.; 2-3/4-inch chamber; 32-inch, 34-inch vent-rib barrel; Invector Plus choke tubes; weighs 8-5/8 lbs.; ivory front sight, middle bead; hand-checkered walnut pistol-grip Monte Carlo or standard stock, forend; gold-plated trigger; automatic ejector; recoil pad. Made in Japan. Introduced 1995; still in production.

Perf: $1200 **Exc:** $710 **VGood:** $580

Stainless model with black ported barrel

Perf: $1450 **Exc:** $825 **VGood:** $650

BROWNING BT-99 TRAP

Same specs as BT-99 Max except Improved, Full fixed choke or Invector Plus chokes (standard 1992); no gold plating; also available in stainless version with black barrel. Made in Japan. Introduced 1969; discontinued 1994. Reintroduced 2001.

Perf: $800 **Exc:** $500 **VGood:** $420

Stainless model with black barrel

Perf: $1275 **Exc:** $850 **VGood:** $650

Pigeon Grade high-grade stock

Perf: $1150 **Exc:** $700 **VGood:** $600

Signature Painted with red, black stock

Perf: $950 **Exc:** $500 **VGood:** $450

Golden Clays with gold inlays

Perf: $1950 **Exc:** $1400 **VGood:** $1150

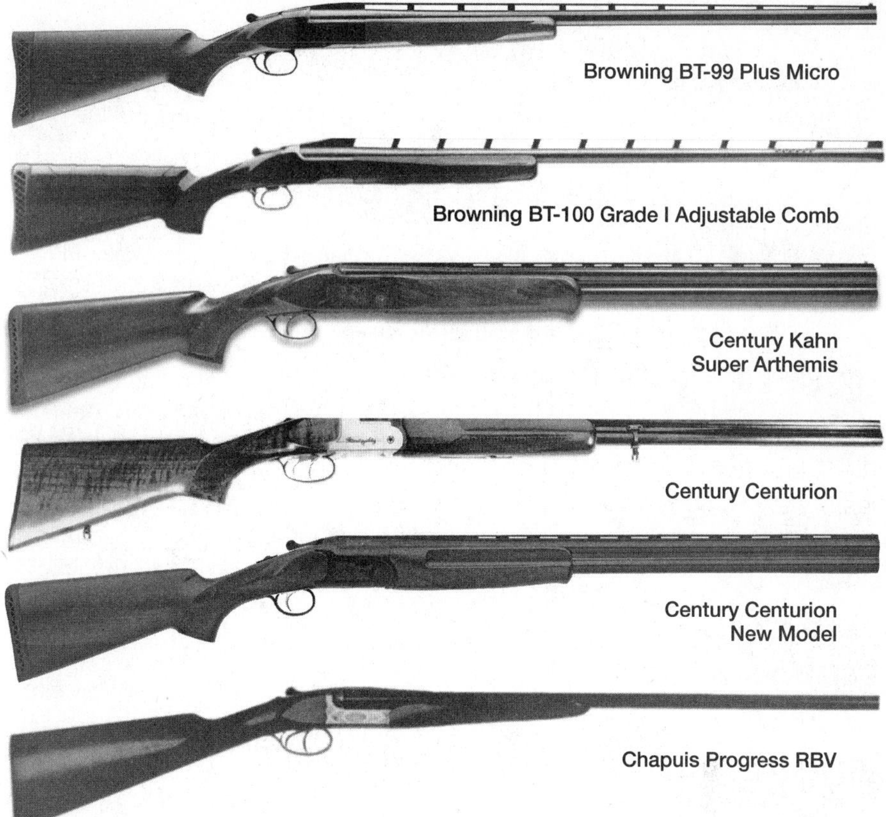

Browning BT-99 Plus Micro

Browning BT-100 Grade I Adjustable Comb

Century Kahn Super Arthemis

Century Centurion

Century Centurion New Model

Chapuis Progress RBV

Conventional stock, 32-inch or 34-inch barrel

Perf: $895 **Exc:** $700 **VGood:** $550

Adj.-comb stock, 32-inch or 34-inch barrel

Perf: $1298 **Exc:** $1063 **VGood:** $938

BROWNING BT-99 PLUS

Same specs as BT-99 Max except high, wide rib, Monte Carlo-style stock. Introduced 1976; Competition name dropped 1978; discontinued 1994.

Perf: $1200 **Exc:** $900 **VGood:** $750

Stainless model with black barrel

Perf: $1475 **Exc:** $900 **VGood:** $750

Pigeon Grade high grade stock

Perf: $1425 **Exc:** $900 **VGood:** $750

Signature Painted with red, black stock

Perf: $1400 **Exc:** $900 **VGood:** $780

Golden Clays with gold inlays

Perf: $2475 **Exc:** $2000 **VGood:** $1775

BROWNING BT-99 PLUS MICRO

Same specs as BT-99 Max except 28-inch, 30-inch ported barrel with adjustable rib system; Invector Plus choke system and back-bored barrel; buttstock with adjustable length of pull range of 13-1/2-inch to 14-inch; Browning's recoil reducer system; scaled down for smaller shooters; marketed in Travel Vault case. Made in Japan. Introduced 1991; discontinued 1994.

Perf: $1325 **Exc:** $900 **VGood:** $750

Stainless model with black barrel

Perf: $1625 **Exc:** $1400 **VGood:** $1200

Pigeon Grade high grade stock

Perf: $1475 **Exc:** $1250 **VGood:** $1000

Signature Painted with red, black stock

Perf: $1475 **Exc:** $1250 **VGood:** $1000

Golden Clays with gold inlays

Perf: $2625 **Exc:** $2000 **VGood:** $1600

BROWNING BT-100 TRAP

Single shot; 12-ga.; 2-3/4-inch chamber; back-bored 32-inch, 34-inch barrel with Invector Plus, or fixed Full choke; weighs 8-5/8 lbs.; 48-1/2-inch overall length (32-inch barrel); cut-checkered walnut Monte Carlo stock, wedge-shaped forend with finger groove; high gloss finish; drop-out trigger adjustable for weight of pull from 3-1/2 to 5-1/2 lbs., and for three length positions; Ejector-Selector allows ejection or extraction of shells; stainless steel or blue finish; optional adjustable comb stock with thumbhole. Made in Japan. Introduced 1995; still imported. Blue finish.

Grade I, blue, Monte Carlo, Invector Plus

Perf: $1835 **Exc:** $1225 **VGood:** $985

Grade I, blue, adj. comb, Invector Plus

Perf: $2073 **Exc:** $1463 **VGood:** $1223

Stainless steel, Monte Carlo, Invector Plus

Perf: $2310 **Exc:** $1475 **VGood:** $1125

Stainless steel, adj. comb, Invector Plus

Perf: $2549 **Exc:** $1714 **VGood:** $1364

CAESAR GUERINI ELLIPSE LIMITED

O/U in 12, 20 or 28 gauge, also 20/28-gauge combo. Barrels: 28 inches, weight is 6.5 lbs. Stock of high-grade walnut. LH stock is available. Built on rounded action. Comes in a fitted case with five choke tubes. The EVO has more elaborate engraving and higher grade of walnut. Prices shown are for base Limited model. Many extra-cost options are available.

Perf: $3600 **Exc:** $3200 **VGood:** $2900

Add 35 percent for EVO model

CAPRINUS SWEDEN

Over/under; 12-ga.; 2-3/4-inch chamber; 28-inch, 30-inch barrel; interchangeable choke tubes; high-grade European walnut, optional Monte Carlo stock; oil finish; checkered butt; single selective trigger ejectors; double safety system; stainless steel construction. Made in Sweden. Introduced 1982; discontinued 1985.

Skeet Special

Perf: $3600 **Exc:** $2700 **VGood:** $2350

Skeet Game

Perf: $3650 **Exc:** $2750 **VGood:** $2400

Game

Perf: $3700 **Exc:** $2800 **VGood:** $2400

Trap

Perf: $3600 **Exc:** $2700 **VGood:** $2350

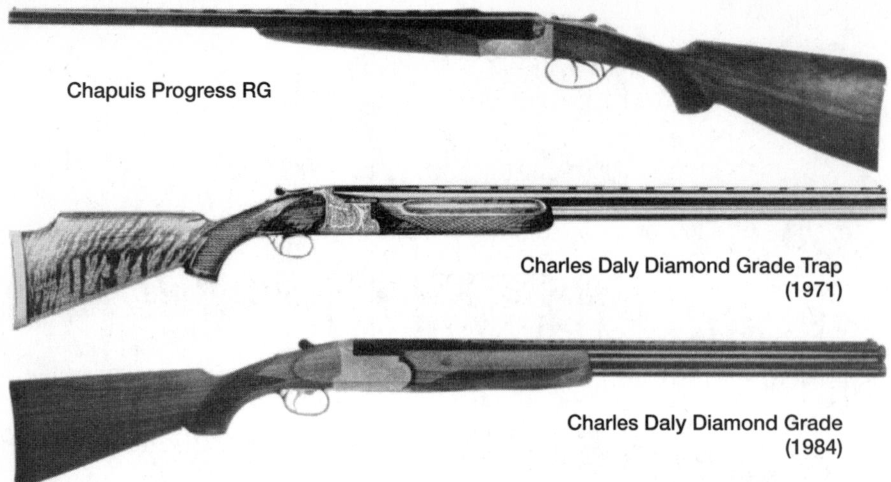

Chapuis Progress RG

Charles Daly Diamond Grade Trap (1971)

Charles Daly Diamond Grade (1984)

CARLO CASARTELLI

Side-by-side; sidelock; various gauges; elaborate game scene and/or scroll engraving was available. Essentially a custom order gun. No longer imported.

Perf: $13,000 **Exc:** $9700 **VGood:** $7900

CENTURION ORDNANCE POSEIDON

Slide action; 12 ga.; 1-3/4-inch chamber (shoots mini-shells and slugs); 18-1/4-inch smoothbore barrel; 13-inch LOP; black synthetic stock and forearm; 6-shot magazine; adjustable rear sight; weighs 5 lbs., 5 oz.. Imported in prototype form only 2001.

Perf: $295 **Exc:** $250 **VGood:** $225

CENTURY KHAN ARTHEMIS (SUPER ARTHEMIS)

Over/under; 12-, 20, 28 ga., .410 bore; 3-inch chambers, 28-inch barrels; vent. Rib; SST; extractors; checkered walnut stock and forearm; weighs 5.3 to 7.4 lbs. Imported from Turkey by Century International Arms, Inc. until late 2004. Importation resumed by Legacy Sports International, early 2005.

Perf: $450 **Exc:** $395 **VGood:** $350

Add $25 to above prices for 20 ga or 28 ga.
Add $50 for .410 bore

CENTURY PHANTOM

Semi-auto.; 12 ga.; 3-inch chamber; 24-inch, 26-inch 28-inch barrel; vent. Rib; 3 choke tubes; black synthetic stock and forearm. Imported from Turkey by Century International Arms, Inc.

Perf: $265 **Exc:** $225 **VGood:** $200

CENTURY SAS-12

Semi-auto.; 12 ga.; 2-3/4-inch chamber; 22-inch, 23-1/2-inch barrel; detachable 3- or 5-shot magazine; black synthetic stock and forearm. Manufactured by PRC in China. Imported by Century International Arms, Inc.

Perf: $225 **Exc:** $185 **VGood:** $165

CENTURY COACH GUN

Side-by-side; 12-, 20-ga., .410 bore; exposed hammers; 20-inch barrels; steel construction; checkered walnut stock and forearm; sling swivels. Imported from China by Century International Arms, Inc.

Perf: $240 **Exc:** $195 **VGood:** $175

CENTURY MODEL YL12

Slide action; 12 ga.; 2-3/4-inch, 3-inch chamber; 19-inch barrel; bead or rifle sights; fixed choke; weighs 7.2 lbs. Imported from China by Century International Arms, Inc.

Perf: $140 **Exc:** $115 **VGood:** $100

CENTURY CENTURION (OLD MODEL)

Over/under; boxlock; 12-ga.; 2-3/4-inch chamber; 28-inch Modofied/Full barrel; weighs 7-1/4 lbs.; European Walnut stock; double triggers; extractors; polished blue finish. Introduced 1993; formerly imported by Century International Arms, Inc.

Perf: $320 **Exc:** $220 **VGood:** $200

CENTURY CENTURION (NEW MODEL)

Over/under; 12-, 20-, 28-ga., .410 bore; bead sight; SST; 3-inch chambers (2-3/4-inch 28 ga.); 5 choke tubes (12 and 20 ga.); gloss finish Turkish walnut stock; automatic safety; hand checkering, extractors; 4140 drilled steel barrel; ventilated recoil pad; weighs 5.3 to 7.35 lbs.; 8mm top rib (12 & 20 ga.), 7mm top rib (28 ga. & .410 bore). Imported from Turkey beginning 2005 by Century International Arms, Inc.

Perf: $390 **Exc:** $295 **VGood:** $235

CENTURY BLACK DIAMOND

Semi-auto.; 12 ga.; 22-inch barrel. Imported from Turkey by Century International Arms, Inc.

Perf: $180 **Exc:** $140 **VGood:** $120

CENTURY TOZ MODEL 34

Over/under; 12-, 20, 28-ga.; full choke over modified; ejectors (20 ga. only); 28-inch barrel (26-inch 28 ga.); overall length 45-inches (28 ga. 43-inches); blued receiver; 1-inch recoil pad; weighs 6.7 to 7.5 lbs. Imported from Russia by Century International Arms, Inc.

Perf: $190 **Exc:** $150 **VGood:** $130

CHAPUIS PROGRESS RBV

Side-by-side; boxlock, sideplates; 12-, 20-ga.; 26-1/2-inch, 27-1/2-inch barrels; ventilated rib; weighs about 6-1/4 lbs.; fine-checkered oil-finished French or American walnut straight or pistol-grip stock; auto ejectors; double triggers; chromed bores; scroll engraving. Made in France. Introduced 1979; discontinued 1982.

Perf: $1800 **Exc:** $1400 **VGood:** $1200

CHAPUIS PROGRESS RG

Same specs as Progress RBV except boxlock. Introduced 1979; discontinued 1982; reintroduced 1989; no longer imported.

Perf: $1200 **Exc:** $900 **VGood:** $750

CHAPUIS PROGRESS SLUG

Same specs as Progress RBV except boxlock; right barrel is rifled for slugs. No longer imported.

Perf: $1200 **Exc:** $900 **VGood:** $750

CHAPUIS ST. BONETT

Side-by-side; 12-, 16-, 20-ga.; boxlock with case colored or coin finished sideplates with fine English scroll or game scene engraving; 27 ½-inch monobloc barrels; ejectors; DTs; checkered straight grip walnut stock and forearm; hardshell case. Limited importation began 1997.

Perf: $2675 **Exc:** $2300 **VGood:** $2000

CHAPUIS O/U

Over/under; sidelock; 12-, 16-, 20-ga.; 22-inch, 23-1/2-inch, 26-2/3-inch, 27-1/2-inch, 31-1/2-inch barrel; choked to customer specs; choice of rib styles; French walnut straight English or pistol-grip stock; auto ejectors or extractors; long trigger guard. Made in France. Introduced 1989; no longer imported.

Perf: $3450 **Exc:** $2250 **VGood:** $1900

NOTE: 20-, 28-gauges bring 25 percent to 35 percent more than prices shown. The .410 is as much as 50 percent higher.

CHARLES DALY AUTO

Recoil-operated autoloader; 12-ga.; 5-shot magazine; 3-shot plug furnished; 26-inch Improved, 28-inch Modified or Full, 30-inch Full barrels; vent rib; hand-checkered walnut pistol-grip stock, forearm; button safety; copy of early Browning patents. Made in Japan. Introduced 1973; discontinued 1975.

Perf: $300 **Exc:** $250 **VGood:** $210

CHARLES DALY DIAMOND GRADE

Over/under; boxlock; 12-, 20-, 28-ga., .410; 26-inch, 28-inch, 30-inch barrels; choked Skeet/Skeet, Improved/Modified, Modified/Full, Full/Full; vent rib; extensive hand-checkered French walnut pistol-grip stock, beavertail forearm; selective single trigger; selective ejection system; safety/barrel selector; engraved receiver, trigger guard. Made in Japan. Introduced 1967; discontinued 1973.

Field model

Perf: $1000 **Exc:** $900 **VGood:** $800

Skeet model

Perf: $1050 **Exc:** $900 **VGood:** $800

Trap model

Perf: $900 **Exc:** $780 **VGood:** $700

CHARLES DALY DIAMOND-REGENT GRADE

Same specs as Diamond Grade except highly figured French walnut stock; profuse engraving; hunting scenes inlaid in gold, silver; firing pins removable through breech face. Made in Japan. Introduced 1967; discontinued 1973.

Perf: $1900 **Exc:** $1350 **VGood:** $1150

CHARLES DALY DIAMOND DL DOUBLE SHOTGUN

Side-by-side; 12-, 20-ga., .410 bore; 3-inch chambers; 28, 2-3/4-inch chambers; 28-inch barrel (Mod. & Full), 26-inch (Imp. Cyl. & Mod.), 26-inch (Full & Full, .410); weighs about 5-7 lbs.; select fancy European walnut; English-style butt; beavertail forend; hand-checkered, hand-rubbed oil finish; drop-forged action with gas escape valves; demiblock barrels with concave rib; selective automatic ejectors; hand-detachable double safety sidelocks with hand-engraved rose and scrollwork; hinged front trigger; color case-hardened receiver. Introduced 1997. Imported from Spain by K.B.I., Inc.

12- or 20-gauge

Perf: $6060 **Exc:** $4950 **VGood:** $4375

28 gauge

Perf: $6160 **Exc:** $4995 **VGood:** $4575

.410

Perf: $6160 **Exc:** $4995 **VGood:** $4575

CHARLES DALY DIAMOND REGENT DL DOUBLE SHOTGUN

Side-by-side; 12-, 20-ga.;.410, bore; 3-inch chambers; 28, 2-3/4-inch chambers; 28-inch barrel (Mod. & Full), 26-inch (Imp. Cyl. & Mod.), 26-inch (Full & Full, .410); weighs about 5-7 lbs.; special select fancy European walnut, English-style butt, splinter forend; hand-checkered; hand-rubbed oil finish; drop-forged action with gas escape valves; demiblock barrels of chrome- nickel steel with concave rib; selective automatic-ejectors; hand-detachable, double-safety

H&H sidelocks with demi-relief hand engraving; H&H pattern easy-opening feature; hinged trigger; coin-finished action. Introduced 1997. Imported from Spain by K.B.I., Inc.

12- or 20-gauge
Perf: $18,950 **Exc:** $15,750 **VGood:** $13,250

28-gauge
Perf: $18,950 **Exc:** $15,750 **VGood:** $13,250

.410
Perf: $18,950 **Exc:** $15,750 **VGood:** $13,250

CHARLES DALY DIAMOND REGENT GTX DL HUNTER O/U

Over/under; 12-, 20-ga.; .410 bore; 3-inch chambers; 28, 2-3/4-inch chambers; 26-inch, 28-inch, 30-inch barrel (choke tubes), 26-inch (Imp. Cyl. & Mod. in 28, 26-inch (Full & Full) in .410; weighs about 7 lbs.; extra select fancy European walnut with 24-inch hand checkering; hand rubbed oil finish; Boss-type action with internal side lumps; deep cut hand-engraved scrollwork and game scene set in full sideplates; GTX detachable single selective trigger system with coil springs; chrome-moly steel barrels; automatic safety; automatic ejectors; white bead front sight; metal bead center sight. Introduced 1997; dropped 1997. Imported from Italy by K.B.I., Inc.

12 or 20
Perf: $19,750 **Exc:** $16,250 **VGood:** $13,750

28; MSR
Perf: $19,750 **Exc:** $16,2500 **VGood:** $13,750

.410
Perf: $19,7500 **Exc:** $16,250 **VGood:** $13,750

Diamond Regent GTX EDL Hunter (as above with engraved scroll and birds, 10 gold inlays), 12, 20 or 28
Perf: $23,000 **Exc:** $19,500 **VGood:** $16,000

As above, .410
Perf: $23,000 **Exc:** $19,500 **VGood:** $16,000

CHARLES DALY DIAMOND GTX SPORTING O/U SHOTGUN

Over/under: 12-, 20-ga.; 3-inch chambers; 28-inch, 30-inch barrel with choke tubes; weighs about 8.5 lbs.; checkered deluxe walnut stock; Sporting Clays dimensions; pistol grip; semi-beavertail forend; hand-rubbed oil finish; chromed, hand-engraved receiver; chrome-moly steel barrels; GTX detachable single selective trigger system with coil springs; automatic safety; automatic ejectors; red bead front sight; ported barrels. Introduced 1997. Imported from Italy by K.B.I., Inc.

Perf: $5260 **Exc:** $4750 **VGood:** $4275

CHARLES DALY DIAMOND GTX TRAP AE-MC O/U SHOTGUN

Over/under; 12-ga.; 2-3/4-inch chambers; 30-inch barrel (Full & Full); weighs about 8.5 lbs.; checkered deluxe walnut stock; pistol grip; trap dimensions; semi- beavertail forend; hand-rubbed oil finish; silvered, hand-engraved receiver; chrome-moly steel barrels; GTX detachable single selective trigger system with coil springs; automatic safety; automatic-ejectors; red bead front sight; metal bead middle; recoil pad. Introduced 1997. Imported from Italy by K.B.I., Inc.

Perf: $5865 **Exc:** $4900 **VGood:** $4400

CHARLES DALY DIAMOND GTX DL HUNTER O/U

Over/under; 12-, 20-ga.; .410 bore; 3-inch chambers; 28, 2-3/4-inch chambers; 26, 28-inch barrels; choke tubes in 12- and 20-ga.; 26-inch (Imp. Cyl. & Mod.), 26-inch (Full & Full) in .410- bore; weighs about 8.5 lbs.; select fancy European walnut stock; 24 lpi hand checkering; hand-rubbed oil finish; Boss-type action with internal side lugs; hand-engraved scrollwork and game scene; GTX detachable single selective trigger system with coil springs; chrome-moly steel barrels; automatic safety; automatic ejectors; red bead front sight; recoil pad. Introduced 1997. Imported from Italy by K.B.I., Inc.

12 or 20
Perf: $11,250 **Exc:** $9000 **VGood:** $7000

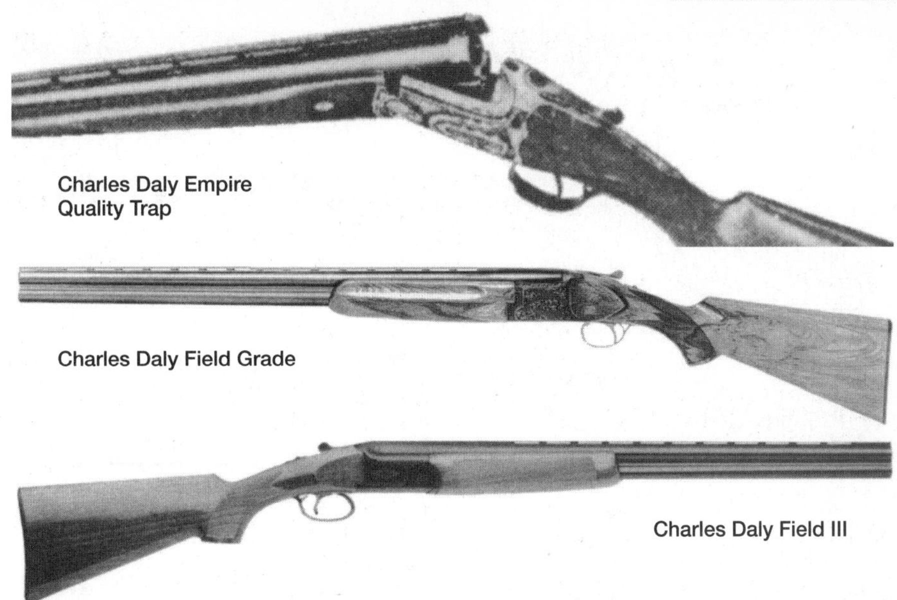

Charles Daly Empire Quality Trap

Charles Daly Field Grade

Charles Daly Field III

28
Perf: $11,250 **Exc:** $9000 **VGood:** $7000

.410
Perf: $11,250 **Exc:** $9000 **VGood:** $7000

GTX EDL Hunter (with gold inlays), 12, 20
Perf: $13,750 **Exc:** $11,250 **VGood:** $9000

As above, 28
Perf: $13,750 **Exc:** $11,250 **VGood:** $9000

As above, .410
Perf: $13,750 **Exc:** $11,250 **VGood:** $9000

CHARLES DALY DIAMOND GRADE (1984)

Over/under; boxlock; 12-, 20-ga.; 27-inch barrels; three choke tubes; hand-checkered oil-finished European walnut stock; single selective competition trigger; selective auto ejectors; silvered, engraved receiver. Made in Italy. Introduced 1984; discontinued 1987.

Perf: $650 **Exc:** $500 **VGood:** $480

CHARLES DALY DIAMOND SKEET (1984)

Same specs as Diamond Grade (1984) except 12-ga.; 26-inch Skeet/Skeet barrels; competition vent rib; Skeet stock; target trigger. Introduced 1984; discontinued 1988.

Perf: $750 **Exc:** $450 **VGood:** $400

CHARLES DALY DIAMOND TRAP (1984)

Same specs as Diamond Grade (1984) except 12-ga.; 30-inch barrels; competition vent top and middle ribs; Monte Carlo stock; target trigger. Introduced 1984; discontinued 1988.

Perf: $800 **Exc:** $500 **VGood:** $450

CHARLES DALY EMPIRE DOUBLE

Side-by-side; boxlock; hammerless; 12-, 16-, 20-ga; 2-3/4-inch (16-ga.), 3-inch (12-, 20-ga.) chamber; 26-inch, 28-inch, 30-inch barrels; standard choke combos; checkered walnut pistol-grip stock, beavertail forearm; plain extractors; non-selective single trigger. Made in Japan. Introduced 1968; discontinued 1971.

Exc: $500 **VGood:** $380 **Good:** $300

CHARLES DALY EMPIRE EDL HUNTER O/U

Over/under; 12-, 20-ga.; .410 bore; 3-inch chambers; 28 ga., 2-3/4-inch; 26-inch, 28-inch barrels (12, 20, choke tubes), 26-inch (Imp. Cyl. & Mod., 28 ga.), 26-inch (Full & Full, .410); weighs about 7 lbs.; checkered walnut pistol grip buttstock; semi- beavertail forend; recoil pad; silvered, engraved receiver; chrome-moly barrels; gold single selective trigger; automatic safety; automatic ejectors; red bead front sight, metal bead middle sight. Introduced 1997. Imported from Italy by K.B.I., Inc.

Empire EDL (dummy sideplates) 12 or 20
Perf: $1365 **Exc:** $1070 **VGood:** $875

Empire EDL
Perf: $1351 **Exc:** $1056 **VGood:** $864

Empire EDL, .410
Perf: $1351 **Exc:** $1056 **VGood:** $864

CHARLES DALY EMPIRE SPORTING O/U

Similar to the Empire EDL Hunter except 12- or 20-gauge only, 28-inch, 30-inch barrels with choke tubes; ported barrels; special stock dimensions. Introduced 1997. Imported from Italy by K.B.I., Inc.

Perf: $1375 **Exc:** $1075 **VGood:** $900

CHARLES DALY EMPIRE QUALITY TRAP

Single barrel; Anson & Deeley-type boxlock; 12-ga.; 30-inch, 32-inch, 34-inch vent-rib barrel; hand-checkered European walnut pistol-grip stock, forearm; automatic ejector. Made in Suhl, Germany. Introduced 1920; discontinued 1933.

Exc: $1200 **VGood:** $900 **Good:** $700

CHARLES DALY EMPIRE TRAP AE MC

Single barrel; 12-ga.; 2-3/4-inch chambers; 30-inch barrel choke tubes; weighs about 7 lbs.; checkered walnut; pistol grip, semi-beavertail forend; silvered, engraved, reinforced receiver; chrome-moly steel barrels; gold single selective trigger; automatic safety; automatic ejector; red bead front sight; metal bead center; recoil pad. Introduced 1997. Imported from Italy by K.B.I., Inc.

Perf: $1415 **Exc:** $1075 **VGood:** $900

CHARLES DALY FIELD AUTO

Autoloader; 12-ga.; 2-3/4-inch, 3-inch chamber; 27-inch, 30-inch barrel; standard chokes or Invector choke tubes; weighs 7 1/4 lbs.; checkered walnut pistol-grip stock, forend; crossbolt safety; alloy receiver; chromed bolt; stainless steel gas piston. Made in Japan. Introduced 1984; discontinued 1987.

Perf: $300 **Exc:** $250 **VGood:** $210

CHARLES DALY FIELD GRADE

Over/under; boxlock; 12-, 20-, 28-ga., .410; 2-3/4-inch, 3-inch chambers (12-, 20-ga.); 26-inch, 28-inch, 30-inch barrels; choked Skeet/Skeet, Improved/Modified, Modified/Full, Full/Full; vent rib; hand-checkered walnut pistol-grip stock, fluted forearm; recoil pad (12-ga. Magnum); selective single trigger; automatic selective ejectors; safety/barrel selector; engraved receiver. Made in Japan. Introduced

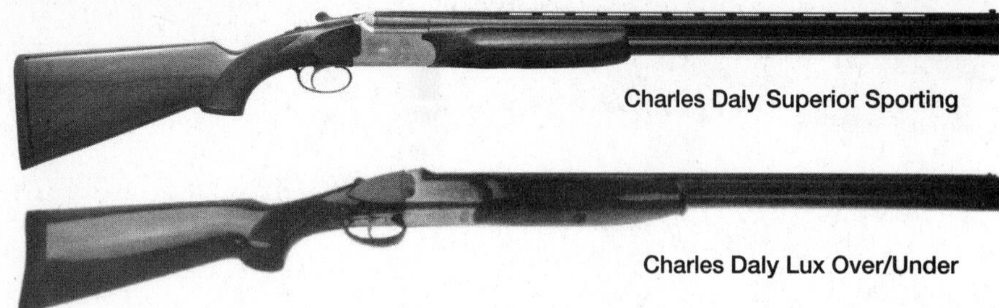

Charles Daly Superior Sporting

Charles Daly Lux Over/Under

1963 (12-, 20-ga.); introduced 1965 (28-ga., .410); discontinued 1976.

Perf: $600 **Exc:** $500 **VGood:** $450

CHARLES DALY FIELD GRADE (1989)

Over/under; boxlock; 12-, 20-ga.; 3-inch chambers; 26-inch, 28-inch barrels; standard fixed choke combos; cut-checkered walnut pistol-grip stock, forend with semi-gloss finish; black vent rubber recoil pad; manual safety extractors; single-stage selective trigger; color case-hardened, engraved receiver. Made in Europe. Introduced 1989; still in production.

Perf: $450 **Exc:** $350 **VGood:** $280

CHARLES DALY FIELD GRADE DELUXE (1989)

Same specs as Field Grade (1989) except 12-, 20-ga.; Improved Cylinder, Modified and Full choke tubes; automatic selective ejectors; antique silver finish on frame. Introduced 1989; still imported.

Perf: $670 **Exc:** $450 **VGood:** $400

CHARLES DALY FIELD III

Over/under; boxlock; 12-, 20-ga.; 26-inch, 28-inch, 30-inch chrome-lined barrels; standard choke combos; vent rib; checkered European walnut stock, forend; single selective trigger extractors; blued, engraved frame. Made in Italy. Introduced 1984; discontinued 1988.

Perf: $375 **Exc:** $320 **VGood:** $295

CHARLES DALY FIELD HUNTER DOUBLE SHOTGUN

Side-by-side; 10-, 12-, 20, 28-ga., .410 bore (3-inch chambers; 28 has 2-3/4-inch); 32-inch barrel (Mod. & Mod.), 28, 30-inch (Mod. & Full), 26-inch (Imp. Cyl. & Mod.), .410 (Full & Full); weighs 6 lbs. to 11.4 lbs.; checkered walnut pistol grip and forend; silvered, engraved receiver; gold single selective trigger in 10-, 12-, and 20 ga.; double triggers in 28 and .410; automatic safety; extractors; gold bead front sight. Introduced 1997. Imported from Spain by K.B.I., Inc.

10-ga.
Perf: $665 **Exc:** $465 **VGood:** $400

12- or 20-ga.
Perf: $665 **Exc:** $465 **VGood:** $400

28-ga.
Perf: $595 **Exc:** $395 **VGood:** $330

.410-bore
Perf: $595 **Exc:** $395 **VGood:** $330

As above, 12 or 20 AE. MC
Perf: $665 **Exc:** $465 **VGood:** $400

CHARLES DALY FIELD HUNTER OVER/UNDER SHOTGUN

Over/under; 12-, 20-, 28-ga. and .410 bore (3-inch chambers, 28 ga. has 2-3/4-inch); 28-inch barrel Mod & Full, 26-inch Imp. Cyl. & Mod (.410 is Full & Full); weighs about 7 lbs.; checkered walnut pistol grip and forend; blued engraved receiver; chrome-moly steel barrels; gold single selective trigger; automatic safety; extractors; gold bead front sight. Introduced 1997. Imported from Italy by K.B.I., Inc.

12- or 20-ga.
Perf: $670 **Exc:** $475 **VGood:** $395

28-ga.
Perf: $750 **Exc:** $555 **VGood:** $475

.410 bore
Perf: $750 **Exc:** $555 **VGood:** $475

CHARLES DALY FIELD HUNTER AE SHOTGUN

Similar to the Field Hunter except 28-gauge and .410-bore only; 26-inch (Imp. Cyl. & Mod., 28-gauge), 26-inch (Full & Full, .410); automatic; ejectors. Introduced 1997. Imported from Italy by K.B.I., Inc.

28
Perf: $865 **Exc:** $745 **VGood:** $640

.410
Perf: $865 **Exc:** $745 **VGood:** $640

CHARLES DALY SUPERIOR HUNTER AE SHOTGUN

Similar to the Field Hunter AE except has silvered, engraved receiver. Introduced 1997. Imported from Italy by F.B.I., Inc.

28-ga.
Perf: $1025 **Exc:** $895 **VGood:** $720

.410 bore
Perf: $1025 **Exc:** $895 **VGood:** $720

CHARLES DALY FIELD HUNTER AE-MC

Similar to the Field Hunter except in 12 or 20 only, 26-inch or 28-inch barrels with five multichoke tubes; automatic ejectors. Introduced 1997. Imported from Italy by K.B.I., Inc.

12 or 20
Perf: $865 **Exc:** $745 **VGood:** $640

CHARLES DALY SUPERIOR SPORTING

Similar to the Field Hunter AE-MC except 28-inch or 30-inch barrels; silvered, engraved receiver; five choke tubes; ported barrels; red bead front sight. Introduced 1997. Imported from Italy by K.B.I., Inc.

Perf: $1130 **Exc:** $955 **VGood:** $790

CHARLES DALY HAMMERLESS DRILLING

Anson & Deeley-type boxlock; 12-, 16-, 20-ga.; rifle barrel chambered for 25-20, 25-35, 30-30; automatic rear sight; hand-checkered European walnut pistol-grip stock, forearm; plain extractors. Made in three grades that differ only in checkering, amount of engraving, wood, overall quality. Made in Suhl, Germany. H.A. Linder models exhibit extensive higher grade engraving, and inlays which affect value. Introduced 1921; discontinued 1933.

Superior Quality
Exc: $2200 **VGood:** $1650 **Good:** $1300

Diamond Quality
Exc: $4000 **VGood:** $3000 **Good:** $2500

Regent Diamond Quality (Linder)
Exc: $7500 **VGood:** $6850 **Good:** $6000

Regent Diamond Quality (Sauer)
Exc: $6500 **VGood:** $4500 **Good:** $3800

CHARLES DALY HAMMERLESS OVER/UNDER

Over/under; Anson & Deeley-type boxlock; 12-, 16-, 20-ga.; 26-inch to 30-inch barrels; any standard choke combo; European walnut stock hand-checkered pistol grip, forearm; double triggers; automatic ejectors. Made in two grades that differ in grade of wood, checkering, amount of engraving, general overall quality. Made in Suhl, Germany. Introduced 1920; discontinued 1933.

Empire Quality
Exc: $2500 **VGood:** $2150 **Good:** $1750

Diamond Quality
Exc: $3600 **VGood:** $2800 **Good:** $2200

CHARLES DALY HAMMERLESS SIDE-BY-SIDE

Side-by-side; Anson & Deeley-type boxlock; 10-, 12-, 16-, 20-, 28-ga., .410; 26-inch to 28-inch barrels; any choke combo; checkered walnut pistol-grip stock, forearm; made in four grades; all have automatic ejectors, except Superior Quality; grades differ in grade of wood, checkering, amount of engraving, general overall quality. Made in Suhl, Germany. Shotguns made by H.A. Linder exhibit extensive higher-grade engraving, inlays and other custom features which affect value. Introduced 1920; discontinued 1933.

Superior Quality
Exc: $700 **VGood:** $500 **Good:** $400

Empire Quality (Linder)
Exc: $4000 **VGood:** $3000 **Good:** $2000

Diamond Quality (Linder)
Exc: $9500 **VGood:** $7000 **Good:** $5000

Regent Diamond Quality (Linder)
Exc: $13,000 **VGood:** $9000 **Good:** $7000

Empire Quality (Sauer)
Exc: $3000 **VGood:** $2000 **Good:** $1500

Diamond Quality (Sauer)
Exc: $5000 **VGood:** $3500 **Good:** $2200

Regent Diamond Quality (Sauer)
Exc: $6500 **VGood:** $4800 **Good:** $3600

CHARLES DALY LUX OVER/UNDER

Over/under; boxlock; 12-, 20-, 28-ga., .410; 26-inch, 28-inch vent rib, chrome-lined barrels; three internal choke tubes; cut-checkered walnut pistol-grip stock, forend with semi-gloss finish; single selective trigger; auto selective ejectors; antique silver-finished frame. Made in Europe. Introduced 1989; no longer in production.

Perf: $600 **Exc:** $440 **VGood:** $390

CHARLES DALY LUX SIDE-BY-SIDE

Side-by-side; boxlock; 12-, 20-ga.; 26-inch barrel; choke tubes; cut-checkered walnut pistol-grip stock, semi-beavertail forend; single selective trigger; ejectors; recoil pad. Introduced 1990; discontinued 1994.

Perf: $520 **Exc:** $370 **VGood:** $300

CHARLES DALY MODEL 100 COMMANDER

Over/under; Anson & Deeley-type boxlock; 12-, 16-, 20-, 28-ga., .410; 26-inch, 28-inch, 30-inch barrels; Improved/Modified, Modified/Full chokes; hand-checkered European walnut straight or pistol-grip stock, forearm; automatic ejectors; double triggers or Miller single selective trigger; engraved receiver. Made in Liege, Belgium. Introduced 1933; discontinued at beginning of WWII.

Exc: $425 **VGood:** $350 **Good:** $275

With single selective trigger
Exc: $450 **VGood:** $370 **Good:** $300

CHARLES DALY MODEL 200 COMMANDER

Over/under; Anson & Deeley-type boxlock; 12-, 16-, 20-, 28-ga., .410; 26-inch, 28-inch, 30-inch barrels; Improved/Modified, Modified/Full chokes; hand-checkered select European walnut straight or pistol-grip stock, forearm; automatic ejectors; double triggers or Miller single selective trigger; elaborate engraved receiver. Made in Liege, Belgium. Introduced 1933; discontinued at beginning of WWII.

Exc: $495 **VGood:** $350 **Good:** $290

With single selective trigger
Exc: $525 **VGood:** $425 **Good:** $360

CHARLES DALY MODEL DSS

Side-by-side; boxlock; 12-, 20-ga.; 3-inch chambers; 26-inch barrels; choke tubes; weighs about 6-3/4 lbs.; cut-checkered figured walnut pistol-grip stock, semi-beavertail forend; black rubber recoil pad; automatic selective ejectors; automatic safety; gold single trigger; engraved, silvered frame. Introduced 1990; no longer imported.

Exc: $550 **VGood:** $400 **Good:** $325

CHARLES DALY MODEL DSS

Side-by-side; boxlock; 12-, 20-ga.; 3-inch chambers; 26-inch barrels; choke tubes; weighs about 6-3/4 lbs.; cut-checkered figured walnut pistol-grip stock, semi-beavertail forend; black rubber recoil pad; automatic selective ejectors; automatic safety; gold single trigger; engraved, silvered frame. Introduced 1990; no longer imported.

Exc: $550 **VGood:** $400 **Good:** $325

CHARLES DALY MULTI-XII

Gas-operated autoloader; 12-ga.; 3-inch chamber; 27-inch vent-rib barrel; Invector choke system; checkered walnut pistol-grip stock, forend; rosewood grip cap; brown vent recoil pad; shoots all loads without adjustment; scroll engraved receiver. Made in Japan. Introduced 1986; discontinued 1987.

Perf: $400 **Exc:** $300 **VGood:** $220

CHARLES DALY NOVAMATIC LIGHTWEIGHT

Autoloader; 12-ga.; 2-3/4-inch chamber; 4-shot tubular magazine; 26-inch, 28-inch barrel; Improved Cylinder or three-tube Quick-Choke system; plain or vent-rib barrel; checkered walnut pistol-grip stock, forearm. Made in Italy by Breda. Introduced 1968; discontinued 1968.

With plain barrel

Exc: $265 **VGood:** $200 **Good:** $150

With vent rib

Exc: $295 **VGood:** $230 **Good:** $180

CHARLES DALY NOVAMATIC LIGHTWEIGHT MAGNUM

Same specs as Novamatic Lightweight except 12-, 20-ga.; 3-inch chambers; 3-shot magazine; 28-inch vent-rib barrel; Full choke. Introduced 1968; discontinued 1968.

Exc: $285 **VGood:** $250 **Good:** $190

CHARLES DALY NOVAMATIC LIGHTWEIGHT TRAP

Same specs as Novamatic Lightweight except 30-inch vent-rib barrel; Full choke; Monte Carlo trap stock; recoil pad. Introduced 1968; discontinued 1968.

Exc: $300 **VGood:** $240 **Good:** $190

CHARLES DALY NOVAMATIC LIGHTWEIGHT SUPER

Same specs as Novamatic Lightweight except 12-, 20-ga.; 26-inch, 28-inch (only 12-ga.) barrel; Skeet choke available; standard vent rib (only 12-ga.); lighter weight. Introduced 1968; discontinued 1968.

Exc: $280 **VGood:** $240 **Good:** $180

CHARLES DALY PRESENTATION GRADE

Over/under; boxlock; 12-, 20-ga.; 27-inch barrel; three choke tubes; hand-checkered, oil-finished European walnut stock; single selective competition trigger; selective auto ejectors; silvered, engraved receiver, sideplates. Made in Italy. Introduced 1984; discontinued 1986.

Perf: $1000 **Exc:** $800 **VGood:** $695

CHARLES DALY SEXTUPLE TRAP

Single barrel; Anson & Deeley-type boxlock; 12-ga.; 30-inch, 32-inch, 34-inch vent-rib barrel; hand-checkered European walnut pistol-grip stock, forearm; six locking bolts; automatic ejector. Made in two grades that differ only in checkering, amount of engraving, grade of wood, improved overall quality. Made in Suhl, Germany. Introduced 1920; discontinued 1933.

Empire Quality

Exc: $1850 **VGood:** $1300 **Good:** $1050

Regent Diamond Quality

Exc: $2500 **VGood:** $1750 **Good:** $1100

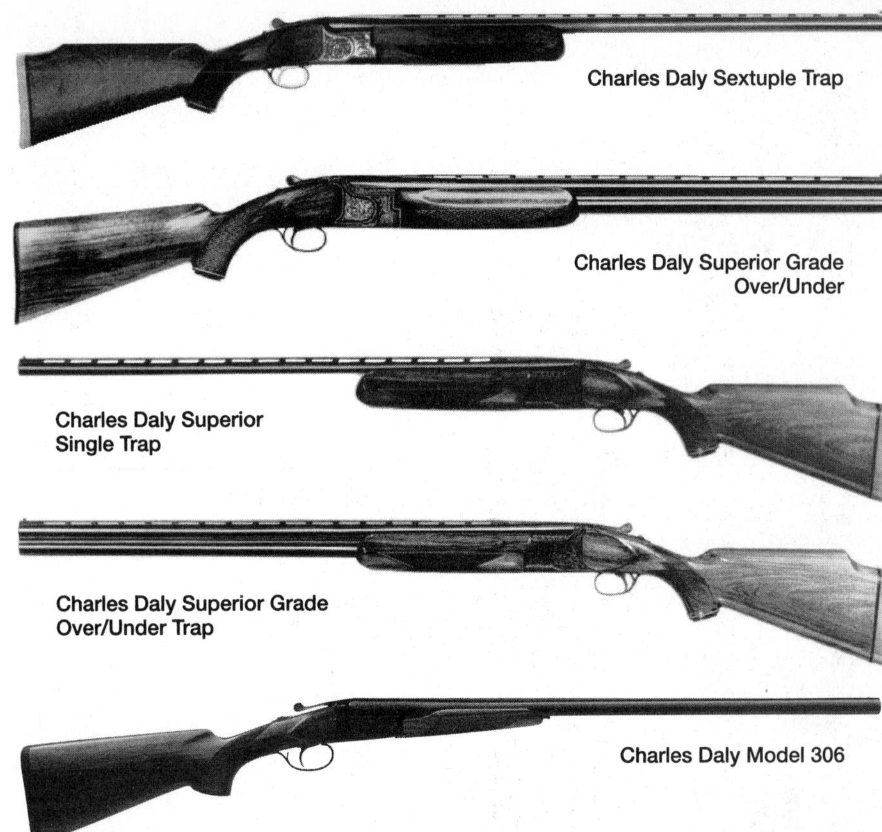

Charles Daly Sextuple Trap

Charles Daly Superior Grade Over/Under

Charles Daly Superior Single Trap

Charles Daly Superior Grade Over/Under Trap

Charles Daly Model 306

CHARLES DALY SUPERIOR GRADE OVER/UNDER

Over/under; boxlock; 12-, 20-, 28-ga., .410; 26-inch, 28-inch, 30-inch barrels; choked Skeet/Skeet, Improved/Modified, Modified/Full, Full/Full; vent-rib; hand-checkered walnut pistol-grip stock, beavertail forearm; selective single trigger; selective ejection system; safety/barrel selector; engraved receiver. Made in Japan. Introduced 1963; discontinued 1976.

Standard model

Perf: $700 **Exc:** $550 **VGood:** $425

Trap model

Perf: $750 **Exc:** $600 **VGood:** $460

CHARLES DALY SUPERIOR GRADE SIDE-BY-SIDE

Side-by-side; boxlock; 12-, 20-ga.; 26-inch, 28-inch, 30-inch chrome-lined barrels; standard choke combos; vent-rib; checkered European walnut stock, forend; single selective trigger. Introduced 1984; discontinued 1985.

Perf: $510 **Exc:** $395 **VGood:** $320

CHARLES DALY SUPERIOR HUNTER DOUBLE SHOTGUN

Side-by-side; 12-, 20-ga.; 3-inch chambers; 28-ga. 2-3/4-inch chambers; 28-inch barrel (Mod. & Full) 26-inch (Imp. Cyl. & Mod.); weighs about 7 lbs.; checkered walnut; pistol grip; splinter forend; silvered, engraved receiver; chrome-lined barrels; gold single trigger; automatic safety; extractors; gold bead front sight. Introduced 1997. Imported from Italy by K.B.I., Inc.

Exc: $890 **VGood:** $775 **Good:** $650

28-ga., 26-inch

Exc: $860 **VGood:** $745 **Good:** $620

470 EL

CHARLES DALY EMPIRE HUNTER DOUBLE SHOTGUN

Similar to Superior Hunter except deluxe wood, game scene engraving, automatic ejectors. Introduced 1997. Imported from Italy by K.B.I., Inc.

12 or 20

Perf: $1165 **Exc:** $975 **VGood:** $790

CHARLES DALY MODEL 306

This 3" side-by-side is offered in 12 and 20 gauge with 26" or 28" barrels. Turkish walnut stock, gold-plated single selective trigger and extractors. Three choke tubes.

NIB: $575 **Exc:** $530 **VGood:** $475

CHARLES DALY SUPERIOR II

Over/under; boxlock; 12-, 20-ga.; 2-3/4-inch, 3-inch chambers (12-ga.); 26-inch, 28-inch, 30-inch chrome-lined barrels; vent-rib; standard choke combos; checkered European walnut stock, forend; single selective trigger; automatic ejectors; silvered receiver; engraving. Introduced 1984; discontinued 1988.

Perf: $650 **Exc:** $440 **VGood:** $390

CHARLES DALY SUPERIOR SINGLE TRAP

Single shot; boxlock; hammerless; 12-ga.; 32-inch, 34-inch barrels; Full choke; vent-rib; checkered walnut Monte Carlo pistol-grip stock, forearm; recoil pad; auto ejector. Made in Japan. Introduced 1968; discontinued 1976.

Perf: $575 **Exc:** $500 **VGood:** $400

CHARLES DALY SUPERIOR TRAP AE MC

Single barrel; 12-ga.; 2-3/4-inch chamber; 30-inch barrel choke tubes; weighs 7 lbs.; checkered walnut stock; pistol grip, semi-beavertail forend; silver engraved receiver; chrome-moly steel barrels; gold single selective trigger; automatic safety; automatic ejectors; red bead front sight; metal bead center;

Charles Daly Model 105

Charles Daly Model 106

Charles Daly VR-MC Semi-Auto

Field Hunter 20-Ga. Youth Pump

Charles Daly VR-MC Pump Youth

Charles Daly Maxi-Mag VR-MC Pump

recoil pad. Introduced 1997. Imported from Italy by K.B.I., Inc.

Perf: $1160 **Exc:** $990 **VGood:** $815

CHARLES DALY VENTURE GRADE

Over/under; boxlock; 12-, 20-ga; 26-inch Skeet/Skeet or Improved/Modified, 28-inch Modified/Full, 30-inch Improved/Full barrels; vent rib; checkered walnut pistol-grip stock, forearm; manual safety; automatic ejectors; single selective trigger. Made in three variations. Made in Japan. Introduced 1973; discontinued 1976.

Standard model

Perf: $575 **Exc:** $500 **VGood:** $400

Trap model, Monte Carlo stock, 30-inch barrel

Perf: $550 **Exc:** $480 **VGood:** $390

Skeet model, 26-inch barrel

Perf: $600 **Exc:** $520 **VGood:** $490

CHARLES DALY MODEL 105

This 3" 12 gauge over-and-under features an engraved nickel-plated steel receiver, double triggers and extractors. Chokes are fixed Modified and Full with 28" barrels or Modified and Improved Cylinder with 26" barrels.

NIB: $375 **Exc:**$335 **VGood:** $295

CHARLES DALY MODEL 106

Available in 12, 20 and 28 gauge and .410 bore, the Model 106 O/U has a blued receiver with raised gold ducks and a rounded pistol grip. All but the .410 include three screw-in chokes. Barrels are 26" or 28" in 12 and 20 gauge and 26" in 28 gauge and .410. Frames are scaled to gauge.

NIB: $400 **Exc:** $365 **VGood:** $300

CHARLES DALY FIELD HUNTER SEMI-AUTO LEFT HAND

Same as above but left hand only.

Perf: $350 **Exc:** $300 **VGood:** $275

CHARLES DALY FIELD HUNTER SEMI-AUTO BLACK CHROME TACTICAL

Same as above but with 22-inch Cylinder-bore smoothbore barrel, rifle sights.

Perf: $350 **Exc:** $300 **VGood:** $275

CHARLES DALY FIELD HUNTER VR-MC

This series of 3" semi-automatic 12 gauges is finished in one of four Realtree/Advantage camo patterns or matte black. Barrels are 24", 26" or 28". Advantage Timber model is available in 20 gauge and black matte is available in 20 and 28 gauge. Add 15 percent for camo.

NIB: $200 **Exc:** $165 **VGood:** $130

CHARLES DALY HUNTER VR-MC YOUTH

As above but with a 1.6-inch shorter stock and 22" barrel. In 20 gauge only.

NIB: $190 **Exc:** $150 **VGood:** $120

CHARLES DALY SUPERIOR II HUNTER

Semi-auto featuring oil-finished Turkish walnut stocks and three chokes. Available in 12 and 20 gauge with 26" or 28" barrel and 28 gauge with 26" barrel.

NIB: $500 **Exc:** $435 **VGood:** $375

CHARLES DALY SUPERIOR II SPORT

Semi-auto in 12 gauge only with 28" or 30" ported barrel and wide rib.

NIB: $525 **Exc:** $460 **VGood:** $400

CHARLES DALY SUPERIOR II TRAP

Semi-auto in 12 gauge, 30" ported barrel only with Monte Carlo comb and wide rib.

NIB: $535 **Exc:** $470 **VGood:** $410

CHARLES DALY FIELD HUNTER MAXI-MAG VR-MC SEMI-AUTO

This 3.5" 12 gauge comes in one of three Realtree/Advantage camos and matte black with 24", 26" or 28" ported barrel. Add 15 percent for camo.

NIB: $550 **Exc:** $500 **VGood:** $395

CHARLES DALY FIELD HUNTER PUMP

Slide-action; 12- and 20-ga.; 24-, 26-, 28- or 30-inch barrels; ventilated rib; black synthetic stock; 3 choke tubes. Still in production.

Perf: $200 **Exc:** $175 **VGood:** $150

Camo

Perf: $250 **Exc:** $200 **VGood:** $175

CHARLES DALY FIELD BLACK CHROME TACTICAL PUMP

Same as above but with 18-1/2-inch Cylinder-bore barrel, rifle sights.

Perf: $175 **Exc:** $150 **VGood:** $125

CHARLES DALY FIELD NICKEL TACTICAL PUMP

Same as above but with nickel finish.

Perf: $185 **Exc:** $160 **VGood:** $135

CHARLES DALY FIELD HUNTER 20-GA. YOUTH PUMP

Same as Field Hunter but in 20-ga. only and 22-inch barrel.

Perf: $200 **Exc:** $175 **VGood:** $150

Camo

Perf: $250 **Exc:** $200 **VGood:** $175

CHARLES DALY FIELD HUNTER MAXI-MAG VR-MC PUMP

Newer versions of the Maxi-Mag are recognized by an updated forend and availability in Timber or Hardwoods camo or matte black. All are 3.5" 12 gauges with a 24", 26" or 28" ported barrel. Add 15 percent for camo.

NIB: $200 **Exc:** $175 **VGood:** $135

CHIPMUNK .410 YOUTH SHOTGUN

Gauge: .410 bore; 18-1/4-inch tapered, barrel; blue finish; weighs 3.25 lbs.; length: 33-inch; walnut stock; manually cocking single shot bolt; blued receiver.

Perf: $185 **Exc:** $160 **VGood:** $145

CHURCHILL, E.J., CROWN

Side-by-side; boxlock; hammerless; 12-, 16-, 20-, 28-ga., .410; 25-inch, 28-inch, 30-inch, 32-inch barrel; any desired choke combo; third-grade, hand-checkered European walnut stock, forearm; pistol grip or straight English-style; ejectors; double triggers or single selective trigger. Introduced 1900; discontinued 1982. Made in England.

Perf: $4750 **Exc:** $3200 **VGood:** $2600

With single selective trigger

Perf: $5200 **Exc:** $3700 **VGood:** $3000

20-ga.

Perf: $5500 **Exc:** $3800 **VGood:** $3000

28-ga.

Perf: $6500 **Exc:** $4500 **VGood:** $3500

.410-bore

Perf: $7500 **Exc:** $5000 **VGood:** $4200

CHURCHILL, E.J., FIELD

Side-by-side; sidelock; hammerless; 12-, 16-, 20-, 28-ga.; 25-inch, 28-inch, 30-inch, 32-inch barrel; any desired choke combo; third grade, hand-checkered European walnut stock, forearm; pistol grip or straight English-style; ejectors; double triggers or single selective trigger; engraving. Introduced 1900; discontinued 1982. Made in England.

Perf: $9500 **Exc:** $7500 **VGood:** $6500

With single selective trigger

Perf: $10,500 **Exc:** $8500 **VGood:** $7500

20-ga.

Perf: $12,500 **Exc:** $9000 **VGood:** $8000

28-ga.

Perf: $14,500 **Exc:** $10,500 **VGood:** $9000

CHURCHILL, E.J., HERCULES

Side-by-side; boxlock; hammerless; 12-, 16-, 20-, 28-ga.; 25-inch, 28-inch, 30-inch, 32-inch barrel; any desired choke combo; top-grade, hand-checkered European walnut stock, forearm; pistol grip or straight English-style; ejectors; double triggers or single selective trigger; engraving. Introduced 1900; discontinued 1982. Made in England.

Perf: $9000 **Exc:** $7000 **VGood:** $6000

With single selective trigger

Perf: $10,000 **Exc:** $8000 **VGood:** $7000

20-ga.

Perf: $12,000 **Exc:** $8500 **VGood:** $7500

28-ga.

Perf: $14,000 **Exc:** $9500 **VGood:** $8000

CHURCHILL, E.J., IMPERIAL

Side-by-side; boxlock; hammerless; 12-, 16-, 20-, 28-ga.; 25-inch, 28-inch, 30-inch, 32-inch barrel; any desired choke combo; second-grade, hand-checkered European walnut stock, forearm; pistol grip or straight English-style; ejectors; double triggers or single selective trigger; engraving. Introduced 1900; discontinued 1982. Made in England.

Perf: $19,500 **Exc:** $13,500 **VGood:** $11,500

With single selective trigger

Perf: $20,000 **Exc:** $14,000 **VGood:** $12,000

20-ga.

Perf: $24,000 **Exc:** $16,000 **VGood:** $13,500

28-ga.

Perf: $28,000 **Exc:** $19,000 **VGood:** $16,000

CHURCHILL, E.J., PREMIER

Over/under; sidelock; hammerless; 12-, 16-, 20-, 28-ga.; 25-inch, 28-inch, 30-inch, 32-inch barrel; hand-checkered European walnut stock, forearm; pistol grip or straight English-style; ejectors; double triggers or single selective trigger; English engraving. Introduced 1925; discontinued 1955. Made in England.

Perf: $18,000 **Exc:** $12,000 **VGood:** $9000

With single selective trigger

Perf: $19,000 **Exc:** $13,000 **VGood:** $10,000

20-ga.

Perf: $22,000 **Exc:** $14,500 **VGood:** $11,000

28-ga.

Perf: $25,000 **Exc:** $16,500 **VGood:** $13,000

CHURCHILL, E.J., PREMIER QUALITY

Side-by-side; sidelock; hammerless; 12-, 16-, 20-, 28-ga.; 25-inch, 28-inch, 30-inch, 32-inch barrel; any desired choke combo; top-grade, hand-checkered European walnut stock, forearm; pistol grip or straight English-style; ejectors; double triggers or single selective trigger; English engraving. Introduced 1900; discontinued 1982. Made in England.

Perf: $17,000 **Exc:** $11,000 **VGood:** $8000

With single selective trigger

Perf: $18,000 **Exc:** $12,000 **VGood:** $9000

20-ga.

Perf: $21,000 **Exc:** $13,500 **VGood:** $10,000

28-ga.

Perf: $24,000 **Exc:** $15,500 **VGood:** $12,000

CHURCHILL, E.J., REGAL

Side-by-side; boxlock; hammerless; 12-, 16-, 20-, 28-ga., .410; 25-inch, 28-inch, 30-inch, 32-inch barrel; any desired choke combo; second-grade, hand-checkered European walnut stock, forearm; pistol grip or straight English-style; ejectors; double triggers or single selective trigger. Introduced during WWII; discontinued 1982. Made in England.

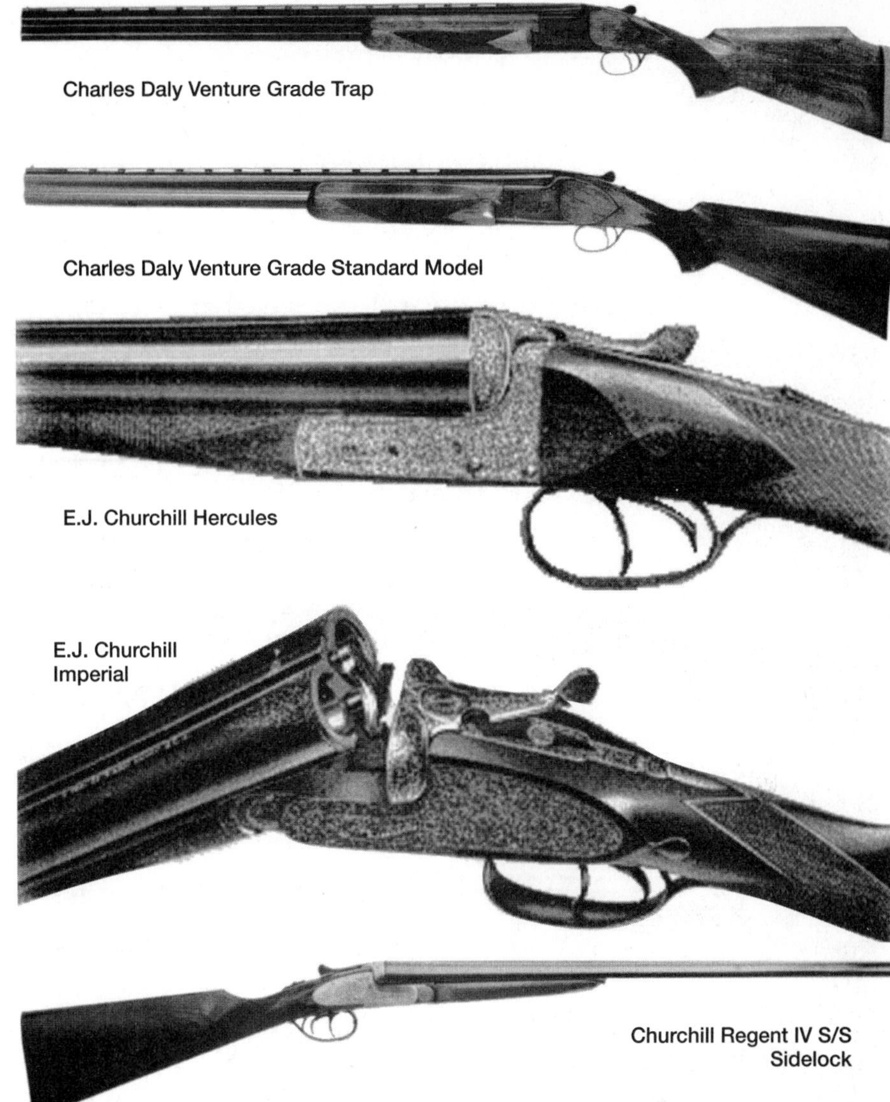

Charles Daly Venture Grade Trap

Charles Daly Venture Grade Standard Model

E.J. Churchill Hercules

E.J. Churchill Imperial

Churchill Regent IV S/S Sidelock

Perf: $5500 **Exc:** $3800 **VGood:** $3200

With single selective trigger

Perf: $6000 **Exc:** $4300 **VGood:** $3700

20-ga.

Perf: $6700 **Exc:** $4500 **VGood:** $3850

28-ga.

Perf: $7500 **Exc:** $4500 **VGood:** $3800

.410-bore

Perf: $8500 **Exc:** $6000 **VGood:** $5000

CHURCHILL, E.J., UTILITY

Side-by-side; boxlock; hammerless; 12-, 16-, 20-, 28-ga., .410; 25-inch, 28-inch, 30-inch, 32-inch barrel; any desired choke combo; second-grade, hand-checkered European walnut stock, forearm; pistol grip or straight English-style; ejectors; double triggers or single selective trigger. Introduced 1900; discontinued WWII. Made in England.

Exc: $5600 **VGood:** $4600 **Good:** $3000

With single selective trigger

Exc: $6000 **VGood:** $5100 **Good:** $3400

20-ga.

Exc: $6300 **VGood:** $5500 **Good:** $3800

28-ga.

Exc: $6500 **VGood:** $6000 **Good:** $5000

.410-bore

Exc: $6700 **VGood:** $6300 **Good:** $5400

Subtract 10 percent for 16 ga.

CHURCHILL DEERFIELD SEMI-AUTO

Autoloader; 12-ga.; 2-3/4-inch, 3-inch chamber; 20-inch slug barrel; standard chokes or ICT choke tubes; weighs 7-1/2 lbs.; checkered select Claro walnut pistol -grip stock, forend; high gloss or matte finish wood; rosewood grip cap; stainless steel gas piston; crossbolt safety; aluminum alloy receiver. Made in Japan. Introduced 1984; discontinued 1986. Previously imported by Ellett Brothers.

Perf: $450 **Exc:** $350 **VGood:** $300

CHURCHILL REGENT IV S/S BOXLOCK

Side-by-side; boxlock; 12-, 20-ga.; 2-3/4-inch chamber; 25 & 28-inch barrels; tapered Churchill rib; hand-checkered European walnut straight stock; double triggers. Made in Spain. Introduced 1984; discontinued 1987. Previously imported by Ellett Brothers.

Perf: $525 **Exc:** $400 **VGood:** $325

Left-hand version

Perf: $575 **Exc:** $450 **VGood:** $375

CHURCHILL REGENT VI S/S SIDELOCK

Same specs as Regent IV S/S except sidelock. No longer in production. Previously imported by Ellett Brothers.

Perf: $800 **Exc:** $600 **VGood:** $500

Churchill Regent O/U Flyweight

Churchill Regent O/U Trap

Churchill Regent O/U Skeet

Churchill Regent VII O/U

Churchill Regent Semi-Auto

Churchill Windsor O/U III

Churchill Windsor S/S

Churchill Windsor Semi-Auto

CHURCHILL REGENT V O/U

Over/under; boxlock; 12-, 20-ga.; 27-inch barrel; interchangeable choke tubes; ventilated rib; ejectors; SST; pewter finish. Made in Italy. Introduced 1984; discontinued 1991.Previously imported by Ellett Brothers.

Perf: $850 **Exc:** $690 **VGood:** $600

CHURCHILL REGENT O/U COMPETITION

Same specs as Regent V except available with trap and Skeet models. 12-ga.; 2-3/4-inch chamber; 26-inch Skeet/Skeet, 30-inch Improved Modified/Full (trap) barrel; checkered European walnut stock, schnabel forend; oil finish; single selective trigger; automatic ejectors; silvered, engraved receiver. Introduced 1991; discontinued 1992. Previously imported by Ellett Brothers.

Trap version

Perf: $800 **Exc:** $575 **VGood:** $550

Skeet version

Perf: $750 **Exc:** $525 **VGood:** $500

CHURCHILL REGENT O/U FLYWEIGHT

Same specs as Regent V except 23-inch barrel; choke tubes. Made in Japan. Introduced 1984; discontinued 1986. Previously imported by Ellett Brothers.

Perf: $850 **Exc:** $790 **VGood:** $700

CHURCHILL REGENT O/U TRAP/SKEET

Same specs as Regent V except sideplates; 26-inch, 30-inch barrel; checkered Monte Carlo stock (trap model); oil-finished wood; vent recoil pad; chrome bores; silvered, engraved receivers. Introduced 1984; discontinued 1991. Previously imported by Ellett Brothers.

Perf: $800 **Exc:** $600 **VGood:** $500

CHURCHILL REGENT VII O/U

Same specs as Regent V except sideplates. No longer imported.

Perf: $850 **Exc:** $690 **VGood:** $600

CHURCHILL REGENT SEMI-AUTO

Autoloader; 12-ga.; 2-3/4-inch, 3-inch chamber; 26-inch, 28-inch, 30-inch barrel; standard chokes or ICT choke tubes; weighs 7-1/2 lbs.; checkered select Monte Claro walnut pistol-grip stock, forend; high gloss or matte finish wood; rosewood grip cap; stainless steel gas piston; crossbolt safety; etched, polished aluminum receiver. Made in Japan. Introduced 1984; discontinued 1986. Previously imported by Ellett Brothers.

Perf: $400 **Exc:** $300 **VGood:** $280

CHURCHILL ROYAL

Side-by-side; boxlock; 10-, 12-, 20-, 28-ga., .410; 3-inch, 3-1/2-inch chamber; 26-inch, 28-inch barrel; standard choke combos; concave rib; checkered European walnut straight-grip stock; double triggers; extractors; chromed bores; color case-hardened finish. Made in Spain. Introduced 1988; discontinued 1991. Previously imported by Ellett Brothers.

10-ga.

Perf: $450 **Exc:** $350 **VGood:** $300

12-, 20-ga.

Perf: $450 **Exc:** $350 **VGood:** $300

28-ga.

Perf: $480 **Exc:** $380 **VGood:** $330

.410

Perf: $525 **Exc:** $425 **VGood:** $375

CHURCHILL TURKEY AUTOMATIC SHOTGUN

Gas-operated autoloader; 12-ga.; 3-inch chamber; 5-shot magazine; 25-inch barrel; Modified, Full, Extra Full choke tubes; weighs 7 lbs.; hand-checkered walnut stock with satin finish; magazine cut-off; non-glare metal finish; gold-colored trigger. Introduced 1990;. Previously imported by Ellett Brothers.

Perf: $480 **Exc:** $360 **VGood:** $300

CHURCHILL WINDSOR O/U III

Over/under; boxlock; 12-, 20-ga., .410; 3-inch chamber; 26-inch, 28-inch, 30-inch barrel; standard choke combos or interchangeable choke tubes; checkered European walnut pistol-grip stock, forend; extractors; single selective trigger; silvered, engraved finish. Made in Italy. Introduced 1984; no longer in production. Previously imported by Ellett Brothers.

Perf: $500 **Exc:** $400 **VGood:** $340

CHURCHILL WINDSOR IV O/U

Same specs as Windsor O/U III except 12-, 20-ga.; ejectors. Introduced 1984; no longer imported.

Perf: $750 **Exc:** $525 **VGood:** $440

CHURCHILL WINDSOR O/U FLYWEIGHT

Same specs as Windsor O/U except 23-inch barrel; ICT choke tubes; checkered walnut straight-grip stock. No longer imported.

Perf: $600 **Exc:** $500 **VGood:** $450

CHURCHILL WINDSOR O/U SPORTING CLAYS

Same specs as Windsor IV except 12-ga.; 28-inch, 30-inch ported, back-bored barrels; choke tubes; tapered ventilated rib, ventilated side rib; select walnut stock, sporting-style forend with finger grooves; palm swell grip; lengthened forcing cones. Introduced 1995; no longer imported.

Perf: $900 **Exc:** $750 **VGood:** $600

CHURCHILL WINDSOR S/S

Side-by-side; boxlock; 10-, 12-, 16-, 20-, 28-ga., .410; 2-3/4-inch (16-ga.), 3-inch chamber; 24-inch, 26-inch, 28-inch, 30-inch, 32-inch barrel; hand-checkered European walnut stock, beavertail forend; rubber butt pad; auto safety; double triggers; extractors; silvered, engraved finish. Made in Spain. Introduced 1984; discontinued 1991.

Perf: $500 **Exc:** $410 **VGood:** $320

10-ga.

Perf: $495 **Exc:** $380 **VGood:** $300

CHURCHILL WINDSOR S/S II

Same specs as Windsor S/S except ejectors. No longer in production.

Perf: $550 **Exc:** $460 **VGood:** $370

CHURCHILL WINDSOR SEMI-AUTO

Autoloader; 12-ga.; 2-3/4-inch, 3-inch chamber; 26-inch to 30-inch barrel; standard chokes or ICT choke tubes; weighs 7-1/2 lbs.; checkered select Monte Claro walnut pistol-grip stock, forend; high gloss or matte finish wood; rosewood grip cap; stainless steel gas piston; crossbolt safety; anodized alloy receiver. Made in Japan. Introduced 1984; discontinued 1991.

Perf: $350 **Exc:** $275 **VGood:** $210

CITADEL LE TACTICAL

Slide-action 12 gauge with 3-inch chamber, 20-inch barrel and rifle type sights. Composite stock is adjustable and comes in standard, pistol grip or thumbhole configuration with Speed Lock ergonomic forearm. Capacity 7+1.

Perf: $440 **Exc:** $385 **VGood:** $325

Add 10 percent for pistol grip stock, 30 percent for thumbhole

CLAYCO MODEL 6

Over/under; 12-ga.; 2-3/4-inch chamber; 26-inch, 28-inch, barrel; vent top rib; checkered walnut-finished hardwood pistol-grip stock, forend; single non-selective trigger; auto safety; vent rubber recoil pad; blued scroll-engraved receiver. Made in China. Introduced 1983; discontinued 1985.

Perf: $200 **Exc:** $150 **VGood:** $100

COGSWELL & HARRISON AMBASSADOR

Side-by-side; boxlock; 12-, 16-, 20-ga.; 26-inch, 28-inch, 30-inch barrel; any choke combo; hand-checkered European walnut straight-grip stock, forearm; ejectors; double triggers; sideplates feature game engraving or rose and scroll engraving. Introduced 1970; no longer in production. Made in England.

Perf: $5500 **Exc:** $4950 **VGood:** $4450

COGSWELL & HARRISON AVANT TOUT KONOR

Side-by-side; boxlock; hammerless; 12-, 16-, 20-ga.; 25-inch, 27-1/2-inch, 30-inch barrels; any desired choke combo; hand-checkered European walnut straight-grip stock, forearm; pistol-grip stock available on special order; sideplates; double, single or single selective triggers; engraving. Introduced 1920s; no longer in production. Made in England.

Exc: $2500 **VGood:** $2200 **Good:** $1800

Add $400 to above prices for SST

Add 20 percent for 20 ga.

Subtract 10 percent for 16 ga.

COGSWELL & HARRISON AVANT TOUT REX

Same specs as Avant Tout Konor except no sideplates; lower grade wood, checkering, engraving, overall finish. No longer in production. Made in England.

Exc: $2150 **VGood:** $1800 **Good:** $1650

COGSWELL & HARRISON AVANT TOUT SANDHURST

Same specs as Avant Tout Konor except less intricate engraving, checkering; lower grade of wood, overall workmanship. No longer in production. Made in England.

Exc: $2500 **VGood:** $2300 **Good:** $2150

COGSWELL & HARRISON HUNTIC MODEL

Side-by-side; sidelock; 12-, 16-, 20-ga.; 25-inch, 27-1/2-inch, 30-inch barrel; any desired choke combo; hand-checkered European walnut straight-grip stock, forearm; pistol-grip stock on special order; ejectors; double, single or single selective triggers. Introduced in late 1920s; no longer in production. Made in England.

Exc: $3500 **VGood:** $3200 **Good:** $3000

Add $400 to above prices for SST

COGSWELL & HARRISON MARKOR MODEL

Side-by-side; boxlock; 12-, 16-, 20-ga.; 27-1/2-inch, 30-inch barrels; any standard choke combo; hand-checkered European walnut straight-grip stock, forearm; double triggers; ejectors or extractors. Introduced in late 1920s; no longer in production. Made in England.

Extractors

Exc: $1475 **VGood:** $1300 **Good:** $1050

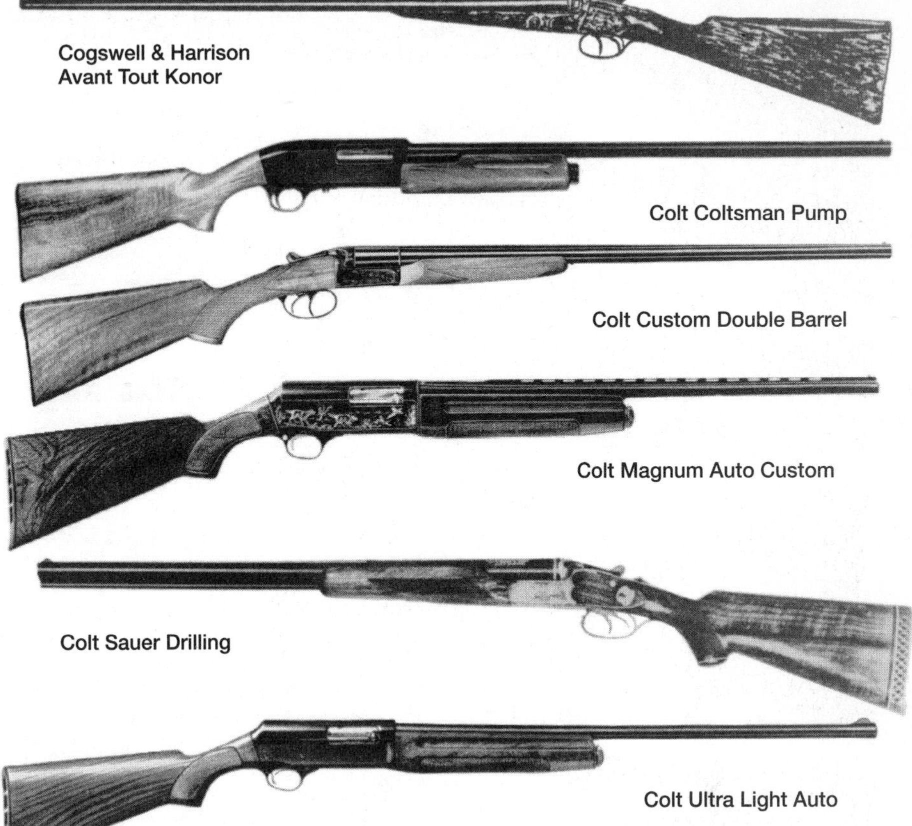

Cogswell & Harrison Avant Tout Konor

Colt Coltsman Pump

Colt Custom Double Barrel

Colt Magnum Auto Custom

Colt Sauer Drilling

Colt Ultra Light Auto

Ejectors

Exc: $1750 **VGood:** $1650 **Good:** $1350

COGSWELL & HARRISON PRIMAC MODEL

Side-by-side; hand-detachable sidelock; 12-, 16-, 20-ga.; 25-inch, 26-inch, 27-1/2-inch, 30-inch barrels; any choke combo; hand-checkered European walnut straight-grip stock, forearm; ejectors; double triggers, single or single selective triggers; English-style engraving. Introduced in 1920s; no longer in production. Made in England.

Exc: $4950 **VGood:** $3750 **Good:** $2400

COGSWELL & HARRISON VICTOR MODEL

Side-by-side; hand-detachable sidelock; 12-, 16-, 20-ga.; 25-inch, 26-inch, 27-1/2-inch, 30-inch barrels; any choke combo; hand-checkered European walnut straight-grip stock, forearm; ejectors; double triggers, single or single selective triggers; high quality English-style engraving. Introduced in 1920s; no longer in production. Made in England.

Exc: $6000 **VGood:** $4000 **Good:** $3000

COLT COLTSMAN PUMP

Slide action; takedown; 12-, 16-, 20-ga.; 4-shot magazine; 26-inch Improved, 28-inch Modified, 30-inch Full choke barrel; weighs about 6 lbs.; uncheckered European walnut stock. Introduced 1961; discontinued 1965.

Exc: $350 **VGood:** $260 **Good:** $230

COLT COLTSMAN PUMP CUSTOM

Same specs as Coltsman Pump except vent rib; hand-checkered pistol grip, forearm. Introduced 1961; discontinued 1963.

Exc: $375 **VGood:** $275 **Good:** $255

COLT CUSTOM DOUBLE BARREL

Boxlock; 12-, 16-ga.; 2-3/4-inch, 3-inch chamber (12-ga.); 26-inch Improved/Modified, 28-inch Modified/Full, 30-inch Full/Full choke barrels; hand-checkered European walnut pistol-grip stock, beavertail forearm. Introduced 1961; discontinued 1961.

Exc: $600 **VGood:** $450 **Good:** $225

COLT MAGNUM AUTO

Autoloader; takedown; 12-, 20-ga.; 3-inch chamber; 28-inch (20-ga.), 32-inch (12-ga.) interchangeable chrome-lined barrels; Full choke; plain, solid or vent rib; weighs 8-1/4 lbs. (12-ga.) or 6 lbs. (20-ga.); walnut stock; steel receiver. Introduced 1964; discontinued 1966.

Exc: $350 **VGood:** $290 **Good:** $230

COLT MAGNUM AUTO CUSTOM

Same specs as Magnum Auto except solid or vent rib; select walnut stock, forearm; engraved receiver. Introduced 1964; discontinued 1966.

Exc: $395 **VGood:** $330 **Good:** $270

COLT SAUER DRILLING

Side-by-side; boxlock; top lever; 30-06 or 243 Winchester under 12-ga.; 25-inch barrels; shotgun barrels choked Modified/Full; folding leaf rear sight, blade front with brass bead; hand-checkered oil-finished American walnut pistol-grip stock, forearm; black pistol-grip cap; recoil pad; cocking indicators; tang barrel selector; automatic sight positioner; set rifle trigger; side safety; crossbolt safety. Made for Colt by Sauer in Germany. No longer imported by Colt.

Perf: $3200 **Exc:** $2300 **VGood:** $1900

COLT ULTRA LIGHT AUTO

Autoloader; takedown; 12-, 20-ga.; 2-3/4-inch chamber; 4-shot magazine; 26-inch Improved or Modified, 28-inch Modified or Full, 30-inch Full chrome-lined interchangeable barrels; plain, solid or vent rib; weighs 6-1/4 lbs. (12-ga.), 5 lbs. (20-ga.); walnut stock; crossbolt safety; aluminum alloy receiver. Introduced 1964; discontinued 1966.

Perf: $280 **Exc:** $250 **VGood:** $195

COLT ULTRA LIGHT AUTO CUSTOM

Same specs as Ultra Light Auto except solid or vent rib; select walnut stock, forearm; engraved with bird scenes. Introduced 1964; discontinued 1966.

Perf: $225 **Exc:** $175 **VGood:** $140

CZ Grouse

CZ Sporting

CZ Wingshooter

CZ 712/720

CONNECTICUT SHOTGUN MANUFACTURING CO. MODEL 21

Side-by-side; 12-, 16-, 20-, 28-ga., .410 bore; 4 frame sizes (12, 16, 20 and 28 ga./.410 bore); barrels lengths up to 32-inch; matte, solid or vent. Rib; fixed chokes; best quality checkered wood; Limited manufacture beginning 2002. Each is built on a custom order basis.

CONNECTICUT SHOTGUN MANUFACTURING MODEL 21-1

Similar to Model 21, except features light scroll engraving patterned after the Winchester no. 1; A fancy wood. Introduced 2002.

Perf: $8750 **Exc:** $7250 **VGood:** $6500

Add $1000 to above prices for 28 ga.
Add $3500 for .410 bore

CONNECTICUT SHOTGUN MANUFACTURING MODEL 21-5

Similar to Model 21, except has both scroll and three hunting scenes engraved patterned after Winchester's No. 5 style on barrels and frame; AA fancy wood. Introduced 2002.

Perf: $12,900 **Exc:** $9950 **VGood:** $8750

Add $2100 to above prices for 28 ga.
Add $2600 for .410 bore

CONNECTICUT SHOTGUN MANUFACTURING MODEL 21-6

Similar to Model 21, except has tight scroll and dog and game bird engraving patterned after Winchester's No. 6 style on frame and barrels; AAA fancy wood. Introduced 2002.

Perf: $13,800 **Exc:** $11,250 **VGood:** $9250

Add $2100 to above prices for 28 ga.
Add $2600 for .410 bore

CONNECTICUT SHOTGUN MANUFACTURING MODEL 21 GRAND AMERICAN

Similar to Model 21, except is top of the line model; 2 sets of barrels; elaborate scroll engraving on barrels and frame; 5 gold inlays; B carved stock and forearm; AAA full fancy feather crotch American walnut. Introduced 2002.

Perf: $16,995 **Exc:** $14,250 **VGood:** $11,650

CONNECTICUT VALLEY CLASSICS CLASSIC SPORTER

Over/under; boxlock; 12-ga.; 3-inch chambers; 28-inch, 30-inch, 32-inch barrels; Skeet, Improved Cylinder, Modified, Full CV choke tubes; weighs 7-3/4 lbs.; hand-checkered American black walnut pistol-grip stock, forend; elongated forcing cones; stainless receiver with fine engraving; chrome-lined bores and chambers suitable for steel shot; receiver duplicates Classic Doubles M101 specifications. Introduced 1993; no longer in production.

Perf: $2450 **Exc:** $2000 **VGood:** $1500

CONNECTICUT VALLEY CLASSICS CLASSIC FIELD WATERFOWLER

Over/under; boxlock; 12-ga.; 3-inch chambers; 30-inch barrels; Skeet, Improved Cylinder, Modified, Full CV choke tubes; weighs 7-3/4 lbs.; hand-checkered American black walnut pistol-grip stock, forend; elongated forcing cones; blued, non-reflective receiver with fine engraving; chrome-lined bores and chambers suitable for steel shot; receiver duplicates Classic Doubles M101 specifications. Introduced 1995; no longer in production.

Perf: $2200 **Exc:** $1300 **VGood:** $1000

COSMI SEMI-AUTOMATIC

Recoil-operated autoloader; break-open; 12-, 20-ga.; 2-3/4-inch, 3-inch chamber; 3-, 8-shot magazine in buttstock; 22-inch to 34-inch barrel to customers specs; choke tubes; weighs 6-1/4 lbs.; hand-checkered exhibition-grade Circassian walnut stock; double ejectors; double safety system; stainless steel construction; various grades of engraving can double price; marketed in fitted leather case; essentially a hand-made custom gun. Made in Italy. Introduced 1985; still imported.

Perf: $12,000 **Exc:** $5000 **VGood:** $4500

COSMI ALUMINUM MODEL

Similar to standard Cosmi, except 12-, 20-ga.; receiver made of machined aluminum; weighs 7 lbs. (12-ga.), 5.9 lbs. (20 ga.).

Perf: $14,000 **Exc:** $5000 **VGood:** $4595

COSMI TITANIUM MODEL

Similar to standard Cosmi, except 12-, 20-ga.; receiver made of machined titanium; weighs 6.8 lbs. (12-ga.), 5.7 lbs. (20-ga.). Introduced in 1990.

Perf: $16,500 **Exc:** $5750 **VGood:** $4950

CROSSFIRE SHOTGUN/RIFLE

Gauge/Caliber: 12, 2-3/4-inch; Chamber: 4-shot/223 Rem. (5-shot). Barrel: 20-inch (shotgun), 18-inch (rifle). Weight: About 8.6 lbs. Length: 40-inch overall. Stock: Composite. Sights: Meprolight night sights. Integral Weaver-style scope rail. Features: Combination pump-action shotgun, rifle; single selector, single trigger; dual action bars for both upper and lower actions; ambidextrous selector and safety. Introduced 1997. Made in U.S. From Hesco.

Perf: $1750 **Exc:** $1550 **VGood:** $1350

With camo finish

Perf: $1850 **Exc:** $1650 **VGood:** $1450

CRUCELEGUI HERMANOS MODEL 150

Side-by-side; Greener triple crossbolt action; exposed hammers; 12-, 20-ga.; 20-inch, 26-inch, 28-inch, 30-inch, 32-inch barrels; hand-checkered European walnut stock, beavertail forend; double triggers; color case-hardened receiver; chromed bores; sling swivels. Made in Spain. Introduced 1979; still in production.

Perf: $350 **Exc:** $290 **VGood:** $240

NOTE: On this model, .410 is worth 50 percent more than prices shown, 28-gauge worth 40 percent more, 20-gauge, 25 percent more.

CZ 581 SOLO OVER/UNDER SHOTGUN

Over/under; 12-ga.; 2-3/4-inch chambers; 27.6-inch barrel (Mod. & Full); weighs 7.37 lbs.; 44.5-inch overall; circassian walnut stock; automatic ejectors; double triggers; Kersten-style double lump locking system. Imported from the Czech Republic by CZ-USA.

Exc: $740 **VGood:** $625 **Good:** $570

CZ 912

Gas-operated 12 gauge with 3-inch chamber. Similar to CZ 712 except 28-inch barrel only, polished black chrome finish, high gloss checkered stock and improved recoil pad. Fiber optic bead front sight.

Perf: $450 **Exc:** $400 **VGood:** $350

CZ GROUSE

New in 2008, the Grouse is a single trigger side-by-side in 12, 20 and 28 gauge and .410 bore with 3" chambers (2.75" in 28 gauge). White chrome-plated receiver with scroll engraving. Prince of Wales grip and semi-beavertail Schnabel forend. Barrels are 28" in 12 and 20 gauge and 26" in 28 and .410. Includes five choke tubes (.410 is choked IC/MOD). Add 20% for 28 gauge and .410 bore.

Exc: $900 **VGood:** $725 **Good:** $600

CZ SPORTING

This dedicated sporting clays over/under is a 12 gauge with an adjustable comb stock and forend of #3 Circassian walnut. It features chrome-lined barrels back-bored to .736 and automatic ejectors. Barrels are 30" or 32". Five choke tubes included. Weight is about 9 lbs.

Exc: $2200 **VGood:** $1125 **Good:** $850

CZ WINGSHOOTER

O/U in 12, 20, 28 gauge or 410 bore with 3-inch chambers. Barrels are 28 inches with ventilated rib, five choke tubes. Checkered Turkish walnut stock. Engraved scroll work depicts upland birds on sideplates. Automatic ejectors on 12 and 20 gauges, extractors on 28 and 410.

Perf: $925 **Exc:** $785 **VGood:** $675

CZ-712/720

Gas-operated autoloader in 12- or 20-gauge (720). 20, 26, or 28-inch barrel with choke tubes, ventilated rib. Matte black finish. Checkered walnut or polymer stock.

Perf: $385 **Exc:** $325 **VGood:** $275

DAKOTA PREMIER GRADE SHOTGUNS

Side-by-side; 12-, 16-, 20-, 28-ga.; .410 bore. 27-inch barrel; exhibition-grade English walnut, hand-rubbed oil finish with straight grip and splinter forend; French grey finish; 50 percent coverage engraving; double triggers; selective ejectors. Finished to customer specifications. Made in U.S. by Dakota Arms.

12-, 16-, 20-gauge

Exc: $8300 **VGood:** $6950 **Good:** $5650

28 gauge and .4105

Perf: $13,950 **Exc:** $10,250 **VGood:** $8300

DAKOTA LEGEND

Similar to Premier Grade except has special selection English walnut, full- coverage scroll engraving, oak and leather case. Made in U.S. by Dakota Arms.

12-, 16-, 20-gauge

Perf: $16,000 **Exc:** $13,000 **VGood:** $11,000

28-gauge and .410

Perf: $17,600 **Exc:** $14,300 **VGood:** $12,100

DARNE MODEL R11 BIRD HUNTER

Side-by-side; sliding breech action; 12-, 20-ga.; 25-1/2-inch Improved Cylinder/Modified barrels; raised rib;

deluxe hand-checkered walnut stock, forearm; double triggers; automatic selective ejection; case-hardened receiver. Made in France. Discontinued 1979.

Perf: $1700 **Exc:** $1550 **VGood:** $1300

DARNE MODEL R15 PHEASANT HUNTER

Side-by-side; sliding breech action; 12-ga.; 27-1/2-inch Modified/Full barrels; raised rib; fancy hand-checkered walnut stock, forearm; double triggers; automatic selective ejection system; case-hardened engraved receiver. Discontinued 1979.

Perf: $2250 **Exc:** $2000 **VGood:** $1850

DARNE MODEL V19 QUAIL HUNTER SUPREME

Side-by-side; sliding breech action; 20-, 28-ga.; 25-1/2-inch Improved/Modified barrels; raised rib; extra-fancy hand-checkered walnut stock, forearm; double triggers; automatic selective ejection; case-hardened receiver; elaborate engraving. Discontinued 1979.

Perf: $4500 **Exc:** $4150 **VGood:** $3700

DARNE MODEL MAGNUM R16

Similar to other Darne models in the R series, but higher grade of wood and greater amount of engraving. Discontinued 1979.

Perf: $3500 **Exc:** $3150 **VGood:** $2650

DARNE MODEL V22

Similar to other Darne models in the V series, except higher grade of wood and greater amount of engraving. Discontinued 1979.

Perf: $5750 **Exc:** $5300 **VGood:** $4600

DAVIDSON MODEL 63B

Double barrel; Anson & Deeley boxlock; 12-, 16-, 20-, 28-ga, .410; 25-inch (.410), 26-inch, 28-inch 30-inch (12-ga.) barrels; Improved Cylinder/Modified, Modified/Full, Full/Full chokes; hand-checkered walnut pistol-grip stock; plain extractors; automatic safety; engraved, nickel-plated frame. Made in Spain. Introduced 1963; no longer in production.

Exc: $275 **VGood:** $260 **Good:** $220

DAVIDSON MODEL 63B MAGNUM

Same specs as Model 63B except 10-, 12-, 20-ga.; 3-inch (12-, 20-ga.), 3-1/2-inch (10-ga.) chambers; 32-inch Full/Full barrels (10-ga. only). Made in Spain. No longer in production.

12-, 20-ga. Magnum

Exc: $360 **VGood:** $340 **Good:** $310

10-ga. Magnum

Exc: $385 **VGood:** $370 **Good:** $340

DAVIDSON MODEL 69SL

Double barrel; sidelock; 12-, 20-ga.; 26-inch, 28-inch barrels; Modified/Improved (26-inch), Modified/Full (28-inch) choke; hand-checkered European walnut stock; detachable locks; nickel-plated, engraved action. Introduced 1963; discontinued 1976.

Perf: $415 **Exc:** $395 **VGood:** $375

DAVIDSON MODEL 73

Side-by-side; sidelock; exposed hammer; 12-, 20-ga.; 3-inch chambers; 20-inch barrels; checkered European walnut pistol-grip stock, forearm; detachable sideplates; plain extractors; double triggers. Made in Spain. Introduced 1976; no longer in production.

Perf: $275 **Exc:** $260 **VGood:** $220

DESERT INDUSTRIES BIG TWENTY

Single shot; 20-ga.; 19-inch Cylinder bore barrel; 31-3/4-inch overall length; weighs 4-3/4 lbs.; bead front sight; fixed formed-wire stock with buttplate; walnut forend, grip; all-steel construction; blued finish. Introduced 1990; no longer in production.

Perf: $180 **Exc:** $155 **VGood:** $125

DIAMOND 12-GA. PUMP SHOTGUN

Pump-action; 12-ga.; 2-3/4-inch and 3-inch chambers; 18-inch-30-inch barrel; weighs 7 lbs.; walnut or synthetic stock; aluminum one-piece receiver sculpted for lighter weight; double locking on fixed bolt; Gold, Elite and Panther series with vented barrels and 3 chokes. Imported from Turkey by ADCO Sales.

Davidson Model 63B

E.A.A./Baikal IZH-43K Bounty Hunter

E.A.A./Baikal IZH-18 Max Single Barrel

E.A.A./Baikal IZH-18 Single Barrel

E.A.A./Baikal IZH-43 Bounty Hunter

Gold, 28-inch, walnut

Perf: $450 **Exc:** $375 **VGood:** $325

Gold, 28-inch, synthetic

Perf: $400 **Exc:** $325 **VGood:** $275

Gold Slug, 24-inch, same as above

Perf: $400 **Exc:** $325 **VGood:** $275

Silver Mariner 20-inch Slug, synthetic

Perf: $425 **Exc:** $350 **VGood:** $300

Elite, 20-inch-28-inch, walnut

Perf: $285 **Exc:** $240 **VGood:** $200

Elite, 20-inch Slug, walnut

Perf: $245 **Exc:** $200 **VGood:** $165

Panther, 20-inch, 28-inch, synthetic

Perf: $225 **Exc:** $200 **VGood:** $165

Panther,18.5-inch Slug, synthetic

Perf: $211 **VGood:** $186 **VGood:** $151

DUMOULIN EUROPA

Side-by-side; 12-, 20-, 28-ga., .410 bore; Anson & Deeley boxlock action; single or double trigger; moderately engraved; oil finished stock and forearm; choice of 6 engraving options. Discontined 1989. Formerly imported from Belgium.

Perf: $3300 **VGood:** $2750 **VGood:** $2350

DUMOULIN LIEGE

Side-by-side; Anson & Deeley boxlock or sidelock; 12-, 16-, 20-, 28-ga.; 2-3/4-inch, 3-inch chambers; 26-inch to 32-inch barrels choked to customers specs; weighs 6-1/4 lbs. Custom-built in Belgium. Introduced 1986; discontinued 1988.

Luxe Model

Perf: $5500 **Exc:** $.4100 **VGood:** $3450

Grand Luxe

Perf: $7200 **Exc:** $5200 **VGood:** $4400

Add 15 percent to above prices for 28 ga.

Add 15 percent for sideplates

EAA/BAIKAL IZH-43 BOUNTY HUNTER

Gauge: 12 (2-3/4-inch, 3-inch chambers), 16 (2-3/4-inch chambers), 20 (2-3/4-inch and 3-inch chambers); 20-inch, 24-inch, 26-inch, 28-inch barrel; Imp., Mod. and Full choke tubes; hardwood or walnut; checkered forend and grip; hammer forged barrel; internal hammers; extractors; engraved receiver; automatic tang safety; non-glare rib. Imported by European American Armory.

12-gauge, 2-3/4-inch chambers, 20-inch bbls., dbl. triggers, hardwood stock

Perf: $260 **Exc:** $225 **VGood:** $200

12- or 20-gauge, 2-3/4-inch chambers, 20-inch bbls., dbl. triggers, walnut stock

Perf: $320 **Exc:** $285 **VGood:** $260

EAA/BAIKAL IZH-43K BOUNTY HUNTER

Gauge: 12 (2-3/4-inch, 3-inch chambers), 20 (3-inch chambers), 28 (2-3/4-inch chambers), .410 (3-inch chambers); 18-1/2-inch, 20-inch, 24-inch, 26-inch, 28-inch barrel, three choke tubes; weighs 7.28 lbs.; walnut, checkered forearm and grip; machined receiver; hammer-forged barrels with chrome-line bores; external hammers; double triggers (single, selective trigger available); rifle barrel inserts optional. Imported by European American Armory.

Perf: $365 **Exc:** $300 **VGood:** $260

EAA/BAIKAL IZH-18 SINGLE BARREL

Single barrel; 12-ga. (2-3/4-inch and 3-inch chambers), 20-ga. (2-3/4-inch and 3-inch), 16-ga. (2-3/4-inch), .410 bore (3-inch); 26-1/2-inch, 28-1/2-inch barrel; modified or full choke (12 and 20 gauge); full only (16-gauge); improved cylinder (20-gauge); full or improved modified (.410); walnut-stained hardwood; rubber recoil pad; hammer-forged steel barrel; machined receiver; cross-block safety; cocking lever with external cocking indicator; optional automatic ejector; screw-in chokes and rifle barrel. Imported by European American Armory.

IZH-18 (12, 16, 20 or .410)

Perf: $80 **Exc:** $65 **VGood:** $55

IZH-18 (20-gauge with Imp. Cyl. or .410 with Imp. Mod.)

Perf: $94 **Exc:** $79 **VGood:** $69

EAA/BAIKAL IZH-18MAX SINGLE BARREL

Single barrel; 12-ga. 3-inch chamber; 20-ga. 3-inch; .410, 3-inch; 24-inch barrel (.410), 26-inch (.410 or 20-ga.) or 28-inch (12-ga.); weighs 6.4 to 6.6 lbs.; walnut stock; polished nickel receiver; ventilated rib; I.C., Mod. and Full choke tubes; titanium-coated trigger; internal hammer; selectable ejector/extractor; rubber butt pad; decocking system. Imported by European American Armory.

12- or 20-ga., choke tubes

Perf: $154 **Exc:** $135 **VGood:** $129

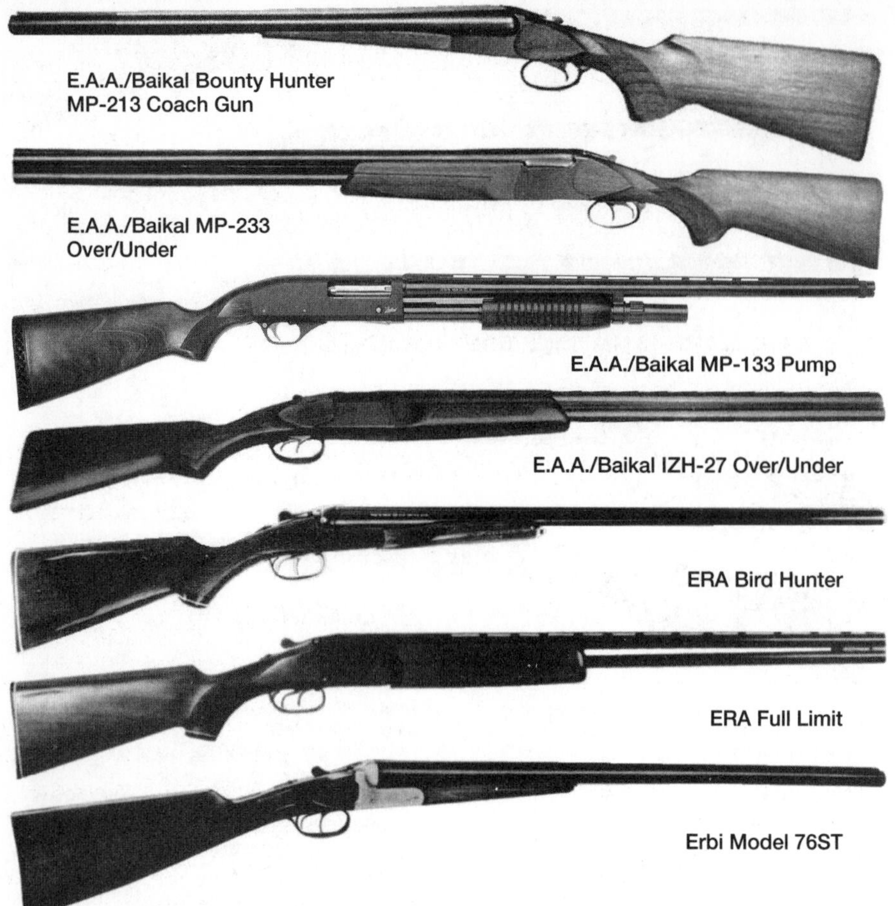
E.A.A./Baikal Bounty Hunter MP-213 Coach Gun

E.A.A./Baikal MP-233 Over/Under

E.A.A./Baikal MP-133 Pump

E.A.A./Baikal IZH-27 Over/Under

ERA Bird Hunter

ERA Full Limit

Erbi Model 76ST

.410 bore, full choke only

Perf: $94 **Exc:** $79 **VGood:** $69

Sporting, 12-ga., ported, Monte Carlo stock

Perf: $185 **Exc:** $160 **VGood:** $135

EAA/BAIKAL MP-133 PUMP

Pump action; 12-ga., 3-1/2-inch chamber; 18-1/2-inch, 20-inch, 24-inch, 26-inch, 28-inch barrel; Imp., Mod. and Full choke tubes; walnut, checkered grip and grooved forearm; hammer-forged, chrome-lined barrel with ventilated rib; machined steel parts; dual action bars; trigger-block safety; 4-shot magazine tube; handles 2-3/4-inch through 3-1/2-inch shells. Introduced 2000. Imported by European American Armory.

Perf: $275 **Exc:** $215 **VGood:** $185

EAA/BAIKAL MP-153 AUTO

Semi-auto; 12-ga., 3-1/2-inch chamber; 18-1/2-inch, 20-inch, 24-inch, 26-inch, 28-inch barrel; Imp., Mod. and Full choke tubes; weighs 7.8 lbs.; walnut stock; gas-operated action with automatic gas-adjustment valve allows use of light and heavy loads interchangeably; 4-round magazine; rubber recoil pad. Introduced 2000. Imported by European American Armory.

Blued finish, walnut stock and forend

Perf: $445 **Exc. $375** **VGood:** $320

Field grade, synthetic stock

Perf: $355 **Exc:** $285 **VGood:** $230

EAA/BAIKAL MP-213

Gauge: 12, 3-inch chambers; 24-inch, 26-inch, 28-inch barrel; Imp., Mod. and Full choke tubes; weighs 7.28 lbs.; walnut, checkered forearm and grip; rubber butt pad; hammer-forged barrels; chrome-lined bores; machined receiver; double trigger (each trigger fires both barrels independently); ejectors. Introduced 2000. Imported by European American Armory.

Perf: $795 **Exc:** $675 **VGood:** $595

EAA/BAIKAL BOUNTY HUNTER MP-213 COACH GUN

Side-by-side; 12-ga., 2-3/4-inch chambers; 20-inch barrel; Imp., Mod. and Full choke tubes; weighs 7 lbs.; walnut, checkered forend and grip; selective double trigger with removable assembly (single trigger and varied pull weights available); ejectors; engraved receiver. Imported by European American Armory.

Perf: $954 **Exc:** $834 **VGood:** $754

EAA/BAIKAL MP-233 OVER/UNDER

Over/under; 12-ga., 3-inch chambers; 26-inch, 28-inch, 30-inch barrel; Imp., Mod. and Full choke tubes; weighs 7.28 lbs.; walnut; checkered forearm and grip; hammer-forged barrels; chrome-lined bores; removable trigger assembly (optional single selective trigger or double trigger); ejectors. Introduced 2000. Imported by European American Armory.

Perf: $795 **Exc:** $650 **VGood:** $575

EAA/BAIKAL IZH-27 OVER/UNDER

Over/under; 12-ga. (3-inch chambers), 16-ga. (2-3/4-inch chambers), 20-ga. (3-inch chambers), 28-ga. (2-3/4-inch chambers), .410 bore (3-inch); 26-1/2-inch barrel, 28-1/2-inch (Imp., Mod. and Full choke tubes for 12 and 20 gauges; Improved Cylinder and Modified for 16 and 28 gauges; Improved Modified and Full for .410; 16 also offered in Mod. and Full); walnut, checkered forearm and grip. Imported by European American Armory.

12-, 16- and 20-gauge

Perf: $420 **Exc:** $350 **VGood:** $295

28-gauge and .410

Perf: $479 **Exc:** $409 **VGood:** $354

EAA IZH-27 SPORTING O/U

Basic IZH-27 with barrel porting, wide vent rib with double sight beads, engraved nickel receiver, checkered walnut stock and forend with palm swell and semi-beavertail, 3 screw chokes, SS trigger, selectable ejectors, auto tang safety

Perf: $500 **Exc:** $430 **VGood:** $375

E.A.A./SABATTI FALCON-MON

Over/under; boxlock; 12-, 20-, 28-ga., .410; 3-inch chambers; 26-inch, 28-inch barrels; standard chokes; ventilated rib; weighs about 7 lbs.; cut-checkered select walnut pistol-grip stock, beavertail forend with gloss finish; gold-plated single selective trigger; extractors; engraved, blued receiver. Made in Italy. Introduced 1993; discontinued 1994.

12- or 20-ga.

Perf: $600 **Exc:** $420 **VGood:** $350

28-ga. or .410

Perf: $650 **Exc:** $470 **VGood:** $400

E.A.A./SABATTI SABA-MON DOUBLE

Side-by-side; boxlock; 12-, 20-, 28-ga., .410; 3-inch chambers; 26-inch, 28-inch barrels; standard chokes; European walnut straight English or pistol-grip stock; single selective trigger; automatic selective ejectors; blue finish. Made in Italy. Introduced 1993; discontinued 1994.

Perf: $920 **Exc:** $680 **VGood:** $500

E.A.A./SABATTI SPORTING CLAYS PRO-GOLD

Over/under; boxlock; 12-ga.; 3-inch chambers; 28-inch, 30-inch barrels; six choke tubes; weighs 7-3/4 lbs.; target-style fluorescent bar front sight; European walnut pistol-grip stock, forend with gloss finish; special Sporting Clays recoil pad; automatic ejectors; gold-plated single selective trigger; engraved, blued receiver with gold inlays. Comes with lockable hard shell plastic case. Made in Italy. Introduced 1993; no longer imported.

Perf: $800 **Exc:** $600 **VGood:** $500

EAA/SAIGA AUTO SHOTGUN

Semi-automatic; 12-ga, 20-ga., .410 bore; 3-inch chamber; 19-inch, 21-inch, 22-inch barrel; weighs 6.6-7.6 lbs.; length: 40-inch-45-inch; synthetic stock; retains best features of the AK rifle by Kalashnikov as a semi-auto shotgun; magazine fed. Imported from Russia by EAA Corp.

.410 bore

Perf: $210 **Exc:** $160 **VGood:** $145

20-ga.

Perf: $340 **Exc:** $300 **VGood:** $275

12-ga.

Perf: $380 **Exc:** $340 **VGood:** $315

E.M.F. HARTFORD MODEL COWBOY

Gauge: 12; 20-inch barrel; checkered walnut; center bead sight; exposed hammers; color-case hardened receiver; blued barrel. Introduced 2001. Formerly imported from Spain (during 2001 and 2002) by E.M.F. Co. Inc.

Perf: $550 **Exc:** $495 **VGood:** $450

E.M.F. STAGECOACH MODEL

Side-by-side; exposed hammers, 12 ga. only; 20-inch brown barrels; made by S.I.A.C.E. Imported 2000-2002.

Perf: $300 **Exc:** $275 **VGood:** $215

E.M.F. MARK V CONQUEST

Side-by-side; 12 ga.; 28-inch barrels; choke tubes. Importation began 2003.

Perf: $385 **Exc:** $325 **VGood:** $275

ERA BIRD HUNTER

Side-by-side; boxlock; 12-, 16-, 20-ga., .410; 26-inch, 28-inch, 30-inch barrels; raised matted rib; hand-checkered walnut stock, beavertail forend; extractors; auto disconnector; double triggers; engraved receiver. Made in Brazil. Introduced 1979; no longer in production.

Perf: $150 **Exc:** $125 **VGood:** $100

ERA FULL LIMIT

Over/under; 12-, 20-ga.; 28-inch barrels; vent, top and middle ribs; hand-checkered walnut-finished hardwood stock; Monte Carlo or straight styles; auto safety, extractors; double triggers; engraved receiver. Made in Brazil. Introduced 1980; no longer in production.

Perf: $250 **Exc:** $200 **VGood:** $180

ERA WINNER

Single barrel; exposed hammer; 12-, 16-, 20-ga.,.410; 28-inch barrel; metal bead front sight; walnut-stained hardwood stock, beavertail forend; triggerguard button opens action; auto ejectors. Made in Brazil. Introduced 1980; no longer in production.

Perf: $125 **Exc:** $100 **VGood:** $75

ERBI MODEL 76AJ

Side-by-side; 10-, 12-, 20-, 28-ga.; 26-inch, 28-inch Modified/Full barrels; medium bead front sight; hand-checkered European walnut straight-grip stock; double triggers; automatic ejectors; engraved, silvered receiver. Made in Spain. Introduced 1982 by Toledo Armas; discontinued 1984.

Perf: $550 **Exc:** $460 **VGood:** $400

ERBI MODEL 76ST

Same specs as Model 76AJ except automatic extractors. Introduced 1982 by Toledo Armas; discontinued 1984.

Perf: $500 **Exc:** $400 **VGood:** $350

ERBI MODEL 80

Side-by-side; sidelock; 10-, 12-, 20-, 28-ga.; 26-inch, 28-inch Modified/Full barrels; medium bead front sight; hand-checkered European walnut straight-grip stock; double triggers; extractors; engraved silvered receiver. Introduced 1982 by Toledo Armas; discontinued 1984.

Perf: $850 **Exc:** $675 **VGood:** $550

ESCORT MODEL AS

Semi-auto.; 12-ga.; 28-inch barrel (choke tubes, M, IM, F); 3-inch chambers; weighs 7 lbs.; Turkish walnut; checkered pistol grip and forend; aluminum-alloy receiver; blued finish; chrome-plated bolt; adjustment for normal and magnum loads; gold-plated trigger; trigger-guard safety; magazine cut-off; choke tube wrench; two stock-adjustment shims; waterfowl plug; 7-shot magazine extender. Introduced 2002. Imported from Turkey by Legacy Sports International.

Perf: $332 **Exc:** $297 **VGood:** $272

Model PS, black polymer stock

Perf: $320 **Exc:** $285 **VGood:** $260

ESCORT SERIES

Slide action; 12-ga.; 3-inch chamber; matte blue or camo finish with polymer stock and forearm;20-inch, 24-inch, 28-inch barrel; alloy receiver with 3/8-inch milled dovetail for sight mounting; trigger guard safety; 5-shot magazine with cut-off button; two stock adjustment shims; weighs 6.4 to 7 lbs. Importation began 2003.

Aimguard Model; 20-inch barrel; black synthetic stock; fixed cyl. Bore choke; 6.4 lbs.

Perf: $160 **Exc:** $135 **VGood:** $120

Field Hunter; 24-inch, 28-inch barrel; 100 percent camo coverage or matte blue finish; includes 3 choke tubes.

Perf: $175 **Exc:** $155 **VGood:** $135

Add $50 to above prices for camo stock
Add $105 for FH TriViz sight combo

ESCORT AVERY WATERFOWL EXTREME

Gas-operated semi-auto in 12 or 20 gauge. Chambered for 2-3/4 and 3-inch loads (both gauges), or for 2-3/4 through 3-1/2 inch loads in 12 gauge. Capacity 5+1. Barrel length is 28 inches, weight 7 to 7.5 pounds. Available in left-hand version. Composite stock features Avery Outdoors' KW1 or Buck Brush camo patterns (12 gauge only) with textured gripping surfaces and is adjustable for length of pull, cast and drop. The 20-gauge has black synthetic stock.

Perf: $550 **Exc:** $465 **VGood:** $400

Add 20 percent for 3.5-inch chamber, 25 percent for camo finish

Escort Aimguard

Escort Field Hunter

Exel Model 101

Exel Model 201

EXEL MODEL 101

Over/under; boxlock; 12-ga.; 2-3/4-inch, 3-inch chambers; 26-inch Improved Cylinder/Modified barrels; vent-rib; checkered European walnut stock; single selective trigger; extractors. Made in Spain. Introduced 1984; discontinued 1987.

Perf: $350 **Exc:** $300 **VGood:** $260

EXEL MODEL 102

Over/under; boxlock; 12-ga.; 2-3/4-inch, 3-inch chambers; 27-5/8-inch Improved Cylinder/ Modified barrels; vent-rib; checkered European walnut stock; single selective trigger; extractors. Made in Spain. Introduced 1984; discontinued 1987.

Perf: $360 **Exc:** $300 **VGood:** $260

EXEL MODEL 103

Over/under; boxlock; 12-ga.; 2-3/4-inch, 3-inch chambers; 29 1/2-inch Modified/Full barrels; vent-rib; checkered European walnut stock; single selective trigger; extractors. Made in Spain. Introduced 1984; discontinued 1987.

Perf: $360 **Exc:** $300 **VGood:** $260

EXEL MODEL 104

Over/under; boxlock; 12-ga.; 2-3/4-inch, 3-inch chambers; 27-5/8-inch Improved Cylinder/Improved Modified barrels; vent-rib; checkered European walnut stock; single selective trigger; selective auto ejectors. Made in Spain. Introduced 1984; discontinued 1987.

Perf: $360 **Exc:** $300 **VGood:** $260

EXEL MODEL 105

Over/under; boxlock; 12-ga.; 2-3/4-inch, 3-inch chambers; 27-5/8-inch barrel with screw-in choke tubes; vent-rib; deluxe checkered European walnut stock; single selective trigger; selective auto ejectors; engraved satin finish. Made in Spain. Introduced 1984; discontinued 1987.

Perf: $525 **Exc:** $410 **VGood:** $380

EXEL MODEL 106

Over/under; boxlock; 12-ga.; 2-3/4-inch, 3-inch chambers; 27-5/8-inch barrel with screw-in choke tubes; vent-rib; deluxe checkered European walnut stock; single selective trigger; selective auto ejectors; engraved blue finish. Made in Spain. Introduced 1984; discontinued 1987.

Perf: $700 **Exc:** $500 **VGood:** $430

EXEL MODEL 107

Over/under; boxlock; 12-ga.; 2-3/4-inch, 3-inch chambers; 29-1/2-inch barrel with Full/ interchangeable tubes; vent-rib; deluxe checkered European walnut stock; single selective trigger; selective auto ejectors; engraved blue finish. Made in Spain. Introduced 1984; discontinued 1987.

Perf: $700 **Exc:** $500 **VGood:** $430

EXEL MODEL 201

Side-by-side; boxlock; 12-, 20-ga.; 2-3/4-inch chambers; 28-inch barrels; high matted rib; metal bead front sight; hand-checkered European walnut straight or pistol-grip stock; double triggers; extractors; color case-hardened finish. Made in Spain. Introduced 1984; discontinued 1987.

Perf: $350 **Exc:** $220 **VGood:** $190

EXEL MODEL 202

Side-by-side; boxlock; 12-, 20-ga.; 2-3/4-inch chambers; 26-inch barrels; high matted rib; metal bead front sight; hand-checkered European walnut straight or pistol-grip stock; double triggers; extractors; color case-hardened finish. Made in Spain. Introduced 1984; discontinued 1987.

Perf: $350 **Exc:** $220 **VGood:** $190

EXEL MODEL 203

Side-by-side; boxlock; 12-, 20-ga.; 3-inch chambers; 27-inch barrels; high matted rib; metal bead front sight; hand-checkered European walnut straight or pistol-grip stock; double triggers; extractors; color case-hardened finish. Made in Spain. Introduced 1984; discontinued 1987.

Perf: $350 **Exc:** $220 **VGood:** $190

EXEL MODEL 204

Side-by-side; boxlock; 12-, 20-ga.; 2-3/4-inch chambers; 28-inch barrels; high matted rib; metal bead front sight; hand-checkered European walnut straight or pistol-grip stock; single or double triggers; automatic selective ejectors; silvered, engraved receiver. Made in Spain. Introduced 1984; discontinued 1987.

Perf: $525 **Exc:** $400 **VGood:** $340

EXEL MODEL 205

Side-by-side; boxlock; 12-, 20-ga.; 2-3/4-inch chambers; 26-inch barrels; high matted rib; metal bead front sight; hand-checkered European walnut straight or pistol-grip stock; single or double triggers; automatic selective ejectors; silvered, engraved receiver. Made in Spain. Introduced 1984; discontinued 1987.

Perf: $525 **Exc:** $400 **VGood:** $340

Exel Model 251

Exel Series 300

Fabarm Camo Turkey Mag

Fabarm Ultra Camo

Fabarm Classic Lion Double Grade I

Fabarm Classic Lion Double Grade II

Fabarm FP6 Pump

Fabarm Classic Lion Double Elite Grade I

EXEL MODEL 206

Side-by-side; boxlock; 12-, 20-ga.; 2-3/4-inch chambers; 27-inch barrels; high matted rib; metal bead front sight; hand-checkered European walnut stock; straight or full pistol-grip; single or double triggers; automatic selective ejectors; silvered, engraved receiver. Made in Spain. Introduced 1984; discontinued 1987.

Perf: $525 **Exc:** $400 **VGood:** $340

EXEL MODEL 207

Side-by-side; sidelock; 12-ga.; 2-3/4-inch chambers; 28-inch barrels; high matted rib; metal bead front sight; hand-checkered European walnut straight or pistol-grip stock; double triggers; extractors or ejectors; color case-hardened finish. Made in Spain. Introduced 1984; discontinued 1987.

Perf: $600 **Exc:** $490 **VGood:** $400

EXEL MODEL 208

Side-by-side; sidelock; 12-ga.; 2-3/4-inch chambers; 28-inch barrels; high matted rib; metal bead front sight; deluxe hand-checkered European walnut straight or pistol-grip stock; double triggers; extractors or ejectors; color case-hardened finish; engraved receiver. Made in Spain. Introduced 1984; discontinued 1987.

Perf: $675 **Exc:** $525 **VGood:** $500

EXEL MODEL 209

Side-by-side; sidelock; 20-ga.; 2-3/4-inch chambers; 26-inch barrel; high matted rib; metal bead front sight; deluxe hand-checkered European walnut straight or pistol-grip stock; double triggers; extractors or ejectors; color case-hardened finish; engraved receiver. Made in Spain. Introduced 1984; discontinued 1987.

Perf: $550 **Exc:** $465 **VGood:** $400

EXEL MODEL 210

Side-by-side; sidelock; 20-ga.; 2-3/4-inch chambers; 27-inch barrel; high matted rib; metal bead front sight; deluxe hand-checkered European walnut straight or pistol-grip stock; double triggers; extractors or ejectors; color case-hardened finish; engraved receiver. Made in Spain. Introduced 1984; discontinued 1987.

Perf: $550 **Exc:** $465 **VGood:** $400

EXEL MODEL 240

Side-by-side; boxlock; .410; 2-3/4-inch chambers; 28-inch barrel; high matted rib; metal bead front sight; hand-checkered European walnut straight or pistol-grip stock; double triggers; extractors; color case-hardened finish. Made in Spain. Introduced 1984; discontinued 1987.

Perf: $425 **Exc:** $280 **VGood:** $210

EXEL MODEL 251

Single shot; exposed hammer; .410; 3-inch chamber; folding stock; splinter forend; non-ejector; case-hardened frame. Made in Spain. Introduced 1985; discontinued 1987.

Perf: $160 **Exc:** $125 **VGood:** $100

EXEL MODEL 281

Side-by-side; boxlock; 28-ga.; 2-3/4-inch chambers; 28-inch barrel; high matted rib; metal bead front sight; hand-checkered European walnut straight or pistol-grip stock; double triggers; extractors; color case-hardened finish. Made in Spain. Introduced 1984; discontinued 1987.

Perf: $400 **Exc:** $295 **VGood:** $250

EXEL SERIES 300

Over/under; boxlock; 12-ga.; 2-3/4-inch chambers; 28-inch, 29-inch barrels; vent-rib; checkered European walnut pistol-grip field or Monte Carlo stock, forend; auto selective ejectors; silvered, engraved finish. Offered in ten variations with differing degrees of ornamentation. Made in Spain. Introduced 1984; discontinued 1987.

Models 301 & 302

Perf: $450 **Exc:** $360 **VGood:** $300

Models 303 & 304

Perf: $520 **Exc:** $430 **VGood:** $390

Models 305 & 306

Perf: $600 **Exc:** $500 **VGood:** $450

Models 307 & 308

Perf: $550 **Exc:** $450 **VGood:** $400

Models 309 & 310

Perf: $600 **Exc:** $500 **VGood:** $450

FABARM CAMO TURKEY MAG

Over/under: 12-ga.; 3-1/2-inch chambers; 20-inch barel TriBore (Ultra-Full ported tubes); weighs 7.5 lbs.; length: 46-inch overall; stock dimensions 14.5 inches by 1.5 inches by 2.29 inches; front bar sight; Picatinny rail scope base; completely covered with Xtra Brown camouflage finish; unported barrels. Introduced 1999. Imported from Italy by Heckler & Koch, Inc.

Perf: $995 **Exc:** $875 **VGood:** $775

FABARM ULTRA CAMO

Similar to Camo Turkey but without front bar sight and Picatinny base.

FABARM CLASSIC LION DOUBLE

Side-by-side; 12-ga.; 3-inch chambers; 26-inch, 28-inch, 30-inch barrel (Cyl., Imp. Cyl., Mod., Imp. Mod., Full choke tubes); weighs 7.2 lbs.; length: 44.5-inch-48.5; English-style or pistol grip oil-finished European walnut; boxlock action with double triggers; automatic ejectors; automatic safety. Introduced 1998. Imported from Italy by Heckler & Koch, Inc.

Grade I

Perf: $1375 **Exc:** $1125 **VGood:** $850

Grade II

Perf: $1875 **Exc:** $1525 **VGood:** $1200

Grade II Bill Hanus Birdgun Model

Similar to Grade II, except has best quality wood. Importation discontinued 2000.

Perf: $2275 **Exc:** $1925 **VGood:** $1550

Elite (color-case hardened finish, 44.5-inch)

Perf: $1395 **Exc:** $1150 **VGood:** $875

FABARM FIELD PUMP

Pump action; 12-ga.; 3-inch chamber; 28-inch barrel (24-inch rifled slug barrel available); weighs 76.6 lbs.;

length 48.25-inch overall; polymer stock; similar to Fabarm FP6 pump shotgun; alloy receiver; twin action bars; available in black or Mossy Oak Break-Up camo finish; includes Cyl., Mod. and Full choke tubes. Introduced 2001. Imported from Italy by Heckler & Koch Inc.

Matte black finish

Perf: $325 **Exc:** $285 **VGood:** $260

Mossy Oak Break-Up finish

Perf: $400 **Exc:** $355 **VGood:** $320

FABARM FP6 PUMP

Pump action; 12-ga.; 3-inch chamber; 20-inch barrel; (Cyl.); accepts choke tubes; weighs 6.6 lbs.; 41.25-inch overall; black polymer stock with textured grip; grooved slide handle; blade front sight; twin action bars; anodized finish; free carrier for smooth reloading. Introduced 1998. Imported from Italy by Heckler & Koch, Inc.

Carbon fiber finish

Perf: $460 **Exc:** $400 **VGood:** $365

With flip-up front sight, Picatinny rail with rear sight, oversize safety button

Perf: $480 **Exc:** $440 **VGood:** $400

FABARM GOLD LION MARK II AUTO

Semi-auto.; 12-ga.; 3-inch chamber; 24-inch, 26-inch, 28-inch barrel; choke tubes; weighs 7 lbs.; length: 45.5-inch overall; European walnut stock with gloss finish; olive wood grip cap; TriBore barrel; reversible safety; gold-plated trigger and carrier release button; leather-covered rubber recoil pad. Introduced 1998. Imported from Italy by Heckler & Koch, Inc.

Perf: $750 **Exc:** $675 **VGood:** $595

FABARM CAMO LION AUTO

Similar to Gold Lion except 24-inch, 26-inch or 28-inch ported TriBore barrel system with five choke tubes, completely covered with Wetlands camouflage pattern. Red front sight bead and mid-rib bead. Introduced 1999. Imported from Italy by Heckler & Koch, Inc.

Perf: $850 **Exc:** $725 **VGood:** $650

FABARM SPORTING CLAYS EXTRA AUTO

Similar to Gold Lion except 28-inch TriBore ported barrel with interchangeable colored front-sight beads, mid-rib bead, 10mm channeled vent rib, carbon- fiber finish, oil-finished walnut stock and forend with olive wood grip cap. Distinctive gold-colored receiver logo. Available in 12-gauge only, 3-inch chamber. Introduced 1999. Imported from Italy by Heckler & Koch, Inc.

Perf: $1025 **Exc:** $895 **VGood:** $775

FABARM MAX LION OVER/UNDER

Over/under: 12-ga.; 3-inch chambers; 20, 3-inch chambers; 26-inch, 28-inch, 30-inch barrel (12 ga.); 26-inch, 28-inch barrel (20-ga.); choke tubes; weighs 7.4 lbs.; 47-1/2-inch overall (26-inch barrel); European walnut; leather-covered recoil pad; TriBore barrel; boxlock action with single selective trigger; manual safety; automatic ejectors; chrome-lined barrels; adjustable trigger; silvered, engraved receiver; locking, fitted luggage case. Introduced 1998. Imported from Italy by Heckler & Koch, Inc.

Perf: $1625 **Exc:** $1350 **VGood:** $1150

FABARM MAX LION PARADOX

Over/under; 12-ga.; 3-inch chambers; 24-inch barrel; weighs 7.6 lbs.; 44.5-inch overall; walnut with special enhancing finish; TriBore upper barrel and lower barrel with paradox rifling; both wood and receiver are enhanced with special finishes; color case-hardened type finish.

Perf: $975 **Exc:** $875 **VGood:** $775

FABARM MONOTRAP

Single barrel; 12-ga.; 2-3/4-inch chamber; 30-inch, 34-inch barrel; weighs 6.7 to 6.9 lbs.; 48-1/2-inch overall length (30-inch bbl.); walnut; adjustable comb competition-style stock; red front sight bar, mid-rib bead; built on 20-gauge receiver for quick handling; silver receiver with blued barrel; special trap rib (micrometer adjustable); includes three choke tubes (M, IM, F). Introduced 2000.

Perf: $1625 **Exc:** $1375 **VGood:** $1150

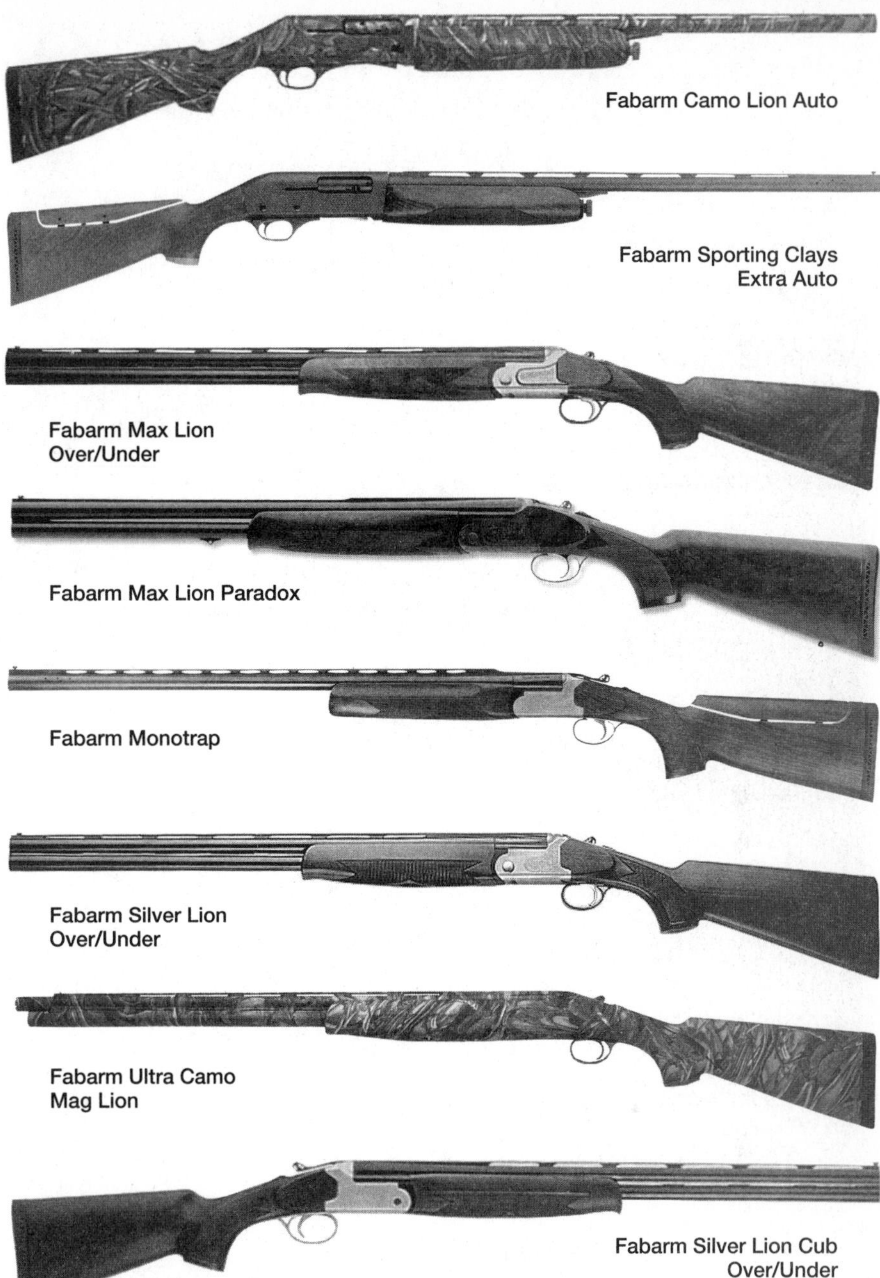

Fabarm Camo Lion Auto

Fabarm Sporting Clays Extra Auto

Fabarm Max Lion Over/Under

Fabarm Max Lion Paradox

Fabarm Monotrap

Fabarm Silver Lion Over/Under

Fabarm Ultra Camo Mag Lion

Fabarm Silver Lion Cub Over/Under

FABARM RED LION

Semi-auto.; 12-ga.; 3-inch chamber; 26-inch, 28-inch barrel; five screw-in chokes; weighs 7 to 7.2 lbs.; premium walnut; olive grip cap; red bar sights; TriBore barrel system. Limited edition Gold Lion, black and silver finish receiver with English-style gold inlaid engraving, Fabarm semi-automatic operating system. Blue finish.

Perf: $710 **Exc:** $635 **VGood:** $550

FABARM SILVER LION OVER/UNDER

Over/under; 12-ga.; 3-inch chambers; 20, 3-inch chambers; 26-inch, 28-inch, 30-inch barrel (12-ga.); 26-inch, 28-inch barrel (20-ga.); choke tubes; weighs: 7.2 lbs.; 47-1/2-inch overall length(26-inch barrels); walnut; leather-covered recoil pad; TriBore barrel; boxlock action with single selective trigger; silvered receiver with engraving; automatic ejectors; locking hard plastic case. Introduced 1998. Imported from Italy by Heckler & Koch, Inc.

Perf: $1075 **Exc:** $925 **VGood:** $825

FABARM SILVER LION CUB OVER/UNDER

Similar to the Silver Lion except has 12.5-inch length of pull, is in 20-gauge only (3-1/2-inch chambers), and comes with 24-inch TriBore barrel system. Weight is 6 lbs. Introduced 1999. Imported from Italy by Heckler & Koch, Inc.

Perf: $1075 **Exc:** $925 **VGood:** $825

FABARM ULTRA CAMO MAG LION

Similar to Silver Lion but with all-camo finish. Introduced 1998. Imported from Italy by Heckler & Koch, Inc. 12- or 20-gauge.

Perf: $1075 **Exc:** $925 **VGood:** $825

FABARM SPORTING CLAYS COMPETITION EXTRA O/U

Over/under; 12-, 20-ga.; 3-inch chambers; 12-ga. has 30-inch barrel; 20 ga. has 28-inch; ported TriBore barrel system with five tubes; weighs 7 to 7.8 lbs.; deluxe walnut; leather-covered recoil pad; single selective trigger; auto ejectors; 10mm channeled rib;

Fabarm Sporting Clays Competition Extra O/U

Fabarm Tactical Semi-Auto

Fausti Caledon

Fausti DEA

Ferlib Model F VII

F.I.E. Hamilton & Hunter

carbon fiber finish. Introduced 1999. Imported from Italy by Heckler & Koch, Inc.

Perf: $1575 **Exc:** $1325 **VGood:** $1100

FABARM TACTICAL SEMI-AUTOMATIC

Semi-auto.; 12-ga.; 3-inch chamber; 20-inch barrel; weighs 6.6 lbs.; length: 41.2-inch overall; polymer or folding stock; ghost ring sights (tritium night sights optional); gas-operated; matte receiver; twin forged action bars; oversized bolt handle and safety button; Picatinny rail; includes cylinder bore choke tube. Introduced 2001. Imported from Italy by Heckler & Koch Inc.

Perf: $865 **Exc:** $750 **VGood:** $650

FAUSTI CALEDON

Over/under in 12-, 16-, 20-, 28-gauge and .410-bore with 26, 28, or 30-inch barrels with interchangeable choke tubes (except .410, which has Modified and Full fixed chokes). A+ oil-finished walnut stock with rounded pistol grip. Automatic ejectors and single selective trigger. Made in Italy. Add 25 percent to prices shown for 16, 28 or .410.

Perf: $1800 **Exc:** $1500 **VGood:** $1300

FAUSTI DEA

Side-by-side double in 12-, 16-, 20-, 28-gauge and .410-bore with 26, 28 or 30-inch barrels with interchangeable choke tubes (except .410 which has modified and full fixed chokes). AAA grade oil-finished walnut stock with English-style straight grip. Trigger is single non-selective, and there are automatic ejectors. Made in Italy. Add 25 percent to prices shown for 16, 28 or .410.

Perf: $2900 **Exc:** $2450 **VGood:** $1800

FERLACH CONSTANT COMPANION

Side-by-side; Anson & Deeley-type action; 12-, 16-, 20-ga.; 28-inch, 30-inch barrels; tapered boring; hand-checkered black walnut pistol-grip stock, cheekpiece; quadruple Greener bolt; auto safety; ejectors; double triggers; engraved receiver. Made in Austria. Introduced 1956; discontinued 1958.

Perf: $875 **Exc:** $775 **VGood:** $700

FERLIB MODEL F VII

Side-by-side; boxlock; 12-, 16-, 20-, 28-ga., .410; 25-inch, 26-inch, 27-inch, 28-inch barrels; standard chokes; oil-finished checkered European walnut straight-grip stock, forend; beavertail forend optional; single or double triggers; silvered, scroll-engraved receiver. Made in Italy. Introduced 1983; still in production.

12-, 16-, 20-ga.

Perf: $9950 **Exc:** $8750 **VGood:** $7600

28-ga., .410

Perf: $10,200 **Exc:** $9100 **VGood:** $7900

FERLIB MODEL F VII/SC

Same specs as Model F VII except elaborate engraving with gold inlays. Made in Italy. Introduced 1983; still in production.

12-, 16-, 20-ga.

Perf: $7500 **Exc:** $6000 **VGood:** $5000

28-ga., .410

Perf: $8100 **Exc:** $6500 **VGood:** $5400

FERLIB MODEL F VII SIDEPLATE

Same specs as Model F VII except sideplates; single trigger; elaborate engraving. Made in Italy. Introduced 1983; still in production.

12-, 16-, 20-ga.

Perf: $12,950 **Exc:** $10,500 **VGood:** $9000

28-ga., .410

Perf: $13,200 **Exc:** $10,750 **VGood:** $9220

FERLIB MODEL F VII SIDEPLATE SC

Same specs as Model F VII except sideplates; single trigger; elaborate engraving with gold inlays. Made in Italy. Introduced 1983; still in production.

12-, 16-, 20-ga.

Perf: $10,000 **Exc:** $8500 **VGood:** $7000

28-ga., .410

Perf: $11,000 **Exc:** $9000 **VGood:** $7500

FIAS MODEL SK-1

Over/under; boxlock; 12-, 20-ga.; 3-inch chambers; 26-inch Improved Cylinder/Modified, 28-inch Modified/Full, 30-inch Modified/Full or Full/Full, 32-inch Full/Full barrels; vent-rib; hand-checkered select European walnut pistol-grip stock, forearm; top lever break; Greener crossbolt; double triggers; extractors. Made in Europe. Introduced 1974; discontinued 1984.

Perf: $275 **Exc:** $230 **VGood:** $190

FIAS MODEL SK-3

Over/under; boxlock; 12-, 20-ga.; 3-inch chambers; 26-inch Improved Cylinder/Modified, 28-inch Modified/ Full, 30-inch Modified/Full or Full/Full, 32-inch Full/Full barrels; vent-rib; hand-checkered select European walnut pistol-grip stock, forearm; top lever break; Greener crossbolt; selective single trigger; extractors. Made in Europe. Introduced 1974; discontinued 1984.

Perf: $290 **Exc:** $240 **VGood:** $200

FIAS MODEL SK-4

Over/under; boxlock; 12-, 20-ga.; 3-inch chambers; 26-inch Improved Cylinder/Modified, 28-inch Modified/Full, 30-inch Modified/Full or Full/Full, 32-inch Full/Full barrels; vent-rib; hand-checkered select European walnut pistol-grip stock; beavertail forearm; top lever break; Greener crossbolt; selective single trigger; selective auto ejectors. Made in Europe. Introduced 1974; discontinued 1984.

Perf: $350 **Exc:** $280 **VGood:** $210

FIAS MODEL SK-4D

Same specs as SK-4 except sideplates; better grade wood; deluxe engraving. Introduced 1974; discontinued 1984.

Perf: $480 **Exc:** $320 **VGood:** $270

FIAS MODEL SK-4S

Same specs as SK-4 except 26-inch Skeet 1/Skeet 2 barrels. Introduced 1974; discontinued 1984.

Perf: $320 **Exc:** $280 **VGood:** $210

FIAS MODEL SK-4T

Same specs as Model SK-4 except 12-ga.; 2-3/4-inch chambers; 30-inch Improved Modified/Full, 32-inch Improved Modified/Full barrels; middle sight; select European walnut Monte Carlo pistol-grip stock, beavertail forearm. Introduced 1974; discontinued 1984.

Perf: $350 **Exc:** $280 **VGood:** $210

F.I.E. BRUTE

Side-by-side; boxlock; 12-, 20-ga., .410; 19-inch barrels; 30-inch overall length; short hand-checkered walnut stock, beavertail forend. Made in Brazil. Introduced 1979; no longer in production.

Perf: $195 **Exc:** $150 **VGood:** $130

F.I.E. CBC

Single shot; takedown; exposed hammer; 12-, 16-, 20-ga., .410; 28-inch Full-choke barrel; metal bead front sight; walnut-stained hardwood stock, beavertail forend; trigger guard button breaks action; auto ejector. Made in Brazil. Introduced 1982; discontinued 1984.

Perf: $90 **Exc:** $75 **VGood:** $50

F.I.E. HAMILTON & HUNTER

Single shot; takedown; exposed hammer; 12-, 20-ga., .410; 3-inch chamber; 28-inch barrel; weighs 6-1/2 lbs.; metal bead front sight; walnut-stained hardwood stock, beavertail forend; break-button on trigger guard; auto ejector. Made in Brazil. Introduced 1986; discontinued 1990.

Perf: $100 **Exc:** $80 **VGood:** $60

F.I.E. S.O.B.

Single barrel; exposed hammer; 12-, 20-ga., .410; 18-1/2-inch barrel; metal bead front sight; short walnut-finished hardwood stock, beavertail forend; auto ejector. Made in Brazil. Introduced 1980; discontinued 1984.

Perf: $110 **Exc:** $80 **VGood:** $60

F.I.E. S.S.S. MODEL

Single barrel; exposed hammer; 12-, 20-ga., .410; 3-inch chamber; 18 1/2-inch Cylinder barrel; weighs 6-1/2 lbs.; walnut-finished hardwood stock, full beavertail forend; auto ejectors; break-button on trigger guard. Made in Brazil. Introduced 1986; discontinued 1990.

Perf: $90 **Exc:** $75 **VGood:** $50

F.I.E. STURDY

Over/under; 12-, 20-ga.; 3-inch chamber; 28-inch vent-rib barrel; walnut stock; double triggers; extractors; engraved silver finished receiver. Introduced 1985; discontinued 1988.

Perf: $300 **Exc:** $275 **VGood:** $250

F.I.E. STURDY DELUXE PRITI

Same specs as Sturdy except deluxe walnut stock. Introduced 1985; discontinued 1988.

Perf: $325 **Exc:** $290 **VGood:** $260

With optional single selective trigger; ejectors; choke tubes

Perf: $395 **Exc:** $360 **VGood:** $330

F.I.E. STURDY MODEL 12 DELUXE

Same specs as Sturdy except only 12-ga.; choke tubes; select walnut stock; single selective trigger; ejectors. Introduced 1988; discontinued 1988.

Perf: $320 **Exc:** $290 **VGood:** $260

FOX FA-1

Autoloader; 12-ga.; 28-inch Modified, 30-inch Full choke barrels; metal bead front sight; walnut pistol-grip stock; rosewood grip cap with inlay; self-compensating gas system; crossbolt safety; chrome-moly barrel, polished receiver. Made in Japan. Introduced 1981 by Savage Arms; discontinued 1982.

Perf: $300 **Exc:** $260 **VGood:** $225

FOX FP-1

Slide action; 12-ga.; 28-inch, 30-inch barrels; vent. rib; metal bead front sight; checkered pistol-grip walnut stock; rosewood pistol-grip cap; crossbolt safety; dual action bars. Made in Japan. Introduced 1981 by Savage Arms; discontinued 1982.

Perf: $290 **Exc:** $250 **VGood:** $210

STEVENS/FOX MODEL B

Side-by-side; boxlock; hammerless; 12-, 16-, 20-ga.,.410; 26-inch, 28-inch, 30-inch barrels; Modified/Full, Improved/ Modified, Full/Full chokes; hand-checkered American walnut pistol-grip stock, forearm; double triggers; plain extractors; case-hardened frame. Introduced 1940; no longer in production.

Exc: $320 **VGood:** $270 **Good:** $225

STEVENS/FOX MODEL B-DE

Same specs as Model B except for checkered select walnut pistol-grip stock, beavertail forearm; non-selective single trigger; satin chrome-finished frame; replaced Model B-DL. Introduced 1965; discontinued 1966.

Exc: $340 **VGood:** $290 **Good:** $215

STEVENS/FOX MODEL B-DL

Same specs as Model B except for checkered select walnut pistol-grip stock, beavertail forearm; non-selective single trigger; satin chrome-finished frame; sideplates. Introduced 1962; discontinued 1965.

Exc: $360 **VGood:** $310 **Good:** $225

STEVENS/FOX MODEL B-SE

Same specs as Model B except single trigger; selective ejectors. Introduced 1966; discontinued 1987.

Perf: $450 **Exc:** $425 **VGood:** $290

STEVENS/FOX MODEL B-ST

Same specs as Model B except non-selective single trigger. Introduced 1955; discontinued 1966.

Exc: $475 **VGood:** $400 **Good:** $320

Fox FA-1

Fox FP-1

Stevens/Fox Model B-DE

Stevens/Fox Model B

Stevens/Fox Model B-DL

Stevens/Fox Model B-SE

Stevens/Fox Model B-ST

A.H. FOX MODEL B LIGHTWEIGHT

Side-by-side; boxlock; hammerless; 12-, 20-ga., .410; 24-inch Improved/Modified (12-, 20-ga. only), 26-inch Full/Full (.410 only), 26-inch Improved/ Modified, 28-inch Modified/Full, 30-inch Modified/ Full (12-ga. only) barrels; vent rib; checkered select walnut pistol-grip stock, beavertail forearm; double triggers; color case-hardened frame. Introduced 1973; no longer in production.

Perf: $350 **Exc:** $320 **VGood:** $200

A.H. FOX HAMMERLESS DOUBLE BARREL (1902-1905)

Side-by-side; boxlock; 12-ga.; 28-inch, 30-inch, 32-inch Krupp fluid steel barrels; Damascus barrels optional in grades C and higher; Whitworth fluid steel barrels optional in Grade H; English walnut stocks; pistol grip in Grade A, straight or pistol grip in others; made by Philadelphia Gun Company, Philadelphia. Introduced 1902; discontinued 1905.

Grade A

Perf: $1250 **Exc:** $875 **VGood:** $700

Grade B

Perf: $2000 **Exc:** $1400 **VGood:** $1100

Grade C

Perf: $2900 **Exc:** $2000 **VGood:** $1600

Grade D

Perf: $6500 **Exc:** $4900 **VGood:** $3600

Grade E

Perf: $10,000 **Exc:** $7500 **VGood:** $5500

Grade F

Perf: $13,500 **Exc:** $10,000 **VGood:** $7400

Grade H

Perf: $15,500 **Exc:** $12,000 **VGood:** $8600

A.H. FOX HAMMERLESS DOUBLE BARREL (1905-1946)

Side-by-side; boxlock; 12-, 16-, 20-ga.; 2-9/16-inch (until mid-1930s), 2-3/4-inch, 3-inch chambers; Krupp fluid steel (until about 1910), Chromox steel barrels (used exclusively after the early 1920s); walnut half-pistol-grip stock standard, straight or pistol grip optional; earliest graded smallbores have snap-on forend latch; standard engraving patterns for all grades except CE were changed 1913-1914; all graded 12-ga. and graded smallbores built after 1913 have Deeley finger-lever forend latch; Fox-Kautzky single trigger available in all grades after 1914; other options included beavertail forend, vent rib, skeleton steel butt, recoil pad, extra sets of barrels, custom stocks. 12-ga. introduced 1905; 16-, 20-ga. introduced 1912 and built on the same, scaled-down frame. Made by A.H. Fox Gun Company,

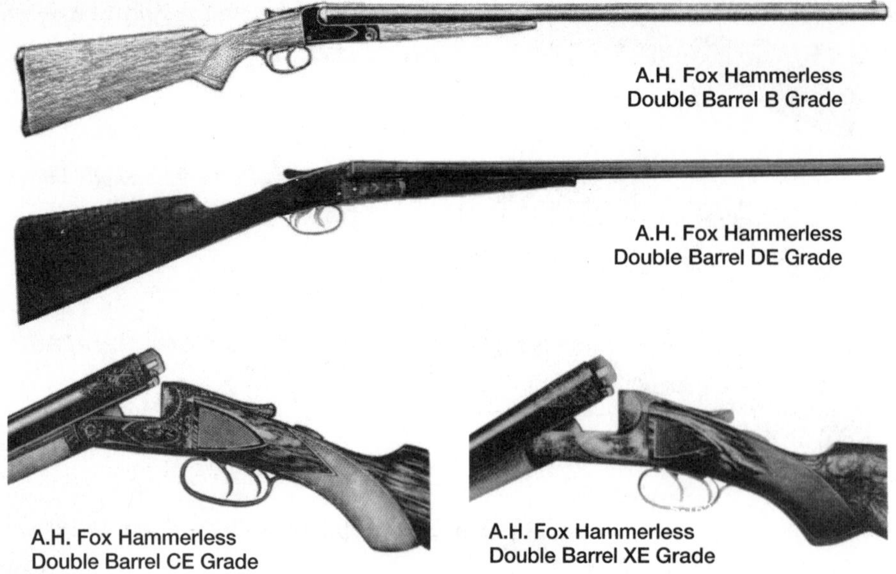

A.H. Fox Hammerless Double Barrel B Grade

A.H. Fox Hammerless Double Barrel DE Grade

A.H. Fox Hammerless Double Barrel CE Grade

A.H. Fox Hammerless Double Barrel XE Grade

Philadelphia, 1905-1929; taken over by Savage Arms Company in late 1929 and production moved to Utica, New York in 1930; production of the original A.H. Fox gun discontinued in 1946. Approximate production totals: graded 12-ga., 35,000; graded 16-ga., 3521; graded 20-ga., 3434.

A.H. FOX HAMMERLESS DOUBLE BARREL A GRADE

Same specs as Hammerless Double Barrel (1905-1946) except 26-inch to 32-inch barrels; American walnut stocks; double or single trigger; extractors. Introduced 1905; discontinued 1942.

Exc: $1400 **VGood:** $950 **Good:** $800

A.H. FOX HAMMERLESS DOUBLE BARREL AE GRADE

Same specs as Hammerless Double Barrel (1905-1946) except 26-inch to 32-inch barrels; American walnut stocks; double or single trigger; ejectors. Introduced 1905; discontinued 1946.

Exc: $1600 **VGood:** $1150 **Good:** $950

A.H. FOX HAMMERLESS DOUBLE BARREL B GRADE

Same specs as Hammerless Double Barrel (1905-1946) except 26-inch to 32-inch barrels; English walnut stocks; double or single trigger; extractors. Introduced 1905; discontinued 1918.

Exc: $2300 **VGood:** $1700 **Good:** $1450

A.H. FOX HAMMERLESS DOUBLE BARREL BE GRADE

Same specs as Hammerless Double Barrel (1905-1946) except 26-inch to 32-inch barrels; English walnut stocks; double or single trigger; ejectors. Introduced 1905; discontinued 1918.

Exc: $2500 **VGood:** $1900 **Good:** $1650

A.H. FOX HAMMERLESS DOUBLE BARREL C GRADE

Same specs as Hammerless Double Barrel (1905-1946) except 26-inch to 32-inch barrels; English walnut stocks; double or single trigger; extractors. Introduced 1905; discontinued 1913.

Exc: $3400 **VGood:** $2900 **Good:** $2400

A.H. FOX HAMMERLESS DOUBLE BARREL CE GRADE

Same specs as Hammerless Double Barrel (1905-1946) except 26-inch to 32-inch barrels; English walnut stocks; double or single trigger; ejectors. Introduced 1905; discontinued 1946.

Exc: $3800 **VGood:** $3100 **Good:** $2600

A.H. FOX HAMMERLESS DOUBLE BARREL D GRADE

Same specs as Hammerless Double Barrel (1905-1946) except 26-inch to 32-inch barrels; Circassian walnut stocks; double or single trigger; extractors. Introduced 1905; discontinued 1913.

Exc: $7700 **VGood:** $5700 **Good:** $4300

A.H. FOX HAMMERLESS DOUBLE BARREL DE GRADE

Same specs as Hammerless Double Barrel (1905-1946) except 26-inch to 32-inch barrels; Circassian walnut stocks; double or single trigger; ejectors. Introduced 1905; discontinued 1945.

Exc: $8000 **VGood:** $6000 **Good:** $4500

A.H. FOX HAMMERLESS DOUBLE BARREL F GRADE

Same specs as Hammerless Double Barrel (1905-1946) except 26-inch to 32-inch barrels; Circassian walnut stocks; extractors; made to order with any available option at no extra charge. Introduced 1906; discontinued 1913.

Exc: $16,000 **VGood:** $11,000 **Good:** $9500

A.H. FOX HAMMERLESS DOUBLE BARREL FE GRADE

Same specs as Hammerless Double Barrel (1905-1946) except 26-inch to 32-inch barrels; Circassian walnut stocks; ejectors; made to order with any available option at no extra charge. Introduced 1906; discontinued 1940.

Exc: $16,500 **VGood:** $12,000 **Good:** $10,000

A.H. FOX HAMMERLESS DOUBLE BARREL GE GRADE

Same specs as Hammerless Double Barrel (1905-1946) except reputedly the highest-grade A.H. Fox gun; included in price lists from 1922 through 1930, but never shown in catalogs.

A.H. FOX HAMMERLESS DOUBLE BARREL SKEETER

Same specs as Hammerless Double Barrel (1905-1946) except 12-, 20-ga.; 28-inch barrels; vent rib; ivory beads; walnut pistol-grip stock, beavertail forend; recoil pad; ejectors; double triggers; single trigger optional. Introduced 1931; discontinued 1931.

Exc: $2500 **VGood:** $1800 **Good:** $1400

A.H. FOX HAMMERLESS DOUBLE BARREL TRAP GRADE

Same specs as Hammerless Double Barrel (1905-1946) except 26-inch to 32-inch barrels; vent rib; ivory beads; walnut pistol-grip stock, beavertail forend; recoil pad; double triggers; single trigger optional. Introduced 1932; discontinued 1936.

Exc: $2500 **VGood:** $1800 **Good:** $1400

A.H. FOX HAMMERLESS DOUBLE BARREL XE GRADE

Same specs as Hammerless Double Barrel (1905-1946) except 26-inch to 32-inch barrels; Circassian walnut stocks; Monte Carlo comb optional; double or single trigger; ejectors. Introduced 1914; discontinued 1945.

Exc: $5750 **VGood:** $4800 **Good:** $3800

A.H. FOX HAMMERLESS DOUBLE BARREL (CURRENT PRODUCTION)

Side-by-side; boxlock; 20-ga.; 26-inch, 28-inch, 30-inch barrels; American walnut stock, splinter forend; stocks made to order; double triggers; optional beavertail forend, skeleton steel butt, recoil pad, checkered butt, single trigger; grades CE, DE, FE, Exhibition. Introduced 1993 by Connecticut Shotgun Manufacturing Company, New Britain, Connecticut; still in production.

CE Grade

Perf: $10,950 **Exc:** $8500 **VGood:** $.6250

DE Grade

Perf: $14,800 **Exc:** $11,500 **VGood:** $9500

FE Grade

Perf: $19,700 **Exc:** $16,500 **VGood:** $12,750

Exhibition Grade

Perf: $22,500 **Exc:** $17,500 **VGood:** $12,500

A.H. FOX SIDE-BY-SIDE SHOTGUNS

Gauge: 16, 20, 28, .410. Barrel: Length and chokes to customer specifications. Rust-blued Chromox or Krupp steel. Weight: 5-1/2 to 6-3/4 lbs. Stock: Dimensions to customer specifications. Hand-checkered Turkish Circassian walnut with hand-rubbed oil finish. Straight, semi or full pistol grip; splinter, schnabel or beavertail forend; traditional pad, hard rubber buttplate or skeleton butt. Features: Boxlock action with automatic ejectors; double or Fox single selective trigger. Scalloped, rebated and color case-hardened receiver; hand finished and hand-engraved. Grades differ in engraving, inlays, grade of wood, amount of hand finishing. Add $1,500 for 28 or .410-bore. Introduced 1993. Made in U.S. by Connecticut Shotgun Mfg.

CE Grade

Perf: $11,000 **Exc:** $8,500 **VGood:** $6,250

XE Grade $12,500.00

Perf: $12,500 **Exc:** 9,250 **VGood:** $6,500

DE Grade

Perf: $15,000 **Exc:** $11,500 **VGood:** $9,500

FE Grade

Perf: $20,000 **Exc:** $16,500 **VGood:** $12,750

Exhibition Grade

Perf: $30,000 **Exc:** $26,000 **VGood:** $22,000

28/.410 CE Grade

Perf: $12,500 **Exc:** $10,000 **VGood:** $7,750

28/.410 XE Grade

Perf: $14,000 **Exc:** $10,750 **VGood:** $8,000

28/.410 DE Grade

Perf: $16,500 **Exc:** $13,000 **VGood:** $11,000

28/.410 FE Grade

Perf: $21,500 **Exc:** $18,000 **VGood:** $14,250

28/.410 Exhibition Grade

Perf: $30,000 **Exc:** $27,000 **VGood:** $23,000

A.H. FOX SINGLE-BARREL TRAP

Single shot; boxlock; 12-ga.; 30-inch, 32-inch barrel; vent rib; American walnut straight, half- or pistol-grip stock; Monte Carlo comb optional for early guns, standard after 1931; ejector; available in four grades. Introduced 1919; discontinued 1939. Approximate production totals: J Grade, 460; K Grade, 77; L Grade, 25; M Grade, 9.

J Grade

Exc: $3860 **VGood:** $3550 **Good:** $3200

K Grade

Exc: $5200 **VGood:** $4650 **Good:** $4000

L Grade

Exc: $6500 **VGood:** $5750 **Good:** $5000

M Grade

Exc: $8000 **VGood:** $7250 **Good:** $6000

A.H. FOX SP GRADE

Side-by-side; boxlock; 12-, 16-, 20-ga.; 26-inch, 28-inch, 30-inch, 32-inch barrels; American walnut pistol-grip stock; double triggers; extractors; optional single trigger, beavertail forend, recoil pad, ivory beads; a distinct model mechanically identical to standard Fox guns but with a squarer, smooth-sided frame and no cheek panels on the stock; originally called Fox Special Grade, changed to SP Grade. Introduced 1932; discontinued 1946.

Perf: $2000 **Exc:** $1400 **VGood:** $1100

A.H. FOX SPE GRADE

Same specs as SP Grade except ejectors. Introduced 1932; discontinued 1946.

Perf: $2100 **Exc:** $1500 **VGood:** $1200

A.H. FOX SPE SKEET GRADE

Same specs as SP Grade except ejectors; double or single trigger. Introduced 1934; discontinued 1934.

Perf: $2100 **Exc:** $1500 **VGood:** $1200

A.H. FOX SPE SKEET AND UPLAND GAME GUN

Same specs as SP Grade except 26-inch, 28-inch Cylinder/Quarter barrels; American walnut straight or pistol-grip stock, beavertail forend; single trigger; ejectors; optional double triggers, vent rib, recoil pad. Introduced 1935; discontinued 1939.

Perf: $2100 **Exc:** $1500 **VGood:** $1200

A.H. FOX SPR GRADE

Same specs as SP Grade except vent rib; ejectors. Introduced 1936; discontinued 1936.

Perf: $2300 **Exc:** $1700 **VGood:** $1400

A.H. FOX STERLINGWORTH

Side-by-side; boxlock; 12-, 16-, 20-ga.; 2-9/16-inch (until mid-1930s), 2-3/4-inch, 3-inch chambers; 26-inch to 32-inch Krupp fluid steel (until about 1910), Chromox steel barrels (used exclusively after the early 1920s); checkered American walnut half-pistol-grip stock, snap-on forend standard; straight or pistol grip optional; snap-on forend latch; double triggers; optional Fox-Kautzky single trigger available in all grades after 1914; extractors; standard engraving patterns for all grades except CE were changed 1913-1914; other options include beavertail forend, vent rib, skeleton steel butt, recoil pad, extra sets of barrels, custom stocks; mechanically same as other A.H. Fox doubles, but purely production-line guns without much handwork. Introduced 1911; discontinued 1946. Made by A.H. Fox Gun Company, Philadelphia, 1905-1929; taken over by Savage Arms Company in late 1929 and production moved to Utica, New York in 1930; production of the original A.H. Fox gun discontinued in 1946. Approximate production totals: 12-ga. Sterlingworth, 110,000; Sterlingworth 16-ga., 28,000; 20-ga. Sterlingworth, 21,000.

Exc: $1000 **VGood:** $700 **Good:** $450

A.H. FOX STERLINGWORTH BRUSH

Same specs as Fox Sterlingworth except 26-inch Cylinder/Modified barrels. Introduced 1911; discontinued 1930.

Exc: $1000 **VGood:** $700 **Good:** $450

A.H. FOX STERLINGWORTH DELUXE

Same specs as Fox Sterlingworth except Lyman ivory beads; recoil pad. Introduced 1930; discontinued 1945.

Exc: $1250 **VGood:** $1000 **Good:** $800

A.H. FOX STERLINGWORTH DELUXE EJECTOR

Same specs as Fox Sterlingworth except Lyman ivory beads; ejectors; recoil pad. Introduced 1931; discontinued 1945.

Exc: $1400 **VGood:** $1150 **Good:** $950

A.H. FOX STERLINGWORTH EJECTOR

Same specs as Fox Sterlingworth except ejectors. Introduced 1911; discontinued 1946.

Exc: $1200 **VGood:** $900 **Good:** $650

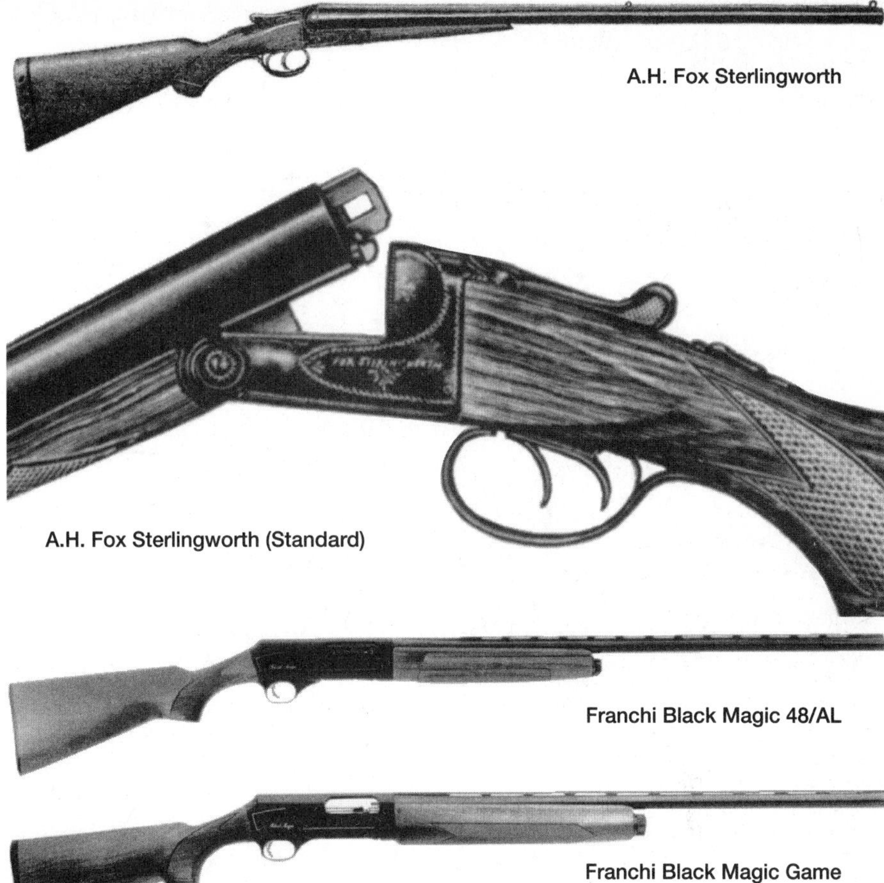

A.H. Fox Sterlingworth

A.H. Fox Sterlingworth (Standard)

Franchi Black Magic 48/AL

Franchi Black Magic Game

A.H. FOX STERLINGWORTH FIELD

Same specs as Fox Sterlingworth except 28-inch Modified/Full barrels. Introduced 1911; discontinued 1930.

Exc: $1000 **VGood:** $700 **Good:** $450

A.H. FOX STERLINGWORTH SKEET

Same specs as Fox Sterlingworth except 26-inch, 28-inch barrels; checkered American walnut straight-grip stock; extractors; double triggers; optional single trigger, beavertail forend, recoil pad. Introduced 1935; discontinued 1945.

Perf: $2200 **Exc:** $1600 **VGood:** $1200

A.H. FOX STERLINGWORTH SKEET EJECTOR

Same specs as Fox Sterlingworth except 26-inch, 28-inch barrels; checkered American walnut straight-grip stock; ejectors; double triggers; optional single trigger, beavertail forend, recoil pad. Introduced 1935; discontinued 1945.

Perf: $2250 **Exc:** $1650 **VGood:** $1250

A.H. FOX STERLINGWORTH STANDARD

Same specs as Fox Sterlingworth except 30-inch Full/Full barrels. Introduced 1911; discontinued 1930.

Exc: $1000 **VGood:** $700 **Good:** $450

A.H. FOX STERLINGWORTH TRAP

Same specs as Fox Sterlingworth except 32-inch Full/Full barrels. Introduced 1911; discontinued 1930.

Exc: $1100 **VGood:** $750 **Good:** $500

A.H. FOX STERLINGWORTH WILDFOWL

Same specs as Fox Sterlingworth except 12-ga.; 30-inch, 32-inch barrels; ejectors; not a true Sterlingworth but rather a Super-Fox engraved and stamped "Fox Sterlingworth." Introduced 1934; discontinued 1940.

Exc: $1300 **VGood:** $850 **Good:** $700

A.H. FOX SUPER-FOX

Over/Under; boxlock; 12-, 20-ga.; over-bored 30-inch, 32-inch Chromox steel barrels; checkered American walnut half-pistol-grip stock, snap-on forend standard; straight or pistol grip optional; snap-on forend latch; double triggers; optional Fox-Kautzky single trigger available; ejectors; standard engraving patterns; built on special, oversized frames; other options include beavertail forend, vent rib, ivory beads; skeleton steel butt, recoil pad, extra sets of barrels, custom stocks; special Fox model designed for long-range shooting; although designated HE Grade, it was also available in any standard Fox grade on special order; high grades rare. A few very early Super-Foxes are stamped "Barrels Guaranteed - See Tag"; most later ones are stamped "Barrels Not Guaranteed - See Tag"; both stamps refer to pattern density, not quality of barrels. 12-ga. introduced 1923; 20-ga. introduced 1925; 20-ga. discontinued 1931; 12-ga. discontinued 1942. Produced in very small numbers, about 300 guns in 12-ga. and only about 60 in 20-ga.

Exc: $2000 **VGood:** $1400 **Good:** $1100

FRANCHI BLACK MAGIC 48/AL

Recoil-operated autoloader; 12-, 20-ga.; 2-3/4-inch chamber; 5-shot magazine; 24-inch rifled, 24-inch, 26-inch, 28-inch barrel; Improved Cylinder, Modified, Full Franchoke tubes; vent rib; weighs 5-1/4 lbs.; checkered walnut pistol-grip stock, forend; chrome-lined bore; crossbolt safety. Made in Italy. Introduced 1950; still in production.

Perf: $585 **Exc:** $530 **VGood:** $430

FRANCHI BLACK MAGIC GAME

Autoloader; 12-, 20-ga.; 3-inch chamber; 24-inch, 26-inch, 28-inch barrel; vent rib; choke tubes; bead front sight; checkered walnut stock, forearm; crossbolt safety; magazine cut-off; recoil pad. Made in Italy. Introduced 1989; discontinued 1991.

Perf: $550 **Exc:** $450 **VGood:** $395

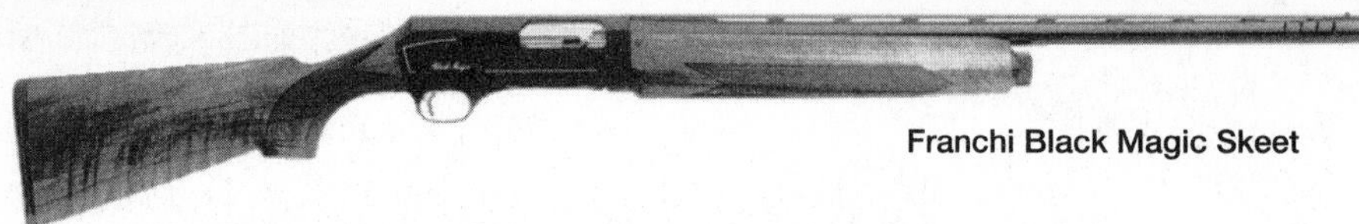
Franchi Black Magic Skeet

Franchi Crown Grade

Franchi Diamond Grade

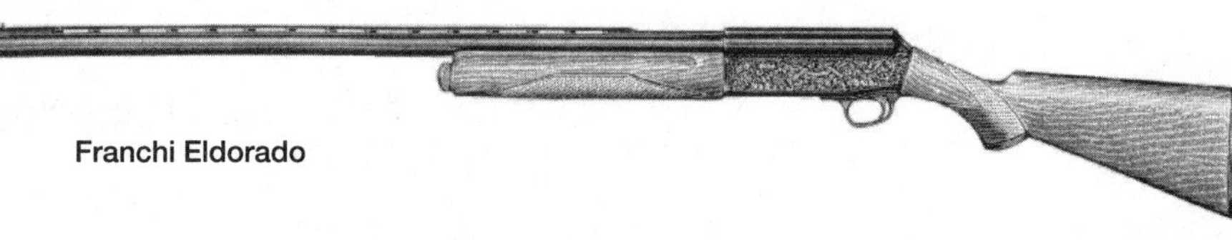
Franchi Eldorado

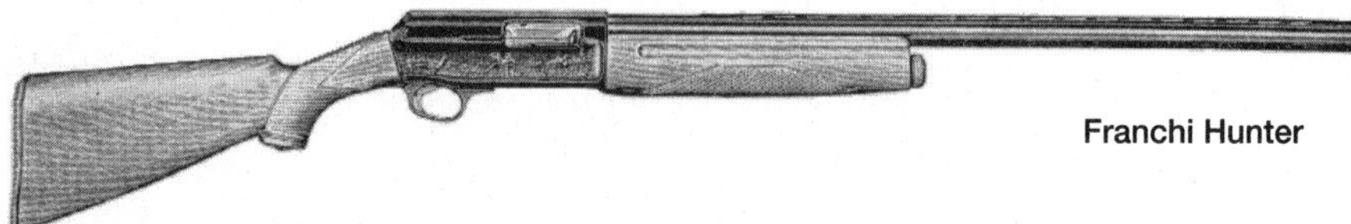
Franchi Hunter

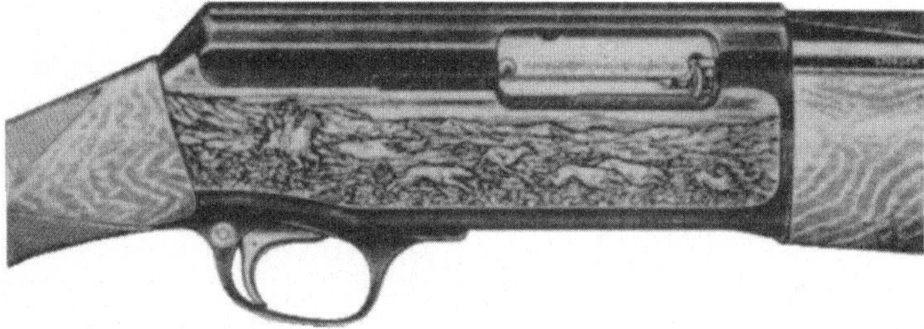
Franchi Imperial Grade

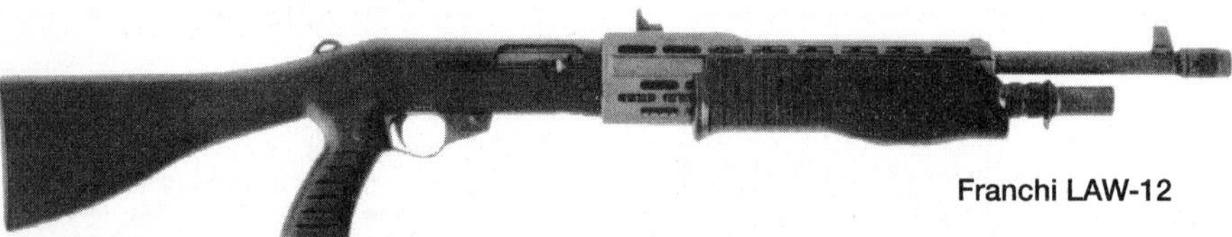
Franchi LAW-12

FRANCHI BLACK MAGIC SKEET

Autoloader; 12-, 20-ga.; 2-3/4-inch chamber; 28-inch barrel; vent rib; choke tubes; bead front sight; checkered walnut stock, forearm; crossbolt safety; magazine cut-off; recoil pad. Made in Italy. Introduced 1989; discontinued 1991.

Perf: $580 **Exc:** $475 **VGood:** $425

FRANCHI BLACK MAGIC TRAP

Autoloader; 12-ga.; 2-3/4-inch chamber; 30-inch barrel; vent rib; choke tubes; bead front sight; checkered European walnut trap-style stock, forearm; crossbolt safety; magazine cut-off; recoil pad. Made in Italy. Introduced 1989; discontinued 1991.

Perf: $615 **Exc:** $.495 **VGood:** $430

FRANCHI CROWN GRADE

Recoil-operated autoloader; 12-, 20-ga.; 5-shot magazine; 24-inch, 26-inch, 28-inch, 30-inch interchangeable vent-rib barrel; Improved, Modified, Full chokes; hand-checkered European walnut pistol-grip stock, forearm; alloy receiver; chrome-lined barrels; simplified takedown; engraved hunting scene. Introduced 1954; discontinued 1975.

Perf: $1540 **Exc:** $1320 **VGood:** $1210

FRANCHI DIAMOND GRADE

Recoil-operated autoloader; 12-, 20-ga.; 5-shot magazine; 24-inch, 26-inch, 28-inch, 30-inch interchangeable vent-rib barrel; Improved, Modified, Full chokes; hand-checkered European walnut pistol-grip stock, forearm; alloy receiver; chrome-lined barrels; simplified takedown; scroll engraved with silver inlay. Introduced 1954; discontinued 1975.

Perf: $1980 **Exc:** $1735 **VGood:** $1540

FRANCHI ELDORADO

Recoil-operated autoloader; 12-, 20-ga.; 5-shot magazine; 24-inch, 26-inch, 28-inch, 30-inch interchangeable vent-rib barrel; Improved, Modified, Full chokes; select hand-checkered European walnut pistol-grip stock, forearm; alloy receiver; chrome-lined barrels; simplified takedown; scroll engraving covering 75 percent of receiver surfaces; gold-plated trigger; chrome-plated breech bolt. Introduced 1955; discontinued 1975.

Perf: $450 **Exc:** $420 **VGood:** $395

FRANCHI ELITE

Gas-operated autoloader; 12-ga.; 2-3/4-inch, 3-inch chamber; 24-inch, 26-inch, 28-inch, 30-inch, 32-inch barrel; 7mm vent rib; all standard chokes; weighs 7-3/8 lbs.; oil-finished, checkered European walnut stock; blued receiver; stainless steel gas piston; engraved receiver. Made in Italy. Introduced 1985; discontinued 1989.

Perf: $595 **Exc:** $500 **VGood:** $425

FRANCHI HUNTER

Recoil-operated autoloader; 12-, 20-ga.; 5-shot magazine; 24-inch, 26-inch, 28-inch, 30-inch interchangeable vent-rib barrel; Improved, Modified, Full chokes; hand-checkered select European walnut pistol-grip stock, forearm; alloy receiver; chrome-lined barrels; simplified takedown; etched receiver. Introduced 1950; discontinued 1990.

Perf: $415 **Exc:** $360 **VGood:** $300

FRANCHI HUNTER MAGNUM

Same specs as Hunter Semi-Automatic except 12-, 20-ga.; 3-inch chamber; 32-inch (12-ga.), 28-inch (20-ga.) vent-rib, Full-choke barrel; recoil pad. Introduced 1955; discontinued 1973.

Perf: $430 **Exc:** $380 **VGood:** $370

FRANCHI IMPERIAL GRADE

Recoil-operated autoloader; 12-, 20-ga.; 5-shot magazine; 24-inch, 26-inch, 28-inch, 30-inch interchangeable vent-rib barrels; Improved, Modified, Full chokes; hand-checkered European walnut pistol-grip stock, forearm; alloy receiver; chrome-lined barrels; simplified takedown; elaborate engraving with gold inlay. Introduced 1954; discontinued 1975.

Perf: $2420 **Exc:** $2090 **VGood:** $1925

FRANCHI LAW-12

Autoloader; 12-ga.; 2-3/4-inch chamber; 5-, 8-shot tube magazine; 21-1/2-inch barrel; synthetic pistol-grip stock; alloy receiver. Introduced 1988; discontinued 1994.

Perf: $575 **Exc:** $485 **VGood:** $400

FRANCHI MODEL 500

Gas-operated autoloader; 12-ga.; 4-shot magazine; 26-inch, 28-inch barrel; vent rib; any standard choke; checkered European walnut pistol-grip stock. Introduced 1976; no longer in production.

Perf: $330 **Exc:** $310 **VGood:** $305

FRANCHI MODEL 520 DELUXE

Gas-operated autoloader; 12-ga.; 4-shot magazine; 26-inch, 28-inch barrel; vent rib; any standard choke; checkered select European walnut pistol-grip stock; engraved receiver. Introduced 1976; no longer in production.

Perf: $385 **Exc:** $365 **VGood:** $330

FRANCHI MODEL 520 ELDORADO GOLD

Same specs as Model 520 Deluxe except high quality of wood; better engraving; gold inlays in receiver. Introduced 1977; no longer in production.

Perf: $990 **Exc:** $770 **VGood:** $715

FRANCHI MODEL 530

Autoloader; 12-, 20-, 28-ga; 2-3/4-inch, 3-inch chamber; 5-shot magazine; 30-inch barrel; interchangeable choke tubes; vent rib; oil finished, hand-checkered French walnut straight or Monte Carlo stock; interchangeable stock drilled, tapped for recoil reducer; specially tuned gas system; target-grade trigger; chrome-lined bore, chamber; matte blue finish. Introduced 1978; discontinued 1982.

Perf: $660 **Exc:** $550 **VGood:** $525

FRANCHI 612 AND 620

Autoloader; 12-, 20-ga.; 3-inch chamber; 24-inch, 26-inch, 28-inch barrel; IC, M, F tubes; weighs 7 lbs.; European walnut, synthetic and Timber HD stocks; alloy frame with matte black finish; gas-operated with Vario System; four-lug rotating bolt. Introduced 1996. Imported from Italy by Benelli U.S.A.

Walnut
Perf: $565 **Exc:** $490 **VGood:** $430

Camo, Timber HD
Perf: $655 **Exc:** $580 **VGood:** $520

Synthetic (black synthetic stock, forend)
Perf: $550 **Exc:** $475 **VGood:** $415

20-ga., 24-inch, 26-inch, 28-inch, walnut
Perf: $565 **Exc:** $490 **VGood:** $430

Variopress 620 (Timber HD Camo)
Perf: $655 **Exc:** $485 **VGood:** $520

FRANCHI 612 DEFENSE

Similar to 612 except has 18-1/2-inch, Cylinder-bore barrel with black, synthetic stock. Available in 12-gauge, 3-inch chamber only. Weighs 6-1/2 lbs. 2-shot magazine extension available. Introduced 2000.

Perf: $525 **Exc:** $450 **VGood:** $375

FRANCHI 612 SPORTING

Similar to 612 except has 30-inch ported barrel to reduce muzzle jump. Available in 12-gauge, 3-inch chamber only. Introduced 2000.

Perf: $825 **Exc:** $750 **VGood:** $625

FRANCHI 620 SHORT STOCK

Similar to 620 but with stock shortened to 12-1/2-inch length of pull for smaller shooters. Introduced 2000.

Perf: $565 **Exc:** $490 **VGood:** $430

FRANCHI 720

Autoloader; 20-ga.; 3-inch chamber; 24-inch, 26-inch, 28-inch barrel; IC, M, F tubes; weighs 6 lbs.; European walnut, Max-4, and Timber HD stocks; four-lug rotating bolt. Imported from Italy by Benelli U.S.A.

Walnut
Perf: $565 **Exc:** $490 **VGood:** $430

Camo, Timber HD/Max-4
Perf: $655 **Exc:** $580 **VGood:** $520

Youth version (12-1/2-inch LOP)
Perf: $550 **Exc:** $475 **VGood:** $415

FRANCHI 712 RAPTOR

Autoloader; 12-ga.; 2-3/4 and 3-inch chamber; 30-inch barrel; IC, M, F tubes; weighs 7.1 lbs.; WeatherCoat stock; four-lug rotating bolt. Imported from Italy by Benelli U.S.A.

Perf: $565 **Exc:** $490 **VGood:** $430

Franchi Model 530

Franchi 612 Defense Shotgun

Franchi 612 Sporting Shotgun

Franchi 620 Short Stock Shotgun

Franchi Model 720

Franchi 712 Raptor

Franchi Model 912 Timber HD Max4 Camo

Franchi Model 912 Timber HD Camo with SteadyGrip

Franchi Prestige

FRANCHI MODEL 720 RAPTOR

Similar to above but in 20-ga., 2-3/4- and 3-inch barrel.

Perf: $565 **Exc:** $490 **VGood:** $430

FRANCHI 912

Autoloader; 12-ga.; 3-1/2-inch chamber; 24-inch, 26-inch, 28-, 30-inch barrel; IC, M, F tubes; weighs 7-1/2 lbs.; European walnut, synthetic, Timber HD and Max-4 HD stocks; gas-operated with Vario System; four-lug rotating bolt. Imported from Italy by Benelli U.S.A.

Walnut
Perf: $665 **Exc:** $590 **VGood:** $530

Camo, Timber HD
Perf: $755 **Exc:** $680 **VGood:** $620

Synthetic (black synthetic stock, forend)
Perf: $650 **Exc:** $575 **VGood:** $515

SteadyGrip (full pistol grip) stock, camo
Perf: $760 **Exc:** $685 **VGood:** $625

FRANCHI PRESTIGE

Gas-operated autoloader; 12-ga.; 2-3/4-inch, 3-inch chamber; 24-inch, 26-inch, 28-inch, 30-inch, 32-inch barrel; 7mm vent-rib; all standard chokes; weighs 7-3/8 lbs.; oil-finished, checkered European walnut stock; blued receiver; stainless steel gas piston. Made in Italy. Introduced 1985; discontinued 1989.

Perf: $600 **Exc:** $390 **VGood:** $290

FRANCHI SKEET GUN

Recoil-operated autoloader; 12-, 20-ga.; 5-shot magazine; 26-inch vent-rib barrel; Skeet choke; hand-checkered fancy European walnut pistol-grip stock, forearm; alloy receiver; chrome-lined barrels; simplified takedown. Introduced 1972; discontinued 1974.

Perf: $385 **Exc:** $370 **VGood:** $350

FRANCHI SLUG GUN

Recoil-operated autoloader; 12-, 20-ga.; 5-shot magazine; 22-inch Cylinder-bore barrel; raised gold bead front sight, Lyman folding leaf open rear; hand-checkered European walnut pistol-grip stock, forearm; sling swivels. Introduced 1955; no longer in production.

Exc: $360 **VGood:** $330 **Good:** $350

FRANCHI 48AL

Autoloader; 20 or 28 ga.; 2-3/4-inch chamber; 24-inch, 26-inch, 28-inch barrel (Full, Cyl., Mod., choke tubes); weighs 5.5 lbs. (20-gauge); length: 44-inch-48-inch; 14- 1/4-inchx1-5/ 8-inchx2-1/2-inch stock dimensions; walnut with checkered grip and forend; long recoil-operated action; chrome-lined bore; cross-bolt safety. Imported from Italy by Benelli U.S.A.

20 ga.
Perf: $585 **Exc:** $530 **VGood:** $430

28 ga.
Perf: $695 **Exc:** $640 **VGood:** $540

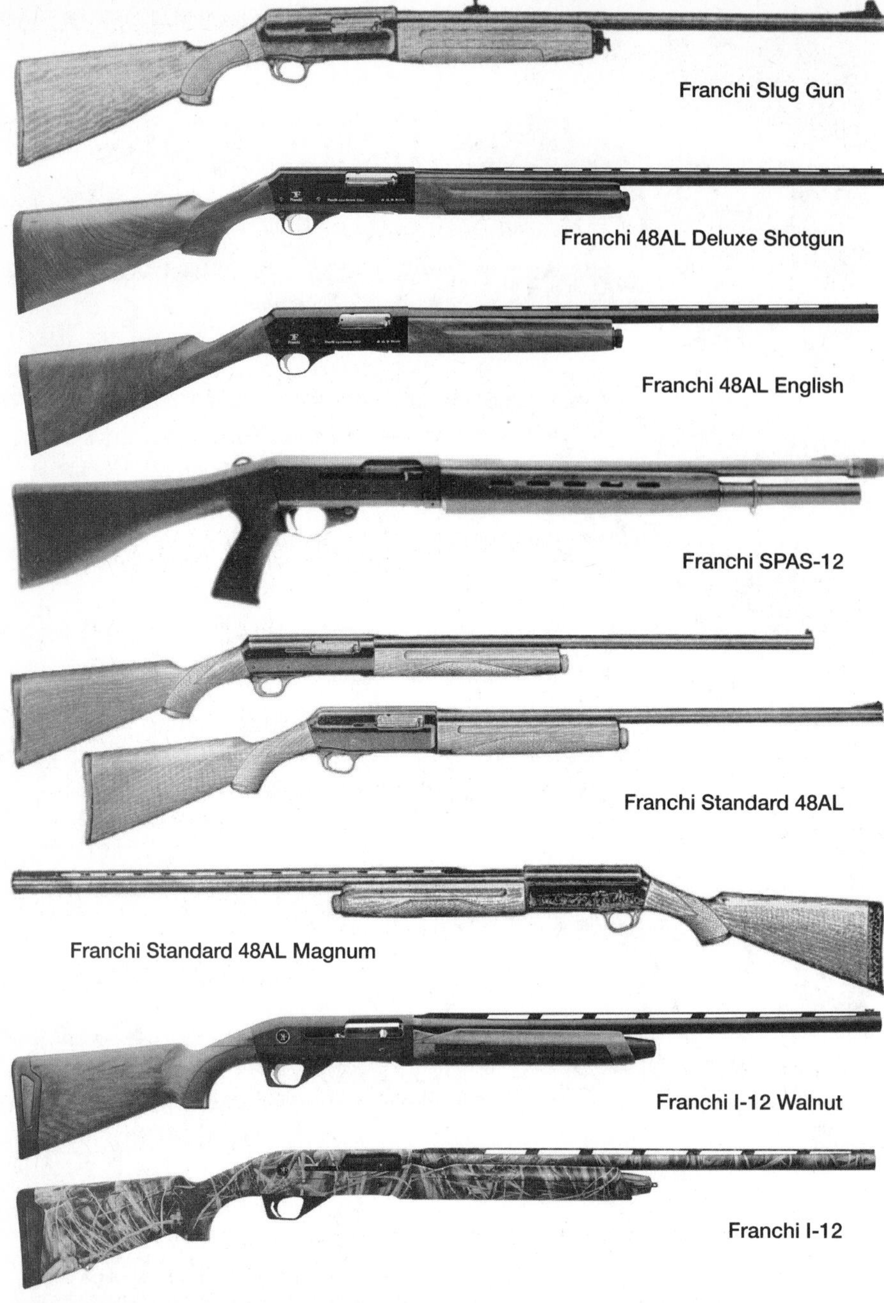

Franchi Slug Gun

Franchi 48AL Deluxe Shotgun

Franchi 48AL English

Franchi SPAS-12

Franchi Standard 48AL

Franchi Standard 48AL Magnum

Franchi I-12 Walnut

Franchi I-12

FRANCHI STANDARD 48/AL

Recoil-operated autoloader; 12-, 20-ga.; 5-shot magazine; 24-inch, 26-inch, 28-inch, 30-inch interchangeable vent-rib barrel; Improved, Modified, Full chokes; hand-checkered European walnut pistol-grip stock, forearm; alloy receiver; chrome-lined barrels; simplified takedown. Introduced 1950; still in production.

Perf: $480 **Exc:** $290 **VGood:** $240

FRANCHI STANDARD 48/AL MAGNUM

Same specs as 48/AL except 12-, 20-ga.; 3-inch chamber; 28-inch (20-ga.), 32-inch (12-ga.) plain or vent-rib barrel; recoil pad. Introduced 1952; discontinued 1990.

Perf: $400 **Exc:** $300 **VGood:** $225

FRANCHI 48AL DELUXE

Similar to 48AL but with select walnut stock and forend and high-polish blue finish with gold trigger. Introduced 2000.

20-gauge, 26-inch barrel

Perf: $775 **Exc:** $625 **VGood:** $525

28-gauge, 26-inch barrel

Perf: $825 **Exc:** $675 **VGood:** $575

FRANCHI 48AL ENGLISH

Similar to 48AL Deluxe but with straight grip "English style" stock. 20-ga., 28-ga., 26-inch bbl.; IC, M, F tubes.

20-gauge

Perf: $775 **Exc:** $625 **VGood:** $525

28-gauge

Perf: $825 **Exc:** $675 **VGood:** $575

FRANCHI 48AL SHORT STOCK

Similar to 48AL but with stock shortened to 12-1/2-inch length of pull. 20-gauge, 26-inch barrel.

Perf: $585 **Exc:** $530 **VGood:** $430

FRANCHI VARIOMAX 912

Introduced in 2001 this model is chambered for the 12 gauge 3.5" shell. It is offered with a choice of 24", 26", 28", or 30" barrels with vent-rib. Black synthetic stock. Weight is about 7.6 lbs. Choke tubes. In 2002 a walnut stock was added as an option.

Perf: $625 **Exc:** $550 **VGood:** $450

FRANCHI VARIOMAX 912 CAMO

Same as above but with Advantage Timber camo finish.

Perf: $650 **Exc:** $575 **VGood:** $475

FRANCHI VARIOMAX 912 STEADYGRIP

Introduced in 2005 this model features a extended pistol grip and Advantage H-D camo stock with 24" vent rib barrel and choke tubes. Weight is about 8 lbs.

Perf: $700 **Exc:** $575 **VGood:** $495

FRANCHI VARIOPRESS 612 SPORTING

This is a 12 gauge semi-automatic gas-operated shotgun with 30" ported barrel. Extended choke tubes. Select walnut stock with stock drop kit. Magazine capacity is 5 rounds. Weight is about 7 lbs. First imported in 2000.

Perf: $675 **Exc:** $595 **VGood:** $450

FRANCHI VARIOPRESS 612 FIELD

This 12 gauge model is offered with barrel lengths from 24" to 28". Stock configurations are walnut, synthetic, or camo. Magazine capacity is 5 rounds. Weight is about 7 lbs. depending on barrel length.

Perf: $500 **Exc:** $425 **VGood:** $350

FRANCHI VARIOPRESS 612 DEFENSE

This 12 gauge gun is fitted with an 18.5" barrel and black synthetic stock. Matte black finish. Choke is cylinder. Weight is about 6.5 lbs. Magazine capacity is 5 rounds. First imported in 2000.

Perf: $425 **Exc:** $350 **VGood:** $275

FRANCHI VARIOPRESS 620 FIELD

This model is offered in 20 gauge with a choice of walnut or camo stock. Barrel lengths from 24" to 28". Magazine capacity is 5 rounds. Weight is about 6 lbs.

Perf: $675 **Exc:** $595 **VGood:** $465

FRANCHI VARIOPRESS 620 SHORT STOCK

Same as above but with 12.5" length of pull and walnut stock. First imported in 2000.

Perf: $675 **Exc:** $595 **VGood:** $465

FRANCHI SPAS-12

Autoloader/slide action; 12-ga.; 2-3/4-inch chamber; 5-, 8-shot tube magazine; 21-1/2-inch barrel; synthetic pistol-grip stock; alloy receiver; button-activated switch to change action type. Introduced 1988; discontinued 1994.

Perf: $675 **Exc:** $575 **VGood:** $475

FRANCHI TURKEY GUN

Recoil-operated autoloader; 12-ga.; 3-inch chamber; 5-shot magazine; 32-inch vent-rib barrel; Extra Full choke; hand-checkered European walnut pistol-grip stock, forearm; alloy receiver; chrome-lined barrels; simplified takedown; engraved turkey scene on receiver. Introduced 1963; discontinued 1965.

Perf: $415 **Exc:** $385 **VGood:** $370

FRANCHI I-12

Introduced in 2005 this 12 gauge model is offered with 3" chambers and choice of 24", 26", or 28" vent rib barrels. Available with synthetic, walnut, Max-4, or Timber H-D stock. Choke tubes. Weight is about 7.5 lbs. depending on barrel length.

Perf: $900 **Exc:** $750 **VGood:** $575

FRANCHI I-12 WHITE GOLD

Similar to Inertia I-12 but with highly figured walnut stock and white gold game bird scene on a satin nickel receiver. Introduced in 2006. Available only with 28-inch barrel. Weight is about 7.7 lbs.

NIB: $1150 **Exc:** $1025 **VGood:** $850

FRANCHI ALCIONE

Over/under; 12-ga.; 2-3/4-inch chamber; 28-inch Modified/Full barrel; cut-checkered French walnut pistol-grip stock, forend; top tang safety; single selective trigger; auto ejectors; chrome-plated bores; silvered receiver; decorative scroll engraving. Made in Italy. Introduced 1982; discontinued 1989.

Perf: $675 **Exc:** $550 **VGood:** $495

FRANCHI ALCIONE SL

Same specs as Alcione except 27-inch Improved/Modified, 28-inch Modified/Full barrels; ivory bead front sight; better engraving; silvered receiver; gold-plated trigger; gold-inlaid receiver; marketed in fitted case. Made in Italy. Introduced 1982; discontinued 1986.

Perf: $1150 **Exc:** $995 **VGood:** $875

FRANCHI ALCIONE FIELD

Over/under; 12-, 20-ga.; 3-inch chambers; 26-inch, 28-inch barrel; IC, M, F tubes; weighs 7-1/2 lbs.; length: 43-inch overall with 26-inch barrels; European walnut; boxlock action with ejectors; barrel selector mounted on trigger; silvered, engraved receiver; vent center rib; automatic safety; interchangeable 20-ga. barrels.; left-hand available. Imported from Italy by Benelli USA.

Perf: $1100 **Exc:** $950 **VGood:** $800
Add $460 for extra 20-gauge barrel

FRANCHI SX

Similar to Alcione Field model with high-grade walnut stock and forend. Gold engraved removable sideplates, interchangeable barrels.

Perf: $1675 **Exc:** $1495 **VGood:** $1275

FRANCHI ALCIONE SPORT SL

Similar to Alcione except 2-3/4-inch chambers, elongated forcing cones and porting for Sporting Clays shooting. 10mm vent rib, tightly curved pistol grip, manual safety, removable sideplates. Imported from Italy by Benelli USA.

Perf: $1400 **Exc:** $1200 **VGood:** $950

FRANCHI ALCIONE TITANIUM

Over/under; 12-, 20-ga.;3-inch chambers; 26-inch, 28-inch barrels; IC, M, F tubes; weighs 6.8 lbs.; 43-inch, 45-inch overall; select walnut; front/mid bead sight; receiver (titanium inserts) made of aluminum alloy; 7mm vent rib; fast locking triggers. Left-hand available.

Perf: $1225 **Exc:** $1050 **VGood:** $950
Add $450 to above prices for 2 barrel set (includes extra 20 ga. barrels)

FRANCHI ARISTOCRAT

Over/under; 12-ga.; 24-inch Cylinder/Improved Cylinder, 26-inch Improved/Modified, 28-inch Modified/Full, 30-inch Modified/Full vent-rib barrel; hand-checkered Italian walnut pistol-grip stock, forearm; selective automatic ejectors; automatic safety; selective single trigger; English scroll engraving on receiver; blue-black finish. Introduced 1960; discontinued 1968.

Exc: $660 **VGood:** $470 **Good:** $440

FRANCHI ARISTOCRAT DELUXE

Same specs as Aristocrat except select walnut stock forearm; heavy relief engraving on receiver, tang and trigger guard. Introduced 1960; discontinued 1965.

Exc: $800 **VGood:** $700 **Good:** $640

FRANCHI ARISTOCRAT IMPERIAL

Same specs as Aristocrat except top-quality European walnut stock; exquisite engraving. Introduced 1967 on customer-order basis; discontinued 1969.

Exc: $2200 **VGood:** $2090 **Good:** $1925

FRANCHI ARISTOCRAT MAGNUM

Same specs as Aristocrat except 3-inch chamber; 32-inch Full choke barrels; recoil pad. Introduced 1962; discontinued 1965.

Exc: $470 **VGood:** $440 **Good:** $395

FRANCHI ARISTOCRAT MONTE CARLO

Same specs as Aristocrat except top-of-the-line European walnut stock; top-of-the-line engraving. Introduced 1967 on customer-order basis; discontinued 1969.

Exc: $3080 **VGood:** $2915 **Good:** $2640

Franchi Alcione Field

Franchi SX O/U

Franchi Alcione Sport SL

Franchi Alcione Titanium

Franchi Aristocrat Deluxe

Franchi Aristocrat Silver-King

Franchi Aristocrat Skeet

FRANCHI ARISTOCRAT SILVER-KING

Same specs as Aristocrat except selected ultra-deluxe walnut stock forearm, cut from the same blank for match of grain, color, finish; hand-checkered pistol grip, forearm; engraved, bright-finish receiver. Introduced 1965; discontinued 1968.

Exc: $750 **VGood:** $560 **Good:** $535

FRANCHI ARISTOCRAT SKEET

Same specs as Aristocrat except 26-inch Skeet/Skeet vent-rib barrel; grooved beavertail forearm. Introduced 1962; discontinued 1968.

Exc: $425 **VGood:** $390 **Good:** $350

FRANCHI ARISTOCRAT SUPREME

Same specs as Aristocrat except select walnut stock, forearm; heavy relief engraving on receiver, tang and trigger guard; gold-inlaid game bird figures on receiver. Introduced 1960; discontinued 1965.

Exc: $1265 **VGood:** $1155 **Good:** $1075

FRANCHI ARISTOCRAT TRAP

Same specs as Aristocrat except 30-inch Modified/Full vent-rib barrels; hand-checkered select deluxe-grade European walnut pistol-grip stock, beavertail forend; Monte Carlo comb; color case-hardened receiver. Introduced 1962; discontinued 1968.

Exc: $550 **VGood:** $525 **Good:** $480

FRANCHI BLACK MAGIC LIGHTWEIGHT HUNTER

Over/under; boxlock; 12-, 20-ga.; 2-3/4-inch chambers; 25-inch barrel; choke tubes; weighs 6 lbs.; cut-checkered figured walnut stock, schnabel forend with semi-gloss finish; solid black recoil pad; single selective trigger auto safety; auto selective ejectors; polished blue finish; gold accents. Made in Italy. Introduced 1989; discontinued 1991.

Perf: $975 **Exc:** $850 **VGood:** $775

FRANCHI BLACK MAGIC SPORTING HUNTER

Over/under; boxlock; 12-ga.; 3-inch chambers; 28-inch barrel; choke tubes; weighs 7 lbs.; cut-checkered figured walnut stock, schnabel forend with semi-gloss finish; solid black recoil pad; single selective trigger auto safety; auto selective ejectors; polished blue finish; gold accents. Made in Italy. Introduced 1989; discontinued 1991.

Perf: $995 **Exc:** $875 **VGood:** $800

FRANCHI FALCONET

Over/under; 12-, 16-, 20-, 28-ga., .410; 24-inch, 26-inch, 28-inch, 30-inch (12-ga. only) barrels; standard choke combos; checkered walnut pistol-grip stock, forearm; epoxy finish; selective

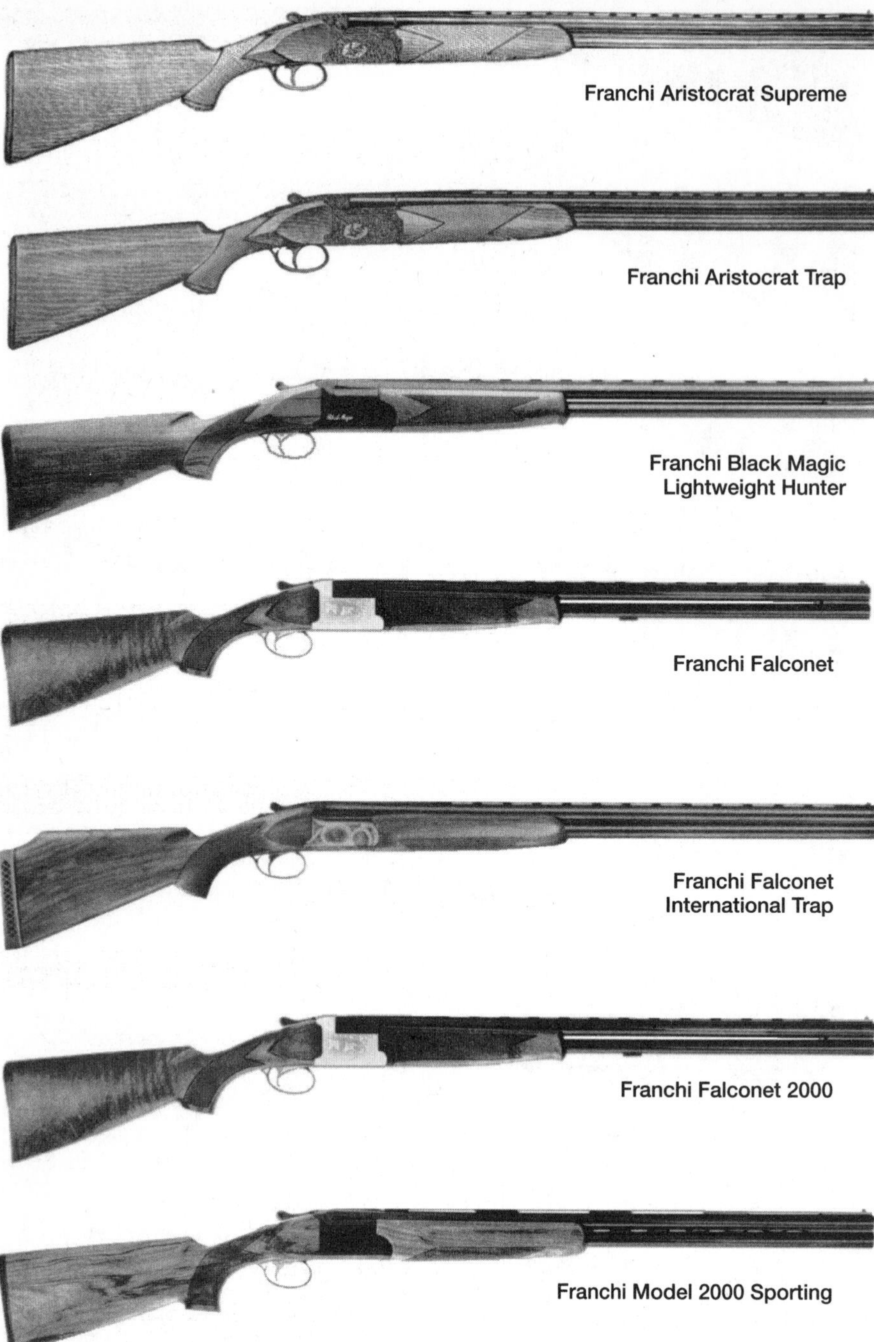
Franchi Aristocrat Supreme

Franchi Aristocrat Trap

Franchi Black Magic Lightweight Hunter

Franchi Falconet

Franchi Falconet International Trap

Franchi Falconet 2000

Franchi Model 2000 Sporting

single trigger; barrel selector; automatic safety; selective automatic ejectors; alloy receiver, fully engraved. Introduced 1969 as Falcon; discontinued 1985.

Perf: $530 **Exc:** $450 **VGood:** $.410

FRANCHI FALCONET INTERNATIONAL SKEET

Same specs as Falconet except 26-inch Skeet-choked barrels; wide vent rib; select Skeet-style stock, forearm; engraved color case-hardened receiver. Introduced 1970; discontinued 1974.

Perf: $935 **Exc:** $865 **VGood:** $825

FRANCHI FALCONET INTERNATIONAL TRAP

Same specs as Falconet except 12-ga.; 30-inch Modified/Full choke barrels; wide vent rib; select checkered trap-style Monte Carlo stock, forearm; engraved color case-hardened receiver; recoil pad. Introduced 1970; discontinued 1974.

Perf: $935 **Exc:** $855 **VGood:** $825

FRANCHI FALCONET SKEET

Same specs as Falconet except 26-inch Skeet-choked barrels; wide vent rib; Skeet-style stock, forearm; color case-hardened receiver. Introduced 1970; discontinued 1974.

Perf: $935 **Exc:** $855 **VGood:** $825

FRANCHI FALCONET SUPER

Same specs as Falconet except 12-ga.; 27-inch, 28-inch barrels; translucent front sight; engraved silver finish lightweight alloy receiver; rubber buttplate. Made in Italy. Introduced 1982; discontinued 1986.

Perf: $825 **Exc:** $610 **VGood:** $525

FRANCHI FALCONET TRAP

Same specs as Falconet except 12-ga.; 30-inch Modified/Full choke barrel; wide vent rib; checkered trap-style Monte Carlo stock, forearm; color case-hardened receiver; recoil pad. Introduced 1970; discontinued 1974.

Perf: $935 **Exc:** $855 **VGood:** $825

FRANCHI FALCONET 2000

Over/under; boxlock; 12-ga.; 2-3/4-inch chambers; 26-inch barrels; Improved Cylinder, Modified, Full Franchoke tubes; weighs 6 lbs.; white fluorescent bead front sight; checkered walnut stock; silvered action with gold-plated game scene; single selective trigger; automatic selective ejectors. Made in Italy. Reintroduced 1992; no longer imported.

Perf: $1245 **Exc:** $975 **VGood:** $850

FRANCHI MODEL 2000 SPORTING

Over/under; boxlock; 12-ga.; 2-3/4-inch chambers; 28-inch ported barrels; Skeet, Improved Cylinder, Modified, Full Franchoke tubes; weighs 7 3/4 lbs.; white fluorescent bead front sight; checkered walnut stock; single selective mechanical trigger; automatic selective ejectors; blued action. Made in Italy. Introduced 1992; no longer imported.

Perf: $1275 **Exc:** $1025 **VGood:** $875

FRANCHI MODEL 2003 TRAP

Over/under; boxlock; 12-ga.; 30-inch, 32-inch, Improved Modified/Full, Full/Full barrels; high vent rib; checkered European walnut straight or Monte Carlo stock, beavertail forearm; single selective trigger; auto ejectors; recoil pad; marketed with carrying case. Introduced 1976; discontinued 1982.

Perf: $1150 **Exc:** $1000 **VGood:** $900

FRANCHI MODEL 2004 TRAP

Single barrel; boxlock; 12-ga.; 32-inch, 34-inch, Full choke barrel; high vent rib; checkered European walnut straight or Monte Carlo stock, beavertail forearm; single selective trigger; auto ejectors; recoil pad; marketed with carrying case. Introduced 1976; discontinued 1982.

Perf: $1205 **Exc:** $1090 **VGood:** $1045

FRANCHI MODEL 2005 COMBINATION TRAP

Over/under; boxlock; 12-ga.; incorporates barrels of Model 2003, single barrel of Model 2004 as interchangeable set; high vent rib; checkered European walnut straight or Monte Carlo stock, beavertail forearm; single selective trigger; auto ejectors; recoil pad. Introduced 1976; discontinued 1982.

Perf: $1815 **Exc:** $1595 **VGood:** $1515

FRANCHI MODEL 2005/3 COMBINATION TRAP

Same specs as Model 2005 Combination Trap except three-barrel set incorporating over/under barrels of Model 2003, single barrel of Model 2004. Introduced 1976; discontinued 1982.

Perf: $2420 **Exc:** $2090 **VGood:** $1980

FRANCHI MODEL 3000/2

Over/under; 12-ga.; 30-inch, 32-inch over and 32-inch, 34-inch under barrel; 3 interchangeable choke tubes; high vent rib; checkered European walnut straight or Monte Carlo stock, beavertail forearm; single selective trigger; auto ejectors; recoil pad. Marketed with fitted case. No longer in production.

Perf: $2600 **Exc:** $2200 **VGood:** $1950

FRANCHI PEREGRIN MODEL 400

Over/under; 12-ga.; 26-1/2-inch, 28-inch vent-rib barrels; standard choke combos; checkered European walnut pistol-grip stock, forearm; steel receiver; auto ejectors; selective single trigger. Introduced 1975; no longer in production.

Perf: $660 **Exc:** $605 **VGood:** $570

FRANCHI PEREGRIN MODEL 451

Over/under; 12-ga.; 26 1/2-inch, 28-inch vent-rib barrels; standard choke combos; checkered European walnut pistol-grip stock, forearm; alloy receiver; auto ejectors; selective single trigger. Introduced 1975; no longer in production.

Perf: $605 **Exc:** $550 **VGood:** $525

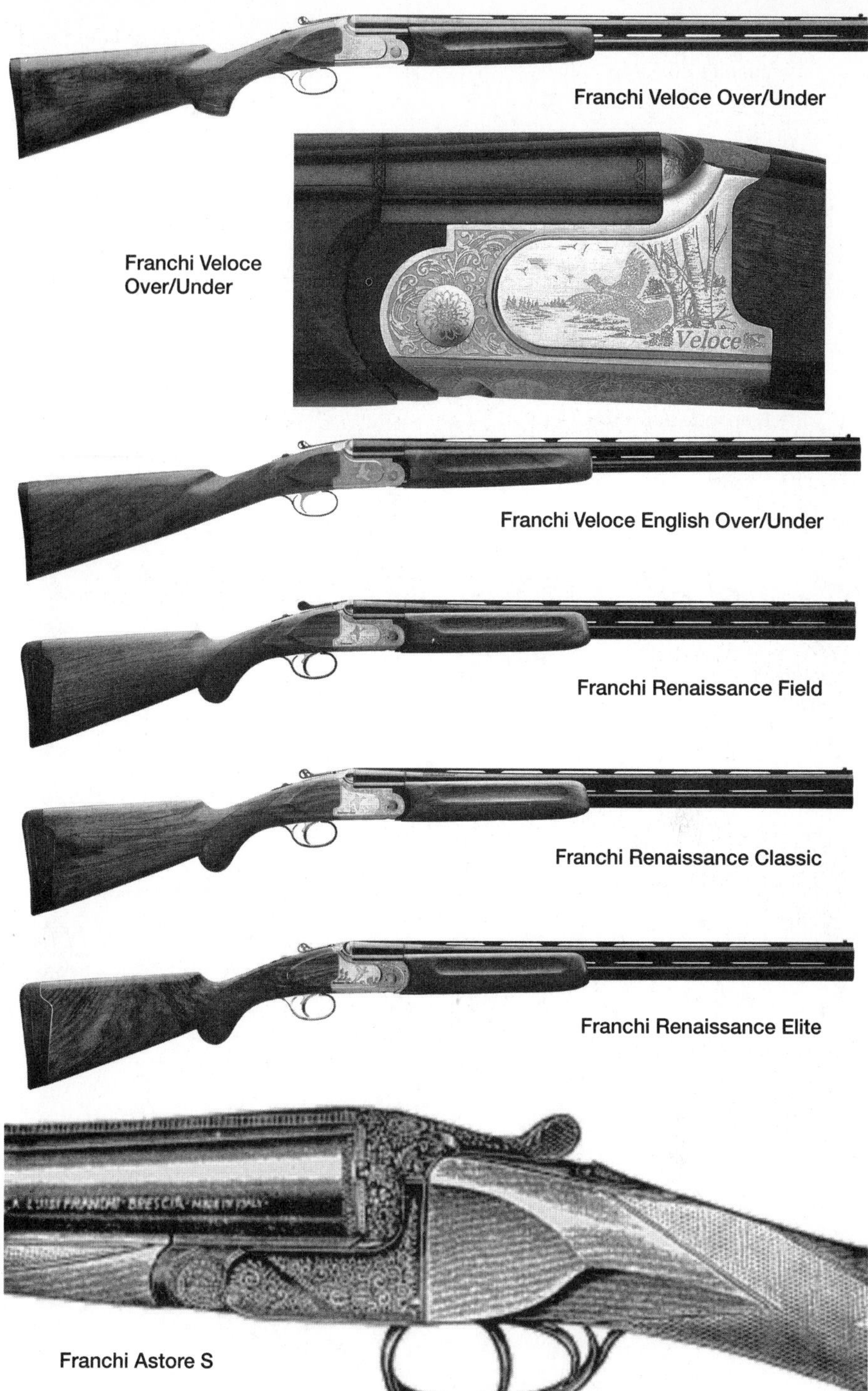

Franchi Veloce Over/Under

Franchi Veloce Over/Under

Franchi Veloce English Over/Under

Franchi Renaissance Field

Franchi Renaissance Classic

Franchi Renaissance Elite

Franchi Astore S

FRANCHI VELOCE OVER/UNDER

Over/under; 20-, 28-ga.; 26-inch, 28-inch barrel; IC, M, F tubes; weighs 5.5 to 5.8 lbs.; 43-inch to 45-inch length; high-grade walnut stock; aluminum receiver with steel reinforcement scaled to 20-gauge for light weight; pistol grip stock with slip recoil pad. Imported by Benelli USA.

Perf: $1250 **Exc:** $1050 **VGood:** $925

28-ga.

Perf: $1325 **Exc:** $1125 **VGood:** $1000

FRANCHI VELOCE ENGLISH OVER/UNDER

Similar to Veloce standard model with straight grip English style stock. Available with 26-inch barrels in 20- and 28-gauge.

Perf: $1250 **Exc:** $1050 **VGood:** $925

28-ga.

Perf: $1325 **Exc:** $1125 **VGood:** $1000

FRANCHI RENAISSANCE FIELD

The Renaissance Series was introduced in 2006. These over-and-unders feature ultra-light alloy receivers, oil-finished walnut stocks, Prince of Wales pistol grips, cut checkering and Twin Shock Absorber recoil pads with gel insert. The 3" 12 and 20 gauges have 26" or 28" barrels; the 28 gauge has a 26" barrel. Weights average 6.2 lbs. in 12 gauge, 5.8 lbs. in 20 gauge and 5.5 lbs. in 28 gauge. Add 5 percent to values shown for 28 gauge.

NIB: $1175 **Exc:** $995 **VGood:** $800

FRANCHI RENAISSANCE CLASSIC

A-Grade walnut with gold inlaid receiver.

NIB: $1250 **Exc:** $1150 **VGood:** $895

FRANCHI RENAISSANCE ELITE

AA-Grade Walnut with gold inlaid receiver.

NIB: $2000 **Exc:** $1700 **VGood:** $1400

FRANCHI RENAISSANCE SPORTING

This 3" 12 gauge model was introduced in 2007. It features a 30" barrel, A-Grade walnut stock, engraved receiver with gold inlay and adjustable comb. Weight is about 7.9 lbs.

NIB: $1750 **Exc:** $1500 **VGood:** $1195

FRANCHI SIDE-BY-SIDE SHOTGUNS FRANCHI AIRONE

Side-by-side; boxlock; 12-ga.; all standard barrel lengths, choke combinations; hand-checkered European walnut straight-grip stock, forearm; automatic ejectors; double triggers. Introduced 1956; special order only; discontinued 1968.

Exc: $1320 **VGood:** $1100 **Good:** $900

FRANCHI ASTORE

Side-by-side; boxlock; 12-ga.; all standard barrel lengths, choke combinations; hand-checkered European walnut straight-grip stock, forearm; plain extractors; double triggers. Introduced 1956; special order only; discontinued 1968.

Exc: $910 **VGood:** $770 **Good:** $715

FRANCHI ASTORE S

Same specs as Astore except high-grade hand-checkered European walnut straight-grip stock, forearm; auto ejectors; fine engraving on frame. No longer in production.

Exc: $1700 **VGood:** $1540 **Good:** $1450

FRANCHI ASTORE II

Same specs as Astore except 27-inch, 28-inch barrels; standard chokes; European walnut pistol-grip stock; plain extractors or auto ejectors; engraving. No longer in production.

Exc: $935 **VGood:** $880 **Good:** $800

FRANCHI CUSTOM SIDELOCK

Side-by-side; 12-, 16-, 20-, 28-ga.; barrel lengths, chokes custom-ordered; hand-checkered European walnut straight or pistol-grip stock, forearm; automatic ejectors; hand-detachable locks; self-opening action; single trigger optional. Made in six grades; variations depending upon quality of wood, amount of engraving, checkering, overall workmanship. For self-opening action, add $75; for single trigger, add $200. Introduced 1956, special order only; discontinued 1968.

Condor

Exc: $6500 **VGood:** $5700 **Good:** $4000

Imperial

Exc: $9000 **VGood:** $7500 **Good:** $6000

Imperial Extra

Exc: $9200 **VGood:** $7900 **Good:** $6500

No. 5 Imperial Monte Carlo

Exc: $12,000 **VGood:** $9500 **Good:** $7500

No. 11 Imperial Monte Carlo

Exc: $12,500 **VGood:** $10,000 **Good:** $9000

Imperial Monte Carlo Extra

Exc: $15,000 **VGood:** $13,000 **Good:** $10,000

FRANCHI SAS-12

Slide action; 12-ga.; 3-inch chamber; 8-shot tube magazine; 21-1/2-inch barrel; synthetic pistol-grip stock; alloy receiver. Introduced 1988; discontinued 1990.

Perf: $415 **Exc:** $360 **VGood:** $300

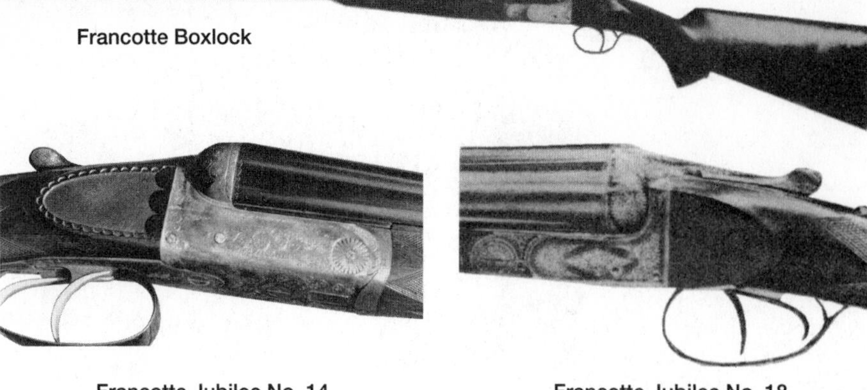

Francotte Boxlock

Francotte Jubilee No. 14

Francotte Jubilee No. 18

Francotte Jubilee No. 20

Francotte Jubilee No. 25

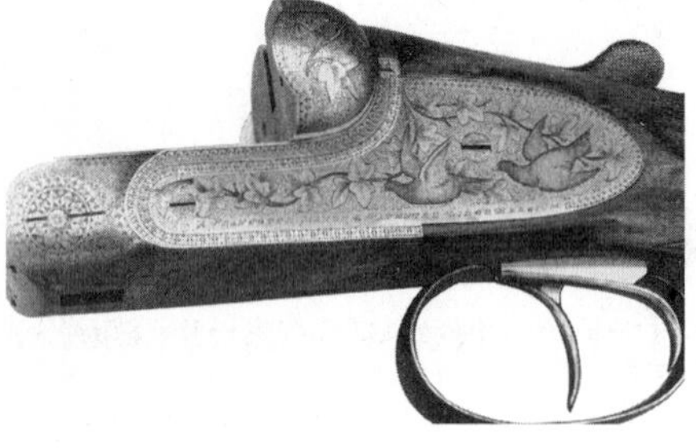

Francotte Jubilee No. 30

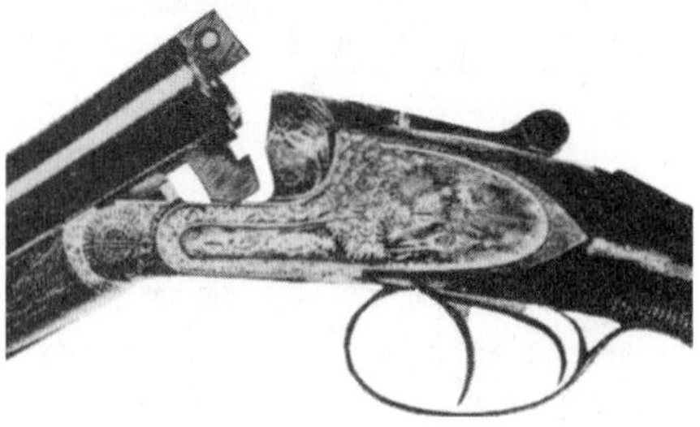

Francotte Jubilee No. 45 Eagle Grade

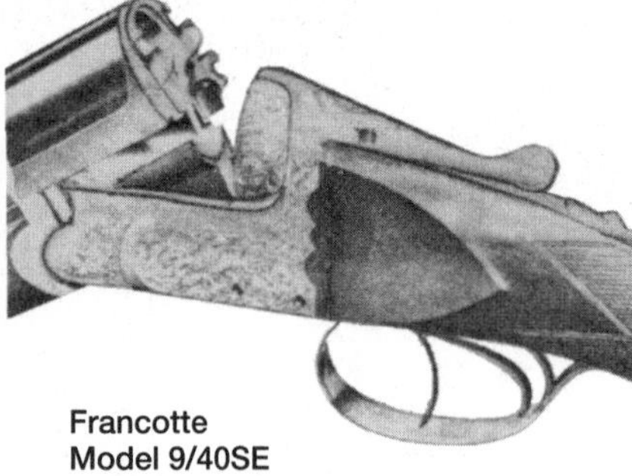

Francotte Model 9/40SE

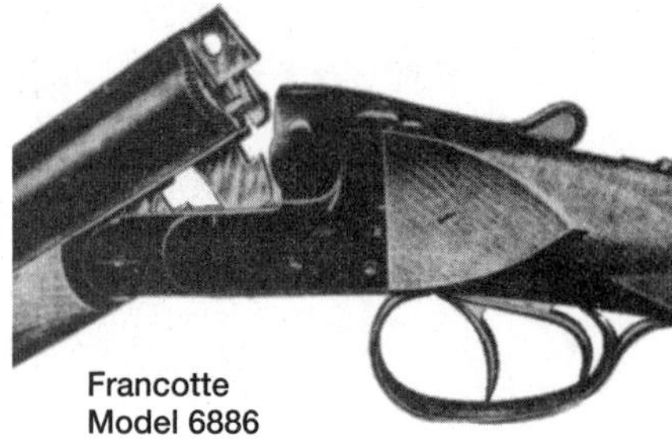

Francotte Model 6886

FRANCOTTE BOXLOCK

Side-by-side; boxlock; 12-, 16-, 20-, 28-ga., .410; 2-3/4-inch, 3-inch chambers; 26-inch to 29-inch barrels; bead front sight; custom deluxe oil-finished European walnut straight or pistol-grip stock, splinter or beavertail forend; checkered butt; double locks, triggers; manual or auto safety; ejectors; English scroll engraving, coin finish or color case-hardening; many custom options. Made in Belgium. Introduced 1989. Considerable premium for small guages.

Perf: $2,650 **Exc:** $1950 **VGood:** $900

FRANCOTTE JUBILEE

Side-by-side; boxlock with sideplates; 12-, 16-, 20-, 28-ga., .410; 2-3/4-inch, 3-inch chambers; customer-specified chokes, triggers and stock style; ejectors; imported in numbered grades 14, 18, 20, 25, 30 and No. 45 Eagle Grade.

No. 14

Exc: $1325 **VGood:** $1100 **Good:** $975

No. 18

Exc: $1925 **VGood:** $1700 **Good:** $1550

No. 20

Exc: $2900 **VGood:** $2525 **Good:** $1950

No. 25

Exc: $3550 **VGood:** $3000 **Good:** $2500

No. 30

Exc: $4975 **VGood:** $4500 **Good:** $4000

No. 45 Eagle Grade

Exc: $5850 **VGood:** $4950 **Good:** $4250

FRANCOTTE KNOCKABOUT

Side-by-side; boxlock; 12-, 16-, 20-, 28-ga., .410; 26-inch to 32-inch (12-ga.), 26-inch to 28-inch barrels in other gauges; any desired choke combo; crossbolt safety; double triggers; ejectors; series was made in several grades for distribution exclusively in this country by Abercrombie & Fitch; grades varied only in overall quality, grade of wood, checkering and engraving. Introduced prior to WWII; discontinued in 1960s. A&F applied the Knockabout name to a different gun imported from Italy.

Exc: $1265 **VGood:** $1100 **Good:** $935

FRANCOTTE MODEL 9/40E/38321

Side-by-side; Anson & Deeley boxlock; sideplates; 12-, 16-, 20-, 28-ga., .410; all standard barrel lengths, choke combos; hand-checkered European walnut stock, straight or pistol-grip design; reinforced frame, side clips; Purdey-type bolt; automatic ejectors; fine English engraving. Introduced about 1950; no longer in production.

Perf: $4200 **Exc:** $3000 **VGood:** $2200

FRANCOTTE MODEL 9/40SE

Over/under; Anson & Deeley boxlock; 12-, 16-, 20-, 28-ga., .410; all standard barrel lengths choke combos; hand-checkered European walnut straight or pistol-grip stock, forearm; automatic ejectors; double triggers; elaborate engraving. Introduced about 1950; no longer in production.

Perf: $8700 **Exc:** $6000 **VGood:** $4800

FRANCOTTE MODEL 10/18E/628

Side-by-side; Anson & Deeley boxlock; 12-, 16-, 20-, 28-ga., .410; all standard barrel lengths, choke combos; hand-checkered European walnut straight or pistol-grip stock, forearm; Purdey-type bolt; Greener crossbolt; side clips; automatic ejectors; double triggers. Manufactured before World War II.

Perf: $3000 **Exc:** $2100 **VGood:** $1650

FRANCOTTE MODEL 11/18E

Side-by-side; Anson & Deeley boxlock; 12-, 16-, 20-, 28-ga., .410; all standard barrel lengths, choke combos; hand-checkered European walnut straight or pistol-grip stock, forearm; Purdey-type bolt; Greener crossbolt; side clips; automatic ejectors; double triggers. Manufactured before World War II.

Perf: $3000 **Exc:** $2100 **VGood:** $1650

FRANCOTTE MODEL 120.HE/328

Side-by-side; sidelock; made in all standard gauges; chokes, barrel lengths to customer's order; hand-checkered European walnut straight or pistol-grip stock, forearm; automatic ejectors; double triggers. Introduced about 1950; no longer in production.

Perf: $8100 **Exc:** $5700 **VGood:** $4450

FRANCOTTE MODEL 4996

Side-by-side; Anson & Deeley boxlock; 12-, 16-, 20-, 28-ga., .410; all standard barrel lengths, choke combinations available; hand-checkered European walnut straight or pistol-grip stock, forearm; Greener crossbolt; side clips; automatic ejectors; double triggers. Manufactured before World War II.

Perf: $2750 **Exc:** $1900 **VGood:** $1500

FRANCOTTE MODEL 6886

Side-by-side; boxlock; 12-, 16-, 20-, 28-ga., .410; all standard barrel lengths, choke combinations available; hand-checkered European walnut straight or pistol-grip stock, forearm; automatic ejectors; double triggers. Manufactured before World War II.

Perf: $2250 **Exc:** $1600 **VGood:** $1250

FRANCOTTE MODEL 6930

Side-by-side; boxlock; 12-, 16-, 20-, 28-ga., .410; all standard barrel lengths, choke combos; hand-checkered European walnut straight or pistol-grip stock, forearm; square crossbolt; automatic ejectors; double triggers. Manufactured before World War II.

Perf: $2350 **Exc:** $1850 **VGood:** $1300

FRANCOTTE MODEL 6982

Side-by-side; Anson & Deeley boxlock; sideplates; 12-, 16-, 20-, 28-ga., .410; all standard barrel lengths, choke combos; hand-checkered European walnut stock, straight or pistol-grip design; reinforced frame, side clips; Purdey-type bolt; automatic ejectors. Introduced about 1950; no longer in production.

Perf: $3125 **Exc:** $2200 **VGood:** $1700

FRANCOTTE MODEL 8446

Side-by-side; boxlock; 12-, 16-, 20-, 28-ga., .410; all standard barrel lengths, choke combinations available; hand-checkered European walnut straight or pistol-grip stock, forearm; Greener crossbolt; side clips; automatic ejectors; double triggers. Manufactured before World War II.

Perf: $2700 **Exc:** $1900 **VGood:** $1500

FRANCOTTE MODEL 8455

Side-by-side; Anson & Deeley boxlock; sideplates; 12-, 16-, 20-, 28-ga., .410; all standard barrel lengths, choke combos; hand-checkered European walnut stock, straight or pistol-grip design; reinforced frame, side clips; Greener crossbolt; Purdey-type bolt; automatic ejectors; engraving. Introduced about 1950; no longer in production.

Perf: $3100 **Exc:** $2200 **VGood:** $1700

FRANCOTTE MODEL 8457

Side-by-side; Anson & Deeley boxlock; 12-, 16-, 20-, 28-ga., .410; all standard barrel lengths, choke combos; hand-checkered European walnut straight or pistol-grip stock, forearm; Greener-Scott crossbolt; side clips; automatic ejectors; double triggers. Manufactured before World War II.

Perf: $3000 **Exc:** $2100 **VGood:** $1700

FRANCOTTE MODEL 9261

Side-by-side; Anson & Deeley boxlock; 12-, 16-, 20-, 28-ga., .410; all standard barrel lengths, choke combos; hand-checkered European walnut straight or pistol-grip stock, forearm; Greener crossbolt; side clips; automatic ejectors; double triggers. Manufactured before World War II.

Perf: $2350 **Exc:** $1650 **VGood:** $1300

FRANCOTTE MODEL 10594

Side-by-side; Anson & Deeley boxlock; sideplates; 12-, 16-, 20-, 28-ga., .410; all standard barrel lengths, choke combos; hand-checkered European walnut stock, straight or pistol-grip design; reinforced frame, side clips; Purdey-type bolt; automatic ejectors. Introduced about 1950; no longer in production.

Perf: $3000 **Exc:** $2100 **VGood:** $1650

FRANCOTTE MODEL SOB.E/11082

Over/under; Anson & Deeley boxlock; 12-, 16-, 20-, 28-ga., .410; all standard barrel lengths, choke combos; hand-checkered European walnut straight or pistol-grip stock, forearm; automatic ejectors; double triggers; engraving. Introduced about 1950; no longer in production.

Perf: $6300 **Exc:** $4400 **VGood:** $3500

FRANCOTTE SIDELOCK

Side-by-side; sidelock; 12-, 16-, 20-, 28-ga., .410; 2-3/4-inch, 3-inch chamber; 26-inch, 29-inch barrel; custom chokes; bead front sight; deluxe oil-finished European walnut straight or pistol-grip stock, splinter or beavertail forend; checkered butt; double intercepting sears; double triggers; ejectors; English scroll engraving, coin finish or color case-hardening; numerous custom options. Made in Belgium. Introduced 1989; imported by Armes de Chasse.

Perf: $24,000 **Exc:** $20,000 **VGood:** $17,500

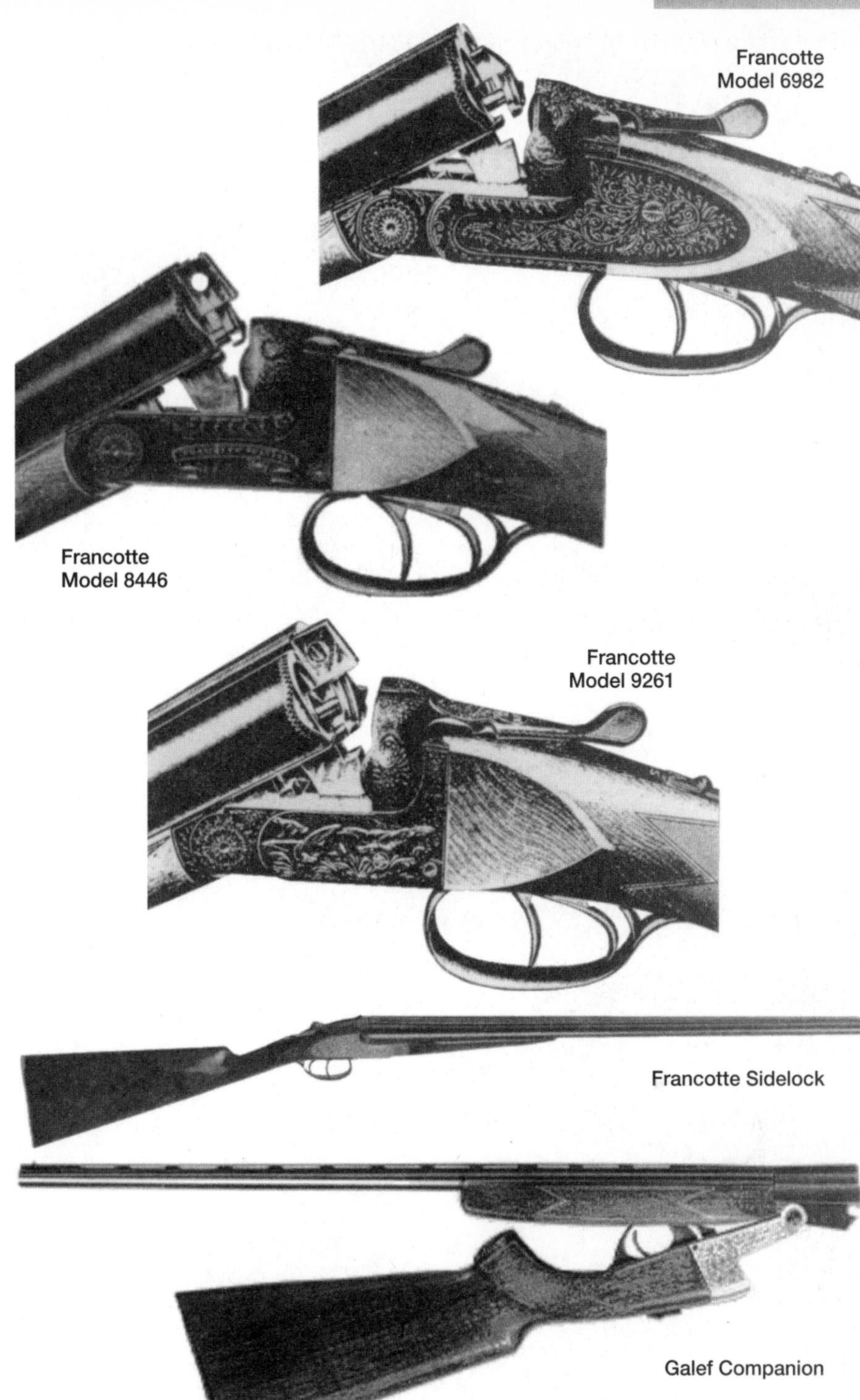

Francotte Model 6982

Francotte Model 8446

Francotte Model 9261

Francotte Sidelock

Galef Companion

GALEF COMPANION

Single shot; 12-, 16-, 20-, 28-ga., .410; 26-inch, 28-inch, 30-inch barrel; plain or vent rib; European walnut pistol-grip stock, forearm; special folding feature. Made in Italy. Introduced 1968; no longer imported.

Exc: $125 **VGood:** $100 **Good:** $85

GALEF MONTE CARLO TRAP

Single shot; underlever; 12-ga.; 32-inch barrel; Full choke; vent rib; checkered European walnut pistol-grip stock, beavertail forearm; extractor; recoil pad. Made in Italy. Introduced 1968; no longer imported.

Exc: $185 **VGood:** $175 **Good:** $150

GALEF/ZABALA

Side-by side; boxlock; 10-, 12-, 16-, 20-, 28-ga., .410; 22-inch (12-ga.) Improved/Modified, 26-inch (12-, 20-, 28-ga.) Improved/Modified or (.410) Modified/Full, 28-inch (10-, 12-, 16-, 20-, 28-ga.) Modified/Full, 30-inch (12-ga.) Modified/Full, 32-inch (10-, 12-ga.) Full/Full barrels; hand-checkered European walnut stock, beavertail forearm; recoil pad; automatic safety; extractors. Made in Spain; no longer in production.

Standard gauges

Exc: $175 **VGood:** $150 **Good:** $130

.410-bore

Exc: $190 **VGood:** $170 **Good:** $140

Galef/Zabala

Galef/Zoli Silver Hawk

Galef/Zoli Silver Snipe

Gamba Daytona

Gamba Daytona Grade 4 Engraving

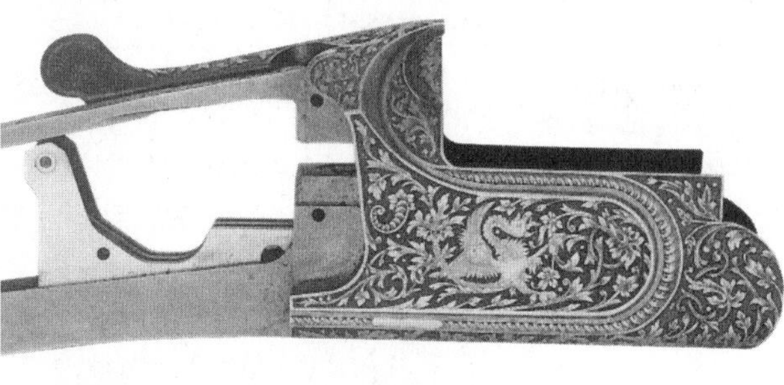

Gamba Daytona Grade 5 Engraving

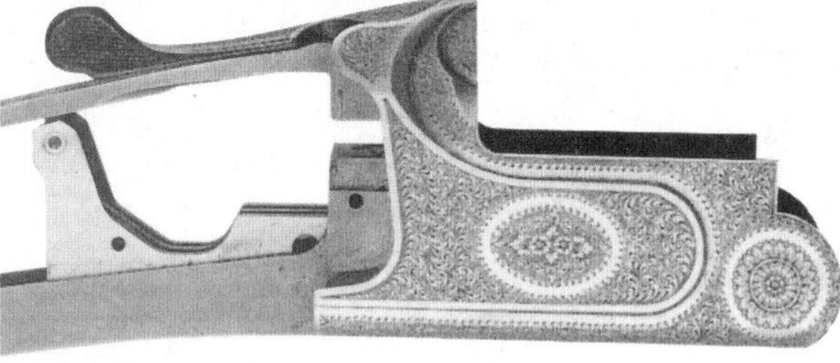

Gamba Daytona Grade 6 Engraving

GALEF/ZOLI GOLDEN SNIPE

Over/under; boxlock; 12-, 20-ga.; 3-inch chambers; 26-inch Improved/Modified, 28-inch Modified/Full, 30-inch Modified/Full (12-ga. only) barrels; vent rib; hand-checkered European walnut pistol-grip stock, forearm; crossbolt safety; automatic safety; automatic selective ejectors; single trigger; chrome-lined barrels. Made in Italy. No longer imported.

Field model

Exc: $400 **VGood:** $300 **Good:** $225

Trap/Skeet models

Exc: $480 **VGood:** $380 **Good:** $310

GALEF/ZOLI SILVER HAWK

Side-by-side; boxlock; 12-, 20-ga.; 3-inch chambers; 26-inch, 28-inch, 30-inch barrels; Improved/Modified, Modified/Full chokes; hand-checkered European walnut pistol-grip stock. Made in Italy. Introduced 1967; discontinued 1972.

Exc: $500 **VGood:** $475 **Good:** $400

GALEF/ZOLI SILVER SNIPE

Over/under; boxlock; 12-, 20-ga.; 3-inch chambers; 26-inch Improved/Modified, 28-inch Modified/Full, 30-inch Modified/Full (12-ga. only) barrels; vent rib; hand-checkered European walnut pistol-grip stock, forearm; crossbolt safety; automatic safety; single trigger; chrome-lined barrels. Made in Italy. No longer imported.

Exc: $500 **VGood:** $475 **Good:** $400

GALEF/ZOLI SILVER SNIPE TRAP

Same specs as Silver Snipe except 30-inch Full/Full barrel; non-automatic safety. No longer imported.

Exc: $395 **VGood:** $295 **Good:** $220

GALEF/ZOLI SILVER SNIPE SKEET

Same specs as Silver Snipe except 26-inch Skeet/Skeet barrels; non-automatic safety. No longer imported.

Exc: $385 **VGood:** $295 **Good:** $220

GAMBA 2100

Slide action; 12-ga.; 7-shot magazine; 20-inch barrel; weighs 7 lbs.; European walnut stock; flat black finish; designed for law enforcement. No longer imported.

Perf: $590 **Exc:** $375 **VGood:** $300

GAMBA AMBASSADOR

Side-by-side; sidelock; 12-, 20-ga.; 2-3/4-inch chamber; 27-1/2-inch barrels; choked to customer's specs; checkered straight English-style root walnut stock; double or single trigger; ejectors; inlaid gold shield in forend; engraved, gold-inlaid blued barrels. Made in Italy. Introduced 1987; discontinued 1987.

Perf: $35,500 **Exc:** $22,500 **VGood:** $15,000

Add $950 to above prices for English scroll engraving

GAMBA AMBASSADOR EXECUTIVE

Same specs as Ambassador except custom built to customer's specs; has better wood; extensive signed engraving. Made in Italy. Introduced 1987; discontinued 1987.

Perf: $47,750 **Exc:** $28,750 **VGood:** $21,250

GAMBA DAYTONA

Over/under; boxlock; 12-, 20-ga.; 2-3/4-inch chambers; 26-3/4-inch, 28-inch, 29-inch, 32-inch barrel; weighs 5-1/2 to 8-1/2 lbs.; European walnut stock in Monte Carlo, traditional, Skeet/Sporting Clays or hunting configuration; interchangeable schnabel, half or full beavertail forend; ejectors; single selective, adjustable or release trigger available. Made in Italy. Introduced 1990. New Daytona series introduced 2000.

Perf: $8500 **Exc:** $6000 **VGood:** $4300

Add $2000 to above prices for Daytona combo package

Add $3700 - $4300 for extra set of barrels

GAMBA DAYTONA SL

Same specs as Daytona except sidelock; cased. Limited importation 1990-1994; reintroduced 2000.

Perf: $26,000 **Exc:** $18000 **VGood:** $11050

GAMBA DAYTONA GRADE 4

Same specs as Daytona, except is the most elaborately engraved number Daytona Model; buyer's choice of fine scroll engraving or eagle panel scene.

Perf: $26,000 **Exc:** $18000 **VGood:** $11050

GAMBA DAYTONA GRADE 5/5E

One grade below Grade 4 in ornamentation.

Perf: $18,000 **Exc:** $15,000 **VGood:** $11,750

GAMBA DAYTONA GRADE 6/6SCE

One grade below Daytona Grade 5 with choice of tight scroll engraving or duck game scene.

Perf: $17,000 **Exc:** $14,000 **VGood:** $10,450

GAMBA DAYTONA GRADE 7

One grade below Grade 6; oval game scene engraving with English scroll around perimeter.

Perf: $16,000 **Exc:** $12,750 **VGood:** $9,750

GAMBA DAYTONA GRADE 8

One grade below Grade 7 with English scroll engraving.

Perf: $14,000 **Exc:** $11,250 **VGood:** $8,950

GAMBA DAYTONA SL HH

Same specs as Daytona except hand-detachable sidelocks; cased.

Perf: $45,500 **Exc:** $30,000 **VGood:** $20,500

GAMBA DAYTONA SL

Over/under; boxlock; 12-ga.; deluxe variation of the Daytona Model; sideplates have extensive engraving; newer manufactured examples have detachable trigger group; includes case. Limited importation 199 to 1994; reintroduced 2000.

Perf: $26,000 **Exc:** $18,000 **VGood:** $11,500

GAMBA DAYTONA GRADE ROYALE

Same features as Daytona SL, except is the top-of-the-line Daytona Model.

Perf: $27,000 **Exc:** $19,750 **VGood:** $12,500

GAMBA DAYTONA GRADE PURDEY

Same features as Daytona SL, except has Purdey locking system.

Perf: $26,000 **Exc:** $19,000 **VGood:** $12,000

GAMBA DAYTONA SLE TIGER

Same features as Daytona SL, except has sideplates engraved with African game scenes.

Perf: $40,500 **Exc:** $27,500 **VGood:** $17,950

GAMBA DAYTONA SLE BEST

Same features as Daytona SL, except has elaborate scroll and 24 Kt. Gold game scene inlays.

Perf: $45,000 **Exc:** $30,000 **VGood:** $20,000

GAMBA DAYTONA SLE VENUS

Same features as Dayton SL, except has elaborate scroll and game scene engraving.

Perf: $41,750 **Exc:** $28,500 **VGood:** $18,750

GAMBA DAYTONA GRADE 1 SL

Same features as Daytona SL, except has elaborate engraving with 24 Kt. Gold game scene engraving.

Perf: $40,000 **Exc:** $26,750 **VGood:** $17,500

GAMBA DAYTONA GRADE 2 SL

Same features as Daytona SL, except has elaborate game scene and scroll engraving without gold inlays.

Perf: $28,250 **Exc:** $21,000 **VGood:** $13,500

GAMBA DAYTONA GRADE 3 SL

Same features as Daytona SL, except has hand engraved sideplates with English scroll and game scenes.

Perf: $26,000 **Exc:** $18,750 **VGood:** $11,750

GAMBA DAYTONA COMPETITION

Over/under; boxlock; 12-, 20-ga.; 2-3/4-inch, 3-inch chambers; 26-3/4-inch Skeet/Skeet, 28-inch Skeet/Skeet, 28-inch Modified/Full (SC model), 30-inch Improved Modified/Full (SC model), 30-inch Improved Modified/Full (trap), 32-inch Modified/Full (trap), 32-inch Full (monotrap) barrels; hand-checkered select walnut stock with oil finish; detachable trigger mechanism; Boss-type locking system; automatic ejectors; anatomical single trigger; optional single selective, release or adjustable trigger; black or chrome frame. Made in Italy. Introduced 1990; still imported.

Trap, 12- or 20-ga.

Perf: $5200 **Exc:** $3200 **VGood:** $2750

Skeet, 12-ga.

Perf: $5250 **Exc:** $3750 **VGood:** $3300

Pigeon, 12-ga.

Perf: $5500 **Exc:** $3500 **VGood:** $3250

Sporting, 12-ga.

Perf: $5800 **Exc:** $3700 **VGood:** $3200

American Trap, 12-ga.

Perf: $5950 **Exc:** $4400 **VGood:** $3850

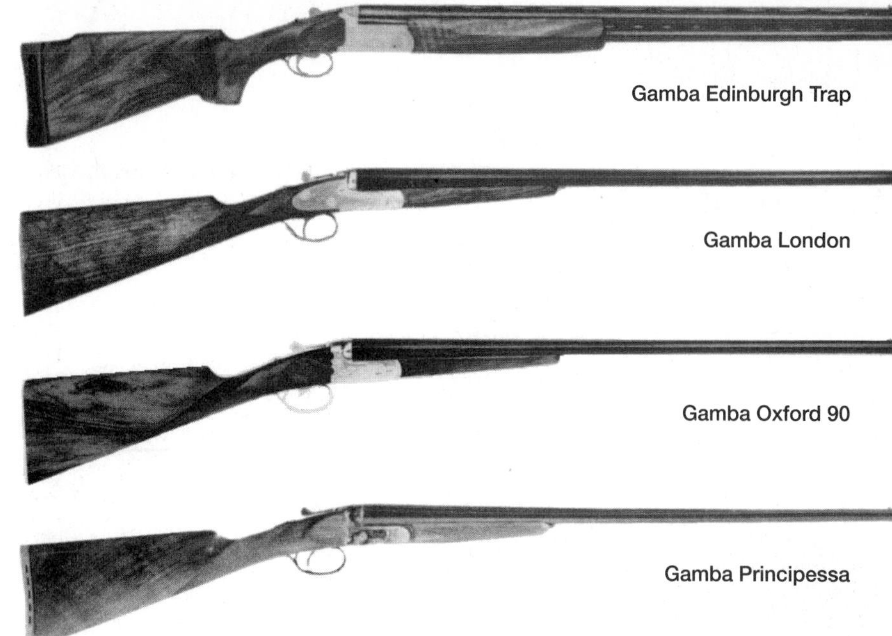

Gamba Edinburgh Trap

Gamba London

Gamba Oxford 90

Gamba Principessa

GAMBA EDINBURGH SKEET

Over/under; 12-ga.; 2-3/4-inch chambers; 26-1/2-inch Skeet/Skeet barrels; European walnut stock with high-gloss lacquer finish; recoil pad; chrome-lined barrels; double vent ribs; single trigger; auto ejectors; scroll border engraving; silver-finished receiver. Made in Italy. Introduced 1980; no longer imported.

Perf: $1450 **Exc:** $1050 **VGood:** $950

GAMBA EDINBURGH TRAP

Same specs as Edinburgh except 30-inch, 32-inch, 34-inch barrels; oil-finished walnut Monte Carlo stock. No longer imported.

Perf: $1450 **Exc:** $1050 **VGood:** $950

GAMBA EUROPA 2000

Over/under; boxlock; 12-ga.; 2-3/4-inch chamber; 27-inch Improved/Modified or Modified/Full barrels; oil-finished, select walnut stock; dummy sideplates; ejectors; anti-recoil buttplate; floral, English engraving patterns. Made in Italy. Introduced 1987; discontinued 1987.

Perf: $1250 **Exc:** $995 **VGood:** $895

GAMBA GRIFONE

Over/under; boxlock; 12-, 20-ga.; 2-3/4-inch chambers; 27-inch Improved/Modified, Modified/Full barrels; weighs 7 lbs.; checkered European walnut stock; ejectors; double or single triggers; silvered receiver engraved game, floral scenes. Made in Italy. Introduced 1987; discontinued 1987.

Perf: $750 **Exc:** $600 **VGood:** $500

GAMBA GRINTA SKEET

Over/under; boxlock; 12-ga.; 2-3/4-inch chambers; 27-inch Skeet/Skeet barrels; weighs 8 lbs.; checkered European walnut Skeet-style stock; ejectors; single selective trigger. No longer imported.

Perf: $1400 **Exc:** $900 **VGood:** $750

GAMBA GRINTA TRAP

Same specs as Grinta Skeet except 29-inch Modified/Full barrels; checkered European walnut trap-style stock. No longer imported.

Perf: $1400 **Exc:** $900 **VGood:** $750

GAMBA HUNTER SUPER

Side-by-side; boxlock; 12-ga.; 2-3/4-inch chambers; 26-3/4-inch Modified/Full, 28-inch Improved/Modified barrels; weighs 6-3/4 lbs.; checkered European walnut stock; double triggers; extractors; silvered, engraved receiver. Made in Italy. Introduced 1987; importation by Armes de Chasse discontinued 1987.

Perf: $1750 **Exc:** $1275 **VGood:** $895

GAMBA LONDON

Side-by-side; sidelock; 12-, 20-ga.; 2-3/4-inch chambers; 26-3/4-inch, 27-1/2-inch barrels; weighs 6-3/4 lbs.; checkered straight English-style root walnut stock; double sear safety; ejectors; double triggers; silvered receiver; fine English-type scroll, rosette engraving. Made in Italy. Originally marketed by Renato Gamba. Introduced 1981; discontinued 1987.

Perf: $8800 **Exc:** $8500 **VGood:** $7000

GAMBA LS2000

Over/under; boxlock; 12-, 20-, 28-ga., .410; 27-1/2-inch Modified/Full barrels; weighs 6-1/4 lbs.; European walnut stock; single trigger extractors; game scene engraving; folding design. Made in Italy. Introduced 1987; discontinued 1987.

Perf: $500 **Exc:** $300 **VGood:** $250

GAMBA MILANO

Single shot; 12-, 16-, 20-, 28-, 32-ga., .410; 27-1/2-inch Full choke barrel; vent rib; weighs 5-3/4 lbs.; checkered European hardwood stock; chromed, photo-engraved receiver; folding design. Made in Italy. Introduced 1987; discontinued 1987.

Perf: $300 **Exc:** $210 **VGood:** $175

GAMBA OXFORD 90

Side-by-side; boxlock with sideplates; 12-, 20-ga.; 26-3/4-inch, 27-1/2-inch barrels; straight English or pistol-grip root walnut stock; double or single trigger auto ejectors; better grade of engraving. Made in Italy. Introduced 1981; discontinued 1987; reintroduced by Heckler & Koch 1990; discontinued 1991.

Perf: $3650 **Exc:** $2700 **VGood:** $2300

GAMBA PRINCIPESSA

Side-by-side; 12-, 20-ga.; 2-3/4-inch chambers; straight English-style walnut stock; double or single trigger; ejectors; fine English-style scroll engraving; silvered receiver. Made in Italy. Introduced 1981; discontinued 1987; reintroduced by Heckler & Koch 1990; discontinued 1991.

Perf: $2750 **Exc:** $1900 **VGood:** $1525

GAMBA VICTORY SKEET

Over/under; boxlock; 12-ga.; 2-3/4-inch chambers; 27-inch Skeet/Skeet barrels; recessed chokes; weighs 7-3/4 lbs.; stippled European walnut Skeet-style stock; removable rubber recoil pad; ejectors; single trigger; blued receiver; light engraving; gold nameplate. Made in Italy. Introduced 1987; discontinued 1987.

Perf: $1450 **Exc:** $1050 **VGood:** $950

Garbi Model 51B

Garbi Model 60A

Garbi Model 71

Garbi Model 100

Garbi Model 102

Garbi Model 101 Engraving

Garbi Model 103A Engraving

Garbi Model 103A

Garbi Model 200

GAMBA VICTORY TRAP

Same specs as Victory Skeet except 29-inch Modified/Full barrels; stippled European walnut trap-style stock. Made in Italy. Introduced 1987; discontinued 1987.

Perf: $1450 **Exc:** $1050 **VGood:** $950

GARBI MODEL 51A

Side-by-side; boxlock; 12-ga.; 2-3/4-inch chambers; 28-inch Modified/Full barrels; hand-checkered European walnut pistol-grip stock, forend; double triggers; extractors; hand-engraved receiver. Made in Spain. Introduced 1980; no longer imported.

Perf: $475 **Exc:** $340 **VGood:** $310

GARBI MODEL 51B

Same specs as Model 51A except 12-, 16-, 20-ga.; automatic ejectors. Introduced 1980; discontinued 1988.

Perf: $800 **Exc:** $540 **VGood:** $500

GARBI MODEL 60A

Side-by-side; sidelock; 12-ga.; 2-3/4-inch chambers; 26-inch, 28-inch, 30-inch barrel; custom chokes; hand-checkered select European walnut custom pistol-grip stock, forend; double triggers; extractors; scroll-engraved receiver. Made in Spain. Introduced 1981; discontinued 1988.

Perf: $735 **Exc:** $550 **VGood:** $495

GARBI MODEL 60B

Same specs as 60A except 12-, 16-, 20-ga.; ejectors; demi-block barrels. Introduced 1981; no longer imported.

Perf: $1150 **Exc:** $800 **VGood:** $700

GARBI MODEL 62A

Side-by-side; sidelock; 12-ga.; 2-3/4-inch chamber; 26-inch-30-inch barrels; Modified/Full chokes; demi-block barrels; gas exhaust valves; extractors; jointed double triggers; plain receiver with engraved border. Made in Spain. Introduced 1981; discontinued 1988.

Perf: $695 **Exc:** $550 **VGood:** $490

GARBI MODEL 62B

Same specs as 62A except 12-, 16-, 20-ga.; ejectors. Introduced 1982; discontinued 1988.

Perf: $1100 **Exc:** $740 **VGood:** $700

GARBI MODEL 71

Side-by-side; hand-detachable sidelock; 12-, 16-, 20-ga.; 26-inch, 28-inch barrels; oil-finished checkered European walnut straight-grip stock, classic forend; ejectors; double triggers; color case-hardened action. Made in Spain. Introduced 1980; discontinued 1988.

Perf: $2100 **Exc:** $1450 **VGood:** $1300

GARBI MODEL 100

Side-by-side; hand-detachable sidelock; 12-, 16-, 20-ga.; 26-inch, 28-inch custom-choked barrels; checkered European walnut straight-grip stock, classic forend; ejectors; double triggers; forged barrel lumps; color case-hardened action; numerous options. Made in Spain. Introduced 1986; still imported.

Perf: $4750 **Exc:** $3800 **VGood:** $3250

GARBI MODEL 100 DOUBLE

Side-by-side; sidelock; 12-, 16-, 20-, 28-ga.; 26-inch, 28-inch barrel choked to customer specs.; weighs 5-1/2 to 7-1/2 lbs.; European walnut stock, straight grip, checkered butt, classic forend; automatic ejectors; double triggers standard; color case-hardened action; coin finish optional; single trigger; beavertail forend, etc. optional. Five other models are available. Imported from Spain by Wm. Larkin Moore.

Perf: $4800 **Exc:** $3850 **VGood:** $3250

GARBI MODEL 101

Side-by-side; hand-detachable sidelock; 12-, 16- , 20-ga.; file-cut Churchill or vent top rib; select European walnut stock; ejectors; Continental-style floral, scroll engraving; 12-ga. pigeon or wildfowl designs available; better quality than Model 71.

Perf: $6200 **Exc:** $4900 **VGood:** $4100

GARBI MODEL 102

Side-by-side; 12-, 16-, 20-, 28-ga.; 25-inch to 30-inch barrels; standard chokes; select European walnut stock; Holland sidelock ejector; chopper lump barrels; scroll engraving; hinged double triggers; non-selective single trigger optional; other options. Made in Spain. Introduced 1982; dropped 1988. Was imported by Wm. Larkin Moore, L. Joseph Rahn.

Perf: $4500 **Exc:** $4000 **VGood:** $3000

GARBI MODEL 103A

Side-by-side; 12-, 16-, 20-ga.; 25-inch to 30-inch barrels; chopper lump barrels; select European walnut stock; ejectors; hinged double triggers; non-selective single trigger optional; Purdey-type scroll, rosette engraving. Made in Spain. Introduced 1982.

Perf: $8000 **Exc:** $6300 **VGood:** $4890

GARBI MODEL 103B

Same specs as 103 except Holland & Holland-type assisted-opening mechanism; nickel-chrome steel barrels. Introduced 1982.

Perf: $11,800 **Exc:** $8850 **VGood:** $7100

GARBI MODEL 103B ROYAL

Same specs. as the 103B, except is a deluxe variation with engraving similar to the H&H Royal style; extra fancy walnut stock; gold oval stock plate; matted concave rib.

Perf: $15,800 **Exc:** $12,300 **VGood:** $10,000

GARBI MODEL 110

Side-by-side; sidelock; 12-, 20-, 28-ga.; barrel lengths, chokes, stocks to custom order. Made in Spain. Introduced 1982 by Toledo Armas; discontinued 1984.

Perf: $7300 **Exc:** $4500 **VGood:** $4000

GARBI MODEL 200

Side-by-side; sidelock; 12-, 16-, 20-, 28-ga.; 26-inch, 28-inch chopper-lump, nickel-chrome steel barrels; finely figured European walnut stock; ejectors; double triggers; heavy-duty locks; Continental-style floral, scroll engraving. Made in Spain. Introduced 1982; still imported.

Perf: $11,200 **Exc:** $8300 **VGood:** $6350

GARBI MODEL 300

Side-by-side; sidelock; 12-, 20-, 28-ga.; barrel lengths, chokes, stocks to custom order; engraving. Made in Spain. No longer imported.

Perf: $8900 **Exc:** $6500 **VGood:** $5000

GARBI SPECIAL MODEL

Side-by-side; sidelock; 12-, 16-, 20-, 28-ga.; 26-inch, 28-inch barrels; fancy European walnut stock; ejectors; game scene engraved in receiver some with gold inlays; top quality metalwork, wood. Made in Spain. Introduced 1982; discontinued 1988.

Perf: $7600 **Exc:** $5000 **VGood:** $4100

GARCIA BRONCO

Single shot; swing-out action; takedown; .410; 18-1/2-inch barrel; weighs 3-1/2 lbs.; one-piece metal frame skeletonized stock, receiver; crinkle finish. Made in USA by Firearms International; later bought by Garcia. Introduced 1968; discontinued 1978.

Perf: $350 **Exc:** $325 **VGood:** $295

GARCIA BRONCO .22/.410

Over/under combo; swing-out action; takedown; 22 LR over, .410 under, 18 1/2-inch barrel; one-piece metal frame stock, receiver; crinkle finish. Introduced 1976; discontinued 1978.

Perf: $325 **Exc:** $300 **VGood:** $285

GOLDEN EAGLE MODEL 5000 GRADE I FIELD

Over/under; boxlock; 12-, 20-ga.; 2-3/4-inch, 3-inch chambers; 26-inch, 28-inch, 30-inch barrels; Improved/Modified, Modified/Full chokes; vent rib; checkered walnut pistol-grip stock, semi-beavertail forearm; selective single trigger; auto ejectors; engraved receiver; gold eagle head inlaid in frame. Made in Japan. Introduced 1975; discontinued 1980.

Perf: $850 **Exc:** $775 **VGood:** $700

GOLDEN EAGLE MODEL 5000 GRADE II FIELD

Same specs as Model 5000 Grade I Field except more elaborate engraving; spread-wing eagle inlaid in gold; fancier wood. Introduced 1975; discontinued 1980.

Perf: $950 **Exc:** $875 **VGood:** $790

GOLDEN EAGLE MODEL 5000 GRADE I TRAP

Same specs as Model 5000 Grade I Field except 30-inch, 32-inch barrels; Modified/Full, Improved Modified/Full, Full/Full choke; wide vent rib; trap-style stock; recoil pad. Introduced 1975; discontinued 1980.

Perf: $875 **Exc:** $800 **VGood:** $725

GOLDEN EAGLE MODEL 5000 GRADE II TRAP

Same specs as Model 5000 Grade I Field except 30-inch, 32-inch barrels; Modified/Full, Improved Modified/Full, Full/Full choke; wide vent rib; vent side ribs; trap-style stock; recoil pad; more elaborate engraving; spread-wing eagle gold inlay; inertia trigger; fancier wood. Introduced 1975; discontinued 1980.

Perf: $975 **Exc:** $895 **VGood:** $810

GOLDEN EAGLE MODEL 5000 GRADE I SKEET

Same specs as Model 5000 Grade I Field except 26-inch, 28-inch Skeet/Skeet barrels; vent rib. Introduced 1975; discontinued 1980.

Perf: $875 **Exc:** $800 **VGood:** $725

GOLDEN EAGLE MODEL 5000 GRADE II SKEET

Same specs as Model 5000 Grade I Field except 26-inch, 28-inch Skeet/Skeet barrels; vent rib; vent side ribs; more elaborate engraving; spread-wing eagle gold inlay; inertia trigger; fancier wood. Introduced 1975; discontinued 1980.

Perf: $975 **Exc:** $895 **VGood:** $810

Garcia Bronco

Garcia Bronco 22/410

Golden Eagle Model 5000 Grade II Field

Golden Eagle Model 5000 Grade III Trap

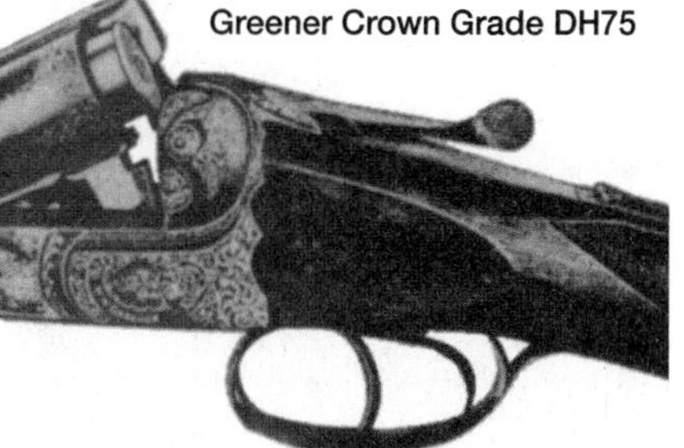

Greener Crown Grade DH75

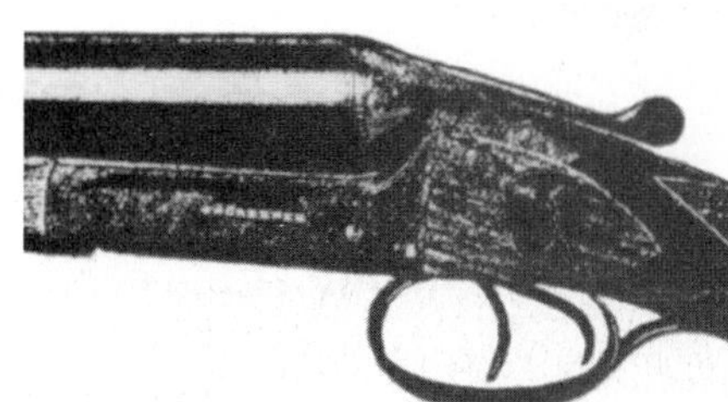

Greener Empire

GOLDEN EAGLE MODEL 5000 GRADE III

Same specs as Grade I Field except game scene engraving; scroll-engraved frame, barrels, sideplates; fancy wood; available in Field, Trap and Skeet versions; Trap model has Monte Carlo comb, full pistol grip, recoil pad. Introduced 1976; discontinued 1980.

Field version

Perf: $2250 **Exc:** $1900 **VGood:** $1600

Trap/Skeet versions

Perf: $2200 **Exc:** $1800 **VGood:** $1500

GOROSABEL 501

Side-by-side; boxlock; 12-, 16-, 20-, 28-ga., .410; 26-inch, 27-inch, 28-inch barrels; standard choke combos; hand-checkered select walnut English or pistol-grip stock, splinter or beavertail forend; ejectors. Introduced 1986; discontinued 1988.

Perf: $700 **Exc:** $590 **VGood:** $500

GOROSABEL 502

Side-by-side; boxlock; 12-, 16-, 20-, 28-ga.,.410; 26-inch, 27-inch, 28-inch barrels; standard choke combos; hand-checkered English or pistol-grip select walnut stock, splinter or beavertail forend; ejectors; engraving. Introduced 1986; discontinued 1988.

Perf: $890 **Exc:** $790 **VGood:** $700

GOROSABEL 503

Side-by-side; boxlock; 12-, 16-, 20-, 28-ga., .410; 26-inch, 27-inch, 28-inch barrels; standard choke combos; hand-checkered fancy walnut English or pistol-grip stock; splinter or beavertail forend; ejectors; scalloped frame; scroll engraving. Introduced 1986; discontinued 1988.

Perf: $1000 **Exc:** $850 **VGood:** $750

GOROSABEL BLACKPOINT

Side-by-side; sidelock; 12-, 20-ga.; 2-3/4-inch, 3-inch chambers; 26-inch, 27-inch, 28-inch barrels; standard choke combos; hand-checkered select European walnut stock, splinter or beavertail forend; Purdey-style scroll, rose engraving; numerous options. Made in Italy. Introduced 1986, discontinued 1988.

Perf: $1550 **Exc:** $1200 **VGood:** $1000

GOROSABEL SILVERPOINT

Side-by-side; sidelock; 12-, 20-ga.; 2-3/4-inch, 3-inch chambers; 26-inch, 27-inch, 28-inch barrels; standard choke combos; hand-checkered European walnut stock, splinter or beavertail forend; large scroll engraving. Made in Italy. Introduced 1986, discontinued 1988.

Perf: $1000 **Exc:** $800 **VGood:** $700

Note: On all variations, add $175 for non-selective single trigger; $350 for selective trigger.

GREENER CROWN GRADE DH75

Side-by-side; boxlock; 12-, 16-, 20-ga.; 26-inch, 28-inch, 30-inch barrels; any choke combo; top-quality hand-checkered European walnut straight or pistol-grip stock, forearm; Greener crossbolt; ejectors; double triggers; non-selective or selective single trigger at added cost; best-grade engraved action. Introduced 1875; discontinued 1965.

Exc: $8200 **VGood:** $6975 **Good:** $5350

GREENER EMPIRE

Side-by-side; boxlock; 12-ga.; 28-inch, 30-inch, 32-inch barrels; any choke combo; hand-checkered European walnut straight or half-pistol-grip stock, forearm; non-ejector; ejectors at additional cost. Introduced about 1893; discontinued 1962.

Exc: $1760 **VGood:** $1540 **Good:** $1300

Add approximately $200 to above prices for auto. ejectors.

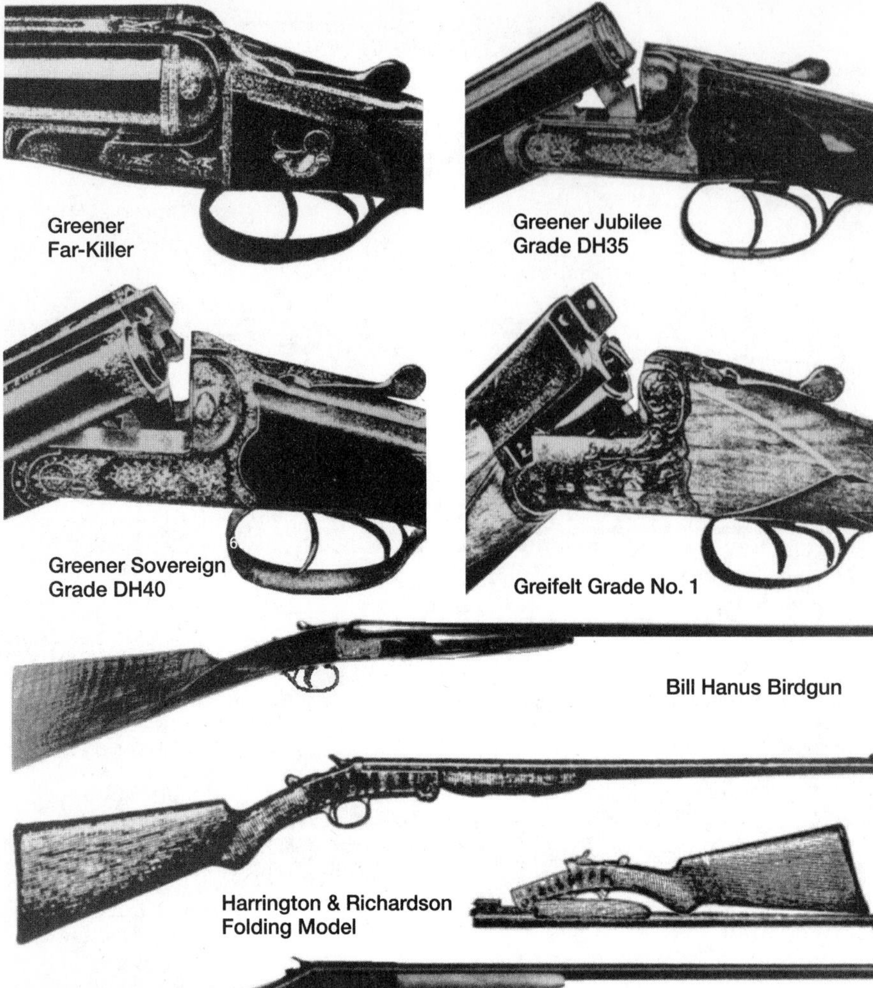
Greener Far-Killer

Greener Jubilee Grade DH35

Greener Sovereign Grade DH40

Greifelt Grade No. 1

Bill Hanus Birdgun

Harrington & Richardson Folding Model

Harrington & Richardson Model 088

GREENER EMPIRE DELUXE

Same specs as Empire except deluxe finish and better craftsmanship.

Exc: $1850 **VGood:** $1660 **Good:** $1500

GREENER FAR-KILLER

Side-by-side; boxlock; 12-, 10-, 8-ga.; 28-inch, 30-inch, 32-inch barrels; any desired choke combination; hand-checkered European walnut straight or half-pistol-grip stock; non-ejectors; automatic ejectors at added cost. Introduced about 1895; discontinued 1962.

12-ga.

Exc: $2300 **VGood:** $1900 **Good:** $1650

10-, 8-ga.

Exc: $2500 **VGood:** $2100 **Good:** $1790

Add approximately $800 to above prices for auto. ejectors.

GREENER GENERAL PURPOSE

Single shot; Martini-type action; takedown; 12-ga.; 26-inch, 30-inch, 32-inch barrel; Modified, Full choke; hand-checkered European walnut straight-grip stock, forearm; ejector. Introduced 1910; discontinued 1964. Subtract 25 percent for 14-ga. police model (shells very rare).

Exc: $400 **VGood:** $325 **Good:** $250

GREENER JUBILEE GRADE DH35

Side-by-side; boxlock; 12-, 16-, 20-ga.; 26-inch, 28-inch, 30-inch barrels; any choke combo; hand-checkered European walnut straight or pistol-grip stock, forearm; Greener crossbolt; ejectors; double triggers; non-selective or selective single trigger at added cost; engraved action. Introduced 1875; discontinued 1965.

Exc: $2400 **VGood:** $1700 **Good:** $1550

GREENER SOVEREIGN GRADE DH40

Side-by-side; boxlock; 12-, 16-, 20-ga.; 26-inch, 28-inch, 30-inch barrels; any choke combo; hand-checkered select European walnut straight or pistol-grip stock, forearm; Greener crossbolt; ejectors; double triggers; non-selective or selective single trigger at added cost; engraved action. Introduced 1875; discontinued 1965.

Exc: $2500 **VGood:** $2000 **Good:** $1895

GREIFELT GRADE NO. 1

Over/under; boxlock; 12-, 16-, 20-, 28-ga., .410; 26-inch, 28-inch, 30-inch, 32-inch barrels; any desired choke combo; solid matted rib standard; vent rib at added cost; hand-checkered European walnut straight or pistol-grip stock; ejectors; double triggers; single trigger at added cost; elaborate engraving. Made in Germany prior to World War II.

Solid rib

Exc: $2850 **VGood:** $2100 **Good:** $1750

Vent rib

Exc: $3100 **VGood:** $2350 **Good:** $2000

.410-bore or 28 ga.

Exc: $3650 **VGood:** $2650 **Good:** $2400

Add approximately $400 to above prices for SST. Subtract about 10 percent from above prices for 16 ga.

GREIFELT GRADE NO. 3

Over/under; boxlock; 12-, 16-, 20-, 28-ga., .410; 26-inch, 28-inch, 30-inch, 32-inch barrels; any desired choke combo; solid matted rib standard; vent rib at added cost; hand-checkered European walnut straight or pistol-grip stock; ejectors; double triggers; single trigger at added cost; engraving. Made in Germany prior to World War II.

Solid rib

Exc: $2250 **VGood:** $1650 **Good:** $1250

Vent rib

Exc: $2400 **VGood:** $1850 **Good:** $1450

.410-bore or 28 ga.

Exc: $2500 **VGood:** $1900 **Good:** $1500

Add about $400 to above prices for SST.
Subtract about 10 percent from above prices for 16 ga.

GREIFELT MODEL 22

Side-by-side; boxlock; 12-, 20-ga.; 28-inch, 30-inch barrels; Modified/Full choke; hand-checkered straight English or pistol-grip stock, forend; cheekpiece; plain extractors; double triggers; sideplates. Introduced about 1950; no longer in production.

Exc: $1760 **VGood:** $1595 **Good:** $1320

GREIFELT MODEL 22E

Same specs as Model 22 except ejectors. Introduced about 1950; no longer in production.

Exc: $2200 **VGood:** $1950 **Good:** $1700

GREIFELT MODEL 103

Side-by-side; boxlock; 12-, 16-ga.; 28-inch, 30-inch barrels; Modified/Full chokes; hand-checkered European walnut straight English or pistol-grip stock, forearm; extractors; double triggers. Introduced about 1950; no longer in production.

Exc: $1650 **VGood:** $1485 **Good:** $1210

GREIFELT MODEL 103E

Same specs as Model 103 except ejectors. Introduced about 1950; no longer in production.

Exc: $1760 **VGood:** $1595 **Good:** $1320

GREIFELT MODEL 143E

Over/under; boxlock; 12-, 16-, 20-ga.; 26-inch, 28-inch, 30-inch barrels; any desired choke; solid or vent rib; hand-checkered European walnut straight or pistol-grip stock; single or double trigger; engraved; post-WWII version of the Grade I but of lower quality. Introduced about 1950. No longer imported.

Exc: $2150 **VGood:** $1850 **Good:** $1550

BILL HANUS BIRDGUN

Side-by-side; boxlock; 16-, 20-, 28-ga.; 26-inch Skeet/Skeet barrels; weighs 6-1/4 lbs. (12-ga.); hand-checkered straight-grip walnut stock, semi-beavertail forend; single non-selective trigger; raised Churchill rib; auto safety; ejectors; color case-hardened action. Made in Spain. Introduced 1991; still imported.

Perf: $1800 **Exc:** $1450 **VGood:** $950

HARRINGTON & RICHARDSON FOLDING MODEL

Single barrel; 12-, 16-, 20-, 28-ga. or .410 with 26-inch barrel (Heavy Frame model); 28-ga., .410 with 22-inch barrel (Light Frame model); Full choke; bead front sight; checkered pistol-grip stock, forearm; gun is hinged at front of frame so barrel folds against stock for storage, transport. Introduced about 1910; discontinued 1942.

Exc: $175 **VGood:** $150 **Good:** $125

Add about 75 percent to above prices for 28 ga. or .410 bore

HARRINGTON & RICHARDSON MODEL 088

Single shot; sidelever; external hammer; takedown; 12-, 16-, 20-, 28-ga., .410; 26-inch, 28-inch, 30-inch, 32-inch, 36-inch barrels; walnut-finished hardwood semi-pistol-grip stock; auto ejector; case-hardened frame. No longer in production.

Exc: $85 **VGood:** $75 **Good:** $55

HARRINGTON & RICHARDSON MODEL 088 JUNIOR

Same specs as Model 088 except 20-ga., .410; 25-inch Modified (20-ga.) or Full (.410) choke barrel; stock dimensions for smaller shooters.

Exc: $75 **VGood:** $60 **Good:** $50

HARRINGTON & RICHARDSON MODEL 099 DELUXE

Single shot; 12-, 16-, 20-ga., .410; 2-3/4-inch, 3-inch chamber; 25-inch, 26-inch, 28-inch barrel; bead front sight; walnut-finished hardwood semi-pistol-grip stock, semi-beavertail forend; electroless matte nickel finish. Introduced 1982; discontinued 1985.

Perf: $85 **Exc:** $60 **VGood:** $50

HARRINGTON & RICHARDSON MODEL 159 GOLDEN SQUIRE

Single barrel; exposed hammer; 12-, 20-ga.; 28-inch (20-ga.), 30-inch (12-ga.) barrel; Full choke; bead front sight; uncheckered hardwood straight-grip stock, schnabel forearm. Introduced 1964; discontinued 1966.

Exc: $75 **VGood:** $65 **Good:** $55

HARRINGTON & RICHARDSON MODEL 162 SLUG GUN

Single barrel; sidelever break-open; exposed hammer; takedown; 12-, 20-ga.; 3-inch chamber; 24-inch Cylinder choke barrel; rifle sights; uncheckered hardwood pistol-grip stock, forend; recoil pad. Introduced 1968; discontinued 1985.

Perf: $105 **Exc:** $85 **VGood:** $75

HARRINGTON & RICHARDSON MODEL 176

Single shot; sidelever break-open; exposed hammer; takedown; 10-, 12-ga.; 3-inch, 3-1/2-inch chamber; 32-inch, 36-inch heavy barrel; Full choke; weighs 9-1/4 lbs.; bead front sight; uncheckered hardwood pistol-grip stock, special long forend; recoil pad. Introduced 1978; discontinued 1985.

Perf: $110 **Exc:** $85 **VGood:** $65

HARRINGTON & RICHARDSON MODEL 176 SLUG GUN

Same specs as Model 176 except 10-ga. rifled slugs; 3-1/2-inch chamber; 28-inch Cylinder barrel; weighs 9-1/4 lbs.; ramp front sight, folding leaf rear; uncheckered hardwood pistol-grip stock, magnum-type forend; recoil pad; sling swivels. Introduced 1982; discontinued 1985.

Perf: $125 **Exc:** $95 **VGood:** $80

HARRINGTON & RICHARDSON MODEL 348 GAMESTER

Bolt action; takedown; 12-, 16-ga.; 2-shot tube magazine; 28-inch barrel; Full choke; uncheckered hardwood pistol-grip stock, forearm. Introduced 1949; discontinued 1954.

Exc: $95 **VGood:** $75 **Good:** $50

HARRINGTON & RICHARDSON MODEL 349 GAMESTER DELUXE

Bolt action; takedown; 12-, 16-ga.; 2-shot tube magazine; 26-inch barrel; adjustable choke device; uncheckered hardwood pistol-grip stock, forearm; recoil pad. Introduced 1953; discontinued 1955.

Exc: $100 **VGood:** $85 **Good:** $60

HARRINGTON & RICHARDSON MODEL 351 HUNTSMAN

Bolt action; takedown; 12-, 16-ga.; 2-shot tube magazine; 26-inch barrel; adjustable choke device; uncheckered American hardwood Monte Carlo stock; recoil pad; push-button safety. Introduced 1956; discontinued 1958.

Exc: $95 **VGood:** $75 **Good:** $55

HARRINGTON & RICHARDSON MODEL 400

Slide action; hammerless; 12-, 16-, 20-ga.; 5-shot tube magazine; 28-inch Full choke barrel; uncheckered pistol-grip stock, grooved slide handle; recoil pad (12-, 16-ga. only). Introduced 1955; discontinued 1967.

Exc: $145 **VGood:** $125 **Good:** $110

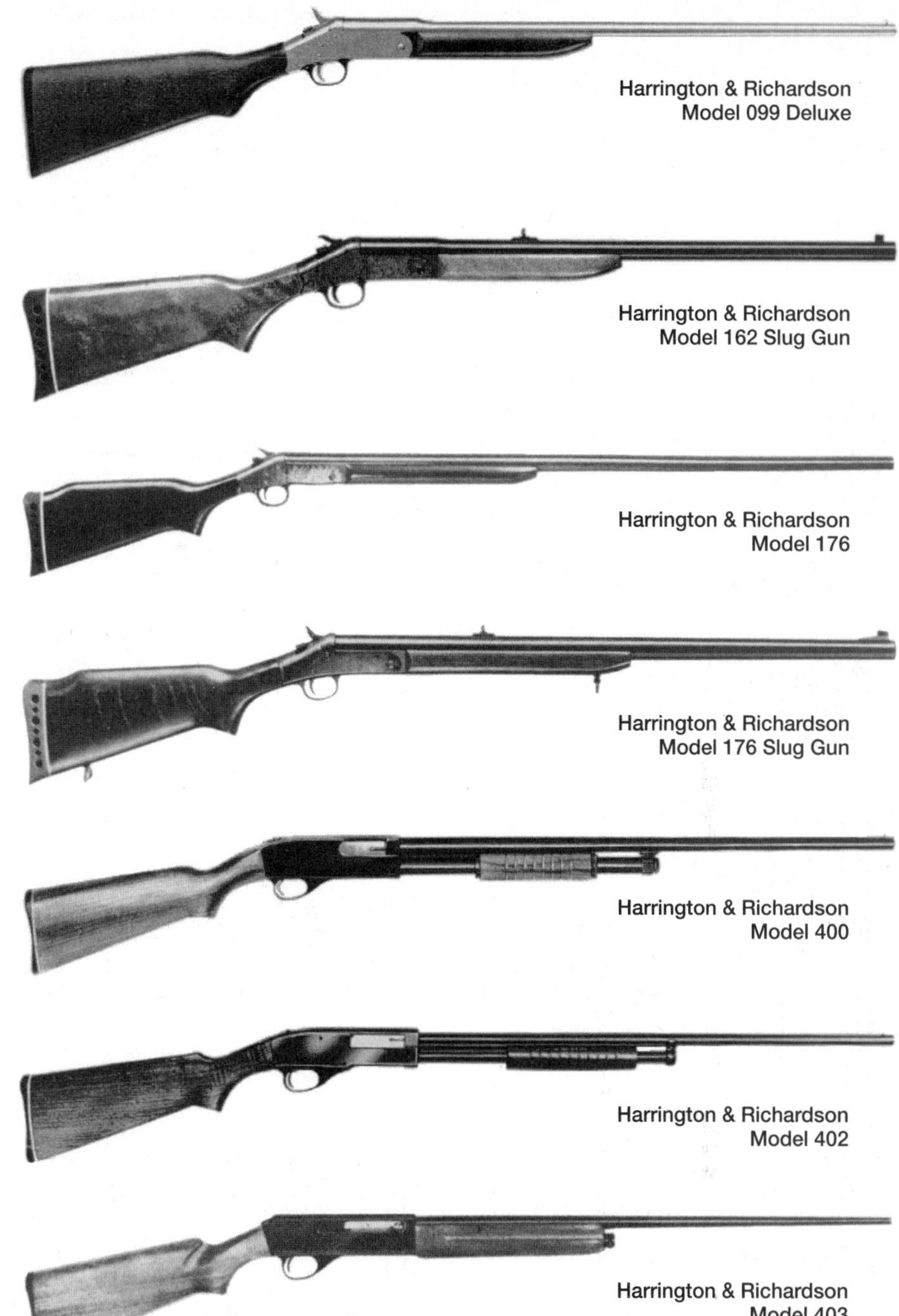

Harrington & Richardson Model 099 Deluxe

Harrington & Richardson Model 162 Slug Gun

Harrington & Richardson Model 176

Harrington & Richardson Model 176 Slug Gun

Harrington & Richardson Model 400

Harrington & Richardson Model 402

Harrington & Richardson Model 403

HARRINGTON & RICHARDSON MODEL 401

Slide action; hammerless; 12-, 16-, 20-ga.; 5-shot tube magazine; 28-inch barrel; adjustable choke device; uncheckered pistol-grip stock, grooved slide handle; recoil pad (12-, 16-ga. only). Introduced 1956; discontinued 1963.

Exc: $155 **VGood:** $140 **Good:** $120

HARRINGTON & RICHARDSON MODEL 402

Slide action; hammerless; .410; 5-shot tube magazine; 28-inch Full choke barrel; uncheckered pistol-grip stock, grooved slide handle; recoil pad (12-, 16-ga. only). Introduced 1959; discontinued 1963. Premium for .410.

Exc: $175 **VGood:** $125 **Good:** $95

HARRINGTON & RICHARDSON MODEL 403

Autoloader; takedown; .410; 4-shot tube magazine; 26-inch barrel; Full choke; uncheckered walnut pistol-grip stock, forearm. Introduced 1964; discontinued 1964.

Exc: $375 **VGood:** $325 **Good:** $260

HARRINGTON & RICHARDSON MODEL 404

Side-by-side; boxlock; 12-, 20-ga., .410; 25-inch Full/Full (.410), 26-inch Modified/Improved (20-ga.), 28-inch Modified/Full (12-ga.) barrels; checkered hardwood pistol-grip stock, forearm; double triggers; plain extractors. Made to H&R specifications in Brazil. Introduced 1968; discontinued 1972.

Exc: $315 **VGood:** $265 **Good:** $245

Harrington & Richardson Model 404

Harrington & Richardson Model 440

Harrington & Richardson Model 442

Harrington & Richardson Model 1212

Harrington & Richardson Model 1212 Waterfowler

Harrington & Richardson No. 1 Harrich

Harrington & Richardson No. 3

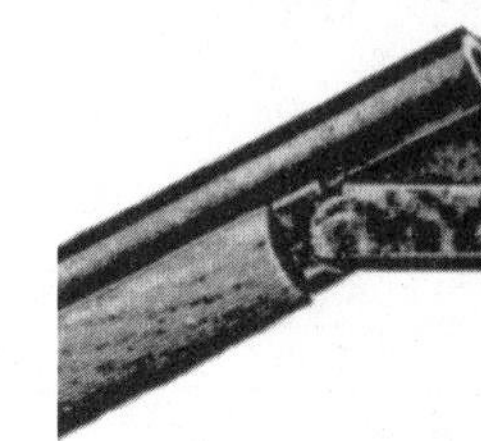

Harrington & Richardson No. 5

Harrington & Richardson No. 6

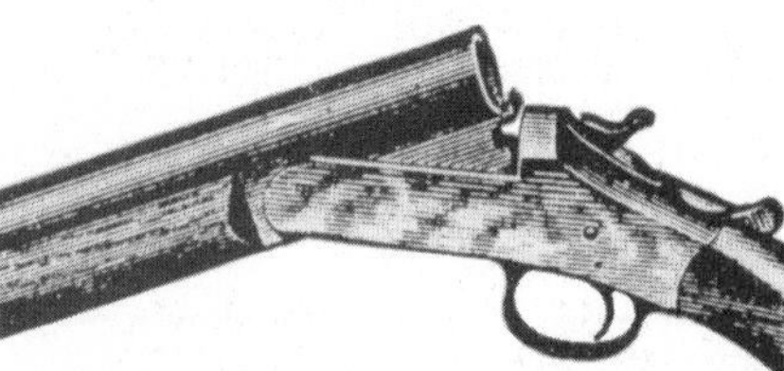

Harrington & Richardson No. 7 Bay State

Harrington & Richardson No. 8

HARRINGTON & RICHARDSON MODEL 404C

Same specs as Model 404 except Monte Carlo stock. No longer in production.

Exc: $325 **VGood:** $275 **Good:** $255

HARRINGTON & RICHARDSON MODEL 440

Slide action; hammerless; 12-, 16-, 20-ga.; 4-shot magazine; 24-inch, 26-inch, 28-inch barrel; standard chokes; uncheckered American walnut pistol-grip stock, forend; recoil pad; slide ejection. Introduced 1972; discontinued 1975.

Exc: $250 **VGood:** $230 **Good:** $180

HARRINGTON & RICHARDSON MODEL 442

Slide action; hammerless; 12-, 16-, 20-ga.; 4-shot magazine; 24-inch, 26-inch, 28-inch barrel; standard chokes; vent rib; checkered American walnut pistol-grip stock, forend; recoil pad; slide ejection. No longer in production.

Exc: $165 **VGood:** $155 **Good:** $140

HARRINGTON & RICHARDSON MODEL 459 GOLDEN SQUIRE JUNIOR

Single barrel; exposed hammer; 20-ga., .410; 26-inch barrel; Full choke; bead front sight; youth-sized uncheckered hardwood straight-grip stock, schnabel forearm. Introduced 1964; discontinued 1964.

Exc: $75 **VGood:** $65 **Good:** $55

HARRINGTON & RICHARDSON MODEL 1212

Over/under; boxlock; 12-ga.; 2-3/4-inch chambers; 28-inch barrels; Improved Cylinder/Improved Modified chokes; vent rib; checkered European walnut pistol-grip stock, fluted forearm; selective single trigger; plain extractors. Made in Spain by Lanber. Introduced 1976; discontinued 1981.

Perf: $300 **Exc:** $270 **VGood:** $240

HARRINGTON & RICHARDSON MODEL 1212 WATERFOWLER

Same specs as Model 1212 except 3-inch chamber; 30-inch barrels; Modified/Full choke; recoil pad. Introduced 1976; discontinued 1981.

Perf: $310 **Exc:** $280 **VGood:** $250

HARRINGTON & RICHARDSON NO. 1 HARRICH

Single shot; 12-ga.; 32-inch, 34-inch barrel; Full choke; high vent rib; hand-checkered European walnut Monte Carlo pistol-grip stock, beavertail forearm; Kersten top locks, double under lugs; recoil pad; trap model. Made in Austria. Introduced 1971; discontinued 1974.

Perf: $1700 **Exc:** $1550 **VGood:** $1400

HARRINGTON & RICHARDSON NO. 3

Single barrel; top-lever break-open; hammerless; takedown; 12-, 16-, 20-, 24-, 28-ga., .410; 26-inch, 28-inch, 30-inch, 32-inch barrels; Full choke; bead front sight; uncheckered American walnut pistol-grip stock, forearm; automatic ejector. Introduced 1908; discontinued 1942.

Exc: $75 **VGood:** $50 **Good:** $40

HARRINGTON & RICHARDSON NO. 5

Single barrel; toplever break-open; exposed hammer; takedown; 28-ga., .410; 26-inch, 28-inch barrel; Full choke; bead front sight; uncheckered American walnut pistol-grip stock, forearm; automatic ejector; lightweight configuration. Introduced 1908; discontinued 1942.

Exc: $90 **VGood:** $65 **Good:** $45

HARRINGTON & RICHARDSON NO. 6

Single barrel; top-lever break-open; exposed hammer; takedown; 10-, 12-, 16-, 20-ga.; 28-inch, 30-inch, 32-inch, 34-inch, 36-inch barrels; bead front sight; uncheckered American walnut pistol-grip stock, forearm; heavy breech; automatic ejector. Introduced 1908; discontinued 1942.

Exc: $85 **VGood:** $65 **Good:** $55

HARRINGTON & RICHARDSON NO. 7 BAY STATE

Single barrel; exposed hammer; takedown; 12-, 16-, 20-ga., .410; 26-inch, 28-inch, 30-inch, 32-inch barrels; Full choke; bead front sight; uncheckered American walnut pistol-grip stock, slim forearm. Also known as Model No. 9. Introduced 1908; discontinued 1942.

Exc: $85 **VGood:** $65 **Good:** $55

HARRINGTON & RICHARDSON NO. 8

Single barrel; exposed hammer; takedown; 12-, 16-, 20-, 28-ga., .410; 26-inch, 28-inch, 30-inch, 32-inch barrel; Full choke; bead front sight;

uncheckered American walnut pistol-grip stock, forearm; different forearm design than No. 5; automatic ejector. Introduced 1908; discontinued 1942.

Exc: $125 **VGood:** $95 **Good:** $75

Add 100 percent to above prices for 28 ga. or .410 bore.

HARRINGTON & RICHARDSON NO. 48 TOPPER

Single barrel; top-lever break-open; exposed hammer; takedown; 12-, 16-, 20-ga., .410; 26-inch, 28-inch, 30-inch, 32-inch barrel; Modified, Full choke; bead front sight; uncheckered American walnut pistol-grip stock, forearm; automatic ejector. Introduced 1946; discontinued 1957.

Exc: $110 **VGood:** $75 **Good:** $65

Add about 15 percent to above prices for Topper Deluxe.

HARRINGTON & RICHARDSON N.W.T.F. SHOTGUNS

Single shot; 12-ga., 3-1/2-inch chamber, fixed full choke; 20-ga., 3-inch chamber, fixed modified choke; 24-inch barrel (12-ga.) or 22-inch (20-ga.); weighs 5 to 6 lbs.; straight-grip camo laminate with recoil pad and sling swivel studs; bead front sight; break-open action with side lever release; hand-checkered stock and forearm; includes trigger lock. National Wild Turkey Federation logo on receiver.

Perf: $145 **Exc:** $120 **VGood:** $100

20-ga. youth gun (12-1/2-inch length of pull, weighs 5 lbs.)

Perf: $140 **Exc:** $110 **VGood:** $95

HARRINGTON & RICHARDSON N.W.T.F TURKEY

Single shot; break-open; sidelever; 12-ga.; 3-1/2-inch chamber; 24-inch barrel; Turkey Full choke tube; weighs 6 lbs.; 40-inch overall length; gold bead front sight; Mossy Oak camouflage hardwood pistol-grip stock, semi-beavertail forend; auto ejector; Mossy Oak sling; swivels; studs; satin-nickel frame; blued barrel. Introduced, 1992; still in production.

Perf: $140 **Exc:** $105 **VGood:** $80

HARRINGTON & RICHARDSON N.W.T.F. TURKEY YOUTH

Same specs as N.W.T.F. Turkey except 20-ga.; 3-inch chamber; 22-inch Full choke barrel; recoil pad. Introduced 1992; still in production.

Perf: $135 **Exc:** $100 **VGood:** $75

HARRINGTON & RICHARDSON SB2-980 ULTRA SLUG

Single shot; 12-ga.; 3-inch chamber; 24-inch fully rifled barrel; weighs 9 lbs.; scope mount; walnut-stained hardwood Monte Carlo stock; sling swivels; black nylon sling; H&R 10-gauge action with heavy-wall barrel. Introduced 1995; still in production.

Perf: $180 **Exc:** $140 **VGood:** $110

HARRINGTON & RICHARDSON MODEL 928 ULTRA SLUG HUNTER DELUXE

Similar to the SB2-980 Ultra Slug except uses 12 gauge action and 12 gauge barrel blank bored to 20 gauge, then fully rifled with 1:35-inch twist. Has hand- checkered camo laminate Monte Carlo stock and forend. Comes with Weaver-style scope base, offset hammer extension, ventilated recoil pad, sling swivels and nylon sling. Introduced 1997. Made in U.S. by H&R 1871 LLC.

Perf: $260 **Exc:** $205 **VGood:** $165

HARRINGTON & RICHARDSON TAMER

Single shot; .410; 3-inch chamber; 19-1/2-inch barrel; Full choke; weighs 5-6 lbs.; 33-inch overall length; high-density black-polymer thumbhole stock holds four spare shotshells; H&R Topper action with matte electroless nickel finish. Introduced 1994.

Perf: $110 **Exc:** $90 **VGood:** $75

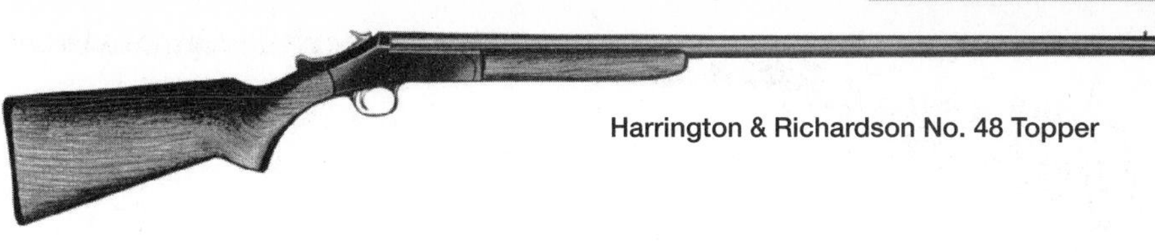

Harrington & Richardson No. 48 Topper

Harrington & Richardson Tamer

Harrington & Richardson Topper Model 098

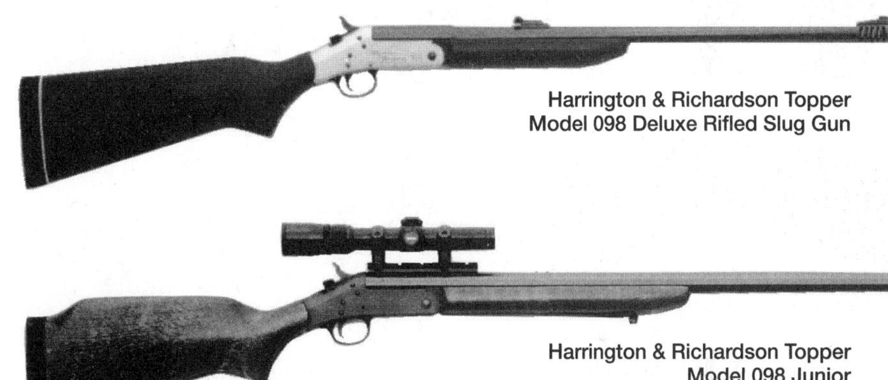

Harrington & Richardson Topper Model 098 Deluxe Rifled Slug Gun

Harrington & Richardson Topper Model 098 Junior

HARRINGTON & RICHARDSON TOPPER MODEL 058

Single shot; sidelever; exposed hammer; takedown; 12-, 16-, 20-, 28-ga., .410; 26-inch, 28-inch, 30-inch barrel; walnut-finished hardwood pistol-grip stock; auto ejector; case-hardened frame. Introduced 1978; discontinued 1981.

Perf: $80 **Exc:** $65 **VGood:** $50

HARRINGTON & RICHARDSON TOPPER MODEL 098

Single shot; break-open; sidelever; 12-, 16- (2-3/4-inch), 20-, 28-ga., .410; 3-inch chamber; 26-inch, 28-inch barrel; Modified, Full choke; gold bead front sight; black-finish hardwood pistol-grip stock, semi-beavertail forend; auto ejector; satin nickel frame; blued barrel. Introduced 1992.

Perf: $90 **Exc:** $75 **VGood:** $60

HARRINGTON & RICHARDSON TOPPER JUNIOR 098

As above except 22-inch barrel, 20 ga. (Mod.), .410-bore (Full), 12-1/2-inch length of pull). Same prices.

HARRINGTON & RICHARDSON TOPPER MODEL 098 CLASSIC YOUTH

Same specs as Topper Model 098 except 20-, 28-ga. (2-3/4-inch), .410; 3-inch chamber; Modified, Full choke; 22-inch barrel; cut-checkered American black walnut pistol-grip stock, forend; ventilated rubber recoil pad with white line spacers; blued barrel, blued frame. Introduced 1992; still produced.

Perf: $115 **Exc:** $90 **VGood:** $65

HARRINGTON & RICHARDSON TOPPER MODEL 098 DELUXE

Same specs as Topper Model 098 except 12-ga.; 3-1/2-inch chamber; 28-inch barrel; Modified choke tube. Introduced 1992; still in production.

Perf: $105 **Exc:** $85 **VGood:** $60

HARRINGTON & RICHARDSON TOPPER MODEL 098 DELUXE RIFLED SLUG GUN

Same specs as Topper Model 098 except 12-ga.; 3-inch chamber; 28-inch fully rifled and ported barrel; ramp front sight, fully adjustable rear; black-finish hardwood pistol-grip stock, semi-beavertail forend; barrel twist is 1:35-inch; nickel-plated frame; blued barrel. Introduced 1995; still produced.

Perf: $150 **Exc:** $125 **VGood:** $100

HARRINGTON & RICHARDSON TOPPER MODEL 098 JUNIOR

Same specs as Topper Model 098 except 20-ga., .410; 22-inch barrel; Modified, Full choke; stock dimensions for smaller shooters. Introduced 1992; still in production.

Perf: $90 **Exc:** $75 **VGood:** $60

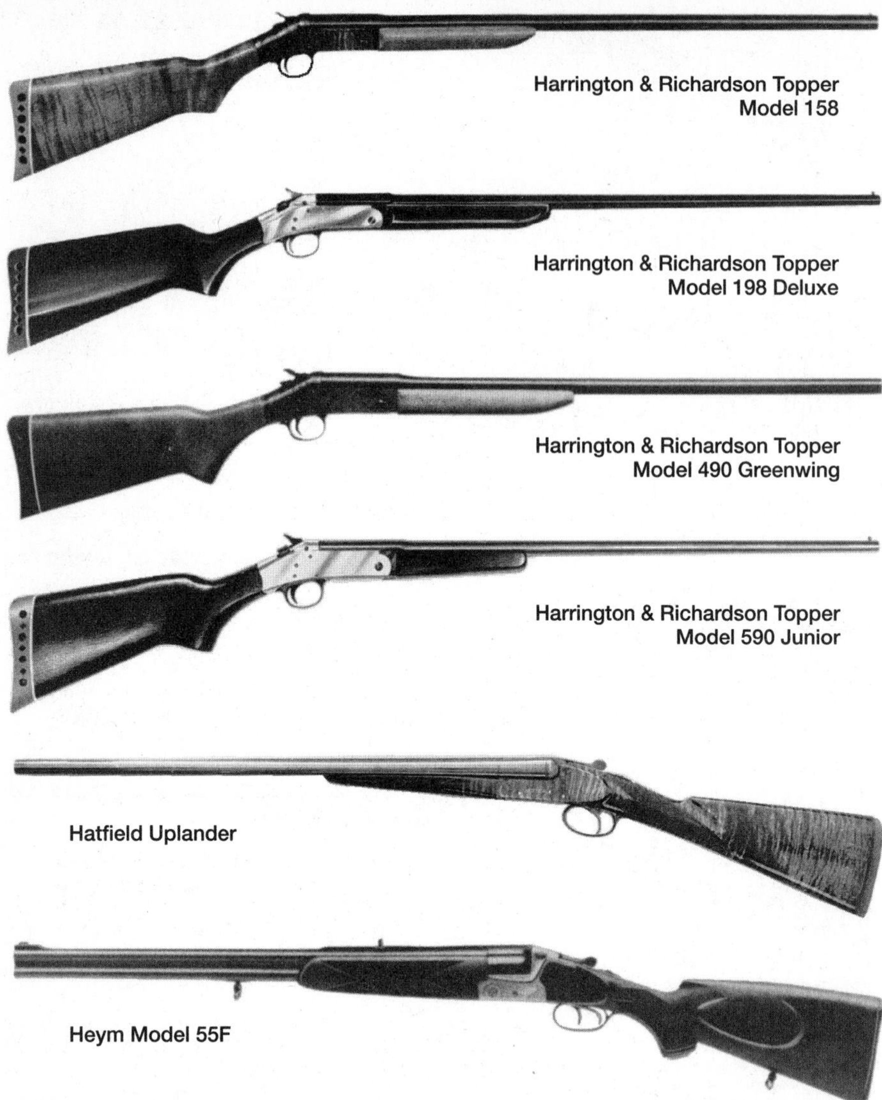
Harrington & Richardson Topper Model 158

Harrington & Richardson Topper Model 198 Deluxe

Harrington & Richardson Topper Model 490 Greenwing

Harrington & Richardson Topper Model 590 Junior

Hatfield Uplander

Heym Model 55F

HARRINGTON & RICHARDSON TOPPER MODEL 148

Single barrel; sidelever; exposed hammer; takedown; 12-, 16-, 20-ga., .410; 28-inch, 30-inch, 32-inch, 36-inch barrel; Full choke; uncheckered American walnut pistol-grip stock, forearm; recoil pad. Introduced 1958; discontinued 1961.

Exc: $100 **VGood:** $75 **Good:** $60

HARRINGTON & RICHARDSON TOPPER MODEL 158

Single barrel; sidelever; exposed hammer; takedown; 12-, 16-, 20-ga., .410; 28-inch, 30-inch, 32-inch, 36-inch barrel; Full, Modified choke; bead front sight; uncheckered hardwood pistol-grip stock, forearm; recoil pad; improved version of Topper Model 148. Introduced 1962; discontinued 1985.

Perf: $90 **Exc:** $75 **VGood:** $60

HARRINGTON & RICHARDSON TOPPER MODEL 188 DELUXE

Single barrel; sidelever; exposed hammer; takedown; .410; 28-inch, 30-inch, 32-inch, 36-inch barrels; Full choke; uncheckered American walnut pistol-grip stock, forearm finished with black, red, yellow, blue, green, pink or purple lacquer; recoil pad; chrome-plated frame. Introduced 1958; discontinued 1961.

Exc: $125 **VGood:** $100 **Good:** $75

HARRINGTON & RICHARDSON TOPPER MODEL 198 DELUXE

Single barrel; sidelever; exposed hammer; takedown; 20-ga., .410; 28-inch barrel; Full, Modified choke; uncheckered American walnut pistol-grip stock, forearm finished with black lacquer; chrome-plated frame. Introduced 1962; discontinued 1985.

Perf: $90 **Exc:** $75 **VGood:** $60

HARRINGTON & RICHARDSON TOPPER MODEL 480 JUNIOR

Single barrel; top-lever break-open; exposed hammer; takedown; .410; 26-inch barrel; Modified, Full choke; bead front sight; youth-sized uncheckered American walnut pistol-grip stock, forearm; automatic ejector. Introduced 1958; discontinued 1960.

Exc: $70 **VGood:** $60 **Good:** $50

HARRINGTON & RICHARDSON TOPPER MODEL 488 DELUXE

Single barrel; top-lever break-open; exposed hammer; takedown; 12-, 16-, 20-ga., .410; 26-inch, 28-inch, 30-inch, 32-inch barrel; Modified, Full choke; bead front sight; uncheckered American walnut pistol-grip stock, forearm with black-lacquer finish; recoil pad; automatic ejector; chrome-plated frame. Introduced 1946; discontinued 1957.

Exc: $75 **VGood:** $65 **Good:** $55

HARRINGTON & RICHARDSON TOPPER MODEL 490 JUNIOR

Single shot; sidelever break-open; takedown; 20-, 28-ga., .410; 26-inch barrel; Modified (20-, 28-ga.), Full (.410) choke; weighs 5 lbs.; bead front sight; youth-sized uncheckered hardwood pistol-grip stock, forend; recoil pad. Introduced 1962; discontinued 1985.

Perf: $90 **Exc:** $75 **VGood:** $60

HARRINGTON & RICHARDSON TOPPER MODEL 490 GREENWING

Same specs as Topper Model 490 Junior except gold-finished trigger; inscription on frame; polished blued finish. Discontinued 1984.

Perf: $100 **Exc:** $85 **VGood:** $75

HARRINGTON & RICHARDSON TOPPER MODEL 580 JUNIOR

Single barrel; top-lever break-open; exposed hammer; takedown; 12-, 16-, 20-ga., .410; 26-inch, 28-inch, 30-inch, 32-inch barrel; Modified, Full choke; bead front sight; uncheckered American walnut pistol-grip stock, forearm with black, red, yellow, blue, green, pink or purple lacquer finish; automatic ejector. Introduced 1958; discontinued 1961.

Exc: $120 **VGood:** $90 **Good:** $70

HARRINGTON & RICHARDSON TOPPER MODEL 590 JUNIOR

Single shot; sidelever break-open; exposed hammer; takedown; 20-, 28-ga., .410; 26-inch barrel; Modified (20-, 28-ga.), Full (.410) choke; weighs 5 lbs.; bead front sight; youth-sized uncheckered hardwood pistol-grip stock, forearm with black lacquer finish; chrome-plated frame; recoil pad. Introduced 1962; discontinued 1963.

Exc: $75 **VGood:** $60 **Good:** $50

HATFIELD UPLANDER

Side-by-side; boxlock; 20-ga.; 3-inch chambers; 26-inch Improved Cylinder/Modified barrel; weighs 5-3/4 lbs.; fancy maple straight English-style stock, splinter forend; double locking underlug; single non-selective trigger; color case-hardened frame; half-coverage hand-engraved action with French gray finish; comes with English-style oxblood leather luggage case with billiard felt interior. Made in eight grades with various levels of engraving, inlays and fancy wood. Introduced 1988; dropped 1996. Production resumed of some models in 2003.

Grade I

Perf: $1700 **Exc:** $1500 **VGood:** $1325

Grade II

Perf: $2650 **Exc:** $2250 **VGood:** $1825

Grade III

Perf: $2350 **Exc:** $1900 **VGood:** $1575

Grade IV

Perf: $3995 **Exc:** $3575 **VGood:** $2900

Grade V

Perf: $4700 **Exc:** $4400 **VGood:** $3350

Grade VI

Perf: $5200 **Exc:** $4850 **VGood:** $3700

Grade VII

Perf: $5250 **Exc:** $4895 **VGood:** $3750

Grade VIII

Perf: $12,000 **Exc:** $9750 **VGood:** $8750

HATFIELD'S UPLANDER 28

Side-by-side; boxlock; 28 ga.; 26-inch monobloc barrels; matte rib; small scalloped frame; extractors; SST or DT; checkered Circassian walnut straight grip stock; splinter forend; case colored frame; weighs 4 lbs. Introduced 2004.

Perf: $1350 **Exc:** $1200 **VGood:** $1000

HEYM MODEL 55 F

Over/under; boxlock; 12-, 16-, 20-ga.; 28-inch barrel; hand-checkered European walnut stock; Kersten double crossbolt; double underlugs; Arabesque or hunting engraving; numerous options at added cost. Introduced 1979; discontinued 1992.

Perf: $5100 **Exc:** $4525 **VGood:** $3950

HEYM MODEL 55 SS

Same specs as Model 55 F except sidelock action; large engraving scenes. No longer in production.

Perf: $4800 **Exc:** $3825 **VGood:** $3300

HEYM MODEL 200

Over/under; boxlock; 20-ga.; 3-inch chambers; 28-inch vent rib barrels; light engraving; no longer imported.

Perf: $895 **Exc:** $795 **VGood:** $700

HHF (HUGLU) MODEL 101 B 12 AT-DT

Over/under; boxlock; 12-ga.; 3-inch chambers; combo set with 30-inch and 32-inch barrels; fixed chokes or choke tubes; 16mm rib; weighs about 8 lbs.; Circassian walnut Monte Carlo stock to trap dimensions; palm swell grip; recoil pad; single selective trigger; manual safety; automatic ejectors or extractors; silvered frame with 50 percent engraving coverage. Many custom features available. Made in Turkey. Introduced 1995; still imported.

With extractors
Perf: $2000 **Exc:** $1750 **VGood:** $1500

With ejectors
Perf: $2100 **Exc:** $1850 **VGood:** $1600

HHF MODEL 101 B 12 ST TRAP

Same specs as Model 101 B 12 AT-DT except 30-inch over/under barrels. Made in Turkey. Introduced 1995; still imported.

With extractors
Perf: $950 **Exc:** $750 **VGood:** $600

With ejectors
Perf: $1025 **Exc:** $825 **VGood:** $675

HHF (HUGLU) MODEL 103 B 12 ST

Over/under boxlock; 12-, 20-, 28-ga., .410; 3-inch chambers; 28-inch barrels; choke tubes or fixed chokes; weighs about 7-1/2 lbs.; Circassian walnut stock; dummy sideplates; double triggers; manual safety; extractors; 80- percent engraving coverage, inlaid animals on blackened sideplates. Made in Turkey. Introduced 1995; still imported.

12-, 20-ga., fixed chokes
Perf: $900 **Exc:** $725 **VGood:** $550

12-, 20-ga., choke tubes
Perf: $950 **Exc:** $775 **VGood:** $600

28-ga., .410, fixed chokes
Perf: $950 **Exc:** $775 **VGood:** $600

HHF (HUGLU) MODEL 103 C 12 ST

Same specs as Model 103 B 12 ST except 12-, 20-ga.; 3-inch chambers; extractors or ejectors; black receiver with 50- percent engraving coverage. Made in Turkey. Introduced 1995; still imported.

With extractors
Perf: $950 **Exc:** $750 **VGood:** $600

With ejectors
Perf: $1025 **Exc:** $825 **VGood:** $675

HHF (HUGLU) MODEL 103 D 12 ST

Same specs as Model 103 B 12 ST except standard boxlock; 12-, 20-ga.; 3-inch chambers; extractors or ejectors; 80 percent engraving coverage. Made in Turkey. Introduced 1995; still imported.

With extractors
Perf: $950 **Exc:** $750 **VGood:** $600

With ejectors
Perf: $1025 **Exc:** $825 **VGood:** $675

HHF MODEL 103 F 12 ST

Same specs as Model 103 B 12 ST except 12-, 20-ga.; 3-inch chambers; extractors or ejectors; 100- percent engraving coverage. Made in Turkey. Introduced 1995; still imported.

With extractors
Perf: $1000 **Exc:** $800 **VGood:** $650

With ejectors
Perf: $1075 **Exc:** $875 **VGood:** $725

HHF (HUGLU) MODEL 104 A 12 ST

Over/under; boxlock; 12-, 20-, 28-ga., .410; 3-inch chambers; 28-inch barrels; fixed chokes or choke tubes; weighs about 7-1/2 lbs.; Circassian walnut stock with field dimensions; manual safety; extractors or ejectors; double triggers; silvered, engraved receiver with 15- percent engraving coverage. Made in Turkey. Introduced 1995; still imported.

12-, 20-ga., fixed chokes, extractors
Perf: $850 **Exc:** $675 **VGood:** $500

12-, 20-ga., choke tubes, ejectors
Perf: $900 **Exc:** $725 **VGood:** $550

28-ga., .410, fixed chokes, extractors
Perf: $900 **Exc:** $725 **VGood:** $550

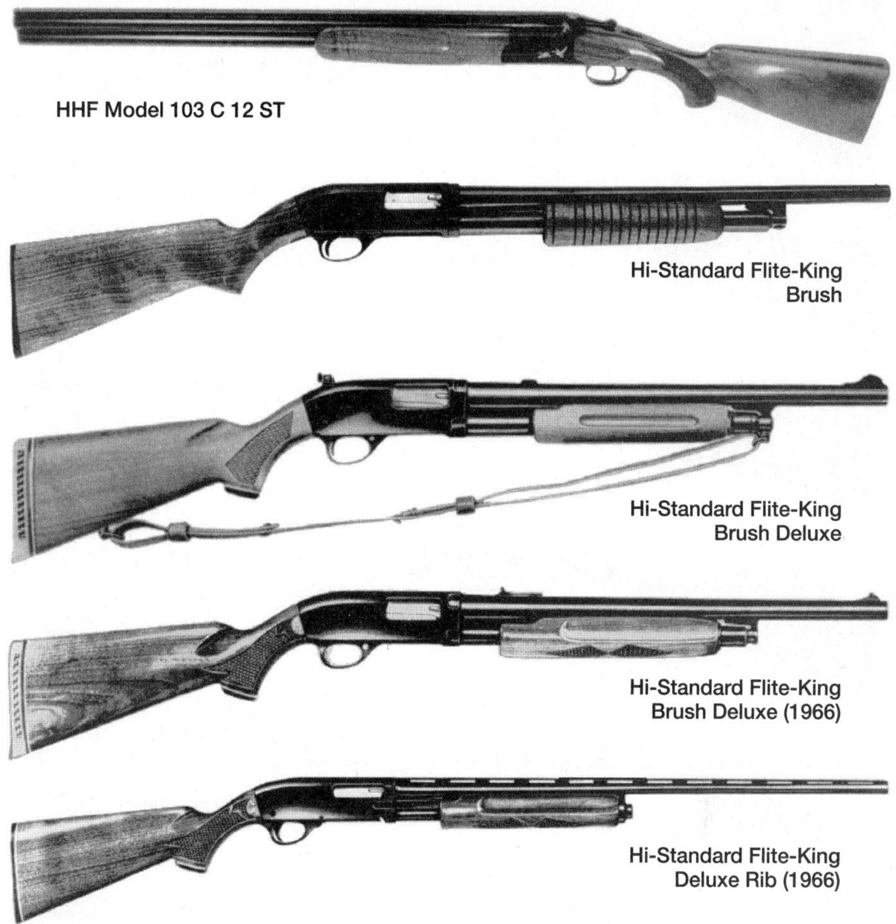

HHF Model 103 C 12 ST

Hi-Standard Flite-King Brush

Hi-Standard Flite-King Brush Deluxe

Hi-Standard Flite-King Brush Deluxe (1966)

Hi-Standard Flite-King Deluxe Rib (1966)

HHF (HUGLU) MODEL 200 A 12 ST DOUBLE

Side-by-side; boxlock; 12-, 20-, 28-ga., .410; 3-inch chambers; 28-inch barrels; fixed chokes or choke tubes; weighs about 7-1/2 lbs.; Circassian walnut stock; single selective trigger; extractors; manual safety; silvered receiver with 15 percent engraving coverage. Made in Turkey. Introduced 1995; still imported.

12-, 20-ga.
Perf: $950 **Exc:** $750 **VGood:** $600

28-ga., .410
Perf: $1025 **Exc:** $825 **VGood:** $675

HHF (HUGLU) MODEL 202 A 12 ST

Side-by-side; boxlock; 12-, 20-, 28-ga., .410; 3-inch chambers; 28-inch barrels; fixed chokes or choke tubes; weighs about 7-1/2 lbs.; Circassian walnut stock; double triggers; extractors; manual safety; silvered receiver with 30 percent engraving coverage. Made in Turkey. Introduced 1995; still imported.

12-, 20-ga.
Perf: $925 **Exc:** $725 **VGood:** $575

28-ga., .410
Perf: $1000 **Exc:** $800 **VGood:** $700

HI-STANDARD FLITE-KING BRUSH

Slide action; 12-ga.; 2-3/4-inch chamber; 4-shot magazine; 18-inch, 20-inch Cylinder-bore barrel; rifle sights; uncheckered walnut pistol-grip stock, slide handle. Introduced 1962; discontinued 1964.

Exc: $160 **VGood:** $150 **Good:** $140

HI-STANDARD FLITE-KING BRUSH DELUXE

Same specs as Flite-King Brush except 20-inch Cylinder barrel; adjustable peep rear sight; checkered pistol grip, fluted slide handle; recoil pad; sling swivels; sling. Introduced 1964; discontinued 1966.

Exc: $190 **VGood:** $160 **Good:** $150

HI-STANDARD FLITE-KING BRUSH (1966)

Slide action; 12-ga.; 2-3/4-inch chamber; 5-shot magazine; 20-inch Cylinder barrel; rifle sights; checkered American walnut pistol-grip stock, slide handle; recoil pad. General specs follow Flite-King series dropped in 1966, except for damascened bolt, new checkering design. Introduced 1966; discontinued 1975.

Perf: $195 **Exc:** $170 **VGood:** $150

HI-STANDARD FLITE-KING BRUSH DELUXE (1966)

Same specs as Flite-King Brush (1966) except adjustable peep rear sight; sling swivels; sling. Introduced 1966; discontinued 1975.

Perf: $270 **Exc:** $200 **VGood:** $180

HI-STANDARD FLITE-KING DELUXE RIB

Slide action; 12-, 16-, 20-, 28-ga., .410; 2-3/4-inch (12-ga.), 3-inch chamber; 3- (20-ga.), 4-shot magazine; 28-inch Full or Modified, 30-inch Full barrel; vent rib; checkered walnut pistol-grip stock, slide handle. Introduced 1961; discontinued 1966. 50% premium for small gauges.

Exc: $215 **VGood:** $195 **Good:** $160

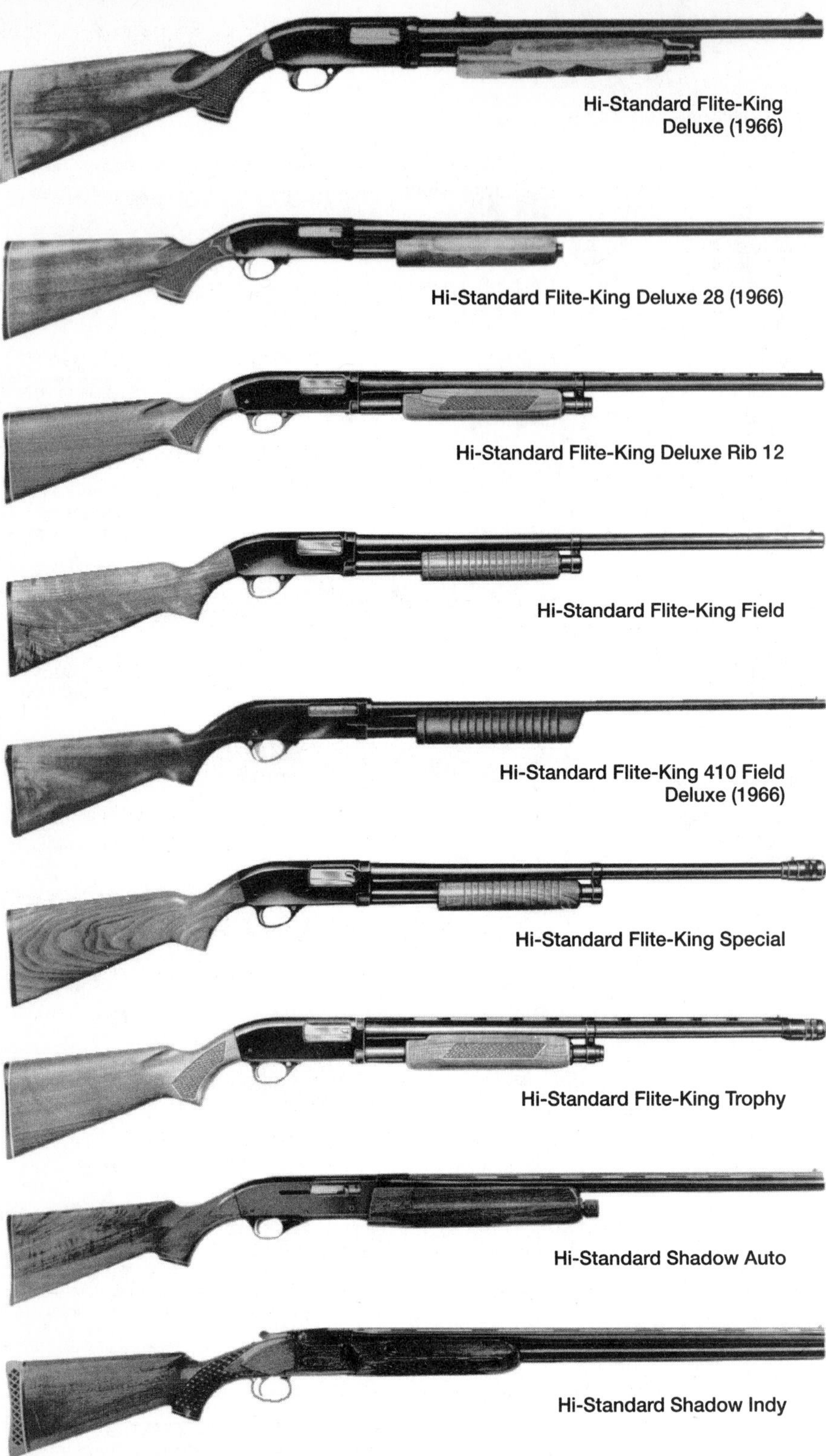

HI-STANDARD FLITE-KING DELUXE (1966)

Slide action; 12-, 20-, 28-ga., .410; 2-3/4-inch (12-ga.), 3-inch chamber; 5-shot magazine; 26-inch Improved Cylinder, 27-inch adjustable choke, 28-inch Modified or Full, 30-inch Full choke barrel; checkered American walnut pistol-grip stock, slide handle; recoil pad. General specs follow Flite-King series dropped in 1966, except for damascened bolt, new checkering design. Introduced 1966; discontinued 1975. 50% premium for small gauges.

Fixed choke

Perf: $195 **Exc:** $175 **VGood:** $150

Adjustable choke

Perf: $200 **Exc:** $180 **VGood:** $160

HI-STANDARD FLITE-KING DELUXE RIB (1966)

Same specs as Flite-King Deluxe (1966) except 27-inch adjustable choke, 28-inch Modified or Full, 30-inch Full choke barrel; vent rib. General specs follow Flite-King series dropped in 1966, except for damascened bolt, new checkering design. Introduced 1966; discontinued 1975. 50% premium for small gauges.

Fixed choke

Perf: $210 **Exc:** $180 **VGood:** $150

Adjustable choke

Perf: $220 **Exc:** $190 **VGood:** $160

HI-STANDARD FLITE-KING DELUXE SKEET (1966)

Same specs as Flite-King Deluxe (1966) except 26-inch vent-rib barrel; Skeet choke; optional recoil pad. General specs follow Flite-King series dropped 1966, except for damascened bolt, new checkering design. Introduced 1966; discontinued 1975. 50% premium for small gauges.

Perf: $270 **Exc:** $200 **VGood:** $175

HI-STANDARD FLITE-KING DELUXE TRAP (1966)

Same specs as Flite-King Deluxe (1966) except 12-ga.; 2-3/4-inch chamber; 30-inch Full choke barrel; vent rib; trap-style checkered walnut pistol-grip stock, slide handle. General specs follow Flite-King series dropped in 1966, except for damascened bolt, new checkering design. Introduced 1966; discontinued 1975.

Perf: $270 **Exc:** $200 **VGood:** $175

HI-STANDARD FLITE-KING FIELD

Slide action; 12-, 16-, 20-, 28-ga., .410; 2-3/4-inch (12-ga.), 3-inch chamber; 3- (20-ga.), 4-shot magazine; 26-inch Improved Cylinder, 28-inch Modified or Full, 30-inch Full barrel; uncheckered walnut pistol-grip stock, grooved slide handle. Introduced 1960; discontinued 1966. 50% premium for small gauges.

Exc: $165 **VGood:** $150 **Good:** $140

HI-STANDARD FLITE-KING SKEET

Same specs as Flite-King Field except 12-, 20-, 28-ga., .410; 2-3/4-inch (12-ga.), 3-inch chamber; 26-inch Skeet-choked barrel; vent rib; checkered walnut pistol-grip stock, slide handle. Introduced 1962; discontinued 1966. 50% premium for small gauges.

Exc: $250 **VGood:** $225 **Good:** $200

Add 35 percent to above prices for 28 ga. or .410 bore.

HI-STANDARD FLITE-KING SPECIAL

Same specs as Flite-King Field except 12-, 16-, 20-, 28-ga.; 2-3/4-inch (12-ga.), 3-inch chamber; 27-inch adjustable choke barrel. Introduced 1960; discontinued 1966. 50% premium for 28 ga.

Exc: $165 **VGood:** $150 **Good:** $140

HI-STANDARD FLITE-KING TRAP

Same specs as Flite-King Field except 12-ga.; 2-3/4-inch chamber; 4-shot magazine; 30-inch barrel; Full choke; vent rib; trap-style checkered walnut pistol-grip stock, slide handle; recoil pad. Introduced 1962; discontinued 1966.

Exc: $190 **VGood:** $150 **Good:** $135

HI-STANDARD FLITE-KING TROPHY

Same specs as Flite-King Field except Slide-action; 12-, 16-, 20-, 28-ga.; 2-3/4-inch (12-ga.), 3-inch chamber; 3- (20-ga.), 4-shot magazine; 27-inch adjustable choke, 28-inch Modified or Full barrel (20-ga.); vent rib; checkered walnut pistol-grip stock, slide handle. Introduced 1960; discontinued 1966. 50% premium for 28 ga.

Exc: $190 **VGood:** $180 **Good:** $170

HI-STANDARD SHADOW AUTO

Gas-operated autoloader; 12-, 20-ga.; 2-3/4-inch, 3-inch chamber; 3- (3-inch), 4-shot magazine; 26-inch Improved Cylinder or Skeet, 28-inch Modified, Improved Modified or Full, 30-inch Trap or Full barrel; magnum available only with 30-inch barrel; checkered walnut pistol-grip stock, forearm. Made in Japan. Introduced 1974; discontinued 1975.

Perf: $375 **Exc:** $345 **VGood:** $330

HI-STANDARD SHADOW INDY

Over/under; boxlock; 12-ga.; 2-3/4-inch chamber; 27-1/2-inch Skeet, 29-3/4-inch Improved Modified/Full or Full/Full barrels; Airflow vent rib; skip-checkered walnut pistol-grip stock, ventilated forearm; selective auto ejectors;

selective single trigger; engraved receiver; recoil pad. Made in Japan. Introduced 1974; discontinued 1975.

Perf: $850 **Exc:** $800 **VGood:** $760

HI-STANDARD SHADOW SEVEN

Same specs as Shadow Indy except 27-1/2-inch Improved Cylinder/Modified or Modified/Full barrels; vent rib; skip-checkered walnut pistol-grip stock, forearm; no recoil pad. Made in Japan. Introduced 1974; discontinued 1975.

Perf: $700 **Exc:** $640 **VGood:** $550

HI-STANDARD SUPERMATIC DEER

Autoloader; 12-ga.; 4-shot magazine; 22-inch Cylinder barrel; rifle sights; checkered American walnut stock, forearm; recoil pad. Introduced 1965; discontinued 1965.

Exc: $225 **VGood:** $205 **Good:** $185

HI-STANDARD SUPERMATIC DELUXE

Autoloader; 12-, 20-ga.; 2-3/4-inch (12-ga.), 3-inch chamber; 3- (20-ga.), 4-shot magazine; 27-inch adjustable-choke barrel (discontinued 1970), 26-inch Improved, 28-inch Modified or Full, 30-inch Full choke barrels; checkered American walnut pistol-grip stock, forearm; recoil pad. Differs from original Supermatic; has new checkering, damascened bolt. Introduced 1966; discontinued 1975. This gun has never received the credit it deserves; although heavy, it was America's first successful gas-operated sporting arm.

Fixed choke

Perf: $240 **Exc:** $225 **VGood:** $195

Adjustable choke

Perf: $255 **Exc:** $240 **VGood:** $215

HI-STANDARD SUPERMATIC DELUXE RIB

Same specs as Supermatic Deluxe except 28-inch Modified or Full, 30-inch Full choke barrels; vent rib. Introduced 1966; discontinued 1975.

Fixed choke

Perf: $260 **Exc:** $245 **VGood:** $215

Adjustable choke

Perf: $275 **Exc:** $260 **VGood:** $230

HI-STANDARD SUPERMATIC DUCK

Autoloader; 12-ga.; 3-inch chamber; 3-shot magazine; 30-inch Full-choke barrel; uncheckered American walnut pistol-grip stock, forearm; recoil pad. Introduced 1961; discontinued 1966.

Exc: $265 **VGood:** $235 **Good:** $190

HI-STANDARD SUPERMATIC DUCK DELUXE

Same specs as Supermatic Duck except checkered American walnut pistol-grip stock, forearm. Introduced 1966; discontinued 1975.

Perf: $280 **Exc:** $250 **VGood:** $205

HI-STANDARD SUPERMATIC DUCK RIB

Same specs as Supermatic Duck except vent rib. Introduced 1961; discontinued 1966.

Exc: $285 **VGood:** $255 **Good:** $210

HI-STANDARD SUPERMATIC DUCK RIB DELUXE

Same specs as Supermatic Duck Rib except vent rib; checkered American walnut pistol-grip stock, forearm. Introduced 1966; discontinued 1975.

Perf: $295 **Exc:** $275 **VGood:** $225

HI-STANDARD SUPERMATIC FIELD

Gas-operated autoloader; 12-, 20-ga.; 2-3/4-inch (12-ga.), 3-inch chamber; 3- (20-ga.), 4-shot magazine; 26-inch Improved, 28-inch Modified or Full, 30-inch Full barrel; uncheckered American walnut pistol-grip stock, forearm. Introduced 1960; discontinued 1966.

Exc: $200 **VGood:** $190 **Good:** $180

Add 5 percent to above prices for 20 gauge.

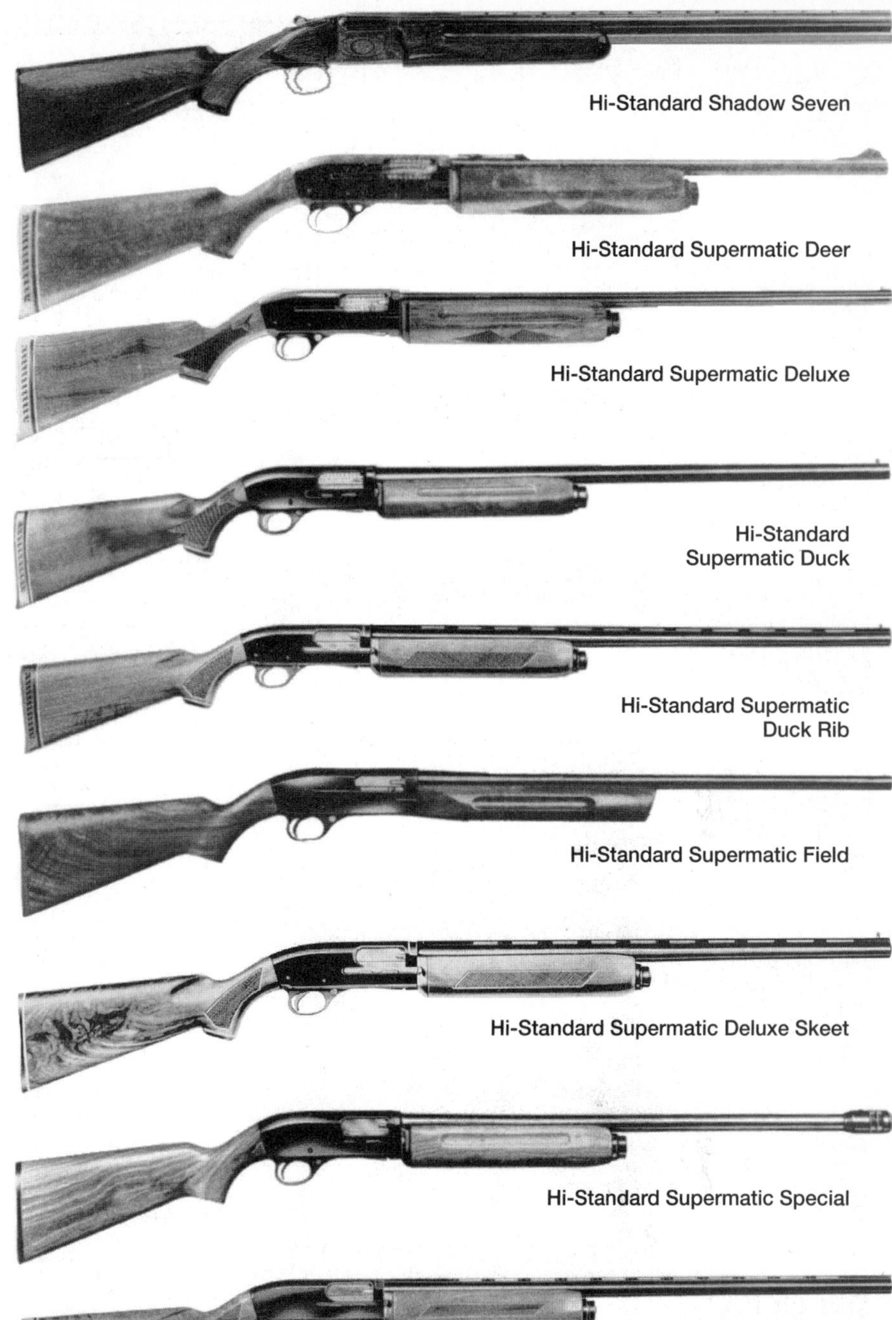

Hi-Standard Shadow Seven

Hi-Standard Supermatic Deer

Hi-Standard Supermatic Deluxe

Hi-Standard Supermatic Duck

Hi-Standard Supermatic Duck Rib

Hi-Standard Supermatic Field

Hi-Standard Supermatic Deluxe Skeet

Hi-Standard Supermatic Special

Hi-Standard Supermatic Deluxe Trap

HI-STANDARD SUPERMATIC SKEET

Autoloader; 12-, 20-ga.; 2-3/4-inch (12-ga.), 3-inch chamber; 3- (20-ga.), 4-shot magazine; 26-inch vent-rib barrel; Skeet choke; uncheckered Skeet-style American walnut pistol-grip stock, forearm; recoil pad. Introduced 1962; discontinued 1966.

Exc: $260 **VGood:** $230 **Good:** $240

HI-STANDARD SUPERMATIC SKEET DELUXE

Same specs as Supermatic Skeet except checkered Skeet-style American walnut pistol-grip stock, forearm. Introduced 1966; discontinued 1975.

Perf: $310 **Exc:** $240 **VGood:** $250

HI-STANDARD SUPERMATIC SPECIAL

Autoloader; 12-, 20-ga.; 2-3/4-inch (12-ga.), 3-inch chamber; 3- (20-ga.), 4-shot magazine; 27-inch barrel; adjustable choke; uncheckered American walnut pistol-grip stock, forearm. Introduced 1960; discontinued 1966.

Exc: $180 **VGood:** $145 **Good:** $125

HI-STANDARD SUPERMATIC TRAP

Autoloader; 12-ga.; 4-shot magazine; 30-inch Full barrel; vent rib; trap-style uncheckered American walnut pistol-grip stock, forearm; recoil pad. Introduced 1962; discontinued 1966.

Exc: $240 **VGood:** $200 **Good:** $150

Hi-Standard Supermatic Trophy

Hoenig Rotary Round Action Game Gun

Holland & Holland Badminton

Holland & Holland Dominion Game Gun

Holland & Holland Royal Game Gun

HI-STANDARD SUPERMATIC TRAP DELUXE

Same specs as Supermatic Trap except trap-style checkered American walnut pistol-grip stock, forearm. Introduced 1966; discontinued 1975.

Perf: $250 **Exc:** $235 **VGood:** $215

HI-STANDARD SUPERMATIC TROPHY

Autoloader; 12-, 20-ga.; 2-3/4-inch (12-ga.), 3-inch chamber; 3- (20-ga.), 4-shot magazine; 27-inch adjustable choke barrel; vent rib; checkered American walnut pistol-grip stock, forearm; recoil pad. Introduced 1961; discontinued 1966.

Exc: $235 **VGood:** $210 **Good:** $195

HOENIG ROTARY ROUND ACTION GAME GUN

Gauge: 28. Barrel: 26-inch, 28-inch, solid tapered rib. Weight: 6 lbs. Stock: English walnut. Features: Round action opens by rotating barrels, pulling forward. Inertia extractor, rotary safety blocks strikers. Simple takedown without removing forend. Elegance and class of guns of yesteryear. Made in U.S.A. by George Hoenig. Price: $19,995

HOLLAND & HOLLAND

NOTE: 20-gauge versions are valued at 20 percent more than indicated prices; 28-gauge, 40 percent additional; .410 at 60 percent higher.

HOLLAND & HOLLAND BADMINTON

Side-by-side; sidelock; hammerless; 12-, 16-, 20-, 28-ga.; barrel lengths, chokes to customer specs; hand-checkered straight-grip or pistol-grip stock, forearm; non-self-opening action; auto ejectors; double triggers or single trigger; engraving. Introduced 1902; no longer in production.

Double triggers

Perf: $10,000 **Exc:** $8000 **VGood:** $7000

Single trigger

Perf: $11,000 **Exc:** $9000 **VGood:** $8000

HOLLAND & HOLLAND BADMINTON GAME GUN

Same specs as Badminton except only 12-, 20-ga. Discontinued 1988.

Double trigger

Perf: $20,000 **Exc:** $15,000 **VGood:** $12,000

Single trigger

Perf: $22,000 **Exc:** $17,000 **VGood:** $14,000

HOLLAND & HOLLAND CAVALIER

Side-by-side; boxlock; 12-, 20-, 28-ga.; 28-inch, 30-inch barrels; any standard choke combo; hand-checkered European walnut pistol-grip or straight-grip stock, forearm; double trigger; auto ejectors; engraving; color case-hardened receiver. Discontinued 1993.

Perf: $9500 **Exc:** $7750 **VGood:** $6350

Add about 10 percent to above prices for 20 ga.
Add approximately 10 percent to above prices for 28 ga.

HOLLAND & HOLLAND CAVALIER DELUXE

Same specs as Cavalier except better engraving and select wood. Discontinued 1993.

Perf: $10,000 **Exc:** $8000 **VGood:** $7000

HOLLAND & HOLLAND DOMINION GAME GUN

Side-by-side; sidelock; hammerless; 12-, 16-, 20-ga.; 25-inch, 28-inch, 30-inch barrels; choked to customer's specs; hand-checkered European walnut straight-grip stock, forearm; double triggers; automatic ejectors. Introduced 1935; discontinued 1989.

Perf: $6750 **Exc:** $6150 **VGood:** $5650

Add approximately 20 percent to above prices for 20 ga.

HOLLAND & HOLLAND NORTHWOOD

Side-by-side; boxlock; 12-, 16-, 20-, 28-ga.; 28-inch, 30-inch barrels; any standard choke combo; hand-checkered European walnut pistol-grip stock or straight-grip stock, forearm; double triggers; auto ejectors; engraving; color case-hardened receiver. Discontinued 1993.

Perf: $6000 **Exc:** $4800 **VGood:** $4400

Add approximately 10 percent to above prices for 20 ga.
Add approximately 20 percent for 28 ga.

HOLLAND & HOLLAND NORTHWOOD DELUXE

Same specs as Northwood except better engraving and select wood. Discontinued 1993.

Perf: $7000 **Exc:** $5500 **VGood:** $4500

Add approximately 10 percent to above prices for 20 ga.
Add approximately 20 percent for 28 ga.

HOLLAND & HOLLAND NORTHWOOD GAME MODEL

Side-by-side; Anson & Deeley boxlock; 12-, 16-, 20-, 28-ga.; 28-inch barrels; any standard choke combo; hand-checkered European walnut straight-grip or pistol-grip stock, forearm; double triggers, automatic ejectors. Introduced prior to World War II; discontinued late 1960s.

Perf: $7000 **Exc:** $5500 **VGood:** $4500

HOLLAND & HOLLAND NORTHWOOD PIGEON MODEL

Same specs as Northwood Game Model except 12-, 16-, 20-ga.; more engraving. No longer in production.

Perf: $8000 **Exc:** $6500 **VGood:** $5000

HOLLAND & HOLLAND NORTHWOOD WILDFOWL MODEL

Same specs as Northwood Game Model except 12-ga.; 3-inch chamber; 30-inch barrels. No longer in production.

Perf: $8000 **Exc:** $6500 **VGood:** $5000

HOLLAND & HOLLAND RIVIERA

Side-by-side; sidelock; hammerless; 12-, 16-, 20-, 28-ga.; barrel lengths, chokes to customer specs; hand-checkered straight-grip or pistol-grip stock, forearm; non-self-opening action; auto ejectors; double triggers; two interchangeable barrels; engraving. Introduced 1945; discontinued 1967.

12 Gauge

Exc: $11,000 **VGood:** $9300 **Good:** $7500

20 Gauge

Exc: $13,000 **VGood:** $11,500 **Good:** $9500

HOLLAND & HOLLAND ROYAL

Side-by-side; sidelock; hammerless; 12-, 16-, 20-, 28-ga.; barrel lengths, chokes to customer's specs; hand-checkered straight-grip or pistol-grip stock, forearm; non-self-opening action; automatic ejectors; double triggers or single non-selective trigger; English engraving. Introduced 1885; no longer in production.

Double triggers

Exc: $20,000 **VGood:** $17,500 **Good:** $7000

Single trigger

Exc: $21,500 **VGood:** $18,500 **Good:** $8000

HOLLAND & HOLLAND ROYAL GAME GUN

Side-by-side; sidelock; hammerless; 12-, 16-, 20-, 28-ga., .410; barrel lengths, chokes to customer's specs; hand-checkered straight-grip or pistol-grip stock, forearm; self-opening action; double triggers or single non-selective trigger; ornate engraving. Introduced 1922; still in production.

Double triggers

Perf: $48,000 **Exc:** $27,000 **VGood:** $19,000

Single trigger

Perf: $48,000 **Exc:** $30,000 **VGood:** $22,000

Add approximately 10 percent for 28 ga. or .410 bore
Add about $3000 for vent. rib.

HOLLAND & HOLLAND ROYAL GAME GUN DELUXE

Same specs as Royal Game Gun except top-of-the-line model with better engraving and wood. Still in production.

Double triggers
Perf: $56,900 **Exc:** $35,000 **VGood:** $20,000

Single trigger
Perf: $56,900 **Exc:** $39,000 **VGood:** $24,000

HOLLAND & HOLLAND ROYAL OVER/UNDER

Over/under; hand-detachable sidelocks; hammerless; 12-ga.; barrel lengths, chokes to customer's specs; hand-checkered European walnut straight-grip stock, forearm; automatic ejectors; double triggers or single trigger. Introduced 1925; discontinued 1950. Seek appraisal.

HOLLAND & HOLLAND ROYAL OVER/UNDER (NEW MODEL)

Same specs as Royal Over/Under except narrower, improved action. Introduced 1951; discontinued 1965. Seek appraisal.

HOLLAND & HOLLAND ROYAL OVER/UNDER GAME GUN

Over/under; hand-detachable sidelocks; hammerless; 12-, 20-ga.; 2-3/4-inch chambers; 25-inch to 30-inch barrels; any standard choke combo; select hand-checkered walnut straight-grip or pistol-grip stock, forearm; automatic ejectors; single or double triggers; engraved color case-hardened receiver. Introduced 1992; still in production.

Double triggers
Perf: $60,375 **Exc:** $35,000 **VGood:** $24,000

Single trigger
Perf: $60,375 **Exc:** $39,000 **VGood:** $28,000

HOLLAND & HOLLAND SINGLE BARREL TRAP

Single barrel; boxlock; 12-ga.; 30-inch, 32-inch barrel; Full choke; vent rib; European walnut Monte Carlo pistol-grip stock, forearm; auto ejector; recoil pad. Discontinued 1992.

Perf: $14,500 **Exc:** $12,000 **VGood:** $10,000

HOLLAND & HOLLAND SPORTING OVER/UNDER

Blitz action; 12-, 20-ga.; 2-3/4-inch chambers; 28-inch to 32-inch barrels; screw-in choke tubes; hand-checkered European walnut straight-grip or pistol-grip stock, forearm; single selective trigger; auto ejectors. Introduced 1993; still in production.

Perf: $25,000 **Exc:** $22,000 **VGood:** $16,000

HOLLAND & HOLLAND SPORTING OVER/UNDER DELUXE

Same specs as Sporting Over/Under except better engraving and select wood. Introduced 1993; still in production.

Perf: $34,775 **Exc:** $23,000 **VGood:** $18,000

HOLLAND & HOLLAND SUPER TRAP

Single barrel; Anson & Deeley boxlock; 12-ga.; 30-inch, 32-inch barrel; Extra-Full choke; European walnut Monte Carlo stock, full beavertail forearm; automatic ejector; no safety; recoil pad. Made in three grades with varying types of engraving and wood. Introduced prior to World War II; discontinued late 1960s.

Standard Grade
Perf: $4500 **Exc:** $4000 **VGood:** $3500

Deluxe Grade
Perf: $7500 **Exc:** $6000 **VGood:** $4500

Exhibition Grade
Perf: $10,250 **Exc:** $8500 **VGood:** $7000

HUNTER FULTON

Side-by-side; boxlock; hammerless; 12-, 16-, 20-ga., .410; 26-inch to 32-inch barrels; standard choke combos; walnut stock; hand-checkered pistol grip, forearm; double triggers or non-selective single trigger. Introduced 1920; discontinued 1948. Made by Hunter Arms Company, Fulton, New York. Considerable premium for .410.

Double triggers
Exc: $500 **VGood:** $390 **Good:** $295

Single trigger
Exc: $600 **VGood:** $425 **Good:** $325

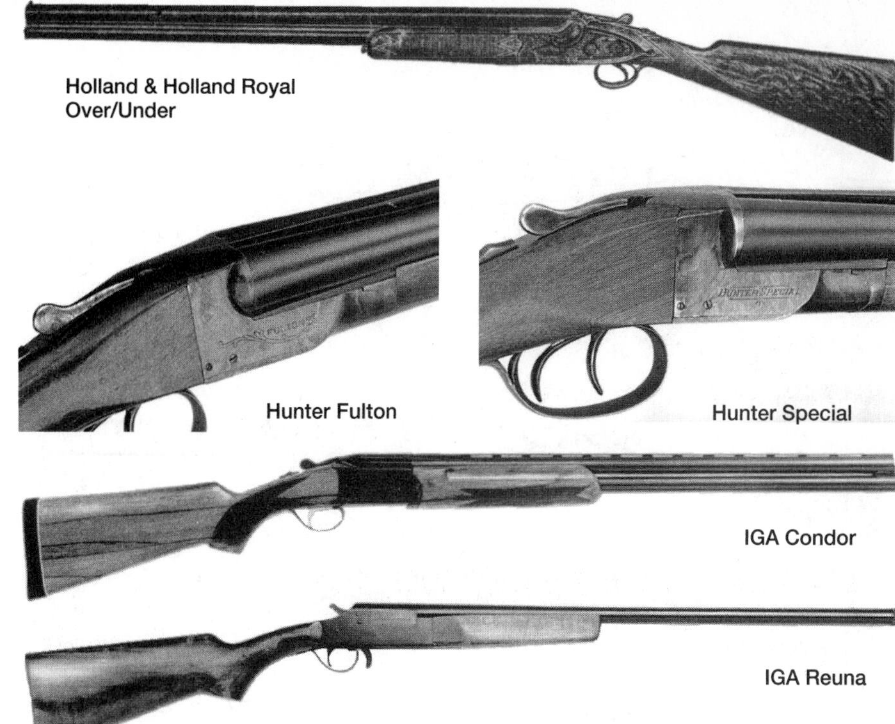

Holland & Holland Royal Over/Under

Hunter Fulton

Hunter Special

IGA Condor

IGA Reuna

HUNTER SPECIAL

Side-by-side; boxlock; hammerless; 12-, 16-, 20-ga.; 26-inch to 30-inch barrels; standard choke combos; hand-checkered walnut pistol-grip stock, forearm; extractors. Introduced 1920; discontinued 1948.

Double triggers
Exc: $525 **VGood:** $425 **Good:** $325

Single trigger
Exc: $625 **VGood:** $525 **Good:** $425

IGA COACH MODEL

Side-by-side; 12-, 20-ga., .410; 2-3/4-inch (12-, 20-ga.), 3-inch (.410) chambers; 20-inch barrels; Improved Cylinder/ Modified chokes; solid matted rib; oil-finished hand-checkered Brazilian hardwood pistol grip stock, forend; extractors; auto safety; double triggers. Made in Brazil. Introduced 1983; still imported by Stoeger.

Perf: $240 **Exc:** $170 **VGood:** $135

IGA CONDOR

Over/under; boxlock; 12-, 20-ga.; 3-inch chambers; 26-inch. 28-inch barrels; Improved Cylinder/Modified, Modified/Full choke tubes; vent top rib; weighs 7 lbs.; oil-finished checkered Brazilian hardwood pistol-grip stock, forend; manual safety; single trigger; extractors. Made in Brazil. Introduced 1983.

Perf: $280 **Exc:** $225 **VGood:** $150

IGA CONDOR I

Same specs as the Condor except single trigger, deluxe checkered walnut stock; vent. rib; separated barrels; choke tubes.

Perf: $295 **Exc:** $250 **VGood:** $175

IGA CONDOR II

Same specs as the Condor except double triggers, molded buttplate. Made in Brazil. Introduced 1983; still imported by Stoeger.

Perf: $295 **Exc:** $250 **VGood:** $175

IGA CONDOR I SPECIAL

Similar to Condor I, except has matte nickel finish, oil finished hardwood stock and forearm. Importation began 2002.

Perf: $355 **Exc:** $300 **VGood:** $240

IGA CONDOR SUPREME

Same specs as the Condor except automatic ejectors. Made in Brazil. Introduced 1983; still imported by Stoeger.

Perf: $395 **Exc:** $250 **VGood:** $195

IGA CONDOR SUPREME DELUXE

Same specs. as the Condor Supreme, except high polish blue; gold SST. Importation began 2000.

Perf: $430 **Exc:** $355 **VGood:** $260

IGA HUNTER CLAYS MODEL

Over/under; 12-ga.; single trigger; ejectors; 28-inch barrels; choke tubes; deluxe checkered stock and forearm; gold trigger. Mfg. 1997-99.

Perf: $495 **Exc:** $415 **VGood:** $335

IGA TURKEY SERIES

Over/under; 12-ga.; 3-inch chambers; 26-inch barrels; vent. rib; choke tubes; single trigger; ejectors; Advantage camo on wood and metal (except receiver. Produced 1997 to 2000.

Perf: $415 **Exc:** $325 **VGood:** $250

IGA WATERFOWL SERIES

Similar to Turkey Series, except has 30-inch barrels; 12-ga.; 3-inch chamber. Produced 1998-2000.

Perf: $415 **Exc:** $325 **VGood:** $250

IGA ERA 2000

Over/under; boxlock; 12-ga.; 3-inch chambers; 26-inch, 28-inch barrels; Full, Modified, Improved Cylinder choke tubes; oil-finished hand-checkered Brazilian hardwood pistol grip stock, forend; single trigger; blue finish. Made in Brazil. Introduced 1992; still imported by Stoeger.

Perf: $385 **Exc:** $275 **VGood:** $195

IGA REUNA

Single shot; exposed hammer; 12-, 20-ga., .410; 2-3/4-inch (12-ga), 3-inch (20-ga., .410) chamber; 26-inch, 28-inch barrel; Full choke tube; weighs 5-1/4 lbs.; metal bead front sight; Brazilian hardwood

stock; half-cock safety; extractor; blued finish. Made in Brazil. Introduced 1987; still imported by Stoeger.

Perf: $95 **Exc:** $70 **VGood:** $60

IGA UPLANDER

Side-by-side; boxlock; 12-, 20-, 28-ga., .410; 2-3/4-inch (12, 20-, 28-ga.), 3-inch (.410) chambers; 26-inch. 28-inch barrels; Improved Cylinder/Modified, Modified/Full, Full/Full (.410) chokes; solid matted rib; oil-finished hand-checkered hardwood pistol-grip stock, forend; extractors; auto safety; double triggers. Made in Brazil. Introduced 1983; still imported by Stoeger.

Perf: $300 **Exc:** $235 **VGood:** $185

INDUSTRIAS DANOK RED PRINCE

Side-by-side; 12-ga.; 2-3/4-inch chambers; Modified/Full barrels; medium bead front sight; checkered European walnut straight-grip stock, forend; double triggers; auto ejectors; hand-engraved action. Made in Spain. Introduced 1982 by Toledo Armas; discontinued 1984.

Perf: $900 **Exc:** $700 **VGood:** $550

ITHACA MAG-10

Gas-operated autoloader; 10-ga.; 3-1/2-inch chamber; 3-shot magazine; various barrel lengths, chokes; plain or vent rib; walnut stock, forearm; recoil pad. Introduced 1977; discontinued 1986.

With plain barrel

Perf: $650 **Exc:** $520 **VGood:** $440

With vent rib

Perf: $700 **Exc:** $570 **VGood:** $490

ITHACA MAG-10 DELUXE

Same specs as Mag-10 except vent rib; checkered semi-fancy walnut stock, forearm; sling swivels. Introduced 1977; discontinued 1986.

Perf: $800 **Exc:** $725 **VGood:** $575

ITHACA MAG-10 SUPREME

Same specs as Mag-10 except vent rib; checkered fancy walnut stock, forearm; sling swivels. Introduced 1974; discontinued 1986.

Perf: $850 **Exc:** $740 **VGood:** $625

ITHACA MAG-10 ROADBLOCKER

Similar to the standard Mag-10, except 22-inch cylinder bore ribless barrel; parkerized finish. Was marketed to police departments as a tactical shotgun for stopping moving cars.

Perf: $750 **Exc:** $625 **VGood:** $575

ITHACA MODEL 51

Gas-operated autoloader; takedown; 12-, 20-ga.; 2-3/4-inch chamber; 3-shot tube magazine; 26-inch Improved or Skeet, 28-inch Full or Modified or Skeet, 30-inch Full barrel; optional vent rib; Raybar front sight; hand-checkered American walnut pistol-grip stock; white spacer on pistol grip; reversible safety; engraved receiver. Introduced 1970; discontinued 1982.

Plain barrel

Perf: $260 **Exc:** $210 **VGood:** $180

Vent rib

Perf: $290 **Exc:** $240 **VGood:** $210

ITHACA MODEL 51A

Same specs as Model 51 except cosmetic improvements. Introduced 1982; discontinued 1986.

Perf: $260 **Exc:** $210 **VGood:** $180

ITHACA MODEL 51A DEERSLAYER

Same specs as Model 51 except special 24-inch slug barrel; Raybar front sight, open adjustable rear; sight base grooved for scope mounts. Introduced 1983; discontinued 1984.

Perf: $355 **Exc:** $300 **VGood:** $260

ITHACA MODEL 51A MAGNUM

Same specs as Model 51 except 12-ga.; 3-inch chamber. Introduced 1984; discontinued 1985.

Perf: $375 **Exc:** $320 **VGood:** $225

Add approximately 10 percent to above prices for vent. rib.

ITHACA MODEL 51A MAGNUM WATERFOWLER

Same specs as Model 51 except 12-ga.; 3-inch chamber; vent rib; matte-finished metal; sling; swivels. Introduced 1985; discontinued 1986.

Perf: $325 **Exc:** $290 **VGood:** $210

Add approximately $50 for camouflage exterior finish.

ITHACA MODEL 51A PRESENTATION

Same specs as Model 51 except 12-ga.; deluxe checkered walnut pistol-grip stock, forearm; elaborate engraving. Introduced 1984; discontinued 1986.

Perf: $850 **Exc:** $775 **VGood:** $675

ITHACA MODEL 51A SUPREME SKEET

Same specs as Model 51 except 12-, 20-ga.; 26-inch Skeet barrel; fancy American walnut Skeet stock. Introduced 1983; discontinued 1986.

Perf: $465 **Exc:** $395 **VGood:** $340

ITHACA MODEL 51A SUPREME TRAP

Same specs as Model 51 except 30-inch Full-choke barrel; fancy American walnut trap stock; Monte Carlo stock optional; recoil pad. Introduced 1983; discontinued 1986.

Perf: $450 **Exc:** $375 **VGood:** $320

ITHACA MODEL 51 DEERSLAYER

Same specs as Model 51 except 12-, 20-ga.; special 24-inch slug barrel; Raybar front sight, open adjustable rear; sight base grooved for scope. Introduced 1972; discontinued 1983.

Perf: $335 **Exc:** $275 **VGood:** $225

ITHACA MODEL 51 FEATHERLIGHT

Same specs as Model 51 except hand-fitted; engraved receiver; weighs 7-1/2 lbs. Introduced 1978; discontinued 1982.

Perf: $375 **Exc:** $300 **VGood:** $275

ITHACA MODEL 51 FEATHERLIGHT DELUXE TRAP

Same specs as Model 51 except 28-inch Full or Improved Modified, 30-inch Full or Improved Cylinder barrel; weighs 7-1/2 lbs.; fancy walnut trap-style stock; hand-fitted, engraved receiver. No longer produced.

Perf: $400 **Exc:** $315 **VGood:** $270

ITHACA MODEL 51 MAGNUM

Same specs as Model 51 except 12-ga.; 3-inch chamber. Introduced 1970; discontinued 1985.

Plain barrel

Perf: $255 **Exc:** $200 **VGood:** $175

Vent rib

Perf: $285 **Exc:** $235 **VGood:** $200

ITHACA MODEL 51 SKEET

Same specs as Model 51 except 12-, 20-ga.; 26-inch Skeet barrel; vent rib; select Skeet-style stock; recoil pad. Introduced 1970; discontinued 1986.

Perf: $360 **Exc:** $310 **VGood:** $260

ITHACA MODEL 51 TRAP

Same specs as Model 51 except 30-inch. 32-inch barrel; Full choke; vent rib; select trap-style stock; recoil pad. Introduced 1970; discontinued 1986.

Perf: $360 **Exc:** $310 **VGood:** $260

ITHACA MODEL 51 TURKEY

Same specs as Model 51 except 12-ga.; 3-inch chamber; 26-inch barrel; sling; swivels; matte finish. Introduced 1984; discontinued 1986.

Perf: $350 **Exc:** $270 **VGood:** $240

ITHACA MODEL 300

Recoil-operated autoloader; takedown; 12-ga.; 26-inch Improved Cylinder, 28-inch Full or Modified, 30-inch Full-choke barrel; optional vent rib; checkered American walnut pistol-grip stock, fluted forearm; crossbolt safety; automatic magazine cutoff allows changing loads without unloading magazine. Introduced 1969; discontinued 1973.

Plain barrel

Perf: $275 **Exc:** $200 **VGood:** $150

Vent rib

Perf: $295 **Exc:** $220 **VGood:** $170

ITHACA MODEL 900 DELUXE

Recoil-operated autoloader; takedown; 12-, 20-ga.; 25-inch Improved Cylinder; 28-inch Full or

Modified, 30-inch Full-choke (12-ga.) vent-rib barrel; hand-checkered American walnut pistol-grip stock, forearm; white spacers on grip cap, buttplate; interchangeable barrels; crossbolt safety; gold-filled engraving on receiver; gold-plated trigger; nameplate inlaid in stock. Introduced 1969; discontinued 1973.

Perf: $420 **Exc:** $340 **VGood:** $270

ITHACA MODEL 900 DELUXE SLUG

Same specs as Model 900 Deluxe except 24-inch barrel; rifle sights. Introduced 1969; discontinued 1973.

Perf: $420 **Exc:** $340 **VGood:** $270

ITHACA MODEL XL 300

Gas-operated autoloader; 12-, 20-ga.; 26-inch Improved Cylinder or Skeet, 28-inch Full or Modified, 30-inch Full or Modified barrel; optional vent rib; checkered American walnut pistol-grip stock, fluted forearm; self-compensating gas system; reversible safety. Introduced 1973; discontinued 1976.

Perf: $325 **Exc:** $250 **VGood:** $200

Add approximately 10 percent to above prices for vent. rib.

ITHACA MODEL XL 900

Gas-operated autoloader; 12-, 20-ga.; 5-shot tube magazine; 26-inch Improved Cylinder or Skeet, 28-inch Full or Modified, 30-inch Full or Improved Cylinder barrels; Bradley-type front sight on target-grade guns; Raybar front sight on vent-rib field guns; checkered walnut-finished stock; self-compensating gas system; reversible safety; action release button. Introduced 1973; discontinued 1978.

Perf: $350 **Exc:** $270 **VGood:** $200

Vent rib

Perf: $370 **Exc:** $290 **VGood:** $220

Skeet grade

Perf: $385 **Exc:** $300 **VGood:** $250

Trap grade

Perf: $385 **Exc:** $300 **VGood:** $250

ITHACA MODEL XL 900 SLUG GUN

Same specs as Model XL 900 except 24-inch slug barrel; rifle sights. Introduced 1973; discontinued 1978.

Perf: $335 **Exc:** $270 **VGood:** $240

ITHACA MODEL 37

Slide action; hammerless; takedown; 12-, 16-, 20-ga.; 4-shot tube magazine; 26-inch, 28-inch, 30-inch barrel; hand-checkered American walnut pistol-grip stock, slide handle, or uncheckered stock, grooved slide handle. Introduced 1937; discontinued 1986.

Checkered stock

Perf: $300 **Exc:** $225 **VGood:** $175

Uncheckered stock

Perf: $275 **Exc:** $250 **VGood:** $175

ITHACA MODEL 37 $3000 GRADE

Same specs as Model 37 except custom-built; hand-finished parts; hand-checkered pistol-grip stock, slide handle of select figured walnut; gold-inlaid engraving; recoil pad. Was listed as $1000 Grade prior to World War II. Introduced 1937; discontinued 1967.

Exc: $4000 **VGood:** $3500 **Good:** $2800

ITHACA MODEL 37 BASIC FEATHERLIGHT

Same specs as Model 37 except plain or vent rib; tung-oil-finished walnut stock, traditional ringtail forend; matte finish on all metal. Introduced 1980; discontinued 1983.

Perf: $295 **Exc:** $190 **VGood:** $150

ITHACA MODEL 37D FEATHERLIGHT

Same specs as Model 37 except 12-, 20-ga.; 5-shot magazine; Ithaca Raybar front sight; checkered American walnut pistol-grip stock, fore-end; decorated receiver; crossbolt safety; recoil pad. Introduced 1954; discontinued 1981.

Perf: $300 **Exc:** $225 **VGood:** $190

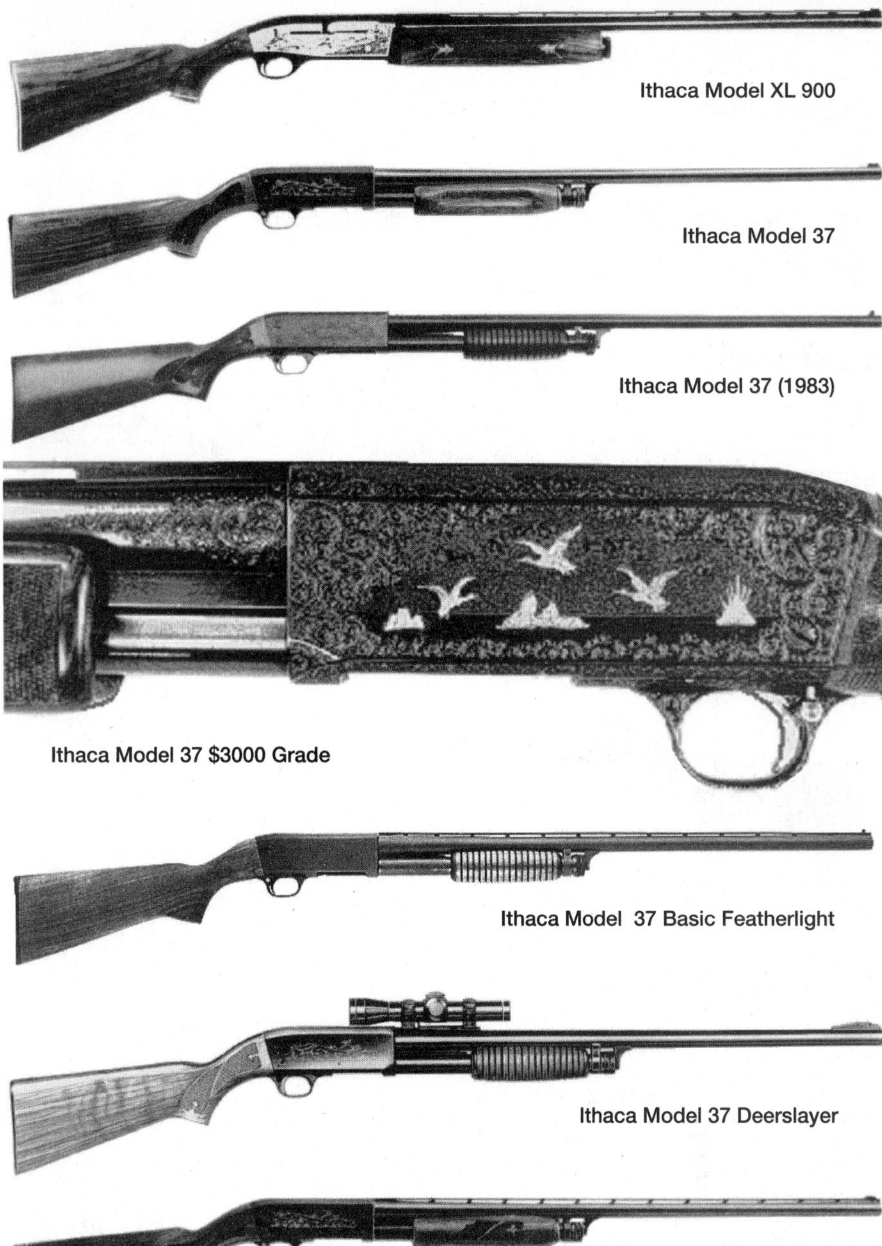

Ithaca Model XL 900

Ithaca Model 37

Ithaca Model 37 (1983)

Ithaca Model 37 $3000 Grade

Ithaca Model 37 Basic Featherlight

Ithaca Model 37 Deerslayer

Ithaca Model 37DV Featherweight

Ithaca Model 37 English Ultralight

ITHACA MODEL 37 DEERSLAYER

Same specs as Model 37 except 20-inch, 26-inch barrel bored for rifled slugs; open rifle-type rear sight, ramp front. Introduced 1969; discontinued 1986.

Perf: $350 **Exc:** $250 **VGood:** $225

ITHACA MODEL 37 DELUXE FEATHERLIGHT

Same specs as Model 37 except vent rib; deluxe oil-finished cut-checkered straight-grip stock, slide handle. Introduced 1981; discontinued 1986.

Perf: $350 **Exc:** $325 **VGood:** $295

ITHACA MODEL 37DV FEATHERWEIGHT

Same specs as Model 37 except 12-, 20-ga.; 5-shot magazine; Ithaca Raybar front sight; vent rib; checkered American walnut pistol-grip stock, beavertail forend; decorated receiver; crossbolt safety; recoil pad. Introduced 1962; discontinued 1981.

Perf: $300 **Exc:** $240 **VGood:** $195

ITHACA MODEL 37 ENGLISH ULTRALIGHT

Same specs as Model 37 except 12-, 20-ga.; 25-inch vent-rib barrel; oil-finished cut-checkered straight-grip stock, slide handle. Introduced 1981; discontinued 1986.

Perf: $475 **Exc:** $400 **VGood:** $350

ITHACA MODEL 37 FEATHERLIGHT

Same specs as Model 37 except 12-, 20-ga.; 5-shot magazine; Ithaca Raybar front sight; checkered American walnut pistol-grip stock; decorated

Ithaca Model 37R Deluxe

Ithaca Model 37 Super Deerslayer

Ithaca Model 37T Target Grade

Ithaca Model 37 Deluxe

Ithaca Ellett Special Model 37 Turkeyslayer

receiver; crossbolt safety. Introduced 1980; discontinued 1986.

Perf: $300 **Exc:** $240 **VGood:** $195

ITHACA MODEL 37 FEATHERLIGHT PRESENTATION

Same specs as Model 37 except 12-ga.; 5-shot magazine; Ithaca Raybar front sight; fancy checkered American walnut pistol-grip stock; gold decorated receiver; engraving; crossbolt safety. Introduced 1981; discontinued 1986.

Perf: $1175 **Exc:** $1000 **VGood:** $890

ITHACA MODEL 37 FIELD GRADE

Same specs as Model 37 except 12-, 20-ga.; 2-3/4-inch chamber; standard or vent rib barrel; Raybar front sight; American hardwood stock, ring-tail forend. Introduced 1983; discontinued 1986.

Perf: $300 **Exc:** $240 **VGood:** $195

ITHACA MODEL 37 FIELD GRADE MAGNUM

Same specs as Model 37 except 12-, 20-ga.; 3-inch chamber; 28-inch, 30-inch vent-rib barrel; Raybar front sight; American hardwood stock, ringtail forend; elongated receiver; grip cap has flying mallard; recoil pad. Introduced 1978; discontinued 1986.

Perf: $370 **Exc:** $340 **VGood:** $310

ITHACA MODEL 37R

Same general specs as Model 37 except raised solid rib. Introduced 1937; discontinued 1967.

Checkered stock

Exc: $275 **VGood:** $250 **Good:** $185

Uncheckered stock

Exc: $265 **VGood:** $240 **Good:** $175

ITHACA MODEL 37R DELUXE

Same specs as Model 37 except raised solid rib; hand-checkered fancy walnut stock, slide handle. Introduced 1955; discontinued 1961.

Exc: $350 **VGood:** $275 **Good:** $250

ITHACA MODEL 37S SKEET GRADE

Same specs as Model 37 except vent rib; checkered stock, extension slide handle. Introduced 1937; discontinued 1955.

Exc: $445 **VGood:** $375 **Good:** $335

ITHACA MODEL 37 SUPER DEERSLAYER

Same specs as Model 37 except 20-inch, 26-inch barrel bored for rifled slugs; open rifle-type rear sight, ramp front; improved wood in stock, slide handle. Introduced 1962; discontinued 1979.

Exc: $330 **VGood:** $250 **Good:** $185

ITHACA MODEL 37 SUPREME GRADE

Same specs as Model 37 except hand-checkered fancy walnut stock, slide handle; available in Skeet or trap configurations. Introduced 1967; discontinued 1979.

Perf: $500 **Exc:** $400 **VGood:** $350

ITHACA MODEL 37T TARGET GRADE

Same specs as Model 37 except vent rib; hand-checkered fancy walnut stock, slide handle; choice of Skeet or Trap stock. Replaced Model 37S Skeet Grade and Model 37T Trap Grade. Introduced 1955; discontinued 1961.

Perf: $425 **Exc:** $375 **VGood:** $325

ITHACA MODEL 37T TRAP GRADE

Same specs as Model 37 except vent rib; checkered select walnut straight trap-style stock, extension slide-handle; recoil pad. Introduced 1937; discontinued 1955.

Perf: $425 **Exc:** $375 **VGood:** $325

ITHACA MODEL 37 ULTRA-LIGHT

Same specs as Model 37 except 12-, 20-ga.; 5-shot magazine; 25-inch vent-rib barrel; checkered American walnut pistol-grip stock; recoil pad; gold-plated trigger; Sid Bell-designed grip cap. No longer in production.

Perf: $390 **Exc:** $275 **VGood:** $220

ITHACA MODEL 37V FEATHERWEIGHT

Same specs as Model 37 except 12-, 20-ga.; 5-shot magazine; vent rib; Ithaca Raybar front sight; checkered American walnut pistol-grip stock; decorated receiver; crossbolt safety. No longer in production.

Perf: $260 **Exc:** $240 **VGood:** $195

ITHACA MODEL 37 DELUXE PUMP

Gauge: 12, 16, 20, 3-inch chamber. Barrel: 26-inch, 28-inch, 30-inch (12 gauge), 26-inch, 28-inch (16 and 20 gauge), choke tubes. Weight: 7 lbs. Stock: Walnut with cut-checkered grip and forend. Features: Steel receiver; bottom ejection; brushed blue finish, vent rib barrels. Reintroduced 1996. Made in U.S. by Ithaca Gun Co.

Perf: $485 **Exc:** $365 **VGood:** $275

With straight English-style stock

Perf: $675 **Exc:** $580 **VGood:** 340

ITHACA MODEL 37 NEW CLASSIC

Ringtail forend, sunburst recoil pad, hand-finished walnut stock, 26-inch or 28-inch barrel)

Perf: $665 **Exc:** $525 **VGood:** $400

ITHACA MODEL 37 WATERFOWLER

Similar to Model 37 Deluxe except in 12-gauge only with 28-inch barrel, special extended steel shot choke tube system. Complete coverage of Advantage Wetlands or Hardwoods camouflage. Introduced 1999. Made in U.S. by Ithaca Gun Co.

Perf: $540 **Exc:** $400 **VGood:** $315

ITHACA MODEL 37 DEERSLAYER II

Gauge: 12, 20, 3-inch chamber. Barrel: 20-inch, 25-inch, fully rifled. Weight: 7 lbs. Stock: Cut-checkered American walnut with Monte Carlo comb. Sights: Rifle-type. Features: Integral barrel and receiver. Bottom ejection. Brushed blue finish. Reintroduced 1997. Made in U.S. by Ithaca Gun Co.

Perf: $500 **Exc:** $375 **VGood:** $295

Smooth Bore Deluxe

Perf: $475 **Exc:** $395 **VGood:** $325

Rifled Deluxe

Perf: $475 **Exc:** $395 **VGood:** $325

ITHACA MODEL 37 DEERSLAYER III

Gauge: 12, 20, 2-3/4-inch and 3-inch chambers; 26-inch rifled barrel free floated; weighs 9 lbs.; Monte Carlo laminate stock; barrel length gives increased velocity; trigger and sear set hand filed and stoned for creep free operation; Weaver-style scope base; swivel studs; matte blue.

Perf: $550 **Exc:** $475 **VGood:** $300

ITHACA MODEL 37 RUFFED GROUSE SPECIAL EDITION

Gauge: 20. Barrel: 22-inch, 24-inch, interchangeable choke tubes. Weight: 5.25 lbs. Stock: American black walnut. Features: Laser engraved stock wtih line art drawing. Bottom eject. Vent rib and English style. Right- or left-hand via simple safety change. Aluminum receiver. Made in U.S.A. by Ithaca Gun Co.

Perf: $715 **Exc:** $565 **VGood:** $435

ITHACA ELLETT SPECIAL MODEL 37 TURKEYSLAYER

Gauge: 12, 3-inch chamber. Barrel: 22-inch ported. Stock: Composite. Sights: Fully adjustable, TruGlo front and rear. Features: Recreated from "Golden Age." Complete camo covering. Drilled and tapped. Extended turkey chokes. Matte metal, Realtree Hardwoods 20/200 or Advantage Timber patterns.

Perf: $500 **Exc:** $375 **VGood:** $295

ITHACA QUAD BORE MODEL 37 TURKEYSLAYER

Gauge: 20. Barrel: 22-inch ported. Weight: 6.25 lbs. Stock: Black walnut stock and forend. Sights: Fully adjustable, TruGlo. Features: Sling swivel studs, matte blue, turkey Full choke tube, 100 percent American made.

Perf: $520 **Exc:** $395 **VGood:** $315

ITHACA MODEL 37 ULTRALIGHT DELUXE

Gauge: 16, 2-3/4-inch chamber. Barrel: 24-inch, 26-inch, 28-inch. Weight: 5.25 lbs. Stock: Standard deluxe. Sights: Raybar. Features: Vent rib, drilled and tapped, interchangeable barrel. F, M, IC choke tubes.

Deluxe

Perf: $475 **Exc:** $380 **VGood:** $340

Classic/English

Perf: $475 **Exc:** $380 **VGood:** $340

Classic/Pistol

Perf: $475 **Exc:** $380 **VGood:** $340

ITHACA MODEL 66

Lever action; single shot; manually cocked hammer; 12-, 20-ga., .410; 26-inch Full (.410), 28-inch Full or Modified (12-, 20-ga.), 30-inch Full (12-ga.) barrel; vent. rib (special order); checkered straight stock, uncheckered forearm. Introduced 1963; discontinued 1979.

Exc: $225 **VGood:** $195 **Good:** $115

Add about 35 percent to above prices for .410 bore.
Add 10 percent for vent. rib.

ITHACA MODEL 66 LONG TOM

Same specs as Model 66 except 12-ga.; 36-inch Full-choke barrel; recoil pad. Introduced 1969; discontinued 1974.

Exc: $265 **VGood:** $235 **Good:** $195

ITHACA MODEL 66RS BUCK BUSTER

Same specs as Model 66 except 12-, 20-ga.; 22-inch Cylinder barrel; rifle sights. Introduced 1967; 12-ga. discontinued 1970; 20-ga. discontinued 1979.

Perf: $265 **Exc:** $250 **VGood:** $175

ITHACA MODEL 66 VENT RIB

Same specs as Model 66 except vent-rib barrel. Introduced 1969; discontinued 1974.

Perf: $250 **Exc:** $210 **VGood:** $125

ITHACA MODEL 66 YOUTH MODEL

Same specs as Model 66 except 20-ga., .410; 25-inch barrel; shorter stock; recoil pad. Introduced 1965; discontinued 1979.

Exc: $150 **VGood:** $125 **Good:** $100

ITHACA MODEL 87

Slide action; 12-, 20-ga.; 3-inch chamber; 5-shot magazine; 26-inch, 28-inch, 30-inch barrel; choke tubes; Raybar front sight; checkered walnut pistol-grip stock, forend; bottom ejection; crossbolt safety. Introduced 1988.

Perf: $350 **Exc:** $220 **VGood:** $180

ITHACA MODEL 87 CAMO

Same specs as Model 87 except 12-ga.; 24-inch, 26-inch, 28-inch vent-rib barrel; Modified choke tube; camouflage finish. Introduced 1988; still in production.

Perf: $410 **Exc:** $240 **VGood:** $180

ITHACA MODEL 87 COMBO

Same specs as Model 87 except 28-inch barrel with choke tubes, 20-inch, 25-inch rifled barrel; no checkering. No longer in production.

Perf: $400 **Exc:** $315 **VGood:** $275

ITHACA MODEL 87 DEERSLAYER

Same specs as Model 87 except 20-inch, 25-inch slug or rifled barrel; Raybar blade front sight on ramp, rear adjustable for windage, elevation; grooved for scope mounting. Introduced 1988; discontinued 1993.

Perf: $325 **Exc:** $210 **VGood:** $180

Ithaca Model 66

Ithaca Model 66 Long Tom

Ithaca Model 66RS Buck Buster

Ithaca Model 66 Youth Model

Ithaca Model 87 Deerslayer

Ithaca Model 87 Deerslayer II

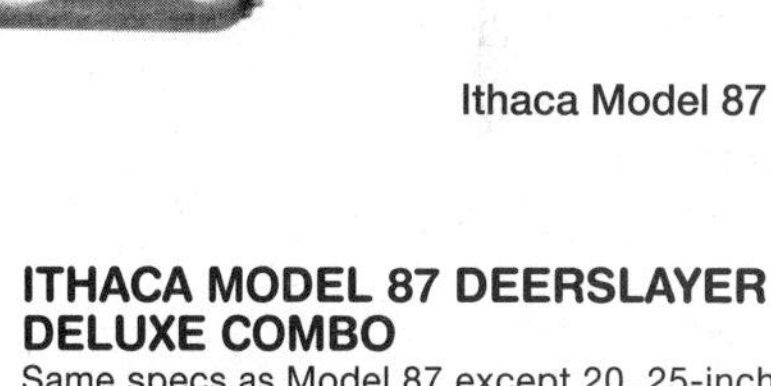

Ithaca Model 87

ITHACA MODEL 87 DEERSLAYER II

Same specs as Model 87 except rifled barrel; Raybar blade front sight on ramp, rear adjustable for windage and elevation; grooved for scope mounting; high-gloss checkered American walnut Monte Carlo stock, forend; solid-frame construction. Introduced 1988.

Perf: $425 **Exc:** $275 **VGood:** $210

ITHACA MODEL 87 DEERSLAYER II FAST TWIST

Same specs as Model 87 except 12-ga.; 25-inch non-removable rifled barrel; Raybar blade front sight on ramp, rear adjustable for windage and elevation; grooved for scope mounting; high-gloss checkered American walnut Monte Carlo stock, forend; solid-frame construction. Introduced 1992; discontinued 1993.

Perf: $420 **Exc:** $300 **VGood:** $250

ITHACA MODEL 87 DEERSLAYER DELUXE

Same specs as Model 87 except 20-inch, 25-inch slug or rifled barrel; Raybar blade front sight on ramp, rear adjustable for windage and elevation; grooved for scope mounting; high-gloss checkered walnut pistol-grip stock, forend; gold trigger. Introduced 1989.

Perf: $375 **Exc:** $240 **VGood:** $195

ITHACA MODEL 87 DEERSLAYER DELUXE COMBO

Same specs as Model 87 except 20, 25-inch slug or rifled barrel; extra 28-inch barrel; Raybar blade front sight on ramp, rear adjustable for windage and elevation; grooved for scope mounting; high-gloss checkered walnut pistol-grip stock, forend; gold trigger. Introduced 1989; still in production.

Perf: $475 **Exc:** $340 **VGood:** $295

ITHACA MODEL 87 DELUXE

Same specs as Model 87 except vent-rib barrel; choke tubes; high-gloss walnut stock, forend; gold trigger. Introduced 1988; still in production.

Perf: $400 **Exc:** $300 **VGood:** $240

ITHACA MODEL 87 DELUXE COMBO

Same specs as Model 87 except extra 28-inch barrel; vent rib; choke tubes; high-gloss walnut stock, forend; gold trigger. No longer in production.

Perf: $450 **Exc:** $350 **VGood:** $290

ITHACA MODEL 87 DELUXE MAGNUM

Same specs as Model 87 except vent-rib barrel; choke tubes; high-gloss walnut stock, forend; gold trigger. Introduced 1981; discontinued 1988.

Perf: $320 **Exc:** $270 **VGood:** $230

Ithaca Model 87 Supreme

Ithaca Model 87 Turkey

Ithaca Model 87 Ultralight

New Ithaca Double (NID) Field Grade

ITHACA MODEL 87 ENGLISH
Same specs as Model 87 except 20-ga.; 3-inch chamber; 24-inch, 26-inch vent-rib barrel; choke tubes; recoil pad. Introduced 1991.

Perf: $.410 **Exc:** $275 **VGood:** $225

ITHACA MODEL 87 M&P
Same specs as Model 87 except 5-, 8-shot magazine; 18-1/2-inch, 20-inch Cylinder bore barrel; weighs 7 lbs.; black polymer pistol-grip stock, forearm; Parkerized finish. Introduced 1988; discontinued 1993.

Perf: $250 **Exc:** $200 **VGood:** $170

ITHACA MODEL 87 SUPREME
Same specs as Model 87 except vent-rib; fancy-grade walnut stock, forend; engraving. Introduced 1988; still in production.

Perf: $650 **Exc:** $400 **VGood:** $300

ITHACA MODEL 87 TURKEYGUN
Same specs as Model 87 except 12-ga.; 24-inch barrel; fixed Full choke or Full choke tube; matte blue or Camoseal finish. Introduced 1988; still in production.

Perf: $375 **Exc:** $280 **VGood:** $200

ITHACA MODEL 87 ULTRA DEERSLAYER
Same specs as Model 87 except 20-inch, 25-inch slug or rifled barrel; Raybar blade front sight on ramp, rear adjustable for windage and elevation; grooved for scope mounting; high-gloss checkered walnut pistol-grip stock, forend; gold trigger; aluminum construction. Introduced 1989; discontinued 1990.

Perf: $325 **Exc:** $225 **VGood:** $180

ITHACA MODEL 87 ULTRALIGHT
Same specs as Model 87 except 12-, 20-ga.; 3-inch chamber; 20-inch, 24-inch, 25-inch, 26-inch barrel; fixed or choke tubes; aluminum construction. Introduced 1988; discontinued 1990.

Perf: $375 **Exc:** $295 **VGood:** $240

ITHACA MODEL 87 ULTRALIGHT DELUXE
Same specs as Model 87 except 12-, 20-ga.; 3-inch chamber; 20-inch, 24-inch, 25-inch, 26-inch barrel; fixed or choke tubes; high-gloss select-grade checkered walnut stock, forend; gold trigger; aluminum construction. Introduced 1989; discontinued 1991.

Perf: $410 **Exc:** $300 **VGood:** $235

ITHACA HOMELAND SECURITY GUNS
Gauge: 12 ga., 2-3/4-inch and 3-inch chambers. Barrel: 18-1/2-inch interchangeable. Weight: 6.5 lbs. Stock: Synthetic deluxe and oil finish. Sights: Bead. Discontinued 2002.

Synthetic/Standard

Perf: $450 **Exc:** $400 **VGood:** $300

Synthetic/Ported

Perf: $465 **Exc:** $415 **VGood:** $315

ITHACA CLASSIC DOUBLES SPECIAL FIELD GRADE SXS
Gauge: 20, 28, 2-3/4-inch chambers, .410, 3-inch. Barrel: 26-inch, 28-inch, 30-inch, fixed chokes. Weight: 5 lbs., 14 oz. (20-gauge). Stock: 14-1/2-inchx2-1/4-inchx1-3/8-inch. High-grade American black walnut, hand-rubbed oil finish; splinter or beavertail forend, straight or pistol grip. Features: Double triggers, ejectors; color case-hardened, engraved action body with matted top surfaces. Introduced 1999. Made in U.S. by Ithaca Classic Doubles. Discontinued.

Perf: $5999 **Exc:** $5200 **VGood:** $4650

ITHACA CLASSIC DOUBLES GRADE 4E CLASSIC SXS SHOTGUN
Similar to Special Field Grade except gold-plated triggers, jeweled barrel flats and hand-turned locks. Feather crotch and flame-grained black walnut hand-checkered 28 lpi with fleur-de-lis pattern. Action body engraved with three game scenes and bank note scroll, color case-hardened. Introduced 1999. Made in U.S. by Ithaca Classic Doubles. Discontinued.

Perf: $7500 **Exc:** $6750 **VGood:** $5750

ITHACA CLASSIC DOUBLES GRADE 7E CLASSIC SXS SHOTGUN
Similar to Special Field Grade except engraved with bank note scroll and flat 24k gold game scenes: gold setter and gold pointer on opposite action sides, American bald eagle inlaid on bottom plate. Hand-timed, polished, jeweled ejectors and locks. Exhibition grade American black walnut stock and forend with eight-panel fleur-de-lis borders. Introduced 1999. Made in U.S. by Ithaca Classic Doubles. Discontinued.

Perf: $11,000 **Exc:** $9900 **VGood:** $8950

ITHACA CLASSIC DOUBLES SOUSA SPECIAL GRADE SXS SHOTGUN
Similar to the Special Field Grade except presentation grade American black walnut, hand-carved and checkered; hand-engraving with 24-karat gold inlays; tuned action and hand-applied finishes. Made in U.S. by Ithaca Classic Doubles.

Perf: $18,000 **Exc:** $16,200 **VGood:** $15,125

ITHACA CRASS MODEL NO. 1
Side-by-side; boxlock; hammerless; (also available with exposed hammers); 10-, 12-, 16-ga. (introduced about 1898); twist barrels; American walnut pistol-grip stock; double triggers; extractors (ejectors optional after 1897). Ithaca's first hammerless model; original grades, No. 1 through No. 7; No. 1 Special and No. 1-1/2 added about 1898. Introduced, about 1888; discontinued, 1901; serial number range: 6981 to 49104.

Exc: $350 **VGood:** $300 **Good:** $240

ITHACA CRASS MODEL NO. 1 SPECIAL
Same specs as Crass Model No. 1 except steel barrels.

Exc: $400 **VGood:** $350 **Good:** $295

ITHACA CRASS MODEL NO. 1-1/2
Same specs as Crass Model No. 1.

Exc: $450 **VGood:** $400 **Good:** $325

ITHACA CRASS MODEL NO. 2
Same specs as Crass Model No. 1 except English walnut pistol-grip stock.

Exc: $570 **VGood:** $425 **Good:** $350

ITHACA CRASS MODEL NO. 3
Same specs as Crass Model No. 1 except twist or steel barrels; English walnut pistol-grip stock.

Exc: $660 **VGood:** $500 **Good:** $400

ITHACA CRASS MODEL NO. 4
Same specs as Crass Model No. 1 except twist or steel barrels; French walnut pistol-grip stock.

Exc: $1350 **VGood:** $1000 **Good:** $800

ITHACA CRASS MODEL NO. 5
Same specs as Crass Model No. 1 except twist or Krupp steel barrels; French walnut pistol-grip stock.

Exc: $1800 **VGood:** $1450 **Good:** $1100

ITHACA CRASS MODEL NO. 6
Same specs as Crass Model No. 1 except twist or Krupp steel barrels; French walnut pistol-grip stock.

Exc: $2200 **VGood:** $1850 **Good:** $1500

ITHACA CRASS MODEL NO. 7
Same specs as Crass Model No. 1 except twist or Whitworth steel barrels; French walnut pistol-grip stock.

Exc: $2500 **VGood:** $2150 **Good:** $1800

NEW ITHACA DOUBLE (NID) FIELD GRADE
Side-by-side; boxlock; hammerless; 10- (3-inch, 3-1/2-inch chambers), 12- (2-3/4-inch, 3-inch chambers), 16-, 20-ga., .410; 26-inch (12-, 16-, 20-ga., .410), 28-inch (12-, 16-, 20-ga., .410), 30-inch (12-, 16-, 20-ga.), 32-inch (10-ga.), 34-inch (10-ga.) fluid-steel barrels; American walnut pistol-grip stock; extractors (ejectors optional); double triggers (single trigger optional); optional recoil pad, ivory sight. Produced in nine grades. Magnum 10-ga. available in any grade, on special-order only, 1932-1942; total production about 887. Magnum 12-ga. available on special-order only, after 1937; total production about 87. Early NIDs (1926-1936) have snail-ear cocking indicators at the top of the frame. Introduced 1926; discontinued 1948; serial number range: 425000 to 470099. Minimum 150% premium for .410.

Exc: $590 **VGood:** $480 **Good:** $400

NEW ITHACA DOUBLE (NID) SKEET MODEL FIELD GRADE

Same specs as New Ithaca Double (NID) Field Grade except ivory sight; American walnut pistol-grip stock, beavertail forend; ejectors; recoil pad. Introduced 1935; discontinued 1948.

Exc: $750 **VGood:** $600 **Good:** $475

NEW ITHACA DOUBLE (NID) NO. 2

Same specs as New Ithaca Double (NID) Field Grade.

Exc: $950 **VGood:** $550 **Good:** $525

NEW ITHACA DOUBLE (NID) NO. 3

Same specs as New Ithaca Double (NID) Field Grade; ejectors standard after 1935.

Exc: $1100 **VGood:** $700 **Good:** $600

NEW ITHACA DOUBLE (NID) NO. 4

Same specs as New Ithaca Double (NID) Field Grade except extractors (ejectors optional until 1935, then standard); double triggers (single trigger optional); optional beavertail forend, vent rib, recoil pad, ivory sight.

Exc: $2250 **VGood:** $1600 **Good:** $1200

NEW ITHACA DOUBLE (NID) NO. 5

Same specs as New Ithaca Double (NID) Field Grade except extractors (ejectors optional until 1926, then standard); double triggers (single trigger optional); optional beavertail forend, vent rib, recoil pad, ivory sight.

Exc: $3000 **VGood:** $2650 **Good:** $1900

NEW ITHACA DOUBLE (NID) NO. 7

Same specs as New Ithaca Double (NID) Field Grade except extractors (ejectors optional until 1926, then standard); double triggers (single trigger optional); optional beavertail forend, vent rib, recoil pad, ivory sight.

Exc: $6000 **VGood:** $5000 **Good:** $4500

NEW ITHACA DOUBLE (NID) SOUSA SPECIAL

Same specs as New Ithaca Double (NID) Field Grade except extractors (ejectors optional until 1926, then standard); double triggers (single trigger optional); optional beavertail forend, vent rib, recoil pad, ivory sight. Extreme rarity precludes pricing.

ITHACA FLUES MODEL FIELD GRADE

Side-by-side; boxlock; hammerless (also available with exposed hammers until about 1915); 10-, 12-, 16-, 20-ga.; 24-inch (20-ga.), 26-inch (12-, 16-, 20-ga.), 28-inch (12-, 16-, 20-ga.), 30-inch (10-, 12-, 16-ga.), 32-inch (10-, 12-ga.) fluid-steel barrels; American walnut half-pistol-grip stock; extractors (ejectors optional); double triggers (Infallible single trigger optional, 1915-1916); produced in eleven grades. Introduced 1908; discontinued 1926; serial number range: 175000 to 398365.

Exc: $750 **VGood:** $500 **Good:** $350

ITHACA FLUES MODEL NO. 1

Same specs as Flues Model Field Grade except also 28-ga. with 24-inch, 26-inch barrels; twist barrels; American walnut pistol-grip stock.

Exc: $800 **VGood:** $650 **Good:** $400

ITHACA FLUES MODEL NO. 1 SPECIAL

Same specs as Flues Model Field Grade except also 28-ga. with 24-inch, 26-inch barrels; American walnut pistol-grip stock.

Exc: $850 **VGood:** $700 **Good:** $500

ITHACA FLUES MODEL NO. 1-1/2

Same specs as Flues Model Field Grade except also 28-ga. with 24-inch, 26-inch barrels; twist barrels; American walnut pistol-grip stock.

Perf: $750 **Exc:** $500 **VGood:** $350

ITHACA FLUES MODEL NO. 2

Same specs as Flues Model Field Grade except also 28-ga. with 24-inch, 26-inch barrels; twist barrels; American walnut pistol-grip stock.

Exc: $750 **VGood:** $500 **Good:** $350

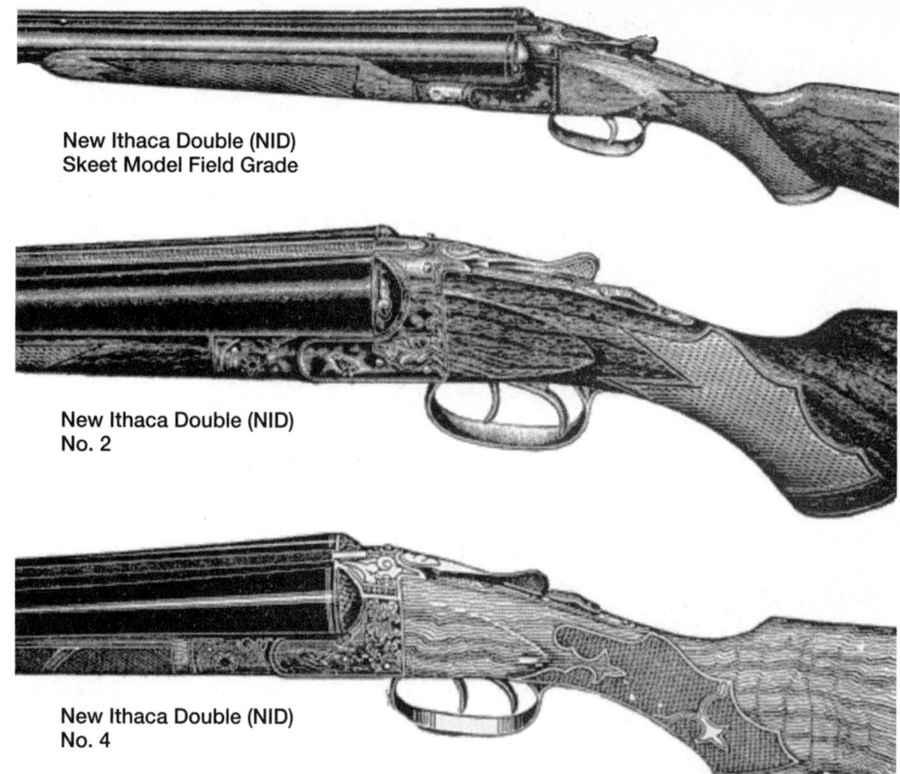

New Ithaca Double (NID) Skeet Model Field Grade

New Ithaca Double (NID) No. 2

New Ithaca Double (NID) No. 4

ITHACA FLUES MODEL NO. 2 KRUPP PIGEON GUN

Same specs as Flues Model Field Grade except also 28-ga. with 24-inch, 26-inch barrels; Krupp steel barrels; European walnut stock; pistol, half-pistol or straight grip.

Exc: $800 **VGood:** $550 **Good:** $400

ITHACA FLUES MODEL NO. 3

Same specs as Flues Model Field Grade except also 28-ga. with 24-inch, 26-inch barrels; twist or Krupp steel barrels; European walnut stock; pistol, half-pistol or straight grip.

Krupp steel

Exc: $825 **VGood:** $550 **Good:** $400

ITHACA FLUES MODEL NO. 4

Same specs as Flues Model Field Grade except also 28-ga. with 24-inch, 26-inch barrels; twist or Krupp steel barrels; European walnut stock; pistol, half-pistol or straight grip.

Krupp steel

Exc: $1350 **VGood:** $1000 **Good:** $800

ITHACA FLUES MODEL NO. 5

Same specs as Flues Model Field Grade except also 28-ga. with 24-inch, 26-inch barrels; twist or Krupp steel barrels; European walnut stock; pistol, half-pistol or straight grip.

Krupp steel

Exc: $1800 **VGood:** $1450 **Good:** $1100

ITHACA FLUES MODEL NO. 6

Same specs as Flues Model Field Grade, except also 28-ga. with 24-inch, 26-inch barrels; twist or Krupp steel barrels; English walnut stock; pistol, half-pistol or straight grip. Extreme rarity precludes pricing.

ITHACA FLUES MODEL NO. 7

Same specs as Flues Model Field Grade, except also 28-ga. with 24-inch, 26-inch barrels; Whitworth steel barrels; English walnut stock; pistol, half-pistol or straight grip. Extreme rarity precludes pricing.

ITHACA FLUES ONE-BARREL TRAP GUN NO. 4

Side-by-side; boxlock; hammerless; 12-ga.; 30-inch, 32-inch, 34-inch Krupp steel barrels; vent rib; American walnut stock; pistol, half-pistol or straight grip; ejector; decoration similar to equivalent grades of Flues Model double guns. Introduced 1914; discontinued 1922; serial number range same as Flues Model doubles; total production about 4700.

Exc: $1050 **VGood:** $800 **Good:** $650

ITHACA FLUES ONE-BARREL TRAP GUN NO. 5

Same specs as Flues One-Barrel Trap Gun No. 4.

Exc: $1350 **VGood:** $1000 **Good:** $800

ITHACA FLUES ONE-BARREL TRAP GUN NO. 6

Same specs as Flues One-Barrel Trap Gun No. 4. Extreme rarity precludes pricing.

ITHACA FLUES ONE-BARREL TRAP GUN NO. 7

Same specs as Flues One-Barrel Trap Gun No. 4.

Exc: $2500 **VGood:** $2200 **Good:** $1900

ITHACA FLUES ONE-BARREL TRAP GUN SOUSA SPECIAL

Same specs as Flues One-Barrel Trap Gun No. 4. Introduced 1918; discontinued 1922. Extreme rarity precludes pricing.

ITHACA FLUES ONE-BARREL TRAP GUN VICTORY GRADE

Same specs as Flues One-Barrel Trap Gun No. 4 except extractor; straight-grip stock. Introduced 1919; discontinued 1922.

Exc: $800 **VGood:** $600 **Good:** $450

ITHACA KNICKERBOCKER ONE-BARREL TRAP GUN NO. 4

Boxlock; hammerless; 12-ga.; 30-inch, 32-inch, 34-inch fluid-steel barrel; vent rib; American walnut straight or pistol-grip stock; recoil pad; ejector; decoration similar to equivalent grades of New Ithaca Double guns; named for its designer, Frank Knickerbocker, it was widely known among shooters as the Knick. Introduced 1922; discontinued 1977, except on special order; serial number range: 400000 to 405739.

Exc: $1495 **VGood:** $995 **Good:** $750

Ithaca Knickerbocker One-Barrel Trap No. 4

Ithaca Minier Model No. 3

Ithaca Minier Model No. 4

Ithaca Lewis Model No. 1 Special

ITHACA KNICKERBOCKER ONE-BARREL TRAP NO. 5
Same specs as Ithaca Knickerbocker One-Barrel Trap Gun No. 4. Introduced 1922; discontinued 1982.
Exc: $3500 **VGood:** $3000 **Good:** $2500

ITHACA KNICKERBOCKER ONE-BARREL TRAP NO. 6
Same specs as Ithaca Knickerbocker One-Barrel Trap Gun No. 4. Though never a catalogue item, a few Knicks in grade No. 6 were built in 1922-1923.
Exc: $3800 **VGood:** $2900 **Good:** $2200

ITHACA KNICKERBOCKER ONE-BARREL TRAP NO. 7
Same specs as Ithaca Knickerbocker One-Barrel Trap Gun No. 4. Introduced 1922; discontinued early 1960s.
Exc: $4200 **VGood:** $3200 **Good:** $2500

ITHACA KNICKERBOCKER ONE-BARREL TRAP SOUSA SPECIAL
Same specs as Ithaca Knickerbocker One-Barrel Trap Gun No. 4. Introduced 1922; discontinued 1937. Extreme rarity precludes pricing.

ITHACA KNICKERBOCKER ONE-BARREL TRAP VICTORY GRADE
Same specs as Ithaca Knickerbocker One-Barrel Trap Gun No. 4 except 32-inch barrel; straight-grip stock. Introduced 1922; discontinued 1937.
Exc: $795 **VGood:** $600 **Good:** $455

ITHACA KNICKERBOCKER ONE-BARREL TRAP $1000 GRADE
Same specs as Ithaca Knickerbocker One-Barrel Trap Gun No. 4. Introduced in 1937 to replace Sousa Special Grade; the name was changed periodically to reflect price increases: $1500 Grade, $2000 Grade, $6500 Grade; after 1980, it was simply Dollar Grade; discontinued 1981.
Perf: $6000 **Exc:** $4800 **VGood:** $4000

ITHACA MINIER MODEL FIELD GRADE
Side-by-side; boxlock; hammerless (also available with exposed hammers); 10-, 12-, 16-ga.; 26-inch. 28-inch. 30-inch. 32-inch fluid-steel barrels; American walnut half-pistol-grip stock, forearm; extractors (ejectors optional except as noted); double triggers; mechanically quite different from the Lewis Model; produced in eleven grades. Introduced 1906; discontinued 1908; serial number range: 130000 to 151770.
Exc: $400 **VGood:** $350 **Good:** $290

ITHACA MINIER MODEL NO. 1
Same specs as Minier Model Field Grade except 10-, 12-, 16-, 20-ga.; twist barrels; American walnut pistol-grip stock.
Exc: $400 **VGood:** $350 **Good:** $290

ITHACA MINIER MODEL NO. 1 SPECIAL
Same specs as Minier Model Field Grade except American walnut pistol-grip stock.
Exc: $425 **VGood:** $375 **Good:** $300

ITHACA MINIER MODEL NO. 1-1/2
Same specs as Minier Model Field Grade except 10-, 12-, 16-, 20-ga.; twist barrels; American walnut pistol-grip stock.
Perf: $400 **Exc:** $350 **VGood:** $290

ITHACA MINIER MODEL NO. 2
Same specs as Minier Model Field Grade except 10-, 12-, 16-, 20-ga.; twist barrels; American walnut pistol-grip stock.
Exc: $470 **VGood:** $400 **Good:** $350

ITHACA MINIER MODEL NO. 2 KRUPP PIGEON GUN
Same specs as Minier Model Field Grade except 10-, 12-, 16-, 20-ga.; Krupp steel barrels; American walnut pistol-grip stock.
Exc: $750 **VGood:** $550 **Good:** $400

ITHACA MINIER MODEL NO. 3
Same specs as Minier Model Field Grade except 10-, 12-, 16-, 20-ga.; twist or Krupp steel barrels; American walnut pistol-grip stock.
Exc: $850 **VGood:** $625 **Good:** $450

ITHACA MINIER MODEL NO. 4
Same specs as Minier Model Field Grade except 10-, 12-, 16-, 20-ga.; twist or Krupp steel barrels; American walnut straight or pistol-grip stock.
Exc: $1400 **VGood:** $1100 **Good:** $900

ITHACA MINIER MODEL NO. 5
Same specs as Minier Model Field Grade except 10-, 12-, 16-, 20-ga.; twist or Krupp steel barrels; American walnut straight or pistol-grip stock.
Exc: $2000 **VGood:** $1650 **Good:** $1400

ITHACA MINIER MODEL NO. 6
Same specs as Minier Model Field Grade except 10-, 12-, 16-, 20-ga.; twist or Krupp steel barrels; American walnut straight or pistol-grip stock.
Exc: $3500 **VGood:** $3000 **Good:** $1500

ITHACA MINIER MODEL NO. 7
Same specs as Minier Model Field Grade, except 10-, 12-, 16-, 20-ga.; twist or Whitworth steel barrels; American walnut straight or pistol-grip stock.
Exc: $3600 **VGood:** $3200 **Good:** $1700

ITHACA LEWIS MODEL NO. 1
Side-by-side; boxlock; hammerless; 10-, 12-, 16-, 20-ga. (intro. 1904); twist barrels; American walnut pistol-grip stock; extractors (ejectors optional); same grades as and slightly redesigned version of Crass Model. Introduced 1901; discontinued 1906; serial number range: 9.4109 to 123677.
Exc: $500 **VGood:** $300 **Good:** $240

ITHACA LEWIS MODEL NO. 1 SPECIAL
Same specs as Lewis Model No. 1 except steel barrels.
Exc: $800 **VGood:** $525 **Good:** $240

ITHACA LEWIS MODEL NO. 1-1/2
Same specs as Lewis Model No. 1.
Exc: $800 **VGood:** $550 **Good:** $240

ITHACA LEWIS MODEL NO. 2
Same specs as Lewis Model No. 1 except English walnut pistol-grip stock.

Exc: $825 **VGood:** $600 **Good:** $350

ITHACA LEWIS MODEL NO. 3
Same specs as Lewis Model No. 1 except twist or steel barrels; English walnut pistol-grip stock.

Exc: $1400 **VGood:** $750 **Good:** $400

ITHACA LEWIS MODEL NO. 4
Same specs as Lewis Model No. 1 except twist or steel barrels; French walnut pistol-grip stock.

Exc: $1900 **VGood:** $1700 **Good:** $800

ITHACA LEWIS MODEL NO. 5
Same specs as Lewis Model No. 1 except twist or Krupp steel barrels; French walnut pistol-grip stock.

Exc: $1800 **VGood:** $1450 **Good:** $1100

ITHACA LEWIS MODEL NO. 6
Same specs as Lewis Model No. 1 except twist or Krupp steel barrels; French walnut pistol-grip stock.

Exc: $4250 **VGood:** $3000 **Good:** $2400

ITHACA LEWIS MODEL NO. 7
Same specs as Lewis Model No. 1 except twist or Whitworth steel barrels; French walnut pistol-grip stock.

Exc: $4250 **VGood:** $3200 **Good:** $2400

ITHACA LSA-55 TURKEY GUN
Over/under combo; exposed hammers; 12-ga./222 Rem.; 24-1/2-inch vent-rib barrels; folding leaf rear sight, bead front; checkered walnut Monte Carlo stock, forearm; plain extractor; single trigger. Made in Finland. Introduced 1970; discontinued 1979.

Perf: $800 **Exc:** $680 **VGood:** $575

ITHACA SINGLE BARREL 5E CUSTOM TRAP
Single barrel; boxlock; 12-ga.; 2-3/4-inch chamber; 32-inch, 34-inch Full choke barrel; weighs about 8-1/2 lbs.; white front bead, brass middle bead sights; checkered fancy American walnut stock, forend; extensively engraved and gold inlaid frame, top lever, trigger guard. Reintroduced 1988; discontinued 1991.

Perf: $3000 **Exc:** $2400 **VGood:** $2000

IVER JOHNSON CHAMPION MATTED RIB MODEL
Single shot; top-lever breaking; 12-, 16-, 20-ga., .410 (intro. 1928); 28-inch, 30-inch, 32-inch barrel; Full choke; solid raised full-length rib finely matted; 45-inch overall length (30-inch barrel); weighs 7-1/4 lbs. (12-ga.), 7 lbs. (16-, 20-ga.); full-checkered pistol-grip stock; automatic extractor; optional automatic ejector; hard rubber pistol-grip cap, buttplate; large knob on forend. Introduced 1913; discontinued 1941.

Exc: $125 **VGood:** $95 **Good:** $65

IVER JOHNSON CHAMPION MODEL 36
Single shot; top lever breaking; 12-, 16-, 20-, 24-, 28-ga., .410; 28-inch, 30-inch, 32-inch barrel; Full choke; 45-inch overall length (30-inch barrel); weighs 6-3/4 lbs.; American black walnut stock, forend; rebounding hammer; barrel and lug forged in one; extractor; optional automatic ejector; case-hardened frame, nickel optional; browned barrel; Introduced 1909; name changed to Champion Single Barrel Shotgun in 1913; .410, 24-, 28-ga. introduced 1913; 24-ga. discontinued 1928; 16-, 20-, 28-ga., .410 discontinued 1941; 12-ga. discontinued 1957.

Exc: $125 **VGood:** $100 **Good:** $85

IVER JOHNSON CHAMPION MODEL 36 JUNIOR
Same specs as Champion Model 36 except 26-inch barrel; shortened stock. Introduced 1909; dropped 1941.

Exc: $115 **VGood:** $100 **Good:** $75

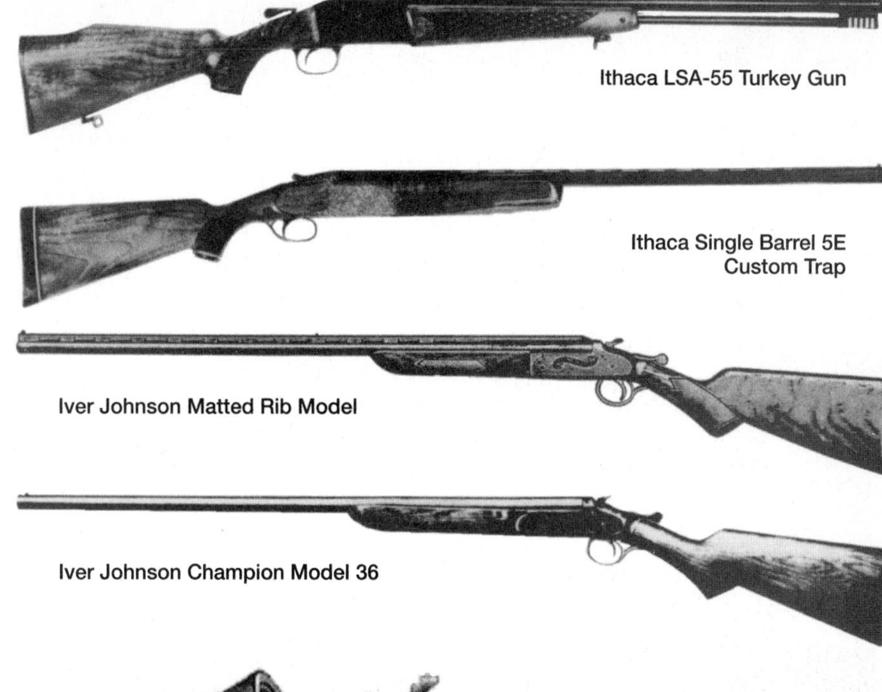

Ithaca LSA-55 Turkey Gun

Ithaca Single Barrel 5E Custom Trap

Iver Johnson Matted Rib Model

Iver Johnson Champion Model 36

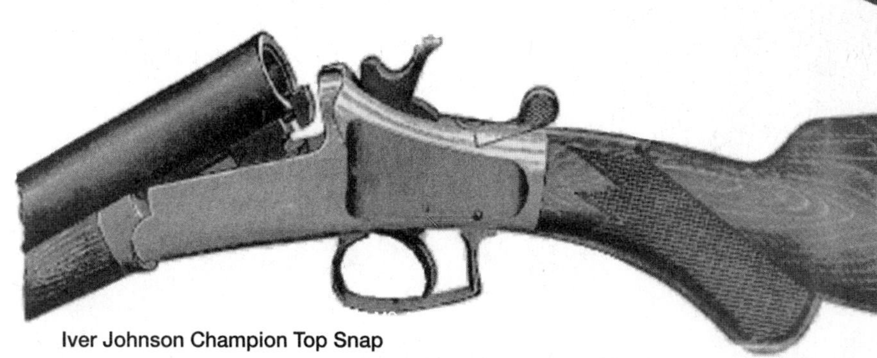

Iver Johnson Champion Top Snap

Iver Johnson Ejector Single

IVER JOHNSON CHAMPION MODEL 39
Single shot; top-lever breaking; 24-, 28-ga.; 28-inch. 30-inch plain barrel; Full choke; 45-inch overall length (30-inch barrel); weighs 5-3/4 lbs.; American black walnut stock, forend; hard rubber pistol-grip cap, buttplate; barrel and lug forged as one; rebounding hammer; extractor; optional automatic ejector; case-hardened frame, nickel optional; brown barrel. Introduced 1909; discontinued 1913.

Exc: $135 **VGood:** $120 **Good:** $100

IVER JOHNSON CHAMPION MODEL 39 JUNIOR
Same specs as Champion Model 39 except 26-inch. 28-inch barrel; shortened stock. Introduced 1909; dropped 1913.

Exc: $135 **VGood:** $120 **Good:** $100

IVER JOHNSON CHAMPION TOP SNAP
Single shot; top lever breaking; 12-ga.; 30-inch plain twist steel barrel; 45-3/4-inch overall length; weighs 6-1/2 lbs.; American black walnut stock, forend; rebounding hammer; double locking bolt; extractor; nickeled frame; browned barrel imported from Belgium. Introduced 1880; discontinued 1905.

Exc: $85 **VGood:** $70 **Good:** $50

IVER JOHNSON CHAMPION TOP SNAP NEW MODEL
Single shot; top lever breaking; 12-, 16-ga.; 28-inch, 30-inch, 32-inch steel barrel; Full choke; 45-inch overall length (30-inch barrel); weighs 6-3/4 lbs.; American black walnut stock, forend; hard rubber pistol grip, buttplate cap; rebounding hammer; automatic extractor; case-hardened frame; browned barrel. Introduced 1900; discontinued 1908.

Exc: $90 **VGood:** $65 **Good:** $55

IVER JOHNSON CHAMPION TOP SNAP NEW MODEL JUNIOR
Same specs as Champion Top Snap New Model except shortened stock. Introduced 1900; dropped 1908.

Exc: $90 **VGood:** $65 **Good:** $55

IVER JOHNSON EJECTOR SINGLE
Single shot; ring trigger break-open; semi-hammerless; 12-, 16-ga.; 28-inch, 30-inch, 32-inch plain twist steel barrel; 43-3/4-inch overall length (28-inch barrel); weighs 7 lbs.; American black walnut stock, forend; bobbed rebounding hammer; automatic ejector; case-hardened frame; browned barrel; after 1900 ring trigger model available with full hammer. Introduced 1885; 16-ga. introduced 1900; discontinued 1905.

Exc: $85 **VGood:** $60 **Good:** $45

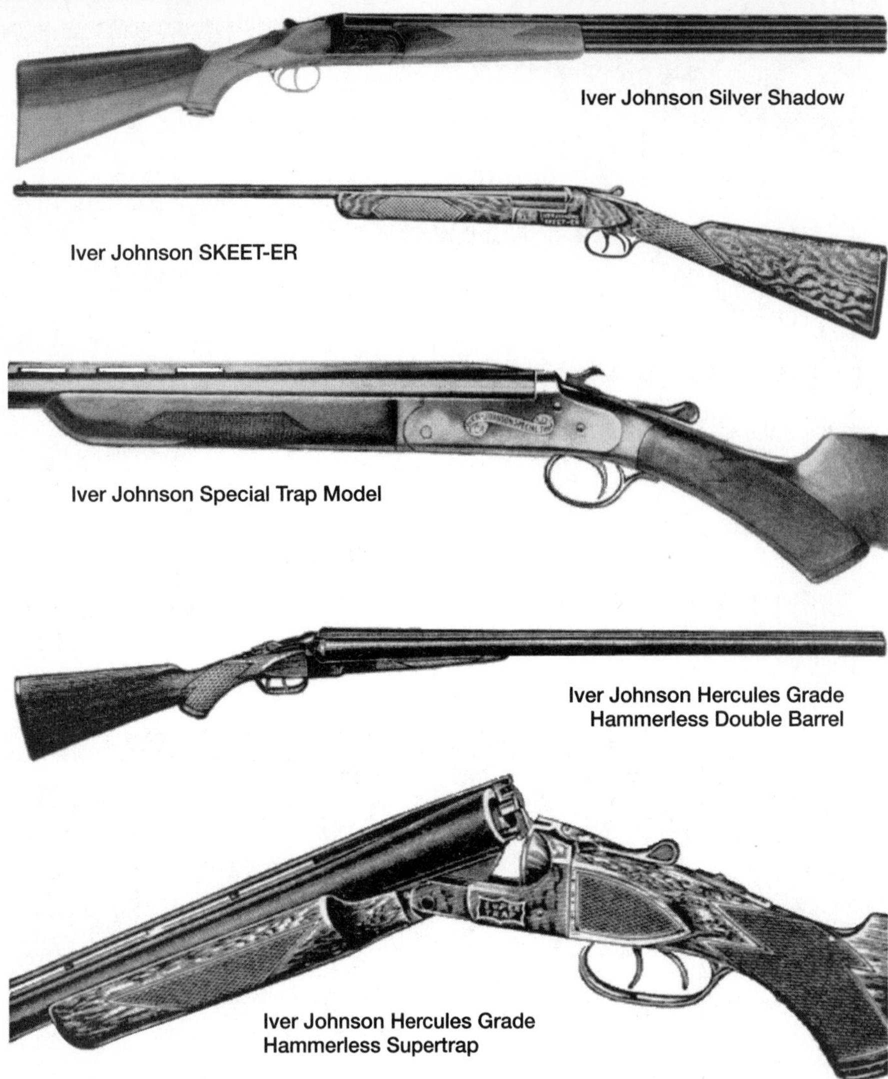

Iver Johnson Silver Shadow

Iver Johnson SKEET-ER

Iver Johnson Special Trap Model

Iver Johnson Hercules Grade Hammerless Double Barrel

Iver Johnson Hercules Grade Hammerless Supertrap

IVER JOHNSON EJECTOR SINGLE JUNIOR

Same specs as Ejector Single except shortened stock. Introduced 1900; dropped 1905.

Exc: $90 **VGood:** $65 **Good:** $55

IVER JOHNSON HAMMERLESS DOUBLE BARREL

Side-by-side; boxlock; 12-ga.; 28-inch, 30-inch, 32-inch barrel; 28-inch, 30-inch Full (left barrel) and Modified (right), 32-inch Full choke; 46-3/8-inch overall length; weighs 7-1/2 lbs.; American black walnut stock, forend; hard rubber buttplate, pistol-grip cap; breech sleeve area is solid drop-forged piece; hammer can be lowered without snapping on empty chambers; automatic safety; automatic ejectors; double triggers. Introduced 1913; discontinued 1923.

Exc: $400 **VGood:** $365 **Good:** $250

IVER JOHNSON HERCULES GRADE HAMMERLESS DOUBLE BARREL

Side-by-side; boxlock; 12-, 16-, 20-ga., .410; 26-inch, 28-inch, 30-inch barrels; 46-3/8-inch overall length (30-inch barrels); hand-checkered American black walnut stock with 14-inch pull; .410 has straight stock with 13-1/2-inch pull; stock drop at comb, 1-3/4-inch; drop at heel, 2-3/4-inch; plain extractor model with slim forend; automatic ejector model with beavertail forend with D&E fastener; hard rubber buttplate and pistol grip cap; barrels, lugs forged as one then joined together; automatic safety; double triggers. Introduced 1924; discontinued 1941.

Exc: $850 **VGood:** $650 **Good:** $400

Add 10 percent to above prices for 16 ga.
Add 20 percent for 20 ga.
Add 100 percent for .410 bore
Add 200 percent for 28 ga.

IVER JOHNSON HERCULES GRADE HAMMERLESS SUPERTRAP

Side-by-side; boxlock; 12-ga.; 32-inch barrel; raised full-length ventilated rib; 48-3/8-inch overall length; 8-1/2 lbs.; two Lyman ivory bead sights; hand-checkered American black walnut stock, wide beavertail forend with Deeley & Edge fastener; 14 1/2-inch length of stock; 1-1/2-inch drop at comb; 2-inch drop at heel; hard rubber buttplate and pistol-grip cap; each barrel and lug forged in one, proof-tested, then joined together; automatic selective ejectors; double triggers; anti-flinch recoil pad; automatic safety. Introduced 1924; discontinued 1941.

Exc: $1100 **VGood:** $800 **Good:** $700

IVER JOHNSON SEMI-OCTAGON BARREL

Single shot; 12-, 16-ga.; 28-inch, 30-inch, 32-inch barrel; top half of barrel 5-inch from breech semi-octagon; top surface of barrel matted; Full choke; 45-inch overall length; weighs 6-3/4 lbs. (12-ga.), 6-1/2 lbs. (16-ga.); American black walnut stock, plain-finished forend with large knob; hard rubber buttplate and pistol-grip cap; extractor; optional

Iver Johnson Hercules Grade Hammerless

Ga.	Barrel (ins.)	Optional Barrels	Choke Lt./Rt.	Wgt./lbs. Extractor	Wgt./lbs. Ejector
12	30	28, 32	Full/Mod.	7	7¼
16	28	30, 32	Full/Mod.	6¾	7
20	28	None	Full/Mod.	6¾	6¾
410	26	None	Full/Full	5¾	6
	32	Full/Full			

automatic ejector; case-hardened frame; browned barrel. Introduced 1913; discontinued 1927.

Exc: $95 **VGood:** $85 **Good:** $75

IVER JOHNSON SILVER SHADOW

Over/under; boxlock; 12-ga.; 3-inch chambers; 26-inch Improved Cylinder/Modified, 28-inch Modified/Full, 30-inch Full/Full barrels; full-length ventilated rib; checkered European walnut pistol-grip stock, forend; plastic pistol-grip cap; plain extractors; double triggers; optional non-selective single trigger. Made in Italy. Introduced 1973; discontinued 1978.

Perf: $400 **Exc:** $350 **VGood:** $300

IVER JOHNSON SKEET-ER

Side-by-side; boxlock; 12-, 16- 20-, 28-ga., .410; 2-3/4-inch, 3-inch (.410) chamber; optional 2-1/2-inch chamber; 26-inch, 28-inch barrel; 8-1/2 lbs. (12-, 16-, 20-, 28-ga.), 7-1/2 lbs. (.410); Skeet choke, 75 percent at 30 yds. (right barrel), 75 percent at 20 yds. (left); hand-checkered, lacquer-finished select fancy figured American black walnut straight (.410) or pistol-grip stock, large beavertail forend with Deeley & Edge fastener; 14-1/2-inch length; drop at heel 2 -5/8-inch; hard rubber grip cap; each barrel, lug forged in one, proofed then joined together; automatic extractors or automatic ejectors; automatic or manual safety. Introduced 1927; discontinued 1941.

Exc: $1800 **VGood:** $1350 **Good:** $1000

Add 20 percent to above prices for automatic ejectors.
Add 50 percent for factory vent. rib.
Add 20 percent for 20 ga.
Add 40 percent for SST.
Add 100 percent for 16 ga., 28 ga. or .410 bore.
Add 200 percent for factory engraving (rare).

IVER JOHNSON SPECIAL TRAP MODEL

Single shot; top-lever breaking; 12-ga.; 32-inch barrel; Full choke; raised full-length ventilated rib, finely matted; 47-inch overall length; weighs 7 lbs.; two Lyman ivory sight beads; hand-checkered American black walnut stock, large trap-style forend; hard rubber buttplate, pistol-grip cap; length of stock, 14-1/2-inch; drop at comb, 1-1/2-inch; drop at heel, 2-inch; automatic ejectors; optional rubber recoil pad. Introduced 1927; discontinued 1941.

Exc: $250 **VGood:** $225 **Good:** $200

IVER JOHNSON TRIGGER ACTION EJECTOR SINGLE

Single shot; 12-, 16-ga.; 28-inch, 30-inch, 32-inch barrel; Full choke; 45-inch overall length (30-inch barrel); weighs 6 lbs.; American black walnut stock, forend; hard rubber pistol-grip cap, buttplate; automatic ejectors; trigger operates locking bolt; fires by small trigger inset in main trigger; case-hardened frame; browned barrel. Introduced 1900; discontinued 1908.

Exc: $100 **VGood:** $80 **Good:** $60

IVER JOHNSON TRIGGER ACTION EJECTOR SINGLE JUNIOR

Same specs as Trigger Action Ejector Single except shortened stock; weighs 5-1/2 lbs.; 42-inch overall length. Introduced 1900; dropped 1908.

Exc: $110 **VGood:** $90 **Good:** $70

KASSNAR FOX

Autoloader; 12-ga.; 26-inch, 28-inch, 30-inch barrels; standard choke combos; vent rib; metal bead front sight; American walnut stock; crossbolt safety; interchangeable barrel. Imported by Kassnar. Introduced 1979; discontinued 1983.

Perf: $275 **Exc:** $240 **VGood:** $200

KASSNAR GRADE I

Over/under; boxlock; 12-, 20-, 28-ga., .410; 3-inch chambers; 26-inch, 28-inch barrels; fixed or choke tubes; vent rib; checkered European walnut stock, forend; extractors; gold-plated single selective trigger; blued, engraved receiver. Introduced 1990; still imported by K.B.I. Inc.

With fixed chokes, extractors

Perf: $500 **Exc:** $400 **VGood:** $350

With choke tubes, extractors

Perf: $550 **Exc:** $450 **VGood:** $400

With choke tubes; automatic ejectors

Perf: $600 **Exc:** $500 **VGood:** $450

KASSNAR GRADE II

Side-by-side; boxlock; 10-, 12-, 16-, 20-, 28-ga., .410; 3-inch, 3-1/2-inch chambers; 26-inch, 28-inch, 32-inch barrels; concave rib; checkered European walnut stock; double triggers; auto top tang safety; extractors; color case-hardened action. Made in Europe. Introduced 1989; discontinued 1990.

Perf: $500 **Exc:** $395 **VGood:** $300

KASSNAR OMEGA

Over/under; .410; 3-inch chambers; 24-inch Full/Full barrels; vent rib; checkered European walnut stock; auto safety; single trigger; folds for storage, transport. Made in Italy. Introduced 1984; discontinued 1985.

Perf: $380 **Exc:** $320 **VGood:** $290

KASSNAR OMEGA PUMP

Slide action; 12-ga.; 2-3/4-inch chambers; 5-, 8-shot magazine; 20-inch, 26-inch, 28-inch, 30-inch barrels; bead front sight; rifle-type on slug gun; stained hardwood or Philippine mahogany stock; damascened bolt; crossbolt safety. Made in the Philippines. Introduced 1984; discontinued 1986.

Perf: $240 **Exc:** $190 **VGood:** $150

KASSNAR OMEGA SXS

Side-by-side; .410; 3-inch chambers; 24-inch barrels; checkered beech (standard) or walnut (deluxe) semi-pistol-grip stock; top tang safety; blued barrels, receiver; folds for storage, transport. Made in Spain. Introduced 1984; discontinued 1985.

Standard

Perf: $210 **Exc:** $185 **VGood:** $150

Deluxe

Perf: $230 **Exc:** $205 **VGood:** $170

KASSNAR OMEGA SINGLE BARREL

Single barrel; 12-, 16-, 20-, 28-ga., .410; 2-3/4-inch, 3-inch chambers; 26-inch, 28-inch, 30-inch Full choke barrel; checkered hardwood (standard) or walnut (deluxe) stock, forearm; chromed (standard) or blued (deluxe) receiver; bottom lever (standard) or top lever (deluxe) break; folds for storage, transport. Introduced 1984; discontinued 1985.

Standard

Perf: $100 **Exc:** $80 **VGood:** $70

Deluxe

Perf: $120 **Exc:** $100 **VGood:** $80

KASSNAR OMEGA STANDARD FOLDING SINGLE BARREL

Single barrel; 12-, 16-, 20-, 28-ga., .410 bore; 28-inch, 30-inch barrel; checkered hardwood stock; matte chrome receiver; weighs 5-1/2 lbs. Importation discontinued 1987.

Perf: $160 **Exc:** $135 **VGood:** $115

KASSNAR DELUXE FOLDING SINGLE BARREL

Similar to the standard, except has checkered walnut stock and forearm; blue receiver. Importation discontinued 1987.

Perf: $195 **Exc:** $160 **VGood:** $135

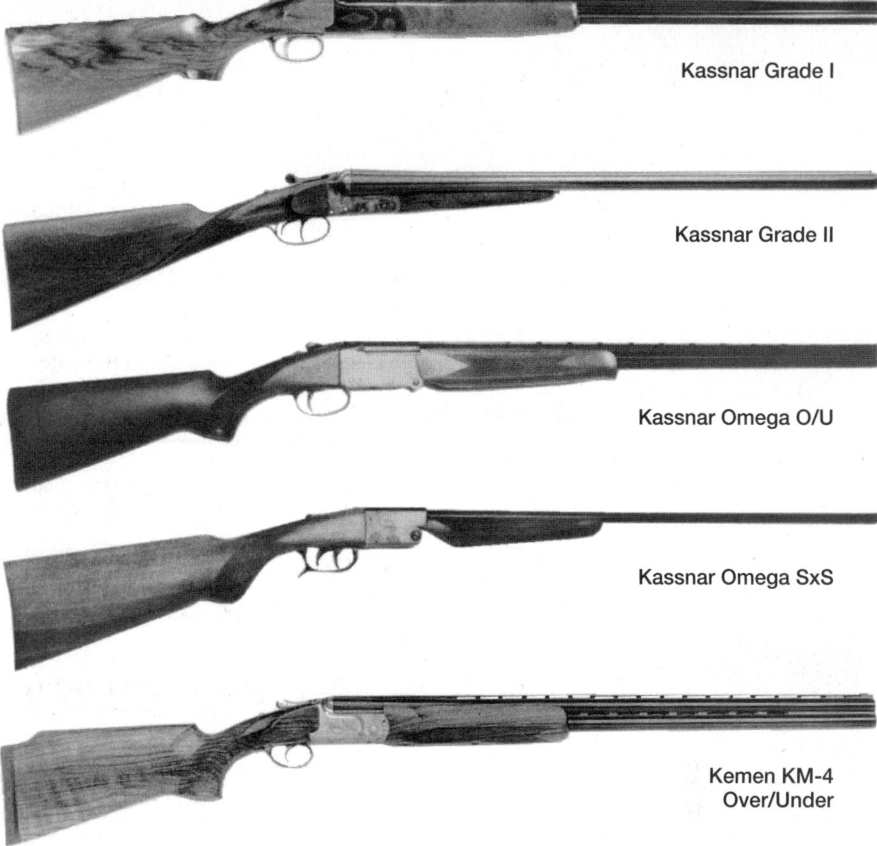

Kassnar Grade I

Kassnar Grade II

Kassnar Omega O/U

Kassnar Omega SxS

Kemen KM-4 Over/Under

KAWAGUCHIYA FG

Over/under; boxlock; 12-ga.; 2-3/4-inch chambers; 26-inch, 28-inch barrels; vent rib; sterling silver front bead sight; high-grade French walnut stock; selective single trigger; selective auto ejectors; chrome-lined bore; chromed trigger. Made in Japan. Introduced 1981 by La Paloma Marketing; discontinued 1985.

Perf: $625 **Exc:** $500 **VGood:** $450

KAWAGUCHIYA M-250

Gas-operated autoloader; 12-ga.; 2-3/4-inch chamber; 26-inch, 28-inch, 30-inch barrel; standard fixed chokes or Tru-Choke System; vent rib; checkered French walnut pistol-grip stock; reversible crossbolt safety. Made in Japan. Introduced 1980 by La Paloma Marketing; discontinued 1986.

With fixed chokes

Perf: $325 **Exc:** $245 **VGood:** $200

With Tru-Choke System

Perf: $375 **Exc:** $300 **VGood:** $250

KAWAGUCHIYA M-250 DELUXE

Same specs as M-250 except silvered, etched receiver. Introduced 1980; discontinued 1986.

With fixed chokes

Perf: $410 **Exc:** $300 **VGood:** $260

With Tru-Choke System

Perf: $460 **Exc:** $350 **VGood:** $310

KAWAGUCHIYA OT-SKEET E1

Over/under; boxlock; 12-ga.; 2-3/4-inch chambers; 26-inch, 28-inch Skeet/Skeet barrels; 13mm vent rib; middle and front bead sights; high-grade French walnut stock; gold-colored wide trigger; plastic buttplate; push-button forend release. Introduced 1981 by La Paloma Marketing; discontinued 1985.

Perf: $900 **Exc:** $750 **VGood:** $690

KAWAGUCHIYA OT-SKEET E2

Same specs as OT-Skeet E1 except super-deluxe French Walnut stock, forend; chromed receiver; better scroll engraving. Introduced 1981 by La Paloma Marketing; discontinued 1985.

Perf: $1350 **Exc:** $1000 **VGood:** $900

KAWAGUCHIYA OT-TRAP E1

Over/under; boxlock; 12-ga.; 2-3/4-inch chamber; 30-inch barrels; 13mm vent rib; bone white middle, front bead sights; high-grade oil-finished French walnut stock; rubber recoil pad; blued scroll-engraved receiver. Introduced 1981 by LaPaloma Marketing; discontinued 1985.

Perf: $910 **Exc:** $725 **VGood:** $650

KAWAGUCHIYA OT-TRAP E2

Same specs as OT-Trap E1 except super-deluxe French walnut stock, forend; chromed receiver; better scroll engraving. Introduced 1981 by LaPaloma Marketing; discontinued 1985.

Perf: $1295 **Exc:** $1000 **VGood:** $900

KDF BRESCIA

Side-by-side; 12-, 20-ga.; Anson & Deeley-type action; 28-inch Full/Modified or Improved/Modified chrome-lined barrels; hand-checkered European walnut pistol-grip stock, forearm; recoil pad; double triggers; engraved action. Made in Italy. No longer imported.

Perf: $330 **Exc:** $290 **VGood:** $250

KDF CONDOR

Over/under; boxlock; 26-inch Improved/Modified or Skeet/Skeet; 28-inch Full/Modified or Modified/Modified, 30-inch (12-ga.) Full/Modified or Full/Full barrels; vent rib; Skeet model has extra-wide rib; hand-checkered European walnut pistol-grip stock, forearm; single selective trigger; automatic ejectors. Made in Italy. No longer imported.

Field Grade

Perf: $600 **Exc:** $570 **VGood:** $525

Skeet Grade

Perf: $625 **Exc:** $595 **VGood:** $550

KDF CONDOR TRAP

Same specs as Condor except 12-ga.; 28-inch Full/Modified, 30-inch, 32-inch Modified/Full or Full/Full barrels; wide vent rib; Monte Carlo stock. No longer imported.

Perf: $625 **Exc:** $595 **VGood:** $550

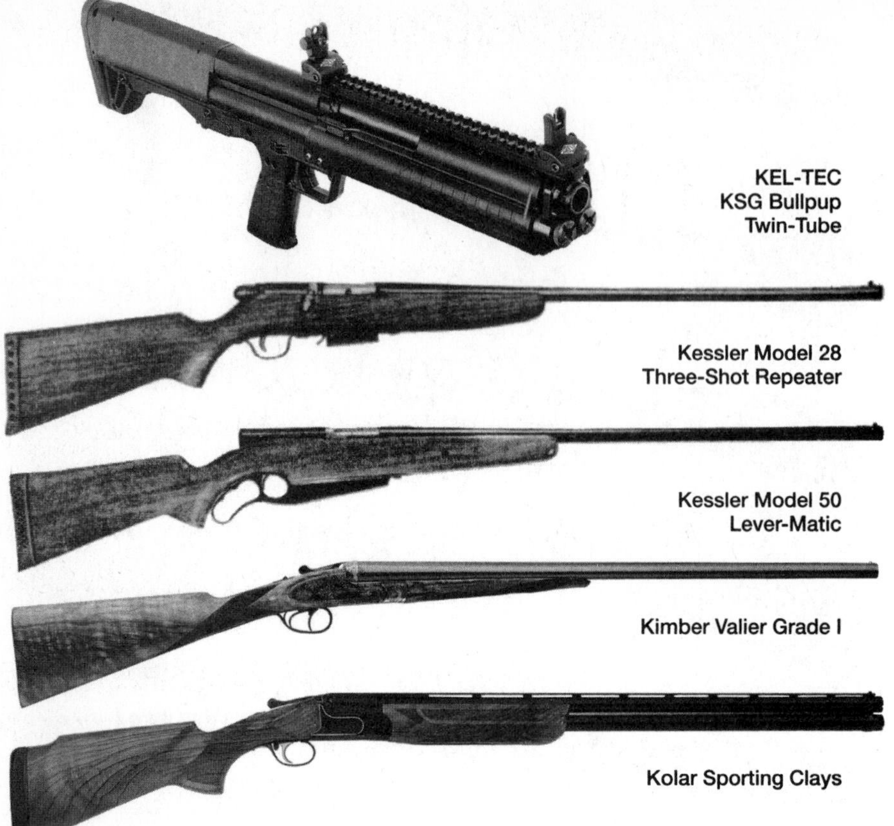
KEL-TEC KSG Bullpup Twin-Tube

Kessler Model 28 Three-Shot Repeater

Kessler Model 50 Lever-Matic

Kimber Valier Grade I

Kolar Sporting Clays

KEL-TEC KSG BULLPUP TWIN-TUBE

Unique slide-action 12 gauge in bullpup configuration with 18.5-inch barrel and 26-inch overall length. Two 7-shot tubular magazines are side-by-side under the barrel for a capacity of 14. A switch near the top of the grip selects which tube is used. Picatinny rail above barrel for various optics. comes with flip-up sights. Another rail is below the barrel for lights, lasers or a forward grip.

Perf: $750 **Exc:** $685 **VGood:** $600

KEMEN KM-4 OVER/UNDER

Over/under; boxlock; 12-ga.; 2-3/4-inch, 3-inch chambers; 27-5/8-inch barrels choked Hunting, Pigeon, Sporting Clays, Skeet; 30-inch, 32-inch barrels choked Sporting Clays, Trap; ventilated flat or step top rib; ventilated, solid or no side ribs; weighs 7-1/4 to 8-1/2 lbs.; high-grade walnut stock made to customer dimensions; drop-out trigger assembly; low-profile receiver with black finish on Standard model, antique silver on sideplate models and all engraved, gold inlaid models; barrels, forend, trigger parts interchangeable with Perazzi. Comes with hard case, accessory tools, spares. Imported from Spain by USA Sporting Clays. Introduced 1989.

KM-4 Standard
Perf: $7450 **Exc:** $5900 **VGood:** $5000

KM-4 Luxe-A (engraved scroll), Luxe-B (game scenes)
Perf: $9000 **Exc:** $7000 **VGood:** $5000

KM-4 Super Luxe (engraved game scene)
Perf: $13,500 **Exc:** $9950 **VGood:** $8250

KM-4 Extra Luxe-A (scroll engraved sideplates)
Perf: $14,000 **Exc:** $10,500 **VGood:** $9000

KM-4 Extra Luxe-B (game scene sideplates)
Perf: $16,000 **Exc:** $15,500 **VGood:** $15,000

KM-4 Extra Gold (inlays, game scene)
Perf: $22,500 **Exc:** $18,000 **VGood:** $15,500

KESSLER MODEL 28 THREE-SHOT REPEATER

Bolt action; takedown; 12-, 16-, 20-ga.; 3-shot detachable box magazine; 26-inch (20-ga.), 28-inch (12-,16-ga.) barrel; Full choke; uncheckered one-piece pistol-grip stock; recoil pad. Introduced 1951; discontinued 1953.

Exc: $95 **VGood:** $75 **Good:** $50

KESSLER MODEL 50 LEVER-MATIC

Lever action; takedown; 12-, 16-, 20-ga.; 3-shot magazine; 26-inch, 28-inch, 30-inch barrels; Full choke; uncheckered pistol-grip stock; recoil pad. Introduced 1951; discontinued 1953.

Exc: $190 **VGood:** $150 **Good:** $125

KIMBER AUGUSTA SHOTGUN

Premium over/under, Boss type action. 12-ga. only. Tri-alloy barrel with choke tubes. Backbored 736. Long forcing cones. HiViz sight with center bead on vent rib. Available with many features. Custom dimensions available. Imported from Italy by Kimber Mfg., Inc.

Perf: $3995 **Exc:** $3500 **VGood:** $3150

KIMBER VALIER GRADE I

A lightweight, properly-scaled side-by-side in 16- and 20-gauge. Double triggers and extractors. Choked IC and Mod. Color case-hardened receiver, straight stock and splinter forend. Hand checkered wood at 24 lpi. Chambered for 2.75-inch shells in 16 gauge and 3-inch shells in 20 gauge.

NIB: $3300 **Exc:** $2900 **VGood:** $2300

KIMBER VALIER GRADE II

Similar to Valier Grade I but with higher grade wood and choice of color case, blued or bone charcoal receiver in 20 gauge; bone charcoal only in 16 gauge. Automatic ejectors.

NIB: $4000 **Exc:** $3350 **VGood:** $2400

KIMBER MARIAS GRADE I

This single-trigger sidelock over-and-under features scroll hand engraving and bone charcoal case colors with 24 lpi checkered wood. Grade I is available with 28-inch barrels and Prince of Wales stock in 12 and 20 gauge. Chambered for 3-inch shells. Automatic ejectors. Comes with 5 choke tubes.

NIB: $4500 **Exc:** $3795 **VGood:** $2600

KIMBER MARIAS GRADE II

Similar to Marias Grade I but with higher grade wood. Available in 12 gauge with PW stock or 20 gauge with PW or straight stock in 26-inch, 28-inch or 30-inch barrels.

NIB: $4995 **Exc:** $4100 **VGood:** $3200

KOLAR SPORTING CLAYS

Gauge: 12, 2-3/4-inch chambers. Barrel: 30-inch, 32-inch; extended choke tubes. Stock: French walnut. Features: Single selective trigger, detachable, adjustable for length; overbored barrels with long forcing cones; flat tramline rib; matte blue finish. Made in U.S. by Kolar.

Standard
Perf: $6100 **Exc:** $5500 **VGood:** $4800

Elite Gold
Perf: $11,100 **Exc:** $9500 **VGood:** $8800

Legend
Perf: $13,100 **Exc:** $12,500 **VGood:** $10,800

Custom Gold
Perf: $23,190 **Exc:** $22,500 **VGood:** $19,900

KOLAR AAA COMPETITION TRAP

Similar to the Sporting Clays gun except has 32-inch O/U; 34-inch Unsingle or 30-inch barrels. Stock: American or French walnut; step parallel rib standard. Contact maker for full listings. Made in U.S. by Kolar.

Over/under, choke tubes, Standard
Perf: $6900 **Exc:** $6200 **VGood:** $5900

Unsingle, choke tubes, Standard
Perf: $7650 **Exc:** $7500 **VGood:** $7200

Combo (30-inch/34-inch, 32-inch/34-inch), Standard
Perf: $9995 **Exc:** $9700 **VGood:** $8900

KOLAR AAA COMPETITION SKEET

Similar to the Sporting Clays gun except has 28-inch or 30-inch barrels with Kolarite AAA sub-gauge tubes; stock of American or French walnut with matte finish; flat tramline rib; under barrel adjustable for point of impact. Many options available. Contact maker for complete listing. Made in U.S. by Kolar.

Standard, choke tubes
Perf: $8500 **Exc:** $7900 **VGood:** $7450

Standard, choke tubes, two-barrel set
Perf: $10,690 **Exc:** $9990 **VGood:** $8900

NOTE: The following values for Krieghoff shotguns are suggested. With Krieghoffs, values are whatever the local market will bear.

KRIEGHOFF K-80 LIVE BIRD

Over/under; 12-ga.; 2-3/4-inch chambers; 28-inch, 29-inch, 30-inch barrels; Improved Modified/Extra-Full chokes; weighs 8 lbs.; checkered European walnut stock; free-floating barrels; steel receiver satin gray finish; engraving; marketed in aluminum case made in four grades with differing wood and engraving options. Introduced 1980; still in production.

Perf: $5100 **Exc:** $3500 **VGood:** $2800

Bavaria Model
Perf: $9200 **Exc:** $6000 **VGood:** $4800

Danube Model
Perf: $15,000 **Exc:** $10,000 **VGood:** $8000

Gold Target Model
Perf: $18,500 **Exc:** $12,000 **VGood:** $9000

KRIEGHOFF K-80 LIVE BIRD LIGHTWEIGHT

Same specs as K-80 Live Bird except lightweight barrels and action. Introduced 1980; still in production.

Perf: $5100 **Exc:** $3500 **VGood:** $2800

Bavaria Model
Perf: $9200 **Exc:** $6000 **VGood:** $4800

Danube Model
Perf: $15,000 **Exc:** $10,000 **VGood:** $8000

Gold Medal Target
Perf: $18,500 **Exc:** $12,000 **VGood:** $9000

KRIEGHOFF K-80 SKEET

Over/under; 12-ga.; 2-1/2-inch chambers; 28-inch Skeet/Skeet barrels; optional Tula or choke tubes; vent rib; Skeet-style checkered European walnut stock; selective adjustable trigger; satin-gray finish receiver; made in four grades with differing wood and engraving options. Made in Germany. Introduced 1980; still in production.

Perf: $5700 **Exc:** $3500 **VGood:** $2900

Bavaria Model

Perf: $14,975 **Exc:** $11,250 **VGood:** $8575

Danube Model

Perf: $22,945 **Exc:** $19,250 **VGood:** $17,750

Gold Medal Target

Perf: $25,975 **Exc:** $20,500 **VGood:** $15,950

Standard, Skeet chokes

Perf: $5700 **Exc:** $3500 **VGood:** $3150

Skeet Special (28-inch or 30-inch, tapered flat rib, Skeet & Skeet choke tubes)

Perf: $6000 **Exc:** $4600 **VGood:** $3500

KRIEGHOFF K-80 SKEET FOUR-BARREL SET

Same specs as K-80 Skeet except comes with four 28-inch barrels for 12-, 20-, 28-ga., .410; marketed in aluminum case; made in four grades with differing wood and engraving options. Introduced 1980; still in production.

Perf: $13,000 **Exc:** $7600 **VGood:** $6200

Bavaria Model

Perf: $18,200 **Exc:** $12,500 **VGood:** $9750

Danube Model

Perf: $26,100 **Exc:** $17,000 **VGood:** $13,000

Gold Medal Target

Perf: $29,650 **Exc:** $17,300 **VGood:** $13,000

KRIEGHOFF K-80 SKEET INTERNATIONAL

Same specs as K-80 Skeet except Tula chokes with gas release ports; 1/2-inch vent Broadway-type rib; International Skeet stock; marketed in fitted aluminum case. Introduced 1980; still in production.

Perf: $6200 **Exc:** $4000 **VGood:** $3400

KRIEGHOFF K-80 SKEET LIGHTWEIGHT

Same specs as K-80 Skeet except weighs 7 lbs.; made in three grades with differing wood and engraving options. Made in Germany. Introduced 1980; still in production.

Perf: $6000 **Exc:** $3800 **VGood:** $3200

Bavaria Model

Perf: $9700 **Exc:** $5500 **VGood:** $5000

Danube Model

Perf: $16,000 **Exc:** $10,500 **VGood:** $9000

KRIEGHOFF K-80 SKEET LIGHTWEIGHT TWO-BARREL SET

Same specs as K-80 Skeet except set of two 28-inch, 30-inch barrels; weighs 7 lbs.; made in four grades with differing wood and engraving options. Made in Germany. Introduced 1988; still in production.

Perf: $9400 **Exc:** $7000 **VGood:** $5150

Bavaria Model

Perf: $14,975 **Exc:** $11,250 **VGood:** $8575

Danube Model

Perf: $22,945 **Exc:** $15,250 **VGood:** $17,750

Gold Medal Target

Perf: $25,975 **Exc:** $20,500 **VGood:** $15,500

KRIEGHOFF K-80 SKEET SPECIAL

Same specs as K-80 Skeet except Skeet/Skeet choke tubes; tapered flat rib. Introduced 1980; still in production.

Perf: $6100 **Exc:** $3900 **VGood:** $3300

Bavaria Model

Perf: $10,000 **Exc:** $7000 **VGood:** $5900

Danube Model

Perf: $16,000 **Exc:** $11,500 **VGood:** $9000

Gold Medal Target

Perf: $19,000 **Exc:** $12,500 **VGood:** $10,000

Krieghoff K-80 Skeet

Krieghoff K-80 Skeet International

Krieghoff K-80 Sporting Clays

Krieghoff K-80 Trap

Krieghoff K-80 Trap Combo

Krieghoff K-80 Trap Topsingle

KRIEGHOFF K-80 SPORTING CLAYS

Over/under; 12-ga.; 2-3/4-inch chambers; 28-inch, 30-inch, 32-inch barrels; choke tubes; tapered flat or step rib styles; checkered European walnut sporting stock for gun-down shooting style; free-floating barrels; standard or lightweight receiver; satin nickel finish; scroll engraving; marketed in aluminum case; made in four grades with differing wood and engraving options. Made in Germany. Introduced 1988; still in production.

Standard grade with five choke tubes

Perf: $6750 **Exc:** $6000 **VGood:** $5500

Bavaria Model

Perf: $10,000 **Exc:** $6400 **VGood:** $5000

Danube Model

Perf: $15,500 **Exc:** $10,000 **VGood:** $8000

Gold Medal Target

Perf: $20,000 **Exc:** $11,500 **VGood:** $9200

KRIEGHOFF K-80 SINGLE BARREL TRAP GUN

Gauge: 12, 2-3/4-inch chamber; 32-inch or 34-inch barrel unsingle; fixed full or choke tubes; weighs about 8-3/4 lbs.; four stock dimensions or adjustable stock available; all hand-checkered European walnut; satin nickel finish; selective mechanical trigger adjustable for finger position; tapered step vent. rib; adjustable point of impact.

Standard grade full Unsingle

Perf: $6600 **Exc:** $5300 **VGood:** $4350

KRIEGHOFF K-80 TRAP

Over/under; 12-ga.; 2-3/4-inch chambers; 30-inch, 32-inch barrels; standard choke combos or choke tubes; vent step rib; weighs 8-1/2 lbs.; checkered European walnut stock; palm swell grip; four stock dimensions or adjustable stock; selective adjustable trigger; satin nickel receiver; made in four grades with differing wood and engraving options. Made in Germany. Introduced 1980; still in production.

Standard

Perf: $7750 **Exc:** $6750 **VGood:** $5300

Bavaria Model

Perf: $10,000 **Exc:** $6200 **VGood:** $5000

Danube Model

Perf: $15,500 **Exc:** $9500 **VGood:** $8500

Gold Medal Target

Perf: $19,500 **Exc:** $12,000 **VGood:** $9000

KRIEGHOFF K-20

Similar to the K-80 except built on a 20-gauge frame. Designed for skeet, sporting clays and field use. Offered in 20-, 28-gauge and .410-bore, 28-inch and 30-inch barrels. Imported from Germany by Krieghoff International Inc.

K-20, 20-gauge

Perf: $8000 **Exc:** $7500 **VGood:** $6500

K-20, 28-gauge

Perf: $8775 **Exc:** $7775 **VGood:** $6775

K-20, .410-bore

Perf: $8775 **Exc:** $7775 **VGood:** $6775

KRIEGHOFF K-80 TRAP COMBO

Same specs as K-80 Trap except two-barrel set cased with standard frame; made in four grades with differing wood and engraving options. Introduced 1980; still in production.

Perf: $9000 **Exc:** $6000 **VGood:** $4000

Bavaria Model

Perf: $12,000 **Exc:** $8200 **VGood:** $7000

Danube Model

Perf: $20,500 **Exc:** $15,000 **VGood:** $11,000

Gold Medal Target

Perf: $24,000 **Exc:** $17,500 **VGood:** $14,000

KRIEGHOFF K-80 TRAP TOPSINGLE

Same specs as K-80 Trap except single top 34-inch barrel; Full choke; made in four grades with differing wood and engraving options. Introduced 1980; still in production.

Perf: $6600 **Exc:** $4500 **VGood:** $3500

Bavaria Model

Perf: $11,000 **Exc:** $6900 **VGood:** $6000

Danube Model

Perf: $19,000 **Exc:** $12,500 **VGood:** $10,000

Gold Medal Target

Perf: $21,000 **Exc:** $14,000 **VGood:** $11,000

Krieghoff K-80 Trap Unsingle

Krieghoff KS-5 Trap

Krieghoff Model 32

Krieghoff Teck

Krieghoff Ulm

KRIEGHOFF K-80 TRAP UNSINGLE

Same specs as K-80 Trap except single lower 32-inch, 34-inch barrel; Full choke; made in four grades with differing wood and engraving options. Introduced 1980; still in production.

Perf: $8400 **Exc:** $6200 **VGood:** $5500

Bavaria Model

Perf: $10,000 **Exc:** $6400 **VGood:** $5000

Danube Model

Perf: $15,500 **Exc:** $10,000 **VGood:** $8000

Gold Medal Target

Perf: $20,000 **Exc:** $11,500 **VGood:** $9200

KRIEGHOFF KS-5 TRAP

Single shot; 12-ga.; 2-3/4-inch chamber; 32-inch, 34-inch barrels; Full choke or choke tubes; vent tapered step rib; weighs 8-1/2 lbs.; high Monte Carlo, low Monte Carlo or factory-adjustable stock of European walnut; adjustable trigger; blued or nickel receiver; marketed in fitted aluminum case. Made in Germany. Introduced 1988; still in production.

With fixed chokes

Perf: $3000 **Exc:** $2000 **VGood:** $1600

With choke tubes

Perf: $3300 **Exc:** $2300 **VGood:** $1900

KRIEGHOFF KS-5 SPECIAL

Same specs as KS-5 Trap except fully adjustable rib; adjustable stock. Made in Germany. Introduced 1990; still in production.

With fixed chokes

Perf: $3300 **Exc:** $2200 **VGood:** $1750

With choke tubes

Perf: $3600 **Exc:** $2500 **VGood:** $2000

KRIEGHOFF KX-5 TRAP GUN

Gauge: 12, 2-3/4-inch chamber. Barrel: 34-inch; choke tubes. Weight: About 8-1/2 lbs. Stock: Factory adjustable stock. European walnut. Features: Ventilated tapered step rib. Adjustable position trigger, optional release trigger. Fully adjustable rib; shooter to adjust point of impact from 50 percent/50 percent to nearly 90 percent/10 percent. Satin gray electroless nickel receiver. Fitted aluminum case. Imported from Germany by Krieghoff International, Inc.

Perf: $3700 **Exc:** $3200 **VGood:** $2650

KRIEGHOFF MODEL 32

Over/under; boxlock; 12-, 20-, 28-ga., .410; 26-1/2-inch, 28-inch, 30-inch, 32-inch barrels; any choke combo; checkered European walnut pistol-grip stock, forend; single trigger; auto ejectors; manufactured in Field, Skeet, Trap configurations; patterned after Remington Model 32. Introduced 1958; discontinued 1980.

Perf: $2500 **Exc:** $2250 **VGood:** $2000

Low-rib two-barrel trap

Perf: $3200 **Exc:** $2500 **VGood:** $2000

High-rib Vandalia two-barrel trap

Perf: $3200 **Exc:** $2500 **VGood:** $2000

Add approximately 20 percent to above prices for two-barrel set.

KRIEGHOFF MODEL 32 FOUR-BARREL SKEET SET

Same specs as Model 32 except four sets of matched barrels (12-, 20-, 28-ga., .410); Skeet chokes, stock design; marketed in fitted case; made in seven grades depending upon quality of wood, amount and quality of engraving. No longer in production.

Standard Grade

Perf: $11,000 **Exc:** $8400 **VGood:** $7300

Munchen Grade

Perf: $12,500 **Exc:** $9200 **VGood:** $8000

San Remo Grade

Perf: $15,800 **Exc:** $10,000 **VGood:** $8500

Monte Carlo Grade

Perf: $18,800 **Exc:** $13,500 **VGood:** $10,500

Crown Grade

Perf: $23,000 **Exc:** $16,500 **VGood:** $13,500

Super Crown Grade

Perf: $28,000 **Exc:** $19,500 **VGood:** $16,000

Exhibition Grade

Perf: $32,000 **Exc:** $23,000 **VGood:** $18,500

KRIEGHOFF MODEL 32 SINGLE-BARREL TRAP

Same specs as Model 32 except single shot; 12-ga.; 32-inch, 34-inch barrel; Modified, Improved Modified, Full choke; high vent rib; checkered Monte Carlo stock, beavertail forend; recoil pad. Introduced 1959; no longer in production.

Perf: $1700 **Exc:** $1100 **VGood:** $900

KRIEGHOFF NEPTUN

Drilling; sidelock; 12-, 20-ga. (2-3/4-inch, 3-inch chamber); 22 Hornet, 222 Remington, 243 Winchester, 270 Winchester, 6.5x57R, 7x57R, 7x65R, 30-06, other calibers available on special order; 25-inch barrels; solid rib; folding leaf rear sight, post or bead front; checkered European walnut pistol-grip stock, forend; cheekpiece; steel or dural receiver; slit extractor or ejector for shotgun barrels; double triggers; sling swivels; engraving. Introduced 1960; still in production.

Perf: $13,500 **Exc:** $9500 **VGood:** $7500

KRIEGHOFF NEPTUN PRIMUS

Same specs as Neptun except detachable sidelocks; fancier figured walnut; higher grade of engraving. Introduced 1962; still in production.

Perf: $18,000 **Exc:** $12,500 **VGood:** $9000

KRIEGHOFF PLUS

Drilling; boxlock; 12-, 20-ga. (2-3/4-inch, 3-inch chamber); 222 Remington, 243 Winchester, 270 Winchester, 6.5x57R, 7x65R, 30-06, other calibers on special order; 25-inch barrels; solid rib; folding leaf rear sight, post or bead front; checkered European walnut pistol-grip stock, forend; cheekpiece; slit extractor or ejector for shotgun barrels; double triggers. Introduced 1988; still in production.

Perf: $4600 **Exc:** $2800 **VGood:** $2000

KRIEGHOFF TECK

Over/under; boxlock; 12-, 16-, 20-ga.; 28-inch vent-rib barrel; Modified/Full choke; checkered European walnut pistol-grip stock, forend; Kersten double crossbolt; auto ejectors; double or single triggers; steel or Dural receiver. Made in Germany. Introduced 1967; still in production.

Perf: $6500 **Exc:** $4400 **VGood:** $3750

KRIEGHOFF TECK COMBINATION

Same specs as Teck except rifle barrel in 22 Hornet, 222 Remington, 222 Remington Magnum, 7x57R, 7x64, 7x65R, 30-30, 300 Winchester Magnum, 30-06, 308, 9.3x-74R; solid rib; folding leaf rear sight, post or bead front; cheekpiece, semi-beavertail forend; sling swivels. Introduced 1967; still in production.

Perf: $6500 **Exc:** $4400 **VGood:** $3750

KRIEGHOFF TRUMPF

Drilling; boxlock; 12-, 16-, 20-ga. (2-3/4-inch, 3-inch chamber); 22 Hornet, 222 Remington, 243 Winchester, 270 Winchester, 6.5x57R, 7x57R, 7x65R, 30-06, other calibers available on special order; 25-inch barrels; solid rib; folding leaf rear sight, post or bead front; checkered European walnut pistol-grip stock, forend; cheekpiece; steel or Dural receiver; slit extractor or ejector for shotgun barrels; double triggers; sling swivels. Introduced 1953; still in production.

Perf: $8000 **Exc:** $5200 **VGood:** $4400

KRIEGHOFF ULM

Over/under; sidelock; 12-, 16-, 20-ga.; 28-inch vent-rib barrel; Modified/Full choke; checkered European walnut pistol-grip stock, forend; Kersten double crossbolt; auto ejectors; double or single triggers; steel or Dural receiver; Arabesque engraving. Introduced 1958; still in production.

Perf: $10,500 **Exc:** $8200 **VGood:** $7000

KRIEGHOFF ULM COMBINATION

Same specs as Ulm except rifle barrel in 22 Hornet, 222 Remington, 222 Remington Magnum, 7x57R, 7x64, 7x65R, 30-30, 300 Winchester Magnum, 30-06, 308, 9.3x74R; solid rib; folding leaf rear sight, post or bead front; cheekpiece; semi-beavertail forend; sling swivels. Introduced 1963; still in production.

Perf: $10,500 **Exc:** $7200 **VGood:** $6000

KRIEGHOFF ULM-PRIMUS

Over/under; detachable sidelock; 28-inch vent-rib barrel; Modified/Full choke; fancy checkered European walnut pistol-grip stock, forend; Kersten double crossbolt; auto ejectors; double or single triggers; steel or dural receiver; high-grade engraving. Introduced 1958; still in production.

Perf: $18,100 **Exc:** $12,850 **VGood:** $9000

KRIEGHOFF ULM-PRIMUS COMBINATION

Same specs as Ulm-Primus except rifle barrel in 22 Hornet, 222 Remington, 222 Remington Magnum, 7x57R, 7x64, 7x65R, 30-30, 300 Winchester Magnum, 30-06, 308, 9.3x74R; solid rib; folding leaf rear sight, post or bead front; cheekpiece; semi-beavertail forend; sling swivels. Introduced 1963; still in production.

Perf: $15,500 **Exc:** $8500 **VGood:** $7000

KRIEGHOFF ULTRA COMBINATION

Over/under; boxlock; 12-ga. over 7x57R, 7x64, 7x65R, 30-06, 308; 25-inch vent-rib barrel; folding leaf rear sight, post or bead front; checkered European walnut pistol-grip stock, forend; Kersten double crossbolt; auto ejectors; double triggers; thumb-cocking mechanism; satin finish receiver. Introduced 1985; still in production.

Perf: $3500 **Exc:** $1750 **VGood:** $1400

KRIEGHOFF ULTRA-B COMBINATION

Same specs as Ultra Combo except barrel selector for front set trigger. Introduced 1985; still in production.

Perf: $4200 **Exc:** $1900 **VGood:** $1500

KRIEGHOFF VANDALIA TRAP

Single barrel or over/under; boxlock; 12-ga.; 30-inch, 32-inch, 34-inch barrels; vent rib; hand-checkered European walnut pistol-grip stock, beavertail forearm; three-way safety; selective single trigger; ejectors; optional silver, gold inlays, relief engraving, fancier wood. Made in Germany. Introduced 1973; discontinued 1976.

Perf: $2200 **Exc:** $1850 **VGood:** $1500

LANBER 82

Over/under; boxlock; 12-, 20-ga.; 3-inch chambers; 26-inch Improved Cylinder/Modified, 28-inch Modified/Full barrels; European walnut stock, forend; double triggers; silvered, engraved receiver. Imported from Spain by Eagle Imports, Inc. Introduced 1994; still imported.

Perf: $480 **Exc:** $375 **VGood:** $325

LANBER 87 DELUXE

Over/under; boxlock; 12-, 20-ga.; 3-inch chambers; 26-inch, 28-inch barrels; choke tubes; single selective trigger; silvered, engraved receiver. Imported from Spain by Eagle Imports, Inc. Introduced 1994; still imported.

Perf: $820 **Exc:** $550 **VGood:** $480

LANBER 97 SPORTING CLAYS

Over/under; boxlock; 12-ga.; 2-3/4-inch chambers; 28-inch barrels; choke tubes; European walnut stock, forend; single selective trigger; silvered, engraved receiver. Imported from Spain by Eagle Imports, Inc. Introduced 1994; still imported.

Perf: $870 **Exc:** $575 **VGood:** $500

LANBER MODEL 844

Over/under; boxlock; 12-ga.; 2-3/4-inch chambers; 28-inch Improved Cylinder/Improved Modified barrels; checkered European walnut pistol-grip stock, forend; single trigger; extractors. Made in Spain. Introduced 1981; discontinued 1986.

Exc: $375 **VGood:** $300 **Good:** $275

LANBER MODEL 844 EST

Same specs as Model 844, except ejectors. Introduced 1981; discontinued 1986.

Exc: $395 **VGood:** $320 **Good:** $295

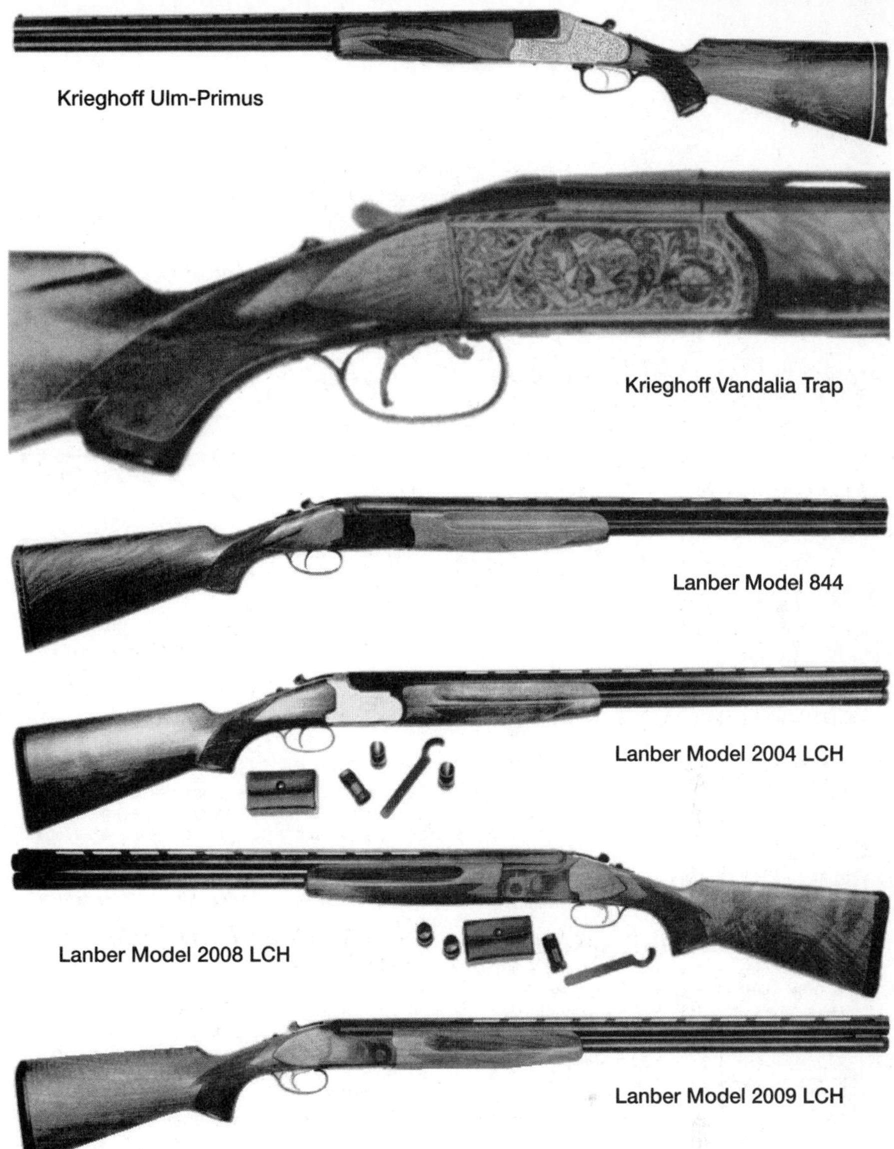

Krieghoff Ulm-Primus

Krieghoff Vandalia Trap

Lanber Model 844

Lanber Model 2004 LCH

Lanber Model 2008 LCH

Lanber Model 2009 LCH

LANBER MODEL 844 MST

Same specs as Model 844, except 12-ga.; 3-inch chambers; 30-inch Modified/Full barrels. Introduced 1981; discontinued 1986.

Exc: $375 **VGood:** $300 **Good:** $275

LANBER MODEL 2004 LCH

Over/under; boxlock; 12-ga.; 2-3/4-inch chambers; 28-inch barrels; interchangeable LanberChoke system; middle rib between barrels; checkered European walnut pistol-grip stock, forend; single selective trigger; ejectors; satin finish. Made in Spain. Introduced 1981; discontinued 1986.

Perf: $650 **Exc:** $500 **VGood:** $390

LANBER MODEL 2004 LCH SKEET

Same specs as Model 2004 LCH, except select walnut stock; engraving; blued finish. Made in Spain. Introduced 1981; discontinued 1986

Perf: $710 **Exc:** $550 **VGood:** $500

LANBER MODEL 2004 LCH TRAP

Same specs as Model 2004 LCH, except 30-inch barrels; trap-style walnut stock; blued finish. Introduced 1981; discontinued 1986.

Perf: $650 **Exc:** $540 **VGood:** $500

LANBER MODEL 2008 LCH

Over/under; boxlock; 12-ga.; 2-3/4-inch chambers; 28-inch barrels; interchangeable LanberChoke system; checkered European walnut pistol-grip stock, forend; single selective trigger; ejectors; blued finish. Introduced 1981; discontinued 1986.

Perf: $750 **Exc:** $625 **VGood:** $410

LANBER MODEL 2009 LCH

Over/under; boxlock; 12-ga.; 2-3/4-inch chambers; 30-inch barrels; interchangeable LanberChoke system; checkered European walnut pistol-grip stock, forend; single selective trigger; ejectors; blued finish. Introduced 1981; discontinued 1986.

Perf: $570 **Exc:** $460 **VGood:** $410

MIGUEL LARRANAGA TRADITIONAL

Side-by-side; exposed hammers; 12-, 20-ga.; 2-3/4-inch chambers; 28-inch Modified/Full barrels; medium bead front sight; hand-checkered European walnut straight-grip stock; checkered butt; hand-engraved locks. Made in Spain. Introduced 1982 by Toledo Armas; discontinued 1984.

Perf: $395 **Exc:** $325 **VGood:** $295

LAURONA 82 SUPER GAME

Over/under; boxlock; 12-, 20-ga.; 2-3/4-inch chambers; 28-inch Full/Modified, Improved Cylinder/Improved Modified barrels; vent rib; checkered European walnut stock, forend; twin single triggers; auto selective ejectors; silvered, engraved frame; black chrome barrels. Made in Spain. Inroduced 1986; discontinued 1989

Perf: $925 **Exc:** $750 **VGood:** $650

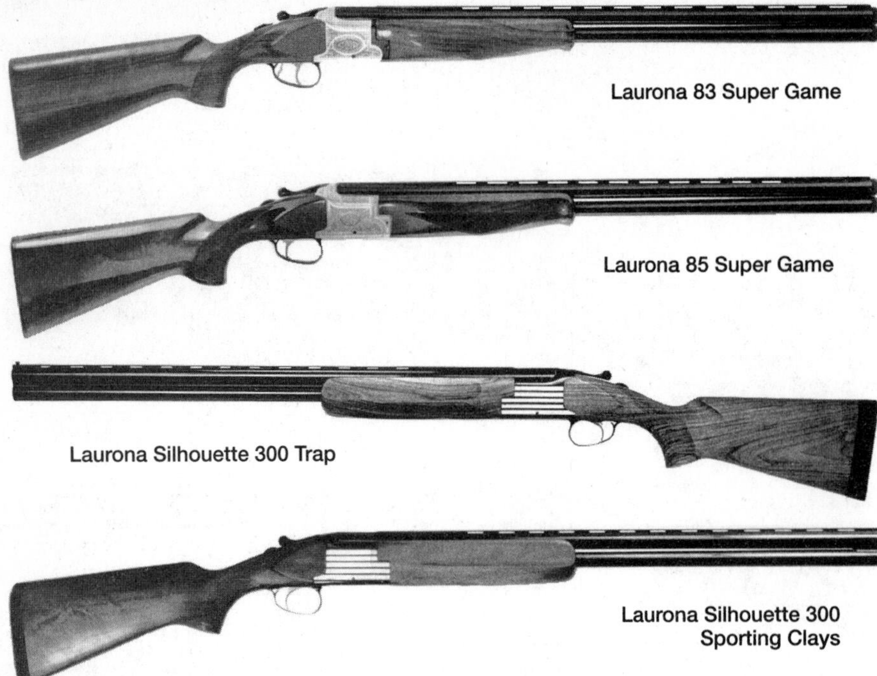
Laurona 83 Super Game

Laurona 85 Super Game

Laurona Silhouette 300 Trap

Laurona Silhouette 300 Sporting Clays

LAURONA 82 TRAP COMPETITION

Same specs as 82 Super Game except 29-inch barrels; checkered European walnut Monte Carlo stock, forend; single trigger; rubber recoil pad. Introduced 1986; discontinued 1986.

Perf: $600 **Exc:** $475 **VGood:** $375

LAURONA 83 SUPER GAME

Over/under; boxlock; 12-, 20-ga.; 2-3/4-inch, 3-inch chambers; 28-inch vent-rib barrels; Multichokes; checkered European walnut stock, forend; twin single triggers; auto selective ejectors; silvered, engraved frame; black chrome barrels. Made in Spain. Introduced 1986; no longer in production.

Perf: $1150 **Exc:** $850 **VGood:** $750

LAURONA 84 SUPER GAME

Over/under; boxlock; 12-, 20-ga.; 2-3/4-inch, 3-inch chambers; 28-inch Full/Modified, Improved Cylinder/Improved Modified barrels; vent rib; checkered European walnut stock, forend; single selective trigger; auto selective ejectors; silvered, engraved frame; black chrome barrels. Made in Spain. Introduce 1986; discontinued 1989.

Perf: $900 **Exc:** $740 **VGood:** $650

LAURONA 84 SUPER TRAP

Same specs as 84 Super Game, except 29-inch Improved Modified/Full, Modified/Full barrels; checkered European walnut pistol-grip stock, beavertail forend; rubber recoil pad. Made in Spain. Introduced 1986; no longer in production.

Perf: $1250 **Exc:** $925 **VGood:** $830

LAURONA 85 SUPER GAME

Over/under; boxlock; 12-, 20-ga.; 2-3/4-inch, 3-inch chambers; 28-inch vent-rib barrels; Multichokes; checkered European walnut stock, forend; single selective trigger; auto selective ejectors; silvered, engraved frame; black chrome barrels. Made in Spain. Introduced 1986; no longer in production.

Perf: $1150 **Exc:** $825 **VGood:** $750

LAURONA 85 SUPER SKEET

Same specs as 85 Super Game, except only 12-ga.; 2-3/4-inch chambers; mechanical triggers. Made in Spain. Introduced 1986; no longer in production.

Perf: $1450 **Exc:** $925 **VGood:** $825

LAURONA 85 SUPER TRAP

Same specs as 85 Super Game, except 29-inch vent-rib barrels; Full/Multichokes; checkered European walnut pistol-grip stock, beavertail forend; rubber recoil pad, Made in Spain. Introduced 1986; no longer in production.

Perf: $1575 **Exc:** $950 **VGood:** $850

LAURONA GRAND TRAP GTO COMBO

Single shot or over/under; 12-ga.; 3-inch chambers; 34-inch single top barrel; 29-inch over/under barrels; Multichokes; 10mm steel rib; European walnut Monte Carlo stock, full beavertail, finger-grooved forend; curved trap recoil pad; elongated forcing cone; bottom chamber area fitted with buffered recoil system. Made in Spain. Introduced 1990; discontinued 1991.

Perf: $2000 **Exc:** $1250 **VGood:** $1000

LAURONA GRAND TRAP GTU COMBO

Same specs as Grand Trap GTO Combo, except single barrel is on bottom; floating steel rib; teardrop forend. Introduced 1990; discontinued 1991.

Perf: $2100 **Exc:** $1350 **VGood:** $1100

LAURONA SILHOUETTE 300 SPORTING CLAYS

Over/under; 12-ga.; 3-inch chambers; 28-inch vent-rib barrels; Multichokes; weighs 7-1/4 lbs.; European walnut pistol-grip stock, beavertail forend; selective single trigger; auto selective ejectors; rubber buttpad; blued finish. Made in Spain. Introduced 1988; no longer in production.

Perf: $1350 **Exc:** $900 **VGood:** $800

LAURONA SILHOUETTE 300 TRAP

Same specs as Silhouette 300 Sporting Clays, except 29-inch barrels; weighs about 8 lbs.; trap-style European walnut pistol-grip stock, forend. Introduced 1988; no longer in production.

Perf: $1500 **Exc:** $950 **VGood:** $850

LAURONA SILHOUETTE SINGLE BARREL TRAP

Single shot; 12-ga.; 2-3/4-inch chamber; top single or bottom single 34-inch vent-rib barrel; Multichokes; European walnut pistol-grip stock, beavertail forend; rubber buttpad. Made in Spain. Introduced 1991; no longer in production.

Perf: $1000 **Exc:** $850 **VGood:** $700

LAURONA SILHOUETTE ULTRA-MAGNUM

Over/under; boxlock; 12-ga.; 3-1/2-inch chamber; 28-inch barrels; Multichokes; checkered European walnut pistol-grip stock, beavertail forend; single selective trigger; auto selective ejectors; rubber buttpad. Made in Spain. Introduced 1990; no longer in production.

Perf: $1350 **Exc:** $925 **VGood:** $825

LEBEAU-COURALLY BOSS-VEREES O/U

Gauge: 12, 20; 2-3/4-inch chambers. Barrel: 25-inch to 32-inch. Weight: To customer specifications. Stock: Exhibition-quality French walnut. Features: Boss- type sidelock with automatic ejectors; single or double triggers; chopper lump barrels. A custom gun built to customer specifications. Imported from Belgium by Wm. Larkin Moore.

Exc: $59,000 **VGood:** $47,000 **Good:** $41,000

LEBEAU-COURALLY BOXLOCK

Side-by-side; Anson & Deeley boxlock; 12-, 16-, 20-, 28-ga.; 26-inch to 30-inch barrels; choked to custom specs; hand-rubbed, oil-finished French walnut stock, forend; double triggers; ejectors; optional sideplates; Purdey-type fastener; choice of rib style, engraving. Made in Belgium to custom order. Introduced 1987; still in production.

Perf: $13,000 **Exc:** $9000 **VGood:** $7500

LEBEAU-COURALLY BOXLOCK SXS SHOTGUN

Gauge: 12-, 16-, 20-, 28-ga., .410-bore. 25-inch to 32-inch barrel; weight to customer specifications; French walnut; Anson & Deely-type action with automatic ejectors; single or double triggers. Essentially a custom gun built to customer specifications. Imported from Belgium by Wm. Larkin Moore.

Exc: $16,750 **VGood:** $14,000 **Good:** $11,500

LEBEAU-COURALLY MODEL 1225

Side-by-side; Holland & Holland sidelock; 12-, 20-, 28-ga.; 2-3/4-inch, 3-inch chambers; 26-inch to 28-inch custom-choked barrels; weighs 6-3/8 lbs.; custom Grand Luxe walnut stock; double triggers; auto ejectors; color case-hardened frame; English engraving. Made to order in Belgium. Introduced 1987; discontinued 1988.

Perf: $25,000 **Exc:** $17,500 **VGood:** $12,000

LEBEAU-COURALLY SIDELOCK

Side-by-side; Holland & Holland sidelock; 12-, 16-, 20-, 28-ga., .410; 26-inch to 30-inch custom-choked barrels; best-quality checkered French walnut custom pistol-grip stock, splinter forend; ejectors; chopper lump barrels; choice of rib type, engraving pattern; some have H&H-type self-opening mechanism. Made to custom order in Belgium. Introduced 1987; no longer in production.

Perf: $32,000 **Exc:** $22,500 **VGood:** $19,000

LEBEAU-COURALLY SIDELOCK SXS SHOTGUN

Gauge: 12-, 16-, 20-, 28-ga., .410-bore; 25-inch to 32-inch barrel; weight to customer specifications; fancy French walnut; Holland & Holland-type action with automatic ejectors; single or double triggers. Essentially a custom gun built to customer specifications. Imported from Belgium by Wm. Larkin Moore.

Exc: $33,000 **VGood:** $26,250 **Good:** $22,500

LEFEVER ARMS AUTOMATIC HAMMERLESS DOUBLES

Side-by-side; sidelock; hammerless; 8-, 10-, 12-, 16-, 20-ga.; 26-inch (only 12-, 16-, 20-ga.), 28-inch (only 10-, 12-, 16-, 20-ga.), 30-inch, 32-inch, 34-inch (only 8-ga.) twist and fluid-steel barrels; ejectors optional in some grades, standard in others; double triggers standard; single trigger catalogue option after 1913; earliest guns semi-boxlock, later ones fully boxlock, both with decorative sideplates. Originally called the Automatic Hammerless, the Lefever Arms gun has an unusual ball-and-socket hinge joint and numerous adjustable features in the action, fastening system, triggers, safety and ejectors. Originally offered in eight grades; several more were added after 1890; grades differ in quality of finish, amount and quality of engraving and checkering, quality of wood, and in some cases simply the addition of ejectors. Introduced 1885; discontinued 1915. Lefever Arms was purchased by Ithaca Gun Company in 1915; all subsequent guns bearing the Lefever name – Nitro Special, Long Range, Grade A, and Single Barrel Trap – were manufactured by Ithaca. None of these was built on the same mechanical system as either the Lefever Arms or D.M. Lefever guns.

LEFEVER ARMS AUTOMATIC HAMMERLESS DOUBLE GRADE I

Same specs as Automatic Hammerless Double except 12-, 16-, 20-ga.; steel barrels; walnut half-pistol-grip stock; double triggers; extractors. The Grade I never appeared in Lefever Arms catalogues and may have been made on contract for Schoverling, Daly & Gales sporting-goods company of New York. It is the only grade Lefever Arms ever discontinued. Introduced 1899; discontinued 1907.

Exc: $1000 **VGood:** $830 **Good:** $700

LEFEVER ARMS AUTOMATIC HAMMERLESS DOUBLE GRADE A

Same specs as Automatic Hammerless Double except 8-, 10-, 12-, 16-, 20-ga.; twist or Krupp steel barrels; Circassian or French walnut stock; pistol, half-pistol or straight grip; horn or skeleton-steel buttplate; ejectors. 8-gauge extremely rare, precludes pricing.

Other gauges

Exc: $14,500 **VGood:** $10,000 **Good:** $9000

LEFEVER ARMS AUTOMATIC HAMMERLESS DOUBLE GRADE AA

Same specs as Automatic Hammerless Double except 8-, 10-, 12-, 16-, 20-ga.; twist or Krupp steel barrels; Circassian or French walnut stock; pistol, half-pistol or straight grip; horn or skeleton-steel buttplate; ejectors. 8-gauge extremely rare, precludes pricing.

Other gauges

Exc: $20,000 **VGood:** $15,000 **Good:** $11,000

LEFEVER ARMS AUTOMATIC HAMMERLESS DOUBLE GRADE B

Same specs as Automatic Hammerless Double except 8-, 10-, 12-, 16-, 20-ga.; twist or Krupp steel barrels; English walnut stock; pistol, half-pistol or straight grip; extractors. 8-gauge extremely rare, precludes pricing.

Other gauges

Exc: $4700 **VGood:** $4000 **Good:** $3000

LEFEVER ARMS AUTOMATIC HAMMERLESS DOUBLE GRADE BE

Same specs as Automatic Hammerless Double except 8-, 10-, 12-, 16-, 20-ga.; twist or Krupp steel barrels; English walnut stock; pistol, half-pistol or straight grip; ejectors. 8-gauge extremely rare, precludes pricing.

Other gauges

Exc: $8000 **VGood:** $6500 **Good:** $5500

LEFEVER ARMS AUTOMATIC HAMMERLESS DOUBLE GRADE C

Same specs as Automatic Hammerless Double except 8-, 10-, 12-, 16-, 20-ga.; twist or Krupp steel barrels; English walnut stock; pistol, half-pistol or straight grip; extractors. 8-gauge extremely rare, precludes pricing.

Other gauges

Exc: $3850 **VGood:** $2650 **Good:** $2400

LEFEVER ARMS AUTOMATIC HAMMERLESS DOUBLE GRADE CE

Same specs as Automatic Hammerless Double except 8-, 10-, 12-, 16-, 20-ga.; twist or Krupp steel barrels; English walnut stock; pistol, half-pistol or straight grip; ejectors. 8-gauge extremely rare, precludes pricing.

LeFever Grade A

Other gauges

Exc: $6500 **VGood:** $4300 **Good:** $3900

LEFEVER ARMS AUTOMATIC HAMMERLESS DOUBLE GRADE D

Same specs as Automatic Hammerless Double except 8-, 10-, 12-, 16-, 20-ga.; twist or Krupp steel barrels; English walnut stock; pistol, half-pistol or straight grip; extractors. 8-gauge extremely rare, precludes pricing.

Other gauges

Exc: $2400 **VGood:** $1900 **Good:** $1750

LEFEVER ARMS AUTOMATIC HAMMERLESS DOUBLE GRADE DE

Same specs as Automatic Hammerless Double except 8-, 10-, 12-, 16-, 20-ga.; twist or Krupp steel barrels; English walnut stock; pistol, half-pistol or straight grip; ejectors. 8-gauge extremely rare, precludes pricing.

Other gauges

Exc: $3900 **VGood:** $3000 **Good:** $2500

LEFEVER ARMS AUTOMATIC HAMMERLESS DOUBLE GRADE DS

Same specs as Automatic Hammerless Double except 12-, 16-, 20-ga.; steel barrels; walnut half-pistol-grip stock; double triggers; extractors; grade stamp on water table.

Exc: $1000 **VGood:** $800 **Good:** $700

LEFEVER ARMS AUTOMATIC HAMMERLESS DOUBLE GRADE DSE

Same specs as Automatic Hammerless Double except 12-, 16-, 20-ga.; steel barrels; walnut half-pistol-grip stock; double triggers; ejectors; grade stamp on water table.

Exc: $1150 **VGood:** $900 **Good:** $790

LEFEVER ARMS AUTOMATIC HAMMERLESS DOUBLE GRADE E

Same specs as Automatic Hammerless Double except 8-, 10-, 12-, 16-, 20-ga.; twist or Krupp steel barrels; English walnut stock; pistol, half-pistol or straight grip; extractors. 8-gauge extremely rare, precludes pricing.

Other gauges

Exc: $2200 **VGood:** $1800 **Good:** $1700

LEFEVER ARMS AUTOMATIC HAMMERLESS DOUBLE GRADE EE

Same specs as Automatic Hammerless Double except 8-, 10-, 12-, 16-, 20-ga.; twist or Krupp steel barrels; English walnut stock; pistol, half-pistol or straight grip; ejectors. 8-gauge extremely rare, precludes pricing.

Other gauges

Exc: $3000 **VGood:** $2500 **Good:** $2200

LEFEVER ARMS AUTOMATIC HAMMERLESS DOUBLE GRADE F

Same specs as Automatic Hammerless Double except 10-, 12-, 16-, 20-ga.; twist or steel barrels; English walnut stock; pistol, half-pistol or straight grip; double triggers; extractors.

Exc: $1650 **VGood:** $1450 **Good:** $1300

LEFEVER ARMS AUTOMATIC HAMMERLESS DOUBLE GRADE FE

Same specs as Automatic Hammerless Double except 10-, 12-, 16-, 20-ga.; twist or steel barrels; English walnut stock; pistol, half-pistol or straight grip; double triggers; ejectors.

Exc: $2200 **VGood:** $1650 **Good:** $1400

LEFEVER ARMS AUTOMATIC HAMMERLESS DOUBLE GRADE G

Same specs as Automatic Hammerless Double except 10-, 12-, 16-, 20-ga.; twist or steel barrels; English walnut stock; pistol, half-pistol or straight grip; double triggers; extractors.

Exc: $1500 **VGood:** $1350 **Good:** $1200

LEFEVER ARMS AUTOMATIC HAMMERLESS DOUBLE GRADE GE

Same specs as Automatic Hammerless Double except 10-, 12-, 16-, 20-ga.; twist or steel barrels; English walnut stock; pistol, half-pistol or straight grip; double triggers; ejectors.

Exc: $2100 **VGood:** $1600 **Good:** $1350

LEFEVER ARMS AUTOMATIC HAMMERLESS DOUBLE GRADE H

Same specs as Automatic Hammerless Double except 12-, 16-, 20-ga.; twist (12-, 16-ga.) or steel (12-, 16-, 20-ga.) barrels; English walnut stock; pistol, half-pistol or straight grip; double triggers; extractors.

Exc: $1250 **VGood:** $1000 **Good:** $900

LEFEVER ARMS AUTOMATIC HAMMERLESS DOUBLE GRADE HE

Same specs as Automatic Hammerless Double except 12-, 16-, 20-ga.; twist (12-, 16-ga.) or steel (12-, 16-, 20-ga.) barrels; English walnut stock; pistol, half-pistol or straight grip; double triggers; ejectors.

Exc: $1700 **VGood:** $1300 **Good:** $1000

LEFEVER ARMS AUTOMATIC HAMMERLESS DOUBLE OPTIMUS

Same specs as Automatic Hammerless Double except 8-, 10-, 12-, 16-, 20-ga.; twist or Whitworth steel barrels; Circassian or French walnut stock; pistol, half-pistol or straight grip; horn or skeleton-steel buttplate.

8-ga.

Exc: $5000 **VGood:** $3700 **Good:** $3000

Other gauges

Exc: $4000 **VGood:** $3000 **Good:** $2000

LEFEVER ARMS AUTOMATIC HAMMERLESS DOUBLE THOUSAND DOLLAR GRADE

Same specs as Automatic Hammerless Double except built to order.

8-ga.

Exc: $10,000 **VGood:** $8000 **Good:** $6500

Other gauges

Exc: $9000 **VGood:** $7000 **Good:** $5500

LEFEVER GRADE A

Side-by-side; boxlock; hammerless; 12-, 16-, 20-ga., .410; 26-inch, 28-inch, 30-inch, 32-inch barrels; standard choke combos; hand-checkered American walnut pistol-grip stock, forend; plain extractors or auto ejectors; double, single triggers. Made by Ithaca. Introduced 1934; discontinued 1942.

With extractors, double triggers

Exc: $700 **VGood:** $500 **Good:** $390

With ejectors, double triggers

Exc: $900 **VGood:** $700 **Good:** $550

With extractors, single trigger

Exc: $760 **VGood:** $560 **Good:** $450

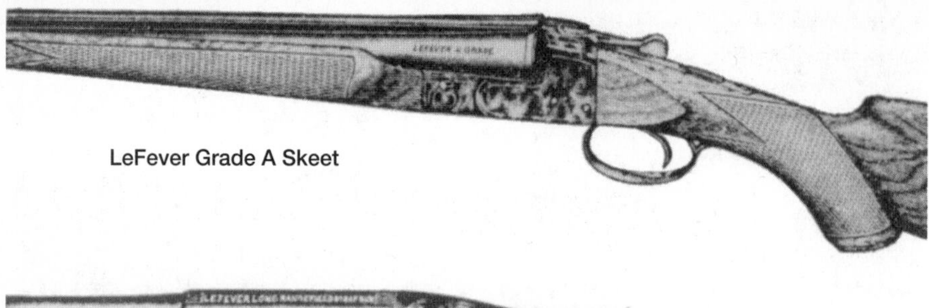
LeFever Grade A Skeet

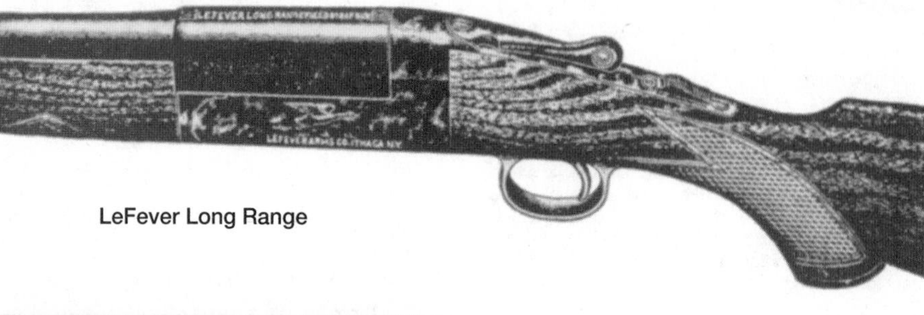
LeFever Long Range

LeFever Nitro Special

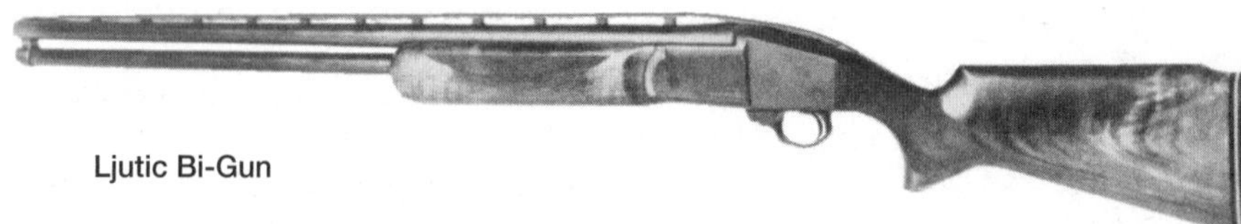
Ljutic Bi-Gun

With ejectors, single trigger

Exc: $900 **VGood:** $700 **Good:** $600

NOTE: 16-gauge 20 percent higher; 20-gauge 50 percent higher; .410 200 percent higher.

LEFEVER GRADE A SKEET

Same specs as Grade A, except 26-inch barrels, Skeet chokes; beavertail forend; integral auto ejector; single trigger. Introduced 1934; discontinued 1942.

Exc: $950 **VGood:** $800 **Good:** $700

NOTE: 16-gauge 50 percent higher; 20-gauge 100 percent higher; .410 200 percent higher.

LEFEVER LONG RANGE

Single shot; boxlock; hammerless; 12-, 16-, 20-ga., .410; 26-inch, 28-inch, 30-inch, 32-inch barrels; standard chokes; vent-rib; bead front sight; hand-checkered American walnut pistol-grip stock, forearm; ejector. Introduced 1923; discontinued 1942.

Exc: $225 **VGood:** $150 **Good:** $100

LEFEVER NITRO SPECIAL

Side-by-side; boxlock; 12-, 16-, 20-ga., .410; 26-inch, 28-inch, 30-inch, 32-inch barrels; standard choke combos; hand-checkered American walnut pistol-grip stock, forearm; single nonselective trigger; optional double triggers; plain extractors. Introduced 1921; discontinued 1948.

With double triggers

Exc: $440 **VGood:** $310 **Good:** $195

With single trigger

Exc: $470 **VGood:** $350 **Good:** $250

NOTE: 16-gauge 20 percent higher; 20-gauge 50 percent higher than prices shown; .410, 200 percent higher.

LEFEVER SINGLE BARREL TRAP

Single shot; boxlock; hammerless; 12-ga.; 30-inch, 32-inch barrels; Full choke; vent rib; bead front sight; hand-checkered American walnut pistol-grip stock, forearm; ejector; recoil pad. Introduced 1923; discontinued 1942.

Exc: $350 **VGood:** $240 **Good:** $200

NOTE: 16-gauge 20 percent higher; 20-gauge 50 percent higher; .410 200 percent higher.

D.M. LEFEVER HAMMERLESS DOUBLE

Side-by-side; boxlock; hammerless; 12-, 16-, 20-ga.; 26-inch, 28-inch, 30-inch 32-inch twist or fluid-steel barrels; double triggers; optional single trigger; ejectors standard in most grades; same ball-and-socket hinge joint as Lefever Arms and most of the same adjustable features; quite rare, only about 1000 were built. Introduced 1901; discontinued 1906. Extreme rarity precludes pricing.

D.M. LEFEVER HAMMERLESS DOUBLE GRADE NO. 4, AA

Same specs as Hammerless Double except twist, Krupp steel or Whitworth steel barrels; French walnut stock; pistol, half-pistol or straight grip; ejectors; double triggers; optional single trigger; skeleton-steel or Lefever buttplate.

With double triggers

Exc: $9000 **VGood:** $8000 **Good:** $6000

With single trigger

Exc: $10,500 **VGood:** $9000 **Good:** $7000

D.M. LEFEVER HAMMERLESS DOUBLE GRADE NO. 5, B

Same specs as Hammerless Double except twist or Krupp steel barrels; English walnut stock; pistol, half-pistol or straight grip; skeleton-steel or Lefever buttplate; ejectors; double triggers; optional single trigger.

With double triggers

Exc: $7500 **VGood:** $6000 **Good:** $5000

With single trigger

Exc: $8000 **VGood:** $7000 **Good:** $6000

D.M. LEFEVER HAMMERLESS DOUBLE GRADE NO. 6, C

Same specs as Hammerless Double except twist or Krupp steel barrels; English walnut stock; pistol, half-pistol or straight grip; skeleton-steel or Lefever buttplate; ejectors; double triggers; optional single trigger.

With double triggers

Exc: $5000 **VGood:** $4000 **Good:** $3000

With single trigger

Exc: $6000 **VGood:** $5000 **Good:** $4000

D.M. LEFEVER HAMMERLESS DOUBLE GRADE NO. 8, E

Same specs as Hammerless Double except twist, steel, or Krupp steel barrels; English walnut stock; pistol, half-pistol or straight grip; ejectors; double triggers; optional single trigger.

With double triggers

Exc: $4000 **VGood:** $3500 **Good:** $2500

With single trigger

Exc: $5200 **VGood:** $4500 **Good:** $3500

D.M. LEFEVER HAMMERLESS DOUBLE GRADE NO. 9, F

Same specs as Hammerless Double except twist, steel or Krupp steel barrels; American walnut stock; pistol, half-pistol or straight grip; ejectors; double triggers; optional single trigger.

With double triggers

Exc: $3000 **VGood:** $2750 **Good:** $2000

With single trigger

Exc: $3750 **VGood:** $3400 **Good:** $3000

D.M. LEFEVER HAMMERLESS DOUBLE GRADE O EXCELSIOR

Same specs as Hammerless Double except twist or steel barrels; American walnut stock; pistol, half-pistol or straight grip; extractors; optional ejectors; double triggers only.

With extractors

Exc: $2500 **VGood:** $2000 **Good:** $1500

With ejectors

Exc: $3100 **VGood:** $2800 **Good:** $2300

D.M. LEFEVER HAMMERLESS DOUBLE UNCLE DAN GRADE

Same specs as Hammerless Double except made to order.

Exc: $7000 **VGood:** $6200 **Good:** $5000

D.M. LEFEVER SINGLE BARREL TRAP

Single shot; boxlock; 12-ga.; 26-inch, 28-inch, 30-inch, 32-inch steel barrel; Full choke; checkered American walnut pistol-grip stock, forend; ejector; presumably available in same grades as double guns; extremely rare, total production fewer than 50; have the gun appraised by an expert. Introduced 1904; discontinued 1906.

Exc: $1000 **VGood:** $850 **Good:** $700

LJUTIC BI-GUN

Over/under; 12-ga.; 28-inch, 33-inch barrels; choked to customer specs; hollow-milled rib; oil-finished, hand-checkered American walnut stock; choice of pull or release trigger; push-button opener in front of trigger guard; custom-made gun. Introduced 1978; no longer in production.

Perf: $9000 **Exc:** $8400 **VGood:** $7000

LJUTIC BI-GUN COMBO

Same specs as Bi-Gun except interchangeable single barrel; two trigger assemblies (one for single trigger, one for double). No longer in production.

Perf: $15,000 **Exc:** $12,500 **VGood:** $8500

LJUTIC BI-GUN FOUR-BARREL SKEET

Same specs as Bi-Gun except comes with matched 28-inch barrels in 12-, 20-, 28-ga., .410; custom checkered fancy American or French walnut stock; Ljutic Paternator chokes integral to barrels. No longer in production.

Perf: $19,000 **Exc:** $17,500 **VGood:** $15,500

LJUTIC BI-MATIC

Autoloader; 12-ga.; 2-3/4-inch chamber; 2-shot magazine; 26-inch, 28-inch, 30-inch, 32-inch barrel; choked to customer's specs; oil-finished, hand-checkered American walnut stock; designed for trap, Skeet; left- or right-hand ejection; many options. Introduced 1983.

Perf: $3500 **Exc:** $2900 **VGood:** $1990

LJUTIC DYNA TRAP

Single barrel; 12-ga.; 33-inch Full barrel; trap-style walnut stock; extractor; push-button opening. Introduced 1981; discontinued 1984.

Perf: $2500 **Exc:** $2150 **VGood:** $1650

Add approximately $300 to above prices for release trigger.

Add $400 for extra release trigger.

Add $250 for extra pull trigger.

LJUTIC LM-6

Over/under; 12-ga.; 2-3/4-inch chambers; 28-inch to 32-inch barrels; choked to customer's specs; hollow-milled rib; custom oil-finished, hand-checkered walnut stock; pull or release trigger push-button opener. Introduced 1988; still in production.

Perf: $19,990 **Exc:** $15,750 **VGood:** $11,800

LJUTIC LM-6 COMBO

Same specs as LM-6 except interchangeable single barrel; two trigger guards (one for single trigger, one for double triggers). Introduced 1988.

Perf: $20,000 **Exc:** $16,000 **VGood:** $12,000

LJUTIC LM-6 FOUR-BARREL SKEET SET

Same specs as LM-6, except matched set of 28-inch barrels in 12-, 20-, 28-ga. and .410; integral Ljutic Paternator chokes; custom-checkered American or French walnut stock. Introduced 1988; still in production to order.

Perf: $28,500 **Exc:** $20,000 **VGood:** $18,000

LJUTIC LM-6 SUPER DELUXE

Gauge: 12. Barrel: 28-inch to 34-inch, choked to customer specs for live birds, trap, International Trap. Weight: To customer specs. Stock: To customer specs. Oil finish, hand checkered. Features: Custom-made gun. Hollow-milled rib, pull or release trigger, pushbutton opener in front of trigger guard. From Ljutic Industries.

Super Deluxe LM-6 O/U

Perf: $19,995 **Exc:** $15,750 **VGood:** $11,000

LJUTIC OVER/UNDER COMBO

Interchangeable single barrel, two trigger guards, one for single trigger, one for doubles)

Perf: $25,995 **Exc:** $21,750 **VGood:** $17,000

Extra over/under barrel sets, 29-inch to 32-inch

LJUTIC MODEL X-73

Single barrel; 12-ga.; 33-inch Full barrel; Monte Carlo walnut stock; extractor; push-button opening. Introduced 1981; no longer in production.

Perf: $2400 **Exc:** $1900 **VGood:** $1800

LJUTIC MONO GUN

Single barrel; 12-ga.; 34-inch barrel; fixed or choke tubes; choice of Olympic, step-style or standard rib; hand-checkered, oil-finished fancy walnut stock; pull or release trigger; removable trigger guard; push-button opening. Introduced 1962; still in production.

With fixed choke

Perf: $5950 **Exc:** $4000 **VGood:** $3500

With choke tubes

Perf: $6300 **Exc:** $4400 **VGood:** $3900

Stainless steel mono gun

Perf: $6995 **Exc:** $5500 **VGood:** $4450

Ljutic Dyna Trap

Ljutic LM-6 Super Deluxe

Ljutic Mono Gun

Ljutic Mono Gun LTX

Ljutic LTX Pro 3 Deluxe Mono Gun

Ljutic Space Gun

Ljutic Space Gun Vent Rib

LJUTIC MONO GUN ADJUSTABLE BARREL

Same specs as Mono Gun, except adjustable choke to adjust pattern. Introduced 1978; discontinued 1983.

Perf: $4600 **Exc:** $3200 **VGood:** $2700

LJUTIC MONO GUN LTX

Same specs as Mono Gun, except 33-inch extra-light barrel; double recessed choking; Olympic rib; exhibition-quality wood; extra-fancy checkering. Introduced 1985.

With fixed choke

Perf: $7400 **Exc:** $5600 **VGood:** $4000

With choke tubes

Perf: $7750 **Exc:** $5950 **VGood:** $4300

LJUTIC MONO GUN LTX SUPER DELUXE

Same specs as Mono Gun, except 33-inch extra-light barrel; double recessed choking; medium rib; exhibition-quality wood; extra-fancy checkering; release trigger. Introduced 1984; still in production.

Perf: $6000 **Exc:** $5000 **VGood:** $3900

With choke tubes

Perf: $6200 **Exc:** $5200 **VGood:** $4100

LJUTIC LTX PRO 3 DELUXE MONO GUN

Deluxe lightweight version of the Mono Gun with high quality wood, upgrade checkering, special rib height, screw in chokes, ported and cased.

Perf: $8995 **Exc:** $7750 **VGood:** $6500

Stainless steel model

Perf: $9995 **Exc:** $8750 **VGood:** $7500

LJUTIC SPACE GUN

Single barrel; 12-ga.; 30-inch barrel; front sight on vent rib; fancy American walnut stock with medium or large pistol grip, universal comb; pull or release button trigger; anti-recoil device. Introduced 1981; still in production.

Perf: $5500 **Exc:** $4500 **VGood:** $3500

LUGER CLASSIC O/U SHOTGUNS

Gauge: 12, 3-inch and 3-1/2-inch chambers; 26-inch, 28-inch, 30-inch barrel; Imp. Cyl. Mod. and Full choke tubes; weighs 7-1/2 lbs.; 45-inch overall (28-inch barrel); select-grade European walnut, hand-checkered grip and forend; gold, single selective trigger; automatic ejectors. Introduced 2000.

Classic (26-inch, 28-inch or 30-inch barrel; 3-1/2-inch chambers)

Classic Sporting (30-inch barrel; 3-inch chambers): limited importation precludes pricing.

LUGER SEMI-AUTO SHOTGUN

Gas-operated 12-ga semi-auto manufactured by Khan in Turkey. Resembles Benelli semi-auto; no longer imported.

Perf: $400 **Exc:** $300 **VGood:** $195

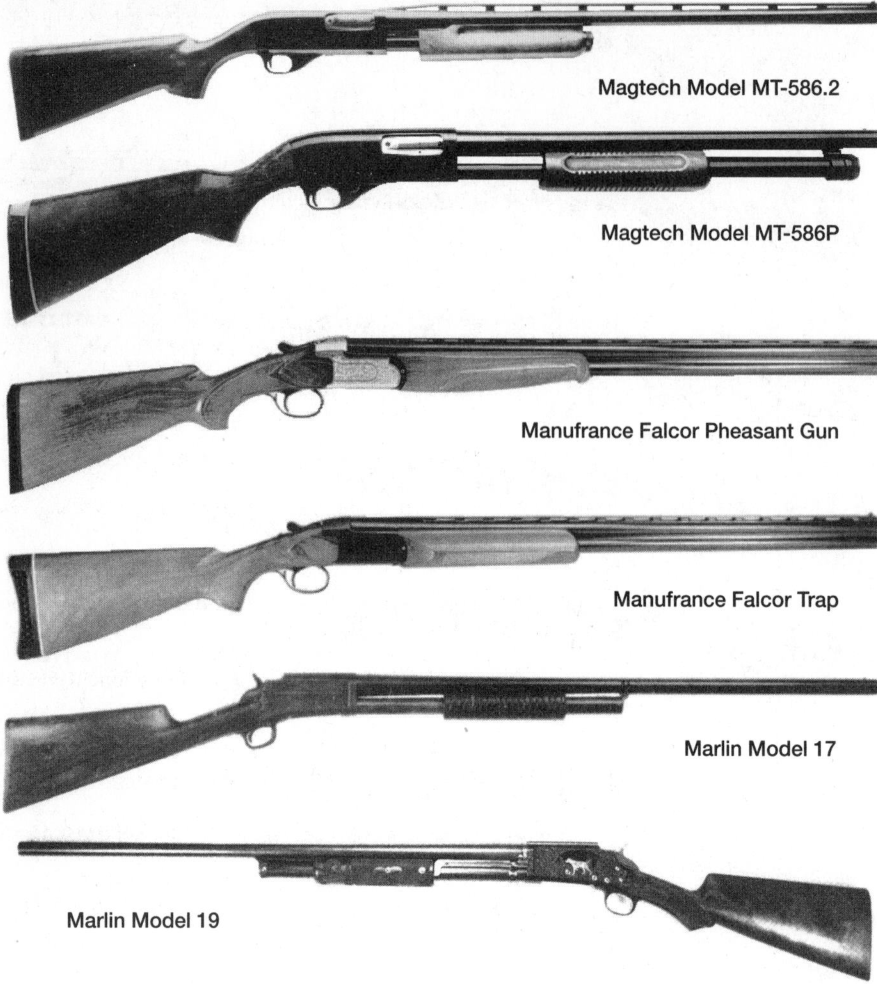
Magtech Model MT-586.2

Magtech Model MT-586P

Manufrance Falcor Pheasant Gun

Manufrance Falcor Trap

Marlin Model 17

Marlin Model 19

MAGTECH MT-151

Single shot; exposed hammer; three-piece takedown; 12-, 16-, 20-ga., .410; 2-3/4-inch (16-ga.), 3-inch chamber; 25-inch (.410 only), 26-inch, 28-inch, 30-inch barrel; weighs about 5 3/4 lbs.; Brazilian hardwood stock, beavertail forend; trigger guard opener button. Made in Brazil. Introduced 1991; dropped 1992.

Perf: $100 **Exc:** $80 **VGood:** $60

MAGTECH MODEL MT-586.2

Slide action; 12-ga.; 2-3/4-inch, 3-inch chamber; 28-inch Full, Modified or Improved Modified barrel; Brazilian Embuia hardwood stock, grooved slide handle; crossbolt safety; dual-action slide bars; blued finish. Made in Brazil. Introduced 1991; discontinued 1995.

Perf: $190 **Exc:** $175 **VGood:** $160

MAGTECH MODEL MT-586.2-VR

Same specs as Model MT-586.2 except 12-ga.; 3-inch chamber; 26-inch, 28-inch barrel; choke tubes; weighs 7-1/4 lbs.; 46-1/2-inch overall length (26-inch barrel); ventilated rib with bead front sight. Made in Brazil. Introduced 1995; no longer imported.

Perf: $230 **Exc:** $180 **VGood:** $150

MAGTECH MODEL MT-586 SLUG

Same specs as Model MT-586.2 except 24-inch Cylinder barrel; rifle sights; Brazilian Embuia hardwood Monte Carlo stock, slide handle; matte finish. Made in Brazil. Introduced 1991; discontinued 1995.

Perf: $180 **Exc:** $150 **VGood:** $130

MAGTECH MODEL MT-586P

Slide action; 12-ga.; 3-inch chamber; 7-shot magazine; 19-inch Cylinder bore barrel; weighs 7-1/4 lbs.; bead front sight; Brazilian hardwood stock, pump handle; crossbolt safety dual-action slide bars; blued finish. Made in Brazil. Introduced 1991; still in production.

Perf: $180 **Exc:** $150 **VGood:** $130

MANUFRANCE AUTO

Gas-operated autoloader; 12-ga.; 2-3/4-inch, 3-inch chamber; 3-shot magazine; 26-inch Improved Cylinder, 28-inch Modified, 30-inch Full choke barrels; vent rib; hand-checkered French walnut pistol-grip stock; black matte finish; quick takedown; interchangeable barrels. Made in France. Introduced 1978; no longer in production.

Perf: $325 **Exc:** $260 **VGood:** $230

MANUFRANCE FALCOR COMPETITION TRAP

Over/under; boxlock; 12-ga.; 2-3/4-inch chambers; 30-inch chrome-lined barrels; alloy high-post rib; 48-inch overall length; ivory bead front sight on metal sleeve, middle ivory bead; hand-checkered French walnut stock, smooth beavertail forend; hand-rubbed oil finish; inertia-type trigger; top tang safety/barrel selector; auto ejectors. Made in France. Introduced 1984; discontinued 1985.

Perf: $700 **Exc:** $600 **VGood:** $540

MANUFRANCE FALCOR PHEASANT GUN

Same specs as Falcor Competition Trap, except 27-1/2-inch chrome-lined barrels; metal bead front sight; checkered forend; single trigger; silver-gray finish, scroll engraving on receiver top lever, trigger guard. Made in France. Introduced 1984; discontinued 1985.

Perf: $800 **Exc:** $700 **VGood:** $640

MANUFRANCE FALCOR SKEET

Same specs as Falcor Competition Trap except 27-1/2-inch Skeet barrels; vent top and middle rib; luminous yellow front bead in metal sleeve; checkered forend; smooth Skeet buttpad. Introduced 1984; discontinued 1985.

Perf: $700 **Exc:** $600 **VGood:** $540

MANUFRANCE FALCOR TRAP

Same specs as Falcor Competition Trap, except vent top and middle rib; luminous yellow front bead in metal sleeve; checkered forend. Made in France. Introduced 1984; discontinued 1985.

Perf: $700 **Exc:** $600 **VGood:** $540

MANUFRANCE ROBUST

Side-by-side; boxlock; 12-ga.; 2-3/4-inch chambers; 20-1/2-inch, 27-1/2-inch barrels; hand-checkered French walnut stock, beavertail forend; double triggers; extractors; top tang safety; color case-hardened receiver. Introduced 1984; discontinued 1985.

Perf: $500 **Exc:** $400 **VGood:** $340

MANUFRANCE ROBUST DELUXE

Same specs as Robust except 27-1/2-inch chrome-lined barrels; auto ejectors; silver-gray finish, scroll engraving on receiver, top lever, trigger guard; optional retractable sling in butt. Made in France. Introduced 1984; discontinued 1985.

Perf: $550 **Exc:** $450 **VGood:** $390

MARLIN MODEL 16

Slide action; visible hammer; takedown; 16-ga.; 5-shot tubular magazine; 26-inch, 28-inch barrel; standard chokes; American walnut pistol-grip stock, grooved slide handle; made in four grades, differing in quality of wood, engraving and checkering on Grades C, D. Introduced 1903; discontinued 1910.

Grade A

Exc: $275 **VGood:** $225 **Good:** $200

Grade B

Exc: $485 **VGood:** $400 **Good:** $375

Grade C

Exc: $715 **VGood:** $635 **Good:** $580

Grade D

Exc: $1120 **VGood:** $1050 **Good:** $900

MARLIN MODEL 17

Slide action; visible hammer; solid frame; 12-ga.; 5-shot tubular magazine; 30-inch, 32-inch barrel; Full choke; uncheckered American walnut straight-grip stock, grooved slide handle. Introduced 1906; discontinued 1908.

Exc: $300 **VGood:** $210 **Good:** $150

MARLIN MODEL 17 BRUSH

Same specs as Model 17, except for 26-inch Cylinder barrel. Introduced 1906; discontinued 1908.

Exc: $275 **VGood:** $150 **Good:** $130

MARLIN MODEL 17 RIOT

Same specs as Model 17, except for 20-inch Cylinder barrel. Introduced 1906; discontinued 1908.

Exc: $260 **VGood:** $150 **Good:** $140

MARLIN MODEL 19

Slide action; visible hammer; 12-ga.; 5-shot tubular magazine; 26-inch, 28-inch, 30-inch, 32-inch barrel; standard chokes; American walnut pistol-grip stock, grooved slide handle; checkering on higher grades; two extractors; matted sighting groove on top of lightweight receiver; made in four grades, differing in quality of workmanship, wood and amount of engraving. Introduced 1906; discontinued 1907.

Grade A

Exc: $325 **VGood:** $240 **Good:** $150

Grade B

Exc: $425 **VGood:** $325 **Good:** $240

Grade C

Exc: $550 **VGood:** $475 **Good:** $325

Grade D

Exc: $1000 **VGood:** $750 **Good:** $650

MARLIN MODEL 21 TRAP

Slide action; visible hammer; 12-ga.; 5-shot tubular magazine; 26-inch, 28-inch, 30-inch, 32-inch barrel; standard chokes; American walnut straight-grip stock, grooved slide handle; checkering on higher grades; two extractors; matted sighting groove on top of lightweight receiver; made in four grades, differing in workmanship, quality of wood and engraving. Introduced 1907; discontinued 1908.

Grade A
Exc: $375 **VGood:** $225 **Good:** $120
Grade B
Exc: $425 **VGood:** $325 **Good:** $225
Grade C
Exc: $550 **VGood:** $450 **Good:** $300
Grade D
Exc: $1175 **VGood:** $1050 **Good:** $600

MARLIN MODEL 24

Slide action; visible hammer; improved takedown; 12-ga.; 5-shot tubular magazine; 26-inch, 28-inch, 30-inch, 32-inch barrel; standard chokes; solid matted rib attached to frame; American walnut pistol-grip stock, grooved slide handle; checkering or higher grades; two extractors; matted sighting groove on top of lightweight receiver; automatic recoil safety lock; made in four grades. Introduced 1908; discontinued 1917.

Grade A
Exc: $325 **VGood:** $275 **Good:** $150
Grade B
Exc: $450 **VGood:** $400 **Good:** $280
Grade C
Exc: $575 **VGood:** $500 **Good:** $350
Grade D
Exc: $1100 **VGood:** $800 **Good:** $600

MARLIN MODEL 25MG GARDEN GUN SHOTGUN

Gauge: 22 WMR shotshell; 7-shot magazine; 22-inch smoothbore barrel; weighs 6 lbs.; 41-inch overall; press-checkered hardwood; high-visibility bead front sight; bolt action; thumb safety; red cocking indicator. Introduced 1999. Discontinued 2002. Made in U.S. by Marlin.

Perf: $190 **Exc:** $155 **VGood:** $130

MARLIN MODEL 26

Slide action; visible hammer; solid frame; 12-ga.; 5-shot tubular magazine; 30-inch, 32-inch Full-choke barrel; solid matted rib attached to frame; American walnut straight-grip stock, grooved slide handle; two extractors; matted sighting groove on top of lightweight receiver; automatic recoil safety lock. Introduced 1909; discontinued 1916.

Exc: $250 **VGood:** $200 **Good:** $120

MARLIN MODEL 26 BRUSH

Same specs as Model 26, except 26-inch Cylinder barrel. Introduced 1909; discontinued 1916.

Exc: $250 **VGood:** $180 **Good:** $120

MARLIN MODEL 26 RIOT

Same specs as Model 26, except 20-inch Cylinder barrel. Introduced 1909; discontinued 1915.

Exc: $250 **VGood:** $175 **Good:** $120

MARLIN MODEL 28

Slide action; hammerless; takedown; 12-ga.; 5-shot tubular magazine; 26-inch, 28-inch, 30-inch, 32-inch barrel; standard chokes; American walnut pistol-grip stock, grooved slide handle; matted barrel top or solid matted rib (28D); made in four grades, differing in quality of wood, amount of engraving on 28C, 28D. Introduced 1913; 28B, 28C, 28D discontinued 1915; 28A discontinued 1922.

Grade A
Exc: $275 **VGood:** $225 **Good:** $175
Grade B
Exc: $475 **VGood:** $325 **Good:** $250
Grade C
Exc: $600 **VGood:** $500 **Good:** $395
Grade D
Exc: $1200 **VGood:** $875 **Good:** $625

MARLIN MODEL 28T

Same specs as Model 28, except 30-inch Full-choke barrel; matted rib; hand-checkered American walnut straight-grip stock; high fluted comb; fancier wood. Introduced 1915; discontinued 1915.

Exc: $500 **VGood:** $420 **Good:** $355

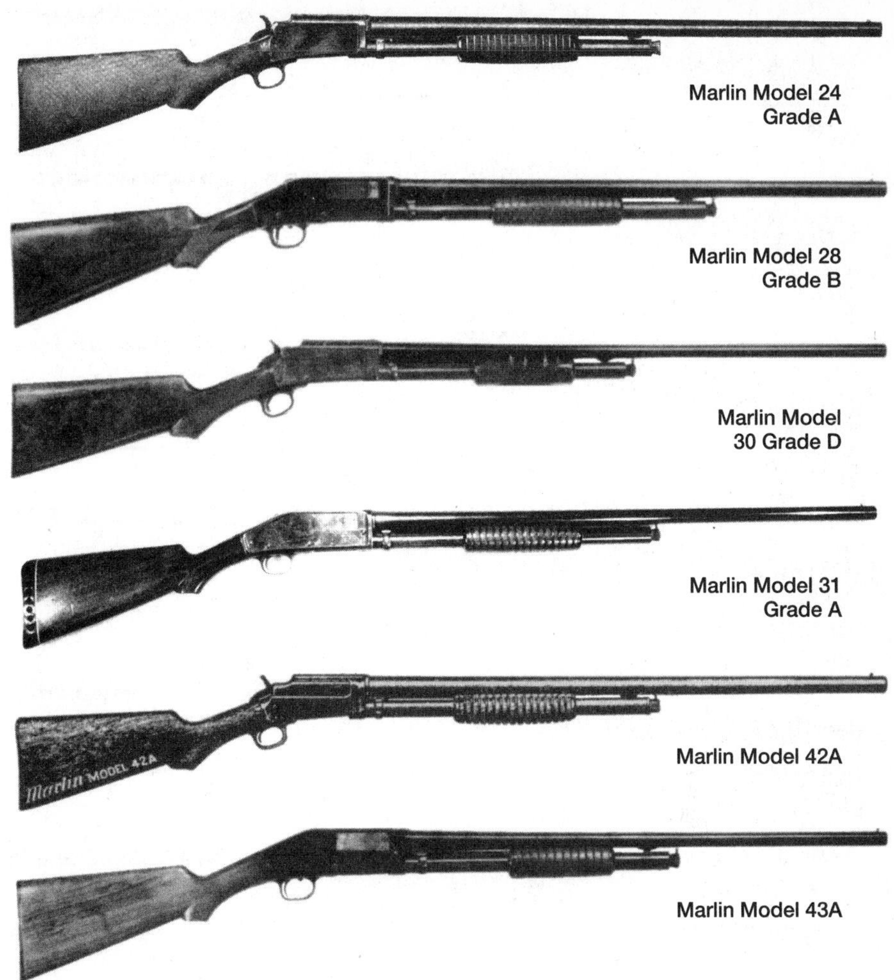
Marlin Model 24 Grade A

Marlin Model 28 Grade B

Marlin Model 30 Grade D

Marlin Model 31 Grade A

Marlin Model 42A

Marlin Model 43A

MARLIN MODEL 28TS

Same specs as Model 28, except 30-inch Full-choke barrel; American walnut straight-grip stock; matted barrel top. Introduced 1915; discontinued 1915.

Exc: $400 **VGood:** $350 **Good:** $250

MARLIN MODEL 30

Slide action; visible hammer; improved takedown; 16-ga.; 5-shot tubular magazine; 26-inch, 28-inch barrel; standard chokes; solid matted rib on frame; American walnut pistol-grip stock, grooved slide handle; auto recoil safety lock; made in four grades depending upon quality of wood, amount and quality of engraving. Introduced 1911; discontinued 1917.

Grade A
Exc: $325 **VGood:** $275 **Good:** $225
Grade B
Exc: $475 **VGood:** $375 **Good:** $300
Grade C
Exc: $575 **VGood:** $495 **Good:** $375
Grade D
Exc: $1200 **VGood:** $975 **Good:** $695

MARLIN MODEL 30 FIELD

Same specs as Model 30, except 25-inch barrel; Modified choke; American walnut straight-grip stock. Introduced 1911; discontinued 1917.

Exc: $300 **VGood:** $200 **Good:** $100

MARLIN MODEL 31

Slide action; hammerless; 16-, 20-ga.; 5-shot tubular magazine; 25-inch, 26-inch, 28-inch barrel; standard chokes; American walnut pistol-grip stock, grooved slide handle; matted barrel top; scaled-down version of Model 28; made in four grades, differing in quality wood, checkering and engraving. Introduced 1914; discontinued 1917.

Grade A
Exc: $350 **VGood:** $250 **Good:** $140
Grade B
Exc: $400 **VGood:** $300 **Good:** $260
Grade C
Exc: $550 **VGood:** $475 **Good:** $350
Grade D
Exc: $1100 **VGood:** $800 **Good:** $500

MARLIN MODEL 31 FIELD

Same specs as Model 31, except 25-inch barrel; Modified choke; American walnut straight- or pistol-grip stock. Introduced 1914; discontinued 1917.

Exc: $350 **VGood:** $325 **Good:** $290

MARLIN MODEL 42A

Slide action; visible hammer; takedown; 12-ga.; 5-shot tubular magazine; 26-inch Cylinder, 28-inch Modified, 30-inch or 32-inch Full barrel; bead front sight; uncheckered American walnut pistol-grip stock, grooved slide handle. Introduced 1922; discontinued 1933.

Exc: $260 **VGood:** $225 **Good:** $175

MARLIN MODEL 43A

Slide action; hammerless; takedown; 12-ga.; 5-shot tubular magazine; 26-inch 28-inch, 30-inch, 32-inch barrel; standard chokes; American walnut pistol-grip stock, grooved slide handle; matted barrel top. Introduced 1922; discontinued 1930.

Exc: $275 **VGood:** $250 **Good:** $200

MARLIN MODEL 43T

Same specs as Model 43A, except 30-inch Full-choke barrel; matted rib; American walnut straight-grip stock. Introduced 1922; discontinued 1930.

Exc: $350 **VGood:** $300 **Good:** $250

MARLIN MODEL 43TS

Same specs as Model 43, except 30-inch Full-choke barrel; American walnut straight-grip stock. Introduced 1922; discontinued 1930.

Exc: $400 **VGood:** $340 **Good:** $290

MARLIN MODEL 44A

Slide action; hammerless; 20-ga.; 5-shot tubular magazine; 25-inch, 26-inch, 28-inch barrel; standard chokes; American walnut pistol-grip stock, grooved slide handle; matted barrel top. Introduced 1922; discontinued 1933.

Exc: $325 **VGood:** $275 **Good:** $225

MARLIN MODEL 44S

Same specs as Model 44A, except select hand-checkered American walnut stock, slide handle. Introduced 1922; discontinued 1933.

Exc: $350 **VGood:** $300 **Good:** $250

MARLIN MODEL 49

Slide action; visible hammer; takedown; 12-ga.; 5-shot tubular magazine; 26-inch Cylinder, 28-inch Modified, 30-inch or 32-inch Full barrel; bead front sight; uncheckered American walnut pistol-grip stock, grooved slide handle. Used by Marlin as a premium, with purchase of four shares of corporate stock; fewerthan 3000 made. Introduced 1928; discontinued 1930.

Exc: $400 **VGood:** $350 **Good:** $275

MARLIN MODEL 50

Bolt action; 12-, 20-ga.; 2-shot clip magazine; 28-inch (12-ga.), 26-inch (20-ga.) barrel; Full or adjustable choke; uncheckered American walnut one-piece pistol-grip stock; thumb safety; sling swivels; leather sling; double extractors; tapped for receiver sights. Introduced 1967; discontinued 1975.

With fixed choke

Perf: $125 **Exc:** $80 **VGood:** $60

With adjustable choke

Perf: $140 **Exc:** $90 **VGood:** $70

MARLIN MODEL 53

Slide action; hammerless; takedown; 12-ga.; 5-shot tubular magazine; 26-inch, 28-inch, 30-inch, 32-inch barrel; standard chokes; American walnut pistol-grip stock, grooved slide handle; matted barrel top. Introduced 1929; discontinued 1931.

Exc: $300 **VGood:** $250 **Good:** $200

MARLIN MODEL 55

Bolt action; takedown; 12-, 16-, 20-ga.; 28-inch (12-, 16-ga.); 26-inch (20-ga.) barrel; Full or adjustable choke; uncheckered American walnut one-piece pistol-grip stock; recoil pad (12-ga.). Introduced 1954; discontinued 1965.

With fixed choke

Exc: $200 **VGood:** $160 **Good:** $140

With adjustable choke

Exc: $250 **VGood:** $190 **Good:** $150

MARLIN MODEL 55 GOOSE GUN

Same general specs as Model 55 except 3" 12-ga.; 2-shot clip magazine; 36-inch barrel; Full choke; thumb safety; sling swivels; leather carrying strap; double extractors; tapped for receiver sights. Introduced 1962.

Perf: $300 **Exc:** $260 **VGood:** $175

MARLIN MODEL 55 SWAMP GUN

Same specs as Model 55, except 12-ga., 3-inch chamber; 20-1/2-inch barrel; adjustable choke; sling swivels. Introduced 1963; discontinued 1965.

Exc: $300 **VGood:** $200 **Good:** $100

MARLIN MODEL 55S SLUG

Same specs as Model 55, except 12-ga.; 2-shot clip magazine; 24-inch Cylinder barrel; rifle sights; tapped for receiver sights; thumb safety; sling swivels; leather carrying strap; double extractors. Introduced 1973; discontinued 1979.

Perf: $275 **Exc:** $250 **VGood:** $185

MARLIN MODEL 59 OLYMPIC

Single shot; bolt action; .410; 2-1/2-inch, 3-inch chamber; 24-inch Full barrel; bead front sight; uncheckered one-piece walnut pistol-grip stock, also available with Junior stock with 12-inch length of pull; self-cocking bolt; automatic thumb safety. Introduced 1959; discontinued 1965.

Exc: $150 **VGood:** $125 **Good:** $100

MARLIN MODEL 59 OLYMPIC JUNIOR

Same specs as Model 59 Olympic except smaller sized stock with 12-inch length of pull. No longer in production.

Exc: $165 **VGood:** $140 **Good:** $115

MARLIN MODEL 60

Single shot; boxlock; visible hammer; takedown; 12-ga.; 30-inch, 32-inch Full barrel; walnut pistol-grip stock, beavertail forend; automatic ejector. Limited production of 600 to 3000. Introduced 1923; discontinued 1923.

Exc: $300 **VGood:** $225 **Good:** $175

MARLIN MODEL 63A

Slide action; hammerless; takedown; 12-ga.; 5-shot magazine; 26-inch, 28-inch, 30-inch, 32-inch barrel; standard chokes; American walnut pistol-grip stock, grooved slide handle; matted barrel top. Replaced model 43A. Introduced 1931; discontinued 1933.

Exc: $300 **VGood:** $225 **Good:** $125

MARLIN MODEL 63T

Same specs as Model 63A, except 30-inch Full-choke barrel; matted rib; American walnut straight-grip stock. Introduced 1931; discontinued 1933.

Exc: $325 **VGood:** $275 **Good:** $225

MARLIN MODEL 63TS TRAP SPECIAL

Same specs as Model 63A, except 30-inch Full-choke barrel; matted rib; American walnut trap-style stock with dimensions to special order. Introduced 1931; discontinued 1933.

Exc: $375 **VGood:** $325 **Good:** $275

MARLIN MODEL 90

Over/under; boxlock; 12-, 16-, 20-ga., .410; 26-inch, 28-inch, 30-inch barrels; Improved/Modified, Modified/Full chokes; full-length rib between barrels; bead front sight; hand-checkered American walnut pistol-grip stock, forearm; double triggers; optional single non-selective trigger; recoil pad. Introduced 1937; discontinued during WWII.

With double triggers

Exc: $440 **VGood:** $280 **Good:** $200

With single trigger

Exc: $550 **VGood:** $380 **Good:** $300

.410 model, double triggers

Exc: $900 **VGood:** $520 **Good:** $350

.410 model, single trigger

Exc: $950 **VGood:** $575 **Good:** $400

MARLIN MODEL 90-DT

Same specs as Model 90 except post-WWII version with double triggers; no rib between barrels; no recoil pad. Introduced 1949; discontinued 1958. Deduct 15 percent for 16-ga.

Exc: $400 **VGood:** $350 **Good:** $295

.410 model

Exc: $1000 **VGood:** $875 **Good:** $550

MARLIN MODEL 90-ST

Same specs as Model 90, except post-WWII version with single non-selective trigger; no rib between barrels; no recoil pad. Introduced 1949; discontinued 1958.

Exc: $500 **VGood:** $380 **Good:** $300

.410 model

Exc: $1050 **VGood:** $925 **Good:** $600

MARLIN MODEL 120 MAGNUM

Slide action; hammerless; 12-ga.; 2-3/4-inch, 3-inch chamber; 26-inch Improved Cylinder, 28-inch Modified, 30-inch Full barrel; vent rib; checkered walnut pistol-grip stock, semi-beavertail forearm; slide release button; crossbolt safety; interchangeable barrels; side ejection. Introduced 1971; discontinued 1984. Add 20 percent for 40-inch "Long Tom" barrel.

Exc: $325 **VGood:** $275 **Good:** $200

MARLIN MODEL 120 TRAP

Same specs as Model 120 Magnum, except 30-inch Full or Modified barrel; hand-checkered Monte Carlo stock, full forearm. Introduced 1973; discontinued 1975.

Exc: $345 **VGood:** $295 **Good:** $220

MARLIN MODEL .410

Lever action; visible hammer; solid frame; .410, 2-1/2-inch shell; 4-shot tubular magazine; 22-inch, 26-inch barrel; Full choke; uncheckered American walnut pistol-grip stock, grooved beavertail forend. Used by Marlin as a promotional firearm for shareholders. Introduced 1929; discontinued 1932.

Exc: $1000 **VGood:** $850 **Good:** $675

MARLIN LEVER ACTION .410 (RECENT)

Lever action shotgun based on 1895 lever action rifle action, chambered for 2-1/2-inch shells. Cylinder bore, rubber buttplate, fold-down rear sight. Discontinued.

Exc: $1100 **VGood:** $850 **Good:** $675

Marlin Model 90-ST

Marlin Model 120 Magnum

Marlin Model 410

Marlin Model 512 Slugmaster

Marlin Model 1898 Grade A

Marlin Model 5510 Goose Gun

Marlin Premier Mark I

Marlin Premier Mark II

MARLIN MODEL 512 SLUGMASTER

Bolt action; 12-ga.; 3-inch chamber; 2-shot detachable box magazine; 21-inch rifled barrel with 1:28-inch twist; weighs 8 lbs.; 44-3/4-inch overall length; ramp front sight with brass bead and removable hood, adjustable folding semi-buckhorn rear; drilled and tapped for scope mounting; press-checkered, walnut-finished Maine birch stock; ventilated recoil pad. Uses Model 55 action with thumb safety. Designed for shooting saboted slugs. Introduced 1994; dropped 1999.

Perf: $295 **Exc:** $220 **VGood:** $195

MARLIN MODEL 1898

Slide action; visible hammer; takedown; 12-ga.; 5-shot tubular magazine; 26-inch, 28-inch, 30-inch, 32-inch barrel; standard chokes; American walnut pistol-grip stock, grooved slide handle; checkering on higher grades; grades differ in quality of woods, amount of engraving; Marlin's first shotgun. Introduced 1898; discontinued 1905.

Grade A

Exc: $325 **VGood:** $250 **Good:** $190

Grade B

Exc: $420 **VGood:** $320 **Good:** $275

Grade C

Exc: $600 **VGood:** $500 **Good:** $420

Grade D

Exc: $1250 **VGood:** $1000 **Good:** $850

MARLIN MODEL 5510 GOOSE GUN

Bolt action; takedown; 10-ga.; 3-1/2-inch chamber; 2-shot clip magazine; 34-inch heavy barrel; Full choke; uncheckered American walnut one-piece pistol-grip stock; recoil pad; sling swivels; leather sling. Introduced 1976; discontinued 1985.

Perf: $395 **Exc:** $350 **VGood:** $290

MARLIN PREMIER MARK I

Slide-action; hammerless; takedown; 12-ga.; 3-shot magazine; 26-inch Improved or Skeet, 28-inch Modified, 30-inch Full barrel; bead front sight; French walnut pistol-grip stock, forearm; bead front sight; side ejection; crossbolt safety. Made in France by Manufrance. Introduced 1961; discontinued 1963.

Exc: $200 **VGood:** $175 **Good:** $100

MARLIN PREMIER MARK II

Same specs as Premier Mark I, except checkered pistol grip, forearm; scroll-engraved receiver. Made in France. Introduced 1961; discontinued 1963.

Exc: $210 **VGood:** $190 **Good:** $110

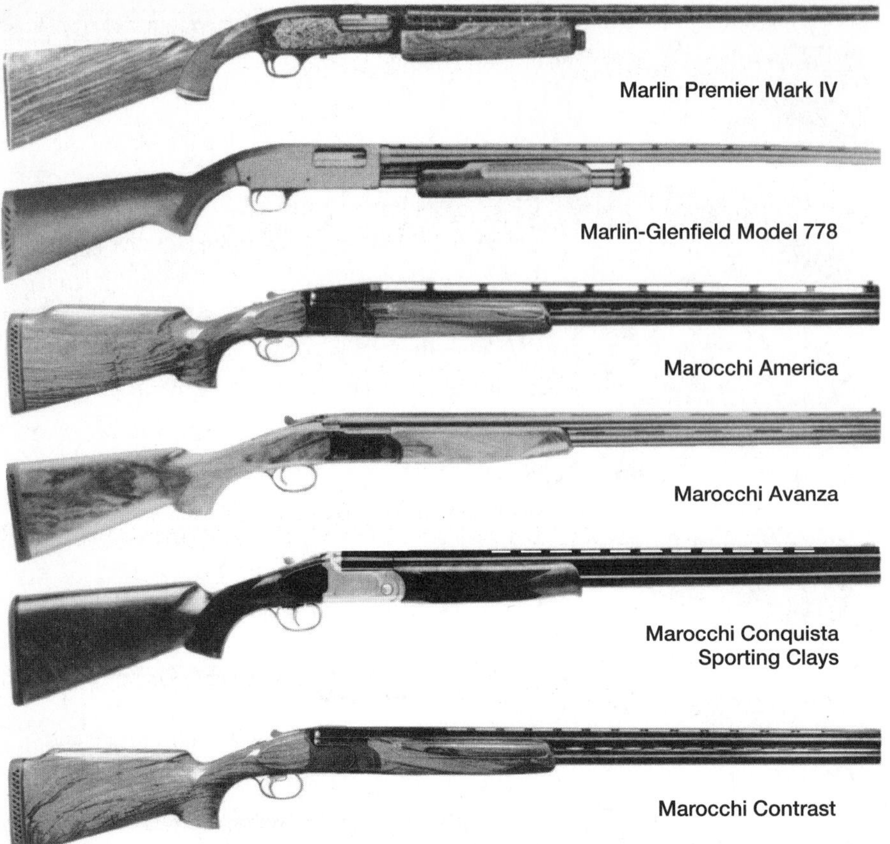

MARLIN PREMIER MARK IV

Same specs as Premier Mark I except optional vent rib; fine checkering; better wood; pistol-grip cap; full-coverage engraved receiver; engraved trigger guard. Made in France. Introduced 1961; discontinued 1963.

Exc: $275 **VGood:** $225 **Good:** $175

With vent rib

Exc: $305 **VGood:** $250 **Good:** $190

MARLIN-GLENFIELD MODEL 55G

Bolt action; takedown; 12-, 16-, 20-ga.; 28-inch (12-, 16-ga.); 26-inch (20-ga.) barrel; Full or adjustable choke; uncheckered walnut-finished hardwood one-piece pistol-grip stock; recoil pad (12-ga.). Introduced 1954; discontinued 1965.

With fixed choke

Exc: $185 **VGood:** $160 **Good:** $140

With adjustable choke

Exc: $195 **VGood:** $170 **Good:** $150

MARLIN-GLENFIELD MODEL 60G

Single shot; bolt action; .410; 2-1/2-inch, 3-inch chamber; 24-inch Full barrel; bead front sight; uncheckered walnut-finished hardwood one-piece pistol-grip stock; also available with junior stock with 12-inch length of pull; self-cocking bolt; automatic thumb safety. Introduced 1960; discontinued 1964.

Exc: $75 **VGood:** $60 **Good:** $40

MARLIN-GLENFIELD MODEL 60G JUNIOR

Same specs as Model 60G except smaller-sized stock with 12-inch length of pull. No longer in production.

Exc: $75 **VGood:** $60 **Good:** $40

MARLIN-GLENFIELD MODEL 778

Slide action; 12-ga.; 2-3/4-inch, 3-inch chambers; 5-shot magazine; 20-inch slug barrel with sights, 26-inch Improved, 28-inch Modified, 30-inch Full barrel; plain or vent rib; walnut-finished hardwood stock, semi-beavertail forend; steel receiver; engine-turned bolt; double action bars; vent recoil pad. Introduced 1979; discontinued 1984. Glenfield-labaled version of Marlin Model 120.

With plain barrel

Perf: $230 **Exc:** $180 **VGood:** $125

With vent rib

Perf: $250 **Exc:** $200 **VGood:** $150

MAROCCHI AMERICA

Over/under; 12-, 20-ga.; 2-3/4-inch chambers; 26-inch to 29-inch Skeet, 27-inch to 32-inch trap, barrels, 30-inch, 32-inch single barrel; hand-checkered select European walnut stock, schnabel or beavertail forend; left- or right-hand palm swell; medium engraving coverage on frame; custom engraving, inlays offered. Marketed in fitted hard case. Made in Italy. Introduced 1983; discontinued 1986.

Perf: $1800 **Exc:** $1550 **VGood:** $1200

With deluxe engraving

Perf: $1950 **Exc:** $1700 **VGood:** $1350

MAROCCHI AVANZA

Over/under; 12-, 20-ga.; 2-3/4-inch chambers; 26-inch, 28-inch barrels; fixed or Interchokes; vent top, middle ribs; weighs 6-3/4 lbs.; cut-checkered select walnut stock; recoil pad; auto mechanical barrel cycling; auto selective ejectors; auto safety; single selective trigger. Made in Italy. Introduced 1990; discontinued 1993.

Perf: $700 **Exc:** $575 **VGood:** $480

MAROCCHI AVANZA SPORTING CLAYS

Same specs as Avanza except 12-ga.; 28-inch vent-rib barrels; Interchokes; trigger adjustable for length. Made in Italy. Introduced 1990; still in production.

Perf: $800 **Exc:** $550 **VGood:** $490

MAROCCHI CONQUISTA SKEET

Over/under; boxlock; 12-ga.; 2-3/4-inch chambers; 28-inch Skeet/Skeet barrels; 10mm concave vent rib; checkered American walnut pistol-grip stock, forend; buttpad. Weighs about 7-3/4 lbs. Introduced 1994. Ergonomically shaped trigger adjustable for pull length and weight; automatic selective ejectors; coin-finished receiver, blued barrels; hard case; stock wrench. Also available as true left-hand model-opening lever operates from left to right; stock has left-hand cast. Made in Italy. Introduced 1994; still imported.

Grade I, right-hand

Perf: $1725 **Exc:** $1475 **VGood:** $1225

Grade II, right-hand

Perf: $1995 **Exc:** $1675 **VGood:** $1450

Grade III, right-hand; MSR

Perf: $3225 **Exc:** $2650 **VGood:** $2250

MAROCCHI CONQUISTA SPORTING CLAYS

Same specs as Conquista Skeet except 28-inch, 30-inch, 32-inch barrels; Contrechoke tubes; Sporting Clays buttpad; no left-hand model. Made in Italy. Introduced 1994; still imported.

Grade I

Perf: $1725 **Exc:** $1450 **VGood:** $1200

Add approximately $125 to above prices for left-hand version.

Grade II

Perf: $1995 **Exc:** $1675 **VGood:** $1425

Add approximately $355 to above prices for left-hand version.

Grade III

Perf: $3225 **Exc:** $2650 **VGood:** $2250

Add approximately $396 to above prices for left-hand version.

MAROCCHI CONQUISTA TRAP

Same specs as the Conquista Skeet except 30-inch, 32-inch barrels; Full/Full; weighs about 8-1/4 lbs.; trap stock dimensions; no left-hand model. Made in Italy. Introduced 1994; still imported.

Grade I (RH)

Perf: $1700 **Exc:** $1450 **VGood:** $1250

Grade II (RH)

Perf: $1890 **Exc:** $1600 **VGood:** $1400

Grade III

Perf: $3225 **Exc:** $2650 **VGood:** $2200

MAROCCHI LADY SPORT

Over/under; boxlock; 12-ga.; 2-3/4-inch chambers; 28-inch, 30-inch barrels; five Contrechoke tubes; 10mm concave vent rib; weighs about 7-1/2 lbs.; checkered American walnut pistol-grip stock, forend; buttpad; ergonomically shaped trigger adjustable for pull length and weight; automatic selective ejectors; coin-finished receiver, blued barrels; hard case; stock wrench; ergonomically designed specifically for women shooters; available with colored graphics finish on frame and opening lever. Also available as true left-hand model-opening lever operates from left to right; stock has left-hand cast. Made in Italy. Introduced 1995.

Grade I

Perf: $1750 **Exc:** $1200 **VGood:** $1100

Grade II

Perf: $1850 **Exc:** $1450 **VGood:** $1250

Grade III

Perf: $2850 **Exc:** $2050 **VGood:** $1850

MAROCCHI CONTRAST

Over/under; 12-, 20-ga.; 2-3/4-inch chambers; 26-inch to 29-inch Skeet, 27-inch to 32-inch trap barrels; select European walnut stock; hand-checkered pistol grip, schnabel or beavertail forend; hand-rubbed wax finish; left or right-hand palm swell; light engraving on standard grade; custom engraving, inlays at added cost. Marketed in fitted hard case. Made in Italy. Introduced 1983; discontinued 1986.

Perf: $1800 **Exc:** $1450 **VGood:** $1100

With deluxe engraving

Perf: $1950 **Exc:** $1600 **VGood:** $1250

MAROCCHI CONQUISTA USA MODEL 92 SPORTING CLAYS

Gauge: 12, 3-inch chambers; 30-inch barrel; back-bored, ported (ContreChoke Plus tubes); 10mm concave ventilated top rib, ventilated middle rib; weighs 8 lbs. 2 oz.; stock dimensions 14-1/4-inch-14-5/8-inchx 2-1/8-inchx1-3/8-inch; American walnut with checkered grip and forend; Sporting Clays butt pad; low profile frame; fast lock time; automatic selective ejectors; three choke tubes; ergonomically shaped trigger adjustable for pull length without tools; barrels are back-bored and ported. Introduced 1996. Imported from Italy by Precision Sales International.

Perf: $1450 **Exc:** $1175 **VGood:** $950

MAROCCHI MODEL 99 SPORTING TRAP AND SKEET

Gauge: 12, 2-3/4-inch, 3-inch chambers; 28-inch, 30-inch, 32-inch barrel; French walnut; Boss Locking system; screw-in chokes; low recoil, lightweight monoblock barrels and ribs. Imported from Italy by Precision Sales International.

Grade I
Perf: $1995 **Exc:** $1750 **VGood:** $1500

Grade II
Perf: $2475 **Exc:** $2125 **VGood:** $1725

Grade II Gold
Perf: $2630 **Exc:** $2280 **VGood:** $1880

Grade III
Perf: $2925 **Exc:** $2400 **VGood:** $2000

Grade III Gold
Perf: $3110 **Exc:** $2585 **VGood:** $2185

Blackgold
Perf: $3650 **Exc:** $3200 **VGood:** $2600

Lodestar
Perf: $4625 **Exc:** $4175 **VGood:** $3575

Brittania
Perf: $4625 **Exc:** $4175 **VGood:** $3575

Diana
Perf: $5850 **Exc:** $5400 **VGood:** $4800

MAROCCHI SM-28 SXS

Side-by-side; 12-, 20-ga.; 2-3/4-inch chamber; totally handmade to customers specs and dimensions. Supplied with fitted leather luggage case. Introduced 1983; discontinued 1986.

Perf: $10,000 **Exc:** $8500 **VGood:** $7500

MAROCCHI PRITI

Over/under; 12-, 20-ga.; 3-inch chambers; 28-inch barrels; vent top and middle ribs; hand-checkered walnut stock; auto safety; extractors; double triggers; engraved antique silver receiver. Made in Italy. Introduced 1984; discontinued 1988.

Perf: $324 **Exc:** $285 **VGood:** $250

MAUSER MODEL CONTEST

Over/under; 12-ga.; 27-1/2-inch chrome-lined barrels; select European walnut stock; receiver engraved with hunting scenes; dummy sideplates; auto ejectors; single selective trigger. Made in Germany. Introduced 1981; no longer in production.

Trap Model
Perf: $1100 **Exc:** $950 **VGood:** $800

Skeet Model
Perf: $1500 **Exc:** $1200 **VGood:** $900

MAUSER-BAUER MODEL 71E

Over/under; Greener crossbolt boxlock; 12-ga.; 28-inch Modified/Full, Improved/Modified barrels; vent rib; hand-checkered European walnut pistol-grip stock, beavertail forearm; double triggers; automatic ejectors. Made in Italy. Introduced 1972; discontinued 1973.

Perf: $375 **Exc:** $250 **VGood:** $200

MAUSER-BAUER MODEL 72E

Over/under; boxlock; 12-ga.; 28-inch Full/Modified, 30-inch Full/Full barrels; wide vent rib; hand-checkered European walnut pistol-grip stock, beavertail forearm; Greener crossbolt; single trigger; automatic ejectors; engraved receiver. Made in Italy. Introduced 1972; discontinued 1973.

Perf: $300 **Exc:** $260 **VGood:** $225

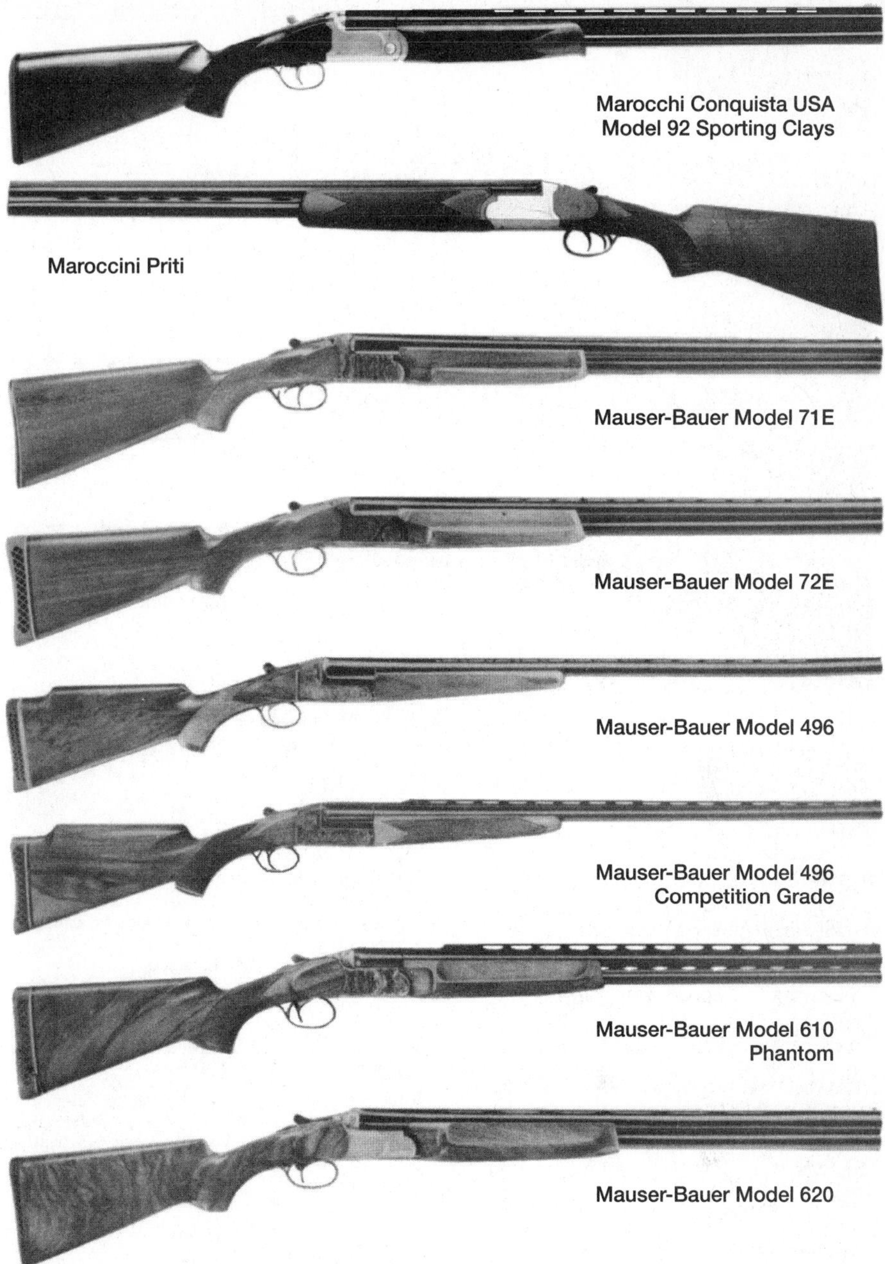

Marocchi Conquista USA Model 92 Sporting Clays

Maroccini Priti

Mauser-Bauer Model 71E

Mauser-Bauer Model 72E

Mauser-Bauer Model 496

Mauser-Bauer Model 496 Competition Grade

Mauser-Bauer Model 610 Phantom

Mauser-Bauer Model 620

MAUSER-BAUER MODEL 496

Single barrel; single shot; boxlock; 12-ga.; 32-inch Modified, 34-inch Full-choke barrel; matted vent rib; hand-checkered European walnut Monte Carlo stock, forearm; recoil pad; automatic ejector; auto safety; Greener crossbolt; double underlocking blocks; color case-hardened action; scroll engraving. Introduced 1972; discontinued 1974.

Perf: $495 **Exc:** $385 **VGood:** $295

MAUSER-BAUER MODEL 496 COMPETITION GRADE

Same specs as Model 496 except high ramp rib; front, middle sight bead; hand finishing on wood and metal parts. Introduced 1973; discontinued 1974.

Perf: $600 **Exc:** $435 **VGood:** $325

MAUSER-BAUER MODEL 580 ST. VINCENT

Side-by-side; Holland & Holland sidelock; 12-ga.; 28-inch, 30-inch, 32-inch barrels; standard choke combos; hand-checkered European walnut straight stock, forearm; split sear levers; coil hammer springs; single or double triggers; scroll-engraved receiver. Introduced 1973; discontinued 1974.

Perf: $900 **Exc:** $795 **VGood:** $695

MAUSER-BAUER MODEL 610 PHANTOM

Over/under; 12-ga.; 30-inch, 32-inch barrels; standard choke combos; raised rib; vent rib between barrels for heat reduction; hand-checkered European walnut stock, forearm; recoil pad; coil springs throughout working parts; color case-hardened action. Introduced 1973; discontinued 1974.

Perf: $695 **Exc:** $580 **VGood:** $500

MAUSER-BAUER MODEL 610 SKEET

Same specs as Model 610 except three Purbaugh tubes to convert gun for all-gauge competition (20-, 28-ga., .410). Introduced 1973; discontinued 1974.

Perf: $1100 **Exc:** $850 **VGood:** $700

MAUSER-BAUER MODEL 620

Over/under; boxlock; 12-ga.; 28-inch Modified/Full, Improved/Modified, Skeet/Skeet, 30-inch Full/Modified barrels; vent rib; hand-checkered European walnut pistol-grip stock, beavertail forearm; Greener crossbolt; single nonselective adjustable trigger;

Maverick Model 88

Maverick Model 88 Security

Maverick Model 91 Accu-Mag

Maverick Model 95

Merkel Model 47S

optional selective or double triggers; automatic ejectors; recoil pad. Made in Italy. Introduced 1972; discontinued 1974.

With double triggers

Perf: $750 **Exc:** $650 **VGood:** $575

With single selective trigger

Perf: $795 **Exc:** $680 **VGood:** $600

MAVERICK MODEL 60

Autoloader; 12-ga.; 2-3/4-inch, 3-inch chamber; 5-shot magazine; 18-1/2-inch (2-3/4-inch chamber only) Cylinder, 24-inch Full and rifled choke tubes, 28-inch vent-rib Modified Accu-Choke barrel; weighs 7-1/4 lbs.; black synthetic stock and forend; designated barrels for magnum and non-magnum loads; action release button; blued receiver. Introduced 1993; limited production; no longer in production.

Perf: $175 **Exc:** $150 **VGood:** $125

MAVERICK MODEL 88

Slide action; 12-ga.; 3-inch chamber; 6-shot magazine; 24-inch with rifle sights, 28-inch, 32-inch barrels; fixed or Accu-chokes; plain or vent rib; 48-inch overall length with 28-inch barrel; weighs 7-1/4 lb.; bead front sight; black synthetic stock, ribbed forend; alloy receiver; interchangeable barrels; crossbolt safety; rubber recoil pad; blue finish. Marketed with Mossberg Cablelock. Introduced 1988.

With plain barrel

Perf: $195 **Exc:** $150 **VGood:** $125

With vent rib

Perf: $200 **Exc:** $160 **VGood:** $140

With 24-inch barrel with rifle sights

Perf: $205 **Exc:** $145 **VGood:** $115

MAVERICK MODEL 88 COMBAT

Same specs as Model 88 except 18-1/2-inch Cylinder barrel with vented shroud; black synthetic pistol-grip stock; built-in carrying handle. Introduced 1990; discontinued 1992.

Perf: $280 **Exc:** $250 **VGood:** $195

MAVERICK MODEL 88 SECURITY

Same specs as Model 88 except 6-, 8-shot magazine; 18-1/2-inch Cylinder barrel; synthetic straight- or pistol-grip stock, unribbed forend. Introduced 1993; still in production.

Perf: $195 **Exc:** $130 **VGood:** $100

Add $10 to above prices for 8-shot model with 20-inch barrel.

Add up to $65 for combo package.

Add $100 for Bullpup configuration (6- to 9-shot); discontinued 1994.

MAVERICK MODEL 91 ACCU-MAG

Slide action; 12-ga.; 3-1/2-inch chamber; 28-inch vent-rib barrel; ACCU-MAG Modified tube; weighs about 7-3/4 lbs.; black synthetic stock, slide handle; dual slide bars; crossbolt safety; rubber recoil pad. Accessories interchangeable with Mossberg Model 835. Introduced 1993; still in production.

Perf: $250 **Exc:** $205 **VGood:** $180

MAVERICK MODEL 95

Bolt action; 12-ga.; 3-inch chamber; 2-shot magazine; 25-inch Modified barrel; weighs 6-1/2 lbs.; full-length textured black synthetic stock with integral magazine; ambidextrous rotating safety; twin extractors; rubber recoil pad; blue finish. Introduced 1995; still in production.

Perf: $160 **Exc:** $120 **VGood:** $100

MERCURY MAGNUM

Side-by-side; boxlock; 10-, 12-, 20-ga.; 3-inch, 3-1/2-inch chambers; 28-inch, 32-inch barrels; checkered European walnut pistol-grip stock; double triggers; auto safety; extractors; safety gas ports; engraved frame. Made in Spain and imported by Tradewinds, Inc. Also called Model G1032. Introduced 1970; discontinued 1989.

10-ga.

Perf: $500 **Exc:** $410 **VGood:** $380

12-, 20-ga.

Perf: $300 **Exc:** $260 **VGood:** $210

MERKEL MODEL 8

Side-by-side; boxlock; 12-, 16-, 20-ga.; 2-3/4-inch chambers; 26-inch, 26 3/4-inch, 28-inch barrels; weighs 6+ lbs.; checkered European walnut English straight-grip or pistol-grip stock, forend; double triggers or single selective trigger; double lugs; Greener crossbolt locking system; automatic ejectors; sling swivels; built to handle steel shot; engraved, color case-hardened receiver. Made in Germany. Discontinued 1994.

Perf: $1250 **Exc:** $900 **VGood:** $750

MERKEL MODEL 47E

Side-by-side; boxlock; hammerless; 12-, 20-ga.; 2-3/4-inch chambers; standard barrel lengths, choke combos; hand-checkered European walnut stock, forearm; pistol grip and cheekpiece or straight English style; double hook bolting; Greener crossbolt; double triggers or single selective trigger; automatic ejectors; cocking indicators; engraving; sling swivels; built to handle steel shot. Still in production.

Perf: $3025 **Exc:** $2150 **VGood:** $1500

MERKEL MODEL 47LSC SPORTING CLAYS

Same specs as Model 47E except 12-ga.; 3-inch chambers; 28-inch barrel; Briley choke tubes; weighs about 7-1/4 lbs.; fancy figured walnut pistol-grip stock, beavertail forend; recoil pad; single selective trigger adjustable for length of pull; H&H-type ejectors; manual safety; cocking indicators; lengthened forcing cones; color case-hardened receiver with Arabesque engraving. Comes with fitted leather luggage case. Made in Germany. Introduced 1993; no longer imported.

Perf: $2600 **Exc:** $1950 **VGood:** $1700

MERKEL MODEL 47S

Same specs as Model 47E except sidelock; 12-, 16-, 20-, 28-ga., .410; 2-3/4-inch, 3-inch chambers; double triggers or single trigger. Introduced prior to WWII; still in production.

Perf: $3950 **Exc:** $2800 **VGood:** $2400

MERKEL MODEL 47SL, 147SL SIDE-BY-SIDES

Similar to Model 122 except H&H style sidelock action with cocking indicators, ejectors. Silver-grayed receiver and sideplates have Arabesque engraving, engraved border and screws (Model 47S), or fine hunting scene engraving (Model 147S). Imported from Germany by GSI.

Model 47SL

Perf: $5650 **Exc:** $4650 **VGood:** $3800

Model 147SL

Perf: $7650 **Exc:** $5350 **VGood:** $4300

Model 247SL (English-style engraving, large scrolls)

Perf: $7700 **Exc:** $5300 **VGood:** $4250

Model 447SL (English-style engraving, small scrolls)

Perf: $9250 **Exc:** $8350 **VGood:** $7500

MERKEL MODEL 280EL AND 360EL SHOTGUNS

Similar to Model 47E except smaller frame. Greener cross bolt with double under-barrel locking lugs, fine engraved hunting scenes on silver-grayed receiver, luxury-grade wood, Anson and Deely box-lock action. H&H ejectors, single-selective or double triggers. Introduced 2000. From Merkel.

Model 280EL (28-gauge, 28-inch barrel, Imp. Cyl. and Mod. chokes)

Perf: $5500 **Exc:** $4400 **VGood:** $3700

Model 360EL (.410-bore, 28-inch barrel, Mod. and Full chokes)

Perf: $5625 **Exc:** $4400 **VGood:** $3700

Model 280/360EL two-barrel set (28-ga. and .410-bore)

Perf: $8050 **Exc:** $6950 **VGood:** $6250

MERKEL MODEL 280SL AND 360SL SHOTGUNS

Similar to Model 280EL and 360EL except has sidelock action, double triggers, English-style Arabesque engraving. Introduced 2000. From Merkel.

Model 280SL (28-gauge, 28-inch barrel, Imp. Cyl. and Mod. chokes)

Perf: $8050 **Exc:** $6850 **VGood:** $6150

Model 360SL (.410-bore, 28-inch barrel, Mod. and Full chokes)

Perf: $8100 **Exc:** $7000 **VGood:** $6150

Model 280/360SL two-barrel set

Perf: $11,650 **Exc:** $10,250 **VGood:** $9250

MERKEL MODEL 100

Over/under; boxlock; hammerless; 12-, 16-, 20-ga.; standard barrel lengths, choke combos; plain or optional ribbed barrel; hand-checkered European walnut stock, forearm; pistol grip and cheekpiece or straight English style; Greener crossbolt safety; double triggers; plain extractors. Made in Germany prior to World War II.

With plain barrel

Exc: $1250 **VGood:** $900 **Good:** $700

With ribbed barrel

Exc: $1350 **VGood:** $1000 **Good:** $900

MERKEL MODEL 101

Over/under; boxlock; hammerless; 12-, 16-, 20-ga.; standard barrel lengths, choke combos; ribbed barrel; hand-checkered European walnut stock, forearm; pistol grip and cheekpiece or straight English style; Greener crossbolt safety; double triggers; separate extractors; engraving. Made in Germany prior to World War II.

Exc: $1850 **VGood:** $1600 **Good:** $1325

MERKEL MODEL 101E

Same specs as Model 101 except ejectors. Made in Germany prior to World War II.

Exc: $2000 **VGood:** $1750 **Good:** $1425

MERKEL MODEL 122

Side-by-side; Anson & Deely boxlock; 12-, 16-, 20-ga.; 3-inch chambers; 26-3/4-inch, 28-inch barrels; any standard choke combo; hand-checkered straight-grip or pistol-grip stock, forend; automatic ejectors; double triggers or single selective trigger; dummy sideplates; Greener crossbolt. Made in Germany. Introduced 1993; still in production.

Perf: $3200 **Exc:** $2000 **VGood:** $1650

MERKEL MODEL 127

Side-by-side; Holland & Holland-type hand-detachable sidelocks; hammerless; 12-, 16-, 20-, 28-ga., .410; standard barrel lengths, choke combos; hand-checkered European walnut stock, forearm; pistol-grip and cheekpiece or straight English style; double triggers; automatic ejectors; elaborately engraved with Arabesque or hunting scene. Manufactured in Germany prior to WWII.

Perf: $13,500 **Exc:** $9000 **VGood:** $7000

MERKEL MODEL 130

Side-by-side; Anson & Deeley-type boxlock; hammerless; 12-, 16-, 20-, 28-ga., .410; standard barrel lengths, choke combos; hand-checkered European walnut stock, forearm; pistol-grip and cheekpiece or straight English style; dummy sideplates; double triggers; automatic ejectors; elaborate Arabesque or hunting-scene engraving. Made in Germany prior to World War II.

Perf: $9,999 **Exc:** $8500 **VGood:** $6000

MERKEL MODEL 147

Side-by-side; Anson & Deeley boxlock; 12-, 16-, 20-ga.; 26-3/4-inch, 28-inch barrels; other lengths on special order; any standard choke combo; hand-checkered straight-grip or pistol-grip stock, forend; extractors; double triggers or single selective trigger. Made in Germany since World War II; still in production.

Perf: $1600 **Exc:** $1100 **VGood:** $900

MERKEL MODEL 147E

Same specs as Model 147 except 12-, 16-, 20-, 28-ga.; automatic ejectors. Made in Germany since World War II; still in production.

Perf: $2150 **Exc:** $1850 **VGood:** $1600

MERKEL MODEL 147S

Same specs as Model 147 except sidelock; 12-, 16-, 20-, 28-ga., .410; 25-1/2-inch, 26-inch, 26-3/4-inch, 28-inch barrels; automatic ejectors; engraved hunting scene on action. Made in Germany since World War II; still in production.

Perf: $5300 **Exc:** $3600 **VGood:** $3100

28-ga.

Perf: $2250 **Exc:** $1950 **VGood:** $1700

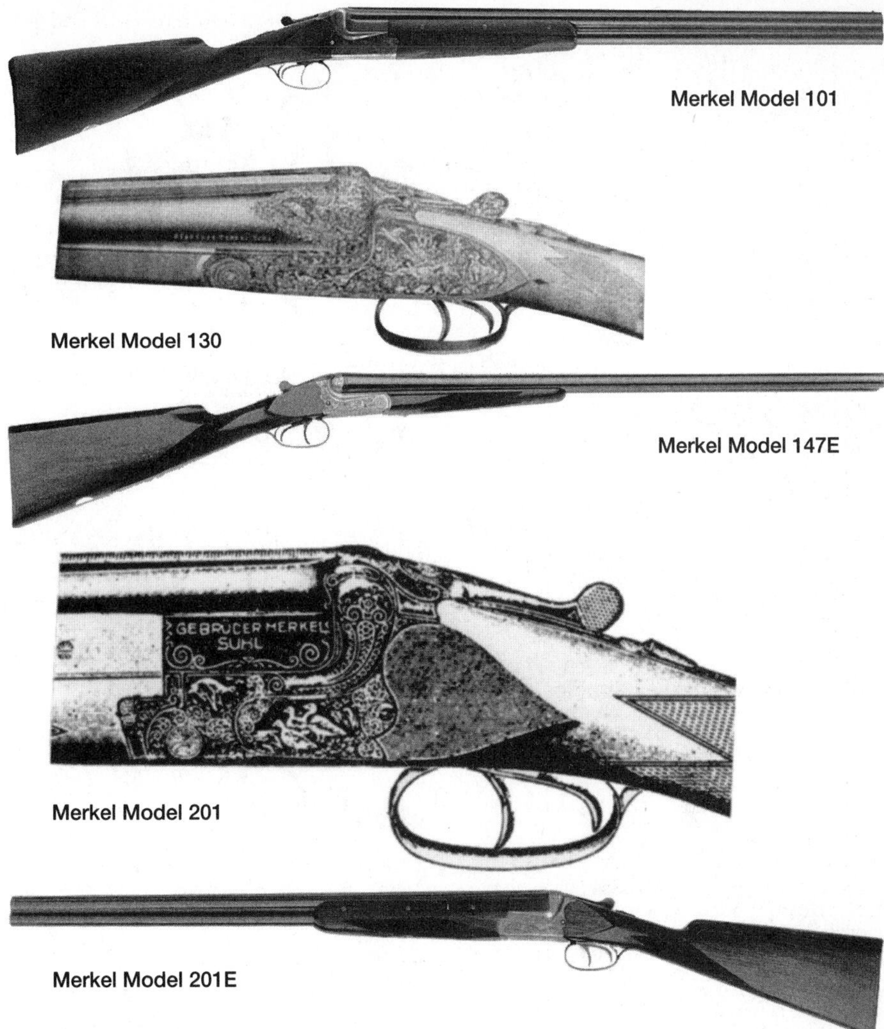

Merkel Model 101

Merkel Model 130

Merkel Model 147E

Merkel Model 201

Merkel Model 201E

MERKEL MODEL 200

Over/under; boxlock; hammerless; 12-, 16-, 20-, 24-, 28-, 32-ga.; standard barrel lengths, choke combos; ribbed barrels; hand-checkered European walnut stock, forearm; pistol grip and cheekpiece or straight English style; Kersten double crossbolt; separate extractors; double triggers; scalloped frame; Arabesque engraving. Made in Germany prior to World War II.

Exc: $1000 **VGood:** $800 **Good:** $700

MERKEL MODEL 200E

Same specs as the Model 200 except ejectors; double, single or single selective trigger. Introduced prior to WWII; 24-, 28-, 32-ga. dropped during WWII; still in production.

Perf: $3300 **Exc:** $2450 **VGood:** $1995

MERKEL MODEL 200E SKEET

Same specs as the Model 200 except 12-ga.; 2-3/4-inch chambers; 26-inch Skeet/Skeet barrels; tapered ventilated rib; competition pistol-grip stock; single selective trigger; half-coverage Arabesque engraving on silver-grayed receiver. Made in Germany. Introduced 1993; still imported.

Perf: $4650 **Exc:** $3700 **VGood:** $3500

MERKEL MODEL 200ET TRAP

Same specs as the Model 200 except 12-ga.; 2-3/4-inch chambers; 30-inch Full/Full barrels; tapered ventilated rib; competition pistol-grip stock; single selective trigger; half-coverage Arabesque engraving on silver-grayed receiver. Made in Germany. Introduced 1993; still imported.

Perf: $4650 **Exc:** $3700 **VGood:** $3300

MERKEL MODEL 200SC SPORTING CLAYS

Same specs as the Model 200 except Blitz action; 30-inch barrels with lengthened forcing cones; fixed or five Briley choke tubes; tapered vent rib select-grade stock; single selective trigger adjustable for length of pull; Kersten double crossbolt lock; competition recoil pad; color case-hardened receiver; fitted luggage case. Made in Germany. Introduced 1995; still imported.

With fixed chokes

Perf: $6700 **Exc:** $3900 **VGood:** $3200

With choke tubes

Perf: $7100 **Exc:** $4300 **VGood:** $3600

MERKEL MODEL 201

Over/under; boxlock; hammerless; 12-, 16-, 20-ga.; standard barrel lengths, choke combos; ribbed barrels; hand-checkered European walnut stock, forearm; pistol grip and cheekpiece or straight English style; separate extractors; double triggers; Greener crossbolt; scalloped frame; engraving. Made in Germany prior to World War II. No longer in production.

Exc: $1600 **VGood:** $1200 **Good:** $990

MERKEL MODEL 201E

Same specs as Model 201 except ejectors. Made in Germany prior to World War II.

Exc: $2550 **VGood:** $2150 **Good:** $1950

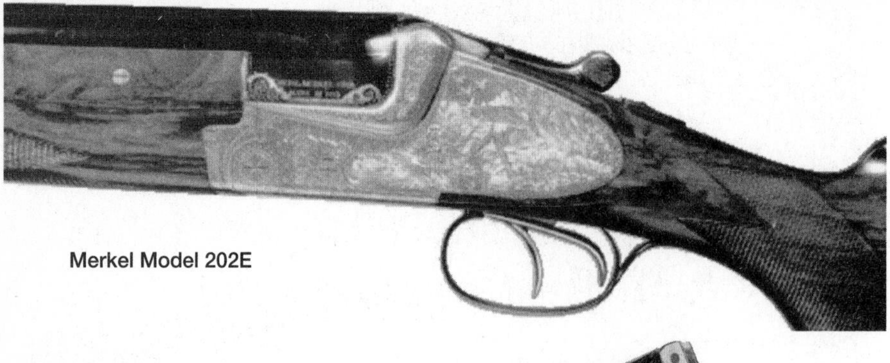

Merkel Model 202E

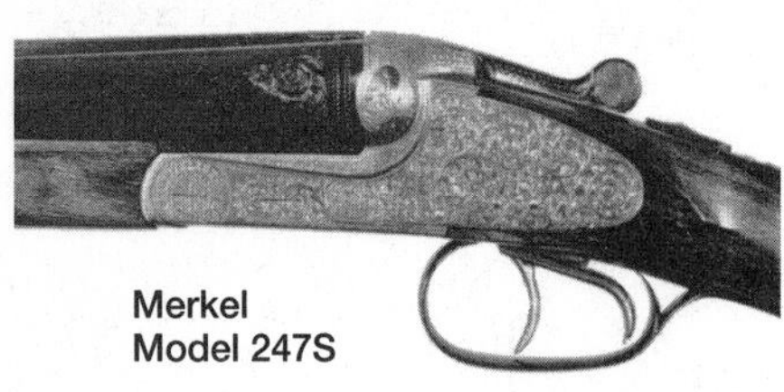

Merkel Model 247S

Merkel Model 303E

Merkel Model 347S

MERKEL MODEL 201E (RECENT)
Same specs as Model 201 except 12-, 16-, 20-, 28-ga.; ejectors; double, single or single selective trigger. Made in Germany. Still in production.

Perf: $4200 **Exc:** $2750 **VGood:** $2200

28-ga. model

Perf: $5000 **Exc:** $3250 **VGood:** $2700

MERKEL MODEL 201ES
Same specs as Model 201 except 12-ga.; 2-3/4-inch chamber; 26-3/4-inch Skeet/Skeet barrels; full-coverage engraving. Made in Germany. Still in production.

Perf: $6800 **Exc:** $4350 **VGood:** $3200

MERKEL MODEL 201ET
Same specs as Model 201 except 12-ga.; 2-3/4-inch chamber; 30-inch Full/Full barrels; full-coverage engraving. Made in Germany. Still in production.

Perf: $3000 **Exc:** $2800 **VGood:** $2600

MERKEL MODEL 202
Over/under; boxlock; hammerless; 12-, 16-, 20-ga.; standard barrel lengths, choke combos; ribbed barrels; selective hand-checkered European walnut stock, forearm; pistol grip and cheekpiece or straight English style; Greener separate extractors; double triggers; dummy sideplates. Made in Germany prior to World War II.

Exc: $2950 **VGood:** $2500 **Good:** $2300

MERKEL MODEL 202E
Same specs as Model 202 except ejectors. Made in Germany prior to World War II.

Exc: $3200 **VGood:** $2750 **Good:** $2400

MERKEL MODEL 202E (RECENT)
Same specs as Model 202, except automatic ejectors; full-coverage engraving. Made in Germany. Introduced 1993; still in production.

Perf: $8200 **Exc:** $5500 **VGood:** $4000

MERKEL MODEL 203
Over/under; hand-detachable sidelocks; hammerless; 12-, 16-, 20-ga.; ribbed barrels in standard lengths, choke combos; hand-checkered European walnut stock, forearm; pistol grip and cheekpiece or straight English style; Kersten double crossbolt; automatic ejectors; double triggers; optional single selective or non-selective trigger; Arabesque or hunting scene engraving. Made in Germany prior to World War II.

With double triggers

Perf: $5000 **Exc:** $3500 **VGood:** $2800

With single trigger

Perf: $5500 **Exc:** $4000 **VGood:** $3000

With single selective trigger

Perf: $6000 **Exc:** $4500 **VGood:** $3500

MERKEL MODEL 203E
Same specs as Model 203 except standard sidelocks. Made in Germany. Still in production.

Perf: $9500 **Exc:** $4900 **VGood:** $3800

MERKEL MODEL 203ES
Same specs as Model 203 except standard sidelocks; 12-ga.; 2-3/4-inch chamber; 26 3/4-inch Skeet/Skeet barrels; full coverage engraving. Made in Germany. No longer imported.

Perf: $13,500 **Exc:** $9500 **VGood:** $7500

MERKEL MODEL 203ET
Same specs as Model 203 except standard sidelocks; 12-ga.; 2-3/4-inch chamber; 30-inch Full/Full barrels; full coverage engraving. Made in Germany. Still in production.

Perf: $12,500 **Exc:** $9500 **VGood:** $7500

MERKEL MODEL 204E
Over/under; Merkel sidelocks; hammerless; 12-, 16-, 20-ga.; ribbed barrels in standard lengths, choke combos; hand-checkered European walnut stock, forearm; pistol grip and cheekpiece or straight English style; Kersten double crossbolt; automatic ejectors; double triggers; fine English-style engraving. Made in Germany prior to World War II.

Exc: $6000 **VGood:** $4200 **Good:** $3400

MERKEL MODEL 210
Over/under; boxlock; hammerless; 12-, 16-, 20-, 24-, 28-, 32-ga.; ribbed barrels in standard lengths, choke combos; select hand-checkered European walnut stock, forearm; pistol grip and cheekpiece or straight English style; Kersten double crossbolt; scalloped frame; elaborate engraving; separate extractors; double triggers. Made in Germany prior to World War II.

Exc: $2150 **VGood:** $1900 **Good:** $1500

MERKEL MODEL 247S
Side-by-side; sidelock; 12-, 16-, 20-ga.; 25 1/2-inch, 26-inch, 26-3/4-inch barrels; standard choke combos; hand-checkered straight-grip or pistol-grip stock, forend; automatic ejectors; double triggers or single selective trigger; engraving. Made in Germany. Still in production.

Perf: $6500 **Exc:** $3800 **VGood:** $3200

MERKEL MODEL 300
Over/under; Merkel-Anson boxlock; hammerless; 12-, 16-, 20-, 24-, 28-, 32-ga.; ribbed barrels in standard lengths, choke combos; hand-checkered European walnut stock; pistol grip and cheekpiece or straight English style; Kersten double crossbolt; two underlugs; scalloped frame; Arabesque or hunting scene engraving; separate extractors. Made in Germany prior to World War II.

Exc: $1950 **VGood:** $1700 **Good:** $1500

MERKEL MODEL 300E
Same general specs as Model 300 except automatic ejectors. Made in Germany prior to World War II.

Exc: $2650 **VGood:** $1950 **Good:** $1650

MERKEL MODEL 301
Over/under; Merkel-Anson boxlock; hammerless; 12-, 16-, 20-, 24-, 28-, 32-ga.; ribbed barrels in standard lengths, choke combos; select hand-checkered European walnut stock; pistol grip and cheekpiece or straight English style; Kersten double crossbolt; two underlugs; scalloped frame; elaborate engraving; separate extractors. Made in Germany prior to World War II.

Exc: $6000 **VGood:** $4500 **Good:** $3400

MERKEL MODEL 301E
Same specs as Model 301 except automatic ejectors. Made in Germany prior to World War II.

Exc: $4200 **VGood:** $3200 **Good:** $2600

MERKEL MODEL 302
Over/under; hammerless; 12-, 16-, 20-, 24-, 38-, 32-ga.; ribbed barrels in standard lengths, choke combos; select hand-checkered European walnut stock; pistol grip and cheekpiece or straight English style; Kersten double crossbolt; two underlugs; scalloped frame; elaborate engraving; automatic ejectors; dummy sideplates. Made in Germany prior to World War II.

Exc: $9000 **VGood:** $7500 **Good:** $6000

MERKEL MODEL 303E
Over/under; Holland & Holland-type hand-detachable sidelocks; hammerless; ribbed barrels in standard lengths, choke combos; select hand-checkered European walnut stock, forearm; pistol grip and cheekpiece or straight English style; Kersten crossbolt; double underlugs; automatic ejectors. Introduced prior to World War II; still in production.

Perf: $18,000 **Exc:** $13,000 **VGood:** $10,000

MERKEL MODEL 304E
Over/under; Holland & Holland-type hand-detachable sidelocks; hammerless; 12-, 16-, 20-, 24-, 28-, 32-ga.; ribbed barrels in standard lengths, choke combos; fancy hand-checkered European walnut stock; pistol grip and cheekpiece or straight English style; Kersten double crossbolt; two underlugs; automatic ejectors; scalloped frame; elaborate engraving. Made in Germany prior to World War II. Optional extras can greatly affect price.

Perf: $20,000 **Exc:** $15,000 **VGood:** $10,000

MERKEL MODEL 310E
Over/under; Merkel-Anson boxlock; hammerless; 12-, 16-, 20-, 24-, 28-, 32-ga.; ribbed barrels in standard lengths, choke combos; hand-checkered European walnut stock; pistol grip and cheekpiece or straight English style; Kersten double crossbolt; two underlugs; automatic ejectors; scalloped frame; Arabesque or hunting scene engraving. Made in Germany prior to World War II.

Exc: $6500 **VGood:** $4900 **Good:** $3500

MERKEL MODEL 347S
Side-by-side; sidelock; 12-,16-, 20-ga.; 25 1/2-inch, 26-inch, 26 3/4-inch barrels; any standard choke combo; select hand-checkered straight-grip or pistol-grip stock, forend; automatic ejectors; double triggers

or single selective trigger; elaborate engraving. Made in Germany. Still in production.

Perf: $7300 **Exc:** $4200 **VGood:** $3500

MERKEL MODEL 400

Over/under; boxlock; hammerless; 12-, 16-, 20-ga.; ribbed barrels in standard lengths, choke combos; hand-checkered European walnut stock, forearm; pistol grip and cheekpiece or straight English style; Kersten double crossbolt; double triggers; separate extractors; Arabesque engraving on receiver. Made in Germany prior to World War II.

Exc: $1850 **VGood:** $1450 **Good:** $1100

MERKEL MODEL 400E

Same specs as Model 400 except for ejectors. Made in Germany prior to World War II.

Exc: $1900 **VGood:** $1500 **Good:** $1250

MERKEL MODEL 410

Over/under; boxlock; hammerless; 12-, 16-, 20-ga.; ribbed barrels in standard lengths, choke combos; select hand-checkered European walnut stock, forearm; pistol grip and cheekpiece or straight English style; Kersten double crossbolt; double triggers; separate extractors; elaborate engraving. Made in Germany prior to World War II.

Exc: $1900 **VGood:** $1600 **Good:** $1250

MERKEL MODEL 410E

Same specs as Model 410 except ejectors. Made in Germany prior to World War II.

Exc: $2175 **VGood:** $1900 **Good:** $1600

MERKEL MODEL 447S

Side-by-side; sidelock; 12-, 16-, 20-ga.; 25-1/2-inch, 26-inch, 26-3/4-inch barrels; standard choke combos; select hand-checkered straight-grip or pistol-grip stock, forend; automatic ejectors; double triggers or single selective trigger; fancy engraving. Made in Germany. Still in production.

Perf: $8500 **Exc:** $4400 **VGood:** $3200

MERKEL MODEL 2001EL

Gauge: 12, 20, 3-inch chambers, 28, 2-3/4-inch chambers. Barrel: 12-28-inch; 20, 28 ga.-26-3/4-inch. Weight: About 7 lbs. (12 ga.). Stock: Oil-finished walnut; English or pistol grip. Features: Self-cocking Blitz boxlock action with cocking indicators; Kersten double cross-bolt lock; silver-grayed receiver with engraved hunting scenes; coil spring ejectors; single selective or double triggers. Imported from Germany by GSI, Inc.

Perf: $7100 **Exc:** $5600 **VGood:** $4250

MERKEL MODEL 303EL

Similar to Model 2001 EL except Holland & Holland-style sidelock action with cocking indicators; English-style Arabesque engraving. Available in 12-, 20-, 28-gauge. Imported from Germany by GSI, Inc.

Perf: $19,750 **Exc:** $16,250 **VGood:** $13,000

MERKEL MODEL 2002 EL

Similar to Model 2001 EL except dummy sideplates, Arabesque engraving with hunting scenes; 12-, 20-, 28-gauge. Imported from Germany by GSI, Inc.

Perf: $10,625 **Exc:** $8000 **VGood:** $6000

MERKEL 1622

Introduced in 2006, this 16-gauge boxlock side-by-side features full sideplates, case hardened receiver with cocking indicators, ejectors, single selective or double triggers and pistol grip or English style stock. Fixed IC and Mod. chokes. Add 50 percent for 2-barrel set (second set is 28-inch 20 gauge).

NIB: $5200 **Exc:** $4600 **VGood:** $3250

MERKEL 1622E

Similar to 1622 but with fine engraved hunting scenes on silver-grayed receiver.

NIB: $6200 **Exc:** $5600 **VGood:** $2250

MERKEL 1622EL

Similar to Model 1622E but with luxury grade wood. Add 30 percent for 2-barrel set (second set is 28-inch 20 gauge).

NIB: $8895 **Exc:** $8175 **VGood:** $7675

Merkel Model 2001EL

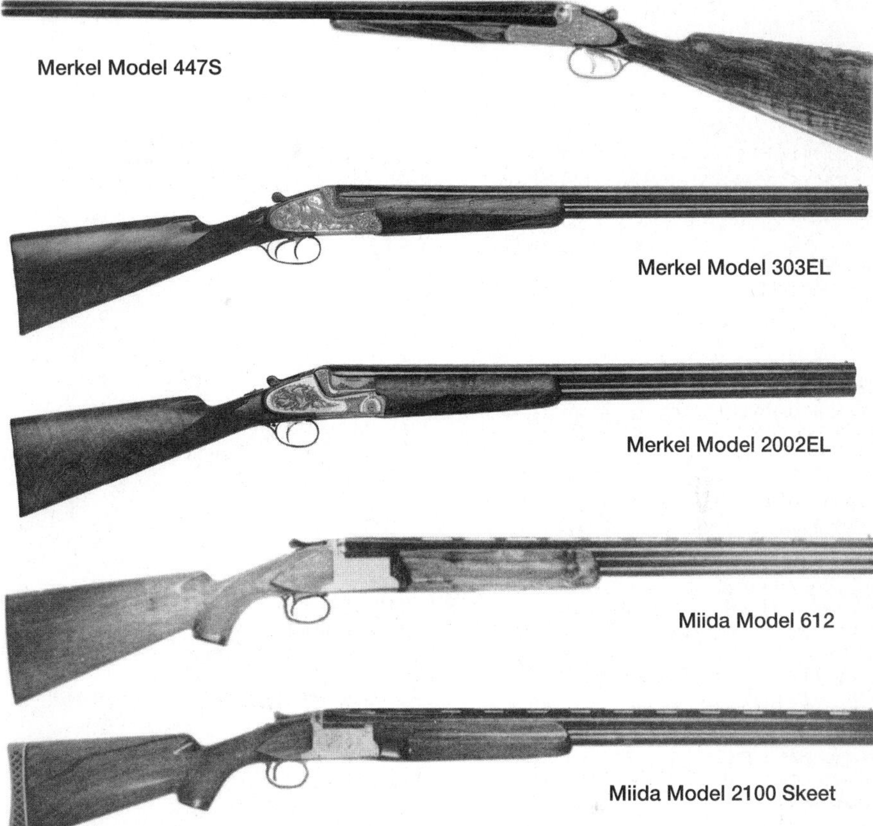

Merkel Model 447S

Merkel Model 303EL

Merkel Model 2002EL

Miida Model 612

Miida Model 2100 Skeet

MERKEL 2000CL

Introduced in 2006, this model is similar to the 2000EL but has a scroll engraved case hardened receiver and luxury grade wood. Semi-pistol grip or English style stock and three-piece forearm. Available in 12, 20 and 28 gauge, all with 28-inch barrel and fixed IC and Mod. chokes.

NIB: $6995 **Exc:** $6250 **VGood:** $5200

MERKEL 2000CL SPORTER

Similar to 2000CL but in following configurations: 12-gauge with 30-inch vent rib barrels; 20-gauge with 28-inch solid rib barrels; and 28-gauge with 28-inch solid rib barrels. All are fixed choke Skeet and IC.

NIB:6995 **Exc:** 6250 **VGood:** 5200

MIIDA MODEL 612

Over/under; boxlock; 12-ga.; 26-inch Improved Cylinder/Modified; 28-inch Modified/Full barrels; vent rib; checkered walnut pistol-grip stock, forearm; auto ejectors; single selective trigger; engraving. Made in Japan; imported by Marubeni America Corp. Introduced 1972; discontinued 1974.

Perf: $825 **Exc:** $700 **VGood:** $600

MIIDA MODEL 2100 SKEET

Over/under; boxlock; 12-ga.; 27-inch vent-rib barrels; 12-ga.; 27-inch Skeet/Skeet barrels; vent rib; select checkered walnut pistol-grip stock, forearm; selective single trigger; auto ejectors; 50 percent engraving coverage. Made in Japan; imported by Marubeni America Corp. Introduced 1972; discontinued 1974.

Perf: $875 **Exc:** $780 **VGood:** $700

MIIDA MODEL 2200S SKEET

Over/under; boxlock; 12-ga.; 27-inch Skeet/Skeet barrels; vent rib; checkered fancy walnut Skeet stock, semi-beavertail forearm; 60 percent engraving coverage. Made in Japan; imported by Marubeni America Corp. Introduced 1972; discontinued 1974.

Perf: $950 **Exc:** $800 **VGood:** $700

MIIDA MODEL 2200T TRAP

Same specs as 2200S, except 29-3/4-inch Improved Modified/Full barrels; trap stock; recoil pad. Made in Japan; imported by Marubeni America Corp. Introduced 1972; discontinued 1974.

Perf: $950 **Exc:** $800 **VGood:** $700

MIIDA MODEL 2300S SKEET

Over/under; boxlock; 12-ga.; 27-inch Skeet/Skeet barrels; vent rib; checkered fancy walnut Skeet stock, semi-beavertail forearm; 70 percent engraving coverage. Made in Japan; imported by Marubeni America Corp. Introduced 1972; discontinued 1974.

Perf: $900 **Exc:** $750 **VGood:** $650

MIIDA MODEL 2300T TRAP

Same specs as Model 2300S Skeet, except 29-3/4-inch Improved Modified/Full barrels; trap stock; recoil pad. Made in Japan; imported by Marubeni America Corp. Introduced 1972; discontinued 1974.

Perf: $900 **Exc:** $750 **VGood:** $650

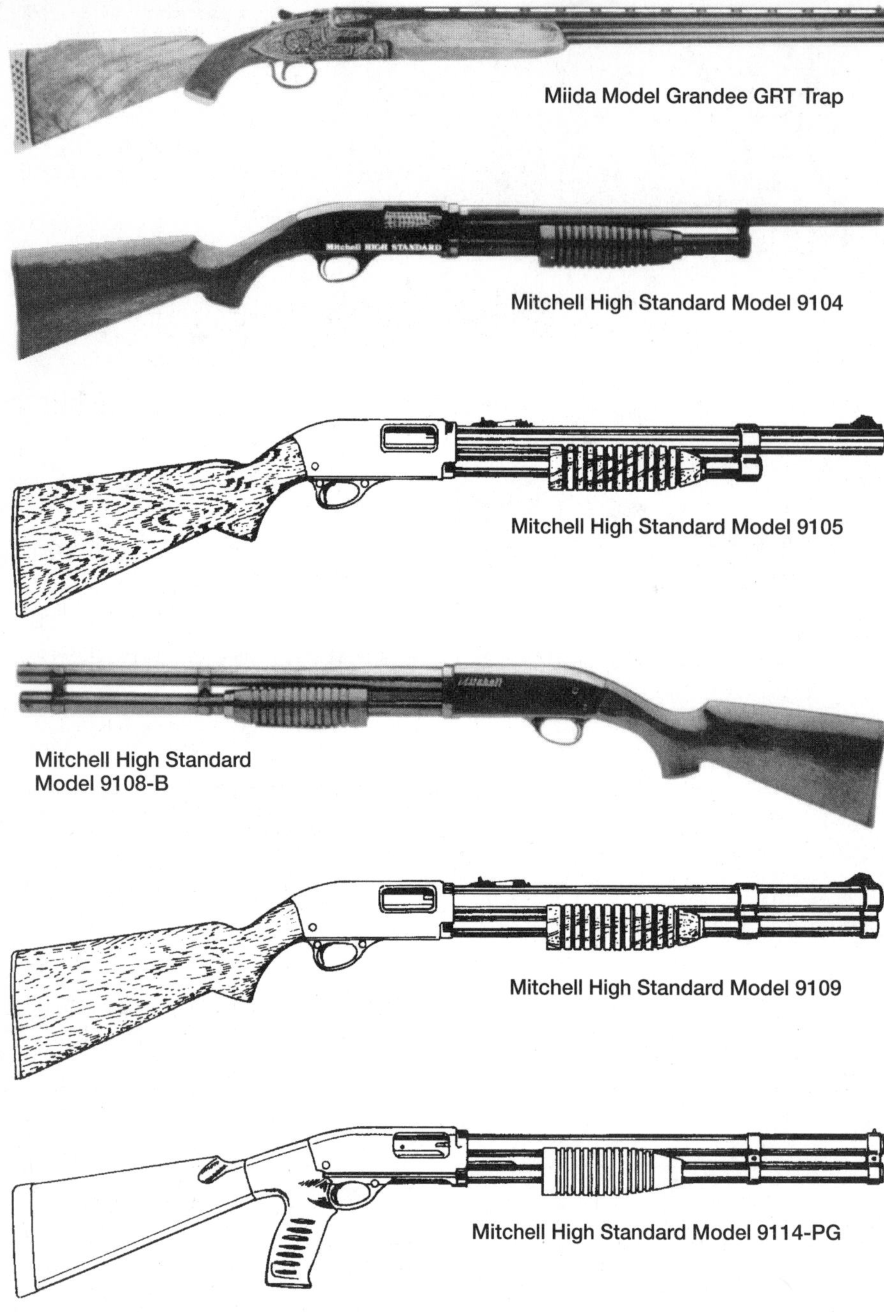

Miida Model Grandee GRT Trap

Mitchell High Standard Model 9104

Mitchell High Standard Model 9105

Mitchell High Standard Model 9108-B

Mitchell High Standard Model 9109

Mitchell High Standard Model 9114-PG

MIIDA MODEL GRANDEE GRS SKEET

Over/under; boxlock; 12-ga.; 27-inch Skeet/Skeet barrels; wide vent rib; extra fancy walnut Skeet stock, semi-beavertail forearm; single selective trigger; auto ejectors; sideplates; gold-inlaid, fully engraved frame, breech ends of barrels, locking lever, trigger guard. Made in Japan; imported by Marubeni America Corp. Introduced 1972; discontinued 1974.

Perf: $2250 **Exc:** $1800 **VGood:** $1600

MIIDA MODEL GRANDEE GRT TRAP

Same specs as Model Grandee GRS Skeet, except 29-3/4-inch Full/Full barrels; trap stock; recoil pad. Made in Japan; imported by Marubeni America Corp. Introduced 1972; discontinued 1974.

Perf: $2250 **Exc:** $1800 **VGood:** $1800

MITCHELL HIGH STANDARD MODEL 9104

Slide action; 12-ga.; 2-3/4-inch chamber; 6-shot magazine; 20-inch Cylinder barrel; bead sight; walnut-finished hardwood stock, slide handle; fixed barrel with steel receiver; polished blue finish. Made in the Philippines. Introduced 1994; discontinued 1996.

Perf: $230 **Exc:** $180 **VGood:** $160

MITCHELL HIGH STANDARD MODEL 9104-CT

Same specs as Model 9104 except Improved Cylinder, Modified, Full choke tubes. Introduced 1994; discontinued 1996.

Perf: $250 **Exc:** $200 **VGood:** $160

MITCHELL HIGH STANDARD MODEL 9105

Slide action; 12-ga.; 2-3/4-inch chamber; 6-shot magazine; 20-inch Cylinder barrel; rifle sights; walnut-finished hardwood stock, slide handle; fixed barrel with steel receiver; polished blue finish. Made in the Philippines. Introduced 1994; discontinued 1996.

Perf: $250 **Exc:** $200 **VGood:** $160

MITCHELL HIGH STANDARD MODEL 9108-B

Slide action; 12-ga.; 2-3/4-inch chamber; 8-shot magazine; 20-inch Cylinder barrel; bead sight; brown-finished hardwood stock, slide handle; fixed barrel with steel receiver; polished blue finish. Made in the Philippines. Introduced 1994; discontinued 1996.

Perf: $230 **Exc:** $180 **VGood:** $140

MITCHELL HIGH STANDARD MODEL 9108-BL

Same specs as Model 9108-B except black-finished hardwood stock, slide handle. Introduced 1994; discontinued 1996.

Perf: $230 **Exc:** $180 **VGood:** $140

MITCHELL HIGH STANDARD MODEL 9108-CT

Same specs as Model 9108-B except Improved Cylinder, Modified, Full choke tubes. Introduced 1994; discontinued 1996.

Perf: $250 **Exc:** $200 **VGood:** $160

MITCHELL HIGH STANDARD MODEL 9108-HG-B

Same specs as Model 9108-B except brown-finished hardwood stock, slide handle. Introduced 1994; discontinued 1996.

Perf: $250 **Exc:** $200 **VGood:** $160

MITCHELL HIGH STANDARD MODEL 9108-HG-BL

Same specs as Model 9108-B except black-finished hardwood stock, slide handle. Introduced 1994; discontinued 1996.

Perf: $250 **Exc:** $200 **VGood:** $150

MITCHELL HIGH STANDARD MODEL 9109

Slide action; 12-ga.; 2-3/4-inch chamber; 8-shot magazine; 20-inch Cylinder barrel; rifle sights; walnut-finished hardwood stock, slide handle; fixed barrel with steel receiver; polished blue finish. Made in the Philippines. Introduced 1994; discontinued 1996.

Perf: $250 **Exc:** $200 **VGood:** $150

MITCHELL HIGH STANDARD MODEL 9111-B

Slide action; 12-ga.; 2-3/4-inch chamber; 7-shot magazine; 18-1/2-inch Cylinder barrel; bead sight; brown-finished hardwood hand-grip stock, slide handle; fixed barrel with steel receiver; polished blue finish. Made in the Philippines. Introduced 1994; discontinued 1996.

Perf: $250 **Exc:** $200 **VGood:** $150

MITCHELL HIGH STANDARD MODEL 9111-BL

Same specs as Model 9108-B except black-finished hardwood stock, slide handle. Introduced 1994; discontinued 1996.

Perf: $250 **Exc:** $200 **VGood:** $150

MITCHELL HIGH STANDARD MODEL 9111-CT

Same specs as Model 9108-B except Improved Cylinder, Modified, Full choke tubes. Introduced 1994; discontinued 1996.

Perf: $250 **Exc:** $200 **VGood:** $150

MITCHELL HIGH STANDARD MODEL 9113-B

Slide action; 12-ga.; 2-3/4-inch chamber; 7-shot magazine; 18-1/2-inch Cylinder barrel; rifle sights; brown-finished hardwood hand-grip stock, slide handle; fixed barrel with steel receiver; polished blue finish. Made in the Philippines. Introduced 1994; discontinued 1996.

Perf: $250 **Exc:** $200 **VGood:** $150

MITCHELL HIGH STANDARD MODEL 9114-PG

Slide action; 12-ga.; 2-3/4-inch chamber; 7-shot magazine; 18-1/2-inch Cylinder barrel; rifle sights; pistol-grip stock; slide handle; fixed barrel with steel receiver; polished blue finish. Introduced 1994; discontinued 1996.

Perf: $290 **Exc:** $220 **VGood:** $180

MITCHELL HIGH STANDARD MODEL 9115

Slide action; 12-ga.; 2-3/4-inch chamber; 7-shot magazine; 18-1/2-inch Cylinder barrel with ventilated heat shield; bead sight; walnut-finished hardwood SAS-style stock, slide handle; stock stores four shells; fixed barrel with steel receiver; Parkerized finish. Made in the Philippines. Introduced 1994; discontinued 1996.

Perf: $290 **Exc:** $220 **VGood:** $180

MITCHELL HIGH STANDARD MODEL 9115-CT

Same specs as Model 9115 except Improved Cylinder, Modified, Full choke tubes. Introduced 1994; discontinued 1996.

Perf: $310 **Exc:** $230 **VGood:** $190

MITCHELL HIGH STANDARD MODEL 9115-HG

Same specs as Model 9115 except walnut finished hardwood SAS-style hand-grip stock, slide handle. Introduced 1994; discontinued 1996.

Perf: $290 **Exc:** $220 **VGood:** $180

MONTE CARLO SINGLE

Single barrel; 12-ga.; 32-inch trap barrel; hand-checkered European walnut pistol-grip stock, beavertail forend; recoil pad; auto ejector; slide safety; gold-plated trigger. Made in Italy. Introduced 1968; no longer in production.

Exc: $275 **VGood:** $240 **Good:** $180

MOSSBERG SEMI-AUTOMATIC SHOTGUNS

MOSSBERG MODEL 1000

Gas-operated autoloader; 12-, 20-ga.; 2-3/4-inch chamber; 4-shot tube magazine; 26-inch, 28-inch vent-rib barrel; standard chokes; optional screw-in choke tubes; front, middle bead sights; checkered American walnut stock; interchangeable crossbolt safety; pressure compensator, floating piston for recoil control; engraved alloy receiver. Made in Japan. Formerly marketed by Smith & Wesson; discontinued 1987.

Perf: $390 **Exc:** $320 **VGood:** $280

Add $30 to above prices for Multi-Choke II.

MOSSBERG MODEL 1000 JUNIOR

Same specs as Model 1000 except 20-ga.; 22-inch Multi-Choke barrel; vent rib; junior-sized stock. Introduced 1986; discontinued 1987.

Perf: $410 **Exc:** $330 **VGood:** $290

MOSSBERG MODEL 1000 SKEET

Same specs as Model 1000 except 26-inch Skeet barrel; vent rib; Skeet-style stock; steel receiver. Introduced 1986; discontinued 1986.

Perf: $375 **Exc:** $300 **VGood:** $250

MOSSBERG MODEL 1000 SLUG

Same specs as Model 1000 except 22-inch barrel; rifle sights; recoil pad. Introduced 1986; discontinued 1987.

Perf: $400 **Exc:** $320 **VGood:** $260

MOSSBERG MODEL 1000 SUPER

Same specs as Model 1000 except gas-metering system for 2-3/4-inch, 3-inch shells; 26-inch, 28-inch, 30-inch Multi-Choke barrel; recoil pad. Introduced 1986; discontinued 1987.

Perf: $480 **Exc:** $375 **VGood:** $315

MOSSBERG MODEL 1000 SUPER SKEET

Same specs as Model 1000 except gas-metering system for 2-3/4-inch, 3-inch shells; 25-inch barrel; recessed-type Skeet choke; oil-finished, select-grade walnut stock, forend; palm swell; recoil-reduction compensator system; contoured trigger; forend cap weights for changing balance. Introduced 1986; discontinued 1987.

Perf: $550 **Exc:** $450 **VGood:** $400

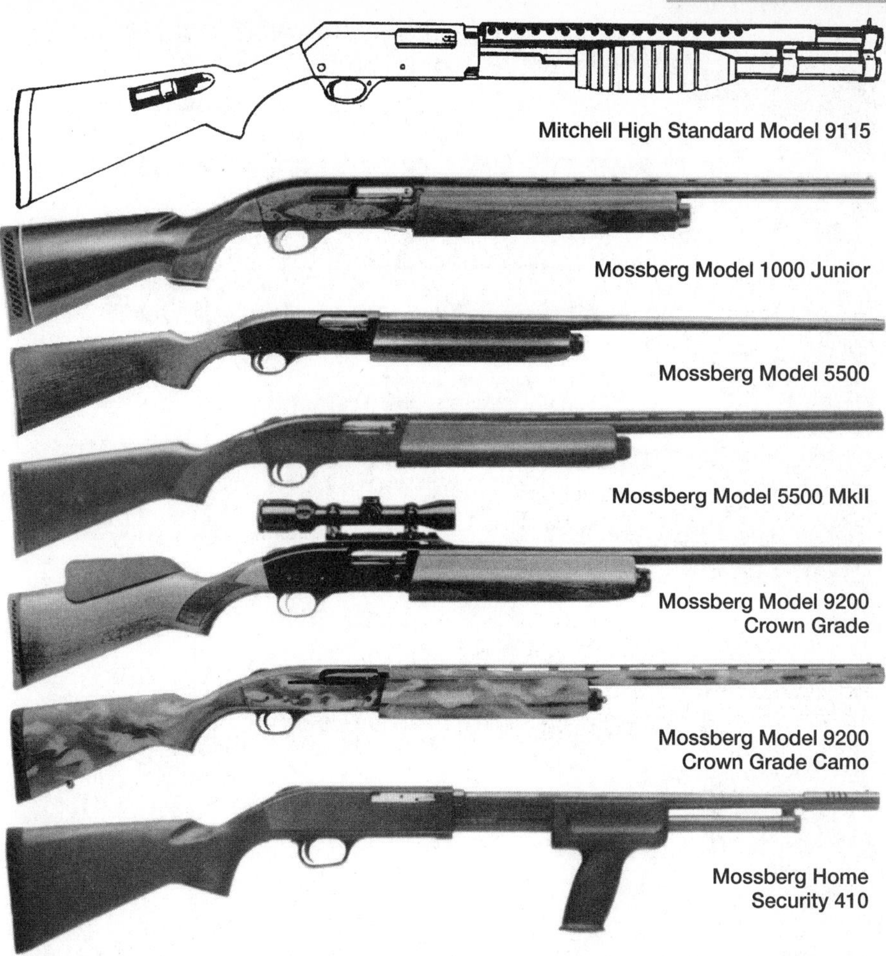

Mitchell High Standard Model 9115

Mossberg Model 1000 Junior

Mossberg Model 5500

Mossberg Model 5500 MkII

Mossberg Model 9200 Crown Grade

Mossberg Model 9200 Crown Grade Camo

Mossberg Home Security 410

MOSSBERG MODEL 1000 SUPER TRAP

Same specs as Model 1000 except 12-ga.; gas-metering system for 2-3/4-inch, 3-inch shells; 30-inch Multi-choke barrel; vent rib; walnut-finished hardwood Monte Carlo stock; recoil pad. Introduced 1986; discontinued 1987.

Perf: $465 **Exc:** $370 **VGood:** $300

MOSSBERG MODEL 1000 SUPER WATERFOWLER

Same specs as Model 1000 except 12-ga.; gas-metering system for 2-3/4-inch, 3-inch shells; 28-inch Multi-choke barrel; sling swivels; camo sling; Parkerized finish. Introduced 1986; discontinued 1987.

Perf: $500 **Exc:** $400 **VGood:** $360

MOSSBERG MODEL 5500

Autoloader; 12-ga.; 2-3/4-inch, 3-inch chamber; interchangeable 18-1/2-inch Cylinder, 24-inch Slugster, 26-inch Improved, 28-inch Modified, 30-inch Full barrel; Accu-Choke tubes; bead front sight; walnut-finished hardwood stock. Introduced 1983; discontinued 1985.

Perf: $235 **Exc:** $200 **VGood:** $170

Slugster model

Perf: $260 **Exc:** $215 **VGood:** $190

MOSSBERG MODEL 5500 MKII

Same specs as Model 5500 except 24-inch rifled, 24-inch, 26-inch, 28-inch vent-rib barrel; Accu-II choke tubes. Also marketed as two-barrel set with both 26-inch (2-3/4-inch) and 28-inch (3-inch) barrels. Introduced 1988; discontinued 1992.

Perf: $250 **Exc:** $200 **VGood:** $175

Combo set

Perf: $300 **Exc:** $250 **VGood:** $225

MOSSBERG MODEL 5500 MARK II CAMO

Same specs as Model 5500 except 28-inch barrel; Accu-II choke tubes; synthetic stock; camouflage finish. Introduced 1988; discontinued 1992.

Perf: $280 **Exc:** $230 **VGood:** $200

MOSSBERG MODEL 6000

Autoloader; 12-ga.; 3-inch chamber; 28-inch barrel; Modified Accu-Choke tube; weighs about 7-1/2 lbs.; walnut-finished stock with high-gloss finish; alloy receiver; shoots all 2-3/4-inch or 3-inch loads without adjustment. Introduced 1993; discontinued 1993.

Perf: $275 **Exc:** $200 **VGood:** $180

MOSSBERG MODEL 9200 CROWN GRADE

Autoloader; 12-ga.; 3-inch chamber; 24-inch rifled, 24-inch, 28-inch vent-rib barrel; Accu-Choke tubes; weighs about 7 1/2 lbs.; cut-checkered walnut stock with high-gloss finish; ambidextrous safety; alloy receiver; shoots all 2-3/4-inch or 3-inch loads without adjustment. Introduced 1992; dropped 2001.

With standard barrel

Perf: $425 **Exc:** $350 **VGood:** $290

With 24-inch rifled barrel; scope base; Dual-Comb stock

Perf: $445 **Exc:** $370 **VGood:** $310

MOSSBERG MODEL 9200 CROWN GRADE CAMO

Same specs as Model 9200 Crown Grade except 24-inch vent-rib barrel; Accu-Choke tubes; synthetic stock, forend; completely covered with Mossy Oak Tree Stand or OFM camouflage finish. Introduced 1993; dropped 1999.

With Mossy Oak finish

Perf: $400 **Exc:** $325 **VGood:** $265

Mossberg Model 500

Mossberg Model 500AHT (Hi-Rib Trap)

Mossberg Model 500 Bantam

Mossberg Model 500 Bullpup

Mossberg Model 500 Camo

With OFM camo finish

Perf: $400 **Exc:** $325 **VGood:** $265

MOSSBERG MODEL 9200 NWTF EDITION

Same specs as Model 9200 Crown Grade except black matte receiver with turkey scenes etched on both sides; Realtree camo finish on rest of gun. Introduced 1994; still in production.

Perf: $490 **Exc:** $395 **VGood:** $350

MOSSBERG MODEL 9200 REGAL

Same specs as Model 9200 Crown Grade except 24-inch rifled, 28-inch vent-rib barrel; Accu-Choke tubes; less fancy wood. Introduced 1992; discontinued 1993.

Perf: $425 **Exc:** $350 **VGood:** $290

MOSSBERG MODEL 9200 USST

Same specs as Model 9200 Crown Grade except 26-inch vent-rib barrel; Accu-Choke tubes (including Skeet); cut-checkered walnut-finished stock, forend; "United States Shooting Team" custom engraved receiver. Introduced 1993; still in production.

Perf: $415 **Exc:** $330 **VGood:** $280

MOSSBERG SLIDE-ACTION SHOTGUNS

MOSSBERG HOME SECURITY 410

Slide action; .410; 3-inch chamber; 18-1/2-inch barrel; spreader choke; 37-1/2-inch overall length; weighs 6-1/4 lbs; synthetic pistol-grip stock, forend; recoil pad; blued finish; also available with laser installed in forend. Marketed with Mossberg Cablelock. Introduced 1990; still in production.

Perf: $260 **Exc:** $195 **VGood:** $165

With laser

Perf: $375 **Exc:** $300 **VGood:** $275

MOSSBERG MODEL HS410 SHOTGUN

Similar to the Model 500 Security pump except chambered for 20 gauge or 410 with 3-inch chamber; has pistol grip forend, thick recoil pad, muzzle brake and has special spreader choke on the 18.5-inch barrel. Overall length is 37-1/2-inch; weight is 6-1/4 lbs. Blue finish; synthetic field stock. Mossberg Cablelock and video included. Introduced 1990.

Perf: $280 **Exc:** $230 **VGood:** $200

MOSSBERG MODEL 200D

Slide action; 12-ga.; 3-shot detachable box magazine; 28-inch barrel; interchangeable choke tubes; uncheckered, walnut-finished hardwood pistol-grip stock, grooved black nylon slide handle; recoil pad. Introduced 1955; discontinued 1959.

Exc: $135 **VGood:** $95 **Good:** $50

MOSSBERG MODEL 200K

Same specs as Model 200D except variable C-Lect-Choke instead of interchangeable choke tubes. Introduced 1955; discontinued 1959.

Exc: $140 **VGood:** $100 **Good:** $50

MOSSBERG MODEL 500

Slide action; hammerless; takedown; 12-, 20-ga., .410; 6-shot tube magazine; 3-shot plug furnished; 24-inch Slugster Cylinder with rifle sights (12-ga. only), 26-inch Improved, 28-inch Modified or Full, 30-inch Full (12-ga. only) barrel; adjustable C-Lect-Choke, Accu-Choke, Accu-II, Accu-Steel tubes; white bead front sight, brass mid-bead; checkered or uncheckered American walnut pistol-grip stock, grooved slide handle; recoil pad; twin extractors; ambidextrous safety; disconnecting safety dual action bars. Marketed with Cablelock. Introduced 1961; still in production.

With fixed-choke barrel

Perf: $220 **Exc:** $150 **VGood:** $130

With adjustable-choke barrel

Perf: $240 **Exc:** $170 **VGood:** $140

Combo with extra barrel

Perf: $280 **Exc:** $210 **VGood:** $180

MOSSBERG MODEL 500AGVD

Same specs as Model 500 except 12-, 20-ga.; 3-inch chamber; 28-inch vent-rib barrel with Accu-Choke system for Improved, Modified, Full. No longer in production.

Perf: $240 **Exc:** $170 **VGood:** $140

MOSSBERG MODEL 500AHT (HI-RIB TRAP)

Same specs as Model 500 except 12-ga.; 28-inch, 30-inch Full-choke barrel; Simmons Olympic-style free-floating rib; built-up Monte Carlo trap stock. Introduced 1978; discontinued 1986.

Perf: $275 **Exc:** $240 **VGood:** $200

MOSSBERG MODEL 500AHTD (HI-RIB TRAP)

Same specs as Model 500 except 12-ga.; 28-inch, 30-inch barrel; three choke tubes; Simmons Olympic-style free-floating rib; built-up Monte Carlo trap stock. Introduced 1978; discontinued 1986.

Perf: $305 **Exc:** $255 **VGood:** $215

MOSSBERG MODEL 500ALD

Same specs as Model 500 except 12-ga.; 2-3/4-inch, 3-inch chamber; 28-inch vent-rib barrel; Accu-Choke or three interchangeable choke tubes; game scene etched in receiver. Introduced 1977; no longer in production.

Perf: $245 **Exc:** $180 **VGood:** $150

MOSSBERG MODEL 500 ALMR (HEAVY DUCK)

Same specs as Model 500 except 12-ga.; 3-inch chamber; 30-inch, 32-inch Full-choke barrel; vent rib. Introduced 1977; no longer in production.

Perf: $250 **Exc:** $185 **VGood:** $155

MOSSBERG MODEL 500ALS SLUGSTER

Same specs as Model 500 except 12-ga.; 2-3/4-inch, 3-inch chamber; 18-1/2-inch, 24-inch Cylinder-bore barrel; rifle sights; game scene etched in receiver. Introduced 1977; no longer in production.

Perf: $230 **Exc:** $160 **VGood:** $130

MOSSBERG MODEL 500ASG SLUGSTER

Same specs as Model 500 except 12-, 20-ga.; 2-3/4-inch, 3-inch chamber; 18-1/2-inch, 24-inch slug barrel; ramp front sight, open adjustable folding leaf rear; running deer etched on receiver. No longer in production.

Perf: $225 **Exc:** $180 **VGood:** $150

MOSSBERG MODEL 500APR PIGEON GRADE TRAP

Same specs as Model 500 except for 30-inch Full-choke barrel; vent rib; checkered walnut Monte Carlo trap-style stock, beavertail slide handle. Introduced 1968; discontinued 1975.

Perf: $425 **Exc:** $310 **VGood:** $240

MOSSBERG MODEL 500 BANTAM

Same specs as Model 500 except 20-ga.; 22-inch vent rib barrel; Modified Accu-Choke tube; 1-inch shorter stock with reduced length from pistol grip to trigger, reduced forend reach. Introduced 1992; still in production.

Perf: $245 **Exc:** $200 **VGood:** $160

MOSSBERG MODEL 500 BULLPUP

Same specs as Model 500 except 12-ga.; 3-inch chamber; 6-, 9-shot magazine; 18-1/2-inch, 20-inch Cylinder-bore barrel; weighs 9-1/2 lbs.; fixed sights mounted in carrying handle; plastic bullpup-design stock; crossbolt, grip safeties; marketed with Cablelock. Designed for law enforcement; may be illegal in some jurisdictions. Introduced 1986; discontinued 1990.

6-shot model

Perf: $480 **Exc:** $390 **VGood:** $350

8-shot model

Perf: $500 **Exc:** $410 **VGood:** $370

MOSSBERG MODEL 500 CAMO

Same specs as Model 500 except 12-ga.; receiver drilled, tapped for scope mount; synthetic field or Speedfeed stock; sling swivels; camo sling; entire surface covered with camo finish; marketed with Mossberg Cablelock. Introduced 1986; still in production.

Perf: $250 **Exc:** $150 **VGood:** $100

Camo Combo with extra barrel
Perf: $340 **Exc:** $220 **VGood:** $170

MOSSBERG MODEL 500 CAMPER
Same specs as Model 500 except .410 bore only; 18-1/2-inch Cylinder-bore barrel; synthetic pistol-grip stock; carry case. Introduced 1988; dropped 1988.
Perf: $325 **Exc:** $280 **VGood:** $250

MOSSBERG MODEL 500CLD
Same specs as Model 500 except 20-ga.; 2-3/4-inch chamber; 28-inch barrel; Accu-Choke or three interchangeable choke tubes; game scene etched on receiver. Introduced 1977; no longer in production.
Perf: $250 **Exc:** $175 **VGood:** $130

MOSSBERG MODEL 500CLDR
Same specs as Model 500 except 20-ga.; 2-3/4-inch chamber; 28-inch vent-rib barrel; Accu-Choke or three interchangeable choke tubes; game scene etched on receiver. Introduced 1977; no longer in production.
Perf: $270 **Exc:** $195 **VGood:** $150

MOSSBERG MODEL 500CLS SLUGSTER
Same specs as Model 500 except 20-ga.; 2-3/4-inch, 3-inch chamber; 24-inch Cylinder-bore barrel; rifle sights; game scene etched in receiver. Introduced 1977; no longer in production.
Perf: $235 **Exc:** $170 **VGood:** $130

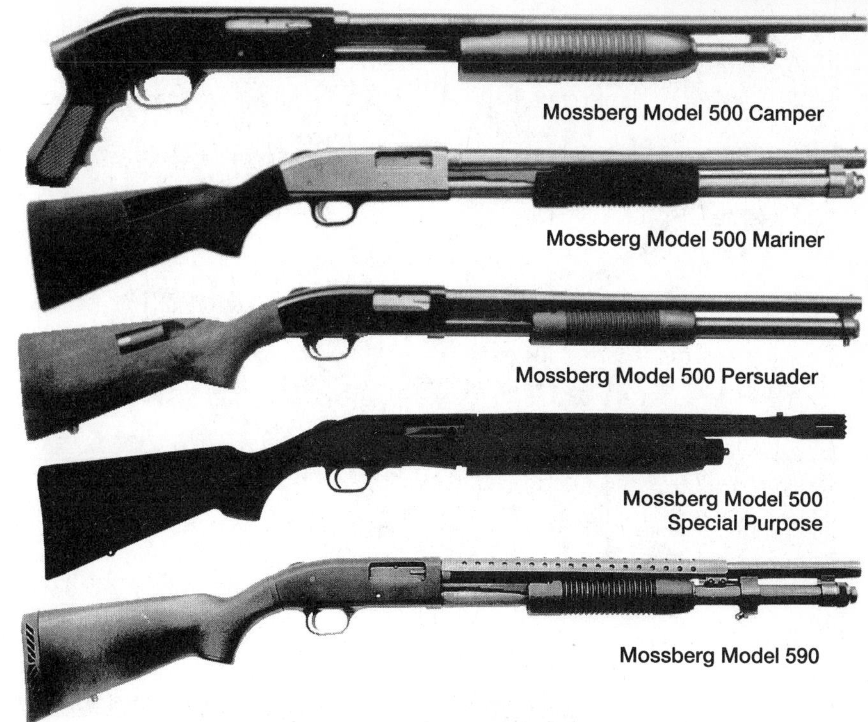

Mossberg Model 500 Camper

Mossberg Model 500 Mariner

Mossberg Model 500 Persuader

Mossberg Model 500 Special Purpose

Mossberg Model 590

MOSSBERG MODEL 500E
Same specs as Model 500 except .410; 26-inch barrel; Full, Modified, Improved chokes; fluted comb. No longer in production.
Perf: $245 **Exc:** $175 **VGood:** $145

Skeet barrel with vent rib, checkering
Perf: $275 **Exc:** $195 **VGood:** $175

MOSSBERG MODEL 500EGV
Same specs as Model 500 except .410; 26-inch Full-choke barrel; vent rib; checkered pistol grip, forend; fluted comb; recoil pad. No longer in production.
Perf: $275 **Exc:** $195 **VGood:** $175

MOSSBERG MODEL 500EL
Same specs as Model 500 except .410; 2 1/2-inch, 3-inch chamber; 26-inch Full-choke barrel; game scene etched in receiver. Introduced 1977; no longer in production.
Perf: $275 **Exc:** $195 **VGood:** $175

MOSSBERG MODEL 500ELR
Same specs as Model 500 except .410; 2-1/2-inch, 3-inch chamber; 26-inch Full-choke barrel; vent rib; game scene etched in receiver. Introduced 1977; no longer in production.
Perf: $275 **Exc:** $195 **VGood:** $175

MOSSBERG MODEL 500 GHOST RING
Same specs as Model 500 except 12-ga., 3-inch chamber; 6-, 9-shot magazine; 18-1/2-inch Cylinder or Accu-Choke barrel; adjustable blade front sight, adjustable Ghost Ring rear with protective ears; synthetic or Speedfeed stock; blue or Parkerized finish. Introduced 1990; dropped 1997.

Blue finish
Perf: $270 **Exc:** $190 **VGood:** $150

Parkerized finish
Perf: $300 **Exc:** $210 **VGood:** $180

Parkerized finish, Accu-Choke barrel
Perf: $350 **Exc:** $260 **VGood:** $225

Add $50 to above prices for 9-shot magazine.
Add $125 for Accu-Choke barrel.
Add $135 for Speedfeed stock.

MOSSBERG MODEL 500 INTIMIDATOR
Same specs as Model 500 except 12-ga.; 3-inch chamber; 6-, 9-shot magazine; 18-1/2-inch Cylinder-bore barrel; integral laser sight incorporated in synthetic forend; blued or Parkerized finish; marketed with Mossberg Cablelock. Introduced 1990; discontinued 1993.

With blue finish
Perf: $450 **Exc:** $360 **VGood:** $300

With Parkerized finish
Perf: $460 **Exc:** $370 **VGood:** $310

MOSSBERG MODEL 500 MARINER
Same specs as Model 500 except 12-ga.; 3-inch chamber; 6-, 9-shot magazine; 18-1/2-inch, 20-inch Cylinder-bore barrel; weighs 7 lbs.; ghost ring or metal bead front sight; walnut-finished hardwood, synthetic or Speedfeed stock; all metal parts are finished with Marinecoat to resist rust, corrosion; marketed with Cablelock. Still in production.
Perf: $350 **Exc:** $220 **VGood:** $180

Mini Combo with extra barrel, handguard, pistol grip
Perf: $450 **Exc:** $320 **VGood:** $280

Add $20 to above prices for 9-shot variation.
Add $70 for ghost ring sights.
Add $25 for Speedfeed stock.

MOSSBERG MODEL 500 MEDALLION
Same specs as Model 500 except 12-, 20-ga.; 28-inch vent-rib barrel; Accu-Choke tubes; game bird medallion inset in receiver: pheasant or duck (12-ga.), grouse or quail (20-ga.); only 5000 made in each category. Introduced 1983; discontinued 1984.
Perf: $260 **Exc:** $190 **VGood:** $175

MOSSBERG MODEL 500 MUZZLELOADER COMBO
Same specs as Model 500 except two-barrel set with 24-inch rifled Slugster barrel with rifle sights and 24-inch fully rifled 50-caliber muzzle-loading barrel with ramrod; Uses #209 standard primer. Introduced 1992; still in production.
Perf: $390 **Exc:** $280 **VGood:** $220

MOSSBERG MODEL 500 PERSUADER
Same specs as Model 500 except 12-, 20-ga.; 6-, 8-shot magazine; 18-1/2-inch, 20-inch barrel; Cylinder bore or Accu-Choke tubes; shotgun or rifle sights; uncheckered wood or synthetic pistol-grip stock, grooved slide handle; blue or Parkerized finish; optional bayonet lug. Designed specifically for law enforcement. Introduced 1977; still in production.
Perf: $245 **Exc:** $175 **VGood:** $150

With bayonet lug
Perf: $260 **Exc:** $190 **VGood:** $165

12 gauge, Parkerized finish, 6-shot, 18-1/2-inch barrel, ghost ring sights.
Perf: $377 **Exc:** $317 **VGood:** $287

Home Security 410 (.410-bore, 18-1/2-inch barrel with spreader choke)
Perf: $280 **Exc:** $230 **VGood:** $200

12- or 20-ga., 18-1/2-inch, blue, wood or synthetic stock, 6-shot.
Perf: $265 **Exc:** $205 **VGood:** $175

Cruiser, 12- or 20-ga., 18-1/2-inch, blue, pistol grip, heat shield.
Perf: $282 **Exc:** $217 **VGood:** $192

As above, .410-bore.
Perf: $270 **Exc:** $205 **VGood:** $180

MOSSBERG MODEL 500 SECURITY SERIES
Same specs as Model 500 except 12-ga.; 3-inch chamber; 6-, 8-shot magazine; 18-1/2-inch, 20-inch Cylinder bore barrel; weighs 7 lbs.; metal bead front sight; walnut-finished hardwood, synthetic or Speedfeed stock; blue, Parkerized or nickel finish.

With blue or nickel finish
Perf: $240 **Exc:** $170 **VGood:** $150

With Parkerized finish
Perf: $260 **Exc:** $190 **VGood:** $170

Mini Combo with extra barrel
Perf: $290 **Exc:** $220 **VGood:** $190

MOSSBERG MODEL 500 SPECIAL PURPOSE
Slide-action in 12 or 20 gauge or 410 bore with 3-inch chamber. Barrel length, 18.5 or 20 inches. Weight is approximately 7 pounds. Walnut-finished hardwood or black synthetic stock. Available in 6- or 9-shot models. Blue, Parkerized, Marinecote finishes. Offered in several variants. HS410 Home Security model chambered for 410 has pistol grip fore-end, thick recoil pad, muzzle brake and special spreader choke on the 18.5-inch barrel. Base price shown is for Persuader/Cruiser model and HS410 model.
Perf: $385 **Exc:** $335 **VGood:** $285

Add 30 percent for Mariner 9-shot model, 50 percent for Tactical Tri-Rail

MOSSBERG MODEL 500 SUPER GRADE
Same specs as Model 500 except vent-rib barrel; checkered pistol grip, slide handle. Introduced 1961; discontinued 1976.

With fixed-choke barrel
Perf: $245 **Exc:** $190 **VGood:** $150

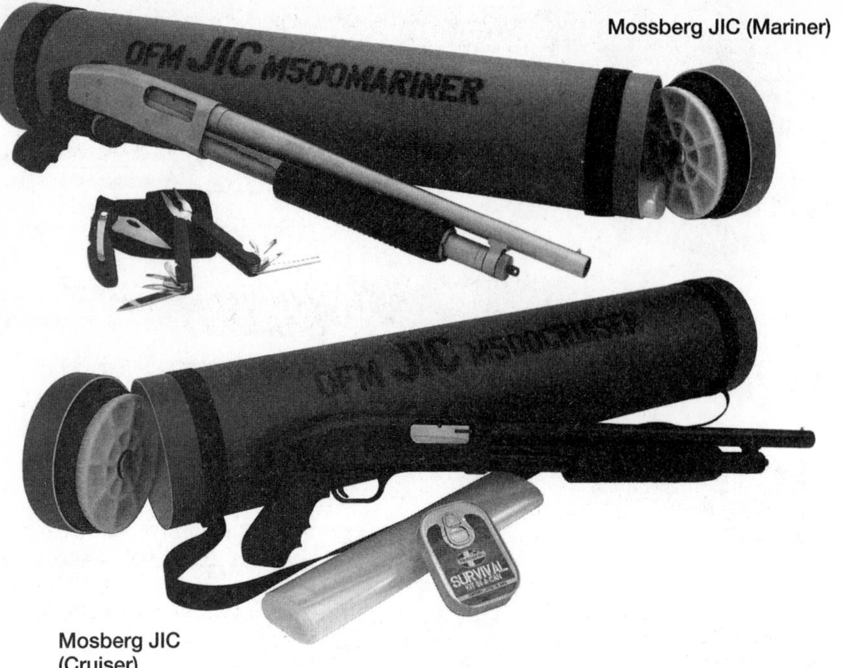

Mossberg JIC (Mariner)

Mosberg JIC (Cruiser)

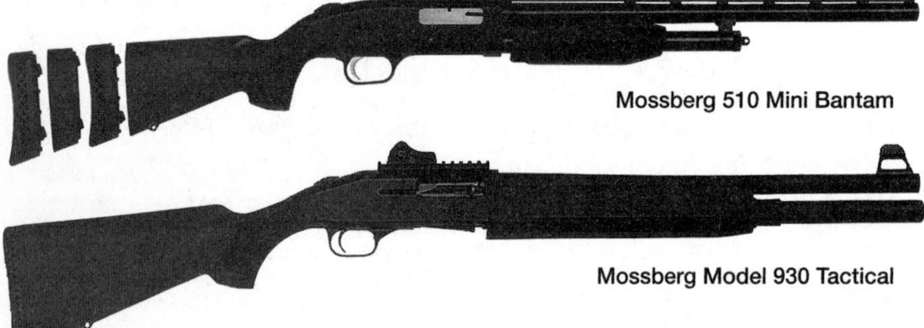
Mossberg 510 Mini Bantam

Mossberg Model 930 Tactical

With adjustable-choke barrel
Perf: $265 **Exc:** $210 **VGood:** $170

MOSSBERG MODEL 500 TROPHY SLUGSTER

Same specs as Model 500 except 12-ga.; 3-inch chamber; 24-inch smooth or rifled bore; 44-inch overall length; weighs 7-1/4 lbs.; scope mount; walnut-stained hardwood stock; swivel studs; recoil pad; Introduced 1988; still in production.
Perf: $285 **Exc:** $200 **VGood:** $180

MOSSBERG MODEL 500 TURKEY

Same specs as Model 500 except 24-inch Accu-Choke barrel with Improved Cylinder, Modified, Full, Extra-Full lead shot choke tubes; Ghost-Ring sights; swivel studs; camo sling; overall OFM camo finish. Introduced 1992. Still in production.
Perf: $300 **Exc:** $240 **VGood:** $200

MOSSBERG MODEL 500 ROLLING THUNDER

This home defense/tactical model is a 3" 12 gauge featuring a pistol grip, 23" barrel with heat shield and recoil-reducing stabilizer and six-round capacity.
Perf: $375 **Exc:** $315 **VGood:** $250

MOSSBERG MODEL 500 JIC (JUST IN CASE)

This survival model is a 3" 12 gauge featuring a pistol grip, 18.5" barrel and a weatherproof pack tube. Three different models available with different finishes and accessory packages.
Perf: $375 **Exc:** $325 **VGood:** $250

MOSSBERG 510 MINI BANTAM

Slide-action 20 gauge or 410 bore with 3-inch chamber. Barrel length is 18.5 inches. Weight is 5 lbs., length 34.75 inches. Designed primarily for younger or smaller statured shooters. Synthetic stock with optional Mossy Oak Break-Up Infinity is adjustable for growing shooters.
Perf: $300 **Exc:** $250 **VGood:** $225

MOSSBERG MODEL 590 SPECIAL PURPOSE SHOTGUNS

Similar to Model 500 except has Parkerized or Marinecote finish, 9-shot magazine and black synthetic stock (some models feature Speed Feed. Available in 12-gauge only with 20-inch, cylinder bore barrel. Weighs 7-1/4 lbs. Still in production.

Bead sight, heat shield over barrel.
Perf: $335 **Exc:** $275 **VGood:** $225

Ghost ring sight, Speedfeed stock.
Perf: $456 **Exc:** $396 **VGood:** $346

Add $60 to above prices for parkerized finish.
Add $90 for heavy barrel variation with metal triggerguard and safety.

MOSSBERG MODEL 590

Slide action; 12-ga.; 3-inch chamber; 9-shot magazine; 20-inch Cylinder-bore barrel; synthetic field or Speedfeed stock with heat shield; bayonet lug; swivel studs; rubber recoil pad; blued or Parkerized finish; marketed with Cablelock. Introduced 1990; still in production.

With blued finish, field stock
Perf: $290 **Exc:** $220 **VGood:** $190

With blued finish, Speedfeed stock
Perf: $310 **Exc:** $240 **VGood:** $210

With Parkerized finish, field stock
Perf: $340 **Exc:** $270 **VGood:** $240

With Parkerized finish, Speedfeed stock
Perf: $360 **Exc:** $290 **VGood:** $260

MOSSBERG 590DA DOUBLE-ACTION PUMP SHOTGUN

Similar to Model 590 except trigger requires a long stroke for each shot, duplicating the trigger pull of double-action-only pistols and revolvers. Available in 12-gauge only with black synthetic stock and Parkerized finish with 14-inch (law enforcement only), 18-1/2-inch and 20-inch barrels. Six-shot magazine tube (9-shot for 20-inch barrel). Front bead or ghost ring sights. Weighs 7 pounds (18 1/2-inch barrel). Introduced 2000; dropped 2003. From Mossberg. Bead sight, 6-shot magazine.
Perf: $450 **Exc:** $415 **VGood:** $360

Ghost ring sights, 6-shot magazine. Still in production.
Perf: $498 **Exc:** $463 **VGood:** $408

Bead sight, 9-shot magazine. Still in production.
Perf: $450 **Exc:** $415 **VGood:** $360

Ghost ring sights, 9-shot magazine. Still in production.
Perf: $498 **Exc:** $463 **VGood:** $408

MOSSBERG MODEL 590 BULLPUP

Same specs as Model 590 except shrouded 20-inch Cylinder-bore barrel; fixed sights mounted in carrying handle; bullpup-configuration plastic stock; crossbolt, grip safties. Designed for law enforcement. Introduced 1989; discontinued 1990.
Perf: $410 **Exc:** $310 **VGood:** $260

MOSSBERG MODEL 590 GHOST RING

Same specs as Model 590 except ghost-ring sights. Introduced 1990; still in production.

With blued finish, field stock
Perf: $310 **Exc:** $240 **VGood:** $210

With blued finish, Speedfeed stock
Perf: $330 **Exc:** $260 **VGood:** $230

With Parkerized finish, field stock
Perf: $360 **Exc:** $290 **VGood:** $260

With Parkerized finish, Speedfeed stock
Perf: $380 **Exc:** $310 **VGood:** $280

MOSSBERG MODEL 590 INTIMIDATOR

Same specs as Model 590 except has integral laser sight built into synthetic field stock, forend; marketed with Mossberg Cablelock. Introduced 1990; discontinued 1993.

With blued finish
Perf: $425 **Exc:** $330 **VGood:** $280

With Parkerized finish
Perf: $450 **Exc:** $365 **VGood:** $300

MOSSBERG MODEL 590 MARINER

Same specs as Model 590 except all parts coated with Marinecoat. Introduced 1989; discontinued 1993.

With field stock
Perf: $300 **Exc:** $210 **VGood:** $170

With Speedfeed stock
Perf: $320 **Exc:** $230 **VGood:** $190

MOSSBERG 930 SPECIAL PURPOSE SERIES

Semiauto 12 gauge with 3-inch chamber. Barrel, 28 inches; weight, 7.3 lbs.; overall length: 49 inches. Composite stock with pistol grip and Speed Lock fore-end with textured gripping surfaces; shim adjustable for length of pull, cast and drop. Mossy Oak Bottomland camo finish and Dura-Touch Armor Coating. Capacity is 7+1 on models with extended magazine tube, 4+1 on models without. Available in a variety of configurations. SPX has full length, pistol-grip stock, ghost ring sight, Picatinny rail, extended magazine tube. Special Purpose Combo has one 28-inch barrel, one 18.5 inches. Tactical has 18.5-inch bbl, extended magazine, M-16 type front sight, ghost-ring rear. Prices shown are for basic Home Security model.
Perf: $515 **Exc:** $440 **VGood:** $375

Add 10 percent for SP Combo, 25 percent for Tactical model, 40 percent for SPX

MOSSBERG MODEL 930 TACTICAL

This 3" 12 gauge has an 18.5" barrel and cylinder bore. Synthetic stock with matte black finish.
Perf: $495 **Exc:** $395 **VGood:** $275

MOSSBERG MODEL 935 MAGNUM

Semi-auto in 12-gauge only with 3½-inch chamber, 24, 26, or 28-inch barrel with choke tubes. Offered in several finish variations including Mossy Oak and Realtree camo. Introduced in 2004. Add 30 percent for camo finish.

Perf: $600 **Exc:** $500 **VGood:** $425

MOSSBERG MODEL 835 AMERICAN FIELD

Slide action; 12-ga.; 3-1/2-inch chamber handles all size shells; backbored 28-inch Accu-Mag Modified choke tube for steel or lead shot; weighs 7-3/4 lbs.; cut-checkered, walnut-stained hardwood stock; ambidextrous thumb safety; twin extractors; dual slide bars. Introduced 1988; still in production.

Perf: $225 **Exc:** $180 **VGood:** $150

MOSSBERG MODEL 835 ULTI-MAG

Same specs as Model 835 American Field except 24-inch rifled bore with rifle sights, 24-inch, 28-inch backbored vent-rib barrel; four Accu-Mag choke tubes for steel or lead shot; cut-checkered, walnut-stained hardwood or camo synthetic stock. Introduced 1988; discontinued 1991.

Perf: $380 **Exc:** $275 **VGood:** $200

MOSSBERG MODEL 835 ULTI-MAG CROWN GRADE

Same specs as Model 835 American Field except 24-inch rifled bore with rifle sights, 24-inch, 28-inch backbored vent-rib barrel; four Accu-Mag choke tubes for steel or lead shot; cut-checkered walnut standard or Dual-Comb, or camo synthetic stock. Introduced 1988; still in production.

With standard barrel; standard walnut stock

Perf: $380 **Exc:** $310 **VGood:** $270

With standard barrel; Dual-Comb walnut stock

Perf: $385 **Exc:** $315 **VGood:** $275

With rifled barrel; scope base; Dual-Comb walnut stock

Perf: $400 **Exc:** $320 **VGood:** $290

Combo with 24-inch rifled, 28-inch barrels; Dual-Comb walnut stock

Perf: $420 **Exc:** $340 **VGood:** $300

Realtree or Mossy Oak Camo with standard barrel; synthetic stock

Perf: $430 **Exc:** $350 **VGood:** $310

Realtree Camo Combo with 24-inch rifled, 24-inch smoothbore barrels; synthetic stock, hard case

Perf: $525 **Exc:** $450 **VGood:** $400

OFM Camo with standard barrel; synthetic stock

Perf: $410 **Exc:** $330 **VGood:** $300

OFM Camo Combo with 24-inch rifled, 28-inch barrels; synthetic stock

Perf: $460 **Exc:** $400 **VGood:** $360

MOSSBERG MODEL 835 ULTI-MAG

Gauge: 12, 3-1/2-inch chamber; ported 24-inch rifled bore, 24-inch, 28-inch barrel; Accu-Mag choke tubes for steel or lead shot; weighs 7-3/4 lbs. ; 48-1/2-inch overall; dual comb; cut-checkered hardwood or camo synthetic; both have recoil pad; white bead front, brass mid-bead sights, fiber optic; shoots 2-3/4-inch, 3-inch or 3-1/2-inch shells; back-bored and ported barrel to reduce recoil, improve patterns; ambidextrous thumb safety; twin extractors; dual slide bars. Mossberg Cablelock included. Introduced 1988.

28-inch vent. rib, hardwood stock

Perf: $375 **Exc:** $310 **VGood:** $265

Combo, 24-inch rifled bore, rifle sights, 24-inch vent. rib, Accu-Mag Ulti-Full choke tube, Woodlands camo finish

Perf: $425 **Exc:** $350 **VGood:** $305

RealTree Camo Turkey, 24-inch vent. rib, Accu-Mag, Extra-Full tube, synthetic stock

Perf: $450 **Exc:** $380 **VGood:** $345

Mossberg Model 835 Ulti-Mag

Mossberg Model 835 Ulti-Mag Crown Grade

Mossberg Model 835 Ulti-Mag Thumbhole Turkey

Mossberg Model 835 Ulti-Mag Tactical Turkey

Mossberg Model SA-20

Mossberg Model 190D

Mossy Oak Camo, 28-inch vent. rib, Accu-Mag tubes, synthetic stock

Perf: $460 **Exc:** $385 **VGood:** $350

OFM Camo, 28-inch vent. rib, Accu-Mag Mod. tube, synthetic stock

Perf: $460 **Exc:** $385 **VGood:** $350

MOSSBERG 835 ULTI-MAG SPECIAL PURPOSE SERIES

Slide-action 12 gauge chambered for all loads from 2-3/4 to 3-1/2 inches. Choice of four barrel lengths, 20, 24, 26 and 28 inches with flat ventilated rib. Several choices of wood, synthetic and camo pattern stocks including thumbhole style. Weight is from 7.25 to 7.75 pounds, depending on barrel length. Prices shown are for Waterfowl model with blue finish. Many other options such as HiViz Tactical fiber optic front sight (Turkey THUG model), X-Factor ported tube (Turkey Tactical), fully rifled barrel (Deer/Turkey combo), can add to prices.

Perf: $415 **Exc:** $375 **VGood:** $300

Add 20 percent for Mossy Oak or Realtree camo, another 20 percent for adjustable stock or HiViz front sight.

MOSSBERG MODEL 835 SYNTHETIC STOCK

Similar to the Model 835, except with 28-inch ported barrel with Accu-Mag Mod. choke tube, Parkerized finish, black synthetic stock and forend. Introduced 1998. Still in production.

Perf: $260 **Exc:** $225 **VGood:** $200

MOSSBERG 835 ULTI-MAG THUMBHOLE TURKEY

New in 2006, this dedicated pump-action 12 gauge turkey gun features a thumbhole stock and overbored barrel. Chambered for 3.5 inch shells. X-Factor ported choke tube. Barrel is 20 inches and has adjustable fiber-optic front and rear sights. Weight is about 7.75 lbs. Available in Mossy Oak New Break-Up camo or Realtree Hardwoods Green camo.

NIB: $400 **Exc:** $350 **VGood:** $295

MOSSBERG 835 ULTI-MAG TACTICAL TURKEY

Same as above but with extended pistol grip stock that is adjustable for length of pull from 10.75-inch to 14.5-inch.

NIB: $425 **Exc:** $375 **VGood:** $320

MOSSBERG MODEL SA-20

This synthetic-stocked, matte black 20 gauge autoloader is chambered for 3-inch shells. It has a 28" or 26" vent-rib barrel and comes with five choke tubes. Weight is about 6 lbs. The Bantam model has a 1-inch shorter length of pull and 24" barrel and weighs about 5.6 lbs. Introduced in 2008.

NIB: $350 **Exc:** $295 **VGood:** $195

MOSSBERG MODEL 70

Bolt action; single shot; takedown; .410; 24-inch barrel; interchangeable Modified, Full choke tubes; uncheckered one-piece, finger-grooved, pistol-grip stock. Introduced 1933; discontinued 1935.

Exc: $100 **VGood:** $75 **Good:** $50

MOSSBERG MODEL 73

Bolt action; single shot; takedown; .410; 24-inch barrel; interchangeable Modified, Full choke tubes; uncheckered one-piece, finger-grooved, pistol-grip stock. Introduced 1936; discontinued 1939.

Exc: $125 **VGood:** $95 **Good:** $75

MOSSBERG MODEL 75

Bolt action; single shot; takedown; 20-ga.; 26-inch barrel; interchangeable Modified, Full choke tubes; uncheckered one-piece, finger-grooved, pistol-grip stock. Introduced 1934; discontinued 1937.

Exc: $125 **VGood:** $95 **Good:** $75

MOSSBERG MODEL 80

Bolt action; takedown; .410; 2-shot fixed top-loading magazine; 24-inch barrel; interchangeable Modified, Full choke tubes; uncheckered one-piece, finger-grooved, pistol-grip stock. Introduced 1934; discontinued 1935.

Exc: $100 **VGood:** $80 **Good:** $60

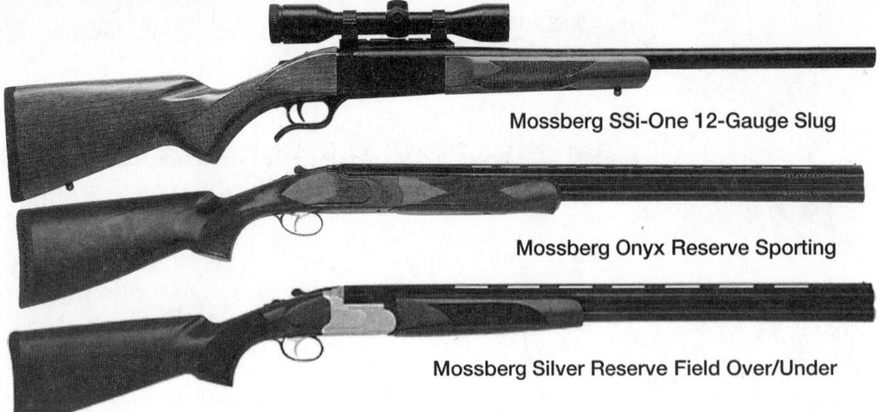

Mossberg SSi-One 12-Gauge Slug

Mossberg Onyx Reserve Sporting

Mossberg Silver Reserve Field Over/Under

MOSSBERG MODEL 83D

Bolt action; takedown; .410; 2-shot fixed top-loading magazine; 23-inch barrel; interchangeable Modified, Full choke tubes; uncheckered one-piece, finger-grooved, pistol grip stock. Introduced 1940; discontinued 1947 replaced by Model 183D.

Exc: $100 **VGood:** $80 **Good:** $60

MOSSBERG MODEL 85

Bolt action; takedown; 20-ga.; 2-shot fixed top-loading magazine; 26-inch barrel; interchangeable Modified, Full choke tubes; uncheckered one-piece, finger-grooved, pistol-grip stock. Introduced 1934; discontinued 1939.

Exc: $90 **VGood:** $60 **Good:** $45

MOSSBERG MODEL 85D

Same specs as Model 85 except 2-shot detachable box magazine; 25-inch barrel; interchangeable Full, Modified, Improved Cylinder choke tubes; black plastic buttplate. Introduced 1940; discontinued 1947 & replaced by Model 185D.

Exc: $80 **VGood:** $60 **Good:** $45

MOSSBERG MODEL 173

Bolt action; single shot; takedown; .410; 2-1/2-inch, 3-inch chamber; 24-inch Full-choke barrel; 43-1/2-inch overall length; weighs 5-1/2 lbs.; uncheckered one-piece, finger-grooved, pistol-grip stock; plastic buttplate. Introduced 1957; discontinued 1973.

Exc: $80 **VGood:** $60 **Good:** $45

MOSSBERG MODEL 173Y

Same specs as Model 173 except 22-inch Full-choke barrel; youth-size uncheckered one-piece, finger-grooved, pistol-grip stock. Introduced 1957; discontinued 1973.

Exc: $80 **VGood:** $60 **Good:** $45

MOSSBERG MODEL 183D

Bolt action; takedown; .410; 2-shot fixed top-loading magazine; 24-inch barrel; interchangeable Modified, Full choke tubes; 43-1/2-inch overall length; weighs 5-1/2 lbs.; uncheckered one-piece, finger-grooved, pistol-grip stock. Introduced 1947; discontinued 1971.

Exc: $90 **VGood:** $60 **Good:** $45

MOSSBERG MODEL 183K

Same specs as Model 183D, except variable C-Lect-Choke instead of interchangeable tubes; 44-1/2-inch overall length. Introduced 1953; discontinued 1985.

Exc: $95 **VGood:** $60 **Good:** $45

MOSSBERG MODEL 185D

Bolt action; takedown; 20-ga.; 2-3/4-inch chamber; 2-shot detachable box magazine; 26-inch barrel; Full, Improved Cylinder choke tubes; 44-1/2-inch overall length; weighs 6-1/4 lbs.; uncheckered one-piece, finger-grooved, pistol-grip stock; black plastic buttplate. Introduced 1947; discontinued 1971.

Exc: $95 **VGood:** $60 **Good:** $45

MOSSBERG MODEL 185K

Same specs as Model 185D except variable C-Lect-Choke instead of interchangeable tubes; 45 1/2-inch overall length. Introduced 1951; discontinued 1963.

Exc: $95 **VGood:** $60 **Good:** $45

MOSSBERG MODEL 190D

Bolt action; takedown; 16-ga.; 2-3/4-inch chamber; 2-shot detachable box magazine; 26-inch barrel; Full, Improved Cylinder choke tubes; 44-1/2-inch overall length; weighs 6-3/4 lbs.; uncheckered one-piece, finger-grooved, pistol-grip stock; black plastic buttplate. Introduced 1955; discontinued 1971.

Exc: $100 **VGood:** $65 **Good:** $50

MOSSBERG MODEL 190K

Same specs as Model 190D except variable C-Lect-Choke instead of interchangeable choke tubes; 45 1/2-inch overall length. Introduced 1956; discontinued 1963.

Exc: $90 **VGood:** $60 **Good:** $45

MOSSBERG MODEL 195D

Bolt action; takedown; 12-ga.; 2-3/4-inch chamber; 2-shot detachable box magazine; 26-inch barrel; interchangeable Full, Improved Cylinder choke tubes; 45-1/2-inch overall length; weighs 7-1/2 lbs.; uncheckered one-piece, finger-grooved, pistol-grip stock; black plastic buttplate. Introduced 1955; discontinued 1971.

Exc: $90 **VGood:** $60 **Good:** $45

MOSSBERG MODEL 195K

Same specs as the Model 195D except variable C-Lect-Choke instead of interchangeable choke tubes; 46-1/2-inch overall length. Introduced 1956; discontinued 1963.

Exc: $95 **VGood:** $65 **Good:** $50

MOSSBERG MODEL 385K

Bolt action; takedown; 20-ga.; 3-inch chamber; 2-shot detachable clip magazine; 26-inch barrel; C-Lect-Choke; walnut-finished hardwood Monte Carlo stock; recoil pad. Introduced 1963; no longer in production.

Exc: $95 **VGood:** $70 **Good:** $50

MOSSBERG MODEL 390K

Bolt action; takedown; 16-ga.; 3-inch chamber; 2-shot detachable clip magazine; 28-inch barrel; C-Lect-Choke; walnut-finished hardwood Monte Carlo stock; recoil pad. Introduced 1963; no longer in production.

Exc: $95 **VGood:** $70 **Good:** $50

MOSSBERG MODEL 395K

Bolt action; takedown; 12-ga.; 3-inch chamber; 2-shot detachable clip magazine; 28-inch barrel; C-Lect-Choke; walnut-finished hardwood Monte Carlo stock; recoil pad. Introduced 1963; no longer in production.

Exc: $95 **VGood:** $70 **Good:** $50

MOSSBERG MODEL 695 SLUGSTER

Gauge: 12, 3-inch chamber; 22-inch barrel, fully rifled, ported; weighs 7-1/2 lbs.; black synthetic, with swivel studs and rubber recoil pad; blade front, folding rifle-style leaf rear sights; fiber optic; Weaver-style scope bases; matte metal finish; rotating thumb safety; detachable 2-shot magazine; Mossberg cablelock. Made in U.S. by Mossberg. Introduced 1996.

Perf: $275 **Exc:** $220 **VGood:** $185

With Fiber Optic rifle sights

Perf: $297 **Exc:** $242 **VGood:** $207

With woodlands camo stock, Fiber Optic sights

Perf: $327 **Exc:** $272 **VGood:** $237

MOSSBERG SSI-ONE 12-GAUGE SLUG

Gauge: 12, 3-inch chamber; 24-inch, fully rifled barrel; weighs 8 lbs.; 40-inch overall length; walnut, fluted and cut checkered stock; sling-swivel studs; drilled and tapped for scope base; no sights (scope base supplied); frame accepts interchangeable rifle barrels (see Mossberg SSi- One rifle listing); lever-opening, break-action design; ambidextrous, top-tang safety; internal eject/extract selector. Introduced 2000.

Perf: $390 **Exc:** $310 **VGood:** $250

MOSSBERG SSI-ONE TURKEY SHOTGUN

Similar to SSi-One 12-gauge Slug Shotgun, but chambered for 12-ga., 3-1/2-inch loads. Includes Accu-Mag Turkey Tube. Introduced 2001.

Perf: $390 **Exc:** $310 **VGood:** $250

MOSSBERG ONYX RESERVE SPORTING

12-ga. O/U with 26- or 28-inch barrels. Similar to Silver Reserve Sporting but with blued receiver.

NIB: $575 **Exc:** $475 **VGood:** $325

MOSSBERG SILVER RESERVE SIDE-BY-SIDE

New in 2008, the side-by-side version of the Silver Reserve comes in 12 gauge with 28" or 26" barrels and 20 and 28 gauge with 26" barrels. The stock and forend is select black walnut with satin finish. The receiver is satin-finished silver with scroll engraving and barrels are blued. Bores are chrome-plated. All models come with five choke tubes. Weight is 6.4 to 6.5 lbs. for 20 and 28 gauges; 7.2 lbs. for 12 gauge.

NIB: $700 **Exc:** $475 **VGood:** $325

MOSSBERG ONYX RESERVE SPORTING SXS

Similar to Silver Reserve Sporting but with blued receiver.

NIB: $700 **Exc:** $475 **VGood:** $325

MOSSBERG SILVER RESERVE FIELD OVER/UNDER

Offered in 12-, 20-, 28-gauge and .410-bore with 26- or 28-inch barrels. Features include scroll engraved receiver with gold inlaid game scenes, single trigger and extractors, checkered walnut stock. Available in sporting model with ported barrels. Made in Turkey and imported from 2005 to 2012. Add 25 percent for sporting model.

Perf: $600 **Exc:** $500 **VGood:** $400

ONYX RESERVE SIDE-BY-SIDE

This model is similar to the Silver Reserve but with a blued receiver.

NIB: $700 **Exc:** 475 **VGood:** 325

NAVY ARMS MODEL 83 BIRD HUNTER

Over/under; boxlock; 12-, 20-ga.; 3-inch chambers; 28-inch barrels; standard choke combos; vent top, middle ribs; weighs 7-1/2 lbs.; metal bead front sight; checkered European walnut stock; double triggers; extractors; silvered, engraved receiver. Made in Italy. Introduced 1984; discontinued 1990.

Perf: $260 **Exc:** $200 **VGood:** $180

NAVY ARMS MODEL 93

Over/under; boxlock; 12-, 20-ga.; 3-inch chambers; 28-inch barrels; standard choke tubes; vent top, middle ribs; metal bead front sight; checkered European walnut stock, forend; double triggers; ejectors; silvered engraved receiver. Made in Italy. Introduced 1985; discontinued 1990.

Perf: $315 **Exc:** $240 **VGood:** $200

NAVY ARMS MODEL 95

Over/under; boxlock; 12-, 20-ga.; 3-inch chambers; 28-inch barrels; five choke tubes; vent top, middle ribs; weighs 7-1/2 lbs.; metal bead front sight; checkered European walnut stock; single trigger; extractors; silvered, engraved receiver. Made in Italy. Introduced 1985; discontinued 1990.

Perf: $365 **Exc:** $300 **VGood:** $270

NAVY ARMS MODEL 96

Over/under; boxlock; 12-, 20-ga.; 3-inch chambers; 28-inch barrels; five choke tubes; vent top, middle ribs; weighs 7-1/2 lbs.; metal bead front sight; checkered European walnut stock; single trigger; ejectors; gold-plated, engraved receiver. Made in Italy. Introduced 1986; discontinued 1990.

Perf: $450 **Exc:** $360 **VGood:** $300

NAVY ARMS MODEL 100 SXS

Side-by-side; 12-, 20-ga.; 3-inch chambers; 28-inch Improved Cylinder/Modified, Modified/Full chrome-lined barrels; weighs 7 lbs.; checkered European walnut stock; extractors; gold-plated double triggers; engraved, hard-chromed receiver. Made in Italy. Introduced 1985; discontinued 1987.

Perf: $300 **Exc:** $290 **VGood:** $225

NAVY ARMS MODEL 100 O/U

Over/under; 12-, 20-, 28-ga., .410; 3-inch chambers; 26-inch vent-rib, chrome-lined barrels; checkered walnut stock; single trigger; extractors; engraved, hard-chrome finished receiver. Introduced 1985; discontinued 1988.

Perf: $375 **Exc:** $290 **VGood:** $260

NAVY ARMS MODEL 105

Single shot; top lever; hammerless; 12-, 20-ga., .410; 3-inch chamber; 26-inch, 28-inch Full-choke barrel; metal bead front sight; checkered walnut-stained hardwood stock; folds for storage, transport; engraved chrome receiver. Made in Italy. Introduced 1987; discontinued 1990.

Perf: $80 **Exc:** $60 **VGood:** $40

NAVY ARMS MODEL 105 DELUXE

Similar to the standard Model 105, except has European walnut stock and vent. rib.

Perf: $95 **Exc:** $85 **VGood:** $75

NAVY ARMS MODEL 150

Side-by-side; 12-, 20-ga.; 3-inch chambers; 28-inch Improved Cylinder/Modified, Modified/Full chrome-lined barrels; weighs 7 lbs.; checkered European walnut stock; ejectors; gold-plated double triggers; engraved, hard-chromed receiver. Introduced 1985; discontinued 1987.

Perf: $465 **Exc:** $375 **VGood:** $315

NAVY ARMS MODEL 600

Single shot; top lever; hammerless; 12-, 20-ga., .410; 26-inch, 28-inch chrome-lined barrel; checkered beech stock; engraved hard-chromed receiver; folds for storage, transport. Made in Italy. Introduced 1986; discontinued 1987.

Perf: $80 **Exc:** $60 **VGood:** $40

NEW ENGLAND FIREARMS CAMO TURKEY SHOTGUNS

Gauge: 10, 3-1/2-inch; 12, 20, 3-inch chamber; 24-inch barrel; Extra-Full, screw-in choke tube (10 ga.); fixed Full choke (12, 20); American hardwood, green and black camouflage finish with sling swivels and ventilated recoil pad; bead front sight; matte metal finish; stock counterweight to reduce recoil; patented transfer bar system for hammer-down safety; includes camo sling and trigger lock. Accepts other factory-fitted barrels. Introduced 2000.

10-, 12-ga.

Perf: $145 **Exc:** $120 **VGood:** $100

20-ga. youth model (22-inch bbl.)

Perf: $150 **Exc:** $115 **VGood:** $95

NEW ENGLAND FIREARMS HANDI-RIFLE

Single shot; break-open; interchangeable rifle, shotgun barrels; 22 Hornet, 223, 243, 30-30, 30-06, 45-70; 12-, 20-ga. with 3-inch chamber; 22-inch barrel; 37-inch overall length; weighs 6-1/2 lbs.; American hardwood stock; rifle barrels have ramp front sight, open rear; drilled, tapped for scope mounts; matte electroless nickel or blued finish. Introduced 1987; still produced.

Perf: $200 **Exc:** $160 **VGood:** $130

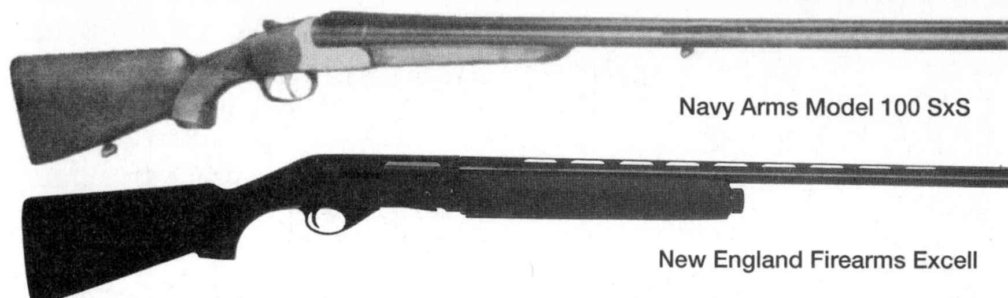

Navy Arms Model 100 SxS

New England Firearms Excell

NEW ENGLAND FIREARMS PARDNER

Single shot; sidelever; 12-, 16-, 20-, 28-ga., .410; 2-3/4-inch, 3-inch chambers; 24-inch, 26-inch, 28-inch, 32-inch barrel; standard chokes; weighs 5-1/2 lbs.; walnut-finished hardwood stock; transfer-bar ignition; blued finish. Introduced 1987; still in production.

Perf: $90 **Exc:** $65 **VGood:** $50

Youth model (12-, 20-, 28-ga., .410, 22-inch barrel, recoil pad)

Perf: $115 **Exc:** $95 **VGood:** $80

12-ga., 32-inch (Full)

Perf: $110 **Exc:** $90 **VGood:** $75

NEW ENGLAND FIREARMS PARDNER DELUXE

Same specs as Pardner except Double Back-up buttstock holding two extra shotshells. Introduced 1987; discontinued 1991.

Perf: $100 **Exc:** $75 **VGood:** $60

NEW ENGLAND FIREARMS PARDNER SPECIAL PURPOSE

Same specs as Pardner except 10-ga.; 3 1/2-inch chamber; 28-inch barrel; weighs 9-1/2 lbs.; recoil pad; blued or camo finish. Introduced 1988; still in production.

Perf: $135 **Exc:** $115 **VGood:** $95

NEW ENGLAND FIREARMS PARDNER YOUTH

Same specs as Pardner except 20-, 28-ga., .410; 22-inch barrel; shorter stock. Introduced 1989; still in production.

Perf: $95 **Exc:** $65 **VGood:** $55

NEW ENGLAND FIREARMS SPECIAL PURPOSE SHOTGUNS

Gauge: 10, 3-1/2-inch chamber; 28-inch barrel (Full), 32-inch barrel (Mod.); weighs 9-1/2 lbs.; 44-inch overall (28-inch barrel); American hardwood with walnut or matte camo finish; ventilated rubber recoil pad; bead front sight; break-open action with side-lever release; ejector; matte finish on metal. Introduced 1992.

Walnut-finish wood sling and swivels

Perf: $135 **Exc:** $115 **VGood:** $95

Camo finish, sling and swivels

Camo finish, 32-inch, sling and swivels

Perf: $238 **Exc:** $218 **VGood:** $198

Black matte finish, 24-inch, Turkey Full choke tube, sling and swivels

Perf: $190 **Exc:** $160 **VGood:** $135

NEW ENGLAND FIREARMS SURVIVOR

Single shot; 12-, 20-ga., .410/45 Colt; 3-inch chamber; 20-inch rifled (.410/45 Colt), 22-inch smoothbore with Modified choke tube; weighs 6 lbs.; 36-inch overall length; black polymer thumbhole/pistol-grip stock, beavertail forend; sling swivels; buttplate removes for extra ammunition storage; forend also holds extra ammunition; black or nickel finish. Introduced 1993.

With black finish

Perf: $100 **Exc:** $75 **VGood:** $50

With nickel finish

Perf: $110 **Exc:** $85 **VGood:** $60

With black finish, .410/45 Colt

Perf: $135 **Exc:** $95 **VGood:** $75

With nickel finish, .410/45 Colt

Perf: $140 **Exc:** $100 **VGood:** $80

NEW ENGLAND FIREARMS TRACKER SLUG GUN

Single shot; break-open; sidelever; 12-, 20-ga.; 3-inch chamber; 24-inch barrel; Cylinder choke; weighs 6 lbs.; 40-inch overall length; blade front sight, fully adjustable rifle-type rear; walnut-finished hardwood pistol-grip stock; recoil pad; blued barrel, color case-hardened frame. Introduced 1992; dropped 2001.

Perf: $100 **Exc:** $60 **VGood:** $55

NEW ENGLAND FIREARMS TRACKER II SLUG GUN

Same specs as the Tracker Slug Gun except fully rifled bore. Introduced 1992; still in production.

Perf: $125 **Exc:** $95 **VGood:** $55

NEW ENGLAND FIREARMS TURKEY/GOOSE GUN

Single shot; break-open; sidelever; 10-ga.; 3-1/2-inch chamber; 28-inch barrel; Full choke; weighs 9 1/2 lbs.; 44-inch overall length; walnut- or camo-finished American hardwood stock; ventilated rubber recoil pad; ejector; matte finish on metal. Introduced 1992; still in production.

Perf: $140 **Exc:** $90 **VGood:** $70

NEW ENGLAND FIREARMS TURKEY/GOOSE N.W.T.F.

Same specs as Turkey/Goose Gun except 10-, 20-ga.; 24-inch barrel; interchangeable choke tubes (comes with Turkey Full, others optional); drilled, tapped for long-eye relief scope mount; completely covered with Mossy Oak camouflage finish; Mossy Oak sling included. Introduced 1992; still in production.

10-ga. model

Perf: $200 **Exc:** $145 **VGood:** $100

20-ga. model

Perf: $125 **Exc:** $70 **VGood:** $50

NEW ENGLAND FIREARMS TURKEY/GOOSE SPECIAL

Same specs as the Turkey/Goose Gun except 12-ga.; 3-inch chamber; 24-inch (fixed Full Turkey choke); weighs 5 to 6 lbs; 40-inch overall length; modified pistol-grip stock; recoil pad; swivel studs; full coverage Realtree camouflage. Introduced 1994; still in production.

Perf: $95 **Exc:** $75 **VGood:** $55

NEW ENGLAND FIREARMS/ H&R 1871 TOPPER

Single-shot, break-open; 12 gauge (SB1-198), 16 gauge (SB1-698), 20 gauge (SB1-298), 28 gauge (SB1-898), .410 bore (SB1-498); American hardwood stock, black finish, pistol grip; barrel lengths: 26- (20 ga., 28 ga., .410 Bore) and 28-inch (12 ga., 16 ga.); chamber: Up to 3-inch (12 ga., 20 ga., .410 bore), 2-3/4-inch (16 ga., 28 ga.); bead front sight; weighs 5-6 lbs.

Perf: $95 **Exc:** $75 **VGood:** $55

NEW ENGLAND FIREARMS TOPPER DELUXE CLASSIC

Similar to the Topper; available in 20 as well as 12 gauge with a ventilated rib and choke tube system (modified tube provided); 28-inch (26-inch in 20

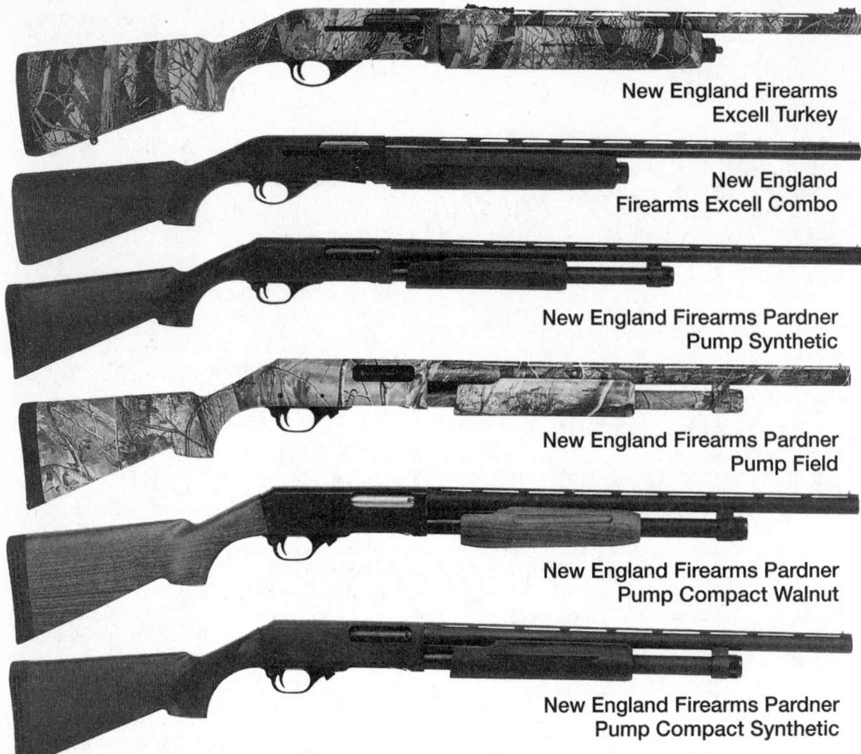

New England Firearms Excell Turkey

New England Firearms Excell Combo

New England Firearms Pardner Pump Synthetic

New England Firearms Pardner Pump Field

New England Firearms Pardner Pump Compact Walnut

New England Firearms Pardner Pump Compact Synthetic

gauge) barrel with bead front sight; nickel-plated receiver; genuine American Walnut stock with ventilated recoil pad.

Perf: $175 **Exc:** $135 **VGood:** $95

NEW ENGLAND FIREARMS TOPPER DELUXE

Similar to Topper; available in 12 gauge with a 3-1/2-inch chamber and a screw-in choke that can handle both lead and steel shot.

Perf: $125 **Exc:** $70 **VGood:** $50

NEW ENGLAND FIREARMS TOPPER JUNIOR

Similar to Topper; 22-inch barrel is scaled ideally for smaller-framed shooters.

Perf: $125 **Exc:** $70 **VGood:** $50

NEW ENGLAND FIREARMS TOPPER JUNIOR CLASSIC

Similar to Topper Jr. but with blued frame, and cut-checkered American black walnut stock and fore-end.

Perf: $125 **Exc:** $70 **VGood:** $50

NEW ENGLAND FIREARMS EXCELL

Introduced in 2005 this model is chambered for the 12 gauge 3" shell and fitted with a 28" vent rib barrel with choke tubes. Checkered black synthetic stock. Magazine capacity is 5 rounds. Weight is about 7 lbs.

Exc: $300 **VGood:** $200 **Good:** $135

NEW ENGLAND FIREARMS EXCELL WATERFOWL

As above but with Real Tree Advantage Wetlands camo finish. Introduced in 2005.

Exc: $350 **VGood:** $250 **Good:** $165

NEW ENGLAND FIREARMS EXCELL TURKEY

This model is fitted with a 22" barrel with choke tubes and fiber optic front sight. Real Tree Advantage Hardwoods camo finish. Weight is 7 lbs. Introduced in 2005.

Exc: $350 **VGood:** $250 **Good:** $165

NEW ENGLAND FIREARMS EXCELL COMBO

This model has a black synthetic stock and two barrels: 28" vent rib with choke tubes, and 24" rifled barrel. Weight is about 7 lbs. depending on barrel length. Introduced in 2005.

Exc: $350 **VGood:** $250 **Good:** $165

NEW ENGLAND FIREARMS PARDNER PUMP WALNUT

12- or 20-gauge pump-actio shotgun with American walnut furniture, 28- or 26-inch vent rib barrel, 3-inch chamber and screw-in choke tube. Weight 7-1/2 lbs.

Perf: $180 **Exc:** $115 **VGood:** $85

NEW ENGLAND FIREARMS PARDNER PUMP SYNTHETIC

Similar to above but with black synthetic buttstock and forend.

Perf: $150 **Exc:** $100 **VGood:** $75

NEW ENGLAND FIREARMS PARDNER PUMP FIELD

Similar to above but with Realtree APG HD camo finish.

Perf: $180 **Exc:** $115 **VGood:** $85

NEW ENGLAND FIREARMS PARDNER PUMP COMPACT FIELD

Similar to above but with 1-1/4-inch shorter length of pull and 21 inch barrel.

Perf: $180 **Exc:** $115 **VGood:** $85

NEW ENGLAND FIREARMS PARDNER PUMP COMPACT WALNUT SHOTGUN

Similar to Pardner Pump Walnut model but with 1-1/4 inch shorter length of pull and 21 inch barrel. Weight 6-1/4 lbs.

Perf: $180 **Exc:** $115 **VGood:** $85

NEW ENGLAND FIREARMS PARDNER PUMP COMPACT SYNTHETIC

Similar to above but with black synthetic buttstock and forend.

Perf: $180 **Exc:** $115 **VGood:** $85

NEW ENGLAND FIREARMS PARDNER PUMP COMBO

Introduced in 2005 this model features two 12 gauge 3" barrels. One 28" with vent rib and choke tubes, and the other 22" rifled slug barrel. Walnut stock. Weight is about 7.5 lbs. depending on barrel length.

Perf: $180 **Exc:** $115 **VGood:** $85

NEW ENGLAND FIREARMS SPECIAL PURPOSE

This is a similar model but it is offered only in 10 gauge. It is available in several different configurations: A 10 gauge model with hardwood stock with 28" barrel, a camo model with 28" barrel, a camo model with 32" barrel choked Modified, and a black matte finish model with 24" barrel with screw-in turkey Full choke. Weight is about 9.5 lbs.

Perf: $180 **Exc:** $115 **VGood:** $85

NEW ENGLAND FIREARMS PARDNER PUMP PROTECTOR

Similar to Pardner Pump but with matte black finish throughout and synthetic buttstock and forend. Also available with carbon fiber dipped stock.

Perf: $180 **Exc:** $115 **VGood:** $85

NEW ENGLAND FIREARMS PARDNER PUMP COMBO

Similar to Pardner Pump but with two barrels: 28-inch smoothbore with vent rib and 22-inch rifled slug barrel with iron sights and drilled and tapped for scope base.

Perf: $150 **Exc:** $100 **VGood:** $75

NEW ENGLAND FIREARMS PARDNER PUMP TURKEY

Similar to Pardner Pump but with Realtree APG HD full-camo dip or Realtree Hardwoods camo finish. Fiber optics front and rear sights. Comes with screw-in XF Turkey choke tube.

Perf: $180 **Exc:** $115 **VGood:** $85

NEW HAVEN MODEL 273

Bolt action; single shot; top-loading; .410; 24-inch tapered barrel; Full choke; oil-finished American walnut Monte Carlo-style, pistol-grip stock; thumb safety. Made by Mossberg. Introduced 1960; discontinued 1965.

Exc: $75 **VGood:** $50 **Good:** $45

NEW HAVEN MODEL 283

Bolt action; takedown; .410; 3-inch chamber; 2-shot clip detachable clip magazine; 25-inch barrel; detachable Full-choke tube; other chokes available at added cost; oil-finished American walnut Monte Carlo-style, pistol-grip stock; thumb safety. Made by Mossberg. Introduced 1960; discontinued 1965.

Exc: $80 **VGood:** $55 **Good:** $45

NEW HAVEN MODEL 285

Bolt action; takedown; 20-ga.; 3-inch chamber; 2-shot clip detachable clip magazine; 25-inch barrel; detachable Full-choke tube; other chokes available at added cost; oil-finished American walnut Monte Carlo-style, pistol-grip stock; thumb safety. Made by Mossberg. Introduced 1960; discontinued 1965.

Exc: $80 **VGood:** $55 **Good:** $45

NEW HAVEN MODEL 290

Bolt action; takedown; 16-ga.; 2-shot detachable clip magazine; 28-inch barrel; detachable Full-choke tube; other choke tubes available at added cost; oil-finished American walnut Monte Carlo-style, pistol-grip stock; thumb safety. Made by Mossberg. Introduced 1960; discontinued 1965.

Exc: $80 **VGood:** $55 **Good:** $45

NEW HAVEN MODEL 295

Bolt action; takedown; 12-ga.; 2-shot detachable clip magazine; 28-inch barrel; detachable Full-choke tube; other choke tubes available at added cost; oil-finished American walnut Monte Carlo-style pistol-grip stock; thumb safety. Made by Mossberg. Introduced 1960; discontinued 1965.

Exc: $80 **VGood:** $55 **Good:** $45

NEW HAVEN MODEL 495

Bolt action; takedown; 12-ga.; 2-shot detachable clip magazine; 28-inch Full-choke barrel; uncheckered walnut-finished hardwood Monte Carlo-style, pistol-grip stock; thumb safety. Introduced 1964; discontinued 1965.

Exc: $80 **VGood:** $55 **Good:** $45

NEW HAVEN MODEL 600

Slide action; takedown; 12-ga.; 2-3/4-inch, 3-inch chamber; 6-shot magazine; 26-inch Improved Cylinder, 28-inch Full or Modified, 30-inch Full-choke barrel; choice of standard or magnum barrel; uncheckered walnut pistol-grip stock, extension slide handle; safety on top of receiver. Same general design as Mossberg Model 500. Introduced 1962; discontinued 1965.

Exc: $140 **VGood:** $110 **Good:** $90

NEW HAVEN MODEL 600AST SLUGSTER

Same specs as Model 600 except 12-, 20-ga.; 18-1/2-inch, 24-inch Slugster barrel; ramp front sight, open adjustable folding leaf rear; running deer scene etched on receiver. Introduced 1978; no longer in production.

Exc: $140 **VGood:** $110 **Good:** $90

NEW HAVEN MODEL 600ETV

Same specs as Model 600 except .410; 26-inch vent-rib barrels; checkered walnut-finished, pistol-grip stock, forend; fluted comb; recoil pad. No longer in production.

Exc: $150 **VGood:** $120 **Good:** $100

NEW HAVEN MODEL 600K

Same specs as Model 600 except C-Lect-Choke feature. No longer in production.

Exc: $150 **VGood:** $120 **Good:** $100

NOBLE MODEL 40

Slide action; solid frame; 12-, 16-ga; 6-shot magazine; 28-inch barrel; Multi-choke; uncheckered American walnut pistol-grip stock, grooved forearm; recoil pad; push-button safety. Introduced 1952; discontinued 1956.

Exc: $150 **VGood:** $110 **Good:** $75

NOBLE MODEL 50

Slide action; solid frame; 12-, 16-ga.; 6-shot magazine; 28-inch barrel; uncheckered American walnut pistol-grip stock, grooved forearm; push-button safety. Introduced 1954; discontinued 1956.

Exc: $150 **VGood:** $110 **Good:** $75

NOBLE MODEL 60

Slide action; solid frame; 12-, 16-ga.; 6-shot magazine; 28-inch barrel; Master choke; uncheckered American walnut pistol-grip stock, grooved slide handle; crossbolt safety; recoil pad. Introduced 1957; discontinued 1969.

Exc: $150 **VGood:** $110 **Good:** $75

NOBLE MODEL 60ACP

Same specs as Model 60 except receiver is machined from single block of steel, all lock surfaces are hardened. Replaced Model 60 and Model 60AF. Introduced 1967; discontinued 1971.

Exc: $160 **VGood:** $120 **Good:** $85

NOBLE MODEL 60AF

Same specs as Model 60 except selected steel barrel; damascened bolt; select walnut stock with fluted comb. Introduced 1965; discontinued 1966.

Exc: $150 **VGood:** $110 **Good:** $75

NOBLE MODEL 65

Slide action; solid frame; 12-, 16-ga.; 6-shot magazine; 28-inch barrel; Full or Modified choke; uncheckered American walnut pistol-grip stock, grooved slide handle; crossbolt safety. Introduced 1967; discontinued 1969.

Exc: $150 **VGood:** $110 **Good:** $75

NOBLE MODEL 66CLP

Slide action; solid frame; 12-, 16-ga.; 3-inch (12-ga.) chamber; 6-shot tubular magazine; 28-inch barrel; adjustable choke; checkered American walnut pistol-grip stock, slide handle; keylock safety mechanism; recoil pad. Introduced 1967; discontinued 1979.

Exc: $155 **VGood:** $115 **Good:** $85

New Haven Model 600AST Slugster

Noble Model 60

Noble Model 60ACP

Noble Model 65

Noble Model 66CLP

Noble Model 66RLP

Noble Model 66XL

Noble Model 70

NOBLE MODEL 66RCLP

Same specs as Model 66CLP except vent-rib barrel. Introduced 1967; discontinued 1970.

Exc: $160 **VGood:** $120 **Good:** $85

NOBLE MODEL 66RLP

Same specs as Model 66CLP except Modified or Full choke. Introduced 1967; discontinued 1970.

Exc: $160 **VGood:** $120 **Good:** $85

NOBLE MODEL 66XL

Same specs as Model 66CLP except Modified or Full choke; checkered slide handle; no recoil pad. Introduced 1967; discontinued 1970.

Exc: $155 **VGood:** $115 **Good:** $85

NOBLE MODEL 70

Slide action; solid frame; .410; 3-inch chamber; 6-shot magazine; 26-inch barrel; Full choke; uncheckered walnut pistol-grip stock, grooved forearm; top safety. Introduced 1959; discontinued 1967.

Exc: $150 **VGood:** $110 **Good:** $75

NOBLE MODEL 70CLP

Same specs as Model 70 except adjustable choke. Introduced 1958; discontinued 1970.

Exc: $150 **VGood:** $110 **Good:** $75

NOBLE MODEL 70RCLP

Same specs as Model 70 except adjustable choke; vent rib. Introduced 1967; discontinued 1970.

Exc: $155 **VGood:** $115 **Good:** $89

NOBLE MODEL 70RLP

Same specs as Model 70 except vent rib. Introduced 1967; discontinued 1970.

Exc: $155 **VGood:** $115 **Good:** $80

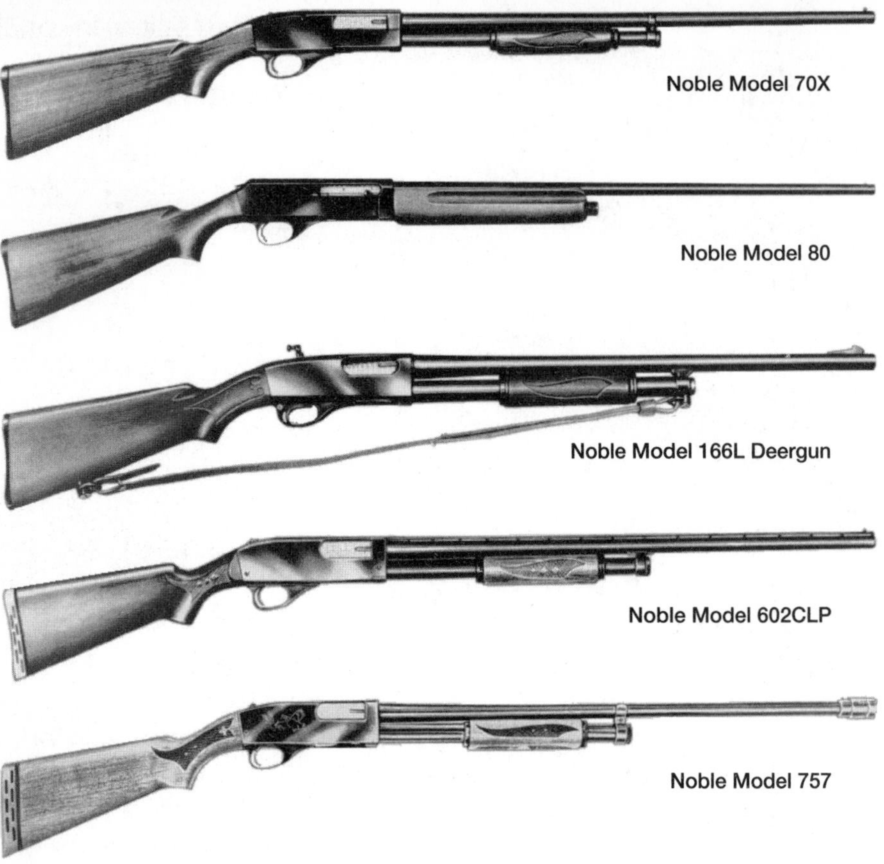
Noble Model 70X

Noble Model 80

Noble Model 166L Deergun

Noble Model 602CLP

Noble Model 757

Noble Model 450E

NOBLE MODEL 70X

Same specs as Model 70 except side ejection; damascened bolt. Replaced Model 70. Introduced 1967; discontinued 1971.

Exc: $160 **VGood:** $120 **Good:** $85

NOBLE MODEL 70XL

Same specs as Model 70 except checkered buttstock. Introduced 1958; discontinued 1970.

Exc: $160 **VGood:** $120 **Good:** $85

NOBLE MODEL 80

Recoil-operated autoloader; .410; 2-1/2-inch, 3-inch chamber; 6-shot magazine; 26-inch barrel; Full choke; uncheckered American walnut pistol-grip stock, grooved forearm; fluted comb; action release button; push-button safety. Introduced 1965; discontinued 1967.

Exc: $225 **VGood:** $200 **Good:** $140

NOBLE MODEL 160 DEERGUN

Slide action; 12-, 16-ga.; 6-shot magazine; 24-inch barrel; Lyman adjustable peep rear sight, ramp post front; tapped for scope; uncheckered American walnut pistol-grip stock, grooved slide handle; hard rubber buttplate; sling swivels; detachable carrying strap. Introduced 1965; discontinued 1966.

Exc: $140 **VGood:** $90 **Good:** $75

NOBLE MODEL 166L DEERGUN

Slide action; 12-, 16-ga.; 6-shot magazine; 24-inch barrel; Lyman adjustable peep rear sight, ramp post front; tapped for scope; uncheckered American walnut pistol-grip stock, grooved slide handle; hard rubber buttplate; sling swivels; detachable carrying strap. Replaced Model 160 Deergun. Introduced 1967; discontinued 1971.

Exc: $185 **VGood:** $150 **Good:** $120

NOBLE MODEL 390 DEERGUN

Slide action; solid frame; 12-ga.; 3-inch chamber; 6-shot magazine; 24-inch rifled slug barrel; Lyman adjustable peep rear sight, ramp post front; impressed-checkered American walnut stock, slide handle; tang safety; sling swivels; detachable carrying strap. Introduced 1972; discontinued 1972.

Exc: $185 **VGood:** $150 **Good:** $125

NOBLE MODEL 420

Double barrel; hammerless; top lever; 12-, 16-, 20-ga.; 28-inch barrels; Full/Modified chokes; matted rib; checkered pistol-grip stock, forearm; double triggers; automatic safety. Introduced 1959; discontinued 1971. Made in Spain.

Exc: $275 **VGood:** $225 **Good:** $95

NOBLE MODEL 420EK

Same specs as Model 420 except demi-block with triple lock; front, middle bead sights; hand-checkered Circassian walnut pistol-grip stock, beavertail forearm; recoil pad; automatic selective ejectors; hand-engraved action; gold inlay on top lever. Introduced 1968; discontinued 1968. Made in Spain.

Exc: $290 **VGood:** $240 **Good:** $125

NOBLE MODEL 450E

Double barrel; demi-block with triple lock; 12-, 16-, 20-ga.; 28-inch barrel; Modified/Full chokes; front, middle bead sights; hand-checkered Circassian walnut pistol-grip stock, beavertail forend; double triggers; engraving; gold inlay; recoil pad. Replaced Model 420EK. Introduced 1969; discontinued 1971. Made in Spain.

Exc: $290 **VGood:** $240 **Good:** $125

NOBLE MODEL 520

Side-by-side; hammerless; 12-, 20-, 16-, 28-ga. .410; 2-3/4-inch chamber; 26-inch, 28-inch barrels; standard choke combos; matted top rib; hand-checkered Circassian walnut stock, forend; double triggers; Holland-design extractors; hand-engraved frame. Introduced 1970; discontinued 1972. Made in Spain.

Exc: $250 **VGood:** $150 **Good:** $125

NOBLE MODEL 550

Side-by-side; hammerless; 12-, 20-ga.; 2-3/4-inch chambers; 28-inch barrels; Modified/Full chokes; front, middle bead sights; hand-checkered Circassian walnut pistol-grip stock, beavertail forend; grip cap; double triggers; double auto selective ejectors; tang safety; rubber recoil pad; custom hand-engraved frame; knight's head medallion inlaid on top snap. Introduced 1970; discontinued 1972. Made in Spain.

Exc: $270 **VGood:** $160 **Good:** $130

NOBLE MODEL 602

Slide action; solid frame; 20-ga.; 3-inch chamber; 6-shot magazine; 28-inch barrel; adjustable choke; uncheckered American walnut pistol-grip stock, grooved slide handle; top safety; side ejection; recoil pad. Introduced 1963; discontinued 1971.

Exc: $175 **VGood:** $140 **Good:** $80

NOBLE MODEL 602CLP

Same specs as Model 602 except keylock safety mechanism; checkered pistol-grip stock, slide handle. Introduced 1958; discontinued 1970.

Exc: $175 **VGood:** $140 **Good:** $85

NOBLE MODEL 602RCLP

Same specs as Model 602 except keylock safety mechanism; vent rib; checkered pistol-grip stock, slide handle. Introduced 1967; discontinued 1970.

Exc: $175 **VGood:** $140 **Good:** $85

NOBLE MODEL 602RLP

Same specs as Model 602 except keylock safety mechanism; vent rib; Full or Modified choke; checkered pistol-grip stock, slide handle. Introduced 1967; discontinued 1970.

Exc: $175 **VGood:** $140 **Good:** $85

NOBLE MODEL 602XL

Same specs as Model 602 except keylock safety mechanism; Full or Modified choke; checkered slide handle; no recoil pad. Introduced 1958; discontinued 1970.

Exc: $165 **VGood:** $125 **Good:** $80

NOBLE MODEL 662

Slide action; solid frame; 20-ga.; 6-shot magazine; 26-inch barrel; Full choke; uncheckered walnut pistol-grip stock, grooved slide forearm; top safety; aluminum alloy barrel, receiver. Introduced 1966; discontinued 1970.

Exc: $170 **VGood:** $140 **Good:** $100

NOBLE MODEL 757

Slide action; solid frame; 20-ga.; 2-3/4-inch chamber; 5-shot magazine; 28-inch aircraft alloy barrel; adjustable choke; impressed-checkered American walnut pistol-grip stock, slide handle; tang safety; barrel, receiver black anodized; decorated receiver. Introduced 1972; discontinued 1972.

Exc: $170 **VGood:** $120 **Good:** $100

NOBLE SERIES 200

Slide action; solid frame; 20-ga.; 3-inch chamber; 6-shot magazine; 28-inch barrel; optional vent rib; adjustable choke or Modified, Full choke; impressed-checkered American walnut stock, slide handle; tang safety; side ejection; keylock safety mechanism; recoil pad. Introduced 1972; discontinued 1972.

With fixed choke

Exc: $150 **VGood:** $100 **Good:** $80

With fixed choke, vent rib

Exc: $155 **VGood:** $105 **Good:** $85

With adjustable choke

Exc: $155 **VGood:** $105 **Good:** $85

With adjustable choke, vent rib

Exc: $160 **VGood:** $110 **Good:** $90

NOBLE SERIES 300

Slide action; solid frame; 12-, 16-ga.; 3-inch (12-ga.) chamber; 6-shot magazine, 3-shot plug furnished; 28-inch barrel; adjustable choke or Modified, Full choke; optional vent rib; impressed-checkered American walnut stock, slide handle; tang safety; side ejection; keylock safety mechanism; damascened bolt. Introduced 1972; discontinued 1972.

With fixed choke
Exc: $150 **VGood:** $100 **Good:** $80

With fixed choke, vent rib
Exc: $155 **VGood:** $105 **Good:** $85

With adjustable choke
Exc: $155 **VGood:** $105 **Good:** $85

With adjustable choke, vent rib
Exc: $160 **VGood:** $110 **Good:** $90

NOBLE SERIES 400

Slide action; solid frame; .410; 3-inch chamber; 6-shot magazine; 25-inch barrel; adjustable choke or Modified, Full choke; optional vent rib; impressed-checkered American walnut pistol-grip stock, slide handle; tang safety; side ejection; keylock safety mechanism; damascened bolt. Introduced 1972; discontinued 1972.

With fixed choke
Exc: $155 **VGood:** $105 **Good:** $85

With fixed choke, vent rib
Exc: $160 **VGood:** $110 **Good:** $90

With adjustable choke
Exc: $160 **VGood:** $110 **Good:** $90

With adjustable choke, vent rib
Exc: $165 **VGood:** $115 **Good:** $95

NORINCO TYPE HL12-203

Over/under; boxlock action; 12-ga. only; 2-3/4-inch chambers; ejectors; 30-inch barrels; vent. rib; single trigger; multi-chokes; checkered stock and forearm; 7-1/2 lbs. Importation began 1989; dropped 1993.

Exc: $350 **VGood:** $300 **Good:** $265

NORINCO MODEL 99 COACH GUN

Side-by-side; 12-ga. only; 2-3/4-inch chambers; exposed hammers; 20-inch barrels; Fjull/Modified choke tubes; blue finish; checkered stock and forearm; weighs 7-1/5 lbs.

Exc: $215 **VGood:** $190 **Good:** $175

NORINCO MODEL 87L

Lever action; 12-ga. only; 2-3/4-inch chamber; styled after Winchester Model 1887; 20-inch barrel; walnut stock and forearm. Importation began 2003.

Exc: $335 **VGood:** $275 **Good:** $235

NORINCO MODEL 2000 FIELD

Autoloader; 12-ga. only; 2-3/4-inch chamber; steel receiver; aluminum alloy triggerguard; 26-inch, 28-inch barrel; vent. rib; Modified choke tube; choice of black synthetic or checkered hardwood stock and forearm; weighs 7-1/2 lbs. Limited importation during 1999 only.

Exc: $230 **VGood:** $200 **Good:** $185

Add $10 to above prices for wood stock and forearm.

NORINCO MODEL 2000 DEFENSE

Similar to Model 2000 Field, except 18-1/2-inch barrel; cyl. Choke tube; choice of bead, rifle or ghost ring sights; matte black metal finish; black synthetic stock and forearm with recoil pad. Limited importation during 1999 only.

Exc: $230 **VGood:** $200 **Good:** $185

Add $10 to above prices for rifle sights.
Add $20 for ghost ring sights.

NORINCO TYPE HL12-102

Slide-action; 12-ga. only; 2-3/4-inch chamber; 28.4-inch barrel; 3-shot mag.; crossbolt safety; fixed chokes; weighs 9.3 lbs. Importation began 1989; dropped 1993.

Perf: $230 **Exc:** $200 **VGood:** $175

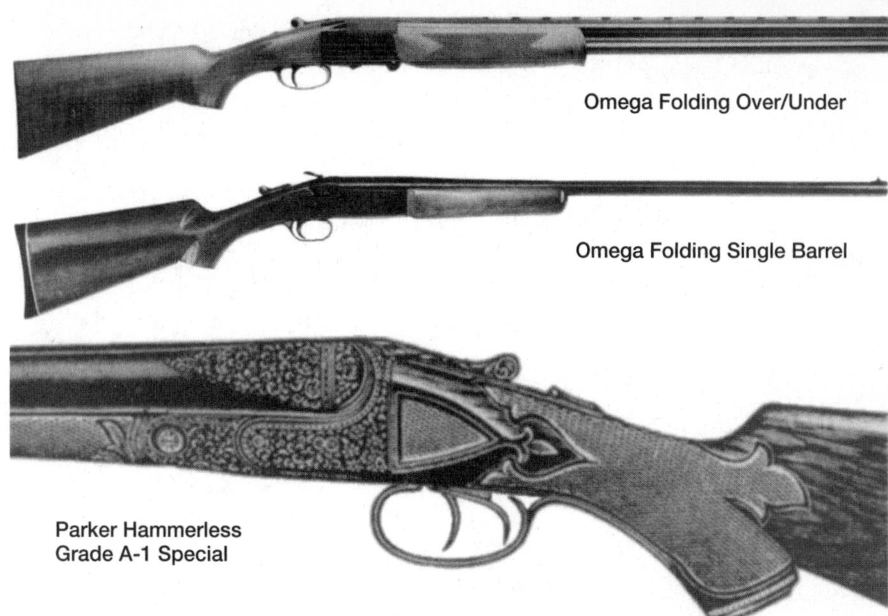

Omega Folding Over/Under

Omega Folding Single Barrel

Parker Hammerless Grade A-1 Special

NORINCO MODEL 984/985/987

Slide-action; 12-ga. only; 3-inch chamber; 26-inch, 28-inch-barrel, vent. rib; Modified choke tube; black synthetic or uncheckered hardwood stock and forearm; matte black metal finish. Importation began 2001; dropped 2002.

Perf: $200 **Exc:** $170 **VGood:** $155

Add $10 to above prices for hardwood stock (models 985 & 987).

NORINCO MODEL 97W HAMMER

Slide-action; 12-ga. only; styled similar to the Winchester Model 97; outside hammer; 20-inch plain barrel; cylinder bore fixed choke; solid frame; hardwood stock with grooved "corn cob" forearm. Importation began 2001.

Perf: $400 **Exc:** $350 **VGood:** $250

NORINCO MODEL 97T TRENCH GUN

Slide-action; 12-ga. only; reproduction of the original Winchester WWI Trench Gun; shrouded barrel; proper markings same as original.

Perf: $500 **Exc:** $400 **VGood:** $300

NORINCO MODEL 981/982T

Slide-action; 12 ga. only; 3-inch chamber; 18-1/2-inch cylinder bore barrel; fixed choke; black synthetic stock and forearm; matte black metal fin ish. Importation began 2001.

Perf: $200 **Exc:** $170 **VGood:** $150

Add $20 to above prices for ghost ring sights (Model 982T).

NORINCO MODEL 983

Slide-action; 12-ga. only; 22-inch barrel; external rifled choke tube; adjustable rifle sights; synthetic black stock. Imported during 2002 only.

Perf: $215 **Exc:** $170 **VGood:** $155

OMEGA FOLDING OVER/UNDER

Over/under; boxlock; 12-, 20-, 28-ga., .410; 3-inch chambers; 26-inch, 28-inch barrels; standard choke combos; vent rib; weighs 5-1/2 lbs.; checkered European walnut stock; auto safety; single trigger; extractors; folding takedown design. Made in Italy. Introduced 1986; discontinued 1994.

Perf: $330 **Exc:** $250 **VGood:** $200

OMEGA FOLDING OVER/UNDER DELUXE

Same specs as Folding Over/Under except select walnut stock. Introduced 1986; discontinued 1990.

Perf: $400 **Exc:** $310 **VGood:** $265

OMEGA FOLDING SIDE-BY-SIDE

Side-by-side; boxlock; 10-, 28-ga., .410; 26-inch barrels; standard choke combos; vent rib; weighs 5 1/2 lbs.; checkered beechwood stock, forearm; auto safety; double triggers; extractors; folding takedown design. Introduced 1986; discontinued 1989.

Perf: $180 **Exc:** $130 **VGood:** $100

OMEGA FOLDING SIDE-BY-SIDE DELUXE

Same specs as Folding Side-By-Side except select walnut stock. Introduced 1986; discontinued 1990.

Perf: $210 **Exc:** $180 **VGood:** $130

OMEGA FOLDING SINGLE BARREL

Single shot; 12-, 16-, 20-, 28-ga., .410; 2-3/4-inch, 3-inch chamber; 26-inch, 28-inch, 30-inch barrel; Full choke; metal bead front sight; checkered beech stock; top opening lever; matte chromed receiver; folds for storage, transport. Made in Italy. Introduced 1984; discontinued 1988.

Perf: $145 **Exc:** $100 **VGood:** $80

OMEGA FOLDING SINGLE BARREL DELUXE

Same specs as Folding Single Barrel except vent rib; checkered walnut stock; blued receiver. Introduced 1984; discontinued 1988.

Perf: $190 **Exc:** $165 **VGood:** $130

PARKER HAMMERLESS DOUBLE

Side-by-side; boxlock; 10-, 12-, 16-, 20-, 28-ga., .410; 26-inch to 32-inch barrels; any standard choke combo; hand-checkered select walnut stock, forearm; choice of straight, half- or pistol-grip stock; automatic ejectors; double or selective single trigger. After Parker Brothers was absorbed by Remington Arms in 1934, shotgun was designated as Remington Parker Model 920. Because of the wide variations in styles and extras, as well as the number of grades-differing in engraving, checkering and general workmanship-there is a wide range of values. The selective trigger was introduced in 1922, with the raised vent rib; the beavertail forend was introduced in 1923; all add to used value. Some guns were put together from available parts and stocks by Remington until 1942. Grades are in descending values, with the A-designated model being worth several times that of the V model. Non-ejector models (pre-1934) are worth about 30 percent less than value shown for ejector models; if gun has interchangeable barrels, it is worth 30 to 35 percent more than shown. Those in 20-ga. are 35

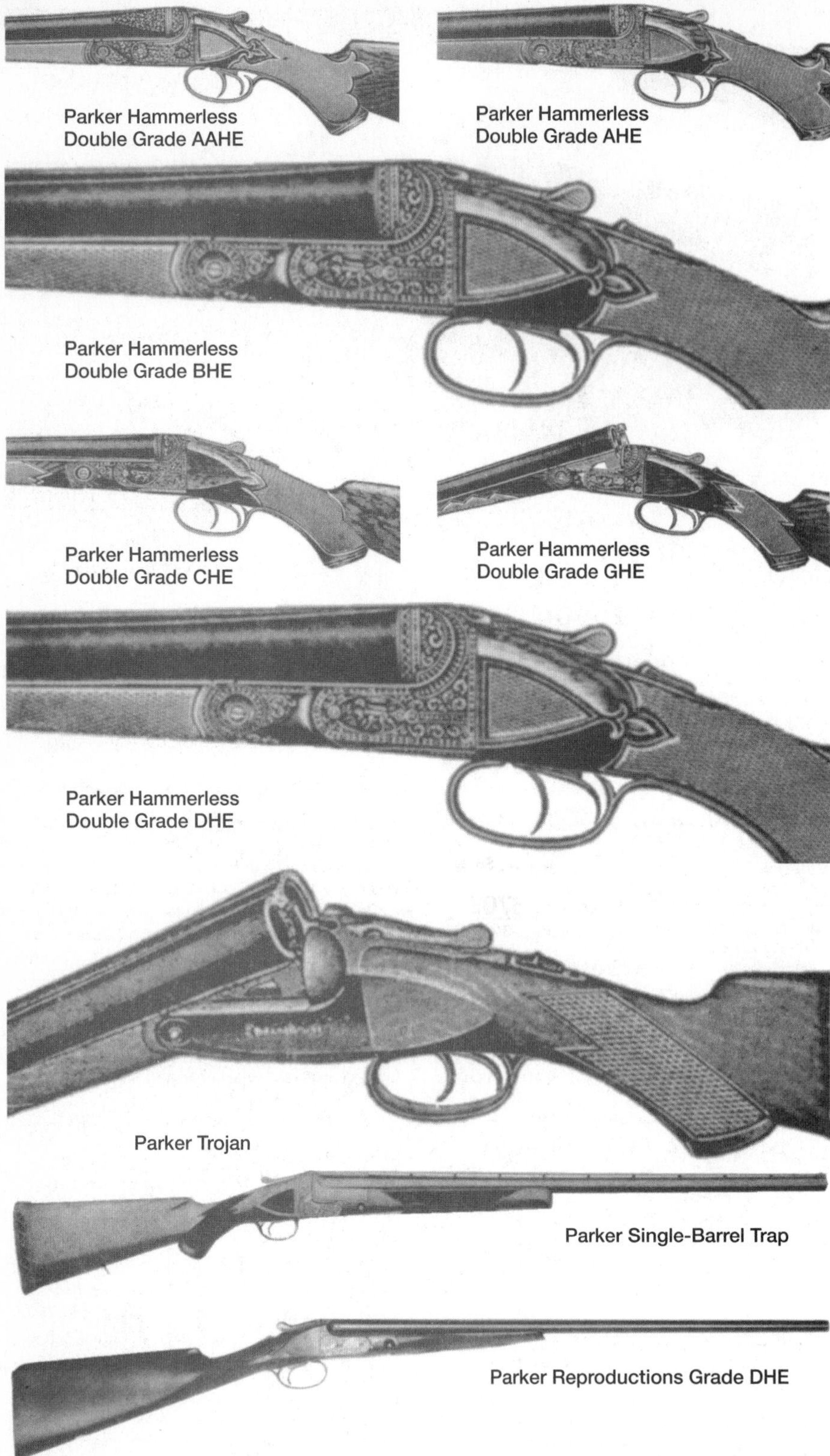
Parker Hammerless Double Grade AAHE

Parker Hammerless Double Grade AHE

Parker Hammerless Double Grade BHE

Parker Hammerless Double Grade CHE

Parker Hammerless Double Grade GHE

Parker Hammerless Double Grade DHE

Parker Trojan

Parker Single-Barrel Trap

Parker Reproductions Grade DHE

percent higher, 28-ga. are 75 percent higher and .410 are 100 percent higher than values shown. Prices shown are for 12-, 16-ga. configurations. For single trigger, add $250; vent rib, add $300; single selective trigger, add $200 to $300; raised vent rib, add $325 to $350; beavertail forearm addition in grades VHE, GHE, DHE, CHE, add $200 to $250 to base price; for grades BHE, AHE, AAHE, add $450 to $500 to base; for A1 Special, add $500 to $750.

Grade A-1 Special

Exc: $65,000 **VGood:** $50,000 **Good:** $42,000

Grade AAHE

Exc: $30,000 **VGood:** $22,500 **Good:** $18,500

Grade AHE

Exc: $17,500 **VGood:** $10,000 **Good:** $8000

Grade BHE

Exc: $7500 **VGood:** $5000 **Good:** $4000

Grade CHE

Exc: $5000 **VGood:** $3500 **Good:** $2500

Grade DHE

Exc: $4000 **VGood:** $2500 **Good:** $2000

Grade GHE

Exc: $3000 **VGood:** $2000 **Good:** $1500

Grade VHE

Exc: $2100 **VGood:** $1250 **Good:** $1000

PARKER SINGLE-BARREL TRAP

Single barrel; boxlock; hammerless; 12-ga.; 30-inch, 32-inch, 34-inch barrel; any designated choke; vent rib; hand-checkered select walnut pistol grip stock, forearm; choice of straight, half- or pistol grip; ejector. Various grades differ with amount of workmanship, checkering, engraving, etc. General specs are the same for all variations. After absorption of Parker by Remington, model was listed as Remington Parker Model 930. Introduced 1917; discontinued 1942.

Grade SA-1 Special

Exc: $12,500 **VGood:** $9500 **Good:** $8000

Grade SAA

Exc: $5200 **VGood:** $4000 **Good:** $3000

Grade SA

Exc: $4000 **VGood:** $3500 **Good:** $2500

Grade SB

Exc: $3500 **VGood:** $3000 **Good:** $2600

Grade SC

Exc: $3000 **VGood:** $2100 **Good:** $1700

PARKER TROJAN

Double barrel; boxlock; hammerless; 12-, 16-, 20-ga.; 26-inch, 28-inch Modified/Full, 30-inch Full barrels; hand-checkered American walnut pistol grip stock, forearm; plain extractors; double or single triggers. Introduced 1915; discontinued 1939.

12-, 16-ga. model with double triggers

Exc: $1600 **VGood:** $1000 **Good:** $800

12-, 16-ga. model with single trigger

Exc: $1900 **VGood:** $1200 **Good:** $950

20-ga. model with double triggers

Exc: $2400 **VGood:** $1650 **Good:** $1400

20-ga. model with single trigger

Exc: $2900 **VGood:** $2000 **Good:** $1700

PARKER REPRODUCTIONS GRADE A-1 SPECIAL

Side-by-side; boxlock; 12-, 20-, 28-ga.; 2-3/4-inch, 3-inch chambers; 26-inch, 28-inch barrels; metal bead front sight; checkered select American walnut straight or pistol-grip stock, forend; double or single trigger; skeleton or hard rubber buttplate; two-barrel set; engraving; reproduction of original; all parts interchange with original. Introduced 1988; no longer in production.

Perf: $10,000 **Exc:** $7500 **VGood:** $7250

PARKER REPRODUCTIONS GRADE BHE

Side-by-side; 12-, 20-, 28-ga.; 2-3/4-inch, 3-inch chambers; checkered fancy American walnut straight or pistol-grip stock, splinter or beavertail forend; checkered butt; double or single selective triggers; selective ejectors; hand engraving; case-hardened frame; marketed in fitted leather trunk-type case; reproduction of original; all parts interchange with original. Made in Japan. Introduced 1984; discontinued 1989. Premium for 28 ga.

Perf: $4500 **Exc:** $3800 **VGood:** $2900

PARKER REPRODUCTIONS GRADE DHE

Side-by-side; boxlock; 12-, 20-, 28-ga.; 2-3/4-inch, 3-inch chambers; 26-inch, 28-inch barrels; metal bead front sight; checkered American walnut straight or pistol-grip stock, forend; double or single trigger; skeleton or hard rubber buttplate; reproduction of original; all parts interchange with original. Made in Japan. Introduced 1984; no longer in production. Premium for 28 ga.

Perf: $3700 **Exc:** $2800 **VGood:** $2500

PARKER-HALE MODEL 630

Side-by-side; boxlock; 12-ga.; 3-inch chambers; 26-inch, 28-inch barrels; standard choke combos; checkered straight-grip English-style stock, forend; auto safety; extractors; double triggers; color case-hardened action. Made in Spain. Introduced 1993; discontinued 1993.

Perf: $600 **Exc:** $425 **VGood:** $380

PARKER-HALE MODEL 640A

Side-by-side; boxlock; 12-, 16-, 20-, 28-ga., .410; 2-3/4-inch, 3-inch chambers; 25-inch, 26-inch, 27-inch, 28-inch barrels; raised rib; hand-checkered, oil-finished walnut pistol-grip stock, beavertail forend; auto safety; extractors; single trigger; buttplate; silvered, engraved action. Made in Spain. Introduced 1986; discontinued 1993.

Perf: $800 **Exc:** $600 **VGood:** $540

PARKER-HALE MODEL 640E

Same specs as Model 640A except concave rib; hand-checkered, oil-finished straight-grip English-style walnut stock, splinter forend; checkered butt; double triggers. Available in a wide variety of styles. Made in Spain. Introduced 1986; discontinued 1993. Name changed to Precision Sports Model 800 Series in 1990.

Perf: $760 **Exc:** $520 **VGood:** $450

PARKER-HALE MODEL 640M

Same specs as Model 640A except 10-ga.; 3-1/2-inch chambers; 26-inch, 30-inch, 32-inch Full/Full barrels; checkered straight-grip English-style stock, forend; auto safety; extractors; double triggers; recoil pad. Made in Spain. Introduced 1989; discontinued 1993.

Perf: $825 **Exc:** $625 **VGood:** $550

PARKER-HALE MODEL 640 SLUG

Same specs as Model 640A except 12-ga.; 25-inch Improved Cylinder/Improved Cylinder barrels. Made in Spain. Introduced 1991; discontinued 1993.

Perf: $900 **Exc:** $700 **VGood:** $600

PARKER-HALE MODEL 645A

Side-by-side; boxlock; 12-, 16-, 20-, 28-ga., .410; 2-3/4-inch, 3-inch chambers; 26-inch, 28-inch barrels; raised rib; hand-checkered, oil-finished walnut pistol-grip stock, beavertail forend; auto safety; ejectors; single trigger; buttplate; silvered, engraved action. Made in Spain. Introduced 1986; discontinued 1993.

Perf: $1000 **Exc:** $725 **VGood:** $600

PARKER-HALE MODEL 645E

Same specs as Model 645A except concave rib; hand-checkered, oil-finished straight-grip English-style walnut stock, splinter forend; checkered butt; double triggers. Made in Spain. Introduced 1986; discontinued 1993.

Perf: $910 **Exc:** $600 **VGood:** $550

PARKER-HALE MODEL 645E-XXV

Same specs as Model 645E except 25-inch barrels; Churchill rib; hand-checkered, oil-finished straight-grip English-style walnut stock, splinter forend; checkered butt; double triggers. Made in Spain. Introduced 1986; discontinued 1993.

Perf: $900 **Exc:** $600 **VGood:** $550

PARKER-HALE MODEL 650A

Side-by-side; boxlock; 12-ga.; 28-inch barrels; choke tubes; raised rib; checkered pistol-grip walnut stock, beavertail forend; auto safety; extractors; single trigger; buttplate; silvered action. Made in Spain. Introduced 1992; discontinued 1993.

Perf: $850 **Exc:** $650 **VGood:** $600

PARKER-HALE MODEL 650E

Same specs as Model 650A except concave rib; straight-grip English-style walnut stock, splinter forend; checkered butt; double triggers. Made in Spain. Introduced 1992; discontinued 1993.

Perf: $800 **Exc:** $600 **VGood:** $550

PARKER-HALE MODEL 655A

Side-by-side; boxlock; 12-ga.; 28-inch barrels; choke tubes; raised rib; checkered pistol-grip walnut stock, beavertail forend; auto safety; ejectors; single trigger; buttplate; silvered action. Made in Spain. Introduced 1992; discontinued 1993.

Perf: $975 **Exc:** $775 **VGood:** $700

PARKER-HALE MODEL 655E

Same specs as Model 655A except concave rib; straight-gip English-style walnut stock, splinter forend; checkered butt; double triggers. Made in Spain. Introduced 1992; discontinued 1993.

Perf: $900 **Exc:** $700 **VGood:** $625

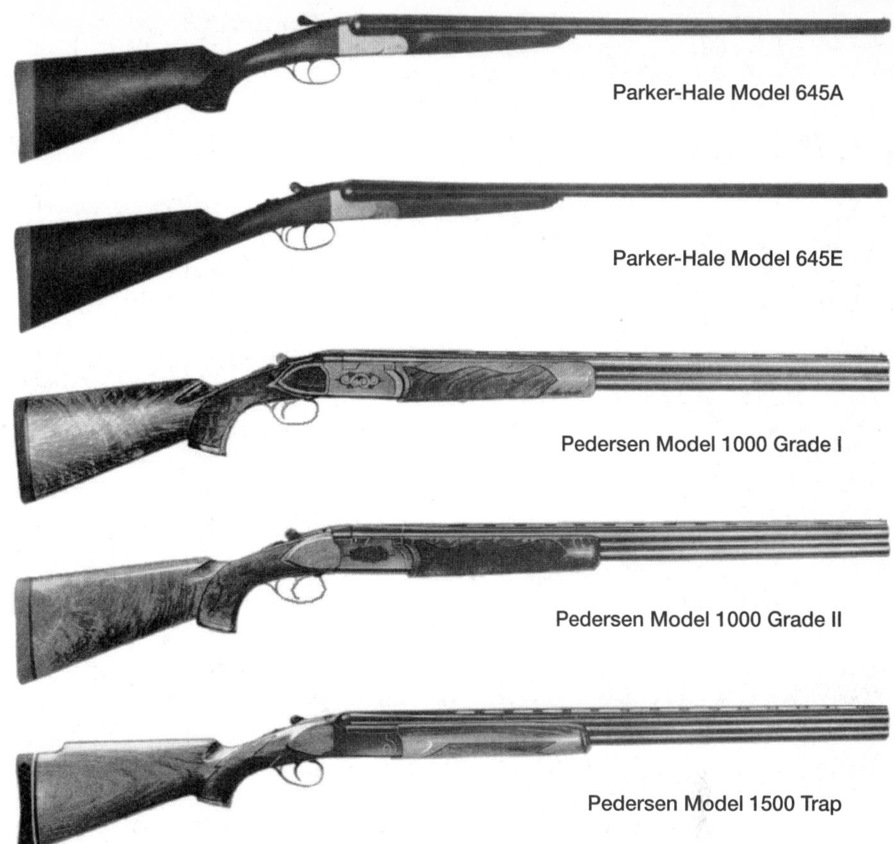

Parker-Hale Model 645A

Parker-Hale Model 645E

Pedersen Model 1000 Grade I

Pedersen Model 1000 Grade II

Pedersen Model 1500 Trap

PARKER-HALE MODEL 670E

Side-by-side; sidelock; 12-, 16-, 20-ga.; 2-3/4-inch, 3-inch chambers; 26-inch, 27-inch, 28-inch barrels; concave rib; hand-checkered, oil-finished straight-grip English-style walnut stock, splinter forend; auto safety; ejectors; double triggers; checkered butt; silvered, engraved action. Made in Spain. Introduced 1986; discontinued 1993.

Perf: $3500 **Exc:** $2500 **VGood:** $1900

PARKER-HALE MODEL 680E-XXV

Side-by-side; sidelock; 12-, 16-, 20-ga.; 2-3/4-inch, 3-inch chambers; 25-inch barrels; Churchill rib; hand-checkered, oil-finished straight-grip English-style walnut stock, splinter forend; auto safety; ejectors; double triggers; checkered butt; color case-hardened action. Made in Spain. Introduced 1986; discontinued 1993.

Perf: $3300 **Exc:** $2300 **VGood:** $1700

PARQUEMY MODEL 48

Side-by-side; .410; 3-inch chambers; Modified/Full barrels; medium bead front sight; hand-checkered straight-grip European walnut stock; double triggers; checkered butt; extractors; hand-engraved locks. Made in Spain. Introduced 1983 by Toledo Armas; discontinued 1984.

Perf: $525 **Exc:** $400 **VGood:** $350

PARQUEMY MODEL 48E

Same specs as Model 48 except 12-, 20-, 28-ga.; 2-3/4-inch chambers; ejectors. Introduced 1982 by Toledo Armas; discontinued 1984.

Perf: $650 **Exc:** $525 **VGood:** $450

PEDERSEN MODEL 1000

Over/under; boxlock; 12-, 20-ga.; 2-3/4-inch chambers; 26-inch, 28-inch, 30-inch barrels; vent rib; hand-checkered American walnut pistol-grip stock, forearm; rubber recoil pad; automatic ejectors; single selective trigger; hand-engraved, gold-filled receiver; silver inlays. Introduced 1973; discontinued 1975.

Grade I

Perf: $2000 **Exc:** $1700 **VGood:** $1600

Grade II

Perf: $1700 **Exc:** $1400 **VGood:** $1200

PEDERSEN 1000 MAGNUM

Same specs as Model 1000 except 12-ga.; 3-inch chamber; 30-inch barrels; Improved Modified/Full chokes. Introduced 1973; discontinued 1975.

Grade I

Perf: $2000 **Exc:** $1700 **VGood:** $1600

Grade II

Perf: $1700 **Exc:** $1400 **VGood:** $1300

PEDERSEN MODEL 1000 SKEET

Same specs as Model 1000 except 12-ga.; 2-3/4-inch chambers; 26-inch, 28-inch barrels; Skeet chokes; Skeet-style walnut stock. Introduced 1973; discontinued 1975.

Grade I

Perf: $2100 **Exc:** $1950 **VGood:** $1700

Grade II

Perf: $1900 **Exc:** $1450 **VGood:** $1300

PEDERSEN MODEL 1000 TRAP

Same specs as Model 1000 except made in 12-ga.; 2-3/4-inch chambers; 30-inch, 32-inch barrels; Modified/Full or Improved Modified/Full chokes; Monte Carlo trap-style walnut stock. Introduced 1973; discontinued 1975.

Grade I

Perf: $2000 **Exc:** $1600 **VGood:** $1400

Grade II

Perf: $1550 **Exc:** $1300 **VGood:** $1100

PEDERSEN MODEL 1500

Over/under; boxlock; 12-ga.; 2-3/4-inch, 3-inch chambers; 26-inch, 28-inch, 30-inch, 32-inch barrels; standard choke combos; vent rib; hand-checkered European walnut pistol-grip stock, forearm; rubber recoil pad; automatic selective ejectors; choice of sights. Introduced 1973; discontinued 1975.

Perf: $650 **Exc:** $450 **VGood:** $350

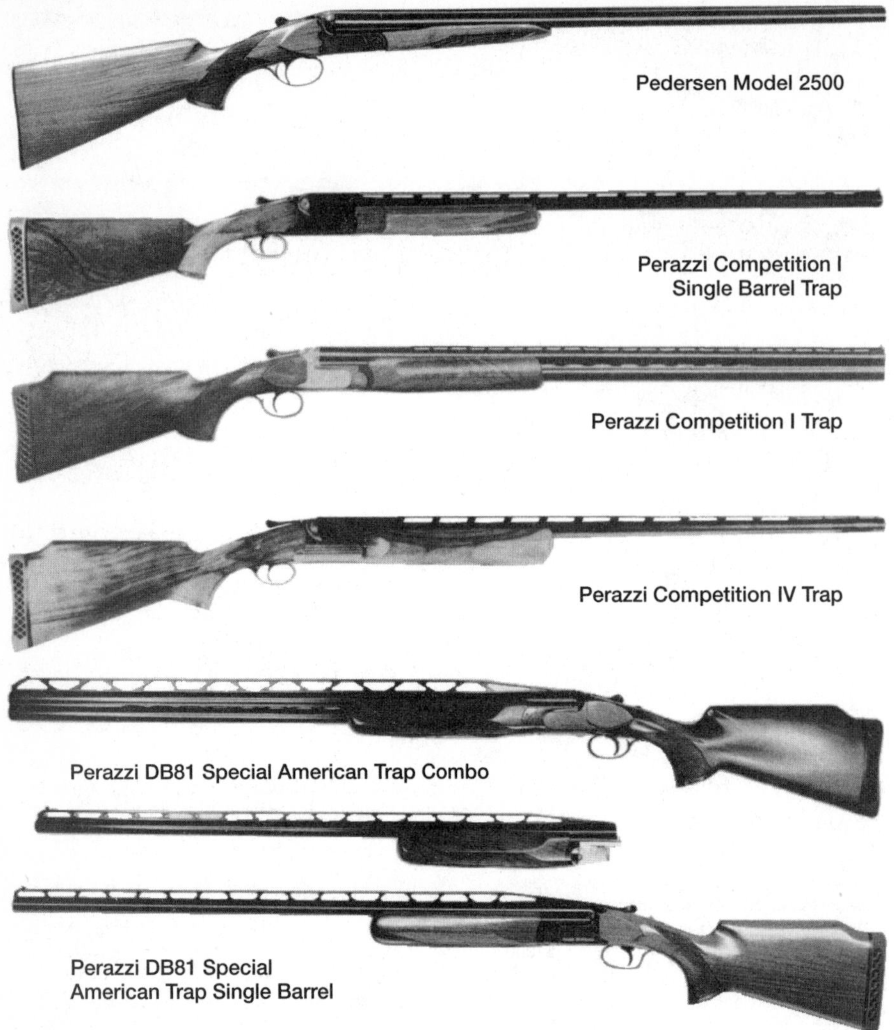

Pedersen Model 2500

Perazzi Competition I Single Barrel Trap

Perazzi Competition I Trap

Perazzi Competition IV Trap

Perazzi DB81 Special American Trap Combo

Perazzi DB81 Special American Trap Single Barrel

PEDERSEN MODEL 1500 SKEET

Same specs as Model 1500 except 27-inch barrels; Skeet choke; Skeet-style walnut stock. Introduced 1973; discontinued 1975.

Perf: $700 **Exc:** $530 **VGood:** $450

PEDERSEN MODEL 1500 TRAP

Same specs as Model 1500 except 30-inch, 32-inch barrels; Modified/Full or Improved Modified/Full chokes; Monte Carlo trap-style walnut stock. Introduced 1973; discontinued 1975.

Perf: $750 **Exc:** $500 **VGood:** $400

PEDERSEN MODEL 2000

Side-by-side; boxlock; 12-, 20-ga.; 26-inch, 28-inch, 30-inch barrels; hand-checkered American walnut pistol-grip stock forearm; automatic selective ejectors; barrel selector/safety; single selective trigger; automatic safety; gold-filled, hand-engraved receiver. Introduced 1973; discontinued 1975.

Grade I

Perf: $2500 **Exc:** $2100 **VGood:** $1800

Grade II

Perf: $2250 **Exc:** $1900 **VGood:** $1650

PEDERSEN MODEL 2500

Side-by-side; boxlock; 12-, 20-ga.; hand-checkered European walnut pistol-grip stock, beavertail forearm; automatic selective ejectors; barrel selector/safety; single selective trigger; automatic safety; no receiver engraving. Introduced 1973; discontinued 1975.

Perf: $450 **Exc:** $375 **VGood:** $300

PEDERSEN MODEL 4000

Slide action; 12-, 20-ga., .410; 3-inch chambers; 26-inch, 28-inch, 30-inch vent-rib barrel; standard chokes; checkered select American walnut stock, slide handle; full-coverage engraving on receiver. Based upon Mossberg Model 500. Introduced 1973; discontinued 1973.

Perf: $450 **Exc:** $375 **VGood:** $300

PEDERSEN MODEL 4000 TRAP

Same specs as Model 4000 except 12-ga.; 30-inch Full-choke barrel; Monte Carlo trap-style walnut stock; recoil pad. Introduced 1975; discontinued 1975.

Perf: $475 **Exc:** $365 **VGood:** $325

PEDERSEN MODEL 4500

Slide action; 12-, 20-ga., .410; 3-inch chamber; 26-inch, 28-inch, 30-inch vent-rib barrel; standard chokes; checkered select American walnut stock, slide handle; some engraving on receiver. Introduced 1975; discontinued 1975.

Perf: $400 **Exc:** $320 **VGood:** $280

PEDERSEN MODEL 4500 TRAP

Same specs as Model 4500 except 12-ga.; 30-inch Full-choke barrel; Monte Carlo trap-style walnut stock; recoil pad. Introduced 1975; discontinued 1975.

Perf: $420 **Exc:** $330 **VGood:** $290

PERAZZI COMPETITION I SINGLE BARREL TRAP

Single shot; boxlock; 12-ga.; 32-inch, 34-inch vent-rib barrel; Full choke; checkered Monte Carlo stock, beavertail forend; auto ejectors; single trigger; recoil pad. Introduced by Ithaca 1973; discontinued 1978.

Perf: $2650 **Exc:** $1950 **VGood:** $1700

PERAZZI COMPETITION I SKEET

Same specs as Competition I Single Barrel Trap except over/under; 26 3/4-inch barrels; integral muzzlebrakes; Skeet chokes; Skeet-style checkered European walnut pistol-grip stock, forend. Introduced by Ithaca 1969; discontinued 1974.

Perf: $4400 **Exc:** $3300 **VGood:** $2800

PERAZZI COMPETITION I TRAP

Same specs as Competition I Single Barrel Trap except over/under; 30-inch, 32-inch barrels; Improved Modified/Full chokes; checkered European walnut pistol-grip stock, forend. Introduced by Ithaca 1969; discontinued 1974.

Perf: $4000 **Exc:** $3200 **VGood:** $2700

PERAZZI COMPETITION IV TRAP

Single barrel; boxlock; 12-ga.; 32-inch, 34-inch barrel; four interchangeable choke tubes; high, wide vent rib; checkered European walnut stock, beavertail forend; auto ejectors; single selective trigger; recoil pad; marketed in fitted case. Introduced by Ithaca 1977; discontinued 1978.

Perf: $2000 **Exc:** $1400 **VGood:** $1100

PERAZZI DB81 SPECIAL AMERICAN TRAP COMBO

Over/under; boxlock; 12-ga.; two-barrel set of 29-1/2-inch or 31-1/2-inch O/U and 32-inch or 34-inch single; fixed or choke tubes; high vent rib; checkered European walnut Monte Carlo stock, beavertail forend; removable trigger group; external selector. Made in Italy. Introduced 1988; still in production.

Standard Grade

Perf: $10,000 **Exc:** $7000 **VGood:** $5000

SC3 Grade

Perf: $16,000 **Exc:** $11,200 **VGood:** $8000

SC0 Grade

Perf: $27,500 **Exc:** $19,250 **VGood:** $13,750

SC0 Gold Grade

Perf: $30,000 **Exc:** $20,000 **VGood:** $15,000

SC0 Sideplates Grade

Perf: $40,000 **Exc:** $28,000 **VGood:** $20,000

SC0 Gold Sideplates Grade

Perf: $45,000 **Exc:** $31,500 **VGood:** $22,500

PERAZZI DB81 SPECIAL AMERICAN TRAP SINGLE BARREL

Same specs as DB81 Special American Trap Combo except only single shot; 32-inch, 34-inch barrel. Made in Italy. Introduced 1988; discontinued 1994.

Standard Grade

Perf: $5800 **Exc:** $3650 **VGood:** $3100

SC3 Grade

Perf: $9500 **Exc:** $6100 **VGood:** $5000

SC0 Grade

Perf: $16,000 **Exc:** $10,000 **VGood:** $8500

SC0 Gold Grade

Perf: $17,500 **Exc:** $11,000 **VGood:** $9000

SC0 Sideplates Grade

Perf: $23,000 **Exc:** $15,500 **VGood:** $12,500

SC0 Gold Sideplates Grade

Perf: $26,500 **Exc:** $20,000 **VGood:** $16,000

PERAZZI DB81 SPECIAL TRAP O/U

Same specs as DB81 Special American Trap Combo except only 29-1/2-inch, 31-1/2-inch O/U barrels. Made in Italy. Introduced 1988; still in production.

Standard Grade

Perf: $8000 **Exc:** $5600 **VGood:** $4100

SC3 Grade

Perf: $12,500 **Exc:** $8500 **VGood:** $6500

SC0 Grade

Perf: $22,000 **Exc:** $14,500 **VGood:** $11,500

SC0 Gold Grade

Perf: $25,500 **Exc:** $17,500 **VGood:** $13,250

SC0 Sideplates Grade

Perf: $34,000 **Exc:** $23,500 **VGood:** $17,500

SC0 Gold Sideplates Grade

Perf: $40,000 **Exc:** $28,000 **VGood:** $21,000

PERAZZI GRAND AMERICAN 88 SPECIAL AMERICAN TRAP COMBO

Over/under; boxlock; 12-ga.; two-barrel set with 29-1/2-inch or 31-1/2-inch O/U and 32-inch or 34-inch single; fixed or choke tubes; vent rib; checkered European walnut Monte Carlo stock, beavertail forend; removable, adjustable trigger group; single selective trigger; external selector. Made in Italy. Discontinued 1992.

Standard Grade
Perf: $9500 **Exc:** $6150 **VGood:** $4950

SC3 Grade
Perf: $15,000 **Exc:** $9750 **VGood:** $7800

SC0 Grade
Perf: $23,000 **Exc:** $15,000 **VGood:** $11,950

SC0 Gold Grade
Perf: $26,000 **Exc:** $16,900 **VGood:** $13,500

SC0 Sideplates Grade
Perf: $33,500 **Exc:** $21,950 **VGood:** $17,500

SC0 Gold Sideplates Grade
Perf: $38,500 **Exc:** $25,000 **VGood:** $20,000

PERAZZI GRAND AMERICAN 88 SPECIAL AMERICAN TRAP SINGLE BARREL

Same specs as Grand American 88 Special American Trap Combo except 32-inch, 34-inch single barrel only. Made in Italy. Discontinued 1992.

Standard Grade
Perf: $6500 **Exc:** $3800 **VGood:** $3000

SC3 Grade
Perf: $12,000 **Exc:** $7000 **VGood:** $5500

SC0 Grade
Perf: $20,000 **Exc:** $11,500 **VGood:** $9000

SC0 Gold Grade
Perf: $22,000 **Exc:** $13,500 **VGood:** $10,000

SC0 Sideplates Grade
Perf: $29,500 **Exc:** $18,000 **VGood:** $13,000

SC0 Gold Sideplates Grade
Perf: $34,500 **Exc:** $21,000 **VGood:** $17,000

PERAZZI GRAND AMERICAN 88 SPECIAL TRAP O/U

Same specs as Grand American 88 Special American Trap Combo except 29-1/2-inch, 30-3/4-inch, 31-1/2-inch O/U barrels; checkered European walnut pistol-grip stock, beavertail forend. Made in Italy. Discontinued 1992.

Standard Grade
Perf: $6900 **Exc:** $4500 **VGood:** $3600

SC3 Grade
Perf: $12,500 **Exc:** $8150 **VGood:** $6500

SC0 Grade
Perf: $20,500 **Exc:** $13,300 **VGood:** $10,500

SC0 Gold Grade
Perf: $23,000 **Exc:** $14,500 **VGood:** $12,000

SC0 Sideplates Grade
Perf: $31,000 **Exc:** $20,000 **VGood:** $16,100

SC0 Gold Sideplates Grade
Perf: $35,500 **Exc:** $23,000 **VGood:** $18,500

PERAZZI LIGHT GAME MODEL

Over/under; boxlock; 12-ga.; 27-1/2-inch barrels; Modified/Full, Improved Cylinder/Modified chokes; checkered European walnut field stock, forend; single trigger; auto ejectors. Introduced by Ithaca 1972; discontinued 1974.

Perf: $4300 **Exc:** $3100 **VGood:** $2750

PERAZZI MIRAGE CLASSIC SPORTING O/U

Over/under; boxlock; 12-ga.; 28-3/8-inch, 29 1/2-inch, 31-1/2-inch barrels; fixed or choke tubes; vent rib; checkered European walnut pistol-grip stock, beavertail forend; single selective trigger; removable trigger group; external selector; engraving. Made in Italy. Still in production.

Perf: $9000 **Exc:** $6300 **VGood:** $4900

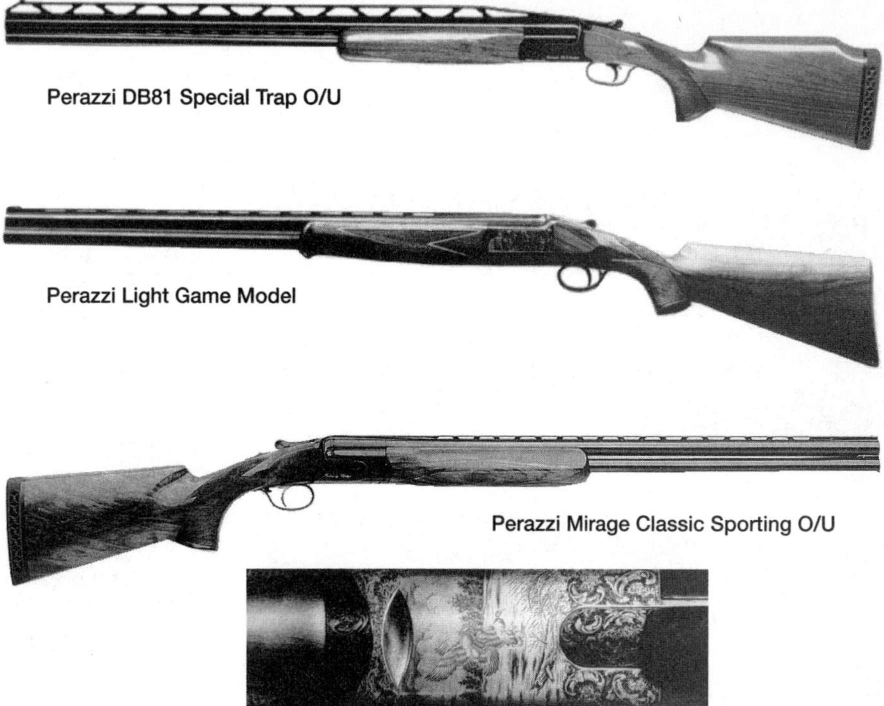

Perazzi DB81 Special Trap O/U

Perazzi Light Game Model

Perazzi Mirage Classic Sporting O/U

PERAZZI MIRAGE LIVE BIRD (EARLY MFG.)

Over/under; boxlock; 12-ga.; 28-inch Modified/Extra-Full barrels; vent rib; checkered European walnut pistol-grip stock, forend; selective ejectors; non-selective single trigger; recoil pad. Introduced by Ithaca 1973; discontinued 1978.

Perf: $2500 **Exc:** $1700 **VGood:** $1300

PERAZZI MIRAGE SKEET (EARLY MFG.)

Same specs as Mirage Live Bird (Early Mfg.) except 28-inch barrels; integral muzzle brakes; Skeet chokes; Skeet-style checkered European walnut pistol-grip stock, forend. Introduced by Ithaca 1973; discontinued 1978.

Perf: $2500 **Exc:** $1700 **VGood:** $1300

PERAZZI MIRAGE TRAP (EARLY MFG.)

Same specs as Mirage Live Bird (Early Mfg.) except 30-inch, 32-inch barrels; Improved Modified/Full chokes; tapered vent rib; checkered European Monte Carlo stock, forend. Introduced by Ithaca 1973; discontinued 1978.

Perf: $2500 **Exc:** $1700 **VGood:** $1300

PERAZZI MIRAGE PIGEON-ELECTROCIBLES O/U

Over/under; boxlock; 12-ga.; 27-1/2-inch, 28-3/8-inch, 29-1/2-inch, 31-1/2-inch barrels; fixed or choke tubes; vent rib; checkered European walnut pistol-grip stock, schnabel beavertail forend; removable trigger group. Made in Italy. Introduced 1995; still in production.

Standard Grade
Perf: $7000 **Exc:** $4500 **VGood:** $3600

SC3 Grade
Perf: $12,500 **Exc:** $8000 **VGood:** $6500

SC0 Grade
Perf: $21,500 **Exc:** $14,000 **VGood:** $11,000

SC0 Gold Grade
Perf: $24,000 **Exc:** $15,500 **VGood:** $12,500

SC0 Sideplates Grade
Perf: $32,500 **Exc:** $21,000 **VGood:** $17,000

SC0 Gold Sideplates Grade
Perf: $38,500 **Exc:** $25,000 **VGood:** $20,000

PERAZZI MIRAGE SKEET O/U

Same specs as Mirage Pigeon-Electrocibles O/U except 26-3/4-inch, 27-1/2-inch barrels; beavertail forend. Made in Italy. Introduced 1993; still in production.

Standard Grade
Perf: $7000 **Exc:** $4500 **VGood:** $3600

SC3 Grade
Perf: $12,500 **Exc:** $8000 **VGood:** $6500

SC0 Grade
Perf: $21,500 **Exc:** $14,000 **VGood:** $11,000

SC0 Gold Grade
Perf: $24,000 **Exc:** $15,500 **VGood:** $12,500

SC0 Sideplates Grade
Perf: $32,500 **Exc:** $21,000 **VGood:** $17,000

SC0 Gold Sideplates Grade
Perf: $38,500 **Exc:** $25,000 **VGood:** $20,000

PERAZZI MIRAGE TRAP O/U

Same specs as Mirage Pigeon-Electrocibles O/U except 29 1/2-inch, 30 3/4-inch, 31-1/2-inch barrels; beavertail forend. Made in Italy. Still in production.

Standard Grade
Perf: $7000 **Exc:** $4500 **VGood:** $3600

SC3 Grade
Perf: $12,500 **Exc:** $8000 **VGood:** $6500

SC0 Grade
Perf: $21,500 **Exc:** $14,000 **VGood:** $11,000

SC0 Gold Grade
Perf: $24,000 **Exc:** $15,500 **VGood:** $12,500

SC0 Sideplates Grade
Perf: $32,500 **Exc:** $21,000 **VGood:** $17,000

SC0 Gold Sideplates Grade
Perf: $38,500 **Exc:** $25,000 **VGood:** $20,000

PERAZZI MIRAGE SPECIAL PIGEON-ELECTROCIBLES O/U

Over/under; boxlock; 12-ga.; 28-3/8-inch, 29 1/2-inch, 31-1/2-inch barrels; fixed or choke tubes; vent rib; checkered European walnut pistol-grip stock; schnabel beavertail forend; removable, adjustable trigger. Made in Italy. Introduced 1995; still in production.

Standard Grade
Perf: $7500 **Exc:** $5000 **VGood:** $3900

SC3 Grade
Perf: $12,500 **Exc:** $8000 **VGood:** $6500

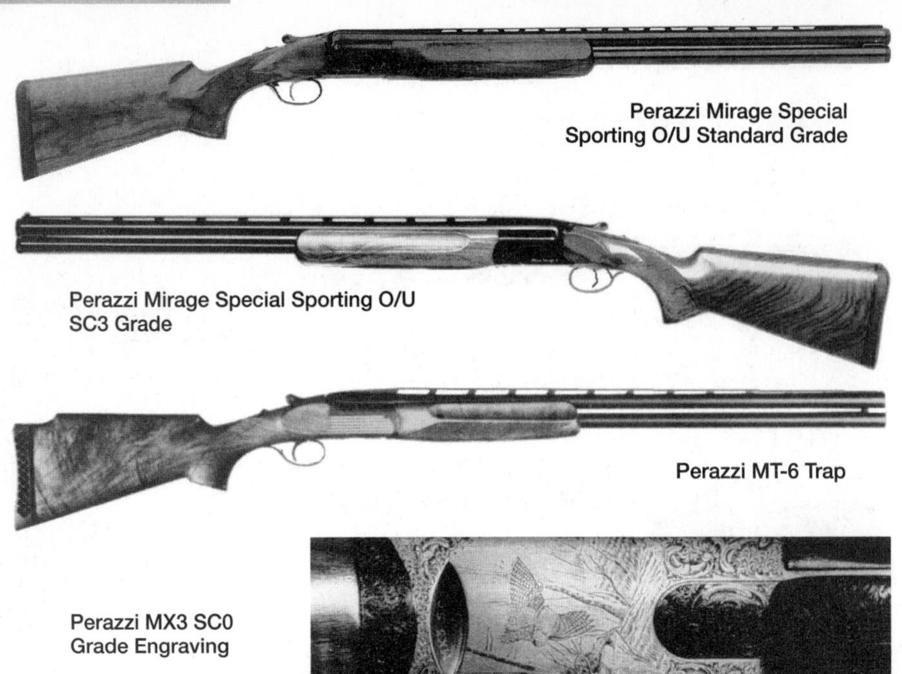

Perazzi Mirage Special Sporting O/U Standard Grade

Perazzi Mirage Special Sporting O/U SC3 Grade

Perazzi MT-6 Trap

Perazzi MX3 SC0 Grade Engraving

SC0 Grade
Perf: $22,000 **Exc:** $14,000 **VGood:** $11,500

SC0 Gold Grade
Perf: $25,000 **Exc:** $16,250 **VGood:** $13,000

SC0 Sideplates Grade
Perf: $33,000 **Exc:** $21,500 **VGood:** $17,000

SC0 Gold Sideplates Grade
Perf: $38,000 **Exc:** $25,000 **VGood:** $19,750

PERAZZI MIRAGE SPECIAL SKEET O/U

Same specs as Mirage Special Pigeon-Electrocibles O/U except 26-3/4-inch, 27-1/2-inch barrels; beavertail forend. Made in Italy. Still in production.

Standard Grade
Perf: $7500 **Exc:** $5000 **VGood:** $3900

SC3 Grade
Perf: $12,500 **Exc:** $8000 **VGood:** $6500

SC0 Grade
Perf: $22,000 **Exc:** $14,000 **VGood:** $11,500

SC0 Gold Grade
Perf: $25,000 **Exc:** $16,250 **VGood:** $13,000

SC0 Sideplates Grade
Perf: $33,000 **Exc:** $21,500 **VGood:** $17,000

SC0 Gold Sideplates Grade
Perf: $38,000 **Exc:** $25,000 **VGood:** $19,750

PERAZZI MIRAGE SPECIAL SPORTING O/U

Same specs as Mirage Special Pigeon-Electrocibles O/U except 28-3/8-inch, 29-1/2-inch, 31-1/2-inch barrels; beavertail forend; single selective trigger; external selector. Made in Italy. Still in production.

Standard Grade
Perf: $7500 **Exc:** $5000 **VGood:** $3900

SC3 Grade
Perf: $12,500 **Exc:** $8000 **VGood:** $6500

SC0 Grade
Perf: $22,000 **Exc:** $14,000 **VGood:** $11,500

SC0 Gold Grade
Perf: $25,000 **Exc:** $16,250 **VGood:** $13,000

SC0 Sideplates Grade
Perf: $33,000 **Exc:** $21,500 **VGood:** $17,000

SC0 Gold Sideplates Grade
Perf: $38,000 **Exc:** $25,000 **VGood:** $19,750

PERAZZI MIRAGE SPECIAL TRAP O/U

Same specs as Mirage Special Pigeon-Electrocibles O/U except 29-1/2-inch, 30-3/4-inch, 31-1/2-inch barrels; beavertail forend. Made in Italy. Still in production.

Standard Grade
Perf: $7500 **Exc:** $5000 **VGood:** $3900

SC3 Grade
Perf: $12,500 **Exc:** $8000 **VGood:** $6500

SC0 Grade
Perf: $22,000 **Exc:** $14,000 **VGood:** $11,500

SC0 Gold Grade
Perf: $25,000 **Exc:** $16,250 **VGood:** $13,000

SC0 Sideplates Grade
Perf: $33,000 **Exc:** $21,500 **VGood:** $17,000

SC0 Gold Sideplates Grade
Perf: $38,000 **Exc:** $25,000 **VGood:** $19,750

PERAZZI MT-6 SKEET

Over/under; boxlock; 12-ga.; 28-inch separated barrels; five interchangeable choke tubes; wide vent rib; Skeet-style checkered European walnut pistol-grip stock, forend; non-selective single trigger; auto selective ejectors; recoil pad; marketed in fitted case. Introduced by Ithaca 1976; discontinued 1978.

Perf: $4000 **Exc:** $3100 **VGood:** $2750

PERAZZI MT-6 TRAP

Same specs as MT-6 Skeet except 30-inch, 32-inch barrels; trap-style checkered European walnut pistol-grip stock, forend. Introduced by Ithaca 1976; discontinued 1978.

Perf: $2500 **Exc:** $1700 **VGood:** $1300

PERAZZI MT-6 TRAP COMBO

Same specs as MT-6 Skeet except two-barrel set with 30-inch or 32-inch O/U and 32-inch or 34-inch single under barrel; seven interchangeable choke tubes; high aluminum vent rib; trap-style checkered European walnut pistol-grip stock, forend; marketed in fitted case. Introduced by Ithaca 1977; discontinued 1978.

Perf: $4200 **Exc:** $3000 **VGood:** $2200

PERAZZI MX1B PIGEON-ELECTROCIBLES O/U

Over/Under; boxlock; 12-ga.; 27-1/2-inch barrels; fixed or choke tubes; vent rib; checkered European pistol-grip walnut stock, schnabel forend; removable trigger group. Made in Italy. Introduced 1995; still in production.

Standard Grade
Perf: $7000 **Exc:** $4500 **VGood:** $3600

SC3 Grade
Perf: $12,500 **Exc:** $8000 **VGood:** $6500

SC0 Grade
Perf: $21,500 **Exc:** $14,000 **VGood:** $11,000

SC0 Gold Grade
Perf: $24,000 **Exc:** $15,000 **VGood:** $12,500

SC0 Sideplates Grade
Perf: $32,500 **Exc:** $21,000 **VGood:** $17,000

SC0 Gold Sideplates Grade
Perf: $38,500 **Exc:** $25,000 **VGood:** $20,000

PERAZZI MX1B SPORTING O/U

Same specs as MX1B Pigeon-Electrocibles O/U except 28-3/8-inch, 29-1/2-inch, 31-1/2-inch barrels; choke tubes; single selective trigger; external selector, Made in Italy. No longer in production.

Standard Grade
Perf: $7000 **Exc:** $4500 **VGood:** $3600

SC3 Grade
Perf: $12,500 **Exc:** $8000 **VGood:** $6500

SC0 Grade
Perf: $21,500 **Exc:** $14,000 **VGood:** $11,000

SC0 Gold Grade
Perf: $24,000 **Exc:** $15,000 **VGood:** $12,500

SC0 Sideplates Grade
Perf: $32,500 **Exc:** $21,000 **VGood:** $17,000

SC0 Gold Sideplates Grade
Perf: $38,500 **Exc:** $25,000 **VGood:** $20,000

PERAZZI MX3 SPECIAL AMERICAN TRAP COMBO

Over/under; boxlock; 12-ga.; two-barrel set with 29-1/2-inch or 31-1/2-inch and 32-inch O/U or 34-inch single; fixed or choke tubes; vent rib; checkered European walnut Monte Carlo stock, beavertail forend; removable, adjustable trigger group; single selective trigger; external selector. Made in Italy. Discontinued 1992.

Perf: $7500 **Exc:** $4900 **VGood:** $3900

SC3 Grade
Perf: $13,000 **Exc:** $8500 **VGood:** $6750

SC0 Grade
Perf: $21,500 **Exc:** $14,000 **VGood:** $11,000

SC0 Gold Grade
Perf: $24,000 **Exc:** $15,500 **VGood:** $12,500

PERAZZI MX3 SPECIAL AMERICAN TRAP SINGLE BARREL

Same specs as MX3 Special American Trap Combo except 32-inch, 34-inch single barrel. Made in Italy. Discontinued 1992.

Standard Grade
Perf: $5500 **Exc:** $3500 **VGood:** $2850

SC3 Grade
Perf: $9500 **Exc:** $6200 **VGood:** $5000

SC0 Grade
Perf: $17,500 **Exc:** $11,500 **VGood:** $9100

SC0 Gold Grade
Perf: $18,000 **Exc:** $11,750 **VGood:** $9500

PERAZZI MX3 SPECIAL SKEET O/U

Same specs as MX3 Special American Trap Combo except 26-3/4-inch, 27-1/2-inch barrels; checkered European walnut pistol-grip stock, beavertail forend. Made in Italy. Discontinued 1992.

Standard Grade
Perf: $6000 **Exc:** $3900 **VGood:** $3100

SC3 Grade
Perf: $10,000 **Exc:** $6500 **VGood:** $5200

SC0 Grade
Perf: $17,500 **Exc:** $11,500 **VGood:** $9100

SC0 Gold Grade
Perf: $20,000 **Exc:** $13,000 **VGood:** $10,500

PERAZZI MX3 SPECIAL SPORTING O/U

Same specs as MX3 Special American Trap Combo except 28-3/8-inch, 29-1/2-inch, 31-1/2-inch barrels; checkered European walnut pistol-grip stock, beavertail forend. Made in Italy. Discontinued 1992.

Standard Grade
Perf: $6200 **Exc:** $4000 **VGood:** $3200
SC3 Grade
Perf: $10,500 **Exc:** $6800 **VGood:** $5500
SC0 Grade
Perf: $18,000 **Exc:** $11,700 **VGood:** $9400
SC0 Gold Grade
Perf: $20,500 **Exc:** $13,500 **VGood:** $10,500

PERAZZI MX3 SPECIAL TRAP O/U

Same specs as MX3 Special American Trap Combo except 29-1/2-inch, 30-3/4-inch, 31-1/2-inch barrels; checkered European walnut pistol-grip stock, beavertail forend. Made in Italy. Discontinued 1992.

Standard Grade
Perf: $6000 **Exc:** $3900 **VGood:** $3100
SC3 Grade
Perf: $10,000 **Exc:** $6500 **VGood:** $5200
SC0 Grade
Perf: $17,500 **Exc:** $11,500 **VGood:** $9100
SC0 Gold Grade
Perf: $20,000 **Exc:** $13,000 **VGood:** $10,500

PERAZZI MX6 AMERICAN TRAP SINGLE BARREL

Single shot; 12-ga.; 32-inch, 34-inch barrel; fixed or choke tubes; raised vent rib; checkered European walnut Monte Carlo stock, beavertail forend; removable trigger group. Made in Italy. Introduced 1995; still in production.

Perf: $4200 **Exc:** $2900 **VGood:** $2200
Combo model with extra O/U barrels
Perf: $6800 **Exc:** $4500 **VGood:** $3600

PERAZZI MX6 SKEET O/U

Same specs as MX6 American Trap Single Barrel except over/under; boxlock; 26-3/4-inch, 27-1/2-inch barrels. Made in Italy. Introduced 1995.

Perf: $5500 **Exc:** $3500 **VGood:** $2650

PERAZZI MX6 SPORTING O/U

Same specs as MX6 American Trap Single Barrel except over/under; boxlock; 28-3/8-inch, 29-1/2-inch, 31-1/2-inch barrels; single selective trigger; external selector. Made in Italy. Introduced 1995; still in production.

Perf: $6000 **Exc:** $4000 **VGood:** $3100

PERAZZI MX6 TRAP O/U

Same specs as MX6 American Trap Single Barrel except over/under; boxlock; 29-1/2-inch, 30-3/4-inch, 31-1/2-inch barrels. Made in Italy. Introduced 1995.

Perf: $5000 **Exc:** $3500 **VGood:** $2650

PERAZZI MX7 AMERICAN TRAP SINGLE BARREL

Single shot; 12-ga.; 32-inch, 34-inch barrel; fixed or choke tubes; raised vent rib; checkered European walnut Monte Carlo stock, beavertail forend; fixed trigger group. Made in Italy. Introduced 1995.

Perf: $4900 **Exc:** $3500 **VGood:** $2600
Combo model with extra O/U barrels
Perf: $7000 **Exc:** $4900 **VGood:** $3700

PERAZZI MX7 SKEET O/U

Same specs as MX7 American Trap Single Barrel except over/under; boxlock; 27-1/2-inch barrels; checkered European walnut pistol-grip stock, beavertail forend; single selective trigger; external selector. Made in Italy. Introduced 1993.

Perf: $5200 **Exc:** $3700 **VGood:** $2800

PERAZZI MX7 SPORTING O/U

Same specs as MX7 American Trap Single Barrel except over/under; boxlock; 28-3/8-inch, 29-1/2-inch, 31-1/2-inch barrels; checkered European walnut pistol-grip stock, beavertail forend; single selective trigger; external selector. Made in Italy. Introduced 1992.

Perf: $5800 **Exc:** $4000 **VGood:** $3000

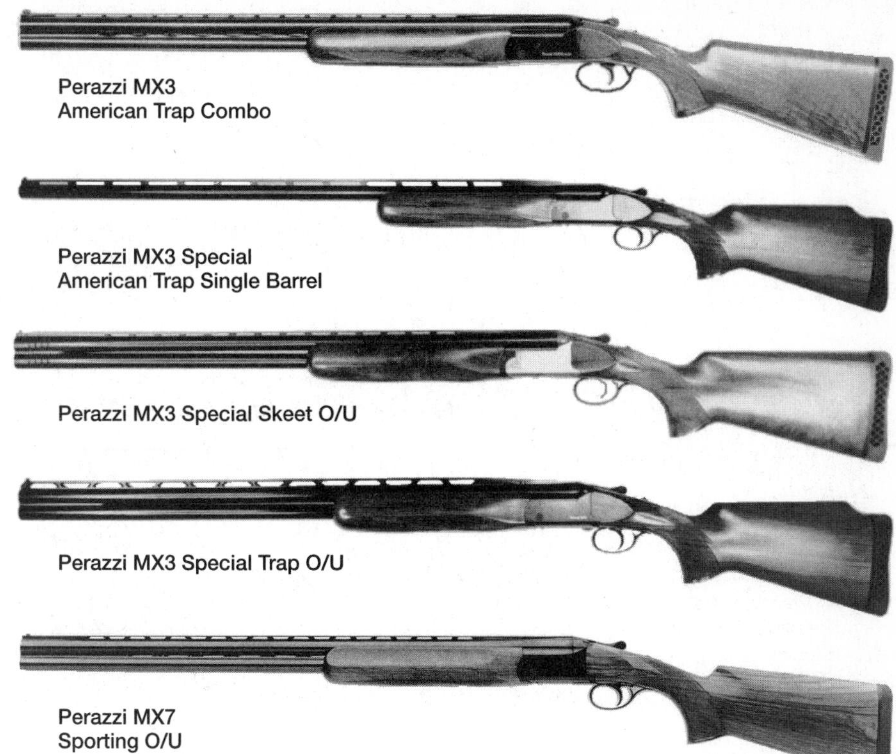

Perazzi MX3 American Trap Combo

Perazzi MX3 Special American Trap Single Barrel

Perazzi MX3 Special Skeet O/U

Perazzi MX3 Special Trap O/U

Perazzi MX7 Sporting O/U

PERAZZI MX7 TRAP O/U

Same specs as MX7 American Trap Single Barrel except over/under; boxlock; 29-1/2-inch, 30-3/4-inch, 31-1/2-inch barrels; checkered European walnut pistol-grip stock, beavertail forend; single selective trigger; external selector. Made in Italy. Introduced 1993.

Perf: $5200 **Exc:** $3700 **VGood:** $2800

PERAZZI MX8 OVER/UNDER SHOTGUNS

Gauge: 12, 2-3/4-inch chambers; 28-3/8-inch barrel (Imp. Mod. & Extra Full), 29-1/2-inch barrel (choke tubes); weighs 7 lbs., 12 oz.; special stock specifications; single selective trigger. Many options available. Imported from Italy by Perazzi U.S.A., Inc.

Sporting
N/A
Trap Double Trap (removable trigger group)
Exc: $3800 **VGood:** $3750 **Good:** $3100
Skeet
Exc: $5900 **VGood:** $4400 **Good:** $3600
SC3 grade (variety of engraving patterns)
SCO grade (more intricate engraving, gold inlays).

PERAZZI MX8 GAME O/U

Over/under; boxlock; 12-, 20-ga.; 26-3/4-inch, 27-1/2-inch barrels; fixed or choke tubes; vent rib; checkered European walnut pistol-grip (12-ga.) or straight-grip (20-ga.) stock; schnabel or tapered forend; removable trigger group; single selective trigger; external selector. Made in Italy. Introduced 1993.

Standard Grade
Perf: $7000 **Exc:** $4500 **VGood:** $3600
SC3 Grade
Perf: $12,500 **Exc:** $8000 **VGood:** $6500
SC0 Grade
Perf: $21,500 **Exc:** $14,000 **VGood:** $11,000
SC0 Gold Grade
Perf: $24,000 **Exc:** $15,500 **VGood:** $12,500
SC0 Sideplates Grade
Perf: $32,500 **Exc:** $21,000 **VGood:** $17,000
SC0 Gold Sideplates Grade
Perf: $38,500 **Exc:** $25,000 **VGood:** $20,000

PERAZZI MX8 SKEET O/U

Same specs as MX8 Game O/U except 26-3/4-inch, 27-1/2-inch barrels; checkered European walnut pistol-grip stock, beavertail forend. Made in Italy. Introduced 1993.

Standard Grade
Perf: $7000 **Exc:** $4500 **VGood:** $3600
SC3 Grade
Perf: $12,500 **Exc:** $8000 **VGood:** $6500
SC0 Grade
Perf: $21,500 **Exc:** $14,000 **VGood:** $11,000
SC0 Gold Grade
Perf: $24,000 **Exc:** $15,500 **VGood:** $12,500
SC0 Sideplates Grade
Perf: $32,500 **Exc:** $21,000 **VGood:** $17,000
SC0 Gold Sideplates Grade
Perf: $38,500 **Exc:** $25,000 **VGood:** $20,000

PERAZZI MX8 TRAP O/U

Same specs as MX8 Game O/U except 29-1/2-inch, 30-3/4-inch, 31-1/2-inch barrels; checkered European walnut pistol-grip stock, beavertail forend. Made in Italy. Introduced by Ithaca 1969; still in production by Perazzi.

Standard Grade
Perf: $7000 **Exc:** $4500 **VGood:** $3600
SC3 Grade
Perf: $12,500 **Exc:** $8000 **VGood:** $6500
SC0 Grade
Perf: $21,500 **Exc:** $14,000 **VGood:** $11,000
SC0 Gold Grade
Perf: $24,000 **Exc:** $15,500 **VGood:** $12,500
SC0 Sideplates Grade
Perf: $32,500 **Exc:** $21,000 **VGood:** $17,000
SC0 Gold Sideplates Grade
Perf: $38,500 **Exc:** $25,000 **VGood:** $20,000

PERAZZI MX8 TRAP COMBO

Same specs as MX8 Game O/U except two-barrel set with 29-1/2-inch or 31-1/2-inch O/U and 32-inch

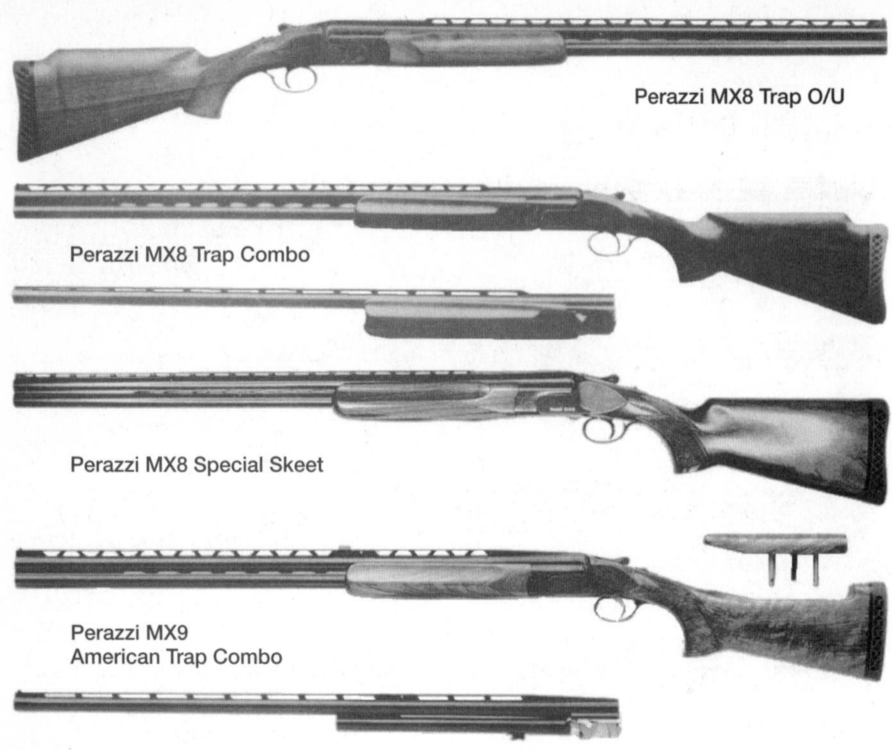

Perazzi MX8 Trap O/U

Perazzi MX8 Trap Combo

Perazzi MX8 Special Skeet

Perazzi MX9 American Trap Combo

or 34-inch single; checkered European walnut pistol-grip stock, forend; two trigger groups. Introduced by Ithaca 1973; discontinued 1978.

Perf: $3500 **Exc:** $2300 **VGood:** $1800

PERAZZI MX8/MX8 SPECIAL TRAP, SKEET

Gauge: 12, 2-3/4-inch chambers; Trap 29-1/2-inch barrel (Imp. Mod. & Extra Full), 31-1/2-inch barrel (Full & Extra Full); choke tubes optional; Skeet 27-5/8-inch barrel (Skeet & Skeet); weighs about 8-1/2 lbs. (Trap); 7 lbs., 15 oz. (Skeet); interchangeable and custom made stock to customer specs; detachable and interchangeable trigger group with flat V springs; flat 7/16-inch ventilated rib. Many options available. Imported from Italy by Perazzi U.S.A., Inc.

Exc: $3900 **VGood:** $3525 **Good:** $3100

MX8 Special (adj. four-position trigger)

Exc: $3900 **VGood:** $3525 **Good:** $3100

MX8 Special Combo (O/U and single barrel sets)

Exc: $9450 **VGood:** $8000 **Good:** $7150

PERAZZI MX8 SPECIAL SKEET OVER/UNDER

Similar to the MX8 Skeet except has adjustable four-position trigger, Skeet stock dimensions.

Exc: $3900 **VGood:** $3525 **Good:** $3100

PERAZZI MX8/20 OVER/UNDER SHOTGUN

Similar to the MX8 except has smaller frame and has a removable trigger mechanism. Available in trap, Skeet, sporting or game models with fixed chokes or choke tubes. Stock is made to customer specifications. Introduced 1993.

Exc: $4350 **VGood:** $4000 **Good:** $3650

PERAZZI MX8 SPECIAL AMERICAN TRAP COMBO

Over/under; boxlock; 12-ga.; two-barrel set of 29-1/2-inch or 31-1/2-inch O/U and 32-inch or 34-inch single; fixed or choke tubes; raised vent rib; checkered European walnut Monte Carlo stock, beavertail forend; adjustable, removable trigger group; external selector. Made in Italy. Introduced 1988.

Standard Grade

Perf: $9200 **Exc:** $6000 **VGood:** $4800

PERAZZI MX8 SPECIAL AMERICAN TRAP SINGLE BARREL

Same specs as MX8 Special American Trap Combo except 32-inch, 34-inch single barrel. Made in Italy. Introduced 1988; discontinued 1994.

Standard Grade

Perf: $6000 **Exc:** $3900 **VGood:** $3100

SC3 Grade

Perf: $11,000 **Exc:** $7100 **VGood:** $5700

SC0 Grade

Perf: $19,000 **Exc:** $12,300 **VGood:** $9900

SC0 Gold Grade

Perf: $21,000 **Exc:** $13,500 **VGood:** $11,000

SC0 Sideplates Grade

Perf: $30,000 **Exc:** $17,500 **VGood:** $15,500

SC0 Gold Sideplates Grade

Perf: $35,000 **Exc:** $22,750 **VGood:** $18,000

PERAZZI MX8 SPECIAL SKEET O/U

Same specs as MX8 Special American Trap Combo except 26-3/4-inch, 27-1/2-inch O/U barrels; checkered European walnut pistol-grip stock, beavertail forend. Made in Italy.

Standard Grade

Perf: $7500 **Exc:** $5000 **VGood:** $3900

SC3 Grade

Perf: $12,500 **Exc:** $8000 **VGood:** $6500

SC0 Grade

Perf: $22,000 **Exc:** $14,000 **VGood:** $11,500

SC0 Gold Grade

Perf: $25,000 **Exc:** $16,250 **VGood:** $13,000

SC0 Sideplates Grade

Perf: $33,000 **Exc:** $21,500 **VGood:** $17,000

SC0 Gold Sideplates Grade

Perf: $38,000 **Exc:** $25,000 **VGood:** $19,750

PERAZZI MX8 SPECIAL SPORTING O/U

Same specs as MX8 Special American Trap Combo except 12-, 20-ga.; 28-3/8-inch, 29-1/2-inch, 31-1/2-inch O/U barrels; checkered European walnut pistol-grip stock, beavertail forend. Made in Italy. Still in production.

Standard Grade

Perf: $7800 **Exc:** $5000 **VGood:** $4000

SC3 Grade

Perf: $13,000 **Exc:** $8500 **VGood:** $6750

SC0 Grade

Perf: $22,500 **Exc:** $14,600 **VGood:** $11,700

SC0 Gold Grade

Perf: $25,500 **Exc:** $16,500 **VGood:** $13,250

PERAZZI MX8 SPECIAL TRAP O/U

Same specs as MX8 Special American Trap Combo except 29-1/2-inch, 30-3/4-inch, 31-1/2-inch O/U barrels; checkered European walnut pistol-grip stock, beavertail forend. Made in Italy.

Standard Grade

Perf: $7500 **Exc:** $5000 **VGood:** $3900

SC3 Grade

Perf: $12,500 **Exc:** $8000 **VGood:** $6500

SC0 Grade

Perf: $22,000 **Exc:** $14,000 **VGood:** $11,500

SC0 Gold Grade

Perf: $25,000 **Exc:** $16,250 **VGood:** $13,000

SC0 Sideplates Grade

Perf: $33,000 **Exc:** $21,500 **VGood:** $17,000

SC0 Gold Sideplates Grade

Perf: $38,000 **Exc:** $25,000 **VGood:** $19,750

PERAZZI MX9 AMERICAN TRAP COMBO

Over/under; boxlock; 12-ga.; two-barrel set of 29-1/2-inch or 31-1/2-inch O/U and 32-inch or 34-inch single; fixed or choke tubes; adjustable rib to change point of impact; checkered European walnut Monte Carlo adjustable stock, beavertail forend; removable trigger. Made in Italy. Introduced 1993; discontinued 1994.

Standard Grade

Perf: $11,500 **Exc:** $7500 **VGood:** $6000

SC3 Grade

Perf: $17,000 **Exc:** $11,000 **VGood:** $8800

SC0 Grade

Perf: $26,500 **Exc:** $17,000 **VGood:** $13,800

SC0 Gold Grade

Perf: $29,000 **Exc:** $19,000 **VGood:** $15,000

SC0 Sideplates Grade

Perf: $37,500 **Exc:** $24,000 **VGood:** $19,500

SC0 Gold Sideplates Grade

Perf: $42,000 **Exc:** $27,000 **VGood:** $21,800

PERAZZI MX9 AMERICAN TRAP SINGLE BARREL

Same specs as MX9 American Trap Combo except 32-inch, 34-inch single barrel. Made in Italy. Introduced 1993; discontinued 1994.

Standard Grade

Perf: $8500 **Exc:** $5500 **VGood:** $4400

SC3 Grade

Perf: $13,000 **Exc:** $8500 **VGood:** $6700

SC0 Grade

Perf: $21,500 **Exc:** $14,000 **VGood:** $11,000

SC0 Gold Grade

Perf: $23,500 **Exc:** $15,000 **VGood:** $12,000

SC0 Sideplates Grade

Perf: $32,500 **Exc:** $21,000 **VGood:** $17,000

SC0 Gold Sideplates Grade

Perf: $37,500 **Exc:** $24,000 **VGood:** $19,500

PERAZZI MX9 TRAP O/U

Same specs as MX9 American Trap Combo except 29-1/2-inch, 30-3/4-inch, 31-1/2-inch O/U barrels; checkered European walnut pistol-grip adjustable stock, beavertail forend. Made in Italy. Introduced 1993; discontinued 1994.

Standard Grade

Perf: $8800 **Exc:** $5700 **VGood:** $4500

SC3 Grade

Perf: $13,400 **Exc:** $8700 **VGood:** $7000

SC0 Grade

Perf: $22,000 **Exc:** $14,000 **VGood:** $11,500

SC0 Gold Grade

Perf: $24,100 **Exc:** $15,600 **VGood:** $12,500

SC0 Sideplates Grade

Perf: $33,200 **Exc:** $21,600 **VGood:** $17,000

SC0 Gold Sideplates Grade

Perf: $38,300 **Exc:** $25,000 **VGood:** $20,000

PERAZZI MX10 OVER/UNDER SHOTGUN

Gauge: 12, 2-3/4-inch chambers; 29-1/2-inch barrel, 31.5-inch barrel (fixed chokes); walnut, cheekpiece adjustable for elevation and cast; adjustable rib; vent. side rib; externally selective trigger; available in single barrel, combo, over/under trap, Skeet, pigeon and sporting models. Introduced 1993. Imported from Italy by Perazzi U.S.A., Inc.

Perf: $9000 **Exc:** $4550 **VGood:** $4400

PERAZZI MX10 AMERICAN TRAP COMBO

Over/under; boxlock; 12-ga.; two-barrel set of 29-1/2-inch or 31-1/2-inch O/U and 32-inch or 34-inch single; fixed or choke tubes; checkered European walnut adjustable stock, beavertail forend; removable trigger group; external selector. Made in Italy. Introduced 1993.

Standard Grade
Perf: $12,000 **Exc:** $7800 **VGood:** $6200
SC3 Grade
Perf: $18,000 **Exc:** $11,700 **VGood:** $9400
SC0 Grade
Perf: $28,000 **Exc:** $18,200 **VGood:** $14,500
SC0 Gold Grade
Perf: $31,000 **Exc:** $20,000 **VGood:** $16,000

PERAZZI MX10 AMERICAN TRAP SINGLE BARREL

Same specs as MX10 American Trap Combo except 32-inch, 34-inch single barrel. Made in Italy. Introduced 1993; discontinued 1993.

Standard Grade
Perf: $8500 **Exc:** $5500 **VGood:** $4400
SC3 Grade
Perf: $13,000 **Exc:** $8500 **VGood:** $6700
SC0 Grade
Perf: $21,000 **Exc:** $13,600 **VGood:** $11,000
SC0 Gold Grade
Perf: $24,000 **Exc:** $15,600 **VGood:** $12,500
SC0 Sideplates Grade
Perf: $32,000 **Exc:** $20,800 **VGood:** $16,500
SC0 Gold Sideplates Grade
Perf: $38,000 **Exc:** $25,000 **VGood:** $20,000

PERAZZI MX10 PIGEON-ELECTROCIBLES O/U

Same specs as MX10 American Trap Combo except 27-1/2-inch, 29-1/2-inch O/U barrels. Made in Italy. Introduced 1995; still in production.

Standard Grade
Perf: $9000 **Exc:** $5800 **VGood:** $4700
SC3 Grade
Perf: $14,000 **Exc:** $9100 **VGood:** $7300
SC0 Grade
Perf: $23,500 **Exc:** $15,000 **VGood:** $12,000
SC0 Gold Grade
Perf: $26,000 **Exc:** $17,000 **VGood:** $13,500

PERAZZI MX10 SKEET O/U

Same specs as MX10 American Trap Combo except 27-1/2-inch, 29-1/2-inch O/U barrels. Made in Italy. Introduced 1995; still in production.

Standard Grade
Perf: $9000 **Exc:** $5800 **VGood:** $4700
SC3 Grade
Perf: $14,000 **Exc:** $9100 **VGood:** $7300
SC0 Grade
Perf: $23,500 **Exc:** $15,000 **VGood:** $12,000
SC0 Gold Grade
Perf: $26,000 **Exc:** $17,000 **VGood:** $13,500

PERAZZI MX10 SPORTING O/U

Same specs as MX10 American Trap Combo except 28-3/8-inch, 29-1/2-inch, 31-1/2-inch O/U barrel. Made in Italy. Introduced 1993; still in production.

Standard Grade
Perf: $10,000 **Exc:** $6500 **VGood:** $5200

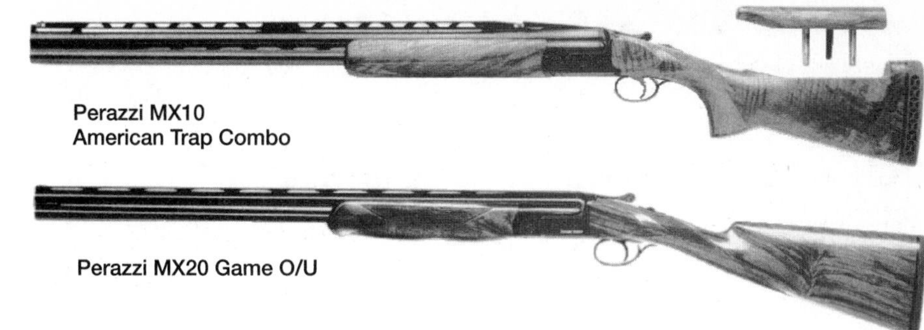

Perazzi MX10 American Trap Combo

Perazzi MX20 Game O/U

SC3 Grade
Perf: $15,000 **Exc:** $9750 **VGood:** $7800
SC0 Grade
Perf: $24,500 **Exc:** $16,000 **VGood:** $13,000
SC0 Gold Grade
Perf: $27,500 **Exc:** $18,000 **VGood:** $14,300

PERAZZI MX10 TRAP O/U

Same specs as MX10 American Trap Combo except 12-, 20-ga.; 29-1/2-inch, 30-3/4-inch, 31-1/2-inch O/U barrels. Made in Germany. Introduced 1993; still in production.

Standard Grade
Perf: $9000 **Exc:** $5800 **VGood:** $4700
SC3 Grade
Perf: $14,000 **Exc:** $9100 **VGood:** $7300
SC0 Grade
Perf: $23,500 **Exc:** $15,000 **VGood:** $12,000
SC0 Gold Grade
Perf: $26,000 **Exc:** $17,000 **VGood:** $13,500

PERAZZI MX11 AMERICAN TRAP COMBO

Over/under; boxlock; 12-ga.; two-barrel set of 29-1/2-inch or 31-1/2-inch O/U and 32-inch or 34-inch single; fixed or choke tubes; vent rib; checkered European walnut Monte Carlo adjustable stock, beavertail forend; removable trigger group; single selective trigger; external selector. Made in Italy. Introduced 1995.

Perf: $8200 **Exc:** $5800 **VGood:** $4300

PERAZZI MX11 AMERICAN TRAP SINGLE BARREL

Same specs as MX11 American Trap Combo except 32-inch, 34-inch single barrel. Made in Italy. Introduced 1995.

Perf: $6200 **Exc:** $4300 **VGood:** $3300

PERAZZI MX11 PIGEON-ELECTROCIBLES O/U

Same specs as MX11 American Trap Combo except 27-1/2-inch O/U barrels; checkered European walnut pistol grip adjustable stock, beavertail forend. Made in Italy. Introduced 1995.

Perf: $6500 **Exc:** $4500 **VGood:** $3400

PERAZZI MX11 SKEET O/U

Same specs as MX11 American Trap Combo except 26-3/4-inch, 27-1/2-inch O/U barrels; checkered European walnut pistol-grip adjustable stock, beavertail forend. Made in Italy. Introduced 1995; still in production.

Perf: $6500 **Exc:** $4500 **VGood:** $3400

PERAZZI MX11 SPORTING O/U

Same specs as MX11 American Trap Combo except 28-3/8-inch, 29-1/2-inch, 31-1/2-inch O/U barrels; checkered European walnut pistol-grip adjustable stock, beavertail forend. Made in Italy. Introduced 1995; still in production.

Perf: $7500 **Exc:** $5000 **VGood:** $4000

PERAZZI MX11 TRAP O/U

Same specs as MX11 American Trap Combo except 29-1/2-inch, 30-3/4-inch, 31-1/2-inch O/U barrels; checkered European walnut pistol-grip adjustable stock, beavertail forend. Made in Italy. Introduced 1995; still in production.

Perf: $6500 **Exc:** $4500 **VGood:** $3400

PERAZZI MX12 HUNTING OVER/UNDER

Gauge: 12, 2-3/4-inch chambers; 26-3/4-inch, 27-1/2-inch, 28-3/8-inch, 29-1/2-inch barrel (Mod. & Full); choke tubes available in 27-5/8-inch, 29-1/2-inch only (MX12C); weighs 7 lbs., 4 oz.; stock to customer specs; interchangeable; single selective trigger; coil springs used in action; schnabel forend tip. Imported from Italy by Perazzi U.S.A., Inc.

Exc: $4650 **VGood:** $4350 **Good:** $3950

PERAZZI MX20 HUNTING OVER/UNDER

Similar to the MX12 except 20 ga. frame size. Non-removable trigger group. Available in 20, 28, 410 with 2-3/4-inch or 3-inch chambers. 26-inch standard, and choked Mod. & Full. Weight is 6 lbs., 6 oz.

Exc: $4500 **VGood:** $4300 **Good:** $3650

PERAZZI MX12 GAME O/U

Over/under; boxlock; 12-ga.; 26-3/4-inch, 27-1/2-inch barrels; fixed or choke tubes; vent rib; checkered European walnut straight-grip stock, schnabel or tapered forend; single selective trigger; non-removable trigger group; engraving. Made in Italy.

Standard Grade
Perf: $6200 **Exc:** $4400 **VGood:** $3500
SC3 Grade
Perf: $12,500 **Exc:** $8000 **VGood:** $6500
SC0 Grade
Perf: $21,000 **Exc:** $13,500 **VGood:** $11,000
SC0 Gold Grade
Perf: $24,000 **Exc:** $15,500 **VGood:** $12,500
SC0 Sideplates Grade
Perf: $33,000 **Exc:** $21,500 **VGood:** $17,000
SC0 Gold Sideplates Grade
Perf: $38,500 **Exc:** $25,000 **VGood:** $20,000

PERAZZI MX14 AMERICAN TRAP SINGLE BARREL

Single shot; 12-ga.; 34-inch barrel; fixed or choke tubes; vent rib; checkered European walnut Monte Carlo adjustable stock, beavertail forend; removable trigger group; unsingle configuration. Made in Italy. Introduced 1995.

Perf: $6200 **Exc:** $4300 **VGood:** $3300
Combo model with extra O/U barrels
Perf: $8500 **Exc:** $5500 **VGood:** $4400

PERAZZI MX20 GAME O/U

Over/under; boxlock; 20-ga.; 26-inch, 26-3/4-inch, 27-1/2-inch barrels; fixed or choke tubes; vent rib; checkered European walnut straight-grip stock, schnabel or tapered forend; single selective trigger; non-removable trigger group; engraving. Made in Italy.

Standard Grade
Perf: $6700 **Exc:** $4400 **VGood:** $3500
SC3 Grade
Perf: $12,500 **Exc:** $8000 **VGood:** $6500

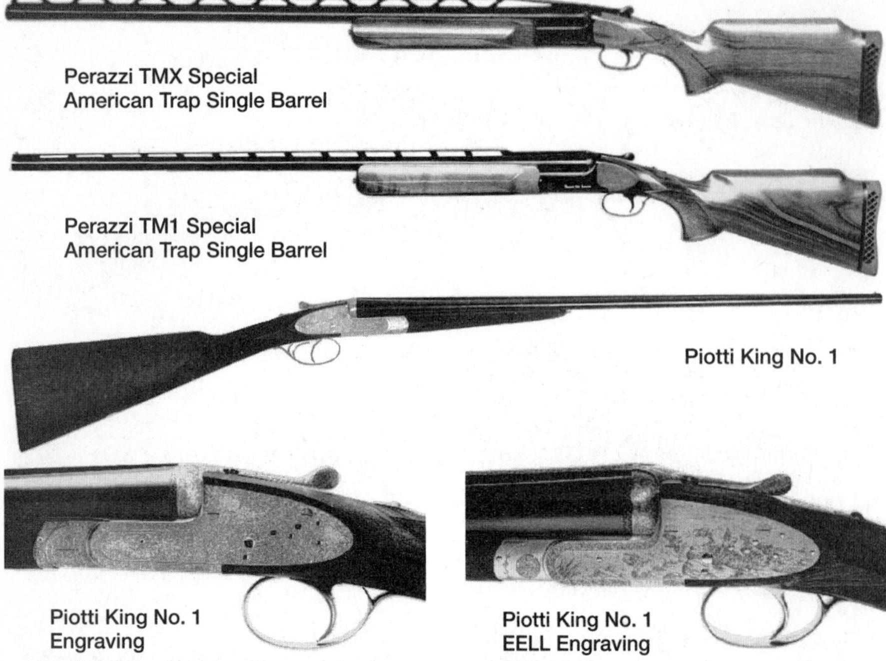

Perazzi TMX Special American Trap Single Barrel

Perazzi TM1 Special American Trap Single Barrel

Piotti King No. 1

Piotti King No. 1 Engraving

Piotti King No. 1 EELL Engraving

SC0 Grade

Perf: $21,000 **Exc:** $13,500 **VGood:** $11,000

SC0 Gold Grade

Perf: $24,000 **Exc:** $15,500 **VGood:** $12,500

SC0 Sideplates Grade

Perf: $33,000 **Exc:** $21,500 **VGood:** $17,000

SC0 Gold Sideplates Grade

Perf: $38,500 **Exc:** $25,000 **VGood:** $20,000

PERAZZI MX28, MX410 GAME O/U SHOTGUNS

Gauge: 28, 2-3/4-inch chambers, 410, 3-inch chambers; 26-inch barrel (Imp. Cyl. & Full); stock to customer specifications; made on scaled-down frames proportioned to the gauge. Introduced 1993. Imported from Italy by Perazzi U.S.A., Inc.

Exc: $8100 **VGood:** $7750 **Good:** $7250

PERAZZI MX28 GAME O/U

Over/under; boxlock; 28-ga.; 26-inch, 26-3/4-inch, 27-1/2-inch barrels; fixed or choke tubes; vent rib; checkered European walnut straight-grip stock, tapered forend; non-removable trigger group; engraving. Made in Italy. Introduced 1993.

Standard Grade

Perf: $11,500 **Exc:** $9700 **VGood:** $7300

SC3 Grade

Perf: $20,000 **Exc:** $13,000 **VGood:** $10,500

SC0 Grade

Perf: $29,000 **Exc:** $19,000 **VGood:** $15,000

SC0 Gold Grade

Perf: $31,500 **Exc:** $20,500 **VGood:** $16,000

SC0 Sideplates Grade

Perf: $40,000 **Exc:** $26,000 **VGood:** $21,000

SC0 Gold Sideplates Grade

Perf: $46,000 **Exc:** $30,000 **VGood:** $24,000

PERAZZI MX410 GAME O/U

Over/under; boxlock; .410; 26-inch, 26-3/4-inch, 27-1/2-inch barrels; fixed chokes; vent rib; checkered European walnut straight-grip stock, tapered forend; non-removable trigger group; engraving. Made in Italy. Introduced 1993; still in production.

Standard Grade

Perf: $11,500 **Exc:** $9700 **VGood:** $7300

SC3 Grade

Perf: $20,000 **Exc:** $13,000 **VGood:** $10,500

SC0 Grade

Perf: $29,000 **Exc:** $19,000 **VGood:** $15,000

SC0 Gold Grade

Perf: $31,500 **Exc:** $20,500 **VGood:** $16,000

SC0 Sideplates Grade

Perf: $40,000 **Exc:** $26,000 **VGood:** $21,000

SC0 Gold Sideplates Grade

Perf: $46,000 **Exc:** $30,000 **VGood:** $24,000

PERAZZI SINGLE BARREL TRAP

Single shot; boxlock; 12-ga.; 34-inch barrel; Full choke; vent rib; checkered European walnut pistol-grip stock, forend; auto ejector; recoil pad. Introduced by Ithaca 1971; discontinued 1972.

Perf: $2200 **Exc:** $1700 **VGood:** $1500

PERAZZI TM1 SPECIAL AMERICAN TRAP SINGLE BARREL

Single shot; 12-ga.; 32-inch, 34-inch barrel; fixed or choke tubes; raised vent rib; checkered European walnut Monte Carlo stock, beavertail forend; removable, adjustable four-position trigger. Made in Italy. Introduced 1988; still in production.

Standard Grade

Perf: $5200 **Exc:** $3400 **VGood:** $2700

SC0 Grade

Perf: $16,000 **Exc:** $10,500 **VGood:** $8300

SC0 Gold Grade

Perf: $18,500 **Exc:** $12,000 **VGood:** $9600

PERAZZI TMX SPECIAL AMERICAN TRAP SINGLE BARREL

Single shot; 12-ga.; 32-inch, 34-inch barrel; fixed or choke tubes; high vent rib; checkered European walnut Monte Carlo stock, beavertail forend; removable, adjustable four-position trigger. Made in Italy. Introduced 1988.

Standard Grade

Perf: $5500 **Exc:** $3600 **VGood:** $2900

SC0 Grade

Perf: $17,000 **Exc:** $11,000 **VGood:** $8900

SC0 Gold Grade

Perf: $19,500 **Exc:** $12,500 **VGood:** $10,000

PERUGINI-VISINI CLASSIC DOUBLE

Side-by-side; sidelock; 12-, 20-ga.; 2-3/4-inch, 3-inch chambers; various barrel lengths, chokes; high-grade oil-finished straight English briar walnut stock; H&H-type hand-detachable sidelocks; internal parts gold-plated; single or double triggers; auto ejectors; numerous options. Made in Italy. Introduced, 1986; discontinued 1989.

Perf: $20,000 **Exc:** $17,000 **VGood:** $15,000

PERUGINI-VISINI LIBERTY DOUBLE

Side-by-side; boxlock; 12-, 20-, 28-ga.; 410; 2-3/4-inch, 3-inch chambers; various barrel lengths, chokes; high-grade oil-finished straight English briar walnut stock; internal parts gold-plated; single or double trigger; auto ejectors; numerous options. Made in Italy. Introduced 1986; discontinued 1989.

Perf: $10,750 **Exc:** $9000 **VGood:** $7750

PERUGINI-VISINI AUSONIA

Side-by-side; sidelock; 12-, 20-ga.; exposed hammers; double Purdey type sidelock action; demibloc barrels; variety of engraving options. No longer produced.

Perf: $7140 **Exc:** $6500 **VGood:** $5750

PERUGINI-VISINI REGINA

Side-by-side; 12-ga.; heavy frame construction intended for hunting and competition; removable trigger group; chopper lump barrels; many options.

Exc: $11,500 **VGood:** $9950 **Good:** $8700

PERUGINI-VISINI ROMAGNA HAMMER GUN

Best quality Zanotti-stylke bar action hammer gun; 12-, 16-, 20-, 28-ga., .410 bore; heavy frame configuration for competition use. Engraved by master engraver.

Exc: $19,500 **VGood:** $16,950 **Good:** $13,000

PERUGINI-VISINI NOVA

Over/under; best quality Boss-style sidelock with back action locks; Boss-style forend iron and side ribs; best quality English rose and scroll engraving is standard.

Exc: $38,500 **VGood:** $32,950 **Good:** $26,000

PIOTTI BOSS OVER/UNDER

Over/under; sidelock; 12-, 16-, 20-, 28-ga.; 26-inch to 32-inch barrels; standard chokes; stock dimensions to customer specs; best quality figured walnut. Essentially a custom-made gun with many options. Made in Italy. Introduced 1993; still imported by William Larkin Moore & Co.

Perf: $48,000 **Exc:** $34,000 **VGood:** $28,750

Add $8,900 to above prices for 28 ga.
Add $3,200 for 16- or 20-ga.
Add $3,100 for single trigger.

PIOTTI KING NO. 1

Side-by-side; H&H sidelock; 12-, 16-, 20-, 28-ga., .410; 25-inch to 30-inch (12-ga.), 25-inch to 28-inch (other gauges) barrels; file-cut or concave vent rib; fine-figured straight-grip European walnut stock, split or beavertail forend; oil or satin luster finish; double triggers; optional single non-selective trigger; coin finish or color case-hardening; full-coverage engraving; gold crown on top lever; name in gold; gold crest on forend. Made in Italy to customer's requirements. Introduced 1983; still in production.

Perf: $29,600 **Exc:** $20,900 **VGood:** $17,750

With single trigger

Perf: $32,000 **Exc:** $22,300 **VGood:** $20,000

PIOTTI KING NO. 1 EELL

Same specs as King No. 1 except highest quality wood, metal work; engraved scenes, gold inlays; signed by master engraver. Made in Italy. Introduced 1983; no longer imported. Extremely rare, precludes pricing.

PIOTTI KING NO. 1 EXTRA

Same specs as King No. 1 except exhibition grade wood; better metal work; Bulino game scene engraving or game scene engraving with gold inlay work signed by master engraver. Made in Italy.

Perf: $35,000 **Exc:** $32,000 **VGood:** $28,250

With single trigger

Perf: $37,000 **Exc:** $34,000 **VGood:** $30,250

PIOTTI LUNIK

Side-by-side; H&H sidelock; 12-, 16-, 20-, 28-ga., .410; 25-inch to 30-inch (12-ga.), 25-inch to 28-inch (other gauges) barrels; fine-figured straight-grip European walnut stock, splinter or beavertail forend; oil or satin luster finish; double triggers; optional single non-selective trigger; Renaissance-style scroll engraving, gold crown on top lever, gold name and gold crest in forend; demi-block barrels. Made in Italy. Introduced 1983.

Perf: $30,900 **Exc:** $21,900 **VGood:** $18,750

With single trigger

Perf: $32,900 **Exc:** $23,900 **VGood:** $20,750

PIOTTI MONTE CARLO

Side-by-side; H&H sidelock; 12-, 16-, 20-, 28-ga., .410; 25-inch to 30-inch (12-ga.), 25-inch to 28-inch (other gauges) barrels; fine-figured straight-grip European walnut stock, split or beavertail forend; oil or satin luster finish; double triggers; optional single non-selective trigger; ejectors; Purdey-type engraving. Made in Italy. Introduced 1983; discontinued 1989.

Perf: $10,500 **Exc:** $9250 **VGood:** $8200

With single trigger

Perf: $11,500 **Exc:** $10,250 **VGood:** $9200

PIOTTI PIUMA

Side-by-side; Anson & Deeley boxlock; 12-, 16-, 20-, 28-ga., .410; 25-inch to 30-inch (12-ga.), 25-inch to 28-inch (other gauges) barrels; file-cut rib; oil-finished, straight-grip European walnut stock, splinter type or beavertail forend; satin luster finish optional; ejectors; chopper lump barrels; double triggers, hinged front; optional single non-selective trigger; coin finish or color case-hardening; scroll, rosette, scallop engraving. Made in Italy. Introduced 1983.

Perf: $14,800 **Exc:** $10,900 **VGood:** $9,500

With single trigger

Perf: $16,000 **Exc:** $12,100 **VGood:** $10,700

PIOTTI WESTLAKE

Side-by-side; H & H sidelock action; 12-, 16-, 20, 28-ga., .410 bore; scroll engraving. Discontinued 1989.

Perf: $8500 **Exc:** $7500 **VGood:** $6000

PIOTTI HAMMER GUN

Side-by-side; 12-ga.; self-cocking; ejector; double triggers; exposed hammers; back action with fine scroll engraving. Importation began 2001.

Perf: $29,800 **Exc:** $23,200 **VGood:** $18,750

PIOTTI KING EXTRA

Side-by-side; sidelock; 12-, 16-, 20-, 28-ga., .410 bore; best quality H&H pattern; ejectors; chopper lump barrels; level-file cut rib; choice of Burlino game scene or standard cameo game scene engraving with gold inlays; signed by a master engraver; exhibition grade wood.

Perf: $35,000 **Exc:** $25,900 **VGood:** $22,000

PRECISION SPORTS MODEL 640A

Side-by-side; boxlock; 12-, 16-, 20-, 28-ga., .410; 2-3/4-inch chambers; 26-inch, 28-inch barrels; Improved Cylinder/Modified or Modified/Full chokes; raised matte rib; hand-checkered walnut pistol-grip stock, beavertail forend with oil finish; checkered butt; buttplate; automatic safety; ejectors or extractors; single non-selective trigger; silvered, engraved action. Made in Spain by Ugartechea. Originally imported as Parker-Hale brand. Introduced 1986; discontinued 1993.

Exc: $800 **VGood:** $650 **Good:** $500

28-ga., .410, ejectors

Perf: $900 **Exc:** $750 **VGood:** $600

PRECISION SPORTS MODEL 640E

Same specs as Model 640A except concave rib; hand-checkered walnut straight-grip stock, splinter forend with oil finish; double triggers. Made in Spain by Ugartechea. Originally imported as Parker-Hale brand. Introduced 1986; discontinued 1993.

Perf: $700 **Exc:** $500 **VGood:** $400

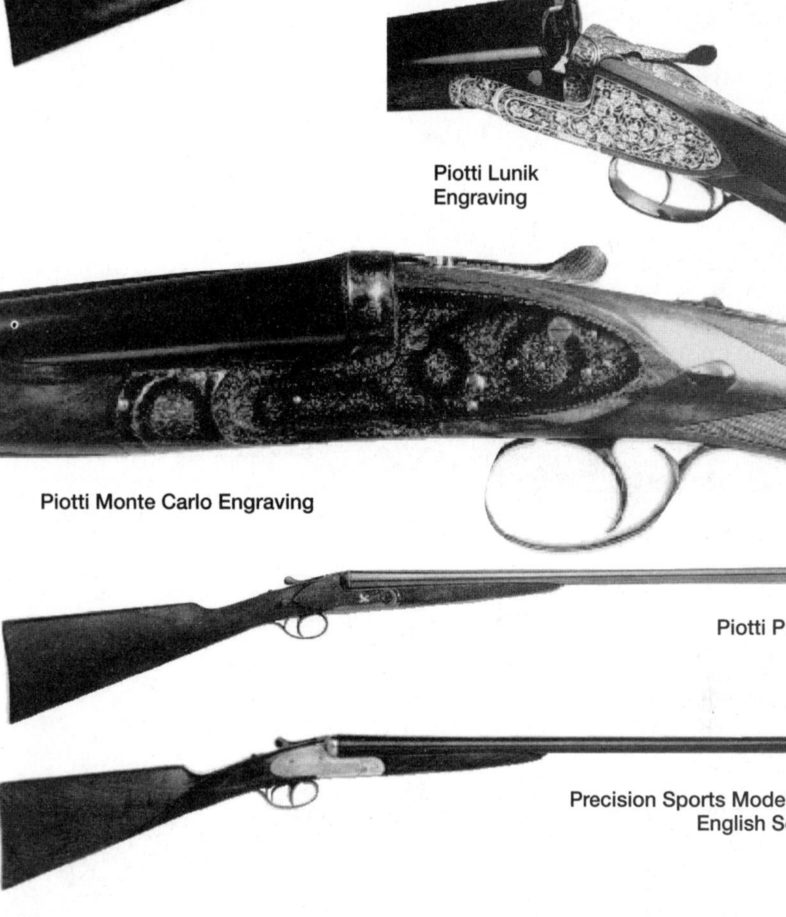

Piotti Lunik

Piotti Lunik Engraving

Piotti Monte Carlo Engraving

Piotti Piuma

Precision Sports Model 600 English Series

28-ga., .410, ejectors

Perf: $800 **Exc:** $600 **VGood:** $500

PRECISION SPORTS MODEL 600 ENGLISH SERIES

Similar to the Model 640E but with oil finished English-style straight stock.

Perf: $900 **Exc:** $800 **VGood:** $650

PRECISION SPORTS MODEL 640M BIG TEN

Same specs as Model 640A except chambered for 10-ga.; 26-inch, 30-inch, 32-inch barrels; Full/Full. Originally imported as Parker-Hale brand. Introduced 1986; discontinued 1993.

Perf: $800 **Exc:** $650 **VGood:** $550

PRECISION SPORTS MODEL 640 SLUG GUN

Same specs as Model 640A except 12-ga. only; 25-inch barrels; Improved Cylinder/Improved Cylinder. Originally imported as Parker-Hale brand. Introduced 1986; discontinued 1993.

Perf: $950 **Exc:** $700 **VGood:** $600

PRECISION SPORTS MODEL 645A

Side-by-side; boxlock; 12-, 16-, 20-, 28-ga., .410; 2-3/4-inch chambers; 26-inch, 28-inch barrels; Improved Cylinder/Modified or Modified/Full; raised matte rib; hand-checkered walnut pistol-grip stock, beavertail forend with oil finish; checkered butt; buttplate; automatic safety; ejectors; single non-selective trigger; silvered, engraved action. Made in Spain by Ugartechea. Originally imported as Parker-Hale brand. Introduced 1986; discontinued 1993.

Perf: $1100 **Exc:** $750 **VGood:**600

28-ga., .410, ejectors

Perf: $1200 **Exc:** $850 **VGood:** $700

PRECISION SPORTS MODEL 645E

Same specs as Model 645A except concave rib; hand-checkered walnut straight-grip stock, splinter forend with oil finish; double triggers. Made in Spain by Ugartechea. Originally imported as Parker-Hale brand. Introduced 1986; discontinued 1993.

Perf: $900 **Exc:** $650 **VGood:** $550

28-ga., .410, ejectors

Perf: $980 **Exc:** $730 **VGood:** $630

PRECISION SPORTS MODEL 645E-XXV

Same specs as Model 645A except 25-inch barrels; Churchill-type rib. Originally imported as Parker-Hale brand. Introduced 1986; discontinued 1993.

Perf: $900 **Exc:** $650 **VGood:** $550

28-ga., .410, ejectors

Perf: $980 **Exc:** $730 **VGood:** $630

PRECISION SPORTS MODEL 650A

Side-by-side; boxlock; 12-ga.; 2-3/4-inch chambers; 26-inch, 28-inch barrels; Improved Cylinder/Modified choke tubes; raised matte rib; hand-checkered walnut pistol-grip stock, beavertail forend with oil finish; checkered butt; buttplate; automatic safety; extractors; single non-selective trigger; silvered, engraved action. Made in Spain by Ugartechea. Originally imported as Parker-Hale brand. Introduced 1986; discontinued 1993.

Perf: $800 **Exc:** $650 **VGood:** $550

PRECISION SPORTS MODEL 650E

Same specs as Model 650A except concave rib; hand-checkered walnut straight-grip stock, splinter forend with oil finish; double triggers. Made in Spain by Ugartechea. Originally imported as Parker-Hale brand. Introduced 1986; discontinued 1993.

Perf: $800 **Exc:** $650 **VGood:** $550

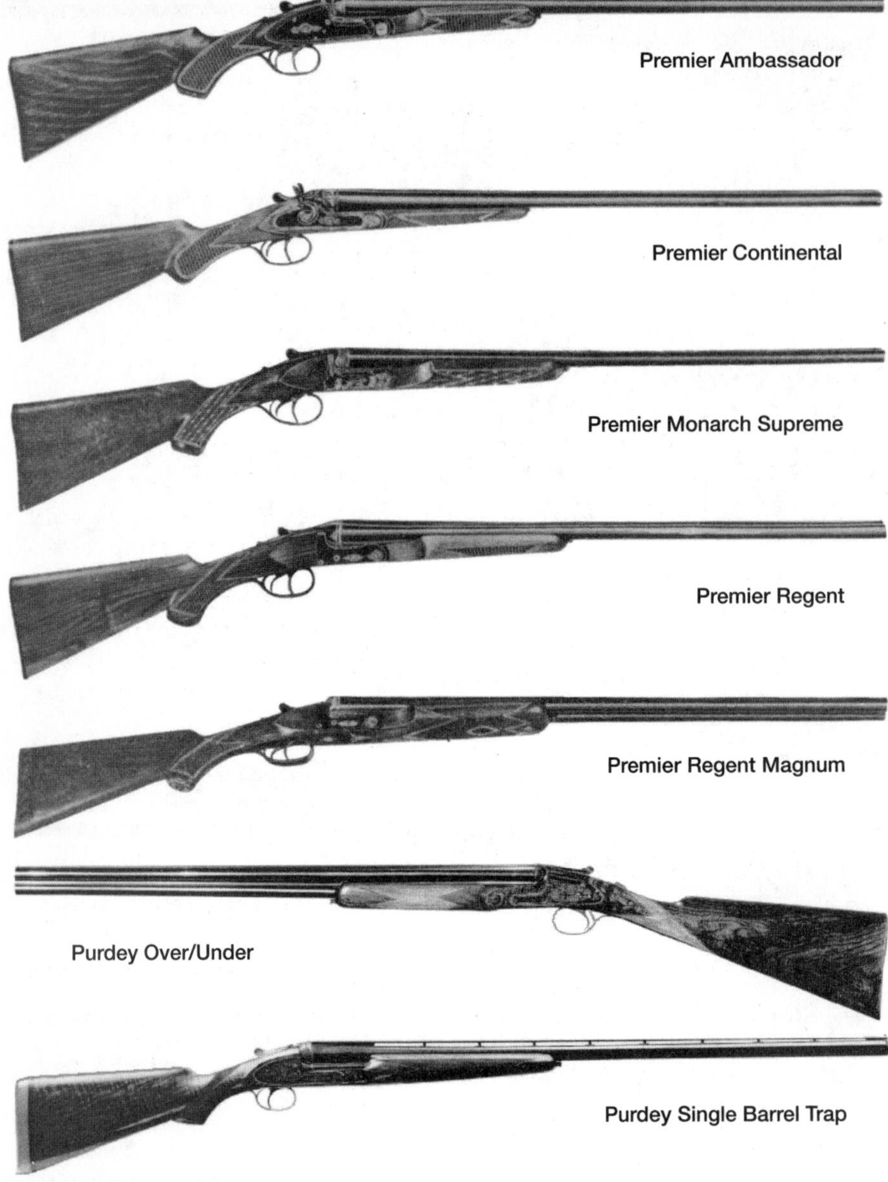
Premier Ambassador

Premier Continental

Premier Monarch Supreme

Premier Regent

Premier Regent Magnum

Purdey Over/Under

Purdey Single Barrel Trap

PRECISION SPORTS MODEL 655A

Side-by-side; boxlock; 12-ga.; 2-3/4-inch chambers; 28-inch barrels; Improved Cylinder/Modified choke tubes; concave rib; hand-checkered walnut pistol-grip stock, beavertail forend with oil finish; automatic safety; ejectors; checkered butt; buttplate; single non-selective trigger; silvered, engraved action. Made in Spain by Ugartechea. Originally imported as Parker-Hale brand. Introduced 1986; discontinued 1993.

Perf: $900 **Exc:** $700 **VGood:** $600

PRECISION SPORTS MODEL 655E

Same specs as Model 655A except concave rib; hand-checkered walnut straight-grip stock, splinter forend with oil finish; double triggers. Made in Spain by Ugartechea. Originally imported as Parker-Hale brand. Introduced 1986; discontinued 1993.

Perf: $900 **Exc:** $700 **VGood:** $600

PRECISION SPORTS MODEL 800 AMERICAN SERIES

Side-by side; boxlock; 10-, 12-, 16-, 20-, 28-ga., .410; 2-3/4-inch, 3-inch, 3-1/2-inch chambers depending upon gauge; 25-inch, 26-inch, 27-inch, 28-inch barrels; raised matte rib; hand-checkered European walnut pistol-grip stock, beavertail forend; buttplate; auto safety; ejectors or extractors; single non-selective trigger; engraved, silvered frame. Made in Spain. Introduced 1986; discontinued 1993.

Perf: $1000 **Exc:** $750 **VGood:** $650

PREMIER AMBASSADOR

Side-by-side; 12-, 16-, 20-ga., .410; 22-inch (except .410), 26-inch barrels; Modified/Full chokes; European walnut stock; hand-checkered pistol-grip stock, forearm; double triggers; cocking indicators; automatic safety. Made in Europe. Introduced 1957; discontinued 1981.

Perf: $385 **Exc:** $360 **VGood:** $295

PREMIER BRUSH KING

Side-by-side; 12-, 20-ga.; 22-inch Improved/Modified barrels; matted tapered rib; hand-checkered European walnut pistol-grip stock, forearm; double triggers; automatic safety. Introduced 1959; discontinued 1981.

Perf: $275 **Exc:** $250 **VGood:** $220

PREMIER CONTINENTAL

Side-by-side; exposed hammers; 12-, 16-, 20-ga.; 22-inch, 26-inch barrels; Modified/Full chokes; hand-checkered European walnut pistol-grip stock, forearm; double triggers; cocking indicators; automatic safety. Made in Europe. No longer in production.

Perf: $225 **Exc:** $190 **VGood:** $170

PREMIER MONARCH SUPREME

Side-by-side; boxlock; 12-, 20-ga.; 2-3/4-inch (12-ga.), 3-inch (20-ga.) chambers; 26-inch Improved Cylinder/Modified, 28-inch Modified/Full barrels; checkered fancy European walnut pistol-grip stock, beavertail forearm; double triggers; auto ejectors. Introduced 1959; discontinued 1981.

Perf: $440 **Exc:** $385 **VGood:** $360

PREMIER PRESENTATION CUSTOM GRADE

Side-by-side; boxlock; 12-, 20-ga.; 2-3/4-inch (12-ga.), 3-inch (20-ga.) chambers; 26-inch Improved Cylinder/Modified, 28-inch Modified/Full barrels; hand-checkered high-grade European walnut pistol-grip stock, beavertail forearm; engraved hunting scene; gold and silver inlays; custom-order gun. Introduced 1959; discontinued 1981.

Perf: $1150 **Exc:** $950 **VGood:** $825

PREMIER REGENT

Side-by-side; 12-, 16-, 20-, 28-ga., .410; 26-inch Improved/Modified, Modified/Full, 28-inch Modified/Full barrels; matted tapered rib; hand-checkered European walnut pistol-grip stock, forearm; double triggers; automatic safety. Introduced 1955; discontinued 1981.

Perf: $280 **Exc:** $250 **VGood:** $210

PREMIER REGENT MAGNUM

Same specs as Regent except 10-, 12-ga.; 3-inch, 3-1/2-inch chambers; 30-inch, 32-inch Full/Full barrels; hand-checkered European walnut pistol-grip stock, beavertail forearm; recoil pad. Discontinued 1981.

10-ga.

Perf: $330 **Exc:** $285 **VGood:** $265

12-ga.

Perf: $305 **Exc:** $275 **VGood:** $250

PURDEY SIDE-BY-SIDE

Side-by-side; sidelock; 12-, 16-, 20-, 28-ga., .410-ga.; 26-inch, 27-inch, 28-inch, 30-inch barrels; 2-1/2, 2-3/4, or 3-inch; any choke combo; choice of rib style; hand-checkered European walnut straight-grip stock, forearm; pistol-grip stock on special order; double triggers or single trigger; automatic ejectors; made in several variations including Game Model, Featherweight Game, Pigeon Gun, with side clips. Prices are identical for all. Introduced 1880.

With double triggers

Perf: $44,000 **Exc:** $35,000 **VGood:** $30,000

With single trigger

Perf: $45,000 **Exc:** $36,000 **VGood:** $31,000

PURDEY OVER/UNDER

Over/under; sidelock; pre-WWII guns are built on Purdey action, post-war versions on Woodward action; 12-, 16-, 20-, 28-ga., .410-bore; 26-inch, 27-inch, 28-inch barrels; any choke combo; any rib style to customer's preference; hand-checkered European walnut straight or pistol-grip stock, forearm; double or single trigger; engraved receiver. Introduced 1925.

With Purdey action, double triggers

Perf: $50,000 **Exc:** $36,000 **VGood:** $33,000

With Purdey action, single trigger

Perf: $52,000 **Exc:** $38,000 **VGood:** $35,000

With Woodward action, double trigger

Perf: $56,000 **Exc:** $40,000 **VGood:** $37,000

With Woodward action, single trigger

Perf: $60,000 **Exc:** $44,000 **VGood:** $40,000

PURDEY SINGLE BARREL TRAP

Single shot; Purdey action; 12-ga.; barrel length, choke to customer's specs; vent rib; hand-checkered European walnut straight or pistol-grip stock, forearm; engraved receiver. Introduced 1917; discontinued prior to WWII.

Perf: $12,500 **Exc:** $9000 **VGood:** $8200

REMINGTON MODEL 11A

Autoloader; hammerless; takedown; 12-, 16-, 20-ga.; 5-shot tube magazine; 26-inch, 28-inch, 30-inch, 32-inch barrel; Full, Modified, Improved Cylinder, Skeet chokes; plain, solid or vent rib; checkered pistol-grip stock, forearm. Introduced 1905; discontinued 1949. Deduct 10 percent for 16-ga.

Plain barrel
Exc: $300 **VGood:** $225 **Good:** $185

Solid rib
Exc: $315 **VGood:** $235 **Good:** $200

Vent rib
Exc: $360 **VGood:** $335 **Good:** $305

NOTE: The following grades of the remington model 11 (11b - 11f) feature progressively higher-quality wood and ornamentation. prices fluctuate but may approach $10,000 for the 11f premiere.

REMINGTON MODEL 11B SPECIAL

Same specs as Model 11A except higher grade of walnut, checkering and engraving. Discontinued 1948.

REMINGTON MODEL 11D TOURNAMENT

Same specs as Model 11A except select grade of walnut, checkering and engraving. Discontinued 1948.

REMINGTON MODEL 11E EXPERT

Same specs as Model 11A except fine grade of walnut, checkering and engraving. Discontinued 1948.

REMINGTON MODEL 11F PREMIER

Same specs as Model 11A except best grade of walnut, checkering and engraving. Discontinued 1948.

REMINGTON MODEL 11R RIOT GUN

Same specs as Model 11A except 12-ga.; special 20-inch barrel; sling swivels. Introduced 1921; discontinued 1948. 100% premium for US Ordnance/ Army markings.

Exc: $360 **VGood:** $295 **Good:** $210

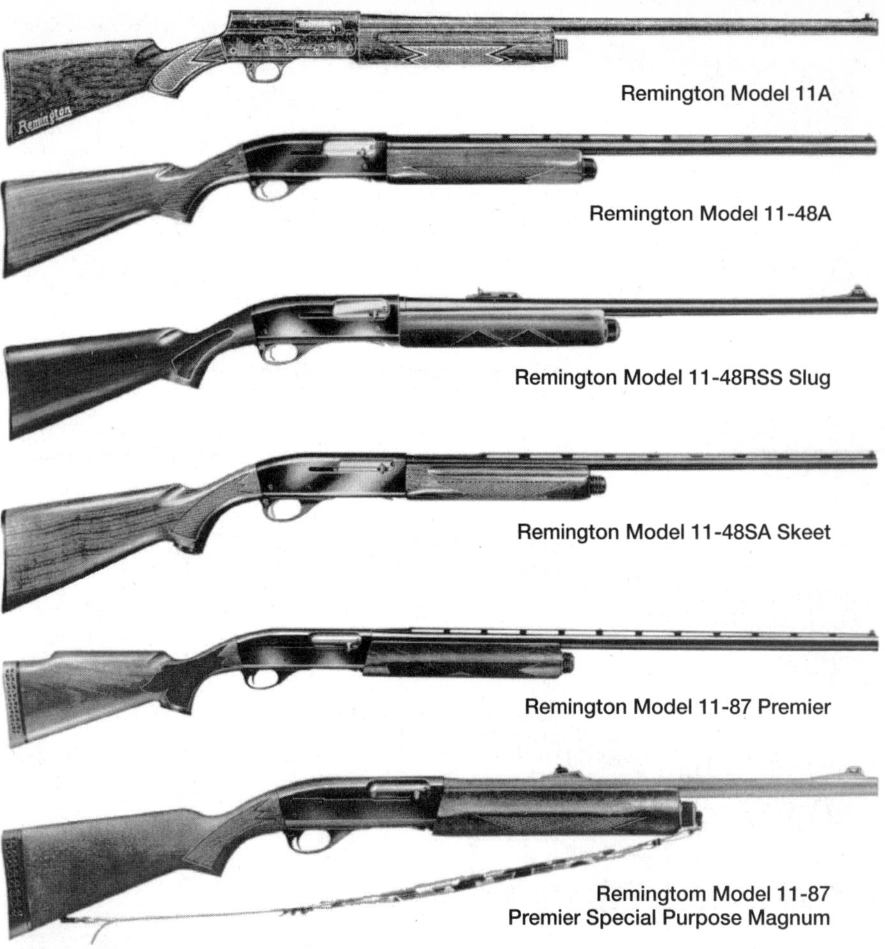

Remington Model 11A

Remington Model 11-48A

Remington Model 11-48RSS Slug

Remington Model 11-48SA Skeet

Remington Model 11-87 Premier

Remingtom Model 11-87 Premier Special Purpose Magnum

REMINGTON MODEL 11-48A

Recoiling-barrel autoloader; hammerless; takedown; 12-, 16-, 20-, 28-ga., .410; 4-, 5-shot tube magazine; 26-inch Improved Cylinder, 28-inch Modified or Full, 30-inch Full barrels; plain matted or vent-rib barrel; hand-checkered half-pistol-grip stock, forend; redesigned version of Model 11. Introduced 1949; discontinued 1969. Designated the 11-48 to draw on the popularity of the previous Model 11; i.e., "the new Model 11 of 1948." Premium for small gauge.

Plain barrel
Exc: $300 **VGood:** $240 **Good:** $195

Vent-rib barrel
Exc: $450 **VGood:** $350 **Good:** $300

REMINGTON MODEL 11-48A RIOT

Same specs as Model 11-48A except 12-ga.; 20-inch plain barrel. Introduced 1949; discontinued 1969.

Exc: $300 **VGood:** $240 **Good:** $195

NOTE: Values for the following higher grades of the Remington 11-48 fluctuate and may approach $10,000 for the 11-48F Premiere grade.

REMINGTON MODEL 11-48B SPECIAL

Same specs as Model 11-48A except higher grade of wood, checkering and engraving. Introduced 1949; discontinued 1969. Premium for small gauge.

REMINGTON MODEL 11-48D TOURNAMENT

Same specs as Model 11-48A except select grade of wood, checkering and engraving. Introduced 1949; discontinued 1969.

REMINGTON MODEL 11-48F PREMIER

Same specs as Model 11-48A except best grade of wood, checkering and engraving. Introduced 1949; discontinued 1969.

REMINGTON MODEL 11-48 RSS SLUG GUN

Same specs as Model 11-48 except 12-ga. slug; 26-inch plain barrel; adjustable rifle-type gold bead front sight, step-adjustable rear. Introduced 1959; no longer in production.

Exc: $350 **VGood:** $265 **Good:** $200

REMINGTON MODEL 11-48SA SKEET

Same specs as Model 11-48A except 25-inch vent-rib barrel; Skeet choke; Skeet-style walnut stock, forend. Introduced 1952; discontinued 1969.

Exc: $550 **VGood:** $480 **Good:** $400

REMINGTON MODEL 11-87 PREMIER

Gas-operated autoloader; 12-ga.; 3-inch chamber; 26-inch, 28-inch, 30-inch vent-rib barrel; Rem-Choke tubes; weighs 8-1/4 lb.; metal bead middle sight, Bradley-type white-faced front; high-gloss or satin-finished, cut-checkered walnut stock, pinned forend; brown buttpad; pressure compensating system handles 2-3/4-inch or 3-inch shells; stainless steel magazine tube; barrel support ring on operating bars; left- or right-hand versions. Introduced, 1987; still in production. Add $150 for nickel plated version.

Right-hand model
Perf: $630 **Exc:** $495 **VGood:** $410

Left-hand model
Perf: $670 **Exc:** $555 **VGood:** $475

REMINGTON MODEL 11-87 PREMIER 175TH ANNIVERSARY

Same specs as Model 11-87 Premier except 28-inch vent-rib barrel; walnut wood with high-gloss finish; receiver engraved with Remington's 175th anniversary scroll design with an American eagle. Introduced 1991; discontinued 1991.

Perf: $650 **Exc:** $505 **VGood:** $335

REMINGTON MODEL 11-87 PREMIER N.W.T.F.

Same specs as Model 11-87 Premier except 21-inch vent-rib barrel; Rem-Choke Improved Cylinder and Turkey Extra-Full tubes; synthetic brown Trebark camouflage-finished stock; camo sling; swivels. Introduced 1992; discontinued 1993.

Perf: $525 **Exc:** $375 **VGood:** $285

REMINGTON MODEL 11-87 PREMIER SKEET

Same specs as Model 11-87 Premier except 12-ga.; 2-3/4-inch chamber; 26-inch vent-rib barrel; cut-checkered, deluxe walnut Skeet-style stock with satin finish; two-piece buttplate, Introduced 1987; still in production.

Perf: $650 **Exc:** $550 **VGood:** $475

REMINGTON MODEL 11-87 PREMIER SPECIAL PURPOSE DEER GUN

Same specs as Model 11-87 Premier except 21-inch barrel; rifled and Improved Cylinder choke tubes; rifle sights; cantilever scope mount, rings; gas system handles all 2-3/4-inch and 3-inch slug, buckshot, high-velocity field and magnum loads; not designed to function with light 2-3/4-inch field loads; dull stock finish, Parkerized exposed metal surfaces; bolt and carrier have blackened color. Introduced 1987; discontinued 1995.

Perf: $690 **Exc:** $495 **VGood:** $425

REMINGTON MODEL 11-87 PREMIER SPECIAL PURPOSE MAGNUM

Same specs as Model 11-87 Premier except black synthetic or satin wood stock; Parkerized metal finish; blackened bolt, carrier; quick-detachable sling swivels; camo padded nylon sling. Introduced 1987; still in production.

Perf: $500 **Exc:** $350 **VGood:** $260

With synthetic stock and forend (SPS).
Perf: $610 **Exc:** $475 **VGood:** $400

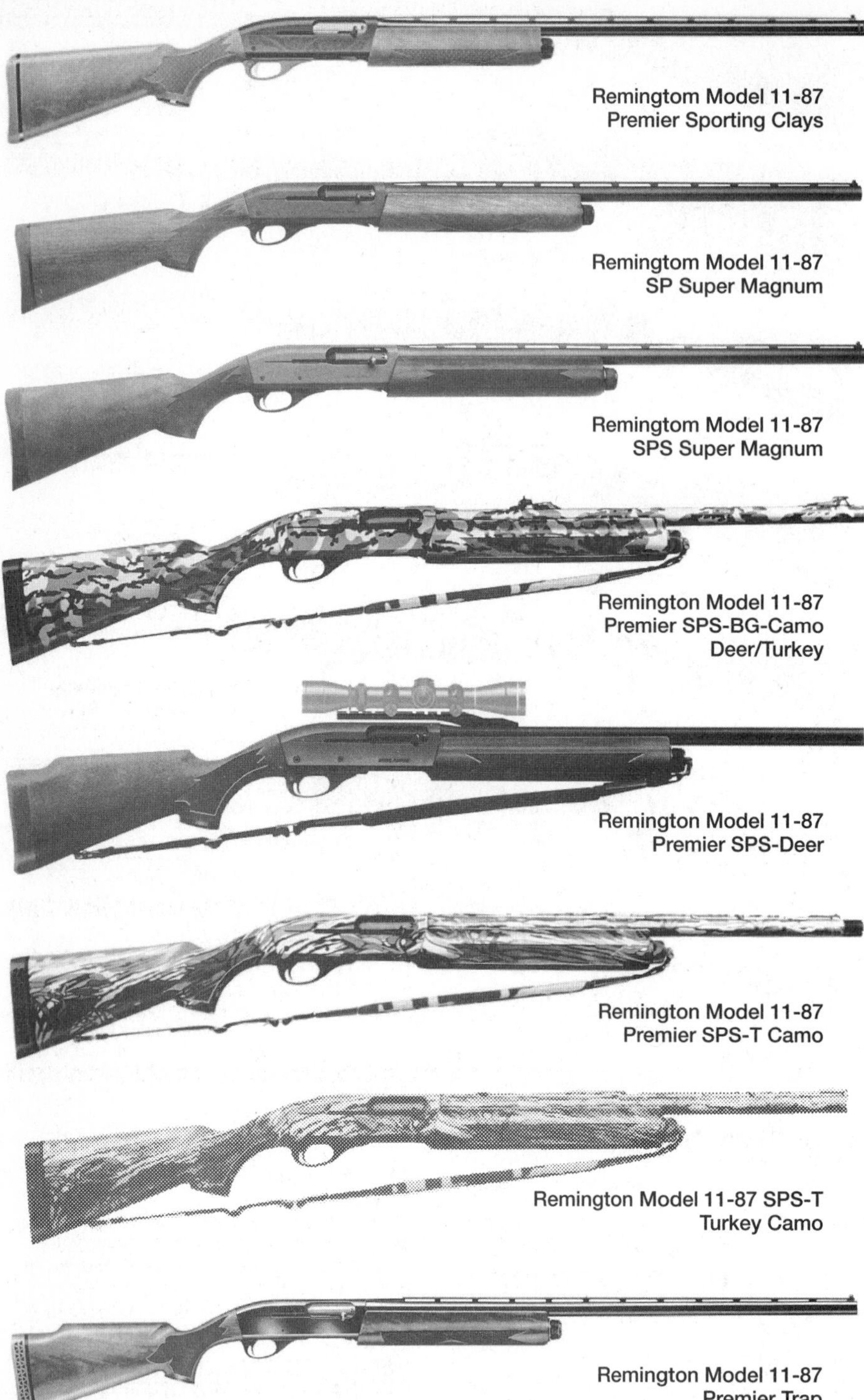

Remingtom Model 11-87 Premier Sporting Clays

Remingtom Model 11-87 SP Super Magnum

Remingtom Model 11-87 SPS Super Magnum

Remington Model 11-87 Premier SPS-BG-Camo Deer/Turkey

Remington Model 11-87 Premier SPS-Deer

Remington Model 11-87 Premier SPS-T Camo

Remington Model 11-87 SPS-T Turkey Camo

Remington Model 11-87 Premier Trap

REMINGTON MODEL 11-87 PREMIER SPECIAL PURPOSE SYNTHETIC CAMO

Same specs as Model 11-87 Premier except 26-inch vent-rib barrel; synthetic stock; camo sling; swivels; all surfaces (except bolt and trigger guard) covered with Mossy Oak Bottomland camo finish. Introduced 1992; still in production.

Perf: $710 **Exc:** $520 **VGood:** $435

REMINGTON MODEL 11-87 PREMIER SPORTING CLAYS

Same specs as Model 11-87 Premier except 12-ga.; 2-3/4-inch chamber; 26-inch, 28-inch medium-height vent-rib Light Contour barrel; Skeet, Improved Cylinder, Modified, Full long Rem-Choke tubes; ivory bead front sight; special stock dimensions; shortened magazine tube and forend; Sporting Clays buttpad; lengthened forcing cone; competition trigger; top of receiver, barrel and rib matte finished; comes in two-barrel fitted hard case. Introduced 1992; still in production.

Perf: $675 **Exc:** $570 **VGood:** $450

REMINGTON MODEL 11-87 SP AND SPS SUPER MAGNUM SHOTGUNS

Similar to Model 11-87 Special Purpose Magnum except has 3-1/2-inch chamber. Available in flat-finish American walnut or black synthetic stock, 26-inch or 28-inch black-matte finished barrel and receiver; Imp. Cyl., Modified and Full Rem-Choke tubes. Overall length 45-3/4-inch, weighs 8 lbs., 2 oz. Introduced 2000.

SP Super Magnum (walnut stock)

Perf: $695 **Exc:** $495 **VGood:** $435

SPS Super Magnum (synthetic stock)

Perf: $610 **Exc:** $475 **VGood:** $400

SPS Super Magnum (camo)

Perf: $710 **Exc:** $510 **VGood:** $435

REMINGTON MODEL 11-87 PREMIER SPS-BG-CAMO DEER/TURKEY

Same specs as Model 11-87 Premier except 21-inch barrel; Improved Cylinder, Super-Full Turkey (.665-inch diameter with knurled extension) Rem-Choke tubes and rifled choke tube insert; rifle sights; synthetic stock, forend; quick-detachable swivels; camo Cordura carrying sling; all surfaces Mossy Oak Bottomland camouflage-finished. Introduced 1993; discontinued 1995.

Perf: $525 **Exc:** $365 **VGood:** $300

REMINGTON MODEL 11-87 PREMIER SPS CANTILEVER

Same specs as Model 11-87 Premier except 20-inch barrel; Improved Cylinder, 3 1/2-inch rifled Rem-Choke tubes; cantilever scope mount; synthetic Monte Carlo stock; sling; swivels. Introduced 1994; still in production.

Perf: $600 **Exc:** $420 **VGood:** $320

REMINGTON MODEL 11-87 PREMIER SPS-DEER

Same specs as Model 11-87 Premier except fully-rifled 21-inch barrel; rifle sights; black non-reflective synthetic stock, forend; black carrying sling. Introduced 1993; still in production.

Perf: $525 **Exc:** $375 **VGood:** $290

With wood stock (Model 11-87 SP Deer Gun) Rem-Choke, 21-inch barrel w/rifle sights

REMINGTON MODEL 11-87 SPS CANTILEVER SHOTGUN

Similar to the 11-87 SPS except has fully rifled barrel; synthetic stock with Monte Carlo comb; cantilever scope mount deer barrel. Comes with sling and swivels. Introduced 1994.

Perf: $650 **Exc:** $525 **VGood:** $453

REMINGTON MODEL 11-87 PREMIER SPS-T CAMO

Same specs as Model 11-87 Premier except 21-inch vent-rib barrel; Improved Cylinder, Super-Full Turkey (.665-inch diameter with knurled extension) Rem-Choke tubes; synthetic stock; all surfaces Mossy Oak Green Leaf camouflage-finished; non-reflective black bolt body, trigger guard and recoil pad. Introduced 1993; still in production.

Perf: $620 **Exc:** $440 **VGood:** $340

REMINGTON MODEL 11-87 SPS-T TURKEY CAMO

Similar to the 11-87 Special Purpose Magnum except with synthetic stock, 21-inch vent. rib barrel with Rem-Choke tube. Completely covered with Mossy Oak Break-Up Brown camouflage. Bolt body, trigger guard and recoil pad are non-reflective black.

Exc: $700 **VGood:** $500 **Good:** $420

Model 11-87 SPS-T RS/TG (TruGlo fiber optics sights)

Exc: $720 **VGood:** $520 **Good:** $440

Model 11-87 SPS-T Camo CL cantilever

Exc: $702 **VGood:** $502 **Good:** $422

REMINGTON MODEL 11-87 SPS-T SUPER MAGNUM SYNTHETIC CAMO

Similar to the 11-87 SPS-T Turkey Camo except has 23-inch vent rib barrel with Turkey Super full choke tube, chambered for 12 ga., 3-1/2-inch, TruGlo rifle sights. Introduced 2001.

Exc: $720 **VGood:** $520 **Good:** $440

REMINGTON MODEL 11-87 PREMIER TRAP

Same specs as Model 11-87 Premier except 12-ga.; 2-3/4-inch chamber; 30-inch vent-rib barrel; checkered deluxe walnut Trap-style stock with satin-finish; straight or Monte Carlo comb; right- or left-hand models. Introduced 1987; dropped 1999.

Right-hand model

Perf: $625 **Exc:** $450 **VGood:** $345

Left-hand model

Perf: $675 **Exc:** $500 **VGood:** $395

REMINGTON MODEL 11-87 UPLAND SPECIAL

Similar to 11-87 Premier except has 23-inch ventilated rib barrel with straight- grip, English-style walnut stock. Available in 12- or 20-gauge. Overall length 43-1/2-inch, weighs 7-1/4 lbs. (6-1/2 lbs. in 20-ga.). Comes with Imp. Cyl., Modified and Full choke tubes. Introduced 2000.

12- or 20-gauge

Perf: $600 **Exc:** $475 **VGood:** $400

REMINGTON MODEL 11-87 SPORTSMAN

No-frills 11-87 with matte black synthetic stock. Available in 12 and 20 gauge with 3-inch chamber and 26-inch or 28-inch barrel. One choke tube included. Youth model 20 gauge with smaller dimensions also available.

NIB: $415 **Exc:** $375 **VGood:** $315

REMINGTON MODEL 11-87 SPORTSMAN NRA EDITION

Similar to 11-87 Sportsman but in 12 gauge only with NRA logo on receiver and Mossy Oak New Break-Up stock and forend.

NIB: $460 **Exc:** $420 **VGood:** $360

REMINGTON MODEL 11-87 SPORTSMAN CAMO

New in 2007, the camo version of the Sportsman comes in 12 and 20 gauge with 26" or 28" barrel. Finished in Mossy Oak Break-Up camo.

NIB: $795 **Exc:** $695 **VGood:** $525

REMINGTON MODEL 11-87 SPORTSMAN CAMO RIFLED

Camo 12 gauge slug gun with 21" barrel and cantilever scope mount.

NIB: $525 **Exc:** $485 **VGood:** $425

REMINGTON MODEL 11-87 SPORTSMAN CAMO YOUTH

Youth model in 20 gauge with shorter length of pull was introduced in 2007. Weight is about 6.5 lbs.

NIB: $725 **Exc:** $665 **VGood:** $575

REMINGTON MODEL 11-87 SPS SUPER MAGNUM WATERFOWL

This 3.5" 12 gauge is finished in Mossy Oak Duck Blind camo. It has a 30" barrel and includes three chokes. Weight is 8.25 lbs.

NIB: $1050 **Exc:** $975 **VGood:** $850

REMINGTON MODEL 11-87 SP-T THUMBHOLE

This 12 gauge with 3.5-inch chamber is made specifically for turkey hunting. Camouflaged in Mossy Oak Obsession with an R3 recoil pad and thumbhole stock. The 23-inch barrel has fiber-optic adjustable rifle sights and is drilled and tapped for scope mounting. Includes a turkey super full choke tube and sling/swivels.

NIB: $725 **Exc:** $675 **VGood:** $575

REMINGTON MODEL 11-87 SP THUMBHOLE

Laminated, thumbhole-stock 12 gauge slug gun with 3-inch chamber and 21-inch fully rifled cantilever barrel.

NIB: $700 **Exc:** $650 **VGood:** $550

REMINGTON MODEL 11-87 SPS-T SUPER MAGNUM

Similar to Model 11-87 SP Thumbhole but with pistol-grip stock and vent rib barrel.

NIB: $650 **Exc:** $550 **VGood:** $450

REMINGTON MODEL 11-87 SPORTSMAN SUPER MAG SHURSHOT TURKEY

New in 2008, this specialized turkey shotgun with ShurShot stock is a 3.5-inch-chamber 12 gauge with a 23-inch non-vent-rib barrel. It comes with fiber-optic rifle-type sights, and a synthetic stock and forend. The gun is fully covered in Realtree APG HD camo. Weight is about 7.6 lbs.

NIB: $800 **Exc:** $675 **VGood:** $550

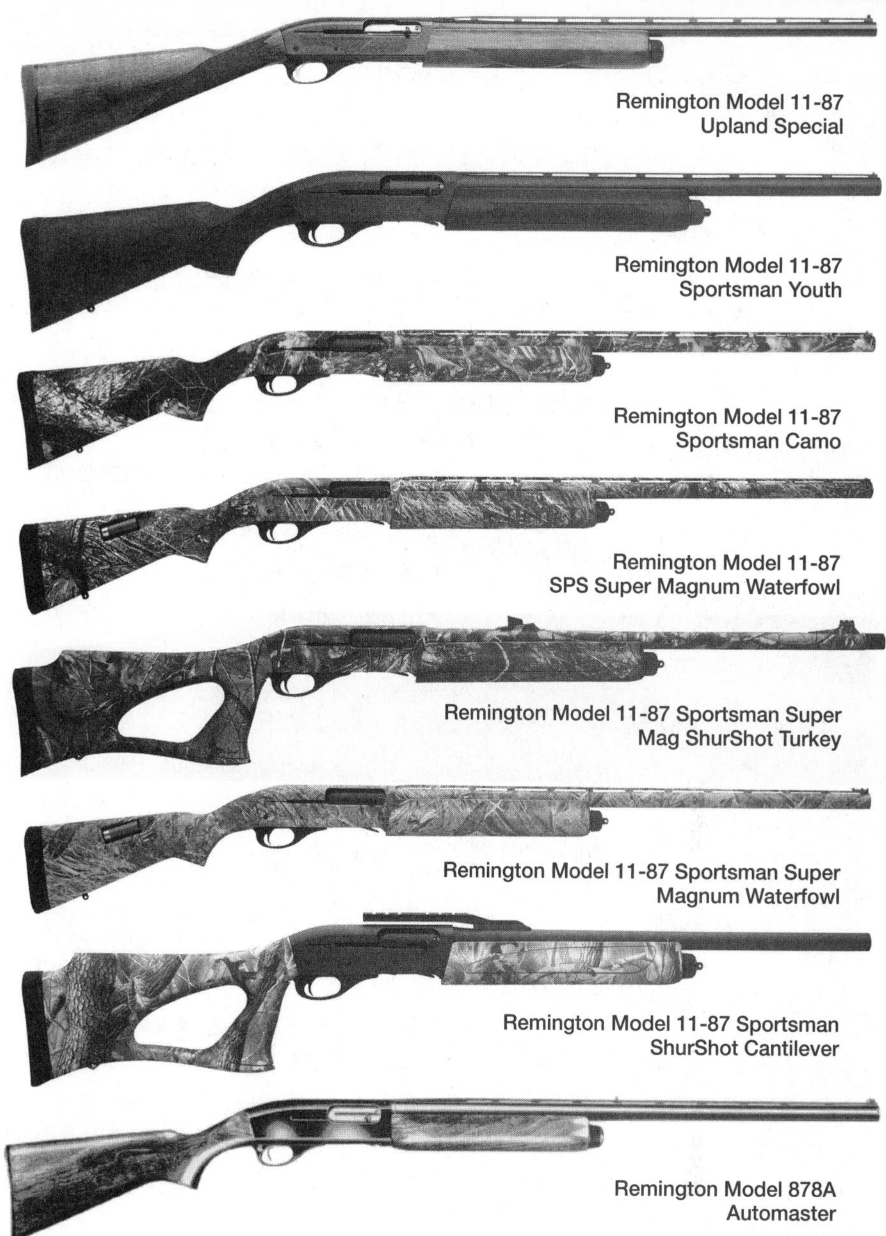

Remington Model 11-87 Upland Special

Remington Model 11-87 Sportsman Youth

Remington Model 11-87 Sportsman Camo

Remington Model 11-87 SPS Super Magnum Waterfowl

Remington Model 11-87 Sportsman Super Mag ShurShot Turkey

Remington Model 11-87 Sportsman Super Magnum Waterfowl

Remington Model 11-87 Sportsman ShurShot Cantilever

Remington Model 878A Automaster

REMINGTON MODEL 11-87 SPORTSMAN SUPER MAGNUM WATERFOWL

As above, but with full coverage in Mossy Oak Duck Blind camo and shell-holding Speedfeed stock and three choke tubes.

NIB: $750 **Exc:** $675 **VGood:** $550

REMINGTON MODEL 11-87 SPORTSMAN SHURSHOT CANTILEVER

This dedicated slug gun in 3-inch 12-gauge features a 23-inch, fully rifled barrel with cantilever scope mount. It is matte black with synthetic stock and forend finished in Realtree Hardwoods HD camo. Weight is about 8 lbs.

NIB: $750 **Exc:** $675 **VGood:** $550

REMINGTON MODEL 11-96 EURO LIGHTWEIGHT

Semi-auto 12-gauge with streamlined receiver. Based on 11-87 action. Fine line engraving on receiver, 26- or 28-inch barrel with Rem Choke tubes. Weight is 7 pounds. Manufactured only in 1996.

Perf: $900 **Exc:** $750 **VGood:** $600

REMINGTON MODEL 878A AUTOMASTER

Gas-operated autoloader; 12-ga.; 3-shot tube magazine; plain or vent rib; 26-inch Improved Cylinder; 28-inch Modified, 30-inch Full choke barrels; uncheckered pistol-grip stock, forend. Introduced 1959; discontinued 1962.

Plain barrel

Exc: $190 **VGood:** $160 **Good:** $130

Vent-rib barrel

Exc: $215 **VGood:** $185 **Good:** $155

REMINGTON MODEL 1100D TOURNAMENT

Gas-operated autoloader; hammerless; takedown; 12-, 16-, 20-, 28-ga., .410; 5-shot magazine; 26-inch, 28-inch, 30-inch vent-rib barrel; fixed or choke tubes; high-grade checkered walnut pistol-grip stock, forend; buttplate; engraving; custom-order gun. Introduced 1963.

Perf: $2900 **Exc:** $2050 **VGood:** $1425

REMINGTON MODEL 1100 DEER

Gas-operated autoloader; hammerless; takedown; 12-, 20-ga.; 5-shot magazine; 20-inch, 21-inch, 22-inch Improved Cylinder barrel; rifle sights; checkered walnut pistol-grip stock, forend; recoil pad. No longer in production.

Perf: $430 **Exc:** $350 **VGood:** $275

Left-hand model

Perf: $450 **Exc:** $370 **VGood:** $295

REMINGTON MODEL 1100 DEER SPECIAL PURPOSE

Same specs as Model 1100 Deer except matte finish on checkered walnut pistol-grip stock, forend; matte metal finish. Introduced 1986; discontinued 1986.

Perf: $335 **Exc:** $295 **VGood:** $275

REMINGTON MODEL 1100 DEER CANTILEVER 20-GAUGE

Same specs as Model 1100 Deer except 20-ga.; fully rifled 21-inch slug barrel; cantilever scope mount; sling; swivels. Introduced 1994; still in production.

Perf: $500 **Exc:** $350 **VGood:** $260

REMINGTON MODEL 1100F PREMIER

Gas-operated autoloader; hammerless; takedown; 12-, 16-, 20-, 28-ga., .410; 5-shot magazine; 26-inch, 28-inch, 30-inch vent-rib barrel; fixed or choke tubes; best-grade checkered walnut pistol-grip stock, forend; buttplate; engraving; custom-order gun. Introduced 1963; still in production.

Perf: $6000 **Exc:** $4400 **VGood:** $2850

REMINGTON MODEL 1100F PREMIER GOLD

Same specs as Model 110F Premier except gold inlays. Introduced 1963.

Perf: $9030 **Exc:** $5150 **VGood:** $3425

REMINGTON MODEL 1100 FIELD

Gas-operated autoloader; hammerless; takedown; 12-, 16-, 20-ga.; 5-shot magazine; 26-inch, 28-inch, 30-inch barrel; fixed or choke tubes; plain or vent rib; checkered walnut pistol-grip stock, forend; buttplate. Introduced 1963; discontinued 1988.

Plain barrel

Perf: $350 **Exc:** $290 **VGood:** $250

Vent-rib barrel

Perf: $395 **Exc:** $340 **VGood:** $295

REMINGTON MODEL 1100 FIELD COLLECTORS EDITION

Same specs as Model 1100 Field except positive cut-checkered, richly figured walnut stock; deep-relief etching; gold highlights; marketed with certificate showing serial number. Only 3000 made. Introduced 1981; discontinued 1981.

Perf: $1000 **Exc:** $650 **VGood:** $550

REMINGTON MODEL 1100 SPECIAL FIELD

Same specs as Model 1100 Field except 12-, 20-ga., .410; 23-inch vent-rib barrel; fixed or choke tubes; checkered walnut straight-grip stock, shortened forend; matte-finished receiver; no engraving. Introduced 1983.

Perf: $510 **Exc:** $410 **VGood:** $360

REMINGTON MODEL 1100 LIGHTWEIGHT MAGNUM

Same specs as Model 1100 Field except 20-ga.; 3-inch chamber; lightweight frame. Introduced 1977; no longer in production.

Plain barrel

Perf: $395 **Exc:** $320 **VGood:** $270

Vent rib

Perf: $425 **Exc:** $360 **VGood:** $310

REMINGTON MODEL 1100 LT-20

Same specs as Model 1100 Field except 20-ga.; 2-3/4-inch chamber; 26-inch, 28-inch plain barrel; 6-1/2 lbs.; satin or high-gloss mahogany pistol-grip stock, forend; lightweight receiver. Still in production.

Perf: $500 **Exc:** $415 **VGood:** $325

REMINGTON MODEL 1100 LT-20 SYNTHETIC

Gauge: 20. Barrel: 26-inch Rem-Chokes. Weight: 6-3/4 lbs. Stock: black synthetic, checkered pistol grip and forend. Features: Matted receiver top with scroll work on both sides of receiver.

Perf: $510 **Exc:** $410 **VGood:** $360

REMINGTON MODEL 1100 YOUTH GUN LT-20

Shortened synthetic stock with 21-inch barrel with Rem-Chokes.

Perf: $500 **Exc:** $400 **VGood:** $350

REMINGTON MODEL 1100 YOUTH SYNTHETIC TURKEY CAMO

Similar to the Model 1100 LT-20 except has 1-inch shorter stock, 21-inch vent rib barrel with Full Rem-Choke tube; 3-inch chamber; synthetic stock and forend are covered with RealTree Advantage camo, and barrel and receiver have non-reflective, black matte finish. Introduced 1999.

Perf: $500 **VGood:** $415 **Good:** $325

REMINGTON MODEL 1100 LT-20 SYNTHETIC DEER

Similar to the Model 1100 LT-20 except has 21-inch fully rifled barrel with rifle sights, 2-3/4-inch chamber, and fiberglass-reinforced synthetic stock. Introduced 1997.

Perf: $495 **Exc:** $375 **VGood:** $300

REMINGTON MODEL 1100 SYNTHETIC

12 gauge, and has black synthetic stock; vent. rib 28-inch barrel on 12 gauge, both with Mod. Rem-Choke tube. Weighs about 7-1/2 lbs. Introduced 1996.

Perf: $430 **Exc:** $340 **VGood:** $275

REMINGTON MODEL 1100 LT-20 TOURNAMENT SKEET

Same specs as Model 1100 except 20-, 28-ga., .410; 26-inch plain barrel; special Skeet choke; vent rib; ivory bead front, metal bead middle sights. No longer in production.

Perf: $500 **Exc:** $380 **VGood:** $300

REMINGTON MODEL 1100 MAGNUM DUCK GUN

Same specs as Model 1100 Field except 12-, 20-ga.; 3-inch chamber; 28-inch (20-ga.), 30-inch (12-ga.) barrel; recoil pad. Introduced 1963; discontinued 1988.

Plain barrel

Perf: $400 **Exc:** $300 **VGood:** $200

Vent-rib barrel

Perf: $425 **Exc:** $270 **VGood:** $225

REMINGTON MODEL 1100 MAGNUM SPECIAL PURPOSE

Same specs as Model 1100 Field except 12-ga.; 3-inch chamber; 26-inch, 30-inch vent-rib barrel; oil-finished wood; dark recoil pad; quick-detachable swivels; padded sling; chrome-lined bore; all exposed metal finished in nonreflective black. Introduced 1985; discontinued 1986.

Perf: $400 **Exc:** $300 **VGood:** $225

REMINGTON MODEL 1100 SPORTING 28

Similar to the 1100 LT-20 except in 28-gauge with 25-inch barrel; comes with Skeet, Imp. Cyl., Light Mod., Mod. Rem-Choke tube. Semi-Fancy walnut with gloss finish, Sporting rubber butt pad. Introduced 1996.

Perf: $750 **Exc:** $600 **VGood:** $525

REMINGTON MODEL 1100 SPORTING 20

Similar to Model 1100 LT-20 except tournament-grade American walnut stock with gloss finish and sporting-style recoil pad, 28-inch Rem-Choke barrel for Skeet, Imp. Cyl., Light Modified and Modified. Introduced 1998.

Perf: $720 **Exc:** $550 **VGood:** $475

REMINGTON MODEL 1100 CLASSIC TRAP

Similar to Standard Model 1100 except 12 gauge with 30-inch, low-profile barrel, semi-fancy American walnut stock, high-polish blued receiver with engraving and gold eagle inlay. Singles, mid handicap and long handicap choke tubes. Overall length 50-1/2-inch, weighs 8 lbs., 4 oz. Introduced 2000.

Perf: $735 **Exc:** $570 **VGood:** $485

REMINGTON MODEL 1100 SPORTING 12

Similar to Model 1100 Sporting 20 Shotgun except in 12-gauge, 28-inch ventilated barrel with semi-fancy American walnut stock, gold-plated trigger. Overall length 49-inch, weighs 8 lbs. Introduced 2000.

Perf: $720 **Exc:** $550 **VGood:** $475

REMINGTON MODEL 1100 SYNTHETIC DEER

Similar to Model 1100 LT-20 except 12-gauge, 21-inch fully rifled barrel with cantilever scope mount and fiberglass-reinforced synthetic stock with Monte Carlo comb. Introduced 1997.

Exc: $495 **VGood:** $375 **Good:** $310

REMINGTON MODEL 1100SA SKEET

Same specs as Model 1100 Field except Skeet boring; vent rib; ivory bead front sight, metal bead middle; cut checkering; new receiver scroll pattern. Introduced 1963; no longer made. Premium for small gauge.

Perf: $460 **Exc:** $375 **VGood:** $300

REMINGTON MODEL 1100SC SKEET

Same specs as Model 1100 Field except Skeet boring; vent rib; ivory bead front sight, metal bead middle; new receiver scroll pattern; selected wood. No longer made. Premium for small gauge.

Perf: $460 **Exc:** $375 **VGood:** $300

REMINGTON MODEL 1100TA TRAP

Same specs as Model 1100 Field except 12-ga.; 30-inch Full-choke barrel; recoil pad; right- or left-hand models. Introduced 1979; discontinued 1986.

Perf: $410 **Exc:** $330 **VGood:** $295

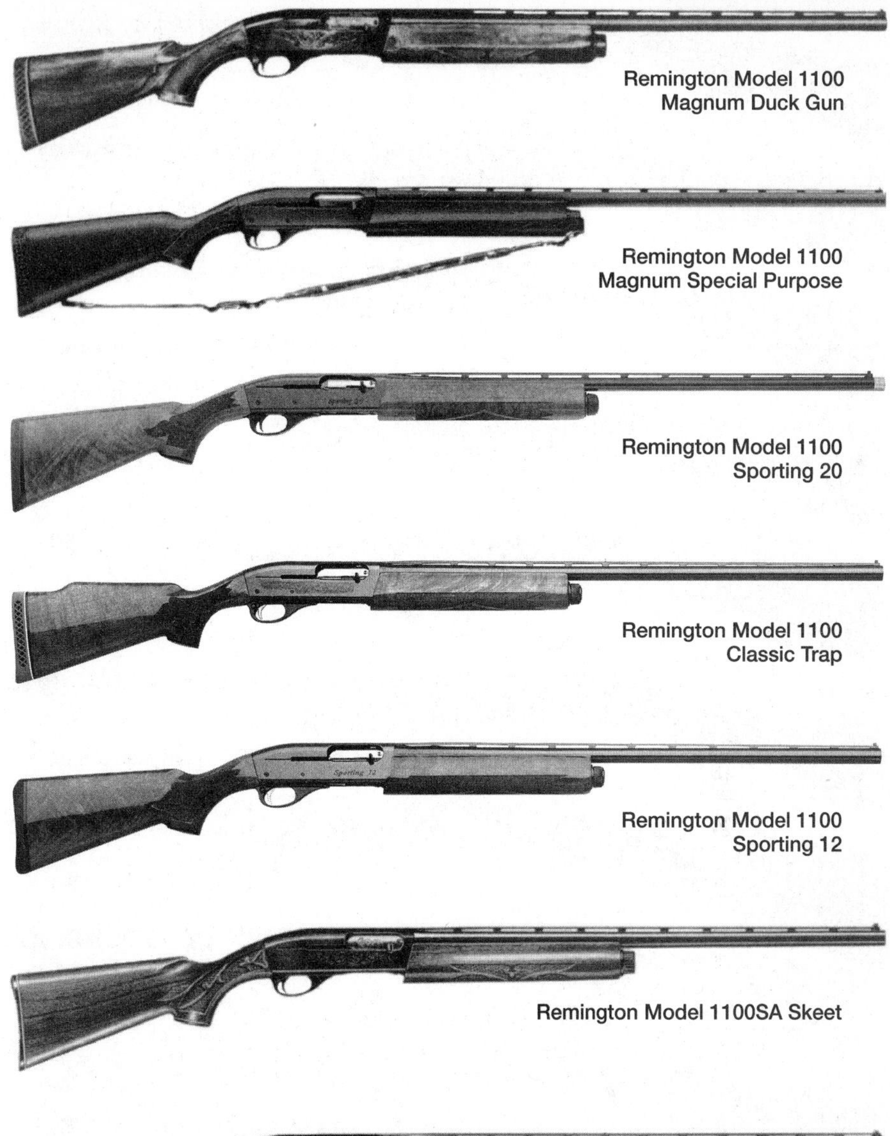

Remington Model 1100 Magnum Duck Gun

Remington Model 1100 Magnum Special Purpose

Remington Model 1100 Sporting 20

Remington Model 1100 Classic Trap

Remington Model 1100 Sporting 12

Remington Model 1100SA Skeet

Remington Model 1100TB Trap

REMINGTON MODEL 1100TB TRAP

Same specs as Model 1100 Field except 12-ga.; 30-inch Full-choke barrel; vent rib; trap-style stock; Monte Carlo or straight comb; recoil pad. Introduced 1963; discontinued 1981.

Straight-comb stock

Perf: $475 **Exc:** $400 **VGood:** $325

Monte Carlo stock

Perf: $495 **Exc:** $415 **VGood:** $340

REMINGTON MODEL 1100TD TRAP TOURNAMENT

Same specs as Model 1100 Field except 12-ga.; 30-inch Full-choke barrel; vent rib; select-grade trap-style stock; Monte Carlo or straight comb; recoil pad. Introduced 1979; discontinued 1986.

Straight-comb stock

Perf: $550 **Exc:** $400 **VGood:** $350

Monte Carlo stock

Perf: $570 **Exc:** $420 **VGood:** $370

REMINGTON MODEL 1100 YOUTH

Same specs as Model 1100 Field except 20-ga.; 2-3/4-inch chamber; 21-inch barrel; youth-sized mahogany stock, forend; lightweight receiver. Still in production.

Perf: $475 **Exc:** $340 **VGood:** $260

REMINGTON MODEL 1100 TACTICAL SPEEDFEED IV

All-black 2.75" 12 gauge has an 18" barrel with fixed Improved Cylinder choke and Speedfeed IV stock. Extended 6-round magazine. Weight is 7.5 lbs.

NIB: $725 **Exc:** $650 **VGood:** $535

REMINGTON MODEL 1100 TACTICAL STANDARD STOCK

Tactical 2.75" 12 gauge has 22" barrel threaded for Remchokes. Extended 8-round magazine.

NIB: $650 **Exc:** $595 **VGood:** $460

REMINGTON MODEL 1100 G3

Introduced in 2006, this updated 1100 features a Realwood high gloss semi-fancy stock and forend. Available in 12 and 20 gauges with 26-inch or 28-inch barrel and chambered for 3-inch shells. Includes five Pro Bore chokes for 12 gauge and five Rem chokes for 20 gauge, R3 recoil pad and high-grade travel case.

NIB: $695 **Exc:** $610 **VGood:** $500

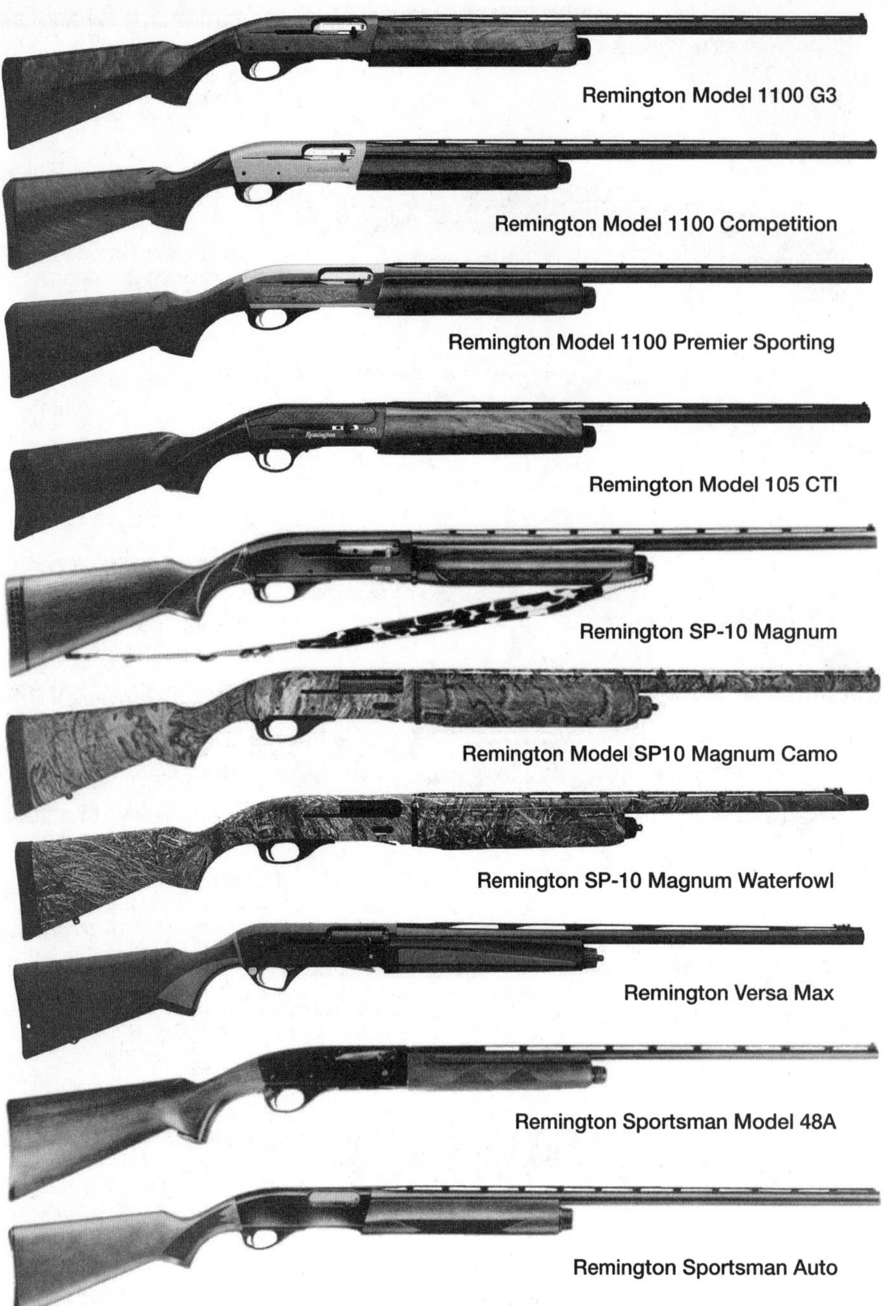

Remington Model 1100 G3

Remington Model 1100 Competition

Remington Model 1100 Premier Sporting

Remington Model 105 CTI

Remington SP-10 Magnum

Remington Model SP10 Magnum Camo

Remington SP-10 Magnum Waterfowl

Remington Versa Max

Remington Sportsman Model 48A

Remington Sportsman Auto

REMINGTON MODEL 1100 COMPETITION

This 12 gauge with 2.75-inch chamber is optimized for target shooting with a 30-inch overbored barrel and R3 recoil pad. Nickel-teflon receiver and semi-fancy walnut stock and forend. Includes five ProBore chokes. Weight is about 8 lbs. Add 10 percent for adjustable-comb model.

NIB: $915 **Exc:** $865 **VGood:** $695

REMINGTON MODEL 1100 PREMIER SPORTING

Introduced in 2008 as a dedicated sporting clays gun, the Premier Sporting comes in 12, 20 and 28 gauge and .410 bore with 2.75" chamber (3" in .410). Polished nickel receiver with fine-line embellishments and gold accents. Stock and forend are semi-fancy American walnut with high-gloss finish. A full line of Briley choke tubes and Premier Sporting hard case are included. Weights are about 8 lbs. in 12 gauge; 7 lbs. in 20 gauge; and 6.5 lbs. in 28 gauge and .410. Add 5 percent for 28 and .410.

BIN: $1250 **Exc:** $1050 **VGood:** $895

REMINGTON MODEL 105CTI

New in 2006, this ultralight gas-operated 12 gauge autoloader features advanced recoil reduction and bottom feed and ejection. Available with 26-inch or 28-inch barrel. Satin finish walnut stock. Chambered for 3-inch shells. Includes three Pro Bore chokes. Weighs about 7 lbs.

NIB: $825 **Exc:** $750 **VGood:** $665

REMINGTON SP-10 MAGNUM

Autoloader; 10-ga.; 3-1/2-inch chamber; 3-shot magazine; 26-inch, 30-1/2-inch barrel; Full, Modified Rem-Choke tubes; 47-1/2-inch overall length with shorter barrel; weighs about 11 lbs.; metal bead front sight; checkered satin-finished American walnut stock; brown recoil pad; padded Cordura sling; stainless steel gas system that lessens recoil; matte-finished receiver, barrel. Introduced 1989; still in production.

Perf: $995 **Exc:** $875 **VGood:** $785

Turkey Camo (26-inch vent rib barrel, Rem-Choke tube, Mossy Oak Break-up)

Exc: $1075 **VGood:** $885 **Good:** $785

REMINGTON SP-10 MAGNUM CAMO

Same specs as Model SP-10 Magnum except 23-inch vent-rib barrel; Extra-Full Turkey Rem-Choke tube; mid-rib bead, Bradley-style front sight; swivel studs; quick-detachable swivels; non-slip camo Cordura carrying sling; Mossy Oak Bottomland camo-finished buttstock, forend, receiver, barrel and magazine cap; matte black bolt body and trigger guard. Introduced 1993.

Perf: $1000 **Exc:** $900 **VGood:** $800

REMINGTON SP-10 MAGNUM TURKEY COMBO

Same specs as Model SP-10 except two-barrel set with 26-inch or 30-inch vent-rib barrel and extra 22-inch rifle-sighted barrel; Modified, Full, Extra-Full Turkey Rem-Choke tubes; camo sling; swivels. Introduced 1991; discontinued 1995.

Perf: $1295 **Exc:** $1125 **VGood:** $925

REMINGTON MODEL SP-10 MAGNUM WATERFOWL

New in 2007, this waterfowl-specific model is a synthetic-stock 3.5" 10 gauge with Mossy Oak Duck Blind camo finish and 26" barrel. Includes three Briley ported choke tubes. Weight is about 10.9 lbs.

NIB: $1475 **Exc:** $1325 **VGood:** $1095

REMINGTON MODEL SP-10 MAGNUM THUMBHOLE CAMO

Special turkey model features a synthetic thumbhole stock and complete Mossy Oak Obsession camo finish. Barrel is 23". Briley ported turkey choke included. Weight is 10.9 lbs.

NIB: $1675 **Exc:** $1595 **VGood:** $1295

REMINGTON VERSA MAX

Semi-auto in 12-gauge only. Designed to shoot all loads from light 2¾-inches to 3½-inch magnums. Synthetic stock in black finish or camo is fully adjustable for length of pull, comb height and cast. Introduced in 2011.

Perf: $1150 **Exc:** $1000 **VGood:** $850

REMINGTON SPORTSMAN AUTO

Autoloader; 12-ga.; 2-3/4-inch chamber; 5-shot tube magazine; 28-inch, 30-inch vent-rib barrel; fixed or choke tubes; 7 3/4-inch lbs.; walnut-stained hardwood pistol-grip stock, forend; buttplate. Introduced 1985; discontinued 1986.

Perf: $300 **Exc:** $260 **VGood:** $220

REMINGTON SPORTSMAN MODEL 48A

Autoloader; hammerless; takedown; 12-, 16-, 20-ga.; 3-shot tube magazine; 26-inch Improved Cylinder, 28-inch Modified or Full, 30-inch Full-choke barrel; plain matted or vent-rib barrel available; hand-checkered American walnut pistol-grip stock, grooved forend; streamlined receiver. Introduced 1949; discontinued 1959. The last of Remington's recoil-operated autoloaders.

Plain barrel

Exc: $210 **VGood:** $165 **Good:** $130

Vent-rib barrel

Exc: $240 **VGood:** $195 **Good:** $160

NOTE: Values for the following higher grades of the Remington 48 fluctuate and may approach $10,000 for the 48F Premiere grade.

REMINGTON SPORTSMAN MODEL 48B SPECIAL

Same specs as Model 48A except high-quality wood, checkering; engraved receiver. Introduced 1949; discontinued 1959.

REMINGTON SPORTSMAN MODEL 48D TOURNAMENT

Same specs as 48A except improved wood; finer checkering; more engraving. Introduced 1949; discontinued 1959.

REMINGTON SPORTSMAN MODEL 48F PREMIER
Same specs as 48A except top-quality wood; fully engraved receiver. Introduced 1949; discontinued 1959.

REMINGTON SPORTSMAN MODEL 48SA SKEET
Autoloader; hammerless; takedown; 12-, 16-, 20-ga.; 3-shot magazine; 26-inch Skeet-choke barrel; plain matted surface or vent rib; ivory bead front sight, metal bead rear; checkered American walnut pistol-grip stock, forend. Introduced 1949; discontinued 1960.

Plain barrel
Exc: $305 **VGood:** $275 **Good:** $255

Vent-rib barrel
Exc: $395 **VGood:** $350 **Good:** $300

REMINGTON SPORTSMAN MODEL 48SC SKEET TARGET
Same specs as Model 48SA Skeet except higher grade of wood, checkering and engraving. Introduced 1949; discontinued 1960.
Exc: $360 **VGood:** $330 **Good:** $290

REMINGTON MODEL 48SF SKEET PREMIER
Same specs as Model 48SA Skeet except best grade of wood, checkering and engraving. Introduced 1949; discontinued 1960.
Exc: $2035 **VGood:** $1500 **Good:** $1200

REMINGTON SPORTSMAN MODEL 58ADL
Gas-operated autoloader; 12-ga.; 3-shot tube magazine; 26-inch, 28-inch, 30-inch barrels; plain or vent rib; Improved Cylinder, Modified, Full choke, Remington Skeet boring; checkered pistol-grip stock, forend. Introduced 1956; discontinued 1964.

Plain barrel
Exc: $250 **VGood:** $220 **Good:** $190

Vent-rib barrel
Exc: $300 **VGood:** $275 **Good:** $250

REMINGTON SPORTSMAN MODEL 58BDL DELUXE SPECIAL
Same specs as Sportsman Model 58ADL except higher grade of walnut wood. Introduced 1956; discontinued 1964.
Exc: $260 **VGood:** $220 **Good:** $190

REMINGTON SPORTSMAN MODEL 58D TOURNAMENT
Same specs as Sportsman Model 58ADL except vent rib; select grade of wood, checkering and engraving. Introduced 1956; discontinued 1964.
Exc: $700 **VGood:** $600 **Good:** $530

REMINGTON SPORTSMAN MODEL 58F PREMIER
Same specs as Sportsman Model 58ADL except vent rib; best grade of wood, checkering and engraving. Introduced 1956; discontinued 1964.
Exc: $1375 **VGood:** $1210 **Good:** $1000

REMINGTON SPORTSMAN MODEL 58SA SKEET
Gas-operated autoloader; 12-ga.; 3-shot tube magazine; 26-inch vent-rib barrel; Skeet choke; special Skeet-style stock, forend. Introduced 1956; discontinued 1964.
Exc: $330 **VGood:** $300 **Good:** $270

REMINGTON SPORTSMAN MODEL 58SC SKEET TARGET
Same specs as Sportsman Model 58SA Skeet except higher grade of wood, checkering and engraving. Introduced 1956; discontinued 1964.
Exc: $400 **VGood:** $325 **Good:** $260

REMINGTON SPORTSMAN MODEL 58SD SKEET TOURNAMENT
Same specs as Sportsman Model 58SA Skeet except select grade of wood, checkering and engraving. Introduced 1956; discontinued 1964.
Exc: $605 **VGood:** $500 **Good:** $430

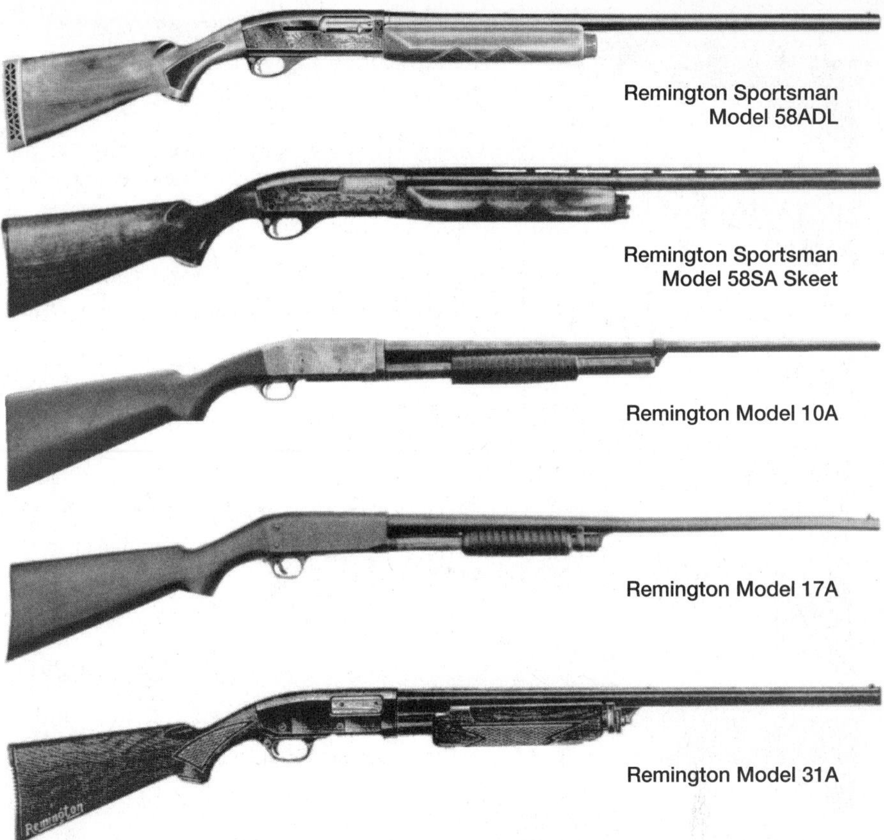
Remington Sportsman Model 58ADL

Remington Sportsman Model 58SA Skeet

Remington Model 10A

Remington Model 17A

Remington Model 31A

REMINGTON SPORTSMAN MODEL 58SF SKEET PREMIER
Same specs as Sportsman Model 58SA Skeet except best grade of wood, checkering and engraving. Introduced 1956; discontinued 1964.
Exc: $1125 **VGood:** $1025 **Good:** $950

REMINGTON MODEL 10A
Slide action; hammerless; takedown; 12-ga.; 6-shot tube magazine; 26-inch, 28-inch, 30-inch, 32-inch barrel; Full, Modified, Cylinder choke; uncheckered pistol-grip stock, grooved slide handle. Introduced 1907; discontinued 1929.
Exc: $270 **VGood:** $195 **Good:** $170

REMINGTON MODEL 17A
Slide action; hammerless; takedown; 26-inch, 28-inch, 30-inch, 32-inch barrel; plain barrel or solid rib; Modified, Full, Cylinder choke; uncheckered stock with pistol grip, grooved slide handle; Browning design. Introduced 1921; discontinued 1933.

Plain barrel
Exc: $275 **VGood:** $220 **Good:** $195

Solid rib
Exc: $375 **VGood:** $325 **Good:** $290

REMINGTON MODEL 29A
Slide action; hammerless; takedown; 12-ga.; 5-shot tubular magazine; 26-inch, 28-inch, 30-inch, 32-inch barrel; plain barrel, solid or vent rib; Full, Modified, Cylinder choke; hand-checkered pistol-grip stock, slide handle. Introduced 1929; discontinued 1933.

Plain barrel
Exc: $250 **VGood:** $230 **Good:** $200

Solid rib
Exc: $290 **VGood:** $265 **Good:** $230

Vent rib
Exc: $310 **VGood:** $275 **Good:** $240

REMINGTON MODEL 29S TRAP SPECIAL
Same specs as Model 29A except ventilated rib; on trap-style straight-grip stock, longer slide handle. No longer in production.
Exc: $450 **VGood:** $425 **Good:** $370

REMINGTON MODEL 31A
Slide action; hammerless; takedown 12-, 16-, 20-ga.; 3-, 5-shot magazine; 26-inch, 28-inch, 30-inch, 32-inch barrel; plain barrel, solid or vent rib; Full, Modified, Improved Cylinder, Skeet choke; early models had checkered pistol-grip stock, slide handle; later styles had plain stock, grooved slide handle. Introduced 1931; discontinued 1949.

Plain barrel
Exc: $345 **VGood:** $300 **Good:** $265

Solid rib
Exc: $385 **VGood:** $345 **Good:** $300

Vent rib
Exc: $415 **VGood:** $375 **Good:** $325

NOTE: Values for the following higher grades of the Remington 31 fluctuate and may approach $10,000 for the 31F Premiere grade.

REMINGTON MODEL 31B SPECIAL
Same specs as Model 31A except higher grade of wood, checkering and engraving. Introduced 1931; discontinued 1949.

REMINGTON MODEL 31D TOURNAMENT
Same specs as Model 31A except select grade of wood, checkering and engraving. Introduced 1931; discontinued 1949.

REMINGTON MODEL 31E EXPERT
Same specs as Model 31A except fine grade of wood, checkering and engraving. Introduced 1931; discontinued 1949.

REMINGTON MODEL 31F PREMIER
Same specs as Model 31A except best grade of wood, checkering and engraving. Introduced 1931; discontinued 1949.

REMINGTON MODEL 31H HUNTER'S SPECIAL
Same specs as Model 31A except 12-ga.; 30-inch, 32-inch solid-rib barrel; Full choke; sporting uncheckered walnut pistol-grip stock, forend. Introduced 1931; discontinued 1949.
Exc: $350 **VGood:** $300 **Good:** $250

Remington Model 31S Trap Special

Remington Model 870 Competition Trap

Remington Model 870 Express

Remington Model 870 SPS Super Slug Deer Gun

Remington Model 870 Express Youth

REMINGTON MODEL 31R RIOT GUN

Same specs as Model 31A except 12-ga.; 20-inch barrel. Introduced 1931; discontinued 1949.

Exc: $365 **VGood:** $325 **Good:** $295

REMINGTON MODEL 31S TRAP SPECIAL

Same specs as Model 31A except 12-ga.; 30-inch, 32-inch solid-rib barrel; Full choke; trap-style uncheckered walnut half-pistol-grip stock, forend. Introduced 1931; discontinued 1949.

Exc: $500 **VGood:** $450 **Good:** $400

REMINGTON MODEL 31 SKEET

Same specs as Model 31A except 26-inch barrel; solid or vent rib; Skeet choke; beavertail forend. Introduced 1931; discontinued 1949.

Solid rib

Exc: $450 **VGood:** $395 **Good:** $365

Vent rib

Exc: $550 **VGood:** $495 **Good:** $425

REMINGTON MODEL 31TC TRAP

Same as Model 31A except 12-ga.; 30-inch, 32-inch vent-rib barrel; Full choke; trap-style checkered walnut pistol-grip stock, beavertail forend; recoil pad. Introduced 1931; discontinued 1948.

Exc: $750 **VGood:** $600 **Good:** $520

REMINGTON MODEL 870ADL WINGMASTER

Slide action; hammerless; takedown; 12-, 16-, 20-ga.; 5-shot tube magazine; 3-shot plug furnished with gun; 26-inch Improved Cylinder, 28-inch Modified or Full, 30-inch Full barrel; choice of plain, matted top surface or vent rib; fine-checkered pistol-grip stock, beavertail forend. Introduced 1950; discontinued 1963.

Plain barrel

Exc: $250 **VGood:** $200 **Good:** $180

Vent rib

Exc: $375 **VGood:** $300 **Good:** $250

REMINGTON MODEL 870 ALL-AMERICAN TRAP

Slide action; hammerless; takedown; 12-ga.; 5-shot tube magazine; 30-inch Full-choke barrel; fancy American walnut straight-comb or Monte Carlo stock, forend; custom-grade engraved receiver, trigger guard, barrel. Introduced 1972; discontinued 1976.

Exc: $600 **VGood:** $500 **Good:** $425

REMINGTON MODEL 870AP WINGMASTER

Slide action; hammerless; takedown; 12-, 16-, 20-ga.; 5-shot tube magazine; 3-shot plug furnished with gun; 26-inch Improved Cylinder, 28-inch Modified or Full, 30-inch Full barrel; choice of plain, matted top surface or vent rib; walnut stock, grooved slide handle. Introduced 1950; discontinued 1963.

Plain barrel

Exc: $300 **VGood:** $250 **Good:** $200

Vent rib

Exc: $375 **VGood:** $300 **Good:** $250

REMINGTON MODEL 870AP WINGMASTER MAGNUM

Same specs as Model 870AP Wingmaster except 12-ga.; 3-inch chamber; 30-inch Full-choke barrel; recoil pad. Introduced 1955; discontinued 1963.

Plain barrel

Exc: $300 **VGood:** $250 **Good:** $200

Vent rib

Exc: $350 **VGood:** $300 **Good:** $250

REMINGTON MODEL 870AP WINGMASTER MAGNUM DELUXE

Same specs as Model 870AP Wingmaster except 12-ga.; 3-inch chamber; 30-inch Full-choke barrel; checkered stock, extension beavertail slide handle; matte top surface barrel.

Exc: $350 **VGood:** $300 **Good:** $250

REMINGTON MODEL 870BDL WINGMASTER

Same specs as Model 870AP Wingmaster except select American walnut pistol-grip stock, forend. Introduced 1950; discontinued 1963.

Plain barrel

Exc: $190 **VGood:** $155 **Good:** $125

Vent rib

Exc: $240 **VGood:** $190 **Good:** $165

REMINGTON MODEL 870 BRUSHMASTER DELUXE

Same specs as Model 870AP Wingmaster except 12-, 20-ga.; 2-3/4-inch, 3-inch chamber; 20-inch barrel; Improved Cylinder or choke tube; adjustable rear sight, ramp front; satin-finished checkered wood stock, forearm; recoil pad; right- or left-hand model. Discontinued 1994.

Right-hand model

Perf: $350 **Exc:** $275 **VGood:** $250

Left-hand model

Perf: $350 **Exc:** $275 **VGood:** $250

REMINGTON MODEL 870 COMPETITION TRAP

Same specs as Model 870AP Wingmaster except single shot; 12-ga.; 30-inch vent-rib barrel; Full choke; select walnut Trap-style stock, forend; gas reduction system to lessen recoil. Introduced 1980; discontinued 1986.

Perf: $480 **Exc:** $390 **VGood:** $300

REMINGTON MODEL 870 EXPRESS

Slide action; hammerless; takedown; 12-, 20-, 28-ga., .410; 5-shot tube magazine; 3-shot plug furnished with gun; 20-inch, 25-inch, 26-inch, 28-inch vent. rib barrel; Modified Rem-Choke tube; press-checkered, walnut-finished hardwood stock, forearm; solid black recoil pad; Parkerized metal surfaces. Introduced 1987.

12-ga., 20-ga.

Perf: $265 **Exc:** $215 **VGood:** $180

Express Combo, 12-ga., 26-inch vent rib with mod. Rem-Choke and 20-inch fully rifled barrel with rifle sights, or Rem. Choke

Perf: $412 **Exc:** $362 **VGood:** $327

Express L-H (left-hand), 12-ga., 28-inch vent rib with Mod. Rem-Choke tube

Perf: $562 **Exc:** $472 **VGood:** $412

Synthetic, 12-ga, 26-inch or 28-inch

Perf: $265 **Exc:** $215 **VGood:** $180

Express Combo (20-ga.) with extra Deer rifled barrel, fully rifled or Rem. Choke

Perf: $412 **Exc:** $362 **VGood:** $327

REMINGTON MODEL 870 EXPRESS SYNTHETIC 18-INCH

Similar to 870 Express with 18-inch barrel except synthetic stock and forend. Introduced 1994.

Perf: $250 **Exc:** $205 **VGood:** $170

REMINGTON MODEL 870 SPS SUPER SLUG DEER GUN

Similar to the Model 870 Express Synthetic except has 23-inch fully rifled, modified contour barrel with cantilever scope mount. Comes with black synthetic stock and forend with swivel studs, black Cordura nylon sling. Introduced 1999.

Perf: $470 **Exc:** $375 **VGood:** $310

REMINGTON MODEL 870 EXPRESS YOUTH GUN

Same as Model 870 Express except 13-inch length of pull, 20-gauge, 23-inch barrel with Mod. Rem-Choke tube. Weighs 6.25 lbs. Hardwood stock with low-luster finish. Introduced 1991.

Perf: $265 **Exc:** $215 **VGood:** $180

Youth Deer 20-inch FR/RS

Perf: $298 **Exc:** $248 **VGood:** $213

REMINGTON MODEL 870 EXPRESS RIFLE-SIGHTED DEER GUN

Same as Model 870 Express except 20-inch barrel with fixed Imp. Cyl. choke, open iron sights, Monte Carlo stock. Introduced 1991.

Perf: $265 **Exc:** $215 **VGood:** $180

W/fully rifled barrel

Perf: $298 **Exc:** $248 **VGood:** $213

Synthetic Deer (black synthetic stock, black matte metal)

Perf: $295 **Exc:** $225 **VGood:** $185

REMINGTON MODEL 870 EXPRESS DEER CANTILEVER

Same specs as Model 870 Express except 12-ga.; 20-inch smooth bore or rifled barrel; fixed Improved Cylinder Rem-Chokes for slugs or buckshot; barrel-mounted cantilever scope mount; scope rings; Monte Carlo stock; sling; swivels; Introduced 1991; discontinued 1992.

Smooth bore barrel

Perf: $300 **Exc:** $235 **VGood:** $200

Rifled barrel

Perf: $330 **Exc:** $265 **VGood:** $230

REMINGTON MODEL 870 EXPRESS HD

Same specs as Model 870 Express except 12-ga.; 18-inch Cylinder barrel; bead front sight; positive-checkered synthetic stock, forend with non-reflective black finish. Introduced 1995; still in production.

Perf: $250 **Exc:** $180 **VGood:** $160

REMINGTON MODEL 870 EXPRESS SYNTHETIC

Same specs as Model 870 Express except 12-, 20-ga.; 26-inch, 28-inch barrel; synthetic stock, forend. Made in U.S. by Remington. Introduced 1994; still in production.

Perf: $265 **Exc:** $215 **VGood:** $180

REMINGTON MODEL 870 EXPRESS TURKEY

Same specs as Model 870 Express except 12-ga.; 3-chamber; 21-inch vent-rib barrel; Extra-Full Rem-Choke turkey tube. Introduced 1991; still in production.

Perf: $275 **Exc:** $215 **VGood:** $185

REMINGTON MODEL 870 EXPRESS YOUTH

Same specs as Model 870 Express except 20-ga.; 21-inch vent-rib barrel; Modified Rem-Choke; low-luster hardwood stock; 12-inch length of pull. Introduced 1991; still in production.

Perf: $265 **Exc:** $215 **VGood:** $180

REMINGTON MODEL 870 EXPRESS TURKEY/ EXPRESS YOUTH

Same as Model 870 Express except 3-inch chamber, 21-inch vent rib turkey barrel and Extra-Full Rem. choke turkey tube; 12-ga. only. Introduced 1991.

Perf: $270 **Exc:** $215 **VGood:** $185

Camo stock w/RealTree Advantage camo, matte black metal

Perf: $324 **Exc:** $269 **VGood:** $239

Youth Turkey camo (as above with 1-inch shorter length of pull)

Perf: $332 **Exc:** $282 **VGood:** $247

REMINGTON MODEL 870 EXPRESS SUPER MAGNUM

Introduced in 1998, this 870 is similar to the 870 Express but is chambered for 3.5" 12 gauge. Offered in walnut stock with blued 28" barrel, matte black synthetic with 26" or 28" barrel or various camo finishes. Also available as a combo with extra 20" rifled deer barrel. Add $100 for camo. Add 20 percent for combo with deer barrel.

Perf: $295 **Exc:** $230 **VGood:** $190

Price: Super Magnum Synthetic

Perf: $308 **Exc:** $243 **VGood:** $203

Remington Model 870 Express Rifle-Sighted Deer

Remington Model 870 Express HD

Remington Model 870 Express Turkey

Remington Model 870 Express Super Magnum

Remington Model 870 Express Deer/Turkey Combo

Remington Model 870 50th Anniversary Classic Trap Shotgun

Turkey Camo (Turkey Extra Full Rem-Choke, full-coverage RealTree Advantage camo)

Perf: $395 **Exc:** $315 **VGood:** $250

Combo (26-inch with Mod. Rem-Choke and 20-inch fully rifled deer barrel with 3-inch chamber and rifle sights; wood stock)

Perf: $442 **Exc:** $377 **VGood:** $337

Synthetic Turkey (black)

Perf: $308 **Exc:** $243 **VGood:** $203

REMINGTON MODEL 870 EXPRESS DEER/TURKEY COMBO

This 3" 12 gauge has a 21-inch barrel threaded for Remchokes for turkey hunting and a 23" rifled slug barrel with cantilever scope mount for deer hunting. Receiver and barrel are matte black; synthetic stock is Mossy Oak Break-Up camo.

NIB: $545 **Exc:** $485 **VGood:** $375

REMINGTON MODEL 870 WINGMASTER

Gauge: 12-, 16-ga., 3-inch chamber; 26-inch, 28-inch, 30-inch barrel (Rem-Chokes); weighs 7-1/4 lbs.; 46-inch, 48-inch overall; walnut, hardwood, synthetic; single bead sight (Twin bead Wingmaster); ballistically balanced performance, milder recoil; light contour barrel; double action bars; cross-bolt safety; blue finish.

Walnut; blued; 26-inch, 28-inch

Exc: $275 **VGood:** $250 **Good:** $220

Super Magnum, 3-1/2-inch chamber

Exc: $295 **VGood:** $230 **Good:** $190

Express, 28-inch, vent rib

Exc: $250 **VGood:** $220 **Good:** $200

Synthetic

Exc: $265 **VGood:** $215 **Good:** $180

REMINGTON MODEL 870 50TH ANNIVERSARY CLASSIC TRAP SHOTGUN

Similar to Model 870 Wingmaster except has 30-inch ventilated rib, light contour barrel, singles, mid and long handicap choke tubes, semi-fancy American walnut stock, high-polish blued receiver with engraving.

Perf: $695 **Exc:** $565 **VGood:** $470

REMINGTON MODEL 870 MARINE MAGNUM

Similar to 870 Wingmaster except all metal plated with electroless nickel, black synthetic stock and forend. Has 18-inch plain barrel (Cyl.), bead front sight, 7-shot magazine. Introduced 1992.

Perf: $430 **Exc:** $355 **VGood:** $275

REMINGTON MODEL 870 WINGMASTER LW SMALL BORE

Similar to Model 870 Wingmaster except in 28-gauge and .410-bore only, 25-inch vent rib barrel with Rem-Choke tubes, high-gloss wood finish. 26-inch & 28-inch barrels/20-ga.

20-gauge

Perf: $535 **Exc:** $445 **VGood:** $385

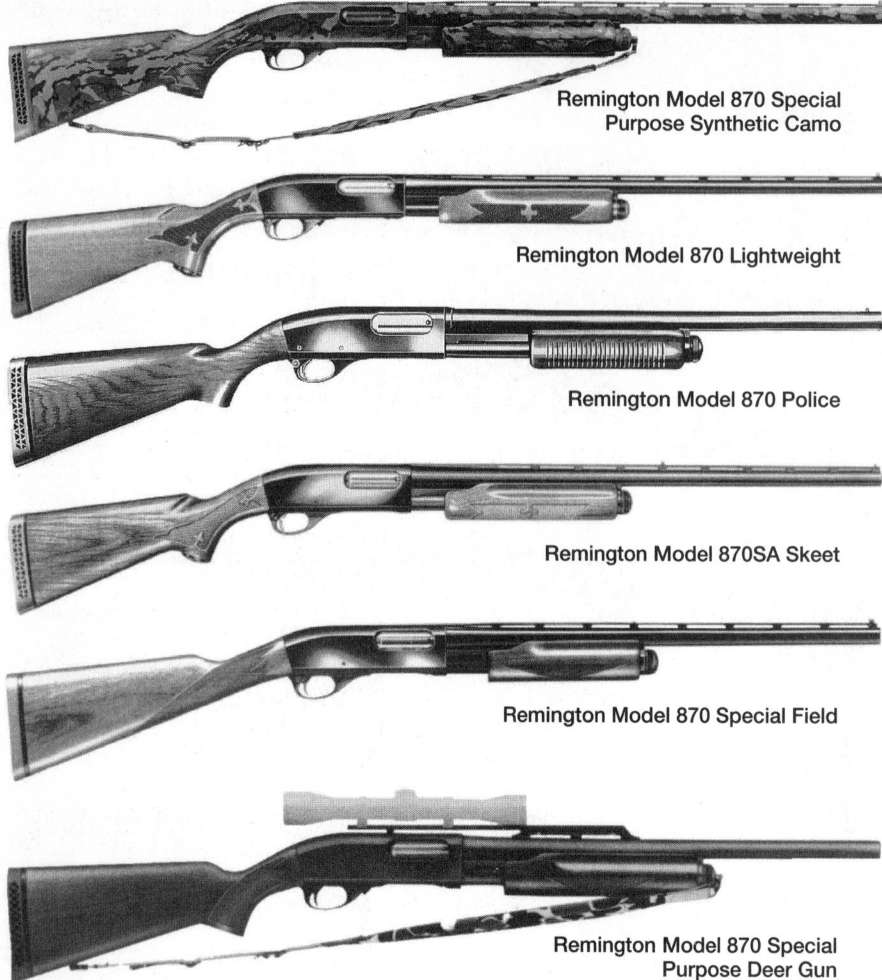

Remington Model 870 Special Purpose Synthetic Camo

Remington Model 870 Lightweight

Remington Model 870 Police

Remington Model 870SA Skeet

Remington Model 870 Special Field

Remington Model 870 Special Purpose Deer Gun

.410-bore

Perf: $535 **Exc:** $445 **VGood:** $385

28-gauge

Perf: $588 **Exc:** $498 **VGood:** $438

REMINGTON MODEL 870 WINGMASTER SUPER MAGNUM

Similar to Model 870 Express Super Magnum except high-polish blued finish, 28-inch vent-rib barrel with Imp. Cyl., Modified and Full choke tubes, 3-1/2-inch chamber, checkered high-gloss walnut stock. Overall length 48-inch, weighs 7 1/2 lbs. Introduced 2000.

Perf: $560 **Exc:** $475 **VGood:** $395

REMINGTON MODEL 870 SPS-T SYNTHETIC CAMO

Chambered for 12-ga., 3-inch shells, has Mossy Oak Break-Up synthetic stock and metal treatment, TruGlo fiber optic sights. Introduced 2001.

20-inch RS, Rem. Choke

Perf: $445 **Exc:** $350 **VGood:** $280

REMINGTON MODEL 870 SPS SUPER MAGNUM CAMO

Has synthetic stock and all metal (except bolt and trigger guard) and stock covered with Mossy Oak Break-Up camo finish. In 12 gauge 3-1/2-inch, 26-inch, 28-inch vent rib, Rem-Choke. Comes with camo sling, swivels.

Perf: $385 **Exc:** $320 **VGood:** $265

REMINGTON MODEL 870 FIELD WINGMASTER

Slide action; hammerless; takedown; 12-, 16-, 20-, 28-ga., .410; 5-shot tube magazine; 25-inch Full or Modified, 26-inch Improved Cylinder, 28-inch Modified or Full, 30-inch Full barrel; fixed or Rem-Choke tubes; choice of plain, matted top surface or vent rib; checkered walnut stock, slide handle with high-gloss or satin finish. Introduced 1965; still in production.

Plain barrel

Perf: $300 **Exc:** $200 **VGood:** $140

Vent rib

Perf: $425 **Exc:** $350 **VGood:** $295

REMINGTON MODEL 870 LIGHTWEIGHT

Slide action; hammerless; takedown; 20-ga.; 5-shot magazine; 23-inch barrel; plain or vent rib; 5 lbs.; lightweight mahogany stock, forearm. Introduced 1972; discontinued 1983.

Plain barrel

Perf: $265 **Exc:** $200 **VGood:** $175

Vent rib

Perf: $300 **Exc:** $235 **VGood:** $210

REMINGTON MODEL 870 LIGHTWEIGHT MAGNUM

Same specs as Model 870 Lightweight except 3-inch chamber; 26-inch, 28-inch barrel; fixed or choke tubes; plain or vent rib; 6 lbs.; lightweight mahogany stock, forearm. Introduced 1972; discontinued 1994.

Plain barrel

Perf: $300 **Exc:** $210 **VGood:** $175

Vent rib

Perf: $350 **Exc:** $250 **VGood:** $200

REMINGTON MODEL 870 MAGNUM DUCK GUN

Slide action; hammerless; takedown; 12-, 20-ga.; 3-inch chamber; 26-inch, 28-inch, 30-inch vent-rib barrel; Full or Modified choke; checkered walnut stock, slide handle; recoil pad. Introduced 1964; still in production.

Perf: $385 **Exc:** $265 **VGood:** $210

REMINGTON MODEL 870 MARINE MAGNUM

Slide action; hammerless; takedown; 12-ga.; 3-inch chamber; 7-shot magazine; 18-inch plain barrel; Cylinder choke; bead front sight; black synthetic stock, forend; electroless nickel-plated metal surfaces. Introduced 1992; still in production.

Perf: $400 **Exc:** $280 **VGood:** $210

REMINGTON MODEL 870 POLICE

Slide action; hammerless; takedown; 12-ga.; 3-inch chamber; 18-inch, 20-inch Police Cylinder or 20-inch Improved Cylinder; weighs 7 lbs.; metal bead front or rifle sights; lacquered hardwood stock; steel receiver; double slide bars; blued or Parkerized finish. Introduced 1994; still in production.

Perf: $350 **Exc:** $295 **VGood:** $230

REMINGTON MODEL 870SA SKEET

Slide action; hammerless; takedown; 12-, 20-, 28-ga., .410; 5-shot tube magazine; 26-inch vent-rib barrel; Skeet choke; ivory bead front sight, metal bead in rear; checkered pistol-grip stock, extension beavertail slide handle. Introduced 1950; discontinued 1982.

Perf: $300 **Exc:** $250 **VGood:** $200

REMINGTON MODEL 870SC SKEET TARGET

Same specs as Model 870SA Skeet except higher grade of wood, checkering and engraving. Introduced 1950; discontinued 1982.

Perf: $350 **Exc:** $300 **VGood:** $250

REMINGTON MODEL 870SD SKEET TOURNAMENT

Same specs as Model 870SA Skeet except select grade of wood, checkering and engraving. Introduced 1950; discontinued 1982.

Perf: $450 **Exc:** $375 **VGood:** $275

REMINGTON MODEL 870SF SKEET PREMIER

Same specs as Model 870SA Skeet except best grade of wood, checkering and engraving. Introduced 1950; discontinued 1982.

Perf: $500 **Exc:** $450 **VGood:** $300

REMINGTON MODEL 870 SPECIAL FIELD

Slide action; hammerless; takedown; 12-, 20-ga.; 3-inch chamber; 21-inch, 23-inch vent-rib barrel; fixed or choke tubes; checkered straight-grip stock, short forend. Introduced 1984.

Perf: $500 **Exc:** $465 **VGood:** $410

REMINGTON MODEL 870 SPECIAL PURPOSE

Slide action; hammerless; takedown; 12-ga.; 3-inch chamber; 26-inch, 28-inch vent-rib barrel; Rem-Choke tubes; oil-finished wood or black synthetic stock, forend; quick detachable sling swivels; padded sling; black metal finish; chrome-lined bore. Introduced 1985.

Synthetic stock

Perf: $325 **Exc:** $250 **VGood:** $200

Wood stock

Perf: $385 **Exc:** $310 **VGood:** $260

REMINGTON MODEL 870 SPECIAL PURPOSE DEER GUN

Same specs as Model 870 Special Purpose except 20-inch barrel; rifled and Improved Cylinder choke tubes; rifle sights or cantilever scope mount with rings; walnut Monte Carlo stock with satin finish; recoil pad; detachable camo Cordura nylon sling; black, non-glare metal finish. Introduced 1989.

With rifle sights

Perf: $350 **Exc:** $250 **VGood:** $200

With scope mount and rings

Perf: $400 **Exc:** $300 **VGood:** $250

REMINGTON MODEL 870 SPECIAL PURPOSE SYNTHETIC CAMO

Same specs as Model 870 Special Purpose except 26-inch vent-rib barrel; Rem-Choke tubes; synthetic stock; all surfaces (except bolt and trigger guard) Mossy Oak Bottomland camo-finished; camo sling; swivels. Introduced 1992.

Perf: $380 **Exc:** $260 **VGood:** $205

REMINGTON MODEL 870 SPS-BG-CAMO DEER/TURKEY

Same specs as Model 870 Special Purpose except 20-inch barrel; Improved Cylinder, Super-Full Turkey (.665-inch diameter with knurled extension) Rem-Choke tubes and rifled choke tube insert; rifle sights, synthetic stock, forend; quick-detachable swivels; camo Cordura carrying sling; all surfaces Mossy Oak Bottomland camouflage-finished. Introduced 1993; discontinued 1995.

Perf: $340 **Exc:** $240 **VGood:** $200

REMINGTON MODEL 870 SPS CANTILEVER

Same specs as Model 870 Special Purpose except 20-inch smooth bore barrel; optional rifled barrel; Improved Cylinder and 3-1/2-inch rifled Rem-Choke tubes; cantilever scope mount; synthetic Monte Carlo stock; sling; swivels. Introduced 1994.

Perf: $350 **Exc:** $250 **VGood:** $200

With fully rifled barrel

Perf: $400 **Exc:** $300 **VGood:** $250

REMINGTON MODEL 870 SPS DEER

Same specs as Model 870 Special Purpose except fully-rifled 20-inch barrel; rifle sights; black non-reflective synthetic stock, forend; black carrying sling. Introduced 1993.

Perf: $340 **Exc:** $240 **VGood:** $190

REMINGTON MODEL 870 SPS SPECIAL PURPOSE MAGNUM

Same specs as Model 870 Special Purpose except 26-inch, 28-inch barrel; Rem-Choke tubes; black synthetic stock, forend; dark recoil pad; padded Cordura 2-inch wide sling; quick-detachable swivels; dull, non-reflective black metal finish. Introduced 1985; still in production as SPS-T Special Purpose Magnum.

Perf: $310 **Exc:** $230 **VGood:** $190

REMINGTON MODEL 870 SPS-T CAMO

Same specs as Model 870 Special Purpose except 21-inch vent-rib barrel; Improved Cylinder and Super-Full Turkey (.665-inch diameter with knurled extension) Rem-Choke tubes; synthetic stock; Mossy Oak Green Leaf camouflage-finished; non-reflective black bolt body, trigger guard and recoil pad. Introduced 1993; still in production.

Perf: $390 **Exc:** $270 **VGood:** $215

REMINGTON MODEL 870TA TRAP

Slide action; hammerless; takedown; 12-ga. 5-shot tube magazine; 30-inch Modified, Full barrel; ivory front bead, white metal middle; deluxe checkered walnut trap-style stock, forend; hand-fitted action, parts; recoil pad; special hammer, sear, trigger assembly. Discontinued 1986.

Perf: $350 **Exc:** $260 **VGood:** $210

REMINGTON MODEL 870TB TRAP

Same specs as Model 870TA Trap except 28-inch, 30-inch vent-rib barrel; Full choke; metal bead front; no rear sight. Introduced 1950; discontinued 1981.

Perf: $425 **Exc:** $300 **VGood:** $225

REMINGTON MODEL 870TC TRAP

Same specs as Model 870TA Trap except 30-inch vent-rib barrel; Rem-Choke; vent rib; optional Monte Carlo stock.

Perf: $550 **Exc:** $355 **VGood:** $295

With Monte Carlo stock

Perf: $570 **Exc:** $375 **VGood:** $310

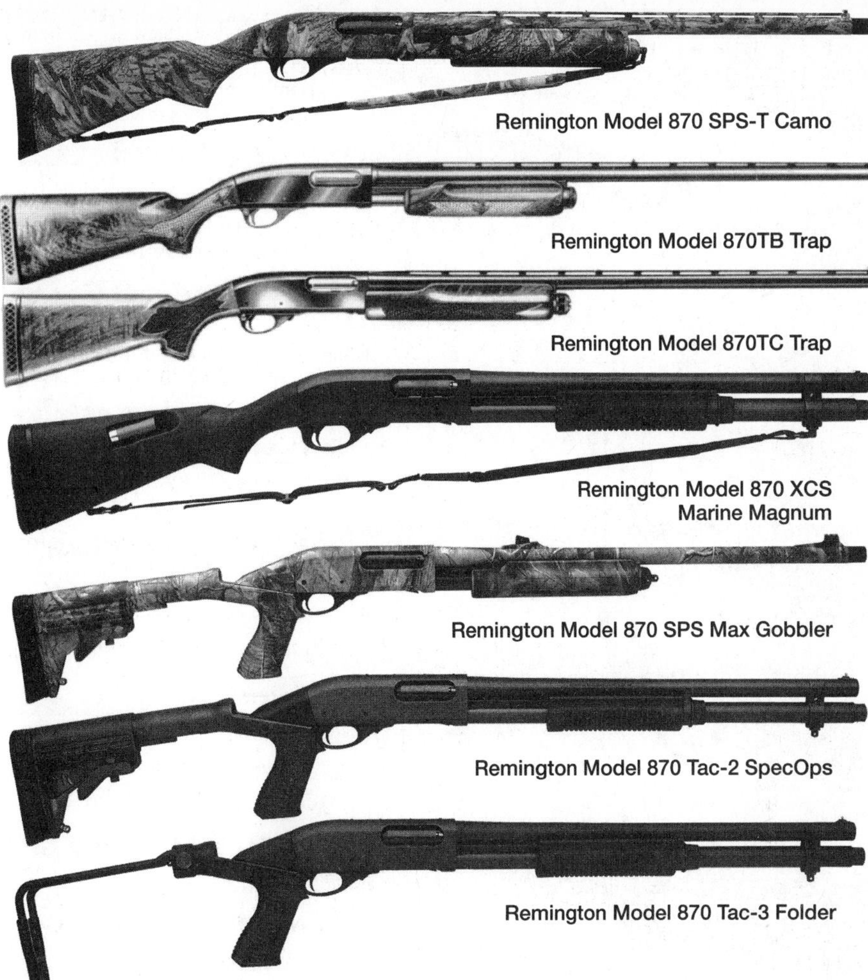

Remington Model 870 SPS-T Camo

Remington Model 870TB Trap

Remington Model 870TC Trap

Remington Model 870 XCS Marine Magnum

Remington Model 870 SPS Max Gobbler

Remington Model 870 Tac-2 SpecOps

Remington Model 870 Tac-3 Folder

REMINGTON MODEL 870 XCS MARINE MAGNUM

New in 2007, this weather-resistant 870 is a 3" 12 gauge with full black TriNyte coverage, 18" fixed Cylinder barrel and 7 round capacity. Weight is 7.5 lbs.

NIB: $750 **Exc:** $695 **VGood:** $575

REMINGTON MODEL 870 SPS MAX GOBBLER

This dedicated turkey gun is a 3.5" 12 gauge featuring a length-adjustable Knoxx SpecOps stock, 23" barrel, fiber-optic rifle sights, Super Full turkey choke tube and full coverage in Realtree APG camo. Drilled and tapped for Weaver style mount. Weight is 8 lbs.

NIB: $700 **Exc:** $635 **VGood:** $525

REMINGTON MODEL 870 TAC-2 SPECOPS

Tactical 3" 12 gauge is available with a Knoxx pistol-grip or folding stock. Barrel is 18" with fixed Cylinder choke. Magazine capacity is 6 shells. Weight is 7 lbs.

NIB: $575 **Exc:** $525 **VGood:** $425

REMINGTON MODEL 870 TAC-3 SPEEDFEED IV

Tactical 3" 12 gauge with pistol-grip stock and 20" barrel. Extended 7-round magazine. Weight is 7.5 lbs.

NIB: $535 **Exc:** $485 **VGood:** $395

REMINGTON MODEL 870 TAC-3 FOLDER

As above but with Knoxx Spec-Ops folding stock. Weight is 7 lbs.

NIB: $595 **Exc:** $545 **VGood:** $475

REMINGTON MODEL 870 SP-T THUMBHOLE

Introduced in 2005, this 3.5-inch 12 gauge is designed specifically for turkey hunting with full coverage in Mossy Oak Obsession camo and thumbhole stock. The 23-inch barrel features fiber-optic adjustable rifle sights and is drilled and tapped for scope mounting. Includes R3 recoil pad, sling, swivels and turkey super full choke tube.

NIB: $435 **Exc:** $395 **VGood:** $300

REMINGTON MODEL 870 SPS-T SUPER MAG

Similar to Model 870 SP-T Thumbhole but with pistol-grip stock and vent-rib barrel.

NIB: $435 **Exc:** $395 **VGood:** $300

REMINGTON MODEL 870 SPS-T/20

This 20-gauge turkey gun features a 3-inch chamber, 23-inch vent rib barrel, R3 recoil pad and full coverage in Mossy Oak New Break-Up camo. Drilled and tapped for scope mount.

NIB: $350 **Exc:** $315 **VGood:** $265

REMINGTON MODEL 870 WINGMASTER NRA EDITION

Special edition with NRA logo on receiver. Available in 12 gauge with 3-inch chamber, 12 gauge Super Mag with 3.5-inch chamber, and 16, 20 and 28 gauges and .410 bore.

NIB: $500 **Exc:** $375 **VGood:** $295

REMINGTON MODEL 870 SPECIAL PURPOSE THUMBHOLE

Laminated stock 12 gauge slug gun with 3-inch chamber and 23-inch fully rifled cantilever barrel.

NIB: $445 **Exc:** $395 **VGood:** $315

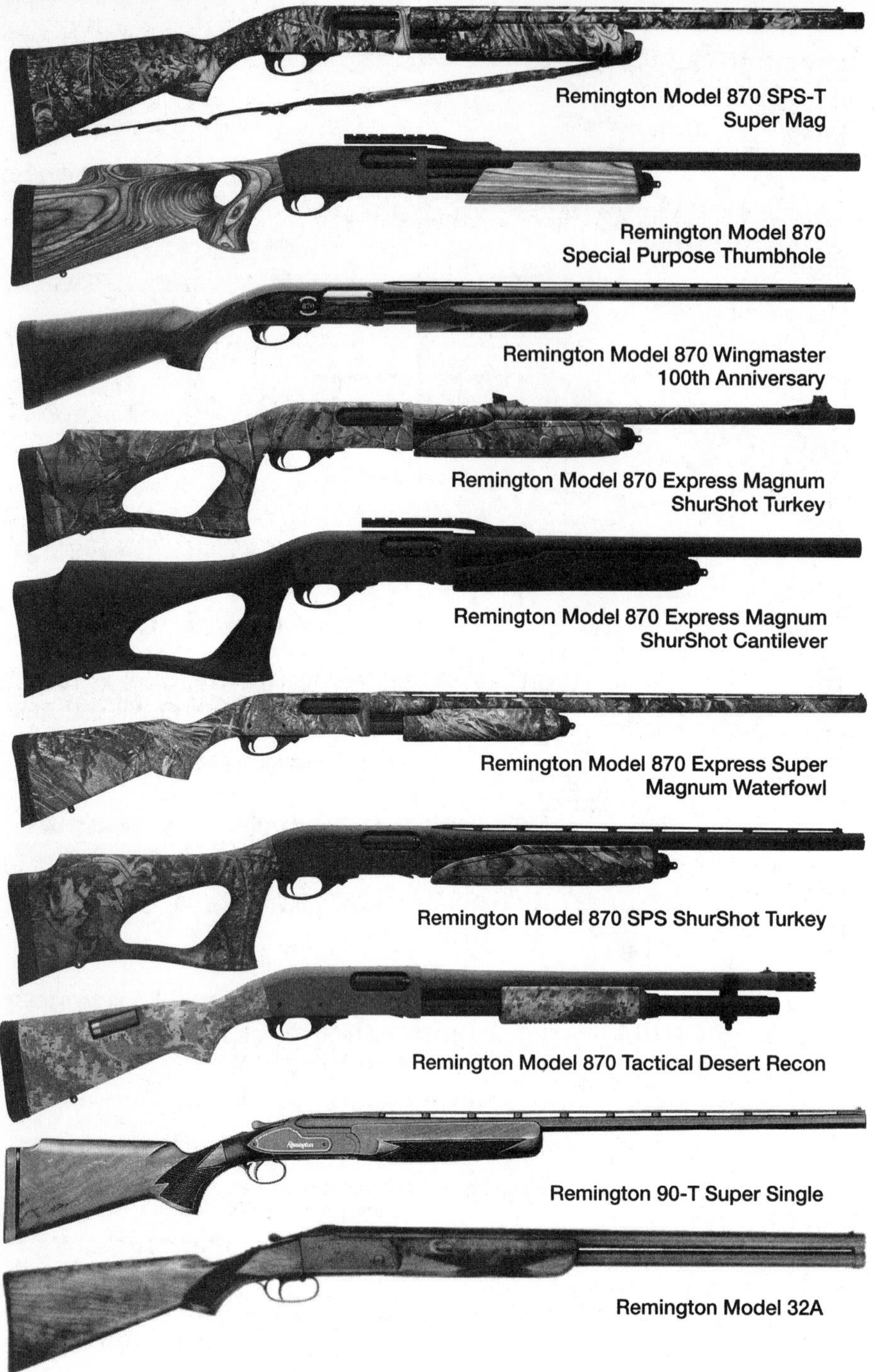
Remington Model 870 SPS-T Super Mag

Remington Model 870 Special Purpose Thumbhole

Remington Model 870 Wingmaster 100th Anniversary

Remington Model 870 Express Magnum ShurShot Turkey

Remington Model 870 Express Magnum ShurShot Cantilever

Remington Model 870 Express Super Magnum Waterfowl

Remington Model 870 SPS ShurShot Turkey

Remington Model 870 Tactical Desert Recon

Remington 90-T Super Single

Remington Model 32A

REMINGTON MODEL 870 WINGMASTER 100TH ANNIVERSARY

This Commemorative Edition 12 gauge celebrating 100 years of Remington pump shotguns (dating from the introduction of the Model 10 in 1908) was introduced in 2008 and offered only for one year. Gold-inlaid logos on both sides of receiver and "B" Grade American Walnut stock with high-gloss finish. Includes three choke tubes. MSRP: $1035.

NIB: $875 **Exc:** $700 **VGood:** $550

REMINGTON MODEL 870 EXPRESS MAGNUM SHURSHOT TURKEY

This turkey-dedicated model has a matte black finish with a ShurShot pistol grip/thumbhole stock and forend finished in Mossy Oak Obsession camo. The 3-inch 12 gauge has a 21-inch barrel. Includes a Turkey Extra Full choke tube. Weight is about 7.5 lbs.

NIB: $500 **Exc:** $375 **VGood:** $295

REMINGTON MODEL 870 EXPRESS MAGNUM SHURSHOT CANTILEVER

This 3 inch 12 gauge has a 23", fully rifled barrel with cantilever scope mount. Matte black finish. Weight is about 7.75 lbs.

NIB: $550 **Exc:** $425 **VGood:** $315

REMINGTON MODEL 870 EXPRESS SUPER MAGNUM WATERFOWL

Introduced in 2008, his dedicated waterfowl gun is completely finished in Mossy Oak Duck Blind camo. The 3.5" 12 gauge has a 28" barrel, HiViz single bead sight and weighs about 7.5 lbs. Includes one choke tube.

NIB: $575 **Exc:** $475 **VGood:** $250

REMINGTON MODEL 870 SPS SHURSHOT TURKEY

New in 2008, this 12 gauge 870 is chambered for shells up to 3.5". It features Remington's ShurShot pistol grip/thumbhole stock and is fully covered in Realtree's APG HD camo. It has a 23-inch non-vent-rib barrel outfitted with fiber-optic rifle-type sights and includes an extended Turkey Rem Choke. Weight is about 7.5 lbs.

NIB: $650 **Exc:** $525 **VGood:** $315

REMINGTON MODEL 870 TACTICAL DESERT RECON

This tactical version 870 features Digital Tiger desert camo on the synthetic stock and forend and an olive-drab powder-coated barrel and receiver. It is available with an 18" (six round mag. capacity) or 20" (seven round mag. capacity) barrel. Speedfeed I (shell holding) or Speedfeed IV (pistol grip) stock. Add 10 percent for Speedfeed IV stock.

NIB: $650 **Exc:** $525 **VGood:** $315

REMINGTON SPORTSMAN

Slide action; 12-, 16-, 20-ga; 5-shot tube magazine; 20-inch, 26-inch barrel; various choke options; walnut pistol-grip stock, forearm; made in Field, Riot and Skeet models. Introduced 1931; discontinued 1948.

Plain barrel

Exc: $295 **VGood:** $180 **Good:** $140

Solid rib

Exc: $310 **VGood:** $225 **Good:** $170

Vent rib

Exc: $375 **VGood:** $290 **Good:** $235

REMINGTON SPORTSMAN PUMP

Slide action; 12-ga.; 3-inch chamber; 28-inch, 30-inch vent-rib barrel; 7 1/2 lbs.; checkered walnut-stained hardwood stock, forend; recoil pad; similar to Model 870. Introduced 1984; discontinued 1986.

Perf: $285 **Exc:** $195 **VGood:** $150

REMINGTON 90-T SUPER SINGLE

Single shot; 12-ga.; 2-3/4-inch chamber; 30-inch, 32-inch, 34-inch barrel; fixed choke or Rem-Chokes; ported or non-ported barrel; weighs 8-3/4 lb.; figured, checkered American walnut stock; cavities in forend, buttstock for added weights; black vented rubber recoil pad; elongated forcing cones; drop-out trigger unit. Introduced 1990; discontinued 1998.

Perf: $2000 **Exc:** $1800 **VGood:** $1600

With adjustable rib

Perf: $2300 **Exc:** $2100 **VGood:** $1850

REMINGTON RIDER NO. 3

Single shot; break-open; hammerless; 10-, 12-, 16-, 20-, 24-, 28-ga.; 30-inch, 32-inch barrel; unchecked American walnut pistol-grip stock, forearm. Introduced 1893; discontinued 1903.

Exc: $425 **VGood:** $360 **Good:** $220

REMINGTON RIDER NO. 9

Single shot; break-open; hammerless; 10-, 12-, 16-, 20-, 24-, 28-ga.; 30-inch, 32-inch barrel; uncheckered American walnut pistol-grip stock, forearm; automatic ejector. Introduced 1902; discontinued 1910.

Exc: $325 **VGood:** $295 **Good:** $260

REMINGTON MODEL 32A

Over/under; double lock; hammerless; takedown; 12-ga.; 26-inch, 28-inch, 30-inch barrels; various fixed chokes; plain barrels, solid or vent rib; walnut checkered pistol-grip stock, forend; double or single trigger; auto ejectors. Introduced 1931; discontinued 1947.

Single trigger, plain barrels

Exc: $1500 **VGood:** $1100 **Good:** $900

Single trigger, solid or vent rib

Exc: $1600 **VGood:** $1200 **Good:** $1000

Double triggers, plain barrels
Exc: $1450 **VGood:** $1050 **Good:** $800
Double triggers, solid or vent rib
Exc: $1500 **VGood:** $1100 **Good:** $900

REMINGTON MODEL 32D TOURNAMENT

Same specs as Model 32A except higher grade of wood, checkering and engraving. Introduced 1931; discontinued 1947.

Single trigger, plain barrels
Exc: $2700 **VGood:** $2350 **Good:** $1400
Single trigger, solid or vent rib
Exc: $3000 **VGood:** $2475 **Good:** $1700
Double triggers, plain barrels
Exc: $2500 **VGood:** $2000 **Good:** $1200
Double triggers, solid or vent rib
Exc: $2700 **VGood:** $2200 **Good:** $1400

REMINGTON MODEL 32 EXPERT

Same specs as Model 32A except select grade of wood, checkering and engraving. Introduced 1931; discontinued 1947.

Single trigger, plain barrels
Exc: $4300 **VGood:** $3200 **Good:** $2600
Single trigger, solid or vent rib
Exc: $4700 **VGood:** $3600 **Good:** $3000
Double triggers, plain barrels
Exc: $3900 **VGood:** $2800 **Good:** $2200
Double triggers, solid or vent rib
Exc: $4300 **VGood:** $3200 **Good:** $2600

REMINGTON MODEL 32F PREMIER

Same specs as Model 32A except best grade of wood, checkering and engraving. Introduced 1931; discontinued 1947.

Single trigger, plain barrels
Exc: $5300 **VGood:** $3900 **Good:** $3000
Single trigger, solid or vent rib
Exc: $5800 **VGood:** $4400 **Good:** $3500
Double triggers, plain barrels
Exc: $4800 **VGood:** $3400 **Good:** $2500
Double triggers, solid or vent rib
Exc: $5300 **VGood:** $3900 **Good:** $3000

REMINGTON MODEL 32 SKEET GRADE

Same specs as Model 32A except 26-inch, 28-inch barrels; Skeet boring; single selective trigger, beavertail forend. Introduced 1932; discontinued 1942.

Plain barrels
Exc: $1400 **VGood:** $1000 **Good:** $750
Solid or vent rib
Exc: $1500 **VGood:** $1100 **Good:** $850

REMINGTON MODEL 32TC TRAP

Same specs as Model 32A except 30-inch, 32-inch vent-rib barrel; Full choke; checkered trap-style pistol-grip stock, beavertail forend.

Double triggers
Exc: $2200 **VGood:** $1500 **Good:** $1100
Single trigger
Exc: $2400 **VGood:** $1700 **Good:** $1200

REMINGTON MODEL 332

Gauge: 12, 3-inch chambers; 26-inch, 28-inch, 30-inch barrel; weighs 7-3/4 lbs.; 42 inches to 47 inches overall; satin-finished American walnut; twin bead sights; light-contour, vent rib; Rem chock barrel; blued; traditional M-32 experience with M-300 Ideal performance; standard auto ejectors; set trigger. Boxlock action.

Perf: $1325 **Exc:** $1025 **VGood:** $895

REMINGTON MODEL 3200

Over/under; boxlock; 12-ga.; 2-3/4-inch chamber; 26-inch Improved Cylinder/Modified, 28-inch Modified/Full, 30-inch Modified/Full barrels; vent rib; checkered American walnut pistol-grip stock, forearm; auto ejectors; selective single trigger. Similar to earlier Model 32. Introduced 1973; discontinued 1984.

Perf: $1100 **Exc:** $995 **VGood:** $900

Remington Model 32 Expert

Remington Model 332

Remington Model 3200 Competition Skeet

Remington Model 3200 Competition Trap

Remington Model 3200 Skeet

Remington Model 3200 Trap

Remington Premier STS Competition

REMINGTON MODEL 3200 COMPETITION SKEET

Same specs as Model 3200 except 26-inch, 28-inch Skeet-choke barrels; select walnut Skeet-style stock, full beavertail forearm; engraved forend latch plate, trigger guard; gilt scrollwork on frame. Introduced 1973; discontinued 1984.

Perf: $1750 **Exc:** $1400 **VGood:** $1200

REMINGTON MODEL 3200 COMPETITION TRAP

Same specs as Model 3200 except 30-inch, 32-inch Improved Modified/Full or Full/Full barrels; select fancy walnut straight comb or Monte Carlo stock, beavertail forend; engraved forend latch plate, trigger guard; gilt scrollwork on frame. Introduced 1973; discontinued 1984.

Perf: $2000 **Exc:** $1300 **VGood:** $1100

REMINGTON MODEL 3200 MAGNUM

Same specs as Model 3200 except 12-ga.; 3-inch chamber; 30-inch Modified/Full or Full/Full barrels. Introduced 1973; discontinued 1984.

Perf: $1950 **Exc:** $1800 **VGood:** $1670

REMINGTON MODEL 3200 SKEET

Same specs as Model 3200 except for 26-inch, 28-inch Skeet-choke barrels; Skeet-style stock, full beavertail forearm. Introduced 1973; discontinued 1984.

Perf: $1250 **Exc:** $1000 **VGood:** $950

REMINGTON MODEL 3200 SPECIAL TRAP

Same specs as Model 3200 except 30-inch, 32-inch Improved Modified/Full or Full/Full barrels; higher grade select walnut straight comb or Monte Carlo trap-style stock, beavertail forearm. Introduced 1973; discontinued 1984.

Perf: $1400 **Exc:** $1350 **VGood:** $1200

REMINGTON MODEL 3200 TRAP

Same specs as Model 3200 except 30-inch, 32-inch Improved Modified/Full or Full/Full barrels; straight comb or Monte Carlo trap-style stock, beavertail forearm. Introduced 1973; discontinued 1984.

Perf: $1375 **Exc:** $1100 **VGood:** $950

REMINGTON PREMIER STS COMPETITION

This 12 gauge O/U with 28-inch or 30-inch barrels has a titanium receiver, overbored barrel, gloss finish stock and 5 extended chokes. Weight is about 7.5 lbs.

Perf: $1975 **Exc:** $1830 **VGood:** $1600

REMINGTON PREMIER FIELD GRADE

O/U available in 12, 20 and 28 gauges with satin finish and nickel receiver. Available with 26-inch or 28-inch barrels. Includes three flush chokes. Weight is about 6.5 lbs. for 20 and 28 gauges and 7.5 lbs. for 12 gauge.

NIB: $1600 **Exc:** $1450 **VGood:** $1175

Remington Premier Field Grade

Remington Premier Upland Grade

Remington Model 1882

Remington Model 1894

Remington Parker (2008)

Remington Peerless

Richland Model 200

Richland Model 707 Deluxe

REMINGTON PREMIER UPLAND GRADE
As above but with oil finish stock and case colored receiver with gold game bird scene.

NIB: $1150 **Exc:** $995 **VGood:** $735

REMINGTON MODEL 1882
Side-by-side; visible hammers; 10-, 12-, 16-ga.; 28-inch, 30-inch, 32-inch steel or Damascus barrels; hand-checkered American walnut pistol-grip stock, forearm; double triggers. Introduced 1882; discontinued 1910.

Damascus barrels

Exc: $1500 **VGood:** $1400 **Good:** $1200

Steel barrels

Exc: $1000 **VGood:** $900 **Good:** $800

REMINGTON MODEL 1889
Side-by-side; visible hammers; 10-, 12-, 16-ga.; 28-inch, 30-inch, 32-inch steel or Damascus barrels; double triggers; hand-checkered American walnut stock, slim forend. Introduced 1889; discontinued 1908. Prices shown are for lowest grade.

Damascus barrels

Exc: $2100 **VGood:** $1800 **Good:** $1700

Steel barrels

Exc: $1350 **VGood:** $1250 **Good:** $900

REMINGTON MODEL 1894
Side-by-side; boxlock; hammerless; 10-, 12-, 16-ga.; 26-inch, 28-inch, 30-inch, 32-inch barrels; hand-checkered American walnut straight-grip stock, forearm; double triggers; auto ejectors. Introduced 1894; discontinued 1910.

Exc: $1350 **VGood:** $1225 **Good:** $1025

REMINGTON MODEL 1894 TRAP
Same specs as Model 1894 except 32-inch Full-choke barrels; trap-style walnut stock. Introduced 1894; discontinued 1910.

Exc: $2750 **VGood:** $2625 **Good:** $2525

REMINGTON MODEL 1900
Side-by-side; boxlock; hammerless; 10-, 12-, 16-ga.; 28-inch, 30-inch barrels; hand-checkered American walnut straight-grip stock, heavy forearm; double triggers; auto ejectors. Introduced 1900; discontinued 1910.

Exc: $1200 **VGood:** $1100 **Good:** $1000

REMINGTON PARKER AAHE 28 GAUGE OVER/UNDER SHOTGUN
A reintroduction of the Charles Parker O/U shotgun. Built to customer specs with a variety of options. Pricing starts at $49,000 (as of 2008).

NIB: $49,000 **VGood:** N/A **Good:** $N/A

REMINGTON MODEL 1900 TRAP
Same specs as Model 1900 except 32-inch Full-Choke barrels; select trap-style walnut stock. Introduced 1900; discontinued 1910.

Exc: $700 **VGood:** $425 **Good:** $390

REMINGTON PEERLESS
Over/under; boxlock; 12-ga.; 3-inch chamber; 26-inch, 28-inch, 30-inch barrels; Improved, Modified, Full Rem-Choke tubes; weighs 7-1/4 lbs.; cut-checkered American walnut pistol-grip stock, forend with Imron gloss finish; black ventilated recoil pad; gold-plated, single selective trigger; automatic safety; automatic ejectors; polished blue finish with light scrollwork on removable sideplates; Remington logo on bottom of receiver. Introduced 1993;.

Perf: $925 **Exc:** $700 **VGood:** $600

RHODE ISLAND ARMS MORONNE MODEL 46
Over/under; boxlock; 12-, 20-ga.; 26-inch Improved Cylinder/Modified, 28-inch Modified/Full barrels; plain barrel or vent rib; checkered straight or pistol-grip stock; non-selective single trigger; plain extractors. Fewer than 500 made. Introduced 1949; discontinued 1953.

12-ga., plain barrel

Exc: $875 **VGood:** $675 **Good:** $600

12-ga., vent rib

Exc: $1000 **VGood:** $825 **Good:** $750

20-ga., plain barrel

Exc: $1000 **VGood:** $825 **Good:** $750

20-ga., vent rib

Exc: $1150 **VGood:** $975 **Good:** $900

RICHLAND MODEL 200
Side-by-side; Anson & Deeley-type boxlock; hammerless; 12-, 16-, 20-, 28-ga., .410; 26-inch Improved/Modified or Modified/Full, 28-inch Modified/Full barrels; hand-checkered European walnut pistol-grip stock, beavertail forearm; cheekpiece; double triggers; plain extractors; recoil pad. Made in Spain. Introduced 1963; discontinued 1985.

Perf: $330 **Exc:** $300 **VGood:** $275

RICHLAND MODEL 202
Side-by-side; Anson & Deeley boxlock; hammerless; 12-, 20-ga.; comes in two-barrel set for a single gauge; 26-inch Improved/Modified and 30-inch Full/Full (12-ga.) or 22-inch Improved/Modified and 26-inch Modified/Full (20-ga.) barrels; hand-checkered European walnut pistol-grip stock, beavertail forearm; cheekpiece; double triggers; plain extractors; recoil pad. Made in Spain. Introduced 1963; discontinued 1971.

Exc: $450 **VGood:** $390 **Good:** $275

RICHLAND MODEL 707 DELUXE
Side-by-side; boxlock; hammerless; 12-, 20-ga.; 26-inch Improved/Modified, 28-inch Modified/Full, 30-inch Full/Full barrels; hand-checkered European walnut stock, forearm; triple bolting system; double triggers; plain extractors; recoil pad. Made in Spain. Introduced 1963; discontinued 1972.

Exc: $300 **VGood:** $275 **Good:** $250

RICHLAND MODEL 711 MAGNUM

Side-by-side; hammerless; Anson & Deeley-type boxlock; Purdey-type triple lock; 10- (3 1/2-inch), 12- (3-inch), 20-ga.; 30-inch, 32-inch Full/Full barrels; hand-checkered European walnut pistol-grip stock, forearm; double triggers; plain extractors; automatic safety; recoil pad. Advertised as Long Range Waterfowl Magnum. Made in Spain. Introduced 1963; discontinued 1985.

10-ga.
Perf: $400 **Exc:** $325 **VGood:** $275

12-ga.
Perf: $340 **Exc:** $295 **VGood:** $265

20-ga.
Perf: $450 **Exc:** $340 **VGood:** $295

RICHLAND MODEL 808

Over/under; boxlock; 12-ga.; 26-inch Improved/Modified, 28-inch Modified/Full, 30-inch Full/Full barrels; vent rib; hand-checkered European walnut stock, forearm; plain extractors; non-selective single trigger. Made in Italy. Introduced 1963; discontinued 1968.

Exc: $425 **VGood:** $375 **Good:** $330

RICHLAND MODEL 828

Over/under; boxlock; 28-ga.; 26-inch Improved/Modified, 28-inch Full/Modified barrels; vent rib; hand-checkered European walnut stock, quick-detachable forearm; sliding crossbolt lock; non-automatic safety; plain extractors; single selective trigger; color case-hardened receiver; rosette engraving. Made in Italy. Introduced 1971; no longer in production. Available on special order only.

Perf: $650 **Exc:** $550 **VGood:** $500

RICHLAND MODEL 844

Over/under; boxlock; 12-ga.; 2-3/4-inch, 3-inch chambers; 26-inch Improved/Modified, 28-inch Modified/Full, 30-inch Full/Full barrels; hand-checkered European walnut pistol-grip stock, forearm; plain extractors; non-selective single trigger. Made in Italy. Introduced 1971; no longer in production.

Perf: $325 **Exc:** $280 **VGood:** $250

RIGBY BEST QUALITY SIDELOCK

Side-by-side; 12-, 20-ga.; various barrel lengths, chokes to customer's specs; hand-checkered European walnut straight-grip stock, forearm; automatic ejectors; double triggers; English engraving. Still in production.

Perf: $36,000 **Exc:** $32,000 **VGood:** $26,000

RIGBY SIDELOCK DOUBLE

Side-by-side; all gauges; various barrel lengths, chokes to customer's specs; hand-checkered European walnut straight-grip stock, forearm; automatic ejectors; double triggers; English engraving; made in two grades, differing in overall quality, amount of engraving. Introduced 1885; discontinued 1955.

Sandringham Grade
Exc: $8500 **VGood:** $6000 **Good:** $5000

Regal Grade
Exc: $12,000 **VGood:** $9000 **Good:** $7500

RIGBY BOXLOCK DOUBLE

Side-by-side; all gauges; various barrel lengths, chokes to customer's specs; hand-checkered European walnut straight-grip stock, forearm; automatic ejectors; double triggers; English engraving; made in two grades, differing in amount and nature of engraving, overall quality. Introduced 1900; discontinued 1955.

Chatsworth Grade
Exc: $4000 **VGood:** $3000 **Good:** $2500

Sackville Grade
Exc: $5500 **VGood:** $4500 **Good:** $4000

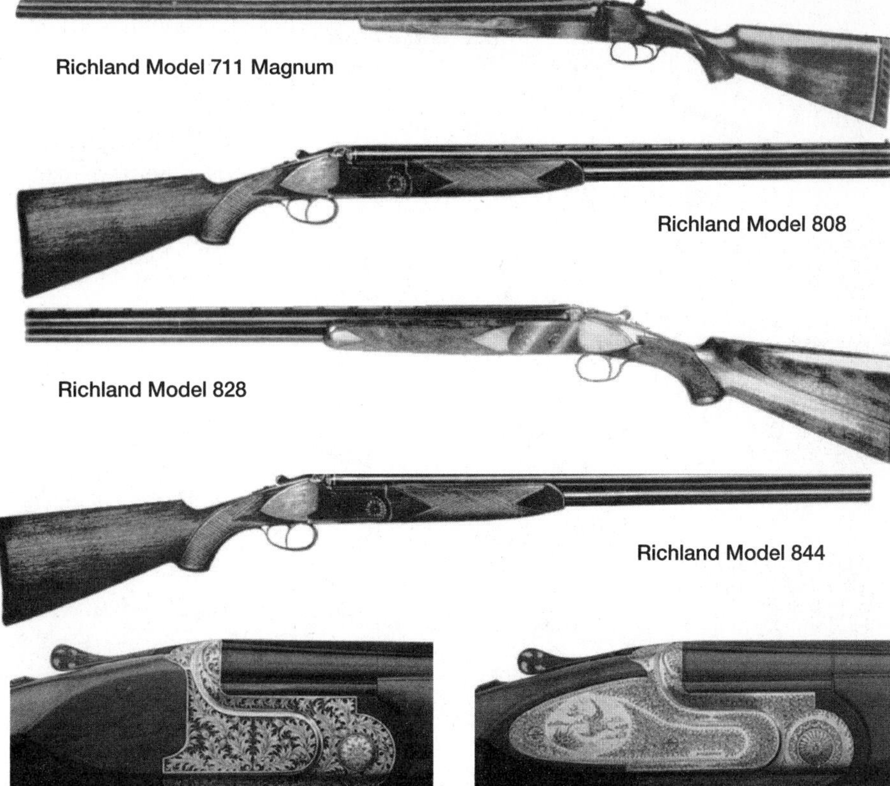

Richland Model 711 Magnum

Richland Model 808

Richland Model 828

Richland Model 844

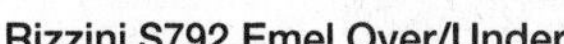

Rizzini S790 Emel Over/Under

Rizzini S792 Emel Over/Under

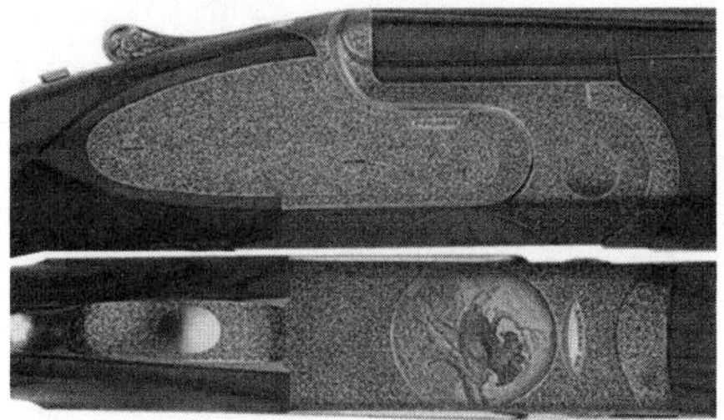

Rizzini Artemis Over/Under

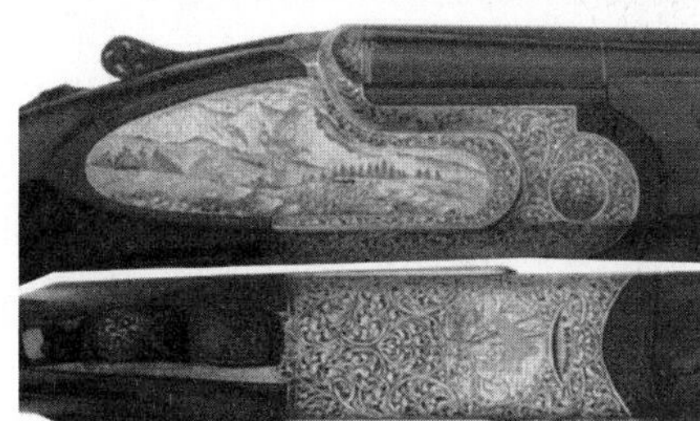

Rizzini S782 Emel Over/Under

RIZZINI S790 EMEL OVER/UNDER

Gauge: 20-, 28-ga., .410; 26-inch, 27.5-inch barrel (Imp. Cyl. & Imp. Mod.); weighs about 6 lbs.; extra-fancy select walnut stock; boxlock action with profuse engraving; automatic ejectors; single selective trigger; silvered receiver. Comes with Nizzoli leather case. Introduced 1996. Imported from Italy by Wm. Larkin Moore & Co.

Perf: $7800 **Exc:** $6800 **VGood:** $5900

RIZZINI S792 EMEL OVER/UNDER

Similar to S790 EMEL except dummy sideplates with extensive engraving coverage. Nizzoli leather case. Introduced 1996. Imported from Italy by Wm. Larkin Moore & Co.0

Perf: $7500 **Exc:** $6600 **VGood:** $5650

RIZZINI UPLAND EL OVER/UNDER

Gauge: 12, 16, 20, 28, .410. Barrel: 26-inch, 27-1/2-inch, Mod. & Full, Imp. Cyl. & Imp. Mod. choke tubes. Weight: About 6.6 lbs. Features: Boxlock action; single selective trigger; ejectors; profuse engraving on silvered receiver. Comes with fitted case. Introduced 1996. Imported from Italy by Wm. Larkin Moore & Co.

Perf: $2800 **Exc:** $2400 **VGood:** $2100

RIZZINI ARTEMIS OVER/UNDER

Same as Upland EL model except dummy sideplates with extensive game scene engraving. Fancy European walnut stock. Fitted case. Introduced 1996. Imported from Italy by Wm. Larkin Moore & Co.

Perf: $1850 **Exc:** $1575 **VGood:** $1300

RIZZINI S782 EMEL OVER/UNDER

Gauge: 12, 2-3/4-inch chambers; 26-inch, 27-1/2-inch barrel (Imp. Cyl. & Imp. Mod.); weighs about 6.75 lbs.; extra fancy select walnut; boxlock action with dummy sideplates; extensive engraving with gold inlaid game birds; silvered receiver; automatic ejectors; single selective trigger; Nizzoli leather case. Introduced 1996. Imported from Italy by Wm. Larkin Moore & Co.

Perf: $9500 **Exc:** $8525 **VGood:** $7200

RIZZINI BOXLOCK

Side-by-side; Anson & Deeley boxlock: 12-, 16-, 20-, 28-ga., .410; 25-inch to 30-inch barrels; file-cut rib;

Rossi Matched Pair

Rossi Overland

Rossi Turkey Gun

Rossi Squire

Rottweil Model 72 American Trap Single

Rottweil Model 72 Field Supreme

Rottweil Model 72 International

weighs 5-1/2 to 6-1/4 lbs., depending upon gauge; hand-rubbed oil finish stock; ejectors; chopper lump barrels; double triggers, single non-selective optional; scroll, rosette engraving on scalloped frame; coin finish; optional color case-hardening; primarily a custom gun with stock, choke tubes to customer specs. Made in Italy. Introduced 1989; still in production.

12-, 16-, 20-ga.

Perf: $22,000 **Exc:** $11,000 **VGood:** $9000

28-ga., .410

Perf: $25,000 **Exc:** $12,000 **VGood:** $10,000

RIZZINI SIDELOCK

Side-by-side; Holland & Holland sidelock; 12-, 16-, 20-, 28-ga., .410; 25-inch to 30-inch barrels; optional rib styles; weighs 6-1/2 to 8 lbs., depending upon gauge; rubbed oil finish or optional satin luster finish stock; auto ejectors; double triggers; single selective trigger optional; coin finish or optional color case-hardening; full coverage scroll engraving, with floral bouquets, gold crown on top lever; customer's name in gold; gold crest inset in forend. Primarily a custom gun with stock, choke tubes to customer specs. Made in Italy. Introduced 1989; still in production.

12-, 16-, 20-ga.

Perf: $35,000 **Exc:** $17,500 **VGood:** $15,000

28-ga., .410

Perf: $40,000 **Exc:** $21,000 **VGood:** $16,500

ROSSI MATCHED PAIR SINGLE-SHOT SHOTGUN/ RIFLE

Gauge: 12,- 20-ga., .410 22-inch barrel (18-1/2-inch Youth), 28-inch barrel (23-inch full); weighs 4 to 6 lbs.; hardwood (brown or black finish); bead front sight; break-open internal transfer bar manual external safety; blued or stainless steel finish; sling-swivel studs; includes matched 22 LR or 22 Mag. barrel with fully adjustable front and rear sight; trigger block system. Introduced 2001. Imported by BrazTech/Taurus.

Blue

Perf: $125 **Exc:** $100 **VGood:** $90

Stainless steel

Perf: $120 **Exc:** $100 **VGood:** $90

ROSSI OVERLAND

Side-by-side; sidelock; 12-, 20-ga., .410; 20-inch, 26-inch, 28-inch barrels; solid raised matted rib; European walnut pistol-grip stock, beavertail forend; double triggers; external hammers; Greener crossbolt. Made in Brazil. Introduced 1978; discontinued 1988.

Perf: $275 **Exc:** $230 **VGood:** $185

ROSSI SINGLE-SHOT SHOTGUN

Gauge: 12-, 20-ga., 2-3/4-inch chamber; .410, 3-inch chamber; 28-inch barrel full, 22-inch barrel Youth; weighs 5 lbs.; stained hardwood; bead sight; break-open, positive ejection; internal transfer bar; trigger block.

Perf: $90 **Exc:** $80 **VGood:** $70

ROSSI TURKEY GUN

Introduced in 2008. A specialized version of Roosi's 12-ga. single-shot shotgun. Features a 3-1/2 inch chamber, fiber optic sights, drilled and tapped barrel, included scope mount base and a removable Briley® Extended Turkey Choke.

Perf: $175 **Exc:** $140 **VGood:** $95

ROSSI SQUIRE

Side-by-side; hammerless; 12-, 20-ga., .410; 20-inch, 28-inch barrels; raised matted rib; walnut-finished hardwood pistol-grip stock, beavertail forearm; double triggers; twin underlugs; synchronized sliding bolts. Made in Brazil. Introduced 1978; discontinued 1990.

Perf: $300 **Exc:** $245 **VGood:** $195

ROTTWEIL MODEL 72 AMERICAN SKEET

Over/under; boxlock; 12-ga.; 26-3/4-inch barrels; vent rib; metal bead front sight; hand-checkered French walnut pistol-grip stock, forend; ejectors; single trigger; engraved. Introduced 1977; discontinued 1986.

Perf: $1800 **Exc:** $1650 **VGood:** $1450

ROTTWEIL MODEL 72 AMERICAN TRAP SINGLE

Same specs as Model 72 American Skeet except 34-inch single barrel; hand-honed chokes; high vent rib; center bead sight, plastic front in metal sleeve; hand-checkered, oil-finished French walnut Monte Carlo stock; muzzle collar changes point of impact; double vent recoil pad; single selective or double triggers. Introduced 1977; discontinued 1986.

Perf: $950 **Exc:** $850 **VGood:** $700

ROTTWEIL MODEL 72 AMERICAN TRAP COMBO

Same specs as Model 72 American Skeet except two-barrel set with 32-inch separated over/under barrels, 34-inch single-barrel; hand-honed chokes; high vent rib; center bead sight, plastic front in metal sleeve; hand-checkered, rubbed European walnut Monte Carlo stock; muzzle collar changes point of impact; double vent recoil pad; single selective or double triggers. Introduced 1977; discontinued 1986.

Perf: $1850 **Exc:** $1700 **VGood:** $1600

ROTTWEIL MODEL 72 AMERICAN TRAP DOUBLE

Same specs as Model 72 American Skeet except 32-inch barrels; hand-honed chokes; high vent rib; center bead sight, plastic front in metal sleeve; hand-checkered, oil-finished Monte Carlo French walnut stock; muzzle collar changes point of impact; double vent recoil pad; single selective or double triggers. Introduced 1977; discontinued 1986.

Perf: $1750 **Exc:** $1400 **VGood:** $1200

ROTTWEIL MODEL 72 FIELD SUPREME

Same specs as Model 72 American Skeet except 28-inch barrels; plastic buttplate; removable interchangeable single trigger assembly; engraved action. Made in Germany. Introduced 1976; discontinued 1986.

Perf: $1750 **Exc:** $1300 **VGood:** $1100

ROTTWEIL MODEL 72 INTERNATIONAL SKEET

Same specs as Model 72 American Skeet except 26-3/4-inch chrome-lined barrels; flared chokes; hand-checkered, oil-finished French walnut stock, modified beavertail forend; retracting spring-mounted firing pins; selective single inertia-type trigger. Introduced 1976; discontinued 1986.

Perf: $1850 **Exc:** $1600 **VGood:** $1400

ROTTWEIL MODEL 72 INTERNATIONAL TRAP

Same specs as Model 72 American Skeet except 30-inch barrels; raised vent rib. Introduced 1976; discontinued 1986.

Perf: $1850 **Exc:** $1600 **VGood:** $1400

ROTTWEIL PARAGON OVER/UNDER

Gauge: 12, 2-3/4-inch chambers; 28-inch, 30-inch barrel; five choke tubes; weighs 7 lbs.; European walnut; boxlock action; detachable trigger assembly; ejectors can be deactivated; convertible top lever for right- or left-hand use; trigger adjustable for position. Imported from Germany by Dynamit Nobel-RWS, Inc..

Perf: $6950 **Exc:** $6500 **VGood:** $5750

ROYAL ARMS MODEL 87SC

Over/under; boxlock; 12-ga.; 2-3/4-inch chambers; 27-5/8-inch barrels; choke tubes; tapered raised rib; weighs 7 3/8 lb.; select walnut stock; auto ejectors; auto safety; single selective trigger; coin-finish receiver; arabesque scroll engraving. Made in Italy. Introduced 1987; discontinued 1987.

Perf: $575 **Exc:** $475 **VGood:** $400

ROYAL ARMS MODEL 87T TRAP

Same specs as Model 87SC except Trap-style stock; other Trap configurations. Introduced 1987; discontinued 1987.

Perf: $600 **Exc:** $440 **VGood:** $340

SAE MODEL 66C

Over/under; 12-ga.; 26-inch Skeet/Skeet, 28-inch Modified/Full barrels; oil-finished Monte Carlo walnut stock, beavertail forearm; selective auto ejectors; auto safety; single mechanical trigger; dummy sideplates; gold inlays; extensive engraving. Made in Spain. Introduced 1987; discontinued 1988.

Perf: $950 **Exc:** $725 **VGood:** $650

SAE MODEL 70

Over/under; boxlock; 12-, 20-ga.; 3-inch chambers; 26-inch Modified/Full, 28-inch Improved/Modified barrels; weighs 6 3/4 lbs.; European walnut stock; selective auto ejectors; auto safety; single mechanical trigger; engraved receiver; blued finish. Made in Spain. Introduced 1987; discontinued 1988.

Perf: $400 **Exc:** $275 **VGood:** $260

SAE MODEL 70 MULTICHOKE

Same specs as Model 70 except 12-ga.; 27-inch barrels; choke tubes; silvered receiver. Made in Spain. Introduced 1987; discontinued 1988.

Perf: $425 **Exc:** $350 **VGood:** $300

SAE MODEL 209E

Side-by-side; sidelock; 12-, 20-ga., .410; 2-3/4-inch chambers; 26-inch Modified/Full, 28-inch Modified/Improved Cylinder barrels; fancy oil-finished checkered select walnut stock, forend; double triggers; selective ejectors; engraved, coin-finished receiver. Made in Spain. Introduced 1987; discontinued 1988.

Perf: $925 **Exc:** $700 **VGood:** $650

SAE MODEL 210S

Side-by-side; boxlock; 12-, 20-ga., .410; 3-inch chambers; 25-inch Modified/Full, 28-inch Modified Improved barrels; weighs 7 lbs.; checkered pistol-grip European walnut stock, splinter forend; auto safety; extractors; double triggers; silver-finished, engraved action. Made in Spain. Introduced 1987; discontinued 1988.

Perf: $420 **Exc:** $300 **VGood:** $210

SAE MODEL 340X

Side-by-side; sidelock; 12-, 20-ga.; 2-3/4-inch chambers; 26-inch Modified/Full, 28-inch Modified/ Improved Cylinder barrels; weighs about 7 lbs.; high-gloss straight-grip select walnut stock, forearm; double triggers; selective ejectors; color case-hardened receiver, engraving. Made in Spain. Introduced 1987; discontinued 1988.

Perf: $700 **Exc:** $550 **VGood:** $495

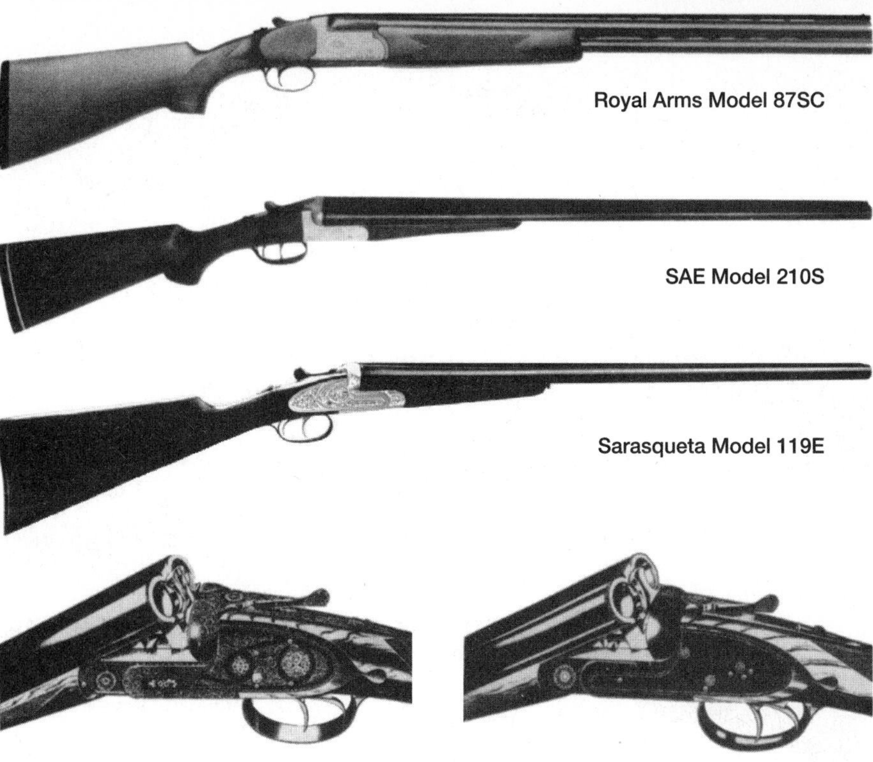

Royal Arms Model 87SC

SAE Model 210S

Sarasqueta Model 119E

Sarasqueta Model Sidelock Double No. 4E

Sarasqueta Sidelock Double No. 4

Sarasqueta Sidelock Double No. 6E

Sarasqueta Sidelock Double No. 7E

SAN MARCO 10-GAUGE

Over/under; boxlock; 10-ga.; 3-1/2-inch chambers; 28-inch Modified/Modified, 32-inch Modified/ Full barrels; chrome-lined bores; solid 3/8-inch barrel rib; weighs 9 to 9-1/2 lbs.; walnut stock with waterproof finish; long forcing cones; double triggers; extractors; Deluxe grade has automatic ejectors; engraved receiver with game scenes, matte finish. Made in Italy. Introduced 1990; discontinued 1994.

Perf: $700 **Exc:** $500 **VGood:** $370

Deluxe grade

Perf: $800 **Exc:** $600 **VGood:** $470

SAN MARCO FIELD SPECIAL

Over/under; boxlock; 12-, 20-, 28-ga.; 3-inch chambers; 26-inch Improved Cylinder/Modified, 28-inch Full/Modified barrels; vented top and middle ribs; weighs 5-1/2 to 6 lbs.; engraved, silvered receiver; single trigger. Made in Italy. Introduced 1990; discontinued 1994.

Perf: $600 **Exc:** $430 **VGood:** $330

SAN MARCO WILDFOWLER

Over/under; boxlock; 12-ga.; 3-1/2-inch chambers; 28-inch Modified/Modified, Full/Modified barrels; chrome-lined bores; vented top and middle ribs; weighs 7-3/4 lbs.; checkered waterproof walnut pistol-grip stock, forend; long forcing cones; single non-selective trigger; extractors on Standard, automatic ejectors on Deluxe; silvered, engraved action. Made in Italy. Introduced 1990; discontinued 1994.

Perf: $525 **Exc:** $380 **VGood:** $300

Deluxe grade

Perf: $600 **Exc:** $430 **VGood:** $330

SARASQUETA BOXLOCK DOUBLE

Side-by-side; boxlock; hammerless; 12-, 16-, 20-, 28-ga.; various standard barrel lengths, choke combinations; hand-checkered European walnut straight-grip stock, forearm; plain extractors; double triggers; Greener crossbolt (No.2); optional ejectors; engraved. Introduced mid-1930s; no longer in production.

No. 2

Perf: $325 **Exc:** $250 **VGood:** $180

No. 2E

Perf: $375 **Exc:** $280 **VGood:** $230

No. 3

Perf: $375 **Exc:** $280 **VGood:** $230

No. 3E

Perf: $425 **Exc:** $330 **VGood:** $280

SARASQUETA MODEL 119E

Side-by-side; 12-ga.; 2-3/4-inch chambers; 28-inch Modified/Full, Improved/Modified barrels; medium bead front sight; European walnut straight-grip stock; auto ejectors; double triggers; hand-engraved locks. Made in Spain. Introduced 1982 by Toledo Armas; discontinued 1984.

Perf: $450 **Exc:** $350 **VGood:** $300

SARASQUETA SIDELOCK DOUBLE

Side-by-side; hammerless; 12-, 16-, 20-, 28-ga., .410; barrel lengths, choke combinations to customer's order; hand-checkered European walnut straight-grip stock, forearm; double triggers; optional automatic ejectors; made in 18 grades, differing in

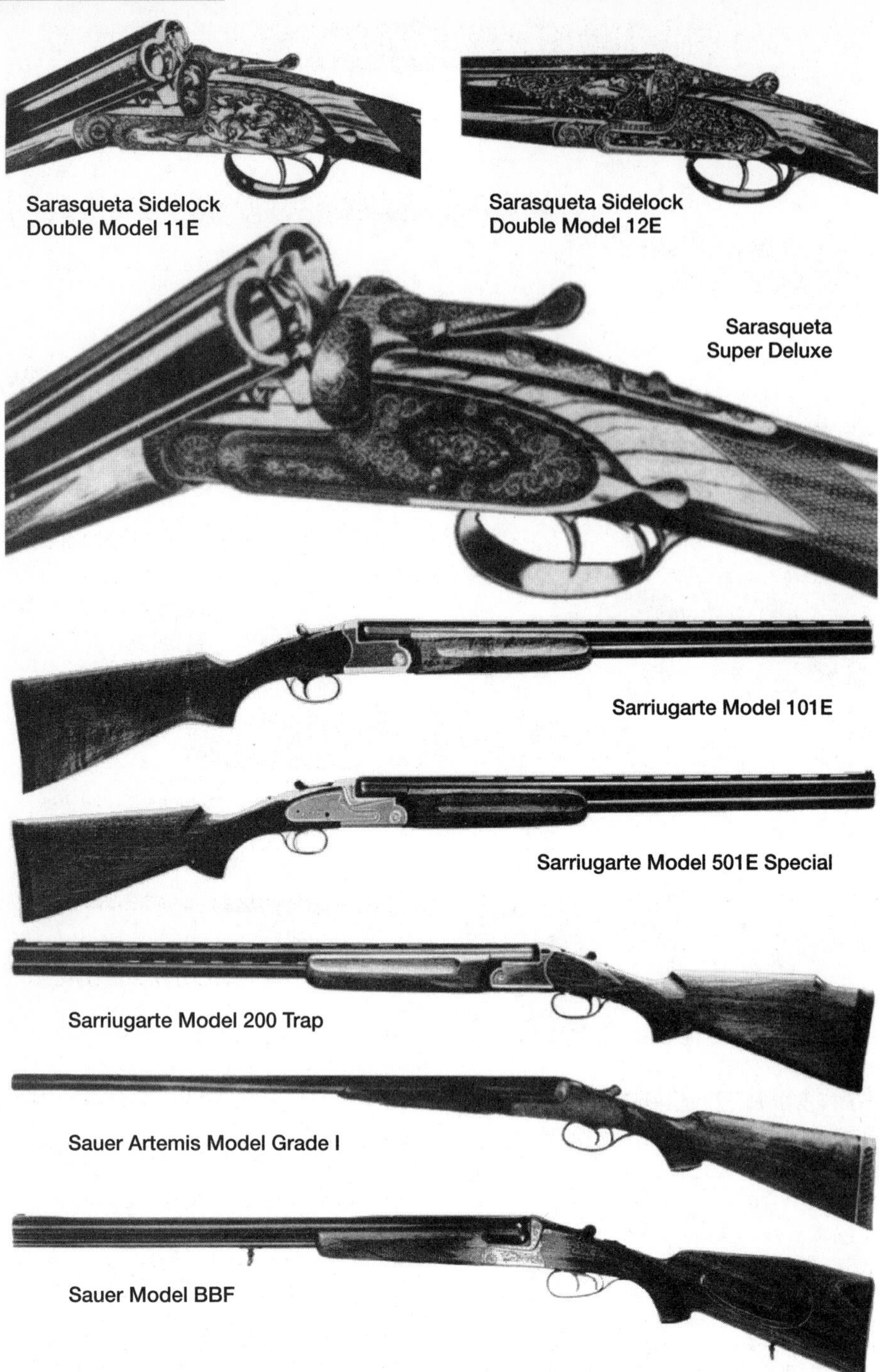
Sarasqueta Sidelock Double Model 11E

Sarasqueta Sidelock Double Model 12E

Sarasqueta Super Deluxe

Sarriugarte Model 101E

Sarriugarte Model 501E Special

Sarriugarte Model 200 Trap

Sauer Artemis Model Grade I

Sauer Model BBF

quality of wood, checkering and engraving. Made in Spain.

No. 4		
Perf: $600	**Exc:** $500	**VGood:** $450
No. 4E		
Perf: $650	**Exc:** $550	**VGood:** $500
No. 6E		
Perf: $780	**Exc:** $680	**VGood:** $600
No. 7E		
Perf: $850	**Exc:** $750	**VGood:** $700
No. 10E		
Perf: $1650	**Exc:** $1400	**VGood:** $1300
No. 11E		
Perf: $1700	**Exc:** $1500	**VGood:** $1400
No. 12E		
Perf: $2000	**Exc:** $1800	**VGood:** $1650

SARASQUETA SUPER DELUXE

Side-by-side; sidelock; hammerless; 12-ga.; barrel lengths, choke combos to customer's order; hand-checkered European walnut pistol-grip stock, forearm; automatic ejectors; double triggers; engraved action. Introduced 1930s; no longer in production.

Perf: $1800 **Exc:** $1600 **VGood:** $1200

SARRIUGARTE MODEL 101DS

Over/under; 12-ga.; 2-3/4-inch chambers; 26-inch Improved/Modified, 28-inch Modified/Full barrels; medium bead front sight; hand-checkered European walnut pistol-grip stock; extractors; selective trigger; border engraving on receiver. Made in Spain. Introduced 1982 by Toledo Armas; discontinued 1984.

Perf: $425 **Exc:** $340 **VGood:** $295

SARRIUGARTE MODEL 101E

Same specs as Model 101DS except single trigger; auto ejectors. Introduced 1982; discontinued 1984.

Perf: $500 **Exc:** $375 **VGood:** $320

SARRIUGARTE MODEL 101E DS

Same specs as Model 101DS except ejectors. Introduced 1982; discontinued 1984.

Perf: $550 **Exc:** $425 **VGood:** $350

SARRIUGARTE MODEL 200 TRAP

Over/under; 12-ga.; 2-3/4-inch chambers; 30-inch Full/Full barrels; vent middle rib; European walnut Monte Carlo stock; single trigger; auto ejectors. Made in Spain. Introduced 1982 by Toledo Armas; discontinued 1984.

Perf: $700 **Exc:** $570 **VGood:** $500

SARRIUGARTE MODEL 501E SPECIAL

Over/under; 12-ga.; 2-3/4-inch chambers; 30-inch Full/Full barrels; vent middle rib; select European walnut Monte Carlo stock; single trigger; auto ejectors; elaborate engraving. Introduced 1982; discontinued 1984.

Perf: $1500 **Exc:** $1150 **VGood:** $900

SARRIUGARTE MODEL 501E SPECIAL EXCELSIOR

Same specs as Model 501E Special except top of the line with best wood available; best grade of engraving. Introduced 1982; discontinued 1984.

Perf: $2000 **Exc:** $1550 **VGood:** $1300

SARRIUGARTE MODEL 501E SPECIAL NIGER

Same specs as Model 501E Special except higher-grade wood; better engraving. Introduced 1982; discontinued 1984.

Perf: $1900 **Exc:** $1400 **VGood:** $1100

SARSILMAZ SEMI-AUTOMATIC SHOTGUN

Gauge: 12, 3-inch chamber; 26-inch or 28-inch barrel; fixed chokes; Walnut or synthetic; handles 2-3/4-inch or 3-inch Magnum loads. Introduced 2000. Imported from Turkey by PMC.

Perf: $325 **Exc:** $250 **VGood:** $180

SARSILMAZ PUMP SHOTGUN

Gauge: 12, 3-inch chamber. Barrel: 26-inch or 28-inch. Stocks: Oil-finished hardwood. Features: Includes extra pistol-grip stock. Introduced 2000. Imported from Turkey by PMC.

Perf: $300 **Exc:** $250 **VGood:** $180

SARSILMAZ OVER/UNDER SHOTGUN

Over/under; 12-ga.; 3-inch chambers; 26-inch, 28-inch barrel; fixed chokes or choke tubes; oil-finished hardwood stock; double or single selective trigger; wide ventilated rib; chrome-plated parts; blued finish. Introduced 2000. Imported from Turkey by PMC.

Perf: $425 **Exc:** $375 **VGood:** $315

SAUER ARTEMIS MODEL

Side-by-side; Holland & Holland-type sidelock; 12-ga.; 28-inch Modified/Full barrels; hand-checkered European walnut pistol-grip stock, beavertail forearm; Greener-type crossbolt; double underlugs; double sear safeties; automatic ejectors; single selective trigger; recoil pad; Grade I has fine-line engraving; Grade II has English arabesque motif. Introduced 1960s; discontinued 1977.

Grade I		
Perf: $5500	**Exc:** $4600	**VGood:** $3800
Grade II		
Perf: $6600	**Exc:** $5500	**VGood:** $4800

SAUER MODEL BBF

Over/under combo; blitz action; Kersten lock; 16-ga. top barrel; choice of 30-30, 30-06, 7x65R rifle barrel; 25-inch barrels; shotgun barrel Full choke; folding leaf rear sight; hand-checkered European walnut pistol-grip stock, forearm; modified Monte Carlo comb, cheekpiece; front set trigger activates rifle barrel; sling swivels; arabesque engraving pattern. Introduced 1950s; discontinued 1985.

Standard Grade

Perf: $2150 **Exc:** $1600 **VGood:** $1250

Deluxe Grade

Perf: $2350 **Exc:** $1800 **VGood:** $1450

SAUER MODEL 66 FIELD

Over/under; Holland & Holland sideplates; 12-ga.; 28-inch Modified/Full barrels; hand-checkered European walnut stock, forearm; automatic safety; selective automatic ejectors; single selective trigger; recoil pad; three grades of engraving. Introduced 1960s; discontinued 1975.

Grade I

Perf: $2200 **Exc:** $1750 **VGood:** $1500

Grade II

Perf: $2995 **Exc:** $2400 **VGood:** $1900

Grade III

Perf: $3850 **Exc:** $3300 **VGood:** $2800

SAUER MODEL 66 TRAP

Same specs as Model 66 Field except 30-inch Full/Full or Modified/Full barrels; wide vent rib; trap-style checkered European walnut stock, ventilated beavertail forearm; non-automatic safety. Introduced 1960s; discontinued 1975.

Grade I

Perf: $2090 **Exc:** $1760 **VGood:** $1540

Grade II

Perf: $3080 **Exc:** $2420 **VGood:** $1980

Grade III

Perf: $3800 **Exc:** $3300 **VGood:** $2800

SAUER MODEL 66 SKEET

Same specs as Model 66 Field except 26-inch Skeet/Skeet barrels; vent rib; Skeet-style checkered European walnut stock, ventilated beavertail forearm. Introduced 1966; discontinued 1975.

Grade I

Perf: $2000 **Exc:** $1650 **VGood:** $1300

Grade II

Perf: $2900 **Exc:** $2000 **VGood:** $1700

Grade III

Perf: $3750 **Exc:** $3000 **VGood:** $2600

SAUER ROYAL MODEL

Side-by-side; Anson & Deeley-type boxlock; 12-, 16-, 20-ga.; 26-inch Improved/Modified, 28-inch Modified/Full, 30-inch Full/Full barrels; hand-checkered European walnut pistol-grip stock, beavertail forearm; Greener crossbolt; single selective trigger; automatic ejectors; automatic safety; double underlugs; scalloped frame; recoil pad; arabesque engraving. Introduced 1955; discontinued 1977.

Perf: $1500 **Exc:** $1100 **VGood:** $900

SAUER/FRANCHI STANDARD GRADE

Over/under; 12-ga.; 28-inch, 29-inch barrels; vent rib; standard choke combos; weighs 7 lbs.; checkered European walnut stock; single selective trigger; selective auto ejectors; blued finish; made in four grades with differing wood, finish and engraving. Made in Germany. Introduced 1986; discontinued 1988.

Standard Grade

Perf: $350 **Exc:** $300 **VGood:** $280

Regent Grade

Perf: $475 **Exc:** $390 **VGood:** $350

Favorite Grade

Perf: $550 **Exc:** $495 **VGood:** $450

Diplomat Grade

Perf: $875 **Exc:** $750 **VGood:** $625

SAUER/FRANCHI SKEET

Over/under; 12-ga.; 28-inch Skeet/Skeet barrels; vent rib; checkered select European walnut stock, forearm; ejectors; single selective trigger; silvered receiver. Introduced 1986; discontinued 1988.

Perf: $900 **Exc:** $690 **VGood:** $600

Sauer Model 66 Field

Sauer Royal Model

Sauer/Franchi Sporting S

Savage Model 24

Savage Model 30

Savage Model 30AC

SAUER/FRANCHI SPORTING S

Over/under; 12-ga.; 28-inch barrels; standard choke combos; vent rib; checkered select European walnut stock, forearm; ejectors; single selective trigger; silvered receiver. Introduced 1986; discontinued 1988.

Perf: $800 **Exc:** $700 **VGood:** $600

SAUER/FRANCHI TRAP

Over/under; 12-ga.; 29-inch barrels; standard choke combos; vent rib; checkered select European walnut trap-style stock, forearm; ejectors; single selective trigger; silvered receiver. Introduced 1986; discontinued 1988.

Perf: $850 **Exc:** $700 **VGood:** $600

SAVAGE MODEL 24

Over/under combo; break-open; 22 Short, Long, LR upper barrel; .410; 3-inch, Full-choke lower barrel; 24-inch barrels; open rear sight, ramp front rifle sight; uncheckered walnut pistol-grip stock; sliding button selector; single trigger. Introduced 1950; discontinued 1965.

Exc: $435 **VGood:** $380 **Good:** $260

SAVAGE MODEL 24DL

Same specs as Model 24 except top lever; 20-ga., .410 lower barrel; checkered Monte Carlo stock, beavertail forearm; satin chrome-finished receiver, trigger guard. No longer in production.

Exc: $425 **VGood:** $325 **Good:** $260

SAVAGE MODEL 24M

Same specs as Model 24 except 22 WMR upper barrel. Introduced 1965; discontinued 1971.

Exc: $525 **VGood:** $450 **Good:** $400

SAVAGE MODEL 24MDL

Same specs as Model 24L except top lever; 20-ga., .410 lower barrel; 22 WMR upper barrel; checkered Monte Carlo stock, beavertail forearm; satin chrome-finished receiver, trigger guard. Introduced 1965; discontinued 1969.

Exc: $500 **VGood:** $405 **Good:** $315

SAVAGE MODEL 28A

Slide action; hammerless; takedown; 12-, 16-, 20-ga.; 5-shot tube magazine; 26-inch, 28-inch, 30-inch, 32-inch plain barrel; Modified, Cylinder, Full choke; uncheckered American walnut pistol-grip stock, grooved slide handle; black plastic buttplate. Introduced 1920s; discontinued 1940.

Exc: $225 **VGood:** $175 **Good:** $150

SAVAGE MODEL 28B

Same specs as Model 28A except raised matted rib. No longer in production.

Exc: $235 **VGood:** $185 **Good:** $160

SAVAGE MODEL 28D

Same specs as Model 28A except Full-choke barrel; matted rib; hand-checkered pistol-grip trap-style stock, slide handle. No longer in production.

Exc: $235 **VGood:** $185 **Good:** $160

SAVAGE MODEL 30

Slide action; hammerless; solid frame; 12-, 16-, 20-ga., .410; 4-shot (.410), 5-shot magazine; 26-inch, 28-inch, 30-inch barrel; Improved Modified, Full chokes; vent rib; uncheckered American walnut stock, grooved slide handle; hard rubber buttplate. Introduced 1958; discontinued 1979.

Exc: $170 **VGood:** $150 **Good:** $130

Savage Model 30D

Savage Model 30 Slug Gun

Savage Model 220

Savage Model 312 Field

Savage Model 333

Savage Model 333T Trap

SAVAGE MODEL 30AC

Same specs as Model 30 except 12-ga.; 26-inch barrel; adjustable choke; checkered stock. Introduced 1959; discontinued 1975.

Exc: $200 **VGood:** $175 **Good:** $160

SAVAGE MODEL 30ACL

Same specs as Model 30 except 12-ga.; 26-inch barrel; adjustable choke; checkered stock; ejection port, safety on left side. Introduced 1960; discontinued 1964.

Exc: $180 **VGood:** $150 **Good:** $120

SAVAGE MODEL 30D

Same specs as Model 30 except takedown; 12-, 20-ga., .410; 3-inch chamber; vent rib; checkered pistol-grip stock, fluted extension slide handle; recoil pad; alloy receiver; etched pattern on receiver. Introduced 1972; discontinued 1979.

Exc: $180 **VGood:** $165 **Good:** $150

SAVAGE MODEL 30FG

Same specs as Model 30 except takedown; 12-, 20-ga., .410; 3-inch chamber; checkered pistol-grip stock, fluted extension slide handle; recoil pad; alloy receiver. Introduced 1970; discontinued 1975.

Perf: $180 **Exc:** $130 **VGood:** $100

SAVAGE MODEL 30 SLUG GUN

Same specs as Model 30 except 12-, 20-ga.; 22-inch slug barrel; rifle sights. Introduced 1964; discontinued 1982.

Perf: $180 **Exc:** $150 **VGood:** $130

SAVAGE MODEL 30T

Same specs as Model 30 except 12-ga.; 30-inch Full-choke barrel; Monte Carlo trap-style stock; recoil pad. Introduced 1964; discontinued 1975.

Perf: $180 **Exc:** $150 **VGood:** $130

SAVAGE MODEL 210F MASTER SHOT SLUG GUN

Gauge: 12, 3-inch chamber; 2-shot magazine; 24-inch barrel 1:35-inch rifling twist; weighs 7-1/2 lbs.; 43-1/2-inch overall; glass-filled polymer with positive checkering; based on the Savage Model 110 action; 60-degree bolt lift; controlled round feed; comes with scope mount. Introduced 1996. Made in U.S. by Savage Arms.

Perf: $495 **Exc:** $325 **VGood:** $280

SAVAGE MODEL 220

Single barrel; single shot; hammerless; takedown; 12-, 16-, 20-ga., .410; 28-inch to 32-inch barrels; Full choke; uncheckered American walnut pistol-grip stock, forearm; automatic ejector. Introduced 1947; discontinued 1965. Separate barrels $100 in Excellent condition.

Exc: $300 **VGood:** $240 **Good:** $150

SAVAGE MODEL 220AC

Same specs as Model 220 except Savage adjustable choke. No longer in production.

Exc: $285 **VGood:** $225 **Good:** $135

SAVAGE MODEL 220L

Same specs as Model 220 except side lever. Introduced 1965; discontinued 1972.

Exc: $285 **VGood:** $220 **Good:** $150

SAVAGE MODEL 220P

Same specs as Model 220 except 12-, 16-, 20-, 28-ga.; Poly Choke; recoil pad. No longer in production.

Exc: $285 **VGood:** $225 **Good:** $135

SAVAGE MODEL 242

Over/under; .410; 24-inch barrels; Full choke; open rear, ramp front sight; single exposed hammer; uncheckered walnut pistol-grip stock; lever barrel selector; single trigger. Introduced 1977; discontinued 1979.

Perf: $425 **Exc:** $375 **VGood:** $255

SAVAGE MODEL 312 FIELD

Over/under; boxlock; 12-ga.; 3-inch chambers; 26-inch, 28-inch barrels; Improved Cylinder, Modified, Full choke tubes; ventilated top, middle ribs; weighs 7 lbs.; checkered walnut stock; ventilated recoil pad; single trigger; satin chrome-finished frame. Introduced 1990; discontinued 1993.

Perf: $475 **Exc:** $365 **VGood:** $300

SAVAGE MODEL 312SC SPORTING CLAYS

Same as the Model 312 Field except 28-inch barrels; Skeet 1, Skeet 2, Improved Cylinder, Modified, Full choke tubes; curved target-type recoil pad; receiver marked "Sporting Clays" on each side. Introduced 1990; discontinued 1993.

Perf: $575 **Exc:** $460 **VGood:** $400

SAVAGE MODEL 312T TRAP

Same as the Model 312 Field except 30-inch barrels; Full, Modified choke tubes; weighs 7-1/4 lbs.; checkered walnut Monte Carlo stock; rubber recoil pad. Introduced 1990; discontinued 1993.

Perf: $500 **Exc:** $425 **VGood:** $430

SAVAGE MODEL 320

Over/under; 20-ga.; 3-inch chambers; 26-inch barrels; choke tubes; vent top, middle ribs; weighs 6-3/4 lbs.; high-gloss, uncheckered stock, forend; recoil pad; single trigger; marketed with gun lock, shooting glasses, ear protection. Introduced 1991; discontinued 1992.

Perf: $500 **Exc:** $425 **VGood:** $325

SAVAGE MODEL 330

Over/under; boxlock; 12- (2-3/4-inch), 20-ga. (3-inch); 26-inch Improved Cylinder/Modified, 28-inch Modified/Full, 30-inch Modified/Full barrels; checkered European walnut pistol-grip stock, forearm; selective single trigger; plain extractors. Made in Finland by Valmet. Introduced 1969; discontinued 1979.

Perf: $500 **Exc:** $400 **VGood:** $325

SAVAGE MODEL 333

Over/under; boxlock; 12- (2-3/4-inch), 20-ga. (3-inch); 26-inch Improved Cylinder/Modified or Skeet/Skeet, 28-inch Modified/Full, 30-inch Modified/Full barrels; vent rib; checkered European walnut pistol-grip stock, broad forearm; single selective triggers; auto ejectors. Made in Finland by Valmet.

Perf: $575 **Exc:** $475 **VGood:** $425

Add 30 percent to above prices for 20-ga.
Add 25 percent for extra set of barrels.

SAVAGE MODEL 333T TRAP

Same specs as Model 333 except 12-ga.; 30-inch Improved Modified/Full barrels; checkered European walnut Monte Carlo pistol-grip trap stock; extractors; recoil pad. Introduced 1972; discontinued 1979.

Perf: $550 **Exc:** $425 **VGood:** $375

SAVAGE MODEL 420

Over/under; boxlock; hammerless; takedown; 12-, 16-, 20-ga.; 26-inch, 28-inch, 30-inch barrels;

Modified/Full or Cylinder/Improved; uncheckered American walnut pistol-grip stock, forearm; double triggers; optional single non-selective trigger; extractors; automatic safety. Introduced 1930s; discontinued 1942.

Double triggers
Exc: $300 **VGood:** $200 **Good:** $175

Single trigger
Exc: $340 **VGood:** $235 **Good:** $200

SAVAGE MODEL 430

Over/under; boxlock; hammerless; takedown; 12-, 16-, 20-ga.; 26-inch, 28-inch, 30-inch barrels; Modified/Full, Cylinder/Improved chokes; matted top barrel; hand-checkered American walnut stock, forearm; double triggers; optional single non-selective trigger; automatic safety; recoil pad. Introduced 1930s; discontinued 1942.

Double triggers
Exc: $350 **VGood:** $250 **Good:** $200

Single trigger
Exc: $395 **VGood:** $300 **Good:** $250

SAVAGE MODEL 440

Over/under; boxlock; 12- (2-3/4-inch), 20-ga. (3-inch); 26-inch Improved Cylinder/Modified or Skeet/Skeet, 28-inch Modified/Full, 30-inch Modified/Full barrels; checkered American walnut pistol-grip stock, forearm; single selective trigger; plain extractors. Introduced 1968; discontinued 1972.

Perf: $480 **Exc:** $400 **VGood:** $375

SAVAGE MODEL 440T TRAP

Same specs as Model 440, except 12-ga.; 30-inch Improved Modified/Full barrels; wide vent rib; checkered select American walnut Monte Carlo trap stock, semi-beavertail forearm; recoil pad. Introduced 1969; discontinued 1972.

Perf: $550 **Exc:** $450 **VGood:** $400

SAVAGE MODEL 444 DELUXE

Over/under; boxlock; 12- (2-3/4-inch), 20-ga. (3-inch); 26-inch Improved Cylinder/Modified or Skeet/Skeet, 28-inch Modified/Full, 30-inch Modified/Full barrels; select checkered American walnut pistol-grip stock, semi-beavertail forearm; single selective trigger; auto ejectors. Introduced 1969; discontinued 1972.

Perf: $550 **Exc:** $450 **VGood:** $400

SAVAGE MODEL 550

Side-by-side; boxlock; hammerless; 12- (2-3/4-inch), 20-ga. (3-inch); 26-inch Improved Cylinder/Modified, 28-inch Modified/Full, 30-inch Modified/Full barrels; checkered American walnut pistol-grip stock, semi-beavertail forearm; non-selective single trigger; auto ejectors. Introduced 1971; discontinued 1973.

Perf: $325 **Exc:** $275 **VGood:** $175

SAVAGE MODEL 720

Autoloader; Browning humpback design; takedown; 12-, 16-ga.; 4-shot tube magazine; 26-inch, 28-inch, 30-inch, 32-inch barrels; Cylinder, Modified, Full chokes; hand-checkered American walnut pistol-grip stock forearm; black plastic buttplate. Introduced 1930; discontinued 1949.

Exc: $345 **VGood:** $275 **Good:** $250

SAVAGE MODEL 726

Autoloader; takedown; 12-, 16-ga.; 2-shot tube magazine; 26-inch, 28-inch, 30-inch, 32-inch barrels; Cylinder, Modified, Full chokes; hand-checkered American walnut pistol-grip stock, forearm; black plastic buttplate; engraved receiver. Introduced 1930; discontinued 1949.

Exc: $345 **VGood:** $275 **Good:** $250

SAVAGE MODEL 740C

Autoloader; takedown; 12-, 16-ga.; 2-shot tube magazine; 24-1/2-inch barrel; Skeet choke; hand-checkered American walnut pistol-grip Skeet-style stock, beavertail forearm; Cutts Compensator; black plastic buttplate. Introduced 1939; discontinued 1949.

Exc: $350 **VGood:** $230 **Good:** $195

Savage Model 430

Savage Model 440

Savage Model 440T Trap

Savage Model 550

Savage Model 720

Savage Model 726

Savage Model 755

SAVAGE MODEL 745 LIGHTWEIGHT

Autoloader; takedown; 12-ga.; 3-, 5-shot tube magazine; 28-inch barrel; Cylinder, Modified, Full chokes; hand-checkered American walnut pistol-grip stock, forearm; black plastic buttplate; alloy receiver. Introduced 1946; discontinued 1949.

Exc: $345 **VGood:** $275 **Good:** $250

SAVAGE MODEL 750

Autoloader; Browning design; takedown; 12-ga. 4-shot tube magazine; 26-inch Improved, 28-inch Full or Modified barrel; checkered American walnut pistol-grip stock, grooved forearm. Introduced 1960; discontinued 1963.

Exc: $345 **VGood:** $275 **Good:** $250

SAVAGE MODEL 750AC

Same specs as Model 750 except 26-inch barrel; adjustable choke. Introduced 1964; discontinued 1967.

Exc: $345 **VGood:** $275 **Good:** $250

SAVAGE MODEL 750SC

Same specs as Model 750 except 26-inch barrel; Savage Super Choke. Introduced 1962; discontinued 1963.

Exc: $225 **VGood:** $150 **Good:** $120

SAVAGE MODEL 755

Autoloader; takedown; 12-, 16-ga.; 2-, 4-shot tube magazine; 26-inch Improved Cylinder, 28-inch Full or Modified, 30-inch Full barrel; hand-checkered American walnut pistol-grip stock, forearm; rounded receiver. Introduced 1949; discontinued 1958.

Exc: $210 **VGood:** $160 **Good:** $120

SAVAGE MODEL 755SC

Same specs as Model 755 except 25-inch barrel; Savage Super Choke. No longer in production.

Exc: $210 **VGood:** $160 **Good:** $120

SAVAGE MODEL 775 LIGHTWEIGHT

Autoloader; takedown; 12-, 16-ga.; 2-, 4-shot magazine; 26-inch Improved Cylinder, 28-inch Full or Modified, 30-inch Full barrel; hand-checkered

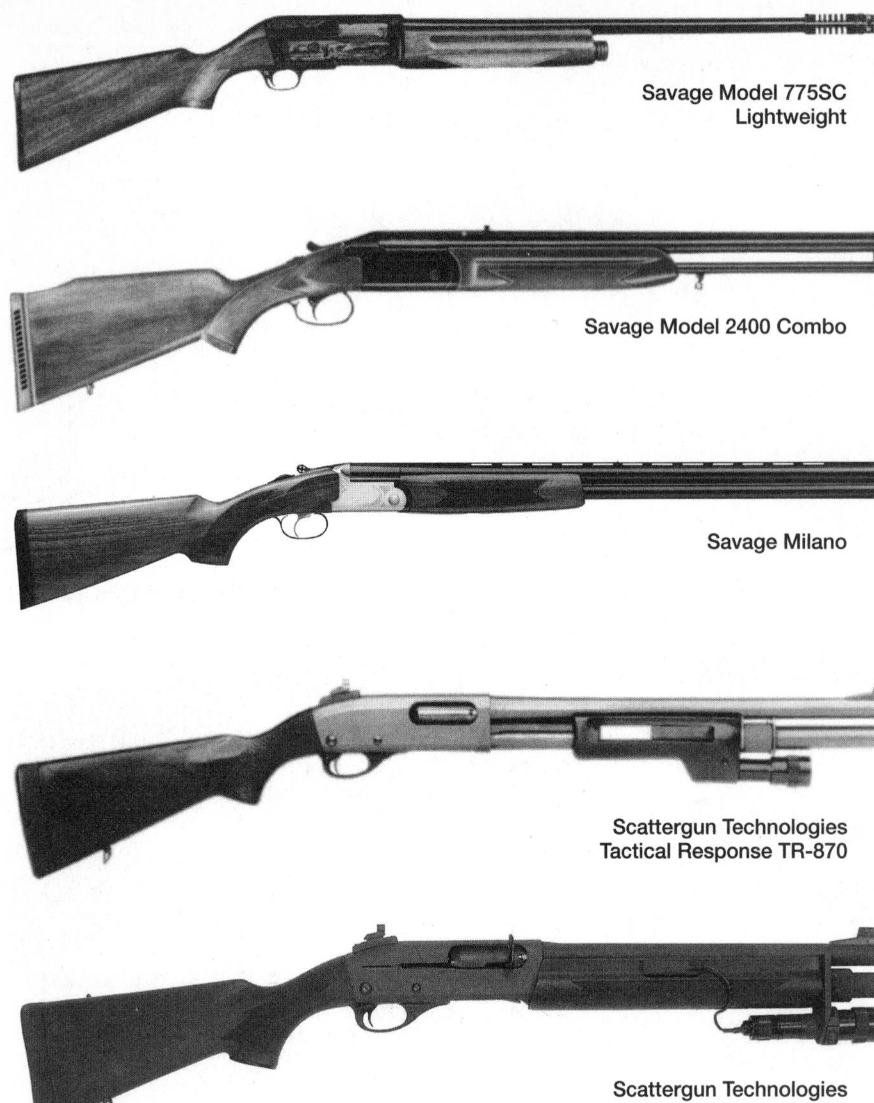
Savage Model 775SC Lightweight

Savage Model 2400 Combo

Savage Milano

Scattergun Technologies Tactical Response TR-870

Scattergun Technologies SWAT

American walnut pistol-grip stock, forearm; alloy receiver. Introduced 1953; discontinued 1960.

Exc: $210 **VGood:** $150 **Good:** $125

SAVAGE MODEL 775SC LIGHTWEIGHT

Same specs as Model 775 Lightweight, except 26-inch barrel; Savage Super Choke. No longer in production.

Exc: $225 **VGood:** $165 **Good:** $120

SAVAGE MODEL 2400 COMBO

Over/under; boxlock; 12-ga.; Full-choke upper barrel, 308 Win. or 222 Rem. lower barrel; 23-1/2-inch barrels; solid matted rib; blade front sight, folding leaf rear; dovetail for scope mounting; checkered European walnut Monte Carlo pistol-grip stock, semi-beavertail forearm; recoil pad. Made by Valmet in Finland. Introduced 1975; discontinued 1979.

Perf: $775 **Exc:** $600 **VGood:** $450

SAVAGE MILANO

This Italian-made over-and-under is available in 12, 20 and 28 gauges and .410-bore on frames scaled to match, all with 28-inch barrels and 3-inch chambers. Single selective trigger. Three choke tubes (fixed IC and Mod. on .410-bore). Automatic ejectors.

NIB: $1225 **Exc:** $1100 **VGood:** $875

SCATTERGUN TECHNOLOGIES TACTICAL RESPONSE TR-870

Slide action; 12-ga.; 3-inch chamber; 7-shot magazine; 18-inch Cylinder-choked barrel; ramp front sight with tritium insert, adjustable Ghost Ring rear; Davis Speed Feed II synthetic stock; adjustable nylon sling; Jumbo Head safety; 6-shot ammo holder on left side of receiver; modified Remington 870P; additions include recoil-absorbing buttplate; nylon forend with flashlight. Made in variety of law enforcement versions. Introduced 1991; still in production.

Perf: $650 **Exc:** $400 **VGood:** $300

FBI model (Discontinued 1999)

Perf: $715 **Exc:** $625 **VGood:** $490

Patrol model (Discontinued 1999)

Perf: $545 **Exc:** $500 **VGood:** $465

Border Patrol model

Perf: $650 **Exc:** $550 **VGood:** $475

Louis Awerbuck model

Perf: $625 **Exc:** $490 **VGood:** $385

Practical Turkey model

Perf: $545 **Exc:** $500 **VGood:** $465

Expert model

Perf: $1200 **Exc:** $995 **VGood:** $775

Professional model

Perf: $895 **Exc:** $735 **VGood:** $580

Entry model

Perf: $995 **Exc:** $800 **VGood:** $600

Compact model

Perf: $575 **Exc:** $510 **VGood:** $420

SCATTERGUN TECHNOLOGIES K-9

Autoloader; 12-ga.; 18-inch barrel; adj. ghost ring sight; 7-shot mag.; side saddle; synthetic buttstock and forearm. Discontinued 2003.

Perf: $1100 **Exc:** $875 **VGood:** $775

SCATTERGUN TECHNOLOGIES SWAT

Similar to K-9 Model, except has 14-inch barrel and forearm with 11,000CP flashlight. Discontinued 2003. This model was available for police and military sales only.

Perf: $1400 **Exc:** $1150 **VGood:** $895

SCATTERGUN TECHNOLOGIES URBAN SNIPER

Autoloader; 12-ga.; 18-inch rifled barrel; scout optics; 7-shot mag.; side saddle; synthetic butt stock and forearm; bipod. Descontinued 1999.

Perf: $1225 **Exc:** $1075 **VGood:** $950

W&C SCOTT (GUNMAKERS) LTD. BLENHEIM

Side-by-side; bar-action sidelock; 12-ga.; 25-inch to 30-inch barrels; choking to order; concave, Churchill or flat rib; figured walnut with 28 lpi checkering; gold oval on belly at stock; fine scroll and floral engraving; optional full or half pistol grip stock, semi-beavertail forend. Introduced 1983; discontinued 1991. A best quality gun. Made in England.

Perf: $25,000 **Exc:** $18,500 **VGood:** $15,000

Deluxe, upgraded wood and metal work

Perf: $30,000 **Exc:** $23,000 **VGood:** $19,000

W&C SCOTT (GUNMAKERS) LTD. BOWOOD DELUXE

Side-by-side; boxlock; 12-, 16-, 20-, 28-ga.; 25-inch to 30-inch barrels; Improved/Modified choking or to order; concave, Churchill or flat rib; hand-checkered custom French walnut stock; scroll engraving. Made in England. Introduced 1980; discontinued 1991.

12-, 16-ga.

Perf: $7500 **Exc:** $6000 **VGood:** $5000

20-, 28-ga.

Perf: $8500 **Exc:** $7000 **VGood:** $6000

W&C SCOTT (GUNMAKERS) LTD. CHATSWORTH GRANDELUXE

Side-by-side; boxlock; 12-, 16-, 20-, 28-ga.; 25-inch to 30-inch barrels; Improved/Modified choking or to order; concave, Churchill or flat rib; fine hand-checkered custom French walnut stock; hand-fitted; extensive scroll engraving. Made in England. Introduced 1980; discontinued 1991.

12-, 16-ga.

Perf: $9500 **Exc:** $7000 **VGood:** $6000

20-, 28-ga.

Perf: $10,500 **Exc:** $8000 **VGood:** $7000

W&C SCOTT (GUNMAKERS) LTD. CROWN

Side-by-side; hammerless boxlock; 12-, 16-, 20-, 28-ga.; 25-inch to 30-inch barrels; Improved/ Modified choking or to order; concave, Churchill or flat rib; checkered French walnut stock with side panels and drop points; engraved case-colored action. Introduced 1982; discontinued 1991. Made in England. Seek appraisal.

W&C SCOTT (GUNMAKERS) LTD. KINMOUNT

Side-by-side; boxlock; 12-, 16-, 20-, 28-ga.; 25-inch to 30-inch barrels; Improved/Modified choking or to order; concave, Churchill or flat rib; checkered

French walnut stock; engraving. Introduced 1981; discontinued 1991. Made in England.

12-, 16-ga.
Perf: $7000 **Exc:** $5500 **VGood:** $4500

20-, 28-ga.
Perf: $8000 **Exc:** $6500 **VGood:** $5500

W&C SCOTT (GUNMAKERS) LTD. TEXAN

Side-by-side; hammerless boxlock with false sideplates; 12-, 16-, 20-, 28-ga.; 25-inch to 30-inch barrels; standard chokes; flat rib; single trigger; ejectors; fancy walnut; pistol grip stock, beavertail forend. Made for the American market. Introduced 1981; discontinued 1991. Made in England.
Perf: $7000 **Exc:** $5500 **VGood:** $4500

W&C SCOTT & SON MONTE CARLO B

Side-by-side; hammerless; bar-action sidelock; 10-, 12-, 16-, 20-ga.; 28-inch to 32-inch Damascus or fluid steel barrels; choking to order; solid flat rib; figured walnut stock and forend; extractors or ejectors; double or single trigger; early examples have crystal (cocking) indicators on sideplate; two grades of engraving; case-colored action. This was the company's most popular sidelock. Introduced 1898; discontinued 1935. Made in England.
Perf: $5000 **Exc:** $3500 **VGood:** $2500

W&C SCOTT & SON PIGEON CLUB GUN

Side-by-side; bar-action sidelock; exposed hammers; 10-, 12-ga.; 27-inch to 32-inch Damascus or fluid steel barrel; choking to order; solid flat rib; figured walnut stock and forend; fully engraved case-colored action; made in grades A, B, C, but not marked. Made in England. Introduced 1879; discontinued 1924.
Perf: $4500 **Exc:** $3500 **VGood:** $2850

W&C SCOTT & SON PREMIER HAMMERLESS

Side-by-side; bar-action sidelock; hammerless; 10-, 12-, 16-, 20-ga.; 28-inch to 32-inch Damascus or fluid steel barrel; choking to order; solid flat rib; figured walnut stock and forend; ejectors; square cross bolt third lock; sideclips; fully engraved case-colored action. Made in England. This was the company's best gun. Introduced 1897; discontinued 1927.
Perf: $9000 **Exc:** $7500 **VGood:** $6000

W&C SCOTT & SON IMPERIAL PREMIER HAMMERLESS

Same specs as the Premier Hammerless except with extensive high-quality engraving; finest Italian walnut with fleur-de-lis checkering. Introduced 1897; discontinued 1932.
Perf: $11,500 **Exc:** $9000 **VGood:** $7000

W&C SCOTT & SON PREMIER QUALITY HAMMER

Side-by-side; bar-action sidelock; exposed hammers; 4-, 8-, 10-, 12-, 16-ga.; 27-inch to 32-inch Damascus or fluid steel barrels; choking to order; solid flat rib; figured walnut stock and forend; fully engraved case-colored action. Made in England. Introduced 1873; discontinued 1921.
Perf: $2800 **Exc:** $2000 **VGood:** $1750

W&C SCOTT & SON RELIANCE/CONTINENTAL

Side-by-side; hammerless boxlock; 10-, 12-, 16-, 20-ga.; 28-inch to 32-inch Damascus or fluid steel barrels; standard choking; solid flat rib; figured walnut; ejectors; double trigger; Greener cross bolt; sideclips fully engraved, case-colored scalloped action. This was the company's best boxlock shotgun. Made in England. Discontinued 1933.
Perf: $3000 **Exc:** $2400 **VGood:** $1900

W&C Scott (Gunmakers) Ltd. Kinmount

W&C Scott (Gunmakers) Ltd. Crown

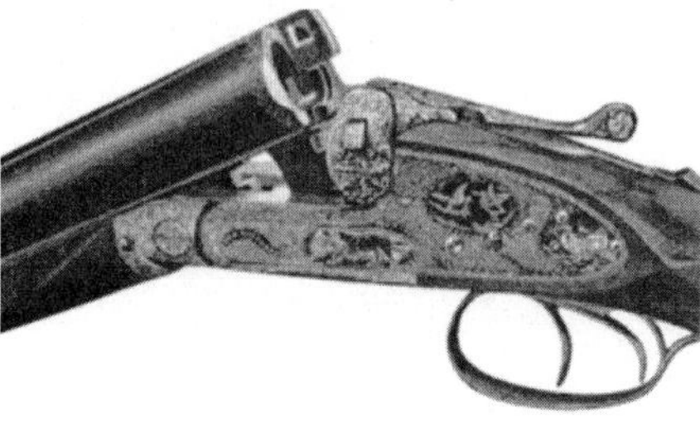

W&C Scott & Son Premier Hammerless

W&C Scott (Gunmakers) Ltd. Texan

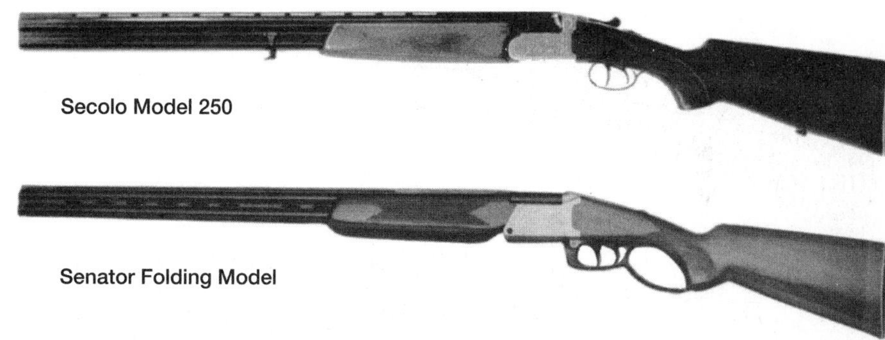

Secolo Model 250

Senator Folding Model

W&C SCOTT & SON SINGLE BARREL TRAP

Single shot; bar-action sidelock; 12-ga.; 27-inch to 36-inch fluid steel barrel; vent-rib with twin ivory sight beads; pistol grip Monte Carlo stock, beavertail forend; recoil pad; engraved action; Italian walnut. Sold for $400 in 1928; 70 guns made. Made in England. Introduced 1914; discontinued 1929. Extreme rarity precludes pricing.

SECOLO MODEL 250

Over/under; 12-ga.; 2-3/4-inch chambers; 28-inch Modified/Full barrels; vent rib; hand-checkered European walnut pistol-grip stock, forend; extractors; single or double triggers; sling swivels; silvered frame; light engraving. Made in Spain. Introduced 1983; discontinued 1984.
Perf: $375 **Exc:** $295 **VGood:** $225

SECOLO MODEL 530

Single barrel; 12-ga.; 2-3/4-inch chamber; 30-inch, 32-inch lower barrel; 5 interchangeable choke tubes; vent rib; European walnut Monte Carlo stock; silvered or case-hardened receiver. Made in Spain. Introduced 1983; discontinued 1984.
Perf: $900 **Exc:** $775 **VGood:** $675

SECOLO MODEL 540 MONO TRAP

Single barrel; 12-ga.; 2-3/4-inch chamber; 30-inch, 32-inch upper barrel; 5 interchangeable choke tubes; vent rib; European walnut Monte Carlo stock; silvered or case-hardened receiver. Made in Spain. Introduced 1983; discontinued 1984.
Perf: $900 **Exc:** $775 **VGood:** $675

SECOLO MODEL 550 TRAP

Over/under; 12-ga.; 2-3/4-inch chambers, 30-inch, 32-inch barrels; 5 interchangeable choke tubes; vent rib; European walnut Monte Carlo stock; silvered or case-hardened receiver. Made in Spain. Introduced 1983; discontinued 1984.
Perf: $800 **Exc:** $625 **VGood:** $540

SECOLO MODEL 560 SKEET

Over/under; 12-ga.; 2-3/4-inch chambers; 30-inch, 32-inch Skeet/Skeet barrels; vent rib; Skeet-style European walnut stock; silvered or case-hardened receiver. Made in Spain. Introduced 1983; discontinued 1984.
Perf: $825 **Exc:** $650 **VGood:** $575

SENATOR FOLDING MODEL

Over/under; boxlock; 12-, 20-ga., .410; 3-inch chambers; 26-inch, 28-inch barrels; vent top, middle ribs; weighs 7 lbs.; European walnut stock; engraved; underlever cocking/opening system. Made in Italy. Introduced 1986; discontinued 1988.
Perf: $210 **Exc:** $160 **VGood:** $110

SIGARMS APOLLO TR AND TT SHOTGUNS

Over-under; boxlock action; 12-, 20-gauge, .410, 3-inch chambers; 28-gauge 2-3/4-inch chambers; 26-inch, 28-inch, 30-inch, 32-inch barrels; weighs 6 to 7-1/4 lbs.; oil-finished European walnut stock; hard-chromed bores; automatic ejectors; single selective trigger; choke tubes (12 and 20 ga. only). Introduced 2000. From Sigarms.

TR 30 Field (color casehardened side plates)
Perf: $2275 **Exc:** $1900 **VGood:** $1675

TR 40 Gold (gold overlays on game scenes)
Perf: $2575 **Exc:** $2125 **VGood:** $1850

TT 25 Competition (wide vent. rib with mid-bead)
Perf: $2475 **Exc:** $2000 **VGood:** $1750

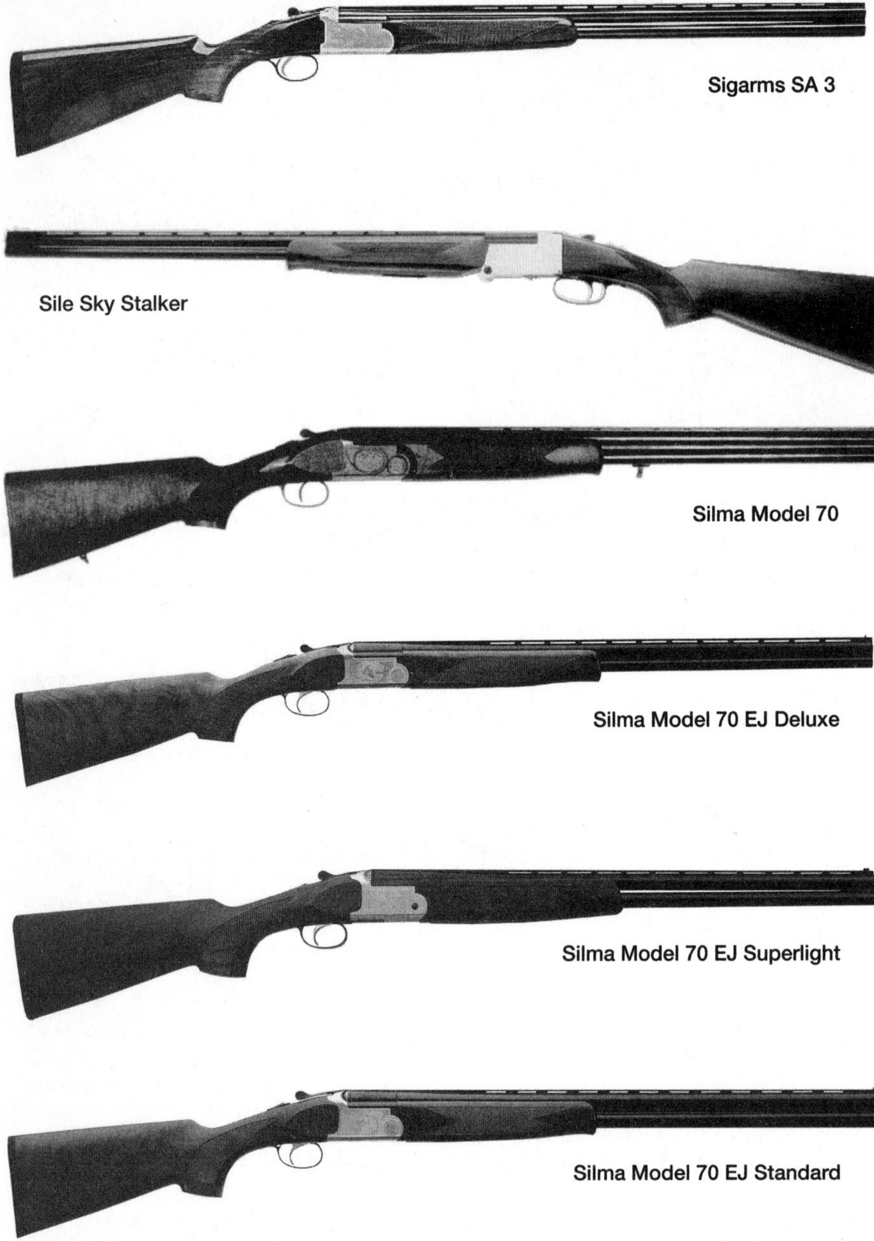
Sigarms SA 3

Sile Sky Stalker

Silma Model 70

Silma Model 70 EJ Deluxe

Silma Model 70 EJ Superlight

Silma Model 70 EJ Standard

SIGARMS SA 3

Over-under; boxlock action; 12-, 20-gauge; 3-inch chambers; 26-inch, 28-inch, 30-inch separated barrels; weighs 7 lbs.; scalloped coin finished monoblock with game scene engraving; field or Sporting Clays (introduced 1998) configuration; vent rib; choke tubes; ejectors; SST; checkered walnut stock and forearm. Introduced 1997; dropped 1998.

Perf: $1175 **Exc:** $925 **VGood:** $775

SIGARMS SA 5

Over-under; boxlock action; 12-, 20-gauge; 3-inch chambers; coin finished monoblock action; hand engraved detachable side plates; ejectors; SST; select checkered walnut stock and forearm; field or Sporting Clays (introduced 1998) configuration; 26-1/2-inch, 28-inch, 30-inch (Sporting Clays only) barrels; vent rib; choke tubes; lockable case; weighs 6 to 7 lbs. Introduced 1997; dropped 1999.

Perf: $2175 **Exc:** $1775 **VGood:** $1450

SILE SKY STALKER

Over/under; .410; 3-inch chambers; 26-inch barrels; checkered walnut stock, schnabel forend; folds for storage, carrying; chrome-lined bores; matted hard chrome finish on receiver. Made in Italy. Introduced 1984; discontinued 1990.

Perf: $275 **Exc:** $230 **VGood:** $185

SILMA MODEL 70

Over/under; boxlock; 12-ga.; 3-inch chambers; 27-1/2-inch barrels; Modified/Improved Cylinder; weighs 7 lbs.; European walnut pistol-grip stock; single trigger; sling swivels; engraved, blued action. Made in Italy. Introduced 1995; still in production.

Perf: $725 **Exc:** $600 **VGood:** $515

SILMA MODEL 70EJ DELUXE

Gauge: 12 (3-1/2-inch chambers), 20, .410 (3-inch chambers), 28 (2-3/4-inch chambers); 28-inch barrel (12- and 20-gauge, fixed and tubed, 28-ga. and .410 fixed), 26-inch barrel (12- and 20-ga. fixed); weighs 7.6 lbs 12-gauge; 6.9 lbs. 20-, 28-ga. and .410; checkered select European walnut, pistol grip, solid rubber recoil pad; monobloc construction; chrome-moly blued steel barrels; raised vent rib; automatic safety and ejectors; single mechanical gold-plated trigger; bead front sight; brushed, engraved receiver. Introduced 2002. Imported from Italy by Legacy sports International.

12-, 20-ga. w/multichokes (IC, M, F)

Perf: $815 **Exc:** $750 **VGood:** $675

28-ga., .410 w/multichokes (IC, M, F), fixed (M&F)

Perf: $868 **Exc:** $813 **VGood:** $733

SILMA MODEL 70 EJ SUPERLIGHT

Similar to Silma 70EJ Deluxe except 12-gauge, 3-inch chambers, alloy receiver, weighs 5.6 lbs.

12-, 20-ga. w/multichokes (IC, M, F)

Perf: $1000 **Exc:** $896 **VGood:** $806

12-, 20-ga. w/fixed chokes (M&F)

Perf: $890 **Exc:** $785 **VGood:** $695

SILMA MODEL 70 EJ STANDARD

Similar to Silma 70EJ Deluxe except 12- and 20-gauge only, standard walnut stock, light engraving, silver-plated trigger.

12-ga. w/multichokes (IC, M, F)

Perf: $686 **Exc:** $611 **VGood:** $576

SKB MODEL 300

Recoil-operated autoloader; takedown; 12-, 20-ga.; 5-shot magazine; 26-inch Improved Cylinder, 28-inch Full or Modified, 30-inch Full barrel; optional vent rib; checkered American walnut pistol-grip stock, fluted forearm; crossbolt safety; automatic magazine cutoff allows changing loads without unloading magazine. Introduced 1969; discontinued 1973.

With plain barrel

Perf: $300 **Exc:** $200 **VGood:** $150

With vent rib

Perf: $325 **Exc:** $225 **VGood:** $175

SKB MODEL 900 DELUXE

Recoil-operated autoloader; takedown; 12-, 20-ga; 5-shot magazine; 25-inch Improved Cylinder, 28-inch Full or Modified, 30-inch Full barrel; vent rib; hand-checkered American walnut pistol-grip stock, forearm; white spacers on grip cap, buttplate; interchangeable barrels; crossbolt safety; gold-filled engraving on receiver; gold-plated trigger; nameplate inlaid in stock. Introduced 1969; discontinued 1973.

Perf: $300 **Exc:** $250 **VGood:** $200

SKB MODEL 900 DELUXE SLUG

Same specs as Model 900 Deluxe except 24-inch slug barrel; rifle sights. Introduced 1969; discontinued 1973.

Perf: $275 **Exc:** $220 **VGood:** $200

SKB MODEL 1300 UPLAND MAG

Gas-operated autoloader; 12-, 20-ga.; 2-3/4-inch, 3-inch chamber; 22-inch Slug barrel, 26-inch, 28-inch vent-rib barrel; Inter-Choke tubes; hand-checkered walnut pistol-grip stock, forend; magazine cut-off system; blued receiver. Made in Japan. Introduced 1988; discontinued 1992.

Perf: $400 **Exc:** $325 **VGood:** $290

SKB MODEL 1900 FIELD

Gas-operated autoloader; 12-, 20-ga.; 2-3/4-inch, 3-inch chambers; 22-inch Slug barrel, 26-inch, 28-inch vent-rib barrel; Inter-Choke tubes; hand-checkered walnut pistol-grip stock, forend; magazine cut-off system; gold-plated trigger; engraved bright-finish receiver. Made in Japan. Introduced 1988; discontinued 1992.

Perf: $450 **Exc:** $375 **VGood:** $300

SKB MODEL 1900 TRAP

Same specs as Model 1900 Field except 12-ga.; 2-3/4-inch chamber; 30-inch barrel; Inter-Choke tubes; 9.5mm wide raised rib. Made in Japan. Introduced 1988; discontinued 1992.

Perf: $450 **Exc:** $375 **VGood:** $300

SKB MODEL XL 100

Gas-operated autoloader; slug gun; 12-ga.; 2-3/4-inch chamber; 4-shot magazine; 20-inch Cylinder barrel; 40-3/8-inch overall length; red ramp front sight with Raybar-type blade, adjustable rifle rear sight; French walnut stock forend; reversible crossbolt safety; marketed with sling swivels; aluminum alloy receiver black anodized finish. Made in Japan. Introduced 1978; discontinued 1980.

Perf: $225 **Exc:** $175 **VGood:** $150

SKB MODEL XL 300

Gas-operated autoloader; 12-, 20-ga.; 5-shot magazine; 26-inch Improved Cylinder or Skeet, 28-inch Full or Modified, 30-inch Full barrel; optional vent rib; checkered American walnut pistol-grip stock, fluted forearm; self-compensating gas system; reversible safety. Introduced 1973; discontinued 1976.

With plain barrel

Perf: $275 **Exc:** $225 **VGood:** $190

With vent rib

Perf: $300 **Exc:** $250 **VGood:** $210

SKB MODEL XL 900

Gas-operated autoloader; 12-, 20-ga; 5-shot tube magazine; 26-inch Improved Cylinder; 28-inch Full or Modified, 30-inch Full barrel; vent rib; Raybar front sight; checkered walnut-finished stock; self-compensating gas system; reversible safety; action release button. Introduced 1973; discontinued 1978.

Perf: $300 **Exc:** $250 **VGood:** $220

SKB MODEL XL 900 SKEET

Same specs as Model XL 900 except 26-inch Skeet barrel; Bradley front sight. Introduced 1973; discontinued 1978.

Perf: $400 **Exc:** $350 **VGood:** $265

SKB MODEL XL 900 SLUG GUN

Same specs as Model XL 900 except 24-inch slug barrel; rifle sights. Introduced 1973; discontinued 1978.

Perf: $350 **Exc:** $295 **VGood:** $260

SKB MODEL XL 900 TRAP

Same specs as Model XL 900 except 12-ga.; 30-inch Full or Improved Cylinder barrel; Bradley front sight. Introduced 1973; discontinued 1978.

Perf: $395 **Exc:** $350 **VGood:** $320

SKB MODEL 500

Over/under; boxlock; hammerless; 12-, 20-, 28-ga., .410; 26-inch Improved/Modified, 28-inch Improved/ Modified or Modified/Full, 30-inch Modified/Full barrels; Raybar front sight; hand-checkered walnut pistol-grip stock, forearm; pistol-grip cap; fluted comb; gold-plated single selective trigger; automatic ejectors; non-automatic safety; chrome-lined barrels, action; scroll-engraved border on receiver. Introduced 1967; discontinued 1979.

Perf: $500 **Exc:** $400 **VGood:** $350

SKB MODEL 500 MAGNUM

Same specs as Model 500 except 12-ga.; 3-inch chambers. Introduced 1967; discontinued 1979.

Perf: $550 **Exc:** $450 **VGood:** $400

SKB MODEL 500 SKEET

Same specs as Model 500 except 12-, 20-ga.; fixed Skeet/Skeet chokes; recoil pad with white line spacer; white front sight with middle bead. Introduced 1979; no longer in production.

Perf: $500 **Exc:** $400 **VGood:** $350

SKB MODEL 505 DELUXE

Over/under; boxlock; 12-, 20-, 28-ga. (2-3/4-inch), 410; 3-inch chambers; 26-inch, 28-inch, 30-inch, 32-inch, 34-inch barrels; all 12-ga. barrels are back-bored, have lengthened forcing cones and longer choke tube system; Inter-Choke tubes or fixed (.410 only) Improved Cylinder/Modified, Modified/Full chokes; ventilated side ribs; weighs 6-1/2 to 8-1/2 lbs.; hand-checkered walnut stock with high-gloss finish; manual safety; automatic ejectors; single selective trigger; silver nitride-finish receiver with Field or Target pattern engraving, gold inlay. Made in Japan. Introduced 1987; discontinued 1993.

Field

Perf: $850 **Exc:** $700 **VGood:** $600

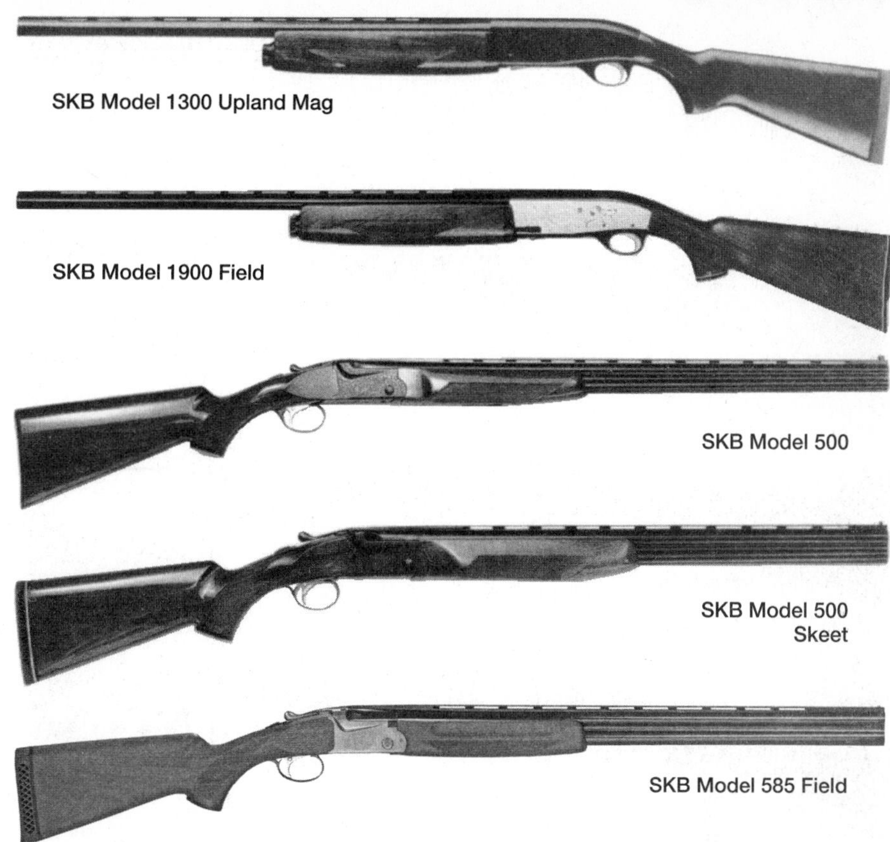

SKB Model 1300 Upland Mag

SKB Model 1900 Field

SKB Model 500

SKB Model 500 Skeet

SKB Model 585 Field

Two-barrel Field Set (12- & 20-ga., 20- & 28-ga. or 28-ga. & .410)

Perf: $1150 **Exc:** $1000 **VGood:** $900

SKB MODEL 505 SKEET

Same specs as the Model 505 Deluxe except 12-, 20-, 28-ga., .410; 26-inch 28-inch barrels; Skeet/ Skeet chokes; Skeet stock dimensions. Made in Japan. Introduced 1987; discontinued 1993.

Perf: $750 **Exc:** $600 **VGood:** $500

SKB MODEL 505 SKEET SET

Same specs as the Model 505 Deluxe except 12-ga. gun comes with 20-, 28-ga. and .410 barrel sets in 26-inch or 28-inch lengths; fixed Skeet/Skeet chokes; Skeet stock dimensions. Made in Japan. Introduced 1987; discontinued 1993.

Perf: $1750 **Exc:** $1400 **VGood:** $1050

SKB MODEL 505 TRAP

Same specs as the Model 505 Deluxe except 12-ga.; 2-3/4-inch chambers; 30-inch barrels; fixed Improved Modified/Full chokes; Trap stock dimensions. Made in Japan. Introduced 1987; discontinued 1993.

Perf: $850 **Exc:** $600 **VGood:** $500

SKB MODEL 505 TRAP COMBO

Same specs as the Model 505 Deluxe except comes with 30-inch or 32-inch over/under barrels and 32-inch or 34-inch top single barrel; standard or Monte Carlo stock. Made in Japan. Introduced 1987; discontinued 1993.

Perf: $1150 **Exc:** $900 **VGood:** $800

SKB MODEL 585 FIELD

Over/under; boxlock; 12-, 20-, 28-ga. (2-3/4-inch), .410; 3-inch chambers; 26-inch, 28-inch, 30-inch, 32-inch, 34-inch barrels; all 12-gauge barrels are back-bored, have lengthened forcing cones and longer choke tube system; Inter-Choke tubes or fixed (.410 only) Improved Cylinder/Modified or Modified/Full chokes; ventilated side ribs; hand checkered walnut stock with high-gloss finish; target stocks available in standard and Monte Carlo; manual safety, automatic ejectors, single selective trigger; silver nitride-finished receiver with Field or Target pattern engraving. Made in Japan. Introduced 1992; still in production.

Perf: $1255 **Exc:** $945 **VGood:** $760

Two-barrel Field Set (12- & 20-ga., 20- & 28-ga. or 28-ga. & .410)

Perf: $2115 **Exc:** $1775 **VGood:** $1475

Trap, Skeet

Perf: $1310 **Exc:** $975 **VGood:** $800

Two-barrel trap combo

Perf: $2110 **Exc:** $1775 **VGood:** $1600

Sporting Clays

Perf: $1410 **Exc:** $1050 **VGood:** $850

Skeet Set (20-, 28-, .410)

Perf: $3175 **Exc:** $2550 **VGood:** $2000

SKB MODEL 585 GOLD PACKAGE

Similar to Model 585 Field except gold-plated trigger, two gold-plated game inlays, schnabel forend. Silver or blue receiver. Introduced 1998. Imported from Japan by G.U. Inc.

12-, 20-ga.

Perf: $1375 **Exc:** $1065 **VGood:** $880

28-ga., .410

Perf: $1445 **Exc:** $1135 **VGood:** $950

SKB MODEL 585 SKEET

Same specs as Model 585 Field except Competition series choke tubes; Skeet-dimensioned stock, radiused recoil pad; oversize bores and lengthened forcing cones (12-ga. models); chrome-plated bores, chambers, ejectors. Made in Japan. Introduced 1992; still in production.

Perf: $1050 **Exc:** $800 **VGood:** $750

Four-barrel Skeet set

Perf: $2400 **Exc:** $1725 **VGood:** $1200

SKB MODEL 585 SPORTING CLAYS

Same specs as Model 585 Field except 12-, 20-, 28-ga.; 28-inch, 30-inch, 32-inch barrels; Competition series choke tubes (12-ga.), standard Inter-Choke tubes (20-, 28-ga.); traditional 3/8-inch narrow stepped rib or semi-wide channeled 15/16-inch stepped rib; nickel center bead, white front; special

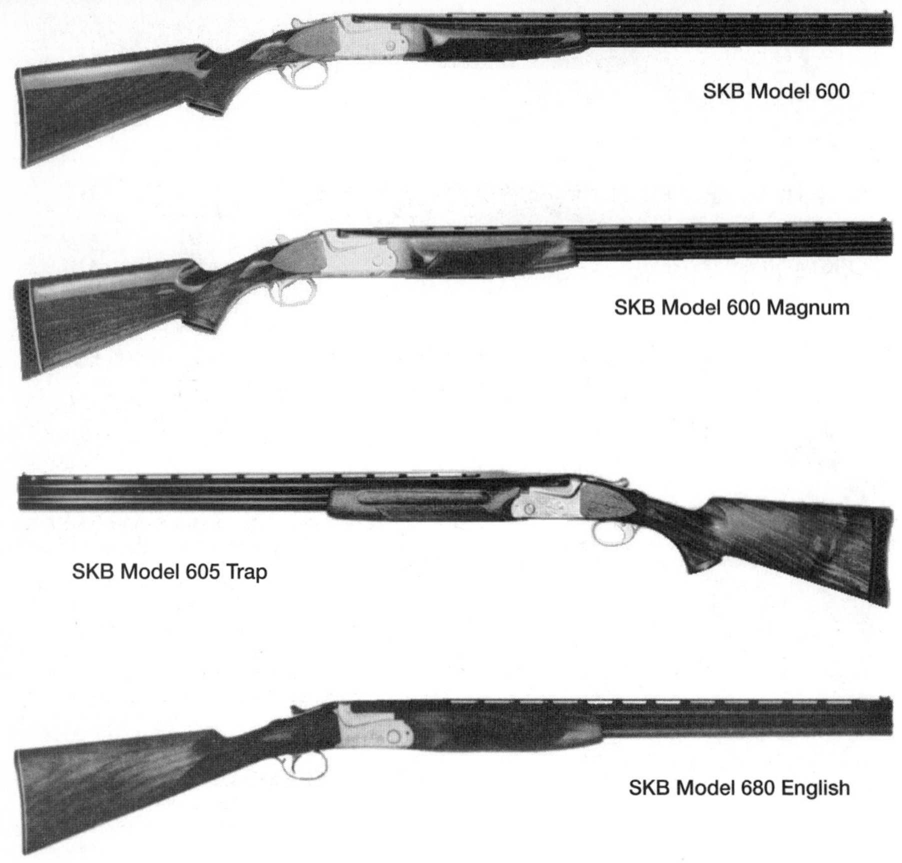
SKB Model 600
SKB Model 600 Magnum
SKB Model 605 Trap
SKB Model 680 English

stock dimensions. Made in Japan. Introduced 1992; still in production.

Perf: $1100 **Exc:** $850 **VGood:** $750

SKB MODEL 585 TRAP

Same specs as Model 585 Field except 12-ga.; 30-inch, 32-inch barrels; Competition series choke tubes; wide step rib; nickel center bead, white front; standard trap stock or Monte Carlo; oversize bores; lengthened forcing cones. Made in Japan. Introduced 1992; still in production.

Perf: $1050 **Exc:** $800 **VGood:** $750

SKB TWO-BARREL COMBO

Perf: $1550 **Exc:** $1300 **VGood:** $1150

SKB MODEL 585 WATERFOWLER

Same specs as Model 585 Field except 12-ga.; 28-inch, 30-inch barrels; Improved Cylinder, Skeet 1, Modified Inter-Choke tubes; oil-finished stock, forend; bead-blasted receiver with silver nitride finish; bead-blasted, blued barrels. Made in Japan. Introduced 1995; still in production.

Perf: $1100 **Exc:** $850 **VGood:** $750

SKB MODEL 585 YOUTH

Same specs as Model 585 Field except 12-, 20-ga.; 26-inch, 28-inch barrels; 13-1/2-inch length of pull; .755-inch bores, lengthened forcing cones and Competition series choke tubes. Made in Japan. Introduced 1994; still in production.

Perf: $950 **Exc:** $750 **VGood:** $650

SKB MODEL 600

Over/under; boxlock; hammerless; 12-, 20-, 28-ga., .410; 26-inch Improved/Modified, 28-inch Improved/Modified or Modified/Full, 30-inch Modified/Full barrel; Raybar front sight; select hand-checkered walnut pistol-grip stock, forearm; pistol-grip cap; fluted comb; gold-plated single selective trigger; automatic ejectors; non-automatic safety; chrome-lined barrels; silver-finished, scroll-engraved receiver. Introduced 1967; discontinued 1979.

Perf: $950 **Exc:** $875 **VGood:** $700

SKB MODEL 600 MAGNUM

Same specs as Model 600 except 12-ga.; 3-inch chamber. Introduced 1969; discontinued 1972.

Perf: $1050 **Exc:** $875 **VGood:** $730

SKB MODEL 600 SKEET GRADE

Same specs as Model 600 except 26-inch, 28-inch Skeet/Skeet barrels; recoil pad. Introduced 1967; discontinued 1979.

Perf: $995 **Exc:** $850 **VGood:** $725

SKB MODEL 600 SMALL BORE

Same specs as Model 600 except 20-, 28-ga., .410; 28-inch Skeet/Skeet three-barrel set; recoil pad. Introduced 1979; discontinued 1979.

Perf: $1400 **Exc:** $1100 **VGood:** $925

SKB MODEL 600 TRAP GRADE

Same specs as Model 600, except 12-ga; 30-inch, 32-inch barrels; Full/Full or Full/Improved; walnut straight or Monte Carlo pistol-grip stock; recoil pad. Introduced 1967; discontinued 1979.

Perf: $990 **Exc:** $850 **VGood:** $700

SKB MODEL 605 FIELD

Over/under; boxlock; 12-, 20-, 28-ga. (2-3/4-inch), .410; 3-inch chambers; 26-inch, 28-inch, 30-inch, 32-inch, 34-inch barrels; all 12-gauge barrels are back-bored, have lengthened forcing cones and longer choke tube system; Inter-Choke tubes or fixed Improved Cylinder/Modified, Modified/Full chokes; ventilated side ribs; weighs 6-1/2 to 8-1/2 lbs.; hand-checkered semi-fancy American walnut stock with high-gloss finish; manual safety; automatic ejectors; single selective trigger; silver nitride-finished receiver with Field or Target pattern engraving, gold inlay. Made in Japan. Introduced 1987; discontinued 1992.

Field

Perf: $1075 **Exc:** $850 **VGood:** $750

Two-barrel Field Set (12- & 20-ga. or 28-ga. & .410)

Perf: $1575 **Exc:** $1300 **VGood:** $1250

SKB MODEL 605 SKEET

Same specs as Model 605 Field except 12-, 20-, 28-ga., .410; 28-inch barrels; Skeet/Skeet chokes; Skeet stock dimensions. Made in Japan. Introduced 1987; discontinued 1992.

Perf: $1100 **Exc:** $850 **VGood:** $750

Four-barrel Skeet set

Perf: $1850 **Exc:** $1500 **VGood:** $1100

SKB MODEL 605 SPORTING CLAYS

Same specs as Model 605 Field except 12-ga.; 2-3/4-inch chambers; 28-inch, 30-inch barrels; Inter-Choke tubes; Sporting Clays stock dimensions. Made in Japan. Introduced 1987; discontinued 1993.

Perf: $1050 **Exc:** $800 **VGood:** $700

SKB MODEL 605 TRAP

Same specs as Model 605 Field except 12-ga.; 2-3/4-inch chambers; 30-inch, 32-inch barrels; Improved Modified/Full choke tubes; trap stock dimensions. Made in Japan. Introduced 1987; discontinued 1992.

Perf: $1000 **Exc:** $750 **VGood:** $650

Two-barrel trap combo

Perf: $1300 **Exc:** $1050 **VGood:** $950

SKB MODEL 680 ENGLISH

Over/under; boxlock; hammerless; 12-, 20-, 28-ga., .410; 26-inch, 28-inch chrome-lined barrels; Full/Modified or Modified/Improved chokes; vent rib; Bradley sights; checkered select walnut English-style straight-grip stock; single selective trigger; automatic selective ejectors; black chromed exterior surfaces. Introduced 1973; discontinued 1979.

Perf: $1300 **Exc:** $1150 **VGood:** $975

SKB MODEL 685 FIELD

Over/under; boxlock; 12- 20-, 28-ga. (2-3/4-inch), .410; 3-inch chambers; 26-inch, 28-inch, 30-inch, 32-inch, 34-inch barrels; all 12-gauge barrels are back-bored, have lengthened forcing cones and longer choke tube system; Inter-Choke tubes or fixed (.410 only) Improved Cylinder/Modified or Modified/Full chokes; hand-checkered walnut stock with high-gloss finish; target stocks available in standard and Monte Carlo; manual safety; automatic ejectors; single selective trigger; jeweled barrel block; silver-finished receiver with fine engraving, gold inlay. Made in Japan. No longer imported.

Perf: $1250 **Exc:** $925 **VGood:** $750

Two-barrel Field set (12- & 20-ga. or 28-ga. & .410)

Perf: $1650 **Exc:** $1350 **VGood:** $1200

SKB MODEL 685 SPORTING CLAYS

Same specs as Model 685 Field except 12-, 20-, 28-ga.; 28-inch, 30-inch, 32-inch barrels; choke tubes; 3/8-inch stepped target-style rib optional; nickel center bead, white front; special stock dimensions; matte finish receiver. Made in Japan. No longer imported.

Perf: $1250 **Exc:** $850 **VGood:** $750

Two-barrel Sporting Clays set (12-, 20-ga.)

Perf: $1650 **Exc:** $1250 **VGood:** $1150

SKB MODEL 685 TRAP

Same specs as Model 685 Field except 12-ga.; 30-inch, 32-inch barrels; wide step rib; nickel center bead, white front; Competition series choke tubes; standard trap or Monte Carlo stock; oversize bores and lengthened forcing cones. Made in Japan. No longer imported.

Perf: $1350 **Exc:** $950 **VGood:** $850

Two-barrel combo

Perf: $1650 **Exc:** $1250 **VGood:** $1150

SKB MODEL 685 SKEET

Same specs as Model 685 Field except Competition series choke tubes; Skeet-dimensioned stock, radiused recoil pad; all 12-ga. models have oversize bores and lengthened forcing cones; chrome-plated bores, chambers, ejectors. Made in Japan. No longer imported.

Perf: $1250 **Exc:** $850 **VGood:** $750

Four-barrel Skeet set

Perf: $1750 **Exc:** $1350 **VGood:** $1200

SKB MODEL 700 SKEET

Over/under; boxlock; hammerless; 12-, 20-, 28-ga., .410; 26-inch, 28-inch Skeet/Skeet chrome-lined barrels; Raybar front sight; select hand-checkered oil-finished walnut pistol-grip stock, forearm; pistol-grip cap; fluted comb; gold-plated single selective trigger; automatic ejectors; non-automatic safety; recoil pad; silver-finished engraved receiver. Introduced 1967; discontinued 1979.

Perf: $800 **Exc:** $700 **VGood:** $625

SKB MODEL 700 TRAP

Same specs as Model 700 Skeet except 12-, 20-ga.; 30-inch, 32-inch barrels; Full/Full or Full/Improved chokes; straight or Monte Carlo walnut pistol-grip stock. Introduced 1967; discontinued 1979.

Perf: $850 **Exc:** $705 **VGood:** $625

SKB MODEL 785 FIELD

Over/under; boxlock; 12-, 20-, 28-ga. (2-3/4-inch), .410; 3-inch chambers; 26-inch, 28-inch, 30-inch, 32-inch barrels; chrome-plated, oversize, back-bored barrels with lengthened forcing cones; Inter-Choke tubes; hand-checkered American black walnut stock, semi-beavertail forend with high-gloss finish; single selective chrome-plated trigger, chrome-plated selective ejectors; manual safety. Made in Japan. Introduced 1995.

Perf: $1750 **Exc:** $1400 **VGood:** $1200

Field set (12- and 20-ga.)

Perf: $2200 **Exc:** $1800 **VGood:** $1500

Field, 12- or 20-ga.

Perf: $1900 **Exc:** $1650 **VGood:** $1400

Field, 28-ga. or .410

Perf: $1980 **Exc:** $1730 **VGood:** $1480

Field set, 20- & 28-ga., 28-ga. & .410

Perf: $2780 **Exc:** $2400 **VGood:** $2025

Sporting Clays, 12- or 20-ga.

Perf: $2000 **Exc:** $1675 **VGood:** $1375

Sporting Clays, 28-ga.

Perf: $2080 **Exc:** $1755 **VGood:** $1455

Sporting Clays set, 12- and 20-ga.

Perf: $2775 **Exc:** $2450 **VGood:** $2125

Skeet, 12- or 20-ga.

Perf: $1940 **Exc:** $1625 **VGood:** $1365

Skeet, 28-ga. or .410

Perf: $1980 **Exc:** $1665 **VGood:** $1405

Skeet, three-barrel set, 20-, 28-ga.,.410

Perf: $3835 **Exc:** $2975 **VGood:** $2350

Trap, standard or Monte Carlo

Perf: $1940 **Exc:** $1625 **VGood:** $1365

Trap combo, standard or Monte Carlo

Perf: $2820 **Exc:** $2505 **VGood:** $2245

SKB MODEL 785 SKEET

Same specs as Model 785 Field except Competition series choke tubes; Skeet-dimensioned stock, radiused recoil pad; all 12-ga. barrels back-bored with lengthened forcing cones. Made in Japan. Introduced 1995; still in production.

Perf: $1750 **Exc:** $1400 **VGood:** $1200

Three-barrel Skeet set (20-, 28-ga., .410)

Perf: $2350 **Exc:** $1800 **VGood:** $1500

SKB MODEL 785 SPORTING CLAYS

Same specs as Model 785 Field except 12-, 20-, 28-ga.; 28-inch, 30-inch, 32-inch barrels; target-style ventilated rib; Sporting Clays stock dimensions; radiused recoil pad. Made in Japan. Introduced 1995; still in production.

Perf: $1800 **Exc:** $1400 **VGood:** $1150

Sporting Clays set (12- and 20-ga.)

Perf: $2400 **Exc:** $2000 **VGood:** $1550

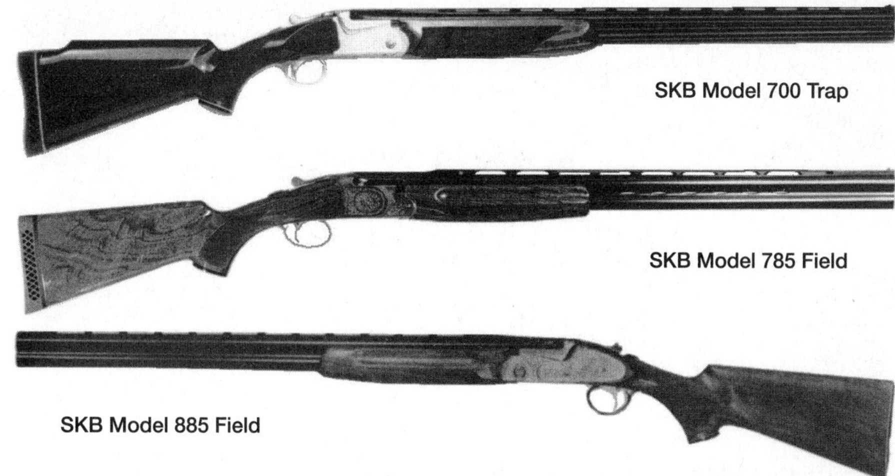

SKB Model 700 Trap

SKB Model 785 Field

SKB Model 885 Field

SKB MODEL 785 TRAP

Same specs as Model 785 Field except 12-ga.; 30-inch, 32-inch barrels; back-bored barrels with lengthened forcing cones, chrome-plated chambers; Competition series choke tubes; standard trap or Monte Carlo stock. Made in Japan. Introduced 1995; dropped 2002.

Perf: $1750 **Exc:** $1400 **VGood:** $1200

Two-barrel combo

Perf: $2200 **Exc:** $1800 **VGood:** $1500

SKB MODEL 800 FIELD

Over/under; boxlock; hammerless; 12-, 20-, 28-ga., .410; 26-inch Improved/Modified, 28-inch Improved/Modified or Modified/Full, 30-inch Modified/Full barrels; Raybar front sight; select hand-checkered walnut pistol-grip stock, forearm; pistol-grip cap; fluted comb; gold-plated single selective trigger; automatic ejectors; non-automatic safety; chrome-lined barrels, action; fine scroll-engraved border on receiver. Introduced 1979; discontinued 1980.

Perf: $1100 **Exc:** $800 **VGood:** $700

SKB MODEL 800 SKEET

Same specs as Model 800 Field except 12-, 20-ga.; 26-inch, 28-inch Skeet/Skeet chrome-lined barrels; recoil pad. Introduced 1969; discontinued 1979.

Perf: $1250 **Exc:** $900 **VGood:** $800

SKB MODEL 800 TRAP

Same specs as Model 800 Field except 12-ga.; 30-inch, 32-inch barrels; Full/Full or Full/Improved; straight or Monte Carlo walnut pistol-grip stock. Introduced 1967; discontinued 1979.

Perf: $1250 **Exc:** $900 **VGood:** $800

SKB MODEL 880 CROWN GRADE

Over/under; boxlock; sideplates; 12-, 20-, 28-ga., .410; 26-inch Skeet/Skeet, 28-inch Skeet/Skeet, 30-inch Full/Improved, 32-inch Full/Improved barrels; Bradley-type front sight; trap or Skeet hand-checkered fancy French walnut pistol-grip stock, forearm; hand-honed action; engraved receiver; gold-inlaid crown on bottom of frame. Introduced 1973; discontinued 1976.

Perf: $1900 **Exc:** $1800 **VGood:** $1600

SKB MODEL 885 FIELD

Over/under; boxlock; dummy sideplates; 12-, 20-, 28-ga. (2-3/4-inch), .410; 3-inch chambers; 26-inch, 28-inch, 30-inch, 32-inch, 34-inch barrels; all 12-gauge barrels are back-bored, have lengthened forcing cones and longer choke tube system; Inter-Choke tubes or fixed (.410 only) Improved Cylinder/Modified or Modified/Full chokes; hand-checkered select-grade walnut stock with high-gloss finish; target stocks available in standard and Monte Carlo; manual safety; automatic ejectors; single selective trigger; jeweled barrel block; silver-finished receiver with fine engraving, gold inlay. Made in Japan. No longer imported.

Perf: $1650 **Exc:** $1200 **VGood:** $900

Two-barrel Field set (12- & 20-ga. or 28-ga. & .410)

Perf: $2100 **Exc:** $1500 **VGood:** $1300

SKB MODEL 885 SPORTING CLAYS

Same specs as Model 885 Field except 12-, 20-, 28-ga.; 28-inch, 30-inch 32-inch barrels; choke tubes; 3/8-inch stepped target-style rib optional; nickel center bead, white front; special stock dimensions; matte finish receiver. Made in Japan. No longer imported.

Perf: $1450 **Exc:** $800 **VGood:** $700

SKB MODEL 885 SKEET

Same specs as Model 885 Field except Competition series choke tubes; Skeet-dimensioned stock, radiused recoil pad; all 12-ga. barrels oversize with lengthened forcing cones; chrome-plated bores, chambers, ejectors. Made in Japan. No longer imported.

Perf: $1450 **Exc:** $800 **VGood:** $700

Four-barrel Skeet set

Perf: $2800 **Exc:** $2000 **VGood:** $1800

SKB MODEL 885 TRAP

Same specs as Model 885 Field except 12-ga.; 30-inch, 32-inch barrels; Competition series choke tubes; wide step rib; nickel center bead, white front; standard trap stock or Monte Carlo; oversize bores and lengthened forcing cones. Made in Japan. No longer imported.

Perf: $1650 **Exc:** $900 **VGood:** $800

Two-barrel combo

Perf: $2100 **Exc:** $1500 **VGood:** $1300

SKB MODEL 5600

Over/under; 12-ga.; 26-inch, 28-inch, 30-inch barrels; vent rib; checkered walnut pistol-grip stock; auto selective ejectors; mechanical single trigger; hand-polished, blued frame, barrels; made in trap and Skeet configurations. Made in Japan. Introduced 1979; discontinued 1980.

Perf: $575 **Exc:** $495 **VGood:** $430

SKB MODEL 5700

Over/under; 12-ga.; 26-inch, 28-inch, 30-inch barrels; vent rib; high-grade checkered walnut pistol-grip stock; auto selective ejectors; mechanical single trigger; hand-polished, blued frame, barrels; engraving; made in trap and Skeet configurations. Introduced 1979; discontinued 1980.

Perf: $695 **Exc:** $530 **VGood:** $455

SKB MODEL 5800

Over/under; 12-ga.; 26-inch, 28-inch, 30-inch barrels; vent rib; best-grade checkered walnut pistol-grip stock; auto selective ejectors; mechanical single trigger; hand-polished, blued frame, barrels; elaborate engraving; made in trap and Skeet configurations. Introduced 1979; discontinued 1980.

Perf: $950 **Exc:** $850 **VGood:** $775

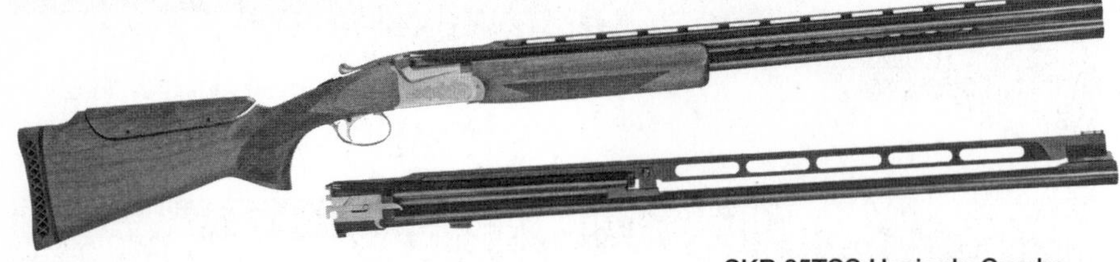
SKB 85TSS Unsingle Combo

SKB Model 150

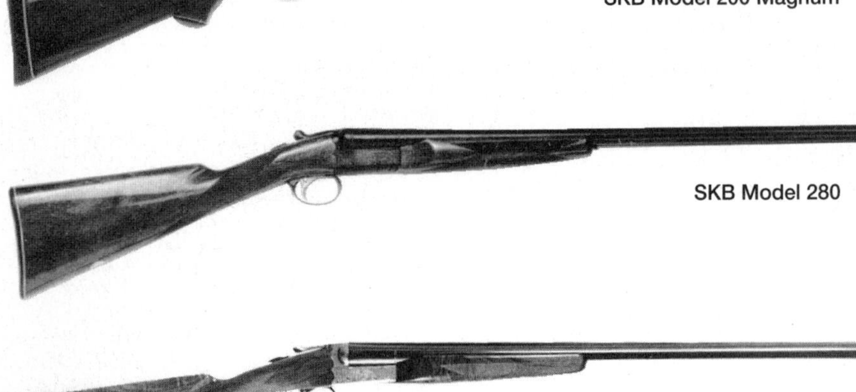
SKB Model 200 Magnum

SKB Model 280

SKB Model 385

SKB MODEL 85 TSS TRAP

Over/under; 12-ga.; 3-inch chamber; 32-inch barrel (Mag-na-ported barrel optional); weighs 8-3/4 lbs.; fixed or adjustable comb; 12 mm step-up rib.

SKB 85TSS UNSINGLE COMBO

Same as 85TSS above but with extra "unsingle" single-shot barrel set.

SKB MODEL 100

Side-by side; boxlock; 12-, 20-ga.; 26-inch Improved/Modified, 28-inch Full/Modified, 30-inch Full/Full barrels; hand-checkered pistol grip stock, forearm; single selective trigger; plain extractors; automatic safety. Made in Japan. Introduced 1967; discontinued 1979.

Perf: $795 **Exc:** $575 **VGood:** $400

Add 20 percent to above prices for 20-ga. Add 10-15 percent for fully engraved receiver with hunting scene.

SKB MODEL 150

Side-by-side; boxlock; 12-, 20-ga.; 26-inch Improved/Modified, 28-inch Full/Modified, 30-inch Full/Full barrels; hand-checkered pistol-grip stock, beavertail forearm; single selective trigger; plain extractors; automatic safety. Introduced 1972; discontinued 1974.

Perf: $895 **Exc:** $645 **VGood:** $425

Add 20 percent to above prices for 20-ga.

SKB MODEL 200E

Side-by-side; boxlock; 12-, 20-ga.; 2-3/4-inch chambers; 26-inch Improved/Modified, 28-inch Full/Modified, 30-inch Full/Full barrels; hand-checkered pistol-grip stock, beavertail forearm; recoil pad; automatic selective ejectors; engraved, silver-plated frame; gold-plated nameplate, trigger. Introduced 1967; discontinued 1979.

Perf: $1100 **Exc:** $995 **VGood:** $875

SKB MODEL 200E SKEET GRADE

Same specs as Model 200E except 25-inch Skeet/Skeet barrels; straight-grip English-style stock; non-automatic safety; recoil pad. Introduced 1967; discontinued 1979.

Perf: $1150 **Exc:** $1025 **VGood:** $900

SKB MODEL 200 MAGNUM

Same specs as Model 200E except 3-inch chambers; 26-inch, 28-inch, 30-inch barrels; white line spacer recoil pad. Introduced 1979; no longer in production.

Perf: $1150 **Exc:** $1025 **VGood:** $900

SKB MODEL 280

Side-by-side; boxlock; 12-, 20-ga.; 2-3/4-inch chambers; 25-inch, 26-inch, 28-inch barrels; standard choke combos; hand-checkered straight-grip stock, forearm; automatic selective ejectors; single selective trigger; gold-plated nameplate, trigger; game scene engraving. Introduced 1971; discontinued 1979.

Perf: $1400 **Exc:** $900 **VGood:** $650

SKB MODEL 385

Gauge: 12, 20, 3-inch chambers; 28, 2-3/4-inch chambers. Barrel: 26-inch (Imp. Cyl., Mod., Skeet choke tubes). Weight: 6-3/4 lbs. Length: 42 1/2-inch overall; American walnut with straight or pistol grip stock, semi-beavertail forend. Features: Boxlock action. Silver nitrided receiver with engraving; solid barrel rib; single selective trigger, selective automatic ejectors, automatic safety. Introduced 1996. Imported from Japan by G.U. Inc.

Perf: $1750 **Exc:** $1425 **VGood:** $1050

Field Set, 20-, 28-ga., 26-inch or 28-inch, English or pistol grip

Perf: $2475 **Exc:** $2100 **VGood:** $1750

SKB MODEL 385 SPORTING CLAYS

Similar to the Field Model 385 except 12-gauge only; 28-inch barrel with choke tubes; raised ventilated rib with metal middle bead and white front. Introduced 1998. Imported from Japan by G.U. Inc.

Perf: $1850 **Exc:** $1425 **VGood:** $1050

Sporting Clays set, 20-, 28-ga.

Perf: $2575 **Exc:** $2100 **VGood:** $1750

SKB MODEL 485

Similar to the Model 385 except has dummy sideplates, raised ventilated rib with metal middle bead and white front, extensive upland game scene engraving, semi-fancy American walnut English or pistol grip stock. Imported from Japan by G.U. Inc.

Perf: $2400 **Exc:** $2050 **VGood:** $1725

Field set, 20-, 28-ga., 26-inch

Perf: $3400 **Exc:** $2825 **VGood:** $2300

SKB MODEL 400E

Side-by-side; boxlock; 12-, 20-ga.; 3-inch chambers; 26-inch Improved/Modified, 28-inch Full/Modified, 30-inch Full/Full barrels; hand-checkered pistol-grip stock, beavertail forearm; recoil pad; automatic selective ejectors; engraved, silver-plated frame, sideplates; gold-plated nameplate, trigger. No longer in production.

Perf: $1595 **Exc:** $1495 **VGood:** $1395

SKB MODEL 400E SKEET GRADE

Same specs as Model 400E except 25-inch Skeet/Skeet barrel; straight-grip English-style stock; non-automatic safety; recoil pad. Introduced 1967; discontinued 1979.

Perf: $650 **Exc:** $500 **VGood:** $450

SKB MODEL 480

Side-by-side; boxlock; 12-, 20-ga.; 3-inch chambers; 25-inch, 26-inch, 28-inch barrels; standard choke combos; hand-checkered straight-grip stock, forearm; automatic selective ejectors; single selective trigger; gold-plated nameplate, trigger; game scene engraving. Introduced 1971; discontinued 1979.

Perf: $1000 **Exc:** $750 **VGood:** $600

SKB CENTURY

Single-barrel trap; boxlock; 12-ga.; 30-inch, 32-inch barrel; vent rib; full choke; checkered pistol-grip walnut stock, beavertail forearm; straight or Monte Carlo comb; recoil pad; auto ejector. Introduced 1973; discontinued 1974.

Perf: $550 **Exc:** $475 **VGood:** $430

SKB CENTURY II

Same specs as Century except redesigned locking iron; Monte Carlo stock, reverse-taper forearm. Introduced 1975; discontinued 1979.

Perf: $575 **Exc:** $495 **VGood:** $455

SKB MODEL 7300

Slide action; 12-, 20-ga.; 2-3/4-inch, 3-inch chambers; 24-inch, 26-inch, 28-inch, 30-inch barrels; vent rib; Ray-type front sights; hand-checkered French walnut stock, beavertail forend; recoil pad; white line spacer; double action bars. Made in Japan. Introduced 1979; discontinued 1980.

Perf: $275 **Exc:** $200 **VGood:** $180

SKB MODEL 7900 TARGET GRADE

Slide action; 12-, 20-ga.; 2-3/4-inch, 3-inch chambers; 26-inch Skeet/Skeet, 30-inch trap-choked barrels; white front sight, middle bead; hand-checkered French walnut stock, beavertail forend; recoil pad (Trap) or composition buttplate (Skeet); blued scroll-etched receiver; made in Trap and Skeet configurations. Introduced 1979; discontinued 1980.

Perf: $325 **Exc:** $275 **VGood:** $225

S&M 10-GAUGE

Over/under; boxlock; 10-ga.; 3-1/2-inch chambers; 28-inch, 32-1/2-inch Full/Full barrels; weighs 9 lbs.; checkered walnut stock; double triggers; extractors; matte-finished metal. Made in Europe. Introduced by Ballistic Products 1986; discontinued 1988.

Perf: $475 **Exc:** $375 **VGood:** $300

L.C. SMITH HAMMERLESS DOUBLE BARRELS (1890-1912)

Side-by-side; sidelock; hammerless; 8-, 10-, 12-, 16-, 20-ga.; 26-inch, 28-inch, 30-inch, 32-inch twist or fluid steel barrels; lowest grades stocked in American walnut, high grades in European walnut; splinter or beavertail forend; straight, half-, or pistol grip; double triggers; selective single trigger optional after 1904; ejectors optional in lower grades, standard in high grades; Featherweight frame was available in certain grades after 1909; only 30 made in 8-ga., 1895 to 1897; made in 12 grades until revised in 1913. Manufactured by Hunter Arms Co., Fulton, New York. Introduced 1890; discontinued 1912.

L.C. SMITH HAMMERLESS DOUBLE BARREL NO. 00 (1890-1912)

Same specs as Hammerless Double Barrel (1890-1912), except 12-, 16-, 20-ga.; fluid steel barrels; double trigger, extractors standard; single trigger, ejectors optional; total production, 57,795; with ejectors, 5,874. Introduced 1889; discontinued 1912.

Exc: $1250 **VGood:** $800 **Good:** $650

L.C. SMITH HAMMERLESS DOUBLE BARREL NO. 0 (1890-1912)

Same specs as Hammerless Double Barrel (1890 to 1912), except twist (10-, 12-, 16-ga.) or fluid steel (10-, 12-, 16-, 20-ga.) barrels; double triggers, extractors standard; ejectors optional after 1898; Featherweight frame available after 1907; total production, 29,360; with ejectors, 6607. Introduced 1895; discontinued 1912.

Exc: $1450 **VGood:** $950 **Good:** $750

L.C. SMITH HAMMERLESS DOUBLE BARREL NO. 1 (1890-1912)

Same specs as Hammerless Double Barrel (1890 to 1912), except twist (10-, 12-, 16-ga.) or fluid steel (10-, 12-, 16-, 20-ga.) barrels; fluid steel barrels available after 1907; double triggers, extractors standard; single trigger, ejectors optional; Featherweight frame available after 1907; in decoration, corresponds to the earlier Quality 2; total production, 10,221; with ejectors, 1640. Introduced 1890; discontinued 1912.

Exc: $1800 **VGood:** $1100 **Good:** $900

L.C. SMITH HAMMERLESS DOUBLE BARREL PIGEON GUN (1890-1912)

Same specs as Hammerless Double Barrel (1890 to 1912), except twist (10-, 12-, 16-ga.) or fluid steel (12-, 16-, 20-ga.) barrels; French walnut straight or pistol grip stock; Monte Carlo comb optional; double triggers, ejectors standard; single trigger optional; lightweight version available in 12- and 16-ga.; total production, 1214. Introduced 1895; discontinued 1912.

Exc: $1950 **VGood:** $1500 **Good:** $1300

L.C. SMITH HAMMERLESS DOUBLE BARREL NO. 2 (1890-1912)

Same specs as Hammerless Double Barrel (1890 to 1912), except 28-inch to 32-inch fluid steel barrels standard; twist barrels optional; European walnut pistol-grip stock; double triggers, extractors standard; ejectors optional; Featherweight frame

SKB Model 7300

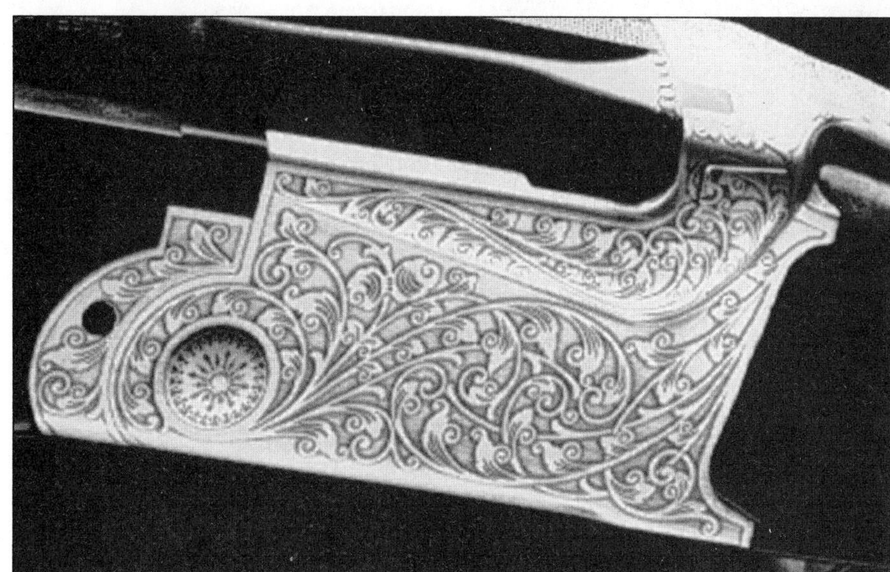

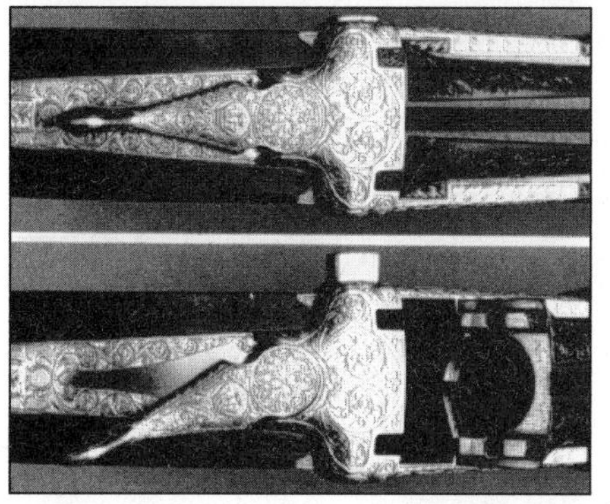

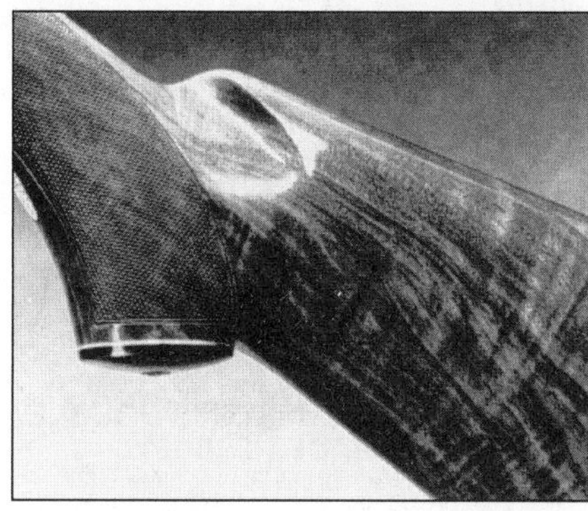

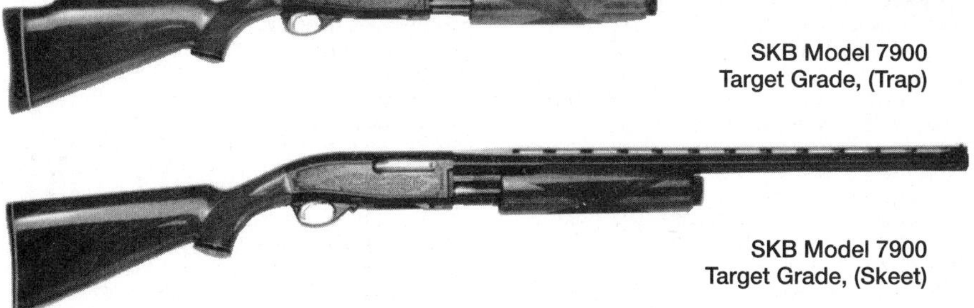

SKB Model 7900 Target Grade, (Trap)

SKB Model 7900 Target Grade, (Skeet)

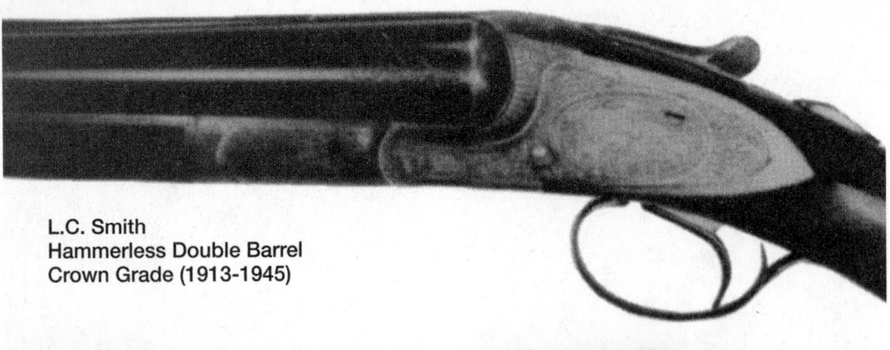

L.C. Smith
Hammerless Double Barrel
Crown Grade (1913-1945)

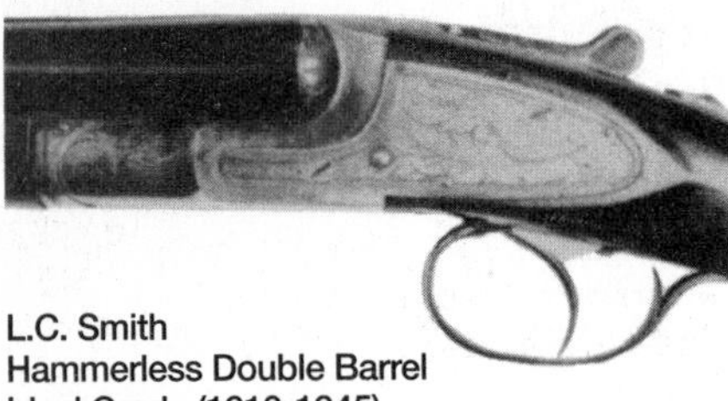

L.C. Smith
Hammerless Double Barrel
Ideal Grade (1913-1945)

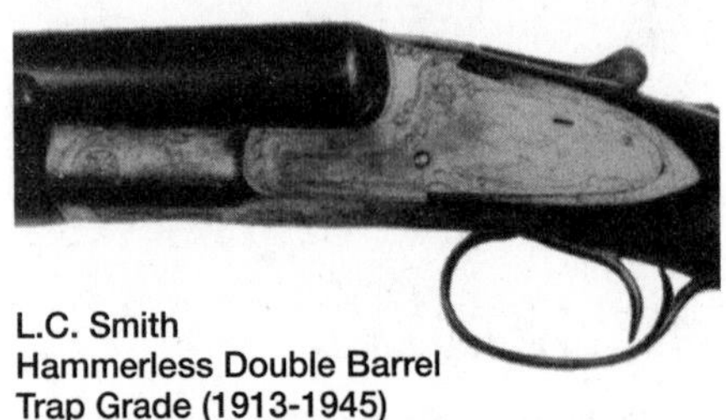

L.C. Smith
Hammerless Double Barrel
Trap Grade (1913-1945)

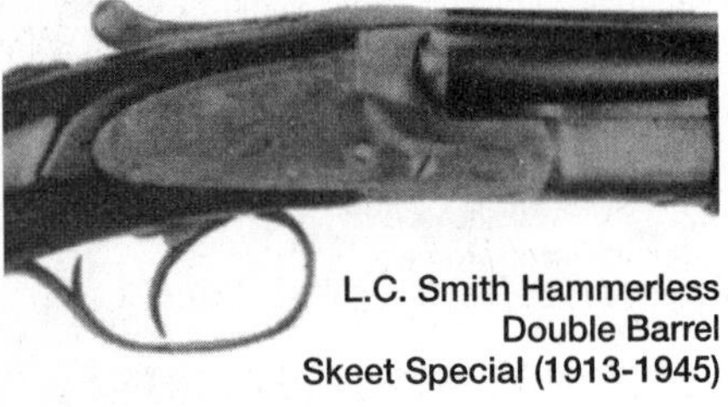

L.C. Smith Hammerless
Double Barrel
Skeet Special (1913-1945)

L.C. Smith Hammerless
Double Barrel
Specialty Grade (1913-1945)

available; total production, 12,887; with ejectors, 5044. Introduced 1892; discontinued 1912.

Exc: $2600 **VGood:** $1800 **Good:** $1400

L.C. SMITH HAMMERLESS DOUBLE BARREL NO. 3 (1890-1912)

Same specs as Hammerless Double Barrel (1890 to 1912), except fluid steel (12-, 16-, 20-ga.) or twist (10-, 12-, 16-, 20-ga.) barrels; English walnut straight or pistol-grip stock; double triggers, extractors standard; single trigger, ejectors optional; total production, 3790; with ejectors, 2093. Introduced 1892; discontinued 1912.

Exc: $2800 **VGood:** $2000 **Good:** $1500

L.C. SMITH HAMMERLESS DOUBLE BARREL NO. 4 (1890-1912)

Same specs as Hammerless Double Barrel (1890 to 1912), except twist (10-, 12-, 16-, 20-ga.) or fluid steel (12-, 16-, 20-ga.) barrels; French or English walnut straight or pistol-grip stock; Monte Carlo comb optional; double triggers, extractors standard; ejectors optional; total production, 455; with ejectors, 321. Introduced 1892; discontinued 1913.

Exc: $7500 **VGood:** $5900 **Good:** $3500

L.C. SMITH HAMMERLESS DOUBLE BARREL A1 GRADE (1890-1912)

Same specs as Hammerless Double Barrel (1890 to 1912), except 10-, 12-, 16-ga.; 28-inch to 32-inch twist barrels; English walnut half-, three-quarter- or pistol-grip stock; double triggers, ejectors standard; total production, 739. Introduced 1890; discontinued 1898.

Exc: $4500 **VGood:** $3100 **Good:** $2500

L.C. SMITH HAMMERLESS DOUBLE BARREL NO. 5 (1890-1912)

Same specs as Hammerless Double Barrel (1890 to 1912), except twist (10-, 12-, 16-ga.) or fluid steel (12-, 16-, 20-ga.) barrels; English or French walnut stocks; double triggers, ejectors standard; extractors, single trigger optional; in 1913, No. 5 was renamed Crown Grade; total production before 1913, 484; with ejectors, 373. Introduced 1892; discontinued 1912.

Exc: $7000 **VGood:** $4200 **Good:** $3300

L.C. SMITH HAMMERLESS DOUBLE BARREL MONOGRAM (1890-1912)

Same specs as Hammerless Double Barrel (1890 to 1912), except twist barrels; Whitworth fluid steel barrels available after 1896; English, French or Circassian walnut straight or pistol-grip stock; Monte Carlo comb optional; ejectors standard after 1896; double triggers standard; single trigger optional; Featherweight frame, with Whitworth steel barrels, available after 1907; Monogram was the only grade not changed in 1913; total production (1895-1912), 102. Introduced 1895; discontinued 1945.

Exc: $9000 **VGood:** $6300 **Good:** $5000

L.C. SMITH HAMMERLESS DOUBLE BARREL A2 GRADE (1890-1912)

Same specs as Hammerless Double Barrel (1890 to 1912), except twist or Whitworth fluid steel barrels; French, English or Circassian walnut straight or pistol-grip stock; Monte Carlo comb optional; ejectors, double triggers standard; single trigger optional; lightweight version with Krupp steel barrels available; total production, 100. Introduced 1892; discontinued 1912.

Exc: $12,000 **VGood:** $8500 **Good:** $6600

L.C. SMITH HAMMERLESS DOUBLE BARREL A3 GRADE (1890-1912)

Same specs as Hammerless Double Barrel (1890 to 1912), except Whitworth steel barrels; Krupp steel barrels optional; ejectors, double triggers standard; single trigger optional; Circassian walnut straight or pistol-grip stock; Monte Carlo comb optional; lightweight version available; total production, 17. Introduced 1896; discontinued 1915. Extremely rare, precludes pricing.

L.C. SMITH HAMMERLESS DOUBLE BARRELS (1913-1945)

Side-by-side; sidelock; hammerless; 10-, 12-, 16-, 20-ga., .410; 26-inch, 28-inch, 30-inch, 32-inch twist or fluid steel barrels; lowest grades stocked in American walnut, high grades in European walnut; straight-, half- or pistol-grip; splinter or beavertail forend. L.C. Smith guns built after 1912 follow the same basic specifications in gauges, barrel lengths, and other features as those made earlier. Their appearance is somewhat different, however, in that the frames and lockplates lack many of the complex, graceful curves and planes that characterize the older guns; this simpler, more straightforward shaping was an attempt by Hunter Arms to reduce the amount of milling and handwork that went into the guns, and thereby reduce the cost of manufacture. Beavertail forends became available in 1920; .410-bore guns in 1926; 10-ga. phased out in early 1920s; Featherweight frame available in some grades up to 1927, in all grades after 1927; special, extra-high solid rib available in all grades after 1939; manufactured by Hunter Arms Co., Fulton, New York. Introduced 1913; discontinued 1945.

L.C. SMITH HAMMERLESS DOUBLE BARREL FIELD GRADE (1913-1945)

Same specs as Hammerless Double Barrel (1913 to 1945), except 12-, 16-, 20-ga., .410; fluid steel barrels; American walnut pistol-grip stock; double triggers, extractors standard; single trigger, ejectors optional; a version featuring ivory sights and recoil pad was introduced in 1939 as the Field Special; total production, 141,844. Introduced 1913; discontinued 1945.

Exc: $995 **VGood:** $700 **Good:** $600

L.C. SMITH HAMMERLESS DOUBLE BARREL IDEAL GRADE (1913-1945)

Same specs as Hammerless Double Barrel (1913 to 1945), except twist or fluid steel barrels; fluid steel barrels only, after 1917; 26-inch, 28-inch barrels only in .410; American walnut pistol-grip stock; straight or half-pistol grip optional; double triggers, extractors standard; single trigger, ejectors optional; total production, 21,862. Introduced 1913; discontinued 1945.

Exc: $1300 **VGood:** $900 **Good:** $800

L.C. SMITH HAMMERLESS DOUBLE BARREL TRAP GRADE (1913-1945)

Same specs as Hammerless Double Barrel (1913 to 1945), except fluid steel barrels standard; twist barrels optional until 1917; American walnut pistol-grip stock standard; straight or half-pistol grip optional; ejectors and single trigger standard; double triggers optional; total production 3335. Introduced 1913; discontinued 1939.

Exc: $1500 **VGood:** $1300 **Good:** $900

L.C. SMITH HAMMERLESS DOUBLE BARREL SKEET SPECIAL (1913-1945)

Same specs as Hammerless Double Barrel (1913 to 1945), except 12-, 16-, 20-ga., .410; 26-inch, 27-inch, 28-inch fluid steel barrels; American walnut straight-grip stock, beavertail forend standard; half- and pistol grip optional; single trigger; ejectors; checkered butt standard; Featherweight frame standard; total production 771. Introduced 1929; discontinued 1944.

Exc: $1950 **VGood:** $1400 **Good:** $1100

L.C. SMITH HAMMERLESS DOUBLE BARREL OLYMPIC GRADE (1913-1945)

Same specs as Hammerless Double Barrel (1913 to 1945), except 12-, 16-, 20-ga.; 28-inch to 32-inch fluid steel barrels; vent rib; ivory bead sight; American walnut pistol-grip stock, beavertail forend standard; straight or half-pistol grip optional; single trigger; recoil pad; total production, 26. Introduced 1932; discontinued 1938. Extremely rare; precludes pricing.

L.C. SMITH HAMMERLESS DOUBLE BARREL SPECIALTY GRADE (1913-1945)

Same specs as Hammerless Double Barrel (1913 to 1945), except fluid steel barrels standard; twist barrels optional until 1917; vent rib optional; American walnut straight-, half- or pistol-grip stock; double triggers, extractors standard; single trigger, ejectors optional; total production, 6,565. Introduced 1913; discontinued 1945.

Exc: $2000 **VGood:** $1400 **Good:** $1100

L.C. SMITH HAMMERLESS DOUBLE BARREL EAGLE GRADE (1913-1945)

Same specs as Hammerless Double Barrel (1913 to 1945), except 10-, 12-, 16-, 20-ga.; fluid steel barrels standard; twist barrels optional until 1917; European walnut straight-, half- or pistol-grip stock; double triggers, extractors standard; single trigger, ejectors optional; total production, 580. Introduced 1913; discontinued 1932.

Exc: $4000 **VGood:** $2800 **Good:** $2200

L.C. SMITH HAMMERLESS DOUBLE BARREL CROWN GRADE (1913-1945)

Same specs as Hammerless Double Barrel (1913 to 1945), except fluid steel barrels standard; twist barrels optional until 1917; made largely to order, with all options: vent rib; European walnut straight-, half- or pistol-grip stock, beavertail forend; single trigger; ejectors; total production, 842. Introduced 1913; discontinued 1945.

Exc: $5000 **VGood:** $3500 **Good:** $2750

L.C. SMITH HAMMERLESS DOUBLE BARREL MONOGRAM GRADE (1913-1945)

Same specs as Hammerless Double Barrel (1913 to 1945), except twist or Whitworth fluid steel barrels; English, French or Circassian walnut straight or pistol-grip stock; Monte Carlo comb optional; ejectors; double triggers standard; single trigger optional; Featherweight frame, with Whitworth steel barrels, available; same specifications as pre-1913 Monogram Grade; total production (1913-1945), 164. Introduced 1895; discontinued 1945.

Exc: $9000 **VGood:** $6300 **Good:** $5000

L.C. SMITH HAMMERLESS DOUBLE BARREL PREMIER GRADE (1913-1945)

Same specs as Hammerless Double Barrel (1913 to 1945), except 12-, 16-, 20-ga.; Whitworth fluid steel barrels; made to order; all options available; total production, 28. Introduced 1913; discontinued 1941. Extremely rare; precludes pricing.

L.C. SMITH HAMMERLESS DOUBLE BARREL DELUXE GRADE (1913-1945)

Same specs as Hammerless Double Barrel (1913 to 1945), except 12-, 16-, 20-ga.; Whitworth fluid steel barrels; made to order; all options available; total production, 30. Introduced 1913; discontinued 1945. Extreme rarity precludes pricing.

L.C. SMITH HAMMERLESS DOUBLE BARREL LONG RANGE WILD FOWL GUN (1913-1945)

Same specs as Hammerless Double Barrel (1913 to 1945), except 12-ga.; 3-inch chambers; 30-inch or 32-inch barrels; European walnut pistol-grip stock; straight- or -pistol-grip optional; extractors or ejectors; double or single trigger; available in any standard grade. Introduced 1924; discontinued 1945.

Exc: $900 **VGood:** $600 **Good:** $500

L.C. SMITH HAMMERLESS DOUBLE BARRELS (1945-1950)

Side-by-side; sidelock; hammerless; 10-, 12-, 16-, 20-ga., .410; 26-inch, 28-inch, 30-inch, 32-inch twist or fluid steel barrels; lowest grades stocked in American walnut, high grades in European walnut; straight-, half- or pistol-grip; splinter or beavertail forend. Marlin Firearms Company purchased Hunter Arms Company in 1945; guns built after 1945 were stamped L.C. SMITH GUN COMPANY; all grades of double gun except Field, Ideal, Specialty and Crown were discontinued; specifications for these grades remained same as before; manufactured by Marlin Firearms, Co. Introduced 1945; discontinued 1950.

L.C. SMITH HAMMERLESS DOUBLE BARREL FIELD GRADE (1945-1950)

Same specs as Hammerless Double Barrel (1945 to 1950), except 12-, 16-, 20-ga., .410; fluid steel barrels; American walnut pistol-grip stock; double triggers, extractors standard; single trigger, ejectors

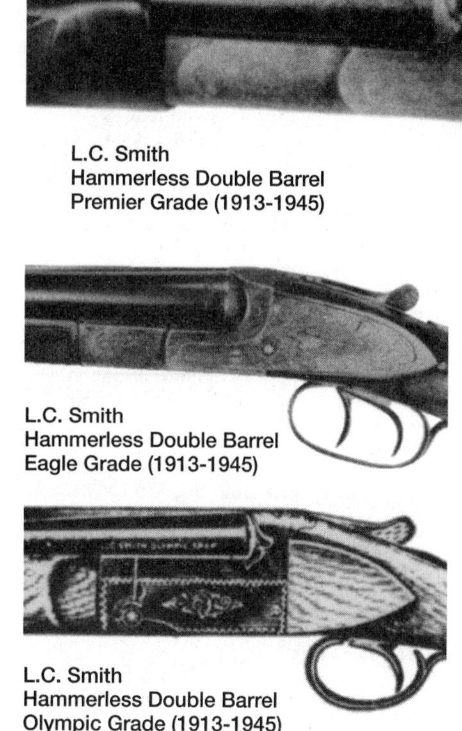

L.C. Smith Hammerless Double Barrel Premier Grade (1913-1945)

L.C. Smith Hammerless Double Barrel Eagle Grade (1913-1945)

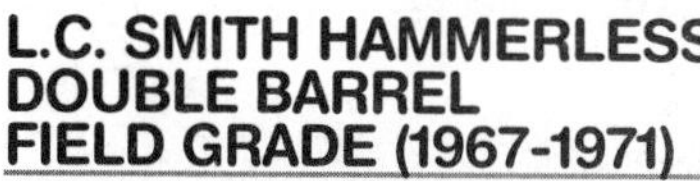

L.C. Smith Hammerless Double Barrel Monogram Grade (1913-1945)

L.C. Smith Hammerless Double Barrel Olympic Grade (1913-1945)

L.C. Smith Hammerless Double Barrel Premier Skeet Grade (1945-1950)

optional; total production, 43,312. Introduced 1945; discontinued 1950.

Exc: $900 **VGood:** $600 **Good:** $500

L.C. SMITH HAMMERLESS DOUBLE BARREL IDEAL GRADE (1945-1950)

Same specs as Hammerless Double Barrel (1945 to 1950), except fluid steel barrels; 26-inch, 28-inch barrels only in .410; American walnut pistol-grip stock; straight or half-pistol grip optional; double triggers, extractors standard; single trigger, ejectors optional; total production, 3950. Introduced 1945; discontinued 1950.

Exc: $1300 **VGood:** $900 **Good:** $700

L.C. SMITH HAMMERLESS DOUBLE BARREL SPECIALTY GRADE (1945-1950)

Same specs as Hammerless Double Barrel (1945 to 1950), except fluid steel barrels standard; vent rib optional; American walnut straight-, half- or pistol-grip stock; double triggers, extractors standard; single trigger, ejectors optional; total production, 109. Introduced 1945; discontinued 1950.

Exc: $2100 **VGood:** $1500 **Good:** $1200

L.C. SMITH HAMMERLESS DOUBLE BARREL CROWN GRADE (1945-1950)

Same specs as Hammerless Double Barrel (1945 to 1950), except fluid steel barrels standard; made largely to order, with all options: vent rib; European walnut straight-, half- or pistol-grip stock, beavertail forend; single trigger; ejectors; total production, 48. Introduced 1945; discontinued 1950.

Exc: $5000 **VGood:** $3500 **Good:** $2750

L.C. SMITH HAMMERLESS DOUBLE BARREL PREMIER SKEET GRADE (1945-1950)

Same specs as Hammerless Double Barrel (1945 to 1950), except 12-, 20-ga.; 26-inch or 28-inch barrels; high solid rib; European walnut straight-grip stock, beavertail forend; ejectors; single trigger; checkered butt; manufactured 1949 to 1950; total production, 507. Introduced 1949; discontinued 1950.

Exc: $1850 **VGood:** $1300 **Good:** $1000

L.C. SMITH HAMMERLESS DOUBLE BARREL FIELD GRADE (1967-1971)

Side-by-side; sidelock; hammerless; 12-ga.; 28-inch barrels; vent rib; American walnut pistol-grip stock, splinter forend; double triggers; extractors. Marlin Firearms Co. briefly reintroduced to L.C. Smith double gun; total production, 2351. Introduced 1967; discontinued 1971.

Exc: $700 **VGood:** $550 **Good:** $450

L.C. SMITH HAMMERLESS DOUBLE BARREL FIELD GRADE DELUXE

Same specs as Hammerless Double Barrel Field Grade (1967 to 1971), except Simmons vent rib; select American walnut pistol-grip stock, beavertail forend; total production, 188. Introduced 1971; discontinued 1971.

Exc: $950 **VGood:** $725 **Good:** $550

L.C. SMITH SINGLE-BARREL TRAP GUN

Single shot; boxlock; hammerless; 12-ga.; 30-inch to 34-inch barrels (Olympic Grade 32-inch only); vent rib; hand-checkered American walnut pistol-grip stock, beavertail forend; ejectors; recoil pad; made in 10 grades with differing quality of workmanship, engraving and wood. Specialty, Eagle, Crown and Monogram grades introduced 1917; other grades introduced later (Olympic in 1928); Eagle Grade discontinued 1932; all others (except Olympic and Specialty) discontinued 1945; Olympic and Specialty grades discontinued 1950. Production totals as follows: Field Grade, 1; Ideal Grade, 5; Olympic Grade, 622; Specialty Grade, 1861; Trap Grade, 1; Eagle Grade, 56; Crown Grade, 88; Monogram Grade, 15; Premier Grade, 2; DeLuxe Grade, 3. The rarity of some grades precludes pricing.

Olympic Grade

Exc: $1900 **VGood:** $1400 **Good:** $1000

Specialty Grade

Exc: $2500 **VGood:** $1800 **Good:** $1400

Crown Grade

Exc: $4500 **VGood:** $3000 **Good:** $2500

Monogram Grade

Exc: $9000 **VGood:** $6000 **Good:** $5000

Smith & Wesson Model 916

Smith & Wesson Model 1000 Waterfowler

Smith & Wesson Model 3000

Smith & Wesson Model 3000 Waterfowler

Smith & Wesson Elite Gold

Sporting Arms Snake Charmer

Stevens Model 22-410

SMITH & WESSON MODEL 916

Slide action; 12-, 16-, 20-ga.; 6-shot magazine; 20-inch Cylinder, 26-inch Improved Cylinder, 28-inch Modified, Full or adjustable choke, 30-inch Full barrel; vent rib (26-inch, 28-inch barrel); uncheckered walnut stock, fluted comb, grooved slide handle; optional recoil pad; satin-finished steel receiver, no-glare top. Introduced 1973; discontinued 1980.

With plain barrel

Perf: $230 **Exc:** $200 **VGood:** $180

With plain barrel, recoil pad

Perf: $235 **Exc:** $205 **VGood:** $185

With vent rib

Perf: $250 **Exc:** $220 **VGood:** $200

With vent rib, recoil pad

Perf: $260 **Exc:** $230 **VGood:** $210

SMITH & WESSON MODEL 916T

Same specs as Model 916 except takedown; 12-ga.; no 20-inch barrel. Introduced 1976; discontinued 1980.

With plain barrel

Perf: $235 **Exc:** $205 **VGood:** $185

With plain barrel, recoil pad

Perf: $240 **Exc:** $210 **VGood:** $185

With vent rib

Perf: $255 **Exc:** $225 **VGood:** $205

With vent rib, recoil pad

Perf: $265 **Exc:** $235 **VGood:** $215

SMITH & WESSON MODEL 1000

Gas-operated autoloader; 12-, 20-ga.; 2-3/4-inch chamber; 4-shot magazine; 26-inch Skeet or Improved Cylinder, 28-inch Improved, Modified or Full barrel; vent rib; front, middle beads; walnut checkered pistol-grip stock, forearm; crossbolt safety; pressure compensator; engraved alloy receiver. Made in Japan. Introduced 1973; discontinued 1984.

Perf: $325 **Exc:** $280 **VGood:** $250

SMITH & WESSON MODEL 1000 MAGNUM

Same specs as Model 1000 except 12-, 20-ga.; 3-inch chamber; 28-inch, 30-inch Modified or Full choke barrel; recoil pad. Introduced 1977; discontinued 1984.

Perf: $330 **Exc:** $285 **VGood:** $255

SMITH & WESSON MODEL 1000S

Same specs as Model 1000 except recessed-type Skeet choke with compensator to soften recoil, reduce muzzle jump; fluorescent red front bead; oil-finished select walnut stock with palm swell. Introduced 1979; discontinued 1984.

Perf: $375 **Exc:** $325 **VGood:** $280

SMITH & WESSON MODEL 1000 TRAP

Same specs as Model 1000 except 30-inch Multi-Choke barrel; stepped rib; white middle bead, Bradley front; Monte Carlo trap-style stock; shell catcher; steel receiver. Introduced 1983; discontinued 1984.

Perf: $550 **Exc:** $400 **VGood:** $350

SMITH & WESSON MODEL 1000 WATERFOWLER

Same specs as Model 1000 except 3-inch chamber; 30-inch Full-choke barrel; dull oil stock finish; quick-detachable swivels; padded camouflage sling; Parkerized finish; black oxidized bolt. Introduced 1982; discontinued 1984.

Perf: $375 **Exc:** $325 **VGood:** $285

SMITH & WESSON MODEL 3000

Slide action; 12-, 20-ga.; 3-inch chamber; 22-inch slug with rifle sights, 26-inch Improved, 28-inch Modified, 30-inch Full plain or vent-rib barrel; Multi-Choke available; American walnut stock; cross-bolt reversible safety for left-handers; dual action bars; chrome-plated bolt; steel receiver; rubber recoil pad. Introduced 1980; discontinued 1984.

Perf: $345 **Exc:** $275 **VGood:** $215

With slug barrel

Perf: $375 **Exc:** $305 **VGood:** $245

SMITH & WESSON MODEL 3000 WATERFOWLER

Same specs as Model 3000 except 3-inch chamber; 30-inch Full-choke barrel; dull oil-finished stock; quick-detachable sling swivels; padded camo sling; Parkerized finish; black oxidized bolt. Introduced 1982; discontinued 1984.

Perf: $355 **Exc:** $285 **VGood:** $225

SMITH & WESSON ELITE GOLD

Side-by-side double chambered only in 20-gauge with scalloped boxlock action and 26- or 28-inch barrels with fixed chokes. Single selective or double triggers, automatic ejectors. Checkered Grade III walnut stock with pistol or straight grip. Color case-hardened frame. Made in Turkey. Imported from 2007 to 2010.

Perf: $1800 **Exc:** $1450 **VGood:** $1100

SPORTING ARMS SNAKE CHARMER

Single barrel; break-open; .410; 3-inch chamber; 18 1/8-inch barrel; no sights; plastic thumbhole stock; storage compartment in buttstock for spare ammo; all stainless steel construction. Introduced 1978; discontinued 1988.

Perf: $110 **Exc:** $85 **VGood:** $70

SPORTING ARMS SNAKE CHARMER II

Same specs as Snake Charmer. Reintroduced 1989; still in production.

Perf: $120 **Exc:** $95 **VGood:** $80

SPORTING ARMS SNAKE CHARMER II NEW GENERATION

Same specs as Snake Charmer I except black carbon steel barrel. Introduced 1989; still in production.

Perf: $130 **Exc:** $90 **VGood:** $75

STEVENS MODEL 22-410

Over/under combo; exposed hammer; takedown; 22 Short, 22 Long, 22 LR barrel over .410 shotgun barrel; 24-inch barrels; Full choke; open rear sight, rifle-type ramp front; original models had uncheckered American walnut pistol-grip stock, forearm; later production had Tenite plastic stock, forearm; single trigger. Introduced 1938; discontinued 1950. Still in production by Savage Arms as Model 24, with variations.

With walnut stock

Exc: $410 **VGood:** $320 **Good:** $170

With Tenite stock

Exc: $405 **VGood:** $315 **Good:** $165

STEVENS MODEL 58

Bolt action; takedown; .410; 3-shot detachable box magazine; 24-inch barrel; Full choke; uncheckered, one-piece, walnut-finished hardwood pistol-grip stock; late models had checkering; plastic buttplate. Introduced 1937; discontinued 1945.

Exc: $125 **VGood:** $100 **Good:** $65

STEVENS MODEL 59

Bolt action; takedown; .410; 5-shot tube magazine; 24-inch barrel; Full choke; uncheckered one-piece walnut-finished hardwood pistol-grip stock; plastic buttplate. Introduced 1934; discontinued 1973.

Exc: $135 **VGood:** $110 **Good:** $75

STEVENS MODEL 67

Slide action; 12-, 20-ga., .410; 3-inch chamber; 5-shot tube magazine; 26-inch, 28-inch, 30-inch barrel; optional vent rib; fixed or choke tubes; metal bead front sight; checkered walnut-finished hardwood pistol-grip stock, tapered slide handle; top tang safety; steel receiver. Introduced 1981; discontinued 1988. Add 25 percent for 410.

Perf: $175 **Exc:** $150 **VGood:** $125

With vent rib

Perf: $185 **Exc:** $160 **VGood:** $135

STEVENS MODEL 67 SLUG

Same specs as Model 67 except 12-ga.; 21-inch slug barrel; rifle sights. Introduced 1986; discontinued 1989.

Perf: $175 **Exc:** $150 **VGood:** $125

STEVENS MODEL 67 VRT-K CAMO

Same specs as Model 67 except 12-, 20-ga.; 28-inch vent-rib barrel; choke tubes; laminated hardwood camouflage stock, slide handle. Introduced 1986; discontinued 1988.

Perf: $225 **Exc:** $180 **VGood:** $160

STEVENS MODEL 67 VRT-Y

Same specs as Model 67 except 20-ga.; 22-inch vent-rib barrel; choke tubes; youth-sized checkered walnut-finish hardwood stock, forearm. Introduced 1987; discontinued 1988.

Perf: $200 **Exc:** $150 **VGood:** $125

STEVENS MODEL 69 RXL

Slide action; 12-ga.; 5-shot tube magazine; 18-1/4-inch Cylinder barrel; checkered walnut-finished hardwood stock, slide handle; recoil pad. Introduced 1981; discontinued 1989.

Perf: $200 **Exc:** $150 **VGood:** $125

STEVENS MODEL 77

Slide action; hammerless; solid frame; 12, 16-, 20-ga.; 5-shot tube magazine; 26-inch Improved; 28-inch Modified or Full barrel; uncheckered walnut-finished hardwood stock, grooved slide handle. Introduced 1954; discontinued 1971.

Exc: $130 **VGood:** $90 **Good:** $70

STEVENS MODEL 77SC

Same specs as Model 77 except Savage Super Choke. No longer in production.

Exc: $130 **VGood:** $90 **Good:** $70

STEVENS MODEL 79-VR

Slide action; 12-, 20-ga.; 26-inch, 28-inch, 30-inch vent-rib barrel; metal bead front sight; checkered walnut-finished hardwood pistol-grip stock, tapered slide handle; top tang safety; interchangeable barrels. Introduced 1981; discontinued 1983.

Perf: $200 **Exc:** $150 **VGood:** $125

STEVENS MODEL 94C

Single barrel; single shot; exposed hammer; break-open; early models side lever breaking; 12-, 16-, 20-ga., .410; 28-inch, 30-inch, 32-inch, 36-inch barrel; Full choke; checkered walnut finished hardwood pistol-grip stock, forearm; automatic ejector; color case-hardened frame. Introduced 1937; discontinued 1984.

Perf: $100 **Exc:** $80 **VGood:** $60

STEVENS MODEL 94Y

Same specs as Model 94C except top lever breaking; 20-ga., .410; 26-inch barrel; youth stock; recoil pad. Discontinued 1984.

Perf: $100 **Exc:** $80 **VGood:** $60

STEVENS MODEL 107

Single barrel; exposed hammer; takedown; 12-, 16-, 20-ga., .410; 26-inch, 28-inch, 30-inch barrel; Full choke; uncheckered walnut-finished hardwood pistol-grip stock, forearm automatic ejector. Introduced 1937; discontinued 1953.

Exc: $75 **VGood:** $50 **Good:** $40

STEVENS MODEL 124

Straight-pull bolt action; solid frame, hammerless; 12-ga.; 2-shot tube magazine; 28-inch barrel; Improved, Modified, Full chokes; checkered Tenite plastic stock, forearm. Introduced 1947; discontinued 1952.

Exc: $175 **VGood:** $140 **Good:** $125

STEVENS MODEL 240

Over/under; takedown; .410; 26-inch barrels; Full choke; early models had uncheckered American walnut pistol-grip stock, forearm; later versions had Tenite plastic stock forearm; double triggers. Introduced 1939; discontinued 1942.

With walnut stock

Exc: $475 **VGood:** $340 **Good:** $240

With Tenite stock

Exc: $470 **VGood:** $335 **Good:** $225

STEVENS MODEL 258

Bolt action; takedown; 20-ga.; 3-shot detachable box magazine; 25-inch barrel; Full choke; uncheckered hardwood, one-piece, pistol-grip stock; black plastic forearm cap, buttplate. Introduced 1937; discontinued 1965.

Exc: $100 **VGood:** $75 **Good:** $50

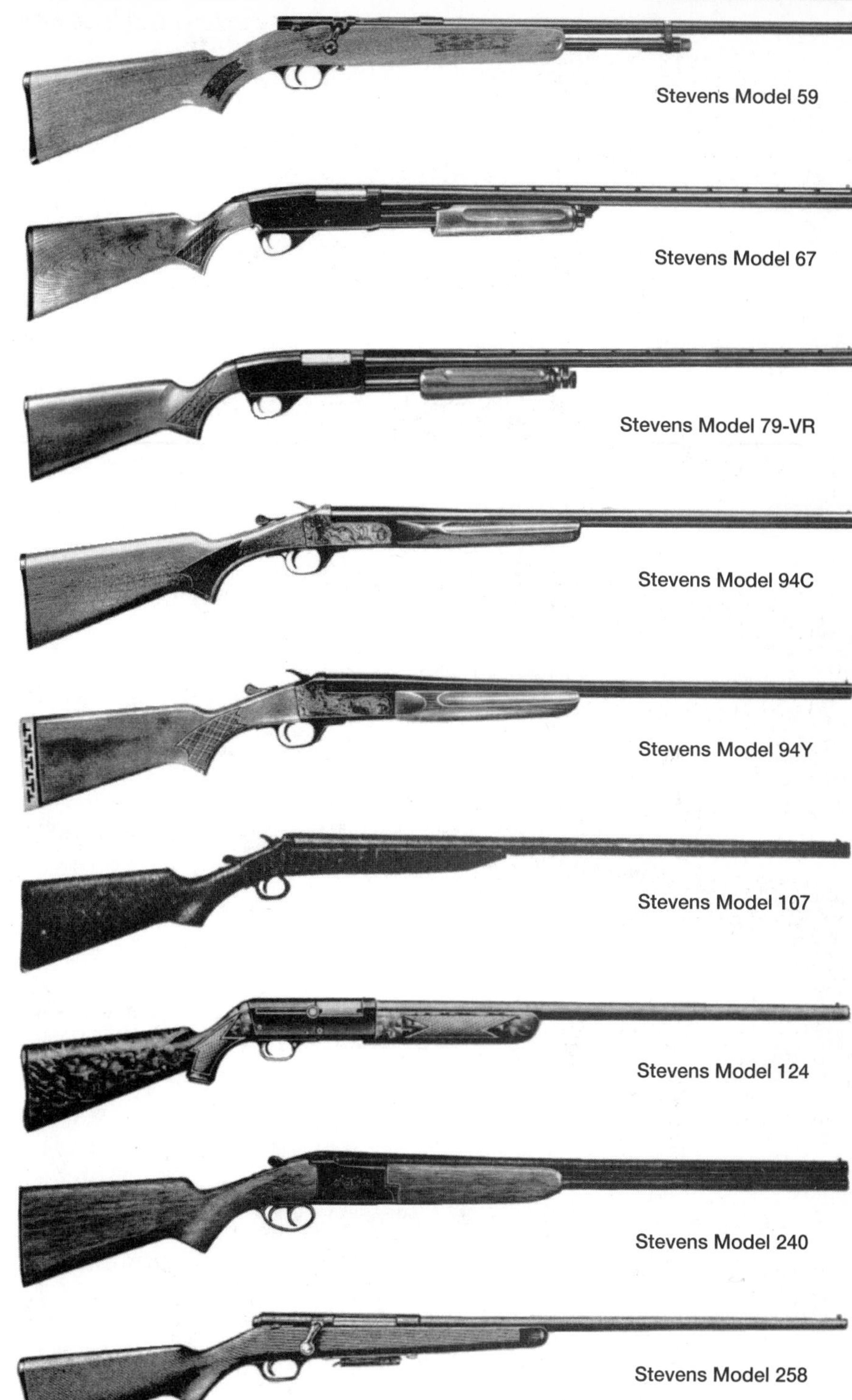

Stevens Model 59

Stevens Model 67

Stevens Model 79-VR

Stevens Model 94C

Stevens Model 94Y

Stevens Model 107

Stevens Model 124

Stevens Model 240

Stevens Model 258

Stevens Model 311

Stevens Model 520

Stevens Model 530

Stevens Model 620

Stoeger P-350

Stoeger P-350 Camo

Stoeger P-350 Defense

STEVENS MODEL 311

Side-by-side; boxlock; hammerless; 12-, 16-, 20-ga., .410; 3-inch chambers; 26-inch, 28-inch, 30-inch, 32-inch barrels; standard choke combos; early models had uncheckered American walnut pistol-grip stock, forearm; later models had walnut-finished hardwood pistol-grip stock, fluted comb; double triggers, auto top tang safety; plastic buttplate; case-hardened finish on frame. Originally introduced 1931 as Model 311, but stamped Model 5000; in 1941 stamp was changed to Model 5100, but still listed in catalog as Model 311A; in 1950 gun marked Model 311; discontinued 1988.

Perf: $375 **Exc:** $325 **VGood:** $250

STEVENS MODEL 520

Slide action; 12-, 16-, 20-ga.; 5-shot magazine; 30-inch barrel; weighs 7-1/2 lbs.; checkered American walnut stock, forend; safety inside trigger guard; made exclusively for Sears, Roebuck; marketed as Sears Ranger. Discontinued about 1930.

Exc: $160 **VGood:** $120 **Good:** $95

STEVENS MODEL 530

Side-by-side; boxlock; hammerless; 12-, 16-, 20-ga., .410; 26-inch, 28-inch, 30-inch, 32-inch barrels; Modified/Full, Cylinder/Modified, Full/Full chokes; hand-checkered American walnut pistol-grip stock, forearm; double triggers; early models have recoil pads. Introduced 1936; discontinued 1954.

Exc: $350 **VGood:** $300 **Good:** $225

STEVENS MODEL 530M

Same specs as Model 530 except Tenite plastic stock, forearm. Introduced before WWII; discontinued 1947.

Exc: $345 **VGood:** $295 **Good:** $220

STEVENS MODEL 530ST

Same specs as Model 530 except single selective trigger. Introduced 1947; discontinued 1954.

Exc: $375 **VGood:** $325 **Good:** $235

STEVENS MODEL 620

Slide action; hammerless; takedown; 12-, 16-, 20-ga.; 5-shot tube magazine; 26-inch, 28-inch, 30-inch, 32-inch barrel; Cylinder, Improved, Modified, Full choke; hand-checkered American walnut pistol-grip stock, slide handle; black plastic buttplate. Introduced 1927; discontinued 1953.

Exc: $250 **VGood:** $185 **Good:** $125

STEVENS MODEL 621

Slide action; hammerless; takedown; 12-, 16-, 20-ga.; 5-shot tube magazine; 26-inch, 28-inch, 30-inch, 32-inch barrel; Cylinder, Improved, Modified Full choke; raised solid matted rib; hand-checkered American walnut pistol-grip stock, slide handle; black plastic buttplate. Introduced 1927; discontinued 1953.

Exc: $250 **VGood:** $185 **Good:** $125

STEVENS MODEL 675

Slide action; 12-ga.; 5-shot tube magazine; 24-inch vent-rib barrel; choke tubes; rifle iron sights; checkered walnut-finished hardwood pistol-grip stock, forearm; recoil pad. Introduced 1987; discontinued 1988.

Perf: $240 **Exc:** $185 **VGood:** $160

STEVENS MODEL 5151

Side-by-side; boxlock; hammerless; 12-, 16-, 20-ga., .410; 3-inch chambers; 26-inch, 28-inch, 30-inch, 32-inch barrels; Ivoroid sights; hand-checkered American walnut pistol-grip stock, forearm; recoil pad. Introduced 1936; discontinued 1942.

Exc: $200 **VGood:** $140 **Good:** $110

STEVENS MODEL 5151-ST

Same specs as Model 5151 except non-selective single trigger. No longer in production.

Exc: $220 **VGood:** $160 **Good:** $120

STEVENS MODEL 9478 SUPER VALUE

Single barrel; exposed hammer; 10-, 12-, 20-ga., .410; 26-inch, 28-inch, 30-inch, 36-inch barrel; walnut-finished hardwood stock; bottom action opening button; auto ejection; color case-hardened frame. Introduced 1979; discontinued 1986.

Perf: $110 **Exc:** $90 **VGood:** $70

STOEGER P-350

This pump-action 12 gauge is chambered for 3.5" shells. It has a 24", 26" or 28" barrel and a matte black, Max-4, Timber or APG finish. There are also some pistol-grip stock offerings with 24" barrels. Includes five choke tubes. Weight is about 6.8 lbs. Add $20 for pistol-grip stock. Add $75 for camo finish.

NIB: $275 **Exc:** $230 **VGood:** $175

STOEGER P-350 DEFENSE

Same as above in a matte black finish with 18.5", fixed cylinder choke barrel. Add $20 for pistol-grip stock.

NIB: $275 **Exc:** $230 **VGood:** $175

STOEGER/IGA UPLANDER

Gauge: 16-, 28-ga., 2-3/4-inch chambers. 12, 20, .410, 3-inch chambers. Barrel: 26-inch, 28-inch. Weight: 7.3 lbs. Sights: Brass bead. Features: Double trigger, IC, Mod. choke tubes with gun.

Perf: $300 **Exc:** $235 **VGood:** $185

With screw-in chokes

Perf: $315 **Exc:** $250 **VGood:** $200

Upland Special

Perf: $340 **Exc:** $300 **VGood:** $260

Upland Supreme with SST, red bar sights

Perf: $395 **Exc:** $355 **VGood:** $300

STOEGER/IGA ENGLISH STOCK SIDE-BY-SIDE

Similar to Uplander except in .410 or 20-ga. only with 24-inch barrels, straight English stock and beavertail forend. Automatic safety, extractors, double triggers. Introduced 1996. Imported from Brazil by Stoeger.

.410 (Mod. chokes)

Perf: $300 **Exc:** $235 **VGood:** $185

20-ga. (IC and Mod. choke tubes)

Perf: $300 **Exc:** $235 **VGood:** $185

STOEGER UPLAND SHORT STOCK SIDE-BY-SIDE

Similar to English stock, only 13-inch length of pull. Excellent for ladies and youth. 20-ga., IC, Mod. fixed, .410 Mod.& Full. Rubber recoil.

Perf: $300 **Exc:** $235 **VGood:** $185

STOEGER MODEL 2000

Semi-auto 12 gauge: 3-inch chamber, set of 5 choke tubes; 24-inch, 26-inch, 28-inch, 30-inch barrel; walnut, deluxe, synthetic, and Timber HD/Max-4 camo stock; white bar sight; inertia-recoil for light target to turkey leads; single trigger combo 26-inch/24-inch pack wtih optional 24-inch slug barrel.

Walnut, 26-inch, 28-inch, 30-inch bbl.

Perf: $355 **Exc:** $315 **VGood:** $285

Deluxe, 26-inch, 28-inch bbl.

Perf: $476 **Exc:** $436 **VGood:** $406

Synthetic, 24-inch, 26-inch, 28-inch bbl.

Perf: $355 **Exc:** $315 **VGood:** $285

Synthetic combo, 26-inch/24-inch bbl.

Perf: $430 **Exc:** $390 **VGood:** $360

Optional slug bbl., 26-inch

Perf: $520 **Exc:** $410 **VGood:** $370

Timber HD, 24-inch, 26-inch, 28-inch bbl.

Perf: $430 **Exc:** $390 **VGood:** $360

STOEGER SILVERADO COACH

Side-by-side 12, 20, and .410 gauge: 2-3/4-inch, 3-inch chambers; 20-inch barrel; weighs 6-1/2 lbs.; brown hardwood, classic beavertail forend; brass bead sight; IC & Mod. fixed chokes; tang auto safety; auto extractors; silvered finish; black plastic butt plate; 12-ga. and 20-ga. also with English style stock.

Perf: $320 **Exc:** $270 **VGood:** $215

STOEGER COACH GUN SUPREME

Similar to Coach Gun but with walnut stock, blued, stainless, or nickeled finish.

STOEGER UPLANDER

Gauge: 12, 20, .410 (3-inch chambers); 28 (2-3/4-inch chambers). Barrel: 24-inch, 26-inch, 28-inch. Weight: 6-3/4 lbs. Length: 40-inch to 44-inch overall. Stock: Brazilian hardwood; checkered grip and forearm. Features: Automatic safety; extractors; handles steel shot. Introduced 1997. Imported from Brazil by Stoeger. With chokes tubes.

Perf: $315 **Exc:** $250 **VGood:** $185

STOEGER UPLANDER SUPREME

Similar to Uplander except American walnut soft black rubber recoil pad, gloss finish. Choke tubes and 3-inch chambers standard 12-, 20-ga.; 28-ga. has 26-inch, 3-inch chambers; chokes, fixed IC and Mod. Single selective gold plated triggers; extractors. Introduced 1997. Imported from Brazil by Stoeger.

Perf: $395 **Exc:** $355 **VGood:** $300

STOEGER 2002 SINGLE-SHOT

Gauge: 12, 20, .410, 2-3/4-inch, 3-inch chambers. Blued. Barrel: 26-inch, 28-inch. Weight: 5.4 lbs. Sights: Brass bead. Features: .410; Full fixed choke tubes, rest Mod. screw-in. .410 24-inch bbl. available (l.o.p. 13-inch). 12-ga. hardwood pistol-grip stock and forend. 20-ga. 26-inch bbl., hardwood forend.

Perf: $90 **Exc:** $75 **VGood:** $65

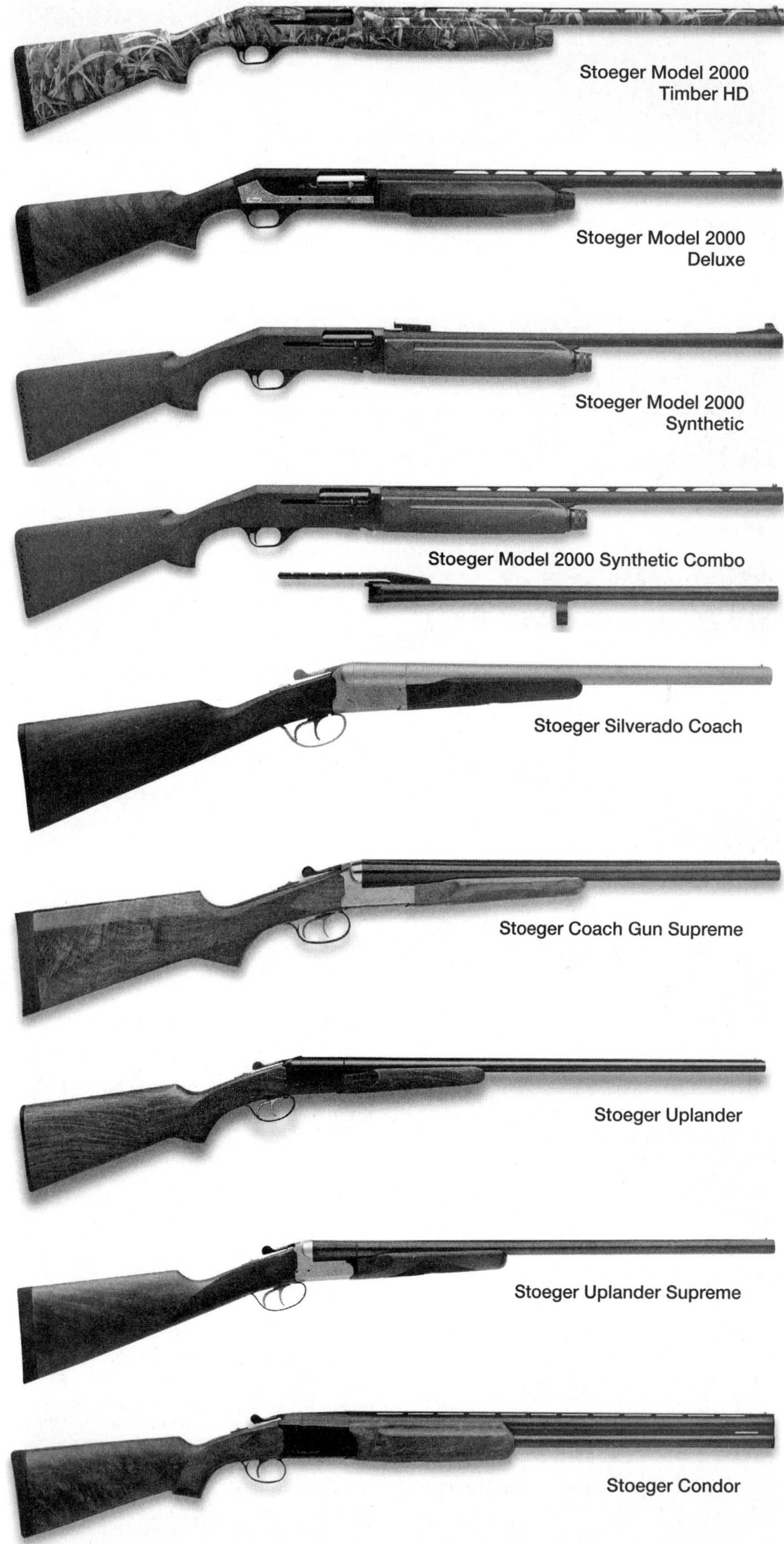

Stoeger Model 2000 Timber HD

Stoeger Model 2000 Deluxe

Stoeger Model 2000 Synthetic

Stoeger Model 2000 Synthetic Combo

Stoeger Silverado Coach

Stoeger Coach Gun Supreme

Stoeger Uplander

Stoeger Uplander Supreme

Stoeger Condor

STOEGER CONDOR

Over/under; boxlock; 12-, 20-ga.; 3-inch chambers; 26-inch. 28-inch barrels; Improved Cylinder/Modified, Modified/Full choke tubes; vent top rib; weighs 7 lbs.; oil-finished checkered Brazilian hardwood pistol-grip stock, forend; manual safety; single trigger; extractors. Introduced 1983; still imported by Stoeger.

Perf: $320 **Exc:** $300 **VGood:** $275

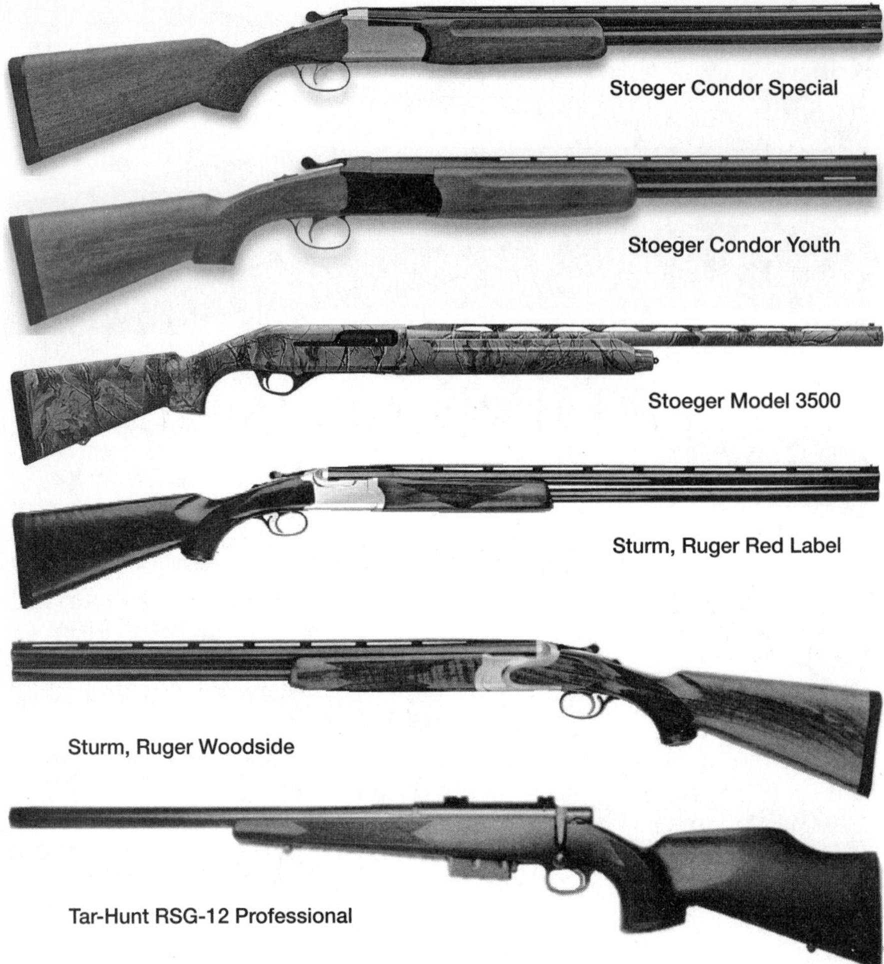
Stoeger Condor Special

Stoeger Condor Youth

Stoeger Model 3500

Sturm, Ruger Red Label

Sturm, Ruger Woodside

Tar-Hunt RSG-12 Professional

CONDOR SPECIAL
Same specs as the Condor except 12- and 20-ga.; deluxe checkered walnut stock; vent. rib; stainless steel receiver; choke tubes.

Perf: $350 **Exc:** $325 **VGood:** $300

CONDOR COMBO
Same specs as the Condor except with matched 12- and 20-ga., 26- and 28-inch barrel set; deluxe checkered walnut stock; vent. rib; separated barrels; choke tubes.

Perf: $400 **Exc:** $380 **VGood:** $355

CONDOR SUPREME
Same specs as the Condor except with single selective trigger.

Perf: $395 **Exc:** $365 **VGood:** $320

CONDOR YOUTH
Similar to Condor but in .410 and 20-ga. only with 13-inch LOP.

Perf: $320 **Exc:** $300 **VGood:** $275

STOEGER CONDOR COMPETITION
These 3" 12 and 20 gauge over-and-unders feature 30" barrels, AA Grade wood and adjustable combs. Three choke tubes. Weight is about 7.3 lbs. in 20 gauge and 7.8 lbs. in 12 gauge.

NIB: $525 **Exc:** $495 **VGood:** $375

STOEGER CONDOR COMPETITION COMBO
As above with 12- and 20-gauge barrels.

NIB: $635 **Exc:** $595 **VGood:** $475

STOEGER CONDOR OUTBACK
New in 2007, the Outback O/Ucomes in 12 and 20 gauge chambered for 3" shells. The finish is either A Grade satin walnut stock with blued barrels and receiver or matte black walnut stock with polished barrels and receiver. Barrels are 20" with rifle sights. Includes two choke tubes. Add $40 for black/nickel.

NIB: $425 **Exc:** $375 **VGood:** $275

STOEGER MODEL 3500
Semi-auto 12 gauge with 3½-inch chamber. Operating system is same as Benelli intertia recoil. Available with 24-, 26-, or 28-inch barrel with five choke tubes. Finish is black or Realtree camo.

Perf: $525 **Exc:** $450 **VGood:** $400

STURM RUGER GOLD LABEL
Side-by-side12 gauge; 12, 3-inch chambers; 28-inch barrel with skeet tubes; weighs 6-1/2 lbs.; 45-inch overall; American walnut straight or pistol grip; gold bead front; full-length rib, serrated top; spring-assisted break-open; SS trigger; auto eject; five interchangeable screw-in choke tubes; combination safety/barrel selector with auto safety reset.

Perf: $2775 **Exc:** $2075 **VGood:** $1450

STURM RUGER KTS-1234-BRE RED LABEL TRAP MODEL
Side-by-side12 gauge; 2-3/4-inch chamber; 34-inch barrel; weighs 9 lbs.; 50-1/2-inch overall; select walnut checkered; adjustable pull length 13-1/2 to 15-inch; fully adjustable rib for pattern position; adjustable stock comb cast for right- or left-handed shooters; straight grooves the length of barrel to keep wad from rotating for pattern improvement; Full and Modified choke tubes; gold-inlaid eagle and Ruger name on receiver. Introduced 2000. Only 300 produced.

Perf: $3000 **Exc:** $2575 **VGood:** $1725

STURM RUGER RED LABEL
Over/under; boxlock; 12-, 20-ga.; 3-inch chambers; 26-inch, 28-inch vent-rib barrels; Full/Modified, Improved Cylinder/Modified, Skeet choke tubes; checkered American walnut pistol-grip stock, forearm; optional straight-grip stock; single selective trigger; auto ejectors. Introduced (20-ga.) 1977; (12-ga.) 1982; still in production.

Perf: $1050 **Exc:** $860 **VGood:** $725

English Field with straight-grip stock

Perf: $965 **Exc:** $775 **VGood:** $685

All-Weather Red Label with black synthetic stock

Perf: $1125 **Exc:** $860 **VGood:** $715

Factory engraved All-Weather models

Perf: $1225 **Exc:** $1050 **VGood:** $815

RUGER ENGRAVED RED LABEL
Similar to Red Label except scroll-engraved receiver with 24-carat gold game bird (pheasant in 12-ga., grouse in 20-ga., woodcock in 28-ga., duck on All-Weather 12-ga.). Introduced 2000.

Engraved, 12 gauge, 30-inch bbls.

Perf: $1225 **Exc:** $1050 **VGood:** $815

Engraved,(12-, 20- and 28-gauge; 26-inch and 28-inch bbls.)

Perf: $1225 **Exc:** $1050 **VGood:** $815

Engraved, All-Weather (synthetic stock, 12-gauge only; 26-inch and 28-inch bbls.)

Perf: $1225 **Exc:** $1050 **VGood:** $815

Engraved, All-Weather (synthetic stock, 12-ga. only, 30-inch bbls.)

Perf: $1300 **Exc:** $1125 **VGood:** $890

STURM RUGER RED LABEL SPORTING CLAYS
Same specs as Red Label except 12-ga.; 3-inch chambers; 30-inch barrels backbored to .744-inch diameter; two Skeet, one Improved Cylinder, one Modified stainless steel choke tubes; optional Full and Extra-Full tubes available; free-floating serrated vent rib; brass front, mid-rib beads; weighs 7-3/4 lbs.; overall length 47-inch; no barrel side ribs. Introduced 1992; still in production.

Perf: $1100 **Exc:** $800 **VGood:** $700

STURM RUGER RED LABEL SPORTING CLAYS 20-GAUGE
Same specs as the Red Label except 20-ga.; 3-inch chambers; 30-inch barrels backbored to .631-inch-.635-inch diameter; four special 2-inch long interchangeable, screw-in choke tubes: two Skeet, one Modified, one Improved Cylinder; optional Full and Extra-Full tubes available; no barrel side spacers. Introduced 1994; still in production.

Perf: $1100 **Exc:** $800 **VGood:** $700

STURM RUGER RED LABEL WOODSIDE
Over/under; boxlock; 12-, 20-ga.; 3-inch chambers; 26-inch, 28-inch, 30-inch backbored barrels; Full, Modified, Improved Cylinder and two Skeet stainless steel choke tubes; serrated free-floating rib; weighs 7-1/2 to 8 lbs.; select Circassian walnut pistol-grip or straight-grip stock; buttstock extends forward into action as two side panels; newly patented Ruger cocking mechanism for easier, smoother opening; single selective mechanical trigger; selective automatic ejectors; blued barrels; stainless steel receiver; optional engraved action. Introduced 1995.

Perf: $1500 **Exc:** $1100 **VGood:** $850

Woodside Sporting Clays (30-inch bbls.)

Perf: $1525 **Exc:** $1250 **VGood:** $1000

TAR-HUNT RSG-12 PROFESSIONAL
Bolt action; 12-, 20-ga.; 2-3/4-inch chamber; 21-1/2-inch fully rifled barrel with muzzlebrake; weighs 7-3/4 lbs.; Weaver-style scope mounting bases and Burris steel rings; matte black McMillan fiberglass stock; Pachmayr Decelerator pad; rifle-style action with two locking lugs; two-position safety; single-stage, adjustable rifle trigger; right- and left-hand models at same prices. Introduced 1991; still in production.

Perf: $1200 **Exc:** $850 **VGood:** $750

Professional 16-ga. Elite model, right- or left-hand

Perf: $1750 **Exc:** $1475 **VGood:** $1150

Millennium/10th Anniversary models (limited to 25 guns): NP-3 nickel/Teflon metal finish, black McMillan Fibergrain stock, Jewell adj. Trigger.

Perf: $2075 **Exc:** $1825 **VGood:** $1500

TAR-HUNT RSG-12 PROFESSIONAL MATCHLESS MODEL

Same specs as RSG-12 Professional except McMillan Fibergrain or camouflage stock; 400-grit gloss metal finish. Introduced 1991.

Perf: $1500 **Exc:** $1100 **VGood:** $950

TAR-HUNT RSG-12 PROFESSIONAL PEERLESS MODEL

Same specs as RSG-12 Professional except McMillan Fibergrain fiberglass stock; NP-3 nickel/teflon metal finish. Introduced 1991.

Perf: $1750 **Exc:** $1200 **VGood:** $1000

TAR-HUNT RSG-12 TURKEY MODEL

Same specs as RSG-12 Professional except smoothbore barrel; Remington Rem-Choke thread system. Introduced 1991.

Perf: $1200 **Exc:** $850 **VGood:** $750

TAR-HUNT RSG-20 MOUNTAINEER SLUG GUN

Similar to the RSG-12 Professional except chambered for 20-ga. (2-3/4-inch) shells; 21-inch Shaw rifled barrel, with muzzle brake; two-lug bolt; one- shot blind magazine; matte black finish; McMillan fiberglass stock with Pachmayr Decelerator pad; receiver drilled and tapped for Rem. 700 bases. Weighs 6 -1/2 lbs. Introduced 1997. Made in U.S. by Tar-Hunt Custom Rifles, Inc.

Perf: $1750 **Exc:** $1475 **VGood:** $1150

TECHNI-MEC MODEL 610

Over/under; boxlock; 10-ga.; 3-1/2-inch chambers; 32-inch barrels; Improved Modified/Full chokes; hand-checkered walnut stock, forend; rubber recoil pad; single selective trigger; silvered and engraved frame, blued barrels. Made in Italy. Introduced 1991; no longer imported.

Perf: $875 **Exc:** $700 **VGood:** $625

TECHNI-MEC MODEL SPL 640

Over/under; boxlock; 12-, 16-, 20-, 28-ga.; 2-3/4-inch chambers; 26-inch chrome-lined barrel; Modified/Full chokes; ventilated rib; weighs 5-1/2 lbs.; European walnut stock; single or double triggers; folds in half for storage, transportation; photo-engraved silvered receiver. Made in Italy. Introduced 1984; no longer imported.

Perf: $440 **Exc:** $300 **VGood:** $250

TECHNI-MEC MODEL SPL 642

Folding over/under; 12-, 16-, 20-, 28-ga., .410; 26-inch Modified/Full barrels; vent rib; checkered European walnut stock, forearm; single or double triggers; chrome-lined barrels; photo-engraved, silvered receiver. No longer in production.

With single trigger

Perf: $440 **Exc:** $300 **VGood:** $250

With double triggers

Perf: $420 **Exc:** $280 **VGood:** $230

TECHNI-MEC MODEL SR 690 SKEET

Over/under; boxlock; 12-ga.; 2-3/4-inch chambers; 25-inch, 28-inch barrels; Skeet/Skeet chokes; Ray-type sights; select European walnut Monte Carlo stock with Skeet dimensions; single selective trigger; automatic ejectors; antique silver finish on receiver. Made in Italy. Introduced 1984; no longer imported.

Perf: $525 **Exc:** $375 **VGood:** $300

TECHNI-MEC MODEL SR 690 TRAP

Same specs as Model SR 690 Skeet except 30-inch barrels; Full/Full chokes; select European walnut Monte Carlo stock with trap dimensions. Made in Italy. Introduced 1984; no longer imported.

Perf: $525 **Exc:** $375 **VGood:** $300

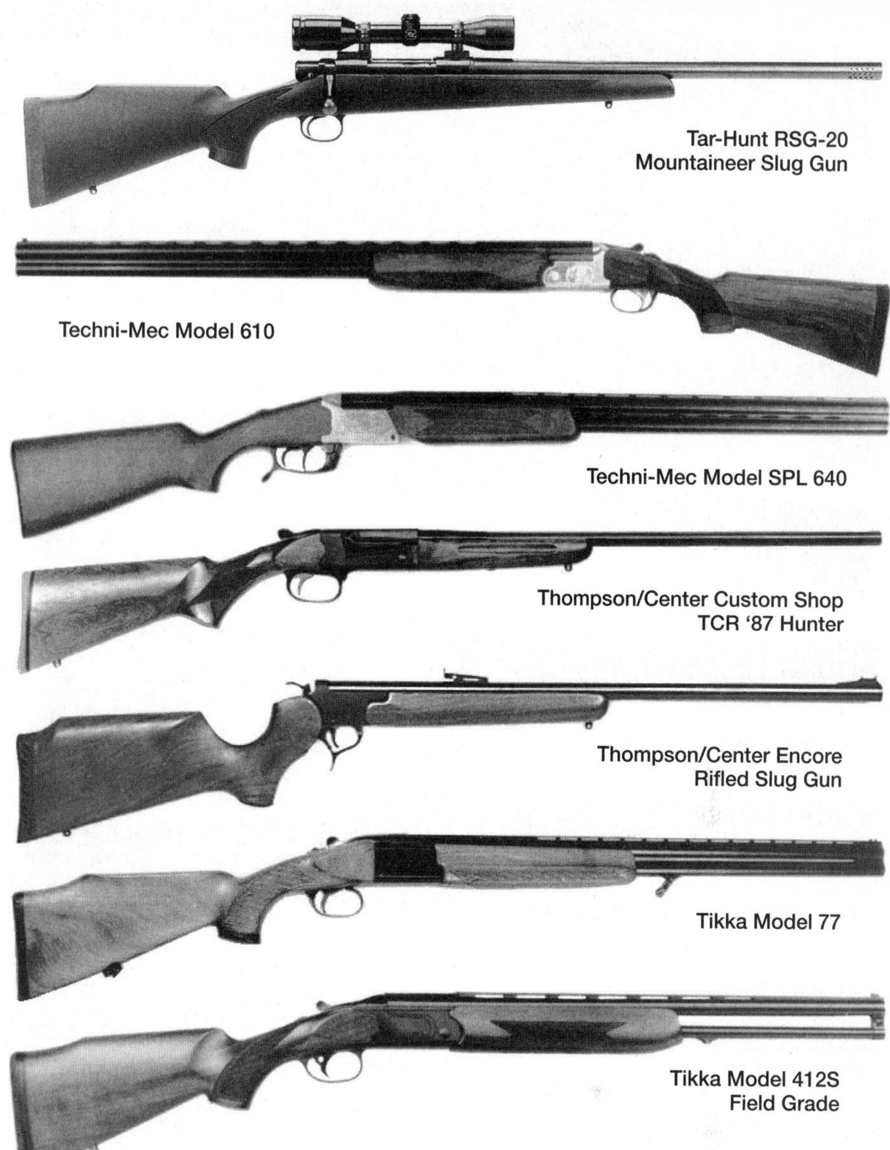

Tar-Hunt RSG-20 Mountaineer Slug Gun

Techni-Mec Model 610

Techni-Mec Model SPL 640

Thompson/Center Custom Shop TCR '87 Hunter

Thompson/Center Encore Rifled Slug Gun

Tikka Model 77

Tikka Model 412S Field Grade

TECHNI-MEC MODEL SR 692 EM

Over/under; boxlock; 12-, 16-, 20-ga.; 2-3/4-inch, 3-inch chambers; 26-inch, 28-inch, 30-inch barrels; Modified, Full, Improved Cylinder, Cylinder chokes; checkered European walnut pistol-grip stock, forend; single selective trigger; automatic ejectors; dummy sideplates with fine game scene engraving. Made in Italy. Introduced 1984; no longer imported.

Perf: $440 **Exc:** $350 **VGood:** $290

THOMPSON/CENTER CUSTOM SHOP TCR '87 HUNTER

Single shot; boxlock; 10-, 12-ga.; 3, 3-1/2-inch chamber; 25-inch barrel; Full choke designed for steel shot; weighs 8 lbs.; uncheckered walnut stock; stock has extra 7/16-inch drop at heel; same receiver as TCR '87 rifle models. Introduced through T/C custom shop 1989; discontinued 1994.

Perf: $725 **Exc:** $495 **VGood:** $325

THOMPSON/CENTER ENCORE RIFLED SLUG GUN

Gauge: 20, 3-inch chamber; 26-inch barrel, fully rifled; weighs about 7 lbs. ; 40-1/2-inch overall; walnut with walnut forearm; steel, click-adjustable rear and ramp-style front, both with fiber optics; break-open design uses interchangeable barrels; composite stock and forearm available. Introduced 2000.

Perf: $620 **Exc:** $465 **VGood:** $395

THOMPSON/CENTER ENCORE TURKEY GUN

Gauge: 12-ga. Barrel: 24-inch. Features: Blued, high definition Adv. Timber camo.

Perf: $575 **Exc:** $500 **VGood:** $430

TIKKA MODEL 77

Over/under; 12-ga.; 27-inch, 30-inch vent-rib barrels; skip-line-checkered European walnut Monte Carlo pistol-grip stock with roll-over cheekpiece, forend; ejectors; barrel selector; single trigger. Made in Finland. Introduced 1979; no longer imported.

Perf: $675 **Exc:** $525 **VGood:** $475

TIKKA MODEL 412S FIELD GRADE

Over/under; boxlock; 12-, 20-ga.; 3-inch chambers; 24-inch, 26-inch, 28-inch, 30-inch barrels; Improved Cylinder, Modified, Improved Modified, Full stainless steel screw-in chokes; weighs about 7-1/4 lbs.; checkered American walnut pistol-grip stock, forend; barrel selector in trigger; automatic top tang safety; barrel cocking indicators; system allows free interchangeability of barrels, stocks and forends

Tikka Model 412S Sporting Clays

Tradewinds H-170

Traditions ALS 2100 Turkey

Traditions Elite Series Side-by-Side

into double rifle model, combination gun, etc. Name changed to Model 512S in 1993. Made in Finland and Italy. Introduced 1980; still imported as Tikka Model 512S.

Perf: $1000 **Exc:** $700 **VGood:** $525

TIKKA MODEL 412S SPORTING CLAYS

Same as the Model 412S except 12-ga.; 28-inch, 30-inch barrels; five choke tubes; manual safety. Made in Finland and Italy. Introduced 1992; still imported as Model 512S.

Perf: $1050 **Exc:** $750 **VGood:** $600

TIKKA MODEL 412ST SKEET

Over/under; 12-, 20-ga.; 28-inch stepped-rib barrels; choke tubes; European walnut Skeet-style stock; mechanical single trigger; auto ejectors; elongated forcing cone; cocking indicators; hand-honed action. Made in Finland. Introduced 1980; discontinued 1990.

Perf: $1000 **Exc:** $750 **VGood:** $650

TIKKA MODEL 412ST SKEET GRADE II

Same specs as Model 412ST Skeet except checkered semi-fancy European walnut Skeet-style stock; drilled for recoil-reducing unit; matte nickel receiver; matte blue locking bolt, lever; gold trigger. Made in Finland. Introduced 1989; discontinued 1990.

Perf: $1200 **Exc:** $850 **VGood:** $775

TIKKA MODEL 412ST TRAP

Same specs as Model 412ST Skeet except 12-ga.; 30-inch, 32-inch barrels; European walnut stock, palm swell. Made in Finland. Introduced 1980; discontinued 1990.

Perf: $1000 **Exc:** $750 **VGood:** $650

TIKKA MODEL 412ST TRAP GRADE II

Same specs as Model 412ST Skeet except 12-ga.; 30-inch, 32-inch barrels; checkered semi-fancy European walnut stock, palm swell; drilled for recoil-reducing unit; matte nickel receiver; matte blue locking bolt, lever; gold trigger. Made in Finland. Introduced 1989; discontinued 1990.

Perf: $1200 **Exc:** $850 **VGood:** $775

TOLEDO ARMAS VALEZQUEZ

Side-by-side; 12-ga. 2-3/4-inch chambers; custom barrel lengths, chokes; custom exhibition-grade European walnut stock; auto ejectors; hand-engraved action; many options. Made in Spain. Introduced 1982; discontinued 1984.

Perf: $2600 **Exc:** $2000 **VGood:** $1700

TRADEWINDS H-170

Recoil-operated autoloader; 12-ga.; 2-3/4-inch chambers; 5-shot tube magazine; 26-inch Modified, 28-inch Full barrel; vent rib; hand-checkered select European walnut pistol-grip stock; light alloy receiver. Made in Japan. Introduced 1970; no longer in production.

Perf: $275 **Exc:** $250 **VGood:** $195

TRADITIONS ALS 2100 SERIES

Side-by-side12 gauge; 12, 3-inch chamber; 20, 3-inch chamber; 24-inch, 26-inch, 28-inch barrel (imp. cyl., mod. and full choke tubes); weighs 5 lbs., 10 oz. to 6 lbs., 5 oz.; 44-inch to 48-inch overall; walnut or black composite; gas-operated; vent-rib barrel with Beretta-style threaded muzzle. Introduced 2001 by Traditions.

12- or 20-ga., 26-inch or 28-inch barrel, walnut stock

Perf: $430 **Exc:** $390 **VGood:** $355

12- or 20-ga., 24-inch barrel Youth Model, walnut stock

Perf: $430 **Exc:** $390 **VGood:** $355

12- or 20-ga., 26-inch or 28-inch barrel, composite stock

Perf: $410 **Exc:** $375 **VGood:** $335

TRADITIONS ALS 2100 TURKEY

Similar to ALS 2100 Field Model except chambered in 12-gauge, 3-inch only with 21-inch barrel and Mossy Oak Break Up camo finish. Weighs 6 lbs., 1 oz.; 41-inch overall.

Perf: $465 **Exc:** $410 **VGood:** $365

26-inch vent rib bbl.

Perf: $455 **Exc:** $400 **VGood:** $360

TRADITIONS ALS 2100 WATERFOWL

Semi-auto 12 gauge; similar to ALS 2100 Field Model, 3-inch only with 28-inch barrel (w/steel chokes for 2002) and Advantage Wetlands camo finish. Weighs 6 lbs., 5 oz.; 48-inch overall.

Perf: $465 **Exc:** $410 **VGood:** $365

TRADITIONS ALS 2100 HUNTER COMBO

Similar to ALS 2100 Field Model except 2 barrels, 28-inch vent rib and 24-inch fully rifled deer. Choice TruGlo adj. sights or fixed cantilever mount on rifled barrel. Multi chokes.

Perf: $590 **Exc:** $535 **VGood:** $500

TRADITIONS CLASSIC SERIES

Over/under 12 ga., 3-inch; 20 ga., 3-inch; 16 ga., 2-3/4-inch; 28 ga., 2-3/4-inch; and .410, 3-inch; 26-inch barrel, 28-inch; weighs 6 lbs., 5 oz. to 7 lbs., 6 oz.; 43-inch to 45-inch overall; walnut stock; single-selective trigger; chrome-lined barrels with screw-in choke tubes; extractors (Field Hunter and Field I models) or automatic ejectors (Field II and Field III models); rubber butt pad; top tang safety. Imported from Fausti of Italy by Traditions.

Field Hunter - blued receiver; 12- or 20-ga.; 26-inch bbl. has I.C. and mod. tubes, 28-inch has mod. and full tubes)

Perf: $710 **Exc:** $655 **VGood:** $580

Field I - blued receiver; 12-, 20-, 28-ga. or .410; fixed chokes (26-inch IC/Mod., 28-inch Mod./Full)

Perf: $675 **Exc:** $555 **VGood:** $485

Field II - coin-finish receiver; 12-, 16-, 20-, 28-ga. or .410; gold trigger; choke tubes)

Perf: $710 **Exc:** $635 **VGood:** $575

Field III - coin-finish receiver; gold engraving and trigger; 12 ga.; 26-inch or 28-inch bbl.; choke tubes

Perf: $1000 **Exc:** $850 **VGood:** $775

Upland II - blued receiver; 12- or 20-ga.; English-style straight walnut stock; choke tubes

Perf: $975 **Exc:** $875 **VGood:** $715

Upland III - blued receiver, gold engraving; 20-ga.; high-grade pistol grip walnut stock; choke tubes

Perf: $1320 **Exc:** $1095 **VGood:** $925

Upland III - blued, gold engraved receiver, 12-ga. Round pistol grip stock, choke tubes

Perf: $1320 **Exc:** $1095 **VGood:** $925

Sporting Clay II - silver receiver; 12-ga.; ported barrels with skeet, I.C., mod. and full extended tubes

Perf: $915 **Exc:** $810 **VGood:** $700

Sporting Clay III - engraved receivers, 12- and 20-ga., walnut stock, vent rib, extended choke tubes

Perf: $1175 **Exc:** $975 **VGood:** $850

TRADITIONS ELITE SERIES

Side-by-side12 gauge; 3-inch; 20, 3-inch; 28, 2-3/4-inch; .410, 3-inch; 26-inch barrel; weighs 5-3/4 to 6-1/2 lbs.; 43-inch overall; walnut stock; chrome-lined barrels; fixed chokes (Elite Field III ST, Field I DT and Field I ST) or choke tubes (Elite Hunter ST); extractors (Hunter ST and Field I models) or automatic ejectors (Field III ST); top tang safety. Imported from Fausti of Italy by Traditions.

Elite Field I DT – 12-, 20-, 28-ga. or .410; I.C. and Mod. fixed chokes (F/F on .410); double triggers

Perf: $780 **Exc:** $720 **VGood:** $595

Elite Field I ST - 12-, 20-, 28-ga. or .410; same as DT but with single trigger

Perf: $860 **Exc:** $750 **VGood:** $625

Elite Field III ST – 28-ga. or .410; gold-engraved receiver; high-grade walnut stock

Perf: $1825 **Exc:** $1550 **VGood:** $1275

Elite Hunter ST – 12- or 20-ga.; blued receiver; IC and Mod. choke tubes

Perf: $995 **Exc:** $850 **VGood:** $775

TRADITIONS MAG 350 SERIES

Gauge: 12, 3-1/2-inch; 24-inch, 26-inch and 28-inch barrel; weighs 7 lbs. to 7 lbs., 4 oz.; 41-inch to 45-inch overall; walnut or composite with Mossy Oak Break-Up or Advantage Wetlands camouflage; black matte, engraved receiver; vent rib; automatic ejectors; single-selective trigger; three screw-in choke tubes; rubber recoil pad; top tang safety. Imported from Fausti of Italy by Traditions.

Mag Hunter II - 28-inch black matte barrels, walnut stock, includes IC, Mod. and Full tubes

Perf: $700 **Exc:** $630 **VGood:** $575

Turkey II - 24-inch or 26-inch camo barrels, Break-Up camo stock, includes Mod., Full and X-Full tubes

Perf: $825 **Exc:** $715 **VGood:** $625

Waterfowl II - 28-inch camo barrels, Advantage Wetlands camo stock, includes IC, Mod. and Full tubes

Perf: $835 **Exc:** $715 **VGood:** $635

TRIDENT SUPERTRAP II

Single shot; 12-ga.; 32-inch, 34-inch ported barrel; Multi-Choke tubes; weighs 8-1/2 lbs.; white front bead, brass middle bead; checkered American walnut stock, forend; vent rubber recoil pad; pull/release-convertible trigger; long forcing cone. Introduced 1990; discontinued 1992.

Perf: $1800 **Exc:** $1400 **VGood:** $1200

TRISTAR BRITTANY

This SxS features a boxlock action with case-colored frame with scroll engraving. Straight grip walnut stock with semi-beavertail forend. Offered in 12, 16, 20 and 28 gauge and .410 bore with 3-inch chambers and choke tubes. Weight is 6.2 - 7.4 lbs. depending on gauge.

NIB: $900 **Exc:** $840 **VGood:** $725

TRISTAR BRITTANY CLASSIC

Enhanced Brittany model features fancy walnut wood and rounded pistol grip, cut checkering, engraved case colored frame and auto selective ejectors. Available in 12, 16, 20 and 28 gauges and .410 bore, all with 3" chambers and 27" barrels. Weight is about 6.7 lbs. in 12 gauge and slightly less in sub-gauges. Deduct 15 percent for standard Brittany model.

NIB: $925 **Exc:** $865 **VGood:** $750

TRISTAR TSA FIELD

Semi-auto with walnut forend and pistol grip stock, 3-inch chamber, 3 choke tubes and magazine cut-off feature. Weight is around 5.7 lbs. in 20 gauge and 6.5 lbs. in 12 gauge depending on barrel length. 20 gauge available in youth model.

NIB: $350 **Exc:** $300 **VGood:** $250

TRISTAR TSA SYNTHETIC AND SYNTHETIC MAG

Same features as TSA Field Model but with non-glare black synthetic stock and forend. Also available with complete Realtree Max-4 coverage. Mag model has 3.5-inch chamber. Add 15 percent for camo.

NIB: $325 **Exc:** $275 **VGood:** $225

TRISTAR DERBY CLASSIC

Side-by-side12 gauge. Barrel: 28-inch Mod. & Full fixed chokes. Features: Sidelock action, engraved, double trigger, auto ejectors, English straight stock. Made in Europe for Tristar Sporting Arms Ltd.

Perf: $1075 **Exc:** $925 **VGood:** $825

TRISTAR MODEL 1887

Lever-action; 12-ga.; 22-inch barrel; weighs 8-3/4 lbs.; 40-1/2-inch overall; walnut w/pistol grip; improved cylinder choke; oil finish. Introduced 2002. Made in Australia. Available through AcuSport Corp.

Perf: $995 **Exc:** $850 **VGood:** $750

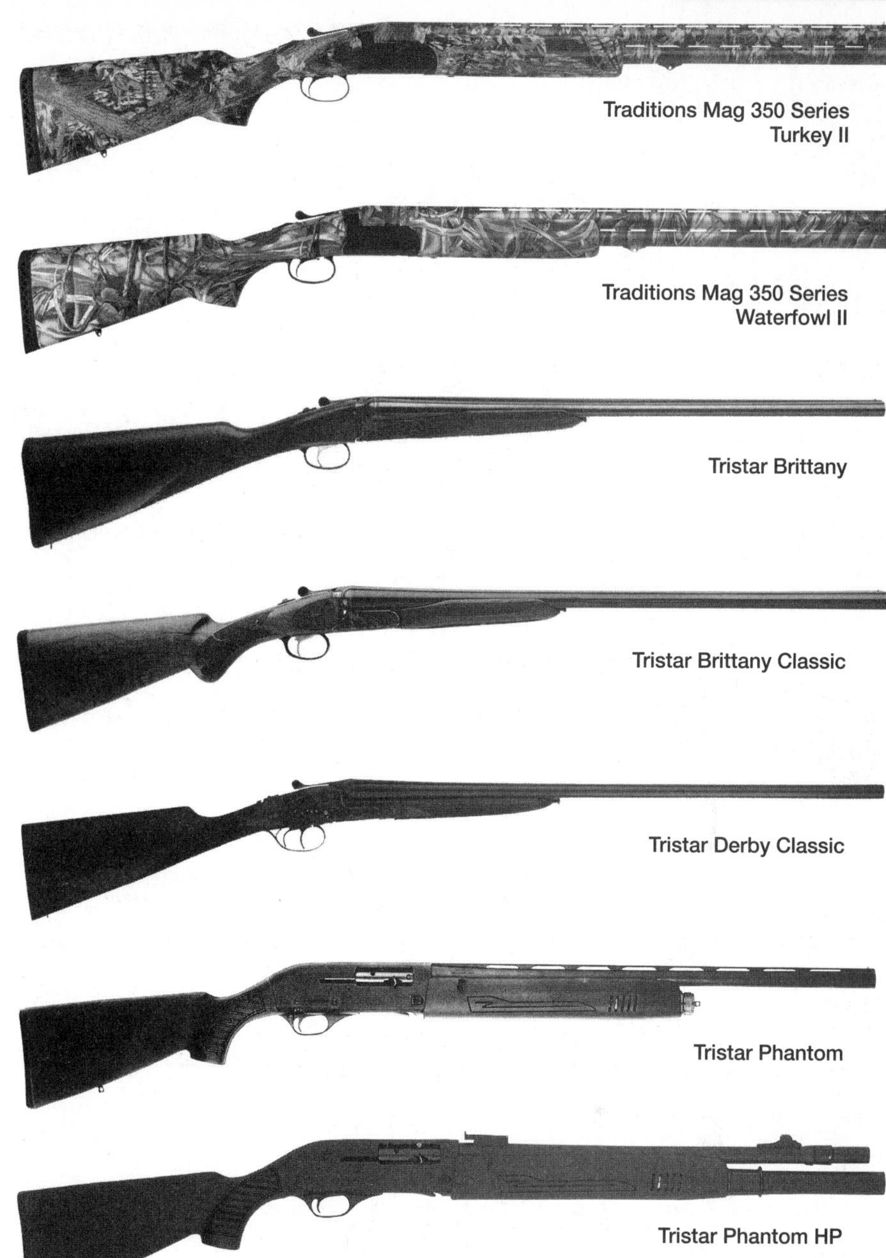

Traditions Mag 350 Series Turkey II

Traditions Mag 350 Series Waterfowl II

Tristar Brittany

Tristar Brittany Classic

Tristar Derby Classic

Tristar Phantom

Tristar Phantom HP

TRISTAR PHANTOM

Semi-auto 12 gauge; shoots 2-3/4-inch or 3-inch interchangeably; 24-inch, 26-inch, 28-inch barrel (Imp. Cyl., Mod., Full choke tubes); European walnut or black synthetic; gas-operated action; blued barrel; checkered pistol grip and forend; vent rib barrel. Introduced 1999. Imported by Tristar Sporting Arms Ltd.

Perf: $385 **Exc:** $350 **VGood:** $315

TRISTAR PHANTOM HP

Semi-auto 12 gauge; 3-inch chamber. Barrel: 19-inch; threaded for external choke tubes. Stock: Black synthetic. Sights: Bead front. Features: Gas-operated action; blue/ black finish; five-shot extended magazine tube. Imported by Tristar Sporting Arms Ltd.

Perf: $341 **Exc:** $306 **VGood:** $271

TRISTAR YORK

This side-by-side with blued engraved receiver and 3-inch chambers comes in 12 and 20 gauge with 26-inch or 28-inch barrels. Walnut, pistol grip stock and rubber recoil pad.

NIB: $825 **Exc:** $765 **VGood:** $600

TRISTAR ROTA MODEL 411

Side-by-side 12, 16, 20, and .410 gauge; 3-inch chambers; 28, 2-3/4-inch; 12-ga., 26-inch barrel; 28-inch; 16-, 20-, 28-ga., 410-bore, 26-inch; 12- and 20-ga. have three choke tubes, 16, 28 (Imp. Cyl. & Mod.), .410 (Mod. & Full) fixed chokes; weighs 6-1/2 to 7-1/4 lbs.; 14-3/8-inch l.o.p.; standard walnut with pistol grip, splinter-style forend; hand checkered; engraved, color case-hardened boxlock action; double triggers, extractors; solid barrel rib. Introduced 1998. Imported from Italy by Tristar Sporting Arms, Ltd.

Perf: $710 **Exc:** $650 **VGood:** $575

TRISTAR ROTA MODEL 411D

Similar to Model 411 except automatic ejectors, straight English-style stock, single trigger. Solid barrel rib with matted surface; chrome bores; color case-hardened frame; splinter forend. Introduced 1999. Imported from Italy by Tristar Sporting Arms, Ltd.

Perf: $915 **Exc:** $800 **VGood:** $700

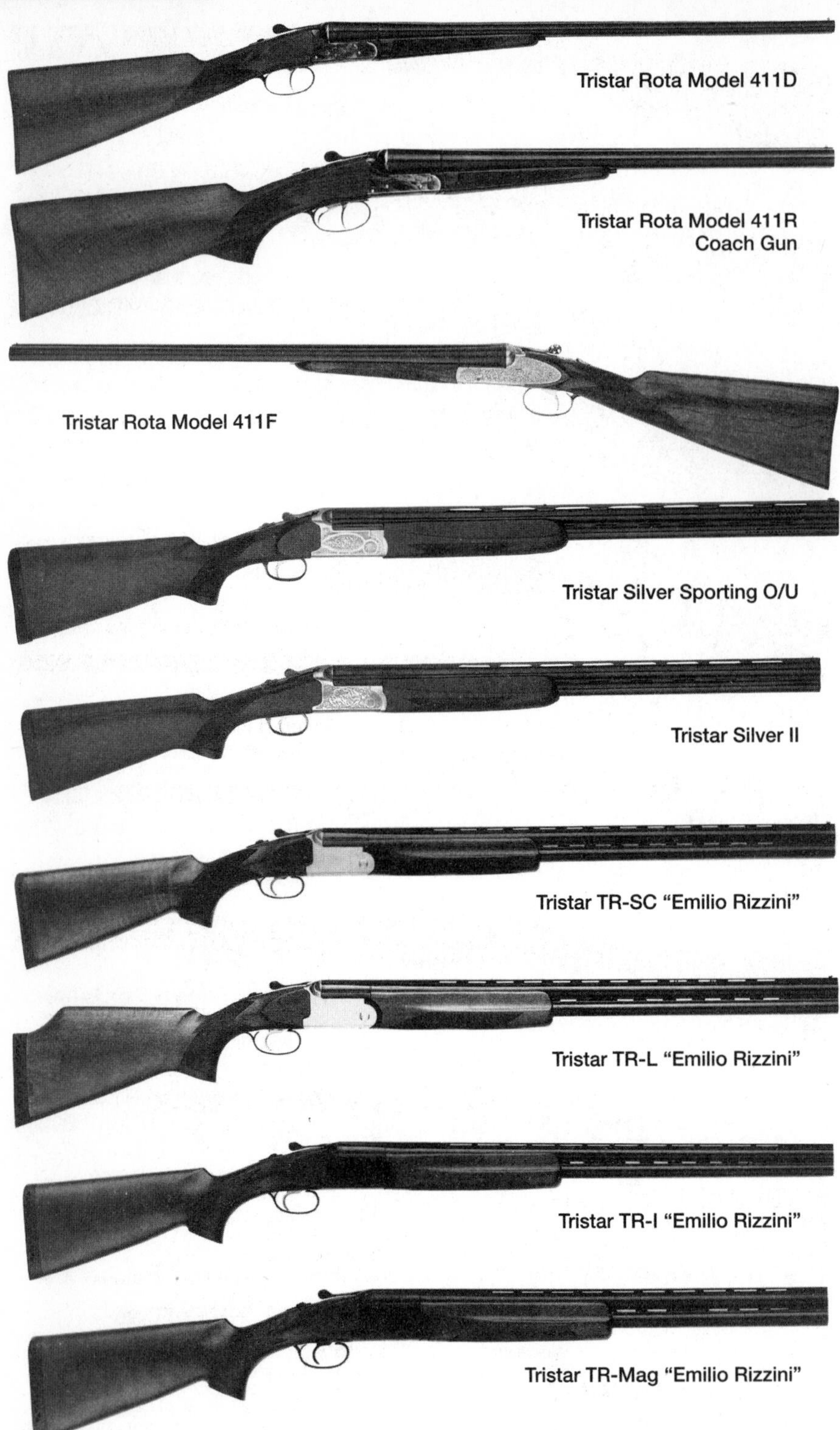

TRISTAR ROTA MODEL 411R COACH GUN

Similar to Model 411 except in 12- or 20-gauge only with 20-inch barrels and fixed chokes (Cyl. & Cyl.). Double triggers, extractors, choke tubes. Introduced 1999. Imported from Italy by Tristar Sporting Arms, Ltd.

Perf: $650 **Exc:** $575 **VGood:** $525

TRISTAR ROTA MODEL 411F

Similar to Model 411 except silver, engraved receiver, ejectors, IC, Mod. and Full choke tubes, English-style stock, single gold trigger, cut checkering. Imported from Italy by Tristar Sporting Arms Ltd.

Perf: $1425 **Exc:** $1200 **VGood:** $995

TRISTAR SILVER SPORTING

Over/under 12 gauge; 2-3/4-inch chambers, 20 3-inch chambers; 28-inch barrel, 30-inch (Skeet, Imp. Cyl., Mod., Full choke tubes); weighs 7-3/8 lbs.; 45-1/2-inch overall; figured walnut, cut checkering; Sporting Clays quick-mount buttpad; target bead front sight; boxlock action with single selective trigger, automatic selective ejectors; special broadway channeled rib; vented barrel rib; chrome bores; chrome-nickel finish on frame, with engraving. Introduced 1990. Imported from Italy by Tristar Sporting Arms Ltd.

Perf: $675 **Exc:** $575 **VGood:** $495

TRISTAR SILVER II

Similar to the Silver I except 26-inch barrel (Imp. Cyl., Mod., Full choke tubes, 12- and 20-ga.), 28-inch (Imp. Cyl., Mod., Full choke tubes, 12-ga. only), 26-inch (Imp. Cyl. & Mod. fixed chokes, 28-ga. and .410), automatic selective ejectors. Weight about 6 lbs., 15 oz. (12-ga., 26-inch).

Perf: $565 **Exc:** $475 **VGood:** $425

TRISTAR TR-SC "EMILIO RIZZINI"

Over/under 12 and 20 gauge; 3-inch chambers; 28-inch barrel, 30-inch (Imp. Cyl., Mod., Full choke tubes); weighs 7-1/2 lbs.; 46-inch overall (28-inch barrel); semi-fancy walnut; pistol grip with palm swell; semi-beavertail forend; black Sporting Clays recoil pad; silvered boxlock action with Four Locks locking system; auto ejectors; single selective (inertia) trigger; auto safety; hard chrome bores; vent. 10mm rib with target-style front and mid-rib beads. Introduced 1998. Imported from Italy by Tristar Sporting Arms, Ltd.

Sporting Clays model

Perf: $885 **Exc:** $775 **VGood:** $675

20 ga.

Perf: $965 **Exc:** $855 **VGood:** $755

TRISTAR TR-ROYAL "EMILIO RIZZINI"

Similar to the TR-SC except has special parallel stock dimensions to give low felt recoil; Rhino-ported, extended 12-, 20-, 28-ga. or .410 choke tubes; solid barrel spacer; has "TR-Royal" gold engraved on the silvered receiver. Available in 12- (28-inch, 30-inch), 20- and 28-gauge (28-inch only). Introduced 1999. Imported from Italy by Tristar Sporting Arms, Ltd.

12-ga.

Perf: $1075 **Exc:** $935 **VGood:** $825

20-, 28-ga.

Perf: $1075 **Exc:** $935 **VGood:** $825

TRISTAR TR-L "EMILIO RIZZINI"

Similar to the TR-SC except has stock dimensions designed for female shooters. Standard grade walnut. Introduced 1998. Imported from Italy by Tristar Sporting Arms, Ltd.

Perf: $890 **Exc:** $780 **VGood:** $680

TRISTAR TR-I, II "EMILIO RIZZINI"

Over/under 12 and 20 gauge; 3-inch chambers (TR-I); 12-, 16-, 20-, 28-ga., .410/3-inch chambers; 12-ga., 26-inch barrel (Imp. Cyl. & Mod.), 28-inch (Mod. & Full); 20-ga., 26-inch barrel (Imp. Cyl. & Mod.); fixed chokes; weighs 7-1/2 lbs.; walnut with palm swell pistol grip, hand checkering, semi-beavertail forend, black recoil pad; boxlock action with blued finish; Four Locks locking system; gold single selective (inertia) trigger system; automatic safety; extractors. Introduced 1998. Imported from Italy by Tristar Sporting Arms, Ltd.

TR-I

Perf: $585 **Exc:** $485 **VGood:** $430

TR-II (automatic ejectors, choke tubes) 12-, 16-ga.

Perf: $795 **Exc:** $675 **VGood:** $575

20-, 28-ga., .410

Perf: $845 **Exc:** $725 **VGood:** $625

TRISTAR TR-MAG "EMILIO RIZZINI"

Similar to TR-I, 3-1/2-inch chambers; choke tubes; 24-inch or 28-inch barrels with three choke tubes; extractors; auto safety. Matte blue finish on all metal, non-reflective wood finish. Introduced 1998. Imported from Italy by Tristar Sporting Arms, Ltd.

Perf: $650 **Exc:** $575 **VGood:** $475

Mossy Oak Break-Up camo

Perf: $820 **Exc:** $745 **VGood:** $645

Mossy Oak Shadow Grass camo

Perf: $820 **Exc:** $745 **VGood:** $645

10 ga., Mossy Oak camo patterns

Perf: $1018 **Exc:** $943 **VGood:** $843

TRISTAR TR SL "EMILIO RIZZINI"

Gauge: 12, 2-3/4-inch chambers; 28-inch, 30-inch barrel; weighs 7-3/4 lbs.; fancy walnut, hand checkering, semi-beavertail forend, black recoil pad, gloss finish; boxlock action with silvered, engraved sideplates; Four Lock locking system; automatic ejectors; hard chrome bores; vent tapered 7mm rib with target-style front bead; hand-fitted gun. Introduced 1999. Imported from Italy by Tristar Sporting Arms, Ltd.

Perf: $1625 **Exc:** $1400 **VGood:** $1125

TRISTAR WS

Gauge: 12, 3 1/2-inch chambers; 28-inch or 30-inch barrel (Imp. Cyl., Mod., Full choke tubes); weighs 6 lbs., 15 oz.; 46-inch overall; European walnut with cut checkering, black vented recoil pad, matte finish; boxlock action with single selective trigger; automatic selective ejectors; chrome bores; matte metal finish. Imported by Tristar Sporting Arms Ltd.

Perf: $550 **Exc:** $475 **VGood:** $425

TRISTAR HUNTER LITE

Over-and-under with silver alloy engraved frame, 3-inch chambers, extractors, choke tubes and walnut pistol grip stock and forearm. 20-gauge with 26-inch barrels weighs 5.4 lbs.; 12 gauge with 28-inch barrels weighs 6 lbs.

NIB: $400 **Exc:** $350 **VGood:** $295

TRISTAR HUNTER

Similar to Hunter Lite But with blued steel frame.

NIB: $390 **Exc:** $340 **VGood:** $275

TRISTAR FIELD HUNTER

Over/under 12-ga with 28-inch barrels, walnut stocks and three interchangeable chokes; this model includes selective auto ejectors and five choke tubes.

NIB: $500 **Exc:** $450 **VGood:** $395

TRISTAR VIPER G2

Gas-operated semi-auto in 12-, 20-, or 28-gauge with 26- or 28-inch barrel, ventilated rib and choke tubes. Wood or synthetic stock. Black or silver alloy receiver. Youth, sporting, tactical and left-hand models available. Sporting model has ported barrel, adjustable comb. Add 20 percent for silver receiver, or 28-gauge. Add 50 percent for sporting model.

Perf: $425 **Exc:** $385 **VGood:** $320

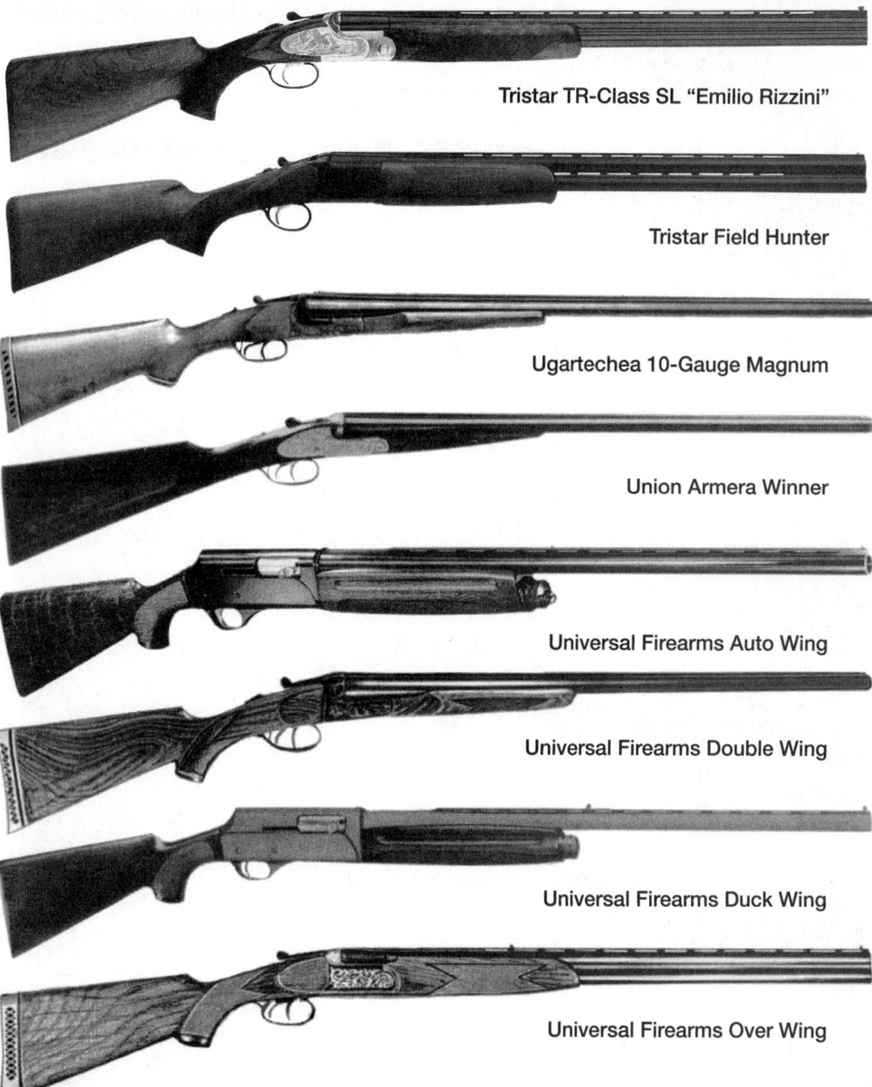

Tristar TR-Class SL "Emilio Rizzini"

Tristar Field Hunter

Ugartechea 10-Gauge Magnum

Union Armera Winner

Universal Firearms Auto Wing

Universal Firearms Double Wing

Universal Firearms Duck Wing

Universal Firearms Over Wing

UGARTECHEA 10-GAUGE MAGNUM

Side-by-side; boxlock; 10-ga.; 3-1/2-inch chambers; 32-inch barrels; matted rib; weighs 11 lbs.; front, center metal beads; checkered European walnut stock; vent rubber recoil pad; Purdey-type forend release; double triggers; color case-hardened action; rest is blued. Made in Spain. Introduced 1990; still in production.

Perf: $725 **Exc:** $645 **VGood:** $545

UNION ARMERA LUXE

Side-by-side; 12-, 20-ga.; 2-3/4-inch chambers; custom built to customer's specs; top-grade European walnut stock; auto ejectors; hand-engraved action; numerous options. Made in Spain. Introduced 1982; discontinued 1984.

Perf: $5200 **Exc:** $3750 **VGood:** $3200

UNION ARMERA WINNER

Side-by-side; 12-, 20-ga.; 2-3/4-inch chambers; custom built to customer's specs; top-grade European walnut stock; auto ejectors; hand-engraved action; numerous options. Made in Spain. Introduced 1982; discontinued 1984.

Perf: $2700 **Exc:** $2250 **VGood:** $1900

UNIVERSAL FIREARMS AUTO WING

Recoil-operated autoloader; takedown; 12-ga.; 2-3/4-inch chamber; 5-shot magazine, 3-shot plug furnished; 25-inch, 28-inch, 30-inch barrel; Improved, Modified, Full chokes; vent rib; ivory bead front, middle sights; checkered European walnut pistol-grip stock, grooved forearm; crossbolt safety; interchangeable barrels. Introduced 1970; discontinued 1974.

Perf: $150 **Exc:** $125 **VGood:** $100

UNIVERSAL FIREARMS DOUBLE WING

Side-by-side; boxlock; 10-, 12-, 20-ga.; 26-inch Improved/Modified, 28-inch or 30-inch Modified/Full barrels; checkered European walnut pistol-grip stock, beavertail forearm; double triggers; recoil pad. Introduced 1970; discontinued 1974.

Perf: $350 **Exc:** $295 **VGood:** $250

UNIVERSAL FIREARMS DUCK WING

Recoil-operated autoloader; takedown; 12-ga.; 2-3/4-inch chamber; 5-shot magazine, 3-shot plug furnished; 28-inch, 30-inch barrel; Full choke; ivory bead front, middle sights; checkered European walnut pistol-grip stock, grooved forearm; crossbolt safety; interchangeable barrels; exposed metal parts coated with olive green Teflon-S. Introduced 1970; discontinued 1972.

Perf: $200 **Exc:** $125 **VGood:** $95

UNIVERSAL FIREARMS MODEL 101

Single shot; top break; external hammer; takedown; 12-ga.; 3-inch chamber; 28-inch, 30-inch Full-choke barrel; uncheckered pistol-grip stock, beavertail forearm. Introduced 1967; discontinued 1969. Replaced by Single Wing model.

Perf: $75 **Exc:** $45 **VGood:** $30

UNIVERSAL FIREARMS MODEL 202

Side-by-side; boxlock; 12-, 20-ga.; 3-inch chambers; 26-inch Improved/Modified, 28-inch Modified/Full barrels; hand-checkered European walnut pistol-grip stock, European-style forearm; double triggers. Introduced 1967; discontinued 1969. Replaced by Double Wing model.

Perf: $275 **Exc:** $195 **VGood:** $145

UNIVERSAL FIREARMS MODEL 203

Side-by-side; boxlock; 10-ga.; 3 1/2-inch chambers; 32-inch Full/Full barrels; hand-checkered European walnut pistol-grip stock, European-style forearm; double triggers. Introduced 1967; discontinued 1969.

Perf: $440 **Exc:** $420 **VGood:** $295

UNIVERSAL FIREARMS MODEL 2030

Side-by-side; boxlock; 10-ga.; 3-1/2-inch chambers; 32-inch Full/Full barrels; checkered European walnut pistol-grip stock, beavertail forearm; double triggers; recoil pad. Introduced 1970; discontinued 1974.

Perf: $440 **Exc:** $420 **VGood:** $295

UNIVERSAL FIREARMS OVER WING

Over/under; boxlock; hammerless; 12-, 20-ga.; 3-inch chambers; 26-inch Improved/Modified, 28-inch or 30-inch Modified/Full barrels; vent rib; front, middle sights; checkered European walnut pistol-grip stock, forearm; double triggers; single-trigger model

with engraved receiver at added cost. Introduced 1970; discontinued 1974.

With double triggers

Perf: $295 **Exc:** $195 **VGood:** $150

With single trigger, engraved receiver

Perf: $325 **Exc:** $220 **VGood:** $175

UNIVERSAL FIREARMS SINGLE WING

Single-shot; top break; external hammer; takedown; 12-ga.; 3-inch chamber; 28-inch Full or Modified barrel; uncheckered European walnut pistol-grip stock, beavertail forearm; automatic ejector. Introduced 1970; discontinued 1974.

Perf: $75 **Exc:** $45 **VGood:** $30

URBIOLA MODEL 160E

Side-by-side; 12-, 20-ga.; 2-3/4-inch chambers; 26-inch Improved/Full, 28-inch Modified/Full barrels; hand-checkered European walnut straight-grip stock; checkered butt; automatic ejectors; double triggers; hand-engraved locks. Made in Spain. Introduced 1982 by Toledo Armas; discontinued 1984.

Perf: $625 **Exc:** $500 **VGood:** $425

VALMET LION

Over/under; boxlock; 12-ga.; 26-inch Improved/ Modified, 28-inch Modified/Full, 30-inch Modified/ Full or Full/Full barrels; hand-checkered walnut stock; single selective trigger; plain extractors. Made in Finland. Introduced 1951; discontinued 1967.

Exc: $360 **VGood:** $300 **Good:** $275

VALMET MODEL 412K

Over/under; 12-, 20-ga.; 26-inch, 28-inch, 30-inch barrels; vent rib; checkered American walnut stock; extractors; interchangeable barrels, stocks, forends; barrel selector on trigger; auto top tang safety; barrel cocking indicators; optional double triggers. Made in Finland. Introduced 1980; discontinued 1990.

Perf: $700 **Exc:** $500 **VGood:** $400

VALMET MODEL 412KE

Same specs as Model 412K except auto ejectors; non-auto safety. Introduced 1980; discontinued 1983.

Perf: $775 **Exc:** $575 **VGood:** $475

VALMET MODEL 412S AMERICAN

Same specs as Model 412K except luminous sights; better wood, checkering; palm swell on pistol grip; new forend latch spring mechanism; improved firing pin; made in Trap, Skeet, Field versions. Made in Finland. Introduced 1980; discontinued 1984.

Perf: $1000 **Exc:** $750 **VGood:** $600

VALMET MODEL 412ST SKEET

Over/under; 12-, 20-ga.; 28-inch stepped-rib barrels; choke tubes; European walnut Skeet-style stock; mechanical single trigger; auto ejectors; elongated forcing cone; cocking indicators; hand-honed action. Made in Finland. Introduced 1980; discontinued 1990.

Perf: $995 **Exc:** $750 **VGood:** $650

VALMET MODEL 412ST SKEET GRADE II

Same specs as Model 412ST Skeet except checkered semi-fancy European walnut Skeet-style stock drilled for recoil-reducing unit; matte nickel receiver; matte blue locking bolt, lever; gold trigger. Made in Finland. Introduced 1989; discontinued 1990.

Perf: $1200 **Exc:** $800 **VGood:** $700

VALMET MODEL 412ST TRAP

Same specs as Model 412ST Skeet except 12-ga.; 30-inch, 32-inch barrels; European walnut stock, palm swell. Made in Finland. Introduced 1980; discontinued 1990.

Perf: $1200 **Exc:** $800 **VGood:** $700

VALMET MODEL 412ST TRAP GRADE II

Same specs as Model 412ST Skeet except 12-ga.; 30-inch, 32-inch barrels; checkered semi-fancy European walnut stock, palm swell; stock drilled for recoil-reducing unit; matte nickel receiver; matte blue locking bolt, lever; gold trigger. Made in Finland. Introduced 1989; discontinued 1990.

Perf: $1200 **Exc:** $800 **VGood:** $700

VENTURA AVANTI SMALL GAUGE

Over/under; boxlock; 28-ga. (2-3/4-inch), .410 (3-inch); 26-inch barrels; vent top, side ribs; weighs 5 3/4 lbs.; straight English-type French walnut stock; single selective trigger; auto ejectors; fully engraved. Made in Italy. Introduced 1987; discontinued 1988.

Perf: $750 **Exc:** $600 **VGood:** $525

VENTURA AVANTI SMALL GAUGE EXTRA LUSSO

Same specs as Avanti Small Gauge except highly figured French walnut stock; more ornate engraving. Introduced 1987; discontinued 1988.

Perf: $1050 **Exc:** $850 **VGood:** $750

VENTURA CONTENTO

Over/under; boxlock; 12-ga.; 26-inch, 28-inch, 29-1/2-inch, 32-inch barrels; high post rib, vent side ribs; hand-checkered European walnut Monte Carlo stock; Woodward side lugs, double internal bolts; selective single trigger; auto ejectors. Introduced 1975, discontinued 1982.

Perf: $1800 **Exc:** $1250 **VGood:** $1000

VENTURA CONTENTO EXTRA LUSSO

Same specs as Contento except best-grade fancy walnut stock; extensive Florentine engraving. No longer in production.

Perf: $2000 **Exc:** $1475 **VGood:** $1200

VENTURA CONTENTO LUSSO GRADE

Same specs as Contento except better wood; engraved action. No longer in production.

Perf: $1900 **Exc:** $1350 **VGood:** $1100

VENTURA MODEL 51

Side-by-side; 12-, 20-ga.; 27-1/2-inch, 30-inch barrels; hand-checkered select European walnut straight or pistol-grip stock, slender beavertail forend; single selective trigger; auto ejectors; hand-engraved action. Made in Spain. Introduced 1980; discontinued 1985.

Perf: $600 **Exc:** $450 **VGood:** $375

VENTURA MODEL 53

Side-by-side; 12-, 20-, 28-ga., .410; 25-inch, 27-1/2-inch, 30-inch barrels; hand-checkered select European walnut straight or pistol-grip stock, slender beavertail forend; single selective or double triggers; auto ejectors; hand-engraved frame. Made in Spain. Introduced 1980; discontinued 1985.

Perf: $640 **Exc:** $490 **VGood:** $410

VENTURA MODEL 62

Side-by-side; H&H sidelock; 12-, 20-, 28-ga.; 25-inch, 27-1/2-inch, 30-inch barrels; select figured

English walnut straight or pistol-grip stock, slender beavertail forend; single selective or double triggers; auto ejectors; cocking indicator; gas escape valve; intercepting safety; double underbolts; Purdey-style engraving. Made in Spain. Introduced 1980; discontinued 1982.

Perf: $1125 **Exc:** $850 **VGood:** $750

VENTURA MODEL 64

Side-by-side; H&H sidelock; 12-, 20-, 28-ga.; 25-inch, 27-1/2-inch, 30-inch barrels; select figured English walnut straight or pistol-grip stock, slender beavertail forend; single selective or double triggers; auto ejectors; cocking indicator; gas escape valve; intercepting safety; Florentine engraving. Introduced 1978; no longer in production.

Perf: $1125 **Exc:** $850 **VGood:** $750

VENTURA MODEL 66

Side-by-side; H&H sidelock; 12-, 20-, 28-ga.; 25-inch, 27-1/2-inch, 30-inch barrels; select figured English walnut straight or pistol-grip stock, slender beavertail forend; single selective or double triggers; auto ejectors; cocking indicator; gas escape valve; intercepting safety; treble bolting; side clips; Florentine engraving. Introduced 1980; no longer in production.

Perf: $1125 **Exc:** $850 **VGood:** $750

VENTURA MODEL XXV

Side-by-side; 12-, 20-, 28-ga., .410; 25-inch barrels; Churchill rib; hand-checkered select European walnut straight or pistol grip stock, slender beavertail forend; single selective or double triggers; auto ejectors; hand-engraved frame. Made in Spain. Introduced 1980; no longer in production.

Perf: $850 **Exc:** $625 **VGood:** $550

VENTURA REGIS MODEL

Side-by-side; H&H sidelock; 12-, 20-, 28-ga., .410; 2-3/4-inch, 3-inch chambers; 26-inch, 28-inch barrels; weighs 6-1/2 lbs.; hand-checkered select figured French walnut stock, sliver beavertail forend; intercepting safeties; triple locks; auto ejectors; single selective, double triggers; floral engraving; several options. Made in Italy. Introduced 1986; discontinued 1988.

Perf: $1500 **Exc:** $1350 **VGood:** $1100

VENTURA VICTRIX

Side-by-side; Anson & Deeley boxlock; 12-, 20-, 28-ga., .410; 2-3/4-inch, 3-inch chambers; 26-inch, 28-inch barrels; fixed chokes; optional screw-in chokes; weighs 6-1/2 lbs.; hand-checkered French walnut stock, beavertail forend; triple locks; auto ejectors; double or single selective trigger; marketed in leather trunk-type case. Made in Italy. Introduced 1986; discontinued 1988.

With fixed chokes

Perf: $800 **Exc:** $600 **VGood:** $500

With choke tubes

Perf: $850 **Exc:** $650 **VGood:** $550

VENTURA VICTRIX EXTRA LUSSO

Same specs as Victrix except better quality wood; full floral engraving. Made in Italy. Introduced 1986; discontinued 1988.

With fixed chokes

Perf: $1125 **Exc:** $850 **VGood:** $750

With choke tubes

Perf: $1175 **Exc:** $900 **VGood:** $800

VERONA LX501 HUNTING

Gauge: 12, 20, 28, 410 (2-3/4-inch, 3-inch chambers); 28-inch barrel; 12-, 20-ga. have Interchoke tubes, 28-ga. and .410 have fixed Full & Mod.; weighs 6 to 7 lbs.; matte-finished walnut with machine-cut checkering; gold-plated single-selective trigger; ejectors; engraved, blued receiver; non-automatic safety; coil spring-operated firing pins. Introduced 1999. Imported from Italy by B.C. Outdoors.

12- and 20-ga.

Perf: $650 **Exc:** $550 **VGood:** $495

Ventura Model 64

Verona LX501 Skeet

Verona LX680 Skeet/Sporting, Trap

Verona LX692 Gold Sporting

Weatherby Athena Grade IV

28-ga. and .410

Perf: $675 **Exc:** $595 **VGood:** $525

Combos 20/28, 28/410

Perf: $1300 **Exc:** $1200 **VGood:** $1150

VERONA LX692 GOLD HUNTING

Similar to Verona LX501 except engraved, silvered receiver with false sideplates showing gold-inlaid bird hunting scenes on three sides; schnabel forend tip; hand-cut checkering; black rubber butt pad. Available in 12- and 20-gauge only, five InterChoke tubes. Introduced 1999. Imported from Italy by B.C. Outdoors.

Perf: $1195 **Exc:** $995 **VGood:** $875

Combo 28/410

Perf: $2100 **Exc:** $1900 **VGood:** $1750

VERONA LX680 SPORTING

Similar to Verona LX501 except engraved, silvered receiver; ventilated middle rib; beavertail forend; hand-cut checkering; available in 12- or 20-gauge only with 2-3/4-inch chambers. Introduced 1999. Imported from Italy by B.C. Outdoors.

Perf: $975 **Exc:** $800 **VGood:** $700

VERONA LX680 SKEET/ SPORTING, TRAP

Similar to Verona LX501 except Skeet or trap stock dimensions; beavertail forend, palm swell on pistol grip; ventilated center barrel rib. Introduced 1999. Imported from Italy by B.C. Outdoors.

Perf: $1100 **Exc:** $900 **VGood:** $800

Gold Competition (false sideplates with gold-inlaid hunting scenes)

Perf: $1475 **Exc:** $1300 **VGood:** $1100

VERONA LX692 GOLD SPORTING

Similar to Verona LX680 except false sideplates have gold-inlaid bird hunting scenes on three sides; red high-visibility front sight. Introduced 1999. Imported from Italy by B.C. Outdoors.

Perf: $1275 **Exc:** $1100 **VGood:** $1000

VERONA LX680 COMPETITION TRAP

Gauge: 12; 30-inch barrel O/U, 32-inch single bbl.; weighs 8-3/8 lbs. combo, 7 lbs. single; walnut stock; white front, mid-rib bead sights; interchangeable barrels switch from O/U to single configurations; 5 Briley chokes in combo, 4 in single bbl.; extended forcing cones, parted barrels 32-inch with raised rib.

Trap Single

Perf: $1499 **Exc:** $1395 **VGood:** $1200

Trap Combo

Perf: $2300 **Exc:** $2200 **VGood:** $2000

VERONA LX702 GOLD TRAP COMBO

Gauge: 20 & 28, 2-3/4-inch chamber; 30-inch barrel; weighs 7 lbs.; Turkish walnut with beavertail forearm; white front bead sight; 2-barrel competition gun; color case-hardened sideplates and receiver with gold inlaid pheasant; ventilated rib between barrels; 5 interchokes. Imported from Italy by B.C. Outdoors.

Combo

Perf: $1475 **Exc:** $1300 **VGood:** $1100

20-gauge

Perf: $1475 **Exc:** $1300 **VGood:** $1100

VERONA MODEL SX400 SEMI-AUTO SHOTGUN

Gauge: 12; 26-inch, 30-inch barrel; weighs 6-1/2 lbs.; walnut, black composite stock; red dot sights; aluminum receivers; gas-operated; 2-3/4-inch or 3-inch Magnum shells (without adj.); 4 screw-in chokes and wrench included; sling swivels; gold trigger; blued barrel. Imported from Italy by B.C. Outdoors.

401S, 12-gauge

Perf: $375 **Exc:** $325 **VGood:** $290

405SDS, 12-gauge

Perf: $570 **Exc:** $495 **VGood:** $395

405L, 12-gauge

Perf: $295 **Exc:** $250 **VGood:** $210

WEATHERBY ATHENA SIDE-BY-SIDE

Side-by-side; 12-, 20-ga.; 26-inch, 28-inch barrel; Turkish walnut, straight grip stock; brass bead front sight; barrel selector independent of crossbolt safety; integral multi-choke system; interchangeable screw-in Briley choke tubes (excepting .410 bored IC & Mod.); receiver engraved with rose and scroll.

Perf: $1285 **Exc:** $1025 **VGood:** $865

WEATHERBY ATHENA GRADE IV

Over/under; boxlock; dummy sideplates; 12-, 20-ga.; 3-inch chambers; 26-inch, 28-inch barrels; three

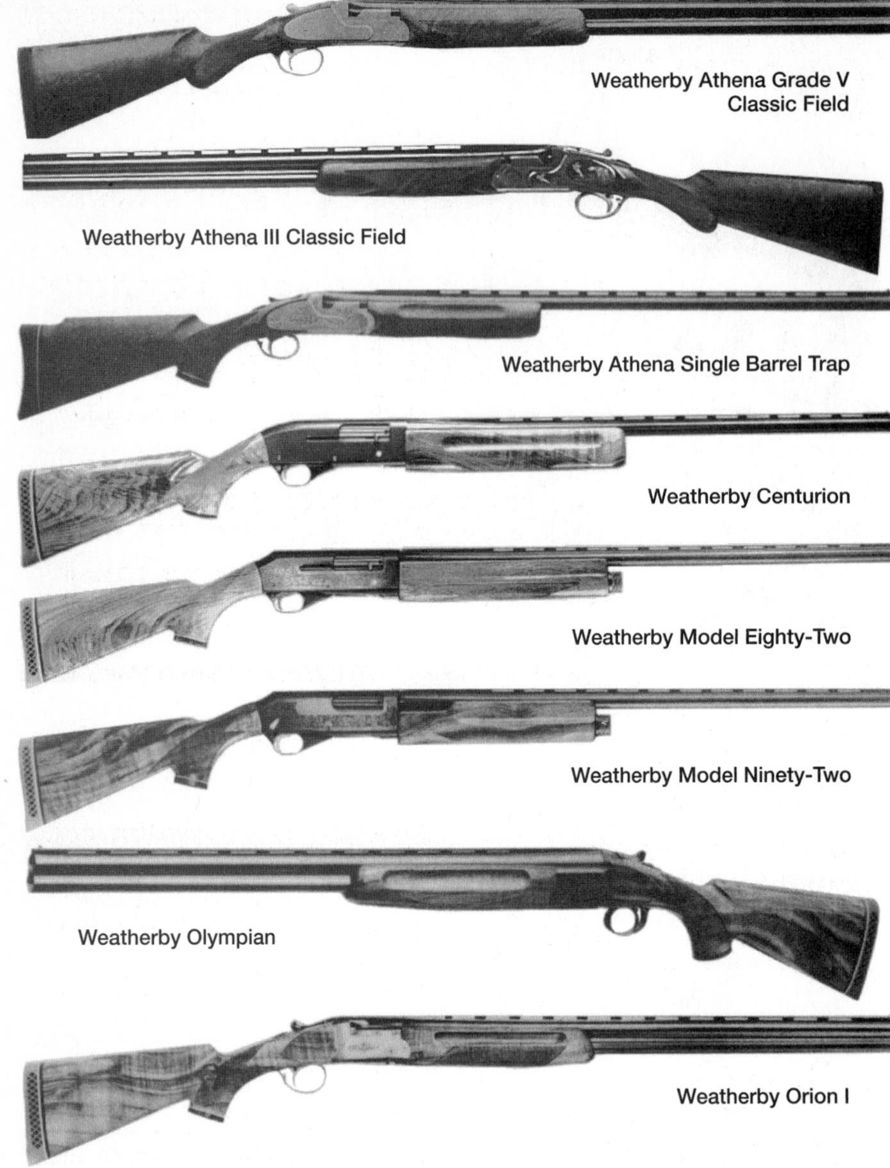

Weatherby Athena Grade V Classic Field

Weatherby Athena III Classic Field

Weatherby Athena Single Barrel Trap

Weatherby Centurion

Weatherby Model Eighty-Two

Weatherby Model Ninety-Two

Weatherby Olympian

Weatherby Orion I

IMC Multi-Choke tubes; checkered American walnut pistol-grip stock, forend; mechanically operated single selective trigger (selector inside trigger guard); selective auto ejectors; top tang safety, Greener crossbolt; fully engraved receiver. Made in Japan. Introduced 1982; still in production.

Perf: $2000 **Exc:** $1495 **VGood:** $1150

WEATHERBY ATHENA GRADE V CLASSIC FIELD

Same specs as the Athena Grade IV except 26-inch, 28-inch, 30-inch barrels; oil-finished, fine-line-checkered Claro walnut, rounded pistol-grip stock w/slender forend; Old English recoil pad; sideplate receiver rose and scroll engraved. Made in Japan. Introduced 1993; still imported.

Perf: $2500 **Exc:** $2000 **VGood:** $1500

WEATHERBY ATHENA III CLASSIC FIELD

Has Grade III Claro walnut with oil finish, rounded pistol grip, slender forend; silver nitride/gray receiver has rose and scroll engraving with gold- overlay upland game scenes. Introduced 1999. Imported from Japan by Weatherby.

12-, 20-, 28-gauge

Perf: $1900 **Exc:** $1550 **VGood:** $1275

WEATHERBY ATHENA SINGLE BARREL TRAP

Same specs as the Athena Grade IV except 12-ga.; 2-3/4-inch chambers; 32-inch, 34-inch single top barrel; Full, Modified, Improved Modified Multi-Choke tubes; white front sight, brass middle bead; trap stock dimensions. Made in Japan. Introduced 1988; discontinued 1992.

Perf: $1550 **Exc:** $950 **VGood:** $850

Combo with extra O/U barrel set

Perf: $2000 **Exc:** $1500 **VGood:** $1200

WEATHERBY CENTURION

Autoloader; 12-ga.; 2-3/4-inch chamber; 26-inch Skeet or Improved Cylinder, 28-inch Improved or Modified or Full, 30-inch Full barrel; vent rib; front, middle bead sights; hand-checkered American walnut pistol-grip stock, forearm; pressure compensator; engraved alloy receiver. Made in Japan. Introduced 1970; discontinued 1982; replaced by Model Eighty-Two.

Perf: $325 **Exc:** $275 **VGood:** $225

WEATHERBY CENTURION DELUXE

Same specs as Centurion except fancy-grade wood; etched receiver. Introduced 1972; discontinued 1982.

Perf: $395 **Exc:** $325 **VGood:** $250

WEATHERBY CENTURION TRAP

Same specs as Centurion except 30-inch Full-choke barrel; trap-style walnut stock. Introduced 1972; discontinued 1982.

Perf: $370 **Exc:** $350 **VGood:** $310

WEATHERBY MODEL EIGHTY-TWO

Gas-operated autoloader; 12-ga.; 2-3/4-inch, 3-inch chamber; 26-inch, 28-inch, 30-inch barrels; 22-inch slug barrel with rifle sights available; fixed or interchangeable choke tubes; hand-checkered pistol-grip stock, forend; rubber recoil pad; floating piston; fluted bolt; crossbolt safety; gold-plated trigger. Made in Japan. Introduced 1982; discontinued 1988.

With fixed choke

Perf: $395 **Exc:** $295 **VGood:** $255

With choke tubes

Perf: $425 **Exc:** $320 **VGood:** $285

WEATHERBY MODEL EIGHTY-TWO BUCKMASTER

Same specs as Model Eighty-Two except 22-inch Skeet barrel; rifle sights. Introduced 1982; discontinued 1987.

Perf: $375 **Exc:** $350 **VGood:** $295

WEATHERBY MODEL EIGHTY-TWO TRAP

Same specs as Model Eighty-Two except 30-inch Full-choke barrel; trap-style walnut stock. Introduced 1982; discontinued 1984.

With fixed choke

Perf: $350 **Exc:** $275 **VGood:** $250

With choke tubes

Perf: $375 **Exc:** $300 **VGood:** $275

WEATHERBY MODEL NINETY-TWO

Slide action; 12-ga.; 2-3/4-inch, 3-inch chamber; 26-inch Modified or Improved or Skeet, 28-inch Full or Modified, 30-inch Full barrel; vent rib; hand-checkered American walnut pistol-grip stock, forend; grip cap; recoil pad; crossbolt safety; engraved black alloy receiver. Made in Japan. Introduced 1982; discontinued 1988.

With fixed choke

Perf: $325 **Exc:** $275 **VGood:** $240

With Multi-chokes

Perf: $350 **Exc:** $325 **VGood:** $270

WEATHERBY MODEL NINETY-TWO BUCKMASTER

Same specs as Model Ninety-two except 22-inch Skeet barrel; rifle sights. Introduced 1982; discontinued 1987.

Perf: $345 **Exc:** $285 **VGood:** $250

WEATHERBY MODEL NINETY-TWO TRAP

Same specs as Model Ninety-Two except 30-inch Full-choke barrel; trap-style walnut stock. Introduced 1982; discontinued 1984.

With fixed choke

Perf: $300 **Exc:** $220 **VGood:** $190

With Multi-chokes

Perf: $325 **Exc:** $240 **VGood:** $200

WEATHERBY OLYMPIAN

Over/under; boxlock; 12-, 20-ga.; 26-inch, 28-inch, 30-inch barrels; checkered American walnut pistol-grip stock; selective auto ejectors; single selective trigger; top tang safety; Greener crossbolt. Made in Italy. Introduced 1978; discontinued 1982; replaced by Athena.

Perf: $875 **Exc:** $750 **VGood:** $650

WEATHERBY OLYMPIAN TRAP

Same specs as Olympian except 12-ga.; 30-inch, 32-inch barrels; vent rib; trap-style walnut stock. Introduced 1978; discontinued 1982.

Perf: $875 **Exc:** $750 **VGood:** $650

WEATHERBY ORION I

Over/under; boxlock; 12-, 20-ga.; 3-inch chambers; 26-inch, 28-inch Full/Modified or Modified/Improved or Skeet/Skeet, 30-inch Full/Modified barrels; Multi-chokes; checkered American walnut pistol-grip stock, forend; rubber recoil pad; selective auto ejectors; single selective trigger; top tang safety;

Greener-type crossbolt. Made in Japan. Introduced 1982.

Perf: $1000 **Exc:** $750 **VGood:** $600

WEATHERBY ORION I SPORTING CLAYS

Same specs as Orion I except 12-ga.; 28-inch barrels; IMC choke tubes; raised rib; center and front beads; special Sporting Clays stock dimensions; rounded buttpad; elongated forcing cones; blued receiver with two 24-Karat gold clay targets on the bottom. Made in Japan. Introduced 1991; discontinued 1992.

Perf: $1200 **Exc:** $950 **VGood:** $800

WEATHERBY ORION UPLAND

Similar to Orion Grade I. Plain blued receiver, gold W on trigger guard; rounded pistol grip, slender forend of Claro walnut with high-gloss finish; black butt pad. Available in 12- and 20-gauge with 26-inch and 28-inch barrels. Introduced 1999. Imported from Japan by Weatherby.

Perf: $1095 **Exc:** $965 **VGood:** $800

WEATHERBY ORION II

Over/under; boxlock; 12-, 20-, 28-ga., .410; 3-inch chambers; 26-inch, 28-inch, 30-inch barrels; fixed or choke tubes; high-gloss checkered American walnut pistol-grip stock, forend; rubber recoil pad; selective auto ejectors; single selective trigger; top tang safety; Greener crossbolt; engraving. Discontinued 1993.

Perf: $1100 **Exc:** $800 **VGood:** $675

WEATHERBY ORION II CLASSIC

Same specs as Orion II except 12-, 20-, 28-ga.; 3-inch chambers; fine-line-checkered Claro walnut rounded-pistol-grip, slender forend with high-gloss finish; Old English recoil pad; silver-gray nitride receiver with engraved waterfowl and upland scenes. Made in Japan. Introduced 1993; still in production.

Perf: $1300 **Exc:** $1095 **VGood:** $875

WEATHERBY ORION II CLASSIC SPORTING CLAYS

Same specs as Orion II except 12-ga.; 28-inch, 30-inch barrels; IMC choke tubes; stepped Broadway-style competition vent top, side rib; Sporting Clays rounded-pistol-grip stock, slender forend with high-gloss finish; rounded buttpad; elongated forcing cones; silver-gray nitride receiver; scroll engraving with clay pigeon monogram in gold-plate overlay. Made in Japan. Introduced 1993; still in production.

Perf: $1450 **Exc:** $1100 **VGood:** $950

WEATHERBY ORION II SPORTING CLAYS

Same specs as Orion II except 12-ga.; 2-3/4-inch chambers; 28-inch, 30-inch barrels; Improved Cylinder, Modified, Full chokes; competition center vent rib; mid-barrel and enlarged front beads; Sporting Clays rounded-pistol-grip stock, slender forend with high-gloss finish; rounded recoil pad; lengthened forcing cones; silver nitride receiver with acid-etched, gold-plate clay pigeon monogram. Made in Japan. Introduced 1992.

Perf: $1550 **Exc:** $1400 **VGood:** $1250

WEATHERBY ORION III

Over/under; boxlock; 12-, 20-ga.; 3-inch chambers; 26-inch, 28-inch, 30-inch barrels; Multi-chokes; high-gloss checkered American walnut pistol-grip stock, forend; rubber recoil pad; selective auto ejectors; single selective trigger; top tang safety; Greener crossbolt; silvered, engraved receiver. Introduced 1989; still in production.

Perf: $1250 **Exc:** $850 **VGood:** $700

WEATHERBY ORION III CLASSIC

Same specs as Orion III except fine-line-checkered Claro walnut rounded-pistol-grip stock, slender forend with oil finish; Old English recoil pad; silver-gray nitride receiver with engraved waterfowl and upland scenes and gold-plate overlay. Made in Japan. Introduced 1993; still in production.

Perf: $1400 **Exc:** $1200 **VGood:** $950

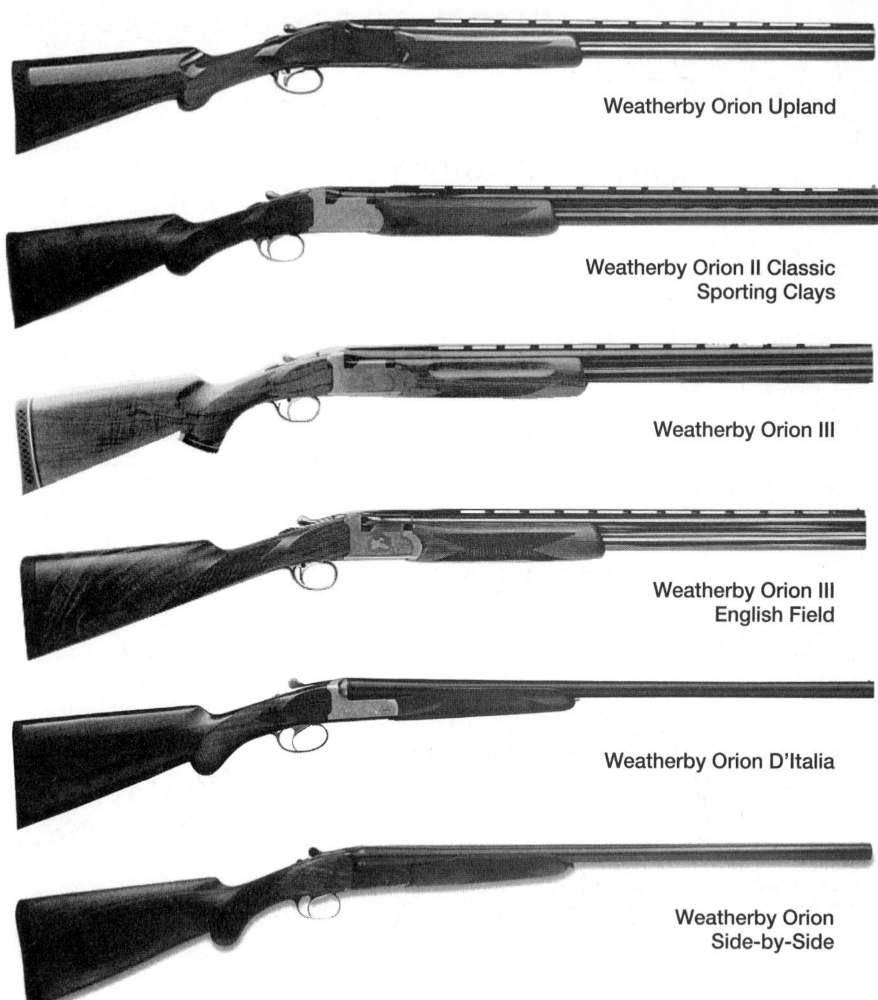

Weatherby Orion Upland

Weatherby Orion II Classic Sporting Clays

Weatherby Orion III

Weatherby Orion III English Field

Weatherby Orion D'Italia

Weatherby Orion Side-by-Side

WEATHERBY ORION GRADE III FIELD

Over/under; 12-, 20-ga.; 3-inch chambers; 26-inch, 28-inch barrel; IMC Multi-Choke tubes; weighs 6-1/2 to 9 lbs.; American walnut, checkered grip and forend; rubber recoil pad; selective automatic ejectors; single selective inertia trigger; top tang safety; Greener cross bolt; silver-gray receiver with engraving and gold duck/pheasant. Imported from Japan by Weatherby.

Perf: $1545 **Exc:** $1225 **VGood:** $965

WEATHERBY ORION GRADE III CLASSIC FIELD

Similar to Orion III Field except stock has rounded pistol grip, satin oil finish, slender forend, Old English recoil pad. Introduced 1993. Imported from Japan by Weatherby.

Perf: $1565 **Exc:** $1250 **VGood:** $1075

WEATHERBY ORION III ENGLISH FIELD

Similar to Orion III Classic Field except straight grip English-style stock. Available in 12-gauge (28-inch), 20-gauge (26-inch, 28-inch) with IMC Multi-Choke tubes. Silver/gray nitride receiver engraved and gold-plate overlay. Introduced 1997. Imported from Japan by Weatherby.

Perf: $1695 **Exc:** $1300 **VGood:** $1175

WEATHERBY ORION GRADE II CLASSIC FIELD

Similar to Orion III Classic Field except stock has high-gloss finish, and bird on receiver is not gold. Available in 12-gauge, 26-inch, 28-inch, 30-inch barrels; 20-gauge, 26-inch 28-inch, both with 3-inch chambers; 28-gauge, 26-inch, 2-3/4-inch chambers. All have IMC choke tubes. Imported from Japan by Weatherby.

Perf: $1300 E **Exc:** $1095 **VGood:** $875

WEATHERBY ORION GRADE I FIELD

Similar to Orion Grade III Field except blued receiver with engraving, and the bird is not gold. Available in 12-gauge, 26-inch, 28-inch, 30-inch; 20-gauge, 20-inch, 28-inch, both with 3-inch chambers and IMC choke tubes. Imported from Japan by Weatherby.

Perf: $1240 **Exc:** $1040 **VGood:** $860

WEATHERBY ORION SIDE-BY-SIDE

Side-by-side 12, 20, 28, and .410 ga. Barrel: 26-inch, 28-inch. Stock: Turkish walnut, half round pistol grip. Sights: Brass bead front. Features: Barrel selector independent of crossbolt safety. Integral multi-choke system, interchangeable screw-in Briley choke tubes (excepting .410 bored IC & Mod.). Receivers engraved with rose and scroll.

Perf: $960 **Exc:** $845 **VGood:** $735

WEATHERBY ORION D'ITALIA

Engraved silver-finish metalwork and fineline, 20 lpi checkering. Turkish walnut stock with high-gloss finish. Available in 12 gauge with 28" barrel and 20 gauge with 26" barrel.

Perf: $1695 **Exc:** $1300 **VGood:** $1175

WEATHERBY ORION SSC

Over/under 12 gauge; 3-inch chambers; 28-inch, 30-inch, 32-inch barrel (Skeet, SC1, Imp. Cyl., SC2, Mod. IMC choke tubes); weighs about 8 lbs.; Claro

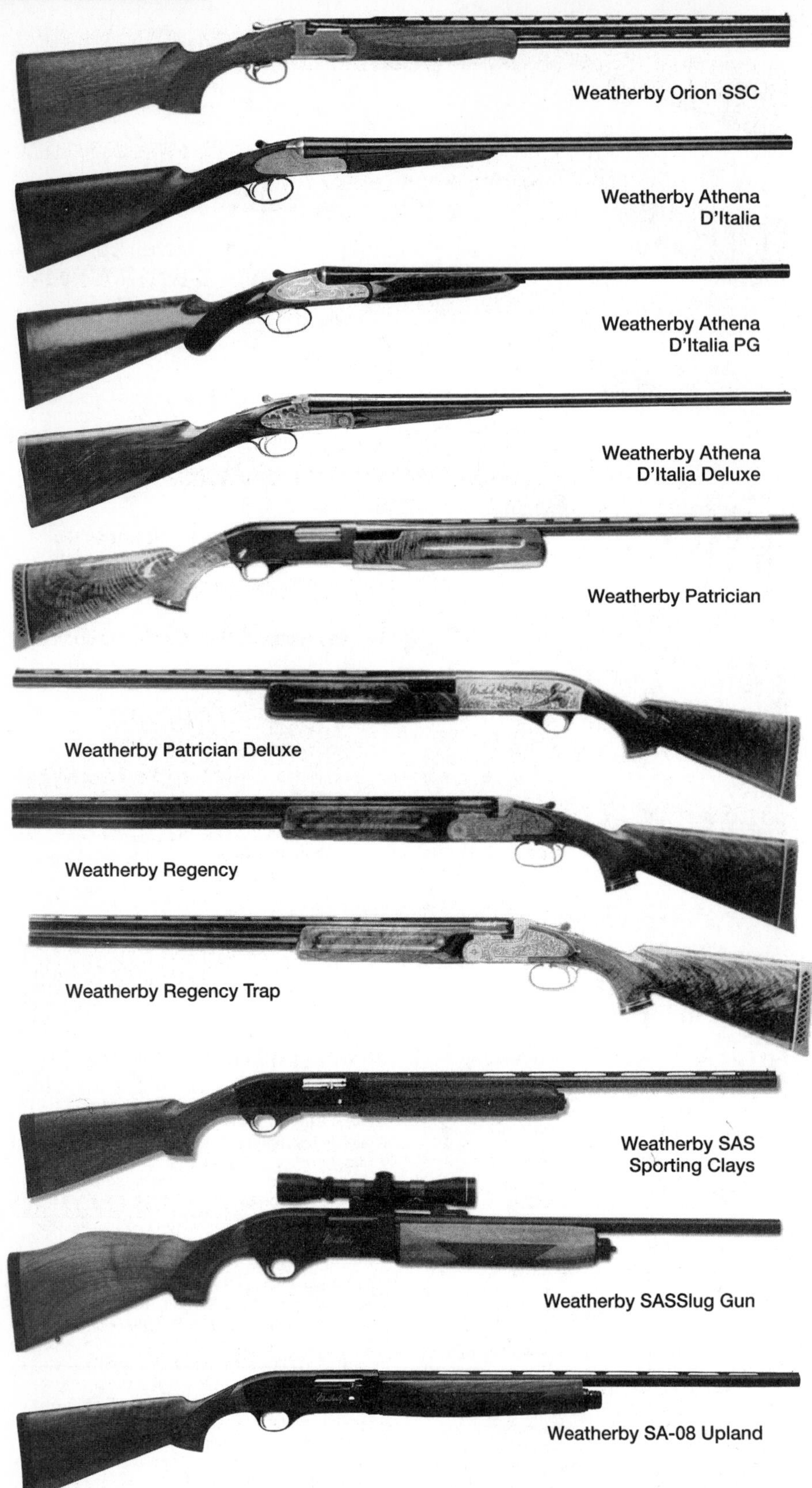
Weatherby Orion SSC

Weatherby Athena D'Italia

Weatherby Athena D'Italia PG

Weatherby Athena D'Italia Deluxe

Weatherby Patrician

Weatherby Patrician Deluxe

Weatherby Regency

Weatherby Regency Trap

Weatherby SAS Sporting Clays

Weatherby SASSlug Gun

Weatherby SA-08 Upland

walnut with satin oil finish; schnabel forend tip; sporter-style pistol grip; Pachmayr Decelerator recoil pad; lengthened forcing cones and back-boring; ported barrels with 12mm grooved rib with mid-bead sight; mechanical trigger is adjustable for length of pull. Introduced 1998. Imported from Japan by Weatherby.

SSC (Super Sporting Clays)

Perf: $1645 **Exc:** $1350 **VGood:** $1125

WEATHERBY ATHENA D'ITALIA

This side-by-side model features a boxlock action with intricately engraved sideplates, straight grip stock and double triggers. Available in 12, 20 and 28 gauges. Three chokes in 12 and 20 gauges; fixed IC and Mod. in 28 gauge. 3-inch chambers in 12 and 20 gauges; 2.75-inch chambers in 28 gauge. Automatic ejectors. Weight 6.75 to 7.25 lbs.

NIB: $2500 **Exc:** $2250 **VGood:** $1695

WEATHERBY ATHENA D'ITALIA PG

Introduced in 2006, this model is offered in the same configurations as the side-by-side Athena D'Italia. It is identical in action and frame to the D'Italia but with a rounded pistol grip stock and single gold trigger. Laser-cut checkering at 20 lpi.

NIB: $2750 **Exc:** $2500 **VGood:** $1825

WEATHERBY ATHENA D'ITALIA DELUXE

Renaissance floral engraving with Bolino style game scene and AAA Fancy Turkish walnut with 24 lpi hand checkering adorn this straight grip stocked side-by-side model. Available in 12, 20 and 28 gauges with 26-inch or 28-inch barrels with fixed IC and Mod. chokes. Single trigger.

NIB: $6700 **Exc:** $5750 **VGood:** $3995

WEATHERBY PATRICIAN

Slide action; 12-ga.; 2-3/4-inch chamber; 26-inch Modified or Improved or Skeet, 28-inch Full or Modified, 30-inch Full barrels; vent rib; hand-checkered stock, pistol-grip & forearm; recoil pad; hidden magazine cap; crossbolt safety. Made in Japan. Introduced 1970; discontinued 1982; replaced by Model Ninety-Two.

Perf: $280 **Exc:** $200 **VGood:** $170

WEATHERBY PATRICIAN DELUXE

Same specs as Patrician except fancy-grade wood; etched receiver. Introduced 1972; discontinued 1982.

Perf: $310 **Exc:** $275 **VGood:** $240

WEATHERBY PATRICIAN TRAP

Same specs as Patrician except 30-inch Full-choke barrel; Trap-style walnut stock. Introduced 1972; discontinued 1982.

Perf: $280 **Exc:** $230 **VGood:** $195

WEATHERBY REGENCY

Over/under; 12-, 20-ga.; boxlock; 28-inch Full/Modified, Modified/Improved, Skeet/Skeet barrels; vent rib; bead front sight; hand-checkered American walnut pistol-grip stock, forearm; recoil pad; selective automatic ejectors; single selective trigger; simulated sidelocks; fully engraved receiver. Made first in Italy; then Japan. Introduced 1972; discontinued 1982; replaced by Orion.

Perf: $950 **Exc:** $800 **VGood:** $725

WEATHERBY REGENCY TRAP

Same specs as Regency except 30-inch, 32-inch barrels; Modified/Full, Improved Modified/Full, Full/Full chokes; vent side, top ribs; walnut Monte Carlo or straight Trap-style stock. Introduced 1965; discontinued 1982.

Perf: $895 **Exc:** $800 **VGood:** $725

WEATHERBY SAS (SEMI-AUTOMATIC SHOTGUN) SPORTING CLAYS/SLUG GUN

6 Models: SAS Field, SAS Sporting Clays, SAS Shadow Grass, SAS Break-Up, SAS Synthetic, SAS Slug Gun Gauge: 12. Barrel: Vent ribbed, 24-inch-30-inch. Stock: SAS Field and Sporting Clays, walnut. SAS Shadow Grass, Break-Up, Synthetic, composite. Sights: SAS Sporting Clays, brass front and mid-point back. SAS Shadow Grass and Break-Up, HiViz front and brass mid. Synthetic has brass front. Features: IMC system includes 3 Briley screw-in choke tubes. Case included.

Sporting Clays

Perf: $695 **Exc:** $595 **VGood:** $495

Slug Gun

Perf: $675 **Exc:** $625 **VGood:** $525

WEATHERBY SA-08 UPLAND

This semi-automatic was new in 2008. It features a walnut stock with oil finish. Available in 12 and 20 gauge with 3" chambers and 28" or 26" barrels. Three choke tubes included.

Perf: $525 **Exc:** $475 **VGood:** $375

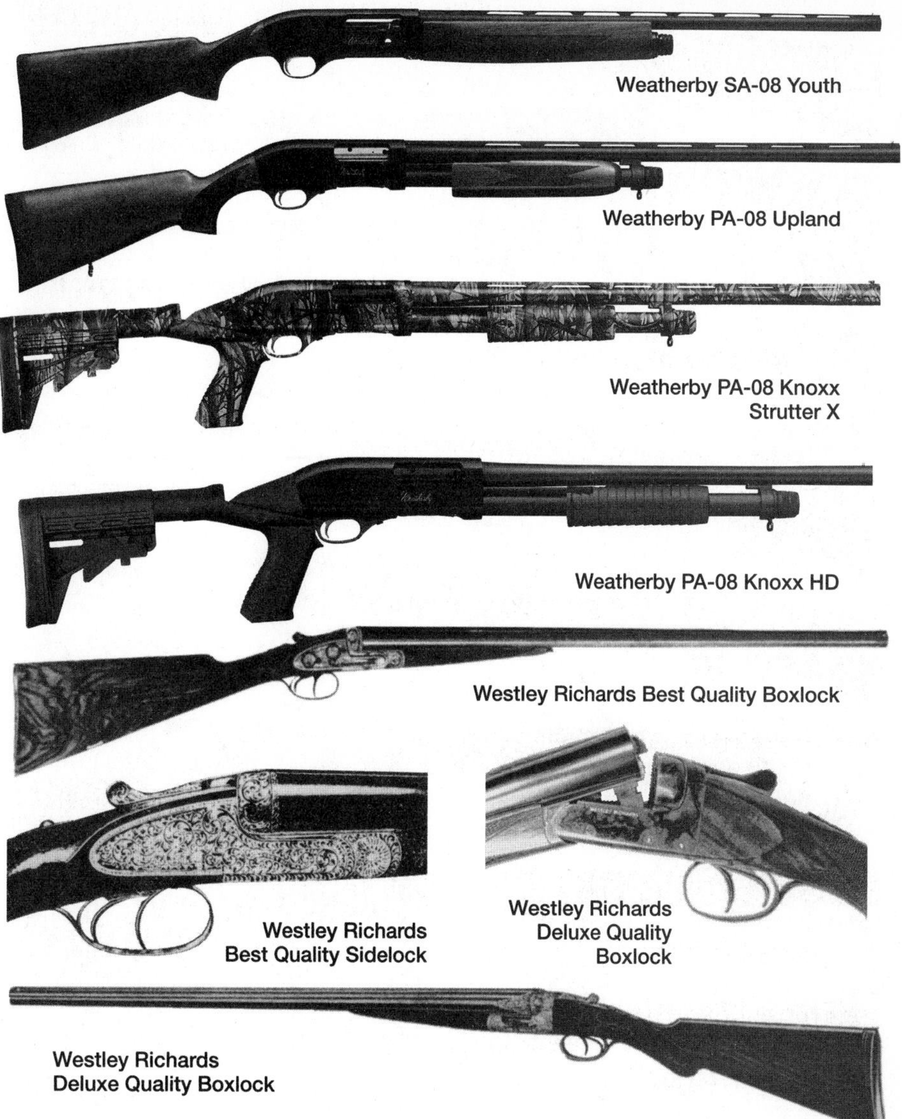

Weatherby SA-08 Youth

Weatherby PA-08 Upland

Weatherby PA-08 Knoxx Strutter X

Weatherby PA-08 Knoxx HD

Westley Richards Best Quality Boxlock

Westley Richards Best Quality Sidelock

Westley Richards Deluxe Quality Boxlock

Westley Richards Deluxe Quality Boxlock

WEATHERBY SA-08 YOUTH

As above but in 20 gauge with 26" barrel only and shorter 12.5" length of pull.

Perf: $525 **Exc:** $475 **VGood:** $375

WEATHERBY PA-08 SERIES

Weatherby introduced this line of pump-action shotguns in 2008. All models come in 12 gauge with 3" chambers and have chrome-lined barrels. Knoxx stock models reduced recoil and are adjustable in length.

WEATHERBY PA-08 UPLAND

This model has a walnut stock and forend with low-lustre finish and matte black metal work. Available with 28" or 26" barrel. Includes three choke tubes.

Perf: $325 **Exc:** $295 **VGood:** $250

WEATHERBY PA-08 KNOXX STRUTTER X

Strutter models feature a synthetic stock and 24" vent rib barrel. Three choke tubes included. Add 15 percent for Apparition Excel camo pattern.

Perf: $435 **Exc:** $325 **VGood:** $295

WEATHERBY PA-08 KNOXX HD

Home defense model features an 18" non-vent-rib barrel and cylinder choke.

Perf: $435 **Exc:** $325 **VGood:** $295

WEATHERBY SA-08 SERIES

Gas-operated semi-auto in 12 or 20 gauge with 3-inch chambers, 26 or 28-inch barrel with three choke tubes. Synthetic or wood stock (Upland model). Deluxe model has higher grade checkered walnut stock. Waterfowler model comes with camo stock. Youth model has shorter synthetic stock and 24-inch barrel. Entre Rios is scaled-down model in 28 gauge.

Perf: $450 **Exc:** $400 **VGood:** $335

Add 35 percent for Waterfowler model, 40 percent for Upland model, 45 percent for Deluxe or Entre Rios.

WESSON & HARRINGTON LONG TOM CLASSIC SHOTGUN

Gauge: 12, 3-inch chamber; 32-inch barrel (Full); weighs 7-1/2 lbs.; length 46-inch overall; American black walnut with hand- checkered grip and forend; color case-hardened receiver and crescent steel buttplate, blued barrel; receiver engraved with the National Wild Turkey Federation logo. Introduced 1998; dropped 2001.

Perf: $275 **Exc:** $240 **VGood:** $195

WESTERN ARMS LONG RANGE HAMMERLESS

Side-by-side; boxlock; 12-, 16-, 20-ga., .410; 26-inch to 32-inch Modified/Full barrels; uncheckered walnut stock, forearm; double or single trigger; plain extractors. Introduced 1924; discontinued 1942. Made by Western Arms Corp., later absorbed by Ithaca Gun Co.

With double triggers

Exc: $250 **VGood:** $175 **Good:** $150

With single trigger

Exc: $275 **VGood:** $200 **Good:** $175

WESTLEY RICHARDS BEST QUALITY BOXLOCK

Side-by-side; hand-detachable boxlock; hammerless; 12-, 16-, 20-, 28-ga., .410; barrel lengths, chokes to order; hand-checkered walnut straight or half-pistol-grip stock, forearm; hinged lockplate; selective ejectors; double or single selective trigger. Still in production.

With double triggers

Perf: $15,500 **Exc:** $9000 **VGood:** $7000

With single trigger

Perf: $16,500 **Exc:** $10,000 **VGood:** $8000

WESTLEY RICHARDS BEST QUALITY SIDELOCK

Side-by-side; hand-detachable sidelocks; hammerless; 12-, 16-, 20-, 28-ga., .410; barrel lengths, chokes to order; hand-checkered walnut straight or half-pistol-grip stock, forearm; selective ejectors; double or single selective trigger. Introduced 1910; still in production.

With double triggers

Perf: $25,000 **Exc:** $18,000 **VGood:** $12,000

With single trigger

Perf: $26,000 **Exc:** $19,000 **VGood:** $13,000

WESTLEY RICHARDS BOXLOCK MODEL DELUXE QUALITY

Side-by-side; hand-detachable boxlock; hammerless; 12-, 16-, 20-, 28-, .410-ga.; barrel lengths, chokes to order; hand-checkered European stock, forearm; straight or half-pistol grip available in Pigeon or Wildfowl Model at same price; triple-bite leverwork; selective ejectors; double triggers or single selective trigger. Introduced 1890; still in production.

With double triggers

Perf: $11,500 **Exc:** $8500 **VGood:** $7000

With single trigger

Perf: $12,500 **Exc:** $9500 **VGood:** $8000

WESTLEY RICHARDS MODEL B

Side-by-side; Anson & Deeley boxlock; hammerless; 12-, 16-, 20-ga.; barrel lengths, choking to order; hand-checkered European walnut straight or half-pistol-grip stock, forearm; Pigeon or Wildfowl Model available at same price; selective ejectors or extractors; double triggers. Introduced late 1920s; still in production.

With ejectors

Perf: $5500 **Exc:** $4000 **VGood:** $3000

With extractors

Perf: $5000 **Exc:** $3500 **VGood:** $2500

WESTLEY RICHARDS OVUNDO

Over/under; hand-detachable boxlock; hammerless; 12-ga.; barrel lengths, chokes to order; hand-checkered European walnut straight or half-pistol-grip stock, forearm; dummy sideplates; single selective trigger. Introduced 1920.

Perf: $17,500 **Exc:** $15,500 **VGood:** $12,000

WINCHESTER MODEL 40

Recoil-operated autoloader; 12-ga.; 4-shot tube magazine; 28-inch, 30-inch barrel; Modified, Full choke; ramp bead front sight; uncheckered pistol-grip stock, semi-beavertail forend; streamlined receiver. Introduced 1940; discontinued 1941.

Exc: $590 **VGood:** $475 **Good:** $350

WINCHESTER MODEL 40 SKEET

Same specs as Model 40 except 24-inch barrel; Cutts Compensator; checkered pistol-grip stock, forearm; grip cap. No longer in production.

Exc: $560 **VGood:** $450 **Good:** $280

WINCHESTER MODEL 50

Autoloader; 12-, 20-ga.; 2-shot magazine; 28-inch, 30-inch barrel; Improved, Modified, Full chokes; optional vent rib; 7-1/4 lbs.; bead-front sight; hand-

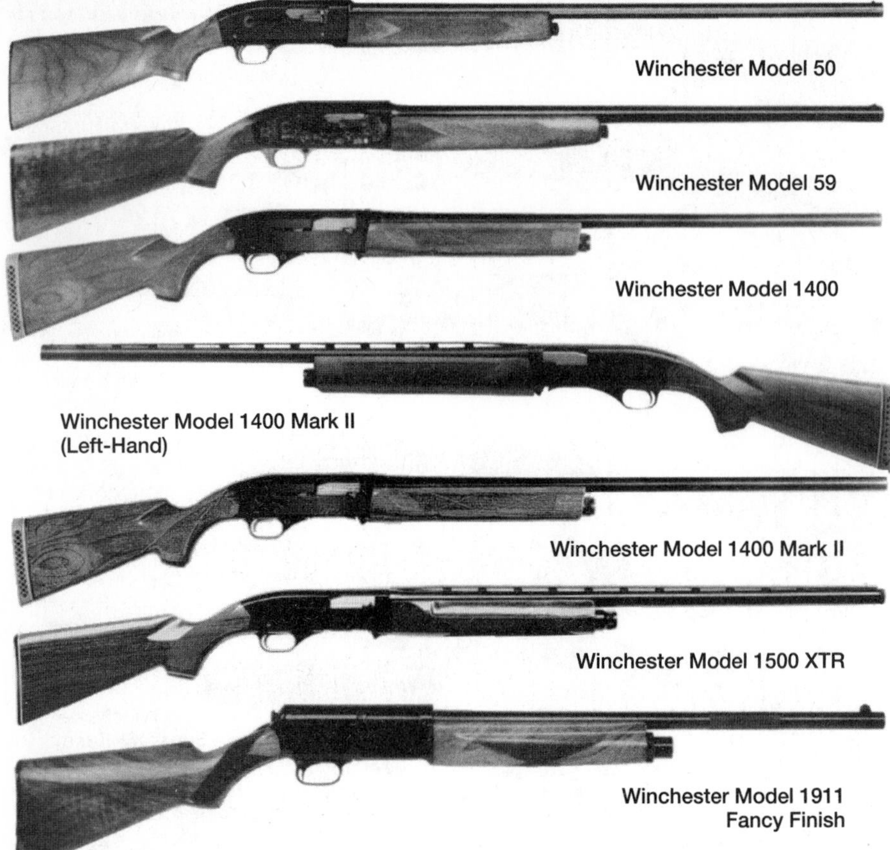
Winchester Model 50

Winchester Model 59

Winchester Model 1400

Winchester Model 1400 Mark II (Left-Hand)

Winchester Model 1400 Mark II

Winchester Model 1500 XTR

Winchester Model 1911 Fancy Finish

checkered American walnut stock; fluted comb; composition buttplate; side ejection; short recoil action; interchangeable barrels. Introduced 1954; discontinued 1961.

Exc: $500 **VGood:** $450 **Good:** $390

With vent rib

Exc: $540 **VGood:** $475 **Good:** $420

WINCHESTER MODEL 50 FEATHERWEIGHT

Same specs as Model 50 except 12-ga. weighs 7 lbs.; 20-ga. weighs 5-3/4 lbs.; alloy construction. Introduced 1958; discontinued 1961.

Exc: $425 **VGood:** $365 **Good:** $310

WINCHESTER MODEL 50 PIGEON

Same specs as Model 50 except best-grade wood, carving and engraving. Introduced 1954; discontinued 1961.

Standard model

Exc: $1000 **VGood:** $825 **Good:** $650

Featherweight model

Exc: $1100 **VGood:** $800 **Good:** $600

Skeet model

Exc: $1100 **VGood:** $900 **Good:** $750

Trap model

Exc: $1100 **VGood:** $900 **Good:** $750

WINCHESTER MODEL 50 SKEET

Same specs as Model 50 except 12-ga.; 26-inch vent-rib barrel; Skeet choke; hand-checkered American walnut Skeet-style stock. Introduced 1954; discontinued 1961.

Exc: $600 **VGood:** $525 **Good:** $420

WINCHESTER MODEL 50 TRAP

Same specs as Model 50 except 12-ga.; 30-inch vent-rib barrel; Full choke; hand-checkered American walnut Monte Carlo stock. Introduced 1954; discontinued 1961.

Exc: $600 **VGood:** $525 **Good:** $420

WINCHESTER MODEL 59

Autoloader; 12-ga.; 3-shot magazine; 26-inch Improved Cylinder, 28-inch Modified or Full, 30-inch Full choke barrel; special-order 26-inch fiberglass-wrapped steel barrel (Winlite) with Versalite choke system of cylinder tubes (introduced in 1961) to allow any choke variation; checkered walnut stock, forearm. (Winchester also made a Model 59 rimfire rifle in 1930-don't be confused by the model numbers.) Introduced 1959; discontinued 1965.

Perf: $600 **Exc:** $500 **VGood:** $400

WINCHESTER MODEL 1400

Gas-operated autoloader; takedown; 12-, 16-, 20-ga.; 2-3/4-inch chamber; 2-shot magazine; 26-inch, 28-inch, 30-inch barrel; fixed Improved Cylinder, Modified, Full chokes or Winchoke tubes; plain or vent rib; checkered walnut stock, forearm; optional Cycolac stock and recoil pad with recoil-reduction system. Introduced 1964; discontinued 1968; replaced by Model 1400 Mark II.

With plain barrel, walnut stock

Exc: $300 **VGood:** $225 **Good:** $190

With vent rib, walnut stock

Exc: $310 **VGood:** $235 **Good:** $195

With plain barrel, Cycolac stock

Exc: $275 **VGood:** $210 **Good:** $180

With vent rib, Cycolac stock

Exc: $325 **VGood:** $245 **Good:** $200

WINCHESTER MODEL 1400 DEER GUN

Same specs as Model 1400 except 12-ga.; 22-inch barrel for slugs or buckshot; rifle sight; walnut stock, forearm. Introduced 1965; discontinued 1974.

Perf: $265 **Exc:** $240 **VGood:** $195

WINCHESTER MODEL 1400 MARK II

Same specs as Model 1400 except restyled walnut stock, forearm; push-button carrier release; front-locking, rotating bolt locking into barrel extension; self-compensating gas system for standard and magnum 2-3/4-inch loads; aluminum receiver; engine turned bolt; push-button action release; crossbolt safety. Made in right- or left-hand versions. Introduced 1968; replaced Model 1400; discontinued 1980.

With plain barrel

Perf: $305 **Exc:** $230 **VGood:** $200

With vent rib

Perf: $315 **Exc:** $255 **VGood:** $230

WINCHESTER MODEL 1400 SKEET

Same specs as Model 1400 except 12-, 20-ga.; 26-inch vent-rib barrel; Skeet choke; semi-fancy walnut Skeet-style stock, forearm; optional Cycolac stock with recoil reduction system. Introduced 1965; discontinued 1968.

With walnut stock

Exc: $350 **VGood:** $260 **Good:** $210

With Cycolac stock with recoil reduction

Exc: $375 **VGood:** $310 **Good:** $245

WINCHESTER MODEL 1400 TRAP

Same specs as Model 1400 except 12-ga.; 30-inch vent-rib barrel; Full choke; semi-fancy walnut Monte Carlo stock, forearm; optional Cycolac stock with recoil reduction system. Introduced 1965; discontinued 1973.

With walnut stock

Exc: $300 **VGood:** $230 **Good:** $190

With Cycolac stock with recoil reduction

Exc: $350 **VGood:** $280 **Good:** $240

WINCHESTER MODEL 1400 (RECENT)

Gas-operated autoloader; 12-, 20-ga.; 2-3/4-inch chamber; 3-shot magazine; 22-inch, 26-inch, 28-inch vent-rib barrel; WinChoke tubes; cut-checkered American walnut stock, forearm. Introduced 1989; discontinued 1994.

Perf: $340 **Exc:** $270 **VGood:** $230

WINCHESTER MODEL 1400 CUSTOM (RECENT)

Same specs as Model 1400 (Recent) except 12-ga.; 28-inch vent-rib barrel; semi-fancy walnut stock, forend; hand-engraved receiver; made in Winchester custom shop. Introduced 1991; discontinued 1992.

Perf: $750 **Exc:** $600 **VGood:** $500

WINCHESTER MODEL 1400 SLUG HUNTER (RECENT)

Same specs as Model 1400 (Recent) except 12-ga.; 22-inch smoothbore barrel; Improved Cylinder, Sabot Winchoke tubes; adjustable open sights; drill, tapped for scope mounts. Introduced 1990; no longer in production.

Perf: $300 **Exc:** $275 **VGood:** $235

WINCHESTER MODEL 1500 XTR

Gas-operated autoloader; 12-, 20-ga.; 26-inch, 28-inch, 30-inch barrel; plain or vent rib; WinChoke tubes; metal bead front sight; cut-checkered American walnut pistol-grip stock; front locking, rotating bolt; nickel-plated carrier, crossbolt safety. Introduced 1978; discontinued 1983.

Perf: $300 **Exc:** $250 **VGood:** $210

WINCHESTER MODEL 1911

Autoloading; hammerless; takedown; 12-ga.; 26-inch, 28-inch barrel standard chokes; uncheckered laminated birch stock, forend. Introduced 1911; discontinued 1925. Popularly called "The Widowmaker" because of its quirky cocking system (i.e., pulling the barrel rearward).

Exc: $425 **VGood:** $325 **Good:** $210

WINCHESTER MODEL 1911 FANCY FINISHED

Same specs as Model 1911 except checkered walnut stock, forend. Introduced 1911; discontinued 1918.

Exc: $525 **VGood:** $425 **Good:** $310

WINCHESTER MODEL 1911 PIGEON

Same specs as Model 1911 except matted barrel; checkered fancy walnut straight-grip stock, forend; pistol grip optional; elaborate engraving. Introduced 1913; discontinued 1926.

Exc: $750 **VGood:** $500 **Good:** $350

WINCHESTER MODEL 1911 TRAP

Same specs as Model 1911 except matted barrel; checkered fancy walnut straight-grip stock, forend; pistol grip optional. Introduced 1913; discontinued 1926.

Exc: $525 **VGood:** $425 **Good:** $310

WINCHESTER SUPER-X MODEL 1

Gas-operated autoloader; takedown; 12-ga.; 2-3/4-inch chamber; 4-shot magazine; 26-inch Improved Cylinder, 28-inch Modified or Full, 30-inch Full-choke barrel; vent rib; checkered American walnut pistol-grip stock, forearm. Introduced 1974; discontinued 1981.

Perf: $500 **Exc:** $450 **VGood:** $400

WINCHESTER SUPER-X MODEL 1 SKEET

Same specs as Super-X Model 1 except 26-inch Skeet-choke barrel; select American walnut Skeet-style stock. Introduced 1974; discontinued 1981.

Exc: $695 **VGood:** $550 **Good:** $450

WINCHESTER SUPER-X MODEL 1 TRAP

Same specs as Super-X Model 1 except 30-inch barrel; Improved Modified or Full choke; select American walnut straight or Monte Carlo trap-style stock, forearm; recoil pad. Introduced 1974; discontinued 1981.

Exc: $525 **VGood:** $400 **Good:** $375

WINCHESTER SUPER X2

Gauge: 12, 3-inch, 3-1/2-inch chamber; 24-inch, 26-inch, 28-inch barrel; Invector Plus choke tubes; weighs 7-1/4 to 7-1/2 lbs.; walnut or black synthetic; gas-operated action shoots all loads without adjustment; vent. rib barrels; 4-shot magazine. Introduced 1999. Made in U.S.A. by U.S. Repeating Arms Co.

Field, 3-inch, walnut or synthetic stock

Perf: $720 **Exc:** $645 **VGood:** $565

Magnum, 3-1/2-inch, synthetic stock, 26-inch or 28-inch bbl.

Perf: $850 **Exc:** $710 **VGood:** $610

Camo Waterfowl, 3-1/2-inch, Mossy Oak Shadow Grass

Perf:: $960 **Exc:** $815 **VGood:** $675

NWTF Turkey, 3-1/2-inch, black synthetic stock, 24-inch bbl.

Perf: $970 **Exc:** $815 **VGood:** $685

NWTF Turkey, 3-1/2-inch, Mossy Oak Break-Up camo

Perf: $970 **Exc:** $815 **VGood:** $685

WINCHESTER SUPER X2 SPORTING CLAYS

Similar to the Super X2 except has two gas pistons (one for target loads, one for heavy 3-inch loads), adjustable comb system and high-post rib. Back-bored barrel with Invector Plus choke tubes. Offered in 28-inch and 30-inch barrels. Introduced 2001. From U.S. Repeating Arms Co.

Perf: $830 **Exc:** $710 **VGood:** $600

WINCHESTER SUPER X2 FIELD 3-INCH

Similar to the Super X2 except has a 3-inch chamber, walnut stock and forearm and high-profile rib. Back-bored barrel (26-inch or 28-inch) and Invector Plus choke tubes. Introduced 2001. From U.S. Repeating Arms Co.

Perf: $720 **Exc:** $645 **VGood:** $565

WINCHESTER SUPER X3

Introduced in 2006, The Super X3 12 gauge features weight and recoil reducing features and a .742-inch back-bored barrel. It is available in a variety of configurations weighing under 7 lbs. in the 3-inch Field model and about 7.5 lbs. in composite, camo and 3.5-inch models. All models except Cantilever Deer include three choke tubes.

NIB: $900 **Exc:** $825 **VGood:** $650

Winchester Super-X Model 1

Winchester Super X2 Magnum

Winchester Super X2 Sporting Clays

Winchester Super X3 Camo

Winchester Super X3 "Flanigun"

Winchester Super X3 Classic Field

Winchester Super X3 Turkey

WINCHESTER SUPER X3 "FLANIGUN" EXHIBITION/SPORTING

With a red receiver and forend cap, this is a duplicate of the gun used by exhibition shooter Patrick Flanigan but with a shorter magazine tube. It has a 3" chamber and 28" barrel.

NIB: $1250 **Exc:** $1025 **VGood:** $750

WINCHESTER SUPER X3 CLASSIC FIELD

Introduced in 2008, the Classic Field is similar to the Super X3 Field but with traditional sharp checkering on pistol grip and forend. Barrel length is 26" or 28".

NIB: $975 **Exc:** $850 **VGood:** $650

WINCHESTER SUPER X3 TURKEY

New in 2008, this dedicated turkey model has a 3.5" chamber, 24" barrel, extra-full choke tube and complete coverage in Mossy Oak New Breakup camo. Price includes a TruGlo red-dot scope. Weight is 7.5 lbs.

NIB: $1200 **Exc:** $1000 **VGood:** $750

WINCHESTER MODEL 12

Slide action; hammerless; 12-, 16-, 20-, 28-ga.; 2-3/4-inch, 3-inch chamber; 5-shot magazine; 26-inch, 28-inch, 30-inch, 32-inch barrel; Improved Cylinder, Modified, Full choke; optional matted or vent rib; uncheckered walnut pistol-grip stock, forearm; blued. Introduced 1912; discontinued 1963.

With plain barrel

Exc: $575 **VGood:** $480 **Good:** $325

With matted rib

Exc: $600 **VGood:** $550 **Good:** $375

With vent rib

Exc: $700 **VGood:** $600 **Good:** $475

WINCHESTER MODEL 12 FEATHERWEIGHT

Same specs as Model 12 except 12-ga.; 26-inch Improved Cylinder, 28-inch Modified or Full, 30-inch Full barrel; alloy guard. Introduced 1959; discontinued 1962.

Exc: $695 **VGood:** $625 **Good:** $490

WINCHESTER MODEL 12 HEAVY DUCK

Same specs as Model 12 except 12-ga.; 3-inch chamber; 3-shot magazine; 30-inch, 32-inch Full barrel; plain, matted or vent rib; recoil pad. Introduced 1937; discontinued 1963.

With plain barrel

Exc: $850 **VGood:** $750 **Good:** $600

With matted rib

Exc: $875 **VGood:** $775 **Good:** $625

With vent rib

Exc: $1000 **VGood:** $800 **Good:** $650

WINCHESTER MODEL 12 PIGEON

Same specs as Model 12 except hand-checkered fancy walnut stock, forearm; engine-turned bolt, carrier; hand-worked action; optional carving and engraving. Introduced 1912; discontinued 1963.

Standard model with plain barrel

Exc: $1250 **VGood:** $800 **Good:** $700

Standard model with vent rib

Exc: $1375 **VGood:** $950 **Good:** $800

Skeet model with plain barrel

Exc: $1250 **VGood:** $800 **Good:** $700

Skeet model with plain barrel, Cutts Compensator

Exc: $1000 **VGood:** $600 **Good:** $500

Skeet model with vent rib

Exc: $1250 **VGood:** $950 **Good:** $800

Trap model with matted rib

Exc: $1200 **VGood:** $900 **Good:** $800

Trap model with vent rib

Exc: $1250 **VGood:** $950 **Good:** $850

WINCHESTER MODEL 12 RIOT

Same specs as Model 12 except 12-ga.; 20-inch Cylinder barrel; vent handguard. Introduced 1918; discontinued 1963.

Military Version

Exc: $1150 **VGood:** $850 **Good:** $600

Civilian Version

Exc: $850 **VGood:** $775 **Good:** $575

WINCHESTER MODEL 12 SKEET

Same specs as Model 12 except 26-inch Skeet barrel; plain barrel or vent rib; red or ivory bead front sight; 94B middle; checkered walnut pistol-grip stock, extension slide handle; recoil pad. Introduced 1937; discontinued 1963.

With plain barrel

Exc: $625 **VGood:** $575 **Good:** $500

With plain barrel, Cutts Compensator

Exc: $475 **VGood:** $375 **Good:** $300

With vent rib

Exc: $825 **VGood:** $775 **Good:** $700

WINCHESTER MODEL 12 SUPER PIGEON

Same specs as Model 12 except 12-ga.; 26-inch, 28-inch, 30-inch vent-rib barrel; hand-checkered fancy walnut stock, forearm; hand-honed and fitted action; engine-turned bolt, carrier; carving; engraving; top-of-the-line custom gun. Introduced 1965; discontinued 1975.

Standard model with plain barrel

Exc: $1750 **VGood:** $1300 **Good:** $1200

Standard model with vent rib

Exc: $1950 **VGood:** $1600 **Good:** $1350

Skeet model with plain barrel

Exc: $1750 **VGood:** $1500 **Good:** $1200

Skeet model with plain barrel, Cutts Compensator

Exc: $1500 **VGood:** $1000 **Good:** $850

Skeet model with vent rib

Exc: $1950 **VGood:** $1600 **Good:** $1350

Trap model with matted rib

Exc: $1800 **VGood:** $1500 **Good:** $1350

Trap model with vent rib

Exc: $1950 **VGood:** $1600 **Good:** $1450

WINCHESTER MODEL 12 TRAP

Same specs as Model 12 except 12-ga.; 30-inch Full-choke barrel; vent or matted rib; checkered walnut pistol-grip stock, extension slide handle; optional Monte Carlo stock; recoil pad. Introduced 1937; discontinued 1963.

With matted rib

Exc: $700 **VGood:** $500 **Good:** $425

With vent rib

Exc: $850 **VGood:** $650 **Good:** $575

With vent rib, Monte Carlo stock

Exc: $975 **VGood:** $775 **Good:** $725

WINCHESTER MODEL 12 (1972)

Same specs as Model 12 except 12-ga.; 26-inch, 28-inch, 30-inch barrels; standard chokes; vent rib; hand-checkered American walnut stock, slide handle; engine-turned bolt, carrier. Introduced 1972; discontinued 1975.

Perf: $575 **Exc:** $525 **VGood:** $425

WINCHESTER MODEL 12 (1993)

Same specs as Model 12 except limited production. Introduced 1993, still in production.

Perf: $950 **Exc:** $800 **VGood:** $650

WINCHESTER MODEL 12 SKEET (1972)

Same specs as Model 12 except 26-inch Skeet-choke barrel; hand-checkered American walnut Skeet-style stock, slide handle; engine-turned bolt, carrier; recoil pad. Introduced 1972; discontinued 1975.

Perf: $900 **Exc:** $650 **VGood:** $525

WINCHESTER MODEL 12 TRAP (1972)

Same specs as Model 12 except 30-inch Full-choke barrel; vent rib; checkered American walnut straight or Monte Carlo trap-style stock; engine-turned bolt, carrier; recoil pad. Introduced 1972; discontinued 1975.

Perf: $700 **Exc:** $575 **VGood:** $475

WINCHESTER MODEL 25

Slide action; hammerless; solid frame; 12-ga.; 4-shot tubular magazine; 26-inch, 28-inch plain barrel; Improved Cylinder, Modified or Full choke; metal bead front sight; uncheckered walnut pistol grip stock, grooved slide handle. Introduced 1950; discontinued 1954.

Exc: $325 **VGood:** $275 **Good:** $225

WINCHESTER MODEL 25 RIOT

Same specs as Model 25 except 20-inch Cylinder barrel. Introduced 1949; discontinued 1955.

Exc: $250 **VGood:** $230 **Good:** $190

WINCHESTER MODEL 42

Slide action; hammerless; .410; 2-1/2-inch, 3-inch chamber; 5- (3-inch), 6-shot (2-1/2-inch) magazine; 26-inch; 28-inch barrel; Full, Modified, Cylinder choke; plain, matted or vent rib; weighs 6 lbs.; uncheckered walnut stock, grooved slide handle. Introduced 1933; discontinued 1963.

With plain barrel

Exc: $850 **VGood:** $700 **Good:** $600

With matted rib

Exc: $1250 **VGood:** $1100 **Good:** $950

With vent rib

Exc: $1450 **VGood:** $1300 **Good:** $1050

WINCHESTER MODEL 42 DELUXE

Same specs as Model 42 except top-of-the-line model with best-grade wood and finish. Introduced 1933; discontinued 1963.

Exc: $2200 **VGood:** $1750 **Good:** $1300

WINCHESTER MODEL 42 SKEET

Same specs as Model 42 except Skeet choke; matted rib; checkered fancy walnut Skeet-style stock, forearm. Introduced 1933; discontinued 1963.

Exc: $1850 **VGood:** $1350 **Good:** $1200

WINCHESTER MODEL 42 TRAP

Same specs as Model 42 except matted rib; checkered fancy walnut trap-style stock, forearm. Introduced 1933; discontinued 1940.

Exc: $1850 **VGood:** $1350 **Good:** $1200

WINCHESTER MODEL 42 HIGH GRADE (1993)

Slide action; hammerless; .410; 2-3/4-inch chamber; 26-inch vent-rib barrel; Full choke; weighs 7 lbs.; checkered high-grade walnut pistol-grip stock, forend; engraved receiver with gold inlays. Only 850 guns made. Made in Japan. Introduced 1993; discontinued 1993.

Perf: $1350 **Exc:** $1000 **VGood:** $850

WINCHESTER MODEL 1200

Slide action; takedown; 12-, 16-, 20-ga.; 2-3/4-inch chambers; 4-shot magazine; 26-inch, 28-inch, 30-inch barrel; Improved Cylinder, Modified, Full fixed choke or interchangeable WinChoke tubes for Cylinder, Modified, Full; plain or vent rib; press-checkered walnut stock, slide handle; optional Cycolac stock with recoil-reduction system; front-lock rotary bolt; recoil pad. Introduced 1964; discontinued 1981.

With plain barrel, walnut stock

Perf: $200 **Exc:** $170 **VGood:** $150

With vent-rib barrel, walnut stock

Perf: $240 **Exc:** $210 **VGood:** $190

With plain barrel, Cycolac stock

Perf: $260 **Exc:** $230 **VGood:** $200

With vent-rib barrel, Cycolac stock

Perf: $300 **Exc:** $270 **VGood:** $240

WINCHESTER MODEL 1200 DEER

Same specs as Model 1200 except 12-ga.; 22-inch barrel for rifled slugs or buckshot; rifle-type sights; walnut stock only; sling swivels. Introduced 1965; discontinued 1974.

Perf: $210 **Exc:** $150 **VGood:** $140

WINCHESTER MODEL 1200 MAGNUM

Same specs as Model 1200 except 12-, 20-, 28-ga.; 3-inch chamber; 28-inch, 30-inch Full-choke barrel; plain or vent rib. Introduced 1964; discontinued 1981.

With plain barrel, walnut stock

Perf: $290 **Exc:** $265 **VGood:** $250

With vent-rib barrel, walnut stock

Perf: $300 **Exc:** $275 **VGood:** $260

With plain barrel, Cycolac stock

Perf: $280 **Exc:** $240 **VGood:** $200

With vent-rib barrel, Cycolac stock

Perf: $325 **Exc:** $260 **VGood:** $230

WINCHESTER MODEL 1200 SKEET

Same specs as Model 1200 except 12-, 20- ga.; 2-shot magazine; 26-inch vent-rib barrel; Skeet choke; semi-fancy walnut stock, forend; optional Cycolac stock with recoil-reduction system; tuned trigger. Introduced 1965; discontinued 1974.

With walnut stock

Perf: $295 **Exc:** $240 **VGood:** $200

With Cycolac stock

Perf: $350 **Exc:** $300 **VGood:** $250

WINCHESTER MODEL 1200 TRAP

Same specs as Model 1200 except 12-ga.; 2-shot magazine; 28-inch WinChoke, 30-inch Full-choke barrel; vent rib; semi-fancy walnut standard or Monte Carlo trap-style stock, forearm; optional Cycolac stock with recoil-reduction system. Introduced 1965; discontinued 1974.

With standard stock

Perf: $325 **Exc:** $275 **VGood:** $200

With Monte Carlo stock
Perf: $345 **Exc:** $300 **VGood:** $220
With Cycolac stock
Perf: $360 **Exc:** $325 **VGood:** $250

WINCHESTER MODEL 1300 DEFENDER PUMP

Gauge: 12, 20, 3-inch chamber, 5- or 8-shot capacity; 18-inch barrel (Cyl.); weighs 6-3/4 lbs.; 38-5/8-inch overall; walnut-finished hardwood stock and ribbed forend, synthetic or pistol grip; metal bead front sight or TRUGLO fiber-optic; front-locking rotary bolt; twin action slide bars; black rubber butt pad.
8-Shot (black synthetic stock, TRUGLO sight)
Perf: $265 **Exc:** $205 **VGood:** $160
8-Shot Pistol Grip (pistol grip synthetic stock)
Perf: $278 **Exc:** $218 **VGood:** $173

WINCHESTER MODEL 1300 STAINLESS MARINE PUMP

Same as the Defender 8-Shot except has bright chrome finish, stainless steel barrel, bead front sight. Phosphate coated receiver for corrosion resistance.
Perf: $435 **Exc:** $360 **VGood:** $265

WINCHESTER MODEL 1300 CAMP DEFENDER

Same as the Defender 8-Shot except has hardwood stock and forearm, fully adjustable open sights and 22-inch barrel with WinChoke choke tube system (cylinder choke tube included). Weighs 6-7/8 lbs. Introduced 2001.
Perf: $295 **Exc:** $225 **VGood:** $175

WINCHESTER MODEL 1300 WALNUT FIELD PUMP

Gauge: 12, 20, 3-inch chamber; 5-shot capacity; 26-inch, 28-inch barrel; vent. rib, with Full, Mod. & Imp. Cyl. Winchoke tubes; weighs 6-3/8 lbs.; 42-5/8-inch overall; American walnut, with deep cut checkering on pistol grip, high luster finish; metal bead front sight; twin action slide bars; front-locking rotary bolt; roll-engraved receiver; blued, highly polished metal; cross-bolt safety with red indicator. Introduced 1984.
Perf: $345 **Exc:** $250 **VGood:** $200

WINCHESTER MODEL 1300 UPLAND PUMP

Similar to Model 1300 Walnut except straight-grip stock, 24-inch barrel. Introduced 1999. Made in U.S.A. by U.S. Repeating Arms Co.
Perf: $325 **Exc:** $240 **VGood:** $195

WINCHESTER MODEL 1300 BLACK SHADOW

Slide action; hammerless; 12-, 20-ga.; 3-inch chamber; 5-shot magazine; 26-inch, 28-inch vent-rib barrel; Modified WinChoke tubes; metal bead front sight; black composite pistol-grip stock, forend; black rubber recoil pad; crossbolt safety; twin action slide bars; front-locking rotating bolt; matte black finish. Introduced 1995.
Perf: $270 **Exc:** $210 **VGood:** $180

WINCHESTER MODEL 1300 BLACK SHADOW DEER

Same specs as Model 1300 Black Shadow except 12-ga.; 3-inch chamber; 22-inch vent-rib barrel; Improved Cylinder WinChoke tube; ramp-type front sight, fully adjustable rear; receiver drilled and tapped for scope mounts. Introduced 1994.
Perf: $270 **Exc:** $210 **VGood:** $180
With rifled barrel
Perf: $301 **Exc:** $231 **VGood:** $186
With cantilever scope mount
Perf: $344 **Exc:** $274 **VGood:** $229
Combo (22-inch rifled and 28-inch smoothbore bbls.)
Perf: $395 **Exc:** $325 **VGood:** $280
Compact (20-ga., 22-inch rifled barrel, shorter stock)
Perf: $295 **Exc:** $225 **VGood:** $165

Winchester Model 1300 Defender 8-shot

Winchester Model 1300 Camp Defender

Winchester Model 1300 Walnut Field

Winchester Model 1300 Black Shadow

Winchester Model 1300 Ranger

Winchester Model 1300 Ranger Combo

WINCHESTER MODEL 1300 BLACK SHADOW TURKEY

Same specs as Model 1300 Black Shadow except 12-ga.; 3-inch chamber; 22-inch vent-rib barrel; Full WinChoke tube; receiver drilled and tapped for scope mounts. Introduced 1994; discontinued 2000.
Perf: $270 **Exc:** $210 **VGood:** $180

WINCHESTER MODEL 1300 N.W.T.F. SERIES I

Slide action; hammerless; 12-ga.; 3-inch chamber; 5-shot magazine; 22-inch vent-rib barrel; Extra Full, Full, Modified WinChoke tubes; checkered green WinCam laminated stock, forend; black rubber recoil pad; crossbolt safety; twin action slide bars; front-locking rotating bolt; camo sling and swivels; receiver roll-engraved with turkey scenes; right side has National Wild Turkey Federation name in script; matte finish metal. Introduced 1989; no longer in production.
Perf: $420 **Exc:** $365 **VGood:** $260
Add approximately $45 to above prices for Buck & Tom Superflauge configuration.

WINCHESTER MODEL 1300 N.W.T.F. SERIES II

Same specs as the Model 1300 N.W.T.F. Series I except 12-, 20-ga.; WinCam green laminated stock, ribbed forend; ladies/youth-sized stock available. Introduced 1990; discontinued 1991.
Perf: $350 **Exc:** $265 **VGood:** $210

WINCHESTER MODEL 1300 N.W.T.F. SERIES III

Same specs as the Model 1300 N.W.T.F. Series I except rifle-type adjustable sights; WinCam green laminated stock, forend. Introduced 1992; discontinued 1993.
Perf: $350 **Exc:** $265 **VGood:** $210

WINCHESTER MODEL 1300 N.W.T.F. SERIES IV

Same specs as the Model 1300 N.W.T.F. Series I except WinTuff black laminated stock, ribbed forend. Introduced 1993; discontinued 1994.
Perf: $350 **Exc:** $265 **VGood:** $210

WINCHESTER MODEL 1300 RANGER

Slide action; hammerless; 12-, 20-ga.; 3-inch chamber; 5-shot magazine; 26-inch, 28-inch vent-rib barrel; Full, Modified, Improved Cylinder WinChoke tubes; checkered walnut-finished hardwood pistol-grip stock, forend; early guns had ribbed forend; black rubber recoil pad; crossbolt safety; twin action slide bars; front-locking rotating bolt. Introduced 1983.
Perf: $280 **Exc:** $220 **VGood:** $185
Model 1300 Compact, 24-inch vent. rib
Perf: $280 **Exc:** $210 **VGood:** $165

WINCHESTER MODEL 1300 RANGER COMBO

Same specs as Model 1300 Ranger except two-barrel set with 22-inch Cylinder smoothbore or rifled deer barrel with rifle-type sights and an interchangeable 28-inch vent-rib barrel with Full, Modified, Improved Cylinder WinChoke tubes; drilled and tapped for scope mounts; rings and bases. Introduced 1983.
Perf: $330 **Exc:** $270 **VGood:** $230

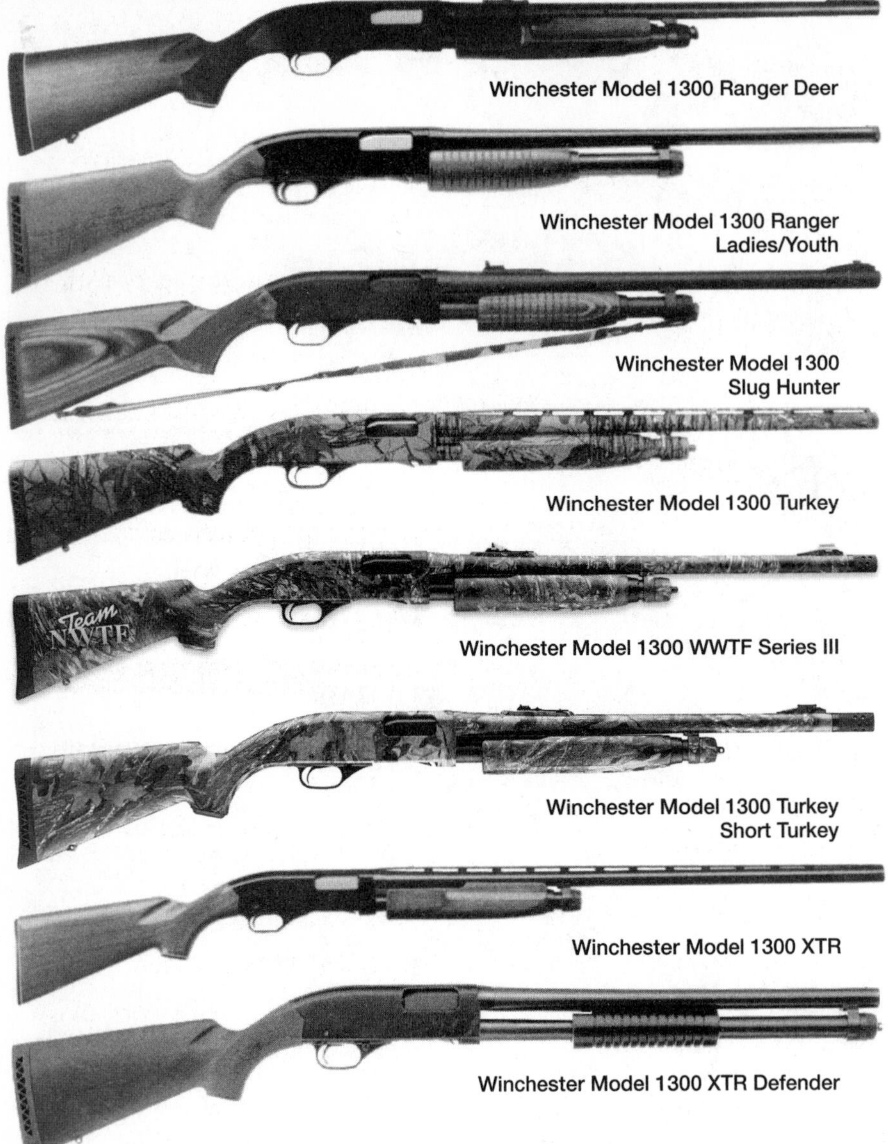

Winchester Model 1300 Ranger Deer

Winchester Model 1300 Ranger Ladies/Youth

Winchester Model 1300 Slug Hunter

Winchester Model 1300 Turkey

Winchester Model 1300 WWTF Series III

Winchester Model 1300 Turkey Short Turkey

Winchester Model 1300 XTR

Winchester Model 1300 XTR Defender

WINCHESTER MODEL 1300 RANGER DEER

Same specs as Model 1300 Ranger except 22-inch Cylinder smoothbore or rifled deer barrel with rifle-type sights; drilled and tapped; for scope mounts; rings and bases. Introduced 1983.

Perf: $300 **Exc:** $245 **VGood:** $200

WINCHESTER MODEL 1300 RANGER LADIES/YOUTH

Same specs as Model 1300 Ranger except 20-ga.; 3-inch chamber; 22-inch vent-rib barrel; Full, Modified, Improved Cylinder WinChoke tubes; weighs 6-1/2 lbs.; overall length 41-5/8-inch; hardwood stock (walnut available) with 13-inch pull length. Introduced 1983.

With hardwood stock

Perf: $280 **Exc:** $220 **VGood:** $185

With walnut stock

Perf: $300 **Exc:** $240 **VGood:** $200

WINCHESTER MODEL 1300 REALTREE TURKEY GUN

Same specs as Model 1300 Ranger except 12-ga.; 3-inch chamber; 22-inch barrel; Extra Full, Full, Modified WinChoke tubes; drilled and tapped for scope mounts; synthetic Realtree(r) camo stock, forend; padded, adjustable sling; matte finished barrel, receiver. Introduced 1994.

Perf: $325 **Exc:** $285 **VGood:** $225

WINCHESTER MODEL 1300 SLUG HUNTER

Same specs as Model 1300 Ranger except 12-ga.; 22-inch smoothbore or rifled barrel; Improved Cylinder, Sabot choke tubes (smoothbore only); adjustable open sights; receiver drilled and tapped for scope mounts; scope bases; cut-checkered walnut stock, forend. Introduced 1990; smoothbore dropped 1992; still in production as Model 1300 Slug Hunter Deer.

Perf: $350 **Exc:** $265 **VGood:** $200

WINCHESTER MODEL 1300 STAINLESS MARINE

Same specs as Model 1300 Ranger except 5-, 8-shot magazine; 18-inch Cylinder stainless barrel; rifle-type sights; bright chrome finish; phosphate-coated receiver for corrosion resistance. Introduced 1989.

Perf: $395 **Exc:** $275 **VGood:** $210

WINCHESTER MODEL 1300 TURKEY

Same specs as Model 1300 Ranger except 12-ga.; 22-inch barrel; Modified, Full, Extra Full WinChoke tubes; WinCam green camo laminated stock; recoil pad, Cordura sling; swivels; matte finish wood and metal. Introduced 1985; discontinued 1988.

Perf: $300 **Exc:** $240 **VGood:** $185

WINCHESTER MODEL 1300 TURKEY AND UNIVERSAL HUNTER MODELS

12-gauge w/3-inch chamber. Rotary bolt action. Mossy oak break-up finish on 26-inch VR barrel Extra Full turkey, Improved Cylinder, Modified and Full WinChoke tubes included.

Universal Hunter

Perf: $365 **Exc:** $315 **VGood:** $280

Buck and Tom

Perf: $401 **Exc:** $351 **VGood:** $316

Short Turkey

Perf: $405 **Exc:** $355 **VGood:** $320

WINCHESTER MODEL 1300 XTR

Slide action; 12-, 20-ga.; 3-inch chamber; 4-shot magazine; 26, 28-inch plain or vent-rib barrel; WinChoke tubes; metal bead front sight; cut-checkered American walnut stock, grooved forearm; twin action bars; crossbolt safety; engine-turned bolt; alloy receiver, trigger guard. Introduced 1978; XTR designation dropped 1989; discontinued 1993.

With plain barrel

Perf: $260 **Exc:** $200 **VGood:** $160

With vent-rib barrel

Perf: $295 **Exc:** $240 **VGood:** $185

WINCHESTER MODEL 1300 XTR DEER GUN

Same specs as Model 1300 XTR except 12-ga.; 24-1/8-inch barrel; rifle-type sights. No longer in production.

Perf: $295 **Exc:** $240 **VGood:** $185

WINCHESTER MODEL 1300 XTR DEFENDER

Same specs as Model 1300 XTR except 5-, 8-shot magazine; 18-inch, 24-inch Cylinder barrel; 38-3/5-inch overall length; weighs 6-3/4 lb.; metal bead front sight; walnut-finished hardwood or synthetic pistol-grip stock, ribbed forend; crossbolt safety; front-locking rotary bolt; twin slide bars; black rubber buttpad. Introduced 1984; XTR designation dropped 1989.

Perf: $240 **Exc:** $165 **VGood:** $120

Defender Combo with extra 28-inch vent-rib barrel

Perf: $320 **Exc:** $240 **VGood:** $180

WINCHESTER MODEL 1300 XTR FEATHERWEIGHT

Same specs as Model 1300 XTR except 22-inch vent-rib barrel; crossbolt safety with red indicator; roll-engraved alloy receiver. Introduced 1984; XTR designation dropped 1989; discontinued 1993.

Perf: $320 **Exc:** $240 **VGood:** $200

WINCHESTER MODEL 1300 XTR LADIES/YOUTH

Same specs as Model 1300 XTR except 22-inch vent-rib barrel; youth-sized walnut stock with high luster finish; crossbolt safety with red safety indicator; highly polished blue finish. Introduced 1983; XTR designation dropped 1989.

Perf: $250 **Exc:** $220 **VGood:** $185

WINCHESTER MODEL 1300 XTR WALNUT

Same specs as Model 1300 XTR 26-inch, 28-inch vent-rib barrel; walnut stock with high luster finish; crossbolt safety with red safety indicator; highly polished blued finish. Introduced, 1984; XTR designation dropped 1989.

Perf: $300 **Exc:** $245 **VGood:** $200

WINCHESTER MODEL 1300 XTR WATERFOWL

Same specs as Model 1300 XTR except 12-ga.; 28-inch, 30-inch vent-rib barrel; matte walnut or brown WinTuff stock, forearm; recoil pad; camo sling; swivels. Introduced 1984; XTR designation dropped 1989; discontinued 1991.

Perf: $280 **Exc:** $230 **VGood:** $200

WINCHESTER SPEED PUMP SERIES

This family of inertia-assisted slide-action shotguns was introduced in 2008 to take the place of the discontinued Model 1300. The 3" 12 gauge is available with a 26" or 28" barrel. Three choke tubes included. Weight is 7 to 7.25 lbs.

WINCHESTER SPEED PUMP WALNUT FIELD

High-gloss walnut with traditional checkering.

Perf: $375 **Exc:** $315 **VGood:** $295

WINCHESTER SPEED PUMP BLACK SHADOW FIELD

Synthetic stock and forend with matte black metal. MSRP:

Perf: $375 **Exc:** $315 **VGood:** $295

WINCHESTER SPEED PUMP DEFENDER

This home-security 12 gauge has an 18", cylinder choke barrel and 5-round magazine tube. Weight is about 6.5 lbs.

Perf: $295 **Exc:** $265 **VGood:** $215

WINCHESTER SXP CAMP/ FIELD COMBO

Slide-action 12 gauge with 3-inch chamber. Capacity is 5+1 with 2-3/4 inch shells. Barrel has ventilated rib and comes in choice of 26 or 28 inches. Three Invector Plus choke tubes (F,M,IC) and ivory bead front sight. Extra 18-inch Defender barrel is included. Weight is approximately 6.8 pounds. Black composite stock with sling swivel studs and Inlex Technology recoil pad. Metal has non-glare matte finish.

Perf: $425 **Exc:** $375 **VGood:** $325

WINCHESTER MODEL 1893

Slide action; exposed hammer; solid frame; 12-ga.; 2-5/8-inch chamber; 5-shot tubular magazine; 30-inch, 32-inch steel barrel; Damascus barrel optional; Full choke standard; Modified or Cylinder bore optional; uncheckered American walnut half-pistol-grip stock; fancy wood, checkering optional. Introduced 1893; discontinued 1897.

Exc: $800 **VGood:** $600 **Good:** $500

With fancy wood, checkering

Exc: $900 **VGood:** $675 **Good:** $550

WINCHESTER MODEL 1897

Slide action; visible hammer; takedown or solid frame; 12-, 16-ga.; 2-3/4-inch chamber; 5-shot tube magazine; 26-inch, 28-inch, 30-inch, 32-inch (12-ga. only) barrel; Full, Modified, Cylinder bore; intermediate chokes added 1931; uncheckered walnut half-pistol-grip stock, grooved forend. Introduced 1897; discontinued 1957.

Exc: $900 **VGood:** $600 **Good:** $435

WINCHESTER MODEL 1897 BRUSH

Same specs as Model 1897 except 26-inch Cylinder bore barrel. Introduced 1897; discontinued 1931.

Exc: $825 **VGood:** $600 **Good:** $335

WINCHESTER MODEL 1897 PIGEON

Same specs as Model 1897 except checkered fancy walnut stock, standard or beavertail forearm; engraving. Introduced 1897; discontinued 1939.

Exc: $3500 **VGood:** $2250 **Good:** $1800

WINCHESTER MODEL 1897 SPECIAL TRAP

Same specs as Model 1897 except checkered fancy walnut trap-style stock, standard or beavertail forearm; engraving. Introduced 1931; discontinued 1939.

Exc: $3500 **VGood:** $2250 **Good:** $1800

WINCHESTER MODEL 1897 STANDARD TRAP

Same specs as Model 1897 except Trap-style stock; replaced Model 1897 Trap. Introduced 1931; discontinued 1939.

Exc: $1100 **VGood:** $700 **Good:** $500

Winchester Model 1300 XTR Waterfowl

Winchester Speed Pump Walnut Field

Winchester Speed Pump Black Shadow Field

Winchester Speed Pump Defender

Winchester Model 1897

Winchester Model 101 Pigeon Grade

WINCHESTER MODEL 1897 TOURNAMENT

Same specs as Model 1897 except checkered fancy walnut stock, standard or beavertail forearm; engraving. Introduced 1910; discontinued 1931.

Exc: $1200 **VGood:** $750 **Good:** $600

WINCHESTER MODEL 1897 TRAP

Same specs as Model 1897 except Trap-style stock. Introduced 1897; discontinued 1931.

Exc: $1100 **VGood:** $700 **Good:** $500

WINCHESTER MODEL 1897 TRENCH

Same specs as Model 1897 except ventilated steel handguard; bayonet stud; built for U.S. Army during WWI. Introduced 1920; discontinued 1935.

Exc: $2500 **VGood:** $1500 **Good:** $1300

WINCHESTER MODEL 101

Over/under; boxlock; 12- (2-3/4-inch), 20- (3-inch), 28-ga. (2-3/4-inch), .410 (3-inch); 26-1/2-inch Improved/Modified, 28-inch Modified/Full, 30-inch Modified/Full (12-ga. only) barrels; vent rib; checkered french walnut stock, forearm; auto ejectors; single selective trigger; combo barrel selector, safety; engraving. Made in Japan by Olin Kodensha. Introduced 1963; discontinued 1978.

12-, 20-ga. model

Perf: $1200 **Exc:** $800 **VGood:** $700

28-ga., .410 model

Perf: $1600 **Exc:** $1275 **VGood:** $850

WINCHESTER MODEL 101 MAGNUM

Same specs as Model 101 except 12-, 20-ga.; 3-inch chambers; 30-inch Full/Full, Modified/Full barrels; recoil pad. Introduced 1966; discontinued 1981.

Perf: $1150 **Exc:** $850 **VGood:** $700

Add approximately 20 percent 9o above prices for 20-ga.

WINCHESTER MODEL 101 PIGEON GRADE

Same specs as Model 101 except best-grade wood, checkering and engraving. Introduced 1963; discontinued 1984.

Field model

Perf: $1500 **Exc:** $1200 **VGood:** $1000

Skeet model

Perf: $1300 **Exc:** $900 **VGood:** $800

Trap model

Perf: $1400 **Exc:** $1000 **VGood:** $900

WINCHESTER MODEL 101 SKEET

Same specs as Model 101 except 26-inch (12-ga.), 26-1/2-inch (20-ga.), 28-inch (28-ga., .410) barrels; Skeet chokes; Skeet-style stock, forearm. Introduced 1966; discontinued 1984. Considerable premium for small gauges.

Perf: $1000 **Exc:** $850 **VGood:** $695

WINCHESTER MODEL 101 TRAP

Same specs as Model 101 except 12-ga.; 30-inch, 32-inch Improved Modified/Full, Full/Full barrels; Trap-style stock; Monte Carlo or straight comb. Introduced 1966; discontinued 1984.

With Monte Carlo stock

Perf: $1250 **Exc:** $900 **VGood:** $800

With straight stock

Perf: $1250 **Exc:** $900 **VGood:** $800

WINCHESTER MODEL 101 TRAP SINGLE BARREL

Same specs as Model 101 except 12-ga.; 32-inch, 34-inch single over barrel; Full choke; Trap-style Monte Carlo stock. Introduced 1967; discontinued 1971.

Perf: $900 **Exc:** $600 **VGood:** $500

WINCHESTER MODEL 101 WATERFOWL

Same specs as Model 101 except 12-ga.; 3-inch chambers; 32-inch barrels; WinChokes. Introduced 1981; discontinued 1982.

Perf: $1350 **Exc:** $1000 **VGood:** $900

WINCHESTER MODEL 101 DIAMOND GRADE SKEET

Over/under; boxlock; 12-, 20-, 28-ga., .410; 27-1/2-inch barrels; WinChokes; tapered, elevated vent rib; hand-checkered select walnut Skeet-style stock, beavertail forearm; auto ejectors; contoured single selective trigger; combo barrel selector, safety;

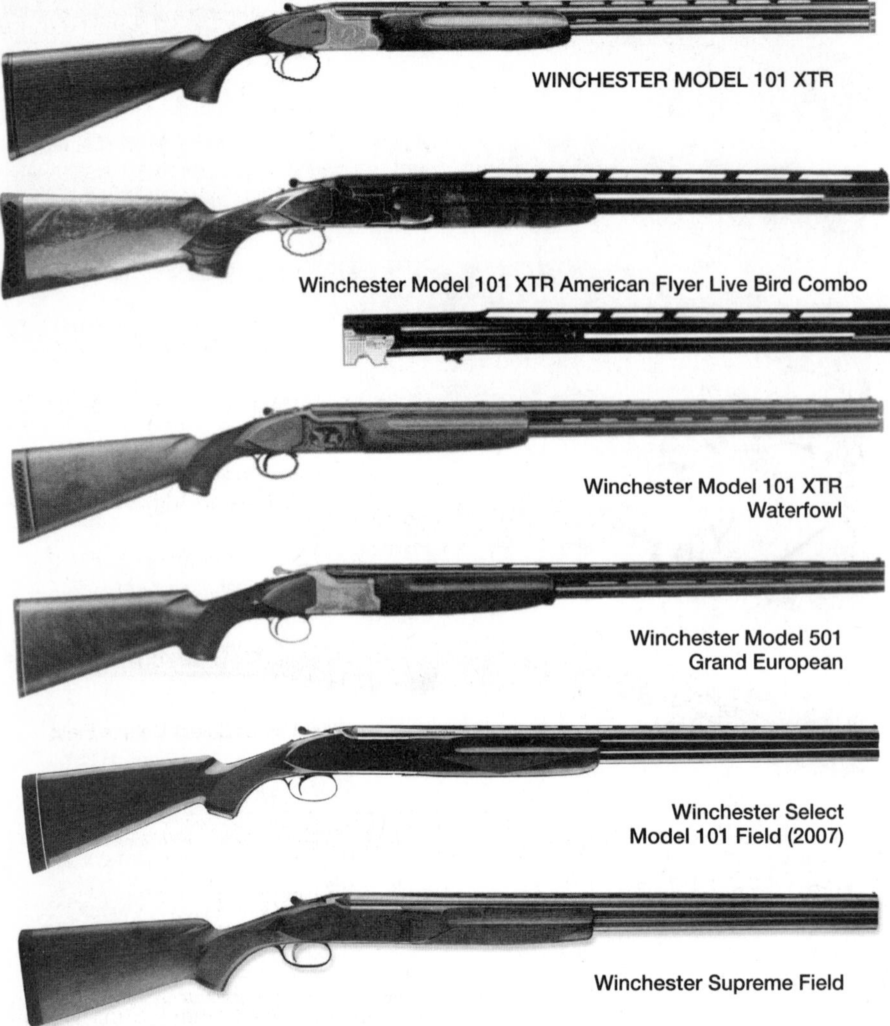

diamond-pattern engraved satin-finished receiver. Made in Japan. Introduced 1982; discontinued 1987.

Perf: $1750 **Exc:** $1300 **VGood:** $1100

WINCHESTER MODEL 101 DIAMOND GRADE TRAP

Same specs as Model 101 Diamond Grade Skeet except 12-ga.; 30-inch, 32-inch barrels; hand-checkered select walnut trap-style stock, beavertail forearm. Introduced 1982; discontinued 1987.

Perf: $1750 **Exc:** $1300 **VGood:** $1100

WINCHESTER MODEL 101 DIAMOND GRADE TRAP COMBO

Same specs as Model 101 Diamond Grade Skeet except 12-ga.; two-barrel set with 30-inch or 32-inch over/under barrels and 32-inch or 34-inch single barrel; hand-checkered select walnut trap-style stock, beavertail forearm. Introduced 1982; discontinued 1987.

Perf: $2600 **Exc:** $2100 **VGood:** $1900

WINCHESTER MODEL 101 DIAMOND GRADE TRAP SINGLE

Same specs as Model 101 Diamond Grade Skeet except 12-ga.; 32-inch, 34-inch single barrel; hand-checkered select walnut Trap-style stock, beavertail forearm. Introduced 1982; discontinued 1987.

Perf: $2000 **Exc:** $1650 **VGood:** $1450

WINCHESTER MODEL 101 XTR

Over/under; boxlock; 12-, 20-ga.; 26-inch, 28-inch, 30-inch barrels; WinChokes; vent rib; metal bead front sight; cut-checkered American walnut pistol-grip stock, beavertail forearm; chrome-plated chambers, bores; manual safety, barrel selector; single selective trigger; auto ejectors; hand engraving; replaced Model 101. Introduced 1978; discontinued 1987.

Perf: $1850 **Exc:** $1400 **VGood:** $1200

WINCHESTER MODEL 101 XTR AMERICAN FLYER LIVE BIRD

Same specs as Model 101 XTR except 12-ga.; 2-3/4-inch chambers; 28-inch, 29-1/2-inch barrels; under barrel fitted for internal WinChokes, over barrel has Extra-Full choke; competition vent-rib; full fancy American walnut stock; blued receiver, gold wire border inlays; matte finish on top of receiver; marketed in luggage-type case. Made in Japan. Introduced 1987; discontinued 1987.

Perf: $2450 **Exc:** $1900 **VGood:** $1700

WINCHESTER MODEL 101 XTR AMERICAN FLYER LIVE BIRD

Same specs as Model 101 XTR except 12-ga.; 2-3/4-inch chambers; two-barrel set with 28-inch, 29-1/2-inch barrels; under barrel fitted for internal WinChokes, over barrel has Extra-Full choke; competition vent rib; full fancy American walnut stock; blued receiver, gold wire border inlays; matte finish on top of receiver. Made in Japan. Introduced 1987; discontinued 1987.

Perf: $3500 **Exc:** $2900 **VGood:** $2600

WINCHESTER MODEL 101 XTR PIGEON GRADE FEATHERWEIGHT

Same specs as Model 101 XTR except 12-, 20-ga.; 25 1/2-inch Improved Cylinder/Improved Modified barrels; checkered walnut straight-grip stock. Introduced 1983; discontinued 1987.

Perf: $1400 **Exc:** $950 **VGood:** $850

WINCHESTER MODEL 101 XTR PIGEON GRADE LIGHTWEIGHT

Same specs as Model 101 XTR except 12-, 20-, 28-ga., .410; 26-inch to 32-inch barrels; hand-checkered French walnut stock; knurled non-slip trigger; alloy construction; hand-engraved satin-finished receiver; marketed in hard case. Made in Japan. Introduced, 1983; discontinued 1987.

Perf: $1800 **Exc:** $1350 **VGood:** $1200

WINCHESTER MODEL 101 XTR PIGEON GRADE SKEET

Same specs as Model 101 XTR except 12-, 20-, 28-ga., .410; select checkered Skeet-style stock. Introduced 1980; discontinued 1987.

Perf: $1200 **Exc:** $950 **VGood:** $850

WINCHESTER MODEL 101 XTR PIGEON GRADE TRAP

Same specs as Model 101 XTR except 12-ga.; select checkered trap-style stock. Introduced 1980; discontinued 1987.

Perf: $1200 **Exc:** $950 **VGood:** $850

WINCHESTER MODEL 101 XTR QUAIL SPECIAL

Same specs as Model 101 XTR except 12-, 20-, 28-ga., .410; 25 1/2-inch vent-rib barrels; Winchokes; checkered American walnut straight-grip stock; silvered engraved receiver. Made in Japan. Introduced 1987; discontinued 1988.

12-ga., .410 models

Perf: $1850 **Exc:** $1400 **VGood:** $1200

20-ga. model

Perf: $2300 **Exc:** $1700 **VGood:** $1450

28-ga. model

Perf: $3000 **Exc:** $2000 **VGood:** $1800

WINCHESTER MODEL XTR WATERFOWL

Same specs as Model 101 XTR except 25-1/2-inch, 27-inch, 28-inch barrels; weighs 8-1/4 lbs.; vent-rib; bead front and middle sights; hand-checkered French walnut stock, forend. Made in Japan. Introduced 1981; discontinued 1982.

Perf: $1900 **Exc:** $1475 **VGood:** $975

WINCHESTER MODEL 501 GRAND EUROPEAN

Over/under; 12-, 20-ga.; 27-inch, 30-inch, 32-inch barrels; tapered vent rib; hand-rubbed oil-finish American walnut stock; Trap model has Monte Carlo or regular stock; Skeevt version has rosewood buttplate; engine-turned breech interior; selective auto ejectors; chromed bores; engraved silvered receiver. Made in Japan. Introduced 1981; discontinued 1986.

Perf: $2195 **Exc:** $1995 **VGood:** $1895

WINCHESTER MODEL 1001

Over/under; 12-ga.; 3-inch chamber; 28-inch barrel; Imp. Cyl., Mod., Imp. Mod., Skeet WinPlus; 45-inch overall length; weighs 7 lbs.; select walnut stock; checkered grip, forend; single selective trigger; automatic ejectors; wide vent rib; matte finished receiver top; blued receiver with scroll engraving. Although carried in the 1993 catalog and advertised for a year, the Model 1001 never reached full production status because of technical and quality control difficulties in Italy. Both Field and Sporting Clays versions were planned. Some guns reached consumers, but in late 1994 all were recalled and the project was cancelled.

Note: Since none are in the marketplace, no sales performance can be established and no values are given.

WINCHESTER SELECT MODEL 101 FIELD (2007)

This Belgian-made version of Winchester's popular Model 101 was introduced in 2007. It features Grade II/III walnut, 26" or 28" barrels and deep-relief engraving on the blued receiver that mimics the original 101. Classic white line spacer and vented recoil pad. Three choke tubes. Weight is about 7.2 lbs.

NIB: $1700 **Exc:** $1495 **VGood:** 1050

MODEL 101 PIGEON GRADE TRAP

This deluxe dedicated trap gun was introduced in 2008. It features a Grade III/IV walnut stock with a high-gloss finish and a raised comb. Barrels are 30" or 32". Three choke tubes included. Weight is 7.5 to 7.75 lbs. Add 5% for adjustable comb stock.

NIB: $1700 **Exc:** $1495 **VGood:** 1050

WINCHESTER SUPREME

Gauge: 12, 2-3/4-inch, 3-inch chambers; 28-inch, 30-inch barrel, Invector Plus choke tubes; weighs 7 lbs. 6 oz. to 7 lbs. 12. oz.; 45-inch overall (28-inch barrel); checkered walnut stock; chrome-plated chambers; back-bored barrels; tang barrel selector/safety; deep-blued finish. Introduced 2000.

Supreme Field (26-inch or 28-inch barrel, 6mm ventilated rib)

Perf: $1075 **Exc:** $895 **VGood:** $825

Supreme Sporting (28-inch or 30-inch barrel, 10mm rib, adj. trigger)

Perf: $1200 **Exc:** $995 **VGood:** $900

WINCHESTER XPERT MODEL 96

Over/under; boxlock; 12-, 20-ga.; 3-inch chambers; 26-inch, 28-inch, 30-inch barrels; vent rib; depending on gauge, barrel length, weighs 6-1/4 to 8-1/4 lbs.; checkered walnut pistol-grip stock, forend; similar to Model 101. Made in Japan. Introduced 1976; discontinued 1981.

Exc: $800 **VGood:** $600 **Good:** $500

WINCHESTER XPERT MODEL 96 SKEET

Same specs as Xpert Model 96 except 2-3/4-inch chambers; 27-inch barrels; Skeet choke; checkered walnut Skeet-style stock. Made in Japan. Introduced 1976; discontinued 1981.

Exc: $825 **VGood:** $625 **Good:** $500

WINCHESTER XPERT MODEL 96 TRAP

Same specs as Xpert Model 96 except 12-ga.; 2-3/4-inch chambers; 30-inch barrels; checkered walnut straight or Monte Carlo trap-style stock; recoil pad. Made in Japan. Introduced 1976; discontinued 1981.

Exc: $775 **VGood:** $595 **Good:** $495

WINCHESTER SELECT DELUXE FIELD

New in 2007, this Belgian-made 3" 12 gauge O/U features an engraved steel receiver with silver nitride finish and Grade II walnut. Barrels are 26", 28" or 30". Three chokes included. Weight is about 7.25 lbs.

NIB: $1325 **Exc:** $1250 **VGood:** $1050

WINCHESTER SELECT PLATINUM FIELD

This 3" 12 gauge O/U was introduced in 2007. It is Belgian-made and comes with 28" or 30" barrels, Grade II/III walnut and deep relief engraving. Includes three Signature extended choke tubes and hard case.

NIB: $1950 **Exc:** $1795 **VGood:** $1395

WINCHESTER SELECT PLATINUM SPORTING

Similar to the Platinum Field with 28", 30" or 32" ported barrels, wide rib, adjustable trigger shoe and five Signature extended choke tubes and hard case.

NIB: $2195 **Exc:** $1995 **VGood:** $1700

WINCHESTER SELECT MIDNIGHT

High-gloss bluing on receiver and barrels with gold accent game bird pattern on both sides and bottom of the receiver. Satin finished Grade II/III walnut. Oval checkering pattern. Choke tubes. Introduced 2006. Available in 26-inch and 28-inch barrels.

NIB: 2000 **Exc:** 1695 **VGood:** 1050

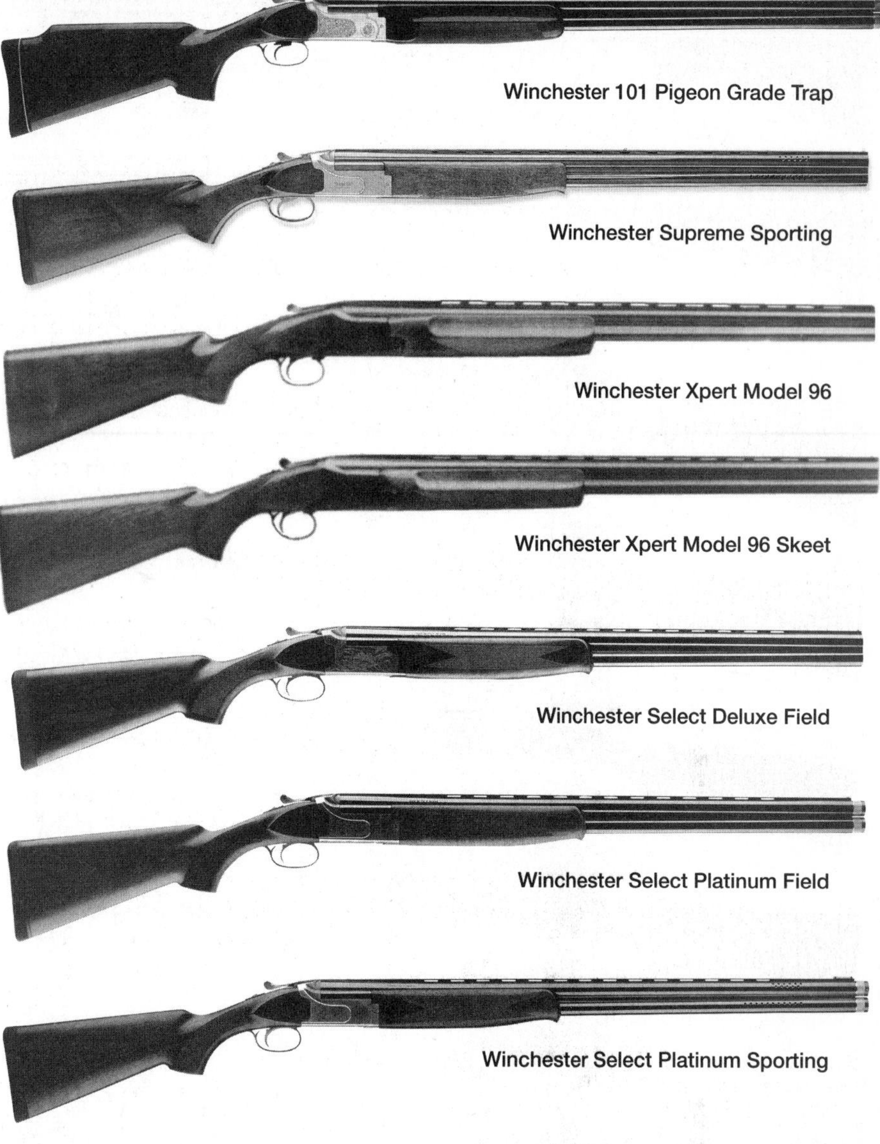

Winchester 101 Pigeon Grade Trap

Winchester Supreme Sporting

Winchester Xpert Model 96

Winchester Xpert Model 96 Skeet

Winchester Select Deluxe Field

Winchester Select Platinum Field

Winchester Select Platinum Sporting

WINCHESTER SELECT WHITE FIELD

An engraved silver nitride receiver is featured on both versions of the White Field. The Traditional model has traditional checkering and the Extreme model features the Select Series' unique oval checkering pattern. Both versions have choke tubes and are available in 26-inch and 28-inch barrels. Introduced 2006.

NIB: 1400 **Exc:** 1050 **VGood:** 795

WINCHESTER MODEL 21

Side-by-side; boxlock; hammerless; 12-, 16-, 20-, 28-ga., .410; 20-inch, 28-inch, 30-inch, 32-inch (12-ga. only) barrels; raised matted or vent rib; Full, Improved Modified, Modified, Improved Cylinder, Skeet chokes; checkered walnut straight or pistol-grip stock, regular or beavertail forend; automatic safety; early models (1931-1944) have double triggers and extractors, single trigger and ejectors optional; later models (1945-1959) have selective single trigger and selective ejectors. Introduced 1931; discontinued 1959.

With double triggers, extractors

Exc: $3500 **VGood:** $2900 **Good:** $2000

With double triggers, selective ejectors

Exc: $4200 **VGood:** $3700 **Good:** $2850

With single selective trigger, extractors

Exc: $5900 **VGood:** $4400 **Good:** $3100

With single selective trigger, selective ejectors

Exc: $6500 **VGood:** $5500 **Good:** $4750

.410 model

Exc: $30,000 **VGood:** $20,000 **Good:** $14,000

28-ga. model

Exc: $20,000 **VGood:** $14,000 **Good:** $9000

WINCHESTER MODEL 21 CUSTOM

Same specs as Model 21 except hand-checkered fancy American walnut stock, forearm; hand-honed internal parts; optional carving, engraving and gold inlays. Introduced 1960; discontinued 1982.

Perf: $7500 **Exc:** $5500 **VGood:** $4500

WINCHESTER MODEL 21 DUCK

Same specs as Model 21 except 12-ga.; 3-inch chamber; 30-inch, 32-inch barrels; Full choke; checkered walnut pistol-grip stock, beavertail forearm; selective ejection; selective single trigger; recoil pad. Introduced 1940; discontinued 1954.

With matted rib

Exc: $6000 **VGood:** $5000 **Good:** $3750

With vent rib

Exc: $6300 **VGood:** $5300 **Good:** $4050

WINCHESTER MODEL 21 GRAND AMERICAN

Same specs as Model 21 except two barrel sets; hand-checkered fancy American walnut stock, forearm; hand-honed internal parts; optional

Winchester Select Midnight

Winchester Select White Field

Winchester Model 21 Grand American

Winchester Model 23 XTR Golden Quail

Winchester Model 23 XTR Pigeon Grade

Winchester Model 23 XTR Pigeon Grade Lightweight

Winchester Model 24

carving, engraving and gold inlays. Introduced 1960; discontinued 1982.

Perf: $49,750 **Exc:** $37,500 **VGood:** $25,000

WINCHESTER MODEL 21 PIGEON

Same specs as Model 21 except hand-checkered fancy American walnut stock, forearm; hand-honed internal parts; optional carving, engraving and gold inlays. Introduced 1960; discontinued 1982.

Perf: $15,500 **Exc:** $14,500 **VGood:** $13,000

WINCHESTER MODEL 21 SKEET

Same specs as Model 21 except 26-inch, 28-inch barrels; Skeet chokes; red bead front sight; checkered French walnut stock, beavertail forearm; selective single trigger, selective ejection; non-auto safety. Introduced 1933; discontinued 1958.

With matted rib

Exc: $1900 **VGood:** $1600 **Good:** $1300

With vent rib

Exc: $2100 **VGood:** $1800 **Good:** $1500

WINCHESTER MODEL 21 TRAP

Same specs as Model 21 except 30-inch, 32-inch barrels; Full choke; checkered walnut pistol-grip or straight stock, beavertail forearm; selective trigger; non-auto safety; selective ejection. Introduced 1932; discontinued 1940.

With matted rib

Exc: $6000 **VGood:** $4995 **Good:** $3000

With vent rib

Exc: $6300 **VGood:** $5295 **Good:** $3150

WINCHESTER MODEL 23 CLASSIC

Side-by-side; 12-, 20-, 28-ga., .410; 26-inch vent-rib barrels; deluxe hand-checkered walnut stock, beavertail forend; auto safety; auto ejectors; single selective trigger; solid recoil pad; gold inlay on bottom of receiver; gold initial plate in stock; ebony inlay in forend; blued, engraved receiver. Made in Japan. Introduced 1986; discontinued 1988.

12-, 20-ga.

Perf: $1600 **Exc:** $1200 **VGood:** $1000

28-ga., .410

Perf: $2100 **Exc:** $1500 **VGood:** $1250

WINCHESTER MODEL 23 CUSTOM

Same specs as Model 23 Classic except 12-ga.; 27-inch WinChoke barrels; chrome-lined bores, chambers for steel shot; high-luster blued receiver, no engraving; marketed in luggage-style case. Made in Japan. Introduced 1986; discontinued 1988.

Perf: $2000 **Exc:** $1200 **VGood:** $1000

WINCHESTER MODEL 23 XTR

Side-by-side; 12-, 20-ga.; 3-inch chambers; 25-1/2-inch, 26-inch, 28-inch, 30-inch barrels; tapered vent rib; WinChokes; tapered vent rib; cut-checkered high-luster American walnut stock, beavertail forend; mechanical single trigger; selective ejectors; silver-gray satin finish on receiver, top lever, trigger guard; fine-line scroll engraving. Made in Japan. Introduced 1978; discontinued 1986.

Perf: $1000 **Exc:** $700 **VGood:** $600

WINCHESTER MODEL 23 XTR GOLDEN QUAIL

Same specs as Model 23 XTR except different chamberings produced each year; 12- (1986), 20- (1984), 28-ga. (1985), .410 (1987); 25-1/2-inch solid-rib barrel; fixed chokes; English-style straight-grip stock, beavertail forearm; engraving; gold inlays. Only 500 made each year. Introduced 1984; discontinued 1987.

12 Gauge

Perf: $2500 **Exc:** $2300 **VGood:** $2000

20 Gauge

Perf: $2850 **Exc:** $2500 **VGood:** $2150

28 Gauge

Perf: $3950 **Exc:** $3750 **VGood:** $3450

.410 Bore

Perf: $3950 **Exc:** $3750 **VGood:** $3450

WINCHESTER MODEL 23 XTR HEAVY DUCK

Same specs as Model 23 XTR except 12-ga; 3-inch chambers; 30-inch Full/Extra-Full barrels; select American walnut stock, beavertail forend; blued receivers, barrels; marketed in hard case. Only 500 made. Made in Japan. Introduced 1983; discontinued 1984.

Perf: $2150 **Exc:** $1750 **VGood:** $1450

WINCHESTER MODEL 23 XTR LIGHT DUCK

Same specs as Model 23 XTR except 20-ga.; 3-inch chambers, 28-inch Full/Full barrels; select American walnut stock, beavertail forend; blued receiver, barrels; marketed in hard case. Only 500 made. Made in Japan. Introduced 1984; discontinued 1985.

Perf: $2495 **Exc:** $2150 **VGood:** $1850

WINCHESTER MODEL 23 XTR PIGEON GRADE

Same specs as Model 23 XTR except higher grade of wood, checkering and engraving; marketed in hard case. Made in Japan. Introduced, 1983; discontinued 1986.

Perf: $2220 **Exc:** $2000 **VGood:** $1750

WINCHESTER MODEL 23 XTR PIGEON GRADE LIGHTWEIGHT

Same specs as Model 23 XTR except 25-1/2-inch barrels; fixed or choke tubes; English-style straight-grip stock, thin semi-beavertail forend; engraved bird scene. Marketed in hard case. Made in Japan. Introduced 1982; discontinued 1988.

Perf: $2250 **Exc:** $2000 **VGood:** $1800

WINCHESTER MODEL 23 XTR TWO-BARREL SET

Same specs as Model 23 XTR except 20-, 28-ga.; two-barrel set in each gauge of 25-1/2-inch barrel, each fitted with its own full fancy American walnut semi-beavertail forend; marketed in handmade leather luggage-style carrying case. Only 500 made. Introduced 1986; discontinued 1986

Perf: $4900 **Exc:** $4100 **VGood:** $3100

WINCHESTER MODEL 24

Side-by-side; hammerless; takedown; 12-, 16-, 20-ga.; 26-inch Improved/Modified, 28-inch Modified/Full or Improved/ Modified, 30-inch Modified/Full (12-ga. only) barrels; uncheckered walnut straight or pistol-grip stock, semi-beavertail forearm; composition buttplate; double triggers; automatic ejectors. Introduced 1940; discontinued 1957.

12-, 16-ga. model.

Exc: $575 **VGood:** $395 **Good:** $275

20-ga. model

Exc: $600 **VGood:** $425 **Good:** $300

WINCHESTER MODEL 20

Single shot; exposed hammer; takedown; .410; 2-1/2-inch chamber; 26-inch Full-choke barrel; checkered pistol-grip stock, forearm. Introduced 1919; discontinued 1924.

Exc: $475 **VGood:** $350 **Good:** $290

WINCHESTER MODEL 36

Single shot; bolt action; takedown; 9mm short shot, 9mm long shot, 9mm ball cartridges interchangeably; 18-inch round barrel; one-piece plain wood stock, forearm; special trigger guard forms pistol grip; composition buttplate; cocks by pulling rearward on knurled firing pin head, same mechanism used in some Winchester single-shot rifles; guns were not serialized. Introduced 1920; discontinued 1927.

Exc: $600 **VGood:** $475 **Good:** $300

WINCHESTER MODEL 37

Single shot; break-open; semi-hammerless; 12-, 16-, 20-, 28-ga., .410; 26-inch, 28-inch, 30-inch, 32-inch barrel; Full, Modified, Cylinder choke; metal bead front sight; uncheckered American walnut pistol-grip stock, semi-beavertail forearm; automatic ejector; checkered composition buttplate. Introduced 1936; discontinued 1968. Some buyers pay a slight premium for "red lettering" on Winchester logo.

12-ga. model

Exc: $350 **VGood:** $275 **Good:** $125

16-ga. model

Exc: $295 **VGood:** $275 **Good:** $115

20-ga. model

Exc: $295 **VGood:** $225 **Good:** $145

28-ga. model

Exc: $950 **VGood:** $650 **Good:** $500

.410 model

Exc: $425 **VGood:** $295 **Good:** $250

WINCHESTER MODEL 37A

Single barrel; break-open; 12- (3-inch), 16- (2-3/4-inch), 20- (3-inch), 28-ga. (2-3/4-inch), .410 (3-inch); 25-inch, 28-inch, 30-inch, 32-inch, 36-inch barrel; Full choke; checkered walnut-stained hardwood pistol-grip stock; concave hammer spur; white spacer between grip cap and buttplate; gold trigger; engraving. Introduced 1973; discontinued 1980.

12-, 16-, 20-ga. model

Perf: $140 **Exc:** $100 **VGood:** $80

28-ga., .410 model

Perf: $190 **Exc:** $140 **VGood:** $120

WINCHESTER MODEL 37A YOUTH

Same specs as Model 37A except 20-ga., .410; 26-inch barrel; Improved Modified, Full chokes; youth-sized hardwood stock. Introduced 1973; discontinued 1980.

Perf: $180 **Exc:** $110 **VGood:** $90

WINCHESTER MODEL 41

Single shot; bolt action; takedown; .410; 2-1/2-inch (pre-1933), 3-inch (post-1933) chamber; 24-inch full-choke barrel; uncheckered one-piece walnut pistol-grip or straight-grip stock; checkering on special order; guns were not numbered serially. Introduced 1920; discontinued 1934.

Exc: $400 **VGood:** $300 **Good:** $250

WINCHESTER MODEL 370

Single barrel; break-open; 12- (3-inch), 16- (2-3/4-inch), 20- (3-inch), 28-ga. (2-3/4-inch), .410 (3-inch); 26-inch, 28-inch, 30-inch, 32-inch, 36-inch barrel; Full choke; weight varies with gauges and barrel lengths, from 5-1/2 to 6-1/4 lbs.; bead front sight; plain American hardwood pistol-grip stock, forearm; hard-rubber buttplate; auto ejectors. Introduced 1968; discontinued 1973, replaced by Model 37A.

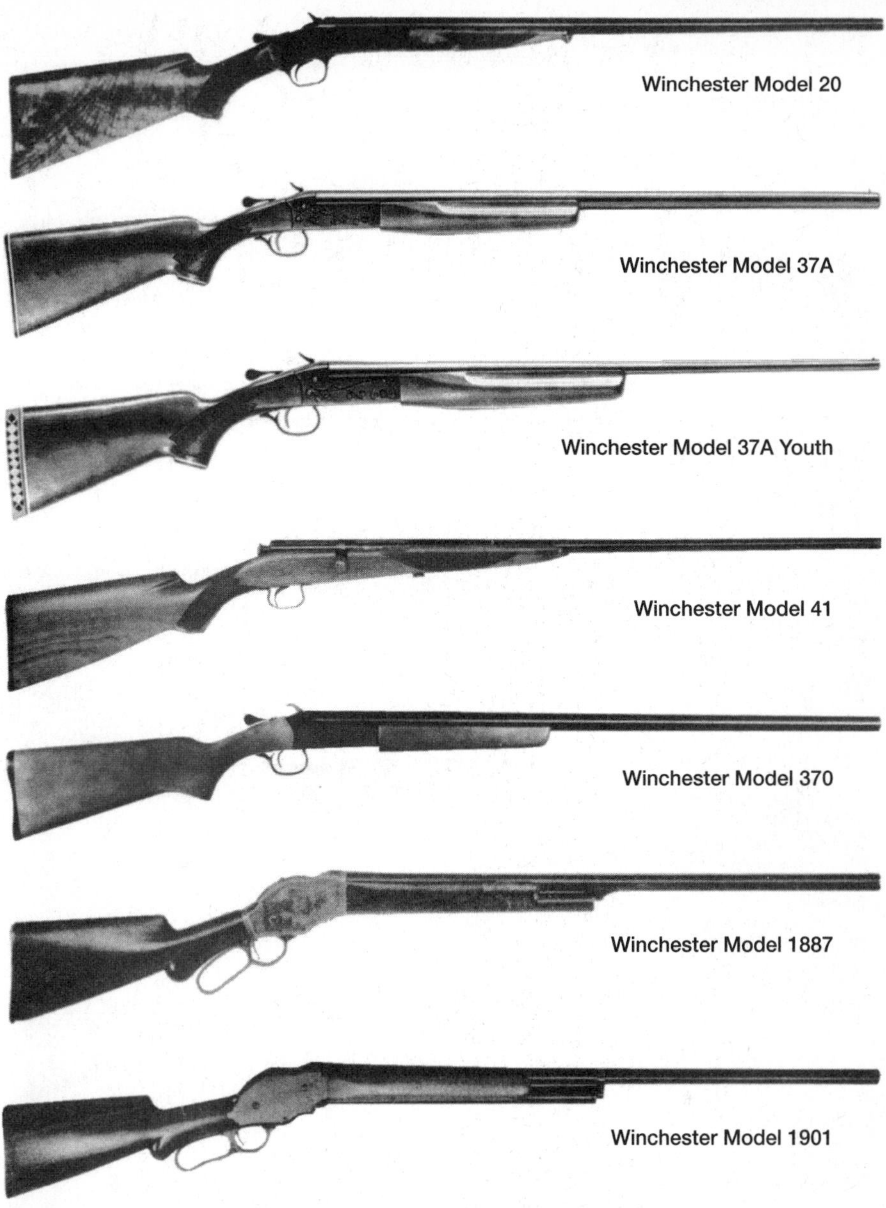

Winchester Model 20

Winchester Model 37A

Winchester Model 37A Youth

Winchester Model 41

Winchester Model 370

Winchester Model 1887

Winchester Model 1901

12-, 16-, 20-ga. model

Perf: $125 **Exc:** $100 **VGood:** $80

28-ga., .410 model

Perf: $175 **Exc:** $140 **VGood:** $120

WINCHESTER MODEL 370 YOUTH

Same specs as Model 370 except 20-ga., .410; 26-inch Improved Modified barrel; youth-sized hardwood stock; rubber recoil pad. Introduced 1969; discontinued 1973.

Perf: $160 **Exc:** $110 **VGood:** $90

WINCHESTER MODEL 1885 SINGLE SHOT

Falling block; takedown or solid frame; 20-ga.; 3-inch chamber; 26-inch nickel-steel barrel; extra barrels or matted top barrels optional; Full choke standard; Modified or Cylinder bore optional; uncheckered walnut pistol-grip stock; shotgun version of Model 1885 Hi-Wall rifle. Introduced 1913; discontinued 1918.

Exc: $3000 **VGood:** $2300 **Good:** $1800

WINCHESTER MODEL 1887

Lever action; solid frame; 10-, 12-ga.; 4-shot tubular magazine; 30-inch, 32-inch barrel; Full choke; uncheckered American walnut half-pistol-grip stock, forend. Introduced 1887; discontinued 1901.

Exc: $1950 **VGood:** $1400 **Good:** $1100

WINCHESTER MODEL 1887 DELUXE

Same specs as Model 1887 except Damascus barrel; hand-checkered stock, forend. Introduced 1887; discontinued 1901.

Exc: $2400 **VGood:** $1850 **Good:** $1400

WINCHESTER MODEL 1901

Lever action; solid frame; 10-ga.; 4-shot tube magazine; 30-inch, 32-inch barrel; Full choke; uncheckered American walnut half-pistol-grip stock, forend; replaced Model 1887 in line with internal redesign features. Introduced 1901; discontinued 1920.

Exc: $1900 **VGood:** $1500 **Good:** $1300

WINCHESTER MODEL 9410 LEVER-ACTION SHOTGUN

Gauge: .410, 2-1/2-inch chamber; 24-inch barrel (Cyl. bore); weighs 6-3/4 lbs.; 42-1/8-inch overall; checkered walnut straight-grip, checkered walnut forearm; V rear sight, TruGlo front; Model 94 rifle action (smoothbore) chambered for .410 shotshell. 9-shot tubular magazine; 13-1/2-

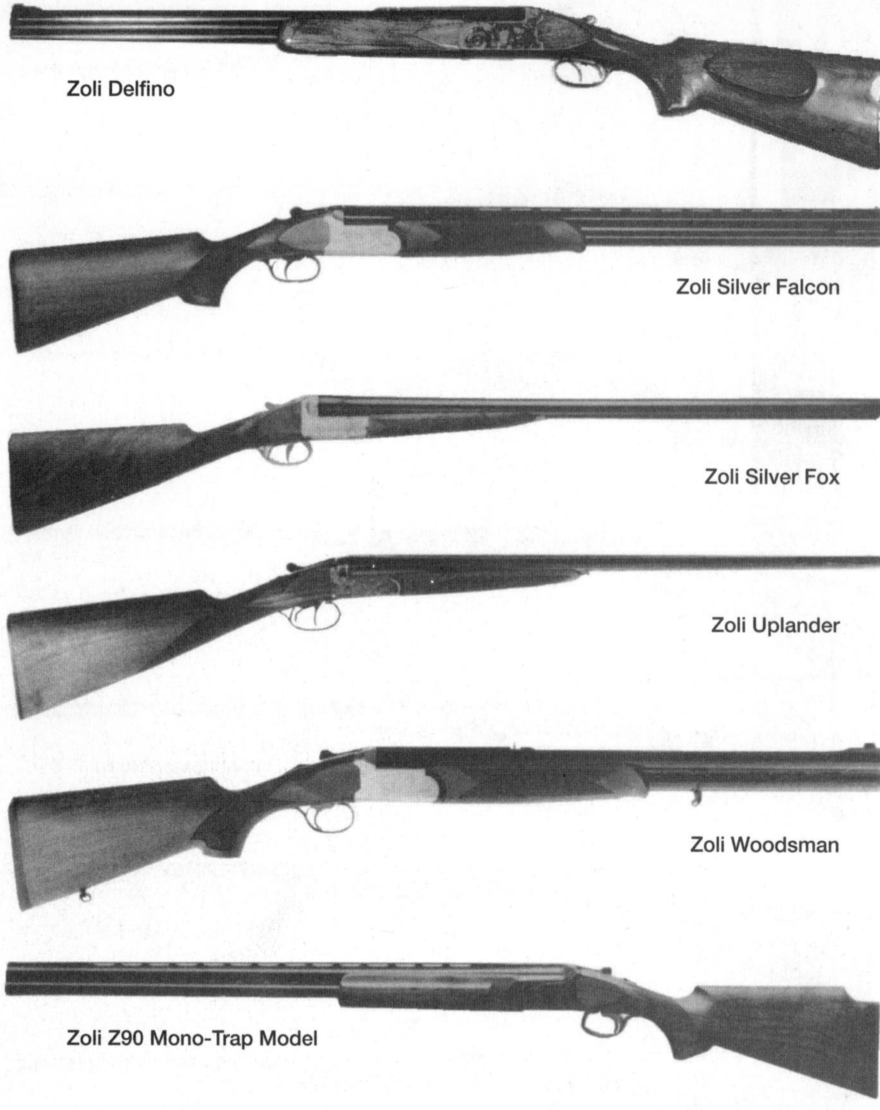
Zoli Delfino

Zoli Silver Falcon

Zoli Silver Fox

Zoli Uplander

Zoli Woodsman

Zoli Z90 Mono-Trap Model

inch length of pull. Introduced 2001. From U.S. Repeating Arms Co.

Price: 9410 Lever-Action Shotgun
Perf: $1100 **Exc:** $875 **VGood:** $600

Price: 9410 Packer Shotgun
Perf: $1100 **Exc:** $875 **VGood:** $600

WOODWARD BEST QUALITY DOUBLE

Side-by-side; sidelock; built to customer order in any standard gauge, barrel length, choke; double or single trigger; automatic ejectors; produced in field, wildfowl, Skeet or Trap configurations. Made in England. Manufactured prior to WWII.

With single trigger
Perf: $28,500 **Exc:** $21,000 **VGood:** $19,500

With double trigger
Perf: $27,500 **Exc:** $20,000 **VGood:** $18,500

WOODWARD BEST QUALITY OVER/UNDER

Over/under; sidelock; built to customer order in any standard gauge, barrel length, choke; plain barrel or vent rib; double or single trigger; auto ejectors. Made in England. Introduced 1909; discontinued WWII.

With single triggers
Perf: $34,000 **Exc:** $25,000 **VGood:** $20,500

With double triggers
Perf: $33,000 **Exc:** $24,000 **VGood:** $19,000

WOODWARD SINGLE BARREL TRAP

Single shot; sidelock; 12-ga.; built to customer order in any standard barrel length, choke; plain barrel or vent rib; single trigger; auto ejectors. Made in England. Manufactured prior to WWII.

Perf: $13,000 **Exc:** $9000 **VGood:** $8000

ZABALA DOUBLE

Side-by-side; 10-, 12-, 20-ga., .410; 26-inch, 28-inch, 30-inch, 32-inch barrels; raised matted solid rib; metal bead front sight; hand-checkered French walnut pistol-grip stock, plastic-finished beavertail forend; double triggers; front trigger hinged; hand-engraved action, blued finish. Made in Spain. Introduced 1980; discontinued 1982. Add 25 percent for 10-ga.

Perf: $475 **Exc:** $395 **VGood:** $325

PIETRO ZANOLETTI MODEL 2000 FIELD

Over/under; boxlock; 12-ga.; 28-inch barrels; gold bead front sight; checkered European walnut pistol-grip stock, forend; auto ejectors; double triggers; engraved receiver. Made in Italy. Introduced 1984; no longer in production.

Perf: $500 **Exc:** $385 **VGood:** $325

ZOLI DELFINO

Over/under; 12-, 20-ga.; 3-inch chambers; 28-inch barrels; vent rib; hand-checkered European walnut pistol-grip stock, cheekpiece; chromed bores; double triggers; auto sliding safety; color case-hardened receiver; light engraving. Made in Italy. Introduced 1980; discontinued 1989.

Perf: $650 **Exc:** $560 **VGood:** $490

ZOLI GOLDEN SNIPE

Over/under; boxlock; 12-, 20-ga.; 26-inch, 28-inch, 30-inch vent-rib barrels; standard choke combos; hand-checkered European walnut pistol-grip stock, forend; single trigger; auto ejectors; engraving. No longer in production.

Perf: $700 **Exc:** $560 **VGood:** $490

ZOLI SILVER FALCON

Over/under; boxlock; 12-, 20-ga.; 3-inch chambers; 26-inch, 28-inch barrels; standard choke combos or Full choke tubes; Turkish Circassian walnut stock; single selective trigger, auto ejectors; silvered finish, floral engraving on frame. Made in Italy. Introduced 1989; discontinued 1990.

Perf: $950 **Exc:** $700 **VGood:** $550

ZOLI SILVER FOX

Side-by-side; boxlock; 12-, 20-ga.; 3-inch chambers; 26-inch, 28-inch barrels; standard choke combos; select Turkish Circassian walnut straight-grip stock, splinter forend; solid recoil pad; single trigger; selective ejectors; engraved, silvered receiver. Made in Italy. Introduced 1989; discontinued 1990.

Perf: $1750 **Exc:** $1425 **VGood:** $1250

ZOLI UPLANDER

Side-by-side; boxlock; 12-, 20-ga.; 3-inch chambers; 25-inch Improved Cylinder/Modified barrels; hand-checkered Turkish Circassian walnut straight English-style stock, splinter forend; single trigger; auto ejectors; color case-hardened frame. Introduced 1989; discontinued 1990.

Perf: $975 **Exc:** $875 **VGood:** $775

ZOLI WOODSMAN

Over/under; boxlock; 12-ga.; 3-inch chambers; 23-inch vent-rib barrels for rifled slugs; five choke tubes; rifle sights on raised rib; skip-line-checkered, oil-finished Turkish Circassian walnut stock; rubber buttpad; single selective trigger; auto selective ejectors; with or without sling swivels; engraved frame. Made in Italy. Introduced 1989; discontinued 1990.

Perf: $1600 **Exc:** $1150 **VGood:** $900

ZOLI Z90 MONO-TRAP

Single barrel; break-open; 12-ga.; 2-3/4-inch chamber; 32-inch, 34-inch single barrel; choke tubes; raised vent rib; two sight beads; checkered Turkish Circassian walnut Monte Carlo pistol-grip stock, forearm; single selective trigger; selective auto ejectors; recoil pad; matte blue finish on receiver. Made in Italy. Introduced 1989; discontinued 1990.

Perf: $2150 **Exc:** $1450 **VGood:** $1200

ZOLI Z90 SKEET MODEL

Same specs as Z90 Mono-Trap except over/under; boxlock; 28-inch barrels; checkered Turkish Circassian walnut Skeet-style stock, forearm. Made in Italy. Introduced 1989; discontinued 1990.

Perf: $2150 **Exc:** $1450 **VGood:** $1200

ZOLI Z90 SPORTING CLAYS

Same specs as Z90 Mono-Trap except over/under; sidelock; 28-inch barrels; weighs 7-1/4 lbs.; checkered Turkish Circassian walnut pistol-grip stock, forend; schnabel forend tip; single selective trigger; selective auto ejectors; solid rubber buttpad; silvered, engraved frame. Made in Italy. Introduced 1989; discontinued 1990.

Perf: $2150 **Exc:** $1450 **VGood:** $1200

ZOLI Z90 TRAP

Same specs as Z90 Mono-Trap except over/under; boxlock; 29-1/2-inch, 32-inch barrels; step-type vent rib; vent center rib; weighs 8-1/2 lbs.; adjustable single selective trigger. Made in Italy. Introduced 1989; discontinued 1990.

Perf: $2150 **Exc:** $1450 **VGood:** $1200

MODERN GUN VALUES
COMMEMORATIVES
Directory of Dates

1960 677
1961....................677
1962 677
1963 678
1964 678
1965 680
1966 681
1967 682
1968 683
1969 684
1970 685
1971....................686
1972 687
1973 687
1974 688
1975 689
1976 689
1977 690
1978 690
1979 691
1980 692
1981....................692
1982 693
1983 694
1984 695
1985 696
1986 696
1987 697
1988 698
1989 699
1990 699
1991....................700
1992 701
1993 702
1994 703
1995 704

Commemoratives & Limited Editions

I will be frank: as far as I know, no one has ever compiled an exhaustive list of all the commemorative, special-issue, and special-order firearms offered during the twentieth and twenty-first centuries. The mere thought of compiling such a list makes my head hurt.

Here's why: back in the sixties and seventies, the only major manufacturers of commemorative guns were Colt and Winchester. Colt's platform was the Single Action Army; Winchester's, the Model 94. The speculation at the time was that these two companies made these guns to spur sales of their two aging flagship models. This explanation is still valid, to some extent at least, four decades later.

Today, however, it's a different story. During the last two decades, most American gunmakers invested in computer-aided manufacturing, which meant that making special-run guns presented no particular problems in terms of tooling and scrap. If, say, the Upper Sandusky Conservation and Hog Roast Club wanted to commemorate their fiftieth anniversary with a special rifle, pistol or shotgun, gunmakers will usually be happy to comply as long as a minimum buy is guaranteed.

Then major gun distributors got into the act. Sales and marketing firms such as TALO began offering exclusives, which they sold to their dealers as non-catalogued specialty items. Most of these special-run guns were, and are, very attractive, but their uncatalogued status makes them very difficult to classify. I get probably two calls a month inquiring about these guns, which don't usually appear in any price guides.

In general, there are four different types of commemorative firearms: those released directly from the manufacturer into their normal distribution channel; those exclusively made for a specific distributor; those made as fund-raisers for non-profit organizations; and those commissioned from a specialty retailer for direct sales to the public. Let's take a look at them.

The Factory Commemorative

The first type is exemplified by the Winchester 94 and Colt SAA commemoratives that we all love – or hate. These firearms have lately acquired a legitimacy among collectors that they didn't always enjoy – in fact, most serious Winchester collectors would have spit in your face 20 years ago if you had asked them if they had a Crazy Horse commemorative among their holdings. Until recently, the NRA commemorative Colt SAA was a pariah among collectors. This situation is changing; the discontinuance of the Model 94 in 2006 has made all 94s collectible, and the value of second-generation SAAs is appreciating rapidly.

The Distributor Special

The second type includes the TALO and Davidson's special-run guns that are released to key retailers who buy from such distributors. As discussed above, these guns are usually uncatalogued, and most of the general gun-owning public is usually unaware of their existence.

The Fund-Raiser

The third type is exemplified by the various not-for-profit guns that we have all seen, often unfired, in the used-gun racks of our local retailers. The Ithaca Model 37 shotgun was a big favorite of Ducks Unlimited some years back, for example, but I know of no comprehensive source that lists all of the variations of these fund-raiser guns or how many were produced.

The Distributor Special

The fourth type of commemorative or special-issue gun includes the various historical and personality-cult commemoratives that are built on the chassis of both domestic and offshore firearms. American Historical Foundation, for example, offers at least 60 commemorative firearms at this writing, ranging from fancy .25 Colt semi-autos to Thompsons. And right now, at this very moment, you can buy an Elvis Presley commemorative Smith & Wesson revolver from a collectibles company doing business as America Remembers. The revolver itself is called the Elvis Presley Taking Care of Business, and it can be yours for a mere $2195. If you're you're the kind of person whose living room motif features imitation velvet Elvis tapestries and Presley collector plates, you might also consider America Remembers' Elvis Presley Western Tribute, which is based on an Italian-made Uberti Single Action Army clone. America Remembers offers dozens of other special-run commemorative or tribute guns should your tastes run in that direction.

Often the definitions of these four types becomes blurred or disappears altogether. Was the Charter Arms "Bonnie & Clyde" matched set of revolvers that was produced 30 years ago a true commemorative, or just a marketing gimmick? Is the Remington Model Seven 25th Anniversary Edition bolt action rifle a true commemorative? The mind boggles.

In this book, we pretty much limit ourselves to factory-built commemoratives that hit the market between 1960 and 1995. We apologize in advance who are searching for, say, a Colt El Capitan or El Presidente in these pages. We might also go ahead and apologize to those who find commemorative firearms listed herein for sale at figures substantially above or below the values shown in this section. These things happen. By the way, values shown are for examples in mint, unfired condition.

One thing is for sure: like all guns, commemorative or special-run firearms are worth precis ely what someone is willing to pay for them, no more or less. The fact that a gun might be a "distributor special," for example, does not inherently add to or detract from its value. If someone is willing to pay a certain amount for the privilege of being the only kid on the block with a [fill in the blank], then that figure is what that gun is worth to that buyer in those circumstances. To generalize beyond that is misleading.

I have always thought that the most fascinating collectors are those who are just slightly mad on the subject of their interest. I once knew a man, for example, who would energetically expound on the RCA/Victor recordings of Spike Jones until he was literally frothing at the mouth. Was he a nut? Yes. Was he MY kind of nut? Absolutely! Passionate people are always the most interesting.

So let us not turn up our noses at someone who's saving his pennies for a Gene Autry, Smiley Burnette and Pat Buttram Tribute Rifle from America Remembers. You may not find such a rifle listed in the following section, but that doesn't mean it's inherently less valuable than some of the guns that are listed.

Besides, I'm kind of a Gene Autry fan myself.

Cheers,

Dan Shideler

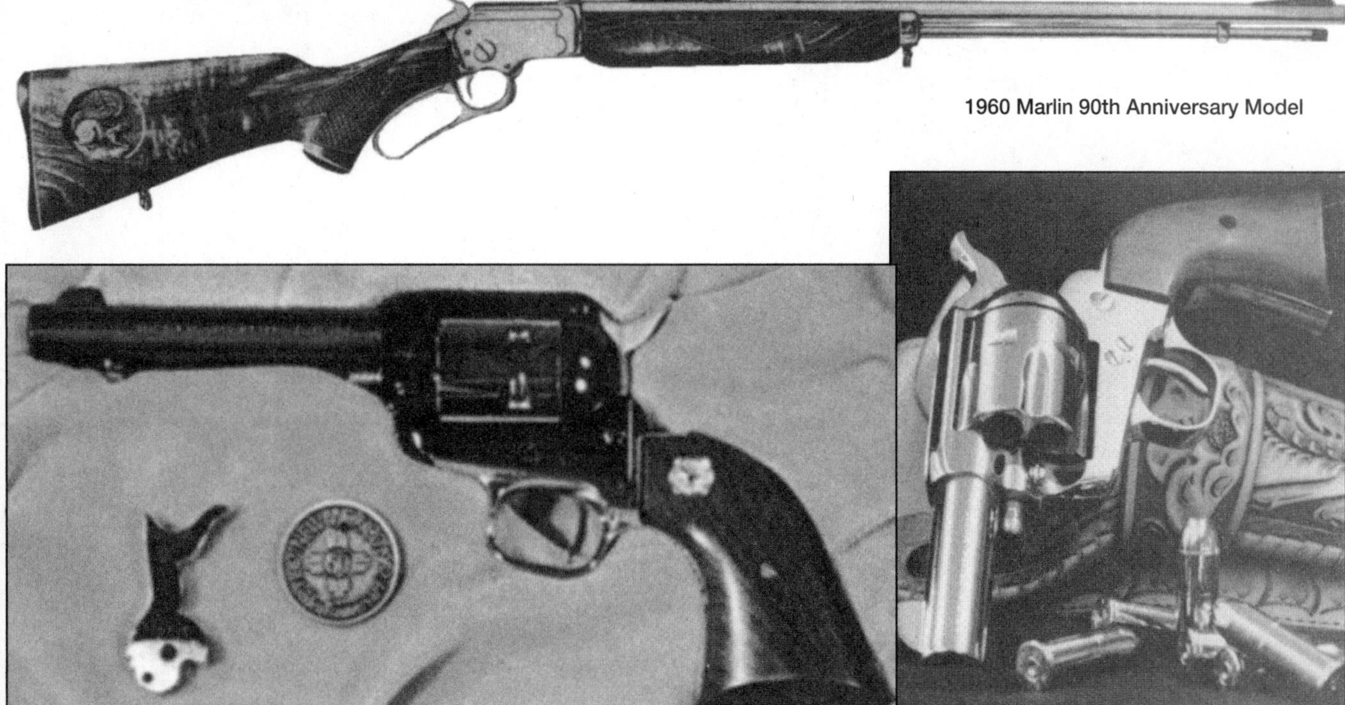

1960 Marlin 90th Anniversary Model

1962 Colt New Mexico Golden Anniversary

1961 Colt Sheriff's Model

1960

MARLIN 90TH ANNIVERSARY MODEL

Model 39A rifle commemorating firm's ninth decade. Has same general specs as Golden 39A, except for chrome-plated barrel, action; stock forearm of hand-checkered select American walnut; squirrel figure carved on right side of butt stock. Manufactured 1960; only 500 made.
Market Value: $995

1961

COLT 125TH ANNIVERSARY MODEL

Single Action Army revolver; "125th Anniversary—SAA Model .45 Cal." on left side of 7-1/2-inch barrel; 45 Colt only; varnished walnut grips; gold-plated Colt medallions; gold-plated hammer, trigger, trigger guard; balance blued. Originally cased in red velvet-lined box; 7390 made in 1961 only.
Issue Price: $150
Market Value: $1495

COLT CIVIL WAR CENTENNIAL

Single shot replica of Colt Model 1860 Army revolver; "Civil War Centennial Model—.22 Caliber Short" on left side of 6-inch barrel; 22 Short only; varnished walnut grips; gold-plated Colt medallions; gold-plated frame, backstrap, trigger guard assembly, balance blued; originally in leatherette case; 24,114 made in 1961 only.
Issue Price: $32.50
Market Value: $175

COLT GENESEO ANNIVERSARY

No. 4 derringer replica; "1836—Geneseo Anniversary Model—1961" on left side of 2-1/2-inch barrel; 22 Short only; walnut grips; gold plated in entirety; originally cased in velvet/satin-lined box; made especially for Cherry's Sporting Goods, Geneseo, Illinois; 104 made in 1961 only.
Issue Price: $27.50
Market Value: $650

COLT KANSAS STATEHOOD CENTENNIAL

Frontier Scout revolver; "1861—Kansas Centennial—1961" on left side of 4-3/4-inch barrel; 22 LR only; walnut grips; no medallions; gold-plated in entirety; originally cased in velvet-lined box with Kansas state seal inlaid in lid; made in 1961 only.
Issue Price: $75
Market Value: $450

COLT PONY EXPRESS CENTENNIAL

Frontier Scout revolver; "1860-61—Russell, Majors and Waddell/Pony Express Centennial Model—1960-61" on left side of 4-3/4-inch barrel; 22 LR only; varnished walnut grips; gold-plated Colt medallions; gold plated in entirety; originally cased in rosewood box with gold-plated centennial medallion in lid; 1007 made in 1961 only.
Issue Price: $80
Market Value: $450

COLT SHERIFF'S MODEL

Single Action Army revolver; made exclusively for Centennial Arms Corp.; "Colt Sheriff's Model .45" on left side of 3-inch barrel; 45 Colt only; walnut grips without medallions; 25 made with nickel finish; 478 blued; made only in 1961.
Issue Price: Nickel, $139.50; Blued, $150

Nickel
Market Value: $5500

Blued
Market Value: $1995

1962

COLT COLUMBUS, OHIO, SESQUICENTENNIAL

Frontier Scout revolver; "1812—Columbus Sesquicentennial—1962" on left side of 4-3/4-inch barrel; 22 LR only; varnished walnut grips with gold-plated medallions; gold-plated in entirety; originally cased in velvet/satin-lined walnut case; 200 made in 1962 only.
Issue Price: $100
Market Value: $550

COLT FORT FINDLAY, OHIO, SESQUICENTENNIAL

Frontier Scout revolver; "1812—Fort Findlay Sesquicentennial—1962" on left side of 4-3/4-inch, barrel; 22 LR, 22 WMR; varnished walnut grips; gold-plated in entirety; originally cased in red velvet/satin-lined walnut box; 110 made in 1962 only.
Issue Price: $89.50
Market Value: $650

Cased Pair, 22 LR, 22 WMR (20 made in 1962)
Market Value: $2500

COLT NEW MEXICO GOLDEN ANNIVERSARY

Frontier Scout revolver; "1912—New Mexico Golden Anniversary—1962" wiped in gold on left side of 4-3/4-inch barrel; 22 LR only; varnished walnut grips; gold-plated medallions; barrel, frame, base pin screw, ejector rod, rod tube, tube plug and screw, bolt and trigger, hammer screws blued; balance gold-plated; originally cased in redwood box with yellow satin/velvet lining; 1000 made in 1962 only.
Issue Price: $79.95
Market Value: $450

COLT ROCK ISLAND ARSENAL CENTENNIAL

Single shot version of Colt Model 1860 Army revolver; "1862—Rock Island Arsenal Centennial Model—1962" on left side of 6-inch barrel; 22 Short only; varnished walnut grips; blued finish; originally in blue and gray leatherette case; 550 made in 1962 only.
Issue Price: $38.50
Market Value: $250

COLT WEST VIRGINIA STATEHOOD CENTENNIAL

Frontier Scout revolver; "1863—West Virginia Centennial—1963" wiped in gold on left side of 4-3/4-inch barrel; 22 LR only; pearlite grips, gold-plated medallions; blued, with gold-plated backstrap, trigger guard assembly and screws, stock screw; originally cased in blonde wood box with gold velvet/satin lining; 3452 made in 1962 only.
Issue Price: $75
Market Value: $450

COLT WEST VIRGINIA STATEHOOD CENTENNIAL SINGLE ACTION ARMY

Same legend on barrel as 22 version; 5-1/2-inch barrel; 45 Colt only; same blue/gold finish as Scout version; same type of casing; 600 made in 1963 only.
Issue Price: $150
Market Value: $1495

1963 Colt Idaho Territorial Centennial

1963 Colt Arizona Territorial Centennial

1963 Colt General John Hunt Morgan Indian Raid

1964 Colt Nevada Battle Born Commemorative Frontier Scout/Single-Action Army Set

1963

COLT ARIZONA TERRITORIAL CENTENNIAL

Frontier Scout revolver "1863—Arizona Territorial Centennial—1963" wiped in gold on left side of 4-3/4-inch barrel; 22 LR only; pearlite grips, gold-plated medallions; gold plated, with blue barrel, frame, base pin screw, ejector rod, rod tube, tube plug and screw, bolt and trigger screws, hammer and hammer screw; originally cased in blonde-finished box with yellow velvet/satin lining; 5355 made in 1963 only.
Issue Price: $75
Market Value: $500

COLT ARIZONA TERRITORIAL CENTENNIAL SINGLE ACTION ARMY

Same as Colt Arizona Territorial Centennial Frontier Scout with same legend on barrel; 5 1/2-inch barrel; 45 Colt only; same blue/gold-plated finish; same type case; 1280 made in 1963 only.
Issue Price: $150
Market Value: $1495

COLT BATTLE OF GETTYSBURG CENTENNIAL

Frontier Scout revolver "1863—Battle of Gettysburg Centennial—1963" wiped in gold on left side of 4-3/4-inch barrel; 22 LR only; walnut grips; gold-plated medallions; gold plated with blued barrel, frame, base pin screw, ejector rod tube, tube plug and screw, and bolt, trigger and hammer screws; originally cased in blonde-finished wood with yellow velvet in bottom, blue satin in lid; 1019 made in 1963 only.
Issue Price: $89.95
Market Value: $800

COLT CAROLINA CHARTER TERCENTENARY

Frontier Scout revolver "1663—Carolina Charter Tercentenary—1963" wiped in gold on left side of 4-3/4-inch barrel; 22 LR only; walnut grips; gold-plated medallions; gold-plated, with barrel, frame, cylinder, base pin screw, ejector rod, rod tube, tube plug, tube screw, bolt, trigger and hammer screws blued; originally cased in blonde-finished box with yellow velvet/satin lining; 300 made in 1963 only.
Issue Price: $75
Market Value: $460

COLT CAROLINA CHARTER TERCENTENARY 22/45 COMBO SET

Includes Frontier Scout described above and Single Action Army revolver, with same legend on 5-1/2-inch barrel, 45 Colt only; same finish on grips as Frontier version; larger case to fit both guns; 251 sets made in 1963 only.
Issue Price: $240
Market Value: $1995

COLT FORT MCPHERSON, NEBRASKA, CENTENNIAL

No. 4 Derringer replica; "Fort McPherson/1863—Centennial—1963" wiped in gold on left side of 2-1/2-inch barrel; 22 Short only; ivorylite grips, no medallions; gold-plated with blued barrel, bolt, trigger screw, hammer and screw, trigger and stock screw; originally cased in walnut-finished box, with gold velvet/satin lining; 300 made in 1963 only.
Issue Price: $28.95
Market Value: $600

COLT FORT STEPHENSON, OHIO, SESQUICENTENNIAL

Frontier Scout revolver "1813—Fort Stephenson Sesquicentennial—1963" wiped in silver on left side of 4-3/4-inch barrel; 22 LR only; laminated rosewood grips, nickel-plated medallions; nickel-plated finish, with blued barrel, frame, base pin screw, ejector rod, rod tube, tube plug and screw, bolt and trigger and hammer screws; originally cased in blonde-finished wood, with yellow velvet/satin lining; 200 made only in 1963.
Issue Price: $75
Market Value: $750

COLT GENERAL JOHN HUNT MORGAN INDIAN RAID

Frontier Scout revolver; "1863—Gen. John Hunt Morgan Indian Raid—1963" wiped in gold on left side of 4-3/4-inch barrel; 22 LR; pearlite grips, gold-plated medallions; gold-plated with blued frame, barrel, cylinder, base pin screw, ejector rod, rod tube, tube plug and tube screw and bolt and trigger screw; originally cased in blonde-finished wood, with gold velvet/satin lining; 100 made in 1963 only.
Issue Price: $74.50
Market Value: $850

COLT H. COOK 1 OF 100

Frontier Scout/Single Action Army revolvers; sold as set; "H. Cook 1 of 100" on left side of barrels; Scout has 4-3/4-inch barrel, 22 LR only; SA Army has 7-1/2-inch barrel, 45 Colt only; pearlite grips; nickel-plated medallions; both nickel-plated with blued frame, base pin, trigger and hammer screws; originally cased in silver-colored box with blue satin/velvet lining; 100 sets made in 1963 only for H. Cook Sporting Goods, Albuquerque, N.M.
Issue Price: $275
Market Value: $1995

COLT IDAHO TERRITORIAL CENTENNIAL

Frontier Scout revolver; "1863—Idaho Territorial Centennial—1963" wiped in silver on left side of 4-3/4-inch barrel; 22 LR only; pearlite grips; nickel-plated medallions; nickel-plated with blue frame, barrel, base pin screw, ejector rod tube, tube plug and screw, and bolt, trigger and hammer screws; originally cased in blonde-finished wood, with gold velvet/satin lining; 902 made in 1963 only.
Issue Price: $75
Market Value: $650

1964

COLT CALIFORNIA GOLD RUSH COMMEMORATIVE

Frontier Scout revolver; "California Gold Rush Model" on left side of 4-3/4-inch barrel; 22 LR only; ivorylite grips; gold-plated medallions; gold-plated in entirety; originally cased in blonde wood box; blue velvet lining in bottom, gold in lid; 500 made in 1964 only.
Issue Price: $79.50
Market Value: $675

COLT CALIFORNIA GOLD RUSH SINGLE ACTION ARMY

Same barrel legend as Frontier Scout version; 5-1/2-inch barrel; 45 Colt only; same finish, grips, casing; 130 made in 1966 only.
Issue Price: $175
Market Value: $1250 to $1500

COLT CHERRY'S SPORTING GOODS 35TH ANNIVERSARY

Frontier Scout/Single Action Army revolvers, sold as set; "1929—Cherry's Sporting Goods 1964" on left side of barrel; Scout has 4-3/4-inch barrel, 22 LR only; SA Army has 4-3/4-inch barrel, 45 Colt only; both have laminated rosewood grips; gold-plated medallions; gold-plated in entirety; originally cased in embossed black leatherette, with black velvet/satin lining; 100 sets made in 1964 only.
Issue Price: $275
Market Value: $1995

1964 Colt
General Hood Centennial

1964 Colt
California Gold Rush
Commemorative

1964 Colt
New Jersey Tercentenary

COLT CHAMIZAL TREATY COMMEMORATIVE

Frontier Scout revolver; "1867 Chamizal Treaty—1964" wiped in gold on left side of 4-3/4-inch barrel; 22 LR only; pearlite grips; gold-plated medallions; gold-plated finish; blued frame, barrel, ejector rod, ejector tube, rod plug and screw, base pin and base pin screw and hammer, trigger and bolt screws; originally cased in blonde-finished wood; yellow velvet/satin lining; 450 made in 1964.

Issue Price: $85
Market Value: $650

COLT CHAMIZAL TREATY SINGLE ACTION ARMY

Same legend on 5-1/2-inch barrel; 45 Colt only; same grips, finish as Frontier Scout version; same type of case; 50 made in 1964.

Issue Price: $170
Market Value: $1595

COLT CHAMIZAL TREATY FRONTIER SCOUT/SINGLE ACTION ARMY COMBO

Includes the two revolvers described above in one oversize case; 50 pairs made in 1965.

Issue Price: $280
Market Value: $1995

COLT COL. SAM COLT SESQUICENTENNIAL PRESENTATION

Single Action Army revolver; "1815—Col. Sam Colt Sesquicentennial Model—1964" on left side of 7-1/2-inch barrel; 45 Colt only; rosewood grips; roll-engraved scene on cylinder; nickel-plated medallions; silver-plated finish, with blued frame, barrel, ejector rod tube and screw, hammer and trigger; originally cased in varnished walnut box with 12 dummy nickel-plated cartridges in cartridge block; burgundy velvet lining; 4750 made in 1964 only.

Issue Price: $225
Market Value: $1595

COLT COL. SAM COLT SESQUICENTENNIAL DELUXE

Same specs as Col. Sam Colt Sesquicentennial Presentation model except hand-fitted rosewood grips with escutcheons rather than medallions; hand-engraved cylinder; case has plate marked "1 of 200"; 200 made in 1964 only.

Issue Price: $500
Market Value: $2600

COLT COL. SAM COLT SESQUICENTENNIAL CUSTOM DELUXE

Same specs as Col. Sam Colt Sesquicentennial Deluxe except facsimile of Samuel Colt's signature engraved on backstrap; lid of case engraved with "1 of 50"; name of purchaser engraved when requested; 50 made in 1965.

Issue Price: $1000
Market Value: $4200

COLT GENERAL HOOD CENTENNIAL

Frontier Scout revolver; "1864—General Hood's Tennessee Campaign—1964" on left side of 4-3/4-inch barrel; 22 LR only; laminated rosewood grips, gold-plated medallions; gold-plated finish, except for blued trigger, hammer, base pin, ejector rod, rod head and screw and screws for base pin, hammer, trigger, backstrap and trigger guard; originally cased in blonde-finished wood box with green velvet/satin lining; 1503 made in 1964 only.

Issue Price: $75
Market Value: $650

COLT MONTANA TERRITORY CENTENNIAL

Frontier Scout revolver; "1864—Montana Territory Centennial—1964" on left side of barrel; "1889—Diamond Jubilee Statehood—1964" on right side; both markings wiped in gold; 4-3/4-inch barrel; 22 LR only; rosewood or pearlite grips; gold-plated medallions; gold-plated finish, except for blued barrel, frame, base pin screw, cylinder, ejector rod, rod tube, tube plug and tube screw, bolt, and trigger and hammer screws; originally cased in walnut-finished box with red velvet/satin lining; 2300 made in 1964 only.

Issue Price: $75
Market Value: $650

COLT MONTANA TERRITORY CENTENNIAL SINGLE ACTION ARMY

Same barrel markings as Frontier Scout version; 7-1/2-inch barrel, 45 Colt only; same grips, finish, except frame is color case-hardened; same casing as Frontier Scout; 851 made in 1964 only.

Issue Price: $150
Market Value: $1595

COLT NEVADA STATEHOOD CENTENNIAL

Frontier Scout revolver "1864—Nevada Centennial—1964" wiped in silver on left side of 4-3/4-inch barrel; 22 LR only; pearlite grips; nickel-plated medallions; nickel-plated finish, with blued barrel, frame, base pin screw, cylinder ejector rod, rod tube, tube plug and tube screw, hammer, bolt, trigger screws; originally cased in gray-finished wood with blue velvet-lined bottom, silver satin-lined lid; 3984 made in 1964 only.

Issue Price: $75
Market Value: $650

COLT NEVADA STATEHOOD CENTENNIAL SINGLE ACTION ARMY

Same legend on barrel as Frontier Scout; 5-1/2-inch barrel; 45 Colt only; grips, medallions, finish identical to Scout; same casing motif; 1688 made in 1964 only.

Issue Price: $150
Market Value: $1595

COLT NEVADA STATE CENTENNIAL FRONTIER SCOUT SINGLE ACTION ARMY SET

Includes the two handguns described above in oversized case; 189 standard sets were made, plus 577 sets featuring extra engraved cylinders; made in 1964 only.

Issue Price: $240
($350 with extra engraved cylinders).

Standard Set
Market Value: $1895

With extra engraved cylinders
Market Value: $1995

COLT NEVADA BATTLE BORN COMMEMORATIVE

Frontier Scout revolver; "1864—Nevada 'Battle Born'—1964" wiped in silver on left side of 4-3/4-inch barrel; 22 LR only; pearlite grips; nickel-plated medallions; nickel-plated, with blued frame, barrel, base pin screw, ejector rod, tube, tube plug and screw, bolt, trigger and hammer screws; cased in blue-finished wood box, with blue velvet/satin lining; 981 made in 1964 only.

Issue Price: $85
Market Value: $650

COLT NEVADA BATTLE BORN COMMEMORATIVE SINGLE ACTION ARMY

Same legend on barrel as Frontier Scout version; 5-1/2-inch barrel; 45 Colt only; same grips, finish, casing as Frontier Scout; 80 made in 1964 only.

Issue Price: $175
Market Value: $1595

COLT NEVADA BATTLE BORN COMMEMORATIVE FRONTIER SCOUT/SINGLE ACTION ARMY SET

Includes the two handguns previously described in oversize case; 20 sets were made in 1964 only.

Issue Price: $265
Market Value: $2695

COLT NEW JERSEY TERCENTENARY

Frontier Scout revolver; "1664—New Jersey Tercentenary—1964" on left side of barrel; 4-3/4-inch barrel; 22 LR only; laminated rosewood grips; nickel-plated medallions; blued finish, with nickel-plated barrel, frame, ejector rod tube, tube plug and screw; originally cased in blonde-finished box with blue velvet lining in bottom, silver satin in lid; 1001 made in 1964 only.

Issue Price: $75
Market Value: $650

COLT NEW JERSEY TERCENTENARY SINGLE ACTION ARMY

Same legend on barrel as Frontier Scout; 5-1/2-inch barrel; 45 Colt only; grips, medallions, finish the same as on Frontier Scout version; same casing; 250 made in 1964 only.

Issue Price: $150
Market Value: $1595

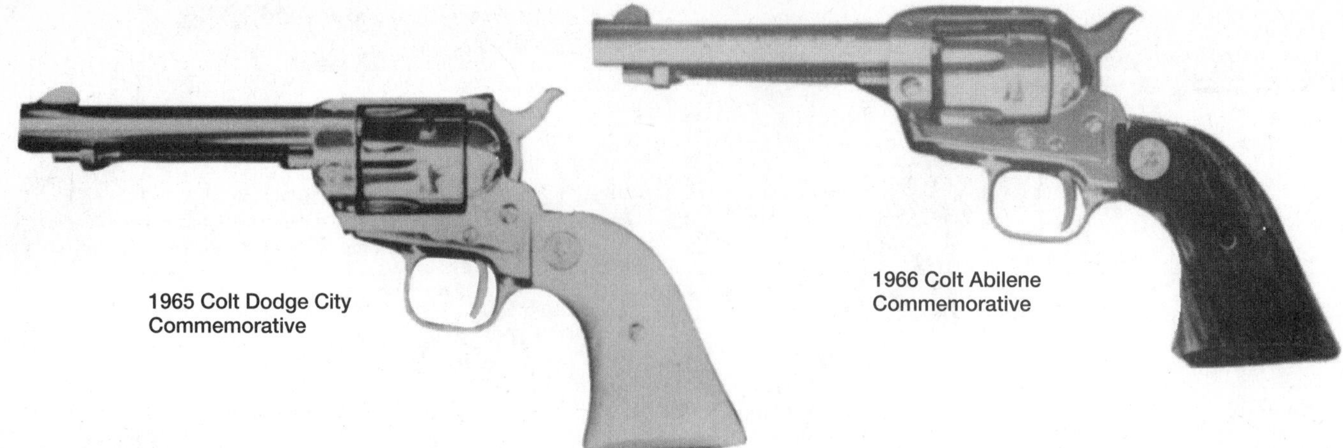

1966 Colt Abilene Commemorative

1965 Colt Dodge City Commemorative

COLT PONY EXPRESS PRESENTATION
Single Action Army revolver; "Russell, Majors and Waddell—Pony Express Presentation Model" on left side of barrel. Various Pony Express stop markings on backstrap; 7-1/2-inch barrel; 45 Colt; walnut grips; nickel-plated medallions; nickel-plated in entirety; originally cased in walnut-finished wood with transparent Lucite lid; lined with burgundy velvet; 1004 made in 1964 only.
Issue Price: $250
Market Value: $1595

COLT ST. LOUIS BICENTENNIAL
Frontier Scout revolver; "1764—St. Louis Bicentennial—1964" wiped in gold on left side of 4-3/4-inch barrel; 22 LR only; laminated rosewood grips; gold-plated medallions; gold-plated, except for blued frame, barrel, cylinder, ejector rod, rod tube, tube plug and screw; non-fluted cylinder: originally cased in blonde-finished wood box; yellow velvet/satin lining; 802 made in 1964 only.
Issue Price: $75
Market Value: $650

COLT ST. LOUIS BICENTENNIAL SINGLE ACTION ARMY
Same legend on barrel as Frontier Scout version; 5-1/2-inch barrel; 45 Colt only; same grips, medallions, finish, casing as Scout version; 200 made in 1964 only.
Issue Price: $150
Market Value: $1595

COLT ST. LOUIS BICENTENNIAL FRONTIER SCOUT/SINGLE ACTION ARMY SET
Includes the two handguns described above in oversize case; 200 sets made in 1964 only.
Issue Price: $240
Market Value: $1995

COLT WICHITA COMMEMORATIVE
Frontier Scout revolver; "1864—Kansas Series-Wichita—1964" wiped in silver on left side of 4-3/4-inch barrel; 22 LR only; pearlite grips; gold-plated medallions; gold-plated in entirety; originally cased in blonde-finished wood; lined with red velvet/satin; 500 made in 1964 only.
Issue Price: $85
Market Value: $650

COLT WYATT EARP BUNTLINE
Single Action Army revolver; "Wyatt Earp Buntline Special" on left side of 12-inch barrel; 45 Colt only; laminated black rosewood grips; gold-plated medallions; gold-plated in entirety; originally cased in black-finished wood, lined with green velvet/satin; 150 made only in 1964.
Issue Price: $250
Market Value: $2850

COLT WYOMING DIAMOND JUBILEE
Frontier Scout revolver "1890—Wyoming Diamond Jubilee—1965" on left side of barrel; 4-3/4-inch barrel; 22 LR only; rosewood grips, nickel-plated medallions; nickel-plated finish, except for blued barrel, frame, ejector rod, rod tube, tube plug and plug screw; cased in blond-finished box, with blue velvet bottom lining, silver satin-lined lid; 2357 made in 1964 only.
Issue Price: $75
Market Value: $650

ITHACA MODEL 48 ST. LOUIS BICENTENNIAL
Lever-action; single shot; hand-operated rebounding hammer; 22 LR, 22 Long, 22 Short; 18-inch barrel; Western carbine-style straight stock; open rear sight, ramp front. Only 200 manufactured in 1964.
Issue Price: $34.95
Market Value: $295

REMINGTON MONTANA CENTENNIAL
Model 600 carbine; bolt action; 6mm Rem. only; deviates from standard Model 600 specs only in better walnut; commemorative medallion inlaid into the stock; barrel inscription reads, "1889-1964/75th Anniversary"; 1000 made in 1964 only.
Issue Price: $124.95
Market Value: $595

WINCHESTER WYOMING DIAMOND JUBILEE COMMEMORATIVE
Model 94 carbine; 30-30 only; 1500 made, distributed exclusively by Billings Hardware Co.; same as standard M94, except for color case-hardened, engraved receiver, commemorative inscription on barrel; brass saddle ring, loading gate; state medallion embedded in stock; made only in 1964.
Issue Price: $100
Market Value: $1495

1965

COLT APPOMATTOX CENTENNIAL
Frontier Scout revolver; "1865—Appomattox Commemorative Model—1965" wiped in silver on left side of 4-3/4-inch barrel; 22 LR only; laminated rosewood grips; nickel-plated medallions; nickel-plated finish, with blued barrel, frame, backstrap and trigger guard screws, ejector rod tube, tube plug and tube screw; originally cased in blonde-finished wood lined with blue velvet on bottom, gray satin in lid; 1001 made in 1965 only.
Issue Price: $75
Market Value: $650

COLT APPOMATTOX CENTENNIAL FRONTIER SINGLE ACTION ARMY
Same legend on 5-1/2-inch barrel; 45 Colt only; grips, finish, casing the same as for Frontier Scout version; 250 made in 1965.
Issue Price: $150
Market Value: $1595

COLT APPOMATTOX CENTENNIAL FRONTIER SCOUT/SINGLE ACTION ARMY COMBO
Same specs as the two revolvers described above in one oversize case; 250 sets made in 1965 only.
Issue Price: $240
Market Value: $1995

COLT COLORADO GOLD RUSH COMMEMORATIVE
Frontier Scout revolver; "1858—Colorado Gold Rush—1878" wiped in silver on left side of 4-3/4-inch barrel; 22 LR only; laminated rosewood grips; nickel-plated medallions; gold-plated finish, with nickel-plated hammer, base pin and screw, ejector rod head, hammer and trigger screws, trigger, grip screw; originally cased in blonde-finished wood; black velvet/satin lining; 1350 made in 1965 only.
Issue Price: $85
Market Value: $675

COLT DODGE CITY COMMEMORATIVE
Frontier Scout revolver; "1864—Kansas Series-Dodge City—1964" wiped in silver on left side of 4-3/4-inch barrel; 22 LR only; ivorylite grips; gold-plated medallions; gold-plated finish, with blued base pin and screw, ejector rod, ejector rod head, bolt and trigger screw, hammer and hammer screw, trigger; originally cased in blonde-finished wood; lined with kelly green velvet/satin; 500 made in 1965 only.
Issue Price: $85
Market Value: $650

COLT FORTY-NINER MINER
Frontier Scout revolver: "The '49er Miner" wiped in gold on left side of 4-3/4-inch barrel; 22 LR only; laminated rosewood grips; gold-plated medallions; gold-plated finish with blued barrel, frame, backstrap and trigger guard assembly, ejector rod, tube and tube plug, ejector tube screw; originally cased in walnut-finished wood; lined with velvet in bottom, blue satin in lid; 500 made only in 1965.
Issue Price: $85
Market Value: $650

COLT GENERAL MEADE CAMPAIGN COMMEMORATIVE
Frontier Scout revolver; "Gen. Meade Pennsylvania Campaign Model" wiped in gold on left side of 4-3/4-inch barrel; 22 LR only; ivorylite grips, gold-plated medallions; gold-plated finish; blued frame, barrel, cylinder, ejector rod tube, tube plug and screw, hammer and trigger screws; originally cased in walnut-finished wood; blue velvet lining in bottom, gold satin in lid; 1197 made in 1965 only.
Issue Price: $75
Market Value: $650

COLT GENERAL MEADE CAMPAIGN SINGLE ACTION ARMY REVOLVER
Same legend on the 5-1/2-inch barrel; 45 Colt only; same finish, casing as Frontier Scout version; 200 made in 1965 only.
Issue Price: $165
Market Value: $1695

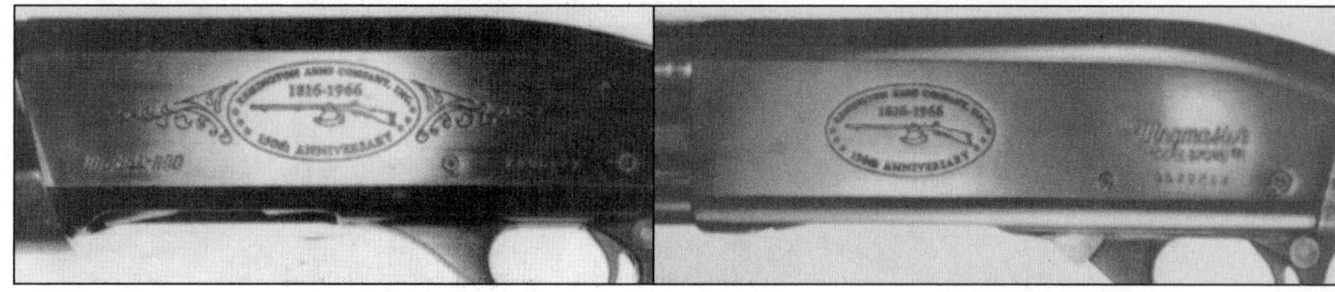

1966 Remington 150th Anniversary Model 1100SA

1966 Remington 150th Anniversary Model 870 SA

COLT OLD FORT DES MOINES RECONSTRUCTION COMMEMORATIVE

Frontier Scout revolver; "Reconstruction of Old Fort Des Moines" wiped in silver on left side of 4-3/4-inch barrel; 22 LR only; pearlite grips; gold-plated medallions; gold-plated in entirety; originally cased in white-finished wood; royal purple velvet lining in bottom; white satin in lid; 700 made in 1965 only.
Issue Price: $89.95
Market Value: $675

COLT OLD FORT DES MOINES RECONSTRUCTION SINGLE ACTION ARMY

Same legend on 5-1/2-inch barrel; 45 Colt only; grips, finish the same as on Frontier Scout version; same casing; 100 made in 1965 only.
Issue Price: $169.95
Market Value: $1695

COLT OLD FORT DES MOINES FRONTIER SCOUT/SINGLE ACTION ARMY COMBO

Same specs as the two revolvers described above, in one oversize case; 100 sets made in 1965 only.
Issue Price: $289.95
Market Value: $2195

COLT OREGON TRAIL COMMEMORATIVE

Frontier Scout revolver; "Oregon Trail Model," wiped in gold, on left side of 4-3/4-inch barrel; 22 LR only; pearlite grips; gold-plated medallions; blued finish with gold-plated backstrap and trigger guard assembly and screws, hammer, trigger and screws, base pin, base pin screw and ejector rod head; originally cased in blonde-finished wood; lined with blue velvet in bottom, gold satin in lid; 1995 made only in 1965.
Issue Price: $75
Market Value: $650

COLT JOAQUIN MURRIETTA 1 OF 100

Frontier Scout/Single Action Army combo; both have "Joaquin Murrietta 1 of 100" on left side of barrels; Scout has 4-3/4-inch barrel, 22 LR only; SAA has 5-1/2-inch barrel, 45 Colt only; grips on both are pearlite, with gold-plated medallions; finish for both is gold-plated with blued barrels, frames, ejector rod tubes; originally in one oversize case of walnut-finished wood; blue velvet/satin lining; 100 sets made in 1965 only.
Issue Price: $350
Market Value: $1995

COLT ST. AUGUSTINE QUADRICENTENNIAL

Frontier Scout revolver; "1565—St. Augustine Quadricentennial—1965" wiped in gold on left side of 4-3/4-inch barrel; 22 LR only; pearlite grips; gold-plated medallions; gold-plated finish, with blued barrel, base pin, ejector rod, tube, tube plug and screw, frame, hammer and trigger screws, backstrap and trigger guard assembly and screws; cased in blonde-finished wood; gold velvet/satin lining; 500 made in 1965 only.
Issue Price: $85
Market Value: $675

1966

COLT ABERCROMBIE & FITCH TRAILBLAZER

New Frontier Single Action Army revolver: "Abercrombie & Fitch Co." wiped in gold on left side of 7-1/2-inch barrel; 45 Colt only; rosewood grips; gold-plated medallions; gold-plated finish, blued barrel, cylinder, hammer, sights, ejector rod tube, ejector rod screw, case-hardened frame; roll-engraved, nonfluted cylinder; originally cased in varnished American walnut with brass-framed glass cover; bottom lined with crushed blue velvet; 200 made in 1966 with "New York" marked on butt, 100 with "Chicago" butt marking; 200 with "San Francisco" butt marking.
Issue Price: $275
Market Value: $1495

COLT ABILENE COMMEMORATIVE

Frontier Scout revolver; "1866—Kansas Series Abilene—1966" wiped in silver on left side of 4-3/4-inch barrel; 22 LR only; laminated rosewood grips; gold-plated medallions; gold-plated in entirety; originally cased in blonde-finished wood; blue velvet/satin lining; 500 made in 1966 only.
Issue Price: $95
Market Value: $650

COLT DAKOTA TERRITORY COMMEMORATIVE

Frontier Scout revolver; "1861—Dakota Territory—1889" wiped in gold on left side of 4-3/4-inch barrel; 22 LR only; laminated rosewood grips; gold-plated medallions; blued finish with gold-plated backstrap and trigger guard assembly and screws, ejector rod and head, base pin, trigger, hammer, stock screw; originally cased in blonde-finished wood; red velvet/satin lining; 1000 made in 1966 only.
Issue Price: $85
Market Value: $650

COLT INDIANA SESQUICENTENNIAL

Frontier Scout revolver; "1816—Indiana Sesquicentennial—1966" wiped in gold on left side of 4-3/4-inch barrel; 22 LR only; pearlite grips; gold-plated medallions; blued finish, with gold-plated backstrap and trigger guard assembly, base pin and screw, ejector rod head, cylinder, bolt and trigger screw, hammer and hammer screw, trigger, stock screw; originally cased in blonde-finished wood; bottom lined with gold velvet, lid with blue satin; 1500 made in 1966 only.
Issue Price: $85
Market Value: $650

COLT OKLAHOMA TERRITORY COMMEMORATIVE

Frontier Scout revolver; "1890—Oklahoma Diamond Jubilee—1965" wiped in gold on left side of 4-3/4-inch barrel; 22 LR only; laminated rosewood grips; gold-plated medallions; blued finish with gold-plated backstrap and trigger guard assembly and screws, cylinder, ejector rod head, base pin and screw, bolt and trigger; cased in blonde-finished wood; red velvet/satin lining; 1343 made only in 1966.
Issue Price: $85
Market Value: $650

REMINGTON 150TH ANNIVERSARY MODEL 552A

Semi-automatic rifle; 22 LR, 22 Long, 22 Short; same specs as standard Model 552 except stamp-engraved legend on left side of receiver: "Remington Arms Company Inc., 1816-1966, 150th Anniversary," with corporate logo; 1000 made in 1966 only.
Issue Price: $58
Market Value: $475

REMINGTON 150TH ANNIVERSARY MODEL 572A

Slide-action rifle; 22 Short, 22 Long, 22 LR; same specs as standard model 572 except stamp-engraved legend on left side of receiver; "Remington Arms Company, Inc., 1816-1966, 150th Anniversary," with corporate logo; 1000 made in 1966 only.
Issue Price: $60
Market Value: $475

REMINGTON 150TH ANNIVERSARY MODEL 742 ADL

Semi-automatic rifle; 30-06 only; impressed basketweave checkering; has same specs as standard 742 ADL, except for stamp-engraved legend on left side of receiver; "Remington Arms Company Inc., 1816-1966, 150th Anniversary" with corporate logo; 1000 made in 1966 only.
Issue Price: $150
Market Value: $500

REMINGTON 150TH ANNIVERSARY MODEL 760 ADL

Pump-action rifle; 30-06 only; same specs as standard 760 BDL Deluxe model except stamp-engraved legend on left side of receiver: "Remington Arms Company Inc., 1816-1966, 150th Anniversary," with corporate logo; 1000 made in 1966 only.
Issue Price: $135
Market Value: $595

REMINGTON 150TH ANNIVERSARY MODEL 870 SA

Slide-action Skeet gun; 12-ga. only; 26-inch barrel; vent rib; specs the same as standard Model 870, except for stamp-engraved legend on left side of receiver: "Remington Arms Company, Inc., 1816-1966, 150th Anniversary" with corporate logo; 1000 made in 1966 only.
Issue Price: $130
Market Value: $550

REMINGTON 150TH ANNIVERSARY MODEL 870 TB

Same specs as Remington 150th Anniversary Model 870 SA except recoil pad; 30-inch barrel; trap stock; same stamp-engraved legend on receiver; 1000 made in 1966 only.
Issue Price: $165
Market Value: $700

REMINGTON 150TH ANNIVERSARY MODEL 1100 SA

Semi-automatic Skeet shotgun; 12-ga. only; 26-inch barrel; vent rib; specs the same as standard Model 1100, except for stamp-engraved legend on left side of receiver: "Remington Arms Company, Inc., 1816-1966, 150th Anniversary" with corporate logo; 1000 made in 1966 only.
Issue Price: $185
Market Value: $700

1966 Winchester Centennial '66 Commemorative 20-inch Barrel

1966 Winchester Centennial '66 Commemorative 26-inch Barrel

REMINGTON 150TH ANNIVERSARY MODEL 1100 TB

Same specs as Remington 150th Anniversary Model 1100 SA except recoil pad; 30-inch barrel; trap stock; same stamp-engraved legend on receiver; 1000 made in 1966 only.
Issue Price: $220
Market Value: $750

REMINGTON 150TH ANNIVERSARY NYLON 66

Semi-automatic; 22 LR; same specs as standard Nylon 66 Apache Black model except stamp-engraved legend on left side of receiver "Remington Arms Company Inc., 1816-1966, 150th Anniversary," with corporate logo; 1000 made in 1966 only.
Issue Price: $50
Market Value: $495

WINCHESTER NEBRASKA CENTENNIAL COMMEMORATIVE

Model 94 carbine; 30-30 only; same as standard M94 except gold-plated loading gate, buttplate, rear barrel band, hammer; commemorative inscription on barrel, medallion in stock; only 2500 made and distributed only in Nebraska; made only in 1966.
Issue Price: $100
Market Value: $1395

WINCHESTER CENTENNIAL '66 COMMEMORATIVE

Model 94; rifle and carbine versions commemorate Winchester's 100th anniversary; produced in 1966 only; 100,478 were made; 30-30 only; rifle version with 26-inch half-octagon barrel; full-length 8-shot magazine; gold-plated forearm cap, receiver; post front sight, open rear; walnut stock forearm with epoxy finish; saddle ring; brass buttplate; commemorative inscription on barrel and top tang. Carbine differs only in shorter forearm; 20-inch barrel; 6-shot magazine.
Issue Price: $125

RIFLE, CARBINE

Market Value: $1206

MATCHED SET WITH CONSECUTIVE SERIAL NUMBERS

Market Value: $2400

1967

COLT ALAMO COMMEMORATIVE

Frontier Scout revolver; "Alamo Model," flanked by stars, wiped in gold on left side of 4-3/4-inch barrel; 22 LR only; ivorylite grips, with inlaid gold-plated Texas star below screw on left grip. Gold-plated finish; blued barrel, frame, ejector rod tube, tube plug and screw; originally cased in blonde-finished wood box; blue velvet/satin lining; 4250 made in 1967 only.
Issue Price: $85
Market Value: $650

COLT ALAMO COMMEMORATIVE SINGLE ACTION ARMY

Same legend on barrel; same grips, finish, but with blued barrel, frame and ejector rod tube and tube screw; same casing; 750 made in 1967 only.
Issue Price: $165
Market Value: $1595

COLT ALAMO COMMEMORATIVE FRONTIER SCOUT/SINGLE ACTION ARMY COMBO

Includes two revolvers described above in one oversize case; 250 sets made in 1967 only.
Issue Price: $265
Market Value: $1995

COLT BAT MASTERSON

Frontier Scout revolver; "Lawman Series—Bat Masterson" on left side of 4-3/4-inch barrel; 22 LR only; checkered rubber eagle grips; nickel-plated finish; cased originally in black leatherette; red velvet/satin lining; 3000 made in 1967 only.
Issue Price: $90
Market Value: $675

COLT BAT MASTERSON SINGLE ACTION ARMY

Same legend on 4-3/4-inch barrel; 45 Colt only; grips, finish, casing are the same as for Frontier Scout version; 500 made in 1967 only.
Issue Price: $180
Market Value: $1600

COLT CHATEAU THIERRY COMMEMORATIVE

Semi-automatic; Model 1911 A1; "1917 World War I Commemorative 1967" on right side of slide; roll-engraved scene on left depicting WWI battle; 5-inch barrel; 45 auto; checkered walnut grips; inlaid commemorative medallions; left grip inlaid with Chateau Thierry battle bar; blued finish with slide scene, serial number, banner, Colt markings wiped in gold; several features including no trigger finger relief cuts, non-grooved trigger, safety lever, adapted from original M1911 design; Standard model cased in olive drab box; Deluxe and Custom models have oiled, waxed teak cases; Deluxe model case inscribed "One of Seventy-Five/Deluxe Engraved/Chateau Thierry Commemoratives"; Custom model case inscribed "One of Twenty-Five/Custom Engraved/Chateau Thierry Commemoratives"; gun bears gold-filled signature of A.A White, engraver; 7400 Standard versions made in 1967-68, 75 Deluxe, 25 Custom.
Issue Price: Standard, $200; Deluxe, $500; Custom, $1000

Standard
Market Value: $995

Deluxe
Market Value: $1450

Custom
Market Value: $2850

COLT CHISHOLM TRAIL COMMEMORATIVE

Frontier Scout revolver; "1867—Kansas Series—Chisholm Trail—1967" wiped with silver on left side of 4-3/4-inch barrel; 22 LR; pearlite grips; nickel-plated medallions; blued finish, with nickel-plated backstrap and trigger guard assembly and screws, trigger, hammer base pin, ejector rod head, stock screw; originally cased in blonde-finished wood, gold velvet/satin lining; 500 made in 1967 only.
Issue Price: $100
Market Value: $650

COLT COFFEYVILLE COMMEMORATIVE

Frontier Scout revolver; "1866—Kansas Series—Coffeyville—1966" wiped in silver on left side of 4-3/4-inch barrel; 22 LR only; walnut grips; gold-plated medallions; gold-plated finish; blued backstrap and trigger guard assembly screws, base pin and screw, ejector rod, ejector rod head, hammer and hammer screw, trigger; originally cased in blonde-finished wood; black velvet/satin lining; 500 made in 1967 only.
Issue Price: $95
Market Value: $650

REMINGTON CANADIAN CENTENNIAL

Model 742 rifle; semi-automatic; 30-06 only; same as standard model except impressed checkering on pistol grip; left side of receiver is engraved with maple leaves, special insignia, "1867-1967—Canadian Centennial Gun," wiped in white; serial number is preceded by letter C; 1000 made in 1967 only.
Issue Price: $119.95
Market Value: $495

RUGER CANADIAN CENTENNIAL 10/22

Standard model of 22 rimfire rifle with silver commemorative medal set in the stock; top of the receiver is engraved with a design composed of the Canadian Exposition symbol, branches of the Canadian maple leaf and the words, "Canadian Centennial Guns." Issued in 1967; 4430 made.
Issue Price: $99.50
Market Value: $550

WINCHESTER ALASKAN PURCHASE CENTENNIAL

Model 94 rifle; sold only in Alaska; receiver engraved in 19th Century filigree for "antique" appeal; centered in stock is the official Alaskan Purchase centennial medallion with totem pole symbol of the state; barrel is 26-inch, with magazine capacity of 8 shots; other facets are standard of Model 94. Introduced, 1967.
Issue Price: $125
Market Value: $1695

WINCHESTER CANADIAN CENTENNIAL

Model 64; action obviously is the Model 94; not to be confused with Winchester's Model 64 boy's rifle discontinued in 1963. Canadian commemorative is in 30-30 caliber; octagonal 26-inch rifle or 20-inch carbine barrel; black-chromed receiver engraved with maple leaf motif; forearm tip black-chromed; straight stock finished with "antique gloss." Both versions have a dovetail bead post front sight, buckhorn rear. Carbine comes with saddle ring; 6-shot magazine; the rifle comes with 8-shot magazine. Gold-filled inscription on barrel reads, "Canadian Centennial 1867-1967." Introduced in 1967.
Issue Price: Rifle or Carbine, $125; Matching Set with consecutive serial numbers, $275

Rifle
Market Value: $1095

Carbine
Market Value: $1075

Matched Set
Market Value: $1950

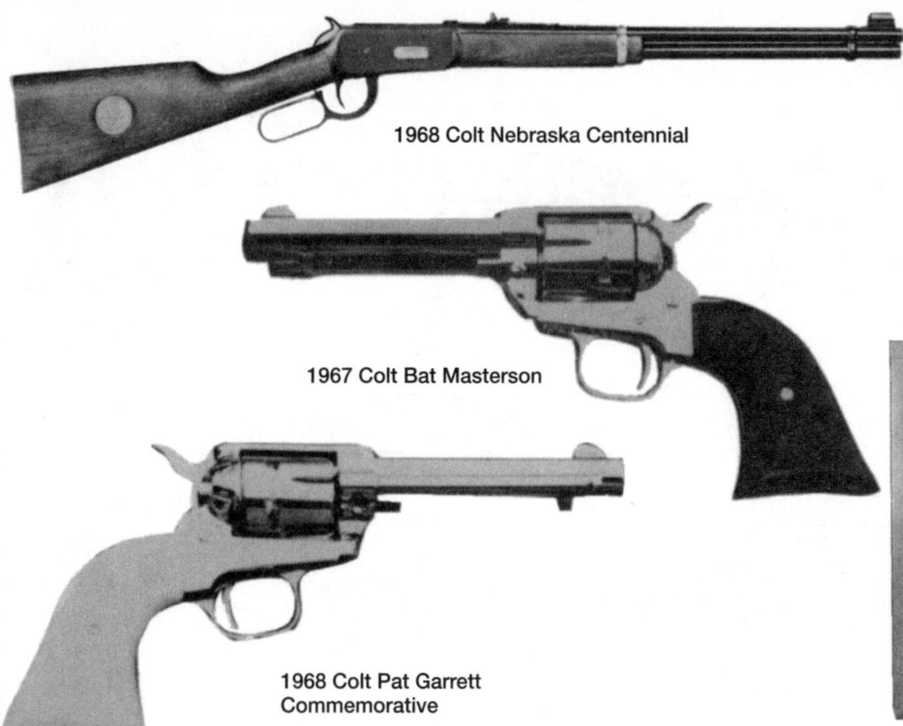

1968 Colt Nebraska Centennial

1967 Colt Bat Masterson

1968 Colt Pat Garrett Commemorative

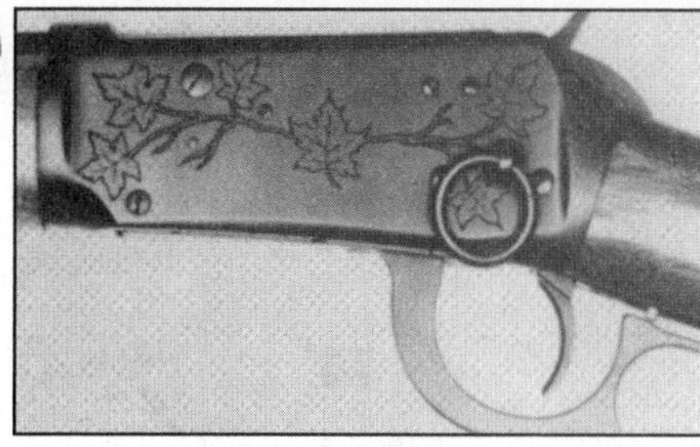

1967 Winchester Canadian Centennial

1968 Colt Belleau Wood Commemorative

1968

COLT BELLEAU WOOD COMMEMORATIVE

Semi-automatic; Model 1911 A1; "1917 World War I Commemorative 1967" on right side of slide; roll engraved scene on left side of machine gun battle; 5-inch barrel; 45 Auto only; rosewood grips inlaid with commemorative medallions; left grip inlaid with Belleau Wood battle bar; blued finish; slide scene, serial number, banner, Colt markings wiped in gold on Standard model; Deluxe version has slide, frame hand engraved, serial numbers gold-inlaid; Custom has more elaborate engraving; the same features of 1911 model adapted to Chateau Thierry model are incorporated; cases are same as Chateau Thierry model, with brass plate for Deluxe engraved "One of Seventy Five/Deluxe Engraved/Belleau Wood Commemorative"; plate on Custom model reads "One of Twenty-Five/Custom Engraved/Belleau Wood Commemoratives"; production began in 1968, with 7400 Standard types, 75 Deluxe, 25 Custom.
Issue Price: Standard, $200; Deluxe, $500; Custom, $1000.

Standard
Market Value: $895

Deluxe
Market Value: $1450

Custom
Market Value: $2850

COLT GEN. NATHAN BEDFORD FORREST

Frontier Scout revolver; "General Nathan Bedford Forrest" on left side of 4-3/4-inch barrel; 22 LR only; laminated rosewood grips; gold-plated medallions; gold-plated finish; blued cylinder, backstrap and trigger guard assembly; originally cased in dark brown leatherette; red velvet/satin lining; 3000 made in 1968-69.
Issue Price: $110
Market Value: $650

COLT NEBRASKA CENTENNIAL

Frontier Scout revolver; "1867—Nebraska Centennial—1967" on left side of 4-3/4-inch barrel; 22 LR; pearlite grips; gold-plated barrel, frame, hammer, trigger, ejector rod head, stock screw; originally cased in blonde-finished wood; lined with blue velvet in bottom, gold satin in lid; 7001 made in 1968 only.
Issue Price: $100
Market Value: $625

COLT PAT GARRETT COMMEMORATIVE

Frontier Scout revolver; "Lawman Series Pat Garrett" on right side of 4-3/4-inch barrel; 22 LR only; pearlite grips; gold-plated medallions; gold-plated finish; nickel-plated barrel, frame, backstrap and trigger guard assembly, ejector rod; loading gate is gold-plated; originally cased in black leatherette with gold velvet/satin lining; 3000 made in 1968 only.
Issue Price: $110
Market Value: $475

COLT PAT GARRETT SINGLE ACTION ARMY REVOLVER

Same barrel legend; 5-1/2-inch barrel; 45 Colt only; same grips, finish, casing as Frontier Scout version; 500 made in 1968.
Issue Price: $200
Market Value: $1595

COLT PAWNEE TRAIL COMMEMORATIVE

Frontier Scout revolver; "1868-Kansas Series—Pawnee Trail—1968" wiped in silver on left side of 4-3/4-inch barrel; 22 LR; laminated rosewood grips; nickel-plated medallions; blued finish; nickel-plated backstrap and trigger guard assembly and screws, cylinder, base pin, ejector rod head, trigger hammer, stock screw; originally cased in blonde-finished wood; lined with blue velvet in bottom, silver satin in lid; 501 made in 1968.
Issue Price: $110
Market Value: $650

COLT SANTA FE TRAIL COMMEMORATIVE

Frontier Scout revolver; "Kansas Series—Santa Fe Trail—1968" wiped in silver on left side of 4-3/4-inch barrel; 22 LR; ivorylite grips; nickel-plated medallions; blued finish with nickel-plated backstrap and trigger guard assembly and screws, hammer, trigger, stock screw, base pin, ejector rod head; originally cased in blonde-finished wood; green velvet/satin lining; 501 made in 1968-69.
Issue Price: $120
Market Value: $650

FRANCHI CENTENNIAL

Semi-automatic take-down rifle; 22 LR only; commemorates 1868-1968 centennial of S.A. Luigi Franchi; centennial seal engraved on receiver; 21-inch barrel; 11-shot buttstock magazine; hand-checkered European walnut stock forearm; open rear sight, gold bead front on ramp. Deluxe model has better grade wood, fully engraved receiver. Made only in 1968.
Issue Price: Standard, $86.95; Deluxe, $124.95.

Standard
Market Value: $425 to $450

Deluxe
Market Value: $550 to $575

WINCHESTER BUFFALO BILL COMMEMORATIVE

Model 94; available with either 20-inch or 26-inch barrel, both with bead post front sights, semi-buckhorn rear sights. Hammer, trigger, loading gate, forearm tip, saddle ring, crescent buttplate nickel-plated. Barrel, tang inscribed respectively, "Buffalo Bill Commemorative" and "W.F. Cody—Chief of Scouts." Receiver embellished with scrollwork. American walnut stock with embedded Buffalo Bill Memorial Assn. medallion; rifle with 8-shot tubular magazine, carbine with 6-shot magazine. Introduced, 1968.
Issue Price: Rifle, Carbine, $129.95 Rifle marked "1 of 300", $1000

Rifle
Market Value: $1200

Rifle marked "1 of 300"
Market Value: $2750

Carbine
Market Value: $1200

WINCHESTER ILLINOIS SESQUICENTENNIAL

Model 94; "Land of Lincoln," and a profile of Lincoln engraved on the receiver, with gold-filled inscription on barrel, "Illinois Sesquicentennial, 1818-1968"; gold-plated metal buttplate, trigger, loading gate and saddle ring. Official souvenir medallion embedded in walnut stock. First state commemorative to be sold outside the celebrating state by Winchester. Introduced in 1968.
Issue Price: $110
Market Value: $1495

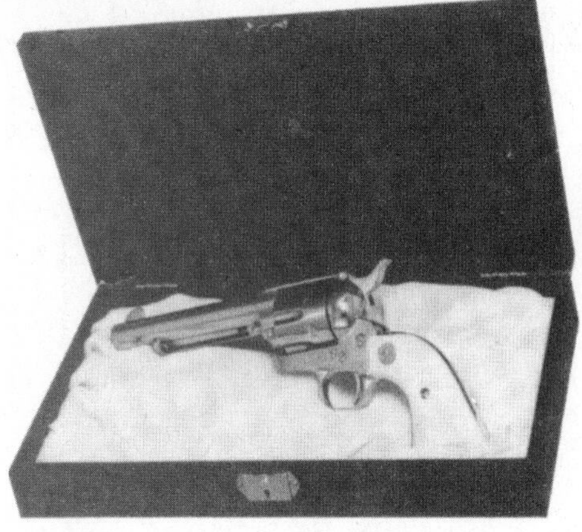

1969 Colt Alabama Sesquicentennial

1969 Colt Second Battle of the Marne Commemorative

1969 Colt Meuse Argonne Commemorative

1969

COLT ALABAMA SESQUICENTENNIAL

Frontier Scout revolver; "1819—Alabama Sesquicentennial—1969" on left side of 4-3/4-inch barrel; 22 LR only; ivorylite grips; gold-plated medallions; gold-plated finish; nickel-plated loading gate, cylinder, ejector rod, rod head, and tube, base pin and screw, bolt and trigger guard assembly screws, hammer and screw, trigger; originally cased in red leatherette covered wood box; white velvet lining in bottom, red satin in lid; 3001 made in 1969.
Issue Price: $110
Market Value: $650

COLT ARKANSAS TERRITORIAL SESQUICENTENNIAL

Frontier Scout revolver; "1819—Arkansas Territory Sesquicentennial—1969" on left side of 4-3/4-inch barrel; 22 LR only; laminated rosewood grips; gold-plated medallions; blued frame, backstrap and trigger guard assembly, ejector rod head; gold-plated stock screw nut; originally cased in blonde-finished basswood; red velvet/satin lining; 3500 made; production began in 1969.
Issue Price: $110
Market Value: $650

COLT CALIFORNIA BICENTENNIAL

Frontier Scout revolver; "1769—California Bicentennial—1969" on left side of 6-inch barrel; 22 LR only; laminated rosewood grips; gold-plated medallions; gold-plated finish; all screws nickel-plated, except base pin, grip screws; hammer, trigger also nickel-plated; originally cased in California redwood; black velvet/satin lining; 5000 made in 1969-70.
Issue Price: $135
Market Value: $650

COLT FORT LARNED COMMEMORATIVE

Frontier Scout revolver; "1869—Kansas Series-Fort Larned—1969" on left side of 4-3/4-inch barrel; 22 LR; pearlite grips; nickel-plated medallions; nickel-plated finish; blued backstrap and trigger guard assembly, base pin and screw, cylinder, ejector rod head and tube screw, hammer and stock screw, bolt and trigger screw; originally cased in blonde finished wood; blue velvet lining in bottom; silver satin in lid; 500 made in 1969-70.
Issue Price: $120
Market Value: $650

COLT GOLDEN SPIKE

Frontier Scout revolver; "1869—Golden Spike—1969" on right side of 6-inch barrel; standard barrel markings on left; both wiped in gold; 22 LR only; sand-blasted walnut-stained fir grips; gold-plated medallions; gold-plated finish; blued barrel, frame, backstrap and trigger guard assembly and ejector tube plug and screw; originally cased in hand-stained, embossed simulated mahogany; 11,000 made in 1969.
Issue Price: $135
Market Value: $650

COLT WILD BILL HICKOK COMMEMORATIVE

Frontier Scout revolver; "Lawman Series—Wild Bill Hickok" wiped in silver on right side of 6-inch barrel; 22 LR only; nonfluted cylinder; pearlite grips; nickel-plated medallions; nickel-plated finish; blued barrel, frame, ejector tube screw; originally cased in black leatherette covered box; bottom lined in blue velvet, lid in silver satin; 3000 made, production began in 1969.
Issue Price: $116.60
Market Value: $675

COLT WILD BILL HICKOK COMMEMORATIVE SINGLE ACTION ARMY

Same legend on 7-1/2-inch barrel; 45 Colt only; same finish as Frontier Scout version, except for nickel-plated loading gate; same casing; 500 made, production beginning in 1969.
Issue Price: $220
Market Value: $1695

COLT MEUSE ARGONNE COMMEMORATIVE

Semi-automatic; Model 1911A1; "1917 World War I Commemorative 1967" on right side of slide; left has roll-engraved charge on pillbox on Standard; slides, frames on Deluxe, Custom models are hand engraved, serial numbers inlaid in gold; Custom model is more elaborately engraved, inlaid; 5-inch barrel, 45 Auto only; varnished crotch walnut grips; inlaid commemorative medallions left grip inlaid with Meuse Argonne battle bar; blued finish; engraving, numbers et. al., gold wiped on Standard model; same case as earlier WWI Commemoratives; brass plate for Deluxe reads "One of Seventy-Five/ Deluxe Engraved/Meuse Argonne Commemoratives"; plate on Custom case is inscribed "One of Seventy Five/Custom Engraved/Meuse Argonne Commemoratives"; production began in 1969; 7400 Standard, 75 Deluxe, 25 Custom.
Issue Price: Standard, $220; Deluxe, $500; Custom, $1000

Standard
Market Value: $495

Deluxe
Market Value: $1550

Custom
Market Value: $2950

COLT SECOND BATTLE OF THE MARNE COMMEMORATIVE

Semi-automatic; Model 1911A1; "1917 World War I Commemorative 1967" on right side of slide; roll-engraved combat scene on left side of slide; 5-inch barrel; 45 Auto; white French holly grips; inlaid commemorative medallions; left grip inlaid with 2nd Battle of the Marne battle bar; blue finish, with slide engraving, serial number on Standard, banner, other markings wiped in gold; Deluxe and Custom models are hand engraved, with serial numbers gold inlaid; work on Custom model is in greater detail; cases are same as others in series, except Deluxe case has brass plate inscribed "One of Seventy-Five/Deluxe Engraved/2nd Battle of the Marne Commemorative"; Custom case has same type of plate inscribed "One of Twenty-Five/Custom Engraved/2nd Battle of the Marne Commemorative"; 7400 Standard guns made in 1969; 75 Deluxe; 25 Custom.
Issue Price: Standard, $220; Deluxe, $500; Custom, $1000

Standard
Market Value: $995

Deluxe
Market Value: $1550

Custom
Market Value: $2950

COLT SHAWNEE TRAIL COMMEMORATIVE

Frontier Scout revolver; "1869—Kansas Series—Shawnee Trail 1969" wiped in silver on left side of 4-3/4-inch barrel; 22 LR only; laminated rosewood grips; nickel-plated medallions; blued finish; nickel-plated backstrap and trigger guard assembly and screws, cylinder, base pin, ejector rod head, hammer, trigger and stock screw; originally cased in blonde-finished wood; red velvet/satin lining; 501 made in 1969 only.
Issue Price: $120
Market Value: $650

COLT TEXAS RANGER COMMEMORATIVE

Single Action Army revolver; "Texas Ranger Commemoratives/One Riot-One Ranger" wiped in silver on left side of barrel; "Texas Rangers" roll engraved on backstrap; sterling silver star, wreath on top of backstrap behind hammer; YO Ranch brand stamped on bottom of backstrap; 7-1/2-inch barrel; 45 Colt only; Standard model has rosewood grips, silver miniature Ranger badge inlaid in left grip; blued finish; case-hardened frame; nickel-plated trigger guard, base pin and screw, ejector rod and head, ejector tube screw; gold-plated stock screw, stock escutcheons, medallions. First 200 are custom models, with finish decoration to customer's desires at increasing prices; custom finished guns had deluxe engraved serial numbers, ivory grips with star inlay; originally cased in special hand-rubbed box with drawers, glass top; red velvet lining; 200 Custom, 800 Standard guns made; production began in 1969.
Issue Price: Custom, varying with customers desires; Standard, $650

Standard
Market Value: $2450

Grade III
Market Value: $5200

Grade II
Market Value: $5700

Grade I
Market Value: $6200

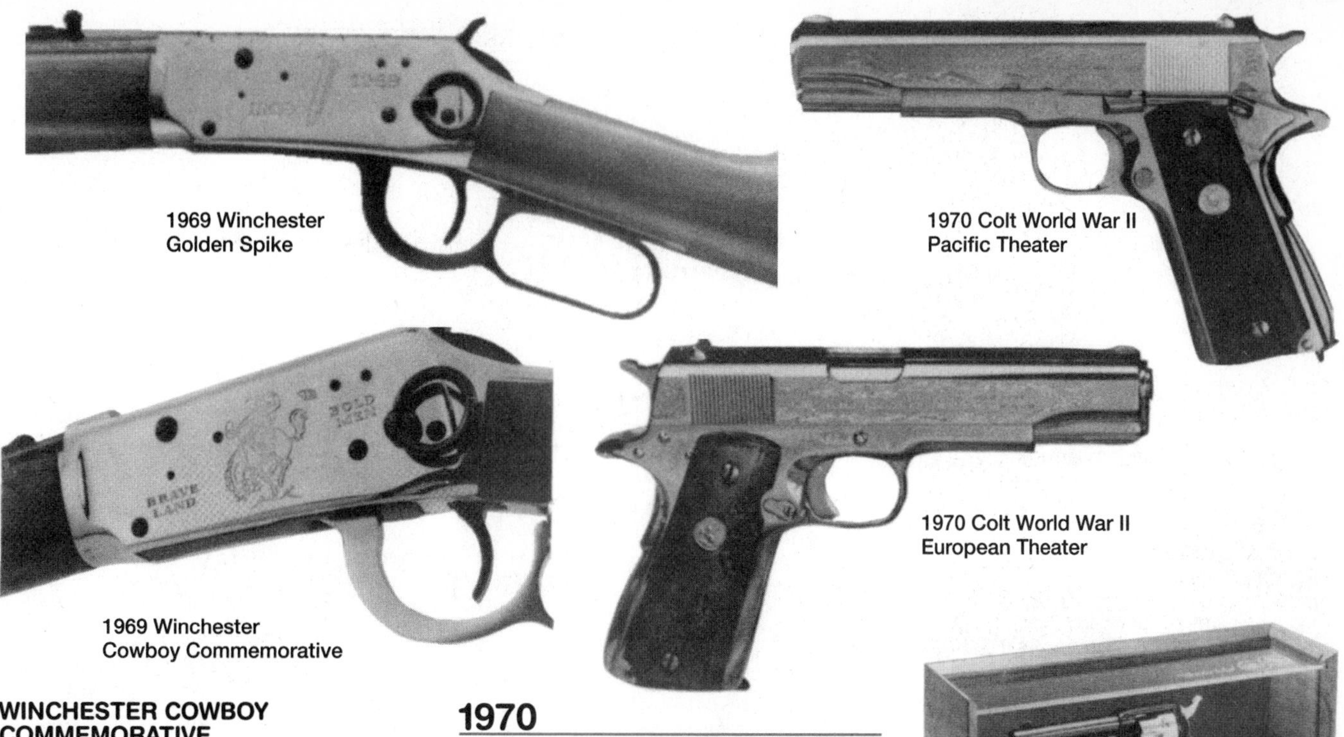

1969 Winchester Golden Spike

1970 Colt World War II Pacific Theater

1969 Winchester Cowboy Commemorative

1970 Colt World War II European Theater

WINCHESTER COWBOY COMMEMORATIVE

Model 94; receiver, upper and lower tang, lever, barrel bands are nickel-plated; butt plate is stainless steel, with tang that extends over top of stock for square comb look; stock is straight grip with extended forearm of American walnut; embedded in right side of stock is medallion of cowboy roping a steer; etched on left side of receiver, "Brave Land—Bold Men." Opposite side is engraved with coiled lariat, spurs; barrel is 20-inch, carrying "Cowboy Commemorative"; upper tang has inscription, "Winchester Model 1894." Has adjustable semi-buckhorn rear sight, blued saddle ring; in 30-30 only. Introduced in 1969.

Issue Price: $125; Marked "1 of 300", $1000
Market Value: $1300

Marked "1 of 300"
Market Value: $2950

WINCHESTER GOLDEN SPIKE

Model 94; features 20-inch barrel with twin barrel bands plated in yellow gold; yellow gold receiver, engraved with decorative scrolled border on right side, inscribed on other side with railroad spike flanked by dates, 1869 and 1969. Barrel carries "Golden Spike Commemorative" inscription; upper tang bears words "Oceans United By Rail." Buttstock, forearm are straight-line design of satin-finished American walnut, with fluted comb. Inset in stock is centennial medallion of engines of Central Pacific, Union Pacific meeting on May 10, 1869. It has straight brass buttplate, blued saddle ring; chambered for 30-30; weight is 7 lbs. Introduced in 1969.

Issue Price: $119.95
Market Value: $1295

WINCHESTER THEODORE ROOSEVELT COMMEMORATIVE

Model 94 rifle and carbine; made in 1969 only; 49,505 manufactured; 30-30 only; rifle has 26-inch octagonal barrel; 6-shot half-magazine; forearm cap, upper tang, receiver plated with white gold; receiver engraved with American eagle, "26th President 1901-1909," Roosevelt's facsimile signature; contoured lever, half pistol grip; medallion in stock. Carbine differs from rifle in shorter forearm, full-length 6-shot tubular magazine; 20-inch barrel.

Issue Price: $125

Rifle
Market Value: $1500

Carbine
Market Value: $1400

Matched set with consecutive serial numbers
Market Value: $2600

1970

COLT FORT HAYS COMMEMORATIVE

Frontier Scout revolver; "1870—Fort Hays—1970" wiped in silver on left side of 4-3/4-inch barrel; 22 LR only; hard rubber grips; nickel-plated finish; blued barrel, backstrap and trigger guard assembly screws, cylinder, base pin screw, ejector tube screw, bolt and trigger screw, hammer screw, trigger; originally cased in blonde finished wood; bottom lined with blue velvet, gold satin in lid; 500 made in 1970.

Issue Price: $130
Market Value: $650

COLT FORT RILEY COMMEMORATIVE

Frontier Scout revolver; "1870—Kansas Series—Fort Riley—1970" wiped in black on left side of 4-3/4-inch barrel; 22 LR only; ivorylite grips; nickel-plated medallions; nickel-plated finish; blued backstrap and trigger guard assembly, cylinder, base pin and screw, ejector rod head and tube screw, bolt and trigger screw, hammer and screw, trigger, stock screw; originally cased in blonde-finished wood; black velvet/satin lining; 500 made in 1970.

Issue Price: $130
Market Value: $650

COLT MAINE SESQUICENTENNIAL

Frontier Scout revolver; "1820—Maine Sesquicentennial—1970" on left side of 4-3/4-inch barrel; 22 LR only nonfluted cylinder; pearlite grips; gold-plated medallions; gold-plated finish; nickel-plated backstrap and trigger guard assembly, cylinder, base pin screw, hammer and hammer screw, ejector rod, ejector rod head, ejector tube screw, bolt and trigger screw; originally cased in natural knotty white pine; lined with royal blue velvet in bottom; light blue satin in lid; 3000 made in 1970.

Issue Price: $120
Market Value: $650

COLT MISSOURI TERRITORIAL SESQUICENTENNIAL

Frontier Scout revolver; "1820-Missouri Sesquicentennial—1970" wiped in gold on left side of 4-3/4-inch barrel; 22 LR only; walnut grips; gold-plated medallions; blued finish; gold-plated cylinder, loading gate, base pin, ejector rod head, ejector tube, tube screw, bolt and trigger screw, hammer, trigger, stock screw, top backstrap screws; originally cased in natural finish willow, lined in red velvet; 3000 made in 1970.

Issue Price: $125
Market Value: $650

1970 Colt Missouri Territorial Sesquicentennial

COLT MISSOURI TERRITORIAL SESQUICENTENNIAL SINGLE ACTION ARMY

Same legend on the 5-1/2-inch barrel; 45 Colt only; grips, medallions, finish and plating are same as Frontier Scout version, except for case-hardened frame, loading gate; same casing; 900 made; production started in 1970.

Issue Price: $220
Market Value: $1695

COLT WORLD WAR II/EUROPEAN THEATER

Semi-automatic; Model 1911A1; slide is marked "World War II Commemorative/European Theater of Operations" on left side; right side is roll-engraved with major sites of activity; 5-inch barrel; 45 Auto only; bird's-eye maple grips; gold-plated medallions; nickel-plated finish in entirety; originally cased in oak box with oak cartridge block; lid removable; seven dummy cartridges included; infantry blue velvet lining; 11,500 made; production began in 1970.

Issue Price: $250
Market Value: $995

COLT WORLD WAR II/PACIFIC THEATER

Semi-automatic; Model 1911A1; slide is marked "World War II Commemorative/Pacific Theater of Operations" on right side; left side roll-engraved with names of ten major battle areas; both sides of slide bordered in roll-marked palm leaf design; 5-inch barrel; 45 Auto only; Brazilian rosewood grips; gold-plated medallions; nickel-plated in entirety; originally cased in Obichee wood; light green velvet lining; seven nickel-plated dummy cartridges in cartridge block; 11,500 made; production began in 1970.

Issue Price: $250
Market Value: $995

1970 Savage Anniversary Model 1895

1971 Harrington & Richardson Anniversary Model 1873

1971 Marlin 39A Article II

1971 Colt NRA Centennial Commemorative Gold Cup

1971 Colt NRA Centennial Commemorative Single Action

COLT WYATT EARP COMMEMORATIVE

Frontier Scout revolver; "Lawman Series—Wyatt Earp" on right side of barrel; standard model markings on left side; 12-inch Buntline barrel; 22 LR only; walnut grips; nickel-plated medallions blued finish; nickel-plated barrel, cylinder, ejector tube plug, ejector tube screw, rod head, base pin and base pin screw, hammer, trigger and backstrap and trigger guard assembly; originally cased in black leatherette-covered box; bottom lined with burgundy velvet; lid with red satin; 3000 made; production started in 1970.

Issue Price: $125
Market Value: $695

COLT WYATT EARP SINGLE ACTION ARMY

Same legend on barrel, but wiped in silver; 16-1/8-inch barrel; 45 Colt only; same grips, medallions as Frontier Scout version; blued finish; case-hardened frame; nickel-plated hammer, trigger, base pin, base pin cross latch assembly; same casing as Frontier Scout; 500 made; production began in 1970.

Issue Price: $395
Market Value: $2950

MARLIN MODEL 39 CENTURY LTD.

Marking the Marlin Centennial, 1870 to 1970; same specs as standard Model 39A except for square lever; fancy walnut straight-grip uncheckered stock; forearm; 20-inch octagonal barrel; brass forearm cap; nameplate inset in stock buttplate. Produced only in 1970.

Issue Price: $125
Market Value: $850

MARLIN CENTENNIAL MATCHED PAIR

Combines presentation-grade Model 336 centerfire, rimfire Model 39, in luggage-type case; matching serial numbers, for additional collector value. Both rifles have fancy walnut straight-grip stocks, forearms; brass forearm caps, brass buttplates, engraved receivers with inlaid medallions. Model 336 is chambered for 30-30 only; Model 39 for 22 LR, 22 Long, 22 Short. Only 1000 sets were manufactured in 1970.

Issue Price: $750
Market Value: $1550

SAVAGE ANNIVERSARY MODEL 1895

Replica of Savage Model 1895; hammerless lever-action; marks 75th anniversary of Savage Arms Corp. (1895-1970); 308 Win. only; 24-inch octagon barrel; 5-shot rotary magazine; engraved receiver, brass-plated lever; brass buttplate; brass medallion inlaid in stock; uncheckered walnut straight grip stock, Schnabel-type forearm. Made only in 1970; 9999 produced.

Issue Price: $195
Market Value: $895

WINCHESTER LONE STAR COMMEMORATIVE

Model 94; produced in rifle version with 26-inch barrel and carbine with 20-inch length. Receiver, upper and lower tang, lever, forearm cap, magazine tube cap all are gold-plated; buttplate is crescent shaped, solid brass. Stocks are American walnut with half pistol grip, fluted comb; commemorative medal with faces of Sam Houston, Stephen F. Austin, William Travis, Jim Bowie and Davy Crockett is inset in right side of stock. Left side of receiver is engraved with star and dates, 1845, 1970; both sides are bordered with series of stars; barrel carries inscription, "Lone Star Commemorative." Upper tang has "Under Six Flags," referring to banners of Spain, France, Mexico, Texas Republic, Confederacy and United States, which have flown over territory. It has bead post front sight, semi-buckhorn rear, plus saddle ring. Introduced in 1970.

Issue Price: Rifle, Carbine, $140; Matched Set with consecutive serial numbers $305

Carbine
Market Value: $1500

Rifle
Market Value: $1600

Matched set
Market Value: $2500

1971

COLT FORT SCOTT COMMEMORATIVE

Frontier Scout revolver; "1871 Kansas Series—Fort Scott—1971" on left side of 4-3/4-inch barrel; 22 LR only; checkered rubber, eagle-style grips; nickel-plated finish; blued barrel, cylinder, base pin screw, ejector tube screw, bolt and trigger screw, hammer, hammer screw, trigger; originally cased in blonde-finished wood; gold velvet/satin lining; 500 made in 1971.

Issue Price: $130
Market Value: $450

COLT NRA CENTENNIAL COMMEMORATIVE SINGLE ACTION ARMY

Single Action Army; "1871 NRA Centennial 1971" wiped in gold on left side of 4-3/4-inch, 5-1/2-inch, or 7-1/2-inch barrels; 357 Magnum, 45 Colt; Goncalo Alves grips; gold-plated NRA medallion inlays; blued finish; case-hardened frame; nickel-silver grip screw escutcheons; originally cased in walnut, with inlaid NRA plate; gold velvet/satin lining; 2412 357 Magnums, 4131 45 Colts made; production began in 1971.

Issue Price: $250

357 Magnum
Market Value: $1495

45 Colt
Market Value: $1695

COLT NRA CENTENNIAL COMMEMORATIVE GOLD CUP

Semi-automatic; Gold Cup National Match model; "1871 NRA Centennial 1971/The First 100 Years of Service/.45 Automatic Caliber" wiped in gold on left side of slide; MK IV barrel; Eliason rear sight; 5-inch barrel; 45 Auto only; checkered walnut grips; gold-plated NRA medallion inlays; blued; same type of case as NRA commemorative SAA; 2500 made; production began in 1971.

Issue Price: $250
Market Value: $1495

1971 Savage Model 71

1971 Winchester National Rifle Association Centennial Model

1972 High Standard Benner Commemorative

1972 Colt Florida Territorial Sesquicentennial

HARRINGTON & RICHARDSON ANNIVERSARY MODEL 1873
Replica of Officer's Model 1873 Trapdoor Springfield commemorating 100th anniversary of H&R (1871-1971); single shot action; 45-70 only; 26-inch barrel; engraved receiver, breech block, hammer, lock plate, buttplate; hand-checkered walnut stock with inlaid brass commemorative plate; peep rear sight, blade front; ramrod. Made only in 1971. Production limited to 10,000.
Market Value: $895

MARLIN 39A ARTICLE II
Same general specs as Model 39A; commemorates National Rifle Association Centennial, 1871-1971. Medallion with legend "The Right to Bear Arms" set on blued receiver; 24-inch octagonal barrel; tube magazine holds 19 LR, 21 Long, 25 Short; fancy uncheckered walnut pistol-grip stock forearm; brass buttplate, forearm cap. Produced only in 1971.
Issue Price: $135
Market Value: $575

MARLIN ARTICLE II CARBINE
Same specs as Marlin 39A Article II rifle except straight grip stock; square lever; shorter magazine; reduced capacity; 20-inch octagonal barrel. Produced only in 1971.
Issue Price: $135; Cased Set, $750

Carbine
Market Value: $175

Cased Set
Market Value: $1100

SAVAGE MODEL 71
Single shot lever-action; replica of Stevens Favorite, issued as commemorative to Joshua Stevens, founder of Stevens Arms Co.; 22 LR only; 22-inch octagonal barrel; brass-plated hammer, lever; uncheckered straight-grip stock, Schnabel forearm; brass commemorative medallion inlaid in stock; brass butt plate; open rear sight, brass blade front. Made in 1971; only 10,000 produced.
Issue Price: $75
Market Value: $395

WINCHESTER NATIONAL RIFLE ASSOCIATION CENTENNIAL MODEL
Introduced in two versions: musket and rifle, both on Model 94 actions; musket resembles Model 1895 NRA musket with military lever to meet requirements for NRA match competition at turn of century; has 26-inch tapered round barrel; full-length American walnut forearm; black-chromed steel buttplate; rear sight has calibrated folding rear leaf, blade front sight; 7-shot magazine. Rifle model resembles Model 64, also made on 94 action with 5-shot half-magazine; 24-inch tapered, round barrel; hooded ramp and bead post front sight; adjustable semi-buckhorn rear sight; contoured lever, blued steel forearm cap. Both models are 30-30; have quick-detachable sling swivels; receivers are black-chromed steel; NRA seal in silver-colored metal is set in right side of stocks; left side of receivers inscribed appropriately with "NRA Centennial Musket" or "NRA Centennial Rifle." Both were introduced in 1971.
Issue Price: $149.95; Matched set with consecutive serial numbers, $325

Musket
Market Value: $1200

Rifle
Market Value: $1300

Cased set
Market Value: $2400

1972

COLT FLORIDA TERRITORIAL SESQUICENTENNIAL
Frontier Scout revolver; "1822—Florida Territory—1972" on left side of 4-3/4-inch barrel; 22 LR only; cypress wood grips; gold-plated medallions, blued finish; case-hardened frame, loading gate; gold-plated base pin, base pin screw, ejector rod head and screws, hammer, trigger and trigger screws; originally cased in cypress wood box; gold velvet/satin lining; 2001 made; production began in 1972.
Issue Price: $125
Market Value: $650

HIGH STANDARD BENNER COMMEMORATIVE
Super Military Trophy auto; 22 Long only; 5-1/2-inch bull barrel; checkered American walnut thumbrest grip; micro rear sight; grip angle is that of the 1911 Government model; engraved with the five-ring Olympic insignia to denote the twentieth anniversary of Huelet O. "Joe" Benner's Olympic Gold Medal win; 1000 guns made; serial numbers, 1 to 1000. Made in 1972.
Issue Price: $550
Market Value: $1650

MARLIN MODEL 336 ZANE GREY
Same specs as Model 336A except 30-30 only; 22-inch octagonal barrel. Commemorates centennial of Zane Grey's birth, 1872 to 1972; commemorative medallion attached to receiver; selected uncheckered walnut pistol grip stock forearm; brass forearm cap, buttplate; 10,000 produced with special serial numbers, ZG1 through ZG10,000. Produced only in 1972.
Issue Price: $150
Market Value: $495

1973

CHURCHILL ONE OF ONE THOUSAND
Bolt-action; 270 Win., 7mm Rem. Magnum, 308, 30-06, 300 Win. Magnum, 375 H&H Magnum, 458 Win. Magnum; 5-shot magazine in standard calibers, 3-shot in magnum; made on Mauser-type action; classic French walnut stock; hand-checkered pistol-grip, forearm; recoil pad, cartridge trap in butt; sling swivels. Manufactured in England in 1973 to commemorate Interarms' 20th anniversary. Only 1000 made.
Market Value: $2500

COLT ARIZONA RANGER COMMEMORATIVE
Frontier Scout revolver; "Arizona Ranger Commemorative" on left side of 4-3/4-inch barrel; 22 LR only; laminated rosewood grips; nickel-plated medallions; blued finish; case-hardened frame; nickel-plated backstrap and trigger guard assembly, hammer trigger, base pin, base pin assembly, screw for backstrap/trigger guard assembly, grips; originally cased in walnut with glass window lid; replica Arizona Ranger badge included in case; lined with maroon velvet; 3001 made; production began in 1973.
Issue Price: $135
Market Value: $650

COLT PEACEMAKER CENTENNIAL
Single Action Army revolver, Frontier Six Shooter configuration; "The Frontier Six-Shooter" etched on left side of barrel, "1873 Peacemaker Centennial 1973" roll-marked on right side; 7-1/2-inch barrel; 44-40 only; checkered rubber eagle-style grips; nickel-plated in entirety; originally cased in leather-covered wood box; brown velvet lining; 1500 made; production began in 1973.
Issue Price: $300
Market Value: $1695

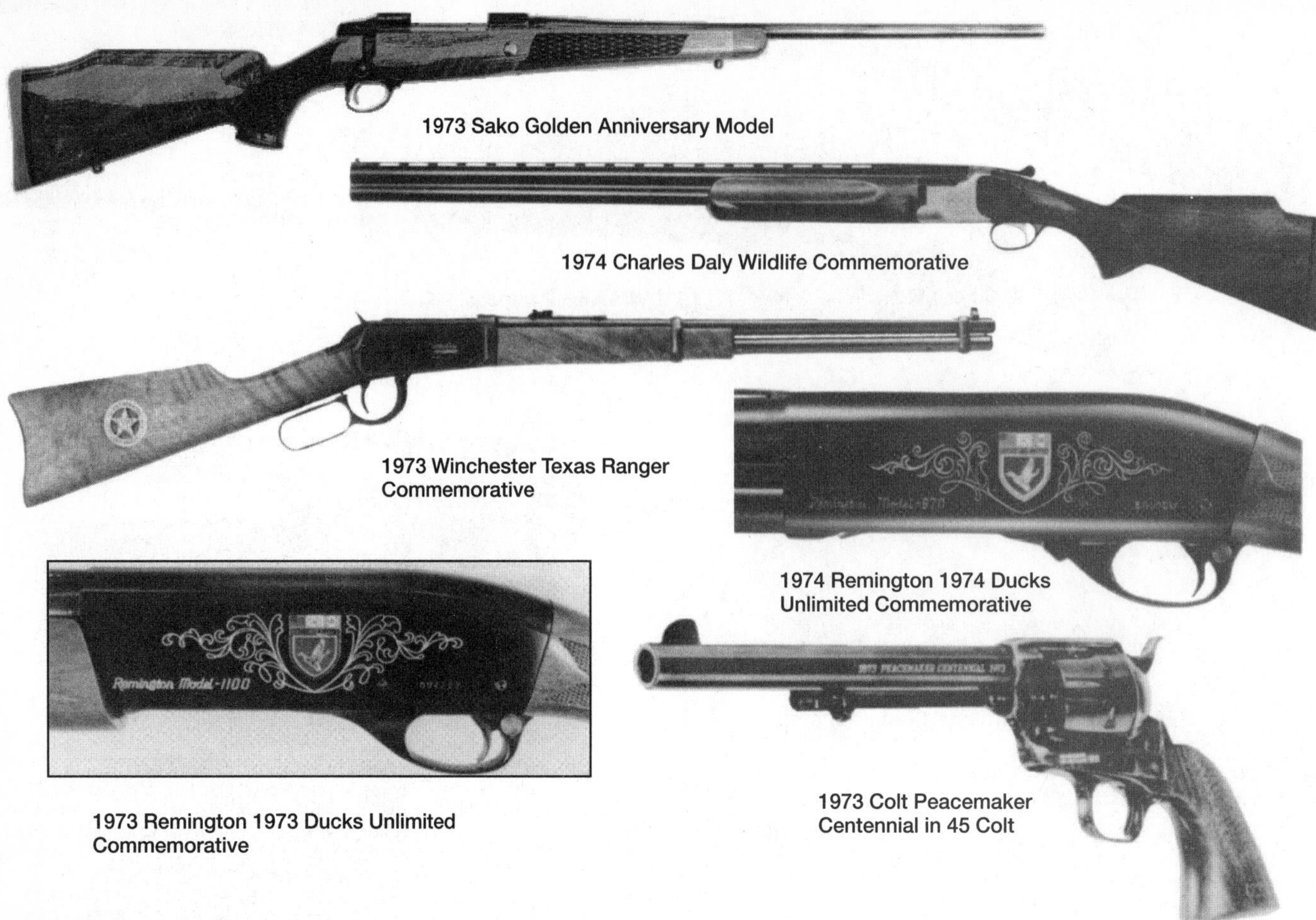

1973 Sako Golden Anniversary Model

1974 Charles Daly Wildlife Commemorative

1973 Winchester Texas Ranger Commemorative

1974 Remington 1974 Ducks Unlimited Commemorative

1973 Remington 1973 Ducks Unlimited Commemorative

1973 Colt Peacemaker Centennial in 45 Colt

COLT PEACEMAKER CENTENNIAL 45 COLT

Configuration has "1873 Peacemaker Centennial 1973" roll marked on left side of 7-1/2-inch barrel; 45 Colt only; one-piece varnished walnut grip; blued finish; case-hardened frame, hammer; originally cased in oiled walnut with brass-framed glass cover; maroon velvet lining; 1500 made; production began in 1973.
Issue Price: $300
Market Value: $1695

COLT PEACEMAKER CENTENNIAL 45 COLT/44-40 COMBO

Includes the two revolvers described above in oversize case of walnut-stained willow; lined with dark maroon velvet; matching serial numbers on guns; 500 sets made in 1973.
Issue Price: $625
Market Value: $3195

HARRINGTON & RICHARDSON CUSTER MEMORIAL EDITION

Replica of blackpowder 1873 Springfield carbine; 54-caliber; inlaid with gold; heavy engraving; fancy-grade walnut stock; marketed in mahogany case. Each rifle bears the name of a cavalryman who died in the Battle of the Little Big Horn. Manufactured, 1973, in two versions; 25 Officers' Model, 243 Enlisted Men's Model.
Issue Price: Officer's Model, $3000; Enlisted Men's Model, $2000

Officer's Model
Market Value: $3995

Enlisted Men's Model
Market Value: $1995

REMINGTON 1973 DUCKS UNLIMITED COMMEMORATIVES

Model 1100 autoloading shotgun; 12-ga. only; 30-inch barrel; Full choke; vent rib. Other specs the same as standard Model 1100, except that serial number is preceded by DU; Ducks Unlimited medallion, surrounded by gilded scrollwork is attached to left side of receiver; 500 made in 1973 only.
Issue Price: $230
Market Value: $595

SAKO GOLDEN ANNIVERSARY MODEL

Same specs as Sako long-action Deluxe sporter; 7mm Rem. Magnum only; floorplate, trigger guard, receiver feature gold oak leaf, acorn decoration; hand-checkered select European walnut stock hand-carved oak leaf pattern. Commemorates firm's 50th anniversary only; 1000 made in 1973.
Market Value: $1095

SMITH & WESSON TEXAS RANGER COMMEMORATIVE

Model 19 357 Combat Magnum; 4-inch barrel; sideplate stamped with Texas Ranger commemorative seal; uncheckered Goncalo Alves stocks; marketed with specially designed Bowie-type knife in presentation case. Commemorated the 150th anniversary of the Texas Rangers. Reported 8000 sets made in 1973.
Market Value: $895

STOEGER LIMITED EDITION LUGER CARBINE

Semi-automatic; 22 LR; 11-inch barrel; forged aluminum frame; walnut pistol grips and forearm. Marketed in a black leatherette, red velvet-lined case. Due to lack of buttstock was classified as a handgun and was legal. Reported 300 made in 1973. Original price unknown.
Market Value: $1000

WINCHESTER TEXAS RANGER COMMEMORATIVE

Model 94; features stock forearm of semi-fancy walnut, with the buttstock having square comb, metal butt plate. Chambered in 30-30; 6-shot tube magazine; a facsimile of Texas Ranger star badge is embedded in the stock; saddle ring is included. Of standard grade, only 4850 were released in April 1973, all of them in the state of Texas. Another 150 Special Edition guns, at $1000 each, were released, in presentation cases, only to the Texas Ranger Association. These were hand-checkered, with full fancy walnut stocks, barrel and receiver highly polished; 4-shot magazine; 16-inch barrel; weighs 6 lbs.; standard model weighs 7 lbs.; 20-inch barrel. With Special Edition guns, commemorative star is mounted inside the presentation case instead of in the stock. Also introduced April 1973. Standard model, Issue Price: $134.95; Special Edition, $1000.

Standard model
Market Value: $1395

Special Edition
Market Value: $2950

1974

CHARLES DALY WILDLIFE COMMEMORATIVE

Over/under; 12-ga.; trap and Skeet models only; same general specs as Diamond Grade over/under; fine scrollwork on left side of receiver, duck scene engraved on right side. Manufactured in Japan 1974. Reported 500 guns made.
Market Value: $795

MOSSBERG MODEL 472 ONE IN 5000

Same specs as Model 472 Brush Gun except brass buttplate; barrel bands and saddle ring; gold-plated trigger; bright blued finish; Indian scenes etched on receiver; select walnut stock and forearm. Limited edition manufactured, 1974 only; numbered 1 through 5,000.
Market Value: $395

REMINGTON 1974 DUCKS UNLIMITED COMMEMORATIVE

Model 870 pump-action, with gilded scroll-engraved receiver; special serial numbers; DU color medallion set in receiver. Made only in 1974 for auction by DU.
Market Value: $495

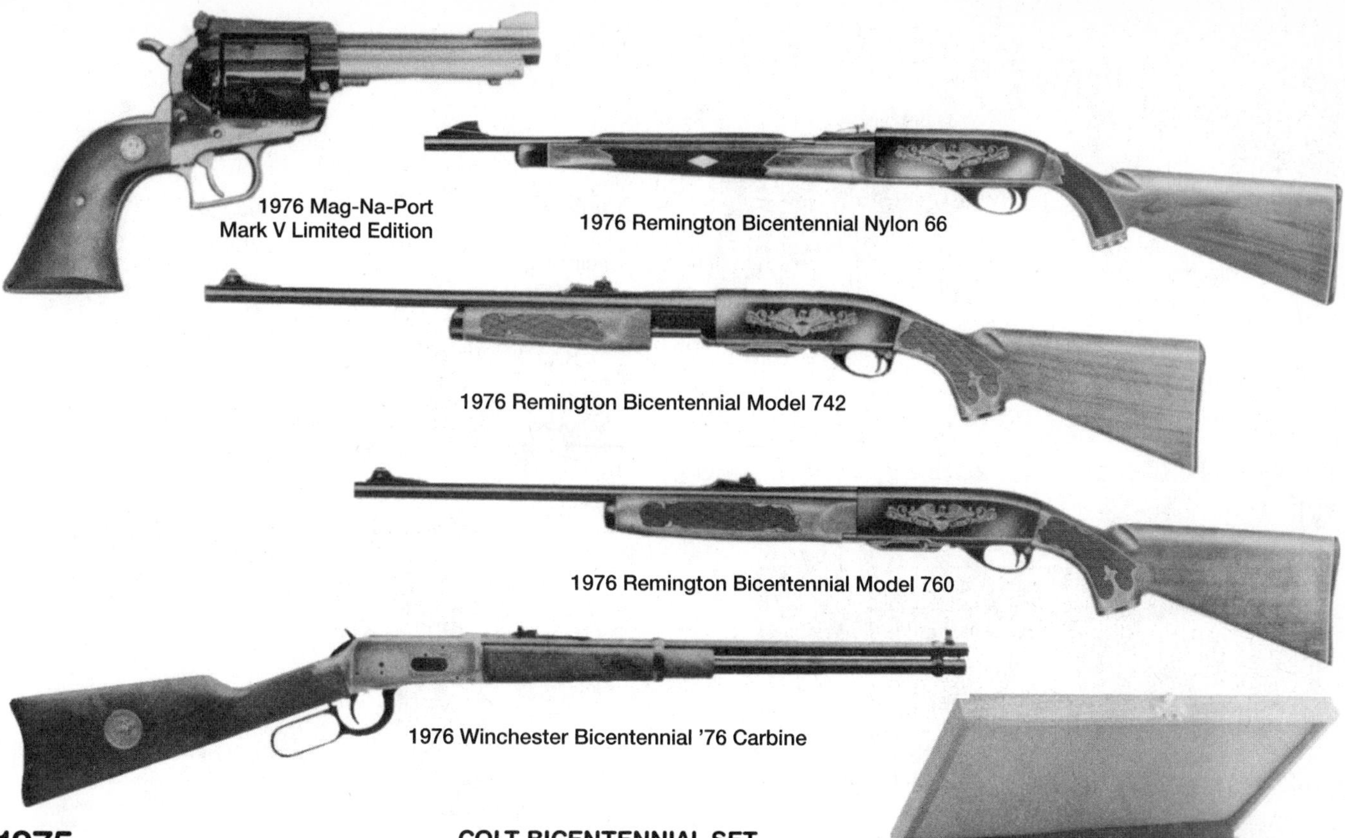

1976 Mag-Na-Port Mark V Limited Edition

1976 Remington Bicentennial Nylon 66

1976 Remington Bicentennial Model 742

1976 Remington Bicentennial Model 760

1976 Winchester Bicentennial '76 Carbine

1975

MOSSBERG DUCK STAMP COMMEMORATIVE

Same specs as the Model 500DSPR Pigeon Grade 12-ga. magnum heavy duck gun; features a heavy 30-inch vent-rib barrel; Full choke only; receiver carries an etching of a wood duck. Gun was marketed with a special wall plaque commemorating, with the shotgun, the Migratory Bird Hunting Stamp Program. Only 1000 made in 1975.
Market Value: $375

RUGER COLORADO CENTENNIAL

Single-Six revolver; 22 LR; stainless steel grip frame; rosewood grip panels; historic scene roll engraved on cylinder; 6-1/2-inch barrel; inscribed to signify its purpose as a centennial commemorative; marketed in walnut presentation case; 15,000 made in 1975.
Issue Price: $250
Market Value: $595

1976

BROWNING BICENTENNIAL 78

Single shot Model 78; 45-70; same specs as standard model, except for bison and eagle engraved on receiver; scroll engraving on lever, both ends of barrel, buttplate, top of receiver; high-grade walnut stock forearm. Manufactured in Japan. Marketed with engraved hunting knife, commemorative medallion, alder presentation case. Gun and knife serial numbers match, beginning with 1776. Only 1000 sets made. Manufactured only in 1976.
Issue Price: $150
Market Value: $1950

BROWNING BICENTENNIAL SUPERPOSED

Over/under; 12-ga.; same basic specs as standard Superposed shotgun, but sideplates engraved, gold-inlaid turkey-hunting scene on right side, U.S. flag, bald eagle on left. State markings are in gold on blue background; hand-checkered American walnut straight-grip stock, Schnabel forearm; marketed in velvet-lined walnut presentation case. Only 51 made; one for each state and District of Columbia. Manufactured in Belgium, 1976.
Market Value: $10,000

COLT BICENTENNIAL SET

Includes Colt SAA revolver, Python revolver and 3rd Model Dragoon revolver, with accessories; all have rosewood stocks, matching roll-engraved unfluted cylinders, blued finish, silver medallion bearing the Seal of the United States; Dragoon has silver grip frame; all revolvers in set have matching serial numbers, 0001 through 1776. Marketed with deluxe three-drawer walnut presentation case, reproduction volume of Armsmear. Made only in 1976.
Market Value: $3195

ITHACA BICENTENNIAL MODEL 37

Slide-action; 12-ga.; basic specs of Model 37 Supreme, except for Bicentennial design etched into receiver; serialized USA 0001 to USA 1976; full fancy walnut stock slide handle. Only 1976 made in 1976. Marketed in presentation case.
Market Value: $795

MAG-NA-PORT MARK V LIMITED EDITION

Revolver; built on Ruger Super Blackhawk; 44 Magnum; 5-inch barrel; jeweled, plated hammer and trigger; smoothed trigger pull; front sight altered with red insert; satin nickel backstrap, trigger guard, ejector rod housing, center pin; deluxe blue finish; Mag-na-ported barrel. Marketed in presentation case; made in 1976.
Issue Price: $395
Market Value: $3500 to $3700

REMINGTON BICENTENNIAL NYLON 66

Rifle; semi-automatic; 22 LR; same specs as standard Nylon 66 except specially marked with eagle, shield flanked with scrollwork and underlined with "1776-1976"; dates are gilded; Mohawk brown stock only; 12,000 made.
Issue Price: $84.95
Market Value: $575

REMINGTON BICENTENNIAL MODEL 742

Same specs as standard Model 742 Woodsmaster except Bicentennial commemorative inscription etched on receiver; different checkering pattern. Manufactured 1976 only.
Market Value: $495

1975 Ruger Colorado Centennial

REMINGTON BICENTENNIAL MODEL 760

Same specs as standard Model 760 Gamemaster except Bicentennial commemorative inscription etched on receiver; different checkering pattern. Manufactured 1976 only.
Market Value: $475

WICKLIFFE '76 COMMEMORATIVE

Single shot; same specs as '76 Deluxe model except filled etching on sidewalls of receiver: 26-inch barrel only; U.S. silver dollar inlaid in stock; marketed in presentation case. Manufactured 1976 only. Only 100 made.
Market Value: $850

WINCHESTER BICENTENNIAL '76 CARBINE

Model 94; same specs as standard model except 30-30 only; engraved antique silver finish; American eagle on left side of receiver, "76" encircled with thirteen stars on right side; engraved on right side of barrel is legend "Bicentennial 1776-1976." Originally marketed with wooden gun rack with simulated deer antlers, gold colored identification plate. Reported 20,000 made in 1976.
Issue Price: $325
Market Value: $1595

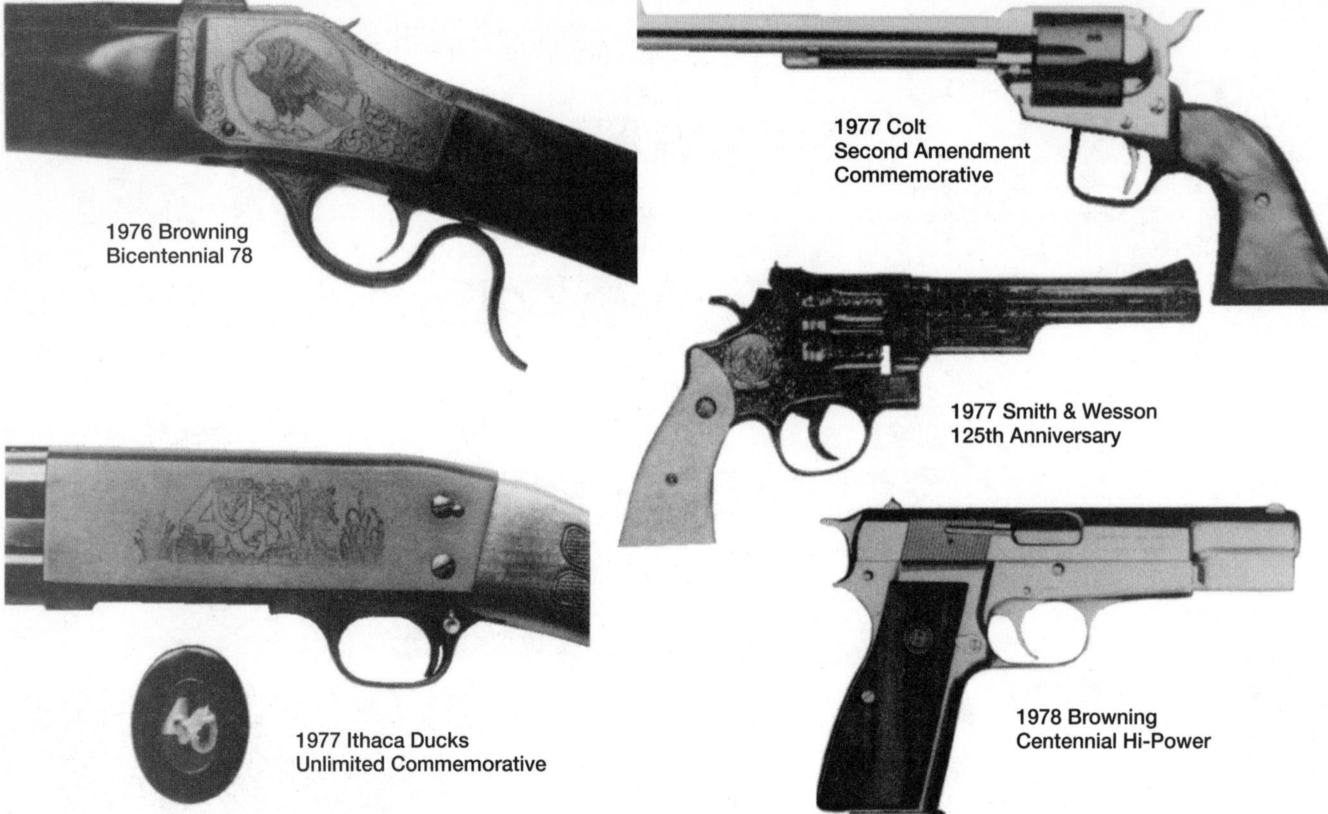
1976 Browning Bicentennial 78

1977 Colt Second Amendment Commemorative

1977 Smith & Wesson 125th Anniversary

1977 Ithaca Ducks Unlimited Commemorative

1978 Browning Centennial Hi-Power

1977

COLT SECOND AMENDMENT COMMEMORATIVE

Peacemaker Buntline revolver; 22 rimfire; 7-1/2-inch barrel bears inscription "The Right To Keep And Bear Arms"; polished nickel-plated barrel, frame, ejector rod assembly, hammer, trigger; blued cylinder, backstrap, trigger guard; black pearlite stocks; fluted cylinder; specially serial numbered; marketed in special presentation case, carrying reproduction copy of Second Amendment to the Constitution. Reported 3000 made in 1977.
Issue Price: $194.95
Market Value: $650

ITHACA DUCKS UNLIMITED COMMEMORATIVE

Limited edition of Model 37 Featherlight pump action; commemorates DU 40th anniversary; 12-ga.; 30-inch Full choke barrel; vent rib; recoil pad; Raybar front sight; commemorative grip cap; receiver engraved with DU anniversary logo, banner commemorating occasion. Also made in high-grade custom version with more elaborate etching, hand-checkered full fancy American walnut stock, custom-fitted carrying case. Reported 5000 made in 1977.
Issue Price: Standard commemorative, $255; Custom model, $600.
Market Value: **Standard:** $500
Market Value: **Custom:** $700

MAG-NA-PORT CUSTOM SIX LIMITED EDITION

Revolver; built on Ruger Super Blackhawk; 44 Magnum; 6-inch barrel; same specs as Mag-na-port Mark V except yellow front sight insert, gold-outlined rear sight blade; gold inlay. 50 made in 1977.
Issue Price: $350
Market Value: $2250

MAG-NA-PORT TOMAHAWK LIMITED EDITION

Revolver; built on Ruger Blackhawk; 44 Magnum; Mag-na-ported 4-3/4-inch barrel; Metalife SS finish; smoothed trigger pull; red front sight insert; white outline rear sight; hammer engraved with Tomahawk logo; topstrap engraved with Mag-na-port and Tomahawk logos; serial numbered 1 to 200; 200 made in 1977. Marketed in carrying case.
Issue Price: $495
Market Value: $2000

SMITH & WESSON 125TH ANNIVERSARY

Model 25 revolver; 45 Colt; 6-1/2-inch barrel; blued finish; Goncalo Alves stocks; "Smith & Wesson 125th Anniversary" gold-filled on barrel; sideplate has gold-filled anniversary seal; marketed in case bearing nickel-silver anniversary seal. Included is book, *125 Years With Smith & Wesson*. Reported 10,000 issued in 1977.
Market Value: $1095

SMITH & WESSON DELUXE EDITION 125TH ANNIVERSARY

Same specs as Smith & Wesson 125th Anniversary except Class A engraving; ivory stocks; anniversary medallion on box is sterling silver; book leather-bound. Reported 50 issued in 1977.
Market Value: $1695

WINCHESTER WELLS FARGO MODEL 94

Same specs as standard Model 94 except 30-30 only; antique silver-finish engraved receiver; nickel-silver stagecoach medallion inset in buttstock; checkered fancy American walnut stock forearm; curved buttplate. Reported 20,000 made in 1977.
Market Value: $1295

WINCHESTER CHEYENNE COMMEMORATIVE

Lever-action rifle; same specs as standard Model 94 carbine except 44-40; made specifically for the Canadian market. Reported 11,220 made in 1977.
Issue Price: $375
Market Value: $1295

1978

BROWNING CENTENNIAL HI-POWER

Commemorates Browning's centennial anniversary; same specs as standard 9mm Hi-Power except oil-finished hand-checkered walnut stocks; Browning medallion inset on both sides; chrome finish; has centennial inscription with date hand-engraved on side; gold-plated trigger; fixed sights. Issued in fitted walnut case with red velvet lining. Only 3500 produced in 1978, with serial #1878D-0001 through 1878D-3500.
Issue Price: $495
Market Value: $895

COLT U.S. CAVALRY COMMEMORATIVE

Based on 1860 Army design; commemorates 200th anniversary of U.S. Cavalry, 1777 to 1977; blued barrel, hammer assembly, cylinder, backstrap, trigger; frame, hammer color case-hardened; brass trigger guard; one-piece walnut stocks; naval engagement scene roll marked on nonfluted cylinder; marketed with detachable walnut shoulder stock, accessories, in oiled American walnut presentation case. Reported 3000 units manufactured 1978.
Issue Price: $995
Market Value: $1450

WINCHESTER ANTLERED GAME COMMEMORATIVE

Built on Winchester 94 action but with polished 20-inch barrel; gold-colored inscription reading "Antlered Game;" gold-plated lever; tang and barrel bands match blue of receiver; 30-30 only. Total of 19,999 made in 1978.
Issue Price: $374.95
Market Value: $1350

WINCHESTER LEGENDARY LAWMAN

Model 94 Carbine; 30-30 only; same specs as standard model except 16-inch barrel; full-length tube magazine; antique silver-finish barrel bands; right side of barrel bears silver-colored inscription, "Legendary Lawman"; extended forearm, straight-grip stock; nickel-silver medallion set in buttstock features sheriff standing on Western street. Reported 20,000 manufactured in 1978.
Issue Price: $375
Market Value: $1495

1979 Winchester Set of 1000 Collector Issue

1979 Winchester Limited Edition II

1979 Winchester Legendary Frontiersman

1979 Mag-Na-Port Bullseye Limited Edition

1979 Mag-Na-Port Safari #1 Cape Buffalo

1979 Colt Ned Buntline Commemorative

1979

COLT NED BUNTLINE COMMEMORATIVE

Single Action Army revolver; 45 Colt; 12-inch barrel; built on New Frontier SAA frame; adjustable rear sight; nickel-plated; black composite rubber grips; marketed in custom presentation case with six nickel-plated 45 cartridges. Reported 3000 manufactured in 1979.
Issue Price: $900
Market Value: $1495

MAG-NA-PORT BACKPACKER LIMITED EDITION

Revolver; built on Charter Arms Bulldog; 44 Special; no front sight; Mag-na-ported 1.875-inch barrel; dehorned, anti-snag hammer; Pachmayr grips; Metalife SS finish; engraved with Mag-na-port logo and Backpacker 1 to 250 serial number; 250 made in 1979. Marketed in carrying case.
Issue Price: $295
Market Value: $400

MAG-NA-PORT BULLSEYE LIMITED EDITION

Semi-automatic; built on Ruger MKI Target Model; 22 LR; Mag-na-ported 5-1/2-inch barrel; gold-outlined rear sight; Clark target trigger; standard black Ruger grips; Metalife SS finish; Mag-na-port logo on end of bolt; lettering, logo gold inlaid; gold bullseye logo on receiver; serial numbered 001-200; 200 made in 1979. Marketed in wild poplar case.
Issue Price: $395
Market Value: $700

MAG-NA-PORT CLASSIC LIMITED EDITION

Revolver; built on Ruger Super Blackhawk; 44 Magnum; Mag-na-ported 7-1/2-inch barrel; yellow insert front sight, gold outline rear; satin nickel finish on backstrap, ejector rod; deluxe blued cylinder, frame, barrel; jeweled, gold-plated hammer, trigger; polished, gold-plated center pin release, ejector rod; "Mag-na-port Classic" engraved, gold inlaid on topstrap; antique grips with gold grip screw; custom tune-up; other lettering, logos gold inlaid; carries Mag-na-port serial numbers 1 through 250; 250 made in 1979. Hammer, trigger were seal-locked to ensure unfired condition. Marketed in case of wild poplar with Mag-na-port logo.
Issue Price: $590
Market Value: $2500

MAG-NA-PORT SAFARI #1 CAPE BUFFALO

Revolver; built on Ruger Super Blackhawk; 44 Magnum; 6-inch barrel; Metalife finish; Mag-na-port vent process; yellow front insert on sight, Omega Maverick rear sight; smoothed action; Mag-na-port logo and serial numbers 001 through 200 engraved; stainless steel ejector rod housing; gold-plated hammer, trigger, center pin, center pin release, ejector rod and grip screws; antiqued factory grips inlaid with 44 Magnum case head; Cape buffalos engraved on cylinder. Only 200 made in 1979.
Issue Price: $995
Market Value: $1500

WINCHESTER LEGENDARY FRONTIERSMAN

Model 94 Carbine; receiver decorated with scenes of the old frontier; silver-plated finish on receiver; polished, blued barrel, finger lever, hammer and trigger; forearm and straight-grip stock of semi-fancy American walnut; cut checkering; "Legendary Frontiersman" in silver on right side of barrel. Reported 19,999 made in 1979
Issue Price: $549.95 each
Market Value: $1595

WINCHESTER LIMITED EDITION II

Rifle; built on standard Model 94 carbine action but with gold-plated receiver with etched game scenes on each side, gold-plated hammer, lever; rest of metal bright blued; top quality fancy walnut stock forend. Only 1500 made in 1979.
Issue Price: $1750
Market Value: $1895

WINCHESTER SET OF 1000 COLLECTOR ISSUE

Combines Model 94 in 30-30 and Model 9422 in 22 WMR; both with game scene engraved on receiver; levers, receivers, barrel bands are gold-plated. Marketed in red velvet-lined wooden case, with brass hardware, lock key. Only 1000 sets made in 1979.
Issue Price: $3000 per set
Market Value: $3000

1980 Wickliffe Big Game Commemorative

1980 Winchester Oliver Winchester Commemorative

1981 Winchester John Wayne Commemorative

1981 Browning Waterfowl/Mallard Limited Edition

1980

ITHACA MODEL 37 2500 SERIES CENTENNIAL

Pump-action shotgun; 12-ga. only; etched receiver; antiqued parts; deluxe walnut stock; silver-plated parts. Commemorated Ithaca's 100th anniversary. Unknown number made, 1977.
Market Value: $595

MAG-NA-PORT SAFARI #2 ELEPHANT

Revolver; built on Ruger Super Blackhawk; 44 Magnum; 7-1/2-inch barrel, with custom inverted crown; includes Mag-na-port venting, satin and bright nickel finish; jeweled and nickeled hammer, trigger; custom rosewood grips with inlaid ivory scrimshaw of elephant; engraved elephant on cylinder; scroll engraving at muzzle; Mag-na-port logo on topstrap; smoothed action; white outline rear sight, red front sight insert. Marketed in walnut presentation case inlaid with ivory elephant scrimshaw. Only 200 made in 1980.
Issue Price: $1395
Market Value: $1800

WICKLIFFE BIG GAME COMMEMORATIVE

Single shot; same specs as Wickliffe Model '76 except glossy stock finish; gold-filled receiver etchings, chambered for 338 Win. Magnum only. Only 200 made. Manufactured 1980 only.
Market Value: $750

WINCHESTER OLIVER WINCHESTER COMMEMORATIVE

Model 94; 38-55 Win. only; gold commemorative plaque featuring Oliver Winchester medallion inlaid in American walnut stock; gold-plated, engraved receiver, forend cap. Reported 19,999 made in 1980.
Issue Price: $595
Market Value: $1895

1981

BROWNING WATERFOWL/MALLARD LIMITED EDITION

Over/under; 12-ga.; 28-inch Modified/Full barrels; other specs same as Lightning Superposed model except each gun is inscribed in gold with the Latin scientific name for the mallard, has gold mallard inlaid in receiver, with two ducks on bottom, one on trigger guard; grayed, engraved receiver; French walnut stock forend; 24 lpi checkering; oil-finished hand-rubbed wood; marketed in velvet-lined black walnut case. Only 500 made in 1981.
Issue Price: $7000
Market Value: $5195

COLT JOHN M. BROWNING COMMEMORATIVE

Model 1911; 45 Auto; standard model to commemorate the 70th anniversary of the model's existence. Gold inlay on right side of slide announces the reason for manufacture, with eagle, scrollwork and Colt stallion; right side of slide also features extensive scrollwork; blued hammer and trigger, hand-checkered walnut grips. Reported 3000 made in 1981.
Issue Price: $1100
Market Value: $1095

MAG-NA-PORT SAFARI #3 LION

Revolver; built on Ruger Blackhawk; 44 Magnum; Mag-na-ported 5-1/2-inch barrel; highly polished blue-black finish; Omega Maverick rear sight, white front sight insert; silver inlay of Mag-na-port logo; custom grip with ivory scrimshaw of lion; lion engraving on cylinder and "Shumba" engraved on backstrap. Marketed in hand-crafted presentation case. Only 200 made in 1981.
Issue Price: $995
Market Value: $1550

REMINGTON 1981 DUCKS UNLIMITED SPECIAL

Model 1100 LT-20; 26-inch Improved Cylinder, vent-rib barrel; 2-3/4-inch chamber; left side of receiver panel carries words "Ducks Unlimited Special" in script lettering. Right receiver panel has DU mallard head logo with scrollwork. Right side of buttstock has laser-etched reproduction of DU crest. Only 2400 made in 1981, with serial numbers 0001-DU81 to 2400-DU81, for auction by DU.
Market Value: $695

REMINGTON 1981 CLASSIC

Bolt-action Model 700; 7mm Mauser only; 24-inch barrel; 44-1/2-inch overall length; cut-checkered American walnut stock of Classic design; satin finish on wood; no sights; hinged floorplate; rubber recoil pad; sling swivel studs. Limited production in this caliber only in 1981.
Issue Price: $364.95
Market Value: $725

REMINGTON ATLANTIC DU COMMEMORATIVE

Model 1100 12-ga. magnum; 32-inch Full-choke, vent-rib barrel; right side of receiver is embossed with "Ducks Unlimited" and DU mallard head symbol; left side carries the words, "The Atlantic," surrounded by scroll markings. Made only in 1981; carries special DU serial numbers.
Issue Price: $552
Market Value: $695

REMINGTON CHESAPEAKE

Ducks Unlimited commemorative for 1981; Model 1100; 12-ga. magnum; 30-inch barrel; Full choke; select American walnut stock; cut checkering; recoil pad; gold-colored trigger; ivory bead front sight; left side of receiver decorated with plaque of flying duck scrollwork engraved gold-filled legend; furnished with foam-lined hard carrying case. Only 2400 made for DU auctions with opening bid of $950.
Market Value: $695

REMINGTON MODEL 1100 COLLECTORS EDITION

Same specs as standard Model 1100 except deep-relief etching, gold highlights, richly figured walnut stock positive cut checkering. Marketed with certificate showing serial number. Only 3000 made in 1981.
Market Value: $995

WINCHESTER JOHN WAYNE COMMEMORATIVE

Model 94 carbine; 32-40 Win. only; pewter-plated receiver; nickel-silver likeness of Wayne inlaid in American walnut stock; cut checkering; receiver engraved with cattle drive scene on one side, stagecoach under attack by Indians on other; scenes are edged with titles of Wayne's films. Reported 50,000 made in 1981, some marketed by U.S. Repeating Arms.
Issue Price: $600
Market Value: $1795

1982 Browning Waterfowl/Pintail Limited Edition

1980 Mag-Na-Port Safari #2 Elephant

1981 Mag-Na-Port Safari #3 Lion

1981 Remington Atlantic DU Commemorative

1981 Colt John M. Browning Commemorative

1981 Remington Ducks Unlimited Special

1981 Remington Chesapeake

1982 Remington Ducks Unlimited Special

1982 Colt John Wayne Deluxe

1982 Colt John Wayne Presentation

1982 Colt John Wayne Commemorative

1982

BROWNING WATERFOWL/PINTAIL LIMITED EDITION

Over/under; 12-ga.; 28-inch Modified/Full barrels; same specs as 1981 Mallard Limited Edition except hand-sculptured inlays of pintails in flight against background of cattails; gold-inlaid head of pintail on trigger; inscribed in gold are "American Pintail" and the scientific name, "Anas Acuta." Stock is of French walnut, with checkered butt. Marketed in velvet-lined black walnut case. Only 500 made in Belgium in 1982.
Issue Price: $8800
Market Value: $5195

COLT JOHN WAYNE COMMEMORATIVE

Single Action; 45 Colt; ivory grips; etched, gold-plated portrait of Wayne on cylinder, eagle and shield on barrel with name; gold-filled Wayne signature on backstrap; marketed in presentation case. Reported 3100 made.
Issue Price: $2995
Market Value: $2195

COLT JOHN WAYNE DELUXE

Same specs as John Wayne Commemorative except silver-plated, hand-engraved finish with 18-karat gold inlaid motif; two-piece ebony grips with ivory insert, gold-plated image of Wayne on horseback etched on right side of cylinder. Only 500 made.
Issue Price: $10,000
Market Value: $7700

COLT JOHN WAYNE PRESENTATION

Same specs as John Wayne Commemorative except blued finish, gold plating, 24-karat gold inlays, two-piece checkered ivory grips with gold inlay. Only 100 made.
Issue Price: $20,000
Market Value: $12,500

REMINGTON 1982 CLASSIC

Same specs as the 1981 Remington Classic except 257 Roberts; limited production of approximately 7000 in this caliber only in 1981.
Issue Price: $381.95
Market Value: $460

1983 Mag-Na-Port Alaskan Series, Grizzly

1983 Mag-Na-Port Alaskan Series, Moose

1983 Mag-Na-Port Alaskan Series, Dall Sheep

1983 Mag-Na-Port Alaskan Series, Caribou

1983 Colt Buffalo Bill Wild West Show Commemorative

1982 Winchester Annie Oakley 22

1982 Ruger Model 1 Limited Edition

1982 Remington River DU Commemorative

REMINGTON 1982 DU SPECIAL

Model 870; 20-ga. lightweight; 2-3/4-inch chamber, 26-inch Improved Cylinder barrel; decorated with gold-filled scrollwork inscribed with mallard logo, words, "Ducks Unlimited Special"; has gold-colored trigger, ivory bead front sight. Only 3000 made; serial numbers are 0001-DU82 to 3000-DU82.
Issue Price: $550
Market Value: $675

REMINGTON MODEL FOUR COLLECTORS EDITION

Same specs as standard Model Four semi-automatic except etched receiver; 24K gold inlays; all metal parts with high-luster finish; 30-06 only. Only 1500 made in 1982.
Market Value: $1195

REMINGTON RIVER DU COMMEMORATIVE

Model 670; 12-ga. magnum; 30-inch Full-choke, vent-rib barrel; dedicated to the Mississippi Flyway; left receiver panel has engraved bronze medallion of mallard duck flanked by script lettering of gun's model and commemorative title, "The River," set off by scroll markings filled in gold color. Special serial numbers are DU82-0001 to DU82-3000. Only 3000 made.
Issue Price: $425
Market Value: $695

RUGER MODEL I LIMITED EDITION

Mark I Target Model semi-automatic pistol of stainless steel introduced January 1, 1982, to mark the end of production of the standard model. Pistol was marketed in the same type of wooden case and printed inner box in which the original Ruger auto was shipped at the beginning of production in 1949. Each pistol was accompanied by an exact reproduction of the original automatic pistol brochure. Barrel of each pistol was marked "1 of 5000" and the receiver roll marked with a replica of the signature of the inventor, William B. Ruger. Only 5000 made in 1982.
Issue Price: $435
Market Value: $695

WINCHESTER ANNIE OAKLEY 22

Rifle; 22 LR, 22 WMR; 20-1/2-inch barrel; based on Model 9422; barrel inscription gold inlaid; receiver roll engraved on right side with portrait of Annie Oakley, on left side with Oakley standing in saddle, shooting from moving horse; available with sling swivels, saddle ring on special order. Reported 6000 manufactured.
Issue Price: $699
Market Value: $1795

1983

BROWNING WATERFOWL/BLACK DUCK LIMITED EDITION

Over/under; 12-ga.; 28-inch Modified/Full barrels; same specs as 1981 Mallard Limited Edition except 24-karat black ducks inlaid in receiver; words, "Black Duck" and Latin designation "Anas Rubripes," engraved in gold within gold banners. Marketed in velvet-lined black walnut case. Only 500 made in Belgium in 1983.
Issue Price: $8800
Market Value: $5195

COLT BUFFALO BILL WILD WEST SHOW COMMEMORATIVE

Single Action Army; 45; 4-3/4-inch barrel etched with gold-plated figure of Colonel Cody on unfluted cylinder, cowboys, Indians and buffalo on barrel with commemorative inscription; two-piece walnut grips; blued finish, color case-hardened frame; marketed in cherry-stained hardwood case. Only 500 made.
Issue Price: $1349.95
Market Value: $2095

MAG-NA-PORT ALASKAN SERIES

Revolver; built on stainless steel Ruger Super Blackhawk; 44 Magnum; four variations in the series; rear sight is original Omega white outline; front sight is C-More by Magnum Sales, with different colored inserts; barrels are Mag-na-ported with Mag-na-port logo etched on each cylinder. "Alaskan Series" is etched into the barrel, "One of 200" into the topstrap, with appropriate animal's profile also etched into the cylinder; each gun was delivered with Mag-na-port seal as guarantee the hammer had never been in cocked position. Each gun marketed in walnut presentation case with appropriate animal's head branded into wood. Introduced, 1983.

MAG-NA-PORT ALASKAN GRIZZLY

Motif included 50 of the 200 guns in series; barrel had been cut to 4 5/8-inch and recrowned; C-More front sight carried a green insert.
Issue Price: $695
Market Value: $850

1983 Winchester Chief Crazy Horse Commemorative

1984 Winchester 9422 Eagle Scout Commemorative

1984 Texas Longhorn
South Texas Army Limited Edition

MAG-NA-PORT ALASKAN DALL SHEEP

Same as Grizzly with 50 guns issued except barrel cut to 5 1/2-inch, recrowned; replacement C-More front sight carries pink insert of high-contrast DuPont acetal.
Issue Price: $695
Market Value: $850

MAG-NA-PORT ALASKAN CARIBOU

Issue includes 50 guns with 6-1/2-inch recrowned barrel; insert of C-More sight is blaze orange in color.
Issue Price: $695
Market Value: $850

MAG-NA-PORT ALASKAN MOOSE

Comprises 50 guns with standard 7-1/2-inch Blackhawk barrel; C-More sight insert is bright yellow.
Issue Price: $695
Market Value: $850

MAG-NA-PORT SAFARI #4 RHINO

Revolver; built on stainless steel Ruger Super Blackhawk; 44 Magnum; 4-5/8-inch Mag-na-ported barrel; velvet hone finish; gold-plated hammer, trigger, ejector rod, center pin, center pin release; Omega white-outline rear sight, red insert front sight; rhino head hand-engraved on cylinder; Mag-na-port serial numbers 001 through 200 hand-engraved on frame. Marketed in walnut presentation case with overlay of African continent and hand-painted head of rhino. Only 200 made in 1983.
Issue Price: $895
Market Value: $1450

REMINGTON 1983 CLASSIC

Same specs as Classic limited issue of previous years except 300 H&H Magnum only. Approximately 3500 made in this caliber only in 1983.
Issue Price: $421.95
Market Value: $675

REMINGTON MISSISSIPPI DU COMMEMORATIVE

Model 870 12-ga. magnum; 32-inch Full-choke, vent-rib barrel; right side of receiver embossed with words, "Ducks Unlimited," DU mallard head symbol; left side of receiver carries title of gun, "The Mississippi," with scrollwork.
Issue Price: $454
Market Value: $650

WINCHESTER CHIEF CRAZY HORSE COMMEMORATIVE

Rifle; built on Model 94 action; 38-55 Win.; 24-inch barrel; stock decorated with brass tacks; medallion in stock symbolizes united Sioux tribes; Chief Crazy Horse inscription engraved in barrel; receiver engraved, gold filled on both sides with Indian scenes, names of Sioux tribes in English, Lakota Sioux; saddle ring. Reported 19,999 made.
Issue Price: $600
Market Value: $1595

1984

AMERICA REMEMBERS BUFFALO BILL CENTENNIAL

Replica of Colt Model 1860 Army blackpowder 44 revolver; 8-inch barrel; extensive gold etching of Western scenes; bonded ivory stocks and powder flask; brass accessories; marketed in lined display case. Reported 2500 manufactured in Virginia gun factory, 1984.
Issue Price: $1950
Market Value: $895

AMERICAN HISTORICAL FOUNDATION KOREAN WAR COMMEMORATIVE THOMPSON

Semi-automatic; 45 ACP; same specs as standard Model 1927 Thompson except highly polished walnut buttstock, pistol grip, forend; gold-plated activator knob, Cutts compensator, rear sight base, trigger, sling swivels; commemorative medallions set in buttstock, pistol grip; special serial numbers, KW0001 through KW1500. Reported 1500 made by Auto Ordnance, 1984.
Issue Price: $1,195
Market Value: $1295

AMERICAN HISTORICAL FOUNDATION M1 GARAND WORLD WAR II COMMEMORATIVE

Reproduction of WWII combat rifle; select-grade walnut stock; highly blued finish; gold plating on smaller parts. Reported 2500 made by Springfield Armory in Illinois under special order; carried serial numbers WW0001 through WW2500. Marketed, 1984, with walnut display case.
Issue Price: $1695
Market Value: $1195

COLT KIT CARSON COMMEMORATIVE

Single action; 22 rimfire; based on Colt New Frontier model; 6-inch barrel; blued, color case-hardened frame; ivory-colored stocks; gold artwork in Western motif on barrel; marketed in custom cherry case with hardbound copy of Kit Carson's Own Story; 950 made.
Issue Price: $549
Market Value: $650

COLT USA EDITION

Single Action Army revolver; 44-40; 7-1/2-inch barrel; fluted cylinder; checkered ivory stocks with fleur-de-lis pattern; gold inlaid frame borders, outline of state or capital city on recoil shield; gold-inlaid rampant colt on loading gate; gold-inlaid "USA" on left side of barrel; two gold-inlaid barrel bands; gold-inlaid ejector tube band; silver- and gold-inlaid stars; only 100 made.
Issue Price: $4995
Market Value: $5000

COLT THEODORE ROOSEVELT COMMEMORATIVE

Single action; based on Colt SAA; 7-1/2-inch barrel; 44-40; hand-fitted ivory stocks; backstrap bears gold TR monogram; barrel, cylinder hand engraved; marketed in oak presentation case; 500 made.
Issue Price: $1695
Market Value: $1995

REMINGTON 1984 CLASSIC

Same specs as earlier Classic Limited issues except 250-3000 Savage. Approximately 2500 made in this caliber in 1984.
Issue Price: $420.80
Market Value: $465

TEXAS LONGHORN SOUTH TEXAS ARMY LIMITED EDITION

Revolver; single action; all centerfire pistol calibers; 6-shot cylinder; 4-3/4-inch barrel; grooved topstrap rear sight, blade front; one-piece fancy walnut stocks; loading gate, ejector housing on left side of the gun; cylinder rotates to left; color case-hardened frame; high polish blue finish; music wire coil springs; hand made; "One of One Thousand" engraved on barrel; marketed in glass-covered display case. Only 1000 made.
Market Value: $1695

WEATHERBY 1984 MARK V OLYMPIC COMMEMORATIVE

Rifle; bolt-action; 300 Weatherby; same specs as standard Mark V except accents gold-plated; top-grade walnut stock with inlaid star. Reported 1000 made in Japan, 1984.
Issue Price: $2000
Market Value: $1100

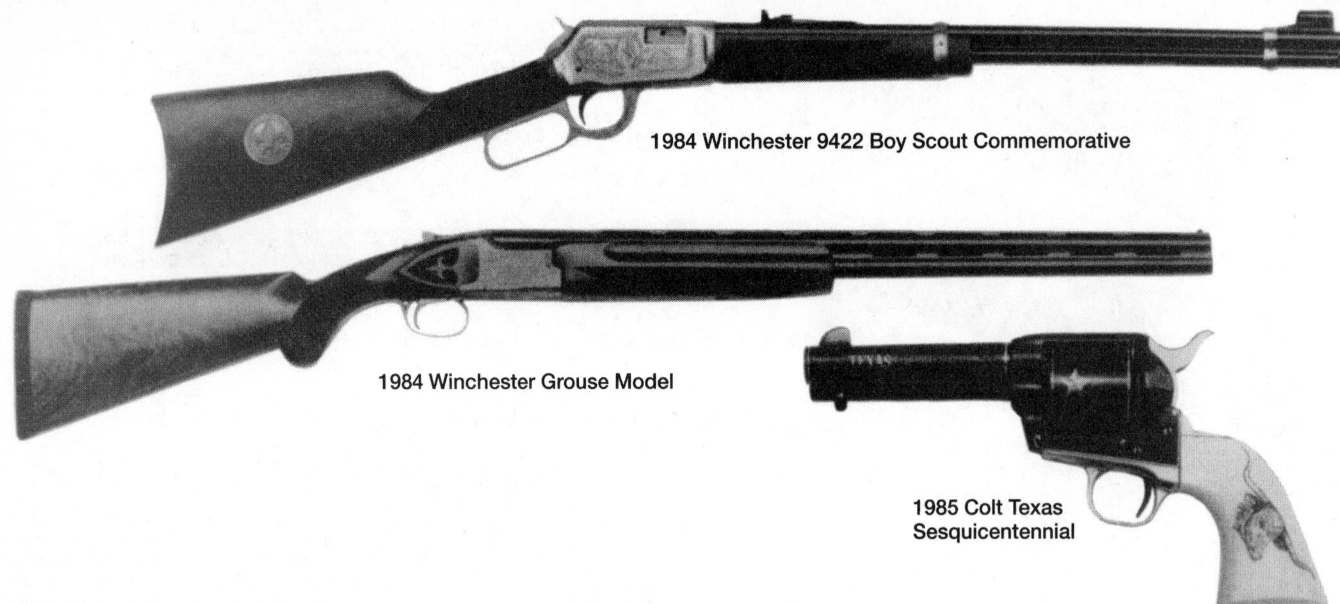
1984 Winchester 9422 Boy Scout Commemorative

1984 Winchester Grouse Model

1985 Colt Texas Sesquicentennial

WINCHESTER 9422 EAGLE SCOUT COMMEMORATIVE

Same specs as Model 9422 XTR except receiver deep etched, plated in gold; left side has Boy Scout law, right side has Boy Scout oath; frame has "1910-1985" inscription; checkered stock, forend, high-luster finish; Eagle Scout medallion embedded in right side of stock; crescent steel buttplate; gold-plated forend cap; jeweled bolt. Marketed in oak presentation case; 1000 made.
Issue Price: $1710
Market Value: $3500

WINCHESTER 9422 BOY SCOUT COMMEMORATIVE

Same specs as Model 9422 except receiver roll-engraved, plated in antique pewter; frame carries "1910-1985" anniversary inscription, Boy Scout oath, law; lever has engraved frieze of scouting knots; "Boy Scouts of America" inscribed on barrel; medallion embedded in stock; 15,000 made.
Issue Price: $495
Market Value: $1195

WINCHESTER GROUSE MODEL

Limited edition over/under based on Model 101 configuration; custom built for the Ruffed Grouse Society; 20-ga. only; engraved scene of grouse on action; fancy walnut woodwork. Only 225 made in 1984.
Market Value: $1450

WINCHESTER/COLT 94 SET

Both guns 44-40 Win.; carbine with 20-inch barrel; tube magazine; 38-1/8-inch overall length; follows basic Model 94 specs except horse-and-rider trademark, WC monogram etched in gold on left side; gold-etched portrait of Oliver Winchester on right; right side of barrel has rendering of original Winchester factory; additional gold scrollwork; crescent buttplate; deep-cut spade checkering; semi-gloss finish on American walnut woodwork. Colt is Peacemaker SAA model with backstrap bearing Sam Colt signature in gold; WC monogram is gold-etched on left side of cylinder; barrel bears serpentine Colt logo in gold; right side of barrel has gold etching of original Colt factory; gold-plated scrollwork; oil-finished American walnut grips; 7-1/2-inch barrel; 4440 sets made.
Issue Price: $3995
Market Value: $2950

1985

AMERICAN HISTORICAL FOUNDATION WWII VICTORY SPECIAL EDITION M1 CARBINE

Semi-automatic; 30 Carbine; same specs as M1 Carbine standard military version except highly polished; American walnut stock; mirror-polished barrel, receiver; gold-plated rear sight, windage knob, front sight, trigger, magazine release, barrel bands, safety, slide stop; special serial numbers are WW0001 through WW2500. Reported 2,500 made under special contract by Iver Johnson Arms, 1985.
Issue Price: $695
Market Value: $595

COLT TEXAS SESQUICENTENNIAL

Single action; 45 Colt; built on SAA Sheriff's Model; 4-inch barrel; Texas legend, dates inlaid on barrel in gold; gold star in shield on cylinder; marketed in French-fitted oak presentation case; 1000 made.
Issue Price: $1836
Market Value: $1695

COLT SESQUICENTENNIAL PREMIER

Same specs as Texas Sesquicentennial; built on SAA design; 45 Colt; 4-3/4-inch barrel; 24-karat gold-plated trigger guard, backstrap; engraved gold-inlaid scenes of Texas history, including the Alamo; scrimshawed ivory grips; marketed in four-sided glass presentation case; 75 made.
Issue Price: $7995
Market Value: $5000

REMINGTON 1985 CLASSIC

Same specs as earlier versions except 350 Rem. Magnum. Approximately 6500 made in this caliber only in 1985.
Issue Price: $474.70
Market Value: $475

RUGER YR-25 CARBINE

Semi-automatic; 44 Magnum; same specs as the standard Ruger Model 44 except medallion in stock commemorating the 25th anniversary of the carbine's manufacture; the last year the model was made. Made only in 1985.
Market Value: $450

SIG MODEL 226 15TH ANNIVERSARY COMMEMORATIVE

Same specs as Model 226 except deep black non-reflective finish; ornately carved wooden grips; trigger, hammer, magazine release, decocking lever and slide stop all are gold-plated, all stampings on slide are gold-filled. Slide marking reads, "125 Jahre SIG Waffen 1860-1985"; marketed in leather presentation case. Only 200 imported into U.S. in 1985.
Issue Price: $2500
Market Value: $1195

WINCHESTER ATA HALL OF FAME COMMEMORATIVE

Combo trap set; 12-ga.; 34-inch single-barrel; 30-inch vent-rib over/under Winchoke barrels; engraved with Amateur Trapshooting Assn. Hall of Fame logo; serial numbered HF1 through HF250; first 60 were auction items at 1985 Grand American; marketed in fitted luggage style case; only 250 made in 1985 in Japan by Winchester-Olin.
Issue Price: $2795
Market Value: $2750

1986

AMERICAN HISTORICAL FOUNDATION VIETNAM WAR COMMEMORATIVE THOMPSON

Semi-automatic; 45 ACP; basic specs of 1927 Thompson except highly polished blued finish; gold-plated rear sight, front sight and Cutts compensator, trigger, sling swivels; American walnut stock, forearm, with inset medallions; receiver carries gold-filled commemorative inscriptions, serial number, issuing organization, Thompson patent numbers. Reported 1500 made by Auto Ordnance Corp., on special order, 1986.
Issue Price: $1,295
Market Value: $1295

AMERICAN HISTORICAL FOUNDATION M1 GARAND KOREAN WAR COMMEMORATIVE

Semi-automatic; 30-06; same specs as M1 Garand military version except polished Fajen select American walnut stock; gold-plated front sight, rear sight base, trigger, windage knob, elevation knob, stacking swivel, sling swivels, safety; barrel, receiver and other metal parts mirror polished; gold-plated medallion inset in stock. Reported 2500 made, 1986, serial numbers KW0001 through KW2500.
Issue Price: $1895
Market Value: $1195

BROWNING BIG HORN SHEEP ISSUE

Same specs as standard Browning A-Bolt rifle except 270 Win. only; checkered stock is high-grade walnut with high-gloss finish; has brass spacers under grip cap, recoil pad; deep relief engraving; big horn displayed in 24-karat gold. Only 600 made in Japan. Introduced, 1986.
Market Value: $1250

BROWNING MODEL 1886 MONTANA CENTENNIAL

Same specs as 1886 High Grade lever-action rifle except different stock design; engraving on receiver reads "Montana Centennial". Only 1,000 made in Japan, 1986.
Issue Price: $995
Market Value: $1895

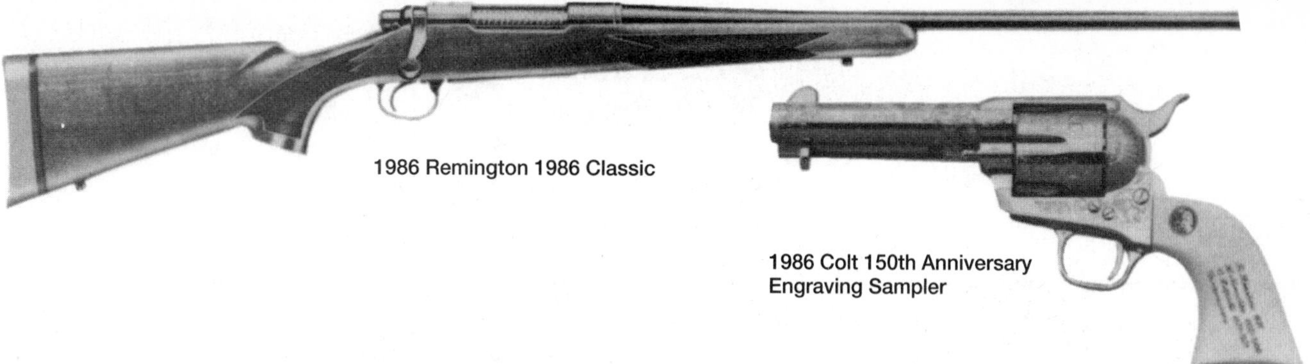
1986 Remington 1986 Classic

1986 Colt 150th Anniversary Engraving Sampler

COLT 150TH ANNIVERSARY COMMEMORATIVE

Single Action Army revolver with 10-inch barrel, royal blue finish, authentic old-style frame with "B" engraving coverage, Goncalo Alves grips; anniversary logo is etched in 24K gold on backstrap, plus gold-etched signature panel. Marketed in an oak case with silver blue velvet lining; top of lid branded "1836-Colt-1986"; inside of the lid has inset 150th anniversary medallion; 1000 made with serial numbers AM-0001 through AM-1000. Made in 1986 only.
Issue Price: $1595
Market Value: $1995

COLT 150TH ANNIVERSARY ENGRAVING SAMPLER

Single Action Army; 4-3/4-inch barrel; blued or nickel finish; carries four styles of hand engraving; Henshaw, Nimschke, Helfricht and Colt Contemporary, with each style contained on one part of the gun; ivory grips are scrimshawed with the names of the four patterns. Made only in 1986.
Issue Price: Blued, $1612.95; Nickel, $1731.50
Market Value: $2500 to $3000 depending on finish, caliber and barrel length.

COLT 150TH ANNIVERSARY DOUBLE DIAMOND

Two-gun set of stainless steel, including the Python Ultimate with 6-inch barrel and a polished Officers Model 45 ACP automatic. Both guns carry matching serial numbers and rosewood grips as well as the Double Diamond logo. Marketed in a cherrywood presentation case with a framed glass lid; lining is black velvet. Serial numbers extend from 0001-DD through 1000-DD. Only 1000 sets made in 1986.
Issue Price: $1574.95
Market Value: $2000

COLT WHITETAILER II

King Cobra AA3080; 357 Magnum; 8-inch barrel, vented rib; red insert in front sight ramp, fully-adjustable white outline rear; rubber combat-style grips; transfer bar safety; brushed stainless steel finish; barrel marked on left side, "Whitetailer II"; furnished with 1-1/2-4x variable Burris scope, with brushed aluminum finish; Millett satin nickel mounts. Marketed in soft-sided custom carrying case. Produced in 1986; 1000 made.
Issue Price: $807.95
Market Value: $1595

KIMBER BROWNELL

Rifle; bolt-action; 22 rimfire; honors stockmaker Len Brownell. Has high-grade, full-length, Mannlicher-type stock. Reported 500 made, 1986.
Market Value: $1500

REMINGTON 1986 CLASSIC

No changes in the basic design except 264 Win. Magnum only.
Issue Price: $509.85
Market Value: $495

TEXAS LONGHORN SESQUICENTENNIAL MODEL

Revolver; single action; same specs as South Texas Army Limited Edition except with 3/4-coverage engraving, antique gold, nickel finish; one-piece ivory stocks. Marketed in hand-made walnut presentation case. Only 150 made in 1986.
Market Value: $2500

WINCHESTER 120TH ANNIVERSARY LIMITED EDITION

Model 94 carbine; 44-40 only; anniversary medallion in left side of receiver, with horse-and-rider trademark; right side of receiver carries gold-etched portrait of Oliver Winchester; signature is on the tang; right side of barrel has rendering of original Winchester factory; gold-plated scrollwork on barrel and receiver; magazine cap, front sight blade are gold-plated; has hoop-type lever, crescent buttplate. Only 1000 made in 1986. Serial numbers are WRA0001 to WRA1000.
Issue Price: $950
Market Value: $1895

WINCHESTER SILVER ANNIVERSARY MODEL 101

Special issue in 12-ga. only; 28-inch barrels, vent rib. Each gun marketed in a custom leather carrying case, complete with snap caps and silver initial plate. Only 101 made in 1986.
Issue Price: $5200
Market Value: $2995

1987

AMERICAN DERRINGER TEXAS COMMEMORATIVE

Same specs as Model 1 Derringer except solid brass frame; stainless steel barrel, stag grips. Made in 38 Special, 44-40, 44 American, 45 Colt. Produced in 1987.
Market Value: $295

AMERICAN HISTORICAL FOUNDATION GENERAL PATTON COMMEMORATIVE

Single Action Army revolver; 45 Colt; 4-3/4-inch barrel; same general specs as Colt Single Action Army but made in Italy by Uberti; all exposed metal silver-plated; engraved frame, cylinder, barrel; faux ivory grips with Patton initials. Serial numbered P0001 through P2500. Reported 2500 made, 1987.
Issue Price: $1495
Market Value: $1495

AMERICAN HISTORICAL FOUNDATION M14 VIETNAM COMMEMORATIVE

Semi-automatic rifle; 7.62mm NATO; version of maker's M1A; 22-inch barrel; highly polished blued metal; some gold-plated parts; select walnut stock. Reported 1500 in Army motif, 1500 in Marine motif made by Springfield Armoury, 1987.
Issue Price: $1600
Market Value: $1195

AMERICAN HISTORICAL FOUNDATION VIETNAM WAR COMMEMORATIVE THOMPSON

Semi-automatic; 45 ACP; polished lacquer American walnut stock; same general specs as standard Model 1927 except gold-plated small parts; roll-engraved; gold-filled legend on receiver. Reported 1500 made by Auto Ordnance with special serial numbers, 1987.
Issue Price: $1295
Market Value: $1295

BROWNING PRONGHORN ANTELOPE ISSUE

Same specs as standard Browning A-Bolt except 243 Win. only; extensive detailed engraving; pronghorn in gold on each side of receiver; stock has skip-line checkering, high-gloss finish, brass spacers under pistol-grip cap, recoil pad. Only 500 made in Japan. Introduced, 1987.
Market Value: $1100

F.I.E. YELLOW ROSE LIMITED EDITION

Same specs as the standard model except polymer grips scrimshawed with map of Texas, Texas state flag, yellow rose with green leaves; other scrimshawed depictions available. Marketed in French-fitted American walnut presentation case. Manufactured in 1987.
Market Value: $200

KIMBER CENTENNIAL

Bolt-action rifle commemorates the 100th anniversary of the 22 Long Rifle cartridge; tastefully engraved; match barrel; select walnut stock; skeleton buttplate. Reported 100 manufactured in 1987 with serial numbers C-1 through C-100.
Market Value: $2600

PARKER B GRADE LIMITED EDITION

Replica of Parker Bros. side-by-side shotgun; 12-, 20- and 28-ga.; extensive engraving follows original pattern. Reported 100 made in Japan, 1987, specifically for Parker Reproductions.
Issue Price: $3975
Market Value: $4800

REMINGTON 1987 CLASSIC

Same specs as other Model 700s in Classic Series except 338 Win. Magnum only. Approximately 3000 made in this chambering only in 1987.
Issue Price: $421
Market Value: $450

WALTHER 100TH YEAR COMMEMORATIVE

Semi-automatic; 9mm Para.; same basic specs as P-5 model except heavy engraving. Marketed in walnut presentation case. Number made, original price unknown. Introduced, 1987.
Market Value: $2350

WINCHESTER MODEL 70 XTR GOLDEN ANNIVERSARY

Similar to sporter magnum except select walnut classic-style stock old-style swivel bases, steel floorplate, grip cap, trigger guard; hand-engraving on barrel, receiver, magazine cover, trigger guard; inscription on barrel, "The Rifleman's Rifle 1937-1987"; hand engraved receiver, floor- plate, trigger guard, grip cap, crossbolt; chambered for 300 Win. Magnum only; 500 made.
Issue Price: $939
Market Value: $1350

1988 Colt Heirloom Limited Edition

1988 American Historical Foundation M14 Vietnam Commemorative

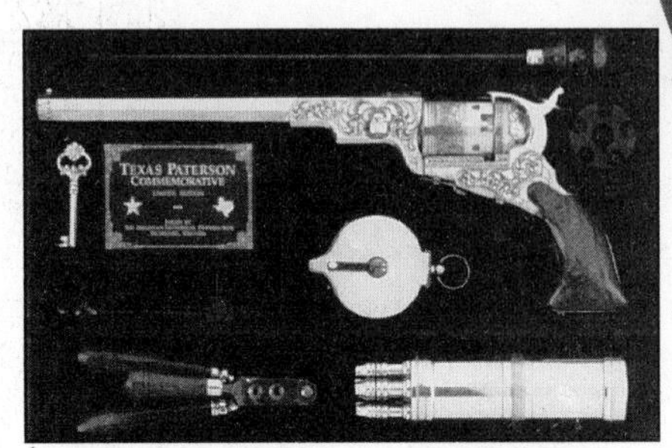

1988 American Historical Foundation Commemorative Texas Paterson

1988 American Historical Foundation Teddy Roosevelt Commemorative

1988

AMERICA REMEMBERS U.S. CAVALRY MODEL

Limited edition blackpowder Colt Model 1860 replica; 44 blackpowder revolver; 8-inch barrel; gold-etched scene on cylinder; stag grips. Marketed in presentation case with replica brass cavalry buckle. Reported 2500 made in U.S., 1988.
Issue Price: $1650
Market Value: $895

AMERICAN HISTORICAL FOUNDATION AMERICAN ARMED FORCES UZI COMMEMORATIVE

Semi-automatic; 9mm Para.; basic specs of standard Uzi except highly polished blued finish; gold-plated magazine release, barrel ring nut, pistol-grip bushing, sear and trigger pivot pins, trigger, stock screws and nuts, sling keepers and cocking knob; furniture-finished woodstock carrying medallion with words, "The American Armed Forces Around The World." Marketed with gold-plated sight-adjustment tool. Reported 1500 made under special Israeli Military Industries contract, 1988.
Issue Price: $2195
Market Value: $1500

AMERICAN HISTORICAL FOUNDATION COMMEMORATIVE TEXAS PATERSON

Five-shot revolver; blackpowder; 36-caliber; part of Samuel Colt Golden Tribute Collection, commemorates 150th anniversary of gun's production; gold-plated, hand-engraved in Italy by Pedersoli; hand-fitted burled walnut grips; 9-inch octagonal barrel. Marketed with combination tool, extra cylinder. Reported 950 made, 1988.
Issue Price: $1495
Market Value: $1495

AMERICAN HISTORICAL FOUNDATION M14 VIETNAM COMMEMORATIVE

Semi-automatic; 7.62mm NATO; same specs as M14 military issue except high-quality Fajen stock; gold-plated components; patriotic inscriptions etched and gold-filled on operating rod and receiver. Made in two configurations, 500 Deluxe Museum Edition and 500 Collector Edition by Federal Arms under special contract, 1988, with special serial numbers.
Issue Price: Deluxe Museum Edition, $1,595; Collector Edition, $1,395

Deluxe Museum Edition
Market Value: $1195

Collector Edition
Market Value: $995

AMERICAN HISTORICAL FOUNDATION LAW ENFORCEMENT COMMEMORATIVE THOMPSON

Semi-automatic; 45 ACP; same specs as standard 1928 Thompson subgun except highly polished American walnut buttstock, grip and vertical foregrip; gold-plated frontsight, Cutts compensator; sling swivels. Receiver roll-engraved, gold-filled legend; police shield medallion in buttstock, rear grip carries medallion with police motto. Marketed with night stick carrying same serial number as gun. Reported 1500 made on special order by Auto Ordnance, 1988.
Issue Price: $1595
Market Value: $1295

AMERICAN HISTORICAL FOUNDATION TEDDY ROOSEVELT COMMEMORATIVE

Revolver; 45 Colt; same specs as Colt Single Action Army except 7-1/2-inch barrel; gold-plated ejector rod housing, trigger, hammer and cylinder; all other external metal parts sterling silver-plated; ivory/polymer grips, with buffalo head raised on right panel; TR monogram on left; extensively engraved in Nimaschke pattern of Roosevelt's original SAA. Reported 750 made in Italy by Uberti, 1988.
Issue Price: $1995
Market Value: $1495

AMERICAN HISTORICAL FOUNDATION U.S. ARMY COMMEMORATIVE

Semi-automatic; 45 ACP; same specs as standard Model 1911A1 except ten gold-plated parts; slide etched, gold-filled with U.S. Army seal, legend; Herrett burled walnut grips with Army medallion. Reported 1911 made on special order by Auto Ordnance, 1988.
Issue Price: $995
Market Value: $750

AMERICAN HISTORICAL FOUNDATION VIETNAM WAR M16 COMMEMORATIVE

Semi-automatic; 5.56mm; same basic specs as M16 military issue except high-gloss black finish; gold-plated flash suppressor, trigger, selector lever, bolt catch, rear sight windage knob, take-down pins, sling swivels; pistol grip and buttstock carry commemorative medallions. Marketed with adjustable black leather military-type sling. Reported 1,500 made by Colt on special order, 1988.
Issue Price: $1995
Market Value: $1795

BROWNING MODEL 12 LIMITED EDITION

Slide-action shotgun; 20-, 28-ga.; 2-3/4-inch chamber; 26-inch barrel; reproduction of the Winchester Model 12; has cut-checkered walnut stock; high-post floating rib, grooved sight plane; crossbolt safety in trigger guard; polished blue finish. Limited edition; 8500 Grade I, 4000 Grade V guns made in Japan in 1988. Imported by Browning.
Issue Price: Grade I, 20-ga., $734.95; Grade I, 28-ga., $771.95; Grade V, 20-ga., $1187; Grade V, 28-ga., $1246.

Mint Grade I
Market Value: $650

Mint Grade V
Market Value: $995

COLT HEIRLOOM LIMITED EDITION

Officers Model 1911A1; 45 ACP; produced in Colt Custom Shop on individual order, with serial numbers to order, combining numbers with family names or initials; full mirror finish; Combat Commander hammer; extended trigger; wide combat grip safety; ambidextrous safety; jeweled barrel, hammer and trigger; ivory grips; special grip medallion. Marketed in mahogany presentation case. Made in 1988-89.
Issue Price: $1500
Market Value: $1395

COLT U.S. MARSHALS BICENTENNIAL COMMEMORATIVE

Single Action Army revolver; 45 Colt; smooth walnut grips; 7-1/2-inch barrel; blued finish; U.S. Marshal medallion set in left grip panel; on left side of the barrel, marking is "U.S. Marshals Bicentennial 1789-1989"; on right side, legend reads "One of Five Hundred." Marketed in glass-topped case, with French blue velvet lining; U.S. Marshal's badge included. Produced for U.S. Marshals Foundation; 500 made in 1988.
Issue Price: $775
Market Value: $1495

KRICO 720 LIMITED EDITION

Bolt-action rifle; 270; 20-1/2-inch barrel; full-length Mannlicher-type stock; gold-plated trim and scrollwork on metal parts; serial number inlaid in gold. Made in Germany. Imported by Beeman Precision Arms, 1988.
Issue Price: $2375
Market Value: $2300

REMINGTON 1988 CLASSIC

Same specs as earlier rifles in the series except 35 Whelen. Approximately 7000 made in this caliber in 1988 only.
Issue Price: $440
Market Value: $495

1989 Mossberg National Wild Turkey Federation Limited Edition

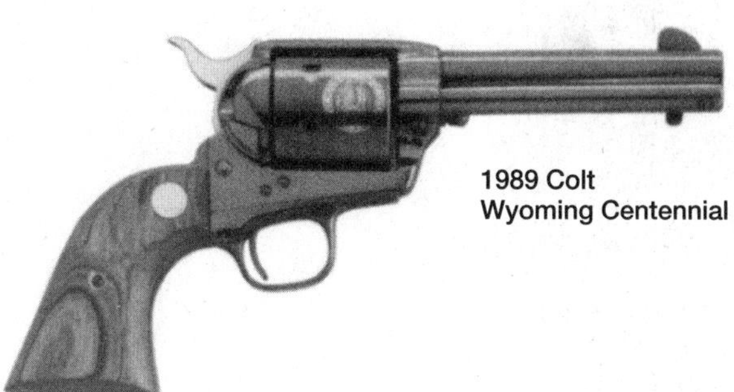
1989 Colt Wyoming Centennial

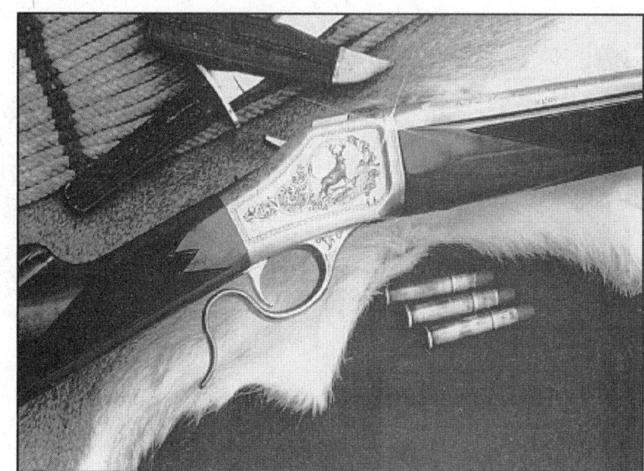
1989 American Historical Foundation Browning Model 1885 Deerhunter Limited Edition

1989

AMERICAN HISTORICAL FOUNDATION BROWNING MODEL 1885 DEERHUNTER LIMITED EDITION

Lever-action; 45-70; same specs as original Winchester 1885 except has complete engraving coverage of receiver featuring a deer in a wreath; hand-finished walnut stock, forearm. Reported 100 made, 1989.
Issue Price: $2775
Market Value: $1750

AMERICAN HISTORICAL FOUNDATION VIETNAM WAR COMMEMORATIVE

Semi-automatic; 45 ACP; same specs as standard Model 1911A1 except gold-plated hammer, trigger, safety, slide stop, magazine catch, magazine catch lock and grip screws; slide engraved with Oriental dragons, carries bannered legend; American oak grips with medallion. Reported 2500 made by Auto Ordnance on special order, 1989.
Issue Price: $1095
Market Value: $795

BROWNING WYOMING CENTENNIAL

Model 1885 lever-action rifle; 25-06; same basic specs as standard model except tapered octagon barrel, No. 5 walnut stock, Wyoming state seal, centennial logo inlaid in gold. Reported 2000 made in 1989. Marketed by Sports, Inc.
Issue Price: $1200
Market Value: $1200

COLT BEVERLY HILLS POLICE COMMEMORATIVE

Colt Combat Government Model; 45 ACP; commemorates the 75th anniversary of California's Beverly Hills Police Department; gold-plated scene on both sides of slide includes city hall, police car, motorcycle officer foot patrolman; city insignia on rear of slide in gold; city seal inset in grips; gold-bannered commemorative buckle included; special serial numbers, BHPD001 to 150; 150 guns made in 1989. Marketed in red velvet-lined presentation case.
Issue Price: $785
Market Value: $950

COLT JOE FOSS LIMITED EDITION

Government Model auto; 45 ACP; blued finish; fixed sights; smooth walnut grips; left side of the slide covers Foss' life through WWII with gold-plated figures of farmhouse, Marine Corps seal, Marine aviator's wings, cannon and Grumman aircraft; at rear of the slide is bordered rampant colt. On the slide's right side, the gold-plated figures represent Foss' post-WWII career, including South Dakota capitol, a hunter, Mount Rushmore figures, and an F16 fighter aircraft, with words "A Tribute To Joe Foss" Serial numbers are JF0001 through JF2500; 2500 made in 1989. Marketed in walnut presentation case with red velvet lining. Included are brass plate and medallion.
Issue Price: $1375
Market Value: $995

COLT SNAKE EYES SET

Colt Python models; 357 Magnum; two guns in set; 2-1/2-inch barrels; one gun has blued finish, other is stainless steel; Snake Eyes name appears on left side of barrels; ivory-like grips with scrimshaw snake eyes dice on left side, royal flush poker hand on right; matching serial numbers EYES001 through EYES500 positioned on butt of each gun; glass-front presentation case is etched with gold letters, trim; interior of case is lined with green felt; interior lighting; Colt-marked poker chips, playing cards are French-fitted. 500 sets made in 1989.
Issue Price: $3500 per set
Market Value: $2700

COLT WYOMING CENTENNIAL

Single Action Army revolver; 45 Colt; 4-3/4-inch barrel; rosewood custom grips; gold-plated rampant colt medallion; left side of barrel carries roll-marked gold-washed logo with "1890 Wyoming Centennial." Unfluted cylinder carries gold-inlaid state seal on one side, centennial logo on the other. Only 200 made in 1989. Marketed in French-fitted walnut case with commemorative plate by Sports, Inc., Lewiston, Montana.
Issue Price: $1250
Market Value: $1395

MOSSBERG NATIONAL WILD TURKEY FEDERATION LIMITED EDITION

Same specs as standard Mossberg Model 835 Ulti-Mag 12-ga. pump-action shotgun, except camo finish; Wild Turkey Federation medallion inlaid in the stock. Marketed with a 10-pack of Federal 3-1/2-inch turkey-load shotshells. Made in 1989.
Issue Price: $477
Market Value: $295

REMINGTON 1989 CLASSIC

Same specs as earlier caliber chamberings in the series except 300 Weatherby Magnum. Approximately 6000 made in this caliber only.
Issue Price: $485
Market Value: $495

1990

AMERICA REMEMBERS FREDERICK REMINGTON MODEL 1886

Revolver; honors the famed Western artist's 100th anniversary as an associate of the National Academy of Design; 44 blackpowder 1886 Army replica; gold etching on 8-inch barrel, trigger, cylinder frame and gripstraps. Marketed with cased accessories. Reported 1000 made, 1990.
Issue Price: $1500
Market Value: $750

AMERICA REMEMBERS LIMITED EDITION TEXAS RANGER DRAGOON

Blackpowder 44 replica revolver; 8-inch barrel; silver-plating on gripstraps, trigger guard and cylinder; colorcase-hardened frame, loading lever; gold etched barrel, frame. Marketed in case with accessories. Reported 1000 made in U.S., 1990.
Issue Price: $1585
Market Value: $995

AMERICA REMEMBERS ROY ROGERS COWBOY EDITION

Single Action Army 45 Colt revolver; 4-3/4-inch barrel; gold-plated cylinder; gold etchings on barrel, gripstrap, frame; stag grips. Marketed in presentation case. Reported 2500 made, 1990.
Issue Price: $1550
Market Value: $1495

AMERICA REMEMBERS ROY ROGERS PREMIER EDITION

Same general specs as Roy Rogers Cowboy Edition except extensive inlays and heavy engraving. Reported 250 made, 1990.
Issue Price: $4500
Market Value: $2995

1991 American Historical Foundation WWII Commemorative Hi-Power

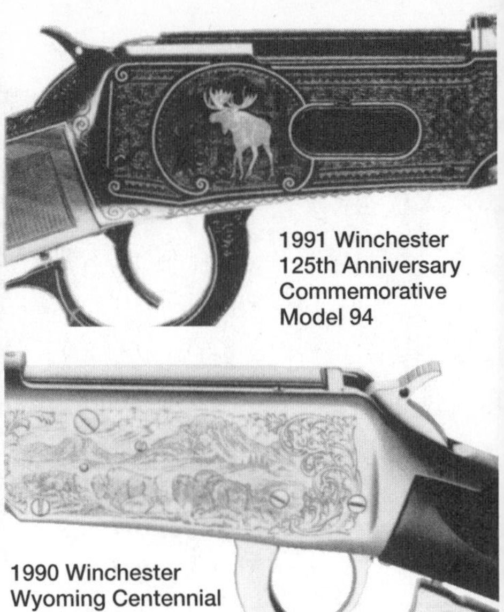

1991 Winchester 125th Anniversary Commemorative Model 94

1990 Winchester Wyoming Centennial Commemorative

AMERICA REMEMBERS ROYAL ARMORIES DRAGOON

Replica of 44 blackpowder 2nd Model Dragoon revolver made in England for Sam Colt; 7-1/2-inch barrel; hand-engraved case-hardened action; walnut grips with sterling silver plaque. Reported 1000 made, 1990.
Issue Price: $2450
Market Value: $1995

BROWNING MODEL 53 LIMITED EDITION

Rifle; 32-20; 7-shot half-length magazine; 22-inch round, tapered barrel; 39.5-inch overall length; weighs 6.8 lbs.; post bead front sight, open adjustable rear; cut-checkered select walnut stock, forend; metal grip cap; blued finish. Only 5000 produced in Japan. Based on Winchester Model 92 design. Introduced, 1990; dropped, 1991.
Issue Price: $675
Market Value: $595

COLT EL PRESIDENTE

Dressed-up version of the Colt Government Model 38 Super; highly polished Ultimate stainless finish; Pearlex grips; "El Presidente" and rampant colt are engraved on left side of the slide. Only 350 made in 1990 for Lew Horton Distributing. Marketed in special soft case with Colt logo.
Issue Price: $800
Market Value: $1695

KIMBER 10TH ANNIVERSARY ISSUE

Bolt-action rifle; 223 Remington; French walnut stock with shadow cheekpiece, slim forend; 22-inch barrel; round-top receiver; steel buttplate; scope mounts furnished. Introduced, 1990 in extremely limited numbers.
Market Value: $1600

REMINGTON 1990 CLASSIC

Same specs as previous 700 Classic models except 25-06 only; 4-shot magazine; 24-inch barrel. Made only in 1990.
Issue Price: $520
Market Value: $495

SMITH & WESSON MODEL 28 MAGNACLASSIC

Same specs as standard Model 29 except 7-1/2-inch full lug barrel; highly polished finish; target hammer, trigger; ergonomic Goncalo Alves grips with carnuba finish. Marketed in cherrywood case with gold-embossed leather lid, fitted velvet interior, black leather sight box, sight assortment, test target, certificate of authenticity; factory accurized; barrel laser-etched, "1 of 3000." 1550 were made in 1990.
Issue Price: $999
Market Value: $1200

SMITH & WESSON MODEL 629 MAGNACLASSIC

Same specs as Model 29 MagnaClassic except stainless steel; same markings; marketed with same accessory package. 1450 were made in 1990.
Issue Price: $999
Market Value: $1200

WINCHESTER WYOMING CENTENNIAL COMMEMORATIVE

Model 94-30-30; features coin-type finish on receiver, barrel bands; receiver engraved both sides with Wyoming scenes; left side carries engraved banners, "1890-1990" and "Wyoming Centennial"; 20-inch barrel; full buckhorn Marble sight; special serial numbers; only 999 made. Marketed exclusively by Cherry's.
Issue Price: $895
Market Value: $1395

1991

AMERICA REMEMBERS INTERPOL COLT SAA

Single Action Army revolver; 45 Colt; 4-3/4-inch barrel; engraving replica of that on Kornblath Interpol Model; silver-plated, with faux ivory grips; marketed in book-like leather case. Only 154 manufactured by Colt on special order, 1991.
Issue Price: $4500
Market Value: $2995

AMERICAN HISTORICAL FOUNDATION WWII COMMEMORATIVE HI-POWER

Semi-automatic; 9mm Para.; same specs as standard Hi-Power model except overall gold plating; carries deep-etched inscriptions, scrollwork; custom-finished walnut grips; inset with victory medallion. Marketed with extra magazine and cleaning rod, both gold-plated. Reported 500 made on special order by Browning 1991.
Issue Price: $1795
Market Value: $1295

GLOCK DESERT STORM COMMEMORATIVE

Built on the Glock 17 9mm Parabellum configuration; legend on the right side of the slide reads, "Operation Desert Storm January 16 - February 17, 1991"; on the left side is "New World Order" and the Glock 17 logo. On top of the slide are listed the 30 countries of the United Nations that took part in the campaign. Marketed with a field knife in a glass case bearing the Desert Storm shield. Only 1000 made in 1991.
Issue Price: $900
Market Value: $900

IVER JOHNSON 50TH ANNIVERSARY M-1 CARBINE

Semi-automatic; 30 U.S. Carbine; same specs as standard version except deluxe American walnut stock; red, white and blue American enameled flag embedded in stock; gold-filled, roll engraving with words "50th Anniversary 1941-1991" on slide; Parkerized finish. Introduced, 1991; still available.
Issue Price: $384.95
Market Value: $375

REMINGTON 1991 CLASSIC

Same Model 700 specs as other rifles in the annual series except 7mm Weatherby Magnum only; 4-shot magazine. Produced only in 1991.
Market Value: $495

REMINGTON 7400 175TH ANNIVERSARY RIFLE

Same specs as the standard Remington Model 7400 except receiver engraved with company's 175th Anniversary scroll design, American eagle; high-gloss American walnut stock; deep-cut checkering; 30-06 only. Introduced, 1991; dropped, 1992.
Market Value: $350

REMINGTON MODEL 11-87 175TH ANNIVERSARY COMMEMORATIVE

Same specs as the Model 11-87 Premier except engraved receiver carries anniversary design with American eagle; walnut stock, forend with high-gloss finish; 28-inch vent-rib barrel; 12-ga. only. Marketed with Rem Choke tubes. Made in 1991.
Issue Price: $618
Market Value: $450

SAVAGE MODEL 110WLE LIMITED EDITION

Same specs as Model 110G except 250-3000, 300 Savage, 7x57; high-luster fancy-grade American walnut stock, cut checkering, swivel studs, recoil pad, polished barrel; Savage logo is laser-etched on bolt. Marketed with gun lock, shooting glasses, ear plugs, sight-in target. Introduced, 1991; still available.
Market Value: $350

WINCHESTER 125TH ANNIVERSARY COMMEMORATIVE MODEL 84

Rifle; 30-30; features John Ulrich-style, full-coverage engraving; right side has 24-karat gold relief bull moose; left side has gold figures of buck and doe; 20-inch octagon barrel, lever are engraved, gold inlaid; full buckhorn rear sight; hand-checkered American walnut stock; marketed in French-fitted walnut presentation case exclusively by Cherry's. Only 125 made in 1991. **Issue Price:** $4995.
Market Value: $5500

1992 Winchester Kentucky Bicentennial Commemorative

1992 Springfield Armory Gulf Victory Special Edition

1992

AMERICAN HISTORICAL FOUNDATION 40TH ANNIVERSARY RUGER COMMEMORATIVE

Semi-automatic; 22 LR; same specs as Ruger Mark II except faux ivory grips with red Ruger medallion inset in right grip, black medallion in left grip; gold-plated trigger, trigger pivot, hammer pivot, gripscrews, bolt handle, bolt stop, scrollwork; 40th Anniversary inset in barrel in gold. Reported 950 made, 1992.
Issue Price: $995
Market Value: $495

AMERICAN HISTORICAL FOUNDATION 50TH ANNIVERSARY WW II COLT

Semi-automatic; 45 ACP; same basic specs as Colt Model 1911A1; blued finish; faux ivory grips; issued in honor of six major battles in Pacific, six in Europe; explanatory legend etched in gold on slide; grips carry historical quotations, details of campaigns, rampant colt insignia. Reported 250 pistols made by Colt, 1992, for each of the twelve campaigns; guns numbered 001 through 250 with prefix appropriate to each campaign. Marketed in OD-lined presentation case with serially numbered Basic Field Manual.
Issue Price: $995
Market Value: $995

AMERICAN HISTORICAL SOCIETY SAMUEL COLT GOLDEN TRIBUTE BUNTLINE

Revolver; 45 Colt; same basic specs of Colt Single Action Army model except 12-inch barrel; all metal parts gold-plated; heavy engraving in Texas scroll pattern; hand-fitted walnut grips. Marketed in walnut wall display case with glass lid, brass hardware. Reported 950 made in Italy by Uberti, 1992.
Issue Price: $2195
Market Value: $1495

AMERICA REMEMBERS COWBOY HALL OF FAME REVOLVER

Single Action Army revolver; 45 Colt; 4-3/4-inch barrel; hand-fitted stag grips; blued steel barrel, trigger guard, gripstraps; gold-plated frame; gold-etched scenes on cylinder. Marketed in velvet-lined display case with glass lid. Marketed in conjunction with the Cowboy Hall of Fame, Oklahoma City. Reported 1000 manufactured in 1992.
Issue Price: $1600
Market Value: $1600

AMERICA REMEMBERS EISENHOWER COMMEMORATIVE

Semi-automatic; 45 ACP; Springfield Armory-made Model 1911A1; 5-inch barrel; 7-shot magazine; checkered walnut grips with inset bronze medallions; blued slide carries gold decoration. Marketed in velvet-lined display case with Eisenhower's signature etched in walnut lid; framed photo of Ike autographed by his son, John. Reported 2500 made, 1992.
Issue Price: $1675
Market Value: $995

AMERICA REMEMBERS MEL TORME COLT SAA

Single Action Army revolver; 45 Colt; 5-1/2-inch barrel; mother of pearl grips; silver-inlaid engraving; gold-inlaid highlights. Marketed in leather-bound display case bearing gold-embossed signature of singer/gun fancier Torme. Reported 100 manufactured by Colt on special contract, 1992.
Issue Price: $4500
Market Value: $2995

AMERICA REMEMBERS RICHARD PETTY SILVER EDITION

Single Action Army revolver; 45 Colt; blued steel; sterling silver decoration; faux ivory grips with incised signature. Reported 1000 made by Colt in 1992.
Issue Price: $1495
Market Value: $1650 to $1700

SPRINGFIELD ARMORY GULF VICTORY SPECIAL EDITION

Semi-automatic; 45 ACP; same specs as Model 1911A1 except decoration; highly blued finish; gold plating on slide, small parts; marketed in padded, embroidered carrying case with jacket patch, window decal and medallion. Number made unknown.
Issue Price: $869
Market Value: $775

WINCHESTER ARAPAHO COMMEMORATIVE

Lever-action carbine; 30-30; same specs as standard Model 94 carbine except varnished select walnut stock, decoration; lever, receiver, barrel bands gold-plated, other metal parts blued; right side of the receiver etched with scene of Arapaho life, left side carries scene of buffalo hunt with a banner reading, "The Arapaho Commemorative." Reported 500 made exclusively for Cherry's by USRAC/Winchester, 1992.
Issue Price: $895
Market Value: $1295

WINCHESTER KENTUCKY BICENTENNIAL COMMEMORATIVE

Lever-action carbine; 30-30; same specs as standard Model 94 except receiver engraved in Italy, then bone charcoal case-colored; checkered stock, forearm. Banner on left side of receiver reads, "Kentucky Bicentennial 1792-1992"; racehorse etchings also featured. On right side is a Kentucky horse barn. Reported 500 made by USRA/Winchester exclusively for Cherry's, 1992.
Issue Price: $995
Market Value: $1295

WINCHESTER ONTARIO CONSERVATION COMMEMORATIVE

Lever-action carbine; 30-30; same specs as standard Model 94 except pewter finish of some parts; fancy walnut stock, decoration; right receiver panel carries Ontario game scene and portrait of conservation officer; left panel carries etching of moose, beavers in wilderness setting; replica of conservation officer's badge is set in stock. Reported 500 made by USRA/Winchester exclusively for Cherry's, 1992.
Issue Price: $795
Market Value: $1295

1994 American Historical Foundation
Smith & Wesson Bank Note Limited Edition

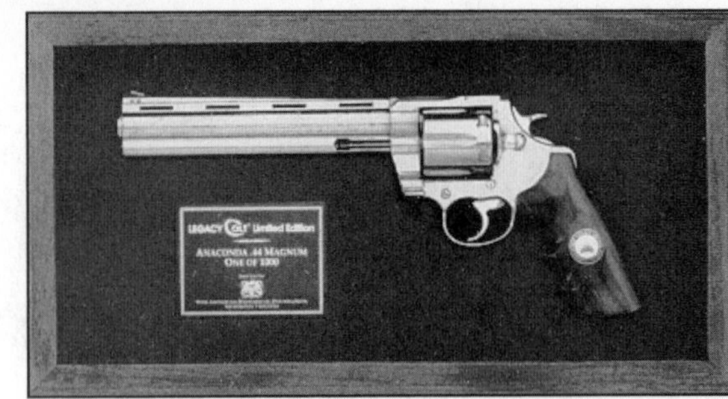

1994 American Historical Foundation
Limited Edition Colt Anaconda

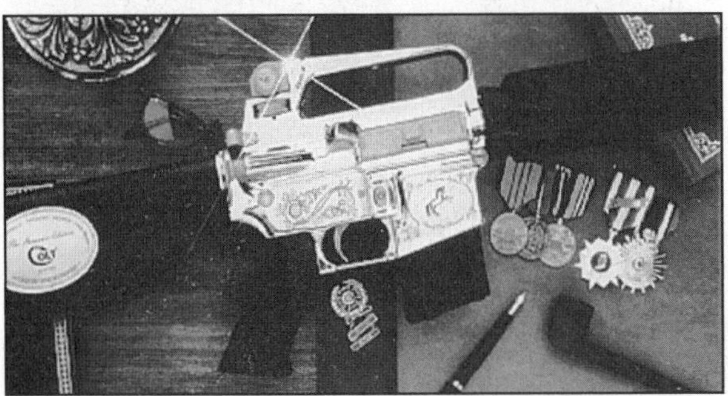

1993 American Historical Foundation
Showcase Edition Colt M16

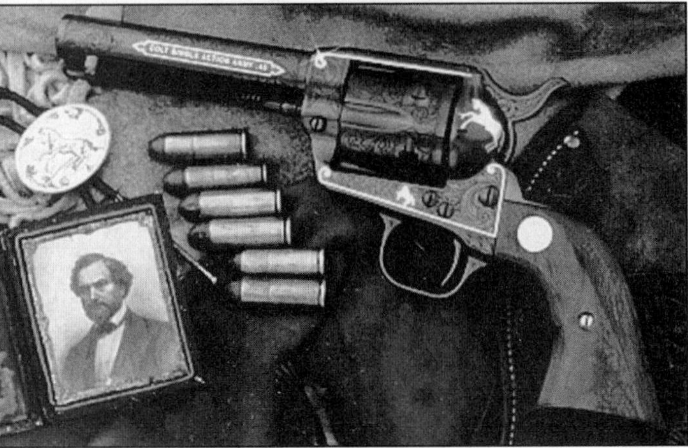

1994 American Historical Foundation
Colt Heritage Edition SAA

1993

AMERICA REMEMBERS AMERICAN EAGLE COLT

Semi-automatic; 45 ACP; Colt-made Model 1911A1; 5-inch barrel; blued finish; gold/silver bald eagle etched on each side; gold-plated safety, sights, hammer, grip screws. Marketed in blue velvet-lined walnutcase with American flag and brass identification plate. Reported 2500 made, 1993.
Issue Price: $1950
Market Value: $1950 to $2000

AMERICA REMEMBERS DON'T GIVE UP THE SHIP MODEL

Semi-automatic; 45 ACP; Colt-made Model 1911A1; 4-inch barrel; blued finish; gold-etched on the slide are USS Constitution, USS Ticonderoga, plus appropriate legend; rosewood grips with Colt medallion. Reported 1997 made, 1993.
Issue Price: $1570
Market Value: $995

AMERICA REMEMBERS GEORGE JONES SAA

Single Action Army revolver; 45 Colt; blued steel finish, decorated with gold inlays of music scores; Jones' name on barrel; bonded pearl grips. Reported 950 made, 1993.
Issue Price: $1575
Market Value: $1495

AMERICA REMEMBERS HOPALONG CASSIDY COWBOY EDITION

Single Action Army revolver; 45 Colt; 5-1/2-inch barrel; grips of black water buffalo horn; blued finish; frame, barrel, cylinder decorated with sterling silver. Marketed in velvet-lined cherrywood display case. Reported 950 manufactured, 1993.
Issue Price: $1675
Market Value: $1650

AMERICA REMEMBERS HOPALONG PREMIERE EDITION

Same specs as Cowboy Edition except in addition to silver decoration it has deep engraving, gold inlays and a leather case embossed with William Boyd's monogram. Only 100 made, 1993.
Issue Price: $4500
Market Value: $2995

AMERICA REMEMBERS "WILL PENNY" CHARLTON HESTON TRIBUTE

Single Action Army revolver; 45 Colt; 5-1/2-inch barrel; blued steel; silver and gold decoration on metal, including cattledrive scene. Minted gold portrait medallion of Heston inset in single-piece walnut grips. Reported 500 manufactured in 1993.
Issue Price: $1850
Market Value: $995

AMERICAN HISTORICAL FOUNDATION GENERAL ROBERT E. LEE HENRY REPEATER

Lever-action rifle; 44-40; 44-inch overall length; same specs as original Henry repeating rifle except receiver scrolled with dogwood, cotton flowers, magnolias; high-gloss blued finish; gold-plated trigger, follower, front sight blade and lifter; oil-finished walnut stock; left side of receiver with gold-filled Confederate seal, right side with portrait of Lee and Confederate flag. Reported 250 made in Italy by Uberti, 1993.
Issue Price: $2495
Market Value: $1500

AMERICAN HISTORICAL FOUNDATION SHOWCASE EDITION COLT M16

Semi-auto; 5.56mm; same specs as standard Colt M16 military version except receiver, sights, barrel mirror polished or glass-beaded, then nickel-plated; plastic stock has heavily textured finish; sterling silver plaque inset in stock reads "The Showcase Edition Colt One of One Hundred"; same legend etched on magazine well, surrounding rampant colt. Reported 100 with special serial numbers made by Colt, 1993.
Issue Price: $1995
Market Value: $1795

AMERICAN HISTORICAL FOUNDATION SPECIAL EDITION M16 VIETNAM TRIBUTE

Semi-auto M16; 5.56mm; HBAR match configuration; heavy barrel; custom-textured buttstock, pistol grip and hand guard; gold-plated trigger, magazine release, safety, pivot pins, windage knob, elevation knob, flash suppressor, sling swivels; medallion in pistol grip displays Vietnam ribbon and legend. Reported 1500 made, 1993, on special order by Colt, serial numbers VI0001 through VI1500.
Issue Price: $1995
Market Value: $1795

AMERICAN HISTORICAL FOUNDATION SPECIAL EDITION S&W MODEL 629 HUNTER

Revolver; 44 Magnum; same specs as standard Model 629 except 6-inch Mag-Na-Ported barrel with integral scope base, variable underweight; heavily engraved; finger-grooved Goncalo Alves grips. Marketed with Tasco scope mounts, 2x Nikon pistol scope, S&W Performance Center shooting bag, Tasco shooting glasses, Silencio ear plugs. Only 50 made by S&W under special order, 1993.
Issue Price: $3795
Market Value: $1795

WINCHESTER NEZ PERCE COMMEMORATIVE

Lever-action carbine; 30-30; same specs as standard Model 94 except for decoration; nickel-finished receiver, lever, barrel bands; other parts blued; left side of the receiver etched with bust of Chief Joseph, map of tribe's travels; right side features Nez Perce encampment against mountain background. Reported 600 made by USRAC/Winchester on special order, 1993. Serial numbered NEZ001 through NEZ600.
Issue Price: $950
Market Value: $1295

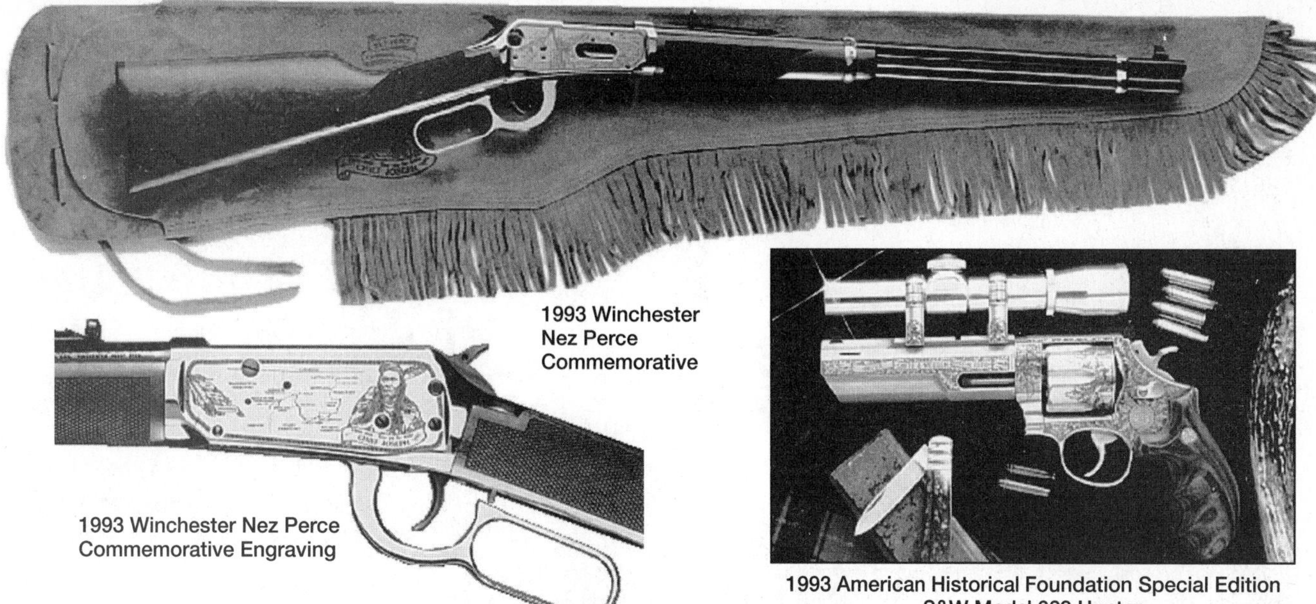

1993 Winchester Nez Perce Commemorative

1993 Winchester Nez Perce Commemorative Engraving

1993 American Historical Foundation Special Edition S&W Model 629 Hunter

1994

AMERICA REMEMBERS AMERICAN INDIAN TRIBUTE CARBINE

Rifle; 45 Colt; same specs as Winchester Model 94 Wrangler except gold-plated loop-style lever; gold-plated barrel bands, action; right side of receiver with buffalo highlighted in nickel, Indian-head penny mounted ahead of ejection port; left side features buffalo hunt in nickel, with buffalo-head nickel adjoining. Reported 300 made by USRA, 1994.
Issue Price: $1295
Market Value: $1195

AMERICA REMEMBERS ARMY AIR FORCES TRIBUTE

Semi-automatic; 45 ACP; Colt-made Model 1911A1; decoration etched on left side of the slide, including Air Corps wings and Master of the Sky legend, nickel-plated; remainder of slide gold-plated; right side carries insignia of all sixteen Army Air combat units of the World War II era; gold-plated safety, sights and grip screws; rosewood custom grips inset with Colt medallion. Reported 500 made, 1994.
Issue Price: $1500
Market Value: $995

AMERICA REMEMBERS GETTYSBURG COMMEMORATIVE

Revolver; 44-caliber replica of Colt 1860 Army Model; 8-inch barrel; blued finish; select walnut grips; cylinder etched with panorama of Pickett's charge; barrel marked with gold, Gettysburg, Pennsylvania, July 1863 and line from Lincoln's address. Marketed in velvet-lined walnut display case; inset leather lid carries silhouette of a general, with "Gettysburg 1863" stamped in gold. Reported 1863 made, 1994.
Issue Price: $1350
Market Value: $995

AMERICA REMEMBERS JOHNNY CASH PATERSON

Revolver; 36-caliber blackpowder Colt Paterson replica; 12-1/2-inch overall length; bonded pearl grips; blued finish; decorated with 24-karat gold; titles of Cash's hit songs on barrel. Marketed in black-finished hardwood display case bearing Cash's signature. Included was a copy of Cash's biography. Reported 1000 made, 1994.
Issue Price: $1350
Market Value: $995

AMERICA REMEMBERS MARINE PACIFIC TRIBUTE

Semi-automatic; 45 ACP; Model 1911A1 design; 5-inch barrel; gold-plated slide, safety, grip screws, sights; slide etched with WWII battles on right side, appropriate legend and Iwo Jima flag raising on left; custom rosewood grips with gold-plated Colt medallion; 500 made by Colt, 1994.
Issue Price: $1500
Market Value: $995

AMERICA REMEMBERS PACIFIC NAVY TRIBUTE

Semi-automatic; 45 ACP; Model 1911A1 design; 5-inch barrel; gold-plated slide, safety, grip screws; slide etched with appropriate inscriptions, classes of ships that participated in the Pacific in World War II; custom-checkered rosewood grips inset with U.S. Navy seal. Reported 500 made on special order by Auto Ordnance,1944.
Issue Price: $1500
Market Value: $995

AMERICA REMEMBERS WWII GOLDEN ANNIVERSARY VICTORY TRIBUTE

Semi-automatic; Model 1911A1 design; 5-inch barrel, gold-plated slide, safety, sights, grip screws; slide etched with regimental badges of units under Eisenhower's command on D-Day; rosewood grips inset with gold commemorative medallion. Reported 500 made on special order by Colt, 1994.
Issue Price: $1500
Market Value: $1995

AMERICAN HISTORICAL FOUNDATION 2ND AMENDMENT BROWNING HI-POWER

Semi-automatic; 40 S&W; dedicated to the right to bear arms; same specs as standard Browning Hi-Power except silver plating overall, with gold-plated hammer, trigger, magazine release, safety, slide release, grip screws; scroll-etched frame, slide; polished rosewood grips, 2nd Amendment medallion inset in left grip. Reported 500 made on special order by Browning, 1994.
Issue Price: $1995
Market Value: $1295

AMERICAN HISTORICAL FOUNDATION COLT HERITAGE EDITION SAA

Revolver; 45 Colt; 4-3/4-inch barrel; honors Sam Colt and company history; same specs as standard Single Action Army model except heavy scroll engraving on frame barrel, cylinder, hammer; gold inlaid decoration, including rampant colt on recoil shield, company insignia on loading gate, bronc rider on frame, Colt 45 Single Action Army bannered in gold inlay on left side of barrel; walnut grips; Colt grip medallions. Marketed in stand-up glass/walnut case. Reported 250 made by Colt, 1995.
Issue Price: $2995
Market Value: $2995

AMERICAN HISTORICAL FOUNDATION LIMITED EDITION COLT ANACONDA

Double-action revolver; 44 Magnum; 8-inch barrel; same specs as standard Anaconda except major parts plated with black and gold titanium; identifying legend, rampant colt trademark etched in left side of barrel, gold-filled; polished rosewood grips inset with special Colt medallion. Reported 1000 made, 1995; serial numbers LE0001 through LE1000.
Issue Price: $1595
Market Value: $1675

AMERICAN HISTORICAL FOUNDATION SMITH & WESSON BANK NOTE LIMITED EDITION

Revolver; 45 ACP; stainless steel construction; same specs as S&W Model 625; 3-inch barrel, underlug; left side of frame has "45" hand-cut, surrounded by Bank Note engraving pattern; right side hand-engraved, "Bank Note .45"; etched on right side of barrel ".45 Cal. Model of 1989"; custom Hogue Bill Jordan grips of patented synthetic. Reported 100 produced, 1995.
Issue Price: $2195
Market Value: $1495

MARLIN CENTURY LIMITED MODEL 1894

Lever-action rifle; 44-40; 12-shot tube magazine; 24-inch tapered octagonal barrel; 407/8-inch overall length; weighs 6-1/2 lbs.; checkered semi-fancy American black walnut stock, forearm; brass buttplate; carbine front sight, adjustable semi-buckhorn rear; lever, bolt, lever engraved in Italy. Commemorates 100th anniversary of model. Reported 2500 made, 1994.
Issue Price: $1087
Market Value: $1150

PEDERSOLI CREEDMORE COMMEMORATIVE

Single shot rifle; 45-70; 34-inch round/octagon barrel; hand-checkered American walnut stock; hand-fitted German silver forend cap; color case-hardened receiver, buttplate; tasteful engraving; hooded front sight, long Vernier tang rear; weighs 12 lbs., 2 oz. Reported 280 made on special order for Cherry's, 1995.
Issue Price: $1495
Market Value: $1795

1995 America Remembers Tom Mix Classic Edition

1995 America Remembers American Indian Tribute

1995 America Remembers Navajo Code Talkers Tribute

1995

AMERICA REMEMBERS 7TH CAVALRY TRIBUTE

Single Action Army revolver; 45 Colt; 7-1/2-inch barrel; blued finish; 24-karat gold etchings of crossed sabers on each side of barrel, unit designation, mixed cavalry and Indian symbols on cylinder; Custer portrait laser-carved in faux ivory grips. Marketed in walnut presentation case with replica cavalry belt buckle. Reported 500 made, 1995.
Issue Price: $1500
Market Value: $1495

AMERICA REMEMBERS AMERICAN INDIAN TRIBUTE

Single Action Army revolver; 45 Colt; 4-3/4-inch barrel; genuine hand-fitted stag grips; blued finish; decorated with gold, nickel; left side of frame with Indian battle scene etched in gold; on right side etching of two bison. Individual edition number is stamped on right side of barrel, "The American Indian" on left. Marketed as a companion piece to 1994 issue American Indian Carbine in glass-topped cherrywood case, with brass plaque. Reported 300 made, 1995.
Issue Price: $1495
Market Value: $1495

AMERICA REMEMBERS BUFFALO BILL SESQUICENTENNIAL

Single Action Army revolver; 45 Colt; 4-3/4-inch barrel; stag grips; blued finish; left side of frame with Buffalo Bill's Wild West etched in gold, right side carries American bison, Chief Scout Cody in Cheyenne territory; cylinder with gold-etched art of Cody's career. Issue commemorates 150th anniversary of his birth. Reported 500 made, 1995.
Issue Price: $1500
Market Value: $1495

AMERICA REMEMBERS CHUCK YEAGER TRIBUTE

Semi-automatic; 45 ACP; 5-inch barrel; checkered rosewood grips; silver-plated with gold and blued decorations; left side carries etching of breaking the sound barrier and Yeager's signature; right side portrays subject as WWII fighter pilot with P-51 and Messerschmitt aircraft. Marketed in blue velvet-lined walnut case with signature laser-carved on lid. Reported 500 made on special order by Colt, 1995.
Issue Price: $1750
Market Value: $995

AMERICA REMEMBERS NAVAJO CODE TALKERS TRIBUTE

Semi-automatic; 45 ACP; Colt-made Model 1911A1; 5-inch barrel; blued finish; stippled slide, with engraved Navajo Code Talkers Commemorative in banner; ironwood grips inlaid with silver, red coral and turquoise, silver figures of code talkers and Iwo Jima flag raising. Marketed in ironwood case with David Yellowhorse custom-made knife featuring stippled, gold-plated bolsters, handle of silver, turquoise, red coral and ironwood inlaid with flag-raising. Reported 300 sets made, 1995.
Issue Price: $3000
Market Value: $1500

AMERICA REMEMBERS NORTH AMERICAN RODEO TRIBUTE

Lever-action carbine; 30-30; loop-style lever; 16-inch barrel; other specs the same as standard Model 94 Winchester except for gold-finished barrel bands, gold etching on trigger, trigger guard, hammer. On left side of receiver, "The Great North American Rodeo" in gold banner, steer wrestling and bronc riding in gold against a nickel background; right side has bull rider and barrel racer featured in gold, nickel. Reported 500 made by USRA/Winchester, 1995.
Issue Price: $1600
Market Value: $1495

AMERICA REMEMBERS ROY ROGERS WINCHESTER TRIBUTE

Lever-action rifle; 30-30; same specs as standard Model 94 Winchester except jeweled hammer and breechbolt, gold-plated lever, barrel bands and front sight hood; left side of receiver features portrait of Rogers in gold and nickel; right side with Rogers on rearing horse, six-guns leveled, also in nickel and gold. Reported 300 made on special order by USRA/Winchester, 1995.
Issue Price: $2100
Market Value: $1395

AMERICA REMEMBERS TOM MIX CLASSIC EDITION

Single Action Army revolver; 45 Colt; blued finish; 5-1/2-inch barrel with TM brand in 24-karat gold; Mix brand also on each chamber of cylinder; gold signature on backstrap, portrait of Mix on recoil shield, repro of monument erected at the sight of his death on left; faux ivory grips carry Mix name, Stetson hat and TM brand. Marketed in walnut case with red velvet lining; included is Tom Mix comic book, circa 1948-1953. Reported 200 made by Uberti in Italy, 1995.
Issue Price: $1395
Market Value: $995

AMERICA REMEMBERS TOM MIX PREMIER EDITION

Same specs as the Classic except barrel carries gold-filled edition numbers 1 through 50. Each gun also furnished with an original-edition Tom Mix Big Little Book of the 1930s. Fifty guns made by Colt, 1995.
Issue Price: $2595
Market Value: $1750

1995 America Remembers
North American Rodeo Tribute

Marlin 1895 Century Limited

1995 America Remembers
Roy Rogers WinchesterTribute

1995 America Remembers
The Confederate Enfield Limited Edition

1995 America Remembers
Buffalo Bill Sesquicentennial

AMERICA REMEMBERS THE CONFEDERATE ENFIELD LIMITED EDITION

Single shot muzzle-loading rifle; 58 caliber; overall length, 55-inch; barrel length, 39-inch; European walnut stock; blued finish; gold-finished buttplate, hammer and lock, trigger guard, barrel bands, barrel design. Replica of Confederate belt buckle inlaid in right side of stock. Marketed in wall-mount display case with Confederate gray lining and uniform buttons of the eleven Rebel states as decoration. Reported 500 made, 1995.
Issue Price: $1695
Market Value: $1250

AMERICA REMEMBERS V-J DAY TRIBUTE

Semi-automatic; 45 ACP; Model 1911A1; 5-inch barrel; checkered rosewood grips inset with gold Colt medallion; blued finish, except for safety, hammer and grip screws; decoration on slide; top of slide carries engraved legend, gold seal; left side with gold portrait of Admiral Nimitz, with dive bomber, battleship; right side with Douglas MacArthur in victory wreath with his words at surrender ceremony. Reported 250 made, 1995.
Issue Price: $1495
Market Value: $995

AMERICAN HISTORICAL FOUNDATION LIMITED EDITION COLT GOLD CUP

Semi-automatic; 45 ACP; same specs as standard Colt Gold Cup but all exterior surfaces gold-plated, except backstrap. Banner carries legend, "Gold Cup Edition" and "One of 100". Reported 100 made, 1995.
Issue Price: $2195
Market Value: $1495

AMERICAN HISTORICAL FOUNDATION SECOND AMENDMENT S&W SIGMA

Semi-automatic; 40 S&W; 4-1/2-inch barrel; same specs as standard Sigma model except gold-filled etched scrollwork on slide, special commemorative medallion inset in grip; special serial numbers. Reported 250 made, 1995.
Issue Price: $1995
Market Value: $750

AMERICAN HISTORICAL FOUNDATION WORLD WAR II 50TH ANNIVERSARY THOMPSON

Semi-automatic; 45 ACP; gold-etched receiver follows military acorn motif; gold-plated trigger, rear sight base, Cutts compensator, actuator knob, sling swivels; American walnut stock inset with three medallions; special serial numbers. Reported 500 made by Auto Ordnance on special order, 1995.
Issue Price: $2495
Market Value: $1295

MARLIN 1895 CENTURY LIMITED

Lever-action; 45-70; commemorates company's 125th anniversary, 100th anniversary of model; same specs as original 1895 model except black walnut stock; French gray-finished receiver, etched with centennial dates; inletted steel buttplate. Unknown number made, 1995.
Issue Price: $1105
Market Value: $1195

MARLIN BAT MASTERSON COMMEMORATIVE

Lever-action carbine; 44 Special/44 Magnum; same specs as standard Marlin Model 1894 except decoration; receiver and bolt engraved in Italy; left receiver panel engraved with old Dodge City street scene with portrait of Masterson inset; right panel carries the names of towns where he enforced the law, with his derby, badge, a buffalo skull and other artwork; gold-plated action, other metal parts blued. Reported 500 made exclusively for Cherry's by Marlin, 1995.
Issue Price: $895
Market Value: $995

WINCHESTER FLORIDA SESQUICENTENNIAL COMMEMORATIVE

Lever-action carbine; same specs as standard Model 94 except decoration; lever, receiver, barrel bands gold-plated; barrel hammer, bolt, magazine tube deep-luster blued; left receiver panel engraved with state seal, state bird and Kennedy Space Center launch; right panel features Everglades with alligator, crane and airboat; checkered semi-fancy French walnut stock; special serial numbers FL001 through FL500. Reported 500 made exclusively for Cherry's, 1995.
Issue Price: $1195
Market Value: $1495

FIREARMS TRADE AND PROPRIETARY NAMES

A.A. Co.: Inexpensive pocket revolvers of unknown manufacture.
Acme: a) Trade name of the W.H. Davenport Firearms Company on shotguns. b) Trade name of the Hopkins and Allen Company on revolvers produced for the Merwin, Hulbert and Company and the Herman Boker Company of New York. c) Trade name of the Maltby, Henley and Company of New York on inexpensive pocket revolvers.
Acme Arms Company: Trade name of the J. Stevens Arms and Tool Company on pistols and shotguns produced for the Cornwall Hardware Company of New York.
Adams, N.R.: Trade name of the N. R. Davis and Company on shotguns.
Aetna: Trade name of the firm of Harrington and Richardson on inexpensive pocket revolvers.
Alaska: Trade name of the Hood Firearms Company on inexpensive pocket revolvers.
Alert: Trade name of the Hood Firearms Company on inexpensive pocket revolvers.
Alexander Gun Company: Trade name believed to have been E.K. Tryon of Philadelphia on imported shotguns.
Alexis: Trade name of the Hood Firearms Company on inexpensive pocket revolvers.
Allen 22: Trade name of the Hopkins and Allen Company on inexpensive pocket revolvers.
America: Trade name of the Crescent Firearms Company on inexpensive pocket revolvers.
American: Trade name of the Ely and Wray on inexpensive pocket revolvers.
American Barlock Wonder: Trade name of the H. & D. Folsom Arms Company on Shotguns made for the Sears, Roebuck Company of Chicago.
American Boy: Trade name used on firearms retailed by the Townley Metal and Hardware Company of Kansas City, Missouri.
American Bulldog: Trade name of the Iver Johnson Arms and Cycle Works on inexpensive pocket revolvers.
American Bulldog Revolver: Trade name of Harrington and Richardson Arms Company on an inexpensive pocket revolver.
American Eagle: Trade name of the Hopkins and Allen Company on inexpensive pocket revolvers.
American Gun Company: Trade name of H. & D. Folsom Arms Company on pistols and shotguns that firm retailed.
American Gun Barrel Company: Trade name of R. Avis of West Haven, Connecticut between 1916 and 1920.
American Nitro: Trade name of H. & D. Folsom Arms Co. on shotguns.
Americus: Trade name of the Hopkins and Allen Company on inexpensive pocket revolvers.
Angel: Trade name found on inexpensive pocket revolvers of unknown manufacture.
Arab, The: Trade name of the Harrington and Richardson Arms Company on shotguns.
Aristocrat: a) Trade name of the Hopkins and Allen Company on inexpensive pocket revolvers.
Armory Gun Company: Trade name of H. & D. Folsom Arms Co. on shotguns.
Aubrey Shotgun: Trade name found on shotguns made for the Sears, Roebuck and Company of Chicago by Albert Aubrey of Meriden, Connecticut.
Automatic: a) Trade name of the Forehand and Wadsworth Company on inexpensive pocket revolvers. b) Trade name of the Harrington and Richardson Arms Company on inexpensive pocket revolvers. c) Trade name of the Iver Johnson Arms and Cycle Works on inexpensive pocket revolvers.
Avenger: Trade name found on inexpensive pocket revolvers of unknown manufacture.
Baby Hammerless: Trade mark used successively by Henry Kolb and R. F. Sedgley on pocket revolvers. **Baby Russian:** Trade name of the American Arms Company on revolvers.
Baker Gun Company: Trade name of the H. & D. Folsom Arms Company on shotguns.
Baker Gun and Forging Company: Trade name of the H. & D. Folsom Arms Company on shotguns.
Bang: Trade name found on inexpensive pocket revolvers of unknown manufacture.
Bang Up: Trade name used on inexpensive pocket revolvers retailed by the Graham and Haines Company of New York.
Barker, T.: Trade name of the H. & D. Folsom Arms Company of New York on shotguns.
Bartlett Field: Trade name used on shotguns retailed by Hibbard, Spencer, Bartlett and Company of Chicago.
Batavia: Trade name used on shotguns produced by the Baker Gun Company.
Batavia Leader: Trade name used on shotguns produced by the Baker Gun Company.
Bay State: Trade name of the Harrington and Richardson Arms Company on both inexpensive pocket revolvers and shotguns.
Belknap: Trade name of the Belknap Hardware Company of Louisville, Kentucky on shotguns made by the Crescent Fire Arms Company, which.
Beilmore Gun Company: Trade name of the H. & D. Folsom Arms Company on shotguns made for them by the Crescent Fire Arms Company.
Berkshire: Trade name of the H. & D. Folsom Arms Company on shotguns made for the Shapleigh Hardware Company of St. Louis, Missouri.
Bicyle: Trade name used on firearms made by the Harrington and Richardson Arms Company.
Big All Right: Trade name used on shotguns manufactured by the Wright Arms Company.
Big Bonanza: Trade name found on inexpensive pocket revolvers of unknown manufacture.
Bismarck: Trade name found on inexpensive pocket revolvers of unknown manufacture.
Black Beauty: Trade name of the Sears, Roebuck and Company on imported shotguns.
Black Diamond: Trade name found on Belgian made shotguns retailed by an unknown American wholesaler.
Black Diana: Trade name of the Baker Gun Company or shotguns.
Blackfield: Trade name of the Hibbard, Spencer, Bartlet and Company of Chicago on shotguns.
Blackhawk: Trade name found on inexpensive pocket revolvers of unknown manufacture.
Black Prince: Trade name of the Hopkins and Allen Company on inexpensive pocket revolvers.
Bliss: Trade name believed to have been of the Norwich Arms Company.
Blood Hound: Trade name found on inexpensive pocket revolvers of unknown manufacture.
Bluefield: Trade name of the W.H. Davenport Firearms Company on shotguns.
Bluegrass: Trade name of the Belknap Hardware Company of Louisville, Kentucky on shotguns.
Bluegrass Arms Company: Trade name of shotguns made by H. & D. Folsom Arms Co. for Belknap Hardware of Louisville, KY.
Blue Jacket: Trade name of the Hopkins and Allen Company on inexpensive pocket revolvers they made for the Merwin, Hulbert and Company of New York.
Blue Leader: Trade name found on inexpensive pocket revolvers of unknown manufacture.
Blue Whistler: Trade name of the Hopkins and Allen Company on inexpensive pocket revolvers they made for the Merwin, Hulbert and Company of New York.
Bogardus Club Gun: Trade name found on Belgian made shotguns retailed by an unknown American wholesaler (possibly B. Kiftredge and Company of Cincinnati, Ohio).
Bonanza: Trade name of the Bacon Arms Company on inexpensive pocket revolvers.
Boom: Trade name of the Shattuck Arms Company on inexpensive pocket revolvers.
Boone Gun Company: Trade name of the Belknap Hardware Company of Louisville, Kentucky on firearms.
Boss: Trade name found on inexpensive pocket revolvers of unknown manufacture.
Boys Choice: Trade name of the Hood Firearms Company on inexpensive pocket revolvers.
Bride Black Prince: Trade name of H. & D. Folsom Arms Co. on shotguns.
Bridge Gun Company: Registered trade name of the Shapleigh Hardware Company, St. Louis, Missouri.
Bridgeport Arms Company: Trade name of H. & D. Folsom Arms Co. on shotguns.
Bright Arms Company: Trade name of H. & D. Folsom Arms Company
British Bulldog: Trade name found on inexpensive pocket revolvers of unknown American, Belgian and English manufacture (foreign makes bear extensive proofmarks).
Brownie: a) Trade name of the W.H. Davenport Firearms Company on shotguns. b) Trade name of the O.F. Mossberg Firearms Company on a four-shot pocket pistol.
Brutus: Trade name of the Hood Firearms Company on inexpensive pocket revolvers.
Buckeye: Trade name of the Hopkins and Allen Company on inexpensive pocket revolvers. a)Trade name of the Supplee - Biddle Hardware Company of Philadelphia.
Buffalo: Trade name of the Western Arms Company on an inexpensive pocket revolver.
Buffalo Bill: Trade name of the Iver Johnson Arms and Cycle Works on an inexpensive pocket revolver.
Bull Dog: Trade name of the Forehand and Wadsworth Company on inexpensive pocket revolvers.
Bull Dozer: a) Trade name of the Norwich Pistol Company on inexpensive pocket revolvers. b) Trade name of the Forehand and Wadsworth Company on inexpensive pocket revolvers. c) Trade name on Hammond Patent pistols made by the Connecticut Arms and Manufacturing Company.
Bull Frog: Trade name of the Hopkins and Allen Company on rifles.
Bulls Eye: Trade name of the Norwich Falls Pistol Company (O.A. Smith) on inexpensive pocket revolvers.
Burdick: Trade name of the H. & D. Folsom Arms Company on shotguns made for the Sears, Roebuck and Company of Chicago.
Butler, General: Trade name found on inexpensive pocket revolvers of unknown manufacture.
Cadet: Trade name of the Crescent Firearms Company on rifles.
Canadian Belle: Trade name of H. & D. Folsom Arms Co. on shotguns.
Cannon Breech: Trade name of the Hopkins and Allen Company on shotguns.
Carolina Arms Company: Trade name of the H. & D. Folsom Arms Company on shotguns produced for the Smith, Wadsworth Hardware Company of Charlotte, North Carolina.
Caroline Arms: Trade name of the H. & D. Folsom Arms Co.
Caruso: Trade name of the Crescent Firearms Company on shotguns made for the Hibbard, Spencer, Bartlett and Company of Chicago.
Centennial 1876: a) Trade name of the Deringer Pistol Company on inexpensive pocket revolv-

ers. b) Trade name of the Hood Firearms Company on inexpensive pocket revolvers.
Central Arms Company: Trade name of the W. H. Davenport Firearms Company on shotguns made for the Shapleigh Hardware Company of St. Louis, Missouri.
Century Arms Company: Trade name of the W. H. Davenport Firearms Company on shotguns made for the Shapleigh Hardware Company of St. Louis, Missouri.
Challenge: a) Trade name found on inexpensive pocket revolvers of unknown manufacture. b) Trade name of the Sears, Roebuck and Company of Chicago on shotguns made by Albert Aubrey of Meriden, Connecticut.
Challenge Ejector: Trade name of the Sears, Roebuck and Company of Chicago on shotguns made by Albert Aubrey of Meriden, Connecticut.
Champion: a) Trade name of H.C. Squires on shotguns. b) Trade name of J.P. Lovell on shotguns. c) Trade name of the Iver Johnson Arms and Cycle Works on shotguns and inexpensive pocket revolvers. d) Trade name of the Norwich Arms Company on inexpensive pocket revolvers.
Chatham Arms Company: Trade name of H. & D. Folsom Arms Company used on shotguns.
Cherokee Arms Company: Trade name of the H. & D. Folsom Arms Company on shotguns made for C.M. Mclung and Company of Knoxville, Tennessee.
Chesapeake Gun Company: Trade name of the H. & D. Folsom Arms Company of New York.
Chicago: Trade name found on shotguns retailed by the Hibbard, Spencer, Bartlett and Company of Chicago.
Chicago Ledger: Trade name of the Chicago Firearms Company on inexpensive pocket revolvers.
Chicago Long Range Wonder: Trade name of the H. & D. Folsom Arms Company on shotguns made for the Sears, Roebuck and Company of Chicago.
Chicopee Arms Company: Trade name of the H. & D. Folsom Arms Company of New York.
Chieftain: Trade name found on inexpensive pocket revolvers of unknown manufacture.
Christian Protector: Trade name found on inexpensive pocket revolvers of unknown manufacture.
Climax XL: Trade name of Herman Boker and Company of New York on revolvers, rifles and shotguns.
Club Gun: Trade name of B. Kittredge and Company of Cincinnati, Ohio on shotguns.
Cock Robin: Trade name of the Hood Firearms Company on inexpensive pocket revolvers.
Colonial: Trade name of H. & D. Folsom Company on shotguns.
Colton Arms Company: Trade name of the Shapleigh Hardware Company of St. Louis, Missouri on imported shotguns.
Colton Firearms Company: Trade name of the Sears, Roebuck and Company of Chicago on shotguns.
Columbia: a) Trade name found on inexpensive pocket revolvers of unknown manufacture. b) Trade name of H.C. Squires on shotguns.
Columbia Arms Company: Registered trade name of Henry Keidel, Baltimore, Maryland.
Columbian: Trade name found on inexpensive pocket revolvers of unknown manufacture.
Columbian Firearms Company: a) Trade name of the Maltby, Henly and Company on inexpensive pocket revolvers. b) Trade name of the Crescent Firearms Company on shotguns.
Comet: Trade name of the Prescott Pistol Company on inexpensive pocket revolvers.
Commander: Trade name of the Norwich Arms Company on inexpensive pocket revolvers.
Commercial: Trade name of the Norwich Falls Pistol Company (O.A. Smith) on inexpensive pocket revolvers.
Compeer: Trade name of the H. & D. Folsom Arms Company on firearms made for the Van Camp Hardware and Iron Company of Indianapolis, Indiana.
Competition: Trade name of John Meunier of Milwaukee, Wisconsin on rifles.
Conestoga Rifle Works: Trade name of Henry Leman, Philadelphia, Pennsylvania.
Connecticut Arms Company: Trade name of H. & D. Folsom Arms Company on shotguns.
Continental: Trade name of the Great Western Gun Works of Pittsburgh, Pennsylvania on firearms.
Continental Arms Company: Trade name of the Marshall-Wells Company of Duluth, Minnesota on firearms.
Cotton King: Trade name found on inexpensive pocket revolvers of unknown manufacture.
Cowboy: Trade name of the Hibbard, Spencer, Bartlett and Company of Chicago on imported, inexpensive pocket revolvers.
Cowboy Ranger: Trade name of the Rohde Spencer Company of Chicago on inexpensive pocket revolvers.
Crack Shot: Trade name of the 3. Stevens Arms and Tool Company on rifles.
Crackerjack: Trade name of the J. Stevens Arms and Tool Company on pistols.
Creedmoore: a) Trade name of the Hopkins and Allen Company on inexpensive pocket revolvers. b) Trade name of the Chicago Firearms Company on inexpensive pocketrevolvers. c) Trade name of William Wunflein on rifles.
Creedmoore Armory: Trade name of A.D. McAusland of Omaha, Nebraska on rifles.
Creedmoore Arms Company: Trade name found on imported shotguns retailed by an unknown American wholesaler.
Crescent: Trade name of the Crescent Arms Company on inexpensive pocket revolvers and shotguns. Later bought by Savage Arms Co.
Crescent International IXL: Trade name of Herman Boker and Company of New York on shotguns.
Creve Coeur: Trade name of the Isaac Walker Hardware Company of Peoria, Illinois on imported shotguns.
Crown: Trade name of the Harrington and Richardson Arms Company on inexpensive pocket revolvers.
Crown Jewel: Trade name of the Norwich Arms Company on inexpensive pocket revolvers.
Cruso: Trade name of the H. & D. Folsom Arms Company on shotguns made for Hibbard, Spencer, Bartlett and Company of Chicago.
Cumberland Arms Company: Trade name of the H. & D. Folsom Arms Company on shotguns made for the Gray and Dudley Hardware Company of Nashville, Tennessee.
Czar: Trade name of the Hopkins and Allen Company on inexpensive pocket revolvers.
Daisy: a) Trade name of the Bacon Arms Company on inexpensive pocket revolvers. b) Registered proprietary trade name engraved on firearms made by the Winchester Repeating Arms Company for the F. Lassefter and Company, Limited of Sydney, Australia.
Daniel Boone Gun Company: Trade name of H. & D. Folsom Arms Company on shotguns made for Belknap Hardware Company of Louisville, Ky.
Daredevle: Trade name of Louis Eppinger of Detroit, Michigan on pistols.
Dash: Trade name found on inexpensive pocket revolvers of unknown manufacture.
Davis Guns: Trade names used successively by N.R. Davis, N.R. Davis & Sons, Davis-Warner and the Crescent - Davis Arms Company on various firearms. Later bought by Savage Arms Co.
Dead Shot: a) Trade name found on inexpensive pocket revolvers of unknown manufacture. b) Trade name of the Meriden Firearms Company on rifles.
Deer Slayer: Trade name of J. Henry and Son of Boulton, Pennsylvania on rifles.
Defender: a) Trade name of the Iver Johnson Arms and Cycle Works on inexpensive pocket revolvers. b) Trade name of the U.S. Small Arms Company on knife pistols.
Defiance: Trade name of the Norwich Arms Company on inexpensive pocket revolvers.
Delphian Arms Company: a) Trade name of the Supplee Biddle Hardware Company of Philadelphia, Pennsylvania on shotguns which were supplied by the H. & D. Folsom Company of New York. b) Trade name of the H. & D. Folsom Arms Company of New York on shotguns.
Delphian Manufacturing Company: Trade name of the H. & D. Folsom Arms Company of New York on shotguns.
Dexter: Trade name found on inexpensive pocket revolvers of unknown manufacture.
Diamond Arms Company: Trade name of the Shapleigh Hardware Company of St. Louis, Missouri on imported shotguns.
Dictator: Trade name of the Hopkins and Allen Company on inexpensive pocket revolvers.
Dominion Pistol: Trade name found on inexpensive pocket revolvers of unknown manufacture.
Double Header: Trade name of E.S. Renwick on Perry and Goddard Patent derringers.
Douglas Arms Company: Trade name of the Hopkins and Allen Company on shotguns.
Dreadnought: Trade name of the Hopkins and Allen Company on shotguns and inexpensive pocket revolvers.
Duchess: Trade name of the Hopkins and Allen Company on inexpensive pocket revolvers.
Duke: Trade name found on inexpensive pocket revolvers which may have been made by the Hopkins and Allen Company.
Dunlop Special: Trade name of the Davis Warner Arms Company on shotguns made for the Dunlop Hardware Company of Macon, Georgia.
Duplex: Trade name of the Osgood Gun Works of Norwich, Connecticut.
Eagle: Trade name of the Iver Johnson Arms and Cycle Works on inexpensive pocket revolvers.
Eagle Arms Company: Trade name of the Iver Johnson Arms and Cycle Works on inexpensive pocket revolvers.
Earlhood: Trade name of E.L. Dickinson on inexpensive pocket revolvers.
Earnest Companion: Trade name found on inexpensive pocket revolvers of unknown manufacture.
Earthquake: Trade name of E.L Dickinson on inexpensive pocket revolvers.
Eastern Arms Company: Trade name of the Sears, Roebuck and Company of Chicago on both shotguns and inexpensive revolvers made by the ver Johnson Arms and Cycle Works.
Eclipse: a) Trade name found on single shot derringers of unknown manufacture. b) Trade name of E.C. Meacham on imported shotguns.
Electric: Trade name found on inexpensive pocket revolvers of unknown manufacture.
Electric City Single Hammer: Trade name found on single shot shotguns retailed by the Wyeth Hardware and Manufacturing Company of St. Joseph, Missouri.
Elector: Trade name found on inexpensive pocket revolvers of unknown manufacture.
Elgin Arms Company: Trade name of the H. & D. Folsom Arms Company on shotguns made for the Strauss and Schram Company of Chicago.
Elita: Trade name of the W.H. Davenport Fire Arms Company on shotguns.
Empire: a) Trade name of the Rupertus Patented Pistol Manufacturing Company on inexpensive pocket revolvers. b) Trade name of the Cresent Firearms Company on shotguns.
Empire Arms Company: Trade name of the H. & D. Folsom Arms Company on firearms made for the Sears, Roebuck and Company of Chicago.
Enders Royal Shotgun: Trade name of the Crescent - Davis Firearms Company on shotguns made for the Simmons Hardware Company of St. Louis, Missouri.
Enders Special Service: Trade name of the Crescent Davis Firearms Company on shotguns made for the Simmons Hardware Company of St. Louis, Missouri.
Enterprise: Trade name of the Enterprise Gun Works on inexpensive pocket revolvers.
Essex Gun Works: Trade name of the Crescent - Davis Firearms Company on shotguns made

for the Belknap Hardware Company of Louisville, Kentucky.

Eureka: Trade name of the Iver Johnson Arms and Cycle Works on inexpensive pocket revolvers.

Excel: Trade name of both the H. & D. Folsom Arms Company and the Iver Johnson Arms and Cycle Works on shotguns made for the Montgomery Ward and Company of Chicago.

Excelsior: a) Trade name found on inexpensive pocket revolvers of unknown manufacture b) Trade name of the Iver Johnson Arms and Cycle Works on shotguns.

Expert: a) Trade name found on single shot derringers of unknown manufacture. b) Trade name of the W.J. Davenport Firearms Company on shotguns made for the Witte Hardware Company of St. Louis, Missouri.

Express: Trade name of the Bacon Arms Company on inexpensive pocket revolvers.

Farwell Arms Company: Trade name of the Farwell, Ozmun, Kirk and Company of St. Paul, Minnesota on shotguns.

Fashion: Trade name found on inexpensive pocket revolvers of unknown manufacture.

Faultless: Trade name of the H. & D. Folsom Arms Company on shotguns made for the John M. Smythe Merchandise Company of Chicago.

Faultless Goose Gun: Trade name of the H. & D. Folsom Arms Company on shotguns made for the John M. Smythe Merchandise Company of Chicago.

Favorite: a) Trade name of the J. Stevens Arms and Tool Company on rifles. b) Trade name of the Iver Johnson Arms and Cycle Works on inexpensive pocket revolvers.

Favorite Navy: Trade name of the Iver Johnson Arms and Cycle Works on inexpensive pocket revolvers.

Featherlight: Trade name of the Sears, Roebuck and Company of Chicago on firearms.

Folks Gun Works: Trade name of William and Samuel Folk of Bryan, Ohio on rifles and shotguns.

Freemont Arms Company: Trade name found on shotguns distributed by an unknown retailer.

Frontier: Trade name of the Norwich Falls Pistol Company (O.A. Smith) on inexpensive pocket revolvers made for the firm of Maitby, Curtis and Company of New York.

Fulton: Trade name of the Hunter Arms Company on shotguns.

Fulton Arms Company: Trade name of the W. H. Davenport Firearms Company on shotguns.

Game Getter: Registered trade mark of the Marble Arms and Manufacturing Company on combination rifle shotguns.

Gem: a) Trade name of the J. Stevens Arms and Tool Company on single shot pocket pistols. b) Trade name of the Bacon Arms Company on inexpensive pocket revolvers.

General: Trade name of the Rupertus Patented Pistol Manufacturing Company on inexpensive pocket revolvers.

Gerrish: Trade name of G.W. Gerrish of Twin Falls, Idaho used on shotguns.

Gibralter: Trade name of Albert Aubrey on shotguns made for the Sears, Roebuck and Company of Chicago.

Gladiator: Trade name of Albert Aubrey on shotguns made for the Sears, Roebuck and Company of Chicago.

Gold Field: Trade name found on inexpensive pocket revolvers of unknown manufacture.

Gold Hibbard: Trade name of Hibbard, Spencer, Bartlett and Company of Chicago on firearms.

Gold Medal Wonder: Trade name of H. & D. Folsom Arms Co. on shotguns.

Governor: Trade name of the Bacon Arms Company on inexpensive pocket revolvers.

Guardian: Trade name of the Bacon Arms Company on inexpensive pocket revolvers.

Gut Buster: Trade name found on inexpensive pocket revolvers of unknown manufacture.

Gypsy: Trade name found on inexpensive pocket revolvers of unknown manufacture.

Half Breed: Trade name found on inexpensive pocket revolvers of unknown manufacture.

Hamilton Arms: Registered trade name of the Wiebusch and Hilger Company, New York.

Hammerless Auto Ejecting Revolver: Trade name of the Meriden Firearms Company used on revolvers made for the Sears, Roebuck and Company of New York.

Hanover Arms Co.: If no foreign proofmarks then trade name of H. & D. Folsom Arms Company.

Harrington, S.H.: If no foreign proofmarks then trade name of H. & D. Folsom Arms Company.

Frank Harrison Arms Company: Trade name of the Sickles and Preston Company of Davenport, Iowa on firearms.

Hart Arms Company: Trade name of a Cleveland, Ohio wholesaler (possibly the George Worthington Company).

Hartford Arms Company: Trade name of the H. & D. Folsom Arms on shotguns made for the Simmons Hardware Company of St. Louis, Missouri.

Harvard: Trade name of the H. & D. Folsom Arms Company on shotguns made for the George Worthington Company of Cleveland, Ohio.

Hercules: Trade name of the Iver Johnson Arms and Cycle Works on shotguns made for the Montgomery Ward and Company of Chicago.

Hermitage Arms Company: Trade name of the H. & D. Folsom Arms Company on shotguns made for the Gray and Dudley Hardware Company of Nashville, TN.

Hero: a) Trade name of the American Stand Tool Company on percussion pistols. b) Trade name of the Manhattan Firearms Manufacturing Company on percussion pistols.

Hexagon: Trade name of the Sears, Roebuck and Company of Chicago on shotguns.

Hinsdale: Trade name of the Hopkins and Allen Company on inexpensive pocket revolvers.

Holt Arms Company, S.: Trade name of the Sears, Roebuck and Company of Chicago on shotguns.

Hornet: Trade name of the Prescott Pistol Company on inexpensive pocket revolvers.

Howard Arms Company: Trade name of the H. & D. Folsom Arms Company on shotguns they distributed.

Hudson: Trade name of the Hibbard, Spencer, Bartlett and Company of Chicago on shotguns.

Hunter: Trade name of the H. & D. Folsom Arms Company on shotguns made for the Belknap Hardware Company of Louisville, Kentucky.

The Hunter: Trade name of the Hunter Arms Company on shotguns.

Hurricane: Trade name found on inexpensive pocket revolvers of unknown manufacture.

Illinois Arms Company: Trade name of the Rohde, Spencer Company of Chicago on firearms.

Imperial: Trade name of the Lee Arms Company on inexpensive pocket revolvers.

Imperial Arms Company: Trade name of the Hopkins and \llen Company on inexpensive pocket revolvers.

Infallible: Trade name of the Lancaster Arms Company of Lancaster, Pennsylvania on shotguns.

Infallible Automatic Pistol: Trade name of the Kirtland Brothers Company of New York on inexpensive pistols.

International: a) Trade name found on inexpensive pocket revolvers of unknown manufacture. b) Trade name of E.C. Meacham on shotguns.

Interstate Arms Company: Trade name of the H. & D. Folsom Arms Company on shotguns made for the Townley Metal and Hardware Company of Kansas City, Missouri.

I.O.A.: Trade name of the Brown, Camp Hardware Companyof Des Moines, Iowa on firearms.

Invincible: Trade name of the Iver Johnson Arms and Cycle Works on both shotguns and inexpensive pocket revolvers.

I.X.L.: a) Trade name of B.J. Hart on percussion revolvers. b) Trade name of the W.H. Davenport Firearms Company on shotguns made for the Witte Hardware Company of St. Louis, Missouri.

J.S.T. & Company: Trade name of the Iver Johnson Arms and Cycle Works on inexpensive pocket revolvers.

Jackson Arms Company: Trade name of the H. & D. Folsom Arms Company on shotguns made for C.M. Mclung and Company of Knoxville, Tennessee.

Jewel: Trade name of the Hood Fire Arms Company on inexpensive pocket revolvers.

Joker: Trade name of the Marlin Firearms Company on inexpensive pocket revolvers.

Joseph Arms Company (Norwich, Conn.): Trade name of H. & D. Folsom Arms Company.

Judge: Trade name found on inexpensive pocket revolvers of unknown manufacture.

KK: Trade name of the Hopkins and Allen Company on shotguns made for the Shapleigh Hardware Company of St. Louis, Missouri.

Keno: Trade name found on inexpensive pocket revolvers of unknown manufacture.

Kentucky: Trade name of the Iver Johnson Arms and Cycle Works on inexpensive pocket revolvers.

Keystone Arms Company: Trade name of the W.H. Davenport Firearms Company on shotguns made for the E.K. Tryon Company of Philadelphia, Pennsylvania.

Kill Buck: Trade name of the Enterprise Gun Works (James Bown), Pittsburgh, Pennsylvania.

Killdeer: Trade name of the Sears, Roebuck and Company of Chicago on firnarms bearing their trade name Western Arms Company.

King Nitro: Trade name of the W.H. Davenport Firearm Company on shotguns made for the Shapleigh Hardware Company of St. Louis, Missouri.

King Pin: Trade name found on inexpensive single shot and volving pocket pistols.

Kingsland Gun Company: Trade name of the H. & D. Folsom Arms Company on shotguns made for the Geller, Ward and Hasner Company of St. Louis, Missouri.

Kirk Gun Company: Trade name of Farwell, Ozmun, and Kirk Company of St. Paul, Minnesota.

Knickerbocker: Trade name of the Crescent-Davis Firearms Company on shotguns.

Knickerbocker Club Gun: Trade name of Charles Godfrey of New York on imported shotguns he retailed. Knockabout: Trade name of the Montgomery Ward and Company of Chicago on shotguns.

Knox-All: Trade name of the Iver Johnson Arms and Cycle Works on firearms they made for the H. & D. Folsom Arms Company of New York.

Lakeside: Trade name of the H. & D. Folsom Arms Company on firearms they made for the Montgomery Ward and Company of Chicago.

Leader: a) Trade name of the Shattuck Arms Company on inexpensive pocket revolvers. b) Trade name of the Harrington and Richardson Arms Company on inexpensive pocket revolvers.

Leader Gun Company: Trade name of the H. & D. Folsom Arms Company on shotguns they made for the Charles Williams Stores, Inc. of New York.

Lees Hummer: Trade name of the H. & D. Folsom Arms Company on firearms they made for the Lee Hardware Company of Salina, Kansas.

Lees Special: Trade name of the H. & D. Folsom Arms Company on firearms they made for the Lee Hardware Company of Salina, Kansas.

Liberty: Trade name of the Norwich Falls Pistol Company (O.A. Smith) on inexpensive pocket revolvers.

Liege Gun Company: Trade name of the Hibbard, Spencer, Bartlett and Company of Chicago on imported shotguns.

Lion: Trade name of the Iver Johnson Arms and Cycle Works on inexpensive pocket revolvers.

Little Giant: Trade name of the Bacon Arms Company on inexpensive pocket revolvers.

Little John: Trade name of the Hood Firearms Company on inexpensive pocket revolvers.

Little Joker: Trade name found on inexpensive pocket revolvers of unknown manufacture.

Little Pal: Registered trade name for knife pistols made by L.E. Polhemus.
Little Pet: Trade name of the Sears, Roebuck and Company of Chicago on inexpensive pocket revolvers.
London Revolver: Trade name found on inexpensive pocket revolvers of unknown manufacture.
Lone Star: Trade name found on inexpensive pocket revolvers of unknown manufacture.
Long Range Winner: Trade name of the Sears, Roebuck and Company of Chicago on shotguns.
Long Range Wonder: Trade name of the Sears, Roebuck and Company of Chicago on shotguns.
Long Tom: Trade name of the Sears, Roebuck and Company of Chicago on shotguns.
Marshwood: Trade name of the H. and D. Folsom Arms Company on shotguns they made for the Charles Williams Stores Inc. of New York.
Marvel: Trade name of the J. Stevens Arms and Tool Company on various firearms.
Massachusetts Arms Company: Trade name of both the J. Stevens Arms and Tool Company and the H. & D. Folsom Arms Company on firearms made for the Blish, Mizet and Silliman Hardware Company of Atchinson, Kansas.
Maximum: Trade name found on inexpensive pocket revolvers of unknown manufacture.
Metropolitan: Trade name of the H. & D. Folsom Arms Company on firearms they made for the Siegal-Cooper Company of New York.
Metropolitan Police: a) Trade name of the Maitby, Curtiss and Company on inexpensive pocket revolvers. b) Trade name of the Rohde-Spencer Company of Chicago on inexpensive pocket revolvers.
Midget Hammerless: Trade name of the Rohde - Spencer Company of Chicago on inexpensive pocket revolvers.
Minnesota Arms Company: Trade name of the H. & D. Folsom Arms Company on shotguns they made for the Farwell, Ozmun, Kirk and Company of St. Paul, Minnesota.
Missaubi Arms Company: Trade name of the Hunter Arms Company, possibly for the Farwell, Ozmun, Kirk and Company of St. Paul, Minnesota.
Mississippi Arms Company: Trade name of the H. & D. Folsom Arms Company on firearms made for the Shapleigh Hardware Company of St. Louis, Missouri.
Mississippi Valley Arms Company: Trade name of the H. & D. Folsom Arms Company on firearms made for the Shapleigh Hardware Company of St. Louis, Missouri.
Mohawk: Trade name of the H. & D. Folsom Arms Company on firearms made for the Blish, Mizet and Silliman Hardware Company of Atchinson, Kansas.
Mohegan: Trade name of the Hood Firearms Company on inexpensive pocket revolvers.
Monarch: a) Trade name of the Hopkins and Allen Company on inexpensive pocket revolvers. b) Trade name of the Osgood Gun Works on Duplex revolvers.
Monitor: a) Trade name of the Whitneyville Armory on inexpensive pocket revolvers. b) Trade name of the H. & D. Folsom Arms Company on firearms made for the Paxton and Gallagher Company of Omaha, Nebraska.
Montgomery Arms Company: Trade name of the H. & D. Folsom Arms Company on a variety of firearms.
Mountain Eagle: Trade name of the Hopkins and Allen Company on inexpensive pocket revolvers.
Mount Vernon Arms Company: Trade name of the H. & D. Folsom Arms Company on firearms made for the Carlin, Hulifish Company of Alexandria, Virginia.
My Companion: Trade name found on inexpensive pocket revolvers of unknown manufacture.
My Friend: Trade name of James Reid of New York.
Napoleon: Trade name of the Thomas J. Ryan Pistol Manufacturing Company of Norwich, Connecticut on inexpensive pocket revolvers.
National Arms Company: Trade name of the H. & D. Folsom Arms Company on firearms made both for the May Hardware Company of Washington, D.C., and the Moskowitz and Herbach Company of Philadelphia, Pennsylvania.
Nevermiss: Trade name of the Marlin Firearms Company on single shot pocket pistols.
New Aubrey: Trade name of Albert Aubrey of Meriden, Connecticut on both revolvers and shotguns made for the Sears, Roebuck and Company of Chicago.
New Britain Arms Company: Trade name of H. & D. Folsom Arms Company. New Elgin Arms Company: Trade name of H. & D. Folsom Arms Company.
New Empire: Trade name of H. & D. Folsom Arms Co.
New England Arms Company: Trade name believed to have been of Charles Godfrey on shotguns made for the Rohde, Spencer Company of Chicago.
New Era Gun Works: Trade name of the Baker Gun Company on firearms made for an unknown retailer.
New Haven Arms Company: Trade name found on Belgian shotguns imported by either E.K.Tryon of Philadelphia or the Great Western Gun Works of Pittsburgh, Pennsylvania.
New Liberty: Trade name of the Sears, Roebuck and Company of Chicago on inexpensive pocket revolvers. New Rival: Trade name of the H. & O. Folsom Arms Company on firearms made for the Van Camp Hardware and Iron Company of Indianapolis, Indiana.
Newport: a) Trade name found on inexpensive pocket revolvers of unknown manufacture. b) Trade name of the H. & D. Folsom Arms Company on shotguns made for Hibbard, Spencer, Bartlett and Company of Chicago.
New Worcester: Trade name of the Torkalson Manufacturing Company of Worcester, Massachusetts.
New York Arms Company: Trade name of the H. & D. Folsom Arms Company on firearms made for the Garnet Carter Company of Chattanooga, Tennessee.
New York Gun Company: Trade name of the H. & O. Folsom Arms Company on firearms made for the Garnet Carter Company of Chattanooga, Tennessee.
New York Club: Trade name of the H. & O. Folsom Arms Company on rifles.
New York Machine Made: Trade name of the H. & D. Folsom Arms Company.
New York Pistol Company: Trade name of the Norwich Falls Pistol Company (O.A. Smith) on inexpensive pocket revolvers.
Nightingale: Trade name found on inexpensive pocket revolvers of unknown manufacture.
Nitro Bird: Trade name of the Richards and Conover Hardware Company of Kansas City, Missouri.
Nitro Hunter: Trade name of the H. & D. Folsom Arms Company on shotguns made for the Belknap Hardware Company of Louisville, Kentucky.
Nitro King: Trade name of the Sears, Roebuck and Company of Chicago on shotguns of unknown manufacture.
Nitro Special: Trade name of the J. Stevens Arms and Tool Company on shotguns.
Northfield Knife Company: Trade name of the Rome Revolver and Novelty Works of Rome, New York on inexpensive pocket revolvers.
Norwich Arms Company: a) Trade name of the Hood Firearms Company on inexpensive pocket revolvers. b) Trade name found on shotguns retailed by the Marshall, Wells Company of Duluth, Minnesota and Winnipeg, Manitoba, Canada.
Norwich Falls Pistol Company: Trade name of the O.A. Smith Company on inexpensive pocket revolvers made for Maltby, Curtis and Company of New York.
Norwich Lock Manufacturing Company: Trade name of.W. Hood Firearms Company on inexpensive pocket revolvers.
Not-Nac Manufacturing Company: Trade name of the H. & D. Folsom Arms Company on firearms made for the Canton Hardware Company of Canton, Ohio.
OK: a) Trade name of the Marlin Firearms Company on single shot pocket pistols. b) Trade name of Cowles and Son of Chicopee Falls, Massachusefts on single shot pocket pistols. c) Trade name found on inexpensive pocket revolvers of unknown manufacture.
Old Hickory: a) Trade name found on inexpensive pocket revolvers of unknown manufacture. b) Trade name of the Hibbard, Spencer, Bartleft and Company of Chicago on shotguns.
Old Reliable: Trade name of the Sharps Rifle Company.
Olympic: a) Trade name of the J. Stevens Arms and Tool Company on rifles and pistols. b) Trade name of the Morley and Murphy Hardware Company of Green Bay, Wisconsin on firearms (possibly made by the J. Stevens Arms and Tool Company).
Osprey: Trade name of Lou 3. Eppinger of Detroit, Michigan on firearms he made.
Our Lake: Trade name of E.L. and 3. Dickinson of Springfield, Massachusefts on inexpensive pocket revolvers.
Oxford Arms Company: Trade name of the H. & D. Folsom Arms Company on firearms made for the Belknap Hardware Company of Louisville, Kentucky.
Pagoma: Trade name of the H. & D. Folsom Arms Company on firearms made for the Paxton and Gallagher Company of Omaha, Nebraska.
Palmetto: Trade name of the Edward K. Tryon Company of Philadelphia, Pennsylvania on various types of firearms.
Panther: Trade name found on inexpensive pocket revolvers of jnknown manufacture.
Paragon: a) Trade name of the Prescoft Pistol Company on inexpensive pocket revolvers. b) Trade name of the Baker Gun Company on shotguns.
Parole: Trade name of the Bacon Arms Company on inexpensive pocket revolvers.
Path Finder: Trade name found on inexpensive pocket revolvers of unknown manufacture.
Patriot: Trade name found on inexpensive pocket revolvers of unknown manufacture.
Peace Maker: Trade name found on inexpensive pocket revolvers of unknown manufacture.
Peerless: Trade name of the Crescent-Davis Firearms Company on shotguns made for various wholesalers.
Pelican: Trade name of the Thomas, Ogilvie Hardware Company of Shreveport, Louisiana.
Penetrator: Trade name of the Norwich Arms Company on inexpensive pocket revolvers.
Peoria Chief: Trade name found on inexpensive pocket revolvers.
Perfect: Trade name of the Foehl and Weeks Firearms Manufacturing Company of Philadelphia, Pennsylvania on inexpensive pocket revolvers.
Perfection: a) Trade name of the H. & O. Folsom Arms Company on firearms made for the H.G. Lipscomb and Company of Nashville, Tennessee. b) Trade name of the John M. Smythe Merchandise Company of Chicago on firearms.
Pet: Trade name found on inexpensive pocket revolvers of unknown manufacture.
Petrel: Trade name found on inexpensive pocket revolvers of unknown manufacture.
Phenix: Trade name of J. Reid of New York on revolvers.
Phoenix: a) Trade name of J. Reid of New York on revolvers. b) Trade name of the Whitneyville Armory on percussion revolvers.
Piedmont: Trade name of the H. & O. Folsom Arms Company on firearms made for the Piedmont Hardware Company of Danville, Pennsylvania.

Pinafore: Trade name of the Norwich Falls Pistol Company (O.A. Smith) on inexpensive pocket revolvers.
Pioneer: Trade name found on inexpensive pocket revolvers of unknown manufacture.
Pioneer Arms Company: Trade name of the H. & O. Folsom Arms Company on firearms made for the Kruse and Baklmann Hardware Company of Cincinnati, Ohio.
Pittsfield: Trade name of the Hibbard, Spencer, Bartlett and Company of Chicago on firearms probably made by the H. & O. Folsom Arms Company.
Plug Ugly: Trade name found on inexpensive pocket revolvers of unknown manufacture.
Plymouth: Trade name of Spear and Company of Pittsburgh, Pennsylvania on firearms.
Pocahontas: Trade name found on inexpensive pocket revolvers of unknown manufacture.
Pointer: Trade name found on single shot pocket pistols of unknown manufacture.
Prairie Fire: Trade name found on inexpensive pocket revolversof unknown manufacture.
Prairie King: a) Trade name of the Bacon Arms Company on inexpensive pocket revolvers. b) Trade name of the H. & O. Folsom Arms company on inexpensive pocket revolvers.
Premier: a) Trade name of the Thomas E. Ryan Company on inexpensive pocket revolvers. b) Trade name of the Harrington and Richardson Arms Company on revolvers. c) Trade name of the Montgomery Ward Company of Chicago on firearms. d) Registered trade name of Edward K. Tryon and Company of Philadelphia, Pennsylvania.
Premium: Trade name of the Iver Johnson Arms and Cycle Works on inexpensive pocket revolvers.
Price, John W.: Trade name of the Belknap Hardware Company of Louisville, Kentucky on firearms.
Progress: Trade name of Charles J. Godfrey of New York on shotguns.
Protection: Trade name of the Whitneyville Armory on revolvers.
Protector: a) Trade name found on inexpensive pocket revolvers of unknown manufacture. b) Trade name of the Chicago Firearms company on inexpensive pocket revolvers.
Protector Arms Company: Trade name of the Rupertus Patented Pistol Manufacturing Company on inexpensive pocket revolvers.
Providence: Trade name found on inexpensive pocket revolvers of unknown manufacture.
Quail: Trade name of the Crescent-Davis Arms Company on shotguns.
Queen: a) Trade name of the Hood Firearms Company on inexpensive pocket revolvers. b) Trade name of the Hyde and Shattuck Company on inexpensive single shot pocket pistols.
Queen City: Trade name of the H. & O. Folsom Arms Company on firearms made for the Elmira Arms Company of Elmira, New York.
Ranger: a) Trade name found on inexpensive pocket revolvers of unknown manufacture. b) Trade name of Eastern Arms Company on various firearms made for Sears And Robuck and Co of Chicago. c) Trade name of the Sears, Roebuck and Company of Chicago on a wide variety of firearms marketed by that firm.
Reassurance: Trade name found on inexpensive pocket revolvers of unknown manufacture.
Red Chieftain: Trade name of the Supplee Biddle Hardware Company of Philadelphia, Pennsylvania on inexpensive pocket pistols.
Red Cloud: Trade name of the Ryan Pistol Manufacturing Company on inexpensive pocket revolvers.
Red Hot: Trade name found on inexpensive pocket revolvers of unknown manufacture.
Red Jacket: a) Trade name of the Lee Arms Company on inexpensive pocket revolvers. b) Trade name of the Hopkins and Allen Company on inexpensive pocket revolvers.
Reliable: Trade name found on inexpensive pocket revolvers of unknown manufacture.
Reliance: Trade name of John Meunier of Milwaukee, Wisconsin on rifles.
Rev-O-Noc: Trade name of the H. & O. Folsom Arms Company on firearms made for the Hibbard, Spencer, Bartlett and Company of Chicago; "Conover" spelled backward.
Rich-Con: Trade name of the H. & O. Folsom Arms Company for shotguns made for Richardson & Conover Hardware Company.
Richmond Arms Company: Trade name of the H. & O. Folsom Arms Company on firearms made for an unknown retailer.
Richter Company, Charles: Trade name of the H. & O. Folsom Arms Company on firearms made for the New York Sporting Goods Company of New York.
Rickard Arms Company: Trade name of the H. & O. Folsom Arms Company on firearms made for the J.A. Rickard Company of Schenectady, New York.
Rip Rap: Trade name of the Bacon Arms Company on inexpensive pocket revolvers.
Rival: Trade name of the H. & O. Folsom Arms Company on firearms made for the Van Camp Hardware and Iron Company of Indianapolis, Indiana.
Riverside Arms Company: Trade name of the J. Stevens Arms and Tool Company on various types of firearms.
Robin Hood: Trade name of the Hood Firearms Company on inexpensive pocket revolvers.
Rocky Hill: Trade name found on inexpensive cast iron percussion pocket pistols made in Rocky Hill, Connecticut.
Rodgers Arms Company: Trade name of the Hood Firearms Company on firearms made for an unknown retailer.
Royal Gun Company: Trade name of the Hollenbeck Gun Co. Wheeling West Virgina.
Royal Service: Trade name of the Shapleigh Hardware Company of St. Louis, Missouri on firearms.
Rummel Arms Company: Trade name of the H. & O. Folsom Arms Company on firearms made for the A.J. Rummel Arms Company of Toledo, Ohio.
Russel Arms Company: Registered trade name of the Wiebusch and Hilger Company of New York.
Russian Model: Trade name of the Forehand and Wadsworth Company on inexpensive pocket revolvers.
Safe Guard: Trade name found on inexpensive pocket revolvers of unknown manufacture.
Safety Police: Trade name of the Hopkins and Allen Company on inexpensive pocket revolvers.
St. Louis Arms Company: Trade name of the H. & O. Folsom Arms Company on firearms made for the Shapleigh Hardware Company of St. Louis, Missouri.
Scott: Trade name of the Hopkins and Allen Company on inexpensive pocket revolvers.
Secret Service Special: Trade name of the Rohde, Spencer Company of Chicago on inexpensive pocket revolvers.
Senator: Trade name found on inexpensive pocket revolvers of unknown manufacture.
Sentinel: Trade name found on inexpensive pocket revolvers of unknown manufacture.
Sheffield, The: Trade name of the A. Baldwin and Company, Limited of New Orleans, Louisiana on shotguns.
Sickels-Arms Company: Trade name of the Sickels and Preston Company of Davenport, Iowa on firearms.
Simson: Trade name of the Iver Johnson Arms and Cycle Works on firearms made for the Iver Johnson Sporting Goods Company of Boston, Massachusetts.
Sitting Bull: Trade name found on inexpensive pocket revolvers of unknown manufacture.
Skues Special: Trade name of Ira M. Skue of Hanover, Pennsylvania on shotguns.
Smoker: Trade name of the Iver Johnson Arms and Cycle Works on inexpensive pocket revolvers.
Smythe & Company, John M.: Trade name of H. & O. Folsom Arms Company for shotguns made for John M. Smythe Hardware Company of Chicago.
Southern Arms Company: Trade name of the H. & O. Folsom Arms Company on firearms made for an unknown retailer.
Southerner: a) Trade name of the Brown Manufacturing Company and the Merrimac Arms Manufacturing Company on single shot pocket pistols. b) Registered trade name of Asa Farr of New York on pistols.
Southron: Trade name found on inexpensive pocket pistols of unknown manufacture.
Special Service: Trade name of the Shapleigh Hardware Company of St. Louis, Missouri on inexpensive pocket revolvers.
Spencer Gun Company: Trade name of the H. & O. Folsom Arms Company. Splendor: Trade name found on inexpensive pocket revolvers of unknown manufacture.
Sportsman, The: Trade name of the H. & O. Folsom Arms Company on firearms made for the W. Bingham Company of Cleveland, Ohio.
Springfield Arms Company: Trade name of the J. Stevens Arms and Tool Company.
Spy: Trade name found on inexpensive pocket revolvers of unknown manufacture.
Square Deal: Trade name of the H. & O. Folsom Arms Company on firearms made for the Stratton, Warren Hardware Company of Memphis, Tennessee.
Stand: Trade name of the Marlin Firearms Company on revolvers.
Stanley Arms: Registered trade name of the Wiebusch and Hilger Company of New York on firearms.
Stanley Double Gun: Trade name of the H. & O. Folsom Arms Company on shotguns.
Star: a) Trade name found on inexpensive single shot pocket pistols of unknown manufacture. b) Trade name of the Prescott Pistol Company on inexpensive pocket revolvers.
State Arms Company: Trade name of the H. & O Folsom Arms Company on firearms made for the J. H. Lau and Company of New York.
Sterling: a) Trade name of E.L. and J. Dickinson of Springfield, Massachusetts on single shot pistols. b) Trade name of the H. & O. Folsom Arms Company on shotguns.
Stinger: Registered proprietary trade name engraved on firearms made by the Winchester Repeating Arms Company for the Perry Brothers Limited of Brisbane, Australia.
Stonewall: a) Trade name of the Marlin Firearms Company on single shot derringers. b) Trade name of T.F. Guion of Lycoming, Pennsylvania on single shot percussion pistols he retailed.
Striker: Trade name found on inexpensive pocket revolvers of unknown manufacture.
Sullivan Arms Company: Trade name of the H. & O. Folsom Arms Company on firearms made for the Sullivan Hardware Company of Anderson, South Carolina.
Superior: Trade name of the Paxton and Gallagher Company of Omaha, Nebraska on revolvers and shotguns.
Super Range: Trade name of the Sears, Roebuck and Company of Chicago on shotguns.
Sure Fire: Trade name found on inexpensive pocket revolvers of unknown manufacture.
Swamp Angel: Trade name of the Forehand and Wadsworth Company on inexpensive pocket revolvers.
Swift: Trade name of the Iver Johnson Arms and Cycle Works on firearms made for the John P. Lovell & Sons, Boston, Massachusetts.
Syco: Trade name of the Wyeth Hardware Company of St. Joseph, Missouri on firearms.
Ten Star: Trade name of the H. & D. Folsom Arms Company on firearms made for the Geller, Ward and Hasner Company of St. Louis, Missouri.
Terrier: Trade name of the Rupertus Pantented Pistol Maufacturing Company on inexpensive pocket revolvers.
Terror: Trade name of the Forehand and Wadsworth Company on inexpensive pocket revolvers.

Texas Ranger: Trade name of the Montgomery Ward and Company of Chicago on inexpensive pocket revolvers.
Thames Arms Company: Trade name of the Harrington and Richardson Arms Company on firearms they made for an unknown wholesaler.
Tiger: a) Trade name of the Iver Johnson Arms and Cycle Works on inexpensive pocket revolvers. b) Trade name of the J.H. Hall and Company of Nashville on shotguns.
Tobin Simplex: Trade name used on shotguns of unknown manufacture which were retailed by the G.B. Crandall Company, Limited of Woodstock, Ontario, Canada.
Toledo Firearms Company: a) Trade name of the Hopkins and Allen Company on inexpensive pocket revolvers. b) Trade name of E.L. and J. Dickinson on inexpensive pocket revolvers.
Toronto Belle: Trade name found on inexpensive pocket revolvers of unknown manufacture.
Townleys Pal and Townleys American Boy: Trade name of H. & D. Folsom Arms Company for shotguns made for Townley Metal and Hardware Company of Kansas City, Missouri.
Tramps Terror: Trade name of the Forehand and Wadsworth Company on inexpensive pocket revolvers.
Traps Best: Trade name believed to have been of the H. & D. Folsom Arms Company on firearms made for the Watkins, Coftrell Company of Richmond, Virginia.
Triumph: Trade name of the H. & D. Folsom Arms Company on shotguns.
Trojan: Trade name found on inexpensive pocket revolvers of unknown manufacture.
True Blue: Trade name found on inexpensive pocket revolvers of unknown manufacture.
Tryon Special: Trade name of the Edward K. Tryon Company of Philadelphia, Pennsylvania on shotguns.
Tycoon: Trade name of the Iver Johnson Arms and Cycle Works on inexpensive pocket revolvers.
Union: a) Trade name found on inexpensive single shot pocket pistols of unknown manufacture. b) Trade name of the Hood Firearms Company on inexpensive pocket revolvers. c) Trade name of the Prescott Pistol Company on inexpensive pocket revolvers.
Union Arms Company: Trade name of the H. & D. Folsom Arms Company on firearms made for the Bostwick, Braun Company of Toledo, Ohio.
Union Jack: Trade name found on inexpensive pocket revolvers of unknown manufacture.
Union N.Y.: Trade name of the Whitneyville Armory on inexpensive pocket revolvers.
Unique: Trade name of the C.S. Shattuck Arms Company on revolvers and four barrel pocket pistols.
United States Arms Company: Trade name of Norwich Falls Pistol Company (O.A. Smith) on inexpensive pocket revolvers.
U.S. Arms Company: Trade name used successively by the Alexander Waller and Company (1877), the Barton and Company (1878) and the H. & D. Folsom Arms Company (1879 forward) on a variety of firearms.
U.S. Revolver: Trade name of the Iver Johnson Arms and Cycle Works on inexpensive pocket revolvers.
U.S. Single Gun: Trade name of the Iver Johnson Arms and Cycle Works on single barrel shotguns.
Universal: Trade name of the Hopkins and Allen Company on inexpensive pocket revolvers.
Utica Firearms Company: Trade name of the Simmons Hardware Company of St. Louis, Missouri on firearms.
Valient: Trade name of the Spear and Company of Pittsburgh, Pennsylvania on firearms.
Veiled Prophet: Trade name of the T.E. Ryan Pistol Manufacturing Company on inexpensive pocket revolvers.
Venus: Trade name of the American Novelty Company of Chicago on inexpensive pocket revolvers.
Veteran: Trade name found on inexpensive pocket revolvers of unknown manufacture.
Veto: Trade name found on inexpensive pocket revolvers of unknown manufacture.
Victor: a) Trade name of the Marlin Firearms Company on single shot pocket pistols. b) Trade name of the Harrington and Richardson Arms Company on inexpensive pocket revolvers. c) Trade name of the H. & D. Folsom Arms Company on inexpensive pocket pistols and revolvers.
Victor Arms Company: Trade name of the H. & D. Folsom Arms Company on firearms made for the Hibbard, Spencer, Bartlett and Company of Chicago.
Victor Special: Trade name of the H. & D. Folsom Arms Company on firearms made for the Hibbard, Spencer, Bartleft and Company of Chicago.
Victoria: Trade name of the Hood Firearms Company on inexpensive pocket revolvers.
Virginia Arms Company: Trade name of the H. & D. Folsom Arms Company and later the Davis-Warner Arms Company on firearms made for the Virginia-Carolina Company of Richmond, Virginia.
Volunteer: Trade name of the H. & O. Folsom Arms Company on inexpensive pocket revolvers ade for the Belknap Hardware Company of Louisville, Kentucky.
Vulcan: Trade name of the H. & O. Folsom Arms Company on firearms made for the Edward K. Tryon Company of Philadelphia, Pennsylvania.
Walnut Hill: Trade name of the J. Stevens Arms and Tool Company on rifles.
Warner Arms Corporation: Trade name of the H. & O Folsom Arms Company on firearms made for the Kirtland Brothers, Inc. of New York.
Wasp: Trade name found on inexpensive pocket revolvers of unknown manufacture.
Wautauga: Trade name of the Whitaker, Holtsinger Hardware Company of Morristown, Tennessee on firearms.
Western: Trade name of the H. & O. Folsom Arms Company on firearms made for the Paxton and Gallagher Company of Omaha, Nebraska.
Western Arms Company: a) Trade name of the Bacon Arms on various types of firearms. b) Trade name of W.W. Marston on revolvers. c) Trade name of Henry Kolb and later R.F. Sedgly of Philadelphia, Pennsylvania on Baby Hammerless revolvers. d) Trade name of the Ithaca Gun Company on shotguns believed to have been made for the Montgomery Ward and Company of Chicago.
Western Field: Trade name of Montgomery Ward and Company of Chicago on shotguns of various makes.
Weston, J.J.: Trade name of the H. & O. Folsom Arms Company on shotguns.
Whippet: Trade name of the H. & O. Folsom Arms Company on firearms made for the Hibbard, Spencer, Bartleft and Company of Chicago.
Whistler: Trade name of the Hood Firearms Company on inexpensive pocket revolvers.
White Powder Wonder: Trade name of Albert Aubrey of Meriden, Connecticut on shotguns made for the Sears, Roebuck and Company of Chicago.
Wildwood: Trade name of the H. & O. Folsom Arms Company for shotguns made for Sears, Roebuck & Company.
Wilkinson Arms Company: Trade name of the H. & O. Folsom Arms Company on firearms made for the Richmond Hardware Company of Richmond, Virginia.
Wiltshire Arms Company: Trade name of the H. & O. Folsom Arms Company on firearms made for the Stauffer, Eshleman and Company of New Orleans, Louisiana.
Winfield Arms Company: Trade name of the H. & O. Folsom Arms Company on various types of firearms.
Winner: Trade name found on inexpensive pocket revolvers of-unknown manufacture.
Winoca Arms Company: Trade name of the H. & O. Folsom Arms Company on firearms made for the N. Jacobi Hardware Company of Wilmington, North Camlina.
Wittes Expert: Trade name of the Witte Hardware Company of St. Louis, Missouri on shotguns.
Wittes IXL: Trade name of the Wifte Hardware Company of St. Louis, Missouri on shotguns.
Wolverine Arms Company: Trade name of the H. & O. Folsom Arms Company on firearms made for the Fletcher Hardware Company of Wilmington, North Carolina.
Woodmaster: Trade name found on Belgian shotguns imported by an unknown wholesaler.
Worlds Fair: Trade name of the Hopkins and Allen Company on shotguns.
Worthington Arms Company: Trade name of the H. & O. Folsom Arms Company on various types of firearms.
Wyco: Trade name of the Wyeth Hardware and Manufacturing Company of St. Joseph, Missouri on firearms.
XL: a) Trade name of the Hopkins and Allen Company on inexpensive pocket revolvers. b) Trade name of the Marlin Firearms Company on single shot pocket pistols.
XPERT: a) Trade name of the Hopkins and Allen Company on inexpensive pocket revolvers. b) Trade name of the Iver Johnson Arms and Cycle Works on inexpensive single shot pocket pistols.
XXX Stand: Trade name of the Marlin Firearms Companyon revolvers.
Young America: Trade name of J.P. Lindsay of New York on superimposed - load percussion pistols.
Young American: Trade name of the Harrington and Richardson Arms Company on revolvers.

Firearms Trade and Proprietary Names
Used with Permission of Dave Fulton
Hoosier Gun Works
457 Park City - Bon Ayr Rd.
Park City, KY 42160
(270-749-2109)
www.HoosierGunWorks.com

Stay on target with

GunDigest
THE MAGAZINE

- GUN REVIEWS
- NEW PRODUCT UPDATES
- GUNS FOR SALE
- FIREARMS INDUSTRY NEWS
- AUCTION AND SHOW LISTINGS

3 EASY WAYS TO SUBSCRIBE NOW

Order your print or digital subscription at
subscribe.gundigest.com

NOW AVAILABLE ON:

CALL **800.829.9127**

Gun Digest Kindle

Gun Digest Nook

Gun Digest® Books

An imprint of F+W Media, Inc.

www.gundigeststore.com

We Know Guns So You Know Guns

From firearms-related references and resources to tools and accessories and instruction and advice, at www.GunDigestStore.com you'll find what you're after, at affordable prices.

SHOP WITH US ANYTIME, DAY OR NIGHT, WE'RE HERE FOR YOU.

www.GunDigestStore.com

ebooks.gundigest.com

GUN DIGEST SHOOTERS GUIDE TO SHOTGUNS
U2146 • $19.99

GD SHOOTER'S GUIDE TO RIFLES
V6631 • $19.99

GUN DIGEST SHOOTER'S GUIDE TO RIFLE MARKSMANSHIP
U2928 • $19.99

GD SHOOTERS GUIDE TO HANDGUNS
V9633 • $19.99

HANDGUN TRAINING FOR PERSONAL PROTECTION
U2147 • $21.99

GLOCK DECONTRUCTED
V9707 • $29.99

ASSORTED TOPICS

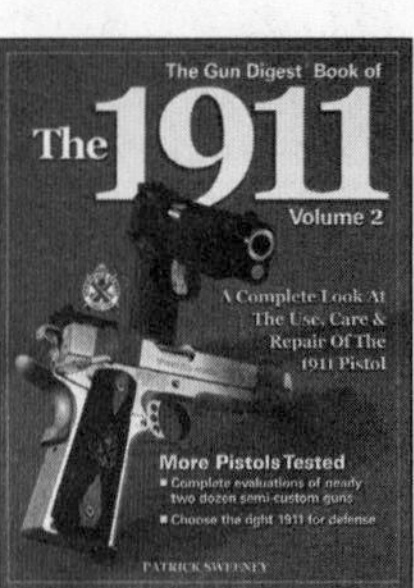

GUN DIGEST BOOK OF THE 1911 VOL 2
VIIPT • $27.99

GUN DIGEST BOOK OF THE REVOLVER
W1576 • $22.99

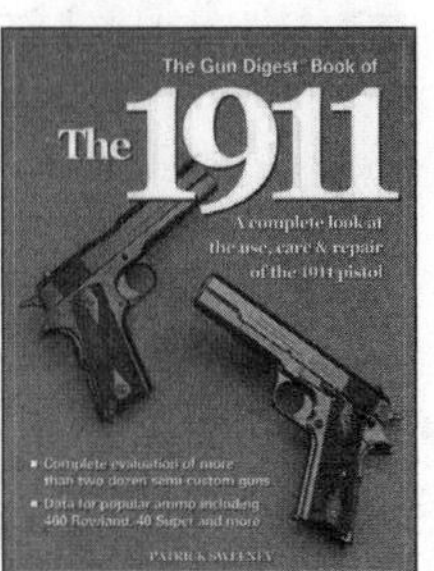

GUN DIGEST BOOK OF THE 1911
PITO • $27.95

CUSTOM RIFLES: MASTERY OF WOOD & METAL
V8196 • $59.99

COMPLETE GUIDE TO 3-GUN COMPETITION
W6536 • $27.99

GD BOOK OF THE REMINGTON 870
V8197 • $32.99

GUN DIGEST BOOK OF MODERN GUN VALUES
W1804 • $32.99

OFFICIAL GUN DIGEST BOOK OF GUNS & PRICES 2013 8TH ED.
U2619 • $24.99

GD ILLUSTRATED GUIDE TO MODERN FIREARMS
V9118 • $32.99

BIG-BORE REVOLVERS
W5866 • $27.99

GUN DIGEST PRESENTS CLASSIC SPORTING RIFLES
W7930 • $24.99

STANDARD CATALOG OF FIREARMS, 2012
X4714 • $39.99

To order, go to www.GunDigestStore.com.

ASSORTED TOPICS

GUN DIGEST SHOOTERS GUIDE TO THE 1911
Y0048 • $19.99

STANDARD CATALOG OF RIFLES & SHOTGUNS
W7939 • $29.99

GD BOOK OF CONCEALED CARRY, 2ND EDITION
V9337 • $27.99

OLD GUNSIGHTS & RIFLE SCOPES
Z2346 • $34.99

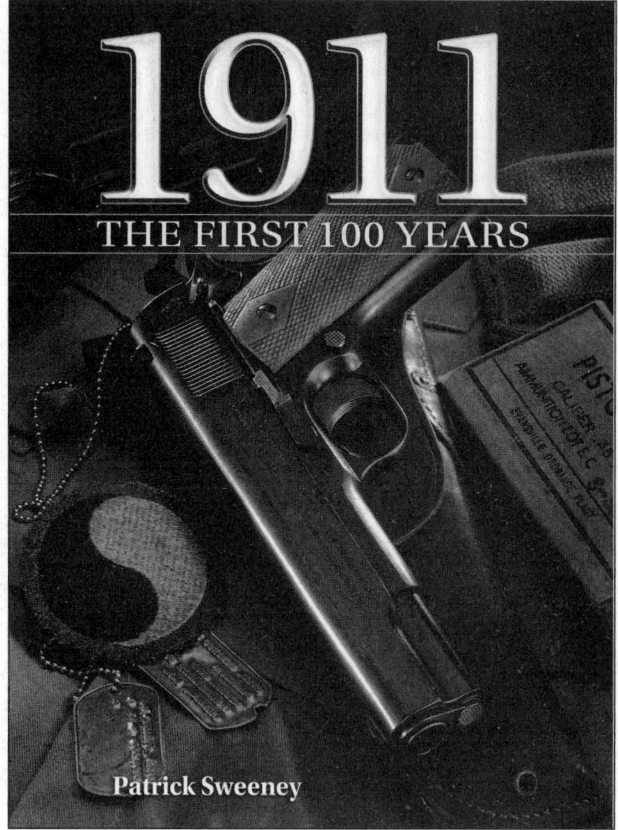

1911 THE FIRST 100 YEARS
Z7019 • $29.99

GUN DIGEST BOOK OF PERSONAL PROTECTION & HOME DEFENSE
Z3653 • $24.99

GUN DIGEST BIG FAT BOOK OF THE .45 ACP
Z4204 • $24.99

OWN THE NIGHT
Z5015 • $29.99

GUN DIGEST BOOK OF TRAP & SKEET SHOOTING
Z5055 • $24.99

PERSONAL DEFENSE FOR WOMEN
Z5057 • $21.99

MASSAD AYOOB'S GREATEST HANDGUNS OF THE WORLD
Z6495 • $27.99

GUN DIGEST BOOK OF SHOTGUNNING
Z7015 • $27.99

ARMED-THE ESSENTIAL GUIDE TO CONCEALED CARRY
W7927 • $24.99

To order, go to www.GunDigestStore.com.

MASSAD AYOOB'S GREATEST HANDGUNS OF THE WORLD, V2
W6538 • $27.99

ASSORTED TOPICS

GUN DIGEST BOOK OF THE .22 RIFLE
Z8581 • $19.99

GUN DIGEST BUYER'S GUIDE TO CONCEALED CARRY HANDGUNS
Z8905 • $24.99

ARMED FOR PERSONAL DEFENSE
Z9404 • $19.99

GREATEST GUNS OF THE GUN DIGEST
Z9830 • $24.99

GUNSMITHING

GUN DIGEST BOOK OF FIREARMS ASSEMBLY/ DISASSEMBLY PART IV
AS4R2 • $24.99

GUN DIGEST BOOK OF RIMFIRE RIFLES ASSEMBLY/DISASSEMBLY
W1577 • $34.99

GUN DIGEST BOOK OF THE AR-15
GDAR • $27.99

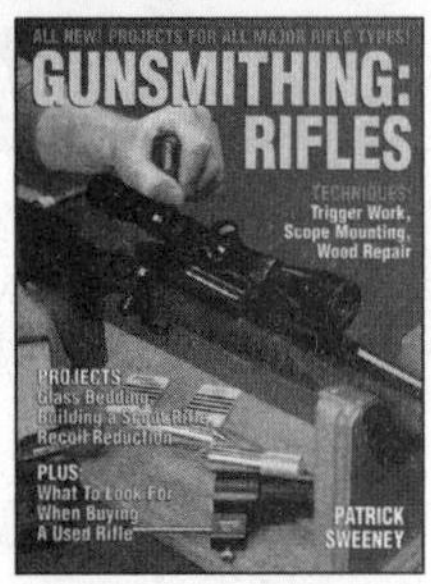

GUNSMITHING RIFLES
GRIF • $26.99

CUSTOMIZE THE RUGER 10/22
NGRTT • $29.99

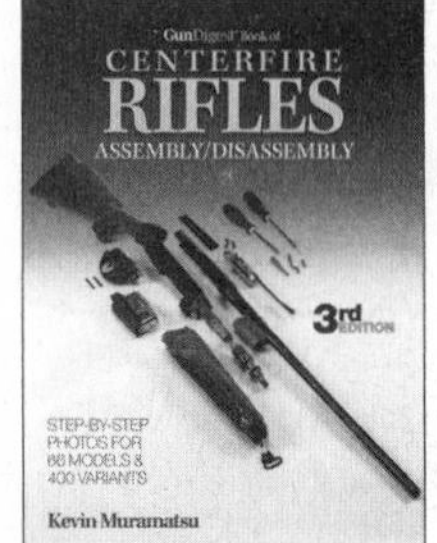

GUN DIGEST BOOK OF CENTERFIRE RIFLES ASSEMBLY/DISASSEMBLY 3RD ED.
U2620 • $34.99

GD BOOK OF SHOTGUNS ASSEM/DISSASEM, 3RD ED.
V6630 • $36.99

GUN DIGEST BOOK OF EXPLODED GUN DRAWINGS
Y0047 • $36.99

GUN DIGEST BOOK OF REVOLVERS ASSEMBLY/ DISASSEMBLY
Y0773 • $34.99

GUN DIGEST BOOK OF AUTOMATIC PISTOL ASSEMBLY/DISASSEMBLY
W7933 • $39.99

To order, go to www.GunDigestStore.com.

GUNSMITHING

GUNSMITHING: PISTOLS & REVOLVERS
Z5056 • $27.99

GUNSMITHING THE AR-15
Z6613 • $27.99

MILITARY & PARAMILITARY

MILITARY SMALL ARMS OF THE 20TH CENTURY
MSA7 • $24.95

COMBAT SHOOTING WITH MASSAD AYOOD
W1983 • $24.99

MILITARY & PARAMILITARY

GUN DIGEST BOOK OF CLASSIC COMBAT HANDGUNS
W4464 • $24.99

GUN DIGEST BOOK OF THE AR-15 VOLUME 4
W6537 • $29.99

GUN DIGEST BOOK OF CLASSIC AMERICAN COMBAT RIFLES
W7942 • $24.99

GUN DIGEST BOOK OF TACTICAL RIFLE
Y0046 • $26.99

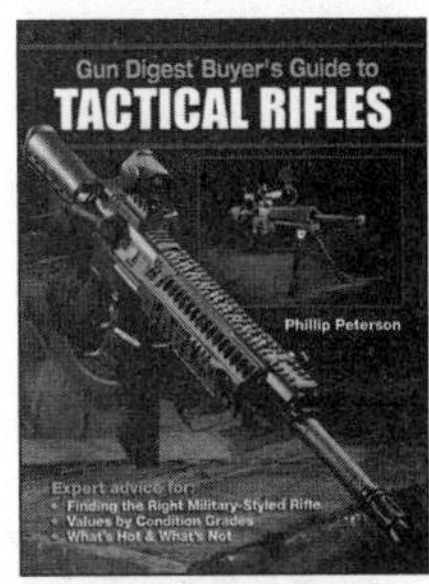

GUN DIGEST BUYER'S GUIDE TO TACTICAL RIFLES
Y0625 • $24.99

STANDARD CATALOG CAT OF MILITARY FIREARMS 6TH EDITION
Y0772 • $32.99

MAUSER MILITARY RIFLES OF THE WORLD 5TH ED
Y1287 • $49.99

GUN DIGEST BOOK OF THE TACTICAL SHOTGUN
Y1448 • $24.99

GUN DIGEST BOOK OF THE AR-15 VOLUME II
Z0738 • $27.99

GUN DIGEST BOOK OF COMBAT GUNNERY
Z0880 • $24.99

GUN DIGEST BOOK OF THE AK & SKS
Z2207 • $24.99

TACTICAL PISTOL SHOOTING
Z5954 • $24.99

To order, go to www.GunDigestStore.com.

THE GUN DIGEST® BOOK OF THE

GLOCK

2nd Edition

How to accessorize and tune your Glock

Performance evaluation of all models and chamberings

Patrick Sweeney

GUN DIGEST BOOK OF THE GLOCK
Z1926 • $27.99

MILITARY & PARAMILITARY

GUN DIGEST BOOK OF THE AR-15 VOL.3
Z8816 • $29.99

DEFENSIVE HANDGUNS SKILLS
Z8883 • $16.99

ANTIQUES & COLLECTIBLES

STANDARD CATALOG OF SMITH & WESSON
FSW03 • $42.99

STANDARD CATALOG OF COLT FIREARMS
Z0931 • $29.99

STANDARD CATALOG OF WINCHESTER FIREARMS
Z0932 • $29.99

STANDARD CATALOG OF CIVIL WAR FIREARMS
Z1784 • $27.99

STANDARD CATALOG OF REMINGTON FIREARMS
Z1828 • $29.99

STANDARD CATALOG OF BROWNING FIREARMS
Z2782 • $29.99

ANTIQUES & COLLECTIBLES

WINCHESTER MODEL 94
Z5058 • $34.99

RELOADING

RELOADING FOR HANDGUNNERS
W0932 • $27.99

9th Edition

The Definitive Guide for Novice to Expert

The ABCs of RELOADING

ABCs OF RELOADING 9TH EDITION
Z9165 • $26.99

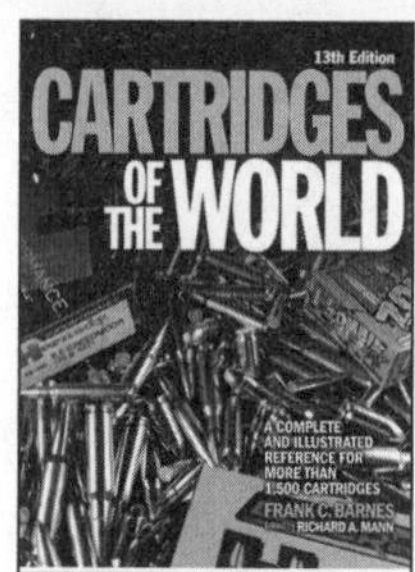

CARTRIDGES OF THE WORLD, 13TH EDITION
V0801 • $34.99

To order, go to www.GunDigestStore.com.

COOKING GAME
U2929 • $9.99

THE SPORTING CHEF'S BETTER VENISON COOKBOOK
U1948 • $24.99

WE KILL IT WE GRILL IT
V6707 • $9.99

301 VENISON RECIPES
VR01 • $10.95

VENISON WISDOM COOKBOOK
Z8928 • $14.99

GUT IT. CUT IT. COOK IT.
Z5014 • $24.99

CURED
Z6078 • $30.00

HUNTING MATURE WHITETAILS THE LAKOSKY WAY
W4542 • $29.99

WHITETAIL LEGENDS
(July 2012)
W7618 • $29.99

MAPPING TROPHY BUCKS
TRTT • $24.99

TROPHY BUCKS IN ANY WEATHER
Z1781 • $21.99

BIG BUCKS THE BENOIT WAY
Z2193 • $29.99

TOM DOKKEN'S ADVANCED RETRIEVER TRAINING
U1863 • $19.99

THE COMPLETE PREDATOR HUNTER
Z3652 • $22.99

PREDATOR CALLING WITH GERRY BLAIR
Z0740 • $19.99

ADVENTURE BOWHUNTER
V9708 • $34.99

DEER & DEER HUNTING'S GUIDE TO BETTER BOW HUNTING
V6706 • $9.99

WHITETAIL RACKS
Z7239 • $29.99

WHITETAILS
Z8906 • $32.00

STRATEGIES FOR WHITETAILS
WTLDD • $24.99

To order, go to www.GunDigestStore.com.

KNIVES

BLADESMITHING WITH MURRAY CARTER
W1852 • $27.99

BLADE'S GUIDE TO MAKING KNIVES, 2ND EDITION
W5865 • $27.99

THE WONDER OF KNIFEMAKING
X3269 • $27.99

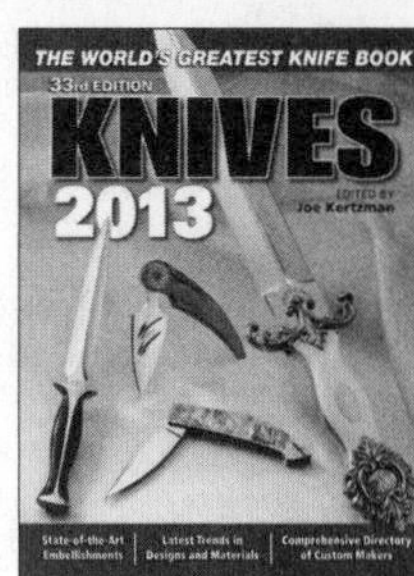

KNIVES 2013, 33RD EDITION
V0802 • $29.99

FLAYDERMAN'S GUIDE TO ANTIQUE AMERICAN FIREARMS
Z0620 • $39.99

AMERICAN PREMIUM GUIDE TO KNIVES & RAZORS
Z2189 • $27.99

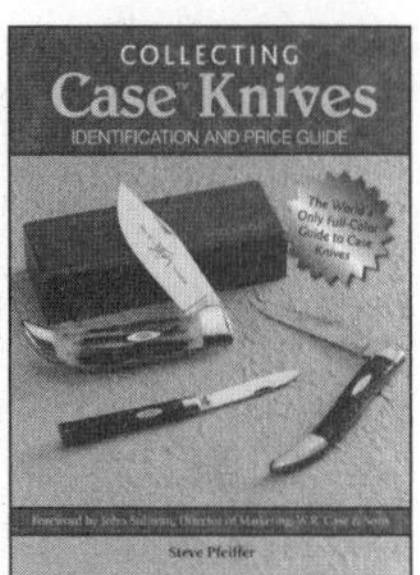

COLLECTING CASE KNIVES
Z4387 • $29.99

BLADE'S GUIDE TO KNIVES & THEIR VALUES
Z5054 • $29.99

KNIFEMAKING WITH BOB LOVELESS
Z7240 • $24.99

SPIRIT OF THE SWORD
Z7241 • $24.99

101 KNIFE DESIGNS
U1059 • $29.99

WAYNE GODDARD'S $50 KNIFE SHOP
WGBWR • $19.99

BLADE'S GUIDE TO MAKING KNIVES
BGKFM • $24.99

HOW TO MAKE KNIVES
KHM01 • $14.99

www.GunDigestStore.com

FREE SHIPPING
On Orders Over $49

100% GUARANTEE
Your Satisfaction is Our Goal

Looking for eBooks, go to ebooks.gundigest.com.